GOOD BEER GUIDE 2010

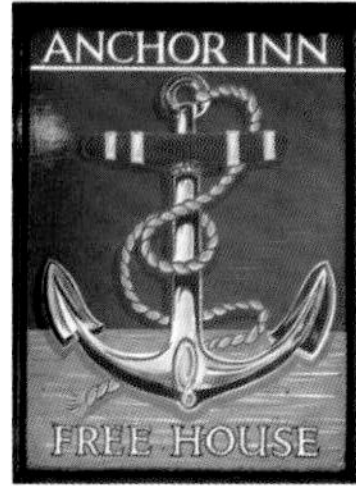

Edited by

Roger Protz

Project Co-ordinator

Emma Haines

Assistant Editors

Ione Brown, Joanna Copestick and Katie Hunt

Managing Editor

Simon Hall

Campaign for Real Ale
230 Hatfield Road, St Albans,
Hertfordshire AL1 4LW

Contents

Special thanks to 100,000 CAMRA members who carried out research for the pubs; Rick Pickup and Steve Westby for advising on new breweries; the Campaign's Regional Directors, who coordinated the pub entries; Paul Moorhouse for assembling the beer tasting notes; Michael Slaughter for checking pubs on the National Inventory; Colin Valentine for compiling the list of beer festivals; the pubs who kindly contributed their photographs; and CAMRA's National Executive for their support.

Thanks also to the following at CAMRA head office: Chief Executive Mike Benner; Campaigns, Marketing and Public Affairs: Louise Ashworth, Tom Blakemore, Tarli Cable; Kim Carvey, Jon Howard, Tony Jerome, Iain Loe, Jonathan Mail, Stuart South; What's Brewing: Claire-Michelle Pearson, Tom Stainer; Administration: Gillian Dale, Cressida Feiler, Robert Ferguson, Gary Ranson, Nicky Shipp; Membership Services: Debbie Campion, Caroline Clerembeaux, John Cottrell, Gary Fowler; Finance and Branch Support: Anita Gibson, Liz McGlynn, Malcolm Harding; Warehouse: Neil Cox, Steve Powell, Barnaby Smith, Ron Stocks.

Photo credits: Photo credits: acestock/Alamy: spine; Alex Segre/Alamy: p4 (b); Cath Harries: p17-21, back cover; Chris Stringer: p16 (b); Chris Wainwright: p16 (t); Frederick Cameron Wilson: p8; Geoff Brandwood: p12 (b); Ian Packham: p16 (t); Karen Hadley/Shutterstock: p880; Mark Dodds: p10; Neil Lloyd: p12 (t, m); The Photolibrary Wales/Alamy: front cover; Reading Evening Post: p9; Roger Protz: p6, p7 (tl), p13, p16 (b).
All other photographs credited where they appear.

Production: Cover design: James Hall; colour section design: Keith Holmes, Thames Street Studio; database, typesetting and beers index: AMA Dataset, Preston, Lancs; maps: David and Morag Perrott, PerroCarto, Machynlleth, Wales.

Printed and bound in the UK by William Clowes, Beccles, Suffolk.

Published by the Campaign for Real Ale Ltd,
230 Hatfield Road, St Albans, Herts, AL1 4LW. Tel 01727 867201.
Email: camra@camra.org.uk Website: www.camra.org.uk

ISBN 978-1-85249-266-3

Groes Inn, Ty'n-y-Groes, North-West Wales

INTRODUCTION

The battle for survival

Pubs rocked by escalating taxes and unfair competition

IT WAS THE BEST OF TIMES, it was the worst of times... Charles Dickens, an inveterate pubgoer, would not object if we take the opening lines of A Tale of Two Cities to underscore the topsy-turvy world of the pub trade and brewing industry at the end of the first decade of the 21st century. At one level, pubs and breweries are in crisis. Around 40 pubs a week are closing while sales of mass-marketed beers are in serious decline. But there is a counter-culture.

In spite of the recession, small craft breweries continue to open and expand – in July 2009, for example, the Thornbridge Brewery in Derbyshire moved to a new custom-built plant that cost £1.6 million and will enable the brewery to produce 30,000 barrels a year. Britain, with around 670, now has more micro breweries per head of population than any other country in the world. British drinkers enjoy greater choice than at any time in the Good Beer Guide's history, dating back to the early 1970s.

New breweries don't open on a wing and a prayer. Their owners carefully test the local market while they scour recipe books to help them devise new and distinctive beers. Their success is driven by a simple and inexorable fact: beer lovers are increasingly tired of "drinking the advertising" that promotes bland global brands. They seek the rich, tempting aromas and flavours of locally-brewed beers made with fresh, wholesome ingredients.

That thirst for good beer is echoed in CAMRA's membership. It stands at more than 100,000, making it far and away the biggest single-issue consumer movement in the world. There has never been greater interest in the subject. Months before the event, beer tastings and talks at CAMRA's 2009 Great British Beer Festival were sold out. New books on the subject pour from the presses. Even television no longer thinks the British consume only wine and broadcasts programmes devoted to beer.

But there are fewer pubs today in which good beer can be enjoyed. The rate of closure is horrific. In some cases, the loss of a pub can rip the heart out of a local community, especially if that community is an isolated rural one.

In a multi-channel age, with so many competing elements of the "leisure industry", some pub closures may have been inevitable. But others are the result of catastrophic failure by government. Pubs are without question pleasanter places today now they are smoke-free. But pleas by CAMRA and other bodies to

Festival-goers at the 2009 Great British Beer Festival celebrate CAMRA's 100,000-member milestone

Supermarkets offer massive discounts on beer to lure shoppers in

make the smoking ban a phased one for pubs – with freedom to set aside one well-ventilated room for smokers for an agreed number of years – were ignored. As a result, many people now prefer to do their drinking at home. They buy their drink from supermarkets and other retail outlets where beer is used as a massively-discounted loss leader to lure shoppers in.

It's not only supermarkets that have come under the spotlight. The activities of the giant national "pubcos" or pub companies have been discussed at parliamentary level, with a call from the Business and Enterprise Committee for a major investigation. CAMRA has lodged a complaint with the Office of Fair Trading concerning the pubcos' policies of high rents, prices and pub closures.

Where the supermarkets are concerned, the Campaign wants the national government to study the Scottish parliament's move to introduce minimum pricing for alcohol and a ban on cheap promotions for beer. It's clear that life can only be breathed back into the pub sector if the yawning gap between on-trade and off-trade pricing is tackled. It makes a nonsense of the "free market" if supermarkets can sell beer for pennies while a pub pint sets you back £3.50.

Taxation is at the root of the pub trade's problems. Excise duty – the tax on alcohol – rose by 19% in 2008 and the first four months of 2009. Pubs are being throttled by the Chancellor, who ignores the blindingly obvious fact that he is losing revenue – duty, income tax and VAT – as a result of his taxation policy that sends drinkers into the arms of the vendors of cheap alcohol in supermarkets.

Drinkers, publicans and brewers are united in their opposition to the crippling levels of duty imposed on beer by the Chancellor of Exchequer

At the time of CAMRA's annual members' meeting in Eastbourne in 2009, national chairman Paula Waters and Miles Jenner of Harvey's Brewery in Lewes displayed a cheque for three billion and sixty-seven million pounds – the annual amount of tax handed over by beer drinkers to the Treasury

The central role of the pub in the lives of communities in town and country can be measured by the encouraging reports in the Guide of determined campaigns to save them from closure. It's clear from reading the descriptions of pubs in this edition that publicans who offer a good choice of cask beer, backed by imaginative food and regular events – mini beer festivals, family events and quiz nights, for example – can not only buck the trend but continue to both make a good living and a vital contribution to their communities.

Remarkably, there are still 57,000 pubs in Britain. We offer our selection of the best, serving the best of British. So let's raise a collective glass to the beleaguered but not defeated British pub. Abuse them and we'll lose them. Go to the pub and take your friends with you. Support the work of craft brewers and publicans serving their products in tip-top condition.

Above all, enjoy!

PUBS IN PERIL

All hands to the pumps!

IN REMOTE VILLAGES AND BUSY TOWN CENTRES, people are uniting to save their local pubs.

Villagers in the Scottish Borders are close to sealing a victory that will save their local pub, the oldest and most historic tavern in the country. The Crook Inn in Tweedsmuir has been shut since 2006 but a revolt by the entire community, with support from the local authority and the Scottish government, should stop a property developer turning the inn into private housing.

The Crook dates from 1604 but is probably older: 1604 was the year it was officially licensed. It has a turbulent history, used as a hiding place in the 17th century by Covenanters, Presbyterian opponents of Charles I, who hunted them down with armed dragoons. One Covenanter was hidden in a peat stack by the landlady.

Robert Burns wrote "Willie Wastle's Wife" in the inn – a bar is named after the poem – and in the 20th century it was often used by John Buchan, author of the The Thirty-Nine Steps, who was born nearby.

The Crook was originally a simple ale house for drovers taking sheep to market. It grew in size and in the 1930s a striking Art Deco extension was added. The ancient ale house and 20th-century additions blend well and as a result the entire site was declared a listed building.

Andrew Mason, one of the leaders of the campaign to save the Crook, says the inn has been a focal point for Tweedsmuir for more than 300 years. It was the only pub for miles around, situated alongside the A701, served excellent food as well as local ales from Broughton Brewery, and was popular with walkers, ramblers and visitors to the John Buchan Centre.

The blow fell in 2006 when Jim Doonan, a local property developer, bought the Crook. According to Andrew Mason, Doonan made the owners of the inn 'an offer they couldn't refuse'. When the inn was closed over Christmas that year, Mason, a local community councillor, asked Doonan when he planned to re-open the Crook. Doonan told Mason the inn was doing no trade, the local community didn't support it and he would seek planning permission to turn the site into flats.

Andrew Mason, who writes computer software and runs a free-holding behind his house, refuted all Doonan's claims. 'The Crook traded profitably under its former owners,' he says. 'With Doonan its opening hours were erratic – it was often closed at busy periods when many visitors were in the area – and the food went from top quality to a restricted menu.'

Mason called a village meeting to discuss the way forward. The turnout proved how strong feelings were about the Crook. 'Only one person in the whole community didn't support the meeting,' he says, 'and that was Jim Doonan! People felt passionately that the pub had to remain a focal point of the village. Tweedsmuir has lost its school and post office. Only the church and pub remain and now we faced the loss of the Crook.

'There's a tea rooms in Broughton eight miles away that now sells beer since the Crook closed, but that's tiny and can only handle a few people.

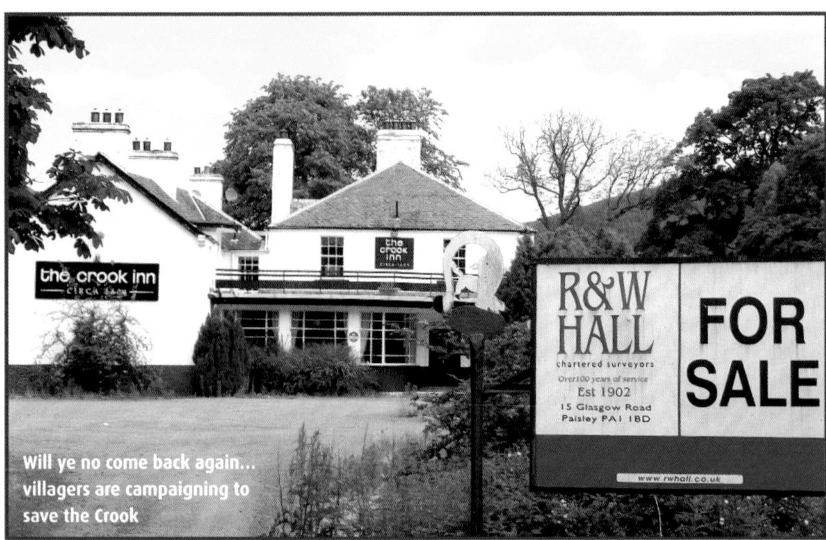

Will ye no come back again... villagers are campaigning to save the Crook

Andrew Mason... leading the fight for the Crook

The nearest real pub is in Moffat and that's a 15-mile drive.' An action group was set up, encouraged by new legislation enacted by the Scottish parliament that gives communities the right to buy important local amenities. The law prevents owners selling a resource without offering it first to the local community.

A long, exhausting planning battle then started. The local planning officer of the Scottish Borders Council supported Doonan's proposals. But the action group took its case to the full council who backed them and rejected Doonan's application. The council even brought in new regulations that recognise the importance of rural resources.

Doonan appealed to the Scottish government in Edinburgh. It sent an official to Tweedsmuir to assess all the arguments. His report said Doonan's application to turn the inn into private dwellings had no merit. Doonan had said he would sell the site for £500,000 but the local planning officer and an independent reviewer both said the complex was worth £200,000.

The action group turned itself into the Tweedsmuir Community Company. Andrew Mason is the vice-chairman of the company and says they are optimistic they can buy the Crook. 'We're a serious business. We want to turn the Crook into the best pub in the Borders. It will make money for Tweedsmuir. Many B&Bs in the area have closed as a result of the Crook being shut. The inn will bring trade back to the village.'

The company's serious intent can be seen by the fact it has already raised and spent £10,000 on surveyor's reports. 'We're close to winning,' Mason says. 'We're applying for a large Lottery Fund donation to buy the inn back.'

The Tweedsmuir company hopes to have the Crook open again in time to mark the 250th anniversary of the birth of Robbie Burns in 1759. There may not be a new poem but you can expect a mighty celebration in the inn he loved.

For up-to-date information, see **www.savethecrook.org.uk**.

Taking the fight to parliament

The Coachmakers Arms in Hanley, Stoke-on-Trent, is another pub where loyal customers are sensing possible victory in a long campaign to stop its closure. The GBG-listed pub was earmarked for the axe by Stoke council as part of a plan to demolish buildings in the area to make way for a car park – despite the fact that the council had called the Coachmakers "a little gem" in its official city guide.

Partners Sue Grocott and Jason Barlow, who boosted the fortunes of the pub with a vigorous guest beer policy, enlisted the support of local CAMRA branches and customers to oppose the council plans. An on-line petition has so far won 10,500 signatures and supporters have also written to the council, calling for the pub to be saved.

The petition has been posted on the Prime Minister's official website – **www.number10.gov.uk** – and the campaigners took their case to the All-Party Parliamentary Save the Pub Group, set up by Liberal Democrat MP Greg Mulholland. The group wants more MPs to support threatened pubs and it says there is an urgent need to change legislation to enshrine in law the future of the British pub. Mr Mulholland said at the launch of the group that some local authorities were failing to recognise the importance of pubs to their communities.

Coachmakers... too good to become a car park

Following a meeting with the parliamentary group, Jason Barlow said he was encouraged by the response he had received. The MPs will write to the Secretary of State for Communities, John Denham, and ask him to call in Stoke council's plans for review.

MP Greg Mulholland

As the Guide went to press, Jason Barlow said neither Stoke council's website nor one used by the developers hired to knock down the Coachmakers had been updated since February 2009. He added that as the council's redevelopment will be funded by money from banks, the scheme could founder for lack of funds.

For up-to-date information see **www.thecoachmakers.co.uk**.

Win some...

CO-OPERATION OF A SPECIAL KIND has saved the Shepherds Inn in Melmerby. The pub, based in the Eden Valley region of Cumbria, dates from 1789 and has featured regularly in the Good Beer Guide.

The pub is owned by national pub company Enterprise Inns, which closed it late in 2008. It reopened six months later thanks to the initiative of the owners of the Old Crown in Hesket Newmarket. For a decade, both the Old Crown and the Hesket Newmarket Brewery behind the pub have been owned by two co-operatives made up of villagers and supporters from further afield.

In June 2009 the doors of the Shepherds Inn reopened again. Sir Chris Bonington, the famous mountaineer and a member of the Old Crown co-op, cut the tape to the cheers of villagers from Melmerby. The pub is now run by the co-op on a leashold arrangement and it has struck a deal with Enterprise Inns that allows six Hesket Newmarket beers to be sold: normally, the pub company would permit only beers from its own list to be sold.

Managers Ceri and Andy Webster say they will offer top-quality food as well as good ale to villagers and tourists. Julian Davey, chairman of the Old Crown co-op, said the Shepherds Inn was the last pub in Melmerby and its reopening would breathe life back into the village.

He hoped that similar deals could be struck in other parts of the country, with local people combining to save threatened pubs.

A large crowd of villagers turned out to celebrate the re-opening of their treasured local. The photo shows Sir Chris Bonington (second from the right) in the front row with other key figures in the success of both the Old Crown and the Shepherds Inn. Pub managers Andy Webster (on the left) and Ceri Webster were joined by Julian Davey (far right) of the Old Crown co-op and, second left, Jim Fearnley, former brewer at Hesket Newmarket.

It was Jim's retirement as the brewer at Hesket Newmarket that inspired the villagers to combine their resources to build co-operatives that run both the brewery and the pub.

Jim and his successors have created a range of beers named after local Cumbrian mountains and fells – many of them scaled regularly by Chris Bonington. The beers include Skiddaw Special Bitter, Haystacks, Sca Fell Blonde and Old Carrocks. Originally brewed just for the Old Crown, they are now available in the free trade – and the revived Shepherds Inn.

Shepherds delight...villagers turned out in force for the pub's re-opening

Local politicians, fellow publicans and CAMRA members show their anger at the decision to board up The Jolly Anglers

...lose some

THE PLOUGH INN in Ashmansworth, Hampshire, closed in September 2008 despite a spirited campaign by locals to save it. The Plough was a regular in the Good Beer Guide. When the landlord declared his intention to close it, he was refused permission by the local authority but said he would appeal against the decision.

The local branch of CAMRA fought the appeal and won. The pub stayed open but remained up for sale. The landlord applied to close it again and this time he was successful. As a result, Ashmansworth now has no shop, post office or pub.

It's not the only town or village to lose its pub. The following regulars in the Guide have closed:

Baker's Arms and the **George,** Buxton, Derbyshire.
Beehive, Upper Basildon, Berks.
Dog & Partridge, Bolton, Lancs (under threat of closure).
Fox & Hounds, Stony Stratford, Bucks.
Green Man, Newport Pagnell, Bucks.
Jolly Anglers, Reading, Berks.
Lord Nelson, Holton, near Halesworth, Suffolk.
Musketeer, Leigh, Greater Manchester.
Nelson, Wheathampstead, Herts.
Plough, Blundeston, Suffolk.
Prince of Wales, Caversham, Berks.
Railway, Heatley, near Lymm, Cheshire.
Red Lion, Theale, Berks.
White Horse, Keysoe, Beds.
Woolpack, Banbury, Oxon.

Even CAMRA's National Inventory of pubs with historic interiors is not immune from closures. The following NI pubs have closed:

Bellefield, Winson Green, Birmingham.
Berkeley Hunt, Purton, Glos.
Colliers Arms, Mossley, Greater Manchester.
Cupids Hill Tavern, Grosmont, Gwent.
Dun Cow, Billy Row, Co Durham.
Fox, Bix, Oxon.
Hop Poles, Risbury, Herefordshire.
Horse & Trumpet, Medbourne, Leics.
Red Lion, Stoke Talmage, Oxon.
Stag & Peasant, Nottingham.
Seven Stars, Halfway House, Shropshire.

WHAT YOU CAN DO

If your pub is under threat and you need advice on how to save it, go to the CAMRA website and click on **Save Our Pubs** and also contact your local branch of CAMRA: Contact details are available from the website or from CAMRA's newspaper What's Brewing.

www.camra.org.uk

Taxing times

Action is needed to prevent more locals closing

IT'S NOT SURPRISING that around 40 pubs are closing every week. Never has one sector of British industry been so battered by government. Beer duty – the tax on beer – is ratcheted up every year, sometimes twice a year.

In 2008, Chancellor Alistair Darling imposed two duty rises, totalling 17 per cent. In his 2009 budget, the Chancellor added a further 2 per cent. That's 19 per cent in just 16 months.

Duty increases are never as simple as they sound. When the Chancellor announces he's increasing beer by a penny a pint, it will amount to at least three or four pence by the time the beer reaches the bar as suppliers add further rises to "maintain their margins". The result is that in many parts of the country a pint will now set you back £3.50.

Warm welcome

Pubs offer more than just beer. A warm welcome, pleasant surroundings, the chance to meet old friends and make new ones, read a newspaper or enjoy lively conversation, eat a snack or a full meal: these are some of the attributes that make the British pub the perfect "leisure experience".

But pubs are being abandoned as drinkers rush for the comfort blanket of cheap supermarket beer. The giant high street multiples are able to sell beer at giveaway prices for a number of reasons. They tell their major suppliers, global brewers such as Carlsberg, Coors, Heineken/S&N and InBev, to absorb duty increases and sell beer at enormous discounts. In some cases, beer is sold as a "loss leader" – at cost price or less – in order to entice people into stores.

CAMRA has called for a minimum pricing policy for beer, similar to a scheme being investigated by the Scottish government. Such a policy would mean that the price of beer in the off-trade would have to reflect costs of production and distribution, bringing them more into line with pub prices. In June 2009, the World Health Organisation endorsed the Scottish government's proposals and urged it to proceed. The Scottish plans would include a minimum price for a unit of alcohol and – equally important – a ban on off-sales promotions.

But action is also needed at pub level. A majority of Britain's pubs are owned by national pub companies – pubcos for short. A top-level investigation in 2009 by the House of Commons Business and Enterprise Committee (BEC) called for urgent action to probe the power of the pubcos. The BEC found that rents for tenants and lessees in pubco houses are far higher than in pubs owned by regional brewers or genuine free traders, leading to higher prices. The committee also reported that licensees pay on average 50 pence a pint more when they source their beer from pubcos rather than the open market.

The result is that consumers who drink in pubs owned by the national pubcos – Enterprise, Punch and Mitchells & Butlers – pay a much higher price for beer than if they used a pub owned by an independent brewer or one run as a free house.

CAMRA is compiling a report for the Office of Fair Trading on the pubcos and their pricing and rents policy. As the Campaign enjoys the status of a "super complainant", the OFT is obliged to make a fast-track investigation of the pubcos within 90 days. CAMRA has made it clear it objects only to the pubcos' policies. It supports

CAMRA's Mike Benner (left) and Jonathan Mail (second right) meet MPs Patrick Hall, Greg Mulholland and Ben Chapman to campaign against high beer duty

the rights of regional and smaller brewers to own "tied estates" of pubs that sell their beers as well as "guests" from other brewers. The campaign has not supported the different tactics of a group called Fair Pint that wants the European Union to consider abolishing the tie completely. The infamous law of "unintended consequences" could lead to disaster, with smaller breweries driven out of business and their pubs bought by the pubcos, the very companies whose policies of escalating rents and high prices need to be curbed.

Guest beers

The Campaign also wants to encourage all pubs, either owned by pubcos or brewers, to offer guest beers – beers outside the tie, from small craft brewers as well as bigger regionals. As pub entries in the Guide show, guest beers are enormously popular with consumers. They offer greater choice and sharper prices and, above all, encourage drinkers back into pubs. They also give entry into the national pub scene for micro brewers, who are effectively barred from the pubcos as a result of the price discounts demanded.

CAMRA has also called for action on the crippling rents burden that pubcos force on hosts. In many cases, rents are bankrupting licensees. In June 2009, David and Anne-Marie Ball lost a court battle to stop Enterprise Inns repossessing the Fleur de Lys in Totley, Sheffield. The Balls owed rent arreas of £8,000 and faced eviction from the pub, which meant losing their home as well. The Balls said Enterprise's annual rent of £30,000 was exorbitant and, based on an annual turnover of £160,000, should have been closer to £16,000. The Balls' case is typical of thousands of pubco licensees throughout the country.

One reason why many pubs close is because the owners – mainly the giant pubcos – place "restrictive covenants" on them. This means that if a pub company closes an outlet with a covenant, the pub ceases to trade, as the terms of the covenant stop any new buyer from running it as licensed premises. It's a breathtaking denial of the free market and accounts for the fact that many pubs have been turned into private houses. It allows the pubcos to stop competition from smaller free traders who have proved repeatedly they can take on a failed pubco outlet and turn it into a thriving pub with a good choice of beers at keen prices.

On the beer duty front, CAMRA is calling on the government to take action that will lead to cheaper pub prices and will encourage drinkers to abandon supermarkets in favour of good draught beer.

The Campaign wants a zero rate of duty on beers of 2.8 per cent alcohol and below. This would encourage more beers such as Welton's Pride & Joy that prove that cask ales of such strength can be rich in flavour and wonderfully refreshing. They are not suitable to be bottled and, available only on draught, would encourage sensible pub-drinking. Such beers would not appeal to the tiny minority of binge drinkers and would stress the healthy attributes of draught beer.

Pride & Joy...at 2.8% it should be zero rated

And CAMRA is lobbying the government with a call for preferential duty on draught beer. This would require a change in EU law and the Campaign wants the British government to raise the issue with the European Commission. CAMRA argues that a lower rate of duty on draught beer will encourage greater use of pubs and stop the blight of pub closures. It says the burden of high beer duty makes no economic sense: pubs make a far greater tax contribution to the treasury than supermarkets as they have to pay not only duty but VAT, employment taxes and business rates. If drinkers switch from the off to the on-trade, then the government will see its tax revenues increase. Preferential duty on draught beer would be of particular benefit to small craft brewers who concentrate on cask beer for the pub trade.

CAMRA says there is nothing natural about the move from pubs to supermarkets. The switch is driven by simple economics: beer sold at giveaway prices. To encourage a vibrant pub sector and stop closures, pubs need a fair crack of the whip through lower duty and other taxes along with an improved choice of beer.

Grassroots action

Beer drinkers can act at community level to save pubs and win improved choice. CAMRA is a keen advocate of the Sustainable Communities Act, supported by more than 100 local authorities in Britain.

It's radical legislation that requires councils to negotiate with local Citizens' Panels on measures to make communities more sustainable. This includes provisions for local pubs and local beers. Councils and the Citizens' Panels take proposals to the Local Government Association, which selects items for discussion with national government. The act has created a mechanism for individuals, groups and CAMRA branches to voice their concerns about lack of pubs in a community, closures of some outlets and the availability of beers from local brewers. For further information about the Sustainable Communities Act see the website **www.localworks.org.uk** or the CAMRA website **www.camra.org.uk**.

Heritage under threat

Geoff Brandwood reports on the campaign to save historic pub interiors

IN THIS GUIDE you will find some pubs marked with a solid or an outline star [★☆]. These are very special pubs where you can savour not only a great pint, but also a genuinely historic pub interior.

Sadly, there aren't many such pubs left. The pub is a great traditional institution, woven into the fabric of the British way of life, so it's ironic that drastic refurbishment over the past few decades means it is not easy to find one where the surroundings are as they were even 40 years ago, never mind 100.

The impressive mosaic bar counter of the Philharmonic

This was becoming apparent in the 1980s and led CAMRA to start identifying pubs throughout the country that still had historic layouts, furnishings and fittings. This epic pub crawl resulted in our National Inventory of Historic Pub Interiors, which is widely recognised as the definitive guide to such pubs and has been put to good use by English Heritage and Historic Scotland in their efforts to protect the best of our built heritage.

The National Inventory comes in two parts. Part One identifies pubs that are wholly or very largely intact since before the Second World War plus a few select examples down to the 1960s. Part Two contains those which, although altered, have particular rooms or features of national significance. The latest list, dated September 2009, records 197 pubs in Part One and 92 in Part Two. That means less than 300 for the whole country out of a total pub stock of some 57,000. These

The Philharmonic, Liverpool – on Part One of CAMRA's National Inventory

precious survivals deserve to be looked after.

The variety is huge. To highlight a few in this Guide, there are country classics such as the Red Lion, Ampney St Peter, Gloucestershire, the Birch Hall Inn, Beck Hole, North Yorkshire, and the Bell, Aldworth, Berkshire.

At the other end of the scale, there is the glitz and glitter from the golden age of pub building around 1900, including the two most spectacular examples in the country, the Crown Bar, Belfast, and the Philharmonic, Liverpool.

Other fantastic pubs from this era include the Victoria, Great Harwood, Lancashire and the Horseshoe Bar, Glasgow. Then there are the more restrained pubs from the inter-war era such as the British Oak, Birmingham, the Hand & Heart, Peterborough, and the Grill, Aberdeen.

There are town locals, too, like the Coachmakers, Stoke-on-Trent, and the Crown & Anchor, Llanidloes, Mid-Wales. The choice goes on. These are what CAMRA describes as Britain's True Heritage Pubs.

Find out about more about True Heritage Pubs by visiting our website **www.heritagepubs.co.uk**

This shows where they are, provides descriptions and pictures, and tells you how you can help in the campaign to identify and save them.

Enjoy your visits.

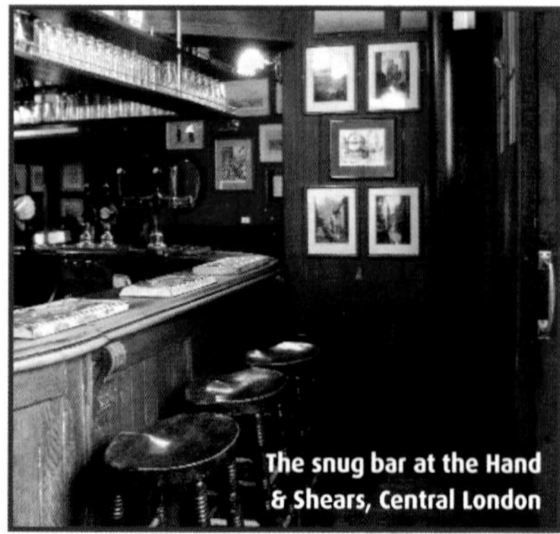
The snug bar at the Hand & Shears, Central London

SERVING UP SUCCESS

Real ale – it's the route to success

'THERE IS NOTHING which has yet been contrived by man by which so much happiness is produced as by a good tavern or inn.' It's a famous quote from the good doctor, Samuel Johnson. He was writing in 1791 and society has moved on. But the value of a good tavern, inn or public house remains a keystone of communities in towns and the countryside.

In Pubs and Places, published by the Institute for Public Policy Research in 2009, author Rick Muir describes the pub as 'more than just a retail business: it plays an important role at the heart of many local communities, providing a hub through which social networks can be maintained and extended.' A national poll carried out by IPPR found that 36 per cent of people considered the pub to be the best location where people meet and get together in their neighbourhood. That figures compared to 32 per cent who preferred other people's homes as a meeting place or 20 per cent who chose cafes and restaurants.

The report said that pubs were important in breaking down social barriers and welcoming people from different backgrounds. At the economic level, pubs inject an average of £80,000 a year into the communities. Pubs add more value to local economies than beer sold through shops and supermarkets because they generate more jobs.

Against that background, it's tragic that so many pubs are closing. But what is clear from all the market research carried out by CAMRA and other bodies is that pubs that serve real ale are more likely to succeed and even grow their business despite the current recession.

It's difficult to imagine a pub in a more difficult area than the Kelham Island Tavern in Sheffield. It's surrounded by empty buildings and factories, a sad sign of 'Steel City's' industrial decline. Yet the tavern is bright and welcoming, its blue-painted exterior decked out with flowers and shrubs.

The tavern, once run-down and neglected, has been open under new owners only since 2002. But since then it has been named CAMRA Sheffield Pub of the Year in 2004, 2005 and 2006, Yorkshire Pub of the Year four times and now, as the pinnacle of success, the current CAMRA National Pub of the Year.

In an unlikely area, it's cask beer that drives the pub's success. It has 11 handpumps and it concentrates in the main on beers from breweries within shouting distance. Owner Trevor Wraith and his manager Lewis Gonda are enthusiastic supporters of CAMRA's LocAle scheme, which encourages licensees to stock beers from breweries not more than 20 or 30 miles way and reduces 'beer miles'. One beer on the bar is the new Sheffield Brewing Co's Porter, brewed yards not miles away, in part of the former Blanco polish works.

Regular beers in the Kelham Island Tavern include Bradfield Farmer's Blonde from just outside Sheffield in the Peak District and Acorn Barnsley Bitter. Guest beers are drawn from, among others, Marston Moor near York and Marble in Manchester.

Kelham Island...breathing life back into the Sheffield beer scene, Trevor Wraith (top right) and Lewis Gonda (bottom right) concentrate on local beers for local drinkers 90% or their sales are cask beer

Trevor Wraith ran the Rutland Arms with great success in Sheffield. It was owned by Allied Breweries and the company allowed Trevor to run a vigorous guest beer policy. But when ownership passed to Punch Taverns the pubco threw out all the guest beers and only allowed Trevor to serve beers from its approved list.

He left the Rutland and bought the Kelham Island Tavern "for a song". It was, he says, in a terrible state. As a result of leaking water, timbers in the pub were rotten and the entire roof had to be rebuilt. He has since spent £150,000 on refurbishing interior and exterior. He's added a new back room that looks out over a pleasant beer garden.

The revamped tavern opened in March 2002. Lewis Gonda, a redundant steel worker, had worked with Trevor at the Rutland and switched to the tavern. Trevor and Lewis wanted a "shiny pub" with a welcoming exterior. They also had to get rid of the old clientele, mainly scrap-metal dealers with a reputation for fighting and drug-taking.

'We cleared them out – just froze them out,' Trevor says. 'I changed the beer range and drinkers started to come down from the Rutland. After just one year we won CAMRA's Sheffield Pub of the Year.'

The tavern has become a magnet for cask ale drinkers. Regulars include groups from Peterborough and Wakefield and now drinkers come from even further afield as a result of its national fame.

In 2002, the pub suffered horrendous flood damage when the whole of the Kelham Island area was several feet under. But it was soon up and running again, not only serving great pints but also simple pie-and-peas type meals for lunchtime regulars.

But beer is the belt-and-braces of the tavern. 'We can do as many as 30 different beers at the weekend,' Trevor says. 'I do three 18-gallon casks of Barnsley Bitter a week and we also sell a lot of mild – it's a big dark beer pub.'

The most astonishing fact about the tavern is that real ale accounts for 90 per cent of sales – most pubs would consider 40 per cent a successful percentage. And it doesn't have the local market to itself. Just a few minutes' walk from the tavern, the Kelham Island Brewery – a separate business – and its adjacent Fat Cat pub offer friendly but vigorous competition.

Thanks to the demand for cask beer – in particular, cask beer from local breweries – both pubs are putting the steel back into Steel City.

John Pascoe runs the Swan at Little Totham in Essex that could not be more different to the Kelham Island Tavern. It's rural, remote, several centuries old, with beamed ceilings and vast gardens. But John, too, bases his success on cask beer, which accounts for 75 per cent of his business. He has notched up the considerable achievement of winning CAMRA's National Pub of the Year trophy twice, in 2002 and 2005.

Swan, Little Totham...twice National Pub of the Year

Like Trevor Wraith, John concentrates on local beers, including Adnams, Crouch Vale, Farmers, Mighty Oak and Woodforde's. 'We give the customers what they want,' John says. 'We serve beer at the correct temperature from a perfect cellar. I'll change a customer's beer if he doesn't like the taste even though there's nothing wrong with it.'

He serves four beers a week and has a list of 10 regular beers and a vast range of guest beers. He stages an annual beer festival in June that ends on Father's Day and he will get through 100 beers during the event.

'The pub trade is going through troubled times,' John says. 'We had a dip in 2008 when the summer was so bad, but we pulled through. All over East Anglia, it's the pubs that sell real ale that are surviving and doing well. We don't sell very much lager and we have no "smooth-flow" keg beers at all.

'It's the pubs that don't serve the beers customers want or can only sell beers supplied by pubcos that are struggling.'

Another secret of John Pascoe's success is a simple but often neglected one: a warm welcome. A pub with the unique name of Land of Liberty, Peace & Plenty – a Chartist slogan from the 19th century – was a finalist in the 2007 National Pub of the Year awards. It was praised by the judges for its welcoming atmosphere.

Based at Heronsgate in Hertfordshire, it's everything a community pub should. It's popular with walkers and cyclists, it has a covered, heated outdoor area for families and stages food nights, beer tastings, quizzes, pubs games and live music. Beer festivals are held most bank holiday weekends and the cask beers are drawn mainly from local breweries, such as Red Squirrel and Tring.

John Pascoe (right) with a happy customer

In the IPPR report, the landlady of another rural pub in Hertfordshire spelt out why pubs are hubs of their communities. She said a wide range of civic activities take place in her pub and customers discuss both local issues and charitable events.

'There's been a lot of discussion recently about the widening of the M25, a big issue locally, mobile phone masts going up – things that affect people as local residents. We've just taken over the Neighbourhood Watch because we are a conduit for information. We advertise local events. There's a local choral group who meet here. We keep programmes for local theatres and cinemas so people can find out what's going on. We have collection boxes to raise money for local charities.'

That's the strength of the pub. It has deep roots in its community. It's the People's Parliament. And it serves living, breathing real ale. It beats supermarkets hands down...and it must be supported.

Land of Liberty, Peace and Plenty...community roots

A NUMBER OF ENTRIES IN THE GUIDE refer to the pubs' support for the LocAle system. This was devised by CAMRA members in Nottingham and is now spreading rapidly to other parts of the country. The aim is to get publicans to stock at least one cask beer that comes from a local brewery no further than 20 miles away. It also encourages publicans to use the Direct Delivery Scheme run by SIBA, the Society of Independent Brewers. SIBA members deliver direct to pubs in their localities instead of going through the central warehouses of pub-owning companies.

The aim is a simple one: to cut down on "beer miles". Research by CAMRA shows that food and drink transport accounts for 25 per cent of all HGV vehicle miles in Britain. Taking into account the miles that ingredients have travelled on top of distribution journeys, an imported lager produced by a multi-national brewery could have notched up more than 24,000 "beer miles" by the time it reaches a pub.

A Licensee's Guide to...
CAMRA
LocAle
CAMRA LocAle is a new accreditation scheme to promote pubs that sell locally-brewed real ale.
LOCAL BREWERY
MASS MARKET
IMPORTS
Reduce the miles the beer you serve travels from Brewery to Bar.
Help the environment and support your local breweries!
We are proud to serve locally-brewed real ale
CAMRA
LocAle
CAMRA accredited 2010

Supporters of LocAle point out that £10 spent on locally-supplied goods generates £25 for the local economy. Keeping trade local helps enterprises, creates more economic activity and jobs, and makes other services more viable. The scheme also generates consumer support for local breweries.

Support for LocAle has grown at a rapid pace. It's been embraced by pubs and CAMRA branches throughout England and has now crossed the border into Scotland.

For more information, see the CAMRA website **www.camra.org.uk** and type "locale" into the search window.

Pub of the Year

THE KELHAM ISLAND TAVERN beat off stiff competition from 200 other nominees to become the 2009 CAMRA National Pub of the Year. The other finalists in the competition were:

CROWN

154 Heaton Lane, Stockport, Great Manchester SK4 1AR

Lee Watts of the Crown said: 'We are both surprised and delighted to be in the final and it's a real testament to the good work everyone's put in'.

TOM COBLEY TAVERN

Spreyton, Devon EX17 5AL

Roger Cudlip, landlord of the Tom Cobley, said: 'We are simply over the moon to be in the final. We're a proper country pub serving 20 real ales and we're bucking the trend'.

ROYAL OAK

Friday Street, Rusper, West Sussex RH12 4QA

Sarah Blunden, landlady of the Royal Oak, said: 'Getting this far is all down to our wonderful local support. We serve a good range of beer from local brewers and their beer is of such good quality all I need to do is get people to drink it!'

KELHAM ISLAND TAVERN

62 Russell Street, Sheffield, Yorkshire S3 8RW

Selected as CAMRA's National Pub of the Year in 2008 after previously picking up many local and regional awards, this small gem was rescued from dereliction as recently as 2002. An impressive 10 permanent handpumps include two that always dispense a mild and a stout/porter, so you are sure to find something to suit your mood. In the warmermonths you can relax in the pub's multi-award winning beer garden.

The Pub of the Year competition is judged by CAMRA members. Each of the CAMRA branches votes for its favourite pub. They are judged on such criteria as customer service, decor, clientele mix, value for money and the quality of the cask beer. The 200 branch winners are entered into 16 regional competitions and then the 16 winners battle it out to reach the final four. Look out for the 🏆 symbol against entries in the Good Beer Guide indicating the branch pubs of the year that will compete for the 2010 title.

FROM BARLEY FIELD TO BAR

Real ale's living journey

HARVEYS BREWERY is quietly steaming at six in the morning. Brewhouse manager Peter Still says he has to "warm the pot" to start the brew. Rather like tea pots, his two mash tuns have been filled with boiling water and then emptied so that barley malt will start its journey in a heated environment.

The brewery is in Lewes, East Sussex. It dates from 1790 but was substantially rebuilt in Victorian times. It's based on the "tower" principle, which means the brewing process – from milling the grain to filling casks with finished beer – flows from floor to floor with the minimum use of pumps.

Today, Peter and his colleagues will make 120 barrels of Sussex Best Bitter and 60 barrels of a summer beer called Olympia. Head brewer Miles Jenner uses only Maris Otter barley malt from East Anglia. Miles, in common with many craft brewers, believes Maris Otter delivers a rich biscuity character to his beers and works in perfect harmony with his yeast culture. It's more expensive than other barley varieties but Miles says firmly: 'You need first-class ingredients to make first-class beer.'

One floor above the mash tuns are grist cases that hold freshly-milled grain. The bottom of the grist cases are shaped like funnels that feed the grain into the mash tuns below.

Miles and Peter consult their watches and a temperature gauge on the wall of the brewhouse. The cry goes up: 'Start the mash!' They pull on levers alongside the domed, stainless steel mash tuns and grain and water pour into the two vessels. The temperature of the mash is 149 degrees Fahrenheit – the old system is still used, equivalent to 65 degrees Celsius. The water used for brewing is known as "liquor" to distinguish it from mains water used for cleaning. Harveys brewing liquor comes from wells on the site and has percolated through the chalky Sussex Downs that surround Lewes. Before brewing starts, the liquor will have sulphates – calcium and magnesium — added. This is known as "Burtonising" and replicates the hard, flinty water of Burton-on-Trent, the historic home of pale ale.

The grain lowers the temperature of the mash. When it reaches 135 degrees F/57 degrees C, the valves are closed and grain and liquor stop flowing into the mash tuns. A rich aroma reminiscent of Ovaltine fills the brewhouse. Temperature is crucial. The malt – partially germinated barley – contains natural enzymes or chemical catalysts that finish germination during mashing, converting starch

in the grain into fermentable sugar. If the temperature is too low, the enzymes will work sluggishly and only partial conversion will take place. If the liquor is too hot it will kill the enzymes. To encourage the enzymes, more hot water is pumped into the tuns half an hour later to maintain the correct temperature.

The mash can now be left to its own devices. Miles goes on his daily rounds of the brewery.

Checking the mash temperature

Two floors down, in the fermentation rooms, he examines the progress of earlier brews. The vessels are high-sided to keep the heaving liquid from over-spilling on to the floor. There are pungent aromas of fruit – raspberries and strawberries – created by fermentation along with the heady tingle of natural carbon dioxide: yeast produces both alcohol and CO_2.

A brew that is 24 hours old has developed a thick white-brown head of yeast. A batch of Harvey's Mild Ale has what Miles describes as a "macaroni head" – less heavy and crusty – that indicates it's ready to be "skimmed": removing the yeast head for future brews while the beer matures. Fermentation lasts for three days, followed by four days cooling and conditioning.

Satisfied with the progress of the brews, Miles heads off to a store room where hops are being weighed for that day's new batch of beer. The room is filled with the piny, spicy and resinous aromas of hops. Miles is loyal to south-east England and buys his hops from Kent, Surrey and Sussex growers. His favoured varieties are Bramling Cross, Fuggles, Goldings and Progress. According to recipe, he will blend one or two varieties together: for example, Fuggles and Goldings are used for the bitterness of the Fuggle and the aroma of the Golding.

It's time to return to the mash tuns where the shout goes up: 'Set taps!' The first stage of the brewing cycle is complete and the run-off of the sweet, sugary liquid begins. Tall glass cylinders – wort receivers – by the sides of the mash tuns suddenly fill with liquid. The mash that will become Olympia is pale while Best Bitter, which is mashed with a proportion of darker crystal malt blended with pale, has a bronze colour.

The liquid, now known as wort, will take 2½ hours to slowly percolate through the thick cake of spent grain and out via the slotted base of the tuns. To ensure that no brewing sugars are left behind, mechanical arms in the roof of the tuns rotate, spraying or "sparging" the spent grain with more hot liquor.

After a break for breakfast, Miles Jenner returns to the brewery to continue checking the brews. In the laboratory next to his office, glass cylinders contain samples of recent brews that are monitored for clarity and yeast count. Any sign of a yeast infection must be detected to stop beers turning sour.

It's time for the copper boil. The worts have flown through the receivers to the coppers a few steps down from the brewhouse. The domed vessels – made as their name suggests from copper – act in a similar manner to coffee percolators. The hot wort gushes up from central columns while hops are emptied through a port hole in the sides of the vessels from large sacks known as pockets. The Ovaltine aroma of the malt turns to a piny and spicy one as the hops start to make an impact. To extract the maximum acids and tannins from the hops, the wort is boiled for 1¼ hours, with hops added late in the boil to add additional aroma and bitterness.

At 12.40 what is now "hopped wort" has been cooled and flows down to the fermenting vessels. Olympia and Best Bitter each get two buckets of thick creamy yeast added. Long paddles are used to vigorously mix the yeast into the wort.

Miles Jenner has one more visit to make – to the racking hall on the ground floor. This is a noisy, clanking area where metal casks are filled or racked with beer from earlier brews. Finings, a thick, glutinous liquid made by boiling isinglass, is added to the casks: finings attract yeast and protein in the beer and will slowly drag them to the foot of the casks in pub cellars.

Racking casks with fresh beer

By 2.30 the magic has started to work. Back in the fermenting room, a quietly heaving head of yeast like ice cream has developed on the brews mashed that morning. Two new batches of living, breathing cask beer are on their way.

Keeping a cool head

IAN SWANSON is meticulous and passionate about beer. He is surrounded by score sheets to mark every beer he tastes. But he breaks one golden rule: he drinks before "the sun is over the yard arm".

There's a good reason for that. Ian is a Cask Marque assessor. His job is to test the quality of real ale in pubs. It requires him to visit several pubs in the course of a day and that explains why he's sipping beer in the Mad Bear & Bishop at 11 in the morning.

Cask Marque is an organisation set-up and supported by most of Britain's brewers who make real ale. They realise that all the efforts made by brewers such as Harvey's into producing perfect pints can be ruined if the beer in the pub is not up to scratch. There's ample evidence to show that drinkers served a pint of warm, cloudy cask beer will move on to the nearest lager fount and never return.

More than 5,000 pubs in Britain now have a Cask Marque plaque, proof for customers that the real ale on tap should be in tip-top condition. But to keep publicans on their toes, Ian Swanson and 50 other assessors – many of them former brewers – descend unannounced twice a year on pubs in the scheme.

The Mad Bear & Bishop is an unusual pub, large, spacious and based above a shopping mall in London's Paddington station. It sells the full range of Fuller's beers and often one Gale's beer, now also brewed in Chiswick.

Ian, who used to work for Fuller's former London rival, Young's of Wandsworth, has to assess each cask beer for temperature, taste, aroma and appearance. The beers must score between 16 and 20 marks in each sector otherwise the pub will fail the assessment.

Temperature is crucial. Cask Marque, along with CAMRA, has been at pains for years to rid the real ale sector of the "warm beer" image. Cask Marque recommends a serving temperature of between 10 and 14 degrees Celsius.

Ian checks temperatures with a digital thermometer and screen. Immediately, he spots a problem. Chiswick Bitter registers 19.5 degrees, way off the Richter Scale. The appearance, he says, is bright rather than "polished" or crystal clear and the taste, not surprisingly, is warm and "estery" – yeasty and bready. He asks for a second half-pint but that is also far too warm at 19 degrees.

Discovery, Fuller's contribution to the new golden ale sector, registers 8.2 degrees C. Cask Marque scores such beers at between eight and 12 degrees. They are meant to be served at a lower temperature than traditional cask beers and Fuller's

All in a day's work...Ian Swanson takes emergency action in the cellar, tests the temperature of the beers and (below) gives marks out of 20

fits special coolers beneath the bar, attached to the beer engine operated by a handpump.

But as soon as Ian returns to the traditional cask beers, the problem is apparent again. London Pride is 20 degrees, ESB 20.1 and Gale's Seafarer 20. Ian suspects there's a problem in the cellar and heads off there with the manager. Cellar inspection is not part of Cask Marque's remit – that's a job for the brewery – but Ian is happy to help out. He swiftly finds the cause of the problem. Cask beer is pulled to the bar through "lines" or plastic tubes from cask to beer engine. The lines are encased in insulating tape and include a thicker tube that holds water at eight degrees, ensuring the beer remains cool on its journey to the bar.

Ian detects that the water from the cooling unit is not circulating, which accounts for warm beer at the bar. The manager immediately phones Fuller's who say that someone from the cellar services department will be at the pub within the hour. Ian has no doubt the beer will soon be restored to the correct temperature. But he will return within a month to check the pub again before he can pass it.

The Victoria in Strathearn Place, London W2, is another Fuller's pub. It's strikingly different to the bar at Paddington station. It's a small, street-corner local, with wood-panelling, leather settles and masses of Victorian bric-a-brac. Ian, needless to say, takes only a small sip of each beer, and finds no problems here. Chiswick, Pride and ESB all register temperatures of 11 degrees. The appearance is polished, the taste fine.

The Victoria passes his assessment with flying colours while back at Paddington Fuller's are already unblocking the water cooler. Nothing must stand in the way of cask beer tasting and looking fine, at a cool and delicious temperature.

In the beginning is the wort...

The brewing process from mash tun to bar

BEFORE YOU CAN RAISE A PINT IN THE PUB, enormous skill and the finest natural ingredients come together in the brewery to turn barley malt, hops, yeast and water into beer. The Good Beer Guide spent a day following the brewing skills at Harveys.

Harveys' classic tower brewery in Lewes, where the brewing process flows from floor to floor.

3 Pure water, known as "liquor", has percolated through the chalk downs of Sussex before reaching the brewery. Hot liquor is mixed in the mash tun with the malt grist. ▶ ▶ ▶

4 Head brewer Miles Jenner checks the temperature of the mash as brewing gets under way. Temperature is crucial to allow malt starch to turn into fermentable sugar. ▶ ▶ ▶

7 The hop store: Harveys uses traditional hop varieties from farmers in Sussex and surrounding counties. ▶ ▶ ▶

8 The copper, where wort is vigorously boiled with hops: the boil extracts acids and tannins from the hops that add aroma and bitterness to the beer. ▶ ▶ ▶

11 To keep the yeast working busily, turning malt sugar into alcohol, the fermenting beer is roused or oxygenated from time to time. ▶ ▶ ▶

12 Beer is racked into casks in preparation for the final destination: the pub cellar where it enjoys a vigorous second fermentation. ▶ ▶ ▶

❶ Malt – partially germinated barley – is stored at the top of the brewery. Harveys uses the classic Maris Otter variety. ◄◄◄

❷ Tom Riley adds malt to a hopper ready to be ground into grist. The grist is then dropped into the mash tun to start the brewing process. ◄◄◄

❺ At the end of the mash, the grain is "sparged" or sprinkled with hot liquor to wash out remaining malt sugars. ◄◄◄

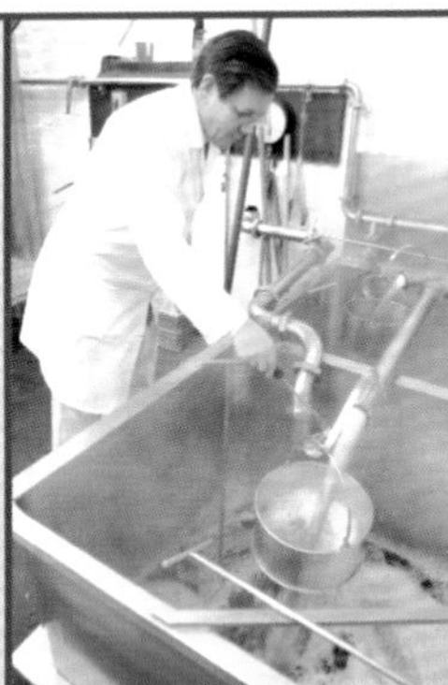

❻ The wort or sugary extract runs out of the mash tun into a receiving vessel where it is checked en route to the copper. ◄◄◄

❾ Some of the hops are added late in the boil for additional aroma and flavour. "Late hopping" restores any aroma lost earlier during the boil. ◄◄◄

❿ After the boil the hopped wort is cooled and transfered to a fermenting vessel. Yeast is "pitched" or blended into the wort to start fermentation. ◄◄◄

⓭ In the racking hall, Joe Tubb adds finings that will clear the beer of yeast and protein in the pub cellar. ◄◄◄

⓮ And finally... checking the quality of the finished beer in the pub. Another perfect pint is poured! ◄◄◄

CASK MARQUE

A word from our sponsor

BEING IN A GROWTH SECTOR has its rewards but also brings with it a few challenges. On the plus side, with more licensees taking cask ale as a serious business opportunity there are more pubs applying for Cask Marque accreditation.

By the end of 2009, over 5,500 pubs will have the award for the quality of their beer, building on an increase of 19% in the previous year.

A recent NOP survey of consumers showed that 46% of cask ale drinkers recognised the plaque, up from 31% in 2007, i.e. nearly one in two of cask ale drinkers. This consumer recognition encourages pubs to focus on their beer quality.

Cask Marque will continue to promote the accredited licensees and pubs to consumers by:

- Sponsoring the CAMRA Good Beer Guide
- Offering a unique text messaging service identifying your two nearest Cask Marque outlets (see below).
- A FREE software package that can be downloaded from the Cask Marque website **www.caskmarque.co.uk** to your satellite navigation system for consumers to locate with ease their nearest Cask Marque pubs while driving.

To find your nearest Cask Marque Pub by mobile sms

1. Text **Cask**
2. Followed by a **Full Stop**.
3. Then **where** (town or full/part postcode) e.g. **Cask.HP18 1PH**
4. Send to **60300**
5. You will receive back the **2** nearest outlets

Texts cost 25p plus your standard operator rate.
Numbers will be retained for future Cask Marque announcements.
To stop, text Cask stop to 60300 at anytime.

TO PASS THE CASK MARQUE VISIT

Cask Marque has 50 assessors covering the whole of the country, normally brewers, who will unannounced visit an outlet twice a year. The assessor will test up to six cask ales on sales for temperature, appearance, aroma and taste and each beer must pass otherwise the inspection is failed. In subsequent years the licensee has two further visits, one in the summer and one in the winter. All pubs are subject to random visits at any time. While visiting the pub the assessor will on a failure offer advice to correct the problem which may relate to equipment failure or poor cellar practices.

- The Cask Marque website instantly regenerates regional guides which can be downloaded by consumers
- Promoting Cask Ale Week – planned for Easter 2010

The challenges we face come from the learnings of the early 1990's when many pubs jumped onto the cask ale bandwagon but failed to deliver a quality pint thus disappointing consumers and contributing ultimately to the downturn of sales in the category. This can only be prevented by education of both the licensee and the consumer. Licensees must have the knowledge to handle cask ale in the cellar (Cask Marque delivered 215 cellar manager courses last year), and have the correct dispense equipment to deliver beer in the glass at 11-13°C (cellar cool). Consumers must learn to complain if they are unhappy about the quality of their beer, something which does not come naturally to many of us.

If you find poor quality cask ale, and in particular if they display the Cask Marque plaque, do contact us by email at **info@cask-marque.co.uk**. Also, why not tell us where you drink a great pint. Together we can become champions of cask ale quality.

NATIONAL
Cask Ale
WEEK
29th - 5th MARCH 2010

Stefan Brady, manager of the Betjeman Arms at St Pancras International, with Oz Clarke and Paul Nunny from Cask Marque toasting his success

BEER FESTIVALS & KEY EVENTS

THE CAMPAIGN FOR REAL ALE'S BEER FESTIVALS are magnificent shop windows for cask ale and they give drinkers the opportunity to sample beers from independent brewers rare to particular localities. Beer festivals are enormous fun: many offer good food and live entertainment, and – where possible – facilities for families. Some seasonal festivals specialise in spring, autumn and winter ales. Festivals range in size from small local events to large regional ones. CAMRA holds two national festivals, the National Winter Ales Festival in January, and the Great British Beer Festival in August; the latter features around 500 beers. The festivals listed are those planned for 2010. For up-to-date information, contact the CAMRA website: **www.camra.org.uk** and click on 'CAMRA Near You'. By joining CAMRA – there's a form at the back of the Guide – you will receive 12 editions of the Campaign's monthly newspaper What's Brewing, which lists every festival on a month-by-month basis. Dates listed are liable to change: check with the website or What's Brewing.

JANUARY

NATIONAL WINTER ALES (MANCHESTER)

Atherton – Bent & Bongs Beer Bash
Cambridge – Winter
Colchester – Winter
Exeter – Winter
Ipswich – Winter
Redditch
Salisbury – Winter

FEBRUARY

Battersea
Chelmsford – Winter
Chesterfield
Derby – Winter
Dorchester
Dover White Cliffs – Winter
Fleetwood
Gosport – Winter
Liverpool
Luton
Pendle
Stockton – Ale & Arty
Tewkesbury – Winter

MARCH

Bradford
Bristol
Burton – Spring
Darlington – Spring
Ely – Elysian (provisional)
Hitchin
Hove – Sussex
Leeds
Leicester
London Drinker
Loughborough
Oldham
Overton (Hampshire)
St Neots
Walsall
Wigan

APRIL

NATIONAL AGM & MEMBER'S WEEKEND – ISLE OF MAN

NATIONAL CASK ALE WEEK

Bexley
Bury St Edmunds – East Anglian
Chippenham
Coventry
Doncaster
Farnham
Glenrothes – Kingdom of Fife
Larbert – Falkirk
Maldon
Mansfield
Newcastle upon Tyne
Paisley
Skipton
Thanet

MAY

Mild Month

Banbury
Cambridge
Colchester
Halifax
Lincoln
Macclesfield
Newark
Newark & Notts Show
Newport (Gwent)
Northampton – Delapre Abbey
Reading
Rugby
Stourbridge
Stratford-upon-Avon
Wolverhampton
Yapton

JUNE

Aberdeen
Braintree
Cardiff – Great Welsh
Edinburgh – Scottish
Ely – Elysian (provisional)
Gibberd Garden – Harlow
Harpenden
Kingston
Lewes – South Downs
Southampton
St Ives (Cornwall)
Stafford
Stockport
Thurrock
Woodchurch – Rare Breeds

JULY

Ardingly
Boxmoor
Bishops Stortford
Bromsgrove
Canterbury – Kent
Chelmsford
Ealing
Derby
Devizes
Hereford – Beer on the Wye
Plymouth
Winchcombe – Cotswold
Woodcote – Steam Fair

AUGUST

GREAT BRITISH, LONDON
Barnstaple
Clacton
Grantham
Harbury
Peterborough
South Shields
Swansea
Watnall – Moorgreen
Worcester

SEPTEMBER

Ascot
Birmingham
Bridgnorth – Severn Valley
Burton
Chappel
Darlington – Rhythm 'N' Brews
Faversham – Hop
Hinckley
Ipswich
Jersey
Keighley
Letchworth
Lytham
Melton Mowbray
Minehead
Nantwich
Newton Abbot
North Cotswolds – Moreton-in-Marsh
Northwich
Rochford – Cider
Shrewsbury
Southport
St. Albans
St Ives (Cambs) – Booze on the Ouse
Tamworth
Ulverston

OCTOBER

CIDER MONTH
Alloa
Barnsley
Basingstoke
Bath
Bedford
Birkenhead
Cambridge – Octoberfest
Carlisle
Chester
Chesterfield – Market
Eastbourne
Heathrow
Huddersfield – Oktoberfest
Kendal
Louth
Milton Keynes
Norwich
Nottingham
Oxford
Poole
Quorn Octoberfest
Redhill
Richmond (N Yorks.)
St Helens

Sawbridgeworth
Sheffield
Solihull
Stoke-on-Trent – Potteries
Troon – Ayrshire
Wallington
Weymouth
Worthing

NOVEMBER

Bury
Dudley
Rochford
Saltburn
Wakefield
Wantage
Watford
Whitehaven
Whitchurch (Hampshire)
Woking
York

DECEMBER

Harwich
London – Pig's Ear

BRITAIN'S CLASSIC BEER STYLES

THE GOOD BEER GUIDE helps you deepen your appreciation of cask ale by detailing the styles listed in the breweries section. This year we single out two styles – Mild and India Pale Ale – that have made a remarkable recovery from near-oblivion.

Mild

Mild is a beer with its roots in the 18th and 19th centuries. It was developed as a result of a demand from drinkers – mainly those engaged in heavy agricultural or industrial labour – for a beer that was sweeter, lighter in body and cheaper than the prevailing dark and heavily-hopped porters and stouts of the time. Drinkers wanted a beer with some unfermented sugar that would act as a restorative after eight hours hard labour in field or factory.

This demand coincided with a growing need for commercial brewers to cut back on storage time for their beers. Beers such as porter, stout and the early IPAs were matured in wood for several months: in the case of Old Ale, for a year or more. They wanted a beer that could be served quickly once the brewing process was finished.

Mild Ale took its name from the fact that it was less heavily hopped than other beers. The name today is often an indication of a beer low in strength but that was not the case when the style developed in the 18th century: in those days it was called mild because it was not exceptionally bitter but strengths could be as high as 5 or 6 per cent alcohol. In 1871, in Herbert's Art of Brewing the typical strength of a Mild Ale was given as 1070 degrees, around 7 per cent in modern measurement.

Mild Ale was brewed with brown or mild ale malt – though this was replaced by most brewers in the 19th century when better-quality pale malt was developed. Brown or pale malts were blended with darker grains, caramel and special brewing sugars. Not all milds were dark in colour: due to demand, many brewers produced several milds, some light, others dark. McMullen's AK – the name derives from a 19th-century form of cask branding – is a now rare example of a light mild, as is Timothy Taylor's Golden Best. At the darker end of the spectrum, Sarah Hughes' Dark Ruby at 6 per cent is a classic example of a true Victorian-style strong Mild Ale.

Mild Ale – called Light in Scotland – remained the most popular style of beer in Britain until the 1950s. The decline of heavy industry and a general move towards lighter-coloured alcohols sent mild into almost terminal decline, replaced in popularity by Bitter and Pale Ale. A few regional brewers – Banks's, Bateman's, Batham, Holden's, Holts, Hydes, McMullen, Robinson's and Tetley, for example – remained true to the style and they have been joined in recent years by scores of new smaller craft brewers, whose large portfolios often include Mild Ale.

In truth, there is no national Mild Ale style: the beer varies from region to region to meet particular demand. Cain's Dark Mild in Liverpool and Holt's in Manchester are more roasty and bitter than is the norm. This reflects the fact that brewers in the North-west of England were competing with imported Irish Guinness and their beers had to reflect in some measure the roasted grain and bitter hop character of Dublin stout.

Mild Ale is back in favour, even though some brewers prefer not to use the term, fearing a "cloth-cap image". Enjoy the rich malty aromas and flavours with hints of dark fruit, chocolate, coffee and caramel and a gentle underpinning of hop bitterness – though hop bitterness will vary.

MILDS TO TRY

BATEMAN'S DARK MILD
BATHAM'S MILD ALE
BECKSTONES BLACK FREDDY
CAINS DARK MILD
HIGHLAND DARK MUNRO
RHYMNEY DARK
ST AUSTELL BLACK PRINCE

Old Ale

Old Ale recalls the type of beer brewed before the Industrial Revolution, stored for months or even years in unlined wooden vessels known as tuns. The beer would pick up some lactic sourness as a result of wild yeasts, lactobacilli and tannins in the wood. The result was a beer dubbed 'stale' by drinkers: it was one of the components of the early, blended Porters. The style has re-emerged in recent years, due primarily to the fame of Theakston's Old Peculier, Gale's Prize Old Ale and Thomas Hardy's Ale, the last saved from oblivion by O'Hanlon's Brewery in Devon. Old Ales, contrary to expectation, do not have to be especially strong: they can be no more than 4% alcohol, though the Gale's and O'Hanlon's versions are considerably stronger. Neither do they have to be dark: Old Ale can be pale and burst with lush sappy malt, tart fruit and spicy hop notes. Darker versions will have a more profound malt character with powerful hints of roasted grain, dark fruit, polished leather and fresh tobacco. The hallmark of the style remains a lengthy period of maturation, often in bottle rather than bulk vessels.

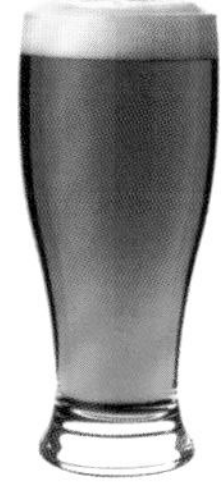

Bitter

Towards the end of the 19th century, brewers built large estates of tied pubs. They moved away from vatted beers stored for many months and developed 'running beers' that could be served after a few days' storage in pub cellars. Draught Mild was a 'running beer' along with a new type that was dubbed Bitter by drinkers. Bitter grew out of Pale Ale but was generally deep bronze to copper in colour due to the use of slightly darker malts such as crystal that give the beer fullness of palate. Best is a stronger version of Bitter but there is considerable crossover. Bitter falls into the 3.4% to 3.9% band, with Best Bitter 4% upwards but a number of brewers label their ordinary Bitters 'Best'. A further development of Bitter comes in the shape of Extra or Special Strong Bitters of 5% or more: familiar examples of this style include Fuller's ESB and Greene King Abbot. With ordinary Bitter, look for a spicy, peppery and grassy hop character, a powerful bitterness, tangy fruit and juicy and nutty malt. With Best and Strong Bitters, malt and fruit character will tend to dominate but hop aroma and bitterness are still crucial to the style, often achieved by 'late hopping' in the brewery or adding hops to casks as they leave for pubs.

Golden Ales

This new style of pale, well-hopped and quenching beer developed in the 1980s as independent brewers attempted to win younger drinkers from heavily-promoted lager brands. The first in the field were Exmoor Gold and Hop Back Summer Lightning, though many micros and regionals now make their versions of the style. Strengths will range from 3.5% to 5%. The hallmark will be the biscuity and juicy malt character derived from pale malts, underscored by tart citrus fruit and peppery hops, often with the addition of hints of vanilla and sweetcorn. Above all, such beers are quenching and served cool.

Pale Ale

The success of IPA in the colonial trade led to a demand in Britain for beer of a similar colour – the new style coincided with commercial glass-blowing and drinkers preferred a pale, clear beer to darker porters and stouts. But IPA, with its heavy level of hopping, was considered to be too strong for the domestic market and the brewers developed a beer dubbed simply Pale Ale that was lower in both levels of alcohol and hops.

Pale Ale was known as "the beer of the railway age", carried around the country from Burton-on-Trent by the new railway system. Brewers from London, Liverpool and Manchester built breweries in Burton to make use of the Trent waters.

Until the arrival of Bitter at the turn of the 19th century, Pale Ale was a dominant form of draught beer. But Bitter's popularity led to Pale Ale becoming mainly a bottled version. London brewers such as Watney and Whitbread grew their fame and fortune on the quality of their bottled Pale Ales. Today the style is overshadowed by Bitter but a true Pale Ale should be different, as pale as an IPA and brewed without the addition of coloured malts. It should have a spicy, resinous aroma and palate, with biscuity malt and tart citrus fruit. Marston's Pedigree, although dubbed a Bitter, is a fine example of a true Burton-style Pale Ale.

IPA

India Pale Ale – IPA – is the beer of the imperial age. It transformed brewing on a world scale and heavily influenced the producers of golden lager in central Europe. Until the Industrial Revolution, beers were coloured brown as a result of malt being gently roasted or "kilned" over wood fires. Once coke was invented, it was possible to control the heat in kilns and produce much paler malt.

Hodgson, a brewer in East London at the turn of the 19th century, used pale malt to develop a beer for export through the London docks to India. There was a strong demand from the Raj in India for a more refreshing beer than the dark porters and stouts being sent to the sub-continent. When Hodgson fell out with the all-powerful East India Company, it encouraged brewers in Burton-on-Trent to fashion beer for the India market. They were desperate for business, as sales of their brown beers to Russia and the Baltic States had been blocked during the Napoleonic Wars.

The Burton brewers found that the spring waters of the Trent Valley, high in sulphates, were ideal for brewing a pale beer, with the salts enhancing the flavours of malts and hops. Soon they were producing large volumes of "India beer", with the likes of Allsopp, Bass and Worthington dominating the market. The beers were truly pale, made with just pale malt and brewing sugar, and massively hopped to withstand the rigors of a three-month sea voyage to India. The strengths of IPA were around 7.5 per cent. International Bitterness Units, a measure of the hop content of beer, are thought to have been as high as 60 or 70 – 40 IBUs would be considered high today. Hops help keep beer free from infection, and infection was a risk on a tempestuous journey from England to India.

Soon IPA was being exported even further afield to the United States and Australasia. The demand was so enormous that by the end of the 19th century, Bass was the biggest brewer in the world.

But IPA's life span was short. The arrival of golden lager, ironically made possible by English pale ale, saw the style driven from most of the colonies and the U.S. Nearly a century has gone by before the style has undergone a major revival. The revival has been led by craft brewers in both the U.S. and Britain, who have delved deep into old recipe books to create genuine interpretations of the style. In Chicago, Goose Island IPA is arguably the finest American version of the style, while in Britain Marston's Old Empire and Meantime's IPA are just two of many modern versions that sizzle and zing with spicy and peppery hops, juicy malt and citrus fruit.

In July 2009, BrewDog of Fraserburgh launched Atlantic IPA, an 8 per cent ABV beer, based on traditional recipes from the 18th and 19th centuries. The beer was racked into wooden casks and then carried on a trawler in the North Sea for two months to replicate the voyage of an India Pale Ale in the 19th century.

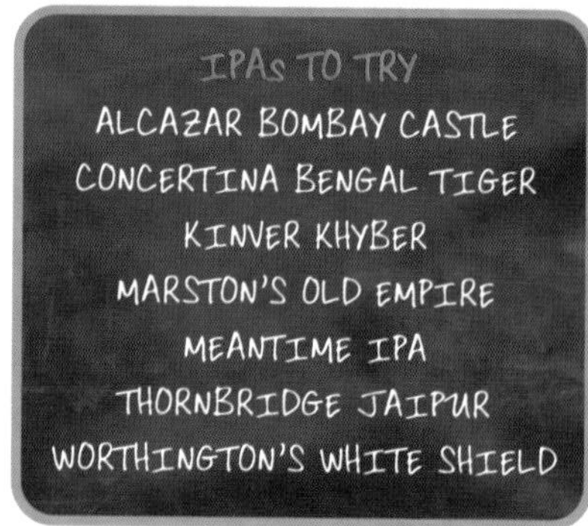

IPAs TO TRY
ALCAZAR BOMBAY CASTLE
CONCERTINA BENGAL TIGER
KINVER KHYBER
MARSTON'S OLD EMPIRE
MEANTIME IPA
THORNBRIDGE JAIPUR
WORTHINGTON'S WHITE SHIELD

Porter and Stout

Porter was a London style that turned the brewing industry upside down early in the 18th century. It was a dark brown beer – 19th-century versions became jet black – that was originally a blend of brown ale, pale ale and 'stale' or well-matured ale. It acquired the name Porter as a result of its popularity among London's street-market workers. The strongest versions of Porter were known as Stout Porter, reduced over the years to simply Stout. Such vast quantities of Porter and Stout flooded into Ireland from London and Bristol that a Dublin brewer named Arthur Guinness decided to fashion his own interpretation of the style. Guinness in Dublin blended some unmalted roasted barley and in so doing produced a style known as Dry Irish Stout. Restrictions on making roasted malts in Britain during World War One led to the demise of Porter and Stout and left the market to the Irish. In recent years, smaller craft brewers in Britain have rekindled an interest in the style, though in keeping with modern drinking habits, strengths have been reduced. Look for profound dark and roasted malt character with raisin and sultana fruit, espresso or cappuccino coffee, liquorice and molasses.

Barley Wine

Barley Wine is a style that dates from the 18th and 19th centuries when England was often at war with France and it was the duty of patriots, usually from the upper classes, to drink ale rather than Claret. Barley Wine had to be strong – often between 10% and 12% – and was stored for prodigious periods of as long as 18 months or two years. When country houses had their own small breweries, it was often the task of the butler to brew ale that was drunk from cut-glass goblets at the dining table. The biggest-selling Barley Wine for years was Whitbread's 10.9% Gold Label, now available only in cans. Bass's No 1 Barley Wine (10.5%) is occasionally brewed in Burton-on-Trent, stored in cask for 12 months and made available to CAMRA beer festivals. Fuller's Vintage Ale (8.5%) is a bottle-conditioned version of its Golden Pride and is brewed with different varieties of malts and hops every year. Expect massive sweet malt and ripe fruit of the pear drop, orange and lemon type, with darker fruits, chocolate and coffee if darker malts are used. Hop rates are generous and produce bitterness and peppery, grassy and floral notes.

Scottish Beers

Historically, Scottish beers tend to be darker, sweeter and less heavily hopped than English and Welsh ales: a colder climate demands warming beers. But many of the new craft breweries produce beers lighter in colour and with generous hop rates. The traditional, classic styles are Light, low in strength and so-called even when dark in colour, also known as 60/-, Heavy or 70/-, Export or 80/- and a strong Wee Heavy, similar to a barley wine and also labelled 90/-. In the 19th century, beers were invoiced according to strength, using the now defunct currency of the shilling.

Only accept perfect pints

Remember, you're the consumer, forking out a high price for beer, so don't be afraid to take your pint back to the bar if:

- It's either too cold or too warm. See the accompanying article on the work of Cask Marque assessors for recommended beer temperatures. Cask beer should be cool, not cold – but bear in mind that some golden ales are meant to be served at a lower temperature than milds and bitters. At the other end of the spectrum, it's a myth that real ale should be served at room temperature. Warm beer tastes bad, as the temperature creates unpleasant off flavours. If your beer smells of acetone, vinegar or stale bread, take it back.
- The pint has no head, is totally flat and out of condition.
- It's not only flat but hazy and has yeast particles or protein floating in the liquid.

If you get the response: "Real ale is meant to be warm and cloudy", invite the publican to join the 21st century. If the offending pub has a Cask Marque plaque, get in touch with Cask Marque. Otherwise let us know at the Good Beer Guide: **www.camra.org.uk**.

And please go back to the bar if you are served short measure – less than a pint of liquid in the glass. Drinkers lose millions of pounds a year as a result of short measure. It's an outrageous rip-off. CAMRA beer festivals serve beer in over-size glasses that ensure drinkers always get a full pint. Most pub owners refuse to use over-size glasses, preferring brim-measure glasses that allow them consistently to serve short measure. It's a scandal. Don't put up with it.

CAMRA'S BEERS OF THE YEAR

THE BEERS LISTED BELOW are CAMRA's Beers of the Year. They were short-listed for the Champion Beer of Britain competition in August 2009 and the Champion Winter Beer of Britain competition in January 2009. The August competition judged Dark and Light Milds; Bitters; Best Bitters; Strong Bitters; Golden Ales, Speciality Beers: and Real Ale in a Bottle. The winter competition judged Old Ales and Strong Milds; Porters and Stouts; and Barley Wines. Each beer was found by a panel of trained CAMRA judges to be consistently outstanding in its category, and they all receive a 'full tankard' [■] in the Breweries section.

DARK AND LIGHT MILDS

B&T Shefford Dark
Bank Top Dark Mild
Brains Dark
Goacher's Dark
Highgate Dark Mild
Highland Dark Munro
Rudgate Ruby Mild
Spire Dark Side of the Moon
St Austell Black Prince

BITTERS

Ashover Poets Tipple
Brimstage Trappers Hat
Butcombe Bitter
Farmer's A Drop of Nelson's Blood
High House Farm Auld Hemp
Humpty Dumpty Little Sharpie
Inveralmond Independence
Jarrow Rivet Catcher
Jennings Bitter
Moor Revival
Orkney Raven Ale
Purity Pure Gold
Purple Moose Snowdonia
Surrey Hills Ranmore Ale
Thornbridge Lord Marples
Triple fff Alton's Pride
Wye Valley Bitter

BEST BITTERS

Bath Gem
Beartown Kodiak Gold
Blythe Staffie
Brampton Best Bitter
Buntingford Britannia
Cairngorm Nessie's Monster Mash
Evan Evans Cwrw
Orkney Red McGregor
Southport Golden Sands
St Austell Tribute
Timothy Taylor Landlord
Vale VPA
West Berkshire Good Old Boy
Wolf Coyote
Wye Valley Butty Bach
Wylam Magic

STRONG BITTERS

Bath Barnstormer
Burton Bridge Stairway to Heaven
Grain Tamarind IPA
Inveralmond Lia Fail
Phoenix Wobbly Bob
Rhymney Export
Thornbridge Kipling
West Berkshire Dr Hexter's Healer
York Centurion's Ghost

GOLDEN ALES

Adnams Explorer
Brains SA Gold
Caledonian XPA
Dark Star American Pale Ale
Elland Beyond the Pale
Nottingham EPA
Salopian Shropshire Gold
St Austell Proper Job

OLD ALES & STRONG MILDS

Adnams Old
Bryncelyn Buddy Marvellous
Great Gable Yewbarrow
Sarah Hughes Dark Ruby
Orkney Dark Island
Theakston Old Peculier
Wells & Young's Winter Warmer

PORTERS AND STOUTS

Acorn Gorlovka Imperial Stout
Ascot Ales Anastasia's Exile Stout
B&T Edwin Taylor Stout
Beowulf Dragon Smoke Stout
Black Isle Organic Porter
Bristol Beer Factory Milk Stout
Bullmastiff Welsh Black
Cairngorm Black Gold
Church End Pews Porter
Elland 1872 Porter
Fuller's London Porter
Marble Stouter Stout
Nethergate Old Growler
RCH Old Slug Porter
Spire Sgt Pepper Stout
Townes Pynot Porter

BARLEY WINES

Hogs Back A over T
Sarah Hughes Snowflake
Oakham Attila
Otley 08

SPECIALITY BEERS

Amber Chocolate Orange Stout
Dark Star Espresso Stout
Dent Rambrau
Nethergate Umbel Magna
Otley O Garden
Skinner's Heligan Honey
Titanic Iceberg
Tryst Zetland Wheatbier
Wentworth Bumble Beer

REAL ALE IN A BOTTLE

Arran Milestone
Bridge of Allan 80/-
Cropton Endeavour
Dark Star Imperial Stout
Durham Temptation
Fox Nelson's Blood
Great Gable Yewbarrow
Green Tye Coal Porter
O'Hanlon's Port Stout
RCH Old Slug Porter
Titanic Stout
Wapping Summer Ale
White Shield Brewery Worthington's White Shield

CHAMPION WINTER BEER OF BRITAIN
Oakham Attila

CHAMPION BEER OF BRITAIN 2009
Rudgate Ruby Mild, 4.4% abv

ACHIEVEMENTS AND THE FUTURE

The price of beer drinkers' freedom is eternal vigilance

CAMRA WAS FORMED IN 1971 and it's fair to say that without such a vigorous and determined organisation we would all be drinking Britain's cold and bland apologies for European lager today.

The Campaign was born at a time when keg beers – filtered, pasteurised and over-carbonated beers – were replacing cask beer. New national brewers were taking over and closing regional plants in order to turn their keg beers into national brands.

The big brewers said drinkers preferred keg. CAMRA proved them wrong. Due to the Campaign's efforts, dreadful beers such as Watney's Red were laughed to oblivion. Regional brewers survived, revived and returned to cask beer production with enthusiasm.

CAMRA's achievements include the birth of the micro or small craft brewers' movement. There are now around 500 small, independent brewers, who bring much-needed diversity to the beer scene. In spite of all the problems facing pubs and brewers today, there's far more choice for beer drinkers now than when CAMRA was launched.

The Campaign has been at the forefront of many major changes during the past 30 years. When CAMRA started, pubs were able to open for only a limited number of hours each day. Now, with less restricted opening hours, we can enjoy a beer when we fancy one, not when the government permits it. In spite of constant sniping from some sections of the media, the new licensing laws have created a more pleasant pub environment with less hurried consumption of alcohol.

As a result of its reports to the British and European parliaments, the Campaign can argue effectively for measures to challenge the power of pub companies to deny drinkers choice and charge exorbitant prices for drinkers and rents for their tenants.

As this edition of the Guide shows, CAMRA is taking up the cudgels on behalf of all beer drinkers to demand an Office of Fair Trading investigation into the behaviour of the giant national pub companies. The pubcos charge higher prices for beer than in pubs run by free traders or independent brewers and their behaviour needs to be curtailed.

And we need urgent action to curb the outrageous behaviour of supermarkets and their "loss leader" beers that are driving pubs out of business.

All this activity is made possible as a result of CAMRA's growing membership. It's the grassroots members – all 100,000 of them – who choose the pubs for this Guide, keep a close eye on local breweries, monitor prices in pubs and organise hundreds of well-run beer festivals that act as shop windows for craft brewers and their beers.

Our voice with brewers, pub owners and government can become even greater if we continue to grow. If, like us, you love good, natural, living real ale and want to see it prosper for future generations to enjoy, then sign up today. Use the forms at the back of the Guide then join us at the bar or the nearest beer festival.

IT'S THE BEER THAT COUNTS

Choosing pubs for the Guide

THE GOOD BEER GUIDE is a masterpiece of local democracy. Unlike most pub guides, where entries are chosen by editors or submitted without checking by members of the public, the Good Beer Guide's strength is CAMRA's 100,000-plus members. CAMRA is divided into several hundred branches and each branch surveys the pubs in its area on a regular basis: not annually but regularly, often weekly. And democracy rules when the Campaign's branches meet to choose their entries from a short list. Votes are taken and the numbers are reduced to meet the allocations for each part of the country. Some members will be allowed to vote by postal ballot if they live in rural areas with poor transport links.

It's a system that has worked well for 37 editions and singles the Good Beer Guide out from pub guides with fewer full entries and a low turnover from one edition to the next. The Good Beer Guide is unique in its methods of selection and the ability to de-list pubs between editions as a result of updates in the Campaign's newspaper What's Brewing and on the CAMRA website.

The Guide is unique in one further and vital way. We begin with the beer. Not roses round the pub lintel, Turkish carpets, sun-dried tomatoes, drizzled olive oil and the temperature of the oak-aged Chardonnay. The Guide is committed to pub architecture, history, food and creature comforts. But, for us, the beer comes first. It has always been our belief that if a publican looks after the cask beer in the cellar then everything else in the pub – from welcome, through food, to the state of the toilets – are likely to receive the same care. CAMRA branches will de-list pubs if during the lifetime of the Guide beer quality falls below an acceptable standard.

All CAMRA members can vote for the quality of beer in pubs throughout the country by using the National Beer Scoring Scheme. The scheme uses a 0-5 scale for quality that can be submitted online. For more information about the scheme, go to **www.beerscoring.org.uk**.

We are especially proud of one aspect of the Guide: its coverage. We do not confine our entries to rural pubs or smart suburbs. We cover towns and cities where most people live and enjoy pubs in abundance. That doesn't mean we neglect rural areas. CAMRA has long campaigned to save village pubs, which are often the centre of life in isolated communities. Village pubs form an important element of the Guide, along with many others in suburban and urban areas. We are wedded to choice and attempt to offer good pubs serving good beer in all parts of the country.

We are also keen to hear from readers with recommendations for possible new entries or if you feel an existing one has fallen below expectations. Please use the Readers' Recommendations forms at the back of the book.

You can keep your copy of the Guide up to date by visiting the CAMRA website: **www.camra.org.uk**. Click on 'Good Beer Guide' then 'Updates to the GBG 2010' where you will find information on changes to pubs and breweries.

England

NORTHUMBER-LAND
TYNE & WEAR
CUMBRIA
DURHAM
NORTH YORKSHIRE
LANCASHIRE
EAST YORKS
WEST YORKS
GREATER MANCHESTER
MERSEYSIDE
SOUTH YORKS
CHESHIRE
DERBYSHIRE
NOTTINGHAM-SHIRE
LINCOLN-SHIRE
STAFFORD-SHIRE
SHROPSHIRE
LEICESTERSHIRE & RUTLAND
NORFOLK
WEST MIDLANDS
CAMBRIDGE-SHIRE
HEREFORD-SHIRE
WORCESTER-SHIRE
WARWICK-SHIRE
NORTHAMPTON-SHIRE
BEDFORD-SHIRE
SUFFOLK
BUCKINGHAM-SHIRE
HERTFORD-SHIRE
ESSEX
GLOUCS & BRISTOL
OXFORD-SHIRE
GREATER LONDON
BERKSHIRE
WILTSHIRE
SURREY
KENT
SOMERSET
HAMPSHIRE
WEST SUSSEX
EAST SUSSEX
DEVON
DORSET
ISLE OF WIGHT
CORNWALL

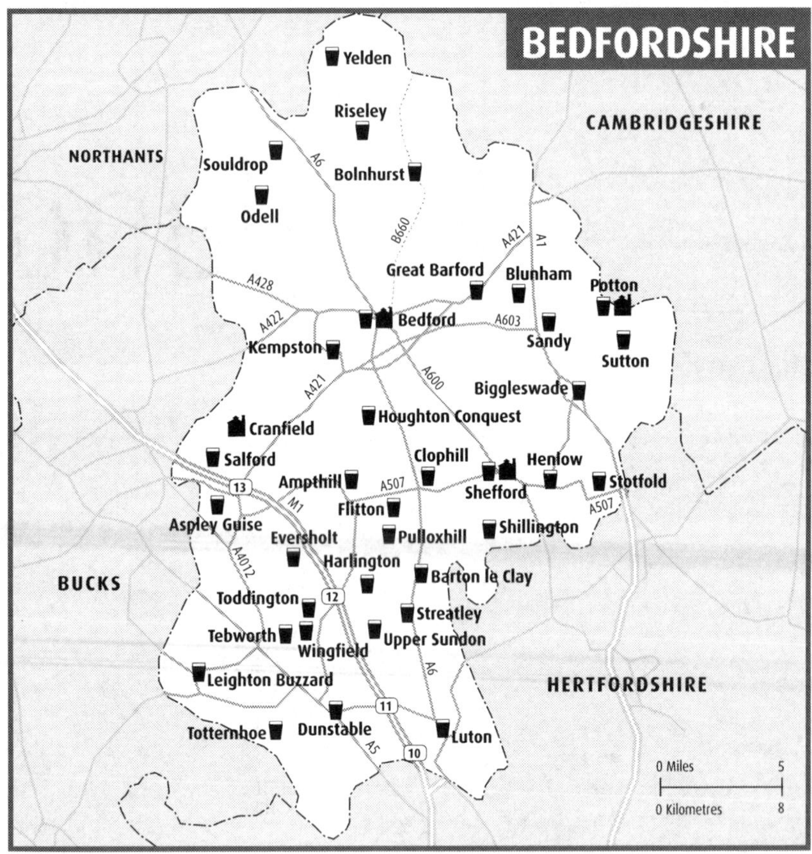

Ampthill

Old Sun

87 Dunstable Road, MK45 2NQ
✪ 12-11.30 (midnight Fri & Sat)
☎ (01525) 405466
Adnams Bitter, Broadside; St Austell Tribute; guest beers Ⓗ
Busy and cosy establishment on Ampthill's main street with two bars and a games room. There is a good selection of regular ales plus two guests. Popular with a good mix of people, and also dog friendly. The walls inside feature pictures of stars of screen and stage and a real fire adds a cosy feel in winter. There are ample decked and lawned areas to the rear and tables to the front. Snacks are served at lunchtimes (not Sun). ⌂❀◐⊟⊡♣P⁻

Queens Head

20 Woburn Street, MK45 2HP
✪ 12-11 (10.30 Sun)
☎ (01525) 405016
Wells Eagle IPA, Bombardier; guest beers Ⓗ
Cosy 18th-century tavern in a historic area of Ampthill close to the park and the Greensand Ridge walk. Inside is a low-beamed saloon bar, lounge and room which can be hired for private functions. Bar snacks are available all day. The pub's name refers to Katherine of Aragon who was imprisoned in Ampthill Castle while Henry VIII dissolved the monasteries and broke from the church of Rome. Regular beer festivals are held. ❀◐◑⊟♿♣⁻

Aspley Guise

Wheatsheaf ✔

Mount Pleasant, MK17 8JZ SP948359
✪ 12-11 (10.30 Sun)
☎ (01908) 583338
Wells Eagle; Young's Special; guest beer Ⓗ
Late Victorian two-bar Charles Wells pub just outside Aspley Guise. A locals' pub, the wood-panelled main bar is always busy and features a Northamptonshire skittles table as well as often interesting banter with the landlord and landlady. Two mini beer festivals a year have become a regular feature. No food is served but a Ramblers Menu can be provided if requested in advance. There is a large garden and camping.
⌂❀⊟▲⊡(10)♣P⁻

Barton-le-Clay

Bull

77 Bedford Road, MK45 4LL
✪ 12-2, 6-1am (2am Fri & Sat); 12-midnight Sun
☎ (01582) 705070

INDEPENDENT BREWERIES

B&T Shefford
Potton Potton
Wells & Young's Bedford
White Park Cranfield

ENGLAND

Adnams Broadside; Sharps Doom Bar; guest beers Ⓗ
Oak-beamed pub in the centre of the village, popular with a varied clientele. Two constantly changing guest beers from the Enterprise Inns' SIBA list are always on offer. Food is served lunchtimes (not Mon or Sat) and Wednesday evening. The pub has dominoes and darts teams and a pool table. A large function room is available to hire where the Barton Folk Club plays on Wednesday, with an audience welcome. Acoustic music is live in the bar every Thursday.
⌂❀♿🚌♣P⚐

Bedford

Cricketers Arms

35 Goldington Road, MK40 3LH (on A428 E of town centre)
⏲ 5 (6.30 Sun)-11
☎ (01234) 303958 🌐 cricketersarms.co.uk
Adnams Bitter; guest beers Ⓗ
Small, friendly, one-bar pub near the Bedford Blues rugby ground, popular with fans of the game and very busy on match days. It opens at noon on Saturday for home games. Live rugby is shown and there is early opening on Sunday for Six Nations games. Guest beers are from Punch Taverns' Finest Cask selection, with a Welsh bias owing to the landlord's origins. There is a covered, heated courtyard for smokers and drinkers. No evening meals are available on Sunday and Monday.
❀◗🚌(5,X5)⚐

Devonshire Arms ✔

32 Dudley Street, MK40 3TB (1 mile E of town centre south of A428)
⏲ 5.30 (2 Fri)-11; 12-11 Sat; 12-11 Sun
☎ (01234) 359329
Wells Eagle IPA, Bombardier; guest beers Ⓗ
Pleasant two-bar local in a quiet residential area east of the town centre near Russell Park and The Embankment. The landlady worked for the Charles Wells brewery for 24 years so knows the trade well and hosts an annual beer festival in May. Good wine is served by the jug. The garden has a smoking area and a lighted and heated covered space for non smokers. Hanging baskets adorn the exterior in summer. ❀⊟🚌(4)♣⚐

Three Cups 🏆

45 Newnham Street, MK40 3JR (200m S of A428 just before rugby ground)
⏲ 11-11; 12-10.30 Sun
☎ (01234) 352153
Greene King XX Mild, IPA, Abbot, seasonal; guest beers Ⓗ
Though just five minutes from the town centre and close to Bedford rugby ground, this 1770s inn with old-style wood panelling has a village pub feel and a welcoming atmosphere. A popular lunchtime menu is available, with a wide range of food served in generous portions. Roast dinners feature on Sunday. The pleasant garden has a heated smoking shelter. Dogs are welcome in the public bar and garden. Quiz night is a highlight on Tuesday. CAMRA North Beds Pub of the Year 2009.
❀◖⊟♿🚌♣P⚐

Wellington Arms ✔

40-42 Wellington Street, MK40 2JX (off A6 north of town centre)
⏲ 12-11 (10.30 Sun)
☎ (01234) 308033
Adnams Bitter; B&T Two Brewers; guest beers Ⓗ
Street-corner B&T house offering a wide range of regional and micro-brewery beers, plus real cider and perry from 14 handpumps. A range of draught and bottled Belgian and imported beers is also available. Breweriana abounds throughout. Filled rolls are on offer (not Sun). The courtyard is partly covered for drinkers and smokers. Street parking is limited but there is a multi-storey car park adjacent. A superb mixed clientele makes this a very friendly pub to visit. Local CAMRA Pub of the Year 2008. ❀🍎⚐

White Horse ✔

84 Newnham Avenue, MK41 9PX (on A5140 off jct with A428)
⏲ 11 (12 Sun)-11
☎ (01234) 409306 🌐 whitehorsebedford.co.uk
Wells Eagle IPA, Bombardier; guest beers Ⓗ
Large suburban pub with a central bar. Good value food is available, with a Sunday roast and occasional themed evenings. Quiz nights are Tuesday and Sunday, and open-mike night is Monday. The licensees and staff have won several brewery and local business awards. A May Day weekend local beer and food festival and a November Beer and Banger Festival are hosted annually. ❀◖◗♿🚌(4)P⚐

Biggleswade

Golden Pheasant 🏆 ✔

71 High Street, SG18 0JH
⏲ 11-11 (midnight Fri & Sat)
☎ (01767) 313653 🌐 goldenpheasantpub.co.uk
Wells Eagle IPA; guest beers Ⓗ
Situated close to the market place and a few minutes' walk from the railway station, the Pheasant has a low ceiling and oak beams contributing to a cosy atmosphere. Local beer enthusiasts enjoy five guest ales sourced from far and wide, many coming from local micro-breweries, alongside the regular Wells & Young's beers. Regular quiz and chess evenings are hosted. Home-cooked Sunday lunches are a highlight.
⌂❀◖⇌🚌⚐

Stratton House Hotel

London Road, SG18 8ED
⏲ 11-11 (midnight Fri & Sat)
☎ (01767) 312442
Wells Eagle IPA, Bombardier; guest beers Ⓗ
Located at the top of the High Street, the Stratton, originally a mansion house, is now a large hotel with 32 bedrooms and a function room. It caters for a mixed clientele, offering a relaxed atmosphere amidst bright decor and comfortable seating. The large restaurant opens daily and meals are also served in the bar area. In addition to ales from Charles Wells, two guest beers change every few weeks, occasionally coming from local micro-breweries. 🛏◖◗♿⇌🚌P⚐

Wheatsheaf ✔

5 Lawrence Road, SG18 0LS
⏲ 11-4, 7-11; 11-11.30 Fri-Sun
☎ (01767) 222220
Greene King XX Mild, IPA Ⓗ
This one-bar, end-of-terrace local is situated on a quiet street and has a small garden at the rear. Inside, the predominantly male clientele contributes to a vibrant atmosphere with the conversation focusing on good beer and sporting

events. The pub is home to dominoes and cribbage teams, and has a large-screen TV for the avid football fans. This is a rare outlet in the area for mild beer. ❀≈♣⊁

Blunham

Salutation

20 High Street, MK44 3NL

⏲ 11-3, 5-midnight (1am Fri & Sat); 11-10.30 Sun

☎ (01767) 640620 🌐 thesalutationblunham.co.uk

Greene King XX Mild, IPA; guest beers Ⓗ

This fine pub is situated in the village centre. The front of the building dates from the early 17th century and features leaded windows. There is a large public bar with skittles and a games room with pool table. Behind the bar is a function room. The five handpumps dispense Greene King beers and guests, some from local micros. Barbecues are hosted in summer and live music plays monthly. ⛰❀◖◗♿🚌(E3)♣🍎P⊁

Bolnhurst

Plough ✔

Kimbolton Road, MK44 2EX (on B660 at S end of village)

⏲ 12-3, 6.30-11; closed Mon; 12-3 Sun

☎ (01234) 376274 🌐 bolnhurst.com

Beer range varies Ⓗ

Full of character, this award-winning pub and restaurant offers excellent food and good service. The main bar features a modern open fireplace with a view through to the kitchen. A second room is set aside for diners. Outside is a large drinking area alongside the car park. Three handpumps dispense a range of beers including local micro-brews. The pub is closed from Christmas until the second week of January. ⛰Q❀◖◗♿🚌(153)P

Clophill

Stone Jug

10 Back Street, MK45 4BY (off A6 at N end of village)

⏲ 12-3, 6-11; 12-11 Fri & Sat; 12-10.30 Sun

☎ (01525) 860526

B&T Shefford Bitter; Black Sheep Best Bitter; Young's Bitter; guest beers Ⓗ

Originally three 16th-century stone cottages, this popular village local has an L-shaped bar that serves two drinking areas and a family/function room. Excellent home-made lunches are served Tuesday to Saturday. There are picnic benches at the front and a rear patio garden for outdoor drinking in fine weather. Parking can be difficult at busy times. Bedfordshire CAMRA Pub of the Year 2006. Q🐎❀◖🚌(J1,S1)♣🍎P⊁

Dunstable

Globe 🏆

43 Winfield Street, LU6 1LS

⏲ 12-11 (midnight Fri & Sat); 12-10.30 Sun

☎ (01582) 512300

B&T Two Brewers, Shefford Bitter, Black Dragon Dark Mild, Dunstable Giant, Edwin Taylor's Extra Stout; guest beers Ⓗ

Acquired and reopened in a rush by B&T in 2005 (the temporary plank in the bar has become a permanent feature), this dog-friendly pub with a chequered past quickly acquired a loyal local and beer destination following. The five guest beers are all from micro-breweries – the Dunstable Giant is named after the popular previous landlord, the late Mel Hall. Twenty plus Belgian bottled beers are also stocked. Folk night is Tuesday. South Beds CAMRA Pub of the Year 2007/08/09. Q❀♿♣🍎⊁

Star & Garter

147 High Street South, LU6 3SQ

⏲ 12-midnight; 11-1am Fri & Sat; 12-10.30 Sun

☎ (01582) 661044

Beer range varies Ⓗ

A friendly locals' pub where the landlord usually serves from a constantly rotating range of real ales including some interesting choices. This traditional two-bar street-corner pub has TV showing sporting events as well as pool, darts, dominoes and crib. Quiz night is Thursday. Freshly-made sandwiches are available all day (to 9pm Fri & Sat). Smokers may use the covered rear courtyard area. ❀◻♿♣⊁

Victoria

69 West Street, LU6 1ST

⏲ 11-12.30am (1am Fri & Sat)

☎ (01582) 662682

Beer range varies Ⓗ

A popular town centre pub which usually offers four ales including a house beer, Victoria Bitter, from Tring Brewery. The ever-changing guest ales are from micro and regional breweries. Good value food is available until early evening Monday-Friday, and Saturday and Sunday lunchtimes. Darts and dominoes are popular and televised sport features in the bar. Quarterly beer festivals are held. There is no admittance after 11pm. ❀◖🚌(61)♣⊁

Eversholt

Green Man

Church End, MK17 9DU SP984325

⏲ 12-2.30 (not Mon), 5-11; 12-11 Sat; 12-3 Sun

☎ (01525) 288111 🌐 greenmaneversholt.com

Fullers London Pride; guest beers Ⓗ

A substantial early Victorian building situated opposite the church, built when the village formed part of the Woburn estate. It is now a genuine, privately-owned free house with two guest ales — one usually from a local brewery. Well supported by the village, it is also popular with walkers. Refurbished recently to a high standard, it has a modern flagstone floor and exposed fireplaces in the main bar area. A separate restaurant area offers good quality meals. Outside is a large patio and garden. ⛰Q❀◖◗♿♣P⊁

Flitton

Jolly Coopers

Wardhedges, MK45 5ED

⏲ 12-3 (not Mon), 5.30-11.30; 12-midnight Sat; 12-11 Sun

☎ (01525) 860626

Wells Eagle IPA; guest beers Ⓗ

Charming Charles Wells village pub with a traditional flagstone floored bar and a restaurant to the rear. Two varying guest beers are sourced from a variety of brewers. The pub is the hub of the little community of Wardhedges and is home to various local interest groups and games teams. The restaurant is closed on Monday evening but hearty, home-cooked meals are available in the bar. ⛰❀◖◗♿♣P⊁

Great Barford

Anchor Inn ✓

High Street, MK44 3LF (by river bridge, 1 mile S of village centre)
12-3, 6 (5.30 Fri)-11; 12-11 Sat; 12-4, 6.30-10.30 Sun
☎ (01234) 870364
Young's Bitter; guest beers Ⓗ
Busy local pub situated next to the church overlooking the River Great Ouse. At least two guest beers are usually available. Good home-cooked food is served in the bar and restaurant as well as a fine selection of wines. The pub is popular with river users in the summer. Occasional themed nights, usually in winter.

Harlington

Carpenters Arms

Sundon Road, LU5 6LS
6-11 Mon; 12-midnight Tue-Sat; 12-10.30 Sun
☎ (01525) 872384 the-carpenters-arms.com
B&T Shefford Bitter; Taylor Landlord; Young's Bitter; guest beer Ⓗ
This authentic low-beamed, friendly local was first licensed in 1790. The wooden-floored traditional village (public) bar, lounge and carpeted snug effectively provide three very different atmospheres in the same pub. Good traditional bar food is cooked and served by the landlady at lunchtime, with a more extensive evening and Sunday menu. The railway station and occasional bus service along with a good range of pleasant county walks make this an ideal place to start or finish your journey. (X42)

Henlow

Engineers Arms ✓

68 High Street, SG16 6AA
12-midnight (1am Fri & Sat)
☎ (01462) 812284 engineersarms.co.uk
Beer range varies Ⓗ
Multiple CAMRA award-winning free house, featuring 10 handpumps with constantly changing beers from across the nation. A firm favourite with real ale buffs, it also offers several real ciders and a perry. This lively community pub provides live music, poker evenings and two large-screen TVs for sports coverage. The pub runs regular beer festivals and organises brewery trips, including visits to its adopted twin town of Dinslaken, Germany.
(82,M1)

Houghton Conquest

Knife & Cleaver

The Grove, MK45 3LA (between B530 and A6, opp church)
12-3, 6.30-11; 12-10.30 Sun
☎ (01234) 740387 theknifeandcleaver.co.uk
Potton Village Bike; guest beer Ⓗ
Dating from 1796 or possibly earlier, this attractive hotel, bar and restaurant has a reputation for friendly staff, good food, fine wines and quality real ales. Light meals and snacks are served in the bar. Seafood is a speciality in the restaurant (booking essential). The delightful garden is an ideal to place to while away an hour or two in the summer. En-suite accommodation is available.
(J2)

Kempston

Half Moon ✓

108 High Street, MK42 7BN
12-3 (4 Sat & Sun), 6 (5 Fri, 7 Sat & Sun)-11
☎ (01234) 852464
Courage Best Bitter; Wells Eagle IPA, Bombardier Ⓗ
This pub, which is well supported by the local community, has a comfortable lounge bar and a public bar with traditional games. It runs a number of teams in local leagues. There is a large garden with a children's play area which is well used in good weather. The River Great Ouse is nearby with its popular walks. Lunches are served Monday to Saturday and evening meals Monday to Friday.

Leighton Buzzard

Hare

10 Southcott Village, Linslade, LU7 2PR
3 (5 Tue)-11.30; 12-midnight Fri & Sat; 12-10.30 Sun
☎ (01525) 373941
Courage Best Bitter; Fuller's London Pride; Tring Buck Bitter; guest beers Ⓗ
Over the years the village of Linslade has expanded and it is now part of the town of Leighton Buzzard. This popular local overlooks the village green, attracting a good mix of drinkers. Two or three regularly changing guest beers, usually from local micros, are on offer. An annual St George's Day beer fest is held in a marquee in the large rear garden. There is a heated smoking area outside.
(36)

White Horse ✓

9 New Road, Linslade, LU7 2LS
12-midnight (11 Sun)
☎ (01525) 635739
Fuller's London Pride; Greene King IPA; guest beers Ⓗ
Genuine back-street free house, close to the Grand Union Canal and railway station. Since reopening in 2007 the owners have built up a good loyal trade. Up to three guest beers are served, often including one from a local brewery. Accommodation is available in a converted stable block and there is a small public car park across the road. Food and additional parking are provided by its sister pub nearby, The Ship. Local CAMRA Most Improved Pub of the Year 2008.

Luton

Black Horse

23 Hastings Street, LU1 5BE
2 (1 Sat)-11; 1-10.30 Sun
☎ (01582) 450994
Beer range varies Ⓗ
Single-room pub with a pool table at one end and home to teams in Monday and Thursday pool leagues. Seven handpumps dispense three to five regularly changing ales as well as Westons Old Rosie cider. A beer festival is held annually in November. A DJ plays gothic rock on the third Thursday of the month, and there is occasional live music. The jukebox has a wide selection of music, but does not appear to have a quiet setting! Dogs are welcome.

Bricklayers Arms ✓

16-18 High Town Road, LU2 0DD
12-11 Mon; 12-3, 5-11 Tue-Thu; 12-midnight Fri & Sat; 12-10.30 Sun

☎ (01582) 611017
Everards Beacon, Tiger; guest beers Ⓗ
This somewhat quirky town centre pub has been run by the same landlady for more than 21 years. Three ever-changing guest beers, displayed on a notice board, are served – on average 10 a week – sourced mainly from micro-breweries. There are also three draught Belgian beers and a modest selection of foreign bottled beers. Popular with Hatters fans, the pub's two TVs show football. Monday is quiz night. Pub lunches are served 12-2pm Monday to Friday. ❀ℂ⇌♣P⁵⁻

English Rose
46 Old Bedford Road, LU2 7PA
✪ 12-11
☎ (01582) 723889 🌐 englishroseluton.co.uk
Beer range varies Ⓗ
Friendly street-corner community local. Four frequently changing guest beers are chosen from a range of breweries nationwide, with more than 500 on offer in 2008. Food is served Tuesday to Friday lunchtime and until early evening on Saturday, with a takeaway service. The quiz on Tuesday evening is a highlight. The garden accommodates both smokers and non-smokers in four specially designed heated huts. An annual beer festival is held. ❀ℂ♿⇌🚌⁵⁻

Globe
26 Union Street, LU1 3AN
✪ 11 (12 Sun)-midnight
☎ (01582) 728681
Caledonian Deuchars IPA; Greene King IPA; guest beers Ⓗ
Popular one-room street-corner local, just out of the town centre. The Caledonian Deuchars is often replaced by Sharps Doom Bar. A frequently changing guest ale is also on offer, generally of a premium strength from a micro or regional brewery. Beer festivals are occasionally staged. Sport is shown on TV and good value food is served Monday to Saturday lunchtime. Outside there is a large patio and heated smoking shelter. ❀ℂ♣P⁵⁻

Odell

Bell
Horsefair Lane, MK43 7AU
✪ 11.30-3 (12-4 Sat), 6-11.30; 12-4, 7-10.30 Sun
☎ (01234) 720254
Greene King IPA, Abbot; guest beers Ⓗ
Handsome, thatched, village pub with a large garden near the River Great Ouse. With the Harrold Odell Country Park just down the lane, this is a popular stop for walkers. Sympathetic refurbishment and a series of linked but distinct seating areas help retain a traditional pub atmosphere. A good food menu offers small portions at lunchtime. ⋒Q❀ℂ◗🚌(125)P⁵⁻

Potton

Rising Sun ✔
11 Everton Road, SG19 2PA
✪ 12-2.30, 6-11 (midnight Fri); 12-midnight Sat; 12-11 Sun
☎ (01767) 260231
St Austell Tribute; Wells Eagle IPA; guest beers Ⓗ
A covered well is the main feature of the wood-beamed bar area, which is divided into many sections creating intimate environments for dining or undisturbed conversation. There is a separate games area, an upstairs function room, a covered patio and rooftop terrace. Up to four guest ales are available featuring smaller micro-breweries. Food is served every day until 9.30pm including weekly specials and Sunday roasts. ❀ℂ◗🚌(E1,E2)♣P⁵⁻

Pulloxhill

Cross Keys ✔
13 High Street, MK45 5HB
✪ 12-3, 5.30-11; 12-10.30 Sun
☎ (01525) 712442
Adnams Broadside; Wells Eagle IPA, Bombardier Ⓗ
This oak-beamed inn is a popular venue for dining due to the good home-made specials. The large restaurant area can also be used for private functions. The pub is well known locally for its live jazz on a Sunday night. Extensive grounds include a children's play area next to the car park and another area where the local archery group practise. Q❀ℂ◗♿⛺🚌♣P⁵⁻

Riseley

Fox & Hounds ✔
High Street, MK44 1DT
✪ 11.30-2.30, 6.30-11; 12-3, 7-10.30 Sun
☎ (01234) 708240
Wells Eagle IPA, Bombardier; guest beers Ⓗ
Old village inn, originally two 16th-century cottages complete with a priest's hiding hole and resident ghosts. It has a reputation for good food, with charcoal-grilled steak a speciality, sold by weight and served with a choice of side orders. The dining room can be reserved for parties, but booking is unnecessary for bar meals – relax over a pint while your food is cooked. The large lawned garden includes a covered patio with heaters. Q❀ℂ◗🚌(152)P⁵⁻

Salford

Red Lion Country Hotel
Wavendon Road, MK17 8AZ (2 miles N of M1 Jct 13)
✪ 11-2.30, 6.30-11
☎ (01908) 583117 🌐 redlionhotel.eu
Wells Eagle IPA, Bombardier Ⓗ
Recently refurbished traditional country hotel serving a fine choice of home-cooked food in the bar and restaurant. The bar, warmed by an open fire in winter, offers a selection of board games. The large garden has a covered area and secure children's play area. Accommodation is in six rooms, some with four-poster beds. ⋒Q❀🛏ℂ◗🛈♿●P⁵⁻

Sandy

Queen's Head
244 Cambridge Road, SG19 1JE
✪ 11.30-11; 12-11 Sun
☎ (01767) 681115
Greene King IPA, Abbot; guest beers Ⓗ
Step back in time to this traditional 18th-century inn located close to the market square and formerly known as the Maidenhead. The interior retains many original features including a large open fire which radiates through the L-shaped bar and separate dining area. The relaxed and friendly atmosphere has an olde world feel to it. Lunches are served daily and the house speciality is Sunday roast. ⋒Q❀ℂ♿⇌🚌P

Sir William Peel ✔

39 High Street, SG19 1AG (opp church)
⏲ 12 (11 Sat)-midnight; 12-10.30 Sun
☎ (01767) 680607
Theakston Best Bitter; guest beers Ⓗ
Large open-plan free house with a single bar split into public and saloon sections. An ever-changing range of three guest ales is supplied by independent breweries. Customer participation is encouraged with regular quiz, disco and open mike nights. Although no food is served, there are restaurant and take-away facilities nearby. The pub name commemorates the local creator of the extended railway line between Sandy and Potton, which no longer operates. ❀♿⇌🚌(178)P⊬

Shefford

Brewery Tap

14 North Bridge Street, SG17 5DH
⏲ 11.30-11; 12-10.30 Sun
☎ (01462) 628448
B&T Shefford Bitter, Dunstable Giant, Dragonslayer; Everards Tiger; guest beers Ⓗ
A short walk from the brewery, the Tap was rescued and renamed by B&T in 1996. Primarily a drinkers' pub, it offers four regular and one guest beer. The open plan interior, featuring a display of breweriana, is divided into two distinct areas plus a family room, all served by a single bar. Pies and filled rolls are available at lunchtime. Outside is a heated patio garden. The car park is through an archway next to the pub. ❀🚌(M1, M2)♣P⊬

Shillington

Musgrave Arms ✔

16 Apsley End Road, SG5 3LX
⏲ 12-11 (midnight Fri & Sat)
☎ (01462) 711286
Greene King IPA, Abbot; guest beer Ⓗ
Original oak beams add to the character of this splendid multi-roomed country pub. Home-cooked meals are served – Tuesday is surf or turf, Thursday is home-made pie night. Live music plays on the last Friday of the month. Dominoes and petanque are also popular. Outside functions are catered for and there is an area for caravans with electric hook-up. Children and dogs are welcome.
Q❀♿▲♣P⊬

Souldrop

Bedford Arms

High Street, MK44 1EY
⏲ 12-3, 6-11 (closed Mon); 12-midnight Sat; 12-11 Sun
☎ (01234) 781384
Adnams Bitter; Black Sheep Best Bitter; guest beers Ⓗ
Large village pub, dating in parts back to the 17th century when it was a hop house and ale house. Guest beers are often from local micro-breweries. The welcoming restaurant has a central open fireplace and serves traditional pub favourites prepared to order, with daily specials and a roast lunch on Sunday (no eve meals Sun). A large games room with skittles runs off the main bar. The spacious garden and play area are popular with families in summer. ❀🚌(125)♣P⊬

Stotfold

Stag

35 Brook Street, SG5 4LA
⏲ 12-11 (midnight Fri & Sat)
☎ (01462) 730261 🌐 thestag-stotfold.co.uk
Adnams Bitter; Fuller's London Pride; guest beers Ⓗ
This charming pub has a horseshoe-shaped bar with two real fires. There is a separate dining room serving daily except Monday evening and a carvery on Sunday. Up to four guest beers often come from micro-breweries including the local Buntingford brewery, alongside the ever-present Adnams and Fuller's ales. There is a car park and two patio areas. Regular events include the Sunday quiz and Friday meat raffle. ❀🚌(97)♣P⊬

Streatley

Chequers

171 Sharpenhoe Road, LU3 3PS (Next to Church)
⏲ 12-11.30 (12.30am Fri & Sat); 12-11 Sun
☎ (01582) 882072
Greene King IPA, Morland Original, Old Speckled Hen, Abbot; guest beers Ⓗ
Village pub of Georgian origin on the green next to the church. It usually has five real ales on handpump and is one of the few hostelries in the region to use oversized, lined pint glasses. Attracting locals and visitors alike, the pub is popular in good weather due to the large patio area. Quiz night is Tuesday and traditional jazz plays on the first Sunday afternoon of the month. Sharpenhoe Clappers is nearby, an area of oustanding natural beauty. ❀♿♣P⊬

Sutton

John O' Gaunt Inn

30 High Street, SG19 2NE
⏲ 12-2.30, 7-11; 12-10.30 Sun
☎ (01767) 260377
Black Sheep Best Bitter; Fuller's London Pride; Greene King Abbot; Woodforde's Wherry Ⓗ
This traditional two-bar pub is the centre of the village community and has appeared in the Guide for more than 20 years. Four regular ales are supported by an excellent menu of home-cooked food. The public bar houses a Northamptonshire skittles table and the large garden features a petanque court. Morris men and folk musicians visit occasionally. A perfect hideaway on a winter's night when the open fire is lit, adding to a cosy and welcoming atmosphere. Q❀🚌♣P

Tebworth

Queen's Head

The Lane, LU7 9QB
⏲ 12-3 (not Mon-Wed), 6 (7 Sat)-11; 12-3, 6-11 Sun
☎ (01525) 874101
Adnams Broadside Ⓖ**; Wells Eagle IPA** Ⓗ**; guest beer** Ⓖ
Traditional two-bar village local with a public bar, popular for darts and dominoes, and a lounge where live music plays on Friday. The pub has featured in the Guide for more than 25 years under the present landlord who also has a career as an actor with appearances on stage, radio and TV.
❀♣P⊬

Toddington

Oddfellows Arms

2 Conger Lane, LU5 6BP

5-11 (midnight Fri); 12-midnight Sat; 12-11 Sun

☎ (01525) 872021

Adnams Broadside; Fuller's London Pride; guest beers Ⓗ

Attractive 15th-century pub facing the village green with a heavily-beamed and brassed bar featuring a vast collection of pump clips and a games room with a pool table. Westons Old Rosie cider, and often a guest cider or perry, are available as well as a good range of bottled ciders. Beer festivals are held in the spring and autumn. The patio garden is popular in summer and has shelter for smokers.

Totternhoe

Cross Keys

201 Castle Hill Road, LU6 2DA

11.30-3, 5-11; 11.30-11 Fri-Sun

☎ (01525) 220434

Adnams Broadside; Greene King IPA Ⓗ

Attractive, thatched, Grade II-listed building dating from 1433, set in a glorious damson orchard with extensive views over Ivinghoe Beacon and the Vale of Aylesbury. Food is served daily (except Sun eve). In the warmer months barbecues are hosted and basket meals served in the garden. Dogs are welcome in the public bar. Q (61)P

Upper Sundon

White Hart

56 Streatley Road, LU3 3PQ

11-11; 12-10.30 Sun

☎ (01525) 872493

Wells Eagle IPA; guest beer Ⓗ

Mock-Tudor, two-bar Charles Wells pub with leaded windows, tucked away from the village centre on the old village green. The walls of the main bar are adorned with football memorabilia, while the second bar houses a pool table. The guest beer comes from the Charles Wells' list and a large selection of malt whiskies is also stocked. A gazebo is provided for smokers. P

Wingfield

Plough

Tebworth Road, LU7 9QH

12-midnight

☎ (01525) 873077

Fuller's London Pride, ESB, Gale's HSB; guest beers Ⓗ

Charming village inn with a thatched roof dating from the 17th century, decorated with paintings of rural scenes and ploughs. Beware the low beams! Good food is available daily except Sunday evening; food tends to dominate until later in the evening at weekends. There are tables outside at the front; to the rear is a conservatory and prize-winning garden which is illuminated at night in summer. There is also a heated gazebo for smokers. P

Yelden

Chequers

High Street, MK44 1AW

12-2 (not Mon & Tue), 5-11 (midnight Fri & Sat); 12-10.30 Sun

☎ (01933) 356383

Black Sheep Best Bitter Ⓖ**; Fuller's London Pride** Ⓗ**; Greene King Abbot** Ⓖ**; Taylor Landlord; guest beers** Ⓗ

Traditional village pub offering five real ales and two ciders. Good home-cooked pub meals are served daily, with occasional ticket-only guest chef days. The extensive rear garden offers petanque and hosts an annual beer and cider festival in July. Yelden lies on the Three Shires Way walkers' route and boasts the impressive earthworks of an abandoned Norman castle.

(125)P

Globe, Dunstable (Photo: Steve Pullan).

A Beer a Day

Jeff Evans

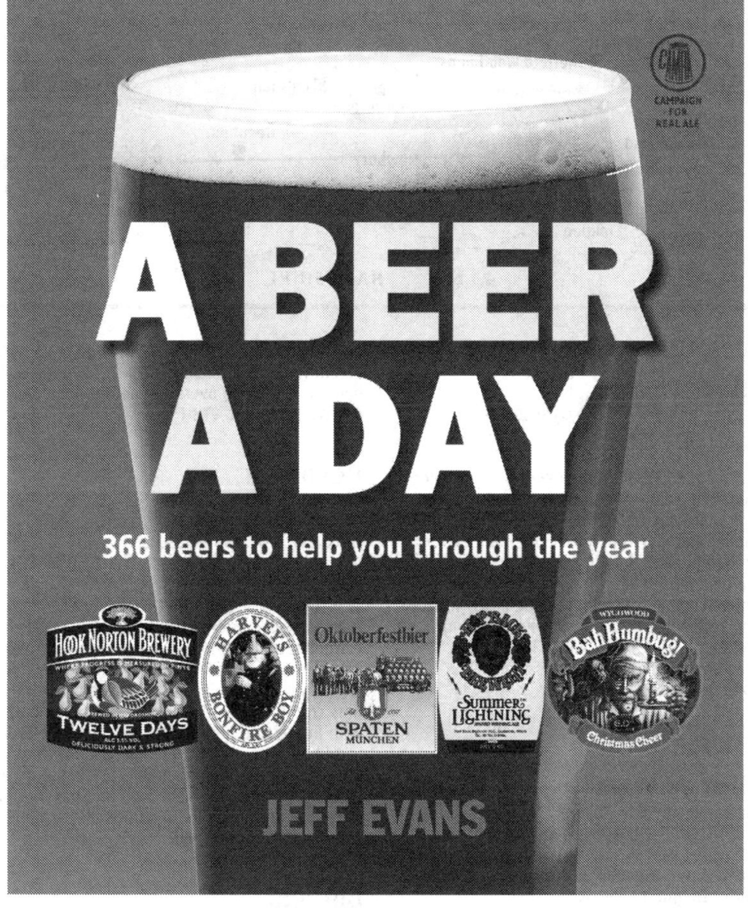

"This book of good pints and bottles is a friendly source of trivia that will help you through any pub quiz... Expert beer writer Jeff Evans finds an event (Battle of Hastings, Brunel's birthday, the last episode of 'Blackadder') for each day of the year and chooses an appropriate tipple with which to celebrate." Time Out magazine.

Written by leading beer writer Jeff Evans, **A Beer a Day** is a beer lover's almanac, crammed with beers from around the world to enjoy on every day and in every season, and celebrating beer's connections with history, sport, music film and television. Whether it's Christmas Eve, Midsummer's Day, Bonfire Night, or just a wet Wednesday in the middle of October, **A Beer a Day** has just the beer for you to savour and enjoy.

£12.99 ISBN 978-1-85249-235-9 Members' price £10.99 384 pages

BERKSHIRE

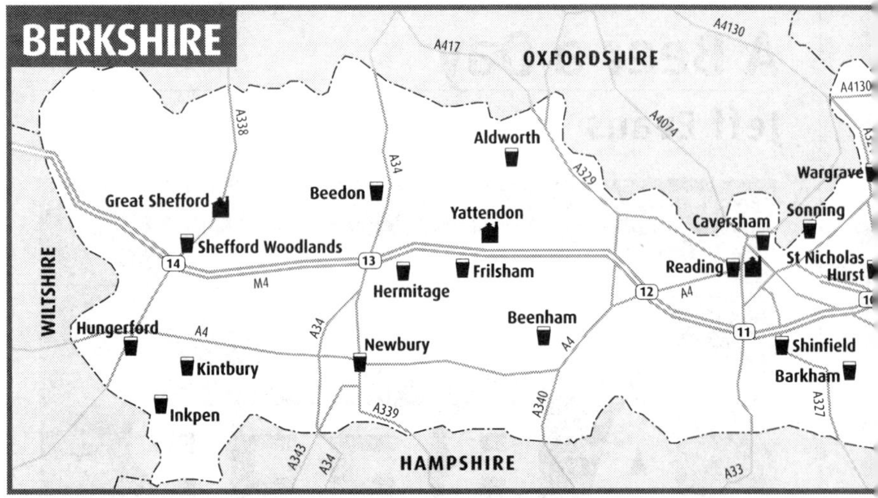

Aldworth

Bell ☆

Bell Lane, RG8 9SE (off B4009) SU555796
⏲ 11-3, 6-11; closed Mon; 12-3, 7-10.30 Sun
☎ (01635) 578272
Arkell's 3B, Kingsdown; West Berkshire Old Tyler, Maggs Mild, seasonal beers 🄷
In the Macaulay family for 200 years, this CAMRA National Inventory pub has a one-handed grandfather clock and an unusual glass walled bar. Situated near the Ridgeway, it is especially popular with walkers as well as locals. Delicious filled rolls complement the beers and award-winning Upton cider. Aunt Sally can be played in the garden. Well-behaved dogs and children are welcome.
♨Q⚲❀⊟♣●P⊡

Barkham

Bull at Barkham ✔

Barkham Road, RG41 4TL (on B3349)
⏲ 11.30-3, 5.30-11; 12-4 Sun
☎ (0118) 976 0324 🌐 thebullatbarkham.com
Adnams Bitter, Broadside; Courage Best Bitter; Fuller's ESB; guest beers 🄷
This 16th-century Grade II-listed building was a working smithy until 1982. It is now an attractive pub with a restaurant and bar area serving home-made dishes (not Sun eve). Local Barkham Blue cheese, which has won national awards, is used in the cooking. The pub's sausages, prepared to the licensee's recipe, are available for sale along with local jams. ♨Q❀◑◗⊟(144)P

Beedon

Langley Hall Inn

Oxford Road, World's End, RG20 8SA (on old Oxford Road 1 mile N of Chieveley) SU483762
⏲ 12-3, 5.30-11, often open all day Saturday; 12-6 Sun
☎ (01635) 248332 🌐 langley-hall-inn.co.uk
West Berkshire Good Old Boy; guest beers 🄷
Single bar pub with a minimal interior divided into areas for drinking and dining. The welcome is warm here and the pub has built up a good reputation for home-made and imaginative food, with seasonal game and fish a speciality. Children and dogs are permitted and the large grass garden accommodates a petanque court. Three en-suite bedrooms provide overnight accommodation.
♨❀⊨◑◗♿Å⊟(6,9)♣P⌐

Beenham

Six Bells

The Green, RG7 5NX SU585688
⏲ 12-2.30 (not Mon & Tue), 6-11; 12-3, 6-11 Sat; 12-3, 6.30-10.30 Sun
☎ (01189) 713368 🌐 thesixbells.co.uk
Fuller's London Pride; guest beers 🄷
Comfortable and popular village pub with two bar areas, a conservatory and well-appointed restaurant that doubles as a function room. Open fires create a cosy feel and the bars are adorned with interesting artefacts from around the world. Local beers are always available, usually from West Berkshire or other small brewers. The pub offers high quality home-cooked food and has four en-suite letting rooms. Board games are available.
♨❀⊨◑◗⊟♿⊟(104)♣P

Binfield

Jack o' Newbury

Terrace Road North, RG42 5PH
⏲ 11-3, 5.30-11; 12-3, 7-10.30 Sun
☎ (01344) 454881 🌐 jackofnewbury.co.uk
Loddon Hoppit; guest beers 🄷
This friendly village freehouse, named after a Tudor cloth merchant, has been run by the same family for many years. It has a bright happy atmosphere, with a friendly landlord, staff and customers. The interior is decorated with brass ornaments and china and pewter mugs, and there is an unusual clock on one wall. No food is served on Sunday and Monday evening. There is a separate skittles alley. Local CAMRA Pub of the Year 2007/08.
♨Q❀◑◗⊟P

INDEPENDENT BREWERIES

Butts Great Shefford
West Berkshire Yattendon
Zerodegrees Reading

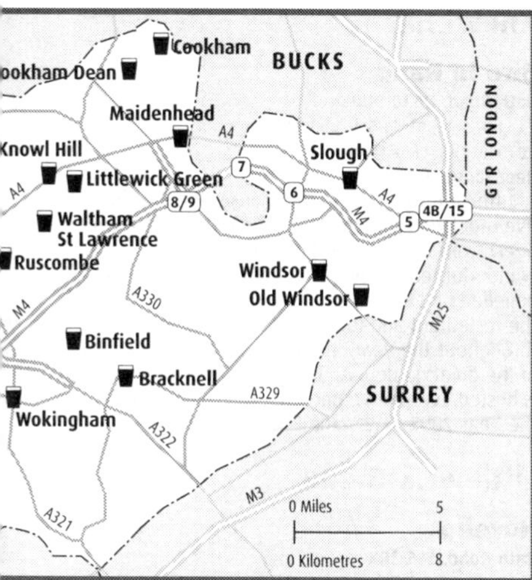

Victoria Arms 🏆

Terrace Road North, RG42 5JA
⏲ 11.30-11 (midnight Fri & Sat); 12-11 Sun
☎ (01344) 483856
Fuller's Discovery, London Pride, ESB, seasonal beer Ⓗ
This busy Victorian Fuller's pub has several seating areas, each with its own atmosphere. See if you can bag one of the most comfortable carvers for many a mile. Perched among the rafters is a collection of more than 800 bottled beers, slowly gathering dust as the years go by. A garden terrace offers protection from the vagaries of the English summer. Quiz night is Sunday. A large sports TV shows all the main fixtures. Local CAMRA branch Pub of the Year 2009. ⌂❀◑◐🚌(53A,53,153)P⊱

Bracknell

Old Manor ✔

Church Road, Grenville Place, RG12 1BP (on inner ring road)
⏲ 9am-midnight
☎ (01344) 304490
Greene King IPA, Abbot; Marston's Pedigree; guest beers Ⓗ
Not a typical Wetherspoon's, this sympathetically refurbished former Tudor manor house is full of character throughout. The Monk's room, where an original priest hole was discovered during restoration, can be booked for private functions. Two bars provide competitively priced and regularly changing guest beers. Ample seating outside. ❀◑◐♿⇌🚌●P⊱

Caversham

Baron Cadogan ✔

22-24 Prospect Street, RG4 8JG
⏲ 9-11 (midnight Fri & Sat); 9-10.30 Sun
☎ (0118) 947 0626
Courage Best Bitter; Greene King IPA; Marston's Pedigree; guest beers Ⓗ
Open plan Wetherspoon's with good disabled access. The range of up to six excellent quality real ales often includes a guest beer from the local Loddon Brewery. Children are welcome during the day. Food is served 9am-10pm all week. No music plays, but TV screens show sports news with subtitles. The pub is named after Baron William Cadogan, noted soldier, politician, diplomat and MP for Reading. Free Wi-Fi access.
Q◑◐♿🚌(9,24,27)●⊱

Cookham

Bounty

Riverside, SL8 5RG (footpath from station car park, across bridge, along towpath) SU907880
⏲ 12-10.30 (winter 12-dusk Sat; closed Mon-Fri)
☎ (01628) 520056
Rebellion IPA, Mutiny; guest beers Ⓗ
Quirky riverside pub that can only be reached on foot (the beer is delivered by boat). Popular with walkers and boaters, it can get very busy at weekends, especially in summer. Dogs, muddy boots and children are all welcome. The boat-shaped bar is decorated with flags and assorted nautical knick-knacks. A blackboard gives details of forthcoming events. Note the winter opening times. ⌂♉❀◑▲⇌(Bourne End)♣

Cookham Dean

Jolly Farmer

Church Road, SL6 9PD
⏲ 11.30-11 (11.45 Fri); 12-10.30 Sun
☎ (01628) 482905 🌐 jollyfarmercookhamdean.co.uk
Brakspear Bitter; Courage Best Bitter; Young's Bitter; guest beers Ⓗ
Situated opposite the local church, the pub is owned by the village. The smaller, adults-only Jolly bar is cosy with its tiled floor and low beams. The larger Dean bar accommodates families, diners and drinkers and features a log burning fire in the winter. There is also a small formal dining area used for the pub's beer festivals on St Georges Day and Halloween (no meals Sun or Mon eve). The large garden has a children's play area. ⌂Q❀◑◐P

Frilsham

Pot Kiln

Bucklebury Road, RG18 0XX (signed from Yattendon) SU554731
⏲ 12-3, 6-11; closed Tue; 12-11 Sat; 12-10.30 (6 winter) Sun
☎ (01635) 201366 🌐 potkiln.org
West Berkshire Mr Chubbs Lunchtime Bitter, Brick Kiln Bitter, Maggs Mild; guest beers Ⓗ
Formerly an ale house for thirsty kiln workers, this is a rural gem, surrounded by meadows and woodland. The public bar remains a traditional area for drinkers who are well served with beers from local micro-breweries. Brick Kiln Bitter is brewed for the inn by West Berkshire Brewery in nearby Yattendon. The separate restaurant features game as a speciality on the menu. Dogs are welcome in the bar and gardens. ⌂Q❀◑◐⊞♣P

Hermitage

Fox Inn ✔

High Street, RG18 9RB (on B4009) SU509731
⏲ 12-2.30, 5-11; 12-2.30, 4.30-midnight Fri; 12-midnight Sat; 12-10.30 Sun
☎ (01635) 201545 🌐 thefoxathermitage.co.uk
Fuller's London Pride; Shepherd Neame Master Brew Bitter, Spitfire; Young's Special; guest beers Ⓗ
This welcoming village pub was converted from three artisan cottages dating from the 16th-century. It has established a wide reputation for

excellent real ales and good affordable food, ranging from bar snacks, including hot and cold filled baguettes, to an a la carte menu in the evening. The regular ales are supplemented by guest beers chosen by customers. Real cider in summer. ⛰❀🛏◐◑⊟🚌(9)♣P⚡

Hungerford

Angel

50 Church Street, RG17 0JH SU336685
⊙ 12-11; closed Mon; 12-4, 7-10.30 Sun
☎ (01488) 681199
Beer range varies Ⓗ
The landlord, previously at the Butlers in Reading, bought the freehold at this back-street multi-area boozer. He chooses beers he likes and offers two or three different ales, with local beers featuring on a regular basis. The ingredients for the home-cooked meals are bought locally. Beer festivals are hosted in summer. ❀◐◑≋🚌(4)P⚡

Downgate

13 Down View, Park Street, RG17 0ED (edge of Hungerford Common) SU341683
⊙ 11-11
☎ (01488) 682708 🌐 the-downgate.co.uk
Arkell's 2B, 3B; guest beer Ⓗ
This Arkell's pub on the outskirts of Hungerford is a shrine to the passions of the landlord. It features memorabilia about planes, automobiles and his beloved Southampton FC. Home-cooked meals include traditional Sunday roasts with special deals for the over 60s. Look for the tropical fish, Sid the 16-year-old parrot and the goals in the Gents. ⛰❀◐◑≋🚌(13)♣P

Inkpen

Crown & Garter

Inkpen Common, RG17 9QR SU378639
⊙ 12-3 (not Mon & Tue), 5.30-11; 12-5, 7-10.30 Sun
☎ (01488) 668325 🌐 crownandgarter.co.uk
Arkell's Moonlight; Ramsbury Gold; Taylor Landlord; West Berkshire Mr Chubb's Lunchtime Bitter Ⓗ
Handsome 17th-century inn, well situated for country walks and overnight stays. The bar rooms and restaurant area are attractively decorated with dark beams, an inglenook and two more fireplaces adding period charm. A side patio leads to a heated smoking shelter and large garden with tables. The food menu uses fresh ingredients from local suppliers. West Berkshire Good Old Boy may sometimes be available when beers rotate. Eight en-suite bedrooms. ⛰Q❀🛏◐◑⊟🚌(13)♣P⚡

Kintbury

Dundas Arms 🏆

53 Station Road, RG17 9UT (opp station) SU385669
⊙ 11-2.30, 6-11; 12-2.30 Sun
☎ (01488) 658263 🌐 dundasarms.co.uk
Adnams Bitter; Ramsbury Gold; West Berkshire Good Old Boy; guest beer Ⓗ
This building has been a pub for more than 100 years and the current landlord has been here since 1967. A lovely multi-room free house, it is situated next to the Kennet & Avon Canal within sight of Kintbury train station. The pub promotes local brewers and is LocAle accredited; where possible the food is local too. Q❀🛏◐◑≋🚌(13)P⚡

Knowl Hill

Bird in Hand

Bath Road, RG10 9UP
⊙ 11-3, 5-11; 11-11 Sat; 12-10.30 Sun
☎ (01628) 826622 🌐 birdinhand.co.uk
Beer range varies Ⓗ
A 14th-century genuine free house, the Bird hosts five regularly changing ales (often featuring a dark beer) from local and distant breweries. A wonderful feature fireplace dominates the wood-panelled bar. Food is available in the bar as well as the restaurant and food themed evenings are held throughout the year, including summer barbecues in the quiet garden. An impressive fireworks event is hosted every November 5th. Local CAMRA Pub of the Year 2008. ⛰❀🛏◐◑⊟🚌(127,239)🍎P⚡

Littlewick Green

Novello

Bath Road, SL6 3RX
⊙ 12-11
☎ (01628) 825753 🌐 greatlittlepub.co.uk
Taylor Landlord; guest beers Ⓗ
A large friendly pub with a baby grand piano – regular special event evenings are held at which a pianist plays. The emphasis is on food here but up to four ales are available in comfortable seating areas. The pub is named after Ivor Novello, a famous composer of the 1930s who lived in Littlewick Green. ❀◐◑♿🚌(127)P⚡

Maidenhead

Craufurd Arms

15 Gringer Hill, SL6 7LY (follow Marlow Road W from town centre)
⊙ 5.30-11; 12-3, 5.30-midnight Fri; 12-midnight Sat; 12-3, 7-midnight Sun
☎ (01628) 625153
Rebellion IPA, seasonal beers Ⓗ
Situated a mile from the town centre, this small red-brick building conceals a cosy one room pub selling two Rebellion beers or an occasional guest. There is a friendly community atmosphere and regular quiz nights are held as well as occasional live music. The pub was originally an ale house for the nearby Craufurd estate, converted from three cottages. Recent alterations include an extra drinking area and a beer garden. ❀🚌(5,6)♣P

Greyhound ✔

92-96 Queen Street, SL6 1HZ
⊙ 9am-midnight (1am Fri & Sat)
☎ (01628) 779410
Greene King Ruddles Best Bitter, Abbot; Marston's Pedigree; guest beers Ⓗ
This large Wetherspoon's Lloyds No 1 near the station is LocAle accredited for stocking Loddon and Rebellion beers among its four guests. Westons Old Rosie and Vintage cider are also available on handpump. The pub's large open plan area has a family section and there is a smaller room which is quiet except for music on Friday and Saturday nights. Outside is a smoking area to the rear. The original Greyhound in the high street (now a bank) was where Charles I met his children the night before his execution. 🐴◐◑🚌⚡

Maidenhead Conservative Club ✔

32 York Road, SL6 1SF
⊙ 11-11 (11.45 Fri & Sat); 12-11 Sun

☎ (01628) 620579 🌐 maidenheadconclub.co.uk
Fuller's Chiswick, London Pride, seasonal beers; guest beers Ⓗ
Friendly club close to the station. The steward is a CAMRA member so it is no surprise that the beer quality is good. Two guest ales from Vale brewery are generally available, plus bottle-conditioned beers. Monday is crib night, Tuesday and Wednesday darts. Hot bar food is available Monday to Friday lunchtimes. Parking is limited. Show this guide or a CAMRA membership card for entry, together with a minimal fee. Recent CAMRA Regional Club of the Year winner.
♨◑♿⇌🚌(7A,7B)♣P⚐

Newbury

Lock, Stock & Barrel ✔
104 Northbrook Street, RG14 1AA
⏲ 11-11 (midnight Fri & Sat); 12-10.30 Sun
☎ (01635) 580550
Fuller's London Pride, ESB, guest ales Ⓗ
Situated just off Newbury's main shopping street, the recently refurbished single bar has a smart, upmarket feel. The riverside patio and rooftop terrace are very popular on sunny days, with views across Newbury Lock and the Kennet & Avon Canal towards St Nicholas Church. Meals served daily.
❀◑◗♿⇌🚌P⚐

Old Windsor

Jolly Gardeners
92-94 St Luke's Road, SL4 2QJ
⏲ 12-11 (midnight Thu-Sat); 12-10.30 Sun
☎ (01753) 830215 🌐 thejollygardeners.org.uk
Courage Best Bitter; Wells Bombardier Ⓗ
Friendly, welcoming locals' pub close to the village shops, with a U-shaped bar serving three distinct areas, one with a large TV and dartboard. Good-value home-made food is available 11-4pm Saturday and roasts are served on Sunday. A quiz is held on Monday evening and Wednesday is open mike night. The landlord is known for taking great care of his beer. Reasonably-priced B&B is available. ❀🛏🚌P⚐

Reading

Allied Arms
57 St Mary's Butts, RG1 2LG
⏲ 12-11; closed Sun
☎ (0118) 958 3323 🌐 allied-arms.co.uk
Fuller's London Pride; Loddon Hullabaloo; guest beers Ⓗ
A genuine family-run house with friendly locals and up to five real ales. Enter via the side passage and choose from two small, cosy bars featuring exposed wooden beams at some interesting angles (the pub seems somewhat older than its 180 years). An eclectic selection of music is on the jukebox. Look for the large, secluded garden to the rear – a quiet oasis in the middle of this busy town. A quiz is held fortnightly on Wednesday, and two beer festivals are hosted annually. ❀⇌🚌⚐

Eldon Arms
19 Eldon Terrace, RG1 4DX
⏲ 11-3, 5.30-11.30 (midnight Fri); 11-3, 7-midnight Sat; 12-3, 7-11.30 Sun
☎ (0118) 957 3857
Wadworth IPA, Horizon, 6X, Bishop's Tipple, seasonal beers Ⓗ
Traditional back-street local in the Eldon Square conservation area, under the care of the same landlords for more than 30 years. The two bars are full of knick-knacks and offer a meeting place for many clubs and groups including local CAMRA. Pub games are played and regular quiz nights are held. In addition to the regular beer range, Pint Size Mild and Wadworth seasonals are often available. Westons Scrumpy also available.
Q❀⊟🚌(9,17,64)♣🍎⚐

Foresters Arms
79-81 Brunswick Street, RG1 6NY
⏲ 4-11; 3-midnight Fri; 12-midnight Sat; 12-11 Sun
☎ (0118) 959 0316
Brakspear Bitter; Harveys Sussex Best Bitter Ⓗ
This two bar urban gem, with a rare side corridor, has managed to avoid being wrecked by 'progress'. It retains a magnificent green tile frontage and, although tightly packed into a terrace, has a country pub ambience. The garden at the rear is a haven of peace and there is also a small seating area at the front. The pub runs a bus (in conjunction with the Nag's Head) to all Reading FC home games. ❀⊟⇌(Reading West)🚌♣⚐

Hobgoblin
2 Broad Street, RG1 2BH
⏲ 11-11; 12-10.30 Sun
☎ (0118) 950 8119
Beer range varies Ⓗ
Larger inside than out, the small front bar of this Georgian building is host to often robust conversation, while the back room is divided into intimate booths where you can sit and chat. Walls and ceilings are covered with pump clips from some of the 6,000 or so brews the Goblin has served since 1992. Three West Berks brews, including seasonals, are supplemented by five constantly-changing guests from micros all over the country. Westons cider and perry are also available. ❀⇌🚌🍎⚐

Hop Leaf
163-165 Southampton Street, RG1 2QZ
⏲ 4-11.30; 12-12.30am Fri & Sat; 12-11.30 Sun
☎ (0118) 931 4700
Hop Back GFB, Odyssey, Crop Circle, Entire Stout, Summer Lightning; guest beers Ⓗ
A friendly community local standing just outside the main town centre. It offers a wide range of cask-conditioned and bottled Hop Back beers alongside two real ciders and a perry from Westons. The cosy L-shaped bar area has daily newspapers, a bar billiards table and dartboard. The pub runs teams in a number of local sports leagues. A quiet back room can be hired for meetings. Look out for the impressive range of super-spicy bar snacks. Dog-friendly. 🚌🍎

Moderation
213 Caversham Road, RG1 8BB
⏲ 12-11
☎ (0118) 375 0767 🌐 spirit-house.co.uk/moderation
Beer range varies Ⓗ
Situated on the main road between Reading and Caversham, the Moderation's refurbished interior is airy and spacious with a modern feel. Three handpumps serve a variety of real ales, often including Cornish beers. The food is locally-sourced and, much like the pub's quirky decor, is a fusion of

east-meets-west. A selection of board games is available. Outside is a large decked garden. ❀◑♿⇌🚌(9,24,27)⚐

Nag's Head 🏆

5 Russell Street, RG1 7XD

⏲ 12-11 (midnight Fri & Sat)

☎ (0118) 957 4649 🌐 nagsheadreading.com

Beer range varies Ⓗ

The Nag's is a thriving real ale haven attracting a wide range of customers. Twelve locally-sourced ales are on offer, always including a stout and a mild, plus cider and perry, as well as an extensive selection of single malt whiskies. The pub runs regular brewery trips and real ale cruises along the Thames. Traditional British cuisine is served during the early evening and weekend lunchtimes. The rear garden now has a variety of hops growing. ♨❀◑⇌(Reading West)🚌♣●P⚐

Red Lion

34 Southampton Street, RG1 2QL

⏲ 12-11 (midnight Fri & Sat); 12-11.30 Sun

☎ (0118) 957 1473

Beer range varies Ⓗ

A pub going from strength to strength since refurbishment and new ownership in February 2008, the Lion has a fresh clean look both inside and out. Lunchtime food is served 12-2.30pm. The pub has a dartboard and pool table as well as sport on TV. For those wishing for more active participation there are teams in local pool, darts and football leagues. A cosy outside garden is available for smokers. Live music is hosted occasionally. ❀◐⚐

Retreat

8 St John's Street, RG1 4EH

⏲ 4.30-11; 12-11.30 Fri & Sat; 12-11 Sun

☎ (0118) 957 1593 🌐 retreatpub.co.uk

Loddon Ferryman's Gold; Ringwood Best Bitter; guest beers Ⓗ

This lively back-street local is very much part of the community. In addition to draught ales the pub is well-known for its selection of foreign bottled beers and a regular choice of two draught ciders or perries – it is current CAMRA Regional Cider Pub of the Year. The Retreat is also popular for live music and community events, including the famous pickled onion competition, most recently won by actress Kate Winslet's mother! 🚌(9,17,64)♣●⚐

Three Guineas

Station Approach, RG1 1LY

⏲ 10-11; 12-10.30 Sun

☎ (0118) 957 2743

Greene King IPA; Thwaites Lancaster Bomber; Young's Bitter; guest beers Ⓗ

A conversion of the old station ticket hall, the Three Guineas is ideal for those travelling to Reading by train – departure times are displayed on monitors inside the pub. There are eight handpumps with two or three regular beers usually available and up to six guest ales. Popular with sports fans when there is a match at the Madjeski Stadium – expect crowds (and plastic glasses) when London Irish or Reading FC play at home. Food is served until 9pm. ❀◑♿⇌🚌⚐

Ruscombe

Royal Oak

Ruscombe Lane, RG10 9JN (on B3024 E of Twyford)

⏲ 12-3, 6 (5 Fri)-11; 12-4 Sun

☎ (0118) 934 5190 🌐 burattas.co.uk

Brakspear Bitter; Fuller's London Pride; guest beers Ⓗ

This pub houses Buratta's bistro, which takes up the majority of the space (booking is strongly advised), but drinkers are just as welcome as diners. The smaller lounge area provides comfortable seating. An antiques shop has been added recently. Beyond the conservatory, where CAMRA branch business meeting are sometimes held, is a large garden. ♨Q❀◑♿⇌🚌(127)P⚐

St Nicholas Hurst

Wheelwrights Arms ✔

Davis Way, RG10 0TR (opp entrance to Dinton Pastures)

⏲ 11-3, 5.30-11; 11.30-11 Sat; 12-10.30 Sun

☎ (0118) 934 4100

Wadworth IPA, Horizon, 6X, JCB Ⓗ**; guest beers** Ⓗ/Ⓖ

This 18th-century wheelwright's shop started selling beer when the railways arrived in the early 1850s. A friendly local attracting both visitors and residents, the licensees have been running the pub for almost 12 years. It retains its stone floors, beamed ceilings, exposed brickwork and a real fire. There are garden benches to the front and rear, which also has a covered patio. Good food is available (not Sun eve). Quiz night is Monday. ♨❀◑♿⇌(Winnersh)🚌(126,128,129)●P⚐

Shefford Woodlands

Pheasant Inn

Ermin Street, RG17 7AA (exit M4 jct 14 N, left onto B4000) SU362733

⏲ 11-12.30am (1am Fri & Sat); 11-midnight Sun

☎ (01488) 648284 🌐 thepheasant-inn.co.uk

Loddon Hoppit, Rin Tin Tin; Wadworth 6X Ⓗ

This 17th-century inn, thought to be the highest in Berkshire, has fine views to the south from the traditional bar and garden. Favoured by the horse-racing fraternity, it screens live races on TV. Photographs and cartoons of horses and jockeys adorn the walls. Tastefully extended in 2008, 11 en-suite rooms have been added and a new restaurant area which is very popular with diners. Ring the bull is played. A convenient stop off for travellers on the M4, with free Wi-Fi. ♨❀🛏◑🚌(90)♣P⚐

Shinfield

Magpie & Parrot

Arborfield Road, RG2 9EA (on A327 E of village) SU737679

⏲ 12-7 (3 Sun)

☎ (0118) 988 4130

Fuller's London Pride; guest beer Ⓗ

The Magpie doesn't shout its presence but manages to remain very busy during its limited opening hours. The reason for its popularity is the unique atmosphere. It has recently been expanded into a two-bar pub by opening up one of the private rooms – but the character has been retained. both rooms are full of unusual knick-knacks. The marquee in the garden hosts weddings and parties. Regular beer festivals often feature hog roasts. ♨Q❀◐🚌(144)♣P⚐

Slough

Rose & Crown

312 High Street, SL1 1NB
⏲ 11-midnight; 12-12.30am Sun
☎ (01753) 521114
Beer range varies Ⓗ
This attractive, blue painted, Grade II-listed inn from the late 16th-century is a pleasant contrast to other more modern buildings on the High Street. Two small bars display an impressive range of pump clips on the walls, reflecting the landlord's passion for real ale and emphasising the variety of beers which have been served. Two ales are generally available and occasionally a real cider. Entertainment includes three TV screens, including one in the garden. ❀≋🚌♣⚡

Sonning

Bull Inn ✔

High Street, RG4 6UP (next to St Andrew's Church)
⏲ 11-11 (11.30 Fri & Sat); 12-10.30 Sun
☎ (0118) 969 3901 🌐 accommodating-inns.co.uk/bullinn
Fuller's Chiswick, Discovery, London Pride; Gale's HSB; guest beers Ⓗ
This cosy 16th-century hostelry, with low dark wood beams throughout, lies at the heart of Sonning village, close to the Thames footpath and Sonning lock. Owned by the neighbouring church, it is leased to Fuller's and run by long-established managers. The Bull is steeped in history and is mentioned in the novel Three Men in a Boat. It now offers first class accommodation, a good menu of home-cooked cuisine and five beers on handpump. ♨Q❀🛏◐🚌(127)P⚡

Waltham St Lawrence

Bell

The Street, RG10 0JJ (opp church)
⏲ 12-3, 5-11; 12-11 Sat; 12-10.30 Sun
☎ (0118) 934 1788 🌐 thebellinn.biz
Beer range varies Ⓗ
Picturesque Grade II-listed building dating back to the 15th century. It has been a pub since the 18th century, owned by the parish. Many interesting features include ornately carved oak panelling, beams, a well in the upper room, and a small room known as the Noggin by the entrance corridor. Five well-kept ales are on offer, along with a popular range of food. Children, dogs and walkers are all welcome. ♨Q🐎❀◐🚌(52A)♣●

Star

Broadmoor Road, RG10 0HY (on B3024 between Twyford and Maidenhead)
⏲ 12-3, 5-11; 12-11 Fri & Sat; 12-10.30 Sun
☎ (0118) 934 3486 🌐 thestar-inn.co.uk
Wadworth IPA, 6X, Bishop's Tipple Ⓗ
A delightful, friendly, country pub with a cosy beamed interior, on the edge of the village. The pub is well known in the local area for the quality of its stone-baked pizzas along with a varied selection of dishes including roasts on Sunday (no food Sun eve). Monthly live music events are held as well as regular pub quizzes. ♨❀◐🚌(52A)P⚡

Wargrave

Wargrave & District Snooker Club

Woodclyffe Hostel, Church Street, RG10 8EP
⏲ 7-11; closed Sat & Sun
☎ (0118) 940 3537
Beer range varies Ⓗ
The Victorian Woodclyffe Hostel, bequeathed to the village by a benefactor, also houses the public library. The independent, volunteer-run Snooker Club has a large L-shaped bar with a friendly club atmosphere. A single ale is stocked – over the years a wide variety has been sold. Show this Guide or CAMRA membership card to gain entry (£3 guest fee to play on the first class snooker tables). Winner of several recent CAMRA branch and regional Club of the Year awards. ≋🚌(127)♣

Windsor

Carpenters Arms ✔

4 Market Street, SL4 1PB
⏲ 11-11 (midnight Fri & Sat)
☎ (01753) 755961
Beer range varies Ⓗ
The ever-changing range of five ales from across Britain makes this pub popular with locals and tourists alike. Situated in a narrow cobbled street between the castle and Guildhall, the entrance to a series of tunnels originally linking the pub to the castle can be seen in the lower drinking area. Mosaic floors in the entrance porches are a reminder of the long since defunct Ashby's Brewery. Pub grub includes an excellent range of pies. Local CAMRA Pub of the Year 2008. ❀◐≋🚌

Duke of Connaught ✔

165 Arthur Road, SL4 1RZ
⏲ 10-midnight (1am Fri & Sat); 12-11.30 Sun
☎ (01753) 840748 🌐 thedukeofconnaught.co.uk
Greene King IPA, Abbot; guest beers Ⓗ
Originally No.1 Connaught Cottages, this pub was the home of Mr Charles Wilkins who was a beer retailer in 1895. Today it is a friendly street-corner tavern with a welcoming atmosphere serving good food. It shows sport on TV and hosts live music most weekends, plus an open mike night on Monday. The interior has bare floorboards and the walls are decorated with old film photos. There is a covered smoking area to the rear. ♨❀◐≋🚌⚡

King & Castle ✔

15-16 Thames Street, SL4 1PL
⏲ 9am-midnight (2am Fri & Sat)
☎ (01753) 625120
Greene King Abbot; Marston's Pedigree; guest beers Ⓗ
Large Wetherspoon's pub set on three floors situated opposite Windsor Castle. The open plan main bar leads to a variety of more intimate areas, some with bar stools, others with comfy sofas. Live jazz plays on Wednesday night. By day the pub is mainly frequented by tourists, by night with a younger crowd attracted by the small dance floor – a dress code applies. The large patio is popular during the summer and partially heated during cooler weather. ❀◐≋🚌⚡

Two Brewers

34 Park Street, SL4 1LB
⏲ 11.30-11 (11.30 Fri & Sat); 12-10.30 Sun
☎ (01753) 855426
Fuller's London Pride; Shepherd Neame Spitfire; Wadworth 6X Ⓗ
This Grade II-listed building was once part of the Crown Estate and is the ideal place to rest up after completing the Long Walk through Windsor Great

Park. Built in the 17th century, it was reputedly a brothel and drinking house on what was then the main London-Windsor road. The frontage was replaced after a fire in the 19th century. The food is very popular here (booking advisable).

Vansittart Arms

105 Vansittart Road, SL4 5DD
12-11 (11.30 Thu; midnight Fri & Sat)
(01753) 865988 vansittartarms.co.uk
Fuller's Discovery, London Pride, ESB, seasonal beers
A consistently good Fuller's house, the two main bar areas have recesses and real fires. Barbecues and special events are hosted in the large garden in summer and there is a covered, heated area for smokers. Sport is keenly followed here with rugby taking priority on the TV screens. Live music plays occasionally. No food Sun evening.

Windsor Castle

98 Kings Road, SL4 2AP
12-11
(01753) 830766 the-windsor-castle-pub.co.uk
Brakspear Bitter; Taylor Landlord; Wadworth 6X; guest beer
Situated a third of the way along the Long Walk from the real Windsor Castle, this pub is a welcoming sight for thirsty locals and tourists. Three regular ales are augmented by a rotating guest beer. A large decked seating area outside is perfect for long summer evenings. There is occasional live music and a large sports TV is in the main bar area. P

Wokingham

Broad Street Tavern

29 Broad Street, RG40 1AU
12-11 (midnight Thu-Sat); 12-10.30 Sun
(0118) 9773706 broadstreettavern.co.uk
Wadworth IPA, Horizon, 6X, Bishops' Tipple, JCB; guest beers, seasonal beers
Popular town-centre pub with the same licensee for more than ten years. Two quiet rooms with wood-panelled walls complement the busy bar and seating area. Outside is a large decked and walled garden. Barbecues are held when the weather permits. Food is available all day and regular beer festivals are hosted, with a good range of guests. Three times winner of local CAMRA Pub of the Year.

Crispin

45 Denmark Street, RG40 2AY
12 - 11 (midnight Fri & Sat); 12-10.30 Sun
(0118) 978 0309
Wells Bombardier; guest beers
Named after the shoemaker St Crispin and considered by some to be the oldest pub in Wokingham, this is a traditional local with a low beamed ceiling and bric-a-brac adorning the walls. The chalk board on the wall allows customers to request their favourite beers. No food is served, but feel free to take your own. A quiz on Thursday evening is very popular, and occasional beer festivals are hosted.

Queen's Head

23 The Terrace, RG40 1BP
12-11 (10.30 Sun)
(0118) 978 1221
Greene King IPA, Morland Original, Abbot, seasonal beer
A rare example of a late medieval timber cruck-framed building, with pairs of curved timbers forming a bowed A-frame supporting the roof independently of the walls. The low ceilings, smouldering fire, panelled walls and bare-boarded floor provide a traditional pub setting for the local darts team (Mon), while the less energetic lounge in comfy leather sofas nibbling on meat or cheese platters served daily. The small beer garden hosts the Aunty Sally team. Occasional guest beers.

Rifle Volunteer

141 Reading Road, RG41 1HD (on A329)
11-11; 12-5.30, 7-11 Sun
(0118) 978 4484
Courage Best Bitter; Fuller's London Pride; Sharp's Doom Bar; guest beers
Community pub a mile west of the town centre with a spacious bar and small alcove for darts. The guest handpump serves a changing beer. Meals are available at lunchtime. Flat-screen TVs show sporting events. There is an enclosed garden with children's play equipment at the rear and heated seating for smokers at the front. (190) P

Ship

104 Peach Street, RG40 1XH (on A329)
12-11 (10.30 Sun)
(0118) 978 0389
Fuller's Discovery, London Pride, ESB, seasonal beers
This Grade II-listed, 17th-century former coaching inn on the eastern edge of the town centre provides a warm welcome for townsfolk and visitors alike. The two main bars, side bar with dartboard, and the refurbished, integrated former stables make for a lively and entertaining atmosphere. Sports are shown on flat screen TVs and there is a popular covered and heated patio area. Good home-cooked food is available every day. P

White Horse

Easthampstead Road, RG40 3AF
12-2.30, 5-11; 12-11 Fri & Sat; 12-10.30 Sun
(0118) 979 7402 thewhitehorse-wokingham.co.uk
Greene King IPA, Ruddles County, Abbot, seasonal beers
Country pub with a relaxed atmosphere, south of Wokingham town centre with views across the fields. A new licensee took over last year who has maintained the high quality of the beers and improved the food menu. Food is available 12-2pm and 6-9pm (12-4pm Sun), including a children's menu. Staff and locals offer a friendly welcome to all. This is a pub which does what it does very well indeed, has no pretensions and serves the best Greene King beers for miles around. P

It was my Uncle George who discovered that alcohol was a food well in advance of modern medical thought.
P G Wodehouse, The Inimitable Jeeves

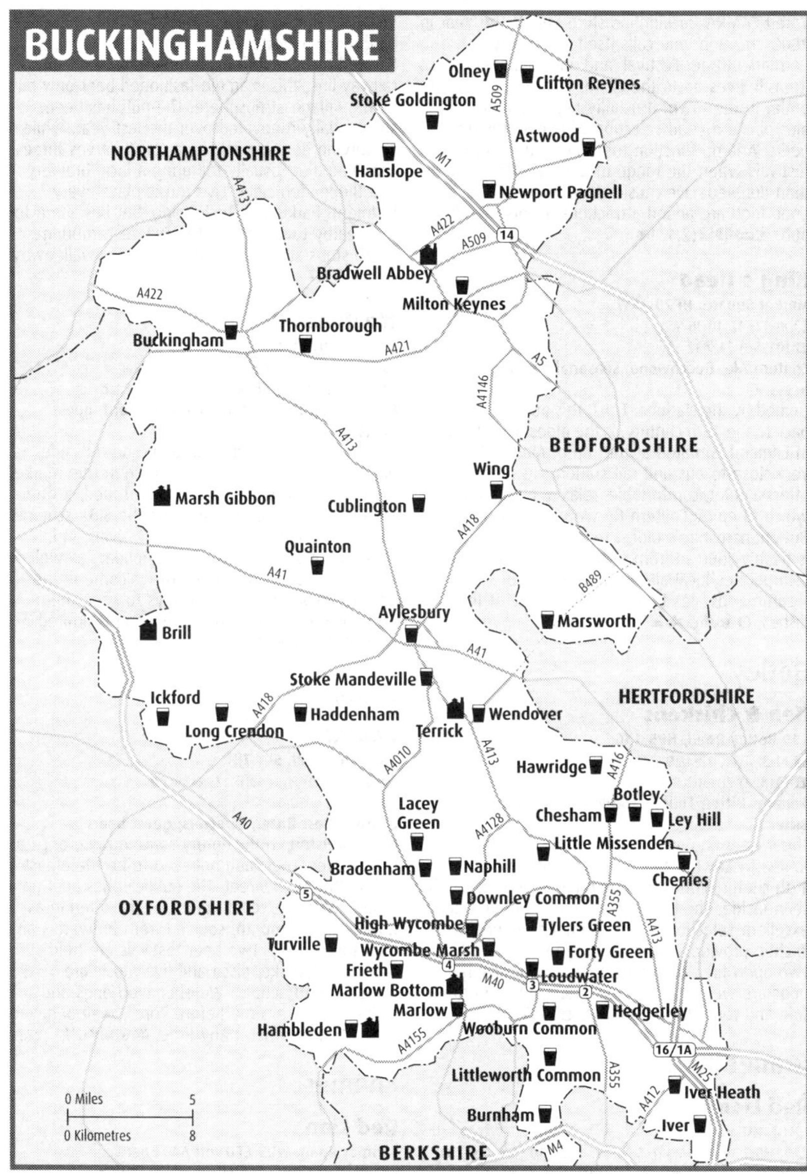

Astwood

Old Swan

8 Main Road, MK16 9JS (off A422)

✪ 11-3, 6-11; closed Mon; 12-3 Sun

☎ (01234) 391351 🌐 oldswanastwood.co.uk

Beer range varies Ⓗ

Seventeenth-century free house in a village just off the northern Milton Keynes-Bedford road. The pub has a superb reputation for high-quality food with fresh fish a speciality on the menu – booking a must. A large blue china collection and an impressive display of water jugs adorn the walls and ceiling. Up to three changing beers are on handpump – ring ahead to ask for the current selection on offer. More than 100 different ales were dispensed last year. ⛫Q❀◐◑♿🚌(1C)P⁻

Aylesbury

Hop Pole

83 Bicester Road, HP19 9AZ

✪ 12-11 (midnight Fri & Sat)

☎ (01296) 482129

Vale Best Bitter, VPA; guest beers Ⓗ

INDEPENDENT BREWERIES

Chiltern Terrick
Concrete Cow Bradwell Abbey
Old Luxters Hambleden
Oxfordshire Ales Marsh Gibbon
Rebellion Marlow Bottom
Vale Brill

Voted CAMRA Buckinghamshire Pub of the Year in 2008, the Hop Pole calls itself 'Aylesbury's Permanent Beer Festival' and with ten handpumps it easily lives up to the claim. Vale Brewery's sole outlet in the town, it usually features four of its ales plus a myriad selection of micro-brewery beers. A large function room hosts two beer festivals when the range of ales on offer is more than doubled. Live music at the weekend plus good food are added attractions at this friendly pub. ❀⛟◐◑⛍(2,16)●

King's Head

Market Square, HP20 2RW

⌚ 11-11; 12-10.30 Sun

☎ (01296) 718812

Chiltern Ale, Beechwood, seasonal beers; guest beers Ⓗ

Owned by the National Trust, this pub, which dates back to the 15th century, is the oldest courtyard inn in England. Situated at the top of Market Square, very close to bus and rail stations, its Farmers Bar offers a quiet, comfortable, relaxed environment in which to enjoy Chiltern Brewery beers from Buckinghamshire's oldest micro-brewery. The food is freshly sourced from local suppliers and often incorporates local ales – the menu also recommends ales to accompany many of the dishes. Q❀◐◑♿⇌⛍⛿

Botley

Hen & Chickens

119 Botley Road, HP5 1XG

⌚ 11-3, 6-11; 12-4.30, 7-10.30 Sun

☎ (01494) 783303

Adnams Bitter; Fuller's London Pride; Young's Bitter Ⓗ

This welcoming pub situated on the old trade route to nearby Ley Hill and Bovingdon occupies a row of 17th century cottages – the original timbers can be seen inside. The lively local clientele enjoys an excellent selection of handpumped beers and the kitchen provides generous portions of good food. Two open fires contribute to a cosy atmosphere. Dogs are welcome. There is a large garden to the side and rear of the pub. ♨Q⛭❀◐◑⛍(373)P

Bradenham

Red Lion

HP14 4HF (on A4010)

⌚ 11.30-2.30 (not Mon), 5.30-11; 11.30-10 (6 winter) Sun

☎ (01494) 562212 🌐 redlionbradenham.co.uk

Brakspear Bitter; Young's Bitter; guest beers Ⓗ

The pub is part of a National Trust-owned hamlet and comprises a snug bar with wood-burning stove and lounge bar/restaurant. The publican provides quality real ales, including guest beers from local breweries and others, and excellent bar meals. Hand-made pies ranging from Aberdeen Angus beef to chicken tikka are specialities. Disraeli, village born, and Bomber Harris, when stationed at nearby Bomber Command, are reputed to have imbibed here. Alternate Sunday evenings are jazz and food nights. ♨Q❀◐◑⊟⇌(Saunderton)P

Buckingham

Mitre ✔

2 Mitre Street, MK18 1DW

⌚ 5-11 (midnight Thu & Fri); 12-midnight Sat; 12-10.30 Sun

☎ (01280) 813080 🌐 themitre.org.uk

Beer range varies Ⓗ

Located to the south of the town, near the old railway line, this is an old-fashioned beer-only pub with a village atmosphere. The pub has been substantially renovated over the last year, while preserving its essential character. It serves three changing ales, usually featuring a local brewery, and Biddenden cider. Live music plays every fortnight. Parking is challenging, but buses run to the nearby town centre. The Oxford-Cambridge X5 coach stops at Tesco about 15 minutes walk away. ♨❀⛍♣●⛿

Woolpack ✔

57 Well Street, MK18 1EP

⌚ 10-11 (midnight Fri & Sat); 12-10.30 Sun

☎ (01280) 817972 🌐 buckinghamwoolpack.co.uk

Black Sheep Best Bitter; Taylor Landlord; guest beers Ⓗ

This pub, with a modern interior and riverside garden, opens early in the morning in true market town style. As well as good, varied food, it offers local guest ales sourced through the SIBA scheme. The pub hosts two annual beer festivals, in late May and over the August bank holiday, as well as live music events. Children are welcome in the back room where there are toys to keep them entertained. Be warned that parking is limited. ♨⛭❀◐◑♿⛍♣P⛿

Burnham

George

18 High Street, SL1 7JH

⌚ 12-11 (1am Fri & Sat); 12-10.30 Sun

☎ (01628) 605047

Courage Best Bitter, Directors; guest beers Ⓗ

Grade II-listed, 16th-century coaching inn, once a magistrates' court and believed to be the oldest pub on the High Street. The publican has built up a reputation for excellent guest beers, offering as many as 30 a month, sourced from breweries all over the country. Two beer festivals are held annually. Karaoke, disco and live music are occasional attractions. Well-behaved dogs and children are welcome before 7pm – well-behaved over-21s welcome at any time. ♨❀⛍♣P⛿

Chenies

Red Lion

Latimer Road, WD3 6ED (off A404 between Chorleywood and Little Chalfont) TQ021980

⌚ 11-2.30, 5.30-11; 12-3, 6.30-10.30 Sun

☎ (01923) 282722 🌐 redlionchenies.co.uk

Vale Best Bitter; Wadworth 6X; guest beers Ⓗ

Long-standing Guide entry with a long-standing landlord. This is a real village gem in idyllic surroundings. A cosy and comfortable pub with a relaxing atmosphere, it has a main bar and a new dining area. Local micro-breweries are a mainstay, with Vale and Rebellion providing the regular house beers alongside a guest ale. This is a beer pub that also serves excellent home-cooked food. Chenies Manor is nearby, along with excellent local walks. ♨Q❀◐◑♿⛍(336)P⛿

Chesham

Queens Head ✔

120 Church Street, HP5 1JD

⏲ 12-11 (midnight Thu & Fri); 11-midnight Sat; 11-10.30 Sun
☎ (01494) 778690
Brakspear Bitter; Fuller's London Pride, ESB; guest beers Ⓗ
The start and finish of the Pednor Loop for walkers, runners and cyclists. The River Chess runs by this street-corner Fuller's Pub of the Year in the old part of town. A central bar serves the public bar, saloon and three more rooms. Thai food is available in the upstairs restaurant or bars, with some traditional choices. There is an interesting whisky menu. Dogs are welcome in the public bar, with a biscuit for good behaviour. Under-18s are allowed until 8.30pm. ⌂Q❀◑◐⊟♿⊖🚌(T1)♣P⅟

Clifton Reynes

Robin Hood
Church Road, MK46 5DR (off A509) SP903512
⏲ 12-3, 6.30-11; closed Mon; 12-3, 7-10.30 Sun
☎ (01234) 711574 🌐 therobinhoodpub.co.uk
Greene King IPA, Abbot; guest beer Ⓗ
A past local CAMRA Pub of the Year, the Robin Hood is all you could wish for in a country pub. Food features highly with dishes ranging from traditional fare to the more unusual. Look out for details of the pub's history in the saloon, including landlords going back to 1577. Northants skittles is played here. The real cider is Westons. A ringing mobile phone will be fined with a £1 donation to charity. The Three Shires Way passes the door, popular with walkers and horse riders.
⌂Q❀◑◐⊟♿🚌(42)♣●P⅟

Cublington

Unicorn
High Street, LU7 0LQ
⏲ 12-3, 5-11; 12-midnight Fri & Sat; 12-10.30 Sun
☎ (01296) 681261
Brakspear Bitter; Greene King IPA; Shepherd Neame Spitfire; guest beers Ⓗ
Picturesque village free house voted Village Pub of the Year in 2008 by Aylesbury Vale Council. The long bar with a low ceiling has open fires at both ends. Food is available every day from an extensive menu and served either in the bar or a small dining area. The large, attractive garden has a covered and heated smoking area. Occasional beer festivals are held from the first weekend in May. Occasional live music features local jazz and rock bands. ⌂❀◑◐🚌(165)♣●P⅟

Downley Common

De Spencer Arms ✔
The Common, HP13 5YQ SU849958
⏲ 12-3, 6-11; 12-midnight Fri & Sat; 12-10.30 Sun
☎ (01494) 535317
Fuller's Chiswick, London Pride, seasonal beers; guest beers Ⓗ
Family oriented and frequented by ramblers, this brick-and-flint building is in a remote location. The interior divides into numerous intimate areas. In summer the pub hosts barbecues and mini beer festivals. Good quality food is served Wednesday to Sunday lunchtime plus Friday and Saturday evenings. Sunday roasts are always popular and booking is advisable. Live music is performed monthly on a Saturday, and a quiz is held weekly on Wednesday night. Dogs are welcome.
⌂Q❀◑◐🚌(31)♣P⅟

Forty Green

Royal Standard of England
HP9 1XT (off Penn Road from Knotty Green) SU924918
⏲ 11-11; 12-10.30 Sun
☎ (01494) 673382 🌐 rsoe.co.uk
Brakspear Bitter; Chiltern Ale; Rebellion Mild, IPA; Marston's Pedigree; guest beer Ⓗ
Ever popular, this rambling, historic free house attracts patrons from all over the world. Visitors converge to experience the ambience of the pub which is reputedly the oldest free house in England. An ale house has resided on this site since Saxon times. Complete with original tiled floors, low beams and period furniture, the interior oozes rustic mystique and charm. Renowned for its award-winning cuisine and local ales, this quaint hostelry should not be missed. Tricky to find, but well signposted. ⌂Q❀◑◐●P

Frieth

Prince Albert
Fingest Road, RG9 6PY
⏲ 11-11; 12-10.30 Sun
☎ (01494) 881683
Brakspear Bitter; Wychwood Hobgoblin Ⓗ
A friendly welcome awaits you at this charming, cloistered Brakspear country local. Sited a stone's throw from Frieth village, this pub is well worth seeking out for its cosy aura. The small bar area boasts a log fire in the winter and leads either way to further rooms and seating. The beer garden offers secluded summer family drinking. A classic example of a quaint, rural inn in good rambling territory for hikers. Evening meals are served Friday and Saturday only. ⌂Q❀◑◐♣P⅟

Haddenham

Rose & Thistle
6 Station Road, HP17 8AJ
⏲ 11-11; 12-10.30 Sun
☎ (01844) 291451
Greene King IPA, H& H Olde Trip; guest beer Ⓗ
This old-fashioned family pub was originally a coaching inn dating back to the 18th century. A large walled garden makes it ideal for families in summer. Most meals, including the good value Sunday lunches, are prepared on the premises and all meat and vegetables are sourced locally. Reduced rates for senior citizens are available Monday to Saturday. A popular quiz night is held on the first Wednesday of the month. Bed and breakfast accommodation is available in two rooms. ⌂Q❀🛏◑◐🚌(280)P

Hambleden

Stag & Huntsman
RG9 6RP (opp churchyard)
⏲ 11-2.30 (3 Sat), 6-11; 12-3, 7-10.30 Sun
☎ (01491) 571227 🌐 stagandhuntsman.co.uk
Rebellion IPA; Wadworth 6X; guest beers Ⓗ
Idealistic and unspoilt traditional inn, situated within a photogenic brick and flint National Trust village. Both pub and village have appeared in countless TV productions, including Midsomer Murders. Cyclists and hikers are among the regular visitors to this rustic gem. Food is served throughout the three bars and dining room. Guest ales favour local and south-west independent

breweries, especially Cottage. An annual beer festival is staged on the first weekend in September. A rare permanent outlet for Thatchers cider on handpump. ♣P

Hanslope

Globe

50 Hartwell Road, MK19 7BZ (N of village, in Long Street) SP794479
12-3.30 (not Mon), 6-11; 12-4 Sun
(01908) 510336 theglobehanslope.co.uk
Banks's Bitter; guest beers H
Visitors can be sure of a warm welcome at this award-winning village pub, located just through the rambling village. The interior comprises two bars: a public bar with a local feel and a small, cosy lounge. The restaurant is renowned for its game dishes and Sunday lunches. Guest beers usually come from the Marston's portfolio. The pub hosts many local events, including three annual beer festivals. The garden has a play area for children. Q (33)P

Hawridge

Full Moon

Hawridge Common, Cholesbury, HP5 2UH SP936069
12-11 (10.30 Sun)
(01494) 758959 thefullmoonpub.co.uk
Adnams Bitter; Brakspear Bitter; Draught Bass; Fuller's London Pride; Taylor Landlord; guest beers H
Originally an alehouse dating from 1693, now serving villages in the Chiltern Hills. Comfortable and spacious beamed seating areas display a collection of water jugs with six beer engines on the decorative bar being the central feature. The beam in the snug above the fireplace bears the carved initials of the first recorded landlord. Separate dining and meeting rooms are to the side and rear. The pub boasts a large garden, pergola covered patio and paddock for those arriving by horse. Q ♣P

Hedgerley

White Horse

Village Lane, SL2 3UY
11-2.30, 5-11; 11-11 Sat; 12-10.30 Sun
(01753) 643225
Greene King IPA; Rebellion IPA; guest beers G
The word 'gem' undersells this rural real ale drinkers' paradise. Seven real ales drawn from the cask (eight at weekends), three real ciders and one Belgian ale are on offer, with more than 1,000 different beers sold over the year (including a Whitsun beer festival with 130 plus ales). Add in two welcoming olde-worlde bars, excellent lunchtime food, a warming real fire in winter and a picture postcard garden in summer, and you have just about the perfect pub. Q ♣P

High Wycombe

Belle Vue

45 Gordon Road, HP13 6EQ (100m from train station, platform 3 exit)
12-2.30, 5-11; 12-midnight Sat; 12-10.30 Sun
(01494) 524728
St Austell Dartmoor Best Bitter; guest beers H
Street-corner locals' pub, the other side of the railway from the main town centre. The pub attracts rail commuters by virtue of its proximity to the station. There are always four ales on offer from the Punch Taverns portfolio. It can get busy when the Wasps play a home rugby match. Regular live music plays including bands and open jam sessions. ♣

Half Moon

103/105 Dashwood Avenue, HP12 3DZ (W of town centre 500 yards from A40)
12-midnight (1am Fri & Sat); 12-11.30 Sun
(01494) 441558
Shepherd Neame Spitfire; Taylor Landlord; guest beers H
This suburban locals' pub has been run by the same licensees for 20 years and was refurbished in 2006. The decor is modern with comfortable seating in one large room. The pub has a strong regular clientele and runs pool and darts teams. Friday night karaoke, entertainment on Saturday and disco/quiz/card games on Sunday evening are all popular. Roast lunch is served on Sunday. Sky Sports and Setanta are screened for sports fans. Each month the guest beer is chosen by customers. (32,33)♣P

Ickford

Rising Sun

36 Worminghall Road, HP18 9JD
12-2.30, 5-11; 12-11 Sat; 12-10.30 Sun
(01844) 339238
Adnams Bitter, Broadside; Black Sheep Best Bitter; Hancock's HB H
After a disastrous fire early in 2006, the pub was rebuilt, rethatched, refurbished and reopened in 2007 with the same popular landlord. Dating originally from the 15th century, the pub has become the hub of the village, hosting local events and games including crib, darts, quizzes and Aunt Sally. Four ales are always available and basic pub food is served at most sessions. Close to the Oxford Way, it attracts many ramblers and cyclists. Families and dogs on leads are welcome. Q (261)♣P

Iver

Bull

7 High Street, SL0 9ND
12-midnight (1am Fri & Sat); 12-10.30 Sun
(01753) 651115
Adnams Bitter; Fuller's London Pride; guest beer H
There has been a pub on this site since 1778, but it was rebuilt in 1817 after a fire. Now a no-nonsense traditional two-bar village pub, the front windows feature bull motifs in the leaded windows. The saloon bar has a Victorian feel with dark wood panelling. Quiz nights are held on alternate Sundays. The pub runs an informal bring and borrow book-swapping facility. Three reasonably priced letting rooms are available. There are heated and covered smoking areas outside. No food is served on Sunday. (58,459)♣P

Iver Heath

Black Horse

95 Slough Road, SL0 0DH (corner of Slough Rd and Bangors Rd)
11-11; 12-10.30 Sun
(01753) 652631

Badger First Gold, Tanglefoot, seasonal beer Ⓗ
Rare in this area, this large Hall & Woodhouse pub/eatery has been completely refurbished in country house style with oak panelling, leather armchairs and extensive library shelves laden with interesting books. It has retained a separate drinking area. A green oak timber conservatory opens onto the patio and garden. Restaurant meals and snacks, including vegetarian, are available all day. The Uxbridge to Slough No 58 bus stops outside the pub (not Sun). (58)P

Lacey Green

Pink & Lily

Pink Road, HP27 0RJ SP826019
11-11; 12-10 (4 winter) Sun
☎ (01494) 488308 pinkandlily.co.uk
Brakspear Bitter; Fuller's London Pride, seasonal beers; guest beers Ⓗ
This large pub has an extensive conservatory-style seating area leading to a pleasant garden. The famous Brooke Bar snug was a favourite of WWI poet Rupert Brooke and has been preserved in keeping with that period. The pub's curious name dates back to a scandal some 200 years ago involving servants at nearby Hampden Hall. Two – or three at Christmas – guest ales are on offer in addition to the regulars, mainly from local breweries Vale, Rebellion, Loddon, Tring and Archers. P

Whip

Pink Road, HP27 0PG
11-11; 12-10.30 Sun
☎ (01844) 344060 whipinn.co.uk
Beer range varies Ⓗ
A real ale cornucopia, over the last year the Whip has dispensed almost 800 different ales from its five handpumps. The beer variety is exceptional, with regulars often balloted for their own favourites. Two beer festivals are held annually including the Alternative Oktoberfest. Perched on top of the Chiltern Hills with an attractive enclosed garden, the pub enjoys splendid views and is a popular destination for ramblers. Good food includes fish freshly landed from Devon. Real cider is always available. Q(300)

Ley Hill

Swan

Ley Hill Common, HP5 1UT (opp cricket pitch) SP990018
12-3, 5.30-11; 12-4, 6-10.30 Sun
☎ (01494) 783075 swanleyhill.com
Adnams Bitter; Brakspear Bitter; Fuller's London Pride; Taylor Landlord; guest beer Ⓗ
Originally three timber-framed cottages, this old style country pub overlooks the local cricket pitch and is close to the golf club. At one time it was the stop-off for condemned prisoners permitted a last request on their way to nearby gallows. Clarke Gable, Glenn Miller and James Stewart visited during WWII from nearby Bovingdon airfield. The interior comprises a restaurant, snug and lounge bar with oak beams and roaring fire. Outside, the small front garden leads to a larger rear garden. No evening meals Sunday or Monday.
Q(373)P

Little Missenden

Crown

HP7 0RD (off A413, between Amersham and Gt Missenden) SU924989
11-2.30, 6-11; 12-3, 7-11 Sun
☎ (01494) 862571
Adnams Bitter; Hook Norton Bitter; St Austell Tribute; guest beer Ⓗ
Run by the same family for almost a century, this village pub has been refurbished to include B&B accommodation and a bigger bar, but retains a cosy, friendly atmosphere. Good pub food, served at lunchtime, is simple and generous. Popular with walkers, the large and attractive garden is a great place to relax and enjoy a peaceful pint. A regular in the Guide for almost 30 years.
QP

Littleworth Common

Blackwood Arms

Common Lane, SL1 8PP SU937862
12-3, 5-11; closed Mon; 12-11 Sat; 12-10 Sun
☎ (01753) 642169 blackwoodarms.com
Brakspear Bitter; guest beers Ⓗ
A secluded country pub to the north of Burnham Beeches, popular with walkers. The landlord has increased the range of guest ales and his strong commitment to real ale won him the local CAMRA Publican of the Year award in 2008. The large garden is deservedly popular in warmer weather and is ideal for families. Good food is available 12-3pm and 6-10pm Tuesday to Friday and all day at the weekend. For special food offers see website.
P

Jolly Woodman

Littleworth Road, SL1 8PF
11-11 (midnight Fri & Sat); 12-10.30 Sun
☎ (01753) 644350 thejollywoodman.co.uk
Fuller's London Pride; Hop Back Summer Lightning; Rebellion IPA; St Austell Tribute; guest beers Ⓗ
A homely country pub close to the northern edge of Burnham Beeches. It is popular for its range of beers and good food, as well as its live Monday night jazz sessions. The bar area contains a large collection of old beer bottles as well as a rowing boat in the rafters. There is a seating area in the garden. Food is available lunchtimes and evenings, with bar snacks only on Sunday evening.
P

Long Crendon

Eight Bells

51 High Street, HP18 9AL
12-3 (not Mon), 5.30-11 (midnight Fri); 12-11 Sat; 12-10.30 Sun
☎ (01844) 208244 eightbellspub.com
Marston's Pedigree; Wadworth IPA Ⓗ**; guest beers** Ⓗ/Ⓖ
A traditional hub of the village local, popular with both drinkers and diners. The quaint interior has some original tiled floors, beams and an alcove dedicated to the pub's Morris dancers. A recently installed stillage blends in perfectly behind the snug bar, giving a six barrel gravity dispense capability. Three guest ales change frequently. Two beer festivals, held on Easter and autumn bank holidays, are hosted in the extensive garden.
(261)P

Loudwater

Derehams Inn

5 Derehams Lane, HP10 9RH (50m off A40 London Road at Station Road jct)

⏲ 11.30-3.30, 5.30-11; 11-midnight Fri & Sat; 12-10.30 Sun

☎ (01494) 530965

Brakspear Bitter; Fuller's London Pride; Loddon seasonal beers; guest beers Ⓗ

Well-established free house, boasting a horseshoe-shaped interior, an intimate ambience and traditional pub fare. It is popular with both locals and pubgoers who enjoy a decent pint in authentic surroundings. Two regular ales are complemented by three guest beers, with a Loddon brew usually available. A regular themed evening is well attended by patrons. The annual beer festival hosting two dozen real ales is staged over the first weekend in July. ⌂❀◖◗🚌♣P⚟

Marlow

Duke of Cambridge

19 Queens Road, SL7 2PS

⏲ 11-11.30 (12.30am Fri & Sat); 10-11 Sun

☎ (01628) 488555

Harveys Sussex Best Bitter; guest beers Ⓗ

Eminent back-street local, now well established as the town's most adventurous real ale pub. Over 400 different beers have been showcased, coming from breweries ranging from large independents to the latest micro. John, the landlord, regularly descends on breweries from Cheshire to Dorset, sourcing the newest brews for the Duke. The first Saturday in the month is steak night, and the popular Sunday roasts are legendary. A beer festival is held in mid June, around the summer solstice. ⌂❀◖♿⇌🚌(2,800,850)♣⚟

Three Horseshoes

Burroughs Grove Hill, SL7 3RA (on High Wycombe-Marlow road)

⏲ 11.30-3, 5-11; 11.30-11 Fri & Sat; 12-5, 7-10.30 Sun

☎ (01628) 483109

Rebellion Mild, IPA, Smuggler, Mutiny, seasonal beers Ⓗ

Favoured by both drinkers and diners who enjoy this brewery tap's six Rebellion beers and the extensive menu (no meals Sun eve). The four regular brews are joined by a seasonal beer and a monthly special. The interior comprises three distinctive areas and the outside boasts an enclosed family-friendly beer garden for summer socialising. The pub is a five minute bus ride from the town centre. Former local CAMRA Pub of the Year. ⌂Q❀◖◗🚌(800,850)P

Marsworth

Anglers Retreat ✔

Startops End, HP23 4LJ (on B489, opp Startops Reservoir car park) SP919141

⏲ 11-11; 12-10.30 Sun

☎ (01442) 822250 🌐 anglersretreatpub.co.uk

Fuller's London Pride; Tring Side Pocket for a Toad; guest beers Ⓗ

A liberal adornment of fishing memorabilia befits the name and location of this pub, situated close to the Grand Union canal and opposite Startops reservoir, renowned for its fishing and bird watching. A single bar serves the main room, and there is a snug with dartboard, conservatory and large garden. Regularly changing guest beers and home-cooked food are available. Seasonal beer festivals are held in spring and autumn. Walkers and dogs welcome. ⌂❀◖◗🚌(61)♣P⚟

Red Lion ✔

90 Vicarage Road, HP23 4LU (off B489, by canal bridge)

⏲ 11-3, 5 (6 Sat)-11; 12-3, 7-10.30 Sun

☎ (01296) 668366

Fuller's London Pride; guest beers, Ⓗ**;** Ⓖ

The Red Lion is a real village pub and long-standing Guide entry. Dating from the 17th century and close to the Grand Union canal, the saloon bar is comfortable, with a small restaurant, while the low-beamed public bar is split into drinking and games areas, including bar biliards, shove ha'penny and skittles (by prior arangement). A real fire adds to the atmosphere. Children are allowed in the games area and dogs are welcome. Outside is a covered patio and garden.
⌂Q❀◖◗⊟♿🚌(61)♣🍎P⚟

Milton Keynes

Plough at Simpson ✔

Simpson Road, Simpson, MK6 3AH

⏲ 12-11 (12-3, 5.30-11 Mon-Thu winter); 12-10.30 Sun

☎ (01908) 691555 🌐 theploughatsimpson.co.uk

Wells Eagle IPA, Bombardier; guest beers Ⓗ

This village pub successfully blends the old with the new with a traditional pub atmosphere, separate games room and an excellent restaurant specialising in fresh seafood and steak. Rebuilt in 1877, a pub has existed here since 1753. Welcoming staff serve superbly kept ales with constantly changing guest beers. A large garden slopes towards the Grand Union Canal. Theme nights are held, raising funds for the local hospice. Charles Wells Area Pub of the Year 2007.
❀◖◗♿🚌(18)♣P⚟

Red Lion

11 Lock View Lane, Fenny Stratford, MK1 1BA (off Simpson Road)

⏲ 12-11 (midnight Fri & Sat); 12-10.30 Sun

☎ (01908) 372317

Beer range varies Ⓗ

The Grade II-listed exterior reflects this small lock-side pub's canal history. It has become a gem of a local since new licensees moved in two years ago and is renowned for well-kept beer and friendly conversation. The smaller of the two bars may be reserved for club meetings. TV screens show sports. The garden is the perfect place to sit and watch the efforts of narrow boat crew negotiating the lock. MK Dons football stadium is less than a mile away. ⌂❀♿⇌(Fenny Stratford)🚌(5,7)♣P⚟

Victoria Inn 🏆

Vicarage Road, Bradwell Village, MK13 9AQ

⏲ 11.30-midnight; 12-11 Sun

☎ (01908) 316355

Beer range varies Ⓗ

The popularity of its quality ales has seen this pub go from strength to strength. Four changing ales are served from water-cooled handpumps. The closest pub to the Concrete Cow Brewery, its beers often feature. Other popular micro-breweries include Tring and Bank Top, although anything from anywhere in the UK may be on offer. Real draught cider is also sold. An annual beer festival is hosted on the August bank holiday weekend. Local CAMRA Pub of the Year 2009. Lunches served weekdays only. ❀◖🚌(2A)♣🍎P⚟

Wetherspoons ✔

201 Midsummer Boulevard, MK9 1EA
9-midnight (1am Fri & Sat)
☎ (01908) 606074
Greene King Ruddles Best Bitter, Abbot; Marston's Pedigree; guest beers Ⓗ
This pub is a long-standing entry in the Guide. Guest beers are sourced directly from micros such as Concrete Cow, Great Oakley and Potton, and are promoted with meal deals such as the Tuesday grills and Thursday curries. The pub wholeheartedly participates in company beer festivals. Staff will remove sparklers if asked. Westons cider is also served. Most buses that go to the city centre from the train station stop outside. There is a covered, heated patio for smokers.
Q&(Central)P

Naphill

Wheel

100 Main Road, HP14 4QA
12.30-2.30 (not Mon), 4.30-11; 12-midnight Fri & Sat; 12-10.30 Sun
☎ (01494) 562210 thewheelnaphill.com
Greene King IPA; guest beers Ⓗ
What was once a run-down pub is now thriving again. The Wheel is popular with locals and walkers, and is handy for passing trade. Muddy boots and well-behaved dogs are both welcome. There are two distinct rooms inside, with a common bar area. Regular beer festivals are held. Lunches are served all week and evening meals from 6-9pm (not Sun). (300)P

Newport Pagnell

Cannon

50 High Street, MK16 8AQ
12-11 (midnight Fri & Sat)
☎ (01908) 211495
Banks's Bitter; Marston's Pedigree; guest beers Ⓗ
A true free house, the Cannon retains the feel of an old town-centre local. Up to two guest beers are often from the Marston's list, but can also be local. Look out for the military memorabilia and various awards adorning the walls. Outside, there is a function room for hire, home to the open mike live music event held on Thursday night. 'Real ale' is written in four languages behind the bar and the landlord speaks them all. (1,2)P

Olney

Swan

12 High Street South, MK46 4AA
11-11 (6 Sun)
☎ (01234) 711111
Adnams Bitter; Fuller's London Pride; Shepherd Neame Kent's Best; Young's Bitter; guest beer Ⓗ
This is an old town-centre pub located not far from the historic Market Square. With wooden floors and bare beamed ceilings, the relaxed atmosphere and friendly locals put visitors at ease. Five handpumps dispense a wide range of ales – the guest beer is sourced locally. Excellent meals (not Mon and Sun eve) add to the bistro feel. A courtyard enables alfresco drinking and dining during the summer. This is the regular haunt of the local MP.
Q(1B)P

Quainton

George & Dragon ✔

The Green, HP22 4AR
12-11 (12-2.30, 5-11 winter); 12-midnight Fri & Sat
☎ (01296) 655436
Hook Norton Hooky Bitter; Shepherd Neame Spitfire; Young's Bitter; guest beers Ⓗ
Two-bar local on the village green overlooked by a restored windmill which provides flour for the pub. An extensive menu of value-for-money food includes vegetarian and children's options. Meal deals are available for older people on Tuesday and steak specials on Tuesday evening (no food Sun eve or Mon lunchtime). Traditional cider is stocked in summer. Post Office facilities are offered in the bar on Wednesday afternoon. The Buckinghamshire Steam Railway Centre is close by.
Q(16)P

Stoke Goldington

Lamb

16-20 High Street, MK16 8NR
12-3, 5-11; 12-11 Sat; 12-8 Sun
☎ (01908) 551233
thelambstokegoldington.moonfruit.com
Beer range varies Ⓗ
This excellent village free house is very much the hub of the local community. Five handpumps offer ales from micros such as Nethergate and Tring, as well as a Westons cider. Northamptonshire skittles and darts teams are based here. Run by the same family for many years, the pub hosts occasional live music events and a jazz and blues festival in September. Good food is available – popular Sunday lunches are served until 5pm. Local CAMRA Pub of the Year 2008. (1B)P

Stoke Mandeville

Bull

5 Risborough Road, HP22 5UP
12-3, 5.30-11; 12-11 Fri & Sat; 12-10.30 Sun
☎ (01296) 613632
Adnams Bitter; Fuller's London Pride; Tetley Bitter Ⓗ
Small two-bar pub situated on a main road, well served by public transport. The public bar at the front is popular with locals who gather to watch football and horse racing on TV. The comfortable lounge bar at the back tends to be quieter. Outside, the large, secure garden is a big attraction, especially in summer. Q(300)P

Thornborough

Two Brewers

Bridge Street, MK18 2DN (off A421, turn by Lone Tree pub)
12-2 Wed & Sat only, 6-midnight; 12-3, 7-11 Sun
☎ (01280) 812020
Black Sheep Best Bitter; Silverstone Pitstop Ⓗ
Run by the same landlord for more than 25 years, this welcoming drinkers' pub is in the centre of the village. You can play darts in the traditional public bar or relax with a pint in the lounge. During the week the pub is closed at lunchtime except on Wednesday when it offers half-price drinks to pensioners. Q

Turville

Bull & Butcher ✔

RG9 6QU (off M40 jct 5 through Ibstone to Turville)

11-11; 12-10.30 Sun

☎ (01491) 638283 🌐 thebullandbutcher.com

Brakspear Bitter, Oxford Gold, seasonal beers; Hook Norton Hooky Dark Ⓗ

Set in an unspoilt village in a beautiful Chiltern valley, this charming 16th-century timbered pub has open log fires and a bar extension that incorporates a table above a 50-foot well. The excellent à la carte menu is reasonably priced (booking is recommended). A function room is available for meetings and there is a very pleasant garden. The village and pub often feature in films and TV series. **Q P**

Tylers Green

Horse & Jockey ✔

Church Road, HP10 8EG

12-3, 5-11; 12-11 Fri & Sat; 12-10.30 Sun

☎ (01494) 815963 🌐 horseandjockeytylersgreen.co.uk

Adnams Bitter, Broadside; Brakspear Bitter; Fuller's London Pride; Greene King Abbot; guest beer Ⓗ

Converted to a pub in 1821, this picturesque, cosy local is near the attractive Tylers Green church. It has been a Guide regular for many years. The single U-shaped room has a games area on the right and the left side is reserved for diners. There are six ales on offer, with tasting notes on boards behind the bar. Food is available all week, lunchtimes and evenings. The main parking area is across the road from the pub. **♣P**

Wendover

Pack Horse

29 Tring Road, HP22 6NR

12-11 (midnight Fri & Sat); 12-10.30 Sun

☎ (01296) 622075

Fuller's London Pride, seasonal beers; Gale's Butser Bitter; guest beers Ⓗ

Small, friendly village free house dating from 1769 and situated at the end of a terrace known as the Anne Boleyn cottages. On the Ridgeway path, it has been owned by the same family for 46 years. The wall above the bar is decorated with RAF squadron badges denoting connections with nearby RAF Halton. The pub runs men's and women's darts teams, dominoes and cribbage.
(54)♣

Wing

Queen's Head ✔

9 High Street, LU7 0NS

11-3, 5.30-11; 11.30-11 Fri & Sat; 12-10.30 Sun

☎ (01296) 688268

Adnams Bitter; Fuller's London Pride; Shepherd Neame Spitfire; guest beers Ⓗ

A village local offering an increasing number of real ales. The 16th-century building features open log fires in the restaurant and main bar and comfortable sofas in the snug. The food is excellent and sensibly priced, with fish dishes a speciality (booking is recommended). Outside is a large attractive garden and patio. Aylesbury Vale Council's Village Pub of the Year 2007.
(100,150)♣P

Wooburn Common

Royal Standard

Wooburn Common Road, HP10 0JS (follow signs to Odds Farm) SU924873

12-11; 12-10.30 Sun

☎ (01628) 521121

Caledonian Deuchars IPA; Hop Back Summer Lightning; St Austell Tribute; guest beers Ⓗ/Ⓖ

Ever-popular, semi-rural country pub that attracts drinkers from afar with the allure of ten real ales and real cider. Five beers are on handpump, five on gravity dispense, with a dark ale usually available. This is a rare source in the area for both Hop Back and Downton brews. Diners are well catered for and Sunday lunchtimes can be busy, especially in the summer. Former local CAMRA Pub of the Year.
Q P

Wycombe Marsh

General Havelock

114 Kingsmead Road, HP11 1HZ (S of M40)

12-2.30, 5.30-11; 12-11 Fri & Sat; 12-10.30 Sun

☎ (01494) 520391

Fuller's Chiswick, London Pride, ESB, seasonal beers; guest beers Ⓗ

A regular entry in the Guide, this imposing pub was converted from a farmhouse. It sits to the rear of the Kingsmead playing fields. The pub has been run by the same family since it was bought by Fuller's. There are now six ales always available. Food is served every lunchtime except Saturday and in the evening on Friday only. The garden is a peaceful haven in summer. **♣P**

The soul of beer

Brewers call barley malt the 'soul of beer'. While a great deal of attention has been rightly paid to hops in recent years, the role of malt in brewing must not be ignored. Malt contains starch that is converted to a special form of sugar known as maltose during the brewing process. It is maltose that is attacked by yeast during fermentation and turned into alcohol and carbon dioxide. Other grains can be used in brewing, notably wheat. But barley malt is the preferred grain as it gives a delightful biscuity / cracker / Ovaltine note to beer. Unlike wheat, barley has a husk that works as a natural filter during the first stage of brewing, known as the mash. Cereals such as rice and corn / maize are widely used by global producers of mass-market lagers, but craft brewers avoid them.

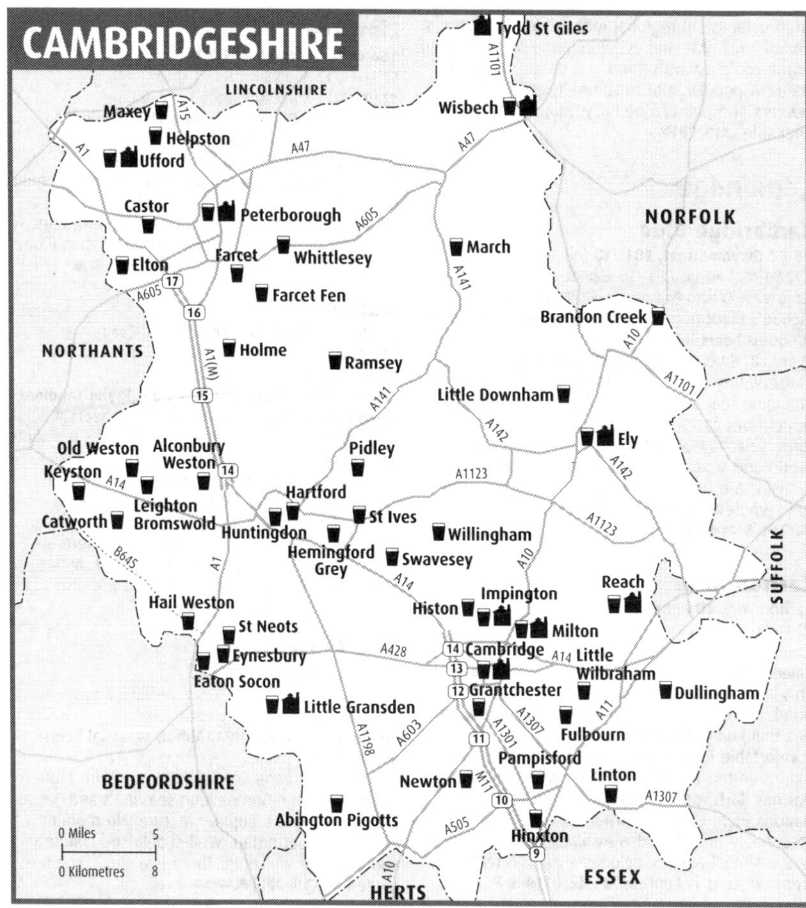

Abington Pigotts

Pig & Abbot

High Street, SG8 0SD (off A505 through Litlington)
⌚ 12-3, 6-11; 12-11 Sat; 12-10.30 Sun
☎ (01763) 853515 🌐 pigandabbot.co.uk
Adnams Bitter; Fuller's London Pride; guest beers Ⓗ
Located in a surprisingly remote part of the south Cambridgeshire countryside, this Queen Anne period pub offers a warm welcome. The interior has exposed oak beams and a large inglenook with a wood-burning stove. A comfortable restaurant offers home-made traditional pub food and specialises in Thai curry made with fresh herbs and spices. Various guest beers are offered, often from Woodforde's or Timothy Taylor. ⌂Q❀◑P

Alconbury Weston

White Hart

2 Vinegar Hill, PE28 4JA
⌚ 12-2.30, 5.30-11; 12-4, 6.30-11 Sat; 12-5.30 Sun
☎ (01480) 890331
Adnams Bitter; Courage Directors Ⓗ
Welcoming 16th-century coaching inn on the old Great North Road with an open plan two-tiered layout providing different drinking sections and a darts area. Home-cooked food is served lunchtimes and evenings, including popular Sunday lunches. International dining nights are a feature and there is occasional live music. This community pub raises funds for local amenities and is supported by villagers, local businesses and passing trade.
❀◑♿🚌♣P⊱

Brandon Creek

Ship

Brandon Creek Bridge, PE38 0PP (just off A10)
⌚ 12-3, 6-midnight (closed Mon winter); 12-11 (12-4, 6-10.30 winter) Sun
☎ (01353) 676228
Adnams Bitter; guest beers Ⓗ
Welcoming free house with pleasant riverside views, serving up to three guest beers, mainly

INDEPENDENT BREWERIES

Cambridge Moonshine Cambridge
Devil's Dyke Reach
Elgood's Wisbech
Hereward Ely
Kilderkin Impington
Milton Milton
Oakham Peterborough
Son of Sid Little Gransden
Tydd Steam Tydd Saint Giles
Ufford Ufford

from established regional independent brewers. A varied lunchtime and evening menu features good home-cooked food served in a choice of dining areas. A popular spot in summer, especially with boaters, the pub can be busy. Moorings are available. ⌂❀◐P⅟

Cambridge

Cambridge Blue

85-87 Gwydir Street, CB1 2LG (off Mill Road)
⊙ 12-2.30, 5.30-11; 12-11 Thu-Sat; 12-10.30 Sun
☎ (01223) 471680 ⊕ the-cambridgeblue.co.uk
Elgood's Black Dog; Woodforde's Wherry Best Bitter [H]; guest beers [H]/[G]
Quiet, traditional, community pub with a conservatory and large garden. Up to 12 ever-changing real ales are available, some served direct from casks in the tap room. There is also a large selection of bottled beers from all over the world and several real ciders and perries. Beer festivals are held in a marquee in February and July. Wholesome home-cooked food is available. ⌂Q❀◐⇶♣●

Carlton Arms

Carlton Way, CB4 2BY
⊙ 11-11; 12-10.30 Sun
☎ (01223) 355717
Caledonian Deuchars IPA; Oakham JHB; guest beers [H]
This large, two-room, community pub has changed hands since its last appearance in the Guide, but has thankfully maintained its form. The comfortable lounge is furnished with sofas alongside the tables and chairs, while the public bar has darts, pool and skittles to offer. A large patio is ideal for the warmer months. Good reasonably priced food is available. The wide beer range almost always includes a mild. A real cider from Westons is kept. ❀◐⊟⊞(C1)♣●P

Castle Inn

38 Castle Street, CB3 0AJ
⊙ 11.30-3, 5-11; 11.30-3.30, 6-11 Sat; 11.30-3.30, 7-10.30 Sun
☎ (01223) 353194
Adnams Bitter, Explorer, Broadside; Fuller's London Pride; Taylor Landlord; guest beers [H]
In the shadow of the mound of the long-gone Cambridge Castle, this Adnams house (its most westerly tied house) offers a great selection of Adnams beers, including seasonals, plus changing guests from all over the country.There is a wide choice of drinking areas on two floors and the sun-trap garden is a delight on warm days. Excellent food is served every session. The landlord was Barry Wom in the Rutles. ⌂❀◐

Champion of the Thames

68 King Street, CB1 1LN
⊙ 11-11 (midnight Fri & Sat) (hours may vary in winter); 11-10.30 Sun
☎ (01223) 352043
Greene King IPA, Abbot; guest beers [H]
This small, two-room, city-centre pub has a truly friendly atmosphere. It is one of four remaining pubs on the infamous King Street Run pub crawl, which historically visited all eight pubs that were once on this street. The oarsmen in the pub's name are also commemorated on the fine etched glazing in the exterior windows. ⌂Q❀⊟⊞♣⅟

Elm Tree

16a Orchard Street, CB1 1JT
⊙ 11-11; 12-10.30 Sun
☎ (01223) 502632 ⊕ elmtreepub.co.uk
B&T Shefford Bitter, Dark Mild; Wells Eagle IPA, Bombardier; guest beer [H]
A relaxed back-street pub where the ever-changing beers, usually including at least one mild, on the ten handpumps are complemented by a large menu of Belgian and other bottled beers. A real cider or perry is also available. Occasional beer tastings and music gigs are held. ❀♿♣●

Empress

72 Thoday Street, CB1 3AX (off Mill Road)
⊙ 4-11.30 (1.30am Fri); 12-1.30am Sat; 12-11.30 Sun
☎ (01223) 247236
Adnams Bitter; Marston's Pedigree; Taylor Landlord; Woodforde's Wherry Best Bitter; guest beers [H]
Back-street local popular with the town's residents and students alike. Three main drinking areas form a U-shape, with the public bar on one side and lounge on the other. There is a large heated gazebo for smokers and a sun-trap patio garden beyond. Pizza is always available and there are regular barbecue and curry nights. Pool, board games and Westons Old Rosie cider are also available. i ❀◐⊟⇶⊞♣●⅟

Free Press

7 Prospect Row, CB1 1DU
⊙ 12-2.30, 6 (4.30 Fri)-11; 12-11 Sat; 12-3, 7-10.30 Sun
☎ (01223) 368337 ⊕ freepresspub.com
Greene King XX Mild, IPA, Abbot, seasonal beers; guest beers [H]
Friendly, traditional, community pub with high-quality food and Greene King seasonals and guests. The tiny snug is a popular feature. No mobile phones are permitted. Well-supervised children and dogs are welcome. There is a small, sheltered garden. ⌂Q❀◐⊞♣⅟▯

Kingston Arms

33 Kingston Street, CB1 2NU (off Mill Rd)
⊙ 12-2.30, 5-11; 12-midnight Fri & Sat; 12-11 Sun
☎ (01223) 319414 ⊕ kingston-arms.co.uk
Crouch Vale Brewers Gold; Elgood's Black Dog; Hop Back Entire Stout, Summer Lightning; Oakham JHB; Taylor Landlord; guest beers [H]
A classic pub, free of any keg products, with four changing guest beers in addition to those listed. The stunning blue exterior adorned with hanging baskets makes it easy to find. Simply furnished, table space is often at a premium. Award-winning food is served lunchtimes and evenings. There are free newspapers, Internet and Wi-Fi access for customers. The walled garden has canopies and heaters and is popular all year round. ⌂Q❀◐⇶⊞●⅟

Live & Let Live

40 Mawson Road, CB1 2EA
⊙ 11.30-2.30, 5.30 (6 Sat)-11; 12-3, 7-11 Sun
☎ (01223) 460261
Adnams Bitter; Nethergate Umbel Ale; guest beer [H]
Modern wood panelling and railway and beer memorabilia contribute to the comfortable atmosphere at this modest street-corner local. Seven handpumps present an array of both regular and guest ales, ranging from a session bitter to a stronger beer, and always a dark beer. The eighth handpump dispenses cider from local producer Cassels. A fine selection of bottled Belgian beers,

and an ever-changing guest Belgian beer on draught, complete the impressive range on offer at this cosy establishment. Q◑⇌🚌(2)♣🍎

Mitre ✔

17 Bridge Street, CB2 1UF

11-11 (midnight Thu; 1am Fri & Sat)

☎ (01223) 358403

Adnams Broadside; Fuller's London Pride; Greene King IPA; Shepherd Neame Spitfire; Taylor Landlord Ⓗ

Standing on the site of two former inns, the Blackmoor's Head and the Cask & Magpie, the pub has been known as the Mitre since 1881. The interior is smart cafe-bar style with cream and salmon walls, parquet flooring and large windows. The stone-flagged floor in the lower area is a remnant of a previous ale house decor. Three changing guest beers come from regionals or bigger micros. Beer and food nights are held on Tuesday plus regular Meet the Brewer sessions. Good value food is available 11am-10.30pm. ◑🚌

Salisbury Arms ✔

76 Tenison Road, CB1 2DW (off Mill Road)

12-2, 5-11 (midnight Fri); 6-midnight Sat (closed lunchtime); 12-2, 7-10.30 Sun

☎ (01223) 576363

Adnams Broadside; St Austell Tribute; Wells Eagle IPA, Bombardier; guest beers Ⓗ

This long end-of-terrace Victorian pub is a short walk from Cambridge railway station. Its recent refurbishment by Charles Wells has maintained its essential character, and it has kept its impressive collection of old folk festival and beer festival posters and decorations. Eight handpumps include four changing guests. Local organic cider is from Crones. No food is available on Saturday and Sunday evenings. ❀◑⇌🚌🍎⊱

St Radegund

129 King Street, CB1 1LD

5 (12 Sat)-11; 12-10.30 Sun

☎ (01223) 311794 🌐 radegund.org.uk

Milton Sackcloth, Nero; Shepherd Neame Spitfire; Woodforde's Wherry Best Bitter Ⓗ

The smallest pub in Cambridge, this unique freehouse is very traditional. The interior is packed with mementos, from steam railway photos to local sporting memorabilia. The pub is also the base of the infamous Hash House Harriers and runs its own sports teams, including rowing and cricket. Occasional background jazz is not intrusive. The pub is a regular outlet for Milton Brewery beers. Q🚌

Castor

Prince of Wales Feathers

38 Peterborough Road, PE5 7AL

12-11.30 (1am Fri & Sat); 12-midnight Sun

☎ (01733) 380222 🌐 princeofwalesfeathers.co.uk

Adnams Bitter; Woodforde's Wherry Best Bitter; guest beers Ⓗ

Refurbished single-room village local run by friendly and welcoming hosts. The interior retains the original stained glass windows, cleverly divided into different areas to cater for a mixed clientele. Lunches are served daily. Live music plays every other Saturday evening and there is a quiz on Sunday evening. Lined glasses are available on request. The pleasant patio to the side of the pub is popular in summer. An annual beer festival is held. ♨❀◐♿🚌♣🍎⊱

Catworth

Fox

Fox Road, PE28 0PW (off A14, near B660 exit)

11-11; 12-10.30 Sun

☎ (01832) 710363 🌐 thefoxcatworth.co.uk

Beer range varies Ⓗ

Perched above the A14 and reached via a slip road to the B660, the pub has a patio outside plus a garden and children's play area. The interior is open plan with a bar in the centre. Real ales regularly come from local micro-breweries such as Digfield and Grainstore. The pub is open for meals all day every day and offers an extensive blackboard menu. A beer festival is held in June or July. A rare appearance in this area for real cider – Westons Old Rosie. ♨❀◑🍎P

Dullingham

Boot

18 Brinkley Road, CB8 9UW

11-2.30, 5-11; 11-11 Sat; 12-3, 7-11 Sun

☎ (01638) 507327

Adnams Bitter, Broadside; guest beers Ⓗ

Basic village inn brought to life by the friendly atmosphere generated by the locals. Saved from closure a few years ago, since then the pub has gone from strength to strength and was a former Cambridge CAMRA Pub of the Year. Sport is high on the agenda, especially horseracing, and many community events are based around the pub. Children are permitted until 8pm. No meals served on Sunday lunchtime. ♨❀◐⇌♣P⊱

Eaton Socon

Rivermill Tavern

School Lane, PE19 8GW

12-11 (midnight Fri)

☎ (01480) 219612

Adnams Broadside; Greene King IPA, Abbot; guest beers Ⓗ

This popular riverside pub at Eaton Socon lock on the River Great Ouse was converted from a flour mill and has a galleried area above the bar. It offers an extensive and varied menu, served all day on Saturday and Sunday. Live music is hosted on Tuesday and Friday evenings and a quiz on Sunday evening. Up to two guest beers are stocked from independent breweries. The patio offers splendid views of the river and marina. Moorings are available. ☙❀◑🚌(X5)♣P⊱

Elton

Crown ✔

8 Duck Street, PE8 6RQ

12 (5 Mon)-11; 12-10.30 Sun

☎ (01832) 280232 🌐 thecrowninn.org

Greene King IPA; guest beers Ⓗ

This listed thatched and stone-built pub overlooking the village green was largely rebuilt in 1845 after a major fire. The landlord takes pride in offering real ales and fine food for which the pub is noted (no food Sun eve or Mon). The house beer, Golden Crown Bitter at 4.3% ABV, is likely to come from the Grainstore Brewery. A beer festival is held in early May. There are five individually furnished letting rooms and free Wi-Fi. ♨Q☙❀🛏◑♿🚌(X4,24)

Ely

Prince Albert

62 Silver Street, CB7 4JF (opp cathedral car park)

11-3.30, 6.30 (6 Fri)-11 (11.30 Fri & Sat); 12-3.30, 7-10.30 Sun

(01353) 663494

Greene King XX Mild, IPA, Abbot; guest beers H

Superb little back-street gem – a traditional local pub with no music or gaming machines, just pleasant bar-room banter. A rare outlet for XX Mild, two guest beers are usually available, mainly from Greene King. Secondhand books and regular events help fundraise for local good causes. Food is served Monday-Saturday lunchtime. Children are permitted only in the pleasant pub garden at the rear but dogs are welcome. A former winner of many local and regional CAMRA Pub of the Year awards. Q

Town House

60-64 Market Street, CB7 4LS

11-11 (1am Fri & Sat); 12-10.30 Sun

(01353) 664338

Beer range varies H

A former Georgian town house, now pleasantly converted to a city-centre pub with the addition of a conservatory at the back. The three guest ales change regularly, mainly sourced from the region, however beers from smaller local micro-brewers sometimes make an appearance. Happy hour is 5-7pm Monday to Friday and a good fun quiz is held on Sunday night. Opens late on Friday and Saturday with a DJ attracting younger customers.

West End House

16 West End, CB6 3AY

12.30-3, 6-11; 12-midnight Fri & Sat; 12-4, 7-11 Sun

(01353) 669718 westendhouseely.co.uk

Adnams Bitter; guest beers H

Built in the 1830s, the pub is located away from the city centre, a short walk from Oliver Cromwell's house. It retains a traditional feel with its low beamed ceiling, rambling between a cosy snug, two bars and a larger saloon. The guest beers are generally from established national independent brewers and occasionally the local Pickled Pig cider is on offer. Light snacks are available at lunchtime. The garden has an enclosed patio area with heating. Well-behaved children are welcome until 8pm. Q

Eynesbury

Cambridgeshire Hunter

64 Berkeley Street, PE19 2NF

12-11

(01480) 216824

Wells Eagle IPA; guest beer H

A community pub with two bars, one a traditional room with rustic beams, the other a modern sports bar with pool, darts and plasma screens for all sporting occasions. The large garden with children's play area is popular in summer. A heated and covered shelter caters for smokers. Good home-cooked food is popular at lunchtimes.

P

Farcet

Black Swan

77 Main Street, PE7 3DF (off B1091)

12-2 (not Mon or winter), 5-11; 12-11 Fri & Sat; 12-10.30 Sun

(01733) 240387

Beer range varies H

Traditional local pub at the bottom of the village next to the river and just ten minutes walk from the church bus stop. Log fires blaze in both the bar and the newly refurbished lounge-restaurant. Food is served Friday to Sunday lunchtimes and Tuesday to Saturday evenings. Three regularly changing cask ales are available. An annual charity beer festival is held in September. Camping available.

Q (3,7) P

Farcet Fen

Plough

Milk & Water Drove, Ramsey Road, PE7 3DR (on B1095)

5-11; 12-3, 6-11 Sat; 12-10.30 Sun

(01733) 844307

Elgood's Black Dog; Fuller's London Pride; Oakham JHB; guest beers H

Remote Fenland pub with a strong reputation for good food and quality beer. It has recently extended its dining area away from the main bars. The lounge bar has a farming theme and a large aquarium. There is a bar billiards table in the public bar. Outside is a play area for children and an enormous events field for weddings and parties. Regular live music and bikers' rallies are hosted.

P

Fulbourn

Six Bells

9 High Street, CB21 5DH

11.30-3, 6-11.30; 12-11.30 Fri & Sat; 12-11 Sun

(01223) 880244

Adnams Bitter; Woodforde's Wherry Best Bitter; guest beers H

Former coaching inn with a thatched roof and low ceilings. An archetypal two-bar village pub with a welcoming log fire, it serves home-cooked, locally-sourced food in the bar and dining room (not Sun or Mon eves). Trad jazz features in the function room on the first and third Wednesday of the month. Quiz night is Thursday. The comfortable patio and sprawling garden to the rear are popular in summer. Real cider is Westons Old Rosie. CAMRA local Pub of the Year for 2008.

(1) P

Grantchester

Blue Ball

57 Broadway, CB3 9NQ

12-3, 6-11 (midnight Thu-Sat); 12-10.30 Sun

(01223) 840679

Adnams Bitter; guest beers H

Small, authentic, traditional and relaxing pub full of interesting and friendly regulars. It holds the oldest licence in Grantchester and displays a list of landlords back to 1767. Good beer, good conversation and old pub games are the order of the day. The piano is still played and there is live music every Thursday. No lager, children or food. At the back is a small walled garden with a heated gazebo for smokers. A past local CAMRA Pub of the Year. Q

Hail Weston

Royal Oak

High Street, PE19 5JW

3-11 Mon & Tue; 12-11 Wed-Sat; 12-10.30 Sun

(01480) 472527

Wells Eagle IPA; Young's Bitter; guest beers H

The Royal Oak is a traditional village pub, the heart, soul and social centre of the village. The building dates from the 16th century. The main bar is dominated by a vast open fire, with many exposed beams and horse brasses. Adjoining the bar is an intimate restaurant offering a varied blackboard menu 12-2.30pm and 6-8.30pm Wednesday to Saturday and Sunday roasts 12-4pm. At the rear of the pub is an extensive garden. Q P

Hartford

King of the Belgians

27 Main Street, PE29 1XU

11-3, 5-11; 11-midnight Fri & Sat; 12-10.30 Sun

(01480) 52030

Beer range varies H

Sixteenth-century pub comprising a bar and dining area, situated in a picturesque village setting. Once the King of the Prussians, it was renamed during WWI. A constantly changing range of three real ales is on offer and good value food is served (not Mon eve). It is believed that Oliver Cromwell used to drop in and some say the pub is haunted – possibly by an ex-serviceman from one of the squadrons whose stickers cover the bar ceiling. (45,55)P

Helpston

Blue Bell

10 Woodgate, PE6 7ED

11.30-2.30, 5 (6 Sat)-11; 12-6 Sun

(01733) 252394

Grainstore Cooking Bitter, Ten Fifty; guest beers H

This stone-built 17th-century village pub has been a Guide entry for many years now and is very popular with locals. The wood-panelled bar in the lounge has been extended into the old cellar, providing a dining area and cosy snug. John Clare, the 18th century English peasant poet, was a pot boy here. The John Clare Bitter is brewed by Grainstore. In summer traditional cider is available. No food is served Sunday evening or all day Monday. Q (201)P

Hemingford Grey

Cock

47 High Street, PE28 9BJ (off A14, SE of Huntingdon)

11.30-3, 6-11; 12-4, 6.30-10.30 Sun

(01480) 463609 cambscuisine.com

Buntingford Highwayman IPA; Wolf Golden Jackal; guest beers H

Situated a short stroll from the River Great Ouse and the Hemingford Meadow, this is an award-winning village local and restaurant. Accessed via a separate door, the restaurant has won many accolades (booking essential at all times). The menu includes an extensive fish board, meat, game and excellent home-made sausages. The beer range features only beers produced within an hour's drive of the pub. During the summer, occasional beer festivals are held in the beer garden. Q (5)P

Hinxton

Red Lion

32 High Street, CB10 1QY

11-3 (3.30 Fri & Sat), 6-11; 12-4, 7-10.30 Sun

(01799) 530601 redlionhinxton.co.uk

Adnams Bitter; Greene King IPA; Woodforde's Wherry Best Bitter; guest beers H

Sixteenth-century coaching inn with a front bar leading around the side to an extensive dining room at the back. There is a choice of comfortable seating areas amid the traditional green and cream decor. Prints of village life, old clocks and stuffed animals add character. The dining room features a vaulted ceiling with exposed oak rafters. The menu is classic English country fare complete with award-winning puddings. (7,139)P

Histon

Red Lion

27 High Street, CB24 9JD

10.30-3, 4-11 (midnight Fri); 10.30-11 Sat; 12-11 Sun

(01223) 564437

Everards Tiger; Mighty Oak Oscar Wilde Mild; Oakham Bishops Farewell; Theakston Best Bitter; Tring Blonde; guest beers H

Both bars in this free house are filled with a magnificent collection of breweriana – bottles, water jugs, signs, mirrors, pump clips, even a malevolently-glowing Watneys Red Barrel. Two ever-changing guest beers plus three Belgian beers are on draught and a huge range of bottled Belgians and Germans is stocked. Food is served every lunchtime and monthly themed food nights are popular. Two beer festivals are held each year – an Easter aperitif then the main event in September with a marquee in the garden and entertainment. (7,104,110)P

Holme

Admiral Wells

41 Station Road, PE7 3PH (jct of B660 & Yaxley Road)

12-2.30, 5-11; 12-11 Sat; 12-10.30 Sun

(01487) 831214

Nethergate Augustinian Ale; Shepherd Neame Spitfire; Woodforde's Wherry Best Bitter; guest beers H

Recently refurbished Victorian inn reputed to be the lowest pub in England and situated close to the Holme Fen nature reserve. Up to six real ales are available including regularly changing guests. Traditional cider is also on offer. This family-run free house has a reputation for good food. The restaurant overlooks the large garden and play area. A function room is available to hire. P

Huntingdon

Market Inn

Market Hill, PE29 3NG

11-11 (midnight Sat); 12-11 Sun

(01480) 431183

Potbelly Beijing Black; Young's Bitter; guest beer H

A 400-year-old traditional pub down an alley off the market square. Once a series of tied cottages serving the former Fountain Hotel Brewery, it still has the original roof and three listed fireplaces. Live music, karaoke on Saturday and quizzes on the first Wednesday of the month are popular. The front bar has an unspoilt wood-panelled decor and stained glass windows. Handy for the bus station. Winner of local CAMRA Most Improved Pub award for 2009.

Old Bridge Hotel

1 High Street, PE29 3TQ

11-11 (10.30 Sun)

(01480) 424300 huntsbridge.com

Adnams Bitter; City of Cambridge Hobson's Choice; guest beers

This handsome hotel is an 18th-century former private bank and enjoys a prominent position on the banks of the Great Ouse. Residents, diners and beer drinkers alike can mix in the relaxed atmosphere of the covered terrace, the main bar or the lounge. Imaginative and high quality food is served and the Old Bridge Wine Shop, opened in 2008, offers wine tasting as an interesting diversion. Located in Oliver Cromwell's birthplace, the bus station is a short walk away.
Q P

Impington

Railway Vue

163 Station Road, CB24 9NP

11.30-3, 5-11; 11.30-11 Thu & Fri; 12-3, 7-11 Sat; 12-3, 7.30-10.30 Sun

(01223) 232426 railwayvue.com

Adnams Broadside; Black Sheep Best Bitter; Greene King IPA; guest beers

Large, thriving pub popular with a wide cross-section of the community. It has a traditional public bar and a quieter, comfy lounge leading to an attractive conservatory with a view of the recently-opened and controversial guided busway between Cambridge and St Ives. (The Histon/Impington stop is across the way from the pub.) Good value home-cooked food is served during the week. The 'customer services' notices in the Gents are worth a look if gender permits.
Q (7,104,110) P

Keyston

Pheasant

Village Loop, PE28 0RE (on B663, 1 mile S of A14, E of Thrapston)

12-11; closed Mon; 12-2.30 Sun

(01832) 710241 thepheasant-keyston.co.uk

Greene King IPA; guest beers

The village is named after Ketil's Stone, probably an Anglo-Saxon boundary marker. Created from a row of thatched cottages in an idyllic setting, the pub offers high quality food, fine wines and well-kept cask ales. There is a splendid lounge bar and three dining areas include the Garden Room in a rear extension overlooking a herb garden. Beers from local micro-breweries usually feature. Food is served 12-2.30pm and 6-9.30pm. Q P

Leighton Bromswold

Green Man

37 The Avenue, PE28 5AW (1 mile N of A14, W of Huntingdon) TL113754

12-2, 7-11; closed Mon; 12-5 Sun

(01480) 890238 greenmanpub.org

Beer range varies

Delightful local in a charming village on a ridge (the 'Bromswold') not far from the Northamptonshire border. The pub provides a congenial focus for a small village community and attracts visitors from a wide area for good food and ale. The interesting, constantly-changing beer range includes beers from Nethergate, Young's, Digfield, Oakham and Buntingford. Food is served 12-2pm and 7-9.30pm Tuesday to Saturday and 12-3pm Sunday. Hood skittles is popular here, and there is a petanque court. A real fire adds atmosphere in winter. P

Linton

Crown

11 High Street, CB21 4HS

11-2.30, 5.30-11; 12-8 Sun

(01223) 891759 crownatlinton.co.uk

Beer range varies

This open plan pub has beams and posts that provide natural divisions between comfortable seating areas. Freshly prepared food from an eclectic menu is served in the bar or the extensive dining room (no food Sun eve). The friendly bar staff, now resplendent in ties, are well-informed about the beers, which often come from local breweries including Nethergate or Buntingford. Accommodation is in five smart en-suite rooms.
P

Little Downham

Plough

106 Main Street, CB6 2SX

12-3 (not Mon); 6-11; 6-midnight Fri & Sat

(01353) 698297

Greene King IPA; guest beers

Small quirky country pub retaining old-fashioned charm complete with local customs including the annual Plough Monday Molly dancing. Other regular events include dwyle flunking or for the less energetic there are film evenings. The two changing guest beers are generally from Woodforde's, Oakham and other regional independent brewers. Excellent authentic Thai food is available to take away. The outdoor area is popular with non-smokers too for its pleasant banter around the wood-burning stove.

Little Gransden

Chequers

71 Main Road, SG19 3DW

12-2, 7-11; 12-11 Fri & Sat; 12-6, 7-10.30 Sun

(01767) 677348

Beer range varies

A true village local run by the same family for the last 59 years. There are three distinct drinking areas – the unspoilt middle bar, with its wooden bench seating and roaring fire, is a favourite spot to pick up on the local gossip. The Son of Sid brewhouse can be viewed from the lounge – it brews for the pub and occasional beer festivals. Fish and chips are a highlight on Friday night (booking essential).
Q (18A) P

Little Wilbraham

Hole in the Wall

2 High Street, CB21 5JY

11.30-3, 6.30-11; closed Mon; 12-3 Sun

(01223) 812282 the-holeinthewall.com

Woodforde's Wherry Best Bitter; guest beers

Quiet, friendly 15th-century village pub named after a real hole in the wall (now filled in), through which agricultural workers going to work in the morning passed empty vessels to be collected, full of beer, when returning in the evening. The pub has a strong emphasis on food, using high quality locally sourced and seasonal ingredients wherever possible, with an extra dining room open at weekends. Two guest beers usually come from local breweries. Q (17)P

March

Oliver Cromwell Hotel

High Street, PE15 9LH

11-11; 11-4, 7-10 Sun

(01354) 602890 olivercromwellhotel.co.uk

Oakham JHB; guest beers H

Situated off the high street behind the registry office, four beers mainly from micro-brewers are on offer, changing on a regular basis. Real cider is dispensed direct from the cellar. Winner of a CAMRA local branch Gold Award in 2008 for reviving the beer selection. Snacks are available 10am-2pm. Q (33)♣P

Maxey

Blue Bell

37-39 High Street, PE6 9EE

5.30 (1 Sat)-midnight; 12-4.30, 7.30-11 Sun

(01778) 348182

Abbeydale Absolution; Fuller's London Pride; Oakham JHB; guest beers H

Built of local limestone and dating back to 1645, the pub has been sympathetically modernised, retaining low beams and flagstones. The long narrow interior has a smaller room to the left decorated with fishing photographs and stuffed game birds. Seven beers are usually available at this popular meeting place. Q♣P

Milton

Waggon & Horses

39 High Street, CB24 6DF

12-2.30, 5-11 (midnight Fri); 12-3, 6-11.30 Sat; 12-3, 7-10.30 Sun

(01223) 860313

Elgood's Black Dog, Cambridge Bitter, Golden Newt; guest beers H

Imposing, mock-Tudor, one-room pub, adorned with a large collection of hats. The Elgood's beers are dispensed via cylinderless handpumps. Meals are good value, and baltis are a speciality on Thursday evening. There is a challenging quiz on Wednesday evening, and bar billiards is ever popular. Real cider is from local producer Cassels. Dogs on a lead are welcome.
(C2,9)♣P

Newton

Queen's Head

Fowlmere Road, CB22 7PG

11.30-2.30, 6-11; 12-2.30, 7-10.30 Sun

(01223) 870436

Adnams Bitter, Broadside, seasonal beers G

One of just a few pubs to have appeared in every edition of the Guide, this two-room village local run by the same family for many years has had just 18 landlords since 1729. Simple but excellent food includes soup and sandwiches at lunchtime. Beer is served from casks behind the bar. The cosy lounge has a welcoming fire. Q(31,139)♣P

Old Weston

Swan

Main Street, PE28 5LL (on B660, N of A14)

12-2.30 (not Mon-Fri), 6.30 (7 Sat)-11; 12-3.30, 7-10.30 Sun 01832 293400

Greene King Abbot; Taylor Landlord; guest beer H

This 16th-century oak-beamed village pub started life as two private houses that were merged, and has grown over the years. At the end of the 19th century the pub had its own brewery. There is a central bar with a large inglenook, a dining area and a games section offering hood skittles, darts and pool. Varied traditional pub food is served at weekends, including home-made puddings.
Q♣P

Pampisford

Chequers

1 Town Lane, CB22 3ER

11-11 (10.30 Sun)

(01223) 833220 chequerspampisford.com

Greene King IPA; Woodforde's Wherry Best Bitter H

A warm welcome and friendly atmosphere await visitors to this archetypal country pub. The character of the place stems from the wealth of exposed timbers and a split-level interior. Speciality food nights are a regular feature and the Sunday quiz is very popular. (7)♣P

Peterborough

Brewery Tap

80 Westgate, PE1 2AA

12-11 (late Fri & Sat)

(01733) 358500

Oakham JHB, White Dwarf, Inferno, Bishops Farewell; guest beers H

Striking modern conversion of a 1930s labour exchange to produce a large airy pub with a mezzanine floor. Twelve real ales always include a mild and Belgian bottled beers are also stocked. Reasonably priced authentic Thai cuisine is available. A new custom-made brew plant has recently been installed for Oakham Ales and this is visible through a glass wall. There is also a new function room available for hire. The Tap is still under threat of demolition when (if) the North Westgate area is redeveloped.

Charters

Town Bridge, PE1 1EH

12-11 (late Fri & Sat); 12-10.30 Sun

(01733) 315700 bluesontheboat.co.uk

Oakham JHB, White Dwarf, Inferno, Bishops Farewell; guest beers H/G

The largest Dutch barge in the country, moored on the Nene at Town Bridge. Twelve real ales generally include a mild, and the latest beers from micros are a speciality. Traditional cider and Belgian bottled beers are also available. A permanent marquee hosts beer festivals at Easter and in May and October. Monthly poetry readings are also held. See the website for details of live music. (1,6,7)♣P

Cherry Tree

9 Oundle Road, PE2 9PB

12-11 (midnight Fri & Sat); 12-10.30 Sun

(01733) 703495

Marston's Pedigree; Taylor Landlord; guest beers H

Local community pub near Railworld and the Nene Valley Railway. The jovial landlady serves excellent home-cooked food at reasonable prices. A popular live music venue at weekends, quiz nights and games are also hosted, and the pub has its own football team. On match days it can get very busy due to the proximity of the football ground. (1)P

Coalheavers Arms

5 Park Street, Woodston, PE2 9BH

12-2 Thu only, 5-11; 12-11 Fri & Sat; 12-10.30 Sun

(01733) 565664

Beer range varies H

Small one-roomed, back-street pub with eight handpumps serving a mix of beers from Milton Brewery together with ever-changing guests. A mild is always available. Traditional cider and a good selection of Belgian bottled beers are also stocked. There is a large garden with a permanent marquee where the May bank holiday and September beer festivals are held. Q(6,7)

Drapers Arms

29-31 Cowgate, PE1 1LZ

9-midnight (1am Fri & Sat)

(01733) 847570

Beer range varies H

This popular city-centre Wetherspoon's has wood-panelled walls that divide the interior into intimate enclosed spaces, displaying pictures of bygone days in the city. Ten handpumps serve the regular beers plus guest ales, often from local breweries. Traditional cider is also stocked. Food is served all day and jazz plays on Sunday lunchtime. TV and Wi-Fi access are available. Local CAMRA Pub of the Year 2007. Q

Hand & Heart ★

12 Highbury Street, Millfield, PE1 3BE

11-11

(01733) 564653

John Smith's Bitter; guest beers H

Community local dating from the 1930s, listed as one of the most unspoilt pubs in the country in CAMRA's National Inventory. Its two rooms are accessed by an impressive black and white tiled corridor. The public bar features a war memorial and real fire while the rear smoke room only has a serving hatch. An original Jug and Bottle serving hatch services the corridor. Q(1)

Palmerston Arms

82 Oundle Road, PE2 9PA

3-11 (midnight Thu & Fri), 12-midnight Sat; 12-11 Sun

(01733) 565865 palmerston-arms.co.uk

Beer range varies G

This stone-built, 17th-century, one-roomed pub is owned by Batemans. It offers up to 12 real ales including three or four of its own and the rest from micros, all served by gravity from the ground floor cellar visible behind the bar through a large window. Traditional cider is also stocked as well as Belgian and German bottled beers. An open plan interior includes the display of a large collection of jugs. (1)

Wortley Almshouses

Westgate, PE1 1QA

12-11 (5 Sun)

(01733) 348839

Samuel Smith OBB H

This busy city-centre pub, recently refurbished to provide six drinking areas was winner of a CAMRA accolade in the process. Historic pictures of Peterborough and the Wortley-Montague family adorn the walls of this former workhouse. Charles Dickens is said to have been inspired by this pub to write his classic Oliver Twist. Q

Pidley

Mad Cat

High Street, PE28 3BX

12-11.30 (10.30 Sun)

(01487) 842245 madcatinn.co.uk

Beer range varies H

Community local on the edge of the fens. The village is the home of the Pidley Mountain Rescue Team, a charity supporting local disabled people. A sociable bar has a welcoming open fire, crib and dominoes. The dining room is popular with villagers and visitors, especially for the Sunday lunchtime carvery. Q(35)P

Ramsey

Jolly Sailor

43 Great Whyte, PE26 1HH

11 (12 Sun)-midnight

(01487) 813388

Adnams Bitter, Broadside; Black Sheep Best Bitter; Greene King Abbot; Wells Bombardier; guest beers H

This Grade II-listed building has been a pub for 400 years. Many of the original wooden beams are still in evidence. The three linked rooms are welcoming and friendly, attracting a mixed age group. A real fire in the small main bar is a major feature. Pictures and paintings of the town from a bygone age adorn the walls. Q(31)P

Railway

132 Great Whyte, PE26 1HS

12-11

(01487) 812597

Greene King Abbot; Wells Bombardier; Woodforde's Wherry Best Bitter; guest beer H

This red-brick building dates from the 1930s and is reasonably unspoilt. Two rooms with real fires separated by a central bar give a warm welcome to drinkers. The public bar has a large trophy case filled with awards dating back to the 1930s. Live music and a quiz night are held on a monthly rota. Very handy for the nearby marina in the summer months. Q(31)P

Reach

Dykes End

8 Fair Green, CB25 0JD

12-3 (not Mon), 6-11; 12-3, 7-10.30 Sun

(01638) 743816

Adnams Bitter; Dykes End Bitter, Mild, Pale, Victorian; Woodforde's Wherry Best Bitter; guest beers H

Quintessential country pub saved from closure by a group of locals. It is now privately owned by a villager with a passion for good beer and real food. A family-run micro-brewery to the rear produces the Dykes End beer range. The interior comprises a

food-free tap-room, bar and attractive, cosy restaurant serving freshly-prepared, home-cooked meals (no food Sun eve or Mon).
⛺Q❀◑♿⛺🚌(10)♣P

St Ives

Oliver Cromwell

13 Wellington Street, PE27 5AZ
⏲ 11-11 (11.30 Thu; 12.30am Fri & Sat); 12-11 Sun
☎ (01480) 465601
Adnams Bitter, Broadside; Oakham JHB; Woodforde's Wherry Best Bitter; guest beers H
Cosy wood-panelled bar near the old St Ives river quay. An old well can be viewed through the floor of one of the drinking areas. There are two guest beers, real local Cromwell cider, a warm lively atmosphere and an imaginative lunch menu. Entertainment includes a monthly quiz and live music on the first and last Thursday evenings of the month plus occasional Sunday afternoons.
❀◑🚌🍎⚊

St. Neots

Lord John Russell

25 Russell Street, PE19 1BA
⏲ 12-11; 9am-midnight Sat
☎ (01480) 406330 🌐 lordjohnrussell.co.uk
Batemans Mild, G**; XB,** H**; Salem Porter** G**; guest beers** H
A small, traditional, back-street pub with a strong local following. The pub centres around the bar, with a recently refurbished dining area leading to a church garden and heated smoking area with umbrella. The food focuses on home-made, good value meals and snacks, with lunchtime specials and steak on the stone in the evening. Beer festivals are held in spring and autumn.
Q❀◑♣🍎P⚊

Swavesey

White Horse 🏆

Market Street, CB24 4QG
⏲ 12-2.30 (not Mon), 6-11 (12.30am Fri); 11.30-12.30am Sat; 12-11 Sun
☎ (01954) 232470 🌐 whitehorseswavesey.com
Caledonian Deuchars IPA; Hall & Woodhouse K&B Sussex Bitter H
A fine old inn whose public bar has polished floor tiles, wood panelling and an elevated fireplace. In later years the pub expanded into adjoining buildings, adding a lounge bar with dining area, pool room and function room. The pub hosts an annual regional pinball meet and has its own fine vintage machine. Entertainment includes occasional live music and a beer festival every May bank holiday. Large garden with play equipment.
⛺❀◑🚌(15)♣⚊

Ufford

White Hart

Main Street, PE9 3BH
⏲ 12-11 (midnight Fri & Sat); 12-9 (6 winter) Sun
☎ (01780) 740250
Ufford White Hart, Nirvana; guest beer H
This restored old stone farmhouse has a public bar with real fire, bar and restaurant, an orangery for diners and a function room. The Ufford Ales brewery is located in the rear car park and its seasonal beers are available in addition to another guest beer. Large gardens with tables overlook the pub, patio area and car park. Accommodation is available in six bedrooms named after Ufford Ales beers. ⛺Q❀🛏◑♿⛺🚌♣🍎P

Whittlesey

Boat 🏆

2 Ramsey Road, PE7 1DR
⏲ 10-midnight
☎ (01733) 202488
Elgood's Black Dog, Cambridge Bitter, Golden Newt, seasonal beers; guest beers G
This 11th century inn is a popular traditional local where visitors are made to feel welcome. The full range of Elgood's beers and a guest ale are on offer as well as up to five real ciders. The lounge has an unusual boat-shaped bar and offers an extensive range of malt whiskies. Saturday night features live music. Popular with anglers. Good value accommodation.
❀🛏♿🚆🚌(31,32,33)♣🍎P⚊

Letter B ✔

53-57 Church Street, PE7 1DE
⏲ 5 (12 Fri & Sat)-11; 12-10.30 Sun
☎ (01733) 206975
Adnams Bitter; Fox Heacham Gold; Oakham JHB; guest beers H
Locals' pub run with a warm welcome. Every weekend is a mini beer fest, with an annual festival held in the spring. Winner of a CAMRA gold award for the range and quality of its ales, it is on the trail of pubs to be visited during the annual Straw Bear weekend in January. A member of the new Oakadamy of pubs offering specially brewed Oakham Ales. Q❀🛏🚆🚌(3,7)♣🍎⚊

Willingham

Duke of Wellington

55 Church Street, CB24 5HS
⏲ 12-3, 5-11 (11.30 Thu & Fri), 12-11.30 Sat; 12-10.30 Sun
☎ (01954) 261622 🌐 doww.co.uk
Greene King XX Mild, IPA; guest beers H
Much improved village local with an attractive public bar plus an L-shaped lounge which has a relaxed, rustic feel, with a low ceiling, big scrubbed tables, bare-boarded floors and exposed beams. Excellent home-cooked food majors on pies and salads. An annual garden party is held over the August bank holiday. Quiz night is Sunday.
⛺❀◑P⚊

Wisbech

Red Lion

32 North Brink, PE13 1JR
⏲ 11.30-2.30, 6-11; 7-11.30 Sat; 12-3, 7-11 Sun
☎ (01945) 582022
Elgood's Black Dog, Cambridge Bitter, Golden Newt; guest beer H
The nearest Elgood's tied pub to the brewery. The present licensee has got the mix of good beer and quality food just right. A newly revamped split level restaurant serves meals every day to discerning drinkers and diners. The drinking area outside is a sun-trap in summer and there is good wheelchair access from the rear car park.
Q❀◑♿🚌(X1)P⚊

CHESHIRE

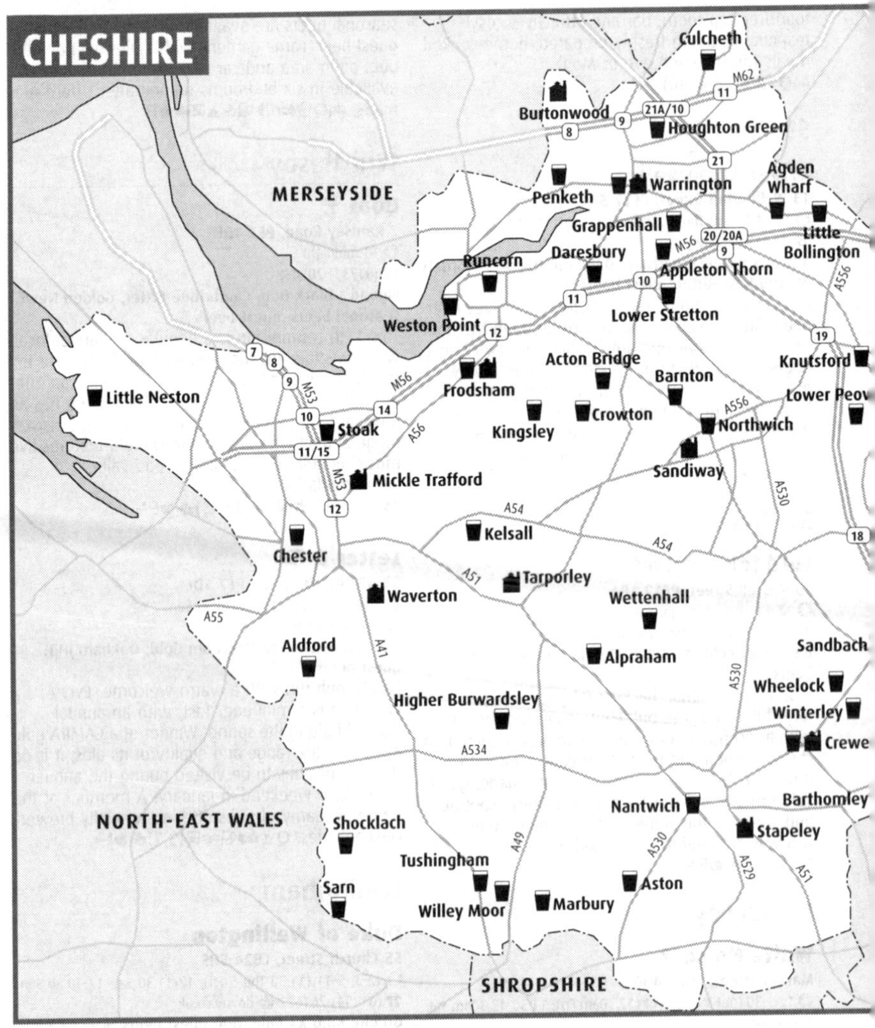

Acton Bridge

Hazel Pear Inn

1 Hill Top Road, CW8 3RA (opp railway station)
12-11 (10.30 Sun)
☎ (01606) 853195
Marston's Pedigree; Taylor Landlord; Tetley Bitter; guest beers Ⓗ
This pub features a mini farm at the rear with goats, rabbits, a pig, owls, ducks and chickens. Eggs from the chickens and ducks are served with meals lunchtimes and evenings and are available for sale to take away. Recently introduced are lunchtime credit-crunch meals for just £1. The bowling green is well used with nine different leagues. The guest beer is from the Punch list.
(48)P

Agden Wharf

Barn Owl

Warrington Lane, WA13 0SW (off A56) SJ707872
11-11; 12-10.30 Sun
☎ (01925) 752020 thebarnowlinn.co.uk
Marston's Burton Bitter, Pedigree; guest beers Ⓗ
Award-winning country pub on the banks of the Bridgewater Canal with extensive views over farmland. A large room accommodates diners and drinkers and a cross-canal ferry is available to walkers. Holder of the Cask Marque Beautiful Beer Gold Award, this pub is a favourite with walkers, cyclists, senior citizens and sailors who can select from three handpumps featuring Marston's beers and three guest beers from craft brewers. A supporter of local ales and former CAMRA branch Pub of the Year. P

Aldford

Grosvenor Arms

Chester Road, CH3 6HJ (on B5130)
11.30-11; 12-10.30 Sun
☎ (01244) 620228 grosvenorarms-aldford.co.uk
Thwaites Original; Weetwood Eastgate; guest beers Ⓗ
Stylish Victorian free house with a large, lively open-plan bar, several well-furnished quieter areas and a pleasant conservatory. As well as the regularly-changing ales there is an extensive wine

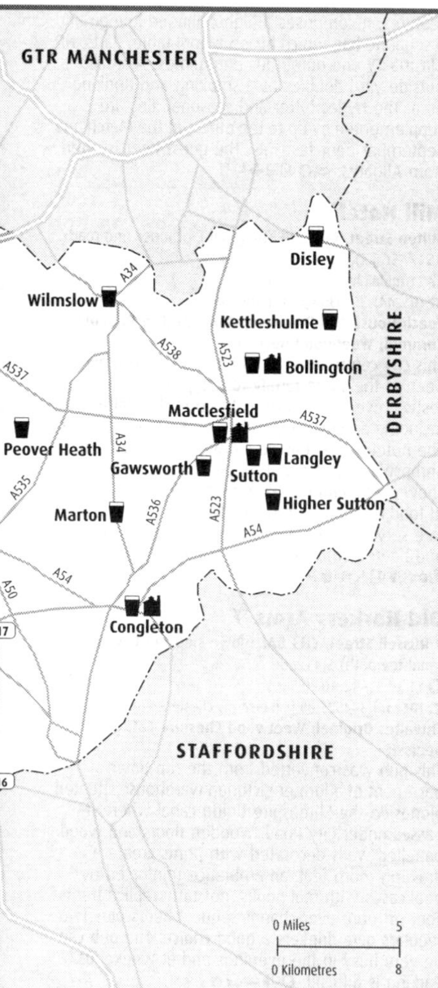

list and a good range of whiskies. Families are welcome and outside there is a large neat lawn with picnic tables. Renowned for well-prepared imaginative food, the pub is popular for dining. Dogs on leads are welcome away from dining areas. ⌂Q❀◐♿🚌P

Alpraham

Travellers Rest ★

Chester Road, CW6 9JA (on main A51 road to Chester)

⏲ 6.30-11; 12-4, 6-11 Sat; 12-3, 7-10.30 Sun

☎ (01829) 260523

Tetley Bitter; Weetwood Eastgate Ⓗ

Traditional, old-fashioned public house on CAMRA's National Inventory of Historic Pub Interiors. Lovely old original furniture includes wicker chairs and cast iron tables. Outside is a large bowling green which is well used in summer. Close to the Shropshire Union Canal, the pub attracts walkers. Look for the swallows nesting in the outside toilets in June, July and August. A great conversation pub, this is a well-deserved twice winner of local CAMRA Pub of the Year. Q❀⊟♿🚌(84)♣P⊱

Appleton Thorn

Appleton Thorn Village Hall

Stretton Road, WA4 4RT

⏲ 7.30-11; closed Mon-Wed; 1-4, 7.30-10.30 Sun

☎ (01925) 261187 🌐 appletonthornvillagehall.co.uk

Beer range varies Ⓗ

CAMRA National Club of the Year 2008, the Village Hall is the hub of the local community. It offers up to seven changing beers from regional and micro breweries, as well as up to four ciders and a perry. There is a comfortable lounge and a larger bar area-cum-function room where regular events are held including live music, quizzes and an annual beer festival in October. Lunches are served 1-3pm Sunday. Buses run only on Friday and Saturday evenings. Q❀♿🚌♣●P⊟

Aston

Bhurtpore Inn

Wrenbury Road, CW5 8DQ SJ610469

⏲ 12-2.30, 6.30-11.30; 12-midnight Fri & Sat; 12-11 Sun

☎ (01270) 780917 🌐 bhurtpore.co.uk

Beer range varies Ⓗ

This family-run free house is a winner of many awards for its beer and food, including CAMRA Regional Pub of the Year. Eleven regularly-changing real ales are sourced from micros, including some LocAle beers. The real cider is frequently from a smaller producer too. Belgian beers and Highland malts are added attractions. The pub is rightfully renowned for its home-made, locally-sourced food, with curries a speciality, served until 9.30pm. Beer festivals in July and November.

⌂Q❀◐♿⅄⇌(Wrenbury)🚌(72)♣●P

Barnton

Barnton Cricket Club

Broomsedge, Townfield Lane, CW8 4LH (200m from A533 via Stoneheyes Lane)

⏲ 6.30-midnight (12.30am Thu & Fri); 12 (4 Oct-Apr)-12.30am Sat; 12-11 Sun

☎ (01606) 77702 🌐 barntoncc.co.uk

Boddingtons Bitter; Hydes Dark Mild, Bitter; Theakston Best Bitter; guest beers Ⓗ

A CAMRA membership card gains entry to this popular club at the edge of Barnton, where four regular beers plus guests are always available. It is home to thriving cricket, bowls, golf, quizzes, darts and dominoes. The club serves excellent value food Thursday to Saturday evenings and Sunday lunchtime. A beer festival is held in November attracting visitors from as far away as Southport and the Wirral. A former CAMRA Regional Club of the Year. ❀◐♿🚌(4)♣P⊱

Barthomley

White Lion ★ ✔

Audley Road, CW2 5PG (jct Audley Road & Radway Green Road) SJ767524

⏲ 11.30-11; 12-10.30 Sun

☎ (01270) 882242

Jennings Sneckliffter; Marston's Burton Bitter; guest beers Ⓗ

Cosy, welcoming thatched pub, dating from 1614, in a small village, popular with locals and visitors alike. The main bar has a quarry tile floor, 17th-century wood panelling and exposed beams. A

smaller simpler room, up two steps, also panelled, has a fine winged settle. An even smaller third room at the back has a solid fuel burner. The River Wulvern, formerly Waldron, borders the pub, named in memory of the last wolf in England, supposedly killed in Barthomley Woods.
Q P

Bollington

Cock & Pheasant ✔

15 Bollington Road, SK10 5EJ
11.30-11 (midnight Fri & Sat); 12-11 Sun
☎ (01625) 573289
Copper Dragon Golden Pippen; Theakston Best Bitter; guest beer H
This large, popular pub on the main road entering Bollington from Macclesfield celebrated its 250th anniversary in 2006. Low ceilings and a stone flagged floor make for a cosy bar with ample dining areas. The conservatory, patio and children's play area caters for all tastes. A good pub to enjoy both beer and food, it offers a well balanced menu every day. The pub runs an active golf society, league darts and dominoes. A regular outlet for local brewer Storm Brewing. The bus stops outside the front door. (10)♣P

Poachers Inn ✔

95 Ingersley Road, SK10 5RE
7-11 Mon; 12-2, 5.30-11 Tue-Thu; 12-midnight Fri & Sat; 12-10.30 Sun
☎ (01625) 572086 thepoachers.org
Sharp's Doom Bar; Taylor Landlord; guest beer H
Friendly and welcoming family run free house on the Gritstone Trail converted from five stone-built terraced cottages, with a lovely sun-trap garden in summer and coal fire in winter. The three guest beers come from local and distant craft breweries, and 18 diverse Belgian beers are available in bottles. Good value, home-prepared food is available. Regular quiz nights and golf days are organised. On Monday night there is a folk jam.
(10)♣P

Vale Inn

29-31 Adlington Road, SK10 5JT
12-2.30, 5.30-11; 12-11 Sat; 12-10.30 Sun
☎ (01625) 575147 valeinn.co.uk
Beer range varies H
Dating from the 1860s, this single room free house is the brewery tap for the Bollington Brewing Company which the landlord and his brother started in 2008 just 50 metres from the pub. A wide variety of guest beers is available from the six handpumps, with a preference for local micros. Seasonal beer festivals are hosted. The pub serves excellent home-cooked food and is popular with the local community and CAMRA group as well as diners, walkers and bikers using the nearby canal and Middlewood Way paths. (10)P

Chester

Carlton Tavern ✔

1 Hartington Street, Handbridge, CH4 7BN (half mile S of city across Old Dee Bridge)
4-11.30; 12-midnight Sat; 12-10.30 Sun
☎ (01244) 674821
Hydes Original, seasonal beers; guest beer H
Set in a residential area, this former Walkers pub has a 1920s feel thanks to its many original features. It comprises a high-ceilinged lounge and a separate bar, which boasts a pool table, darts, HD plasma TV and numerous pub games. A small outside yard doubles as a smoking and drinking area. The Hydes bitter and seasonal ales are supplemented by up to ten others at the March and September beer festivals. The guest beer is often from Allgates. Q♣

Mill Hotel

Milton Street, CH1 3NF (by canal E of inner ring road/ A51/A56 jct)
11-midnight (11.30 Sun)
☎ (01244) 350035 millhotel.com
Coach House Mill Premium; Oakham JHB; Phoenix Cornmill; Weetwood Best, H
This city centre hotel in a former 1830 cornmill has been in the same family for 21 years. It is a beer festival every day here, with up to 15 real ales including a guest mild, cider and two house beers. The hotel offers real ale cruises on the adjacent Shropshire Union Canal. Three plasma screens show sports and the bar runs a quiz team. A range of food is on offer from bar snacks to full restaurant fare served in five dining areas. There is a covered and heated smoking area outside.
P

Old Harkers Arms 🏆

1 Russell Street, CH3 5AL (down steps off City Road to canal towpath) SJ412666
11.30-11; 12-10.30 Sun
☎ (01244) 344525 harkersarms-chester.co.uk
Thwaites Original; Weetwood Cheshire Cat; guest beers H
This pub was converted from the run-down basement of a former Victorian warehouse situated alongside the Shropshire Union canal where it passes under City Road. Wooden floors and wood panelled walls decorated with prints create a drawing room feel, an ambience reinforced by bookcases with real books, not tatty replica fronts. Four or more ever-changing guest beers plus two regulars give drinkers a good choice. The pub can be very busy in the evenings and at weekends. Parking is difficult. Q

Telford's Warehouse ✔

Tower Wharf, CH1 4EZ
12-11 (1am Wed; 12.30am Thu; 2am Fri & Sat); 12-1am
☎ (01244) 390090 telfordswarehouse.com
Thwaites Original; Weetwood Cheshire Cat; guest beers H
Large picture windows with splendid views of the adjacent Shropshire Union Canal give a light and airy feel to this converted warehouse. Bare boards and brickwork abound, with prints and enamel signs, plus an old hoist that dominates the lower

INDEPENDENT BREWERIES

Beartown Congleton
Bollington Bollington (NEW)
Borough Arms Crewe
Burtonwood Burtonwood
Coach House Warrington
Frodsham Frodsham
Northern Sandiway
Spitting Feathers Waverton
Storm Macclesfield
WC Mickle Trafford
Weetwood Tarporley
Woodlands Stapeley

bar. The upstairs restaurant serves a wide variety of Thai, Italian and traditional dishes. An outdoor drinking area is situated next to the canal. Admission charges may apply after 10pm on Friday and Saturday evenings, when live indie music is performed. Q P

Congleton

Beartown Tap

18 Willow Street, CW12 1RL
12-2, 4-11; 12-11 Fri & Sat; 12-10.30 Sun
(01260) 270990 beartownbrewery.co.uk/tap.htm
Beartown Kodiak Gold, Bearskinful, Polar Eclipse, Black Bear, Ursa Major; guest beer H
A real ale flagship pub, just across the road from the Beartown Brewery. Twice winner of the Regional CAMRA Pub Of The Year award, the Tap offers not only a selection from the full range of Beartown beers but also a regularly-changing guest beer sourced from a micro-brewery, real cider and a good range of Belgian bottled beers. With no piped music, this is a pub for good conversation and excellent beer. Q

Congleton Leisure Centre

Worrall Street, CW12 1DT (off A54 Mountbatten Way)
7-10.30 (11 Sep-Apr); 7-10.30 Fri; closed Sat; 8-10.30 Sun
(01260) 271552 congleton.gov.uk/default.asp?t=213
Beer range varies H
Celebrating 10 consecutive years in the Guide, this bar manages to create a pub atmosphere within the town's leisure centre, with no requirement for membership or use of the sporting facilities. Beers on offer include a rotating Copper Dragon beer and two ever-changing micro-brewery ales. Two four-day real ale festivals are held in March and October. A visit can be combined with a trip to the Beartown Tap which is in close proximity. P

Queens Head Hotel

Park Lane, CW12 3DE (on A527)
11 (4 Mon)-11
(01260) 272546 queensheadhotel.org.uk
Greene King Abbot; Wells Bombardier; guest beer H
Canalside pub with its own moorings, popular with locals and canal users. It has twice earned a local CAMRA Pub of the Season award in recent years. Guest beers change regularly and are often sourced from local micro-brewers, including Woodlands and Titanic. Real cider is available in the summer months. Bar meals are inexpensive and include vegetarian options. The large garden includes a children's play area. (9,99)

Crewe

Angel

2 Victoria Centre, CW1 2PU (below street level in Victoria Centre)
10-7 (10 Fri & Sat); closed Sun
(01270) 212003
Oakwell Barnsley Bitter H
A rare outlet for Barnsley Bitter in the area, this large, one-room pub is set below street level in the main shopping area. Very comfortable inside, it has a dartboard and pool table. The beer is competitively priced and good value home-cooked food is served at lunchtime. Note that the pub may close early on quiet evenings. Near the bus station, and a short bus ride or 20 minute walk from the railway station.

Borough Arms

33 Earle Street, CW1 2BG (on Earle Street Bridge)
5 (3 Fri; 12 Sat)-11; 12-10.30 Sun
(01270) 254999 boroughармscrewe.co.uk
Beer range varies H
Popular town-centre free house with an excellent range of real ales dispensed from nine handpumps. Most of the beers come from micro- brewers with paler hoppy beers predominating, as well as a good Belgian beer range. The open plan ground floor has three distinct seating areas where conversation is the main entertainment thanks to the absence of gaming machines, music and pool. More drinking space is provided in a large room downstairs and a sheltered beer garden. Home to Borough Arms Brewery, now brewing regularly. Q

Hops

8-10 Prince Albert Street, CW1 2DF (by Christ Church Steeple)
11 (5 Mon)-11.30; 12-11.30 Sun
(01270) 211100
Beer range varies H
Formerly a bistro and wine bar, this family run pub has a bar area and upstairs room – there is no pool, bandits, jukebox or TV. The pub is totally free of tie from brewery or pub chain. It serves three real ales, usually LocAle, seven draught and more than 100 bottled Belgian beers. Real cider is available straight from the barrel in the cellar. The Looza fruit juices are excellent too. Card carrying CAMRA members receive a discount on Monday. Q P

Crowton

Hare & Hounds

Station Road, CW8 2RN
12-3 (not Tue), 5-11; 12-3, 7-10.30 Sun
(01928) 788851
Greene King IPA; guest beers H
Village hub offering a warm welcome to all. First licensed in 1737, the current licensees have been here since 1991. Three rotating guest beers include the occasional cider or perry. Excellent quality food is prepared by the licensee-chef, with a bar menu for lighter meals and a popular restaurant (booking recommended). Local CAMRA Community Pub of the Year 2007, an annual charity plastic duck race takes place on the stream behind the pub. (48)P

Culcheth

Cherry Tree

35 Common Lane, WA3 4EX (on B5207 400m from A574)
11-11 (midnight Fri & Sat); 12-11 Sun
(01925) 762624
Greene King Abbot; Tetley Bitter; guest beers H
Large, recently refurbished, open-plan pub popular with families, with separate areas to suit diners, drinkers and sports fans. It was rebuilt in the 1970s after the previous pub was demolished by a wayward lorry. Three rotating guest beers supplement the two regulars. A wide variety of food is served all day in the bar and restaurant. Meal deals are available and Fairtrade coffee served. Quiz night is Wednesday, Friday is disco night and karaoke is hosted on Saturday. Free Wi-Fi available. (19,28A)

Daresbury

Ring o' Bells

Chester Road, WA4 4AJ
11-11 (midnight Fri & Sat summer); 12-10.30 Sun
(01925) 740256
Courage Directors; Theakston Best Bitter; Wells Bombardier; guest beers H
Multi-roomed pub in the heart of the village dating back to the 18th century. One of the rooms was the location for the local parish court in days gone by. Extensive beer gardens offer a view of the church across the way, where Lewis Carroll's father was the vicar – related memorabilia is prominently displayed. Food is served all day. Dogs are welcome in a seating area in front of the bar. P

Disley

White Lion

135 Buxton Road, SK12 2HA
11.30 (6.30 Mon)-11 (12.30am Fri & Sat); 12-11 Sun
(01663) 762800 whitelion-disley.co.uk
Jenning's Cumberland Ale; Theakston Best Bitter; guest beers H
Large white roadside pub on the A6 towards the eastern end of the village. Eight real ales are on offer including six constantly-changing beers from SIBA member micro-breweries. The contemporary open-plan interior has a separate 'dog room' (walkers also welcome). A comprehensive and varied menu is on offer with food served all day (except Mon) until 9pm. Live entertainment is hosted on the last Saturday of the month and quiz night is Thursday. (199)P

Frodsham

Helter Skelter

31 Church Street, WA6 6RW
11-11 (11.30 Sat); 12-10.30 Sun
(01928) 733361 helterskelter-frodsham.co.uk
Weetwood Best Cask; guest beers H
A stalwart of real ale choice in the town, this single room bar continues to thrive. There is a choice of seating, with a raised deck area toward the back. Five regularly changing guest beers are on handpump and a changing real cider. One local beer is always on offer and other Cheshire breweries are often represented. Food is available in the bar and an upstairs restaurant. (48)

Gawsworth

Harrington Arms

Church Lane, SK11 9RJ (off A536)
12-3, 5-11.30 (midnight Thu-Sat); 12-4, 7-11 Sun
(01260) 223325
Robinson's Hatters Mild, Unicorn, seasonal beer H
A former working farmhouse/pub, this Grade II-listed building is a superb example of a largely unspoilt country pub. The current tenants have overseen a sympathetic makeover of some of the public rooms which has helped to secure the pub's place on CAMRA's National Inventory. Several small rooms are furnished with simple wooden tables and chairs. Good food is on offer (no food Sun eve), often made using locally-sourced products. The bus stop is 100 metres from the pub. Q

Grappenhall

Bellhouse Club

Bellhouse Farm, Bellhouse Lane, WA4 2SG (200m off A50) SJ642862
5-11.30; 4-midnight Fri; 12-midnight Sat; 12-11.30 Sun
(01925) 268633 grappenhall.com
Theakston Best Bitter; guest beers H
The Club is at the centre of the charming Grappenhall Village. The bar serves a lounge area and a games room, providing dominoes, darts, pool and quizzes. Activities range from watercolour painting to traditional jazz. There is a beer festival each May and drinkers can enjoy a range of guest beers in the garden throughout the summer. Access is via the nearby Bridgewater Canal or buses from Warrington. CAMRA members are welcome at this private club. Q P

Higher Burwardsley

Pheasant Inn

Barracks Lane, CH3 9PF (follow signs on A41 and A49 for Cheshire Workshops)
12-midnight (11.30 Sun)
(01829) 770434 thepheasantinn.co.uk
Weetwood Best, Eastgate; guest beers H
Nestling in the Peckforton Hills, halfway along the sandstone trail, the Pheasant is a delightful collection of 300-year-old sandstone buildings popular with walkers, diners and visitors to the nearby Candle Workshops. Inside are oak-beamed ceilings, wood-panelling and real fires. The flower-filled courtyard with panoramic views across the Cheshire plain is delightful in summer. Excellent food is served and accommodation is available in 12 en-suite rooms. Q P

Higher Sutton

Hanging Gate

SK11 0NG
12-3, 5-11; 11-11 Fri-Sun
(01260) 252238
Hydes Original Bitter, Jekyll's Gold, seasonal beer H
Gritstone Trail pub dating from 1621 on four levels, with low ceilings and wood beams creating a cosy atmosphere. The lovely intimate snug is encountered after passing through the porch containing the main bar. The bottom room commands a magnificent panoramic view over the Cheshire plain to the Welsh hills. Poachers from the Royal Macclesfield Forest are reputed to have been hanged here. Three Hydes beers are available, plus popular high-quality food. P

Houghton Green

Millhouse

Balater Drive, WA2 0LX
12-11 (11.30 Tue & Thu; midnight Fri & Sat)
(01925) 831189
Holts Mild, Bitter, seasonal beers H
A modern-style community pub built to service the estates of northern Warrington, featuring a large open-plan lounge and separate public bar. Popular quiz nights are run on Tuesday and Thursday evenings, with live music playing at weekends. Sports fans come for the large screen in the public bar, where you can also play pool and darts. (23,26) P

Plough

Mill Lane, WA2 0SU (off Delph Lane)
11.30-11 (11.30 Thu & Sat; midnight Fri); 12-11 Sun
(01925) 815409
Weetwood Best Cask, Cheshire Cat; Wells Bombardier; guest beers
This increasingly popular inn is proof that pub companies can get it right. As well as three regular beers, there are another three rotating ales (one from Weetwood). There is a strong emphasis on food here – available seven days a week. Outside is a bowling green next to the car park which overlooks the M62. The pub is a regular finalist in local CAMRA's branch Pub of the Year competition. (23,26)P

Kelsall

Morris Dancer

Chester Road, CW6 0RS
12-11 (midnight Fri & Sat)
(01829) 751291 morrisdancerkelsall.co.uk
Weetwood Ales,
Converted former stable block that offers something for everyone – a homely bar, comfortable lounge, separate restaurant and a function room. The wooden-floored lounge and traditional public bar retain many original features and are separated by a central bar offering three Weetwood ales. These travel less than two miles up the hill from the brewery in nearby Oscroft. The Chester Folk Festival is held next to the pub at the end of May each year. Q♣P

Kettleshulme

Swan

Macclesfield Road, SK23 7QU (on B5470)
12 (5.30 Mon)-11; 12-10.30 Sun
(01663) 732943 the-swan-kettleshulme.co.uk
Marston's Burton Bitter; guest beers
Previously owned by locals to save it from closure, this small 15th-century, whitewashed stone building has a quaint interior with timber beams, stone fireplaces and a real fire. Two or three frequently-changing guest beers, usually from micros, are always available and a small beer festival takes place in autumn. Food is of a high quality with an interesting ever-changing menu (booking advisable). Situated in the Peak District National Park surrounded by good walking country, families and walkers are welcome. There are two patios outside. (60,64)P

Kingsley

Red Bull

The Brow, WA6 8AN (100m from B5153)
5.30 (5 Fri)-midnight; 12-3, 6-midnight Sat; 12-3, 7-midnight Sun
(01928) 788097 redbullpub.co.uk
Thwaites Bitter, Wainwrights; guest beers
Located in the village centre, just off the main road, this local CAMRA Pub of the Year 2008 offers up to four rotating guest beers from all over the UK. Award-winning home-cooked food including real chips is available at all sessions except Sunday evening. Home to several local sporting clubs as well as a drama society, Tuesday is quiz night while Saturday nights feature occasional live music along with murder mystery and close up magic. Q(48)♣P

Knutsford

Cross Keys Hotel

52 King Street, WA16 6DT
11.30-3, 5.30-11; 11.30-midnight Fri-Sun
(01565) 750404 crosskeysknutsford.com
Caledonian Deuchars IPA; Taylor Landlord; Tetley Bitter; guest beer
This lively town-centre 18th-century coaching inn has modern accommodation. The lounge and vault are separated by an unusual wood and glass partition. This is the town's only free house, with three guest beers – one from the Enterprise list, the others from independent breweries. Bar meals are available Tuesday to Sunday. The quieter restaurant area is through a barrel-vaulted passageway. For a peaceful pint, try a lunchtime visit, as the pub can fill up in the evening. ♣P

Lord Eldon

27 Tatton Street, WA16 6AD
11-11 (midnight Thu-Sat); 12-10.30 Sun
(01565) 652261
Tetley Bitter; guest beer
This historic 300-year-old pub has a lovely exterior with a sundial and hanging baskets. The cosy, rambling and attractive interior comprises three rooms plus a bar. Roaring fires, low beams and a riot of brass and pictures provide the background to a friendly local pub. Outside is a pleasant, little known, enclosed beer garden, well worth a visit. Live entertainment features regularly, usually on a Thursday or Saturday. Two guest beers are often Cheshire LocAles. Q(300)♣

Langley

St Dunstan Inn

Main Road, SK11 0BU
5-midnight (1am Fri); 12-1am Sat; 12-midnight Sun
(07801) 818868
Banks's Bitter; guest beer
Two room, traditional terraced pub built in 1825, where the locals choose the guest beer. Food is not available but customers may bring their own or order a takeaway (crockery, cutlery and washing up free!). There is a separate room for pool and darts. Although closed lunchtimes, the pub will open specially if booked for large parties. A real community pub, the landlord runs the beer tent at the village fete. Previous CAMRA Pub of the Season. (14)♣

Little Bollington

Swan with Two Nicks

Park Lane, WA14 4TJ (off A56) SJ730871
12-11 (10.30 Sun)
(0161) 928 2914
Dunham Massey Dark Mild, Big Tree Bitter, Stamford Bitter; Greene King Abbot; Taylor Landlord
A classic country pub near the National Trust Dunham Park and convenient for boaters on the Bridgewater Canal. The cosy front rooms are welcoming to drinkers, with real fires, beams, brasses and quiet background music – no TV or games. Dogs are welcome. The spacious restaurant at the rear serves meals all day. Typically seven cask ales are on offer including four, constantly-changing, from the local Dunham Massey Brewery, and the house beer, Swan with Two Nicks, from nearby Coach House. A recent CAMRA Pub of the Season winner. Q(37,37A)P

Little Neston

Harp

19 Quayside, CH64 0TB (turn left at bottom of Marshlands Road, pub is 400m on left overlooking marshes) SJ290761
✪ 12-midnight; 12-11.30 Sun
☎ (0151) 336 6980
Holt Bitter; Taylor Landlord; Titanic Iceberg Ⓗ
A former coal miners' inn near to the site of Neston Colliery which closed in 1927. Set in a glorious location, the pub overlooks the Dee Marshes and North Wales. Access by car can be a bone-shaking experience along an unadopted road. Converted from two cottages, it has a public bar with real fire in winter and a lounge/family room. There is a garden and a drinking area abutting the edge of the marshes. ⌂Q☋◐⊟♿P⁵⁻

Lower Peover

Crown

Crown Lane, WA16 9QB (on B5081)
✪ 11.30-3, 5.30-11; 12-10.30 Sun
☎ (01565) 722074
Caledonian Deuchars IPA; Flowers IPA; Taylor Landlord; Tetley Bitter Ⓗ
This traditional 17th-century country pub has an L-shaped bar which divides the stone flagged bar from the comfortable lounge. Darts and dominoes are played. Good home-cooked local food is available and the pub has a small restaurant (no food Sun eve). The pub has one changing guest beer to complement the regular beers, often a mild. There is a cobbled area for outdoor drinking. ⌂Q❀◐◑🚌(47)♣P

Lower Stretton

Ring o' Bells

Northwich Road, WA4 4NZ (on A559 just off jct 10 M56)
✪ 12-2.30 (not Mon), 5.30-11; 12-11 Thu; 12-3, 5.30-midnight Fri; 12-3, 7-11 Sat; 12-10.30 Sun
☎ (01925) 730556
Fuller's London Pride; Tetley Bitter; guest beer Ⓗ
An unspoilt, traditional, village local where the emphasis is on conversation – no jukebox, fruit machines or background music. The main bar is the focal point of the pub and there are two smaller rooms where the good beer can be savoured more quietly. A quiz night is held twice a month and boules is played in summer. Local CAMRA Pub of the Year 2007. ⌂Q❀🚌P⁵⁻

Macclesfield

Dolphin

76 Windmill Street, SK11 7HS
✪ 12-2:30, 5-11; 12-11 Sat; 12-10.30 Sun
☎ (01625) 616179
Robinson's Hatters Mild, Unicorn; guest beer Ⓗ
A friendly, traditional, family-run local pub. The main drinking area has a real fire and there is a separate public bar plus a function room for small gatherings. Home-cooked food is served Monday to Saturday lunchtime. There are three local Robinson's ales on offer including the brewery's current seasonal beer. In winter award-winning Old Tom is stocked. Pub games are popular throughout the week. Do not ignore the malt whiskies. ⌂Q◐⊟♣

Old Ship Inn

61-63 Beech Lane, SK10 2DS
✪ 4-11.30; 12-2 Sat; 12-midnight Sun
☎ (01625) 261909
Storm Bosley Cloud, Ale Force; Worthington Bitter; guest beer Ⓗ
Friendly and welcoming pub with two blazing open hearth fires in winter. Although a 15-minute walk from the town centre, it is well worth seeking out as it is a premier outlet for the local Macclesfield brewery, Storm Brewing. Five different Storm beers are usually on offer in addition to Worthington Bitter on handpump. Behind the bar is another room mainly occupied by a pool table. The pub caters for all ages and has a mixed clientele. ⌂❀⇌🚌(10)♣P⁵⁻

Railway View

1 Byrons Lane, SK11 7JW
✪ 6 (4 Fri; 12 Sat & Sun)-11
☎ (01625) 423657
Beer range varies Ⓗ
Attractive local freehouse which offers a good selection of four to eight cask ales from local micros and national breweries. Storm features on a regular basis at a good price. Fires are lit during winter time. There are several beer festivals, music evenings and a Sunday night quiz. Free pool and reduced beer prices are on offer on Monday. A small beer garden is available for smokers. Popular with football fans when Macclesfield Town are at home. ⌂❀♿🚌(9,14)♣●⁵⁻

Society Rooms ✔

Park Green, SK11 7NA
✪ 9-midnight (11 Jan); 9-1am (midnight Jan) Fri & Sat
☎ (01625) 507320
Greene King IPA, Abbot; Marston's Pedigree; guest beer Ⓗ
Large, centrally located, stone-built Wetherspoon's conversion of an 18th-century vicarage and college from which the pub gets its name. The pub is well divided internally with a mix of seating from stools to sofas. Throughout the day the pub is popular with shoppers and families enjoying the good value food and drinks. Management and staff favour cask ale and the pub holds regular beer festivals and sponsors local micros. Five guest beers include at least one local ale. ☋❀◐◑♿⇌🚌●P⁵⁻

Waters Green Tavern

96 Waters Green, SK11 6LH
✪ 12-3, 5.30-11; 11-3, 7-11 Sat; 12-3, 7-10.30 Sun
☎ (01625) 422653
Taylor Landlord; guest beer Ⓗ
This popular and friendly town centre pub offers up to seven beers, with guests from independent breweries such as Pictish, Titanic, Roosters and Thornbridge, as well as from micros. In the winter there is often a dark beer at the weekend. The interior has two distinct drinking areas plus a pool room at the rear. Good value traditional home-cooked food is served at lunchtimes. Winner of many local CAMRA branch awards. ⌂◐⇌🚌♣

Marbury

Swan at Marbury

Wrenbury Road, SY13 4LS
✪ 12-3.30, 6.30-11 (closed Mon) winter; 12-3.30, 6.30-11; 12-11 Sat & Sun summer

☎ (01948) 662220 🌐 theswanatmarbury.co.uk
Beer range varies Ⓗ
This farmhouse pub started selling real ale over 250 years ago. Set in the centre of a picturesque village, it is right on the village green. It has a comfortable bar, candlelit restaurant, real fires, good conversation and easy-going laughter. Two local ales are usually available and two beer festivals are held during the year, one to coincide with the May country fair. The food is not to be missed. **⌂Q❀◐◑P**

Marton

Davenport
Congleton Road, SK11 9HF (on A34)
⏲ 11.45-3 (not Mon), 6-11; 11.45-11 Fri & Sat; 12-11 Sun
☎ (01260) 224269 🌐 thedavenportarms.co.uk
Courage Directors; Theakston Best Bitter; guest beer Ⓗ
Originally a farmhouse, the Davenport is becoming an established bar restaurant, with curry night on Tuesday. Guest beers often come from Cheshire micro-breweries such as Weetwood or Storm. The restaurant is popular with booking advisable at weekends, and bar meals are also available (no food Mon). The large adjoining garden includes a children's play area. **⌂Q❀◐◑♿ΔP⚟**

Nantwich

Globe
100 Audlem Road, CW5 7EA
⏲ 12-11
☎ (01270) 623374
Woodlands Light Oak, Oak Beauty, Midnight Stout, Bitter, Bees Knees, Redwood Ⓗ
Local brewery Woodlands' first tied house usually offers up to nine beers, with seasonal ales complementing the regular choices. This traditional pub was acquired and renovated in 2007 and has an open plan interior with a comfortable bar area where conversation dominates. Home-cooked food is served until 9pm (8pm Sun). A wide range of social activities is supported, including a football team and a summer beer festival. Draught cider is available at times. **⌂❀◐◑⇌🚌(73)●P⚟🍺**

Oddfellows
97 Welsh Row, CW5 5ET
⏲ 12 (5 Mon)-11; 12-11 Sat & Sun
☎ (01270) 624758
Jennings Cumberland Ale, Cocker Hoop; Marston's Mansfield Cask; guest beers Ⓗ
The Oddies, as it is known, is a welcoming hostelry, it was beautifully renovated a few years ago. This is a community pub with darts, dominoes, table skittles and a quiz night on alternate Thursdays. The Dabbers acoustic players perform on the first Thursday of the month while the enthusiastic landlord entertains on Saturday night. A large secluded garden is at the rear. Meals are served at weekends. **⌂❀◐◑⇌🚌(84)♣⚟**

Northwich

Penny Black
110 Witton Street, CW9 5AB
⏲ 9am-11 (1am Fri & Sat)
☎ (01606) 42029
Greene King Abbot; Marston's Pedigree; Tetley Bitter; guest beers Ⓗ
Purpose built as a post office in 1914, this Grade II listed building is now a Wetherspoon's outlet. It has a large open-plan central area in what was once the sorting office together with two side rooms for families in the previous public area and counter of the post office. The beer list usually features a darker beer (mild, stout or porter) and a local Cheshire beer. Free Wi-Fi. **Q☺❀◐◑♿⇌🚌(1,45,289)●P⚟**

Penketh

Ferry Tavern
Station Road, WA5 2UJ
⏲ 12-3.30, 5.30-11 (11.30 Fri); 12-11.30 Sat; 12-10.30 Sun
☎ (01925) 791117 🌐 theferrytavern.com
Greene King Abbot; Lees Bitter; Ruddles County; guest beers Ⓗ
Opened in 1762, the Ferry Tavern is accessed by crossing the railway to Fiddlers Ferry Power Station and the St Helens Canal. The pub itself looks out over the River Mersey. Home-cooked lunches complement the range of six real ales, with three changing regularly. The pub is also renowned for its selection of malt whiskies. Popular events include the music festival Glastonferry. **⌂❀◐P⚟**

Peover Heath

Dog Inn
Wellbank Lane, WA16 8UP (off A50)
⏲ 11.30-3, 4.30-11; 11.30-11 Sat; 12-10.30 Sun
☎ (01625) 861421 🌐 doginn-overpeover.co.uk
Copper Dragon Scotts 1816; Hydes Mild, Bitter; Weetwood Best Bitter Ⓗ
This picturesque pub has a tap room for pool and darts, a comfortable lounge bar with a real fire and an extensive restaurant (meals served all day Sun). There is an attractive heated patio at the front which provides cover for smokers, and a small beer garden next to the car park. Quizzes on Thursday and Sunday are popular, and live music is usually hosted once a month on a Friday. A beer festival is held at the end of July. **⌂❀🛏◐◑🀫♿♣P⚟**

Runcorn

Ferry Boat ✔
10 Church Street, WA7 1LR
⏲ 9-midnight (1am Fri & Sat)
☎ (01928) 583380
Greene King Abbot; Marston's Pedigree; Ruddles Best; guest beers Ⓗ
Located in the centre of the old town, this Wetherspoon shop conversion takes its name from the 12th-century ferry service that once linked Runcorn with Widnes. An attractive, spacious, open-plan pub, it is a welcome find in the real ale desert that is the old town. The interior is divided into several distinct seating areas and food is served all day. **◐◑♿🚌⚟**

Sandbach

Cricketers
54 Crewe Road, CW11 4NN
⏲ 4.30 (4 Fri, 12 Sat)-12.30am; 12-11.30 Sun
☎ (01270) 766960
Hydes Owd Oak, Original Bitter; Moorhouse's Blond Witch; guest beers Ⓗ
This bustling town pub has been a bastion of real ale since the current enterprising owners took over

a few years back. The three staple beers are supplemented by two changing guests, usually from micro-breweries. The pub is divided into two rooms by a central corridor, with a dartboard and three screens showing music or sports – and gets very busy at times. A real fire provides a warm welcome in winter. (38)♣

Sarn

Queens Head

Sarn Road, SY14 7LN SJ440446

6-midnight Tue-Sat; closed Mon; 12-midnight Sun

(01948) 770244

Marston's Burton Bitter; Taylor Golden Best; guest beer H

A welcome return to the Guide for this small unchanging village local. The Sarn, as it is known locally, is just a few yards from the Welsh border and is renowned for its home-made locally sourced food. The homely lounge is next to a separate dining area, and there is a small games room where pool is played. The guest beer is usually from a local micro-brewery and the pub provides a rare outlet for Taylor's light mild.

Q♣P

Shocklach

Bull

SY14 7BL

12-3, 5-11; 12-11 Fri & Sat; 10-10.30 Sun

(01829) 250239 thebullshocklach.com

Stonehouse Station Bitter; guest beers H

Old, recently refurbished country pub that combines good beer, excellent food and community activities. Note the tiled patchwork floor. The enthusiastic owners keep five real ales with at least one from a local brewer. Beer festivals are held and brewery tours are organised.

QP

Stoak

Bunbury Arms

Little Stanney Lane, CH2 4HW

12-11 (10.30 Sun)

(01244) 301665

Beer range varies H

With parts of the building dating from the 16th century, this appealing red-brick pub has moorings on the Shropshire Union Canal, 400 metres away. The interior comprises a small bar and stylish open-plan lounge, and there is a heated patio outside. The pub is popular with cyclists and walkers who fill the tranquil gardens in the summer months. The usual pub games are on offer.

Q(4)♣P

Sutton

Sutton Hall

Bullocks Lane, SK11 0HE

11.30-11; 12-10.30 Sun

(01260) 253211 suttonhall.co.uk

Thwaites Original; Weetwood Cheshire Cat; guest beer H

Splendid 480-year-old manor house set in its own grounds, close to the Macclesfield Canal, recently tastefully refurbished by Brunning & Price at a cost of £1.6m. The interior is notable for its many nooks and crannies including a snug, library and seven dining areas. While there is a strong food focus with an excellent menu, drinkers are most welcome – there are five real ales to enjoy, often from local breweries. With its lovely gardens, Sutton Hall is a real gem. QP

Tushingham

Blue Bell Inn

SY13 4QS

12-3 (not Mon), 6-11 (midnight Fri & Sat); 12-3, 7-11 Sun

(01948) 662172 bluebellinn.net

Oakham JHB; Salopian Shropshire Gold; guest beers H

Wonderful, black and white timber-framed, 17th-century Cheshire pub with plenty of atmosphere. A cobbled front leads to an ancient heavy front door. The main bar is popular with regulars who welcome visitors into their conversations. Well behaved dogs are permitted in the bar. One of the walls in a room used by diners reveals the pub's original wattle and daub. Caravans are allowed. Real cider is on offer in summer only.

Q♣P

Warrington

Albion

94 Battersby Lane, WA2 7EG

12-midnight (1am Fri); 10-1am Sat; 12-11 Sun

(01925) 231820

Beer range varies H

Large, friendly pub near the town centre with a multi-room interior including a reading lounge. Up to five real ales, mainly from micros, often include a mild. The pub's own brewery should be operational by July 2009. Food is served every lunchtime and in the evening Tuesday to Friday. Laurel and Hardy films are shown on the second Wednesday of the month. The pub supports a variety of sports and community events. Well behaved children and pets are welcome. No Sky TV. Q(Central)♣

Lower Angel

27 Buttermarket Street, WA1 2LY

11-11 (midnight Fri & Sat); 12-8 Sun

(01925) 572973

Tetley Bitter; Theakston Dark Mild; guest beers H

Renowned in the 90s as the must visit pub in Warrington, the Lower Angel has now returned to its former glory. This friendly two-roomed town centre pub offers up to six guest beers at any one time. A new one-barrel brewery plant is another reason to visit. (Central)♣

Porters Ale House

78 Buttermarket Street, WA1 2NN

11-midnight; 12-2am Fri & Sat; 1-midnight Sun

(01925) 632885

Beer range varies H

Long, single room, town-centre local where the emphasis is on drink and music. There is a raised seating area, with the bar to the left and a pool table towards the rear. Live classic rock music plays on Friday and Saturday nights with an acoustic session on Sunday. Quiz night is Wednesday with a free barbecue. (Central)♣

Tavern

25 Church Street, WA1 2SS

2-11; 12-11.30 Fri & Sat; 12-11 Sun

(01925) 577990

Beer range varies Ⓗ
A true free house, the Tavern is long established on the Warrington cask ale scene and is a favourite among tickers of new and different beers. This single-roomed pub can get very busy when rugby league is shown on TV (the outside covered smoking area also has its own screen), or when Warrington Wolves are playing at home.
❀≹(Central)🚌⅟–

Weston Point

Weaver Hotel 🏆
South Parade, WA7 4HS
⌚ 12-midnight (12.30am Fri & Sat)
☎ (01928) 572239
Oakwell Old Tom Mild, Barnsley Bitter Ⓗ
A deserved winner of the CAMRA Refurbishment Award and English Heritage Conservation Award in 2008. This Edwardian gem has a small lounge with a smart separate room adorned with historic local photographs. A separate bar with TV leads to a large family seating area outside. Excellent cask beers are served at very reasonable prices. Please ring for food availability. ♨Q♉❀🀄🚌♣P⅟–

Wettenhall

Little Man
Winsford Road, CW7 4DL SJ625605
⌚ 12.30-4 (not Tue), 7 (7.30 Tue)-11; 12.30-4, 7.30-10.30 Sun
☎ (01270) 528203
Beer range varies Ⓗ
This rural inn serves the local farming community. One side of the pub has a public bar feel, with televised sport, the other opens out into a comfortable lounge/dining area, traditionally decorated, with a welcoming fire. Five real ales are usually available, sourced from all over the country. The management is passionately devoted to real ale and good value food. ♨❀◐◑🀄♿♣P⅟–▯

Wheelock

Nags Head
504 Crewe Road, CW11 3RL (at A534/Mill Lane jct)
⌚ 12-2.30, 4-midnight; 12-midnight Sat & Sun
☎ (01270) 762457
Beer range varies Ⓗ
Three or four changing beers from local micros are usually available at this friendly pub. Storm and Weetwood ales are served regularly, with mini beer festivals held two or three times a year. The main front bar is flanked by a dining room and a further lounge area, each with its own real fire, and a public bar is at the rear. Home-cooked food.
♨❀◐◑🀄🚌(38)♣⅟–

Willey Moor

Willey Moor Lock Tavern
Tarporley Road, SY13 4HF (300m from A49) OS534452
⌚ 12-2.30 (3 summer), 6-11; 12-2.30 (3 summer), 7 (6 summer)-10.30 Sun
☎ (01948) 663274
Theakston Best Bitter; guest beers Ⓗ
Reached by a footbridge over the Llangollen Canal, the Willey Moor is a former lock keeper's cottage and is popular with canal boaters and walkers on the nearby Sandstone Trail. This genuine free house always has a good range of up to six beers on offer. The interior is comfortable, with padded wall seats, local watercolour paintings, a collection of teapots and real fires in winter. ♨❀◐◑P

Wilmslow

Bollin Fee ✔
6-12 Swan Street, SK9 1HE
⌚ 10-midnight (1am Thu; 2am Fri & Sat)
☎ (01625) 441850
Greene King Abbot; Marston's Pedigree; guest beer Ⓗ
This smart and modern Lloyds No 1 bar from Wetherspoon is situated in the centre of town and attracts a mixed clientele. The open plan layout includes family and dining areas. Sky TV is screened and weekend nights are very busy. Three regularly changing guest beers are on offer, plus a monthly a beer festival. Q❀◐◑♿≹🚌(88,130,378)♣⅟–

Coach & Four ✔
69-71 Alderley Road, SK9 1PA
⌚ 11.30-11 (midnight Thu-Sat); 12-11 Sun
☎ (01625) 525046
Hydes Original, Jekyll's Gold, Owd Oak; guest beer Ⓗ
This large and comfortable old coaching house is a Hydes Heritage Inn and caters for a wide clientele. The large single room is heavily subdivided by decorative screens to give a measure of intimacy and prevent the dominance of dining areas. Food is served all day and includes a carvery at lunchtime. The pub has its own lodge-style accommodation.
❀🛏◐◑♿≹🚌(130)♣🍎P⅟–

Winterley

Foresters Arms
473 Crewe Road, CW11 4RF SJ748576
⌚ 12-11
☎ (01270) 762642
Greene King Abbot; Tetley Bitter; Theakston Mild; Weetwood Eastgate Ⓗ
Very popular village pub with a strong community focus, where visitors are made welcome. Three cottages were knocked through in the mid-19th century to form the present pub and the interior shows evidence of this. Excellent home-cooked and locally-sourced lunches are available daily. Quiz night is Thursday. ♨❀◐🚌(37,38)🍎P⅟–

> Wer Kein Bier hat, Hat nichts zu trinken.
> **Martin Luther**
> When you have no beer, You have nothing to drink.
> Luther (1483-1546), was an Augustinian friar who rebelled against the excesses of the Papacy and sparked the Protestant reformation. When he was put on trial for heresy at the Diet of Worms in 1521, he was refreshed with supplies of beer from Einbeck in Lower Saxony. Einbeck gave its name to the strong German beer style known as Bock.

CORNWALL

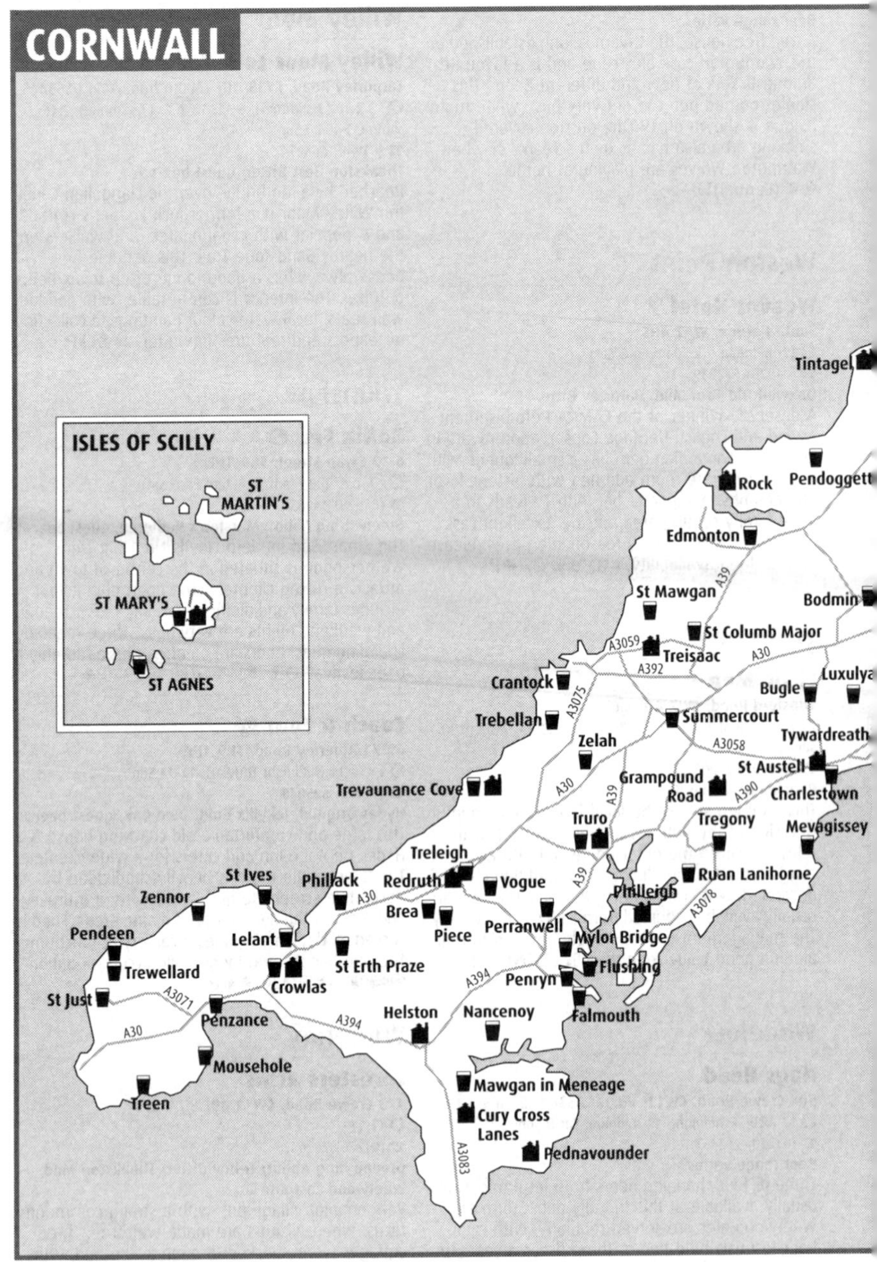

Blisland

Blisland Inn

The Green, PL30 4JF (off A30) SX100733

⌚ 11.30-11; 12-10.30 Sun

☎ (01208) 850739 🌐 bodminmoor.co.uk/blislandinn

Beer range varies Ⓗ/Ⓖ

Winner of numerous CAMRA awards, including National Pub of the Year in 2001, the Blisland Inn sits beside the only village green in Cornwall. A friendly community pub with a plain granite exterior and a warm, welcoming atmosphere, it is famous for the range and quality of its six ever-changing ales, often from Cornish breweries. The cider also varies and tends to be one of the less well-known names. The decor is eclectic, featuring barometers, toby jugs and coffee mugs suspended from the ceiling. ⛰Q🛏❀◑♣●P⁵–

Bodmin

Bodmin Jail

Berrycoombe Road, PL31 2NR (bottom of town near Camel Trail) SX066673

⌚ 11-11 (midnight Sat); 12-11 Sun

☎ (01208) 76292

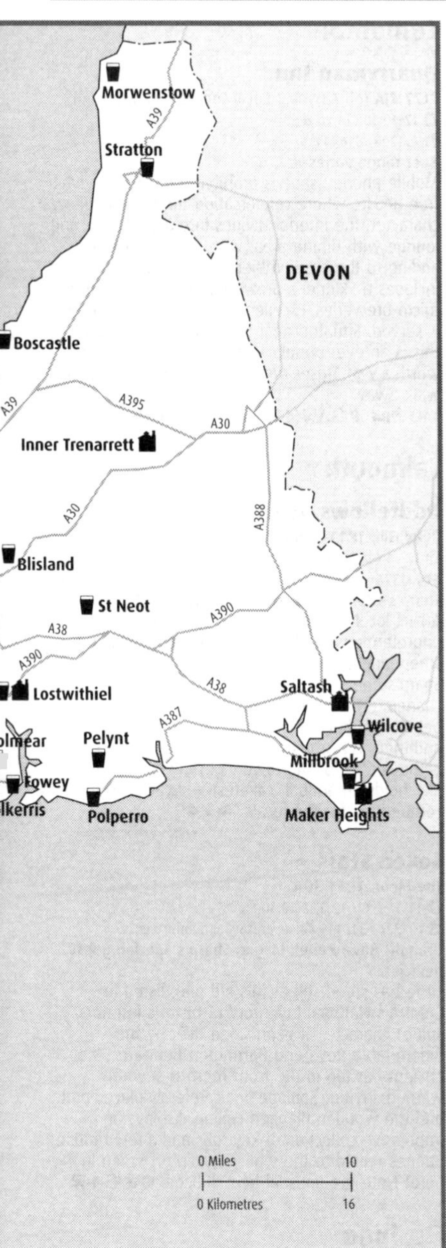

Brains Rev James; Dartmoor Jail Ale; Otter Ale; guest beer Ⓗ

Once the site of the forbidding and infamous jail, a tour of the attached prison museum is a must. The pub has recently been refurbished to create a comfortable lounge/dining area. The guest ale varies regularly, although it is usually from a Cornish brewery. The restaurant offers freshly-cooked, locally-sourced food including daily specials and a Sunday roast. Popular with cyclists and walkers, the pub is close to the Camel Trail. Children and dogs are welcome.
Q❀◐▲🚌(529,555,593)**P**

Boscastle

Napoleon Inn ✔

High Street, PL35 0BD

11-2.30 (3 summer), 5.30-11; 11-11 summer Sat; 12-10.30 Sun

☎ (01840) 250204

St Austell Tinners, Tribute, HSD Ⓖ

Comfortable 16th-century inn at the top of Boscastle, set back from the road. It has two bars set at right angles – the smaller bar is simply furnished and hosts the dartboard, the larger lounge has three separate drinking areas and a restaurant. The decor is a mix of drinking pots and assorted bric-a-brac. The pub has a colourful history – it was a 'recruiting centre' for press gangs during the Napoleonic wars and enjoyed a reputation as a bawdy house. **Q**❀◐🚌(594,595)**P**

Brea

Brea Inn

Higher Brea, TR14 9DA (off Four Lanes-Pool road) SW666404

12-3, 6.30-midnight; 12-3, 7-11 Sun

☎ (01209) 713706

Sharp's Doom Bar; guest beers Ⓗ

Small, split-level, cottage-style pub dating from the 18th-century, with the bar on the lower level and a separate drinking/dining area on the higher level offering an imaginative food menu. Set in the thick of Camborne's copper mining district, the pub was once a mine captain's residence before becoming a miners' ale house. It has been attractively modernised and displays an interesting collection of old mining, farming and other artefacts on the walls and shelves. The two guest ales are mainly local brews. **Q**❀◐🚌(42)**P**

Bugle

Bugle Inn ✔

57 Fore Street, PL26 8PB (on A391)

11-midnight; 12-10.30 Sun

☎ (01726) 850307 bugleinn.co.uk

St Austell IPA, Dartmoor Best, Tribute Ⓗ

Lively, welcoming, village-centre local, named after the sound of the horn of passing stagecoaches of yesteryear. It is situated in the

INDEPENDENT BREWERIES

Ales of Scilly St Mary's
Atlantic Treisaac
Blackawton Saltash
Blue Anchor Helston
Castle Lostwithiel
Chough Cury Cross Lanes
Coastal Redruth
Driftwood Trevaunance Cove
Forgotten Corner Maker Heights (NEW)
Keltek Redruth
Lizard Pednavounder
Penpont Inner Trenarrett (NEW)
Penzance Crowlas
Roseland Philleigh (NEW)
Sharp's Rock
Skinner's Truro
St Austell St Austell
Tintagel Tintagel (NEW)
Warrior Redruth
Wooden Hand Grampound Road

heart of the China Clay district. The comfortable interior has a large Z-shaped bar displaying an interesting collection of carved coconuts and witch effigies. Meals including breakfast are served all day. Live music plays most Sunday evenings. A family-friendly pub with five en-suite rooms, it is an ideal base for touring Cornwall or visiting the nearby Eden Project. (529)P

Charlestown

Harbourside Inn

Charlestown Road, PL25 3NJ (on harbour front)
11-11 (midnight Fri & Sat)
(01726) 76955 pierhousehotel.com/harbourside_inn_in_cornwall.htm
Draught Bass; St Austell Tribute; Sharp's Doom Bar, Special; Skinner's Betty Stogs, Cornish Knocker H
Attached to the Pier House Hotel, this former harbourside warehouse has been stylishly converted to a lively sports-oriented modern pub. Its glass frontage affords views of the tall ships moored in Charlestown's historic harbour. The single bar interior is charming, with exposed stonework, wood flooring and wooden furnishings throughout. The beer menu varies with up to seven real ales available. Good value food is served all day. Popular sporting events are screened, and there is entertainment on Saturday evening. (25)

Crantock

Old Albion

Langurroc Road, TR8 5RB
12-midnight (4-11 Mon-Thu winter); 12-11 Sun
(01637) 830243
Courage Best Bitter; guest beers H
'Find the church and you will find the pub' rings true for this partly-thatched picture postcard inn, which has a history of smuggling via secret tunnels to the church and beach. Up to three guest ales are on offer here, including one from Skinners or another local brewery. The pub is busier when nearby camping and caravan sites are open; midweek meals are available only during the summer months. There is a pleasant outdoor drinking area, and the pub is dog-friendly. (585,587)P

Crowlas

Star Inn

TR20 8DX (on A30 just E of Penzance)
11-11.30; 12-10.30 Sun
(01736) 740375
Penzance Crowlas Bitter, Potion No 9; guest beers H
Voted Cornwall CAMRA Pub of the Year in 2007 and 2008, this is a real pub with the emphasis on beer quality and presentation. Easily accessible by bus, this friendly free house with its own micro-brewery is an ale-drinkers' paradise. A quiet pub where conversation flourishes, the attractive single bar interior features wood and slate furnishings. The ever-changing beer menu includes up to three house brews, with guest ales generally from other micros. No food is served.
Q(17,18,X18)P

Edmonton

Quarryman Inn

PL27 7JA (off A39 near Royal Cornwall Showground)
12-10.30 (11 Fri & Sat)
(01208) 816444
Beer range varies H
Mobile phone usage is prohibited in this convivial free house, where conversation thrives. Full of character, the interior divides into a public bar and lounge with dining area, with an eclectic decor adding to the cosy ambience. The beer menu includes a Skinner's brew and guests from other micro-breweries. Excellent food using local produce is served. Situated near the county showground, this is an ever-popular gem of a pub and well worth a visit. Buses run along the A39, a 10 minute walk away.
Q(510,555,594)P

Falmouth

Oddfellows Arms

Quay Hill, TR11 3HG (off Arwenack Street)
12-11 (10.30 Sun)
(01326) 318530
Sharp's Eden Ale, Special H**; guest beer** G
A real locals' local, this small, basic and unpretentious single-bar free house is hidden up a steep lane off the main shopping street. The Sharp's beers are supplemented by an ever-changing guest ale straight from a cask racked behind the bar. Games include euchre and darts, and there is a small pool room to the rear. The pub is the centre for the town's gig rowing activities, and holds an annual 'cakefest' - a cake-baking competition for the locals.

Seven Stars ★

The Moor, TR11 3QA
11-3, 6-11; 12-3, 7-10.30 Sun
(01326) 312111 sevenstarsfalmouth.co.uk
Draught Bass; Keltek Magik; Sharp's Special; guest beer G
Time has stood still at this old pub, listed in CAMRA's National Inventory of historic interiors. Full of character, it is presided over by the indomitable Reverend Barrington Bennetts. The ancient bar top in the front room is severely warped, inviting spillage of a carelessly placed pint, and the wooden planked ceiling displays an impressive collection of key fobs and a few mobile phones nailed to the wall - switch off when in here! Note the unusual beer stillage. Q

Flushing

Seven Stars

3 Trefusis Road, TR11 5TY (off A393 at Penryn)
11 (12 Sun)-11
(01326) 374373
Sharp's Doom Bar; Skinner's Betty Stogs, Cornish Knocker; guest beer H
Central village pub attracting locals and visitors alike. Tables outside on a narrow patio overlook the Penryn River. Inside is a large, well-furnished L-shaped bar, and a restaurant area serving good, reasonably-priced food, with fresh fish a speciality. Fish 'n' chips and curry themed nights are also popular. Parking is difficult - the easiest daytime access is via a short trip on the foot passenger ferry from Falmouth. Q(400)

Fowey

Galleon Inn

12 Fore Street, PL23 1AQ
⏲ 11 (12 Sun)-11 (midnight summer)
☎ (01726) 833014 🌐 galleon-inn.co.uk
Sharp's Cornish Coaster, Doom Bar; guest beer Ⓗ
Centrally-located waterside inn, reached through a glass-covered corridor off Fore Street decorated with a colourful marine life mural. The only free house in Fowey, it features mainly Cornish real ales, and boasts delightful estuary views from the modernised main bar and dining area. Exposed stone walls are set off by polished woodwork. Tables outside overlook the water and there is a heated, sheltered courtyard. A wide range of meals is available daily. Accommodation is en-suite, most rooms with river views. ⌂Q❀🛏◑♿▲🚌(25)⊬

Safe Harbour ✔

58 Lostwithiel Street, PL23 1BQ
⏲ 11-11; 12-10.30 Sun
☎ (01726) 833379 🌐 cornwall-safeharbour.co.uk
St Austell Tinners, Tribute, Proper Job Ⓗ
Old, split-level pub at the top of town, with low ceilings and exposed stonework, decorated with historic local photos from the age of sail. The public bar hosts the pool table and dartboard. The quiet upper lounge bar, with its polished copper bar top, has been refurbished and brightened, with overstuffed chairs and a sofa. The pub enjoys fine views over the town and estuary, and outside there is a small heated patio. The varied menu features locally-sourced ingredients.
Q❀🛏◑🀫▲🚌(25)♣P⊬

Lelant

Watermill Inn

Old Coach Road, TR27 6LQ (off A3074, on secondary St Ives road) SW541364
⏲ 12-11
☎ (01736) 757912
Sharp's Doom Bar; guest beer Ⓗ
A short walk from Lelant Saltings station, this family-friendly, two-storey free house stands in beautiful surroundings. A former 18th-century mill house, the original working waterwheel, complete with millstones, features downstairs in the traditionally-styled single bar. The comfortable interior is divided into drinking and dining areas where bar meals are served. Upstairs, the former mill loft is an evening-only restaurant, specialising in local seafood. Outside, an expansive beer garden surrounds the mill stream. Annual beer festivals are held in June. ⌂Q❀◑▲≷🚌(14,17)P⊬

Lostwithiel

Globe Inn

3 North Street, PL22 0EG
⏲ 12-2.30, 6-11 (5-midnight Fri); 12-midnight Sat & summer; 12-11.30 Sun
☎ (01208) 872501 🌐 globeinn.com
Sharp's Doom Bar; Skinner's Betty Stogs; guest beers Ⓗ
In the narrow streets of this old stannary town, close to the railway station, nestles this cosy 13th-century pub, named after the ship on which a relative of a former owner died in a 19th-century sea battle. The old rambling building features a single bar with several drinking and dining areas. Towards the rear is a stylish sun-trap patio. A second guest ale appears in summer. Fish and game are specialities on an extensive menu of excellent home-cooked food.
⌂Q❀🛏◑♿▲≷♣⊬

Luxulyan

King's Arms ✔

Bridges, PL30 5EF
⏲ 10-midnight; 12-11 Sun
☎ (01726) 850202
St Austell Tinners, Tribute, HSD Ⓗ
Granite village pub, locally known as Bridges, offering a friendly, no-nonsense welcome to all, including children and dogs. Tastefully refurbished, the spacious room is still partially divided into its original sections by an archway – the bar area is mainly for drinking, the lounge mainly for food. A pool table and skittle alley are housed in a separate building across the road. The pub can be reached via the beautiful Luxulyan Valley, where many remnants of the area's industrial past remain.
⌂Q❀◑♿▲≷🚌(24)♣P⊬

Mawgan-in-Meneage

Ship Inn

Mawgan, TR12 6AD (off B3293) SW709250
⏲ 11-3, 5-11; 12-11 Sun
☎ (01326) 221240
Sharp's Doom Bar; Skinner's Betty Stogs; guest beer Ⓗ
Well worth seeking out, this friendly country pub is located down a steep leafy lane off the Helston to St Keverne road. The welcoming and attractively-furnished interior features a single bar, snug and raised dining area. Full of character and charm, the decor is distinctly rural. Wood-burning stoves add warmth to the cosy ambience. The food menu offers quality meals made from local produce. A guest ale appears in summer only. The bus stop is up the hill. ⌂Q❀◑▲🚌(2,3)●P⊬

Mevagissey

Fountain Inn ✔

3 Cliff Street, PL26 6QH
⏲ 12-midnight
☎ (01726) 842320
St Austell Tinners, HSD Ⓗ
Friendly, two-bar, 15th-century inn with slate floors, stone walls, historic photographs and low ceilings – the tunnel to the side door is particularly low. The Smugglers Bar features signs of the pilchard press that was once housed here, a glass plate in the floor covering the pit where the oil was caught, which doubled as a store for contraband. The meat was compressed to feed Nelson's navy. Buses run to St Austell and the Lost Gardens of Heligan. ⌂Q🛏◑🀫🚌(26,526)

Millbrook

Devon & Cornwall ✔

West Street, PL10 1AA (near B3247) SX422520
⏲ 12 (3 Mon-Wed)-11; 12-10.30 Sun
☎ (01752) 822320
Butcombe Bitter; Courage Best Bitter; Skinner's Betty Stogs Ⓗ
Convivial single-bar local in the centre of the village. The L-shaped open-plan interior has one end comfortably furnished with sofas and wing

chairs, presided over by a piano, and the other end partially screened, providing scope for more private dining and drinking. Essentially a locals' pub, visitors are nonetheless warmly welcomed, with conversation the main entertainment. Food is limited in the winter months, when you may bring your own. ❀🛏◐ ⛺🚌(81)♣

Morwenstow

Bush Inn

Cross Town, EX23 9SR (5km off A39 N of Kilkhampton) SS209150

⏲ 11-midnight

☎ (01288) 331242 🌐 bushinn-morwenstow.co.uk

St Austell Proper Job, HSD; Skinner's Betty Stogs Ⓗ

This pub is an ancient former chapel dating in parts from 950AD. Unassuming externally, it is a gem inside, simply furnished with slate floors, granite walls and exposed beams in the two separate bar rooms. Conversation is the main entertainment here. There is a smokers' area in the courtyard at the front of the pub, and a large garden at the back offering outstanding views over the valley and out to sea. ♨Q❀🛏◐⊟⛺🚌♣P⁄–

Mousehole

Ship Inn ✔

South Cliff, TR19 6QX

⏲ 11-11.30 (11 Sun)

☎ (01736) 731234

St Austell IPA, Tinners, Tribute, HSD Ⓗ

Traditional, 18th-century, harbourside inn, set in a picturesque Cornish fishing village. The unspoiled interior has floors of scrubbed wood and huge granite flags, and ceilings of low black wood beams. Pictures decorating the walls reflect its long association with the sea and the Penlee lifeboat disaster of 1981. The inn was a favoured haunt of Dylan Thomas when he lived in Mousehole. The large restaurant serves freshly-cooked food made with the best local produce.
♨❀🛏◐⊟🚌(6,504)♣⁄–

Mylor Bridge

Lemon Arms ✔

Lemon Hill, TR11 5NA (off A393 at Penryn) SW804362

⏲ 11-3, 6.30-11; 12-3, 7-11 Sun

☎ (01326) 373666

St Austell Tinners, Tribute, HSD Ⓗ

There has been a hostelry on this site since 1765. Once called the Griffin Inn, it became the Red Lion in 1829 and took its present name in 1837. A friendly one-bar pub in the centre of the village, it is popular with local sports teams. Good home-cooked food is available – booking is advisable for the popular Sunday lunches. Families with children are made most welcome. Daytime buses run from Falmouth during the week. ♨❀◐🚌(400)♣P⁄–

Nancenoy

Trengilly Wartha Inn

TR11 5RP (off B329) SW732283

⏲ 11-3, 6.30-11; 12-3, 7-10.30 Sun

☎ (01326) 340332 🌐 trengilly.co.uk

Beer range varies Ⓗ

Well-run, versatile inn sitting in a steeply-wooded valley near the village of Constantine. Converted from a farmhouse, it has a bar, snug and restaurant, with a later conservatory extension serving as the family room. Up to three real ales are offered from Cornish breweries. Winner of many awards, the Trengilly's main emphasis is on fresh food, with a wide-ranging and imaginative menu prepared where possible with Cornish produce. Accommodation is above the pub or in the garden rooms nearby. ♨Q👶❀🛏◐♣P

Pelynt

Jubilee Inn ✔

Jubilee Hill, PL13 2JZ

⏲ 11-11; 12-10.30 Sun

☎ (01503) 220312 🌐 jubilee-inn.co.uk

St Austell Tribute; guest beer Ⓗ

Originally a 17th-century farmhouse, this comfortable village inn has been sympathetically extended. First called The Axe, it was renamed in 1887 to celebrate 50 years of Queen Victoria's reign. It has low ceilings, Delabole slate flags, antique furnishings and a collection of royal jubilee and other memorabilia. The guest beer comes from the St Austell brewery range. An extensive menu features locally-sourced produce and daily specials. Outside, there is a part-covered patio and spacious beer garden. ♨❀🛏◐⊟⛺🚌(573)♣P⁄–

Pendeen

North Inn ✔

TR19 7DN (on B3306)

⏲ 11-midnight (1am Fri & Sat); 12-11 Sun

☎ (01736) 788417

St Austell Tinners, Tribute, Proper Job Ⓗ

Welcoming village inn in an area of outstanding natural beauty, close to the coastal path and cliffs, and Geevor tin mining museum. Pictures and artefacts from the mining industry decorate the large single bar. The St Austell real ales vary according to seasonal demand. Quality home-cooked food is served daily – the curries are locally famous. There is a small overflow restaurant upstairs. B&B and camping are both available. Former Cornwall CAMRA Pub of the Year.
♨Q❀🛏◐⛺🚌(17A,507)♣P⁄–

Pendoggett

Cornish Arms

PL30 3HH (on B3314) SX024794

⏲ 11-2.30, 6-11; 11-11 Fri-Sun

☎ (01208) 880263 🌐 cornisharms.com

Sharp's Doom Bar Ⓗ

Welcoming, family-friendly coaching inn with a main bar, snug, two drinking and dining areas and a restaurant. Charming and full of character, the flagstone floors, open beams, wood-panelled walls, partitions and furnishings reflect the pub's 16th-century origins. Open fires add to the cosy ambience. Caricatures of locals adorn the walls and a collection of handbells hangs above the bar. The house beer, PSB (4.7%), is brewed by Sharp's. Locally-sourced quality food is available, and popular speciality themed nights are held (booking advised). Q❀🛏◐⛺♣●P⁄–

Penryn

Seven Stars

73 The Terrace, TR10 8EL

⏲ 11 (12 Sun)-11

☎ (01326) 373573
Blue Anchor Spingo Middle; Skinner's Betty Stogs, Heligan Honey, Cornish Knocker, Figgy's Brew Ⓗ
The nearest thing Penryn has to an ale house, this single-bar town pub is run by a jovial Dutchman. Decorated with foreign cash, postcards and beer-related clippings, the spacious interior has a raised and comfortably-furnished drinking annexe at the rear, dominated by a huge ship's wheel. The pub is home to the Penryn Community Theatre which entertains with plays and pantos. A piano is available for competent pianists and occasional live music is performed. The Skinner's beer selection may vary.

Penzance

Crown Inn
Victoria Square, TR18 2EP
12-midnight (12.30am Fri & Sat)
☎ (01736) 351070 thecrownpenzance.co.uk
Otter Ale; Skinner's Heligan Honey; guest beer Ⓗ
Small community local with a relaxing atmosphere situated a short walk from bus and rail stations, just off the main shopping street. It has a tidily furnished single bar and a small back room that provides extra dining space with a welcoming open fire. Two regular real ales, one local, are complemented by a varying guest beer. Quality home-cooked food is served daily during the summer (Thursday to Saturday evenings and Friday to Sunday lunchtimes in winter).
Q

First & Last Inn
24 Alverton Road, TR18 4TN
10.30-11; 12-10.30 Sun
☎ (01736) 364095
Beer range varies Ⓗ
In Victorian times this traditional Cornish inn was referred to as Mr Tonkin's Beer House. It once served as a staging post for the Royal Mail in the Land's End area. The small public bar has a wooden floor, wood-panelled walls and a beamed ceiling, and offers three ever-changing real ales, one Cornish. The lounge has a small bar and carpeted dining area. Quality home-cooked food is served at lunchtime (not Mon), with discounted prices on Tuesday and Thursday. **Q**(5,6,512)

Pirate Inn
Alverton Road, TR18 4PS
10.30-11.30; 12-10.30 Sun
☎ (01736) 366094 pirateinn.co.uk
Sharp's Doom Bar; Skinner's Betty Stogs; guest beer Ⓗ
Typical granite Cornish inn, converted from a 17th-century farmhouse in the 1950s. There is an almost rural feel to this pub on the edge of town, with its plentiful trees and shrubs, and spacious, pleasant beer garden. The lounge has an impressive stone fireplace and raised dining area, and both large bars are carpeted throughout. Two local ales are complemented by a guest beer, and real cider is served from the cellar. Buses stop outside the door.
Q(5,6)**P**

Perranwell

Royal Oak
TR3 7PX
11-3, 6-11; 12-3, 7-10.30 Sun
☎ (01872) 863175
Skinner's Betty Stogs; guest beer Ⓗ
Small and friendly 18th-century cottage-style village pub renowned for good ale and food. The emphasis here is on food and most of the tables are laid up for meals, but drinkers are made welcome at the bar. Booking ahead for food is recommended as the pub often gets busy with diners. The guest beer is usually a Cornish brew. Bus services stop outside, connecting with Truro and Helston. The railway station is 15 minutes' walk away. **Q**(88,T1,T2)**P**

Phillack

Bucket of Blood
14 Churchtown Road, TR27 5AE SW563383
12-2.30 (3 Sat, not Mon), 6-11 (midnight Fri & Sat); 12-4, 7-11 Sun
☎ (01736) 752378
St Austell Dartmoor Best Bitter, Proper Job IPA, HSD Ⓗ
Gory local legend (involving a well and a murdered revenue officer at the bottom of it) explains the name of this old pub near the dunes of Hayle Towans. Recently refurbished, the single bar houses a cosy drinking and dining area at one end with settles, an old fireplace, and a pool table at the other. A mural depicting St Ives Bay overlooks the pool table. 'Familiarity breeds contempt', written on one of the unusually low beams, serves as a warning rather than a proverb. No food is served in winter. **P**

Piece

Countryman Inn
TR16 6SG (on Four Lanes-Pool road) SW679398
11-11 (midnight Sat); 12-11 Sun
☎ (01209) 215960
Courage Best Bitter; Greene King Old Speckled Hen; Sharp's Doom Bar; Skinner's Betty Stogs, Heligan Honey; guest beer Ⓗ
Lively, welcoming country pub set high among the copper mines near Carn Brea, once a grocery shop for the miners. The larger bar hosts live entertainment every night, and on Sunday lunchtime there is a raffle in support of local charities. A range of nine ales is offered, including two brews each from Sharp's and Skinner's breweries, and a guest beer or two from various sources. Good value food is available all day.
(42)**P**

Polkerris

Rashleigh Inn
PL24 2TL (off A3082 Par-Fowey road) SX094522
11-11; 12-10.30 Sun
☎ (01726) 813991 therashleighinnpolkerris.co.uk
Taylor Landlord; guest beers Ⓗ
Excellent, family-run, 18th-century free house, once a pilchard boathouse, situated beside a secluded beach near the Saint's Way footpath. The cosy, atmospheric main bar features exposed stonework, beamed ceilings, open fires and comfortable furnishings, and there are piano-accompanied singalongs on Saturday evening. Additional guest ales are on offer in the summer. First-rate food is served in the bar and split-level restaurant. A sheltered terrace affords panoramic views of St Austell Bay and the setting sun.
QP

Polmear

Ship Inn

Polmear Hill, PL24 2AR (on A3082 Par-Fowey road)
⊙ 11 (12 Sun)-11.30
☎ (01726) 812540 ⊕ theshipinnpar.co.uk
Fuller's London Pride; Sharp's Doom Bar; Skinner's Cornish Knocker; guest beer Ⓗ

Homely, family-friendly free house next to Par beach, popular with tourists and locals alike. The spacious single-bar interior is divided into numerous seating areas, with old wagon wheels forming an unusual partition. Wooden furnishings and open fires, including a Cornish range, create a cosy atmosphere. Food is served all day either in the bar or upstairs restaurant. Occasional mini beer festivals are held. Outside, tidy gardens include a play area for children. A self-catering log cabin is available for weekly summer rental.
⛫Q❀⇌◐◑♿Å♣●P⅍

Polperro

Blue Peter Inn

Quay Road, PL13 2QZ
⊙ 11-11; 12-10.30 Sun
☎ (01503) 272743 ⊕ thebluepeterinn.co.uk
St Austell Tribute; guest beers Ⓗ

Named after the naval flag, this friendly family-run free house is found up a flight of steps near the outer harbour. Up to four guest beers from West Country breweries are on offer, with cider from Cornish Orchards. Built on two levels, the old pub has low ceilings, wooden floors and hidden corners. The decor features foreign breweriana, unusual souvenirs and work by local artists. The pub is popular with locals, visitors, fishermen and dogs – ask for a biscuit! ⛫♉◐◑Å⊟(573)♣●⅍

Crumplehorn Inn

The Old Mill, PL13 2RJ (on A387)
⊙ 11-11; 12-10.30 Sun
☎ (01503) 272348 ⊕ crumplehorn-inn.co.uk
Sharp's Doom Bar; Skinner's Betty Stogs; guest beer Ⓗ

Once a working mill and mentioned in the Domesday Book, this 18th-century inn at the entrance to the village retains its fine waterwheel. Inside, it has three comfortable low-beamed rooms on split levels. The guest ale is usually Cornish, and the menu features locally-caught seafood. A spacious patio offers gazebos to shade customers from the elements. Accommodation is B&B or self-catering. In summer, you can catch a horse-drawn bus or tram to the village centre.
⛫Q❀⇌◐◑Å⊟(573)♣⅍

Ruan Lanihorne

Kings Head

TR2 5NX SW895420
⊙ 12-2.30, 6-11 (closed Mon winter); 12-2.30, 6-10.30 summer (12-4 winter) Sun
☎ (01872) 501263 ⊕ kingsheadruan.co.uk
Skinner's Betty Stogs, Cornish Knocker Ⓗ

Delightful family-run free house nestling in the Fal estuary on the Roseland Peninsula. Quiet, traditional and full of character, the homely interior comprises a single bar and two dining areas, the decor reflecting country life. The pub is renowned locally for quality ales and superb, locally-sourced food. The house beer is Skinner's Kings Ruan, and a fourth Skinner's ale appears in summer. Cider is Skinner's Press Gang. A sun terrace and quaint sunken garden cater for alfresco drinking and dining. ⛫Q❀◐◑Å●P⅍

St Agnes: Isles of Scilly

Turk's Head

TR22 0PL
⊙ 11-4.30, 7-11 (11-11 Jul & Aug; winter hours restricted); 12-4.30, 7-10.30 (12-11 Jul & Aug; winter hours restricted) Sun
☎ (01720) 422434
St Austell Tribute; guest beer Ⓗ

The only pub on the island, well-loved by locals and visitors, with an outdoor drinking area unrivalled for its scenic beauty. Opening hours vary according to boat times – the jetty is only a couple of minutes walk away and you can watch your boat approaching from the bar. In summer, evening boat trips run from St Mary's to sample the ale and food. The Tribute is rebadged as the house beer Turk's Ale. Order lunchtime pasties early! ♉❀◐◑Å

St Columb Major

Ring O' Bells

3 Bank Street, TR9 6AT
⊙ 12-2.30, 5-11; 12-3, 7-10.30 Sun
☎ (01637) 880259
Sharp's Doom Bar, Eden Ale Ⓗ**; guest beer** Ⓖ

A former brewhouse built to commemorate the parish church tower, this is the oldest pub in town. The narrow frontage of this charming 15th-century free house belies the capacious interior, which comprises three bars and a restaurant, formerly the brewery. Open beams, slate floors and wooden furnishings create a traditional atmosphere, each bar having its own character and custom. A guest ale is available in summer only. A fine cosmopolitan menu is served in the restaurant and rear bar. ⛫Q❀◐◑⊟Å⊟(557,593,594)♣●⅍

St Erth Praze

Smugglers Inn

3 Calais Road, TR27 6EG (on B3302, 3km from Hayle)
⊙ 12-11
☎ (01736) 850280
Skinner's Betty Stogs; guest beers Ⓗ

Families and dogs are welcome at this spacious roadside hostelry. The entrance corridor leads to a good-sized bar room with an enormous fire in winter, a smaller games room, a light, airy restaurant and a function room, and there is a large garden and plenty of parking space. Food is available all day on Sunday. Occasional live entertainment includes visiting jazz bands on Sunday lunchtimes. The two guest ales may be sourced from either national or local breweries.
⛫❀⇌◐◑ÅP⅍

St Ives

Golden Lion ✔

Market Place, TR26 1RZ
⊙ 11 (12 Sun)-1am
☎ (01736) 793679
Beer range varies Ⓗ

In the town centre near the church, this former coaching inn is a popular locals' pub. It has two rooms: the smaller horseshoe-shaped front lounge attracts drinkers who enjoy convivial conversation,

while the larger and more boisterous 'public' at the rear, with pool table, is favoured by younger customers. The beer menu always includes one brew from the Sharp's and Skinner's ranges, plus a guest ale. Good quality and value food is home cooked using local produce.
Q❀◑⊟Å⇌(St Ives)⊟♣●⁻

St Just

Star Inn ✔

1 Fore Street, TR19 7LL
11-midnight
☎ (01736) 788767
St Austell IPA, Tinners, Dartmoor Best Bitter, Tribute Ⓗ
This 18th-century inn near the Square is reputedly the oldest pub in St Just. Its single bar displays pictures and artefacts reflecting its long association with mining and the sea. A separate snug also serves as a family room. This is a proper drinkers' pub – conversation (or singing) is the main entertainment for locals and visitors. The range of St Austell ales varies with seasonal demand. Monday is 'Fiddly-Dee' night, and there is live music on Saturday. No food. ⛰Q❀Å⊟♣⁻

St Mary's: Isles of Scilly

Old Town Inn

Old Town, TR21 0NN
12-2.30, 5-11 (closed Mon-Thu lunchtime winter)
☎ (01720) 422301
Ales of Scilly Firebrand; Sharp's Doom Bar; guest beer Ⓗ
This modern and roomy pub lies just below the airport, on the road towards Hugh Town. Wood panelling and flooring dominate the two bars. The front bar is for day-to-day drinking, while the rear bar is a dining and function room. Home to the Islands Folk Club, the pub offers occasional live entertainment. Food is served daily including takeaway pizzas and curries. About 20 minutes' walk from Hugh Town, it has good wheelchair access. ⛰❀⊟◑♿

St Mawgan

Falcon Inn ✔

TR8 4EP (near Newquay airport) SW873658
11-3, 6-11 (midnight Fri & Sat); 12-11 Sun
☎ (01637) 860225 🌐 thefalconinn-stmawgan.co.uk
St Austell Tinners, Tribute, HSD; guest beer Ⓗ
Charming 16th-century pub set in the idyllic Lanherne Valley. Centrally located in a picturesque village, the family-friendly pub is the hub of local activities. The quiet, single-bar interior has a cosy, relaxed atmosphere with decor reflecting country life. Excellent meals are served in the bar and dining room. Outside there is a large well-kept garden with covered areas for dining alfresco.
⛰Q❀⊟◑Å⊟(556)♣P⁻

St Neot

London Inn

PL14 6NG
12-3, 6-midnight (12-midnight Sat & summer); 12-midnight Sun
☎ (01579) 320263
Sharp's Doom Bar; John Smith's Bitter; guest beer Ⓗ
Former 16th-century coaching inn near Colliford Lake, now a lively village local and focal point for village activities, with occasional beer festivals held in support of local cricket teams. Its beamed and flagstoned interior accommodates a single bar, restaurant and traditional skittles alley. Welcoming and family-friendly, its wood furnishings, real fires and rustic decor create a cosy ambience. Quality pub grub and an evening a la carte menu are on offer, but beer quality is the prime concern in this no-frills pub. ⛰Q❀⊟◑♿Å♣P⁻

Stratton

King's Arms ✔

Howells Road, EX23 9BX
12-11
☎ (01288) 352396
Exmoor Ale; Sharp's Doom Bar; Shepherd Neame Spitfire; guest beer Ⓗ
Popular 17th-century coaching inn with two simply-furnished bars retaining many original features including well worn Delabole slate flagstone floors. During renovation of the large open fireplace in the lounge, a small bread oven was exposed. Draught cider is available in summer. The building has good disabled access. The pub's name reflects the town's political loyalties after the Civil War – the battle of Stamford Hill took place near here in 1643. ⛰Q❀⊟◑♿⊟♣●P

Summercourt

London Inn

1 School Road, TR8 5EA (off A30)
12-2 (not Mon-Thu winter), 5 (6 Sat)-midnight; 12-2, 7-11 Sun
☎ (01872) 510281
Beer range varies Ⓗ
A warm welcome is assured at this lively, family-friendly free house. On the old London road, this former 17th-century coaching inn is central to the annual village fair celebrations in September. Wooden screens divide the spacious single bar interior into drinking and dining areas. Coach lamp lighting, wooden furnishings and Laurel and Hardy figurines feature among the eclectic decor. Quality counts with the ever-changing beer menu, and traditional home-cooked food is served. Buses stop nearby. ⛰Q❀◑Å⊟(527,597)●P⁻

Trebellan

Smugglers Den Inn

TR8 5PY (off Cubert road from A3075) SW783574
11-11 (12-3, 6-11 Thu-Sat winter); 12-11 Sun
☎ (01637) 830209 🌐 thesmugglersden.co.uk
St Austell Tribute; Sharp's Cornish Coaster; guest beer Ⓗ
An idyllic location down a narrow country lane makes this former farmhouse a popular place for food and drink. Oak beams, paved yards and a thatched roof all add to its charm. Four locally-brewed beers are usually available, sometimes rebadged as house beers. Occasional jazz or folk evenings are hosted, and an ale and pie festival held over the May Day weekend. The pub is convenient for nearby caravan sites. Truro-Newquay buses stop at the top of the lane.
⛰Q❀◑Å⊟(585,587)P⁻

Treen

Gurnard's Head

TR26 3DE SW436376
⏲ 11.30-midnight (11.30 Sun)
☎ (01736) 796928 🌐 gurnardshead.co.uk
St Austell Tribute; Skinner's Ginger Tosser, Betty Stogs Ⓗ
Impressive free house near the coastal path, named after the headland nearby. A growing reputation for fine ales and excellent food draws custom from near and far. The expansive wood-floored interior comprises a spacious single bar, cosy snug and stylish dining room. Wooden furnishings, comfy sofas and open fires create a relaxed, comfortable atmosphere, with local art featuring on the walls. The pub is community oriented and holds weekly Cornish song and poetry evenings and monthly folk evenings.
⛫Q❀🛏◑▲🚌(507,508,300)P⚡

Tregony

King's Arms ✔

55 Fore Street, TR2 5RW
⏲ 12-3, 5.30-midnight; 12-3, 6-midnight Sun
☎ (01872) 530202
St Austell Tinners, Tribute, Proper Job, seasonal beer Ⓗ
This 16th-century former coaching inn is situated in the village centre on reputedly the widest street in Cornwall. Recently refurbished, it has a long bar area and two dining rooms, one also used for functions. There is an old well at the far end of the bar, now covered with a glass plate. Morning coach parties are welcome for coffee and snacks by arrangement. St Austell's premium ale, HSD, features on the bar in summer.
⛫Q❀◑♿🚌(50,51)♣P⚡

Treleigh

Treleigh Arms

TR16 4AY (beside old Redruth bypass) SW704435
⏲ 11-11 (11-3, 6-11 Mon-Thu winter)
☎ (01209) 315095
Draught Bass; Keltek Golden Lance; Sharp's Doom Bar; Skinner's Betty Stogs; guest beer Ⓗ
Easily accessible just off the old Redruth bypass, this cosy pub features comfortable seating around a wood-burning fire, tables for dining, and bar seats if you fancy a chat with the regulars in the 'Grumpy Gits' corner. There are no intrusive machines or music. Highlights include themed meal nights and the popular Tuesday quiz. There is a small patio and, round the back, a petanque pitch used mostly in summer. Dogs are welcome.
⛫Q❀◑▲🚌(T20,T21)P⚡

Trevaunance Cove

Driftwood Spars 🏆 ✔

Quay Road, TR5 0RT SW721513
⏲ 11-11 (1am Fri & Sat)
☎ (01872) 552428 🌐 driftwoodspars.com
Driftwood Blue Hills Bitter; St Austell Tinners; Sharp's Doom Bar; Skinner's Betty Stogs; guest beer Ⓗ
Built from granite, slate and enormous ships' spars, this coastal free house is popular and vibrant. The nautically-themed interior includes three stylish bars, a dining room with sea views and a sun terrace. Outside there are two beer gardens and ample parking. Brews from Driftwood, St Austell, Sharp's and Skinner's feature and vary across their ranges. Good pub food is made with locally-sourced seasonal produce. Entertainment includes weekly live music and occasional live theatre. Cornwall CAMRA Pub of the Year 2009.
⛫Q❀🛏◑⊟♿▲🚌(85,403,583)🍎P⚡

> That ale is a wholesome drinke contrary to many men's conceits.
> **Panala Alacatholica**, 1623

Trewellard

Trewellard Arms

Trewellard Road, TR19 7TA (on B3318/B3306 jct)
⏲ 12-1am (midnight Sun)
☎ (01736) 788634
Sharp's Doom Bar; guest beer Ⓗ
Former home of the owner of nearby Geevor Tin Mine, this is now a thriving, welcoming, family-run free house. The cosy interior accommodates a large, open-beamed single bar and pleasant restaurant, comfortable furnishings throughout creating a homely atmosphere. A varying beer menu includes up to four guest ales. The quality home-cooked food is good value. Popular with locals, families and tourists alike, it has a patio beer garden and ample parking. Regular bus services pass the door. ⛫Q❀🛏◑▲🚌(17A,507,300)P⚡

Truro

Bunter's Bar ✔

58 Little Castle Street, TR1 3DL
⏲ 11-midnight
☎ (01872) 241220
St Austell Tribute; Sharp's Doom Bar; Skinner's Betty Stogs Ⓗ
Thriving, sports-oriented, city centre pub. Always busy, it is popular with drinkers of all ages during the day, though in the evening the crowd tends to be younger. Local real ales are available at good value prices, usually from St Austell, Sharp's and Skinner's, with occasional promotions linked to major sporting events. The unique decor includes a red telephone box and large screens adorn the capacious drinking area. Live music is hosted most weekends. No food is served, but you may bring your own. ♿⇌🚌

City Inn ✔

Pydar Street, TR1 3SP
⏲ 12-11.30 (12.30am Fri & Sat)
☎ (01872) 272623
Courage Best Bitter; Sharp's Doom Bar; Skinner's Betty Stogs; guest beer Ⓗ
Close to the city centre near the railway viaduct, this community-focused pub has the feel of a village local. The two-bar interior comprises a comfortable lounge with several drinking areas, decorated with an impressive collection of water jugs, and the more functional public bar which is determinedly sports-oriented. Up to four guest beers change regularly, and good pub grub is available. The spacious beer garden at the rear is a real suntrap. Regular charity events include the annual conker championships.
⛫Q❀🛏◑⊟⇌🚌♣⚡

Tywardreath

New Inn

Fore Street, PL24 2QP
12-11
(01726) 813901
Draught Bass G; St Austell Dartmoor Best Bitter, Tribute, Proper Job H
Built in 1752 by local copper mine owners, this classic local is the hub of village life, and holds many functions in its large, secluded garden. A slotted brass plate remains in the bar where miners inserted their beer tokens. Good conversation is the entertainment here, and sometimes singing in the bar. The games room houses the jukebox so the noise is confined to the rear of the pub. A good bus service passes the door.
(25)P

Vogue

Star Inn

TR16 5NP SW724424
12-midnight (1am Fri & Sat); 12-11 Sun
(01209) 820242
Draught Bass; Skinner's Ginger Tosser; guest beers H
Plenty of local character can be found in this old mining village inn. Converted cottages provide a multi-roomed interior for either quiet dining (Sunday lunch a speciality) or livelier drinking. Entertainment includes big-screen sports, live music, quizzes, karaoke and pool. The Skinner's beer varies with house or seasonal brews, and other Cornish micros are well-represented. A boules pitch outside is popular, and a beer festival Bash Out The Back is staged on St Day Feast in May.
(T7)P

Wilcove

Wilcove Inn

PL11 2PG (off A374, 2km from Torpoint ferry) SX430563
12-2.30, 6.30-midnight; 12-midnight Sun
(01752) 812381
Sharp's Doom Bar; Skinner's Betty Stogs; guest beer H
Friendly village pub, tucked away beside a secluded creek off the River Tamar and handy for woodland walks around nearby Anthony House. Children and dogs on leads are welcome. At least two real ales are usually available. Community-oriented, the pub hosts an annual regatta with a canoe race as the main event. On fine days, enjoy the palm trees in the garden and views across the river. Beware, though, spring tides may sometimes flood the road and car park. P

Zelah

Hawkins Arms

High Road, TR4 9HU (off A30)
11.30-3, 6-11; 12-3, 6-10.30 Sun
(01872) 540339
Otter Bitter; guest beers H
Easy to find off the A30 (follow the brown signs), this traditional village free house offers a welcome to locals and visitors alike. Exposed stone walls, wood furnishings and an open fire in winter create a cosy ambience, and there are plenty of quiet, partitioned nooks and crannies in which to enjoy a beer. Excellent home-cooked meals promote local produce, with home-made pies a speciality. Guest beers are usually from Cornish breweries. Daytime Newquay-Truro buses stop close by.
(585,586)P

Zennor

Tinners Arms

TR26 3BY (off B3306) SW454385
11.30-3.30, 6.30-11 (11.30-11 Sat & summer); 12-10.30 Sun
(01736) 796927 tinnersarms.com
St Austell Tinners; Sharp's Own, Special H
Near the windswept northern cliffs and granite moors of the Penwith Peninsula stands this ancient granite village pub, reputedly dating from 1271. The cosy, homely, single-bar interior with separate dining areas exudes a timeless atmosphere. Near the coastal path, it is popular with walkers and families – dogs are also welcome. Food availability in winter is variable – phone first. The south-facing sheltered garden is ideal for fair-weather drinking. The Sharp's Special is badged as Zennor Mermaid – ask about the legend!
(508,300)P

Crumplehorn Inn, Polperro.

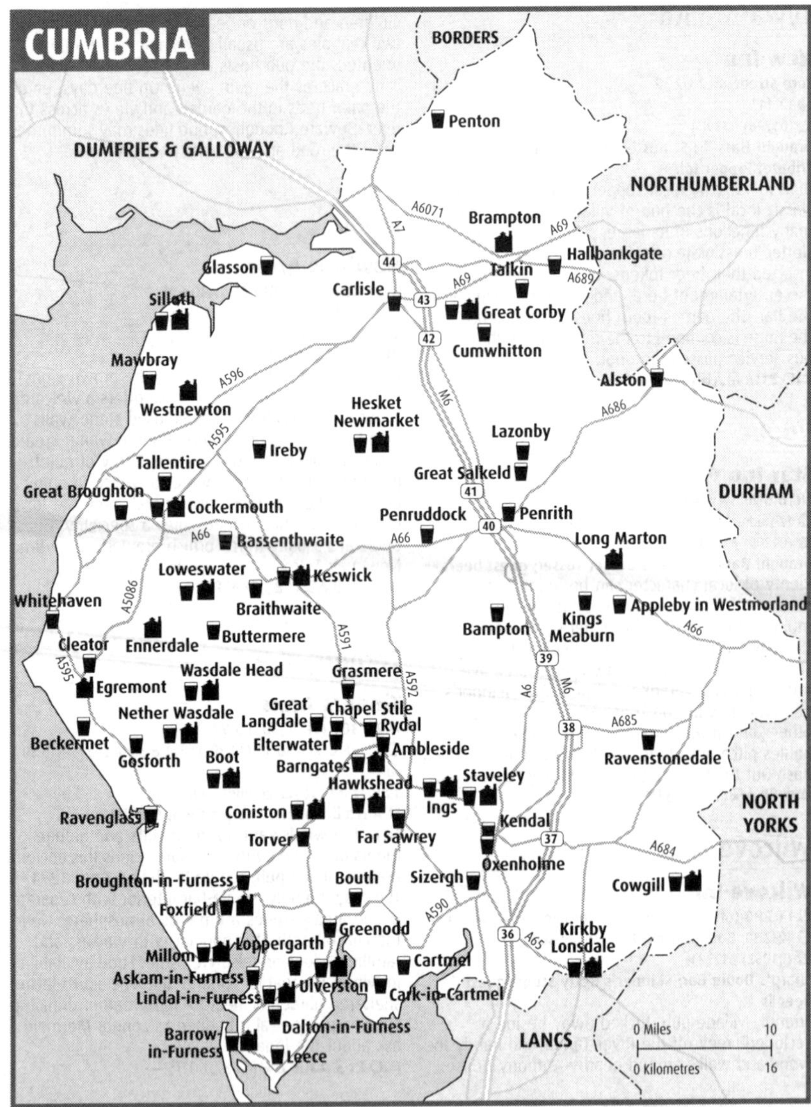

Alston

Cumberland Inn

Townfoot, CA9 3HX

12-11

(01434) 381875 alstoncumberlandhotel.co.uk

Yates Bitter; guest beers H

Owned by CAMRA members, this family-run 19th-century five bedroom inn overlooks the South Tyne River. Situated on the Coast to Coast cycle route and the Pennine Way, it is an ideal base to explore England's highest market town, South Tynedale Railway and the North Pennines. At least two Cumbrian beers are on handpump with others coming from Northumbria or further afield. Known as Alston's real cider venue, it serves Westons Old Rosie, occasional Cumbrian ciders and perry. There is a separate restaurant and food is served all day. Awarded local CAMRA Pub of the Year 2009.

(680) P

Ambleside

Golden Rule

Smithy Brow, LA22 9AS (100m off A591 towards Kirkstone)

11 (12 Sun)-midnight

(01539) 432257

Robinson's Hatters, Hartleys XB, Cumbria Way, Unicorn, Dizzy Blonde, Double Hop H

A traditional pub which is rapidly becoming a time warp. The major thrust here is the beer – no meals, piped sound, plasma TV or pool. It appeals to locals, visitors and students attending the nearby Ambleside campus of the University of Cumbria. Outside at the rear is a heated shelter and a patio area which catches the best of any sunshine. A seasonal beer may replace one of the regular ales. Well-behaved dogs are welcome. The pub has appeared in every edition of the Guide except one.

Q (555,599)

White Lion Hotel ✔
Market Place, LA22 9DB
⏲ 11-11; 12-10.30 Sun
☎ (01539) 439901
Hawkshead Bitter; Thwaites Original; guest beers Ⓗ
Originally a coaching inn, the former stables and grooms' quarters are now garages and staff accommodation. The paved bar area is adjoined by several dining areas. Guest beers are selected from the wide-ranging monthly Cask Fresh list. There is no jukebox or pool. The patio area with large umbrellas is an ideal spot for watching the busy passing scene. ⛰❀🛏◐♿🚌(555,599)⚊

Appleby-in-Westmorland

Midland Hotel
25 Clifford Street, CA16 6TS
⏲ 11 (12)-midnight
☎ (01768) 351524
Beer range varies Ⓗ
Across the road from the station on the Settle-to-Carlisle line, this is a must for the steam enthusiast. An extended end-of-terrace pub dating from the mid-19th century, it has four handpumps offering a range of mainly Cumbrian beers. The bar area has motor sport and railway pictures on the walls; there are separate games and dining rooms. Food is served all day, a Thursday quiz evening and live music on some Fridays are popular.
❀🛏◐♿⛺⇌(Appleby-in-Westmorland)♣P⚊

Royal Oak Inn ✔
Bongate, CA16 6UN
⏲ 11 (12 Sun)-midnight
☎ (01768) 351463 🌐 royaloakappleby.co.uk
Black Sheep Best Bitter; Hawkshead Bitter Ⓗ
Situated on the edge of this historic former county town and originally a coaching inn, the pub has an attractive exterior with separate entrances for two bars. To the left is a traditional tap room with wooden panelling and framed group photographs. Between this and a pleasantly furnished dining room is a lounge with a small snug and bar counter. A different beer from Hawkshead or one from Taylor may be on offer. Q❀🛏◐🀫⇌♣P⚊

Askam-in-Furness

London House
Duddon Road, LA16 7FB
⏲ 7 (4 Thu)-midnight; 3-1am Fri & Sat; closed Mon & Tue; 3-midnight Sun
☎ (01229) 463838
Copper Dragon Golden Pippin; guest beer Ⓗ
Friendly family-run village pub popular with locals and visitors from the nearby caravan site and golf course. The main bar area has a real wood-burning stove and there are two other rooms, one with a pool table. Television is available for sporting events, mainly Rugby League.The friendly landlord has worked hard to promote real ale in a village that was formerly a desert for well-kept beer.
⛰❀♿⛺⇌🚌(X7)♣⚊

Bampton

Mardale Inn ✔
CA10 2RQ
⏲ 11-11
☎ (01931) 713244 🌐 mardaleinn.co.uk
Coniston Bluebird; guest beers Ⓗ
Situated on the eastern edge of the Lake District near to Haweswater, the Coast to Coast walk and the location of Withnail and I, this early 18th-century hostelry, formerly the St Patrick's Well Inn, was recently refurbished and offers a guest selection from Cumbrian and Taylor beers. The pub serves good food and makes an excellent base for walking, biking, fishing and other outdoor activities. Dogs are warmly welcomed.
⛰Q❀🛏◐⛺♣

Barngates

Drunken Duck Inn ✔
LA22 0NG NY351013
⏲ 11.30-11; 11.30-10.30 Sun
☎ (01539) 436347 🌐 drunkenduckinn.co.uk
Beer range varies Ⓗ
Home of the Barngates Brewery, the Duck always serves four of the ten beers brewed here and brewery tours can be arranged. The bar has been extensively renovated to create a pleasing mix of local and modern styles. Bar meals served at lunchtime and the a la carte menu available in the dining room in the evening are of an exceptionally high standard. The outside seating area at the front offers magnificent views of the fells to the north east. ⛰Q❀🛏◐⛺●P⚊

Barrow-in-Furness

Duke of Edinburgh Hotel
Abbey Road, LA14 5QR
⏲ 11-11.30 (midnight Fri & Sat); 11-11 Sun
☎ (01229) 821039 🌐 thedukehotelandbar.co.uk
Lancaster Amber, Gold, Red, Black; Thwaites Original; guest beers Ⓗ
Situated on the edge of the town centre near the station, the Duke doesn't get as noisy as similar large bars in the town. The room has an airy feel with modern, comfortable furniture and a fine open fire. Paintings by local artists are displayed around the walls. Good quality, reasonably priced

INDEPENDENT BREWERIES

Abraham Thompson Barrow-in-Furness
Barngates Barngates
Beckstones Millom
Bitter End Cockermouth
Blackbeck Egremont (NEW)
Coniston Coniston
Cumberland Great Corby (NEW)
Cumbrian Legendary Hawkshead
Dent Cowgill
Derwent Silloth
Foxfield Foxfield
Geltsdale Brampton
Great Gable Wasdale Head
Hardknott Boot
Hawkshead Staveley
Hesket Newmarket Hesket Newmarket
Keswick Keswick
Kirkby Lonsdale Kirkby Lonsdale (NEW)
Loweswater Loweswater
Strands Nether Wasdale
Stringers Ulverston (NEW)
Tirril Long Marton
Ulverston Lindal in Furness
Watermill Ings
Whitehaven Ennerdale
Yates Westnewton

bar meals are available as well as fine dining in the separate bistro. Beers are mainly from Lancaster and Thwaites, with a guest ale too.

Bassenthwaite

Sun

CA12 4QP (from A591 head for village centre)
4.30-11 Mon; 12-11.30 (10.30 Sun)
(01768) 776439
Jennings Bitter, Cumberland Ale; guest beers H
Built as a farmhouse, this multi-roomed pub is mostly open plan and was converted to a coaching inn in the 19th century. It retains the original low ceilings, exposed beams and old stone floor. A single bar is located in the front area. There is a games room with a pool table and TV to the rear, and a selection of board games is on offer. Popular with locals and tourists alike, food is served lunchtimes (not Mon) and evenings. Occasional live music plays in the evening.
Q (73,73A,74) P

Beckermet

Royal Oak

CA21 2XB (1 mile off A595 2 miles S of Egremont) NY022066
12-2.30, 6-11; 12-10.30 Sun
(01946) 841551 royaloakbeckermet.com
Jennings Bitter, Cumberland Ale, seasonal ale H
Typical Cumbrian village pub with a low timber roof. It has a traditional cosy snug and front bar with real fire, plus friendly bar staff working two handpumps which serve excellent Jennings Bitter and a guest, usually from the Jennings list. A separate dining area is at the rear. Beckermet is close to the seaside and, although you wouldn't guess it, near to the Sellafield nuclear power plant.
Q (6,6X) P

Boot

Brook House Inn

CA19 1TG
11-11
(01946) 723288 brookhouseinn.co.uk
Hawkshead Bitter; Jennings Cumberland Ale; Taylor Landlord; guest beer H
Eskdale – a 365-day beer festival! And the two Boot pubs serve great beers the whole year round, instigating the annual June Boot Beer Festival, when the valley throngs with good-natured real ale lovers, Morris dancers and walkers, enjoying up to 100 beers. Brook House, family-run, with up to seven real ales and cider, popular with both locals and visitors, has lovely views of surrounding fells, including Sca Fell. Log fires, stained glass windows, stuffed animals and old gin traps reflect historic country sports and farming.
(Dalegarth) P

Woolpack Inn

CA19 1TH (1 mile E of Boot) SD102999
11-11 Mar-Oct (ring to check at other times); 12-10.30 Sun
(01946) 723230 woolpack.co.uk
Beer range varies H
It is a delightful seven-mile ride on the Ratty narrow-gauge steam railway through glorious scenery to Dalegarth station, then an easy one and a half mile walk to this wonderfully-located traditional Cumbrian inn, nestling at the western foot of the terrifying 1:3 Hardknott Pass. Walkers are welcome – a huge painted board recommends the Woolpack walk 39 (just under 19 miles around Upper Eskdale) for working up a thirst for the Hardknott beers brewed here, many of which are low ABV and very suitable for slaking the thirst. The peaceful beer garden has wonderful mountainous views. Q P

Bouth

White Hart

LA12 8JB (off A590, 6 miles NE of Ulverston)
12-11 (10.30 Sun)
(01229) 861229 bed-and-breakfast-cumbria.co.uk
Black Sheep Bitter; Coniston Bluebird; Ulverston Another Fine Mess; guest beers H
Quaint old country inn festooned with farming and hunting implements and stuffed animals. Exposed beams, a slate-flagged floor and real fires give the place a welcoming, traditional atmosphere. At the rear is a newly refurbished lounge/dining room. The food is of a high standard and uses locally-sourced ingredients. Outside, a large patio area adjoins the car park. P

Braithwaite

Coledale Inn

CA12 5TN
11-11 summer; 12-3, 6-midnight winter; 12-3, 6-11 Sun
(01768) 778272 coledale-inn.co.uk
Yates Best Bitter; guest beers H
Nestled above Braithwaite in a hillside position with a good view of Skiddaw and off the road to the Whinlatter Pass, this former wool mill and pencil factory is popular with walkers. An outlet for Yates beers for many years, and now frequently for Keswick Brewing Co, its two bars are decorated with Victorian prints, furniture and antiquities. There is a popular beer garden – a real joy in the summer months following exertions on the fells.
Q (X5,74,74A) P

Middle Ruddings Hotel

CA12 5RY (just off A66 at Braithwaite)
12-2.30, 6-11
(01768) 778436 middle-ruddings.co.uk
Beer range varies H
On first impression, an unlikely venue for quality cask ales, but this fair-sized hotel boasts three handpumps and a landlord who happily goes the extra mile to please locals and visitors and is keen on promoting Cumbrian brews – the local Keswick Brewing Co supplies Middle Ruddings Ale. It's close to the A66 just north of the main turning for Braithwaite village, with great views across to the Skiddaw massif.
Q (X5,74,74A) P

Broughton-in-Furness

Manor Arms

The Square, LA20 6HY
12-11.30 (midnight Fri & Sat); 12-11 Sun
(01229) 716286
Copper Dragon Golden Pippin; Yates Bitter; guest beers H
This outstanding inn, where the Varty family have celebrated 20 years in charge, looks to have a rosy future, with the pub's reins being handed from father to son. The beer range is supportive of

independent breweries and the pub's eight handpumps are in themselves a mini beer festival. A winner of numerous CAMRA awards, including reaching the latter stages of National Pub of the Year three times, this is the perfect place to discover real ale. (X7,511)

Buttermere

Fish Hotel

CA13 9XA (9 miles SE of Cockermouth on B5289)
10.30-3, 6-11; 11-11 Sat & Sun; closed Jan
(01768) 770287 fish-hotel.co.uk
Jennings Bitter; guest beers H
Run by the same family for 40 years, the hotel is situated between Buttermere and Crummock Water in the centre of the village. The large bar welcomes walkers and fills up with thirsty hikers on a summer afternoon. Good value bar meals are served in a family friendly atmosphere along with six real ales from the Lakeland breweries. A terrace outside provides good views of the local fells. Check opening hours out of season.
Q (77,77A) P

Cark-in-Cartmel

Engine Inn

LA11 7NZ (3 miles W of Grange-over-Sands)
11.30 (12 Sun)-1.30am
(01539) 558341 engineinn.co.uk
Beer range varies H
Seventeenth century family-run traditional inn which takes its name from the steam engines that used to service the local mills in Cark. The pub is multi-roomed, including a games room and restaurant area. Five en-suite letting rooms get booked very early for Cartmel Races and events at nearby Holker Hall. An extensive menu includes finest locally sourced and produced ingredients. Three regularly changing Cask Marque ales are from the Enterprise list. Walkers and ramblers are welcome. Closes earlier if quiet.
Q (532) P

Carlisle

Griffin

Court Square, CA1 1QX
9-11 (midnight Fri & Sat); 10-midnight Sun
(01228) 598941
Jennings Cumberland Ale; guest beers H
This former Midland Bank building has been transformed by the John Barras chain into a two-storey pub. Several large-screen TVs show different sports for all tastes. Guest beers rotate on four handpumps. A separate area is available for private functions. Meals are served all day but no children are allowed. Situated next to the railway station, it is handy for travellers waiting for trains. Popular as an away supporters' pub when Carlisle United play at home.

Howard Arms

107 Lowther Street, CA3 8ED
11-midnight (1am Fri & Sat); 12-10.30 Sun
(01228) 532926
Black Sheep Best Bitter; Theakston Best Bitter H
An ex-State Management pub with a beautiful tiled exterior that predated the scheme. Inside there are lots of small rooms radiating from the horseshoe bar. The tenant has been here for 25 years and 20 years in the Guide shows the quality of the beer and service. Old photos and posters on the walls show past links with the old city theatre which once stood opposite. Q

King's Head

Fisher Street, CA3 8RF
10 (11 Sat)-11 (midnight Fri & Sat); 12-11 Sun
(01228) 533797 kingsheadcarlisle.co.uk
Yates Bitter; guest beers H
One of the oldest pubs in the city centre, with the castle, cathedral and Lanes shopping centre nearby. Pictures of Carlisle through the ages are displayed inside and a plaque outside explains why Carlisle is not in the Domesday Book. A covered all-weather yard has a large-screen TV and barbecue area. Good value lunches are served but please note that children are not allowed. A carry-out service is available for real ales at this local CAMRA award winner.

Linton Holme

82 Lindisfarne Street, CA1 2NB
5 (4 Fri; 12 Sat)-11; 12-10.30 Sun
(01228) 532637
Yates Bitter; guest beer H
Former hotel retaining many original features including tiled mosaic floors, etched windows and a wonderful marble pillar outside. Situated in a quiet residential area, it is well worth making the effort to seek out. Inside, a variety of rooms all open out to a bar area where there is a large pool table suitable for use by wheelchair users. The guest ale is frequently from a micro-brewery. TVs show sporting events and regular darts, pool and quiz nights are held. Local CAMRA award winner.

Spinners Arms

Cummersdale Road, Cummersdale, CA2 6BD (1 mile W of Carlisle off B5299)
6 (12 Sat & Sun)-midnight
(01228) 532928
Beer range varies H
Refurbished and cosy family-friendly Redfern pub with unique animal-decorated gutters and a welcoming real fire. Situated at the heart of the village, it is close to the Cumbrian Way and National Cycle Path 7 which run alongside the River Caldew. The landlord and locals ensure there is a good variety of guest ales, mostly from local Cumbrian micro-breweries. Lunches are served on Sunday only. Well-behaved dogs are welcome.
(75)

Woodrow Wilson

48 Botchergate, CA1 1QS
9-midnight (12.30am Fri & Sat)
(01228) 819942
Greene King IPA, Abbot; Marston's Pedigree; guest beers H
Wetherspoon's pub in a former Co-op building, offering the largest range of real ales in Carlisle and a regular outlet for local beers including Geltsdale and Derwent. Food is available all day. At the rear there is a spacious heated patio for smokers and there is also some seating in the main street at the front. Children are welcome in some areas until 8pm. Five minutes walk from the railway station, local buses stop outside the front door.
Q P

Cartmel

King's Arms

The Square, LA11 6QB

⌚ 11-11 (10.30 Sun)

☎ (01539) 536220 🌐 kingsarmscartmel.co.uk

Hawkshead Red; Barngates Tag Lag; Draught Bass; Hawkshead Bitter Ⓗ

There has been a drinking establishment on this site near Cartmel Priory for 900 years. The current pub serves good-value, locally-sourced food in the bar or in the Paddock Restaurant overlooking the River Eea. If you arrive by car, park at the racecourse and walk through the village, as Cartmel gets very busy on race days. The outdoor area, overlooking the square, is popular in summer. A bus links Cartmel with the railway stations at Grange and Cark (check latest timetables).

⛰Q✿◐◑🚌(532)♣⊱

Chapel Stile

Wainwrights Inn ✔

LA22 9JH (on B5343 from Skelwith Bridge)

⌚ 11.30 (12 Sun)-11

☎ (01539) 438088 🌐 langdale.co.uk/wainwrights

Beer range varies Ⓗ

Originally a farmhouse near a former gun powder works, the pub is now well known not only for its location in one of the most popular Lake District valleys, but also for the quality of service and variety of real ales offered. The stone flag-floored bar area, where owners with dogs are welcome, has a changing variety of Thwaites and four guests usually from smaller northern and particularly Cumbrian breweries. There is also a separate dining area. ⛰✿◐◑♿⛺🚌(516)P

Cleator

Brook

Trumpet Terrace, CA23 3DX (on A5086 between Cleator Moor and Egremont) NY021140

⌚ 11-midnight (1am Fri & Sat)

☎ (01946) 811635

Taylor Landlord; Yates Bitter; guest beers Ⓗ

A popular community pub where well-kept cask ale, excellent food and a warm welcome are always on tap. The Coast to Coast route is a short distance away and walkers and cyclists have been known to take a taxi to the next stop after a relaxing time here. Live music and birthday parties make the pub lively but a quiet pint is possible outside food times. Landlord and Yates are on all the time and guests, sometimes from Salopian and Scottish breweries, often delight.

⛰Q◐◑🚌(22)♣●

Cockermouth

Bitter End

15 Kirkgate, CA13 9PS

⌚ 12-2.30, 6-11.30 (11 Sun)

☎ (01900) 828993 🌐 bitterend.co.uk

Coniston Bluebird; Hawkshead Bitter; Jennings Bitter, Cumberland Ale; guest beer Ⓗ

Attached to the pub is a small brewery, which brews the Lakeland range of beers, and this can be viewed through a window at the back of the pub. In addition to its own beers, Coniston Bluebird and a couple of Jennings beers are always available with at least one other guest ale. Food is served at lunchtimes and evenings, with most tables reseved for diners in the evening. Traditional pub food is supplemented with a daily specials board.

⛰◐◑🚌(X4,X5,600)

Bush ✔

Main Street, CA13 9JS

⌚ 11-11 (midnight Fri & Sat); 12-11 Sun

☎ (01900) 822064

Jennings Bitter, Cumberland Ale, Cockerhoop, Sneck Lifter, seasonal beer; guest beer Ⓗ

This traditional town-centre pub offers a full range of Jennings' beers alongside a Jennings' seasonal beer and a guest ale from the Marston's list. The front bar has a low ceiling with a real fire and newspapers to read. There is always a good handful of locals in the pub. The back room has its own bar with a bit of a sports bar feel, with Sky Sports on a large-screen TV. Food is served daily at lunchtimes, except on Sunday.

⛰✿◐🚂🚌(X4,X5,600)⊱

Coniston

Sun Hotel

LA21 8HQ

⌚ 12-11.30

☎ (01539) 441248 🌐 thesunconiston.com

Coniston Bluebird; Copper Dragon Golden Pippin; Hawkshead Bitter; Yates Fever Pitch; guest beers Ⓗ

The pub and hotel date back to the 16th century, built on the old Walna Scar packhorse trail, situated up the hill and overlooking the village. A typical welcoming Lakeland bar, it has a slate floor, low beams and an open fire housed in an iron range which also heats the hotel's water. There is a separate dining room, conservatory and a spacious terrace on the sunny side overlooking the garden. The bar, with its eight cask ales, is popular with both locals and walkers.

⛰Q✿🛏◐◑⛺🚌(X12,505)P⊱

Cowgill

Sportsman's Inn

LA10 5RG SD767864

⌚ 12-3 (not Mon), 7-11; 12-11 Sat; 11-3, 7-11 Sun

☎ (01539) 625282

Tetley Mild; guest beers Ⓗ

This friendly pub has been run by the same family for 21 years and is very much the hub of the community, as well as committed to co-operative working in the locality. Guest beers often include those from Copper Dragon and/or Dent. Themed seasonal events are popular and ensure that this very rural pub continues to buck the general economic trend. The impressive Arten Gill railway viaduct is nearby and ascending the steep road up to Dent station is well worth the effort.

⛰✿🛏◐◑🚂♣P⊱

Cumwhitton

Pheasant Inn ✔

CA8 9EX (4 miles SE of A69 at Warwick Bridge)

⌚ 6-11 (midnight Sat); closed Mon

☎ (01228) 560102 🌐 thepheasantinncumwhitton.co.uk

Black Sheep Best Bitter; guest beers Ⓗ

Situated at the end of a pleasant small village, this pub has a big reputation, winning the local CAMRA Pub of the Year award twice recently. A wintertime log fire adds to the general ambience of the bar with its flagged floor and exposed beams sporting a collection of water jugs. With an excellent reputation for quality food, booking is advised on week nights and essential at weekends. Twice-monthly quiz nights and regular special events are always well attended by locals and visitors.

Dalton-in-Furness

Black Dog Inn

Holmes Green, Broughton Rd, LA15 8JP SD233761
4 (11 Wed-Sat)-11; closed Mon; 12-10.30 Sun
(01229) 462561
Beer range varies H
A quiet, unassuming country pub that is just a 20-minute walk from Dalton town centre. It hosts regular beer festivals throughout the year and serves up to nine beers between times. In essence it is a one-roomed pub with quarry tiled floor, beams and two real fires. The snug in front of the bar provides a focal point for the locals, and visitors will invariably be drawn in to the conversation. Popular with diners as well as drinkers.

Brown Cow

Goose Green, LA15 8LQ (just off A590)
11.30-midnight
(01229) 462553 browncowinndalton.co.uk
Beer range varies H
A warm and friendly atmosphere greets visitors to this 400-year-old coaching house which has retained many original features including original beams, brasses, local prints and an open fire. A winner of many awards for its five real ales, the pub also serves excellent food from a full and varied menu. Meals can be enjoyed in the large, separate dining room or on warmer days on the charming patio with heating and lighting. Well worth a visit.

Elterwater

Britannia Inn

LA22 9HP
11-11; 12-10.30 Sun
(01539) 437210 britinn.co.uk
Coniston Bluebird; Jennings Bitter; guest beers H
This attractive pub is set next to a small triangular village green in a location with superb views. An entrance lobby with seating leads to a small bar area to the right. Guest beers are chosen from near and far and include a specially blended beer with a unique pump clip from Coniston Brewery. There is a separate dining room and a back room with seating. See website for details of the annual Champion of Champions beer festival.
(516)

Far Sawrey

Claife Crier

Sawrey Hotel, LA22 0LQ (B5285 SE of Hawkshead, 1 mile from Windermere ferry) SD379955
11-11; 12-10.30 Sun
(01539) 443425 sawrey-hotel.co.uk
Hawkshead Bitter, Gold, Red; Jennings Cumberland Ale, Snecklifter; Theakston Bitter H
The bar of the Sawrey Hotel, a short steep walk from the ferry, bears all the hallmarks of its former existence as stables. Whitewashed walls, exposed beams and long bench tables create a convivial atmosphere. The name Claife Crier comes from a local ghost. Lunchtime meals are served in the bar while evening meals are available in the hotel dining room. A shove ha'penny board supplements other games. The bar is served by the cross lakes shuttle bus service in summer.

Foxfield

Prince of Wales

LA20 6BX (opp station)
2.45 (12 Fri & Sat)-11; closed Mon & Tue; 12-10.30 Sun
(01229) 716238 princeofwalesfoxfield.co.uk
Beer range varies H
This gem of a pub is testament to what can be achieved through passion and hard work. It has been newly extended without losing any of its charm, and in winter its two fires give a homely feel. The guest beers come from a combination of the two house breweries, Foxfield and Tigertops, plus ales from throughout the country, always including a mild. Frequent beer festivals throughout the year are an added bonus. There are bus and rail stops outside. Discount on B&B for CAMRA members.
(X7,511)

Glasson

Highland Laddie

Water Street, CA7 5DT
12-midnight
(01697) 351839 highlandladdieinn.co.uk
Jennings Best Bitter; guest beers H
Small village local with a good reputation for homely food. Situated on the Hadrian's Wall route and close to the Solway Firth and bird watching reserve, it is open all day for walkers, bird watchers and other recreational users. The regular Jennings bitter is not all that common in this part of north Cumbria and the guest ale is usually from the Marston's range. Meals are served daily except Tuesday. (93)

Gosforth

Gosforth Hall Inn

CA20 1AZ
12 (4 Mon & Tue)-11; 11-11 Sat; 12-11 Sun
(01946) 725322 gosforthhallinn.co.uk
Beer range varies H
Built on the site of a 10th-century Norse hall, this historic Grade II-listed former Peel tower and fortified farmhouse has a winding stone staircase and the widest span sandstone hearth in England, so it is proclaimed. Archaeological digs have revealed a Viking longhouse in the beer garden. Rod and Barbara hold enchanting medieval banquets in the dining room. Rod's famous pies are served in the bar. Three constantly changing guest beers favour Cumbrian breweries.
(6,6X)

Grasmere

Dale Lodge Hotel (Tweedies Bar)

Langdale Road, LA22 9SW
12-11 (midnight Thu-Sun)
(01539) 435300 dalelodgehotel.co.uk
Caledonian Deuchars IPA; Theakston Old Peculier; guest beers H

This former tweed shop has become a popular bar offering an excellent range of beers from nearby (Yates Brewery) and further afield (Scotland). The bar area has a solid stone floor and a welcome stove in winter. The adjoining room is used for dining and as an additional bar during beer festivals. Quality meals are served, owners with dogs are welcome in the bar area and there are extensive lawned grounds with plenty of bench seating. ⛰❀⇌◐♿🚌(555,599)♣●P⁵–

Great Broughton

Punchbowl Inn

19 Main Street, CA13 0YJ
⏲ 7 (12 Fri & Sat)-11; 12-11 Sun
☎ (01900) 824708
Jennings Bitter; guest beers H
Built in the 17th century, this traditional village pub has beams, open fires and is full of character. The walls are covered in tokens of local esteem and sporting memorabilia creating a welcoming atmosphere. Two well-kept, regularly changing ales include Jennings and a guest from anywhere in Britain. ⛰Q🚌(58)♣

Great Corby

Queen Inn

CA4 8LR (1 mile off A69 at Warwick Bridge)
⏲ 12-2.30, 5.30-12.30am (1am Fri-Sun); closed Tue
☎ (01228) 562088 🌐 queeninngreatcorby.co.uk
Beer range varies H
Situated at the heart of a picturesque village, this friendly pub is a true supporter of locally-brewed ales. Three pumps serve real ale from a range of local micro-breweries including the Cumberland just across the green. The spacious bar area has floor tiles, beams, open log fires at either end plus an adjacent family room. Lunchtime and evening meals are served in the bar and restaurant made with best quality local produce. Regular speciality food events and seasonal mini beer festivals are held. ⛰Q❀◐⊟♿⇌(Wetheral)🚌♣P⊡

Great Langdale

Old Dungeon Ghyll Hotel

LA22 9JY (over bridge at end of B5343)
⏲ 11-11 (10.30 Sun)
☎ (01539) 437272 🌐 odg.co.uk
Black Sheep Best Bitter, Ale; Jennings Cumberland Ale; Theakston XB, Old Peculier; Yates Bitter; guest beers H
Converted from a cowshed in the late 1940s, this pub is now a haven for walkers and climbers, offering an especially friendly welcome to those in muddy boots and wet weatherproofs. The fire in the range is much appreciated in winter, while views of the impressive surrounding fells can be enjoyed from the patio benches. An excellent range of Cumbrian beers is complemented by good home-made pub food. Meals in the hotel need to be booked in advance.
⛰Q❀⇌◐⊟Ⓐ🚌(516)●P⁵–

Great Salkeld

Highland Drove

CA11 9NA (off B6412 between A686 and Lazonby)
⏲ 12-3 (not Mon), 6-11; 12-midnight Sat; 12-3, 6-11 Sun
☎ (01768) 898349 🌐 highland-drove.co.uk
John Smith's Bitter; Theakston Black Bull Bitter; guest beer H
Tastefully decorated throughout, this popular inn has twice been local CAMRA Pub of the Year in recent times. There is a well-stocked bar and an upstairs restaurant known as Kyloes, a comfortable lounge offering a varying food selection and a games room. The pub name derives from the olden days when highland cattle were driven down from Scotland to markets in the midlands and south, when it was an overnight stopping-off point. No lunchtime meals on Monday.
⛰❀⇌◐⊟♿Ⓐ♣P⁵–

Greenodd

Ship Inn

Main Street, LA12 7QZ
⏲ 12-2.30, 6-midnight; closed Mon; 12-10.30 Sun
07782655294 (mobile)
Lancaster Amber; guest beers H
Traditional village pub, blending the old and the new. Beamed ceilings contrast with leather suites, and real fires enhance the ambience of the relaxing lounge and bar areas. A separate games room houses a pool table, dart board and jukebox. Guest beers often come from local breweries. There is usually a good selection of cider and perry available. ⛰◐♣●P⊡

Hallbankgate

Belted Will

CA8 2NJ (on A689 Alston road 4 miles E of Brampton)
⏲ 12-2 (summer only), 5-midnight; 12-midnight Sat & Sun
☎ (01697) 746236 🌐 beltedwill.co.uk
Jennings Cumberland Ale; guest beers H
Popular pub with three real ales on offer, at least one from a local brewery. Lunchtime meals are served weekends all year round and all week in summer. Located at the foot of the Northern Pennines, this is an ideal base for fans of outdoor pursuits including walking and hiking, mountain biking and cycling, fishing, golfing, bird watching and pony trekking. The pub's unusual name refers to William Howard of nearby Naworth Castle whose nickname was mentioned in a poem by Sir Walter Scott. ⛰❀⇌◐⊟♿🚌(680)♣⁵–

Hawkshead

King's Arms Hotel

The Square, LA22 0NZ
⏲ 11-midnight
☎ (01539) 436372 🌐 kingsarmshawkshead.co.uk
Hawkshead Bitter; Coniston Old Man; guest beers H
Owned by the same family for nealy 30 years, this cosy, often busy pub dates back to Elizabethan times and is popular with locals and visitors alike. It has an open fire and traditional beamed ceilings – note the hand-carved native American figure supporting one of the beams. A spacious dining room ensures that diners can usually find a table if the bar area is busy. The outside seating area overlooks the village square. Guest beers are usually from local breweries. ⛰❀⇌◐Ⓐ🚌(505)♣

Hesket Newmarket

Old Crown ✔

Main Street, CA7 8JG
⏲ 12-2.30 (Fri-Sun), 5.30-11 (10.30 Sun)

☎ (01697) 478288 🌐 theoldcrownpub.co.uk
Hesket Newmarket Great Cockup Porter, Blencathra Bitter, Skiddaw, Hellvellyn Gold, Doris's 90th Birthday Ale, Old Carrock Strong Ale Ⓗ
On the edge of the northern Lakeland fells, this pub is at the centre of village life. It is owned as a co-operative by the local community, who are dedicated to maintaining its original character. It offers the full range of Hesket Newmarket beers from the brewery in the barn at the rear of the pub. Brewery tours are usually followed by samples, and a meal can be arranged by contacting the pub. A firm favourite of Prince Charles and Sir Chris Bonington, the pub is popular with visitors and locals.

Ings

Watermill Inn 🏆
LA8 9PY (off A591 by church)
12-11 (10.30 Sun)
☎ (01539) 821309 🌐 watermillinn.co.uk
Hawkshead Bitter; Moorhouse's Black Cat; Theakston Old Peculier; Watermill Collie Wobbles, Wruff Night, A Bit'er Ruff; guest beers Ⓗ
Upgraded from a guest house in 1990 and since then the recipient of many awards, several extensions and its own brewery, the pub is now firmly established as a top favourite by lovers of a wide beer choice and the absence of distractions from conversation. Very popular with dog owners. Meals are served 12-9pm every day.
Q(555)P

Ireby

Lion
Market Place, CA7 1EA
6-11 (midnight Sat); 12-3, 7-11 Sun
☎ (01697) 371460 🌐 irebythelion.co.uk
Derwent Carlisle State Bitter; Jennings Bitter; guest beers Ⓗ
The pub sits at the centre of a quiet rural town which is really just a village with a market cross. It features wood panelling from local churches but the bar itself came from a pub in Leeds. The pub supplies beer for the annual folk festival in May. Four beers are usually available, mostly from local breweries. No meals served on Monday evening.
Q

Kendal

Burgundy's Wine Bar
19 Lowther Street, LA9 4DH
11.30-3 (not Tue & Wed), 6.30-midnight; closed Mon; 7-11 Sun
☎ (01539) 733803 🌐 burgundyswinebar.co.uk
Yates Fever Pitch; guest beers Ⓗ
This Grade II-listed building was a labour exchange and, although called a wine bar, the accent is on an interesting range of mainly local beers and on offering several continental lagers on draught and in bottle. Building work in progress to the rear will add a first floor patio. The pub hosts a live music evening on Thursday and a popular Spring Cumbria Beers Challenge. (41,555)

Castle Inn
Castle Street, LA9 7AA
11.30-midnight (1am Sat); 12-11.30 Sun
☎ (01539) 729983
Black Sheep Best Bitter; Jennings Bitter; Tetley Bitter; guest beers Ⓗ
A community pub, once part of the former Duttons Brewery estate, which boasts an original etched window pane (now mounted inside). The lounge to the left has an impressive fish tank and offers good value lunchtime meals. The bar to the right has TV and a raised games area with pool and a jukebox. Regular quiz evenings are held and the pub is close to the remains of Kendal castle, the river Kent and public transport connections.
(43,42)

Riflemans Inn
4 Greenside, LA9 4LD
6 (12 Sat & Sun)-midnight 07939434341
Tetley Bitter; guest beers Ⓗ
Take the bus or walk up to this village pub in the town. Overlooking a pleasant sloping green, the entrance leads into a partly divided room where the bar offers three regularly changing guest beers from the Cellarman's Reserve list. The pub is well supported by the local community, with several sport and quiz teams as well as folk musicians who play on a Thursday evening. There is a separate games room and a room upstairs for meetings. Dogs are welcome, and families until 9pm.
Q(44,48)

Keswick

Bank Tavern ✔
47 Main Street, CA12 5DS
11-midnight (11 Sun)
☎ (01768) 772663 🌐 cumberlandtaverns.co.uk
Jennings Bitter, Cumberland Ale, Sneck Lifter; guest beers Ⓗ
One of a number of Jenning's tied houses in Keswick, the Bank Tavern always keeps its range of beers in good condition, including seasonal brews. Other Marston's breweries' ales are served too, forming what is often an extensive selection. Wholesome food is served to restore the walker tired out by the fells or outdoor shops. CAMRA Pub of the Year 2009. (73,73A,79)

Dog & Gun ✔
2 Lake Road, CA12 5BT (off Market Place at top of Main Street)
11-midnight (11 Sun)
☎ (01768) 773463
Coniston Bluebird; Keswick Thirst Pitch, Thirst Run; guest beers Ⓗ
The busiest of Keswick's pubs, with the best selection of real ales. Full of character, it has flagged floors, low oak-beamed ceilings and an open fire. The beams are crammed with coins – donations to Keswick Mountain Rescue. Good food, including the highly-regarded goulash, is served. Well-behaved dogs are allowed to snooze under tables. An interesting collection of climbing photographs and pump clips decorates the walls in this outlet for the Keswick Brewing Co.
(X4,X5,X3)

Kings Meaburn

White Horse
CA10 3BU NY620211
7 (6 Thu & Fri)-11; 12-2am Sat; 12-2, 6-11 Sun
☎ (01931) 714256
Beer range varies Ⓗ

A fine example of a rural pub that is genuinely at the heart of the community. A cosy single room welcomes with equal warmth both locals and visitors. Beers are chosen, often even collected, by the enthusiastic owner to provide an ever-changing choice. The pub hosts the Eden Valley beer festival under canvas in July and an indoor festival in March. Meals are prepared using local ingredients. Weekday hours may extend in summer when there is sufficient demand.
⛰Q❀◐◑♿♣●P⁵⁻

Kirkby Lonsdale

Orange Tree

9 Fairbank, LA6 2BD
⏲ 11-11
☎ (01524) 271965
Jennings Bitter; Kirkby Lonsdale Ruskin's Bitter; Taylor Landlord; guest beers Ⓗ
A friendly, family-run pub where sporting pictures adorn most of the wall space. It is now the brewery tap to the newly created Kirkby Lonsdale Brewery and the beer range is steadily increasing. Good value food, also served in the rear dining room, includes popular specials evenings on Monday and Wednesday. The Lake District and Yorkshire Dales National Parks are nearby and Devil's Bridge over the River Lune is just a pleasant walk away. A self-catering cottage is available to rent.
⛰Q🛏◐◑♿⛺🚌(567)♣⁵⁻

Lazonby

Joiners Arms

Townfoot, CA10 1BL
⏲ 12-3 (Wed-Sun), 6-11 (1.30am Fri & Sat)
☎ (01768) 898728
Beer range varies Ⓗ
On first sight, little appears to have changed at this pub but an extended restaurant to the rear and new cellar and kitchen facilities have made a big difference. Situated in the Eden Valley and just down the hill from the station on the Settle-Carlisle railway, it attracts tourists as well as locals who come for the homely, welcoming atmosphere and excellent meals (available Wed to Sun). There is a games room on a lower level. ⛰Q❀🛏◐◑⛺≷♣

Leece

Copper Dog

LA12 0QP (3 miles E of Barrow) SD244695
⏲ 11.30-3, 5.30-11 (midnight Fri); 11.30-midnight Sat; 12-11 Sun
☎ (01229) 877088
Beer range varies Ⓗ
Spacious pub on the outskirts of the village with a large bar with an open fire, plus a room suitable for families. The beautiful conservatory dining room, with superb views over surrounding countryside, is also available for private functions. Food is freshly prepared to a very high standard, but at reasonable prices. An annual charity beer festival is held during the first weekend in June. Run by the same ownership as the White House Hotel in Barrow.
⛰Q🐴❀◐◑🚌(10)P

Lindal-in-Furness

Railway Inn

London Road, LA12 0LL
⏲ 4 (3 Fri)-midnight; 12-midnight Sat; 12-11 Sun
☎ (01229) 462889
Ulverston Lonesome Pine; guest beers Ⓗ
A welcoming single-room pub with a beamed ceiling and comfortable seating at one end in front of an open fire. The centrally positioned bar is made from old church pews. Good value meals are served on candlelit tables on Saturday and Sunday lunchtime and every evening until 8pm. Booking is advisable, and essential on Friday evening. A quiz night is held each Thursday evening.
⛰❀◐◑🚌(6,6A)⁵⁻

Loppergarth

Wellington

Main Street, LA12 0JL (1 mile from A590 between Lindal and Pennington) SD260772
⏲ 6-midnight (1am Fri & Sat)
☎ (01229) 582388
Beer range varies Ⓗ
Family-run local in a picturesque hamlet. The central three-sided bar is surrounded by four distinct drinking areas, with a TV in one corner by a cosy fire. A separate games/family room at the side features a warming stove, pool, darts, a fruit machine and books, but noise is well controlled. Four to five handpumps dispense mainly local beers, particularly from Ulverston, Stringers and Foxfield (dark mild). The pub hosts gents and ladies darts and pool teams, plus a popular quiz on alternate Saturdays, and occasional whist evenings. No food is served. ⛰Q🐴❀♣●

Loweswater

Kirkstile Inn 🏆

CA13 0RU (signed off B5289) NY140210
⏲ 10-11 (10.30 Sun)
☎ (01900) 85219 🌐 kirkstile.com
Loweswater Melbreak Bitter, Kirkstile Gold, Grasmoor Dark Ale, seasonal beers; Yates Bitter; guest beer Ⓗ
Award-winning 16th-century Lakeland inn with a spectacular setting between Loweswater and Crummock Water. Low ceilings and stone walls add character to this deservedly popular inn, which can be very busy at peak times. The home of Loweswater Brewery, three regular award-winning beers are available as well as two bottle-conditioned beers from the brewery which are only sold in the pub. Dogs welcome until 6pm. Local CAMRA Pub of the Year 2003-2005 and 2008.
⛰Q🐴❀🛏◐◑♿P🍺

Mawbray

Lowther Arms

CA15 6QT (off B5300)
⏲ 12-midnight; closed 3-5pm Mon & Tue, Jan-Feb
☎ (01900) 881337 🌐 lowtherarms.co.uk
Beer range varies Ⓗ
Traditional family-oriented country pub built in 1790 catering for both holidaymakers and locals. The bar area has a stone floor and an open fire. A local brewery, either Yates or Derwent, usually provides one of the ales dispensed from the two handpumps. Dogs are permitted only before and after food is served. There is a caravan park attached to the pub and accommodation, including a self-contained flat, is available.
⛰❀◐◑⛺🚌(60)♣P

Millom

Punch Bowl

The Green, LA18 5HJ SD178846
6-11; 12-3, 6-10.30 Sun
☎ (01229) 772605
Beckstones range; guest beers Ⓗ
This village pub has a family connection with the nearby Beckstones Brewery and is effectively its tap house, with up to nine beers on handpump including guest ales from other local breweries. There is a large open plan bar area and a separate games/TV room. Real fires make for a convivial atmosphere.
Q❀≠(Green Road)🚌(511,X7)♣

Nether Wasdale

Strands

CA20 1ET
12 (4 winter)-11; 12-10.30 Sun
☎ (01946) 726237 🌐 strandshotel.com
Jennings Bitter; Strands Errmmm, Red Screes, T'Errmm-inator Ⓗ
This family-run hotel in the village of Nether Wasdale is well off the beaten track but is close to Wastwater, officially Britain's Favourite View, and has its own brewery. Strands Brewery offers a growing range of cask ales, the original being the excellent and popular Errmmm – its title arising out of the family not being able to make up its mind what to call it. The second one was called T'Errmmm-inator after dozens of suggestions from customers. This pub prides itself on its food as well as the real ale. Children and dogs are welcome.
❀♣P

Oxenholme

Station Inn

LA9 7RF
12-11 (10.30 Sun)
☎ (01539) 724094
Jennings Cumberland Ale; Moorhouse's Blond Witch; Tirril 1823; guest beers Ⓗ
Originally a farmhouse and still surrounded by pleasant countryside, it became a hostelry soon after the arrival of the main London to Glasgow railway line. An alternative Tirril beer may be offered. The large garden includes extensive facilities for children including crazy golf and a llamas' paddock. Owners with dogs are welcome and touring caravans can be parked on an adjoining site. Q❀≠🚌(108)♣P

Penrith

Agricultural Hotel

Castlegate, CA11 7JE
11-11 (midnight Sat); 12-10.30 Sun
☎ (01768) 862622
Jennings Bitter, Cumberland Ale, Sneck Lifter; guest beers Ⓗ
Old, well-established pub on the edge of the Lake District, a short walk from the town centre near Penrith railway station. It is overlooked by the ruins of Penrith Castle – a throwback to the Border disputes with the Reivers of old. Warm and welcoming, the Aggie, as it is known locally, serves food all day. Q❀♿≠🚌P

Gloucester Arms

Great Dockray, CA11 7DE
11-midnight; 12-10.30 Sun
☎ (01768) 863745
Greene King Old Speckled Hen; Hawkshead Bitter; guest beers Ⓗ
The oldest pub in Penrith, claiming links as far back as Richard III, is a short walk from the main bus station. Bar meals are also served throughout the pub and there is a separate restaurant offering good home-cooked food. The main bar/lounge area has dark panelled wood, made cosy and welcoming by good lighting, and warmed by a real fire. There is an outdoor heated smoking area to the rear. ❀≠♣

Lowther Arms

3 Queen Street, CA11 7XD
11-3, 6-11; 11-midnight Sat; 12-3, 6-10.30 Sun
☎ (01768) 862792
Caledonian Deuchars IPA; Fuller's London Pride; guest beers Ⓗ
Visitors are assured of a warm welcome at this coaching inn next to the A6 in a busy market town. A sympathetic extension has added more space without losing the character of the old building. Drinkers are spoiled for choice with a range of up to six real ales usually available. Good food is served and the pub can get busy at meal times. A past winner of awards from CAMRA and Britain in Bloom. Q≠🚌

Penruddock

Herdwick Inn

CA11 0QU
12-3, 5.30-11; 12-midnight Sat; 12-10.30 Sun
☎ (01768) 483007 🌐 herdwickinn.com
Jennings Bitter, Cumberland Ale Ⓗ
This 400-year-old pub is named after a hardy breed of Cumbrian sheep. Situated just north of the A66, between Penrith and Keswick, it benefits from the North Lakes tourist trade and is also popular with locals enjoying the ambience and excellent food. The premises includes a bar, games room, large furnished garden and a mezzanine restaurant converted from the adjoining stables and hayloft. Accommodation is recommended.
❀🚌(105)♣P

Penton

Bridge Inn

CA6 5QB NY438764
7-11
☎ (01228) 577041
Marston's Pedigree; guest beers Ⓗ
The closest real ale pub to Scotland in the area, this quiet countryside drinking establishment is spread over three rooms. It is frequented by locals and is home to several teams competing in darts and pool leagues. The regulars choose the guest ale from the list provided. There is renowned fishing nearby on the River Esk. Q❀♣P

Ravenglass

Holly House

CA18 1SQ
11-midnight summer; 3-11 winter (closed Wed); 12-midnight Sun
☎ (01229) 717230

Jennings Cumberland Ale; Moorhouse's Blond Witch; Taylor Landlord; guest beer Ⓗ
One of three pubs all serving good real ale in this historic Viking/Roman village and harbour. A free house, its five handpumps offer a range of individually chosen beers during the summer. The small hotel has a seaside café ambience and a nautical theme, with stunning views over a peaceful haven with a few small boats, a profusion of birdlife, and glorious sunsets. Nearby attractions include a castle and a steam railway.
⛰Q⛟❀🛏◐▲⇌🚌(6,6X)P

Ravenstonedale

Black Swan Inn ✔
CA17 4NG (village signed off A685)
🕓 11-midnight (1am Fri & Sat); 12-midnight Sun
☎ (01539) 623204 🌐 blackswanhotel.com
Black Sheep Best Bitter; John Smith's Bitter; guest beers Ⓗ
Situated in a conservation area between the Lake District and Yorkshire Dales National Parks, this is a perfect example of the CAMRA Pub is the Hub campaign, and was visited by the Prince of Wales. Guest beers are usually from Cumbria and quality meals are served. Breakfasts are offered from 8am. Across the road is an extensive garden beside a stream. The pub shop has local produce and household items. Accommodation includes facilities for the disabled as well as owners with dogs. ⛰Q❀🛏◐⊞♿🚌(564,569)♣P

Rydal

Glen Rothay Hotel (Badger Bar)
LA22 9LR
🕓 11-11 (10.30 Sun)
☎ (01539) 434500 🌐 theglenrothay.co.uk
Beer range varies Ⓗ
This roadside inn dates from 1624 and is especially popular with walkers. The bar area has copper-topped tables and a welcoming winter log fire. The five beers on offer are exclusively from Cumbrian brewers, reflecting the importance placed here on the environment. The separate Oak Room has a fireplace with a superb overmantle. Pictures and models of badgers are in abundance. A well-appointed dining room looks out towards Rydal Water. ⛰Q❀🛏◐🚌(555,599)♣P

Silloth

Albion
Eden Street, CA7 4AS
🕓 3 (7 Mon; 4.30 winter)-midnight; 2-midnight Fri; 11-midnight Sat & Sun
☎ (01697) 331321
Derwent Parsons Pledge; Tetley Mild Ⓗ
A traditional one-bar pub with a separate family room featuring a pool table and TV that is well supported by friendly locals and summer visitors. Pictures of old Silloth decorate the walls, along with two models of whaling trawlers. There are also numerous photos celebrating the Isle of Man TT races alongside old motoring memorabilia. The pub serves as a meeting place for several local groups. The nearby Derwent Brewery often brings in new beers for trial periods. A holiday cottage is available to let. ⛰⛟❀🛏▲🚌(38,60)♣P⍽

Sizergh

Strickland Arms
LA8 8DZ (follow signs to Sizergh Castle off A590)
🕓 11.30-3, 5.30-11; 11.30-11 Sat, Sun & summer
☎ (01539) 561010
Thwaites Original; guest beers Ⓗ
Now bypassed by the London to Carlisle Roman road (A6), the pub is part of the Sizergh Castle estate, owned by the National Trust. The interior features refurbished stone and wood flooring as well as quality furniture and fittings. Excellent meals major on the use of local produce. The Thwaites beer choice varies, complemented by guests from local breweries. Rooms are available upstairs for meetings, functions or dining. Dog friendly. ⛰Q❀◐♿▲🚌(X35,555)♣P⍽

Staveley

Beer Hall ✔
Mill Yard, LA8 9LR
🕓 12-5 (6 Wed-Sun)
☎ (01539) 822644 🌐 hawksheadbrewery.co.uk
Hawkshead Bitter, Red, Lakeland Gold, Brodie's Prime Ⓗ
Now well established as a showcase not only for Hawkshead beers – watch the brewing process through large windows – but also as an ambassador for other real ales. Festivals offering category winners of Society of Independent Brewers (SIBA) beers are held twice yearly. Tours of the brewery are available on any Saturday lunchtime or by prior arrangement. Private functions and music evenings are a regular feature. Food is available from the interconnecting Wilf's Cafe. Q❀⇌🚌(555)●P

Eagle & Child
Kendal Road, LA8 9LP
🕓 11-11; 12-10.30 Sun
☎ (01539) 821320 🌐 eaglechildinn.co.uk
Hawkshead Bitter; guest beers Ⓗ
A long-standing Guide entry noted for its choice of beers and its beer festivals. Exceptional value meals are much appreciated by lunchtime customers and evening quizzes are popular with the whole community. An upstairs function room can be hired, a riverside garden is across the road and there is another to the rear. Interesting artefacts are displayed on shelves around the horseshoe-shaped bar area.
⛰❀🛏◐⇌🚌(555)●P⍽

Talkin

Blacksmith's Arms
CA8 1LE
🕓 12-3, 6-11
☎ (01697) 73452 🌐 blacksmithstalkin.co.uk
Black Sheep Best Bitter; Geltsdale Cold Fell, Brampton Bitter; Yates Bitter Ⓗ
A regular entry in the Guide, the Blackies, as it is known locally, continues to attract its longstanding loyal customers as well as many visitors drawn by its reputation for a warm welcome and the host of outdoor attractions in the vicinity. These include a nearby golf course and country park, with Hadrian's Wall in easy reach. The well-stocked bar with four real ales is supplemented by three further rooms, including a restaurant. ⛰Q❀🛏◐⊞♿▲♣P⍽

Tallentire

Bush Inn

CA13 0PT
⏲ 6-midnight; closed Mon; 12-2.30, 7-11 Sun
☎ (01900) 823707
Jennings Bitter; guest beers Ⓗ
Traditional village inn at the heart of many community activities. Stone-flagged floors and original fireplaces contribute to a simple uncluttered atmosphere in the bar area. There are always two changing guest beers, often from northern and Scottish breweries, with real cider available in summer. The restaurant serves high-quality meals Thursday to Saturday evenings and Sunday lunchtime. A past winner of CAMRA branch Pub of the Season and Pub of the Year runner-up. Q❀🚌(58)♣●P⁂–

Torver

Church House Inn

LA21 8AZ (2 miles SW of Coniston) SD285942
⏲ 11 -11 summer; 12-3, 5 -11 winter Sun
☎ (01539) 441282
Barngates Tag Lag; Hawkshead Bitter; guest beers Ⓗ
Offering a friendly welcome and good quality food, served in the bar or dining room, this unspoilt 14th-century inn features low beams, flagged floors and a magnificent open fire. A welcome sight whether you have just walked up Coniston Old Man or simply come in search of a fine pint – there are five to choose from – and a bit of craic with the locals. Occasional live folk music plays at weekends. The garden at the rear boasts fine views of the surrounding fells. 🔥Q❀🛏◐▲🚌(X12)♣P⁂–

Ulverston

Devonshire Arms

Braddyll Terrace, Victoria Road, LA12 0DH
⏲ 4-11; 3-midnight Fri; 12-midnight Sat; 12-11 Sun
☎ (01229) 582537
Beer range varies Ⓗ
A proper free house, just away from the town centre, and the nearest pub to both the bus and train stations. Sports oriented, it has darts and pool teams, and live sporting events are shown on a large-screen TV. Although open plan, the games and TV are all at one end of the bar, leaving the other end for civilised conversation. Five handpumps feature mainly local beers. No food is served. ❀▲⇌🚌♣P⁂–

Stan Laurel Inn

The Ellers, LA12 0AB
⏲ 12-2, 6-midnight; 12-3, 5-midnight Sun
☎ (01229) 582814 🌐 thestanlaurel.co.uk
Thwaites Original; Ulverston Lonesome Pine; guest beers Ⓗ
Named after the town's most famous son who lived only a few yards away, this bright and spacious local just outside the town centre sources its guest beers from local breweries. Good quality, reasonably priced meals are served daily except Monday. There is a separate pool/darts room, a function/private room, and an outside seating area. ❀🛏◐▲⇌🚌♣P⁂–🗍

Swan Inn

Swan Street, LA12 7JX
⏲ 3.30-11; 12-midnight Fri & Sat; 12-11 Sun
☎ (01229) 582519
Coniston Bluebird; Hawkshead Bitter, Lakeland Gold, Brodie's Prime; Yates Bitter; guest beers Ⓗ
Free house offering up to nine beers, with guest ales coming from far and wide. A good mix of regulars ensures the craic is always lively. Although open plan, the interior divides into three distinct areas: a bar with feature picture window, a seating area with an open fire and a darts area off to the side. Two TVs screen sporting fixtures. The elevated beer garden at the rear catches the sun all day. Dogs and well-behaved children are welcome. 🔥❀♿▲⇌🚌(6,6A,X35)♣●⁂–🗍

Wasdale Head

Wasdale Head Inn

CA20 1EX (E off A595 at Gosforth) NY187085
⏲ 11-11; 12-10.30 Sun
☎ (01946) 726229 🌐 wasdaleheadinn.co.uk
Great Gable Burnmoor Pale, Wasd'ale, Illgill IPA, Yewbarrow; guest beer Ⓗ
With a dramatic location at the foot of England's tallest mountains in the Lake District National Park, this famous pub is miles from anywhere at the birthplace of climbing. It boasts its own brewery producing excellent real ale. Although determined winter visitors are able to savour the full range of 10 ales, summer visitors may have to settle for other superb Cumbrian cask beers as the brewery struggles to cope with demand. Local produce features in the hearty pub food. Local, Cumbrian and regional CAMRA Pub of the Year in 2006. 🔥Q🚸❀🛏◐🍴▲♣●P⁂–🗍

Whitehaven

Bransty Arch ✔

9 Bransty Row, CA28 7XE
⏲ 9-midnight (1am Fri & Sat)
☎ (01946) 517640
Greene King IPA, Abbot; Marston's Pedigree; guest beers Ⓗ
A smart Wetherspoon's pub with a modern interior. Opened in March 2003, the pub's name is a tribute to the Bransty Arch, built around 1800 to transfer coal to the dockside, and demolished in the late 1920s. The pub has strong ties with local CAMRA and guest beers often comes from local Cumbrian breweries. Polypin and occasional draught Westons cider are available. ◐♿⇌🚌(1,2,6)

Whittington Cat

21 Lowther Street, CA28 7DG
⏲ 10.30-11.15 (11.45 Fri & Sat); 11.30-11 Sun
☎ (01946) 67170
Jennings Bitter; guest beer Ⓗ
A lively pub with the attributes of a traditional local in a busy part of Whitehaven. A short walk from the harbour, the pub is opposite the church of St Nicolas – all of which apart from the still-standing clocktower was destroyed by fire on 31 August 1971. Popular for lunch with CAMRA members during beer festival set-up and take-down. Major sports matches are screened and the pub boasts two pool teams. ❀◐⇌🚌(1,2,6)♣⁂–

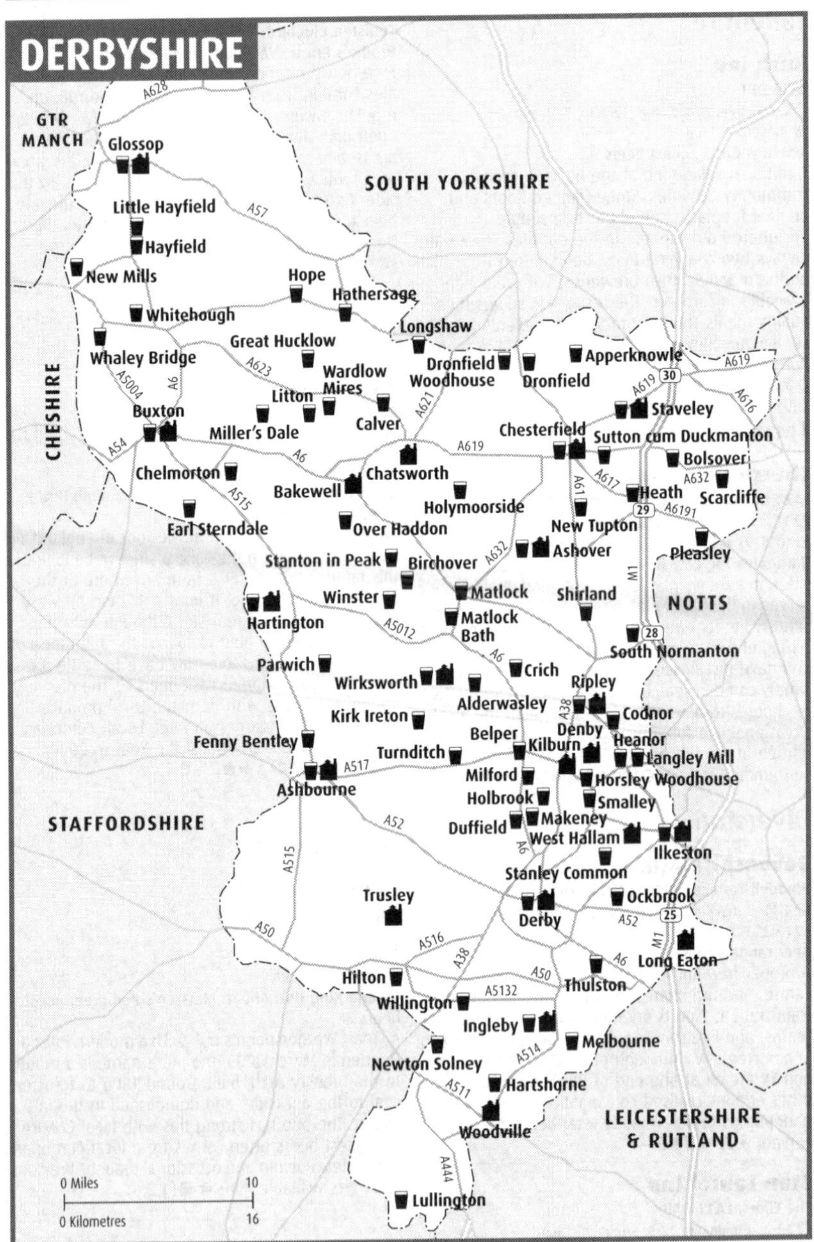

Alderwasley

Bear Inn & Hotel

DE56 2RD SK314527

12-midnight

(01629) 822585 bear-hotel.com

Draught Bass; Greene King Old Speckled Hen Ⓗ; Taylor Landlord Ⓖ; Thornbridge Jaipur; Whim Hartington Bitter; guest beers Ⓗ

Originally a farmhouse, this pub first opened as the Brown Bear Inn in 1735. Three stone-framed hatchways form the bar, backed by paintings of bears. Rooms sub-divided by settles lead off from the bar, filled with old curios, including many on the bear theme. Bear Hall occupies the other end of the inn, where a carvery is served on Sunday lunchtime. Three beers from the Thornbridge range are usually available. The garden offers panoramic views of Derbyshire countryside towards Crich Stand. ♨Q✿⇄◑♣P

Apperknowle

Barrack Hotel

Barrack Road, S18 4AU (turn left off New Road from Unstone) SK381782

6-midnight; 7-1am Sat; 12-5, 7 (8 winter)-midnight Sun

(01246) 416555

Abbeydale Moonshine; Kelham Island Pale Rider; Tetley Bitter; guest beers Ⓗ
This stone-built pub has a front terrace with extensive views over the surrounding countryside. The main room has an L-shaped bar with ornamental glass screen and fittings. To the rear is a separate dining room and a small games room with pool table. Home-cooked bar meals are served (Tue-Fri, plus Sun lunch). Two guest beers are usually available, often from local breweries. No dogs allowed. (14,253)P

Ashbourne

Green Man & Black's Head Royal Hotel

St John's Street, DE6 1GH
11-11 (midnight Thu; 1am Fri; 2am Sat); 12-11 Sun
☎ (01335) 345783 gmrh.com
Greene King Abbot; Leatherbritches Dr Johnson, seasonal beer; guest beers Ⓗ
Warmly praised by Boswell in his famous biography of Samuel Johnson, the Green Man still has its old gallows sign across Ashbourne's main street. A rambling 300-year-old former coaching inn, it has welcoming fires in winter. It is close to where the ball is 'turned up' for the start of the Royal Shrovetide football game and mementos feature throughout the pub. Leatherbritches Brewery and shop are situated in outbuildings and an August bank holiday beer festival is held.
Q

Ashover

Old Poets' Corner

Butts Road, S45 0EW (downhill from church)
12-11
☎ (01246) 590888 oldpoets.co.uk
Ashover Light Rale, Poets Tipple; Taylor Landlord; guest beers Ⓗ
The home of Ashover Brewery, this is a mock-Tudor building that has been fully refurbished creating a warm, welcoming atmosphere with open fires, candlelit tables and hop-strewn beams. Choose from nine handpumps, six traditional ciders, draught and bottled Belgian beers and country wines. The pub was CAMRA national Cider Pub of the Year 2006 and local CAMRA Pub of the Year 2009. Live music features, together with poetry readings, a weekly quiz and regular beer festivals.
Q(63,64)P

Belper

Cross Keys

35 Market Place, DE56 1FZ
11 (12 Sun)-11
☎ (01773) 599191
Batemans XB, XXXB, seasonal beers, Draught Bass; guest beers Ⓗ
This early 19th-century pub was formerly used as accommodation for visiting theatre troupes, and as a meeting place for Druids and Oddfellows; it has also witnessed at least one murder in its time. Two roomed, with a central bar, the pub has enjoyed a renaissance since it was bought by Batemans, whose beers have proved popular locally; regular beer festivals are held. A selection of whiskies is also available and a real fire warms the lounge. Bar billiards and shove-ha'penny are played and there is occasional live music.

George & Dragon

117 Bridge Street, DE56 1BA
3 (11 Thu-Sat)-11.30; 12-10.30 Sun
☎ (01773) 880210
Greene King Abbot; Tetley Bitter; guest beers Ⓗ
A fine Georgian roadside pub on the town's main thoroughfare featuring an unusual covered pillared entrance. Formerly a coaching inn, it has an archway that now provides access to the car park. A deep open-plan pub, it has unusual airline-style seating in the back area that comes from the old Derby Rugby Club. Outside is a skittle alley. Belper Town Football Club, River Gardens and Derwent Valley Mills World Heritage Site visitors' centre are all nearby. P

Birchover

Red Lion

Main Street, DE4 2BN
12-2, 7 (6 Fri)-11; 12-11 Sat; closed Mon; 12-10.30 Sun
☎ (01629) 650363 birchoverredlion.com
Peak Ales Swift Nick; Peakstones Rock 9 Ladies, Nemesis; guest beers Ⓗ
This traditional gritstone-built free house is located in the centre of the village, close to the historic Stanton Moor and Nine Ladies stone circle (after which one of the pub's regular beers is named). Recently refurbished with log-burning stoves in both rooms, it is popular with walkers, tourists and locals alike. Serving excellent food, it has a minimum of three real ales (more in busy summer periods), normally sourced from local micros.
QP

Bolsover

Blue Bell

57 High Street, S44 6HF
12-3.30 (3 Sun), 6.30 (7 Sun)-midnight
☎ (01246) 823508 bolsover.com

INDEPENDENT BREWERIES

Amber Ripley
Ashover Ashover
Blue Monkey Ilkeston (NEW)
Bottle Brook Kilburn
Brampton Chesterfield
Brunswick Derby
Buxton Buxton (NEW)
Derby Derby
Derventio Trusley
Falstaff Derby
Funfair Ilkeston
Globe Glossop
Haywood Bad Ram Ashbourne
Headless Derby
Howard Town Glossop
John Thompson Ingleby
Leadmill Denby
Leatherbritches Ashbourne
Muirhouse Long Eaton (NEW)
Nutbrook West Hallam
Peak Ales Chatsworth
Spire Staveley
Thornbridge Bakewell
Tollgate Woodville
Townes Staveley
Whim Hartington
Wild Walker Derby (NEW)
Wirksworth Wirksworth

Banks's Bitter; guest beers Ⓗ
This traditional family-run, two-roomed alehouse was Chesterfield & District CAMRA's Pub of the Year 2007. A gem of a pub with a cosy atmosphere, it is tucked away just behind the market place near the historic Bolsover Castle. The beer garden sits on top of a cliff face offering views across to the Peak District. An ever-changing choice of five guest ales regularly includes favourites from Jennings. Watch out for the Neglected Shed beer festivals, and other activities such as the weekly Tap Room Cinema. Q❀◑⊟⊞♣P

Buxton

Beltane

8A Hall Bank, SK17 6EW
⏲ 10-11 (midnight Thu; 1am Fri & Sat); closed Mon; 11-11 Sun
☎ (01298) 26010
Beer range varies Ⓗ
This café bar in converted shop premises proves you can serve good quality beer alongside wonderful locally-sourced food and coffee in a relaxed family-friendly atmosphere. During the day the emphasis is on food, but at night the bar becomes a popular local venue with three ever-changing beers on at all times, usually from micro-breweries. There is live music on Thursday evening when the bar becomes packed. ◑⛺⇌⊞

Ramsey's Bar

Buckingham Hotel, 1 Burlington Road, SK17 9AS
⏲ 6-midnight
☎ (01298) 70481 🌐 buckinghamhotel.co.uk
Howard Town Wren's Nest; guest beers Ⓗ
This large public bar and adjoining restaurant are part of the Buckingham Hotel. The name originates from No 1 Burlington Road, home and studio to local artist George Ramsey in the early part of the last century. With up to seven beers from micro-breweries, often including one from Thornbridge, the bar is very popular despite prices that are high for the area. A wide choice of food includes simple bar meals and a full restaurant menu. There is folk music each Thursday. ❀🛏◑♿⛺⇌⊞P

Swan

40 High Street, SK17 6HB
⏲ 11-1am
☎ (01298) 23278
Greene King Old Speckled Hen; Tetley Bitter; guest beers Ⓗ
This is a hostelry that prides itself on being a drinkers' pub, and has a friendly, welcoming atmosphere. Three rooms surround a central bar and major sports matches are shown on the TVs, otherwise background music plays. The tartan room is a former whisky bar. There is always a Storm beer from nearby Macclesfield on handpump and the pub has thriving darts and dominoes teams. Quiz night is Thursday and a small outdoor patio area is available. ❀⊟⇌⊞♣P

Calver

Bridge Inn

Calver Bridge, Hope Valley, S32 3XA (on A623)
⏲ 11.30-3 (3.30 Sat), 5.30-11; 12-3.30, 7-10.30 Sun
☎ (01433) 630415
Greene King H&H Bitter, Abbot, seasonal beer Ⓗ
Sturdy, stone-built and traditionally-designed pub with a central bar area separating two rooms. These are both comfortably furnished and include a collection of local guide books, some antique fire-fighting equipment and an array of hats. The extensive garden overlooks the River Derwent and Arkwright's Calver Mill, now apartments. The landlord has been here since Bass owned the pub in the 1980s. Meals are not served on Monday or winter Sunday. A third beer from Greene King is often available. ♨Q❀◑♿⛺⊞(214,240)P⊟

Chelmorton

Church Inn ✔

Main Street, SK17 9SL
⏲ 12-3.30, 6.30 (7 winter)-11
☎ (01298) 85319
Adnams Bitter; Marston's Burton Bitter, Pedigree; guest beers Ⓗ
Set in beautiful surroundings opposite the local church, this traditional village pub caters for both locals and walkers. The main room is laid out for dining and good home-cooked food is on offer, however a cosy pub atmosphere is maintained with a low ceiling and real fire. Guest beers are usually from local micros. Parking is available at the end of the road in front of the pub and there is a patio area outside. Monday is quiz night. ♨Q❀🛏◑⛺♣

Chesterfield

Derby Tup

387 Sheffield Road, Whittington Moor, S41 8LS
SK382735
⏲ 11.30-3, 5-11; 11.30-11 Wed; 11.30-midnight Fri & Sat; 12-11 Sun
☎ (01246) 454316
Castle Rock Harvest Pale; York Brewery Terrier; guest beers Ⓗ
Voted Chesterfield CAMRA's Pub of the Season for winter 2008, the Tup offers a wide range of up to 10 guest beers, including a stout or porter, plus continental beers, traditional cider and a large range of Irish whiskey. On the way into the main room with its roaring fire, you pass a proper little snug on the left. At the rear is a secluded, quieter area. A true drinkers' pub with no music or other distractions – conversation and camaraderie rule here. ♨Q◐⊟⊞(50,43)♣🍎

Grouse

136 Chatsworth Road, Brampton, S40 2AR (on A619)
⏲ 3-midnight; 12-1am Fri & Sat; 12-midnight Sun
☎ (01246) 279632
Beer range varies Ⓗ
Friendly main road pub with one U-shaped room around a central bar area. Situated very close to Brampton Brewery, it features their beers. The many TV screens make this venue a popular place for viewing sporting events; it also features regular live music. Outside, behind the pub is a small beer garden. A 15-minute walk from the town centre, it also benefits from a frequent bus service. ❀♿⊞♣⚍

Market

95 New Square, S40 1AH
⏲ 11-11; 7-10.30 Sun
☎ (01246) 273641

Greene King Abbot; Taylor Landlord; Tetley Bitter; guest beers H
This popular, town-centre local makes a welcome re-entry to the Guide, mainly due to the enthusiasm of its young proprietors, Douglas and Emma, for good quality real ale and food. Several small beer festivals are held here and it attracts locals and marketeers alike. There are occasional live music events and a quiz night is held on Thursday evening. A small patio to the rear is available for fair-weather drinking. ❀◑⇌▭●⚍

Portland Hotel ✔
West Bars, S40 1AY
9-midnight (1am Fri & Sat)
☎ (01246) 245410
Greene King IPA, Abbot; Marston's Pedigree; guest beers H
This JD Wetherspoon outlet originally opened in 1899 as the station hotel for the Lancashire, Derbyshire & East Coast Railway. A big, mock-Tudor hotel with an ornate exterior, its prime position is handy for Chesterfield's busy market. The bar serves up to four guest beers, which often include local ales, especially from Spire Brewery.
❀⊫◑⇌▭(25)⚍

Red Lion
570 Sheffield Road, Whittington Moor, S41 8LX
SK381737
12-11 (10.30 Sun)
☎ (01246) 450770
Old Mill Mild, Bitter, Bullion, seasonal beers H
Locals' pub where visitors are made welcome. A large-screen TV dominates the public bar but there are enough alcoves for quiet conversation. The separate lounge bar is quieter and ideal for the many groups that meet here. This is the only outlet for Old Mill's excellent beers in Chesterfield, and offers the only guaranteed mild all year round. Frequent fundraising charity evenings are held, notably for the Edale Mountain Rescue.
Q❀⊟▭(43,50)♣P⚍

Rutland Arms ✔
23 Stephenson Place, S40 1XL (adj to church)
11-11 (midnight Thu-Sat)
☎ (01246) 205857
Brampton Golden Bud H/P**; Caledonian Deuchars IPA; Greene King Abbot; John Smith's Magnet Ale; Taylor Landlord; guest beers** H/G
This popular family-run pub has the widest selection of real ale in the town centre and continues to offer the best value food with large portions (Yorkshire puddings are huge). Vegetarians are catered for, mini beer festivals are hosted regularly and a beer-token pub quiz is held on Tuesday night. The main bar area has a good rock jukebox, TV and electronic games. Party events are catered for on occasions, and there is seating outside for smokers. ⋒❀◑⇌▭●⚍

Codnor

Poet & Castle
2 Alfreton Road, DE5 9QY
12-11
☎ (01773) 744150 🌐 poetandcastle.co.uk
Ashover Castle Light, Poet's Tipple; Everards Original; Taylor Landlord; guest beers H
The former Clock pub, rescued from closure by Everards and run by the Ashover Brewery, has become a thriving real ale venue with eight handpumps in constant use. Cider, perry, fruit wines and draught continentals also feature. Quiz Wednesday, acoustic Thursday and live bands on Friday or Saturday form the regular entertainment. The upstairs function room becomes the Poet's Pantry Restaurant on Friday and Saturday evenings and for the Sunday Night Takeaway you provide the food, the pub supplies plates, cutlery and washing-up. No food Monday evening.
⋒❀◑♿⛺▭(R1,H1)♣●P⚍

Crich

Cliff Inn ✔
Town End, DE4 5DP
12-2 Wed, Thu & Sat, 6-midnight; 12-midnight
☎ (01773) 852444
Black Sheep Best Bitter; Taylor Landlord; guest beers H
This former Greene King pub has blossomed since becoming a free house in 2008. It is situated on the edge of the village, close to the National Tramway Museum, and has superb views down the valley. The landlady is a staunch supporter of local beers, often featuring the likes of Amber Ales and Wirksworth Brewery as part of the LocAle scheme. Local societies meet here including cyclists, motorcyclists and horticulturalists. Live music jam Sunday evening.
Q❀◑⊟⛺⇌(Whatstandwell)▭♣P⚍

Derby

Alexandra Hotel
203 Siddals Road, DE1 2QE
3 (11 Thu-Sat)-11; 12-3, 7-10.30 Sun
☎ (01332) 293993
Castle Rock Harvest Pale; guest beers H
Named after the Danish princess who married the Prince of Wales (later Edward VII) in 1863, the Alex was originally called the Midland Coffee House. The end wall once advertised Zacharia Smith's Shardlow Ales, but both sign and brewer have long gone. Long a Shipstones house, then a Batemans pub, it has latterly gone to Tynemill (Castle Rock). Continental beers also feature here. Two-roomed with a central bar, the pub was the birthplace of Derby CAMRA in 1974. ⋒Q❀⊫♿⇌▭♣●P⚍

Babington Arms ✔
11-13 Babington Lane, DE1 1TA
9-11 (midnight Fri & Sat)
☎ (01332) 383647
Greene King Ruddles Best, Abbot; Marston's Burton Bitter, Pedigree; Wyre Piddle Marcoe's King of the Watusi; guest beers H
Probably the best Wetherspoon's house in the country, winning the company's prestigious Cask Ale Pub of the Year and local CAMRA City Pub of the Year twice. It showcases an amazing range of 18 beers on handpump, with permanent guest beers from Derby and Falstaff Breweries, and regular themed brewery weekends. The pub stands in the former grounds of Babington House. The first performance of Bram Stoker's Dracula was given in the neighbouring Grand Theatre in 1924.
Q◑♿▭●

Brewery Tap – Derby's Royal Standard 🏆
1 Derwent Street, DE1 2ED
11-11 (midnight Thu; 1am Fri & Sat)

☎ (01332) 366283 🌐 derbybrewing.co.uk/brewery_tap.htm
Derby Triple Hop, Business As Usual, Dashingly Dark, Double Mash; guest beers [H]
The brewery tap for Derby Brewing Company is the completely renovated Royal Standard. The open-plan interior has an attractive curved bar as the focal point in two distinct drinking areas, with bare brick and wooden floors lending a contemporary feel. In fine weather, the roof terrace affords a view across the River Derwent. Tasting racks of five x third-of-a-pint plus a bowl of cheese are very popular and food is served until 7pm (5pm Sunday). Q❀◑♿🚌⁵–

Brunswick Inn

1 Railway Terrace, DE1 2RU
⏲ 11-11; 12-10.30 Sun
☎ (01332) 290677 🌐 brunswickinn.co.uk
Brunswick White Feather, Triple Hop, Second Brew, Station Approach, Railway Porter, Father Mike's [H]/[G]**; Everards Beacon; Marston's Pedigree** [H]
Originally built in 1842 as the centrepiece of a railway village, the pub was closed in 1974 and fell into disrepair. Eventually rescued and restored, it opened as Derby's first multiple real ale house some 13 years later. A purpose-built brewery was added and it rapidly became one of the best-known free houses in the country, before being sold to Everards in 2002 – and the high standards remain unchanged. ⌂Q❀◑♿🚆🚌♣🍎⁵–

Falstaff

74 Silverhill Road, DE23 6UJ
⏲ 12-11 (midnight Fri & Sat)
☎ (01332) 342902 🌐 falstaffbrewery.co.uk
Falstaff Fistful of Hops, Phoenix, Smiling Assassin, seasonal beer [H]
Known locally as The Folly and reputedly haunted, this was originally a coaching inn before the surrounding area was built up, closing it in. Now a free house, its on-site brewery has made it the best real ale house in Normanton. The curved bar is flanked on one side by a small lounge with a real fire where Offilers Brewery memorabilia is on display. Other collectables can be viewed throughout the games room and second bar room. ⌂Q❀⊟⁵–

Flowerpot

23-25 King Street, DE1 3DZ
⏲ 11 (12 Sun)-11 (midnight Fri & Sat)
☎ (01332) 204955
Headless KSA, First Bloom, [H]**; seasonal beers; Oakham Bishop's Farewell; Whim Hartington IPA; guest beers** [H]/[G]
Dating from around 1800 but much expanded from its original premises, the building reaches far back from the small, roadside frontage and divides into several interlinking rooms. One room provides the stage for regular live bands and another has a glass cellar wall, revealing row upon row of stillaged firkins. The new Headless Brewery is at the rear. A real ale showcase with up to 25 beers on offer every weekend, this was local CAMRA Pub of the Year 2007. Q❀◑⊟♿🚌🍎⁵–

Horse & Groom

48 Elms Street, DE1 3HN
⏲ 12-11
☎ (01332) 384775
Draught Bass; Marston's Pedigree; guest beers [H]
Situated in the City's old West End and dating from c1850 but much modernised latterly, this former Bass pub is now a free house, always serving beer from Thornbridge Brewery. Rescued from certain closure by enthusiastic new licensees, the pub has been transformed into a thriving community local featuring live music at the weekend, jazz on Wednesday, wide-screen TV for sports events and traditional pub games in its two split-level rooms. ❀♣

Mr Grundy's Tavern

32-34 Ashbourne Road, DE22 3AD
⏲ 11 (12 Sat)-11; 12-10.30 Sun
☎ (01332) 340279 🌐 mrgrundystavern.info
Burton Bridge Golden Delicious; Hop Back Summer Lightning; Marston's Pedigree; Taylor Landlord; guest beers [H]
Public bar within the Grade II-listed Georgian House Hotel, serving up to seven real ales. Champion of the LocAle scheme, it features micro-breweries from the Derby/Burton area. Wood panelled throughout, it has open fires, low lighting, wooden bench seating and a bar area featuring hanging hops, breweriania, film memorabilia and an unusual collection of hats. An old red telephone box, a saxophone and a Laurel & Hardy sign add to its charm. Outdoors is a large covered area and beer garden. No evening meals on Sunday. ⌂❀🛏◑♿🚌(29)P⁵–

Olde Dolphin Inne ★ ✔

5A Queen Street, DE1 3DL
⏲ 10.30-midnight; 12-11 Sun
☎ (01332) 267711
Adnams Bitter; Black Sheep Best Bitter; Caledonian Deuchars IPA; Draught Bass; Greene King Abbot; Marston's Pedigree; Taylor Landlord; guest beers [H]
Standing below the great gothic tower of the cathedral, the timber-framed Dolphin is Derby's most picturesque and oldest surviving pub, although much restored. Reputed to be haunted, the beamed interior divides into bar, upper and lower lounges, a snug and an upstairs steak bar, each with its own character. Regular themed evenings are supplemented by a beer festival in July, which spreads out on to a splendid, raised rear patio. A real gem that is not to be missed. ⌂Q❀◑⊟🚌P⁵–

Rowditch Inn

246 Uttoxeter New Road, DE22 3LL
⏲ 12-2 Sat & Sun, 7-11
☎ (01332) 343123
Marston's Pedigree; guest beers [H]
A no-frills pub with first-class beer; winner of local CAMRA City Pub of the Year in 2006. A plain fronted but warmly welcoming roadside hostelry, its unexpectedly deep interior divides into two drinking areas and a small snug. The long rear garden is a positive haven in warmer weather. Pump clips adorning the walls of the bar are evidence of myriad guest ales. A cheese evening is held each Monday. Its own micro-brewery is set to open at the rear of the pub during 2009. ⌂❀🚌♣⁵–

Smithfield

Meadow Road, DE1 2BH
⏲ 11-11; 12-10.30 Sun
☎ (01332) 370429 🌐 thesmithfield.co.uk
Draught Bass; Headless seasonal beers; Oakham Bishop's Farewell; Whim Arbor Light, Hartington IPA; guest beers [H]

Bow-fronted riverside pub built to serve the cattle market, which has long since moved to a new site, leaving the Smithy in a bit of a backwater. A long, basic bar is flanked on one side by a games room with dartboard and on the other by a cosy lounge with stone fireplace and old settles, overlooking a pleasant riverside patio where a beer festival is held at the end of August. Headless Brewery's second city pub is also a former local CAMRA Pub of the Year winner. ❀◐⊟⇌🚌♣P⅃▭

Dronfield

Coach & Horses 🏆

Sheffield Road, S18 2GD
⏲ 5-10 Mon; 12-11 (midnight Fri & Sat); 12-10.30 Sun
☎ (01246) 413269
Thornbridge Jaipur, seasonal beers Ⓗ
Roadside pub north of the town centre, with one comfortably furnished open-plan room. It is owned by Sheffield FC, the world's oldest football club, founded in 1857, whose ground is adjacent. There are usually up to five Thornbridge beers available. Good home-cooked food is made with locally sourced ingredients where possible, served in a friendly, relaxed atmosphere. Evening meals are available until 8.30pm, but no food Monday or Sunday evening. Q❀◐◑⇌🚌(43,44)♣P⅃

Dronfield Woodhouse

Jolly Farmer ✔

Pentland Road, S18 8ZQ
⏲ 12-midnight (1am Fri & Sat)
☎ (01246) 418018
Black Sheep Best Bitter; John Smith Magnet; Taylor Landlord; Tetley Bitter; guest beers Ⓗ
Community pub built on a large housing estate in 1976 by Shipstones and turned into a themed ale house in the 1990s. The cask beers are stillaged in a glass-fronted cellar behind the bar, which is free of the usual ostentatious lager pumps. The pub is open plan but has distinct areas including a tap room with pool table and a raised dining area. Two guest beers feature, usually from small independents, and a beer festival is held in November. Q❀◐◑⊟♿🚌(43,89)♣P⅃

Duffield

Pattenmakers Arms

4 Crown Street, DE56 4EY
⏲ 12-2, 5-midnight; 12-midnight Fri-Sun
☎ (01332) 842844 🌐 pattenmakersarms.co.uk
Draught Bass Ⓖ**; Taylor Landlord; Marston's Pedigree; guest beers** Ⓗ
Pleasant 19th-century inn, five minutes' walk from the main road. The pub is open plan, with a central horseshoe bar. Guest beers are chosen from the SIBA list. This lively, family-friendly hostelry offers a warm welcome to all, and runs skittles, darts and dominoes teams, as well as quizzes and meat raffles. Older architectural features survive, including quarry tiled and parquet floors, and stained glass and etched windows. Simple, nourishing lunchtime meals are served from Wednesday to Sunday. ❀◐⇌🚌♣P⅃

Earl Sterndale

Quiet Woman

SK17 0BU (off B5053)
⏲ 12-3 (4 Sat; 5.30 Sun), 7-1am
☎ (01298) 83211
Jennings Dark Mild; Marston's Burton Bitter, Pedigree; guest beers Ⓗ
This unspoilt local set in the heart of the Peak District National Park is opposite the church and village green. Inside is a low-beamed room with a real fire on the left and a small bar to the right plus a separate games room with a pool table. Local fresh eggs and traditional pork pies can be purchased at the bar. The pub offers its own selection of naturally conditioned bottled beers brewed by Leek Brewery. 🔥Q🐴❀⛺🚌(442)♣P

Fenny Bentley

Coach & Horses ✔

DE6 1LB (on A515)
⏲ 11-11; 12-10.30 Sun
☎ (01335) 350246
Marston's Pedigree; guest beers Ⓗ
This traditional 16th-century coaching inn has retained many original features such as old flagged floors and very low beams. Coal and log burning stoves, set in brick, combine with comfortable wooden chairs and settles to create a cosy atmosphere in the bar. The dining room and garden room cater for fabulous home-cooked food made from local produce. The number of guest beers increases in the summer. Some of Derbyshire's major tourist attractions, including Dovedale and Tissington Hall, are nearby. 🔥Q◐◑⛺P

Glossop

Crown Inn ★

142 Victoria Street, SK13 8JF (on Hayfield Road)
⏲ 5 (11.30 Fri & Sat)-11; 12-10.30 Sun
☎ (01457) 862824
Samuel Smith OBB Ⓗ
This end of terrace local, a few minutes from the town centre and Glossop station, was built in 1846 and has been the only Smith's house in the High Peak area since 1977. An attractive curved bar serves two side snugs, each with a real fire in winter, and a pool/games room. Old pictures of Glossop's past add to the traditional character. Prices are keen and Smith's bottled beers are also available. An enclosed outdoor drinking area is provided in the rear yard. 🔥Q❀♿⇌🚌♣⅃

Friendship

3 Arundel Street, SK13 7AB
⏲ 4 (3 Fri)-midnight; 12-midnight Sat; 12-11 Sun
☎ (01457) 855277
Robinson's Hatters, Unicorn Ⓗ
Traditional local retaining 1950s-style panelling and exuding a warm ambience. The semi-circular bar serves the open-plan front lounge, while the rear tap room is served from a hatch. One corner is dedicated to local cricket and also used by supporters of Glossop North End FC – both clubs are nearby. Old Tom in bottles is sold in addition to a range of malt whiskies. Note the impressive lamp over the front door circa 1900 and the award-winning beer garden. 🔥Q❀⊟⇌🚌♣⅃

Star Inn ✔

2 Howard Street, SK13 7DD (next to railway station)
⏲ 2 (4 Mon & Tue)-11 (midnight Fri & Sat); 12-10.30 Sun
☎ (01457) 853072

Black Sheep Best Bitter; guest beers Ⓗ
Often the first and last stop-off for visitors by public transport, as Glossop train station and bus stops are very close by. This highly-regarded local is currently run by long-standing CAMRA members. Six handpumps offer a range of ales along with real cider, served from the cellar. Pictures of bygone Glossop, wood floors and a rear tap room served by a hatch add to the traditional atmosphere. A covered and heated outdoor smoking area is available.

Great Hucklow

Queen Anne

Main Road, SK17 8RF
12-2.30, 5-11; closed Mon; 12-11 Fri & Sat; 12-10.30 Sun
(01298) 871246 queenanneinn.co.uk
Tetley Bitter; guest beers Ⓗ
Recently refurbished, this pub was first granted a licence in 1704, although it was functioning as an ale house as early as 1577. The village thrived on lead mining in the 18th century and there is a Unitarian chapel dating from this period. Inside the pub, the recently refurbished rooms have low ceilings, beams and brasses, and there is a high-backed settle. Walkers are welcome and good value lunches are available. The pub is closed all day Monday. (65)P

Hartington

Charles Cotton Hotel

Market Place, SK17 0AL
12-11
(01298) 84229 charlescotton.co.uk
Whim Hartington Bitter, Hartington IPA; guest beers Ⓗ
This 17th-century coaching inn is situated just off the village green and duck pond. The comfy bar and adjacent overspill/dining area, according to the landlord, has no 'beer factory beers' and all ales are local. A fine selection of gin and malt whiskies is maintained by the landlady, and the restaurant focuses on locally-produced food. There is an annual beer festival in October and a good community atmosphere prevails with local stonewallers and bellringers meeting regularly.
QP

Hartshorne

Admiral Rodney Inn

65 Main Street, DE11 7ES (on A514) SK325211
12-midnight; 6-11.30, 5-midnight Fri
(01283) 216482
Marston's Pedigree; guest beers Ⓗ
This traditional village pub dates back to the early 19th-century, but was substantially rebuilt in 1959, and more recently refurbished to provide an open-plan L-shaped drinking area, retaining the original oak beams in the former snug. A small raised area behind the bar is served through a hatch. Up to four guest beers are available, often from SIBA members. Meals are limited to traditional Sunday lunches. The grounds include a cricket pitch and the pub is open during Sunday afternoon matches.
(68)P

Mill Wheel

31 Ticknall Road, DE11 7AS (on A514) SK326213
12-3, 5.30-11; 12-10.30 Sun
(01283) 550335 themillwheel.co.uk
Greene King Abbot; Marston's Pedigree; guest beers Ⓗ
This attractive and comfortable free house incorporates a 24-foot diameter 19th-century iron water wheel, visible from both the main open-plan bar area and the upstairs restaurant. Originally the site of a corn mill, various industrial uses followed. Radical reconstruction saw the conversion into a pub in 1987, with further sensitive and extensive restoration work in 1999. Guest beers are usually from SIBA members. Food is available all day Sunday. Accommodation is in an attached cottage.
(68)P

Hathersage

Millstone Inn ✔

Sheffield Road, S32 1DA (on A6187 E of village)
11.30-11; 12-10.30 Sun
(01433) 650258 millstoneinn.co.uk
Abbeydale Moonshine; Black Sheep Best Bitter; Fuller's Discovery; Taylor Landlord; guest beers Ⓗ
This pub originally served the nearby millstone quarry and is now popular with walkers and climbers. Smartly decorated, it has a large bar, ballroom/dining area and an extensive outdoor area partly under cover. Guest beers are from local breweries. There is a quiz on Friday evening. The landlord runs his own taxi service to the nearby station for residents. Meals are available throughout the day every day. The traditional cider is Black Rat. (272)P

Hayfield

Royal Hotel

Market Street, SK22 2EP
12-11
(01663) 742721 theroyalhayfield.co.uk
Hyde's Bitter; guest beers Ⓗ
A former vicarage, this imposing stone pub stands near the church and cricket ground alongside the River Sett. The interior boasts original oak panels and pews, with real fires in winter. A restaurant and function room complete the facilities and an annual beer festival is hosted in October. The village is the base for many leisure activities in the Dark Peak area and was also the birthplace of Arthur Lowe, the immortal Captain Mainwaring in Dad's Army. QP

Heanor

Red Lion ✔

2 Derby Road, DE75 7QG
9am-11 (1am Fri & Sat)
(01773) 533767
Greene King Abbot; Marston's Pedigree; guest beers Ⓗ
A pub bearing this historic name has stood on this site since 1700. This late Victorian incarnation is now a Wetherspoon house, and as popular as ever despite the smoking ban. A bank of handpumps dispenses the broadest range of beer in town, and there is usually something to interest the discerning drinker. A small patio area to the side is a fair-weather haven and provides sanctuary for smokers.

Heath

Elm Tree

Mansfield Road, S44 5SE SK446672
11.30-3, 5-midnight; 11.30-midnight Sat; 12-10.30 Sun
(01246) 850490 theelmtreeheath.co.uk
Jennings Sneck Lifter; guest beers H
This two-roomed hostelry has a spacious main bar complemented by a smaller public bar at the rear. A fine menu offers food that is all freshly cooked to order. Well-maintained gardens surround the pub, offering fine views of the Derbyshire countryside. With an ever growing range of beers this pub goes from strength to strength.

Hilton

Old Talbot

1 Main Street, DE65 5FF
3.30 (3 Fri; 12.30 Sat)-11.30 (12.30am Fri & Sat); 12-11.30 Sun
(01283) 733728 oldtalbot.co.uk
Draught Bass; Marston's Pedigree; guest beers H
This welcoming Grade II-listed pub dates from the early 1500s. The existence of a malt drying kiln on the back of the main fireplace suggests it was probably first built as an ale house. By local repute, the ale for the nearby Tutbury Castle was brewed at the Talbot and was thus drunk by Mary Queen of Scots. A social centre for activities including motorcycling, angling, Sunbeam Talbot owners and other clubs, it also hosts an annual beer festival in September. Q(V1,V2)P

Holbrook

Dead Poets Inn

38 Chapel Street, DE56 0TQ
12-2.30, 5-11; 12-11 Fri & Sat; 12-10.30 Sun
(01332) 780301
Marston's Pedigree; Greene King Abbot G**; guest beers** H
Built in 1800 and formerly known as the Cross Keys, the pub has undergone a remarkable transformation to become an inn with a real medieval feel within. Its two rooms contain high-backed pews, stone-flagged floors, low lighting, a real fire and an inglenook. Once a free house but now owned by Everards, it offers up to 25 guest beers a week (six at any one time), and usually includes at least one from Abbeydale and Whim breweries. Q(71,71A,138)P

Holymoorside

Lamb

16 Loads Road, S42 7EU SK339694
5 (4 Fri)-11; 12-3, 7-11 Sat & Sun
(01246) 566167
Daleside Blonde; Theakston Black Bull; guest beers H
A locals' pub, unspoilt by progress, with a mixed clientele where all are welcome including dogs and walkers – but take your boots off before going in. The public bar (a valued survivor of the craze for one-room pub conversions) is warmed by a real fire. The paved outdoor drinking area is ideal for warm, dry summer evenings and hosts a jazz session as part of the annual Holymoorside Festival. Frequent winner of Chesterfield CAMRA awards. Q(50,99)P

Hope

Cheshire Cheese

Edale Road, S33 6ZF
12-3, 6.30-11.30; 12-11.30 Sat; 12-10.30 Sun
(01433) 620381
Black Sheep Best Bitter; Copper Dragon Best Bitter; guest beers H
This cosy pub dating from 1578 has an open-plan bar area and a smaller room at a lower level that was probably originally used to house animals; nowadays it is used as a dining area (no evening meals Sun). The pub is situated in walking country but parking is limited and the road outside narrow. There is a strong regular trade from nearby villages, and a sloe gin-making competition is among the activities centred on the pub. At the rear is a refurbished beer garden. QP

Horsley Woodhouse

Old Oak Inn

176 Main Street, DE7 6AW (on A609)
4 (3 Thu & Fri; 12 Sat & Sun)-midnight
(01332) 881299
Bottle Brook seasonal beers; Leadmill seasonal beers; guest beers H
Once a farmhouse, the Old Oak was under threat of demolition when, in 2003, it was acquired and renovated by the Denby-based Leadmill Brewery. Four rooms of individual character, two with real fires and low beams, provide a homely atmosphere for regulars and visitors alike. Nine handpumps plus a real cider, beer festivals and occasional live music help to make this a successful village pub. Dogs are welcome. QP

Ilkeston

Dewdrop

24 Station Street, DE7 5TE (50m from A6096)
12-11 (10.30 Sun)
(0115) 9329684
Castle Rock Harvest Pale; Oakham Bishops Farewell; Taylor Best Bitter; guest beers H
Built in 1884, when named for local landowner Lord Middleton, this Victorian traditional corner house was a three-storey hotel serving the old time colliery and mill workers. Now named the Dewdrop, it still boasts its three-roomed format and a grand lobby, where a plaque hangs commemorating the wartime stay of Ripley born Barnes Wallis, inventor of the bouncing bomb. LocAle affiliated and winner of local CAMRA Pub of the Year 2009, there are not many pubs like this left. Q(27)

Good Old Days

93 Station Road, DE7 5LJ (on A6096)
12-3, 6-midnight; 12-1am Fri & Sat; 12-midnight Sun
(0115) 8751103
Beer range varies H
Situated by the Erewash Canal, this former local CAMRA Club of the Year is a perennial Guide entry that continues to champion the cause of real ale by stocking micro-brewery beers sourced from near and far, often showcasing new brewers. Traditional pub games include snooker, and a pianist makes an occasional guest appearance. The large garden is landscaped and there are adjacent narrowboat moorings. (27)

Poacher ✓

69 South Street, DE7 5QQ

11 (12 Mon-Wed)-11 (midnight Fri & Sat); 12-10.30 Sun

(0115) 9325452

Nottingham EPA; Taylor Landlord; guest beers H

A shining example of pub refurbishment that successfully marries tasteful, contemporary style with a traditional, three-roomed layout. This former Shipstones house boasts a modern public bar with an attractive, curved bar as its focal point. To one side is a lounge with comfortable banquettes. Another lounge to the rear has welcoming sofas. A member of the LocAle scheme, the pub promotes real ale by constantly changing its guest beers, sourced from Scottish & Newcastle's Cellarmans Choice.

Spanish Bar

76 South Street, DE7 8QJ

10-11 (midnight Fri & Sat); 11-10.30 Sun

(0115) 9308666

Mallard Quacker Jack; Whim Hartington IPA; guest beers H

Bustling, friendly locals' pub with a cafe-bar style that attracts all ages. Regular customers enjoy cards and dominoes schools, and Tuesday is quiz night. The colourful main bar has comfy chairs surrounding a log burner, and a second room, open in the evenings, has a large-screen TV showing important events. The pleasant rear garden features a heated skittle alley. There is a range of bottled continental beers and the guest ales are often sourced from micro-breweries.
(15)

Ingleby

John Thompson Inn

DE73 7HW (off A514)

11-2.30, 6-11 (midnight Sat); 12-midnight Sun

(01332) 862469 johnthompsoninn.com

John Thompson seasonal beers; guest beers H

The oldest brewery in Derbyshire now sits alongside six four-bed self-catering chalets in the grounds of the pub, now run by the son of its eponymous founder. With rural views over the River Trent, this delightful setting is enhanced by the carefully crafted interior, featuring works by the local Gresley family of artists. A modern extension offers TV and pool. Lunches are served daily except Monday. P

Kirk Ireton

Barley Mow ★

Main Street, DE6 3JP (off B5023)

12-2, 7-11 (10.30 Sun)

(01335) 370306

Whim Hartington IPA; guest beers G

Set in a village overlooking the Ecclesbourne Valley, this gabled Jacobean building features a sundial dated 1683. Several interconnecting rooms of different size and character have low, beamed ceilings, mullioned windows, slate-topped tables, well-worn woodwork and open fires. A small serving hatch reveals a stillage with up to six beers dispensed straight from the cask. This pub is well worth a visit as there are not many rural gems like this left. Local CAMRA Pub of the Year 2008.
Q

Langley Mill

Railway Tavern

188 Station Road, NG16 4AE

12-midnight

(01773) 764711

Alcazar Ale, Foxtale Ale H

This classic white stuccoed 1920s building was once a Home Brewery pub, and is enjoying a renaissance following a skilful refurbishment. The multi-roomed interior is largely intact and some original fittings, including the settles in the bar area, have been retained. The Tavern is an active participant in traditional pub games, which remain popular in this area. It has the added attraction of Alcazar bottle-conditioned ales and is well served by bus and rail. DH Lawrence was born in nearby Eastwood.

Little Hayfield

Lantern Pike

45 Glossop Road, SK22 2NG

12 (5 Mon winter)-11

(01663) 747590 lanternpikeinn.co.uk

Black Sheep Best Bitter; Howard Town Wren's Nest; Taylor Landlord H

Picturesque ivy-clad stone pub nestling in a small hamlet within the Dark Peak area of the High Peak. The comfortable, traditional lounge bar, with real fire in winter, connects to separate dining areas. Coronation Street originator Tony Warren lived nearby and wrote some of the first episodes of the soap while in the pub, hence the display of photographs of original characters and a letter from Warren in the lounge. The rear patio area has superb views across Lantern Pike Hill.
(61)P

Litton

Red Lion ✓

Church Lane, SK17 8QU

12-11 (midnight Fri & Sat); 12-10.30 Sun

(01298) 871458

Abbeydale Absolution; Oakwell Barnsley Bitter; guest beers H

The only pub in the village, the Red Lion is a focus of local activity and a welcome refuge for visitors. The village green opposite is complete with punishing stocks and resplendent with daffodils in spring. There is an enormous fireplace serving three cosy rooms and a fourth room has recently been opened up to create extra space. The pub keeps a collection of local guide books. A monthly quiz is held on Monday and food is available all day Thursday to Sunday. Q(65)

Longshaw

Grouse Inn

S11 7TZ (on A625)

12-3, 6-11; 12-11 Sat; 12-10.30 Sun

(01433) 630423

Banks's Bitter; Caledonian Deuchars IPA; Marston's Pedigree; guest beer H

In the same family since 1965, this free house stands in isolation on bleak moorland south west of Sheffield, and is deservedly popular with walkers and climbers. There are some fine photographs of nearby gritstone edges, as well as collections of bank notes and cigarette cards on display. The comfortable lounge is situated at the front, a smaller bar area is at the rear and a conservatory in between. ⌂Q⊘❀◑♣P⊟

Lullington

Colvile Arms

Main Street, DE12 8EG SK249131
⏲ 6-11; 12-3, 7-10.30 Sun
☎ (01827) 373212
Draught Bass; Marston's Pedigree; guest beer Ⓗ
Popular 18th-century free house, leased from the Lullington Estate, at the heart of an attractive hamlet at the southern tip of the county. The public bar has an adjoining hallway and snug, each featuring high-backed settles with wood panelling. The bar and a comfortable lounge are situated on opposite sides of a central serving area. A second lounge/function room overlooks the garden and a bowling green. Two quiz teams and the local cricket and football teams meet here. ❀⊟♣P⊱

Makeney

Holly Bush Inn ☆

Holly Bush Lane, DE56 0RX
⏲ 12-3, 4.30-11; 12-11 Sat; 12-10.30 Sun
☎ (01332) 841729 🌐 hollybush-inn.co.uk
Fuller's London Pride; Greene King Abbot Ⓗ**;**
Marston's Pedigree Ⓖ**; Taylor Landlord; guest beers** Ⓗ
This late 17th-century Grade II-listed pub oozes character. It was once a farmhouse with a brewery on the Strutt Estate and stood on the Derby turnpike before the new road opened in 1818 – Dick Turpin drank here. The enclosed wooden snug is sandwiched between two bars with real fires, and beer festivals are held in March and October. The Milford bus stop by the King William IV is a ten-minute walk. Local CAMRA Country Pub of the Year 2007. ⌂Q⊘❀◑⊟⊡♣●P⊱

Matlock

Thorn Tree

48 Jackson Road, DE4 3JQ (off Bank Rd) SK300608
⏲ 12-2 (not Mon), 6-11; 12-midnight Fri & Sat; 12-11 Sun
☎ (01629) 580295
Black Sheep Best Bitter; Draught Bass; Greene King Ruddles Best, Morland Original; Taylor Landlord; guest beer Ⓗ
Perched high on the hill on the north side of Matlock, the pub enjoys excellent views from the delightful patio over the town and the Derwent Valley. This compact two-roomed pub is popular with office workers at lunchtime and locals in the evening. Lunches are available Tuesday to Friday, evening meals Wednesday and Thursday. Sunday lunches and barbecues are on offer in summer. Q❀◑⊟⊡♣⊱

Matlock Bath

Temple Hotel 🏆

Temple Walk, DE4 3PG (off A6)
⏲ 6-10.30; 12-11 Sat; 12-10 Sun
☎ (01629) 583911 🌐 templehotel.co.uk
Amber Ales Amber Pale; Howard Town Wrens Nest; guest beers Ⓗ
Historic Georgian hotel with a public bar situated above the hustle and bustle of the Matlock Bath riverside promenade, with good views across the Derwent Valley. Nearby are the popular cable car rides and the Peak District Mining Museum. Past visitors include Lord Byron, who etched a poem on a window. The landlord focuses on beers from Derbyshire micro-breweries, and up to three beers from Thornbridge, Whim and Leatherbritches often feature. ⌂Q❀⊨◑♿⇌⊡(6)P⊱

Melbourne

Alma Inn

59 Derby Road, DE73 8FE
⏲ 4 (11 Sat)-11 (12.30am Fri & Sat); 11-12.30am Sun
☎ (01332) 695200
Marston's Pedigree; guest beers Ⓗ
The delightful small town of Melbourne is best known for its Antipodean cousin, which actually took its name from the 2nd Viscount Melbourne, whose family still lives here. The pub gets its name from the Crimean War battle, so it is only to be expected that beers from Marston's are in winning form. The hostelry is usually lively, often catering for a younger clientele, and holds two beer festivals a year. ⌂⊘❀▲⊡(68)♣P⊱

Milford

King William IV

The Bridge, DE56 0RR (on A6)
⏲ 5 (12 Sat)-11.30; 12.30-11 Sun
☎ (01332) 840842
Taylor Landlord; guest beers Ⓗ
Next to the bridge in the centre of a historic mill village, backed by sandstone cliffs, this is a small, narrow, single-roomed local. It has exposed interior stone walls, a welcoming fireplace, low-beamed ceiling, quarry tiled floor and wooden settles. On handpump Bass and Pedigree rotate, plus two other guests, often including a local micro-brewery ale. There are beer festivals in April and September. An ideal base for exploring the Derwent Valley World Heritage site. ⌂⊨⊡♣●

Miller's Dale

Angler's Rest ✔

SK17 8SN (on B6049)
⏲ 12-3, 6.30-11; 12-11 Sat & Sun
☎ (01298) 871323 🌐 theanglersrest.co.uk
Marston's Pedigree; Tetley Bitter; guest beers Ⓗ
Ivy-clad pub on the banks of the River Wye, with a cosy lounge bar with coal fire, comfortable dining room and hikers' bar where walking boots and dogs are welcome. Thursday night is pie night. Local attractions include Ravenstor Cliff for rock climbers and the spectacular walk along the Monsal Trail between Litton Mill and Cressbrook Mill, both of historical interest and now converted to apartments. Accommodation is a self-catering apartment. Guest beers are mostly LocAle. ⌂Q⊨◑⊟▲⊡(65)♣P

New Mills

Pack Horse Inn

Mellor Road, SK22 4QQ
⏲ 12-3, 5-11; 12-midnight Sat; 12-10.30 Sun
☎ (01663) 742365 🌐 packhorseinn.co.uk
Phoenix Arizona; Tetley Bitter; guest beers Ⓗ
A much-extended pub built from local stone, with a recent matching extension incorporating an elegant dining room and high standard accommodation. The traditional bar room interior,

however, remains largely unaltered, with an open fire plus a stove for the winter. Two regularly-changing guest beers, often from local micros, are available. Outside there are two stone patio areas, one imaginatively built into the hillside, the other offering sweeping Pennine views. ⩕Q❀⇄◑P⁻

New Tupton

Britannia Inn

Ward Street, S42 6XP SK397661
⌚ 4-11; 3-midnight Fri; 11.30-midnight Sat; 12-10.30 Sun
☎ (01246) 861438 🌐 spirebrewery.co.uk/britannia.html
Beer range varies Ⓗ
This LocAle accredited community pub, is the brewery tap for nearby Spire Brewery. Featuring eight cask ales, a stout or a porter and a mild are always available on the bar, along with real cider, perry and locally-produced Czech-style lager, Moravka. A big supporter of local CAMRA campaigns, The Brit has regular quizzes, an outdoor skittle alley and is a supporter of charities. Easily accessible by bus. Q❀⊟⊡(51,98)♣●P⁻⊓

Newton Solney

Unicorn Inn

Repton Road, DE15 0SG (on B5008) SK283257
⌚ 12-midnight (1am Fri & Sat)
☎ (01283) 703324 🌐 unicorn-inn.co.uk
Draught Bass; Marston's Pedigree; guest beers Ⓗ
This popular local was originally a farmhouse on the Ratcliffe family estate (of Bass, Ratcliffe & Gretton brewery fame), but became a pub in the late 19th century. The attractive bar area, featuring a wooden bar counter and bar stools, is linked to a small, cosy lounge on one side and a separate dining room on the other. Beer festivals are held in February and August, jointly with the Bull's Head in nearby Repton. The garden includes a children's play area. ❀⇄◑⊟⊡(V3)♣P⁻

Ockbrook

Royal Oak

55 Green Lane, DE72 3SE
⌚ 11.30-2.30 (3 Sat), 5.30-11 (11.30 Sat); 12-4, 7-11 Sun
☎ (01332) 662378
Draught Bass; guest beers Ⓗ
Approached across a cobbled courtyard, this was CAMRA regional Pub of the Year 2000 and has featured in the Guide since 1976. Run by the same family since Coronation year, it is little changed, with each of the six rooms preserving its own distinctive character and customers. Three ever-changing guest beers, including a LocAle, are supplemented by beer festivals in May and October. Excellent home-cooked food is served every lunchtime, and evenings Monday to Friday (except Tue). Q❀◑♿⊡(9)♣●P⁻

Over Haddon

Lathkil Hotel

DE45 1JE SK206665
⌚ 11.30-3, 6-11; 11.30-11 Sat; 12-10.30 Sun
☎ (01629) 812501 🌐 lathkil.co.uk
Everards Tiger; Whim Hartington Bitter; guest beers Ⓗ
The pub overlooks a masterpiece of Peak District scenery, marvellous in any weather. Walking in, one side is an old-fashioned bar room with real fire and oak beams, while the larger room opposite is where diners enjoy superb home-cooked meals. A covered beer garden is the perfect place to while away summer evenings with a pint. Well-equipped rooms are available for staying over; dogs are welcome in the bar but walkers should take off their boots at the door. ⩕Q❀⇄◑⊟Å⊡P⁻⊓

Parwich

Sycamore Inn

DE6 1QL
⌚ 12-2 (4 Sat), 7 (6 Thu & Fri)-11; 12 -11 Sun
☎ (01335) 390212
Robinson's Double Hop, seasonal beers Ⓗ
Residing in a small, remote Peak District village, this inn, named after nearby cottages, is next to the village green, duck pond and church. It hosts the village shop and won a national award for Community Pub of the Year 2008. The bar has a real fire and warm greetings from staff and locals. It has separate rooms for pool and darts, and dominoes is also played. Regular and seasonal beers come from the Robinson's range – Old Tom features in winter. ⩕Q❀◑⊟Å♣P

Pleasley

Nags Head

Chesterfield Road, NG19 7PA (400m off A617)
⌚ 5 (4 Fri)-midnight; 12-midnight Sat & Sun
☎ (01623) 810235
Greene King XX Mild, H&H Bitter, Morland Original Bitter; guest beers Ⓗ
Family-run pub with an enthusiastic cask ale licensee who ensures that a traditional mild is always available – locals still enjoy a pint of mixed. This is a family-oriented pub where darts and dominoes are played, and where the traditional multi-room format has been retained. Although not open during the day, except at weekends, there are buses that pass the door until 11pm. No food is available. ⩕Q❀⊟⊡(23,53)♣P⁻

Ripley

George Inn

20 Lowes Hill, DE5 3DW
⌚ 6 (2.30 Fri; 1 Sat)-1am; 1-11 Sun
☎ (01773) 512041
Amber seasonal beers; guest beers Ⓗ
It is just a ten-minute walk to this former Batemans house from the town centre, and well worth the effort. Amber Ales Brewery is not much further down the road and its brews often feature, along with those from Tollgate and other guests. A community pub, it supports teams for football, pool, dominoes and skittles. The locals are friendly and treat the pub as their home-from-home. Live bands feature on Saturday night. ⊡(2,9)♣P

Scarcliffe

Horse & Groom

Rotherham Road, S44 6SU (on B6417) SK490687
⌚ 12-midnight
☎ (01246) 823152
Black Sheep Best Bitter; Greene King Abbot; Stones Bitter; Tetley's Bitter; guest beers Ⓗ
A regular in the Guide for the past 10 years and run by the same family for the past 13 years, this stone-built pub is over 480 years old and now has three modern self-catering holiday cottages

attached. No hot food is available, but the local pork pie is a must. An impressive range of malt whisky is stocked, complementing up to seven real ales. The lounge is a mobile-free room. (53,82)P

Shirland

Shoulder of Mutton

Hallfieldgate Lane, DE55 6AA (on B6013, Wessington-Shirland crossroad) SK393582

12 (7 Tue)-11; 12-10.30 Sun

(01773) 834992

John Smith's Bitter; guest beers H

Genuinely friendly and welcoming pub, with a strong community feel. It is situated in an attractive stone building, once two cottages. Set in semi-rural surroundings, it features a pleasant side garden with lovely views over the Amber Valley. There is a large lounge with open fire and comfortable seating. The constantly changing guest beers, up to 10 per week, sourced from local micro-breweries and further afield, will satisfy the ardent ale drinker. QP

Smalley

Bell Inn

35 Main Road, DE7 6EF (on A608)

11.30-3, 5-11; 11.30-11 Fri-Sun

(01332) 880635

Adnams Broadside; Marston's Pedigree; Oakham JHB; Whim Hartington Bitter, Hartington IPA; guest beer H

Situated near Shipley Country Park, this mid 19th century inn has three rooms where brewing memorabilia adorn the walls, and a large attractive garden. The food is very good, with the mixed grill being a veritable meat feast, but it is still a drinkers' pub and won Derbyshire CAMRA Pub of the Year in 2006. Accommodation is offered in three flats, in converted stables to the rear. Weekday opening hours may be extended in the summer. Q(H1)P

South Normanton

Devonshire Arms

137 Market Street, DE55 2AA

12-midnight

(01773) 810748 the-devonshire-arms.co.uk/index.htm

Sarah Hughes Dark Ruby; guest beers H

This local CAMRA Pub of the Season is a family-run free house with restaurant, games room and adjoining bar area. Sky Sports is shown on three large-screen TVs in the main bar and games room. Home-cooked meals are available daily (except Sun eve), with vegetarians, vegans and coeliacs all catered for, and a Sunday carvery is served 12-3pm (booking advised). Up to three guest beers are on offer along with Westons traditional cider. Live entertainment plays on Friday evening. (9.1,9.2,331)P

Stanley Common

White Post Inn

237 Belper Road, DE7 6FT (on A609)

12-3 (not Mon), 6-11; 12-1am Sat; 12-11 Sun

(0115) 9300194

Jennings Cocker Hoop; Marston's Pedigree; guest beers H

This large, white-painted roadside inn is on the main road through Stanley Common. Three interlinking rooms, one used as a family-friendly dining area, are served by a central bar. A conservatory at the back leads to a heated smoking area that overlooks the large garden. Seven handpumps dispense up to five changing guest beers, usually including locally brewed Funfair ales. The pub hosts live Saturday evening entertainment and regular beer festivals. (59)P

Stanton in Peak

Flying Childers

Main Road, DE4 2LW (off B6056 Bakewell-Ashbourne Rd) SK240643

12-2 (not Mon & Tue), 7-11; 12-3, 7-11 Sat & Sun

(01629) 636333

Black Sheep Best Bitter; Wells Bombardier; guest beers H

Created from four cottages during the 18th century, this is an unspoilt village pub named after a famous 18th-century racehorse owned by the Duke of Devonshire. It is located near the historic Stanton Moor and is popular with walkers, tourists and locals alike. Both rooms are welcoming with real fires, and there is a pleasant beer garden outside. Home-made soups and snacks are available at lunchtime and the guest beer changes regularly. Dogs are welcome. QP

Staveley

Speedwell Inn

Lowgates, S43 3TT

6-11 (10.30 Sun)

(01246) 474665

Townes IPA, Speedwell Bitter, Staveley Cross, Pynot Porter; guest beer H

Twice winner of Chesterfield CAMRA Pub of the Year, this is the brewery tap for Townes beers, which have been brewed here for the last 11 years. The regular ales and additional specials are supplemented by a small range of bottled and continental beers. Those who like the opportunity to join in (sometimes) lively conversation while propping up the bar and enjoying a pint or two will appreciate this modest pub. Q

Sutton Cum Duckmanton

Arkwright Arms

Chesterfield Road, S44 5JG (on A632)

11-11 (midnight Fri); 11-10.30 Sun

(01246) 232053 arkwrightarms.co.uk

Beer range varies H

There is always a warm welcome at this mock Tudor-fronted free house. All three rooms are made cosy with open fires. An excellent range of ever-changing guest ales, many from local micros, is complemented by ten ciders and two perries. Beer festivals are held at Easter and bank holidays, as well as mini events throughout the year. Winner of many CAMRA awards including East Midlands Pub of the Year 2008. (81,84)P

Thulston

Harrington Arms

4 Grove Close, DE72 3EY (off B5010)

11.30-3 (not Mon), 5-11; 11.30-11 Sat; 12-10.30 Sun

(01332) 571798

Draught Bass; Tollgate Earl of Harrington; guest beers H
Two former cottages, re-fronted to stand out and brightly lit after dark, have been smartly modernised without losing a cottagey feel. The pub has low, beamed ceilings, wooden-clad interior walls and open fires in winter. Regular beer festivals are held and an adjoining restaurant serves good food. Elvaston Castle Country Park, former estate of the Earls of Harrington (hence the names of the house beers) is close by. No food Sunday evening or Monday. P

Turnditch

Tiger Inn
232 Asbourne Road, DE56 2LH (on A517)
12-midnight (2am Fri & Sat)
(01773) 550200
Marston's Pedigree; guest beers H
Turnditch is a small village on a steep hill straddling the main road between Belper and Ashbourne, and the inn enjoys far reaching views over Ecclesbourne Valley. This former Ind Coope house is now a Marston's pub with five handpumps, usually all in full use. Thoughtful use of the open-plan layout has the dining area to one side and drinkers next to the bar. The landlord's cricket and tankard collection is on display. (113)P

Wardlow Mires

Three Stags Heads ★
SK17 8RW (A623/B6465 jct)
7 (11 Sat)-11; 12-10.30 Sun
(01298) 872268
Abbeydale Matins, Absolution, Black Lurcher; guest beers H
A quaint 300-year-old pub with two small rooms, stone-flagged floors and low ceilings. It is one of the few inns in the area on CAMRA's National Inventory of unspoilt pubs. An ancient range warms the bar and the house dogs – the house beer, Black Lurcher, takes its name from a former resident. No draught lager, but imported bottled lagers are available. QP

Whaley Bridge

Shepherd's Arms
7 Old Road, SK23 7HR
3-11 (1am Fri); 12-1am Sat; 12-11 Sun
(01663) 732384
Marston's Burton Bitter, Pedigree; guest beers H
This attractive, whitewashed stone-built pub has been preserved unspoilt, conveying the feel of the farmhouse it once was. The unchanged tap room, the best for miles around, is a delight, with open fire, flagged floor and scrubbed-top tables. Additionally there is a comfortable lounge and a small drinking area in the garden. A short walk from Whaley Bridge station, the pub is also on the 199 (Manchester Airport-Buxton) and other bus routes. Q(60,62,199)P

Whitehough

Old Hall Inn
SK23 6EJ (off B6062)
12-2, 5-11 (midnight Sat); 12-10.30 Sun
(01663) 750529 old-hall-inn.co.uk
Beer range varies H
Nestling in the attractive hamlet of Whitehough near Chinley, this charming 16th-century inn offers a warm welcome. Food and drink focuses on local produce, with two beers from local micros in addition to a Jennings ale and one from a regional brewer. The adjacent 14th-century Whitehough Hall, with minstrels gallery and mullioned windows, can be accessed directly from the inn and is used for medieval banquets and informal dining. (Chinley)P

Willington

Green Man
1 Canal Bridge, DE65 6BQ (by railway station)
11.30-11 (11.30 Wed & Thu; midnight Fri & Sat); 12-11 Sun
(01283) 702377
Draught Bass; Marston's Pedigree H**; guest beers** H/G
An attractive two-roomed pub at the heart of the village and not far from the canal. Dating back some 150 years, it features oak beams throughout, and traditional bench seating. Note the picture gallery of local landmarks in the lounge. The child-friendly rear garden is complemented by tables and chairs at the front. Live music is hosted regularly and good home-cooked food is served daily (not Sun eve). (V3)P

Winster

Old Bowling Green
East Bank, DE4 2DS
6-11 (midnight Fri & Sat); closed Mon, and Tue winter; 12-11.30 Sun
(01629) 650219 peakparkpub.co.uk
Beer range varies H
Popular 15th-century pub, located close to the market hall at the heart of this attractive Peak District village. A central bar serves a long main room with cosy log fire, and two smaller rooms. Up to four ever-changing beers from local micro-breweries are available, often coming from Bradfield and Abbeydale. Wholesome food is served evenings (Thu-Sat) and all day Sunday. Q(172)P

Wirksworth

Royal Oak
North End, DE4 4FG (off B5035)
8-11.30 (midnight Fri & Sat); 12-3, 7.30-11 Sun
(01629) 823000
Draught Bass; Taylor Landlord; Whim Hartington IPA; guest beers H
Excellent ultra-traditional local in a stone terrace near the market place, highlighted at night by fairy lights. The bar features old pictures of local interest and there is also a pool room and smoking grotto. The Oak combines a long-standing reputation for serving Bass alongside a choice of guest beers. The Ecclesbourne Valley railway line visitor attraction is not far away. Q(6.1)

What care I how time advances: I am drinking ale today. **Edgar Allan Poe**

Cider

Photography by Mark Bolton

NEW FOR 2009

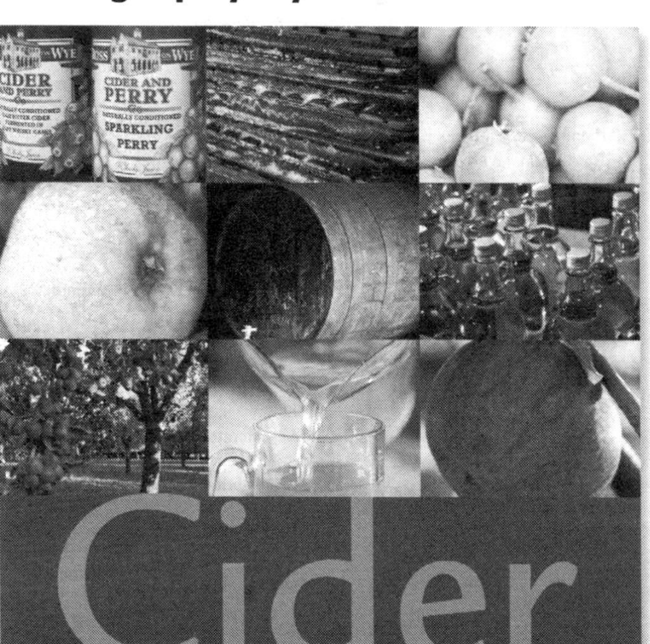

Proper cider and perry – made with apples and pears and nothing but, is a wonderful drink – but there's so much more to it than that. **Cider** is a lavishly illustrated celebration of real cider, and its close cousin perry, for anyone who wants to learn more about Britain's oldest drink. With features on the UK's most interesting and characterful cider and perry makers, how to make your own cider, foreign ciders, and the best places to drink cider – including unique dedicated cider houses, award-winning pubs and year-round CAMRA festivals all over the country – **Cider** is the essential book for any cider or perry lover.

"This book, clearly a work of devotion by its authors, represents a tour de force of the world of cider, covering history, recipes, museums, and a compendium of sources for both drink and trees. Lovingly written (with several critiques of the abomination of carbonised cider), the chapters are compiled by different experts in clear, accessible prose. Mark Bolton's warm images capture the emotional involvement of those involved in its production." BBC Countryfile Magazine

£14.99 ISBN 978-1-85249-259-5 Members' price £12.99 192 pages

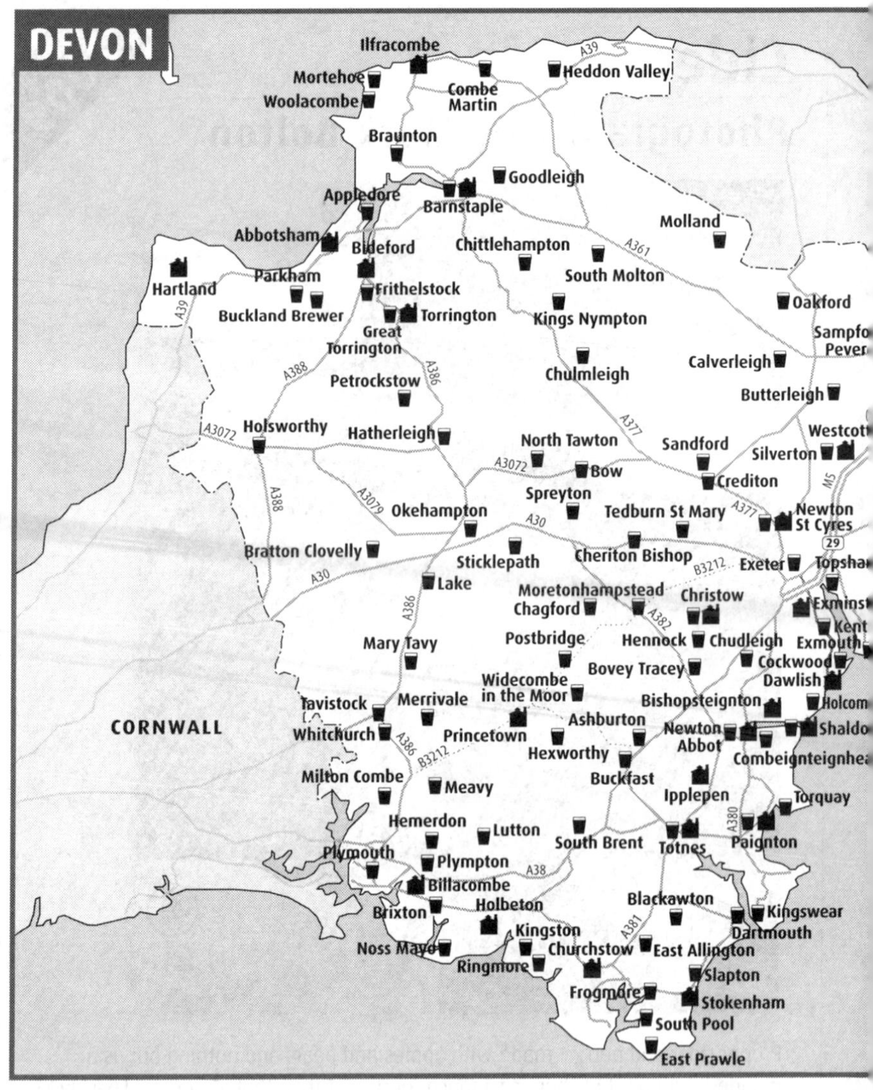

Appledore

Beaver Inn

2 Irsha Street, EX39 1RY SS462308
⏲ 11-midnight; 11.30-10.30 Sun
☎ (01237) 474822 🌐 beaverinn.co.uk
Beer range varies Ⓗ
Situated in the old part of a small fishing village with a long history of seafarers and shipbuilding, the pub enjoys superb views of the Taw and Torridge estuaries entering the Bristol Channel, particularly from the riverside patio. Nearby are attractive walks along the sands and quay towards Bideford and Westward Ho! The single bar has a choice of beers from three handpumps, mainly from West Country brewers, and Sam's cider from Winkleigh. Well-behaved children and dogs are welcome. Excellent pub food is available either in the bar or in the raised restaurant. Locally caught fish and chips is a speciality. ❀◐🚌(16,16A)♣●

Ashburton

Dartmoor Lodge ✔

Peartree Cross, TQ13 7JW (just off A38 at Peartee junction)
⏲ 11-11 (10.30 Sun)
☎ (01364) 652232 🌐 dartmoorlodge.co.uk
Dartmoor Jail Ale; O'Hanlon's Firefly; Teignworthy Old Moggie; guest beer Ⓗ
Friendly and comfortable roadside hotel, now back in private ownership, on the edge of the Dartmoor National Park and the town of Ashburton. A beamed bar and restaurant area with a log fire in winter make for a welcoming visit, while a good selection of local real ales and food is served, with plenty of seating in the bar area. Rooms are available for meetings and conferences, in addition to overnight accommodation in 24 bedrooms. An ideal base for exploring this breathtaking part of the country. ⛰Q🍺❀🛏◐♿▲🚌(X38,88)P⁴–

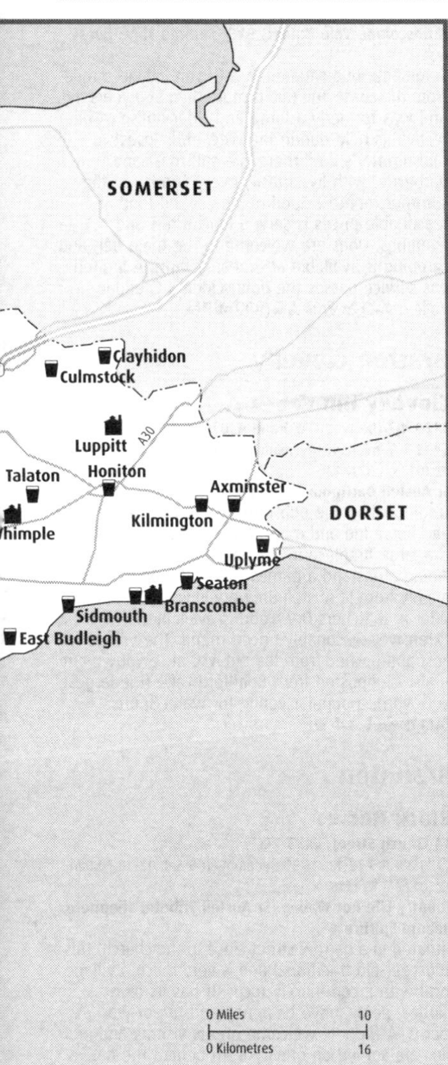

Exeter Inn

26 West Street, TQ13 7DU (opp church)
⏲ 11-2.30, 5-11 (midnight Fri & Sat); 12-3, 7-10.30 Sun
☎ (01364) 652013
Badger First Gold; Dartmoor IPA; guest beer Ⓗ
This friendly local, built in 1131, is the oldest pub in Ashburton, with additions in the 17th century. It was built to house the workers that constructed the nearby church and the inn was used by Sir Francis Drake on his journeys to London. The main bar is L-shaped, rustic and wood panelled, with a canopy. There are two main drinking areas either side of the entrance hallway and a further bar at the back, served via a small hatch and counter.
Q❀◑⊟(X38,88)♣⁻

Axminster

Lamb Inn

Lyme Road, EX13 5BE
⏲ 11.30-midnight (1am Fri; 2am Sat)
☎ (01297) 33922
Branscombe Vale Branoc; guest beers Ⓗ
A traditional local half a mile from the town centre. The single-room interior has a comfortable bar, areas for dining and playing pool, plus a large-screen TV that often shows sport. There is a large garden with two boules pistes and a heated smokers' shelter. The landlady's pub grub is very good and great value. The WCs are not to full disabled standard, but have a good level of access, and are worth a visit just for the pictures. No dogs please because the resident pub dog gets very jealous. ❀◑⊟(31)P⁻

Barnstaple

Panniers ✔

33-34 Boutport Street, EX31 1RX
⏲ 9-midnight (1am Fri & Sat)
☎ (01271) 329720
Greene King IPA, Abbot; Marston's Pedigree; Shepherd Neame Spitfire; guest beers Ⓗ
Popular Wetherspoon's in the town centre close to the Queens Theatre, cinema, shops and pannier market. The selection of real ales is unrivalled in the area, with the majority of guest beers coming from Devon/West Country breweries. There is a large selection of continental and bottled beers and the cider is from Westons. Regular beer festivals offer discounted real ales with food and drink offers on themed food days. The rear garden area is a suntrap and offers covered seating for less clement weather. ♞❀◑♿⊟●⁻

Rolle Quay Inn ✔

Rolle Quay, EX31 1JE
⏲ 11 (12 Sun)-midnight (1am Fri & Sat)
☎ (01271) 345182
St Austell IPA, HSD, Dartmoor Best; guest beers Ⓗ
Two minutes from Barnstaple town centre, yet close to the River Yeo and adjacent to the Tarka Trail and its cycle-hire facility, this spacious, well

INDEPENDENT BREWERIES

Barum Barnstaple
Bays Paignton
Beer Engine Newton St Cyres
Branscombe Vale Branscombe
Bridgetown Totnes
Clearwater Torrington
Country Life Abbotsham
Dartmoor Princetown
Dartmouth Newton Abbot
Devon Earth Paignton
Exe Valley Silverton
Exeter Exminster
Forge Hartland (NEW)
Gargoyles Dawlish
Gidleys Christow
Hunter's Ipplepen (NEW)
Jollyboat Bideford
O'Hanlon's Whimple
Otter Luppitt
Quercus Churchstow
Red Rock Bishopsteignton
Ringmore Shaldon
South Hams Stokenham
Summerskills Billacombe
Teignworthy Newton Abbot
Union Holbeton
Wizard Ilfracombe

run two-bar pub is also handy for the local rugby and football grounds. The landlord, a previous local CAMRA Pub of the Year winner, is passionate about real ale so the guest beers change regularly. A good quality menu, including children's portions, is available, with Sunday lunch a particular favourite among the locals. Super-league darts, skittles, pool and euchre are played here.
(3,303)

Blackawton

George Inn

Main Street, TQ9 7BG
12-3, 5 (7 Sun)-11
(01803) 712342
Dartmoor Jail Ale; Teignworthy Springtide; guest beers H
A friendly local in the heart of the village, this two-room pub has a lot of character and is said to be haunted. An annual beer festival in May coincides with the village's worm-charming festival. Three cask ales are always available, with more in summer months. There is a separate room for family dining. QP

Bovey Tracey

Cromwell Arms

Fore Street, TQ13 9AE
11-11; 12-10.30 Sun
(01626) 833473 thecromwellarms.co.uk
St Austell IPA, Tribute, Proper Job; guest beers H
A roomy, comfortable 17th-century town centre pub with plenty of character, a ghost and beams throughout. Popular with locals and visitors alike, it has one large room with three separate areas, one of which is specifically for drinkers. In addition there is a smart dining room where good value, wholesome food is served seven days a week. Guest beers tend to be seasonal. In this busy town the car park is very useful. (39)P

Bow

White Hart Hotel

EX17 6EN
12-3 (not Mon), 6-11; 12-11 Sat; 12-3, 6.30-10.30
(01363) 881287 whitehartbow.co.uk
Greene King Old Speckled Hen; Skinner's Betty Stogs; guest beers H
Sixteenth-century coaching inn with stone flagstones and wooden panelling surrounded by wood beams throughout, plus a roaring log fire, creating a warm, welcoming ambience. The pub is popular with locals, including the village football and pool teams, and there are many photographs of village and sporting life. A large garden features hog roasts and an annual firework display. Dogs and children are welcome if well-behaved. Quiz night is every third Thursday, and Irish folk music plays every first Wednesday. Food is locally sourced from within 20 miles. Cider is Sam's Medium.
(51,315)P

Branscombe

Fountain Head Inn

EX12 3BG
11-3, 6-11; 12-10.30 Sun
(01297) 680359 thefountainheadinn.com
Branscombe Vale Branoc, BVB, Summa That; guest beers H
Traditional pub situated in a Devon village a mile from the coast. The pub is more than 500 years old, and was formerly a forge and cider house. A beer festival is held during the weekend closest to Midsummer's day. There is a spit roast and barbecue, with live music, every Sunday in the summer months. Good home-cooked food at reasonable prices is served lunchtimes and evenings. Dogs are welcome in the main bar, and camping is available at a nearby farm. A limited bus service passes the door. Cider is Cheddar Valley. Q(899)P

Bratton Clovelly

Clovelly Inn

EX20 4JZ (between A30 and A3079) SX465920
12-3, 6-midnight; 12-midnight Sat & Sun
(01837) 871447
St Austell Dartmoor Best; guest beers H
Traditional village pub formerly known as the Old Packhorse Inn and more than 150 years old. There is a large fireplace in the bar, plus two separate dining areas and a games room. The beers are mainly from St Austell Brewery in Cornwall and the cider is Thatchers Dry. Food is available from an extensive, reasonably-priced menu. The village is best approached from the old A30 at Lewdown but is also signposted from Roadford Lake (the largest in Devon), a popular venue for water sports.
QP

Braunton

Black Horse

34 Church Street, EX33 2EL
11.30-2, 5.30-11; 11.30-midnight Fri & Sat; 12-10.30 Sun
(01271) 812386
Country Life Pot Wallop; St Austell Tribute; Shepherd Neame Spitfire G
Situated in a narrow street close to the church, this 400-year-old traditional pub is very much a village local with a community focus. It has its own skittles, pool, shove ha'penny and tug-of-war teams. A friendly welcome greets visitors and all ales are served on gravity from behind the bar. Three small, popular beer festivals are held every year. There is an unobtrusive flat-screen TV and a separate dining area where food is served every evening in summer, but weekends only in winter.
(3,3A,303)P

Brixton

Foxhound

Kingsbridge Road, PL8 2AH
11 (12 Sun)-11 (midnight Fri & Sat)
(01752) 880271 foxhoundinn.co.uk
Courage Best Bitter; guest beers H
This late 18th-century roadside inn was recently briefly known as the Foxhound Clipper, reflecting the disputed claim that it was given to the captain of a customs ship as his reward for successful capture of local pirates. Now back to its original name, it is a popular two-bar village pub serving good food, with a darts team, jazz evenings and a monthly quiz night. Guest beers include at least one from the local Summerskills Brewery, alongside Thatchers Cheddar Valley cider.
(93,94)P

Buckfast

Abbey Inn ✔

TQ11 0EA (off A38, follow signs to Buckfast Abbey)
11 (12 Sun)-11
(01364) 642343
St Austell Dartmoor Best, Tribute, HSD H
Large inn within Dartmoor National Park, close to the famous Buckfast Abbey. The pub is situated in a beautiful setting next to the River Dart and has an outside terrace with seating and views overlooking the river, including glimpses of the Abbey. Inside, the warm and welcoming oak-panelled bar is spacious, with traditional furniture. The large dining room serves an excellent range of food and there any many visitor attractions within close vicinity of the pub. (X38,88)P

Buckland Brewer

Coach & Horses

Buckland Brewer, EX39 5LU SS423206
12-3, 5.30 (6.30 Sun)-11.30
(01237) 451395
Skinner's Betty Stogs; Cotleigh Golden Seahawk Premium Bitter; Shepherd Neame Spitfire H
A 13th-century, low beamed, thatched two-storey inn reputedly used as a court room in the 17th century, with the cellars as a gaol and an execution drop in the main bar. There is a woodburner with antique settle and a small back room where darts and pool are played. The skittle alley doubles as a function room. Quizzes are held three times a year and the frontage is used for drinking and dining alfresco. An old innkeeper's house is available to rent nearby. QP

Butterleigh

Butterleigh Inn

EX15 1PN (opp church)
12-2.30, 6-11; 12-3, 6-11 Sun
(01884) 855407
Cotleigh Tawny; O'Hanlon's Yellowhammer; guest beers H
An excellent country pub in a quaint village, this splendid 17th-century Devon cob building is full of character for all ages. Nice and quiet during the week for the mature clientele, and busy at the weekends for the younger generation, when a great atmosphere creates more diverse conversation. There is always a choice of three ales in house. The pub has a main bar and lounge with a modern, sympathetically styled dining room. Drink inside or outside, with lovely surroundings either way. QP

Calverleigh

Rose & Crown Inn

EX16 8BA (on old Rackenford Road)
11.30-midnight; 12-11.30 Sun
(01884) 256301
Otter Ale; Taylor Landlord; guest beers H
Traditional 17th-century country pub not far from the town of Tiverton, with a restaurant, beer garden and skittle alley that doubles as a function room and library with more than 600 books. Excellent home-cooked food, made with local produce where possible, is available, together with local cider from Palmershayes across the road. P

Chagford

Sandy Park Inn ✔

Sandy Park, TQ13 8JW (on A382 Moretonhampstead-Whiddon Down road)
12-11
(01647) 433267 sandyparkinn.co.uk
O'Hanlon's Yellowhammer; Otter Bitter; St Austell Tribute H**; guest beer** H/G
Thatched free house, thought to be 17th century, in a hamlet within Dartmoor National Park. The main bar has a large open fireplace, ancient beams, stone flooring and pews at the tables, while a small snug is set around a large table. Another bar becomes an intimate restaurant serving excellent home-cooked food at weekends. Castle Drogo (National Trust), Fingle Bridge and the village of Chagford are nearby. At the front of the pub is parking for up to six cars. QP

Cheriton Bishop

Old Thatch Inn

EX6 6JH (¼ mile off A30, 10 miles W of Exeter) XS775930
11.30-3, 6-11 (not Sun eve)
(01647) 24204 theoldthatchinn.com
O'Hanlon's Royal Oak; Otter Ale; guest beer H
Totally and sympathetically refurbished throughout 2007 following a fire, this is a traditional Grade II-listed thatched free house, originally built as a coaching house. On the eastern edge of Dartmoor, it is popular with walkers and welcomes dogs. Four handpumps serve West Country ales. Exmoor Brewery supplies the popular third pint glasses. The restaurant-style menu offers a good selection, and there is a specials board too, all using local produce, and a choice of two roasts on Sunday. Q(X30,173)P

Chittlehampton

Bell Inn

The Square, EX37 9QL (opp church)
11-3, 6-midnight; 11-midnight Sat; 12-11 Sun
(01769) 540368 thebellatchittlehampton.co.uk
Beer range varies H/G
Local CAMRA Pub of the Year 2007, this 18th-century village-centre inn is popular with locals and visitors alike. The landlord is passionate about real ale and offers West Country beers at attractive prices along with Thatchers cider and a large range of whiskies. Good value food using local produce is served in the bar, the dining conservatory or the attractive garden. The garden has a children's play area with views of alpacas in the adjacent orchard. A music jam night is held on the second Monday of each month.

Christow

Teign House Inn

Teign Valley Road, EX6 7PL (on B3193)
12-3, 5-11.30; 12-11.30 Sat & Sun
(01647) 252286 teignhouseinn.co.uk
Dartmoor Jail Ale; Sharp's Doom Bar; guest beers H
This welcoming, atmospheric country pub, with lots of beams and a warming log fire, has strong local community support. The sizeable garden attracts the families of locals and visitors alike, while an adjoining large field has space for four caravans as well as campers. An annual beer festival with up to 30 beers is held on the second weekend in July.

Great pub food, all home-cooked, includes a gluten-free menu. Two guest beers are available, both from West Country breweries.
♨❀◑♿⛺🚌(360)P⚐

Chudleigh

Bishop Lacy

52-53 Fore Street, TQ13 0HY
⏲ 12-midnight (1am Fri & Sat); 12-10.30 Sun
☎ (01626) 854585
O'Hanlon's Yellowhammer; Sharp's Doom Bar; guest beers Ⓗ
Welcoming and historic pub with a Grade II-listing and a recently discovered medieval window. The left-hand bar has a magnificent fireplace and witches adjoining the bar (ask the landlady to explain). The right hand bar or 'real ale bar' attracts members of a well-supported real ale club on Wednesday evening. West Country beers predominate while excellent home-cooked food is served in both bars and the restaurant area. Sensible dogs and well-behaved children are always welcome. ♨Q◑🚌(39,182)●

Chulmleigh

Old Court House

South Molton Street, EX18 7BW
⏲ 11.30-midnight
☎ (01769) 580045 🌐 oldcourthouseinn.co.uk
St Austell Tribute; guest beers Ⓗ
Grade II-listed historic thatched local where Charles I held court in 1634. A huge coat of arms commemorating the event dominates one of the bedrooms. Guest beers, mostly from the South West area, change regularly, and the cider is Thatchers Dry. Thursday quiz night supports local charities and a folk night is held every second Tuesday of the month. The harvest festival includes a religious service held in the bar by the local vicar. Food is served all day up until 9.30pm.
♨❀🛏◑🚌(377)♣●⚐

Clayhidon

Half Moon Inn

EX15 3TJ
⏲ 12-3, 6-11 (not Mon); 12-3, 7-10.30 Sun
☎ (01823) 680291 🌐 halfmoondevon.co.uk
Otter Bitter; guest beers Ⓗ
Traditional country inn set in the Blackdown Hills near the Somerset border, with spectacular views over the Culm Valley. It was probably built originally as a cottage in the 13th century for stonemasons to live in while they constructed the nearby church. The menu offers fresh, locally-sourced foods, plus themed evenings such as a pie night on Tuesday. Live musical entertainment plays on most Wednesdays. Two guest beers are available and a beer festival is held each May.
♨❀◑⛺♣P

Cockwood

Anchor Inn

Starcross, EX6 8RA (on A379, outside Starcross, next to small harbour)
⏲ 11-11 (10.30 Sun)
☎ (01626) 890203 🌐 anchorinncockwood.com
Draught Bass; Otter Bright, Bitter, Ale; Taylor Landlord Ⓗ
Opposite a picturesque harbour, this ancient inn has a wealth of old settles, timber panelling, very low beams and snug areas. It has been extended into the old village hall, with an impressive display of old nautical memorabilia, and now features live music of various genres at least three times a week. The pub is best known for its national award-winning and very extensive seafood menu. This is a most atmospheric inn, a real Devon gem.
♨Q❀◑♿⛺⇌(Starcross)🚌♣P⚐

Combe Martin

Castle Inn

High Street, EX34 0HS (opp church)
⏲ 12-1.30am
☎ (01271) 883706 🌐 castleinn.info
Worthington Bitter; guest beers Ⓗ
Main-street pub with wood-panelled walls and a huge fireplace with a log fire in winter. The pool room leads to a large purpose-built function room which holds a fortnightly folk club and hosts live music to suit other tastes in between. The cider is from Winkleigh and good value pub food is served daily. The large rear garden holds summer barbecues and a small annual beer festival takes place during carnival week in August. Skittles, darts, table football, pool and big-screen Sky TV are available here. ♨🐎❀◑♿⛺🚌(3,30)♣●P⚐

Combeinteignhead

Wild Goose

TQ12 4RA
⏲ 11-2.30, 5.30-11; 12-2.30, 7-10.30 Sun
☎ (01626) 872241
Sharp's Doom Bar; guest beers Ⓗ
A 17th-century free house in an attractive village. There are always six regularly changing real ales on handpump, with one at a lower price. The long bar with a genuine beamed ceiling has seating, tables and fireplaces at each end. A charming dining area overlooks the large rural garden. Freshly-cooked food is served with fresh fish, local produce and vegetarian options available. A beer festival is held within the pub each September.
♨Q❀◑♿⛺♣●P

Crediton

Crediton Inn

28A Mill Street, EX17 1EZ
⏲ 11-11; 12-3, 7-10.30 Sun
☎ (01363) 772882 🌐 crediton-inn.co.uk
Fuller's London Pride; Sharp's Doom Bar; guest beers Ⓗ
A 19th-century inn according to the framed deeds of 1878, with windows etched with the ancient seal of the town. This genuine free house is well supported by locals. Following recent refurbishment it now has eight handpumps dispensing ale from local breweries, and hosts an ale festival in November. The skittle alley doubles as a function room, and good home-cooked food is served at weekends, with snacks available at other times. The bubbly owner is the longest serving landlady in Crediton, having been here for 30 years. ♨❀◑⇌🚌(50,51,315)♣P⚐

Culmstock

Culm Valley Inn

EX15 3JJ
12-4, 6-11; 11-11 Sat; 12-10.30 Sun
☎ (01884) 840354
Beer range varies G
Three hundred-year-old village inn situated by the river Culm, near to where it emerges from the Blackdown Hills. The car park was formerly the railway sidings of the Tiverton Light Railway, and the pub was previously called the Railway Inn. Local produce, often organic and free range, features on the menu, while Bollhayes and Tricky ciders are served from the cask. There is a beer festival every end of May bank holiday weekend. Q ♣ P

Dartmouth

Cherub Inn

13 Higher Street, TQ6 9RB
11-11 summer; 11-2.30, 5.30-11 winter; 12-10.30 summer, 12-2.30, 5.30-10.30 winter Sun
☎ (01803) 832571 the-cherub.co.uk
St Austell Proper Job; guest beers H
This nautical town is famous for its Tudor buildings and the Cherub is one of the best. Grade II-listed, it is the oldest house in Dartmouth and in the 14th century was a merchant's home. The bar is small and cosy with many original features including some old ships' timbers as beams. A lovely old staircase leads to the next two floors which house the restaurant. Three cask ales are available (two in winter). Q

Royal Castle Hotel

The Quay, TQ6 9PS
9-11
☎ (01803) 833033 royalcastle.co.uk
Bays Gold; Dartmoor Jail Ale; Sharp's Doom Bar H
The Galleon Bar offers three real ales (no sparklers used) in a comfortable, large but cosy lounge. Wood panelling and beams dominate the decor and give the room a traditional feel, while old firearms adorn the walls. Situated in the town centre, on the quay, the bar is very popular with visitors but retains the support of the locals.

East Allington

Fortescue Arms

TQ9 7RA
12-2.30 (not Mon), 6-11; 12-2.30, 6-10.30 Sun
☎ (01548) 521215 fortescue-arms.co.uk
Butcombe Bitter; Quercus Shingle Bay; guest beers H
Divided into two distinct parts with a welcoming, traditional bar on one side and a restaurant on the other, both with real fires, this attractive village pub is well supported by residents and local organisations. Beers are from West Country brewers and this is a welcome outlet for the Quercus Brewery. The garden has an abundance of flowers in summer and an alfresco dining area. The bar menu includes highly recommended stews and curries. Q P

East Budleigh

Sir Walter Raleigh

22 High Street, EX9 7ED (on B3170)
11.45-2.30, 6-11; 7-11 Sun
☎ (01395) 442510
Adnams Broadside; Otter Bitter; St Austell Tribute H
A pleasant 16th-century pub located at the top of the village at the junction with Hayes Lane which leads to the birthplace of Sir Walter Raleigh. Due to the demographic nature of the local community, the pub is busiest at lunchtime and in the early evening. There is a varied selection of good food in this quiet friendly pub. No gaming machines or muzak, but dogs are welcome in the main bar. Q (157) ♣

East Prawle

Pig's Nose Inn

TQ7 2BY SX781364
12-2.30, 7-11 (closed Mon and Sun eve winter)
☎ (01548) 511209 pigsnoseinn.co.uk
Bays Gold; South Hams Devon Pride, G**; Eddystone** H
An old three-roomed smugglers' inn on the village green in an area that attracts birdwatchers and coastal walkers. Gravity beers are stored on a specially made rack in an alcove behind the bar and wholesome home-cooked food made with local ingredients is available. Children and dogs are welcome in the cluttered interior with its maritime theme. Occasional live music is performed at weekends in a hall adjoining the pub. ♣

Exeter

City Gate Hotel

Iron Bridge, North Street, EX4 3RB
11-11 (midnight Fri & Sat); 12-11 Sun
☎ (01392) 495811 citygatehotel.co.uk
Wells Bombardier; Young's Bitter, Special; guest beers H
Now Wells and Young's, this attractively-refurbished city centre hotel has pleasant and well-furnished outdoor courtyard areas beneath the ancient city wall, with ample covered space for smokers. Beers are restricted to the Wells and Young's range, including Courage, with a good selection of bottled beers to take home. Food is served throughout the day, a function room is available and a cellar bar provides occasional live music. (Central/St David's)

Fat Pig

2 John Street, EX1 1BL (near Corn Exchange)
12-3, 5-11; 12-midnight Sat & Sun
☎ (01392) 437217
Exeter Avocet; Hop Back Crop Circle; O'Hanlon's Yellowhammer H
Originally dating from the 1800s, this small freehold pub was refurbished in 2007, exposing original woodwork. The emphasis is on original and locally sourced food and drink, including a Farmers Organic monthly market. Apart from local ales, ciders and own produced perry, other draught products include Budvar Dark and Light. A light, airy feel is complemented by a friendly and warm welcome. Well behaved children and dogs are allowed, daytime only. There is live music on Sunday lunchtime. Q (Central)

First & Last

90 Cowick Street, St Thomas, EX4 1HL
11-11; 12-10.30 Sun
☎ (01392) 439403/438437

Hop Back GFB, Odyssey, Crop Circle, Summer Lightning, seasonal beers 🄷
Genuine community pub with a diverse clientele, acquired by Hop Back in 2007. It lies about a quarter of a mile from Exeter St Thomas rail station and is well served by several bus routes. It has darts and pool teams, and features old photos of the area on the walls. Acoustic music sessions are held fortnightly and guest beers come from the Hop Back and Downton range. Westons cider is also available, and biannual beer festivals are held.
⛼⇌(St Thomas)🚌●P⚐

Great Western Hotel

St David's Station Approach, EX4 4NU
⏲ 11-11; 12-10.30 Sun
☎ (01392) 274039 🌐 greatwesternhotel.co.uk
Branscombe Vale Branoc; Dartmoor Jail Ale; Exeter Avocet; O'Hanlon's Yellowhammer, Port Stout; RCH Pitchfork 🄷
Featuring a large range of ales from around the country, in addition to the regular beers, this traditional two-bar railway hotel has a good community spirit. It has twice won a local CAMRA Pub of the Year award. Beer festivals are usually held over the bank holidays. Well-priced meals with a varied menu are available in the bar or the Brunel restaurant, including a Sunday carvery and steak and curry nights. Children and dogs are welcome. ⛼Q❀⛾◑♿⇌(St David's)🚌(H)

Imperial ✔

New North Road, EX4 4AH
⏲ 9-midnight (1am Fri & Sat)
☎ (01392) 434050
Greene King Abbot; Marston's Pedigree; guest beers 🄷
This large Wetherspoon pub, converted from the Imperial Hotel, is close to the city centre, college and university, and to both of Exeter's main railway stations. It has a very wide clientele of families, OAPs and students. The ale range is very good, supporting micros both local and nationwide; there is always a choice of up to ten ales. The beautiful, mature gardens sweep down the hill towards St David's Station. The Orangery is an architectural delight, and festivals are frequent and extensive. This is one of the best pubs in the area.
Q❀◑⛾♿⇌(Central/St David's)🚌●P⚐

Old Fire House

50 New North Road, EX4 4EP
⏲ 12-2.30, 5-2am; 12-3am Fri; 5-3am Sat; 12-1am Sun
☎ (01392) 277279
Sharp's Doom Bar; Wychwood Hobgoblin; guest beers 🄶
Situated close to the bus and Exeter Central rail stations, this popular city centre pub serves good value food at lunchtime and evenings, including late-night pizzas available until 1am, plus roasts on Sunday. Two regular beers plus up to eight ever-changing guests are from South West breweries. Two draught ciders and bottled ciders are always available. Live music plays on Friday and Saturday evenings. Beer festivals are held on all bank holidays. A dress code applies – no sports wear or baseball caps. This gem is well worth seeking out.
❀◑⇌🚌●⚐

Well House Tavern

16-17 Cathedral Yard, EX1 1HD
⏲ 11-11 (midnight Fri & Sat); 12-10.30 Sun
☎ (01392) 223611 🌐 michaelcaines.com/taverns
O'Hanlon's Yellow Hammer; Sharp's Doom Bar; guest beers 🄷
In an historic setting overlooking the Cathedral and converted from two shops in an ancient building, this tavern is at the heart of Exeter's tourist trade. It is part of the Royal Clarence Hotel owned by two-star Michelin chef Michael Caines, but stands on its own as a place to sup ale while watching the world go by. The two regular ales are augmented by four more, usually from local brewers. Beer and cider festivals are a regular feature, and live music plays on the last Sunday of the month. Cider is Rich's Farmhouse. ◑♿⇌🚌♣●

Exmouth

First & Last Inn

10 Church Street, EX8 1PE (off B3178 Rolle Street)
⏲ 11-11 (11.30 Sat); 12-10.30
☎ (01395) 263275
Courage Directors; O'Hanlon's Yellowhammer; Otter Ale 🄷**; guest beer** 🄶
This late Victorian pub is just a few minutes from the shopping centre, with a public car park opposite. A genuine free house much enlarged by the present owners, it provides three distinct drinking areas. Outside is a patio area with heated awnings. Games, including table football, are prominent, as is televised sport. Live music is performed on Sunday. Well-behaved dogs are welcome. The guest beer is normally from the West Country and the cider is Thatchers Dry.
❀♿⇌🚌♣●⚐

Frithelstock

Clinton Arms

EX38 8JH (signed from A386 between Torrington & Bideford) SS464194
⏲ 12-3, 6-11; 12-11 Sat; 12-10.30 Sun
☎ (01805) 623279 🌐 clintonarms.co.uk
Clearwater Cavalier; St Austell Tribute; guest beers 🄷
Nestling behind the village green of a pleasant hamlet, this popular country inn has been sympathetically improved by the owners. The semi-circular bar is at one end of a deceptively spacious, yet cosy L-shaped room, while steps lead down to an intimate restaurant area. The cider is Sam's from Winkleigh and outside, in front of the pub, the village green doubles as a beer garden. Live music sessions are held regularly. Permits are available for fly fishing on the River Torridge. Accommodation is en-suite. ⛼Q❀⛾◑●P

Frogmore

Globe Inn

TQ7 2NR
⏲ 12-2.30 (not Mon), 6-11; 12-3, 6.30-10.30 Sun
☎ (01548) 531351 🌐 theglobeinn.co.uk
Otter Ale; Skinners Betty Stogs; South Hams Eddystone; guest beer 🄷
This pub can be reached by car, bus or boat (tidal Frogmore creek). Very popular with locals and visitors, the Globe has ample places to sit and enjoy the fine West Country beers. Full meals and light snacks are served in the restaurant area which has room for families. There is folk music on the third Thursday of each month. Eight en-suite rooms are available. Look out for the amusing comments on boards at the front of the pub.
⛼♉❀⛾◑🚌(93)P

Goodleigh

New Inn

EX32 7LX SS599341
12-2.30, 6-11; 12-3, 7-10.30 Sun
(01271) 342488
Sharp's Cornish Jack, Special; guest beer H
The rural setting of this traditional old village inn is a pleasant contrast to the expanding area of Barnstaple less than two miles away. A warm welcome awaits from the friendly licensees. There is one large bar on two levels boasting an eclectic range of decor and furnishings, with a wood-burning fire and old beams. High quality, home-cooked, locally-sourced food is served, with the emphasis on meat, game and fish. Facilities include skittles and darts, with a beer garden for warmer months. Well-behaved dogs are welcome.

Great Torrington

Torrington Arms

170 New Street, EX38 8BX (on A386)
11-11; 12-10.30 Sun
(01805) 622280
Clearwater Cavalier; St Austell Dartmoor Best; guest beers H
Traditional open plan pub in a town with historic links to the Civil War. Note the photos of local Cavalier bonfire events which have been taking place for over 40 years, and archive prints of regulars. There is a good atmosphere, and a real fire, in the main part of the bar and a small dining area at the rear. At the back of the pub, on the way to the patio where occasional live music events take place, is a spacious function room/restaurant with real ale. (70,71,315)

Hatherleigh

Tally Ho!

14 Market Street, EX20 3JN (opp church)
12 (11 Tue)-11; 12-11 Sun
(01837) 810306 tallyhohatherleigh.co.uk
Clearwater Cavalier; St Austell Tribute; guest beers H
Oak-beamed 15th-century inn with a single bar which has two wood-burning fires. There are three real ales available, which are significantly reduced in price from 11-3pm on Tuesday market day. Cider is Sam's from Winkleigh. Good quality food made with local produce is served in the bar or separate dining room. The garden also has a barbecue and covered smoking area. A disused railway line is available nearby for walkers, and fishing is available on the River Torridge.
(86)

Heddon Valley

Hunters Inn

EX31 4PY (signed from A399) SS655483
10-11
(01598) 763230 thehuntersinn.net
Exmoor Ale, Hart, Gold, Stag, Beast; guest beers H
Expansive building set in the spectacularly beautiful Heddon Valley with a large front garden. More gardens to the rear lead to paths accessing the surrounding countryside and Heddon's Mouth cove. The single bar has two adjacent rooms (there are plans to restore the old bar) plus a large function room. A welcoming atmosphere means the pub is popular with walkers/hikers, families with children and dog owners. A popular beer festival takes place over three days in September and themed evenings are held each Sunday. A remote, unique inn that is well worth searching out.

Hemerdon

Miners Arms

PL7 5BU
12-3, 5.30-midnight; 12-midnight Sun
(01752) 336040 theminersarmspub.co.uk
Draught Bass; guest beers H
Dating from 1783, this gastro pub is well worth seeking out. The friendly atmosphere and delightful location ensure its family-friendly popularity. A spacious children's play area enables parents to relax and enjoy bar snacks and meals alfresco on a summer's day. The Garden Restaurant, in the conservatory, has a dining area and patio with views towards Plymouth Sound, but the bar remains traditional and features a locally-mined slate floor. Look out for the authentic wishing well hidden in the snug.
(58,59)

Hennock

Palk Arms

Church Road, TQ13 9QB
7-midnight Mon, Tue & Fri; 11.30-2.30, 6-11 Wed, Thu & Sat; 12-10.30 Sun
(01626) 836584
Bays Gold; Otter Bitter; St Austell Tribute; guest beers H
Slightly off the beaten track, involving a climb up the Dartmoor Hills, but well worth the effort. The pub was named after the local landowner who gave his name to the straits between India and Sri Lanka. It was originally a 16th-century building with an adjoining cider house and, allegedly, a Victorian ghost. The front bar is dominated by a magnificent fireplace and no-nonsense furniture, while the rear has a collection of musical instruments. From here there are superb views of the Teign Valley.

Hexworthy

Forest Inn

PL20 6SD (on unclassified road linking Holne & B3357)
11-2.30, 6-11
(01364) 631211 theforestinn.co.uk
Teignworthy Reel Ale; guest beers H
A country inn situated in the Dartmoor Forest that welcomes walkers, horse riders, anglers, canoeists, dogs and children. Two Teignworthy beers and a varying local cider are available year-round, with a further guest ale in summer. Good home-made food, using local produce wherever possible, and accommodation, including en-suite guest rooms and a bunkhouse, are offered. The bar area has recently been attractively refurbished. Horses can be stabled by prior arrangement, and Duchy of Cornwall fishing permits are available for holders of a current NRA licence.

Holcombe

Smugglers Inn

27 Teignmouth Road, EX7 0LA (on A379 between Dawlish and Teignmouth)

11-11; 12-10.30 Sun

☎ (01626) 862301 thesmugglersinn.net

Draught Bass; Teignworthy Reel Ale; guest beers Ⓗ

With splendid coastal views, this roadside free house has an excellent reputation for food. The bar area has a wood-burning stove and the beer policy is to rotate West Country ales with one national brew. The outside area is popular and there is a separate smokers' canopy. Families are welcome in a dedicated area, and disabled facilities are excellent. Beer festivals are held. There is a large car park, and buses pass the door.

(2)P

Holsworthy

Old Market Inn

Chapel Street, EX22 6AY (on A388 S of town square)

11-midnight (1am Fri & Sat); 12-11 Sun

☎ (01409) 253941 oldmarketinn.co.uk

Bays Gold; Sharp's Doom Bar; Skinner's Betty Stogs; guest beers Ⓗ

Situated on the outskirts of this historic market town mentioned in the Domesday Book, this is a family-run inn and free house that has been tastefully renovated by the current owners. There are usually four real ales available, the majority of West Country origin, and the favoured cider is Autumn Scrumpy from Winkleigh. The restaurant is relaxed and informal, serving locally-sourced food to a high standard. Wednesday is very busy with a thriving outdoor Pannier Market nearby in the town. (X9,X90)P

Rydon Inn

Rydon Road, EX22 7HU (half mile W of Holsworthy on A3072 Bude road) SS335041

11.30-3, 6-11 (closed Mon winter); 12-3, 6-10.30 (not winter eve) Sun

☎ (01409) 259444 rydon-inn.com

Sharp's Doom Bar; guest beers Ⓗ

A spacious, modern extension to an original Devon longhouse. This free house and licensed wedding venue is ideally situated for the market town of Holsworthy and just a few miles from the north Cornish coast around Bude. The bar area has a thatched bar and a high vaulted ceiling, making it light and airy, with a cosy fire in winter. It also has a large conservatory restaurant serving excellent award-winning food. Well-behaved children are welcome. Q(X9,X90)P

Honiton

Holt

178 High Street, EX14 1LA

11-3, 5.30-11; 5.30-midnight Sat; closed Sun & Mon

☎ (01404) 47707 theholt-honiton.com

Otter Bitter, Bright, Ale, Head Ⓗ

Otter Brewery's first pub has been converted from a former wine bar. The cosy bar at street level is popular with locals, and there is a dining area upstairs – both are smartly decorated, with plenty of exposed wood that adds character. The kitchen is in full view of the clientele – in addition to the regular restaurant food, there are lunchtime specials plus tapas-style snacks. Seasonal music festivals are held.

Kenton

Dolphin Inn

Fore Street, EX6 8LD (on A379 in village centre)

11-11 (11.30 Fri); 11 (12 winter)-midnight Sat; 12-10.30 Sun

☎ (01626) 891371

Exmoor Ale; guest beers Ⓗ

Now the only pub in the village, this quaint and welcoming village inn features a lovely old black kitchen range. There is a warren of little rooms off the main bar for chatting, dining and games. Live music features on Saturday evenings, and there is a quiz every Thursday. The regular Exmoor Ale averages five kils a week, augmented by one guest in winter, and more in summer. Sunday roast is very popular, and disabled facilities are good. For children there is a games room with toys.

QP

Kilmington

New Inn

The Hill, EX13 7SF

11-2.30, 7-11; 11.30-3, 6-11 Sat; 12-4, 7-10.30 Sun

☎ (01297) 33376

Palmer Copper, IPA, seasonal beers Ⓗ

This cosy, thatched Devon longhouse has appeared in every edition of the Guide. After a major fire in 2004, it was sympathetically rebuilt, with the WCs completely modernised to meet current disabled standards. Local members confined to wheelchairs voted it the pub with the best facilities in the branch area. Outside there is a large secluded garden. A skittle alley, quizzes and other events help maintain this pub at the heart of village life.

P

Old Inn

EX13 7RB

11-3, 6-11; 11-11 Fri & Sat summer; 12-3, 7-10.30 Sun

☎ (01297) 32096 oldinnkilmington.co.uk

Branscombe Vale Branoc; Otter Bitter, Ale; guest beer Ⓗ

Thatched 16th-century inn on the A35 with a cosy bar, lounge with a good log fire and a restaurant area. Outside there is a sun-trap patio and raised lawn. Food is sourced locally, and the blackboard menu is changed daily. A skittle alley is available for functions. There are regular theme nights, and the landlord has introduced a loyalty card scheme, allowing regular customers to obtain discounts on food and drink. QP

Kings Nympton

Grove Inn

EX37 9ST

12-3 (not Mon), 6-11; 12-3, 7-10.30 Sun

☎ (01769) 580406 thegroveinn.co.uk

Exmoor Ale; guest beers Ⓗ

Seventeenth-century, Grade II-listed thatched pub situated within this picturesque village. The single bar has low beams, local historical information and photographs on the walls, with an open fire in winter. Awarded Taste of the West South West Dining Pub of the Year 2008, Tuesday's fish and chips in Exmoor Ale batter is a particular favourite. The cider is Sam's Dry from Winkleigh. A quiz night is held on the first Monday of the month. Well-behaved children and dogs are welcome. A self-catering cottage opposite is available for hire.

Q

Kingston

Dolphin Inn

TQ7 4QE (next to church)
⏲ 12-3, 6-11; 12-3, 7-10.30 Sun
☎ (01548) 810314 🌐 dolphin-inn.co.uk
Courage Best Bitter; Otter Ale; Sharp's Doom Bar; Teignworthy Spring Tide Ⓗ
A focal point for the local community, this pub is popular with tourists during the summer. On one side of the road is the main part of the pub – converted from three 16th-century cottages – with the family room, the garden and the gents' WC on the other. In winter, open inglenook fires blend well with the pleasant low lighting. The food is home-cooked with the emphasis on locally-sourced ingredients. Cornwall's Haye Farm and the local Heron Valley provide the real cider.
♨❀🛏◐♣●P⁄

Kingswear

Ship Inn

Higher Street, TQ6 0AG
⏲ 12-midnight (closed 3.30-6 Mon-Thu winter)
☎ (01803) 752348 🌐 theshipinnkingswear.co.uk
Adnams Bitter; Greene King IPA; guest beers Ⓗ
Tucked away at the side of the village church and overlooking the River Dart and Dartmouth, this friendly pub has its bar in the middle of a horseshoe shaped room. The restaurant is renowned for its fish dishes, and is reached through an arch in a three foot thick wall. There are log fires and nautical memorabilia, with wonderful views from the patio. Three to four beers are always available. ♨Q❀◐⇌🚌⁄

Lake

Bearslake Inn

EX20 4HQ (on A386 between Okehampton and Tavistock) SX528888
⏲ 11-3, 6-11; 12-4 Sun
☎ (01837) 861334 🌐 bearslakeinn.com
Otter Bitter; Teignworthy Old Moggie; guest beers Ⓗ/Ⓖ
Grade II-listed family-run inn on the edge of Dartmoor by the Granite Way making it ideal for walkers and cyclists. This former Devon longhouse was originally a working farm, the bar area is believed to have 13th-century origins. The interior features flagstone floors with exposed beams and timbers. It has an excellent restaurant offering a menu that changes daily and features local produce. Accommodation is of a high standard and there are stunning views of the highest peaks on Dartmoor from the rear garden.
♨Q❀🛏◐♿🏠🚌(86)♣P⁄

Lutton

Mountain Inn

Old Chapel Road, PL21 9SA SX595594
⏲ 12 (6 Tue)-11
☎ (01752) 837247
Dartmoor Jail Ale; guest beers Ⓗ
Two-roomed village pub on the edge of Dartmoor with simple cob walls and real fires in each room. At the bar, the Jail Ale is accompanied by three wide-ranging guest ales and occasional real ciders. Additionally, up to eight bottled ciders are also available and 2007 saw the introduction of an annual beer festival at this Cask Marque pub. The pub's name is a corruption of a local landowner's family name, Montain. Simple pub food is available daily except Tuesday. ♨Q❀◐🚌(58,59)●P

Mary Tavy

Elephant's Nest

Horndon, PL19 9LQ
⏲ 12-3, 6.30-11 (10.30 Sun)
☎ (01822) 810273 🌐 elephantsnest.co.uk
Palmer Best Bitter; guest beers Ⓗ
Intriguingly renamed from the New Inn by a previous landlord, this 16th-century pub affords magnificent views over Dartmoor from its large garden. The bar remains traditional despite featuring many elephantine items, including a mural, figures, curios; note the word 'elephant' spelt in many languages on the beams. Two further rooms off the bar are suitable for children. The pub has its own cricket ground and club, with regular fixtures throughout the season. Real cider is served, from local producer Countryman.
♨Q❀🛏◐●P

Meavy

Royal Oak

PL20 6PJ
⏲ 12-3, 6-11; 12-11 Sat & Sun
☎ (01822) 852944 🌐 royaloakinn.org.uk
Dartmoor IPA, Jail Ale Ⓗ**; guest beers** Ⓖ
This classic inn by a village green is an archetype of Olde England. In the comfortable, relaxed lounge, good and often adventurous food is available, whereas the public bar – with flagstones, roaring fire and interesting characters – offers the more bucolic experience. The three or four beers are sourced from the West Country; Westons Scrumpy and Old Rosie real ciders also feature. There are occasional beer festivals and live music. A bus from Yelverton runs Monday to Saturday, daytime only.
♨Q❀◐⊟🚌(56)●

Merrivale

Dartmoor Inn

Merrivale Bridge, PL20 6ST
⏲ 11.30-2.30, 6.30-11.30
☎ (01822) 890340
Beer range varies Ⓗ
Set in a wonderful Dartmoor location between Tavistock and Princetown, this excellent 17th-century freehouse is popular with tourists and walkers. The decor is rustic, warm and welcoming, as is the glorious fire on chilly days. The four West Country beers usually include two from Skinner's. Good bar food is served; there is also a full a la carte menu. On a clear day, the Eddystone Lighthouse may be visible from some 30 miles away. There is no bus service on winter Sundays.
♨❀◐Å🚌(98,272)P⁄

Milton Combe

Who'd Have Thought It

PL20 6HP
⏲ 12-3, 6-11; 12-11 Sat and summer; 12-3, 7-10.30 (12-10.30 summer) Sun
☎ (01822) 853313 🌐 whodhavethoughtitdevon.co.uk
Beer range varies Ⓗ

A picturesque 16th-century pub in a peaceful, secluded village location, featuring a cosy bar with wood-burner, two further rooms and three outdoor patio drinking areas, one of which is covered. Three or four ales are offered, usually from Devon and Cornwall. Good home-cooked food is also served – there is an emphasis on local produce, including game. The bus service from Yelverton terminates right by the front door approximately hourly during the day, weekdays and Saturday. Buckland Abbey (National Trust) is nearby. Q(55)P

Molland

London Inn

EX36 3NG (next to church) SS807283

12-3, 6.30-11; 12-3 Sun

(01769) 550269 mollandinn.co.uk

Cotleigh Tawny Owl; Exmoor Ale; guest beers G

Set in a village mentioned in the Domesday book, this is a delightful 15th-century former coaching inn on the edge of Exmoor that still boasts open log fires, inglenooks and beamed ceilings, attracting locals and visitors alike. The pub comprises several small rooms, all full of displays connected to field sports, with beers and cider from Winkleigh all on gravity. The restaurant offers fresh fish and meat from local farms. Skittles and darts are played and the establishment of a micro-brewery in an adjacent property is now planned. B&B is available but credit cards are not accepted. Q

Moretonhampstead

Union Inn

10 Ford Street, TQ13 8LN

11 (12 Sun)-11

(01647) 440199 theunioninn.co.uk

Fuller's London Pride; guest beers H

Sixteenth-century town-centre free house in the village centre named after the 1801 Act of Union. Inside, the bar is clad in 19th-century panelling with old photographs of the village on display. The function room is reached via a corridor displaying historic artefacts relating to the inn's history. Home-cooked food is good value and a carvery is served on Sunday. Guest beers include one lighter and one darker variety, with Gray's cider also available. The outside seating area is next to a small rear car park. P

Mortehoe

Chichester Arms

Chapel Hill, EX34 7DU (next to church)

12-3, 6.30-11; 12-11 Sat and summer; 12-10.30 Sun

(01271) 870411

Barum Original; Cottage Golden Arrow; Exmoor Fox; St Austell Dartmoor; guest beers H

Unique and popular 16th-century village free house in a picturesque location with seating at the front for dining and drinking alfresco. From here there are views of Lundy Island and the expansive beaches of Woolacombe Bay nearby. Once the old vicarage, it still has gas lighting in the bar. Normally there are four real ales available, with up to two occasional guests. Busy during holiday times, quality food is served all week except Monday in winter. There is a separate skittle alley and children's room for families.
Q(303)P

Newton Abbot

Richard Hopkins

34-42 Queen Street, TQ12 2EW (400m from railway station)

9-midnight

(01626) 323930

Greene King Abbot; Marston's Pedigree; guest beers H

This friendly Wetherspoon's pub offers ten hand-pumped ales, many from South West breweries, including Bays, Cotleigh, Cottage, Exmoor and O'Hanlon's. Converted from a furniture store, the spacious interior is divided into a number of areas, some with comfortable sofas and TV screens. On the walls are illustrations of famous local men, historic events and places. Children are welcome until 9pm. A covered area with seating and tables runs along the front of the pub. The cider is Westons Organic.

Union Inn

6 East Street, TQ12 1AF

10-11 (midnight Fri & Sat); 12-10.30 Sun

(01626) 354775

Draught Bass; Greene King IPA; Sharp's Doom Bar; guest beers H

Escape from the hurly burly of local retail experiences to this welcome retreat in a newly pedestrianised street between the Clock Tower and Magistrates Court. Here you will find a happy mixture of shoppers enjoying good value food and regulars who form the football, darts and euchre teams. Five beers are normally available, often including a guest from Teignworthy and another West Country brewer. It can sometimes be a little crowded and noisy, with a large-screen TV and occasional live music.

Wolborough Inn

55 Wolborough Street, TQ12 1JQ

12 (4 Mon)-midnight; 12-11.30 Sun

(01626) 334511

Teignworthy Reel Ale; guest beers H/G

The front of the pub is old-fashioned, with etched windows on each side of a doorway that leads into an L-shaped bar. Here you can relax on pews and in leather armchairs. The decor is plain, with a wooden floor. The beers include one from the Teignworthy range plus guests from other West Country brewers. There is a small split-level outdoor terrace with a cover for smokers. Also known as the First & Last, this pub is certainly worth a visit.

Newton St Cyres

Beer Engine

EX5 5AX (N of A377, next to station)

11-11; 12-10.30 Sun

(01392) 851282 thebeerengine.co.uk

Beer Engine Rail Ale, Silver Bullet, Piston Bitter, Sleeper Heavy, seasonal beer H

Busy and popular with locals and visitors alike, this brewery pub is situated a mile from the A377, north of the village of Newton St Cyres, and beside the Exeter to Barnstaple Tarka railway line. The open-plan bar with attached restaurant area is festooned with dried hops. The ales reflect the railway theme, as do village and railway scenes in photographs. The pub makes its own bread, and the wholesome food is from locally-sourced suppliers. Q(50,51,315)P

North Tawton

Railway Inn

Whiddon Down Road, EX20 2BE (1 mile S of town)
SS666001
12-3 Fri & Sat, 6-11; 12-3, 7-11 Sun
☎ (01837) 82789
Teignworthy Reel Ale; guest beers Ⓗ
Family-run single-bar local that is part of a working farm. There is a translation of the landlord's Devon dialect displayed in the bar area for the benefit of confused visitors. Situated next to the former North Tawton Railway Station (closed 1971), the bar decor includes railway memorabilia and old photos of the station. The beer range changes regularly, normally West Country based, with Thatchers cider stocked in summer. The dining room is popular in the evening (no food Thu eve), with light meals served at lunchtime. P

Noss Mayo

Ship Inn

PL8 1EW (W side of Noss Creek)
11-11; 12-10.30 Sun
☎ (01752) 872387 nossmayo.com
Dartmoor Jail Ale; St Austell Tribute; Summerskills Tamar; guest beer Ⓗ
Popular with ramblers and seafarers alike, this fine pub is situated on an inlet off the idyllic Yealm estuary. A former local CAMRA Pub of the Year, it is an ideal start/finish point for a walk to sample the breathtaking river and sea views along the route of Lord Revelstoke's Drive. If sailing, ring ahead to ascertain the tide table and moorings. Like the beer, food served all day is locally sourced. There is no bus service evenings or Sunday.
Q (94)P

Oakford

Red Lion

Rookery Hill, EX16 9ES
12-2.30 (not Tue & Wed), 6-11; closed Mon; 12-3, 6-10.30 Sun
☎ (01398) 351219 theredlionhoteloakford.co.uk
Exeter Lighterman; Otter Ale Ⓗ
Welcoming free house set in a quiet village in undulating countryside on the fringes of Exmoor. The main bar features a large inglenook fireplace, and excellent value food is served in a separate, recently restyled, dining room. Westons cider is available in the summer months only. A small car park and garden area can be found across the road. Overnight accommodation comprises four comfortable en-suite rooms, including one with a four-poster bed. P

Okehampton

Plymouth Inn

26 West Street, EX20 1HH (W end of town near West Okement Bridge)
11-midnight
☎ (01837) 53633
Beer range varies Ⓖ
A friendly village-style local situated on the west edge of town. The constantly-changing ales are served on gravity from stillage behind the bar and Sam's cider from Winkleigh is available in summer. There are two popular beer festivals held every year, one coinciding with the Ten Tors Challenge in May. Reasonably-priced locally-sourced food and bar snacks are available. A quiz night is held on the first Sunday of the month and musician/folk evenings on the last Sunday. Children and dogs are welcome. (X9,X90)

Paignton

Isaac Merritt

54-58 Torquay Road, TQ3 3AA
9-midnight
☎ (01803) 556066
Bays Gold; Courage Directors; Greene King Abbot; Marston's Pedigree; guest beers Ⓗ
Busy and popular town-centre Wetherspoon's pub themed around the man who invented the Singer sewing machine. It has a good reputation for ever-changing guest beers, augmented by mini beer festivals on Sundays and Mondays. Friendly surroundings with cosy alcoves and helpful staff make this hostelry appealing to all ages. Good value meals are served all day in this former local CAMRA Pub of the Year and Wetherspoon's award winner. There is easy access for wheelchair users, with a designated ground-floor WC.
(12)

Parkham

Bell Inn

Rectory Lane, EX39 5PL (1m S of the A39 at Horns Cross)
SS387212
12-3, 5.30-11; 5-11 Fri; 12-3, 6-10.30 Sun
☎ (01237) 451201 thebellinnparkham.co.uk
Exmoor Fox; Greene King IPA; Sharp's Doom Bar; guest beers Ⓗ
This 13th-century thatched free house was originally a forge and two cottages and up until recently housed the village store. The single bar serves two distinct areas, with a wood burner and coal fire for colder months. A well-attended beer festival takes place yearly at the end of May/beginning of June and spit roasts in the summer have become a popular feature. Locally-produced food is cooked to order and served in the bar or the raised dining area. P

Petrockstowe

Laurels Inn

EX20 3HJ (S of church on main road through village)
SS512091
12-midnight summer; 12-3, 6-midnight (1am Sat) winter
☎ (01837) 810578 petrockstowe.co.uk/laurels
Otter Bitter; St Austell Tribute; Sharp's Doom Bar; guest beers Ⓗ
Situated in a picturesque village with several 'chocolate box' thatched cottages, this 17th-century coaching house has historic links to the Civil War. The single bar has three handpumps with the guest ale often leaning towards the stronger side, plus Autumn Scrumpy cider from Winkleigh. There is a cosy restaurant offset near the entrance and a pool table in the bar area. Outside there are wooden benches and tables with parasols for eating and drinking alfresco. The Tarka Trail, convenient for walkers and cyclists, is one mile away. P

Plymouth

Artillery Arms

6 Pound Street, Stonehouse, PL1 3RH (opp RM barracks gate)
11 (12 Sun)-midnight
(01752) 262515
Draught Bass; guest beers [H]
Located behind the Brittany Ferries terminal, this pub comprises a single bar with a separate dining area where good value, home-made food is served (except Sun). Very much a community pub, it sponsors many charity events, with a Beach Party in February, and the ever-popular monkey races. Not the easiest pub to find in the back streets of Stonehouse, but the effort is well rewarded with a warm and friendly welcome. Real cider, rotating through the Thatchers range, is available.

Blue Peter

68 Pomphlett Road, Plymstock, PL9 7BN
12-11 (midnight Fri & Sat); 12-4, 7-10.30 Sun
(01752) 402255
Beer range varies [H]
Twice local CAMRA Pub of the Year, this unpretentious and friendly two-bar establishment in Plymouth's south-east suburb would surprisingly appear to have been named after the 1939 Epsom Derby winner, rather than for more obvious maritime connections. The public bar features a games area which can also be used for live entertainment, while the lounge has alcove seating and doubles as the main dining area. Roast dinners are served Wednesday and Sunday lunchtimes. The pub also hosts occasional beer festivals.

Boringdon Arms

13 Boringdon Terrace, Turnchapel, PL9 9TQ
11-midnight
(01752) 402053 bori.co.uk
Draught Bass; Butcombe Bitter; RCH Pitchfork; Sharp's Doom Bar; guest beers [H]
This is a light, airy, two-roomed waterside pub, popular with locals and walkers using the South West Coast Path. The Bori, local CAMRA Pub of the Year in 2006, is well served by road as well as water taxis from the Barbican to Mount Batten Pier. Regular beer festivals are held on the last weekend of odd-numbered months. The pub has an excellent reputation for home-cooked food which may be enjoyed alfresco in the garden, planted up in a former quarry. (2,17)

Britannia

1 Wolseley Road, Milehouse, PL2 3AA
9am-midnight (1am Fri & Sat)
(01752) 607596
Greene King IPA, Abbot; Marston's Pedigree; Shepherd Neame Spitfire; guest beers [H]
An imposing Wetherspoon conversion of a run-down Edwardian inn, the Brit is a fine local which serves a large community well. Although mainly attracting a regular clientele, it can be busy in the evenings, and even more so when Plymouth Argyle are playing at home. Numerous buses pass from the city centre and railway station – the pub is located opposite the Citybus depot on one of the city's busiest road junctions. Two real ciders from the Westons range are served.

Clifton

35 Clifton Street, Greenbank, PL4 8JB
2-11.30 (12.30am Fri); 12-12.30am Sat; 12-11.30 Sun
(01752) 266563 cliftonpub.com
Dartmoor Jail Ale; Draught Bass; Summerskills Clifton Classic; guest beers [H]
Rejuvenated, spacious back-street local just to the north of the burgeoning university quarter, where a warm-hearted welcome awaits. This comfortable pub was once considered to be the luckiest in Britain, as there was a time when no fewer than three National Lottery millionaires could be counted among its regulars. Two large-screen TVs provide entertainment, especially major rugby matches. As well as the house beer, local brewer Summerskills supplies a seasonally-changing guest. Outside is a large heated patio area.

Clovelly Bay Inn

11 Boringdon Road, Turnchapel, PL9 9TB
11-3, 6-11; 12-4, 7-10.30 Sun
(01752) 402765 clovellybayinn.co.uk
Beer range varies [H]
Formerly the New Inn, this family-run free house is situated on the waterfront of the historic fishing village of Turnchapel, accessible by half-hourly water taxi from the Barbican to Mount Batten Pier, as well as by bus. Renowned for special events throughout the year, the landlord sources beers upon request from all breweries and also offers over 30 malt whiskies. A diverse menu can be enjoyed within a warm and convivial atmosphere, while listening to a free Wurlitzer vinyl jukebox. (2,17)

Dolphin Hotel

14 The Barbican, PL1 2LS
10-11 (midnight Fri & Sat); 11-11 Sun
(01752) 660876
Draught Bass; St Austell Tribute [G]
Most recently made famous as the local of late artist Beryl Cook, no visit to the Barbican can be considered complete without a pint at the Dolphin. The interior is minimalist, but you are assured of a wealth of conversation with some of the colourful regulars. Well-behaved dogs are welcome and an attractive fireplace completes the scene. The Tolpuddle Martyrs stayed here on their return from transportation. Look out for the logo of the city's old Octagon Brewery on the windows. (25)

Fawn Private Members Club

39 Prospect Street, Greenbank, PL4 8NY
2 (12 Sat)-11; 12-10.30 Sun
(01752) 660540 thefawnclub.co.uk
Courage Best Bitter; Sharp's Fawn Ale; guest beers [H]
Named after the now-scrapped HMS Fawn, the club welcomes CAMRA members with a current valid membership card – although regular visitors will be required to join. Many of the members live locally and are keen followers of rugby and other televised sports, are members of the darts and euchre teams, or simply enjoy the friendly ambience and reasonable prices. Three guest ales are usually available as well as Sam's real cider from Winkleigh. The covered smoking area is on the patio.

Fortescue

37 Mutley Plain, Mutley, PL4 6JQ
11-11 (midnight Fri & Sat); 12-10.30 Sun
(01752) 660673 fortescueonline.co.uk

Butcombe Bitter; Dartmoor Jail Ale; Greene King Abbot; Highgate Irish Whiskey Ale; Taylor Landlord; guest beers Ⓗ
Conversation flourishes at this lively local, frequented by a broad section of the community. Cricket memorabilia adorns the walls at the back of the Fort as you make your way through to the heated patio beer garden. Sundays idled away here are near-perfect: a good-value home-cooked roast, washed down with Spingo, followed by a quiz in the cellar bar in the evening. CAMRA branch Pub of the Year in 2009, eight or more beers are offered, together with real Thatchers cider.

Lounge

7 Stopford Place, Devonport, PL1 4QT
11.30-3 (not Mon), 6-11 (midnight Fri); 11.30-11 Sat; 12-11 Sun
☎ (01752) 561330
Draught Bass; guest beers Ⓗ
This street-corner local, near Devonport Park, is something of a haven in a part of the city where real ale is increasingly scarce. Food, popular with local workers during the week, is served every lunchtime except Monday. Saturdays can be particularly busy, with Plymouth Albion RFC's Brickfields ground nearby. To satisfy the demands of both lunchtime and evening patrons, in terms of strength, the guest beers always fall either side of the Bass. Children are welcome for lunch.
Q (Devonport)

Prince Maurice ✓

3 Church Hill, Eggbuckland, PL6 5RJ
11-3, 7-11; 11-11 Fri & Sat; 12-10.30 Sun
☎ (01752) 771515
Courage Best Bitter; Dartmoor Jail Ale; O'Hanlon's Royal Oak; St Austell HSD; Sharp's Doom Bar; Summerskills Best Bitter; guest beer Ⓗ
Before the post-war northern expansion of the city, Eggbuckland was a village, and both the character of the pub and its location between the church and the green emphasise this. A four-times local CAMRA Pub of the Year, it is named after the Royalist General, the King's nephew, who during the siege of Plymouth in the Civil War had his headquarters nearby. Seven beers are always available, as is Thatchers Cheddar Valley cider. No food served at weekends.

Thistle Park Brewhouse

32 Commercial Road, Coxside, PL4 0LE
11-1am (4am Fri & Sat); 12-1am Sun
☎ (01752) 204890
South Hams Devon Pride, Re-Session, XSB, Eddystone, seasonal beers Ⓗ
Despite the name, don't expect to find a kettle or mash tun here, as the former Sutton Brewery underwent relocation (and renaming) to the more verdant South Hams five years ago. This pub effectively remains the brewery tap, showcasing its full range of ales, and has been extensively refurbished and expanded to include a Thai restaurant and roof garden upstairs. Thatchers Cheddar Valley cider is also served. Visitors should note that the bridge from the Barbican closes nightly (9.30pm – 4.30am).

Yard Arm ✓

159 Citadel Road, PL1 2HU
12-midnight
☎ (01752) 202405 yardarmplymouth.co.uk
Beer range varies Ⓗ
A short walk from either the Barbican or city centre, this busy street-corner pub lies opposite the picturesque Plymouth Hoe – famed for Sir Francis Drake's game of bowls – and serves up to four real ales, with local and national breweries represented. Maritime memorabilia adorns the walls, with the wood-panelled, raised and lower deck seating areas adding to the nautical flavour. Popular for live sports shown on the large screen TV, and for good food cooked to order.

Plympton

Foresters Arms

44 Fore Street, PL7 1NB
12.30 (2 Tue)-11; 12-10.30 Sun
☎ (01752) 336018
Dartmoor Jail Ale; guest beers Ⓗ
A non-ostentatious single-roomed pub, situated in the St Maurice area of this ancient stannary town. The building – with acanthus carvings under the eaves – was formerly the holding cells for the adjacent old Guildhall, and is reputed to be haunted. Beers are sourced primarily from the West Country, although others from outside the region may be ordered upon request: the pub welcomes suggestions. Live music plays on Sunday evening, with a quiz on Monday. Dogs are welcome.

George Inn

191 Ridgeway, PL7 2HJ
11.30-11; 11.30-midnight Fri & Sat; 12-11 Sun
☎ (01752) 342674
Courage Best Bitter; Greene King Abbot; guest beers Ⓗ
Situated on the old Plymouth to Exeter road, this welcoming and friendly former 17th-century coaching house is popular with locals and visitors alike. The inn offers an extensive menu – served all day Sunday – supplemented by blackboard specials, with booking advisable at the weekend. In fine weather, meals or snacks can be eaten on the florally-bedecked patio outside. The flagstone-floored bar has a warm atmosphere for colder days, with dogs also welcome. Popular acoustic sessions are held on most Sunday evenings.
Q P

Postbridge

Warren House Inn

PL20 6TA (2 miles NE of Postbridge on B3212) SX674809
11-11 (5 Mon & Tue winter); 11-10.30 Sun
☎ (01822) 880208 warrenhouseinn.co.uk
Otter Ale; Sharp's Doom Bar; guest beers Ⓗ
High and isolated, this pub is a welcome sight for walkers, riders and drivers. The interior features exposed beams, wood panelling, rustic benches and tables and the famous fire. Lunch and evening menus offer home-cooked dishes using locally-sourced ingredients including Dartmoor beef and lamb, plus vegetarian options. There is a large family room and tables outside with good views over the moor. Countryman cider is available, with carry-outs; guest beers include many from local breweries and usually feature one strong ale.
Q P

Ringmore

Journey's End

TQ7 4HL SX650460

12-3, 6-11, closed Mon; 12-3, 6-10.30 Sun

☎ (01548) 810205 journeysendinn.co.uk

Sharp's Doom Bar; guest beers Ⓖ

Taking its name from RC Sherriff's famous play, which he started writing while staying here, this is a homely 13th-century village pub. Three ales are dispensed on gravity, although up to five may feature in summer. Bottled Belgian beers are also available, with a real cider from Thatchers; a winter ale festival is held in October. A separate lounge/dining room offers a daily-changing menu and caters for children. There is a car park 200 metres away, opposite All Hallows Church.

❀♣P

Sampford Peverell

Globe Inn ✔

16 Lower Town, EX16 7BJ

8-midnight

☎ (01884) 821214 the-globeinn.co.uk

Exmoor Fox; O'Hanlon's Yellowhammer; Otter Bitter, Head Ⓗ

This traditional Devon village inn is situated in the heart of Sampford Peverell, near Tiverton, backing on to the Grand Western Canal, which is popular with both walkers and cyclists. All the food products are locally sourced and the meat is farm-assured with full traceability. A carvery is served Friday, Saturday evening, all day Sunday and Monday lunchtime. There are two private function rooms and six accommodation rooms. Two beer festivals are held, one in April for cask ale week and the other during the third week in November.

❀(Tiverton Parkway)(1)♣P

Sandford

Lamb Inn

The Square, EX17 4LW

9-midnight; 11-11 Sun

☎ (01363) 773676 lambinnsandford.co.uk

Cotleigh Tawny Ⓗ**; guest beers** Ⓗ/Ⓖ

This 16th-century genuine free house is in the centre of the village and enjoys a traditional inviting atmosphere. It is popular for both its beer and food, and is well supported by both local and city folk. Although food does not dominate, the menu is varied and comprises local and organic produce wherever possible. Skittles is played four nights a week in the alley and there are regular themed nights, including live music and open mike comedy evenings. Three rooms are available for B&B accommodation. Sandford Orchards cider is stocked. Q❀(369)♣

Seaton

King's Arms

55 Fore Street, EX12 2AN

11-3, 6-midnight; 11-midnight Sat; 12-10.30 Sun

☎ (01297) 23431

Branscombe Vale Branoc, BVB Best Bitter; guest beers Ⓗ

A busy local away from the tourist area, located in the original fishing village of Seaton. The pub has one large bar where very popular, reasonably priced food is available every lunchtime and evening, except Sunday. There is a separate restaurant where children are welcome. A large garden at the rear, hidden from the road, affords good views over the River Axe estuary. ❀

Shaldon

Clifford Arms

34 Fore Street, TQ14 0DE

11-2.30, 5-11.30; 11.30-3, 6-11 Sun

☎ (01626) 872311

Dartmoor Dartmoor IPA; Greene King Abbot; Ringmore Craft Oarsome; guest beers Ⓗ

Village centre pub with an attractive, modern interior and a warming log fire in winter. This is the only draught outlet for the local Ringmore Craft Brewery, with guest and seasonal beers sourced mainly from West Country breweries. The low-level restaurant area at the rear serves good quality food every day and leads out onto a sunny, decked patio. Special menus are available on modern jazz evenings on Monday, monthly trad jazz sessions on Sunday lunchtime, and Thursday charity quiz nights. ❀(32)

Sidmouth

Swan Inn

37 York Street, EX10 8BY

11-2.30 (3 Sat), 5.30-11; 12-3, 7-10.30 Sun

☎ (01395) 512849

Young's Bitter, Special; guest beers Ⓗ

This traditional and quiet back-street inn, established around 1770, lies just off the centre of this quaint town, a short walk from the seafront and bus terminus. A cosy, old-style wood-panelled bar with an open fire attracts a strong local trade and leads to a dedicated dining area. Three beers, all from the Wells & Young's range, are normally available. Dogs, but not children, are welcome indoors, and various sports teams are supported.

Q❀♣

Silverton

Lamb Inn

Fore Street, EX5 4HZ

11.30-2.30, 6-11 (1am Thu; 2am Fri); 11.30-2am Sat; 12-11 Sun

☎ (01392) 860272

Dartmoor IPA; Exe Valley Dob's Best Bitter; Otter Ale; guest beers Ⓖ

Broadly popular family-run village pub with stone flooring, stripped timber and old pine furniture inside. It has a good sized bar and a strong local trade. Three or more regular ales, plus various guests, are served by gravity from a temperature-controlled stillage behind the bar. A multi-purpose function room plus skittle alley and bar are well used by local teams. Good value home-cooked food is served, together with popular Sunday roasts and a specials board which changes weekly.

❀♣

Slapton

Queen's Arms

TQ7 2PN

12-3, 6-11 (7-10.30 Sun)

☎ (01548) 580800 slapton.org/queensarms

Dartmoor Jail Ale; Otter Bright; Teignworthy Reel Ale; guest beer Ⓗ

A large open fire welcomes you in the bar, which has photographs on the wall depicting the wartime evacuation. A beer festival is held in late March/early April. Food offerings include the fish and chips special on Friday lunchtime and Sunday roast lunch, both well worth booking. Otherwise a full menu, including the chef's home-made pies and a takeaway service, is available. There is a flower-filled garden and a patio. Children and dogs are very welcome inside and outside.
(93)♣P

South Brent

Royal Oak

Station Road, TQ10 9BE
12-2.30, 5.30-11 (12-11 summer); 12-midnight Fri & Sat; 12-11 Sun
(01364) 72133 oakonline.net
St Austell Tribute; Teignworthy Reel Ale; guest beers H
Busy village-centre pub on the edge of Dartmoor. The main L-shaped bar is surrounded by a large open-plan area, while the wood-panelled bar is the place for an excellent range of real ales. At the rear a restaurant serves good quality food and a new function room can be found upstairs. There is a no-smoking courtyard outside and accommodation is available. Occasional beer festivals are held at this current local CAMRA Pub of the Year. CAMRA members receive a discount on real ales. Q

South Molton

Town Arms Hotel

124 East Street, EX36 3BU (100m E of town square)
11-midnight (1am Fri & Sat); 12-midnight Sun
(01769) 572531
Draught Bass; Marston's Burton Bitter; guest beers H
Main street local with interesting old photographs on the walls. This small historic market town is ideally suited for exploring Exmoor and north Devon. The main bar has a pool table and an open fire, and there is a back room. The pub can get very lively on occasions with friendly locals, particularly on Thursday market day. The owners are proud of their real ales and usually have three available, with a West Country guest plus one other that is ever changing and occasionally a mild. Dogs are welcome. (X12,155,337)♣P

South Pool

Millbrook Inn

TQ7 2RW (off A379 at Frogmore) SX774402
12-11 (10.30 Sun)
(01548) 531581 millbrookinnsouthpool.co.uk
Red Rock Red Rock; guest beers H
Situated in the picturesque village of South Pool, most of the pub's summer trade comes from walkers and boaters on South Pool creek. Devon beers are available to be tasted every Sunday. At 2pm, Sunday roasts are served (booking recommended) before the jazz band starts at 3pm. A summer barbecue is provided, mainly for use by the boating fraternity. Meals are home cooked using local ingredients. Aylesbury ducks swim by the back terrace. Q

Spreyton

Tom Cobley Tavern

EX17 5AL (on A3124)
12-3, 6-midnight (6.30-11 Mon); 12-3, 6-1am Fri & Sat; 12-3, 7-11 Sun
(01647) 231314
Clearwater Cavalier; Cotleigh Tawny; Otter Ale; Quercus Stormbrew; St Austell Proper Job, Tribute H
Still riding high on the success of winning National CAMRA Pub of the Year in 2006, the pub attracts visitors from all over the country who come to witness the remarkable turnover of up to 22 ales at any one time, mainly on gravity. This 16th-century village inn always gives a warm welcome in the homely bar and spacious dining room. The beers are great, but so is the wonderful home-cooked food and extensive menu. Booking is advisable, especially for Sunday lunch. Q♣P

Sticklepath

Taw River Inn

EX20 2NW SX641941
12-midnight (11 Sun)
(01837) 840377 tawriver.co.uk
Draught Bass; Greene King Abbot; St Austell Tribute; Sharp's Doom Bar; guest beers H
A lively pub in an active village on the edge of Dartmoor offering picturesque walks and historical attractions. A past local CAMRA Pub of the Year winner, the large single bar houses numerous sports and pub games played by friendly locals. The ever-changing real ales are available at very attractive prices and good value pub food is served. Popular with walkers and visitors to the Finch Foundry Museum (NT) opposite, children and dogs are welcome, and there is plenty of garden space.
(X9,X90)♣P

Talaton

Talaton Inn

EX5 2RQ
12-3, 7-11 (10.30 Sun)
(01404) 822214
Otter Bitter, Bright; guest beer H
This family-run free house is an excellent example of a traditional village country pub. The 16th-century building has a good-sized bar frequented by locals and a separate lounge with dining area (booking recommended). Meals are good value (not served Sun or Mon eve), with lunchtime specials and offers for senior citizens. The skittle alley adjoining the public bar is very popular. Winner of the Kennel Club 2008 Open for Dogs award, the public bar attracts a large canine clientele. Q(382)♣P

Tavistock

Trout & Tipple

Parkwood Road, PL19 0JS
12-2.30 (not Tue), 6-11; 12-2.30, 6-10.30 (7-10.30 winter) Sun
(01822) 618886 troutandtipple.co.uk
Dartmoor Jail Ale; guest beers H
Near a trout fishery a mile north of the town, this friendly hostelry features a traditional hop-draped bar, with a plethora of pump clips from past guest ales on the ceiling, plus a large conservatory, games room and patio. Seasonal beers from

Teignworthy and two changing real ciders are served. Beer festivals in February and October are complemented by frequent single-brewery events in between. Dogs and children are welcome, the latter until 9pm. Local CAMRA Pub of the Year 2007. Q P

Tedburn St Mary

Kings Arms Inn

EX6 6EG

11-3, 6-11; 11-midnight Fri & Sat; 12-11 Sun

(01647) 61224 kingsarmsinn.co.uk

Otter Ale; St Austell Tribute; guest beer H

A lively and welcoming village local with good home-cooked food and quality rooms, just off the A30 in the middle of the village on the edge of Dartmoor. There is a good mixed clientele, a lively public bar and a real fire in winter. Families are welcome and there is a function room. Outside is a lovely patio and garden area. Accommodation is in six rooms. P

Topsham

Bridge Inn ★

Bridge Hill, EX3 0QQ (by River Clyst)

12-2, 6-10.30 (11 Fri & Sat); 12-2, 7-10.30 Sun

(01392) 873862 cheffers.co.uk

Branscombe Vale Branoc; guest beers G

Wonderful 16th-century pub with up to nine ales, served in thirds of a pint on request, including dark and strong beers, all gravity dispensed from the cellar. This real gem, run on traditional lines by the same family owners for 112 years, recently welcomed its sixth generation with baby Amelia. In 1998 the Queen made her only official UK pub visit here, and ten years later Caroline, the landlady, was presented at Buckingham Palace. There are stunning views over the River Clyst from the outside seating area. Snacks are available at lunchtime. Q (57)P

Exeter Inn

68 High Street, EX3 0DY

11-11 (midnight Fri & Sat); 12-10.30 Sun

(01392) 873131

Blackawton Exhibition; guest beers H

This 17th-century former coaching house has a vast choice of real ales, 14 in total, on a rotational basis, with a selection of seasonal ales throughout the year. A very friendly couple, who have a lot of interest in the local community, runs the pub. They are members of SIBA, and they also support the local cider maker Green Valley, who won best cider in 2008. (57,T)

Globe Hotel

Fore Street, EX3 0HR

11-11 (midnight Fri & Sat); 12-11 Sun

(01392) 873471 globehotel.com

Butcombe Bitter; Otter Ale; St Austell Tribute; Sharp's Doom Bar; guest beers H

Originally a 17th-century coaching house, this atmospheric, genuine free house retains its historic feel. The wood beamed and panelled interior is warm and welcoming, with a good range of up to five ales available, plus guests, qualifying as a LocAle pub. The restaurant offers good traditional English food specialising in locally-sourced produce. The Topsham folk club is held on Sunday evening, while the malt house room is available for functions and skittles. Q (57,T)P

Torquay

Crown & Sceptre ✔

2 Petitor Road, St Marychurch, TQ1 4QA

12-4, 5.30-11; 12-midnight Fri; 12-4, 6.30-midnight Sat; 12-4, 7-11.30 Sun

(01803) 328290

Badger Tanglefoot; Otter Ale; St Austell Tribute; Young's Special; guest beers H

A 200-year-old coaching house with over 30 years of unbroken entries in this Guide while under the stewardship of the same landlord. A collection of chamberpots and pennants plus a real fire lend character inside, while outside there are two small enclosed gardens. This well-supported community pub, with six regular beers and three guests, supports live music, with jazz on Tuesday evening and folk on Friday. Traditional cider is available most bank holiday weekends. Food is served lunchtimes, Monday to Saturday. Q P

Hole in the Wall

6 Park Lane, TQ1 2AU

11 (12 winter)-midnight

(01803) 200755 hole-in-the-wall.co.uk

Bays Best; Butcombe Bitter; Otter Bitter; Sharp's Doom Bar; Shepherd Neame Spitfire; guest beers H

Tucked away in the town centre and a few yards from the harbour, this is Torquay's oldest inn (circa 1540). A real ale haven with a listed cobbled floor and low-beamed ceilings, this pub has a truly nautical feel and a welcoming atmosphere. Very popular with seafarers, businessmen, holidaymakers and locals, it has a busy, roomy 70-seat restaurant serving highly-regarded food. A narrow passageway outside, adorned with floral displays, makes a pleasant alfresco drinking area. Dogs on leads are welcome. Q (12,32)

Totnes

Bay Horse Inn

8 Cistern Street, TQ9 5SP

11.30-11.30 summer; 4 (5 Mon)-11.30 winter; 12-2.30, 5-11.30 Sat; 12-2.30, 7-11 Sun

(01803) 862088 bayhorsetotnes.com

Dartmoor Jail Ale; Otter Bitter; Sharp's Eden Ale; guest beers H

South Devon CAMRA 2008 Pub of the Year, this 15th-century coaching inn at the top of the town is a roomy pub with a traditional snug bar. A large, attractive garden, with heated patio, is used for annual beer festivals. There is a jazz night on the last Sunday of each month and real fires in the winter. Good home-cooked food and comfortable accommodation are available. Four beers, normally from local breweries, are on offer. Q

Uplyme

Talbot Arms

Lyme Road, DT7 3TF

11-2.30 (not Mon & Tue), 6-11; 11-11 Sat & Sun

(01297) 443136 talbotarms.com

Beer range varies H

A friendly pub, named after Admiral Sir John Talbot, just inside the Devon/Dorset border, with a cosy lounge and separate dining area. The WCs and games/family room are downstairs, with access to a large garden. Food is popular but not always available on weekday lunchtimes out of season, so ring to check. Sunday lunch is a carvery and on Tuesday night there is a limited take-out menu including fish and chips – with a two-pint cooking time, many locals take advantage of this. A summer beer festival is held near the end of June – see website. Q (31)P

Westcott

Merry Harriers

EX15 1SA (on B3181, 2 miles S of Cullompton)

12-3, 6-11; 12-11 Sun

(01392) 881254 themerryharriers.co.uk

Cotleigh Tawny; guest beers H

Traditional Devon hostelry with a friendly atmosphere, a welcoming log fire, and the old ambience of oak beams. Families are welcome in the award-winning restaurant. This is one of only two pubs to have won silver medals in the Taste of the West pub-dining category. So whether you choose to eat inside or outside, you know the food will be good. There is also ample parking.

QP

Whimple

New Fountain Inn

Church Road, EX5 2TA

12-3, 6.30-11; 12-3, 7-10.30 Sun

(01404) 822350

Bays Gold; Teignworthy Reel Ale; guest beer G

Small, friendly two-bar local in a lovely village, converted from cottages around 1890, with new toilets added in 2009. A genuine free house, this pub has been owned by the current licensees for 19 years. The handpumps are not in use; ale is fetched from the cellar. Extremely good value home-cooked food is served daily. A village heritage centre is in the car park. QP

Whitchurch

Whitchurch Inn

Church Hill, PL19 9ED

11-11; 12-10.30 Sun

(01822) 612181 thewhitchurchinn.co.uk

Dartmoor Jail Ale; Otter Bitter; St Austell Tribute H**; guest beer** G

Lying just a few hundred metres outside the Dartmoor National Park, this is a small, single-bar pub situated next to a 15th-century village church. Wood-burners at either end help to maintain a homely atmosphere. A glass case on one wall displays a small silk slipper, originally hidden to ward off evil spirits – a custom dating from Plantagenet times. In addition to the three regular beers, a local ale may be available at weekends, dispensed on gravity behind the bar. (84)

Widecombe in the Moor

Ruggleston Inn

TQ13 7TF (quarter mile from village centre) SX721760

11.30-3, 6-midnight; 11.30-midnight Sat; 12-11 Sun

(01364) 621327 rugglestone.co.uk

Butcombe Bitter; St Austell Dartmoor Best; guest beer G

Unspoilt, cosy pub in a splendid Dartmoor setting, named after a local 'logan' stone. The small bar area has seating and a stone floor, with beer served through a hatch in the passageway. An open fire warms the lounge. Across the stream is a large grassed seating area with a shelter for bad weather. A wide selection of home-cooked food is available and children are welcome. There is a holiday cottage in the grounds available to let, and a large car park just down the road.

QP

Woolacombe

Red Barn

Barton Road, EX34 7DF (opp beach car park)

11-11 (midnight Fri); 9.30-midnight Sat; 9.30am-11 Sun

(01271) 870264

St Austell HSD, Proper Job, Tribute; guest beers H

Situated at the north end of Woolacombe beach in an area that is a tourists' paradise, the pub can get very busy in the holiday season. At one time this used to be a cafe, and from the outside it still looks like one, but inside is a large, welcoming establishment serving superb food in good-sized portions. Four real ales are always available, with regularly changing guest beers. A small ale and music festival is held in December and local live music is supported regularly.

(3B,303)

Beers suitable for vegetarians and vegans

A number of cask and bottle-fermented beers in the Good Beer Guide are listed as suitable for vegetarians and vegans. The main ingredients used in cask beer production are malted grain, hops, yeast and water, and these present no problems for drinkers who wish to avoid animal products. But most brewers of cask beer use isinglass as a clearing agent: isinglass is derived from the bladders of certain fish, including the sturgeon. Isinglass is added to a cask when it leaves the brewery and attracts yeast cells and protein, which fall to the bottom of the container. Other clearing agents – notably Irish moss, derived from seaweed – can be used in place of isinglass and the Guide feels that brewers should take a serious look at replacing isinglass with plant-derived finings, especially as the sturgeon is an endangered species.

Vegans avoid dairy products: lactose, a bi-product of cheese making, is used in milk stout, of which Mackeson is the best-known example.

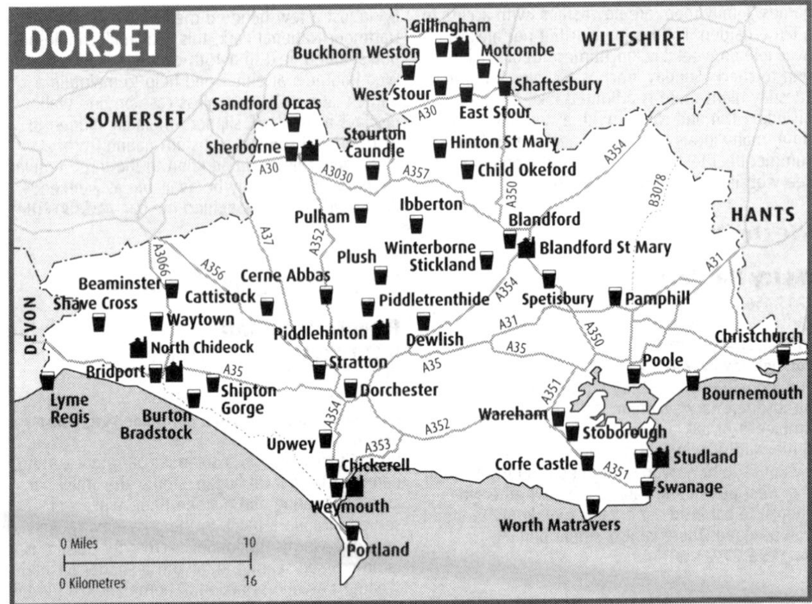

Beaminster

Knapp Inn

Clay Lane, DT8 3BU

12-2.30, 5-late (Mon, Tue & Thu), 12-late (Wed, Fri-Sun)

☎ (01308) 862408

Theakston Best Bitter; guest beers Ⓗ

Small, traditional free house on the edge of the town, popular with the locals. Guest beers are usually from the West Country. Bar snacks made by the landlady using local breads are a speciality. There is live music monthly and the pub offers traditional games as well as lending its support to the local cricket team. Dogs are welcome and there are seven types of Jack Daniels available for the rye enthusiast.

Blandford

Dolphin

42 East Street, DT11 7DR

11.30-3, 5.15-11; 11.30-11 Wed; 11.30-midnight Thu-Sat; 12-11 Sun

☎ (01258) 456813

Hopback Summer Lightning; Ringwood Best Bitter, Fortyniner; guest beers Ⓗ

Expect a warm welcome in this single bar, town-centre pub. Originally a cottage built in the 1750s, it was first licensed in the 1840s and refitted in 1996 by ex-brewers Gibbs Mew. The 18th-century dark wood panelled walls and low ceiling create a cosy atmosphere. Six ales are always on handpump and a range of malt whiskies and fruit wines is available. Evening meals are served Monday-Thursday only. Dogs on leads are welcome. (X8)

Railway ✔

Oakfield Street, DT11 7EX (off B3082)

11-3am; 10.30-12.30am Sun

☎ (01258) 456374

Badger First Gold; Ringwood Best Bitter; guest beers Ⓗ

Lively, community, back-street local in the heart of Blandford offering a wide range of entertainment for all, including a skittle alley. The single central bar once served commuters using the adjacent railway, but now plays host to numerous darts, pool and shove ha'penny teams. Good food is served well into the evening, four local ales are always available and there is a beer festival every May bank holiday. (X8)

Bournemouth

Brunswick

199 Malmesbury Park Road, Charminster, BH8 8PX

11-11 (midnight Fri)

☎ (01202) 290197

Greene King IPA, Ruddles Best, Old Speckled Hen, Abbot; guest beers Ⓗ

Friendly character pub in a residential area offering two constantly changing guest ales. Good, reasonably priced food is available, with a choice of roasts on Sunday. The smoking area at the back of the pub has been tastefully renovated to resemble an open air Victorian lounge complete with log-burning stove. Check out the Atrium function room with its oak panelling and inglenook fireplace. Q(5a,5b)

Cricketers Arms

41 Wind Ham Road, Springbourne, BH1 4RN

11-11; 12-10.30 Sun

☎ (01202) 551589

Fuller's London Pride; guest beer Ⓗ

Bournemouth's oldest pub, dating from 1847. The bar backs and other interesting original features. It once had stables and a separate boxing gym where the former world boxing champion Freddie Mills trained, but the room has now been opened up into the main bar. The two changing guest beers are chosen from the distributor's list. A good community pub with occasional live entertainment and a Tuesday night quiz. Sunday lunches only. P

Goat & Tricycle ✔
27-29 West Hill Road, BH2 5PF
12-11 (11.30 Fri & Sat); 12-10.30 Sun
☎ (01202) 314220
Wadworth IPA, 6X, JCB, seasonal beers; guest beers Ⓗ
The green tiled Victorian exterior adjoining a plainer frontage reveals the merger of two pubs into one, creating this large single bar pub. The full Wadworth range is always available alongside an ever-changing selection of five guests plus draught cider. The pub has an extensive food menu and a chalkboard details forthcoming guest beers. Notice the walking stick collection on the ceiling. A take-out service and Wadworth's bottled beers are available. The heated patio area is popular on balmy summer evenings.
❀◐◑♿🚌♣🍎

Porterhouse
113 Poole Road, Westbourne, BH4 9BG
11-11 (midnight Fri & Sat); 12-11 Sun
☎ (01202) 768586
Ringwood Best Bitter, Fortyniner, Old Thumper, seasonal beers; guest beers Ⓗ
Ringwood Brewery's only tied house in Bournemouth sells the full range of its award-winning ales plus ever-changing guests. Recently refurbished but retaining its original character, this is a pleasant, cosy pub with a strong local following – conversation as well as card and board games dominate. Simple wholesome food is offered at lunchtime and a quiz night is held on Tuesday. East Dorset CAMRA Pub of the Year seven times, and winner of many Pub of the Season awards.
Q◐≉(Branksome)🚌♣🍎

Royal Oak
Wimborne Road, Kinson, BH10 7BB
10.30-11; 12-6 Sun
☎ (01202) 572305
Dorset Piddle Yogi; Isle of Purbeck Fossil Fuel; Sharp's Doom Bar; guest beers Ⓗ
Traditional two-bar locals' pub in the centre of the north Bournemouth district of Kinson. The basic public bar is decorated with a range of curios and has a dartboard and shove ha'penny. The walls of the comfortable lounge bar feature motor racing prints and there is an open log fire. A previous CAMRA Spring Pub of the Season winner, the landlord plans to increase the beer range to five. Occasional live entertainment is hosted and there is a disco most weekends. ⛫❀◐🚌(many)♣P

Bridport

Crown Inn ✔
59 West Bay Road, DT6 4AX (on A35 roundabout between Bridport and West Bay)
11.30-late
☎ (01308) 786811
Palmers Copper, IPA, 200, Tally Ho! Ⓗ
Welcoming single-bar pub frequented by locals as well as beer and live music lovers from further afield. Food is available throughout the day from noon until 9pm. The full range of Palmer's beers is usually available. There is a great live music scene at the pub at weekends. A large TV screen, which can be seen from around the bar, shows sports events. Outside is a beer garden and dogs are welcome. ❀◐◑🚌P

Tiger Inn
14-16 Barrack Street, DT6 3LY
12-11; 11-midnight Sat; 12-9 Sun
☎ (01308) 427543
Beer range varies Ⓗ
This bright and cheerful Victorian ale house offers a frequently-changing beer list from across the UK, featuring breweries from Cornwall to the Orkney Isles. The single bar, with TV screening major sports events, and table skittles, is complemented by a small, attractive restaurant, a pretty garden and a full-size skittle alley. Close to the town centre and shops, the Tiger is well worth seeking out if you like a traditional public house. Thatchers cider is available. ⛫❀◐◑🚌(31)♣🍎

Woodman Inn
61 South Street, DT6 3NZ
11 (12 Sun)-11
☎ (01308) 456455
Branscombe Vale BVB; guest beers Ⓗ
Just a short stroll from the town centre, this small but bright and attractive pub offers all the features a real ale enthusiast could want. The single bar makes space for drinkers and diners to enjoy delicious home-cooked food. A full-size skittle alley leads to the garden —an oasis for a pint in the sun. Regular live music and a pub quiz on Sunday night are added attractions at this happy little pub. ⛫Q❀◐◑🚌(X53)♣

Buckhorn Weston

Stapleton Arms 🏆
Church Hill, SP8 5HS (between A303 and A30) ST757247
11-3, 6-11; 11-11 Sat & Sun
☎ (01963) 370396 thestapletonarms.com
Butcombe Bitter; Cheddar Potholer; guest beers Ⓗ
Imposing and stylish village pub with a single spacious bar and adjacent dining area. It has a relaxed, friendly atmosphere with a quiet, secluded garden. The beer range varies, often sourced from local micros. Real ciders are complemented by interesting apple juices and a wide selection of draught and bottled foreign beers. Excellent food includes hand-made pork pies and scotch eggs. Monthly beer and food tasting evenings are held. Children, dogs and muddy boots are welcome. ⛫Q❀🛏◐◑♿🍎P

Burton Bradstock

Three Horseshoes ✔
Mill Street, DT6 4QZ
11 (12 Sun)-11
☎ (01308) 897259 three-horseshoes.com
Palmers Copper, IPA, Tally Ho! Ⓗ
Old, thatched-cottage-style stone pub in an attractive village a mile from the sea. The L-shaped bar has a large inglenook with a log fire in winter and beams, pictures, local photos and rustic

INDEPENDENT BREWERIES
Art Brew North Chideock (NEW)
Dorset (DBC) Weymouth
Dorset Piddle Piddlehinton
Hall & Woodhouse/Badger Blandford St Mary
Isle of Purbeck Studland
Palmers Bridport
Sherborne Sherborne
Small Paul's Gillingham

furniture including a table with bench seats that was originally a double bed. Good value pub food with friendly service is available in the bar, with a more extensive menu in the restaurant. There is a small rear garden and dogs are welcome. A popular hostelry for locals, walkers and tourists. ⌂❀◑P

Cattistock

Fox & Hounds Inn ✔

Duck Street, DT2 0JH

12-3 (not Mon), 7-late (12-late Sat & Sun summer)

☎ (01300) 320444 foxandhoundsinn.com

Palmers Copper, IPA, Gold H

A warm welcome is assured at this delightful village pub set in picturesque countryside. Three well-kept Palmer's ales and Thatchers cider are on handpump and excellent home-cooked food (booking advised) is served from a choice that changes daily. You can enjoy Steak Night every Thursday and Folk Music Night on the second Monday of the month. The pub is home to various teams and clubs including skittles, crib, bowls, football, cricket and tennis. A function room is available. Dogs are very welcome – they even have their own section on the bar snacks menu. Wonderful accommodation. ⌂Q❀◑♣

Cerne Abbas

Giant Inn

24 Long Street, DT2 7JF

12-3 (not Tue), 6–11; 12-11 Sat; 12-10.30 Sun

☎ (01300) 341441 thegiantinncerneabbas.co.uk

St Austell Tribute; Dorset Piddle Piddle H

Lively village inn – the only free house in Cerne Abbas – formerly known as the Red Lion and rebuilt after a fire in 1898. The 16th-century stone fireplace remains, making it cosy in winter. Home to darts and skittles teams, this is a popular meeting place for all and regularly welcomes local Morris sides. The open-plan bar has a dining area with good pub food on offer (telephone for times). Cream teas are also served. All major football, rugby and F1 fixtures are screened. Outside is a patio with awning and garden. ⌂❀◑♣

Chickerell

Lugger

30 West Street, DT3 4DY (just off B3157)

8.30-midnight (11 Sun)

☎ (01305) 766611 theluggerinn.co.uk

Dorset Lugger Ale; Dorset Piddle Piddle; Palmers IPA; guest beers H

An attractive, family-friendly inn with a large split-level bar and separate dining room. Open for breakfast onwards and serving food all day, the pub offers a choice of excellent ales from an enthusiastic landlord who champions local beer. The house beer is brewed by DBC just up the road. Holiday cottages overlooking the beer garden can be booked through the pub and beer-lovers' breaks include brewery tours.

⌂Q❀◑♿Λ♣P

Child Okeford

Saxon Inn

Gold Hill, DT11 8HD

12-3, 7-11; 12-11 Sun

☎ (01258) 860310 saxoninn.co.uk

Butcombe Bitter; guest beer H

The external approach to this village free house is unusual as it is set back from the road, reflecting its origins as three separate cottages dating from the 17th century. The charming rustic exterior belies a refurbished and extended interior designed to provide more dining space and now incorporating four en-suite bedrooms. Guest beers are usually regional. A log fire warms the bar area and there is a large patio and garden popular with families in summer. ⌂Q❀◑♣P

Christchurch

Olde George Inn 🏆 ✔

2A Castle Street, BH23 1DT

11-11.30 (midnight Fri & Sat); 10.30-11 Sun

☎ (01202) 479383

Dorset Piddle Jimmy Riddle, Piddle, Yogi Beer, Silent Slasher; guest beer H

This former coaching inn was rebuilt after the civil war – some of its stone foundations were looted from the nearby castle. Today the inn serves as the brewery tap to Dorset Piddle, and is popular with locals and tourists alike. Excellent food is served all day, plus a Sunday carvery. Facilities include a heated courtyard and skittle alley. The menu includes Pedigree (Chum, not Marston's) for canine visitors. Handy for the castle, quay and historic priory. Local CAMRA pub of the year 2008.

❀◑♿⇌(1b,1c)♣

Thomas Tripp

10, Wick lane, BH23 1HX

10-11; 12-10.30 Sun

☎ (01202) 490498

Ringwood Best Bitter, Fortyniner H

Lively local just off Church Street, named after a ledendary local smuggler. This historic inn has a large main bar with a quieter room at the front. An excellent variety of food ranges from the full English breakfast to gourmet fresh seafood for which the pub is renowned. The large patio garden has bench seating. Local bands play on Wednesday and Sunday evenings. ❀◑♿⇌(1b,1c)♣

Corfe Castle

Greyhound Inn

The Square, BH20 5EZ

11-12.30am; 12-10 Sun

☎ (01929) 480205 greyhoundcorfe.co.uk

Ringwood Best Bitter; Sharp's Doom Bar; guest beers H

Situated at the gateway to the Purbecks, the gardens provide beautiful views of Corfe Castle's imposing ruins and the Swanage Steam Railway, both of which are within easy walking distance. The pub hosts regular live music with beer festivals in May and August as well as a sausage and cider festival in October. Food holds centre-stage in this village pub with an extensive menu on offer. Cyclists, walkers and dogs are welcome.

Q❀◑Λ⇌(Steam railway)(40)♣

Royal British Legion Club

East Street, BH20 5EQ (on A351)

12-3, 6-11; 12-midnight Sat; 12-10.30 Sun

☎ (01929) 430591

Ringwood Best Bitter; Taylor Landlord; guest beer H

This Purbeck stone building has a small bar and comfortable raised seating area. The guest beer is often Taylor Landlord and Thatchers cider is available. Occasionally there is entertainment on Saturday evening and major sporting events are screened. The outside drinking area includes a boules court. Sandwiches are available but no hot meals. Entry is with a valid CAMRA membership card or a copy of this Guide. ❀≋⊟(40)♣●P⅍

Dewlish

Oak

DT2 7ND

⏲ 11.30-2.30, 6-11.30; 12-3, 7-10.30 Sun

☎ (01258) 837352

Beer range varies [H]

Unpretentious village local with a public bar where you can enjoy darts or pool while sampling one of the ever-changing local ales. It has a small dining area off the main bar and a separate dining room opening onto the patio and large garden. Food ranges from all-day breakfasts to Sunday roasts – don't miss the home-made puds. Dogs are allowed in the bar. Monthly jazz nights are hosted. Accommodation is available in the converted coach house next door. Dewlish is of much interest to archaeologists and some of the sites are within walking distance of the Oak. ♨Q⊭◐◑♣

Dorchester

Blue Raddle 🏆

9 Church Street, DT1 1JN

⏲ 11.30-3 (not Mon), 6.30-midnight; 12-3, 7-10.30 Sun

☎ (01305) 267762

Butcombe Bitter; Dorset Piddle Piddle; Otter Bitter; guest beers [H]

Genuine, popular town-centre free house with friendly, helpful staff. The pub has a long narrow bar with plush seating at polished tables where home-cooked food sourced from local ingredients and real ales sit well together. Guest beers come from several local brewers. The pub takes part in local events and hosts regular live music with local musicians, including Irish and folk nights. Note the piped comedy and Private Eye available in the conveniences! CAMRA West Dorset Pub of the Year 2009. ◐◑♿≋(South)⊟♣●

Colliton Club ✔

Colliton House, Colliton Park, DT1 1XJ (opp County Hall & Crown Court)

⏲ 9-3, 7-11.30; closed Sun and bank holidays

☎ (01305) 224503

Greene King Abbot; Hop Back Odyssey; Palmers Copper Ale, IPA; guest beers [H]

Thriving club opposite County Council HQ with a reputation for good service. Formed in 1950, the club is housed in the mainly 17th-century Grade II-listed Colliton House and welcomes CAMRA members – just show your membership card to gain entry. Six real ales are always available. Busy in and out of office hours, this is a popular meeting place for a number of local associations. CAMRA Wessex Region Club of the Year 2008. Q◐≋(South/West)⊟

Kings Arms Hotel

30 High East Street, DT1 1HF

⏲ 11-11 (10.30 Sun)

☎ (01305) 265353 🌐 kingsarmsdorchester.com

Dorset Piddle Piddle, Cocky Hop, Silent Slasher; guest beers [H]

This 288-year-old coaching inn situated on the original London to Exeter route has recently undergone a £1 million facelift but retains much original character. Now the Dorset Piddle Brewery tap, the plush lounge bar is the perfect place to enjoy one of three well-kept Dorset Piddle ales or a guest beer. Good quality meals are served in the bar and the restaurant across the hall. Victorian scenes and portraits hang on the walls along with country sport and travel memorabilia. Accommodation is available all year round. Q♉⊭◐◑⊞♿≋(West/South)⊟P⅍

Tom Browns

47 High East Street, DT1 1LU

⏲ 11-11 (2am Fri & Sat); 12-11 Sun

☎ (01305) 264020

Beer range varies [H]

Previously home to the Goldfinch Brewery, the pub is now the Dorset Brewing Company tap. Four handpumps rotate through the full range of Goldfinch (now brewed by DBC) and DBC ales, alongside interesting guests. Refurbished but retaining the feel of a town centre ale house, the hostelry plays host to mini beer festivals, live music and other events. Simple locally-sourced pub grub is available at a reasonable price. It boasts a large garden ideal for lazy pints in the sun. Bottled DBC beers and presentation packs are on sale. ♨♉❀◐◑≋(West/South)⊟♣●⅍

East Stour

King's Arms

East Stour Common, SP8 5NB (on A30, W of Shaftesbury)

⏲ 12-3, 5.30-11; 12-midnight Sat; 12-10.30 Sun

☎ (01747) 838325 🌐 thekingsarmsdorset.co.uk

Palmers Copper Ale; St Austell Tribute; Wadworth 6X [H]

Imposing and recently extended roadside pub. This multi-roomed establishment is served by a single bar, with many areas provided for diners. A popular locals' pub, regulars recommend their favourite beers. Excellent food is made with locally sourced ingredients where possible and the monthly chef's challenge provides for a varied menu. There is a patio and enclosed garden as well as comfortable accommodation. Dogs and muddy boots are welcome in the bar. ♨Q❀⊭◐◑♿P⅍

Gillingham

Phoenix Inn ✔

The Square, SP8 4AY

⏲ 10-2.30 (3 Sat), 7-11 (not Mon eve); 12-3, 7-10.30 Sun

☎ (01747) 823277

Badger K&B Sussex, First Gold, seasonal beers [H]

Popular town centre pub built in the 15th century, originally a coaching inn complete with its own brewery. A cosy, one-bar inn, it has no games machines, just occasional background music. It is renowned for good value home-cooked food, including magnificent breakfasts, served in the bar and a separate dining area. A small courtyard for drinking alfresco is next to the quaint town square. ♨Q❀◐◑♿⛺≋♣

Hinton St Mary

White Horse

DT10 1NA (off B3092)
✪ 12-3, 6-11; closed Mon; 12-3, 7-11 Sun
☎ (01258) 472723
Beer range varies 🄷
This 16th-century stone building is a genuine old-fashioned public house at the heart of the village community. With wooden beams throughout, the public bar features stone flooring and an open fire, while the lounge is comfortable, cosy and home to a resident ghost. A warm, friendly welcome is extended to all including families and pets. No music, games machines or TV spoil the atmosphere. Excellent home-prepared food is served and there is a small but pretty garden. ♨Q❀◐◑♿🚌(309)♣P⚟

Ibberton

Crown

Church Lane, DT11 0EN ST787077
✪ 12-3, 6-11; closed Mon; 12-3, 7-10.30 Sun
☎ (01258) 817448
Beer range varies 🄷
Situated in the heart of the Dorset countryside below Bulbarrow Hill, this fine rural 16th-century pub retains many original features including its flagstone floor, oak doors and inglenook fireplace. The hillside garden with a small stream is a pleasure on a summer's day. Good food and locally-sourced ales attract regulars and visitors. Ideal for walkers, the Wessex Ridgeway is nearby. The village church of St Eustace is well worth a visit, offering views over the Blackmore Vale. ♨Q🐴❀◐◑P

Lyme Regis

Nag's Head

32 Silver Street, DT7 3HS
✪ 11-midnight
☎ (01297) 442312
Otter Ale; guest beers 🄷
Old coaching inn with magnificent views along the Jurassic Coast, offering an ever-changing choice of ales in two linked bar areas warmed by a wood burner, plus a games room. The house beer Sark Lark is brewed by Otter. Live music plays on Saturday and most Wednesdays. No meals are available but regular barbecues are held in summer. The garden has a covered terrace heated by a wood burner where smoking is allowed. Good quality en-suite B&B accommodation is available upstairs. ♨❀🛏▲P⚟

Volunteer Inn

31 Broad Street, DT7 3QE (on A3052)
✪ 11-11; 12-10.30 Sun
☎ (01297) 442214
Fuller's London Pride; guest beers 🄷
Historic two-room pub in the heart of town, a few steps from the seafront, with a lovely olde-worlde atmosphere. Popular with locals, the main bar buzzes with jolly banter and conversation. The house beer, Donegal, is stillaged behind the bar and named by long-serving landlord Joe after his homeland. A rotating choice of West Country ales is on offer. The pub is renowned for freshly-cooked meals including fish, served in the bar and dining room, where families are welcome. No food is served on Monday. 🐴◐◑▲

Motcombe

Coppleridge Inn ✔

SP7 9HW (signed from village)
✪ 12-3, 6-11; 12-11 Sun
☎ (01747) 851980 🌐 coppleridge.com
Butcombe Bitter; Greene King IPA; guest beer 🄷
A family-run country inn and restaurant, the main building is a converted farmhouse set in 15 acres of woodland, meadow and gardens. There is a cosy wood-panelled bar and a number of discrete dining areas. A continually rotating guest beer is offered, often quite unusual for the area. Local produce is sourced for the excellent meals and there are occasional theme nights. Accommodation is provided in chalet-style rooms around a courtyard. Function and conference facilities are available and the pub is licensed for weddings. ♨Q❀🛏◐◑♣P

Pamphill

Vine Inn ★

Vine Hill, BH21 4EE (off B3082) ST994003
✪ 11 (12 Sun)-3, 7-10.30
☎ (01202) 882259
Fuller's London Pride 🄷; **guest beers** 🄶
This 200-year-old bakehouse was converted into an inn in 1900 by the present landlady's grandfather and features in CAMRA's National Inventory of historic pub interiors. Popular with cyclists, walkers and their dogs, it comprises an intimate public bar, lounge area and a family/games room upstairs. The sun-trap garden, resplendent with grape vine, has heaters for the winter and play equipment for children. Westons cider and perry is available. Sandwiches and a hearty ploughman's lunch are offered at lunchtime. Q🐴❀◐🚆♣🍐⚟🍺

Piddletrenthide

Piddle Inn

DT2 7QF
✪ 11-midnight; 12-11 Sun
☎ (01300) 348468 🌐 piddleinn.co.uk
Dorset Piddle Piddle; Hop Back GFB; Ringwood Best Bitter 🄶
Once known as the Green Dragon, the Piddle is now named after the river on whose banks it stands. It is the closest pub to the Dorset Piddle Brewery serving its ales. A large, cheery single bar, brightly decorated and carpeted throughout, it serves three ales straight from the cask. The large restaurant seats 50, with dining also available in the bar for a more informal occasion. Popular locally, with a sunny garden and riverside patio seating, AA 4-star accommodation is available. ♨❀🛏◐◑♿🚌♣P⚟

Plush

Brace of Pheasants ✔

DT2 7RQ
✪ 12-3, 7-11; closed Mon; 12-3 Sun
☎ (01300) 348357 🌐 braceofpheasants.co.uk
Dorset Piddle Jimmy Riddle; Palmers Copper; Ringwood Best Bitter; guest beers 🄶
Cosy village pub with a friendly welcome for all (including dogs). The main bar, with a real fire in winter, serves regularly-changing ales dispensed direct from the cask. Superb food is available in the newly refurbished bar and restaurant areas. A large

sloping cottage garden to the rear has tables and a covered, heated area for smokers. Widely renowned for well-kept ales and good food, the pub can get busy and booking is a must for meals. Four comfortable and stylish designer bedrooms are available. ⛰Q❀🛏◐◑P⚟

Poole

Angel

28 Market Street, BH15 1NF

⏲ 11-11 (11.30 Thu-Sat); 11-10.30 Sun

☎ (01202) 666431

Ringwood Best Bitter, Fortyniner, Old Thumper, seasonal beers; guest beers Ⓗ

Ringwood Brewery's only tied house in Poole, sitting in the shadow of the historic Guildhall where an inn has stood since 1789. This is a large, friendly pub, served by a central bar and offering a good range of entertainment including a quiz night on Tuesday, music quiz on Wednesday and occasional live music evenings. Home-made food is served all week. There are views into the cask ale cellar and, outside, an attractive sun-trap drinking terrace. ⛰❀◐◑♿⇌♣⚟

Bermuda Triangle

10 Parr Street, Lower Parkstone, BH14 0JY

⏲ 12-2.30, 5-11 (midnight Fri); 12-midnight Sat; 12-11 Sun

☎ (01202) 748087

Beer range varies Ⓗ

This lively single bar local is a Guide regular and summer 2008 CAMRA Pub of the Season. Themed around the Bermuda Triangle mystery, one drinking area resembles a timber boat while part of an aircraft wing hangs from the ceiling in the main bar. The ever-changing selection of four real ales is cellared separately from the keg beers, assuring consistent quality and temperature. Foreign beer includes a variety of German lagers, wheat beers and Budvar Dark. Sadly, disabled access is impossible. ❀⇌(Parkstone)🚌(M1)

Branksome Railway Hotel

429 Poole Road, Branksome, BH12 1DQ (opp train station)

⏲ 11-11 (midnight Fri & Sat); 12-3, 7-10.30 Sun

☎ (01202) 769555 🌐 branksomerailwayhotel.co.uk

Hop Back Summer Lightning; Otter Ale; guest beer Ⓗ

Typical Victorian station pub with high ceilings built in 1894 to service the rail network and still benefiting from excellent links with public transport. Although essentially open plan in layout, the bar is partitioned into three distinct drinking areas, one with a pool table. Very popular with locals and commuters, as well as visitors availing themselves of the excellent accommodation, it plays host to a Friday night DJ, live music on Saturday, and screens major sporting events throughout the year.
🛏⇌(Branksome)🚌(M1,M2)♣P

Brewhouse

68 High Street, BH15 1DA

⏲ 11-11; 12-10.30 Sun

☎ (01202) 685288 🌐 milkstreetbrewery.co.uk

Milk Street Mermaid, Beer, seasonal beers Ⓗ

Originally the site of the Dolphin Brewery, the Brewhouse is now owned by Milk Street Brewery and operates as a drinkers' local. The front of the pub overlooks the high street and the games area at the back features pool, darts, pinball and a classic jukebox. Outside is a patio and smoking area. 2009 saw the introduction of a pub grub menu and occasional real cider.
❀◐◑⇌(Poole)♣⚟

Bricklayers Arms

31, Parr Street, Ashley Cross, BH14 0JX

⏲ 12-2.30, 5-11.30; 12-11.30 Sat & Sun

☎ (01202) 740304

Fuller's London Pride; Hop Back Summer Lightning; Ringwood Best Bitter, Fortyniner Ⓗ

In winter, a lovely real fire provides a warm welcome at this one-roomed pub with an L-shaped bar. Light and airy, it is popular with locals and visitors alike. Adorning the walls are pictures of bygone days, many of local interest. At the rear is a large garden with seating and a covered smoking area. Raised decking at the front provides a pleasant place to sit and watch the world go by.
⛰Q❀⇌(Parkstone)🚌(M1)

Portland

Royal Portland Arms

40 Fortuneswell, DT5 1LZ

⏲ 11-11.50 (12.50am Fri & Sat); 12-11.30 Sun

☎ (01305) 862255

Beer range varies Ⓖ

Full of character, this Portland stone pub stands alongside the main road with public car parks opposite and adjacent. More than 200 years old, inside you will find basic, homely furnishings and a friendly welcome for all. An ever-changing range of mainly West Country ales and ciders is available on gravity dispense. Live music is a regular feature and the pub hosts locally-attended events. King George III is noted to have stopped here for a drink on a visit to the island. Q🚌(1)●🗑

Pulham

Halsey Arms

DT2 7DZ

⏲ 11-11

☎ (01258) 817344 🌐 halseyarms.co.uk

Beer range varies, Ⓗ

A warm welcome awaits you at this family-friendly free house where young and old find something to smile about. The public bar boasts an ever-changing selection of real ales chosen by the enthusiastic landlady. Good food is on offer daily with the Sunday carvery very good value and always popular. For entertainment there is live music on Sunday, bingo in the evening and karaoke every fortnight. Traditional pub games include a skittle alley, pool table and table football. A function room hosts weddings, parties, skittles evenings, group meetings and village events. Dogs and coach parties are welcome. ⛰Q❀◐◑♿♣P

Sandford Orcas

Mitre Inn

DT9 4RU

⏲ 11.30-2.30 (3 Sat), 7-11; 12-3, 7-10.30 Sun

☎ (01963) 220271

Beer range varies Ⓗ

Set in a picturesque valley just outside Sherborne, run by the same landlord for the last 16 years, this cosy inn with wood burners and flagstone flooring remains unspoilt and original. A welcoming establishment, it offers a delicious home-cooked menu from a regularly changing blackboard. Three real ales are available and the pub often offers local produce for sale in the bar. The village itself is famous for its haunted manor house. Q❀P

Shaftesbury

Mitre

23 High Street, SP7 8JE
10.30-midnight; 12-11 Sun
(01747) 853002
Wells Bombardier; Young's Bitter, Special, seasonal beers H
Historic pub close to the town hall at the top of Gold Hill, with grand views overlooking the beautiful Blackmore Vale. Popular with younger drinkers but catering for all, an extensive food menu ranges from morning coffee to cream teas to good pub food. The Mitre runs crib and darts teams and hosts charity quizzes as well as occasional live music nights. ❀♣

Shave Cross

Shave Cross Inn

DT6 6HW (W of B3162 Bridport-Broad Windsor road) SY416980
11-3, 6-11; closed Mon; 12-3, 7-10.30 Sun
(01308) 868358 theshavecrossinn.co.uk
Beer range varies H
This 700-year-old rural inn, stone-built with a thatched roof, was rescued from oblivion by the local owners who have now added impressive accommodation. Historically a busy stop-off point for pilgrims and monastic visitors, it is now an award-winning free house with a small flagstoned bar serving a regularly changing and interesting selection of real ales and ciders. The bar leads to the restaurant where Caribbean-influenced dishes feature. A remote rural idyll with an attractive and mature garden, it is well worth the extra mileage. Q❀P

Sherborne

Digby Tap

Cooks Lane, DT9 3NS
11-11; 12-3, 7-11 Sun
(01935) 813148 digbytap.co.uk
Beer range varies H
Sherborne's only free house, the Digby is a supporter of West Country ales with beers coming from Teignworthy, Sharp's and Dorset Brewing Company. Well worth seeking out for the building alone – dating back to the 16th century, it was once the parish workhouse and many features of the original building remain. There are benches on a paved area outside for summer drinking. Food is served at lunchtime (Mon-Sat). Q❀

Shipton Gorge

New Inn

Shipton Road, DT6 4LT SY498927
11-3 (not Mon), 6-11; 12-3 Sun
(01308) 897302
Palmers IPA, Copper, 200 H
Well off the beaten track, this pub was saved from permanent closure in 2006 by a group of local people. In the last two years it has become the focal point for a range of village activities. The pub has a single bar serving three Palmers ales and an adjoining dining room. Those seeking food Sunday to Tuesday evenings should telephone ahead. Q❀P

Spetisbury

Drax Arms

High Street, DT11 9DJ
12-3, 7 (6 Wed & Thu)-10.30; 12-3, 6-11 Fri; 12-11 Sat & Sun
(01258) 452658
Beer range varies H
Situated on the A350 close to Spetisbury hill fort, this friendly ex-Hall & Woodhouse pub is now a free house. It keeps a range of four keenly and clearly priced beers, usually including one from the Dorset Piddle Brewery. The Drax also offers a real cider. There may be extended opening at weekends. An ideal base for a countryside walk. East Dorset CAMRA Rural Pub of the Year 2008. ❀(X8)♣P

Stoborough

King's Arms

3 Corfe Road, BH20 5AB (adjacent to B3075)
11-3, 5-11; 11-11 Fri-Sun
(01929) 552705
Black Sheep Best Bitter; Ringwood Best Bitter; guest beers H
This 400-year-old listed thatched building played host to Cromwell's troops in 1642 at the time of the siege of Corfe Castle. The pub is renowned for its food, and holds popular themed evenings. A long, slim pub with a split-level bar, its riverside dining area is always busy in summer. Up to four real ales and a cider from Cheddar Valley are available. An annual beer festival is held in summer. Q❀(40)P

Stourton Caundle

Trooper Inn

Golden Hill, DT10 2JW ST715149
12-2.30 (not Mon), 7 (6 Wed & Thu)-midnight; 12-3.30, 7-midnight Sun
(01963) 362405
Otter Bitter; guest beers H
Stone-built, single-room village centre pub with a separate function room featuring a bar and skittle alley. Two large inglenook fireplaces have been converted to seating areas and there is a children's area next to the beer garden. A popular fish & chips (in paper) night is held each Friday. The pub hosts an annual beer festival and real cider is served in summer. Dogs are welcome. Q❀♣P

Stratton

Saxon Arms

The Square, DT2 9WG
11-3, 5.30-11; 11-11 Sat; 12-10.30 Sun
(01305) 260020
Ringwood Best Bitter; Taylor Landlord; guest beers H
Built in recent years, this flint and thatch pub has the feel of a country inn. Outside, a patio area overlooks the village green. Inside, the bar divides into three areas —one a dining space where locally-sourced produce is served. Already an integral part of the local community, this attractive pub is very popular with regulars and visitors in summer months. ❀P

Studland

Bankes Arms

Watery Lane, BH19 3AU
🕔 11-11
☎ (01929) 450225 🌐 bankesarms.com
Isle of Purbeck Best, Fossil Fuel, Solar Power, Studland Bay Wrecked, IPA; guest beers Ⓗ
Built over 200 years ago, owned by the National Trust and run by the same family for more than 25 years, this famous country inn is home to the Isle of Purbeck Brewery. Nine handpumps dispense the entire range plus guest ales. The huge beer garden with views across the bay hosts a beer festival every August. The pub has an adjacent car park (free after 5pm and in winter) and moorings for 12 boats. Local CAMRA Rural Pub of the Year 2008. ⛰Q❀🛏◐⛺🚌(50)🍎

Swanage

Red Lion

63 High Street, BH19 2LY
🕔 11-11.30; 12-11 Sun
☎ (01929) 423533 🌐 redlionswanage.co.uk
Caledonian Deuchars IPA; Ringwood Best Bitter; Taylor Landlord Ⓗ**; guest beers** Ⓖ
This 17th-century hostelry retains many traditional features and serves up to six real ales in the summer, supporting local breweries. What makes the pub special are the ciders – Westons' full range and a variety of bottled ciders and perry are all on offer here. The restaurant provides an extensive selection of good food. Live music occasionally features. The garden is busy in the summer. Situated in a scenic seaside town, the pub is handy for the Swanage Steam Railway and the South West Coastal Path. ❀🛏◐⊟⇌🚌(50)♣🍎P⁵⁄–

White Swan

31 High Street, The Square, BH19 2LJ
🕔 11-11
☎ (01929) 423804 🌐 whiteswanswanage.co.uk
Dorset Piddle Piddle; Ringwood Best Bitter; guest beers Ⓗ
Fifty yards from the sea and opposite the small town square, this is a traditional old pub with modern touches set over four levels. It offers a range of food from pub grub to daily chef's specials including fresh fish. Guest beers are usually locally sourced. There is a walled garden at the rear for fine weather. Live music plays on Friday and Saturday nights and during Swanage jazz, folk and blues festivals, with a late licence. En suite rooms are available. ♨❀🛏◐⇌🚌(50)♣P⁵⁄–

Upwey

Royal Standard

700 Dorchester Road, DT3 5LA (on A354)
🕔 12-3, 6-midnight; 12-midnight Sat; 12-11 Sun
☎ (01305) 812558
Butcombe Bitter; Hop Back GFB; Ringwood Fortyniner; guest beers Ⓗ
Comfortable and homely two-roomed pub on the outskirts of Weymouth, well-known and well-loved by locals for its excellent beer and friendly welcome. The interior is dominated by a GWR railway theme. The wood-panelled public bar is complemented by a lounge bar area. Although customers are welcome to use the Internet facilities here, it is a mobile phone-free zone. ⛰Q⊟♿⇌🚌(10,31,145)♣P▯

Wareham

Black Bear Hotel

14 South Street, BH20 4LT
🕔 7.30am-midnight
☎ (01929) 553339
Ringwood Best Bitter, Fortyniner; Wychwood Hobgoblin; guest beer Ⓗ
Award-winning, Grade II-listed, 18th-century coaching inn full of period features set close to the River Frome in beautiful Wareham. It offers two bars, a restaurant, 11 en-suite bedrooms, a TV room and a fabulous, covered and heated smoking area and beer garden. A large chained bear stands proudly above the entrance. The pub offers regular entertainment and great food. An excellent base when visiting local Dorset attractions and the famous Purbeck coast. ❀🛏◐♿⇌🚌(40)⁵⁄–

Kings Arms

41 North Street, BH20 4AD
🕔 11-11; 12-10.30 Sun
☎ (01929) 552503
Ringwood Best Bitter; guest beers Ⓗ
Friendly, welcoming 15th-century thatched inn close to the town centre, with the original flagstone floors and fireplace in the main bar. This gem has two bars and a small restaurant where 'proper pub food' is served. The Brewers Bar is ideal for darts or a quiet drink. Traditional cider and perry are available. Live music features monthly. At the rear is a large beer garden, a heated, covered smoking area and a car park (off Mill Lane). Opening times are sometimes extended. ⛰❀◐⇌🚌(40,X53)♣🍎P⁵⁄–

Waytown

Hare & Hounds ✔

DT6 5LQ SY470978
🕔 11-3, 6.30 (6 summer)-11; 12-3, 7-11 Sun
☎ (01308) 488203
Palmers Copper Ale, IPA, Dorset Gold Ⓗ
Tucked away, this rural gem of an unspoilt village local is well worth seeking out. The garden, with stunning views across the Brit Valley, is a major attraction in summer with seating, a play area and grassy expanse for small folk to let off steam. Taunton cider is a regular and an attractive food menu features home-cooked meals and fresh local produce. Palmers 200 ale is available during the winter months. ⛰Q❀◐♣🍎P

West Stour

Ship Inn

SP8 5RP (on A30)
🕔 12-3, 6-11; 12-11 Sun
☎ (01747) 838640 🌐 shipinn-dorset.com
Ringwood Best Bitter; St Austell Tribute; guest beer Ⓗ
Built in 1750 as a coaching inn, this popular roadside pub has fine views across the Blackmore Vale. The public bar features a flagstone floor and low ceiling; the lounge and restaurant area are light and airy with stripped oak floorboards and farmhouse furniture. There is a pretty patio and large garden to the rear. This family-friendly pub is renowned for superb home-cooked food and comfortable accommodation. Dogs are welcome in the bar. ⛰Q❀🛏◐♣P⁵⁄–

Weymouth

Boot Inn

High Street, DT4 8JH
11-11; 12-10.30 Sun
☎ (01305) 770327
Ringwood Best Bitter, Fortyniner, Old Thumper, seasonal beers Ⓗ
Weymouth's oldest inn is tucked away behind the fire station. A fabulous, old-fashioned pub where conversation dominates, the single wood-floored bar area leads to small rooms at both ends with comfortable seating and warming coal fires. The full Ringwood range is supplemented by the landlord's choice of guest beer and a real cider. Local CAMRA Pub of the Year 2008.
Q

Duke of Cornwall

St Edmund Street, DT4 8AS
10-2am summer; 11-2am winter; 12-2am Sun
☎ (01305) 776594
Dartmoor Jail Ale; guest beers Ⓗ
This popular local is close to the harbour and the registry office. Open all day, it's ideal for that quick drink before the wedding ceremony! The only pub in the area serving Dartmoor Jail Ale, the Duke has a spacious wooden interior. Some fishing memorabilia and cartoons of local characters are displayed on the walls. Live music plays frequently and there is a lively atmosphere on weekend evenings, especially in summer.

Old Rooms Inn

Cove Row, DT4 8TT (on harbourside)
11-11 (midnight Fri); 12-10.30 Sun
☎ (01305) 771130
Dorset JD; Sharp's Doom Bar, IPA Ⓗ
Just around the corner from the Dorset Brewing Company and Brewers Quay overlooking the harbour, this is a very popular spot in summer months. No longer offering 'rooms for weary travellers' of course but the oldest part of the building dates back to Elizabethan times and its claim to fame is that the Duke of Gloucester took tea(!) here in 1771. Family-friendly, there is a large room off the bar where sports are screened. Quiz night is Tuesday and live music plays every second week.

Weatherbury

7 Carlton Road North, DT4 7PX
12-midnight
☎ (01305) 786040
Fuller's London Pride; guest beers Ⓗ
Down-to-earth free house in a residential part of town. The single bar interior is divided into different areas with a TV screen in each one. The London Pride is accompanied by frequently changing guest beers. Outside, the patio has a covered, heated area for smokers. Well-behaved children are welcome. Food may not always be available on Sunday – phone first to check.
Q P

Winterborne Stickland

Crown

North Street, DT11 0NJ (2 miles N of A354)
12-2.30, 6-11; 12-11 Sat; 12-10.30 Sun
☎ (01258) 880838
Ringwood Best Bitter, Fortyniner, seasonal beers Ⓗ
This 18th-century Grade II-listed inn is situated in the centre of the village set in pleasant walking country. There is an outdoor seating area and garden complete with original well. Excellent home-cooked food is available and can be enjoyed in front of the inglenook fireplace or in the beamed dining room at the back. Damory coaches run the bus service Mon to Sat from Blandford.
(311) P

Worth Matravers

Square & Compass ★

BH19 3LF (off B3069) SY974777
12-3, 6-11; 12-11 summer; 12-11 Sun
☎ (01929) 439229
Palmers Copper Ale; Ringwood Best Bitter; guest beers Ⓖ
This Good Beer Guide regular (one of only nine pubs nationwide that has featured in every edition) has added National Cider Pub of the Year 2008 to its growing list of awards. Offering excellent views across the Purbecks, the ever popular gem serves its own cider from the small serving hatch. The stone floors and modest furnishings add character, and a small museum containing fossils found along the famous Jurassic Coast is worth a visit.
Q (44) P

Spores for thought

Yeast is a fungus, a single cell plant that can convert a sugary liquid into equal proportions of alcohol and carbon dioxide. There are two basic types of yeast used in brewing, one for ale and one for lager (the yeasts used to make the Belgian beers known as gueuze and lambic are wild spores in the atmosphere). It is often said that ale is produced by 'top fermentation' and lager by 'bottom fermentation'. While it is true that during ale fermentation a thick blanket of yeast head and protein is created on top of the liquid, while only a thin slick appears on top of fermenting lager, the descriptions are seriously misleading. Yeast works at all levels of the sugar-rich liquid in order to turn malt sugars into alcohol. If yeast worked only at the top or bottom of the liquid, a substantial proportion of sugar would not be fermented. Ale is fermented at a warm temperature, lager at a much cooler one. The furious speed of ale fermentation creates the yeast head and with it the rich, fruity aromas and flavours that are typical of the style. It is more accurate to describe the ale method as 'warm fermentation' and the lager one as 'cold fermentation'.

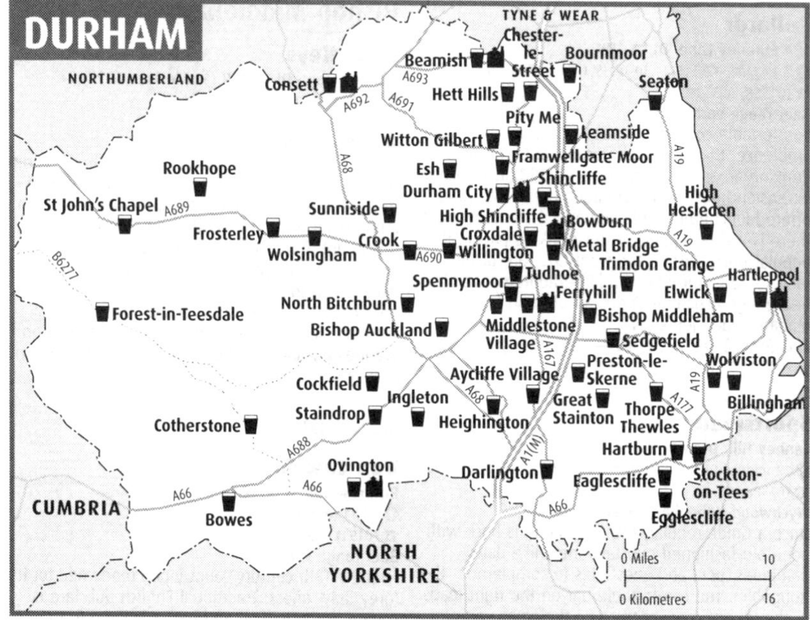

Co Durham incorporates part of the former county of Cleveland

Aycliffe Village

County

13 The Green, DL5 6LX
12-3, 6-11
☎ (01325) 312273 the-county.co.uk
Beer range varies H
Overlooking the award-winning green in a picturesque village, this attractive free house was originally three 17th-century cottages, and is now open plan with the bar and three dining areas unified by bright modern decor, complemented by older beams and log fireplaces. The owners took over in January 2008, with a passion to marry good food with excellent beers. The house beer, County Best Bitter, is brewed by Yard of Ale, just up the road. Up to three guests from northern micros are also on offer. ⁂Q❀◑◗⊟P⁑–⊡

Beamish

Shepherd & Shepherdess

DH9 0RS (follow signs for Beamish Museum)
11.30-11.30 (11 Sun)
☎ (0191) 370 0349
Black Sheep Best Bitter; guest beer H
Friendly village pub undergoing refurbishment, with interesting photos and pictures, many with a fox-hunting theme. Note the sign outside depicting a shepherd and shepherdess, and the mural in oil behind the bar of old Durham County. Wednesday is quiz night. One guest ale is available in the winter, two in summertime. The pub serves generously portioned meals offering good value for money. Baby changing facilities are available and outside is a play area for children. Buses to Newcastle and Sunderland pass close to the pub. ❀◑◗♿⊟(28,78)P⁑–

Billingham

Catholic Club

37 Wolviston Road, TS23 2RU (on E side of old A19, just S of Roseberry Rd roundabout)
7-11 (midnight Fri); 12-midnight Sat; 12-10.30 Sun
☎ (01642) 551137
Copper Dragon Best Bitter; guest beers H
Described as Teesside's best kept secret by one regular, this Victorian mansion and former Catholic junior school is now a thriving, friendly private members club. Card-carrying CAMRA members are always welcome. Dedicated and enthusiastic volunteers ensure that the club's reputation for serving fine real ales continues to grow. One regular and one guest ale are supplemented by up to six cask beers. Single brewery beer festivals held over a weekend or bank holiday have become a club speciality. Monthly blues/R&B nights are a highlight. ❀♿⊟(36)♣P⁑–

Bishop Auckland

Grand Hotel

Holdforth Crest, DL14 6DU (on A6072)
6-11; 12-3 Sun
☎ (07810) 751425
Beer range varies H
Well regarded throughout the region for its live music on Saturday nights, the pub now also enthusiastically promotes local young talent on Thursday and Friday nights (telephone for details). A big screen shows football. Lunches are served on Sunday only. The smoking area in the yard is covered and heated. The pub is a five-minute walk from the railway station, past Asda. ❀◑⇌(Bishop Auckland)♣●P⁑–

Pollards

104 Etherley Lane, DL14 6TW
⏲ 7-11 Mon; 12-2, 5-11.30 Tue-Sat; 12-2, 7-10.30 Sun
☎ (01388) 603539
Beer range varies Ⓗ
Comfortable community pub with a good ambience, two fires, pub games and four distinct drinking areas served from a central bar. A recent extension houses a large dining area, with food offered lunchtimes and evenings. On Sunday night there is a free supper for those taking part in the popular quiz. Outside the front door are picnic tables and to the rear is a large heated patio. The beer range usually includes an offering from Marston's and Jennings.
Q (94) P

Sportsman

Canney Hill, DL14 8QN
⏲ 12-midnight Mon, Wed & Thu; 12-1am Fri & Sat; 12-3 Sun
☎ (01388) 603847
Wychwood Hobgoblin; guest beers Ⓗ
Once a Guide regular, the Sportsman is back with good old-fashioned pub favourites like darts, dominoes, pool and guest ales to complement the Hobgoblin. The comfortable bar on the right leads to the lounge/pool room, and the small snug on the left leads to the restaurant. Good-value meals include a popular Sunday lunch, and there is occasional live music and various other entertainment including regular Scottish football thanks to landlord's origins. A music quiz is held on the last Sunday of the month. P

Stanley Jefferson ✔

5 Market Place, DL14 7NJ
⏲ 9am-midnight (1am Fri & Sat)
☎ (01388) 542836
Greene King IPA, Abbot; Marston's Pedigree; guest beers Ⓗ
This interesting conversion of a former solicitors' offices offers the typical range of Wetherspoon's facilities. Several comfortable drinking areas are served from one long bar, with an impressive glass roof above and a large heated patio outside. The eponymous Mr Jefferson lived in the town, was schooled nearby and was better known as Stan Laurel. Ciders are Westons Old Rosie and Organic. Food is served all day, and children are welcome if dining until 9pm. The Bishop of Durham's palace and adjacent park are nearby.

Tut 'n' Shive ✔

68 Newgate Street, DL14 7EQ
⏲ 11-11 (1am Thu-Sat); 12-11 Sun
☎ (01388) 603252
Beer range varies Ⓗ
Single-room pub with a popular jukebox and busy pool table, right in the heart of the town. It attracts a varied clientele thanks to its eclectic range of ales, mostly from independent and local breweries, preaching the cask gospel to younger drinkers. Old Rosie is regularly backed up with another real cider. Bagatelle and shove-ha'penny are played, there is a general knowledge quiz on Monday, music quiz on Thursday, and regular live music. An outdoor drinking area is next to the small car park.
P

Bishop Middleham

Cross Keys

9 High Street, DL17 9AR (1 mile from A177)
⏲ 12 (5 Mon)-11; 12-10.30 Sun
☎ (01740) 651231
Wells Bombardier Ⓗ
Busy, family-run, village pub with a warm, friendly atmosphere and a good reputation for excellent meals (booking advised). The spacious open-plan lounge/bar is complemented by a large restaurant/function room serving an extensive menu of freshly-prepared meals. Situated in excellent wildlife and walking country, a three-mile circular walk starts opposite. Quiz night is Tuesday, Teesside Tornadoes Bike Club meets on Wednesday and the pub has its own football team.

Bournmoor

Dun Cow ✔

Primrose Hill, DH4 6DY
⏲ 12-11 (midnight Fri & Sat)
☎ (0191) 385 2631
Beer range varies Ⓗ
Friendly 18th-century country pub renowned for its 'grey lady' ghost. Traditional English pub fare is served in the lounge and bar, a la carte in the restaurant and gastro in the new conservatory. Family friendly, there is a bouncy castle in the extensive gardens. Beer festivals in March and October promote local beers and live music festivals (first Saturday in June, last in September) feature local folk and rock bands. There is a function room for up to 100 and a marquee for up to 400 people. P

Bowes

Bowes Club (CIU)

Arch House, The Street, DL12 9HR
⏲ 7 (3 Sat & Sun)-midnight
☎ (01833) 628477
Beer range varies Ⓗ
This 18th-century gem was previously the village lock-up. The stone building is now a small, thriving club and hosts many community events, including quoits in the rear garden. There are two downstairs rooms – one with pool and darts, the other with a cosy fire in the fine old fireplace – and a meeting room upstairs. The beers are often sourced locally. Guests are welcome – show your CAMRA membership card. Opening hours may vary.

Chester-le-Street

Butchers Arms

Middle Chare, DH3 3QD
⏲ 11 (12 Sun)-3, 7-11; 11-midnight Sat
☎ (0191) 386 3605

INDEPENDENT BREWERIES

Camerons Hartlepool
Consett Ale Works Consett
Durham Bowburn
Four Alls Ovington
Hill Island Durham City
Stables Beamish (NEW)
Yard of Ale Ferryhill

Jennings Cumberland Ale; Marston's Pedigree; guest beers Ⓗ
The only real ale venue left in Chester town, this pub is recognised for the quality and quantity of its beers. It is also noted for its food, with fish freshly delivered and home-cooked pies a speciality. Sunday lunches are very popular and offer good value for money. Coffee and tea are usually available. Note the plates and tea pots on display. Small meetings can be accommodated. An awning is provided outside for smokers. Convenient for Chester-le-Street railway station and all buses through the town. Q◐◑⇌🚌⌐

Chester-le-Street Cricket Club ✔

Hawthorn Terrace, DH3 3PE
⏲ 12-11 (later at weekends)
☎ (0191) 3883684
Beer range varies Ⓗ
A well-appointed club house with two main rooms downstairs and an area of decking outside for warm-weather drinking – all with splendid views over the cricket ground. Light refreshments of sandwiches and pies are usually available from the bar. Functions for up to 90 people (including wheelchair users) can be accommodated in the brand new function room on the first floor. There is an external smoking shelter. Durham CAMRA branch Club of the Year 2008. ❀♿🚌P⌐

Pelaw Grange Greyhound Stadium

Drum Road, DH3 2AF (signed from Barley Mow roundabout on A167)
⏲ 6.30-11 (closed Mon, Wed & Thu); 12-4 Sun
☎ (0191) 410 2141 🌐 pelawgrange.co.uk
Beer range varies Ⓗ
Managed by a CAMRA member, this is the only greyhound stadium in Britain with real ales. The large open bar, Panorama restaurant and a concert room all overlook the track. There is a lively atmosphere on race nights (Tue, Fri & Sat) when CAMRA members are admitted free. An annual beer festival is held on the Easter weekend and trips to local micro-breweries are organised. Children are welcome and the trackside terrace is available for smokers. Twice Durham CAMRA branch Club of the Year. ❀◑♿🚌(21,22,50)P⌐

Smiths Arms

Brecon Hill, Castle Dene, DH3 4HE NZ299507
⏲ 4 (12 Fri & Sat)-11; 12-10.30 Sun
☎ (0191) 385 6915 🌐 smithsarms.com
Black Sheep Best Bitter; Courage Directors; Jarrow Rivet Catcher; guest beers Ⓗ
Next to the Brecon woods, this traditional pub was described by one regional newspaper as being 'miles from anywhere, minutes from everywhere'. It has a small, cosy bar with a log-burning stove and a larger lounge with an open fire. Smartly decorated in period style, the popular restaurant is on the second floor (booking recommended at the weekend). Food is also available in lounge. A folk club is hosted on Monday. The pub is reputed to be haunted. ⛼Q◐◑🀫♣P

Cockfield

Queen's Head

106 Front Street, DL13 5AA
⏲ 5 (1 Thu & Fri; 12 Sat & Sun)-11
☎ (07792) 413352
Beer range varies Ⓗ
Popular, community-focused local towards the south end of the village, with two constantly-changing guest ales. The single-room, open-plan drinking area is divided into various sections. The historic Cockfield Fell is just out the back, and visitors to this interesting area will find a warm welcome here. ◐🚌(8)♣P

Consett

Grey Horse

115 Sherburn Terrace, DH8 6NE
⏲ 12-midnight
☎ (01207) 502585
Consett Aleworks Steel Town Bitter; Consett Ale Works White Hot, Red Dust; guest beers Ⓗ
An oasis in a cask beer desert, this traditional pub dates back to 1848. With Consett Aleworks Brewery at the rear, the inn is one of a chain of four including the White Swan in Stokesley which brew Captain Cook ales. The interior comprises a lounge and L-shaped bar, with a wood-beamed ceiling. Beer festivals are held twice a year, live entertainment is hosted on Thursday and there is a quiz on Wednesday. Cider is Westons Old Rosie. The coast-to-coast cycle route is close by.
⛼Q❀🀫🚌♣🍎⌐

Cotherstone

Red Lion

Main Street, DL12 9QE
⏲ 12-3 Sat only, 7-11; 12-4, 7-10.30 Sun
☎ (01833) 650236
Jennings Cumberland Ale; Caledonian Deuchars IPA; guest beer Ⓗ
Nestling in a terrace of stone buildings dating from around 1738, this traditional local has changed little since the 1960s. It has a long main room with a serving hatch-style bar, and still has outside toilets. There is no TV or jukebox, just good beer and conversation. Guest beers are from local micros. CAMRA branch Community Pub of the year 2008, the pub is used by various clubs. Children and dogs are welcome and there is a small beer garden. ⛼Q🐕❀⛺🚌♣P

Crook

Colliery

High Jobs Hill, DL15 0UL (on A690 at E edge of town) NZ177351
⏲ 12-2 (not Tue & Wed), 6.30-midnight; closed Mon; 12-3, 7-midnight Sun
☎ (01388) 762511
Camerons Strongarm Ⓗ
Situated on the Durham road out of the town, with panoramic views over Wear Valley, this is a popular pub offering good quality, inexpensive food from a varied menu. The traditional interior features interesting ceramics and pottery. It serves as a meeting place for the local riding club and as a convenient location for nearby allotment holders to slake their thirst. The smoking area outside is covered. Q❀🛏◐◑♿🚌(46)P⌐

Croxdale

Daleside Arms

Front Street, DH6 5HY (on B6288, 3 miles S of Durham, off A167)
⏲ 3 (7 Tue; 12 Sat)-11 (midnight Thu-Sat); 11-8 Sun

☎ (01388) 814165

Beer range varies Ⓗ

Up to two beers, often from local brewers, can be found in this comfortable roadside rural setting. Visitors are greeted by stunning award-winning floral displays. Sporting memorabilia adorns the cosy main bar. Food is served in the spacious lounge but pre-booking is advised. A previous CAMRA branch Pub of the Year winner, it remains an oasis in a village ideally situated for country walks but well served by public transport. Worth making the effort for the simple things done properly. Q❀⇌◐♿🚌♣P⁄–

Darlington

Britannia

1 Archer Street, DL3 6LR (next to ring road W of town centre)

⌚ 11.30-3, 5.30-11; 11.30-11 Thu-Sat; 12-10.30 Sun

☎ (01325) 463787

Camerons Strongarm; John Smith's Bitter; guest beers Ⓗ

Friendly, popular, local CAMRA award-winning pub – a bastion of cask beer for over 150 years. The pub retains much of the appearance and layout of the private house it once was – a modestly enlarged bar and small parlour (used for meetings) sit either side of a central corridor. There are prize-winning external floral displays in summer. Listed for its historic associations, it was the birthplace of teetotal 19th-century publisher JM Dent. Four countrywide guest beers are available.
❀≋🚌♣P⁄–

Darlington Snooker Club

1 Corporation Road, DL3 6AE (corner of Northgate)

⌚ 11-midnight (late Fri & Sat); 12-midnight Sun

☎ (01325) 241388

Beer range varies Ⓗ

This first floor, family-run and family-oriented private snooker club offers a warm, friendly welcome. Four guest beers from micros countrywide are on offer. A small, comfortable TV lounge is available for those not playing on one of the 10 top-quality snooker tables. Twice yearly the club plays host to a professional celebrity and two beer festivals are held annually. Winner of CAMRA regional Club of the Year 2004-2008, it welcomes CAMRA members with a membership card or a copy of this Guide. ≋(North Rd)🚌♣

Number Twenty-2 ✔

22 Coniscliffe Road, DL3 7RG

⌚ 12-11; closed Sun

☎ (01325) 354590 🌐 villagebrewer.co.uk

Burton Bridge Bitter; Village Brewer White Boar, Seasonabull, Old Raby; guest beers Ⓗ

Town-centre ale house with a passion for real ale and winner of many CAMRA awards. It has up to 13 handpumps along with nine draught European beers. Huge curved windows, stained glass panels and a high ceiling give the interior an airy, spacious feel. To the rear, the Canteen serves upmarket but inexpensive lunches in a convivial surrounding. The pub comes alive in the early evening as people leave work. This is the home of Village Brewer beers, commissioned from Hambleton by the licensee. Q◐♿≋🚌

Old Yard Tapas Bar

98 Bondgate, DL3 7JY

⌚ 10-11; 12-10.30 Sun

☎ (01325) 467385 🌐 tapasbar.co.uk

John Smith's Magnet; Theakston Old Peculier; guest beers Ⓗ

Interesting mixture of a town centre bar and Mediterranean-style taverna offering a range of real ales alongside a fascinating blend of international wines and spirits. Four guest beers from micros countrywide are stocked. Although this is a thriving restaurant, you are more than welcome to simply pop in for a pint – and maybe a tapa or two (Greek and Spanish). The excellent south-facing pavement café is popular in good weather. TV is for sport only. ❀◐≋🚌⁄–

Quakerhouse 🏆

1-3 Mechanics Yard, DL3 7QF (off High Row)

⌚ 11 (12 Sun)-midnight

☎ (07817) 108756 🌐 quakerhouse.net

Beer range varies Ⓗ

Often the first point of call for CAMRA members visiting Darlington, this lively, award-winning free house is situated in one of the old yards just off the pedestrianised town centre. It opened in 1998 in the former Quaker Coffee House and has the feel of a cellar bar. Up to 10 guest beers are available from regional and micro-breweries countrywide. Live rock music features on Wednesday (there is a door charge after 7.30pm). An upstairs function room is available for hire. ♿≋🚌

Tanners Hall ✔

62-64 Skinnergate, DL3 7LL

⌚ 9-midnight (1am Fri & Sat)

☎ (01325) 369939

Marston's Pedigree; Greene King IPA, Abbot; guest beers Ⓗ

A popular Wetherspoon's town pub with a varied clientele. Its 12 handpumps provide a good selection of real ales including up to five guests at value for money prices, often from local micros. Converted from a furniture shop in 1998, its spacious interior makes it an ideal venue for holding its own beer festivals as well as the chain's national events. It gets very busy at weekends, in fact occasionally boisterous. Reasonably priced food is served until 10pm. Q❀◐♿≋🚌⁄–

Durham City

Bridge Hotel

40 North Road, DH1 4SE (200m from Durham rail station)

⌚ 11 (12 Sun)-11

☎ (0191) 386 8090 🌐 bridgehoteldurham.co.uk

Morland Speckled Hen; Theakston Best Bitter; guest beer Ⓗ

Originally built in the 1850s as lodgings for the Irish navvies constructing the railway viaduct under which it sits, it evolved into a public house a few years after completion of the railway. Three immaculately kept ales are always available, including a weekly changing guest. The comfortable dining area offers a diverse, high quality menu of home-cooked food throughout the day at reasonable prices. It can get busy at weekends, but you are always assured a warm welcome and excellent service from the attentive staff. ⇌◐♿≋🚌

Colpitts Hotel

Colpitts Terrace, DH1 4EL

⌚ 2 (12 Thu-Sat)-11; 12-10.30 Sun

☎ (0191) 386 9913

Samuel Smith OBB Ⓗ

An unspoilt gem, this late Victorian pub has changed little since it was first built. Occupying a corner site, the building has an unusual A shape with three rooms – a small lounge, a snug used as a pool room and the comfortable main bar partially divided by a fireplace. Like all Sam Smith's, the noise comes from conversation not jukebox or games machines. A must-visit hostelry for anyone who appreciates pubs as they used to be. ⩞Q❀⊟⇌⊟⚐

Dun Cow ✔

37 Old Elvet, DH1 3HN

11-11; 12-10.30 Sun

☎ (0191) 386 9219

Black Sheep Best Bitter; Camerons Castle Eden Ale; Jennings Cumberland Ale Ⓗ

In 995AD Lindisfarne monks were searching for a resting place for the body of St Cuthbert when they came across a milkmaid looking for her lost cow. She directed them to Dun Holm (Durham). This pub, dating back to the 16th century, is named after the historic animal. At the front of the building is a friendly snug and there is a larger lounge to the rear. The story of the monks' legendary journey is told on the wall of the corridor alongside the two rooms. Q⊟⇌⊟(20)⚐

Half Moon ✔

86 New Elvet, DH1 3AQ (opp Royal County Hotel)

11-11 (midnight Fri & Sat); 12-11 Sun

☎ (0191) 383 6981

Draught Bass; Taylor Landlord; guest beer Ⓗ

A long-term regular in the Guide, this city-centre pub is named after the crescent-shaped bar that runs from the front room through to the lounge area. Run by the same landlord for 25 years, the interior is largely unchanged with traditional decor throughout and interesting photos of the pub at the beginning of the 20th century on the walls. Attracting a lively crowd on Friday and Saturday evenings, it has a large backyard outdoor area next to the river which is popular in summer. The guest beer is from Durham Brewery. ❀⇌⊟(21)⚐

Market Tavern

27 Market Place, DH1 3NJ

11-11 (midnight Thu; 1am Fri & Sat); 12-11 Sun

☎ (0191) 3862069

Beer range varies Ⓗ

Situated in Durham's historic market place, this single-roomed, L-shape bar offers an array of six ales from all over the UK. The management makes full use of its guest list and has featured Mordue, Hydes, Beartown and Oakleaf beers, to name but a few. This venue is improving all the time, and good food is available up to 9pm. The interior is basic wooden ale house style, and friendly staff provide a warm welcome to regular and casual visitors alike. ◐♿⇌

Olde Elm Tree

12 Crossgate, DH1 4PS

12-11; 11-midnight Fri & Sat; 12-10.30 Sun

☎ (0191) 386 4621

Adnams Bitter; Camerons Strongarm; guest beers Ⓗ

One of Durham's oldest pubs, dating back to at least 1600 – as befits its age it is reputed to have two ghosts. The interior comprises an L-shaped bar room and a 'top' room linked by a set of stairs. A popular pub, it attracts a good mix including students, locals and bikers. Arrive early for the quiz on Wednesday or folk group on Monday and Tuesday. Ask the landlord for details of the scenic walk to the river banks and cathedral. The bus station in North Road is just 200m away. ❀⇌P⚐

Shakespeare Tavern ★

63 Saddler Street, DH1 3NU (100m from Market Place)

11-midnight (11 Sun)

☎ (0191) 384 3261 🌐 shakespearedurham.co.uk

Caledonian Deuchars IPA; Fullers London Pride; guest beers Ⓗ

A CAMRA heritage pub in the city centre on the way to the cathedral. The small bar has a side snug and a back lounge which was enlarged in 2008 by utilising an old adjacent storage room. It was originally a haunt for 19th-century theatre actors and patrons, hence the name. Despite the recent alterations and other ill-judged attempts at change over the years, it has largely maintained its character – though purists may disagree. Popular with locals and students. Q⊟⇌

Victoria Inn 🏆 ★

86 Hallgarth Street, DH1 3AS

11.45-3, 6-11; 12-2, 7-10.20 Sun

☎ (0191) 386 5269 🌐 victoriainn-durhamcity.co.uk

Big Lamp Bitter; guest beers Ⓗ

This friendly, welcoming and authentic Victorian pub remains almost unaltered since it was built in 1899. The quaint decor, coal fires, tiny snug and a genuine Victorian cash drawer help create an olde-worlde feel. Five superb real ales, mainly from local breweries, are on sale alongside a wide selection of whiskies. There is no food menu but toasties are available. The excellent en-suite accommodation is renowned. Voted local CAMRA Pub of the Year for the fifth time in 2007. ⩞Q⛟⊟⇌⊟(21)♣

Water House ✔

65 North Road, DH1 4SQ

9am-11.30

☎ (0191) 370 6540

Greene King IPA, Abbot; Marston's Pedigree; guest beers Ⓗ

Situated in former water board offices and a short distance from the bus station, this pub is popular with young and old alike and extremely busy at weekends. A selection of beers from regional and micro-brewers awaits, with single brewery weekends now a feature. The modern decor is complemented by coal-effect open fires. Good value food is served. An excellent Wetherspoon's pub. ◐♿⇌⊟

Eaglescliffe

Cleveland Bay

718 Yarm Road, TS16 0JE (jct of A67 and A135)

11-1am

☎ (01642) 780275

Taylor Landlord; guest beers Ⓗ

Dating from the arrival of the world's first public railway, the Stockton & Darlington, the gate pillars from the goods yard now adorn the entrance to the car park. An ever-popular pub, you can be sure of a friendly and genuine welcome. A previous CAMRA Pub of the Season winner, its reputation for fine cask beers continues to grow. With a separate bar, lounge and large function room, it is bustling on big sports occasions. ❀⊟⊟(7)P⚐⊡

Egglescliffe

Pot & Glass

Church Road, TS16 9DQ (300m from A135, opp church)
12-2 (not Mon), 6-11 (5.30-midnight Fri; 6-midnight Sat); 12-11 Sun
(01642) 651009
Draught Bass; Black Sheep Best Bitter; Caledonian Deuchars IPA; guest beers H
A previous CAMRA Pub of the Season winner, this classic and popular multi-roomed village pub is situated in a quiet cul-de-sac opposite the village church. Former licensee and cabinet maker Charlie Abbey, whose last resting place overlooks the pub, left his legacy in the form of the ornate bar fronts fashioned from old country furniture. Tasting notes are available for the five handpumps, which include two guests. Outside is a large south-facing garden. Themed food evenings support the good value, home-cooked menu. Q (7)P

Elwick

McOrville Inn

34 The Green, TS27 3EF (300m off A19)
12-2.30, 5-11; 12-3, 7-10.30 Sun
(01429) 273344
Camerons Mcorville Ale; guest beers, seasonal beers H
This ancient inn, situated on the village green and named after a local horse that won the 1902 St Leger, is popular with locals and visitors alike. A previous CAMRA award winner, it has deep damp cellars that ensure the beers are kept in excellent condition, while real fires and old village photos add to the traditional ambience. The seasonal ales are sourced from Camerons' micro-brewery, the Lion's Den. A popular menu, sourced from local produce wherever possible, represents good value. Q (516,518)P

Esh

Cross Keys

Front Street, DH7 9QR (3 miles W of A691) NZ197440
12-2, 5.30-11; 12-3, 7-11 Sun
(0191) 373 1279
Black Sheep Best Bitter; guest beer H
Pleasant 18th-century pub in a picturesque village offering a varied food menu including vegetarian and children's choices. A comfortable locals' bar is complemented by a lounge overlooking the Browney Valley. Delft racks display porcelain artefacts, some of which portray the old village. The village is commonly known as Old Esh to distinguish it from nearby Esh Winning. Q P

Ferryhill

Surtees Arms

Chilton Lane, DL17 0DH
4-11; 12-midnight Fri & Sat; 12-11 Sun
(01740) 655724 thesurteesarms.co.uk
Yard of Ale One Foot in the Yard, Black as Owt Stout; guest beers H
Large multi-roomed traditional pub owned by CAMRA members – a rare nitrokeg-free cask ale outlet in the town. Guest beers are sourced from local and national breweries. The real cider also changes regularly. Annual beer festivals are held in the summer and at Hallowe'en. Live music and charity nights are regular events. Lunches are served on Sunday only. A function room is available for private gatherings. The pub is also home to the Yard of Ale micro-brewery, established in 2008, and its beers are always on offer here. Q

Forest in Teesdale

Langdon Beck Hotel

DL12 0XP (on B6277, 8 miles NW of Middleton in Teesdale) NY853312
11-11 (closed Mon Nov 1-Easter); 12-10.30 Sun
(01833) 622267 langdonbeckhotel.com
Black Sheep Best Bitter; Jarrow Rivet Catcher; guest beers H
Situated high in the Pennines, in some of the finest countryside in England, this inn has long been a destination for walkers, fishermen and those seeking tranquillity. This gem offers excellent food plus a range of beers that includes a guest from a local micro. A beer festival is held in May. The spectacular High Force and Cauldron Snout waterfalls are not too far away and the Pennine Way passes close by. Q P

Framwellgate Moor

Tap & Spile

Front Street, DH1 5EE (off A167 by-pass)
12-3 (Fri & Sat only), 6 (5 Fri)-11.30; 12-3, 7-10.30 Sun
(0191) 386 5451
Beer range varies H
Offering one of the best selections of ales in Durham, this ever-popular CAMRA award-winning pub continues to fly the flag for local micros. A typical ale house divided into four rooms with wooden flooring, it offers a warm welcome and good conversation. With its display of old pump clips, some bearing testament to breweries long departed, this is a must visit for any real ale fan. Why not try your luck at the Wednesday night quiz? Q (1A,21)

Frosterley

Black Bull

Bridge End, DL13 2SL (100m S of A689 at W end of village)
10.30-11; closed Mon; 10.30-5.30 Sun
(01388) 527784
Beer range varies H
Four ales from north-eastern independent breweries, plus up to four ciders and perries, set the tone for this unique pub. Stone and bare wooden floors throughout, plus a kitchen range and piano in the bar, add to the rustic decor and real old-fashioned pub ambience. High-quality food is from locally-sourced ingredients. There are tables outside the front door and a covered yard to the side. The only pub in the country to have its own peal of bells. Winter hours may vary. Q (101)P

Great Stainton

King's Arms

The Green, TS21 1NA
11.30-3, 6-11; 12-3.30, 6.30-midnight Sun
(01740) 630361 kingsarmspub.co.uk
Beer range varies H
The pub is situated five miles north-east of Darlington, just off an old Roman road in a small,

quiet village. The bay-windowed 18th-century main building on the tiny green accommodates the old public bar, the extensions to the right a lounge and dining room. There are plenty of seats outside at the front of the pub. Mainly a food venue, the pub also prides itself on its two ever-changing guest ales from majors and micros countrywide. Spot the VR post box.

Hartburn

Masham Hotel

87 Hartburn Village, TS18 5DR
11-11 (11.30 Fri & Sat); 12-4, 7-10.30 Sun
☎ (01642) 645526
Black Sheep Ale; Draught Bass; Greene King IPA
Set in a leafy residential area, the Masham still retains the appearance of the Victorian house it once was. Step inside and it is like walking into someone's front room. The multi-room interior has a central bar serving the range of real ales, some of which may change from time to time. Food is all home made, good value and deservedly popular. Outdoor facilities are impressive and extensive, with a shelter for smokers. Q(20)P

Parkwood

64-66 Darlington Road, TS18 5ER
12-11 (midnight Fri & Sat); 12-11 Sun
☎ (01642) 587933 theparkwoodhotel.com
Adnams Broadside; Camerons Strongarm; Greene King Abbot; guest beers
This magnificent red brick Victorian building, with its imposing porch, tiled hallway, staircase and public rooms, is the former home of the Ropner family – local shipbuilders, ship owners and civic benefactors. The licensee has been a real ale enthusiast for many years and is determined to keep the large, friendly bar for drinkers, though there is a strong emphasis on food. The guest beer is usually a rarity for the area. Accommodation is in six high-quality en-suite bedrooms.
Q(20)P

Hartlepool

Brewery Tap

Stockton Street, TS24 7QS (on A689 in front of Camerons Brewery)
11-4; closed Sun
☎ (01429) 868686 cameronsbrewery.com
Camerons Strongarm, seasonal beers
When Camerons Brewery discovered that it owned the adjacent derelict Stranton Inn, its future was secured by turning it into a visitor centre. Visitors to this award-winning development can sample Strongarm, the brewery's flagship brand, together with quarterly specials from the main brewery and Camerons' own Lion's Den micro-brewery. The Brewery Tap also acts as a shop, museum and starting point for brewery tours. Conference facilities and evening opening for groups and other social events can be arranged. Q(36)P

Causeway

Vicarage Gardens, Stranton, TS24 7QT (beside Camerons Brewery)
3-11 (11.30 Thu); 11-midnight Fri & Sat; 12-10.30 Sun
☎ (01429) 273954 myspace.com/thecausewaypubhartlepool
Banks's Bitter; Camerons Strongarm; Wychwood Hobgoblin; guest beers
This marvellous multi-roomed red-brick Victorian building has been Camerons' unofficial brewery tap for decades. Though owned by Marston's, the sales of Strongarm remain huge. This CAMRA multi-award winning pub even gets a mention in Hansard for the quality of its Strongarm. The licensee, a keen musician, hosts an eclectic mix of live music most evenings. Good value home-cooked lunches are served Friday to Sunday. Two guest beers are always available. The covered beer garden is, not surprisingly, a smokers' paradise.
Q

Jackson's Arms

Tower Street, TS24 7HH (100m S of railway & bus stations)
12-midnight (2am Fri & Sat)
☎ (01429) 862413
Beer range varies
Close to the Grand Central and Northern railway station and the bus station, and also to Hartlepool United football ground, this warm and friendly street-corner local was once offered as the prize in a raffle. However, at £100 a ticket, there were few takers! There are two busy bars, one for convivial conversation and one for pool and darts. The upstairs function room is newly refurbished. At least three, generally four, premium guest beers are on offer, sourced from throughout the country.

Tall Ships

Mulberry Rise, Middle Warren, TS26 0BF (on A179, 3km NW of town)
10-11 (midnight Thu-Sat); 11-11 Sun
☎ (01429) 273515
John Smith's Bitter; guest beers
Aptly named in readiness for the town's Tall Ships festivities during the summer of 2010, this newly built, out-of-town, prestigious pub is all set for you to embark on your own mini beer festival in a friendly and comfortable environment. Four guest beers are always available, with the regular ale sold at a discounted price. Third-of-a-pint tasting racks come complete with tasting notes, and details of forthcoming beers are also listed. Quality, value for money food is served all day, every day.
(6)P

Heighington

Bay Horse

28 West Green, DL5 6PE
11-11.30 (11.45 Fri & Sat); 12-10.30 Sun
☎ (01325) 312312
Black Sheep Best Bitter; Greene King Old Speckled Hen; John Smith's Magnet; Taylor Landlord; guest beer
Picturesque, historic, 300-year-old pub overlooking the village's largest green. It has a traditional feel inside with exposed beams and stone walls, partitioned into distinct drinking and dining areas, with a large restaurant extending from the lounge. Food plays a prominent role, with home-cooked meals available as well as bar snacks. The bar area gives drinkers the chance to enjoy the beer range in the evening, along with Old Rosie cider.
P

George & Dragon

4 East Green, DL5 6PP
12-3 (not Mon & Tue), 5-11; 12-midnight Fri & Sat; 12-11 Sun

☎ (01325) 313152
Wells Bombardier; Black Sheep Best Bitter; John Smith's Magnet; guest beers H
Friendly village pub where locals warmly welcome visitors, situated in a fine position on the smaller green. An old coaching inn complete with stables, it has been refurbished in a modern style with a bar and spacious lounge. Meals are served in the lounge, while a conservatory-style restaurant area offers excellent home-cooked food. There are tables outside, weather permitting. Two guest ales, often from the Wylam Brewery, help to ensure this is a pub for lovers of good beer. ♔Q❀◐▶⊟♿♣P

Hett Hills

Moorings

DH2 3JU NZ240513
⏲ 12-11.30 (10.30 Sun)
☎ (0191) 370 1597 🌐 themooringsdurham.co.uk
Taylor Landlord; guest beers H
A large, well-appointed, nautically-themed pub on two levels, recently extended by the addition of quality hotel accommodation – some rooms with hot tubs. The bar and bistro serve food all day with a wide choice of traditional home-cooked English dishes. Upstairs, with splendid views, the Prime Rib restaurant offers quality meals including seafood and fine cuts of local meats – ideal for special occasions. A smoking cabin is available outside. Wheelchair users can only access the ground floor. ❀🛏◐▶♿🚌(28)P⁄–

High Hesleden

Ship Inn

TS27 4QD NZ453381
⏲ 12-3 (Sat only), 6-11; 12-9 Sun
☎ (01429) 836453 🌐 theshipinn.net
Beer range varies H
Remote gem of a country free house in the south east of the county. Up to seven ales, mainly from micro-breweries, are on handpump in the comfortable bar. An award-winning selection of superb food is served in the lounge and restaurant. A nautical theme runs through the pub with pictures of warships on display in the bar and models of sailing ships in the lounge/restaurant. Adjacent to the large rear garden are six chalets plus a family apartment. There is ample parking and a good view of the North Sea on a clear day. ♔Q❀🛏◐▶⊟P

High Shincliffe

Avenue Inn ✔

Avenue Street, DH1 2PT (150m from A177)
⏲ 12-11 (10.30 Sun)
☎ (0191) 3865954 🌐 theavenue.biz
Black Sheep Best Bitter; Camerons Strongarm; guest beer H
A friendly out of town pub. The food menu offers traditional home-cooked fare on weekday evenings, as well as specials and Sunday lunch. A dominoes competition on Thursday evening and the Monday night quiz are popular with locals and guests. Darts is also played. Many public footpaths nearby make this a handy base for walkers and cyclists exploring the surrounding countryside. Regular bus services link it to historic Durham City only a mile away. ❀🛏▶🚌♣P⁄–

Ingleton

Black Horse

Front Street, DL2 3HS
⏲ 7-midnight Mon & Tue; 6-midnight Wed-Sat; 12-3.30, 8-midnight Sun
☎ (01325) 730374
Jennings Cocker Hoop; guest beers H
Traditional, family-run village free house set back from the road with a large car park. A leaded glazed screen separates the dining area from the lounge bar. The two guest ales come from local micros. Thai food is served Wednesday to Saturday evenings, with traditional lunch on Sunday. A taxi service is available for groups of four to eight people. This popular community pub has had the same landlord for more than 15 years and also serves as a village shop. Q❀◐▶🚌(88)♣P⁄–

Leamside

Three Horseshoes

Pit House Lane, DH4 6QQ
⏲ 11 (12 Sun)-11
☎ (0191) 5842394 🌐 threehorseshoesleamside.co.uk
Taylor Landlord; guest beers H
Three years ago this pub underwent extensive alterations and building work, and is now well worth a visit. The landlord is a past winner of CAMRA branch and regional Pub of the Year competitions with previous pubs. The traditonal bar has a large open fire and to the rear is a smart, modern restaurant and a spacious garden area. Fresh food is served in both rooms with a varied menu in the restaurant. Booking is advisable. The pub hosts local cycle and clay pigeon clubs. Traditional cider comes from Westons. ♔◐▶⊟🍎P

Metal Bridge

Old Mill Hotel

Thinford Road, DH6 5NX (off A177) NZ303351
⏲ 12-11 (10.30 Sun)
☎ (01740) 652928 🌐 theoldmill.uk.com
Beer range varies H
Originally built as a paper mill in 1813, this is now the venue of choice for discerning locals and visitors alike. Renowned for its good-quality food and well-kept ales, three handpumps serve an ever-changing range, with the nearby Durham Brewery often supplying one of the beers. The food menu is extensive with daily specials written on a board above the bar. Larger groups are welcome in the conservatory. Accommodation is of a high standard, with all rooms en-suite. ✪❀🛏◐▶♿P

Middlestone Village

Ship Inn 🍸 ✔

Low Road, DL14 8AB (on B6287)
⏲ 4 (12 Fri-Sun)-11
☎ (01388) 810904 🌐 shipinnmiddlestone.co.uk
Beer range varies H
The epitome of a village pub, this bustling local is very much at the heart of the community, though regulars come from miles around. Entertainment includes darts and dominoes on Monday, a quiz on Thursday, plus regular themed nights and twice-yearly beer festivals. The open plan bar has three drinking areas and there is an upstairs function room with two roof-top patios – from here you can enjoy spectacular views south to the North

Yorkshire Moors. Food is available lunchtimes and evenings Friday-Sunday, evenings only Monday-Thursday. (2,3)

North Bitchburn

Red Lion

North Bitchburn Terrace, DL15 8AL (just off A689)
12-2 (not Mon), 6.30-11; 12-3, 6.30-11 Sun
(01388) 763561 theredlionbitchburn.co.uk
Black Sheep Best Bitter; Taylor Landlord; guest beers H

Popular 250-year-old village pub with fine south-easterly views over the Wear Valley from the dining room. Originally a farm, it then became a way station for drovers on the way to Bishop Auckland market. The cheerful, refurbished interior is light and bright, with a comfortable bar room, small pool room and larger restaurant with a second dining area down a couple of steps. The pub has a well-deserved reputation for good food, available lunchtime and evening. Guest beers tend to come from smaller north-eastern breweries, with a monthly 'feature brewery' such as Mordue or Jarrow. (1C)P

Ovington

Four Alls

The Green, DL11 7BP (2 miles S of Winston & A67)
7 (6 Fri; 3 Sat)-11; 12-10.30 Sun
(01833) 627302 thefouralls-teesdale.co.uk
Beer range varies H

Friendly 18th-century inn opposite the village green in what is known as 'the maypole village'. A Victorian sign denotes the four alls: 'I govern all (queen), I fight for all (soldier), I pray for all (parson), I pay for all (farmer)'. The pub has a bar, games room and restaurant serving excellent value food. Home of the Four Alls Brewery, is the only place to sample beers. It also offers comfortable country inn accommodation in a lovely setting.
QP

Pity Me

Lambton Hounds

Front Street, DH1 5DE 100m from A167 by-pass roundabout
11-11 (midnight Fri & Sat); 12-11 Sun
(0191) 386 4742 lambtonhoundsinn.com
Beer range varies H

Situated on the Great North Road, this 250-year-old former coaching inn offers comfortable en-suite accommodation. It has a basic bar and cosy lounge with a small back room. Good home-made food is served in all rooms (not Sun eve) and there is also a separate restaurant. The ales can be found in the lounge bar, where part of the counter is from the cocktail bar of the Titanic's sister ship the Olympic. Local brewers are usually well represented.
(21)P

Preston-le-Skerne

Blacksmiths Arms

Preston Lane, DL5 6JH (off A167 at Gretna Green)
11.30-2, 6-11; closed Mon; 12-10.30 Sun
(01325) 314873
Beer range varies H

Welcoming free house known locally as the Hammers, situated in a rural location. A long corridor separates the bar, lounge and restaurant. The beamed lounge is furnished in a farmhouse style. The pub has an excellent reputation for home-cooked food and up to three guest beers are available, sourced mainly from local micros. A former local CAMRA Rural Pub of the Year, it even has a helicopter landing pad. QP

Rookhope

Rookhope Inn

Rear Hogarth Terrace, DL13 2BG
12-midnight
(01388) 517215
Black Sheep Best Bitter H

Off the beaten track in the north Pennines, this Grade II-listed building dating from 1680 retains the original open fires and wood beams. A welcome rest stop on the Coast to Coast cycle route, this friendly two-roomed community pub also offers accommodation. Spectacular views of upper Weardale can be enjoyed from the garden. Situated in a pretty former lead-mining village, the surrounding area provides ample opportunity for exploration.

St John's Chapel

Blue Bell

12 Hood Street, DL13 1QJ
5 (12 Sat & Sun)-1am
(01388) 537256
Caledonian Deuchars IPA; guest beers H

This small, homely village local is situated in beautiful Upper Weardale, and is very much at the heart of the community. The pub hosts ladies and gents darts and pool teams, and runs a quiz on Sunday night. It also has a leek club which holds an annual show, and there is a small library. The local angling club is based here and fishing licences are on sale at the bar. The guest beer often comes from the local Allendale Brewery. There is a covered and heated outdoor area.
(101)P

Seaton

Seaton Lane Inn

SR7 0LP (on B1404 W of A19)
11.30-midnight (1am Fri & Sat); 12-midnight Sun
(0191) 581 2038 seatonlaneinn.com
Taylor Landlord; Wells Bombardier; guest beers H

This roadside inn can trace its origins to an 18th-century blacksmith's – the basic stone-walled bar was the original building and a pictorial history is displayed on the walls. Behind this room is a small lounge next to a popular restaurant area. Quiz nights are Wednesday and Thursday. What was once a large decked garden has been lost to the construction of a 18-room hotel. QP

Sedgefield

Ceddesfeld Hall

Sedgefield Community Association, Rectory Row, TS21 2AE
7.30-10.30; 8-11 Fri & Sun; 9-11 Sat
(01740) 620341
Beer range varies H

Built in 1791 as the local parsonage, the hall comes complete with resident ghost 'the Pickled Parson'. Set in extensive grounds, ideal for a summer's evening, this is a private club but CAMRA members are most welcome. There is a bar, comfortable lounge and large function room. Run by volunteers from the Sedgefield Community Association, it is used by a wide variety of groups. An annual beer festival is held on the first weekend in July with reasonably-priced ale. Q❀⊟♿🚌P⚲▯

Nag's Head

8 West End, TS21 2BS
⏲ 6 (5 Wed-Fri; 12 Sat)-midnight; 12-11 Sun
☎ (01740) 620234
Taylor Landlord; guest beers Ⓗ
Situated at the centre of the village, close to Sedgefield racecourse, this free house is a traditional local attracting all age groups – families with well-behaved children are very welcome. There is a comfortable bar and a smaller lounge as well as a restaurant serving traditional Sunday lunch prepared with fresh local produce. Meals are also available in the bar (no food Sun & Mon eve). The landlord and landlady both come from the village. ❀◗⊟♿🚌♣P⚲

Shincliffe

Seven Stars Inn

High Street North, DH1 2NU (on A177, S of Durham)
⏲ 11-11 (10.30 Sun)
☎ (0191) 384 8454 🌐 sevenstarsinn.co.uk
Black Sheep Best Bitter; Taylor Landlord; guest beers Ⓗ
Dating from 1724, this small, cosy, beamed pub is situated on the edge of a pleasant village. Local country walks and the long Weardale Way pass nearby. Walkers are welcome in the bar – just make sure your boots are clean. Well-behaved dogs are also permitted. Meals are served in the bar and traditional restaurant. Comfortable accommodation makes the pub a great base for visiting the city and other attractions in the area. See the website for details. ❀🛏◖◗⊟🚌

Spennymoor

Frog & Ferret

Coulson Street, DL16 7RS
⏲ 12-midnight (11.30 Sun)
☎ (01388) 818312
Beer range varies Ⓗ
This friendly family-run free house offers four constantly changing real ales sourced from far and wide, with local and northern micro-breweries well represented. A welcoming atmosphere greets you on arrival at the three-sided bar in the comfortably-furnished lounge. Darts and dominoes are played and bar snacks are available. Well-behaved children are permitted until 4pm. A quiz is held on Sunday evening. 🔥❀◖♿♣P⚲

Staindrop

Wheatsheaf

42 South Green, DL2 3LD
⏲ 12-11 (10.30 Sun)
☎ (01833) 660129
Black Sheep Ale; Camerons Strongarm; guest beer Ⓗ
Welcoming, Tudor-style former coaching inn with 1930s stained glass windows overlooking the green in a picturesque Teesdale village. The interior has a linked bar and lounge with a separate pool room, and is home to many clubs and games including quoits, darts, dominoes and pool. The village carnival committee meets here. A quiz is held every Tuesday. The garden is fabulous, with water features and a covered, heated smoking shelter. Handy for exploring Teesdale, the bus stop is right outside the door. Q❀♿⛺🚌(8,75)♣⚲

Stockton-on-Tees

Sun Inn ✔

Knowles Street, TS18 1SU
⏲ 11-11; 12-10.30 Sun
☎ (01642) 611461
Draught Bass Ⓗ
Popular town-centre drinkers' pub, reputed to sell more Draught Bass than any other pub in the country. It was rescued from an uncertain future six years ago by a regular at the pub who became the licensee and quickly increased sales of Bass to 12 18-gallon casks a week – his son-in-law is the current licensee. The pub supports darts teams, a football team and charitable causes. On Monday evening the large function room is home to the famous Stockton Folk Club. ⇌🚌♣⚲

Thomas Sheraton 🏆 ✔

4 Bridge Road, TS18 1BH
⏲ 9-midnight (1am Fri & Sat)
☎ (01642) 606134
Greene King Ruddles Best Bitter, Abbot; Marston's Pedigree; guest beers Ⓗ
This local CAMRA 2008 Pub of the Season and 2009 Pub of the Year is a fine Wetherspoon conversion of the extensive Victorian law courts, and named after one of the country's great Georgian cabinet makers and furniture designers who was born in the town in 1751. It comprises several separate dining and drinking spaces downstairs, while upstairs a balcony and a sheltered patio are accessed by palatial staircases. There is an ever-varying selection of up to nine guest beers, several sourced from local craft breweries.
🐴❀◖◗♿⇌🚌🍎⚲

Sunniside

Moss Inn

78 Front Street, DL13 4LX (W end of village on B6299)
⏲ 6-11; 12-10.30 Sun
☎ (01388) 730447
Black Sheep Best Bitter; guest beer Ⓗ
Homely freehouse situated closed to Tow Law serving good food and ale. As well as the beers an extensive selection of malt whiskies is available to the connoisseur, perfect for enjoying in front of the open fire on a winter's evening. Friday is dominoes night and visitors are welcome to join the friendly locals. Food is served on Sunday lunchtime, and there is a quiz on the first Saturday of the month.
🔥◖◗⊟🚌(1B)♣P⚲

Thorpe Thewles

Hamilton Russell Arms

Bank Terrace, TS21 3JW (100m off A177)
⏲ 12-11; 12-10.30 Sun
☎ (01740) 630757 🌐 hamiltonrussell.com
Marston's Pedigree; guest beers Ⓗ
Customers come from far and wide to this busy, impressive village pub. While the emphasis here leans towards good-value, top-quality food, served all day every day, real ale continues to remain the

licensee's lasting passion and drinkers are always made most welcome. Three handpumps include two guest beers, usually premium or strong bitters, which change weekly. The extensive south-facing patio areas have fine views. ⌂❀◐♿🚌(69)P

Trimdon Grange

Dovecote Inn

Salters Lane, TS29 6EP (on B1278)
⏲ 7 (12 Fri & Sat)-11; 12-11 Sun
☎ (01429) 880967
Beer range varies Ⓗ
This free house's licensees hail from Charles Wells country and the pub's twin passions are Rugby Union and real ale. Situated on the outskirts of a former mining village, the building dates back to at least 1820, growing an extra storey in 1927, resulting in its distinctive tall but narrow appearance. There used to be a dovecote on one corner, hence the name. Inside, the single large room houses a popular pool table and dartboard. Quiz night is Tuesday. ⌂🚌

Tudhoe

Black Horse Inn

4 Attwood Terrace, DL16 6TD (on B6288)
⏲ 11.30-11
☎ (01388) 420662
Caledonian Deuchars IPA; Courage Directors; guest beers Ⓗ
Once closed down by a pubco as unviable, this pub was reopened by the current owners in October 2008 and is now a busy, atmospheric and friendly free house. Two changing guest ales are always available. Excellent food is served at lunchtimes and evenings in the restaurant and the bar. Buses from Durham city pass the door. A family-friendly pub, it is well worth a visit. ❀◐♿🚌♣P⊬

Willington

Burn Inn

14 West End Terrace, DL15 0HW (jct B6286 & A690 at W end of village)
⏲ 11-11 (midnight Sat); 12-11 Sun
☎ (01388) 746291
Beer range varies Ⓗ
This cosy establishment has become a first-class community hostelry, serving three ales from the Punch Taverns Finest Cask range. Various pub games are played here throughout the week and a quiz is held on Wednesday. The pub also runs its own golf society and provides a meeting point for village junior football teams and local Labour Party meetings. There is a heated outdoor area for smokers. ❀🚌♣P⊬

Witton Gilbert

Glendenning Arms ✔

Front Street, DH7 6SY (off A691 bypass, 3 miles from city centre)
⏲ 4 (12 Sat)-midnight; 12-10.30 Sun
☎ (0191) 371 0316
Black Sheep Best Bitter; guest beer Ⓗ
Typical village community local and Guide regular with a small, comfortable lounge and a lively and welcoming bar with the original Vaux 1970s red and white handpulls. The bar is attractively decorated in a contemporary style while the lounge remains more traditional. The pub runs darts, dominoes and football teams. Situated on the village's main road, there is ample car parking. ⌂Q❀⊟🚌♣P

Travellers Rest

Front Street, DH7 6TQ (off A691 bypass, 3 miles from city centre)
⏲ 11-11; 12-10.30 Sun
☎ (0191) 371 0458
Theakston Best Bitter; guest beers Ⓗ
Open-plan, country-style pub, popular with diners. The bar area is split into three sections with a conservatory off to the side where families are welcome. There is also a more private dining room. An extensive food menu suits all tastes, with food served throughout the pub. Quiz nights are Tuesday and Sunday. The restaurant has recently been redesigned and the kitchen upgraded to modern standards. Q♉❀◐🚌P⊬

Wolsingham

Bay Horse Hotel

59 Uppertown, DL13 3EX (on B6296 to Tow Law) NZ078378
⏲ 11-midnight (11-3, 5-midnight Mon-Fri winter)
☎ (01388) 527220
Camerons Strongarm; guest beer Ⓗ
Large Cameron's house on the north edge of the village. Excellent quality, good-value food is served in the bar and a la carte restaurant. The guest beer is usually from the Cameron's range. Quiz night is Sunday. Good quality B&B accommodation is available, providing an ideal base for exploring Weardale. ⌂♉❀🛏◐⊟♿🚌(101)♣P⊬

Black Bull

27 Market Place, DL13 3AB
⏲ 12-11 (11.30 Sun)
☎ (01388) 527332
Caledonian Deuchars IPA; guest beer Ⓗ
Imposing hotel in the centre of the village, providing excellent food and accommodation. The pub runs various games nights and serves as headquarters for the village cricket team in the summer, hosting its social events. A good base for walkers and cyclists, it is convenient for the Weardale Railway, which has a station in the village. The garden is a real surprise, especially in summer. ⌂Q❀🛏◐⊟♿⛺🚌(101)♣⊬

Wolviston

Ship Inn

50 High Street, TS22 5JX
⏲ 12-3, 5-11; 12-3.30, 7-11 Sun
☎ (01740) 644420 🌐 theshipinnwolviston.co.uk
Beer range varies Ⓗ
In a picturesque village this impressive pub was rebuilt during the 19th century on the site of an old coaching inn. The licensee follows a vigorous real ale policy, with three handpumps providing a constantly-changing range of premium bitters. Only freshly-cooked, good value, traditional pub food is served (not Sun eve), including the Captain's Whopper Cod. There is a large beer garden and a function room available free of charge. Q❀◐P⊬

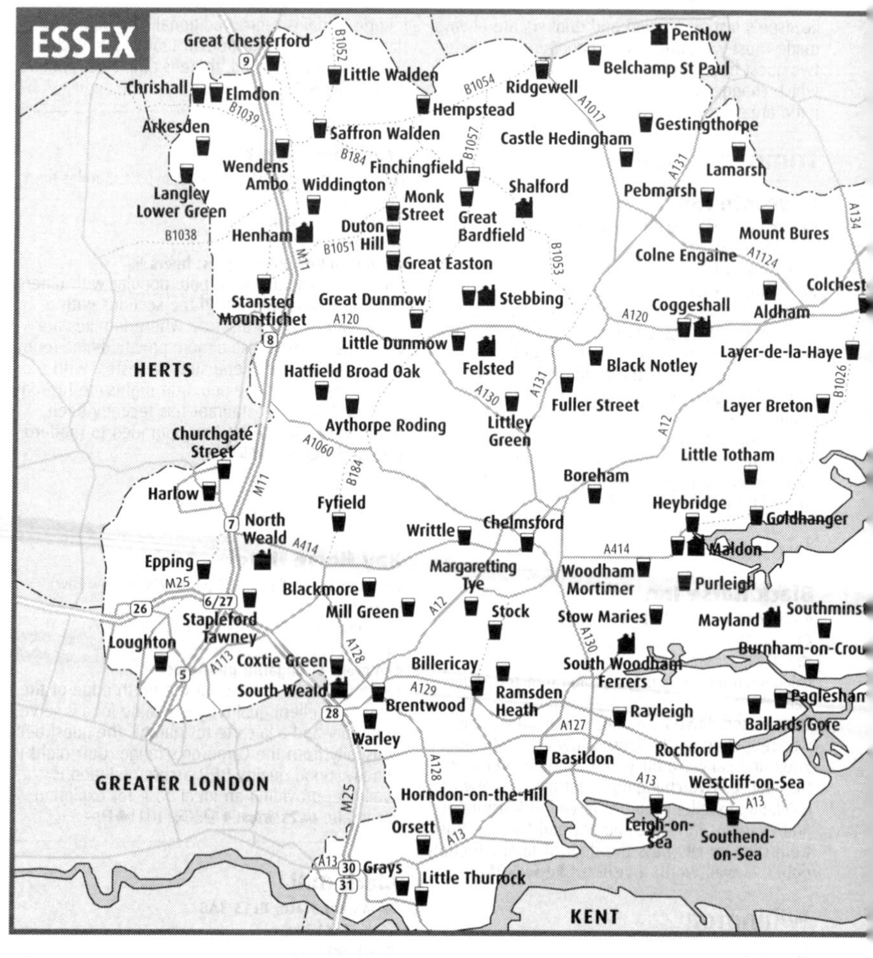

Aingers Green

Royal Fusilier

Aingers Green Road, CO7 8NH

11-1 (Wed & Fri only), 6-11; 11-11 Sat; 12-10.30 Sun

(01206) 250001

Beer range varies Ⓗ

This delightful village pub has recently been acquired by a local couple and makes a welcome return to the Guide. Starting life as a beer house over 50 years ago, it retains its traditional appearance, with brickwork and timber from a previous era. There are three rooms, one with a welcoming fire in winter, another with a well-used pool table. The pub has teams in darts and pool leagues and hosts special themed evenings. (Great Bentley)P

Aldham

Old Queens Head

Ford Street, CO6 3PH (on A1124)

11.30-11; 12-10.30 Sun

(01206) 241584

Greene King IPA Ⓗ**; guest beers** Ⓗ/Ⓖ

This large, friendly village inn is popular with locals and walkers, situated close to the Essex Way footpath. The 16th-century pub has two bar areas and a separate restaurant, serving a wide range of food including a popular Sunday lunch. Live music plays occasionally, including an acoustic open mike night, and a quiz is held on the second Sunday of the month. A marquee is erected in summer, used for barbecues, music and private functions. Two to three guest ales are usually available, sometimes on gravity dispense. (88)P

INDEPENDENT BREWERIES

Brentwood South Weald
Crouch Vale South Woodham Ferrers
Famous Railway Tavern Brightlingsea
Farmer's Ales Maldon
Felstar Felsted
Hart of Stebbing Stebbing
Harwich Town Harwich
Mersea Island East Mersea
Mighty Oak Maldon
Nethergate Pentlow
Pitfield North Weald
Red Fox Coggeshall (NEW)
Saffron Henham
Shalford Shalford
Sticklegs Great Bromley (NEW)
Wibblers Mayland

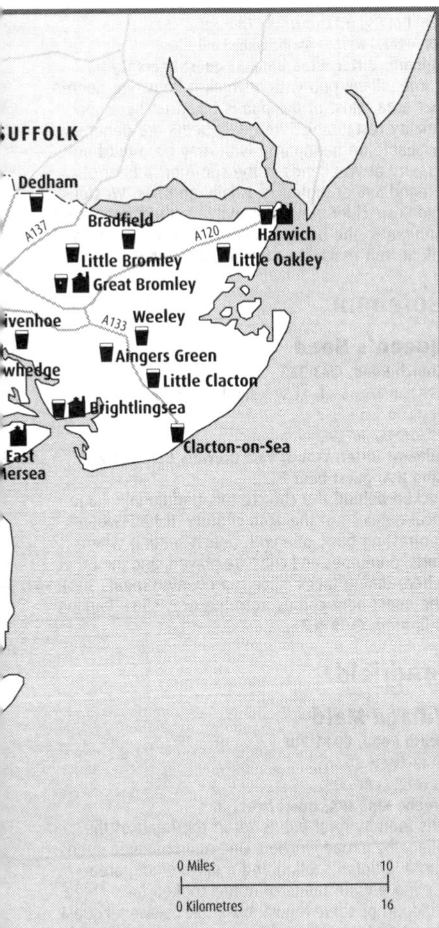

Arkesden

Axe & Compasses

Wicken Road, CB11 4EX (2 miles N of B1038) TL483344
11.30-2.30, 6-11 (11.30 Sat); 12-3, 7-10.30 Sun
(01799) 550272 axeandcompasses.co.uk
Greene King IPA, Old Speckled Hen, Abbot H
Partly thatched 17th-century village inn with a public bar and an award-winning restaurant. This friendly community hostelry is at the centre of village life – the locals in the public bar tend to be interested in, and talk to, strangers. The pub is frequented by walkers on the extensive footpath network in this pleasant area where three counties meet. The patio/garden is pleasant in summer and the Harcamlow Way long distance path passes nearby.

Aythorpe Roding

Axe & Compasses

Dunmow Road, CM6 1PP (on B1845 5 miles SW of Dunmow) TL594154
11-11 (midnight Fri & Sat); 12-10.30 Sun
(01279) 876648 theaxeandcompasses.co.uk
Nethergate IPA H**; Sharp's Doom Bar; guest beers** G
Refurbished and reopened in 2007 after being closed for some time, this friendly thatched pub, frequented by many local drinkers, provides both good beer and good food, from lunchtime snacks to elegant dining in the separate restaurant. In winter there is an open fire and in summer a pleasant garden, with views over farmland to the nearby windmill and open countryside. Winner of the Best Traditional Pub 2008, sponsored by BBC Radio Essex.

Ballards Gore (Stambridge)

Shepherd & Dog

Gore Road, SS4 2DA (between Rochford and Paglesham)
12-3, 6-11; 12-11 Sat; 12-10.30 Sun
(01702) 258279
Beer range varies H
This excellent, cottage-style pub was voted local CAMRA Pub of the Year 2004 and Rural Pub of the Year in 2008. The four changing real ales generally come from micro-breweries and are often unusual for the area. Cider is stocked in summer. The comfortable restaurant serves high-quality meals and a wide range of good food is also available at the bar. Traditional pub games including Shut the Box are available on request. Walkers, cyclists and coach groups are welcome. (60)P

Basildon

Selex Sports & Leisure Club

Gardiners Way, SS14 3AP (small turning off Gardiners Lane, easily missed) TQ721908
11-11; 12-10.30 Sun
(01268) 523773
Beer range varies H
Members' social club in an industrial estate area, two miles from Basildon town centre. Three changing low-priced guest ales are available from local and distant brewers. The club has a quiet lounge bar and a separate games room with pool table and satellite TV. There is a patio seating area overlooking a park area with football pitches. Bar snacks are available at most times during the week. The club has a covered smoking area. Card-carrying CAMRA members are welcome.
QP

Belchamp St Paul

Half Moon

Cole Green, CO10 7DP TL792423
12-3, 7-11; closed Mon
(01787) 277402
Greene King IPA; guest beer H
Beautiful thatched rural pub opposite the village green and dating from circa 1685, with a cosy interior and attentive landlord and landlady. A good selection of real ales is served, with the second handpump rotating Adnams, Black Sheep and Timothy Taylor Landlord; the third pump varies. There is good local trade and excellent bar and restaurant food (no meals Sun eve). In the past the pub provided one of the locations for the Lovejoy television series. A pub definitely not to be missed.
P

Billericay

Blue Boar

39 High Street, CM12 9BA
9am-11.30
(01277) 655552

Courage Best Bitter, Directors; Greene King Abbot; Marston's Pedigree; Shepherd Neame Spitfire; guest beers Ⓗ
A popular Wetherspoon's, especially at weekends, with the usual suspects on handpump, plus guests from micro-breweries, often local ones such as the Brentwood Brewing Co. The pub has its own pay and display car park at the rear, and the train station and bus stops are close by. Breakfast is available until midday, plus main meals and snacks until 10pm. There is no music, but there are fruit machines and muted TVs. An outside area at the rear is designated for drinking and smoking. Q❀◐◑♿⇌🚌(100)●P⚟

Chequers

44 High Street, CM12 9BQ
⏲ 12-11.30 (12.30am Fri & Sat); 12-10.30 Sun
☎ (01277) 650500 🌐 thechequersbillericay.com
Young's Bitter; guest beers Ⓗ
Once a row of cottages, this 500-year-old pub is the focal point of the High Street and one of the historic buildings on the town trail. There are two bar areas, with three guest beers usually on at a time, supplied by Scottish & Newcastle. Music is a prominent attraction, with acoustic night on Monday and other live music on Thursday. Karaoke also features, as do charity nights. Food is served Monday to Friday at lunchtimes only. Ask how to play the Joker Board. ⛰❀◐♿⇌🚌(100)♣P⚟

Coach & Horses

36 Chapel Street, CM12 9LU
⏲ 10-11; 12-10.30 Sun
☎ (01277) 622873
Adnams Bitter; Greene King IPA, Abbot; guest beers Ⓗ
Close to the High Street, this welcoming one-bar pub with an inviting atmosphere is a regular in the Guide. Guest beers, from the Gray's portfolio, change weekly. Breakfast is served 10-11.30am (not Sun) and good quality food is available lunchtimes and evenings, with curry night on Wednesday and fish night on Friday. The bar and food service is efficient and friendly, enhancing the feel-good factor. The walls are adorned with prints and decorative plates, and a fine collection of jugs hangs from the ceiling. Q❀◐◑⇌🚌(100)P

Black Notley

Vine Inn

105 Witham Road, CM77 8LQ OS767208
⏲ 12-2.30 (4 Sun), 6.30-11
☎ (01376) 324269
Adnams Bitter; guest beers Ⓗ
Sixteenth-century open-plan free house with a central bar, a drinking/lounge area to the left, a restaurant area to the right and log-burning stoves at both ends. An unusual feature is the six-person mezzanine above the lounge, accessible via a steep staircase. The two guest beers are usually of East Anglian origin and one is often from Mighty Oak. Cressing railway station is a 15-minute walk away down country lanes. A heated, covered smoking area is provided outside.
⛰Q❀◐◑🚌(21)P⚟

Blackmore

Leather Bottle

Horsefayre Green, CM4 0RL
⏲ 11 (12 Sun)-11 (midnight Fri & Sat)
☎ (01277) 821891 🌐 theleatherbottle.net
Adnams Bitter, Broadside Ⓗ**; guest beers** Ⓗ/Ⓖ
Large village pub with a smallish flagstone-floored bar area. Most of the pub is taken up by a good quality restaurant. Two guest beers are generally available on handpump with may be a third on gravity at weekends in the summer; a beer of around 5% or higher is usually on offer. Westons Old Rosie cider may be available in the summer. An annexe to the bar has a pool table, dartboard and silent fruit machine. ⛰❀◐◑🀫🚌(32)♣P

Boreham

Queen's Head

Church Road, CM3 3EG
⏲ 11.30-2.30, 5-11; 11.30-midnight Fri; 12-midnight Sat; 12-11.30 Sun
☎ (01245) 467298
Adnams Bitter; Crouch Vale Brewers Gold; Greene King IPA; guest beer Ⓗ
Tucked behind the church, this traditional village local dates from the 16th century. It has two contrasting bars, one with bench seating where darts, dominoes and cribs are played, and the other where dining takes place (no evening meals Sun). The guest beer comes from the Gray's list. Parking is limited. Q◐◑♣P⚟

Bradfield

Village Maid

Heath Road, CO11 2UZ
⏲ 12-11 (10.30 Sun)
☎ (01255) 870329
Greene King IPA; guest beers Ⓗ
This friendly rural pub is set in the heart of the village by a road junction. One main bar area opens into additional seating and a large dining area serving a wide range of home-cooked fare. Three handpumps serve regular bitter plus seasonal guest ales. A beer garden and seating area are to the side of the pub. Sport is shown on a large-screen TV in the bar. ❀🛏◐🚌P⚟

Brentwood

Rising Sun

144 Ongar Road, CM15 9DJ (on A128, at Western Rd jct)
⏲ 3 (12 Sat)-11.30 (midnight Fri & Sat); 12-10.30 Sun
☎ (01277) 213749
Taylor Landlord; Woodforde's Wherry Best Bitter; guest beers Ⓗ
Comfortable, friendly local which brings a good selection of real ales to an area where beer choice can be limited. The pub is a rare (but regular) outlet for Taylor's Landlord and Woodforde's Wherry, as well as one or two ever-changing guest beers, usually including a Brentwood ale. This is a community-focused pub that hosts a charity quiz on Monday evening, cribbage on Sunday evening and frequent darts matches. Framed prints of the local area decorate the walls. Outside is a covered, heated smokers' area, plus a shellfish stall at weekends. ⛰❀🀫🚌♣P⚟

Brightlingsea

Railway Tavern

58 Station Road, CO7 0DT (on B1029)
⏲ 5 (3 Fri)-11; 12-11 Sat; 12-3, 7-10.30 Sun

☎ (01206) 302581
Railway Tavern Crab & Winkle Mild, Bladderwrack; guest beers Ⓗ
Enthusiastic regulars make every night special here. The three favourite house beers reign supreme. The surrounds would be fitting for a French bar, with Monet and local artists' works demanding attention at all times. The bar is a clatter of chatter, especially on Friday nights. Without doubt the Famous Railway Tavern is a simple classic pub. Music and cider rule the roost at a festival in May and Dave's brews squeeze their way on to beer festival stillages throughout the year. ⌂Q❀🚌(78)♣🍎

Burnham-on-Crouch

Queen's Head

26 Providence, CM0 8JU (opp clock tower)
⏲ 12-11
☎ (01621) 784825 🌐 queensheadburnham.com
Mighty Oak IPA; guest beers Ⓗ
Tucked away from the High Street in a popular yachting town, this pub is known as the place for real ale. Normally three or four changing guests can be found at the bar, in addition to real cider. The landlord has been a CAMRA member for many years and his ideals are well suited to the campaign. Folk nights are held monthly. Traditional Essex Huffers are available, among other culinary delights. An August beer festival is one of several events held for the local community and visitors. Q❀◐▶⇌🚌(31X)♣🍎

Castle Hedingham

Bell

10 St James Street, CO9 3EJ (off A1017 signed Castle Hedingham)
⏲ 11.45-3, 6-11; 11.45-12.30am Fri; 12-11.30 Sat; 12-11 Sun
☎ (01787) 460350
Adnams Bitter; Mighty Oak IPA, Maldon Gold; guest beers Ⓖ
This 15th-century coaching inn is well worth a visit. It has small rooms for drinking and dining beside the two main bars. Beers are served direct from the casks, which are all on view in the public bar. Summer and winter beer festivals are held. Live jazz is played on the last Sunday of the month and folk and pop are played every Friday evening, with a quiz on Sunday night. Local Devlin End Storm cider is served alongside Mighty Oak Oscar Wilde, usually at weekends. ⌂Q❀◐▶⊟♿🚌♣🍎P⊱

Chelmsford

Angel ✔

160 Broomfield Road, Broomfield, CM1 7AH
⏲ 11-11 (10.30 Sun)
☎ (01245) 444917 🌐 vintageinns.co.uk
Adnams Bitter, Broadside; guest beer Ⓗ
A Grade II-listed, attractive, recently-refurbished inn with a large car park, in the village of Broomfield just north of Chelmsford. There is a large beer garden and open fires in the winter. The Adnams ales are very well kept by an ex-Southwold landlord and the guest ale is generally from a regional brewery. A wide selection of traditional pub food, including Sunday roasts, is served all day, with meat, fish and vegetarian specials daily. Frequent buses stop outside. ⌂❀◐▶♿🚌P

Cricketers

143 Moulsham Street, CM2 0JT
⏲ 11 (12 Sun)-11
☎ (01245) 261157
Adnams Bitter; Greene King Abbot; guest beers Ⓗ
Friendly street-corner pub at the southern end of the main shopping area. The front bar has a pool table and jukebox with a good selection covering 1950s classics to recent hits, and live sport on TV at certain times. The back bar is quieter and has more comfortable seating – and a reasonable piano. Generally one guest beer is served during the week and two at weekends, with an emphasis on Essex breweries. There is a covered patio area outside for smokers. ❀◐⊟🚌(42,100)♣⊱

Orange Tree

6 Lower Anchor Street, CM2 0AS
⏲ 12-11 (11.30 Fri & Sat)
☎ (01245) 262664 🌐 the-ot.com
Mighty Oak Oscar Wilde, Maldon Gold; Sharp's Doom Bar Ⓗ**; guest beers** Ⓗ/Ⓖ
The Orange Tree has established its place as one of the top real ale pubs in Chelmsford. There are usually six or seven beers on handpump (often including a stout or porter), with two on gravity from casks behind the bar. The cider is from the Westons' range. There is a charity quiz on Tuesday evening and Sunday lunch is very popular. Rock/blues bands play one Saturday each month. Q❀◐⊟♿🚌♣🍎P⊱

Original Plough ✔

28 Duke Street, CM1 1HY
⏲ 11-11 (midnight Fri & Sat); 12-10.30 Sun
☎ (01245) 250145
Beer range varies Ⓗ
Busy pub opposite the bus station and next to Chelmsford railway station, split into three areas – a quieter, comfortable area to the left, a wooden floored area to the centre and a flagstone-laid area with larger tables. Rugby takes preference over soccer on the TV, which can dominate on match days. Six to eight beers, mainly from regionals and larger micros, are served, with mild frequently available and sometimes other dark beers. There is a heated, partly-covered patio outside. ❀◐▶⇌🚌P⊱

Queen's Head

30 Lower Anchor Street, CM2 0AS
⏲ 12-11 (11.30 Fri & Sat)
☎ (01245) 265181 🌐 queensheadchelmsford.co.uk
Crouch Vale Essex Boys Bitter, Best Bitter, Brewer's Gold, Amarillo; guest beers Ⓗ
A welcome return to the Guide under a new landlord for this six-times former CAMRA Branch Pub of the Year. Crouch Vale's only pub, it sells four of its beers, occasionally supplemented or replaced by a beer from its seasonal list. The four guest ales, from far and wide, are ever-changing and often include a stout or porter. The cider is Westons. ⌂Q❀◐♿🚌♣🍎P

Woolpack

23 Mildmay Road, CM2 0DN
⏲ 12-11 (midnight Fri-Sun)
☎ (01245) 259295 🌐 thewoolpackchelmsford.com
Greene King Abbot Ⓖ**; guest beers** Ⓗ
This award-winning pub makes the most of the extended range of beers available from Greene King, generally offering six ales including seasonal and dark brews. Darts and pool are available in a

small public bar while the spacious main lounge leads to a leather-seated annexe with a large-screen TV. There is a popular quiz on Tuesday and folk music once a month. An ever-changing range of speciality sausages complements the food menu, served Monday-Friday and Sunday lunchtime. An annual Easter beer festival is held.
❀◑⊟⊟♣P⁄–

Chrishall

Red Cow

11 High Street, SG8 8RN (2 miles N of B1039) TL445394
12-3 (not Mon), 6-11; 12-10.30 Sun
☎ (01763) 838792 theredcow.com
Adnams Bitter; guest beers Ⓗ
Thatched 14th-century pub, close to an 11th-century tithe barn in a small village very close to the Cambridge and Hertfordshire borders. Guest beers are usually from East Anglia. The enthusiastic owners welcome visitors and many local groups including the cricket club (who run regular quizzes), the village book group, stall holders from the farmers' market and the WI. Special occasions can be celebrated with meals from the extensive and intelligent menu, either in the tiled bar or restaurant separated by original open timbering.
⌂❀◑P

Churchgate Street

Queen's Head

26 Churchgate Street, near Old Harlow, CM17 0JT
TL483114
11.45-3, 5 (6 Sat)-11; 12-4, 7-10.30 Sun
☎ (01279) 427266
Adnams Bitter, Broadside; Crouch Vale Brewers Gold; Nethergate IPA Ⓗ
The new town of Harlow seems a long way from this traditional village pub. It was originally built as two cottages in 1530, then joined together and converted into a pub in 1750. Wooden beams feature throughout and there is a welcoming open fire during the winter months. Guest beers are usually from East Anglian breweries. A full range of food is served (not Sun eve).
⌂Q❀◑⊟⊟(7,59)P⁄–

Clacton-on-Sea

Moon & Starfish ✔

1 Marine Parade East, CO15 1PU
9-11 (midnight Thu-Sat)
☎ (01255) 222998
Greene King IPA, Abbot; Marston's Pedigree; Courage Directors; guest beers Ⓗ
This Wetherspoon pub is situated on the ground floor of the Royal Hotel, which is in the middle of a major facelift. It is conveniently situated opposite the famous Clacton pier and very handy for the annual August air show. In common with its other establishments, the pub holds two beer festivals each year and the manager strives to provide all of the ales available during the festival period.
❀◑⇌⊟⁄–

Coggeshall

Queens Head

Old Road, CO6 1RS (on A120, ½ mile E of Coggeshall)
12-11 (midnight Fri & Sat)
☎ (01376) 564999
Red Fox Fox & Hind Bitter, seasonal beers; guest beers Ⓗ
Rescued from dereliction thanks to a major investment after many years of closure, the Queens Head has a light and airy, modern interior, but retains the feeling of a real pub. The restaurant area offers an excellent daily carvery 12-2pm and 7-9pm (12-7pm Sun), plus bar meals. A full range of beers from the nearby Red Fox Brewery is complemented by occasional guest ales. The landlord heads a national campaign to amend the smoking ban, and a separate old-style bar is planned to take advantage of the change if it happens. ⌂Q❀◑♿⊟(70)P

Colchester

Bricklayers

27 Bergholt Road, CO4 5AA (jct A134/B1508 nr North Station)
11-3, 5.30-11; 11-midnight Fri; 11-11 Sat; 12-3, 7-11 (not winter eve) Sun
☎ (01206) 852008
Adnams Bitter, Explorer, Broadside, seasonal beers; Fuller's London Pride; guest beers Ⓗ
The 'Brick' is a friendly, busy local, very close to North Station. Darts and pool are played in the public bar, the lounge bar is very popular, and there is a light and airy conservatory. Run by a family who have won awards, excellent food is served at lunchtime and booking for the famous Sunday roast is recommended. Frequented by a lively mix of commuters and locals, three guest ales and Crones cider are available, in addition to the full Adnams range.
❀◑⊟⇌(North)⊟(65)♣●P⁄–

British Grenadier

67 Military Road, CO1 2AP (½ mile SW of Colchester Town station)
12-2.30 (not Wed), 5-11.30; 11-midnight Sat; 12-3, 7-11.30 Sun
☎ (01206) 500933
Adnams Bitter, Broadside, seasonal beers; guest beers Ⓗ
A warm welcome is guaranteed at this award-winning traditional local, recently saved from closure by the persistence of the landlord and landlady. The pub makes the most of Adnams' generous guest beer policy, as can be seen by the numerous pump clips around the walls, and the tempting Beers to Come board. Darts is popular in the main bar, with pool played in a separate room. The pub hosts a quiz each Sunday and has a real fire in winter. CAMRA Branch Pub of the Year 2008.
⌂❀⊟⇌(Town)⊟(66)♣⁄–▯

Fat Cat

65 Butt Road, CO3 3BZ (on B1026, nr police station)
12-11 (midnight Fri); 11-midnight Sat
☎ (01206) 577990
Crouch Vale Brewers Gold; Fat Cat Bitter, Honey Ale; Mauldons Silver Adder; Woodforde's Wherry Best Bitter Ⓗ**; guest beers** Ⓖ
Classing itself as a 'free mouse', this single-bar local offers up to 16 real ales and takes pride in sourcing locally, which is reflected in the choice of guest ales from the cold room. Regular events include live acoustic music on Saturday and a Sunday night quiz. There is a thriving golf society, beer festivals and Meet the Brewer nights. Home-made food includes Sunday roasts, and you can even order your own takeaway to be delivered

here – the staff do the washing up. A real ale club on Sunday features three beers at very reasonable prices. ❀◑≹(Town)⊟◆⚟

Forester's Arms

1-2 Castle Road, CO1 1UW
⊙ 12-11 (12.30am Fri & Sat; 10.30 Sun)
☎ (01206) 224059
Beer range varies Ⓗ
Small but welcoming back-street local situated in a residential area close to the High Street and Castle Park. Dating from the Edwardian era, the single bar has a two-bar atmosphere. Three to four ales, including the house beer, from the local Shalford Brewery are complemented by occasional guests. Good-value food is served, which can be eaten alfresco in summer on the quiet street front. Pub games are keenly contested, but conversation usually prevails. Local musicians play occasionally at the weekend. ⛟◐≹(Town)⊟♣⚟

Fox & Fiddler

1 St John's Street, CO2 7AA (jct of Head Street)
⊙ 12-11 (midnight Fri & Sat; 10.30 Sun)
☎ (01206) 560520
Mighty Oak IPA, English Oak; guest beers Ⓗ
Friendly town-centre pub with a deceptively small frontage disguising a long single bar with three separate drinking and dining areas. The pub dates from 1420 and is heavily timbered, with a relaxing atmosphere and comfortable seating inside. Mighty Oak beers are always available, with regularly changing guests from micro-breweries. Excellent home-cooked food using local produce is served Wednesday (steak night) to Sunday lunchtime; Sunday roasts are particularly good value. Weekend evenings can be lively, with occasional music on Saturday. The smoking area is heated and covered. ❀◐≹(Town)⊟P⚟

Odd One Out 🏆

28 Mersea Road, CO2 7ET (on B1025)
⊙ 4.30-11; 12-11 Fri; 11-11 Sat; 12-10.30 Sun
☎ (01206) 513958
Beer range varies Ⓗ
Seemingly ever-present in this Guide, a worthy winner of CAMRA Branch Pub of the Year 2009, and National Cider Pub of the Year finalist, the 'Oddie' is a step back in time to the traditional English local. Five ever-changing guest ales usually include a dark beer, at least three ciders are served from casks on the bar, and there is a good range of Scottish and Irish whisky. Conversation is king, interrupted by the occasional card school and trip to the bar to refill and partake of a nourishing cheese roll. Don't expect glamour – just enjoy! ⛼Q❀≹(Town)⊟(8A,67)♣◆⚟

Colne Engaine

Five Bells

Mill Lane, CO6 2HY (2 miles E of Halstead) TL851303
⊙ 12-3, 6-11; 12-1am Fri & Sat; 12-11.30 Sun
☎ (01787) 224166 🌐 fivebells.net
Greene King IPA; guest beers Ⓗ
This 16th-century free house with original beams is set in a peaceful village where the enthusiastic landlord has transformed the pub. Selling more than 400 different ales each year, local breweries and micros are well represented. Several small dining and drinking areas plus a separate restaurant serve locally-sourced quality food. The community is well represented, with pool and football teams, live music on Friday night and Jazz on Sunday afternoons, plus a November beer festival. The smoking area is covered and heated. ⛼Q❀◑⊞♿♣P⚟

Coxtie Green

White Horse

173 Coxtie Green Road, CM14 5PX (1 mile W of A128, jct with Mores Lane) TQ564959
⊙ 11.30-11 (midnight Fri & Sat); 12-11 Sun
☎ (01277) 372410 🌐 whitehorsecoxtiegreen.co.uk
Fuller's London Pride; guest beers Ⓗ
There is always a relaxed, friendly atmosphere at this excellent, small country free house. The varied clientele will find a well-appointed saloon bar and a public bar with dartboard and TV. Six handpumps are in constant use, featuring beers from all over, including the local Brentwood Brewery, plus either Adnams Bitter or Greene King IPA. A beer festival is held each July in the large rear garden, which has a children's play area. Local CAMRA branch Pub of the Year 2004 and 2006. ❀◐⊞♿⊟♣◆P

Dedham

Sun Inn

High Street, CO7 6DF (on B1029, opp Church)
⊙ 12-11 (6 Sun)
☎ (01206) 323351 🌐 thesuninndedham.com
Adnams Broadside; guest beers Ⓗ
This 15th-century inn comprises a bar area, side lounge, restaurant and garden. The lounge, open to non-residents, has a range of comfortable furniture, and board games are available. Guest ales change frequently, featuring micros and local brewers. The restaurant serves an award-winning range of food and fine wines, with regular culinary lectures and tasting sessions (booking advised). One of the four well-appointed guest bedrooms has a four poster bed for that romantic weekend. ⛼Q❀⛟◑⊟♣P⚟

Duton Hill

Three Horseshoes

CM6 2DX (½ mile W of B184 Dunmow-Thaxted road) TL606268
⊙ 12-2.30 (not Mon-Wed; 3 Sat), 6-11; 12-3, 7-10.30 Sun
☎ (01371) 870681
Mighty Oak IPA; guest beers Ⓗ
Cosy village local with a large garden, wildlife pond and terrace overlooking the Chelmer Valley and open farmland. The landlord is a former pantomime dame, and the pub hosts a weekend of open-air theatre in July. A millennium beacon in the garden, breweriana and a remarkable collection of Butlins memorabilia are features. A beer festival is held on the late spring bank holiday in the Duton Hill Den. Look for the pub sign depicting a famous painting, The Blacksmith, by former local resident Sir George Clausen. ⛼❀⊟(313)♣P

Elmdon

Elmdon Dial

Heydon Lane, CB11 4NH TL461397
⊙ 12-3, 6-11; closed Mon; 12-4, 6-10.30 Sun
☎ (01763) 837386 🌐 theelmdondial.co.uk
Adnams Bitter, Broadside; Taylor Landlord; guest beers Ⓗ

CAMRA local Pub of the Year 2008, this friendly, welcoming pub dating from 1450 is owned by a real ale enthusiast. Previously called the Kings Head, the pub was closed in 1998 and became a private house. After a seven-year planning battle and support from villagers and CAMRA, it was reopened with a new name and pub sign to reflect a window sundial in the village church. The building was carefully extended in 2006 to provide a modern kitchen and restaurant in addition to a tasteful bar. ⌂Q✿◐◑♿🚌♣P⅟–

Epping

Forest Gate

111 Bell Common, CM16 4DZ (opp Bell Hotel) TL450011
⏲ 10-2.30, 5-11; 12-3, 7-10.30 Sun
☎ (01992) 572312
Adnams Bitter, Broadside; Nethergate IPA [H]**; guest beers** [H]/[G]
This 17th-century pub is a genuine free house specialising in traditional ales. On the edge of Epping Forest and a short walk from Epping, it attracts locals and hikers, and is free from TV and fruit machines. Food is usually available, with the long standing house speciality turkey broth always popular. A large lawn at the front is used for summer drinking – just look out for the geese. ⌂Q✿◐◑⊖●P

Finchingfield

Red Lion

6 Church Hill, CM7 4NN (on B1053, opp church)
⏲ 12-11 (midnight Fri & Sat)
☎ (01371) 810400 🌐 theredlionfinchingfield.com
Greene King IPA, Old Speckled Hen; guest beers [H]
This 15th-century coaching inn is a friendly local in a famously picturesque village, with a warm atmosphere, a heavily beamed area with an open fire and a separate restaurant. There is also a garden for better weather. Situated opposite the church just up the hill from the pond, the pub is popular with cyclists, walkers and locals; families are also welcome. Good value bar and restaurant menus featuring home-cooked food are available at all times except Sunday evening. High quality accommodation is available – see website for more information. ⌂Q✿🛏◐◑🚌P⅟–

Fuller Street

Square & Compasses

Fairstead, CM3 2BB (1½ miles E off A131 at Gt Leighs, St Anne's Castle) TL748161
⏲ 11.30-3, 6-11; 12-11 Sat & Sun
☎ (01245) 361477 🌐 thesquareandcompasses.co.uk
Beer range varies [G]
Seventeenth-century, three-roomed free house with a first floor meeting/private dining room. Known locally as the Stokehole, it reopened in 2007 having been closed for two years. There are exposed beams throughout and two inglenook fireplaces, one housing a woodburner. Old local woodworking tools adorn the public bar. Up to four ever-changing beers are sold from behind the bar, including Stokers Ale brewed by Nethergate. Westons cider and perry are sold. Food is prepared from locally sourced produce, including game, from the surrounding estates (no food Sun eve or Mon). ⌂✿◐◑⊟●P

Fyfield

Queen's Head

Queen Street, CM5 0RY (off B184)
⏲ 11-3.30, 6-11; 11-11 Sat; 12-10.30 Sun
☎ (01277) 899231 🌐 thequeensheadfyfield.co.uk
Adnams Bitter, Broadside; Crouch Vale Brewers Gold; guest beers [H]
The emphasis here is on dining, though with only nine tables to chose from, reservations are recommended at this friendly pub. The beer is reasonably priced and customers popping in just for a drink are made very welcome. The garden goes down to the River Roding, and outside tables are popular in summer. Children and dogs are not allowed inside. The pub is closed between Christmas and New Year. ⌂Q✿◐◑●P

Gestingthorpe

Pheasant

Church Street, CO9 3AU (off B1058 Castle Hedingham-Sudbury road) TL813375
⏲ 12-3, 6-11 (not Mon); 12-3 Sun
☎ (01787) 461196
Mauldons Pleasant Pheasant; guest beers [H]
Set in a tiny village, this traditional pub enjoys good local trade and a reputation for fine food, ale and cider. Recently refurbished, it has three separate rooms with two bars and a large garden. Occasional quiz nights and music evenings make this hostelry an ideal venue for summer evenings and long winter nights. The house beer is brewed by Mauldons. Guest beers are frequently from local breweries. ⌂Q✿◐◑⊟●P⅟–

Goldhanger

Chequers ✔

The Square, CM9 8AS (500m from B1026) TL904088
⏲ 11-11; 12-10.30 Sun
☎ (01621) 788203 🌐 thechequersgoldhanger.co.uk
Caledonian Deuchars IPA; Everards Tiger; Flowers IPA; guest beers [H]
A regular finalist and frequent winner of CAMRA local Pub of the Year, the Chequers guarantees a warm welcome and a great atmosphere. The inn dates from the 15th century and remains largely untouched, with two main bars and several smaller rooms including a games room with bar billiards. Exceptional food is served, ranging from bar snacks to a full restaurant menu. An ever-changing choice of guest ales is on offer, and beer festivals are hosted in March and September. Frequent community events are held – see website for details. ⌂Q✿✿◐◑⊟▲🚌(95)♣P⅟–

Grays

Theobald Arms

141 Argent Street, RM17 6HR
⏲ 11-11 (midnight Fri & Sat); 12-11 Sun
☎ (01375) 372253 🌐 theobaldarms.com
Beer range varies [H]
Genuine, traditional pub with a public bar that has an unusual hexagonal pool table. The changing selection of four guest beers features local independent breweries and a range of British bottled beers is also stocked. Regular St George's Day weekend and summer beer festivals are held in the old stables and on the rear enclosed patio; the summer festival has been running for more

than 10 years. Lunchtime meals are served 12-2pm Monday to Friday. Darts and cards are played. A former local CAMRA Branch Pub of the Year. ❀◐⊞♿⇌⊟♣P⚍

White Hart 🏆 ✔

Kings Walk, Argent Street, RM17 6HR
⊙ 12-11.30 (midnight Fri & Sat); 12-11 Sun
☎ (01375) 373319 🌐 whitehartgrays.co.uk
Crouch Vale Brewers Gold; guest beers Ⓗ
Under new ownership since 2006, this traditional local just outside the town centre has been transformed and rejuvenated. The three guest ales usually include a mild or other dark beer and there are 20+ Belgian bottled beers. Pool is played and a meeting/function room is available. Live blues bands play every other Thursday and there is a large beer garden. An annual beer festival is usually held in February. Local CAMRA Branch Pub of the Year 2007/08/09. ⌂❀⊭◐⊞⇌⊟♣P⚍

Great Bardfield

Bell

Dunmow Road, CM7 4SA
⊙ 12-3, 6-11; 12-4 Sun
☎ (01371) 811097
Greene King IPA; guest beers Ⓗ
This friendly village local features interesting guest beers from all over the country. Easily found in the centre of the village, it has a beamed bar and restaurant area with an open fire and a separate public bar with TV and darts. A patio area caters for the better weather. The pub offers good value bar and restaurant food, all locally sourced. Specials such as pheasant casserole or stuffed pork fillets are available at all sessions except Sunday evening and Monday lunchtime. There is a wine list too. ⌂❀◐◑⊞♿⊟♣P

Great Bromley

Cross Inn

Ardleigh Road, CO7 7TL (on B1029 between Great Bromley and Ardleigh)
⊙ 12-2 (not Mon), 6.30-11; 12-3, 7-10.30 Sun
☎ (01206) 230282 🌐 bromleycrossinn.co.uk
Sticklegs Malt Shovel Mild, Prize Fighter, Best Bitter; Wadworth Henry's IPA; Woodforde's Wherry Best Bitter; guest beers Ⓖ
Quiet, cosy and warm free house featuring a single bar that feels like a private front room, with a wood burner and comfortable seating, as well as fresh flowers. The landlord has run previous pubs listed in the Guide and hosts an annual beer and folk festival, usually in May. Booking is advised for meals (served Wed to Sat). There is a large car park, enclosed beer garden and a heated and covered smoking area. The Cross Inn now has an on-site brewery, Sticklegs, situated in a former letting room. Its beers are only available here. ⌂Q❀◐◑♣P⚍

Snooty Fox

Frating Road, CO7 7JN (on B1029, 500m from A133)
⊙ 12-3, 6-11 (5.30-midnight Sat); 12-midnight Sun
☎ (01206) 251065
Beer range varies Ⓗ
This village inn is a beer lover's paradise, with a constantly changing range of real ales on offer from micro-breweries around the country. A warm welcome is always provided by the staff. The public bar includes a real fire which enhances the ambience of the wood-beamed interior. Excellent value for money food, ranging from the traditional to the exotic, is served in the bar and large dining room. A monthly quiz brings in customers from far and wide. ⌂Q❀◐◑♣●P⚍

Great Chesterford

Crown & Thistle

High Street, CB10 1PL (near B1383, close to M11/A11 jct)
⊙ 12-3, 6-midnight; 12-3, 7-11 (not winter eve) Sun
☎ (01799) 530278
Greene King IPA; Woodforde's Wherry Best Bitter; guest beers Ⓗ
Popular inn in an interesting village, frequented by locals, including the cricket team. The pub, built in 1528 and called The Chequers, was extended in 1603 to serve as a coaching inn and renamed at that point. According to legend, James I stopped here on his way to London for his coronation. The magnificent inglenook in the bar is the earliest example of its type in Essex. A patio has seating for outdoor drinking and dining, with a heated smoking area. ⌂Q❀◐◑⛺⇌⊟P⚍

Great Dunmow

Boars Head

37 High Street, CM6 1AB
⊙ 11-midnight (1am Fri & Sat); 12-11 Sun
☎ (01371) 873630
Adnams Bitter; Greene King IPA; guest beers Ⓗ
Four hundred year old traditional town-centre pub on the corner of the main public car park. This timber-framed lathe and plaster building tends to 'give' a little when lorries 'bump it' while negotiating the tight bend outside. Inside are beamed low ceilings and three large-screen TVs for sport. Live music is performed on Saturday evenings. A large decking area at the rear includes covered seating for smokers. Traditional Sunday roasts use locally-sourced meat and a fresh fish van visits on Thursday. ❀◐⊟(33,133)P⚍

Great Easton

Swan

The Endway, CM6 2HG (3 miles N of Dunmow, off B184) TL606255
⊙ 12-3, 6-11; 12-3, 7-10.30 (not winter eve) Sun
☎ (01371) 870359 🌐 swangreateaston.co.uk
Adnams Bitter; guest beers Ⓗ
A warm welcome is assured at this 15th-century free house in an attractive village. A log-burning stove, exposed beams and comfortable sofas feature in the lounge, while pool and darts are played in the public bar. Featuring in CAMRA's Good Pub Food Guide, all meals are freshly prepared to order from fresh local produce, including the chips. The chef looks after the beers, chosen to complement the food. Accommodation is now available in four superb double rooms. ⌂Q❀⊭◐◑⊞♣P

Harlow

William Aylmer ✔

Aylmer House, Kitson Way, CM20 1DG
⊙ 9am-midnight (1am Fri & Sat)
☎ (01279) 620630

Greene King IPA; Marston's Pedigree; Shepherd Neame Spitfire; guest beers Ⓗ
Situated in the centre of Harlow and converted from a 1960s office building, there is usually an interesting selection of guest beers here. The pub can get very busy before clients go on to nightclubs at weekends, but is usually roomy. The walls feature pictures relating to the development of Harlow and the local medical pioneer, William Aylmer. ❀◐◑♿🚌●

Harwich

New Bell Inn

Outpart Eastward, CO12 3EN (200m from E end of A120)
✪ 11-3, 7-11 (midnight Sat); 12-4, 7-11 (12-11 summer) Sun
☎ (01255) 503545
Greene King IPA; guest beers Ⓗ
Situated in the old town at the back of the former Naval Dockyard, this buzzing community pub attracts people from all walks of life including famous jazz musicians and film stars, thanks to its proximity to the Electric Palace Cinema. Three separate drinking areas and a walled garden give the pub a cosy feel. Hearty lunchtime food includes fantastic home-made soups. Beers come mainly from East Anglian micro-breweries including the nearby Harwich Town Brewery, and a mild is always available. ❀◐⊟⇌(Town)🚌P

Hatfield Broad Oak

Cock Inn

High Street, CM22 7HF
✪ 12-11 (12.30am Fri & Sat); 12-10.30 Sun
☎ (01279) 718306
Adnams Bitter; Woodforde's Wherry Best Bitter; guest beers Ⓗ
The Cock has had a new landlord for the past two years, during which time the pub has been refurbished in a modern style, within a Grade II-listed building. It was originally a much larger coaching inn, stretching to the corner of the road. It has a friendly family atmosphere and is popular with walkers visiting nearby Hatfield Forest. ♨Q♘◐◑🚌(5,347)♣P

Hempstead

Bluebell Inn

High Street, CB10 2PD (on B1054, between Saffron Walden and Haverhill)
✪ 12-3, 6-11; 12-11 Fri & Sat (winter opening varies); 12-10.30 Sun
☎ (01799) 599199
Adnams Bitter, Broadside; Woodforde's Wherry Best Bitter; guest beers Ⓗ
Late 16th-century village pub with 18th-century additions, reputed to be the birthplace of Dick Turpin; the bar displays posters about his life. Six beers are usually available. The restaurant serves excellent meals from an extensive menu and the large bar has a log fire. Ample seating is provided outside, plus a children's play area.This local CAMRA Pub of the Year 2005 hosts a folk evening on Tuesday. ♨Q❀◐◑🚌(I)♣P⚟

Heybridge

Maltsters Arms

Hall Road, CM9 4NJ (nr B1022)
✪ 12-midnight (1am Fri & Sat); 12-10.30 Sun
☎ (01621) 853880
Greene King IPA, Abbot; guest beers Ⓖ
This traditional Gray's house is a single-bar local, where a warm welcome is extended to drinkers and their dogs. The pub can be busy at lunchtimes with locals and ramblers. The pleasant atmosphere is enhanced by a collection of mirrors and some breweriana. Two guest beers are usually available, one from Mighty Oak. A rear patio overlooks the old course of the tidal river. Occasional mini beer festivals are held. A selection of rolls and hot pasties is usually available. Q❀🚌♣⚟

Horndon-on-the-Hill

Bell Inn

High Road, SS17 8LD (nr B1007 opp Woolmarket)
✪ 11-2.30 (3 Sat), 5.30 (6 Sat)-11; 12-4, 7-10.30 Sun
☎ (01375) 642463 🌐 bell-inn.co.uk
Draught Bass Ⓖ**; Greene King IPA; guest beers** Ⓗ
Busy 15th-century coaching inn, where the beamed bars feature wood panelling and carvings. Note the unusual hot cross bun collection; a bun is added every Good Friday. The hilltop village, much more peaceful since the bypass was completed, has a restored Woolmarket. Up to five guest ales are stocked, including beers from Essex breweries. The award-winning restaurant is open daily, lunchtime and evening. Accommodation includes five honeymoon suites.
♨Q❀🛏◐◑⊟🚌(11,374)P⚟

Lamarsh

Lamarsh Lion

Bures Road, CO8 5EP (1¼ miles NW of Bures) TL892355
✪ 12-11 (10.30 Sun)
☎ (01787) 227918
Greene King IPA; guest beers Ⓗ
This attractive 14th-century inn is situated in a quiet country lane, with tables outside offering a wonderful view over the Stour Valley. Popular with locals and ramblers, the wealth of beams and a roaring log fire in winter make this a genuinely welcoming free house. Four guest beers are normally on offer, including a dark beer and at least one on gravity, mainly from local micros. A full menu is available daily. Attached to the large single bar is a room with a pool table and TV.
♨Q❀◐◑⛺♣●P⚟

Langley Lower Green

Bull

CB11 4SB (off B1038 at Clavering) TL436345
✪ 12-2 (3 Sat), 6-11; 12-3, 7-10.30 Sun
☎ (01279) 777307
Adnams Bitter; Greene King IPA; guest beers Ⓗ
Classic Victorian village local with original cast-iron lattice windows and fireplaces. It sits in a tiny isolated hamlet less than a mile from the Hertfordshire border and just a bit further from Cambridgeshire. The pub has a devoted band of local regulars including cricket and football teams. This friendly pub in beautiful rolling countryside, two miles from the highest point in Essex, is worth seeking out. A long distance footpath passes within a mile. Meals can be arranged with advance notice.
♨Q❀⊟P

Layer Breton

Hare & Hounds

Crayes Green, CO2 0PN TL944188
11.30-11; 12-10.30 Sun
(01206) 330459
Greene King IPA, Abbot; guest beers [H]
This village pub provides pleasant surroundings to enjoy good beer and food. The beers are from local and regional breweries. The bar contains a wood-burning stove and the separate restaurant area features a glass-topped 'well table'. Home-made pub food is served at lunchtimes (not Mon) and weekend evenings, including value meals for two. The Sunday carvery (12-5pm) is very popular. Two B&B rooms are available. P

Layer-de-la-Haye

Donkey & Buskins

Layer Road, CO2 0HU (on B1026 S of Colchester) TL974208
11.30-3, 6-11; 11.30-11.30 Sat; 12-11 Sun
(01206) 734774
Greene King IPA; guest beers [H]
This village freehouse has a welcoming atmosphere and a strong reputation for good beer, wines and food. A wide range of dishes can be enjoyed in the front or rear bars and guest beers, often from local micros, are regularly available. A variety of local clubs and societies meets at the pub, and Sunday quiz night is very popular. A secluded garden offers relaxed summertime drinking and a beer festival is held each July.
Q P

Leigh-on-Sea

Broker

213-217 Leigh Road, SS9 1JA
11-11 (midnight Fri & Sat); 12-11 Sun
(01702) 471932 brokerfreehouse.co.uk
Everards Tiger; Fuller's London Pride; St Austell Tribute; Shepherd Neame Spitfire; Young's Bitter; guest beers [H]
Friendly, family-run free house that has featured in every edition of this Guide since 1996, now refurbished following the smoking ban. This sporty, community pub organises local charity events including quizzes or live music on Sunday evenings. Two guest beers are stocked, normally from small East Anglian breweries. Bar and restaurant meals are served at lunchtime (children welcome until 6.30pm). It has a garden with a covered and heated area for smokers and a pavement seating area. (Chalkwell) (5,24)

Elms

1060 London Road, SS9 3ND (on A13)
9am-midnight (1am Fri & Sat)
(01702) 474687
Courage Directors; Greene King IPA, Abbot; Marston's Pedigree; guest beers [H]
Old mock-Tudor coaching inn converted by JD Wetherspoon into a large, traditional-style pub decorated with old photos of the local area. Breakfast is available until midday, main meals and snacks until 10pm. Children are admitted until 9pm. Up to four constantly changing guest ales and two Westons real ciders are served. There is no music but there are TVs and fruit machines. Outside is a paved, heated and covered area for smokers and a large, hedged front garden. P

Little Bromley

Haywain

Bentley Road, CO11 2PL
6-11; 12-2.30, 6-11 Thu (midnight Fri & Sat); 12-6 Sun
(01206) 390004
Adnams Bitter; Greene King Old Speckled Hen; Nethergate Essex Border; guest beers [H]
An 18th-century pub that reopened in 2007 after a lengthy period as a nightclub. The new owners, both CAMRA members, have been warmly welcomed by the local villagers. Dawn provides generous portions of home-made food which is sourced locally whenever possible. Her steak and ale pie is thoroughly recommended. Dawn's father Ernie ensures that the beer is in excellent condition, with up to four ales available. Local CAMRA Pub of the Year 2009. P

Little Clacton

Apple Tree

The Street, CO16 9LF
12-11.30 (midnight Fri & Sat); 12-11 Sun
(01255) 861026
Beer range varies [H]
This is a friendly village local. Quality ales are mostly locally sourced, often from Mighty Oak and Mauldon's, with seasonal ales featuring strongly. The beer menu on a chalkboard lists brewery, strength and price. The pub plays host to pool and darts teams and has a thriving real ale club. It also holds charity pub quiz nights and other fund-raising activities supporting local charities. There is live music on Saturday night and the large-screen Sky Sports TV attracts many sports fans. P

Little Dunmow

Flitch of Bacon

The Street, CM6 3HT (850m S of B1256)
12-3 (not Mon), 5.30 (6 Sat)-11; 12-10 Sun
(01371) 820323
Fuller's London Pride; Greene King IPA; guest beers [H]
A traditional country inn which is the focal point of this rural village. The sign depicts a side, or 'flitch' of bacon – the prize awarded to a happily-married couple in an ancient contest still held every four years. Inside, there are exposed timbers and an open fire in winter. Note the old signs advertising Bass and Worthington in bottles. A menu of locally-sourced food is available in the bar or the rear restaurant area (not Sun eve). (133)

Little Oakley

Olde Cherry Tree

Clacton Road, CO12 5JH (by B1414)
12-3, 5-midnight; 12-midnight Sat & Sun
(01255) 886290
Adnams Bitter; guest beers [H]
This historic and multi-award winning village pub has a great following among the local community and has been recently refurbished by enthusiastic owners. Four handpumps serve one regular and three guest real ales, mostly sourced from local micro-breweries. Food is good value home-cooked fare served in the bar or a separate restaurant. A roaring fire in winter and a spacious garden in summer make this a great pub to visit at any time of the year. P

Little Thurrock

Traitor's Gate

40-42 Broadway, RM17 6EW (on A126, 1 mile E of Grays town centre)

⏲ 3 (1 Fri)-11; 12-11 Sat & Sun

☎ (01375) 372628

Beer range varies Ⓗ

This friendly hostelry with a wide and varied clientele, mostly local, shows how a good pub attracts a good trade. Two ever-changing guest beers are served; look out for forthcoming beers displayed on the blackboard above the bar. An amazing collection of more than 1500 pump clips shows ales that have featured over the last few years. Sport is screened most nights on TV. The beer garden has won Thurrock in Bloom awards in recent years. Local CAMRA Branch Pub of the Year 2005. ❀🚌(66)♣⚐

Little Totham

Swan 🏆

School Road, CM9 8LB (1 country mile SE of B1022) TL889117

⏲ 11-11; 12-10.30 Sun

☎ (01621) 892689 🌐 theswanpublichouse.co.uk

Crouch Vale Brewers Gold; Farmer's Pucks Folly; Mighty Oak Oscar Wilde Mild, Maldon Gold, Totham Parva; Red Fox Fox & Hind Bitter; guest beers Ⓖ

The epitome of the traditional village pub, with original beams and some exposed internal wattle and daub. Warm and welcoming, it has roaring fires in the winter and a walled garden for better weather. An ever-changing beer selection of guest ales and listed beers includes mild plus cider and perry. An annual beer festival is held, with live music and Morris dancing. A varied menu is available, including basket meals and takeaways. Twice winner of CAMRA National Pub of the Year among many other accolades.

⛫Q❀◐◑🚂♿⛺♣🍎P⚐🗑

Little Walden

Crown

High Street, CB10 1XA (on B1052)

⏲ 11.30-2.30 (3 Sat), 6-11; 12-10.30 Sun

☎ (01799) 522475

Adnams Broadside; Greene King IPA, Abbot; Woodforde's Wherry Best Bitter; guest beers Ⓖ

Charming 18th-century beamed pub in a quiet hamlet. The pub has a large walk-through fireplace. It is popular with diners, especially at weekends, when booking is advisable. Evening meals are available Tuesday to Saturday. Racked cask stillage is used for dispensing an excellent range of beers. The pub is used for club meetings and hosts traditional jazz on Wednesday evening.

⛫Q❀◐◑🚌P

Littley Green

Compasses ✔

CM3 1BU (turn off B1417 at former Ridley's Brewery, Hartford End) TL699172

⏲ 12-3, 5.30-midnight; 12-midnight Thu-Sun

☎ (01245) 362308 🌐 compasseslittleygreen.co.uk

Adnams Bitter; guest beers Ⓖ

The former Ridley's Brewery tap is a picturesque country pub in a quiet hamlet. Beers are drawn direct from the cask and carried up to the bar from a half-cellar. Huffers (giant baps) and jacket potatoes, both with a wide variety of fillings, are available every lunchtime and evening. There are seats and tables outside the bar and in the large gardens. No electronic games or piped music here but a folk evening is held monthly. Cider and perry come from Double Vision and others. ⛫Q❀◐◑♣🍎

Loughton

Victoria Tavern

165 Smarts Lane, IG10 4BP (off A121 at edge of forest)

⏲ 11-3, 5-11; 12-11 Sun

☎ (0208) 5081779

Adnams Bitter; Greene King IPA; Taylor Landlord; guest beers Ⓗ

A large, friendly regulars' pub where glasses and surfaces gleam with constant polishing. It has a single horseshoe-shaped bar, with a raised area for dining, offering a wide selection of food. Visitors who drop in for a drink are made very welcome in the bar, or in the large garden with a shady tree and a covered smoking area. The pub does not accept credit cards. Situated on the edge of Epping Forest, it welcomes many walkers.

Q❀◐◑♿⊖🚌(20,167)P⚐

Maldon

Blue Boar Hotel

Silver Street, CM9 4QE (opp All Saints church)

⏲ 11 (12 Sun)-11

☎ (01621) 855888 🌐 blueboarmaldon.co.uk

Adnams Bitter; Farmer's Drop of Nelson's Blood, Puck's Folly, Golden Boar, seasonal beers Ⓖ

Fifteenth-century coaching inn in the historic heart of Maldon. Farmer's Ales are brewed in the stable block across the yard, with seasonal beers often available. This fine medieval hotel building has two bars and a meeting room upstairs. A range of meals and bar snacks is served. Folk music and jazz evenings are hosted on a regular basis and many community groups hold meetings here. The church next door has a unique triangular tower and a memorial window to a local ancestor of George Washington buried within.

⛫Q❀🛏◐◑🚂🚌(31X)P⚐🗑

Queen Victoria

Spital Road, CM9 6EP

⏲ 10.30 (11.30 Sun)-midnight

☎ (01621) 852923

Greene King IPA, Abbot; Mighty Oak Maldon Gold Ⓗ

Opened in 1845, this comfortable, welcoming Gray's local offers well-kept beers, a friendly service and excellent home-cooked food. The single bar provides separate areas for darts, dominoes, music, TV and a quiet dining area. The extensive menu and ever-changing specials board provides good value for the heartiest appetite. Meals are served 12-9pm Monday-Saturday and 12-5pm Sunday. A car park and beer garden are to the side and superb hanging flower baskets adorn the exterior. Q❀◐◑♿🚌(31X)♣P⚐

Queen's Head

The Hythe, CM9 5HN

⏲ 10-11 (midnight Fri & Sat); 12-10.30 Sun

☎ (01621) 854112 🌐 thequeensheadmaldon.co.uk

Adnams Broadside; Farmers Pucks Folly; Greene King Abbot; Sharp's Doom Bar; Taylor Landlord; guest beers Ⓗ

This pleasant old pub is situated north of the River Blackwater adjacent to the quay which is home to some of the Thames barges. There is a spacious riverside outdoor seating area and outside bar, plus a barbecue that operates in summer. The cosy front bar has a log fire in winter. Food is served in either the bar or the restaurant with fish and seafood extensively featured on the menu. Children are allowed in the restaurant. There is good disabled access and WC facilities. ⛫❀◑⊟♿⚡

Margaretting Tye

White Hart Inn

Swan Lane, CM4 9JX TL684011
⏲ 11.30-3, 6-midnight; 11.30-midnight Sat; 12-11 Sun
☎ (01277) 840478 🌐 whitehart.uk.com
Adnams Bitter, Broadside; Mighty Oak Oscar Wilde, IPA; Red Fox Hunters Gold; guest beers Ⓖ
The ideal home for well-kept real ale and good food, slightly off the beaten track but still accessible, this fine pub has it origins in the 17th century. The recent sympathetic restoration created an atmosphere conducive to both diners and drinkers. Regular club meetings are held here for cyclists, car clubs, ramblers and Young Farmers. Very much community focused, a book stall raises money for charities and beer festivals are held in June and November. CAMRA branch Pub of the Year 2007 and 2008. ⛫Q❀◑♿♣P⚡

Mill Green

Viper ☆

Mill Green Road, CM4 0PT TL641018
⏲ 12-3, 6-11; 12-11 Sat; 12-10.30 Sun
☎ (01277) 352010
Mighty Oak Oscar Wilde; Viper Ales Jake The Snake, VIPA; guest beers Ⓗ
The only pub in the country with this name, the Viper is an isolated, unspoilt country pub with a lounge, public bar and wood-panelled snug. Jake the Snake is occasionally replaced by another Viper ale. Viper Ales are commissioned from Mighty Oak and Nethergate, who also sometimes supply the two guest beers, but these may come from anywhere. Good home-cooked food is served at lunchtime, and Westons cider is sold. Beer festivals are held at Easter and August bank holiday.
⛫Q❀◑⊟♣●P⚡

Monk Street

Farmhouse Inn

CM6 2NR (off B184, 2 miles S of Thaxted) TL612287
⏲ 11-midnight
☎ (01371) 830864 🌐 farmhouseinn.org
Greene King IPA; Mighty Oak Oscar Wilde, Maldon Gold; guest beers Ⓗ
Built in the 16th century, this former Dunmow Brewery pub has been enlarged to incorporate a restaurant in the old cart shed and accommodation; the bar is in the original part of the building. The quiet hamlet of Monk Street overlooks the Chelmer Valley, two miles from historic Thaxted, and is convenient for Stansted Airport and the M11. A well in the garden is no longer used, but it supplied the hamlet with water during WWII. Outside there is a rear patio, front garden and field. Draught cider from Westons is usually sold in the summer.
❀◑🚌(313)●P⚡

Mount Bures

Thatchers Arms ✔

Hall Road, CO8 5AT (1½ m S of Bures, 1½ m N of Chappel) TL905319
⏲ 12-3, 6-11; closed Mon; 12-11 Sat & Sun
☎ (01787) 227460 🌐 thatchersarms.co.uk
Adnams Bitter; Crouch Vale Brewers Gold; guest beers Ⓗ
This family-friendly pub on the Essex-Suffolk border is popular with locals and visitors alike. Its two main bar areas and extensive garden overlook the Stour Valley. Up to five real ales are available, mainly from local micro-breweries, together with an extensive selection of British, Belgian and American bottled beers. Winter and spring beer festivals are held at the pub, which is renowned for its quality food made with locally-sourced produce.
❀◑⅄P

Orsett

Foxhound

18 High Road, RM16 3ER (on B188)
⏲ 11-11.30 (midnight Fri & Sat); 12-10.30 Sun
☎ (01375) 891295
Courage Best Bitter; Greene King IPA; guest beers Ⓗ
Two-bar village local that is at the centre of social life in Orsett. It has a comfortable saloon and a basic but characterful public bar. The three guest beers are usually sourced from independent breweries. Excellent bar meals are available on weekday lunchtimes. The Fox's Den restaurant is open Friday and Saturday evenings and Sunday lunchtime (booking advisable). It is also available for functions and business meetings. Regular quiz nights are held. ⛫❀◑⊟♿🚌♣P

Paglesham

Punch Bowl

Churchend, SS4 2DP
⏲ 11.30-3, 6.30-11; 12-10.30 Sun
☎ (01702) 258376
Adnams Bitter; guest beers Ⓗ
South-facing, white painted, weatherboarded pub dating from the 16th century, situated in a quiet one-street village. A former bakery and sailmaker's house, it has been an ale house since the mid 1800s, when it was reputedly frequented by smugglers. The low beamed single bar displays a large collection of mugs, brassware and old local pictures. There is a small restaurant to one side serving excellent, good value food, together with picnic tables at the front and in the rear garden. Ample parking is available. Q❀◑P

Pebmarsh

King's Head

The Street, CO9 2NH (4 miles NE of Halstead) TL853336
⏲ 12-3, 6-11; closed Mon; 12-midnight Fri & Sat; 12-8 Sun
☎ (01787) 269306 🌐 kingshead.pebmarsh.com
Greene King IPA; Woodforde's Wherry Best Bitter; guest beers Ⓗ
This friendly 500-year-old village pub is popular with locals and walkers alike. It features heavy oak beams and a central open fire in winter and there are plenty of benches at the front and in the rear garden. Guest beers from micro-breweries are featured regularly. Home-cooked food can be eaten in the main bar or separate restaurant area,

with Mexican and American styles a speciality. Autumn beer festivals are held in the detached barn, which is also available for functions.

Purleigh (Roundbush)

Roundbush

Roundbush Road, CM9 6NN (on left just off B1010 between North Fambridge and Maldon)
11-2.30, 6-midnight; 12-midnight Sun
(01621) 828354
Adnams Bitter; Greene King IPA; guest beers G
This 300-year-old pub is visible from the old Roman road from North Fambridge to Maldon. It is popular with locals from the village and has a warm, friendly atmosphere. Guest beers are often from one of the excellent local breweries in this part of Essex. A hearty breakfast can be enjoyed at the adjoining café which belongs to the pub, and good bar meals are supplemented by fish and chips on Friday to eat in or take away. Q P

Ramsden Heath

Nags Head

50 Heath Road, CM11 1HS
12-11 (2am Fri & Sat)
(01268) 711875 thenagshead-ramsdenheath.co.uk
Greene King IPA, Old Speckled Hen, Abbot; guest beers G
Traditional local with a friendly welcome. The beers, which are dispensed by gravity, can be viewed in their 'cellar' through the picture window to the side of the bar. There is regular entertainment including jazz, karaoke and quizzes. Major sporting events are shown on the TVs. The pub is very community-oriented and supportive of local charities and societies, as well as sponsoring the local football team. Home-cooked lunches are served throughout the afternoon, and barbecues are held on the patio in summer. P

Rayleigh

Roebuck

138 High Street, SS6 7BU
9-midnight (1am Fri & Sat)
(01268) 748430
Courage Directors; Greene King IPA, Abbot; Marston's Pedigree; guest beers H
Friendly high-street Wetherspoon's pub located on the site of the Reverend James Pilkington's baptist school and close to the shops. It stocks an excellent range of guest beers. Meals are served all day until 11pm and children are welcome during the day in a sectioned-off dining area. Outdoor drinking and smoking are permitted in a cordoned-off area at the front of the pub. Rayleigh is served by many buses and has a rail station.

Ridgewell

White Horse Inn

Mill Road, CO9 4SG (on A1017 between Halstead and Haverhill) TL736407
12-3 (not Mon & Tue), 6-11; 12-10.30 Sun
(01440) 785532 ridgewellwh.com
Beer range varies G
This old established pub dating from circa 1860 has an atmosphere that is second to none. It offers an ever-changing range of beers, usually six, including a mild, stout or porter from a wide variety of local and national breweries, all dispensed by gravity from the cellar. Real ciders from Biddenden, Hecks and Westons are also from the cellar. A second 'dark' winter beer festival was held in February 2009 in addition to the pub's regular summer festival. A large dining room/restaurant offers excellent food and luxury accommodation is available. Essex CAMRA Pub of the Year 2006 and local CAMRA Pub of the Year 2009.
P

Rochford

Golden Lion

35 North Street, SS4 1AB
11-11.30 (11 Tue; midnight Fri & Sat); 11-11 Sun
(01702) 545487
Adnams Bitter; Crouch Vale Brewers Gold; Greene King Abbot; guest beers H
Small, often busy, 16th-century traditional Essex weatherboarded freehouse complete with stained glass windows. Many times local CAMRA Pub of the Year, including 2008, it serves six ales including three changing guests, one a dark beer, plus real cider at all times. A large-screen TV shows major sporting events. Bar snacks are available. The decor includes hops above the bar and a fireplace with traditional log burner. A patio garden at the back is suitable for smokers. (7,8,60)

Horse & Groom

1 Southend Road, SS4 1HA
11.30-11 (midnight Fri & Sat); 12-11 Sun
(01702) 544015
Mighty Oak Maldon Gold; Sharp's Special; guest beers H
A fine locals' pub, a few minutes walk from the town centre, winner of local CAMRA Pub of the Year 2009. The ever-changing guest ales always include a selection from Essex breweries as well as from further afield, and real cider is always available. Occasional beer festivals are held and the pub also hosts CAMRA SE Essex branch's annual cider festival in September. A separate restaurant provides good value food, especially on Fridays, when a varied menu of fish is available.
(7,8) P

King's Head Inn

11 West Street, SS4 1BE
12-midnight
(01702) 531741
Shepherd Neame Kent's Best, Spitfire, Bishop's Finger; guest beer H
Originally a coaching inn, this is now a comfortable pub split into three bars, and features a log fire in winter. Shepherd Neame beers are always served in excellent condition by friendly staff, and a guest ale is now available too. The pub is situated in the market square, close to good public transport links. There is no jukebox but live music plays on three evenings. This is a non-TV establishment so conversation is possible on most evenings.
(7,8)

Rowhedge

Olde Albion

High Street, CO5 7ES (3 miles S of Colchester)
12-3 (not Mon), 5-11; 12-11 Thu-Sat; 12-10.30 Sun
(01206) 728972 yeoldealbion.co.uk

Beer range varies Ⓗ/Ⓖ
Traditional free house with a strong community spirit, the Albion has an ever-changing range of ales from micro-breweries. Forthcoming beers are featured above the bar – annoyingly, so are those you've just missed. In summer, visitors can sit in front of the pub and laze away the hours next to the River Colne. The upstairs function room can be hired out and provides useful extra space for regular beer festivals, including on St George's Day and during the village regatta in June. Look out for the pub's impossibly friendly dog in this small but perfectly formed local. ❀🚌(66)♣

Saffron Walden

Old English Gentleman

11 Gold Street, CB10 1EJ (E of B184/B1052 jct)
⏲ 11-11 (2am Tue-Thu; 1am Fri & Sat); 11-11 Sun
☎ (01799) 523595
Adnams Bitter; Woodforde's Wherry Best Bitter; guest beers Ⓗ
This 18th-century town-centre pub has log fires and a welcoming atmosphere. It serves a selection of guest ales and an extensive menu of bar food and sandwiches which changes regularly. Traditional roasts and chef's specials are available on Sunday in the bar or the dining area, where a variety of works of art are displayed. Saffron Walden is busy on Tuesday and Saturday market days. The pub has a pleasant patio at the rear.
⛼❀◐⚟

Railway

Station Road, CB11 3HQ (300 yds SE of war memorial)
⏲ 12-3, 6-11 (midnight Thu-Sat); 12-11 Sun
☎ (01799) 522208
Brakspear Bitter; Fuller's London Pride; Woodforde's Wherry Best Bitter; guest beer Ⓗ
Typical 19th-century town-centre railway tavern, recently refurbished to a high standard with railway memorabilia, including model trains, above the bar. The single, large bar features a mix of furniture and fittings that helps to convey a relaxed, comfortable atmosphere. An extensive menu of good food is available lunchtimes and evenings. ❀◐◑P⚟

Southend-on-Sea

Borough Hotel

10-12 Marine Parade, SS1 2EJ (on seafront, opposite Adventure Island)
⏲ 10am-midnight (2am Fri & Sat)
☎ (01702) 466936
Courage Best Bitter; Taylor Landlord; guest beers Ⓗ
This welcoming, spacious and comfortable pub is situated close to Southend's famous pier, and was refurbished two years ago when it reverted to its former name (previously called The Liberty Belle). It features up to six cask ales and is especially popular on sunny summer weekends. It has a jukebox and Sky TV, with a sports area at the rear for pool and darts matches. There is a seating area on the pavement to the front. Close to Southend bus station. ⛾❀🛏⇌(Central)🚌♣⚟

Cornucopia

39 Marine Parade, SS1 2EN (on seafront)
⏲ 10-11
☎ (01702) 460770 🌐 cornucopia.county-of-essex.com
Mighty Oak Maldon Gold, seasonal beer Ⓗ
A big welcome awaits from the best-dressed barman on the seafront at one of the smallest pubs in Essex. This street-corner local, on Southend's Golden Mile, usually serves two Mighty Oak beers and is popular with punters who watch Sky TV. Music is provided from a huge CD collection and there is karaoke on Saturday evening. Seats out front are available for smokers. Can you spot the Victorian three-bar layout among the lead-light windows? ❀⇌(Central)🚌⚟

Southminster

Station Arms

39 Station Road, CM0 7EW (near B1021)
⏲ 12-2.30, 6 (5.30 Thu & Fri)-11; 2-11 Sat; 12-4, 7-10.30 Sun
☎ (01621) 772225 🌐 thestationarms.co.uk
Adnams Bitter; Mighty Oak Oscar Wilde; guest beers Ⓗ
Approaching this tradional Essex weatherboarded pub, you can't miss the friendly hubbub from within. A regular award winner, it provides an excellent range of ales with guests changing frequently. Simply decorated and furnished with an attractive patio garden, it has a rustic barn with woodburning stove used for beer festivals twice a year. Regular live music nights and a weekly meat raffle are held. Local CAMRA branch 2008 and Essex county Pub of the Year are among its accolades.
⛼Q❀⇌(Southminster)🚌(31X)♣●⚟

Stansted Mountfitchet

Rose & Crown

31 Bentfield Green, CM24 8HX (½ mile W of B1383)
TL507255
⏲ 12-3, 6-11 (midnight Fri & Sat); 12-10.30 Sun
☎ (01279) 812107
Adnams Bitter; guest beers Ⓗ
Typical family-run Victorian pub near a duck pond on the edge of a small hamlet, now part of Stansted Mountfitchet village. This free house has been modernised to provide one large bar but retains the atmosphere of a village inn and is well used by locals. The front of the pub is brightened by floral displays. Food is traditional and good value (not Sun or Mon evenings). The guest beers are sourced locally. The smoking area is covered and heated. ⛼❀◐◑🚌(7)♣P⚟

Stapleford Tawney

Moletrap

Tawney Common, CM16 7PU (3 miles E of Epping)
TL500013
⏲ 11.30-2.30, 6-11; 12-3.30, 7-10.30 Sun
☎ (01992) 522394 🌐 themoletrap.co.uk
Fuller's London Pride; guest beers Ⓗ
Former McMullen pub, now a small free house, this old inn enjoys superb views over the surrounding countryside. There are usually three guest beers from small independent breweries on offer, and good food is served (not Sun and Mon eve). The bar can get crowded, but the large garden is delightful in good weather. Despite being close to the M25, the pub can be hard to find, but worth the effort. It is a popular cycle ride from nearby towns.
⛼Q❀◐◑P

Stebbing

White Hart

High Street, CM6 3SQ (2 miles N of old A120 Dunmow-Braintree road)
11-3, 5-11; 11-11 Sat; 12-10.30 Sun
(01371) 856383 pickapub.co.uk/whitehartstebbing
Greene King IPA; Hart of Stebbing Hart Throb, Harts Content; guest beer H
Friendly 15th-century timbered inn in a picturesque village. This comfortable pub features exposed beams, an open fire, eclectic collections from chamber pots to cigarette cards, an old red post box in an interior wall and a section of exposed lathe and plaster wall behind a glass screen. A new micro-brewery, Hart of Stebbing, opened in December 2007, producing three or four beers including Hart & Soul and Black Hart, currently only available in the pub and at local beer festivals. Good value food is served daily. A patio features a covered gazebo with heater. Q P

Stock

Hoop

High Street, CM4 9BD (on B1007)
11-11 (midnight Fri & Sat); 12-10.30 Sun
(01277) 841137 thehoop.co.uk
Adnams Bitter; Brentwood Hoop, Stock & Barrel H**; guest beers** H/G
A long-standing Guide entry, the interior of this 15th-century timber-framed building retains plenty of character. A traditional, friendly drinkers' pub, this award-winning hostelry has at least four guest beers on gravity dispense and a cider or perry is usually available. Home-made food is served in the bar and in the upstairs restaurant. The large garden is the setting for the Hoop's renowned beer festival held over the spring bank holiday. During the summer months there is an outside bar and barbecue. Q (100)

Stow Maries

Prince of Wales

Woodham Road, CM3 6SA (near B1012) TL830993
11-11 (midnight Fri & Sat); 12-11 Sun
(01621) 828971 prince-stowmaries.co.uk
Beer range varies H/G
One of the county's long-standing real ale free houses, offering a varied selection of beers plus Westons Old Rosie cider and an extensive bottled and draught range from Belgium, where the pub has many friends. This 17th-century inn was once a bakery and has three open-plan drinking areas, all with real fires. The annual November fireworks display is renowned internationally. Fine meals are available, featuring local fish or seafood specialities to complement the ales on offer. Stylish farmhouse accommodation is a recent addition.
Q P

Benjamin Wilson's Burton beer was better known in Russia, where he did a large trade, than it was in the metropolis. The Empress Catherine, and the grand old savage Tsar Peter, freely drank the beer at their respective courts long before it became popular at St James's under the four Georges. **Dr Bushman**, 1852

Warley

Brave Nelson

138 Woodman Road, CM14 5AL (½ mile E of B186)
12-3, 5.15-11 (11.30 Fri); 12-11.30 Sat; 12-3.30, 7-11 Sun
(01277) 211690
Greene King IPA; Nethergate Suffolk County; guest beer H
Cosy local, featuring wood-panelled bars with understated nautical memorabilia including pictures, drawings and plates. A rare, regular outlet in the area for Nethergate Suffolk County Bitter, the guest beer is usually from Brentwood Brewery or Cottage. The Sunday evening quizzes, which are usually well-attended, start soon after 9pm. Darts, pool and crib are played, and widescreen TVs show sport. Live music features twice a month. No food is served on Sunday. There is a sheltered smoking area in the garden. P

Weeley

White Hart

Clacton Road, Weeley Heath, CO16 9ED (on B1441)
12-2.30, 4-11; 12-11 Fri-Sun
(01255) 830384
Beer range varies H
Friendly, well-run local. Four handpumps are normally in use, serving both local Harwich Town ales and micro-brewery beers from all parts of the country, often including a mild. The pub's thriving real ale club helps to influence the landlord in his choice of beers. There is a covered smoking area near the car park. Although somewhat isolated, the pub is on regular village bus routes and Weeley railway station is less than a mile away. No food is available. (76) P

Wendens Ambo

Bell

Royston Road, CB11 4JY (on B1039, 1 mile W of B1383/old A11 jct)
11.30-3, 6-11; 11.30-12.30am Fri & Sat; 12-11.30 Sun
(01799) 540382
Adnams Bitter; Woodforde's Wherry Best Bitter; guest beers H
Classic country pub at the centre of a picturesque village near Saffron Walden. A charity fundraising event is held in summer and small beer festivals take place throughout the year. Quality beers can be drawn from the cask on request. A chalkboard features beer tasting notes and forthcoming guest beers. Traditional pub food is served at lunchtimes and main meals in the evenings. Roast lunches on Sunday include a vegetarian option. Outside is a large garden with play area, a petanque pitch and a nature walk near the river. A weekly quiz is held on Thursday. Dogs are welcome.
(Audley End) P

Westcliff-on-Sea

Cricketers

228 London Road, SS0 7JG (on A13)
11 (12 Sun)-midnight (2am Fri & Sat)
(01702) 343168
Greene King Abbot; Sharp's Doom Bar; guest beers H
This large street-corner pub on the edge of Southend with an attractive facade is very popular and, with its late licence, is especially busy at weekends. A Gray's pub, it serves two regular ales,

up to four constantly changing guest ales mainly from Essex breweries and at least one guest cider. The excellent music venue Club Riga adjoining the premises adds to the feel-good factor and occasional beer festivals are held. Good value meals are available lunchtimes and evenings.
❀◐◑♿⇌(Southend Victoria/Westcliff)🚌🍎⚡

Widdington

Fleur de Lys

High Street, CB11 3SG TL538316

🕘 12-3 (not Mon), 6-11, 12-midnight Fri & Sat; 12-11 Sun

☎ (01799) 543280

Adnams Bitter; Greene King IPA; guest beer Ⓗ

A welcoming 400-year-old village local which is reputed to be haunted, with a large open fireplace and wood beams. Note the 'hole' in the seat by the door for the traditional game of pitch penny. The pub is close to the source of the River Cam and Priors Barn, an English Heritage site. This was the first pub to be saved from closure by the North West Essex branch of CAMRA after the branch's formation many years ago. No meals on Monday.
🔥Q❀◐◑♿🚌(322)♣P

Wivenhoe

Horse & Groom ✔

55 The Cross, CO7 9QL (on B1028)

🕘 10.30-3, 5.30-11 (midnight Fri); 10.30-3, 6-11 Sat; 12-4.30, 7-10.30 Sun

☎ (01206) 824928

Adnams Bitter, seasonal beers; guest beers Ⓗ

Friendly locals' pub on the outskirts of Wivenhoe with a proper two-bar layout featuring a public bar that is popular for darts. Adnams beers are on offer, with changing guests often including a mild. Very good home-cooked food is served lunchtimes Monday to Saturday – the curries are well worth sampling. At the rear is a garden with a covered and heating smoking area, plus a small car park. The pub is accessible by bus and a one-mile walk from Wivenhoe station. ❀◐🀫🚌(78)♣P⚡

Woodham Mortimer

Hurdlemakers Arms

Post Office Road, CM9 6ST (off A414)

🕘 12-11 summer; 12-3, 6-11 winter; 12-10.30 (12-3, 7-10.30 winter) Sun

☎ (01245) 225169 🌐 hurdlemakersarms.co.uk

Greene King Abbot; Mighty Oak IPA; guest beers Ⓗ

Popular 400-year-old Gray's country pub offering an excellent range of ales, real cider and good food. Mine hosts are CAMRA members and keenly promote local breweries with regular ales and at least three guests. Cider is stocked and home-cooked food is locally sourced and available daily. An open log fire in winter, cosy restaurant, huge beer garden, children's outdoor play area and summer barbecues provide a perfect venue for locals, walkers, diners and families. Special events take place throughout the year.
🔥Q❀◐◑🀫♿🚌(D2,31)♣🍎P⚡

Writtle

Wheatsheaf 🏆

70 The Green, CM1 3DU (S of A1060)

🕘 11-3, 5-11; 11-midnight Fri & Sat; 12-11 Sun

☎ (01245) 420695 🌐 wheatsheafph-writtle.co.uk

Adnams Bitter; Farmer's Drop of Nelson's Blood; Greene King Abbot; Mighty Oak Oscar Wilde, Maldon Gold; Sharp's Doom Bar Ⓗ

Traditional village pub with a small public bar, an equally small lounge and a small roadside patio covered for smokers. Winner of CAMRA Branch Pub of the Year 2009, it serves a guest seventh beer on gravity from the wide Gray's list. The atmosphere is generally quiet, as Sky TV in the public bar is only switched on for occasional sporting events. A folk night is held on the third Friday of the month. Note the Gray & Sons sign in the public bar.
Q🀫🚌(45)♣P⚡

Red Cow, Chrishall.

GLOUCESTERSHIRE & BRISTOL

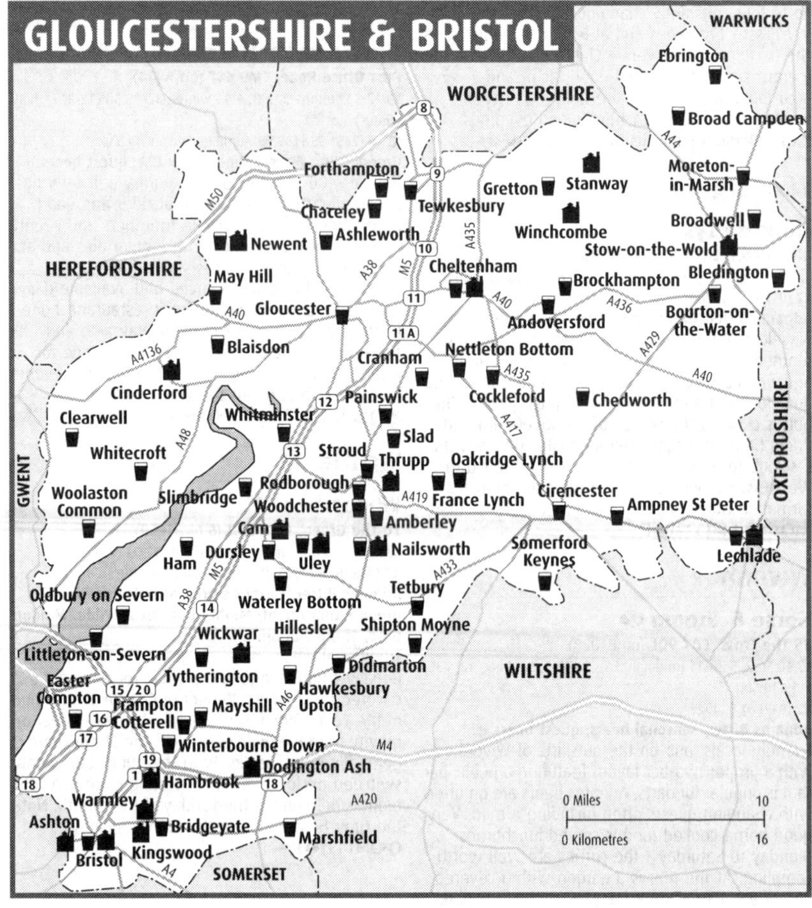

Amberley

Black Horse

GL5 5AL ST848016

12-11 (midnight Fri & Sat)

(01453) 872556 blackhorseamberley.co.uk

Otter Bright; RCH Old Slug Porter; Stroud Tom Long, Budding; Taylor Landlord H

Busy, friendly, family-run pub on the edge of Minchinhampton Common. The L-shaped bar ends in a conservatory with stunning views across the Nailsworth Valley to Selsley Common. Good value food is served until 10pm daily. There are regular music and quiz nights, and other themed evenings. A separate room houses a pool table and jukebox. The terraced gardens command views of the River Severn and the Forest of Dean. Barbecues are held in summer, and occasional beer festivals. Black Rat cider is served.

Ampney St Peter

Red Lion ★

London Road, GL7 5SL (on A417)

6-8.30 (10 Fri & Sat); 12-2.30 (closed eve) Sun

(01285) 851596

Hook Norton Hooky Bitter; Taylor Golden Best, Landlord H

Possibly the quintessential example of a basic, no-frills pub, with its promise of a cracking log fire and crystal clear ale. This CAMRA National Inventory-listed building is a gem, and has welcomed travellers (and their tales) for more than 400

INDEPENDENT BREWERIES

Arbor Bristol: Kingswood
Avon Bristol
Bath Ales Bristol: Warmley
Battledown Cheltenham
Bristol Beer Factory Bristol: Ashton
Cotswold Spring Dodington Ash
Donnington Stow-on-the-Wold
Festival Cheltenham
Freeminer Cinderford
Goff's Winchcombe
Great Western Bristol: Hambrook
Halfpenny Lechlade (NEW)
Nailsworth Nailsworth
Prescott Cheltenham (NEW)
Severn Vale Cam
Stanway Stanway
Stroud Thrupp
Uley Uley
Whittington's Newent
Wickwar Wickwar
Zerodegrees Bristol

continuous years. Benches adorn both small rooms off the narrow wood-panelled entrance corridor – the bar itself has no counter, just two handpumps in the corner. The friendly landlord and the locals make this a difficult place to leave. ⛪Q❀⊟⊟P

Andoversford

Royal Oak

Gloucester Road, GL54 4HR (on A436) SP023195
11-3, 5-11; 12-10.30 Sun
☎ (01242) 820335
Sharp's Doom Bar; Stanway Stanney Bitter; guest beers Ⓗ
Popular, well-run local pub offering up to five quality real ales including two from local Cotswold brewers. A large open log fire creates a homely atmosphere, visible from both the comfortable lounge area and a two-level restaurant with gallery. Attractive refurbishment has created a comfortable environment for both real ales and home-cooked meals. A patio area at the rear of the pub provides access to the large car park. Andoversford is an expanding village between Cheltenham and the North Cotswolds, in good walking country. ⛪Q❀◑⊟(801,803)♣●P⁵–

Ashleworth

Boat Inn

The Quay, GL19 4HZ (follow sign for Quay from village) SO819251
11.30-2.30 (3 Sat; not Wed), 7-11; closed Mon; 12-3, 7-10.30 Sun
☎ (01452) 700272 🌐 boat-inn.co.uk
Beer range varies Ⓖ
This unspoilt, tranquil haven on the banks of the River Severn is an absolute gem. It has been owned by the same family for 400 years and serves micro-brewery beers direct from the cask, making it a frequent winner of local CAMRA awards. It has an old fireplace with a bread oven. Several rooms are furnished with antiques. There are some tables under cover and on the river bank. Rolls are available at lunchtime and the pub has its own mooring for river visitors. Q❀♣●P

Blaisdon

Red Hart

GL17 0AH SO703169
12-3, 6 (7 Sun) -11
☎ (01452) 830477
Hook Norton Hooky Bitter; guest beers Ⓗ
A charming old inn with flagstone floors, low beams and a welcoming open fire, plus a warm, friendly atmosphere. It offers up to five beers on handpump, four constantly changing. There is an excellent choice of good value, quality food on the menu. The permanent barbecue and outdoor seating make this a lovely venue on a summer's evening. ⛪Q❀◑P

Bledington

Kings Head ✔

The Green, OX7 6XQ (on village green) SP243228
11-3, 6-11; 12-10.30 Sun
☎ (01608) 658365 🌐 kingsheadinn.net
Hook Norton Hooky Bitter; guest beers Ⓗ
North Cotswold CAMRA Pub of the Year 2008, this delightful 16th-century honey-coloured stone inn overlooks the village green, with its brook and ducks. The original old beams, inglenook with kettle plus military brasses, open wood fire, flagstone floors and high-back settles and pews create a heart-warming atmosphere. Quality food is served in a separate dining area, while 12 rooms offer charming accommodation. Guest ales are varied but are often from Gloucestershire. ⛪Q❀❀⊟◑⊟Å⇌(Kingham)♣P⁵–

Bourton on the Water

Mousetrap Inn

Lansdowne, GL54 2AR (300m W of village centre)
11.30-3, 6-11; 12-3, 6-10.30 Sun
☎ (01451) 820579 🌐 mousetrap-inn.co.uk
North Cotswold Pigbrook Bitter; Wickwar Cotswold Way; guest beers Ⓗ
This attractive, traditional and friendly Cotswold stone pub is a family-run free house, situated in the quieter Lansdowne part of Bourton. It is popular with the local community and offers 10 en-suite letting rooms for visitors. Three Gloucs beers and good-value home-cooked meals are served. A welcoming, cosy atmosphere is created with a feature fireplace and coal-effect fire. A patio area in front provides a sheltered suntrap in summer. Q❀⊟◑⊟(801,855)♣P

Bridgeyate

White Harte

111 London Road, BS30 5NA
11-2.45 (3 Sat), 5 (6 Sat)-11; 11-11 Fri; 12-10.30 Sun
☎ (0117) 9673830
Bath Ales Gem; Butcombe Bitter; Courage Best Bitter; Marston's Pedigree Ⓗ
Traditional inn dating from 1860 and extended in 1987. Situated with the large village green at the front, it is also know as the 'Inn on the Green'. An unusual bar counter incorporates old wooden spice drawers. Reasonably priced food attracts lunchtime diners, and the pub also gets busy in the evening with people out for a drink. Pub games and sporting activities are likely conversation topics, and a quiz features on Monday evening. Black Rat cider is served. ⛪❀◑⊟(634,635)♣●P⁵–

Bristol (Central)

Bag O'Nails

141 St George's Road, Hotwells, BS1 5UW (5 mins walk from cathedral)
12-2 (Thu only), 5.30-11; 12-11 Fri & Sat; 12-10.30 Sun
☎ (07717) 846560 🌐 thebagonails.co.uk
Beer range varies Ⓗ
Small, friendly, gas-lit terraced free house which showcases the beers of small breweries from all over, often from the newer brewers. Up to six constantly-changing guest ales are served and regular beer festivals take place twice a year, usually in April and November. The basic interior features wood panelling and bare floorboards, with port holes providing a view into the cellar. A good range of British and foreign bottled beers is available. Bristol to North Somerset buses stop nearby, as does the river ferry from Temple. Quiz night is Wednesday. Q⊟

Bank

8 John Street, BS1 2HR
12-midnight (1am Thu-Sat)

☎ (0117) 9304691
Beer range varies Ⓗ
After many incarnations and several closures, The Bank has emerged as a tremendous new addition to the Bristol real ale scene. A compact, one-bar pub, it is situated in the city centre but well hidden down a small lane by the old city wall. A strong supporter of south-west micro-brewers, the three or four featured ales come from many sources. The pub is not afraid to sell dark or very strong beers, always at keen prices. Expect a lot of quirky humour and to find the Gents on the second attempt. Food is served 12-4pm daily, including popular Sunday roasts. The cider is Thatchers plus guests. ❀◐≹(Temple Meads)🚌●⁻

Barley Mow

39 Barton Road, The Dings, BS2 0LP (400m from rear exit Temple Meads station over footbridge)
⏲ 12-3 (not Mon), 5-11; 12-11 Fri-Sun
☎ (0117) 9304709 🌐 myspace.com/barleymowbristol
Bristol Beer Factory Red, No. 7, Sunrise, seasonal beer Ⓗ
A short walk from the rear exit of Temple Meads station brings you to this excellent pub, saved from closure by Bristol Beer Factory in 2008. Located in the Dings renovation area, it has an open plan layout with a pleasant courtyard outside. Pictures of the area and local art feature strongly. Live music is held on Thursday and Saturday evenings and good food is served lunchtime and evening. Seasonal ales include the award-winning Milk Stout when available. Worth getting a later train for. ⌂❀◐◑≹(Temple Meads)🚌⁻

Bell ✔

Hillgrove Street, Stokes Croft, BS2 8JT (off Jamaica St)
⏲ 12-2 (not Sat), 5-midnight (1am Thu-Sat); 1-11.30 Sun
☎ (0117) 909 6612 🌐 bell-butcombe.com
Bath Ales Gem; Butcombe Bitter, Gold, seasonal beer Ⓗ
Pleasant, eclectic, two-roomed pub where DJs spin their discs from 10pm nightly in the back room. Friday evenings in particular attract drinkers on their way to nearby clubs. Local workers are regular customers for the lunchtime and early evening food. Sunday lunches are popular too. A surprising feature is the pleasant rear garden with a patio which is heated in colder weather. Local art on the wood-panelled walls and artistic graffiti in the toilets add character and a bohemian feel. Plenty of buses serve the Gloucester Road nearby.
❀◐◑🚌⁻

Colston Yard ✔

Colston Street, BS1 5BD
⏲ 12-midnight (1am Fri & Sat)
☎ (0117) 376 3232 🌐 colstonyard-butcombe.com
Butcombe Bitter, Gold, seasonal beers; Fuller's London Pride; guest beer Ⓗ
A tremendous renovation of the old Smiles Brewery and tap site, reopened by Butcombe in late 2007. Unrecognisable internally and decorated to a high standard, it has a pleasant, upmarket feel. In addition to the Butcombe range there are one or two guest beers, a number of interesting foreign draught beers from Europe and the US, plus around 30 quality bottled brews from elsewhere. An extensive bar and restaurant menu features local organic produce and fresh pizzas. Very handy for the Colston Hall and BRI. ◐◑🚌

Commercial Rooms ✔

43-45 Corn Street, BS1 1HT
⏲ 8am-midnight (1am Fri & Sat); 9am-midnight Sun
☎ (0117) 927 9681
Butcombe Bitter, Gold; Courage Best Bitter; Greene King Abbot; Marston's Pedigree; guest beers Ⓗ
Grade II-listed building dating from 1810 and impressively converted to Bristol's first Wetherspoon pub in 1995. It is currently one of its top national real ale pubs, with up to seven guest beers. The interior features Greek revival-style decor, a stunning ceiling with dome, portraits and memorabilia from its days as a businessmen's club. There is a quieter galleried room, although the main bar can be very busy at peak times. Disabled access is via the side entrance in Small Street. The pub always gets fully involved with JDW festivals and CAMRA events. Q◐◑♿≹(Temple Meads)🚌●

Eldon House

6 Lower Clifton Hill, BS8 1BT (off Jacobs Wells Rd)
⏲ 12-3, 5-11; 12-midnight Fri & Sat; 12-11 Sun
☎ (0117) 922 1271 🌐 theeldonhouse.co.uk
Bath Ales Gem, Barnstormer, seasonal beers; guest beer Ⓗ
This delightful Grade II-listed pub has two bars and a rear snug, and plans to extend the building further. Good honest pub food is served daily at lunchtime and until 9pm on Friday and Saturday. Sunday roasts, served 12-4pm, are very popular. Entertainment includes free Wi-Fi, poker on Monday and a quiz on Tuesday. Close to the city museum and the QEH theatre, buses run nearby: get off at the top of Park Street. ⌂Q◐◑🚌

Grain Barge

Hotwells Road, Hotwells, BS8 4RU (moored on the opposite bank to the SS Great Britain)
⏲ 12-11.30; closed Mon
☎ (0117) 929 9347 🌐 grainbarge.co.uk
Bristol Beer Factory Red, No. 7, Sunrise, seasonal beers Ⓗ
This permanently moored boat, built in 1936 and until recently a restaurant, was purchased by the Beer Factory in 2007 and converted into a floating pub offering good food. Great views of the SS Great Britain and the floating harbour are available from the top two decks. Live music plays on Friday, and popular themed food nights are held on Tuesday and Wednesday. No food is served Sunday evening. The cider is Thatchers. A downstairs bar and function room are available. ❀◐◑🚌●⁻

Highbury Vaults

164 St Michaels Hill, Kingsdown, BS2 8DE (next to Bristol Royal Infirmary)
⏲ 12-midnight (11 Sun)
☎ (0117) 973 3203
Bath Ales Gem; Brains SA; St Austell Tribute; Wells Bombardier; Young's Bitter, Special, seasonal beers; guest beer Ⓗ
A long-standing Guide entry and in the same hands for many years, this is a popular haunt of university students and hospital staff. Dating from the mid-19th century, its interior is dark, and features a small front snug bar, a main drinking area and a bar billiards table. Outside is a large heated patio and garden. Good quality, great value food is served lunchtimes and weekday evenings. A new feature is an enclosed model railway running the length of the pub. Toilets are reached via steep stairs. No entry after 11pm.
Q❀◐◑≹(Clifton Down)🚌(8,9)♣⁻

Hillgrove Porter Stores
53 Hillgrove Street North, Kingsdown, BS2 8LT
⏲ 4-midnight (1am Fri & Sat); 2-1am Sun
☎ (0117) 944 4780 🌐 thehillgroveporterstores.com
Cheddar Best; Goff's Tournament; Matthews Brassknocker; guest beers Ⓗ
This was the first of the Dawkins Taverns, the brainchild of a local entrepreneur. An excellent community pub, it is free of tie and making the most of it, usually dispensing five guest ales including dark beers and rare styles. The interior is horseshoe shaped with a wonderfully comfy lounge area hidden behind the bar. Outside is a pleasant patio. Sunday night is quiz night. Frequent themed mini beer festivals are held in conjunction with the other Dawkins pubs. Local CAMRA Pub of the Year 2007. ❀◑⇌(Montpelier)🚌♣🍎⛳

Hope & Anchor
38 Jacobs Well Road, BS8 1DR (between Anchor Rd and top of Park St)
⏲ 12-11 (10.30 Sun)
☎ (0117) 929 2987
Beer range varies Ⓗ
Popular and friendly city local frequented by students, diners and drinkers, all enjoying the chance to choose from up to six changing real ales, mostly from West Country micro-breweries. The pub has achieved a happy balance between those who come to eat the high-quality food, served all day, and those who just want a pint. Subdued lighting, candles on the tables and hanging hop bines over the bar create atmosphere. On summer days the terraced garden at the rear is very pleasant. Street parking is limited, but buses pass nearby. ❀◑🚌⛳

Kings Head ★
60 Victoria Street, BS1 6DE
⏲ 11-11; 12-5, 7-11 Sat; 12-3, 7-11 Sun
☎ (0117) 927 7860
Sharp's Doom Bar, Atlantic IPA; Wadworth 6X; Wickwar BOB Ⓗ
Classic small pub, dating from pre-1660 and listed on CAMRA's National Inventory. A narrow area around the bar leads to the tramcar snug to the rear. Multiple historic pictures of Bristol as it was long ago make fascinating viewing. A resident ghost, said to be an earlier landlady, is reputed to haunt the pub. Popular food is served weekday lunchtimes only. A few minutes walk from Temple Meads station on the way to town, the pub is also well served by buses. There are tables outside for summer drinking. Q❀◐⇌(Temple Meads)🚌

Old Fishmarket ✔
59-63 Baldwin Street, BS1 1QZ
⏲ 12-11.30 (midnight Fri & Sat)
☎ (0117) 921 1515
Butcombe Bitter; Fuller's Discovery, London Pride, ESB, seasonal beers Ⓗ
Spacious Fuller's pub which has become the main venue for those who enjoy a great pint with their TV sport; all main events are screened. As the name suggests, this was once a fish market. It has a large front bar and an indoor patio to the side, as well as several discrete seating booths behind the bar for those wishing to avoid the sport. Thai and English meals are served lunchtime and evening. Temple Meads station is a ten-minute walk. ◑♿⇌(Temple Meads)🚌

Seven Stars
1 Thomas Lane, Redcliffe, BS1 6JG (just off Victoria St nr Bristol Bridge)
⏲ 12-11 (10.30 Sun)
☎ (0117) 376 3970
Beer range varies Ⓗ
Small one-bar pub with poignant links to the abolition of the slave trade in Bristol. The enthusiastic management team offers a warm welcome and very competitive prices. The pub has kicked on from its debut in the Guide last year and now offers eight changing beers, with generous discounts at certain times. A pool table is in one corner and a silent TV is set to sport channels. A rock-oriented jukebox is well used and there is outdoor seating in fine weather. Handy location between the centre and the station.
⇌(Temple Meads)🚌♣

White Lion
Quay Head, Colston Avenue, BS1 1EB
⏲ 11 (12 Sat)-11; 12-10.30 Sun
☎ (0117) 9277744
Draught Bass Ⓟ**; Wickwar Coopers, BOB, Cotswold Way, seasonal beers** Ⓗ
This small city-centre pub is Wickwar's only tied house. The room curls around the central bar and the dizzying spiral staircase to the Gents is not for the faint-hearted. Five handpumps feature a selection of Wickwar beers, sometimes accompanied by guests from far and wide. Bristol's 'smallest beer festival' is held here twice yearly when casks on stillage appear by the bar. Hearty sandwiches are served weekday lunchtimes. The pumps usually feature either Station Porter or Mr Perretts Stout. In better weather take a seat outside and watch the frenetic city-centre activity.
❀🚌⛳

Bristol (East)

Chelsea Inn
60-62 Chelsea Road, Easton, BS5 6AU
⏲ 1-midnight
☎ (0117) 9029186 🌐 pickofthepubs.co.uk/thechelsea
Jennings Cocker Hoop, Sneckfilter; guest beers Ⓗ
Street-corner community local with one large room and a collection of vintage sofas, armchairs and other furniture. Pictures and pottery from local artists are for sale or commission. In a very cosmopolitan area, it attracts a varied crowd, many relatively young. Free internet facilities and a small exchange library operate here. Up to five beers are sold, not always from the Marston's range, as the landlord loves to offer guest ales, and one real cider too. Live jazz plays on Tuesday, plus more live music on Wednesday and Saturday.
❀⇌(Stapleton Road)♣🍎⛳

Bristol (North)

Annexe
Seymour Road, Bishopston, BS7 9EQ (behind Sportsman pub)
⏲ 11.30-11.30; 12-11 Sun
☎ (0117) 9493931
Adnams East Green; Courage Best Bitter; Sharp's Doom Bar; Shepherd Neame Spitfire; Skinner's Cornish Knocker; guest beer Ⓗ
A community pub tucked away down a residential street close to the county cricket ground and a short walk from the Memorial football and rugby

stadium. Inside is a converted skittle alley with a large conservatory/family room on one side and a partially covered patio on the other. Large-screen TVs show sport at both ends of the bar and out on the patio, while good simple food, including quality pizzas, is served. Quiz night is Monday and pool and darts are played. Q❀◑▶♿🚌♣⚐

Duke of York

2 Jubilee Road, St Werburghs, BS2 9RS (behind Mina Road Park close to M32 jct 3)

⏲ 5 (4 Sat)-11 (midnight Thu-Sat); 3.30-11 Sun

☎ (0117) 941 3677

Beer range varies Ⓗ

This well-hidden, genuine free house is a traditional community local serving an eclectic clientele. The exterior features an enchanted forest mural which continues inside. Visit in daylight for the mural, then at night experience the warm glow of the grotto-like interior. Expect many fairy lights, odd memorabilia, wooden floors, 1940s newspapers, a rare skittle alley and much more. Check out the two rooms and extra bar upstairs. Three handpumps offer unusual beers, plus Westons cider and a good range of bottled ales. Local CAMRA Pub of the Year 2008.
❀⊟⇌(Montpelier)🚌(5,25)♣●⚐

Miners Arms

136 Mina Road, St Werburghs, BS2 9YQ (400m from M32 jct 3)

⏲ 4 (2 Sat)-11 (midnight Fri-Sat); 12-11 Sun

☎ (0117) 955 6718

Fuller's London Pride; St Austell Tribute; guest beers Ⓗ

Located close to St Werburghs City Farm and Bristol Climbing Centre, this is an excellent two-roomed street corner local, part of the local Dawkins chain. The split-level interior houses a hop-adorned bar where three or four guest beers, including a beer of the month, join the regulars. Another small quiet bar lies to the side. The pub dogs, Nelson and Morris, welcome other well-behaved canines. Parking nearby can be tricky but buses 5 and 25 stop nearby. ♨❀⊟⇌(Montpelier)🚌(5,25)♣

Robin Hood's Retreat

197 Gloucester Road, Bishopston, BS7 8BG (on A38)

⏲ 12-11

☎ (0117) 9248639

Beer range varies Ⓗ

This Victorian red brick pub has been transformed into a smart, sophisticated dining and drinking venue, and a refuge from the bustling Gloucester Road outside. Eight handpumps offer a changing range of brews from independent outfits, often local. Award-winning food is produced by the chef/co-owner at all sessions. The pub can get very busy, especially at weekends. An outside decked area to the rear is open until 10.30pm. Children are welcome during the daytime.
Q❀◑▶♿⇌(Montpelier)🚌

Wellington

Gloucester Road, Horfield, BS7 8UR (on jct Gloucester Rd and Wellington Hill)

⏲ 12-11 (midnight Fri & Sat)

☎ (0117) 9513022 🌐 bathales.com

Bath Ales SPA, Gem, Barnstormer, seasonal; guest beer Ⓗ

The largest of Bath Ales' pub portfolio, situated at a busy junction on the A38. This imposing building, with B&B accommodation above, has a long, light and airy L-shaped bar, with various drinking areas arranged around it. A recently added lounge area has access to the extensive patio/garden. Close to the Memorial Stadium for rugby and football fans, only home fans are admitted at policed football games. A good selection of bottled beers and traditional home-cooked food is on offer. An annual beer festival is hosted in late May.
Q❀🛏◑▶♿🚌P⚐

Bristol (South)

Coronation

18 Dean Lane, Southville, BS3 1DD

⏲ 3-1am (midnight Sat); 12-10.30 Sun

☎ (0117) 940 9044

Hop Back GFB, Odyssey, Crop Circle, Summer Lightning, seasonal beer; guest beer Ⓗ

Hop Back's only Bristol pub, this busy street-corner local is a stone's throw from the River Avon, a 10-minute walk from the centre. It usually serves five Hop Back beers plus a guest from the associated Downton Brewery. The full range of Hop Back bottle-conditioned beers and a guest cider are also sold. Low-volume background music is played and a small TV is switched on for major sports events only. Quiz night is Monday. Pizzas are served 6-9pm every evening and Westons cider is on offer from a changing list. ▶🚌(24)●

Windmill

14 Windmill Hill, Bedminster, BS3 4LU (next to Bedminster railway station)

⏲ 11 (12 Sat)-11 (midnight Fri & Sat); 12-10.30 Sun

☎ (0117) 963 5440 🌐 thewindmillbristol.com

Bristol Beer Factory Red, No. 7, Sunrise Ⓗ

Completely refurbished in 2006, with pastel colours and wooden flooring throughout. Three beers from the nearby Bristol Beer Factory are always on offer, with the range changing occasionally. Westons cider and a few foreign bottled beers are also stocked. The pub is on two levels, with a family room on the lower one. There is also a small outside patio area to the front. Good quality home-cooked tasty food is served all day, and board games are available. Many buses pass nearby.
♨❀◑▶⇌(Bedminster)🚌●⚐

Bristol (West)

Cambridge Arms

Coldharbour Road, Redland, BS6 7JS

⏲ 12-11 (12.30am Fri & Sat)

☎ (0117) 9739786

Butcombe Bitter; Fuller's Discovery, London Pride, ESB, seasonal beer Ⓗ

Large, recently refurbished red brick Fuller's pub, not far from the Downs, with wooden floors and pastel-coloured walls. It can get very busy with diners but drinkers are also welcome around the L-shaped room. There is a large south-facing low-level garden behind the pub. Fuller's seasonal beers and those from the former Gale's brewery are often available. ❀◑▶🚌(20)P⚐

Lansdown

8 Clifton Road, Clifton, BS8 1AF

⏲ 4-11 (midnight Fri); 12-midnight Sat; 12-10.30 Sun

☎ (0117) 9734949

Bath Ales Barnstormer; Cheddar Ales Potholer; St Austell Tribute; guest beers Ⓗ

Traditional pub that now specialises in a great choice of real ale. Four of the five beers come from within 20 miles and the range always features an excellent mix of styles including a dark beer and a golden ale. The selection will change from time to time. There is an upstairs function room and live acoustic music events. Food is available evenings except Sunday and lunchtimes when open. The courtyard garden is heated and covered.
❀◐◑🚌(8,9)⚌

Merchants Arms

5 Merchants Road, Hotwells, BS8 4PZ
🕓 10.30-2, 5-11; 10.30-11.30 Sat; 11-11 Sun
☎ (0117) 9040037
Bath Ales SPA, Gem, Barnstormer, seasonal beer Ⓗ
Traditional local located just before the Cumberland Basin, on all the main Bristol to North Somerset bus routes. It won a national CAMRA award for its refurbishment a few years ago, when Bath Ales first took it on. Conversation dominates in the two drinking areas, although live music is held on some Tuesdays and a quiz night on Thursday. The concealed TV is brought out occasionally to show football. Food is limited to bar snacks. Well-behaved dogs are welcome. **Q🚌P**

Portcullis

3 Wellington Terrace, Clifton, BS8 4LE
🕓 12-2 Fri, 4.30-11; 12-11 Sat; 12-10.30 Sun
☎ (0117) 9085536
Cheddar Potholer; Matthews Brassknocker, Green Barrel; guest beers Ⓗ
A pub since 1821, the Portcullis was rescued from closure by the Dawkins chain in early 2008. A downstairs bar complements a quieter lounge upstairs that can be used for functions. The pub is close to the suspension bridge and to Clifton village. The landlord is totally anti large brewers and all pumps are occupied by small micro beers, including at least three changing guest ales and varying ciders plus foreign beers. Four beer festivals are held each year, including one with a Belgian theme. The Thursday quiz is popular. Good quality food is served. **Q**❀◐◑🚌(8,9)●⚌

Post Office Tavern

17 Westbury Hill, Westbury on Trym, BS9 3AG
🕓 11-11 (11.30 Fri); 12-11 Sun
☎ (0117) 9401233 🌐 buccaneer.co.uk
Bath Ales Gem; Butcombe Bitter; Courage Best Bitter; Draught Bass; Otter Bitter Ⓗ
Impressive single storey pub at the top of Westbury Hill which was originally a mail coach house, with a gaol opposite. The bars are air-conditioned and display much post office memorabilia. A large-screen TV shows sports events. Although bar food and teas are served lunchtime and evening, the pub is famed for its pizzas (two for one on Mon eve). Dogs are welcome here – as is the pub's reappearance in this Guide. ❀◐◑🚌(1)♣⚌

Royal Oak

50 The Mall, Clifton, BS8 4JG
🕓 12-11 (4 Sun)
☎ (0117) 973 8846
Butcombe Bitter; Courage Best Bitter; Fuller's London Pride; Sharp's Doom Bar Ⓗ
A short walk from the downs and suspension bridge in the heart of Clifton village, this is a busy, split-level pub. Crowds tend to gather around the bar on one level, while quiet seats can be found in the rear area. The pub is popular with local sports clubs and the TV shows major sports, especially rugby. Lunchtime food and a Sunday roast are offered. Count how many puffer fish you can spot among the dried hops around the bar and walls. Moles Black Rat cider is sold. ◐🚌(8,9)●⚌

Victoria ✔

20 Chock Lane, Westbury on Trym, BS9 3EX (in small lane behind churchyard)
🕓 12-2.30, 6-11; 12-3, 7-10.30 Sun
☎ (0117) 950 0441 🌐 thevictoriapub.co.uk
Butcombe Bitter; Draught Bass; Wadworth Henrys IPA, 6X, seasonal beers, Ⓗ
Quiet, relaxed and welcoming Wadworth-owned traditional pub that was once a courthouse and has been in the same hands for many years. The beer is well recommended by Bertie the pub's beer hound. A raised garden to the rear is a suntrap in summer. Pictures of Westbury as a village adorn the walls, and popular home-cooked food is available daily including pizzas. Entertainment includes quizzes, themed meals and live blues featuring the landlord on Sunday evening. Various societies meet here. **Q**❀◐◑🚌(1,20)⚌

Victoria

2 Southleigh Road, Clifton, BS8 2BH (off St Pauls Rd)
🕓 4 (12 Sat)-11; 12-10.30 Sun
☎ (0117) 974 5675
Goffs Jouster; Matthews Brassknocker; guest beers Ⓗ
The third Dawkins Tavern to open, and now in the safe hands of Paul and Dee (ex-licensees of the Hare on the Hill), tucked away just off the bottom of Whiteladies Road and next to the newly reopened Clifton Lido. Eight pumps offer a changing selection of independent beers and ciders. There are plans to open the upstairs function room, introduce food and run themed beer festivals. A film club and live acoustic music are also to come. Parking close by is very difficult.
♨**Q**◐◑⇌(Clifton Down)🚌●

Broad Campden

Bakers Arms

GL55 6UR (signed from B4081) SP158378
🕓 11.30-2.30, 4.45-11; 11.30-11 Fri, Sat & summer; 12-10.30 Sun
☎ (01386) 840515
Donnington BB; Stanway Stanney Bitter; Wells Bombardier; guest beers Ⓗ
This genuine free house, where the owners are celebrating their 10th year, is characterised by Cotswold stone walls, exposed beams, an inglenook fireplace and an attractive oak bar counter where the local Stanney Bitter is a popular choice. Home-cooked meals prepared by the landlady can be enjoyed in the bar or dining room. A framed handwoven rug is a feature of this CAMRA county Pub of the Year 2005. This is a traditional Cotswold pub at its very best.
♨**Q**❀◐◑♣●**P**

Broadwell

Fox Inn

The Green, GL56 0UF (off A429) SP202276
🕓 11-2.30, 6-11; 12-2.30, 7-10.30 Sun
☎ (01451) 870909 🌐 pubs2000.com
Donnington BB, SBA Ⓗ
This attractive stone-built pub overlooking the large village green was deservedly North Cotswold

CAMRA Pub of the Year 2007. Donnington Beers are popular with visitors. The pub is a true local centre where good home-cooked food is enjoyed. Features include original flagstone flooring in the main bar area, jugs hanging from beams and the Aunt Sally game played in the garden. Behind the garden is a camping and caravan site. A special experience is assured at this attentive family-run pub. ♛Q✿◐◑▲🚌♣P⛔

Brockhampton

Craven Arms

Kingsbury Street, GL54 5XQ (off A436) SP035224
⌚ 12-3, 6-11; 12-11 Sat; 12-10.30 (4 winter) Sun
☎ (01242) 820410
Otter Bitter; Wye Valley Bitter; guest beers Ⓗ
This spacious 17th-century pub is a proper free house, with a variety of selected guest beers. Set in an attractive hillside village with oustanding views and walks, it has an open fire bar area and excellent dining. Bank notes from numerous countries adorn the low beams. A beer festival is held annually in August in the sizeable garden, with live music in a marquee. Handy for nearby Sudeley Castle, this is a well-managed gem, with friendly family service. ♛Q✿🛏◐◑▲♣P

Chaceley

Yew Tree Inn

Stock Lane, GL19 4EQ SO865298
⌚ 12-2.30 (3 Sat), 6-11.30 (midnight Fri & Sat); 12-3, 7-11 Sun
☎ (01452) 780333
Wye Valley Butty Bach; guest beers Ⓗ
This riverside pub is set on the west bank of the Severn with visitor moorings. It has been altered and extended over 200 years and now has a large public bar, comfortable lounge and a restaurant serving good value food. Both the seating on the river bank in the summer and the real fire in the winter draw customers to this friendly hostelry. It holds a beer festival in the summer. Caravans are permitted. ♛🐾✿◐◑🀫♿▲P⛔

Chedworth

Seven Tuns

Queen Street, GL54 4AE (NE of village opp church) SP053121
⌚ 12-3.30, 6-11; 11-11 Sat & summer; 12-10.30 Sun
☎ (01285) 720242
Wells Bombardier, seasonal beers; Young's Bitter, seasonal beers Ⓗ
Unspoilt and atmospheric pub, attractively located in one of England's longest villages and a rare outlet for Young's beers served by attentive staff. The various rooms and dining areas are tastefully furnished and display local photographs and artefacts. Upstairs the skittle alley doubles as a function room and is available for hire. Outside, water cascades noisely from the stream opposite into a stone reservoir. This pub, close to the Roman Villa at Chedworth, is set in outstanding Cotswold walking country. ♛Q✿◐◑♣P⛔

Cheltenham

Adam & Eve

8 Townsend Street, GL51 9HD
⌚ 10-2 (not Thu), 4-11; 10-11 Sat; 12-2, 4-10.30 Sun
☎ (01242) 690030
Arkell 2B, 3B, seasonal beers Ⓗ
Run by the same landlady for 32 years, this friendly and unpretentious terraced local is home to skittles, darts and quiz teams. It is a 15-minute walk from the town centre and, while parking is very limited, the pub is readily accessible by public transport and buses stop at the end of the street. There is a separate lounge and the public bar forms a strong community focus. Charity events are often hosted. Q🚌(C,H,41)♣⛔

Bath Tavern

68 Bath Road, GL53 7JT
⌚ 11-11; 12-10.30 Sun
☎ (01242) 256122
Arbor Brigstow Bitter; Sharp's Cornish Coaster, Doom Bar Ⓗ
Located close to the town hall and nearby Cheltenham College with its cricket festival, there is always a warm welcome in this friendly and busy single bar free house. Run for more than 100 years by the Cheshire family, it now has young owners. Local produce is freshly cooked on the premises and Sunday lunch is especially popular (booking is advisable). Music is played at a background level, but the volume may rise during weekend evenings. ◐

Cheltenham Motor Club

Upper Park Street, GL52 6SA (access from A40 London Road via Crown Passage)
⌚ 6 (12 Sat; 7 Sun)-midnight
☎ (01242) 522590 🌐 cheltmc.com
Donnington SBA; guest beers Ⓗ
Card-carrying CAMRA members are welcome at this friendly club, in the former Crown pub, just outside the town centre. A finalist in the CAMRA National Club of the Year 2007, it offers an interesting range of three regularly changing ales, mainly from micro-breweries, alongside Donnington SBA and Thatchers cider. There is also a range of bottled porters and foreign beers, and often a perry. Local league quiz, darts and pool teams are based here. Parking is limited, but the club is served by Stagecoach B service. Q🀫🚌(B)🍎P⛔

Jolly Brewmaster

39 Painswick Road, GL50 2EZ
⌚ 12-11 (10.30 Sun)
☎ (01242) 772261
Beer range varies Ⓗ
The six handpumps in Cheltenham CAMRA's 2009 Pub of the Year regularly feature beers from local brewers, alongside Black Rat, Thatchers Heritage, Cheddar Valley and Westons Old Rosie ciders. Booking is advised for the excellent value Sunday lunch. Relaxed and friendly, this busy pub appears in CAMRA's Good Cider Guide and features original etched windows and open fires. The very attractive beer garden serves as an extra room in the summer and offers winter warmth for smokers. ♛Q✿🚌(10)🍎⛔

Kemble Brewery Inn

27 Fairview Street, GL52 2JF
⌚ 11-11 (midnight Fri & Sat)
☎ (01242) 243446
Beer range varies Ⓗ
This small, popular, back-street local is hard to find but well worth the effort. It can get very busy on race days or if nearby neighbours Cheltenham Town FC are at home. Six real ales are usually

available, often including local brews, with traditional ciders available between March and August. Booking is necessary for the excellent Sunday lunch (12-3.30pm) and a special is served daily at lunchtime. Smoking is permitted in an attractive walled area outside. Q❀◐●⁻

Royal Oak

43 The Burgage, Prestbury, GL52 3DL
11-2.30, 5.30 (6 Sat)-11; 12-10.30 Sun
☎ (01242) 522344 🌐 royal-oak-prestbury.co.uk
Taylor Landlord; guest beers Ⓗ
Cotswold stone-built local in Prestbury village with limited parking, but handy for the racecourse. The quiet public bar features oak beams, parquet flooring, equine prints and a log fire. Good quality food is served in the lounge bar with daily specials (booking advised). The Pavilion, a skittle alley and function room in the garden, hosts an annual beer festival in May and a cider festival in August. Beers are listed on the website. ⌂Q❀◐◑🚌(A)●P

Cirencester

Corinium Hotel

12 Gloucester Street, GL7 2DG (N of town centre)
11-11 (10.30 Sun)
☎ (01285) 659711 🌐 coriniumhotel.co.uk
Uley Laurie Lee's Bitter; guest beers Ⓗ
An agreeable two-star hotel with a discreet frontage that you enter through a narrow courtyard leading to a stylish interior, where the comfortable lounge area with its small, flagstoned bar adjoins an attractive restaurant. The varying thickness of the original walls shows where it was once an Elizabethan wool merchant's house and the resultant layout occasionally confuses new customers. There is a pleasant garden area at the rear of the premises. ⌂❀🛏◐◑♿P

Waggon & Horses ✔

11 London Road, GL7 2PU
11.30-3, 6-11 (midnight Fri & Sat); 12-3, 7-11 Sun
☎ (01285) 652022 🌐 thewaggonandhorses.co.uk
Skinner's Betty Stogs; Wye Valley HPA; guest beers Ⓗ
Pure enthusiasm from the young licensees has helped drive through a remarkable transformation at this once staid hostelry, with little left unchanged for the better. With the bar counter now back in front of the entrance, a welcome balance between the drinking and dining sides of the pub has been achieved. A separate function room leads off to the rear. Comfy sofas, a real fire and some subtle decorating make this a pleasant place to drink. ⌂◐◑🚌

Clearwell

Lamb

High Street, GL16 8JU SO570081
12-3 Sat, 6-11; closed Mon-Wed; 12-3, 7-10.30 Sun
☎ (01594) 835441
Wye Valley Bitter; guest beers Ⓖ
This pub is an absolute delight. It has two bars with open fires and two large settles flank the fire in the snug bar. The atmosphere is warm and welcoming and the beer, served by gravity, is always excellent. This friendly village pub has been a long-time favourite with CAMRA members and is well worth a visit. One resident ale and three ever-changing guests are sourced from local micros.
⌂Q❀🚂♣●P

Cockleford

Green Dragon

GL53 9NW (take Elkstone turn off A435)
11-11; 12-10.30 Sun
☎ (01242) 870271
Butcombe Bitter; Courage Directors; Otter Bitter Ⓗ
This delightful Cotswold stone inn dating from the 17th century features two bars with log fires, a restaurant and a function room/skittle alley as well as nine en-suite rooms. The bar and furniture are all hand-crafted by Robert Thompson, the Mouse Man of Kilburn – look for his trademark mice carved into the furniture. Excellent food is available lunchtime and evening and the pub can get very busy at weekends. There is a large car park across the road. ⌂Q🐎🛏◐◑●P⁻

Cranham

Black Horse

GL4 8HP (off A46 or B4070) SO896129
12-3, 6.30-11; closed Mon; 12-3, 8-10.30 Sun
☎ (01452) 812217
Hancock's HB; Stroud Tom Long; guest beer Ⓗ
A delightful 17th-century free house in popular wooded walking country. The bumpy car park, the main entrance's low lintel and the landlord's corny humour may present newcomers with challenging surprises. There is no doubting the quality of the ales and the generous portions of country-style dishes chosen from a packed blackboard. There is a small lounge and two extra rooms upstairs for dining. Quoits and shove ha'penny are played. No food is served on Sunday evening. ⌂Q❀◐◑🚂♣P

Didmarton

King's Arms

The Street, GL9 1DT (on A433)
11-11; 12-10.30 Sun
☎ (01454) 238245 🌐 kingsarmsdidmarton.co.uk
Otter Ale; Uley Bitter; guest beer Ⓗ
A smart, low-key frontage gives just a hint at the stylish refurbishments inside this 17th-century coaching inn. Copious amounts of reclaimed wood give the public bar, games area and central counter a warmth and comfort that are echoed by the smart furnishings of the popular restaurant. If you can tear yourself away from the friendly staff and chatty locals, take time to admire the tidy, walled garden with a smokers' pavilion. ⌂❀🛏◐◑🚌♣P⁻

Dursley

Old Spot 🏆

Hill Road, GL11 4JQ (next to bus station)
11 (12 Sun)-11
☎ (01453) 542870 🌐 oldspotinn.co.uk
Severn Vale Session; Uley Old Ric; guest beers Ⓗ
This Cotswold Way free house dates from 1776. It was named after the Gloucestershire Old Spot Pig and a porcine theme blends with the extensive brewery memorabilia. Low ceilings and log fires provide a cosy atmosphere and friendly staff offer a warm welcome. The pretty garden is perfect for summer and has a heated, covered area. Wholesome, freshly prepared dishes complement the pub's enthusiasm for real ale and cider. CAMRA National Pub of the Year 2007. There is a free car park opposite. ⌂Q❀◐♿🚌♣⁻

Easter Compton

Fox

Main Road, BS35 5RA (on B4055)
11-3, 6-11; 11-11 Sat summer; 12-10.30 (5.30 winter) Sun
☎ (01454) 632220
Bath Ales Gem; Otter Ale; guest beer Ⓗ
Run by the same family for more than 20 years, this pub has two distinct rooms. The comfortable, quiet lounge is popular for food (not Sun eve), much of it home-cooked, and offers a children's menu. The more lively public bar attracts locals and darts players. The skittle alley has three regular teams and can also be hired for functions. A single guest beer changes monthly and Exmoor Fox often appears but may not be available at quieter times of year. A large garden at the rear incorporates a safe children's play area. ♨Q❀◑▶⊟🚌(625)♣P⁻–

Ebrington

Ebrington Arms 🍷 ✔

GL55 6NH SP186399
12-3, 6-11; closed Mon; 12-11 Fri & Sat summer; 12-6 Sun
☎ (01386) 593223 🌐 theebringtonarms.co.uk
Stroud Tom Long; Uley Bitter; guest beers Ⓗ
Very friendly, unspoilt, 17th-century Cotswold stone free house serving four carefully sourced, mainly Gloucestershire, beers. An attractive low-beamed bar area and a cosy separate dining room both have feature fires. This family-run inn serves home-cooked meals from a varied menu using local ingredients. Situated two miles from Chipping Campden and popular with the local community, it has three en-suite letting rooms. In summer, enjoy the beautiful walled garden and visit the famous nearby estates of Hidcote and Kifsgate. North Cotswold CAMRA Pub of the Year 2009.
♨Q❀🛏◑▶Å●P

Forthampton

Lower Lode Inn

GL19 4RE (follow sign to Forthampton from A438 Tewkesbury-Ledbury road) SO878317
12-midnight (2am Fri & Sat)
☎ (01684) 293224 🌐 lowerlodeinn.co.uk
Cotswold Spring Gloucestershire Glory; Donnington BB; Sharp's Doom Bar; guest beers Ⓗ
This brick-built pub has been licensed since 1590. Standing in three acres of lawned river frontage, it looks across the River Severn to Tewkesbury Abbey. It has its own moorings and a private slipway. Day-fishing permits are available and the pub is also a licensed touring park site. The regular ales are complemented by two changing guests (three in summer). There is en-suite accommodation, lunch and evening meals are served and the Sunday lunch carvery is popular.
♨Q🐎❀🛏◑▶♿Å♣P⁻–

Frampton Cotterell

Live and Let Live

Clyde Rd, BS36 2EF
12-11 (midnight Fri-Sun)
☎ (01454) 772254 🌐 bathales.co.uk
Bath Ales SPA, Gem, Barnstormer, seasonal beers Ⓗ
Situated in a residential part of the village, this Bath Ales pub is open plan, with two distinct areas. It has a large car park and two landscaped gardens. Pictures adorn the walls and a TV is available. Food is served lunchtime and evening. The pub is well served by local bus routes.
♨❀◑▶♿🚌(X40,342)♣P⁻–

Rising Sun

43 Ryecroft Road, BS36 2HN
11.30-11.30 (midnight Fri & Sat); 12-11 Sun
☎ (01454) 772330
Butcombe Bitter; Draught Bass; Great Western Maiden Voyage, seasonal beer; Wadworth 6X; guest beer Ⓗ
This excellent free house is now the brewery tap for the Great Western Brewery, owned by the same family for many years. At least two GWB beers are normally on, together with one guest ale. The three-roomed interior comprises the main flagstoned bar, a small snug and a conservatory that acts as the restaurant during food hours. There is also a skittle alley/function room and a covered smoking area. Now open all day so there is no reason to leave. Q❀◑▶🚌(581)♣P⁻–

France Lynch

King's Head

France Lynch, Stroud, GL6 8LT
12-3, 6-11; 12-11 Sun
☎ (01453) 882225
Butcombe Bitter; Otter Bitter; Sharp's Doom Bar Ⓗ
Friendly single-bar pub hidden away at the heart of a village surrounded by winding lanes, but well worth finding. The village name implies Huguenot connections – French and Flemish weavers came to this wool-rich part of the Cotswolds in search of work. The pleasant garden has a safe play area for children and a creche is provided on Friday evening (7-9pm). No food Sunday evening. ♨Q❀◑▶P

Gloucester

Cross Keys Inn

Cross Keys Lane, GL1 2HQ
11-11 (midnight Fri & Sat); 7-midnight Sun
☎ (01452) 523358 🌐 crosskeysinngloucester.co.uk
Beer range varies Ⓗ
A fine 17th-century free house off Southgate Street. The front door opens immediately into a warm and welcoming main bar, where mature ale drinkers converse by day and towards the weekend a younger clientele enjoys an evening mix of live and recorded music. Bistro-style food is served every day, and the two ales always include a local one. There is a cocktail bar for small parties and an attractive sun terrace with heated cover for smokers. Closed Sunday lunchtime. ❀◑▶⇌⁻–

Greyhound

Greyhound Gardens, Longlevens, GL2 0XH (near Elmbridge roundabout at jct of A40/A417)
12-11 (midnight Fri & Sat)
☎ (01452) 506107
Banks's Original; Jennings Cumberland Ale Ⓗ
Built in 1985 on the site of a former greyhound stadium, this highly popular and welcoming community pub's quirky architecture is timeless. Recycled bricks from the demolished 18th-century infirmary blend externally with gently sloping slate roofs and internally with a warm colour scheme and furnishings. Food is available 12-9pm (8pm Sun). The small garden has a covered, heated area for smokers. Two guest ales are from Marston's national list. ❀◑▶♿🚌(94)♣P⁻–

Linden Tree

73-75 Bristol Road, GL1 5SN (on A430 S of docks)
⏲ 11.30-2.30, 6-11; 11.30-11.30 Sat; 12-11 Sun
☎ (01452) 527869
Wadworth IPA, Horizon, 6X, JCB, Bishop's Tipple; guest beers Ⓗ
The end property in a Grade II-listed Georgian terrace, this popular community pub has beamed ceilings, exposed stone walls, an open log fire with unusual canopy, carriage lamps and even a carriage wheel as a room divider. A skittle alley opens up to provide extra space when required. Eight ales are usually stocked, with guests coming mainly from family brewers. Substantial home-cooked meals are offered except Saturday and Sunday evening. The accommodation is reasonably priced. ♨Q❀⛟◑◐🚌(12)♣⁻

Pig Inn The City

121 Westgate Street, GL1 2PG
⏲ 11-midnight (1.30 Fri & Sat); 12-midnight Sun
☎ (01452) 421960
Brakspear Bitter; Wychwood Hobgoblin; guest beers Ⓗ
An imposing listed 19th-century facade belies the vibrant and youthful atmosphere within. Humorous piggy bric-a-brac is displayed and pig portraits adorn the walls. Four guest ales are from local brewers and occasionally from Black Country craft brewers. Excellent home-made food is available each lunchtime and on Monday, Wednesday, Thursday and Saturday evenings. There is entertainment on Tuesday, Friday and Sunday evenings. A large function room is available for hire upstairs. Gloucester CAMRA City Pub of the Year 2009. ❀◑◐⇌♣⁻

Water Poet ✔

61-63 Eastgate Street, GL1 1PN
⏲ 9-midnight
☎ (01452) 783530
Greene King IPA, Abbot; Marston's Pedigree; guest beers Ⓗ
Opened in 2007, this is a highly successful second venue for Wetherspoon in the city. An abundant use of wood and a warm colour scheme give a quality feel. A large paved and bricked garden surrounded by mature trees and shrubs has a spacious heated shelter for smokers. There is no music and the silent TV shows only news. Up to four guest ales come from craft brewers, some local. Food is served until 11pm. Q❀◑◐♿⇌⁻

Gretton

Royal Oak

Gretton Road, GL54 5EP SP014305
⏲ 12-3, 6-11; 12-4, 6-10.30 Sun
☎ (01242) 604999
Brakespear Bitter; Goff's Jouster; Stanway Stanney Bitter; guest beers Ⓗ
A very popular Cotswold pub where a warm welcome is assured from the family owners. Two regular beers are from Gloucestershire breweries with varied guests. Excellent home-cooked food can be enjoyed in the two bars and conservatory, with outstanding views across the vale. Bar areas have a mix of wood and flagstone floors, while the large sloping garden hosts an annual beer and music festival in July. There is a tennis court for hire and the Gloucestershire-Warwickshire Railway runs nearby. ♨❀◑◐♣P⁻

Ham

Salutation

Ham Green, Berkeley, GL13 9QH (from Berkeley take road signed to Jenner Museum) ST681984
⏲ 12-2.30 (not Mon), 5-11; 11-11 Sat; 12-10.30 Sun
☎ (01453) 810284
Cotswold Spring Old English Rose; Severn Vale Dursley Steam Bitter; guest beers Ⓗ
Rural free house situated in the Severn Valley within walking distance of the Jenner Museum, Berkeley Castle and Deer Park. This friendly local sources its beers from nearby breweries and is popular with walkers and cyclists. The pub has two cosy bars with a log fire and a skittle alley/function room. Food is served lunchtimes and early evening. There is a child-friendly garden at the front of the pub. ♨Q❀◑◐⊟♿♣P

Hawkesbury Upton

Beaufort Arms

High Street, GL9 1AU (off A46, 6 miles N of M4 jct 18)
⏲ 12-11 (10.30 Sun)
☎ (01454) 238217 🌐 beaufortarms.com
Wickwar BOB; guest beers Ⓗ
This 17th-century Grade II-listed Cotswold stone free house is close to the historic Beaufort Monument. It has public and lounge bars, a dining room and skittle alley/function room. The pub contains a plethora of ancient brewery and local memorabilia. Four ales and Wickwar Screech cider are served. The attractive garden is busy in summer. The pub is at the hub of community activities and a warm welcome is assured in this local CAMRA-award winner. ♨Q❀◑◐⊟♿🚌♣●P

Fox Inn

High Street, GL9 1AU (off A46, 6 miles N of M4 jct 18)
⏲ 12-11
☎ (01454) 238219 🌐 thefoxinnhawkesburyupton.co.uk
Beer range varies Ⓗ
The Fox is situated in an 18th-century building in the centre of this historic village. Originally a coaching inn, today it is a typical village pub with a warm and friendly atmosphere, enhanced by a real fire in winter. Food is served every lunchtime and evening. There is a large enclosed garden and a covered smoking area. It stands close to the Cotswold Way, in ideal walking country. ♨Q❀◑◐🚌♣P⁻

Hillesley

Fleece Inn

Chapel Lane, GL12 7RD
⏲ 12-3, 6-11 (closed Mon Jan & Feb), 12-midnight Sat; 12-11 Sun
☎ (01453) 843189
Butcombe Bitter; Sharp's Doom Bar; guest beer Ⓗ
Quaint 200-year-old whitewashed pub in the village of Hillesley. Its tastefully renovated interior is modern in flavour with a restaurant that serves a la carte meals in the evening and traditional pub fare at lunchtime. All produce is sourced from surrounding farms. The pub has something for everyone – it is popular with locals, passing trade and walkers on the Cotswold Way. ♨Q⛄❀◑◐🚌P⁻

Lechlade

Crown Inn

High Street, GL7 3AE (opp traffic lights at jct of A417/ A361)
12-midnight (11 Sun)
(01367) 252198 crownlechlade.co.uk
Halfpenny Old Lech; Wells Bombardier; guest beer H
Fans of wooden-floored boozers will delight in this confidently run, twin-room brew pub, from the open fire to the myriad array of paraphernalia decorating the walls and ceiling. Already known locally for its parties and unusual choice of games, the enthusiasm which greets each new brew from 'out the back' can make for a memorable drinking experience. A large wooden settle dominates the pool room, while smokers can watch the brewing from their patio.

Littleton on Severn

White Hart

BS35 1NR (signed from B4461 at Elberton)
12-11
(01454) 412275
Bath Ales Gem; Young's Bitter, Special, seasonal beers H
Young's pub characterised by low ceilings, oak beams, flagstone floors and many nooks and crannies to hide in. Food is served throughout the pub. Outside there is a sunny patio and a large front garden with views over the Severn Estuary. The pub plans to produce its own cider from apples from the orchard at the rear. Young's seasonal and occasional guest beers complement the regular beers. **QP**

Marshfield

Catherine Wheel

High Street, SN14 8LR (off A420)
12-3, 6-11 (midnight Sat); 12-11 Sun
(01225) 892220 thecatherinewheel.co.uk
Courage Best Bitter; Cotswold Spring Codrington Codger; guest beers H
Beautifully-restored Georgian-fronted pub on the village High Street with a pretty dining room. An extensive main bar leads down from the original wood-panelled area, via stone-walled rooms, to the patio area at the rear. A superb open fire warms in winter. Up to two local guest ales are on offer and imaginative and well presented food is served in the bar or garden (no meals Sun eve). Children are allowed and free Wi-Fi access is available. **Q**(635)**P**

May Hill

Glasshouse

GL17 0NN (off A40 W of Huntley) SO710213
11.30-3, 6.30-11; 12-3 Sun
(01452) 830529
Butcombe Bitter; Fuller's London Pride G
This village pub has been sympathetically extended using reclaimed building materials to blend in with the surroundings. It has three areas, with an old black range in one and a log fire in another. Flagstone floors, nooks and crannies, good beer, fine food and a friendly atmosphere make this a popular venue. An historic yew hedge with its own seat cut into it, and a safe, fenced garden make the pub popular with families. **QP**

Mayshill

New Inn

Badminton Road, BS36 2NT (on A432)
11.45-2.30, 6-10.30 (11 Wed-Sat); 12-10 Sun
(01454) 773161
Beer range varies H
This 17th-century inn is hugely popular for its food, so booking is advised. Expect one beer from the nearby Cotswold Spring Brewery and two changing guests from far and wide. One of the guests is likely to be dark, because it is the genial Scottish landlord's favourite - expect sudden outbreaks of Scottish beer, too. The main bar is warmed by a real fire in winter, and the rear area is more of a restaurant. Children are welcome until 8.45pm. The garden is pleasant in summer. There are generous beer discounts for card-carrying CAMRA members on Sunday and Monday evenings.
Q(X42,342)**P**

Moreton-in-Marsh

Inn on the Marsh

Stow Road, GL56 0DW (on A429 at S end of town)
12-2.30, 7-11; 11-3, 6-11 (Thu-Sat & summer); 12-3, 7-11 Sun
(01608) 650709
Banks's Original; Marston's Burton Bitter, Pedigree; guest beer H
This charming Marston's pub, a rare outlet locally, has an interesting in-house guest ale, often from Ringwood. Situated next to a duckpond, this former bakery has hanging woven baskets on display. The bar area has a dedicated locals' section and the welcoming lounge area features an open fire and comfortable seating. A unique large conservatory is ideal for dining and parties. Food is of a Dutch East Indies influence, prepared by the landlady chef. The landlord, with 11 years in residence, guarantees the experience.
QP

Nailsworth

Village Inn

The Cross, Fountain Street, GL6 0HH (N end of town)
11-11 (midnight Thu-Sat); 12-10.30 Sun
(01453) 835715
Nailsworth Artist's Ale, Mayor's Bitter, Town Crier, Vicar's Stout, seasonal beers; guest beers H
The Village Inn, which reopened in late 2006 as the Nailsworth Brewery brew pub, is unrecognisable from the pub that closed in the mid 1990s; truly an ugly duckling reborn as a swan. An intricate warren of rooms and spaces has been created with care and flair, where salvaged furniture combines with new joinery. CAMRA Stroud Sub Branch Pub of the Year 2008. **Q**

Nettleton Bottom

Golden Heart

GL4 8LA (on A417)
11-3, 5.30-11; 11-11 Fri & Sat; 12-10.30 Sun
(01242) 870261 thegoldenheart.co.uk
Brakspear Bitter; Festival Gold; guest beers H
The peaceful, rustic charm of this unspoilt 300-year-old wayside inn contrasts greatly with the bustle of traffic outside. Visitors are greeted by a huge open fire beyond which hides a small, unobtrusive bar. Highest quality meats make for

popular eating and it has won many prizes for its food (served all day Sun). A stone paved patio and lawn to the rear lead to open meadows. The pub has two en-suite guest bedrooms.

Newent

George

Church Street, GL18 1PU (opp church)
11-11 (midnight Fri & Sat); 12-10.30 Sun
☎ (01531) 820203 georgehotel.uk.com
Butcombe Bitter; Cottage Golden Arrow; Freeminer Bitter; guest beers Ⓗ
This mid-17th-century hotel has a quiet bar at the front with a central serving area. A dartboard, fruit machines and TV screens are at the rear. The former coach house is now the restaurant. A beer festival is held in September to coincide with Newent Onion Fair. Accommodation comprises en-suite bedrooms and a two-bedroom mews flat. Local attractions include the National Birds of Prey Centre.

Oakridge Lynch

Butchers Arms ✔

GL6 7NZ
6-8.30 Mon; 12-2.30, 6-11 (8.30 Fri), 12-3, 6-11 Sat; 12-3 6-10.30 Sun
☎ (01285) 760371
Wadworth Henry's IPA, 6X, JCB, seasonal beers; guest beers Ⓗ
A popular Cotswold village pub with exposed beams and log fires. Two bars serve the full range of Wadworth's beers plus a varying guest. There is a skittle alley, which is also used for meetings and private functions. This pub is noted for its excellent garden in summer and its well-kept beers, of which the landlady is justly proud. Children and dogs are welcome. No meals on Mondays or Sunday evenings.

Oldbury on Severn

Anchor Inn

Church Road, BS35 1QA
11.30-2.30, 6.30-11; 11.30-11 Sat; 12-10.30 Sun
☎ (01454) 413331
Butcombe Bitter; Draught Bass; Otter Bitter; guest beers Ⓗ
Excellent converted riverside mill with two bars and a restaurant. People come from afar for the food, which is served in all areas when busy. The lounge has an L-shaped bar, wooden beams and an open fire. The more spartan public bar is popular with locals. One guest beer is supplemented by a strong dark beer each Thursday – usually from Theakston, Severn Vale or Wickwar – until it runs out. The large enclosed garden has a boules piste and access to the river footpath. Children are welcome in the restaurant.

Painswick

Royal Oak

St Mary's Street, GL6 6QG (100m from Painswick Church)
11-3, 5.45-midnight; 12-3, 6.30-10.30 Sun
☎ (01452) 813129 theroyaloakpainswick.co.uk
Stroud Budding, Teasel, Tom Long Ⓗ
A small, two-bar, 16th-century Cotswold inn with low ceilings, old beams and an open fire. Renowned for its high-quality, locally-sourced, freshly-prepared food, fish such as hake and marlin are a speciality alongside home-made bangers and mash and local game. The family and staff are so committed to local produce that they only sell real ales from the award-winning Stroud Brewery, including seasonal beers such as an organic ale. Regular monthly musical events also feature.
(46)

Rodborough

Prince Albert ✔

GL5 3SS (corner of Rodborough Hill & Walkley Hill)
4-11.30 (12.30am Fri & Sat); 12-10.30 Sun
☎ (01453) 755600 theprincealbertstroud.co.uk
Fuller's London Pride; Otter Bitter; Stroud Budding; guest beers Ⓗ
This lively, cosmopolitan, stone-built pub near Rodborough Common manages to be simultaneously bohemian, homely and welcoming. It has an imaginative colour scheme and an eclectic mix of furniture and fittings, with chandeliers from a French chateau and a Dutch brothel. Art exhibitions and themed nights are held, including a pub quiz, backgammon, crib and scrabble, folk music and live bands. Children and dogs are welcome. Bar meals are served Thursday to Saturday. Sunday lunch is followed by a film matinee. There is free Internet access and Wi-Fi.
(Stroud)

Shipton Moyne

Cat & Custard Pot

The Street, GL8 8PN (on Tetbury rd)
11-3, 6-11.30; 11.30-3, 6-11 Sun
☎ (01666) 880249
Flowers Original; Taylor Landlord; Wadworth Henry's IPA, 6X; guest beer Ⓗ
The interior of this pretty village pub is mainly open plan, revealing where rooms have been opened out for extra space to cope with the increasing number of diners who come to enjoy the varied menu. The main bar is the hub of the village, especially for dog walkers, with a quiet snug behind it for families. The prints on the walls reflect the equestrian bent of the local community, with the origins of the unusual pub sign also explained. Parking can be an issue during busy periods.

Slad

Woolpack

GL6 7QA (on B4070)
12-3, 5-11.30; 12-10.30 Sun
☎ (01452) 813429 thewoolpackinn-slad.com
Uley Bitter, Old Spot, Pig's Ear; guest beer Ⓗ
This popular 16th-century village inn affords superb views over the Slad Valley. It achieved fame through the late Laurie Lee, author of Cider With Rosie, who was a regular customer. The building has been thoughtfully restored and the bar extends to each of the four rooms, with wooden settles in the end room of three, where children are welcome. The guest beer is usually from a local small brewery and cider and perry are available.

Slimbridge

Tudor Arms

Shepherd's Patch, GL2 7BP
⏲ 11-11; 12-10.30 Sun
☎ (01453) 890306
Uley Pig's Ear; Wadworth 6X; guest beers Ⓗ
Large, family-owned free house reached by a winding road that leads to the famous Wildfowl and Wetlands Trust site. It incorporates two bars and a number of dining areas, with a modern lodge alongside. A separately-owned caravan and camping site is adjacent. Four guest ales come from craft or family brewers: the cider is Moles Black Rat. Excellent home-cooked food is available all day and children are welcome. Local CAMRA Country Pub of the Year 2007 and 2008.
❀🛏◐◑⊞♿Ă♣●P⁵—

Somerford Keynes

Bakers Arms

GL7 6DN (northern end of the village)
⏲ 11-11 (midnight Fri & Sat); 12-10.30 Sun
☎ (01285) 861298 🌐 thecompletechef.co.uk
Courage Best Bitter; Butcombe Bitter; Stroud Budding Ⓗ
A thriving village local where the main bar has been carefully opened out over the years to create additional dining space and a function room. A piano delineates the drinking area, where a well-balanced range of ales, served by enthusiastic staff, proves increasingly popular. Basic rustic furniture merges well with the decor to give a homely feel to both rooms. The large, shaded garden is popular with families. ♛❀◐◑ĂP

Stroud

Queen Victoria

5 Gloucester Street, GL5 1QG
⏲ 11-11 (later Fri & Sat); 12-10.30 Sun
☎ (01453) 762396
Beer range varies Ⓗ
This imposing building formerly housed the Gloucester Street forge and records show that it was owned by the Nailsworth Brewery in 1891. The large single bar offers a constantly changing range of at least four beers from micro-breweries. This community pub fields quiz, darts and pool teams in local leagues. Across the courtyard, the spacious function room holds a beer festival at least once a year and hosts live music on Thursday, Friday and Saturday evenings. ♛❀⇌♣⁵—

Tetbury

Priory Inn Hotel

London Road, GL8 8JJ (on A433)
⏲ 11-11 (midnight Fri & Sat)
☎ (01666) 502251 🌐 theprioryinn.co.uk
Uley Bitter; guest beers Ⓗ
Proudly advertising that all food is sourced within a 30-mile radius, this flourishing pub and pizzeria shows what can be achieved with some imagination. Little remains of the transport café era; a stylish array of exposed stonework, flagstones and a large central hearth now greets the eye, with local artists proudly displaying their work on the walls. The bar is at the back, through the arches, and there is live acoustic music most Sunday evenings. ♛❀🛏◐◑♿🚌P

Tewkesbury

Royal Hop Pole ✔

94 Church Street, GL20 5RS
⏲ 7 (8 Sat & Sun)-11
☎ (01684) 274039
Greene King IPA, Abbot; Marston's Pedigree; guest beers Ⓗ
This well-known landmark is an amalgamation of historic buildings from the 15th and 18th centuries. It has been known as the Royal Hop Pole since a visit in September 1891 from Princess Mary of Teck (Queen Mary Royal Consort of George V) and was mentioned in The Pickwick Papers. It was purchased by JD Wetherspoon to join its list of lodges and reopened in May 2008, following a £4 million refurbishment.
♛Q♘❀🛏◑♿Ă🚌(41,42,72)●⁵—

Tudor House Hotel

51 High Street, GL20 5BH (3 miles from M50 jct 9)
⏲ 11-11 (midnight Fri & Sat)
☎ (01684) 297755 🌐 tudorhousetewkesbury.co.uk
Greene King Old Speckled Hen; guest beers Ⓗ
Situated on the High Street, this delightful Tudor building oozes charm and dignity. The Tudor House Bar offers a selection of four real ales, three constantly changing, with Speckled Hen a favourite with locals. Pub meals are served in the bar; more upmarket cuisine is available either in the eatery or the garden in summer. A delightful coffee shop opens on to the secret garden. The Tudor House has been tastefully redecorated in keeping with the theme of the Battle of Tewkesbury.
♛Q❀🛏◐◑⊞♿🚌♣●P⁵—

White Bear

Bredon Road, GL20 5BU (N of High St)
⏲ 10-11
☎ (01684) 296614
Draught Bass; guest beers Ⓗ
Family-run free house on the edge of the town centre, close to the river and marina. A multi-space bar, which was completely renovated following the floods of 2007, provides four handpumps with ever-changing guest beers plus local ciders. Crib, darts, skittles and local league pool all feature here. There is a separate skittle alley which can double as a function room. Live music is performed most Sunday afternoons. A small library includes children's books. ❀Ă🚌♣●P⁵—🗍

Tytherington

Swan ✔

Duck Street, GL12 8QB
⏲ 12-2.30 (not winter Mon), 6-11; 12-10.30 (6 winter) Sun
☎ (01454) 412380 🌐 swan-inn.com
Bath Gem; Fuller's London Pride; guest beer Ⓗ
This 16th-century coaching inn is situated in the quaint village of Tytherington. Its friendly, welcoming atmosphere is enhanced by low ceilings and wood-burning inglenook fireplaces in the main bar. The pub has a reputation for good food, freshly cooked and often sourced locally. The separate Village Bar has a dartboard and table games. There is also a large function room, a spacious, child-friendly garden with umbrellas and an extensive car park. ♛❀◐⊞♿♣P⁵—

Uley

Old Crown

The Green, GL11 5SN (at top end of village)
12-11
(01453) 860502
Uley Bitter, Pig's Ear; guest beers H
This attractive 17th-century whitewashed coaching inn with a pleasant walled garden is situated in the pretty village of Uley on the edge of the Cotswold Way. The village local, it is also popular with passing walkers. The low-beamed single bar has a welcoming open fire. Beers are sourced mainly from micro-breweries. The pub offers four en-suite double bedrooms and food is served lunchtime and evenings. **Q P**

Waterley Bottom

New Inn

North Nibley, GL11 6EF (signed from North Nibley)
ST758964
12-2.30 (not Mon), 6-11; 12-11 Sat; 12-10.30 Sun
(01453) 543659
Beer range varies H
This welcoming free house, once a 19th-century cider house frequented by mill workers en route to Dursley, nestles in a tiny hamlet in a scenic valley. It has a cosy lounge/dining area and an enlarged public bar where darts and cards are played. A child-friendly, attractive garden includes a large decked area with a pool table. Draught cider and perry, served by gravity, are from Westons. The menu offers quality food cooked to order by the landlord (no food Mon). Local CAMRA Cider Pub of the Year 2007. **Q P**

Whitecroft

Miners Arms

The Bay, GL15 4PE (on B4234 near railway crossing)
SO619062
12-11 (10.30 Sun)
(01594) 562483 minersarms.org
Banks's Original; guest beer H
A classic free house offering good value and high quality food including Sunday lunches. Voted CAMRA Cider & Perry Pub of the Year in 2005, it dispenses a range of draught ciders as well as five ever-changing guest beers. The skittle alley doubles as a blues music venue once a month, and quoits is played in the bar. The back garden is safe for children and steam trains from the Dean Forest Railway stop behind the pub. **P**

Whitminster

Old Forge Inn

GL2 7NP (on A38, close to M5 jct 13)
12-11 (10.30 Sun)
(01452) 741306
Butcombe Bitter; Greene King IPA; Shepherd Neame Spitfire; guest beer H
This mainly timber-framed building, bearing a strange mix of window styles, dates from the 16th century and was a forge during the last century. The smartly furnished interior with an aquarium, horse brasses and a collection of commemorative spoons (437 at the last count) reflects the landlady's character and interests. Excellent home-cooked food is served lunchtimes (not Mon in winter) and evenings. Outside is a large patio with games including chess. **Q P**

Winterbourne Down

Cross Hands

85 Down Road, BS36 1BZ
12-11
(01454) 850077
Courage Best Bitter; guest beers H
Friendly, 17th-century, stone-built free house with a spacious main bar, snug area and an alcove used by darts players. Old sewing machines feature as decoration, together with an interesting selection of old pump clips on a dummy beer engine near the entrance. A large rear garden includes a children's play area and a smoking shelter. Parking can be tricky outside, but there is a daytime bus service and the Frome Valley walkway is nearby. Guest beers often include Timothy Taylor's Landlord. The cider is Thatchers.

Woodchester

Ram Inn

Station Road, GL5 5EQ (signed from A46)
11-11; 12-10.30 Sun
(01453) 873329
Butcombe Bitter, Gold; Stroud Budding, Organic; Uley Old Spot; guest beers H
More than 400 years old and standing in superb walking country near Woodchester Mansion, this is a dog-friendly village pub which stocks an excellent range of ales, including those from the local Nailsworth or Stroud breweries. The food is highly recommended. There is good wheelchair access and the pub is a regular venue for the Stroud Morris men. **Q P**

Woolaston Common

Rising Sun

GL15 6NU (1 mile off A48 at Woolaston) SO590009
12-2.30 (not Tue or Wed), 6.30-11; 12-3, 7-11 Sun
(01594) 529282
Wye Valley Bitter; guest beers H
This 350-year-old stone-built pub with a cosy snug and main bar area has had the same landlord for the last 30 years. Spectacular views over the Forest of Dean from the front of the pub and its situation on the circular pub walks of the Forest have made it a must for ramblers. Good home-cooked food is available except Tuesday and Wednesday lunchtimes. **Q P**

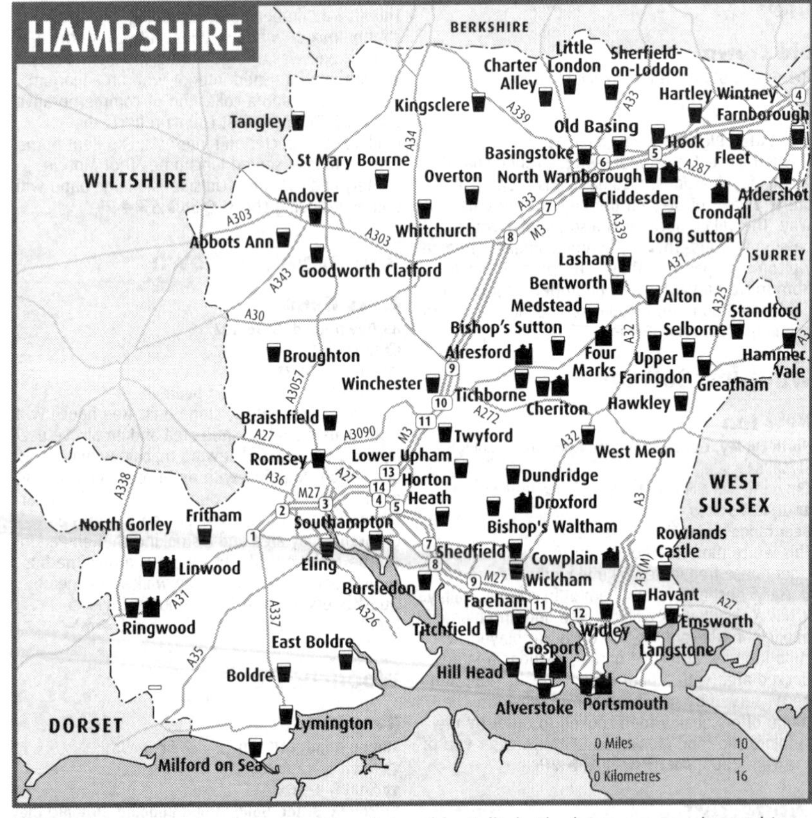

NOTE: Gale's Brewery has been bought and closed by Fuller's. The beers are now brewed in London at Fuller's Chiswick brewery. When a Guide entry serves only Gale's beer we list the beers as shown on pumpclips i.e. Gale's HSB, rather than Fuller's Gale's HSB. Please see Fuller's entry in the Independent Breweries section. Please note that Ringwood is now owned by Marston's – see New Nationals section.

Abbotts Ann

Eagle

Red Rice Road, SP11 7BG SU328435

11.30-11; 12-10.30 Sun

☎ (01264) 710339 eagleabbottsann.co.uk

Skinner's Betty Stoggs; guest beers

This superb village pub, two miles SW of Andover, is at the heart of the community. Similarly, real ale is at the heart of the pub. The regular Betty Stoggs is supplemented by three changing southern and south western guests, plus Westons Old Rosie cider on handpump. The separate public bar features a pool table and there is a skittle alley at the back of the pub. Food is not available Tuesday or Sunday evenings. Q (77,87)♣P

Aldershot

Garden Gate

Church Lane East, GU11 3BT

4.30-midnight; 2.30-1am Fri; 12-1am Sat; 12-10.30 Sun

☎ (01252) 321051 gardengatepub.com

Greene King IPA, Abbot, seasonal beer

Cosy and friendly local pub with one bar split into two areas. Good value home-cooked food is served and B&B offered in two twin en-suite rooms. A covered smoking area is provided, with a sheltered garden to the side. Real pork scratchings and local free range eggs are sold. Quiz night is Thursday and bluegrass music plays on the first Monday of the month. There is a piano, darts and Sunday meat draw featuring a local butcher's meat.

(15,18,46)♣

White Lion

20 Lower Farnham Road, GU12 4EA (200m from jct of A331/A323)

1-10.30; 12-midnight Fri & Sat; 12-10.30 Sun

☎ (01252) 323832

INDEPENDENT BREWERIES

Andwell North Warnborough (NEW)
Bowman Droxford
Crondall Crondall
Flowerpots Cheriton
Havant Cowplain (NEW)
Irving Portsmouth
Itchen Valley Alresford
Oakleaf Gosport
Red Shoot Linwood
Ringwood Ringwood
Triple fff Four Marks

Triple fff Alton's Pride, Pressed Rat & Warthog, Moondance, seasonal beers; guest beers Ⓗ
Genuine small two-bar locals' pub a mile east of the town centre, run by the Triple fff Brewery; so traditional you can even close the door behind you in a quiet side bar. The publican's enthusiasm for scooters is evident in the display of items behind the bar, while substantial bar stools complement the no-nonsense plain wooden tables and church pews. Open mike night is every other Thursday, quiz night is Monday and live music plays some Saturdays. Board games are available. Pizzas on offer at all times. ⌂Q❀⊟⊟(3,20)♣⁻

Alton

Eight Bells
33 Church Street, GU34 2DA
⏲ 11-11; 12-10.30 Sun
☎ (01420) 82417
Ballard's Best Bitter; Bowman Swift One; guest beers Ⓗ
A popular free house, dating back to 1640, just outside the town centre on the Old Odiham Road turnpike. Opposite lies St Lawrence Church, site of the Civil War Battle of Alton. The pub has an original oak-beamed interior with a main bar and smaller drinking area, plus a restored listed smoking shelter incorporating a 17th-century well in a secluded paved garden. Dogs are welcome with well-behaved owners. Noted as being the village pub in the town. ⌂Q❀⇌⊟⁻

French Horn
The Butts, GU34 1RT
⏲ 12-11 (10.30 Sun)
☎ (01420) 83269 🌐 frenchhorn.co.uk
Butcombe Bitter; Fuller's London Pride; Ringwood Best Bitter; guest beers Ⓗ
Once part of Chawton, to the west of the town, this delightful, historic pub overlooks the medieval archery Butts and is within sight and sound of the Watercress Line. The beamed bar has a roaring fire in winter, while excellent food may be enjoyed in the restaurant. Outside, there is a garden, skittle alley and heated smoking area. The pub has gained an excellent reputation for its real ales which include three guests, often from local breweries. ⌂Q❀⊨◑♿⊟(28,X64)P⁻

King's Head
Market Street, GU34 1HA
⏲ 10 (11 Mon, Wed & Thu)-11; 12-10.30 Sun
☎ (01420) 82313
Courage Best Bitter; guest beers Ⓗ
Popular market-town free house, retaining its two-bar layout, which has been run by the same family for 20 years. The ever popular Wells & Young's Courage Best is complemented by two guest beers, often from local breweries; recommendations from customers are welcome. Dominoes, darts and shove ha'penny are played and the pub regularly participates in local charity and sporting events. No food is served on Sunday. ⌂❀◖⊟⇌⊟♣⁻

Railway Arms
26 Anstey Road, GU34 2RB
⏲ 12-11; 11-midnight Fri & Sat
☎ (01420) 82218
Triple fff Alton's Pride, Pressed Rat & Warthog, Moondance, Stairway, seasonal beers; guest beers Ⓗ
Friendly pub close to the Watercress Line and mainline station. It is owned by Triple fff Brewery, whose own beers are supplemented by ales from a host of micros. The extension at the rear has its own bar which is available for hire. A new patio area, designed with a traditional railway theme, is ideal for barbecues and incorporates a covered, heated smoking area. There are tables outside the front of the pub, under a striking sculpture of a steam locomotive. Q❀⊟⇌⊟♣⁻

Alverstoke

Alverbank
Stokes Bay Road, PO12 2QT
⏲ 11-11; 12-10.30 Sun
☎ (023) 9251 0005 🌐 alverbankhotel.co.uk
Caledonian Deuchars IPA; guest beers Ⓗ
Overlooking Stokes Bay, this hotel was built in 1842 as a country house for JW Croker, a Victorian political figure. Early visitors included the Duke of Wellington, Sir Robert Peel, Lily Langtry and members of the royal family. Up to two guest beers from the Courage portfolio are available. Summer Lightning appears regularly in the summer and Fuller's ESB in the winter. The function suite is a modern extension used for weddings and other events and there is a quiz night every Monday. ⌂❀⊨◑♿▲⊟(88)P⁻

Andover

Lamb Inn
21 Winchester Street, SP10 2EA (opp police station)
⏲ 12-2.30 (not Tue), 6-midnight (1am Fri & Sat); 12-2.30, 7-11 Sun
☎ (01264) 323961
Wadworth Henry IPA, 6X; guest beer Ⓗ
A traditional pub dating from the 1600s on the edge of the main shopping area. The small lounge retains a cosy and homely atmosphere, while the lower public bar is more sports oriented, with pool and darts. A third, smaller area separates the two, and there is a compact outside patio. Live music and folk evenings are held regularly. The pub sign depicting the Lamb refers to the Knights Templar. ⌂Q❀⊟⊟♣

Lardicake
19 Adelaide Road, SP10 1HF
⏲ 11-11; 12-10.30 Sun
☎ (01264) 337782
Courage Best Bitter; Fuller's London Pride; Taylor Landlord Ⓗ
Once known as the War Office, this traditional back-street style pub has gone through several incarnations. The single bar has two levels, the lower with many historic pictures of old Andover. Just off the shopping area, it attracts a local clientele including some characters who will involve you in light-hearted banter. A friendly atmosphere pervades the pub, which makes a great escape from the anonymous circuit pubs of the town centre. Nearby is the Andover Museum of the Iron Age, well worth a visit. ⌂❀⊟⊟⁻

Wyke Down Country Pub & Restaurant ✔
Picket Piece, SP11 6LX (signed from A303)
⏲ 12-2.30, 6-11; 6-10.30 Sun
☎ (01264) 352048 🌐 wykedown.co.uk
Taylor Landlord; guest beer Ⓗ
This spacious country pub is based around an extended barn with exposed beams, in which

many old agricultural implements are displayed. The large restaurant with real fire draws customers from afar and is also used for functions. A comfortable conservatory and adjacent games room complete the facilities in the main building. Outside there is a campsite, children's play area, golf driving range and swimming pool. Various annual events take place in the grounds. The house ale is from West Berks Brewery. ⚶♘❀◑▲♣P⚟

Basingstoke

Basingstoke Sports & Social Club

Mays Bounty, Fairfields Road, RG21 3DR

🕒 12-3, 5-11; 12-11 Fri & Sat; 12-10.30 Sun

☎ (01256) 331646 🌐 basingstoke-sports-club.co.uk

Adnams Bitter; Fuller's Discovery, London Pride; Ringwood Best Bitter; guest beers Ⓗ

Home to the Basingstoke and North Hants Cricket Club, the club also has squash, football, rugby and other sports facilities. Opening hours may vary when there are major cricket matches outside. Two or more guest beers from smaller breweries are usually available and lunchtime snacks are served Monday to Friday. As you would expect, the TV usually shows cricket or football. Although a private members' club, CAMRA members are welcome on production of a membership card. Local CAMRA Pub of the Year 2009. ❀◐P

Chineham Arms ✔

Hanmore Road, Chineham, RG24 8XA (off old Reading Rd)

🕒 11-11 (11.30 Fri); 12-10.30 Sun

☎ (01256) 356404

Fuller's Discovery, London Pride, ESB Ⓗ

Modern public house situated in the village of Chineham, a suburb north of Basingstoke off the old Reading Road. The village has been populated with an Anglo-Saxon settlement dating back to 800BC. The standard range of Fuller's beers is served, with the seasonals also occasionally available. Food is served every day, with a varying range of dishes including a children's menu. There is a separate dining area and outside a seating area under cover. The Jazz1 bus stop is 100m away. ⚶❀◑♿🚌P⚟

Queens Arms ✔

Bunnian Place, RG21 7JE (150m from rail station)

🕒 11-11 (10.30 Sun)

☎ (01256) 465488

Courage Best Bitter; Sharp's Doom Bar; Wadworth 6X; guest beers Ⓗ

A welcoming beacon of excellence, the 'Queens' attracts a wide-ranging clientele of all ages and from all walks of life. The choice of guest beers is imaginative and the turnaround is such that a free text-alert service, tailored to customers' tastes, is available. Good-value home-cooked food is of high quality and locally sourced, available weekday lunchtimes and evenings (except Mon), and at weekends (Sat 12-3pm, Sun 12-4pm). During warmer weather the shady courtyard garden is a popular attraction. Q❀◑⇌🚌♣⚟

Way Inn

Chapel Hill, RG21 5TB (behind station opp Holy Ghost chapel) SU634526

🕒 12-11 (10.30 Sun)

☎ (01256) 321520 🌐 thewayinn.org.uk

Caledonian Deuchars IPA; Greene King Abbot; Taylor Landlord; guest beers Ⓗ

This extensively refurbished pub provides a comfortable environment for the 20+ age group. It has a spacious family room and dining area at the rear with access to the large car park, outside patio and south-facing sun-drenched garden. There is no TV or bar games but there is an online jukebox. Menus offer a wide range of home-cooked traditional food available lunchtime and evening, with a good vegetarian range. The guest beers are sourced via SIBA. ⚶♘❀◑♿⇌🚌P⚟

Bentworth

Star Inn

GU34 5RB

🕒 12-3.30, 5-11.30; 12-11.30 Fri & Sat; 12-11.30 Sun

☎ (01420) 561224 🌐 star-inn.com

Fuller's London Pride; Palmers Copper Ale; guest beers Ⓗ

Dating back to 1841, this friendly free house has a bar warmed by open fires and an adjacent, quiet restaurant offering freshly-cooked meals during all sessions. The pub is a social hub for the village community, its enthusiastic staff providing an active social calendar, including Tuesday curry evening, live music on Friday and a blues jam session on Sunday evening. Visitors, especially walkers, are always made welcome. Local bottled cider is available. A bus stops outside the door. ⚶❀◑🚌(28)♣P⚟

Bishop's Sutton

Ship Inn

Main Road, SO24 0AQ (on B3047)

🕒 12-2.30 (not Mon), 6-11; 12-3, 7-10.30 Sun

☎ (01962) 732863

Palmers Copper Ale; guest beers Ⓗ

Cosy, genuine free house with a split-level bar and a real log fire providing a quiet, relaxing atmosphere. An adjoining room acts as a restaurant and games area while the Crow's Nest bar doubles as a family/dining room. Home-cooked food features on the daily specials board – try the watercress soup. Sunday roasts (with vegetarian option) are popular. The pub is an ideal stopping-off point for visitors to the Watercress Line steam railway, just over a mile away. Frequent Winchester-Alton buses stop outside. ⚶Q♘❀◑🚌(64)♣P⚟

Bishop's Waltham

Bunch of Grapes

St Peter's Street, SO32 1AD (follow signs to church)

🕒 12-2, 6-11; 12-2 Sun

☎ (01489) 892935

Courage Best Bitter; Goddards Ale of Wight; guest beer Ⓖ

This tiny pub is part of a row of cottages on the narrow street leading to St Peter's Church. The low door leads into the small comfortable bar and there is another small room beyond. The garden gives extra space in the summer. Local wine is available from a vineyard in which the landlord has an involvement. Golf is a popular topic of conversation in the bar due to the pub's flourishing golf society. Closing time can be a little flexible if there are no customers. Q❀🚌♣

Boldre

Red Lion

Rope Hill, SO41 8NE (on Rope Hill/Boldre Lane crossroads)
11-3, 5.30-11; 12-4, 6-10.30 (12-10.30 summer) Sun
☎ (01590) 673177 theredlionboldre.co.uk
Marston's Pedigree; Ringwood Best Bitter, Fortyniner; guest beer H
A quintessentially cosy, beamed, New Forest pub that is an amalgamation of olde-worlde public house, two cottages and stables. It is both dog and horse friendly. Its New Forest Marque denotes that local produced is served. Often busy, it is advisable to book for food, but drinkers are always welcome in the central ale snug. The rapidly changing guest ales are from the Marston's group list. Three self-contained, en-suite accommodation units are due for completion by 2010. (112)P

Braishfield

Newport Inn

Newport Lane, SO51 0PL (take lane opp phone box) SU373249
12-2.30 (not Mon), 6-11; 12-2.30, 7-10.30 Sun
☎ (01794) 368225
Gale's Butser Bitter, HSB, seasonal beers H
Owned by the same family for 68 years, this pub is in a time-warp, where the world has stood still for so long that you expect to be charged in shillings and pence. A two-bar local, tucked away down a narrow lane, it has a fiercely loyal, cosmopolitan clientele drawn from miles around. The landlady presides, on the piano, over the Saturday evening singalong, and Thursday often features impromptu folk sessions. Although no meal symbols are shown, you cannot go hungry here – the fabulous sandwiches (just ham or cheese) and the ploughman's are memorable. P

Wheatsheaf

Braishfield Road, SO51 0QE
11 (12 Sun)-11
☎ (01794) 368372 wheatsheafbraishfield.co.uk
Ringwood Best Bitter; guest beers H
The Wheatsheaf is close to the Hillier Arboretum and the Monarch's Way. Its decor mixes rusticity with eccentricity, and its large garden offers views of fields, wooded hills and the pub's smallholding, home to rare-breed pigs. Gourmet burger night (every Wednesday) and pie night (first Monday of the month) are popular events, as are the quizzes and occasional live music. The last bus to Braishfield (Monday-Saturday only) arrives at lunchtime; others come within two miles, but not evenings or Sunday. P

Broughton

Tally Ho!

High Street, SO20 8AA
11-3, 6-11; 11-11 Sat; 12-10.30 Sun
☎ (01794) 301280
Ringwood Best Bitter; guest beers H
Cheerful, lively pub within a few yards of the Monarch's and Clarendon Ways. Situated in a handsome village, it stands opposite the church which has a large dovecote in the grounds, the key to which is held in the pub. Good quality food is served, much of it sourced locally and all of it reasonably priced. Some dishes are available in small portions on request. On 'Cheeky Tuesday' a special main course is available at a low price. There is additional parking by the village hall. (68)

Bursledon

Vine Inn

High Street, SO31 8DJ (½ mile SW of station)
12-2 (Fri only), 5.30-11; 12-4, 7.30-10.30 Sun
☎ (023) 8040 3836
Greene King IPA, Abbot G
Unspoilt traditional village pub – a rare outlet serving Greene King beers by gravity. The oak-beamed bar has a plethora of hanging copper kettles and artefacts, an interesting collection of old beer bottles and many local prints. Tuesday is quiz night, a meat draw is held on Sunday and the piano is available for aspiring musicians and occasional music sessions. There are river views from the garden. Parking is difficult but the station car park is a hilly 10-minute walk. Dogs are welcome. P

Charter Alley

White Hart

White Hart Lane, RG26 5QA (1 mile W of A340) SU593577
12-2.30 (3 Sat), 7-11; 12-3, 7-10.30 Sun
☎ (01256) 850048 whitehartcharteralley.com
Palmers Best Bitter; Triple fff Alton's Pride; guest beers H
The oldest building in the village, this was the place where folk used to natter, hence 'chatter alley' (Charter Alley). Oak beams and log fires enhance the welcoming atmosphere of the pub. The bar now houses six pumps and the range of beers is forever changing. Good-quality food is served in a very pleasant restaurant converted from the original skittle alley. There is also a lovely terraced garden where water features make for a peaceful drink. En-suite guest rooms are available. Local CAMRA Pub of the Year 2009.
P

Cheriton

Flower Pots

SO24 0QQ (½ mile N of A272 between Winchester and Petersfield) SU581283
12-2.30 (3 Sat), 6-11; 12-3, 7-10.30 Sun
☎ (01962) 771318 flowerpots-inn.co.uk
Flowerpots Bitter, Goodens Gold, seasonal beers G
Four-square, warm, red-brick pub with two separate bars, dating from 1820; popular with walkers and cyclists. A large rear marquee provides welcome overflow space on busy days. Two outbuildings house the pub's famous 10-barrel brewery and the four comfortable B&B rooms. All the brewery's current beers (usually at least three) are served directly from their casks. Good, home-cooked food is available daily (except Sun evening) with Wednesday evening featuring curries from a Punjabi chef. Westons Old Rosie cider is available. (67)P

Cliddesden

Jolly Farmer

Farleigh Road, RG25 2JL (on B3046)
12-11 (10.30 Sun)
☎ (01256) 473073

Beer range varies Ⓗ
Busy, listed village pub close to Basingstoke, offering an interesting selection of beers from the Punch Taverns list. A cider such as Westons Old Rosie is usually available from the cellar. The quieter second bar may be used by families when not reserved for functions. At the rear a large garden provides a secluded area for a peaceful drink, with a heated, covered area with table football for cooler evenings. The kitchen closes at 4pm on Sunday. ☸❀◑♣●P⅟

Dundridge

Hampshire Bowman

Dundridge Lane, Bishop's Waltham, SO32 1GD (1 mile E of B3035) SU578184
✪ 12-11 (10.30 Sun)
☎ (01489) 892940 ⊕ hampshirebowman.com
Bowman Swift One, Wallops Wood, Quiver; Palmers 200; guest beers Ⓖ
A pub people may think no longer exists, situated in an idyllic spot and catering for almost everyone. The old front bar retains its charm and leads to a larger extension, mainly used by diners enjoying the excellent food – families are welcome here until 9pm. Outside, a patio and large garden are the perfect place to pass summer afternoons and evenings. In winter the pub has three real fires and in the summer real cider. Camping is available to groups by prior arrangement. Disabled access is by the rear patio door. ♨Q❀◑♿▲♣●P

East Boldre

Turfcutters Arms

Main Road, SO42 7WL (1½m SW of Beaulieu, off B3054 at Hatchet Pond) SU374004
✪ 11-3, 6-11; 11-11 Fri & Sat; 12-10.30 Sun
☎ (01590) 612331 ⊕ theturfcutters.co.uk
Ringwood Best Bitter, Fortyniner; guest beers Ⓗ
This rustic pub is located in the heart of the southern New Forest and welcomes allcomers including well-behaved children and dogs. The pub boasts a selection of 80 whiskies on display behind the bar, which is adorned with antique cameras. The self-styled 'scruffy' landlord is proud of the demanding library and offers customers free Wi-Fi. A converted thatched stable block provides accommodation. Home-cooked food (not Sun evening) features game, and snacks include locally-produced biltong. ♨Q❀⛼◑🚌(112)♣P⅟

Eling

King Rufus

Eling Hill, SO40 9HE (at T-jct 400m S of the Tide Mill) SU368121
✪ 11.30-3, 6-11; 12-10.30 Sun
☎ (023) 8086 8899
Ringwood Best Bitter; guest beers Ⓗ
Compact 19th-century pub at the southern end of the village, near the country's only working tide mill. The welcoming single bar, full of intriguing Victorian decoration, has a small dining room adjoining. Reasonably priced food, including several vegetarian choices, is served daily except Sunday and Monday nights, with roast lunches on Sunday. Family games are played on Monday. The sheltered garden has a boules piste and play area. A tiny car park is at the front of the pub. ♨◑♣P⅟

Emsworth

Coal Exchange ✔

21 South Street, PO10 7EG
✪ 10.30-3, 5.30-11; 10.30-midnight Fri & Sat; 12-11 Sun
☎ (01243) 375866 ⊕ thecoalexchange-emsworth.co.uk
Fuller's Discovery, London Pride, seasonal beers; Gale's Seafarers, HSB; guest beers Ⓗ
A cosy one-bar pub in the town centre and near to the harbour. Its location prompted the pub's name as it was used by local farmers trading their produce with merchants delivering coal by sea. The harbour is no longer commercial but is popular with the yachting community and people enjoying walks along the shoreline. The pub hosts excellent curry and international food evenings on Tuesday and Thursday respectively, so an early arrival for these is essential. ♨❀◐⇌🚌(700)♣⅟

Lord Raglan

35 Queen Street, PO10 7BJ
✪ 11-3, 6-11; 11-11 Sat; 12-11 Sun
☎ (01243) 372587 ⊕ thelordraglan.com
Fuller's London Pride; Gale's Seafarers, HSB Ⓗ
This flint-built pub at the eastern edge of the town has a single bar and small restaurant. The garden to the rear offers views of the tidal-filled Slipper Mill Pond, a habitat for many species of bird, fish and plant life. The pub itself serves excellent home-cooked food and hosts live music from local bands every Sunday evening thanks to the enthusiastic landlord and staff. The cider is Bulmers Traditional. ♨❀◑⇌🚌(700)♣●

Fareham

Lord Arthur Lee ✔

100-108 West Street, PO16 0EP
✪ 9am-11 (midnight Fri & Sat)
☎ (01329) 280447
Courage Directors; Greene King IPA, Abbot; Marston's Pedigree; guest beers Ⓗ
Popular with office workers and shoppers, this Wetherspoon's pub is conveniently located near the bus station and shopping centre. The walls are lined with photographs and historical details of the pub's namesake and other local figures. Up to five guest beers mainly from small independent breweries are available, including dark and foreign beers, although this number goes up significantly during beer festivals. The usual range of food is available all day. ❀◑♿⇌🚌⅟

Farnborough

Prince of Wales ✔

184 Rectory Road, GU14 8AL
✪ 11.30-2.30, 5.30-11; 11.30-11 Fri & Sat; 12-10.30 Sun
☎ (01252) 545578
Dark Star Hophead; Fuller's London Pride; Hop Back Summer Lightning; Ringwood Fortyniner; Young's Bitter; guest beers Ⓗ
Popular free house, unsurpassed for choice and quality in the area. A single bar is flanked by separate drinking areas, with tables under cover outside at the rear. Dark Star Hophead is now a permanent fixture among the five regular beers. Up to five guest beers are also served from mainly local breweries, including a keenly priced session beer. Milds feature in May, strong beers around Christmas time, and a very popular beer festival is held in October. Lunches are available Monday to Saturday. ❀◐⇌(North)🚌(73)P⅟

Fleet

Prince Arthur ✔

238 Oatsheaf Parade, Fleet Road, GU51 4BX
⏲ 9-midnight (12.30am Fri & Sat)
☎ (01252) 622660
Greene King IPA, Abbot; Marston's Pedigree; Shepherd Neame Spitfire; guest beers Ⓗ
A Wetherspoon's situated at the southern end of Fleet's high street, a mile from Fleet station. It offers all the usual Wetherspoon facilities and has a changing range of guest beers including ales from small, local breweries.The real cider is Westons Old Rosie. A former Guide entry, the Prince Arthur has recently shown a welcome return to form in a town where good real ale has sometimes been hard to find. ❀◖◗♿🚌(71,72,73)🍎🚬

Queen's Hotel

143 Queen's Road, PO12 1LG
⏲ 11.30-2.30 Fri only, 5-11; 11.30-11 Sat; 12-3, 7-10.30 Sun
☎ (023) 9258 2645
Ringwood Fortyniner; Rooster's Yankee; Young's Bitter; guest beers Ⓗ
Award-winning locals' pub where, in November 2008, Sue Lampon celebrated 25 years as licensee. Two guest beers are normally available, with dark beers appearing regularly in the winter months, and Westons Old Rosie cider features all year round. A regular beer festival takes place in October. Snacks are served Friday lunchtime. Weekend opening hours are often extended by up to half an hour. Stoke Road buses pass nearby. ♨❀🚌♣🍎🚬

Fritham

Royal Oak

SO43 7HJ (1 mile S of B3078) SU232141
⏲ 11.30-2.30 (3 summer), 6-11; 11-11 Sat; 12-10.30 Sun
☎ (023) 8081 2606
Bowman Wallops Wood; Hop Back Summer Lightning; Ringwood Best Bitter, Fortyniner; guest beers Ⓖ
This thatched gem at the end of a New Forest track is worth finding. The main bar leads into several interconnected areas featuring low beams, log fires and wooden floors, all served via a hatchway. Guest ales are always from small local brewers; Wallops Wood (Royal Oak) is the house beer. Simple but excellent food includes local cheeses. The vast tabled garden hosts barbecues, hog roasts and occasional beer festivals. A perfect welcome awaits walkers, cyclists and equestrians (facilities provided) – dogs abound. ♨Q❀◖⛺

Goodworth Clatford

Clatford Arms

Village Street, SP11 7RN
⏲ 12-3, 5.30-11 Wed-Fri; 12-11 Sat; 12-10.30 Sun
☎ (01264) 363298
Wadworth 6X, seasonal beers; guest beers Ⓗ
A traditional local pub boasting a strong sporting following, with pool, darts and cribbage teams, as well as a golf and cricket team. The local shoot also meets here. The pub serves several guest ales in the traditional bar. The large garden incorporates a football goal and childrens' play area. Walkers and dogs are encouraged and live music is held once a month. Q❀◖◗♿♣P🚬

Gosport

Clarence Tavern

1 Clarence Road, PO12 1BB
⏲ 11-11; 12-3, 7-10.30 Sun
☎ (023) 9252 9726 🌐 clarencetavern.co.uk
Oakleaf Bitter, Hole Hearted, Blake's Gosport Bitter Ⓗ
The brewery tap for the nearby Oakleaf Brewery, this pub is within walking distance of the Gosport ferry and local buses. Adjoining the main bar is a room whose roof came from an old chapel on the Isle of Wight. Seasonal beers from Oakleaf appear occasionally, and there are two well-established beer festivals over the Easter and August bank holiday weekends. The pub sometimes closes on winter weekday afternoons. Food is served until 6pm on Saturday and 4pm on Sunday. ♨❀🛏◖◗♿🚌♣P🚬

Greatham

Greatham Inn

Petersfield Road, GU33 6AD SU778310
⏲ 12-11 (10.30 Sun)
☎ (01420) 538016 🌐 thegreathaminn.co.uk
Ringwood Best Bitter, Fortyniner; guest beers Ⓗ
A delightful, dog-friendly pub in the centre of the village. As well as the regular beers, there are two guests, mainly from southern England. You may dine in the restaurant or bar lunchtime and evening (booking advisable at weekends). Fish dishes are available; check the specials board. The proprietor has ambitious plans to swap round the dining room and bar area. As you enter the pub you will see a decorative coat of arms from Lady Carol, who is buried in the nearby churchyard. ♨Q❀◖◗♿🚌(72)P🚬

Hammer Vale

Prince of Wales

GU27 1QH SU868325
⏲ 12-midnight (11 Sun)
☎ (01428) 652600
Gale's HSB, seasonal beer Ⓗ
Set in a lovely valley, this large roadhouse-style pub with three distinct drinking areas is in an out-of-context location as it was built speculatively for the nearby A3, which took a different route. The pub boasts some attractive glass windows, including one from the original owners, Ameys. Children are welcome; no food on Monday. ♨❀◖◗🚌(59)♣P🚬

Hartley Wintney

Waggon & Horses

High Street, RG27 8NY
⏲ 11 (12 Sun)-11 (midnight Fri & Sat)
☎ (01252) 842119
Courage Best Bitter Ⓗ**; Gale's HSB** Ⓖ**; guest beer** Ⓗ
A village pub whose landlord of 28 years has won several local CAMRA awards. HSB is served from a cask in the cellar and the guest beer changes constantly. The lively public bar contrasts with a quieter lounge, and tables outside on the pavement enable guests to enjoy the atmosphere of the village, renowned for its antique shops. At the rear of the pub is a pleasant courtyard garden and a heated, covered smokers' area. Food is served lunchtimes only, not Sunday. ♨Q❀◖⊟🚌(72,200)🚬

Havant

Old House At Home ✔

2 South Street, PO9 1DA

11-11 (11.30 Fri & Sat); 12-10.30 Sun

(023) 9248 3464

Fuller's Chiswick Bitter, London Pride, ESB; Gale's HSB Ⓗ

Although the date on the front wall is about 200 years too early, this is still one of the oldest buildings in town, having survived the fire of 1760. Beams recovered from the Spanish Armada were used in the construction of what were five cottages. They were first converted to a bakery and then a pub. In the lounge bar are the remains of the bakery oven and the public bar reputedly showed the last dancing bear in England.

Robin Hood

6 Homewell, PO9 1EE

11-midnight; 12-11 Sun

(023) 9248 2779

Fuller's Chiswick Bitter, London Pride; Gale's HSB; guest beers Ⓗ

In the early days, this pub was more like the landlord's front room. Over the years it has expanded to cope with increasing trade but still retains its original character. The front drinking area has a stone floor, while to the rear is a comfortable lounge area with large settees and low tables. A short walk from the pub is a spring which provided water for the town's now defunct parchment-making industry.

Hawkley

Hawkley Inn

Pococks Lane, GU33 6NE SU747291

12-3, 5.30-11; 12-11 Sat; 12-10.30 Sun

(01730) 827205 hawkleyinn.co.uk

Beer range varies Ⓗ

Small, comfortable but basic village pub well off the beaten track. It has between five and nine beers on draught, depending on the time of year, mainly from small breweries. One bar serves three rooms; the main room has an open fire with a moose's head above. The Hangers Way is nearby, so the pub is popular with walkers. Locally sourced fresh produce is used for the interesting menu. One regular but changing cider is available and accommodation comprises five en-suite rooms.

Hill Head

Crofton

48 Crofton Lane, PO14 3QF

11-11; 12-10.30 Sun

(01329) 314222

Adnams Broadside; Caledonian Deuchars IPA; guest beers Ⓗ

This modern award-winning estate pub looks unimposing from the outside but is well worth a visit. Although owned by Punch Taverns, the four guest beers include offerings from SIBA, with Oakleaf Hole Hearted and Hop Back Summer Lightning appearing regularly. The function room has a skittle alley where special events are held including a beer festival in October. Home-cooked food is available all day at weekends. Real cider (Westons Scrumpy) is now available regularly. (33)

Hook

Crooked Billet ✔

London Road, RG27 9EH (on A30 1 mile E of Hook)

11.30-3, 6-11; 11.30-11 Sat; 12-10.30 Sun

(01256) 762118 thecrookedbillethook.co.uk

Courage Best Bitter; guest beers Ⓗ

Recently extended and air-conditioned, this spacious pub beside the river Whitewater has been run by the same landlord for the past 20 years. The hostelry is renowned for its good food as well as its beer. One of the guests is always from Andwell Brewery. An open log fire is welcoming in winter and there is plenty of space for both drinkers and diners, especially in summer when the riverside garden is at its best. Thatchers cider is stocked and a covered area is available for smokers. Families are welcome. Q (200)P

Horton Heath

Lapstone

Botley Road, SO50 7AP (on B3354)

11.30-2.30, 5-11; closed Mon; 11.30-11.30 Fri & Sat; 12-9 Sun

(023) 8060 1659 thelapstone.co.uk

Gale's HSB; Ringwood Best Bitter; Sharp's Doom Bar Ⓗ

Friendly and lively pub located in a dip between two villages, known as Lapstone Bottom. The building was originally two cottages built circa 1740 and has been a hostelry for more than 100 years. Inside, the bar serves a single split-level room. The large beer garden has a covered patio area and a good children's play area. A wide range of traditional pub food is available plus a popular tapas menu. Quiz night is Tuesday and live music plays on Saturday. P

Kingsclere

Swan Hotel

Swan Street, RG20 5PP

11-3, 5.30 (6 Sat)-11 (11.30 Fri & Sat); 12-3.30, 7-10.30 Sun

(01635) 298314 swankingsclere.co.uk

Theakston XB; Young's Bitter; guest beers Ⓗ

Traditional inn frequented by an eclectic mix of customers, serving four beers including two frequently-changing local guests. The 400-year-old pub is one of the county's oldest coaching inns, dating from 1449 and associated with the Bishop of Winchester for 300 years. The Grade II-listed building, close to the Watership Down beauty spot, retains original oak beams and fireplaces and offers nine en-suite bedrooms. Good food is served in both the dining room and the bar. No food on Sunday. Q (32,32A)

Langstone

Ship Inn ✔

Langstone Road, PO9 1RD

11-11; 12-10.30 Sun

(023) 9247 1719

Fuller's Discovery, London Pride; Gale's Seafarers, HSB Ⓗ

Located adjacent to the bridge to Hayling Island that separates Langstone and Chichester harbours, this pub is an ideal place to start or end a walk along the shoreline or the much-missed railway line to Havant. There is plenty here to interest

nature and yacht enthusiasts as well as walkers, and the more intrepid explorer may discover the remains of the berth of the Isle of Wight train ferry or the Roman Wade Way to Hayling.
(30,31)P

Lasham

Gliding Club

Lasham Airfield, GU34 5SS (signed from A339)
12-2, 5.30-11; 12-11 Sat summer; 12-11 Sun
(01256) 384900
Sharp's Doom Bar; guest beers H
This club has a friendly, comfortable lounge bar and an excellent restaurant with a resident chef. Check in advance for availability of evening meals. The establishment is open to the public at all times and children are welcome. An extensive patio area is a good place to enjoy your pint while watching the aircraft. It was voted local CAMRA Club of the Year in 2007, 2008 and 2009. P

Royal Oak

GU34 5SJ (off A339 between Alton and Basingstoke)
12-11 (10.30 Sun)
(01256) 381213 royaloak.uk.com
Gale's HSB; Ringwood Best Bitter; Triple fff Moondance; guest beers H
Situated in the centre of a quiet village next to Lasham Airfield, well known for its gliding club, the pub is more than 200 years old and has two bars. Food is served daily at lunchtime and in the evening (not Mon), plus all day on Sunday. A large car park, beautiful garden and picturesque surroundings make this pub popular with ramblers and cyclists. Children are welcome.
Q(28)P

Linwood

Red Shoot

Tom's Lane, BH24 3QT (4m NE of Ringwood) SU187094
11-3, 6-11; 11-11 Sat & Sun
(01425) 475792 redshoot.co.uk
Red Shoot Forest Gold, Muddy Boot, Tom's Tipple; Wadworth Henry's IPA, 6X H
Located amid idyllic, remote New Forest countryside, ideal for a healthy walk, the pub is a very relaxed family and dog-friendly place. The large L-shaped bar is simply furnished in wood, with a good view of the pub's micro-brewery (qv Red Shoot Brewery) at the west end. Regular events include beer festivals in April and October, a quiz on Thursday, and live music on Sunday. Food is served all day and there is a camping and caravan site behind the pub. P

Little London

Plough Inn

Silchester Road, RG26 5EP (1 mile off A340, S of Tadley)
12-2.30 (3 Sat), 5.30 (6 Sat)-11; 12-3, 7-10.30 Sun
(01256) 850628
Ringwood Best Bitter, seasonal beers H**; guest beers** G
Wonderful village pub where in winter you can enjoy a glass of porter in front of one of the log fires or play a game of bar billiards instead. Live music is hosted on the second Tuesday of the month and quiz night is the third Monday of the month. A good range of baguettes is available (not Sun eve). There is a secluded garden at the side of the pub. Ideal for ramblers and cyclists visiting the Roman ruins at nearby Silchester or Pamber Wood.
Q(44)P

Long Sutton

Four Horseshoes

RG29 1TA (1 mile E of village centre) SU748471
12-2.30 (not Mon & Tue), 6.30-11; 12-2.30 Sun
(01256) 862488 fourhorseshoes.com
Beer range varies H
Next to Lord Wandsworth College, this friendly local has a single bar divided by a fireplace. A small enclosed veranda at the front offers fine views over the surrounding countryside. Accommodation is provided and there is a grassed area for camping; enquire in advance. Home-cooked meals are tasty and reasonably priced. Up to three beers are available, usually one local and one under 4% ABV. Opening hours can vary and there is only one bus per day, although the 1940s timetable on the wall recalls better times! QP

Lower Upham

Woodman

Winchester Road, SO32 1HA (on B2177)
12-2.30 (6.15 Sat & Sun), 7.15-11
(01489) 860270
Greene King IPA; guest beers H
The landlord has lived in the pub for more than five decades – his parents ran it before him. A cosy lounge and a more basic public bar serve guest ales from the Greene King list with some on gravity dispense. The pub has a choice of over 150 whiskies. Sandwiches and ploughman's are normally available at lunchtime. Events include 'Sausage Saturday' in March, a mini beer festival on the nearest Saturday to St George's Day and live blues the first Wednesday of each month.
(69)P

Lymington

Borough Arms

39 Avenue Road, SO41 9GP
4-11 Mon; 11-11 (midnight Fri & Sat); 12-10.30 Sun
(01590) 672814
Ringwood Best Bitter, Fortyniner; guest beer H
Welcoming, family-run community pub with a mixed but friendly clientele. Pool, darts, jukebox and TV for live sport are all available, but a quieter lounge area also enables good conversation. The developing guest beer list is sourced from the SIBA and Admiral portfolios. Simple bar snacks are available at all times, supplemented by Sunday roasts. Smokers have a partly covered, heated patio. Handy for the St Barbe Museum, high street and library. Shove ha'penny and dominoes are played. P

Bosun's Chair

Station Street, SO41 3BA
11.30-3, 5.30-midnight; 11.30-midnight Sat; 12-midnight Sun
(01590) 675140
Wadworth Henry's IPA, 6X, JCB H
A former Station Hotel, this tied Wadworth house has been run by Roger and Cheryl for over 15 years. Handy for both the historic town quay and the Saturday market, this pub with a nautical theme and a multi-seated, award-winning garden

has a strong local trade. Sky TV provides sport coverage. A separate, 30-seat dining area hosts private functions and evening meals (by prior appointment only). An attractive, heated and covered patio links the bar and garden. Accommodation comprises two single and seven double en-suite rooms. ❀🛏◑◗♿⇌P⅟–

Wheel Inn

Sway Road, Pennington, SO41 8LJ
⌚ 10-midnight (1am Fri & Sat); 12-11 Sun
☎ (01590) 676122 🌐 thewheelinn.co.uk
Ringwood Best Bitter; guest beers Ⓗ
Friendly and traditional, you will be warmly welcomed by the landlord and jovial landlady at this rare true free house with a large public bar and cosy lounge. Good value home-prepared food is served lunchtime and evening, with breakfast available 10am-midday, Monday to Saturday. A LocAle accredited pub, its guest ales are sourced from small local breweries. Live music night is Friday, acoustic night is Monday and jam night is the third Wednesday of the month. Other fun events are detailed on the website. Small functions are catered for and dogs are welcome.
⛰❀◑◗🚌(X12)P⅟–

Medstead

Castle of Comfort

Castle Street, GU34 5LU
⌚ 11.30-2.30 (3 Sat), 6-11; 12-3, 7-10.30 Sun
☎ (01420) 562112 🌐 castleofcomfort.co.uk
Black Sheep Best Bitter; Courage Best Bitter, Directors; guest beer Ⓗ
Tucked behind the church, this 17th-century village local has a public bar and a small lounge which feels more like a family living room, with a wood-burning stove set in a large fireplace. The pub has a large garden and a sun-trap drinking area outside at the front, and bar food is available at lunchtime (not Mon). The Castle is a perfect stopping-off place for ramblers. ⛰Q❀◑🎯🚌(28)♣P⅟–

Milford on Sea

Red Lion

32 High Street, SO41 0QD (on B3058, off A337 at Everton)
⌚ 11.30-2.30, 5-11; 12-3 (7-10.30 summer only) Sun
☎ (01590) 642236 🌐 redlionpubmilfordonsea.co.uk
Fuller's London Pride; Ringwood Best Bitter; guest beers Ⓗ
Imposing 18th-century inn, comfortable, friendly and relaxing, with a notable feature fireplace. The single bar area is split up and arranged on several levels, with carpeting throughout. One area is reserved for pool and darts, with a quiet, unobtrusive gaming machine. The dining area can be used by drinkers after food service ends. Up to two guest ales, free of tie, are from smaller breweries. Cheddar Valley cider is served May-September. Overnight accommodation consists of three en-suite rooms and caravans are allowed.
⛰Q❀🛏◑◗♿⛺🚌(X12)🍎P🗑

North Gorley

Royal Oak

Ringwood Road, SP6 2PB (1½m S of Fordingbridge, ½m E of A338) SU161119
⌚ 11.30-11; 12-11 Sun
☎ (01425) 652244
Beer range varies Ⓗ
This attractive, thatched-roof building started life as a royal hunting lodge, becoming a pub in 1820. Inside is a spacious bar, with an annexe that is used as a family room, music venue or skittle alley as required. Often quiet in winter (no food Sun and Mon eves), in summer the pub caters well for many visitors. The landlord, once a professional musician, ensures that Friday night is live music night. The beers are usually locally brewed and often include Downton and Hop Back ales.
⛰Q🐎❀◑◗🚌(X3)♣P⅟–

North Warnborough

Lord Derby ✔

Bartley Heath, RG29 1HD (on A287 towards Farnham at jct 5 M3)
⌚ 11.30-3, 5.30-11; 11.30-11 Wed-Sat; 12-10.30 Sun
☎ (01256) 702283
Fuller's London Pride; Moorhouse's Pendle Witches Brew; guest beers Ⓗ
A well-presented country roadside pub situated in a no-through road. Its central bar, with a flagstone floor, services the bar and restaurant. Two regular ales plus up to two guests are normally available, usually including one from the very local Andwell Brewery. The restaurant area is open plan but still cosy, with an open fireplace and hop-covered oak beams. It serves quality meals, including local game dishes. ⛰Q❀◑◗P⅟–

Old Basing

Crown Inn ✔

The Street, RG24 7BW (next to Old Basing House)
⌚ 11-3, 5-11; 11-11.30 Fri & Sat; 11.30-10.30 Sun
☎ (01256) 321424 🌐 thecrownoldbasing.co.uk
Fuller's London Pride; guest beers Ⓗ
Grade II-listed building dating from the Civil War when Oliver Cromwell's Roundheads laid siege to Basing House. The inn is home to the Hawkins Regiment of the re-enactment society and a microlight club. There are two bars, one a cosy snug and one with wheelchair access. Food is available every day and includes tapas, which are very popular. Two of the three guest beers are always from local micro-breweries. Glasses are oversized, except branded ones, and smokers have a covered area. At the rear is a garden with a children's play area. ⛰Q🐎❀◑◗🎯♿🚌(12)P⅟–🗑

Overton

Red Lion

37 High Street, RG25 3HQ (200m W of village centre on B3400)
⌚ 11.30-3, 6-11; 12-4, 6-10.30 (closed eves Nov-Mar) Sun
☎ (01256) 773363
Flowerpots Bitter; Triple fff Moondance; guest beer Ⓗ
Just a short walk from the centre of the village, the Red Lion is gaining a good reputation for high quality food at reasonable prices. As well as the main menu, which includes a vegetarian dish, there are daily specials. Three tastefully decorated separate areas include a restaurant (bookings advisable) and a cosy snug, with the main bar sandwiched between the two. A good-sized garden with a covered wooden patio overlooks the car park. The staff are friendly, extremely efficient and attentive. ❀◑◗🚌P

Portsmouth

Barley Mow

39 Castle Road, Southsea, PO5 3DE

12 (11 Sat)-midnight; 12-11 Sun

(023) 9282 3492

Fuller's London Pride; Gale's HSB; guest beers

Good-sized Victorian street corner pub with pool and darts in the public bar and a wood-panelled lounge bar with plenty of seating – but beware of the settees as they can be difficult to get out of after a hard day. Five guest beers are usually on sale, including a dark beer. This is a lively community pub which hosts a wide range of events, from theme nights to quizzes and live music. (1,23,40)

Duke of Devonshire

119 Albert Road, PO5 2SR

11-midnight (12.30am Fri & Sat); 12-11.45 Sun

(023) 9282 3682

Fuller's London Pride; Greene King Old Speckled Hen

A busy little street-corner locals' pub affectionally known as Mollies, in the Albert Road area of Southsea. A richly-deserved first time entry into the Guide, the hostelry has hardly changed over the years and is a real step back in time. The pub is very big on ladies darts, and a warm welcome with some fine real ale await you. (17,18)

Eastfield Hotel

124 Prince Albert Road, Southsea, PO4 9HT

11-11 (midnight Fri & Sat); 12-11 Sun

(023) 9275 0102

Fuller's London Pride; Oakleaf Oakleaf Bitter; guest beers

An imposing Edwardian pub in the back streets of Eastney, still displaying the original tiled exterior and windows from its construction in 1906 by AE Cogswell. The boisterous public bar shows sport and supports darts and pool teams, while the quieter lounge has original wood panelling. Guest beers are sourced from many independent local breweries.

Fifth Hants Volunteer Arms

74 Albert Road, Southsea, PO5 2SL

3-midnight (1am Fri); 12-1am Sat & Sun

(023) 9282 7161

Fuller's London Pride; Gale's Seafarers, HSB

Although a traditional street-corner drinkers' local, this pub is popular with both young and old thanks to the lively and enthusiastic manager and staff. The public bar has stripped floorboards and boasts probably the best jukebox in town. The smaller lounge is decorated with military memorabilia and certificates commemorating the pub's many years in this Guide. A popular quiz is held Wednesday evening and the pub supports both darts and cricket teams. (17,18)

Florence Arms

18-20 Florence Road, Southsea, PO5 2NE

12-midnight (11 Sun)

(023) 9287 5700

Adnams Bitter, Broadside; Shepherd Neame Spitfire; guest beers

One of Southsea's hidden gems, the Flo has a genuine public bar, a more select lounge and a dining room serving excellent home-cooked food (not weekends except Sun lunch). Live entertainment includes jazz and folk music. Guest beers come from local independent breweries, each featuring for a month at a time. One of the main attractions is the excellent range of cider and perry, with at least 12 real ciders and perries on draught and more than 40 in bottles.

Hole in the Wall

36 Great Southsea Street, Southsea, PO5 3BY

4-11; 12-2, 4-midnight Fri; 4-midnight Sat

(023) 9229 8085 theholeinthewallpub.co.uk

Oakleaf Hole Hearted; guest beers

Converted from a wine bar by Geoff Hartridge as part of his now defunct Winchester Ale House chain, the Hole is one of the smallest pubs in Portsmouth but, for its size, has one of the best ever-changing beer ranges sourced from both local breweries and agencies. Hole Hearted, which is named after the pub, is on sale by gravity from the back of the bar. Cider is also available. No admittance after 11pm. Local CAMRA Pub of the Year 2009. (1,23,40)

Leopold Tavern

154 Albert Road, Southsea, PO4 0JT

10-11 (midnight Fri & Sat); 12-11 Sun

(023) 9282 9748

Bowman Swift One; Greene King Abbot; Hop Back Summer Lightning; Oakleaf Hole Hearted; guest beers

A green-tiled exterior to this street-corner pub belies its modernised interior. The pub has however has retained its two distinctive drinking areas. The one closest to Albert Road can become extremely busy on a weekend evening when the Albert Road crawls visit. The inner area is quieter but still busy. The provision of an outdoor heated beer garden for both smokers and non-smokers means that the interior drinking areas are less crowded than before. (Fratton)(17,18)

Marmion Tavern

20 Marmion Road, PO5 2BA

11-11 (midnight Thu-Sat); 12-11 Sun

(023) 9273 7765

Beer range varies

A lovely pub situated just off the Palmerston Road shopping precinct, back in the Guide after a long absence. Four constantly changing guest real ales, budget bar snacks and a separate dining area are available. For cheese lovers, a fine selection is on offer. The upstairs restaurant doubles as a local artists' gallery, which is worth seeking out.

Pembroke

20 Pembroke Road, Southsea, PO1 2NR

10-midnight (11 Mon); 12-4, 7-11 Sun

(023) 9282 3961

Draught Bass; Fuller's London Pride; Greene King Abbot

Street-corner local close to the Cathedral. The original pub was built in 1711 as the Little Blue Line and changed its name to the Pembroke more than 100 years ago. Apparently unchanging, this haven for beer drinkers attracts a varied clientele, serving what has been described as 'the best pint of Pride in Portsmouth'. (6)

Phoenix

13 Duncan Road, Southsea, PO5 2QU

10-midnight (1am Fri & Sat); 12-midnight Sun

(023) 9278 1055

Beer range varies

A typical back-street drinkers' pub with two bars. The pub is next to the old Dock End Brewery which burnt down and was rebuilt as the Phoenix Brewery (now also closed). The lounge bar has many posters from the nearby Kings Theatre while the public bar is largely devoted to the local football team. Smokers are catered for with a small walled patio garden and there is a separate games room which used to be part of the old brewery. ❀⊟⊟(17,18)♣⁻

Rose In June ✓

102 Milton Road, PO3 6AR

⏲ 12-11.30

Fuller's London Pride; Gale's HSB; Hogs Back TEA; Otter Otter Ale Ⓗ

Large, imposing pub next to the prison and only five minutes' walk from Fratton Park. It can get very busy on match days but is always friendly, even to away supporters. It has two very different bars and a huge well-kept garden which hosts an annual beer festival in the last week of June. A guest beer is served at reduced prices each weekend. If arriving by bus ask for the prison bus stop. The cider is Cheddar Valley. Q❀⊟(1,6)♣●

Royal Marines Artillery Tavern

58 Cromwell Road, Eastney, PO4 9PN

⏲ 6-midnight (1am Fri-Sun)

☎ (023) 9282 0896

Fuller's London Pride; Gale's Seafarers, HSB Ⓗ

A back-street drinking local right outside what used to be the old main gate to the Royal Marines barracks, from which the pub takes its name. The beer range comes from Fuller's and the old Gale's portfolio. The pub provides free live entertainment most weekends and is home to the last remaining skittle alley in Portsmouth. Its location is within walking distance of the seafront at Eastney and the Royal Marines museum. ❀▲⊟♣⁻

Sir Loin Of Beef

152 Highland Road, PO4 9NH

⏲ 11-11.30 (midnight Fri & Sat); 12-11.30 Sun

☎ (023) 9282 0115

Hop Back Summer Lightning; guest beers Ⓗ

A true free house, the extensive beer range served here is mainly taken from southern independent breweries, and a fine range of bottle-conditioned beers is also stocked. The pub has a Mediterranean-style café feel with a nautical theme. Submarine paraphernalia adorns the walls and a klaxon is used to call time. The pub hosts a brewery evening once a month, featuring a different local brewery. ▲⊟♣●

Taswell Arms ✓

42 Taswell Road, Southsea, PO5 2RG

⏲ 12-midnight (11 Sun)

☎ (023) 9285 1301

Shepherd Neame Spitfire; Oakleaf Hole Hearted; Hop Back Summer Lightning; guest beers Ⓗ

A well-appointed community pub close to the Albert Road and Southsea shopping areas of town. The split-level design incorporates traditional tables and comfortable settees for seating. The pub provides a wide range of activities for local residents but also offers a warm welcome to new visitors. Table football, pool and darts are played, and good food includes an extensive range of home-cooked meals (available until 8.30pm weekdays and 6pm weekends). ❀◐◑♿⊟(17,18)♣

Winchester Arms

99 Winchester Road, Buckland, PO2 7PS

⏲ 2 (4 Mon)-11; 12-11 Sat & Sun

☎ (023) 9266 2443

Oakleaf Hole Hearted; Shepherd Neame Spitfire; guest beers Ⓗ

Friendly two-bar local concealed among the terraced back streets of Portsmouth. A guest cider or perry on handpump complements the real ales. There are live music performances on Sunday evenings. The pub has its own darts and football teams and hosts the local science-fiction group on the second Tuesday of the month. There is a covered smoking area in the garden. The pub may stay open until midnight on Friday and Saturday if busy. ⚘Q❀⊟♣●⁻

Ringwood

Inn on the Furlong ✓

12 Meeting House Lane, BH24 1EY

⏲ 11-11 (midnight Fri & Sat); 12-11 Sun

☎ (01425) 475139

Ringwood Best Bitter, Fortyniner, Old Thumper, seasonal beers; guest beers Ⓗ

This cream-painted Victorian building escaped demolition in 1985 to become Ringwood Brewery's first pub. Centrally situated, it has a single, large, flagstoned bar that serves several linked areas including a sunny conservatory and a family area. Although generally a quiet pub, it can be a busy and lively meeting place for more mature customers. All the Ringwood brews are available, augmented with several other Marston's guests. Tuesday and Saturday are live music nights. No meals Sunday or Tuesday evenings. ⚘Q♉❀◐◑♿▲⊟♣⁻

Romsey

Abbey Hotel

11 Church Street, SO51 8BT

⏲ 11-3, 6-11; 12-3, 7-10.30 Sun

☎ (01794) 513360 ⊕ abbeyhotelromsey.co.uk

Courage Best Bitter, Directors; Young's Bitter Ⓗ

The dining room and lounge of this pub look out on to the east end of Romsey Abbey, which was founded in 907, almost 1,000 years before the building of its secular namesake. The handsome exterior, with black and white gables and confident Courage lintel, is enhanced in summer by floral displays. The interior is a matrix for conversation and contemplation. On fine days you may enjoy the attractive garden beyond the car park and adjacent to the medieval, but inappropriately named, King John's House. No food served on Sunday. ⚘Q❀⊨◐◑⇌⊟P⁻

Old House at Home

62 Love Lane, SO51 8DE

⏲ 11-3, 5-11 (11.30 Sat); 12-4, 7-10.30 Sun

☎ (01794) 513175

Fuller's Discovery, London Pride; Gale's HSB Ⓗ

Just five minutes' walk from the town centre and Broadlands, Romsey's only thatched inn is spacious and full of olde-worlde charm. A busy pub, it is popular with locals at lunchtime. Interesting memorabilia adorns the walls and Toby jugs hang above the bar. A separate side room off the bar is used mainly for diners. Food is made with local ingredients and cooked to order (no meals Sun eve, when a quiz is held). Outside is a large walled

garden with a heated smoking area to the rear. Friendly staff make you welcome.
⛫Q❀◐◑⇌▣P⚟

Rowlands Castle

Castle Inn ✔

1 Finchdean Road, PO9 6DA
⏲ 11 (12 Sun)-midnight
☎ (023) 9241 2494
Fuller's London Pride; Gale's Seafarers, HSB 🄷
Hidden behind the railway bridge at the eastern edge of the village, this cosy two-bar pub offers a welcoming atmosphere to all. One bar is partly used as a restaurant serving good home-cooked food while the other is an excellent place to relax by an open fire after enjoying a walk in the local countryside. Unusually, the pub has two garden areas, one dedicated to those who prefer a quiet drink in the summer. ⛫❀◐◑⊟♿⇌♣P

St Mary Bourne

Coronation Arms

The Street, SP11 6AR (NW end of village)
⏲ 11.30-2.30 (not Mon), 6.30-11; 12-3, 7-10.30 Sun
☎ (01264) 738432 🌐 thecoronationarms.com
Fuller's London Pride; Ringwood Best Bitter; guest beers 🄷
This comfortable free house sits in the picturesque Bourne Valley, home to some of the county's famous watercress beds. The roomy bar attracts locals and visitors alike and is always a place for friendly conversation. Two further rooms serve as small dining areas, where familes are always welcome. Good quality home-cooked food is a speciality, but check for food times.
⛫❀🛏◐◑▣(C3)♣P

Selborne

Selborne Arms ✔

High Street, GU34 3JR
⏲ 11-3, 6 (5.30 Fri)-11; 11-11 Sat summer; 12-11 Sun
☎ (01420) 511247 🌐 selbornearms.co.uk
Ringwood Fortyniner; Courage Best Bitter; guest beers 🄷
Traditional village pub in a building that dates back to the 1600s, retaining original features including a log fire. It is situated at the bottom of Selborne Hanger and the famous zigzag path carved by naturalist Gilbert White. The guest beer range showcases local micro-breweries and local Mr Whitehead's Cider is available, while the award-winning menu also features local produce. Extensive outside facilities include a covered patio heated with wood-burning fires, a play area for children and a fantastic barbecue.
⛫Q❀◐◑⊟▣(72,X72)●P⚟

Shedfield

Wheatsheaf Inn

Botley Road, SO32 2JG (on A334)
⏲ 12-11 (10.30 Sun)
☎ (01329) 833024
Flowerpots Bitter, Gooden's Gold, seasonal beer; guest beers 🄶
When visiting this increasingly popular country pub, customers will find a selection of six real ales served directly from the casks behind the bar. Thatchers Cheddar Valley cider is also available. The home-cooked food is excellent value for money, although evening meals are only served on Tuesday and Wednesday. Blues, jazz or folk music is played live on most Saturday evenings. An annual beer festival is held on the late spring bank holiday weekend. Parking is across a busy road.
⛫Q❀◐◑⊟▣(69)♣●P⚟

Sherfield-on-Loddon

White Hart

Reading Road, RG27 0BT (off A33)
⏲ 11 (12 Sun)-11
☎ (01256) 882280 🌐 whitehartsherfield.co.uk
Wells Bombardier; Young's Bitter, Special, seasonal beers 🄷
Traditional 17th-century coaching inn situated in the heart of the village, opposite the green. The pub has a pleasant garden area to the rear and a heated smoking area to the front. Inside, although it has had a makeover, there are oak beams, brick fireplaces and many reminders of days gone by, including the mail rack above the fireplace, said to be one of only four remaining in England. The pub is a good base for walkers using the three suggested routes listed on the pub's website.
⛫Q❀◐◑♿▣P⚟

Southampton

Bitter Virtue (off-licence)

70 Cambridge Road, SO14 6US (take Alma Rd from The Avenue, by church, 200m)
⏲ 10.30-8.30 (2 Sun); closed Mon
☎ (023) 8055 4881 🌐 bittervirtue.co.uk
Beer range varies 🄶
This award-winning beer shop has been in the Guide since opening 12 years ago. A range of some 400 bottled beers from Belgium, Germany, Czech Republic, US micros, Netherlands and Great Britain are stocked, including many from local breweries. At least one draught beer is on sale and occasionally draught cider. Bottled cider is also sold. Polypins from local breweries can be ordered upon request. An extensive selection of T-shirts, books and glasses is also available. ▣

Fleming Arms ✔

Wide Lane, Swaythling, SO18 2QN
⏲ 11-11; 12-10.30 Sun
☎ (023) 8058 4358
Fuller's London Pride; Gale's HSB 🄷
Large single room pub but with a range of separate areas – dining area, lounge bar and large public bar area, complete with pool and sports TV. Outside is a patio overlooking a small river – Monks Brook. The interior is mainly decorated with attractive contemporary art, but there is also a corner featuring old photographs of Swaythling. Good lunchtime and evening food is served until 9pm, all day on Sunday. There is a function room upstairs.
❀◐◑♿⇌(Swaythling)▣P⚟

Guide Dog 🏆

38 Earl's Road, Bevois Valley, SO14 6SF (100m W of Bevois Valley Rd, opp Aldi)
⏲ 3 (12 Sat)-11; 12-10.30 Sun
☎ (023) 8022 5642
Bowman Swift One; Fuller's ESB; guest beers 🄷
With up to eight real ales you are spoilt for choice here; a bright blue exterior makes it hard to miss, too. The pub is within walking distance of St Mary's

Stadium so can be busy on match days. It hosts a variety of charity events during the year and a meat draw is held on Friday. Jugs of ale are available as carry-outs and there is a selection of Belgian bottled beers. A regular autumn beer festival is always well attended. Local CAMRA Pub of the Year 2007 and 2008. ≢(St Denys)♣⁵–

Hop Inn

Woodmill Lane, SO18 2PH (corner of Oak Tree Road and Woodmill Lane)

11-11; 12-10.30 Sun

☎ (023) 8055 7723

Gale's HSB; guest beers Ⓗ

Good urban local in a residential area. This 1930s pub has two bars with separate entrances, and interesting internal architecture in which it seems no two walls meet at right angles. The lounge bar is divided by a central fireplace and is decorated with jugs, painted plates, pictures and china ornaments. The more modern public bar leads to a covered patio area and a garden which has a small aviary. Guest beers usually include Sharp's and Bowman Ales. Food is served daily at lunchtime except Sunday. ❀0⊟⊟(3,8,U9)♣P⁵–

Humble Plumb ✔

Commercial Street, Bitterne, SO18 6LY

11.30 (12 Mon)-2.30, 5-11; 11.30-11 Fri & Sat; 12-10.30 Sun

☎ (023) 8043 7577

Jennings Sneck Lifter; Wadworth Henry IPA, Horizon, Ⓗ**; 6X,** Ⓖ**; Bishop's Tipple; guest beers** Ⓗ

Friendly local in Bitterne, a quiet suburb of Southampton, with an excellent range of ales that changes regularly; one guest is often from Wadworth's Red Shoot micro-brewery. A rare outlet for 6X gravity dispensed from wooden casks. All beers are on a 'try before you buy' basis. Good quality food is available lunchtime and early evening, daily except Sunday evening. Outside is a colourful garden and a covered, heated patio for smokers. A meat draw is held on Sunday afternoon and quiz night is Monday. Parking is behind the pub. ❀0D♿⊟(18)P⁵–

Junction Inn

21 Priory Road, St Denys, SO17 2JZ (50m from St Denys station)

12-11 (midnight Fri & Sat)

☎ (023) 8058 4486 🌐 thejunction-inn.co.uk

Greene King XX Mild, IPA, Abbot; guest beers Ⓗ

Two minutes' walk from St Denys station, the Junction is a Grade-II listed building, dating from the 1860s. It retains many original features including the Victorian bar back and eyelid windows. Popular with football fans walking to matches at St Marys, this is a friendly local with good home-cooked food and pub games, including bar billiards. It deservedly won Southampton's Community Pub of the Year in 2008. In addition to the regular beers, up to four guest ales are from Greene King's list. ⚠❀0D⊟≢(St Denys)♣⁵–

Park Inn ✔

37 Carlisle Road, Shirley, SO16 4FN (jct of Shirley Park Road)

11.30 (12 Sun)-midnight

☎ (023) 8078 7835 🌐 parkinn.org.uk

Wadworth Henry IPA, 6X, Bishop's Tipple, seasonal beers; guest beer Ⓗ

This Wadworth pub is characteristic of the small community pubs built at the end of the 19th century – a locals' pub with a friendly welcome for visitors. Although converted into one bar, it retains a two-bar feel. The walls are adorned with a collection of brewery memorabilia mirrors. A quiet pub where the timeless activities of reading the paper, enjoying conversation, playing darts or, more recently, accessing the internet through free Wi-Fi, all co-exist in harmony. Q❀♿⊟(8a,10)♣⁵–

Platform Tavern

Town Quay, SO14 2NY

12-11.30; 11-12.30am Sat

☎ (023) 8033 7232 🌐 platformtavern.com

Fuller's London Pride; Itchen Valley Godfathers; guest beers Ⓗ

Free house in the heart of the historic dockland of Southampton incorporating part of the original city wall. This small, comfortable pub has a relaxed atmosphere ideal for escaping from the hurly-burly of modern life. It also has a reputation as an intimate live-music pub. With an emphasis on blues, there is live music every Sunday and Thursday night. Sunday lunchtimes feature live jazz along with roast dinners. There is a wide pavement area for summer drinking. 0D♿⊟

Waterloo Arms

101 Waterloo Road, Freemantle, SO15 3BS (next to church)

12-11

☎ (023) 8022 0022

Hop Back GFB, Crop Circle, Entire Stout, Summer Lightning, seasonal beers; guest beer Ⓗ

This friendly local dates from the 1860s, becoming a Hop Back tied house in 1991. It has a single L-shaped bar, a rear conservatory and beyond that a paved garden for drinkers and smokers. Eight handpumps serve the full Hop Back range plus seasonal and guest beers. Hot food is served Tuesday to Saturday lunchtimes and evenings and there is a Sunday roast from 12-2pm. Families are welcome in the conservatory until 9pm. Tuesday evening features a popular quiz. Milbrook station is 500m away.

❀0D≢(Millbrook/Central)⊟(10,11,12)⁵–

Wellington Arms

56 Park Road, Freemantle, SO15 3DE (jct of Mansion Road)

12-11.30 (12.30am Fri & Sat)

☎ (023) 8022 0356

Adnams Bitter; Fuller's London Pride, ESB; Ringwood Best Bitter; Wychwood Hobgoblin; guest beers Ⓗ

This two-bar, friendly local dates from the 1860s. A third room with seating leads to a paved patio area for smokers and outside drinking. Eleven handpumps serve six regular beers and up to five guests, with Hoegaarden and Leffe Blonde also featuring. The bar counters have many old coins set in them and there is much Iron Duke memorabilia to be seen. A popular quiz is held each Thursday and a Find the Joker raffle on Sunday afternoon. ❀⊟≢(Millbrook/Central)⁵–

Standford

Robin Hood

Standford Lane, GU35 8RA SU815346

11-11; 12-6 Sun

☎ (01428) 751508

Brakspear Bitter; Otter Bitter; Sharp's Doom Bar; guest beers Ⓗ

Roadhouse pub near Bordon and the A3, the Robin Hood is situated in walking country near Passfield Common and Woolmer Forest, and has a large garden and car park. It has been extended over the years and, although it is no longer divided into separate rooms, there are still distinct bar, restaurant and drinking areas. There are usually a couple of guest beers on offer, including a strong one. May close early on Sunday if trade is slow. ❀◐♿🚌(13)P⚟

Tangley

Cricketers Arms

SP11 0SH (in village, towards Lower Chute) SU327528
⏲ 11-3 (not Mon & Tue), 6-11; 12-3, 7-10.30 Sun
☎ (01264) 730283 🌐 thecricketers.eu
Bowman Swift One, Wallops Wood Ⓖ
Situated in attractive countryside, this dog-friendly (with three resident black labs) 16th-century drovers' inn sits below the Berkshire Downs, on the border with Wiltshire. The two Bowman ales, served from stillage behind the bar, may be supplemented in summer months by a local guest. The front bar, with its huge inglenook fireplace, is used mainly for drinking, while traditional home-cooked food is served in the flagstoned dining area at the rear. Behind the pub is a large Scandinavian-style wooden chalet with 10 en-suite bedrooms. 🔥Q❀🛏◐♿P⚟

Tichborne

Tichborne Arms

SO24 0NA SU571304
⏲ 11.30-3, 6-11 (1am Fri; midnight Sat); 12-3 Sun
☎ (01962) 733760
Palmers Copper Ale; guest beers Ⓖ
Friendly and unpretentious, this compact two-bar pub is steeped in fascinating local history. The cosy wood-panelled public bar offers traditional pub games such as darts and shove ha'penny. The larger bar has a welcoming wood-burning stove for the walkers, cyclists and locals who come here to enjoy the good food and three or four gravity-dispensed beers, often from local breweries. The garden includes an unusually comfortable covered smoking area with chairs and tables. Whiteheads cider is served in summer. 🔥Q❀◐🅖♣●P⚟

Titchfield

Wheatsheaf

1 East Street, PO14 4AD
⏲ 12-3, 6-11; 12-11 Fri & Sat; 12-10.30 Sun
☎ (01329) 842965
Flowerpots Bitter; guest beers Ⓗ
This 17th-century free house is in a conservation area in the village centre. The interior has been tastefully altered to include a tiny snug and a family dining room alongside the main bar, and there is also a large garden. There are two guest beers which sometimes include other beers from the Flowerpots' range. The licensee is a qualified chef who has established a reputation for his cuisine. No food is served on Sunday night or on Monday. 🔥❀◐🚌P⚟

Twyford

Bugle

Park Lane, SO21 1QT (jct of Park Lane and High St)
⏲ 11.30-11; 12-10.30 Sun
☎ (01962) 714888
Bowman Swift One; Flowerpots Bitter; guest beer Ⓗ
This pub was closed for several years as 'developers' fought opposition from planners, a vigorous village action group and CAMRA to turn it into housing. Happily, in a rare campaigning victory, they finally gave up and the Bugle reopened in 2008, modernised as a large, light and airy single bar. A high-quality daily food menu is on offer as well as Sunday roast, with eight wines available by the glass (no food Sun eve). The guest beer is often another Bowman or Flowerpots brew. Wi-Fi is available. 🔥Q❀◐🚌(49A,69)P⚟

Phoenix

High Street, SO21 1RF
⏲ 11.30-2.30, 6-11; 11.30-11 Fri & Sat; 12-11 Sun
☎ (01962) 713322 🌐 thephoenixinn.co.uk
Greene King XX Mild, IPA, Old Speckled Hen; guest beer Ⓗ
Old coaching inn in the village centre, dating in parts from the 17th century. Once many-roomed, the pub is now one long, multi-level bar. To the rear is a large, bookable skittle alley with bar that doubles as a family area. It's a rare rural outpost for Mild. Food is a major feature, with a number of themed evenings – Monday is curry, Wednesday is steak and Thursday fish and chips. The bar also hosts occasional live music sessions and quiz nights. Check the website for details. 🔥Q❀◐🚌(49A,69)♣P⚟

Upper Farringdon

Rose & Crown

Crows Lane, GU34 3ED (signed off A32 at Farringdon Crossroads)
⏲ 12-3, 6-11; 12-11 Sat; 12-10.30 Sun
☎ (01420) 588231
Hogs Back TEA, HBB; Triple fff Alton's Pride, Pressed Rat and Warthog, Moondance; guest beer Ⓗ
This off-the-beaten-track pub was built in 1810 by the Knight family of Chawton. On entry to this friendly pub you find an L-shaped bar with a cosy seating area warmed by a log fire. Deeper inside is a dining area leading to a modern restaurant (no food Mon eve). An imaginative menu is supplemented with lunchtime bar snacks. Families, walkers and dogs are always welcome and there is a spacious garden. A monthly traditional jazz evening is held. 🔥Q❀🛏◐♣P⚟

West Meon

Thomas Lord

High Street, GU32 1LN (300m E of A32)
⏲ 11-3, 6-11.30 (6.30-midnight Fri); 11-midnight Sat; 12-11 Sun
☎ (01730) 829244 🌐 thethomaslord.co.uk
Ringwood Best Bitter; guest beers Ⓖ
A welcoming country pub that is the hub of village life. High-quality food is served, with a special emphasis placed on local produce, and most ingredients are sourced locally. Beers come only from Hampshire or the Isle of Wight – one guest is usually from Bowman – and three beers are available on gravity. The extensive garden is laid out in a formal style and provides some of the kitchen's ingredients. The garden has an outside bar and cooking area. 🔥Q❀◐🚌(67)P

Whitchurch

Bell Inn

Bell Street, RG28 7DD
⏲ 10-11; 12-10.30 Sun
☎ (01256) 893120
Courage Best Bitter; Gale's HSB; Goddards Special Ⓗ
Whitchurch is renowned for its community pubs and the half-timbered, family-run Bell is one of the town's oldest and most traditional. Two bars and a separate higher area off the lounge provide exposed beams and space for enjoying a quiet pint in this rare outlet for Goddards beers from the Isle of Wight. Conversation and local gossip rule here. There is a small, pleasant patio at the rear and a pool table in the public bar. **Q❀◐⊟🚌**(76,86)

Whitchurch Sports & Social Club

Longmeadow Sports Centre, Winchester Road, RG28 7RB (S edge of town, by football ground)
⏲ 7-11; 12-7 Sun
☎ (01256) 892493
Bowman Swift One; guest beer Ⓗ
Tucked away opposite the tranquil Millennium Meadow, this excellent club features two large bars – a lounge and function room. As well as being home to Whitchurch United Football Club, the venue is shared by the indoor Bowling Club whose impressive green can be viewed from the comfortable lounge bar. It also has two squash courts. Regular events include parties, discos and the annual Whitchurch Beer Festival, which focuses on beers from Hampshire breweries. CAMRA members are welcome on production of a membership card. Opening hours may vary.
❀⊟♿🚌(86)**P⚟**

White Hart Hotel ✔

The Square, RG28 7DN
⏲ 11-11; 12-10.30 Sun
☎ (01256) 892900
Arkell's 3B, Moonlight Ale, Kingsdown Ale Ⓗ
Impressive, comfortable 15th-century historic coaching inn owned by Arkell's Brewery, with several separate areas. The popular public bar is lively at weekends, and occasional live music/discos are held. To the rear is a restaurant and quiet dining area. Breakfast is available from 8am, and cream teas are served in summer. Local artists' work adorns the walls and there is a small outside patio. The Square outside is where the 'right to demonstrate' was won for the country – the event is marked by a plaque. **Q❀🛏◐◑⊟♿🚌**(76,86)**P⚟**

Wickham

Greens

The Square, PO17 5JQ
⏲ 11-3, 6-11; closed Mon; 12-4 Sun
☎ (01329) 833197 🌐 greensrestaurant.co.uk
Bowman Swift One; guest beer Ⓗ
Overlooking Wickham Square, the building is around 100 years old, with a modern interior providing good disabled access. The guest beer is sometimes another Bowman Ales beer, and all ales are served in oversize glasses. The garden overlooks Wickham Water Meadows and hosts special events in the summer. The gourmet menu uses fresh locally-sourced ingredients and in 2008 the restaurant was among The Times' top Sunday lunch and top solo dining outlet recommendations.
Q❀◐◑♿🚌🗑

Wickham Wine Bar

The Square, PO17 5JN
⏲ 12-2.30, 6-11; closed Sun
☎ (01329) 832732 🌐 wickhamwinebar.com
Bowman Eldorado Ⓗ
This wine bar and restaurant are in a listed 15th-century building featuring medieval wall paintings and original oak beams. Sometimes a different Bowman beer is substituted for Eldorado. The two-storey upstairs restaurant extends over the next building, and the garden has its own vine. Food includes fresh fish and game, and other locally sourced produce. Live jazz on Wednesday evening is a regular event. **Q❀◐◑🚌⚟**

Widley

George Inn

Portsdown Hill Road, PO6 1BE
⏲ 11-11.30 (11 Sun)
☎ (023) 9222 1079
Adnams Broadside; Flowers Original; Fuller's London Pride; Greene King Old Speckled Hen, Abbot; Ringwood Best Bitter; guest beer Ⓗ
With extensive views over Portsmouth on Portsdown Hill, this pub is a popular lunch stop. An island bar has six regular beers and one guest, usually from a local and/or micro-brewery. Pub games including skittles and shove ha'penny are available. A regular calendar of social events includes quizzes and charity events; the pub even boasts its own golf group, which caters for all abilities. **❀◐🚌**(40,41,45)**♣P⚟**

Winchester

Bell Inn

83 St Cross Road, St Cross, SO23 9RE (on B3335 at edge of city)
⏲ 11-11; 12-10.30 Sun
☎ (01962) 865284
Greene King IPA; guest beers Ⓗ
Solid, comfortable pub retaining two separate rooms: a large public bar with a cricketing theme (the St Cross ground is just metres away), and a small conversational lounge at the rear. Two guest beers are from Greene King's list. Glazed doors lead through to a sheltered, walled garden, with several gazebos and a play area. Home-cooked food is served every day. The Bell adjoins the Hospital of St Cross, Britain's oldest almshouse (1132), which is reached via a lovely riverside walk from the city centre. **🔥Q❀◐◑⊟🚌P⚟**

Black Boy

1 Wharf Hill, SO23 9NQ (just off Chesil St, B3330)
⏲ 12-11 (midnight Fri & Sat); 12-10.30 Sun
☎ (01962) 861754 🌐 theblackboypub.com
Flowerpots Bitter; Hop Back Summer Lightning; Ringwood Best Bitter; guest beers Ⓗ
A centuries-old set of rambling buildings comprising many interconnected rooms serviced from a central bar. One room is themed as a country kitchen complete with working Aga, another simulates a butcher's, with papier-mâché joints of meat, while other areas look like tradesmen's workshops. Food is pub-grub style (not served on Sun eve or Mon). Two or more guest beers come from small local breweries, often including Bowman. A fine, newly-built, medieval-style smoking shelter graces the patio/garden. Good dogs are welcome. **🔥Q❀◐◑⚟**

Eclipse

25 The Square, SO23 9EX (just off pedestrianised High St)

11-11 (1am Fri & Sat); 12-10.30 Sun

(01962) 865676 eclipseinn.co.uk

Flowers Original; Fuller's London Pride; Ringwood Best Bitter, Old Thumper, seasonal beers H

The Eclipse (there is uncertainty about the name's origin) is a tiny, ancient tavern in the heart of Winchester, dating from 1540 – its extensive history is well described on the website – finally becoming a pub about 1890; yet the convincing Tudor frontage is the result of a 1920s rebuild. Inside is a timeless front bar with an excellent timber ceiling, plus a basic back room. There is a comprehensive lunchtime menu, with Sunday roasts a speciality. Wednesday night is quiz league night. Q

Fulflood

28 Cheriton Road, SO22 5EF (take Western Rd off Stockbridge Rd)

11-3, 5-11 (11-midnight Fri & Sat); 12-11 Sun

(01962) 842996

Flowerpots Bitter; Greene King IPA; Itchen Valley Godfathers; Triple fff Moondance H

The original dark-green tiled facade and etched windows are evidence of this 19th-century pub's former Winchester Brewery ownership. Situated in a residential conservation area, a recent makeover has given the single bar a fresh new look with comfy sofas, newspapers and flowers. The loyal following of locals, their banter, quizzes, occasional live music and special events all make for a good atmosphere. Bar billiards is played. Outside, drinkers and smokers have small patios at both the front and the rear.

Hyde Tavern

57 Hyde Street, SO23 7DY (on B3047)

12-3, 5-11.30 (12.30am Fri); 12-12.30am Sat; 12-11 Sun

(01962) 862592

Beer range varies H/G

In a street formerly known for breweries and watering holes, the exterior of this small, medieval, timber-framed building is dominated by a double gable frontage. The two-roomed pub is below street level – beware of low ceilings and undulating floors. The cellar bar is used for literature evenings and functions. A conversationalists' haven, an open log fire is a recent addition. Up to six beers come from small local breweries, usually including a mild. No food is available, but customers may bring in takeaways. The secluded garden is delightful. Q

Old Vine

8 Great Minster Street, SO23 9HA (opp Cathedral Green)

11-11 (10.30 Sun)

(01962) 854616 oldvinewinchester.com

Ringwood Best Bitter; Taylor Landlord; guest beers H

Located in the heart of Winchester, with a vine growing up its front, this pub overlooks the Cathedral green. The contemporary yet cosy traditional bar area features an oak-beamed ceiling, artwork from a local design house, welcoming leather sofas and an extensive selection of games. A heavy curtain divides the pub from the award-winning restaurant, where home-cooked food made from local produce is served. Accommodation is available. Well-behaved dogs are welcome and a no-smoking partially-covered terrace is at the rear.

St James' Tavern

3 Romsey Road, SO22 5BE

12-midnight

(01962) 861288

Butcombe Bitter; Wadworth Henry IPA, 6X, JCB, Bishop's Tipple, seasonal beer H

Located on the steep Romsey Road, this pub was purpose built on a triangular site at the end of a Victorian terrace. The long bar has a raised extension, and the wooden panelling and fires create a cosy pub. This is matched by friendly service – the names of the staff are on a board behind the bar. An enterprising menu is available daily, except Sunday, when roast lunches rule. There is a pub quiz on Tuesday, and a quiz league on Wednesday night. Q

Wykeham Arms

75 Kingsgate Street, SO23 9PE (by entrances to Cathedral Close and college)

11-11; 12-10.30 Sun

(01962) 853834

Fuller's Chiswick, London Pride; Gale's HSB; guest beer H

Rambling Georgian inn dating from 1755 with many interlinked rooms, immediately outside the city's ancient Kingsgate. A vast array of memorabilia, much of it Nelsonian, crams every available space. The Wykeham features in many Guides as well as this one, and is frequently busy but always utterly civilised – a conversationalist's haven, away from 21st-century pressures. The guest beer may be another Fuller's seasonal. Advance booking is advised for meals at busy times. More than 20 wines are available by the glass. Accommodation is highly rated. Q

> Ah! My beloved brother of the rod, do you know the taste of beer – of bitter beer – cooled in the flowing river? Take your bottle of beer, sink it deep, deep in the shady water, where the cooling springs and fishes are. Then, the day being very hot and bright, and the sun blazing on your devoted head, consider it a matter of duty to have to fish that long, wide stream. An hour or so of good hammering will bring you to the end of it, and then – let me ask you avec impressement – how about that beer? Is it cool? Is it refreshing? Does it gurgle, gurgle and 'go down glug' as they say in Devonshire? Is it heavenly? Is it Paradise and all the Peris to boot? Ah! If you have never tasted beer under these or similar circumstance, you have, believe me, never tasted it at all.
>
> **Francis Francis**, By Lake and River, 16th century

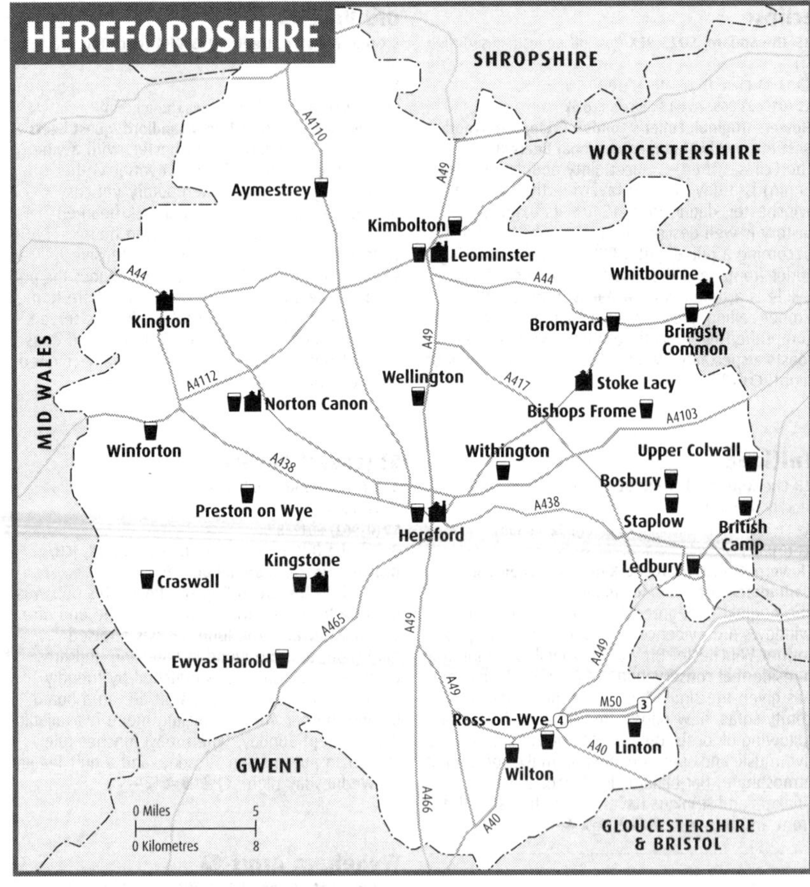

Aymestrey

Riverside Inn

HR6 9ST

11-3 (not Mon), 6-11; 12-3 Sun

(01568) 708440 theriversideinn.org

Wye Valley Bitter, HPA; Hobsons Best H

A well-established venue for evening and weekend diners with a large restaurant, the Riverside does not neglect drinkers with its comfortably furnished bar areas. An interesting menu of well-presented dishes using local meat and home-grown produce is available, with the accent on traditional English cuisine. Delightfully situated on the River Lugg, with its own mile of fishing rights.

Bishops Frome

Green Dragon

WR6 5BP

5 (4 Fri; 12 Sat)-11.30; 12-4, 7-11 Sun

(01885) 490607

Snowdonia Purple Moose; Taylor Golden Best; Theakston Best Bitter; Wye Valley Butty Bach; guest beers H

The quintessential 17th-century English country inn – it features low beams, a warren of flagstone-floored rooms and a real fire in every bar. Run with real verve and enthusiasm, a warm welcome and a bank of six handpumps greet the visitor. Continuing improvements include a new paved garden area. Steaks are the highlight of a limited but tasty evening menu (no food Sun). Herefordshire CAMRA Country Pub of the Year three years running, and joint Pub of the Year for 2008. Real cider is available in summer and two beer festivals are held each year.

Bosbury

Bell Inn

HR8 1PX

12-2.30 (not Mon & Tue), 6-11 (midnight Thu-Sat); 12-2.30, 7-10.30 Sun

(01531) 640285 thebellatbosbury.co.uk

Adnams Broadside; Hancocks HB; Taylor Landlord H

Two-bar, black and white timbered, terraced inn opposite the imposing village church whose bells give the place its name. A restaurant area serving

INDEPENDENT BREWERIES

Arrow Kington
Golden Valley Kingstone (NEW)
Mayfields Leominster
Shoes Norton Canon
Spinning Dog Hereford
Willoughby Whitbourne
Wye Valley Stoke Lacy

food (not Mon or Sun eve) contrasts with a basic yet comfortable public bar, with a grand fireplace, alcoves, books and newspapers. Friendly and welcoming, the pub lies at the heart of its community. A large garden features at the rear. Plenty of on-street parking is usually available. (417)

Bringsty Common

Live & Let Live

WR6 5UW (off A44 – at cat & mouse sign follow right-hand track down to common) SO699547

12-2.30, 5-11 (not Mon); 12-11 Sat; 12-10.30 Sun

(01886) 821462 liveandletlive-bringsty.co.uk

Beer range varies

With CAMRA help, Bringsty residents successfully saw off four planning applications to convert this 17th century Grade-II listed ex-cider house into a private dwelling. Finally, after 11 years of closure, the pub reopened in November 2007 serving three locally-brewed ales. Herefordshire's only thatched pub, it is accessed via a short track across the bracken-clad common. The owners have lovingly renovated the pub to a high standard – downstairs is much exposed timber, flagstone floors, settles and a fine fireplace with oak overmantle. Upstairs is the restaurant where diners enjoy excellent quality locally-sourced food including Bringsty lamb. Q(420)P

British Camp

Malvern Hills Hotel

Jubilee Drive, WR13 6DW (A449 and B4232 jct)

11-11

(01684) 540690 malvernhillshotel.co.uk

Beer range varies

Perched high on the Malvern Hills, this constantly-improving landmark hotel is run with a quiet passion, serving five local ales to the many drinkers who enjoy the atmosphere in the wood-panelled main bar. Popular with walkers for generations (the Herefordshire Beacon is nearby), dry dogs and children are welcome – the latter until 4.30pm. Two stylish restaurants with affordable dining complement a good range of bar meals. Plenty of outside seating. (244)P

Bromyard

Rose & Lion

5 New Road, HR7 4AJ

11-3, 5-11; 11-midnight Fri & Sat; 12-10.30 Sun

(01885) 482381

Wye Valley Bitter, HPA, Butty Bach; guest beer

Another from the successful Wye Valley stable – the Rosie was refurbished in a contemporary style in 2007 but retains the atmosphere of a traditional village pub moved into the town. It has always enjoyed a loyal local following, and is never anything but friendly. The three small original rooms are complemented by a further bar to the rear plus fully-equipped disabled toilets. A venue for live folk music on Sunday night, there is always a buzz about the place. Q

Craswall

Bull's Head ☆

HR2 0PN (on Longtown-Hay road) SO278360

12-11 summer; 12-3, 6.30-11 Wed-Sat winter; 12-3, 6.30-11 Sun

(01981) 510616 thebullsheadcraswall.co.uk

Wye Valley Bitter, Butty Bach

Remarkable and remote inn, perched on the foothills of the Black Mountains. This is one of the last unspoiled drovers' inns in England. Until 1998 it was in the same farming family for 125 years. Ancient stone steps lead into a main bar with settles, an old range, serving hatches and a fine stone floor. Food served in the adjacent dining room is pitched at the fine dining market, with a very limited budget offer for walkers. The Gwatkins Cider is a special blend. Q

Ewyas Harold

Dog Inn

HR2 0EX

10-midnight (1am Fri & Sat); 10-11 Sun

(01981) 240598 thedoginn.net

Beer range varies

A stone-built village inn dating from the early 16th century with a main bar plus games room and restaurant. Three ever-changing beers come from micro-breweries, mainly local. Home prepared and locally sourced meals are served in the restaurant, and snacks in the bar at lunchtime. Live music features from time to time, and a beer festival is held annually in the autumn. Two cricket teams and a football team have their social base here. Q(440)

Hereford

Barrels ✔

69 St Owen Street, HR1 2JQ

11-11.30 (midnight Fri & Sat)

(01432) 274968

Wye Valley Bitter, HPA, Butty Bach, DG Golden Ale; guest beers

Five times local CAMRA Pub of the Year, most recently in 2008, this pub enjoys a cult following. Four distinct rooms are based around a central bar servery – one room has a pool table, another a pull-down TV screen (strictly for major sports events) – otherwise banter and laughter rule. Popular with old and young alike, a stylish new bar now occupies the space where once Wye Valley Brewery brewed. The cobbled and decked courtyard is popular, and home to an annual charity beer and music festival held over the August bank holiday weekend.

Victory ✔

88 St Owen Street, HR1 2QD

3 (11 summer)-11 (midnight Fri & Sat); 12-11 Sun

(01432) 274998

Spinning Dog Hereford Original Bitter, Herefordshire Owd Bull, Celtic Gold, Mutley's Revenge; guest beers

Home to the Spinning Dog Brewery, most of the brewery's range is usually available, along with the most extensive range of cider and perry in Herefordshire. The main bar in the shape of a galleon dates back to a pirate-themed refurbishment in the late 1980s. Further back is a long and narrow rear seating area that incorporates a minstrels' gallery, pool table and skittle alley. The place buzzes when pub teams play at home or local bands gig, but it can be quiet at other times.

Kimbolton

Stockton Cross

HR6 0HD (on A4112, W of village)
12-3, 7-11 (not Mon); 12-3 Sun
(01568) 612509
Wye Valley HPA, Butty Bach; guest beer H
This single-bar, black and white pub dates from the 16th century and has some interesting features. Drinkers and diners mingle throughout the long narrow bar, with its two cosy alcoves set either side of the large fireplace. The interesting food, including a good vegetarian choice, is mainly sourced locally and freshly prepared. Regular events include an open mike night (second Wednesday of the month) and a curry and quiz night (last Wednesday). P

Kingstone

Bull Ring

HR2 9HE
12-3, 5.30-11; 11-11 Fri & Sat; 12-11 Sun
(01981) 252998
Golden Valley Bitter, Hop Stock and Barrel; guest beers H
Living proof that failing pubs can be turned round. Located on a crossroads at the centre of the village, this large, two-room, roadside pub is home to Herefordshire's newest brewery – Golden Valley Ales – in an outbuilding at the front. Noteworthy as you enter is the stained glass in the porch from the long-defunct Alton Court Brewery of Ross. The public bar has a pool table and there is a dining area in the lounge. Honest and simple food includes an excellent value curry night on Tuesday. Q (449) P

Ledbury

Prince of Wales ✔

Church Lane, HR8 1DL
11-11 (10.30 Sun)
(01531) 632250
Banks's Bitter; Sharp's Doom Bar; Wye Valley Butty Bach; guest beer H
Sixteenth century, timber-framed pub set in a cobbled alley leading up to the church. It has front and back bar areas with exposed timber, and a low-ceilinged alcove to one side. Always bustling with locals and visitors, it is first and foremost a community pub, with pub games teams and a folk jam session on Wednesday night. It stocks the best range of foreign beers in Herefordshire (draught and bottled), as well as Westons cider and perry. Bar meals are excellent value including very popular Sunday roasts.

Talbot Hotel

14 New Street, HR8 2DX
11-11 (midnight Fri & Sat)
(01531) 632963 visitledbury.co.uk/talbot
Wadworth IPA, 6X; Wye Valley Butty Bach; guest beer H
Outstanding, black and white, half-timbered building dating back to the 1590s, with direct links to the Civil War. The bar area was restored following a major fire in March 2009. Three comfortably furnished seating areas, with discreet corners for the drinker to hide away, are based around a central bar which boasts a splendid fireplace. The restaurant, with its fine wood panelling, offers affordable fine cuisine made with locally-sourced ingredients, but bar snacks are available too. Accommodation makes this a great venue for a short break.

Leominster

Bell Inn

39 Etnam Street, HR6 8AE
12-midnight
(01568) 612818
Greene King Abbot; Wye Valley Bitter, HPA, Butty Bach; guest beer H
A friendly pub with a single U-shaped bar and light and modern decor, plus a pleasant garden to the rear. Run by a young and enthusiastic licensee who enjoys his beer, the guest ale is from a national brewery. Live folk music features every Tuesday evening and a live band plays on Thursday evening. Reasonably priced home-made pub food is served at lunchtime.

Grape Vaults

2-4 Broad Street, HR6 8BS
11 (12 Sun)-11
(01568) 611404
Hobsons Best; Ludlow Gold; guest beers H
A welcome return to this Guide for a pub freed from its pubco beer tie. In days of yore this was a hard-core cider house, but today it offers a warm welcome in its two delightful small bars. The main bar area has a fireplace, bench seating and much original woodwork, and a small snug, tucked away to one side behind a part-glazed screen, is truly something to cherish. The pub has the smallest Gents in the county. Conventional English pub food is served at affordable prices. Live music plays on Sunday evening. Q

Linton

Alma Inn

HR9 7RY (off B4221, W of M50 jct 3) SO659255
12-3 (not Mon-Fri), 6.30 (6 Fri & Sat)-11; 12-3, 7-10.30 Sun
(01989) 720355
Butcombe Bitter; Oakham JHB; guest beer H
This pub explodes the myth that all country pubs have to sell food to survive – the Alma doesn't, and it has thrived for years. A CAMRA multi-award winner, it is run with true dedication and passion. A welcoming lounge, with real fire, and another wood-panelled room, contrast with the more basic pool room. A real beacon in the community, there is often something happening here – the highlight of the year is the Linton Blues & Ale Festival, held over the June solstice weekend. Q P

Norton Canon

Three Horseshoes

HR4 7BH (on A480)
12-3 (Wed & Sat only), 6-11; 12-3, 7-10.30 Sun
(01544) 318375
Shoes Norton Ale, Canon Bitter, Peploe's Tipple, Farriers Beer, Lin's Lager H
Isolated Herefordshire red-brick home of the Shoes Brewery. The timeless and relaxing, unspoilt interior includes a public bar leading through to a large pool room, contrasting with a small lounge, furnished with an ad hoc collection of comfortable sofas and chairs. A friendly landlord and locals ensure a great atmosphere.
Q (461,462) P

Preston on Wye

Yew Tree

HR2 9JT

⏲ 7-midnight (1am Fri & Sat); 12-3, 7-11 Sun

☎ (01981) 500359

Beer range varies Ⓖ

A basic and pleasantly eccentric village pub in the old mould, this is very much a drinkers' establishment. Comfortable and welcoming, it is popular with fishermen and canoeists from the nearby River Wye, as well as home to boules, pool and quiz teams. The beer, from local or regional breweries, is served direct from the cask behind the small bar, and draught Thatchers and Westons cider are also stocked. Evening meals are available in summer if ordered in advance. Live music plays monthly on Saturday. **⌂Q❀▲♣●P⁄**

Ross-on-Wye

Mail Rooms ✔

Gloucester Road, HR9 5BS

⏲ 9-midnight (1am Fri & Sat)

☎ (01989) 760920

Greene King Abbot; Marston's Pedigree; Ruddles Best Bitter; guest beers Ⓗ

The only clue that this Wetherspoon's conversion was once the town's main post office is its fine red-brick and stone facade. The modern bar area with vaulted ceiling and a rear conservatory has a light and airy feel. At night the place comes into its own – good design and decor combine with subtle lighting to create a genuinely intimate atmosphere. An eclectic range of guest beers, including some from local micros, is backed up by the usual good-value food. **Q❀◑♿⊟●⁄**

Staplow

Oak Inn

HR8 1NP (on B4214)

⏲ 12-3, 5.30 (7 Sun)-11

☎ (01531) 640954 🌐 oakinnstaplow.co.uk

Brakspear Oxford Gold; Wye Valley Bitter; guest beers Ⓗ

This roadside inn has been stylishly refurbished and is rapidly establishing a county-wide reputation for first class, affordable dining – without ignoring drinkers. The comfortable and modern main bar divides into two areas: one with sofas and low tables to relax and enjoy a drink, the other strictly for diners with an open kitchen. Booking is advisable for food, especially at weekends. **⌂Q❀◑♿⊟(417)P⁄**

Upper Colwall

Chase Inn

Chase Road, WR13 6DJ

⏲ 11.30-3, 5-11; 11.30-11 Sat; 12-10.30 Sun

☎ (01684) 540276

Batham Best Bitter; Hobsons Best Bitter; St George's Dragon's Blood; Wood Shropshire Lad; guest beers Ⓗ

Hidden away in a tranquil wooded backwater on the slopes of the Malvern Hills, this very traditional, long-standing free house is very much a locals' pub. The narrow L-shaped public bar is always buzzing and has much character, while a more genteel lounge is primarily focused on good affordable dining. The rear pub garden is a delight, with views out across Herefordshire on a clear day. Guest beers include a second beer from St George's. **Q❀◑⊟(675)♣●P⁄**

Wellington

Wellington Inn

HR4 8AT (½ mile W of A49)

⏲ 12-3 (not Mon), 6-11; 12-3, 7-10.30 (not winter eve) Sun

☎ (01432) 830367 🌐 wellingtonpub.co.uk

Hobsons Best Bitter; Wye Valley HPA, Butty Bach; guest beer Ⓗ

A thriving, traditional village inn which also serves fine food. The welcoming public bar complements a separate barn-style restaurant. Run by the Pub Chef of the Year 2008, food is a speciality, with bar snacks, an adventurous lunchtime and evening menu, and Sunday roasts. The bar has interesting local photographs, board games and newspapers. Guest beers are mainly from micro-breweries. A beer festival is held in July. **⌂❀◑⊟(492)●P⁄**

Wilton

White Lion ✔

Wilton Lane, HR9 6AQ (just off B4260)

⏲ 12-11 (10.30 Sun)

☎ (01989) 562785 🌐 whitelionross.co.uk

Brains Reverend James; Otter Ale; Wye Valley Bitter; guest beer Ⓗ

This pleasant riverside hostelry commands fine views across the River Wye to the town of Ross from its patio and garden. The 16th-century building has a single open-plan main bar area, complete with original beams, stonework and fireplace. Upstairs is a small restaurant – once part of a neighbouring prison house – serving traditional English recipes made with locally-sourced produce. Draught cider from Broome Farm is stocked. Canoe hire is available. **⌂❀◑▲⊟(38)♣●P⁄**

Winforton

Sun Inn

HR3 6EA (on A438)

⏲ 12-3, 6.30-11 (not Mon; not Mon & Tue winter); 12-4 Sun

☎ (01544) 327677

Taylor Landlord (summer); Wye Valley Butty Bach, Bitter Ⓗ

Roadside village inn with a single long bar room that divides into two areas: the larger end is for dining, the other end for drinking. White-painted walls contrast with sections of bare stone, giving a modern feel. Food ranges from sandwiches and snacks to an enterprising menu of home-prepared dishes, highly-commended in the Flavours of Herefordshire awards in 2007. **⌂❀◑P⁄**

Withington

Cross Keys

HR1 3NN (on A465 in Withington Marsh)

⏲ 5-11; 12-11 Sat; 12-4.30, 7-10.30 Sun

☎ (01432) 820616

Greene King Abbot; Wye Valley Butty Bach; guest beers Ⓗ

A traditional and straightforward village inn. Built of stone, it is blessed with original beams, basic bench seating, exposed stonework and real fires at both ends of a long and narrow bar. At the heart of an active community, there is a folk jam session held on the last Thursday of the month. **⌂Q❀▲⊟(420)♣P⁄**

HERTFORDSHIRE

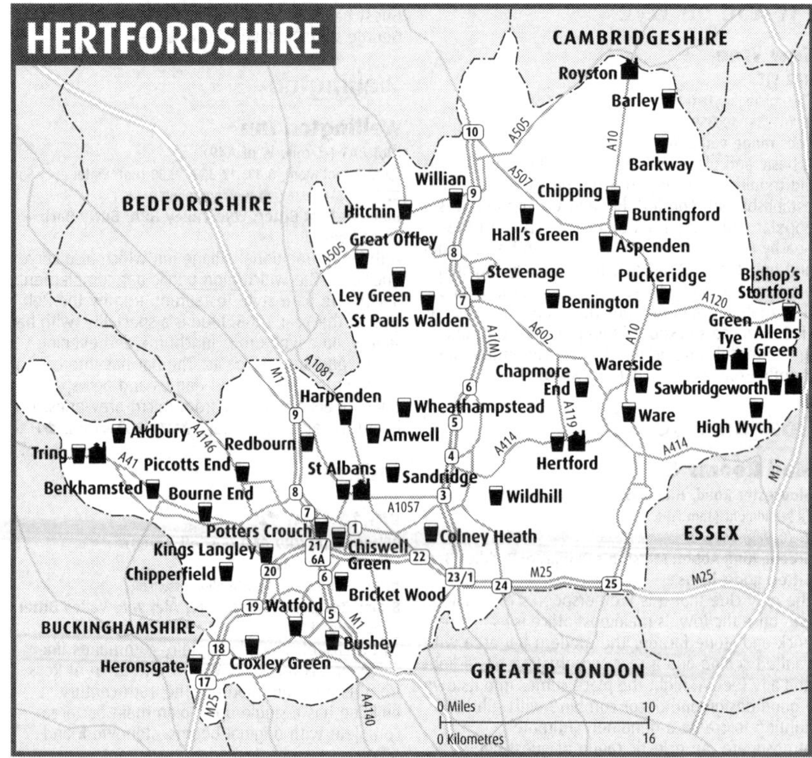

Aldbury

Valiant Trooper

Trooper Road, HP23 5RW (2 miles E of Tring)

11.30-11; 12-10.30 Sun

(01442) 851203 thevalianttrooper.co.uk

Brakspear Bitter; Fuller's London Pride; Tring Trooper, Jack O' Legs; guest beers H

This great Guide stalwart has gained even more appeal following a recent takeover. The new owner's enthusiasm is infectious, with six beers on offer taking pride of place. Food is an ever changing feast, from bar snacks to themed evenings in the separate restaurant. Every need is catered for, from champagne to dominoes, making the pub a haven for truly everyone, while keeping its olde worlde charm, set in a classic woodland village. Local CAMRA Pub of the Year 2009. Q (30,31,387) P

Allens Green

Queens Head

CM21 0LS TL455170

12-2.30 (not Mon & Tue), 5-11; 12-11 Sat; 12-10.30 Sun

(01279) 723393 shirevillageinns.co.uk

Fuller's London Pride H**; Mighty Oak Oscar Wilde,** G**; Maldon Gold** H**; guest beers** H/G

Small traditional village inn with a large garden, popular with locals, cyclists and walkers. Although the location is deeply rural, the pub is well worth seeking out. Hot snacks are always available unless the bar is very busy. Every third weekend of the month is for 'beer lovers', with up to seven local and unusual ales on offer. Beer festivals take place on most bank holidays. Q P

Amwell

Elephant & Castle

Amwell Lane, AL4 8EA TL167131

12-2.30, 5.30-11; 12-11 Sat; 12-10.30 Sun

(01582) 832175

Greene King IPA, H&H Bitter, Abbot; guest beer H

Welcoming and deservedly popular pub, dating from 1714, hidden away in a beautiful and peaceful setting. Two real fires warm the pub in colder weather and there is a 200-feet deep well in the back bar. With the added asset of two large gardens (one is for adults only), this is an excellent example of a successful country pub. Lunches are served daily and evening meals Tuesday-Saturday. The pub hosts Amwell Day – a local charity fundraising event – in June each year. P

Aspenden

Fox

SG9 9PD (off A10 SW of Buntingford) TL360282

12-3 (not Tue), 5.30-11; 12-6 Sun

(01763) 271886

Greene King XX Mild, IPA; guest beer H

A pretty two bar village pub with a large fireplace for the winter and a large garden for the summer. The pub has a petanque team and is home to the village cricket team. The uncommon Greene King XX Dark Mild is a regular beer, along with guests from the Greene King list. There is a beer festival, usually over the Whitsun weekend. Charity quiz nights and themed food evenings feature regularly. P

Barkway

Tally Ho

London Road, SG8 8EX TL383350
11.30-11; 12-3 Sun
(01763) 848389 tallyho-barkway.co.uk
Buntingford Highwayman IPA; Rebellion IPA; guest beers H
This friendly rural free house usually offers two real ales, sometimes three when demand picks up. Dark beers, mild and porters can often be found here. Bar snacks and home-made meals are available in the restaurant. The spirits menu has 58 whiskies, 11 gins and 9 rums. Look out for the large collection of cartoons, newspaper clippings and apocryphal stories. P

Barley

Chequers

London Road, SG8 8JQ TL395382
12-3, 5.30-midnight (6-midnight Fri & Sat); 12-11 Sun
(01763) 848378
Greene King IPA, Abbot; guest beers H
Dating back to 1811, this one bar village pub has an emphasis on food. The small restaurant and the larger bar are both used for dining but you are welcome to just come and enjoy a drink. Pub games, particularly petanque and darts, are popular. There are occasional beer festivals as well as family oriented and charity events.
(331)P

Benington

Lordship Arms

42 Whempstead Road, SG2 7BX TL307228
12-3, 6 (7 Sun)-11
(01438) 869665
Black Sheep Best Bitter; Crouch Vale Brewers Gold; guest beers H
Single bar pub situated at the southern end of the village. A very tidy bar is decorated with telephone memorabilia – even some of the handpumps are modelled on telephones. Good quality sandwiches and the like are available every lunchtime except Sunday. Wednesday evening curries and Sunday roasts are popular. The well maintained garden sports superb floral displays in the summer. A repeat winner of local and county CAMRA Pub of the Year. Q(384)P

Berkhamsted

Lamb

277 High Street, HP4 1AJ
11-11; 12-10.30 Sun
(01442) 862615
Adnams Bitter; Fuller's London Pride; Greene King IPA; Tring Ridgeway H
The two front doors of this traditional pub lead to a public bar and lounge, joined inside by an open doorway. A welcoming and friendly local, the emphasis is on drinking with generously portioned, good value meals served only at lunchtime Monday to Friday. There is a dartboard in the public bar, a small garden and dogs are welcome. This cosy hostelry is one of the few local outlets for Tring Ridgeway bitter. (500,501)

Bishop's Stortford

Castle

38 Castle Street, CM23 3TG
4.30 (12 Sat)-11; 12-10.30 Sun
(01279) 652578
St Austell Tribute; guest beers H
Family-run local, established in 1840. The public bar adjoins a cosy snug with wooden settles, bookshelves and a fireside cat. The south facing patio is inviting in fair weather. Bill, the landlord, is untied and offers two rotating beers alongside the Tribute. His home-made steak pie is a favourite on the menu, available Monday-Saturday evenings and weekend lunchtimes. This gem is hidden away in the old town and is well worth seeking out.
P

Half Moon

31 North Street, CM23 2LD
12-11 (midnight Wed-Sun)
(01279) 834500
Caledonian Deuchars IPA; Courage Directors; Wells Bombardier; guest beers H
Lively town-centre pub housed in a 16th-century building of genuine character. Up to six beers are offered, with a good balance between pale, amber and dark brews. An additional handpump serves Old Rosie cider. A good variety of sandwiches is available at lunchtime Monday-Saturday. There are three bars, a patio and a garden, plus a large function room for regular acoustic, blues and jazz music, as well as for hire.

Jolly Brewers

170 South Street, CM23 3BQ
12-1.30am (2am Fri; 1am Sat)
(01279) 836055
Greene King IPA; Taylor Landlord; guest beers H
At the southern edge of the town centre, the Jollies has a lively sports bar with a pool table and satellite TV, a contrastingly quiet lounge and a garden. There is usually a choice of four or five beers which may include ales from Black Sheep and Adnams. The pub has handy accommodation for Stansted Airport, serviced by the 24-hour 510 bus. The pub's name recalls that Stortford was once a brewing town – might history repeat itself one day? Q(308,333,510)

Bourne End

White Horse

London Road, HP1 2RH (½ mile from A41 jct) TL022063
11-11 (11.30 Fri & Sat); 12-10.30 Sun
(01442) 863888
McMullen AK, Country H
Large roadside hostelry that has been tastefully expanded with an open-plan bar and a large real fire. This old beamed inn has a relaxed cosy feel with corners to hide in. A rare McMullen's pub for

INDEPENDENT BREWERIES

Alehouse St Albans
Buntingford Royston
Green Tye Green Tye
McMullen Hertford
Old Cross Hertford (NEW)
Red Squirrel Hertford
Sawbridgeworth Sawbridgeworth
Tring Tring

the area, it makes the most of its two well-crafted beers, complemented by a varied food menu that is always available. A popular and always welcoming venue, customers obviously appreciate the care and attention as it has a very loyal regular clientele. (500)P

Bricket Wood

Black Boy

79 Old Watford Road, AL2 3RU TL122025
11-11 (12.30am Fri & Sat); 12.30-10.30 Sun
(01923) 672444
Black Sheep Best Bitter; Fuller's London Pride; guest beers H
Dating from 1751, this Grade II-listed building was extended in the 1930s. The bar area has original oak beams and a flagstone floor, with two seating areas at either end. It is a community pub with four football teams and a flourishing golf society. Outdoor drinking can be enjoyed in the sloping garden, which is set on three levels.
(321,724,757)P

Buntingford

Brambles

117 High Street, SG9 9AF TL360298
12-11 (10.30 Sun)
(01763) 273158
Buntingford Highwayman IPA; Fuller's London Pride; Gale's HSB; guest beers H
Brambles has two bars, both warmed by real fires, and eight handpumps dispensing the ales. Beers from local brewers Buntingford and Red Squirrel are usually available, with guests from Tring and Church End. The clientele is very varied, and can get exuberant at weekends. It's one of the few pubs in the area to use oversized glasses.
(331,700)P

Bushey

Swan

25 Park Road, WD23 3EE
11-11; 12-10.30 Sun
(020) 89502256
Black Sheep Best Bitter; Greene King Abbot; Jennings Cumberland Ale; Young's Bitter H
Genuine, cosy, one-bar local sited in a side street, full of character and characters. After a couple of years' hiatus, it now makes a welcome return to this Guide. Bar snacks are available all day. A quiz night is held every other Tuesday. Access to the rear garden (and ladies toilets) is via a side gate. No children under 14 are allowed in the bar.
(142,258)

Chapmore End

Woodman

30 Chapmore End, SG12 0HF TL328164
12-2.30 (not Mon), 5.30-11; 12-11 Sat & Sun
(01920) 463143 woodmanware.co.uk
Greene King IPA, Abbot G**; guest beers** H
Classic two-bar country pub in a quiet hamlet off the B158, popular with walkers. This small unspoilt gem has beer served direct from cooled casks in the cellar behind the public bar. Good home-made food is available, with traditional roasts in the winter. Evening meals (served up to 7.30pm) include a Taste of Britain themed menu on the fourth Thursday of the month. The large rear garden has a safe children's play area and petanque. Look out for beer and music festivals.
QP

Chipperfield

Royal Oak

1 The Street, WD4 9BH
12-3, 6-11 (7-10.30 Sun)
(01923) 266537
Adnams Broadside; Fuller's London Pride; Young's Bitter; guest beer H
Genuine street-corner local with public and saloon areas served by a central bar. The public bar has a real fire, local photographs, historic car pictures and a collection of matches and foreign currency. Some of the seating is upholstered beer casks; the tables are covered with beaten copper. The larger saloon is furnished with dark wood and brasses. Home-made lunches are served daily except Sunday. Children are welcome for meals, dogs at the landlord's discretion. Outside is a patio and there is a meeting room available by arrangement.
Q(R9,352)P

Chipping

Countryman

Ermine Street, SG9 0PG TL356319
12-11 Fri & Sat only; 12-10.30 Sun
(01763) 272721
Beer range varies H
Built in 1663 and a pub since 1760, the Countryman is a one bar split-level pub. The interior boasts some well executed carvings on the bar front, an impressive fireplace and some obscure agricultural implements. Just one real ale is usually available – the beer itself will vary, but tends to be brown and around 4-4.5%ABV. A second may be added during the summer months. Note the restricted opening hours.
Q(331)P

Chiswell Green

Three Hammers

210 Watford Road, AL2 3EA (on B4630) TL133045
12-11 (midnight Fri & Sat)
(01727) 846218
Fuller's London Pride; Taylor Landlord; Wadworth 6X; guest beers H
Well maintained 18th-century inn, originally a blacksmith's, with a contemporary interior and large garden, situated on the main Watford Road near the National Gardens of the Rose. Six real ales include five ever-changing guests. Meals are served 12-9pm every day. The pub hosts regular beer festivals and quiz nights on Sunday and Tuesday for a small cash prize. There is a bus stop outside and the pub is well placed for access to the M25, M1 and M10.
Q(321,621,724)P

Colney Heath

Cock

18 High Street, AL4 0NU TL206058
11-11; 12-3, 7-11 Sun
(01727) 822000
Greene King IPA; Tetley Bitter; Wadworth 6X; guest beers H

Run by the same family since 1962, this is a friendly community two bar pub built in 1822 and perfectly preserved. Several pictures of bygone days in the village adorn the walls of the lounge. There are ladies and gents darts teams and two dominoes teams. Situated by the common, the pub is popular with dog walkers and cyclists. The patio features award-winning floral displays. Lunches are available weekdays only. The small entrance lobby includes a hatch for off-sales. Q◖⊟⊞(304)♣P

Crooked Billet

88 High Street, AL4 0NP TL202060
✪ 11-2.30, 4.30-11; 11-11 Sat; 12-10.30 Sun
☎ (01727) 822128
Tring Side Pocket for a Toad; guest beers Ⓗ
Popular and friendly cottage-style village pub dating back over 200 years. A genuine free house, it stocks three or four guest beers from national, regional and micro-breweries. A wide selection of good value home-made food is served lunchtimes and Friday and Saturday evenings. Summer barbecues and Saturday events are held occasionally. This is a favourite stop-off for walkers on the many local footpaths. Families are welcome in the large garden where there is play equipment. Open all day Saturday in summer.
⛫♘❀◖◗⊟⊞(304)♣P⅟–

Croxley Green

Sportsman

2 Scots Hill, WD3 3AD (on A412 at jct with The Green)
✪ 12-11 (10.30 Sun)
☎ (01923) 443360 ⊕ croxleygreen.com/202.asp
Red Squirrel Conservation; Tring Side Pocket for a Toad; guest beers Ⓗ
Friendly and welcoming family-run pub which has been transformed by new management. The interior has been sensitively refurbished, with comfortable seating. Now firmly committed to real ale, the beer range has been extended to six handpumps and includes three varied guest beers. The LocAle scheme is actively supported and the house beer is brewed by Red Squirrel. Real cider is a new feature and bottled Belgian beers are available. Beer festivals are held and live music continues to be a major attraction at weekends.
❀◖⊖⊞(5,6)♣●P⅟–▯

Great Offley

Red Lion

Kings Walden Road, SG5 3DZ TL145266
✪ 12-midnight (10.30 Sun)
☎ (01462) 768281 ⊕ redlionoffley.co.uk
Fuller's London Pride; Young's Bitter; guest beers Ⓗ
Traditional country pub set in idyllic Hertfordshire countryside with a good reputation for food complementing the beer. A LocAle beer from Buntingford or Tring is usually available. Highlights of the varied food menu include fresh fish on Wednesday, exceptional chips made from locally grown potatoes, and the speciality Red Lion pancake, served in the conservatory restaurant. A large real fire warms the cosy main bar during the colder months. Friday evenings often feature live music. ⛫♘❀◖◗♣P⅟–

Green Tye

Prince of Wales

SG10 6JP TL443184
✪ 12-3, 5.30-11 (1am Fri); 12-11 Sat; 11.15-10.30 Sun
☎ (01279) 842517 ⊕ thepow.co.uk
Greene Tye Union Jack; Wadworth IPA; guest beers Ⓗ
Gary and Jenny welcome you to their traditional and friendly village local, whether you are a walker, cyclist, dog owner or just plain thirsty. Smaller East Anglian breweries are featured throughout the year, as well as the Green Tye Brewery, situated at the rear of the pub. Beer festivals are held on the May Day weekend and in September. Hearty sandwiches are available at lunchtime. Regular live folk and other musical events are staged. ⛫❀◖♿♣●P⅟–

Hall's Green

Rising Sun

SG4 7DR (2 miles SE of Weston via Maiden Street) TL275287
✪ 11-2.30 (not Mon), 6-11; 11-11 Sat; 12-10.30 Sun
☎ (01462) 790487
McMullen AK, Cask Ale, Country, seasonal beer Ⓗ
Traditional country pub in a small hamlet in the beautiful Hertfordshire countryside. A real fire in the winter and a large garden in the summer make it the ideal location for a pint of real ale all year round. The pub plays host to the local petanque league and classic car club. Good pub food is served in the conservatory and bar at lunchtime and in the evening Monday to Saturday and all day Sunday.
⛫Q♘❀◖◗⊟♿♣P⅟–

Harpenden

Carpenters Arms

14 Cravells Road, AL5 1BD TL144133
✪ 11-3, 5.30-11; 12-3, 7-10.30 Sun
☎ (01582) 460311
Adnams Bitter; Courage Best Bitter; Greene King Abbot; guest beers Ⓗ
Harpenden's smallest hostelry is cosy, comfortable and welcoming. No fruit machines, just good beer in a convivial and conversational atmosphere. Five real ales are available. The pub is beautifully furnished and an open fire warms the bar in colder weather. Occasional themed food nights are held throughout the year (booking essential). In summer barbecues are hosted outside on the secluded patio area. ⛫◖≹⊞(321,620)P⅟–

Cross Keys ✔

39 High Street, AL5 2SD (on Bowers Parade)
✪ 11-11 (1am Thu-Sat); 12-10.30 Sun
☎ (01582) 763989
Fuller's London Pride; Rebellion IPA; Taylor Landlord; guest beer Ⓗ
This two-bar pub has retained its traditional charm with a fine pewter bar top and flagstoned floors. The original oak-beamed ceiling has tankards from past and present customers hanging from it. In spring and summer enjoy your pint in the secluded, attractive rear garden and in autumn or winter savour your pint in front of the saloon bar's real fire. Traditional home-cooked lunches are served. From Thu-Sat 11pm is the last entry time, with bar open up until 1am. ⛫Q❀◖⊟≹⊞(321,620)♣

Heronsgate

Land of Liberty, Peace & Plenty 🏆

Long Lane, WD3 5BS TQ023949
⏲ 11-11 (midnight Fri & Sat); 12-11 Sun
☎ (01923) 282226 🌐 landoflibertypub.com
Red Squirrel Conservation Bitter; guest beers Ⓗ
Welcoming single-bar community pub popular with walkers, cyclists and real ale enthusiasts. It features six or more beers, typically from independent micro-breweries, cider, perry and Belgian bottled beers. There is a large garden and a covered pavilion (no children are allowed in the bar). Regular events include book, film and knitting clubs, beer tastings, quizzes, darts and pub games. Beer festivals are held and CAMRA's annual campaigning events supported. Tring Brock Bitter is badged as Liberty Ale. Regular CAMRA branch and county Pub of the Year and National runner-up in 2007. ⛰❀◑🚌(R4)♣●P⊟

Hertford

Old Barge ✔

2 The Folly, SG14 1QD TL326128
⏲ 11-11 (midnight Fri & Sat); 12-11 Sun
☎ (01992) 581871 🌐 theoldbarge.co.uk
Caledonian Deuchars IPA; Shepherd Neame Spitfire; Taylor Landlord; Woodforde's Wherry Best Bitter; guest beers Ⓗ
Pleasantly situated on Folly Island at the head of the Lee Navigation. Home-made food – the landlady's skillet meals are a speciality – is available every lunchtime and evening, with roasts on Sunday up to 4pm. Beer festivals are hosted in the spring and November, and quizzes on Sunday. The TV is restricted to rugby international matches and Wimbledon fortnight. There are quality jazz nights on the second and last Thursday of the month and film nights on the first Thursday. Watch the narrowboats and enjoy a pint.
⛰❀◑◐⇌(East/North)🚌♣●P⊱

Old Cross Tavern 🏆

8 St Andrew Street, SG14 1JA TL323126
⏲ 12 (4 Mon)-11; 12-10.30 Sun
☎ (01992) 583133
Dark Star Hophead; Fuller's London Pride; Old Cross Tavern Laugh n' Titter; Red Squirrel RSB; York Yorkshire Terrier; guest beers Ⓗ
Superb town free house offering a friendly welcome. Eight real ales, usually including a dark beer of some distinction, come from brewers large and small, with one from the pub's own micro-brewery. There is also a fine choice of Belgian bottle-conditioned beers. Beer festivals are held on the covered patio over the spring bank holiday and in October. No TV or music here, just good old-fashioned conversation. Filled rolls and home-made pies are available well into the evening.
⛰Q❀⇌(East/North)🚌♣

White Horse

33 Castle Street, SG14 1HH TL326124
⏲ 11-11 (midnight Fri & Sat); 12-10.30 Sun
☎ (01992) 501950
Adnams Bitter; Fuller's Chiswick, Discovery, London Pride, ESB; guest beers Ⓗ
Charming old timber-framed building with two downstairs bars and additional rooms upstairs, one for bar billiards, one for meetings and one where children are welcome. Guest beers come from small independent brewers. Beer festivals are usually held over the early May and August bank holiday weekends. Home-made lunches are served daily and Monday night features the renowned Gastronomic Tour, a set menu of worldwide dishes. Wednesday is pie and mash night. The TV is strictly for rugby international matches only. Dog friendly.
⛰Q⛀◑⊟⇌(East/North)🚌♣⊱

High Wych

Rising Sun 🏆

CM21 0HZ (2 miles SW of Sawbridgeworth) TL465142
⏲ 12-2.30, 5.30-11; 12-3, 6-11 Sat; 12-3, 7-10.30 Sun
☎ (01279) 724099
Courage Best Bitter; Mighty Oak Maldon Gold, Oscar Wilde; guest beers Ⓖ
A long-time entrant in the Guide, this small village pub has been recently refurbished. It has a stone floor in the main bar and a smaller side bar with a serving hatch. Popular with walkers and friendly locals, it holds monthly quizzes and an annual vegetable competition. There is even a deep sea angling club. Parking is in the village car park across the road. Q❀♣●⊱

Hitchin

Half Moon 🏆

57 Queen Street, SG4 9TZ TL186288
⏲ 12-2.30, 6-midnight; 12-1am Fri & Sat; 12-11 Sun
☎ (01462) 452448
Adnams Bitter; Young's Special; guest beers Ⓗ
Thriving one-bar pub dating back to 1748 and once owned by Hitchin brewer W&S Lucas. It offers two regular beers and up to four guests, often from local breweries. Two ciders and a perry are also available plus a good choice of wines. Twice yearly beer festivals, one with a Nelson theme, are hosted. Home-prepared food is available (not Tue eve). Monthly quiz nights and curry nights are popular. Winner of CAMRA North Hertfordshire Community Pub of the Year 2007 and branch Pub of the Year 2009. ⛰⛀❀◑◐⇌♣P

Nightingale

Nightingale Road, SG5 1RL TL192293
⏲ 12-midnight (10.30 Sun)
☎ (01462) 457448
Nethergate Old Growler, Umbel Magna; Tring Colley's Dog; guest beers Ⓗ
This friendly pub is around 150 years old and reputed to have three ghosts. It was formerly owned by Fordhams of Ashwell, whose name is set into the exterior stonework. The interior is open plan but retains the layout of the original rooms, with distinct seating areas. Five beers are on offer from Nethergate, Tring and Wychwood, usually including a porter or a mild. Traditional entertainment includes darts, pool and board games. Sport is occasionally shown on the four TV screens. ⛀❀◑◐⇌♣P⊱

Kings Langley

Saracens Head

47 High Street, WD4 9HU
⏲ 11-2.30, 5-11.30; 12-4, 7-10.30 Sun
☎ (01923) 400144
Fuller's London Pride, ESB; Tring Ridgeway; guest beer Ⓗ
Early 17th-century community-oriented pub proud of its status as a regular in the Guide and popular

with a mixed clientele. The single room interior has a collection of Saracens' heads, old beer bottles, pottery jugs, bottles and old telephones on display. The landlord often wins 'In Bloom' prizes for his hanging baskets. Food is only available at lunchtime Monday-Saturday. There are pavement benches for roadside drinking and smoking. No facilities for children. ⛺❀◑🚌(500,501)P⚡

Ley Green

Plough

Plough Lane, SG4 8LA TL162243
4 (12 Wed & Thu)-11; 12-midnight Fri & Sat; 12-10.30 Sun
☎ (01438) 871394
Greene King IPA, Abbot; guest beer H

An ale house as far back as 1846, this friendly traditional pub in rolling farming country is a popular stop-off for walkers and cyclists. The large patio has idyllic views of the countryside – look out for the red kites. Join in the acoustic music sessions on Tuesday evenings. Hot and cold snacks, with real chips, are served Wednesday to Sunday lunchtimes. The snug bar is available for small functions. ⛺Q❀◑🚌(88)♣P⚡

Piccotts End

Boars Head

HP1 3AT
12-midnight
☎ (01442) 240084
Fuller's London Pride; Tring Side Pocket for a Toad, seasonal beers H

Friendly single bar pub on the outskirts of Hemel Hempstead old town. It has three distinct areas for drinking and dining – two of these are formed by a double-sided open fireplace. English and Thai food is available. A small TV, dartboard, chess and a mixture of board games along with live music, quizzes and themed nights provide entertainment. There are roadside benches and a large rear garden overlooking the Gade Valley for alfresco drinking. ⛺❀◑🚌(30,X31,327)♣P

Potters Crouch

Holly Bush ✔

Bedmond Lane, AL2 3NN (at jct of Potters Crouch Lane and Ragged Hall Lane off B4630 or A4147) TL116052
12-2.30, 6-11
☎ (01727) 851792 theh ollybushpub.co.uk
Fuller's Chiswick, London Pride, ESB, seasonal beers H

An attractive early 18th-century pub in rural surroundings beautifully and tastefully furnished to a high standard and boasting large oak tables and period chairs. Spotless throughout, there are no jukeboxes, slot machines or TVs to disturb the drinker in any of the three drinking areas. The food menu is not extensive but is of high quality. The garden is ideal in summer – children are welcome in the garden only. ⛺Q❀◑🚌(300,301)P⚡

Puckeridge

Crown & Falcon

33 High Street, SG11 1RN TL386233
12-3, 5.30-11 (midnight Fri); 12-4, 6.30-midnight Sat; 12-5, 7-11 Sun
☎ (01920) 821561 crown-falcon.demon.co.uk
Adnams Bitter; McMullen AK; guest beers H

A public house since 1530, the Crown part of the name was adopted much later from another pub in the village. Changes to the interior layout can be traced on plans displayed in the bar – it is now one large open plan room with a separate restaurant. A collection of Allied Breweries memorabilia is on display. Darts is popular. The Falcon is mentioned in Samuel Pepys' diary of 1662 – he bought the landlord's shoes for four shillings. ⛺❀◑🚌(331,700)♣P⚡

Redbourn

Cricketers

East Common, AL3 7ND TL104119
12-11 (midnight Fri & Sat); 12-10.30 Sun
☎ (01582) 620612 thecricketersofredbourn.com
Fuller's London Pride; Greene King IPA; guest beers H

Attractive and recently refurbished pub dating from 1725, overlooking the common and historic cricket pitch established in the 18th century. A true free house, it offers up to four real ales. The pub has a 60-seater dining area serving top class food freshly prepared with the finest ingredients. ❀◑P⚡

St Albans

Cross Keys ✔

2a Chequer Street, AL1 3XZ TL148072
9-11.30 (midnight Sun)
☎ (01727) 839917
Greene King IPA, Abbot; Marston's Pedigree; guest beers H

A Wetherspoon's conversion of an old Army recruitment office close to the city centre. The pub features local history panels and old photographs of pub scenes in St Albans. There are regular guest ales from local brewers Alehouse, Tring and Potton, and keen participation in company beer festivals. Three themed food events are held weekly – grill, curry and Sunday club – alongside the standard menu. Cider is Weston's Old Rosie and Vintage on handpump, and Weston's scrumpy from polycask in the fridge. ◑♿⇌(Abbey/City)

Farmers Boy

134 London Road, AL1 1PQ
12-11 (midnight Wed & Thu, 2am Fri & Sat)
☎ (01727) 860535 farmersboy.net
Alehouse Clipper IPA, Farmers Joy; Fuller's London Pride; Taylor Landlord; guest beer H

Cosy, cottage-style pub, home of the Alehouse (formerly Verulam) Brewery, which has continued to brew following a change of management. The food menu has been extended with home-made meals available every day – the home-cut chips are renowned. Music plays every Thursday night with open mike on the first Sunday of the month. One guest ale is on offer plus a selection of Belgian bottled beers. The recently renovated pub sign features the licensee's son as the 'farmer's boy'. ❀◑⇌(City)♣⚡

Farriers Arms

32-34 Lower Dagnall Street, AL3 4PT (off A5183 Verulam Road)
12-2.30 (not Mon), 5.30-11, 12-11 Sat; 12-10.30 Sun
☎ (01727) 851025
McMullen AK, Cask Ale, Country H

Originally a grocer's and butcher's shop, the building became a pub in the 1920s and is now a classic back-street local. It is the only pub in the city never to have forsaken real ale. A plaque on the wall outside marks the first meeting of the Hertfordshire branch of CAMRA. Both bars are free of gaming machines but there is a TV for sports, and darts and cards are played. Dog friendly, with Wi-Fi access and outside toilets. Parking nearby can be difficult. ◑⊟≡(Abbey)♣⁵–

Goat Inn

37 Sopwell Lane, AL1 1RN (off Holywell Hill)

12-3, 5-11 Mon; 12-11 Tue-Thu & Sun; 12-midnight Fri & Sat

☎ (01727) 833934 goatinn.co.uk

St Austell Tribute; guest beers Ⓗ

Welcoming, traditional 15th-century pub, a short walk from the cathedral. Situated on the old coaching route from London, it still retains the old carriage arch. Food is served in a dining area at the back – the pub won third prize in the St Albans Restaurant of the Year competition in 2008. Weston's Old Rosie cider is available. Jazz plays on Sunday afternoon and quiz night is Sunday. Bar billiards, dominoes, shove ha'penny and board games are all played here. Families are welcome. ❀◑≡(Abbey/City)🚌(city centre)♣⁵–

Mermaid ✔

98 Hatfield Road, AL1 3RL

12-11 Mon, Tue & Thu; 12-midnight Wed, Fri & Sat; 12-10.30 Sun

☎ (01727) 837758 mermaidalehouse.com

Alehouse Sauvin So Good; Dark Star Hophead; guest beers Ⓗ

Friendly cottage-style pub, a short walk from the city centre, with a community focus. A backgammon group, darts team and three football teams are based here. Live music plays every Saturday. Well presented interesting guest beers are sourced from micro- and small regional breweries, and four regular beer festivals are held. The licensee also runs the local Alehouse Brewery. For wheelchair users there is step free access from the car park and level access to both toilets. ◑≡(City)🚌♣P

Six Bells

16-18 St Michaels Street, AL3 4SH

12-11 (11.30 Fri & Sat); 12-10.30 Sun

☎ (01727) 856945 the-six-bells.com

Black Sheep Best Bitter; Caledonian Deuchars IPA; Fuller's London Pride; Greene King Abbot; Taylor Landlord Ⓗ

Sixteenth-century pub within walking distance of the town centre and cathedral. The only licensed premises within the walls of Roman Verulamium, the park and museum are close by. Five regular beers are served in lined glasses – it is the only pub in St Albans to do so. Food is served lunchtimes and evenings (not Sun) – Monday is fish and chip night. Occasional quiz nights are hosted on Sunday and live music features at this popular friendly pub. ◑🚌(300,301)♣P⁵–

White Hart Tap

4 Keyfield Terrace, AL1 1QJ

12-11

☎ (01727) 860974

Caledonian Deuchars IPA; Fuller's London Pride; guest beers Ⓗ

Welcoming one-bar back-street local which features guest beers from the Punch Taverns range. Good value, home-made food is served every lunchtime and Tuesday-Friday evenings, with fish and chips on Friday, international food night on Thursday and roasts on Sunday. Quiz night is Wednesday. Occasional live music plays on Saturday night. There is a heated, covered smoking area outside and a public car park opposite. Dogs are welcome and Wi-Fi access is available. ❀◑≡(Abbey)⁵–

White Lion

91 Sopwell Lane, AL1 1RN (off Holywell Hill)

12-11

☎ (01727) 850540 thewhitelionph.co.uk

Black Sheep Best Bitter; Young's Special; guest beers Ⓗ

South Herts CAMRA Pub Of The Year in 2006, and St Albans winner for the last three years, this is a traditional two-bar pub close to the Abbey. Seven handpumps dispense two regular and five guest beers from the Punch Taverns Finest Cask range. Weston's Old Rosie cider is available occasionally. The beer garden has a smokers' area, barbecue and petanque piste. High quality home-made food is served daily. Live bands play on Tuesday, folk music on Wednesday and there is a beer festival in August. Wi-Fi access available. Q❀◑≡(Abbey/City)🚌(320,321,724)♣⁵–

St Pauls Walden

Strathmore Arms

London Road, SG4 8BT TL193222

6-11 Mon; 12-2, 5-11 Tue-Thu; 12-11 Fri & Sat; 12-10.30 Sun

☎ (01438) 871654

Buntingford Golden Plover; Fuller's London Pride; guest beers Ⓗ

Situated on the Bowes-Lyon estate, this rural pub is divided into drinking, dining and games areas. The pub does a lot of fundraising and was North Hertfordshire's Community Pub of the Year 2006. A beer ticker's paradise, it offers a constantly changing choice of beers supplemented by regular beer festivals. A range of foreign bottled beers, particularly Belgian, is also stocked. A past winner of CAMRA Hertfordshire Pub of the Year. Q❀◑⊟🚌(304)♣P

Sandridge

Green Man

31 High Street, AL4 9DD TL169104

11-3, 5.30-11; 11-midnight Fri & Sat; 12-11 Sun

☎ (01727) 854845

Greene King IPA, Ⓗ**; Abbot; Tetley Dark Mild** Ⓖ**; guest beer** Ⓗ

Now a regular GBG entry, this classic Victorian red-brick pub is located in the middle of the High Street. This locals' pub extends a warm welcome to all discerning ale drinkers, with the landlord now in his 23rd year of residence. Up to five real ales are available, four served straight from the cask from a separate cellar area located nearby at floor level, so don't be surprised if your server disappears briefly. Q❀◑⊟🚌(304,620)♣P

Sawbridgeworth

Gate

81 London Road, CM21 9JJ

11.30-2.30, 5.30-11; 11.30-11 Fri & Sat; 12-11 Sun

☎ (01279) 722313

Rebellion IPA Ⓗ**; guest beers** Ⓗ/Ⓖ

Unspoilt beer drinkers' pub with pump clips adorning the beams. It is home to several sports teams and the Real Ale Club of Sawbridgeworth. The loyal regulars enjoy a changing range of countrywide ales and the small brewery at the back provides an occasional house beer. Large beer festivals are held on the Easter and August bank holidays. Local CAMRA Pub of the Year 2007. ❀◐⇌🚌(333,510)♣🍎P⚟

Stevenage

Marquis of Lorne

132 High Street, SG1 3DB TL234249

⏲ 12-11 (10.30 Sun)

☎ (01438) 223928

Greene King XX Mild, IPA, Old Speckled Hen, Abbot Ⓗ

Although located on the Stevenage old town High Street, this pub feels like a very friendly local, with a warm welcome for all. The pub is home to three darts teams, a football team and cribbage teams during the summer. Every Sunday the pub hosts a meat raffle and a buffet is laid on by the landlord. There is a covered patio/smoking area at the rear and a large patio and seating area at the front. ♿⇌♣⚟

Our Mutual Friend

Broadwater Crescent, SG2 8EH TL249226

⏲ 12-11 (11.30 Fri & Sat); 12-3, 8-11 Sun

☎ (01438) 312282

Beer range varies Ⓗ

Discerning real ale enthusiasts from far and wide come to sample the seven ever-changing cask beers available at this thriving community pub on the edge of Stevenage. It has appeared in every issue of the Guide since the current licensee took over in 2002. Real cider, perry plus some Belgian bottled beers complement the real ale. A regular beer festival brightens up January. Winner of many local CAMRA awards including Pub of the Year 2006/07/08. Q◐♣P

Tring

King's Arms

King Street, HP23 6BE

⏲ 12-2.30 (3 Fri), 7-11; 11.30-3, 7-11 Sat; 12-4, 7-10.30 Sun

☎ (01442) 823318

Wadworth 6X; guest beers Ⓗ

This 1830s back-street local is ever popular with all age groups. The striking fuchsia pink building is a former local and regional CAMRA Pub of the Year and a regular Guide entry. Run by the same licensees for 28 years, it offers an ever-changing range of five real ales. Two real fires are welcoming in winter, and outside is a secluded heated patio with canopies. Home-cooked food is based on an imaginative international menu. Children are welcome at all times. ⛰Q❀◐◑🚌(61,500,501)🍎⚟

Robin Hood ✔

1 Brook Street, HP23 5ED (jct B4635/B486)

⏲ 11.30-3, 5.30-11 (11.30 Fri); 12-4, 6-11.30 Sat; 12-4, 7-11 Sun

☎ (01442) 824912 🌐 therobinhoodtring.co.uk

Fuller's Chiswick, Discovery, London Pride, ESB, seasonal beers; guest beer Ⓗ

Olde-worlde, end of town pub with a split-level bar and a warming stove giving the place a cosy and characterful feel. A busy pub with a popular patio courtyard for extra drinking space. One of Fuller's flagship outlets, it serves good food with a fish bias and offers six beers to a mixed clientele. A quiz is held on Wednesday in aid of a local charity. The enthusiastic landlords demonstate a dedication to good beer and food. Local CAMRA Pub of the Year 2008. ⛰◐◑♿🚌(61,500,501)♣⚟

Ware

Crooked Billet

140 Musley Hill, SG12 7NL TL362150

⏲ 12-2.30 (Tue & Fri), 5.30-11.30 (midnight Fri); 12-11.30 Sun

☎ (01920) 462516

Beer range varies Ⓗ

This justifiably popular local is well worth tracking down. There are two bars – one cosy and relaxed, the other more lively with pool and TV sport. The landlord is a staunch Carlisle United supporter so stray Carlisle fans can expect the red carpet treatment. With an ever-changing range of cask ales, this is a rare outlet for dark mild during the cooler months, and additional beers are sometimes drawn direct from the cellar. Bar snacks are available at weekends. ⛰♿⇌🚌(395)♣⚟

Worppell ✔

35 Watton Road, SG12 0AD TL353147

⏲ 12-2.30, 5-11; 12-midnight Fri & Sat; 12-10 Sun

☎ (01920) 411666

Greene King IPA, Abbot; guest beers Ⓗ

Hertfordshire's longest-serving landlords are now in their 26th year at the Worppell – named after the man who built the pub in the 19th century. The pub is a much-loved and comfortable single bar local where conversation and banter are the name of the day. The regulars recognise the quality of the beer, while an occasional guest ale comes from the Greene King stable. Food is served lunchtimes Monday to Friday only. Sunday is often busy with football on TV. ◐⇌♣

Wareside

Chequers

SG12 7QY (on B1004) TL394157

⏲ 12-3, 6-11; 12-4, 6-10.30 Sun

☎ (01920) 467010

Adnams Bitter; Taylor Landlord; guest beers Ⓗ

Dating from the 15th century, this traditional free house was originally a coaching inn. It has been run by the same family for 14 years. One guest beer is usually from a small brewery. The interior has three distinct bar areas plus a restaurant. There are no machines or music and a ban on swearing. All food is home-made, with vegetarian options. A good base for a country ramble; walkers and cyclists are welcome. ⛰Q❀🛏◐◑♿🚌(M3,M4)P⚟

Watford

Estcourt Arms ✔

2 St Johns Road, WD17 1PT (on jct with Woodford Rd)

⏲ 10-11.30 (midnight Fri & Sat); 10-10.30 Sun

☎ (01923) 220754

Adnams Bitter; Fuller's London Pride; guest beer Ⓗ

A small, friendly, two bar, back-street town pub. There is a paved seated area at the front of the pub. It hosts traditional Irish music on a Sunday evening when the pub can get very busy. It is known locally as Lynch's after the present tenants who have been at the pub since 1978. Food is available at lunchtime, Monday to Friday, 12-2.30pm, and on Monday to Thursday evenings 5.30-8pm. ❀◑◐⇌(Junction)🚌

One Crown

156 High Street, WD17 2EN
⏲ 12-11 (12.30am Fri & Sat); 12-10 Sun
☎ (01923) 222626
Tring Jack O' Legs; guest beers 🄷
The oldest licensed pub in Watford, dating from the 16th century. The interior divides into several areas, one with a pool table and dartboard. There is a patio with seating behind the pub. The clientele is a mixture of locals, visitors to the town centre and after-work business people. The guest beers are often seasonal beers from Tring Brewery and change on a monthly basis. Sandwiches and light meals are available at lunchtime on weekdays. ❀◑⇌(High Street)🚌♣P⚐

Southern Cross ✔

41-43 Langley Road, WD17 4PP
⏲ 11-11 (11.30 Thu-Sat); 12-10.30 Sun
☎ (01923) 256033
Adnams Broadside; Caledonian Deuchars IPA; Wells Bombardier; guest beers 🄷
Well-located, large, open-plan pub with a central bar and comfortable seating areas. Food from an extensive menu (look for the specials board) is served up to 9pm. The present managers have now served up more than 1000 different beers since they took over – three guest beers from the Beer Seller list are usually on handpump. A general knowledge quiz takes place on Thursday and Saturday evenings and there are board games available. No children under 14 are allowed in the bar. ❀⊏◑◐♿⇌(Junction)🚌♣P⚐

West Herts Sports Club

8 Park Avenue, WD18 7HP (off Rickmansworth Road)
⏲ 4-11; 12-11 Fri & Sat; 12-10.30 Sun
☎ (01923) 229239 🌐 westhertssports.co.uk
Fuller's London Pride; Young's Bitter; guest beers 🄷
Former CAMRA Club of the Year located on the site of Watford FC's original ground. The clubhouse has a spacious modern bar with large windows overlooking the sports field. Up to three guest beers are on offer, with oversized glasses reserved for real ale. The function room has hosted the CAMRA Watford Beer Festival for the past 14 years and is available for hire. Non-members of the club can visit up to three times a year – show a current CAMRA membership card or a copy of this Guide for entry. ❀♿⊖♣P⚐🥛

Wheathampstead

Swan ✔

56 High Street, AL4 8AR TL177139
⏲ 11-11 (midnight Fri & Sat); 12-10.30 Sun
☎ (01582) 833110
Greene King IPA; St Austell Tribute; guest beers 🄷
An old village inn dating from 1744 with exposed beams and three fireplaces including an inglenook. This community village pub has wide appeal with entertainment including live bands and a quiz on Wednesday evening hosted by the landlord. The upper bar has Sky TV and a dartboard, the lower bar is quieter for lunches and drinking in the evening. There is a pool room to the rear. A beer festival with a good choice of ale and cider is held in the autumn in the car park behind the pub. ♨◑♿🚌(304,366,620)♣P⚐🥛

Wildhill

Woodman

45 Wildhill Road, AL9 6EA (between A1000 and B158) TL264068
⏲ 11.30-2.30, 5.30-11; 12-2.30, 7-10.30 Sun
☎ (01707) 642618
Greene King IPA, Abbot; McMullen AK; guest beers 🄷
Small, friendly village pub with a strong community focus. Three regular and three guest beers are on handpump, with at least one from a Herts brewery. Lined glasses are available on request. Good pub grub is served at lunchtime (no food Sun). The large garden is ideal in summer. Saracens fans get the red carpet treatment – the landlord is a keen supporter. The pub has won numerous awards including local CAMRA Pub of the Year a record seven times. An all-round superb boozer! ⛺♨❀◑⇌♣P⚐🥛

Willian

Fox

Baldock Lane, SG6 2AE TL224306
☎ (01462) 480233 🌐 foxatwillian.co.uk
Adnams Bitter; Fuller's London Pride; Woodforde's Wherry Best Bitter; guest beer 🄷
Built in 1860, this village free house enjoys a pleasant location beside the main street. Extensively refurbished in 2004, the single room interior is now light and airy with a restaurant area to the rear. The ethos of the pub is to serve good beer, wine and food to a discerning clientele. Seafood is a speciality on the menu and freshly made bar food is available Monday to Saturday lunchtimes. ❀◑◐♿⇌P

Cask breathers

Where an entry states that some beers in a pub are served with the aid of cask breathers, this means that demand valves are connected to both casks and cylinders of gas. As beer is drawn off, it is replaced by applied gas (either carbon dioxide, nitrogen or both) to prevent oxidation. The method is not acceptable to CAMRA as it does not allow beer to condition and mature naturally. The Campaign believes brewers and publicans should use the size of casks best suited to the turnover of beer in order to avoid oxidation. If a pub in the Good Beer Guide uses cask breathers, we list only those beers that are free of the device.

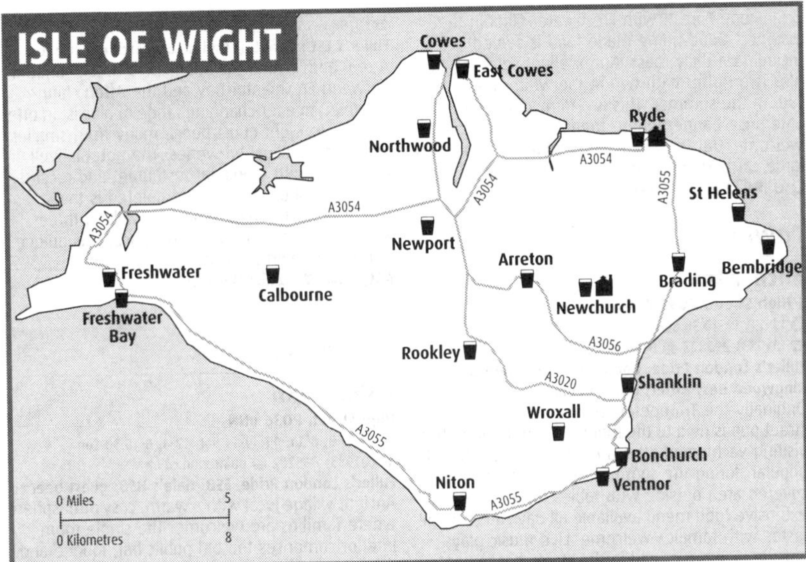

Arreton

White Lion

Main Road, PO30 3AA

11-11; 12-10.30 Sun

(01983) 528479

Timothy Taylor Landlord; guest beers H

A lovely old country pub a stone's throw from St George's 11th-century church and still managing to maintain much character and charm. Beamed ceilings and interesting brassware complement the assortment of old signs and bric-a-brac. The pub has a fine reputation for food with an interesting specials board and a popular curry night on Wednesday. One of the two guest beers is usually local. Families are welcome and there is a quiz every fortnight in winter. Q (8)P

Bembridge

Olde Village Inn

61 High Street, PO35 5SF

11 (12 Sun)-11

(01983) 872616

Draught Bass; Greene King IPA, Abbot H

Comfortable village local with a warm, friendly atmosphere. The one-bar interior is expansive but cosy. Live music plays on occasional Fridays with a popular quiz the first Saturday in the month. Older people can enjoy lunchtime meals at reduced prices Monday to Friday. There are two letting rooms, a patio to the rear and a petanque terraine. (10,14) P

Bonchurch

Bonchurch Inn

The Shute, PO38 1NU (off Shanklin-Ventnor road)

11-3, 6.30-11; 12-3, 7-10.30 Sun

(01983) 852611 bonchurch-inn.co.uk

Courage Best Bitter, Directors; guest beer G

Superbly preserved stone pub in a Dickensian courtyard, formerly the stables of the adjacent manor house. Little has changed since it gained its licence in the 1840s, making this one of the most unspoilt pubs on the Island. As well as featuring in an episode of The Detectives, the pub displays mementoes and keepsakes from many famous names who have popped in. The fine menu reflects an Italian influence and all dishes are cooked to order. Up to two Greene King Ruddles beers are occasional summer guests. Q

Brading

Yarbridge Inn

Yarbridge, PO36 0AA (on the main Brading-Sandown road)

11-11.30; 12-11 (12-3, 5-11 winter) Sun

(01983) 406212 yarbridgeinn.co.uk

Ringwood Best Bitter; guest beers H

Previously known as the Anglers, this is a pleasant single bar pub with a changing range of nine beers, often from obscure, hard to find breweries. The dining area offers a fixed menu plus specials board and a choice of roasts on Sunday. Outside is a safe area for children and a paved area with parasols. Filled with railway memorabilia, the pub has its own model train and the Brading to Sandown line at the bottom of the garden. Live music is hosted occasionally. CAMRA Isle of Wight Pub of the Year 2006/07/08, it was also runner up in the Wessex region for the last two years.
Q (2,3) P

Calbourne

Sun Inn

Sun Hill, PO30 4JA (at Calbourne crossroads)

11-midnight

(01983) 531231 sun-calbourne.co.uk

Beer range varies H

Friendly village pub with a traditional public bar, enjoying splendid views of Westover and

INDEPENDENT BREWERIES

Goddards Ryde
Stumpy's Newchurch
Yates' Newchurch

Brighstone Forest, with Freshwater Cliffs in the distance. Good home-made food is served including a daily roast. An excellent selection of ales is on offer with two in the winter and up to four in the summer. This is a family pub under the Enterprise banner where friendly dogs are welcome. Outside is a garden and patio with a very large car park. Occasional live music plays.
Q❀◑⊟Ă🚌(7,11)♣P

Cowes

Anchor Inn

1 High Street, PO31 7SA
✪ 11-11; 12-10.30 Sun
☎ (01983) 292823 🌐 theanchorcowes.com
Fuller's London Pride; Goddards Fuggle-Dee-Dum; Ringwood Best Bitter; guest beers Ⓗ
Originally the Trumpeters back in 1704, this high-street pub is next to the marina and ferry, tempting visiting yachtsmen after a hard day at sea. Hugely popular during the summer months, it has a covered area outside with tables for smokers. An extensive food menu available all day caters for all tastes with families welcome. Live music plays outside in summer and in the stable bar in winter. Room-only accommodation comprises seven comfortable rooms. ⛫❀🛏◑🚌(1)♣⚐

East Cowes

Ship & Castle

21 Castle Street, PO32 6RB (opp Red Funnel Terminal)
✪ 11 (12 Sun)-midnight
☎ (01983) 290522
St Austell Dartmoor Best; guest beer Ⓗ
Adorned with seafaring memorabilia, the Ship & Castle is just how street-corner pubs used to be – and very cosy in the winter when the wind whistles across the Red Funnel car park. Easy to find – turn left off the floating bridge or once around the block if arriving from Southampton. Despite the small bar there are always at least three beers on offer. Bustling on games nights, four darts teams and Sky TV keeps the locals happy.
❀🚌(4,5)♣⚐▯

Freshwater

Prince of Wales

Princes Road, PO40 9ED
✪ 3-11; 11-11.30 Fri & Sat; 12-11 Sun
☎ (01983) 753535
Greene King XX Mild, IPA, Abbot; Wells Bombardier; Yates Best Bitter, Undercliff Experience Ⓗ
Fine unspoilt gem of a town pub run by possibly the longest serving landlord on the Isle of Wight. Situated just off the main Freshwater shopping centre, it has a large garden to relax in and pleasant public and lounge bars in which to sample the well-kept ales. A popular games area adds to the lively atmosphere. Should you have one too many during the evening, no need to phone for a taxi home – the landlord has one.
Q❀⊟Ă🚌(11)♣P⚐▯

Freshwater Bay

Fat Cat

Sandpipers, Coastguard Lane, PO40 9QX (through main Freshwater Bay car park)
✪ 11-11; 12-10.30 Sun
☎ (01983) 758500 🌐 sandpipershotel.com
Fuller's ESB; Timothy Taylor Landlord; guest beers Ⓗ
A real gem within the Sandpipers Hotel, situated between Freshwater Bay and the Afton Nature Reserve. An ever-changing range of ales is on offer with up to eight guest beers, many from smaller and more unusual breweries. The hotel is well appointed with a popular restaurant and recently added gift shop. Recently completed is the extension of the bar, removing walls of three adjoining rooms to give more space. This unique pub is well worth a visit.
⛫Q❀🛏◑♿Ă🚌(7)♣●P⚐

Newchurch

Pointer Inn

High Street, PO36 0NN
✪ 11.30-3, 6-11; 11.30-11 Sat; 12-4, 6-10.30 Sun
☎ (01983) 865202 🌐 pointerinn.co.uk
Fuller's London Pride, ESB; Gale's HSB; guest beer Ⓗ
Ancient village local with a warm, cosy atmosphere where families are welcome. The single-room interior comprises the old public bar, lounge and dining area. The restaurant has a fine reputation for its home-cooked food, prepared by a chef with 35 years' experience (booking is essential). There is a large garden with a petanque terrain. For smokers there is a covered area. Awarded Dining Pub of the Year by Island Life magazine. Q❀◑Ă🚌(23)P⚐

Newport

Castle Inn

91 High Street, PO30 1BQ
✪ 11-11 (midnight Fri & Sat); 12-10.30 Sun
☎ (01983) 522528 🌐 thecastleiow.co.uk
Fuller's London Pride; Shepherd Neame Spitfire; guest beers Ⓗ
Stone-built 17th-century pub, full of character with flagstones and beams. Two guest beers normally include one from the Island. Reputed to be the last pub in England to allow cock fighting, it was also once authorised to conduct marriages. Standing in an area called Castlehold – referring to nearby Carisbrooke Castle – it was once renowned as the home for every thief, rogue and beggar in Newport. Two big public car parks are within 100 metres. Families are welcome and food is served all day. Q❀◑🚌♣⚐

Niton

White Lion

High Street, PO38 2AT
✪ 11 (12 Sun)-11
☎ (01983) 730293
Ringwood Fortyniner; guest beer Ⓗ
Picturesque pub, full of character, in the centre of the village. The landlord has made a great impression since his arrival with a complete overhaul of the premises. The pub has a fine reputation for food and the Sunday roast is a sell-out. From the cellar comes a succession of two changing ales from the Enterprise portfolio and either Undercliff Experience or Best from the local Yates brewery. There is a covered, decked area outside for smokers. Live music plays occasionally. ⛫Q☋❀◑⊟♿🚌(6)♣P⚐

Northwood

Horseshoe Inn

353 Newport Road, PO31 8PL
✪ 11-4.30, 7-midnight; 11-2am Fri & Sat; 11-midnight Sun
☎ (01983) 292349
Beer range varies Ⓗ
Pleasant 17th-century coaching inn, originally known as the Halfway Inn until the adjacent blacksmith gained precedence with a name change. There is a proper public bar with darts and pool and a saloon that boasts a well. Sit in comfort and take your pick from the four excellent ales. Always expect to see the latest big game on the two massive TV screens. Well-behaved children are welcome. ♛Q♉❀⊟⚠🚌(1)♣P⅟

Travellers Joy

85 Pallance Road, PO31 8LS (on A3020 Yarmouth Road out of Cowes)
✪ 11-2.30, 5-11; 5-11.30 Thu; 11-11.30 Fri & Sat; 12-3, 7-11 Sun
☎ (01983) 298024 🌐 tjoy.co.uk
Goddards Special Bitter; guest beers Ⓗ
Offering one of the best choices of cask ale on the Isle of Wight, this well renovated and extended country inn was the Island's first beer exhibition house. It has been voted CAMRA branch Pub of the Year on five occasions. Seven carefully chosen and interesting ales supplement the ever faithful GSB and seasonal beers from the Island brewers are always popular – if you have mastered the 'Northwood nod' you may even get a special from the cellar. A good range of home-cooked food is available lunchtime and evening.
♛♉❀◐◗⚠🚌(1,30)♣P⅟

Rookley

Chequers

Niton Road, PO38 3NZ (off A3020 Niton road)
✪ 11-11; 12-10.30 Sun
☎ (01983) 840314 🌐 chequersinn-iow.co.uk
Ringwood Best Bitter, Fortyniner; guest beer Ⓗ
This country pub dating back to the mid-1800s is situated at the heart of the Island, enjoying beautiful views of the surrounding countryside. Formerly a Whitbread pub, it is astonishing that the brewery closed it and sold it free of tie considering its present popularity after an extensive rebuild. Once a custom and excise house, these days it is heavily food and family oriented. Beers are mainly from the Marston's portfolio with one local ale and draught cider in the summer. It has good children's facilities including a large outdoor play area and changing room. ♛Q♉❀◐◗⊟♿♣P⅟

Ryde

Simeon Arms

21 Simeon Street, PO33 1JG (opp Canoe Lake)
✪ 11-midnight (11 Tue & Wed); 12-11.30 Sun
☎ (01983) 614954
Courage Directors; Goddards Special Bitter; guest beer Ⓗ
Thriving yet unlikely gem tucked away in a Ryde back street with a Tardis-like interior and annexed function hall. The pub is immensely popular with the local community who come to participate in various leagues including darts, crib and pool, and petanque on the enormous floodlit terrain in summer. Food is available weekend evenings and lunchtime and you can always expect to find a local ale. Live music plays on Saturday and Sunday night. The smoking area outside is heated and covered.
❀◐◗⥈(Esplanade)🚌♣⅟

Solent Inn ✔

7 Monkton Street, PO33 1JW
✪ 11-11 (midnight Thu-Sat); 12-10.30 Sun
☎ (01983) 563546 🌐 solentinn.com
Banks's Bitter; Oakleaf Blake's Gosport; guest beers Ⓗ
Excellent street-corner local with a warm, welcoming atmosphere. There is live music at least three times a week and a very friendly weekly quiz. An interesting range of ales, including four guests, comes mainly from the Punch portfolio, with one local ale. Good home-cooked food is served at lunchtime and barbecues are hosted in summer. Themed and karaoke nights are always popular. A local challenge is shove-ha'penny – Ryde is one of the few places with a local league.
♛❀◐⊟⥈(Esplanade)🚌♣⅟

St Helens

Vine Inn

Upper Green Road, PO33 1UJ
✪ 11-11 (12.20am Fri & Sat); 11-11.30 Sun
☎ (01983) 872337 🌐 the-vine-inn.co.uk
Fuller's London Pride; guest beer Ⓗ
The front of the pub overlooks what is possibly the biggest village green in the kingdom and known locally as Goose Island. Although now a single bar, there is definitely a feel of saloon and public about the interior of this enormously successful enterprise. An eclectic selection of memorabilia reflecting local history, from railways to hunting to breweries to maritime, decorates the walls. From Easter to late summer there is a tented area to the rear of the pub. Three guest beers include one from an Island brewery, with two more in summer. A public car park is nearby. ❀◐◗♿⚠🚌(10,14)♣⅟

Shanklin

Chine Inn

Chine Hill, PO37 6BW
✪ 12-4, 7-11; 12-10.30 Sun
☎ (01983) 865880
Fuller's London Pride; Taylor Landlord; guest beer Ⓗ
This inn is a classic. The pub, which has stood since 1621, must have some claim to being one of the oldest buildings with a licence on the island. Completely refurbished, it has retained plenty of the original charm for which it was well known. On a summer's day when the sky is blue and the sun's rays are dancing on Sandown Bay, there is no finer view in England than from here. Live music plays Saturday night and Sunday afternoon.
♛Q❀◐◗⊟🚌(3,16)♣

King Harry's Bar

Glenbrook Hotel, 8 Church Road, PO37 6NU
✪ 12-11
☎ (01983) 863119
Fuller's ESB; guest beer Ⓗ
Charming 19th-century thatched property with two Tudor bars, restaurants, decked gardens and the Chine walk. Three guest beers are on offer in winter, often more in summer. The long-established Henry VIII kitchen specialises in steaks to die for. There are function facilities and entertainment in the summer months.

Accommodation is available and there is car parking front and rear. Well worth a visit for good beer and food. ❀🛏️◑◗♿🚌(3,16)♣P

Ventnor

Volunteer

30 Victoria Street, PO38 1ES
⏲ 11-11.30 (midnight Fri & Sat); 12-11 Sun
☎ (01983) 853537 🌐 volunteer-inn.co.uk
Courage Best Bitter; Greene King Abbot; guest beers 🄷
Built in 1866, the Volunteer is probably the smallest pub on the Isle of Wight. It operated as a beer house between 1869 and 1871 and retains many original features of a traditional drinkers' pub. A past winner of local CAMRA Pub of the Year, between four and six guest beers are usually available including a local ale. No chips, no children, no fruit machines, no video games —just a pure adult drinking house and one of the few places where you can still play rings and enjoy a traditional games night. Live music plays on Sunday afternoon. **Q🚌(3,6)♣🍎⚟**

Wroxall

Four Seasons

2 Clarence Road, PO38 3BY
⏲ 11-11
☎ (01983) 854701 🌐 the-fourseasons-inn.co.uk
Gale's HSB; Ringwood Best Bitter; guest beer 🄷
Formerly known as the Star, this pub was brought back to life after a disastrous fire when it could easily have been lost to housing. Now a successful village pub, it has an Island-wide reputation for good food with all produce sourced locally and cooked fresh to order. Food is served all day and under 10s eat free. There is a covered, heated smokers' area and small car park.
⚜Q❀◑◗♿⛺🚌(3)♣P⚟

Pointer Inn, Newchurch.

A Life on the Hop: Memoirs from a career in beer

NEW FOR 2009

Roger Protz

The entertaining highlights and challenging low points of acclaimed beer-writer Roger Protz's busy and influential career in beer. Well known and admired within the world of beer, Protz has written many indispensible books on the subject and travelled to most of the great beer-drinking nations – from Britain, through Europe to Russia, Mexico and the USA – and commentated as microbrewers bring back taste and flavour to countries dominated by bland national brands.

£12.99 ISBN 978-1-85249-256-4 Members' price £10.99 240 pages

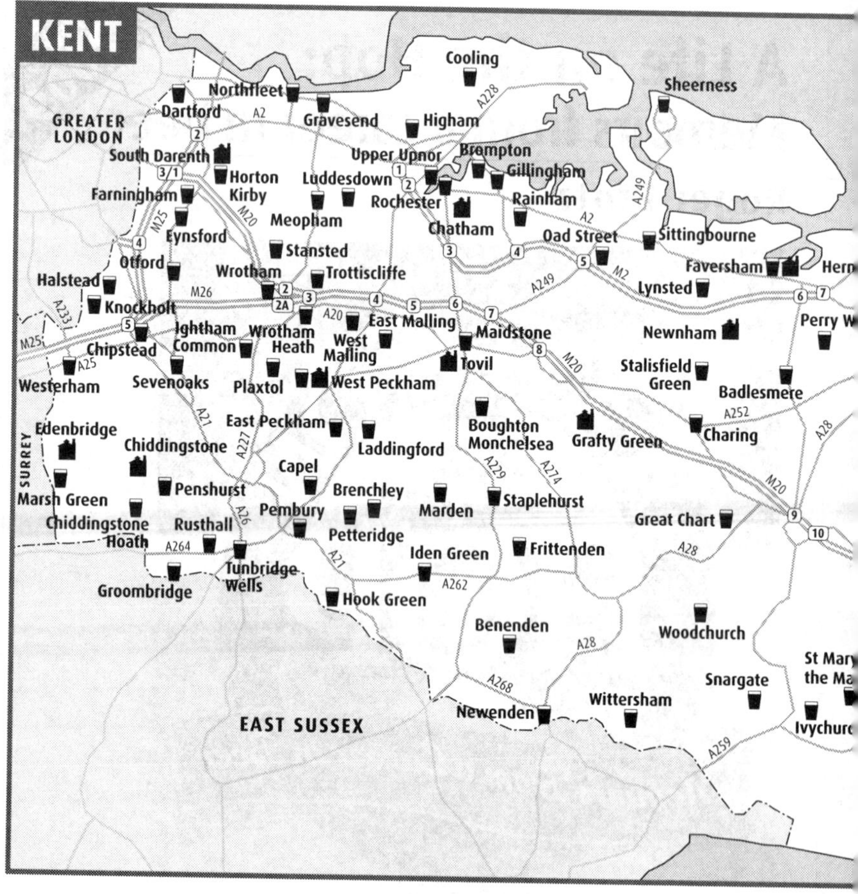

Badlesmere

Red Lion

Ashford Road, ME13 0NX

⏲ 12-3, 5-11; 12-midnight Fri & Sat; 12-10.30 Sun

☎ (01233) 740320 🌐 redlionbadlesmere.co.uk

Shepherd Neame Master Brew Bitter; guest beers Ⓗ

Friendly free house five miles south of Faversham on the A251 to Ashford. Inside it has exposed beams and low ceilings. Beer festivals are held over the Easter and August bank holiday weekends when on-site camping is available. A range of good home-cooked food is served (no eve meals Fri, Sun and Mon). Varied live music is performed every Friday night when the pub gets very busy. The large garden is popular with families in summer. ⛰❀◑▲🚌(666)♣P⅟–

Barfrestone

Yew Tree

CT15 7JH (signed off A2, near Shepherdswell)

⏲ 12-3, 6-11 winter (12-11 summer); 12-11 Sat; 12-10.30 Sun

☎ (01304) 831000 🌐 yewtree.info

Beer range varies Ⓗ

Family-friendly three room pub/restaurant in a picturesque Kent village, next to a beautiful Norman church. Recently refurbished, the pub offers a contemporary environment for drinkers and diners. The pub showcases beers from Kent micro-breweries and usually has three on offer. The award-winning restaurant specialises in good, genuine home-cooked food using locally sourced ingredients, supported by an extensive and good value wine list. Live music plays on Sunday evening. A pleasant two mile country walk from Shepherdswell railway station. ⛰Q🐎❀◑🚂▲●P

Benenden

Bull

The Street, TN17 4DE

⏲ 12 (4 Mon)-midnight; 12-11 Sun

☎ (01580) 240054 🌐 thebullatbenenden.co.uk

Dark Star Hophead; Harveys Sussex Best Bitter; Larkins Traditional; guest beers Ⓗ

Sizeable 17th-century free house, by the green in the centre of a picturesque village. The interior features multi-level wooden floors, exposed oak beams and a large inglenook fireplace. The pub has a separate restaurant, although meals using the same locally-sourced ingredients are also served in the public bar. Sunday lunchtime features a popular carvery with two sittings at 12.30 and 2.30pm (booking is advisable). Once a month on a Thursday the pub holds an acoustic music club. ⛰❀🛏◑♿▲🚌(297)♣●P⅟–

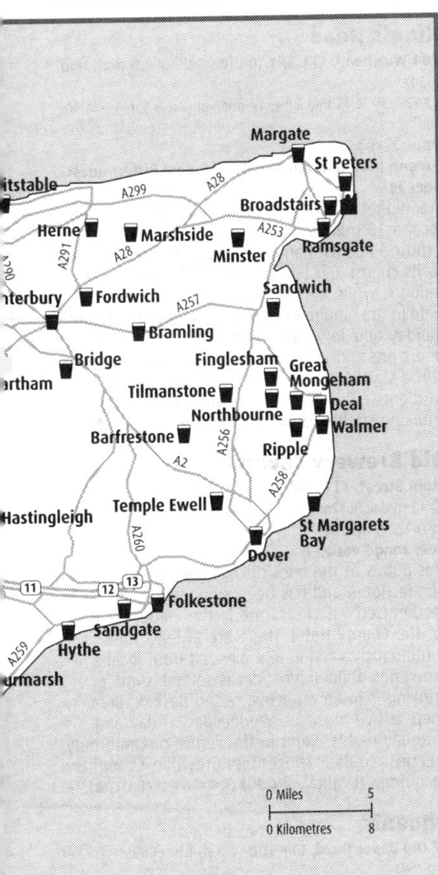

Boughton Monchelsea

Cock Inn ✔

Heath Road, ME17 4JD

⏲ 11-11; 12-10.30 Sun

☎ (01622) 743166 🌐 cockinnboughtonmonchelsea.com

Young's Bitter, Special, seasonal beers; guest beers Ⓗ

Impressive old 16th-century coaching inn, full of character, with oak beams and an inglenook fireplace. Built to provide lodgings for Canterbury pilgrims, it now offers up to four real ales and fine food served in the bar or large restaurant. The atmosphere is friendly and welcoming with no loud music or Sky TV. Darts and board games are available. Children are only allowed in the restaurant, but the pub is dog-friendly.
⛫Q❀◑◐♿🚌(59)♣P⅟–

Bramling

Haywain

Canterbury Road, CT3 1NB (on A257)

⏲ 7-11 Mon; 12-3, 6-11 (midnight Fri & Sat); 12-4 Sun

☎ (01227) 720676 🌐 thehaywainpubbramling.co.uk

Fuller's London Pride; Shepherd Neame Master Brew Bitter; Wells Bombardier; guest beers Ⓗ

The welcoming main bar features hanging hop bines and assorted curios, while the tiny snug is mainly used for diners and meetings. Traditional games include darts and bat and trap, and there is a regular Monday night quiz. Guest beers usually come from small regional breweries, and two annual beer festivals are hosted in marquees in the attractive garden, on the spring bank holiday and in the last week in September. Excellent home-cooked food using local produce is served (not Mon). A regular bus service passes the door.
⛫Q❀◑◐🚌(13,13A,14)♣P⅟–

Brenchley

Halfway House ✔

Horsmonden Road, TN12 7AX (½ mile SE of village) TQ 682413

⏲ 12-11.30 (10.30 Sun)

☎ (01892) 722526

Goacher's Fine Light Ale; Harveys Sussex Best Bitter; Larkins Chiddingstone; Rother Valley Mild; guest beers Ⓖ

Kent CAMRA Pub of the Year 2007 and runner-up 2008, this excellent former coaching inn has been extensively improved by the current landlord and now serves up to 12 ales by gravity. Built in 1740 in Kentish weatherboard and tile-hung, it was once a morgue and is reputed to be haunted. Beer festivals on Whitsun and August bank holidays feature up to 50 beers and a hog roast. The large garden has a children's play area and separate adults-only space. ⛫Q🐴❀🛏◑◐🚌(297)♣🍎P⅟–

Bridge

Plough & Harrow

86 High Street, CT4 5LA

⏲ 12 (11 Sat & Sun)-11

☎ (01227) 830455

Shepherd Neame Master Brew Bitter, seasonal beers; guest beers Ⓗ

Set in a large village, this building was once a brewery but became a pub in 1832. Its history is documented with photographs on the walls of the three traditionally furnished bars. The back room houses a display of Shepherd Neame's famous advertising posters, while a function room hosts many local clubs and has a bar billiards table. Walkers (and dogs) are welcome and often buy a snack at the nearby bakery to enjoy with their pint. There is a patio with a smoking shelter.
⛫Q❀⛺🚌(16,17)♣⅟–

Broadstairs

Neptune's Hall

1-3 Harbour Street, CT10 1ET

⏲ 12-11 (midnight Fri & Sat); 12-10.30 Sun

☎ (01843) 861400

INDEPENDENT BREWERIES

Goacher's Tovil
Hopdaemon Newnham
Larkins Chiddingstone
Millis South Darenth
Nelson Chatham
Ramsgate Broadstairs
Shepherd Neame Faversham
Swan on the Green West Peckham
Westerham Edenbridge
Whitstable Grafty Green

Shepherd Neame Master Brew Bitter, Spitfire, seasonal beers Ⓗ
A Guide regular for many years, this fine early 19th-century watering hole stands in the heart of historic Broadstairs. It retains many original features – especially notable is the superb carved mahogany bar back. The pub is a particularly popular venue for musicians and followers of the annual Folk Week held in August, where the barbecue in the rear garden draws an enthusiastic crowd. A good range of well-kept – if pricey – Sheps beers are on offer to locals and welcome visitors alike. ₥Q❀(ⓐ♿⁂

Brompton

King George V ✔
1 Prospect Row, ME7 5AL
✪ 11.45-11; 12-10.30 Sun
☎ (01634) 842418 🌐 kgvpub.com
Adnams Bitter; guest beers Ⓗ
Built in 1690, close to Chatham historic dockyard, this pub is bedecked with naval and military memorabilia. Four ales including a dark mild – which is rare in this area – are on offer. Magic Bus cider is ferried from the cellar. There is a selection of 70 different Belgian bottled beers. Pizza and two-pint carry outs are available. Live music plays on the last Sunday of the month. The pub supports whiskey, rum and wine societies. No food on Sunday evening or Monday. Accommodation is limited to four rooms. Q⇔(🚌⁂

Burmarsh

Shepherd & Crook ✔
Shear Way, TN29 0JJ (road signed from A259 to E of Dymchurch)
✪ 11.30-4, 6.30-11; 11.30-11 Fri & Sat; 12-11 Sun
☎ (01303) 872336 🌐 shepherdandcrook.co.uk
Adnams Bitter; guest beer Ⓗ
Small and friendly country pub where dogs are welcome. The bar and dining area share a single room in this family-run free house. One guest ale is always available which changes frequently. Traditional English food, all home-cooked using locally-sourced ingredients where possible, is served every day except Tuesday when only light snacks (sandwiches/baguettes) are available. This pleasant popular pub is situated on the Romney Marsh Cycle Route and thus makes a very welcome cyclists' stop. ₥Q❀❀(◗♿♣●P⁂

Canterbury

Bell & Crown
10-11 Palace Street, CT1 2DE (150m from cathedral)
✪ 12-12.30am (1.30am Fri & Sat)
☎ (01227) 784639
Hopdaemon Incubus; Ramsgate Gadds No 3; Whitstable Native, East India Pale Ale Ⓗ
Grade II-listed, characterful city pub with original signage, window etchings and lanterns. It features a fully-beamed interior. The outside seating is on the pavement in front of the pub and has excellent views of the cathedral, as well as the ancient King's School opposite. The pub stocks a range of continental bottled beers as well as its choice of local real ales. Palace Street is part of the King's Mile, with many small shops. ❀(⇌(West)⁂

King's Head
204 Wincheap, CT1 3RY (on the A28, 600m from ring road)
✪ 12-2.30, 4.45-midnight; 12-midnight Fri & Sat; 12-11.30 Sun
☎ (01227) 462885
Greene King IPA; Harveys Sussex Best Bitter; guest beer Ⓗ
Traditional and friendly Grade II-listed 15th-century local a 15-minute walk from the city centre. Exposed beams, hanging hops and bric-a-brac add to its charm. Bar billiards and darts are played indoors, while bat and trap league matches are held in the garden in summer. There is a fortnightly Sunday quiz in winter: September to April. Guest beers are normally sourced from micro-breweries. Three-star B&B is available, with parking for residents only. There is a heated and covered smoking shelter. ❀⇔(◗⇌(East)🚌(28,652)♣⁂

Old Brewery Tavern
Stour Street, CT1 2RX
✪ 11-midnight (2am Fri & Sat); 11-11 Sun
☎ (01227) 826682
Beer range varies Ⓗ
This pub is at the back of chef Michael Caine's Abode Hotel, and has been sympathetically modernised – it was formerly the indoor car park for the County Hotel. There are at least three continuously varying real ales, all from local breweries. Biddenden cider is served. Outdoor drinking is in an attractive raised decking area. There is live music on Wednesday, Friday and Saturday nights. Right in the centre of Canterbury, it is close to the 13th-century Greyfriars Chapel and Eastbridge Hospital. ❀⇔(◗♿⇌(West/East)●P⁂

Phoenix
67 Old Dover Road, CT1 3DB (200m from County Cricket Ground)
✪ 12-1am (10.30 Sun)
☎ (01227) 464220
Young's Bitter; guest beers Ⓗ
Cosy corner pub full of cricket memorabilia and handy for the cricket ground. A changing range of up to eight guest beers comes from all over Britain and includes a mild. A well-attended beer festival is held in December, showcasing a wide range of seasonal beers. Live music is performed monthly on a Saturday night. Good value food is served in generous portions (not Thu). The outdoor patio includes a covered smoking area.
₥❀(◗♿⇌(East)🚌(16,17,89)P⁂

Thomas Ingoldsby ✔
5-9 Burgate, CT1 2HG (200m from cathedral gateway)
✪ 9-midnight (1am Fri & Sat)
☎ (01227) 463339
Greene King Abbot; Marston's Pedigree; Shepherd Neame Spitfire; guest beers Ⓗ
Large JD Wetherspoon's converted from a furniture shop. It stands very close to the main entrance to the cathedral, also on the Burgate. All the main shops and the bus station are nearby. The pub's name is the nom de plume of novelist Richard Barham, author of The Ingoldsby Legends. Limited outdoor seating is available on the pavement outside. A wide range of guest ales is stocked, mostly from small breweries. (◗♿⇌(East)🚌

Unicorn Inn
61 St Dunstan's Street, CT2 8BS
✪ 11.30-11 (midnight Fri & Sat)

☎ (01227) 463187 🌐 unicorninn.com
Caledonian Deuchars IPA; Shepherd Neame Master Brew Bitter; guest beers Ⓗ
This comfortable pub, established in 1604, stands near the historic Westgate and boasts an attractive sun-trap garden. Bar billiards is played, and a quiz, set by regular customers, is held weekly on Sunday evening. The two guest beers often include a Kent micro-brewery ale. Imaginative food, available lunchtimes and evenings, ranges from pub favourites to exotic specials, and is excellent value (no food Sun). There is a covered and heated area for smoking. ♨❀◐◑⇌(West)🚌(3,4,6)♣🚬

Capel

Dovecote Inn

Alders Road, TN12 6SU (½ mile W of A228) TQ643441
⏲ 5.30-10.30 Mon; 12-3, 5.30-11.30 Tue-Sat; 12-11 Sun
☎ (01892) 835966
Gale's HSB; Harveys Sussex Best Bitter; guest beers Ⓖ
This attractive and well-kept traditional pub is situated in a rural hamlet in countryside popular with walkers. The cosy and welcoming one-bar interior has a separate dining area, exposed red-brick walls and beams. Outside there is a large garden with children's play area and a covered, decked patio for dining. Four to six real ales plus Westons Old Rosie cider are served by gravity. Good food is available except Mondays and Sunday evenings. A popular quiz night is held every other Wednesday. ♨Q❀◐◑♣P🚬

Charing

Bowl

Egg Hill Road, TN27 0HG (at jct of 5 Lanes) TQ950514
⏲ 4 (12 summer)-11.30; 12-midnight Fri & Sat; 12-11 Sun
☎ (01233) 712256 🌐 bowlinn.co.uk
Fuller's London Pride; guest beers Ⓗ
Remote and historic pub on the crest of the North Downs, signposted from the A20 and A251. Adnams and Harveys provide the guest beers, in addition to Kentish brewers. Mid-July sees a weekend beer festival. Snacks are available until 9.30pm. A huge old inglenook fire heats the pub during winter. The exceptionally large garden can be used for camping (booking essential) and there are now five letting rooms. ♨Q❀🛏⛺♣P

Chartham

Artichoke

Rattington Street, CT4 7JE (by paper mill)
⏲ 11.30-2.30 (4 Sat), 7-11; 12-5, 7-11 Sun
☎ (01227) 738316
Shepherd Neame Master Brew Bitter, seasonal beers Ⓗ
A quaint, half-timbered exterior hints at the age of this pub, built in the 14th century as a Hall House. There is a cosy, beamed bar with a large fireplace, and in the dining room one table is the glass-topped well. Bat and trap is played in summer, and there are three dartboards and four darts teams. Quiz and race nights are held, dogs are allowed and there is a covered and heated smoking shelter. ♨❀◐⇌🚌(652)♣P🚬

Chiddingstone Hoath

Rock

Near Edenbridge, TN8 7BS (1½ miles S of Chiddingstone, via Wellers Town) TQ498432
⏲ 11.30-3, 6-11; closed Mon; 12-4 Sun
☎ (01892) 870296
Larkins Traditional, Chiddingstone, Best, seasonal beer Ⓗ
Attractive pub in an isolated hamlet to the west of Penshurst. The pub takes its name from one of the local rock outcrops, and is owned by the nearby Larkins Brewery. The full range of the brewery's beers is available, along with good home-cooked food. The floor in the main bar is of well-worn brick which means walkers in muddy boots or people with dogs are welcome. The rare game of 'ringing the bull' can be played. ♨Q❀◐◑⊟♣P

Chipstead

Bricklayers Arms ✔

39 Chevening Road, TN13 2RZ
⏲ 11.30-3.30, 5.30-11; 11.30-11 Fri-Sun
☎ (01732) 743424 🌐 the-bricklayers-arms.co.uk
Harveys Sussex Best Bitter, seasonal beers Ⓗ
A warm and friendly village pub in a row of cottages with a lakeside view. The owners have much improved this pub and it is now popular with locals as well as the many sailors who use the lake. A good range of food is served. Steak and curry nights are held. Thursday is regular quiz night. Live music is on offer from time to time.
♨❀◐◑♿🚌(402)🚬

Cooling

Horseshoe & Castle

The Street, ME3 8DJ
⏲ 11.30 (5.30 Mon)-11 (12.30am Fri & Sat); 12-11.30 Sun
☎ (01634) 221691 🌐 horseshoeandcastle.co.uk
Shepherd Neame Master Brew Bitter; guest beer Ⓗ
Nestling in the quiet village of Cooling, this pub is near a ruined castle once owned by Sir John Oldcastle, on whom Shakespeare modelled his Falstaff character. The local graveyard was used in the film version of Great Expectations, where young Pip met the convict Magwitch. Food is served in a separate dining area (no food Mon). Draught Addlestones cider is available. The pub has a Quality in Tourism four-star inn award for its accommodation. ♨Q❀🛏◐◑♿●P🚬

Dartford

Malt Shovel

3 Darenth Road, DA1 1LP
⏲ 12-11 (midnight Fri); 12-10.30 Sun
☎ (01322) 224381
St Austell Tribute; Young's Bitter, Special, seasonal beers; guest beer Ⓗ
Attractive country cottage-style pub just outside the town centre. The low-ceilinged tap room dates from 1673 and still exudes a rustic charm. The main bar displays a collection of old cameras and other items including a large wooden malt shovel. The modern conservatory houses an original Dartford Brewery mirror. Good food is available every lunchtime and Wednesday to Saturday evening,

including Friday fish night. Quiz night is Monday. A pleasant garden overlooks the parish church. ⛫❀◑◐⊟⇌🚌♣P⚟

Wat Tyler

80 High Street, DA1 1DE

⊙ 9-11 (midnight Fri & Sat); 10.30-11 Sun

☎ (01322) 272546 ⊕ wattylerinn.co.uk

Courage Best Bitter; John Smith's Bitter; guest beers [H]

This historic town-centre pub next to the parish church, originally dating from the 15th century, is named after the leader of the 1481 peasants' revolt. Three constantly-changing guest beers from local and micro-breweries tend towards darker and stronger ales, as favoured by the regular patrons. This long, narrow pub has a secluded mezzanine-level seating area at the far end, while high-backed wooden settles surround the bar. Handy for the railway station and buses to Bluewater Shopping Centre and Ebbsfleet International station. **Q**🛏♿⇌🚌♣⚟

Deal

Bohemian

47 Beach Street, CT14 6HY

⊙ 11am-close; closed Mon winter; 9am-close

☎ (01304) 374843 ⊕ bohemianbythesea.com

Beer range varies [H]

Located on Deal sea front with great views, this pub has a modern but welcoming interior. The landlord selects the finest bottled and draught beers from Europe and beyond. Up to six real ales, often from local breweries, plus perry and cider are on offer. Friday and Saturday nights are busy, the food is superb and unusual, and a sunny beer garden adds to the appeal. The smokers' space is heated. ❀◑◐⇌🚌🍎P⚟

Prince Albert

187-189 Middle Street, CT14 6LW

⊙ 6-11; 12-11 Sun

☎ (01304) 375425

Beer range varies [H]

Victorian pub situated in Deal's conservation area, 100 metres from the sea front. A small cosy bar serves a constantly changing range of three real ales from the smaller breweries, often local ones. The compact restaurant serves evening meals Wednesday to Saturday, and a roast lunch on Sundays. Outside a small sheltered garden makes a pleasant refuge in summer. The pub is 10 minutes' walk north of the town centre, bus and railway stations. ⛫❀🛏◑◐⇌🚌

Ship

141 Middle Street, CT14 6JZ

⊙ 11-11.30; 12-11 Sun

☎ (01304) 372222

Caledonian Deuchars IPA; Ramsgate Gadds' No. 7, Gadds' Seasider; guest beers [H]

You'll find this unspoilt public house just off the seafront, on historic Middle Street, about 10 minutes walk north of Deal's town centre. A good range of beers from micro-breweries is on offer, including Gadds of Ramsgate. The cosy back bar overlooks a small garden. Both bars contain fine displays of nautical memorabilia. If you're seeking fruit machines or juke boxes look elsewhere as this is a pub where conversation prevails. Occasional live music mid-week. ⛫**Q**❀⇌🚌⚟

Dover

Blakes of Dover

52 Castle Street, CT16 1PJ

⊙ 11.30-11; closed Sun

☎ (01304) 202194 ⊕ blakesofdover.com

Harveys Sussex Best Bitter [H]**; guest beers** [H]/[G]

Fine cellar bar easily missed, but don't! Genial hosts assure a haven of civilisation below the busy town centre. A wide selection of beers is on offer from all over, served from handpumps or stillage. Two real ciders come from Thatchers and Broomfield, plus an excellent range of whiskies. Good value food is served at lunchtimes – this is also a handy venue for functions. Tuesday is quiz night. The bar offers popular B&B for those departing from, or arriving on, our shores. Visitors are most welcome, adding to the ambience. **Q**❀🛏◑⇌(Dover Priory)🚌🍎

Eight Bells ✔

19 Cannon Street, CT16 1BZ

⊙ 9-midnight (1am Fri & Sat)

☎ (01304) 205030

Courage Best Bitter; Greene King IPA, Abbot; Marston's Pedigree; Shepherd Neame Spitfire; guest beers [H]

Named after the bells of St Mary's Parish Church opposite, this Wetherspoon's pub was converted from a former cinema and has a split level bar. Most of the 12 handpumps are normally in use. A welcome new entry to the Guide, it is one of relatively few pubs in Dover's town centre. A footpath by the side of the church and across a park leads to the nearby bus station which provides services to local towns and villages. ◑◐♿⇌(Dover Priory)🚌🍎⚟

Louis Armstrong

58 Maison Dieu Road, CT16 1RA

⊙ 4 (7 Sun)-1am

☎ (01304) 204759

Hopdaemon Skrimshander IPA; guest beers [H]

A live music venue for over 40 years, the bar is L-shaped with a stage at the rear. Pictures and posters of bands and musicians adorn the walls. Regular live music plays on Friday, Saturday and Sunday, with jazz every Sunday evening and occasionally at other times. Two or three local real ales are normally available, from Ramsgate, Hopdaemon, Westerham, Goacher's and Whitstable. There is a fine garden at the rear and a large car park opposite. Frequent bus services pass by. ❀🚌⚟

White Horse

St James Street, CT16 1QF

⊙ 4-close

☎ (01304) 242974

Taylor Landlord; guest beers [H]

A 14th-century inn adjoining the ruins of the old St James Church, this is a convenient stop for visitors to Dover Castle and cross-Channel travellers. The main bar is at the front with a raised rear bar area. Details of channel swimmers decorate the walls. At the back, steps lead up to a first-floor garden. The pub has a strong local following, good conversation and up to four real ales, mainly from micro-breweries. Cider is from Biddendens, Thatchers and Moles. Close to public transport. ❀⇌(Dover Priory)🚌🍎

East Malling

King & Queen

1 New Road, ME19 6DD
10 (11 Sat)-11; 11-9 Sun
(01732) 842752
Harveys Sussex Best Bitter; Sharp's Doom Bar; guest beers H
This 16th-century beamed inn, at the centre of a village mentioned in the Domesday Book, is noted for the quality of its meals and snacks. There are rooms at either end with the bar in the central area. The licensee now offers three guest ales, mostly from Kent micro-breweries. There is a monthly quiz night and live music plays on some Sunday evenings. Three self-contained double en-suite rooms have recently been added. (58)P

Rising Sun

125 Mill Street, ME19 6BX
12-11 (10.30 Sun)
(01732) 843284
Goacher's Fine Light Ale; guest beers H
A terraced, family-run village local, popular with sports clubs, where thriving darts league teams play in the back room, with trophies proudly displayed. The front lounge is popular for live football matches, and a compact horseshoe-shaped central bar serves all areas. This is a genuine free house, with a keen pricing policy that ensures regular custom from local clientele and real ale connoisseurs. Simple but tasty food is available Monday to Friday lunchtimes and an extensive rear garden is ideal for summer visits. (58)

East Peckham

Bush, Blackbird & Thrush

194 Bush Road, Peckham Bush, TN12 5LW (1 mile NE of East Peckham, via Old Rd and Pond Rd) TQ664500
11-3 (not Mon), 6-11; 12-3, 6-10.30 Sun
(01622) 871349
Shepherd Neame Master Brew Bitter, Spitfire, H**; seasonal beers** G
Large 15th-century tile-hung traditional country pub situated on a lane leading out of the village. The bar and dining areas are separated by a large working brick fireplace. Shepherd Neame beers are served from the cask. Bat and Trap is played in the garden and there is also darts and cribbage. Tasty home-cooked food is served lunchtimes and Tuesday to Saturday evenings. QP

Eynsford

Malt Shovel

Station Road, DA4 0ER (on A225)
11-midnight (1am Sat); 12-midnight Sun
(01322) 862164
Fuller's London Pride; guest beers H
Imposing main road pub dating from 1607 and licensed since 1880. It has been brightly refurbished throughout, but retains some original beams. It is known locally for good food which is available lunchtimes and evenings, and all day Sunday. Two guest beers are sourced from local and regional independent breweries. Quiz night is Tuesday. The car park is located on the opposite side of the busy A225. Q(408,421)P

Farningham

Chequers

87 High Street, DA4 0DT (250m from A20 jct 3 M25)
12-midnight (11 Sun)
(01322) 865222
Fuller's London Pride, ESB; Taylor Landlord; guest beers H
Bustling one-bar corner local in an attractive riverside village. Ten handpumps offer three regular beers and up to seven guests. Inside, the decor includes murals depicting local scenes plus decorative candelabra. Food is served Monday to Saturday lunchtimes. Parking can be difficult. (408,421)

Faversham

Anchor

52 Abbey Street, ME13 7BP
12-11 (midnight Fri & Sat)
(01795) 536471 theanchorinnfaversham.com
Shepherd Neame Master Brew Bitter, Kent's Best, Spitfire, seasonal beers H
The sailing craft of Standard Quay are just around the corner from this 17th-century pub. Old ships' timbers form the beams and there is a nautical feel throughout the pub. There is a wood-burning stove in the bar and a large fireplace in the dining room. Food is available lunchtimes and evenings (not Sun), except Monday and Tuesday during the winter. Live music plays on most Sunday evenings. Outside, there is a large garden.

Bear Inn

3 Market Place, ME13 7AG
10.30-3, 5.30-11 (11.30 Thu); 10.30-midnight Fri & Sat; 11.30-10.30 Sun
(01795) 532668
Shepherd Neame Master Brew Bitter, Kent's Best, Spitfire, seasonal beers H
Opposite the historic Guildhall in Market Place, the Bear has three small but distinct bars leading off a long side corridor. All have wood panelling and their own separate character. The back bar has an unusual clock – instead of numbers it uses the pub's name spelt out around the dial. Wholesome home-cooked lunches are served. The venue is also popular with local folk musicians.

Chimney Boy

59 Preston Street, ME13 8PG
12 (11 Sat)-11 (midnight Fri & Sat); 12-7.30 Sun
(01795) 532007
Shepherd Neame Master Brew Bitter, Kent's Best, Bishops Finger H
Popular pub dating from the mid-18th century, which was once a convent. It became a hotel around 1885, and was called the Limes. It was acquired by Shepherd Neame during the 1930s. The discovery of steps within the chimney accounts for its current name. Clubs and societies meet in the upstairs function room including the Faversham Folk Club. There are also soul and rock nights. It has a pool room and two wide-screen TVs show Sky Sports. P

Elephant

31 The Mall, ME13 8JN
3-11.30; closed Mon; 12-midnight Sat; 12-7 Sun
(01795) 590157

Beer range varies Ⓗ
There are normally five ever-changing beers, including a mild, on offer in this friendly pub. The licensee aims to offer the best ale selection in town. Beers are sourced, almost exclusively, from micro-breweries, including several in Kent. The single bar has a warming open fire in the winter months and there is a well-tended walled garden which is busy in summer. There is a separate function room. Swale CAMRA Pub of the Year 2007/08/09. Wi-Fi is available upon request. ⚠︎♘❀⇌⊟(333,666)♣⁻

Railway Hotel

Preston Street, ME13 8PE (opp station)
12-11 (10.30 Sun)
☎ (01795) 533173 🌐 railwayhotelfaversham.co.uk
Shepherd Neame Master Brew Bitter, seasonal beers Ⓗ
Opposite the station, the Railway is the pub many visitors to Faversham see first. It is a true hotel with letting rooms. An original and imposing Victorian bar back dominates the interior, and there are also beautiful etched windows. Tables are set outside at the side during the summer. It has a bar billiards table. The breakfast served to residents includes the proprietor's home-made marmalades and jams. Archie, the pub dog, will welcome you, and he gets on well with other dogs. ⚠︎Q❀⇌⊟♣P

Shipwright's Arms

Ham Road, Hollowshore, ME13 7TU (1½ miles N of Faversham) TR017636
11-3 (4 Sat), 6-11; closed Mon; 12-4, 6-10.30 Sun
☎ (01795) 590088
Goacher's Real Mild, Best Dark, Shipwrecked; guest beers Ⓖ
At a remote location by the sea, at the confluence of Faversham and Oare creeks, this lovely old pub oozes atmosphere. Nearby yacht moorings are reflected in interior decor which has much nautical ephemera and also a large number of CAMRA awards. The public bar is warmed by a log fire in winter. There is an extensive rear garden. Beers are sourced mostly from Kentish small and micro-breweries, with the house beer, Shipwrecked, brewed by Goacher's. ⚠︎Q❀◑♣P⁻

Windmill Inn

Canterbury Road, Preston, ME13 8LT (on A2, opp football club)
12-11 (midnight Fri & Sat); 12-5 Sun
☎ (01795) 536505
Shepherd Neame Master Brew Bitter, seasonal beers Ⓗ
Located on what is now the A2, once Watling Street – the Roman road from Dover to Chester – this two-bar pub has many original features. The Preston windmill, from which the pub's name originates, was across the road until the 1940s. The pub has four letting rooms. Meals are available to residents or by prior arrangement. Faversham Football Club's ground is almost opposite. Bus services to the pub are fairly infrequent. ⚠︎⇌⊟♣P⁻

Finglesham

Crown

The Street, CT14 0NA
12-3, 6-11; 11-11.30 Fri & Sat; 12-10.30 Sun
☎ (01304) 612555 🌐 thecrownatfinglesham.co.uk
Shepherd Neame Master Brew Bitter; guest beers Ⓗ
Situated in a quiet rural hamlet, this welcoming village pub and 16th-century restaurant specialises in beers from Kent and south-east brewers. Real cider from Westons and Biddenden is offered regularly. The pub is proud of its award-winning, freshly-prepared, home-cooked food. Themed food nights and quizzes are held throughout the year, and beer festivals are planned for May and August. Bat and trap is played. Well-behaved dogs are welcome outside meal times. Caravan Club certified. Local CAMRA Pub of the Year 2007. ⚠︎❀◑⛺⊟(13,14)●P⁻

Folkestone

British Lion ✔

10 The Bayle, CT20 1SQ (close to the church, off the pedestrian part of Sandgate Road)
12-4, 7-11; 12-10.30 Sun
☎ (01303) 251478
Greene King IPA, Abbot; guest beers Ⓗ
The building dates from 1460, and is now the oldest pub in Folkestone. Charles Dickens visited this former Hanbury, Mackeson and Whitbread house when writing Little Dorrit – the room he used is now the Dickens Room. Situated close to the town centre, adjacent to the church, a comfortable and relaxed atmosphere prevails. Two guest beers are always available, usually from the Finest Cask selection. Good pub food is served in generous portions. ⚠︎❀◑⇌(Central)⊟♣⁻

Chambers

Radnor Chambers, Cheriton Place, CT20 2BB (off the Hythe end of Sandgate Rd)
12-11 (midnight Fri & Sat); 7-10.30 Sun
☎ (01303) 223333
Adnams Bitter; Hopdaemon Skrimshander IPA; Ramsgate Gadd's No 5; Ringwood Old Thumper; guest beers Ⓗ
Surprisingly spacious cellar bar with a café upstairs under the same ownership. Beer festivals are held over the Easter and August bank holiday weekends. The food includes Mexican and European choices plus daily specials. Guest ales are normally from local micro-breweries and the pub attracts a very varied clientele. CAMRA branch Pub of the Year in 2008. ◑⇌(Central)⊟♣●

East Cliff Tavern

13-15 East Cliff, CT19 6BU
5 (12 Sun)-11; 1-midnight Sat
☎ (01303) 251132
Beer range varies Ⓗ
Friendly terraced back-street pub near a footpath across the railway line. The main bar is to the right of the entrance and there are usually two beers, often from Kent or Sussex micro-breweries, with Biddenden cider on gravity behind the bar. Old photographs of Folkestone decorate the walls and community events include weekly raffles. The entrance to the Little Switzerland camp site overlooking the sea is about a mile north east. Q❀⛺♣●⁻

Guildhall ✔

42 The Bayle, CT20 1SQ (close to St Augustine's Church)
12-11 (midnight Fri & Sat); 12-10.30 Sun
☎ (01303) 251393
Greene King IPA; guest beers Ⓗ

A welcoming Cask Marque-accredited traditional pub with a single bar, situated close to the town centre in The Bayle, an attractive old area of town where Charles Dickens once lived. This is a pleasant place to enjoy good ale and to seek a break from the usual hustle and bustle of the town-centre shops. ❀◐♣P⁵–

Lifeboat

42 North Street, CT19 6AF

2-10 (9 Sun & Mon); 1-midnight Fri & Sat

☎ (01303) 252877

Harveys Sussex Best Bitter; Taylor Landlord; Wells Bombardier; guest beers Ⓗ

Friendly corner pub, opened in 1861 – the last example of a timber-framed pub in this part of Folkestone. The building dates back to 1750. This is a fine back-street pub, offering a wide range of guest beers, and decorated with photographs of lifeboats and crews over the years. An RNLI gift shop is incorporated in the pub and the clientele supports the local inshore lifeboat. Q❀♿♣⁵–

Fordwich

Fordwich Arms

King Street, CT2 0DB

11-midnight (1am Fri & Sat)

☎ (01227) 710444 fordwicharms.co.uk

Flowers Original; Shepherd Neame Master Brew Bitter; Wadworth Henry's IPA, 6X Ⓗ

Classic 1930s building listed in Kent CAMRA's Regional Inventory. It has a large bar with a superb fireplace, a wood-block floor and a dining room with wood panelling; excellent meals are served in both areas (not Sun eve). The garden and terrace overlook the River Stour, close to the popular Stour Valley Walk. The pub hosts regular themed evenings including a popular pudding night on the second Wednesday of the month, plus folk music at least every second and fourth Sunday night. The landlord can provide keys to the church and tiny town hall. ♨Q❀◐◑⇌(Sturry)🚌P⁵–

Frittenden

Bell & Jorrocks ✔

Biddenden Road, TN17 2EJ

12 (11 Sat & Sun)-11

☎ (01580) 852415 thebellandjorrocks.co.uk

Adnams Bitter; Black Sheep Best Bitter; Harveys Sussex Best Bitter; guest beer Ⓗ

Fine community village pub incorporating the post office. The unusual name is a combination of the two villlage pubs: the present pub, the former Bell, and John Jorrocks (named after a fictional fox-hunting Cockney created by RS Surtees in the 19th century), which closed in 1969. This old coaching inn has an L-shaped main bar and a small back room. Ask about the Heinkel propellor hanging over the fireplace. Beer festivals are held in April and September. No food on Wednesday. ♨❀◐◑Ⲁ♣⁵–

Gillingham

Dog & Bone

21 Jeffrey Street, ME7 1DE

12 (11 Sat)-11; 12-10.30 Sun

☎ (01634) 576829

Beer range varies Ⓗ

Just off Gillingham High Street, handy for the station and football ground, this pub boasts up to four ever-changing ales. There is a flagstone floor, beamed ceiling, and a separate conservatory with seating for diners. Food is served daily until 3.30pm and there is a carvery on Sunday. Outside is a large patio with picnic tables. The pub also has a large-screen TV inside. ❀◐⇌🚌⁵–

Frog & Toad ✔

38 Burnt Oak Terrace, ME7 2DR

12-11 (10.30 Sun)

☎ (01634) 852231 thefrogandtoad.com

Fuller's London Pride; guest beers Ⓗ

A typical back-street pub, located half a mile from the station. Four frequently changing ales are served on handpump, plus Magic Bus cider from the cask, and a selection of bottled Belgian beers. There is a large garden with picnic tables, and the outside bar is used for up to four beer festivals each year. Food is served until 7pm Tuesday to Saturday, with a traditional roast available on Sunday. The pub supports various sports teams including a golf society. Q❀◐◑⇌🚌●⁵–

Upper Gillingham Conservative Club

541 Canterbury Street, ME7 5LF (160m from jct of Canterbury Street and A2)

11-2.30, 7-11; 11-11 Sat; 12-10.30 Sun

☎ (01634) 851403

Shepherd Neame Master Brew Bitter; guest beers Ⓗ

Expect a friendly welcome at this former army storehouse. A club since 1922, handy for Gillingham Football Stadium, it was a finalist in the CAMRA National Club of the Year awards in 2001. To gain entry, show this Guide or a CAMRA membership card. The U-shaped bar stocks three reasonably priced real ales at up to 4.5% ABV. There is a snooker room with two tables and a large-screen TV in the bar. ♿🚌♣

Will Adams

73 Saxton Street, ME7 5EG

12.30-4 Sat, 7-11; 12-4, 8-11 Sun

☎ (01634) 575902

Hop Back Summer Lightning; guest beers Ⓗ

This friendly one-bar local enjoys a well-deserved reputation for good beer – it was winner of CAMRA Medway branch Pub of the Year in 2008, and many times a runner up. A good choice of ales from micro-breweries is normal, as are two draught ciders and a perry. The pub is named after a local navigator/adventurer whose exploits are depicted on the mural inside. Good value lunches are served when Gillingham football team is playing at home, but the opening hours vary on those days. ❀◐⇌🚌♣●⁵–

Gravesend

Crown & Thistle

44 The Terrace, DA12 2BJ

12-11 (10.30 Sun)

☎ (01474) 326049 crownandthistle.org.uk

Dark Star Hophead; Loddon Shrimpers; guest beers Ⓗ

Situated between the town centre and the river, this narrow pub is a former CAMRA National Pub of the Year and offers four frequently-changing guest beers. Near to the river, it has four rowing teams, for both men and women. Chinese or Indian takeaway orders can be phoned through from the

bar and eaten on the premises. The pub is close to Gravesend Station and central bus services.
❀⇌🚌♣🚬

Jolly Drayman

1 Love Lane, Wellington Street, DA12 1JA
⏲ 12-midnight (1am Thu-Sat); 12-11 Sun
☎ (01474) 352355 🌐 jollydrayman.com
Caledonian Deuchars IPA; guest beers Ⓗ
Low-beamed town-centre pub and small hotel that formed part of the Walker's Brewery. The pub hosts two darts teams and two rowing teams. Occasional live music can be heard on Saturday evenings. Dadlums (Kentish skittles) is played on alternate Sunday evenings. A smoking area is covered and heated. The restaurant serves good food most of the day – please check beforehand.
❀🛏◖◗♿⇌🚌♣P🚬

Ship & Lobster

Mark Lane, Denton, DA12 2QB
⏲ 11-11; 12-4 Sun
☎ (01474) 324571 🌐 shipandlobster.co.uk
Loddon Shrimpers; guest beers Ⓗ
An historic pub set in an industrial area in Denton, past the canal basin at the end of Mark Lane, used by locals fishing the River Thames and by walkers on the Saxon Shore Way. It features as the Ship in Dickens' Great Expectations and has a nautical theme. The Sunday roasts are always popular so booking is essential. ❀◖P🚬

Somerset Arms

9-10 Darnley Road, DA11 0RU
⏲ 11-11 (2am Thu-Sat); 12-11 Sun
☎ (01474) 533837
Greene King IPA; Young's Bitter; guest beers Ⓗ
Town-centre corner pub which is very close to the station. This single bar has nooks and crannies, with wooden seats which were formerly church pews. Film posters and photographs of film stars adorn the walls, together with sporting and music memorabilia. Four constantly rotating guest beers often come from Hop Back and other independent breweries. There is a diverse clientele and the pub has a late licence for discos Thursday to Saturday. No food Sunday lunchtime. ◖⇌🚌

Great Chart

Hoodeners Horse

The Street, TN23 3AN (just off A28)
⏲ 11-11 (midnight Fri & Sat); 12-11 Sun
☎ (01233) 625583
Fuller's London Pride; Wells Bombardier, guest ales Ⓗ
A former Hoodeners Horse chain pub, which has been transformed to its former glory – a basically furnished pub with wooden floors and bar furniture, a good, varied selection of real ales and an interesting menu, which includes Mexican dishes and a range of fresh pizzas. Outside, its unusual garden terraces mingle with the surrounding cottages. 🐴❀◖◗🚬

Great Mongeham

Three Horseshoes

139 Mongeham Road, CT14 9LL
⏲ 12 (11 Sun)-midnight
☎ (01304) 375812 🌐 threehorseshoes.synthasite.com
Beer range varies Ⓗ
Small, welcoming community pub offering two to three regularly changing beers, often from local breweries, and a beer festival in August. The pub supports local charities throughout the year and holds a charity fun day, in aid of Guide Dogs. Food is available Thursday to Saturday lunchtimes, with a roast on Sunday. Themed meals are served one Saturday night every month. The pub has men and women's darts and pool teams, a large, secure, child-friendly garden and is dog-friendly. Camping is available at Solley's Farms. ❀◖⛺🚌(14,82)♣P🚬

Groombridge

Crown Inn

TN3 9QH (A264 from Tunbridge Wells, then B2110)
⏲ 11-3, 6-11; 11-11 Sat; 12-10.30 (5 winter) Sun
☎ (01892) 864742 🌐 thecrowngroombridge.co.uk
Greene King IPA; Larkins Traditional; guest beers Ⓗ
According to English Heritage this is one of Britain's oldest pubs, dating back to 1585. It looks on to the village green and the view is beautiful at any time of the year. Inside, the low ceiling, tiled floor, very old oak beams and inglenook fireplace give it a very traditional atmosphere. This gem of a pub is popular with walkers for its generous helpings of real home-cooked food, and their dogs for the always-available bowl of water.
🔥Q❀◖◗⇌🚌(291)

Halstead

Rose & Crown 🏆

Otford Lane, TN14 7EA
⏲ 12-11
☎ (01959) 533120
Larkins Traditional; Whitstable East India Pale Ale; guest beers Ⓗ
A regular Guide entry, this two-bar, flint-faced free house from the 1860s has a strong local following. The bars are part wood-panelled and display pictures of the pub and village. It hosts a monthly quiz night and a number of darts teams. Four regularly-changing guests ales from smaller breweries are served, including a mild. Home-cooked food is offered with a takeaway option. Booking for Sunday lunch is advisable. Voted local CAMRA Pub of the Year in 2008.
🔥Q🐴❀◖◗♿🚌(402,R5,R10)♣P🚬

Hastingleigh

Bowl

The Street, TN25 5HU TR095449
⏲ 5 (12 Sat)-midnight; closed Mon; 12-10.30 Sun
☎ (01233) 750354 🌐 thebowlonline.co.uk
Adnams Bitter; Fuller's London Pride; Harveys Sussex Best Bitter; guest beer Ⓗ
Lovingly-restored village pub, this listed building retains many period features, including a tap room that is now used for playing pool, and is free from jukebox and games machines. Quiz night is Tuesday. The lovely garden has a cricket pitch to the rear where matches are played most Sundays in summer. A beer festival is held during the August bank holiday weekend. Excellent sandwiches are available at weekends.
🔥Q❀♿🚌(620)♣🍎P

Herne

Butcher's Arms 🏆

29A Herne Street, CT6 7HL (opp church)
12-1.30, 6-9 (or later); closed Sun & Mon
☎ (01227) 371000 🌐 micropub.co.uk
Dark Star Hophead; Harveys Sussex Best; Fuller's ESB; guest beers Ⓖ
The smallest pub in Kent and a real ale gem. It contains the original butcher's chopping tables, plus hooks and other implements. There is seating for 12 customers and standing room for about 20, the compact drinking area ensuring lively conversation. An ever-changing variety of guest beers is on offer alongside a takeaway service. The landlord regularly consults customers about which beers he should stock. The car park is nearby. CAMRA's Kent Pub of the Year in 2008. Q🚌(4,6)

Smugglers Inn

1 School Lane, CT6 7AN (opp church)
11-11 (1am Fri & Sat)
☎ (01227) 741395
Shepherd Neame Master Brew Bitter, Spitfire, seasonal beers Ⓗ
Quaint village local with a smuggling history, situated just inland from Herne Bay. Parts of the pub date back 400 years, and it has been run by the same landlord for 15 years. The comfortable saloon bar has a low ceiling, hanging hops and panelling. The more modern public bar has a pool table and dartboard. Between the bars is a ship's binnacle. The garden has a Bat and Trap pitch and hanging flower baskets. Q❀◐⊟♿🚌(4,6)♣⁼

Hernhill

Three Horseshoes

46 Staple Street, ME13 9UA TR060601
12-3, 6-11; 12-11 Fri & Sat; 12-3, 7-10.30 Sun
☎ (01227) 750842 🌐 3shoes.co.uk
Shepherd Neame Master Brew Bitter, Ⓖ**; Kent's Best, seasonal beers** Ⓗ
Set in a hamlet amid orchards and hop gardens, this hospitable and traditional pub has been run by the same husband and wife team for the past 10 years. Note that the Master Brew Bitter is served direct from the cask, very rare in a Shepherd Neame house. It has a well-deserved reputation for good home-cooked food – meals are not available on Sunday evening or Monday. Live music is played on alternate Saturday nights. A wheelie-bin grand prix race is held in mid-July. ♨Q❀◐◑⛺🚌(638)♣P

Higham

Stonehorse

Dillywood Lane, ME3 8EN (off B2000 Cliffe Road)
12-11 (10.30 Sun)
☎ (01634) 722046
Courage Best Bitter, guest beers, Ⓗ
A country pub with a large garden situated on the edge of Strood, surrounded by fields and handy for walkers. The unspoilt public bar sports a wood-burning range, and a rare bar billiards table. Good value food is served. The pub is dog-friendly but no children are allowed in the bar. Up to three guest beers are usually available. ♨Q❀◐◑⊟♣P

Hook Green

Elephant's Head ✔

Furnace Lane, TN3 8LJ
12-3, 4.30-11; 12-1am Sat; 12-10.30 Sun
☎ (01892) 890279
Harveys Hadlow Bitter, Sussex Best Bitter, Armada Ale, seasonal beers Ⓗ
A lovely Tudor building in a rural setting, constructed in 1489 and a pub since 1768. Its interesting history is displayed by the large tropical fish tank. The well-presented interior includes an inglenook fireplace burning logs in winter and oak beams hung with hop bines. Outside there is a garden and children's play area. A Harvey's pub, it serves a variety of food including a children's menu. A darts team plays regularly. Bayham Abbey ruins and Scotney Castle are nearby.
♨Q❀◐◑🚌(256)♣P

Horton Kirby

Bull 🏆

3 Lombard Street, DA4 9DF
12 (4 Mon)-11 (midnight Fri & Sat); 12-10.30 Sun
☎ (01322) 862274 🌐 thebullpub.co.uk
Beer range varies Ⓗ/Ⓖ
Comfortable and friendly one-bar village pub with a large landscaped garden affording views across Darent Valley. The range of beers includes one on gravity stillage and eight on handpump, often from Dark Star, Oakham or local micro-breweries, plus a micro-brewery showcase on the first Thursday to Sunday of the month. Magic Bus cider is available on gravity. Good-quality food is served at lunchtime (not Mon) and in the evening (Tue-Sat). Monday is quiz league, Tuesday cribbage league and Wednesday darts league. Local CAMRA branch Pub of the Year 2008 and 2009.
♨Q❀◐◑♿🚌(414)♣🍎⁼🥛

Hythe

Red Lion Hotel

Red Lion Square, CT21 5AU (opp main Hythe bus stop on A259)
11-3, 6-11.30; 12-6 Sun
☎ (01303) 266686 🌐 redlionhotelhythe.co.uk
Ramsgate Gadds' No. 3; Whitstable Bay Native Ⓗ
Re-opened April 2008 after major refurbishment as a quiet pub/restaurant/hotel with no fruit machines, pool table or jukebox – but providing board games for customers. This revitalised 17th-century house provides up to four beers, primarily from local Kent breweries, and excellent food sourced from local suppliers whenever posible. Quiz nights Mondays.
♨Q❀🛏◐◑♿⇌(Sandling)🚌♣P⁼

Three Mariners

37 Windmill Street, CT21 6DH (off Stade Street)
12 (4 Mon)-11 (midnight Fri & Sat); 12-11 Sun
☎ (01303) 260406
Young's Bitter; guest beers Ⓗ
A traditional two-bar, back-street local which has recently been extensively refurbished. The friendly and relaxed atmosphere makes this well worth finding, as does its ever-changing range of guest ales. Beer festivals are usually held on the spring and August bank holidays. ♨Q❀⊟♿🍎⁼

Iden Green (Goudhurst)

Peacock Inn

Goudhurst Road, TN17 2PB (1½ miles E of Goudhurst at A262/B2085 jct)
12-11 (6 Sun)
(01580) 211233
Shepherd Neame Master Brew Bitter, Kent's Best, Bishops Finger, seasonal beers Ⓗ
Attractive country inn with a large garden, built in the 17th-century as a hunting lodge for the nearby Glassenbury estate. It became a pub about 150 years ago. There are two simply-furnished bars, one in the original building, the other in a 1960s extension which has been sympathetically refurbished to match the original. The old bar has an inglenook fireplace, low beams and a dining room. Excellent food with varying specials is served throughout. (297)P

Ightham Common

Old House ★

Redwell Lane, TN15 9EE (½ mile SW of Ightham village, between A25 & A227) TQ591558
7-11 (9 Tue); 12-3 Sat; closed Mon; 12-3, 7-11 Sun
(01732) 882383
Loddon Shrimpers; guest beers Ⓖ
Kentish red-brick and tile-hung cottage dating from the 17th century. Tucked away down a steep, narrow country lane, the pub is hard to spot as it has no sign. The larger room to the left features a Victorian wood-panelled bar and a large inglenook fireplace. The smaller room is an old-fashioned parlour complete with ornate armchairs and a retired cash register. Beers are served from a stillage in a room behind the bar. QP

Ivychurch

Bell Inn

TN29 0AL (signed from A2070 between Brenzett and Hamstreet) TR028275
12-11 (10.30 Sun)
(01797) 344355 thebellinnromneymarsh.co.uk
Black Sheep Best Bitter; Wadworth Henry's Original IPA; guest beers Ⓗ
Picturesque 16th-century inn situated in the shadow of the village church. The large bar has a dining area to the left and a games room to the right, with a serving area. This is a welcoming pub in which to relax and enjoy the four well-kept real ales on offer. There are many options for walking and cycling in the surrounding Romney Marsh area. Convenient for the Brenzett Aeronautical Museum. QP

Knockholt

Three Horseshoes

The Pound, TN14 7LD
11.30-3, 6-11; 12-4, 7-11 Sun
(01959) 532102
Adnams Bitter; Harveys Sussex Best Bitter; guest beer Ⓗ
This strong community pub offers great hospitality on every visit. An interesting selection of brass band pictures decorates the walls as the landlord was once a playing member. Home-cooked food is available, plus a takeaway and senior citizens' menu. A good selection of real ales is always available. There is a large garden to the rear of the pub and dogs are welcome. Q(402,R5,R10)P

Laddingford

Chequers

Lees Road, ME18 6BP (1 Mile SW of Yalding) TQ689481
12-3, 5-11; 12-11 Sat; 12-10.30 Sun
(01622) 871266 chequersladdingford.co.uk
Adnams Bitter; Fuller's London Pride; guest beers Ⓗ
Attractive, community-spirited, oak-beamed pub dating from the 15th century, situated in the village centre. During the summer the frontage is adorned with colourful window boxes and hanging baskets. A warm welcome is assured in the simply-furnished bar and split-level dining area. A beer festival is held in late April, showcasing around 30 ales. The food is excellent and features daily specials. Thursday is sausage night and pie nights are monthly. Themed food nights are held regularly. The large garden has children's play areas. Q(26)P

Luddesdown

Cock Inn

Henley Street, DA13 0XB (1 mile SE of Sole Street station) TQ664672
12-11 (10.30 Sun)
(01474) 814208 cockluddesdowne.com
Adnams Bitter; Goacher's Mild; Whitstable East India Pale Ale; guest beers Ⓗ
Superb, traditional English free house dating from 1713 and located in a pleasant rural setting, under the same ownership since 1984. It has two bars and a conservatory. The pub plays host to many local clubs and societies. Outside is a specially designed undercover heated smoking area complete with dartboard. Petanque is played in the garden. The landlord hosts a devious quiz every Tuesday. No food Sunday evening. Local CAMRA Pub of the Year 2005-2007. QP

Lynsted

Black Lion

Lynsted Lane, ME9 0RJ (close to church)
11-3, 6-11; 12-3, 7-10.30 Sun
(01795) 521229
Goacher's Mild, Light, Dark, Crown Imperial Stout Ⓗ
This free house is a shrine to Goacher's of Maidstone, with three or four of its beers on offer. The main bar room includes real fires, while a second bar is home to darts and bar billiards. Wood floors throughout the pub add to its character. Food is available daily. There is a large garden at the side. The 345 bus runs every two hours or so from Sittingbourne via Teynham (not evenings or Sun). Q(345)P

Maidstone

Flower Pot

96 Sandling Road, ME14 2RJ (off A229 N of town centre)
12 (11 Sat)-11; 12-10.30 Sun

☎ (01622) 757705 🌐 flowerpotpub.com
Young's Bitter; guest beers Ⓗ
Six handpumps now adorn the bar of this increasingly popular free house featuring diverse beers from all over the country. Biddenden cider is served on gravity. The pub's top bar has listed interior wall panelling with mouldings from HMS Victory and the lower bar has an original Wurlitzer jukebox and a pool table. Regular events include Tuesday jam night, free pool on Wednesday and frequent live music. Shut-the-box and shove-ha'penny are played. Sandwiches are available. A short walk from County Hall and the railway station. ⌂❀≠(East)⊟(101,155)♣●⊱

Rifle Volunteer

28 Wyatt Street, ME14 1EU
⊙ 11-3 (may vary), 6 (7 Sat)-11; 12-3 (may vary), 7-10.30 Sun
☎ (01622) 758891
Goacher's Real Mild, Crown Imperial Stout, Fine Light Ale Ⓗ
A quiet, street-corner, single-bar pub owned by the local Goacher's brewery. It retains most of its original features and has been a regular in this Guide for several years. The pub fields two quiz teams in the local league. Note the display of interesting old bottled beers and the unusual toy soldiers used to indicate a beer 'in the wood'. A good, old-fashioned pub, free from music and fruit machines. Simple, good value lunches are available in the week. Q◐≠(East)♣

Swan

2 County Road, ME14 1UY
⊙ 12-11
☎ (01622) 751264
Shepherd Neame Master Brew Bitter, Kent's Best, seasonal beers Ⓗ
Town-centre pub close to the County Hall and opposite the main prison entrance. Beers from the Shepherd Neame pilot micro-brewery are stocked when available as well as occasional guests. Hand-cut sandwiches, tea and coffee are always for sale. Hot food may be provided on request if ordered in advance. League and fun quizzes feature as well as darts. Live music nights are held monthly. Special events such as Burns Night and St Patrick's Day are celebrated. The smoking area is heated and covered. ❀◐♿≠(East)♣⊱

Wheatsheaf

301 Loose Road, ME15 9PY (S of Maidstone at jct of A229/A274)
⊙ 4-11; 12-11.30 Fri & Sat; 12-10.30 Sun
☎ (01622) 752624
Courage Best Bitter; guest beers Ⓗ
Spacious inn at the junction of a busy road heading south out of town. The building dates back to 1830, with an earlier structure first licensed in 1786. The pub hosts a thriving golf society with an honours board in the lower section and memorabilia on proud display. Decoration also includes an interesting plate collection. Paperbacks are on sale for charity. Quiz night is Saturday. Shove-ha'penny is played. No food on Monday. Regular beer festivals are held. ❀◐◑♿⊟(5,89)♣⊱

Marden

Stile Bridge Inn

Staplehurst Road, TN12 9BH (S of Maidstone on A229)
⊙ 12-11; 5-10 Mon (club members only); 12-6 Sun
☎ (01622) 831236 🌐 stile.co.uk
Shepherd Neame Master Brew; guest beers Ⓗ
A large roadside pub – the front is part divided, with a wood- panelled dining area to the right and comfortable sofas to the left, where there is a roaring log fire in winter. A third bar to the rear is popular with the regulars and leads to the large tithe barn restaurant/function room. A range of excellent-quality genuinely home-made food is served, with special offers on Friday and Saturday evenings. Live music plays on Friday. Guest ales are mainly from local micro-breweries and continental bottled beers are stocked. ⌂Q❀◐◑⊟(5)●P⊱

Margate

Mechanical Elephant ✔

28-30 Marine Terrace, CT9 1XJ
⊙ 9-midnight (1am Fri & Sat)
☎ (01843) 234100
Greene King IPA; Marston's Pedigree; guest beers Ⓗ
Ideally located opposite Margate main sands with a balcony offering famous summer sunset views. A quiet daytime and evening pub during the week, it becomes a Lloyds No. 1 bar on Friday and Saturday evenings. The name derives from a large roving mechanical elephant that was used to give rides along the seafront in the 1920s. An ever-changing range of ales is on offer and regular beer festivals in line with Wetherspoon's national promotions. Kentish beers are usually available. ⚲❀◐◑♿≠⊟

Northern Belle

4 Mansion Street, CT9 1HE
⊙ 11-11; 12-10.30 Sun
☎ (07810) 088347
Shepherd Neame Master Brew Bitter, Kent Best, seasonal beers Ⓗ
This small, down-to-earth seafarers' tavern is situated down a tiny lane opposite the stone pier. The town's oldest standing pub, it resulted from combining two fishermen's cottages, built around 1680. It was first known as the Aurora Borealis; its present name derives from a merchant ship that ran aground in 1857. Allegedly used by JMW Turner, it is close to the Turner Contemporary Centre (currently under construction). Live music is performed on some Sunday afternoons. ≠♣

Marsh Green

Wheatsheaf Inn

Main Road, TN8 5QL
⊙ 11-11; 12-10.30 Sun
☎ (01732) 864091 🌐 thewheatsheaf.net
Harveys Mild, Sussex Best Bitter; Larkins Traditional; guest beers Ⓗ
Attractive tile-hung pub in a small village close to the Surrey border. Up to five frequently changing ales are sold, together with Biddenden cider. The landlord reckons he has served over 2,500 different beers over the years, and these together with a good range of home-cooked food make the pub a regular Guide entry. Internally, the pub is divided into several distinct drinking and dining areas, including a large conservatory at the rear. A beer festival is held during the summer, usually coinciding with the village fete.
⌂Q⚲❀◐◑⊟⊟(236)♣●P

Marshside

Gate Inn

Boyden Gate, CT3 4EB (off A28 at Upstreet)
🕒 11-2.30 (4 Sat), 6-11; 12-4, 7-10.30 Sun
☎ (01227) 860498
Shepherd Neame Master Brew Bitter, Spitfire, seasonal beers Ⓖ
Chris Smith is probably the longest-serving Guide landlord: the Gate has featured every year since 1977. A focal point for the community, the pub's fund-raising events and traditional entertainment include mummers' plays, hoodeners and morris dancing. The bars have tiled floors, a log fire and hanging hops, while the garden includes a stream, apple trees and ducks. The excellent food includes hotpots and black pudding sandwiches (not Mon eve, or Tue eve in winter). ⛰Q♉❀◐▲♣P

Meopham

George

Wrotham Road, DA13 0AH (on A227 near church)
🕒 11-11; 12-10.30 Sun
☎ (01474) 814198
Shepherd Neame Master Brew Bitter, Bishops Finger, seasonal beers Ⓗ
Former coaching inn – the oldest part dating from the 15th century – with an attractive Kentish weatherboard exterior. There are two bars and a separate restaurant serving good food daily until 9pm. Outside is a spacious drinking and smoking area to the rear. The pub has a large car park and a floodlit petanque piste. A passageway under the road links the inn with the parish church.
⛰❀◐🚌(306,308)♣P⚟

Minster

Bell Inn

2 High Street, CT12 4BU
🕒 11-3, 6-11 (11.30 Fri & Sat); 12-4, 7-11 Sun
☎ (01843) 821274
Brakspear Bitter; Shepherd Neame Master Brew Bitter; Young's Bitter; guest beer Ⓗ
Large, welcoming old oak-beamed public house, built in 1576 as part of a row of farm cottages. Formerly a coaching inn and tea gardens, the interior retains some original features although much alteration has taken place over the years. A rare outlet for Brakspear in East Kent, although all beers tend to be at the lower end of the gravity scale. ⛰Q❀◐⇌🚌(42,51)P⚟

New Inn

2 Tothill Street, CT12 4AG
🕒 11.30-11 (midnight Fri & Sat); 12-10.30 Sun
☎ (01843) 821294
Greene King IPA, Abbot; guest beer Ⓗ
Not far from Minster station, this friendly village local was built in 1837 as a replacement for an 18th-century enterprise which included a landscaped garden and pleasure complex. The old Cobbs Brewery windows are retained and a sympathetic extension houses the pool table, dartboard and space for live music. The garden has probably the most luxurious smoking area in Thanet, along with ample seating and an aviary. No food Sunday evening.
♉❀◐⇌🚌(42,51)♣P⚟

Newenden

White Hart

Rye Road, TN18 5PN (on A268 in centre of village)
TQ834273
🕒 11-11; 12-10.30 Sun
☎ (01797) 252166
Fuller's London Pride; Harveys Sussex Best Bitter; Rother Valley Level Best; guest beers Ⓗ
This lovely, 500-year-old oak-beamed inn is reputedly haunted and stands just within Kent's boundary with East Sussex. Regular customers mark the two guest ales for quality. Seasonal cider is sometimes available. The pub has six guest rooms and is a short walk from Northiam station on the Kent and East Sussex Railway. Runner up CAMRA branch Pub of the Year 2009.
⛰Q♉❀🛏◐▲🚌(340,341)♣P

Northbourne

Hare & Hounds

The Street, CT14 0LG
🕒 12-3, 6-11.30; 12-4 Sun
☎ (01304) 365429 🌐 thehareandhounds.net
Greene King IPA; Harveys Sussex Best Bitter; guest beers Ⓗ
This friendly, traditional local is situated in a pleasant village location. It has a carpeted main bar and restaurant with a raised, smaller seating area. The food menu specialises in local and free-range produce with innovative vegetarian dishes. Events are held throughout the year, including themed dinners and live music, a beer festival in July and quizzes in winter in aid of local charities. A large, enclosed garden includes children's play equipment. Dogs are welcome. ⛰❀◐🚌(14)P⚟

Northfleet

Earl Grey

177 Vale Road, DA11 8BP (off Perry St)
🕒 12-11 (10.30 Sun)
☎ (01474) 365240
Shepherd Neame Master Brew Bitter, Spitfire, seasonal beers Ⓗ
Distinctive late 18th-century cottage-style building with a Kentish brick-and-flint exterior that is rarely seen in this area. The interior consists of an L-shaped bar, with a raised seating area at one end. It exudes a homely, convivial atmosphere. The pub is located near the Cygnet Leisure Centre in Perry Street. ❀🚌(498,499)♣P⚟

Oad Street

Plough & Harrow

Oad Street, Borden, ME9 8LB (opp craft centre)
TQ870620
🕒 12-11 (midnight Sat)
☎ (01795) 843351 🌐 theploughandharrowpub.co.uk
Goacher's Real Mild; Shepherd Neame Master Brew Bitter; guest beer Ⓗ
This is a free house in a small North Downs village. The craft centre opposite is well signposted from several directions. A large main bar and a small public bar are adorned with breweriana and other ephemera on the walls. Goacher's beers feature prominently, although there is always at least one

other cask ale. An ideal location to start or finish a walk through the surprisingly pretty local countryside.

Otford

Crown

10 High Street, TN14 5PQ (adjacent to duckpond)
12-11 (11.30 Fri); 11-11.30 Sat; 11-11 Sun
(01959) 522847 crownpubandrestaurant.co.uk
Harveys Sussex Best Bitter; St Austell Dartmoor Best; guest beers H

Attractive whitewashed cottage-style pub dating from the 16th century. Two distinct bars include one that houses a suit of armour under a bygone stairwell, and banknotes and hotel keys adorn the beams. Excellent home-cooked meals are served (check times beforehand). The Sunday roasts are particularly popular. Two regular beers are supplemented by an interesting changing range of two guests, often from Westerham Brewery, and Westons Traditional Scrumpy. The pub hosts many community activities and occasional beer festivals. (431,432)

Pembury

Black Horse

12 High Street, TN2 4NY
11-11 (midnight Sat & Sun)
(01892) 822141 blackhorsepembury.co.uk
Greene King Old Speckled Hen; Fuller's London Pride H

The Black Horse is a traditional local pub with a cosy, friendly atmosphere, offering a good selection of real ales. The pub features a large log fire and lots of sporting pictures and memorabilia – especially golf and cricket. Home-cooked food is served lunchtimes and evenings. Outside there is an attractive beer garden which has a big heated umbrella and an additional heated area for smokers. (6,276,287)

Penshurst

Spotted Dog

Smarts Hill, TN11 8EE (follow signs from the B2188 S of Penshurst)
11-11 summer; 11-2.30, 5.30-11 winter; 11-11 Sat & Sun
(01892) 870253
Larkins Traditional; Westerham Seasonal; guest beers H

A beautiful 15th-century inn full of character, located on Smarts Hill in the picturesque village of Penshurst – six miles from Tunbridge Wells and close to local tourist attractions such as Penshurst Place and Hever Castle. You can sit by a roaring fire in winter or on patios located at the front and rear in summer. The pub also has its own farm shop selling locally-grown produce. Excellent beer, good food and friendly staff.

Perry Wood

Rose & Crown

ME13 9RY (1½ miles from Selling Station, signed to Perry Wood) TR042552
11.30-3, 6.30-11 (closed Mon eve); 12-3, 7-10.30 Sun (later in summer)
(01227) 752214 roseandcrownperrywood.co.uk
Adnams Bitter; Harveys Sussex Best Bitter; guest beers H

Perry Wood is a council-owned conservation area and is quite unspoilt. This historic free house was once a woodcutter's cottage and is in the middle of the wood, which is East Kent's highest point. Popular with walkers and cyclists, it is well-regarded for its food and, of course, beer. The bar room has a large fireplace and is decorated with old wood-cutting tools and corn dollies. The large garden has a children's play area. No food is available Monday.

Petteridge

Hopbine

Petteridge Lane, TN12 7NE (½ mile down lane to E of Brenchley)
12-2.30, 6-11; 12-3, 7-10.30 Sun
(01892) 722561
Badger First Gold, K&B Sussex Bitter, seasonal beer H

A cosy, traditional pub with a typical Kentish white weatherboarded and tile-hung exterior, appearing in the Guide for its 22nd consecutive year under the same landlord. Inside it has wood panelling and oak beams, and lives up to its name with hop bines slung above the bar along with a yard of ale. A varied menu of traditional home-cooked food (not Wed) and takeaways is available. Outside there is a small garden and tables at the side and front of the building. (296)

Plaxtol

Golding Hop

Sheet Hill, TN15 0PT (N from Plaxtol Church, past Yopps Green) TQ600547
11-3 (2.30 Mon), 6 (5.30 Fri)-11; 11-11 Sat; 12-3.30, 7-10.30 Sun
(01732) 882150
Adnams Bitter, Broadside; guest beers G

Timeless, secluded pub, surrounded by orchards and woodland, serving good value beers direct from the cask, with changing guest beers sourced from far and wide. Four real ciders are also on offer including Westons Vintage and a house rough. The sunny garden slopes down to a children's play area and stream for summer enjoyment. Log-burning stoves keep customers warm in winter. Games played include petanque and bar billiards. Hearty pub grub is available at all sessions except Sunday, Monday and Tuesday evenings. (222)

Rainham

Angel

Station Road, ME8 7UH
12-11 (midnight Fri & Sat)
(01634) 360219 theangelrainham.com
Adnams Bitter; guest beers H

The Angel is a traditional drinkers' pub situated at the bottom of Station Road, where you will be greeted by Buster the dog. A fine pint of Adnams awaits, plus two changing guest beers, making this a little gem, well worth seeking out. The pub was CAMRA Medway branch Pub of the Year in 2004, 2005 and 2007. Smokers are catered for in the large garden.

Ramsgate

Churchill Tavern

19-22 The Paragon, CT11 9JX
11.30-11 (1am Fri & Sat); 12-11 Sun
(01843) 587862 churchilltavern.co.uk
Fuller's London Pride; Ringwood Old Thumper; guest beers H
A large corner house with superb views across the English channel. Formerly the Paragon Hotel, the Van Gogh and Steptoes, the Churchill is now 'the country pub in town', combining a brasserie-style restaurant with a traditional pub atmosphere. The bar was built from 19th-century oak church pews. Some ales are served from the cask including varying guest beers from a wide portfolio. Popular with locals, visitors and fans of live music which features regularly. (34,88)

Comfort Inn (San Clu)

Victoria Parade, CT11 8DT
11 (12 Sun)-11
(01843) 592345 comfortinnramsgate.co.uk
Greene King Abbot; Ramsgate Gadds' No3; Wells Bombardier H
A Victorian listed building on the town's East Cliff, with stunning views across the sea. The hotel's public area has recently been revamped in a startlingly modern style, with the bar immediately adjacent to the hotel restaurant where food is served daily. The bar presents a mixture of national real ale brands and a beer from the local Ramsgate Brewery. The garden is always busy in good weather with an uninterrupted panorama of the French coast. LocAle accredited.
(9,42)P

Foy Boat

8 Sion Hill, CT11 9HZ
11-11; 12-10.30 Sun
(01843) 591198
Young's Bitter; guest beers H
Overlooking the only Royal Harbour in England, the Foy Boat is reputedly the model for the Channel Packet Inn referred to by Ian Fleming in his book Goldfinger. The current building is a post-war replacement for the old Foy Boat Tavern, a Tomson & Wotton house which fell victim to WWII bombing in 1941. Good value food is available, including the popular Sunday carvery. Stunning views from the hotel rooms upstairs.

Montefiore Arms

1 Trinity Place, CT11 7HJ
12-2.30 (not Wed), 7-11; 12-3, 7-10.30 Sun
(01843) 593265
Ramsgate Gadds' No 7; guest beers H
A locals' pub with plenty of wood panelling creating an olde-worlde feel, where you are likely to be served by the friendly landlord. A long, narrow bar, games room and a small snug create a Tardis-like effect behind the exterior corner pub facade. The pub is named after Sir Moses Montefiore (1784-1885), a local Jewish philanthropist who was greatly beloved in Ramsgate. A keen supporter of mild month and other CAMRA initiatives, the Montefiore Arms was local Pub of the Year 2009 and the first pub in Kent to be LocAle accredited. Biddenden cider is always on draught.
Q(Dumpton Park)(9X,9)

Sir Stanley Gray

Pegwell Bay Hotel, 81 Pegwell Road, CT11 0NJ
11-11 (midnight Fri & Sat); 11.30-10.30 Sun
(01843) 599590 pegwellbayhotel.co.uk
Greene King Abbot; Ramsgate Gadds' No7; guest beers H
Located in picturesque Pegwell Bay and boasting spectacular views across the English Channel, the Sir Stanley Gray is part of the Thorley Taverns chain. Low beams and reclaimed panelling evoke an atmosphere redolent of the time when Pegwell was a hotbed of smuggling. Four real ales are usually on offer from both regionals and independents. A selection of home-cooked specials augments the main food menu. A tunnel links the pub to the Pegwell Bay Hotel, a former convalescent home. LocAle accredited.
P

Ripple

Plough Inn

Church Lane, CT14 8JH
12 (2 Mon-Wed winter)-11; 12-10.30 Sun
(01304) 360209
Courage Best Bitter; Fuller's ESB; Shepherd Neame Master Brew Bitter; guest beers H
A traditional pub in a tranquil, rural village setting, seemingly in the middle of nowhere but just outside Deal. A managed house, it is privately owned by Sutton Vale Caravan Park, about a mile away. Popular with walkers, it is easily accessible by field paths from Walmer. This is a renowned outlet for Fuller's ESB, a bit of a rarity in these parts. Do not be put off by six handpumps on the bar in such a quiet pub. Somehow it works! Quiz night is Wednesday. P

Rochester

Britannia Bar Café

376 High Street, ME1 1DJ
10-11 (2am Sat); 12-11 Sun
(01634) 815204 britannia-bar-cafe.co.uk
Goacher's Fine Light Ale; guest beers H
Situated between Rochester and Chatham railway stations, this bar can be busy at lunchtimes, attracting a mainly business clientele. The bar offers an extensive and popular daily menu, including breakfast (10am-noon). Evening meals are served Monday to Thursday and there is a traditional Sunday lunchtime roast. A stylish bar leads out into a small walled garden that is a sun trap in summer. Occasional special events and quizzes are held. Q

Cooper's Arms

10 St Margarets Street, ME1 1DJ
11-2.30, 5.30-11; 11-11 Fri & Sat; 12-10.30 Sun
(01634) 404298
Courage Best Bitter; guest beers H
Just off the High Street, in the shadows of the cathedral and castle, this ancient inn features in the Domesday Book, and is a contender for the oldest pub in Kent. The two bars contain items of historical interest including the original fireplace, which was uncovered a few years ago during renovation work. Good-quality lunches are served. If you happen to see a monk during your visit, it could be the resident ghost. QP

Good Intent
83 John Street, ME1 1YL
12-midnight (11 Sun)
(01634) 843118
Beer range varies G
This two-bar ale house is for real beer enthusiasts. An invaluable local asset, it caters for traditional and contemporary drinkers, with up to eight beers sourced from regional and national micro-breweries. Amenities include large-screen sport, live music and a south-facing garden. Medway CAMRA Pub of the Year for 2008, it hosts regular beer festivals. All real ales are served by gravity.
Q P

Man of Kent
6-8 John Street, ME1 1YN (200m off A2 from bottom of Star Hill)
2 (3 Mon)-11 (midnight Fri); 12-midnight Sat; 12-11 Sun
(0777) 2214315
Goacher's Fine Light Ale, Gold Star; Whitstable East India Pale Ale; guest beers H
This pub serves up to eight Kent brewery beers on handpump, and offers both Biddenden and Pawley Farm ciders in bottles. Dedicated to offering Kentish produce, even the wines come from the Biddenden and Meopham Valley vineyards. For those wanting to try different tastes and beer styles, the pub also offers over 30 bottled German and Belgium beers. Live music features on several evenings during the week.

Rusthall

Beacon
Tea Garden Lane, TN3 9JH (400m off A264 opp Rusthall cricket pitch) TQ563392
11-11; 12-10 Sun
(01892) 524252 the-beacon.co.uk
Harveys Sussex Best Bitter; Larkins Traditional; Taylor Landlord H
Set in 17 acres of grounds on a sandstone outcrop, the decking area has a 180 degree panoramic view of the Spa Valley below. The front bar is comfy with leather seating, surrounded by a collection of old wirelesses. The varied menu is of locally-sourced produce as the pub is a member of Kentish Fayre, and food can be enjoyed in one of four dining rooms. The downstairs bar caters for functions and is licensed for weddings. Fishing and camping are possible in the grounds.
Q (231,291) P

St Margaret's Bay

Coastguard
The Bay, CT15 6DY
11-11; 11-10.30 Sun
(01304) 853176 thecoastguard.co.uk
Beer range varies H
This pub's superb location at the foot of the White Cliffs merits the descent of the cliff path, and even the climb back afterwards. Lounge on the terrace and watch the shipping on the Strait of Dover while enjoying the view and good ale too. An ever-changing beer selection is always on offer, featuring the smaller breweries of Kent and Scotland. Westons cider is served alongside a wide range of continental bottled beers, and the pub has won several food awards. (15) P

St Mary in the Marsh

Star Inn
TN29 0BX TR065279
12-11 (10.30 Sun)
(01797) 362139 thestarinn-themarsh.co.uk
Shepherd Neame Master Brew Bitter; Young's Bitter; guest beers H
Situated in the heart of Romney Marsh, this Grade II-listed building was constructed in 1476 and became an ale house in 1711. A cosy, pretty village inn, where a warm and friendly welcome awaits, it offers real ale from four handpumps, home-cooked food and en-suite accommodation. Opposite is St Mary the Virgin church where author Edith Nesbit is buried. Noel Coward lodged in the adjacent cottages while writing his first play.
P

St Peters

White Swan
17 Reading Street, CT10 3AZ
11.30-2.30, 6 (5 Wed-Fri)-11; 11.30-11 Sat; 11.30-5 Sun
(01843) 863051
Adnams Bitter; guest beers H
Situated in a quiet, historic part of Broadstairs, steeped in smuggling tradition, this popular, welcoming local offers an ever-changing roster of six real ales. Formerly tied to Tomson & Wotton, the present building dates from the early 1900s, rebuilt after the original 17th-century structure burned down. The cosy lounge bar has an assortment of tables and chairs, with the public bar housing the pool table. The old tradition of different prices between the two bars is still observed here. Home-cooked food is served lunchtimes and evenings, Monday to Saturday.
Q

Sandgate

Ship Inn
65 Sandgate High Street, CT20 3AH (on A259)
11.30-11.30 (1am Fri & Sat); 12-11.30 Sun
(01303) 248525
Greene King IPA, Abbot; Hop Back Summer Lightning; Hopdaemon Incubus H**; guest beers** H/G
A good selection of ales is on offer from the long-established landlord. The beer range is considerably increased during holiday periods and a real ale festival takes place over the August bank holiday. The choice of real ciders has also increased, two of which come from Biddenden. This community pub also offers overnight accommodation in rooms with sea views.
(10,101,102)

Sandwich

Fleur de Lis
6-8 Delf Street, CT13 9BZ
10-11 (10.30 Sun)
(01304) 611131 verinitaverns.co.uk
Badger K&B Sussex Bitter; Greene King IPA; guest beer H
A popular and friendly pub, situated in the middle of this Cinque Port, catering for all types of customer. Each of the three areas that make up the

pub has its own character, and there is a separate restaurant space with an unusual painted cupola ceiling. Good pub food is supported by a specials board. Live bands play every Friday, pictures painted by local artists are displayed for sale, and dogs are welcome. Close to public transport. ⛿ ◐ ♿ ⇌ ▣ (13,14,88)

Sevenoaks

Anchor

32 London Road, TN13 1AS

11-3, 6-11.30; 10-4, 6-midnight Fri; 10-4, 7-midnight Sat; 12-5, 7-11 Sun

☎ (01732) 454898

Harveys Sussex Best Bitter; guest beer Ⓗ

A friendly town-centre pub with the area's longest serving licensee, popular with all ages. After entering the pub through the unusual circular lobby, look for the signs on the walls that reflect the landlord's sense of humour. Harveys is the regular beer – guest beers are sourced through the SIBA direct delivery scheme. Live blues music is performed monthly, usually the first Wednesday (check for additional dates). Good food is available Monday to Friday lunchtimes, a smaller range at other times. ◐ ▣ ♣ ⚊

Sheerness

Red Lion

61 High Street, Blue Town, ME12 1RW

10-midnight (1am Thu, Fri & Sat); 12-midnight Sun

☎ (01795) 664354

Beer range varies Ⓗ

An oasis with choice in Sheppey. Facing the former naval dockyard wall, this is the only real ale outlet remaining in the old Blue Town area of Sheerness, with its cobbled High Street. Three beers from regional and micro-breweries are served, with local customers having a say in which beers are ordered. No meals, but there is a free buffet all day on Sunday. Outside are tables and a covered and heated smoking area next to the pub. ♨ ❀ ⇌ ▣ ♣ ⚊

Sittingbourne

Long Hop

80 Key Street, ME10 1YU (on A2)

11.30-11 (1am Fri & Sat)

☎ (01795) 425957

Shepherd Neame Master Brew Bitter; guest beers Ⓗ

On the busy A2, almost two miles west of the centre of town. Once inside, however, you would hardly know the road is there. Parts of this rustic-looking pub date back 200 years and it was once known as the British Queen. Its new name was chosen in a competition around 20 years ago, and refers to the Gore Court cricket ground opposite. There is a covered smoking area. No meals Monday lunchtime. ♨ ❀ ◐ ▣ (333,334) ♣ P ⚊

Snargate

Red Lion 🏆 ★

TN29 9UQ (on A2080, 1 mile W of Brenzett) TQ990285

12-3, 7-10.30

☎ (01797) 344648

Beer range varies Ⓖ

Beautiful, unspoilt, award-winning pub on the remote Welland Marsh. The interior is decorated with WWII and Women's Land Army posters and features in CAMRA's National Inventory of pubs of outstanding historical interest. A haven for good conversation, it is also a friendly place to play one of the traditional games available. Several beer festivals are hosted annually, with the main festival in June. CAMRA branch Pub of the Year 2009. ♨ Q ❀ ⇌ (Appledore) ▣ (11B) ♣ ● P

Stalisfield Green

Plough Inn

ME13 0HY TQ955529

12-3, 6-11 (12.30 Fri); 12-midnight Sat; closed Mon; 12-8 (11 Summer) Sun

☎ (01795) 890256 🌐 stalisfieldgreen.com

Beer range varies Ⓗ

A historic multi-room pub set in attractive rural surroundings. Beers from most of Kent's micro-breweries are featured on a rotating basis, together with Biddenden cider. There is an extensive menu (no food is served Sun eve or Mon lunchtime). Varied live music is played on some Fridays – phone for details. The pub has a large enclosed garden and is a popular starting/finishing point for walks over the North Downs. There is a beer festival over the August bank holiday. ♨ ❀ ◐ Å ♣ ● P

Stansted

Black Horse

Tumblefield Road, TN15 7PR (1 mile N of A20 jct 2) TQ606621

11-11; 12-10.30 Sun

☎ (01732) 822355

Larkins Traditional; guest beers Ⓗ

Nestling in a secluded downland village, this plain Victorian building is the centre of the local community and also popular with visiting walkers and cyclists. A large natural garden with a children's play area is well used by families in summer. Biddenden cider is available and local breweries are supported. A Thai restaurant operates in the evenings (Tue to Sat) and Sunday lunches are recommended. ♨ Q ❀ ⛿ ◐ ♿ Å ● P ⚊

Staplehurst

Bell Inn ✔

High Street, TN12 0AY

12-3, 5-11; 12-11 Fri & Sat; 12-10.30 Sun

☎ (01580) 893366 🌐 bellinn-staplehurst.co.uk

Westerham Finchcocks Original; guest beers Ⓗ

This late-Victorian pub was fully refurbished in 2006, revealing the original floor tiling, half-timbered panelling and wooden floors. The bar area has comfortable seating and a log fire with a fireback featuring a Charles I motif. A second room on a raised level provides additional seating. A split-level restaurant serves bar snacks and meals featuring local produce every day. The large garden includes a children's play area. The two guest beers are mainly from SIBA brewers. Biddenden Bushells cider is available. ♨ Q ❀ ⛿ ◐ Å ⇌ ▣ (5) ♣ ● P ⚊

Lord Raglan

Chart Hill Road, TN12 0DE (½ mile N of A229) TQ786472
⏲ 12-3, 6.30-11.30; closed Sun
☎ (01622) 843747
Goacher's Light; Harveys Sussex Best Bitter; guest beer Ⓗ
An unspoilt, welcoming pub in a typical Kentish location. The bar is warmed by two log fires and a stove. A large orchard garden catches the evening sun. Bar snacks and full meals are always available. The guest beer changes frequently and local Double Vision cider is sold. A good example of a traditional pub serving excellent food.
⌂Q❀◐◑🚌(5)●P

Temple Ewell

Fox

High Street, CT16 3DU
⏲ 11.30-3.30, 6-11; 12-4, 7-11 Sun
☎ (01304) 823598
Caledonian Deuchars IPA; Greene King Abbot; guest beers Ⓗ
The pub is situated in the Dour Valley on the edge of Dover, in scenic countryside close to Kearsney Abbey. The chalk downs rise behind the pub garden which has a side-stream from the river flowing through it. In a congenial atmosphere, four real ales are served, with food lunchtimes and evenings (not Sun eve). Traditional pub games include darts, dominoes and skittles, and the pub runs regular events including quizzes, bingo and curry nights.
⌂❀◐◑♿⇌(Kearsney)🚌(15,15A,68)♣P⁵̶

Tilmanstone

Plough & Harrow

Dover Road, CT14 0HX (signed off A256 between Dover & Sandwich)
⏲ 11-11; 12-10.30 Sun
☎ (01304) 617582 🌐 ploughandharrowtilmanstone.co.uk
Shepherd Neame Master Brew Bitter, Spitfire, seasonal beers Ⓗ
The bar of this rural pub has a traditional feel to it, with wooden floors, sofas, a bar billiards table and an interesting collection of Kent coalfield memorabilia on the walls. Traditional home-cooked food is served in the conservatory restaurant overlooking the garden (no food Sun eve; booking recommended). The pub is popular with ramblers and walkers, families are also welcome, as are dogs. Traditional folk music is performed monthly. ⌂❀🛏◐◑🚌(88)♣P⁵̶

Trottiscliffe

Plough

Taylor's Lane, ME19 5DR TQ640602
⏲ 11.30-3, 6 (6.30 Sat)-11; 12-3 Sun
☎ (01732) 822233
Adnams Bitter, Broadside; Harveys Sussex Best Bitter Ⓗ
Weatherboarded pub situated just below the Pilgrims Way on the North Downs, providing a welcome stop for all, including walkers, families and dogs. The village, pronounced locally as 'Trosley', is noted for the Coldrum Stones, a Neolithic burial chamber. Beams with horse brasses reflect the 1483 origin of this pub and there are rumours of a friendly ghost called Alice. There are several drinking areas to choose from, as well as a small patio. The restaurant offers good-quality home-cooked food. ⌂Q❀◐◑🚌(58)♣P

Tunbridge Wells

Grove Tavern ✔

19 Berkley Road, TN1 1YR
⏲ 12-11
☎ (01892) 526549 🌐 grovetavern.co.uk
Harveys Sussex Best Bitter; Taylor Landlord; guest beer Ⓗ
Possibly the friendliest pub in Tunbridge Wells, this is certainly one of the oldest. Visitors are made very welcome and often stay for just another hour to enjoy the excellent ales and partake of snooker, crosswords, or just friendly chatter. The Grove is a locals' pub in the older part of town with free wireless Internet access for laptops. Dogs are always welcome and there is a lovely park nearby with swings and slides for children. ⌂⇌🚌♣

Royal Oak

92 Prospect Road, TN2 4SY
⏲ 12-11.30 (10.30 Sun)
☎ (01892) 542546 🌐 theroyaloak.food.officelive.com
Harveys Sussex Best Bitter; Larkins Traditional; guest beers Ⓗ
Large, traditional pub with an island bar, wood panelling, and comfy leather chairs in a secluded area. Quiet during the day, the pub is five minutes from the town centre and railway station, and also handy for Dunorlan Park. Good-quality food at good prices is on offer, all home made by the landlady, who is a professional chef of 25 years standing. Jazz plays some Sunday lunchtimes and a quiz night once a month. 🐴◐◑🚌(285)P⁵̶

Sankeys

39 Mount Ephraim, TN4 8AA
⏲ 10.30-11 (midnight Fri & Sat); 12-midnight Sun
☎ (01892) 511422 🌐 sankeys.co.uk
Sankeys Halfway to Paradise, Joey's Bite Ⓗ
Busy most nights, this interesting bar, two minutes' walk from the town centre, offers beers brewed specially for the pub plus the best selection of continental ales in west Kent, some on draught. A good collection of retro metal advertisments on the walls makes for an interesting read. An excellent restaurant downstairs specialises in fish dishes (booking recommended). The outside patio is very popular, especially in the summer months.
⌂❀◐◑♿⇌🚌●⁵̶

Upper Upnor

King's Arms 🏆

2 High Street, ME2 4XG
⏲ 11 (12 Sun)-11
☎ (01634) 717490
Beer range varies Ⓗ
This village local has two bars – one for drinking and the other a restaurant. The pub enjoys a good local reputation for food and the menu provides plenty of choice. Meals are served lunchtimes and evenings (except Sun and Mon). The large garden is lively in the summer and holds regular beer festivals. Medway CAMRA branch Pub of the Year 2009. Cider and perry come from Westons.
❀◐◑🎯🚌(197)●⁵̶

Tudor Rose

29/31 High Street, ME2 4XG
⏲ 11 (12 Sun)-11
☎ (01634) 715305
Shepherd Neame Master Brew Bitter, Kent's Best, Spitfire, Bishops Finger, seasonal beers Ⓗ
This multi-roomed pub is situated at the bottom of the cobbled High Street next to Upnor Castle, overlooking the River Medway and the former dockyard. The garden is partly surrounded by the castle's 17th-century wall. Meals are served at all times except Monday evening. Master of Beer award winner in 2008, this pub serves the full range of Shepherd Neame beers, including some produced in the micro-brewery. Occasional live music plays on Sunday afternoon. Use the car park at the top of the village. ⛫❀◐◑🚌(197)⛳

Walmer

Berry 🏆

23 Canada Road, CT14 7EQ
⏲ 11.30-2.30 (Mon, Wed & Fri), 5.30-11.30; 11-11.30 Sat; 11.30-11 Sun
☎ (01304) 362411 🌐 theberrywalmer.co.uk
Harveys Sussex Best Bitter; guest beers Ⓗ
Be sure to seek out this superb local just off Walmer Green and the seafront. Five handpumps dispense an excellent selection of beers from regional and micro-breweries. Two real ciders and a real perry are usually available. February is real ale festival time and the autumn Oktoberfest introduces a German theme. A good range of pub games is kept, and darts, pool, football and quiz teams keep things busy. Outside is a pleasant drinking area. CAMRA branch Pub of the Year 2008. ⛫❀🚌(13,14,82)♣🍎P⛳

West Malling

Bull

1 High Street, ME19 6QH (S from A20 on left after railway bridge)
⏲ 12-2.30, 5-11; 12-11 Fri & Sat; 12-10.30 Sun
☎ (01732) 842753
Young's Bitter; guest beers Ⓗ
Unpretentious but rightly popular local dating from the 15th century with a friendly, knowledgeable landlord – ask about his special guest beers. A cosy corner with sofa and TV at the far end does not intrude on the conversation around the bar. To the left is a quiet, simply-furnished room where darts is played and beers are ordered through a serving hatch. There is a large patio/beer garden at the rear. Good value Sunday lunches, no food Monday. ⛫Q❀◐⊟⇌🚌(72,151)♣⛳

> Upon both mind and body, then, beer exercises a gracious and salutary influence. It civilises and sustains; it feeds and refreshes; it soothes and humours. As an influence no other drink can compare with it in humanity and companionability. It adjusts the human machine to its optimum working conditions.
> **Anon**, 1934

West Peckham

Swan on the Green

The Green, ME18 5JW (1 mile W of B2016 at Mereworth)
⏲ 11-3 (4 Sat), 6-11 (8 Mon); 12-9 (5 winter) Sun
☎ (01622) 812271 🌐 swan-on-the-green.co.uk
Swan Bewick, Cygnet, Fuggles, Trumpeter, seasonal beers Ⓗ
Opposite the village green and the church, at the end of a no-through road, this pub was first licensed in 1685. A more recent refurbishment has created a modern interior with a wooden floor and a ceiling adorned with hops. Renowned for its food, the menu features locally-sourced ingredients (not Sun and Mon eves). The beers come from a micro-brewery behind the pub. It is a good idea to know the difference between Cobs and Pens before visiting the toilet! ⛫Q❀◐◑P

Westerham

General Wolfe

High Street, TN16 1RQ
⏲ 12-11 (12.30 Fri & Sat); 12-10.30 Sun
☎ (01959) 562104
Greene King IPA, Old Speckled Hen, Abbot Ⓗ
Traditional weatherboarded pub named after a famous resident of the town, General Wolfe of Quebec fame. The garden forms part of the former Black Eagle Brewery. The interior comprises a long room divided into a number of areas, one with a log fire in winter. The pub serves a varied food range (no meals Sun eve) and a good choice of malt whiskies. Quiz night is Wednesday. ⛫Q❀◐◑🚌(246,401,410)♣P

Whitstable

Four Horseshoes

62 Borstal Hill, CT5 4NA (A290 on edge of town)
⏲ 4.45 (11 Sat)-11; 12-10.30 Sun
☎ (01227) 273876
Shepherd Neame Master Brew Bitter, Kent's Best Ⓗ
Small, traditional local pub, originally a forge in 1636. An unusual three-bar layout is built stepwise up the hillside. Bat and Trap, darts and board games are played, while amenities include an in-house poker league on Tuesday – all welcome. Takeaway meals can be delivered to the pub, and the landlady will supply plates and cutlery after 6pm. By arrangement, you can have your own barbecue in the beer garden. Dogs are welcome, but children only in the garden. ⛫Q❀⊟🚌(4,6)♣P⛳

Pearson's

Sea Wall, CT5 1BT (on seafront at end of High Street)
⏲ 12-11 (midnight Fri & Sat)
☎ (01227) 272005
Ramsgate Gadds' No 3, Gadds' No 5, Gadds' No 7, Seasider Ⓗ
Pearson's Crab and Oyster House was built in 1577 and is just behind the sea wall. It has undergone many changes but retains the charm of an old-fashioned seaside inn and restaurant. There are two interlinking bar areas and an upstairs restaurant with stunning views over the Thames estuary. This is a rare outlet for Gadds' beers in Whitstable. Outdoor drinking is on the pub forecourt or on the sea wall itself. 🐴❀◐◑⇌🚌(4,6)

Ship Centurion ✓
111 High Street, CT5 1AY
⏲ 11-11 (11.30 Fri & Sat); 12-7 Sun
☎ (01227) 264740
Adnams Bitter; Elgood's Black Dog; guest beers Ⓗ
Kent CAMRA Pub of the Year 2007 is the only pub in town always serving mild, along with ever-changing guest beers and Biddenden cider. This centrally located free house is festooned with colourful hanging baskets in summer. Fascinating photographs of old Whitstable hang in the comfortable bar. Live entertainment is hosted on Thursday evenings (except Jan). Home-cooked bar food often features authentic German produce – the only food on Saturday is schnitzel. A public car park is close by in Middle Wall. ◑⇌🚌(4,6)●⚐

Wittersham

Swan Inn
1 Swan Street, TN30 7PH (on B2080 between Rye & Tenterden) TQ897275
⏲ 11-midnight (2am Fri & Sat); 12-midnight Sun
☎ (01797) 270913 🌐 swan-wittersham.co.uk
Goacher's Fine Light Ale; Greene King Abbot; Harveys Sussex Best Bitter; Rother Valley Smild Ⓗ**; guest beers** Ⓖ
A regular local CAMRA Pub of the Year, extensively altered in 2007. It has retained its two bar character but has added extra comfort for its varied clientele. Up to eight beers are on offer, including a mild and six ciders. There are summer and winter beer festivals and a cider festival in May as well as regular live music. Good value food is available.
♨Q❀◑⊞♿⇌🚌(312)●P⚐

Woodchurch

Six Bells
Bethersden Road, TN26 3QQ (close to village green opp church) TQ942349
⏲ 11 (12 Sun)-midnight
☎ (01233) 860246
Fuller's London Pride; Harveys Sussex Best Bitter; Woodforde's Wherry Best Bitter; guest beers Ⓗ
A popular village local, welcoming and unspoilt, and dog friendly. It has a separate public bar and a saloon bar which also has a dining area but still has plenty of space for drinkers. A good range of freshly-prepared meals is available Wednesday to Sunday. A large enclosed beer garden at the rear is ideal for families. ♨Q❀◑⊞♿🚌(297)●P

Wrotham

Bull Hotel
Bull Lane, TN15 7RF
⏲ 12-3, 6-11; 12-8 Sun
☎ (01732) 789800 🌐 thebullhotel.com
Dark Star Best Bitter, Hophead, seasonal beers Ⓗ
Former 15th-century coaching inn that once formed part of the stable block of the former archbishop's palace. It has been tastefully refurbished but kept three fireplaces in the restaurant and bar areas. The function room was originally the village bakery. The restaurant uses local produce in all dishes. The pub specialises in Dark Star beers. ♨❀🛏◑♿🚌(306,308,408)P⚐

Wrotham Heath

Moat
London Road, TN15 7RR (on A20 near M26 jct)
⏲ 12-11 (midnight Fri & Sat); 12-10.30 Sun
☎ (01732) 882263
Badger First Gold, Tanglefoot, seasonal beers Ⓗ
A totally refurbished roadhouse on the A20 comprising a pub and restaurant. The interior is bright and airy, although some original features have been retained, including four log-burning fires and some beams. Food is served all day every day and a quiz is hosted on Thursday evening. The outdoor seating area to the rear has heated lamps and umbrellas. ♨❀◑♿P⚐

Red Lion, Sheerness (Photo: Chris Hunt).

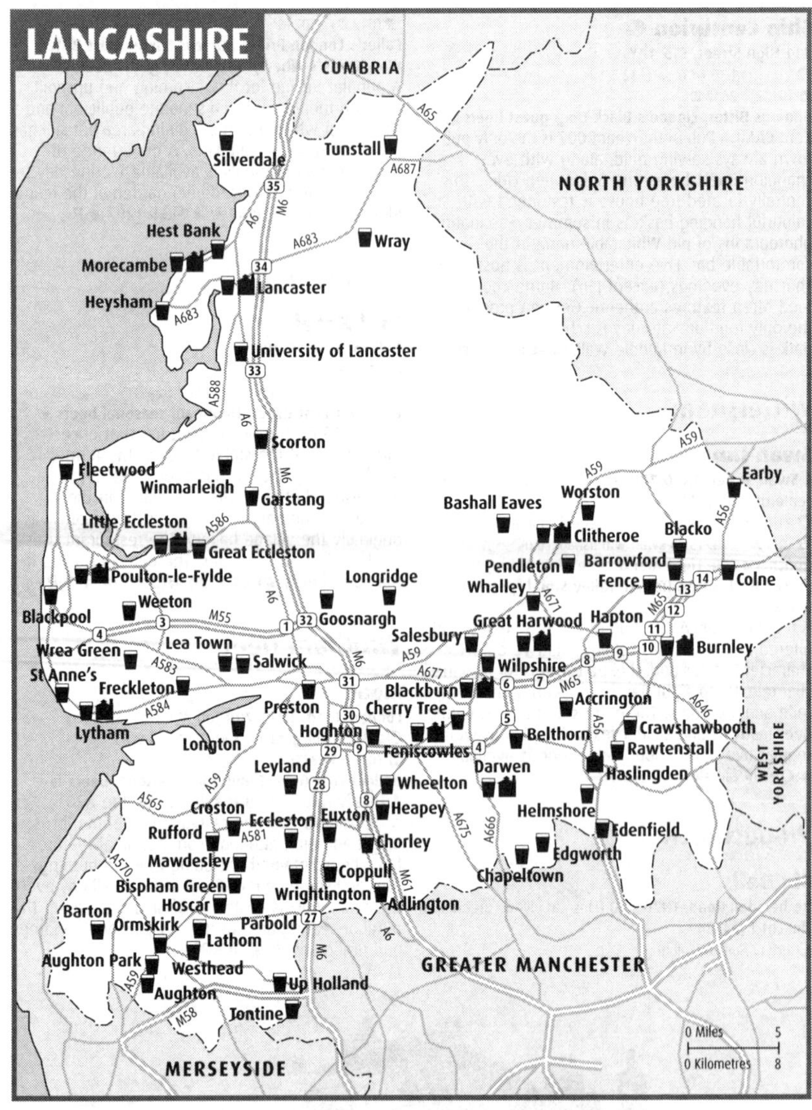

Accrington

Park Inn

68 Manchester Road, BB5 2BN (on A680 to Haslingden)
2-midnight; 1-2am Fri; 12-2am Sat; 12-midnight Sun
(01254) 237043
John Smith's Bitter; guest beers H
A local community pub with a narrow bar area with seating section, a separate back room, and a pool room at the front. The pub is very popular with the locals and can be busy at times. There is one guest beer alongside the regular John Smith's Bitter. (X40,484,464)

Peel Park

Turkey Street, BB5 6EW (200m from A679, adj to Peel Park school)
12-11.30
(01254) 235830
Tetley Bitter; guest beers H
A genuine free house opposite the site of the old Stanley football ground. Eight beers are sold, mainly from micros. The main bar is a large open front room which is divided into two sections. There is a separate little pool room, and a rear room used for dining or meetings. Two beer festivals a year are held, on the spring bank holiday and in November. Outside is a covered smoking area. (23,263)P

Adlington

Spinners Arms

23 Church Street, PR7 4EX
12-11 (midnight Fri & Sat)
(01257) 483331
Coniston Bluebird; Moorhouse's Black Cat; Taylor Landlord; guest beers H
Welcoming and friendly pub known as the Bottom Spinners to differentiate it from the other Spinners

Arms in the village. A single bar serves three seating areas and there is a pleasant outdoor drinking area to the front of the pub. There is no pool table, TV or gaming machine, just an open log fire. The bar menu offers home-cooked food. Guest beers, often sourced from local breweries, always include a mild. A CAMRA Pub of the Season plaque is proudly displayed. ⚠Q❀◖⇌🚌P⁄–

Aughton

Derby Arms

Prescot Road, L39 6TA (at Bowker's Green on B5197, S of Ormskirk) SD407043

⏲ 11.30-11 (midnight Fri & Sat); 11.30-10.30 Sun

☎ (01695) 422237

Tetley Mild, Bitter; guest beers Ⓗ

A multi-award winning CAMRA pub with a local, street-corner feel. Its recent refurbishment is a great example of how it should be done. Guest beers come from micro-breweries and are always interesting, while the food is excellent. Outside there is a pleasant garden to enjoy in the summer. Two real fires offer yet more warmth in winter in this hugely enjoyable hostelry. The pub supports many charities and holds regular quiz nights. ⚠❀◖◗⊟♣P

Aughton Park

Dog & Gun ✔

233 Long Lane, L39 5BU (near railway station) SD413064

⏲ 12 (4 Mon & Tue)-midnight

☎ (01695) 423303

Banks's Bitter; Jennings Bitter; Marston's Pedigree; guest beers Ⓗ

The Dog & Gun has been serving the residents of Aughton with top class ales for many years. With the demise of Burtonwood beers, the pub is now serving ales from the more extensive Marston's range. Although some alterations have taken place to partly open out the pub layout, it retains its intimacy, with old portraits on the walls and, in winter months, a real open fire. A pet parrot is usually present to interest visitors. ⚠Q♘❀◖◗♿⇌P⁄–

Barrowford

George & Dragon ✔

217 Gisburn Road, BB9 6JD (at jct of A682 & B6247 near jct 13 of M65)

⏲ 3 (12 Thu)-midnight; 12-1am Fri & Sat; 12-midnight Sun

☎ (01282) 612929 🌐 gndbarrowford.co.uk

Moorhouse's Premier; guest beers Ⓗ

A community village pub supporting several sports teams, situated near the Pendle Heritage Centre, Barrowford Park and a short walk from Barrowford Locks on the Leeds-Liverpool Canal. The pub is often busy at weekends and live music is played on the last Saturday of the month. The guest beers always include one from Bowland Brewery, plus another sourced from a local micro. ❀🚌(P70,P71,109)♣⁄–

Barton

Blue Bell

Southport Road, L39 7JU (on A5147 S of Halsall) SD362088

⏲ 12-11 (10.30 Sun)

☎ (01704) 841406

Beer range varies Ⓗ

A friendly pub in the heart of the countryside, which caters for the needs of locals and passing visitors. Many of the rural walks in the area should include a stop here, as good value food is available, along with traditional games, and occasional live music in the evening. An unusual feature is the animal farm at the rear of the car park where you will find an assortment of sheep, goats, rabbits and hens. ⚠♘❀◖◗🚌(300)♣P⁄–

Bashall Eaves

Red Pump Inn

Clitheroe Road, BB7 3DA

⏲ 12-2, 6-11; closed Mon and alternate Tue in winter; 12-9 Sun

☎ (01254) 826227 🌐 theredpumpinn.co.uk

Black Sheep Best Bitter; Moorhouse's Cauldron; Tirril Old Faithful Ⓗ

Situated on the edge of the small village of Bashall Eaves – enjoying views over the Ribble Valley to Pendle Hill – is the award-winning Red Pump. Locally-sourced produce is served in this excellent dining pub with renowned and comfortable accommodation. The high standards are also reflected in the quality and choice of beer, usually including a brew from Moorhouse's as well as changing guests. Residents can also enjoy private fishing on the well-stocked River Hodder nearby. ⚠Q❀🛏◖◗♿🚌(B11)P

Belthorn

Dog Inn

61 Belthorn Road, BB1 2NN SD716248

⏲ 12-2 (not Mon), 5.30-11; 12-11 Sat; 12-10.30 Sun

☎ (01254) 690794

Caledonian Deuchars IPA; guest beers Ⓗ

A traditional multi-level village inn, featuring a part stone-flagged floor, wooden beams and open stonework warmed by a real fire. The restaurant serving home-cooked food affords fine views over the moors. Originally one of nine beer and ale houses locally, this is one of just three that survive. Three beers are on handpump, one from a LocAle micro. Noteworthy are the display case between the old wooden staircases that lead to the toilets and the wooden tables and chairs. ⚠❀◖◗🚌(244)P

INDEPENDENT BREWERIES

Bowland Clitheroe
Bryson's Morecambe
Fallons Darwen
Fuzzy Duck Poulton-le-Fylde
Garthela Blackburn (NEW)
Hart Little Eccleston
Hopstar Darwen
Lancaster Lancaster
Lytham Lytham
Moonstone Burnley
Moorhouse's Burnley
Pennine Haslingden
Red Rose Great Harwood
Three B's Feniscowles
Thwaites Blackburn

Bispham Green

Eagle & Child

Maltkiln Lane, L40 3SG (off B5246)
⏲ 12-3, 5.30-11; 12-10.30 Sun
☎ (01257) 462297
Beer range varies Ⓗ
Outstanding 16th-century local that overlooks the village green, with antique furniture and stone-flagged floors. The pub is renowned for its food and features occasional themed menu evenings (booking advisable). An annual beer festival is held on the first May bank holiday in a marquee on the lawn behind the pub. Tables around the bowling green offer wonderful views of the surrounding countryside. The pub stocks a guest cider range, as well as an ever-changing choice of ales. Winner of Wigan CAMRA branch Pub of the Season 2008.
♨Q❀◐◑♿●P

Blackburn

Adelphi Hotel

33 Railway Road, BB1 1EZ (next to bus & train stations)
⏲ 11-11; 12-10.30 Sun
☎ (01254) 681128
Black Sheep Best Bitter; guest beers Ⓗ
A friendly town-centre, open-plan, split-level pub with up to five real ales. Other attractions include large-screen TV showing sport and music, and a '60s-'90s disco each Saturday night. A favourite with visiting football supporters, next to the railway and bus stations, the hostelry hosts pub league pool, darts and dominoes, and is an ideal spot for a quick pint while awaiting travel connections. The window inscription says it all: 'Ye Wines and Ales that make Ye Merry!' ⇌🚌♣🚬

Postal Order ✔

Darwen Street, BB2 2BH
⏲ 9-midnight
☎ (01254) 676400
Courage Directors; Greene King IPA; Marston's Pedigree; guest beers Ⓗ
Former general post office, rumoured to be haunted upstairs. A very lively Wetherspoon's, it has what must be the longest bar in Blackburn, plus raised seating areas at each end of the main hall and a smaller back room with fire. With three banks of handpumps and often a real cider, the pub does a great deal to support local micros and has joined the LocAle scheme, with two or more local brews available at any one time. ◐◑♿⇌●

Blacko

Cross Gaits ✔

Beverley Road, BB9 6RF (off A682) SD867414
⏲ 12-3 (not Mon & Tue), 5-midnight; 12-midnight Sat; 12-10.30 Sun
☎ (01282) 616312
Jennings Cumberland Ale; Marston's Burton Bitter; guest beers Ⓗ
A pleasant country inn serving home-made food 5-9pm Tuesday to Thursday, 12-2, 5-9pm Friday, 12-9pm Saturday and Sunday. The guest beers come from the Marston's list and the pub won the top beer quality award from the Marston's estate in 2008. Note the inscription over the front door dating from 1730: 'Good ale tomorrow for nothing!' ♨Q🛏❀◐◑P

Blackpool

Auctioneer ✔

235-237 Lytham Road, FY1 3AF
⏲ 9-midnight (12.30am Fri & Sat)
☎ (01253) 346412
Greene King IPA, Abbot; guest beers Ⓗ
Wetherspoon's pub, converted from a supermarket but originally an auction room – hence the name. Decorated in a café style, the walls feature many pictures of old Blackpool. There are outside drinking areas to the rear and front.
Q❀◐◑♿⇌(South)⊖🚌(11)🚬

Dunes Hotel

561 Lytham Road, FY4 1SA (500m from airport on B5262)
⏲ 11-11 (midnight Thu-Sat)
☎ (01253) 403854
Black Sheep Best Bitter; Theakston Best Bitter; Wells Bombardier Ⓗ
A regular in the Guide, this local community pub still has a separate vault. It hosts quiz nights on Thursday and Sunday. At the front of the pub, a heated, flower-decked patio allows for outdoor summer drinking. Smokers are catered for too. The meals served here are basic pub fare and finish at 7.30pm. Several buses pass the pub. Handy for Blackpool Airport. ❀◐◑🗔♿⇌🚌(11,16,68)♣P🚬

No 4 & Freemasons ✔

Layton Road, FY3 8ER (jct with Newton Drive)
⏲ 12-11 (midnight Tue, Fri-Sun)
☎ (01253) 302877
Thwaites Nutty Black, Original, Wainwright, Lancaster Bomber Ⓗ
This smart suburban pub fronts on to Newton Drive and is located a mile inland from the seafront with bus stops directly outside. The main lounge has both dining and drinking areas with TV screens and pictures of Blackpool's heyday. The rear games room has pool and darts. Beers are served in top condition and meals are available 12-2.30, 5-8pm Monday to Friday, 12-8pm Saturday and 12-6pm Sunday. ❀◐◑🗔♿🚌(2,15)♣P🚬

Pump & Truncheon

Bonny Street, FY1 5AR (behind Louis Tussauds Waxworks)
⏲ 11-11
☎ (01253) 624099
Boddingtons Bitter; guest beers Ⓗ
Situated opposite Bonney Street police station, this bare-brick and wood former-Hogshead makes the most of its local connections. An impressive display of police badges from around the world is displayed over the bar, while specially-painted friezes give a wry and amusing reflection on the pub's connections. Hearty and generous home-cooked meals are served. Six beers are available in summer, three in winter, with Algates and the local Fuzzy Duck featuring regularly in this genuine free house. ♨◐◑♿⊖(Central Pier)🚌♣

Saddle Inn ✔

286 Whitegate Drive, FY3 9PH (at Preston Old Road jct)
⏲ 12-11 (midnight Fri & Sat)
☎ (01253) 767827
Draught Bass; Thwaites Original; guest beers Ⓗ
Blackpool's oldest pub, established in 1770, and CAMRA local Pub of the Year 2007 and 2008. The Saddle comprises a main bar and two side rooms, plus a large patio for outside drinking during the

summer. This excellent, friendly pub usually has six guest beers on offer. A good menu of food is served all day. ♨❀◐◑♿🚌(2,4,61)P⚟

Shovels

260 Common Edge Road, FY4 5DH (on B5261, ½ mile from A5230 jct)
⏲ 12-11 (midnight Thu-Sat)
☎ (01253) 762702
Beer range varies Ⓗ
A large, open-plan pub which has won CAMRA Local Pub of the Year on more than one occasion. Six handpumps are on at any time, offering a range from micros and changing on a daily basis. The pub screens most sporting events and there is a quiz every Thursday. The annual beer festival in October attracts people from all over the country. Good food is very popular with diners, served from 12 to 9.30pm daily. ♨❀◐◑♿🚌(14)♣P⚟

Burnley

Bridge Bier Huis 🏆

2 Bank Parade, BB11 1UH (behind shopping centre)
⏲ 12-midnight (2am Fri & Sat); closed Mon & Tue; 12-11 Sun
☎ (01282) 411304 🌐 thebridgebierhuis.co.uk
Hydes Bitter; guest beers Ⓗ
This free house has a large open bar area and a small separate snug to one side. Part of the LocAle initiative, it features up to five guest beers, usually from micro-breweries. A good range of Belgian and other foreign beers is on offer, with five on tap and a large selection of bottles plus real cider. The pub hosts a regular Wednesday night quiz and occasional weekend live music. Live acts feature throughout the Easter Burnley Blues Festival (check website for details). CAMRA West Pennines Region Pub of the Year 2007. ❀◐⇌(Central)🚌♣🍎

Cross Keys ✔

170 St James Street, BB11 1NR
⏲ 11 (12 Sat)-11 (midnight Fri & Sat); 12-7 Sun
☎ (01282) 424660
Taylor Landlord; guest beers Ⓗ
Situated at the bottom end of St James Street, opposite the site of the old Masseys Brewery, this large, imposing pub was Masseys' pride and joy. Signed up to East Lancs CAMRA LocAle initiative, all four ales are from local breweries, with Moorhouse's always on the bar. The pub offers football on satellite TV, with a screen in the covered and heated outdoor smoking area. There are also six letting rooms, each with digital TV. 🛏⇌(Central)♣⚟

Gannow Wharf

168 Gannow Lane, BB12 6QH
⏲ 7 (5 Fri)-11; 3-11 Sat & Sun
☎ (07855) 315498
Beer range varies Ⓗ
Next to the Leeds-Liverpool canal at Gannow Bridge, this pub offers a warm and friendly welcome with four beers to choose from. Signed up to CAMRA's East Lancs LocAle initiative, all four beers are usually sourced from local breweries. A biker-friendly venue with a comfortable covered and heated smoking area. Facilities include live music, quizzes and satellite TV sports. ⇌(Rosegrove)🚌(111)⚟

Ministry of Ale

9 Trafalgar Street, BB11 1TQ (100m from Manchester Road railway station)
⏲ 5-11 Wed & Thu; 12.30-midnight Fri; 11-midnight Sat; 12-11 Sun
☎ (01282) 830909 🌐 ministryofale.co.uk
Beer range varies Ⓗ
The home of the Moonstone Brewery, this is the only free house to showcase the range in Burnley. You can see the 2½ barrel plant in the front room of this small local. Two Moonstone beers are available always, alongside two constantly changing guests from micro-breweries. Enjoy a friendly welcome, with an emphasis on good beer and conversation. The walls feature regular art exhibitions. There is a popular quiz on Thursday night. ❀⇌(Manchester Road)🚌(X43,X44)⚟

Chapletown

Chetham Arms

83 High Street, BL7 0EW (on B6391) SD734157
⏲ 12 (5 Mon & Tue)-11 (1am Thu-Sat); 12-11 Sun
☎ (01204) 852279
Bank Top Flat Cap; Moorhouse's Pendle Witches Brew; Taylor Landlord; guest beer Ⓗ
Dating from the 18th century, this village inn has been extended to provide a lounge for dining. Winter and summer opening times vary, so check first. LocAle is available in the bar, which has a through hatch to the rear hide-away room, with flagged floors in parts and a real fire. A popular meeting place for locals, visitors and walkers, live music often plays. Nearby are the Wayoh Reservoir and Turton Tower -originally a medieval pele tower set in nine acres of woodland gardens. ♨❀◐◑P

Cherry Tree

Station

391 Preston Old Road, BB2 5LW (at railway station)
⏲ 3-12.30am; 11-1.30am Fri & Sat; 11-12.30am Sun
☎ (01254) 201643
Thwaites Nutty Black, Original, Wainwright, Lancaster Bomber, seasonal beers Ⓗ
A friendly pub about two miles from Blackburn, selling the full range of Thwaites beers – four regulars and two changing seasonals/specials. Open and modern with a central bar, facilities include satelite TV and a jukebox. There is karaoke on Thursday and a DJ on Friday and Saturday, plus facilities for cards, darts, dominoes and pool. The Station has a pub football team and regularly hosts charity events. ❀♿⇌🚌(152)♣P

Chorley

Malt 'n' Hops

50-52 Friday Street, PR6 0AH (behind railway station)
⏲ 12-11 (10.30 Sun)
☎ (01257) 260967
Beartown Kodiak Gold, Bearskinful, seasonal beers; guest beers Ⓗ
Situated close to Chorley railway and bus stations, this pub has a long-standing reputation in the local area for fine cask ales. Originally converted from an old shop in 1989, it became a haven for local drinkers due to a fine selection of guest beers. Now owned by Beartown Brewery of Congleton, it still has up to seven guest beers plus permanent beers from Beartown. It keeps to traditional licensing hours and is a short walk from the town centre. ❀⇌🚌🍎⚟

Potters Arms

42 Brooke Street, PR7 3BY (next to Morrisons)
☼ 3-11.30 (midnight Fri); 12-4, 7-midnight Sat; 12-5, 7-11 Sun
☎ (01257) 267954
Black Sheep Best Bitter; Three B's Doff Cocker; guest beers Ⓗ
Small, friendly free house named after the owners, Mr & Mrs Potter, situated at the bottom of Brooke Street alongside the railway bridge. The central bar serves two games areas, while two comfortable lounges are popular with locals and visitors alike. The pub displays a fine selection of photographs from the world of music, as well as vintage local scenes. Regular darts and dominoes nights are well-attended and the chip butties go down a treat. The smoking area is covered.
⛰≉🚌(10,11)♣P⚟

Prince of Wales ✔

9-11 Cowling Brow, PR6 0QE (off B6228)
☼ 12-11.30 (midnight Fri-Sun)
☎ (01257) 413239
Jennings Bitter, Cumberland Ale, seasonal beers; guest beers Ⓗ
Stone terraced pub in the south-eastern part of town, not far from the Leeds-Liverpool Canal. An unspoilt interior incorporates a traditional tap room, games room, large lounge and a comfortable snug with real fire. There is photographic evidence of the licensee's love of jazz, and collections of brewery artefacts and saucy seaside postcards are also on display. A large selection of malt whiskies is behind the bar and sandwiches are served on request. No swearing policy. ⛰❀⊟🚌(10,11)♣⚟

Swan With Two Necks

Hollinshead Street, Chorley Bottoms, PR7 1EP (at foot of steps off Park Road behind St Lawrence church)
☼ 12-12.20am (1am Thu); 12-2.30am Fri & Sat; 12-1am Sun
☎ (01257) 266649
Lancaster Blonde, Black; Moorhouse's Black Cat, Pride of Pendle, Blond Witch, Pendle Witches Brew Ⓗ
Chorley's hidden gem, which prides itself on catering for all generations in enjoyable harmony. Five handpumps serve quality ales from LocAle breweries. Food, served in the bar and picturesque Cygneture bistro, is of the highest standard, ranging from homely to exotic. Booking is recommended. High-quality entertainment is assured: jazz, bluegrass, folk, pop, karaoke and disco. ⛰❀◐♿≉🚌P⚟

White Bull

135 Market Street, PR7 2SG
☼ 4-11; 2-1am Fri; 11-1am Sat
☎ (01257) 275300
Bank Top Flat Cap; Greene King Old Speckled Hen; Theakston Best Bitter Ⓗ
Situated next to the Big Lamp at the south end of Market Street, the White Bull remains a beacon for real ale when so many traditional pubs around it are closing down, retaining a convivial atmosphere. A small beer garden can be found to the rear of the pub, which is used in the summer months. ❀≉🚌♣

Clitheroe

New Inn

Parson Lane, BB7 2JN (close to Clitheroe Castle)
☼ 12-midnight (10.30 Sun)
☎ (01200) 443653
Coach House Gunpowder Mild; Moorhouse's Premier Bitter; guest beers Ⓗ
Nestling just below the 12th-century castle, the New Inn regularly has ten handpumps in operation. As well as the two regular beers, you may discover others from a range of breweries that includes Tirril, Cottage, Phoenix and Goose-Eye, all keenly priced for the Ribble Valley. The pub is often used for meetings of local groups and has a real community feel. A central bar serves four separate rooms, all with fires, one with a TV. Occasional live music plays. ⛰Q❀≉🚌P

Colne

Admiral Lord Rodney ✔

Mill Green, Waterside, BB8 0TA
☼ 12 (4 Mon & Tue)-midnight
☎ (01282) 870083 🌐 admirallordrodneycolne.co.uk
Beer range varies Ⓗ
This old community pub was built in 1910 and is set in Colne's historic South Valley. The popular Fern Dean Way starts outside the building. Four to six constantly changing beers are offered, with the emphasis on local breweries. Quality home-cooked food is served Wednesday to Sunday, complementing the excellent range of beers.
⛰◐≉🚌(16)♣

Coppull

Red Herring

Mill Lane, PR7 5AN (off B5251 next to Coppull Mill)
☼ 3-11; 12-11.30 Fri & Sat; 12-11 Sun
☎ (01257) 470130
Beer range varies Ⓗ
This oasis of real ale is situated in the former offices of the imposing next-door mill. It was converted to a pub some years ago and the bar is a large single room plus an extension, usually offering three micro-brewed beers. TV sports fans are catered for, as are anglers who use the mill pond opposite. The pub hosts regular music nights and barbecues and has a large first-floor function room. Trainspotters will enjoy close proximity to the West Coast Main Line. ⛰❀🚌(7,362)♣P⚟

Crawshawbooth

Masons Arms ✔

6 Co-operation Street, BB4 8AG
☼ 4 (12 Sat & Sun)-midnight
☎ (01706) 218993
Moorhouse's Pride of Pendle; Theakston Best Bitter; guest beer Ⓗ
A newly reopened pub, the landlord is dedicated to real ales. The interior is divided into three small rooms with natural stone floors, one dedicated to games and the others with their own TVs. The pub holds small events once or twice a month, including whisky tasting. There is good access with a nearby car park and a major bus route just down the road. ⛰🚌⊡

Croston

Wheatsheaf ✔

Town Road, PR26 9RA
☼ 12-11 (10.30 Sun)
☎ (01772) 600370

Taylor Landlord; guest beers [H]
Situated next to the village green, this former barn specialises in gastro food, especially fish dishes. However, the ale is certainly not neglected, with one regular and three guests beers. Candles adorn each table to give a cosy feel and there is an outdoor drinking area to the front. Live music is on alternate Fridays. Food is served all day Friday to Sunday. The cider is Westons Old Rosie.
(7,112)P

Darwen

Black Horse

72 Redearth Road, BB3 2AF
12-11
(01254) 873040 theblackun.co.uk
Fallons seasonal beers; guest beers [H]
Lively, friendly community local – the brewery tap for Fallons, just down the road. Beer festivals are held on the last weekend of the month, with themed new and rare beers. Cider is available from the cellar, and there are meal deals on Saturday and Sunday afternoons. Live music on a Thursday night is popular, with jazz on the first Thursday in the month and groups/jam sessions otherwise. TV sport, a satellite jukebox and a games room offer something for everyone, with teams in local leagues. At the rear is a paved, seated and tented smoking area.

Earby

Punch Bowl

Skipton Road, BB18 6JJ (on main road between Earby and Skipton) SD906473
12-midnight (1am Fri & Sat)
(01282) 843017
Marston's Pedigree; Moorhouse's Cauldron; guest beers [H]
Popular pub and restaurant on the edge of the village with an open-plan main room with bar area and Sky/Setanta sports TV, and a separate dining area. Frequented by locals and passing trade, there is always a demand for the good home-made food created from fresh local ingredients (served 12-3, 5-8pm). Sunday roast beef comes in small, medium and large portions. To the rear is a spacious garden and ample parking. Two changing guest beers are offered, possibly three in summer. Look out for the comedy and cask ale nights.
(215)P

Eccleston

Original Farmers Arms

Towngate, PR7 5QS (on B5250)
12-midnight
(01257) 451594
Boddingtons Bitter; Phoenix Arizona; Tetley Bitter; guest beers [H]
This white-painted village pub has expanded over the years into the cottage next door, adding a substantial dining area. However, the original part of the pub is still used mainly for drinking. There are two or three frequently-changing guest ales. Meals are available throughout the day seven days a week (12-10pm), and there is accommodation in four good-value guest rooms.
(113,347)P

Edenfield

Horse & Jockey

85 Market Street, BL0 0JQ (on main road from Edenfield to Bury)
5 (12 Sat)-11; 12-11 Sun
(01706) 822655
Moorhouse's Pride of Pendle; Theakston Best Bitter; guest beer [H]
The pub has a large and originally decorated interior, separated into two vast rooms. With more than enough space, this is the main meeting place for many of Edenfield's amateur sporting groups and still has room left over for other events – often on the same night. A gas fire in the main room adds to the atmosphere. The car park, like the building, looks small from the road but is in fact quite big. Regular buses pass by during the day.
Q(243,473,481)P

Edgworth

White Horse

2-4 Bury Road, BL7 0AY (corner of Bolton and Bury Roads) SD742168
12-3 (not Mon & Tue), 5-11 (midnight Thu & Fri); 12-midnight Sat; 12-11 Sun
(01204) 852929
Caledonian Deuchars IPA; Marston's Pedigree; guest beers [H]
Situated prominently at the Bury to Bolton crossroads, this is a large, decorative corner building. An impressively decorated interior has tables fully laid-out for exquisite cuisine and real ale, and a good selection of wines. Ales are dispensed from five handpumps and include some LocAle brews. The pub name has heraldic origins dating back to the 18th century, as explained on the wall plaque outside. P

Euxton

Euxton Mills

Wigan Road, PR7 6JD (at A49/A581 jct)
11.30-3, 5-11; 11.30-11.30 Fri & Sat; 12-10.30 Sun
(01257) 264002
Jennings Bitter; guest beers [H]
A village inn that has won several Best Kept Pub awards, as well as the local CAMRA branch Pub of the Season. Outside, a large collection of hanging baskets and flowerpots is particularly attractive during the summer months. The pub is renowned for the quality of its food and serves up to three guest beers from the extensive Marston's range. Two beer festivals are held each year, with eight ales on offer at any one time. Quiz night is Wednesday at 9.30pm.
(Balshaw Lane)P

Fence

White Swan

300 Wheatley Lane, BB12 9QA (off A6068) SD835381
11.30-2.30 (not Mon), 5-11 (midnight Fri); 11.30-midnight Sat; 12-10.30 Sun
(01282) 611773 whiteswanatfence.co.uk
Taylor Golden Best, Best Bitter, Landlord [H]
Known locally as t'Mucky Duck, this is one of only two Timothy Taylor tied houses in Lancashire. Good, wholesome food is served daily, lunchtimes and evenings, all day Sunday, but not Monday. The fourth handpump regularly dispenses another beer

from Taylor. A warm welcome awaits, especially in winter when two fires heat this small pub.
Q (65)P

Feniscowles

Feildens Arms

673 Preston Old Road, BB2 5ER (at A674/A6062 jct)
12-12.30am (1.30am Fri & Sat); 12-11.30 Sun
(01254) 200988
Black Sheep Best Bitter; Flowers IPA; guest beers H
A welcoming, largely stone-built pub at a busy road junction about three miles west of Blackburn, not far from junction 3 of the M65. There are up to six real ales, including a mild. A supporter of LocAle, at least two of the beers come from local breweries. The Leeds-Liverpool Canal is a short stroll away. Buses stop outside and Pleasington railway station is close by. Live TV football is screened regularly and the pub has facilities for darts, dominoes and pool.
(Pleasington) (124,152)♣P

Fleetwood

Mount Hotel

The Esplanade, FY7 6QE (on the seafront, close to the Mount clock)
12-11 (midnight Fri & Sat)
(01253) 874619
Adnams Bitter; guest beers H
Opposite the local landmark from which it takes its name, this modernised Victorian building overlooks Morecambe Bay and is close to the beach. The hotel side of the business is now closed, but when plans were announced to remove its upper storeys there was local opposition and these have now been converted into flats. Sunday is quiz night. Darts and pool are played in a separate sports bar. Regular live football matches are shown.
(London Street) (1,14,16)

Steamer

1-2 Queens Terrace, FY7 6BT (opp market)
10-midnight (1am Fri & Sat); 12-midnight Sun
(01253) 771756
Wells Bombardier; guest beers, H
This former Matthew Brown outlet is situated opposite Fleetwood market and is convenient for bus and tram routes. There is an old blacksmith's workshop at the rear, dating from the time when the yard was used to stable police horses. Snooker, pool, darts and dominoes can be played. Children are welcome until 7pm. A poker club is held every Monday night and Fleetwood Folk Club meets on Thursday. Winner of local CAMRA Pub of the Season. (Ferry Terminal) (1,14,16)

Thomas Drummond ✔

London Street, FY7 6JY (between Lord St and Dock St)
9-midnight (1am Fri & Sat)
(01253) 775020
Greene King Abbot; Marston's Pedigree; guest beers H
This former church hall and furniture warehouse is named after Thomas Atkinson Drummond, a builder who helped with the construction of Fleetwood. The pub has displays about the founder of the town, Sir Peter Hesketh Fleetwood, and his architect Decimus Burton. Children are welcome until 8pm. Food is served until 10pm daily. There is a covered and heated area for smokers. A past winner of a local CAMRA silver award and Pub of the Season.
(London Street) (1,14,16)

Wyre Lounge Bar

Marine Hall, The Esplanade, FY7 6HF
12-4, 7-11 (Fri-Sun only)
(01253) 771141 marinehall.co.uk
Beer range varies H
This recently refurbished bar is usually open at weekends only, unless there is a function in the Marine Hall. During the week check with the venue. The outside drinking area is yards from the beach and offers panoramic views over Morecambe Bay to the distant Lakeland fells. Crown green bowls and crazy golf are played in the nearby gardens. Show your CAMRA membership card for a 10% discount. Home of the annual Fleetwood Beer Festival in February.
(1,14,16)P

Freckleton

Coach & Horses

PR4 1PD
11-midnight (1am Fri & Sat); 12-midnight Sun
(01772) 632284
Boddingtons Bitter; guest beers H
This community village local has retained its cosy atmosphere. It is home to Freckleton's award-winning brass band and a cabinet displays its impressive collection of trophies. A special place is reserved for mementoes of the US Eighth Air Force who served locally during WWII. The pub also has a golfing society. Lunchtime meals are served Monday to Friday 12-2pm, and Saturday 12-6pm.
(2,68)♣P

Ship Inn

Bunker Street, PR4 1HA
12-11 (midnight Fri & Sat); 12-10.30 Sun
(01772) 632393
Moorhouse's Pride of Pendle; Theakston Best Bitter H
Known to have been licensed since 1677, but probably dating back to the 14th century, the Ship may be the oldest pub in the Fylde. It formerly served local maritime trade and was reputed to be involved in smuggling. The large room at the rear and the beer garden with wildlife identification guides have extensive views over Freckleton marsh and the River Ribble. Lunchtime and evening meals are available daily, all day at the weekend. Quiz night is Tuesday.
Q (68)P

Garstang

Wheatsheaf

Park Hill Road, PR3 1EL
10-midnight (1am Fri & Sat); 11.30-11.30 Sun
(01995) 603398
Black Sheep Best Bitter; Courage Directors; Moorhouse's seasonal beers; guest beers H
Built as a farmhouse in the late 18th century, this is now a Grade II-listed building and was greatly extended in 2002. A disco is held every Sunday, and live music is staged monthly on a Monday. The pub serves breakfast, lunch and supper and there is a covered outdoor smoking area.
(40,42)♣P

Goosnargh

Stag's Head ✔

990 Whittingham Lane, PR3 2AU
12-11 (10.30 Sun)
☎ (01772) 864071 thestagshead.co.uk
Theakston Best Bitter; guest beers H
Large public house and restaurant situated close to the haunted Chingle Hall. Inside there are four seating areas served by a central bar, with a huge garden and a heated area for smokers. Up to four guest beers are taken from the Scottish & Newcastle Cellarman's Reserve list. A mild is usually available. There is often live music and a beer festival is held annually. All food is sourced from local producers and home-made pickles and chutneys are available to take away.
(4)P

Great Eccleston

Black Bull Hotel

The Square, PR3 0ZB (on main street)
3 (12 Sat & Sun)-midnight
☎ (01995) 670224
Moorhouse's Blond Witch; Taylor Landlord; Thwaites Original H
This traditional pub won CAMRA Pub of the Season for summer 2008. The bar has a pool table and an open fire. The tap room has another pool table and upstairs is a full size snooker table. There is an outside seating area and separate covered heated area for smokers. The pub has alternating quiz and poker nights each week. There are facilities for darts and dominoes. Live music plays on one Saturday per month. ♣P

Great Harwood

Royal Hotel ✔

2 Station Road, BB6 7BE (opp jct of Queen St and Park Rd)
4-11; 12-midnight Fri & Sat; 12-10.30 Sun
☎ (01254) 883541
Beer range varies H
The pub is the brewery tap for the Red Rose Brewery, which is in the cellar. Eight beers are on offer including ales from the brewery and guests from near and far. There is a good selection of bottled beers and usually at least two dark ales. A beer festival is held over the May bank holiday. The pub is well served by public transport from Accrington, Blackburn and Manchester.
(6,7)♣

Victoria ★ ✔

St John's Street, BB6 7EP
4-midnight; 3-1am Fri; 12-1am Sat; 12-midnight Sun
☎ (01254) 885210
Beer range varies H
Built in 1905 by Alfred Nuttall and known locally as Butcher Brig, the pub features a wealth of original features. The lobby has floor-to-ceiling glazed tiling and there is dark wood throughout the five rooms. On the horseshoe-shaped bar are eight handpumps dispensing beers sourced from small breweries throughout Northern England and Scotland. There is an annual beer festival. The pub sits on a cycle way. The smoking area is covered and heated.
Q♣

Hapton

Hapton Inn ✔

2 Accrington Road, BB11 5QL (on A679, about ½ mile from station)
11.30-3, 5-11.30; 11.30-midnight Fri & Sat; 12-11.30 Sun
☎ (01282) 771152 thehaptoninn.co.uk
Boddingtons Bitter; Taylor Landlord; guest beers H
A family run and oriented pub situated in a semi-rural position, with rabbits, goats and chickens adjacent to the rear beer garden. Traditional food is served 12-2, 5-8pm Monday to Thursday and 12-8.30pm Friday to Sunday. There are fine views over to Pendle Hill from this friendly inn that offers draught cider – currently Westons Old Rosie.
(23, X63)♣P

Heapey

Top Lock 🏆

Copthurst Lane, PR6 8LS (alongside canal at Johnson's Hillock)
11.30-11; 12-10.30 Sun
☎ (01257) 263376
Beer range varies H
Excellent canal-side pub with an upstairs dining room and up to nine real ales, mostly from micros, which always include a mild and either a porter or stout, together with a Timothy Taylor and a Coniston beer. Up to three real ciders are also on offer. There is an annual beer festival in October with approximately 100 ales available in the pub and marquee. There is a covered smoking area. Winner of local CAMRA Pub of the Year.
QP

Helmshore

Robin Hood Inn

280 Holcombe Road, BB4 4NP (follow signs for Helmshore Textile Museum)
4-11; 12-midnight Sat & Sun
☎ (01706) 213180
Copper Dragon Black Gold, Golden Pippin, Scotts 1816, Challenger IPA; guest beers H
Just down the road from Helmshore Textile Museum, the Robin Hood is a small heritage pub with an original interior and a well-kept range of Copper Dragon beers. The inside is divided into three rooms so it is easy to find a quiet corner near the pub's two open fires in the winter. This is a warm, friendly pub with a lot of character and a large selection of spirits. Quiet, unless there is a big match on! (11)♣

Hest Bank

Hest Bank

2 Hest Bank Lane, LA2 6DN
12-11 (10.30 Sun)
☎ (01524) 824339
Black Sheep Best Bitter; Taylor Landlord; guest beers H
An historic pub dating from 1554 with a canal-side garden, this was formerly a coaching inn for travellers crossing Morecambe Bay to Grange-over-Sands. One of the older rooms in the pub functions as a locals' bar, while another smaller bar plus other rooms on differing levels are mostly used by diners. Wednesday is quiz night. Food is served from the award-winning menu until 9pm.
Q(5,55)♣P

Heysham

Royal

7 Main Street, LA3 2RN (70 yd towards St Patrick's Chapel from Heysham Village bus terminus)
⏲ 12-11.30 (12.30am Fri & Sat); 12-11 Sun
☎ (01524) 859298 🌐 heyshamonline.co.uk/royal/royal.html
Thwaites Lancaster Bomber; York Guzzler; guest beers Ⓗ
A 15th-century inn in the heart of the village. As you enter the pub, a tiny locals' bar is on the right and a restaurant is on the left – the main bar is accessed via a winding passage and opens onto a large landscaped garden. Five handpumps provide the regular beers and there is often a beer from Coniston, Moorhouse's, Dent or Bowland. Forthcoming guest beers are usually listed on the website. Outside is a covered and heated smoking area. **Q**🐴❀◐◑⊟♿🚌(4,5)**P**⸗

Hoghton

Royal Oak

Blackburn Old Road, Riley Green, PR5 0SL (at A675/A674 jct)
⏲ 11.30-11; 12-10.30 Sun
☎ (01254) 201445
Thwaites Nutty Black, Original, Wainwright, Lancaster Bomber, seasonal beers Ⓗ
Stone-built pub on the old road between Preston and Blackburn, near the Riley Green basin on the Leeds-Liverpool Canal. The Royal Oak is popular with diners and drinkers. Rooms, including a dining room, and alcoves radiate from the central bar. Low-beamed ceilings and horse brasses give the pub a rustic feel. This Thwaites tied house is a regular award winner and acts as an outlet for its seasonal beers. Hoghton Towers is nearby, steeped in history and worth visiting. ♨**Q**❀◐◑🚌(152)**P**

Sirloin

Station Road, PR5 0DD (off A675 near level crossing)
⏲ 4-11; 12-midnight Fri & Sat; 12-11 Sun
☎ (01254) 852293
Moorhouse's Jackie's Tea Thyme Tipple; guest beers Ⓗ
This 250-year old, family-run country inn is near Hoghton Tower, where King James I knighted a loin of beef. His coat of arms hangs over one of the fireplaces. Sirloin steak is, of course, a speciality here and in the adjoining restaurant. Three handpumps dispense a choice of beers, often from independent brewers. Moorhouse's brew Jackie's Tea Thyme Tipple, named after the owner's dog, especially for the pub. Pub food is served Friday to Sunday lunchtime only. ♨◐🚌(152)**P**⸗

Hoscar

Railway Tavern

Hoscar Moss Road, L40 4BQ (1 mile from A5209) SD468116
⏲ 12-2 (not Mon winter), 5.30-11; 12-11 Sat; 12-10.30 Sun
☎ (01704) 897503
Black Sheep Best Bitter; Tetley Bitter; Wells Bombardier; guest beers Ⓗ
The pub is immediately adjacent to the tiny Hoscar station on the Southport-Manchester line and dates back to the same time as the railway was built. There are few reasons for alighting here, other than to enjoy the ales and food the tavern provides. Cyclists and rural road users also enjoy the premises – there is a quiet garden at the back, ideal for summer drinking or trainspotting. Please note that no trains stop on Sunday at present. ♨**Q**❀◐◑⊟♿⇌**P**⸗

Lancaster

Boot & Shoe

171 Scotforth Road, LA1 4PU (on A6)
⏲ 11-11 (midnight Sat); 12-11 Sun
☎ (01524) 63011
Black Sheep Best Bitter; Coniston range; Everards Beacon; York range; guest beers Ⓗ
A village inn until Lancaster grew around it, though it still has a fairly rural aspect. Most of the old rooms have been converted into one large lounge. A chunk of this is set aside for diners during food hours – meals are served daily and until 6pm on Sunday. However, there is also a public bar and two tiny snugs, one with a TV. Quiz night is Thursday, piano evening (nowadays a rare feature) Saturday. The garden has a play area. ❀◐◑⊟🚌♣**P**⸗

Borough ✔

3 Dalton Square, LA1 1PP (near town hall)
⏲ 12-12.30 (11.30 Sun)
☎ (01524) 64170 🌐 theboroughlancaster.co.uk
Bank Top range; Black Sheep Best Bitter; Bowland Hen Harrier; Hawkshead Bitter; Lancaster Amber; Thwaites Wainwright Ⓗ
An upmarket town house built in 1824 but with a Victorian frontage. The pub succeeds in appealing to both food lovers and ale aficionados. The front area resembles a gentlemen's club with deep-buttoned chairs and chandeliers; the large back room is a restaurant and the bar is in a passage between them. Outside is a sheltered patio with beer festivals in summer. CAMRA members get a 30p discount on a pint. Poker night is Monday. The regular beers may be replaced by another from the same brewery or Brysons. ❀◐◑♿⇌🚌⸗

Sun

63 Church Street, LA1 1ET
⏲ 10-midnight
☎ (01524) 66006 🌐 thesunhotelandbar.co.uk
Lancaster Amber, Blonde, Black, Red; Thwaites Wainwright; guest beers Ⓗ
The decor here combines a mixture of exposed stonework, wood panelling and solid furniture with ambient candlelight in the evenings. Various original features remain including stone fireplaces and a well. Quality is the name of the game here in all the pub offers. It is the primary outlet for Lancaster Brewery in the city, as well as offering up to four guest beers. Brewery nights are held regularly, featuring numerous national independent breweries. Wi-Fi Internet access is available. Outside is a heated smoking area. ❀🛏◐◑♿⇌🚌⸗

White Cross 🏆

Quarry Road, LA1 4XT (behind town hall, on canal towpath)
⏲ 11.30-11 (12.30am Fri & Sat); 12-11 Sun
☎ (01524) 33999
Caledonian Deuchars IPA; Tirril Old Faithful; guest beers Ⓗ
A modern renovation of an old canalside warehouse with an open-plan interior and a light, airy feel. French windows open onto extensive canalside seating, making this a popular location

for summer afternoons and evenings. The 14 ales available concentrate on Lancastrian, Cumbrian and Pennine brewers plus Old Rosie cider. Meals are available throughout the week, with a Sunday roast. There is a popular Tuesday night quiz and a Beer and Pie Festival each April. ❀◑◗⇌🚌♣🍎P⚐

Yorkshire House

2 Parliament Street, LA1 1DB (opp Greyhound Bridge)
⏲ 7-midnight (1am Thu & Fri); Sat 2-1am; 2-11.30 Sun
☎ (01524) 64679 🌐 yorkshirehouse.enta.net
Everards Tiger; Moorhouse's Premier; guest beers Ⓗ
This is known as a regulars' music pub, with possibly the best jukebox in town and bands playing most evenings in the big room upstairs. The mix of ages, friendly service and intimate drinking spaces, including a cosy corner with a wood-burning stove, help to explain this pub's appeal. One handpump dispenses Westons Perry, Organic Cider, 1st Quality and Scrumpy on rotation. A popular quiz is held on the first Sunday of the month. The courtyard garden is recommended for summer drinking. ♨❀⇌♣🍎⚐

Lancaster University

Graduate College Bar

Barker House Village, LA2 0PF
⏲ 7-11; 6-11.30 Fri; 8-11 during vacations; 8-11 Sun
☎ (01524) 592824 🌐 gradbar.co.uk
Beer range varies Ⓗ
The Graduate College can be found in the complex of buildings at Alexandra Park to the south-west of the main campus. As its name suggests, the 'Gradbar' on Barker Square attracts an age range higher than an average student bar. The choice of beer is good, with eight handpumps often offering Copper Dragon and Barngates beers. The bar is open to university members, staff, guests and people carrying a copy of this Guide. Westons cider and perry are also served. There is a beer festival in June and a cider festival in October. ❀🚌♣🍎⚐

Lathom

Ship

4 Wheat Lane, L40 4BX
⏲ 12-midnight (1am Fri & Sat); 12-11.30 Sun
☎ (01704) 893117
Moorhouse's Pride of Pendle, Pendle Witch's Brew Ⓗ
The Ship is to be found at the junction of the Rufford Branch Canal and the Leeds-Liverpool Canal and nestles amongst picturesque cottages, locks, a dry dock and barges. Reputedly haunted (presumably by a discerning ghost), it is over 200 years old but does not feel in the least bit like a museum. Food is important but doesn't dominate. The pub is a short and pleasant towpath walk from the centre of Burscough and Burscough Bridge Interchange station. **Q**❀◑◗♿⇌♣🍎**P**⚐

Lea Town

Smith's Arms

Lea Lane, PR4 0RP
⏲ 12-midnight
☎ (01772) 760555
Thwaites Nutty Black, Original, Wainwright, Lancaster Bomber, seasonal beers Ⓗ
Open-plan country pub situated near the Preston-Lancaster Canal and adjacent to an atomic fuel factory. It is also known as the Slip Inn from a time when Fylde farmers would walk past on the way to Preston market and slip in for a drink. The five handpumps see plenty of use in this Thwaites house – also a regular winner of awards for its quality food. It can get busy, especially on Sunday when food is served all day. Home to darts and dominoes teams, it has a covered smoking area outside. ♨**Q**❀◑◗♿🚌(77)♣**P**⚐

Leyland

Eagle & Child

30 Church Road, PR25 3AA
⏲ 11.45-11 (11.30 Fri-Sat); 12-11 Sun
☎ (01772) 433531
Banks's Bitter; Marston's Pedigree; guest beers Ⓗ
Attractive, 16th-century inn which is justifiably popular with drinkers aged 18 to 80. This prominent pub is something of a cask beer oasis on the fringe of the town centre. Two guest ales drawn from the Marston's list are offered, plus the two regular brews. A large beer garden to the side of the pub is popular in summer and a crown bowling green lies adjacent to the car park across the road. No food on Monday.
❀◑🚌(111,113)♣**P**⚐

Railway at Leyland

1 Preston Road, PR25 4NT
⏲ 12-11.30 (1am Fri & Sat); 12-10.30 Sun
☎ (01772) 458427 🌐 therailwayatleyland.co.uk
Black Sheep Ale; Wychwood Hobgoblin; guest beers Ⓗ
An outstanding example of a community local, The Railway has gone from strength to strength. Huge investment from Punch Taverns has transformed the interior and the new licensees have made this landmark Leyland pub a welcoming hostelry with something for everyone. Four cask ales including two rotating guests make a fine accompaniment to the excellent food. Live music, beer festivals, quiz nights and fine ales all feature. Little wonder then it was CAMRA West Lancashire branch's Summer Pub of the Season. ❀◑◗⇌🚌(111)**P**⚐

Little Eccleston

Cartford Inn

Cartford Lane, PR3 0YP (½ mile from A586)
⏲ 11-11 (midnight Fri & Sat); 11-10 Sun
☎ (01995) 670166
Theakston XB, Old Peculier; guest beers Ⓗ
The Cartford Inn is a 17th-century coaching inn nestling on the banks of the River Wyre on Lancashire's Fylde Coast. Refurbished in 2007, the Cartford combines traditional features with contemporary style, plus seven stunning bedrooms, all unique and en-suite. The restaurant is closed on Monday but is open lunchtimes and evenings the rest of the week. Guest beers include various ales from the Hart Brewery, which is based out back. ♨❀🛏◑◗⛺🚌(42,80)**P**

Longridge

Corporation Arms

Lower Road, PR3 2YJ (near jct B6243/B6245)
⏲ 11-midnight; 12-11 Sun
☎ (01772) 782644 🌐 corporationarms.co.uk
Beer range varies Ⓗ
Eighteenth-century country inn close to the Longridge reservoirs and a handy base for local

walks. A free house, it has a deserved reputation for excellent ale, food, service and accommodation. Beers are sourced from local breweries, with Moorhouse's, Bowland and Three B's some of the favourites. Luxurious overnight rooms are popular, so booking is advised. Note the old horse trough outside, now used as a planter, which was reputably used by Oliver Cromwell on his way to the Battle of Preston. ⛬❀🛏◑♿🚌P⚡

Old Oak

111 Preston Road, PR3 3BA
⏲ 5-11 Mon; 11-midnight (1am Fri & Sat); 11-11.30 Sun
☎ (01772) 783648
Theakston Best Bitter; guest beers Ⓗ
Situated on the B6243 from Preston, the Old Oak is a large, multi-area, family-run community pub with a friendly, welcoming and traditional feel. Regular theme nights are held, and a number of local organisations, including the Old Oak Beer Appreciation Society, make it their home. Live music is often featured. Up to four guest ales are available, together with good local food, which includes 'hangover breakfasts' (Sat & Sun) and 'credit crunch lunches' (Tue-Thu) at around £2.50! ⛬❀◑♿🚌(4)♣P⚡

Longton

Dolphin

Marsh Lane, PR4 5SJ (down Marsh Lane 1 mile, take right fork)
⏲ 12 (10.30 Sun)-midnight
☎ (01772) 612032
Beer range varies Ⓗ
An isolated former farmhouse, this local CAMRA award-winning marshland pub lies at the start of the Ribble Way. Inside comprises a main bar (no children), a family room, a conservatory and a function room. The four or five ales on offer always include a mild and are sourced from micros near and far. An annual beer festival takes place in August. Food is served daily until 8pm. Outside there is a children's play area and a covered smoking area. A free minibus service is provided from local villages – contact the pub for details. ⛬🐴❀◑🚐P⚡

Lytham

Ship & Royal ✔

91 Clifton Street, FY8 5EH
⏲ 11-11 (midnight Fri & Sat); 12-11 Sun
☎ (01253) 732867
Wells Bombardier; guest beers Ⓗ
Named after a business merger in the past, this Grade II listed Victorian building is a prominent feature on the town's main street. The interior was refurbished in 2007 and has an L-shaped bar with many original fittings. There are discrete areas on two levels with gas fires and large-screen TV, but also a quieter area. Up to five ever-changing beers include ones from a local micro and a house beer from Hart. Music nights are Friday and Saturday, quiz night is Sunday. Food is served every day. ❀◑♿⇌🚌⚡

Taps 🏆 ✔

Henry Street, FY8 5LE
⏲ 11-11 (midnight Fri & Sat); 12-11 Sun
☎ (01253) 736226 🌐 thetaps.net
Greene King IPA; Titanic Taps Bitter; guest beers Ⓗ
Winner of many awards, including several Pub of the Year prizes, this cosy one-roomed local is always popular. The Taps gives enthusiastic support to the local lifeboat station as well as the rugby team, and proudly displays memorabilia of both. Landlord Ian Rigg is a member of SIBA and his own brews occasionally feature among the six regularly changing guest beers, including the only cask mild in town, and a regularly changing real cider. ⛬Q❀◑♿⇌🚌♣🍎⚡

Mawdesley

Black Bull ✔

Hall Lane, L40 2QY (off B5246)
⏲ 12-11 (midnight Fri & Sat); 12-7 winter Mon
☎ (01704) 822202
Black Sheep Best Bitter; Jennings Cumberland Ale; Robinson's Unicorn; Taylor Landlord; guest beer Ⓗ
A pub since 1610, this low-ceilinged stone building boasts some magnificent oak beams. Older village residents know the pub as 'Ell 'Ob, a reference to a coal-fired cooking range. Certificates on display record the pub's success in Lancashire's Best Kept Village competition. It has also earned awards for its numerous hanging baskets. During summer months the well-kept beer garden is popular with both drinkers and diners. The guest beer is usually from a regional brewery. No evening meals on Monday. ⛬❀◑🚌(347)♣P

Robin Hood

Bluestone Lane, L40 2QY (off B5252)
⏲ 11.30-11; 12-10.30 Sun
☎ (01704) 822275 🌐 robinhoodinn.co.uk
Black Sheep Best Bitter; Jennings Cumberland Ale; Taylor Landlord; guest beers Ⓗ
Charming, white-painted inn, at the crossroads between the three old villages of Mawdesley, Croston and Eccleston. The 15th-century building was substantially altered in the 19th century. Run by the same family for 40 years, it enjoys a reputation for good food. The recently renovated Wilsons restaurant upstairs is open Tuesday to Sunday evenings. Bar food is served all day at the weekend. There is always room for those who come just for a drink, with three guest ales from regional brewers and local micros. 🐴❀◑🚌(347)P

Morecambe

Eric Bartholomew ✔

10 Euston Road, LA4 5DD
⏲ 9-11 (midnight Fri & Sat)
☎ (01524) 405860
Greene King Abbot Ale; Marston's Pedigree; guest beers Ⓗ
Opened in April 2004, this Wetherspoon's pub is dedicated to Eric Morecambe. Near the seafront, the pub functions on two levels with an upstairs lounge and dining area. The long bar services an open-plan pub with pictures of 19th-century Morecambe and some artwork with a Morecambe and Wise theme. Westons Vintage and Organic ciders are available. Close to shops and a public car park. ◑⇌🚌🍎

Palatine ✔

The Crescent, LA4 5BZ (overlooking prom, opp Clock Tower)
⏲ 10.30-midnight (1am Fri & Sat); 10.30-11.30 Sun

☎ (01524) 410503
Lancaster Amber, Blonde, Black, Red; Thwaites Lancaster Bomber; guest beers Ⓗ
An Edwardian mid-terraced pub. The ground floor – quite a small bar-room with some intimate corners – was completely transformed in late 2008 with much bare stone and woodwork. An upstairs room is rather different. Cosy and carpeted, many of the fittings – leaded lights, shelving and fireplace – appear to be original. Do not miss the views across the Bay from the bay window. ◐≠🚌

Ranch House
Marine Road West, LA4 4DG (on the front between West End Rd and Aldi)
⌚ 11-midnight
☎ (01524) 851531
Beer range varies Ⓗ
Large, open-plan seaside pub with adjoining amusement arcade, built in 1930 as part of what later became the Frontierland amusement park – now largely demolished. Its facade still features a Wild West theme, but inside it is barely noticeable. The Ranch House faces the promenade and is close to the major 1930s landmark Midland Hotel which reopened in 2008. It is popular with locals, day-trippers and holidaymakers alike. Four ever-changing brews and sandwiches are always available. A very lively pub at weekends. Outside is a covered and heated smoking area. ❀≠🚌♣⊬

Smugglers' Den ✔
56 Poulton Road, LA4 5HB
⌚ 12-midnight (11.30 Sun)
☎ (01524) 421684 🌐 thesmugglersden.com
Adnams Bitter; guest beers Ⓗ
A family-run business that welcomes all, this is the oldest pub in Morecambe, circa 1640s, though remodelled. Four stained-glass windows date from the 1960s. The interior features some interesting maritime artefacts and brass shellcases. Six handpumps have three lines for guest ales and Westons Old Rosie cider and perry are available. Regular live folk music plays throughout the year. An impressive open fire adds warmth in the colder months. Home to a ladies and gents darts team, plus a pub quiz team. Meals are served Tuesday and Wednesday 6-8pm. The pub offers a discount to CAMRA members. ♨❀◑≠🚌(5,430)♣●P⊬

Ormskirk

Eureka ✔
78 Halsall Lane, L39 3AX
⌚ 4 (12 Fri & Sat)-midnight; 12-midnight Sun
☎ (01695) 570819
Black Sheep Best Bitter; Fuller's London Pride; Taylor Landlord; Tetley Bitter; guest beer Ⓗ
It may sound like a trendy bar selling nothing but fizzy lagers, but the Eureka is in fact an attractive local in a residential area of Ormskirk, which has been successfully meeting the social (and cask ale) needs of the surrounding community for many years. The pub is only a short walk from the 375/385 Southport-Wigan bus route, and is well worth stopping off for. ❀◐♿🚌(375,385)♣P⊬

Greyhound
100 Aughton Street, L39 3BS
⌚ 12-11.30 (10.30 Sun)
☎ (01695) 576701
Tetley Dark Mild, Bitter Ⓗ
The Greyhound is a classic community pub, a short walk from the centre of town and Ormskirk train/bus interchange, with a number of small bars and a real local atmosphere. The vault takes you back a century, though the other rooms are more modern. Even if you are a visitor, you will be made to feel like a local. Served by several Aughton Street bus routes, and at the Ormskirk Bus Rail Interchange. ⚲❀⊞♿≠🚌(75,311,351)♣P⊬

Queens Head ✔
30 Moor Street, L39 2AQ
⌚ 11-midnight (1am Fri); 10-1am Sat
☎ (01695) 574380
Tetley Mild, Bitter; guest beers Ⓗ
The Queens Head is a Victorian town pub in the main shopping street of this market town. Apart from offering relief from the market and the shops, the pub is also one of the most adventurous in the area as regards its beer selection policy, with excellent beers drawn from a variety of sources including some of the smaller breweries, as well as from Tetley's. Children are welcome until 7pm. ❀◐♿≠(Ormskirk)🚌(Ormskirk Bus Station)♣⊬

Parbold

Wayfarer
1-3 Alder Lane, WN8 7NL (on A5209)
⌚ 12-3, 5.30-midnight; 12-11 Sun
☎ (01257) 464600
Beer range varies Ⓗ
Restaurant conversion from a row of 18th century cottages, featuring low beamed ceilings and cosy little nooks and crannies. Now a pub, the focus is still very much on fine dining. A popular stop, particularly in the summer and weekends, close to the Leeds-Liverpool Canal and Parbold Hill with its panoramic views stretching from the Welsh Hills to Blackpool Tower and beyond. Food is served 12-3, 5-9.30pm Monday-Saturday, 12-8.30pm Sunday. ❀◐♿≠P

Windmill
3 Mill Lane, WN8 7NW (off A5209 Wigan-Ormskirk road)
⌚ 12-11 (midnight Fri & Sat)
☎ (01257) 462935
Tetley Bitter; guest beers Ⓗ
A former grainstore to the adjacent windmill, parts of the building date back to 1794. Recently sympathetically refurbished introducing clean lines and period furniture in keeping with the building's history. It focuses on fine dining, yet welcomes the casual drinker. LocAle accredited, it features mainly beers from the excellent Prospect and George Wright breweries. Note the snug to the right of the doorway with delightful carved animals in the wooden panels. ♨Q◐≠P

Pendleton

Swan With Two Necks
Main Street, BB7 1PT (½ mile E of A59 turn-off)
⌚ 12 (1 Fri)-3 (not Mon), 7 (6 Fri)-11; closed Tue; 12-2.30, 6-11 Sat; 12-10.30 Sun
☎ (01200) 423112
Beer range varies Ⓗ
Close to Pendle Hill walking country and deservedly popular, the Swan sells a range of beers from micros on four handpumps. One beer is usually from Phoenix, the others might be from Hopstar, George Wright, Copper Dragon or

Grindleton. Food here is good but check in advance that it will be available. Very comfortable, with fires at both ends of the main room in winter – and run by two CAMRA members. The aged white cat guards a wide selection of teapots. ⛰Q❀◐◑P

Poulton-le-Fylde

Old Town Hall ✔

5 Church Street, FY6 7AP

⏲ 11-11 (11.30 Fri & Sat); 12-11 Sun

☎ (01253) 890601

Beer range varies 🄷

Formerly known as The Bay Horse, this building was used as council offices for much of the 20th century but is now a pub once more. Inside, its numerous TV screens are favoured by football and racing followers. Guest beers frequently come from Thwaites, Moorhouse's, J W Lees and Hart. The games area features a frieze depicting old flora and fauna, while a quieter upstairs bar opens on Friday and Saturday and serves two cask ales. No food is available. ♿⇌🚌

Thatched House ✔

12 Ball Street, FY6 7BG

⏲ 11-11 (midnight Fri & Sat); 12-11 Sun

☎ (01253) 891063

Bank Top Flat Cap; Copper Dragon Best Bitter; Lytham Gold; guest beers 🄷

The present pub stands in the grounds of a Norman church, built on the site at the beginning of the 20th century. It also has the honour of being the oldest continuously licensed premises in the Fylde. In the bar, various sporting heroes of the past are on display on the walls. Often busy and loud with the chatter of customers. ⛰Q⊕⛺⇌🚌(2,80,82)⊢

Preston

Anderton Arms ✔

Longsands Lane, Fulwood, PR2 9PS (near Eastway and M6 J31A)

⏲ 11.45-11 (midnight Thu-Sat)

☎ (01772) 700104

Thwaites Original; guest beers 🄷

One of the Ember Inns chain, the Anderton Arms is a modern estate pub to the north of Preston, popular with residents and commuters alike. The interior is light and airy, with seating to a very high standard of comfort. Examples of modern art are on display. Up to six guest beers are usually dispensed, often from small breweries, and third pint 'tasters' are available. Good value food is served. No children under 14, please. Preston Orbit bus services stop outside. ⛰❀◐◑♿🚌P⊢

Bitter Suite

53 Fylde Road, PR1 2XQ

⏲ 12-3, 6 (7 Mon)-11 (11.30 Wed); 12-11 Sat; 7-11 Sun

☎ (01772) 827007 🌐 bittersuitepreston.co.uk

Beer range varies 🄷

Single-room bar converted from a keg-only club four years ago. It is set back from Fylde Road at the side of the unrelated Mad Ferret bar. A genuine free house, it serves six guest beers from micro-breweries that change almost hourly. There are at least four regular beer festivals each year and home-cooked lunches are served Monday to Friday. Although opposite the Students Union and surrounded by university buildings, it is not primarily a student bar. ❀◐🚌(31,35,61)

Black Horse ★

166 Friargate, PR1 2EJ

⏲ 10.30-11 (midnight Fri & Sat); 12-4.30 Sun

☎ (01772) 204855

Robinson's Old Stockport, Cumbria Way, Unicorn, Double Hop, Old Tom, seasonal beers 🄷

Classic Grade II listed pub in the main shopping area, close to the historic open market. With its exquisite tiled bar and walls and superb mosaic floor, it is an English Heritage/CAMRA award winner. The two front rooms bear photos of old Preston; the famous 'hall of mirrors' seating area is to the rear. See the memorabilia of a previous landlord set in a glass partition. Up to seven Robinson's beers are regularly on sale. A new covered smoking area has been built upstairs through the modern non real ale bar. ❀⇌⊢

Continental

South Meadow Lane, PR1 8JP (off Fishergate Hill)

⏲ 12-midnight (1am Fri & Sat); 12-11.30 Sun

☎ (01772) 499425 🌐 newcontinental.net

Marble Continental Bitter; guest beers 🄷

Beside the River Ribble and next to the main rail line, adjacent to Miller Park, the pub was extensively refurbished, and reopened in 2008 after a period of closure. The main room is complemented by a cosy lounge with a real fire in winter, and no TV or games. Live music features regularly in the separate events space, also used for beer festivals. Up to six beers are on offer, including the house beer Continental Bitter from Marble Brewery. Fresh cooked meals are served lunchtime and evening. ⛰❀◐◑♿P⊢

Grey Friar ✔

144 Friargate, PR1 2EE (jct of Ringway)

⏲ 9-midnight (1am Fri & Sat)

☎ (01772) 558542

Greene King Abbot; Marston's Pedigree; Theakston Best Bitter, Old Peculier; guest beers 🄷

Wetherspoon's pub which plays an active role in encouraging young people to appreciate real ale. Preston's students flock here for the range of ales and food at the best prices around, mixing with workers and locals who between them create a bustling atmosphere. The pub plays an active role in CAMRA recruiting. Situated in a fine real ale drinking area on the edge of the city centre. ◐◑♿⇌🚌

Market Tavern

33-35 Market Street, PR1 2ES

⏲ 10.30-9 (midnight Fri & Sat); 12-9 Sun

☎ (01772) 254425

Beer range varies 🄷

Popular city-centre local overlooking the Victorian outdoor market. Three handpumps serve an ever-changing range of guest beers, usually from micros from all over the UK. A superb selection of imported bottled beers is also on offer, plus a German Weisse and French blonde on draught. Outside seating is available in summer. Conversation rules in this former local CAMRA Pub of the Year. No food is served, but you are welcome to bring your own. ❀⇌

New Britannia

6 Heatley Street, PR1 2XB (off Friargate)

⏲ 11-11 (midnight Wed, Fri & Sat); 12-11 Sun

☎ (01772) 253424

Bradfield Farmers Blonde; Greene King Old Speckled Hen; Marston's Pedigree; guest beers 🄷

Single-bar, city centre pub attracting real ale enthusiasts from far and wide with the quality and choice of its beers. Four guest ales, usually from micros or small independents, are usually on offer and occasional beer festivals are hosted. The cider range varies. Tasty home-cooked meals are served at lunchtime (not Sat), representing good value. The pub can get crowded but the service is swift. There is a small patio for smokers. ❀◖⇌⊟♣●⚡–

Old Vic

78 Fishergate, PR1 2UH

⏲ 11.30-11 (midnight Fri; 1am Sat); 12-midnight Sun

☎ (01772) 254690

Caledonian Deuchars IPA; Courage Directors; Marston's Pedigree; Theakston Best Bitter; guest beers Ⓗ

Situated opposite the railway station and on bus routes into the city, the Old Vic can be rather busy at times. There are seven handpumps, with up to three guest ales, often including a beer from a local brewer. Big screens show sports events and there is a large pool table. The pub hosts a keen darts team. Meals are served 12-5pm (4pm Sun). A rear car park is available weekends and evenings. ❀◖⇌⊟♣⚡–

Olde Dog & Partridge

41 Friargate, PR1 2AT

⏲ 11-3, 6-11.30 (1am Sat); 12-5, 7-11.30 Sun

☎ (01772) 252217

Draught Bass; Taylor Landlord; Tetley Dark Mild; guest beers Ⓗ

Down-to-earth city centre pub that specialises in rock music. The student union RockSoc meets here. Five real ales often include one from the White Shield Brewery. The landlord has been at the pub for over 30 years and there is a monthly live music night, a weekly quiz on Thursday and a rock DJ on Sunday evening. Excellent value pub lunches are served (not Sun) and a covered 'Smokey-O Joes' smoking area is provided at the rear. ❀◖⇌⊟♣●⚡–

Preston Grasshoppers Rugby Club

Lightfoot Green, Lightfoot Lane, PR4 0AP

⏲ 4 (12 Sat)-11 (midnight Fri & Sat); 12-10.30 Sun

☎ (01772) 863546

Thwaites Nutty Black, Original, Wainwright, Lancaster Bomber, seasonal beers Ⓗ

You do not have to be rugby-oriented to enjoy the friendly atmosphere in the clubhouse bar. Its premises licence means it is also a family-friendly local for the immediate area. The bar is part of a multi-roomed complex, used for a variety of activities, from dancing and bridge to squash. There is an admission charge up until 3.30pm on First XV match-day Saturdays, but this is waived for people only wanting to use the bar. ❀♿⊟(4)P⚡–

Rawtenstall

White Lion

72 Burnley Road, BB4 8EW

⏲ 4.30 (2 Fri; 12 Sat)-midnight; 12-midnight Sun

☎ (01706) 213117

Black Sheep Best Bitter; Copper Dragon Golden Pippin; Tetley Bitter; Wells Bombardier; guest beers Ⓗ

The beer is always well kept here and the landlord is more than happy to talk about the latest guest he is putting on. The pub and bar is split in two, with a dartboard, large screen and pool table in one half, leaving the other half for drinkers and weekend diners. Events include a Tuesday night quiz and occasional amateur bands. Sitting on a main bus route (X43, Manchester to Burnley), buses pass here every few minutes. ⊟(X43)♣

Rufford

Hesketh Arms

81 Liverpool Road, L40 1SB (on A59)

⏲ 12-11 (midnight Fri & Sat)

☎ (01704) 821002

Jennings Cumberland Ale; Moorhouse's Pride of Pendle; guest beers Ⓗ

A 250-year-old listed building, closed for many years and painstakingly restored in 2005. The Georgian frontage faces the extensive car park – the A59 now passes to the rear. The pub was originally built by the Hesketh family for its foresters – the forest has now all but vanished – and it was altered and added to during the 19th and 20th centuries. Drinkers and diners are both catered for, especially at weekends, with at least two guest beers. ❀◖◗♿⇌⊟(202)P⚡–

St Anne's

Trawl Boat ✔

Wood Street, FY8 1QR

⏲ 9-midnight (1am Fri & Sat)

☎ (01253) 783080

Greene King IPA, Abbot; Marston's Pedigree; guest beers Ⓗ

The Trawl Boat is a Wetherspoon's bar located just off the main square, inside a converted solicitors' offices. The ambience is very much in the coffee bar mould; the interior is decorated in pale colours to offset the lack of natural light. The bar offers three permanent beers with three guests, as well as two real ciders. There is a large patio at the front of the building. ♨Q❀◖◗♿⇌●⚡–

Salesbury

Bonny Inn

68 Ribchester Road, BB1 9HQ (on B6245)

⏲ 12-3, 6-11; 12-11 Sun

☎ (01254) 248467

Thwaites Nutty Black, Original, Wainwright Ⓗ

This village inn is more akin to a restaurant than a pub. One large room is mainly occupied by diners and there is a smaller room with a games machine. The large central bar has four handpumps, one never in use. All Thwaites cask beers are available including a mild, plus a continental lager and a draught cider. A patio and smoking area have been added at the rear of the pub, with a large car park adjacent. ❀◖◗♿P

Salwick

Windmill Tavern

Clifton Lane, PR4 0YE (off A583)

⏲ 12-11 summer; 12-3, 5-11 winter; 12-10.30 Sun

☎ (01772) 687203 🌐 windmill-clifton.co.uk

Beer range varies Ⓗ

Built around 1778, Clifton Windmill is the Fyldes oldest and tallest windmill, constructed with stone from around the county. The restaurant was, until recently, a fully working corn mill, and has only been a pub since 1974. There are up to five guest ales and a selection of continental bottled beers.

An ideal place to sit and enjoy a drink or highest-quality traditional fayre served in a cosy dining area. You are always guaranteed a warm welcome at the Windmill Tavern.
Q❀◐◗⛺≋🚌(77,75)♣P⚟🥤

Scorton

Priory

The Square, PR3 1AU
⏲ 11-11.30 (midnight Fri); 9-midnight Sat; 9-11.30 Sun
☎ (01524) 791255 🌐 theprioryscorton.co.uk
Bowland Nicky Nook; Thwaites Wainwright, Lancaster Bomber; guest beers Ⓗ
Scorton is not a tourist destination as such, yet trippers, coach parties and cycle club runs regularly converge on the place, many ending up in the Priory. This is first and foremost a restaurant, but the former blacksmith's shop at one end of the rambling range of buildings houses a fully-licensed bar (signed 'Stout's Bar'), where the furniture is mostly dining-room style. In the evenings a fair number of locals gather. There is generally no music or amusements, so nothing interrupts the flow of conversation.
♨Q♘❀🛏◐◗♿⛺🚌(Super 8)♣P

Silverdale

Woodlands

Woodlands Drive, LA5 0RU
⏲ 7-11; 12-11.30 Sat; 12-11.30 Sun
☎ (01524) 701655
Beer range varies Ⓗ
Large country house on an elevated site, circa 1878, converted to a pub with only minimal alterations. Most of the trade is provided by locals. The bar has a large fireplace – as big as the counter – and great views across Morecambe Bay. Beer pumps are in another room with a list of the four available ales on the wall facing the bar. Home-made sandwiches are served at weekends. The smoking area is covered and sheltered.
♨Q♘❀🚌(L1)♣P⚟

Tontine

Delph

Sefton Road, WN5 8JU (off B5206)
⏲ 12-midnight (1am Fri & Sat); 12-11.30 Sun
☎ (01695) 622239
Beer range varies Ⓗ
There is always a warm welcome and friendly atmosphere in this pub, which retains a separate vault with a pool table. Good-value meals complement the real ales in a relaxed environment. Children are welcome, although not in the vault area. Darts and dominoes are played in the local league and a quiz night is held on Wednesday. The beers are usually pale ones. Good value meals are available. Wigan CAMRA Pub of the Season Autumn 2006/08.
♘❀◐◗♿≋(Orrell)♣P

Tunstall

Lunesdale

LA6 2QN (on A683)
⏲ 11-3, 6-midnight; closed Mon
☎ (01524) 274203 🌐 thelunesdale.co.uk
Black Sheep Best Bitter; guest beers Ⓗ
The emphasis is on locally-produced food and ales in this bright, clean pub with its pine furniture, cosy settees and log fires. There is a small servery surrounded by several rooms: one has pool and table football, but food dominates everywhere. Pictures by local artists adorn the walls. A pub quiz is held on Sunday and the first Friday of the month is a music night with local groups performing.
♨Q♘❀◐◗♿🚌(81B)♣P

Up Holland

Old Dog

6 Alma Hill, WN8 0NW (off A557, near parish church)
⏲ 5 (1 Sat & Sun)-11
☎ (01695) 632487
Banks's Bitter; guest beers Ⓗ
This stone pub's four heavily beamed rooms are on different levels, with the rear rooms affording superb views towards the Pennines. Apparently local highwayman George Lyon was laid to rest in the lounge. Sensitive refurbishment has retained many original features, including etched windows and a small bar area. The pub only serves cask ales, and pump clips from many past guest beers are on display. It also possesses a fine collection of ornamental dogs, and has a wine-tasting group and quiz team. Q❀🚌

Weeton

Eagle & Child ✔

Singleton Road, PR4 3NB (from Fleetwood, follow the B5260 past Weeton army barracks)
⏲ 12-11
☎ (01253) 836230 🌐 theeagleandchild.co.uk
Caledonian Deuchars IPA; Theakston Best Bitter; guest beers Ⓗ
Dating back to 1585, this pub is one of the oldest in Lancashire. Oliver Cromwell is reputed to have stayed here and the cellars have bricked-up tunnels, used to avoid capture during the Civil War. Some oak beams can be traced to York Minster. There is a resident ghost and regular psychic nights are held. It has a good reputation for quality home-cooked food. Outside is a large beer garden and a children's play area. ♨Q❀◐◗♿⛺🚌(75)P

Westhead

Prince Albert ✔

109 Wigan Road, L40 6HY (on A577 between Ormskirk & Skelmersdale) SD444076
⏲ 12-11.30 (10.30 Sun)
☎ (01695) 573656
Tetley Mild, Bitter; guest beers Ⓗ
A small, traditional, well-kept pub on the Wigan Road from Ormskirk to Skelmersdale, the Prince Albert has a small central bar that serves three snug rooms around it. Excellent home-cooked meals can be enjoyed in these restful surroundings where, on cold days, real fires blaze. Southport to Ormskirk and Wigan buses stop outside.
♨❀◐♿⛺🚌(375,385)♣P⚟

Whalley

Swan Hotel

62 King Street, BB7 9SN
⏲ 12-11 (midnight Fri & Sat)
☎ (01254) 822195 🌐 swanhotelwhalley.co.uk
Bowland Hen Harrier; Taylor Landlord; guest beer Ⓗ

Built in 1781, this haunted inn is situated, like all four Whalley pubs, in the heart of the historic village. The hostelry has a deceptively modern but comfortable interior and serves two local Bowland beers as well as Taylor Landlord. The central bar and lounge area are often lively, especially at weekends. The dining room is a relaxing place to enjoy good pub food, as well as the hearty breakfasts served to guests staying in the six en-suite bedrooms. ❀🛏◐▶⇌🚌(26,225,280)P

Wheelton

Red Lion

196 Blackburn Road, PR6 8EU
⏲ 3-11.30; 12-1am Fri & Sat; 12-11.30 Sun
☎ (01254) 830378 🌐 redlionwheelton.com
Beer range varies Ⓗ
Traditional pub in the heart of the village, close to the Leeds-Liverpool Canal. The interior has a long single room with the bar at one end, and a raised pool room. The landlords pride themselves on the wide selection of cask conditioned ale, with real ales sourced from regionals and micros. A wide range of delicious home-cooked meals is served featuring, where possible, the best of local produce (4-8pm Mon-Thu, 1-6pm Fri & Sat, 12-6pm Sun). ♨◐▶🚌P⚟

Wilpshire

Rising Sun

797 Whalley New Road, BB1 9BE (on A666)
⏲ 1 (12 Fri-Sun)-11.30
☎ (01254) 247379
Theakston Best Bitter; guest beers Ⓗ
A friendly, compact, traditional pub, situated just over a mile from Blackburn town centre, with a separate tap room where patrons play cards and dominoes. In the lounge there is a coal fire and a piano, which is played on Saturday night. The pub is very popular with locals. The names of long-closed local breweries can still be seen in the pub windows: 'Lion Ales' and 'Nuttall & Co Double Stout'. Smokers will find a covered and heated area for their use. ♨⊟⇌(Ramsgreave & Wilpshire)♣⚟

Winmarleigh

Patten Arms

Park Lane, PR3 0JU
⏲ 4 (12 Sun)-11
☎ (01995) 791484
Black Sheep Best Bitter; Courage Directors; Jennings Cumberland Ale; Tetley Bitter; guest beers Ⓗ
Genuine isolated freehouse situated on a B road away from villages, yet enjoying regular local custom. This early 19th-century Grade II listed building includes a single bar with a country pub feel, high-backed bench seats, cream-painted walls and open fires. There is a separate restaurant and terraced seating overlooking a bowling green. ♨❀◐▶♣P⚟

Worston

Calf's Head

West Lane, BB7 1QA (in village off A59)
⏲ 11-11
☎ (01200) 441218 🌐 calfshead.co.uk
Jennings Bitter, Cumberland Ale; guest beers Ⓗ
Large Victorian pub situated at the foot of Pendle Hill. Deservedly popular for good value food, the pub is often very busy at meal times and in summer the garden quickly fills with families. Jennings Bitter and Cumberland are the regular beers, while the two guests are from local breweries. The bar has a comfortable lounge area and a large conservatory for diners. A large dining/function room is available for weddings and other events. Accommodation is good value. ♨Q♉❀🛏◐▶♿ÅP

Wray

George & Dragon

Main Street, LA2 8QG (off B6480)
⏲ 6-11 Mon; 12-2.30, 5-11; 12-11 Sat & Sun
☎ (01524) 221403 🌐 wrayvillage.co.uk/george/home.htm
Everards Beacon Ⓗ
A genuine village local which also has an excellent reputation for its food. Inside there are two bar rooms of quite different sizes and a restaurant. Unusual pub games are available, as is Wi-Fi broadband. Home of the famous maggot race, there is also a Wednesday night quiz. The extensive beer garden has an aviary and a covered smoking area. ♨Q❀◐▶🚌(80,81B)♣⚟

Wrea Green

Villa

Moss Side Lane, PR4 2PE (¼ mile outside village on B5259)
⏲ 12-11 (10.30 Sun)
☎ (01772) 684347
Copper Dragon Best Bitter, Scotts 1816; Jennings Bitter, Cumberland Ale Ⓗ
A 23-room hotel in the extensive grounds of a former 19th-century gentleman's residence. The original house features an à la carte restaurant and a large bar. In winter the best seats are the leather sofas by the real fire in the oak-panelled area. For summer there is an outside drinking and dining area. Jazz nights are monthly on a Friday, and the hotel holds wine tastings and murder mystery events. To encourage staying over, accommodation is offered at a reduced rate. ♨❀🛏◐▶♿🚌(76)P⚟

Wrightington

White Lion

117 Mossy Lea Road, WN6 9RE
⏲ 12-midnight (11 Mon & Wed); 12-10.30 Sun
☎ (01257) 425977
Banks's Bitter; Jennings Cumberland Ale; guest beers Ⓗ
Extremely popular country pub which has undergone extensive but sympathetic refurbishment. It attracts many locals, with a good mix of drinkers and diners. Four handpumps are in constant use, serving beers from the Marston's range. A weekly quiz takes place on Tuesday and a poker league on Thursday. Occasional themed evenings are held in the restaurant and booking is recommended for weekends. The pub is family friendly with a large garden. ❀◐▶⊟♿🚌P⚟

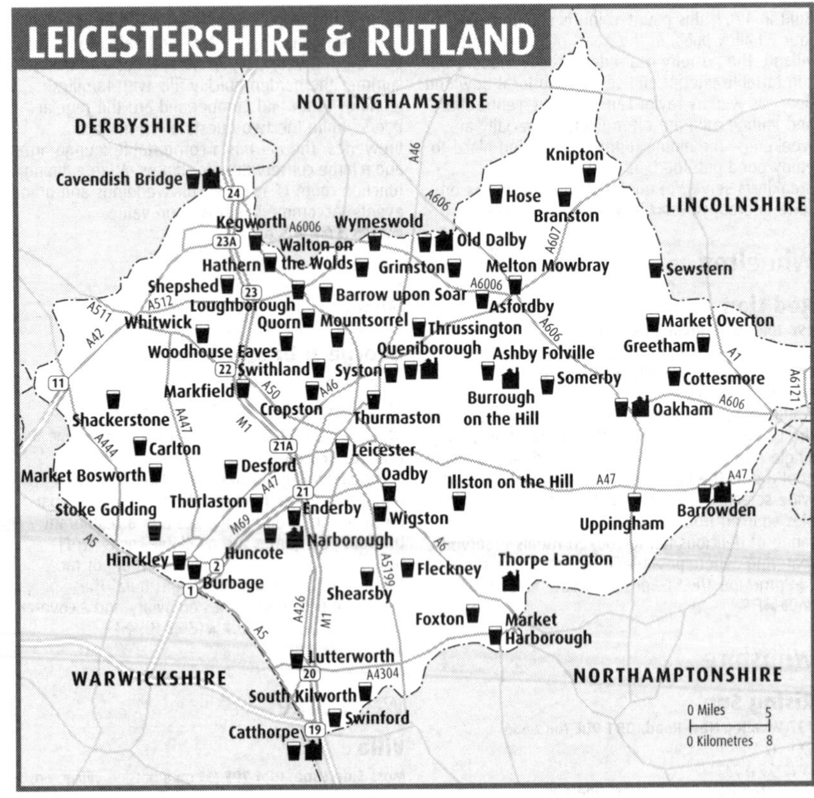

LEICESTERSHIRE

Asfordby

Horseshoes

128 Main Street, LE14 3SA

12-4, 7-11; 11.30-midnight Sat; 12-11 Sun

☎ (01664) 813392

Bateman XB; Tetley Bitter, seasonal beers Ⓗ

Friendly locals' pub in the centre of the village. A Bateman's house, it offers at least one of the brewery's ales plus seasonal beers and occasional guests. Buses from Leicester and Melton Mowbray stop outside the front door, with a frequent daytime weekday service. Regular weekday daytime buses from Grantham and Loughborough also pass the pub. ⌂Q❀🚌

Ashby Folville

Carington Arms

2 Folville Street, LE14 2TE (on main road at NW end of village)

12-2.30, 5-midnight; 12-10.30 Sun

☎ (01664) 841234

Greene King IPA; Taylor Landlord, Ⓗ

Spacious country-village pub with several distinct seating areas and a small recently-refurbished restaurant. A warm welcome is assured at this pub, which can be very busy at times. Guest beers are often from local micro-breweries. Snacks and light meals are available and an a la carte menu is served in the restaurant. ⌂Q❀◐♿🚌(100)P

Barrow upon Soar

Soar Bridge Inn

29 Bridge Street, LE12 8PN

12 (3 Mon)-11; 12-10.30 Sun

☎ (01509) 412686

Everards Beacon, Tiger, Original; guest beer Ⓗ

Situated next to the bridge that gave it its name, this pub is popular with drinkers and diners (no food Sun and Mon). The large single room interior divides into distinct areas, with a separate room for meetings or skittles. Children are welcome and there is a beer garden. ❀◐⛺≋🚌(K2,CB27)P

Branston

Wheel

Main Street, NG32 1RU

11-11; closed Mon; 12-10.30 Sun

☎ (01476) 870376 🌐 thewheelinnbranston.co.uk

Bateman XB; guest beers Ⓗ

Like most of the buildings in the village, this attractive 18th-century pub is built using local stone. There is a small bar with some seating and a larger restaurant area that was originally two small rooms, now sympathetically renovated. The extensive food menu uses locally-sourced ingredients where possible, including produce from the nearby Belvoir Estate. ⌂Q❀◐♿●P

Burbage

Cross Keys

13 Hinckley Road, LE10 2AF

11-11; 11-midnight Fri & Sat; 12-10.30 Sun
(01455) 239443
Marston's Burton Bitter, Pedigree; guest beers H
A traditional pub at the heart of Burbage. One central bar serves all four rooms, including public bar, lounge and a gossip corner with oak panelled walls, settles, servery and beamed ceilings. Log fires warm the pub in winter. Outside a large patio and garden leads to the cricket field. Within the pub, cricket memorabilia is much in evidence. Cricket and football teams are fielded. Numerous pub games include shove ha'penny. Smokers have a heated outdoor area.

Carlton

Gate Hangs Well
Barton Road, CV13 0DB (1 mile N of Market Bosworth)
12-3, 6-11 (midnight Fri & Sat); 7-10.30 Sun
(01455) 291845
Draught Bass; Greene King Abbot; Marston's Burton Bitter, Pedigree H
A friendly, award-winning traditional village inn with seating areas served by a central bar. Popular with walkers and cyclists, there is a pleasant garden and conservatory where families with children are welcome until mid-evening. Sandwiches and rolls are made to order. Darts is played and live music hosted on Wednesday and Saturday evenings. A smoking shelter is available. Convenient for Bosworth Battlefield, Bosworth Water Trust – with camping facilities, Ashby Canal, the Leicestershire Round and The Battlefield Line at Shackerstone.

Catthorpe

Cherry Tree
Main Street, LE17 6DB
12-2.30, 5-11 Mon; 5-11.30 Tue-Thu; 12-2.30, 5-12.30am Fri; 12-12.30am Sat; 12-10.30 Sun
(01788) 860430 cherrytree-pub.co.uk
Adnams Bitter; guest beers H
This popular village free house is adorned with a large old Phipps Brewery sign, now painted and adapted by the landlord. Four real ales are available, regularly including offerings from Catthorpe's own brewery Dow Bridge. Excellent locally-sourced food is served from a varied and extensive menu, including Sunday roast, a vegetarian option and, in summer, a cold table. Railway and aviation memorabilia adorn the walls, while in the corner is a jet fighter ejection seat. Beer festivals are held in summer and winter.

Cavendish Bridge

Old Crown
DE72 2HL
11-midnight (1am Fri & Sat); 12-midnight Sun
(01332) 792392
Jennings Cocker Hoop; Marston's Pedigree, Old Empire; guest beers H
Coaching inn dating from the 17th century with the original oak-beamed ceiling displaying an extensive collection of old jugs. The walls are covered with pub mirrors, brewery signs and railway memorabilia which even extend into the toilets. The cosy open plan interior is divided into two areas with a large inglenook on the right.

Cropston

Bradgate Arms
15 Station Road, LE7 7HG
11.30-11; 12-10.30 Sun
(0116) 234 0336
Banks's Bitter; Marston's Pedigree H
Comfortable village pub popular with locals and tourists. Though extended to the rear in the early 1990s, it retains many original features, with five drinking areas and a dining room on two levels. Food is served all day. Darts and long alley skittles are played. The pub is handy for the Great Central Railway at Rothley and Bradgate Country Park.
P

Desford

Blue Bell Inn
39 High Street, LE9 9JF
11-midnight (1am Fri & Sat); 12-midnight Sun
(01455) 822901
Everards Beacon, Tiger, Original, seasonal beers; guest beers H
Welcoming pub in the centre of the village with two rooms and a restaurant area with a central servery. A general knowledge quiz is held on Tuesday night. Food is available lunchtimes and evenings throughout the week, including the traditional Sunday lunch. Dominoes and darts are played. Outside, the garden has a children's play area and there is a heated and covered space for smokers. Close to Mallory Park, B&B accommodation is provided.
Q (152,153) P

Enderby

New Inn
51 High Street, LE19 4AG
12-2.30 (not Mon; 3pm Sat), 6 (5.30 Fri)-11 (11.30 Thu-Sat); 12-3, 7-11 Sun
(0116) 286 3126
Everards Beacon, Tiger, Original, seasonal beers; guest beers H
Friendly, thatched village local dating from 1549, tucked away at the top of the High Street. Everards' first tied house, the pub is well know locally for the quality of its beer, and often frequented by Everards brewery staff. Three rooms are served by a central bar, with long alley skittles and a snooker room to the rear. Outside is a patio area and garden. Plentiful and imaginative lunches are served Tuesday to Saturday.

Fleckney

Golden Shield
46 Main Street, LE8 8AN

INDEPENDENT BREWERIES

Barrowden Barrowden
Bees Queniborough
Belvoir Old Dalby
Dow Bridge Catthorpe
Everards Narborough
Grainstore Oakham
Langton Thorpe Langton
Parish Burrough on the Hill
Shardlow Cavendish Bridge

12-2.30 (not Mon & Tue), 5-11; 12-midnight Fri & Sat; 11.30-11 Sun
☎ (0116) 2402366
Banks's Bitter; Greene King IPA, Abbot; John Smith's Bitter; Taylor Landlord; guest beer
First opened as an inn named the Dun Cow in 1789, the pub additionally served the community as both a butcher's and a barber's. This popular village local, with a good reputation for locally sourced, freshly prepared food, has six handpumps dispensing beers from nationals and local micro-brewers alike. The pub is keenly active in its support of local football, cricket and golf. Lunch is served daily except Monday and Tuesday – evening meals Tuesday to Saturday. P

Foxton

Bridge 61

Bottom Lock, LE16 7RA
10-11
☎ (0116) 279 2285 🌐 foxtonboats.co.uk
Adnams Bitter; Banks's Original; guest beers
Canal-side pub situated at the bottom of the famous flight of 10 staircase locks at Foxton. The two-roomed interior has a small bar in the snug area and a larger conservatory with wide doors that open out onto the water in summer. The patio is an ideal spot for watching the canal boats pass by. Meals are available all day. Nearby is a boatyard and canal shop with passenger trips and boats to hire; book in advance.
Q

Foxton Locks Inn

Bottom Lock, Gumley Road, LE16 7RA
11-11 (10.30 Sun)
☎ (0116) 279 1515
Caledonian Deuchars IPA; Greene King Old Speckled Hen; Theakston Black Bull, Old Peculier; guest beers
Refurbished canal-side inn situated at the foot of Foxton Locks, a major attraction on the Grand Union Canal. The canal director's office, once upstairs, has been recreated at the rear of the pub, complete with a collection of original share certificates on display. Outdoor seating runs down to the canal bank where boats may be moored. Families are welcome inside the pub and blankets are available for outdoor drinkers.
Q P

Grimston

Black Horse

Main Street, LE14 3BZ
12-3, 6-11; 12-4 Sun
☎ (01664) 812358
Adnams Bitter; Marston's Pedigree; St Austell Tribute; guest beer
Overlooking the village green, this pub is very popular and busy both lunchtimes and evenings. It has a large open plan bar on two levels where a wide range of good food is available. Real cider usually replaces one of the ales in summer. A petanque court hosts several local teams. A regular weekday daytime bus service from Melton Mowbray stops outside the pub.
Q (23)

Hathern

Dew Drop

49 Loughborough Road, LE12 5HY
12-3, 6-midnight; 12-3, 7-1am Fri-Sun
☎ (01509) 842438
Greene King XX Mild, H&H Bitter; guest beers
Traditional two-roomed local with a large bar and comfortable small lounge with real fires. Do not miss a visit to the totally unspoilt toilets with their tiled walls and original features. A large range of malt whiskies is stocked and cobs are available at lunchtime. Q P

Hinckley

Ashby Road Sports and Social Club

Hangmans Lane, LE10 3DA (On N edge of town off Ashby Rd, near A47)
7 (5 Fri)-11; 12-11.30 Sat; 12-10.30 Sun
☎ (01455) 615159
Worthington's Bitter; guest beers
CAMRA members are welcome at this private sports and social club. Its six acres of grounds have good facilities for team activities and camper vans are welcome. A large family-friendly bar area hosts traditional pub games and there are two function rooms. The two guest beers change every Thursday, including LocAles and national beers. Cobs are served. Activities range from cricket, football, dominoes, darts, chess, rifle shooting and table tennis to line, modern, jive and sequence dancing. A smoking shelter is available outside.
P

Hose

Black Horse

21 Bolton Lane, LE14 4JE
12-2 (Fri & Sat only), 7-midnight; 12-4, 7-10.30 Sun
☎ (01949) 860336
Adnams Bitter; Castle Rock Harvest Pale; Fuller's London Pride; guest beers
Traditional pub with a lounge featuring wooden beams and a brass-ornamented brick fireplace. Blackboard menus for food and drink surround a wooden corner bar. The unspoilt public bar, decorated with pictures and mirrors, has a tiled floor, wooden furniture and a brick fireplace. The rustic, wood-panelled restaurant serves good food made with local produce. Q P

Huncote

Red Lion

Main Street, LE9 3AU
12-2.30 (not Mon & Sat), 5 (4 Sat)-11; 12-10.30 Sun
☎ (0116) 286 2233 🌐 red-lion.biz
Everards Beacon, Tiger; guest beers
Built in 1892, the Red Lion is a friendly local offering a warm welcome. With beamed ceilings throughout, it has a cosy lounge with a wooden fireplace and log fire. The bar has an adjoining dining area and a separate pool room. The sizeable garden has picnic tables and a children's play area. Good value home-cooked lunches are served plus evening meals on Tuesday and Wednesday only. Skittles can by played by prior arrangement.
P

Illston on the Hill

Fox & Goose

Main Street, LE7 9EG

⏲ 12-2 (not Mon & Tue), 5.30 (7 Mon)-11; 12-3, 7-11 Sun

☎ (0116) 259 6430

Everards Beacon, Tiger, Original; guest beers [H]

Cosy, unspoilt pub with a timeless feel, tucked away in the village and well worth seeking out. A fascinating collection of local mementos and hunting memorabilia is on display including original Mclaughlan cartoons. Popular annual events include conkers, an onion-growing championship and a fund-raising auction for local charities. ⌂Q❀⊟♣

Kegworth

Red Lion

24 High Street, DE74 2DA

⏲ 11.30-11; 12-10.30 Sun

☎ (01509) 672466

Adnams Bitter; Banks's Original; Courage Directors; Greene King Abbot; guest beers [H]

Georgian building standing on the 19th-century route of the London to Glasgow road (A6). It has three small bars and a separate restaurant, plus a skittle alley and petanque courts. Up to four guest beers are available as well as various flavoured Polish and Ukrainian vodkas and a good selection of malt whiskies. Outside there is a large, secure children's play area. ⌂Q❀⊨◑◗⊟🚌♣🍎P⁼

Knipton

Manners Arms

Croxton Road, NG32 1RH

⏲ 11-11; 12-10.30 Sun

☎ (01476) 879222 🌐 mannersarms.com

Belvoir Beaver Bitter; guest beers [H]

Impressive Georgian hunting lodge beautifully renovated by the Duke and Duchess of Rutland with furniture and prints taken from Belvoir Castle. Served by one long bar, the lounge, with tall bookshelves and comfortable seating, and bar room are warmed by a huge open fireplace. Light bar dishes are available plus a wide range of interesting food made with local produce in the restaurant. There is a live music programme every Thursday evening. A wonderful patio and garden area, overlooked by the conservatory, is ideal for lazing on a hot summer's day. ⌂Q❀⊨◑◗♿P

Leicester

Ale Wagon

27 Rutland Street, LE1 1RE

⏲ 11-11; 12-3, 7-10.30 Sun

☎ (0116) 2623330 🌐 alewagon.co.uk

Hoskins Hob, Best Mild, Brigadier, Bitter, EXS; guest beers [H]

Run by the Hoskins family, this city-centre pub with a 1930s interior, including an original oak staircase, has two rooms with tiled and parquet floors and a central bar. There is always a selection of Hoskins Brothers ales and guests available. The pub is popular with visiting rugby fans and real ale drinkers. It has a function room available with catering and is handy for the new Curve Theatre. ⌂⊟⇌🚌♣

Black Horse

65 Narrow Lane, Aylestone, LE2 8NA

⏲ 12-2.30 (not Mon), 5-11; 12-midnight Fri & Sat; 12-11 Sun

☎ (0116) 2832811 🌐 philspub.co.uk

Everards Beacon, Sunchaser, Tiger, Original, seasonal beers; guest beers [H]

Welcoming, traditional, three-room Victorian pub with a distinctive bar servery in the Aylestone Village Conservation Area, three miles from the city centre. Home-cooked food is served lunchtimes Tuesday to Friday plus Friday evenings. Outside is a large beer garden with a children's play area. The skittle alley hosts a monthly comedy club and acoustic night, and is available for private parties. A popular quiz is held every Sunday and regular beer festivals and community events are hosted. Dogs welcome. ⌂Q❀◑◗⊟🚌♣⁼

Criterion 🏆

44 Millstone Lane, LE1 5JN

⏲ 12-11

☎ (0116) 262 5418

Oakham Inferno, Bishops Farewell; guest beers [H]

Two-roomed 1960s city-centre pub offering up to ten guest ales from micros and regionals at weekends. Beer festivals are held regularly, with many beers on gravity from the cellar. More than 100 international bottled beers are also stocked. A pop quiz is hosted on Tuesday, general knowledge quiz on Wednesday and live music on Thursday and Saturday. Darts and dominoes are played in the bar. Pub food is available Sunday and Monday, Italian style pizzas Tuesday to Saturday. Leicester CAMRA Pub of the Year 2006/07/08/09, and regional Runner Up 2007. ❀◑◗♣🍎⁼

Globe

43 Silver Street, LE1 5EU

⏲ 11-11 (1am Fri); 12-10.30 Sun

☎ (0116) 262 9819

Everards Beacon, Sunchaser, Tiger, Original, seasonal beers; guest beers [H]

More than 30 years ago this city-centre pub was hailed as Everards' first pub to return to a full real ale range after seven years as keg only. Major renovations in 2000 moved the bar to the centre of the pub. There is a snug and gas lighting throughout (electric too). An upstairs room is available for meetings. Leicester CAMRA first met here in 1974. Bar meals and snacks are served until 7pm. A warm welcome awaits from the landlady and staff. ◑⊟♿⇌🚌

Shakespeare's Head

Southgates, LE1 5SH

⏲ 12-midnight (1am Fri & Sat); 12-11 Sun

☎ (0116) 262 4378

Oakwell Old Tom Mild, Barnsley Bitter [H]

This two-roomed local was built alongside the underpass in the 1960s and has changed little since then, retaining all the charm of a typical town pub of its era. Two large glass doors lead to an off-sales area with a bar to the left and lounge to the right. Formerly a Shipstones pub, it now sells Oakwell beers at very reasonable prices. A selection of cobs is available Friday and Saturday, and Sunday lunch is very popular (12-2pm). ◑♿🚌♣

Swan & Rushes

19 Infirmary Square, LE1 5WR

⏲ 12-3, 5-11 (midnight Thu); 12-midnight Fri & Sat; 12-11.30 Sun

☎ (0116) 233 9167 🌐 swanandrushes.co.uk

Batemans XB; Oakham JHB, Bishops Farewell, seasonal beers; guest beers Ⓗ
Comfortable, triangular, two-roomed pub in the city centre with a relaxed atmosphere, filled with breweriana and framed photos on the wall. Up to nine real ales (no nationals) are available, or you can choose from the bottled beer menu featuring more than 100 international classics. Several food-linked beer festivals are held each year plus cider and cheese events. Thursday is quiz night and live gigs take place on some Saturdays. Good value home-cooked food is served lunchtimes and Wednesday and Friday evenings.

Tom Hoskins

131 Beaumanor Road, LE4 5QE
12-11; 11.30-midnight Fri & Sat
(0116) 2669659
Black Sheep Best Bitter; Greene King IPA; Hook Norton Bitter; M&B Mild; guest beers Ⓗ
Hospitable, two-room, suburban pub catering for the mature drinker. There are up to six cask ales on (a minimum of four at any one time) including a mild. Freshly-made cobs are always available. Darts is played in the bar and the pub is very popular with local football and rugby teams. A regular Sunday evening quiz is held. P

Vin IV

24 King Street, LE1 6RL
12-11 (2am Fri & Sat); 12-10.30 Sun viniv.co.uk
Oakham JHB, Bishops Farewell Ⓗ**; guest beers** Ⓗ/Ⓖ
Formerly known as Out of the Vaults, this friendly city centre free house showcases real ales from micro-breweries. Frequent beer festivals keep an eclectic mix of locals and visitors happy. Popular with football and rugby fans, away supporters are especially welcome. Food is served at lunchtime. Occasional live music plays on Saturday night and there are weekly Sunday afternoon acoustic sessions. Traditional pub games are available from the bar. A regular haunt of Leicester Morris dancers.

Western

70 Western Road, LE3 0GA
12-3, 5-11; 12-midnight Fri & Sat
(0116) 2545287
Steamin' Billy Bitter, Skydiver, Last Bark Ⓗ**; guest beers** Ⓗ/Ⓖ
A traditional two-roomed local with a bar and lounge in a residential location, attracting a good mixed clientele of all ages. Old pub signs decorate the walls. Food is served, with a carvery on Sunday. The pub gets busy on match days.

Loughborough

Albion Inn

Canal Bank, LE11 1QA
11-3 (4 Sat), 6-11; 12-3, 7-10.30 Sun
(01509) 213952
Sharp's Doom Bar; Wicked Hathern Doble's Dog Mild; guest beers Ⓗ
Canal-side pub built in the late 18th century at the same time as the Loughborough Canal. It has a bar, darts room and quiet lounge, and outside the patio has an aviary. The house beer, Albion Special, is supplied to the pub by the local Wicked Hathern Brewery. Care should be taken if driving to the pub along the tow path. QP

Moon & Bell

6 Wards End, LE11 3HU
9-midnight
(01509) 241504
Greene King Ruddles Best, Abbot; Marston's Pedigree Ⓗ
The buildings of the former Loughborough Tax Office are the location for this traditionally-styled Wetherspoon's pub. One interesting feature is the bell behind the bar which was cast at Taylors Bellfounders in Loughborough. There is an outdoor seating area at the rear where you can occasionally hear the bells of Loughborough Carillon being played. QP

Paget Arms

41 Oxford Street, LE11 5DP
12-midnight
(01509) 266216 myspace.com/thepaget
Steamin' Billy Bitter, Skydiver; guest beers Ⓗ/Ⓖ
Located on a corner at the end of a row of terraced houses, this former Everards pub has been refurbished and is now one of Steamin' Billy's locals. It offers six real ales with some served by gravity, direct from the cellar. Home-cooked food includes pizzas and doorstep sandwiches. There are two attractive rooms with ample seating and a large, enclosed garden with a heated, covered area for smokers. Regular beer festivals are held.

Peacock

26 Factory Street, LE11 1AL
10-12.30am (1.30am Fri & Sat); 12-midnight Sun
(01509) 214215
Draught Bass; M&B Mild Ⓗ
Traditional, back-street, no-frills local, with a walled beer garden outside. Formerly a multi-roomed pub, it now has an open-plan bar area while retaining cosy nooks and crannies. A true community pub, it supports most pub games including long alley skittles. P

Swan in the Rushes

21 The Rushes, LE11 5BE
11-11 (midnight Fri & Sat); 12-11 Sun
(01509) 217014 castlerockbrewery.co.uk/pub-swanintherushes.html
Adnams Bitter; Castle Rock Harvest Pale, Hemlock; Hop Back Summer Lightning; guest beers Ⓗ
Traditional three-room Castle Rock pub comprising two quiet, comfortable bars and the Charnwood Vaults, a lively room with a jukebox and wooden bench seating. There is a constantly-changing range of up to six guest beers, always including a mild, as well as real cider and perry, a limited range of continental bottled and draught beers, and a good range of malt whiskies and country wines. Upstairs is a skittle alley and function room which hosts live music and twice-yearly beer festivals. QP

Tap & Mallet

36 Nottingham Road, LE11 1EU
5 (11.30 Sat & Sun)-2am
(01509) 210028
Jennings Mild; Marston's Burton Bitter; guest beers Ⓗ
Genuine free house conveniently situated on a direct route from the railway station to the town centre. The five guest beers are from micro-breweries, often from the east or north-east midlands area, but usually beers not commonly found in the Loughborough area. The interior has a

single room split into two distinct drinking areas. The lounge can be partitioned off for private functions. Outside there is a secluded walled garden with children's play equipment and a pet's corner. Cobs are available all day. Note that the pub closes early if quiet. ⛫❀⇌🚌♣●

Lutterworth

Unicorn

27 Church Street, LE17 4AE
⏲ 11-11 (midnight Fri & Sat); 12-11 Sun
☎ (01455) 552486
Black Sheep Best Bitter; Draught Bass; Greene King IPA; M&B Brew XI Ⓗ
The Unicorn is a traditional market town-centre pub. The main room is a hive of activity and is home to many games teams. Table skittles can be played. The back room is cosy, decorated with a collection of old town pictures. Good quality, reasonably-priced food is available.
⛫Q🛏◐◑⊟🚌♣P

Market Bosworth

Olde Red Lion Hotel

1 Park Street, CV13 0LL
⏲ 11 (10 Wed & Sat)-11
☎ (01455) 291713
Banks's Bitter; Jennings Bitter, Sneck Lifter; Marston's Pedigree; guest beers Ⓗ
The Olde Red Lion Hotel is located in the heart of historic Market Bosworth. It prides itself on offering a wide range of real ales, home-cooked food and en-suite B&B accommodation. More than 400 years old, it remains very traditional with a cosy atmosphere, original oak beams and an open fireplace. Excellent food is sourced from local suppliers and home cooked. The first Sunday of the month is quiz night. Smokers have a heated area outside. ⛫❀🛏◐◑♿🚌♣P⚊

Market Harborough

Admiral Nelson

49 Nelson Street, LE16 9AX
⏲ 12-2, 5-midnight; 12-midnight Fri & Sat; 12-11 Sun
☎ (07999) 655550
Wells Eagle IPA, Bombadier; guest beers Ⓗ
Welcoming, friendly locals' pub, built in 1900, situated a short stroll from the centre of the historic market town. Just off the beaten track, this pub is the town's best kept secret, offering a lounge with TV (where they like their rugby) and bar with darts, pool, jukebox and another TV. Home-cooked food is served Monday-Saturday lunchtimes. A function room is available and there is a heated, covered smoking area outside with seating. Dogs are welcome. ❀◐⊟♣P⚊

Markfield

Bulls Head

23 Forest Road, LE67 9UN
⏲ 3 (11 Sat)-11.30 (2am Fri); 12-10.30 Sun
☎ (01530) 242541
Marston's Burton Bitter, Pedigree Ⓗ
Long-established two-roomed local tucked away in the corner of the village. A typical country inn full of character, it offers a friendly welcome to all. Darts and dominoes are played here.
Q❀⊟♿🚌♣P⚊

Melton Mowbray

Anne of Cleves

12 Burton Street, LE13 1AE (Just S of St Mary's Church)
⏲ 11-11; 12-4, 7-10.30 Sun
☎ (01664) 481336
Everards Tiger, Original, seasonal beers; guest beers Ⓗ
One of Everards' most historic pubs and an icon for the town. Part of the property dates back to 1327 when it was home to monks. The house was gifted to Anne of Cleves by Henry VIII as part of her divorce settlement. It is now a popular and busy hostelry following a sympathetic conversion and restoration of the building, with stone-flagged floors, exposed timber roof beams and wall tapestries. The building is said to be haunted and psychic research evenings feature regularly. Up to three guest ales may be available.
⛫Q❀◐◑⇌🚌P⚊

Harboro' Hotel

49 Burton Street, LE13 1AF (opp railway station)
⏲ 11-11 (midnight Fri & Sat); 12-11 Sun
☎ (01664) 560121 🌐 harborohotel.co.uk
Fuller's ESB; Taylor Landlord; Tetley Bitter; guest beers Ⓗ
Eighteenth-century coaching inn conveniently located between the town centre and railway station. The hotel is often very busy and can be a little noisy. The open plan bar has comfortable seating, serving food ranging from bar snacks to restaurant meals. Guest beers vary, real cider is always available and a wide range of draught and bottled Belgian and German beers is on offer. An Easter beer festival is held. There is a petanque court in the rear car park.
❀🛏◐◑♿⇌(Melton Mowbray)🚌♣●P⚊

Kettleby Cross ✔

Wilton Road, LE13 0UJ (opp library)
⏲ 9-midnight
☎ (01664) 485310
Greene King IPA, Abbot; Marston's Pedigree; guest beers Ⓗ
Standing close to the bridge over the nearby River Eye, and named after the cross that once directed travellers towards Ab Kettleby, this is Wetherspoon's recently built flagship 'green' pub with numerous energy saving design features including a prominent wind turbine on the roof. There are ten handpumps on the long bar, with five regular beers supplemented by up to five ever-changing guests, often locally-brewed beers from Langton and Grainstore. ❀◐◑♿⇌🚌⚊

Mountsorrel

Swan Inn

10 Loughborough Road, LE12 7AT
⏲ 12-2.30, 5.30-11; 12-11 Sat; 12-3, 7-10.30 Sun
☎ (0116) 2302340
Black Sheep Best Bitter; Ruddles County; Theakston Best Bitter, XB, Old Peculier; guest beers Ⓗ
Traditional, 17th-century, Grade II-listed coaching inn, formerly called the Nag's Head, under the present ownership since 1990. The split-level bar has stone floors and low ceilings and there is a small dining area with a polished wood floor. Good quality, interesting food is cooked to order, with the menu changing every two weeks. Monthly themed nights are popular. Outside is a secluded riverside garden with moorings. ⛫❀🛏◐◑🚌P

Oadby

Cow & Plough

Stoughton Farm Park, Gartree Road, LE2 2FB

12-3, 5-11; 12-11 summer

(0116) 2720852 steamin-billy.co.uk

Fuller's London Pride; Steamin' Billy Scrum Down, Bitter, Skydiver; guest beers H

Situated in a converted farm building with a conservatory, this pub is decked out with breweriana. A large restaurant has been added in the former Victorian dairy buildings. It is home to Steamin' Billy beers, named after the owner's now departed Jack Russell who features on the logo and pump clips. All beers are brewed at Tower Brewery. A mild and Sheppy's cider are always available. Twice CAMRA Pub of the Year for the East Midlands area and Leicester branch winner 2007/08. Q P

Wheel Inn

99 London Road, LE2 5DP

12-midnight (10.30 Sun)

(0116) 271 2231 wheelinn.biz

Draught Bass; Marston's Pedigree; guest beers H

Sports-oriented community pub where there is always something going on. As well as darts, dominoes and skittles teams there are football, cricket, golf and fishing matches, casino nights, jazz evenings, train trips, cycle rides and anything else the landlord and customers can think of. Tasty home-cooked food and an extensive selection of wines and spirits add to the appeal. The Leicester bus stops outside. (31)P

Old Dalby

Crown Inn

Debdale Hill, LE14 3LF

5-11; closed Mon; 12.30-3, 6-11 Sat; 12-11 Sun

(01664) 823134 crownolddalby.co.uk

Belvoir Beaver Mild; Castle Rock Harvest Pale; guest beer H

Dating from 1590, this charming ivy-clad pub is situated in delightful gardens. There is a quirky selection of rooms including the original brewing room, now used as the bar. The extensive bar and restaurant menu uses local produce. The outdoor pentanque court is popular during the summer months. Q P

Sample Cellar

Belvoir Brewery, Station Road, LE14 3NQ

12-11 (10 Sun)

(01664) 823455

Belvoir Star Mild, Beaver Bitter, seasonal beers H

The brick-fronted Sample Cellar on the outskirts of the village incorporates a bar, visitors' centre and function room. The comfortable, spacious interior, filled with brewing artefacts, has a traditional bar area, and there is even room for long alley skittles and a bar billiard table. Two large internal windows provide views into the brewery. A full menu is served daily, with the focus on good wholesome food made with local produce. P

Queniborough

Britannia

47 Main Street, LE7 3DB

12-2.30, 6-11; 12-11 Sun

(0116) 260 5675

M&B Brew XI; Taylor Landlord; guest beers H

Two-roomed, comfortable village local with a traditional bar and restaurant leading off the lounge. Both rooms have an open fire providing welcome warmth on cold winter evenings. Food is available seven days a week. Old pictures of the village are on the lounge wall. Guest beers come from the Punch list. P

Quorn

Manor House

Woodhouse Road, LE12 8AL

12-11 (midnight Sat); 12-10 Sun

(01509) 413416 themanorhouseatquorn.co.uk

Draught Bass; Taylor Landlord H

Built in 1899 by the Great Central Railway, the Manor House (formerly Manor House Hotel) was built to serve passengers arriving at Quorn & Woodhouse Station, which it still does today. It was refurbished in 2005 and is now an open-plan bar plus award-winning restaurant. From the large beer garden you can watch preserved steam (and diesel) hauled trains pass by, on what is now the Great Central Preserved Railway. P

Sewstern

Blue Dog

Main Street, NG33 5RQ

11-11; 12-10.30 Sun

(01476) 860097

Greene King IPA; guest beers H

Friendly and welcoming pub at the west end of the village, handy for walkers at the southern end of the Viking Way. The unusual name reflects the tradition of local farm workers on the Tollemache estate being paid partly in blue tokens. The 300-year-old building was once a war hospital and has a ghost – a boy drummer called Albert. Guest ales often come from local breweries and a beer festival is held in late May. A popular fish and chip menu is available on Wednesday evening. Q (55)P

Shackerstone

Rising Sun

Church Road, CV13 6NN (3 miles E of Twycross, 3 miles SW of Ibstock)

12-2.30, 6-midnight; 12-midnight Sat & Sun

(01827) 880215 risingsunpub.com

Marston's Pedigree; Taylor Landlord; guest beers H

A family-run free house since 1987 with a large, traditional wood-panelled bar area. Two guest ales change regularly and Old Rosie real cider is sold. A separate sports room has pool and Sky TV. Children are welcome in the conservatory and attractive beer garden. Meals are served daily in the bar and barn-conversion restaurant, with Sunday lunches always popular. The Battlefield Railway and Ashby Canal are nearby. Walkers are welcome. Regular charity fund-raising walks support Guide Dogs for the Blind. P

Shearsby

Chandlers Arms

Fenny Lane, LE17 6PL (close to A5199)

12-3 (not Mon), 7 (6 Fri)-11; 12-4, 6-11 Sat; 12-4, 7-10.30 Sun

(0116) 2478384 chandlersatshearsby.co.uk

Dow Bridge Acris; guest beers H

Classic, quaint old country pub overlooking the village green. Popular with walkers, cyclists, diners and visitors from the city, it also has strong local support. It was the first pub in Leicester Branch to become LocAle accredited. Micro-brewery beers are always on the bar (often locally sourced), and draught cider is available in summer. No food is served on Sunday evening or Monday. Leicester CAMRA County Pub of the Year 2009.

Shepshed

Black Swan

21 Loughborough Road, LE12 9DL

7-midnight; 12-3, 5-1am Fri; 12-3, 6-1am Sat; 12-midnight Sun

(01509) 502659

Adnams Broadside; Draught Bass; Greene King Abbot; Taylor Landlord H

Situated in a prominent position close to the town centre, this multi-roomed pub has been modernised and rejuvenated by the present licensees. The main room has two drinking areas, both with comfortable seating. A further small room can be used by families. The upstairs restaurant serves good quality food (Thu eve, Fri and Sat lunch and eve). Shepshed Dynamo football ground is nearby. Q P

Somerby

Stilton Cheese

Main Street, LE14 2PZ

12-3, 6-11 (7-10.30 Sun)

(01664) 454394

Grainstore Ten Fifty; Marston's Pedigree; Tetley Bitter; guest beers H

Late 16th-century pub built in local ironstone, as are most of the buildings in the village. The interior comprises two bars and a function room. Tall customers will note the wide range of pump clips on the low beams as they bang their heads on them. A popular and lively village pub, booking is advised for dining. Q (113) P

South Kilworth

White Hart

Rugby Road, LE17 6DN

12-2.30 (not Wed), 5.30-11; 12-3, 6-11 Sat; 12-6, 7-11 Sun

(01858) 575416

Banks's Bitter; Jennings Cumberland Ale; guest beer H

Legend has it that Oliver Cromwell had a meal here after the Battle of Naseby in 1645. Good food can still be enjoyed today in the bar or cosy restaurant, specialising in tasty char-grilled steaks, all sourced from the village butcher. The three beers include one guest from the Marston's portfolio. An ideal stopping point for visitors to nearby Stanford Hall. P

Stoke Golding

George and Dragon

Station Road, CV13 6EZ

12-midnight (11 Sun)

(01455) 213268

Wells Bombardier; guest beers H

The oldest pub in the village – a traditional two-roomed local – occupying a prominent central position. The comfortable, old-fashioned interior includes a lounge bar which has been extended to allow space for a small restaurant without affecting the area around the bar. Guest beers are mainly LocAles from nearby micro-breweries, including Church End, and the range changes regularly. Food is home cooked and includes vegetarian dishes (no food Tue or Sun eve). P

Swinford

Chequers

High Street, LE17 6BL

7-11 Mon; 12- 2.30, 6-11 Tue-Sat; 12-3, 7-11 Sun

(01788) 860318 chequersswinford.co.uk

Adnams Bitter; Ansells Mild; guest beer H

This welcoming village local is a mile from the 16th-century Stanford Hall, which hosts many motoring events throughout the summer. Originally three cottages, it is now open plan but keeps the low ceilings and wood floor bar area. A changing guest complements the two regular beers. Traditional pub games are played and quiz nights are held. Good food is served, with vegetarian option and specials. The large garden has a children's play area and hosts an annual 'worm charming' event during the summer. A beer festival is held in July. P

Swithland

Griffin Inn

174 Main Street, LE12 8TJ

11-11 (10.30 Sun)

(01509) 890535 swithland.info

Everards Beacon, Tiger, Original; guest beers H

Friendly and welcoming local with three comfortable rooms. Set in the heart of Charnwood Forest, there are many walking and cycling routes nearby. Swithland Reservoir, Bradgate Park and the preserved Great Central Railway are also close. As well as the regular food menu, light snacks are available every afternoon including Melton Mowbray pork pies. Three guest ales are chosen from Everards Old English Ale Club.
Q P

Syston

Queen Victoria

76 High Street, LE7 1GQ

2 (12 Wed & Thu)-11; 12-midnight Fri & Sat; 12-11 Sun

(0116) 2605750

Everards Sunchaser, Beacon, Tiger; guest beers H

Large bar which has benefited from the recent addition of a very cosy snug, plus a separate restaurant to the side. The large patio and garden area are popular with families in summer. Guest beers come from the Everards Old English Ale Club, very often including a Brunswick Brewery beer. There is plenty of street parking nearby.
P

Thrussington

Blue Lion

5 Rearsby Road, LE7 4UD

12-2.30 (not Wed), 5.30-11; 12-3, 6-11 Sat; 12-3, 7-10.30 Sun

(01664) 424266

Marston's Burton Bitter, Pedigree, seasonal beers; guest beers H

Late 18th-century rural inn, once two cottages. Good value pub grub, using meat supplied by the local butcher, is served in the comfortable lounge. However, the bar is the heart of the pub, where locals meet for high-pressure darts and dominoes matches, kept under control by licensees Mandy and Bob. ⌂Q❀◖◗⊟⛺🚌(128)♣P

Thurlaston

Elephant & Castle

26 Main Street, LE9 7TP 503991
⏲ 12-2.30 (not Mon & Tue), 5-11; 12-3, 7-10.30 Sun
☎ (01455) 888213
Everards Beacon, Tiger, Original; guest beers Ⓗ
A friendly, welcoming local in the heart of the village. It has two comfortable rooms with beamed ceilings and a traditional bar area. The licensees are real ale enthusiasts and CAMRA members. Three Everards ales are on handpump as well as two changing guest ales. The landlady produces good value home-cooked food – her pies are a speciality and Sunday lunches a treat. There is an outdoor patio and seating area. Walking and cycling routes pass through the village. Q❀◖◗⊟♿🚌♣P⚟

Thurmaston

Harrow Inn

635 Melton Road, LE4 8EB
⏲ 11-11.30 (midnight Fri & Sat)
☎ (0116) 2602240 🌐 harrow-inn.com
Belvoir Star Mild, Star Bitter; Taylor Landlord Ⓗ
A traditional community pub with local ales, live entertainment, live sports and traditional bar games. All are welcome to share the jovial and relaxed atmosphere. Good value food is served lunchtimes and evenings. The pub is the home of Glastonbudget Music Festival which features 130 bands from across Europe and nearly 200 real ales and ciders. It is also the home of the Tie Club which meets regularly and raises money for children with special needs. ♞❀◖◗⊟♿🚌♣P⚟

Walton on the Wolds

Anchor Inn

2 Loughborough Road, LE12 8HT
⏲ 12-3 (not Mon), 7-11 (10.30 Sun)
☎ (01509) 880018
Adnams Bitter; Marston's Pedigree; Taylor Landlord; guest beer Ⓗ
Situated in an elevated position in the centre of the village, the pub has an open plan, comfortable lounge with a real fire. Prints and photographs of classic cars and village scenes adorn the walls. Good quality food is served Tuesday to Saturday and roasts on Sunday lunchtime. Self-catering or B&B accommodation is available in four self-contained units. ⌂Q❀🛏🚌P⚟

Whitwick

Three Horseshoes ★

11 Leicester Road, LE67 5GN
⏲ 11-3, 6.30-11; 12-2, 7-10.30 Sun
☎ (01530) 83731
Draught Bass; Marston's Pedigree Ⓗ
Listed on CAMRA's National Inventory of unspoilt pubs, the nickname 'Polly's' is thought to come from a former landlady, Polly Burton. The pub was originally two separate buildings and now has two rooms. To the left is a long bar with quarry-tiled floor and open fires, wooden bench seating and pre-war fittings; to the right is a similarly furnished small snug. ⌂Q⊟🚌♣

Wigston

Star & Garter

114 Leicester Road, LE18 1DS
⏲ 11-11 (midnight Fri & Sat); 12-11 Sun
☎ (0116) 288 2450
Everards Beacon, Tiger; guest beers Ⓗ
This pub has two rooms and a central bar. Very much a locals' pub, skittles can be played by prior arrangement. Lunchtime meals are served 11.30-3.30pm, no evening meals except on Thursday which is curry night. ❀◖🚌♣P⚟

Woodhouse Eaves

Curzon Arms

44 Maplewell Rpad, LE12 8QZ
⏲ 12-2.30 (not Mon), 5.30-11; 12-11 Sat; 12-10.30 Sun
☎ (01509) 890377 🌐 thecurzonarms.com
Beer range varies Ⓗ
Situated in the centre of a pretty village, this granite-built pub set back from the road is the place where the locals drink. It has a single room bar with a separate dining room. Formerly an old coaching inn called the Admiral (no one knows why), the pub is said to be 350 years old but has been much modified over time.
⌂Q❀◖◗♿🚌♣P⚟

Wymeswold

Three Crowns ✔

45 Far Street, LE12 6TZ
⏲ 12-11 (10.30 Sun)
☎ (01509) 880153
Adnams Bitter; Marston's Pedigree; guest beers Ⓗ
A late 18th-century pub standing opposite the church. This friendly village local has a beamed ceiling in the bar and a split level snug/lounge. Two guest beers are stocked, always one from a micro-brewery. There is a regular daytime bus service. ⌂Q♞❀◖◗♿🚌♣P⚟

RUTLAND

Barrowden

Exeter Arms

28 Main Street, LE15 8EQ (1 mile S of A47)
⏲ 12-2.30 (not Mon), 6-11; 12-3.30, 6-11 Sat; 12-5 Sun
☎ (01572) 747247
Barrowden Beech, Attitude, Hop Gear, Bevin, seasonal beers; Greene King IPA Ⓗ
Collyweston stone-built pub with a fantastic view overlooking the village green, duck pond and Welland Valley. It offers a warm welcome and serves highly regarded food. The patio drinking area outside is a wonderful place to spend a summer's day. The Barrowden Brewery is situated in a barn behind the pub. Petanque is played in summer, dominoes in winter, and darts all year round. Live folk music and a quiz night alternate on Monday evenings. ⌂Q❀🛏◖◗♿🚌(12)♣P⚟

Cottesmore

Sun Inn

25 Main Street, LE15 7DH

11-2.30, 5-11; 11.30-3, 5-11 Fri; 11.30-11 Sat; 12-10.30 Sun

(01572) 812321

Adnams Bitter; Everards Sunchaser, Tiger; guest beer H

Traditional whitewashed and thatched pub in the centre of the village. The cosy oak-beamed interior has a log-burning stove, central bar with an area for drinkers, a separate dining area and a function room. A wide choice of food is served, with vegetarian options available. The dog-friendly pub is popular with locals and personnel from the nearby RAF base. Rutland Railway Museum, Barnsdale Gardens and Rutland Water are all close by. Guest ales are supplied by Everards. (RF2)**P**

Greetham

Plough

23 Main Street, LE15 7NJ (1 mile off A1 on B668)

11-11 summer; 11-3, 5-11 Mon-Wed; 11-11 Thu-Sat winter; 12-10.30 Sun

(01572) 813613

Taylor Golden Best; guest beers H

A true village pub with friendly staff and a warm atmosphere, serving excellent beer including a mild along with real cider. It also offers good pub food, table skittles and dominoes. With the Viking Way just a minute away, it is a popular spot for walkers to stop for refreshments. There are two camp sites and Rutland Water within easy reach by car or bicycle. This pub upholds traditional values for visitors and locals alike, and dogs are welcome. **Q** **P**

Market Overton

Black Bull Inn

2 Teigh Road, LE15 7PW (jct of Main St and Teigh Rd)

12-3, 6-11; 12-midnight Sat; 11.30-5, 7-11 Sun

(01572) 767677 blackbullrutland.co.uk

Adnams Bitter; Black Sheep Bitter; guest beers H

Situated close to the church, the Black Bull has been a traditional village pub for more than 200 years. It has a cosy, low-beamed bar and a separate dining area serving good quality food with delicious home-made desserts. With B&B accommodation, it is ideally placed for visitors to nearby Rutland Water. One guest beer is usually from the Grainstore Brewery. (RF2)**P**

Oakham

Grainstore

Station Approach, LE15 6RE (next to Oakham Station)

11-11 (midnight Fri & Sat); 12-11 Sun

(01572) 770065 grainstorebrewery.com

Grainstore Rutland Panther, Cooking, Triple B, 1050, seasonal ales; guest beers H

A classic brew pub hosting Grainstore Brewery award-winning bitters and milds. The spacious open plan bar has wooden seats and benches. The building is a converted grainstore backing onto Oakham Station, with the bar on the ground floor and the brewery taking the two floors above. Brewery tours are available but must be booked in advance, with knowledgeable staff. Take out beer is available in jugs. A regular beer festival is held in August. Occasional live music sessions are hosted. **Q** (RF1,RF2,19) **P**

Wheatsheaf

2-4 Northgate, LE15 6QS (opp church)

11.30-3, 6-11; 12-3, 7-10.30 Sun

(01572) 756797 rutnet.co.uk/Wheatsheaf

Adnams Bitter; Everards Beacon, Tiger; guest beers H

An attractive thatched pub opposite the church, near the Market Place and medieval castle. It has a traditional, cosy feel with an open fire and comfortable chairs, and a solid reputation for good ales. The building is listed and has some steps between levels, which may create difficulties for wheelchair users. A small, prized garden has dining and smoking areas. Food is only served at lunchtime. Two stronger guest ales are usually available. **Q** (RF1,RF2,19)

Uppingham

Crown Inn

19 High Street East, LE15 9PY

11-11; 12-10.30 Sun

(01572) 822302

Everards Tiger, Beacon, Original, seasonal beers; guest beers H

A warm welcome is assured at this traditional market town pub which offers good quality, reasonably priced home-cooked food in the bar and restaurant. Dogs are permitted in the bar area. The licensee has been awarded Everards Gold Master of Beer status and holds regular beer festivals in April and October. Live music is hosted monthly or more often. En-suite accommodation is available. (RF1,12,747) **P**

Choosing pubs

CAMRA members and branches choose the pubs listed in the Good Beer Guide. There is no payment for entry, and pubs are inspected on a regular basis by personal visits; publicans are not sent a questionnaire once a year, as is the case with some pub guides. CAMRA branches monitor all the pubs in their areas, and the choice of pubs for the Guide is often the result of a democratic vote at branch meetings. However, recommendations from readers are welcomed and will be passed on to the relevant branch: write to Good Beer Guide, CAMRA, 230 Hatfield Road, St Albans, Hertfordshire, AL1 4LW; or send an email to **gbgeditor@camra.org.uk**

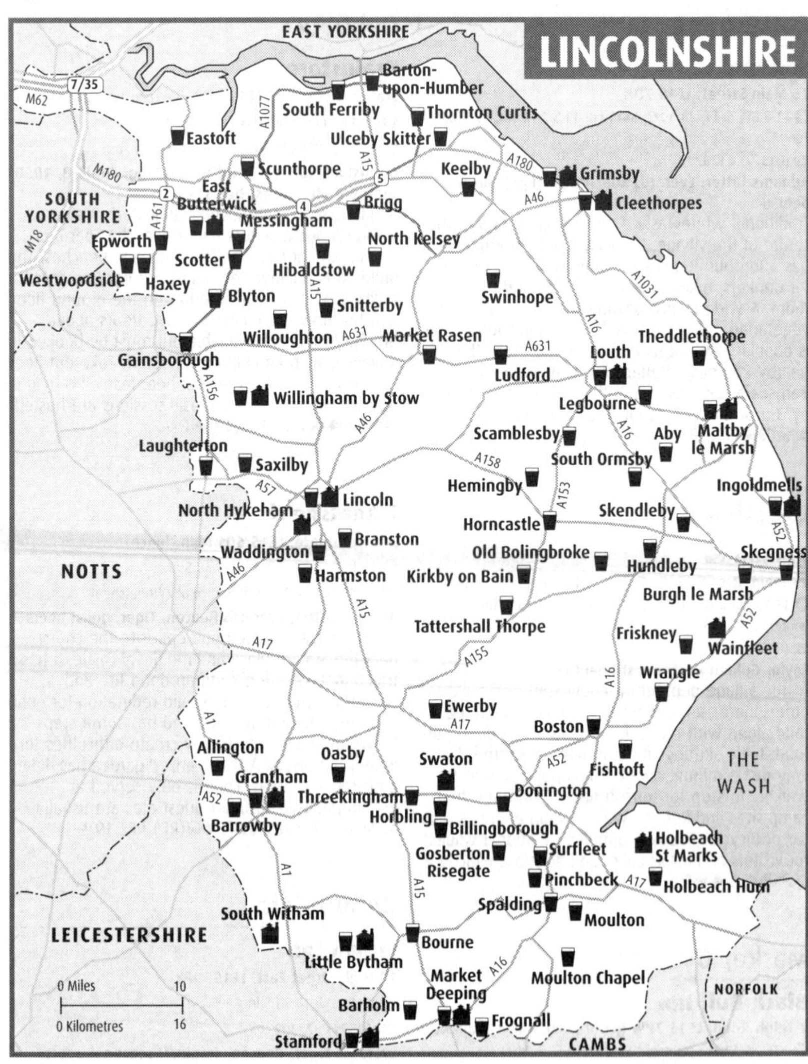

Aby

Railway Tavern

Main Road, LN13 0DR (off A16 via S Thoresby)

12-12.30am; closed Tue winter

☎ (01507) 480676

Beer range varies Ⓗ

This cosy village pub is worth searching out for its ever-changing beer list and excellent food. Plenty of railway memorabilia includes the original Aby platform sign, and even the lighting is railway-oriented. A real community pub with a warm welcome for all, an open fire and a Wednesday quiz night. Dogs are permitted and there are plenty of good walks close by. Food is available most of the time until 8.30pm. ⌂Q❀◑♿⋀♣P⁻

Allington

Welby Arms ✔

The Green, NG32 2EA (1 mile from A1 Gonerby Moor jct)

12-2.30, 6-11; 12-10.30 Sun

☎ (01400) 281361

Draught Bass; Jenning's Cumberland Ale; John Smith's Bitter; Taylor Landlord; guest beers Ⓗ

This attractive ivy-clad village inn is all that a pub should be. It always has six cask ales in superb condition, excellent bar meals are served and a large dining area offers well-cooked meals to suit all tastes. At the heart of the village, the Welby hosts the local Morris dancers and runs the best monthly quiz in the area. Three en-suite letting rooms overlook the charming patio and there is ample parking. A must-visit village inn with a warm welcome in cosy surroundings.

⌂Q❀⇌◑♿P

Barholm

Five Horseshoes

Main Street, PE9 4RA

5 (1 Sat)-11; 12-10.30 Sun

☎ (01778) 560238

Adnams Bitter; Oakham JHB; guest beers Ⓗ

This rustic 18th-century, multi-roomed inn situated in a quiet hamlet is popular enough to support five real ales. The pub is constructed from locally quarried Barnack stone and has a creeper-covered patio and large attractive gardens. The pub concentrates on its real ales and the guests always include a session ale and a strong beer of at least 5% ABV. The third guest beer is normally from one of the local micros. ♨Q♞✿⊟♿▲♣P⊘

Barrowby

White Swan 🏆 ✔

High Road, NG32 1BH
⏲ 12-11 (10.30 Sun)
☎ (01476) 562375
Adnams Bitter, Broadside; guest beers Ⓗ
An old-fashioned traditional village pub within easy reach of the A1 and A52, with two separate bars and a friendly landlord. The public bar offers TV, darts and cribbage plus a pool table in an adjoining space. The lounge is a place to relax with comfortable seating round the walls and without the distractions of piped music or TV. Typical bar meals, prepared by the landlord, are served in either bar at lunchtime. Q✿◖⊟▣♣P⊘

Barton-upon-Humber

Sloop Inn

81 Waterside Road, DN18 5BA (follow Humber Bridge viewing signs)
⏲ 11-11; 12-10.30 Sun
☎ (01652) 637287 🌐 sloopinn.net
Tom Wood Shepherd's Delight, Bomber County; guest beers Ⓗ
Welcoming pub with nautical-themed decoration and areas named after parts of a ship. The central bar serves a games section with a pool table and darts, plus a drinking/dining area and two further rooms. Real ales from the local Tom Wood Highwood Brewery are on offer plus rotating guests. A good range of home-cooked food, with many specials including the pub's own sausages, is popular with locals and walkers. The Far Ings Nature Reserve, Waterside Visitor Centre and Humber Bridge are nearby.
Q✿◖◗♿▲⇌▣(350)♣P

Wheatsheaf

3 Holydyke, DN18 5PS
⏲ 12-11.30 (12.30am Fri & Sat); 12-11 Sun
☎ (01652) 633292
Black Sheep Best Bitter; Theakston Best Bitter; Wells Bombardier; guest beer Ⓗ
Occupying a prominent position on the main road through Barton, this pub dates back to the 18th century, with a list of former licensees going back to 1791. It has an unspoilt, traditional atmosphere, with regulars enjoying classic bar games of dominoes and crib. The pub has a bar, snug and large drinking/dining area, plus a summer beer garden and private car park. A range of excellent home-cooked food is served at lunchtimes and in the evenings. ♨Q✿◖◗⇌▣(250,350)♣P

Billingborough

Fortescue Arms

27 High Street, NG34 0QB
⏲ 12-2, 5.30-11, 12-11 Sat & Sun
☎ (01529) 240228
Fuller's London Pride; Greene King IPA, Abbot Ⓗ
Fine Grade II-listed inn with an interesting multi-roomed interior and a rustic feel. The pub is also popular with diners, with a large patio to the rear providing a pleasant outdoor drinking area. The guest beer is often from a local brewery. Nearby is the site of Sempringham Abbey and its monument to Gwenllian, daughter of the Prince of Wales, who was confined to the priory in the 12th century. Stone from the abbey was used to build part of the inn. ♨Q✿◖◗⊟▣P⊘

Blyton

Black Horse

93 High Street, DN21 3JX
⏲ 12-2, 5-midnight; 12-midnight Fri-Sun; closed Mon
☎ (01427) 628277
Black Sheep Best Bitter; guest beers Ⓗ
Recently extended, refurbished and updated, this pub is now a very well-appointed and comfortable locals' pub but with a clean, fresh twist. Good home-cooked food is prepared using fresh locally-sourced meat, fish and vegetables in a five-star-hygiene rated kitchen. Guest beers often come from Lincolnshire's micro-breweries. Darts and quiz nights are regular events and there is a pool room. The pub has a real community feel, while remaining very welcoming to visitors.
♨Q✿◖◗⊟♿▣♣●P⊘

Boston

Coach & Horses

86 Main Ridge, PE21 6SY
⏲ 4 (12 Sat & Sun)-midnight
☎ (01205) 362301
Batemans XB; Greene King Abbot Ⓗ
Winner of Batemans 2008 pub award in the category of best community pub and runner up in the publican and customer services categories, all during the landlord's first year as licensee. An open plan lounge include tables with candles and soft lighting throughout. The pub hosts pool, darts, poker, football and quiz teams, and is popular with football supporters as it is close to United's ground. Regular entertainment is held at the weekend – well worth the short walk out of the town centre to get here. ♨✿♿♣P⊘▯

INDEPENDENT BREWERIES

Bateman Wainfleet
Blue Bell Holbeach St Marks
Blue Cow South Witham
Brewsters Grantham
Cathedral Lincoln
DarkTribe East Butterwick
Fulstow Louth
Grafters Willingham by Stow
Highwood/Tom Wood Grimsby
Hopshackle Market Deeping
Leila Cottage Ingoldmells
Malt B Maltby le Marsh
Melbourn Stamford
Newby Wyke Little Bytham
Oldershaw Grantham
Poachers North Hykeham
Riverside Wainfleet
Swaton Swaton
Willy's Cleethorpes

Cowbridge

Horncastle Road, PE22 7AX (on B1183 N of Boston)
11 (7 Mon)-11
☎ (01205) 362597
Greene King Old Speckled Hen; Theakston Black Bull Bitter; guest beers
Just out of town, this pub is popular with drinkers and diners. It splits into three main areas: the public bar is a no-nonsense drinking bar with darts, dominoes and a large collection of football scarves; the smaller lounge is cosy with a welcoming open fire; beyond the lounge is a restaurant serving excellent home-cooked food. The pub is popular with fishermen and handy for the local golf club. Q P

Eagle

144 West Street, PE21 8RE (300m from railway station)
11 (11.30 Thu)-11 (midnight Fri & Sat)
☎ (01205) 361116
Banks's Bitter; Castle Rock Harvest Pale; Everards Tiger; guest beer
Part of the Tynemill chain, the Eagle is known as the real ale pub of Boston. This two-roomed, friendly pub has an L-shaped bar with a large TV screen for live sports events. The pub stocks an ever-changing range of guest ales, usually including one or more from Castle Rock, and at least one cider. A function room upstairs is home to Boston Folk Club on a Monday. Thursday is quiz night – allegedly the most challenging quiz in town. Q

Kings Arms

13 Horncastle Road, PE21 9BU
5-11; 12-1am Sat & Sun
☎ (01205) 364296
Batemans Dark Mild, XB, XXXB, Salem Porter; Draught Bass; guest beer
This delightful, mid 18th-century, Grade II-listed, red brick and pantile pub was constructed to slake the thirsts of the navvies digging the Maud Foster drain. The internal layout has been altered over the years and now comprises a single bar and two snug dining rooms (for Sunday lunch only). The beers are on traditional stillage in the original and immaculate brick-vaulted cellar. Across the drain from the pub is the tallest working windmill in the country; both are worth a visit. P

Bourne

Smith's

25 North Street, PE10 9AE
10 (12 Sun)-11 (midnight Fri & Sat)
☎ (01778) 426819
Fuller's London Pride; Ufford Ales White Hart, Nirvana; guest beers
Formerly a grocer's shop from which its name derives, this three-storey building is a past winner of the national CAMRA/English Heritage Conversion to Pub Use award. The ground floor bars have a variety of seating areas to suit all tastes and there are further seating areas upstairs. A well-equipped patio is at the rear of the building. Breakfast is served 8-11am, however no alcohol before 10am. A beer festival is held in mid-summer. Live music plays every Saturday evening. Q (101,102)

Branston

Waggon & Horses

High Street, LN4 1NB
12-2, 5-midnight; 12-1am Fri & Sat; closed Mon; 12-midnight Sun
☎ (01522) 791356
Draught Bass; John Smith's Bitter; Taylor Landlord; guest beers
A welcoming community pub in the heart of the village. The public bar is home to darts and pool teams; spot the moose head if you can. The comfortable lounge hosts Monday quiz night, Tuesday jam night and live entertainment on Saturday night. Regular fundraising events for local charities are often held. Excellent food is available until 8pm on weekdays (later on Thu & Fri) and 6pm at weekends. Outside is a covered, partially heated smoking area. (2) P

Brigg

White Hart

57 Bridge Street, DN20 8NS
11 (12 Sun)-11
☎ (01652) 654887
Banks's Bitter; Jennings Cumberland Ale; guest beers
The pub is in the centre of Brigg, located next to the old River Ancholme, with its beer garden running alongside the riverbank. The interior is traditionally decorated with photos on the walls depicting old Brigg. The lounge bar is located at the front, with the bar area towards the rear, where there is a pool table. The regular beers are quite unusual for the area, and the guest is usually seasonal. Quiz night is Thursday. Food is served lunchtime every day and evenings Monday to Friday. (365) P

Burgh le Marsh

Red Lion

East End, PE24 5LW
11-midnight; 12-11 Sun
☎ (01754) 810582
Beer range varies
This low-ceilinged pub, located off the main road, offers two constantly changing beers. The landlord is enthusiastic about his ales and for a small pub there is quite a high weekly turnover of casks. One of the rare pubs nowdays not to provide food, the Red Lion concentrates instead on beer quality. P

Cleethorpes

No. 2 Refreshment Room

Station Approach, DN35 8AX (on station)
8am-1am (midnight Sun)
☎ (07905) 375587
Greene King H&H Olde Trip; Hancock's HB; M&B Mild; Worthington Bitter; guest beers
A pleasant welcome awaits visitors to this single-roomed free house on Cleethorpes ralway station, known locally as Under the Clock because of its location beneath the station clock tower. It has been a regular Guide entry over many years and CAMRA local Pub of the Year several times. A quiz night is held on Thursday and there is a free buffet provided on Sunday evening. A covered, heated area is available on the station concourse.

Nottingham House

7 Sea View Street, DN35 8EU
12-11 (midnight Fri & Sat)
(01472) 505152
Tetley Mild, Bitter; guest beers H
Prominently located at the town's highest point and at the end of a narrow, timeless street, the pub is dwarfed by adjacent new luxury apartments, which provide a startling contrast with the pub's frontage, positively inviting you to enter. Once inside, you will find two distinctive rooms either side of the entrance lobby, while at the rear is a room with all-round wall seating. A bistro is a recent addition, where service is daily except Mondays and Sunday evening. Q (9,14)

Willy's Pub & Brewery

17 Highcliff Road, DN35 8RQ
11-11 (2am Fri & Sat); 12-10.30 Sun
(01472) 602145
Willy's Original; guest beers H
Vibrant seafront bar, popular with all ages and a long-term entry in the Guide. The attached micro-brewery can be viewed from the bar. Good value home-cooked food is available every lunchtime and on Monday, Tuesday and Thursday evenings. Guest beers from micro-breweries complement real ciders from a varying range and bottled Belgian beers. Outside is a patio.
(9,14)

Donington

Black Bull

Marketplace, PE11 4ST
11-11; 12-10.30 Sun
(01775) 822228
John Smith's Bitter; guest beers H
Busy village local just off the A52. Four handpumps feature a constantly changing selection of guest beers from small brewers as well as larger regionals. Westons cider is on handpump. A comfortable bar has low, beamed ceilings, wooden settles and a cosy fire in winter. The restaurant serves a good choice of reasonably priced evening meals; lunches are served in the bar. Tables in the car park are used for outdoor drinking. Buses run from Boston and Spalding (not Sun). P

East Butterwick

Dog & Gun

High Street, DN17 3AJ (off A18 at Keadby Bridge)
SE837058
5 (12 Sat)-11; 12-11 Sun
(01724) 782324 darktribe.co.uk
DarkTribe Full Ahead, Twin Screw; John Smith's Bitter H
This is a small but busy village pub with a friendly atmosphere, usually quite full of locals and visitors from nearby villages. With three rooms, it accommodates children in the games room up until 9pm. Two excellent DarkTribe beers from the on-site brewery are served alongside John Smith's Cask. These can be enjoyed in winter by a welcoming fire or, in summer, outside on the pleasant river bank. P

Eastoft

River Don Tavern

Sampson Street, DN17 4PQ (on A161 Goole-Gainsborough road)
7.30 (5 Wed-Fri; 12 Sat)-midnight; 12-midnight Sun
(01724) 798040
Beer range varies H
A friendly welcome is assured at this traditional village local, decorated in rustic style with ceiling beams and pictures of village life, past and present, and warmed by real fires. A lively bar area is separated from a more sedate lounge by a wall with open access. Two rotating real ales (three in summer) are sourced mainly from Yorkshire, Lincolnshire and Nottinghamshire breweries. The pub is renowned for good quality food, including a Sunday carvery and meal deals on some nights. An annual beer festival is held in summer. The pub is a short ride from Blacktoft Sands RSPB reserve.
(356) P

Epworth

Queen's Head

19 Queen Street, DN9 1HG (off A161)
12 -11 (midnight Sat & Sun)
(01427) 872306
John Smith's Bitter; guest beers H
A locals' local, catering for a mixed-age clientele in a popular tourist destination. The introduction of rotating guest beers has proved a popular move and the Queen's has gained an excellent reputation for the quality of its ales. At least two are always available, often sourced from micro-breweries. Quizzes and pub games are a regular feature of this community inn, which was named local CAMRA district Pub of the Season for winter 2008. P

Ewerby

Finch Hatton Arms

43 Main Street, NG34 9PH
12-3, 6-11
(01529) 460363 thefinchhattonarms.com
Everards Tiger; guest beers H
Substantial country inn built in the 1870s and later owned by the Finch Hatton family, hence the family crest and motto Nil Conscire Sibi. The pub lies in a quiet village and retains its comfortable charm. Guest beers are usually sourced from local micros and often includes a house beer brewed for them by Riverside. The pub provides a wide range of meals and has in recent years introduced accommodation, with en-suite rooms.
Q P

Fishtoft

Red Cow

Gaysfield Road, PE21 0SF
11-11
(01205) 367552
Batemans Dark Mild, XB, GHA H
A well established village inn extending a warm welcome to customers old and new. This small but charismatic pub is home to various teams including darts, pool and dominoes. Close to the Pilgrim Fathers Memorial and RSPB site at Freiston Shore, it is an ideal place to stop off after a spot of angling, walking or birdwatching. Q P

Friskney

Barley Mow

Sea Lane, PE22 8SD
12-11; closed Mon & Tue
☎ (01754) 820883
Bateman XB; Mordue Mullet Ⓗ
This 300-year-old hostelry known locally as the Barley Mow, to rhyme with cow, is situated on the busy A52 Boston-Skegness road and is particularly busy in the summer months. An imaginative selection of home-cooked meals is available. A lovely conservatory leads to a well-kept garden and adds to the welcoming atmosphere of this gem of a pub. Q❀◑♿⇌♣P

Frognall

Goat

155 Spalding Road, PE6 8SA
11.30-3, 6-11; 12-10.30 Sun
☎ (01778) 347629 🌐 thegoatfrognall.com
Beer range varies Ⓗ
Cosy, welcoming pub with a real fire. Good quality food is served in two dining areas. The ever-changing range of five cask ales always includes a strong beer of at least 6% ABV. The pub supports local micro-breweries and has an extensive menu of American and European bottled beers. Real draught cider is available and also a selection of 70-plus single malt whiskies. The pub holds an annual beer festival in the summer.
❀◑♿(100)P

Gainsborough

Blues Club

North Street, DN21 2QW (adj to Gainsborough Trinity football ground)
7 (3 Fri)-midnight; 11.30-midnight Sat; 12-midnight Sun
☎ (01427) 613688
Beer range varies Ⓗ
A short walk from the town centre, the club is next to the football ground. A welcome return to the Guide for Ian and Gill, who have increased the real ale to two rotating guest beers from a wide range of micros and small brewing outlets, and are planning to introduce beers from local breweries. There is a lounge, a bar with large-screen TVs, a pool table, plus the spacious concert room. Bar food is available at reasonable prices. Show a CAMRA membership card or a copy of this Guide for entry. ◑♿♣

Canutes

12-14 Silver Street, DN21 2DP (50m S of Market Place)
9am (11 Sun)-midnight
☎ (01427) 678715
Springhead Puritan Porter; Wells Bombardier; guest beers Ⓗ
A typical lively town-centre pub with between three and five real ales available. While Bombardier is a regular beer, the Springhead ale varies when Puritan Porter is unavailable. TV screens, live music and quiz nights are part of the pub's week. A wide variety of food is available all day. The pub can get very busy on Friday and Saturday nights or when football is on.
❀◑♿P

Eight Jolly Brewers

Ship Court, Silver Street, DN21 2DW
11 (12 Sun)-midnight
☎ (07767) 638806
Beer range varies Ⓗ
Award-winning real ale venue based in a former carpenter's yard overlooking the River Trent and gardens. This Grade II-listed town-centre building houses a country pub with a patio area, main downstairs bar and two drinking areas upstairs. An ever-changing beer range features Glentworth, Castle Rock and Abbeydale breweries, with one ale usually heavily discounted. Leffe Blonde, real cider on draught and a wide selection of continental bottled beers are also available. Quality live music plays on Thursday night. Q❀♿P

Elm Cottage

139 Church Street, DN21 2JU (100m W of Gainsborough Trinity football ground)
12 (9 Tue)-2.30 (not Mon), 6-midnight; 12-midnight Fri-Sun
☎ (01427) 615474
Jennings Cumberland Ale; guest beers Ⓗ
This attractive old building has a central bar featuring two bay windows with seating, and a separate dining area where good value lunches are available daily. Breakfast is served on Tuesday from 9am to cater for the local auction. The walls show pictures of the local area and a cabinet of trophies won by the sports teams based at the pub. A charity fun quiz is held every other Tuesday with live music on the first Saturday of the month.
❀◑P

Gosberton Risegate

Duke of York

105 Risegate Road, PE11 4EY
12 (6.30 Mon)-11; 12-3.30, 7-10.30 Sun
☎ (01775) 840193
Batemans XB; Black Sheep Best Bitter; guest beers Ⓗ
A long-standing Guide entry, this friendly pub has a well-deserved reputation for value-for-money beers and food. Guest ales generally come from independent brewers and the landlord makes great efforts to ensure an ever-changing and interesting range. A centre for the local community, the pub supports charities, sports teams and other social events. A large secure garden with children's amusements makes it popular for families. The arched bar opening indicates a former Batemans' house, modernised during the 1950s. ❀◑♿♣P

Grantham

Blue Pig

9 Vine Street, NG31 6RQ (near St Wulfram's Church)
11 (10.30 Sat)-11 (1.30am Fri & Sat); 12-11 Sun
☎ (01476) 563704
Caledonian Deuchars IPA; Taylor Landlord; guest beers Ⓗ
The last of over 40 pubs in Grantham with the prefix 'Blue', once belonging to the Manners family. This Tudor building with three distinct rooms is served by a central bar. LocAle-accredited, the Pig is a must-visit when in Grantham, with low ceilings, a roaring fire, good, well-priced food and a great atmosphere. Artefacts abound, with traditional stone-flagged floors, a good outside smoking area with TV, and for those long summer evenings, a beer garden. Real ciders are available.
❀◑

Chequers

25 Market Place, NG31 6LR (on narrow side street between High St and Market Place)
⏲ 12-midnight (1am Fri & Sat)
☎ (01476) 570149
Beer range varies Ⓗ
Fashionable yet unpretentious independently-owned bar, tucked away on a narrow side street close to the marketplace. The single room, comfortably furnished with leather sofas and low tables, is divided into a number of smaller drinking areas. Popular with all ages, it is particularly lively at the weekend. The beers available on the two handpumps change regularly and the landlord supports LocAle.

Lord Harrowby

65 Dudley Road, NG31 9AB
⏲ 4 (12 Sat & Sun)-11
☎ (01476) 563515
Tom Wood Best Bitter; Milestone Rich Ruby; guest beers Ⓗ
One of the few remaining traditional back-street pubs in Grantham, and a supporter of LocAle. A two-roomed local with a separate bar and lounge, the lounge has a real log fire in winter and is decorated with RAF memorabilia. Darts, crib, pool and football teams bring a community atmosphere to this welcoming pub. Live jazz plays on the third Friday of each month, and there is a regular Sunday-night quiz. ⌂❀⊟♿♣⚽

Nobody Inn

9 North Street, NG31 6NU (on corner, opp Asda car park)
⏲ 12-11 (10.30 Sun)
☎ (01476) 565288 🌐 nobodyinn.com
Greene King IPA; Newby Wyke Bear Island, White Squall, Grantham Gold; guest beers Ⓗ
Vibrant, friendly and popular pub with ales from the local Newby Wyke brewery featuring prominently in the beer range. TV screens and projectors make this place a haven for sports fans of all ages. Table football and a pool table are available. Look out for the spider, and allow time to find the hidden entrance to the toilets. ♣⚽

Tollemache Inn 🏆 ✔

17 St Peter's Hill, NG31 6PY
⏲ 9-midnight (1am Fri & Sat)
☎ (01476) 594696
Banks's Original; Greene King Abbot; Marston's Pedigree; guest beers Ⓗ
This well-established, popular Wetherspoon's pub has deservedly won the Grantham CAMRA Town Pub of the Year award for both 2008 and 2009. Serving ten real ales, frequently including beers from local breweries Brewster's, Newby Wyke and Oldershaw, plus micros from further afield, it is easy to understand the pub's popularity with local real ale drinkers. Both the bus and railway stations are a short walk away. Q❀◐◑♿⇌🚌⚽

Grimsby

County Hotel

Brighowgate, DN32 0QU
⏲ 12-11 (midnight Thu-Sun)
☎ (01472) 354422
Beer range varies Ⓗ
Formerly known as the Olde Musician, this one-room pub near the Salvation Army Hostel attracts a mixed clientele. The constantly-changing cask ales on up to four handpumps come from the S&N guest list, with Fugelestou and Tom Wood making regular appearances. There is often a changing cider either on handpull or gravity. Live music features regularly from Friday to Sunday. A lower alcove provides some relative quiet. Poker is played on Monday night. ⊟⇌(Town)●

Ice Barque ✔

Unit 4, Riverhead, Frederick Ward Way, DN31 1XZ
⏲ 9am-midnight (2am Thu-Sat)
☎ (01472) 243720
Greene King IPA, Abbot; Marston's Pedigree; guest beers Ⓗ
Two-level Lloyd's No 1 bar at the Riverhead, opposite the central bus station and Freshney Place mall. Its name refers to the former use of the area for landing ice from Norway. The bar can become busy (DJs, live entertainment) and offers mod cons such as large-screen TVs for sports and wireless Internet. As a Wetherspoon's house it stocks up to four guest beers from micro-breweries and participates in the chain's beer festivals. The food is Wetherspoon's typical value-for-money fare. An enclosed patio area overlooks the river basin. Food is served until 10pm. ❀◐◑♿⇌(Grimsby Town)🚌⚽

Rose & Crown ✔

Louth Road, DN33 2HR (2 miles from town on A16)
⏲ 11-11 (midnight Fri & Sat); 11.30-11 Sun
☎ (01472) 278517
Batemans XXXB; Caledonian Deuchars IPA; Taylor Landlord; Tetley's Bitter; guest beers Ⓗ
Part of the Ember Inns chain and beautifully modernised, this friendly pub typically has an emphasis on good food but the selection of real ales is also very much to the fore. One large bar serves various seating areas. There is a beer festival twice-yearly featuring ales from small breweries. Outside is a patio with heating. ⌂❀◐◑♿🚌(8,51)P⚽

Rutland Arms

26-30 Rutland Street, DN31 3AF (behind Ramsden's superstore)
⏲ 11-11; 12-10.30 Sun
☎ (01472) 268732
Old Mill Mild, Bitter, seasonal beers Ⓗ
Celebrating its 20-year anniversary during 2008, this once run-down social club is now a well-appointed, one-roomed local, catering mainly for the immediate vicinity. It is the only pub for miles around serving real ale and the only Old Mill tied house in the region. There are resident pool and soccer teams, while Grimsby Town FC performs its regular shenanigans at Blundell Park, a 10-minute walk from here. ❀⇌(New Clee)🚌(9,13)♣

Swigs

21 Osborne Street, DN31 1EY
⏲ 9.30-11; 12-10.30 Sun
☎ (01472) 354773
Willy's Original; guest beers Ⓗ
Swigs is the second outlet for Willy's Cleethorpes brewery. A café bar atmosphere makes this pub popular with all ages. Willy's Original is always available alongside three regularly changing guest beers. Home-cooked food is served every lunchtime and the Sunday lunches are always in demand. Located just a few minutes' walk from both rail and bus stations. ◐⇌(Town)🚌

Yarborough Hotel

29 Bethlehem Street, DN31 1JN (opp Grimsby Town rail station)

9am-midnight (1am Fri & Sat)

(01472) 268283

Batemans Dark Mild; Greene King IPA, Abbot; Marston's Pedigree; guest beers H

Local CAMRA Pub of the Year 2008. This spacious Wetherspoon's pub uses the ground floor of an imposing former railway hotel, with two separate bar areas and a rear snug. It gets very busy, particularly at weekends. Up to seven guest beers, many from small breweries, augment the regular ales. Good value meals are served daily until late evening. There is a patio at the rear. The cider is Westons Old Rosie. Located in the town centre, close to all the main bus routes.

Harmston

Thorold Arms

High Street, LN5 9SN

12-3 (not Mon & Tue), 6-11; 12-11 Sun

(01522) 720358 thoroldarms.co.uk

Beer range varies H

This small but welcoming pub is situated in a small village approximately six miles from Lincoln, easily reached by bus. It specialises in beers from micro-breweries on its four handpumps. The pub hosts several unique events during the year, with Harmstock over the August bank holiday weekend undoubtedly the highlight. The building dates from the 17th century, and the bar area has a cosy and comfortable atmosphere. Q(1)P

Haxey

Loco

31-33 Church Street, DN9 2HY (from A161 follow B1396 into village)

4-midnight (1am Fri & Sat); 12-midnight Sun

(01427) 752879 thelocohaxey.co.uk

John Smith's Bitter; guest beers H

Converted from the village Co-op during the 1980s, this pub was originally decorated with railway memorabilia. Following extensive refurbishment only a locomotive smoke box remains of the original design. The Loco is now a fine example of diversity, offering four-star accommodation and a restaurant specialising in English and Indian cuisine (lunches Sun only). At least one guest beer is always available. The Loco participates in the annual Haxey Hood game every January.

Hemingby

Coach & Horses

Church Lane, LN9 5QF (1 mile from A158)

12-2 (not Mon & Tue), 7 (6 Wed-Fri)-11; 12-3, 7-10.30 Sun

(01507) 578280

Riverside Dixon's Major; guest beers H

Low beams provide a clue to the age of this former coaching inn, which stands prominently opposite the parish church. Very much the hub of the small community, the free house hosts pool, darts and dominoes teams. The playroom is well used, as are the Internet-connected computer and book exchange service. Guest beers always include a mild. Recent awards include CAMRA Lincoln Pub of the Year and runner-up in the Tastes of Lincolnshire pub category. A field used for camping overlooks rolling countryside. QP

Hibaldstow

Wheatsheaf

15 Station Road, DN20 9EB (off A15, 4 miles S from M180/A15 jct)

12-midnight (1am Fri & Sat; 11 Sun)

(01652) 658386

Adnams Broadside; Shepherd Neame Spitfire; guest beer H

Large village pub with three spacious rooms comprising a public bar with pool table and TV, a lounge bar with an open fire, and a restaurant area. All are decorated in contemporary style, with slate, wooden and carpet flooring. Generously portioned fresh-cooked meals are available, and can be eaten in any room in the pub. A large car park leads to a rear entrance via a patio area with a wooden smoking shelter, and a front entrance is located off the roadside. QP

Holbeach Hurn

Rose & Crown

Low Road, PE12 8JN (off Marsh Road on N edge of village) TF 395273

10-midnight (1am Fri & Sat)

(01406) 426085 roseandcrown.co.uk

Elgoods Black Dog, Cambridge Bitter G

A charming landlady and her extrovert team of husband, brother-in-law and chef combine to maintain a lively and welcoming atmosphere at this friendly village pub. Vinyl evenings and birthday parties are frequent events. A handpump is used to show what is on offer but the ales are drawn straight from the cask. Good value food is served in an adjoining dining area.

P

Horbling

Plough Inn

Spring Lane, NG34 0PF

12-3, 5-11 (11.30 Thu); 12-midnight Fri & Sat; closed Mon; 12-11 Sun

(01529) 240263 theploughinnhorbling.co.uk

Beer range varies H

Low-beamed pub built in 1832 in a quiet village and owned by the parish council. In addition to the lounge and bar, it has a snug that is surely one of the smallest and most intimate of its kind. Beers are usually from local micro-breweries and change regularly. Home-cooked meals are available in the bar and restaurant. A true community pub. Spring wells are a feature just a few yards down the lane.

P

Horncastle

Angel Inn

65 North Street, LN9 5DX

12-2.30, 7-11 (10.30 Sun); closed Mon eve

(01507) 522214

Highwood Angel Inn, Bomber County H

This 250-year-old local on the fringe of the town has an interesting Tudor frontage and stained glass pub sign above the front door. The tidy U-shaped room provides lounge seating and dining areas. The guest beer changes regularly and home-made food and special themed nights are an attraction. Booking for meals is advised. Unusual pub games include mahjong, pictionary, cribbage, backgammon and table skittles. Q

Red Lion

Bull Ring, LN9 5HT
11- 11 (midnight Fri & Sat); 12-11 Sun
(01507) 523338
Oakwell Barnsley Bitter H
Large town-centre bar/lounge with old bay windows overlooking the Bull Ring. Above the bar a collection of 800 assorted keyrings hangs on display, while framed photographs of Lion Theatre productions from 1988 adorn the walls. The theatre is part of the pub premises, situated at the rear, and run by the Horncastle Theatre Company – productions sometimes star the landlord. A snug and a dining room also feature.

Hundleby

Hundleby Inn

73 Main Road, PE23 5LZ
12 (4 Mon & Tue)-11 (midnight Fri & Sat); 12-11 Sun
(01790) 752577 hundlebyinn.co.uk
Batemans XB; Black Sheep Best Bitter; guest beers H
This welcoming and cosy free house features a wood-panelled bar/lounge decorated with pictures of aeroplanes and sport. The dining room provides excellent, good value home-cooked food. A large outdoor space includes a children's play area, camping and caravanning, a patio and seating. The pub is located on the edge of the Wolds and has excellent walks. It is also in easy striking distance of the nearest town, Spilsby. Plans are in hand for en-suite letting rooms.

Ingoldmells

Countryman

Chapel Road, PE25 1ND
12-3.30, 7-midnight
(01754) 872268 countryman-ingoldmells.co.uk
Leila Cottage Ace Ale, Lincolnshire Life H
The Countryman is the brewery tap for the adjoining Leila Cottage Brewery and has a friendly welcome for locals and visitors alike. The large building has a spacious lounge bar, pool room and dining room, where tasty home-made meals are served. The pub provides welcome relief from the hustle and bustle of nearby visitor attractions and the landlord and brewer are pleased to discuss their beer and brewing.

Keelby

Nag's Head

8 Manor Street, DN41 8EF
12-midnight
(01469) 560660
John Smith's Bitter; Theakston Mild; guest beer H
Friendly bar staff and customers alike welcome you at this cosy pub. The Nag's has two rooms: a lounge adorned with brass and copper on a Tudor-style wall, and a bar with a wood-burning stove and a darts area at one end. Smokers have a large, heated outdoor area.

Kirkby on Bain

Ebrington Arms

Main Street, LN10 6YT
12-3, 6-midnight; 12-11 Sun
(01526) 354560
Batemans XB; Black Sheep Best Bitter; Highwood Ebrington Bitter; Woodforde's Wherry Best Bitter H
This delightful hostelry is situated close to the River Bain and quiet countryside, making it an ideal place to start and finish a pleasant walk. The pub was used by aircrew during World War II – coins remain slotted into the ceiling beams which were intended to pay for beer when the men returned from their missions. Ebrington Bitter is a house beer brewed by Tom Wood. Booking is advisable for the very popular restaurant. A campsite is nearby.

Laughterton

Friendship Inn

Main Road, LN1 2JZ
12-2 (not Mon), 6-11; 12-4, 7-10.30 Sun
(01427) 718681
Banks's Bitter; Jennings Cumberland Ale; Marston's Pedigree; guest beers H
This popular local pub in the heart of the village has an open fire, a cosy seating arrangement and excellent home-cooked food available until 8.30pm. It is also in an ideal location for visitors to nearby Torksey Lock. Golfers from the nearby Millfield course can be found here completing their 19th hole. A pipe-smoking ghoul reputedly haunts the pub. Well-behaved dogs are welcome.

Legbourne

Queens Head

Station Road, LN11 8LL
12-3 (not Tue), 6-midnight; 12-1am Fri & Sat; closed Mon; 12-midnight Sun
(01507) 603839
Batemans XB; guest beers H
Refurbished and reopened in summer 2008, the Queens Head is now well established once again as a welcoming village pub. On a main route from the coast to Lincoln, it caters for tourists as well as locals, with a large garden and playground area for children. It offers occasional themed events, traditional pub food, games and a weekly quiz night. Guest beers often come from micro-breweries. Opening hours may vary in winter.

Lincoln

Dog & Bone

10 John Street, LN2 5BH (off Monks Rd)
12-3 (not Mon), 7-11 (midnight Fri & Sat)
(01522) 522403 dogandbonelincoln.co.uk
Batemans XB, GHA, seasonal beers; guest beers H
Always a friendly welcome from Batemans' Publicans of the Year in this pleasant local which is also Lincoln CAMRA Pub of the Year 2009. The single bar serves two drinking areas decorated with changing art exhibitions and featuring a book exchange. The garden with its heated shelter is a pleasure. Folk music or jam sessions take place on the first and third Sundays of the month, when the pub is open all afternoon. Ask to play the slate push-penny board or other traditional games.

Golden Eagle

21 High Street, LN5 8BD
11-11 (11.30 Fri & Sat); 12-11 Sun

☎ (01522) 521058 🌐 goldeneagle.org.uk
Castle Rock Harvest Pale, Preservation; guest beers Ⓗ
This friendly, traditional pub has up to seven guest ales including local brews. Open mike nights are held on alternate Tuesdays, with a Wednesday lunchtime session once a month. The Eagle hosts crib and dominoes teams, a quiz on Friday night and weekly fishing matches. It is popular with football supporters travelling to nearby Sincil Bank. Food is prepared using fresh local produce. The dining/function room is available for hire and the well-kept beer garden is child friendly and welcoming. ⩩Q❀◖⊟⊟♣●P⚟

Green Dragon
Magpie Square, Broadgate, LN2 5DH
⏲ 10-11 (1.30am Fri & Sat)
☎ (01522) 567155 🌐 greendragonpub.co.uk
Beer range varies Ⓗ
After an extensive and sympathetic refurbishment, this three-storey, 14th-century, timber-framed building located close to the main shopping areas has risen phoenix-like from years of neglect. Now a haven for real ale drinkers, the 12 handpumps in the Waterside bar offer up to four Milestone beers and eight guests (including ales from Cathedral Ales brewed on site). High-quality, good-value food ranging from snacks to a carvery is available daily 12-9pm. ❀◖◗⇌⊟●P⚟

Joiners Arms
4-6 Victoria Street, West Parade, LN1 1HU
⏲ 11-midnight; 12-10.30 Sun
☎ (01522) 805403
Banks's Original; guest beers Ⓗ
This friendly mid 19th-century pub on a hill-side street has been refurbished and extended over the years and is now open plan but retains separate drinking areas. Plans of older layouts adorn the walls, together with pictures of locals. The larger room, with pool table, is on the lower level, with the bar and smaller drinking areas up a couple of steps. Up to two changing guest beers are served from the Cellarman's Reserve list. ❀⇌♣⚟

Jolly Brewer
27 Broadgate, LN2 5AQ
⏲ 12-11 (midnight Wed & Thu; 1am Fri & Sat); 12 (3 winter)-11 Sun
☎ (01522) 528583 🌐 thejollybrewer.co.uk
Tom Wood Best Bitter; Wells Bombardier; guest beers Ⓗ
A city-centre pub with a friendly atmosphere and an eclectic clientele, located not far from the Drill Hall. Live music is hosted on Saturday evening and sometimes outdoors in summer. There is a jukebox and table football plus five pumps dispensing cask ale. As well as the beers there is also a Westons perry on handpump and an alternating real cider on gravity. Out the back is a large heated and sheltered smoking area. ⩩❀◖⇌⊟♣●P⚟⊔

Morning Star
11 Greetwell Gate, LN2 4AW
⏲ 11-midnight; 12-11 Sun
☎ (01522) 527079
Caledonian Deuchars IPA; Draught Bass; Greene King Ruddles Best Bitter, Abbot; Taylor Golden Best; Wells Bombardier Ⓗ
Reputed to have become an inn in the 18th century, this busy pub situated close to the cathedral relies on conversation for its main source of entertainment. Memorabilia from WWI adorns the walls within the main bar area, commemorating Lincoln's association with the development of the first tank. The garden to the rear has a covered, heated area and hosts occasional live music throughout the summer. Q❀◖⊟(2)♣P⚟

Ritz ✔
143-147 High Street, LN5 7PJ
⏲ 9am-midnight (1am Fri & Sat)
☎ (01522) 512103
Greene King IPA, Abbot; Marston's Pedigree Ⓗ
A JD Wetherspoon pub, Ritz was opened in May 1998 in the city's former cinema. Easy to spot at night due to its neon lights which date back to its days as a cinema, the pub's interior is reminiscent of a 1920s speakeasy – all that's missing is the stage and the dancing girls. The walls feature signed photos of celebrities who performed here in its days as an entertainment venue. Local micro-breweries are represented in a changing range of beers. ♉◖◗♿⇌⚟

Strugglers
83 Westgate, LN1 3BG
⏲ 10-11 (1am Thu-Sat); 11-11 Sun
☎ (01522) 535023
Black Sheep Best Bitter; Draught Bass; Fuller's London Pride; Greene King Abbot; Taylor Landlord; guest beers Ⓗ
Nestling beneath the north-west corner of the castle walls, this small and cosy two-bar pub makes a welcome return to the Guide under new management. There is a surprisingly large garden area to the rear – part of it is for the use of smokers – covered by a heated marquee in winter. One of the two guest beers is usually a mild. Good value food is served at lunchtime. ⩩Q❀◖⊟⊟(7,8)⚟

Tap & Spile ✔
21 Hungate, LN1 1ES
⏲ 4-midnight; 12-1am Fri & Sat
☎ (01522) 534015 🌐 tapandspilelincoln.co.uk
Wychwood Hobgoblin; guest beers Ⓗ
Previously known as the White Horse, a friendly atmosphere welcomes young and old alike. A haven for the real ale drinker, there are three drinking areas with a central bar, adorned by eight handpumps often serving Oldershaw, Tom Woods and Everards. Friday nights feature live music and early Sunday evenings a jam session, followed by a popular general knowledge quiz. A music quiz is held on the second Wednesday of the month, with circular chess on a Thursday. ⇌♣●⚟

Victoria
6 Union Road, LN1 3BJ
⏲ 11-midnight (1am Fri & Sat); 12-midnight Sun
☎ (01522) 541000 🌐 victoriapub.net
Batemans XB; Castle Rock Harvest Pale; Taylor Landlord; guest beers Ⓗ
Cosy Victorian pub under the castle wall, in uphill Lincoln's Cathedral quarter and surrounded by historic sites, close to the Lincs Life Museum. This is a long-standing drinkers' pub which, despite recent changes to the interior, retains high standards of service and produce. Off the long bar is a comfortable, newly-upholstered lounge. Outside is a patio with a play area and covered seating. The pub hosts occasional beer festivals and a general knowledge quiz on alternate Wednesdays. Q❀◖⊟⊟(7,8)⚟

Little Bytham

Willoughby Arms ✔

Station Road, NG33 4RA
12-11 (10.30 Sun)
☎ (01780) 410276 🌐 willoughbyarms.co.uk
Batemans XB; Ufford White Hart; guest beers Ⓗ
A true free house offering six real ales. House ales are Batemans XB and local brew Ufford White Hart, with four changing guest beers, one dark ale and a real cider at all times. This 150-year-old beamed, traditional stone country inn offers stunning views from the large garden. Tasty, home-made food is available every lunchtime and evening. The pub hosts regular live music and three annual beer festivals. Four-star en-suite B&B accommodation is offered all year. ❀◑ ▲P

Louth

Boars Head 🏆

12 Newmarket, LN11 9HH (next to cattle market)
12 (9.30 Thu)-2 (not Mon & Tue), 5-11; 12-11 Fri-Sun
☎ (01507) 603561
Batemans Dark Mild, XB; guest beers Ⓗ
A Bateman's pub situated next to the cattle market, a short walk from the town centre, with an ever-changing guest beer list. The interior includes two main rooms plus the old snug, which is now the games room. Warmed by real fires in the winter, it always provides a friendly welcome. Pub games include darts and dominoes. Thursday is cattle market day, when the pub opens earlier. Lunches are served Wednesday to Sunday (no food Mon or Tue). Q◑♣

Newmarket Inn

133 Newmarket, LN11 9EG
12-3 (not Mon & Tue), 5-midnight; 12-midnight Sat & Sun
☎ (01507) 605146
Adnams Bitter; Taylor Landlord; guest beer Ⓗ
This is a very busy, pleasantly decorated, two-roomed inn formerly known as the Brown Cow. The family-run pub is set in an urban location five minutes' walk from the town centre. A free quiz is held every Sunday night, and the local folk club meets here on a Tuesday. The Hurdles bistro is very popular and booking is recommended; lunches are served daily, including Sunday. A guest beer is always available. Q❀P

Wheatsheaf

62 Westgate, LN11 9YD
11-3, 5-11; 12-11 Sat & Sun
☎ (01507) 606262
Black Sheep Best Bitter; Flowers Original; Highwood Tipsy Toad; guest beers Ⓗ
A traditional-style inn situated in a Georgian terrace close to St James' Church which boasts the tallest spire of any parish church in England. All three rooms are warmed by coal fires in winter. Daily home-cooked specials are offered on the menu and the pub holds a beer and bangers festival at the end of May. Quiz night is Sunday. Well-behaved dogs are welcome outside. ❀P

Ludford

White Hart Inn 🏆

Magna Mile, LN8 6AD
12-2 (not Mon-Thu), 5.30-11, 12-2.30, 6-11 Sat; 12-4, 7-10.30 Sun
☎ (01507) 313489
Beer range varies Ⓗ
This 18th-century coaching house was CAMRA Louth & District Country Pub of the Year 2008. A two-roomed rural village pub close to the Viking Way, it is very popular with hikers and ramblers. It offers four changing guest beers and the licensees pride themselves on serving real ale from micro-breweries. All food served here is home made, using ingredients from local suppliers, and meals are available daily. There is guest accommodation separate from the pub. Q❀◑♣P

Maltby le Marsh

Crown Inn

Beesby Road, LN13 0JJ (jct of A157 and A1104)
12-11.30 (11 Sun)
☎ (01507) 450100
Batemans XB; Malt B Old Reliable, Smarty's Night Porter, PEA; guest beers Ⓗ
Up to six beers are on offer, as well as ciders including Westons Old Rosie. A small micro-brewery has been installed to supply mainly the Crown and its first beers have been well received. The inn and its outdoor tables are well situated for the nearby coastal strip with its many visitors, especially in summer. Bar skittles and shove ha'penny are played. Meals are available in the bar and restaurant. ❀◑♿▲(10)♣P

Market Deeping

Bull

Market Place, PE6 8EA
11-midnight
☎ (01778) 343320
Adnams Bitter; Everards Tiger, Old Original; guest beer Ⓗ
Olde-worlde 16th-century coaching inn named after the papal bull relating to Crowland Abbey. The flagstone-floored lounge can be busy so seek out the cosy Dugout bar with its low beams and wooden casks behind the bar, now unfortunately only for decoration. The licensee used to play football for both Chelsea and Peterborough United. Q❀(101,102)♣P

Market Rasen

Aston Arms

18 Market Place, LN8 3HL
11-11 (11.30 Fri & Sat); 12-11 Sun
☎ (01673) 842313
John Smith's Bitter; Wells Bombardier; guest beer Ⓗ
This popular, deceptively large former Younger's house has a heated, covered patio area at the side, with ramp access to the pub. Famous songwriter Bernie Taupin's old haunt is now open plan with a central bar and three drinking areas. The games area is to the rear and features shove ha'penny, pool, darts and a large-screen TV. The guest ale changes frequently. Good value home-cooked food is served daily. A quiz is held on Sunday evening. ❀◑(3)♣P

Red Lion

45 King Street, LN8 3BB
11.30-11 (11.30 Fri & Sat); 12-11 Sun
☎ (01673) 842424 🌐 tom-wood.com
Tom Wood Best Bitter, Bomber County; guest beers Ⓗ

This mock-Tudor pub is the oldest in town, with the bar to the left of the traditional entrance. Tastefully refurbished and reopened by Tom Woods in 2008, it is now open plan, with three drinking areas that retain an olde worlde feel. Old wooden desks for tables, a hogshead, a sixpenny cigarette machine, cellar viewing window and old advertising slogans create atmosphere. Spot the old toy car and German tri-plane too. Beer comes from seven handpumps, plus 50 malts, continental beers – and no mainstream lagers. ⌂❀◐⇌▣(3)P⁄–

Messingham

Bird in the Barley

Northfield Road, DN17 3SQ (½ mile from Messingham on A159)

✪ 11.30-3, 5.30-11; closed Mon; 12-3, 6-11 Sun

☎ (01724) 764744

Jennings Snecklifter; Marston's Pedigree; guest beers Ⓗ

A mix of traditional and modern design, the interior features oak beams and wooden flooring, with a purpose-built 30-seat conservatory dining area (booking advisable). A seating area at one end of the pub includes leather sofas and armchairs, and low tables specifically for drinkers. There are two beer gardens, one with a large umbrella-type canopy and heater. Cyclops tasting notes are on the handpumps. Two regular real ales are stocked, plus two guest beers, often from the Marston's/ Jennings range. ⌂❀◐◑♿▣(100,101,353)P⁄–

Moulton

Swan ✔

13 High Street, PE12 6QB

✪ 11 (11.30 Sun)-2am

☎ (01406) 370349

Tetley Bitter; Wells Bombardier; guest beers Ⓗ

Family-run pub opposite the church and windmill in an attractive village which enjoys a very good daytime bus service. Generally two guest beers are on offer and Tydd Steam beers often feature. The pub also has a good reputation for its meals and now offers a credit crunch menu all day Monday-Wednesday. Be in before 11pm if you wish to take advantage of late evenings. ⌂☺❀⇔◐◑⊟▣(505)●P⁄–

Moulton Chapel

Wheatsheaf

4 Fengate, PE12 0XL

✪ 12-2.30 (not Mon), 5.30-11; 12-2, 7-11 Sat; 12-2, 7-10.30 Sun

☎ (01406) 380525

Beer range varies Ⓗ

A sensible policy of one ale at a time ensures a perfect pint, and the landlord's adventurous spirit means it is never a run-of-the-mill brand. The home cooking is highly regarded, as is the lack of TV, muzak and machines. A splendid range is a feature in the bar as are an open fire and a stove in the two dining rooms. Local artists are keenly supported and their work is displayed throughout. Jazz evenings are also held. ⌂Q❀◐◑Ă▣♣●P

North Kelsey

Butcher's Arms

Middle Street, LN7 6EH

✪ 4-midnight; 12-1.30am Sat; 12-midnight Sun

☎ (01652) 678002

Tom Wood Hop & Glory, Harvest Bitter; guest beer Ⓗ

A traditional single-room country pub located in a quiet village with rustic furnishings and adorned with black and white photographs of village life. An impressive hop bine overhangs the bar. A small games area is reserved for darts and table skittles is also played. Two beers from the local Tom Wood Brewery are always available (three at busy times), plus an ever-changing guest beer. An outdoor drinking area with mature trees is popular during the spring and summer months. ⌂❀♿♣P⁄–

Oasby

Houblon Arms

Village Street, NG32 3NB

✪ 12-2.30, 6.30 (6 Sat)-11; closed Mon; 12-3.30, 7-10.30 Sun

☎ (01529) 455215

Everards Tiger; guest beers Ⓗ

Situated at the centre of the village, this former Grantham CAMRA Country Pub of the Year is well worth a visit. Its flagstone floor, open real fire, large inglenook and cosy atmosphere make this a popular destination. Excellent home-cooked food is served every day except Sunday. B&B accommodation is provided in four cottages. The pub is named after the first Governor of the Bank of England, John Houblon – a local landowner. Local micro-breweries featured include Newby Wyke, Oldershaw and Brewster's. ⌂Q❀⇔◐◑♿P

Old Bolingbroke

Black Horse Inn

Moat Lane, PE23 4HH

✪ 12-3, 7-11; 8.30-11 Tue; closed Mon

☎ (01790) 763388

Wold Top Wold Gold; Young's Bitter; guest beers Ⓗ

A warm welcome is assured at this old country inn with history on its doorstep. The village features castle remains and the roses of Henry IV and the Duke of Lancaster dating from 1366. The pub stages regular beer festivals. Excellent food is served made with local organic produce and booking is advised. Ploughman's lunches are available at the weekend. Ring to check food availability and opening times. ⌂Q❀◐◑♿♣●P⁄–

Pinchbeck

Bull Inn ✔

1 Knight Street, PE11 3RA (on B1356)

✪ 12-2.30, 5.30-11; 12-midnight Sat; 12-11 Sun

☎ (01775) 723022

John Smith's Bitter; guest beers Ⓗ

Situated on the main junction in the village, opposite the green which still has the old stocks. The Bull has two comfortable bars: the public bar with a log fire, and the lounge used mainly for dining. A carved bull's head features on the long bar front, with the bar rail representing its horns. The pub has a reputation for good food, from bar snacks to meals in the upstairs restaurant. Guest beers change regularly, often coming from local micros. ⌂Q❀◐◑⊟♿▣P⁄–

Saxilby

Anglers

65 High Street, LN1 2HA
11-11.30; 12-11 Sun
(01522) 702200
Greene King IPA; Theakston Best Bitter; guest beers H
A village pub popular with sporting locals, as can be seen by the memorabilia, and home to many sports teams. A large TV screen is used for major sporting events. Local societies meet in the lounge bar, which has many photos of old Saxilby. Situated close to the Fossdyke Canal, the name changed from the Railway in the 1840s to reflect its popularity with anglers. Guest beers are from the ScotCo list. P

Scamblesby

Green Man

Old Main Road, LN11 9XG (off A153 Louth to Horncastle road)
12-2.30, 5-midnight; 12-midnight Thu-Sun
(01507) 343282
Young's Bitter; guest beers H
Welcoming village pub in picturesque Wolds countryside, popular with walkers and visitors to Cadwell Park race circuit one mile away. Accommodation is available together with traditional good value meals served until 8.30pm. A spacious main bar and a quiet lounge are both patrolled by Harry the pub dog. Lots of motorcycle memorabilia is on display. The guest beer usually changes every month. QP

Scotter

Sun & Anchor

54 High Street, DN21 3RX
12-midnight (1am Fri & Sat)
(01724) 763444
Courage Best Bitter; guest beer H
Friendly pub close to the A159. A local CAMRA Pub of the Season, it has a bar featuring traditional pub games, plus a large, L-shaped lounge with a log fire in winter. A patio and beer garden contains a barbecue where customers can cook their own food. The pub has several sports teams and a film club is planned. One regular real ale and a guest beer from the SIBA list are kept in excellent condition. (100,101,353)P

Scunthorpe

Berkeley

Doncaster Road, DN15 7DS (½ mile from end of M181)
11.30-2.30, 5-11; 11-11 Fri & Sat; 12-10.30 Sun
(01724) 842333
Samuel Smith Old Brewery Bitter H
Large 1930s Samuel Smith's hotel offering accommodation 30 minutes' walk from the town centre. The interior is decorated in period style and comprises four rooms: a dining room, function room, lounge and public bar at the rear of the building with a separate entrance. Landscaped at the front, it has a beer garden at the back. Lunchtime meals are available Monday to Sunday, evening meals Monday to Saturday. Located close to Glanford Park football ground, the pub may close on some football match days.
Q(31A,32A,37)P

Blue Bell

1-7 Oswald Road, DN15 7PU
9am-midnight (1am Fri & Sat)
(01724) 863921
Greene King IPA, Abbot; Marston's Pedigree; guest beers H
Popular Wetherspoon pub with an open-plan design on two levels. The upper level is a designated family area, with tables for dining. The lower level has wooden flooring with a mix of high and low tables and chairs and leather sofas. The pub holds its own beer festivals twice a year plus events nights such as Valentine's and Hallowe'en. Food is served daily lunchtime and evening. A patio area at the rear has picnic tables and an area with overhead heaters can be used by smokers.
Q

Honest Lawyer

70 Oswald Road, DN15 7PG (10 mins walk from railway station)
11-11 (midnight Fri & Sat); 12-11 Sun
(01724) 849906
Daleside Bitter; Taylor Landlord; guest beers H
Town-centre real ale haven designed on a legal theme with a long, narrow bar area, which opens out into a wider seated area. The bar boasts eight handpulls and offers two regular real ales and six guest beers, plus a real cider and Gales fruit wines. Upstairs the Gallows restaurant serves excellent food and can be hired out. Outside the pub frontage are tables with overhead heaters for cooler weather.

Malt Shovel

219 Ashby High Street, Ashby, DN16 2JP
10-11 (midnight Fri & Sat)
(01724) 843318
Exmoor Gold; Greene King Old Speckled Hen; Tom Wood Dark Mild, Best Bitter; guest beers H
Self-styled country pub in the town, those in the know travel considerable distances to drink at this real ale haven. Three ever-changing guest beers, bottled and draught Belgian beers and real cider and perry straight from the cellar are served here. The pub holds twice-yearly beer festivals and is busy lunch and dinner times for excellent value home-cooked food. Magazines and newspapers are provided and a book swap is offered. Quiz nights are Tuesday and Thursday. Members-only snooker facilities are available. Handy for the shops, but do your shopping first, otherwise you just might not bother.

Skegness

Vine Hotel

Vine Road, Seacroft, PE25 3DB
11 (12 Sun)-11
(01754) 610611/763018 bw-vinehotel.co.uk
Batemans XB, XXXB; guest beers H
A delightful building, one of the oldest in Skegness, dating from the 18th century and set in two acres of pleasant grounds. Inside are comfortable wood-panelled bars in which to enjoy a quiet pint or two after experiencing some of the the noisier attractions and bustle of Skegness. Within striking distance of the Gibraltar Point National Nature Reserve, walking trails, beach and golf links, the inn has reputed Tennyson connections.
P

Skendleby

Blacksmiths Arms
Main Road, PE23 4QE
12-midnight; 12-3, 5.30-midnight winter; 12-2, 7-11 Sun
☎ (01754) 890662
Batemans XB; guest beers [H]
Dating back to the 18th century, this country pub is set in an attractive Wolds village. Ducking beneath the low lintled front door, which is fortunately well-padded, into the quarry-tiled snug bar complete with period fireplace, you discover a cosy and friendly atmosphere despite the former back door now opening into a modern dining room. The cellar is visible through a glass panel behind the bar. There are fine views of the Lincolnshire Wolds from the dining rooms. A cottage is available for overnight accommodation. Q P

Snitterby

Royal Oak
High Street, DN21 4TP
5-11; 12-1am Sat; 12-10.30 Sun
☎ (01673) 818273
Fuller's Chiswick Bitter; Wold Top Bitter, Wold Gold; guest beers [H]
Good old-fashioned community pub, offering up to six real ales and a friendly, warm welcome. A traditional light and airy interior includes wooden floors and real fires. Outside a seating area overlooks the stream. High-quality food, sourced locally, is served Thursday to Sunday, and B&B is available in three en-suite double rooms. This pub was in the first edition of the Guide in 1973 and won local CAMRA Pub of the Season within six months of new ownership. Q P

South Ferriby

Nelthorpe Arms
School Lane, DN18 6HW (off A1077)
12 (3 Mon)-midnight
☎ (01652) 635235
Tetley Bitter; guest beer [H]
Village local tucked away from the main road. The pub has two rooms comprising a public bar with wood panel surround, leather sofas, pool and darts at one end, and a comfortable dining room set out for meals. Two real ales are offered, with a changing guest usually from the SIBA list. Popular for its range of home-cooked food, live music features on Saturday evening, plus an open mike music night on the first Thursday of every month. Accommodation is available in three en-suite rooms. (350) P

South Ormsby

Massingberd Arms
Brinkhill Road, LN11 8QS
12-2.30, 6-11; 12-11 Wed-Sat; 12-10.30 Sun
☎ (01507) 480492
Beer range varies [H]
This pub, named after the local lord of the manor, is not on a main thoroughfare but lovers of good food and beer manage to follow a well-beaten track to its doors. The ale range is constantly changing. The pub is a great stopping-off point for walkers and cyclists in a beautiful area of the country, on the edge of the Lincolnshire Wolds. Guide dogs only are admitted. Q P

Spalding

Lincoln Arms
4 Bridge Street, PE11 1XA
11-3, 7-12.30am; 11-12.30am Fri & Sat; 11-4, 7-midnight Sun
☎ (01775) 710017
Marston's Mansfield Cask Ale; guest beers [H]
Traditional 13th-century local overlooking the River Welland, popular with drinkers of all ages, some of whom can boast over 25 years patronage. Although a town pub there is a relaxed atmosphere, with the emphasis on conversation and pub games – darts, cribbage and pool are played. Spalding Folk Club meets informally on the second Thursday of the month for a jamming session.

Red Lion Hotel
Market Place, PE11 1SU
10 (12 Sun)-midnight
☎ (01775) 722869 redlionhotel-spalding.co.uk
Draught Bass; Fuller's London Pride; Greene King Abbot; Marston's Pedigree [H]
Consistantly well-kept cask ales have made this cosy and welcoming hotel bar a regular Guide entry. Popular with locals and visitors, it makes an ideal base for exploring the town and local area. Bar snacks and meals are available, with a separate dining room open evenings except Sunday. Fine weather will see tables and chairs on the pavement outside for an alfresco pint. The pub's claim to fame is that Jimi Hendrix stayed here in 1969 after playing a local gig.

Stamford

Green Man
29 Scotgate, PE9 2YQ
11 (12 Sun)-midnight
☎ (01780) 753598
Caledonian Deuchars IPA; guest beers [H]
This stone-built former coaching inn dates from 1796 and features a split-level L-shaped bar serving beers mainly from micros together with up to seven traditional ciders and a range of European bottled beers. The secluded patio contains one of only five such stepping stones in the country, dating back to its coaching days. Good pub food is made using local produce. Beer festivals are held at Easter and during September.
(201)

Jolly Brewer
1 Foundry Road, PE9 2PP
11-midnight; 12-11.30 Sun
☎ (01780) 755141
Oakham JHB; Sharp's Doom Bar; guest beers [H]
Three-hundred-year-old stone-built pub with one L-shaped room around the bar and a small dining area. The pub has a strong community spirit and is home to dominoes, darts, pool and crib teams. Push penny is also played. Food is served lunchtime and evening, with Sunday lunch being particularly popular. A good range of single malts is offered. Wi-Fi available. Local CAMRA Pub of the Year 2009. P

Tobie Norris
12 St Paul's Street, PE9 2BE
12-11 (10.30 Sun)
☎ (01780) 753800 tobienorris.com
Adnams Bitter; Ufford Ales range; guest beers [H]

Parts of this stone building date back to circa 1280, and in 1617 it was bought by Tobie Norris and used as a bell foundry. More recently a RAFA club, it was then converted into a pub by Mick Thurlby, for which it won CAMRA's Best National Pub Restoration Award in 2008. It has seven rooms over two floors which have been restored to their former glory. This must-visit gem has five handpumps serving beer from local micro-breweries. ♨Q❀◐◑⇌♣🚬

Surfleet

Ship Inn

154 Reservoir Road, PE11 4DH (off A16, S of A152 jct)
⏲ 11-3, 5-midnight; 11-midnight Sat & Sun
☎ (01775) 680547 🌐 shipinnsurfleet.com
Tom Woods Best Bitter; guest beers 🄷
Standing on the banks of the River Glen, this pub was rebuilt in 2004. All that remains of the original are some flagstones in the entrance and a model in the bar. A popular area for dinghy sailors and walkers, the McMillan Way footpath passes close by. Lunchtime meals are served in the comfortable bar with a wood-burning stove. The upstairs restaurant has views over the river. Tables on the terrace are provided for outdoor drinkers. Four guest bedrooms are available. ♨🛏◐◑♿P

Swinhope

Click'em Inn 🏆

LN8 6BS (2 miles N of Binbrook on B1203)
⏲ 5 (7Mon)-11; 12-3, 5-11 Thu; 12-11.30 Fri & Sat; 12-10.30 Sun
☎ (01472) 398253
Batemans XXXB; Shepherd Neame Spitfire; guest beers 🄷
Country pub set in the picturesque Lincolnshire Wolds. The unusual name originates from the counting of sheep through a nearby clicking gate. Its location makes it a popular stopping point for walkers and cyclists. Good home-cooked food is served in the bar and conservatory, attracting both locals and diners. The pub stocks Terry's Tipple, a house beer, and the guest ales change regularly. A covered but unheated outside area is provided for smokers. Q❀◐◑♣P🚬

Tattershall Thorpe

Blue Bell Inn

Thorpe Road, LN4 4PE
⏲ 12-3, 7-11 (10.30 Sun)
☎ (01526) 342206
Greene King IPA; Highwood Bomber County, Dambuster; guest beers 🄷
You step back in time when you enter this lovely 13th-century inn, one of Lincolnshire's oldest, with a large open fire and very low beamed ceilings. The walls are covered with signed photographs from WWII RAF squadrons who used the pub, including the famous 617 Dambusters. Three ales are usually on offer plus ever-changing guest beers. A gem of a pub in a delightful location. ♨Q❀◐◑♿⛺♣P🚬

Theddlethorpe

Kings Head Inn

Mill Road, LN12 1PB (signed from A1031)
⏲ 12-11 (closed winter Mon); 12-10.30 Sun
☎ (01507) 339798 🌐 kingsheadinn.com
Batemans XB; guest beers 🄷
Set on the edge of a picturesque village near the North Sea coast, this pub is the longest single-thatched public house in the UK. Built in 1623, entering is like stepping back in time. Keep a look out for two thrones situated in the restaurant. The two bars are warmed by roaring open fires in the winter months and the front bar's ceiling is, to say the least, low. There is a restaurant and large garden area. ♨Q❀◐◑⊟♿P

Thornton Curtis

Thornton Hunt Inn

17 Main Street, DN39 6XW (on A1077 between Wooton and Barton)
⏲ 12-3, 6.30-11
☎ (01469) 531252 🌐 thornton-inn.co.uk
Taylor Landlord; Tom Wood Harvest Bitter 🄷
One mile from the ruins of Thornton Abbey, this village local dates from the 1850s, its rustic charm enhanced by wood panelling, beams, brasses and prints of rural life. It has won Tastes of Lincolnshire 2007 for its traditional bar menu consisting of home-cooked, locally-sourced food. Meals are served in a separate dining room in the evening. Two real ales are offered – Taylor Landlord and a rotating Tom Wood beer. The garden area includes a children's fun trail. Accommodation is in six en-suite rooms. ❀🛏◐◑♿P🚬

Threekingham

Three Kings Inn

Saltersway, NG34 0AU
⏲ 12-3, 6-11 (10.30 Sun); closed Mon
☎ (01529) 240249 🌐 threekingsinn.co.uk
Draught Bass; Taylor Landlord; guest beers 🄷
A true country inn that retains its charm and character while managing to be progressive. Its comfortable lounge/bar with attractive and bright rural prints and its panelled dining room serving locally-sourced food are deservedly popular with locals and visitors. The pub name refers to the slaying of three Danish chieftains in 870 in battle at nearby Stow; look for the effigies above the entrance. Threekingham was established where the Roman Mareham Lane crossed the Salter's Way, the trade route linking Droitwich's salt production to the Wash. ♨❀◐◑⛺P🚬

Ulceby Skitter

Yarborough Arms

Killingholme Road, DN39 6TZ
⏲ 11.30-2.30, 5-11; 11-11 Sat; 12-10.30 Sun
☎ (01469) 588383
Tetley Bitter; Tom Wood Best Bitter; guest beer 🄷
This imposing pub started its life as offices to the nearby railway in 1847. It has a large public bar with pool table and a small lounge area that doubles up as overspill for the adjoining dining room. The food here is reasonably priced and good accommodation is available. There is a massive car park to the rear. Q🛏◐◑⊟♿⇌♣P🚬

Waddington

Three Horseshoes

High Street, LN5 9RF
⏲ 3 (12 Fri, 11 Sat)-midnight; 12-11 Sun

☎ (01522) 720448
John Smith's Bitter; guest beers Ⓗ
Situated in a large village approximately five miles from Lincoln, the pub is at the heart of the community and home to numerous sports teams. Up to five handpumps dispense beers from micro-breweries. The busy bar area is complemented by a small cosy side bar with a real fire in the winter. The village is on two bus routes, making it easy to get back to Lincoln after an evening at the pub.
(1,13) P

Westwoodside

Carpenters Arms

Newbigg, DN9 2AT (on B1396)
2 (12 Sun)-midnight
☎ (01427) 752416 thecarps.co.uk
Caledonian Deuchar's IPA; John Smith's Bitter; Wells Bombardier; guest beers Ⓗ
A popular village local, there has been a pub on this site since 1861. The lounge is spread over two levels. Under the present licensees, the range of real ales has increased significantly. Five are now available, including two guest ales, which are usually sourced from micro-breweries. There is a covered and heated smokers' area. P

Willingham by Stow

Half Moon

23 High Street, DN21 5JZ (200m from B1241 jct)
6 (5 Thu)-11; 12-3, 5-11 Fri; 12-11 Sat; 12-10.30 Sun
☎ (01427) 788340 graftersbrewery.com
Grafters Traditional, Over the Moon, Brewers Troop, Moonlight Ⓗ
Home to the award-winning Grafters Brewery, this popular village pub goes from strength to strength. Four regular Grafters ales plus occasional seasonal beers are available. The pub's renowned home-cooked fish and chip suppers are a must (served Thu-Fri eve and Sat & Sun lunch). The pub is home to the local football team and is involved in many local fund-raising events. It also hosts a beer festival in summer. Q (100)

Willoughton

Stirrup Inn

1 Templefield Road, DN21 5RZ
5 (12 Sat)-11; 12-11 Sun
☎ (01427) 668270
John Smith's Bitter; guest beers Ⓗ
Built from local Lincolnshire limestone, this hidden gem in an out of the way location is well worth seeking out. The enthusiastic landlord keeps two constantly changing guest ales to complement the regular beer. The pub attracts locals from the village as well as visitors from further afield and offers a warm welcome to CAMRA members. Pub quizzes are always popular. Q P

Wrangle

Angel Inn

Church End, PE22 9EW (opp church)
12-midnight
☎ (01205) 870315
Batemans XB; Everards Tiger Ⓗ
A welcoming village local, this free house has separate public and lounge bars plus a restaurant. Pool and darts are played. The walls of the quiet lounge bar are covered with photographs of old Wrangle and the surrounding area. Excellent value home-cooked food can be served in the bars if requested, with full meals available in the restaurant. Sunday lunch is a carvery (booking advised) and there is a senior citizens' lunch on Friday. The outdoor smoking area is heated.
Q (7) P

Thornton Hunt Inn, Thornton Curtis.

London Index

* Shown on Inner London map

GREATER LONDON

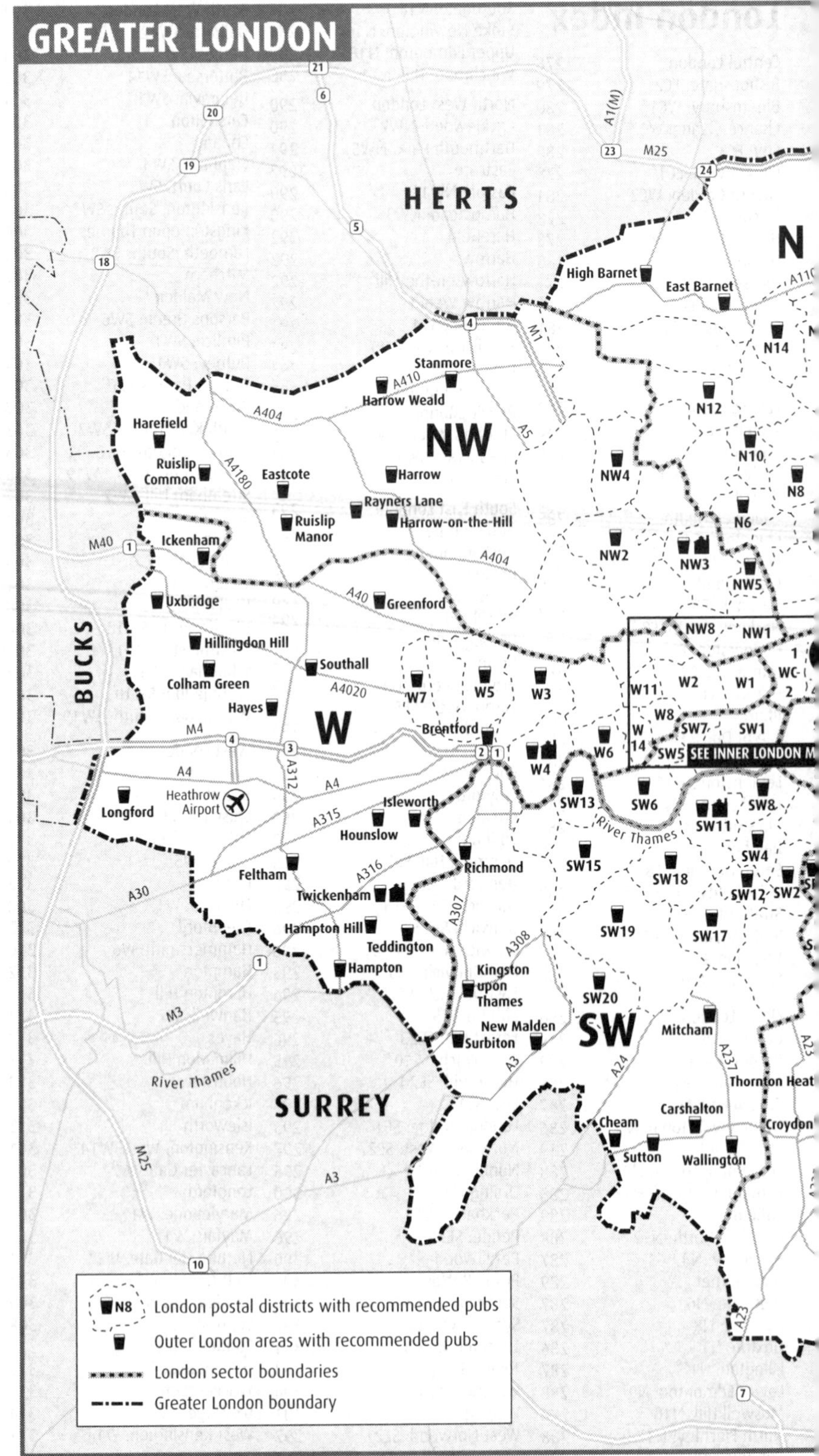
HERTS
BUCKS
SURREY
NW
W
SW
N
M25
A1(M)
M1
A5
A410
A404
A4180
A40
A4020
M40
M4
A4
A312
A315
A316
A30
A307
A308
A3
A24
A237
A23
M3
River Thames
High Barnet
East Barnet
N14
N12
N10
N8
N6
NW4
NW2
NW3
NW5
Stanmore
Harrow Weald
Harefield
Ruislip Common
Eastcote
Harrow
Rayners Lane
Ruislip Manor
Harrow-on-the-Hill
Ickenham
Uxbridge
Greenford
Hillingdon Hill
Colham Green
Southall
Hayes
W7
W5
W3
Brentford
W4
W6
NW8
NW1
W11
W2
W1
WC-1
WC-2
W8
W 14
SW7
SW1
SW5
SEE INNER LONDON M
Longford
Heathrow Airport
Isleworth
Hounslow
Feltham
Twickenham
Hampton Hill
Teddington
Hampton
Richmond
SW13
SW6
SW11
SW8
SW15
SW18
SW4
SW12
SW2
SW19
SW17
Kingston upon Thames
SW20
New Malden
Surbiton
Mitcham
Thornton Heat
Carshalton
Croydon
Cheam
Sutton
Wallington
N8
London postal districts with recommended pubs
Outer London areas with recommended pubs
London sector boundaries
Greater London boundary

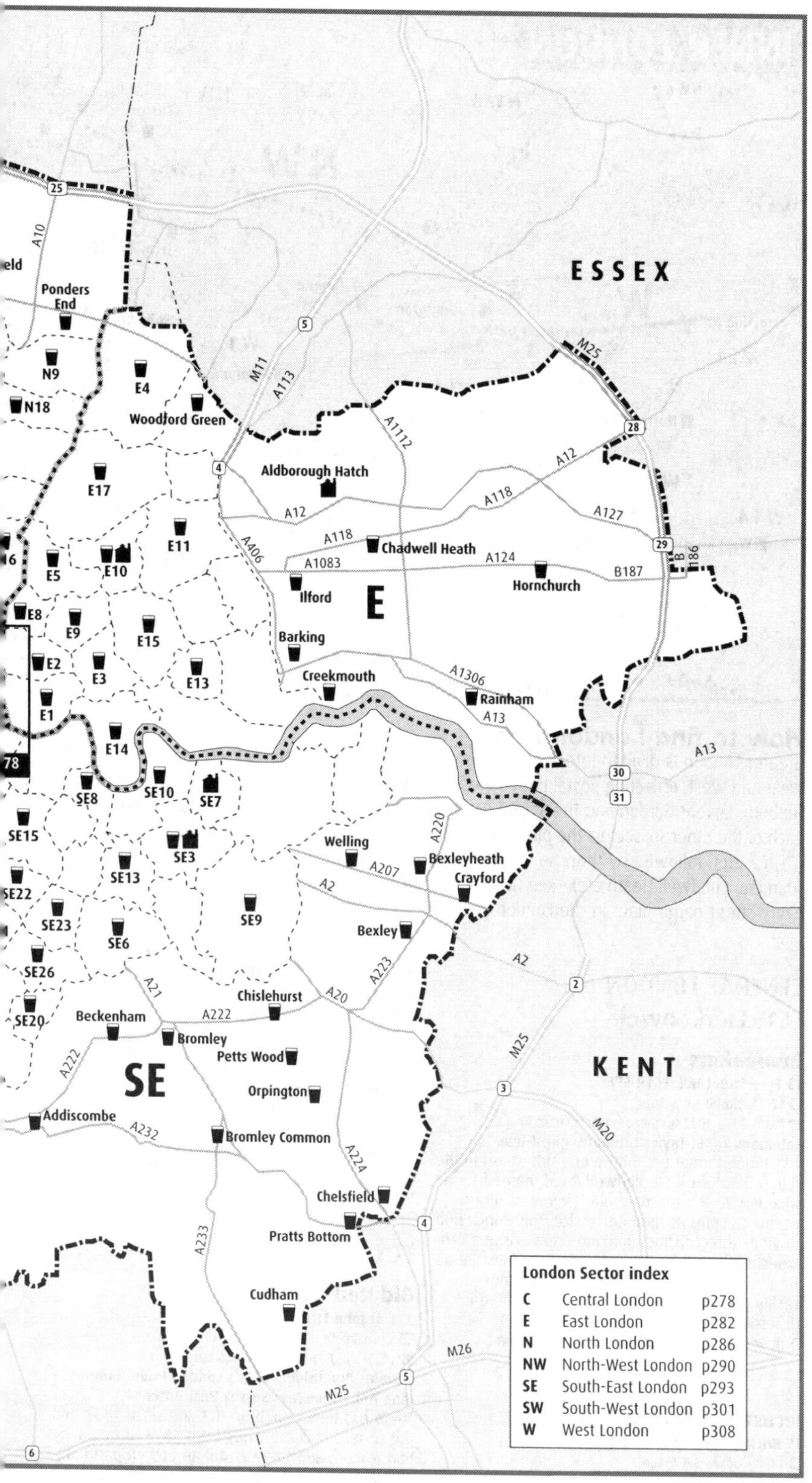

ESSEX
KENT
E
SE
Ponders End
N9
N18
E4
Woodford Green
E17
Aldborough Hatch
E11
E5
E10
E8
E9
E15
E2
E3
E13
E1
E14
Ilford
Barking
Creekmouth
Chadwell Heath
Hornchurch
Rainham
SE8
SE10
SE7
SE15
SE3
SE13
SE22
SE23
SE6
SE9
SE26
SE20
Welling
Bexleyheath
Crayford
Bexley
Chislehurst
Beckenham
Bromley
Petts Wood
Orpington
Addiscombe
Bromley Common
Chelsfield
Pratts Bottom
Cudham
A10
A12
A118
A127
A124
B187
B186
A1083
A406
A1112
A113
M11
M25
A1306
A13
A220
A207
A2
A223
A20
A21
A222
A232
A224
A233
M20
M26
London Sector index
C Central London p278
E East London p282
N North London p286
NW North-West London p290
SE South-East London p293
SW South-West London p301
W West London p308

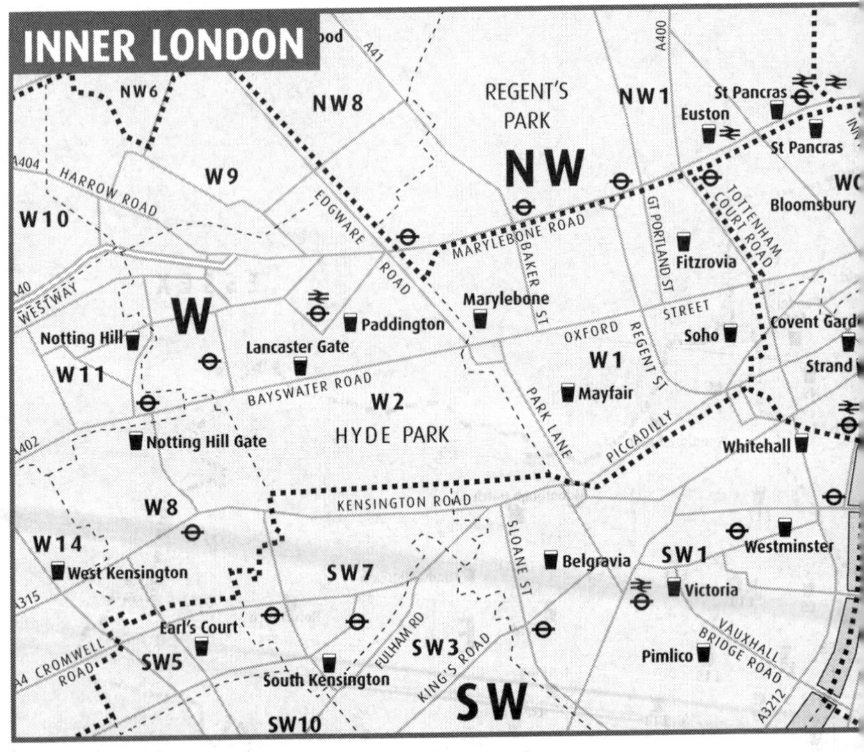

How to find London pubs

Greater London is divided into seven areas: Central, East, North, North-West, South-East, South-West and West, reflecting postal boundaries. The Central sector includes the City (EC1 to EC4) and Holborn, Covent Garden and The Strand (WC1/2), where pubs are listed in postal district order. In each of the other six sectors the pubs with London postcodes are listed first in postal district order (E1, E2 etc), followed by those in outer London districts, which are listed in alphabetical order (Barking, Chadwell Heath etc) – see Greater London map. Postal district numbers can be found on every street name plate in the London postcode area.

CENTRAL LONDON

EC1: Clerkenwell

Gunmakers

13 Eyre Street Hill, EC1R 5ET
12-11; closed Sat & Sun
☎ (020) 7278 1022 thegunmakers.co.uk
Batemans XXXB; Taylor Landlord; guest beer Ⓗ
A Victorian former beerhouse in a side street in the Italian Quarter off Clerkenwell Road, named for its proximity to the machine gun factory of Hiram Maxim. Despite its diminutive size, this Punch pub provides three distinct drinking areas. Visitors can expect well-kept beers, including two guest beers from a varying range, a cider from Westons and freshly prepared food in an intimate, candle-lit atmosphere.
Q (Farringdon) (Chancery Lane)

Jerusalem Tavern

55 Britton Street, EC1M 5UQ
11-11; closed Sat & Sun
☎ (020) 7490 4281
St Peter's Best Bitter, Mild, Organic Best, Golden Ale, Grapefruit Beer, seasonal beers Ⓗ
This small and intriguing pub, with lots of nooks and crannies for the discreet drinker, is named after the 12th-century priory of St John of Jerusalem. It is managed by friendly and knowledgable staff, and is the only pub tied to St Peter's Brewery in Suffolk. Bar food, served every weekday lunchtime and Tuesday to Thursday evenings, includes vegetarian and organic dishes. A traditional pub without music or TV.
Q (Farringdon)

EC1: Finsbury

Old Red Lion ✔

418 St John Street, EC1V 4NJ
12-midnight (1am Fri & Sat); 12-11 Sun
☎ (020) 7837 7816 oldredliontheatre.co.uk
Adnams Broadside; Fuller's London Pride; Greene King Abbot; Harveys Sussex Best Bitter Ⓗ
There has been a pub on this site since 1453 and the current building dates from 1898. It originally had a snug, and there is still an etched partition, although not in its original position, dividing the

bar into two areas. This Punch pub also has a fringe theatre specialising in new writing. Thomas Payne wrote part one of The Rights Of Man in the previous building. Board games are available and a big screen TV for sport. A real pub with a large, friendly dog. ❀♿⊖(Angel)🚌⚡

EC1: Hatton Garden

Olde Mitre ★ ✔

1 Ely Court, Ely Place, EC1N 6SJ

⏲ 11-11; closed Sat & Sun

☎ (020) 7405 4751

Adnams Broadside; Caledonian Deuchars IPA; Fuller's London Pride, seasonal beer; guest beer 🄷

This gem, sold to Fuller's by Punch in 2009, also has a gem of a landlord whose enthusiasm for his well kept beer runs to several mini beer festivals throughout the year. Easily missed by those not in the know, this ancient hostelry hides down a narrow alley between Hatton Garden and Ely Place, where a pub has existed since 1546. Constantly changing guest beer, reasonably priced snacks and the fascinating interior make this a must for visitors to London.
Q❀⊟≠(Farringdon)⊖(Chancery Lane)🚌⚡

EC1: Old Street

Artillery Arms ✔

102 Bunhill Row, EC1Y 8ND

⏲ 12-11 (10.30 Sun)

☎ (020) 7253 4683

Fuller's Chiswick Bitter, Discovery, London Pride, ESB, seasonal beers 🄷

A managed pub with six handpumps treating customers from the city and the local area to Fuller's full range and seasonals in excellent condition. High stools along a window shelf split by snob screens occupy the main drinking area while two half-panelled areas to the rear feature old prints and large mirrors respectively. The function room upstairs has a real fire. Evening meals are only served from Monday to Thursday.
⛬◐◑≠⊖(Moorgate/Old St)🚌♣

Old Fountain

3 Baldwin Street, EC1V 9NU

⏲ 11-11; closed Sat & Sun

☎ (020) 7253 2970 🌐 oldfountain.co.uk

Fuller's London Pride; guest beers 🄷

This free house has entrances on two streets, but do not be tempted to use it as a short cut – it's hard to leave. Seven guest beers are served, often featuring favourites Dark Star, Red Squirrel and Mighty Oak. At least one dark beer is usually available. Salt beef sandwiches are served at lunchtime and pizzas between 5-9pm. The TV is only used to show major sporting events on terrestrial channels. ❀◐◑⊟≠⊖🚌

EC1: Smithfield

Fox & Anchor

115 Charterhouse Street, EC1M 6AA

⏲ 7am (8am Sat)-11; 8.30-7 Sun

☎ (020) 7250 1300 🌐 foxandanchor.com

Fuller's London Pride; Sharp's Doom Bar; guest beer 🄷

Across the road from Smithfield Market, this former M&B pub was rescued after disposal and has been restored to its Victorian design by its new independent owner. The one narrow bar can be difficult to squeeze past when busy, but at the end you will find some tiny rooms seating four to six people, for those who want to get away from the masses standing at the bar. More gastro than pub, it has built up a good local following.
🛏◐≠(Farringdon)⊖(Barbican)🚌●

Hand & Shears ★ ✔

1 Middle Street, EC1A 7JA

⏲ 11-11; closed Sat & Sun

☎ (020) 7600 0257

Courage Best Bitter, Directors; Wadworth 6X 🄷

Situated down a narrow street, this tenanted Trust Inns pub still has the trappings and feel of a 19th-century ale house. The bar area is pleasantly divided into several areas, all creating a cosy feel. There is a real fire in the winter. Full English breakfast, home-made pies and sausage and mash are available at pub prices. Locals and commuters enjoy the ambience side by side.
⛬Q◐⊖(Barbican)🚌

EC2: Bishopsgate

Hamilton Hall ✔

Unit 32, The Concourse, Liverpool Street Station, EC2M 7PY

⏲ 7.30am-11.30; 9am-11.30 Sun

☎ (020) 7247 3579

Fuller's London Pride; Greene King Ruddles Best, Abbot; Marston's Pedigree; guest beers 🄷

This very busy Wetherspoon's has a downstairs bar with eight handpumps serving four regular beers and two guest beers, and an upstairs mezzanine bar with four handpumps serving doubles from downstairs. The spacious bar has

ornate cornices. A large mirror over the fireplace gives a light and airy atmosphere. There are plenty of tables and chairs inside and out, and also upstairs for a cosier dining feel. Two large TVs flank the fireplace for sporting events.
(Liverpool St)

Magpie

12 New Street, EC2M 4TP
11-11; closed Sat & Sun
(020) 7929 3889
Fuller's London Pride; Greene King IPA; Taylor Landlord; guest beer
Tucked away behind Bishopsgate police station, off the far side of Bishopsgate from Liverpool Street Station, this M&B pub sells more of Taylor's Landlord than any other beer. It is very popular with city workers for its pies which are sold at the bar – the restaurant upstairs has an enlarged menu. A hard to find pub, but well worth the effort.
(Liverpool St)

EC3: City

Crosse Keys

9 Gracechurch Street, EC3V 0DR
9-11 (midnight Fri; 7 Sat); closed Sun
(020) 7623 4824
Greene King Ruddles Best, Abbot; Marston's Pedigree; guest beers
Catholic by name and with a catholic choice of beers, this Wetherspoon Grade II-listed conversion of a City bank is a must for anyone wanting a vast choice of real ale. Of the 24 handpumps on the island bar, 21 are reserved for guest beers which change daily. Spring and autumn beer festivals are held and a guest brewery is invited to showcase its range of beers once a month. A function room is available. The door is staffed on Friday evening.
(Cannon St)(Monument)

East India Arms

67 Fenchurch Street, EC3M 4BR
11.30-11; closed Sat & Sun
(020) 7265 5121
Shepherd Neame Master Brew Bitter, Kent's Best, Spitfire, Bishop's Finger
Run by the well-liked character Bob, this small, friendly, single-bar Shepherd Neame pub has wooden floors with a shelf bar and stools around the walls. It gets very busy at lunchtime and early evening. There are tables and chairs outside, where heating is provided. The toilets are downstairs, but facilities for the disabled are available at Fenchurch Street Station nearby.
(Fenchurch St)(Aldgate/Tower Hill)

Elephant

119 Fenchurch Street, EC3M 5BA
11-9; closed Sat & Sun
(020) 7623 8970 elephantpub.co.uk
Wells Bombardier; Young's Bitter, Special, seasonal beer
A lively City Young's pub split into two areas. Upstairs, with an entrance on Fenchurch Street, is a wooden floored bar mainly for drinking while downstairs, which can also be accessed from Hogarth's Alley, is partitioned seating ideal for dining from an extensive menu.
(Fenchurch St)(Monument)

EC3: Tower Hill

Peacock

41 Minories, EC3N 1DT
12-midnight; closed Sat & Sun
(020) 7488 3630
Black Sheep Ale; Butcombe Bitter; Harveys Sussex Best Bitter; guest beer
A busy Punch pub in the north-west corner of Ibex House – the largest Grade I Art Deco building in the City and reputed to have been the Gestapo HQ first choice when they got to London. The leaseholder who runs it is a keen real ale drinker himself, which shows in his choice of beers. The pool table and dartboard are upstairs; table-top games are behind the bar. The pub is available to hire at the weekend.
(Fenchurch St)(Aldgate/Tower Hill/Tower Gateway DLR)

WC1: Bloomsbury

Calthorpe Arms

252 Grays Inn Road, WC1X 8JR
11-11.30 (midnight Fri & Sat); 12-10.30 Sun
(020) 7278 4732
Wells Bombardier; Young's Bitter, Special, seasonal beers
Friendly single-bar Young's pub, popular with locals and office workers, once used as a temporary magistrates court after the first recorded murder of an on-duty policeman in 1830. The upstairs dining room opens at lunchtime and can be booked for meetings and functions. No music and unobtrusive TV. Evening meals are served 6-9.30pm Monday to Friday. Outside seating is available, weather permitting, in a paved patio area. Three times local CAMRA Pub of the Year. Occasional guest beers.
(King's Cross)(Russell Sq)

Jeremy Bentham

31 University Street, WC1E 6JL
11.30-11, closed Sat & Sun
(020) 7387 3033
Caledonian Deuchars IPA; guest beers
Despite appearing to be a one-bar corner pub, stairs lead up to both the Ladies and an upstairs lounge, providing welcome extra seating. Renamed in 1982, it commemorates the 150th anniversary of the death of the recognised spiritual founder of University College London – his mummified head is kept in the college vaults. A Punch pub, it offers three regularly changing guests and a cider from Westons. Although in the heart of academe, prices are not pitched at the student market.
(Euston)(Euston Sq/Warren St)

INDEPENDENT BREWERIES

Brew Wharf SE1
Brodie's E10: Leyton (NEW)
Florence SE24: Herne Hill
Fuller's W4: Chiswick
Ha'penny Aldborough Hatch (NEW)
McLaughlin NW3: Hampstead
Meantime SE7: Greenwich
Sambrook's SW11: Battersea (NEW)
Twickenham Twickenham
Zerodegrees SE3: Blackheath

Museum Tavern ✔

49 Great Russell Street, WC1B 3BA
11-11.30 (midnight Fri & Sat); 12-10 Sun
☎ (020) 7242 8987
Fuller's London Pride; Sharp's Doom Bar; Taylor Landlord; Theakston Old Peculier; guest beers H
The British Museum provides a stream of tourists that mixes with the locals in this Regional Inventory-listed Punch pub. The long bar-back dating from 1889 sets the scene for an essential British experience. A mixture of tables and long benches provides ample space to appreciate the history, to sample a balanced range of beers and to try some traditional food. For hard-line continentals, pavement seating completes the scene. ⊖(Tottenham Ct Rd)

WC1: Holborn

Cittie of Yorke ★

22 High Holborn, WC1V 6BS
11.30 (12 Sat)-11.30; closed Sun
☎ (020) 7242 7670
Samuel Smith OBB H
A pub has stood on this site since 1430. In 1695 it was rebuilt as Gray's Inn Coffee House. Now an extensive three-bar Sam Smith's pub and Grade II-listed building, the huge main bar includes small wooden drinking booths, a high beamed ceiling and large disused oak barrels over the bar. The front bar is more intimate, with wood panelling and an original chandelier, and the cellar bar is the former cellarage of the original 17th-century coffee house. Q⊖(Chancery Lane)

Penderel's Oak ✔

286-288 High Holborn, WC1V 7HJ
9-11 (midnight Thu; 1am Fri & Sat)
☎ (020) 7242 5669
Greene King IPA, Abbot; Marston's Pedigree; guest beers H
Occupying the ground floor and basement of a modern office building, this large, L-shaped Wetherspoon's pub has a quiet ground floor room and a downstairs bar screening sport with sound or music videos. At least four regularly changing guest beers and a cider are available. French windows face out on to the street, where there are seats for the hardy and the smoker. A family area at the back of the main bar opens until 7pm, with last food orders at 6pm.
Q⊖(Chancery Lane/Holborn)

WC1: St Pancras

Mabels Tavern

9 Mabledon Place, WC1H 9AZ
11-11 (midnight Thu-Sat); 12-10.30 Sun
☎ (020) 7387 7739
Shepherd Neame Master Brew Bitter, Kent's Best, Spitfire, Bishop's Finger, seasonal beers H
Busy pub between Euston and St Pancras, attracting office workers at lunchtime and early evening, and tourists and locals evenings and weekends. Its long, single bar room with elevated sections at either end is popular for watching football and rugby on TV screens. There is limited pavement seating for smokers and summertime diners. Good-value food is available (until 9.30pm Mon-Thu, 8.30pm Fri-Sun). The beer range can be limited on a Sunday. Local CAMRA Pub of the Year 2006. ⊖

Skinners Arms

114 Judd Street, WC1H 9NT
12-11; closed Sat & Sun
☎ (020) 7837 6521
Greene King IPA, Old Speckled Hen, Abbot; Taylor Landlord; guest beer H
Taking its name from the City Livery Company, this popular free house has a long room in traditional dark woods with an elevated section on the left as you enter. A smaller section at the rear has a more private feel, while pavement seating is also available. Good-value food is served but the kitchen closes Friday evenings. Although Greene King brews predominate, guests appear occasionally and mini beer festivals occur from time to time. ⊖

WC2: Chancery Lane

Knights Templar ✔

95 Chancery Lane, WC2A 1DT
9-11.30; 11-5 Sat; closed Sun
☎ (020) 7831 2660
Courage Best Bitter; Fuller's London Pride; Greene King Abbot; Marston's Pedigree; guest beers H
A large and successful Wetherspoon's bank conversion with a Knights Templar motif adorning the ceiling and walls. Upstairs seating is available when busy. There are 12 handpumps with a good range of beers and two ciders usually available. Free Wi-Fi is on offer and a large TV screen is used for major sporting events. ⊖

Seven Stars

53 Carey Street, WC2A 2JB
11 (12 Sat)-11; 12-10.30 Sun
☎ (020) 7242 8521
Adnams Bitter, Broadside; Dark Star Hophead; guest beers H
Busy with legal trade midweek, this Enterprise pub gets uncomfortably full at weekends, having been put on a tourist website (to the landlady's displeasure). There is a small central drinking area and two side rooms not much larger. The pub is well decorated with Vanity Fair/Spy legal prints and posters from films with a legal theme. Food is available but hours are at the landlady's discretion. The two loos, up a steep staircase, appear to be interchangeable between Ladies and Gentlemen!
Q⊖

WC2: Covent Garden

Freemasons Arms

81-82 Long Acre, WC2E 9NG
12-11 (11.30 Fri & Sat); 12-10.30 Sun
☎ (020) 7836 3115
Shepherd Neame Master Brew Bitter, Spitfire, seasonal beers H
A busy pub attracting locals, office workers and sports fans. There are five TV screens and Sky is available. The connection with football is historic as this was the place where the rules of the Football Association were drawn up – a copy adorns the wall. There are two function rooms which may be hired. ⊖

Harp ✔

47 Chandos Place, WC2N 4HS
10.30-11; 12-10.30 Sun
☎ (020) 7836 0291

Black Sheep Best Bitter; Harveys Sussex Best Bitter; Taylor Landlord; guest beers Ⓗ
Acquired from Punch by the landlady in 2009, this pub – near the National and Portrait Galleries – has walls adorned with portraits from Shakespeare and Florence Nightingale to Elizabeth Taylor and James Mason (with pet cat). There are no fruit machines, loud music or TVs – so you can enjoy the perfectly kept real ales, ciders or perries and malt whiskies in peace. Local CAMRA Pub of the Year 2006 and 2008, the friendly and helpful staff make it a joy to visit. The comfortable upstairs room can be booked for functions.
Q◑⇌(Charing Cross)⊖(Charing Cross/Leicester Sq)🚌●

Nell of Old Drury
29 Catherine Street, WC2B 5JS
12-3, 5-11.30; 5 (12 Sat)-midnight Fri & Sat; closed Sun
☎ (020) 7836 5328 nellofolddrury.com
Adnams Bitter; Badger Tanglefoot Ⓗ
Small but cosy one bar Enterprise pub conveniently situated opposite the Royal Opera House, decorated with West End theatre posters, with a good mix of locals, tourists, opera-goers and after work drinkers. Additional seating is available in the first floor room but the best seat by far is in the engraved bow window overlooking Drury Lane. Theatre-lovers can take advantage of the pub's interval drinks service. ⊖🚌

WC2: Strand

Edgar Wallace ✔
40 Essex Street, WC2R 3JF
11-11; closed Sat & Sun
☎ (020) 7353 3120 edgarwallacepub.com
Adnams Bitter; Nethergate Edgar's Pale Ale; guest beers Ⓗ
Situated in the heart of the legal area of the Temple, this Enterprise pub is a real gem with eight ales always available including six rotating guests sourced from micro-breweries all over the country. An up-to-date list of available beers is on the website. Good food is served all day and, with such a range of ales, what better way to while away a few hours. The landlord is always on hand to help you choose your beer. Q◑⊖(Temple)🚌

Ship & Shovell
2-3 Craven Passage, WC2N 5PH
11-11; closed Sun
☎ (020) 7839 1311
Badger K&B Sussex Bitter, Tanglefoot, seasonal beers Ⓗ
A gem of an old pub, almost 'underneath the arches', and self-proclaimed as the only pub in London in two halves: its two parts are either side of the passageway. The eponymous Admiral Shovell's portrait hangs over the fireplace. With bevelled mirrors, engraved glass, naval and stage pictures, extensive wood panelling, and gleaming bar, brass hand rail and footrest, this is proudly a Hall & Woodhouse flagship. TV is available in the main bar, and the musak is not too intrusive.
◖⇌(Charing Cross)⊖(Charing Cross/Embankment)🚌

EAST LONDON

E1: Aldgate

Dispensary 🏆
19A Leman Street, E1 8EN
12-11; closed Sat & Sun
☎ (020) 7977 0486 thedispensarylondon.co.uk
Adnams East Green; Caledonian Deuchars IPA; guest beers Ⓗ
In pleasant, contemporary surroundings, this free house caters for the many office employees in this area, with a large range of wines and spirits and an extensive food menu. Sympathetically restored, the pub is split-level, with a couple of separate areas for small groups. The perfect place to enjoy a relaxing drink after work. Local CAMRA 2009 Pub of the Year. ◑⊖(Aldgate E)🚌

White Swan
21-23 Alie Street, E1 8DA
11-11; closed Sat & Sun
☎ (020) 7702 0448
Shepherd Neame Master Brew Bitter, Spitfire, seasonal beer Ⓗ
A short walk from the heart of the City, the Swan offers a warm welcome, hot home-made traditional food at lunchtimes, cold snacks and, most importantly, cool Shepherd Neame beer. Upstairs is a small room used by diners or small groups for meetings. Sit at an immaculately polished wooden table, chill out on a sofa or discuss stocks and shares at the bar.
◖⇌⊖(Aldgate/Aldgate E)🚌

E1: Spitalfields

Pride of Spitalfields
3 Heneage Street, E1 5LJ
11-midnight (1am Thu; 2am Fri & Sat); 11-11 Sun
☎ (020) 7247 8933
Crouch Vale Brewers Gold; Fuller's London Pride, ESB; guest beer Ⓗ
Tucked away, traditional and unspoilt, the reception in this genuine free house is always welcoming. Cosy on winter days when the fire is roaring, and during the summer months with the front door open, the pub's friendly and lively atmosphere spills out to the street with several benches, and plenty of kerb space to occupy. Home cooked food is served weekday lunchtimes, plus Sun roast. ✿◖⇌(Liverpool St)⊖(Aldgate E)🚌

E1: Wapping

Town of Ramsgate ✔
62 Wapping High Street, E1 2PN
12-midnight (11 Sun)
☎ (020) 7481 8000
Adnams Bitter; Fuller's London Pride; Young's Bitter Ⓗ
Friendly riverside local whose historic surroundings contribute to an inviting atmosphere: the first inn on the site is believed to date from 1460 and the present pub, now leased from Enterprise, took its name in 1811 from the fishermen of Ramsgate who would land their catch at nearby Wapping Old Stairs to avoid river taxes at Billingsgate. A delightful patio overlooks the river. Home-made food is served with daily specials every day until 9pm. Wapping overground station is due to open in 2010. ✿◑🚌(100,D3)♣

E2: Bethnal Green

Camel

277 Globe Road, E2 0JD
5 (12 Sat)-11; 12-10.30 Sun
(020) 8983 9888 thecamele2.co.uk
Crouch Vale Brewers Gold; Harvey's Sussex Best Bitter H
Small in size, big in atmosphere, it is hard to believe this thriving, heart-of-the-community free house nearly ended up as a block of flats after closing in 2000. Local residents campaigned to save it and, since reopening, it has gone from strength to strength. Various meat and vegetarian pies and mash are served until 9.30pm. Occasional live music includes a local pianist and a banjo player.

Carpenters Arms

73 Cheshire Street, E2 6EJ
12 (4 Mon)-11.30 (12.30 Fri & Sat)
(020) 7739 6342 carpentersarmsfreehouse.com
Adnams Bitter, seasonal beer; Taylor Landlord H
Atmospheric and well-restored free house, retaining many original features and with local pictures on the walls. This corner pub survives in an area where many have closed and are lost forever. It is mostly glass fronted with a single bar; there are other rooms off the bar area that make it an adventure. It has a wide selection of bottled beers (English and European) and ciders to choose from. Home-made food is available 1-10pm from a menu that changes daily.
(Liverpool St/Bethnal Green) (Liverpool St)

E2: Haggerston

Albion in Goldsmiths Row

94 Goldsmiths Row, E2 8QY
12-11
(020) 7739 0185
Pitfield Epping Forest Bitter; Taylor Landlord H
A welcoming place for everyone – but especially the true football fan. Decorated with football scarves and other memorabilia, the Albion is a safe and friendly place to view matches on Sky. The name refers to West Bromwich, the team supported by the landlord and a surprising number of regulars. There are darts and football teams, as well as a social club for senior citizens. Soccer aside, this is a proper community free house.
(Cambridge Heath)

E3: Bow

Eleanor Arms

460 Old Ford Road, E3 5JP
12-midnight (1am Sat); 12-10.30 Sun
(020) 8980 6992
Shepherd Neame Kent's Best, seasonal beer; guest beer H
A warm welcome awaits you at this wood-panelled, traditional, family-run pub near Victoria Park and the Hertford Union Canal, transformed in just over a year by its current landlord from an uninspiring, down-at-heel pub into a comfortably refurbished hostelry. It usually serves three beers from the Shepherd Neame range or occasionally a guest ale. There is a range of bar snacks and a small beer garden, and it is dog-friendly.
(Bow Rd/Bow Church DLR) (8)

Palm Tree

127 Grove Road, E3 5RP
12-midnight (2am Fri); 12-1am Sun
Beer range varies H
Step back in time to a free house which has had the same owner for 33 years. Originally a street-corner pub alongside the Grand Union Canal, rebuilt in 1930, it now stands isolated. With one bar and a smaller room at the rear, it serves two ever-changing beers, often from micros. The surrounding area became a park in 1983 and access is best via Haverfield Road. Live jazz evenings take place at weekends, with no admission after 11pm. Local CAMRA Pub of the Year 2007. (Mile End) P

E4: Chingford

Kings Head

2B Kings Head Hill, E4 7EA
11.30-11 (midnight Thu-Sat)
(020) 8529 6283
Courage Best Bitter; Fuller's London Pride; Taylor Landlord; Young's Bitter; guest beers H
With a very much altered interior since the last time it was in the Guide, this pub, now run by M&B (Ember Inns), has six handpumps, two of them for guest ales. A great place for a quiet drink in comfortable surroundings, it is used by local clubs and societies. Quiz nights are Wednesday and Sunday evenings at 9pm, steak night is Tuesday and curry night Thursday. Children are allowed only in the patio area. P

E5: Clapton

Anchor & Hope

15 High Hill Ferry, E5 9HG (800m N of Lea Bridge Rd, along river path)
1 (12 Easter-mid October)-11; 12-10.30 (11 summer) Sun
(020) 8806 1730
Fuller's London Pride, ESB; guest beers H
Wonderful testimony to the East London heritage, overlooking the River Lea, with the appeal and warm spirit of an old-time working community. This Fuller's pub has two bars inside and one on the river bank. Popular with locals, it also attracts walkers and cyclists in droves, mainly for the impeccably kept beers. Stroll along the river and refresh yourself with a perfect pint and cheerful company. (393)

Elderfield

57 Elderfield Road, E5 0LF
4 (1 Sat)-11 (midnight Thu-Sat); 1-11 Sun
(020) 8986 1591
Adnams Broadside; Fuller's London Pride; Harveys Sussex Best Bitter; Taylor Landlord H
A Punch pub which was originally multi-roomed with an off-licence. It has been opened up into two separate areas, retaining some 1930s features. Once called the Priory Tavern and then the Eclipse, it sits in a part of Hackney not generally known for its real ales. There is live jazz every other Tuesday and a quiz on alternate weeks. Board games and a range of teas are available, and occasional TV sport, such as England games. (242,308)

E8: Hackney

Pembury Tavern

90 Amhurst Road, E8 1JH

⏲ 12-11
☎ (020) 8986 8597 🌐 individualpubs.co.uk/pembury
Milton Minotaur, Sparta, Nero; guest beers Ⓗ
Beer heaven in Hackney! Sixteen handpumps, three regulars plus rotating guests and a real cider, are supplemented with extra ales and two more ciders for beer festivals in March, July and November. There is no music, TV or games machine, but plenty of board games behind the bar. A spacious one-room free house, it is popular with young professionals. Even the lagers are only premium quality brands. Good quality food is served all day, the menu updated on the website. Q◑◐♿⇌(Hackney Downs/Central)🚌♣🍎

E8: South Hackney

Dove
24-28 Broadway Market, E8 4QJ
⏲ 12-11 (midnight Fri & Sat)
☎ (020) 7275 7617 🌐 dovepubs.co.uk
Crouch Vale Brewers Gold; Taylor Landlord; guest beers Ⓗ
Unique – the only British pub or bar to be an Orval ambassadeur. This benediction from the famed Trappist monastic brewer recognises a dedication to the Belgian beer. The selection of 101 Belgian beers includes always one on draught. No wonder this free house holds regular beer tastings. The highly creative menu is additionally beer-infused: Bouef Carbonnade is but one of the many offerings. There is no music but, more practically, Wi-Fi and Internet access.
Q◑◐♿⇌(London Fields)🚌(394)

E9: Homerton

Globe in Morning Lane
20 Morning Lane, E9 6NA
⏲ 12 (11 Sat)-midnight (3am Thu-Sat); 11-8.30 Sun
☎ (020) 8985 6455
Fuller's London Pride; Young's Bitter Ⓗ
Increasingly a vibrant part of the emerging Hackney entertainment scene, this Enterprise pub is famous for live music sessions with contrasting themes, all free, on Monday, Thursday, Friday and Saturday, plus a Sunday lunchtime trad jazz gig that is a great favourite for real ale drinkers. Not just a music venue, the Globe also serves two perfectly kept beers and good value daytime meals. Fifteen different buses pass nearby.
◑♿⇌(Hackney Central)🚌♣🎯

E10: Leyton

Leyton Orient Supporters Club
Matchroom Stadium, Oliver Road, E10 5NF
⏲ match days from 12.30 Sat, 5.30 weekdays, not during game. Closing time varies
☎ (020) 8988 8288 🌐 orientsupporters.org
Mighty Oak Oscar Wilde; guest beers Ⓗ
You do not have to follow football to enjoy this shrine to real ale with its six ales, including a mild, plus a cider or perry. Everyone is welcomed by the volunteer staff, whether home or away supporters or just casual drinkers. Home of the Piglet Beer Festivals twice a year, it is open Thursday evenings, before a Saturday home game, and for most major games on TV: phone to check. Local CAMRA Club of the Year 2009, national winner 2008. ♿⊖🚌🍎🎯

E11: Leytonstone

North Star
24 Browning Road, E11 3AR
⏲ 4 (12 Sat)-11; 12-10.30 Sun
☎ (020) 8989 5777
Adnams Bitter; Butcombe Gold; Wells Bombardier; guest beers Ⓗ
There is much debate over whether this Enterprise pub is named after a train or a ship, but either way it is a welcome sight, hidden down a small side turning off Leytonstone High Road. Awaiting you is a friendly local serving three regular beers plus one or two guest ales at weekends. It has one bar with serving hatches to the other room. There is music every third Sunday of the month. ✿⊟⊖🚌♣

E13: Plaistow

Black Lion ✔
59-61 High Street, E13 0AD
⏲ 11-11; 12-10.30 Sun
☎ (020) 8472 2351
Courage Best Bitter; guest beers Ⓗ
A true free house in an area where they are rare. The guest beers are increased to four or five when West Ham United are playing at home, only 15 minutes' walk away. The landlord was Mighty Oak's first customer and continues to sells its ales. The pub was rebuilt about 280 years ago. Some original features are still visible such as the cobbled yard, stables (now a boxing club) and low ceilings with oak beams. There is a separate function room.
✿◑◐⊟⊖🚌P🎯

E14: Isle of Dogs

George
114 Glengal Grove, E14 3ND
⏲ 11-midnight
☎ (020) 7987 4433
Caledonian Deuchars IPA; Fuller's London Pride; Taylor Landlord; Young's Bitter; guest beer Ⓗ
Dating from 1864, this Enterprise pub has a rich history linked to the docks and the local community. The present, early '30s building comprises three distinct bars, each with its own special character, plus a large conservatory and patio garden. There are numerous photographs of local dock scenes and characters throughout, all in a welcoming, comfortable environment. An excellent choice of food is provided, vegetarians catered for, fish and chips a speciality.
♔◑◐⊟⊖(Crossharbour DLR)🎯

Gun ✔
27 Coldharbour, E14 9NS
⏲ 11-midnight (11 Sun)
☎ (020) 7515 5222 🌐 thegundocklands.com
Adnams Broadside; Greene King Abbot; Young's Bitter Ⓗ
A beautifully restored, Grade II-listed riverside tavern where Lord Nelson and Lady Hamilton are thought to have conducted their secret assignations. The name refers to the cannon fired to celebrate the opening of the West India Dock in 1802. Highly acclaimed British food is available daily in a separate dining room, as are bar snacks. The inside of this Punch pub is wonderfully atmospheric and outside are impressive river views from the terrace, with the O2 dome on the far bank. ♔✿◑◐⊖(Blackwall DLR)🚌🎯

North Pole

74 Manilla Street, E14 8LG
11-3, 5-11; closed Sat & Sun
☎ (020) 7987 5443
Black Sheep Best Bitter; Fuller's London Pride; Taylor Landlord H
A typical local back-street pub in the heart of Docklands, serving print workers and locals, this Enterprise pub can get very busy at lunchtimes and early evenings. There are three regular ales with Black Sheep now joining the flock. Unusually, it still holds with the afternoon closing between 3-5pm. Enjoy a truly welcome haven from the busy city life outside. ❀◐⊖(South Quay DLR)🚌♣

E14: Limehouse

Grapes ✔

76 Narrow Street, E14 8BP
12-3, 5.30-11; 12-11 Thu-Sat; 12-10.30 Sun
☎ (020) 7987 4396
Adnams Bitter; Marston's Pedigree; Taylor Landlord; guest beer H
There has been an inn here since the 16th century, with the present building dating from 1720. Dickens based the Six Jolly Fellowship Porters in Our Mutual Friend on this pub. Formerly the haunt of dockers and watermen, this Punch pub now caters for locals from the riverside apartments and the estate nearby. It is understandably very popular with tourists, with quality bar meals and a highly regarded fish restaurant upstairs.
Q◐◑⊖(Westferry DLR)

E15: Stratford

King Edward VII

47 Broadway, E15 4BQ
12-11 (midnight Thu-Sat); 12-11.30 Sun
☎ (020) 8534 2313 🌐 kingeddie.co.uk
Nethergate Eddies Best, Suffolk County; Sharp's Doom Bar; Wells Bombardier H
Signed as and affectionately known as King Eddie's, this old Enterprise pub on Stratford Broadway, often busy with a youngish, professional clientele, consists of two bars and a restaurant. The front bar is unspoilt with flagstone floor and wooden pews; the back bar has settles and chairs and is next to the restaurant. Food is also available at the bars. There are no TVs or games machines. Four handpumps serve real ales which change occasionally. ❀◐◑⊟⇌⊖🚌⚡

E17: Walthamstow

Nags Head

9 Orford Road, E17 9LP
4 (2 Fri, 12 Sat)-11; 12-10.30 Sun
☎ (020) 8520 9709
Adnams Broadside; Fuller's London Pride; Mighty Oak Oscar Wilde; Taylor Landlord; guest beers H
Located in Walthamstow Village conservation area, this Enterprise pub has five handpumps, with a mild always on, also a Belgian fruit beer on tap and a selection of bottled Belgian beers. A very comfortable and welcoming one-bar establishment with a relaxed atmosphere, it attracts a young professional clientele. Outside is a patio beer garden and a heated tented area for smokers. With tablecloths, modern decor and excellent service, the landlords have transformed this into a gem of a pub. ❀⇌⊖(Walthamstow Central)🚌(W12)⚡

Olde Rose & Crown ✔

53-55 Hoe Street, E17 4SA
10-11 (midnight Fri & Sat); 12-11 Sun
☎ (020) 8509 3880 🌐 yeolderoseandcrowntheatrepub.co.uk
Adnams seasonal beers; Fuller's London Pride; guest beers H
An Enterprise lease, this large, friendly community theatre pub has everything you would want from your local: a fantastic changing guest ale policy, a range of different seating from small snug-like areas to a raised area with tables and chairs, and entertainment such as E17 Jazz, quiz nights, film nights, comedy nights, live theatre, open mike nights and live music in the bar or in the theatre upstairs (all dates and events are on the website).
⇌⊖(Walthamstow Central)🚌

Barking

Britannia 🏆

1 Church Road, IG11 8PR
11-3, 5-11; 12-11 Fri & Sat; 12-11 Sun
☎ (020) 8594 1305
Young's Bitter, Special, seasonal beers H
As you approach this large, friendly Young's local you see the seven plaster figureheads (caryatids), a reminder that Barking was once home to England's largest fishing fleet. The normally quiet saloon bar offers a comfortable 'home from home', while the public bar has bare boards, darts, pool, jukebox and TV. Good, hearty lunchtime food is served, with roasts on Sunday (booking advisable). The area has been extensively rebuilt with white, Spanish-style, low-level housing. Local CAMRA Pub of the Year 2009. Q❀◐⊟⇌⊖🚌♣P⚡

Chadwell Heath

Eva Hart ✔

1128 High Road, RM6 4AH (on A118)
9-midnight
☎ (020) 8597 1069
Courage Best Bitter, Directors; Greene King Abbot; Marston's Pedigree; guest beers H
Large, comfortable Wetherspoon's pub, previously the local police station but now a real ale oasis. Named after a local singer and music teacher who was one of the longest-living survivors of the Titanic disaster, photographs and memorabilia are on display. Up to four guest ales are usually on handpump together with a Westons cider. Food is served all day, starting with breakfast from 9am. There are patio seating areas at the front and side.
❀◐◑♿⇌🚌●P⚡

Creekmouth

Crooked Billet

113 River Road, IG11 0EG (1½ miles S of A13)
11-midnight; 12-11 Sun
☎ (020) 8507 0126
Fuller's London Pride H
Pleasant, traditional Enterprise pub in an industrial area, featuring three bars: a public bar with pool table, a saloon bar where lunch is served Monday to Friday, and a small wood-panelled bar known as the 'middle bar'. The garden is open during the summer months. The pub is the base for the Creekmouth Preservation Society. Bus route 387 terminates about half a mile away but extends to pass the pub four times during peak periods Monday-Friday. 🔥❀◐⊟🚌(387)P

Hornchurch

JJ Moons ✔

Unit 3, 46-62 High Street, RM12 4UN (on A124)
9-midnight (12.30am Fri & Sat); 9-11.30 Sun
☎ (01708) 478410
Greene King Ruddles Best, Abbot; Marston's Pedigree; guest beers Ⓗ
An impressive range of guest beers greets you in this busy Wetherspoon's pub near the end of the High Street. The usual collection of local historic photographs and information includes a feature on John Cornwall, the boy hero of the Battle of Jutland. Breakfast is served until midday and food up to 11pm. A family area is available until 6pm. Outside at the back is a covered smoking area.
Q◑◐♿⇌(Emerson Pk)🚌

Ilford

Prince of Wales

63 Green Lane, IG1 1XJ (on A1083)
12-11.30
☎ (020) 8478 1326
Fuller's London Pride; Greene King IPA; Young's Bitter; guest beers Ⓗ
This very pleasant local has a small, cosy saloon bar and a larger L-shaped public bar. Regular beers are supplemented by three or four guests. The public bar houses a dartboard and there is an outdoor pool table. Regular quiz nights are held. The rear garden is comfortable and well maintained and there is ample parking. This S&N pub is a welcome addition to an area dominated by 'keg' pubs.
❀◑◐♿🚌P

Rainham

Phoenix

Broadway, RM13 9YW (on B1335 near clock tower)
11-11; 12-3, 7-10.30 Sun
☎ (01708) 553700
Courage Directors; Greene King Abbot; John Smith's Bitter; Wells Bombardier; guest beer Ⓗ
Busy, spacious Enterprise town pub, very close to Rainham Station and convenient for the RSPB Rainham Marshes nature reserve. It has two bars: a public bar with dartboard and a saloon for dining (no food Sun). Quizzes and live entertainment/music alternate on Thursday; entertainment also features on Saturday. The large garden has five aviaries and a barbecue area. Family fun days are held every bank holiday Monday. Accommodation comprises seven twin rooms and one single room.
❀◑◐⇌🚌♣P

Woodford Green

Cricketers

299-301 High Road, IG8 9HQ
11-11 (midnight Fri & Sat); 12-11 Sun
☎ (020) 8504 2734
McMullen AK, Cask Ale, Country Bitter Ⓗ
Comfortable and friendly local with a cosy saloon bar and a slightly more basic public bar with dartboard. The saloon has insignia plaques for all 18 first-class cricket counties, together with a number of photographs of Sir Winston Churchill, for many years the local MP, whose statue stands on the green almost opposite. Good value meals (including pensioners' specials) are served Monday to Saturday lunchtimes. There is a small patio seating area at the front. ❀◑♿🚌(179,W13)P

Traveller's Friend

496-498 High Road, IG8 0PN (by A104)
12-11; 12-4, 7-11 Sun
☎ (020) 8504 2435
Adnams Broadside; Courage Best Bitter; Wells Bombardier; guest beer Ⓗ
An absolute gem of a local, on a slip road off the busy main road. This friendly, comfortable Barracuda pub features oak-panelled walls and rare original snob screens. The beer is served in tip-top condition – there are normally two guest ales available and beer festivals are held in April and September. Several bus routes pass the door. Local CAMRA Pub of the Year 2008.
Q❀♿🚌(20,179,W13)P

NORTH LONDON

N1: Canonbury

Lord Clyde

340-342 Essex Road, N1 3PB
12-11 (midnight Fri & Sat); 12-10.30 Sun
☎ (020) 7288 9850 🌐 thelordclyde.com
Harveys Sussex Best Bitter; guest beer Ⓗ
The original Charrington's woodwork, enhanced with complementary modern decor, makes this revitalised Enterprise pub a clean, welcoming space, with a separate public bar. Food is important but drink leads the way with an ever-changing guest beer from the SIBA (Society of Independent Brewers) direct delivery scheme, emphasising local beers if possible. A garden with decking provides a suntrap in the summer and benches on the pavement complete the picture. Five buses serve the Angel, Islington stop opposite. No food after 7pm on Sunday evening.
❀◑◐⇌(Essex Rd)🚌♣

N1: De Beauvoir Town

Scolt Head

107A Culford Road, N1 4HT
12-midnight (10.30 Sun)
☎ (020) 7254 3965 🌐 thescolthead.com
Caledonian Deuchars IPA; Fuller's London Pride; Hop Back Summer Lightning; guest beer Ⓗ
A light, spacious Punch gastropub with a traditional drinking area in front of the L-shaped bar. Occupying a triangular site, there is a large patio at the front and a restaurant and a sports/function room off the bar. The main bar includes an original bar back and eclectic decorations ranging from pressure gauges to a large china dog. If the roaring fire does not warm you up, the reasonably-priced home-cooked food will.
❀◑◐♿⇌(Dalston Kingsland)🚌(76,141)♣

N1: Hoxton

Prince Arthur

49 Brunswick Place, N1 6EB
11-midnight; 12-6.30 Sun
☎ (020) 7253 3187
Shepherd Neame Canterbury Jack, Master Brew Bitter, Kent's Best, Spitfire, seasonal beers Ⓗ
Handy for both Old Street and Pitfield Street, this small and very friendly pub has a split feel with ample seating at the front and a prominent darts area behind. Photos of landlord Dixie Dean's

days as a boxer adorn the walls together with plenty of horse racing pictures. Food is simple and the pub can get quite lively, but luckily the music and TV are not allowed to drown out the customers. Kent's Best alternates with seasonal ales. Outside seating is available.
❀⇌⊖(Old St)🚌♣

Wenlock Arms
26 Wenlock Road, N1 7TA
🕓 12-midnight (1am Thu-Sat)
☎ (020) 7608 3406 🌐 wenlock-arms.co.uk
Adnams Bitter; Harveys Sussex Best Bitter; guest beers Ⓗ
With a constantly-changing range of seven guest ales, including a mild, from across the country supporting one of the two regulars, a cider or perry and a selection of continental bottled beers, this free house is one of North London's premier real ale pubs. Four times local CAMRA Pub of the Year, it stands near the site of the former Wenlock Brewery and has a strong community focus, home to its own cricket team and regular jazz sessions. Snacks include the legendary salt beef sandwedges.
♨⇌⊖(Old St)🚌♣●

N1: Islington

Charles Lamb
16 Elia Street, N1 8DE
🕓 12 (4 Mon & Tue)-11 (midnight Thu-Sat); 12-10.30 Sun
☎ (020) 7837 5040 🌐 thecharleslambpub.com
Butcombe Bitter; Dark Star Hophead; guest beer Ⓗ
The building dates from 1839, when it contained three shops. Converted into a pub in the 1920s, this is a small, cosy free house in a residential area just south of the Regent's Canal. Food is distinctive but does not dominate. The pub supports local artists. There is a shove-ha'penny board, and boules is played in the street outside on Bastille Day. There are covered smokers' tables on the pavement. Cider is sold fresh in summer and mulled in winter.
Q❀◐⊖(Angel)🚌♣●⌐

Compton Arms
4 Compton Avenue, N1 2XD
🕓 12-11 (10.30 Sun)
☎ (020) 7359 6883
Greene King IPA, Abbot, seasonal beers; guest beer Ⓗ
Built in the country cottage style in the 1960s, the pub has exposed beams and bull's-eye glass in the windows. There is a small rear space with room for functions, which is a quieter place to eat. This is an Arsenal supporters' pub, with two large TVs tuned to sports, and it opens at 11am on weekend match days. There is a covered and heated patio at the rear where children are welcome until 8pm.
❀◐⇌⊖(Highbury & Islington)🚌⌐

N4: Harringay

Salisbury ★
1 Grand Parade, Green Lanes, N4 1JX
🕓 5-midnight (1am Thu; 2am Fri); 12-2am Sat; 12-11.30 Sun
☎ (020) 8800 9617
Fuller's Discovery, London Pride, ESB; guest beer Ⓗ
This CAMRA National Inventory, Grade II-listed pub was built in 1899 by JC Hill, who also designed the Queens Hotel in nearby Crouch End. A wealth of high Victorian features is evident: stained glass windows, tiled walls, floor mosaics and the ever popular skylights in the former saloon and billiards rooms. Run by Remarkable Restaurants, Fuller's beers are supplemented with occasional guests from micro-breweries and genuine Czech lagers. Excellent food is served and regular salsa, quiz and jazz nights are hosted.
◐⇌(Harringay Green Lanes)🚌

N6: Highgate

Gatehouse ✔
1 North Road, N6 4BD
🕓 9-midnight (12.30am Fri & Sat); 12-10.30 Sun
☎ (020) 8340 8054
Greene King Ruddles Best, Abbot; Marston's Pedigree; guest beers Ⓗ
Imposing Tudor-style Wetherspoon's pub at the heart of the village. A spacious bar and separate dining area lead to an enclosed garden, with ramped access for disabled users and heating provided. A former toll house, this is one of Highgate's oldest pubs and was once the court house for St Pancras and Hampstead boroughs, whose boundary it straddles. There is a thriving theatre upstairs and the actors often join the audience after the show. Q❀◐♿⊖🚌●⌐

Prince of Wales
53 Highgate High Street, N6 5JX
🕓 12-11 (midnight Fri & Sat)
☎ (020) 8340 0445
Butcombe Bitter; guest beers Ⓗ
Squeezed between the bustle of Highgate High Street and the calm of Pond Square, this S&N leased pub offers up to three guest beers and an interior relatively unchanged for years. It can get busy, particularly on Tuesday quiz night, perhaps because the quiz itself is one of the most testing in the capital. Thai food is served 12-3 and 6-10pm Monday-Friday, and 12-10pm Saturday. Sunday roasts are available 12-9pm. At the back is an outdoor drinking/smoking area. Q❀◐⊖🚌♣⌐

Red Lion & Sun
25 North Road, N6 4BE
🕓 12-midnight (2am Thu-Sat); 12-1am Sun
☎ (020) 8340 1780 🌐 theredlionandsun.com
Greene King IPA, Morland Original, Abbot; guest beer Ⓗ
Recessed from the roadside and fronted by a large, open patio, the interior has been opened out to create an L-shaped room, leading to a garden at the rear. Two bay windows at the front add character, as do candles, subtle lighting, mixed tables, chairs and sofas, a log fire in winter and wood panelling. Dogs and children are welcome until 8pm and there is wireless Internet access. Food from an imaginative menu is served until 10pm (9pm Sun). The guest beer changes every week. ♨❀◐♿⊖🚌⌐

N8: Crouch End

Harringay Arms
153 Crouch Hill, N8 9QH
🕓 12-11.30 (midnight Fri & Sat)
☎ (020) 8340 4243
Adnams Broadside; Caledonian Deuchars IPA; Courage Best Bitter; Wells Bombardier Ⓗ
Small, cosy, narrow Enterprise pub at the foot of Crouch Hill. Walls adorned with old photos and maps of the area during its growing years add to the quiet, friendly, conversational atmosphere,

undisturbed by a small-screen TV for sports events at one end. Three of the four listed beers are available at any time. A small rear yard caters for smokers. Darts is possible midway through the day and chess boards are available on request. Quiz night is Tuesday. ❀≠(Crouch Hill)🚌♣⁻

N8: Hornsey

Three Compasses ✔

62 High Street, N8 7NX

✪ 11-11 (midnight Fri & Sat); 12-11 Sun

☎ (020) 8340 2729

Caledonian Deuchars IPA; Fuller's London Pride; Taylor Landlord; guest beers Ⓗ

Deservedly popular, well-managed Punch pub in the middle of Hornsey village, catering for diners and large-screen sports fans as well as the real ale drinker. In recent times it has been declared a National Community Pub of the Year and CAMRA local branch Pub of the Season. Three changing guest beers from micros supplement the three regular ales. Food is available until 10pm Monday to Saturday, 9.30pm Sunday. Monday is quiz night. ♨◐◑♿≠🚌(144)♣⁻▯

N9: Lower Edmonton

Beehive 🏆

24 Little Bury Street, N9 9JZ

✪ 12-midnight (1am Fri & Sat); 12-11 Sun

☎ (020) 8360 4358

Draught Bass; Fuller's London Pride; Greene King IPA, Old Speckled Hen; guest beer Ⓗ

A one-bar Punch pub where the licensee has continued to make improvements to all aspects of the trade. Home-cooked meals with vegetarian options include specials of pie & mash Monday to Saturday, steak on Tuesday, fish Tuesday to Saturday and roast dinners until 6pm on Sunday. Live music is performed on Saturday evening. There is a heated, covered, outside smoking area. Local CAMRA Pub of the Year 2009. ♨❀◐◑🚌(329,W8)♣P⁻

N10: Muswell Hill

John Baird ✔

122 Fortis Green Road, N10 3HN

✪ 11-11 (midnight Fri & Sat); 12-10.30 Sun

☎ (020) 8444 8830 🌐 johnbaird-muswellhill.co.uk

Black Sheep Best Bitter; Wells Bombardier; Young's Special; guest beers Ⓗ

A busy Punch local in the heart of Muswell Hill built on a former bombsite, named after a pioneer of television and popular with sports fans, shoppers and cinema goers alike. The pub has wide-screen TV, a thriving Thai restaurant to the side and a secluded patio area to the rear which doubles as a heated smoking area in winter. Roasts are served all day Sunday. There is disabled access via the mews and rear patio. Three guest beers vary. Occasional beer festivals are hosted. ❀◐◑♿🚌(102,234)⁻

N12: North Finchley

Elephant Inn

283 Ballards Lane, N12 8NR

✪ 11-11 (midnight Fri & Sat); 12-10.30 Sun

☎ (020) 8343 6110

Fuller's London Pride, ESB, seasonal beer; guest beer Ⓗ

Comfortable three-bar Fuller's pub with a large front patio. There is a Thai restaurant upstairs where children are allowed until 8pm, and food is also available in the main bar. The service is friendly and efficient, with a landlady and staff who promote real ale. Theme, charity, quiz and poker nights are hosted, and occasional live music. ❀◐◑♿🚌♣⁻

N14: Southgate

New Crown ✔

80-84 Chase Side, N14 5PH

✪ 9-11.30 (12.30am Fri & Sat)

☎ (020) 8882 8758

Greene King Ruddles Best, Abbot; Marston's Pedigree; guest beers Ⓗ

With an ideal town-centre location, this Wetherspoon's pub is handily placed for shops, buses and tube. There are four rapidly changing guest beers always available and clips of past brews are on display above the bar. Occasional brewery beer festivals are held. Pictures and information about Southgate from days gone by decorate the walls. Though the pub is often busy, quieter alcoves may be available. ◐◑⊖🚌

N16: Stoke Newington

Daniel Defoe ✔

102 Stoke Newington Church Street, N16 0LA

✪ 12 (4 Mon-Fri, Oct-May)-midnight

☎ (020) 7254 2906 🌐 thedanieldefoe.com

Courage Directors; St Austell Tribute; Wells Bombardier; guest beer Ⓗ

A busy single-bar Victorian corner local with a reputation for convivial drinking and dining. The guest beer changes fortnightly and food is served from opening until 9.30pm. This Charles Wells pub has the opportunity to stay open late, beyond midnight closing, and frequently does. It offers an impressive list of malt whiskies, Wi-Fi access and a pleasant, walled garden. The name acknowledges the area's literary heritage. ❀◐◑≠🚌⁻

N18: Upper Edmonton

Gilpin's Bell ✔

50-54 Fore Street, N18 2SS

✪ 9-11.30 (12.30am Fri & Sat)

☎ (020) 8884 2744

Greene King IPA, Abbot; Marston's Pedigree; guest beers Ⓗ

John Gilpin was due to meet his family at the Bell Inn in Edmonton but the horse bolted and took him on to Ware – an incident immortalised in a poem by William Cowper. Nowadays it is worth getting off the bus to visit this oasis in a real ale desert – a spacious Wetherspoon's conversion with three separate areas. The busy main bar has Sky Sports, but the other two are quieter. The large back patio has partial cover and heaters. Itchen Valley beers are regular guests. ❀◐◑♿≠(White Hart Lane)🚌🍎P⁻

N21: Winchmore Hill

Dog & Duck

74 Hoppers Road, N21 3LH

✪ 12-11 (10.30 Sun)

☎ (020) 8886 1987 🌐 dogandduck.info
Greene King IPA; Taylor Landlord; Wadworth 6X; guest beer Ⓗ
Welcoming local with attractive etched glass in its front doors indicating previous public and saloon bars. Now open plan with a single bar, this small, characterful Enterprise pub has a loyal following and visitors are made very welcome by the friendly landlord and staff. Sporting events are shown on a large screen TV. Photographs are a reminder of how the pub looked half a century ago. A courtyard garden contains a covered and electrically heated area for smokers. ❀≋🚌(W9)⚐

Orange Tree
18 Highfield Road, N21 3HA
⏲ 12-midnight (1am Fri & Sat)
☎ (020) 8360 4853
Greene King XX Mild, IPA, Old Speckled Hen; guest beer Ⓗ
Traditional back-street Punch local with three distinctive drinking areas, one of which houses a pool table and dartboard. The large family-friendly garden has a children's play area and barbecues in the summer. A wide selection of home prepared food includes traditional roast Sunday lunches. Football and other sporting events are shown on large screen TVs. No admission after 11pm. Parking at the pub is limited but on-street parking is available. ❀◐≋🚌(329)♣P⚐

East Barnet

Prince of Wales ✔
2 Church Hill Road, EN4 8TB
⏲ 11-11; 12-midnight Fri & Sat; 12-11 Sun
☎ (020) 8440 5392
Adnams Bitter; Fuller's London Pride; guest beer Ⓗ
A popular and friendly M&B pub at the centre of East Barnet village, which aims to provide something for everyone. There are one or two guests, often from micros, and all beers are competitively priced. A wide choice of reasonably priced food is served until 8pm. Curry night is Wednesday. Local football teams meet after matches on Sundays. There are poker nights and a Sunday evening quiz. Disabled access is at the rear through the car park.
❀◐◑♿≋(Oakleigh Pk)🚌(184,307)P⚐

Enfield

King & Tinker
Whitewebbs Lane, EN2 9HJ (¾ mile W from A10/A1055 jct) TQ331998
⏲ 12-11 (10.30 Sun)
☎ (020) 8363 6411
Adnams Broadside; Fuller's London Pride; Greene King IPA; guest beer Ⓗ
A Punch pub on the edge of rural Enfield, close to Theobalds House which was one of King James's hunting lodges. He is the king who met the tinker – read the history in the foyer. Food is a varied, home-cooked menu. Very popular with walkers on White Webbs Country Park, and with riders: there is a hitching rail. The garden has a separate children's play area and a covered smoking area. A campsite within half a mile allows caravans. 🔥Q❀◐⛺🍎P⚐

Moon Under Water ✔
115-117 Chase Side, EN2 6NN
⏲ 9-11 (midnight Fri & Sat)
☎ (020) 8366 9855
Courage Best Bitter; Greene King Ruddles Best, Abbot; Marston's Pedigree; guest beers Ⓗ
This spacious Wetherspoon's pub was converted from a dairy over 20 years ago and was formerly a school. It has two main seating areas – one with open booth seating – a U-shaped bar and two banks of handpumps. A pleasant ambience attracts a regular clientele. Breakfasts are served until noon, meals until 10pm. Westons Old Rosie cider is served on gravity.
❀◐◑♿≋(Gordon Hill)🚌(191,W9)🍎P⚐

Old Wheatsheaf
3 Windmill Hill, EN2 6SE
⏲ 12-11.30 (12.30am Fri & Sat)
☎ (020) 8363 0516
Adnams Bitter, Broadside; Brains Reverend James; Greene King IPA; guest beer Ⓗ
A Punch two-bar local: TV screens in one, the other generally quieter. A keen landlord and friendly staff have led to an increased local interest in cask ales. There are award-winning floral displays outside in the warmer months and the pub has old frosted windows. Occasional quiz nights take place and board games are also popular. Outside there is a heated and covered smoking area.
❀≋(Enfield Chase)🚌♣P⚐

Wonder
1 Batley Road, EN2 0JG (near jct of Chase Side and Lancaster Road)
⏲ 11 (12 Sun)-11 (midnight Fri & Sat)
☎ (020) 8363 0202
McMullen AK, Cask Ale, Country Bitter, seasonal beer Ⓗ
Wonderful back street two-bar local with a regular clientele. The landlord and his wife have run this pub for over 15 years and it has the feel of a local from 30 or more years ago. Sing-along around the piano at weekends – watch out for the chap on spoons and the landlady on tea chest double bass or washboard. A local CAMRA Pub of the Year for three consecutive years, it is a football-free zone.
🔥Q❀🍺♿≋(Gordon Hill)🚌(191,W8)P⚐

High Barnet

Hadley Hotel
113 Hadley Road, EN5 5QN
⏲ 11-11; 12-10.30 Sun
☎ (020) 8449 0161
Fuller's London Pride; Hook Norton Old Hooky; Taylor Landlord; guest beer Ⓗ
Comfortable, open-plan free house with murals of the nearby Battle of Barnet on the walls. A modest lunchtime menu offers fresh haddock and chips on Friday but is otherwise renowned for salt beef sandwiches - people travel for miles for them! With a varied clientele of all ages, this family-run pub has a lovely warm welcome for visitors. Dogs are welcome but no children allowed.
❀🛏◐🚌(184)♣P⚐

Lord Nelson
14 West End Lane, EN5 2SA
⏲ 12-11 (midnight Fri & Sat); 12-10.30 Sun
☎ (020) 8449 7249 🌐 thelordnelsonph.co.uk
Wells Bombardier; Young's Bitter, Special, seasonal beers Ⓗ
A cosy, dog-friendly Young's pub just off Wood Street, with a loyal local clientele. It is welcoming, well kept and decorated with model ships and a

display of condiments. There is an extensive range of food available until 8.30pm, including specials. Quiz night is Thursday. Outside there are front and rear patios. ❀◑🚌♣

Olde Mitre ✔
58 High Street, EN5 5SJ
⏲ 12-11 (midnight Fri & Sat)
☎ (020) 8449 5701
Adnams Bitter; guest beers Ⓗ
There has been a pub on this site since 1553. The interior has extensive wood panels; the front area has wood flooring and basic seating and tables. The friendly licensee has taken advantage of Punch Taverns' guest beer list and has put the emphasis on conversation, not TV-based entertainment. The courtyard at the rear and side has tables and chairs for the warmer months. ❀◑♿⊖🚌♣⚐–

Olde Monken Holt ✔
193 High Street, EN5 5SU
⏲ 12-11 (midnight Thu & Sun; 12.45am Fri & Sat)
☎ (020) 8449 4280
Adnams guest beer; Courage Directors; Greene King IPA; Sharp's guest beer Ⓗ
Close to Hadley Green and named after a medieval monk's cell. Although it has a single bar, this Capital Pub Co pub is divided into three distinct areas: a wood-panelled front section with historic photos of Old Barnet, a central area for sports TV, and a raised rear space leading to a secluded garden. Entertainment includes a quiz on Thursday, DJ on Friday, band on Saturday and acoustic on Sunday evening. Food is good value (not available Mon and Sat eves). ❀◑🚌(84)⚐–

Sebright Arms
9 Alston Road, EN5 4ET
⏲ 12-11 (11.30 Sat); 12-10.30 Sun
☎ (020) 8449 6869
McMullen AK, Country Bitter, seasonal beer; guest beer Ⓗ
A two-bar pub in a residential area a short distance from Barnet High Street on a hail and ride bus route. One bar has TV, the other is a quiet haven – although there is a quiz every Wednesday. The CAMRA member licensee welcomes the local branch for meetings. Fish and chips are available early Friday evenings. There is a covered and heated area for smokers and a real fire in one bar. ♨Q❀🛏🚌(384)♣P⚐–

Ponders End

Picture Palace ✔
Howards Hall, Lincoln Road, EN3 4AQ (jct with Hertford Rd)
⏲ 9-11 (midnight Fri & Sat)
☎ (020) 8344 9690
Greene King Ruddles Best, Abbot; Marston's Pedigree; guest beers Ⓗ
Converted to a Wetherspoon's in 2001 from a derelict council community hall built in the 1920s that had originally been a small cinema, and is now listed. The tasteful decor commemorates its heritage with murals to cinema legends. The main area has some comfy sofas as well as tables and chairs, and there are two smaller, quieter sections. Here is a welcome oasis in an area with no other real ale pubs.
❀◑♿⇌(Ponders End/Southbury)🚌●P⚐–

NORTH-WEST LONDON

NW1: Euston

Bree Louise 🏆
69 Cobourg Street, NW1 2HH
⏲ 11.30 (12 Sat & Sun)-midnight
☎ (020) 7681 4930 🌐 thebreelouise.com
Harveys Sussex Best Bitter; Taylor Landlord Ⓖ**; guest beers** Ⓗ/Ⓖ
With a recently installed, cooled stillage behind the bar, the two regular beers are joined by up to another nine on gravity and five on handpump, one always a dark mild, plus a cider. Beers are sourced from all over the country from breweries of all sizes and regular beer festivals are held in this free-of-tie Enterprise leased pub. Food, majoring on home-made pies, is served from 12 to 9pm every day. CAMRA members presenting a membership card get a discount on food and 50p off every pint. ❀◑⇌⊖(Euston/Euston Sq)🚌●⚐–

Doric Arch
1 Eversholt Street, NW1 2DN
⏲ 12-11 (10.30 Sun)
☎ (020) 7383 3359
Fuller's Chiswick Bitter, Discovery, London Pride, ESB; Gale's HSB; Hop Back Summer Lightning; guest beers Ⓗ
Located east of the bus station and in front of the railway station, the pub's first floor, split-level single bar is reached by two entrances. Fuller's continues to promote a range of up to three guest beers plus its own seasonals as well as two to three Westons ciders. TV screens feature live sporting events. Food is served all day until 9pm during the week and 12-3pm on Saturday. There is an impressive display of railway artefacts from when it was the Head of Steam. ◑⇌⊖🚌●

NW1: St Pancras

Euston Flyer ✔
83-87 Euston Road, NW1 2RA
⏲ 10-11 Mon (midnight Tue-Wed; 1am Thu-Sat); 10-11.30 Sun
☎ (020) 7383 0856
Fuller's Discovery, London Pride, ESB, seasonal beers; Gale's HSB Ⓗ
Across the road from the British Library, this is a popular spot for office workers, commuters, sports fans and travellers using the St Pancras Eurostar terminal. A large open-plan Fuller's pub divided into different sections and levels, it can be boisterous in the evenings and during major football matches. Two large-screen TVs plus a smaller one are always on for sporting events, often showing different matches. Meals are served all day until 10pm. At times guest beers may be available. ◑⇌⊖🚌

NW2: Cricklewood

Beaten Docket ✔
50-56 Cricklewood Broadway, NW2 3ET
⏲ 9-11 (12.30am Fri & Sat)
☎ (020) 8450 2972
Courage Directors; Greene King Ruddles Best, Abbot; Marston's Pedigree; guest beer Ⓗ
Thanks to a long period under the same management, this typical Wetherspoon's conversion of retail premises is a local beacon for

real ale. A series of well-defined drinking areas disguises the pub's vastness. The name refers to a losing betting slip, often associated with horse racing which was a feature of this area in the late 19th century; prints and paraphernalia reinforce the theme. There are benches outside all year and a children's certificate. Q❀◐◑♿⇌🚌🚭

NW3: Hampstead

Duke of Hamilton

23-25 New End, NW3 1JD
⌚ 11-11; 12-11 Sun
☎ (020) 7794 0258
Fuller's London Pride, ESB; guest beers Ⓗ
Built in 1721 to celebrate a high profile figure during the English Civil War, this is a free house although Fuller's beers are prominent; guests usually come from Adnams and smaller breweries and the pub stages its own festivals. The cider is Westons Old Rosie. Popular with sports fans, the pub shows televised football and rugby and runs a cricket team – a bat signed by England's 1985 Ashes-winning team hangs in the bar. Three times local CAMRA Pub of the Year.
❀⇌(Hampstead Heath)⊖🚌♣🍎🚭

Holly Bush ✔

22 Holly Mount, NW3 6SG
⌚ 12-11 (10.30 Sun)
☎ (020) 7435 2892 🌐 hollybushpub.com
Adnams Broadside; Brakspear Bitter; Harveys Sussex Best Bitter; Hook Norton Old Hooky; guest beer Ⓗ
An attractive multi-roomed Grade II-listed building in a charming location, the Holly Bush started life as the stables of the artist George Romney's house. It has been a pub for 200 years and many original features are still evident. Traditional British food is served in this Punch pub and in the upstairs restaurant, which opens Tuesday to Sunday and is available for private hire. The licensee is Mexican, the pub quintessentially English. Well worth seeking out. 🔥❀◐◑⊖🚌♣🚭

Olde White Bear

1 Well Road, NW3 1LJ
⌚ 12 (11.30 Sat)-11 (11.30 Thu-Sat)
☎ (020) 7435 3758
Beer range varies Ⓗ
With three interconnected rooms full of old furniture and bric-a-brac, this Punch community pub sits in an historic area: Well Road takes its name from a tributary of the River Fleet and opposite is the former site of the New End Hospital, where Karl Marx died in 1883. More recently a popular haunt for local actors, it serves a constantly changing range of up to six beers, and good food every day 12-9pm. There are outdoor drinking areas both front and rear.
❀◐◑⇌(Hampstead Heath)⊖🚌♣🚭

Spaniards Inn ✔

Spaniards Road, NW3 7JJ
⌚ 11 (10 Sat & Sun)-11
☎ (020) 8731 6571
Adnams Bitter; Fuller's London Pride; Harveys Sussex Best Bitter; St Austell Tribute; guest beer Ⓗ
Few London pubs match the history of the Spaniards Inn – it dates back to 1585, with two stories of how it got its name – or its location among the acres of Hampstead Heath. Close to Kenwood House, this M&B pub is invariably packed in summer, but the range of beers draws the crowds all year round, as do regular beer festivals. Draught cider and perry are supplied by Westons. Food (12-10pm) is traditional British. Behind is a large, heated garden. 🔥Q❀◐◑🚌(210,H3)♣🍎P🚭

NW4: Hendon

Greyhound

52 Church End, NW4 4JT
⌚ 12-midnight (1am Fri & Sat); 12-11 Sun
☎ (020) 8457 9730
Courage Best Bitter; Wells Bombardier; Young's Bitter, Special; guest beers Ⓗ
This popular, friendly, three bar Young's local comes complete with the occasional eccentrics. The pub is next door to St Mary's Church and a museum of local history in the centre of Old Hendon village. The site has been licensed since 1675, the current building rebuilt in 1896. Apart from the well-kept beers – a tribute to the dedication of the landlord – there is a choice of 14 single malt whiskies and wholesome, home-prepared food. 🔥◐◑🚌

NW5: Dartmouth Park

Dartmouth Arms

35 York Rise, NW5 1SP
⌚ 11 (10 Sat)-11; 10-10.30 Sun
☎ (020) 7485 3267 🌐 dartmoutharms.co.uk
Adnams Bitter, Broadside; Caledonian Deuchars IPA; guest beers Ⓗ
A two-room Punch pub in a residential area which can get very noisy when Arsenal are playing, as fans flock to the TV screens. The pub's entertainment schedule includes many themed evenings: quizzes and comedy nights are staged on a rota basis. A small selection of new and secondhand books are for sale. There is also a barber's shop service on Thursday afternoon. The pub offers a wide range of bottled ciders and perries.
🔥Q🐄◐◑⇌(Gospel Oak)⊖(Tufnell Pk)🚌♣🍎🚭

Lord Palmerston

33 Dartmouth Park Hill, NW5 1HU
⌚ 12-11 (10.30 Sun)
☎ (020) 7485 1578
Adnams Bitter, Broadside; Sharp's Doom Bar; Taylor Landlord Ⓗ
Large Victorian corner pub owned by Geronimo Inns, named after the Prime Minister who served two terms between 1855 and 1865, though the interior is firmly 21st century after a 2006 refurbishment. As well as the main bar there are a dining room, conservatory and function room available for hire. Modern British food is served Monday to Friday lunchtimes and evenings and Sunday 12-9pm. Plentiful outdoor space includes pavement tables at the front and a garden behind. Quiz Wednesday, live music Sunday.
🔥❀◐◑⇌(Gospel Oak)⊖(Tufnell Pk)🚌(4)♣🚭

NW5: Kentish Town

Junction Tavern

101 Fortess Road, NW5 1AG
⌚ 12-11 (10.30 Sun)
☎ (020) 7485 9400 🌐 junctiontavern.co.uk
Caledonian Deuchars IPA; guest beers Ⓗ
With up to four guest beers, this well established Enterprise pub was local CAMRA Pub of the Year in

2008. Its beer festivals in May and August feature a wide range of cask beers. The side door leads into a wood-panelled and mirrored bar, all part of the classic Victorian design. Overlooking the main road, the restaurant serves gastro-style food. Behind the bar room is a beautiful conservatory and a flourishing garden with seating. Dogs are welcome. **Q✿◐◑♿⇌⊖🚌⚍**

Oxford
256 Kentish Town Road, NW5 2AA
⏲ 12-11.30 (midnight Fri & Sat)
☎ (020) 7485 3521
Beer range varies Ⓗ
A large, welcoming corner pub run by Realpubs Ltd. Few original period features remain; the interior has the stripped-back style of some gastro-pubs, including an open kitchen and a dining area, but it still retains the atmosphere of a proper pub. The selection of up to three real ales changes regularly. Upstairs is a function room used for live jazz and a weekly comedy night. Quiz night is Tuesday. **Q✿◐◑♿⇌⊖🚌⚍**

Pineapple
51 Leverton Street, NW5 2NX
⏲ 12-11 (10.30 Sun)
☎ (020) 7284 4631
Adnams Bitter; Draught Bass; guest beer Ⓗ
Grade II-listed and on CAMRA's London Regional Inventory, this free house was saved by local action after threats of closure and demolition, and is now expanded and improved under new management. The traditional front bar has original Victorian mirrors and carved woodwork. Side rooms have the feel of an old London club, one leading to a conservatory and garden. Thai food is served every day. Eccentrics, children and dogs welcome, if kept on a lead. Quiz night is Monday. Occasional beer festivals are hosted. **Q✿◐◑♿⇌⊖🚌⚍**

NW8: St John's Wood

Clifton
96 Clifton Hill, NW8 0JT
⏲ 12-11 (10.30 Sun)
☎ (020) 7372 3427 🌐 cliftonstjohnswood.com
Adnams Bitter; Fuller's London Pride; Sharp's Doom Bar; guest beer Ⓗ
A merchant's hunting lodge 200 years ago, then a licensed bar – reputedly King Edward VII granted this pub hotel status so that he could visit Lily Langtry here, as royalty could not visit pubs. Owned by Capital Pub Co, it serves good food using choice ingredients to match the beer. There is a traditional drinking area around the island bar plus separate conservatory and restaurant areas. A hidden gem in a quiet backwater, well worth the short walk from Kilburn High Road.
✿◐◑⇌(Kilburn High Rd)⊖(Kilburn Pk)🚌

Eastcote

Black Horse ✔
Black Horse Parade, Eastcote High Road, HA5 2EN
⏲ 12-11 (midnight Fri & Sat); 12-10.30 Sun
☎ (020) 8866 9106 🌐 theblackhorseeastcote.co.uk
Fuller's London Pride; guest beers Ⓗ
A friendly, comfortable Punch local set slightly back from Eastcote High Road. There are usually two cask beers available plus a rotating guest. Pub games include pool, darts, cribbage, draughts and chess. Major sporting events are shown here. Live music is a feature and Sunday afternoon sessions often get crowded. There is a terraced family garden behind and a decking patio area at the front. ✿◐♿🚌(282,H13)♣P⚍

Case is Altered
Eastcote High Road, HA5 2EW
⏲ 11-11
☎ (020) 8866 0476 🌐 caseisalteredpinner.co.uk
Adnams Bitter; Sharp's Doom Bar; Young's Special Ⓗ
A 17th-century pub set in the attractive village of Old Eastcote next to the cricket pitch, acquired from Punch (Spirit) by the McManus Pub Co. Inside, there is one bar with three seating areas. The barn to the back is a recent refurbishment and provides extra seating. An interesting array of photos on the walls depicts local life in the early 20th century. There is a large beer garden to the front.
♨✿🛏◐◑♿🚌(282,H13)P⚍

Harefield

Harefield
41 High Street, UB9 6BY
⏲ 12-11; 11-10.30 Sun
☎ (01895) 820003
Taylor Landlord; guest beers Ⓗ
This free house, which was given its current name in 2007 after a complete refurbishment, prides itself on the quality of its real ale and its food. The two guest beers, which come from numerous breweries, always include at least one session beer. All the meals are freshly prepared using locally produced ingredients. The real ales are reduced in price all day on Wednesday. There are quizzes on the first and third Thursdays of each month. ♨✿◐◑♿🚌(331,U9)P

Harrow

Moon on the Hill ✔
373-375 Station Road, HA1 2AW
⏲ 9-midnight (12.30am Fri & Sat)
☎ (020) 8863 3670
Courage Best Bitter; Greene King Abbot; Marston's Pedigree; guest beers Ⓗ
Small, busy Wetherspoon's pub located close to Harrow-on-the-Hill station and served by numerous bus routes. It is popular with price-conscious regulars, office workers and students from the nearby University of Westminster. The usual range of meals is served all day. The pub gets extremely busy when there are sporting events on at the nearby Wembley stadium and plastic glasses may be used on these occasions.
Q◐◑⇌⊖(Harrow-on-the-Hill)🚌

Harrow Weald

Case is Altered
Old Redding, HA3 6SE
⏲ 11-11 (10.30 Sun)
☎ (020) 8954 1002 🌐 morethanjustapub.co.uk/thecaseisaltered/
Beer range varies Ⓗ
A comfortable, much-extended country pub franchised from M&B that now concentrates mainly on dining. Three constantly changing guest beers make this a worthwhile stop for the ale connoisseur. The view from the large garden over to Harrow makes it a very popular summer

watering hole. Parking is available 20 metres to the west of the pub. Children are most welcome; the garden sports a play area, perfect for worn out parents. Q❀◑♿🚌(258)

Harrow-on-the-Hill

Castle ★ ✔

30 West Street, HA1 3EF
✪ 12-11 (midnight Fri-Sun)
☎ (020) 8422 3155
Fuller's Discovery, London Pride, ESB, seasonal beers; Gale's HSB Ⓗ
A welcome return to the Guide for this Fuller's house in the heart of Harrow-on-the-Hill, where the friendly welcome is enhanced in winter months by three real coal fires. A secluded beer garden is popular during warmer times of the year. The pub was built in 1901, is Grade II-listed and is in CAMRA's National Inventory. Traditional and popular pub fare is served until 9pm every day. ♨Q❀◑🚌(258,H17)⚽

Rayners Lane

Village Inn ✔

402-408 Rayners Lane, Pinner, HA5 5DY
✪ 9-midnight (12.30am Fri & Sat); 9-11 Sun
☎ (020) 8868 8551
Greene King Ruddles Best, Abbot; Marston's Pedigree; guest beers Ⓗ
Near the Underground and well served by buses, this L-shaped Wetherspoon's pub can get very busy at weekends. The walls are adorned with pictures mainly relating to the development of the area in the 1930s; until then Rayners Lane, like most of Metroland, was mainly fields. There is a pleasant, paved and heated garden to rear and a small patio at the front. Weston's Old Rosie alternates with Weston's Organic Vintage cider. Q❀◑♿⊖🚌●⚽

Ruislip Common

Woodman

Breakspear Road, HA4 7SE
✪ 11-midnight (1am Fri & Sat); 12-midnight
☎ (01895) 635763
Courage Best Bitter; Sharp's Eden Pure Ale; guest beer Ⓗ
A clean and comfortable Enterprise local set on the northern outskirts of Ruislip close to Ruislip Lido and woods, opposite Hillingdon Borough Football Club. The lounge bar has no fruit machines or electronic music although the TV may be turned on for rugby matches. Note the selection of different bottled beers on display above the bar. There is also a selection of single malt whiskies. Q❀◐⊟♿🚌(331)♣P⚽

Ruislip Manor

JJ Moons ✔

12 Victoria Road, HA4 0AA
✪ 9-midnight (1am Fri & Sat)
☎ (01895) 622373
Courage Directors; Fuller's London Pride; Greene King Ruddles Best, Abbot; Marston's Pedigree; guest beers Ⓗ
A large Wetherspoon's conversion conveniently located opposite Ruislip Manor tube station, popular and often very busy in the evenings and at weekends. Food and beer are good value, with the usual promotions. At the rear is an elevated section leading to a small garden patio, while the front now sports a pleasant alfresco area. Three guest ales are available, usually including one from Twickenham, plus Westons Old Rosie and Organic Vintage ciders. Q🐴❀◑♿⊖🚌(114,H13)●⚽

Stanmore

Man in the Moon ✔

1 Buckingham Parade, The Broadway, HA7 4EB
✪ 9-11 (1am Fri & Sat)
☎ (020) 8954 6119
Greene King Ruddles Best, Abbot; Marston's Pedigree; guest beers Ⓗ
A smaller Wetherspoon's shop conversion with pictures and stories from Stanmore's past adorning the walls. Three guest ales are usually offered, one normally from Rebellion. Besides the chain's twice yearly festivals, the pub also has its own occasional festivals, again with more guest ales, in conjunction with other local Wetherspoon pubs. Two TV screens usually show Sky Sports news with the sound turned off (except for major matches). Q◑⊖🚌

SOUTH-EAST LONDON

SE1: Borough

Market Porter

9 Stoney Street, SE1 9AA
✪ 6-8.30am, 11-11; 12-11 Sat; 12-10.30 Sun
☎ (020) 7407 2495 🌐 markettaverns.co.uk/The-Market-Porter
Harveys Sussex Best Bitter; guest beers Ⓗ
This Market Taverns pub is a classic boozer, with plenty of signage outside, ground floor pilasters and woodwork painted dark green, and dimpled, leaded windows creating interior cosiness. Inside is functional, unpretentious and always busy. The bar winds round into an extended rear seating area. This pub always boasts an unrivalled range of real ales and has won several CAMRA awards. ◑⇌⊖(London Bridge)●

Rake

14 Winchester Walk, SE1 9AG
✪ 11 (12 Sat)-11; 12-10.30 Sun
☎ (020) 7407 0557
Beer range varies Ⓗ
Originally an 1840s pub called the Old King's Head, this small and very popular independent free house opened in August 2006 after many years as a greasy spoon cafe. Sometimes very busy, even in the spacious courtyard outside, it always has two ever-changing beers from British micro-breweries. It was voted Best Bar in 2007 by readers of Time Out magazine. ❀◑♿⇌⊖(London Bridge)

Royal Oak ✔

44 Tabard Street, SE1 4JU
✪ 11 (12 Sat)-11; 12-6 Sun
☎ (020) 7357 7173
Harveys Sussex XX Mild, Pale, Sussex Best Bitter, seasonal beers Ⓗ
Very traditional local, with two bars done out in Victorian style including decorative glass and carved woodwork, with subdued corner lighting creating a cosy atmosphere which thankfully is not marred by noisy music or fruit machines. A rarity in London, this is owned by Harveys, and many interesting photos of the brewery hang on the

walls. Draught cider is available, excellent food is offered and there is a handy meeting room upstairs. ⛫Q◐◑⇌(London Bridge)⊖🚌🍎

SE1: London Bridge

Barrowboy & Banker ✔

6-8 Borough High Street, SE1 9QQ

⌚ 11-11; 12-4 Sat; closed Sun

☎ (020) 7403 5415

Fuller's Chiswick Bitter, Discovery, London Pride, ESB, seasonal beer Ⓗ

Situated right at the southern tip of London Bridge, this magnificent 1996 conversion by Fuller's of an old bank has a long, curving bar counter, a grand staircase sweeping up to a mezzanine gallery, high windows and giant murals. Lots of mock-old woodwork includes many small screens that add some cosiness. It can get very busy with city workers and those on their way to nearby London Bridge Station. Q◐◑⇌⊖🚌

Horniman at Hay's ✔

Unit 26, Hay's Galleria, Counter Street, SE1 2HD

⌚ 11-11 (midnight Thu-Sat); 12-10.30 Sun

☎ (020) 7407 1991

Fuller's London Pride; Jennings Cumberland Ale; Sharp's Doom Bar; Taylor Landlord; guest beers Ⓗ

Occupying the former site of a tea warehouse owned by the eponymous Mr Horniman, this 1987 M&B (Nicholson's) pub is a feast of recreated Victoriana with its dark, carved mahogany woodwork, etched mirrors, mosaic tiling on the floor and grand chandeliers hanging from the ornately corniced ceiling. A grand staircase with wrought iron bannisters leads up to a gallery bar looking down on this magnificence. The wonderful riverside location and good range of ales are the icing on the cake. ◐◑⇌⊖🚌⚐

Horseshoe Inn

26 Melior Street, SE1 3QP

⌚ 11-midnight; 12-10.30 Sun

☎ (020) 7403 6364 🌐 horseshoepubse1.co.uk

Brakspear Bitter; Fuller's London Pride; guest beer Ⓗ

Tucked away, a stone's throw from London Bridge Station and Guy's Hospital, this free house dates from 1897 but there has been an inn on the site for much longer; it was a stopping-off point from the south to London. The pub plays host to a small Mongolian community with at least one Mongolian dish on the menu at any time. As well as a roof garden, from where London Bridge Station platforms are visible, an upstairs conference/function room is available for hire. ❀◐◑⇌⊖🚌⚐

SE1: Southwark

Mad Hatter ✔

3-7 Stamford Street, SE1 9NY

⌚ 11-11; 12-10.30 Sun

☎ (020) 7401 9222 🌐 madhatterhotel.com

Fuller's Chiswick Bitter, Discovery, London Pride, ESB, seasonal beer Ⓗ

This was originally an old Victorian hat factory, converted in 1998 by Fuller's into an Ale and Pie House and a hotel with 24 rooms. The interior is enjoyably traditional but fully air-conditioned, with comfortable seating throughout including sofas in the back room. Staff are friendly and large-screen TVs are used on football nights. 🛏◐◑♿⇌(Blackfriars)⊖🚌

SE1: Tower Bridge

Bridge House ✔

218 Tower Bridge Road, SE1 2UP

⌚ 12-11 (midnight Fri & Sat)

☎ (020) 7407 5818

Adnams Bitter, Explorer, Broadside; guest beer Ⓗ

More bar and restaurant than pub, but one of very few Adnams tied houses in London, situated in a terrace of old shops immediately south of Tower Bridge. Interior walls are brightly painted, furniture is modern and wine glasses are already set out on tables: this is not a place for dyed-in-the-wool traditionalists. The only link to its former pub days is the retention of high stools at the bar. Two more modern bars occupy the cellar and the first floor. ◐◑♿⇌(London Bridge)⊖(Tower Hill/London Bridge)🚌

SE1: Waterloo

Hole in the Wall

5 Mepham Street, SE1 8SQ

⌚ 11-11 (10.30 Sun)

☎ (020) 7928 6196

Adnams Bitter; Hogs Back TEA; Purity Pure Gold; Sharp's Doom Bar; Young's Bitter Ⓗ

Tucked under the railway arches, this two-bar free house is very popular with locals and commuters alike and something of an institution, having served an impressive range of real ales for longer than most people can remember. It gets very busy most nights, and also shows sporting events. The word 'unpretentious' was never more apt: this is a terrific basic boozer that cheerfully ignores modern trends. ❀◐◑⊟♿⇌⊖🚌

SE3: Blackheath

Princess of Wales ✔

1a Montpelier Row, SE3 0RL

⌚ 12-11 (10.30 Sun)

☎ (020) 8852 5784 🌐 princessofwalespub.co.uk

Adnams Broadside; Brains SA; Caledonian Deuchars IPA; Fuller's London Pride Ⓗ

A listed building, this large, attractive Georgian M&B pub is just out of the centre of Blackheath Village. It offers a good range of well kept real ales and has friendly and helpful staff as well as serving decent food. It can be a little crowded at the busiest times, but has the advantage of facing on to Blackheath Common, providing patrons with space to spill out on sunny days. ❀◐◑♿⇌🚌P⚐

SE5: Camberwell

Bear

296a Camberwell New Road, SE5 0RP

⌚ 4 (12 Sat)-11 (midnight Fri); closed Mon; 12-10.30 Sun

☎ (020) 7274 7037 🌐 thebear-freehouse.co.uk

Beer range varies Ⓗ

Upmarket free house popular with a young clientele who appreciate three ever-changing beers in an area that used to be a real ale desert. Its decor combines traditional style and French bistro influences. Meals are British/French fusion, cooked by the head chef who is also the owner. Wednesday is Pie and Ale night. The upstairs function room, available for hire, hosts art and short film exhibitions by artists from a nearby college. 🐎◐◑🚌🗑

Hermit's Cave
28 Camberwell Church Street, SE5 8QU
11-midnight (2am Fri & Sat); 12-midnight Sun
(020) 7703 3188
Adnams Broadside; Gravesend Shrimpers Bitter; guest beer H
Lively, down to earth Enterprise boozer with a traditional look, complete with frosted glass and shining brass (a rarity for the area) and a landlord who is always present and knowledgeable about the excellent beers and ciders on offer. With a good mix of locals and students from the nearby art college, it can get very busy at weekends.
(Denmark Hill)

SE5: Denmark Hill

Fox on the Hill
149 Denmark Hill, SE5 8EH
9-midnight (12.30am Fri & Sat)
(020) 7738 4756
Courage Best Bitter; Greene King Ruddles Best, Abbot; Marston's Pedigree; guest beers H
Large Wetherspoon's pub offering two family areas, one available for private hire, and many screened booths. Outside is a large garden with playground – separate tables at the front are convenient for smokers – and there is another green area beyond the car park. John Ruskin and other local notables are remembered in wall displays. There are ever-changing guest ales and seasonal beers and a twice-yearly beer festival. Students and hospital workers receive 20% food discount. QP

SE5: East Dulwich

Hoopers
28 Ivanhoe Road, SE5 8DH
5.30-11; 5-midnight Fri; 12-midnight Sat; 12-11 Sun
(020) 7733 4797 hoopersbar.co.uk
Beer range varies H
Tucked away in back streets off Dog Kennel Hill, this independent free house is worth seeking out for micro-brewery ales from across the country. The bottled range includes nearly 40 German and Belgian beers as well as Polish porter. Frequent live music nights and beer festivals are held and free Wi-Fi is available. A snug bar is handy for meetings and parties. Quiz night is Thursday and major sports events are shown. En-suite accommodation is now available.
(Denmark Hill/E Dulwich)(P13)

SE6: Catford

Catford Ram
9 Winslade Way, SE6 4JU
11-11 (midnight Fri & Sat); 12-10.30 Sun
(020) 8690 6206
Wells Bombardier; Young's Bitter, Special H
Behind the Broadway Theatre, at an entrance to the Catford Centre, this Young's pub was purpose-built in the 1970s. The beers are kept not down in a cellar but in a room above and are carefully delivered through special gravity-controlled pumps to prevent flooding when a pint is poured. There is easy access to this large, fully carpeted, traditional pub and the open-plan interior allows space for quizzes, televised sports and weekend entertainment.
(Catford/Catford Bridge)

SE8: Deptford

Dog & Bell
116 Prince Street, SE8 3JD
12-11.30
(020) 8692 5664 thedogandbell.com
Fuller's London Pride, seasonal beers; guest beers H
A former CAMRA Greater London Pub of the Year, this popular, moderately-sized Victorian back-street free house has survived the closure of the wharves and dockyard it was built to serve. It has three guest ales, plus seasonals from Fuller's, and an impressive range of foreign bottled beers. Cuisine is uncomplicated and matches the traditional pub atmosphere. It boasts the rarity of a bar billiard table and has a walled back yard for outdoor drinking. Q

SE9: Eltham

Park Tavern
45 Passey Place, SE9 5DA
11-11 (midnight Fri & Sat); 12-8 (11 Apr to Sep) Sun
(020) 8850 8919
Harveys Sussex Best Bitter; St Austell Tribute; Taylor Landlord; guest beers H
Good-looking Victorian Enterprise pub with tiled Truman brewery signage to the front and side. Inside is a complete transformation: the proprietors' elegant refurbishment with beautiful lamps, chandeliers and drapes creating a French ambience. A real log fire and vases of fresh flowers adorn an immaculately kept bar that stocks a great range of ales, whiskies and wines. Lunches, morning coffee and pastries, afternoon tea and cakes are available. Outside is a rear garden and seating to the front and side. Q

SE10: Greenwich

Richard I (Tolly's)
52-54 Royal Hill, SE10 8RT
11-11; 12-10.30 Sun
(020) 8692 2996
Wells Bombardier; Young's Bitter, Special; guest beer H
Warm and welcoming Young's pub. Split into a saloon and a public bar, it boasts a well kept beer garden and a tremendous menu. 'Tolly's' was once run by the erstwhile Tolly Cobbold brewery of Ipswich. It was refurbished in 2008, giving it a modern face lift without losing its unpretentious, quiet atmosphere.
Q(Greenwich DLR)

SE13: Lee

Dacre Arms
11 Kingswood Place, SE13 5BU
12-11 (10.30 Sun)
(020) 8852 6779
Courage Best Bitter; Greene King IPA; Harveys Sussex Best Bitter; Taylor Landlord H
This delightful, quiet back-street Enterprise pub is small and cosy, filled with charming odds and ends. The licensee is proud of his well kept ales; the Landlord alone is worth visiting for. On occasion, tasty rolls are given out to customers free. This little pub has some unique features, including a dog that greets patrons when they arrive and also bids them farewell.
Q(Blackheath)

SE15: Nunhead

Old Nun's Head
15 Nunhead Green, SE15 3QQ
⏲ 12-midnight (1am Fri & Sat); 12-11.30 Sun
☎ (020) 7639 4007 🌐 oldnunshead.com
Beer range varies Ⓗ
This timber-framed pub, built in 1934 and overlooking Nunhead Green, was reopened in 2006 and leased from Punch by the people who run the Gowlett. Its name derives from the site, a former nunnery. Four guest beers are served, always including a session beer. Food is top quality but if you just want to come for a drink you will be made very welcome. The interior has pleasant wood panelling, with a function room upstairs available for hire. ♨❀◐◑♿⇌🚌(78,P12)⚡

SE15: Peckham

Gowlett
62 Gowlett Road, SE15 4HY
⏲ 12-midnight (1am Fri & Sat); 12-11.30 Sun
☎ (020) 7635 7048 🌐 thegowlett.com
Beer range varies Ⓗ
Popular with people of all ages, and their dogs, this Punch-leased pub was once described as 'the jewel in Peckham's crown' and remains so. Four rotating guest beers are available. Excellent stone-baked pizzas are cooked on the premises lunchtimes and evenings in the week and all day at weekends. Quiz night is Monday, there is a pool tournament on Tuesday and a DJ on Sunday. Free Wi-Fi and newspapers are available. The enclosed, sunny back patio is a delight.
❀◐◑⇌(East Dulwich/Peckham Rye)🚌⚡

SE20: Penge

Moon & Stars ✔
164-166 High Street, SE20 7QS
⏲ 9-11 (10.30 Sun)
☎ (020) 8776 5680
Courage Directors; Greene King Abbot; Marston's Pedigree; Ringwood Fortyniner; guest beers Ⓗ
This Wetherspoon's pub greets you with an impressive statue of a 'Wizard of Oz' lion, a remnant of the Odeon cinema that once stood on the site. The split-level interior has wood panelling and private booths along the sides, with photos of old Penge lining the walls. It is hugely popular for its choices of beer and food, served by friendly staff. A chalkboard lists ales that will be available soon. Behind is a large outdoor seating area.
Q❀◐◑♿⇌(Kent House)⊖(Beckenham Rd Tramlink)🚌🍎P⚡

SE21: Dulwich

Crown & Greyhound ✔
73 Dulwich Village, SE21 7BJ
⏲ 11-11 (midnight Thu-Sat); 11-10.30 Sun
☎ (020) 8299 4976 🌐 thecrownandgreyhound.co.uk
Fuller's London Pride; Greene King Old Speckled Hen; Harveys Sussex Best Bitter; Young's Bitter Ⓗ
Built around 1900 but extensively refurbished since then, this M&B pub remains one of the loveliest Victorian pubs in south London, with many separate areas inside, a large room upstairs for private functions, a split-level garden and a conservatory. Families are welcome in some areas. A welcome pint in a friendly atmosphere, a short walk from the Dulwich Picture Gallery.
♨Q❀◐◑⇌(North Dulwich)🚌(P4)♣

SE22: East Dulwich

Herne Tavern
2 Forest Hill Road, SE22 0RR
⏲ 12-11 (1am Sat)
☎ (020) 8299 9521 🌐 theherne.net
Taylor Landlord; St Austell Tribute; guest beers Ⓗ
The preservation of features from the inter-war refit earns this Punch pub a place in the London Inventory of historic pub interiors. The left hand, former public bar is reserved for diners while the former saloon bar has a more informal atmosphere enjoyed by families in daytime and locals in the evening. Thursday is rock soul night and Sunday is quiz night. A conservatory at the back leads out to a large garden with a children's play area.
♨❀◐◑🀫🚌(63,363)

SE23: Forest Hill

Blythe Hill Tavern
319 Stanstead Road, SE23 1JB
⏲ 11-midnight
☎ (020) 8690 5176
Courage Best Bitter; Fuller's London Pride; Westerham Black Eagle; guest beers Ⓗ
Local CAMRA Pub of the Year 2008, at the foot of beautiful Blythe Hill which boasts wonderful London views, this is a three-bar, traditional wood-panelled Enterprise boozer manned the old way, by friendly staff in smart attire. The banter here is second to none, especially on Thursday evening – Irish music night. The beer is kept in tip-top condition at all times and the old tiled hearth makes a great centrepiece.
Q❀🀫⇌(Catford/Catford Bridge)🚌(171,185)♣P⚡

Capitol ✔
11-21 London Road, SE23 3TW
⏲ 9-midnight (1am Fri & Sat)
☎ (020) 8291 8920
Greene King Ruddles Best, Abbot; Marston's Pedigree; guest beers Ⓗ
Much credit goes to Wetherspoon for restoring this 1929 cinema to its original grandeur, rather than demolishing it and replacing it with a bland modern development. Layout and decor of the split-level interior are unique and spacious, with the former ticket office now serving as a small coffee bar. Although largely open plan, there are a few cosy corners to be found. Ask about the occasional guided tours of the circle and projectionist's booth. ❀◐◑♿⇌🚌⚡

SE24: Herne Hill

Florence
133 Dulwich Road, SE24 0NG
⏲ 12 (11 Sat)-midnight (1am Fri & Sat); 11-midnight
☎ (020) 7326 4987 🌐 capitalpubcompany.com/the-florence/
Adnams Broadside; Florence Bonobo, Weasel; guest beer Ⓗ
Attractively refurbished Capital Pub Co gastropub where Weasel and Bonobo are brewed on the premises. It can be especially busy on Sundays when booking for lunch is recommended. Families are welcome until 7pm in designated areas and

there is smoking provision in the back garden and at tables out front. Exposed brickwork is interleaved with modern wall surroundings, with tables well spaced on wooden floors.
Q

Prince Regent

69 Dulwich Road, SE24 0NJ
12-11 (midnight Thu-Sat); 12-10.30 Sun
(020) 7274 1567 theprinceregent.co.uk
Adnams Broadside; Black Sheep Bitter; Brains Reverend James; guest beers H
Substantial Victorian corner pub overlooking Brockwell Park, with an ornate exterior boasting a life-size statue of the Prince Regent himself. Inside, some modern refurbishment took place four years ago, but impressive full-height wood-and-glass screens remain, creating two separate rooms. The upstairs bar is available for hire. With four real ales at any time, good food and occasional beer festivals, the current Punch landlord has established an attractive, family-friendly destination, and a very busy place at weekends.

SE26: Sydenham

Dolphin

121 Sydenham Road, SE26 5HB
12-midnight (11 Mon); 12-10.30 Sun
(020) 8778 8101 thedolphinsydenham.com
Adnams Broadside; Fuller's London Pride; Taylor Landlord H
There has been a pub on this site for more than 250 years. Rebuilt by Courage in 'brewers' Tudor' style in the 1930s and now an Enterprise pub, it is airy, open plan and family friendly. The wood-panelled walls display work by local artists. The spacious, designed garden can accommodate at least 80 drinkers and diners in summer and provides the backdrop for live theatre and the occasional hog roast. P

Windmill

125-131 Kirkdale, SE26 4QJ
10-midnight; 12-10.30 Sun
(020) 8291 9281 windmillsydenham.co.uk
Courage Best Bitter; guest beers H
Once a Wetherspoon's pub, newly built on the site of a furniture store, this is now an independent free house. A first-floor 'cellar' is just a part of the quirky design. Tribute artists perform on Saturday night – anything from Rat Pack crooners to Amy Winehouse. Friday is curry night. Regular customers get to nominate the three guest beers. This pub offers all round good value, particularly Sunday lunch.

SE27: West Norwood

Hope

49 Norwood High Street, SE27 9JS
11-11.30 (midnight Fri & Sat); 12-11 Sun
(020) 8670 2035
Young's Bitter, Special, seasonal beer H
A warm, friendly and welcoming pub dating from 1850, this unpretentious Young's boozer on a corner in the West Norwood one-way system is just how a small community local should be. The cosy, U-shaped bar has small round drinking tables with stools and wall-fitted bench seating, and a real fire to entice you on a cold day. Photographs on the walls reflect the diverse sporting and social interests of the area over the years; the South London Theatre is nearby.

Addiscombe

Claret Free House

5A Bingham Corner, Lower Addiscombe Road, CR0 7AA
11.30-11 (11.30 Thu; 11.45 Fri); 12-11 Sun
(020) 8656 7452
Palmer IPA; guest beers H
Just metres from tram and bus stops, this true free house chalks up its 22nd consecutive appearance in this Guide. Over the years it has dispensed three-quarters of a million pints of Palmer's IPA, its one regular beer. Five more handpumps provide an ever-changing range of well-kept beer – mainly from southern breweries, with strong representation from micros. A beer menu lists up to 18 forthcoming ales, and real ciders are always stocked. Conversation dominates, and the TVs cover sporting events.

Cricketers

47 Shirley Road, CR0 7ER
12-11 (10.30 Sun)
(020) 8655 3507
Dark Star Hophead; Harveys Sussex Best Bitter; guest beers H
Robust, friendly Enterprise local with a mock-Tudor exterior and a large collection of pump clips on the walls. The keen landlord promotes brewery nights and runs mini beer festivals when the six handpumps are supplemented by additional beers on gravity. Guest beers are often from micro-breweries. The pub can get very crowded when major sports events are shown on TV. The large garden has a marquee for smokers. Food is available until 7pm (not Sun). Local CAMRA Pub of the Year in 2007.
(Addiscombe/Blackhorse Lane Tramlink) (130,367)P

Beckenham

Jolly Woodman

9 Chancery Lane, BR3 6NR
12 (4 Mon)-11 (midnight Fri & Sat); 12-11 Sun
(020) 8663 1031
Adnams Bitter; Harveys Sussex Best Bitter; Taylor Landlord; Young's Bitter H**; guest beers** H/G
This little, traditional, locally-listed Enterprise pub can be found in a pretty back-street conservation area. A friendly local serving a regular clientele, it has one bar with two areas, timber-panelled walls, beamed ceilings and leaded windows. Secondhand books are for sale around the cosy fireplace. Home-cooked lunches are available weekdays. There is pleasant outside seating at the front and side, with hanging baskets, and a rear patio.
Q(Beckenham Jct)(Beckenham Jct Tramlink)(227,367)

Oakhill

90 Bromley Road, BR3 5NP
10-11 (midnight Fri & Sat); 12-11 Sun
(020) 8650 1279
Courage Best Bitter; St Austell Tribute; Westerham 1965 H
Popular, spacious Faucet Inns pub. Timber and stone effect flooring covers the two modern public

bar areas, with traditional and leather sofa seating, and there is a separate, quiet, carpeted lounge bar. Period features are half-timbered panelling and Victorian fireplaces with gas fires. Local artists' work is displayed and for sale. A large garden is behind and outdoor seating in front. Meals served lunchtimes and evenings include stonebaked pizzas. Q❀◑⊟⇌🚌(227,367)♣P⍀

Bexley

Black Horse

63 Albert Road, DA5 1NJ

⏲ 12-11 (midnight Fri; 11.30 Sat)

☎ (01322) 523371

Courage Best Bitter; guest beers Ⓗ

Four bus routes stop within five minutes' walk of this friendly back-street Enterprise local which offers good-value lunches on weekdays. The open-plan bar is split into two: to the left is an open space with a dartboard while to the right is a smaller, more intimate area. The pub supports a local golf society. The publican aims to put on a different beer every time one of his two guest ales runs out. ❀◐⇌🚌♣⍀

Old Wick

9 Vicarage Road, DA5 2AL

⏲ 12-12.30am

☎ (01322) 524185

Shepherd Neame Canterbury Jack, Master Brew Bitter, Spitfire, seasonal beers; guest beers Ⓗ

This excellent pub on the road from Bexley to Dartford Heath changed its name from the Rising Sun in 1996. The welcoming, cosy interior is enhanced by subdued lighting and friendly staff who make everyone feel welcome. Shepherd Neame porter is served, along with other seasonal beers. Food is served lunchtimes and evenings on weekdays, plus Sunday lunch. Accommodation and on-site camping are available.
⛰❀🛏◑⇌🚌(492,B15)♣P⍀

Bexleyheath

Furze Wren ✔

6 Market Place, DA6 7DY

⏲ 9-11.30 (midnight Thu-Sat)

☎ (020) 8298 2590

Courage Best Bitter; Greene King Abbot; Marston's Pedigree; Shepherd Neame Spitfire; guest beers Ⓗ

This new-build Wetherspoon's pub opened in 2002 as a Lloyds No 1 before becoming the Furze Wren (Dartford Warbler) in 2007. Its location in the heart of the shopping centre ensures the pub has a broad clientele. Everything is on the ground floor, including the award-winning toilets. This is a great place to sit and watch people and buses go by.
◑♿🚌🍎

Robin Hood & Little John 🏆

78 Lion Road, DA6 8PF

⏲ 11-3, 5.30 (7 Sat)-11; 12-4, 7-10.30 Sun

☎ (020) 8303 1128

Adnams Bitter, Broadside; Brains Rev James; Brakspear Bitter; Fuller's London Pride; Harveys Sussex Best Bitter; guest beers Ⓗ

Dating from the 1830s, this delightful little back-street Enterprise pub is well worth a visit. Eight real ales include guest beers from small, independent breweries. It has a well-deserved reputation for its home-cooked food at lunchtimes (not Sun), with themed specials and regular Italian dishes. Dining tables are made from old Singer sewing machines. Voted local CAMRA Pub of the Year 2000-2009 and London winner three times. Over 21s only.
❀◐🚌(B13)

Bromley

Bitter End Off Licence

139 Masons Hill, BR2 9HW

⏲ 12 (11 Sat)-9; 12-2, 7-9 Sun

☎ (020) 8466 6083 🌐 thebitterend.biz

Beer range varies Ⓖ

This off-licence, selling a constantly-changing range of gravity-dispensed real ale by the pint at significantly less than pub prices, is a local treasure. Larger volumes, from minipins to firkins, of over 500 beers can be ordered and delivered, as can real cider. There is also an impressive range of bottled beers and ciders on offer. The website reference to this 'offy' being a 'beer festival in a shop' is an apt description. ⇌(Bromley South)🚌🍎

Bromley Labour Club

HG Wells Centre, St Marks Road, BR2 9HG (behind police station)

⏲ 2-11; 12-10.30 Sun

☎ (020) 8460 7409

Shepherd Neame Master Brew Bitter; guest beer Ⓗ

This friendly community club and former SE London Club of the Year, five minutes' walk from Bromley South Station and the busy high street, has a main bar plus a function room for hire for meetings and social events. It has a good seating area, darts is played in the main bar, with a separate pool area adjacent. Card-carrying CAMRA members are welcome at all times.
❀⇌(Bromley North/South)🚌P⍀

Partridge ✔

194 High Street, BR1 1HE

⏲ 12-11 (midnight Fri & Sat); 12-10.30 Sun

☎ (020) 8464 7656

Fuller's Discovery, London Pride, ESB, seasonal beers; Gale's HSB Ⓗ

Though the interior looks very much like most people's idea of the archetypal English pub, this building used to be a bank. The tasteful conversion by Fuller's retains the sumptuous Edwardian interior and is popular with shoppers, while the large-screen TVs attract sports fans. Although it is often busy, there are two quieter areas off the main bar. A bit pricey, but the splendid food and ales come with excellent service and clean tables.
❀◑♿⇌(Bromley North)🚌

Prince Frederick ✔

31 Nichol Lane, BR1 4DE

⏲ 11-11 (11.30 Fri & Sat); 12-11 Sun

☎ (020) 8466 6741

Greene King IPA, Ruddles County, Abbot Ⓗ

This is apparently the only pub in the country to have this name. A traditional Victorian back-street pub with 1930s panelled interior, it was popular with agricultural workers in the 1890s (see photo in bar) but is now within a post-war housing estate. A quiet Greene King pub with a pleasant atmosphere, mainly frequented by locals, it is half a mile from Bromley town centre and so accessible to adventurous shoppers and real ale enthusiasts.
Q❀⊟⇌(Sundridge Park)🚌♣⍀

Red Lion

10 North Road, BR1 3LG
11 (12 Sun)-11
(020) 8460 2691
Greene King IPA, Abbot; Harveys Sussex Best Bitter; guest beers Ⓗ
This little Greene King gem in the back streets is run by a husband and wife team who are passionate about their ales and won the local CAMRA Pub of the Year award in 2007. The traditional interior is split into two areas, with a real fire, timber flooring and Victorian tiling. Heaving bookshelves line one wall, making it a cosy pub in which to sit, read and enjoy the superb beers. The front benefits from flower displays all year and attractive seating.
Q ≈(Bromley North) (314)

Bromley Common

Two Doves

37 Oakley Road, BR2 8HD
12-3, 5.30-11; 12-midnight Fri-Sun
(020) 8462 1627
Courage Best Bitter; St Austell Tribute; Young's Bitter, Special Ⓗ
The only Young's pub in Bromley, and the home pub of the Ravensbourne Morris Men, appears to have been converted from a pair of farm labourers' cottages by the addition of a rather grand mid-19th century frontage. Located in what is still a semi-rural part of London, it is best accessed via the footpath across Bromley Common from George Lane, Hayes. It has a surprisingly large, picturesque beer garden at the rear, and a good collection of saucy seaside postcards in the Gents.
Q (320)

Chelsfield

Five Bells

Church Road, BR6 7RE
11-11 (midnight Fri & Sat); 12-10.30 Sun
(01689) 821044 thefivebells-chelsfieldvillage.co.uk
Courage Best Bitter; Harveys Sussex Best Bitter; Sharp's Doom Bar; guest beers Ⓗ
A warm welcome awaits you as you enter this gem of a pub set in an unspoilt part of Chelsfield village. Built in 1668, this traditional Enterprise pub has been refurbished and offers two bars and a restaurant. It has a cosy atmosphere with photographs and plates decorating the walls. The large, pleasant garden means walkers, families and dogs are welcome, and the bus stop is right outside. Q (R3) P

Chislehurst

Ramblers Rest ✔

Mill Place, BR7 5ND (off Old Hill)
11.30-11; 12-10.30 Sun
(020) 8467 1734
Brakspear Bitter; Wells Bombardier; guest beers Ⓗ
A superb weatherboarded building in a lovely location on the edge of Chislehurst common, this S&N Pub Enterprises pub has two levels and two bars. The upper bar is most popular with locals. On hot summer days there is always a crowd outside on the grass slope in front. A very handy stop after a visit to the famous caves nearby.
Q ≈ (162,269)

Crayford

Charlotte

38 Station Road, DA1 3QG
9-11 (1am Fri & Sat); 12-10.30 Sun
(01322) 310005
Ringwood Fortyniner; Shepheard Neame Spitfire; guest beer Ⓗ
An Enterprise pub refurbished in a café style but with a homely, friendly atmosphere. Two regular beers are accompanied by a rotating guest. The pub hosts a quiz night on Tuesday and various other events during the year. Numerous prints adorn the walls. The pub staff produce their own calendar in aid of charity. ≈ (492)

Crayford Arms

37 Crayford High Street, DA1 4HH
12-11.30 (midnight Fri & Sat)
(01322) 521467
Shepherd Neame Master Brew Bitter, Kent's Best, Spitfire, Bishops Finger, seasonal beer Ⓗ
Following a sympathetic refurbishment, this pub boasts five handpumps and retains a traditional atmosphere with many original features. To the right is a cosy public bar and to the left a saloon bar with an oak staircase leading up to a large function room. Occasional live music is performed. Although a Shepherd Neame tied house, the pub hosts at least one mini-festival a year. ≈ P

Croydon

Dog & Bull

24 Surrey Street, CR0 1RG
11-11 (midnight Thu-Sat); 12-10.30 Sun
(020) 8667 9718
Wells Bombardier; Young's Bitter, Special, seasonal beers; guest beer Ⓗ
Standing in the heart of Croydon's historic street market, this Grade II-listed pub was rebuilt during the 18th century and was first leased to Young and Bainbridge in 1832. Its history however can be traced back to 1595 and possibly earlier. The main bar with its island servery is augmented by two further rooms and a large, well kept garden. Food is available 12-4 daily, and 6-9 (except Sun). A function room is available for hire.
≈(E/W Croydon) ⊖(George St/Church St Tramlink)

George ✔

17-21 George Street, CR0 1LA
9am-midnight (1am Fri & Sat)
(020) 8649 9077
Greene King Ruddles Best; Marston's Pedigree; guest beers Ⓗ
An old Croydon pub name was revived when this Wetherspoon's pub was opened in 1993, converted from former shop premises. A single room with two bars (one at the rear), situated in the main shopping area, it can be busy at any time. New management has put the focus back on the range of beers available. Guest beers are likely to come from micro-breweries. Beer festivals are held in spring and autumn with other promotions throughout the year.
≈(E/W Croydon) ⊖(George St Tramlink)

Glamorgan

81 Cherry Orchard Road, CR0 6BE
12-11 (midnight Fri); 4-midnight Sat; 3-8 (earlier if quiet) Sun

☎ (020) 8688 6333
Harveys Sussex Best Bitter; guest beers Ⓗ
A welcoming Punch corner pub five minutes' walk from East Croydon Station, divided into three areas, one of which is reserved for diners. Good quality food (sometimes including South African bunny chow) is served at lunchtimes (except weekends) and evenings. Darts and pool are available and there is a TV, but not for live football. The pleasant patio at the rear also serves as a smoking area. It can get busy at times with local office workers.
❀◐◑⇌(East Croydon)⊖(East Croydon Tramlink) 🚌⛳

Green Dragon ✔

58-60 High Street, CR0 1NA
⏲ 10-midnight (1am Fri & Sat); 12-10.30 Sun
☎ (020) 8667 0684 🌐 myspace.com/greendragonpub
Dark Star Hophead Ⓗ**; Hogs Back TEA** Ⓖ**; Wells Bombardier** Ⓗ**; guest beers** Ⓗ/Ⓖ
This vibrant Town & City Pub Co pub at the heart of South London's 'capital city' caters for all. Winner of the local CAMRA Pub of the Year award in 2008, the Dragon is a well-run alehouse whose young staff are efficient and attentive. Expect around six draught beers including locally-brewed options and a regular draught cider. On weekend evenings it will be busy and noisy. Food is available all day including the celebrated Dragon soup and sarnie.
◐◑♿⇌(East/West Croydon)⊖(George St Tramlink) 🚌●

Royal Standard ✔

1 Sheldon Street, CR0 1SS
⏲ 11-midnight; 11-11 Sun
☎ (020) 8688 9749
Fuller's Chiswick Bitter, London Pride; Gale's HSB; Fuller's ESB, seasonal beers Ⓗ
Traditional street-corner Fuller's local, close to the bustle of Croydon town centre but providing a peaceful retreat with its sensitively restored interior. There are three distinct drinking areas, each with its own character – note the misericord and Victorian fireplace. The beers are consistently fine thanks to landlord Martin's assured cellarmanship. Opposite is a surprisingly quiet garden area, almost beneath the Croydon flyover. No lunchtime food at weekends.
Q❀◐◑⊖(George St Tramlink)🚌♣

Skylark ✔

34-36 South End, CR0 1DP
⏲ 9-midnight (1am Fri & Sat)
☎ (020) 8649 9909
Courage Best Bitter; Greene King Abbot; Marston's Pedigree; guest beers Ⓗ
Spacious, open-plan Wetherspoon's pub laid out on two floors, with an interesting view between the two through the unique balcony arrangement. The upper bar has a TV showing sport, but no real ale. There is a mezzanine area adjoining the ground floor. The name and decoration reflect Croydon's aviation history. Micro-brewery guest beers are often promoted; Westerham beers are regularly available. Away from the town centre, the pub usually stays uncrowded at weekends.
◐◑♿⇌(South Croydon)🚌

Spreadeagle ✔

39-41 Katharine Street, CR0 1NX
⏲ 11-11 (midnight Fri & Sat); 12-10.30 Sun
☎ (020) 8781 1134
Fuller's Chiswick, London Pride, ESB, seasonal beers; guest beers Ⓗ
Large two-floor conversion of former 1893 bank premises, in the town centre beside Croydon's old town hall. The interior has wood-panelled walls and wooden floors and function rooms, and is tastefully decorated with local street scenes from the last two centuries. Branded by Fuller's as an Ale and Pie house and with a corresponding standard menu, it is busy after office hours, and has an outdoor canopied area catering for smokers.
❀◐◑♿⇌(East/West Croydon)⊖(George St Tramlink)🚌⛳

Cudham

Blacksmiths Arms

Cudham Lane South, TN14 7QB (opp New Barn Lane)
TQ446598
⏲ 11-midnight
☎ (01959) 572678 🌐 theblacksmithsarms.co.uk
Adnams Bitter; Courage Best Bitter; Harveys Sussex Best Bitter; Taylor Landlord Ⓗ
This friendly, spacious Enterprise country pub, looking out over the steep Cudham valley, has a large, prize-winning garden and patio including a smoking area with a wood-burning stove. A blue plaque declares it the birthplace of Harry Relph 'Little Tich', Music Hall Comedian on 21 July 1867. Close by is a recreation ground with a children's play area. ⛰**Q**❀◐◑🚌(R5)**P**⛳

Orpington

Cricketers

93 Chislehurst Road, BR6 0DQ
⏲ 12-3, 5-midnight; 12-11 Sat; 12-10.30 Sun
☎ (01689) 812648
Adnams Bitter, Broadside; guest beer Ⓗ
Traditional Enterprise pub, run by the same family for over 30 years. Inside it has a friendly, homely atmosphere and is decorated with cricket and boxing memorabilia. Outside there is a unique horse's head on a stable door near the entrance and a pleasant patio and garden at the back. A short walk uphill from the High Street, the Cricketers offers a welcome break for shoppers; dogs are made very welcome too. **Q**🐕❀🚌(61)**P**

Petts Wood

Sovereign of the Seas ✔

109-111 Queensway, BR5 1DG
⏲ 10-11 (11.30 Fri & Sat)
☎ (01689) 891606
Greene King Ruddles Best, Abbot; Marston's Pedigree; Shepherd Neame Spitfire; guest beers Ⓗ
Originally a furniture shop, this attractive, modern Wetherspoon's has varied seating areas: sofas, cosy alcoves and high tables. Mixed decor includes local history panels, modern art and bookshelves at the back. The pub takes its name from a naval warship built in 1638 by local shipbuilder Peter Pett – presumably from the local wood that bears his family name. Sit in one of the five alcoves with a book and a pint and enjoy a really comfortable atmosphere.
❀◐◑♿⇌🚌(208,R3)

Pratts Bottom

Bulls Head
Rushmore Hill, BR6 7NQ
⏲ 11-11 (midnight Fri); 12-10.30
☎ (01689) 852553 🌐 thebullsheadpub.net
Courage Best Bitter; Shepherd Neame Spitfire; guest beers Ⓗ
Friendly, cosy, welcoming local with history, atmosphere and character. Local folklore has Dick Turpin frequenting this pub before being caught for horse stealing and hanged in 1739. Two changing guest ales from the S&N list complement the two regulars and an annual beer festival showcases a wider range. Of three rooms, two are for dining, the other for standing by the bar. There is entertainment every evening: quiz night, karaoke, pub sports etc – details are listed on the website. ♛❀◑◗🚌(402,R5)♣⛳

Thornton Heath

Victoria Cross
228 Bensham Lane, CR7 7EP
⏲ 12-11 (midnight Sat)
☎ (020) 8684 3022
Courage Best Bitter; guest beers Ⓗ
Brewers' Tudor-style two bar pub owned by Sarumdale Ltd. The unspoilt 1937 interior has earned it a place in CAMRA's London Regional Inventory. Both bars have wooden panelling, with prints depicting scenes of local historic interest. The public bar has a pool table and dartboard, and there are large TVs showing sports. There are always plenty of activities going on, such as quiz nights. Hot food can be ordered from local takeaway outlets. ❀◗🚌(450)♣⛳

Welling

New Cross Turnpike ✔
55 Bellgrove Road, DA16 3PB
⏲ 9-midnight
☎ (020) 8304 1660
Courage Best Bitter; Greene King Abbot; Marston's Pedigree; Shepherd Neame Spitfire; guest beers Ⓗ
Exemplary Wetherspoon's pub with an attractive layout on four levels including a gallery and two patios. Disabled access includes a wheelchair lift. Varied guest ales are served by helpful staff. Note Monday Club and Ale Wednesday special offers. The smoking area is heated and covered.
Q❀◑◗♿⇌🚌⛳

SOUTH-WEST LONDON
SW1: Belgravia

Antelope
22-24 Eaton Terrace, SW1W 8EZ
⏲ 12-11; closed Sun
☎ (020) 7824 8512
Fuller's Chiswick Bitter, Discovery, London Pride, ESB, seasonal beers Ⓗ
Attractive 1827 mews pub with etched glass windows and a fine island bar. There is a comfortable rear section with a fire. Wood-panelled walls feature old photos of rugby and football scenes and one wall is dedicated to the pub's cricket team with photos and records. The upstairs and downstairs snug areas can be booked and the main upstairs room (with bar) can be hired for functions. Q◑◗⊖(Sloane Sq)🚌

Horse & Groom
7 Groom Place, SW1X 7BA
⏲ 11-11; closed Sat & Sun
☎ (020) 7235 6980
Shepherd Neame Master Brew Bitter, Kent Best, Spitfire, seasonal beers Ⓗ
You may have a little search to find this traditional mews pub but it is well worth seeking out. The main wood-panelled downstairs room has etched glass front windows. There is also an upstairs room that is mainly used for dining. Although closed on Saturday and Sunday, the pub is available for private hire. ◑◗⇌⊖(Hyde Pk Corner)🚌⛳

Nag's Head
53 Kinnerton Street, SW1X 8ED
⏲ 11-11; 12-10.30 Sun
☎ (020) 7235 1135
Adnams Bitter, Broadside Ⓗ
Small, unspoilt establishment with bars on two levels, the front one boasting the lowest bar counter in London, if not the country. Built circa 1833, it was first licensed as a beer house, was later acquired by Benskins and has now been run for several years as a free house by actor Kevin Moran. A treasure trove of collectibles, it has a 'What the Butler Saw' machine which still works. It attracts tourists, local residents – one of whom is 'Casino John' – and various other celebrities.
♛Q❀◑◗⊖(Hyde Pk Corner/Knightsbridge)🚌

Star Tavern ✔
6 Belgrave Mews West, SW1X 8HT
⏲ 11-11; 12-10.30 Sun
☎ (020) 7235 3019
Fuller's Chiswick Bitter, Discovery, London Pride, ESB, seasonal beers Ⓗ
A Grade II-listed pub dating from 1848, the Star underwent a sensitive refurbishment in early 2008. No glass and chrome here – the ambience takes you back to when a pub looked like a pub. The landlord often organises a posse of regulars to take part in fundraising events to raise money for cancer research. A former local CAMRA Pub of the Year, the Star has featured in every edition of the Guide.
Q◑◗⊟♿⊖(Hyde Pk Corner/Knightsbridge)🚌

SW1: Pimlico

Jugged Hare ✔
172 Vauxhall Bridge Road, SW1V 1DX
⏲ 11-11 (11.30 Fri); 12-10.30 Sun
☎ (020) 7828 1543 🌐 juggedhare.co.uk
Fuller's Chiswick Bitter, Discovery, London Pride, ESB, seasonal beers Ⓗ
Converted in 1996 from a bank dating from the 19th century, the Hare is a 'traditional' Fuller's Ale and Pie House, oak panelled and complete with faux Corinthian colums, a wonderful chandelier, bright brass fittings and Art Deco lights. A comfortable back room and an upstairs gallery can be booked. A busy, well-lit retreat from the roar of the traffic, but with rather insistent musak, it attracts a good mix of young and old, locals and office workers.
◑◗⇌(Victoria)⊖(Pimlico/Victoria)🚌

SW1: Victoria

Cask & Glass
39 Palace Street, SW1E 5HN
⏲ 11-11; 12-9 Sat; closed Sun

☎ (020) 7834 7630
Shepherd Neame Master Brew Bitter, Kent's Best, Spitfire, Bishops Finger, seasonal beers Ⓗ
This attractive one-room pub between Buckingham Palace and Westminster Cathedral, adorned with flowers in summer, is a haven for tourists and local residents. First licensed in 1862 as the Duke of Cambridge, the wood-panelled bar has pictures of local scenes and politicians, plus two gold-framed mirrors. Look out for the bullseye windows and the two paintings of the pub on the way to the toilets. A cosy place for a well-earned pint after seeing the sights.

Willow Walk ✔

25 Wilton Road, SW1V 1LW
9-midnight; 10-11.30 Sun
☎ (020) 7828 2953
Greene King Ruddles Best; Marston's Pedigree; guest beers Ⓗ
A Wetherspoon's conversion dating from 1999, busy with commuters and local workers. The interior makes a nod towards the area's rich history. Two rows of handpumps offer a guest beer range better than the average Wetherspoon's. Regular deals and promotions are available. The pub has a children's certificate and offers Wi-Fi access.

SW1: Westminster

Buckingham Arms

62 Petty France, SW1H 9EU
11-11; 12-6 Sat; 12-10.30 Sun
☎ (020) 7222 3386
Caledonian Deuchars IPA; Wells Bombardier; Young's Bitter, Special, seasonal beers Ⓗ
Opposite the headquarters of the Battalion Grenadier Guards, this ever-popular Young's establishment has featured in every edition of the Guide. Recent refurbishments have retained the etched glass mirrors behind the fine curving bar and added attractive stained glass screens. The side corridor may well have been an alley between the adjoining buildings and was used by servants to drink away from their masters' observations. Ladies, your facilities are now on the ground floor, so no more climbing the Himalayas!
Q(St James's Pk)

Sanctuary House Hotel ✔

33 Tothill Street, SW1H 9LA
11-11; 12-10.30 Sun
☎ (020) 7799 4044 sanctuaryhousehotel.com
Fuller's Chiswick Bitter, London Pride, ESB, seasonal beers Ⓗ
A Fuller's Ale and Pie House plus 34-bedroom hotel in a building said to have formerly housed MI5. With plenty of wood panelling, bevelled mirrors, bright brass fittings at the bar, big tall windows, and generous, split-level hardwood or carpeted seating areas, it is comfortable and warm with a welcoming buzz, though the musak may be irritating. A curious medieval style 'Book of Hours' mural on the back wall is said to represent 'Sanctuary' at the nearby Westminster Abbey.
(St James's Pk)

Speaker ✔

46 Great Peter Street, SW1P 2HA
12-11; closed Sat & Sun
☎ (020) 7222 1749
Shepherd Neame Spitfire; Young's Bitter; guest beers Ⓗ
Located near the heart of Westminster, this Enterprise pub is popular with civil servants and MPs and, like many bars in the area, has its own division bell. There are caricatures of MPs and clay pipes throughout the wood-panelled interior. Regular themed beer festivals are held, utilising two handpumps. Q(St James's Pk)

St Stephen's Tavern

10 Bridge Street, SW1A 2JR
10-11.30 (midnight Fri); 10.30-10.30 Sun
☎ (020) 7925 2286
Badger First Gold, Tanglefoot, seasonal beers Ⓗ
Built in 1875 and reopened in 2003 by Hall & Woodhouse after a period of restoration, this pub, located opposite the Houses of Parliament, is frequented by civil servants and tourists. Grade II-listed, the interior has many features of historical interest with an impression of discreet grandeur. Particularly of note are the high bar back, etched mirrors and splendid hanging brass lamps. The upstairs room has views to the main bar below and distinctive curved leather seating. Q

SW1: Whitehall

Lord Moon of the Mall ✔

16-18 Whitehall, SW1A 2DY
9-11.30 (midnight Fri & Sat); 9-11 Sun
☎ (020) 7839 7701
Greene King Ruddles Best, Abbot; Marston's Pedigree; guest beers Ⓗ
In a listed building dating from 1872, this 1995 Wetherspoon's bank conversion has one large, open-plan room. The long bar normally has up to ten real ales and two draught ciders available. It is popular with passing tourists visiting the surrounding sights and galleries. The walls have paintings and prints of local views and historical information. Also note the statuettes in the alcoves.
Q(Charing Cross)(Charing Cross/ Westminster)

SW2: Streatham Hill

Crown & Sceptre ✔

2A Streatham Hill, SW2 4AH
9-midnight (1am Fri & Sat)
☎ (020) 8671 0843
Courage Best Bitter; Greene King Ruddles Best, Abbot; Marston's Pedigree; guest beers Ⓗ
Although spacious, this is a relatively small Wetherspoon's pub; the split-level interior creating separate, cosy areas. The first such conversion in south west London, it retains its Truman fascia, thanks to the local history society. Cask beer is very important here, generally in a good range of strengths and styles. The pub tries to maintain four guest beers and also sells Westons Old Rosie cider. Children are allowed until 9pm in the family area.
P

SW4: Clapham

Manor Arms

128 Clapham Manor Street, SW4 6ED
12-11 (midnight Fri & Sat)
☎ (020) 7622 2894

Everards Tiger; Sharp's Doom Bar; Taylor Landlord; guest beers Ⓗ
There is a feeling of calm here after the rush of Clapham High Street, despite the TV screens showing major sporting events. Both the bar and the marquee at the back are packed for rugby matches; in 2007 this Enterprise pub was voted the best place in London to watch international rugby. The front area is a good place to watch the world go by. The beer range may vary, but a Downton and a Westerham beer will usually be available alongside the three regulars.
⇌(Clapham High St)⊖(Clapham Common/North)

SW5: Earl's Court

Blackbird ✓
209 Earls Court Road, SW5 9AN
11-11; 12-10.30 Sun
☎ (020) 7835 1855
Fuller's Chiswick Bitter, Discovery, London Pride, ESB Ⓗ
Converted from bank premises in 1993, this large, bright Fuller's pub has excellent beer and a large menu that includes speciality pies, sandwiches, sides and sharers. The atmosphere is welcoming, with unobtrusive music. The staff are very pleasant and willing to give you advice on your ale selection. Meals are served 12-2.45 and 4-9.30pm.
♿⊖

Courtfield ✓
187 Earls Court Road, SW5 9AN
8am-12.30am; 9am-11.30 Sun
☎ (020) 7370 2626
Fuller's London Pride; guest beers Ⓗ
Spacious Punch pub with a good atmosphere, right outside Earl's Court tube station. The staff really try to make your visit as pleasant as possible, with excellent service. Six ales are on handpump. Customers are invited to try the varied food menu throughout the day, and enjoy the guest ales that are available. ♿⊖

SW6: Parsons Green

White Horse 🏆 ✓
1-3 Parsons Green, SW6 4UL
11-11.30 (midnight Thu-Sat); 11-11 Sun
☎ (020) 7736 2115 🌐 whitehorsesw6.com
Adnams Broadside; Harveys Sussex Best Bitter; guest beers Ⓗ
Large, light and airy M&B pub in a very upmarket area, offering up to seven cask ales on handpump and a variety of bottle conditioned and continental beers from an impressive rosewood horseshoe bar. An ornate gilded mirror decorates the bar back. Comfortably furnished, there are wooden benches and leather sofas. The extensive menu includes delights such as Calvados pot roast pheasant with recommended accompanying ales. The outside seating area with barbecue, fronting Parsons Green, gets very busy in summer.
⊖(22,424)

SW7: South Kensington

Anglesea Arms ✓
15 Selwood Terrace, SW7 3QG
11-11; 12-10.30 Sun
☎ (020) 7373 7960
Adnams Bitter, Broadside; Fuller's London Pride; guest beers Ⓗ
This Capital Pub Co establishment has the appearance of a country pub with hanging baskets and benches outside. Walk through the foliage and you discover a hidden gem. Numerous features from the past are apparent including an etched glass panel with the pub's name. A prominent wooden clock hangs above the bar. The front bar has a large brewery mirror and a diverse collection of paintings. A good range of cask ales is served.
⊖

SW8: South Lambeth

Mawbey Arms
7 Mawbey Street, SW8 2TT
11-11; 12-10.30 Sun
☎ (020) 7622 1936
Young's Bitter; guest beers Ⓗ
This listed 19th-century free house, tucked away on the edge of a modern housing estate, attracts a mainly local clientele. The cosy single-bar interior is decorated with traditional framed prints and mirrors as well as Chelsea FC memorabilia. There is a strong darts following here, and an impressive display of trophies. Lunches are served Monday to Friday only. ⇌(Vauxhall)⊖(Stockwell)♣

Priory Arms ✓
83 Lansdowne Way, SW8 2PB
12-11 (10.30 Sun)
☎ (020) 7622 1884
Hop Back Summer Lightning; guest beers Ⓗ
Vibrant free house serving good food and guest beers from a wide range of micro-breweries, attested by the vast number of pump clips on display. It attracts a regular, mixed clientele who enjoy the free newspapers or watching big match sport. There are many German and Belgian bottled beers as well as 25 malt whiskies. Upstairs is a function room. The listed frontage is a riot of colourful hanging baskets in summer.
⇌(Wandsworth Rd)⊖(Stockwell)

SW11: Battersea

Beehive ✓
197 St John's Hill, SW11 1TH
11-11 (midnight Fri & Sat); 12-11 Sun
☎ (020) 7564 1897
Fuller's London Pride, ESB Ⓗ
A rare Fuller's tied house in this part of London, this small, friendly, one-room local has a public bar feel to it. Unobtrusive background music gives way to live performances on Thursday evening. Wholesome lunches are served on weekdays. Everyone is welcome, including well-behaved children. Ten minutes' walk from Clapham Junction, it has six Wandsworth-bound bus routes passing close by. ⇌(Clapham Jct)

Eagle Ale House
104 Chatham Road, SW11 6HG
12-11 (10.30 Sun)
☎ (020) 7228 2328
Westerham seasonal beers; guest beers Ⓗ
A real ale haven with seven ever-changing beers from Westerham and other micro-breweries as well as a real cider. This is an unspoilt, dog-friendly Enterprise local; the somewhat chaotic interior featuring big leather sofas, old bottles and dusty

books. A loyal, mixed clientele is welcoming to all. The large-screen TV shows major sporting events. Curry night is Wednesday and on Sunday there are roasts plus a quiz in the evening. There is a heated marquee in the garden for special occasions.
⛰❀◐◑♿🚌(319,G1)🍎⚡

Falcon ☆ ✔

2 St John's Hill, SW11 1RU
⏲ 10-11 (midnight Thu-Sat); 10-10.30 Sun
☎ (020) 7228 2076
Fuller's London Pride; Taylor Landlord; guest beers Ⓗ
Grand corner pub whose impressive Victorian interior merits a place on CAMRA's National Inventory. Also impressive are the number and variety of real ales available – often up to 12. Although mainly drawn from the M&B (Nicholson's) seasonal list, they often include beers from breweries hard to find elsewhere in the area. Food is served all day. Firmly re-established at the heart of Clapham Junction, this bustling pub serves a wide cross-section of the local resident and working community. ◐◑♿⇌(Clapham Jct)🚌

Westbridge

74-76 Battersea Bridge Road, SW11 3AG
⏲ 12 (11 Sat)-11 (midnight Fri & Sat); 11-10.30 Sun
☎ (020) 7228 6482 🌐 thewestbridge.co.uk
Adnams Bitter; Sambrook's Wandle; guest beer Ⓗ
Many pubs in this area have followed the gastropub trail but the Westbridge stands out from the crowd. A free house, it has in effect become the brewery tap for the local Sambrook's micro-brewery, while the guest beer often comes from a brewery unusual for the area. Moreover, the food is definitely a cut above the average. The decor of the bar and the adjoining dining room is eclectic and funky, featuring modern art prints and LP covers from such classics as Mambo for Cats.
❀◐◑🚌⚡

SW12: Balham

Nightingale

97 Nightingale Lane, SW12 8NX
⏲ 11 (12 Sun)-midnight
☎ (020) 8673 1637
Wells Bombardier; Young's Bitter, Special; guest beer Ⓗ
The 'Bird' is an utterly traditional Young's house where a warm welcome is guaranteed as well as top quality beers which sell in vast quantities. This is a true community local which raises huge sums for charity, especially with its renowned annual walk. A dog-friendly pub, it has a heated family area and new and upgraded facilities often in evidence. Food is served all day, every day. Not to be missed.
⛰Q👪❀◐◑♿⇌(Wandsworth Common)
⊖(Clapham South)🚌(G1)⚡

SW13: Barnes

Red Lion ✔

2 Castelnau, SW13 9RU
⏲ 11-11; 12-10.30 Sun
☎ (020) 8748 2984
Fuller's Discovery, London Pride, ESB, seasonal beer Ⓗ
Large Georgian landmark pub, situated at the entrance to the Wetland Centre. It has been opened out in recent years, although the rear room still has a more exclusive feel. From here guests reach a decked patio area and the spacious garden. Excellent food is always available from a varied, modern menu, and children are welcome during the day. ⛰❀◐◑♿🚌P⚡

SW15: Putney

Bricklayer's Arms 🏆

32 Waterman Street, SW15 1DD
⏲ 12-11 (10.30 Sun)
☎ (020) 8789 0222 🌐 bricklayers-arms.co.uk
Sambrook's Wandle; Taylor Dark Mild, Golden Best, Best Bitter, Landlord, Ram Tam; guest beers Ⓗ
Dating from 1826 and rescued from closure in 2005, this delightful free house was voted local CAMRA Pub of the Year in 2006 and 2008 and the Greater London winner in 2007. Besides the full Taylor range, it serves a Sambrook's beer, guests from other micro-breweries and Westons cider, and holds regular beer festivals. Decorated with old photos and Putney-related cartoons, this community pub, with its shove-ha'penny and bar skittles, is busy when Fulham FC are at home.
⛰❀◐◑⇌⊖(Putney Bridge)🚌♣🍎⚡

Green Man

Putney Heath, SW15 3NG
⏲ 11-11 (midnight Fri & Sat); 12-10.30 Sun
☎ (020) 8788 8096
Wells Bombardier; Young's Bitter, Special; guest beer Ⓗ
This charming, warm and welcoming Young's pub, on the edge of the heath opposite the bus terminus on Putney Hill, retains an intimate atmosphere through sensitive refurbishment. Ring the bull is played in one of various rooms leading off the small bar. Outside are a sheltered front patio and a large, split level back garden ideal for families in summer. Meals are served 12-3 and 6-9pm Monday to Thursday and all day Friday to Sunday. ⛰❀◐◑♿🚌♣⚡

SW17: Tooting

JJ Moons ✔

56A Tooting High Street, SW17 0RN
⏲ 10-midnight
☎ (020) 8672 4726
Courage Best Bitter; Greene King Abbot; Marston's Pedigree; guest beers Ⓗ
Long, narrow Wetherspoon's pub opposite the tube station and handy for the area's many South Asian restaurants. The wood-panelled interior features photos of Edwardian Tooting. There are two large TV screens for sport, but the sound is usually turned down. This is a vibrant community pub; move to the rear for a quieter drink. Westons Old Rosie or Organic Vintage cider is available.
◐◑⊖(Tooting Broadway)🚌🍎

SW18: Wandsworth

Alma

499 Old York Road, SW18 1TF
⏲ 11-midnight; 12-11 Sun
☎ (020) 8870 2537 🌐 thealma.co.uk
Wells Bombardier; Young's Bitter, Special; guest beer Ⓗ
Named after the famous battle of the Crimean War, this busy Young's pub is hard to miss with its green tiled facade right opposite the station. Inside, some fine painted mirrors featuring birds such as herons

survive, hence the pub's inclusion on CAMRA's London Regional Inventory. Bar food is served throughout the day but it is advisable to book for the restaurant area at the rear, a former billiard room with an impressive plaster frieze. ⌂❀◑♿⇌(Wandsworth Town)🚌P⅟–

Grapes

39 Fairfield Street, SW18 1DX

⏲ 12-11 (midnight Fri & Sat); 12-10.30 Sun

☎ (020) 8874 3414 🌐 thealma.co.uk

Young's Bitter, Special Ⓗ

Friendly, traditional Young's local, a stone's throw from the now defunct Ram Brewery. In the summer customers can relax in the delightful garden, a rare oasis, and smokers can enjoy the heated patio all year round. This lively establishment welcomes well-behaved children and shows major sporting events on several TV screens. Excellent lunches are served on week days. Local CAMRA Pub of the Year in 2005, this is definitely not one to miss. ❀◑⇌(Wandsworth Town)🚌⅟–

Le Gothique

Royal Victoria Patriotic Building, John Archer Way, SW18 3SX (off Windmill Road)

⏲ 12-midnight; weekend hours vary

☎ (020) 8870 6567 🌐 legothique.co.uk

Downton seasonal beer; Sambrook's Wandle; Shepherd Neame seasonal beer Ⓗ

Built in 1857 as an orphanage and used by intelligence services in WWII, this gothic building now houses apartments and studios along with this well established free house: a split-level French restaurant and bar stocking up to three real ales and hosting weddings in the adjacent Grand Hall. The large 'Bacchus' sculpture, atmospheric paintings and the furniture were all produced in-house. Many early 20th-century photographs adorn the walls. Diners can eat alfresco in the garden in warm weather. ❀◑♿🚌(77,219)P⅟–

Spread Eagle

71 Wandsworth High Street, SW18 2PT

⏲ 11-11 (midnight Fri & Sat); 12-11 Sun

☎ (020) 8877 9809

Young's Bitter, Special; guest beer Ⓗ

A Young's and a Wandsworth landmark, opposite the former brewery, the present building dates from 1898 and is included on CAMRA's London Regional Inventory for its many surviving internal features including marvellous cut and etched glass partitions and bar-back. Three distinct rooms include a public bar, now a rarity in London, while the main room is decorated with some interesting prints and photographs of old Wandsworth, including the earlier pub. ⌂◑⊟⇌(Wandsworth Town)🚌

SW19: South Wimbledon

Sultan

78 Norman Road, SW19 1BT

⏲ 12-11 (midnight Fri & Sat)

☎ (020) 8544 9323

Hop Back GFB, Entire Stout, Summer Lightning; guest beer Ⓗ

London's only Hop Back tied house, this is a well-run, traditional, two-bar corner local with a friendly welcome for all. It retains a dartboard in the smaller bar (only open evenings) and there is a quiz on Tuesday. Beer club is Wednesday 6-9pm, with reduced prices. A guest ale is normally available from the Hop Back seasonal or Downton range and the pub holds a weekend beer festival in the autumn. ❀⊟♿⊖(Colliers Wood)🚌(200)♣⅟–

Trafalgar

23 High Path, SW19 2JY

⏲ 3 (12 Fri & Sat)-11; 12-11 Sun

☎ (020) 8542 5342 🌐 thetraf.com

Pilgrim Thru'ppenny Hop; guest beers Ⓗ

CAMRA Greater London Pub of the Year 2008, this homely, one-bar community corner pub, the smallest and oldest free house in the Borough of Merton, is a real ale haven: six handpumps offer an ever-changing choice of micro-brewery beers, often milds, including at least one local ale. Nelson-related prints decorate the walls and a wooden spoked wheel from an old Thames barge divides the bar area. Curry night is Thursday, live music plays most Saturdays and some other evenings, plus traditional jazz on Sunday afternoon. An October beer festival is held around Trafalgar Day. ⌂⊖🚌♣●

SW19: Wimbledon

Hand in Hand

6 Crooked Billet, SW19 4RQ

⏲ 11-11 (midnight Fri & Sat); 12-10.30 Sun

☎ (020) 8946 5720

Courage Directors; Wells Bombardier; Young's Bitter, Special, seasonal beer; guest beer Ⓗ

Originally a bakehouse in buildings owned by Daniel Watney, whose grandson founded that brewery, this award-winning pub was a beer house belonging to the Holland family until Young's bought it in 1974. Much altered and extended, it retains an intimate atmosphere in the drinking areas around the central bar, a separate family room and a suntrap patio. Opposite, the grass triangle provides a summer drinking, picnic and play area. ⌂Q⊱❀◑🚌(200)⅟–

SW20: Raynes Park

Edward Rayne ✔

8-12 Coombe Lane, SW20 8ND

⏲ 9-11.30

☎ (020) 8971 0420

Greene King Ruddles Best, Abbot; Marston's Pedigree; Shepherd Neame Spitfire; guest beers Ⓗ

Opened in 2006 on the site of a Co-op supermarket, this cavernous, single bar Wetherspoon's pub commemorates the 19th-century farmer whose estate became Raynes Park. Decorated in pastel shades, with wood panelling, half-mirrored pillars and soft lighting, it attracts local families. TV news is shown with subtitles but no sound, sport is screened (but no football), and games machines are silent. Westons Old Rosie and Organic Vintage ciders are served from a fridge behind the bar. ◑⇌🚌●⅟–

Carshalton

Railway Tavern ✔

47 North Street, SM5 2HG

⏲ 12-2.30, 5-11; 12-11 Sat; 12-10.30 Sun

☎ (020) 8669 8016

Fuller's London Pride, ESB, seasonal beers Ⓗ

Built in Victorian times to serve the nearby station, this small corner local has featured many times in this Guide. The landlord has won the Master Cellarman award from Fuller's. A U-shaped bar has walls adorned with railway memorabilia, together with certificates awarded for beer quality and outdoor floral displays. A small patio garden is situated at the rear. Sporting events are screened on the TV. Lunches are served weekdays only.

Windsor Castle

378 Carshalton Road, SM5 3PT

11-11 (11.30 Fri & Sat); 12-11 Sun

(020) 8669 1191 windsorcastlepub.com

Harveys Sussex Best Bitter; Shepherd Neame Spitfire; guest beers H

Acquired by Shepherd Neame from Punch in 2009, this prominent pub has been CAMRA Sutton Pub of the Year on many occasions. It continues to provide good meals in the restaurant area (except Sun and Mon eve). Thursday night quizzes and Saturday night live music add to the variety. A covered courtyard leads to the function room and garden. Two guest beers are to be sourced from micro-brewers. An annual beer festival is held over the spring bank holiday weekend.
(Carshalton Beeches) P

Cheam

Claret Wine Bar

33 The Broadway, SM3 8BL

11.30-11.30 (12.30am Fri & Sat); 12-11.30 Sun

(020) 8715 9002

Shepherd Neame Master Brew Bitter, Spitfire; guest beers H

Small family-owned pub/wine bar, independently run for the last 25 years, in a pretty village location. A successful shop conversion with idiosyncratically divided space, its mock-Tudor interior is adorned with breweriana. Real ale is promoted, with discounted four pint jugs. Quiz night is Monday and curry night Thursday. Food is locally sourced, including Sunday roasts and a vegetarian option; parties are catered for. Pleasant bar staff, free Wi-Fi, live sport on Sky TV. Credit cards accepted.

Kingston upon Thames

Boaters Inn

Lower Ham Road, KT2 5AU (off A307 via Woodside Rd) TQ180699

11-11; 12-10.30 Sun

(020) 8541 4672

Beer range varies H

Large, open-plan, modern style pub on the bank of the River Thames, just outside the town centre in Canbury Gardens. Operated by Capital Pub Co, it usually has five beers on draught, often from local breweries. Home-made traditional pub food is offered plus more adventurous daily specials. Outside, the spacious drinking area often overflows into the Gardens on sunny summer days (plastic glasses must be used). Families are very welcome inside and dogs too. Live jazz plays on Sunday evenings. (65)

Park Tavern

19 New Road, KT2 6AP

11-11; 12-10.30 Sun

Fuller's London Pride; Taylor Landlord; Young's Bitter; guest beers H

Thriving 19th-century back-street free house, formed from two houses, situated near the Kingston Gate of Richmond Park, half a mile from Norbiton Station. Inside you will find a real log fire for winter, dominoes, cards and a changing range of three guest beers, often from micro-breweries. Dogs on a lead are welcome, as are well-behaved children, until 7pm. The small patio at the front is covered by a trellis. Snacks are available lunchtimes Monday to Saturday. (371)

Willoughby Arms

47 Willoughby Road, KT2 6LN

10 (12 Sun)-midnight

(020) 8546 4236 thewilloughbyarms.com

Fuller's London Pride; Surrey Hills Shere Drop; Twickenham Naked Ladies; Wells Bombardier; guest beers H

Friendly Victorian back-street Enterprise local, divided into a sports bar with games and large-screen TV, and a quieter lounge area. An upstairs function room can be hired for events. Four beer festivals are held every year. Outdoor barbecues are staged in the summer. Folk music is played on the last Friday of the month. The garden has its own TV screen and a covered, heated smoking area. Local CAMRA Pub of the Year 2009.
(371,K5)

Wych Elm

93 Elm Road, KT2 6HT

11-3, 5-midnight; 11-midnight Sat; 12-11 Sun

(020) 8546 3271

Fuller's Chiswick Bitter, London Pride, ESB, seasonal beer H

Welcoming and friendly back-street local, with one of the longest-surviving landlords in the area. It has a smart saloon with a glass partition, and a basic but tidy public bar. Local CAMRA Pub of the Year in 2005, it has also won many prizes for its garden and floral displays out front. Good-quality home-cooked lunches are served daily except Sunday. Jazz sessions are held on the last Saturday of the month. Q (K5)

Mitcham

Queens Head

70 Cricket Green, CR4 4LA

11-midnight (1am Fri & Sat); 11-11 Sun

(020) 8648 3382

Shepherd Neame Master Brew Bitter, Spitfire, seasonal beer H

Early 20th-century pub on the edge of Mitcham's historic cricket green. The comfortable lounge bar has some interesting pictures relating to the pub's name; the smaller public bar has Setanta Sports and a dartboard. Excellent food is served 12-2.30pm (3pm Sat & Sun) and 8 (7 Fri)-10pm (not Sat & Sun eves), plus wonderful fish and chips to eat in or take away on Friday. The pub hosts several darts teams and holds charity events, plus a Saturday quiz night.
(Mitcham Tramlink) (127) P

New Malden

Woodies

Thetford Road, KT3 5DX TQ206673

11-11; 12-10.30 Sun

(020) 8949 5824 woodiesfreehouse.co.uk

Adnams Broadside; Fuller's London Pride, ESB; Young's Bitter; guest beers 🄷
New Malden's hidden gem. This competitively-priced, dog and family-friendly open-plan free house in a former sports pavilion was the local CAMRA Pub of the Year 2006-2008. Showbusiness and sporting artefacts cover the walls and ceiling. Three guest beers are sourced from local breweries with forthcoming beers listed on the website. The large outdoor patio incorporates a heated and covered smoking area. Highlights include the Sunday carvery, fortnightly quiz night, summer weekend barbecues and an annual beer festival in August. ⛼❀◐♿🚌(265)P⚡

Richmond

Shaftesbury Arms
121 Kew Road, TW9 2PN
🕒 12 (11 Sat)-11 (midnight Fri & Sat)
☎ (020) 8255 2419 🌐 shaftesburyarms.com
Wells Bombardier; Young's Bitter, Special, seasonal beer; guest beer 🄷
Friendly, comfortable Victorian pub, popular with the London Welsh RFC a short walk away. At the rear is a covered, heated patio garden. The two original bars were merged in 1988 with the addition of a restaurant area (ex 'chippy' shop) in 2001 serving Thai food all week (closed Sun). Acquired by Young & Bainbridge in 1860, this distinctive building was originally known as the Wheatsheaf, becoming the Shaftesbury Arms in 1878 and rebuilt in 1899. Wi-Fi and Sports TV. ❀◐◑⇌⊖🚌⚡

White Cross
Riverside, Off Water Lane, TW9 1TH
🕒 11-11; 12-10.30 Sun
☎ (020) 8940 6844
Wells Bombardier; Young's Bitter, Special, seasonal beer; guest beer 🄷
Recently refurbished, this prominent Young's pub on Richmond's waterfront dates from 1835. A stained glass panel is a reminder that it stands on the site of a former convent of the Observant Friars, whose insignia was a white cross. It is reached by steps for good reason: the river often floods here. An island bar serves two side rooms (one a mezzanine); an unusual feature is a working fireplace beneath a window. The ground-level patio bar opens at busy times. ⛼Q❀◐◑⇌⊖🚌

Surbiton

Cap in Hand ✔
174 Hook Rise North, KT6 5DE (at A3/A243 jct)
🕒 10-midnight (10 Sun)
☎ (020) 8397 3790
Greene King Ruddles Best; King Red River; Marston's Pedigree; guest beers 🄷
Originally the Southborough Arms, this spacious 1930s roadhouse is located on the Hook junction of the A3. A varied beer range often features ales from Itchen Valley, Hogs Back, WJ King, Pilgrim, Twickenham and Triple fff, with Westons cider also available. Local mini beer festivals complement those organised nationally by Wetherspoon's. Food is served until an hour before closing time. Smokers are catered for with patio heaters. An airy conservatory is designated a family area until 9pm. ⛼Q❀◐◑♿🚌●P⚡

Coronation Hall ✔
St Marks Hill, KT6 4LQ
🕒 9-midnight
☎ (020) 8390 6164
Greene King Ruddles Best, Abbot; Marston's Pedigree; Shepherd Neame Spitfire; guest beers 🄷
A splendid Wetherspoon's conversion of a former music hall that has also seen life as a cinema, bingo hall and nudist health club. Inside there is a movie theme with pictures of film stars and artefacts from yesteryear along with pictures of George V's coronation. Guest beers change regularly with a preference for locally-brewed beers from Hogs Back and Pilgrim among others. Westons Old Rosie and Organic Vintage ciders are served from polypins. Q◐◑♿⇌🚌●

Lamb
73 Brighton Road, KT6 5NF (on A243)
🕒 12-11 (midnight Thu-Sat)
☎ (020) 8390 9229
Ringwood Best Bitter; Wychwood Hobgoblin; guest beer 🄷
Small one-bar free house with a genuine, friendly feel. The beer range may change from time to time, but will usually consist of two session beers and one 'premium'. Behind is a pleasant patio and beer garden. The Gents toilet is on the site of a former pub brewery. Very much a family pub, all are welcome including babes in arms. There is a cheese board on offer every day, with a selection of English cheeses to choose from. ❀⇌🚌⚡

Sutton

Cock & Bull ✔
26 High Street, SM1 1HF
🕒 11-11 (midnight Fri-Sat); 12-10.30 Sun
☎ (020) 8652 9910
Fuller's London Pride, ESB, seasonal beers; Gale's HSB 🄷
A Fuller's managed house in a Grade II-listed former bank premises on a lively corner at the entrance to Sutton's bustling high street. Four plasma screens show all major sporting events. There are carpeted and parquet floor areas, wood panelling and a variety of seating, and a covered and heated smoking area. The pub is popular with the more affluent office crowd through the day and has a local following during the evening. The disabled entrance is from Sutton Court Road. ◐◑♿⇌🚌⚡

Little Windsor ✔
13 Greyhound Road, SM1 4BY
🕒 12-11.30 (midnight Fri & Sat); 12-11 Sun
☎ (020) 8643 2574
Fuller's Discovery, London Pride, ESB, seasonal beers; Gale's HSB; guest beers 🄷
This small street-corner Fuller's local in the heart of the New Town area, east of Sutton town centre, is busy at weekends when the TV is on for sport. The L-shaped bar leads to a covered terrace, which is heated for smokers, and a garden. Quizzes and live music events are held as well as charity fund-raising. A former CAMRA Pub of the Year for Sutton. Good food is served at lunchtimes. ❀◐⇌🚌⚡

Robin Hood
52 West Street, SM1 1SH
🕒 11 (12 Sun)-11

☎ (020) 8643 7584 🌐 robinhoodsutton.co.uk
Courage Directors; Young's Bitter, Special, seasonal beers Ⓗ
A warm welcome awaits you at this fine community pub located close to Sutton's main shopping street. The experienced bar staff have been here for years and the pub was overall winner in The Publican's 'Proud of Your People' awards in 2008. Many local groups meet here, and the pub is home to two cribbage teams. Board games are also available. The full range of Young's bottled beers supplements the draught ales.
❀◑♿⇌(Sutton/West Sutton)🚌♣⚊

Wallington

Whispering Moon ✔

25 Ross Parade, SM6 8QF
🕒 9-midnight (1am Fri-Sat)
☎ (020) 8647 7020
Greene King Ruddles Best, Abbot; Marston's Pedigree; guest beers Ⓗ
A smaller than average Wetherspoon's pub in a former Odeon cinema, across the road from the station, with a split level L-shaped drinking area offering a continually changing range of micro-brewery guest beers plus Westons Old Rosie cider. Pictures of old Wallington (when the railway arrived in 1843 the station was named for nearby Carshalton) line the walls. It is handy for Wallington Hall, home of the local CAMRA annual October beer and cider festival. ◑♿⇌🚌🍎

WEST LONDON

W1: Fitzrovia

King & Queen ✔

1-2 Foley Street, W1W 6DL
🕒 11-11; 7-10.30 Sun
☎ (020) 7636 5619
Adnams Bitter; St Austell Tribute; guest beers Ⓗ
This imposing Grade II-listed red brick Edwardian Gothic building was first licensed in 1767. Now a free house now, although the exterior still displays a 1980s circular Watneys sign. The spacious ground floor bar doubles as a portrait gallery of British royalty and sports teams. The function room upstairs houses an impressive collection of brewery-themed mirrors. The pub also sports a fine selection of whiskies. ◑⊖(Goodge St)🚌⚊

W1: Marylebone

Carpenters Arms

12 Seymour Place, W1H 7NE
🕒 11-11; 12-10.30 Sun
☎ (020) 7723 1050
Adnams Broadside; Harveys Sussex Best Bitter; guest beers Ⓗ
Known locally as 'The Carp', the building was first licensed in 1776 and rebuilt by Meux Brewery in 1872. The U-shaped bar has an area of green leather bench seating by the window. There are six handpumps in this Market Taverns pub, with a varied choice of beers. Three TV screens show most sporting events and it can get crowded. There is a dartboard at the back as alternative entertainment. A function room upstairs can be hired out.
❀⊖(Marble Arch)🚌♣⚊

W1: Mayfair

Coach & Horses ✔

5 Bruton Street, W1J 6PT
🕒 11-11; 12-8 Sat; closed Sun (open 12-8 Dec)
☎ (020) 7629 4123
Fuller's London Pride; Greene King IPA; Taylor Landlord; guest beers Ⓗ
Situated close to the exclusive Bond Street shopping area in the heart of Mayfair, this Punch pub has a prominent mock-Tudor exterior with leaded windows featuring Wm Younger insignia. The comfortable interior incorporates much wood panelling. The bar occupies a central position and the high gantry festooned with pump clips and beer mats demonstrates commitment to real ale. Traditional British food is available and the upstairs room with its own bar can be enjoyed by diners and drinkers.
◑⊖(Bond St/Green Pk/Oxford Circus)🚌

Coach & Horses

5 Hill Street, W1J 5LD
🕒 12-11; closed Sat & Sun
☎ (020) 7355 1055
Shepherd Neame Kent's Best, Spitfire Ⓗ
The oldest surviving pub in Mayfair, built in 1744 and Grade II-listed. The side porch, now bricked in, serves as part of the lounge bar area. This was for a few years a Shepherd Neame managed house but is now run as a tenancy. A popular, one bar pub, busy at lunchtimes and early evenings, it attracts office staff in the area. It has leaded windows and the walls display prints and photographs illustrating the local area and a famous former landlady. Q◑⊖(Bond St/Green Pk)🚌⚊

W1: Soho

Crown ✔

64 Brewer Street, W1F 9TP
🕒 10am-11 (11.30 Fri & Sat); 12-10.30 Sun
☎ (020) 7287 8420
Fuller's London Pride; Taylor Landlord; guest beers Ⓗ
Popular M&B pub in the heart of Soho on the site of the Hickford Rooms, which were London's main concert rooms in the 1740s and '50s. The front bar, with its banquettes, is a welcome retreat from the bustling street. Changing guest beers make for an interesting range of ales. The plush upstairs dining room has its own bar. Breakfast is served from 10am every day. ◑⊖(Piccadilly Circus)🚌

Dog & Duck ☆ ✔

18 Bateman Street, W1D 3AJ
🕒 11-11 (11.30 Fri & Sat); 12-10.30 Sun
☎ (020) 7494 0697
Fuller's London Pride; Taylor Landlord; guest beers Ⓗ
In the bustling heart of Soho, this CAMRA National Inventory M&B pub was built in 1897. Elaborate mosaic tiles depict dogs and ducks, and wonderful advertising mirrors adorn the walls. The upstairs Orwell Bar is a great place to watch the frenetic streets of West One. ◑⊖(Tottenham Ct Rd)🚌

Glassblower ✔

42 Glasshouse Street, W1B 5JY
🕒 11-11 (midnight Thu-Sat); 12-10.30 Sun
☎ (020) 7734 8547
Fuller's London Pride; Wells Bombardier Ⓗ
This Punch (Spirit) pub consists of a wedge-shaped room with the bar against the far wall. There is a large lantern hanging from the centre of the

beamed ceiling, and high tables and chairs. The first floor dining area, with its own bar, can be hired for functions. The pub dates from 1868 and was originally named the Bodega. Food is available until 9. ◑⊖(Piccadilly Circus)🚌

Pillars of Hercules

7 Greek Street, W1D 4DF

⌚ 11-11; 12-10.30 Sun

☎ (020) 7437 1179

Adnams Bitter, Broadside; Caledonian Deuchars IPA; Theakston Old Peculier; Wells Bombardier; guest beer Ⓗ

A pub has been on this site since the early 18th century and Dickens mentions it in A Tale of Two Cities. It was rebuilt around the turn of the 20th century in mock-Tudor and is now run by Faucet Inns. There are Hogarth prints on the walls and pictures of London that will make anyone over 100 years old feel nostalgic. Wednesday is music night. ◑⊖(Tottenham Ct Rd)🚌

Ship ✔

116 Wardour Street, W1F 0TT

⌚ 11-11; closed Sun

☎ (020) 7437 8446

Fuller's Discovery, London Pride, ESB, seasonal beers Ⓗ

Pre-deregulation, this rare Fuller's outlet in the West End was a welcome respite from the big brewers' products. It has some wonderful etched and leaded glass, decorative mirrors and an ornate wooden bar back. The story goes that the building was damaged by a gas explosion during World War II and then carefully repaired using the original 1895 fittings. The clientele reflects the local music and entertainment industry and the pub specialises in its own collection of indie music. ◖⊖(Tottenham Ct Rd)🚌

W2: Lancaster Gate

Leinster Arms ✔

17 Leinster Terrace, W2 3EU

⌚ 12-11; 12-10.30 Sun

☎ (020) 7402 4670

Fuller's London Pride; Taylor Landlord; guest beer Ⓗ

Built in 1856, this M&B pub is Grade II-listed. The facade is impressive, with the pub's name extending across the arch to the adjacent mews. Inside there is a fascinating collection of prints, portraits and paintings. The rear area has a notable brewery mirror. The beer range features a changing guest ale – beer mats and pump clips on display are evidence of previous brews. A vintage car club meets here every month. ❀◑⊖(Lancaster Gate/Queensway)🚌⚐

Mitre

24 Craven Terrace, W2 3QH

⌚ 11-11; 12-10.30 Sun

☎ (020) 7262 5240 🌐 mitrelancastergate.co.uk

Wells Bombardier; Young's Bitter, Special, seasonal beer Ⓗ

Built in 1859 and Grade II-listed, with the interior mostly intact, this pub features some original etched glass. The entrance on the corner has unusual rounded front doors. There are four interconnecting rooms, an upstairs dining room that can be hired for private parties and also a small seating area outside. Children are welcome. Taken over by Young's in 2008, it caters for many tourists and discerning drinkers. ◑⇌(Paddington)⊖🚌⚐

W2: Paddington

Cleveland Arms

28 Chilworth Street, W2 6PT

⌚ 11-11.30 (midnight Fri & Sat); 12-10.30 Sun

☎ (020) 7706 1759

Draught Bass; Greene King IPA; guest beer Ⓗ

A few minutes' walk from Paddington Station, this lovely Grade II-listed pub is named after William Vane, First Duke of Cleveland, and was built by DM Austin in 1852. Note the tiles at both ends on the front. A friendly free house serving local residents as well as passing tourists, it has two rooms; the rear one with dartboard and pool table can be hired for functions. Quiz night is Tuesday, bar buffet Sunday lunchtime. Children and dogs are welcome. ◑⇌⊖🚌⚐

Mad Bishop & Bear ✔

Upper Level, Paddington Station, W2 1HB

⌚ 8-11 (11.30 Fri); 10-10.30 Sun

☎ (020) 7402 2441

Fuller's Chiswick Bitter, Discovery, London Pride, ESB, seasonal beers; guest beers Ⓗ

Opened in 1999 on the second floor of a modern shopping complex attached to the station concourse. No smoking is allowed inside or out. The traditional pub interior features a long bar, mirrors, good prints and a rather grand chandelier. Even in the rush hour, it is not too crowded. There is a screen for train information and a TV for sports events. The raised drinking area can be hired for functions. Q❀◑⇌⊖🚌

Victoria ☆ ✔

10A Strathearn Place, W2 2NH

⌚ 11-11; 12-10.30 Sun

☎ (020) 7724 1191

Fuller's Chiswick, London Pride, ESB, seasonal beers Ⓗ

The pub, with its stucco exterior, dates from 1839 and is Grade II-listed. The impressive bar back inclues a clock, large decorated mirrors and columns. The two distinct bar areas both have fireplaces. Upstairs are the Library, with comfortable furnishings, and the Theatre Bar with fittings from the Gaiety. Reputedly visited by Queen Victoria after the opening of the rebuilt Paddington Station in 1854. Quiz night is Tuesday. Q❀◑⇌⊖(Lancaster Gate/Paddington)🚌⚐

W3: Acton

George & Dragon

183 High Street, W3 9DJ

⌚ 12-11 (midnight Fri & Sat); 12-10.30 Sun

☎ (020) 8992 3712 🌐 georgeanddragonacton.com

Fuller's Chiswick Bitter, London Pride; Gale's HSB Ⓗ

This 18th-century pub was wonderfully restored and improved by Remarkable Restaurants in 2006 and is now a welcoming venue with three bars of real character. A traditional public bar – with a list of landlords dating back to 1759 – leads into a heritage bar with exposed original features and a stylish back room. At the heart of the historic Acton town centre, the pub is opposite the main High Street bus stop (King Street/The Mount) and a short walk from local stations. ♨❀◑♿⇌(Acton Central)⊖(Acton Town)🚌♣⚐

W4: Chiswick

Duke of Sussex

75 South Parade, Acton Green, W4 5LF
☼ 12-11 (midnight Fri & Sat); 12-10.30 Sun
☎ (020) 8742 8801
Beer range varies Ⓗ
With three handpumps serving rotating guest beers, this Grade II-listed pub run by Realpubs Ltd openly welcomes families and dogs. Although it does not regularly show televised sport, it will make an exception for events of national interest. The large restaurant area specialises in English and Spanish cuisine. The bar and restaurant can be booked for parties.
Q❀◐◑♿⊖(Chiswick Pk)🚌(94,440)⚐

Fox & Hounds and Mawson Arms ✔

110 Chiswick Lane South, W4 2QA
☼ 10-8; closed Sat & Sun
☎ (020) 8994 2936
Fuller's Chiswick Bitter, Discovery, London Pride, ESB, seasonal beers Ⓗ
On the corner of the Griffin Brewery, and its de facto brewery tap, this pub is a popular start for the Fuller's brewery tour. Hot food is available at lunchtime, including the pub's renowned home-made steak and ale pies – the ale changes from week to week. The walls feature memorabilia of the brewery's history plus portraits of ancestors of the Fuller, Smith and Turner founders. The pub can be hired out at weekends. 🔥Q◐🚌(190)P

George & Devonshire ✔

8 Burlington Lane, W4 2QE
☼ 12-11; 11-midnight Fri & Sat; 12-10.30 Sun
☎ (020) 8994 1859 🌐 georgeanddevonshire.co.uk
Fuller's Chiswick Bitter, London Pride, ESB, seasonal beers Ⓗ
An alternative Fuller's brewery tap, off a roundabout at the far corner of the Griffin Brewery, this pub has featured in TV programmes of the 70s and 80s, notably The Sweeney. Hot food stops in the late afternoon but the staff are willing to provide a cold platter on request in the evening. The multi-purpose function room has a piano and there are plans for viewing films of local interest. One novelty of the pub is a shandy menu – the 'Randy Shandy', for example, contains cherryade. ❀◐◑🗨🚌(190)P⚐

Old Pack Horse ✔

434 Chiswick High Street, W4 5TF
☼ 10.30-11 (11.30 Thu & Sat; 1am Fri); 10.30-10.30 Sun
☎ (020) 8994 2872
Fuller's Chiswick Bitter, Discovery, London Pride, ESB Ⓗ
A well-preserved corner pub rebuilt in 1910, with a fine Edwardian frontage and retaining impressively ornate wood and glasswork. Five drinking areas include a snug and a large Thai restaurant at the back. The walls are adorned with theatre memorabilia. Two TVs show sports events. The late Tommy Cooper was a regular here.
❀◐◑⊖(Chiswick Pk)🚌⚐

W5: Ealing

Fox & Goose ✔

Hanger Lane, W5 1DP
☼ 12-11 (midnight Fri & Sat); 12-10.30 Sun
☎ (020) 8998 5864 🌐 foxandgoosehotel.com
Fuller's London Pride, ESB, seasonal beer Ⓗ
A long-standing Fuller's house whose frontage dates back to the 1830s. There has been a pub on this site for over 300 years, it being one of the original boundary houses for Ealing. Some interesting architectural points still survive and evidence of the past can be seen in the framed pictures in the front bar. A hotel block is attached, making this an ideal place to stay when visiting London or Wembley Stadium.
🔥❀🛏◐◑♿⊖(Hanger Lane)🚌P⚐

Questors (Grapevine Bar) ✔

12 Mattock Lane, W5 5BQ
☼ 7-11; 12-2.30, 7-10.30 Sun
☎ (020) 8567 0011 🌐 questors.org.uk/grapevine
Fuller's London Pride, seasonal beer; guest beers Ⓗ
This friendly theatre bar is set opposite Walpole Park just south of the town centre. Though regularly serving guest beers it also runs CAMRA-themed festivals twice a year. Books and board games are available, as are Belgian beers and obscure whiskies. The club is run by enthusiastic volunteers and is the current local CAMRA Club of the Year. Q❀♿⇌⊖(Ealing Broadway)🚌♣P⚐

Red Lion 🏆

13 St Mary's Road, W5 5RA
☼ 11-11 (midnight Thu-Sat); 12-11 Sun
☎ (020) 8567 2541
Fuller's Chiswick, London Pride, ESB, seasonal beer; guest beer Ⓗ
The pub is situated opposite Ealing Studios and is affectionately known as Stage 6. Many photographs of TV programmes and films produced at the studios adorn the walls. With the refurbishment several years ago, the licensee was able to add facilities for preparing homemade food while retaining the feel of the original building. At the front the decor is traditional; a more modern extension at the back leads to a covered patio. Winner of many local CAMRA awards.
Q❀◐◑♿⇌(Ealing Broadway)⊖(Ealing Broadway/ South Ealing)🚌(65)

W6: Hammersmith

Andover Arms ✔

57 Aldensley Road, W6 0DL
☼ 12-11.30
☎ (020) 8748 2155
Fuller's Chiswick Bitter, London Pride, ESB, seasonal beers Ⓗ
Built in 1853 and acquired by Fuller's in 1991, this pub in Brackenbury Village, between Goldhawk Road and King Street, was the local of 'Beer Hunter' Michael Jackson. A comfortably furnished room surrounds an attractive central bar that retains snob screens and spiral supporting pillars. There are interesting old photographs and prints on the walls. Look out for beer festivals in spring and autumn. Food is available lunchtimes (11-3pm) and evenings (6-10pm).
◐◑⊖(Ravenscourt Pk)🚌

Brook Green Hotel

170 Shepherds Bush Road, W6 7PB
☼ 11-midnight (11 Mon); 11-11 Sun
☎ (020) 7603 2516 🌐 brookgreenhotel.co.uk
Wells Bombardier; Young's Bitter, Waggledance; guest beers Ⓗ
An excellent Young's pub that hosts welcoming live jazz sessions every Tuesday night. Well-known for showing all the rugby internationals, this

pub delights its customers with well-conditioned beer and friendly bar staff banter. There is a separate basement bar that opens on Saturdays and for functions, and 14 en-suite rooms for a London stay over.

Dove

19 Upper Mall, W6 9TA
11-11; 12-10.30 Sun
(020) 8748 9474
Fuller's Discovery, London Pride, ESB, seasonal beers H
Traditional Fuller's pub, overlooking the Thames, with a quaint dark wood interior, and dining tables and sofa tucked away. Classic food with a slight twist is served every day; it can take up to 45 minutes to arrive at busy times, but is definitely worth the wait. Well-kept beer and a pleasant atmosphere make this one of the best pubs in the area. It also holds the Guinness world record for the smallest bar area.
Q (Ravenscourt Pk)

Plough & Harrow

120-124 King Street, W6 0QU
9-11.30
(020) 8735 6020
Courage Best Bitter, Directors; Fuller's London Pride; Greene King Abbot; Marston's Pedigree; guest beers H
Opened in 2002 in a former car showroom that had occupied the site since the demise of the original Plough & Harrow in 1959, this Wetherspoon's pub has a massive, open interior with tiled floors and an Art Deco touch. There is a carpeted rear area for families and diners and a small enclosed back lounge. A Holiday Inn hotel occupies the upper floors. Q (Hammersmith/Ravenscourt Pk)

Salutation

154 King Street, W6 0QU
11-11; 12-10.30 Sun
(020) 8748 3668
Fuller's Discovery, London Pride, ESB, seasonal beers H
A coaching inn first licensed in 1727, the present Fuller's pub, with its unusual tiled exterior, dates from 1910. The interior has been altered over the years: the large lounge bar now has some raised seating areas and a fine fireplace, and at the rear is an enclosed patio. Children are allowed on the premises until 9pm. The late Queen Mother visited in 1989 as Patron of the London Garden Society to inspect the floral display.
(Ravenscourt Pk)

W7: Hanwell

Fox

Green Lane, W7 2PJ
11-11; 12-10.30 Sun
(020) 8567 3912 thefoxpub.co.uk
Fuller's London Pride; Sharp's Doom Bar; Taylor Landlord; guest beers H
Spacious free house at the south end of Green Lane and a short walk from the Hanwell Locks on the Grand Union Canal, popular with walkers and narrowboat enthusiasts. Beer festivals are held at Easter and in October every year. Lunches are served daily, evening meals Tuesday-Saturday. A regular winner of local CAMRA Pub of the Year.
(195,E8)

W8: Notting Hill Gate

Churchill Arms

119 Kensington Church Street, W8 7LN
11-11 (midnight Thu-Sat); 12-10.30 Sun
(020) 7727 4242
Fuller's Chiswick Bitter, Discovery, London Pride, ESB, seasonal beers H
The winner of awards ranging from Boozers in Bloom to the Griffin Award for Fuller's pub of the year. As you enter it looks as if there is the contents of an antique market hanging from the ceiling. There is even a signpost in the middle of the pub just in case you get lost. The Thai food is to be recommended as well as the beer. Q

Uxbridge Arms

13 Uxbridge Street, W8 7TQ
12-11 (10.30 Sun)
(020) 7727 7326
Fuller's London Pride; St Austell Tribute; Wells Bombardier H
A popular back-street Enterprise local dating from 1836. Wood-panelled and carpeted throughout, the welcoming bar has a warm feel, with lots of photographs and plates, as well as a Lieutenant-Colonel's dress tunic. The best seats are at the end of the bar by the Nicola Sunshine Fund charity collection bottle. The pub has raised £6,400 since April 1990. Q

W11: Notting Hill

Cock & Bottle

17 Needham Road, W11 2RP
11-11; 12-10.30 Sun
(020) 7229 1550
Fuller's London Pride; Hogs Back TEA H
This CAMRA Regional Inventory Enterprise pub has a fine bar back, Corinthian columns and stained glass panels with swans above the windows. Dating from 1851, it was originally called the Swan Tavern. There are two comfortable seating areas plus a small area at the rear. The walls display paintings, including one of the Charge of the Light Brigade, together with prints and photos. The pub is very popular with locals and visiting drinkers alike, and there is a quiz on Tuesday evening.
Q (Notting Hill Gate)

W14: West Kensington

Crown & Sceptre

34 Holland Road, W14 8BA
11-11 (midnight Fri & Sat); 12-11 Sun
(020) 7602 1866
Butcombe Bitter; Hogs Back TEA; guest beers H
A quiet, unassuming corner pub in the affluent suburb of West Kensington, this S&N Pub Enterprises venture was local CAMRA Pub of the Year 2007. Modern decor and artwork on the inside blend successfully with a traditional London pub ambience, and Mexican food goes further to extend the feeling of old meets new. The beer range varies enormously.
Q (Kensington Olympia) (Olympia)

Brentford

Brewery Tap

47 Catherine Wheel Road, TW8 8BD
12-midnight

☎ (020) 8560 5200
Fuller's Chiswick Bitter, Discovery, London Pride, seasonal beer; guest beer Ⓗ
Popular with locals, this Victorian pub is renowned for its regular jazz on Tuesday and Thursday evenings. Live music features every evening of the week except Monday, which is quiz night. Meals are served until 7.30pm on weekdays, plus Sunday lunch. The rear patio is covered and heated, while the front terrace overlooks steps down to the street – the river used to flood here. It was originally the tap for the William Gomm Brewery, acquired by Fuller's in 1909. ❀◐◑⇌🚌♣⁄–

Express Tavern ✔
56 Kew Bridge Road, TW8 0EW
🕘 11.30-3pm, 5.30 (6.30 Sat)-11pm (midnight Thu-Sat); 12-10.30 Sun
☎ (020) 8560 8484
Draught Bass; Young's Bitter; guest beers Ⓗ
This historic and friendly free house at the north end of Kew Bridge is a short walk from both the Kew Bridge Steam Museum and the Musical Museum, and just over the river from Kew Gardens. There are usually two guests alongside the regular ales, and home-cooked food is served lunchtimes and most evenings (not Tue & Sun). The pub offers two cosy bars, one with a piano, plus a mock-manorial lounge and a beer garden with covered and heated area. Q❀◐◑⊕♿⇌(Kew Bridge)🚌⁄–

Magpie & Crown
128 High Street, TW8 8EW
🕘 11-midnight (1am Thu-Sat); 12-midnight Sun
☎ (020) 8560 4570
Beer range varies Ⓗ
This mock-Tudor free house was recently declared by the Robert Rankin fan club to be 'The Flying Swan' of his Brentford Trilogy comic novels. It usually offers four real ales (2,200 have been served since 1996), at least one cider or perry, draught Budvar, Paulaner and Stiegl, Fruli fruit beer and continental and British bottled beers. Thai food is available except Monday. Bar billiards and other games are played. There are tables and a cycle-rack at front, and a rear patio. ❀◑⇌🚌♣●

O'Brien's ✔
11 London Road, TW8 8JB (near canal bridge at W end of High St)
🕘 11-11; 12-10.30 Sun
☎ (020) 8560 0506 🌐 obrienspub.co.uk
Fuller's London Pride; guest beers Ⓗ
Formerly the Northumberland Arms, this compact and popular free house on the main road through Brentford features an ever-changing range of cask beers, frequently from the local Twickenham Brewery, as well as some Belgian specialities. Acoustic music sessions are held on Tuesday evening and a quiz night on Wednesday. TV coverage of sporting events provides regular entertainment. ❀◐◑⇌🚌⁄–

Colham Green

Crown
Colham Green Road, Uxbridge, UB8 3QH
🕘 12-11 (10.30 Sun)
☎ (01895) 442303 🌐 thecrowncolhamgreen.co.uk
Fuller's London Pride; Gale's HSB; guest beers Ⓗ
A comfortable, welcoming Fuller's local approximately five minutes walk from Hillingdon Hospital. The one-room lounge bar has pictures of celebrities adorning the walls and a separate dining area away from the bar. Occasional theme evenings are held. A large Spanish-style garden with a covered heated area allows for good outdoor drinking whatever the weather. Hearty, good value meals are cooked fresh to order lunchtimes and evenings, with roast lunches served on Sunday. Q❀◐◑♿🚌(U5)♣P⁄–

Feltham

Moon on the Square ✔
30 The Centre, High Street, TW13 4AU
🕘 9-midnight (1am Fri & Sat); 9-10.30 Sun
☎ (020) 8893 1293
Courage Best Bitter, Directors; Greene King Ruddles Best, Abbot; Shepherd Neame Spitfire; guest beers Ⓗ
This real ale oasis continues to flourish in a changing Feltham. The interior is early Wetherspoon: wood panels and glass partitioned booths, with pictures and local history panels. The welcome is warm and genuine. At least eight real ales feature continuously varying guests, including local brews. Westons cider is also available. The usual Wetherspoon's value-for-money fare is served all day. Families and children are welcome until early evening. ◐◑♿⇌🚌●

Greenford

Black Horse ✔
425 Oldfield Lane North, UB6 0AS
🕘 11.30-11 (midnight Fri & Sat); 12-11 Sun
☎ (020) 8578 1384
Fuller's London Pride, ESB; guest beers Ⓗ
This friendly, 250-year-old pub, on the bank of the Grand Union Canal, was extended in 1994 and tastefully refurbished by Fuller's in 2007. Children and dogs are welcome. There is a large garden with 28 tables, at the side of which boats can legally moor. Sport is always shown on Sky, but it is not seen (or heard) throughout the pub. Poker night is Tuesday and quiz night Thursday.
❀◐◑♿⇌⊖🚌(92)♣P⁄–

Bridge Hotel
Western Avenue, UB6 8ST
🕘 12-11 (midnight Fri & Sat)
☎ (020) 8566 6246 🌐 thebridgehotel.com
Wells Bombardier; Young's Bitter, Special; guest beer Ⓗ
A small Young's pub inside a hotel with beers served from behind a pleasant corner bar. There is plenty of seating and the bar is well staffed by friendly people. The food is of a great quality, the menu varying daily. The pub has a friendly atmosphere with a good mix of locals, guests and ale drinkers.
❀🛏◐◑♿⇌(Greenford/S Greenford)⊖🚌P⁄–

Hampton

Railway Bell
Station Road, TW12 2AP
🕘 11-11; 12-10.30 Sun
☎ (020) 8979 1897 🌐 therailwaybell.ph
Courage Best Bitter; guest beers Ⓗ
Known locally as 'The Dip', this smallish white-painted cottage-style Enterprise pub is approached across a pleasant patio area down a driveway beside the railway bridge (Tudor Road) just to the east of the station. Both public and saloon bars are

simply furnished and the latter is decorated with authentic old photos of the Hampton area. Four guest beers always include one from the nearby Twickenham Brewery. Evening meals are served Monday to Friday. ❀◑≹▭(111,216)⁞–

Hampton Hill

Roebuck 🏆

72 Hampton Road, TW12 1JN

11-11 (11.30 Fri & Sat); 12-4, 7-10.30 Sun

☎ (020) 8255 8133

Sharp's Doom Bar, Special; Young's Bitter; guest beers Ⓗ

The interior of this street-corner free house is rather like an Aladdin's cave. Highlights range from the wickerwork Harley Davidson at one end to the cigar store Indian at the other. All of the tables have old newspapers, bank notes or coins under glass tops. The traffic lights in the bar which indicate closing time are now replicated in the award-winning garden which also has a heated gazebo for smokers. Local CAMRA Pub of the Year for 2008. ⛫❀⇆◑≹(Fulwell)▭♣⁞–

Hayes

Botwell Inn ✔

25-29 Coldharbour Lane, UB3 3EB

9-midnight

☎ (020) 8848 3112

Greene King Ruddles Best, Abbot; Marston's Pedigree; guest beers Ⓗ

A Wetherspoon's shop conversion with family-friendly areas for dining. The decor is fairly dark but with a comfortable ambience. There is a small patio to the rear with a huge market-style canopy and heaters to cater for smokers, plus a roadside pavement area at the front. Food is served all day until 10pm. Westons Old Rosie cider is available on handpump.
Q❀◑♿≹(Hayes & Harlington)▭●⁞–

Hillingdon Hill

Prince of Wales

1 Harlington Road, Uxbridge, UB8 3HX

10-midnight (2am Fri & Sat)

☎ (01895) 254416

Fuller's London Pride, ESB Ⓗ

Grade II-listed Fuller's pub which retains a number of wooden panels, creating a warm and cosy atmosphere. A quiet, traditional local pub on the A4020, close to Hillingdon cricket ground and village, it has separate lounge and public bars and a secluded patio garden. Bar snacks are available lunchtimes, plus well-kept cask ale and a good range of wines. Q❀◐⊟♿▭(427,A10)♣P⁞–

Hounslow

Moon Under Water ✔

84-88 Staines Road, TW3 3LF (W end of High St)

10 (12 Sun)-11

☎ (020) 8572 7506

Greene King Ruddles Best, Abbot; guest beers Ⓗ

Early Wetherspoon's shop conversion, enlarged recently, in typical original style and still displaying a few local history panels and photos. Very popular, it has a diverse customer base. There are normally five guest ales – far more at festival times, when all 12 handpumps offer different beers. Children are welcome until 8.30pm; the rear is considered the family area, with a patio outside. Q❀◑♿⊖(Hounslow Central)▭⁞–

Ickenham

Tichenham Inn ✔

11 Swakeleys Road, UB10 8DF

9-11 (midnight Thu-Sat)

☎ (01895) 678916

Fuller's London Pride; Greene King Ruddles Best, Abbot; Marston's Pedigree; Rebellion seasonal beers; guest beers Ⓗ

This small and friendly Wetherspoon's pub was once a garage before it took on its new life. It has a strong local following and offers at least two Rebellion beers from Marlow, including Rebellion Red during October. One of the largest outlets for the Rebellion Brewery, Rebellion Ickenham was brewed specially for the local Ickenham Festival. Two or three other guest beers are also available.
Q❀◑♿≹(West Ruislip)⊖(Ickenham/West Ruislip)▭(U1,U10)⁞–

Isleworth

Red Lion ✔

92-94 Linkfield Road, TW7 6QJ

11-11.30 (midnight Fri & Sat); 12-10.30 Sun

☎ (020) 8560 1457 🌐 red-lion.info

Fuller's London Pride; Hogs Back TEA; Young's Bitter; guest beers Ⓗ

Spacious two-bar free house with a strong community focus. There is often something going on: a production on stage or in the garden performed by its own theatre group, live music (Sat eve, Sun afternoon), a quiz on Thursday, or darts and pool competitions. Up to six beers complement the three regulars, and twice-yearly beer festivals feature champion beers. Lunches are offered daily, and evening meals (except Sun). Local CAMRA Pub of the Year 2003 and 2004. ❀◑⊟♿≹▭●⁞–

Longford

White Horse

530 Bath Road, UB7 0EE

11-11

☎ (01753) 682520 🌐 whitehorselongford.com

Courage Best Bitter; Fuller's London Pride; Wells Bombardier; guest beer Ⓗ

A 17th-century building, with some of its front windows bricked up to avoid the window tax. This Enterprise pub has two bars – the Barn Bar is not always open. The main bar inside the pub is split by a chimney, as is the main room. Low ceilings and whitewashed walls create an atmosphere of an old country pub. The walls are decorated with horse brasses and other knick-knacks, along with pictures of historic Longford. ❀◑⊟▭(81,423)

Southall

Conservative & Unionist Club

Fairlawn, High Street, UB1 3HB

11.30-2.30, 7-11; 11.30-3, 6-11 Fri & Sat; 12-3, 7-10.30 Sun

☎ (020) 8574 0261

Rebellion IPA, seasonal beers; guest beers Ⓗ

Virtually the last real ale outlet in this historic market town, situated behind the former town hall. Access can be gained with this Guide or a CAMRA membership card. A selection of beers from the Rebellion range is to be found inside. Meals are served at lunchtimes and various events are held most evenings. This is an ideal meeting place before enjoying a curry in one of the many local restaurants. ❀◐⇌🚌♣P🚬

Teddington

Adelaide

57 Park Road, TW11 0AU
⌚ 12-11 (midnight Fri & Sat); 12-10.30 Sun
☎ (020) 8977 3616
Shepherd Neame Master Brew Bitter, Kent's Best, Spitfire, seasonal beer Ⓗ
Popular and friendly one-room community pub a short walk from the station and Bushy Park, with a dominant central bar. Some seating is provided outside, and at the rear is a secluded, covered patio extending to a grassed garden area. An extensive selection of good food including chef's specials is served 12-3 (not Mon) and 6-9pm; Sunday 12-5pm. A folk club meets twice a month in the upstairs function room. ❀◐◑⇌🚌(481,X26)🚬

Builders Arms

38 Field Lane, TW11 9AS
⌚ 12-2.30, 4.30-11; 12-11 Sat & Sun
☎ (020) 8255 4220
Fuller's London Pride; Sharp's Doom Bar; Twickenham Sundancer; Young's Bitter Ⓗ
Featured in CAMRA's London Regional Inventory, this Enterprise pub is a delightful back-street two-room Edwardian corner house off the High Street. It has been sympathetically redecorated, with the landlady adding her personal touch. Both rooms have beamed ceilings. The side room has a pool table and there is a small secluded patio garden. The walls are wood panelled, with two original fireplaces. Brown glazed brick is used on the outside walls. Outside there is seating on a small front terrace. ♨❀◐♿⇌🚌(281,285,R68)♣🚬

Lion

27 Wick Road, TW11 9DN
⌚ 12-11.30 (11 Sun-Tue)
☎ (020) 8977 3199 🌐 thelionpub.co.uk
Fuller's London Pride; Sharp's Doom Bar; Twickenham seasonal beer; guest beer Ⓗ
Victorian single bar Enterprise pub a short walk from Hampton Wick Station, sympathetically modernised and extended, with a choice of high-quality food until 9pm. Wednesday is quiz night and there is live music most Saturdays. The landlord has continued the tradition of holding an annual beer festival. There is a large patio and garden with a children's play area, also a pool table, sports TV and a function room. Greater London CAMRA Pub of the Year 2006.
♨❀◐◑♿⇌(Hampton Wick)🚌(281,285)♣🚬

> It is gratifying, in these days of hop and malt substitutes and other abominations, to know that the princes of the trade still adhere to malt and hops. For those who sell adulterated beer, no punishment can be too great. **W T Marchant**, 1888

Twickenham

Ailsa Tavern

263 St Margarets Road, TW1 1NJ
⌚ 11-11 (11.30 Fri & Sat); 12-10.30 Sun
☎ (020) 8892 1633 🌐 ailsatavern.com
Fuller's London Pride; Shepherd Neame Canterbury Jack, Kent's Best, Spitfire; guest beer Ⓗ
A traditional community pub acquired by Shepherd Neame in 2009, named after a Victorian landlady. This listed building is in a residential area within sight of the Twickenham rugby ground. Outside, wisteria vines decorate the walls to the front and the beer garden is a favourite haunt, as there are not many in this area. Three separate drinking areas offer fine ales and food from around the world, prepared by an award-winning cellarman and chef. Regular beer festivals are held.
♨Q❀◐◑⇌(St Margarets)🚌(H37)🚬

Prince Albert ✔

30 Hampton Road, TW2 5QB
⌚ 11-11 (midnight Fri & Sat)
☎ (020) 8894 3963
Gale's HSB; Fuller's Chiswick Bitter, Discovery, London Pride, ESB, seasonal beer Ⓗ
Originally opened by the Star Brewery in 1840, the pub was later unofficially known as 'Wiffen's' as it was run by three generations of the same family whose name is still displayed behind the bar. Nowadays it is divided into three areas and has a sports screen, and is popular for its convivial atmosphere and Thai restaurant. The attractive garden and patio are pleasant in summer. Live music is played on Saturday evening. Two annual beer festivals feature small brewers.
♨Q❀◐◑♿⇌(Strawberry Hill)🚌🚬

Prince Blucher ✔

124 The Green, TW2 5AG
⌚ 11-11 (midnight Fri & Sat); 12-11 Sun
☎ (020) 8894 1824
Fuller's Chiswick Bitter, Discovery, London Pride, ESB, seasonal beer; Gale's Seafarer Ⓗ
Historic 1815 inn, the first to be built on the newly enclosed Twickenham Green and reputedly the only pub in the UK still to pay homage to the Duke of Wellington's left flanker at Waterloo. Four separate bar areas suit most tastes. The enthusiastic landlord of 12 years' standing offers home-cooked food all day and in summer hosts hog roasts and barbecues in the ample, child-friendly garden. Food and real ale festivals also feature. ♨Q❀◐◑⇌(Strawberry Hill)🚌P🚬

Prince of Wales

136 Hampton Road, TW2 5QR
⌚ 12 (4 Mon)-11
☎ (020) 8894 5054
Adnams Bitter; St Austell Tribute; Twickenham Sundancer, seasonal beers; guest beers Ⓗ
An inn on this site was the final staging post on the Windsor to London stagecoach route over 150 years ago. The original, surviving stables are listed. Once an Isleworth Brewery pub and now run by S&N Pub Enterprises, this is an unspoilt one-room community pub with a restaurant/function room serving French style cuisine (no food Mon and Tue). Acoustic music plays on Tuesday and quiz night is Thursday. Outside is an attractive garden and heated smoking area. Local Twickenham Brewery beers are always available.
♨Q❀◐◑⇌(Fulwell/Strawberry Hill)🚌🚬

Turk's Head ✓

28 Winchester Road, St Margarets, TW1 1LF

12-11 (11.30 Thu; midnight Fri & Sat); 12-10.30 Sun

☎ (020) 8892 1972

Fuller's Discovery, London Pride, ESB, seasonal beer H

A local corner pub built in 1902, offering fine beers, food, and live music on Friday. Beatles fans used to flock here to see the pub location for a scene from A Hard Day's Night. The Bearcat Comedy Club has been inviting top comedians to the function room every Saturday night for more than 20 years. Rugby fans form human pyramids on match days and try and stick their tickets on the high ceiling! The smoking area outside is heated.

Q(St Margaret's)(H37)

Uxbridge

Load of Hay

33 Villier Street, UB8 2PU

11-midnight

☎ (01895) 234676

Fuller's London Pride; guest beers H

Originally the officers mess of the Elthorne Light Militia, this became a pub in the 1870s. A genuine free house, it usually sells three guest beers, mostly from small and micro-breweries. The pub hosts darts matches, there is an open cribbage competition on Thursday and a quiz on Tuesday. Live music on Saturday includes folk and traditional modern jazz. A recent addition is Millwhites cider on the bar. Car parking is limited.

(U3)P

Queens Head ✓

54 Windsor Street, UB8 1AB

11-11 (10.30 Sun)

☎ (01895) 258750

Brains SA; Wadworth 6X; Young's Bitter; guest beers H

Rebuilt after an arson attack in 1986 and now run by Punch, this Grade II-listed building in the old part of town retains the feeling of an old English pub with its low ceilings and exposed brick. The bar is an irregular L-shape in the main part of the pub and there is a small area to the back which is a little quieter. It was named after Anne Boleyn, whose head is shown on the sign outside.

Bridge Hotel, Greenford, West London (Photo: Geoff Brandwood).

GREATER MANCHESTER

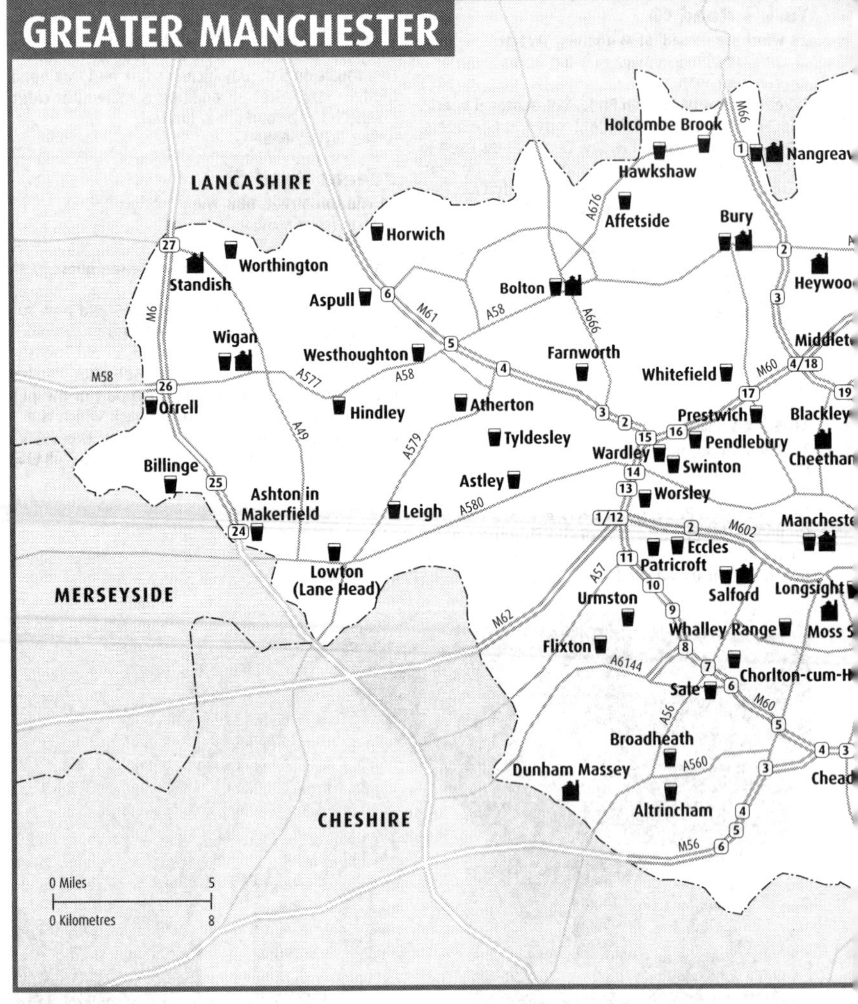

Affetside

Pack Horse

52 Watling Street, BL8 3QW SD755136

12-3, 6-11 (12-11 summer); 12-midnight Fri-Sun

(01204) 883802 packhorseaffetside.co.uk

Hydes Owd Oak, Original Bitter, seasonal beers

This country pub benefits from superb panoramic views thanks to its situation high up on a Roman road. The bar areas and cosy lounge with real fire are part of the original pub, dating from the 15th century. It has a function room and pool room, while the Hightop bar is used as a family room. Many a tale is told about the ghost of a local man whose skull is on view behind the bar. Good quality food is served.

Altrincham

Old Market Tavern

Old Market Place, WA14 4DN (on A56)

12-11 (midnight Wed-Sat)

(0161) 927 7062 oldmarkettavern.co.uk

Bank Top Volunteer; Caledonian Deuchars IPA; Phoenix Arizona; guest beers

Well-deserved winner of CAMRA branch Pub of The Year 2008. Formerly a bank, temporary town hall and coaching inn, this pub has been opened out into four distinct areas together with a beer garden and meeting room. A lively entertainment programme is always on offer including rock bands on Saturday, an open acoustic session on Thursday and a regular quiz night with a free buffet.

Orange Tree

15 Old Market Place, WA14 4DE (on A56)

12-midnight (1am Fri & Sat)

(0161) 928 2935

Caledonian Deuchars IPA; Copper Dragon Golden Pippin; guest beer

Standing in front of the stocks at the Old Market Place, legend has it that a man sold his wife here for a shilling and sixpence in 1823. Meals are served lunchtimes and evenings daily. Sky Sports is shown, karaoke takes place weekly. The pub is dog friendly, children are welcome until 6pm and there is a heated smoking shelter and barbecue area to the rear. Rumour has it that the pub is haunted!

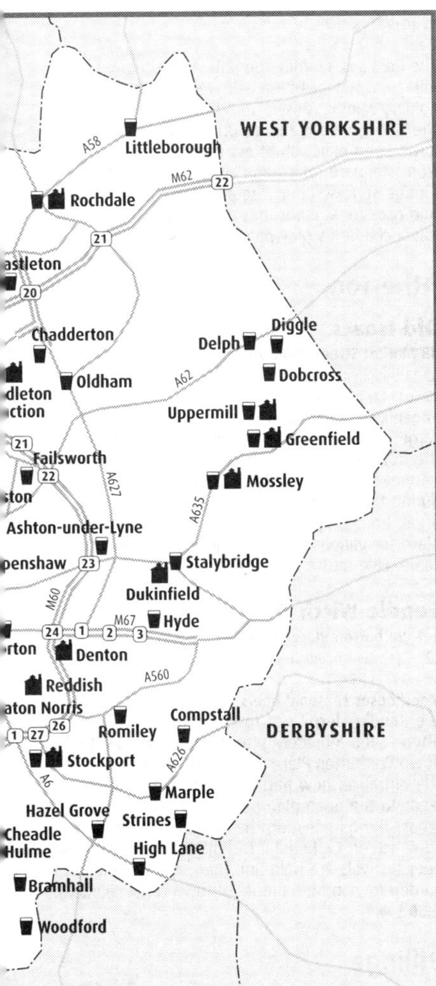

Ashton-in-Makerfield

Jubilee Club

167-169 Wigan Road, WN4 9ST
8 (7.30 Fri & Sat)-midnight
(01942) 202703 jubileeclubashton.co.uk
Beer range varies H
A warm, friendly social club with a welcoming atmosphere. It has a small games room and lobby bar area, a main lounge bar available for functions, plus a small function room upstairs. At least one ever-changing cask ale, often from a local micro-brewery, is served at a competitive price. The club raises money for charity. Non-members are welcome subject to constraints on frequency of visits and payment of a nominal admission charge. Outside is a covered smoking area.
≠(Bryn)(600,601)♣P

Park Lane

159-163 Downall Green Road, Bryn, WN4 0DW (on B5207 off A49)
12-midnight
(01942) 727872
Tetley Bitter; guest beer H
A former social club, this free house offers it's large function room free for special occasions and for band practice by a local brass band. It has a very popular games room with snooker table, darts and large TV screen. Teams feature in local sports leagues. The regular beer is Tetley Bitter and guests vary. Q≠♣

Sir Thomas Gerrard ✓

2 Gerrard Street, WN4 9AN (on A58)
9-midnight (1am Fri & Sat)
(01942) 713519
Greene King Ruddles County, Abbot; Marston's Pedigree; guest beers H
Known locally as the Tom & Jerry, this Wetherspoon pub is a former supermarket. Interesting features including a tiled mural depicting aspects of Ashton-in-Makerfield's history. There are two raised areas away from the busy main floor and small booths to the rear which are good for a cosy drink. Guest beers usually include a LocAle. The pub gets busy at weekends and on race days as it is within walking distance of Haydock Park Racecourse.
(320,600,601)P

Ashton-under-Lyne

Dog & Pheasant

528 Oldham Road, OL7 9PQ
12-11 (11.30 Fri & Sat); 12-10.30 Sun
(0161) 330 4894
Banks's Original; Marston's Burton Bitter, Pedigree; guest beers H
This popular, friendly local near the Medlock Valley Country Park has been a regular Guide entry over the years and is nicknamed the Top Dog. It has a large bar serving three areas, plus another room at the front. The menu of good value food includes vegetarian options. On Tuesday and Thursday evenings a quiz is hosted. Up to three guest beers from the Marston's portfolio are available at all times. Home to a local hiking group known as the Bog Trotters. (409,419)P

INDEPENDENT BREWERIES

3 Rivers Reddish
All Gates Wigan
Bank Top Bolton
Bazens' Salford
Boggart Hole Clough Moston
Cellar Rat Reddish
Dane Town Denton (brewing suspended)
Dunham Massey Dunham Massey
Green Mill Rochdale
Greenfield Greenfield
Holt Cheetham
Hornbeam Denton
Hydes Moss Side
Lees Middleton Junction
Leyden Nangreaves
Marble Manchester
Mayflower Wigan
Millstone Mossley
Outstanding Bury
Phoenix Heywood
Pictish Rochdale
Prospect Standish
Robinson's Stockport
Saddleworth Uppermill
Shaws Dukinfield

Junction Inn

Mossley Road, Hazelhurst, OL6 9BX (on A670)
12-3 (not Mon), 5-midnight; 12-midnight Sat & Sun
☎ (0161) 343 1611
Robinson's Hatters, Unicorn, seasonal beers H
Built from local stone, this pub of great character has remained little changed since the 19th century. It is situated close to Ashton golf course and open country. Small, cosy front rooms serve as a lounge and make it welcoming; the recently converted tap room is a small restaurant. The famous home-made rag puddings, a Lancashire speciality, are on the menu at lunchtime, along with other pub food which is also served Thursday to Saturday evenings until 9pm. Traditional Sunday lunch is popular.
Q❀◑▶🚌(350)♣

Oddfellows Arms

1-7 Alderley Street, Hurst, OL6 9LJ
12-1am
☎ (0161) 330 6356
Robinson's Hatters, Unicorn, seasonal beers H
Within a terrace of former cottages, after 90 years the Oddies has ceased to be in the hands of the same family. However, the interior has changed little, with its small hatch and screen, polished bar and stained glass. Drinkers can still select their favourite nook or cranny or use the more spacious lounge areas. In the walled garden there is a smokers' den and a koi carp fish pond. The tenants have won a Robinson's Brewery food award.
Q❀◑▶🚌(38,39)⚐

Aspull

Victoria

50 Haigh Road, WN2 1YA (on B5239)
1-midnight
☎ (01942) 830869
Beer range varies H
All Gates Brewery's first pub, this is a traditional two-room local. The smart yet intimate lounge displays photographs depicting the history of Aspull and Haigh. Two large-screen TVs cater for sports fans. The pub is well located for Haigh Hall Country Park and is halfway between Bolton Wanderers and Wigan Athletic football grounds. Guest beers come from All Gates and other micro-breweries. LocAle accredited. The smoking area is covered.
🚌(575,715)♣P⚐

Astley

Cart & Horses

221 Manchester Road, M29 7SD
12-11 (1am Fri & Sat); 12-10.30 Sun
☎ (01942) 870751
Holt Mild, Bitter H
Popular, friendly local with an open-plan lounge that was formerly two rooms and still retains a divided feel. There is also a busy tap room to the side of the bar, and a raised seating area that leads to the patio, large walled garden and rear car park. The pub's frontage is worth a look, with etched windows either side of the front door and a Holt's roof sign. Regular quiz nights are held; the local golf society and the Leigh Premier Cycling Club meet here. ❀◑▶♣P⚐

Ross's Arms ✔

130 Higher Green Lane, Higher Green, M29 7JB
12-11 (midnight Fri & Sat); 12-10.30 Sun
☎ (01942) 874405
Beer range varies H
The Ross's is a family-run pub and restaurant in the village of Higher Green, situated next to the Astley Colliery Mining Museum and the Leigh Branch of the Bridgewater Canal at Bridge 58. Inside, the large open plan pub offers various seating areas from standard tables and chairs to comfortable lounge-style seating. Regular food theme nights and occasional barbecues are hosted. The garden has a children's play park. ❀◑▶♿🚌P⚐

Atherton

Old Isaacs

48 Market Street, M46 0DG
11-midnight; 12-11 Sun
☎ (01942) 882885
Phoenix seasonal beers H
Large, popular town centre pub with two rooms at the front for dining or chatting. The main lounge has several comfortable seating areas. Handy during the day for a quiet drink and a snack and a break from shopping, it is also a popular meeting place for various societies, including the Round Table. Live music plays. Q◑▶

Pendle Witch 🏆

2-4 Warburton Place, M46 0EQ
11 (12 Sun)-midnight
☎ (01942) 884537
Moorhouses seasonal beers; guest beers H
The Pendle, despite its town centre location, is often called a hidden gem, tucked away as it is down Warburton Place (access from Market Street). The entrance, now part of a large conservatory, leads to the open plan bar with various seating areas. The games room has a pool table and a large-screen TV. Regular rock nights plus occasional beer festivals are held and there is a well-kept garden for summer. Plenty of town centre parking.
❀◑▶♿♣⚐

Billinge

Holts Arms

Crank Road, WN5 7DT (off B5206)
12 (3 Mon)-11.30; 12-12.30am Sat & Sun
☎ (01695) 622705
Beer range varies H
Known locally as the Foot due to its location at the foot of an old causeway, this is a listed building dating from 1721. It features a central bar in the main lounge and a separate dining area. The pleasant bowling green to the rear overlooks Billinge Hill, with an adjacent children's play area. Meals are available 12-2.30pm and 5-8.30pm Friday and Saturday, 12-7.30pm Sunday. Q❀◑P

Masons

99 Carr Mill Road, WN5 7TY (off A571)
2-1am (midnight Sun)
☎ (01744) 603572
Black Sheep Best Bitter; Courage Directors; Taylor Landlord; guest beers H
Local CAMRA Pub of the Season, Masons has been owned by the same family for as long as anyone can remember. It offers a cosy atmosphere with a welcoming coal fire and pleasant background music. Rugby artefacts adorn the walls in the main bar and movie memorabilia in the rear lobby. Impromptu folk music sessions are held on Thurday

evenings and occasional quiz nights. No regular food is available but it dishes up the infamous Burchalls pies on Fridays and Cottoms hotpots on Thursday evenings. There is a luxurious smoking shelter at the rear. ♨Q❀P⚐

Blackley

Golden Lion

47 Old Market Street, M9 8DX (off Rochdale Road)
⊙ 11-11 (midnight Fri & Sat)
☎ (0161) 740 1941
Holt Mild, Bitter Ⓗ
This fine community pub is the hub of Blackley village. The once separate rooms in the lounge area have been opened out and a quieter side room added – a separate vault and side entrance remain. This is one of a few rare pubs that still has a crown green bowling green and a veranda, which acts as a covered and heated smoking shelter. The mild handpump can be found in the vault. Quiz night is Thursday, with hot food available. ❀⊟▣(51,112)♣P⚐

Bolton

Barristers

7 Bradshawgate, BL1 1HJ (on A575, near Market Cross)
⊙ 12-1am (2am Fri & Sat)
☎ (01204) 365174
Black Sheep Best Bitter; Moorhouse's Blond Witch, Barristers Brief; Wychwood Hobgoblin; guest beers Ⓗ
Barristers Bar is part of the Swan Hotel, a listed building dating from 1845. The wood-panelled interior has been retained and tastefully decorated to recreate a traditional pub atmosphere. The regular range of real ales is supplemented by guest ales which are primarily from local independent breweries. A heated courtyard with tables is used as a smoking area, and disabled toilet facilities are available. A pianist plays on Saturday and Sunday evenings. ❀⇌⚐

Doffcocker

780 Chorley Old Road, BL1 5QE (on B6226)
⊙ 11-11 (midnight Fri & Sat)
☎ (01204) 497426
Holt Mild, Bitter, seasonal beers Ⓗ
This grand, imposing local landmark dated 1901 is in every sense a pillar of the local community. It is a rare 'calendar pub' designed with a mysterious numerical precision (365 panes of glass, 52 doors, etc). The upstairs function room is home to nine local clubs including a metal detector enthusiasts club. In the spacious bar the walls are decorated with Bolton Wanderers memorabilia. On Wednesday afternoon there is a quiz in the comfortable lounge. Food is served 12-5.30pm. ❀◐⊟▣(125,519)♣P⚐

Flag Inn ✔

Arnold Road, Egerton, BL7 9HL (off B6472 Darwen Road) SD717138
⊙ 12-11 (midnight Fri & Sat)
☎ (01204) 598267
Bank Top Flat Cap; Greene King IPA; Moorhouse's Blond Witch; Titanic Iceberg; guest beers Ⓗ
Close to the Last Drop village, walkers are attracted to this pub for its proximity to good countryside. Ten handpumps include rotating Bank Top beers. The Saturday beer club must include a pint of traditional cider. Locally-produced home-cooked specials complement an already comprehensive menu. Live TV sport is shown on multi-screens. Note the unusual viewing cellar. Sporadic and spontaneous piano sessions are hosted and there is a quiz on Sunday. Visitors come to this pub from far and wide.
♨❀◐⇌(Bromley Cross)▣(225,563)♣●⚐

Hen & Chickens ✔

143 Deansgate, BL1 1EX (on B6204 opp post office)
⊙ 11.30 (7 Sun)-11 (extended hours on request)
☎ (01204) 389836
Tetley Dark Mild, Bitter; guest beers Ⓗ
Cask beers are promoted enthusiastically here – in addition to the Tetley ales, several regularly changing guest beers are supplied from the Punch Taverns portfolio. The pub is renowned for its friendly atmosphere and excellent home-cooked lunchtime food. Popular quiz nights are held during the week. The pub is available for private hire during the day on Sunday. There are steps at the door but staff are happy to assist. ◐⇌▣⚐

Hope & Anchor

147 Chorley Old Road, BL1 5QH (on B6226)
⊙ 12-midnight (1am Fri & Sat)
☎ (01204) 842650
Lees Bitter; Taylor Landlord; Tetley Bitter Ⓗ
Situated less than two miles from Bolton town centre, just near Doffcocker Lodge, a well-known nature reserve, this traditional local dating from the late Victorian era attracts walkers and bird watchers. A central bar serves two distinct snugs used for different functions (quiz nights, etc). Locals call the pub the Little Cocker, to distinguish it from the big Doffcocker Inn across the road. A new extension with disabled access and a pool room does not affect the original pub layout. TV sports are shown. Sandwiches are always available.
Q♘❀▣(125,519)♣P⚐

House Without A Name

75-77 Lea Gate, Harwood, BL2 3ET (on B6196, near A676 jct) SD737121
⊙ 12-11.30 (12.30am Fri & Sat); 12-11.30 Sun
☎ (01204) 304750
Holt Bitter; guest beers Ⓗ
Traditional village pub dating from 1810 with a two room layout. Memorabilia from the local Trafalgar Day group is on display in the lounge and there are poignant pictures of the local area throughout. Now the pub is free of tie, it supplements its regular Holt's with an ever-changing selection of ales. The beer terrace is a sun-trap on a summer's evening, with a covered area for smokers provided. The pub also holds occasional beer festivals.
❀⊟▣(506,507)♣⚐

Kings Head

52 Junction Road, Deane, BL3 4NA (just off A676)
⊙ 3.30 (12 Sat & Sun)-11
☎ (01204) 62609
Bank Top Flat Cap; Wells Bombardier Ⓗ
Set back off the road in a lovely setting close to the oldest church in Bolton, Deane Parish Church. A stone built Grade II-listed building from the 17th century, it was named the Kings Head in 1824 and used primarily as a travellers' overnight stop. It has three rooms, two with low timber framed ceilings, the other featuring a cast iron range. At the rear is a bowling green, children's play area and outdoor seating. Q❀▣P⚐

Masons Arms

156-158 Blackburn Road, Egerton, BL7 9SB (on A666)
⏲ 4 (3 Fri) -11 (midnight Thu & Fri); 12-midnight Sat; 12-11 Sun
☎ (01204) 303517
Greene King Ruddles Best; Theakston Best Bitter; guest beers Ⓗ
This inviting pub with its brick-and-stone facade is situated about three miles from Bolton and dates from the late Victorian era. Good value beers, including two constantly changing guests, are dispensed from four handpumps on an imposing bar. The bar is always packed on Tuesday night for the quiz and on Wednesday evening when folk music plays. This is the place for those looking for a genuine friendly local. ❀🚌♣⊬

Spinning Mule ✔

Unit 2, Nelson Square, BL1 1JT
⏲ 9-midnight (1am Fri & Sat)
☎ (01204) 533339
Greene King Ruddles Best; Marston's Pedigree; guest beers Ⓗ
Newly built in 1998, this town-centre pub, just off Bradshawgate, is an open-plan split-level building with a comfortable dining area in a modern Wetherspoon style. It is named after Samuel Crompton's Mule, a revolutionary invention in cotton spinning that made Bolton famous throughout the world. The original device can be seen in the town's museum and Crompton himself is immortalised by the statue in the square. The Mule supports Bank Top, Moorhouse's and other local breweries. Q◐◑♿⇌

Volunteer

276 Radcliffe Road, Darcy Lever, BL3 1RS (on B6209)
⏲ 1-11; 12-midnight Sat & Sun
☎ (01204) 524271
Holt Bitter, Ⓗ
This once thriving village close to Leverhulme Park still has its own cricket ground. The pub was once a Victorian beer house – part of the original red sandstone frontage can be seen alongside a brick built extension. Inside, the single large room is divided by a central bar and there are areas for darts and pool. A very popular local, it supports a pool team and four darts teams. A quiz is held on Tuesday evening. ❀🚌♣P⊬

Bramhall

Ladybrook Hotel

Fir Road, SK7 2NP
⏲ 11.30-11 (11.30 Fri & Sat)
☎ (0161) 440 0176
Boddingtons Bitter; Wells Bombardier; guest beers Ⓗ
Large, striking mock-Tudor house built in the 1930s situated beside local shops. Relaxing sofas at the front of the bar prove a popular spot. Elsewhere there is plush upholstered seating in the semi open plan rooms off the main bar. Beyond the bar in the back room is a large vault. Function room/ conference facilities are available. Ideally situated for a visit to nearby Bramall Hall and its park. Food is served 12-9pm daily. ❀◐◑⊟♿🚌(378)♣P⊬

Broadheath

Railway ★

153 Manchester Road, WA14 5NT (on A56)
⏲ 11-11 (midnight Fri & Sat); 3-7 Sun
☎ (0161) 941 3383
Holt Mild, Bitter Ⓗ
Small, three-room pub built in the angle of a long-gone railway viaduct. The Railway was saved from demolition in the 1990s by a campaign involving CAMRA and local people. The surrounding area has been extensively redeveloped. The car park behind does not belong to the pub and is locked up outside shopping hours. The snug little rooms are named after Manchester's railway stations (and the toilets after one of London's). Children are welcome until 6pm.
♨Q❀⊟⇌(Navigation Rd)⊖(Navigation Rd)🚌♣⊬

Bury

Dusty Miller

87 Crostons Road, BL8 1AL (jct B1263 & B1264) SD 796112
⏲ 1-midnight (1am Fri); 12-1am Sat; 12-midnight Sun
☎ (0161) 764 1124
Moorhouse's Black Cat, Premier Bitter, Blond Witch, Pendle Witches Brew; guest beers Ⓗ
A local landmark, this is a proudly traditional pub catering for a loyal mixed clientele. Divided into two distinct rooms and served by a central bar, there is also a glass covered courtyard, and a fully enclosed outdoor area for summer drinking. The Dusty Miller is one of just a small number of Moorhouse's tied pubs (six at the last count). Its position at a busy road junction makes parking difficult, but it is well worth making the effort to visit. A 10-minute stride from Bury town centre.
❀⊟🚌♣⊬

Lamb Inn

533 Tottington Road, BL8 1UB (on B6123)
⏲ 4.30-11 (midnight Fri); 1-midnight Sat; 1-10.30 Sun
☎ (0161) 764 2714
Beer range varies Ⓗ
Built in 1831, the Lamb is a popular family-run pub. A stone fireplace with open fire and seating with plenty of scatter cushions helps to create a traditional and comfortable ambience. The landlord is enthusiastic about his real ale and regularly features beers from George Wright, Bank Top, Outstanding and HB Clark. A varied menu of excellent pub fare is available early evening and at the weekend. The large enclosed garden gets busy during the summer months.
♨❀◐◑🚌(468,469)P⊬

Old Blue Bell

2 Bell Lane, BL9 6AR (corner of Bell Lane and Wash Lane)
⏲ 12-midnight (2am Fri & Sat)
☎ (07864) 147827
Holt Mild, Bitter Ⓗ
Traditional Holt's public house. One bar area serves three rooms – a spacious L-shaped vault with TV, a large lounge and a smaller room which can be used for meetings. There is a separate pool room. Outside, looking upwards, on the parapet is an eight-pointed star over the date 1899. This is a reminder of the original owner of the pub – Alfred Crowther of the Star Brewery on 66 Brook Street, long defunct. Q❀⊟⊖🚌(468,469,475)♣⊬

Trackside

East Lancashire Railway, Bolton Street Station, BL9 0EY
⏲ 5 (12 Thu)-11; 12-midnight Fri; 10-midnight Sat; 10-11 Sun

☎ (0161) 764 6461
Beer range varies, Ⓗ
This true free house boasts nine handpumps, various real ciders and perries direct from the cellar, and a good range of foreign bottled beers. The vast array of pump clips on display is a testament to the many beers that have been sold in the past. Simple wooden tables and chairs create a traditional, albeit rather austere, railway buffet feel. The bar can be busy at weekends when the ELR holds special events. There are tables and chairs on the platform all year round.
❀≋(Bolton St)⊖🚌●P⁵–

Castleton

New Inn

818 Manchester Road, OL11 3AW (200m from railway station)
⏲ 3 (12 Sat & Sun)-1am
☎ (01706) 667533 🌐 thenewinncastleton.co.uk
Robinson's Hatters, Hartley's Cumbria Way, seasonal beers Ⓗ
Traditional Robinson's pub on a main street where two standard beers plus a changing seasonal are always available. The young, enthusiastic landlady has developed this pub into a busy, friendly and comfortable venue where all are made welcome. The pleasant interior is attractively decorated, with plenty of wood panelling. Toilet facilities are immaculate, having been completely rebuilt with disabled access. Quiz and darts nights are held, along with Irish folk or Lancastrian nights. Children are welcome until 8pm. ♨Q♿≋🚌(17)♣⁵–

Chadderton

Horton Arms

19 Streetbridge Road, OL1 2SZ (on B6195)
⏲ 12 (11.30 Sat)-midnight; 12-11.30 Sun
☎ (0161) 624 7793
Lees Brewer's Dark, Bitter Ⓗ
Neat and attractive roadside pub located in a pleasant area. Inside, one large room is divided into several discrete areas and a side room used mainly for sports fans watching TV. Horse brasses, plates and various interesting prints decorate the walls. The pub serves good home cooked food with lunches always popular. There are two car parks. A recent winner of the Lees Best Kept Cellar competition. ❀◐◑🚌(64)P⁵–

Rifle Range Inn

372 Burnley Lane, OL1 2QP (200m from A663/A627M jct)
⏲ 2 (12 Sat & Sun)-11; 12-11 Sun
☎ (0161) 678 6417
Lees Brewer's Dark, Bitter, seasonal beers Ⓗ
This pub was originally a farmstead, first licensed around 1860. It has a family-friendly atmosphere with an open-plan lounge and separate vault. Sports fans visiting nearby Boundary Park are welcome at all times. TV sports are shown. The pub runs football, darts and pool teams, plus a quiz night on Tuesday. It hosts live entertainment on Saturday evening and barbecues on the heated patio in summer. A pub that caters for all the community. ❀⊟🚌(24,181)♣P⁵–

Rose of Lancaster

7 Haigh Lane, OL1 2TQ (A69/B6195 jct)
⏲ 11.30-11; 11-midnight Fri & Sat; 12-11 Sun
☎ (0161) 624 3031
Lees Brewer's Dark, Bitter Ⓗ
The Rose is one of Lees' busiest pubs with a high ale turnover. Situated by the Rochdale Canal and overlooking countryside, it is a popular watering hole and eatery for walkers, canal boat enthusiasts and locals alike. The covered patio is popular during the summer months, as is the open fire in winter. A thriving vault, friendly management and an eclectic clientele always ensure a memorable visit to the Rose. Buses, trains and boats stop nearby.
♨❀◐◑⊟♿≋(Mills Hill)🚌(59,64)♣P⁵–

Cheadle

Red Lion

83 Stockport Road, SK8 2AJ (on A560, jct Jackson St)
⏲ 12-11 (10.30 Sun)
☎ (0161) 428 5507 🌐 frederic-robinson.com
Robinson's Hatters, Unicorn, Old Tom, seasonal beers Ⓗ
Large, solid-looking, half-rendered building on the fringe of the village. Good management has turned this place round. It has a mixed clientele of varying ages who enjoy the well-appointed surroundings – plenty of dark wood, traditional fittings, fireplaces, toby jugs, old bottles and snug, cosy corners to nestle in. Low ceilings add to a feeling of homeliness. Much used by the community, who come for the weekly quiz and the good, home-cooked food served 12-9pm most days, with a carvery on Sunday. A heated outside drinking and dining area is provided too.
♨Q⚭❀◐◑♿🚌(310, 371)♣P⁵–

Cheadle Hulme

Church

90 Ravenoak Road, SK8 7EG (jct A5149/B5095)
⏲ 11-11 (midnight Fri & Sat); 12-10.30 Sun
☎ (0161) 485 1897
Robinson's Hatters, Unicorn, seasonal beers Ⓗ
Once known as the Knapsack Inn, this friendly, family-run pub is the oldest in Cheadle Hulme. Its cottage-like appearance reflects a cosy interior with low ceilings, wood panelling and brass plates. The busy restaurant serves excellent, freshly prepared food evenings and weekends (booking recommended). Darts is played in the snug, while the lounge boasts a real fire and quiet conversation. ♨Q❀◐◑⊟🚌(313,X57)♣P⁵–

Kings Hall ✔

11-13 Station Road, SK8 5AF (on A5149 near station)
⏲ 9-midnight (1am Fri & Sat)
☎ (0161) 482 0460 🌐 jdwetherspoon.co.uk
Greene King IPA, Abbot; Marston's Pedigree; guest beers Ⓗ
Originally built in 1937 as a dance hall, the Kings Hall served latterly as a restaurant before being acquired by JD Wetherspoon, opening as a pub in 1998. A comfortable modern pub, the rear conservatory area appeals to diners. Food is served daily 9am-11pm. Popular with cask ale drinkers, up to four guest beers are normally available, usually including some from local micros.
Q❀◐◑♿≋(Cheadle Hulme)🚌(313,X57)P⁵–

Chorlton-cum-Hardy

Bar

531-533 Wilbraham Road, M21 0UE

⏲ 12-11.30 (12.30am Fri & Sat)
☎ (0161) 861 7576
Marble Manchester Bitter, Ginger Marble; guest beers ⊞
The Bar offers a modern twist on the traditional pub, with separate areas and differing styles of seating. An outlet for Marble beers, it also offers a selection of ales from other local breweries as well as foreign bottled and draught beers. The food is sourced from local suppliers – an interesting menu will suit most tastes at a reasonable price. A number of beer festivals are held throughout the year, often with a choice of up to 25 local beers. ❀◑▶🚌(55)⇌

Dulcimer

567 Wilbraham Road, M21 0AE
⏲ 12-12.30am (1.30am Fri & Sat)
☎ (0161) 860 0044
Thwaites Dark Mild, Wainwright; guest beers ⊞
Set in the heart of Chorlton, Dulcimer provides an extensive selection of cask ales, bottled beers, wines and spirits as well as an exciting, vibrant atmosphere set to a soundtrack of folk music. The building has been stripped back to bare brick which complements the large oak bar, cast iron radiators and a brand new blue and yellow frontage that opens onto the street in summer. The kitchen can supply a generous cheese and pâté platter served with home-made bread, chutney and fruit. ❀◑▶♿🚌⇌

Marble Beer House

57 Manchester Road, M21 9PW
⏲ 12-11 (midnight Thu-Sun)
☎ (0161) 881 9206 🌐 marblebeers.co.uk
Marble Manchester Bitter, Ginger Marble, Lagonda, Stouter Stout; guest beers ⊞
Marble Beer House was converted from a real ale off-licence 11 years ago and has featured in this Guide for the last 10. Serving a selection of beers from Marble Brewery, it also stocks a number of guest ales from local breweries as well as a good choice of bottled beers. Itt is expertly run by sisters who are rightly proud of their beers and informal atmosphere. Dogs are welcome, with reading material also available. **Q**❀🚌♣●⇌

Pi

99 Manchester Road, M21 9GA
⏲ 5 (12 Sat)-11; 12-10.30 Sun
☎ (0161) 882 0000 🌐 pi-chorlton.co.uk
Bank Top Flat Cap; guest beers ⊞
A great mix of traditional and modern, Pi is a café bar that sells excellent gourmet pies as well as a selection of local micro beers from its four handpumps. The ales are sourced from local breweries, with Bank Top the house regular. Mouthwatering meat and veg pies come with mash, mushy peas and onion gravy. The bar is renowned for its extensive beer knowledge and collection of foreign bottles and wines. **Q**❀◑▶🚌(84,85,86)⇌

Compstall

Andrew Arms

George Street, SK6 5JD
⏲ 12-midnight
☎ (0161) 484 5392
Robinson's Hatters, Hartley's Cumbria Way, Unicorn ⊞
Traditional, detached, stone-built pub in a quiet former mill village, constructed in the 1820s by George Andrew for his workers. Etherow Country Park is close by, with its wildlife and river valley walks. The pub features a comfortable lounge and a small traditional games room in addition to a separate dining room. A community local, popular with all ages, it is the centre for many social activities. A good kitchen serves traditional food and holds themed nights such as Tuesday chippy night. ⛰**Q**❀◑▶⊟🚌(383,384)♣**P**

Delph

Royal Oak (Th' Heights)

Broad Lane, Heights, OL3 5TX SD982090
⏲ 7 (5 Fri)-11; closed Mon; 12-6, 7-10.30 Sun
☎ (01457) 874460
Black Sheep Best Bitter; guest beers ⊞
Isolated, 250-year-old stone-built pub on a packhorse route overlooking the Tame Valley. In a popular walking area, it benefits from outstanding views. The pub comprises a cosy bar and three rooms, each with an open fire. The refurbished side room boasts a hand-carved stone fireplace, while the comfortable snug has exposed beams and old photos of the inn. Good home-cooked food is served Friday and Saturday evenings. The house beer is brewed by Copper Dragon and guests include a beer from Millstone. ⛰**Q**❀▶**P**

Diggle

Diggle Hotel

Station Houses, OL3 5JZ (off A670) SE007081
⏲ 12-3, 5-midnight (1am Fri); 12-1am Sat; 12-midnight Sun
☎ (01457) 872741
Black Sheep Best Bitter; Copper Dragon Black Gold; Taylor Landlord; guest beers ⊞
Stone pub in a pleasant hamlet close to the Standedge Canal Tunnel under the Pennines. Built as a merchant's house in 1789, it became an ale house and general store during construction of the nearby railway tunnel in 1834. Affording fine views of the Saddleworth countryside, the Diggle is a convenient base in a popular walking area. With a bar area and two rooms, the accent is on home-cooked food (served all day Sat and Sun). Brass bands play on alternate summer Sundays. ❀◑▶🚌(184)**P**

Dobcross

Navigation Inn

21-23 Wool Road, OL3 5NS (on A670)
⏲ 12-2.30, 5-11 (midnight Fri); 12-11 Sat; 12-10.30 Sun
☎ (01457) 872418
Lees Bitter; Moorhouse's Black Cat, Pendle Witches Brew; Taylor Landlord; Wells Bombardier; guest beers ⊞
Next to the Huddersfield Narrow Canal, this stone pub was built in 1806 to slake the thirst of the navvies cutting the Standedge Tunnel. It comprises an open-plan bar and L-shaped interior. Live brass band concerts are staged on alternate Sundays in summer. The pub is the venue for annual events such as the Beer Walk in spring and the Rushcart Festival in August. Home-cooked meals including special offer weekday lunches are popular (no food Sun eve). **Q**❀◑▶🚌(184,350)**P**⇌

ENGLAND

Eccles

Drop Inn

204-206 Monton Road, M30 9LJ (on B5229)
12-11.30 (midnight Thu & Fri), 11-midnight Sat; 12-10.30 Sun
☎ (7831) 343 410
Beer range varies H
Village pub with a smart conversion – the unusual H shape is the result of two former shops being joined together, retaining a separate staircase. Each wing has its own bar, but only one is in regular use. Both wings are on two levels and there is a rear games area. Two beers at any time include Black Sheep Best Bitter, Wells Bombardier and Taylor Landlord. Live music and karaoke feature regularly. Many restaurants are in close proximity.

Eccles Cross

13 Regent Street, M30 0BP (opp Metrolink station)
9-midnight (1am Fri & Sat)
☎ (0161) 788 0414
Greene King IPA, Abbot; Marston's Pedigree; guest beers H
A Wetherspoon's pub converted from an old cinema in 1999, retaining the original fine stone and brick frontage. The interior has an open plan layout on four levels including three sunken snugs. The ceiling also reflects the building's former use. The pub is named after the historical Eccles Cross, which is nearby in the centre of the town.
P

Lamb Hotel ★

33 Regent Street, M30 0BP (opp tram terminus)
11.30-11 (11.30 Fri & Sat); 12-11 Sun
☎ (0161) 787 7297
Holt Mild, Bitter H
An imposing, red brick, Edwardian heritage building, this is a classic, traditional pub with a loyal local following. The interior includes a vault, two lounges and a separate billiard room. The central bar and main room feature much traditional woodwork and etched glass fittings. The pub's interior has featured in several TV programmes over the years. Q P

Royal Oak ★

34 Barton Lane, M30 0EN
9.30-11; 9.30-12.30am Sat; 7-10 Sun
☎ (7971) 835 029
Holt Mild, Bitter H
Well-run heritage Edwardian pub in the town centre with a handsome red brick and terracotta exterior. Inside, the superb original oak central bar is best viewed from the equally magnificent vault. Note the unusual fireplace alcove – apart from the removal of the door for the now defunct outdoor sales, the vault remains unchanged, including its etched glass partition. There is a bar parlour, large side lounge and the Newsroom (now the games room). A pub steeped in history.
Q (Eccles) (Eccles Metro)

Failsworth

Willow Tavern

278 Ashton Road East, M35 9HD SD906013
12-3, 7-midnight (5-12.30am Fri); 12-12.30am Sat; 12-midnight Sun
☎ (0161) 681 1698
Black Sheep Best Bitter; Greenfield Dobcross Bitter; guest beers H
Originally built as an ale house in 1870, paintings of the former building can be seen over the fireplace. This community hub serves as a home for local football and cricket teams, plus the Failsworth branch of the Manchester City Supporters' Club. There is a separate tap room, beer garden and family room. The lounge has a large engraved glass window featuring a willow tree. Good value food is available weekdays 12-2pm.
(52,76,159) P

Farnworth

Britannia

34 King Street, BL4 7AF (opp bus station, off A6053)
11-11 (midnight Fri & Sat); 12-11 Sun
☎ (01204) 571629
Beer range varies, H
Thriving local next to the market and bus station with a basic L-shaped vault and a slightly smaller lounge, both served by a central bar. The pub offers inexpensively priced guest beers from Moorhouse's and Coach House. Good value home-cooked lunches are popular. Well attended, mini outdoor beer festivals are held on the May bank holidays and in August. Behind the pub is a free car park. Children are welcome untill 4.30pm.

Flixton

Church Inn

34 Church Road, M41 6HS
11-11 (11.30 Tue & Thu; midnight Fri & Sat); 12-11 Sun
☎ (0161) 748 2158
Taylor Landlord; Theakston Best Bitter; guest beers H
An old, traditional pub on the southern edge of Flixton. It has been opened up internally over the years but retains distinct and separate drinking spaces, with the two areas to the left of the main entrance perhaps the quietest. Guest beers vary. Food from the Spirit Group menu is served between 12-8pm daily but this remains very much a pub rather than a restaurant: darts, dominoes and (sometimes) cribbage are played here.
(247,255) P

Gorton

Vale Cottage

Kirk Street, M18 8UE (off Hyde Rd A57, east of jct with Chapman St)
12-3 (4 Sun), 5 (7 Sat & Sun)-11
☎ (0161) 223 2477
Taylor Landlord; Theakston Black Bull; guest beers H
Well hidden in the Gore Brook conservation area, Vale Cottage has the feel of a country pub. Parts date from the 17th century, hence the low beamed ceilings, multiple drinking areas and a reputed ghost. A relaxed friendly atmosphere, where conversation is the main entertainment, is disturbed only by the ever-popular lively quizzes (Tuesday —general knowledge, Thursday —music). Indulge in an excellent home-cooked meal (available lunch and early evening) in the garden to round off a visit. Don't miss this hidden gem.
Q (Ryder Brow) (201,203) P

Greenfield

King William IV
134 Chew Valley Road, OL3 7DD
12-midnight
☎ (01457) 873933
Caledonian Deuchars IPA; Lees Bitter; Tetley Bitter; guest beers Ⓗ
Detached stone pub at the village centre, comprising a central bar area and two rooms. The benched, cobbled forecourt allows for outdoor drinking with a back yard for smoking. Two or three changing beers are offered, often including a local ale. Food is served Wednesday to Sunday until 7.30pm. A handy base for local walks, the 'King Bill' is the centre of village life, participating in annual beer walks and August's Rushcart Festival, and hosting a Greenfield's Whit Friday brass band contest. ❀◑⇌🚌(180,350,354)♣P⍽

Railway
11 Shaw Hall Bank Road, OL3 7JZ (opp station)
12-midnight (1am Thu-Sat)
☎ (01457) 872307
Caledonian Deuchars IPA; Elland Beyond the Pale; Millstone Tiger Rut; Theakston Old Peculier; Wells Bombardier; guest beer Ⓗ
Unspoilt pub where the central bar and games areas draw a good mix of old and young. The tap room boasts a log fire and old photos of Saddleworth. In a picturesque area, the pub provides a good base for various outdoor pursuits and affords beautiful views across Chew Valley. The venue for live Cajun, R&B, jazz and pop music on Thursday, Friday (unplugged night) and Sunday, it also hosts top class entertainment in the large function room. Weston's and Thatchers cider are served on gravity. Caravans are allowed.
♨❀🛏⊟⛺⇌🚌(180,184)♣●P

Hawkshaw

Red Lion
81 Ramsbottom Road, BL8 4JS (on A676)
11-3, 6-11; 12-11 Sat; 12-10.30 Sun
☎ (01204) 856600 🌐 redlionhawkshaw.com
Jennings Bitter, Cumberland Ale; guest beers Ⓗ
Attractive stone pub nestling in a picturesque village. Inside is a single, large room that is poplar with locals and visitors alike. The excellent menu of freshly prepared dishes has made the inn popular with diners, too, who can opt to eat in the pub or the adjacent restaurant. Meals are served all day at the weekend. The landlord is enthusiastic about his real ales and regularly features beers from Phoenix, Bank Top and Copper Dragon as guests. 🛏◑⊟🚌P

Hazel Grove

Grapes
196 London Road, SK7 4DQ (on A6, jct with Hatherlow Lane)
11.30-11 (midnight Fri & Sat); 12-10.30 Sun
☎ (0161) 4834479
Robinson's Hatters, Unicorn Ⓗ
This very old building has retained its classic town pub layout. The central bar separates the large vault from the three-roomed lounge, which features some original looking wooden beams. The back room displays images of old Hazel Grove, and pictures of local sports teams appear throughout. To the rear is a small beer garden with well-kept flower tubs. Mild is on offer at two different temperatures according to taste.
❀⊟⇌🚌(192,199)♣P⍽

Heaton Norris

Nursery ★ ✔
258 Green Lane, SK4 2NA (off A6, jct with Heaton Rd)
11.30-11 (11.30 Fri; midnight Sat); 12-11.30 Sun
☎ (0161) 432 2044 🌐 hydesbrewery.co.uk
Hydes Mild, Owd Oak, Original Bitter, Jekyll's Gold, seasonal beers; guest beers Ⓗ
CAMRA's National Pub of the Year 2001 and a Guide regular, the Nursery is a classic unspoilt 1930s pub, hidden away in a pleasant suburb. The multi-roomed interior includes a traditional vault with its own entrance and a spacious wood-panelled lounge, used by diners at lunchtime. The home-cooked food draws customers from miles around – children are welcome if dining. The pub's immaculate bowling green – an increasingly rare feature – is well used by local league teams.
Q❀◐⊟🚌(22,364)♣P⍽

High Lane

Royal Oak
Buxton Road, SK6 8AY
12-3, 5-11; 12-10.30 Sun
☎ (01663) 762380
Jennings Cocker Hoop; Marston's Burton Bitter; guest beers Ⓗ
A well-appointed pub with a pleasing exterior. Although it has an open-plan layout, there are three distinct drinking areas, one used for games. Live entertainment is hosted most Fridays and an innovative food menu is served all sessions. The garden and outdoor play area make this a good summer and family pub. Beer is sourced from the Marston's range. Q❀◑♿🚌(199,394)P⍗

Hindley

Edington Arms
186 Ladies Lane, WN2 2QJ (off A58)
12-11.30 (12.30am Fri & Sat)
☎ (01942) 259229
Holt Mild, Bitter, seasonal beers Ⓗ
Also known as the Top Ale House, the Edington is a cosy, welcoming pub. The single bar is centrally situated in the front lounge. There is also a games room with pool table that leads to the beer garden at the rear. An upstairs function room is available by arrangement. Standing next to the Liverpool-Manchester rail line, the pub is ideally situated for any 'rail ale crawl' into Wigan or Manchester.
❀⇌♣P⍽

Holcombe Brook

Hare & Hounds ✔
400 Bolton Road West, BL0 9RY (on A676)
12-11 (midnight Thu-Sat)
☎ (01706) 822107 🌐 hareandhoundsbury.com
Beer range varies, Ⓗ
Winner of the Publican Awards Cask Ale Pub of the Year, this large rural community pub has a bright friendly atmosphere where young, old and their dogs are all welcome. Ten cask ales are on handpump with beers from across the country plus a range of continental lagers on tap. Two beer festivals are held annually in March and October.

Food is served 12-9pm every day. Part of the pub can be used for small functions. Free Wi-Fi access. (472,474)P

Horwich

Crown

1 Chorley New Road, BL6 7QJ (jct A673/B6226)
11-11 (midnight Fri & Sat); 12-11.30 Sun
(07505) 607661
Holt Mild, Bitter, Joey Bitter, seasonal beers H
Spacious pub on the edge of town handy for the Reebok Stadium (away fans welcome), Rivington Pike and the West Pennine Moors. Lever Park across the road was a gift from Lord Leverhulme, the soap magnate and great benefactor to his home town. The pub has a vault and games room at the rear where dogs are allowed. Darts and dominoes teams play on Tuesday evening. Various artistes provide entertainment on Sunday evening. Children are welcome at lunchtime when dining. (125,575)P

Original Bay Horse

206 Lee Lane, BL6 7JF (on B6226, 200m from A673)
1-midnight; 12-12.30am Fri & Sat; 12-midnight Sun
(01204) 696231
Bank Top Flat Cap; Coach House Gunpowder Mild; Lees Bitter; guest beers H
Dating from 1777, this stone-built pub with small windows and low ceilings has been run by the same family for many years and is locally known as the 'Long Pull'. In the lounge, pool and darts are played and live sports coverage on TV is popular, while a cosy traditional vault displays some interesting football memorabilia. A Moorhouse's beer is usually available. Nearby Lever Park is ideal for lovely woodland walks. (125,575)

Hyde

Cheshire Ring

72 Manchester Road, SK14 2BJ
2 (1 Thu & Fri)-11; 12-11 Sat; 12-10.30 Sun
(07917) 055629
Beartown Kodiak Gold, Bearskinful, seasonal beers; guest beers H
A warm welcome is assured at this friendly pub, one of the oldest in Hyde and comprehensively overhauled by Beartown. Seven handpumps offer a range of Beartown beers and guest beers from micros in addition to ciders, perries and continental beers. A range of bottled beers is also stocked and beer festivals periodically offer additional drinking choice. Gentle background music plays and occasional live bands perform. Lunchtime opening hours may vary. (Central)

Queens Inn

23 Clarendon Place, SK14 2ND
11-11
(0161) 368 2230
Holt Mild, Bitter, seasonal beers H
A real town centre community pub with a warm welcome. Home to several sports teams, the interior is divided into four distinct areas to cater for all needs, including a large function room that is a favourite for wedding receptions. Situated close to Hyde bus station and the market, the Queens is popular with shoppers during the day. A late licence is used for special events throughout the year. (Central/Newton for Hyde)

Sportsman

57 Mottram Road, SK14 2NN
11-11; 12-10.30 Sun
(0161) 368 5000
Moorhouse's Black Cat; Pennine Floral Dance, Railway Sleeper, Pitch Porter, White Owl, Sunshine H
A Pennine Ales tied house that also offers three guest beers from micros. Bar snacks are served and there is a restaurant upstairs specialising in home-cooked Cuban food and tapas. This former CAMRA Pub of the Region has recently had a makeover but retains its original character. There is a full-size snooker table upstairs. The rear patio features a covered and heated smoking area. Railway stations are within walking distance. Q(Central/Newton for Hyde)P

Leigh

Boars Head

2 Market Place, WN7 1EG
11-11 (1am Thu-Sat)
(01942) 673036
Beer range varies H
Situated opposite Leigh's parish church, the imposing red brick exterior contains clues to the pub's history, from the Bedford Brewing Company to Walkers Warrington Ales. Behind the pub are unusual two-storey listed stables now converted for local business use. The large pool room houses a collection of rugby league team photographs from various eras, while the lounge contains a collection of Lancashire colliery plates. The main room is divided by a fireplace and live music sessions are held most Saturdays.

Thomas Burke ✔

20A Leigh Road, WN7 1QR
9-midnight (1am Fri & Sat)
(01942) 685640
Greene King IPA, Abbot; Marston's Pedigree; guest beers H
The pub is named after a renowned tenor, known as the Lancashire Caruso, who was born in Leigh and sang in the building when it was the Hippodrome Theatre. The pub splits into three areas: the main long bar, a raised dining area and, in what was once the cinema foyer, lounge-style seating. Ten handpumps offer a changing range of beers from the Wetherspoon range.

Waggon & Horses ✔

68 Wigan Road, WN7 5AY
7 (4 Fri)-midnight; 12-1am Sat; 12-11 Sun
(01942) 673069
Hydes Light, Mild, Original Bitter H
Friendly community pub that attracts all ages. The main lounge is hidden behind a large hearth and includes a large-screen TV for sporting events. The bar, hub of the pub, is a good spot for conversation, while a snug leads off to one side. A large games room includes a pool table, darts and dominoes, and is host to the pub's various teams. Regular theme nights are held throughout the year. Children are welcome until 8pm.

Littleborough

Moorcock

Halifax Road, OL15 0LD (on A58)
11.30-midnight (11.30 Sun)
(01706) 378156

Taylor Landlord; guest beers Ⓗ
Built as a farmhouse in 1681 and first licensed in 1840, this traditional pub in the Pennine foothills features an 80-seat restaurant with separate pub space. Families, ramblers and equestrians are all welcome in the pub, which also caters for football fans with large-screen TVs. Outside there are fantastic panoramic views while inside there are always one or two guest beers, usually from local micro-brewers such as Pictish, plus six rooms offering accommodation. (528)P

White House
Halifax Road, OL15 0LG (on A58)
12-3, 6.30-midnight; 12.30-10.30 Sun
☎ (01706) 378456
Theakston Best Bitter; guest beers Ⓗ
The Pennine Way passes this 17th-century coaching house, situated 1300 feet above sea level. It is a landmark that benefits from panoramic views of the surrounding hills and as far away as Cheshire and Wales. A family-run inn extending a warm, friendly welcome, it has two bars, both with log fires. Local guest ales, continental bottled beers and a good range of wines complement the excellent menu and daily specials board. Meals are served all day Sunday. Q(528)P

Longsight

New Victoria
38 Kingfisher Close, M12 4PW (on Stockport Rd, N of A6/A5184 jct)
12-11 (10.30 Sun)
☎ (0161) 274 4280
Oakwell Old Tom, Bitter Ⓗ
'Never judge a book by its cover' - externally, the '70s architecture does not inspire, yet inside is a different story. Within lies openness, warmth and friendliness. This is exemplified by the greetings and farewells from the regulars. Expect to be engaged in friendly conversation. This really is a local community pub in the true sense of the words, where it is no surprise to walk in and be greeted by a wake or birthday party. Oakwell beers are rare for the area. (192,197)P

Lowton

Travellers Rest
443 Newton Road, WA3 1NX
12-11 (midnight Fri & Sat)
☎ (01925) 224391
Marston's Pedigree; guest beers Ⓗ
Comfortable, friendly roadside local with a separate restaurant that leans towards the Greek style. Meals are available throughout the pub, with the low-ceilinged lounge containing various discrete seating areas. The bar is the social focal point of the hostelry, while a large patio and garden to the rear provide plenty of seating.
QP

Manchester City Centre

Angel
6 Angel Street, M4 4BQ (off Rochdale Rd)
12-midnight; closed Sun
☎ (0161) 833 4786 theangelmanchester.co.uk
Beer range varies Ⓗ
Formerly the Beer House, now reopened as the Angel, this gastro pub owned by chef Robert Owen Brown is renowned for dishes made with local produce. Four real ales come from local breweries such as Dunham Massey and Prospect. The house beer is brewed by Facer's. Situated in the fast developing Northern Quarter, the candlelit pub attracts serious diners, but there is an area for drinkers. Food, served lunchtimes and evenings, is predictably excellent.
(Victoria)(Shudehill)P

Ape & Apple
28-30 John Dalton Street, M2 6HQ (off Cross St corner of Albert Sq)
12-11 (midnight Fri & Sat); 12-9 Sun
☎ (0161) 839 9624
Holts Mild, Bitter, seasonal beer Ⓗ
This old building has seen many incarnations but has been a pub for 11 years. It boasts a fabulous upstairs dining/function room. Wednesday is curry night and it hosts the longest running free comedy club in Manchester. The decor is a mixture of old and new, creating an unusual feeling of opulence for a Holts house. The large number of regulars help to give it a very friendly atmosphere. Winner of Manchester Evening News Pub of the Week in September 2008.
(Deansgate/Victoria)(St Peters Sq)

Bar Fringe
8 Swan Street, M4 5JN (Next to Oldham Rd/Oldham St interchange)
12-midnight (11 Sun)
☎ (0161) 835 3815
Beer range varies Ⓗ
Established 12 years ago, the bar provides a home for the discerning drinker with the emphasis on good beer. Up to five handpumps come from local micro-breweries such as Allgates, Bank Top, Boggart and Hornbeam. Thatchers Cheddar Valley Cider is always available. Belgian beers take centre stage with seven on draught and 50 in bottle, while German and Czech beers provide support. Beer festivals are held in April and November. An eclectic mix of artefacts adorns the walls and ceilings. (Victoria)(Shudehill)

Bulls Head
84 London Road, M1 2PN
11.30-11; 12-10.30 Sun
☎ (0161) 236 1724
Jennings Cumberland Ale; Marstons Pedigree; guest beers Ⓗ
Dating from 1894 and dominating the corner opposite Piccadilly Station, the Bulls Head is the nearest real ale pub to the station entrance and taxi rank, and attracts plenty of passing trade. A single roomed establishment, the large open plan interior allows plenty of standing room. Around the periphery are tables and bench seating. There is the usual scattering of old Manchester pictures adorning the walls. A good starting point for city centre nights out, it gets busy at weekends.
Q(Piccadilly)(Piccadilly)(192,201)

City Arms
46-48 Kennedy Street, M2 4BQ
11-11 (midnight Fri); 12-midnight Sat; 12-8 Sun
☎ (0161) 236 4610
Tetley Bitter; guest beers Ⓗ
Busy little two-roomed pub situated behind the Waterhouse. In 2008 it received a local CAMRA award for 13 consecutive years in this Guide and it was also winner of Spring Pub of the Season. It can

be hectic at lunchtime with office workers who come for the good food. Early doors can be busy, then it settles down and gives way to a quieter period with a local feel. Seven widely sourced guest beers make this a very popular city centre pub. ◑⇌(Oxford Rd)⊖(St Peters Square)🚌

Crown & Kettle

2 Oldham Road, Ancoats, M4 5FE (corner of Oldham St & Great Ancoats St)
⏲ 11-11 (midnight Fri & Sat); 12-10.30 Sun
☎ (0161) 236 2923 🌐 crownandkettle.com
Beer range varies Ⓗ
Historic Grade II-listed pub, reopened in 2005 after a closure of 16 years. Up to four handpumps serve real ales from an ever-updated list of six beers from All Gates, Bank Top, Ossett, Phoenix and Dunham Massey among other breweries. Crown & Kettle Ale from Greenfield micro-brewery is a regular. Note the fine restored ceiling in the separate vault and a yet-to-be-restored ceiling in the main room. A fair-sized modern snug doubles as a lounge. Good value food is served.
◑◐♿⇌(Victoria)⊖(Shudehill)🚌🍎⛿

Dutton Hotel

37 Park Street, Strangeways, M3 1EU (back of MEN Arena, corner of Dutton St)
⏲ 11.30-2am; 12-midnight Sun
☎ (0161) 834 4508
Hydes Original Bitter, seasonal beer Ⓗ
Virtually triangular in shape, this street corner pub is a hidden gem. It displays an extensive collection of brass ornaments and artefacts, with the emphasis on blow lamps – the granddaddy of these sits atop a full sized anvil (the Hydes' symbol) in the snug and could well be used by Desperate Dan to remove his five-o'clock stubble! Late night hours are at the discretion of the publican.
❀⊟⇌(Victoria)⊖(Victoria)🚌(89,135)♣⛿

Jolly Angler ✔

47 Ducie Street, M1 2JW (corner of Pigeon St)
⏲ 12-3, 5.30-11; 12-11 Sat; 12-6, 8-10.30 Sun
☎ (0161) 236 5307
Hydes Original Bitter, Hydes XXXX Ⓗ
Tucked away behind Piccadilly Railway Station, this tiny, genuine Irish pub has been in the same family for nearly 25 years. The Reynolds have built up a reputation for live music at the Jolly. One small room includes the bar, with a second room to the side. The fireplace burns peat when supplies permit. After Manchester City home matches, entry is restricted, as the pub is en-route to the ground.
🔥⇌(Piccadilly)⊖(Piccadilly)🚌(1,2,3)♣

Knott 🏆

374 Deansgate, M3 4LY
⏲ 12-11.30 (midnight Thu; 12.30am Fri & Sat)
☎ (0161) 839 9229
Marble Manchester Bitter, Ginger Marble; guest beers Ⓗ
Built into a railway arch opposite Deansgate station, the pub has a balcony upstairs that doubles as a heated smoking area. Mini beer festivals are held throughout the year. Three guest beers mostly come from local micros and Addlestones traditional cider is stocked. There is also a range of bottled Belgian beers. Meals are available until 8pm daily with interesting vegan and vegetarian options. Unusually for the city centre, children are allowed until 8pm. ❀◑◐♿⇌(Deansgate)⊖(G-Mex)🚌⛿

Lass o' Gowrie

36 Charles Street, M1 7DB (off Oxford Rd B5117)
⏲ 12-11 (midnight Thu-Sat); 12-10.30 Sun
☎ (0161) 273 6932 🌐 thelass.co.uk
Black Sheep Best Bitter; Greene King XX Mild, IPA, Ruddles Best; Outstanding Betty's Bitter; guest beers Ⓗ
This famous Manchester institution goes from strength to strength. Despite its location in the heart of the city, the Lass has the feel of a real community pub with a monthly computer club, book club and regular music and comedy nights. There is also a big screen for major sporting events. Guest beers come from the Greene King list and independent sources, with ales from Conwy Brewery often featuring. The smoking balcony was opened by pub regular Johnny Vegas and there is a plaque on the wall marking the event.
◑◐⇌(Oxford Rd)⊖(St Peters Sq)🚌(42,43)⛿

Marble Arch ☆

73 Rochdale Road, M4 4HY (on A664 200m from A665 jct)
⏲ 12-11 (midnight Fri & Sat)
☎ (0161) 832 5914 🌐 marblebeers.co.uk
Marble Pint, Manchester Bitter, JP Best Bitter, Lagonda IPA, Ginger Marble, seasonal beers; guest beers Ⓗ
Spectacular heritage premier pub noted for its in-house micro-brewery and 11 handpumps with guest beers from all over the country and real cider. Ales can be found from Whim, Pictish, Dunham Massey, Phoenix and Hornbeam. An enthusiastic bar staff provides friendly service. The Marble brewery team can often be seen mixing with customers who come here from all walks of life and all over the world. Quality food is available from 12-9pm (8pm Sun).
🔥❀◑◐⇌(Victoria)⊖(Shudehill)🚌🍎P⛿

Old Wellington Inn ✔

4 Cathedral Gates, M3 1SW (next to Cathedral)
⏲ 10-11 (10 Sun)
☎ (0161) 830 1440
Jennings Cumberland Ale; guest beers Ⓗ
Dating from the 17th century, this timber-framed inn was moved to its present location as part of a redevelopment of the city centre, following the explosion of a terrorist bomb in 1996. Split over three levels, the Nicholson's house has up to four handpumps in use, dispensing guest ales selected from Waverley TBS. Pies are a speciality on the extensive food menu. There is a large courtyard for outdoor drinking and children are allowed inside until 8pm. Q❀◑◐♿⇌(Victoria)⊖(Victoria)🚌⛿

Paramount ✔

33-35 Oxford Street, M1 4BH
⏲ 9-midnight (1am Fri & Sat)
☎ (0161) 233 1820
Greene King Abbot; Marston's Pedigree; guest beers Ⓗ
This extensive and very busy Wetherspoon's pub stands out from the crowd due to its positive attitude to cask beers, with many coming from local micros. It gets its name from its location in Manchester's old theatre land. Handy for local entertainment venues including the Library and Palace theatres, Bridgewater Hall and Manchester Central conference centre, the Paramount has a more relaxed atmosphere than other comparable pubs in the city centre. Food is served 9-10pm daily. ◑◐⇌(Oxford Rd)⊖(St Peter's Sq)🚌(1,3)⛿

ENGLAND

Sand Bar

120-122 Grosvenor Street, All Saints, M1 7HL (off Oxford Rd A34/B5117 jct)
12 (4 Sat)-midnight (1am Thu; 2am Fri & Sat); 4-10.30 Sun
(0161) 273 8449 sandbaronline.net
Moorhouse's Black Cat; Phoenix All Saints; Taylor Landlord; guest beers H
Adjacent to All Saints Metropolitan University Campus and near to Manchester University, Sand Bar attracts lecturers and more mature students. All Saints, specially brewed for the pub by Phoenix, is on offer alongside a fairly permanent bitter and a guest. The guest cider changes fortnightly. An extensive range of draught and bottled foreign beers is also stocked. If using the special glasses, a shoe must be deposited in exchange for flip-flops. Jazz is played on Tuesday evening, and monthly Arts Council-funded art classes are held. Food is served from lunchtime until 6.30pm.
(Oxford Rd)(42,43)

Smithfield Hotel & Bar

37 Swan Street, M4 5JZ (On A665 between Rochdale Rd and Oldham Rd)
12-midnight
(0161) 839 4424
Robinson's Dark Mild; guest beers H
Close to the famous Band On The Wall live-music venue lies this haven for real ale lovers. Enter the long, one-room bar and you will find at least seven ales on handpump, sourced from all over the UK. A balanced mix of milds, bitters and strong ales makes up the beer range, complemented by an expanding range of bottled beers. Facer's brews the house beer, while up to eight beer festivals are held annually. (Victoria)(Shudehill)

Unicorn

26 Church Street, M4 1PW
11.30-11; 12-7 Sun
(0161) 834 8854
Copper Dragon Golden Pippin, Challenger IPA; Draught Bass H
Four roomed Edwardian pub with extensive waxed oak wall panelling in the main room and upstairs function room, a favourite for CAMRA meetings. Downstairs, the island bar serves an L-shaped vault on two sides and a narrow lobby opposite. There's a separate snug at the rear, while two further rooms offer a degree of seclusion. One of the few Draught Bass outlets in the city, it was for decades the HQ for the Honourable Order of Bass Drinkers which pre-dated CAMRA.
(Victoria)(Shudehill)(59,135)

Waterhouse

67-71 Princess Street, M2 4EG
9am-midnight (1am Fri & Sat)
(0161) 200 5380
Phoenix Wobbly Bob; guest beers H
Unusually, this Wetherspoon's is split into multiple rooms with some character. There are 10 handpumps featuring local micro-breweries, with Phoenix Wobbly Bob and Westons Old Rosie cider always available. Due to its excellent transport links this venue is a good place to start or finish a pub crawl in Manchester city centre. As with most Wetherspoon's, you know what you are going to get, but this is definitely one of the better ones.
(Oxford Road)(St Peter's Sq)

Marple

Hare & Hounds

Dooley Lane, Otterspool, SK6 7EJ
11.30-11; 12-10.30 Sun
(0161) 427 0293
Green King Abbot; Hydes Bitter, Jekyll's Gold H
An attractive pub by the River Goyt on the Marple-Romiley road. It is difficult to imagine that when this pub was first built it was at the end of a row of terraced cottages demolished long ago when the road was realigned. It has an open-plan interior with a separate dining area and conservatory plus an improved and pleasant outdoor area. The pub's Hydes' beers provide some welcome variety in the area. Good value food caters for all tastes. QP

Hatters Arms

81 Church Lane, SK6 7AW
12-midnight
(0161) 427 1529 hattersmarple.co.uk
Robinson's Hatters, Unicorn, seasonal beers H
At the end of a row of stone-built hatters' cottages, this tiny pub was enlarged only a few years ago and retains its intimate atomosphere. There are three small rooms and an attractive panelled bar area. Numerous photographs reflect the pub's brass band connections. Much is done to attract regular custom with games evenings and quizzes on Thursdays. (Rose Hill)

Railway

223 Stockport Road, SK6 3EN
12-11 (11.30 Fri & Sat)
(0161) 427 2146
Robinson's Hatters, Unicorn, seasonal beers H
This impressive pub first opened in 1878 alongside Rose Hill Station and many rail commuters still number among its customers. The pub is little changed externally, and is handy for walkers and cyclists on the nearby Middlewood Way. Two open-plan airy and relaxing rooms are complemented by an outside veranda and drinking area in this deservedly popular pub. (Rose Hill)P

Middleton

Old Boar's Head

111 Long Street, M24 6UE
12-11 (10.30 Sun)
(0161) 643 3520
Lees Brewer's Dark, Bitter H
This venerable half-timbered, stone-flagged pub dates back to at least 1632. The interior is divided up into several discrete drinking areas. The large sessions room, once used as a court, now hosts the local slimming club as well as occasional brass band concerts. The pub offers good value food with hot lunches a popular attraction. Try and spot the glass panel revealing part of the original wattle and daub walls. No evening meals are available at weekends. (17)P

Tandle Hill Tavern

14 Thornham Lane, M24 2SD (1 mile along unmetalled road off A664 and A627) SD907094
5 (12 Sat & Sun)-midnight; closed Mon
(01706) 345297
Lees Brewer's Dark, Bitter, seasonal beers H
Run by an award-winning licensee, this remote two roomed gem is reached by a potholed lane from either Middleton (A664) or Royton (A627).

The pub is popular with walkers from the nearby country park and the local farming community. Dogs are welcome. The interior features local photographs and witch paraphernalia. Good home-cooked food including real chips is available until 8pm. Lees Cask Ale Pub 2008-09 and local CAMRA Pub of the Year 2008.

Mossley

Britannia Inn

217 Manchester Road, OL5 9AJ
3 (11 Sat)-11; 12-11 Sun
(01457) 832799
Marston's Burton Bitter; guest beers H
Mossley's closest real ale outlet to the station. Thanks to SIBA, the pub now includes many local breweries' beers in its constantly changing range of five guests. Next to the Britannia Mills, which only recently ceased spinning, the 'Brit' is semi open plan inside with a secluded dining area. Meals are served from opening until 7.30pm (5pm on Sunday). A partially covered front patio is available for smokers and drinkers.
(343,350)

Church Inn

82 Stockport Road, OL5 0RF
4 (2 Fri & Sat)-midnight (1am Fri & Sat); 12-1am Sun
(01457) 832021
Thwaites Original, Wainwright, Lancaster Bomber; guest beers H
This pub retains its tap room, which is becoming increasingly rare. Note the splendid tilework just inside the front door. Mossley Morris dancers frequent this traditional local, which is also dog friendly. Once the Hardman's Arms, it takes its current name from the nearby St John the Baptist church, which can be seen from the rear windows. There is a pavement patio for warmer weather. (353)P

Dysarts Arms

Huddersfield Road, OL5 9BT (on B6175 half a mile S of A635)
12-midnight (1am Sat)
(01457) 832103
Robinson's Unicorn, seasonal beers H
Close to the pre-1974 Lancashire/Yorkshire border and backing onto open farmland, this pub was acquired by Robinson's in 1926, when it had another storey. The present steeply-pitched roof with its deep eaves dates from 1928. Inside there is a comfortable bar area and cosy lounge. A partially covered patio to the side of the pub is available for drinkers and smokers. Food is not served at weekends. (350)P

Woodend Tavern

Manchester Road, OL5 9AY
12-10 (11.30 Fri & Sat)
(01457) 833133
Beer range varies H
Standing in its own grounds with a large garden, the pub usually serves two guest beers mainly from local micro-breweries. The interior is spacious, not unlike a hotel lounge. Outside a partially enclosed shelter is available for smokers and there is ramped access from the car park. The pub specialises in home-cooked food, which is available all day until 7.30pm. The garden has a slide for children. (354)P

Nangreaves

Lord Raglan

Mount Pleasant, BL9 6SP
12-2.30, 6 (5 Fri)-11; 12-11 Sat; 12-10.30 Sun
(0161) 764 6680
Leyden Rammy Rocket, Forever Bury, Crowning Glory, seasonal beers; guest beers H
A country inn at the end of a cobbled lane with open views of the surrounding hills, this is the home of the Leyden Brewery and an impressive selection of its beers always features on the bar. The Leyden family has run this friendly pub for half a century. Good food is served in both restaurant and bar, prepared by the chef who is also the head brewer. The interior is decorated with antique glass and pottery, and old photographs. Q(477)P

Oldham

Ashton Arms

28-30 Clegg Street, OL1 1PL
11.30-11 (11.30 Fri & Sat)
(0161) 630 9709
Beer range varies H
There is something for everyone at this friendly free house situated opposite the old town hall within the conservation area of Oldham. The Ashton welcomes new and established breweries – seven excellent constantly-changing ales come from a range of local micros and include seasonal beers. Traditional cider and a selection of interesting continental bottled beers are served. Themed and annual beer festivals are held regularly. Quiz night is Tuesday. The food is highly recommended. Notice the 200-year-old stone fireplace. (Mumps)

Royal Oak

178 Union Street, OL1 1EN
11-11.30 (midnight Sat); 11.30-11.30 Sun
(0161) 633 2642
Robinson's Unicorn, Old Tom, seasonal beers H
Welcoming town-centre local situated at the Mumps roundabout end of Union Street. Its impressive mahogany horseshoe bar dates from 1928 and forms a central feature. It also has a snug, pool room and a large upstairs function room. Its mature clientele ensures a varied conversation at all times. Look for the unique metron electric metered beer pump, still working. The most improved pub in Oldham town centre in the last 12 months.

Openshaw

Legh Arms

741 Ashton Old Road, M11 2HD (on A635, opp college)
11 (12 Sun)-11
(0161) 223 4317
Moorhouse's Black Cat; guest beers H
An oasis in a real ale desert, run by a licensee who is passionate about both his beer and nearby Manchester City FC. An eclectic local clientele extends a warm welcome at this once multi-roomed pub which still retains quiet nooks and crannies. With games of pool and darts (played on a Manchester log-end board), plus an enclosed beer garden that hosts barbecues and bouncy castles in summer, the Legh Arms has something for everyone. House beers Blue from Moorhouse's and Middle Eastlands from Hydes emphasise the MCFC connection. (Ashburys)(53,219)

Orrell

Robin Hood

117 Sandy Lane, WN5 7AZ

3-midnight; 12-1am Thu-Sat; 12-midnight Sun

☎ (01695) 627479

Beer range varies Ⓗ

Well worth finding, this small sandstone pub tucked away in a residential area has a reputation for serving good home-cooked food (Thu-Sun, lunchtime and evenings booking advisable). The lounge is used for dining at meal times. Three handpumps provide semi-regular beers including Deuchars IPA, Old Speckled Hen and Taylor Landlord. Not surprisingly, the decor has a Robin Hood theme. ❀◑⇌♣P

Running Horses

St James Road, WN5 7AA

4 (12 Fri & Sat)-midnight; 1-11.30 Sun

☎ (01942) 512604

Banks's Bitter; guest beers Ⓗ

Dating back to the 1800s, with a large extension added in 1920 and further modernisation in 2004, the pub offers a warm, cosy interior, with sofas arranged around a fireplace. There is a separate pool and darts room. Sports events are shown on large-screen TVs. Lunches are served on Sunday only (booking advisable). A regular Sunday night quiz and charity events are organised. Quality guest ales cover all tastes. The smoking area is heated and covered. ❀◐♿⇌P⌐

Patricroft

Stanley Arms ★

895 Liverpool Road, M30 0QN (opp fire station on A57)

12-11 (10.30 Sun)

☎ (0161) 788 8801

Holt Mild, Bitter Ⓗ

In 2008 this pub won local CAMRA's unspoilt traditional local award, which describes it exactly. One of Holt's tiniest pubs, it is always busy. The vault is at the front, but its corner entrance is usually shut – use the entrance on Liza Ann Street to enter the small lobby. There is another room at the end of the green-tiled corridor marked 'private', but open to the public, where there is a mock cast iron range. Q❀⊟⇌🚌(10,22,67)♣⌐

Pendlebury

Lord Nelson

653 Bolton Road, M27 4EJ (A666/B5231 jct)

11-11 (midnight Sat)

☎ (0161) 794 3648

Holt Mild, Bitter Ⓗ

Rebuilt in the early 1970s, this pub typifies buildings of the era. The large concert room style lounge has a stage where live music is performed on Sunday. In the corner by the bar is a small offshoot snug. There is also a spacious vault with a large-screen TV popular with football fans. At the back is an outdoor drinking area with a heated smoking shelter. Holt's seasonal beers are occasionally available. ❀⊟⇌(Swinton)🚌(8)♣P⌐

Prestwich

Friendship

Scholes Lane, M25 0PD (on A6044 near Heaton Park)

12-11 (11.30 Fri & Sat); 12-11.30 Sun

☎ (0161) 773 2645

Holt Mild, Bitter, seasonal beers Ⓗ

An imposing red-brick building on the main Prestwich to Agecroft road, the pub comprises a dining area, neat snug bar and a comfortable, well appointed lounge area. Both snug and lounge are served by an impressive semi island bar with wooden surrounds and hatches. Food is served every day until 8pm (9pm Fri). Outside, there is a patio and large bench area for smokers. The car park is small. ❀◐⊟♿P⌐

Rochdale

Baum 🏆

33-37 Toad Lane, OL12 0NU (follow signs for Co-op Museum)

11.30-11 (midnight Fri & Sat); 11.30-10.30 Sun

☎ (01706) 352186 🌐 thebaum.co.uk

Beer range varies Ⓗ

A hidden gem within a conservation area, the Baum occupies part of the same building as the Pioneer Museum, the world's first Co-op. A split level inn with old world charm, the conservatory to the rear overlooks a large secluded beer garden. Friendly staff serve ever-changing real ales plus a rolling variety from Phoenix Brewery, a large choice of bottles of the world and five Belgians on draft including kriek fruit beer. Fresh food and international tapas are served daily. Outside is a heated and covered smoking area. ❀◑⇌⌐

Cask & Feather

1 Oldham Road, OL16 1UA (jct Oldham Rd/Drake St)

11-midnight (1am Fri & Sat); 12-midnight Sun

☎ (01706) 711476

Beer range varies, Ⓗ

This busy pub is situated near a road junction on the way to the railway station. The main entrance is a stone castellated affair leading to an open plan interior with a long bar and pool area. Three cask beers are on offer, usually including one from Phoenix. The pub has a traditional feel and friendly staff make you feel at home. Good value lunches are served 11-2.30pm every day. Pool and poker are played on Monday and Tuesday. There is a heavy rock disco on Friday and live music on Sunday. Good oldies jukebox. ◐⇌♣⌐

Cemetery Hotel ★ ✔

470 Bury Road, OL11 5EU (on B622)

12-2am (1am Sat); 12-10.30 Sun

☎ (01706) 645635

Beer range varies Ⓗ

Rochdale's original free house from the early 1970s, this pub is listed in CAMRA's National Inventory for its many original features including the tilework. It has maintained its multi- roomed layout and has two lovely snugs. Upstairs is a large function room available for hire. There are usually four or five beers available, as well as good value home-cooked lunches. Quiz night is Monday. The pub can get very busy with Rochdale AFC fans on match days. Real cider is served during the summer months. ⚠Q☕◐🚌(469)♣P⌐

Flying Horse Hotel

37 Packer Street, OL16 1NJ (opp town hall)

11 (12 Sun)-midnight

☎ (01706) 646412 🌐 theflyinghorsehotel.co.uk

Lees Bitter; Phoenix Arizona; Taylor Best Bitter, Landlord; guest beers Ⓗ

Impressive stone building opposite an equally impressive town hall, the Flying Horse was opened as a hotel in the early 20th century. A popular pub, it is centrally located, close to all amenities. The well decorated open-plan lounge attracts a mixed clientele and gets very busy at weekends. An extensive food menu is offered daily. The licensed function room is available to hire. Easy to find with the bus station a two-minute walk and rail links close by. 🛏◐◑⇌🚌⍻

Merry Monk ✔

234 College Road, OL12 6AF (Jct A6060/B6222)
⌚ 12-11; 12-5, 7-10.30 Sun
☎ (01706) 646919
Hydes Owd Oak, Original Bitter, Jekyll's Gold, seasonal beer; guest beers Ⓗ
First licensed in 1850, this brick-built detached local has had a varied history, as can be seen from the fine pair of Phoenix tile sets in the entrance. The inn passed to Bass/Cornbrook and was sold as a free house in 1984. The open plan pub is home to strong darts and quiz teams, and ring the bull is played. Outside are two full sized petanque pistes. A wide range of Hydes beers is served alongside an occasional guest. ❀🚌(469)♣⍻

Regal Moon ✔

The Butts, OL16 1HB (next to bus station)
⌚ 9-midnight (1am Fri & Sat); 11-midnight Sun
☎ (01706) 657434
Beer range varies Ⓗ
Imposing former cinema in the middle of town. Many original art deco features remain and pictures of old Rochdale add a local touch. Spot the large mannequin complete with organ above the bar. There is a raised area for families and diners. Up to ten handpumps dispense a wide variety of beers – local breweries are supported as well as Yorkshire brewers. Westons real cider is also on handpump. Food is available all day with breakfast served until noon. Q❀◐◑🚌⍻

Romiley

Duke of York

Stockport Road, SK6 3AN
⌚ 11-midnight (1am Fri-Sat); 12-11.30 Sun
☎ (0161) 430 2806 🌐 dukeofyorkromiley.co.uk
Caledonian Deuchars IPA; John Smith's Bitter; Sharp's Doom Bar; Wells Bombardier; guest beers Ⓗ
Situated on the B6104 and close to Bridge 14 on the Peak Forest Canal, this cosy traditional village pub, built in 1786 as the King's Head and renamed in Victorian times, still retains its character and historical feel. Food is served seven days a week, either in the bar or the Mediterranean restaurant offering Turkish and other dishes. A fun pub quiz is held on Monday, with mellow jazz music on Tuesday evening. A successful beer festival is hosted in September.
🔥Q❀◐◑⊟⇌🚌(383,384)●P⍻

Sale

Volunteer Hotel

81 Cross Street, M33 7HH
⌚ 12-midnight (11 Sun)
☎ (0161) 973 5503
Holts Mild, Bitter, seasonal beers Ⓗ
Dating back to the late 19th century, this once multi-roomed pub has been opened up into one large room served by a single bar. The interior is warm and welcoming, with friendly, helpful staff. Three darts teams are based here, which makes for some lively evenings, while quiz night takes place most Thursdays. There is a fine oak-panelled room upstairs which is available for meetings.
❀♿⊖🚌(16,18,263)P⍻

Salford

Crescent

20 The Crescent, M5 4PF
⌚ 12-midnight (11 Sun)
☎ (0161) 736 5600
Bazens Black Pig Mild, Pacific; guest beers Ⓗ
A plain exterior hides an eclectic selection of drinking areas. Various comfortable rooms are populated with students, academics, beer lovers and locals. The low main bar has a warming fire in an iron range. This long-standing champion of ale has up to 13 on handpump and one for cider. Guest beers come from all over the UK and there are regular beer festivals. Note the refurbished back yard and music room. 🔥❀◐◑⊟⇌⊖🚌♣●P⍻

King's Arms

11 Bloom Street, M3 6AN (off Chapel St)
⌚ 12-11 (midnight Fri & Sat); 12-6 Sun
☎ (0161) 839 8726
Bazens Pacific; Moorhouse's Blond Witch; guest beers Ⓗ
Traditional pub with a thriving bohemian arts scene, including award-winning theatre groups and eclectic live music. The unusual oval shaped lounge and Grade II-listed features are enhanced by an ever-changing collection of bric-a-brac. With up to six beers on handpump, this is well worth seeking out for the real ale drinker looking for something different. The decorated and heated smoking shelter in the back yard is of note.
❀◐◑⇌🚌P⍻

New Oxford 🏆 ✔

11 Bexley Square, M3 6DB (by magistrates court)
⌚ 12-midnight
☎ (0161) 832 7082 🌐 thenewoxford.co.uk
Bazens Flatbac; guest beers Ⓗ
In a historic square, this well-appointed two-room pub is dedicated to serving quality beer. Rescued from an unpromising past by a committed management team, it was crowned CAMRA Greater Manchester Pub of the Year in 2007. Up to 16 ales are on handpull, including guest beers and two house beers from Mallinsons and Moorhouse's, supplemented by a superlative range of Belgian beers, many rare for the UK, with several on draught. Regular popular beer festivals are held. Food serving times vary. ❀◐⇌🚌●⍻

Racecourse Hotel

Littleton Road, Lower Kersal, M7 3SE (next to River Irwell)
⌚ 12-midnight (1am Fri & Sat); 12-11 Sun
☎ (0161) 792 1420
Oakwell Barnsley Bitter Ⓗ
This imposing pub dates from 1930. It was built to cater for visitors to the nearby Manchester racecourse which ran its last race in 1963. A characterful interior is enhanced by lots of wooden panelling and a revolving entrance door. The large central bar serves several distinct drinking areas. Racing mementoes and historic information adorn the walls. Q🐎❀⊟🚌(93,95)♣P⍻

Star Inn

2 Back Hope Street, Higher Broughton, M7 2FR (off Great Clowes St)
⊛ 2-11.30 (11.45 Sat); 1.30-10.30 Sun
☎ (0161) 792 4184
Robinson's Unicorn [H]
Crowned with a local CAMRA award in 2008, this is a fine example of a traditional unspoilt pub. It was built in the 1860s, became a Robinson's house in the 1920s, and very little has changed since. Patronised by welcoming locals, it is run by a dedicated management team. Situated in the Cliff conservation area and surrounded by cobbled streets, the Star has the feel of an original back street pub that was commonplace half a century ago. ❀⊟⊡(98)♣⌐

Welcome

2 Robert Hall Street, Ordsall, M5 3LT (opp community centre)
⊛ 12-midnight; 12-3, 7.30-10.30 Sun
☎ (0161) 872 6040
Lees Mild, Bitter [P]
This two-room community pub comprises a large lounge with comfortable furnishings and a smaller games room where pool and darts can be enjoyed. The pub runs several pool and darts teams. It is situated by the Oldfield Road end of Robert Hall Street and is a short walk from Salford's Grade I-listed Tudor mansion, Ordsall Hall. An unusual python dispense system is used.
♿⊖(Anchorage)⊡(69)♣P

Stalybridge

Stalybridge Labour Club

Acres Lane, SK15 2JR
⊛ 12-4.30, 7.30-11; 12-6, 7.30-10.30 Sun
☎ (0161) 338 4796
Taylor Landlord; Wells Bombardier; guest beers [H]
This modern social club incorporates a lounge, TV room, function/concert room and a small meeting room. The comfortable and friendly atmosphere can be enjoyed while playing a variety of games including billiards and snooker. Guest beers are mainly sourced from local micros. Show a copy of this Guide or a CAMRA membership card for entry.
❀♿⇌⊡P⌐

Stalybridge Station Refreshment Rooms (Buffet Bar) ☆

Rassbottom Street, SK15 1RF (Platform 1)
⊛ 9.30 (alcohol from 11)-11; 11 (alcohol from 12)-10.30 Sun
☎ (0161) 303 0007 🌐 buffetbar.freewebspace.com
Boddingtons Bitter; Flowers IPA; guest beers [H]
Nobody minds delayed or missed trains at Stalybridge. This institution for educated drinkers serves an ever-changing range of up to nine cask beers, usually from micros, plus often rare brews. These can be enjoyed in convivial Victorian splendour by the roaring fire while enjoying simple traditionally cooked meals, or perched outside watching the world and the trains go by. The recently refurbished conservatory adds to the charm and character of this gem. Foreign bottled beers are also available and a folk club plays on Saturday. ♨Q❀◐◑⊟♿⇌⊡●P⌐

Stockport

Arden Arms 🏆 ★

23 Millgate, SK1 2LX (jct of Corporation St)
⊛ 12-11
☎ (0161) 480 2185 🌐 arden-arms.co.uk
Robinson's Hatters, Unicorn, Double Hop, Old Tom, seasonal beers [H]
Grade-II listed and on CAMRA's National Inventory, the Arden's distinctive curved, glazed bar, hidden snug, chandeliers and grandfather clock conjure up a Victorian ambience. Gourmet lunches, quiz nights and wine tastings, however, add a contemporary touch. Conveniently close to Stockport's historic market, the place is abuzz at lunchtimes, but more intimate in the evenings. Formerly a mortuary, the cellars retain body niches in the walls. A beautiful courtyard shows off the old stables and outbuildings. Voted CAMRA branch Pub of the Year 2009, this is an unmissable gem. ♨♉❀◐⊟⊡♣⌐

Armoury

31 Shaw Heath, SK3 8BD (on B5465)
⊛ 10.30-midnight (2am Fri & Sat); 11-midnight Sun
☎ (0161) 477 3711 🌐 frederic-robinson.com
Robinson's Hatters, Unicorn, Old Tom [H]
Busy local with a strong community involvement and friendly and knowledgeable staff. Original glass panels remain in the internal doors bearing the old Bells Brewery logo, while the walls feature memorabilia relating to the Cheshire Regiment. Convenient for Edgeley Park football ground, bar food is often available when Stockport County or Sale Sharks are at home. Darts matches are a feature here, with two leagues often playing on the same night. Live folk music sessions are hosted in an upstairs room. CAMRA branch Pub of the Year 2007 runner-up. Q❀⊟⇌⊡(310,369)♣⌐

Blossoms

2 Buxton Road, Heaviley, SK2 6NU (at A6/A5102 jct)
⊛ 12-3, 5-11 (11.30 Fri); 12-11.30 Sat; 12-10.30 Sun
☎ (0161) 477 2397 🌐 frederic-robinson.com
Robinson's Hatters, Unicorn, [H]**; Old Tom** [G]
Built as a coaching house in the 18th century, the multi-roomed interior includes a lobby bar and three rooms. The snug has an elegant carved fireplace surround, stained glass panels, and features pictures of the town's history. A more basic room has a pinball machine and TV, and is popular when soccer matches are screened. The games room has a well kept pool table. Of historical note, a tunnel connects the pub to nearby St George's Church. Food is served noon-2.30pm Monday to Friday.
Q❀◐⊟⇌(Davenport)⊡(192,199)♣P⌐

Crown

154 Heaton Lane, SK4 1AR (jct of King St West under viaduct)
⊛ 12-11 (10.30 Sun)
☎ (0161) 480 5850 🌐 thecrowninn.uk.com
Beer range varies [H]
CAMRA National Pub of the Year 2009 runner-up, and local branch winner 2008, the Crown is a busy pub, especially in the evening. A choice of around 16 ever-changing beers is usually to be had, including brews from Pictish and Copper Dragon, making it probably the town's foremost cask ale outlet. Real cider is sourced by Merrylegs. Four rooms radiate from the busy bar – two compact snugs, a large lounge with feature overmantle, and a plainer pool room. Lunches are served Monday to Friday. Live music is a feature too, with the rear yard often showcasing local rock, folk, acoustic and more. Barbecues are held in summer. A rare outlet for Cellar Rat beers. ♨❀◐⊟⇌⊡♣●⌐

Olde Vic
1 Chatham Street, SK3 9ED (jct of Shaw Heath)
5 (7 Sat)-late (last entry 10.15); closed Mon; 7-10.30 Sun
(0161) 480 2410 yeoldevic.com
Beer range varies H
'Multum in Parvo' (much in little) goes the motto. One-roomed characterful pub with an ongoing refurbishment programme. Beware the licensee's wicked sense of humour. A strict no-swearing rule belies the easy-going, friendly nature of the pub, which can be particularly busy when Sale Sharks are at home. Five handpumps dispense an ever-changing range of guest beers, usually from Millstone, Hornbeam and Facers. One handpump is reserved for guest ciders (supplied by Merrylegs). Supervised Internet access is available. Note Sunday evening closing time may vary.
(310,369)

Olde Woolpack
70 Brinksway, SK3 0BY (on A560 jct of Hollywood Way)
12-11 (12-3, 8-11 Sat); 12-3, 8-11 Sun
(0161) 476 0688
Thwaites Wainwright; guest beers H
Fully refurbished, the Woolpack has retained a traditional comfortable feel with a vault and two lounges, one with a TV for sport. Behind the pub, separating it from Stockport's most modern landmark – the massive blue Pyramid, is the River Mersey. On a summer's evening there is nothing better than sitting at the tables perched at the end of the now defunct Brinksway Bridge and watching the river rolling by. Guest beers are usually from local independent breweries.
(307,312)P

Pineapple
159 Heaton Lane, SK4 1AQ (off A6)
12-11 (10.30 Sun)
(0161) 480 3221 frederic-robinson.com
Robinson's Hatters, Hartley's Cumbria Way, Unicorn, seasonal beer H
Old, low-set building with three rooms including a smart lounge and a bar area with walls festooned with dozens of plates gathered from travels around the globe. Quite a talking point. At the rear is a spacious lower-level games room. A friendly welcome is offered to all, from regulars to shoppers to business people. Lunches are served 12-2pm daily except Sunday. One of very few Robinson's houses in the town to offer Hartleys beer. (192)

Queens Head (Turner's Vaults) ☆
12 Little Underbank, SK1 1JT
11-11; 12-7 Sun
(0161) 480 0725
Sam Smith Old Brewery Bitter H
The Queens is a much-prized Stockport hostelry dating back to at least the 1790s. It still maintains its original three-room layout, with a narrow bar room at the front with interesting spirit taps, a small snug tucked in the middle, and a quieter more intimate room at the back. The decor includes plenty of wooden panels and wood flooring, while around the walls are pictures of Victorian characters, old advertisements and mirrors. The snug has a stove wood burner which helps to keep things cosy on cold days. Q

Railway
1 Avenue Street, SK1 2BZ (jct of Great Portwood St/A560)
12-11 (10.30 Sun)
(0161) 429 6062
Pennine Floral Dance, Hambeldon Bitter, Railway Sleeper, Porter, Sunshine, seasonal beers; guest beers H
Bustling street-corner house with 11 handpumps showcasing the full Pennine Brewery range, plus three guests at weekends. A changing real cider is also stocked, plus a wide range of Belgian, German and other bottled beers. Home-made lunches are served Monday to Saturday. Look out for the model railway atop the bar canopy, and the amusing loco mural at the back. Enjoy it while you can as it may face demolition if a planned redevelopment ever resurfaces. Branch CAMRA Pub of the Year 2007.
Q(325,330)

Thatched House
74 Churchgate, SK1 1YJ (jct Wellington St)
closed Mon & Tue; 8-11 Wed; 8-1am Thu; 7-2am Fri; 3-11 Sat; 3-11
(0161) 335 1910 thatched-live.co.uk
Black Sheep Best Bitter; Wychwood Hobgoblin; guest beers H
For live music it is one of the town's premier venues for rock, metal and punk bands playing Thursday, Friday and Saturday nights. A quiet pub it is not. Remaining architectural details of note are a mosaic floor in the porch and rare windows featuring Showell's Brewery. The large, open-plan main bar leads to a pool room and beer garden. Two guest beers are usually available along with a changing guest cider, plus a good range of bottled beers. Check the website for details of forthcoming live acts. (314)

Tiviot
8 Tiviot Dale, SK1 1TA
12-11 (4 Sun)
(0161) 480 4109 frederic-robinson.com
Robinson's Hatters, Unicorn P
Lively, town-centre, three-room pub that keeps busy serving food (available 12-2pm Tue-Sat) and ale to a mainly lunchtime trade. Despite the somewhat careworn feel it is warm and welcoming inside. The decor includes some interesting old photos and drawings of the town together with steam loco paintings commemorating the time when Tiviot Dale station stood nearby. P

Strines

Sportsman's Arms
105 Strines Road, SK6 7GE (on B6101)
12-3, 5-11; 12-11 Sat & Sun
(0161) 427 2888 the-sportsman-pub.co.uk
Beer range varies H
Standing on the edge of the Goyt Valley, a superb picture window gives views over the wooded countryside. A monumental fireplace accommodates log fires in winter. Five ever-changing guest beers, mainly from micros, are available and the landlord welcomes beer suggestions. There is a small separate tap room. Outside, a terrace and balcony are popular in summer and the pub is close to the Peak Forest Canal. The bus stops outside and runs until after midnight. QP

Swinton

White Horse ✔

384 Worsley Road, M27 0FH
❂ 12-11 (midnight Fri & Sat)
☎ (0161) 794 2404
Boddingtons Bitter; Wells Bombardier; guest beers Ⓗ
This is Swinton's oldest pub, dating back to the early 17th century when it was converted from a farmhouse. Sadly only the exterior has been listed. The left side of the building, which now contains the main lounge, was added in the 18th century. On the right is the bar and four alcoves, each with a TV. There is ample outdoor seating, covered and heated. Good value food is served until 9pm every day. ✿◑◗♿🚌(12,26)P⁄–

White Swan

186 Worsley Road, M27 5BN (close to jct A572/A580 East Lancashire Road)
❂ 12-11 (11.30 Fri); 12-10.30 Sun
☎ (0161) 794 1504
Holt Mild, Bitter Ⓗ
Large, red-brick, 1920s pub with extensive wooden wall panels and stained glass windows. The five rooms include a vault with its own separate entrance and Gents, a large lounge behind the central bar, an even bigger room at the back used for football on TV, darts, and for families at lunchtimes, and two rooms on the left which have been opened up by partial removal of a dividing wall. Many original features including fireplaces have been left intact. ♘✿⊟🚌(12,26,73)♣P⁄–

Tyldesley

Half Moon

115-117 Elliot Street, M29 8FL
❂ 11-4, 7-midnight; 12-midnight Sat; 12-11 Sun
☎ (01942) 883481
Holt Bitter; guest beers Ⓗ
Town-centre two-room local popular with a clientele of all ages. The main lounge, with its display cabinets, has various seating and standing areas, while the second lounge is comfortable and ideal for get-togethers. In summer the patio is a good place to catch the sun and take in the views of Winter Hill. ✿♣⁄–

Mort Arms

235-237 Elliot Street, M29 8DG
❂ 12-midnight (1am Fri & Sat); 12-11 Sun
☎ (01942) 883481
Holt Mild, Bitter Ⓗ
This 1930s pub has changed little over the years. From the facade to the interior, it is recognisable as a Holt's hostelry. The entrance has two etched doors directing you into the tap room or the lounge. The bar serves both rooms. In the lounge, walls are wood panelled, with seating and tables all around. At the rear, behind the fireplace, is what was once part of the pub's private quarters. The tap room is a bright contrast and just how a tap room should be. ⊟♣

Uppermill

Cross Keys

OL3 6LW (off A670, up Church Road)
❂ 12-11.30 (midnight Fri & Sat)
☎ (01457) 874626
Lees Brewer's Dark, Bitter, seasonal beers Ⓗ
Overlooking Saddleworth Church, this attractive 18th-century stone building has exposed beams throughout. The public bar features a stone-flagged floor and Yorkshire range. The pub is the centre for many activities including mountain rescue and the Saddleworth Runners and mountain bikers. It is especially busy during annual events such as the Road and Fell Race and Rushcart Festival (both August). A folk night is hosted on Wednesday. Home-cooked food includes puddings, pies and real chips (not Mon but all day Sun). Dogs are welcome. There is a covered patio for smokers. ⌂Q♘✿◑◗⊟♣P⁄–

Waggon Inn

34 High Street, OL3 6HR
❂ 11.30-11 (12.30am Fri & Sat); 12-10.30 Sun
☎ (01457) 872376 🌐 thewaggoninn.co.uk
Robinson's Unicorn, Ⓗ**; Old Tom,** Ⓖ**; seasonal beers** Ⓗ
This mid-19th-century stone pub stands in a picturesque village opposite Saddleworth museum and the Huddersfield Narrow Canal. With a central bar, three rooms and a restaurant, it also offers high quality en suite B&B. It is the venue for many annual events including the Whit Friday Brass Band Contest, July Folk Festival and, in August, the Wartime Weekend and Rushcart Festival. Good home-cooked food includes senior specials and themed events (no evening meals Sun or Mon). The Old Tom is served in winter only. Q✿⛾◑◗Å⇌(Greenfield)♣P⁄–

Urmston

Lord Nelson

49 Stretford Road, M41 9LG
❂ 11-11 (11.30 Fri & Sat); 12-11 Sun
Holt Mild, Bitter, seasonal beer Ⓗ
The Nellie is everything you would expect from a Holt's pub, selling beer in volumes that demand hogsheads to a varied clientele, mainly regulars, but no food beyond crisps and nuts. Always busy, it gets particularly crowded for sports events and on quiz night (Tuesday). Despite changes over the years it still retains some of its original multi-room character, notably in the Snug to the right of the entrance. Smokers are catered for with a substantial heated shelter in the yard. ⊟⇌🚌♣P⁄–

Wardley

Morning Star

520 Manchester Road, M27 9QW (on A6 between Swinton and Walken)
❂ 12-11 (11.30 Fri & Sat); 12-10.20 Sun
☎ (0161) 794 4927
Holt Mild, Bitter, seasonal beers Ⓗ
A fine example of a pub that can trace its roots back to Edwardian times. In recent years it has been modernised and an extension added to cater for an increased clientele. It has several rooms including a popular vault, large lounge and a small snug on the right as you enter. A favourite with the local community, it also attracts passing trade from the bust A6. A friendly welcome from the bar staff is assured. ✿⊟⇌(Moorside)🚌♣P⁄–

Westhoughton

Brinsop Country Inn

584-592 Chorley Road, BL5 3NJ (on A6 just S of Blackrod)

12-3, 5.30-11.30; 12-11.30 Fri & Sat; 12-10.30 Sun
(01942) 811113
Thwaites Original; guest beers H
This upmarket roadside hostelry is a genuine privately owned free house. Its name links with the original Brinsop Hall, owned by the Abbots of Cockersand until the dissolution of the monastries. The pub has a very good reputation for food and six handpumps on the bar dispense at least four continually changing beers from Lancashire micro-breweries. The bar area has a modern decor and plush upholstered chairs and sofas. The Brinsop Comedy Club meets here once a month.
P

Whalley Range

Hillary Step

199 Upper Chorlton Road, M16 0BH
4-midnight (1am Fri); 12-1am Sat; 12-midnight Sun
(0161) 881 1978
Beer range varies H
Lively, modern bar where conversation dominates. Wonderful bar snacks are available but no meals. Live jazz features on a Sunday night and broadsheet newspapers are on offer most of the time. Guest beers are generally sourced from micro-breweries and there is also a good choice of wines and whiskies. Freshly ground coffee is always available. Q

Whitefield

Eagle & Child

Higher Lane, M45 7EY (on A665, 300m from A56)
12-11 (midnight Fri & Sat)
Holt Mild, Bitter, seasonal beers H
Detached, imposing double fronted pub with a floodlit bowling green and patio at the rear. Set back from the road, the existing pub dates from 1936 although the site has been in use since the 1800s. This large building has a spacious lounge and a public bar, both served by a central bar. A smaller room is ideal for meetings or private parties. The bowling green is superbly maintained and well used by the pub's 11 teams. There is a covered patio for smokers.
(Besses o'th' Barn)(98,135)P

Wigan

Anvil

Dorning Street, WN1 1ND (next to bus station)
11-11; 12-10.30 Sun
(01942) 239444 allgatesinns.co.uk
Hydes Mild, Bitter; guest beers H
Popular town-centre pub and a frequent winner of local CAMRA seasonal and Pub of the Year awards – note the array of certificates adorning the 'wall of fame'. Six handpumps offer beers from the nearby Allgates brewery, guest beers plus six draught continental ales. There is also a range of bottled beers. The pub can be busy on match days as it is close to the JJB Stadium, home to Wigan Athletic and Wigan Warriors. It has a heated smoking terrace. (Wallgate/North Western)

Berkeley

27-29 Wallgate, WN1 1LD (opp Wallgate station)
11.30-11 (midnight Fri & Sat); 12-10.30 Sun
(01942) 242041 berkeleybar.co.uk
Theakston Mild, Old Peculier; guest beer H
The Berkeley, a former coaching house, has a friendly, comfortable atmosphere, offering something for everyone. Regular sporting fixtures are shown on large-screen TVs in the open-plan bar. The pub's clever design means that the comfortable, split-level areas give the impression of distinct seating sections. Food is served daily until 7pm. A first-floor function room is available for hire. There is a dress code on Saturday night.
(Wallgate/North Western)

Boulevard

Wallgate, WN1 1LD
2-2am (2.30am Fri & Sat); 2-midnight Sun
(01942) 497165
Prospect Nutty Slack; guest beers H
This surprisingly large basement pub (look for a yellow and black sign indicating the entrance) opened in 2006. From the bar you enter a large back room that features regular entertainment. Live music is performed on Friday and Saturday. Open until very late, it is close to both Wigan Wallgate and North Western train stations. Winner of CAMRA Wigan New Cask Outlet award for 2007 and Pub of the Season Autumn 2007, it is LocAle accredited. (Wallgate/North Western)

Bowling Green

106 Wigan Lane, WN1 2LS
3 (12 Sat & Sun)-11 (1am Fri & Sat); 12-11 Sun
(01942) 519871
Caledonian Deuchars IPA; Greene King Old Speckled Hen; Tetley Bitter; Thwaites Lancaster Bomber; guest beers H
This red-brick pub, built in 1904, was once used as a soup kitchen. The building has received some sympathetic internal alterations, creating a comfortable lounge with two distinct drinking areas. There is a separate games and pool room, and a beer garden to the rear with a covered smoking area. A function room is available for hire. In addition to the regular beers, there are changing guest ales. Daily newspapers are available in the lounge.

Brocket Arms

Mesnes Road, Swinley, WN1 2DD
9-midnight (1am Fri & Sat)
(01942) 403500
Greene King Ruddles County, Abbot; Marston's Pedigree; guest beers H
The Brocket is one of the few Wetherlodges in the country. The interior is spacious, light and airy. While open plan, there are intimate booths and flexible seating to accommodate groups of all sizes. The usual Wetherspoon's food and conference rooms are available and a patio area to the front of the pub caters for smokers. Guest beers from local micro-breweries feature regularly. LocAle accredited. Two small function/conference rooms are available for hire. P

Royal Oak

Standishgate, WN1 1XL (on A49 N of town centre)
4-midnight; 12-1am Fri & Sat; 12-midnight Sun
(01942) 323137 royaloakwigan.co.uk
Caledonian Deuchars IPA; Mayflower Dark Oak, seasonal beer; guest beers H
The Royal Oak was built in the early 17th century and is now a listed building. It has always been a landmark inn on the pub circuit due to its location on the A49 and close proximity to Wigan town centre. The multi-roomed pub is served by a long

bar stocking foreign draught and bottled beers. The tap for the Mayflower Brewery, it hosts live music, beer and food festivals. The pleasant beer garden is ideal for summer barbecues.

Woodford

Davenport Arms (Thief's Neck)

550 Chester Road, SK7 1PS (on A5102, jct Church Lane)
11-3.30, 5.15-11; 11-11 Sat; 12-3, 7-10.30 Sun
(0161) 439 2435 frederic-robinson.com
Robinson's Hatters, Unicorn, Old Tom, seasonal beers
Unspoilt, red-brick, farmhouse-style pub where the licence has been in the same family for more than 75 years. The cosy rooms are warmed by real fires, and children are welcome at lunchtimes in the right-hand snug. Excellent food is mostly home-made, with some adventurous specials. Outside, the spacious forecourt and attractive garden, set well away from the road, are popular in summer, when impressive floral displays are on show.
Q (X57) **P**

Worsley

Barton Arms

2 Stablefold, M28 2ED (at side of Bridgewater Canal on Barton Rd)
12-11
(0161) 728 6157
Black Sheep Best Bitter; guest beer
Situated in the old village by the Bridgewater Canal is this modern and comfortable establishment with a spread of rooms and alcoves radiating out from the bar. One of the guest beers is usually Taylor Landlord and mini beer festivals are held occasionally. Food is served throughout the day until 9pm and six tables have been customised to accommodate wheelchair users. Children over 14 are permitted with adults. (33,68)**P**

Worthington

Crown Hotel

Platt Lane, WN1 2XF
12-11 (10.30 Sun)
(08000) 686678 thecrownatworthington.co.uk
Prospect Silver Tally; guest beers
Local CAMRA Pub of the Year 2006 and 2008, this country inn offers seven cask beers and acts as the brewery tap for Prospect beers. High quality home-cooked food is served in the bar and conservatory restaurant, while a large decked sun terrace at the rear has patio heaters for cooler evenings. There are also regular themed evenings and 10 en-suite rooms for staying over. Mini beer festivals are held about four times a year, using all handpumps and cellar runs. LocAle accredited. **P**

Food for thought

Ale is an enemy to idlenesse, it will worke and bee working in the braine as well as in the barrel; if it be abused by any man, it will trip up his heeles, and give him either a faire or fowle fall, if hee bee the strongest, stowtest, and skilfullest wrastler either in Cornwall or Christendome. But if ale bee moderately, mildly, and friendly dealt withall it will appease, qualifie, mitigate, and quench all striffe and contention, it will lay anger asleepe, and give a furious man or woman a gentle nap, and therefore it was rightly called nappy ale, by our learned and reverend fore-fathers.

Besides it is very medicinable, (as the best physitians doe affirme) for beere is seldom used or applyed to any inward or outward maladies, except sometimes it bee warmed with a little butter to wash the galled feete, or toes of a weary Traveller; but you shall never knowe or heare of a usuall drinker of ale, to bee troubled with the hippocondra, with hiopocondragacall obstructions or convulsions, nor are they vexed (as others are) with severall paines of sundry sorts of gowts, such as are the gonogra, podegra, chirocgra, and the lame hop-halting sciatica, or with the intollerable griefe of the stone in the reines, kidneys, or bladder.

Beere is a dutch boorish liquor, a thing not knowne in England, till of late dayes an alien to our nation, till such time as hops and heresies came amongst us, it is a fawcy intruder into this land, and it's sold by usurpation; for the houses that doe sell beere onely, are nickname ale-houses; marke beloved, an ale-house is never called a beere-house, but a beere-House would have but small custom, if it did not falsely carry the name of an ale-house; also it is common to say a stand of ale, it is not onely a stand, but it will make a man understand, or stand under; but beere is often called a hogshead, which all rational men doe knowe is but a swinish expression.

John Taylor (1580-1653), Ale ale-vated into the ale-titude, 1651

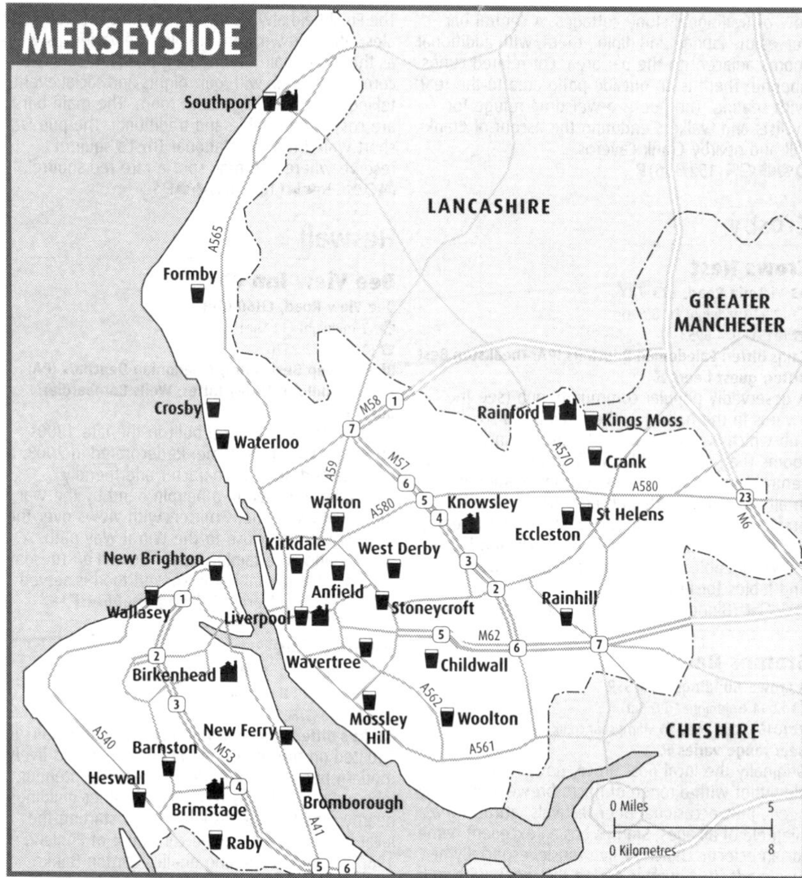

Barnston

Fox & Hounds ✔

107 Barnston Road, Wirral, CH61 1BW

11-11; 12-10.30 Sun

☎ (0151) 648 7685 the-fox-hounds.co.uk

Brimstage Trappers Hat; Theakston Best Bitter, Old Peculier; Webster's Yorkshire Bitter; guest beers Ⓗ

Village pub with bar, lounge and snug full of bric-a-brac, clocks, flying ducks, horse brasses, local photos and other memorabilia. The lounge, converted from tea rooms, is quiet with no music or games machines. The pub retains its original character including real fires in the bar and snug. The stone courtyard is a profusion of colour in the summer. Popular for its cask ales and real lunchtime food, with a fish dish of the day, daily specials and traditional Sunday roasts. CAMRA Wirral Pub of the Year 2008.

Q ♣P

Bromborough

Knockaloe Bar & Restaurant

28 Bridle Road, Wirral, CH62 6AR

12-11 (midnight Fri & Sat)

☎ (0151) 328 5690

Brimstage Trapper's Hat; Tetley Bitter; guest beer Ⓗ

Formerly the Associated Octel Social Club, the 'OC' is now open to all, although members receive a 10% discount on beer and food. The club has undergone a tasteful refurbishment attracting a wide variety of drinkers. There are extensive sports facilities, function and meeting rooms, plus a newly constructed patio area. A well-attended quiz night is a regular feature. Local beers from Brimstage are popular, with the guest beer usually from that brewery. Children are welcome until 9.30pm. No food Monday, Tuesday or Sunday evening. P

Crank

Red Cat

Red Cat Lane, WA11 8RU

12-11 (10.30 Sun)

☎ (01744) 882422 theredcatcrank.co.uk

Beer range varies Ⓗ

Situated in the rural hamlet of Crank, between Rainford and Billinge, the Red Cat is at the end of a

INDEPENDENT BREWERIES

Betwixt Birkenhead
Brimstage Brimstage
Cains Liverpool
Cambrinus Knowsley
George Wright Rainford
Southport Southport
Wapping Liverpool

row of traditional stone cottages. A central bar serves the lounge and dining room, with additional rooms adjacent to the bar area. Cat-related curios abound. There is an outside patio area to the rear with seating. The pub is a welcome refuge for cyclists and walkers enduring the ascent of Crank Hill and nearby Crank Caverns.
Q❀◐◑⊞(152,356)**P**

Crosby

Crows Nest

63 Victoria Road, L23 7XY
12-11 (midnight Fri & Sat)
☎ (0151) 924 6953
Cains Bitter; Caledonian Deuchars IPA; Theakston Best Bitter; guest beers H
A deservedly popular community pub (see the awards in the hallway), the Crow's is a smallish pub which has three separate and distinctive rooms (bar, snug and lounge) arranged around a central serving area. A buzz of conversation thrives in all the rooms, although newspapers are provided for those who just want to sit and enjoy the changing range of guest beers chosen by the knowledgeable staff. There are outside benches and tables for fine weather.
Q❀⇌(Blundellsands/Crosby)⊞**P**

Stamps Bar

4 Crown Buildings, L23 5SR
12-11 (midnight Fri & Sat)
☎ (0151) 286 2662 stampsbar.co.uk
Beer range varies H
Originally the local post office, now a popular real ale outlet with a range of micro-brewery and local beers, plus occasional beer festivals, attracting a clientele of all ages. Stamps has an excellent name for an eclectic choice of live music, especially at weekends. It is quieter during the week with free newspapers and Internet access. Good food with an international flavour is served until early evening, and speciality gourmet nights held upstairs on Tuesday. Compact in size, very lively at times, but always a pleasant ambience.
◑&⇌(Blundellsand/Crosby)⊞**P**

Eccleston

Griffin Inn

Church Lane, St Helens, WA10 5AD
12-11 (10.30 Sun)
☎ (01744) 27907 griffininn.co.uk
Cains Bitter; Jennings Cumberland Ale; guest beer H
Located in Eccleston village and two miles from St Helen's centre, the Griffin has a distinctive sandstone frontage dating from 1812. It offers en suite accommodation and a popular restaurant. A central bar serves two lounges, one with TV. There are comfortable modern furnishings, a rear grassed area with a children's play structure, a decked patio and a rear car park. Q❀◑⊞**P**

Formby

Freshfield Hotel ✔

1A Massams Lane, Freshfield, L37 7BD
12-11 (midnight Fri & Sat)
☎ (01704) 874871
Greene King IPA, Morland Original, Ruddles County, Abbot; Titanic Freshie Mild, Freshie Bitter H
The Freshfield always has a good array of well-kept ales, often drawn from smaller breweries, as well as the three main Greene King brews. It serves the community well, with quiz nights and social events taking place in a large back room. The main bars are cosy, comfortable and traditional. The pub is a short walk from the National Trust's squirrel reserve where you may spot a rare red squirrel.
Q❀◐&⇌⊞(162,165)♣**P**

Heswall

Dee View Inn ✔

Dee View Road, CH60 0DH
12-midnight (11 Sun)
☎ (0151) 342 2320
Black Sheep Best Bitter; Caledonian Deuchars IPA; Taylor Landlord; Tetley Bitter; Wells Bombardier; guest beers H
Homely, traditional local built in the late 1800s offering a warm welcome. Redecorated in 2008, it has retained both its character and friendly atmosphere. It sits on a hairpin bend by the war memorial and famous mirror, with views over the Dee Estuary and close to the Wirral Way path. A popular and entertaining quiz is hosted on Tuesday evening. Traditional home-cooked food is served – children are welcome if dining. ❀◑⊞♣**P**

Johnny Pye

Pye Road, CH60 0DB (next to bus station)
11-11 (11.30 Thu; midnight Fri & Sat); 12-11 Sun
☎ (0151) 342 8215
Banks's Bitter; Marston's Burton Bitter; guest beers H
Situated on the site of an old bus depot, this lively modern pub is named after a local entrepreneur. Johnny Pye is also associated with other buildings nearby, and he was responsible for starting the local bus service. A signed caricature of England's 1966 World Cup winning goalie, Gordon Banks, adorns the bar. The pub has wide screen TVs, a strong football following, and ladies and gents darts teams. Children are welcome on the patio area. No food is available on Sunday.
❀◑&⊞♣**P**

Kings Moss

Colliers Arms

Pimbo Road, WA11 8RD (follow signs to Houghwood Golf Club)
12-11 (10.30 Sun)
☎ (01744) 892894 theredcatcrank.co.uk/colliersarms.html
Black Sheep Best Bitter; guest beers H
Sister pub to the Red Cat, the Collier's is situated in Kings Moss at the foot of Billinge Hill, with the austere sounding Hangman's Wood on the hill above. It is part of a row of miners cottages next to the former site of the Hillside colliery. A central bar serves four distinct areas. Unsurprisingly, it has mining memorabilia as well as a selection of books to accompany a relaxing visit. The small enclosed children's play area is accessed through premises to rear. Q❀◑⊞(152,356)**P**

Liverpool: Anfield

Strawberry Tavern

Breckfield Road South, L6 5DR (off ASDA car park)
12-11 (1am Fri & Sat); 12-10.30 Sun
☎ (0151) 261 9364

Oakwell Old Tom Mild, Barnsley Bitter Ⓗ
This Oakwell pub continues to serve both Oakwell beers. Lying near a housing estate between Breck Road and West Derby Road, close to the old Ogden's tobacco factory, the pub is a welcome oasis for thirsty fans visiting Liverpool Football Club. Usefully, it may open early on match days with a lunchtime kick-off. The interior is divided to create a separate games area with a pool table and dartboard. Food is served until 6pm.
❀◑♿🚌(14)♣P

Liverpool: Childwall

Childwall Abbey

Score Lane, L16 5EY (off Childwall Valley Road)
12-11 (11.30 Mon; midnight Fri)
☎ (0151) 722 5293
Jennings Cumberland Ale; guest beers Ⓗ
An imposing Marston's pub situated opposite Childwall Church. Popular with families, it has large umbrellas and tables next to the bowling green, and a children's play area. There is a grand view to the east on a clear day. With the Liverpool Loop cycle track nearby, bicycle stands are provided. Closing time is later on Monday after the quiz. Last orders for food are taken at 8.15pm. Accommodation is available in seven en-suite rooms. Q❀◑♿🚌♣P

Liverpool: City Centre

Augustus John

Peach Street, L3 5TX (off Brownlow Hill)
11-11 (11.30 Thu; midnight Fri); 12-midnight Sat; closed Sun
☎ (0151) 794 5507
Greene King Abbot; Tetley Bitter; guest beers Ⓗ
This '60s-style open-plan pub run by the University of Liverpool can be very busy, with an eclectic mix of students, lecturers and locals. The artist Augustus John was a lecturer at the university in 1901 and the pub was opened by his son. Up to three guest beers are available. Ask for real cider which is kept in a cooler. There is an annual beer festival. Sky Sports is shown on TV. The pub closes over Christmas and the New Year.
❀♿⇌(Lime St)⊖(Central)🚌(78,79)●

Baltic Fleet

33 Wapping, L1 8DQ
12-11 (midnight Wed-Fri); 11-midnight Sat; 12-midnight Sun
☎ (0151) 709 3116 🌐 wappingbeers.co.uk
Wapping Baltic Gold, Bitter, Stout, Summer, seasonal beers Ⓗ
Located near the Albert Dock, Liverpool's only brew pub is based on a flat-iron shape resembling the bow of a ship. It is named after a 19th-century timber-importing fleet and the interior reflects this with displays of nautical memorabilia. Mysterious tunnels reaching out under the building add to the intrigue, but any link to smuggling and activities of press gangs is probably anecdotal. Food is available from a chalkboard menu but it is best to check ahead for serving times.
Q◑⊖(James St)🚌(500)●

Belvedere Arms

8 Sugnall Street, L7 7EB (off Falkner Street)
12-11 (midnight Fri & Sat)
☎ (0151) 709 0303
Beer range varies Ⓗ
Although close to the city centre, this is very much a community hostelry. A few years ago permission was granted to convert the 1830s listed building into a house, but fortunately it has remained a pub. Many of the original fixtures and fittings feature in the two small rooms, including some interesting glasswork. Its proximity to the Philharmonic Hall has made it a popular watering hole for members of the orchestra. Q❀🚌

Cracke

13 Rice Street, L1 9BB (off Hope St)
12-11.30 (midnight Fri & Sat)
☎ (0151) 709 4171
Phoenix Wobbly Bob; Thwaites Original; guest beers Ⓗ
Typical of pubs that came into existence following the passing of the Beer Act in 1830, this was originally a one-room hostelry consisting of what is now the public bar. Originally called the Ruthin Castle, it rapidly acquired the nickname of the Cracke because of its small size. Since then, it has extended into two houses next door but still remains relatively compact. Food is served until 6pm daily except Monday.
❀◐⇌(Lime St)⊖(Central)🚌●

Crown Hotel ☆

43 Lime Street, L1 1JQ
8-11 (midnight Fri & Sat); 10-midnight Sun
☎ (0151) 707 6027
Cains Bitter; Tetley Bitter; guest beers Ⓗ
Just a few seconds walk from Lime Street Station, this Grade II-listed building boasts an Art Nouveau-style interior with ornate plasterwork ceilings. Many of the original features are retained in the two downstairs rooms, including some impressive wood panelling and original push bells. There is also an ornate glass dome above the staircase. Reasonably priced food is served until 10pm. The outside of the pub is adorned with a stucco 'Walkers Ales, Warrington' frieze.
◑⇌(Lime St)⊖(Central)🚌

Dispensary

87 Renshaw Street, L1 2SP
12-11 (midnight Fri & Sat); 12-11
☎ (0151) 709 2180
Cains Dark Mild, Bitter, IPA, FA, seasonal beers; guest beers Ⓗ
In the shadow of St Luke's Church, the Grapes (as it was previously known – the old name can still be seen over the bar) was bought, converted and renamed the Dispensary by Cains. It won a CAMRA/English Heritage refurbishment award, and celebrated its 10th anniversary in 2008. A popular place for watching sports fixtures on TV, or enjoying a drink before or after dining at one of the many restaurants nearby.
◐♿⇌(Lime St)⊖(Central)🚌●

Doctor Duncan's

St John's House, St John's Lane, L1 1HF (opp St George's Gardens)
10am-11 (midnight Fri & Sat); 10-10.30 Sun
☎ (0151) 709 5100
Cains Dark Mild, IPA, Bitter, FA, seasonal beers Ⓗ
This flagship Cain's pub has an impressive Victorian interior with four distinctively different drinking areas – the green tiled room is particularly handsome. The pub's name commemorates Doctor Duncan, the first chief medical officer of Liverpool

and a ruthless campaigner against poor living conditions in Victorian Liverpool – medical memorabilia can be found throughout. Unsurprisingly, the pub offers the full range of Cains beers. 🔥❀◑♿≠(Lime St)⊖(Lime St)🚌⛳

Everyman Bistro ✔

5-9 Hope Street, L1 9BH (beneath Everyman Theatre)
⏲ 12-midnight (2am Fri & Sat); closed Sun
☎ (0151) 708 9545 🌐 everyman.co.uk
Cains Bitter; Caledonian Deuchars IPA; guest beers Ⓗ
The Everyman Bistro is as much a Liverpool institution as the theatre above it. Much thought is given to the award-winning, home-produced food and equally the ale range which concentrates on Yorkshire and north west beers, with regulars from York, Derwent, George Wright and Brimstage. The bar can be busy early evening before a performance, attracting an eclectic mix of students, professors, media types and locals.
Q◑◐≠(Lime St)⊖(Central)🚌🍎

Fly in the Loaf ✔

13 Hardman Street, L1 9AS
⏲ 11-11 (midnight Fri & Sat)
☎ (0151) 708 0817
Okells Bitter, seasonal beers; guest beers Ⓗ
The second Manx Cat inn to be opened on the mainland by the IoM brewer Okells. The previous Kirkland's bakery – slogan 'no flies in the loaf' – was tastefully refurbished in 2004. There are usually up to seven guest beers from micro-breweries alongside Okells ales and a good selection of foreign bottled beers. The pub is very popular and busy on weekends and evenings and when Sky shows sports fixtures, notably rugby league. There is an upstairs function room with handpumps. ◑◐♿≠(Lime St)⊖(Central)🚌⛳

Globe ✔

17 Cases Street, L1 1HW (opp Liverpool Central Station)
⏲ 11 (10 Sat)-11; 12-10.30 Sun
☎ (0151) 707 0067
Black Sheep Best Bitter; Cains Bitter; Caledonian Deuchars IPA; guest beers Ⓗ
A small, traditional, two-roomed local in the city centre, handy for the main shopping area and stations. A lively pub, it attracts both regulars and visitors to the area. An unusual sloping floor leads you through to the quiet back room, where a brass plaque commemorates the inaugural meeting of the Mersyside branch of CAMRA, held here in 1974.
≠(Lime St)⊖(Central)🚌

Lady of Mann

19 Dale Street, L2 2EZ
⏲ 11.30-8 (11 Thu-Sat); 12-10.30 Sun
☎ (0151) 236 5556
Okells Bitter; guest beers Ⓗ
Formerly the Courtyard Restaurant, the Lady adjoins Thomas Rigby's and they share a large outside drinking area. The pub is named after the eponymous Manx ferry and owned, like Rigby's, by Okells. The interior is open plan with a single bar located in a separate drinking area approached from the Courtyard via a flight of steps. There is live music on Sunday 6-9pm, and cold food is served at all times. ◑◐≠⊖(Moorfields)🚌⛳

Lion Tavern ☆ ✔

67 Moorfields, L2 2BP
⏲ 11-11; 12-10.30 Sun
☎ (0151) 236 1734
Caledonian Deuchars IPA; Lees Bitter; Young's Bitter; guest beers Ⓗ
The Grade II-listed Lion is named after the locomotive that worked the Liverpool to Manchester railway. In 1915, the original building was amalgamated with the adjoining licensed premises, creating the existing layout. The interior features exquisite tilework, etched and stained glass, carefully restored wooden panelling and an ornate glass dome in one of the two lounges. The pub attracts a mixed clientele, including office staff and journalists. Bar food is available, with cheeses and hand-made pork pies particularly recommended. ◑🖃≠(Lime St)⊖(Moorfields)🍎

Monro

92 Duke Street, L1 5AG
⏲ 12-11.30 (1am Fri & Sat); 12-9.30 Sun
☎ (0151) 707 9933 🌐 themonro.com/themonro-dukestr.html
Jennings Cumberland Ale; guest beers Ⓗ
The Monro is a Grade II listed building named after the 19th-century three-masted sailing ship James Monro and the fifth President of the United States, James Monroe (1817-1825). The interior has two main dining areas and a small bar. The Monro has rapidly established a reputation for excellent food while serving up to four cask ales from the Marston's range. Food attractions are too numerous to mention but there is a notable monthly pudding club. ◑◐⊖(Central)🚌(82)⛳

Peter Kavanagh's ★

2-6 Egerton Street, L8 7LY (off Catharine St)
⏲ 12-midnight (1am Fri & Sat)
☎ (0151) 709 3443
Greene King Abbot; guest beers Ⓗ
This gem features on CAMRA's National Inventory – a splendid back-street local located in an area once occupied by rich merchants. It boasts stained glass windows with wooden shutters, and two snugs with wooden benches – note the carved arm rests, allegedly caricatures of the politically incorrect Peter Kavanagh. There are also murals by Eric Robinson, allegedly commissioned to cover a debt, and a varied collection of bric-a-brac. Up to four rotating guest beers are offered. In a word, unmissable. **Q**❀🚌(86)⛳

Philharmonic ★

36 Hope Street, L1 9BX
⏲ 11-midnight (1am Fri & Sat)
☎ (0151) 707 2837
Caledonian Deuchars IPA; guest beers Ⓗ
Featuring in CAMRA's National Inventory, this magnificent Grade II listed building was described by historic pub expert Geoff Brandwood as the finest of its kind. Adjacent to the Philharmonic Hall, the interior is divided into several discrete and highly ornate drinking areas, notably the splendidly refurbished Grand Lounge. There is an upstairs restaurant and food is served until 10pm. While ladies are invited to visit the amazingly ornate Gents, it is polite to check before doing so.
Q◑◐🖃♿≠(Lime St)⊖(Central)🚌(86)

Pilgrim

34 Pilgrim Street, L1 9HB
⏲ 10-11
☎ (0151) 709 2302 🌐 thepilgrimpub.co.uk
Beer range varies Ⓗ
Popular student pub set on two floors, although usually only the basement is open. It has a

jukebox, open-mike nights, jazz and TVs screening sport. Food is served until 4pm Monday to Saturday and 5pm on Sunday. There is a function room upstairs with its own bar and private access. A Phoenix beer is generally available alongside a range of ales, often from the north of England.
❀◖⇌(Lime St)⊖(Central)🚌⚟

Richard John Blackler ✔

1-2 Charlotte Row, L1 1HU
⏲ 8am-midnight (1am Fri & Sat)
☎ (0151) 709 4802
Greene King Abbot; Marston's Pedigree; guest beers Ⓗ
Situated on the site of the old Blackler's department store, this spacious one-room Wetherspoon's is decorated with photos depicting the Liverpool of a bygone era. Two bookshelves to the rear of the pub offer reading material to enjoy while relaxing over a pint. There are a large number of handpumps and a wide range of foreign bottled beers and ciders available. Football is shown on a big screen and the pub can get crowded on match days.
◖◗♿⇌(Lime St)⊖(Central)🚌●

Richmond Hotel

32 Williamson Street, L1 1EB (in pedestrian precinct off Williamson Square)
⏲ 10-11; 11-midnight Fri-Sun
☎ (0151) 709 2614
Draught Bass; Cains Bitter; Taylor Landlord; guest beers Ⓗ
Formerly a Bass house – hence the original Bass mirror – this lively corner house offers up to three guest beers from local breweries. More than 50 malt whiskies are generally available, and satellite TV shows sports fixtures. The pub sign, simply saying 'Richmond Pub', depicts WWII veteran Paddy Golden, a much-missed regular and one of the first to land on the Normandy beaches.
❀♿⇌⊖(Central)🚌⚟

Roscoe Head

24 Roscoe Street, L1 2SX
⏲ 11.30-11 (midnight Fri & Sat); 12-11 Sun
☎ (0151) 709 4365
Jennings Bitter; Marston's Burton Bitter; Tetley Mild, Bitter; guest beers Ⓗ
Welcoming side-street local where conversation is king. One of only 10 pubs in the country to appear in every edition of the Guide, this traditional hostelry has been run by the same family for more than 20 years. The interior retains the original small rooms and snugs, with a sensitive redecoration. Guest beers may come from micros. Quiz night is Tuesday and cribbage night Wednesday. Children are welcome until 6pm.
♔Q◖⇌(Central)⊖(Lime St)🚌(86)♣

Ship & Mitre 🏆

133 Dale Street, L2 2JH (by Birkenhead tunnel entrance)
⏲ 11-11 (midnight Thu-Sat)
☎ (0151) 236 0859 🌐 theshipandmitre.com
Beer range varies Ⓗ
The Ship, as it is known locally, has an impressive Art Deco exterior retaining some original features in the upstairs room. Inside is equally impressive, with a bar that boasts 13 handpulls dispensing real ale at all times, plus a similar number of fonts for continental and foreign brews, and a large selection of German and Belgian bottled beers. Nearby can be found some of Liverpool's more famous landmarks, such as St George's Hall, and various museums and galleries.
Q◖◗♿⇌(Lime St)⊖(Moorfields)🚌♣●P

Swan Inn

86 Wood Street, L1 4DQ
⏲ 12-11 (2am Thu-Sat); 12-10.30 Sun
☎ (0151) 709 5281 🌐 myspace.com/swaninn
Hydes Original; Phoenix Wobbly Bob; guest beers Ⓗ
Established in 1898, the Swan has changed little over the years, retaining its unique character with its blue tile facade and stained glass windows. The pub, renowned for its famous rock jukebox, is known locally as a rockers and bikers pub, although everyone is made welcome. Up to six guests are available which can include various Scottish brews, plus bottled Belgian beers. Orange lighting illuminates the rear of the pub, where old pews and wooden stools provide seating.
♿⇌(Lime St)⊖(Central)🚌●

Thomas Rigby's ✔

23-25 Dale Street, L2 2EZ
⏲ 11.30-11 (10.30 Sun)
☎ (0151) 236 3269
Okells Bitter, Dr Okell's IPA, seasonal beers; guest beers Ⓗ
Within this multi-roomed Grade II-listed building, bearing the name of wine and spirit dealer Thomas Rigby, you will find an extensive world beer range, on draught and in bottles, and at least four changing guest ales. Food is highly recommended, served daily, with one room offering a friendly and efficient table service. The pub is formely a Publican magazine national award winner and has won numerous other accolades for its beer and food. ❀◖◗⇌⊖(Moorfields)

White Star ✔

2-4 Rainford Gardens, L2 6PT
⏲ 11.30-11; 12-10.30 Sun
☎ (0151) 231 6861 🌐 thewhitestar.co.uk
Bowland White Star IPA, seasonal beers; Caledonian Deuchars IPA; Draught Bass Ⓗ
A rare traditional Victorian public house located among the trendier establishments of the Mathew Street area, the White Star is full of fascinating local memorabilia and pictures of White Star liners. A sporting theme is highlighted by an abundance of boxing photography and the regular broadcasting of football matches on screens in two rooms. The pub is linked with bars in the Czech Republic and Norway. Additional seasonal beers from the Bowland range are available.
◖⇌(Lime St)⊖(Central/Moorfields)⚟

Liverpool: Kirkdale

Thomas Frost ✔

177-187 Walton Road, Kirkdale, L4 4AJ (opposite Aldi and Iceland on A59)
⏲ 9-11.30
☎ (0151) 207 8210
Beer range varies Ⓗ
This Wetherspoon's pub occupies the ground floor of a former drapery store owned by Thomas Robert Frost, who had a shop on this site from 1885. The layout is open plan with framed photographs showing scenes from local historic events. The pub is convenient for both Goodison Park and Anfield football grounds.There is a popular quiz on Monday night when there is no football. Food is served until 10pm. ◖◗♿🚌⚟

Liverpool: Mossley Hill

Storrsdale ✔

43-47 Storrsdale Road, L18 7JY
⏲ 3-11 (11.30 Fri); 12-11.30 Sat; 12-11 Sun
☎ (0151) 724 3464
Caledonian Deuchars IPA; Taylor Landlord; Tetley Bitter; guest beers Ⓗ
This stylish two-roomed pub is a 1930s construction and keeps the original attractive exterior tiling and leaded windows. There is a comfortable, music-free, wood-panelled lounge and a stone-floored bar with dartboard and jukebox. A mix of locals, students and thirsty sports people from the nearby playing fields are drawn here by the friendly, relaxed atmosphere. Football matches are shown on TV screens. There is a quiz on Wednesday and a small yard to the side doubles as a smoking area.
Q❀⊟⇌(Mossley Hill)🚌(86)♣⚟

Liverpool: Stoneycroft

Navigator ✔

694 Queens Drive, L13 5UH
⏲ 9-11.30
☎ (0151) 220 2713
Greene King IPA; guest beers Ⓗ
This branch of Wetherspoon's occupies a former showroom. The Navigator refers to St Brendan the Navigator, who is reputed to have discovered America. The interior has an open plan layout punctuated with alcoves along one side and a raised area set aside for families. Children are welcome until 9pm when dining. A welcome oasis for real ale on the edge of a busy shopping area, the pub participates enthusiastically in the company's national beer festivals.
❀◐◑♿🚌(10,61,81)⚟

Liverpool: Walton

Raven ✔

72-74 Walton Vale, L9 2BU (on A59)
⏲ 9-midnight (1am Fri & Sat)
☎ (0151) 524 1255
Greene King IPA, Ruddles County, Abbot; Marston's Pedigree; guest beers Ⓗ
Open from breakfast until late every day, this large, open-plan Wetherspoon's is busy with a local crowd most days but particularly at weekends. Opened in 1998, it is themed on Edgar Allan Poe's The Raven in honour of a local, James William Carling, who produced illustrations for the famous poem in the late 19th century and is buried in Walton Cemetery. There are also plenty of references on the walls to the Grand National, which is run at Aintree, less than a mile away.
Q◐◑♿⇌(Orrell Park)🚌⚟

Liverpool: Waterloo

Stamps Too

99 South Road, L22 0LR (opp Waterloo Station)
⏲ 12-11 (midnight Fri & Sat); 12-11.30 Sun
☎ (0151) 280 0035
Beer range varies; Ⓗ
A welcoming haunt for real ale enthusiasts, Stamps Too is a long, narrow pub with cafe-style seating at the front. There is a stage for live music which plays Thursday to Sunday evenings, and a monthly comedy night. Lively banter often prevails at the bar towards the rear, which sports an ever-changing inventive range of beers, often from local breweries. A daytime tapas menu can be enjoyed (except Mon) and Internet access is available.
❀◐◑♿⇌(Waterloo)🚌(53)⚟

Volunteer Canteen ★

45 East Street, L22 8QR
⏲ 12-11 (10.30 Sun)
☎ (0151) 928 4676
Black Sheep Best Bitter; Tetley Bitter; guest beers Ⓗ
The 'Volly' has been a pub since 1871 and is at the heart of the local community. It has a central servery for a public bar and comfortable lounge. The public bar has a small TV for sports events and is home to a number of societies. The lounge has table service, a warm, convivial atmosphere, good banter and daily newspapers. Much of the glasswork and exterior detailing reflects the building's former ownership by Higson's Brewery.
Q❀⊟⇌(Waterloo)🚌(53)

Liverpool: Wavertree

Edinburgh

4 Sandown Lane, L15 8HY
⏲ 12-midnight
☎ (0151) 733 3533
Cains Mild, Bitter, FA, seasonal beers Ⓗ
This pub was part of the original Cains tied estate that is now owned by the new company. It was awarded Best Community Pub 2008 by the local CAMRA branch, in recognition of its popularity with locals and its support of charities. Irish music can be heard on Monday night and there is a quiz on Tuesday. Sports are shown on TV. ❀🚌♣⚟

Willowbank ✔

329 Smithdown Road, L15 3JA
⏲ 12-11 (11.30 Wed & Thu; midnight Fri & Sat)
☎ (0151) 733 5782
Black Sheep Best Bitter; Tetley Bitter; guest beers Ⓗ
Previously a Walker Heritage Inn, this Victorian pub is now part of the Spirit group and offers guest ales from local breweries. Usefully, taster samples are available, and beer festivals are held throughout the year. There is also a helpful monthly newsletter. A winner of the CAMRA branch Community Pub award in 2007, it is popular with students. Sports are shown on various TV screens and darts is played. Food is available 12-7pm and a quiz night hosted on Wednesday.
⚯❀◐◑⊟♿🚌(86)♣●P⚟

Liverpool: West Derby

Halton Castle

86 Mill Lane, L12 7JD
⏲ 12 (11.30 Sat)-11 (midnight Fri & Sat)
☎ (0151) 270 2013
Black Sheep Best Bitter; guest beers Ⓗ
Traditional Victorian pub divided into several rooms including a public bar. An outside area provides a pleasant place for drinking in decent weather. A rare outlet for real ale in the suburbs of Liverpool, the pub has one regular beer and two changing guests. It is well serviced by bus routes from the city centre. ❀⊟♣P⚟

Liverpool: Woolton

Gardeners Arms ✔

101 Vale Road, L25 7RW

⏲ 4 (2 Fri; 12 Sat & Sun)-11.30
☎ (0151) 428 1443
Cains Bitter; Caledonian Deuchars IPA; guest beers Ⓗ
Friendly, one-room, community village pub situated over the hill from Woolton village and separated from Menlove Avenue by blocks of flats. Recently awarded the Cask Marque plaque, it now serves evening food with a curry club. A popular quiz is held on Tuesday evening and Sky Sports is screened. Look out for details of the monthly live music. There are numerous sports teams based at the pub. Q◗🚌(76,77)⍉

New Brighton

Queen's Royal

Marine Promenade, Wirral, CH45 2JT
⏲ 10.30-11 (10.30 Sun)
☎ (0151) 691 0101 🌐 thequeensroyal.com
Brimstage Trapper's Hat; guest beers Ⓗ
An airy, modern bar in an imposing Victorian building overlooking New Brighton promenade, Marine Lake and Fort Perch Rock. The drinking area outside affords superb views over Liverpool Bay. Only local beers are sold from the three handpumps, with Brimstage and Betwixt favoured. Good value bar meals are available until 7pm. The adjoining restaurant, offering an excellent carvery, opens until 9pm. ❀◖◗⊟♿⇌(New Brighton)🚌⍉

Stanley's Cask

212 Rake Lane, Wirral, CH45 1JP
⏲ 11.30-11.00; 12-10.30 Sun
☎ (0151) 691 1093
John Smith's Bitter; guest beers Ⓗ
This pub's welcome return to the Guide after an absence of 14 years is due in no small part to its present landlady who has a track record of serving good beer. The traditional, single-roomed community local hosts various sports teams, quiz nights and entertainment. Up to four guest beers are served, mainly from national and regional breweries. ❀🚌(410)♣⍉

Telegraph Inn 🏆 ✔

25-27 Mount Pleasant Road, Wirral, CH45 5EW
⏲ 11.30-11.30; 12-10.30 Sun
☎ (0151) 639 1508
Wells Bombardier; Wychwood Hobgoblin; guest beers Ⓗ
This traditional, friendly, multi-roomed local is believed to be New Brighton's oldest pub. It has a conservatory extension where good value home-cooked food is served daily. The handpumps are in the main bar area, with three guests on offer, often from local micro-breweries. An annual beer festival is hosted in the rear garden. A regular live folk music venue. ❀◖◗⊟🚌(410)♣⍉

New Ferry

Freddies Club

36 Stanley Road, Wirral, CH62 5AS
⏲ 5 (12 Sat & Sun)-11
Beer range varies Ⓗ
A former Conservative Club converted into a comfortable lounge bar with adjoining snooker room (with two full-size tables), situated in the back streets of New Ferry. A former Wirral CAMRA Club of the Year, entry is available to members carrying either a membership card or a current copy of the Guide. A keen supporter of local micro-breweries, up to two beers are available from Brimstage and/or Betwixt. Friday features Freddies' ever-popular, fun quiz and there is regular live entertainment. ⛺🚌(401)♣●P⍉

Raby

Wheatsheaf Inn

Raby Mere Road, Wirral, CH63 4JH (from M53 jct 4 take B5151)
⏲ 11.30-11
☎ (0151) 336 3416
Brimstage Trappers Hat; Greene King Old Speckled Hen; Tetley Bitter; Thwaites Original, Wainwright, Lancaster Bomber Ⓗ
Ancient thatched inn of great character rebuilt after a fire in 1611. Wirral's oldest hostelry, the original building dates from the 13th century and it has been a pub for more than 350 years. It is reputed to be haunted by 'Charlotte', who died here. The walls are decorated with old photographs of Raby. A main bar with eight handpumps serves two rooms and a dining room in a converted cowshed. No evening meals Sunday and Monday.
Q♨❀◖◗⊟♿P⍉

Rainford Junction

Junction

News Lane, WA11 7JU (from A570 follow Rainford Junction station signs)
⏲ 4-midnight; 12-1am Fri & Sat; 12-midnight Sun
☎ (01744) 882876
Weetwood Old Dog Bitter; guest beers Ⓗ
Situated next to Rainford Junction Station, with fine views of the rural area, this popular community local is a meeting place for a mixed clientele of all ages. Live music plays on Wednesday evening and folk on Sunday. Popular with clubs and societies, a separate bar area has a dartboard and pool table. Rotating beers from Weetwood complement the guest beers. Wi-Fi Internet access is available and there is a function room upstairs. ❀◖◗⊟⇌🚌♣P

Rainhill

Commercial Hotel

L35 0LL
⏲ 12.30 (12 Sat)-11; 12-10.30 Sun
☎ (0151) 4305473
Cains Bitter; Tetley Mild, Bitter; guest beers Ⓗ
Originally owned by defunct Joseph Jones Brewery, whose livery can still be seen, the original bar has been preserved. The pub is adjacent to Rainhill railway station, home of the Railway Trials of 1829, won by Stephenson's Rocket. The event is depicted pictorially inside the pub alongside scenes of old Rainhill and Prescot. The pub is always busy, with the provision of sports channels on large-screen TVs positioned throughout. A worthy stop-off on the journey from Liverpool to Manchester. Quiz night is Tuesday. ⇌(rainhill)🚌(6B,137,198)P⍉

St Helens

Abbey

1 Hard Lane, Denton's Green, WA10 6TL (off A570 one mile N of St Helens town centre)
⏲ 12-midnight (11 Sun)
☎ (01744) 25649
Holt's Mild, Bitter, seasonal beers Ⓗ

A former coaching inn, just off the A570 to the north of the town, this Holt's pub has been tastefully refurbished, retaining many original features. The central bar area serves five rooms, each with its own character. Traditional pub games including dominoes and pool are played in the games room, and in another room a large screen shows most popular sporting events. Private parties can be accommodated. Curry night is Wednesday. ❀◑⊟(38,356)♣P⚟–

Royal Tavern

21-23 Westfield Street, WA10 1QF
⏲ 11.30-midnight (1.30am Fri & Sat); 12-10.30 Sun
☎ (01744) 756868
Beer range varies Ⓗ
A welcome refuge from the surrounding trendy bars of the Westfield locality, the L-shaped open-plan interior has a bar and comfortable lounge, and retains some of the original etched windows. There is also a large bar and games room leading to the outside patio with a covered smoking area. A rotating guest beer from the Enterprise Inns range is always of interest. Good value lunchtime food is popular, especially Sunday lunch. There is a disco on Friday and Saturday plus occasional live music. ❀◐⊞⇌⊟♣⚟–

Turks Head ✔

49-51 Morley Street, WA10 2DQ
⏲ 2-11.30 (12.30am Fri); 12-12.30am Sat; 12-11.30 Sun
☎ (01744) 751289 🌐 mysthelens.com/entertainment/Turks/turks.html
Beer range varies Ⓗ
A short distance from the town centre, the Turk's is a popular community local built in the 1870s with a distinctive turret and half-timbers. Note the Ellis, Warde Brewery tiled mosaic at the entrance, and etched stained glass. The beer range changes frequently due to high turnover, with up to 12 beers at the weekend, plus draught and bottled foreign beers, real ciders and perry. Darts and pool are played and there is a free quiz on Tuesday night. Curry night is Thursday. CAMRA branch Pub of the Year 2007/08 and runner-up national Pub of the Year in 2007. ⛰❀⊞⊟(32)●⚟–⊓

Southport

Baron's Bar (Scarisbrick Hotel) 🏆 ✔

239 Lord Street, PR8 1NZ (on main A565, opp Eastbank St)
⏲ 11-11 (11.30 Fri & Sat); 12-11 Sun
☎ (01704) 543000 🌐 baronsbar.com

> The job of filling tankards was not one that could be done in a hurry, for he liked them full, with just the right amount of head on them. I was not allowed to pour beer for the old man as one day I had jogged the barrel and had made the contents cloudy. This was, I think, the only sin which he had not forgiven me. Anything else was pardonable, but to make beer undrinkable was a very high blasphemy.
> **Ruthven Todd**, Bodies In A Bookshop, 1946

Flag & Turret; Moorhouses Pride of Pendle; Tetley Bitter; guest beers Ⓗ
This award-winning bar in the Scarisbrick Hotel provides an extensive choice of ales often from micro-breweries, plus its own house bitter, Flag & Turret. Real cider is usually stocked, a rarity for the town. Two significant beer festivals are held – the SIBA Northern Beer Festival in mid-January and another at the beginning of May. The local community is well-served with two league quiz teams, monthly quizzes and live music. Good value barm cakes are available at lunchtime. ❀⛟♿⇌⊟●⚟–

Bold Hotel

583-585 Lord Street, PR9 0BE
⏲ 9.30am-midnight
☎ (01704) 532578
Flowers IPA; Fuller's London Pride; Greene King Old Speckled Hen, Abbot Ⓗ
An attractive hotel with a light, spacious area for drinking on the ground floor. A newcomer to the Guide, it offers well-kept beers at some of the lowest prices in Southport, and is ideally placed for shoppers who are seeking relief for their feet (or their purses). It offers an excellent and varied food menu. In summer comfortable seating outside is an ideal spot to sit and watch Lord Street life. ⛟◑♿⇌⊟

Cheshire Lines

81 King Street, PR8 1LQ
⏲ 11.30-midnight (1am Thu-Sat); 12-midnight Sun
☎ (01704) 532178
Tetley Dark Mild, Bitter Ⓗ
A small, half-timbered, Tudor-style hostelry with attractive hanging baskets and original windows. Inside, the L-shaped bar serves a small front room and a snug opposite. A large room at the rear is used for dining, serving excellent good-value local food. Many railway locomotive prints decorate the walls. The stone hearth comes from the original Cheshire Lines railway terminus on nearby Lord Street (a grand building in front of Morrisons). ⛰Q❀◑⇌⊟♣⚟–

Guest House ✔

16 Union Street, PR9 0QE
⏲ 11-11 (11.30 Fri & Sat); 10.30-10.30 Sun
☎ (01704) 537660
Cains Bitter; Caledonian Deuchars IPA; Courage Directors; Theakston Best Bitter; guest beers Ⓗ
Superb Edwardian town centre pub festooned with flower baskets in summer, with a delightful flower-bedecked courtyard to the rear. The pub has three traditionally-styled rooms furnished with wood panelling, rustic paintings and brass ornaments. The interior retains original features including a tiled entrance lobby, glass-fronted bar and elegant fireplaces. Guest beers may vary according to Pub Co policy. Q❀⊞⇌⊟⚟–

Lakeside Inn

Marine Lake, Promenade, PR9 0EA
⏲ 11-11; 12-10.30 Sun
☎ (01704) 530173
Fuller's London Pride; Tetley Bitter Ⓗ
Reputedly the smallest pub in England (with a Guinness Book of Records certificate on the wall to prove it), the Lakeside Inn is like Dr Who's Tardis in feeling much more spacious inside than seems possible from the outside. The pub is a comfortable local with great views of the marina – the perfect

place to watch the yachts on the water. A listed building, it is well placed for a drink after a visit to Southport Theatre, only a short walk away along the Promenade. Q❀⇌🚌(40)

Mason's Arms

44 Anchor Street, PR9 0UT
☼ 11-1am
☎ (01704) 534123
Robinson's Unicorn, seasonal beers Ⓗ
The Mason's is a small back-street local behind the post office and next to a new development of flats. It is the only outlet for Robinson's ales in the area. A traditional snug is shoehorned into a corner of the building, ideal for couples. The main bar is where the lively regulars congregate to put the world's problems to rights. The sunny roof garden is a fine place to enjoy some peace in this town centre location – access is by request from the bar staff. Regular live music by volunteer performers. ♨❀⇌🚌♣

Sir Henry Segrave ✔

93-97 Lord Street, PR8 1RH (on main A565 road)
☼ 9-midnight
☎ (01704) 530217
Greene King Abbot; Marston's Pedigree; guest beers Ⓗ
Town-centre Wetherspoons situated on Southport's famous Lord Street in an 1880s building, formerly a furniture emporium. The pub is named after a local hero who broke the world land speed record of 152mph on nearby Birkdale Sands in 1926. Segrave was also the first British driver of a British car to win the French Grand Prix in 1923. A pub that caters for all tastes, it usually features beers from local breweries such as Cains and George Wright. Real cider is occasionally available.
Q🐴❀◐◑♿⇌🚌⚊

Volunteer Arms

57-59 Eastbank Street, PR8 1DY
☼ 11 (12 Sun)-midnight
☎ (01704) 543794
Thwaites Lancaster Bomber, Wainwright Ⓗ
An unpretentious, friendly and popular pub on Eastbank Street and just a short walk from Lord Street. The Volunteer serves Thwaites ales – one of only two pubs in Southport to do so on a regular basis. Despite its proximity to the main shopping area, the Volunteer is very much a community pub and is usually buzzing inside with regulars, but visitors are assured of a warm welcome too. Live music often features here. ❀◐◑♿⇌🚌♣⚊

Windmill Inn

12-14 Seabank Road, PR9 0EL (off Lord St)
☼ 11.30-11 (midnight Thu-Sat); 12-10.30 Sun
☎ (01704) 547319
Moorhouses Black Cat; Theakston Best Bitter; guest beers Ⓗ
A community pub situated between Lord Street and the Promenade, the Windmill boasts a league-winning ladies' darts team and a sociable men's darts team. Activities include a Wednesday quiz, live Irish music on Thursday, plus live middle-of-the-road music on Friday. Excellent value, quality food is served lunchtimes and evenings except Wednesday. The only regular outlet for Black Cat Mild, the landlord claims to be the town's longest serving publican. ❀◐◑♿⇌🚌♣⚊

Wallasey

Cheshire Cheese ✔

2 Wallasey Village, Wirral, CH44 2DH
☼ 11.30-11 (midnight Fri & Sat); 12-11 Sun
☎ (0151) 638 3641
Theakston Mild, Best Bitter; guest beers Ⓗ
This friendly, multi-roomed local has a separate bar, snug and lounge. Outside, there is a walled beer garden where regular beer festivals are held. The handpumps are located in the lounge, with three guest beers usually available. Excellent home-cooked food is served until early evening (not Thu). Wirral CAMRA Pub of the Year 2007 and runner-up 2008. Q❀◐◑⊞⇌🚌♣⚊

Ship & Mitre, Liverpool (Photo: Neil Lloyd).

NORFOLK

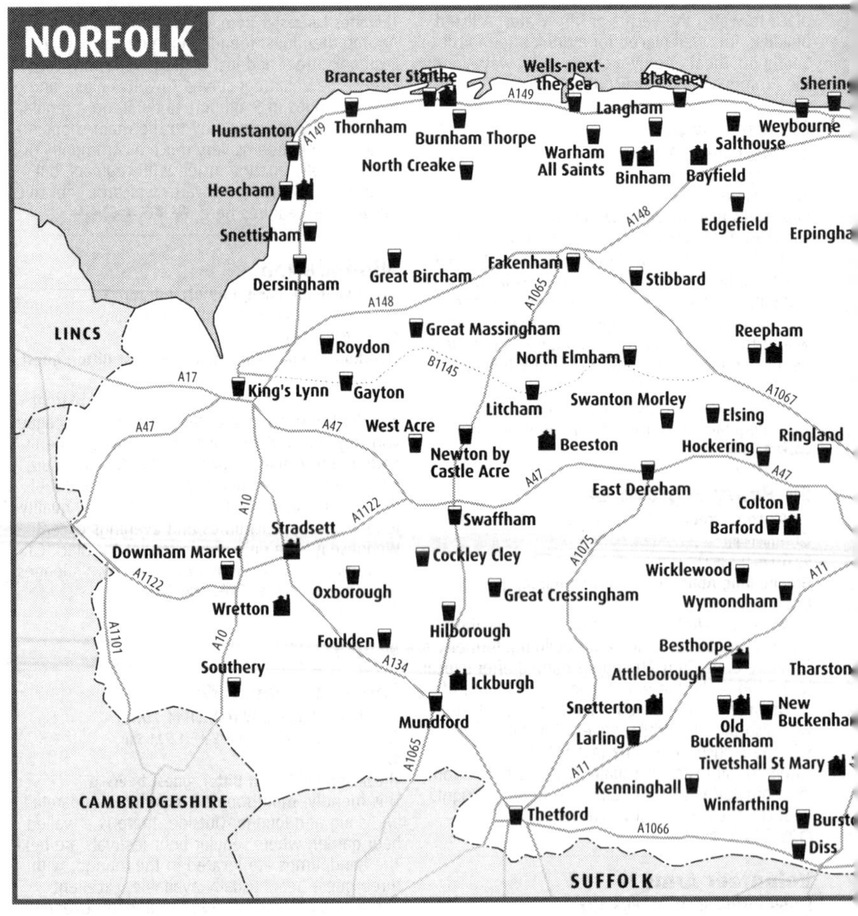

Alby

Horse Shoes

Cromer Road, NR11 7QE (on A140 halfway between Cromer & Aylsham) TG208324
12-2.30 (not Wed), 7-11
(01263) 761378 albyhorseshoes.co.uk
Woodforde's Wherry Best Bitter; guest beers Ⓗ
This 19th-century inn is situated in the heart of rural Norfolk on the main Norwich-Cromer road. It offers four real ales including Woodforde's Wherry and three guests, usually from local brewers. The interior has two bars plus a separate restaurant. One of the bars has an unusual low-level ceiling that incorporates the traditional game of Ring the Bull. Many pictures of old cars adorn the walls as the landlord is a classic car enthusiast. Food is available lunch and evenings, with meat sourced from a local butcher. (X5,50)P

Attleborough

London Tavern

Church Street, NR17 2AH
11-11
(01953) 547415
Fuller's London Pride; Wolf Werewolf; guest beers Ⓗ
A family-friendly pub in the town centre situated opposite the main bus stops. It caters for all tastes and types and has an easy-going atmosphere. The interior, with its stone floors, has a London theme, including atmospheric framed photographs of the capital city. Real ales include Werewolf (Wolf's Golden Jackal rebadged), plus two rotating guests, one of which is from Wolf Brewery. The pub has a dining room, an upstairs function room and a large covered smoking area. P

Banningham

Crown Inn

Church Road, NR11 7DY (adjacent to village green just off B1145) TG217294
12-2.30, 6.30-11; 12-11 Sat; 12-10.30 Sun
(01263) 733534
Adnams Broadside; Greene King IPA, Abbot Ⓗ
Traditional locals' pub situated in the heart of the village opposite the parish church and close to the village green. The interior is modern with carpeted floors, but old beams and a large fireplace at one

> Good ale is the true and proper drink of Englishmen. He is not deserving of the name of Englishman who speaketh against ale, that is good ale.
> **George Borrow**, Lavengro

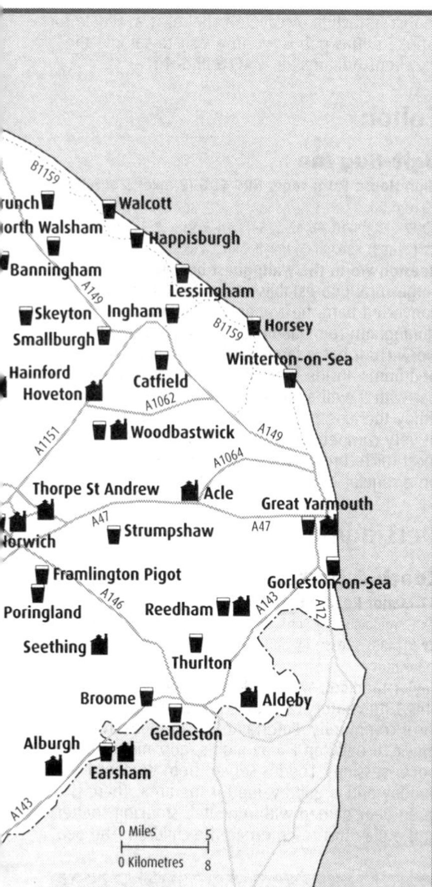

end remind you that you are in an old inn. The rear door leads out onto a patio with a covered smoking shelter and to a large garden. Food, often prepared with locally sourced products, is available lunchtimes and evenings. ⚐❀◐⚟

Barford

Cock Inn

Watton Road, NR9 4AS (on B1108) TG111074
⏲ 12-3, 6 (7 Sun)-11
☎ (01603) 759266
Blue Moon Easy Life, Sea of Tranquillity, seasonal beers Ⓗ
Comfortable two-roomed pub with a real fire in winter in the main room and a separate restaurant. The pub is famed for its food, with the menu featuring fish and game in season (booking essential at weekends). There is an interesting selection of East Anglian breweriana on display. The garden includes a bowling green, while skittles can be played in the bar. Blue Moon beers are brewed for the pub by Winters of Norwich.
⚐Q❀◐🚌♣P

Binham

Chequers Inn

Front Street, NR21 0AL (2 miles S of Stiffkey) TF983396
⏲ 11.30-2.30, 6-11 (11.30 Fri); 11.30-11.30 Sat; 12-11 (12-2.30, 7-11 winter) Sun
☎ (01328) 830297 🌐 binhamchequers.co.uk
Front Street Binham Cheer, Callums Ale, Unity; guest beers Ⓗ
A very popular hostelry with locals and visitors alike, this single-room pub includes roaring fires at each end. It hosts its own micro-brewery, Front Street, which produces a range of 17 excellent ales. Three are always available, together with guest ales and an unrivalled range of German and Belgian specialist beers to sample too. Excellent and varied meals are provided by the extremely personable chef, all made from local produce.
⚐Q❀◐♿🚌(46)P⚟

Blakeney

Kings Arms

Westgate Street, NR25 7NQ TG026440
⏲ 11-11; 12-10.30 Sun
☎ (01263) 740341
Adnams Bitter Ⓖ**; Greene King Old Speckled Hen; Marston's Pedigree; Theakston Best Bitter; guest beer** Ⓗ
Situated close to the harbour in one of Norfolk's most picturesque coastal villages, this old building has an interesting interior comprising a series of interconnecting rooms. Note the plaque halfway up the wall denoting the water level of the 1953 flood. Real ales are dispensed by handpump and gravity. There is a patio and a large garden to the side of the pub. Children and dogs are welcome and food is served all day. En-suite rooms are available. ⚐Q❀🛏◐⛺🚌(36)P

Brancaster Staithe

White Horse

Main Road, PE31 8BY
⏲ 11-11; 12-10.30 Sun
☎ (01485) 210262 🌐 whitehorsebrancaster.co.uk
Adnams Bitter; Fuller's London Pride; Woodforde's Wherry Best Bitter Ⓗ
This large, modern pub sits on the edge of the salt marshes on the beautiful north Norfolk coast. The village is a wonderful place to explore and is home to many seafood stalls. The pub bridges the gap between local and tourist hostelry, catering well for both types of pubgoer. Three beers are always available and the seafood is, of course, very fresh indeed. ⚐Q❀🛏◐♿🚌♣P⚟

Broome

Artichoke 🏆

162 Yarmouth Road, NR35 2NZ (just off A143) TM352915
⏲ 12-11 (midnight Fri & Sat); closed Mon
☎ (01986) 893325 🌐 theartichokeatbroome.co.uk
Adnams Bitter; Elgood's Black Dog; guest beers Ⓗ/Ⓖ
Situated just off the A143, this early 19th-century inn was the original home of the long-defunct Crowfoot Brewery. Flagstone and wood floors, wooden settles, scrubbed tables and a real fire give a rural ambience to the bar area of this welcoming, friendly pub. Home-cooked food is available in a dining area and conservatory. Up to eight beers feature regularly, with an emphasis on local breweries. Some are served by gravity from the tap room. The pub also boasts a range of about 70 malt whiskies. ⚐Q❀◐⛺🚌(580,588)P⚟

Burnham Thorpe

Lord Nelson

Walsingham Road, PE31 8HN (off B1355)
⏲ 11-11 summer; 12-3, 6-11, closed Mon, winter; 11-11 (12-3, 6.30-10.30 winter) Sun
☎ (01328) 738241 🌐 nelsonslocal.co.uk
Greene King Abbot; Woodforde's Wherry Best Bitter Ⓖ
Situated in the village of Nelson's birth and used by the Norfolk hero to throw a farewell party in 1793, this pub was the first to be named in his honour. The dispense is all gravity from a traditional tap room; the beer is served in a bar that contains the original settles. Live bands perform on Thursdays to bring it right up-to-date. There is a Nelson memorabilia shop and Nelson historical walks. Evening meals are not served on Sunday.
♨Q❀◐◑♣P⚡

Burston

Crown Inn

Crown Green, IP22 5TW (2 miles W of A140) TM138834
⏲ 12-11 (10.30 Sun)
☎ (01379) 741257 🌐 burstoncrown.com
Adnams Bitter; Greene King Abbot Ⓖ**; guest beer** Ⓗ
Comfortable, 16th-century, Grade II-listed pub, featuring exposed beams, deep sofas and a blazing fire in the inglenook fireplace in the main bar. The two regular ales are served directly from the cask. Guest beers come from East Anglian breweries including Elmtree, Earl Soham and Oak. A small restaurant serves locally-sourced, freshly-cooked food (no food Sun eve). Live music is every other Sunday and a buskers' night, when anyone can do a turn, takes place on Thursday. ♨❀◐◑P⚡

Catfield

Crown Inn

The Street, NR29 5AA TG387218
⏲ 12-2.30 (3 Sat), 7-11; 12-3, 7-10.30 Sun
☎ (01692) 580128
Greene King IPA; guest beers Ⓗ
Tastefully furnished 300-year-old traditional village inn which is cosy, comfortable and welcoming, with a real fire in winter and a secluded garden in summer. A range of guest beers is changed regularly. Excellent food is prepared by the enthusiastic landlord using fresh, local ingredients where possible, with Italian dishes a speciality. There is a function/dining room and en-suite accommodation is provided in a separate converted hall that was once the doctor's surgery. Close to the Broads and the north Norfolk coast.
♨Q❀🛏◐◑🚌(54)P

Cockley Cley

Twenty Churchwardens

Swaffham Road, PE37 8AN
⏲ 11-3, 7-11; 12-10.30 Sun
☎ (01760) 721439
Adnams Bitter Ⓗ
This unusually named pub in a converted village schoolhouse performs many other functions in this pretty village. The food is locally sourced, home-made pies are a speciality – reasonably priced and excellent (no food Sun eve). The atmosphere is slightly eccentric but friendly and the pub can be very busy at weekends. Nearby is the Iceni Village tourist attraction. A covered shelter is available for smokers. This pub is worth a visit to sample the excellent Adnams ale. ♨Q❀◐◑♿♣P⚡

Colton

Ugly Bug Inn

High House Farm Lane, NR9 5DG (2 miles S of A47) TG104908
⏲ 12-2.30, 5-10.30; 12-2, 5-11 Fri & Sat; 12-3 Sun
☎ (01603) 880794 🌐 uglybuginn.co.uk
Beeston Worth the Wait; guest beer Ⓗ
Large rural pub established in 1991 from a converted barn, best approched from the Honingham roundabout on the A47 west of Norwich. It has a large garden and eight en-suite bedrooms. Inside there is a large, rambling, single bar with a well-appointed dining room in which to enjoy the extensive menu of locally-sourced food at very competitive prices. Regular ale comes from local micro-brewery Beeston. Live jazz takes place on a regular basis. ❀🛏◐◑♿P🗑

Dersingham

Coach & Horses

77 Manor Road, PE31 6LN
⏲ 12-midnight (11 Sun)
☎ (01485) 540391 🌐 norfolkinns.co.uk/coachhorse/index.htm
Taylor Landlord; Woodforde's Wherry Best Bitter Ⓗ
This 19th-century carr stone pub is at the hub of the local community. Entertainment includes live music, usually on Friday nights, quiz nights and poker sessions. Food is served from Wednesday to Sunday and is good value for the area. There is a large beer garden with a heated smoking shelter and a play fort to entertain the children. The pub

INDEPENDENT BREWERIES

Beeston Beeston
Blackfriars Great Yarmouth
Blue Moon Barford
Brancaster Brancaster Staithe
Buffy's Tivetshall St Mary
Bull Box Stradsett
Chalk Hill Norwich
Elmtree Snetterton
Fat Cat Norwich
Fox Heacham
Front Street Binham
Grain Alburgh
Humpty Dumpty Reedham
Iceni Ickburgh
Norfolk Cottage Norwich
Norfolk Square Great Yarmouth
Ole Slewfoot Hainford (NEW)
Opa Hay's Aldeby (NEW)
Reepham Reepham
Spectrum Tharston
Tindall Seething
Tipples Acle
Uncle Stuarts Hoveton
Wagtail Old Buckenham
Waveney Earsham
Why Not Thorpe St Andrew
Winter's Norwich
Wissey Valley Wretton
Wolf Besthorpe
Woodforde's Woodbastwick
Yetman's Bayfield

also has three en-suite rooms to let. Look out for the beer festival in the summer. ⌂❀🛏◐◑🚌(40,41A)P⚐

Feathers Hotel ✔

Manor Road, PE31 6LN

⏲ 10.30-11 (midnight Fri & Sat); 10.30-10.30 Sun

☎ (01485) 540207 🌐 thefeathershotel.co.uk

Adnams Bitter; Draught Bass; guest beers Ⓗ

This carr stone hotel close to Sandringham has three distinctive bars. The main bar has a large open fire and access to a patio area and extensive landscaped gardens, which are split into a fun play area for children and a quiet adults-only pond garden. The Saddle Bar is used for quiz nights and meetings, while, in a separate building, the Stable Bar hosts live music and TV sport. Add to this the restaurant, accommodation and, of course, the three beers on offer, and there is truly something for everyone here. ⌂Q🐎❀🛏◐◑Ⴜ🚌(41)♣P⚐

Diss

Cock Inn

63 Lower Denmark Street, IP22 4BE (off A1066) TM112795

⏲ 12-11 (midnight Fri & Sat); 12-10.30 Sun

☎ (01379) 643633

Adnams Bitter; Fuller's London Pride; Taylor Landlord; guest beers Ⓗ

The Grade II-listed pub dates from 1520 and faces a large green on the outskirts of Diss where it provides an excellent spot for watching the sun go down. One bar serves four distinct comfortably-furnished drinking areas. In winter a large log fire welcomes customers. Live music sessions take place every three weeks. Meals are served lunchtimes except Saturday and Thursday to Saturday evenings. Adnams Broadside is a regular guest ale. ⌂◐◑P⚐

Downham Market

Crown Hotel

12 Bridge Street, PE38 9DH

⏲ 9.30 (11 Sun)-11

☎ (01366) 382322

Adnams Bitter; Greene King IPA, Abbot; guest beers Ⓗ

This 17th-century coaching inn at the heart of the old town is popular with locals and visitors alike. The single bar has a beamed ceiling, large fireplace and four handpumps, one of which dispenses a guest ale, usually from a local brewer. There is a restaurant and a separate function room which caters for parties and weddings. A smoking area is located under the coaching arch. ⌂❀🛏◐◑⇌🚌P⚐

Earsham

Queens Head

Station Road, NR35 2TS

⏲ 12-3, 5-11; 12-11 Sat; 12-10.30 Sun

☎ (01986) 892623

Waveney East Coast Mild, Lightweight; guest beers Ⓗ

The pub, which dates back to the 17th century, overlooks the village green. The main bar features stone floors, wooden beams, an old fireplace and a ceiling decorated with pump clips of guest ales that have previously featured in the pub. Home to the Waveney Brewing Company, there is usually a range of two Waveney beers plus two guests from other brewers. Food is available Wednesday-Sunday lunchtimes. Successful darts, pool and football clubs are based here. The smoking area is unheated. ⌂🐎❀◐🚌(580)♣P⚐

East Dereham

George Hotel

Swaffham Road, NR19 2AZ (near war memorial)

⏲ 10-11 (midnight Fri & Sat); 12-11 Sun

☎ (01362) 696801 🌐 lottiesrestaurant.co.uk

Adnams Bitter, Broadside; Beeston Worth the Wait; Fuller's London Pride; Woodforde's Wherry Best Bitter Ⓗ

The hotel is an 18th-century coaching inn situated in the busy Norfolk market town of Dereham. A well-designed bar is open to non-residents, with alcoves, wood panelling, leather chairs and pictures of local historical interest. The landlord is a promoter of local beers. A fine air-conditioned conservatory has disabled access, and a heated outdoor patio is lined with bamboo plants, with a separate smokers' corner. The George is handy for the Mid-Norfolk Railway and has a secure car park. Q🐎❀🛏◐◑♿⇌🚌(X1)P⚐

Edgefield

Pigs

Norwich Road, NR24 2RL (on B1149) TG098343

⏲ 11-3, 6-11; closed Mon; 12-4 Sun

☎ (01263) 587634 🌐 thepigs.org.uk

Adnams Bitter, Broadside; Woodforde's Wherry Best Bitter; guest beers Ⓗ

Extensively refurbished with a bovine theme throughout. 'The Pig Issue' menu and newssheet advises you of forthcoming events as well as the extensive range of food available, including 'iffits'. The pub operates a unique barter system where you can swap locally caught or grown produce for pints of beer. Quiz night is Wednesday and a traditional pub games night, including billiards, dominoes and shove-ha'penny, is on Thursday. Outside is a safe play area for younger visitors. The house beer Edgefield Old Spot is brewed by Wolf. ❀◐◑♿🚌♣P⚐

Elsing

Mermaid Inn

Church Street, NR20 3EA TG053165

⏲ 12-3.30, 7 (6 Fri & Sat)-midnight; 12-3, 6.30-11.30 Sun

☎ (01362) 637640

Adnams Broadside; Wolf Golden Jackal; Woodforde's Wherry Best Bitter; guest beers Ⓖ

This 17th-century pub is located opposite a large 14th-century parish church in a small village in the charming upper Wensum Valley. The interior has a large bar with a log fire at one end and a pool table at the other. There is also a dining area. Cask ales sold here are mainly from local breweries and are gravity dispensed. Home-made traditional English food is served, with steak & kidney pie and jam roly-poly a local speciality. Occasional quiz nights are held. ⌂❀◐◑♿Ⴜ🚌♣P⚐

Erpingham

Spread Eagle

Eagle Lane, NR11 7QA (1 mile from A140 Aylsham-Cromer road) TG 191319

11-3, 6.30-11; 11-11 Fri & Sat; 12-4, 7-11 Sun
(01263) 761591
Adnams Bitter; Woodforde's Wherry Best Bitter; guest beers H
A family and dog-friendly pub that has recently been enlarged with the addition of a spacious function/dining area. Located on the long-distance footpath known as Weavers Way, it is popular with walkers. There is a regular Thursday night knitting group and live music once a month. In the summer months frequent barbecues and hog roasts are held. There are plans for B&B accommodation in the near future. P

Fakenham

Bull

Bridge Street, NR21 9AG TF856264
10 (12 Sun)-midnight
(01328) 853410 thefakenhambull.co.uk
Woodforde's Wherry Best Bitter; guest beers H
The pub has one open-plan space forming separate areas on differing levels, complete with comfortable leather settees and a welcoming log fire in winter. Four real ales are always available, sourced from brewers countrywide, including lesser known micro-breweries. Over 200 different ales are served each year as well as real cider such as Old Rosie or Crones Organic. Excellent lunchtime meals are also delivered locally and Wednesday is steak night.

Foulden

White Hart

White Hart Street, IP26 5AW
4 (8 Sun)-midnight
(01366) 328638 travelpublishing.co.uk/whitehartfoulden
Buffy's Bitter, Pollys Folly, seasonal ale; guest beers H
A 19th-century pub situated between the A134 and the A1065, not far from Thetford. This is a Buffy's house in which the beers are excellent value for money. Unpretentious pub meals as well as a good selection of wines are also served. Accommodation is available too, making the White Hart a good base for walkers and car owners, with Thetford Forest right on the doorstep. Themed food nights also feature as does live music in this great country pub.
QP

Framingham Pigot

Gull

Loddon Road, NR14 7PL (on A146) TG285038
12-3, 5.30-11
(01508) 492039
Greene King Abbot; Woodforde's Wherry Best Bitter; guest beer G
A 250-year-old pub on the Norwich-Beccles road. This long building is divided into four distinct areas with two for dining and two for drinking, plus a pool room. All beers are served on gravity with the guest beer coming from Oakham, Green Jack or Brandon. The pub is noted for its food – an interesting mix of English and continental dishes, served at all sessions. (X2)P

Gayton

Crown

Lynn Road, PE32 1PA
12-11 (midnight Fri & Sat)
(01553) 636252
Greene King XX Mild, IPA, Old Speckled Hen, Abbot; guest beers H
This true village gem, voted local CAMRA Pub of the Year in 2004, is a rare outlet for XX Mild. The food is excellent in both the pub and dining rooms. Live music evenings and special events are well supported by locals. The pub walls features many wildlife pictures by a local photographer. An inn for all seasons, there are gardens front and back and huge log fires in winter. Dogs are welcome.
Q(48)♣P

Geldeston

Locks Inn

Locks Lane, NR34 0HW (through village to Ellingham Mill, turn left onto track across marshes) TM390908
12-midnight summer; 5-11 (midnight Fri & Sat) Wed-Sat winter; 12-midnight summer (12-7 winter) Sun
(01508) 518414
Green Jack Canary, Orange Wheat, Grasshopper, Mahseer IPA, seasonal beers; guest beers H
Rural community gem located on the banks of the River Wensum, accessed by a long, meandering track between dykes and marshes. The pub has expansive gardens that lead to overnight moorings. The small main bar, with a low-beamed ceiling and clay pamment floor, retains an authentic, welcoming feel, while modern extensions allow the pub to maintain an active live music scene. Owned by Green Jack Brewery, the pub also offers guests from other brewers. A selection of real ciders and perries is also available. The pub hosts two beer festivals a year.
Q♣P

Gorleston-on-Sea

Mariners Compass

21 Middleton Road, NR31 7AJ
11-1.30am (2.30am Thu-Sat); 12-12.30am Sun
(01493) 659494
Beer range varies H
Set back from the Lowestoft Road, this large two-bar pub was opened in the 1930s and fitted out in 'brewer's Tudor' style. It was saved from oblivion in 2008 and has become one of the major real ale meccas for the area. It retains many of its original fittings, and has been sympathetically decorated inside. Beers are an eclectic range, with many from local breweries, always changing and invariably interesting. The locally-produced cider is a superb house speciality, but should be treated with considerable respect. Occasional live music.
Q♣P

New Entertainer

80 Pier Plain, NR31 6PG
12-11
(01493) 441643
Greene King IPA; guest beers H
A pub that has a unique triangular design peculiar to the old Yarmouth Lacons Brewery. This roadside local could easily be overlooked, with no pavements on the surrounding streets. Close to the harbour, it retains a lot of character, and offers a varying selection of ales, many from Norfolk

brewers and the nearby Lowestoft micros. A selection of bottled Belgian beers completes the line-up. Q

Great Bircham

King's Head

Lynn Road, PE31 7RJ
11-11; 12-10.30 Sun
(01485) 578265 the-kings-head-bircham.co.uk
Adnams Bitter; Fuller's London Pride; Woodforde's Wherry Best Bitter; guest beers Ⓗ
The cream and purple decor, pale wood and a stainless steel bar indicate that this is a modern, stylish hotel. There are 12 individually designed bedrooms and the King's Head has been listed as having one of the top restaurants in the country. Don't let this put you off though. There is always a friendly welcome and four top-quality beers on offer. Prices are cheaper than you might expect and with events such as jazz evenings and race nights, this pub is very much part of the local community. CAMRA Branch Pub of the Year 2007. P

Great Cressingham

Windmill Inn

Water End, IP25 6NN (off A1065 S of Swaffham) TF846019
9-midnight; 11.30-2.30, 5-9.30 Sun
(01760) 756232 oldewindmillinn.co.uk
Adnams Bitter, Broadside; Greene King IPA Ⓗ**; guest beers** Ⓗ/Ⓖ
Full of character, this rambling multi-roomed country inn provides a different atmosphere in each of its drinking areas, ranging from olde worlde with open fires and real beams to a modern extension. A good selection of real ales includes the house beer, Windy Miller, by Hancock's, while guest beers are rotated weekly. Thirty different malt whiskies are also stocked alongside bottled and keg lagers. The pub features live music and a talent night. Good home-cooked food is available. A worthwhile detour from the Peddars Way walk. Q P

Great Massingham

Dabbling Duck

11 Abbey Road, PE32 2HN
12-11 (10.30 Sun)
(01485) 520827 thedabblingduck.co.uk
Adnams Broadside; Beeston Worth the Wait; Greene King IPA; Taylor Landlord; Woodforde's Wherry Best Bitter; guest beers Ⓗ
Picturesque pub in a typical rural Norfolk village. This refurbished multi-roomed pub boasts two drinking areas and several cosy nooks for dining, as well as a restaurant. The pub supports many activities including darts and quiz nights, and can cater for all occasions. A large beer garden at the rear makes this a family-friendly place and whether you are simply relaxing in front of one of the log fires or spending a weekend in one of the four guest rooms, a warm welcome awaits you. Dogs welcome. (48)

Great Yarmouth

Gallon Pot

Market Place, NR30 1NB
10-11; 12-10.30 Sun
(01493) 842230
Adnams Bitter; Fuller's London Pride; Greene King Old Speckled Hen; Woodforde's Wherry Best Bitter Ⓗ
An ex-Lacons pub that was built in 1772 by William Burroughes and sadly destroyed by enemy fire in 1943 when this area of the town was heavily bombed. The present pub dates from 1959 and it still retains many Lacons features including a wall frieze. The interior is dark wood with comfortable seating. Situated very close to the market place, near the largest parish church in England, this pub welcomes families in the spacious cellar bar. It can be busy on market days Wednesday and Saturday. (Vauxhall)

Mariners Tavern

69 Howard Street South, NR30 1LN
11-11 (1am Fri & Sat); 12-11 Sun
(01493) 332299
Greene King IPA, Abbot; guest beers Ⓗ
A former Lacons pub with a pleasant red brick and flint exterior. This family-run local comprises a main bar and a smaller wood-panelled lounge which has recently been converted to a cider bar, where at least three real ciders are available. An annual beer festival is held to coincide with the Yarmouth maritime weekend in September. Many of the seven guest ales come from local micro-breweries and there is a small selection of foreign beers.

Red Herring

24-25 Havelock Road, NR30 3HQ
12-3, 6.30-midnight; 12-midnight Sat & Sun
(01493) 853384
Blackfriars Yarmouth Bitter; guest beers Ⓗ
Situated near the award-winning Time and Tide Museum, this friendly back-street one-bar corner local has a separate area with a pool table and TV. A rotating range of guest beers is available, including ales from local brewer Blackfriars. The walls are decorated with photos of Old Yarmouth from its herring fishing days when the town was host to many Scottish boats. Evidence of the old smoke house is still visible in the area. The cider is Westons Old Rosie.

St Johns Head

53 North Quay, NR30 1JB
12-midnight
(01493) 843443
Elgood's Cambridge Bitter; guest beers Ⓗ
This pub is reputed to be built on land confiscated from monks of the Carmelite Order and was acquired by Lacons Brewery in 1787. Its traditional flintstone facade includes oval windows at the front of the pub. A single bar houses a large TV screen and sport is very popular here. There is a pool table in a separate area. Four real ales include three regularly-changing guests. The smoking shelter is minimalist but heated.
(Vauxhall)

Happisburgh

Hill House

NR12 0PW (just off B1159) TG381311
12-11.30 summer; 12-3, 7-11.30 Mon-Wed, 12-11.30 Thu-Sat winter; 12-11.30 Sun
(01692) 650004
Beer range varies Ⓗ

Sixteenth-century inn situated very close to the sea in an attractive north Norfolk coastal village. The pub always offers a range of six real ales including many from local brewers. This rural retreat was a favourite with author Sir Arthur Conan Doyle in the late 19th century. It hosts a mid-summer beer festival each June that offers around 80 real ales plus ciders and perries, and attracts visitors from near and far. ⛫Q⚇❀⛆◐◑♿🚌♣P

Heacham

Fox & Hounds

22 Station Road, PE31 7EX

⏲ 12-11 (10.30 Sun)

☎ (01485) 570345 🌐 foxbrewery.co.uk

Adnams Broadside; guest beers 🄷

Home of the Fox Brewery and CAMRA's West Norfolk Branch Pub of the Year 2008, this pub always offers six beers – four from Fox, one guest and a house ale. Bottled beer is also available including the brewery's own, plus a range of foreign brews. The restaurant offers beer recommendations to match the cuisine. Live music is staged on Tuesday and a quiz is held on Thursday. Beer festivals are hosted throughout the year. The toilets are very posh in this real-ale mecca. ❀◐◑♿🚌(40,41)♣P⚋

Hillborough

Swan

Brandon Road, IP26 5BW (on A1065)

⏲ 11-3 (11 Fri-Sun)

☎ (01760) 756380 🌐 thehillboroughswan.co.uk

Greene King IPA; guest beers 🄷

A welcoming pub on the A1065 between Mundford and Swaffham that also offers B&B. An extensive menu features a good Sunday carvery. Greene King IPA sits alongside two guest ales, regularly including beers from Beeston Brewery. There is always something good to sample at the Swan, with a better choice of ales than can be found in the whole of nearby Swaffham. If you're passing on the way to the coast it's a good stopover for a pint or a meal. ⛫Q❀⛆◐◑♣P⚋

Hockering

Victoria

The Street, NR20 3HL (just off A47) TF863355

⏲ 12-3 (closed Mon-Wed), 6-11; 12-6 Sun

☎ (01603) 880507

Beer range varies 🄷

In the centre of the village just off the A47, this friendly pub offers a warm welcome. The pub has two ever-changing guest beers, rising to four in the summer. The bar has a dartboard and wide-screen TV at one end and a real fire at the other. The walls are adorned with old photos of the village, framed beer mats and Arsenal memorabilia. Bar snacks are available at all sessions. An annual beer festival is held in July. ⛫❀◑♿🚌(X1)♣🍏P⚋

Horsey

Nelson Head

The Street, NR29 4AD (300m N of B1159 coast road) TG460228

⏲ 11-11; 12-10.30 Sun

☎ (01493) 393378 🌐 nelsonheadhorsey.co.uk

Woodforde's Wherry Best Bitter, Nelson's Revenge; guest beers 🄷

A friendly pub close to the coast, Horsey Nature Reserve, Broad and Mill. It has a quiet, timeless atmosphere with a log fire in winter and a large collection of marshman's implements. A good selection of home-cooked meals made with locally-sourced produce is available lunchtime and evenings. Families are welcome in the bar and dining room. The pub is popular with artists, walkers, boaters and locals alike, and the large garden area welcomes children. ⛫Q⚇❀◐◑P⚋

Hunstanton

Wash & Tope Hotel

10-12 Le Strange Terrace, PE36 5AJ

⏲ 11-11

☎ (01485) 532250 🌐 thewashandtope.co.uk

Beer range varies 🄷

This large town pub is close to the seafront and is popular with tourists and locals. The bar has two handpumps dispensing ever-changing beers – an additional handpump is soon to be installed. There is a smaller sports bar behind the main bar which boasts a pool table, dartboard and large-screen TV. The pub also has a restaurant and a separate function room. A beer festival is held annually in September. Dogs are welcome. ⛫❀⛆◐◑⛟⛺🚌(40,41)♣P⚋

Ingham

Swan Inn

Swan Corner, Sea Palling Road, NR12 9AB (1 mile NE of Stalham on B1151) TG390260

⏲ 12-3, 6-11 (10.30 Mon-Fri winter); 12-3.30, 6-10.30 Sun

☎ (01692) 581099

Woodforde's Wherry Best Bitter, Nelson's Revenge; guest beers 🄷

Rural 14th-century thatched and flint-built pub situated close to the church. The interesting split-level, beamed interior has a wealth of warm brick and traditional flint. Beers are selected from the full Woodforde's range. Freshly prepared meals are made with local produce and may be enjoyed in the bar, the restaurant area or, in summer, the secluded courtyard. High quality en-suite rooms in a separate block are available all year round, with short-break rates that include dinner, bed and breakfast. ⛫Q❀⛆◐◑🚌P

Kenninghall

Red Lion ☆

East Church Street, NR16 2EP (opp church) TM042859

⏲ 12-3, 5.30-11; 12-11 Fri & Sat; 12-10.30 Sun

☎ (01953) 887849 🌐 redlionkenninghall.co.uk

Greene King IPA, Old Speckled Hen, 🄷**; Abbot** 🄶**; Woodforde's Wherry Best Bitter; guest beer** 🄷

Dating back more than 400 years, the beautifully-restored interior comprises a bar with log fire, a pine-panelled snug and a separate restaurant. Abbot is available from a cask behind the bar and Elmtree Bitter is one of the regular guest beers. Good quality, home-cooked food with interesting vegetarian options is served every day. There are regular themed nights and live music events. Directions for a short local walk can be obtained from the bar. Four double rooms are available for B&B. ⛫❀⛆◐◑P⚋

King's Lynn

Globe Hotel ✔

Tuesday Market Place, King Street, PE30 1EZ
7.30am-midnight; 8am-1am Fri & Sat; 8am-midnight Sun
☎ (01553) 668000
Greene King Abbot; Marston's Pedigree; guest beers H
A good example of a Wetherspoon's Lloyds No 1 Bar, this sympathetic conversion of a town-centre former coaching inn is on the corner of the larger of the town's two market places. Several screens show a variety of music videos and live sport. Food is served all day until 10pm. The bar can get very busy during evenings and weekends. The outdoor drinking area goes down towards the river and has heaters and parasols. Wetherspoon Lodge accommodation includes rooms adapted for disabled guests. ❀🛏◑♿⚊

Stuart House Hotel

35 Goodwins Road, PE30 5QX
6-11; 7-10.30 Sun
☎ (01553) 772169 stuart-house-hotel.co.uk
Beer range varies H
Find the hotel along a gravel drive from Goodwins Road, not far from King's Lynn FC and the Walks park. Three ales, often local, are available. The pleasant hotel bar has a roaring fire in winter, and there is a beer garden for the summer months. The owner is a real beer enthusiast. There is regular live music on Friday evening and an annual beer festival each July. The bar is open evenings only (except by arrangement). Q❀🛏◑♣P

Langham

Bluebell

22-24 Holt Road, NR25 7BX (take B1156 S from Blakeney, turn right into village) TG012411
11-3, 7-11; 11-11 Fri; 12-4, 7-11 Sat & Sun
☎ (01328) 830502
Greene King IPA; guest beer H
Situated two miles inland from the A149 at Blakeney and slightly off the main tourist route, this is a traditional village local pub that likes visitors. The interior comprises a main bar and a split-level dining area. This pub is family and dog friendly, and home-cooked food using locally-sourced produce where possible is available each day lunchtime and evening except Wednesday. There is a large garden at the rear of the pub.
❀◑♿♣P

Larling

Angel Inn

NR16 2QU (off A11 between Thetford and Norwich, signed by B1111 East Harling) TL983890
10-midnight; 11-11 Sun
☎ (01953) 717963 larlingangel.moonfruit.com
Adnams Bitter; guest beers H
A treasure just off the A11 with a warm welcome. The Angel features a superb range of ales from micro-breweries across the country, favouring Orkney beers and always including a mild. An excellent range of home-cooked food is available and both the lounge and bar have open fires. The bar is frequented by friendly locals and passers by. A summer beer festival features more than 70 ales and the pub also hosts a whisky week, serving a good selection of malts.
Q❀🛏◑♿⛺⇌(Harling Rd)P⚊

Lessingham

Star Inn

School Road, NR12 0DN (300m off B1159 coast road) TG388283
12-3, 7-midnight
☎ (01692) 580510 thestarlessingham.co.uk
Buffy's Bitter; Greene King IPA; guest beers H
An excellent village pub with an easy-going feel. The wood burner in the inglenook fireplace at one end of the bar is especially welcoming on cold winter days. The large beer garden is a great place to relax in summer. A display of beer mats on the bar timbering is testament to the many guest beers offered in the past. The guest beer is often from an East Anglian micro. The cider is Westons Old Rosie and dogs are welcome in the bar.
Q❀🛏⛺(34,36)♣P

Litcham

Bull Inn

Church Street, PE32 2NS (at crossroads at centre of B1145 and Church St) TG886177
12 (5 winter)-midnight; 12-10.30 Sun
☎ (01474) 702170
Beeston Worth the Wait; guest beer H
Situated in a picturesque central Norfolk village and close to the village green, this 17th-century coaching inn abounds with low wood ceiling beams and wooden floorboards. The original timber frame structure is still visible in the restaurant. The cask ales sold here are from the local Beeston micro-brewery. There is a separate dining room and a small patio drinking area at the rear. The pub offers accommodation in nine rooms, all en-suite and some converted for disabled use.
❀🛏◑♿⛺(1,8,32)♣P⚊

Mundford

Crown Hotel

Crown Road, IP26 5HQ
11-11 (10.30 Sun)
☎ (01842) 878233
Courage Directors; Marston's Pedigree; guest beers H
The Crown is a lovely old building, right in the heart of the pretty village centre. With tiny rooms and split levels it really is a maze, with a beautifully appointed restaurant up the narrow stairs. It provides a high standard of accommodation for visitors to the Breckland area but is still very much a village pub. It used to be a regular entry in the Guide and it is good to see it back. Q❀🛏◑⚊

New Buckenham

King's Head

Market Place, NR16 2AN (opp village green) TM088905
12-3, 7-11 (10.30 Sun)
☎ (01953) 860487
Adnams Bitter; guest beer H
This friendly free house faces the market cross in the centre of this orthogonal medieval grid pattern village. A wood burner in the large inglenook fireplace warms the rear drinking area which is furnished with pine tables and wooden chairs. Traditional home-cooked food is available and Sunday lunch is especially popular with pub goers. Quiz night is every second Thursday. The guest beer mostly comes from a local brewery. Q◑⚊

Newton by Castle Acre

George & Dragon

Newton Swaffham Road, PE32 2BX (on main road between Fakenham and Swaffham)
12-2.30, 6-11; 12-5 Sun
(01760) 755046
Beer range varies H

The pub is situated beside a busy road and has a very large car park. Although it has been modernised it retains a lot of its old character, with wooden beams and an open fire. The interior is split into four cosy rooms including a bar and a restaurant. Two ever-changing real ales are available from local breweries. Regular events are staged here. P

North Creake

Jolly Farmers

1 Burnham Road, NR21 9JW
11-2.30, 7-11; closed Mon & Tue; 12-3, 7-10.30 Sun
(01328) 738185 jollyfarmers-northcreake.co.uk
Woodforde's Wherry Best Bitter, Nelson's Revenge; guest beers G

This cosy pub has small rooms with beams and tiled floors which are enhanced on a cold day by a roaring log fire. The beer is on gravity and the menu features both interesting main meals and a range of lighter snacks and sandwiches, with much of the produce coming straight from local suppliers. You may just notice the classical music above the buzz of contented conversation. P

North Elmham

Railway Hotel

Station Road, NR20 5HH TF995202
11-11
(01362) 668300
Beer range varies H/G

Situated in central Norfolk near the ancient Anglo-Saxon North Elmham Cathedral, this rural pub is a fine example of a community local. Many of the beers on sale here are from local breweries such as Beeston, Humpty Dumpty and Wolf. Home-cooked meals using mainly locally sourced ingredients are available at lunchtimes and in the evenings. The recently added function room has been extended to include a first-floor balcony and there is a new patio at the rear of the pub. P

North Walsham

Bluebell

Bacton Road, NR28 0RA (on B1150 Bacton Rd opp Bluebell Rd) TG291310
11 (12 Sun)-11
(01692) 404800
Adnams Bitter, Broadside; Greene King IPA, Abbot; Woodforde's Wherry Best Bitter H

This pub is situated on the north-west side of a bustling north Norfolk market town. The interior is mainly open plan, comprising a comfortable bar/lounge with a separate dining area serving traditional English food. There is an attractive large garden at the back of the pub which includes a spacious covered beer terrace with seats and tables. A regular quiz takes place on Sunday evening to raise money for local charities. (6)P

Norwich

Alexandra Tavern

16 Stafford Street, NR2 3BB (off Dereham Road or Earlham Road)
10.30-11 (midnight Fri & Sat); 12-11 Sun
(01603) 627772 alexandratavern.co.uk
Chalk Hill Tap, Best; guest beers H

A friendly Victorian corner local situated in Norwich's Golden Triangle area. It has a traditional bar with a log fire and much brewery and nautical memorabilia on the walls, leading to a games area with pool table and large wide-screen TV. There is also a comfortable lounge and small outside seating area. Real ales come from the local Chalk Hill Brewery plus guests, mainly from other local micros. Hot and cold food is available from 12.30-7pm, with Mexican dishes a speciality. Q(19,20)

Beehive

30 Leopold Road, NR4 7PJ
12 (5 Mon)-11; 12-midnight Fri & Sat; 12-11 Sun
(01603) 451628
Fuller's London Pride; Wolf Wolf Ale, Golden Jackal; guest beers H

Situated between Unthank and Newmarket Roads, this recently redecorated hostelry is certainly worth a visit. It has two rooms, one leading to a garden area and a smoking shelter. The beer range consists of two regular Wolf ales and up to three guests. The pub has a real community feel to it, with a quiz night on Wednesday, as well as playing host to darts, crib and pool teams. A small function room is available.

Coachmakers

9 St Stephen's Road, NR1 3SP
11-11; 12-10.30 Sun
(01603) 662080
Greene King IPA; Wolf Golden Jackal; Woodforde's Wherry Best Bitter G

A former coaching inn dating from the 17th century, with an attractive floral display above the spacious courtyard entrance. Outside, there is a patio/garden area with a separate space for smokers. Beer is served on gravity dispense from behind the bar so don't miss it when you come in. There is Sky TV and an excellent food menu. Look out for the ghost, as the pub is built on an old asylum. (12,12A)

Duke of Wellington

91-93 Waterloo Road, NR3 1EG
12-11.30 (10.30 Sun)
(01603) 441182 dukeofwellingtonnorwich.co.uk
Elgood's Black Dog; Fuller's London Pride; Oakham JHB, Bishop's Farewell; Wolf Golden Jackal, Straw Dog; guest beers H/G

A friendly and welcoming community pub which serves a wide range of real ales from around the country. It holds a very popular late summer beer festival in the rear garden area. An extension to the tap room, which can be viewed, is being added later in the year to cater for increased demand. There is a folk evening on Tuesday night and the pub supports a bowls team. (9A,16)P

Eaton Cottage

75 Mount Pleasant, NR2 2DQ
12-11 (midnight Fri & Sat)
(01603) 453048

Fuller's London Pride; Tipples Moon Rocket; Wolf Golden Jackal; guest beers Ⓗ
A traditional, friendly, suburban local situated south west of the city centre. A single bar serves the pub's two rooms and there is also a small lounge. A choice of three regular beers is served, plus four guests and a house beer brewed by Winter's. The pub hosts jazz and blues bands on Thursday night and occasionally at the weekend. The building is reputed to be haunted by two ghosts: an elderly lady and a cat. ❀♿🚌(25,35)●

Fat Cat

49 West End Street, NR2 4NA (20 mins walk from city centre, just off Dereham Road)
⏲ 11-11 (midnight Fri & Sat); 12-10.30 Sun
☎ (01603) 624364 🌐 fatcatpub.co.uk
Adnams Bitter; Elgood's Black Dog Ⓗ; Fat Cat Bitter, Top Cat, Honey Cat, Marmalade Cat Ⓗ/Ⓖ; Woodforde's Wherry Best Bitter Ⓗ; guest beers Ⓗ/Ⓖ
A mecca for beer lovers from around the country, hosting 30-plus real ales from all points of the compass as well as the pub's own award-winning Fat Cat range. The long-serving staff are friendly to customers both old and new. Brewery memorabilia adorn the walls in the many nooks and crannies. Major sporting events are shown, and a back room is available for hire. Twice winner of CAMRA's National Pub of the Year. A classic. ❀🚌♣●⚡

Gate House

391 Dereham Road, NR5 8QJ
⏲ 12-11 (midnight Fri & Sat)
☎ (01603) 620340
Grain Oak Ⓖ; Greene King IPA, Abbot; Woodforde's Wherry Best Bitter Ⓗ
Situated two miles west of Norwich city centre, this warm and welcoming traditional 19th-century pub was built on the site of an old tollhouse. Four real ales dispensed by handpump and gravity are available. The interior comprises two oak-panelled bars and there is a roaring log fire in winter. It has a large garden that backs on to the River Wensum. The pub fields three pool teams, a crib team and a ladies' darts team. Occasional live folk music plays on some Sunday afternoons. ⛰Q👶❀◐🚌♣●P⚡

Ketts Tavern

29 Ketts Hill, NR1 4EX
⏲ 12-midnight
☎ (01603) 449654
Blackfriars Mitre Gold; Norfolk Square Winkle Picker, Sunshiny; Tipples Lady Evelyn; Woodforde's Wherry Best Bitter, Nelson's Revenge Ⓗ
This friendly free house is in easy reach of the railway station and close to riverside moorings. It has a large, partitioned bar and a conservatory which houses the pool table. The current management policy is to provide a good range of locally-produced beers and ciders and the pub hosts four beer festivals a year. Lunchtime meals and bar snacks are available. In addition, an arrangement with the local Indian takeaway allows customers to order excellent, reasonably priced meals in the evening, with the pub providing plates and cutlery. ❀◑▶⇌🚌●P⚡

King's Arms

22 Hall Road, NR1 3HQ
⏲ 11-11 (midnight Fri & Sat); 12-10.30 Sun
☎ (01603) 766361 🌐 kingsarmsnorwich.co.uk
Adnams Bitter; Batemans XB Bitter, XXXB; Beeston Worth the Wait; Hop Back Summer Lightning; guest beers Ⓗ
Now a Batemans hostelry, this pub has a well-deserved reputation for quality real ale. The range includes the regular Bateman's beers plus a wide selection of guests from around the country. The pub holds a very popular beer festival in November, as well as themed nights for St George's Day and Burn's Night celebrations. If you are hungry you can 'bring yer own' food – plates and condiments provided. Major sports events are shown and a regular quiz night is held.
❀◑♿🚌(9,10A)♣⚡

King's Head

42 Magdalen Street, NR3 1JE
⏲ 12-midnight (11 Sun)
☎ (01603) 620468 🌐 kingsheadnorwich.co.uk
Winter's Kings Head Bitter Ⓗ; Woodforde's Nelson's Revenge; guest beers Ⓗ/Ⓖ
CAMRA Branch Pub of the Year in 2006 and 2008, this keg-free hostelry stocks only beers from East Anglian micro-breweries – there can be up to 16 available. Friendly, knowledgeable staff will guide you to a beer that suits your palate. A range of bottled ales and lagers caters for those who like to try an alternative. Bar billiards can be played in an area at the back of the pub. Q🚌♣●⚡🍺

Ribs of Beef ✔

24 Wensum Street, NR3 1HY
⏲ 11-12.30am (1am Fri & Sat); 12-12.30am Sun
☎ (01603) 619517 🌐 ribsofbeef.co.uk
Adnams Bitter; Courage Best Bitter; Elgood's Black Dog; Woodforde's Wherry Best Bitter; guest beers Ⓗ
This popular city-centre local, which has recently been refurbished, is situated on the banks of the River Wensum, close to the Cathedral. The Ribs is famous for its range of cask ales, local cider and traditional English food sourced locally. There is a nearby jetty which is popular in the summer, attracting visiting boats that moor up to enjoy the pub's facilities. Sports enthusiasts can enjoy live matches on the large screens in the bar. A room is available for private hire. ◑▶⇌🚌(21,22)●

Take 5

17 Tombland, NR3 1HF
⏲ 11-11
☎ (01603) 763099
St Peter's Organic Ale, guest ales Ⓗ
This Grade-II listed building, parts of which date from the 17th century, is situated at the north end of Norwich's historic Tombland, near the Erpingham Gate entrance to the Cathedral. It was formerly known as the Louis Marchesi before being refurbished and reopened under its present name in 2004. Today it has a continental café bar feel to it, especially at lunchtime. Real ales come from St Peter's and Woodforde's, and the guests are often from local brewers too. There is a large function room upstairs. ◑▶🚌(21,22)●

Trafford Arms ✔

61 Grove Road, NR1 3RL
⏲ 11-11 (11.30 Fri & Sat); 12-10.30 Sun
☎ (01603) 628466 🌐 traffordarms.co.uk
Adnams Bitter; Tetley Bitter; Woodforde's Wherry Best Bitter; guest beers Ⓗ
A welcoming, well-run local close to the city centre. On entering the pub, the row of handpumps that greets you is testimony to the

extensive choice and quality of the beers on offer. There are two main areas for dining and watching sporting events, with TV and pool. Delicious food is available, which makes this a popular pub with the local community. The Valentines Beer Festival is a highlight not to be missed. The pub was a previous CAMRA Pub of the Year winner.
❀◑◗🚌(9,17)♣●P⅟–

Whalebone ✔

144 Magdalen Road, NR3 4BA
⏲ 11-11 (midnight Fri & Sat); 12-11 Sun
☎ (01603) 425482
Adnams Bitter; Fuller's London Pride; Hop Back Summer Lightning; Oakham JHB; Shepherd Neame Spitfire; Woodforde's Wherry Best Bitter Ⓗ
The Whalebone is a fine example of a community local, serving a range of around 10 cask ales. The pub has recently undergone much internal refurbishment and is broken up into a number of drinking areas. The original front bar is connected to an upper level which has been fitted out with soft furnishings. The lounge and new conservatory bar lead to a covered and heated terraced area which is very popular, with barbecues hosted in the summer. ❀🚌(10,18)♣P⅟–

White Lion

73 Oak Street, NR3 3AQ (just off inner link rd, near Barn Rd roundabout)
⏲ 12-2.30, 5.30-11; 12-11 Fri & Sat; 12-10.30 Sun
☎ (01603) 632333 🌐 individualpubs.co.uk/whitelion
Milton Dionysus, Minotaur, Sparta, guest ales Ⓗ
Recently reopened by the Milton Brewery, this small two-roomed back-street local is now the only pub in Oak Street – 100 years ago there were 30 or more. The pub offers a range of ever-changing Milton beers from its vast portfolio, plus two or three guest ales, all at keen prices. A welcome addition to the Norwich pub scene, sympathetically redecorated. Q🚌

Wig & Pen ✔

6 St Martins Palace Plain, NR3 1RN
⏲ 11.30-11 (midnight Fri & Sat); 11.30-6 Sun
☎ (01603) 625891 🌐 thewigandpen.com
Adnams Bitter; Caledonian Deuchars IPA; Fuller's London Pride; guest beers Ⓗ
A renowned, friendly, 17th-century free house, which provides six local and national guest beers. It also hosts a number of themed beer festivals throughout the year. The owner is proud of his Cask Marque accreditation and offers a 'try before you buy' policy. A small back room can be used for meetings. Major sporting events are shown on a large-screen TV and a comprehensive lunchtime and evening menu is served. The spacious outside patio area is well frequented in the summer.
⌂❀◑◗⇌🚌⅟–

Old Buckenham

Gamekeeper

The Green, NR17 1RE (on B1077, by village pond) TM064915
⏲ 11.30-3, 6-11; 12-5 Sun
☎ (01953) 860397 🌐 thegamekeeperfreehouse.com
Adnams Bitter; Taylor Landlord; Woodforde's Wherry Best Bitter Ⓗ
Seventeenth-century Grade II-listed free house overlooking the 40-acre village green – the biggest in the country. A detailed history of the building is on display. The interior is split into a main bar with log fire and two separate dining areas. Now under new management, high quality food is available daily lunchtimes and evenings. There is a large garden with ample seating and an adjacent brick and timbered hall which can be hired for private functions. ⌂❀◑◗P⅟–

Oxborough

Bedingfeld Arms

PE33 9PS
⏲ 12 (11 summer)-midnight
☎ (01366) 328300 🌐 bedingfeldarms.com
Adnams Bitter; guest beers Ⓗ
This 17th-century coaching inn, formerly called the Oxborough Eagle, is now named after the family who reside at the adjacent Oxburgh Hall. Their coat of arms adorns the wall in the bar, which sports three handpumps, two of which dispense ever-changing guest beers. There are two restaurants which provide home-cooked meals with lots of specials (excluding Tue). The old stable block has recently been converted into five bedrooms. Beer festivals and themed monthly bottled-beer tastings are featured. Dogs welcome. ⌂❀🛏◑◗♿♣P⅟–

Poringland

Royal Oak

The Street, NR14 7JT (on B1332) TG267023
⏲ 12-3, 5-11; 12-midnight Fri & Sat; 12-11 Sun
☎ (01508) 493734
Beer range varies Ⓗ
The Oak is unashamedly a beer-oriented pub, and is warmly and invitingly laid out, with numerous nooks and small seating areas for drinkers. It offers a rural beer exhibition which provides a mix of interesting brews from regional brewers across the UK, together with a number of the best local breweries. Eight to ten ales are available at any one time. An excellent fish and chip shop adjoins the pub, for those in need of more solid fare.
⌂Q❀♿🚌(587,588)♣●P⅟–🍺

Reedham

Lord Nelson

38 Riverside, NR13 3TE (on banks of River Yare) TG418016
⏲ 12-midnight (closed Mon winter)
☎ (01493) 701548 🌐 lordnelsonpub.com
Greene King IPA; Humpty Dumpty Little Sharpie; guest beers Ⓗ
This welcoming village freehouse is located by the River Yare overlooking reed beds and grazing marsh. Free moorings are available next to the riverside seating area for the boating trade. The main bar has a roaring open fire in winter and dogs are welcome. The beer range increases in summer and always includes locally-brewed ales. The menu is wholesome, locally sourced and includes vegetarian options. Regular folk sessions and periodic live music enliven this already vibrant pub.
⌂Q🐴❀◑◗♿⛺⇌♣●P

Ship

19 Riverside, NR13 3TQ (on banks of River Yare by railway swing bridge) TG422016
⏲ 11-11; 12-10.30 Sun
☎ (01493) 700287
Adnams Bitter, Broadside; Woodforde's Wherry Best Bitter; guest beers Ⓗ

The pub is in a beautiful location on the River Yare, underneath the famous railway swing bridge. The riverside garden includes a children's play area and a smoking shelter. There is a main bar with a separate public bar and two dining areas where families are welcome. The rear dining room is full of historic paraphernalia with accordions and brass instruments, bedwarmers and chamber pots. Good food is part of the pub's trade. P

Reepham

King's Arms

Market Place, NR10 4JJ TG099231

11.30-3, 5.30-11; 12-3, 7-10.30 Sun

(01603) 870345

Adnams Bitter, Broadside; Elgood's Cambridge Bitter; Greene King Abbot; Taylor Landlord; Woodforde's Wherry Best Bitter H

Parts of this former coaching inn situated in the picturesque market square date from the 17th century. There are several drinking and dining areas on split levels. Charm and character have been retained with many original beams, brickwork and open fires. An original glass-topped well can be viewed in the conservatory. The comprehensive menu includes food sourced from nearby butchers and bakers. On summer Sundays live jazz plays in the rear courtyard. Dogs are welcome. Parking is available on the market square. Q P

Ringland

Swan Inn

The Street, NR8 6AB TG140138

11-11 (1am Fri & Sat); 12-11 Sun

(01603) 868214

Adnams Bitter, Explorer; Courage Best Bitter H

This 400-year-old traditional country local situated close to the banks of the River Wensum. Adjoining the pub is the Australian themed restaurant The Taste of Oz offering Australian and Asian cuisine. Traditional English-style bar snacks can be purchased in the pub area. Although the beer menu in the restaurant concentrates mainly on Australian beers, a choice of at least two real ales, usually from local brewers, is available in the pub. Disabled access is via the restaurant. P

Roydon

Union Jack

30 Station Road, PE32 1AW

12 (4 Tue-Thu)-midnight; 12-midnight Sun

(01485) 601347

Beer range varies H

This is a rare village drinkers' pub that relies solely on its wet trade. It offers up to four guest beers, mostly around 4.2% ABV, with a mild often featuring. Ales are chosen in consultation with the regulars. Occasional beer festivals are held. The pub supports many sports activities and a good quantity of trophies is on display. Live music is performed some weekends and dogs are welcome in the bar. Voted CAMRA local branch Pub of the Year 2009. (48)

Salthouse

Dun Cow

Coast Road, NR25 7XA (on A149 north Norfolk coast road) TG073439

11 (12 Sun)-11

(01263) 740467 duncow-salthouse.co.uk

Adnams Bitter; Greene King Abbot; Taylor Landlord; Woodforde's Wherry Best Bitter H

This old inn is situated on the north Norfolk coast adjacent to Salthouse Marshes, a popular location for bird watchers. The main bar has great views of the marshes. From the car park you enter the pub via a courtyard with a fountain. The pub's two bars and en-suite self-catering accommodation surround this courtyard. Inside there are many old exposed beams and flintstones. An extensive food menu offering many local dishes is available all day. (36)P

Sheringham

Windham Arms

15-17 Wyndham Street, NR26 8BA (just off High St)

11 (12 Fri-Sun)-midnight

(01263) 822609 thewindhamarms.co.uk

Greene King Abbot; Woodforde's Wherry Best Bitter; guest beers H

Situated on a narrow back street just behind the High Street, this cosy two-bar local with Dutch-style gables dates from the early 19th century. There is a main bar plus restaurant and separate function room. Outside is a small drinking area with views of the North Sea. Up to five cask ales are available, mainly from local brewers including Wolf and Blackfriars. Greek food is the speciality, available lunchtimes and evenings.

Q

Skeyton

Goat Inn

Long Road, NR10 5DH (on unclassified road N of ex-RAF Coltishall) TG251244

12-2, 6-11; 12-11 summer Sun

(01692) 538600 skeytongoatinn.co.uk

Adnams Bitter; Shepherd Neame Spitfire; Woodforde's Wherry Best Bitter H

A greatly extended 16th-century thatched country pub. It is set in seven acres of grounds, allowing space for gardens, a play area, a campsite and a marquee for weddings. Some of the grounds are left as wildlife areas. Inside there are many old farm implements, and aviation-themed pictures decorate the walls. Events range from a weekly curry night on Thursday to a classic car and motorbike show in May. P

Smallburgh

Crown

North Walsham Road, NR12 9AD TG330245

12-3 (closed Mon), 5.30 (7 Sat)-11; 12-3 Sun

(01692) 536314

Adnams Bitter; Greene King IPA, Abbot; guest beers H

Thatched village pub with a friendly atmosphere. Once a 15th-century coaching inn, some original timbers inside lend character and charm, while a log fire makes the bar cosy in winter. A fine selection of five ales plus high-quality, home-cooked food using seasonal local produce is served.

Meals may be enjoyed in the dining room, the bar or, in summer, the peaceful, tree-fringed garden. Outside is a covered, heated smoking area. The pub is close to the Broads and the north Norfolk coast. A warm welcome awaits at this popular gem. ♨Q❀🛏◑◗🚌♣P⚟

Snettisham

Rose & Crown

Old Church Road, PE31 7LX

⏲ 11-11; 12-10.30 Sun

☎ (01485) 541382 🌐 roseandcrownsnettisham.co.uk

Adnams Bitter, Broadside; Woodforde's Wherry Best Bitter; guest beers 🄷

This village inn dating back from the 14th century has a modern hotel facility at the rear with 16 rooms. The front bars are small and unspoilt with old fireplaces, tiled floors, exposed beams and low ceilings. A larger back bar is reached through a narrow passage. Home-cooked meals are prepared using local produce. Dogs are welcome. Very busy during the summer months. ♨Q👶❀🛏◑◗⊟🚌(40,41)P⚟

Southery

Old White Bell

20 Upgate Street, PE38 0NA

⏲ 12 (3 Wed)-midnight; 12-10.30 Sun

☎ (01366) 377057 🌐 oldwhitebell.co.uk

Tom Woods Bitter; guest beers 🄷

Just off the A10 between Ely and King's Lynn, the Bell is a true community pub with a friendly welcome. The pub has its own football team (White Bell Wanderers), the ceiling above the pool table is adorned with football shirts, and football fixtures are screened on TV. A single bar serves three real ales. There is good food available in the dining room and the Sunday roast comes highly recomended. The landlord is a biker, and there is a monthly bike meet. ❀◑◗🚌(37)♣P

Stibbard

Ordnance Arms

Guist Bottom, NR20 5PF (on A1067) TF987267

⏲ 12-3 (Sat only), 5.30-midnight; 12-10.30 Sun

☎ (01328) 829471 🌐 ordnancearms.co.uk

Greene King IPA; Woodforde's Wherry Best Bitter; guest beer 🄷

Situated on the main Norwich to Fakenham road, this old local gem is one of the few remaining estate-owned public houses in the county. The front area of the building is very traditional, with log fire, stone floors and wooden furniture. One room has a pool table. At the rear you may feel as though you have been transported to the Far East as there is a traditional Thai restaurant offering excellent food in the evening (closed Sun and Mon). ♨Q◗🚌(X29)P⚟

Strumpshaw

Shoulder of Mutton

Norwich Road, NR13 4NT (on Brundall to Lingwood road S of A47) TG349078

⏲ 11-11; 12-10.30 Sun

☎ (01603) 712274

Adnams Bitter, Broadside; guest beers 🄷

Popular village-centre pub catering for all – locals and visitors, young and old. Adnams beers, including Regatta in summer, and regular guest ales are on offer, plus wines from a local importer. An extensive choice of freshly-prepared meals is served in the separate restaurant – booking advisable, especially for the regular themed evenings. The spacious public bar has pool, darts and crib, and the large rear garden is home to petanque in summer. Close to an RSPB reserve with nature walk and the boating centre of Brundall. ❀◑◗⊟♣P⚟

Swaffham

Lydney House Hotel

Norwich Road, PE37 7QS

⏲ 7-10.30; closed Sun

☎ (01760) 723355 🌐 lydney-house.demon.co.uk

Woodforde's Wherry Best Bitter 🄶

Lydney House is a real ale oasis in an area that is a beer desert. This small, privately-owned hotel is situated next to the town's medieval church and within walking distance of the market place. The hotel bar serves excellent ales on gravity and occasional guest ales from local breweries. A supper menu is available. Traditional pub games are played. Q❀🛏◗♿🚌(X1)♣P

Swanton Morley

Angel

66 Greengate, NR20 4LX (on B1147 towards S edge of village) TG012162

⏲ 12-11; 12-10 (8 winter) Sun

☎ (01362) 637407 🌐 theangelpub.co.uk

Hop Back Summer Lightning; Mighty Oak Oscar Wilde; Woodforde's Wherry Best Bitter; guest beers 🄷

Parts of this large-fronted old inn date back to 1610 and boast a connection with Abraham Lincoln. The present owners are keen CAMRA members and five beers are available. The pub has three rooms – a spacious main bar with real fire, a dining room serving food lunchtimes and evenings, and a small games room with pool and darts. The extensive garden includes a bowling green. The pub now hosts two beer festivals each year at Easter and in November. ♨❀◑◗🚌(4)♣P⚟

Thetford

Albion

93-95 Castle Street, IP24 2DN (opp Castle Hill)

⏲ 12-11 (11.30 Thu); 11-12.30am Fri & Sat; 12-11 Sun

☎ (01842) 752796

Greene King IPA, Abbot 🄷

Small, comfortable pub in a row of flint cottages, in a quiet area close to the town centre, which looks out over scenic Castle Park and the earthworks of Castle Hill. A friendly welcome is always to be found, either in the conversational main bar or the lower room with a pool table and darts. There is an intimate patio for relaxed drinking in good weather, with quiz nights twice a week. No food is served but you can eat takeaways in the pub. ♨❀⚟

Thornham

Lifeboat

Ship Lane, PE36 6LT (signed off A149 coast road)

⏲ 11-11 (10.30 Sun)

☎ (01485) 512236 🌐 lifeboatinn.co.uk

Adnams Bitter; Greene King IPA, Abbot; Woodforde's Wherry Best Bitter; guest beers Ⓗ
On the edge of the saltmarsh, just off the coast road, the Lifeboat retains the dark and cosy atmosphere of a smugglers' inn despite being part of an up-to-date hotel. Log fires and cosy oil lamps create a welcoming feel in winter; in summer the bar attracts many visitors. Whether sheltering from a northerly gale in January or relaxing after a day on the beach, this is a very comforting place for a pint. ⌂Q❀⌧◐▲⊟♣P

Thurlton

Queen's Head

Beccles Road, NR14 6RJ TM414984
5-11; 12-midnight Sat; 12-10 Sun
☎ (01508) 548667 queensheadthurlton.co.uk
Beer range varies Ⓗ
Large L-shaped single-roomed village pub with a separate restaurant. The pub is owned by a group of local residents who purchased it some years ago and leased it to two villagers. The three guest beers are constantly changing with at least one coming from a local brewery. Food is served Saturday lunchtime and evening and from 12-5pm on Sunday. ⌂❀◐P⁄–

Trunch

Crown

Front Street, NR28 0AH (opp church) TG287348
12-3, 5.30-11; 12-11 Fri & Sat; 12-11 Sun
☎ (01263) 722341 trunchcrown.co.uk
Batemans Dark Mild, XB Bitter, Valiant; Greene King IPA; guest beers Ⓗ
Trunch village is well worth taking a stroll around, with its ancient flint cottages and larger houses. Set in the middle of the village, the Crown is Bateman's only pub in the area and offers an excellent choice of beers, as well as frequently changing guests. The restaurant is open Wednesday to Sunday. The website has details of beer festivals and forthcoming events such as the monthly quiz night. Dogs are welcome in the bar. ⌂Q❀◐♿⊟(5,34)P

Walcott

Lighthouse Inn ✔

Coast Road, NR12 0PE (on B1159) TG359319
11-11
☎ (01692) 650371 lighthouseinn.co.uk
Beer range varies Ⓗ
This large family-friendly pub is located on the coast road between Cromer and Great Yarmouth. It has been owned and run by the same landlord for the past 20 years. Situated in a tourist area, the trade here is fairly seasonal, and the range of real ales is limited in winter months. In the summer, however, a rotating range of four real ales is available. The spacious garden has a family marquee during the high season. Hot food is available all day every day, including a children's menu. ⌂❀◐▲♣P

Warham All Saints

Three Horseshoes

Bridge Street, NR23 1NL (2 miles SE of Wells) TF948417
12-2.30, 6-11 (10.30 Sun)
☎ (01328) 710547
Greene King IPA; Woodforde's Wherry Best Bitter; guest beers Ⓗ/Ⓖ
Stone floors, scrubbed pine furniture and gas lighting set the tone for this pub which has been serving beers for nearly 300 years and is included in CAMRA's National Inventory. Its three connected rooms are filled with a jumble of antiques and pictures, with the traditional game of Norfolk Twister in the first bar. The pub is renowned for good plain cooking, featuring soups, pies and puddings. It can be busy with diners at lunchtime and in the early evening in summer, but is often quieter at other times. ⌂Q❀⌧◐♿▲♣●P

Wells-next-the-Sea

Albatros

The Quay, NR23 1AT (moored on quayside)
12-11 07979 087228 albatros.eu.com
Woodforde's Wherry Best Bitter, Nelson's Revenge Ⓖ**; guest beer** Ⓗ
The Albatros is a North Sea clipper sailing ship built in 1899 and is the last commercial sailing boat of this type in the UK. It has been based in Wells harbour since 2001. The bar situated in the hold of the ship is adorned with much nautical memorabilia including many shipping maps. Live bands regularly perform here. The boat can be hired out for private charters, so please note it is occasionally at sea. Also, being a 19th-century vessel, there is no disabled access. ⌧◐⊟(36)

West Acre

Stag

Low Road, PE32 1TR
12-3, 6.30-11 (closed Mon winter); 12-11 Fri; 6.30-11 Sat; 12-3, 6.30-11 Sun
☎ (01760) 755395 westacrestag.co.uk
Beer range varies Ⓗ
The pub is situated at the east end of picturesque West Acre, a village renowned for its theatre in the priory ruins. Voted local CAMRA Pub of the Year 2005, a choice of three ever-changing real ales is available, mostly from local micro-breweries. Regular events are staged here, including beer festivals. Camping is available by prior arrangement. No dogs are allowed in the bar. There are water troughs for horses at the back of the large car park. A good walking and cycling area in summer. ⌂Q❀◐⊕♿▲♣P

Weybourne

Ship

The Street, NR25 7SZ (on A149 coast road) TG111430
11-3, 6-11; 11-midnight Fri & Sat; 11-11 Sun
☎ (01263) 588721 shipinnweybourne.co.uk
Woodforde's Wherry Best Bitter; guest beers Ⓗ
Situated at the heart of this attractive north Norfolk coastal village, the pub comprises three dining areas and a bar, all decorated with seaside-themed photos and ornaments. Three to six ales are on offer, usually from local brewers such as Woodforde's, Grain, Humpty Dumpty and Yetman's. Home-cooked food is available lunchtimes and evenings. There is also a function room. The pub is close to the Muckleburgh Military Vehicle Museum, and North Norfolk Railway's Weybourne Station is about a mile up the hill. ⌂◐▲⊟P⁄–

Wicklewood

Cherry Tree

116 High Street, NR18 9QA TG075022
12-2.30, 6-11; 12-1am Fri & Sat; 12-midnight Sun
(01953) 606962 thecherrytreewicklewood.co.uk
Buffy's Bitter, Polly's Folly, Hopleaf, Norwegian Blue H/G; **guest beers** H
Buffy's first tied house. The L-shaped bar boasts an unusual naturally curved bar top made from planks of solid oak. Home-cooked food is available lunchtimes and evenings and all day at weekends. The pub hosts evening entertainment including a monthly quiz night, bingo, jam session and folk night, and a Chase the Ace game on Sunday lunchtime. P

Winfarthing

Fighting Cocks

The Street, IP22 2ED (on B1077) TM108858
12-3 (closed Mon), 6-11; 12-5 Sun
(01379) 643283
Adnams Bitter H/G; **guest beer** H
This comfortable pub comprises a large beamed bar with an open log fire in winter and a separate games room which has a pool table and dartboard. There is a small outside seating area at the back of the pub. The inn is noted for its food, available Tuesday to Saturday. The Adnams can be served from the cask behind the bar or by handpump. The house beer is brewed by Elgood's and is complemented by a regularly-changing guest ale. P

Winterton-on-Sea

Fisherman's Return

The Lane, NR29 4BN (off B1159) TG495194
11-2.30, 6-11; 11-11 Sat; 12-10.30 Sun
(01493) 393305 fishermans-return.com
Adnams Bitter, Broadside; Woodforde's Wherry Best Bitter, Norfolk Nog; guest beers H
Friendly 17th-century pub in an attractive coastal village. A traditional brick and flint exterior gives way to interesting memorabilia inside. Log fires add to the ambience in winter and the range of beers is complemented by Westons Old Rosie cider. Meals are home prepared using local produce when available and may be enjoyed in the bar or the cosy dining room. A separate function/family room caters for all occasions. Three en-suite bedrooms are available all year. Close to the beach, the Broads and the resort of Great Yarmouth. QP

Woodbastwick

Fur & Feather Inn

Slad Lane, NR13 6HQ (just off B1140) TG328151
11.30-3, 6-11; 12-10.30 Sun
(01603) 720003 thefurandfeatherinn.co.uk
Woodforde's Mardlers, Wherry Best Bitter, Sun Dew, Nelson's Revenge, Norfolk Nog, Admiral's Reserve, Headcracker G
This charming thatched pub is set in the heart of the Broadland countryside, with friendly staff providing a warm welcome. The enticing decor is complemented by oak furniture and leather sofas. The long bar boasts two dining areas, one at each end, where high quality home-cooked food is available lunchtimes and evenings. Located next to Woodforde's Broadland Brewery, the full range of its award-winning ales is served straight from the cask. QP

Wymondham

Feathers Inn

13 Town Green, NR18 0PN
11-2.30, 7-11; 11-2.30, 6-midnight Fri; 11-2.30, 7-11.30 Sat; 12-2.30, 7-10.30 Sun
(01953) 605675
Adnams Bitter; Fuller's London Pride; Greene King Abbot; guest beers H
Situated just a short walk from Wymondham Abbey, the Feathers is an excellent local pub dating from the early 18th century. It has a cosy bar with alcoves and walls adorned with farming and other memorabilia including an old bicycle. The real ale range includes two guest beers plus the house beer, Feathers Tickler, brewed by Elgood's.

Railway

Station Road, NR18 0JY (next to station)
11.30-11; 12-10.30 Sun
(01953) 605262 therailwaypub.com
Adnams Bitter, Broadside; guest beers H
A short walk from the town centre brings you to this pub next to the railway station. The walls of the comfortable split-level interior feature many photos, railway memorabilia and other pictures. Four real ales, two from Adnams and two guests, are available. This food-oriented pub offers a bar and restaurant menu including many vegetarian dishes. Recent additions include a large covered patio at the rear where customers can smoke. P

Choosing pubs

CAMRA members and branches choose the pubs listed in the Good Beer Guide. There is no payment for entry, and pubs are inspected on a regular basis by personal visits; publicans are not sent a questionnaire once a year, as is the case with some pub guides. CAMRA branches monitor all the pubs in their areas, and the choice of pubs for the guide is often the result of democratic vote at branch meetings. However, recommendations from readers are welcomed and will be passed on to the relevant branch: write to Good Beer Guide, CAMRA, 230 Hatfield Road, St Albans, Hertfordshire, AL1 4LW; or send an email to **gbgeditor@camra.org.uk**

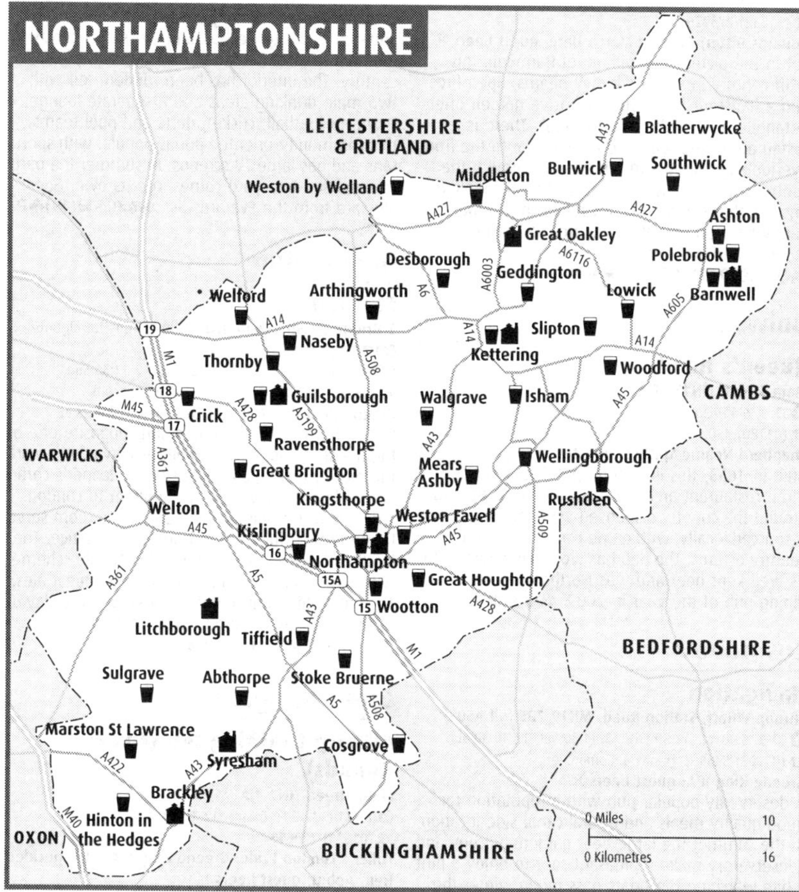

Abthorpe

New Inn

Silver Street, NN12 8QR SP648465

12-2.30 (not Mon & Tue), 6-11 (11.30 Sat); 12-4, 7-10.30 Sun

☎ (01327) 857306

Hook Norton Hooky Bitter, Old Hooky Ⓗ

This quintessentially English pub is hard to find, tucked away on a back street, though it is definitely worth the search. The dining room offers a venue for fine dining in the evening. Much of the food is locally sourced, including meat from the owners' farm. Dating back to the early 19th century, the pub is built from local stone and has an inglenook fireplace. Ales come from Hook Norton, including the house beer Abthorpe Ale, as well as occasional guest beers.

Arthingworth

Bull's Head

Kelmarsh Road, LE16 8JZ (off A508)

12-3, 6-11; 12-10.30 Sun

☎ (01858) 525637 thebullsheadonline.co.uk

Thwaites Original, Lancaster Bomber; guest beers Ⓗ

The Bull's Head is a 19th-century converted farmhouse set in a rural village in rolling countyside. Inside is an L-shaped bar, log fires and secluded drinking areas, together with a separate dining room with a menu utilising local produce in home-cooked meals. The pub was threatened with closure a few years ago but was saved by a local campaign and now goes from strength to strength. Two guest ales are usually available and a popular August bank holiday beer festival is held each year. Q P

Ashton

Chequered Skipper

The Green, PE8 5LD

11.30-3, 6-midnight; 11.30-midnight Sat; 12-11.30 Sun

☎ (01832) 273494 chequeredskipper.co.uk

Brewster's Hophead; guest beers Ⓗ

This stone and thatch pub is set in the centre of the Rothschild's model village of Ashton. The pub comprises a 70-seater restaurant, reception area, roof-top terrace, modern pub/family area and a function room. The village green outside is the scene of the annual World Conker Championship held in October. The pub also hosts two annual beer and cider festivals. Q P

Barnwell

Montagu Arms ✓

PE8 5PH

12-3 (not Mon), 6-11; 12-11 Sat; 12-10.30 Sun

☎ (01832) 273726
Adnams Bitter; Digfield March Hare; guest beers Ⓗ
Set in the picturesque village of Barnwell, this 16th-century inn boasts heavy beams, open fires and a flagstone floor. The extensive garden offers petanque and children's play areas. There is a restaurant to the rear, and a public bar to the front overlooking the stream which runs through the centre of the village. Good use of local suppliers ensures that the food is always fresh. A regular happy hour on real ales runs from 6-7pm on Monday and Wednesday.
⩕Q❀◑♿(24)♣P

Bulwick

Queen's Head

Main Street, NN17 3DY
⏲ 12-3, 6-11; closed Mon; 12-4.30, 7-10.30 Sun
☎ (01780) 450272
Shepherd Neame Spitfire; guest beers Ⓗ
Built in 1653, this limestone pub has a bar and three restaurant areas. It offers five real ales from around the country dispensed via handpump. Food is sourced locally, with game coming from the local country estates. The pub has won many awards for its well kept beer and was Northamptonshire dining pub of the year in 2009. ⩕Q❀◑♣P

Cosgrove

Navigation

Thrupp Wharf, Station Road, MK19 7BE (off A508)
⏲ 12-3, 5.30-11 (11.30 Fri); 12-11.30 Sat; 12-10.30 Sun
☎ (01908) 543156 🌐 navigationinn.net
Greene King IPA; guest beers Ⓗ
A deservedly popular pub with a reputation for good quality meals and a rural canal-side location. In the summer the large beer garden, balcony and conservatory make a pleasant spot to enjoy a pint while watching the boats pass by. In winter the real fire creates a cosy atmosphere inside. Drinkers and diners mix in the spacious bar and there is a separate restaurant. A seasonal and guest beer are available. On Friday there are two additional guest beers and live music is hosted. ⩕❀◑P

Crick

Royal Oak

22 Church Street, NN6 7TP
⏲ 2-11; 12-midnight Sat; 12-10.30 Sun
☎ (01788) 822340
Black Sheep Best Bitter; guest beers Ⓗ
Near the village church, this welcoming, wood-beamed, cottage-style free house is hidden away from the main A428. The interior features a large collection of pump clips from an ever-changing beer range, with up to 12 guest ales available weekly. Open fires warm the two main drinking areas, giving the pub a cosy feel. Northants skittles and darts are played in the games room, and there is a function room which can be booked with catering on request. Chinese takeaway food is available. ⩕Q❀◑♣

Desborough

George

79 High Street, NN14 2NB
⏲ 11-midnight (1am Fri & Sat); 12-midnight Sun
☎ (01536) 760271
Everards Beacon, Tiger; guest beer Ⓗ
Situated opposite Desborough Cross, this coaching inn built in local ironstone dates from the 17th century. The interior has been modernised with two main drinking areas and a separate lounge. Home to football, cricket, darts and pool teams, this community-oriented pub is popular with sports fans and has large TV screens. In summer the part-covered sun-trap yard comes into its own. Guest ales are from the Everards list. ❀◑♿(19)♣P

Geddington

Star Inn

2 Bridge Street, NN14 1AZ (follow signs for Eleanor Cross)
⏲ 12-3, 6-11.30 (midnight Fri & Sat); 12-11.30 Sun
☎ (01536) 742386 🌐 star-inn-geddington.com
Greene King IPA; Nobby's Best; guest beers Ⓗ
Dating from 1817, the pub stands opposite one of the finest Eleanor crosses, built by Edward I to mark the nightly resting places of Queen Eleanor's coffin on her last journey from Nottingham to London. Three areas including a separate dining room serve home-cooked food made from local produce. The landlord is a keen supporter of the LocAle scheme, with two local beers among the three guest ales. The pub holds a quiz night every second Tuesday of the month, and an annual beer festival in September. ⩕❀◑♿♣P

Great Brington

Althorp Coaching Inn (Fox & Hounds)

Main Street, NN7 4JA
⏲ 11-11 (11.45 Fri & Sat); 12-10.30 Sun
☎ (01604) 770651
Fuller's London Pride; Greene King IPA, Old Speckled Hen, Abbot; guest beers Ⓗ
This wonderful stone-built, thatched pub has been serving the public since 1620. The bar is largely unspoilt with oak beams, a flagstone floor and open fireplace, and the dining area has a large inglenook. Outside there is an enclosed courtyard with tables leading to a flower-filled garden. Excellent food is served along with up to four guest ales. Althorp House, the former home of Princess Diana, is nearby. Very popular in the summer.
⩕Q❀◑P

Great Houghton

White Hart

39 High Street, NN4 7AF (off A428)
⏲ 12-3, 5.30 (6 Sat)-11.30; 12-4, 7-10.30 Sun
☎ (01604) 762940
Everards Tiger; Greene King IPA; guest beers Ⓗ

INDEPENDENT BREWERIES

Cherwell Valley Brackley
Digfield Barnwell
Frog Island Northampton
Great Oakley Great Oakley
Hoggleys Litchborough
Julian Church Kettering (NEW)
Nobby's Guilsborough
Potbelly Kettering
Rockingham Blatherwycke
Silverstone Syresham (NEW)

An inn, tavern or ale house of some kind has stood on the site of the existing White Hart since the late 14th century. Parts of the existing building are thought to be 17th century. Today this stone-built, thatched pub is warm and welcoming. Good, reasonably priced food is served daily in three dining and drinking areas. The excellent garden is popular in warmer weather. Q❀◑⊟P

Guilsborough

Ward Arms

High Street, NN6 8PY

⏲ 12-2.30, 5-11; closed Mon & Tue winter; 12-midnight Fri & Sat; 12-11 Sun

☎ (01604) 740265

Brakspear Bitter; Nobby's Best, Guilsborough Gold; guest beers Ⓗ

This 17th-century pub is situated in the heart of the village next to the old grammar school, and has been visited by royalty. Built from local ironstone with white rendering and a thatched roof, the old stables have been converted into Nobby's Brewery, with a visitor centre planned. A selection of Nobby's beers plus guest ales from the SIBA direct delivery scheme are on handpump. Traditional home-cooked food is served, sourced from local suppliers. Live music plays on the last Saturday of the month. ⌂Q♨❀◑⊟♣●P⁄–⊓

Hinton in the Hedges

Crewe Arms

Sparrow Corner, NN13 5NF (off A43/A422)

⏲ 6-11 (midnight Thu-Sat); 12-11 Sun

☎ (01280) 705801

Hook Norton Hooky Bitter; guest beers Ⓗ

Tucked away down a lane in a village that can be hard to find, this is a genuine gem. Following a two year closure, the pub was bought by two local villagers who refurbished and redecorated throughout. The interior is divided into four comfortable areas and retains a traditional bar. Dining is popular here and guest beers often come from local micro-breweries. ⌂❀◗♿P

Isham

Lilacs ✔

39 Church Street, NN14 1HD (off A509 at church)

⏲ 12-3, 5.30-midnight; 12-1am Fri & Sat; 12-midnight Sun

☎ (01536) 723948

Greene King IPA, Ruddles Best, Abbot; guest beers Ⓗ

Named after a breed of rabbit, this hard-to-find village pub is at the heart of the community – popular with locals, diners and drinkers enjoying a well kept pint. The pub has a lounge and cosy snug at the front, complemented by a large games room towards the rear with two pool tables, darts and Northants skittles. Quiz and live music nights are held regularly. The guest beers are from the Greene King range. ⌂Q♨❀◐⊟🚌(X4)♣P⁄–

Kettering

Alexandra Arms

39 Victoria Street, NN16 0BU

⏲ 2-11; 12-midnight Fri & Sat; 12-11 Sun

☎ (01536) 522730

Beer range varies Ⓗ

Several times local CAMRA Pub of the Year, this back-street local just gets better and better. It now has 14 handpumps serving an interesting range of beers from new and unusual micros. Julian Church Brewery is now brewing in the cellar on the former Nobby's plant and at least one of its beers is available at all times. The front bar is covered with pump clips and the larger back bar is home to Northants skittles and pool. No under 14s are permitted. If you visit just one pub in Northants, make it this one. Q❀⊨⊟⇌🚌♣⁄–

Beeswing

226 Rockingham Road, NN16 9AL (on A6003)

⏲ 11.30-11 (midnight Fri & Sat); 12-11 Sun

☎ (01536) 481790

Everards Beacon, Tiger, Sunchaser, Original, seasonal beers Ⓗ

A large, two-roomed, estate pub with the front bar divided into three areas – a lounge with large leather sofas and TV for football, a bar area and a dining area. A smaller room at the back, the Vault, is usually quiet, but no beer is served in this room. Not far from Kettering Town Poppies Football ground, well-behaved away fans are welcomed. ❀◑♿🚌(B,X1,X4)P⁄–

Cherry Tree ✔

Sheep Street, NN16 0AN (opp church)

⏲ 12-midnight; 11-1am Fri & Sat

☎ (01536) 514706

Wells Eagle IPA, Bombardier; guest beers Ⓗ

A short walk from the railway station, the Cherry Tree is a welcome new entry to the Guide. A single-room pub with a low ceiling, it is the oldest pub in town. Alongside the Wells' beers it offers two changing guests from the local Potbelly Brewery. Live music plays on Friday and Saturday nights, with jam sessions on Sunday. Drinking is permitted outside at the front of the pub. All buses into town stop opposite. Renowned for good-value lunches. ❀◐⇌🚌♣

Piper ✔

Windmill Avenue, NN15 6PS

⏲ 11-3, 6-11; 12-11 Sun

☎ (01536) 513870

Hook Norton Hooky Bitter; guest beers Ⓗ

This 1950s two-roomed pub is run by an enthusiastic CAMRA member who offers six changing beers from the Enterprise Inns direct delivery scheme. There is a quiet lounge serving home-cooked food until 10pm complemented by a more lively bar/games room. Sunday night is quiz night, and two beer festivals are held each year. An outdoor area opposite the pub is ideal during the summer months. Ideal for visitors to Wicksteed Park, Britain's first theme park. Q❀◑⊟♿🚌(X4)♣●P⁄–

Shire Horse

18 Newland Street, NN16 8JH

⏲ 11-11; 12-10.30 Sun

☎ (01536) 519078

Tetley Bitter, Burton Ale; guest beers Ⓗ

Down-to-earth locals' pub providing a welcome respite from the busy town centre. Traditional games are played in the open-plan bar where numerous pump clips are displayed, reflecting the many frequently-changing guest beers that have been through the two guest ale handpumps. Motorcycle prints adorn the walls. A wide selection of music is played. Bus stops are next door and across the road. ❀⇌🚌♣●⁄–

Kingsthorpe

Queen Adelaide

50 Manor Road, NN2 6QJ (off A519)
✪ 11.30-11; 12-10.30 Sun
☎ (01604) 714524 ⊕ queenadelaide.com
Adnams Bitter, Broadside; Copper Dragon Golden Pipin; guest beers [H]
The 'Ade' was once a village inn but has now been swallowed up by the expansion of Northampton. This friendly, three-roomed pub has retained an olde-worlde feel in the public bar area with low beams and an uneven floor. Four guest ales often include local micro-brewery beers, and a cider or perry is always available. A beer festival is held on the first weekend in September. Sunday is quiz night. Local CAMRA Pub of the Year runner-up in 2007. ❀◑⊟♿⊡♣●P⁄–

Kislingbury

Sun Inn

6 Mill Road, NN7 4BB
✪ 11.30-2.30, 5-11; 11.30-3, 6-midnight Sat; 11.30-3.30, 7-11.30 Sun
☎ (01604) 833571
Hoggleys Kislingbury Bitter; Phipps IPA; Wadworth 6X; guest beers [H]
This thatched building has four cosy areas inside, adorned with pub memorabilia. Alongside the regular beers, six further handpumps offer guest ales and traditional cider from Thatchers or Rich's in summer. Northants skittles and darts can be played in addition to other traditional table games. A family-friendly garden, complete with barbecue, small koi-filled pond and aviary, is popular in warmer weather. ❀◑⊡♣●P⁄–

Lowick

Snooty Fox

Main Street, NN14 3BH (off A6116)
✪ 12-11 (midnight Fri & Sat); closed Tue; 12-6 Sun
☎ (01832) 733434 ⊕ snootyinns.com
Greene King IPA; guest beers [H]
This lovely stone building was a dower house on part of the Drayton Manor Estate until 1700 when it became the White Horse inn. Gutted and then renamed in the 1980s, the interior is flagstoned throughout with low beams. There are several inter-connecting areas on different levels, separated by large inglenooks and stone walls. The three guest beers are sourced from local micros including Digfield, Potbelly and Great Oakley. An open mike session is held on the first Wednesday of the month. ⩩❀◑♿P

Marston St Lawrence

Marston Inn

The Green, OX17 2DB (off A422/B4525)
✪ 12 (12.30 Sat)-2.30 (not Mon), 5-11 (midnight Fri & Sat); 12-5 Sun
☎ (01295) 711906
Hook Norton Hooky Bitter, Old Hooky, seasonal beer [H]
You are guaranteed a lively, enthusiastic welcome from the magician landlord and landlady at this family-friendly pub. Well worth seeking out, it has two small linked rooms, one with a piano, the other with a bar billiards table. A further two rooms are used as dining areas. The pub blossoms in the summer with extended hours, live entertainment in the large garden and an Aunt Sally skittles alley. There are camping/caravan facilities within the grounds. Guest ales come from Hook Norton.
⩩❀◑⅄♣P⁄–

Mears Ashby

Griffin's Head

28 Wilby Road, NN6 0DX
✪ 12-3, 5-11; 12-midnight Fri & Sat; 12-11 Sun
☎ (01604) 812945
Black Sheep Best Bitter; guest beers [H]
Set back from the road behind a garden, this 19th-century, Victorian-style village pub is popular with locals and visitors alike. It has a central bar and several drinking areas, including a comfortable room to the rear with leather sofas. A Northants skittles table has recently been reinstated, complementing the darts and shove ha'penny board. The four guest beers are normally from family brewers and a local micro-brewery.
Q❀◑♣P

Middleton

Red Lion

7 The Hill, LE16 8YX (off A427)
✪ 12-3, 6-11; 12-midnight Sat & Sun
☎ (01536) 771268
Great Oakley Wot's Occuring; guest beers [H]
A traditional village pub with four rooms and a central bar, located close to East Carlton Country Park. Popular with families, it has a large garden, good food and comfortable seating. There is a games area including Northants table skittles. The pub is a member of the LocAle scheme, offering regular beers from Great Oakley and Potbelly breweries. The pub participates in the unique Welland Valley Beer Festival in June.
⩩Q❀⊨◑⊡♣P⁄–

Naseby

Royal Oak

Church Street, NN6 6DA
✪ 4.30-11.30; 3-midnight Sat; 12-7 Sun
☎ (07985) 408240
Beer range varies [H]
This traditional brick-built village pub is close to the site where the famous Battle of Naseby was fought in 1645. The pub dates from the 1930s, with an L-shaped single room interior divided into three separate spaces. The lounge area is adorned with shelves of knick-knacks and plates on the wall. Northants skittles, pool and darts are played in the games area. Five ever-changing beers are on offer at all times, often from local micro-breweries. Adjoining barns host popular beer festivals in April on the St George's Day weekend and in October.
⩩Q♘❀⊟♿⅄♣●P⁄–

Northampton

Lamplighter

66 Overstone Road, NN1 3JS
✪ 5 (4 Fri)-11 (midnight Fri); 12-midnight Sat; 12-6 Sun
☎ (01604) 631125
Beer range varies [H]
Delightful, traditional, street-corner local near the town centre, just a short walk from the bus station. The welcoming single bar/lounge is on a split level

with soft furnishings. Above the bar is a soft canopy bearing the pub's name. Quizzes are held on Wednesday and Friday nights. Four changing guest beers are available, mostly from micro-breweries. Food is available until 8pm Monday to Saturday and 4pm on Sunday. ❀◑⊟♣≒

Malt Shovel Tavern

121 Bridge Street, NN1 1QF (opp Carlsberg Brewery)
⊙ 11.30-3, 5-11; 12-3, 7-10.30 Sun
☎ (01604) 234212
Frog Island Natterjack; Fuller's London Pride; Great Oakley Wot's Occurring, Harpers; Tetley Bitter; guest beers Ⓗ
Popular, award-winning pub just off the town-centre drinking circuit. The brewery tap for the Great Oakley Brewery, its beers are prominent among the 14 handpumps. Bottled and draught Belgian beers are available as well as a real cider. Breweriana adorns the pub, much of it from Phipps NBC Brewery which once stood opposite the pub. Beer festivals are held at least twice a year, and blues gigs on Wednesday evening. A quiz night is held on the first Thursday of the month. Well worth a visit. Q❀◐♿⇌⊟♣●≒

Racehorse

15 Abington Square, NN1 4AE
⊙ 12-midnight (1am Sat)
☎ (01604) 631997
Beer range varies Ⓗ
A relaxed and friendly pub attracting an eclectic clientele of all ages. The wood-panelled bar has bench seating and Dickensian-style bow windows to the street front. A varied range of up to eight real ales regularly includes local micro-brewery beers. Draught and bottled continental beers also feature, and cider may be available from the barrel. A quiz is held on a Monday and live bands play on the stage in the remote back bar. ❀⊟●≒

Road to Morocco

Bridgewater Drive, Abington Vale, NN3 3AG (off A4500 near Abington)
⊙ 12-11 (midnight Fri & Sat); 12-10.30 Sun
☎ (01604) 632899
Greene King IPA, Abbot; Theakston Old Peculier; guest beers Ⓗ
A popular and welcoming two-roomed estate pub run by a landlord who enthusiastically promotes real ale. There are up to four guests beers available at any one time as well as three regulars. Numerous themed events are held, with pool and darts played in the lively public bar, and a Tuesday night quiz and Thursday night poker game held in the quieter lounge bar. ❀⊕⊟♣P≒

Romany

Trinity Avenue, NN2 6JN (½ mile E of Kingsthorpe)
⊙ 11.30-11.30; 12-11 Sun
☎ (01604) 714647
Beer range varies Ⓗ
Large, two-roomed, 1930s pub offering up to eight changing ales, with beers from local breweries often featuring as well as brews from Newby Wyke. Westons cider and perry are also available. The lounge has live music on Thursday and Saturday, karaoke on Friday and a quiz night on Monday. Now owned by the McManus Pub Co, the commitment to real ale remains. CAMRA members receive a discount on Tuesday and Wednesday. ❀⊕⊟♣●P≒

Victoria Inn

2 Poole Street, NN1 3EX
⊙ 12-midnight (1am Fri & Sat)
☎ (01604) 633660
Vale VPA; guest beers Ⓗ
Difficult to find but well worth it, the Victoria is owned by Vale Brewery but its eight handpumps offer mostly guest beers, and three bottled Chimay beers are also stocked. The single-roomed Victorian corner local is always bustling, with curry and cask ale nights, and quizzes on Tuesday and Wednesday. On Thursday, Friday and Saturday live music features, and Sunday lunch is ever popular. There is a small outside decked area to the rear to get a breath of fresh air. Thursday is the only evening food is served. ❀♣≒

Polebrook

Kings Arms ✔

Kings Arms Lane, PE8 5LW
⊙ 12-3, 6-11 (midnight Fri); 12-11.30 Sat; 12-11 Sun
☎ (01832) 272363 🌐 thekingsarms-polebrook.co.uk
Adnams Bitter; Digfield Barnwell Bitter; guest beers Ⓗ
Traditional, thatched, stone public house in the middle of the small village of Polebrook. The three-sided bar boasts four handpumps with unusual wooden handles. The drinking area is open with an inglenook fireplace dividing the restaurant and bar area. A good-sized enclosed garden is ideal for children to play. There is an extensive food menu with specials and a tapas board. Guest beers from Digfield Ales are a permanent fixture.
⌂Q❀◑♿⊟(15,25)♣P

Ravensthorpe

Chequers

Chequers Lane, NN6 8ER (between A428 and A5199)
⊙ 12-3, 6-11; 12-11 Sat; 12-3, 7-10.30 Sun
☎ (01604) 770379
Greene King IPA; Jennings Bitter; guest beers Ⓗ
Brick-built Grade II-listed free house situated opposite the church in this quite sprawling village, popular with locals, walkers and fishermen. The hosts, who have been here many years, always give a warm welcome. An extensive menu of good value food is served, along with two guest ales. Outside, there is an adventure play area for children and a building for Northants skittles.
♞❀◑⊟♣

Rushden

Rushden Historic Transport Society

Station Approach, NN10 0AW
⊙ 7.30 (12 Sat)-11; 12-3, 7.30-10.30 Sun
☎ (01933) 318988 🌐 rhts.co.uk
Fuller's London Pride; Oakham Bishops Farewell; guest beers Ⓗ
A hidden gem, this is a converted railway station waiting room. The unique lounge with a Northants skittles table is in part of a former Royal Mail parcel van. Many times Local CAMRA Club of the Year and National Winner in 2000, the Station offers five guest ales. Visitors are charged £1 per person or couple. Open weekends are held in the summer and there is a steam rally in May. The museum is open on summer Sundays. ⌂Q❀♿♣≒▯

Slipton

Samuel Pepys

Slipton Lane, NN14 3AR (off A6116)
12-3, 6-11; 12-11 Sat & Sun
☎ (01832) 731739 🌐 samuel-pepys.com
Greene King IPA [H]**; Hop Back Summer Lightning** [G]**; Oakham JHB** [H]**; Potbelly Aisling** [G]**; guest beers** [H]/[G]
A popular ironstone pub dating from the 16th century and encompassing several drinking and dining areas. To the front is a traditional low beamed bar with brick flooring and leather chairs, while the main lounge bar is to the side. There are further intimate drinking areas to the rear, with the main restaurant in the conservatory. The guest beer on handpump is either from Digfield or Potbelly, and two futher guests are on gravity, often from other local micro-brewers.
Q❀◑▶ (16)P

Southwick

Shuckburgh Arms

Main Street, PE8 5BL
12-2, 6-11; closed Mon; 12-3, 6-9 Sun
☎ (01832) 274007
Fuller's London Pride; guest beers [H]
Adjacent to the village hall, this pub has two rooms – one with the bar and a large real fire, the other a restaurant for diners. The spacious enclosed garden at the rear is adjacent to the village cricket pitch and used by campers in summer. Food is popular and well priced. Two beers are available during winter and three in summer.
Q❀◑▶ ♿ (24)P

Stoke Bruerne

Boat Inn

Shutlanger Road, NN12 7SB (opp canal museum)
11-11; 12-10.30 Sun
☎ (01604) 862428 🌐 boatinn.co.uk
Banks's Bitter; Frog Island Best Bitter; Jennings Cumberland Ale; Marston's Burton Bitter, Pedigree, Old Empire [H]
Situated on the banks of the Grand Union Canal opposite the canal museum, the Boat Inn has been run by the same family since 1877. The delightful tap bar comprises several small interconnecting rooms, with open fires, wooden seats in the windows and paintings of canal scenes on the walls. A large, modern extension houses the lounge bar with its vaulted wooden ceiling, restauarant and bistro. Northants skittles is played. A guest beer is often available.
Q❀◑▶ ♿ (86)♣P

Sulgrave

Star Inn

Manor Road, OX17 2SA
11-3, 6-11; 12-5, 6-9.30 Sun
☎ (01295) 760389
Hook Norton Hooky Bitter, Old Hooky, seasonal beers [H]
Set in the beautiful village of Sulgrave, this lovely 300-year-old stone pub is picturesque in the summer with its hanging baskets. It is situated almost opposite Sulgrave Manor, the ancestral home of the George Washington family. The traditional front bar area is relatively unchanged with a flagstone floor, beamed ceiling and inglenook fireplace, and there is also a small, intimate dining area. To the rear is the restaurant where quality home-cooked food is prepared by the French owners. Q❀◑▶P

Thornby

Red Lion

Welford Road, NN6 8SJ (on A5199)
12-2.30, 5-11; 12-11 Sat & Sun
☎ (01604) 740238
Greene King IPA; Smiles Old Tosser; Wadworth IPA; guest beers [H]
Friendly, traditional village pub dating back over 400 years. The three-roomed interior features wooden beams and a wood-burning open fire set up the chimney breast in the cosy lounge. There is also a compact restaurant. Collections of beer steins, tankards and paintings are displayed throughout. Five to seven handpumps offer regularly changing guest beers. Bottled beers are also on sale, including Samuel Smith Oatmeal Stout. Occasional entertainment includes live music. During the summer, classic car meetings are held along with pig roasts. ❀◑▶ ♣P

Tiffield

George Inn ✔

21 High Street, NN12 8AD (off A43)
12-3 (not Tue), 6-midnight; 5.30-1am Fri; 12-1am Sat; 12-7 Sun
☎ (01327) 350587 🌐 thegeorgeattiffield.co.uk
Greene King IPA; guest beers [H]
A popular village pub just outside Towcester dating from the 16th century with Victorian and more recent additions. Three rooms comprise a cosy bar, games room with Northants skittles and a larger room with an eclectic range of furniture and artwork. The bar stocks two changing guest beers and a real cider. Details of beers on tap and those coming on can be found on the pub's website. The George was voted local CAMRA Pub of the Season Spring 2008. ❀◑▶♣P

Walgrave

Royal Oak

Zion Hill, NN6 9PN (2 miles N of A43)
11.30-2.30, 5.30 (5 Fri & Sat)-11; 12-10.30 Sun
☎ (01604) 781248
Adnams Bitter; Greene King Abbot; guest beers [H]
A classic Northamptonshire stone village pub. The front steps lead to a central bar area flanked by two dining areas. The traditional interior features beams with hanging jugs and a stone inglenook fireplace. To the rear is a small, comfortable lounge bar, which leads to the function room. Across the yard is a games room with Northants skittles. The garden has children's play equipment. Three guest beers often come from Northamptonshire breweries. ❀◑▶ (39)♣P

Welford

Wharf Inn ✔

NN6 6JQ (on A5199 N of village)
12-11 (1am Thu-Sat); 12-10.30 Sun
☎ (01858) 575075
Banks's Bitter; Marston's Pedigree; guest beers [H]
This brick-built inn is situated at the end of the Welford Arm of the Grand Union Canal and is

popular with narrow boat travellers, locals and tourists alike. Several footpaths run close by, including the Jurassic Way. Three rotating guest beers often include one from a local micro-brewery. Beer festivals and themed events are held throughout the year. Wireless Internet access is available. ⌂❀⊭◐◑♿P

Wellingborough

Coach & Horses 🏆

17 Oxford Street, NN8 4HY

⏲ 12-midnight (6 Sun)

☎ (01933) 441848

Beer range varies [H]

Town-centre local fully committed to quality real ales. Up to 10 are available, with Adnams beers and local micros featuring regularly. Good, traditional home-cooked food is served lunchtimes and evenings. Lots of breweriana can be found in the front bar area which has a real fire. Sport on Sky TV is screened in the back bar area. The large garden has a heated smoking shelter. Free Wi-Fi is available. ⌂❀◐◑🚌♣⚲

Locomotive

111 Finedon Road, NN8 4AL (on A510)

⏲ 11 (12 Sun)-11

☎ (01933) 276600

Beer range varies [H]

Converted from three cottages, this is a popular locals' pub on the outskirts, not far from the railway. The railway theme runs throughout, with a display of classic '00' gauge locomotives behind the bar and a railway running above the bar. With three rooms, the front bar has a relaxed atmosphere with armchairs and a piano, while the other rooms are more traditional. A themed beer festival is held every bank holiday, and there is always an unusual beer among the seven ever-changing ales, including many from local breweries. ⌂❀◐⊟⇌🚌(45)♣P⚲

Welton

White Horse

High Street, NN11 2JP (off A361 betwen Rugby and Daventry)

⏲ 12-3, 5-11; 12-midnight Sat; 12-midnight Sun

☎ (01327) 702820

Black Sheep Best Bitter; Purity Gold; guest beers [H]

Rugby CAMRA Country Pub of the Year 2008, this two bar inn has a split level public bar in which darts and skittles are played. The lounge, with traditional beams, leads to a restaurant where the original brickwork of the building can be seen. Both bars are heated with wood burners. A large patio area with a canopy overlooks the garden. Restaurant and bar food are available, and children and dogs are welcome. Traditional cider is served in the summer. ⌂Q❀◐◑🚌♣●P⚲

Weston by Welland

Wheel & Compass

Valley Road, LE16 8HZ

⏲ 12-3, 6-11; 12-11 Fri & Sat; 12-10.30 Sun

☎ (01858) 565864

Banks's Bitter; Greene King Abbot; Marston's Burton Bitter, Pedigree; guest beers [H]

A multi-roomed pub in a rural location, popular with locals and visitors alike. This comfortable hostelry has a reputation for good quality food at reasonable prices: 'We do not serve fast food, we serve good food as fast as we can', is its motto. The large rear garden attracts families in summer, with benches and seats plus swings and slides for children. The pub offers two changing guest beers as well as the regular ales. ⌂Q❀◐◑P

Weston Favell

Bold Dragoon

48 High Street, NN3 3JW

⏲ 11.30-11.30; 12-3, 6-11.30 Sat; 12-10.30 Sun

☎ (01604) 401221

Fuller's London Pride; Greene King IPA, Abbot; guest beers [H]

This 1930s pub is situated in the heart of a village that was absorbed by the expansion of Northampton. Seven beers are always available, with four ever-changing guests regularly coming from local breweries. The lively bar has a pool table, darts and a sports TV. The lounge is quieter and the restaurant in the rear conservatory is a peaceful haven. The menu offers a wide choice of good quality food and bar snacks. Q❀◐◑⊟♿🚌♣P

Woodford

Duke's Arms

83 High Street, NN14 4HE (off A14/A510)

⏲ 12-11

☎ (01832) 732224

Greene King IPA, H&H Olde Trip, Abbot; guest beer [H]

This popular village pub overlooking the village green was once called the Lord's Arms, named after the Duke of Wellington, who was a frequent visitor to the village. A games-oriented pub, it features Northant skittles, darts and pool. Home-cooked food is served daily except Sunday evening. A beer festival is held on Whit Sunday bank holiday weekend. ⌂ᘓ❀◐◑⊟♿🚌(16)♣●P

Wootton

Wootton Working Men's Club

High Street, NN4 6LW (off A508 near jct 15 of M1)

⏲ 12-2 (not Wed & Thu), 7-11; 12-3, 7-11.30 Fri & Sat; 12-10.30 Sun

☎ (01604) 761863

Great Oakley Wot's Occurring; guest beer [H]

This ironstone building was rescued from closure by the regulars. It is now an award-winning club, with drinking areas including a bar, quiet lounge, live music room and games room with Northants skittles. Up to six changing guest beers are available. Show this Guide or a CAMRA membership card for admittance. Local CAMRA Club of the Year 2008. Q🚌♣P

> There can't be a good living where there is not good drinking.
> **Benjamin Franklin**

NORTHUMBERLAND

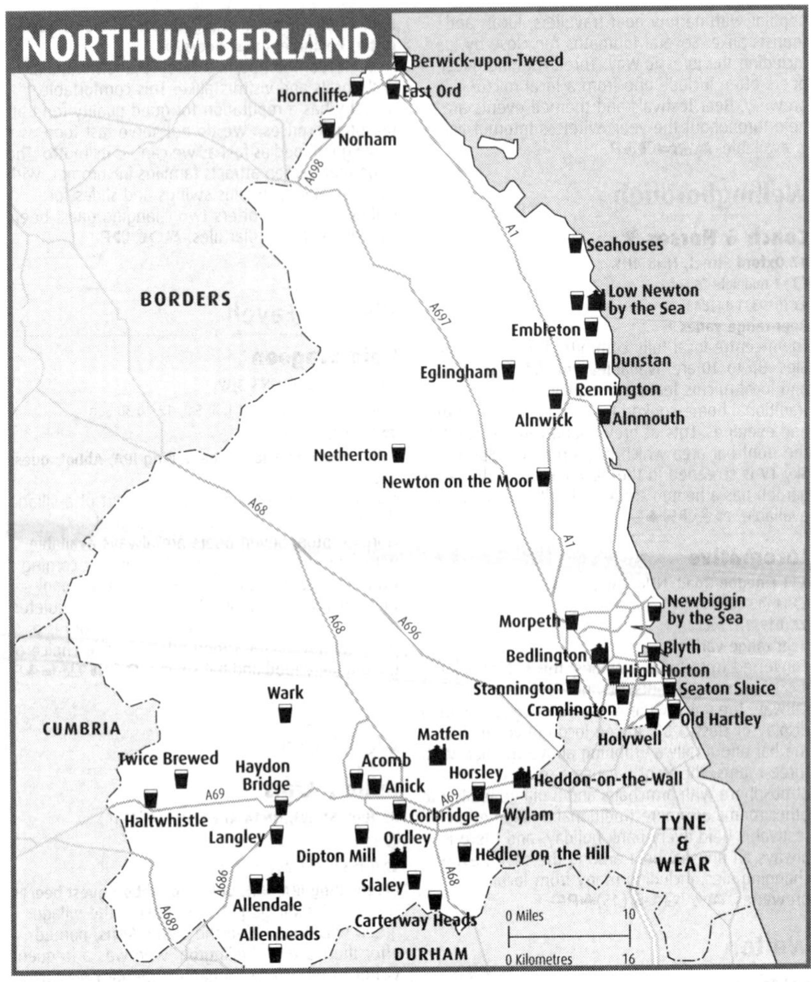

Acomb

Miners Arms

Main Street, NE46 4PW

5 (12 Sat & Sun)-midnight

☎ (01434) 603 909 theminersacomb.com

Mordue Five Bridge Bitter; Yates Bitter; guest beers [H]

Superb, traditional 1746 inn. Family run, the staff empathise with real ale drinkers. Ale is served in oversize glasses. The pub hosts regular music and folk nights. The bar, divided by a central staircase, has a genuine, cosy feel. The miners have long gone but this pub is a superb legacy that lives on in this popular hamlet. (880,882)

Sun Inn

Dene View, Main Street, NE46 4PW

12-11 (1am Fri & Sat)

☎ (01434) 602934

Beer range varies [H]

Updated stone pub located on Main Street. Not far from Hadrian's Wall, it attracts tourists as well as locals. Home to darts, dominoes, pool, football and quoits teams, the pub also has four B&B rooms. (880,882)

Allendale

Allendale Inn

NE47 9BY

12-midnight

☎ (01434) 683246

Greene King Old Speckled Hen; guest beers [H]

Pleasant pub nestling in the corner of Market Square – popular with visitors and locals. The pub is well supported and has darts, dominoes and pool teams. The nearby Allen Banks and superb countryside attract ramblers. Food served lunchtimes and early evenings. (688)

Golden Lion

Market Place, NE47 9BD

12-1.30am (2.30am Sun)

☎ (01434) 683225

Allendale Best Bitter, Wolf; Black Sheep Best Bitter; Wylam Gold Tankard [H]

A friendly and hospitable pub in the market place, home to sociable locals and their dogs. The walls are adorned with photographs of the annual tar barrel procession, an experience in itself. The pub has a late licence at the weekend, and is an outlet for Allendale Brewery's full range of bottled beers.

The local choir practises here on Tuesday evening, and there is live Irish music on the last Wednesday of the month. (688)

Kings Head

Market Place, NE47 9BD
12-midnight
(01434) 683681
Banks's Original; Jennings Cumberland Ale H
A welcoming, upmarket inn situated in the town square, next door to the Golden Lion. The refurbished bar retains original features including an open log fire. Traditional pub food is served all day. The hostelry is popular with ramblers, cyclists and day trippers taking advantage of the nearby countryside walks. Rail and bus links to Allendale are good, and this small market town is well worth seeking out. (688)

Allenheads

Allenheads Inn

NE47 9HJ
12-4, 7-11; 12-11 Sat & Sun
(01434) 685200
Black Sheep Best Bitter; Greene King Abbot; guest beers H
Superb rural pub, very popular with locals, ramblers and tourists. Originally the home of Sir Thomas Wentworth, the 18th-century multi-room building has a public bar with log fire, games room and dining room. Good bar meals are available at a decent price. The premises are adorned with memorabilia and knick-knacks from a bygone age. (688)P

Alnmouth

Red Lion Inn

22 Northumberland Street, NE66 2RJ
11 (12 Sun)-11
(01665) 830584 redlionalnmouth.com
Black Sheep Best Bitter; guest beers H
Listed in CAMRA's regional inventory of historic pub interiors, this charming 18th-century coaching inn features a cosy lounge bar with attractive woodwork. Three guest beers often come from northern English or Scottish micro-breweries. Panoramic views across the Aln estuary can be enjoyed from the decked area at the bottom of the garden. Occasional live music plays – open air in summer. Dogs are welcome. En-suite B&B accommodation is available. (518)P

Alnwick

John Bull Inn

12 Howick Street, NE66 1UY
12-3 (Sat only) 7-11; 12-3, 7-10.30 Sun
(01665) 602055 john-bull-inn.co.uk
Beer range varies H
Current CAMRA North Northumberland Pub of the Year winner, this 180-year-old inn thrives on its reputation as a 'back street boozer'. The passionate landlord offers four cask-conditioned ales at varying ABVs, real cider, the widest range of bottled Belgian beers in the county and 120 different single malt whiskies. There is a newly inaugurated darts team in the local league and the pub upholds the north-east tradition of an annual leek show. Q

Anick

Rat Inn

NE46 4LN (signed from Hexham A69 roundabout)
12-3, 6-11; 12-11 Sat & Sun
(01434) 602814 theratinn.com
Caledonian Deuchars IPA; Draught Bass; guest beers H
Superb 1750 country inn with spectacular views across Tyne Valley and a welcoming and friendly feel to it. An open log fire is surrounded by several chamber pots hanging from the ceiling. The pub has an excellent local reputation for good food prepared with locally sourced ingredients, now enhanced by inclusion in the prestigious Michelin Red Guide. Well worth the short taxi ride from Hexham Rail Station. QP

Berwick upon Tweed

Barrels Ale House

59-61 Bridge Street, TD15 1ES
11.30 (3 winter)-midnight; 11.30-1am (1-midnight winter) Fri & Sat; 12-midnight Sun
(01289) 308 013 thebarrels.co.uk
Shepherd Neame Spitfire; Stewart Pentland IPA; guest beers H
Characterful pub located in the old part of Berwick next to the original road bridge over the Tweed. Excellent real ale no doubt plays its part in encouraging customers to brave the dentist's chair at the side of the bar. The downstairs bar is used by DJs and bands at weekends. The unique rear open drinking area is surrounded by very high walls. A regular winner of local CAMRA Pub of the Year.

Pilot

31 Low Greens, TD15 1LX
12 (11 Sat)-midnight
(01289) 304214
Caledonian Deuchars IPA; guest beers H
Well patronised by locals and sought out by train trippers who have discovered this gem. The stone-built end of terrace pub dates from 19th century and is noted in CAMRA's Regional Inventory. It retains the original small room layout and boast several nautical artefacts over 100 years old. The pub runs darts and quoits teams and hosts music nights. The bar staff are welcoming and friendly.

Blyth

Olivers

60 Bridge Street, NE24 2AP
12 (2 Sat)-11; 12-10.30 Sun
(01670) 540356
Beer range varies H
This warm and friendly one-roomed hostelry was converted from a former newsagent's and is now an oasis within a real ale desert. It is situated close to the regenerated quayside of a port better known

INDEPENDENT BREWERIES

Allendale Allendale
Hexhamshire Ordley
High House Farm Matfen
Northumberland Bedlington
Ship Inn Low Newton by the Sea
Wylam Heddon on the Wall

for the FA Cup exploits of its famous Spartans Football Club. Three real ales are available, one usually locally sourced. (308)♣

Carterway Heads

Manor House Inn

DH8 9LX (on A68 S of Corbridge)
12-11 (11.30 Sun)
☎ (01207) 255268
Beer range varies Ⓗ
Excellent country inn run by a licensee keen on supporting local micros. The multi-room interior with three open fires has a comfortable and welcoming feel. Just off the A68, the pub is very popular with tourists. Proper home-cooked food is served made with local produce. Accommodation is available in four en-suite rooms.
♣P

Corbridge

Angel Inn

Main Street, NE45 5LA
11-11 (midnight Fri & Sat); 12-10.30 Sun
☎ (01434) 632119
Black Sheep Best Bitter; Durham Magus; Hadrian & Border Tyneside Blonde; Taylor Landlord; guest beers Ⓗ
Superb former 1726 coaching inn with a bar and separate lounge area with comfy leather seating. Family friendly, it has a reputation for good food as well as a wonderful selection of malt whiskies. Outside is a seating area for relaxed summer drinking. The town has strong links with the Romans and Hadrian's Wall is nearby. Located on the main road with good transport links, the pub is popular with tourists, ramblers and locals.
Q(602,604)P

Black Bull

Middle Street, NE45 5LE
11-11
☎ (01434) 632261
Greene King IPA, Ruddles County, Old Speckled Hen; guest beers Ⓗ
Traditional stone-built pub retaining several original features, with a separate dining area. Popular with the locals as well as visitors, it is situated in the heart of this much loved town, which has strong links to the Romans. It is well served by good transport links including Hadrian's Wall Tyne Valley Railway operated by Northern Rail. If there are two of you travelling by train ask for a duo return ticket – the second ticket is half price. (685)P

Dyvel's Inn ✔

Station Road, NE45 5AY (by railway station)
12-11
☎ (01434) 633633 dyvelsinn.co.uk
Caledonian Deuchars IPA; guest beers Ⓗ
Family-friendly country pub in an historic Tyne Valley town, easily accessible by train along the beautiful Tyne Valley, 20 minutes from Newcastle. It has a public bar and a separate dining area, but food is served throughout. The interior feels cosy in winter yet open and sunny in summer. There is a secluded garden and private car park. An ideal stop-off for visitors exploring the beautiful town and country walks on the doorstep. Three letting rooms are available. (602,685)P

Cramlington

Plough

Middle Farm Buildings, NE23 1DN
11-3, 6-11; 11-11 Fri & Sat; 12-10.30 Sun
☎ (01670) 737633
Greene King Ruddles County; guest beers Ⓗ
Owned by the Fitzgerald pub chain and located within the old village centre of Cramlington, now surrounded by new town development, this is a sympathetic conversion of what used to be farm buildings into a traditional pub, with a separate bar and lounge. Among the interesting architectural features is the former gin-gan in the lounge – a circular area in which a horse would be harnessed to a wheel to grind corn. The bar is smaller and busy, with doors leading to the outdoor seating area. Children are welcome during the day only.
P

Dipton Mill

Dipton Mill Inn

Dipton Mill Road, NE46 1YA
12-2.30, 6-11; 12-3 Sun
☎ (01434) 606577
Hexhamshire Devil's Elbow, Shire Bitter, Devil's Water, Whapweasel, Old Humbug Ⓗ
The tap for Hexhamshire Brewery, this small inn is run by a keen landlord who brews his own excellent beers. To complement the ales there is great home-cooked food. A cosy atmosphere and warm welcome make this pub well worth seeking out. The large garden has a stream running through it and there is plenty of countryside to explore.
QP

Dunstan

Cottage Inn

Dunstan Village, NE66 3SZ
12-11 (10.30 Sun)
☎ (01665) 576658 cottageinnhotel.co.uk
Beer range varies Ⓗ
A few minutes from the spectacular Northumbrian coastline, this inn set in woodland offers something for everyone. Surprisingly spacious, it has a bar, restaurant, conservatory and covered and open patios. Good food complements the excellent beer. Craster village, famed for its kippers, is half a mile away. The inn is ideally located for birdwatchers, walkers, golfers and tourists. Q

East Ord

Salmon Inn

TD15 2NS
11-3, 5-11; 11-11 Fri-Sun
☎ (01289) 305227
Caledonian Deuchars IPA, 80; Wells Bombardier Ⓗ
A prominent building situated on the main road by the impressive green. The L-shaped single-room village local has separate dining and drinking areas plus a welcoming real fire at its heart. The pub is proud of its locally-sourced food. There is a marquee in the garden, quoits team, leek club, barbecues and quiz nights. The hostelry is also well placed for the Tweed Cycle Way and fishing on the River Tweed. The 67 bus passes the door.
(67)P

Eglingham

Tankerville Arms

15 The Village, NE66 2TX
12-11 (12.30am Fri & Sat); 12-10.30 Sun
(01665) 578444
Black Sheep Best Bitter; Hadrian & Border Tyneside Blonde; guest beers H
Well-appointed, traditional country pub dating from 1851. The bar has several framed pictures that enhance the surroundings, and is complemented by an excellent open beam restaurant. Popular with tourists and ramblers, the pub also hosts meetings for local golf and cricket clubs. Dog and family friendly, it is well worth a visit. **Q P**

Embleton

Greys Inn ✔

Stanley Terrace, NE66 3XJ
12-11; winter hours vary; 12-10.30 Sun
(01665) 576983
Black Sheep Best Bitter; guest beers H
Pleasant, traditional pub located in this lovely seaside hamlet. The pub has three open fires and a framed 1904 grocery list hanging on the wall. This is an excellent venue to catch a bite to eat washed down with a locally-sourced real ale – hopefully sitting outside on the superb patio. A short walk takes you to a wonderful beach.
(501,518)

Haltwhistle

Black Bull

Market Square, NE49 0BL
7-11 Mon; 12-3, 6-11 Tue-Thu; 12-11 Wed-Sun
(01434) 320463
Caledonian Deuchars IPA; Fuller's London Pride; guest beers H
Warm, friendly two-room pub located just off Market Place down a cobbled lane. Close to Hadrian's Wall, it is popular with locals and ramblers. Inside, it has a traditional ambience with a low-beamed timber ceiling, horse brasses and an open fire. There are six handpulls to dispense the ales. Opening hours and food times vary – telephone first to check. **Q** (685)

Haydon Bridge

Railway

Church Street, NE47 6JG
11-midnight; 12-10.30 Sun
(01434) 684254
Black Sheep Best Bitter; Caledonian Deuchars IPA H
Homely, traditional one-room pub with an open fire and friendly customers and staff. Home-cooked food is available at reasonable prices. The pub is home to two cricket teams, and darts and domino teams. Folk and R&B evenings are hosted on the second and fourth Monday of the month.
(685)

Hedley on the Hill

Feathers

NE43 7SW
12 (6 Mon)-11
(01661) 843607 thefeathers.net
Hadrian & Border Gladiator; Mordue Workie Ticket; guest beers H
Much acclaimed country pub set in a pleasant hamlet with superb views of three counties. It has a genuine, comfy feel, with exposed stone walls and beams. The young and welcoming staff serve high quality home-cooked food that complements the real ales. A beer festival is held every Easter weekend with an uphill barrel race on the Monday. The pub has won awards for food quality – booking is recommended for Sunday lunch. **Q P**

High Horton

Three Horse Shoes

Hathery Lane, NE24 4HF (off A189 N of Cramlington, follow A192) N7276793
11-11 (midnight Fri & Sat); 12-11 Sun
(01670) 822410 3horseshoes.co.uk
Greene King Abbot; guest beers H
Extended former coaching inn at the highest point in the Blyth Valley, with views of the Northumberland coast. The pub is open plan with distinct bar and dining areas plus a conservatory. Privately owned and dedicated to real ale, it holds regular beer festivals, with real cider and perry also available. Guest ales are on offer from all over the country as well as local micro-breweries. Ask to see the impressive, modern cellar. An extensive range of meals and snacks is available. **Q P**

Holywell

Olde Fat Ox Inn

Hollywell Village, NE25 0LJ
12-11
(0191) 237 0964
Caledonian Deuchars IPA; guest beers H
Family-friendly, well-appointed former coaching inn, popular with cyclists and walkers. It holds regular theme nights and offers a selection of books if you fancy a quiet read while relaxing in the comfy leather seating. No meals are served but snacks – try a hot beef sandwich – tea and coffee are available, as well as a range of whiskies. The award-winning beer garden leads down to a local beauty spot, Holywell Dene, and there is a heated area for smokers. Dog friendly.

Horncliffe

Fishers Arms

Main Street, TD15 2XW
12-3 (2 Sun), 6-10.30
(01289) 386866
Beer range varies H
Traditional terraced pub in the village centre at the heart of community life, offering a monthly buskers' session, food themed nights, quiz nights, OAP lunch on Thursday, and the 'Hooky Mats' club on Wednesday lunchtime. The interior has separate dining and drinking areas, and reasonably priced home-cooked food is very popular. The Tweed Cycle Way is nearby. B&B accommodation is available. (67)

Horsley

Lion & Lamb ✔

NE15 0NS
12-11 (10.30 Sun)
(01661) 832952

Black Sheep Best Bitter; Caledonian Deuchars IPA; guest beers [H]
Originally a farmhouse in 1718, nearby Hadrian's Wall provided the stone to construct this building. It was converted to a coaching inn in 1744. 'Mind ya heed' is the greeting on entry to the low-beamed bar area, and wooden tables enhance the traditional ambience. Small rooms provide plenty of space including a comfy seating area with leather sofas. The pub has an excellent reputation for good food. ♨Q✿◐◑⊞🚌(685)P

Langley

Carts Bog Inn

NE47 5NW (3 miles off A69 on A686 to Alston)
⏲ 12-2.30 (not Mon), 5-11, 12-11 Sat; 12-10.30 Sun
☎ (01434) 684338
Beer range varies [H]
Excellent rural pub serving the local community at Langley as well as tourists. Built on the site of an ancient brewery (circa 1521), the building dates from 1730. The name is derived from a steeply banked corner on the old road where on wet days the horse-drawn carts were invariably bogged down. A large open fire divides the two rooms. The walls proudly display pictures of bygone days.
♨Q🐴✿◐◑P

Low Newton by the Sea

Ship Inn

Newton Square, NE66 3EL
⏲ 11-11; 12-10.30 Sun (winter hours vary)
☎ (01665) 576262 🌐 shipinnnewton.co.uk
Ship Inn Sandcastle at Dawn, Sea Coal, Sea Wheat, Ship Hop, Dolly Daydream [H]
Nestling at the corner of a three-sided row of former fishermen's cottages, this inn has a unique location virtually on the beach and graced by a small village green. The pub brews its own beer and does get busy. The excellent food menu makes good use of fresh, locally sourced ingredients. Opening times vary in winter so telephone first to check. The car park is a short walk away.
♨Q✿◐◑⊞🚭

Morpeth

Tap & Spile

23 Manchester Street, NE61 1BH
⏲ 12-2.30, 4.30-11; 12-11 Fri & Sat; 12-10.30 Sun
☎ (01670) 513 894
Everards Tiger; guest beers [H]
Cosy, popular local, welcoming to all and handy for the nearby bus station. It has a busy, narrow bar to the front and quieter lounge to rear. A good choice of ales is on offer, with brews from Northumbrian breweries often available. The real cider is Westons Old Rosie, and a selection of fruit wines comes from Lindisfarne Winery. A winner of local CAMRA awards. Q⊞⇌(Morpeth)🚌(Morpeth)♣🚭

Netherton

Star ★

NE65 7HD
⏲ hours vary
☎ (01669) 630238
Camerons Castle Eden Ale [G]
Entering this gem, the only pub in Northumberland to appear in every issue of the Guide, is like entering the private living room of a large house. Beer is served on gravity from the cellar at a hatch in the panelled entrance hall. The bar area is basic with benches around the walls. The walls display the many awards won by the pub. Children are not allowed in the bar. Please telephone to check opening hours. **QP**

Newbiggin by the Sea

Queens Head (Porters) ✔

7 High Street, NE64 6AT
⏲ 9.45 to midnight
☎ (01670) 817293
Beer range varies [H]
Featuring in CAMRA's North East inventory of historic pub interiors, the original Edwardian layout of the pub has been retained, with a public bar area, lounge area displaying many photographs of bygone Newbiggin, and snug to the rear. Outstanding features include the curved bar counter, bench seating, fireplace, etched windows and mosaic floors. The landlord sells competitively priced real ales and displays an ever-growing collection of guest beer pump clips. 🚌♣

Newton on the Moor

Cook & Barker Inn ✔

NE65 9JY (5 miles S of Alnwick, off A1)
⏲ 11 (12 Sun)-11
☎ (01665) 575234 🌐 cookandbarkerinn.co.uk
Black Sheep Best Bitter; guest beers [H]
Old dwelling tastefully updated but still including part of the original blacksmith's forge that was next door. Quite large inside, the interior has exposed beams and stone walls, and has a separate snug and various other rooms to complement the comfortable seating areas. Real ales are both locally and nationally sourced. The pub has an excellent reputation for food.
♨🐴✿◐◑⊞P🚭

Norham

Mason's Arms

17 West Street, TD15 2LB
⏲ 12-3, 7-11; 12-10.30 Sun
☎ (01289) 382326 🌐 tweed-sports.co.uk
Belhaven 80/-; Caledonian Deuchars IPA [H]
The cosy wood-panelled public bar with a real fire at its heart is the centre of this pub, complemented by a separate diing room. An eclectic collection of artefacts adorns the interior including an old Younger's brewery mirror, fishing gear and joinery tools, and photos of bygone Norham. Traditional music nights are hosted. Guest beers are from Greene King and the experienced landlord has made this pub a rare north Northumberland outlet for Budweiser Budvar. ♨✿◐◑⊞🚌(67)♣

Old Hartley

Delaval Arms

NE26 4RL (jct of A193/B1325 S of Seaton Sluice)
⏲ 12-11 (10.30 Sun)
☎ (0191) 237 0489
Caledonian Deuchars IPA; guest beers [H]
Multi-roomed Grade II-listed building dating from 1748, with a listed WWI water storage tower beyond the beer garden. To the left as you enter there is a room served through a hatch from the

ENGLAND

bar and to the right a room where children are welcome. Good quality, affordable meals complement the beer, with guest ales coming from local micros. Current South East Northumberland CAMRA Pub of the Year. Q❀◐☐P

Rennington

Horse Shoes Inn
NE66 3RS
12-3, 7-11; closed Mon
(01665) 577665
Hadrian & Border Farne Island, Tyneside Blonde H
Traditional family-run village pub dating from 1851. The bar is warm and friendly with hop bines hanging over the serving area, and there is a large restaurant serving good, locally-sourced food. The pub hosts a scarecrow competition every August bank holiday Saturday. Outside at the front is a pleasant beer garden. ❀◐◑♣

Seahouses

Olde Ship Hotel
7-9 Main Street, NE68 7RD
11 (12 Sun)-11
(01665) 720200 seahouses.co.uk
Black Sheep Best Bitter; Draught Bass; Courage Directors; Greene King Ruddles County, Old Speckled Hen; Hadrian & Border Farne Island; guest beers H
Featuring in CAMRA's North East regional inventory, this 1745 farmhouse was converted to licensed trade in 1812 and has been in same family since 1910. The pub's three quality bars feature an abundance of maritime memorabilia. It offers a unique menu of fish, fresh crab meals and snacks. ⌂Q❀◐◑☐♿♣P

Seaton Sluice

Melton Constable
Beresford Road, NE26 4DA
12-11 (10.30 Sun)
(0191) 237741
Theakston Best Bitter; Wells Bombadier; guest beers H
Large roadside pub a few minutes' walk from the beach. The pub overlooks a small harbour cut out of rock by early members of the famous Delaval family, which is still in use today. It is named after the southern seat of Lord Hastings, also a Delaval. A popular quiz is held on Wednesday evening. ◐◑🚌(308)P

Slaley

Travellers Rest
NE46 1TT (on B6306 1 mile N of village)
12-11 (10.30 Sun)
(01434) 673231
Black Sheep Best Bitter; guest beers H
Former farmhouse dating from the 16th century, licensed for more than 150 years. The pub has an excellent reputation for good food and accommodation. The bar has a large open fire, flagstone floors and comfortable furniture. Children are welcome and there is a safe play area alongside the pub. Q◑♣P

Stannington

Ridley Arms
NE61 6EL
11.30-11; 12-10.30 Sun
(01670) 789 216
Beer range varies H
Another excellent Fitzgerald's pub and dining house dating back to the 18th century. Divided into several distinct areas, the interior has a calm and relaxed ambience. Eight handpulls offer a good choice of local and countrywide breweries. Well regarded for it quality food, the pub offers a comprehensive menu featuring classic British dishes. ⌂Q❀◐◑♿🚌(X45,416)♣P

Twice Brewed

Twice Brewed Inn
Military Road, Bardon Mill, NE47 7AN (on B6318)
11 (12 winter)-11.30; 12-10.30 Sun
(01434) 344534 twicebrewedinn.co.uk
Yates Twice Brewed Bitter; guest beers H
Superb, remote inn, well patronised by tourists and ramblers, with Hadrian's Wall nearby. There are five ales on offer and nationally sourced guest beers, plus a range of bottled beers from around the world. Good disabled access and 14 en-suite bedrooms. ⌂Q❀◐◑☐♿🚌P

Wark

Battlesteads Hotel
NE48 3LS
11-11; 12-10.30 Sun
(01434) 230209 battlesteads.com
Black Sheep Best Bitter; Durham Magus; Wylam Gold Tankard H
Well-appointed former 1747 farmhouse with a superb walled garden and large conservatory. The pub supports local micros but also offers guest ales. Ingredients for the excellent food menu are obtained from local farms and traders. Live folk nights are popular. Excellent accommodation. ⌂❀◐◑☐♿P

Wylam

Black Bull
Main Street, NE41 8AB
4 (12 Fri-Sun)-11
(01661) 853112 blackbull-wylam.co.uk
Wylam Gold Tankard; guest beers H
Cheerful pub with a friendly landlord and staff, located on the main street in Wylam, very popular with the locals. Regular themed nights are hosted, raising money for charities. Local home-cooked specialities feature in the newly redecorated restaurant area. ◑≠♣

Boathouse Inn
Station Road, NE41 8HR
11-11 (midnight Sat); 12-10.30 Sun
(01661) 853431
Wylam Gold Tankard; guest beers H
Superb, well-managed, two-room real ale emporium with 14 handpulls, two dedicated to cider all year round. Beers are sourced nationwide and every bank holiday there is a themed beer festival. The pub acts as the brewery tap for the highly respected Wylam Brewery. Winner of several CAMRA and food awards. ⌂Q❀◐≠P

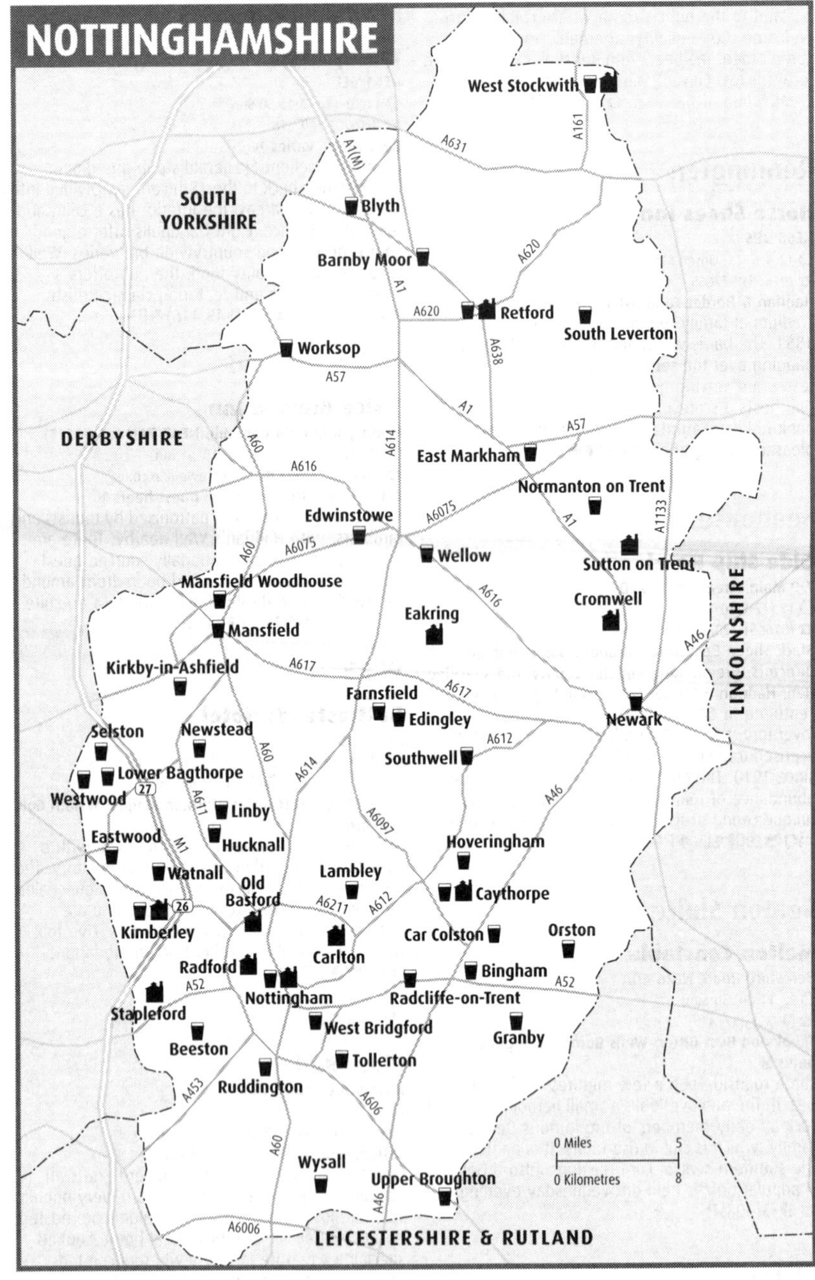

Barnby Moor

White Horse

Great North Road, DN22 8QS (on A638)

11-3, 6-11; 11-11 Sat; 12-11 Sun

(01777) 707721

Beer range varies H

This attractive village pub situated at the side of the A638 has a large lounge bar, a separate dining area and a smaller public bar area. Regularly changing cask ales are available depending on the time of the year, most originating from local micro-breweries. The walls in the lounge are covered with paintings, some connected to the local Grove & Rufford Hunt which has its kennels across the road. ⌂Q❀◑⇌P⁵–

Beeston

Malt Shovel ✓

1 Union Street, NG9 2LU

11 (12 Sun)-11 (11.30 Fri & Sat)

(0115) 922 2320

Nottingham Rock Mild, Rock Bitter; guest beers H

Just off the pedestrianised High Road, this one-room pub offers a friendly welcome. A modern interior makes thoughtful use of furnishings and decor to provide a sense of separate drinking areas. Bright colours and comfortable leather sofas create a light, airy ambience with a cosy atmosphere. There is a good-value food menu (no meals Sun eve), a quiz night on Wednesday and live music on Friday. Guest beers are from micro/regional brewers. ⌂✿◑♿🚌♣●P⍉

Victoria Hotel

85 Dovecote Lane, NG9 1JG (off A6005 by station)
⏲ 10.30 (12 Sun)-11
☎ (0115) 925 4049 🌐 victoriabeeston.co.uk
Castle Rock Harvest Pale; Everards Tiger; guest beers Ⓗ
Buzzing Victorian architectural gem – note the fine windows. This former Nottingham CAMRA Pub of the Year is popular with drinkers and diners alike. The multi-roomed layout includes a dining area, public bar and covered heated outside drinking space, fully non-smoking. Twelve beers are served including a local ale, mild, stout and two real ciders from regional and micro-brewers. High quality freshly-cooked food, with a wide vegetarian choice, is available all day. Regular music festivals are held, outside in summer. ⌂Q✿◑⊟♿⇌🚌●P

Bingham

Horse & Plough ✔

25 Long Acre, NG13 8AF
⏲ 11-11 (11.30 Fri & Sat); 12-11 Sun
☎ (01949) 839313 🌐 horseandploughbingham.com
Caledonian Deuchars IPA; Fuller's London Pride; Wells Bombardier; guest beers Ⓗ
Situated in the heart of a busy market town, this warm, friendly one-room free house was a former Methodist chapel and has a cottage-style interior and flagstone floor. Six cask ales are always available including three guests, with a 'try before you buy' policy. The first floor a la carte restaurant offers a seasonal menu and steak night on Tuesday. A fresh bar menu is served weekday lunchtimes and a traditional roast on Sunday. Local CAMRA Pub of the Year 2007. ◑♿⇌🚌

Blyth

Red Hart

Bawtry Road, S81 8HG
⏲ 12-midnight (11.30 Sun)
☎ (01909) 591221
Beer range varies Ⓗ
An attractive pub situated in the centre of Blyth, a previous winner of best-kept village. It has separate lounge and bar areas and a reasonably sized dining room. The walls in the lounge are decorated with photos and paintings of various locations around the village. Guest ales change regularly, with beers from several micro-breweries usually available. Restaurant quality food at pub prices is served daily. ⌂Q✿◑⊟🚌P⍉

Car Colston

Royal Oak 🏆 ✔

The Green, NG13 8JE
⏲ 11.30-3 (not Mon), 5.30-midnight; 11.30-midnight Fri & Sat; 12-10.30 Sun
☎ (01949) 20247
Jennings Cumberland Ale; Marston's Burton Bitter, Mansfield Cask Bitter; guest beer Ⓗ
Impressive country inn situated on England's largest village green. The two-room interior includes a lounge and restaurant on one side and a bar with comfortable seating on the other. Note the bar's interesting brickwork ceiling – a legacy from the building's previous life as a hosiery factory. Good quality, traditional food is served lunchtimes and evenings. There is a skittle alley to the rear. Local CAMRA Pub of the Year 2009 – the landlord maintains his 100 per cent record of appearances in the Guide. ⌂Q✿◑⊟♿⛺♣P⍉

Caythorpe

Black Horse

29 Main Street, NG14 7ED
⏲ 12-2.30, 6-11; closed Mon; 12-5, 8-11 Sun
☎ (0115) 9663520
Caythorpe Dover Beck, One Swallow; guest beers Ⓗ
Classic, unspoilt 18th-century country inn run by the same family for 37 years and reputedly a former haunt of Dick Turpin. Little has changed inside over the years – there is a comfortable lounge, a tiny snug bar with hatch servery, inglenook, bench seats, beams and wood panelling. A dining room is available for dinner parties (but no children allowed). Bar food is very popular, mostly cooked to order using fresh ingredients (booking essential). The home of Caythorpe Brewery, guest beers are often from other local micros. ⌂Q✿◑⊟🚌(103)♣P

East Markham

Queen's Hotel

High Street, NG22 0RE
⏲ 12-11 (10.30 Sun)
☎ (01777) 870288
Adnams Bitter; guest beers Ⓗ
One of two pubs in East Markham selling cask ales, this cosy house has a friendly atmosphere enhanced by an open fire in the winter. A single bar serves the lounge, pool room and dining area. Food, ranging from hot and cold snacks to full home-cooked meals, is available Tuesday-Sunday. There is a large garden area at the rear where you can enjoy a drink on a warm summer's day. Regular winner of North Notts CAMRA awards. ⌂Q✿◑🚌♣P⍉

Eastwood

Three Tuns

58 Three Tuns Road, NG16 3EJ (near fire station)

INDEPENDENT BREWERIES

Alcazar Nottingham: Old Basford
Castle Rock Nottingham
Caythorpe Caythorpe
Full Mash Stapleford
Grafton Retford
Holland Kimberley
Idle West Stockwith
Magpie Nottingham
Mallard Carlton
Maypole Eakring
Milestone Cromwell
Nottingham Nottingham: Radford
Springhead Sutton-on-Trent

⏲ 11-midnight (1am Fri & Sat)
☎ (01773) 713377
Brains SA; Courage Directors; Wychwood Hobgoblin; Young's Special; guest beers Ⓗ
This large pub has a modern feel, with a historic past. Located in the heart of DH Lawrence country, it was known as the 'Moon and Stars' in his controversial novel 'Sons and Lovers'. A central bar features six handpumps dispensing beers from larger regionals and occasional micros. Several large screen TVs and a pool table cater for sports fans. Visit the spacious gardens and look out for the Sultan tortoise, the landlord's pride and joy.
❀◐♿🚌♣P⊱

Edingley

Old Reindeer

Main Street, NG22 8BE (on main road from Farnsfield to Southwell)
⏲ 11 (12 Sun)-11
☎ (01623) 882253 🌐 oldreindeer.co.uk
Marston's Pedigree, Old Empire; guest beers Ⓗ
Eighteenth-century village pub, modernised inside to provide a comfortable dining space and cosy bar area without losing the essence of a country pub. With up to six real ales from Marston's in tip-top condition and an exceptional daily carvery, this is a popular pub, with games and activities organised for regulars. Quiz nights are Wednesday and Sunday. There is an attractive garden for families and B&B accommodation. A pub for beer connoisseurs, this is one to savour.
⛰Q❀🛏◐⊟♿🚌(29)♣P⊱

Edwinstowe

Forest Lodge Hotel ✔

2 Church Street, NG21 9QA (on A6075 Mansfield-Ollerton road)
⏲ 11.30-3, 5.30 (5 Fri)-11; 12-3, 6-10.30 Sun
☎ (01623) 824443 🌐 forestlodgehotel.co.uk
Cottage Normans Conquest; Kelham Island Easy Rider; Wells Bombardier; guest beer Ⓗ
Dating from the 17th century, this family-run coaching inn has been tastefully restored by the Thompsons and makes a welcome return to the Guide. Situated in the heart of Sherwood Forest, riding and golf are a five-minute drive away. Themed nights are a frequent feature. The pub features a wide range of ever-changing guest beers and has a first class food menu. Accommodation is in 13 en-suite rooms.
⛰Q♉❀🛏◐♿🚌(10,14,16)P⊱

Farnsfield

Red Lion

Main Street, NG22 8EY
⏲ 11-3, 6-11; 12-3, 7-11 Sun
☎ (01623) 882304
Jennings Cocker Hoop; Marston's Mansfield Cask Bitter, Pedigree; Ringwood Fortyniner; guest beer Ⓗ
Locals' pub, family run for many years. It has an open plan lounge with plenty of seating around a large bay window. Up to five well kept real ales are on offer from the Marston's range. Home-cooked food is available lunchtimes and evenings. The welcoming open fire is lit during the winter months and dominoes is played on Sunday and Monday evenings. ⛰Q❀◐♿🚌(29)♣P⊱

Granby

Marquis of Granby

Dragon Street, NG13 9PN
⏲ 11.30-2.30 (not Mon), 5.30-midnight; 11.30-midnight Fri-Sun
☎ (01949) 859517
Brewster's Hophead, Marquis; guest beers Ⓗ
Believed to be the original Marquis of Granby, dating back to 1760 or earlier, this small, two-roomed pub is now the brewery tap for Brewster's Brewery. York stone floors complement the yew bar tops and wood-beamed rooms, period wallpaper features throughout and the lounge has a welcoming open fire in winter months. Guest beers complement the Brewster's range and come from micros, usually including a mild, stout or porter. All food is home-made and sourced locally. Local CAMRA Pub of the Year 2008. ⛰❀◐⊟♿♣P

Hoveringham

Reindeer Inn

Main Street, NG14 7JR SK699469
⏲ 12-2, 5-midnight; 12-midnight Sat & Sun
☎ (0115) 966 3629
Blue Monkey Original; Castle Rock Harvest Pale; Caythorpe Stout Fellow; guest beers Ⓗ
Genuine free house in a pleasant country village with traditional beams and a log fire for cold winter nights. A central servery divides the bar and restaurant areas. Good home-cooked food includes vegetarian and vegan choices. The outside drinking area overlooks a cricket pitch. The local Caythorpe stout replaces Guinness on the bar. Dog friendly.
⛰Q❀◐⇌(Thurgaton)♣P⊱

Hucknall

Green Dragon ✔

Watnall Road, NG15 7JW
⏲ 12-11.30 (11 Sun)
☎ (0115) 964 0941
Beer range varies Ⓗ
Situated just out of the town centre, this traditional pub has five ever-changing ales. An airy open plan interior comprises a lounge with a raised area for food (served 12-4pm Mon-Sat), games area with pool and darts, and separate ground floor family room available for dining, parties and functions. There is a quiz night on Wednesday, karaoke on Thursday, pool knockout on Tuesday and darts league on Monday. Sports are shown on plasma TV and there is live music on Saturday night.
♉❀◐♿⇌⊖🚌♣P⊱

Kimberley

Nelson & Railway ✔

12 Station Road, NG16 2NR
⏲ 11-midnight; 12-11 Sun
☎ (0115) 938 2177 🌐 nelsonandrailway.co.uk
Greene King H&H Bitter, Olde Trip; guest beers Ⓗ
Formerly the brewery tap for Hardys & Hansons, this popular pub lies in the shadow of the defunct brewery buildings. Beers are mainly from the Greene King portfolio but guest ales also appear. The interior, refurbished with several shades of wood, has plenty of character. A friendly local, the pub is renowned for good quality food and accommodation. Unusually, the pub has gardens front and back. ❀🛏◐⊟♿🚌(1)♣P⊱

Stag Inn ✔

67 Nottingham Road, NG16 2NB
✪ 5 (1.30 Sat)-11; 12-10.30 Sun
☎ (0115) 938 3151
Adnams Bitter; Black Sheep Best Bitter; Marston's Pedigree; Taylor Landlord; guest beer Ⓗ
This historic two-room pub is situated on the main road, next to Kimberley Town FC's ground, which is named after the pub. It has low wooden beams adorned with old photographs of Shipstones, the former brewery that once owned the pub. The spacious rear garden includes a children's play area and ample seating. Traditional games such as table skittles and dominoes are played, but at most times conversation reigns. An annual beer festival on the late May bank holiday weekend raises money for charity. Q❀♿🚌(1)♣P⊱

Kirkby-in-Ashfield

Badger Box ✔

Derby Road, NG17 9BX
✪ 11-11.30 (11 Mon); 11.30-11 Sun
☎ (01623) 752243
Greene King XX Mild, IPA, H&H Best Bitter, Old Speckled Hen, Abbot; guest beer Ⓗ
Food-oriented former Hardys & Hansons pub, with an excellent choice of good food served all day. However, the drinker is not neglected – the beers, including a traditional mild, are always in good condition and the pub features on the Nottingham CAMRA Mild Trail. Although open plan, pillars break up the room, giving a cosy feel. There is a large garden and families are welcome until 9pm.
❀◐◑♿🚌(3)♣P

Lambley

Woodlark

Church Street, NG4 4QB
✪ 12-3, 5.30-11; 12-6, 7-11 Sun
☎ (0115) 931 2535
Castle Rock Harvest Pale; Fuller's London Pride; Taylor Landlord; guest beers Ⓗ
Tucked away on the edge of the village, this delightful red-brick local is mercifully free of electronic machines. The bare brick and beamed bar is welcoming and dog friendly while the comfortable lounge has earned a reputation for excellent home cooking (booking recommended). A popular downstairs steak bar is also open on Friday and Saturday evenings from 7-9pm. Folk music nights are held on alternate Mondays.
♨Q❀◐◑⊟🚌(7,61)♣●P⊱

Linby

Horse & Groom

Main Street, NG15 8AE
✪ 12-11 (10.30 Sun)
☎ (0115) 963 2219
Greene King IPA, Old Speckled Hen; Theakston Mild; Wells Bombardier; guest beers Ⓗ
Charming and unspoilt village pub dating back to 1800. This multi-roomed establishment is Grade II-listed and has an inglenook in the public bar, a snug and roaring open fires. The Green Room welcomes families. Food is available at lunchtime from an extensive and varied menu. Evening dining is on Friday and Saturday only. There is a conservatory and the large garden has a children's play area. ♨Q♘❀◐◑⊟🚌(141)♣P⊱

Lower Bagthorpe

Dixies Arms

School Road, NG16 5HF
✪ 12-11
☎ (01773) 810505
Greene King Abbot; Theakston Best Bitter; guest beer Ⓗ
Built in the late 1700s, this pub offers a friendly welcome to all. Locals and visitors alike can be found warming themselves around the real fires in the public rooms, playing darts or dominoes, or gossiping in the snug. Live music plays on Saturday, a quiz is held on Sunday. No food is available. A haven for real ale drinkers.
♨❀⊟🚌(1,331)♣P⊱

Mansfield

Bold Forester 🏆 ✔

Botany Avenue, NG18 5NF
✪ 11-11 (midnight Fri & Sat); 12-11.30 Sun
☎ (01623) 623970
Greene King IPA, Ruddles County, Old Speckled Hen, Abbot; guest beers Ⓗ
The flagship real ale pub in Mansfield, this is a modern, ex-Whitbread pub, 10 years old, run by the same landlord. It became a Hungry Horse in November 2008 and offers good value food. The large open-plan layout is on spilt levels with a raised dining area. There are large flat screen TVs for sporting events and background music. The pub has two beer festivals a year, featuring micros from near and far. A popular quiz night is hosted on Tuesday, and live music on Sunday. Local CAMRA Pub of the Year 2005/06/07. ❀◐◑♿⇌🚌P⊱

Court House ✔

Market Place, NG18 1HX
✪ 9-11 (midnight Fri & Sat)
☎ (01623) 412720
Greene King Old Speckled Hen, Abbot; Marston's Pedigree; guest beers Ⓗ
This friendly pub in the town centre is busy, especially at weekends, offering a comprehensive selection of at least five real ales, with beers from local micro-breweries such as Milestone, Springhead and Derventio regularly available. There is a small separate family dining area and the rest of the pub is split into sections. Food is served all day until 10pm, offering the typical excellent value associated with Wetherspoon's. Local CAMRA Pub of the Season. Q♘◐◑♿⇌🚌●⊱

Nell Gwyn

117 Sutton Road, NG18 5EX
✪ 2 (12 Sat & Sun)-midnight
☎ (01623) 659850
Beer range varies Ⓗ
Friendly pub, formally a social club, offering two ever- changing guest beers from local micros – Full Mash of Stapleford features regularly. Traditional pub games are played in both the lounge and games room, both served from a central bar. No food is served and there is quiet background music only. The new licensee has installed a brand new cellar at the rear. A welcome return to the Guide.
♨❀🚌♣⊱

Railway Inn

9 Station Street, NG18 1EF
✪ 11-11 (8 Tue); 12-6 Sun
☎ (01623) 623086

Beer range varies Ⓗ
Saved from being turned into offices, this is a true independent real ale gem in an area of themed pubs and keg outlets. A genuine community pub, it offers a constantly changing choice of mainly paler beers, some from LocAle breweries, plus a good selection of bottled beers. Excellent value home-cooked food is available every lunchtime and Tuesday to Thursday evenings, 5-8pm. There is a small walled garden and heated smoking area in the courtyard. Local CAMRA Pub of the Season.
Q⊃❀◑◐⊟≠⊟⁂–

Widow Frost ✔

41 Leeming Street, NG18 1NB
9-midnight (1am Fri & Sat)
☎ (01623) 666790
Greene King Ruddles County, Abbot; Marston's Pedigree; guest beers Ⓗ
Spacious pub not far from the town centre. It gets very busy, especially at weekends, but it is possible to find a quiet corner. The full range of Wetherspoon's meals is served all day throughout the pub, including a separate family dining area, offering typical good value for money. There is always a good selection of beers – usually five are available – served by friendly staff from a large bar. Local CAMRA Pub of the Season. Q⊃◑◐♿≠⊟●⁂–

Mansfield Woodhouse

Greyhound

82 High Street, NG19 8BD
12-midnight (10.30 Sun)
☎ (01623) 464403
Adnams Broadside; Caledonian Deuchars IPA; Greene King Abbot; Theakston Mild; Wells Bombardier Ⓗ
Built around 1700, this stone-built, two-roomed pub has been a regular entry in the Guide for more than 15 years – the licensee has run the pub for the last 14 years. Up to five real ales, always including a traditional mild, are stocked, but no food is available. The public bar has a pool table and traditional pub games, with a quiet lounge area for families and group meetings. Two small beer festivals feature annually. Quiz nights are Monday and Wednesday. Q❀⊟≠⊟(1,10)♣P⁂–

Newark

Castle

5 Castlegate, NG24 1AZ (opp Newark Castle)
11-midnight (1am Thu to Sat); 12-midnight Sun
☎ (01636) 640733 ygpc.co.uk
Sharp's Doom Bar; guest beers Ⓗ
Warm and welcoming pub opposite Newark Castle, with an unusual interior offering many nooks and crannies to enjoy the ever-changing guest beers on six handpumps, served by the friendly landlord and landlady. Its rapidly increasing reputation for live music makes it one of the busiest town centre pubs. A staunch supporter of CAMRA's LocAle scheme, it also holds occasional beer festivals.
≠(Castle)

Castle & Falcon

10 London Road, NG24 1TW
12-3 (not Mon-Thu), 7-11.30
☎ (01636) 703513
John Smith's Bitter; guest beers Ⓗ
Busy locals' local, situated under the old James Hole Brewery. Close to the town centre, it attracts old and young alike, and is home to many sports teams. Two guest beers from an imaginative portfolio usually guarantees something different on every visit. A large, comfortable room is available for functions. Local CAMRA Pub of the Year 2008. ❀⊟♿≠(Castle)♣⁂–

Fox & Crown

4-6 Appletongate, NG24 1JY
10.30 -11 (12 Fri & Sat); 12-11 Sun
☎ (01636) 605820
Bateman XXXB; Castle Rock Harvest Pale, Hemlock, Sherriff's Tipple; Everards Tiger; guest beers Ⓗ
A member of the LocAle scheme, this Castle Rock managed house boasts 10 handpumps as well as Belgian bottled beers and a varied selection of malt whiskies and flavoured vodkas. The pub is mainly open plan but split into separate drinking areas. There is occasional live music on Thursday and Saturday. Food is sourced locally and reasonably priced. ◑◐♿≠(Castle/Northgate)

Vine

117 Barnbygate, NG24 1QZ
4 (12 Sat & Sun)-11
☎ (01636) 704333 thevinenewark.co.uk
Springhead Liberty, Roaring Meg; guest beers Ⓗ
Owned by Springhead Brewery and managed by Paul, an enthusiastic CAMRA member, this no frills pub is situated five minutes' walk from the town centre. The public bar has a pool table and gaming machines, to the rear the lounge has a dartboard. The pub's motto is: 'Where normal things don't happen very often.' ❀⊟♿≠(Northgate)♣⁂–

Newstead

Station Hotel

Station Road, NG15 0BZ
11-3, 5 (7 Sat)-11.30 (midnight Sat); 12-3, 7-11 Sun
☎ (01623) 753294
Oakwell Old Tom Mild, Barnsley Bitter Ⓗ
Built in 1881 as a hotel serving the mining village, this is now a traditonal pub with three drinking areas and a function room to the rear. It retains much of its original character, with wood panelling in the lounge and polished wood flooring in the tap room. A focal point for the local community, its location on the Robin Hood Line means it also attracts vistors from further afield. Railway memorabilia and pictures of Newstead Abbey feature. No meals are served except on Thursday which is curry night.
⛼Q❀◐⊟♿≠(Newstead)⊟(3A)♣⁂–

Normanton on Trent

Crown

South Street, NG23 6RQ (exit A1 at B1164 and follow signs to Normanton) SK 792688
12-11
☎ (01636) 821973
Milestone Dark and Stormy, Lions Pride; guest beer Ⓗ
This attractive, newly refurbished village pub used to incorporate the post office. It serves as the brewery tap for Milestone and also features brews from the sister brewery, Cathedral, based at the Green Dragon in Lincoln (also worth a visit). It offers a lounge and an a la carte menu, focusing on locally produced meat and vegetables. A safe children's play area and a heated, covered smoking area are outside. ⛼❀◑◐♿⊟(39)●P⁂–

Nottingham: Central

Canalhouse

48-52 Canal Street, NG1 7EH
⏲ 12-11 (midnight Thu; 1am Fri & Sat); 12-10.30 Sun
☎ (0115) 955 5060
Castle Rock Harvest Pale; guest beers Ⓗ
This listed three-storey Castle Rock pub has a surprise. The canal basin runs through the inside, traversed by wooden walkways. It used to house a canal museum before being converted into an open-plan pub that retains a certain cosiness. One floor doubles as a function room. The canal-side decked patio is very popular in summer, half-covered and heated for those overcast evenings. Food, available daily, is offered in simple or exotic choices. ❀◐◑♿⇌(Nottingham)⊖(Station St)🚌⚲

Kean's Head

46 St Mary's Gate, NG1 1QA (opp St Mary's Church)
⏲ 11.30-midnight (12.30am Fri & Sat); 12-10.30 Sun
☎ (0115) 947 4052 🌐 castlerockbrewery.co.uk
Bateman XB; Castle Rock Harvest Pale, Screech Owl; guest beers Ⓗ
Cosy, one-room pub opposite the imposing St Mary's Church in the historic Lace Market district. Named in honour of the 19th-century actor Edmund Kean, it is busy at weekends and attracts a diverse and varied clientele. Owned by the Castle Rock group, it offers inventive, freshly prepared food from an ever-changing menu. Three guest beers are usually available, including a brew from Castle Rock's Natural Selection series. Occasional live music and themed brewery nights are held. ◐◑♿⇌⊖(Lace Market)🚌

King William IV

6 Eyre Street, Sneinton, NG2 4PB
⏲ 11-11 (10.30 Sun)
☎ (0115) 958 9864
Oakham Bishops Farewell, JHB; guest beers Ⓗ
Known as the King Billy, this cosy Victorian gem nestling on the edge of town is just a stone's throw from the Trent FM Arena. A family-run free house that oozes charm and character, it is a haven for real ale drinkers, with a choice of seven micro-brewery ales from near and far, and a cider. Occasional live music and unusual televised sports feature. A fine selection of rolls is available. This is one pub not to miss on a visit to Nottingham. ❀♿⇌🚌🍎⚲

Lincolnshire Poacher

161-163 Mansfield Road, NG1 3FR (on A60 N of city centre)
⏲ 11-11 (midnight Thu-Sat); 12-11 Sun
☎ (0115) 941 1584
Bateman XB; Castle Rock Harvest Pale, Screech Owl; Everards Tiger; guest beers Ⓗ
Atmospheric two-roomer with a conservatory and enclosed patio to the rear. The choice of ales from 11 handpumps is ever changing, mainly from micro-breweries, always including a local ale, mild, stout or porter and cider. There are also Belgian bottled beers and 80 different whiskies. Popular home-cooked food uses locally sourced fresh ingredients. There is live music on Sunday night, brewery evenings and micro-brewery trips. All NCT Brown, Purple, Yellow and Lime Line buses pass the door. Nottingham CAMRA Pub of the Year 2007/08. ❀◐◑♿🚌♣🍎⚲

Newshouse 🏆

123 Canal Street, NG1 7HB
⏲ 12-11 (midnight Fri & Sat)
☎ (0115) 950 2419
Castle Rock Harvest Pale; Everards Tiger; guest beers Ⓗ
Comfortable, friendly, two-roomed Castle Rock local, decorated with memorabilia from BBC Radio Nottingham and the local Evening Post. Note the brewery names etched into wall tiles in the public bar where sport is shown, sometimes on a large screen. Darts, bar billiards and table skittles can also be played. Quiz night is Thursday. Up to eight cask beers from micro/regional brewers always include a mild and a local ale. A regular winner of local CAMRA awards, especially for the mild. ❀◐🀫⇌⊖🚌♣🍎⚲

Olde Trip to Jerusalem ★ ✔

1 Brewhouse Yard, NG1 6AD (below castle)
⏲ 11-11 (midnight Sat)
☎ (0115) 947 3171 🌐 triptojerusalem.com
Greene King XX Mild, IPA, H&H Olde Trip, Ruddles County, Old Speckled Hen, Abbot; guest beers Ⓗ
This world-famous pub is reputed to date from 1189. It has a number of rooms, some cut out of the castle rock. Upstairs, the rock lounge is home to the Cursed Galleon. A museum room houses a tapestry depicting Nottingham's history. A covered courtyard and a seated pavement drinking area with waitress service are available Easter to August. The rock and museum bars can be reserved for private functions. Cellar tours by appointment. Children are welcome until 7pm. Guest beers tend to come from the Nottingham area. ♨Q❀◐◑🀫⇌⊖🚌♣⚲

Salutation Inn

Houndsgate, Maid Marian Way, NG1 7AA
⏲ 11-midnight (2am Fri & Sat); 12-midnight Sun
☎ (0115) 988 1948 🌐 myspace.com/thesalutationnottingham
Beer range varies Ⓗ
Steeped in history, this lively 17th-century inn with oak beams and stone floor is a favourite venue with young and old. Regular live rock music plays upstairs while downstairs there are quiet snugs for drinking and conversation. The pub sells a range of ciders and promotes local beers. The Halloween beer festival is an annual highlight. Good food is based on local produce and cooked on the premises. The labyrinth of caves under the pub is reputed to be haunted. ♨❀◐◑⊖🚌🍎⚲

Sir John Borlase Warren

1 Ilkeston Road, Canning Circus, NG7 3GD
⏲ 11-11.30 (midnight Fri & Sat); 12-11 Sun
☎ (0115) 947 4247
Everards Sunchaser, Tiger; Greene King IPA; Taylor Landlord; guest beers Ⓗ
A short hop on the bus uphill from the city centre, this pub makes an excellent meeting place. Warm and friendly, the cosy seating provides comfort and relaxation. Although open plan, there are four distinct areas plus the bar. Original artwork decorating the walls is for sale. Good food, usually sourced locally, is served until 10pm (9pm Sun). In summer, the outside seating is a real gem. Q❀◐◑🚌⚲

VAT & Fiddle

12-14 Queen's Bridge Road, NG2 1NB
⏲ 11-11 (midnight Fri & Sat); 12-11 Sun

☎ (0115) 985 0611
Castle Rock Harvest Pale, Hemlock, Preservation, Elsie Mo; guest beers Ⓗ
A stone's throw from the railway station, the Castle Rock brewery tap welcomes both regulars and visitors to the city. Primarily a drinkers' pub, home-cooked food is served at weekday lunchtimes, with sandwiches available most other times. Real cider and up to seven guest beers, mainly from micros, are available, always including a mild. The Art Deco frontage boasts an attractive flower display and there is ample street-side seating.
Q❀◐♿⇌⊖🚌●⁵–

Nottingham: East

Bread & Bitter

153 Woodthorpe Drive, Mapperley, NG3 5JL
⏲ 10-11 (midnight Fri & Sat); 11-11 Sun
☎ (0115) 960 7541
Castle Rock Harvest Pale, Preservation; Everards Tiger; Thornbridge Jaipur; guest beers Ⓗ
New 2007 pub from Castle Rock built on the premises of the old Judge's bakery on Mapperley Top. The original baker's oven fronts are still embedded in an inside wall, giving the place a warm and welcoming feel. The pub has been responsible for a revival of real ale pubs in Mapperley. Up to 12 beers, always including a local ale and a mild, are available, along with an extensive foreign bottled beer list. Food is all home cooked and varies frequently – look for the specials board. Q❀◐◑♿🚌(25,44,45)⁵–

Queen Adelaide

99 Windmill Lane, Sneinton, NG3 2BH
⏲ 12-11
☎ (0115) 958 0607 🌐 queenadelaidenottingham.com
Beer range varies Ⓗ
Great community pub in a residential area affording panoramic views of Nottingham. Up to four beers are available, including one from Magpie and one named after Monty, the pub's pet Weimaraner dog, famous for catching and crunching up ice cubes. The home-cooked fresh food is very popular and booking is advised for the legendary Sunday lunches that come with a huge selection of fresh vegetables. Darts and pool are played in the bar. ❀◐◑⊟🚌(23,24)♣⁵–

Nottingham: North

Chestnut Tree

482 Mansfield Road, Sherwood, NG5 2EL
⏲ 11-11 (midnight Fri & Sat); 12-11 Sun
☎ (0115) 985 6388
Nottingham Rock Bitter; guest beers Ⓗ
Recently rebuilt on the site of a former hotel on the south side of Sherwood, this large open-plan community pub has a friendly and comfortable atmosphere. The pub is a supporter of the LocAle scheme – a regular Nottingham ale is supplemented with four ever-changing SIBA guest beers. Entertainment includes weekly quizzes, regular live music and multi-screens show Setanta and Sky Sports. Honest, good-value traditional pub food is served all day until 9pm (6.30pm Sun).
❀◐◑♿🚌P⁵–

Gladstone ✔

45 Loscoe Road, Carrington, NG5 2AW (off A60)
⏲ 5 (3 Fri, 12 Sat)-11 (11.30 Thu-Sat); 12-11 Sun
☎ (0115) 912 9994
Castle Rock Harvest Pale; Courage Directors; Fuller's London Pride; Greene King Abbot; Taylor Landlord; guest beers Ⓗ
Two-roomed back-street local in the middle of a Victorian terrace. Memorabilia is on display in the narrow public bar, and the TV shows sporting events. A similarly shaped lounge is pleasantly decorated with old bottles, brass ornaments and classic pictures. A shelf of books is available for customers to peruse. The Carrington Folk Club has been meeting in the upstairs function room on a Wednesday night for the last 25 years. ❀⊟🚌♣⁵–

Horse & Groom ✔

462 Radford Road, Basford, NG7 7EA
⏲ 12-11; 11-11.30 Fri & Sat
☎ (0115) 970 3777 🌐 horseandgroombasford.com
Fuller's London Pride; guest beers Ⓗ
The former Shipstones Brewery stands just a few yards south of this popular pub. Access is via steps up to the front door, with disabled access available on request. The small bar area accommodates nine handpumps serving mainly micro-brewery beers, at least one a local ale and one a mild. The split-level pub has several distinct areas and a function room. On Monday night there is a quiet quiz and backgammon club. ♨◐⊖(Shipstone St)🚌(80/81)

Nottingham: South

Globe

152 London Road, NG2 3BQ
⏲ 11.30 (11 Sat)-11; 12-10.30 Sun
☎ (0115) 986 6881 🌐 theglobenottingham.com
Nottingham EPA, Legend; guest beers Ⓗ
Light, airy, popular pub near Nottingham's cricket, football and rugby grounds. Cold snacks are served on match days only. Sport features regularly on several large screens. Six handpumps serve ales mainly from micro-breweries, with Nottingham beers usually available. Ask about the CAMRA discount. An upstairs function room can hold up to 100 people, with catering facilities available.
⇌🚌P⁵–

Nottingham: West

Johnson Arms ✔

59 Abbey Street, Dunkirk, NG7 2NZ
⏲ 12-midnight (1am Fri & Sat)
☎ (0115) 978 6355 🌐 johnsonarms.co.uk
Adnams Bitter; Castle Rock Harvest Pale; guest beers Ⓗ
This former Shipstones house still proudly displays the defunct brewery's name in its etched windows, to complement the green brick tiled frontage. The split level main bar is popular with students, locals and nearby QMC hospital staff. The free jukebox plays at a volume that will not deter good conversation. Quarterly beer festivals are not to be missed, along with the yearly Johnsonbury Music Festival, held in the magnificent beer garden. A quiz is held each Tuesday.
❀◐◑🚌(NCT 13,14 TB Indigo)♣●⁵–

Plough ✔

17 St Peters Street, Radford, NG7 3EN
⏲ 12-midnight (11.30 Sun)
☎ (0115) 970 2615 🌐 nottinghambrewery.com/plough.html
Nottingham Rock Mild, Extra Pale Ale, Legend, Rock Bitter, Supreme; guest beers Ⓗ

This traditional 1840s two-roomed pub is the brewery tap for Nottingham Brewery, situated at the rear. Five Nottingham and up to four guests are usually available. The traditional layout allows for Sky TV in one room and quiet drinking in the other. Curry and a pint night is Tuesday and a quiz with free chilli is hosted on Thursday. Sunday lunches are served. ♨Q❀◐⊟⊞♣P⊱

Orston

Durham Ox

Church Street, NG13 9NS
⊙ 12-3, 6-11 (not Mon); 11.30-11 Sat; 12-3, 7-10.30 Sun
☎ (01949) 850059
Fuller's London Pride; Greene King IPA; Marston's Mansfield Cask Bitter; Wells Bombardier Ⓗ
A delightful pub for locals and visitors alike, situated opposite the village church. Outside, there are hitching rails for horses and ferrets. The large but cosy bar area features many equine pictures and prints, reflecting the landlady's interest in the local area. No hot meals are served but delicious filled rolls can be made to order. Regular well-attended charity fund-raising events are held at the pub all year round. An attractive garden and outdoor drinking space are popular in summer. Q❀♿P⊱

Radcliffe-on-Trent

Horse Chestnut ✔

49 Main Road, NG12 2BE
⊙ 12 (11 Sat)-11 (11.30 Fri & Sat)
☎ (0115) 933 1994 🌐 horsechestnutradcliffe.com
Bateman XB; Castle Rock Harvest Pale; Fuller's London Pride; guest beers Ⓗ
Formerly named the Cliffe Inn, this excellent LocAle accredited pub was refurbished in 2006 in a smart 1920s style. The impressive interior has an attractive bar area and a separate library room furnished with comfortable leather seating. Up to eight reasonably priced ales are served including ever-changing guests. The food menu offers good quality, imaginative dishes utilising local ingredients. Thursday is quiz night, Wednesday is themed food night and Monday is curry night. ❀◐♿⇌⊞P⊱

Retford

Galway Arms

Bridgegate, DN22 7UZ
⊙ 12-11 (midnight Fri & Sat)
☎ (01777) 702446
Beer range varies Ⓗ
Just 250 metres from the main Retford Market, this pub has a pleasant atmosphere with friendly service – a fine example of a typical olde-worlde English inn. The interior is split into three separate areas with two bars – the public bar area has two large plasma TVs showing all the main sporting events. The lounge area is screen-free for a more peaceful drink. There is also a quaint snug area with seating for up to 12 people. ♨❀◐⊟♿⊞P

Rum Runner 

Wharf Road, DN22 6EN (by fire station)
⊙ 12-11
☎ (01777) 860788
Batemans XB, XXB; guest beers Ⓗ
Formerly home to the now-closed Broadstone Brewery, the pub has a long room warmed by a real fire and a second room, formerly the restaurant, with its own serving hatch through to the bar. A quiz night is held on Wednesday as well as frequent music nights. Mini beer festivals are a regular feature. Outside is a large, enclosed beer garden. ♨Q❀◐⊞♣P⊱

Turks Head ✔

Grove Street, DN22 6LE
⊙ 11-4, 7-11; 11-11 Sat; 12-11 Sun
☎ (01777) 702742
Beer range varies Ⓗ
A welcome return to the Guide for this pub after an absence of several years. Situated close to the main Market Square, entry is via two large oak doors which both lead to an open plan area served by an L-shaped bar. The interior features lots of oak panelling and there is a large, warming open fire, and a pool table at the far end. Four real ales are served. ♨⊞♣

Ruddington

Three Crowns

23 Easthorpe Street, NG11 6LB
⊙ 12-3 (11 Sat), 5-11; 12-10.30 Sun
☎ (0115) 921 3226 🌐 ruddingtonbeer.co.uk
Fuller's London Pride; Nottingham Rock Mild, EPA; guest beers Ⓗ
Modern, single-bar village local. The Three Crowns gets its name from its roof-top chimneys, but is known locally as the Top House because of its location at the top end of a street with three pubs. Regular beer festivals are held, often in conjunction with another village local. The Gallery restaurant at the rear of the pub serves locally-sourced home-cooked food and features local art. ◐⊞(10)

White Horse

60 Church Street, NG11 6HD
⊙ 12-11 (11.30 Thu-Sat); 12-10.30 Sun
☎ (0115) 984 4550 🌐 whitehorseruddington.co.uk
Black Sheep Best Bitter; Wells Bombadier; guest beers Ⓗ
Spacious village local with two rooms – the lounge has settles around the sides and is free of background music, the public bar has a pool table and large-screen sports. Up to three guest beers including a LocAle are available. Excellent, locally-sourced, home-cooked food is served Monday to Friday lunchtimes only. A large paved outdoor area is used for barbecues and the annual village beer festival on the last weekend in May. Quiz night is Thursday. CAMRA members should ask for a discount. Q❀◐⊟⊞(10)♣P⊱

Selston

Horse & Jockey

Church Lane, NG16 6FB SK459535
⊙ 12-3, 5-11; 12-4, 7-11 Sun
☎ (01773) 781012
Greene King Abbot; Taylor Landlord Ⓖ**; guest beers** Ⓗ/Ⓖ
Friendly village local dating back to 1664, reputed to be haunted, with a main bar, snug and lounge. Flagstone floors, open fires, an iron range and low-beamed ceilings create a cosy feeling throughout. You are welcome to play pool or a selection of pub games. Up to nine real ales and a cider are

available at all times. Lunchtime meals are served weekdays only. Winner of several local CAMRA awards and Nottinghamshire Pub of the Year 2004 and 2008. Q(90,331)♣P

South Leverton

Plough

Town Street, DN22 0BT (opp village hall)
10-1am (midnight Sun)
☎ (01427) 880323
Greene King Ruddles County; guest beers H
You could drive through the village and not see this pub opposite the village hall, but then you would miss out on a little gem. Some of the seating appears to be old church pews. The small, friendly local also houses the post office – there cannot be many pubs where you can have a pint and buy your stamps at the same time. A recent winner of local CAMRA Pub of the Season. Q♣P

Southwell

Bramley Apple

51 Church Street, NG25 0HQ
12-midnight (1am Fri & Sat; 11 Sun)
☎ (01636) 813675
Springhead Liberty; guest beers H
Situated near the historic Minster, this welcoming Springhead house serves five guest ales alongside two of its own beers. The original Bramley tree still bears fruit and can be seen in a private garden nearby. Southwell comes alive in June when it holds a folk festival and the pub hosts various entertainments as part of the celebrations. Karaoke night is Saturday and jazz and blues bands play every second Sunday. A good, all-round pub with something for everyone. Q(90,100)♣

Old Coach House

69 Easthorpe, NG25 0HY
5 (4 Fri, 12 Sat & Sun)-midnight (1am Fri & Sat)
☎ (01636) 813289
Wells Bombardier; guest beers H
This traditional free house dating back to the 17th century stands in the shadow of the famous minster. A LocAle pub, it serves six different ales, mainly from micros. The pub is split into separate cosy areas boasting three real fires, with oak beams and low ceilings adding to the atmosphere.Traditional pub games are on offer and a quiz on Sunday. An outside patio area is a welcome change in the summer months. Dogs are welcome. (101)♣

Tollerton

Air Hostess

Stanstead Avenue, NG12 4EA
12-11.30 (midnight Fri & Sat)
☎ (0115) 937 7388 airhostesspub.co.uk
Everards Beacon, Original, Tiger; guest beer H
This excellent community village pub gets its name because of its proximity to Nottingham airport, and sports a large carved trolley dolly as its sign. The traditional public bar with darts, dominoes and pool is complemented by a comfortable lounge with a piste for playing petanque outside. Quiz night is Wednesday, good value food evenings are hosted occasionally, and live music features early on Sunday evening. The Tollerton Plough Play is performed here annually. P

Upper Broughton

Golden Fleece

Main Street, LE14 3BG
12-11 (10.30 Sun)
☎ (01664) 822262
Belvoir Beaver; guest beers H
Large, attractive pub situated just off the main A606 Nottingham to Melton road. Food is the main focus here – the spacious interior has a small area for drinkers and a larger dining space and conservatory. The wide and varied menu receives very good reports locally. A guest ale often comes from a micro-brewery and occasional beer festivals are hosted. (19)♣P

Watnall

Queens Head

40 Main Road, NG16 1HT
12-11.30
☎ (0115) 938 6774
Adnams Broadside; Everards Original, Tiger; Greene King Old Speckled Hen; Wells Bombardier; guest beers H
A 17th-century rural gem comprising a lounge/dining area, small snug hidden behind the bar and an unusual locals' area with a grandfather clock. The extensive garden has a children's play area, making it popular with families in summer. The internal fittings around the bar are original and old photos adorn the walls, adding to the pub's ambience. Home-cooked English food is available at lunchtimes and weekday evenings. The pub is reputedly haunted. Q(331)P

Wellow

Olde Red Lion

Eakring Road, NG22 0EG (opp maypole)
12-11
☎ (01623) 861000
Beer range varies H
This 400-year-old pub is situated opposite the village green with its maypole and participates in a large event on May Day. The traditional wood-beamed interior includes a restaurant, lounge and bar area with photographs and maps depicting the history of the village. Sherwood Forest and Clumber Park are nearby. QP

West Bridgford

Stratford Haven

2 Stratford Road, NG2 6BA
10.30-11 (midnight Thu-Sat); 12-11 Sun
☎ (0115) 982 5981
Batemans XB, XXXB; Castle Rock Harvest Pale, Sherriff's Tipple; Everards Tiger; Hop Back Summer Lightning; guest beers H
Busy, gimmick-free Castle Rock pub, tucked down a side street next to the Co-op and handy for Trent Bridge cricket ground. A former pet shop, it was named as a result of a local newspaper competition. The large beer range includes a rotating mild and Castle Rock house beers. Monthly brewery nights are hosted with live music. A good food menu including vegetarian options is available. Q

West Stockwith

White Hart

Main Street, DN10 4ET
⏲ 12-11
☎ (01427) 890176
Beer range varies Ⓗ
Small country pub with a little garden overlooking the River Trent, Chesterfield Canal and West Stockwith Marina. One bar serves the through bar, lounge and dining area. The beer range features regularly changing brews from micro-breweries. Idle Brewery is situated in outbuildings at the rear of the pub and a selection of its beers is always available. The area is especially busy during the summer, due to the volume of river traffic where the Chesterfield Canal joins the River Trent.
Q◐◑♿Å🚌♣P

Westwood

Corner Pin

75 Palmerston Street, NG16 5HY (off B6016)
⏲ 1 (12 Sat)-11 (midnight Fri & Sat); 12-midnight Sun
☎ (01773) 528781
Beer range varies Ⓗ
Corner pub with a lounge and public bar, both with open fires. This is a genuine free house, with beers sourced from local micro-breweries – Amber Ales, Blue Monkey, Bottle Brook, Leadmill, Thornbridge and others, dispensed from three handpulls. The landlady regularly brews special beers for the pub at Amber Ales. There is also a pool room, function room and indoor skittles alley – table skittles can be played in the bar. A Sunday afternoon poker league is hosted. Dogs are welcome.
⛫❀⊟♿🚌(1,90)♣⚊

Worksop

Grafton Hotel

Gateford Road, S80 1UQ (close to railway station)
⏲ 11-11
☎ (01909) 500342
Beer range varies Ⓗ
This single-bar pub is situated on the edge of town and less than 400 metres from Worksop Railway Station. It comprises a bar, lounge and separate dining area. The pub serves a number of Grafton Beers which are brewed at its brewery situated in outbuildings at its sister pub the Packet Inn on Grove Street in the nearby town of Retford.
⛫Q⛺❀◐◑⊟♿⇌🚌P

Mallard

Station Approach, S81 7AG (on railway platform)
⏲ 5 (2 Fri)-11 (midnight Sat); 12-11 Sun
☎ (01909) 530757
Beer range varies Ⓗ
Formerly the Worksop station buffet, this pub offers a warm welcome. Two real ales are always available together with a large selection of foreign bottled beers and country fruit wines. A room is available downstairs for special occasions including the three beer festivals the pub holds each year. Local CAMRA Pub of the Year 2004/05, and a regular winner of Pub of the Season awards.
QÅ⇌🚌P

Shireoaks Inn

Westgate, S80 1LT
⏲ 11.30-4, 6-11; 11.30-11 Sat; 12-10.30 Sun
☎ (01909) 472118
Beer range varies Ⓗ
Warm, friendly pub converted from cottages. The interior has a public bar with a pool table and large-screen TV, a comfortable lounge bar, and a dining area where tasty home-cooked food represents good value for money. The two handpulls dispense regularly-changing guest ales. A small outside area with tables is available in the summer. Q❀◐⊟Å⇌🚌♣⚊

Station Hotel

Carlton Road, S80 1PS (opp railway station)
⏲ 11-11 (10.30 Sun)
☎ (01909) 474108
Acorn Barnsley Bitter; guest beers Ⓗ
Situated opposite Worksop Railway Station, on the edge of the town centre, this pub was formerly the Regency Hotel but its new owners have returned it to its original name. The large hotel has one bar and two dining areas. Food is served at lunchtime and in the evening – Sunday lunch is especially popular. Four changing guest ales are available alongside the Barnsley Bitter. ❀◐◑Å⇌🚌P

Wysall

Plough Inn

Main Street, Keyworth Road, NG12 5QQ (jct of Widmerpool Rd and Main St)
⏲ 12-midnight
☎ (01509) 880339 🌐 ploughatwysall.co.uk
Draught Bass; Fuller's London Pride; Greene King Abbot; Taylor Landlord; guest beers Ⓗ
This pleasing, traditional village free house, run by the same family for more than 10 years, occupies an elevated position overlooking the main road. Once three cottages, it retains the original beamed ceilings. The comfortable interior has several separate alcoves creating a welcoming atmosphere. Guest beers are sourced from local micro-breweries. Quiz night is Tuesday.
⛫❀◐♣P⚊

Noted ales

At one time or another nearly every county town in England of any size has been noted for its beers or ales. Yorkshire claims not only stingo but also Hull and North Allerton ales whilst Nottingham, Lichfield, Derby, Oxford and Burton have almost branded their ales. During the eighteenth century the fame of Dorchester beer almost equalled the popularity of London porter.
Frank A. King, Beer has a History, 1947

OXFORDSHIRE

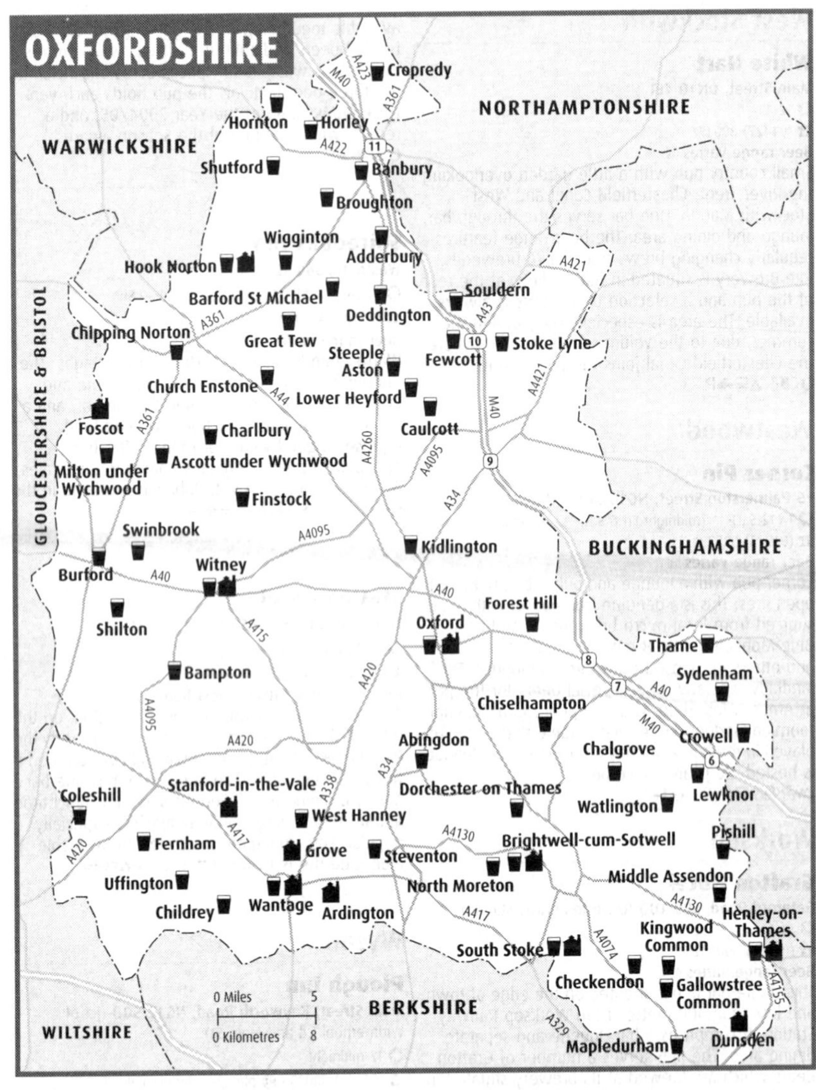

Abingdon

Brewery Tap

40-42 Ock Street, OX14 5BZ

11-11 (1am Fri & Sat); 12-4, 7-11 Sun

☎ (01235) 521655 thebrewerytap.net

Greene King H&H Bitter, Morland Original; guest beers H

Morland created a tap for its brewery in 1993, in an award-wining conversion of three Grade II-listed town houses. The brewery closed and its site was redeveloped in 2000 following a takeover by Greene King, but the pub, run by two generations of the same family since it first opened, has thrived. The attractive interior features panelled walls and stone floors. Although the bar stays open until 1am on Friday and Saturday nights, last admission is midnight. ⌂Q❀⇌◐♿♣P⁻

Crown & Thistle (Stocks Bar)

Bridge Street, OX14 3HS

11-11 (1am Fri & Sat); 12-10.30 Sun

☎ (01235) 522566 crownandthistle.com

Marston's Old Empire; guest beers H

The Stocks Bar is a free house within the 17th-century Crown and Thistle Hotel. Popular with tourists and locals alike, the publican is a keen

INDEPENDENT BREWERIES

Adkin Wantage
Appleford Brightwell-cum-Sotwell
Best Mates Ardington
Brakspear Witney
Cotswold Foscot
Hook Norton Hook Norton
Loddon Dunsden
Lovibonds Henley-on-Thames
Old Bog Oxford
Pitstop Grove (NEW)
Ridgeway South Stoke
White Horse Stanford-in-the-Vale
Wychwood Witney

supporter of local ales and sources his guest beers mainly from local breweries including Hook Norton and White Horse. The bar has many original features including a cobbled courtyard, galleried bar, authentic cannon and working stocks. A varied pub menu is offered, and there is a restaurant for more formal dining. Live music plays at the weekend and occasional beer festivals are held. ❀🛏◐⊟♿🚌(X3)♣●P⚡

Adderbury

Bell Inn

High Street, OX17 3LS

⏲ 12-2.30, 6-11 (midnight Fri & Sat); 12-3, 7-11 Sun

☎ (01295) 810338 🌐 the-bell.com

Hook Norton Hooky Dark, Hooky Bitter, Hooky Gold, seasonal beers; guest beers Ⓗ

Located in the heart of this beautiful village, close to the famous church, this Tardis-like 18th-century ale house retains its character with oak beams, panelling and inglenook fireplace. A Beautiful Beer award-winning pub, and branch Pub of The Year 2008, discounts are available to CAMRA members who join the cask ale drinkers club. Freshly-cooked quality food is served and there are no games machines, pool table or jukebox to disturb your enjoyment. Well-behaved dogs, children and walkers are welcome. ⛰Q🐕❀🛏◐♿🚌(59)♣⚡

Ascott under Wychwood

Swan Inn

4 Shipton Road, OX7 6AY

⏲ 12-3, 5.30-11; closed Mon; 12-4 Sun

☎ (01993) 832332

Brakspear Bitter; guest beers Ⓗ

This two-bar village local offers a warm welcome and a great ambience. The interior is furnished in keeping with a pub that offers something for everyone, including dogs, families and walkers, and features a wood burning stove. Three real ales in good condition are available, and outside there is a large garden area. A separate restaurant offers an imaginative, reasonably priced menu. The perfect pub to enjoy good food and drink and conversation without intrusive TV, jukebox or fruit machines. ⛰Q❀🛏◐⛺⇌🚌(X8,C1)P⚡

Bampton

Morris Clown

High Street, OX18 2JW

⏲ 5 (1 Sat)-11; 12-10.30 Sun

☎ (01993) 850217

Brakspear Bitter; West Berkshire Good Old Boy; guest beers Ⓗ

The 600-year-old Morris dancing tradition thrives in this village and in this pub. A true free house, it has been run by two generations of the same family for years, and features regularly in the Guide. Guest ales are usually sourced directly from smaller breweries. The interior of the pub is decorated with murals featuring past customers, and the pub is heated by a huge log fire. Bar billiards and Aunt Sally are played. Perry is available in the summer months. ⛰❀🚌(18)♣●P⚡

Banbury

Bell Inn

12 Middleton Road, OX16 4QJ

⏲ 12.30-3.30 (not Mon & Tue), 7-11; 12.30-11 Fri & Sat; 12-5.30, 8-11 Sun

☎ (01295) 253169

Black Sheep Best Bitter; guest beers Ⓗ

This friendly and thriving community pub close to the railway station is a regular entry in the Guide. It has a comfortable lounge with a blazing fire in winter, a traditional bar with pool table, and a patio area outside. At least two guest ales are regularly served. The pub hosts traditional pub games such as darts and Aunt Sally. CAMRA North Oxon Pub of the Year in 2007. ⛰❀◐⊟⇌🚌♣P⚡

Barford St Michael

George Inn

Lower Street, OX15 0RH (off B4031)

⏲ 7 (6 Fri)-11; 12-3, 7-11 Sat; 12-4 Sun

☎ (01869) 338226

Beer range varies Ⓗ

This delightful thatched free house dating from 1672 stands in the centre of the village. Stepping inside, a warm welcome awaits from the landlord and Dillon the Labrador. There is an ever-changing range of beers available and a beer festival is held in summer. Outside, there is a large, inviting beer garden. Food is not served but visitors are welcome to bring their own. Weddings, parties and other functions can be catered for. Dillon welcomes other well-behaved dogs. Q❀⊟⛺♣●P⚡

Brightwell-cum-Sotwell

Red Lion

Brightwell Street, OX10 0RT

⏲ 11-3, 6-11.30; 12-3, 7-10.30 Sun

☎ (01491) 837373 🌐 redlion.biz

Appleford Power Station; Loddon Hoppit; guest beers Ⓗ

This 16th-century pub goes from strength to strength, firmly establishing itself as one of the outstanding pubs in south Oxfordshire. Excellent ales from local brewers are always available and food is usually sourced locally if possible. This is an attractive pub in a lovely Oxfordshire village, where all visitors are warmly greeted and treated like locals. Worth seeking out. Local CAMRA Pub of the Year 2009. ⛰Q❀◐🚌(131)P⚡

Broughton

Saye & Sele Arms

Main Road, OX15 5ED (3 miles W of Banbury on B4035)

⏲ 11.30-2.30 (3 Sat), 7-11; 12-5 Sun

☎ (01295) 263348 🌐 sayeandselearms.co.uk

Beer range varies; Ⓗ

A friendly welcome is assured at this 17th-century free house at the edge of Broughton castle grounds. Four real ales are always available in the beamed and flagstone bar, with guest beers often coming from local breweries. There is something for everyone on the menu – including landlord Danny's excellent 'proper' pies and wonderful desserts. In summer the beautiful landscaped garden is perfect for alfresco dining. Inside there is a proud display of water tubs. Don't drive past. Q❀◐♿🚌(480)♣P⚡

Burford

Royal Oak

26 Witney Street, OX18 4SN (off A361)

⌚ 11-2.30 (not Tue), 6.30-11; 11-11 Sat; 11-3, 7-10.30 Sun
☎ (01993) 823278
Wadworth IPA, 6X; guest beer Ⓗ
Tucked away down a side street in this tourist town, this is a genuine local with a traditional pub atmosphere. The flagstone front bar leads to a long carpeted side bar with a bar billiards table at the far end. The walls are covered with interesting pictures and memorabilia. An ancient clock chimes melodiously and around 1,000 tankards hang from the ceiling. Excellent home-made food featuring local produce is served. Walkers are welcome and a boot scraper is provided. ⌂Q❀⛾◐◑⛺🚌♣●**P**

Caulcott

Horse & Groom

Lower Heyford Road, OX25 4ND (on B4030 between Middleton Stoney and Lower Heyford)
⌚ 12-3, 6-11; 12-3, 7-10.30 Sun
☎ (01869) 343257
Hook Norton Hooky Bitter; guest beers Ⓗ
A cosy pub with a warm welcome. The French landlord/chef offers excellent food and the Bastille Day celebrations are not to be missed. A genuine free house, the three guest ales could come from any part of the country – the pub is a supporter of the LocAle scheme and local micros feature strongly. Real cider is sold in summer. No under 10s are admitted and booking is advisable for meals, especially the popular Sunday lunch. The garden is an attraction in summer and car parking is available nearby. A gem. ⌂Q❀◐◑♿

Chalgrove

Red Lion

115 The High Street, OX44 7SS
⌚ 11.30-3, 6-1am; 11.30-11 (11.30-4, 6.30-11 winter) Sun
☎ (01865) 890625
Adnams Bitter; Fuller's London Pride; Taylor Landlord; guest beers Ⓗ
Enter this picturesque village local by crossing the small brook that runs alongside the road. It is owned by the Church of England and dates from the 16th century. Inside, the comfortable bar is split into 'near', 'middle' and 'far', with an open fire and plenty of exposed wood beams. There is a garden to the front with seating for drinkers, and a large child-friendly garden to the rear. Car parking is available opposite. ⌂❀◐◑♿🚌♣⚊

Charlbury

Rose & Crown 🏆 ✔

Market Street, OX7 3PL
⌚ 12-11 (midnight Wed & Thu; 1am Fri) 11-1am Sat
☎ (01608) 810103 🌐 myspace.com/theroseandcrownpub
Ramsbury Bitter; guest beers Ⓗ
Traditional town-centre free house, 23 years in this Guide, with a simply furnished split-level bar and a large lounge with patio courtyard. A pub for the discerning drinker who enjoys an excellent pint, with seven real ales it offers one of the best selections in the area and strongly supports micro-breweries. Fortnightly music nights feature some of the best touring artists around. On the Oxfordshire Way, walkers are welcome to bring their own food. Three times CAMRA North Oxon Pub of the Year. ⌂❀⛺⇌🚌(20A/X9)●⚊

Checkendon

Black Horse

Burncote Lane, RG8 0TE SU666841
⌚ 12-2, 7-11 (10.30 Sun)
☎ (01491) 680418
West Berkshire Mr Chubbs, Ⓗ**; Old Father Thames, Good Old Boy** Ⓖ
This olde worlde pub has been in existence for more than 300 years and, for the last century, run by generations of the same family. A treasure of a public house, it is situated along a lane that initially appears to lead to nowhere, and attracts ramblers, horse riders and visitors who care to seek it out as there is always a good pint waiting. There is no hot food but filled baguettes are available at lunchtimes. ⌂Q❀⛺🚌(142,145)**P**

Childrey

Hatchet Inn

Main Street, OX12 9UF (on B4001)
⌚ 12-2.30 (not Mon & Tue; 3 Sat), 7-11; 12-3.30, 7-10.30 Sun
☎ (01235) 751213
Greene King Morland Original; guest beers Ⓗ
One-room, split-level pub with a small, quiet area off to one side, offering a warm welcome to all. At the centre of this small village community, it is close to the historic Uffington White Horse. Thriving and well-supported quiz and Aunt Sally teams represent the pub in local leagues. Well-behaved dogs are welcome. A regular entry in the Guide, the pub is a previous winner of local CAMRA branch Pub of the Year. ❀◑♿⛺🚌(38,67)♣**P**

Chipping Norton

Chequers ✔

Goddards Lane, OX7 5NP (next to theatre)
⌚ 11-11 (11.30 Fri & Sat); 11-10.30 Sun
☎ (01608) 644717
Fuller's Chiswick, London Pride, ESB, seasonal beers Ⓗ
Traditional, rambling, low-ceilinged pub offering various nooks and crannies in which to enjoy the excellent ales and tasty bar meals. Four distinct seating areas allow the friendly, mixed clientele of visitors and locals of all ages to soak up the old-fashioned atmosphere without TV, jukebox or games machines to disturb the buzz of conversation. An old covered courtyard is now an attractive restaurant, offering a good and varied range of meals (not Sun eve). ⌂Q◐◑🚌

Chiselhampton

Coach & Horses

Watlington Road, OX44 7UX
⌚ 11-11 (10.30 Sun)
☎ (01865) 890255 🌐 coachhorsesinn.co.uk
Hook Norton Hooky Bitter; guest beers Ⓗ
This 16th-century hotel and restaurant provides visitors with good quality ales and an a la carte menu in a bar area and several good sized dining areas. For those staying over, there are nine en-suite bedrooms and free Wi-Fi. The large, attractive patio has ample room for summer drinking. The River Thame is not far away, providing excellent local walking. ⌂❀⛾◐◑♿🚌(101)**P**

Church Enstone

Crown

Mill Lane, OX7 4NN (off A44, on B4030)
12-3, 6-11; 12-4 Sun
(01608) 677262
Hook Norton Hooky Bitter; guest beers H
This picturesque 17th-century stone free house, with wrought iron seating at the front overlooking a quiet village green, is a real gem. Inside, it has an inglenook and old village photographs on the walls. Conversation thrives with no background music or games machines. The restaurant features award-winning menus including fresh fish, seafood, game (in season) and local produce wherever possible. The pub is popular with locals and walkers keen to explore the beautiful surrounding countryside. Q❀◐◑(20)P

Coleshill

Radnor Arms

32 Coleshill, SN6 7PR
11.30-3, 6-11; closed Mon; 12-3, 7-10.30 Sun
(01793) 861575 theradnorarms.co.uk
Beer range varies G
Set in a beautiful National Trust village, the 18th-century building was the former blacksmith's to the Coleshill estate. Old smithy tools are displayed in the dining room, and there is a main bar and cosy snug. The emphasis here is on quality, reasonably-priced, locally-sourced food served in a pub atmosphere. At least two beers are available, dispensed by gravity from behind the bar. There are close links with the countryside – walkers (boots off), children and well-behaved dogs are welcome. Q❀◐◑♣P

Cropredy

Red Lion ✔

8 Red Lion Street, OX17 1PB (opp church)
12-2.30 (3.30 Sat), 6 (5.30 Tue & Fri)-11 (midnight Fri & Sat); 12-10.30 Sun
(01295) 750224 redlioncropredy.co.uk
Hook Norton Hooky Bitter; guest beers H
Tucked away opposite the church in the village, this well-run thatched inn is well worth finding. Four separate areas are served from a central bar, including two dining rooms and a family room. Four handpumps dispense a variety of beers and the regularly-changing lunch and dinner menus are very popular. Two wood-burning fires provide a warming ambience during the winter months, an established garden is available in the summer. The pub is popular with visitors from the nearby canal. Q❀◐◑♿P

Crowell

Shepherd's Crook

The Green, OX39 4RR (off B4009 between Chinnor and M40 Jct 6) SU744997
11.30-3, 5-11; 11-11 Sat; 12-10.30 Sun
(01844) 351431
Enville Enville Ale; Taylor Golden Best; guest beers H
Nestling in the foothills of the Chilterns, this comfortable inn is renowned for its wide selection of beers – the landlord is a real ale fanatic as well as a horse-racing and cricket enthusiast. The pub menu specialises in fish which comes direct from the coast, and meat from the local butcher. Beers from local breweries are often available and a 25-barrel beer festival is held on the August bank holiday weekend, along with ferret racing. Dogs are welcome. Q❀◐◑(40)P

Deddington

Crown & Tuns

New Street, OX15 0SP (on A4260)
12-3 (not Mon), 5.30-11; 12-11 Sun
(01869) 337371 puddingface.com
Hook Norton Hooky Bitter; guest beers H
Originally a coaching inn, this 16th-century building overlooks the main Oxford to Banbury road. It has been sympathetically redecorated with simple wood furnishings to complement the building's original features and has a real fire in winter. The pub attracts a mixed clientele of all ages. Its speciality is good home-made pies with a variety of fillings, however if pies are not your thing, other food is available on the 'But not Pies' menu. ❀◐◑(59)♣

Dorchester on Thames

Fleur De Lys

9 High Street, OX10 7HH (off A4074) SU578942
11.30-3, 6-midnight; 11.30-midnight Sat; 11.30-11.30 Sun
(01865) 340502 fleurdelys-dorchester.co.uk
Brakspear Bitter; Hook Norton Hooky Bitter; guest beer H
The Fleur is situated in the historic village of Dorchester opposite the Abbey, and there are nearby Thames and Thame walks. Once a coaching inn, parts of the pub date from the 16th century. A free house, it offers a friendly welcome with three handpumps, excellent, affordable bar and a la carte menus, a roaring fire in winter and newspapers on the bar. There is a large enclosed rear garden where Aunt Sally is played in the summer. A dog and family friendly pub. ❀◐◑(138)♣P

Fernham

Woodman Inn

SN7 7NX (on B4508)
11-11; 12-10.30 Sun
(01367) 820643 thewoodmaninn.net
Taylor Landlord; guest beers G
First licensed in 1652, this delightful and spacious inn caters for all. Most of the building's internal walls were removed years ago but it retains many original features including the huge roaring fire. There are close links with horse racing. Renowned locally for its food, there is always a warm welcome for those who want to sample the four ever-changing cask ales stored behind the bar and dispensed by gravity. Thatchers cider is available in summer. Q❀◐◑♿(67)♣P

Fewcott

White Lion

Fritwell Road, OX27 7NZ (1 mile from jct 10 of M40)
7 (5.30 Fri; 12 Sat)-11; 12-6.30 Sun
(01869) 346639
Beer range varies H
A true free house and hub of the community, offering a constantly-changing choice of four ales from micros and larger brewers near and far. Stout and porter often feature. This popular village pub is ideal for enjoying conversation, watching sport on

TV or playing pool, though it can get busy on darts nights. One en suite room has recently been added. The large garden is popular in summer, but is closed for the winter. P

Finstock

Plough Inn

The Bottom, OX7 3BY (Off B4022)
12-2.30, 6-11; closed Mon; 12-11 Sat; 12-6 Sun
(01993) 868333 theplough-inn.co.uk
Adnams Broadside; Young's Bitter; guest beer H
Thatched free house dating from the mid-18th century with a simply furnished flagstone-floored public bar. Attractive features include old local photos, a piano and a library. A carpeted, low beamed dining room offers excellent food from a small but interesting menu. The snug bar has comfortable settees around an inglenook fireplace. Walkers (with boots off), well behaved children over five and dogs on leads are welcome. The large well-kept garden is a pleasant place to relax in summer. Q(X8)P

Forest Hill

White Horse

Wheatley Road, OX33 1EH
12-3, 6-11; closed Mon
(01865) 873927
Goldfinch Tom Brown's; guest beers H
Situated on the main road in a small village a couple of miles east of Oxford, the White Horse is a freehold pub selling Goldfinch beers. The stone-built pub has one long room inside divided by a huge fireplace, with a wealth of oak beams. There are some tables set aside for drinkers. This popular eatery sells authentic Thai cuisine, and lunchtime meals are very good value for money. Booking is advisable if you are dining. P

Gallowstree Common

Reformation

Horsepond Road, RG4 9BP (between Cane End and Peppard Common) SU690801
12-3; 5.30-11 (midnight Fri & Sat); 12-8 Sun
(0118) 972 3126 the-reformation.co.uk
Brakspear Bitter, seasonal beers H
The enthusiastic landlord and landlady have revitalised the fortunes of this country pub since their arrival in 2007. The pub is divided into three distinct areas, and boasts a large garden with separate children's play area. Families and well-behaved dogs are welcome, and the pub hosts many local village functions. Food is available at every session, all home-made, using local produce wherever possible. However, there is always an area kept free for those who just want to enjoy a drink. QP

Great Tew

Falkland Arms

19 The Green, OX7 4DB (off A361 and B4022)
11.30-3, 6-11; 11.30-midnight Sat; 12-10.30 Sun
(01608) 683653 falklandarms.org.uk
Wadworth IPA, 6X, seasonal beers; guest beers H
A welcome return to the Guide for this award-winning, quintessential 16th-century English country pub. The beer garden overlooks the picturesque thatched Great Tew estate. Simple wooden furniture on flagstones and bare board floors, old jugs hanging from beams and brewers' memorabilia adorning the walls lend character inside. A large inglenook fireplace warms in winter. Eight handpumps dispense real ale and cider. Good quality food, accommodation and a range of snuffs are available. The annual July beer festival is always popular. Q

Henley-on-Thames

Bird in Hand

61 Greys Road, RG9 1SB SU760824
11.30-2, 5-11; 11.30-11 Sat; 12-10.30 Sun
(01491) 575775 henleybirdinhand.co.uk
Brakspear Bitter; Fuller's London Pride; Hook Norton Hooky Dark; guest beers H
Just out of the town centre, Henley's only genuine free house has a friendly atmosphere and is popular with locals and visitors alike. The one bar pub has a large, secure garden with an aviary, pond and pets. Guest beers are usually from two micro-breweries, and good value lunches are served Monday to Friday. Local CAMRA Pub of the Year 2006 and 2008.

Hook Norton

Pear Tree

Scotland End, OX15 5NU (off A361, follow signs to brewery)
11.30-11.30 (1.30am Fri & Sat); 11.30-11.30 Sun
(01608) 737482
Hook Norton Hooky Dark, Hooky Bitter, Hooky Gold, Old Hooky; guest beers H
This much-loved village local is the brewery tap for Hook Norton, situated just a few hundred metres from the Victorian tower brewery and visitor centre. The full range of Hooky beers is served. There is a cosy log fire in winter and a large family-friendly beer garden for the summer. Acoustic music plays on the first Tuesday of the month. With three guest rooms, this is the ideal base for a brewery tour and/or to explore the Cotswolds. Open all day, every day. (488)P

Horley

Red Lion

OX15 6BQ
6-11; closed Mon; 12-6 Sun
(01295) 730427
Hook Norton Hooky Bitter; Taylor Landlord H
At the heart of the village community, this popular locals' pub offers a friendly welcome to visitors. Little changed over the years, it is a traditional beer-only pub where games and sport feature. Poker, darts and dominoes are played on Tuesday to Thursday nights and sport is regularly shown on TV. Aunt Sally is also played. An additional beer is offered from time to time when music or other events are held, and occasional beer festivals are hosted. P

Hornton

Dun Cow

West End, OX15 6DA (signed from village green) SP391449
6 (12 Sat)-11; 12-10.30 Sun
(01295) 670524

Hook Norton Hooky Bitter; Wells Bombardier; guest beers 🄷
A thatched, low-beamed and flagstone-floored Grade II-listed pub, located in a quiet and attractive village. There is good walking locally and ramblers and dogs are welcome. The family runs the Vitis Wines and Drunken Monk outlets, and stocks historical ales, meads and fruit and country wines. Beer festivals are held in February and July. Freshly-cooked food is available lunchtimes (weekdays by arrangement) and evenings. A previous North Oxfordshire CAMRA Cider and Perry Pub of the Year. ⛫❀◗♣●P⚋

Kidlington

King's Arms

4 The Moors, OX5 2AJ
⏲ 11-3, 5.30-11.30; 11-midnight Fri & Sat; 12-11.30 Sun
☎ (01865) 373004
Greene King IPA; Wells Bombardier; guest beers 🄷
Traditional community pub with two small front rooms in what claims to be England's largest village. Guest beers are a major attraction and can be any style from any brewery, with dark beers often making an appearance. The heated, covered patio is used for playing Aunt Sally and also for a twice-yearly beer festival. Darts is also popular. An outside seating area includes a heated smoking shelter. Good value pub lunches are served Monday to Saturday. ⛫❀◖⊟♿🚌(2A)♣P⚋

Kingwood Common

Unicorn

Colmore Lane, RG9 5LX (on road to Stoke Row) SU701817
⏲ 12-3 (not Mon), 6-11; 12-3.30, 6.30-11 Sun
☎ (01491) 628452 🌐 the-unicorn.co.uk
Brakspear Bitter, seasonal beers; Hook Norton Hooky Dark 🄷
Since it was saved from closure a few years ago, this delightful country pub continues to go from strength to strength. Deep leather seats and a real fire help to create a cosy and welcoming atmosphere. The pub hosts cricket, darts and cribbage teams, and holds a regular Monday night quiz. Food is served at every session except Sunday evening and Monday. A one-room letting suite is an ideal weekend getaway or business stopover. Free wireless Internet is available.
⛫❀🛏◖◗🚌(2,145)♣P⚋

Lewknor

Leathern Bottle

1 High Street, OX49 5TW SU716976
⏲ 11-2.30 (3.30 Sat), 6-11; 12-3.30, 7-10.30 Sun
☎ (01844) 351482 🌐 theleathernbottle.co.uk
Brakspear Bitter, seasonal beers 🄷
This 450-year-old pub (the current proprietors have been there for only 30 of these) is situated on the edge of the beautiful Chilterns, where the M40 crosses the ancient Icknield Way. Featuring in all but one edition of this Guide, this pub and the Red Lion at Britwell Salome were acquired by William Brakspear from Haywards' Watlington Brewery in 1850 for £1460. Handy for the Oxford Tube with its frequent services to and from London and Oxford.
⛫Q♘❀◖◗♿🚌P

Lower Heyford

Bell

21 Market Square, OX25 5NY
⏲ 12-3, 5-11; 12-11 Fri & Sat; 12-10.30 Sun
☎ (01869) 347176
Beer range varies 🄷
Large, multi-roomed pub at the centre of the village, a short walk from Heyford station over the canal bridge. Four regularly-changing ales, which can come from nationals or micros, include a guest ale which rotates monthly. A real cider is occasionally available in summer. Food is served lunchtimes and in the evening from 5pm daily. Occasional live music nights are hosted. The pub is popular with boaters from the nearby Oxford Canal.
⛫❀◖◗♿⇌🚌(25A)♣

Mapledurham

Pack Saddle

Chazey Heath, RG4 7UD (on A4074) SU696772
⏲ 11-3, 6-11; 11-11 Fri & Sat; 12-10.30 Sun
☎ (0118) 946 3000 🌐 thepacksaddleinn.co.uk
Wadworth IPA, 6X, Horizon, Bishop's Tipple, seasonal beers; guest beer 🄷
This is a genuine pub with all the traditional features – large fireplace, wood beams and horticultural memorabilia. It is located between two golf courses on the Mapledurham estate just a few miles from the main house. The bar area is divided into two – the lower part primarily for drinkers. Food is freshly made, of high quality and excellent value, with the emphasis on traditional fare. Outside is an enclosed garden with a children's play area. ⛫Q❀◖◗♿🚌(X39,X40)♣P⚋

Middle Assendon

Rainbow

RG9 6AU (on B480) SU738858
⏲ 12-3, 6-11 (not Mon eve winter); 12-3, 7-10.30 Sun
☎ (01491) 574879
Brakspear Bitter, seasonal beers 🄷
Small and easily missed pub hidden away in the Stonor Valley. Ideally situated for Chiltern walks, it is a popular stop for local horse-drawn carriage tours. There is always a warm and friendly welcome from the landlords and locals. The bar is divided into two – the lounge serving quality home-cooked fresh food including locally-sourced game. This is a lively local pub, very much the hub of the village. Q❀◖◗⊟♣P

Milton under Wychwood

Quart Pot

3 High St, OX7 6LA
⏲ 5 (12 Fri-Sun)-midnight
☎ (01993) 830589
Loddon Hullabaloo; guest beers 🄷
Traditional village local with a friendly, welcoming atmosphere. One bar is carefully furnished with a real fire. The side bar has a pool table, darts, dominoes and TV while a separate dining room has access to the bar. The pub supports local activities and is a popular meeting place for the village community. Three well kept ales focusing on micro-breweries feature. Good quality, reasonably priced pub food is available. Near the Oxfordshire Way path, walkers are welcome.
⛫Q❀◖◗♿🚌(X8,233)♣P

North Moreton

Bear at Home
High Street, OX11 9AT SU561894
12-3, 6-11 (midnight Thu); 12-11 Sat
☎ (01235) 811311 bear-at-home.co.uk
Taylor Landlord; West Berks Bear Beer; guest beers Ⓗ
This friendly village local dates back to the 15th-century when it was a coaching inn. The main bar features sofas, an open fire and plenty of tables for diners. The wide range of mostly local beers includes Bear Beer, brewed exclusively for the pub by West Berks. The pub adjoins the village cricket ground and holds a beer and cricket festival at the end of July. The licensees also run an antiques business, with many items on display in the pub available to buy. Oxfordshire CAMRA Pub of the Year in 2007. (31,95)♣P

Oxford

Far from the Madding Crowd ✔
10-12 Friars Entry, OX1 2BY (down alleyway off Magdalen Street)
11.30-11 (midnight Thu-Sat); 12-10.30 Sun
☎ (01865) 240900 maddingcrowd.co.uk
Brakspear Bitter; guest beers Ⓗ
An independent free house tucked away down an alleyway in the centre of Oxford. The pub opened in 2002 as a conversion of three shop units, and has been popular with real ale drinkers ever since as there is always a good selection of beers available. In addition, the pub runs four mini real ale festivals a year, and occasionally hosts live music and other special events. Convenient for Oxford's theatres and shopping areas, the pub is a welcome retreat from the bustle of George Street. ♿♣

Harcourt Arms
Cranham Terrace, Jericho, OX2 6DG (off Walton Street)
12-2, 5.30-11 (midnight Fri & Sat); 12-2, 7-11 Sun
☎ (01865) 310630
Fuller's Chiswick, Discovery, London Pride, ESB; guest beers Ⓗ
Situated just outside the city centre in Jericho, which is still a good area for pubs, this typical 1930s brick pub has an atmospheric interior with subdued lighting and background jazz. The walls are decorated with modern art prints and an impressive selection of international bank notes. Toasted sandwiches are available, as is Fuller's 1845 bottle conditioned ale. While away the time playing games such as Scrabble or reading the New Scientist or Private Eye. (17)♣

King's Arms
40 Holywell Street, OX1 3SP
10.30-midnight; 12-midnight
☎ (01865) 242369 kingsarmsoxford.co.uk
Caledonian Deuchars IPA; St Austell Tribute; Young's Bitter, Special, seasonal beers; guest beers Ⓗ
Dating from 1607, the pub is set among the university buildings of central Oxford and owned by Wadham College, with students housed on the upper floors. Internally, a warren of rooms includes two bars and much wood panelling. Popular with the academic community, locals and tourists, it is often very busy but the bar service remains efficient. Food is served until 9pm daily. Outside are pavement tables and benches. This city centre pub is open until midnight throughout the week. Q(Oxford)

Lamb & Flag
12 St Giles, OX1 3JS
12-11 (10.30 Sun)
☎ (01865) 515787
Palmers IPA; Shepherd Neame Spitfire; Skinner's Betty Stoggs; Theakston Old Peculier; guest beers Ⓗ
Saved from conversion to student accommodation in a vigorous local campaign some years ago, the pub is now run as a free house by St John's College. Now a flagship for real ale in the city, it draws its clientele equally from the academic, tourist and local communities. Many of the regular beers and guests come from the west country; the Lamb & Flag Gold house beer is brewed by Palmers of Bridport. Q

Masons Arms ✔
2 Quarry School Place, Headington Quarry, OX3 8LH
5 (11 Sat)-11; 12-4, 7-10.30 Sun
☎ (01865) 764579 masonsquarry.co.uk
Brains Reverend James; Caledonian Deuchars IPA; West Berkshire Good Old Boy; guest beers Ⓗ
Family-run, community pub full of character, a meeting place for local darts and Aunt Sally teams. Guest ales change weekly and a popular annual beer festival is held in September. A selection of bottled Belgian beers is also stocked and cider on handpump. Ales from the pub's own micro-brewery, the Old Bog, are generally available at weekends and sell out fast – contact the pub to check availability. A heated decking area is popular all year round and a function room can be booked for private functions. ♣P

Old Bookbinders 🏆
17-18 Victor Street, Jericho, OX2 6BT
5 (12 Fri & Sat)-midnight; 12-11 Sun
☎ (01865) 553549 oldbookbinders.co.uk
Greene King IPA, seasonal beers; guest beers Ⓗ
Situated in a maze of back streets, this pub is well worth finding. Furnished in ale house style with plenty of bric-a-brac and a collection of pump clips, it has a pleasant atmosphere and extends a warm welcome. The food is good and well priced. Guest beers feature alongside those from Greene King and there are beer festivals in the spring and autumn. Well-behaved children, dogs and students are welcome and there is free wireless internet access. Local CAMRA Pub of the Year 2008. (17)♣

Rose & Crown
14 North Parade Avenue, OX2 6LX (off Banbury Road ½ mile N of city centre)
10-midnight (1am Fri & Sat); 12-11 Sun
☎ (01865) 510551 rose-n-crown.com
Adnams Bitter, Broadside; Hook Norton Old Hooky Ⓗ
Well-known Victorian pub on a busy, vibrant north Oxford street, comprising three small rooms with a heated, covered courtyard at the back and a small room that can be booked for functions. It attracts a good mix of students, locals and academics, drawn here by the warm hospitality, lively conversation and excellent beer. Mobile phones are banned and there is no intrusive music – children and dogs are not admitted. Opening times can vary outside term time. Q

Royal Blenheim
13 St Ebbe's Street, OX1 1PT
11-11
☎ (01865) 242355

White Horse Village Idiot, Wayland Smithy; guest beers H
This street-corner, city-centre pub is owned by Everards but leased to the White Horse Brewery. There are 10 handpumps dispensing a well-kept range of White Horse beers and one from Everards, plus guests from all over the country. The interior feels light and airy, with plenty of natural wood. Live sport is shown on the large TV screen, with rugby and American football regularly pulling in the crowds. Food is available at lunchtime.

White Horse

52 Broad Street, OX1 3BB
11-midnight
(01865) 204801 whitehorseoxford.co.uk
Hook Norton Old Hooky; St Austell Tribute; Taylor Landlord; White Horse Wayland Smithy; Wychwood Hobgoblin; guest beer H
Claiming to be the smallest pub in Oxford and sandwiched between the two entrances to Blackwell's famous bookshop, this classic, Grade II listed, 16th-century pub has a single long and narrow bar and a small snug at the rear. Up to six cask ales are dispensed. Popular with students and tourists, the city centre pub regularly featured in Inspector Morse and more recently Lewis. Both Winston Churchill and Bill Clinton are reputed to have frequented the pub during their Oxford days.
Q

Pishill

Crown Inn

RG9 6HH (on B480) SU718902
11.30-2.30, 6-11; 12-3, 7-10.30 Sun
(01491) 638364 crownpishill.co.uk
Brakspear Bitter; guest beers H
Originally a 15th-century coaching inn, the building may have origins dating back as far as the 11th century. There is a 400-year-old barn that complements the brick and flint main pub and holds functions and music nights. Brakspear ales feature alongside one or two regularly-changing guest beers, although this is a free house.
Q P

Shilton

Rose & Crown

OX16 4AB
12-3, 6-11; 12-11 Fri & Sat; 12-10 Sun
(01993) 842280
Young's Bitter; Hook Norton Old Hooky; guest beer H
This authentic 17th-century Cotswold stone pub has two rooms – the front bar features a log fire in winter to welcome visitors, while the rear room is the focal point for diners and has a wood-burning stove. The pub is the focus of the local community, with food sourced locally and prepared by the chef/landlord. The rotating guest beer often comes from a local brewer. Well-behaved dogs are welcome in the front bar. Q P

Shutford

George & Dragon

Church Lane, OX15 6PG (3 miles off A422 next to church)
12-2.30, 5.30-11; closed Mon; 12-10.30 Sun
(01295) 780320 thegeorgeanddragon.com
Hook Norton Hooky Bitter; guest beers H
This welcoming 13th-century listed building in the heart of the village is built into the hill beside the church. Four real ales are available in the lively bar, with its inglenook fireplace and tiled flooring. Hooky Bitter is always on handpump as well as three guest ales, regularly including a local ale. The pub hosts traditional games including darts and Aunt Sally. For the adventurous there is a yard of ale hanging above the bar. Q

Souldern

Fox Inn

Fox Lane, OX27 7JW
12-3, 5-11; 12-11 Sat; 12-4, 6-11 Sun
(01869) 345284 thefoxatsouldern.co.uk
Hook Norton Hooky Bitter; guest beers H
A warm welcome is guaranteed at this friendly free house situated in the centre of the village. Two guest ales come from national as well as local breweries, and occasionally Lancashire and Yorkshire micros. A beer festival is held on the last weekend of July when northern micros feature strongly. The large garden is popular in good weather and Aunt Sally is played. The car park is small, but on-road parking is available nearby. Accommodation is in four en suite rooms.
P

South Stoke

Perch & Pike

The Street, RG8 0JS (off B4009)
12-3, 5-11, 11.30-11 Sat; 12-10.30 Sun
(01491) 872415 perchandpike.co.uk
Brakspear Bitter, Oxford Gold H
A traditional 17th-century brick-and-flint pub at the hub of the village, with an adjoining barn that has been converted into a restaurant and four en-suite bedrooms. A varied menu includes homely pub food at lunchtime, a la carte in the evening and the traditional roast on Sunday. The original part of the pub has three separate areas with low beams, a real fire and comfortable seating.
Q (134,135) P

Steeple Aston

White Lion

Southside, OX25 4RR
12-midnight
(01869) 340307
Taylor Golden Best, Landlord; guest beers H
Family-run, single-room, community pub dating from the 19th century. There is always something going on here, with chess by the fire, satellite TV, pool, occasional live music and free Wi-fi internet access. Fresh food is served all day every day and a heated shelter is provided for smokers in the garden. The Oxford to Banbury bus stops outside.
(59)

Steventon

Cherry Tree Inn

33 High Street, OX13 6RS
11.30 (12 Sat)-11.30; 12-11 Sun
(01235) 831222
Wadworth Horizon, IPA, JCB, 6X, seasonal beers; guest beers H
The building dates back to the 17th century, becoming a pub in the mid 1800s with the coming

of the GWR. This friendly Wadworth managed house has two bars, a dining room and patio area. It is popular with villagers and attracts a busy lunchtime trade from the nearby trading estate. An annual beer festival is held in May as well as monthly folk music sessions. Families, walkers and well behaved dogs are welcome.
⛰Q❀🛏◐◑♿▲🚌(35A)♣P⚟

Stoke Lyne

Peyton Arms

Main Street, OX27 8SD (off B4100)
🕘 12-2, 5-11; closed Mon; 12-11 Sat; 12-7 Sun
☎ (01869) 345285
Hook Norton Hooky Bitter, Old Hooky Ⓖ
This classic old pub, two miles from junction 10 of the M40, is a 'must visit', set in an idyllic rural setting. The legendary hosts and regulars from the local farming community provide much of the pub's character, as well as memorabilia from the 1950s and 1960s on the walls of the bar. The Hook Norton beers are gravity fed from the cellar behind the bar. Freshly prepared rolls are available. No children or dogs are allowed. Good company and conversation guaranteed. ⛰Q❀⚟

Swinbrook

Swan Inn

OX18 4DY (1 mile off A40)
🕘 11-3, 6-11; 12-11 Sun
☎ (01993) 823339 🌐 theswanswinbrook.co.uk
Hook Norton Hooky Bitter; guest beers Ⓗ
This 17th-century pub owned by the Duchess of Devonshire boasts an idyllic setting by the River Windrush. Copies of the Mitford family photographs adorn the walls. An attractive small bar furnished with settees and benches features three well-kept real ales from micro-breweries along with Westons cider. Two comfortable dining areas open off the bar and there is a large, airy garden room. Contemporary food is served. There is an attractive garden with an orchard. Dogs, children and walkers are welcome. ⛰Q❀🛏◐◑♿🍎P

Sydenham

Crown Inn

Sydenham Road, OX39 4NB
🕘 12-3, 5-11; 12-11 Sat; 12-4 Sun
☎ (01844) 351634 🌐 crownsydenham.co.uk
Brakspear Bitter; Fuller's London Pride; guest beer Ⓗ
In a rustic setting at the heart of the village, opposite the church, the Crown was purchased by a group of locals in 2008 to save it from closure. The low-beamed 16th-century pub retains a traditional, welcoming atmosphere with large, sturdy wooden tables and a separate bar area. The food is freshly prepared by the landlord to a high standard. There is a garden to the rear with an Aunt Sally pitch.
⛰❀◐◑🚌(40)♣

Thame

Falcon ✔

1 Thame Park Road, OX9 3JA
🕘 12-11 (10.30 Sun)
☎ (01844) 212118
Hook Norton Hooky Bitter, seasonal beer; guest beers Ⓗ
Thriving, unspoilt community local rescued from possible oblivion by Hook Norton in 2006, run by two enthusiastic families. Refurbished in early 2009, the walls are adorned with a collection of reproduction pub signs. There is a separate dining area where the daily specials, steak offers and themed food evenings can be enjoyed. Children are welcome in the bar until 8pm. Situated a small distance from the town centre, the Thame/Risborough Phoenix Cycle Trail runs along the old railway track nearby. ⛰❀◐◑▲🚌(40,280)♣P⚟

Uffington

Fox & Hounds

High Street, SN7 7RP
🕘 12-3, 5-midnight; 12-midnight Sat & summer; 12-10.30 Sun
☎ (01367) 820680
Ringwood Best Bitter; guest beers Ⓗ
The last remaining pub in the village, this cosy 200-year-old community inn has panoramic views of the Ridgeway and the White Horse. Fresh, made to order food sourced from local suppliers is available. The pub has close links with the countryside. Families, walkers and well-behaved dogs are welcome. Beer festivals are held in the summer.
❀🛏◐◑🚌(67)P

Wantage

Royal Oak Inn 🏆

Newbury Street, OX12 8DF (S of Market Square)
🕘 5.30-11; 12-2.30, 7-11 Sat; 12-2, 7-10.30 Sun
☎ (01235) 763129 🌐 royaloakwantage.2ya.com
Wadworth 6X; West Berkshire Maggs Mild, Dr Hexter's Wedding Ale, Dr Hexter's Healer; guest beers Ⓖ
Photographs of ships bearing the pub's name adorn the walls in this street-corner pub. The lounge bar features a wrought-iron trelliswork, largely hidden by over 300 pump clips. The smaller public bar attracts a younger crowd. A mecca for the discerning drinker, the pub is the primary outlet for Pitstop and West Berks ales in the area – two beers carry the landlord's name. A changing range of ciders and perrys is also available. Current local, county and regional CAMRA Pub of the Year.
🛏🍺🚌♣🍎

Shoulder of Mutton

38 Wallingford Street, OX12 8AX
🕘 12-11 (10.30 Sun)
☎ (07788) 190822
Butts Traditional; guest beers Ⓗ
Corner pub renowned for its friendly atmosphere. It has a cosy snug that accommodates half a dozen at a pinch plus public and lounge bars with traditional decor and furnishings. The lounge has a computer with Internet access. If you prefer to stand you may also drink in the 'lay-by' in the corridor leading to a small outdoor patio which in summer is adorned with an abundance of hanging baskets. ⛰❀🍺🚌♣

Watlington

Carriers Arms

Hill Road, OX49 5AD (off B4009) SU692944
🕘 10-midnight; 10-11 Sun
☎ (01491) 613470
Adnams Bitter; Brains The Rev. James; guest beers Ⓗ
This thriving local has four darts teams and plays Aunt Sally in the summer. There is a quiz and a

curry every Saturday evening. The pub offers a late breakfast and serves food every lunchtime and evening (except Sun eve, Mon and Tue). Situated close to the Ridgeway long distance footpath, from the garden there is a good view of the White Mark, a chalk triangle on Watlington Hill. You will also see large numbers of the once rare red kites whirling overhead. P

West Hanney

Plough

Church Street, OX12 0LN

12-3, 6-11; 12-10.30 Sun

(01235) 868674 ploughwesthanney.co.uk

Brakspear Bitter; Taylor Landlord; guest beers H

Atmospheric, Grade II-listed, 16th-century thatched inn with a cosy, beamed and alcoved split-level bar and a separate dining room serving locally renowned traditional British food. A large garden plays host to Aunt Sally and outdoor skittles in summer. Two beer festivals are held annually. The late May bank holiday festival features Oxfordshire ales. The August festival is a real village and family occasion – a weekend of live music and a variety of entertainments for everyone. QP

Wigginton

White Swan

Pretty Bush Lane, OX15 4LE (off A 361 Chipping Norton-Banbury road)

12-2.30, 6 (5 Fri)-11 (midnight Sat); 12-midnight Sun

(01608) 737322

Hook Norton Hooky Bitter, seasonal beers H

On the northern edge of the village, this 17th-century traditional inn, built of locally quarried ironstone, commands magnificent views across the valley. The bar area features a large inglenook fireplace, a welcome sight for walkers in winter. The garden is peaceful and relaxing. The Hook Norton dray delivers on Wednesday morning, weather permitting. There is a varied menu of locally sourced produce, with senior citizens' lunches on Tuesday and Friday. An acoustic music night is held on the fourth Tuesday of the month. Q(488)P

Witney

Eagle Tavern

22 Corn Street, OX28 6BL

11-3, 5-midnight (2am Fri); 11-2am Sat; 12-midnight

(01993) 849564

Hook Norton Hooky Bitter, Hooky Gold, Old Hooky, seasonal beers H

Run by a highly experienced, real ale drinking landlord and bar staff, this pub has been awarded Best Kept Cellar by Hook Norton Brewery. Plenty of interesting photos and paintings on the walls and a real fire lend a friendly atmosphere, with quiet background music provided by an excellent jukebox. The highlight of the lunchtime menu is the ham cooked by the landlady in Hook Norton beer. There is an unusual hexagonal pool table at the rear of the pub. (S1)

House of Windsor

31 West End, OX28 1NQ

6-11.30 (midnight Fri); 12-3, 6-midnight Sat; 12-11 Sun

(01993) 704277

St Austell Tinners; guest beers H

Excellent local pub with welcoming bar staff. The bar is in the front room, with plenty of seating at both the bar and tables. Quiet music, a friendly atmosphere and the absence of TVs and fruit machines make it a great place to enjoy a pint with friends or chat with the regulars. The room at the back, leading to the large beer garden, is quieter and is home to the resident chameleon (who occasionally makes an appearance on the bar). (S1)

Plough

98 High Street, OX28 6HL

11.30-11 (1am Fri-Sun)

(01993) 704430

Butts Barbus Barbus; Ringwood Best; Taylor Landlord; guest beer H

The enthusiastic publican is committed to both quality beers and good food. The pub was refurbished after flooding in 2007 and is light and airy, with beams, pews and candles contributing to the ambience. A separate restaurant at the rear opened in 2008. An open mike night held every Tuesday for local musicians can be a raucous affair, but the pub is generally quiet with background music and no TV or fruit machines. (S1)

When Sean Franklin, who runs Roosters Brewery in Yorkshire, described hops as the 'grapes of brewing' he opened a debate that has led to a much greater appreciation of the role of the small green plant in brewing.

There are many varieties of hops: global brewers use 'high alpha' varieties (high in alpha acids) purely for bitterness. Craft brewers prefer to use varieties that deliver aroma and flavour as well as bitterness. The two most widely used English hops are Fuggles and Goldings, often blended together in the same beer; the Fuggle primarily for bitterness but with earthy and smoky notes, the Golding for its superb resiny, spicy and peppery character. Bramling Cross delivers rich fruity (blackcurrant) notes, Challenger has a citrus/lime edge while the workhorse of the hop fraternity, Target, offers citrus and pepper. First Gold is the most successful of the new 'hedgerow' varieties that grow to only half the height of conventional hops and are therefore easier to pick. It offers piny and apricot notes. American varieties used in Britain include Willamette (an offshoot of the Fuggle) and Cascade, both of which give rich citrus/grapefruit aromas and flavours. The Styrian Golding (actually a type of Fuggle) from Slovenia is widely used as an aroma hop in Britain for its luscious floral and citrus character.

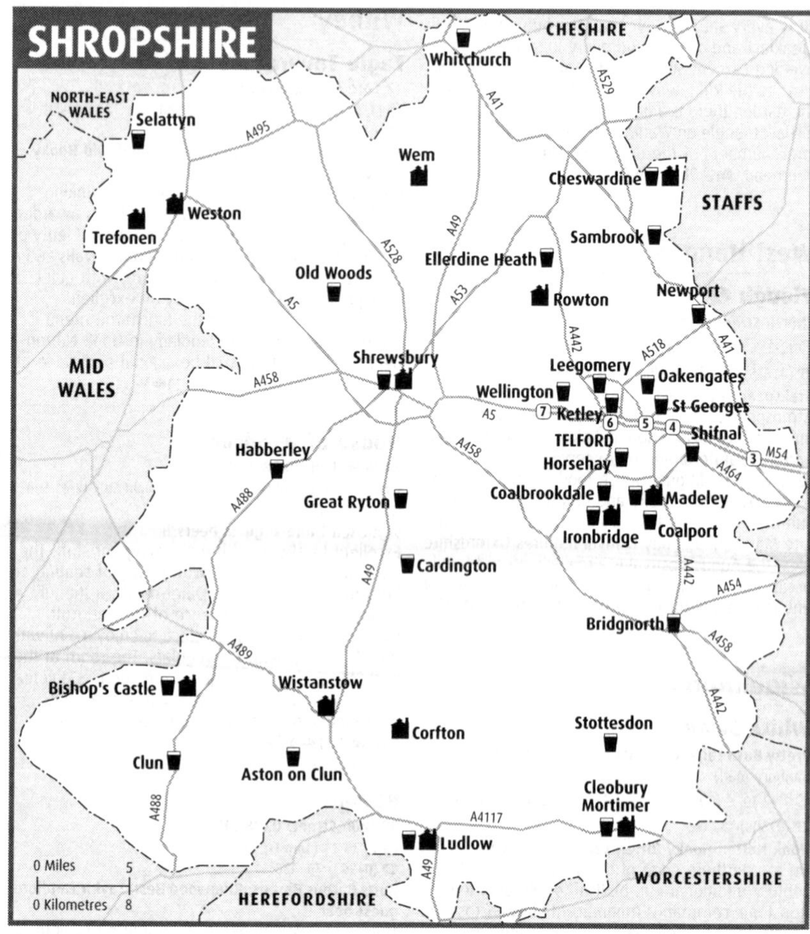

Aston on Clun

Kangaroo

Clun Road, SY7 8EW

⌚ 12-3 (not Mon & Tue), 6-11; 2-11 Fri; 12-11 Sat & Sun

☎ (01588) 660263 🌐 kangarooinn.co.uk

Ludlow Best Bitter; Wells Bombardier; Wye Valley HPA; guest beers 🄷

The unusual name of this cosy village free house comes from a 19th-century steam ship – it is thought to be the only pub of this name in Britain. It has a small lounge, public bar, games room, dining area, large garden and patio. The pub supports the nearby annual Arbour tree redressing ceremony at the end of May, the Clun Valley Beer Festival at the beginning of October and hosts a beer festival on the August bank holiday.

⛫Q❀◐◑⛺⇌(Broome)🚌♣P⁵–🍺

Bishops Castle

Castle Hotel

Market Square, SY9 5BH

⌚ 12-2.30, 6-11; 12-2.30, 7-10.30 Sun

☎ (01588) 638403 🌐 thecastlehotelbishopscastle.co.uk

Hobsons Best Bitter; Six Bells Goldings, Big Nevs; guest beers 🄷

For 20 years now Nikki and Dave, supported by their attentive staff, have lavished loving care on their 17th-century hotel. Magnificently landscaped terraced gardens benefit from fine views over the South Shropshire Hills. Three comfortable bar areas retain much original woodwork and furnishings, to provide the perfect setting to enjoy excellent home-cooked food and local beer. A beer festival in July is actively supported.

⛫Q❀🛏◐◑🍴♿⛺🚌(553,773)♣P

Six Bells

Church Street, SY9 5AA

⌚ 12-2.30 (not Mon), 5-11; 12-11 Sat; 12-3.30, 7-10.30 Sun

☎ (01588) 638930

Six Bells Big Nevs, Goldings, 1859, Cloud Nine; guest beers 🄷

This is the Six Bells brewery tap – the adjoining Six Bells Brewery was re-established on the site of the original one, which closed in the early 1900s. You can be sure of a friendly greeting in the wooden beamed bar, where four real ales are on handpump plus monthly specials and Montgomery Cider in summer. Excellent fresh food is served in the dining/lounge bar (not Sun eve or Mon except bank holidays). A local beer festival in July offers around 20 ales and real ciders plus live music in the courtyard. ⛫Q❀◐◑🍴⛺🚌(553)♣♣⁵–

Three Tuns
Salop Street, SY9 5BW
⏲ 12-11 (10.30 Sun)
☎ (01588) 638797
Three Tuns Clerics Cure, 1642, XXX; guest beer Ⓗ
One of the truly historic pubs in the country, this is one of the Famous Four who were still brewing in the early 1970s. Together with the adjoining, but separately owned, Three Tuns Brewery, from where it gets all its beers, it has been on this site since 1640. As well as serving good food it hosts regular music sessions, including jazz, in the top room. Dogs are welcome.
♨Q❀◑⊞♿🚌(443,745)♣●⁴—

Bridgnorth

Bell & Talbot
2 Salop Street, High Town, WV16 4QU
⏲ 5-midnight; 5.30-11 Sun
☎ (01746) 763233 🌐 odleyinns.co.uk
Batham Best Bitter; Hobsons Town Crier; guest beers Ⓗ
This old coaching inn is the beer drinker's and musician's local. In the larger bar the 'once seen never forgotten' ceiling display of records and musical instruments reflects the long tradition of live music, hosted on Fridays and Sundays. The foliage-adorned conservatory leads to an umbrella-covered smoking area. Guest beers are always LocAle bitters selected from Shropshire or Black Country breweries; cider is occasionally served in summer. ♨🛏⇌(SVR)🚌♣⁴—

Black Horse
4 Bridge Street, Low Town, WV15 6AF
⏲ 12-midnight
☎ (01746) 762415
Banks's Original, Bitter; Batham Best Bitter; Enville Ale; Hobsons Town Crier; guest beers Ⓗ
A mid-1700s ale house with cuisine and fully ensuite accommodation. The small front bar has antique bar fittings and dartboard. The large wood-panelled lounge bar leads to a dining room and conservatory. Wide-screen TVs show mainly sporting events. The external smoking area leads to a long courtyard, pleasant for outdoor drinking, with access to the nearby River Severn. Guest beers include seasonal ales. ❀🛏◑⊞♿⇌(SVR)🚌P⁴—▯

Golden Lion ✔
83 High Street, High Town, WV16 4DS
⏲ 11.30-2.30,5-11; 11-11 Fri & Sat; 12-10:30
☎ (01746) 762016 🌐 goldenlionbridgnorth.co.uk
Greene King IPA; Hobsons Town Crier; guest beers Ⓗ
A traditional town-centre inn with accommodation, and home-cooked (chip free) food served only at lunchtime. The history of this 17th-century coaching inn is displayed on the walls of the two pleasant quiet lounge bars. Dominoes, darts and quiz teams are based in the public bar, and quoits are also available. Q❀🛏◐⊞⇌(SVR)🚌♣P⁴—

Kings Head
3 Whitburn Street, High Town, WV16 4QN
⏲ 11-11 (midnight Fri & Sat); 12-10.30 Sun
☎ (01746) 762141 🌐 kingsheadbridgnorth.co.uk
Bridgnorth Apley Ale, Best; Hobsons Best Bitter, Town Crier; guest beers Ⓗ
Grade II-listed, 16th-century coaching inn sympathetically renovated featuring timber beams, flagstone floor, leaded windows and roaring log fires in winter. Local beers are always available and there is a constantly-changing selection of guest beers. Lunch and evening menus offer plenty of variety, with char-grills featuring local produce a speciality. The Stable Bar to the rear, with seven handpulls, is the Bridgnorth Brewery tap.
♨Q❀◑♿⇌(SVR)🚌⁴—▯

Railwaymans Arms
Hollybush Road, WV16 5DT (follow signs for SVR)
⏲ 11.30-4, 6-11; 11.30-11 Fri; 11-11 Sat; 12-10.30 Sun
☎ (01746) 764361 🌐 bridgnorthstation.co.uk/5
Batham Best Bitter; Hobsons Best Bitter; guest beers Ⓗ
A licensed refreshment room since 1861, owned by SVR, this is an exceptionally busy drinking spot, attracting beer drinkers and steam buffs from around the country. The platform drinking area is perfect for soaking up the atmosphere of the steam era, with plenty of fine railway memorabilia on display. A free house, the three guest beers tend to be from smaller, often local, brewers, plus one changing Belgian beer. A large selection of local and European bottled beers is also available. Sandwiches and pies are occasionally on offer. A CAMRA beer festival is hosted in the car park every September. ♨Q❀⇌(SVR)🚌●P⁴—▯

White Lion ✔
3 West Castle Street, WV16 4AB
⏲ 10.30-11 (midnight Fri & Sat); (closed winter 3-5 Tue-Thu); 10.30-10.30 Sun
☎ (01746) 763962 🌐 whitelionbridgnorth.co.uk
Banks's Bitter; St Austell Tribute; Titanic Mild; Wye Valley Bitter; guest beers Ⓗ
This 18th-century coaching inn boasts a simple interior with an open fire in winter, a lawned beer garden with paved terrace, a children's play area, and a covered and heated smoking area. Locally sourced products provide the basis for its popular lunchtime menu and speciality food nights. With seven handpulls, LocAle beers are always available, along with those from further afield, and Thatchers traditional cider. The pub regularly hosts live folk, folk/rock or blues music sessions and a summer music/beer festival in August.
♨Q❀🛏◑⊞⇌(SVR)🚌♣●⁴—

Cardington

Royal Oak
SY6 7JZ
⏲ 12-2.30, 7-midnight (1am Fri & Sat); closed Mon

INDEPENDENT BREWERIES

Bridgnorth Bridgnorth (brewing suspended)
Corvedale Corfton
Dolphin Shrewsbury
Hobsons Cleobury Mortimer
Ironbridge Ironbridge
Lion's Tail Cheswardine
Ludlow Ludlow
Offa's Dyke Trefonen
Rowton Rowton (NEW)
Salopian Shrewsbury
Shires Madeley
Six Bells Bishop's Castle
Stonehouse Weston
Three Tuns Bishop's Castle
Wem Wem
Wood Wistanstow

☎ (01694) 771266 🌐 at-the-oak.com

Draught Bass; Hobsons Best Bitter; guest beers Ⓗ

This ancient 15th-century free house in a conservation village is reputedly the oldest continuously licensed pub in Shropshire. It retains the character of a country pub – the low-beamed bar has a roaring fire in winter in a vast inglenook fireplace and the dining room has exposed old beams and studwork. Guest beers predominantly come from local breweries. The menu includes Fidget Pie made to a Shropshire recipe that has been handed down from landlord to landlord. Dogs are welcome during non-dining times – phone for details. ⛫Q❀◑▲♣P⁵–

Cheswardine

Red Lion

High Street, TF9 2RS

⏲ 6 (5 Thu & Fri)-11; 12-11 Sat; 12-3, 7-10.30 Sun

☎ (01630) 662234

Lion's Tail Blooming Blonde, Bru, Chesbrewnette; Marston's Burton Bitter Ⓗ

Home of the Lion's Tail Brewery, three of its beers are always available. The main bar area runs down the length of the pub, and there is a small snug and a further room next to the bar. In addition to the fine beers, there are more than 120 whiskies on sale. A true rural gem, this pub has a homely feel and is well worth seeking out. ⛫Q❀⊟♿P⁵–

Cleobury Mortimer

Kings Arms

6 Church Street, DY14 8BS

⏲ 10-11 (midnight Thu-Sat); 10-10.30 Sun

☎ (01299) 271954

Hobsons Mild, Best Bitter, Town Crier; guest beer Ⓗ

This pub, now the brewery tap, was the recipient of Hobsons' first beer delivery. It retains many traditional features, particularly the original wooden floors and beamed ceilings. Although open plan, it has distinct bar and tap room areas and lounges with comfy sofas. The accommodation has recently been refurbished. Food includes full English breakfast and a set lunch menu with daily-changing specials and home-made pies. A heated, covered terrace is provided for smokers. ⛫❀🛏◑♿🚌♣⁵–

Clun

White Horse Inn ✔

The Square, SY7 8JA

⏲ 11 (12 Sun)-midnight

☎ (01588) 640305 🌐 whi-clun.co.uk

Hobsons Mild, Best Bitter; Salopian Shropshire Gold; Three Tuns XXX, 1642; Wye Valley Butty Bach; guest beers Ⓗ

Comfortable, 16th-century coaching inn and post house standing in the old market square at the centre of a wonderfully timeless town, described by A E Housman as 'one of the quietest places under the sun'. It now has its own 'nano' brewery. A friendly local, it has an L-shaped bar with low beams and new adjoining dining room serving excellent, reasonably priced food. Westons First Quality cider, perry and an interesting range of foreign bottled beers are stocked. Outside is a secluded garden. Jam nights are held once a month. Previous winner of local CAMRA Pub of the Year. ⛫Q🐎❀🛏◑▲🚌♣●⁵–🍺

Ellerdine Heath

Royal Oak

TF6 6RL (2 miles off A442 towards A53) SJ604225

⏲ 12-midnight (10.30 Sun)

☎ (01939) 250300

Hobsons Best Bitter; Salopian Shropshire Gold; Wye Valley HPA; guest beers Ⓗ

The Tiddly, as it is known locally, has been in the Guide since 1992 under the management of Barry and Rose, though sadly Barry passed away in early 2009. Rose is continuing the good work and her cooking attracts diners from far and wide (note that the kitchen is closed on Monday and Tuesday). The locals are very friendly and the beer is keenly priced. A cider festival is held annually in July. ⛫Q🐎❀◑♿▲♣●P⁵–

Great Ryton

Fox Inn

Nr Dorrington, SY5 7LS

⏲ 12-2.30 (not Mon), 7-11 (midnight Sat); 12-3.30, 7-1am Sun

☎ (01743) 718499

Jennings Cumberland Ale; Salopian Shropshire Gold; Stonehouse Station Bitter; guest beer Ⓗ

Country pub nestling under the Stretton Hills. At the heart of the local community, the Fox is popular with locals and visitors from neighbouring villages. Local beers are always stocked and the pub hosts an annual beer festival. The lunchtime bar menu is good and in the evening an extensive high-quality food choice is offered. ⛫Q❀◑⊟♿🚌♣●P⁵–🍺

Habberley

Mytton Arms

SY5 0TP (S of Pontesbury off A488) SH398035

⏲ 4 (12 Fri-Sun)-11

☎ (01743) 792989

Hobsons Best Bitter; Three Tuns XXX; guest beers Ⓗ

A rare example of a country pub thriving on mainly beer sales, this pub has survived despite recent closures and is now at the heart of the small village. Off the entrance lobby are a separate lounge and U-shaped bar, subdivided into various nooks and crannies, and home to several pub teams. Outside there are seats to the front and a paved area with a pagoda. Guest beers come from local and national breweries and tend to be around the 4% ABV mark. ⛫Q❀⊟♣P⁵–

Ludlow

Charlton Arms

Ludford Bridge, SY8 1PJ

⏲ 11-midnight (1am Fri & Sat)

☎ (01584) 872813 🌐 thecharltonarms.co.uk

Hobsons Mild, Twisted Spire, Best Bitter; Ludlow Gold; Wye Valley Butty Bach; guest beers Ⓗ

Now extensively refurbished, this fine building is situated to the south of Ludlow, overlooking the River Teme and across the historic Ludford Bridge up towards the town's last remaining fortified gate and the town centre. It has an attractive bar and spacious lounge as well as a separate dining room with a terrace. The impressive function suite and roof bar have fine views across the river. Accommodation is in 10 en-suite rooms. Dogs are allowed in the bar. ⛫Q🐎❀🛏◑⊟♿▲🚌P⁵–🍺

Church Inn
The Buttercross, SY8 1AW
11-11 (11.30 Fri & Sat); 12-11 Sun
(01584) 872174 thechurchinn.com
Hobsons Mild, Town Crier; Ludlow Boiling Well, Gold; Weetwood Eastgate Ale; Wye Valley Bitter; guest beers H
Situated in the centre of Ludlow, close to the castle and market square, the Church is the only free house within the town walls and now has a resident ale conner to ensure the quality of the beer. The landlord, a former mayor of Ludlow, is a great advocate of real ale and also owns the Charlton Arms at Ludford Bridge. Guests ales are usually from national micro-breweries. The upstairs bar affords a wonderful view of the South Shropshire Hills and the church. Dogs are welcome.
Q

Nelson Inn
Rocks Green, SY8 2DS (on A4117 Kidderminster road from Ludlow bypass)
5 (7 Tue)-11; 1-midnight Fri & Sat; 12-midnight Sun
(01584) 872908
St Austell Tribute; guest beers H
On the outskirts of Ludlow, the Nelson dates back some 300 years and is a good example of a traditional beer house. The bar has a pool table, darts, quoits and a jukebox featuring '70s and '80s music. The lounge is decked out with musical instruments. The pub has beer festivals at Easter and late summer. Real cider, and from time to time perry, are stocked. The tasty chips on the menu are highly recommended. Camping is available in nearby fields by prior arrangement.
Q (192,292) P

Newport

Fox
Pave Lane, Chetwynd Aston, TF10 9LQ
12-11 (10.30 Sun)
(01952) 815940 fox-newport.co.uk
Salopian Shropshire Gold; Thwaites Original; Wood Shropshire Lad; guest beers H
Welcoming rural hostelry. Although long and low from the outside, once inside its open-plan interior, cosy corners and spacious rooms provide a pleasant atmosphere. In winter the warming fires are popular, while in summer the terrace provides pleasing views over the rolling hills. An excellent menu of mainly local produce is served all day until 10pm (9.30pm Sun). The pub hosts regular Shropshire beer and food weeks. Q P

Wheatsheaf
Chetwynd Aston, TF10 9LF
4.30 (12 Sat)-midnight; 12-11.30 Sun
(01952) 811447 wheatsheafinn.co.uk
Banks's Original; Marston's Burton Bitter, Pedigree; Wychwood Hobgoblin; guest beer H
A splendid locals' local, owned by the same family for many years – the current licensee has run it since 2006. A Marston's pub, it can get extremely busy despite its remote location. Four cask beers are normally on tap. The pub hosts 'best pickled onions/damson/sloe gin' competitions that are popular with the regulars. A true community pub.
Q P

Old Woods

Romping Cat
SY4 3AX (off B5067 Baschurch Road)
4.30-11; 12-3, 6-11 Sat & Sun
(01939) 290273
Hobsons Best Bitter; Salopian Hoptwister; Stonehouse Cambrian Gold; guest beers H
A warm welcome awaits at this traditional roadside country pub. Six handpumps dispense a selection from mainly independent breweries. Shropshire beers are a permanent feature and Moles Black Rat cider is also available. A bonus following recent changes to the bar layout is the addition of a snug, complete with open fire. A garden has been created at the rear with wonderful floral displays. A range of rolls and baps is usually available.
Q (576) P

Sambrook

Three Horseshoes
TF10 8AP (½ mile E of A41)
5 (4 summer)-11 Mon; 12-2, 5 (4 summer)-11 Tue-Sat; 11-10.30 (11 summer) Sun
(01952) 551133
Banks's Original; St Austell Tribute; Salopian Shropshire Gold; guest beers H
In the Guide for the fourth year and justifiably so, this welcoming country pub attracts customers from near and far. Traditional music is played inside, and there is the occasional outside function within the extensive grounds, ideal in fine weather. The quarry tiled bar is great for a game of darts, or if you just want to talk sit down in the lounge, or enjoy a meal with a good pint. No food on Sunday. Q P

Selattyn

Cross Keys ★
Glyn Road, SY10 7DH (on B4579 Oswestry-Glyn Ceiriog road)
7(6 Fri)-11; closed Mon & Tue; 12-5, 7-11 Sun
(01691) 650247
Stonehouse Station Bitter; guest beers H
Dating from the 17th century, this building has been a pub since 1840 and is CAMRA National Inventory listed. It is situated next to the church in a small village close to the Welsh border and Offa's Dyke. The cosy, small bar has a quarry tiled floor and real fire, and features a large topical cartoon redrawn each December. There are two further rooms and a function room. Two guest beers are always on offer. Open at lunchtime Monday to Saturday by prior arrangement only.
Q P

Shifnal

White Hart
4 High Street, TF11 8BH
12-11
(01952) 461161
Enville Ale; Holden's Mild; Salopian Shropshire Gold; Tetley Burton Ale; Wye Valley HPA; guest beers H
This Grade II-listed, half-timbered free house received the first Cask Marque accreditation in Shropshire and provides a warm welcome in its beamed, traditional bars. Good, wholesome pub grub is offered every lunchtime except Sunday. The pub feels warm and cosy, with the evening

devoted to good conversation and a range of superb beers. Regular quiz, darts and dominoes matches are held during the winter. Groups and coaches are welcome but telephone in advance. Q❀◑≉🚌♣P⚟

Shrewsbury

Abbey Hotel ✓

83 Monkmoor Road, SY2 5AZ (15 mins walk from Shrewsbury railway station via Castle footbridge)
⏲ 11.30-11 (midnight Fri & Sat); 12-11 Sun
☎ (01743) 236788
Fuller's London Pride; Holdens Black Country Mild; M&B Brew XI; guest beers Ⓗ
This large, imposing pub on a suburban road offers a range of up to nine cask ales. Gary the landlord runs what must be Ember Inns flagship real ale house – this is the only outlet within the pub group to offer a permanent cask mild. Quiz nights are hosted twice a week. Children under 14 years are not permitted. ♨Q❀◑◐♿🚌P⚟

Admiral Benbow

24 Swan Hill, SY1 1NF (just off main square)
⏲ 5 (12 Sat)-11; 7-10.30 Sun
☎ (01743) 244423
Greene King IPA; Ironbridge Gold; Ludlow Gold; Six Bells Cloud Nine; Wye Valley HPA; guest beer Ⓗ
Situated just off the town's main square, this spacious free house specialises in a variety of Shropshire and Herefordshire ales and ciders. Ciders are Gwatkin's Foxwhelp and Yarlington Mill, together with Golden Valley Perry. A good range of Belgian beers is available. A small room off the bar can be used for private functions and there is a seating and smoking area outside. Children are not permitted and under 30s are served at the management's discretion. CAMRA West Midlands Cider Pub of the Year 2007. ♨Q❀🛏≉♣🍎⚟

Coach & Horses ✓

Swan Hill, SY1 1NF (near Music Hall)
⏲ 11.30-midnight (12.30am Fri & Sat); 12-11.30 Sun
☎ (01743) 365661 🌐 odleyinns.co.uk/coach&horses.htm
Salopian Shropshire Gold; Wye Valley HPA; guest beers Ⓗ
Set in a quiet street off the main shopping area, the Coach & Horses provides a quiet haven. In summer it has magnificent floral displays. Victorian in style, the pub has a wood-panelled bar, a small side snug area and a large lounge where meals are served at lunchtime and in the evening. Cheddar Valley cider is sold. Tasteful live music, electro-acoustic in the main, plays most Sunday evenings in the lounge/restaurant. Q◑◐🛏♿≉🚌🍎⚟

Loggerheads ★

1 Church Street, SY1 1UG (off St Marys Street)
⏲ 11 (12 Sun)-11
☎ (01743) 355457
Banks's Bitter; Draught Bass; guest beers Ⓗ
Situated in the town centre, this 18th-century Grade II-listed establishment is a classic among urban pubs and features in CAMRA's National Inventory of pub interiors. The small bar provides a servery to three rooms – the one to the left with its scrubbed table tops was up until 1975 reserved for 'gents only'. Q◑🛏≉🚌♣

Montgomery's Tower ✓

Lower Claremont Bank, SY1 1RT
⏲ 9-midnight (1am Fri & Sat)
☎ (01743) 239080
Greene King IPA, Abbot; Marston's Pedigree; Salopian Shropshire Gold; Wood Shropshire Lad; guest beers Ⓗ
Located close to the Quarry Park and handy for Theatre Severn, this Lloyds No.1 conversion from a former nightclub offers a choice of two bars. To the left is a large open area with plenty of natural light, to the right, in contrast, are quieter surroundings more intimately lit. The pub does get lively on Friday and Saturday evenings when a DJ plays. Many prints are displayed illustrating local history and famous Salopians. Food is available 9am to 10pm. ◑◐♿≉⚟

Nags Head

Wyle Cop, SY1 1XB (on RH side of Wyle Cop)
⏲ 11.30-midnight (1am Fri & Sat); 12-midnight Sun
☎ (01743) 362455
Caledonian Deuchars IPA; Courage Directors; Greene King IPA; Taylor Landlord; guest beers Ⓗ
Situated on the historic Wyle Cop, the main features of this timber-framed building are best appreciated externally, in particular the upper storey jettying and to the rear the timber remnants of a 14th-century hall house including a screened passage which provided protection from draughts (and now provides shelter for smokers). The old-style interior has remained unaltered for many years. The pub can be very busy at times attracting a mixed clientele. The Nags Head features on the Shrewsbury Ghost Trail. ❀🛏≉🚌♣⚟

Prince of Wales

Bynner Street, Belle Vue, SY3 7NZ
⏲ 12-2 (not Mon & Tue), 5-midnight; 12-midnight Fri-Sun
☎ (01743) 343301 🌐 princeofwaleshotel.co.uk
Greene King IPA; St Austell Tribute; Salopian Golden Thread; Theakston Mild; guest beers Ⓗ
Welcoming two-roomed community pub with a large decked sun-trap, heated smoking shelter and bowling green overlooked by an 18th-century maltings. Darts, dominoes and bowls teams abound. Two beer festivals are held each year – a winter ales festival in February and another festival in May. The cider is usually Westons Old Rosie. Local CAMRA branch Pub of the Year 2006 and runner up in 2005-9. ♨❀◑🛏♿♣🍎⚟🥛

Salopian Bar 🏆

Smithfield Road, SY1 1PW
⏲ 12-11 (midnight Fri & Sat); closed Mon
☎ (01743) 351505 🌐 thesalopianbar.co.uk
Dark Star Hophead; Oakham Bishops Farewell; Stonehouse Station Bitter; guest beers Ⓗ
This pub has a modern, comfortable atmosphere with tasteful, non-invasive decor. Real cider and perry are provided by Westons and Thatchers and an ever-increasing range of bottled beer (Belgian, American and British) is also available. Live acoustic music plays every Friday and major sports events are screened on TV. Local CAMRA Pub of the Year and Shropshire CAMRA Pub of the Year 2008. ♿≉🚌♣🍎⚟

Three Fishes ✓

Fish Street, SY1 1UR
⏲ 11:30-3, 5-11; 11:30-11:30 Fri & Sat; 12-4; 7-10:30
☎ (01743) 344793
Sharps Doom Bar; Taylor Landlord; guest beers Ⓗ
This 15th-century building stands in the shadow of two churches in the medieval quarter of the town. Freshly prepared food is available at lunchtime and early evening (except Sun eve). Six local and

national beers, with some occasional dark beers are served, together with real cider and perry. Local CAMRA Pub of the Year runner-up 2007, 2008 and 2009. Q◐◑⇌🚌🍎

Wheatsheaf

Frankwell, SY3 8JY (between Welsh Bridge and Frankwell Roundabout)
⏲ 12-midnight (10.30 Sun)
☎ (01743) 354523
Beer range varies Ⓗ
Located in the historic area known as the 'Little Boro', this black-and-white, two-roomed, former coaching inn features an inglenook fireplace, beamed ceiling and bay windows. Two handpulls dispense local and regional micro beers. Home to thriving darts and dominoes teams, plus a ladies rounders team, it holds live music nights, a real ale festival in July and barbecues on the large beer garden decking in summer. The pub is reputed to be haunted. ♨❀⊟♿⇌🚌♣P⚟

Wheatsheaf ✔

50 High Street, SY1 1ST
⏲ 11-midnight; 12-11 Sun
☎ (01743) 272702
Banks's Bitter; Brakspear Oxford Gold; Jennings Cumberland Ale; Marston's Old Empire; Ringwood Old Thumper; guest beers Ⓗ
Comfortable town-centre, street-corner pub with a view to St Julian's Church. Three distinct bar areas for regulars, visitors and shoppers display many pictures of old Shrewsbury. Good lunches are cooked from locally sourced produce (not Sun). Beer festivals are hosted in March and October. Live electro-acoustic music often plays on Thursday and Sunday evenings (check in advance). ◐⇌🚌

Woodman Inn

Coton Hill, SY1 2DZ (on Ellesmere road A528)
⏲ 4 (2 Sat)-11; 12-11 Sun
☎ (01743) 351007
Hobsons Town Crier; Salopian Shropshire Gold; Wye Valley Butty Bach; guest beers Ⓗ
A corner pub originally built in the 1800s but destroyed by fire in 1923 and rebuilt in 1925. The pub is reputedly haunted by an ex-landlady who died when the pub burnt down. It has a wonderful oak-panelled lounge with two real log fires and traditional settles. Local CAMRA Pub of the Year runner-up in 2006 and 2007.
♨Q♉❀⊟♿⇌🚌♣🍎⚟⊓

Stottesdon

Fighting Cocks

1 High Street, DY14 8TZ
⏲ 6-midnight; 5-1am Fri; 12-midnight Sat; 12-11.30 Sun
☎ (01746) 718270
Hobsons Mild, Best Bitter, Town Crier; guest beer Ⓗ
The pub, with its shop and Internet access, is a hub of activity for the local community. An ale house since 1830, there are beamed ceilings, a cosy bar with a log fire, two dining areas and a function room. Excellent award-winning locally-sourced food is served in the evening (not Sun). Monday evening is 'curry and jam' (open mike), and there is live music on alternate Thursday evenings and occasional Saturdays. A beer festival is held in the autumn. ♨Q❀◑Δ♣P⚟

Telford: Coalbrookdale

Coalbrookdale Inn

12 Wellington Road, TF8 7DX (opp Museum of Iron)
⏲ 12-3 (not Mon-Thu), 5-midnight; 12-midnight Sat & Sun
☎ (01952) 433953 🌐 coalbrookdaleinn.co.uk
Hobsons Town Crier; Ironbridge Gold; John Roberts XXX; Wye Valley Butty bach; guest beers Ⓗ
Situated opposite the museums of Enginuity and Iron, the pub's location is also central for all nine Ironbridge Gorge museum sites. This impressive, friendly pub is a former national CAMRA winner with six handpulls serving local beers and food produced in the bar and restaurant. B&B in six lavish en-suite bedrooms is very popular with locals and vistors. ♨Q🛏◐◑Δ🚌♣🍎P⚟

Telford: Coalport

Shakespeare Inn

High Street, TF8 7HT
⏲ 5-11; 12-midnight Sat & Sun
☎ (01952) 580675 🌐 shakespeare-inn.co.uk
Enville Ale; Everards Tiger; guest beers Ⓗ
Warm, welcoming family-run pub with wonderful views of the Severn Gorge and River. The pub offers a good selection of guest ales, often from local brewers – favourites include Exmoor Gold and Three Tuns XXX. Excellent home-cooked food is always popular, so book ahead.
Q❀🛏◐◑♿🚌♣P⚟

Telford: Horsehay

Station Inn

Station Road, TF4 2NJ
⏲ 6-midnight (closed Mon); 12-1am Fri & Sat; 12-11 Sun
☎ (01952) 503006
St Austell Tribute; guest beers Ⓗ
This family-run free house dates back to 1860 and is near to Telford Steam Railway. It has four handpumps and always at least one local guest ale. Regular beer, cider and wine and cheese festivals are held throughout the year, and live bands play on some nights. Meals are home made and feature locally-sourced ingredients where available.
Q❀◐◑⊟P⚟

Telford: Ironbridge

Golden Ball

Newbridge Road, TF8 7BA (off B4373 Madeley Road Hill)
⏲ 12-11 (10.30 Sun)
☎ (01952) 432179 🌐 goldenballinn.com
Everards Tiger; Hobsons Town Crier; guest beers Ⓗ
Hidden away off the Telford to Ironbridge road, this historic inn is well worth seeking out. Friendly and welcoming, it has three main areas set around a central bar plus a separate dining area. Good food is served along with an ever-changing range of guest beers in addition to the two regulars. Foreign bottled beers are served. ♨Q❀🛏◐◑🚌♣P

Robin Hood Inn

33 Waterloo Street, TF8 7HQ
⏲ 10-midnight
☎ (01952) 433100
Holden's Mild, Bitter, Golden Glow, Special; Sarah Hughes Dark Ruby; guest beers Ⓗ
Overlooking the River Severn opposite the Jackfield Bridge, this 18th-century building is situated in the

birthplace of the Industrial Revolution. Warm and welcoming, it has three rooms with oak beamed interiors. There's an excellent home-made carvery daily. Live folk music plays twice a month.
Q❀🛏◑♿🚌♣🍎P⊽

Telford: Ketley

Compasses

72 Beveley Road, TF2 6SD (just off Holyhead road at Ketley)
☼ 12-11 (10.30 Sun)
☎ (01952) 617997 🌐 jenkos.co.uk
Hobsons Best Bitter; Ludlow Gold; Salopian Hop Twister; guest beer Ⓗ
This pub and restaurant was originally a coaching inn and dates back around 350 years. An outstanding free house, it offers quality beer and excellent food – the extremely popular 'eat as much as you can' Mongolian restaurant has recently been extended with a large log cabin and offers a buffet-style Sunday carvery. A family business with happy, efficient staff – marvellous!
❀◗🚌♣P⚡

Telford: Leegomery

Malt Shovel

Hadley Park Road, TF1 6QG
☼ 12-2.30, 5-11; 12-11 Fri-Sun
☎ (01952) 242963
Banks's Original; Marston's Burton Bitter, Pedigree; guest beers Ⓗ
Classic friendly two-roomed hostelry attracting a varied clientele. The lively bar room features televised sport and pub games are also popular. As a contrast, the lounge is large, light and airy. A huge collection of tankards, mugs and jugs hang from the beamed ceiling. Best of all, the beer is always spot-on. ♨Q◑⊟🚌♣P

Telford: Madeley

All Nations

20 Coalport Road, TF7 5DP
☼ 12-midnight
☎ (01952) 585747
Worfield Coalport Dodger Mild, Dabley Ale, Dabley Gold; guest beers Ⓗ
This classic, single-room, traditional pub is in a semi-wooded setting, offering tantalising glimpses and sounds of the Blists Hill Museum across the valley. The attached brewhouse continues the long tradition of brewing at the premises. Its superbly kept ales are available here alongside guest beers and real cider. B & B accommodation is available.
♨Q♘❀🛏⛺🚌♣🍎P

Telford: Oakengates

Crown Inn ✔

Market Street, TF2 6EA
☼ 12-11
☎ (01952) 610888 🌐 crown.oakengates.net
Hobsons Best Bitter, Twisted Spire; guest beers Ⓗ
Warm, friendly town pub dating from 1835 – and easy to find as it is bright yellow. A Cask Marque pub, it has served more than 10,000 guest beers. Handpulled beer festivals are held in May and October, with up to 60 beers. Mild and stout or porter are always available.
♨Q❀⊟♿⇌🚌♣🍎P⚡

Telford: St Georges

St Georges Sports & Social Club

Church Road, TF2 9LU
☼ 7-midnight (12.30am Fri); 12-12.30am Sat & Sun
☎ (01952) 612911
Banks's Original, Bitter; guest beers Ⓗ
A fine example of a club that doubles as a community pub. Most of the beers come from a radius of 30 miles, including the Black Country and beyond. Sporting facilities include cricket, bowls and national league hockey. A large function room is available for hire. ♘❀🚌P

Telford: Wellington

Cock Hotel 🏆

148 Hollyhead Road, TF1 2DL
☼ 4 (12 Thu)-11.30; 12-midnight Fri & Sat; 12-4, 7-11 Sun
☎ (01952) 244954 🌐 cockhotel.co.uk
Hobsons Mild, Best Bitter; guest beers Ⓗ
Local CAMRA Pub of the Year 2009, this imposing 18th-century coaching inn has enjoyed 13 years in the Guide. Lively conversation is the norm in the hop-festooned main bar where eight handpulls dispense changing ales and Black Rat cider. A selection of draught and bottled foreign beers is also available. ♨Q❀🛏⊟⇌🚌♣🍎P⚡

Whitchurch

Old Town Hall Vaults

SY13 1QU (off High Street)
☼ 10-2.30, 6 (7 Sun)-11
☎ (01948) 662251
Brains Rev James; Hancocks HB; M&B Mild; guest beers Ⓗ
Known locally as 'the Backstreets', Whitchurch's only established real ale pub has seven handpulls on the bar, offering three regular beers and four rotating guests from local and national brewers. It has a cosy real fire in the winter and serves locally sourced, home-cooked food. ♨Q❀◑♿⇌♣🍎⚡

Recipe for buttered beer

Take a quart of more of Double Beere and put to it a good piece of fresh butter, sugar candie an ounce, or liquerise in powder, or ginger grated, of each a dramme, and if you would have it strong, put in as much long pepper and Greynes, let it boyle in the quart in the maner as you burne wine, and who so will drink it, let him drinke it hot as he may suffer. Some put in the yolke of an egge or two towards the latter end, and so they make it more strength-full.

Thomas Cogan, The Haven of Health, 1584

Good Bottled Beer Guide

NEW FOR 2009

Jeff Evans

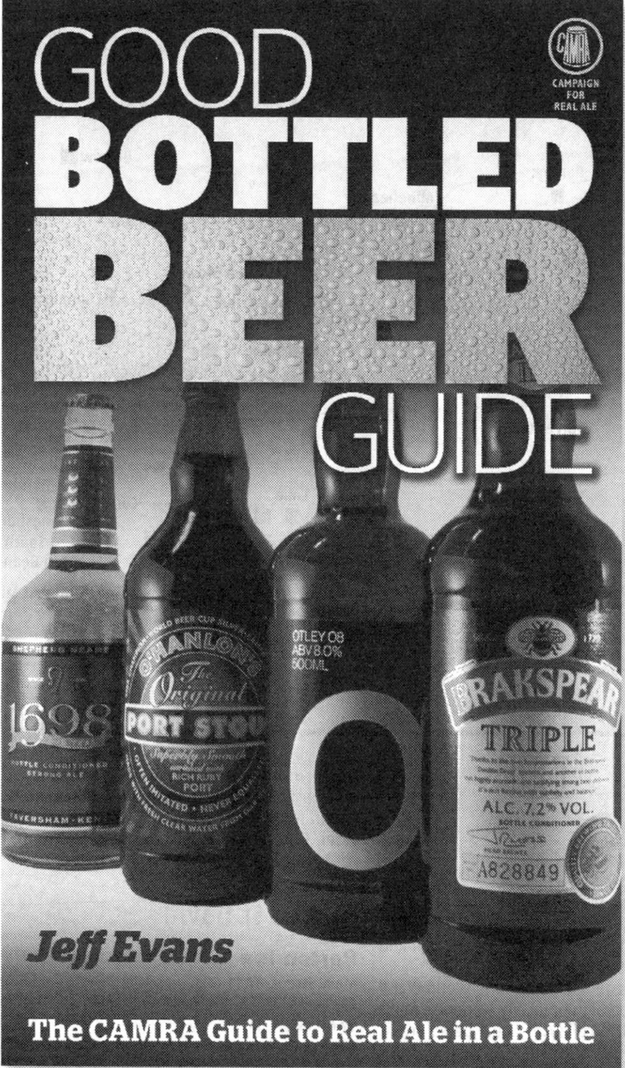

A pocket-sized guide for discerning drinkers looking to buy bottled real ales and enjoy a fresh glass of their favourite beers at home. The 7th edition of the **Good Bottled Beer Guide** is completely revised, updated and redesigned to showcase the very best bottled British real ales now being produced, and detail where they can be bought. Everything you need to know about bottled beers; tasting notes, ingredients, brewery details, and a glossary to help the reader understand more about them.

£12.99 ISBN 978-1-85249-262-5 Members' price £10.99 384 pages

SOMERSET

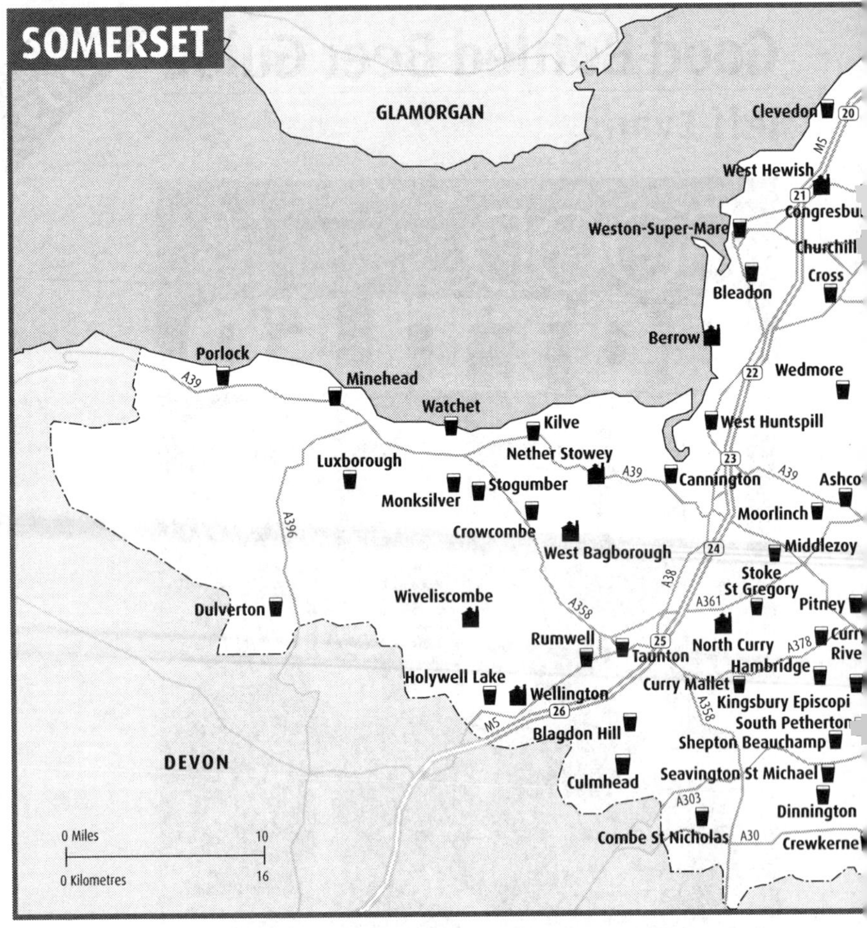

Ash

Bell Inn

3 Main Street, TA12 6NS
12-midnight
☎ (01935) 822727 thebellinnash.co.uk
Fuller's London Pride; Wickwar BOB; guest beers H
A comfortable village local with plenty of bric-a-brac to add interest. Although parts of the building date back to the 15th century, the unusual butressed front was an addition during World War II after the constant passing of locally stationed tanks caused the original to collapse. Guest beers are usually from Somerset breweries. Live music is a regular feature. (52)♣P

Ashcott

Ring O' Bells

High Street, TA7 9PZ (off A39 in village, near church)
12-2.30, 7-11; 12-2.30, 7.30-10.30 Sun
☎ (01458) 210232 ringobells.com
Beer range varies H
Comfortable 18th-century free house with a friendly welcome, in the same family ownership since 1988. The single bar has three distinct areas on different levels. A large function room/skittle alley has disabled access. This Somerset CAMRA Pub of the Year 1998 has won awards for its food. A beer from Moor or Glastonbury is usually available, together with regularly changing guests from around the country as well as local Wilkins cider. Quiz nights and live music sessions are held. (29,375)♣P

Barton St David

Barton Inn

Main Street, TA11 6BZ
12-2.30, 4.30-11 (midnight Sat & Sun)
☎ (01458) 850451
Beer range varies G
A pub full of both character and characters, where eccentricity appears to be the norm. The only red brick pub in the area, the bar has been sympathetically enlarged but has kept its cosy feeling and, while the hostelry may be somewhat off the beaten track, it is worth making the effort to find. Sample some of the mainly West Country ales racked behind the counter or a local cider if you prefer. (667)♣P

Bath

Bell

103 Walcot Street, BA1 5BW
11.30-11; 12-10.30 Sun

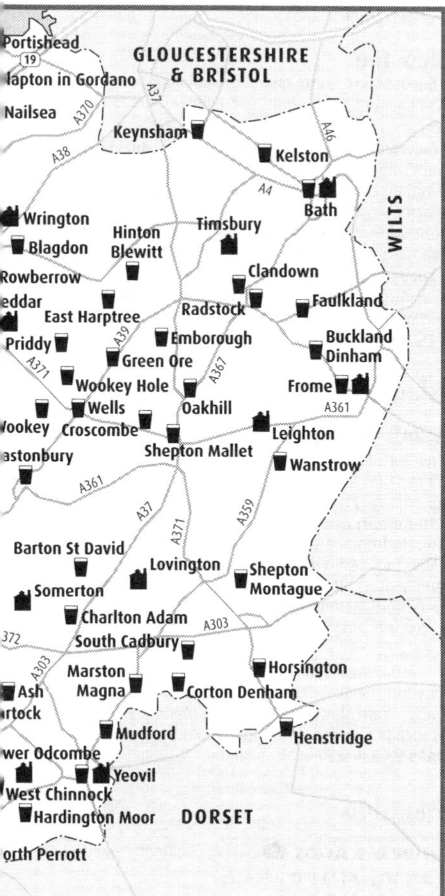

(01225) 460426 walcotstreet.com

Abbey Bellringer; Bath Ales Gem; Hop Back Summer Lightning; Otter Bitter; RCH Pitchfork; Stonehenge Danish Dynamite; guest beers H

The Bell features live bands on Monday and Wednesday evenings and Sunday lunchtime. It has a long main bar and a number of seating areas. The wall space inside is taken up with posters for gigs and other events in the Walcot area. A computer is available for free Internet access and Wi-Fi facilities are available. At the back of the pub is a garden with plenty of covered seating. Local CAMRA Pub of the Year 2004.

Coeur de Lion

17 Northumberland Passage, BA1 5AR

11-11 (1am Fri & Sat); 12-10.30 Sun

(01225) 463568 coeur-de-lion.co.uk

Abbey Ales Bellringer; guest beers H

Situated in a passageway opposite the Guildhall in the centre of town, this pub claims to be the smallest in Bath. As it contains only four tables in the single small bar, this may well be true. Food is served between 12 and 6pm every day upstairs in the newly-added dining room. Seating capacity is increased in summer with tables outside. The stained glass window at the front of the pub is a good example of its kind. (Bath Spa) (2,4,6)

Garrick's Head

8 St John's Place, BA1 1ET (next to Theatre Royal)

12-11.30 (midnight Sat); 12-10.30 Sun

(01225) 318368 garricksheadpub.com

Palmers IPA; guest beers H

Once the home of Beau Nash, Bath's 18th-century master of ceremonies, this palatial building has been a pub for over 200 years. Situated next to the Theatre Royal, and reputedly the most haunted pub in Bath, the Garrick's Head has four beers from local micros and two Somerset ciders. Traditional food made with local ingredients is served lunchtimes and evenings. The outdoor terrace is an ideal spot to sit and watch the world go by. (Bath Spa)

King William

36 Thomas Street, London Road, BA1 5NN (on A4 London Road around 1 mile NE of city centre)

12-3 (not Mon), 5-11 (midnight Fri); 12-midnight Sat; 12-11 Sun

(01225) 428096 kingwilliampub.com

Beer range varies H

This tiny, two-bar Victorian pub has kept the look and feel of a bustling street-corner local while garnering awards for the quality of its home-cooked, locally-sourced food. The ever-changing range of local beers generally includes one from Palmer's and three from local micro-breweries. Local cider is also available. A monthly book club meets in the restaurant upstairs.

Old Green Tree ★

12 Green Street, BA1 2JZ

11-11; 12-10.30 Sun

(01225) 448259

Blindmans Green Tree Bitter; RCH Pitchfork; Wickwar Mr Perretts Stout; guest beers H

Classic, unspoilt pub in a 300-year-old building. An atmosphere of quiet cosiness pervades all three of the small oak-panelled rooms, where the panelling dates from the 1920s. The lounge bar at the front is decorated with pictures of World War II aircraft. The pub can get very crowded, but space can sometimes be found in the comfortable back bar. The range of beers is complemented by an occasional perry and a choice of malt whiskies. Q (Bath Spa)

Pig & Fiddle

2 Saracen Street, BA1 5BR

11-11; 12-10.30 Sun

(01225) 460868

Abbey Bellringer; Butcombe Bitter; guest beers H

A large and busy town-centre pub with a varied clientele and friendly atmosphere. One end is an old shop front, the other an outside courtyard with drinking benches and covered heaters. The decor is an esoteric collection of sports memorabilia such as signed rugby shirts, a pair of signed Olympic skis and an Olympic oar from the Coxed Eight gold medallists. Up to three guest beers come from local breweries. Table football is available. Handy for the rugby ground. (Bath Spa)

Raven

6-7 Queen Street, BA1 1HE

11.30-11 (midnight Fri & Sat); 12-10.30 Sun

(01225) 425045 theravenofbath.co.uk

Blindmans Raven, Raven Gold; guest beers H

Local CAMRA Pub of the Year 2006, this busy city-centre free house has bars on the ground and first floors. House beers Raven and Raven Gold are brewed by Blindmans. An ever-changing selection of guest beers includes many rarities. Mini beer festivals are held throughout the year. The pub hosts regular music sessions and a monthly science cafe. One of the few pubs in Bath to serve food on Sunday evening. ◐◑≉(Bath Spa)♣

Royal Oak 🏆

Lower Bristol Road, Twerton, BA2 3BW (one mile W of city centre on A36)

⏲ 12-11 (midnight Fri & Sat); 12-10.30 Sun

☎ (01225) 481409 ⊕ theroyaloak-bath.co.uk

Beer range varies Ⓗ

Local CAMRA Pub of the Year 2007 and 2008, an ever-changing range of up to 10 beers from micro-breweries near and far includes beer from the pub's own brewery Art Brew. Local ciders and bottled Belgian beers are also available. Beer festivals are held in December and February, with a folk and beer festival in July. There is an Irish session on Wednesday and live music some weekends. Outside is a secluded garden. The pub is around 200m from Oldfield Park station.

Q ◐◑≉(Bath Oldfield Park) ♣ P

Royal Oak

Summerlays Place, BA2 4HN

⏲ 12 (5 Mon)-11 (11.30 winter); 12-10.30 Sun

☎ (01225) 335220 ⊕ theroyaloakbath.co.uk

Bath Ales Gem; Butcombe Gold; Courage Best Bitter; Otter Ale; guest beers Ⓗ

Less than 10 minutes walk from the city centre, this lively pub was originally a row of three cottages. Today it is an airy, open-plan local, popular for food and sport. The rugby and cricket ground are both close by and the pub is currently sponsoring Bath rugby's Matt Banahan. The large beer garden has a boules piste and the skittle alley doubles as a function room with regular music nights.

◐◑≉(Bath Spa) ♣

Star ★

23 The Vineyards, BA1 5NA (on the 14 Paragon 750m N of city centre)

⏲ 12-2.30, 5.30-midnight (1am Fri & Sat); 12-midnight Sun

☎ (01225) 425072 ⊕ star-inn-bath.co.uk

Abbey Bellringer, Heritage Ⓗ**; Draught Bass** Ⓖ**; guest beers** Ⓗ

Now the tap for Abbey Ales this classic town pub was fitted out by Gaskell & Chambers in the 1850s. Its four small rooms have benches around the walls, wood panelling and roaring fires. The smallest has just a single bench called 'Death Row', while the pub, which dates from around 1760, is coffin-shaped. Bass is served from the barrel and complimentary snuff is available. Celtic Band Sulis perform most Tuesdays and there are regular shove-ha'penny matches. Q ≉(Bath Spa) ♣

White Horse

Shophouse Road, Twerton, BA2 1EF

⏲ 2 (12 Sat)-midnight; 12-11 Sun

☎ (01225) 340668 ⊕ thewhitehorsebath.com

Otter Ale; Sharp's Doom Bar; guest beers Ⓗ

This friendly community pub, high on a hill overlooking the city, has made great strides since it was taken over by an enthusiastic landlord three years ago. Up to four real ales are on offer, with guests generally coming from local micro-breweries. There are regular mini beer festivals, live music and weekly quiz nights. The garden features a boules piste. Children are welcome and boxed games are available. ◑ ♿ ♣ P

Blagdon

New Inn

Church Street, BS40 7SB (100m off A368)

⏲ 11-3, 6-11.30; 12-3, 6-10.30 Sun

☎ (01761) 462475

Wadworth Henry's Original IPA, 6X, seasonal beers Ⓗ

Superbly located with panoramic views over Blagdon Lake and the Mendip Hills. This Wadworth-owned 16th-century inn has a strong emphasis on food sales, but not to the detriment of those just wanting a drink. With no music, comfortable sofas, exposed beams and real fires, the pub has a welcoming and characterful ambience. Dogs are allowed. Limited local bus service nearby.

Q ◐◑ ♣ P

Blagdon Hill

Lamb & Flag

TA3 7SL (4 miles S of Taunton)

⏲ 11-11 (midnight Fri); 12-10.30 Sun

☎ (01823) 421736 ⊕ lambandflag.co.uk

Otter Bitter; guest beers Ⓗ

Situated on the northern slopes of the Blackdown Hills, this 16th-century pub is frequented by locals and visitors. The open main bar area has the original flagstone floor and a large fireplace separating the bar and candlelit dining area. The four ales come from south-west micro-breweries. A skittle alley and function room are situated beyond the bar. The large garden has panoramic views from the Brendon to the Mendip Hills. Food is locally sourced and home cooked.

◐◑ ♣ P

Bleadon

Queen's Arms ✔

Celtic Way, BS24 0NF (off A370)

⏲ 11.30-11; 12-10.30 Sun

☎ (01934) 812080

Butcombe Bitter, Gold, seasonal beers; guest beer Ⓗ

The oldest pub of three in Bleadon, situated in the centre of the village. Three rooms converge on the bar and there is a garden/patio sales hatch. Two real fires add to the atmosphere. Food sales are strong, but beer is a popular attraction too. Thatchers cider is sold. Until 2008 the beers were always served on gravity but handpumps have

INDEPENDENT BREWERIES

Abbey Ales Bath
Berrow Berrow
Blindmans Leighton
Butcombe Wrington
Cheddar Ales Cheddar
Cotleigh Wiveliscombe
Cottage Lovington
Exmoor Wiveliscombe
Glastonbury Somerton
Matthews Timsbury
Milk Street Frome
Moor Pitney
North Curry North Curry
Odcombe Lower Odcombe
Quantock Wellington
RCH West Hewish
Stowey Nether Stowey
Taunton West Bagbrough
Yeovil Yeovil

now taken over. A family area is available. Morris men entertain on May Day Monday.
⚑Q♉❀◑◐⊟(83)●P⁄–

Buckland Dinham

Bell

High Street, BA11 2QT (on A362 Frome – Radstock road) ST752512
⊙ 12-3 (not Mon & Tue), 6-midnight; 12-2.30, 7-11.30 Sun
☎ (01373) 462956 ⊕ bellatbuckland.co.uk
Butcombe Bitter; Fuller's London Pride; Wychwood Hobgoblin; guest beers H
This warm and cosy local pub is involved in community activities. It holds film nights, has produced a village recipe book and uses local beers in its dishes. It also offers a facility to order and pay for beer online. A three-day summer beer festival is run with live music each August. There is also a cider festival in October. The pub is convenient for on-site campers. Boules is played.
⚑♉❀◑◐⊟♿⛺⊟♣●P⁄–

Cannington

Rose & Crown

30 High Street, TA5 2HF (off A39)
⊙ 12-11 (10.30 Sun)
☎ (01278) 653190
Caledonian Deuchars IPA; Greene King IPA, Old Speckled Hen, Abbot; guest beers H
An atmospheric, friendly 17th-century pub with a loyal local following. Original beams are covered with interesting objects donated by locals and there is a collection of clocks. The single bar has a pool table, table skittles and a collection of games hand-made by locals. The 'Outside Inn' is a covered, comfortable smoking area in an award-winning large garden. ⚑❀⊟(14)♣P⁄–

Charlton Adam

Fox & Hounds

Broadway Road, TA11 7AU (off A37)
⊙ 12-3, 6-11; 12-3, 6.30-10.30 Sun
☎ (01458) 223466
Beer range varies H
Friendly pub on the east side of the village. The single bar has a large collection of tankards hanging from the ceiling, as well as a former pub sign. Popular with locals and always busy, darts and skittles are played. Good food is served in the bar and conservatory, with steak on Thursday and special offers on Monday. Three handpumps serve mainly West Country beers. An accredited camping site is at the rear. The family-friendly garden has a Wendy house. ⚑❀◑◐♿⛺⊟(667)♣P⁄–

Cheddar

White Hart

The Bays, BS27 3QW
⊙ 10-12.30am (1.30am Fri & Sat)
☎ (01934) 741261 ⊕ thewhitehartcheddar.co.uk
Butcombe Bitter; Greene King Abbot; St Austell Tribute; guest beers H
A delightfully welcoming local pub situated near Cheddar Gorge and licensed since 1842. A large open log fireplace features, complemented by photos depicting the regulars' day trips out, organised by the pub. Breakfast is served from 10am and a wide menu available until 9.30pm which includes authentic Italian ice cream. A free quiz is hosted on Wednesday and a cider festival each June. Guest beers are available in summer only. A function room is well used by local clubs. Thatchers ciders are served. Dogs welcome.
⚑Q❀◑◐⛺⊟(126)♣●P

Churchill

Crown Inn

The Batch, Skinners Lane, BS25 5PP (off A38, ¼ mile S of A368 jct)
⊙ 11.30-11 (midnight Fri & Sat); 12-10.30 Sun
☎ (01934) 852995
Bath Ales Gem; Butcombe Bitter; Cotleigh Batch; Palmers IPA; RCH Hewish, PG Steam; guest beers G
This long-time Guide regular and winner of many CAMRA awards has been in the same hands for 23 years. It is tucked away down a small lane, yet close to the village centre. Several small rooms with stone-flagged floors are warmed by two log fires and offer an assortment of seating. Excellent food is provided at lunchtime only, using local ingredients. Up to nine beers are served straight from the cask, usually sourced from local breweries. There is outside drinking to the front and rear. ⚑Q❀◑⛺⊟(121)P⁄–

Clandown

Lamb Inn

Chapel Road, Radstock, BA3 3BP (off A267 Bath – Wells road) ST683558
⊙ 11-midnight
☎ (01761) 435777
Hogs Back Hop; Palmers Copper Ale; Quantock Sunraker; guest beers H
A very friendly local with an involved and enthusiastic landlord, serving an excellent variety of real ales and good bar food. The pub is home to local skittles, darts and cribbage teams, and table tennis. Live entertainment is also provided. This hostelry is popular with a mixed clientele of all ages. The village is on the Bath to Radstock bus route. Regular guest beers are sourced mainly from micro-breweries in the south and south west.
⚑❀◑⊟♿⊟♣P⁄–

Clapton in Gordano

Black Horse

Clevedon Lane, BS20 7RH (2 miles from M5 jct 19) OS473739
⊙ 11-11; 12-10.30 Sun
☎ (01275) 842105 ⊕ thekicker.co.uk
Butcombe Bitter G**; Courage Best Bitter** H**; Shepherd Neame Spitfire** G**; Wadworth 6X; Websters Green Label** H**; guest beer** G
Excellent 14th-century pub hidden away down a small lane. The snug was once the village lock-up. A large fireplace with a display of old rifles dominates the main bar. Beers are served from a small serving hatch. The games room doubles as a family room, and there is a children's play area in the pleasant garden. The Gordano Valley cycle route is nearby. Dogs are welcome. Thatchers Dry and Moles Black Rat cider are sold. Bar meals are available 12-2pm Monday to Saturday.
⚑Q♉❀◑⛺♣●P⁄–

Clevedon

Old Inn ✔

9 Walton Road, BS21 6AE (on Portishead road)
11-11.30 (midnight Fri & Sat); 12-10.30 Sun
☎ (01275) 340440 theoldinnclevedon.co.uk
Courage Best Bitter; guest beers Ⓗ
A warm welcome is assured at this delightful 15th-century inn with a wonderful community feel that once served the carriage trade from Weston to Portishead. Three guest beers are often adventurous or unusual. Excellent pub food is on offer with generous portions and good value prices, including a children's menu. Six B&B rooms are available, together with a pleasant beer garden and children's play area. Popular National Trust attraction Tynsfield is close by. The cider is Westons. ♣P

Combe St Nicholas

Green Dragon

TA20 3NG
12-2.30 (not Mon), 6-midnight; 12-midnight Sat; 12-4, 7-11 Sun
☎ (01460) 63311 greendragon-combe.co.uk
Otter Bitter; guest beer Ⓗ
A large green dragon carved by the landlord greets visitors to this friendly free house which has origins in the 17th century. The guest beer usually comes from a West Country brewery. A varied menu of good-value, tasty, home-cooked food using local ingredients is served Tuesday to Sunday with a popular 'pie and a pint' night on Wednesday. Wood carvings adorn both bars and there is live music once a fortnight on Fridays. Q(99)P

Congresbury

Old Inn

18 St Pauls Causeway, BS49 5DH (200m from A370/B3133 jct)
11.30-11.30 (12.30am Fri & Sat); 12-11.30 Sun
☎ (01934) 832270
Wells Bombardier; Young's Bitter, Special; guest beer Ⓗ
Popular 16th-century village local, owned by Wells & Young's and tucked away in the heart of the village. This cosy pub has a wonderful inglenook fireplace that burns chunky logs during the winter. There are low ceilings throughout the main bar area and two smaller rooms – one with a TV and the other used for families. The main bar has leather straps hanging from the ceiling to steady yourself after one too many! No food is served.
Q(X1,353)♣P

Plough

High Street, BS49 5JA (off A370 at B3133 junction)
11.30-2.30, 4.30-11 (midnight Thu & Fri); 12-3, 7-11 Sun
☎ (01934) 877402
Butcombe Bitter; St Austell Tribute; guest beers Ⓗ
Friendly, characterful village pub with flagstone floors and many original features, decorated with interesting local artefacts. Sunday is quiz night and is very popular. Three or four guest beers are available, served from a row of old barrel heads behind the bar, and are sourced mainly from local breweries. No food is served on Friday or Sunday evenings. The regular Bristol to Weston buses pass on the A370 nearby. Mendip Morris men meet here. Real fires, no TV and dogs welcome. The cider is Thatchers. Q(X1,353)♣P

Corton Denham

Queen's Arms

DT9 4LR (3 miles from A303)
11-3, 6-11; 11-11 Sat; 12-10.30 Sun
☎ (01963) 220317 thequeensarms.com
Butcombe Bitter; Taylor Landlord; guest beers Ⓗ
What a fantastic village establishment snuggled below the steep hills of south Somerset – just follow the signs from the A303 for South Cadbury and then Corton Denham. The sign at the door welcoming dogs and muddy boots entices you into the flagstoned interior with a range of beers that is only matched by the extensive list of wines by the glass. Food ranges from the locally made pork pies on the bar to some really special creations.
QP

Crewkerne

Old Stagecoach

Station Road, TA18 8AL (next to station)
11-2 (not Sat), 6-11; 12-2, 6-11 Sun
☎ (01460) 72972 stagecoach-inn.co.uk
Glastonbury Mystery Tor; guest beers Ⓗ
Pleasant, comfortable pub very near the station, formerly called The Queens Hotel. The real ales are supplemented by a large selection of Belgian beers, reflecting the friendly landlord's nationality. An extensive food menu includes dishes made with Belgian beer. At the rear is a large garden and an accommodation block. The landlord is a motorcycle enthusiast and visiting bikers are welcome. Opening hours can be varied if notice is given. Q(47,61)P

Croscombe

George Inn

Long Street, BA5 3QH (on A371 between Wells and Shepton Mallet)
12-3, 7 (6 Fri)-11; 11.45-3, 7-11 Sat
☎ (01749) 342306
Blindmans King George the Thirst; Butcombe Bitter; Cheddar Gorgeous George; guest beers Ⓗ
This 17th-century inn, sympathetically refurbished by the landlord, serves at least two guest ales and hosts two beer festivals a year at Whitsun and late October. There is a large main bar with a smaller bar attached, and a separate dining room. The food is home cooked using locally sourced ingredients. At the rear is a skittle alley and a garden with a covered terrace. Guest ales are from local independents. (Gorgeous George is a 3.8% late-hopped semi-regular guest.)
Q♣P

Cross

New Inn ✔

Old Coach Road, BS26 2EE (on A38/A361 jct)
12-11
☎ (01934) 732455
Otter Ale; guest beers Ⓗ
Roadside inn on the A38, close to the historic medieval town of Axbridge. Popular for its extensive food menu and its twice yearly beer festivals, it offers up to three guest beers which can often be adventurous and unusual for the area. There is a separate dining area and a pool room on the first floor. A large hillside garden with children's play facilities offers a fine view of the

Mendip Hills and Somerset Levels. Limited parking, but street parking is possible further into the village. ❀◑🚌P

Crowcombe

Carew Arms

TA4 4AD (off A358)
⌚ 11-11.30 (1am Sat); 12-4, 7-11.30 Sun
☎ (01984) 618631 🌐 thecarewarms.co.uk
Exmoor Ale; Otter Bright; guest beers [H]
Village inn situated in a picture-postcard village at the bottom of the Quantock Hills. The ancient flagstoned public bar includes benches and an inglenook, and is popular with locals and their dogs. A larger lounge/restaurant overlooks a spacious patio garden and the Brendon Hills. Real cider is served and a music and beer festival is held in August. Food is sourced locally where possible, and the ales are mostly from the West Country. Q❀◑♿Λ🚌(18,28)♣●P

Culmhead

Holman Clavel

TA3 7EA (¼ mile off B3170)
⌚ 12-11; 12-3, 7-11 winter Sun
☎ (01823) 421432
Butcombe Bitter, Gold; guest beers [H]
The only pub in England with this name. A clavel is a beam across the fireplace made from holm oak. Fresh fish and game when in season feature on the food menu, which has choices to suit all tastes and budgets. Guest beers come from both micro-breweries and regional brewers. The pub is allegedly haunted by the ghost of a defrocked monk. Q❀◑Λ♣P

Curry Mallet

Bell Inn

Higher Street, TA3 6SY (near post office and village hall)
⌚ 11.30-3, 5.30-11 (midnight Fri); 11.30-11 Sat; 12-10.30 Sun
☎ (01823) 480310
Exmoor Gold; Sharp's Doom Bar; guest beer [H]
Pleasant, remote pub with a friendly welcome. Although essentially one room, a large fireplace divides the pub into two spaces. The pub hosts a darts team and a regular quiz night. Guest ales are from the south west and much of the food is also locally produced. There are meal deals at lunchtime and evening sessions on weekdays. This pub plays a full part in the life of the village. ❀◑♣P

Curry Rivel

King William IV

High Street, TA10 0EZ (on A378 in Curry Rivel)
⌚ 12 (7 Mon)-midnight; 12-11 Sun
☎ (01458) 259200
Otter Bright; Teignworthy Beachcomber, guest beers [G]
Reopened after a period of three years, this 18th-century Somerset cider house has been improved and is now a free house village pub. The real ales are served straight from the casks. All the meals are home cooked using locally sourced produce where possible (no food Mon). A glass-covered illuminated well is a feature in the dining room and a small snug serves as a family room. Q❀◑♿Λ🚌(54)♣P

Dinnington

Dinnington Docks

TA17 8SX
⌚ 11.30-3.30, 6-midnight; 11-midnight Sat; 12-10.30 Sun
☎ (01460) 52397
Butcombe Bitter; Teignworthy Reel Ale; Wadworth 6X; guest beers [H]
A popular village pub which offers a lot more than just beer and skittles. A transport society meets here and it is even possible to get your hair cut on the fourth Tuesday of the month. Dogs and walkers are welcome in the L-shaped bar. There is a varied menu of home-cooked food available and also a specials board. Q❀◑♣●P

Dulverton

Bridge Inn ✔

20 Bridge Street, TA22 9HJ (by river bridge, near town centre)
⌚ 12-3, 6-11 (not winter Mon); 12-11 Fri-Sun
☎ (01398) 324130 🌐 thebridgeinndulverton.com
Exmoor Ale; Otter Ale; guest beers [H]
Situated close to the River Barle, this warm, welcoming pub dating from 1845 has a cosy single room bar decorated with Exmoor memorabilia and features a wood-burning stove. Good food is available at both lunchtime and evening sessions. The pub participates in local promotions and a beer festival is held in July at the time of the local fete. Situated at the southern gateway to Exmoor, there are opportunities for walking and country pursuits. ❀◑🚌(25B,398)♣●P

East Harptree

Castle of Comfort

BS40 6DD (on B3134 just N of jct with B3135)
⌚ 12-3, 6-11; 12-11 Sun
☎ (01761) 221321 🌐 castleofcomfort.com
Butcombe Bitter; Sharp's Doom Bar; guest beers [H]
Splendid sprawling inn on the Mendip Hills, not really in East Harptree, but within reach of both Cheddar Gorge and Wookey Hole caves. The name is said to derive from the time when the pub housed condemned criminals on their last night before execution. A hostelry since 1684, it is popular for its locally-sourced and generously-portioned food. Two guest beers are from south west breweries, or sometimes further afield. The child-friendly garden is busy in summer. Dogs are allowed in the lower bar. The cider is Moles Black Rat. Q❀◑♣●P

Emborough

Old Down Inn

BA3 4SA ST628513
⌚ 12-2 (3 Sun), 6.30-11.30
☎ (01761) 232398 🌐 olddowninn.co.uk
Butcombe Bitter; Draught Bass; guest beers [G]
A free house first licensed in 1640, this pub was once an important coaching inn. The spirit of the past lives on in the pub's wood-panelled main bar, where beer is served straight from the barrel. Guests from local breweries are generally available. Bar snacks are excellent value, likewise main meals. This friendly and popular hostelry has recently been refurbished throughout. A classic example of a traditional Somerset inn. ❀◑P

Faulkland

Tucker's Grave ★

BA3 5XF (on A366 1 mile E of village) ST751551
11.30-3, 6-11; 12-3, 7-10.30 Sun
☎ (01373) 834230
Butcombe Bitter; Draught Bass Ⓖ
This pub was built in the mid-17th century and has changed very little since then. It was named after Tucker, who hanged himself and was buried at the crossroads outside. Beers and Thatchers cider are served from an alcove rather than a bar. Shove-ha'penny is played and there is a skittle alley. Camping is available in the grounds. A warm welcome is guaranteed in this traditional pub, which featured in a song by the 1970s punk band The Stranglers. ⌂Q❀Ā♣●P⅊

Frome

Griffin Inn

Milk Street, BA11 3DB
4-11 (1am Fri & Sat); 1-7 Sun
☎ (01373) 467766 ⊕ milkstreetbrewery.com
Milk Street Nick's, Beer; guest beers Ⓗ
Situated in the older part of Frome known as Trinity or Chinatown and owned by Milk Street Brewery, the small brewhouse out the back is based in a former adult cinema. It produces a wide range of ales, served alongside guests and seasonal beers. The single bar retains original features including open fires, etched windows and wooden floors. Live music plays regularly. A small garden opens in summer. ⌂❀≋🚌♣P⅊

Lamb

1 Christchuch Street East, BA11 1QA
12-11 (10.30 Sun)
☎ (01373) 472042 ⊕ thelambinnfrome.co.uk
Blindmans Buff, Lamb Gold, Lamb Ale, Mine Beer, Icarus; guest beers Ⓗ
Reopened by Blindmans Brewery after a long closure, this pub, once the brewery tap for the defunct Lamb Brewery, has been refurbished to a very high standard, including hotel accommodation and a restaurant. The pub, which is very near the town centre, is now light and spacious throughout, with a slate floor and local artwork on the walls. Cider is from Rich's and guest beers are from local breweries. ⊭◐◑≋🚌●P

Glastonbury

Riflemans Arms

4 Chikwell Street, BA6 8DB (just E of Country Life Museum)
11-11; 12-10.30 Sun
☎ (01458) 831023
Butcombe Bitter; Skinner's Cornish Knocker; guest beers Ⓗ
Ancient tavern with a well-worn 16th-century facade, a wide, low doorway, deep wooden bar and bare floors. Behind the pub is an ample patio for sun worshippers and smokers. The interior is split between the old and the relatively young, with customers tending to gravitate one way or the other depending on their age. The old bar is often filled with white-haired folk, while the relatively new extension features live music for the younger generation. Wilkins Cider is served.
⌂❀◐◑Ā🚌(29,375,377)●P⅊

Green Ore

Ploughboy Inn

BA5 3ET (on A39/B3135 crossroads)
11 (12 Sat)-2.30, 6.30 (7 Sat)-11; closed Mon; 12-3, 7-10.30 Sun
☎ (01761) 241375 ⊕ ploughboyinn.com
Butcombe Bitter; Otter Ale; guest beers Ⓗ
In the same safe hands for over 20 years, this substantial stone free house to the north of Wells occupies a large corner plot by the traffic lights in the hamlet of Green Ore. The 376 Wells to Bristol bus runs nearby and there is a large car park and pleasant beer garden to the rear. A single good-sized L-shaped bar provides reasonably priced, excellent food and the local butcher's huge, meaty sausages are recommended. Up to two guest beers are available. ⌂Q❀◐◑🚌P

Hambridge

Lamb & Lion

The Green, TA10 0AT (on B3168 in village)
11-3, 5-11; 11-11 Sat; 12-11 Sun
☎ (01460) 281355
Otter Bitter Ⓖ**; guest beers** Ⓗ
Friendly, 17th-century village inn with some parts dating from the 16th century. There are low beamed ceilings in the main bar and small side room. Good value home-cooked food, including takeaway, is available. Guest beers often come from St Austell and Teignworthy. The Otter Bitter is normally served straight from the cask at the back of the bar. Darts and skittles play a major role at this pub which is a true part of the local community. ⌂❀◐◑♣P⅊

Hardington Moor

Royal Oak

Moor Lane, BA22 9NW (off A30 at Yeovil Court Hotel)
11.30-3.30 (not Mon), 6.30-11; 11.30-5, 6.30-10.30 Sun
☎ (01935) 862354
Beer range varies Ⓗ
Sonny's, nicknamed after a previous landlord, is a village pub popular throughout the surrounding district, not just with the resident darts and skittle teams. Beer festivals in May and October are among many village events hosted here. Cider comes from the adjacent farm. Please try to avoid stepping on the dogs on entry. ⌂❀◐◑♿♣●P⅊

Henstridge

Bird in Hand

2 Ash Walk, BA8 0RA (100m S of A30/A357 jct)
11-2.30, 5.30-11; 11-11 Sat; 12-3, 7.30-10.30 Sun
☎ (01963) 362255
Beer range varies Ⓗ
This cosy village pub, with thick stone walls and low ceilings, is a real gem. The bar is attractively set in a beamed room with a fire at each end. Although main meals are not served, the bar snacks are superb and real value for money. To the rear is a skittle alley and games room. Three real ales are usually available as well as Taunton Cider. Well worth a visit. ⌂Q❀◐◑♿🚌♣●P

Hinton Blewitt

Ring O' Bells ✔

Upper Road, BS39 5AN (2 miles W of A37 at Temple Cloud) ST594569

12-3, 5-11 (midnight Fri); 12-midnight Sat; 12-11 Sun

☎ (01761) 452239

Butcombe Bitter, Gold, seasonal beer; Fuller's London Pride; guest beer Ⓗ

At the heart of the village and of village life, this pub dates from the 19th century. Enter via a small yard with a pleasant garden to the side and you are soon in the warmth of the intimate bar where many cricketing mementos feature – indeed the pub runs its own team. The food is popular and can be enjoyed in the smaller snug area or outside in good weather. Children and dogs are welcome. Thatchers Cheddar Valley Cider and a shove-ha'penny board also feature. ⌂Q✿◑♣●⚐

Holywell Lake

Holywell Inn

TA21 0EJ (1 mile N of A38 W of Wellington)

12-2.30 (Sat), 6-11; closed Mon; 12-3 Sun

☎ (01823) 672770 ⊕ theholywell.com

Beer range varies Ⓗ

Fifteenth-century village inn retaining cob walls in the main bar but enlarged to include a restaurant and skittle alley/function room. Ales normally include one each from Cotleigh and Exmoor breweries and a guest beer, usually from a West Midlands micro. Although near the A38 trunk road, this is a quiet, charming country pub. Well-behaved dogs are welcome, as are walkers – the pub lies on the Land's End to John O'Groats walking route. The Holy Well is opposite the pub entrance. ⌂Q✿◑♿♣⚐

Horsington

Half Moon

BA8 0EF (200m off A357)

12-2.30 (3 Sat), 6-11; 12-3, 7-10.30 Sun

☎ (01963) 370140 ⊕ horsington.co.uk

Wadworth 6X; guest beers Ⓗ

Real ale is a passion for the owners with more than 1,000 different beers sold over the past 10 years. Up to six ales are on handpump with the range of guests changing continuously. As well as the well-known nationals, local micros are always represented and feature prominently in an annual beer festival held each May. Friendly staff welcome locals and visitors alike. Reasonably priced food is available and there is accommodation in chalets to the rear. ⌂Q✿⊨◑♿🚌♣●P

Kelston

Old Crown ✔

Bath Road, BA1 9AQ (3 miles from Bath on A431)

11.30-11; 12-10.30 Sun

☎ (01225) 423032

Bath Gem; Butcombe Bitter, Gold, seasonal beers; Draught Bass Ⓗ

This attractive multi-roomed 18th-century coaching inn is owned by Butcombe Brewery. The old beer engine in the bar, flagstone floors, open fires and settles all help to create a friendly atmosphere. A choice of quality, imaginative food is served in the restaurant and bar areas (no food Sun or Mon eves). In summer, barbecues are occasionally held in the large attractive garden and the front of the pub is bedecked with colourful flowers. Occasional live music plays on Sunday afternoon. ⌂Q✿⊨◑🚌(319,332)P⚐

Keynsham

Old Bank

20 High Street, BS31 1DG

10-11; 12-9 Sun

☎ (0117) 9046356

Sharp's Doom Bar; guest beers Ⓗ

Located at one end of the High Street, this is a basic and welcoming pub with a single bar decorated with pictures of bygone Keynsham. Quiz night is Monday. The two or three guest beers are often unusual and interesting and there is a small selection of foreign beers too. Full English breakfast is served 9.30-2.45pm Monday to Saturday. The car park is accessed via a narrow entrance to the side of the pub. ✿◐⇌🚌(318,339,649)♣P⚐

Ship ✔

93 Temple Street, BS31 1ER

12-3, 6-11; 12-11 Fri-Sun

☎ (0117) 9869841

Marston's Burtonwood Bitter, Mansfield Cask Ale, Pedigree; guest beers Ⓗ

This Grade II-listed, 17th-century coaching inn, said to be listed in the Domesday Book, is one of the oldest buildings in Keynsham. It retains some original features with a number of areas in different sizes for dining and drinking and a garden at the rear overlooking the park and the River Chew beyond. No food is available Sunday or Monday evenings. The car park is very small, but local buses pass close by. The three or four guests tend to be mainly from other Marston's-owned breweries. ✿◑⊟⇌🚌(318,349,339)♣P⚐

Kilve

Hood Arms

TA5 1AE (on A39)

11-11

☎ (01278) 741210 ⊕ thehoodarms.com

Otter Head; guest beers Ⓗ

17th-century former coaching inn in the centre of the village beside the main road with oak beams, an open fireplace, a comfortable bar and separate restaurant. It has a landscaped walled garden with a well and there are also 12 en-suite guest rooms and a lodge available to rent. A bar billiards knockout is held every Friday night. Well-behaved dogs are welcome. ⌂✿⊨◑♿⛺🚌(14)♣⚐

Kingsbury Episcopi

Wyndham Arms

TA12 6AT

12-11 (midnight Sun)

☎ (01935) 823239 ⊕ wyndhamarms.com

Butcombe Bitter; guest beers Ⓗ

Large old pub – most of the building is believed to be over 400 years old – with a dining area off the bar featuring a log fire. There are antique settles in the public bar which also has an open fire. Outside is a skittle alley/function room and another function room upstairs offering the occasional live music evening. The pub is justifiably proud of its outdoor smoking area with patio heaters and a pool table. ⌂Q✿◑🚌(632,633)♣●P⚐

Luxborough

Royal Oak Inn of Luxborough

TA23 0SH (2½ miles from B3224, Wheddon Cross-Raleigh's Cross)

12-2.30, 6-11; 12-11 Sat & Sun

(01984) 640319 theroyaloakinnluxborough.co.uk

Cotleigh Tawny; Exmoor Ale; Palmers IPA; guest beers H

Exmoor pub and hotel with a strong local following. The flagstoned public bar has a large inglenook fire, there is a child-friendly lounge and separate dining rooms. The pub hosts a monthly folk night known as 'The Blazing Stump' as well as darts and quizzes. Located in a pretty village in the Exmoor National Park, there are many footpaths and bridleways to explore nearby. Beers are mainly local and the ciders are served by gravity. Watch out for the low headroom in places.

Q P

Marston Magna

Red Lion

Rimpton Road, BA22 8DH (200m from A359)

12-3, 6 (7 Sun)-11; closed Mon & Tue

(01935) 851723

Sharp's Doom Bar; guest beers H

Friendly, welcoming former Eldridge Pope house (note the Huntsman Ales plaque outside), now free of tie, just outside the centre of this pretty village. The furnishings of the single bar are homely and comfortable, with wooden chairs and tables, a wooden china cabinet and paintings on the walls. Two guest beers are stocked, usualy from West Country brewers. Good value food is served at all sessions, including a daily roast. Regular quiz nights are held. (1)P

Martock

White Hart Hotel

East Street, TA12 6JQ

12-2 (3 Sat), 5.30-midnight (2am Fri & Sat); 12-3 Sun

(01935) 822005 whitehartotelmartock.co.uk

Otter Bitter; guest beers H

Martock contains many excellent examples of buildings constructed using ham stone from the imposing escarpment to the south, and is just five minutes from the A303. The White Hart provides accommodation, an interesting menu offering both traditional pub food and the more unusual, and an excellent range of local ales. A Guide regular, it also features on the local branch's pub trail.

(N9,52,633)P

Middlezoy

George Inn

42 Main Street, TA7 0NN (off A372, 1 mile NW of Othery)

12-3 (not Mon), 7-midnight (11.30 Sun)

(01823) 698215

Butcombe Bitter; guest beers H

Dating from the 17th century, little seems to have changed here, with exposed beams and a huge fireplace along with a stone-flagged floor. All visitors are warned of the step in the middle of the bar by the booming South African voice of the landlord. Guest ales and wines complement a popular grill-based menu for which booking is essential. Ostrich and kangaroo are particular favourites. Food is not served Sunday to Tuesday. A beer festival is held at Easter. Dogs are welcome.

Q(16)P

Minehead

Queen's Head

Holloway Street, TA24 5NR (off the Parade)

12-3, 5.30-11 (midnight Fri); 12-midnight Sat; 12-3, 6.30-11 Sun

(01643) 702940

Draught Bass; Exmoor Gold; Otter Ale; St Austell Tribute; guest beers H

Popular town pub situated in a side street off the Parade. Six beers are usually sold, guest ales coming mainly from local breweries. Beer festivals are held in spring and autumn with eight or more beers on sale at any time. There is a large single bar room, with a raised seating area for dining and families at one end. Good-value food is served – try the delicious home-made pies. There is also a games room. The West Somerset Railway is 10 minutes walk away.

(West Somerset Railway)(18,28,39)

Monksilver

Notley Arms

TA4 4JB (on B3188)

12-2.30 (not Mon), 6.30-11

(01984) 656217 thenotleyarms.co.uk

Exmoor Ale; Wadworth 6X; guest beers H

Positioned in the walkers' paradise of Exmoor, this stone-floored pub, naturally, allows dogs and boots, and offers wholesome food. The pictures around the walls vary from photographs of locals past and present to watercolours of southern Africa – the landlord's previous home. The rosettes and certificates show that farming in Zimbabwe was his previous love. Talk local or overseas – you will be more than welcome. QP

Moorlinch

Ring O' Bells

Pit Hill Lane, TA7 9BT (between A39 and A361 near Street)

12-2 (not Mon), 5-11; 12-11 Sat & Sun

(01458) 210358 ringobellsmoorlinch.co.uk

Flowers IPA; guest beers H

This traditional village pub serves two constantly changing West Country beers. Locally-sourced home-cooked food is available in the public bar, big lounge bar or the separate dining room. Vegetarian meals are also available. The pub does not open on Monday lunchtime. Although a bit off the beaten track, it is well worth seeking out.

Q(19)P

Mudford

Half Moon

Main Street, BA21 5TF (on A359 between Yeovil and Sparkford)

12-11 (10.30 Sun)

(01935) 850289 thehalfmooninn.co.uk

RCH Pitchfork, seasonal beers; guest beers G

The Half Moon is primarily a restaurant, but drinkers are far from discouraged, as the stillage behind the bar shows. The division of the large building into small dining/drinking areas makes for a comfortable atmosphere. Good food and snacks are available all day and the former skittle alley has been converted into 14 en-suite rooms. The pub has good disabled facilities throughout. (1)P

Nailsea

Blue Flame

West End, BS48 4DE (1 mile off A370 at Chelvey) OS449691
12-3, 6-11; 12-10.30 Sun
(01275) 856910
Fuller's London Pride; RCH East Street Cream G**; guest beer** H

Lovely, rustic 19th-century free house, unaltered for many years, comprising two rooms, one with a bar and a snug. Coal fires help create a cosy atmosphere in winter. Simple, almost spartan decor and outside toilets feature. Food is limited to filled rolls. The cider is Thatchers. Live music plays on the first and third Tuesday of the month. The large rear garden is ideal for families in summer. Camping is available but phone first. Well worth a visit. QP

North Perrott

Manor Arms

Middle Street, TA18 7SG
11 (12 Sun)-11
(01460) 72901
Butcombe Bitter; Fuller's London Pride; O'Hanlon's Yellowhammer; guest beers H

This comfortable, friendly, 16th-century village pub with a one-room layout is divided into four distinct areas, one with an inglenook fireplace. The pub has flagstoned floors, oak beams and exposed stonework. Five beers are always in stock, with extras added at busy seasons, most coming from the West Country. There is a pleasant garden for the summer. Quality food and accommodation are offered, with meal deals at times. The bus stops outside. (60)P

Oakhill

Oakhill Inn

Fosse Road, BA3 5HU (on A37 between Radstock and Shepton Mallet) ST635472
12-3, 5-11 (midnight Fri); 12-midnight Sat & Sun
(01749) 840442 theoakhillinn.com
Beer range varies H

Formerly very much a village local, this has been completely refurbished over the last 12 months and is now a family-friendly gastro pub with a strong emphasis on organic and locally-sourced food. The ambience is more French bistro than country pub, however up to three guest ales are ever changing along with a range of ciders. Regular quiz nights and occasional music nights are held. No food Sunday evening. P

Pitney

Halfway House

Pitney Hill, TA10 9AB (on B3153)
11.30-3.30, 5.30-11 (midnight Fri & Sat); 12-3.30, 7-11 Sun
(01458) 252513 thehalfwayhouse.co.uk
Branscombe Vale Own; Butcombe Bitter; Hop Back Crop Circle, Summer Lightning; Otter Bright; guest beers G

Thriving traditional village pub serving a wide variety of local ales all on gravity alongside a range of international bottled beers. Superb home-cooked food is based on local produce (no food Sun). No background music or fruit machines disturb the buzz of conversation in this multiple award-winning pub. Somerset CAMRA Pub of the Year for 2008, CAMRA National Pub of the Year in 1996 and the Telegraph Pub of the Year in 2007. A real gem. Q(54)P

Porlock

Ship Inn

High Street, TA24 8QD
11-midnight
(01643) 862507 shipinnporlock.co.uk
Exmoor Ale; Otter Ale; St Austell Tribute; guest beers H

Known locally as the Top Ship, this 13th-century inn was recorded in Richard Blackmore's Lorna Doone. The bar appears not to have changed much since then, with flagstoned floors, inglenook fires and a good selection of real ales and cider. Located at the bottom of the notorious Porlock Hill, this gem offers good home-cooked food, a three-tiered patio garden, skittle alley and four en-suite bedrooms. This dog-friendly hostelry also welcomes well-behaved children. Q(39,300)P

Portishead

Windmill Inn

58 Nore Road, BS20 6JZ (next to municipal golf course)
11-11; 12-10.30 Sun
(01275) 843677
Butcombe Gold; Courage Best Bitter; Draught Bass; RCH PG Steam; guest beers H

Formerly a mill, this large split-level free house has a spacious tiered patio to the rear. Situated on the edge of town above the coastal path with panoramic views over the Severn estuary, both Severn bridges can be seen on clear days. A varied menu is served all day and is enormously popular. One large area is set aside for families. The two guest ales are often locally sourced and there is an Easter beer festival. Thatchers Cider is stocked. Q(359)P

Priddy

Hunters Lodge

BA5 3AR (at isolated crossroads 1 mile from A39 at Green Ore) ST549500
11.30-2.30, 6.30-11; 12-2, 7-11 Sun
(01749) 672275
Blindmans Mine Beer; Butcombe Bitter; Cheddar Potholer G**; guest beers** H

Timeless, classic roadside inn near Priddy, the highest village in Somerset, popular with cavers and walkers. The landlord has been in charge for more than 40 years. Three rooms include one with a flagged floor, a good atmosphere and barrels behind the bar. Local guest beers come from brewers such as Cheddar Ales. The simple home-cooked food is excellent and exceptional value. A folk musicians' drop-in session is held on Tuesday evening in the back room. Wilkins cider is served. The garden is pleasant and secluded. Mobile phones are not welcome. QP

Queen Victoria Inn ✔

Pelting Drove, BA5 3BA (on minor road to Wookey Hole, S of village centre)

✪ 12-3, 6-11; 12-11.30 Sat; 12-11 Sun

☎ (01749) 676385

Butcombe Bitter, Gold; guest beer Ⓗ

Traditional creeper-clad inn, a pub since 1851. Four rooms feature low ceilings, flagged floors and three log fires. This is a wonderfully warm and relaxing haven on a cold winter night and is popular during the Priddy Folk Festival in July and the annual fair in August. Reasonably priced, home-cooked food is a speciality. Children and dogs are allowed. Cheddar Valley cider is sold. Beers are now via handpump, not gravity as before. ⌂Q❀◐◑⛺♣●P⁄–

Radstock

Fromeway

Frome Road, BA3 3LG (¾ mile from Radstock centre on A362 Frome Road)

✪ 12-3, 6 (7 Sun)-11

☎ (01761) 432116 ⊕ fromeway.co.uk

Butcombe Bitter; Wadworth 6X; guest beer Ⓗ

This friendly free house has been in the same family for five generations. The present landlord has been in charge for 33 years. The pub is combined with a butcher's shop, which supplies all the meat for the excellent bar and restaurant meals. Well-used by locals, the Fromeway has a warm and relaxing atmosphere. Guest beers are sourced from local and national breweries. Q⛵❀🛏◐◑♿🚌P⁄–

Rowberrow

Swan Inn ✔

Rowberrow Lane, BS25 1QL (signed off A38)

✪ 11.30-3, 6-11; 11.30-11 Fri & Sat; 12-11 Sun

☎ (01934) 852371

Butcombe Bitter, Gold, seasonal beer; guest beer Ⓗ

Believed to date from around the late 17th century, this Butcombe Brewery-owned country pub enjoys an attractive setting, nestling beneath the nearby Dolebury Iron Age Hill Fort. A convenient refreshment stop for walkers on the Mendip Hills, the emphasis is on home-cooked food with unusual specials, but customers who just want a drink are very welcome. There is an interesting collection of artefacts around the walls and a grandfather clock. Thatchers cider is available. The large, attractive beer garden and car park are opposite. ⌂Q❀◐◑●P⁄–

Rumwell

Rumwell Inn

TA4 1EL (on A38 between Taunton and Wellington)

✪ 11-3, 6 (7 Sun)-11

☎ (01823) 461662 ⊕ therumwellinn.co.uk

Otter Bitter; guest beers Ⓗ

This 16th-century coaching inn is on the A38 – the old coaching road from Bristol to Exeter. An atmospheric, friendly pub, you can be sure of a warm welcome. The guest ales normally include one from the south west and one sourced nationally. A varied menu uses ingredients mainly from local suppliers, as well as fish from Brixham. A good stop en route to or from the west, the pub is just five minutes from junction 26 of the M5. ⌂Q❀◐◑🚌(22,92)P⁄–

Seavington St Michael

Volunteer ✔

New Road, TA19 0QE (on former A303, 2 miles E of Ilminster)

✪ 12-2.30, 6.30-11; 12-3, 7-11 Sun

☎ (01460) 240126 ⊕ thevolly.co.uk

St Austell Tribute; guest beers Ⓗ

Pies on Wednesday evenings and good ale always encourage the visitor to this pub, situated on what used to be the main route to the west, before the Ilminster bypass was built. Involved with most village events, the Volunteer can certainly be summed up by Prince Charles' phrase: 'the pub is the hub'. There are stone floors – dogs, as well as walkers, are welcome. ⌂Q❀🛏◐◑⊟♿♣P⁄–

Shepton Beauchamp

Duke of York

North Street, TA19 0LW

✪ 12-11 (midnight Sat)

☎ (01460) 240314 ⊕ thedukeshepton.co.uk

Otter Bright; Teignworthy Reel Ale; guest beers Ⓗ

A friendly, comfortable pub right in the centre of an attractive village. Home to several darts and skittles teams, there is a separate games room with a pool table. Tables on the raised pavement at the front are popular in warmer weather. The ales are mainly from the West Country. Excellent, good-value food is served using local ingredients where possible (no food Sun eve or Mon). Accommodation is provided in recently built units to the rear of the pub. ⌂⛵❀🛏◐◑🚌(633)♣P⁄–

Shepton Mallet

Swan Inn

27 Town Street, BA4 5BE

✪ 11-midnight

☎ (01749) 344995 ⊕ stumbles-inn.co.uk

Matthews Bob Wall; guest beers Ⓗ

Formerly called The Stumbles Inn until it was renamed in 2008, this pub is situated in a terrace of small shops. Inside, the front area is arranged mainly for diners (no meals Mon afternoon or Sun, Mon and Tue eves), with chairs and tables extending out onto the pavement. The bar area at the rear offers darts and shove-ha'penny. Live music is hosted once or twice a month. Guest ales are chosen from local small brewers. 🛏◐◑🚌♣P

Shepton Montague

Montague Arms

BA9 8JW (signed off A359 and A371) ST675315

✪ 12-3, 6-11; closed Mon; 12-3 Sun

☎ (01749) 813213

Bath Ales Gem; Greene King Abbot; Wadworth IPA; guest beers Ⓖ

This attractive pub is in a sparsely populated village between Wincanton, Castle Cary and Bruton and is well known in the region for its outstanding cuisine, complemented by its real ales kept in pins in an anteroom behind the bar. Thatchers cider is usually available. The single bar is cosy and welcoming, with diners now catered for in the newly-opened restaurant at the rear of the building. From here there is access to a wide terrace and garden which enjoys spectacular countryside views towards the famous folly Alfred's Tower. ⌂Q⛵❀🛏◐◑♿●P🍺

South Cadbury

Camelot

Chapel Road, BA22 7EX (just off A303 between Sparkford and Wincanton)
11-3, 5-11; 11-midnight Fri-Sun
(01963) 440448 thecamelotpub.com
Beer range varies H
Located in the village of South Cadbury, this deceptively large pub with flagstoned bar has a most informative glass case containing the history of Cadbury Castle and artefacts found there. The ancient hill fort is a short walk away. Flagstones continue to the dining area which has a log burner at either end. Local ales such as those from Yeovil Ales are always available and usually a local cider as well. A blackboard tempts you with a 'next available' list. QP

South Petherton

Brewers Arms

18 St James Street, TA13 5BW (½ mile off A303)
11.30-2.30, 6-11 (midnight Fri); 12-11 Sun
(01460) 241887
Otter Bitter; guest beers H
Extended licensing hours now give more opportunity to visit this excellent village pub, 2009 Somerset CAMRA Pub of the Year. Guest beers are sourced from all over the UK and beer festivals are held during the late May and August bank holidays in the courtyard, which also houses the smokers' area. Always at the centre of its community, all are welcome (including dogs). Well worth the short detour off the busy A303.
(81,633)

Stogumber

White Horse

High Street, TA4 3TA (turn left off A358 at Crowcombe)
11 (12 Sun)-11
(01984) 656277 whitehorsestogumber.co.uk
Cotleigh Tawny; guest beers H
Friendly Grade II-listed village pub in the centre of this pretty village nestling beneath the Quantock Hills. Guest beers are normally from the West Country and St Austell beers are regularly sold, including a house beer called 'Orse'. Food is freshly prepared using locally sourced ingredients. There is a skittle alley that doubles as a function room and en-suite accommodation is also available. This was one of the first five pubs to sell Exmoor Ale in June 1980 when it was introduced.
(West Somerset Railway)P

Stoke St Gregory

Royal Oak

TA3 6EH (opp church in village centre)
closed Mon; 7.30-11 Tue; 7-11.30 Wed; 12-3, 7-11.30 (midnight Fri & Sat); 12-3, 7-11 Sun
(01823) 490602
St Austell Tribute; guest beers H
A warm, friendly pub in the centre of the village. It has become a real part of the community, with several skittles teams plus darts and pool. A family concern since 2005, you will probably meet most of its members when you visit. The pub is ideally positioned for taking a break when walking the Somerset Levels or the long distance Parrett Trail.
(51)P

Taunton

Plough

75 Station Road, TA1 1PB (300m from railway station)
11-12.30am (3am Thu-Sat; 1am Sun)
(01823) 324404 theploughtaunton.co.uk
Beer range varies G
Previously known as Harpoon Louies, this has reverted back to its original name. Four locally-brewed ales are served along with seven Somerset ciders. Wooden floored and stone walled, the split-level bar areas are furnished with sofas and armchairs, and a selection of board games is available. Ideally situated close to the railway station and cricket ground, it is a favourite haunt of cricket fans. Pub food includes a varied selection of pies and granary baguettes.
(1,28,29)

Racehorse

East Reach, TA1 3HT
12-3, 6-11; 12-midnight Fri & Sat; 12-5, 7-11 Sun
(01823) 327513
St Austell Dartmoor Best Bitter, Tribute, Proper Job H
Friendly pub just off the town centre at the top of East Reach. Multi-roomed, with a front and rear bar, a small lounge with comfortable armchairs and two other indoor drinking areas as well as a large walled beer garden, this traditional town hostelry is the place to go for good conversation and a great atmosphere. The walls are adorned with memorabilia such as old tin signs, musical instruments and a collection of Guiness items. No food is served. (4,21,30)

Wings Club (RAFA)

68 Cheddon Road, TA2 7DW
4 (12 Fri & Sat)-11; 12-11 Sun
(01823) 284883
Beer range varies H
Taunton's branch of the Royal Air Force Association, this club has a comfortable lounge bar at the front and a separate bar at the back used for darts, skittles and functions, where children are welcome until 8pm. The real ales come mainly from West Country breweries, but occasionally from other parts of the country. Show this Guide or a CAMRA membership card to be signed in as a guest.
(1,1A,3)P

Wyvern Club

Mountfields Road, TA1 3BJ
7-11; 12-3, 7-10.30 Sun
(01823) 284591 wyvernclub.co.uk
Exmoor Ale; guest beers H
Large, busy sports and social club offering a variety of West Country beers, with guest ales changing frequently – beers from three different breweries are usually on offer, at club prices. Meals are available each evening until 9pm, plus Sunday lunchtime. The club premises are available for daytime meetings and evening functions. Show this Guide or your CAMRA membership card to be signed in as a guest. A real ale festival is held in October. (1A,99)P

Wanstrow

Pub

Station Road, BA4 4SZ
6.30-11 Mon; 12-2.30 (3 Fri & Sat), 6-11; 12-3, 7-10.30 Sun
(01749) 850455
Draught Bass; Hop Back GFB; guest beers H

An absolute gem, this friendly village local has a lounge bar with open fire and flagstone floors that leads to a small restaurant. The pub serves up to six guest ales and Cheddar Valley and Thatchers ciders are also stocked. Games include skittles, bar billiards and ring the bull. A small but imaginative menu is offered and all food is home cooked.
Q P

Watchet

Esplanade Club

The Esplanade, TA23 0AJ (opp marina)
7-midnight; 12 (2 winter)-midnight Sun
(01984) 634518
St Austell Tribute; Sharp's Doom Bar; guest beers H
A warm welcome awaits you at this local club with views over the marina and Bristol Channel. Built in the 1860s as a sail-making factory, it has been a club since the 1930s. There is live entertainment every weekend, with folk and open mike nights in the week. Just a short walk from the West Somerset Railway, visitors showing this Guide or a CAMRA membership card are very welcome and will be signed in by the staff. Also home to the boat owners club.
(West Somerset Railway)(14,18,28)

Star Inn

Mill Lane, TA23 0BZ
12-3.30, 6.30-midnight (1am Fri & Sat); 12-4, 7-midnight Sun
(01984) 631367
Cotleigh Tawny; guest beers H
The Star has four (five in summer) ever-changing beers from both local and regional breweries. There is a cosy main bar with small side rooms and a large, pleasant garden. Mouth-watering food, including seafood – locally sourced where possible – is served. There are quiz teams, skittle teams and the infamous Sunday bad boys club. Close to the marina, West Somerset Railway and bus routes, it is also handy for walks on the Quantock hills and sea fishing. Dogs are welcome.
(West Somerset Railway)(14,18,28)

Wedmore

New Inn

Combe Batch, BS28 4DU
12-2.30, 5-midnight; 12-2am Fri; 12-1am Sat; 12-10.30 Sun
(01934) 712099
Butcombe Bitter; Cheddar Potholer; guest beers H
Traditional pre-1800s village inn and the current venue for the Turnip Prize. Other annual competitions include conkers, spoof, penny chuffin' and apple bobbin'. There are three main areas – public, lounge and dining – beer gardens front and rear and a skittle alley/function room. A chalkboard lists forthcoming guest ales from breweries including Bath Ales, Exmoor Ales, Hop Back, Timothy Taylor and Yeovil Ales. Local award-winning Wilkins cider is also served. Traditional pub food is available lunchtimes and evenings (not Sun). Q (668,670) P

Wells

City Arms

69 High Street, BA5 2AG
10-11; 9-midnight Fri & Sat; 10-10.30 Sun
(01749) 673916 thecityarmsatwells.com
Butcombe Bitter; Cheddar Gorge Best, Pot Holer; Greene King IPA; guest beers H
In 1810 the city jail closed and became the City Arms. The main bar retains the small barred windows and low vaulted ceilings of its former existence. The Keepers Bar has been refurbished as a patisserie and bistro, and has a modern coffee bar feel. Up to five guest beers are on handpump, and the cider is from Taunton.

West Chinnock

Muddled Man

Lower Street, TA18 7PT
11-2.30 (not Mon winter), 7-midnight; 11-midnight Fri & Sat; 12-10.30 Sun
(01935) 881235
Beer range varies H
This excellent, cosy free house has been run by its friendly, family owners for 10 years. Only beers from the West Country are served, together with Burrow Hill cider. Brewery visits are a regular feature, and many drinkers have been converted to real ale here. Excellent, locally-sourced food is served at reasonable prices – Sunday lunch must be pre-booked. The newly-built skittle alley can be hired for functions and conferences. Newcomers are quickly made to feel at home here.

West Huntspill

Crossways Inn

TA9 3RA (on A38)
11-3, 5.30-midnight (Mon-Fri & winter Sat); 11-midnight summer Sat; 12-11 Sun
(01278) 783756 crossways-inn.com
Fuller's London Pride; guest beers H
This 17th-century inn has recently been refurbished by the new landlord, but retains its cosy atmosphere. An ever-changing selection of guest beers is always available, frequently including beers from Somerset breweries as well as others from the West Country. In addition to the regular menu, specials are listed on the blackboard. There are four rooms available for overnight accommodation. (15,21,21A) P

Royal Artillery Arms

2 Alstone Lane, TA9 3DR (on A38)
12-11.30 (11 Sun)
(01278) 783553
Beer range varies H
This recently refurbished roadside hostelry provides a warm, cosy welcome, with eight handpumps offering a wide selection of real ales. A skittle alley doubles as a function room and an annual beer festival takes place on the August bank holiday weekend. Regular theme nights are held during the year, listed behind the bar.
(15,21,670) P

Weston-super-Mare

Off the Rails

Station Approach, BS23 1XY (on railway station concourse)
7am (9am Sun)-11
(01934) 415109
RCH Hewish IPA; guest beers H

This genuine free house conveniently situated at the railway station doubles up as the station buffet, with snacks, sandwiches and magazines available. The two guest beers usually come from West Country micro-breweries, with the occasional beer and guest ciders from further afield. The landlord is happy to receive suggestions from his regulars for which beers to stock. Two-pint carry-out containers are a handy feature for train travellers. Three TVs show sporting events – often silently. Quiz night is Tuesday and there is a free jukebox.
(112,126)

Raglan

42-44 Upper Church Road, BS23 2DX (100m from sea front)
4 (12 Sat & Sun)-midnight
(01934) 429942
Beer range varies H
Two-room, back-street local close to the sea front, between the piers (or what is left after the fire in 2008). It has two bars – one with a TV and pool table but no handpumps on view. The lounge bar has handpulls plus bar billiards and a piano. The beers are usually, but not always, from south west micros, and surprises do pop up. Live folk music plays in the lounge most Sunday evenings and at other times too. May close earlier than midnight if quiet.

Wookey

Burcott Inn

Wookey Road, BA5 1NJ (on B3139, 2 miles W of Wells)
11-2.30 (3 Sat), 6-11; 12-3, 7-10.30 Sun
(01749) 673874 burcottinn.co.uk
Beer range varies H
Cosy country pub featuring a copper-covered, L-shaped bar always serving two or more ales, mostly from the West Country. This stone-built roadside inn is characterised by low beams, pine tables and flagstone flooring, all heated by a log-burning stove. The chef makes freshly-prepared food with daily specials served throughout the pub (no food Sun eve or Mon). Outside, the garden has an old flower-adorned cider press.
Q(670)P

Wookey Hole

Wookey Hole Inn

High Street, BA5 1BP (opp Wookey Hole caves)
12-11 (6 Sun)
(01749) 676677 wookeyholeinn.com
Beer range varies H
Charismatic, picturesque gastro-pub with a unique contemporary style, situated opposite the famous caves. It offers two to four changing guest beers from small, often unusual brewers, plus a local cider and a wide choice of draught continental beers and lagers. Top-quality food is served at restaurant prices, ideal for special occasions (booking recommended at weekends). The huge rear garden is superb in summer. A lurid pink function room and six highly individual bedrooms complete the picture. P

Wrington

Golden Lion

Broad Street, BS40 5LA
2.30-11.30; 12-midnight Fri & Sat; 12-11.30 Sun
(01934) 862205 goldenlionwrington.co.uk
Butcombe Bitter; guest beers H
Family-run, genuine free house which prides itself on offering a warm welcome. In the centre of the village, it runs its own football team, golfing society and shooting syndicates. No food is served, but great attention is paid to quality beer. Three guest ales are usually sourced from West Country brewers and the landlord will consider customers' suggestions. Events include a beer festival on the late May bank holiday weekend, a summer hog roast and live music on Saturday night.
(121)

Yeovil

Quicksilver Mail

168 Hendford Hill, BA20 2RG
10.30-midnight (1am Sat); 12-11 Sun
(01935) 424721 quicksilvermail.com
Adnams Broadside; Butcombe Bitter; guest beers H
Friendly, well-run pub in a prominent position at the junction of the A30 and A37. It is the only pub in the country with this name, commemorating the original Quicksilver mail coach, which attached extra horses for greater speed in dangerous areas. Displayed in the bar are old photographs of the inn, and sporting memorabilia. Good value food includes Sunday lunches. Well behaved children and dogs are allowed. There is a large function room with regular live music.
(Pen Mill)(4,60,61)P

The sign of the Bell

Mr Jones and Partridge travelled on to Gloucester. Being arrived here, they chose for their house of entertainment the sign of the Bell; an excellent house, and which I do most seriously recommend to every reader who shall visit this ancient city. The master of it is brother to the great preacher, Whitfield, but is absolutely untainted with the pernicious principles of Methodism, or of any other heretical sect. He is indeed a very honest, plain man, and in my opinion not likely to create any disturbance either in Church or State. His wife hath, I believe, had much pretension to beauty, and is still a very fine woman. Her person and deportment might have made a shining figure in the politest assemblies; but though she must be conscious of this and many other perfections, she seems perfectly contented with, and resigned to the state of life to which she is called – To be concise, she is a very friendly, good-natured woman; and so industrious to oblige that the guests must be of a very morose disposition who are not extremely well satisfied in her house.
Henry Fielding (1707-54), The History of Tom Jones, 1749

Abbots Bromley

Coach & Horses

High Street, WS15 3BN

12-2.30 (not Mon), 5.30-11; 12-10.30 Sun

(01283) 840256

Greene King Abbot; Marston's Pedigree H

Grade II-listed old coaching inn dating back to 1745, although the building is even older, with links to Burton Abbey. Inside, the long narrow lounge bar features a beamed ceiling and an assortment of memorabilia and bric-a-brac, such as brasses and old photographs, and some settees for the comfort of the more laid-back drinker. There are several dining areas, including a dedicated dining room to the rear. Abbots Bromley is famous for its annual Horn Dance (see website abbotsbromley.com/horn_dance).

(428) P

Alrewas

George & Dragon

120 Main Street, DE13 7AE

11 (12 Sun)-11

(01283) 791476

Marston's Burton Bitter, Pedigree; guest beer H

Imposing, three-storey, welcoming village local, thought to be a former coaching inn and dating back to the early 1700s. The comfortable main bar area is split into three cosy sections and there is a lounge/dining room to one side. The guest beer is usually from the Marston's list. No meals are served Sunday evening. The Trent & Mersey Canal runs along the edge of the village, and the National Memorial Arboretum is a mile away. Reasonably-priced accommodation is available in one family room and two double rooms.

P

Barton under Needwood

Royal Oak ✔

74 The Green, DE13 8JD (½ mile from B5016 via Wales Lane) SK182180
12-midnight (1am Fri & Sat); 12-11 Sun
☎ (01283) 713852
Marston's Pedigree; guest beers Ⓗ/Ⓖ
Bustling, community local situated on the southern edge of the village, home to many traditional pub games and an over-40s football team. While parts of the building date back to the 16th-century, the pub has only existed since the mid-1800s. Public bar and lounge customers are served from a central sunken bar, set below the level of the rest of the ground floor. Beers are available on handpump or on gravity, direct from the cask, on request.
(7,112)♣P

Shoulder of Mutton ✔

16 Main Street, DE13 8AA SK189186
12-midnight (1am Fri & Sat)
☎ (01283) 712568 shoulderofmutton.com
Draught Bass; Marston's Pedigree; guest beer Ⓗ
This 17th-century former coaching inn, with some 19th-century additions, is located at the centre of the village, opposite the church. Two rather smart Bass lanterns illuminate the front entrances that lead directly to the simple public bar and comfortable lounge, the latter featuring a low-beamed ceiling, wood panelling and inglenook, plus a dining area to one side. There is a delightful landscaped garden to the rear, with a children's play area beyond the car park. Live music nights are popular. (7,112)♣P

Waterfront

Barton Marina, DE13 8DZ (off B5016) SK197181
11-11 (12.30am Fri & Sat); 11-10.30 Sun
☎ (01283) 711500 bartonmarina.co.uk
Burton Bridge XL Bitter; Marston's Pedigree; St Austell Tribute; guest beers Ⓗ
Large, new pub that opened in 2007 within a new retail complex and leisure park by the Barton Marina, which is linked to the nearby Trent & Mersey canal. The main open-plan room features a low ceiling with wooden beams, and has lounge and dining areas amid wood partitioning. There is a separate dedicated restaurant, the Quarterdeck. An outdoor terrace overlooks the marina, where short stay moorings are available and a large function room is located upstairs. No meals after 6pm on Sunday. (7,112)P

Bignall End

Bignall End Cricket Club

Boon Hill, ST7 8LA (off B5500)
12-3 (Tue only), 7-midnight; 12-midnight Sat & Sun
☎ (01782) 720514
Beer range varies Ⓗ
Very welcoming cricket club established for more than 100 years in a village outside Newcastle-under-Lyme. Rural views over Cheshire can be seen from the pitch side. The club hosts popular beer festivals every year in November and August, and many other events in a large upstairs function room which overlooks the pitch. A public bar and snooker room with a full-sized table are downstairs. A wide range of cask beers is supplied by an independent wholesaler. CAMRA members are welcome as guests. (34)P

Plough

2 Ravens Lane, ST7 8PS (on B5500)
12 (5 Mon)-11; 12-11.30 Fri & Sat; 12-10.30 Sun
☎ (01782) 720469
Black Sheep Best Bitter; Hydes Original; guest beers Ⓗ
This pub makes a welcome return to the Guide, now owned by Hydes Brewery. There are eight handpumps offering a range of beers from Hydes, with guests often coming from All Gates of Wigan. The busy public bar is complemented by a split-level lounge and dining area. Home-cooked food and snacks are available from the menu. Car parking is available at the front and rear, and a pleasant beer garden is located at the back. Sky Sports and pub games are also on offer.
(34)♣P

Swan 🏆

Chapel Street, ST7 8QD
12-11 (10.30 Sun)
☎ (01782) 720622
Draught Bass; guest beers Ⓗ
Winner of CAMRA Potteries Pub of the Year for 2007 and 2008, this traditional pub has a bar and lounge, both with real fires, and a pleasant garden to relax in during the warmer months. Eight handpumps serve a range of ever-changing guest beers; two real ciders and a perry are also on offer, usually from Thatchers and Westons. The Swan hosts a beer festival and the pub's Real Ale Club runs regular events. Bar snacks are available.
(34)

Blythe Bridge

One Legged Shunter (Foxfield Railway Bar)

Caverswall Road, ST11 9EA
closed Mon-Fri; 12-1pm Sat; 12-9 Sun
☎ (01782) 396210 foxfieldrailway.co.uk
Beer range varies Ⓗ
A single bar inside the Foxfield Light Railway, run by volunteers. Steam trains run from Easter every year along the former colliery line, and the walls of the bar are adorned with historic memorabilia about the old railway. The beer range changes continuously and is sourced from micro-breweries both near and far. The cider is Westons. Regular beer festivals and themed weekends are held

INDEPENDENT BREWERIES

Beowulf Brownhills
Black Hole Burton upon Trent
Blythe Hamstall Ridware
Burton Bridge Burton upon Trent
Enville Enville
Kinver Kinver
Leek Cheddleton
Lymestone Stone (NEW)
Marston's Burton upon Trent
Morton Essington
Old Cottage Burton upon Trent
Peakstones Rock Alton
Quartz Kings Bromley/Swinfen
Shugborough Milford
Slater's Stafford
Titanic Burslem
Tower Burton upon Trent
Town House Audley
Wincle Rushton Spencer (NEW)

throughout the year; check the website for details. A must for real ale drinkers and steam aficionados alike. P

Brewood

Bridge Inn

22 High Green, ST19 9BD
10-midnight (1am Fri & Sat)
(01902) 851999
Jennings Dark Mild, Cocker Hoop; Mansfield Cask Bitter; guest beers H

Popular with boaters and walkers, the inn stands on the Shropshire Union Canal and the Staffordshire Way. Dogs are welcome in the small traditional bar which can get busy when national sporting events are shown on terrestrial television. Home-cooked food is available in the comfortable lounge and rear restaurant. Note the covered smoking shelter overlooking the canal in the style of a narrow boat. Q(3,76)P

Swan Hotel

15 Market Place, ST19 9BS
11.45-11 (11.30 Thu & Sat); 12-11 Sun
(01902) 850330
Caledonian Deuchars IPA; Courage Directors; Theakston Black Bull; guest beers H

Comfortable village centre coaching inn with low beamed ceilings and log fires, within easy walking distance of the Shropshire Union canal. The bar is flanked by two cosy snugs displaying pictures of old Brewood, and there is a skittle alley upstairs. Hourly buses from Wolverhampton stop outside, with occasional buses from Penkridge and Stafford. This 2008 CAMRA branch rural Pub of the Year displays an unusual collection of witches' figures. Guest beers are often from local breweries. Q(3,76)P

Bridgtown

Stumble Inn

264 Walsall Road, WS11 0JL (just off A34/A5/M6 toll jct)
12-3, 6 (5 Fri)-11; 7-midnight Sat; 12-10.30 Sun
(01543) 502077 thestumbleinn.eu
Beer range varies H

Famed for its hospitality and fun-loving nature, the Stumble has become one of Cannock's best loved watering holes. The comfortable one-room split-level interior includes a pool/darts area and a small function room. An emphasis on music is reflected in the Friday night disco, jam sessions on the second and last Tuesdays of every month, plus the famed Saturday gigs with live bands. Now offering free broadband access.
(Cannock)(1,351)P

Burton upon Trent

Alfred

51 Derby Street, DE14 2LD (on A5121)
11-2, 4.30-11; 11-11 Fri & Sat; 11-4.30, 7-10.30 Sun
(01283) 562178 bbb-thealfred.co.uk
Burton Bridge Golden Delicious, Bridge Bitter, Burton Porter, Stairway to Heaven, Bramble Stout, Festival Ale; guest beer H

This double-fronted terrace pub, now part of the Burton Bridge estate, was once the long-gone Trumans Brewery tap. A central bar counter serves two rooms, each featuring wood partitions topped with leaded stained glass. The raised area in the left-hand room is generally used for dining. There is also a small snug/family room to the rear. The pub is known locally for its range of English fruit wines, Monday poker night and Wednesday quiz night. No meals Wednesday or Sunday evening. P

Burton Bridge Inn

24 Bridge Street, DE14 1SY (on A511, at town end of Trent Bridge)
11.30-2.15, 5-11; 12-2, 7-10.30 Sun
(01283) 536596 burtonbridgebrewery.co.uk
Burton Bridge Golden Delicious, Sovereign Gold, Bridge Bitter, Burton Porter, Festival Ale, seasonal beer; guest beer H

This 17th-century pub is the flagship of the Burton Bridge Brewery estate and fronts the brewery itself. Sensitively renovated and extended in 2000, it has two rooms served from a central bar: a smaller front room with wooden pews displaying awards and brewery memorabilia, and a back room featuring oak beams and panels. The beer range is supplemented by a fine selection of malt whiskies and fruit wines. No meals are served Sunday. A small dining/function room and a skittle alley are upstairs. Q

Coopers Tavern

43 Cross Street, DE14 1EG (off Station Street)
12-2.30 (not Mon or Tue), 5 (7 Mon)-11; 12-midnight Fri & Sat; 12-11 Sun
(01283) 532551
Castle Rock Harvest Pale H**; Draught Bass** G**; guest beers** H/G

Originally the Bass Brewery bottle store, this classic, unspoilt 19th-century ale house was once the Bass Brewery tap and is now a free house. The intimate inner tap room has barrel tables and bench seats. The beer is served from a small counter, next to the cask stillage, using a mixture of gravity and handpumps. Up to four draught cider and perries plus fruit wines are available. The more comfortable lounge, sometimes hosting impromptu folk music, leads to a third small room. Q

Old Cottage Tavern

36 Byrkley Street, DE14 2EG (off Derby Street A5121, behind town hall)
12-11 (10.30 Sun)
(01283) 511615
Old Cottage Oak Ale, Stout, Halcyon Daze; guest beers H

This welcoming local is now a privately owned free-house, but still operates as the Old Cottage Brewery tap, although no longer owned by the brewery. The main public bar at the front and the wood-panelled lounge to the rear are served from a central bar. There is also a cosy snug to one side of the public bar, a small restaurant beyond the lounge, and a games/function room, with a demountable skittle alley upstairs. No meals Monday, or Wednesday and Sunday evenings.

Plough

7 Ford Street, DE15 9LE (off Rosliston Road)
11-midnight
(01283) 516486
Burton Bridge Mystery Mild, Bridge Bitter, Stairway to Heaven; guest beers H/G

Popular recent addition to the Burton Bridge estate, located in the suburb of Stapenhill, on the other side of the River Trent from the town centre. The pub dates back to the 19th century and is thought to be a converted farm building. The single large room is partitioned into distinct areas served from a central counter, with the available guest beers listed on a board. Live entertainment is hosted on Friday and Saturday evening. Occasional beer festivals are held during the year. ❀◐⊟♣P⅟

Cauldon

Yew Tree

ST10 3EJ (1 mile S of A523 at Waterhouses)
11-3, 6 (7 Sun)-11
☎ (01538) 308348
Burton Bridge Bitter; Draught Bass; Grays Dark Mild Ⓗ
Over 300 years old, this gem of a country pub is full of antiques and memorabilia, such as polyphons, pianolas and grandfather clocks. Run by the same family for the past 45 years, it is close to the Manifold Valley and not far from Alton Towers. Pub games are very popular here and the pub fields several darts teams. Live music is staged and bar snacks such as sandwiches and pork pies are always available. There cannot be another pub like this. Q❀♿▲♣P

Chasetown

Uxbridge Arms

2 Church Street, WS7 3QL
12-3, 5.30-11; 12-11 Fri & Sat; 12-10.30 Sun
☎ (01543) 677852
Draught Bass; guest beers Ⓗ
Situated near to Chasetown Country Park and Chasetown Football Club, this is a busy, traditional corner local. The large public bar and lounge features five hand pulls that serve around 300 beer choices each year, many from micro-breweries. A large selection of country wines and malt whiskies is offered, plus one real cider. Meals are available throughout the pub, as well as in the well-regarded Hayloft restaurant upstairs (no food served Sun eve). ❀◐⊟♣●P

Church Eaton

Royal Oak

High Street, ST20 0AJ
5 (12 Sat)-midnight; 12-10.30 Sun
☎ (01785) 823078 🌐 churcheaton.org.uk
Banks's Original, Bitter; guest beer Ⓗ
The only pub in the village was, a few years ago, threatened with closure but was saved by a small consortium of local people and is now the hub of the community. It has a modern interior split into four-interconnecting rooms – a bar, restaurant, TV room and pool room. Children are welcome until 7pm or later if eating in the restaurant. The ever-changing guest beers are mostly sourced from local micro-breweries. ❀◐♿P⅟

Codsall

Codsall Station

Chapel Lane, WV8 2EH
11.30-2.30, 5-11; 11.30-11.30 Fri & Sat; 12-10.30 Sun
☎ (01902) 847061
Holden's Mild, Bitter, Golden Glow, Special, seasonal beers; guest beers Ⓗ
Former stationmaster's house and waiting room converted by Holden's Brewery in 1999. The interior, displaying worldwide railway memorabilia, comprises a bar, lounge, snug and conservatory. Outside a raised terrace overlooks the working platforms on the Wolverhampton-Shrewsbury line. The floodlit boules piste is the site of a beer festival held over the August bank holiday week. Good value home-cooked food is served daily (not Sun eve). Occasional free live acoustic sessions feature on Sunday afternoon.
Q❀◐♿⇌⊟P

Dayhills

Red Lion

Uttoxeter Road, ST15 8RU (3 miles E of Stone on B5027)
5 (4 Fri)-11; 2-midnight Sat; 12-10.30 Sun
☎ (01889) 505474
Draught Bass; Worthington's Bitter; guest beer Ⓗ
Welcoming country pub known locally as the Romping Cat. Unspoilt and full of character, along with the adjoining farm, it has been in the same family since 1920. The main room has a timeless feel with a quarry tile floor, meat hooks in the ceiling and inglenook fireplace. The atmosphere is undisturbed by music, gaming machines or TV.
Q♣P⅟

Dosthill

Fox Inn ✔

105 High Street, B77 1LQ
4 (6 Mon)-11; 12-midnight Fri-Sun
☎ (01827) 280847
Banks's Bitter; Greene King Abbot; Wychwood Hobgoblin; guest beer Ⓗ
Welcoming local to the south of Tamworth, around three miles from the town centre. This three-roomed pub has a traditional bar and very comfortable lounge. The separate Fox's Lounge is quiet and may be used for meetings by local groups and societies. The guest beer is often from a local micro-brewery. A real cider is always available and a very popular quiz night is held on Sunday. The pub is close to the West Midland Water Ski Centre and Kingsbury Water Park.
Q❀◐♿⊟♣●P⅟

Eccleshall

George Hotel

Castle Street, ST21 6DF
11-11; 12-10.30 Sun
☎ (01785) 850300 🌐 thegeorgeeccleshall.com
Slater's Bitter, Original, Top Totty, Premium, Supreme, seasonal beers; guest beer Ⓗ
Slater's Brewery has moved to Stafford, but six handpulls serving nearly the full range of its award-winning ales remain the main attraction at the George. Originally a 17th-century coaching inn, but sadly neglected for much of the last century, the George has thrived under the Slater family's ownership. It now boasts attractive bar and lounge areas. Q◐⊟P⅟

Kings Arms Hotel

Stafford Street, ST21 6BL
12-3, 5-11; 12-11 Sat; 12-3, 7-10.30 Sun
☎ (01785) 850294

Fuller's London Pride; Greene King Old Speckled Hen; Marston's Burton Bitter; Shepherd Neame Spitfire; guest beer
Former coaching inn and local inland revenue office known as the Unicorn. Parts of the original building are still visible and various rooms are served by a small central bar. A monthly farmers market is held close to the pub.
Q P

Enville

Cat
Bridgnorth Road, DY7 5HA (on A458)
12-2.30, 6.30-11 (not Mon); 12-3, 6.30-11 Sat; 12-6 Sun
(01384) 872209 thecatinn.com
Enville Ale; guest beers
Parts of this traditional country pub date back to the 16th century. It has three oak-beamed rooms, two with real fires, together with a family/function room. Hanging baskets adorn the beer garden and courtyard during the summer months. Up to five guest ales are served, including other beers from local breweries. Home-made dishes and daily specials, made with local produce wherever possible, are served. A separate menu is offered in the restaurant. The pub is closed on Monday except bank holidays. P

Gnosall

Boat
Wharf Road, ST20 0DA
12-2.30, 5-midnight; 12-midnight Fri-Sun
(01785) 822208
Banks's Original, Bitter; Marston's Burton Bitter, Pedigree; guest beer
This pleasantly decorated canalside pub is popular with the boating trade. Good home-cooked food is served (not Mon). In order to preserve the traditional atmosphere and conversation, the small TV in the bar area is only switched on for big sporting occasions. The pub runs both darts and dominoes teams. P

Royal Oak
Newport Road, ST20 0BL (on A518)
12-midnight
(01785) 822362
Ansells Mild; Greene King IPA, Abbot; guest beer
Popular village local that was once a coaching inn although the exact date of the building is unknown. The pub has an upstairs function room with a skittle alley for hire and every other Tuesday evening is music night. A large beer garden has swings, a climbing frame and a large heated smoking area. No food on Monday, Tuesday and Sunday evening. Dogs are welcome.
P

Great Haywood

Clifford Arms
Main Road, ST18 0SR (off A51 4 miles NW of Rugeley)
12-11.30 (midnight Fri & Sat); 12-11 Sun
(01889) 881321
Adnams Broadside; Draught Bass; Greene King Old Speckled Hen; guest beers
Village-centre inn with a large bar providing plenty of seating and a restaurant adorned with old photographs of the pub. A lively local, home to cribbage, dominoes and quiz teams, it also has a tug 'o' war team. It attracts walkers, cyclists, boaters, and visitors to the nearby Shugborough Estate (National Trust). The Staffordshire Way and bridge 73 of the Trent and Mersey canal are 200 metres along Trent Lane. The pub is dog-friendly.
P

Harriseahead

Royal Oak
High Street, ST7 4JT
7 (5 Fri & Sat)-11; 12-4, 7-10.30 Sun
(01782) 513262 royaloak-harriseahead.com
Courage Directors; Fuller's London Pride; Samuel Smith OBB; guest beers
Popular, two-roomed village free house situated in an excellent walking area, one mile away from Mow Cop Folly. The three guest beers on offer hail from a wide selection of micro-breweries both near and far, and there is a small meeting room upstairs, which plays host to a beer festival every December. There is also a range of bottled Belgian beers available, plus one on draught; pork pies and baps fill the stomachs of hungry walkers.
Q P

Hednesford

Cross Keys Hotel
42 Hill Street, WS12 2DN
12-midnight
(01543) 877285
Greene King Old Speckled Hen; guest beers
An 18th-century former coaching inn serving five different real ales, including four that are ever changing. Hednesford Town Football Club used to play behind the pub until it was relocated nearby in 1994. Links are still strong as the licensee, in charge since 1997, used to play for, and later managed, the team. Voted local CAMRA Pub of the Year 2008, it also has Cannock Chase area of outstanding natural beauty in close proximity. Sky and Setanta sports are available to view on TV.
(33,60) P

High Offley

Anchor Inn
Peggs Lane, Old Lea, ST20 0NB (by bridge 42 of the Shropshire Union Canal) SJ775256
12-3, 7-11 (10.30 Sun); winter hours vary
(01785) 284569
Wadworth 6X
On the Shropshire Union Canal, this Victorian inn has changed little since the days of commercial waterways and has been run by the same family since 1870. Not easily reached by road but well worth finding, it remains a rare example of an unspoilt country pub, with two small bars where cask ale and cider are served from jugs. Freshly-made sandwiches are always available. There is a large award-winning garden with a canalware gift shop at the rear. Q P

Hilderstone

Roebuck Inn
Sandon Road, ST15 8SF (on B5066)
3-midnight; 12-1am Sat; 12-11 Sun
(01889) 505255
Greene King Abbot; Taylor Golden Best; Wadworth 6X; guest beers

This friendly and comfortable pub has a cosy lounge/bar with two real fires and a dartboard. A separate room, also with a real fire, has a large-screen TV showing Sky Sports. Two guest beers from the SIBA scheme are offered and Thatchers cider is usually available in summer. Live music or karaoke is hosted on Saturday night and live music on Sunday. Well-behaved dogs are welcome but no children under 13 years old. ⛺❀♣P⁵–

Kidsgrove

Blue Bell

Hardingswood, ST7 1EG (off A50 near Tesco)
7.30-11; closed Mon; 1-4, 7-11 Sat; 12-10.30 Sun
☎ (01782) 774052 bluebellkidsgrove.co.uk
Beer range varies Ⓗ
Genuine free house that benefits from the absence of TV, games machines and other nonsense with its lively conversational atmosphere that draws everyone in. Informal and spontaneous live music is played on Sunday evening and the pub attracts customers from a wide area, together with visitors from the Trent & Mersey and Macclesfield canals, which meet one another a few yards away. Six handpumps deliver an ever-changing range of beers from independent and micro-brewers; Belgian and German ales, real cider and perry are always available. Dog friendly. Q❀⇌♣P

Kinver

Constitutional Social Club

119 High Street, DY7 6HL
5-11; 4-midnight Fri; 11.30-midnight Sat; 12-10.30 Sun
☎ (01384) 872044
Draught Bass; Enville Ale; Hobsons Best Bitter, Town Crier; Wye Valley HPA; guest beers Ⓗ
Built in 1902 on the site of an old pub, this converted hotel has three main areas: a smart restaurant, a large snooker room and a bar dispensing up to six guest beers, from myriad breweries, at reasonable prices. The club enjoys an enviable sporting reputation and hosts regular quiz and music nights. Meals are served Sunday lunchtime and Thursday to Saturday evenings, booking advised. Card-carrying CAMRA members are welcome but must be signed in. Local CAMRA Branch Club Of The Year 2007/08/09.
❀◐♿(227,228)♣P⁵–

Plough & Harrow

82 High Street, DY7 6HD
4 (12 Sat & Sun)-midnight
☎ (01384) 872659
Bathams Mild Ale, Best Bitter, XXX (winter) Ⓗ
Situated on the main high street, this characterful community pub, affectionately nicknamed The Steps, is deservedly popular with locals, cyclists and walkers alike. The front bar sees locals and visitors intermixing and engaging in lively conversation while the plusher lounge is more comfortable. Note the usual Bathams breweriana and old advertising hoardings bedecking the walls. Snacks are available. ❀(227,228)♣P

Vine 🏆

1 Dunsley Road, DY7 6LJ (next to canal)
12-11
☎ (01384) 877291 thevineinnkinver.co.uk
Enville Ale; Fuller's London Pride; Kinver Edge; guest beer Ⓗ
The Vine was opened in 1863 in competition with the Lock Inn that once stood opposite. Originally two converted cottages, it extended into adjacent cottages over the years and most internal walls were removed in 1980. Now a one-roomed pub, it retains distinct areas on different levels, with the restaurant overlooking Kinver lock on the Staffs & Worcs canal. There are extensive canalside gardens. Food, all home-made, is served all day on Saturday. The bus from Stourbridge stops nearby. CAMRA local branch Rural Pub of the Year 2009.
❀◐♿(227,228)♣P

Knighton

Haberdasher's Arms

ST20 0QH (between Adbaston and Knighton) SJ753275
12.30 (7 Wed & Thu)-midnight; 12.30-1am Fri & Sat; 12-midnight Sun
☎ (01785) 280650
Banks's Original, Bitter; guest beer Ⓗ
Traditional country pub built about 1840, offering a warm and friendly welcome. This former local CAMRA Pub of the Year has four compact rooms, all served from a small bar. The large garden is used for events including the annual Potato Club Show and occasional music festivals. It is also available for private hire. Well worth the drive through leafy country lanes to get here. ⛺Q❀♿Å♣P⁵–

Leek

Den Engel

Stanley Street, ST13 5HG (off St Edward St)
5-11 Mon & Tue; 11-11.30 Wed & Thu; 11-midnight Fri & Sat; 12-11.30 Sun
☎ (01538) 373751
Courage Directors; guest beers Ⓗ
An authentic Belgian bar located in the heart of the Staffordshire Moorlands with around ten Belgian beers on draught, and an even larger bottled selection, for which a menu is provided. It also offers three varying British beers, usually from micro-breweries, favouring those in Yorkshire, such as Ossett and Rudgate. A quiet hostelry with a varied clientele, heartily recommended for both summer and winter evenings. A warm welcome awaits all who enter. Q❀⁵–

Wilke's Head

15 St Edward Street, ST13 5DS
12 (3 Mon)-midnight; 12-11 Sun
☎ (07976) 59278
Whim Arbor Light, Hartington Bitter, IPA, Flower Power; guest beers Ⓗ
Named after an 18th-century politician, whose biography is on display in the bar. One of the oldest pubs in Leek, it has deeds available dating back to 1705 but a pub was present on the site long before this. This Whim Brewery tap stocks many of its beers plus guests. The licensee is a skilled musician and hosts acoustic nights on Mondays and three live music festivals every summer in the beer garden. Best jukebox in the area. ⛺Q♣⁵–

Lichfield

Acorn ✔

12-18 Tamworth Street, WS13 6JJ
9-11 (1am Fri & Sat)
☎ (01543) 263261

Greene King IPA, Abbot; Marston's Pedigree; guest beers Ⓗ
The Acorn is a credit to the Wetherspoon chain, with a deservedly loyal clientele that enjoys the regularly changing selection of up to seven guest ales, including micros. The cavernous open-plan interior includes a dining area to the rear and a couple of drinking spaces opposite the bar. Ale is delivered to the upstairs stillage via a purpose-built bridge across the centre of the pub. The Acorn tends to become very busy on Friday and Saturday evenings. ◑♿⇌(City)🚌●

Bowling Green ✔
Friary Road, WS13 6QJ
⏲ 11.30-11 (midnight Fri & Sat)
☎ (01543) 257344
Banks's Bitter; guest beer Ⓗ
A large 1930s-style mock-Tudor inn located on a large traffic island which it shares with an independently owned bowling club. A large central bar serves several distinct drinking areas. Up to three guest ales are sourced from the Ember Inns list and a full range of bar meals is available all day until 9pm. The imposing, old stone clock tower opposite the site was relocated there in the 1920s from the other end of the street. ⛫❀◑⇌(City)🚌

Duke of Wellington
Birmingham Road, WS14 9BJ
⏲ 4 (12 Thu-Sun)-11
☎ (01543) 263261
Fuller's London Pride; Marston's Pedigree; guest beers Ⓗ
A deservedly popular haunt for the real ale fan, well worth the 15-minute walk from the city centre. Up to six constantly changing guest beers frequently include local micro brews. The comfortable, open-plan interior comprises three separate drinking areas, with the dartboard and pool table sensibly located at opposite ends from one another. The long rear garden is very popular during the summer months and includes a large open-fronted, smokers' pavilion complete with TV. ⛫❀🚌♣P⚟

Queens Head ✔
4 Queen Street, WS13 6QD
⏲ 12-11 (11.30 Fri & Sat); 12-3, 7-11 Sun
☎ (01543) 410932
Marston's Pedigree; Taylor Landlord; guest beers Ⓗ
The Queens Head has long been a mecca for real ale fans, offering more than 200 guest beers throughout the year. The art of conversation is the main focus among staff, locals and visitors, and contributes to the friendly, welcoming atmosphere. Good value home-cooked food is served Monday to Saturday lunchtime. Bread, cheese and paté are available during all sessions. The Whisky Club offers an ever changing selection of single malts. Dogs are welcome if accompanied by well-behaved owners. Q❀◐⇌(City)🚌⚟

Longdon

Swan with Two Necks ✔
40 Brook End, WS15 4PN (250m off A51)
⏲ 12-3, 6-11; 12-10.30 Sun
☎ (01543) 490251
Adnams Bitter; Taylor Landlord; guest beers Ⓗ
A meeting place for locals from the village and surrounding countryside, this fine pub has been in the guide for more than 29 years. Two regular beers are supplemented by a guest, usually from a micro, as well as a fourth guest at weekends. Meals are of a very high quality and the restaurant area is open on Friday and Saturday evenings. The pleasant outdoor terrace is popular during the summer months. ⛫Q❀◑P⚟

Milwich

Green Man
ST18 0EG (on B5027)
⏲ 12-2.30 Thu & Fri, 5-11; 12-11 Sat; 12-10.30 Sun
☎ (01889) 505310 🌐 greenmanmilwich.com
Adnams Bitter; Draught Bass; Wells Bombardier; guest beers Ⓗ
A pub since 1775, this free house offers guest beers from regional and micro-breweries nationwide – see website for forthcoming guests. The current licensee is in his 19th year at the pub and a list of his predecessors dating back to 1792 is displayed. A popular pub with walkers and cyclists, there is a 16-seat restaurant section within the bar (lunch served Thu-Sun, evening meals Wed-Sat). Westons or Thatchers cider is stocked. Local CAMRA Pub of the Year 2006 and 2007. ⛫❀◑♣●P⚟

Newcastle-under-Lyme

Museum
29 George Street, ST5 1JU
⏲ 12-11
☎ (01782) 623866
Draught Bass; Everards Tiger; Marston's Pedigree; Worthington's Bitter; guest beer Ⓗ
Traditional, two-roomed pub located just outside the centre of Newcastle, with a basic bar and a more comfortable lounge, plus a pleasant smoking area to the rear. The pub is a supporter of Stoke City, running coaches to the ground on match days, and also has its own dominoes, crib and darts teams. Live entertainment is provided on Saturday night and lunches are served during the week. Q◐⊟🚌

Old Brown Jug ✔
Bridge Street, ST5 2RY
⏲ 3pm-midnight (1am Wed); 12-midnight Fri-Sun
☎ (01782) 711393
Marston's Pedigree; guest beers Ⓗ
Located down a side street at the top of the town centre, a short walk from Newcastle bus station, this lively, traditional pub offers five rotating guest ales from the Marston's portfolio; there is also a good selection of cider, both on draught and bottled. The pub is renowned for its live music sessions every Wednesday and Sunday evening, for which a small charge may be levied. The largest beer garden in Newcastle is located at the rear. ❀🚌●⚟

Newtown

Ivy House
62 Stafford Road, WS6 6AZ (on A34)
⏲ 12-2.30, 5-11.30; 12-11.30 Fri & Sat; 12-11 Sun
☎ (01922) 476607 🌐 ivyhousepub.co.uk
Banks's Original, Bitter; Marston's Pedigree; guest beers Ⓗ
Walsall CAMRA (Staffs) Pub of the Year 2005 to 2007 was first listed as an ale house in 1824. This traditional pub comprises three rooms plus a purpose-built restaurant. The beer garden, backing

on to open farm land, retains a country feel. A visit is highly recommended and a warm welcome is assured. Q❀◐◑♿🚌(1,351)P⅄–

Norton Canes

Railway Tavern ✔

63 Norton Green Lane, WS11 9PR (off Walsall Road)
⏲ 12-midnight (1am Fri & Sat); 12-11.30 Sun
☎ (01543) 279579
Banks's Original, Bitter; Greene King IPA; guest beers H
Twice CAMRA Pub of the Year, this friendly, traditional local has been tastefully refurbished to provide a large open-plan lounge bar with dining area. Live entertainment, quiz nights and sports TV are regular highlights. Westons real cider is served during the summer months. ❀◐◑♿♣●P⅄–

Onecote

Jervis Arms

ST13 7RU (on B5053 N of A53 Leek-Ashbourne road)
⏲ 12-3, 7 (6 Sat)-midnight; 12-midnight Sun
☎ (01538) 304206
Sharp's Doom Bar; Titanic Iceberg; Wadworth 6X; guest beers H
A pub for all the family set within the Peak District National Park and close to Alton Towers. On entering the pub via the footbridge, you find yourself in the large beer garden which runs down to the river; wonderful for relaxing on a warm summer's day. Two beer and cider festivals are held every year, when camping is available. Home-cooked food is served and the guest beers hail from a variety of micro-breweries. A true gem. ♨Q🐎❀◐◑▲♣P⅄–

Oulton

Brushmakers Arms ✔

8 Kibblestone Road, ST15 8UW (500m W of A520, 1 mile NE of Stone)
⏲ 12-3, 6-midnight (1am Fri & Sat); 12-3, 7-11 Sun
☎ (01785) 812062
Thwaites Original, Lancaster Bomber; guest beer H
Named after a local cottage industry, the Brush is a pub where time stands still. It has a traditional quarry-tiled bar and a small ornate lounge. Pictures and postcards adorn the walls, reflecting a bygone era. The small rear patio garden is a real suntrap and doubles as the smoking area. With no games machines or jukebox, conversation flows in this excellent village local. Well-behaved dogs are welcome. Guest ales are often sourced from local micros. ♨Q❀⊟♿🚌♣P⅄–

Penkridge

Star Inn

Market Place, ST19 5DJ (150m from A449)
⏲ 12-11 (11.30 Thu; midnight Fri & Sat)
☎ (01785) 712513
Banks's Bitter, Original; Jennings Cocker Hoop; guest beer H
A one-room pub with a patio and seating area outside. Situated in an old market place, it first traded as an inn as far back as 1827. It became a Co-op store early in the 20th century, then a private residence, and was restored to the licensed trade in the second half of the 20th century. Market days are Wednesday and Saturday. Food is available lunchtimes and evenings Monday to Thursday and lunchtime only Friday to Sunday. ♨Q❀◐◑🚌P⅄–🗑

Penn Common

Barley Mow 🏆

Pennwood Lane, WV4 5JN (follow signs to Penn Golf Club from A449) SO901949
⏲ 12-2.30, 6-11; 12-11 Sat; 12-10.30 Sun
☎ (01902) 333510
Caledonian Deuchars IPA; Greene King Abbot; Taylor Landlord; guest beers H
Small, low-beamed pub dating from the 1600s, on the border of Wolverhampton and Staffordshire. A small extension was added in the 1990s. This hidden gem has a well-deserved reputation for food, with the meat supplied from the landlord's own award-winning butcher's shop. Next to the local golf course, the pub is a short walk over the Seven Cornfields from Wolverhampton. Q❀◐◑P

Salt

Holly Bush Inn

ST18 0BX (off A518 opp Weston Hall) SJ959277
⏲ 12-11 (midnight Fri & Sat)
☎ (01889) 508234 🌐 hollybushinn.co.uk
Adnams Bitter; Marston's Pedigree; guest beer H
The Holly Bush is believed to be the second English inn to be granted a licence and the oldest part is still thatched. With extensions and alterations over the centuries there are now three distinct areas: a bar towards the middle of the pub, a dining room and a snug which is mainly occupied by diners. Food is available 12-9.30pm (9pm Sun). Meals are superb quality yet reasonably priced and have won many awards. ♨Q❀◐◑▲🚌P⅄–

Silverdale

Bush

High Street, ST5 6JZ
⏲ 12-11 (midnight Fri & Sat); 12-10.30 Sun
☎ (01782) 713096
Wells Bombardier; guest beers H
An imposing pub in a former mining village, the Bush comprises three rooms and a large enclosed beer garden. Six beers are on handpump, including five ever-changing guest ales, mainly from regional breweries, plus a few occasional appearances from local micros. Good value food is available lunchtime and evening; Wednesday night is steak night, while Sunday lunch is especially popular. Entertainment is provided on Friday and Saturday nights and the pub is home to dominoes, pool and football teams. 🐎❀◐◑⊟♿🚌♣P⅄–

Stafford

Greyhound 🏆

12 County Road, ST16 2PU (opp jail)
⏲ 4 (2 Fri)-11; 12-11 Sat & Sun
☎ (01785) 222432
Wells Bombardier; guest beers H
A short walk from the town centre, sited opposite Stafford's gaol, this site has housed a pub since the 1830s. A separate bar and lounge were retained after a sensitive 2002 refurbishment. The pub was threatened with closure a few years ago and the car park was lost to make way for a block of flats. However, the Greyhound has lost none of its

vitality and energy. Eight hand-pulled ales are usually available, most of them from local micro-breweries and regional brewers. Cold snacks are available. ♣

Lamb Inn ✔

Broad Eye, ST16 2QB (opp Sainsbury's on Chell Rd)
12-11 (midnight Fri & Sat); 12-10.30 Sun
☎ (01785) 603902
Fuller's London Pride; Wells Bombardier H
A traditional street corner local situated right in the town centre and within easy distance of the train station, making it a prime stop-off for those looking for a quality pint. The nearby lorry park and bus stops also generate walk-in trade. Its warm, friendly and welcoming atmosphere lends the pub great charm and community spirit. A small car park is complemented by numerous nearby council parking areas. (1,9,101)♣P

Picture House ✔

Bridge Street, ST16 2HL
9-midnight (1am Fri & Sat)
☎ (01785) 222941 jdwetherspoon
Greene King IPA, Abbot; Marston's Pedigree; guest beers H
A tasteful Wetherspoon conversion from a 1914 cinema, it first opened as a pub in spring 1997. Many original features are retained, including the entrance foyer, projection booth and a profusion of posters from the golden age of cinema. Often busy in the evenings, a good selection of real ales is offered to the county town's mixed clientele. CAMRA LocAle accredited in 2009.
Q♣

Railway Inn

23 Castle Street, ST16 2EB
5-midnight; 4-1am Fri; 12-1am Sat; 12-11 Sun
☎ (01785) 601237
Draught Bass; Greene King Abbot; guest beer H
A traditional end-of-terrace Victorian pub which has changed very little over the years. The landlord is a rugby player and enthusiast therefore rugby takes precedence over football on Sky Sports channels. A variety of clubs is based here, notably a fencing club and walking club which meet on Thursday evening. Due to popular demand an extensive selection of whiskies has been reintroduced and there are currently 60 different malts on offer. Q♣

Spittal Brook ✔

106 Lichfield Road, ST17 4LP (off A34)
12-3, 5-11; 12-11 Sat; 12-4, 7-10.30 Sun
☎ (01785) 245268
Black Sheep Best Bitter; Everards Tiger; Fuller's London Pride; Jennings Cumberland Ale; Marston's Pedigree; guest beer H
A thriving traditional two-roomed alehouse supporting a variety of pub games and sporting clubs and societies including water polo, netball and golf. Accommodation can also be provided for dogs travelling with their owners. Entertainment includes a folk night on Tuesday and a quiz on Wednesday. Q(1,3,6)♣P

Stoke-on-Trent: Burslem

Bulls Head

St John's Square, ST6 3AJ
3-11 (11.30 Wed & Thu); 12-11.30 Fri & Sat; 12-11 Sun
☎ (01782) 834153 titanicbrewery.co.uk/bulls
Titanic Steerage, Anchor, Iceberg, White Star; guest beers H
Traditional two-roomed pub, 10 minutes' walk from Port Vale Park and popular with both home and away fans. The original Titanic pub and still acting as its tap, guest beers are often themed to local events or moments in history. Thatchers cider is also served on draught. The bar has a selection of pub games including bar billiards, plus a jukebox; the lounge is a quieter area, containing a real fire. ♣

Leopard ✔

Market Place, ST6 3AA
11-11 (midnight Fri & Sat)
☎ (01782) 819644
Beer range varies H
Formerly a large hotel, the Leopard is one of the oldest pubs in the area and the location of the first meeting to arrange the cutting of the Trent and Mersey canal. Nine handpumps offer a constantly-changing selection from micro-breweries, with an emphasis on local ales; Westons Cider is also available. The pub has appeared on many TV programmes including Most Haunted. Food is served midday-2pm Monday-Saturday and 7-9pm Wednesday-Saturday. A beer festival is held in July.
Q

Post Office Vaults

Market Place, ST6 3AA
10-10.45pm (Fri 12.45am); 11-12.45am Sat; 12-10.30 Sun
☎ (01782) 811027
Fuller's London Pride; Greene King Abbot; Thornbridge Jaipur; guest beers H
This is a small, one-roomed pub in the centre of Burslem, popular with the local football club and community. The guest beers may hail from a wide variety of micro-breweries; real cider is dispensed off handpump. Sport and live music feature on the many TV screens, and there is also a heated smoking area to the rear, complete with its own TV. Post office memorabilia adorn the walls, including an old factory clocking-in machine.
(20,21,98)

Stoke-on-Trent: Fenton

Malt 'n' Hops

295 King Street, ST4 3EJ
12-4, 7-11; 12-3, 7-10.30 Sun
☎ (01782) 313406
Greene King Abbot; guest beers H
This family-owned ale house is one of the true free houses left in the city, situated in the heart of a local potteries community. The pub is split level, with TV screens in the lower area which show regular sporting events. The upper level offers a quieter and more relaxed atmosphere. The house beers, Bursley Bitter and Dark Mild, are brewed by Tower and there is a selection of bottled Belgian beers available, plus at least one on draught.
(Longton)

Stoke-on-Trent: Hanley

Coachmakers Arms ★

Lichfield Street, ST1 3EA (off A5008 Potteries Way ring road)
12-11.30 (midnight Fri & Sat); 12-11 Sun
☎ (01782) 262158 thecoachmakers.co.uk
Draught Bass; guest beers H

Multi-award winning pub, now celebrating its recent inclusion in CAMRA's National Inventory. One of the very few pubs of its type left in the Potteries, it has four separate rooms spanning off a tiled drinking corridor. The Bass is suplemented by six changing guests beers, which will always include a mild and a stout or porter. Get there while you can though, as the pub is targeted for demolition to make way for a new shopping centre. A true gem. ⌂Q⊞⊟♣⬤⚟

Unicorn ✔

Piccadilly, ST1 1EG

12-1am (12.30am Sun)

(01782) 281809 myspace.com/theunicorninn

Fuller's London Pride; guest beers H

A small, friendly, city-centre pub located in the heart of the cultural quarter, across the road from the Regent Theatre; theatre-goers can order their interval drinks here. Above the bar is a large collection of Toby jugs and there are numerous brasses decorating the cosy room and adjoining seating area. Sandwiches are available at lunchtime. Two guest beers are served in rotation, usually from regional or micro-breweries. A traditional pub at the centre of the club scene. ⊟⚟

Stoke-on-Trent: Hartshill

Greyhound

George Street, ST5 1JT

12-midnight (10.30 Sun)

(01782) 635814

Titanic Anchor, Iceberg, White Star; Everards Tiger; guest beers H

Reopened in 2007 after a long period of closure, this is the first pub to result from a collaboration between Titanic and Everards. The refurbishment is modern but comfortable, comprising an L-shaped bar and a smaller room to the rear. Quality food is served until early evening, and the pub is on major bus routes from Stoke, Hanley and Newcastle. Seasonal specials from Titanic feature, along with guest beers from many an interesting brewery, plus Westons cider. Q◑⊟⬤⚟

Stoke-on-Trent: Longton

Congress

Sutherland Road, ST3 1HJ (opp police station)

12-11 (8 Mon); 12-midnight Fri & Sat; 12-4, 7-11 Sun

(01782) 763667

Hydes Original; Holden's Mild; Townhouse Gladstone's Strong Ale H**; guest beers** H/G

Spacious, two-roomed pub just off the main road through Longton town centre, comprising a large bar area and a meeting room. In the short period of time that the landlord has been in the pub, he has transformed it into one of the best real ale establishments in the Potteries, and it is a regular stalwart near the top of CAMRA's Pub of the Year list. A beer festival is held every April, when the main bar is supplemented by two others. This pub is a pleasure to drink in, a place where you can relax with a great range of traditional ales. ⇌(Longton)⊟♣⬤⚟

Stoke-on-Trent: Penkhull

Beehive

103 Honeywall, ST4 7HU

4-1am; 2-2am Fri & Sat; 12-11.30 Sun

(01782) 846947 beehiveinn.com

Marston's Burton Bitter, Pedigree; guest beers H

Deservedly popular local community pub with a warm and welcoming atmosphere situated on the hill above Stoke. It attracts many Stoke City supporters on match days and has a collection of club memorabilia. A quiz is held on Tuesday evening. Four guest beers change weekly and are sourced from the Marston's portfolio. The licensees also run the nearby Marquis of Granby. ⌂❀⊟P⚟

Stoke-on-Trent: Stoke

Wheatsheaf ✔

84 Church Street, ST4 1BU

9am-midnight (1am Fri & Sat)

(01782) 747462

Greene King IPA, Abbot; Marston's Pedigree; guest beers H

This convivial town centre Wetherspoon's has a well-earned reputation as one of the best real ale outlets in the regional chain. A cosy pub that firmly believes in supporting the LocAle scheme, beers from breweries such as Titanic and Slater's can be found on the bar. The enthusiastic and knowledgeable staff are always searching for ales from further afield, as can be seen from the array of pump clips displayed on the wall behind the bar. A small pavement area is provided for smokers. ◑♿⇌(Stoke-on-Trent)⊟⚟

White Star

63 Kingsway, ST4 1JB (off Church Street, nr King's Hall)

11-11 (midnight Fri & Sat); 12-11 Sun

(01782) 848732 titanicbrewery.co.uk/thewhitestar.html

Everards Tiger; Titanic Steerage, Anchor, White Star, Iceberg, Captain Smiths; guest beers H

A new addition to the Guide, this reopened and refurbished pub is a joint venture by Titanic and Everards breweries. There are 10 handpumps on the bar, dispensing a range of Titanic, Everards and rotating guest beers. Home-cooked food and snacks are available from the menu. Entertainment includes live music on Wednesday and Friday evenings. There are pub and board games available to play, plus a book exchange scheme. There is also a function room available for hire upstairs, with its own bar. ❀◑⇌(Stoke-on-Trent)⊟(23,25,26)♣⬤⚟

Stone

Poste of Stone ✔

1 Granville Square, ST15 8AB

9-midnight (1am Fri & Sat)

(01785) 827920

Greene King IPA, Abbot; Marston's Pedigree; guest beers H

Large open-plan Wetherspoon pub, formerly a post office. Breakfast and beer are served from 9am daily. Children are welcome in the restaurant area until 9pm. With Tuesday grills and Thursday curries complementing a good range of food at all times at competitive prices, the pub is understandably popular. Lymestone, Titanic, Black Hole and Slater's ales often feature. There is a disabled lift to the restaurant. A short walk from the Trent and Mersey canal, south-bound buses pass outside, north-bound 250 metres away. Car parking is nearby. ⌂☕❀◑♿⇌⊟⬤P⚟

Royal Exchange

Radford Street, ST15 8DA (corner of Northesk Street and Radford Street)
⏲ 12-11 (midnight Fri & Sat)
☎ (01785) 812685
Everards Tiger; Titanic Steerage, Iceberg, White Star; guest beers 🄷
A welcome addition to the town's real ale scene, this single-room 2008 refurbishment from Everards and Titanic includes four distinct drinking areas. Up to six guest ales, many from micros, and a real cider, complement ales from the Titanic and Everards ranges. Basic locally-sourced lunchtime food is good value, and there is a good selection of single malts. Well-behaved dogs are welcome. Children are allowed until 9pm. Town car parks are nearby. ♨Q🐴◐≹🚌♣🍎⚡

Swan Inn

18 Stafford Street, ST15 8QW (on A520 by Trent and Mersey canal)
⏲ 11-midnight (1am Thu-Sat); 12-11 Sun
☎ (01785) 815570
Coach House John Joule Old Knotty, John Joule Old Priory, John Joule Victory; guest beers 🄷
Grade II listed and carefully renovated in 1999, this thriving free house is Stone's premier real ale venue, with over 450 breweries so far represented via six guest handpulls. A local Lymestone beer is often available as are ales from Thornbridge, Abbeydale, Townhouse, Sharp's, Blythe and Dark Star. Tuesday is quiz night, live music plays on four nights and on Sunday there is a free buffet. An annual beer festival is held during the second week of July. Real cider is available. Over 18s only.
♨❀♿≹🚌🍎⚡

Summerhill

Boat ✔

Walsall Road, WS14 0BU
⏲ 12-3, 6-11; 12-11 Sun
☎ (01543) 361692 🌐 oddfellowsintheboat.com
Beer range varies 🄷
A heaven for lovers of gourmet food and quality beer, with a large car park and enclosed garden. Sit in the Mediterranean-style reception area and watch the chefs prepare the menu's exciting delights, and be surprised by the range of guest beers. The beer may be from a local brewery or sourced nationally but be assured of the quality; check the website for the current list and tasting notes. ♨Q❀◐◑♿P⚡

Tamworth

Globe Inn

Lower Gungate, B79 7AT
⏲ 11-11; 12-3, 7-10.30 Sun
☎ (01827) 60455 🌐 theglobetamworth.com
Draught Bass; Holden's Mild; Worthington's Bitter; guest beer 🄷
Very comfortable town centre hotel bar, split into three areas, including a raised dining area. A separate function room is available for hire. There is a changing guest beer, with a regular appearance from Archer's. Karaoke nights are held on Sunday and Thursday. The pub can get very busy when live sporting events are shown on the two large-screen TVs. A public car park is next door to the pub. 🛏◐◑≹♣

Sir Robert Peel 🏆

13-15 Lower Gungate, B79 7BA
⏲ 2-11 (midnight Fri); 12-midnight Sat; 12-11.30 Sun
☎ (01827) 300910
Beer range varies 🄷
Local CAMRA Pub of the Year 2007. Run by a family who take pride in the quality of their beers, this busy town centre pub is a regular haunt for CAMRA members. Up to five guest beers and a regular real cider are available. Guest ales vary with many coming from micro-breweries and regular appearances of beers from local breweries including Church End, Beowulf and Blythe. Weekends can be busy, with Monday and Wednesday ideal nights for a quiet pint. ≹🍎

Trysull

Bell

Bell Lane, WV5 7JB SO852940
⏲ 11.30-3, 5-11; 11.30-11 Sat; 12-11 Sun
☎ (01902) 892871 🌐 holdensbrewery.co.uk
Bathams Best Bitter; Holden's Bitter, Golden Glow, Special, seasonal beers; guest beer 🄷
Standing next to the medieval church in the centre of the village, this 18th-century building is on the site of a much older pub. There are three rooms: a pleasant bar, a comfortable lounge and a restaurant/dining room. The ever-changing guest beer usually comes from a micro-brewery and the good value meals are mostly home made. Cod in Bathams batter is particularly popular (no food Sun eve). The Staffordshire & Worcestershire canal is a 15-minute walk away. 🐴◐◑🍺♿P

Tutbury

Cross Keys

39 Burton Street, DE13 9NR SK215287
⏲ 10-3, 5.30 (6 Sat)-11; 12-3, 7-10.30 Sun
☎ (01283) 813677
Tetley Burton Ale; guest beer 🄷
Popular, privately-owned, late 19th-century free house, overlooking the Dove Valley and with a fine view of Tutbury Castle along Burton Street. Its two split-level rooms – public bar and lounge – have a homely feel and are served from a similarly split-level bar. There is a separate 40-seat restaurant (Wendy's) to the rear. One of the few pubs in the area to have remained loyal to Draught Burton Ale since its launch in Burton in 1975. No meals Sunday evening. ❀◐◑🍺♿🚌(1,V1)P

Two Gates

Bull's Head

446 Watling Street, B77 1HW (on crossroads of A51 & B5404)
⏲ 11-3, 5-11; 12-11 Fri-Sun
☎ (01827) 287820
Marston's Pedigree; guest beer 🄷
Popular locals' pub situated on the old Roman road of Watling Street. Just a few minutes walk from Wilnecote railway station, it is also served by regular bus services from Tamworth. The two-roomed pub has a split-level lounge leading to the patio and an outside smoking area, and a small, friendly bar with a large-screen TV. It is home to many games and sports clubs including the long-standing Golf Society. The guest beer changes frequently.
Q❀◐◑🍺≹(Wilnecote)🚌(116,767)♣P⚡

Uttoxeter

Old Swan ✔

Market Place, ST14 8AN
9-midnight (1am Fri-Sat)
☎ (01889) 598654
Greene King IPA, Abbot; Marston's Pedigree; guest beers [H]
Opened by JD Wetherspoon in December 2006, this excellent example of a one-room pub has rapidly become a favourite among Uttoxeter drinkers. Low level background music is played Friday and Saturday evenings. Seven real ales are regularly offered and two Wetherspoon Ale festivals are held annually. Pub games are not discouraged. CAMRA LocAle accredited 2009. Q♿⇌🚌

Weston

Saracens Head

Stafford Road, ST18 0HT (on A518)
12-3 (not Mon), 5-11; 12-11 Fri & Sat; 12-10.30 Sun
☎ (01889) 270286
Greene King IPA; Marston's Burton Bitter, Pedigree; guest beer [H]
Very friendly family hostelry situated in a delightful village. The pub caters for visitors en route to Alton Towers, narrowboats on the nearby Trent and Mersey canal, and the local community. The name of the pub commemorates the grant of a Saracens Head crest to local landowner Lord Ferrers during the Third Crusade. Diners can enjoy views over open countryside in the conservatory. Drinkers can make themselves at home in the public bar or more comfortable in the lounge.
Q❀Λ🚌♣P

Whiston

Swan Inn

ST19 5QH SJ895144
12-3 (not Mon), 5-11; 12-11 Sun
☎ (01785) 716200
Holden's Mild, Bitter; Morton Jelly Roll; Oulton Bitter; guest beer [H]
Although remotely situated, high quality, well-kept ales and superb food make this a thriving pub. Built in 1593, burnt down and rebuilt in 1711, the oldest part today is the small bar housing an inglenook fireplace. The lounge features an intriguing central double-sided log fire. Six acres of grounds include a children's obstacle course, aviary and rabbits.
Q❀♿Λ🚌♣P

Wilnecote

Globe Inn

91 Watling Street, B77 5BA (on B5404)
1-3.30, 7-11 (11.30 Fri & Sat); 12-3, 7-11 Sun
☎ (01827) 280885
Marston's Pedigree [H]
A real community pub where a warm welcome is guaranteed. A regular Guide entry, the pub is renowned for the quality of its Pedigree. Like a good pilsener, it takes the landlord around seven minutes to pull – but is well worth the wait. Situated on an old Roman road, it is a 15-minute walk from Wilnecote railway station. A regular bus service from Tamworth passes close to the pub. Words of wisdom are always assured from a very popular landlord. Q❀🚌(9)♣

Prince of Wales

70 Hockley Road, B77 5EE
1-3 (not Tue & Thu), 7-11; 1-11 Fri; 12-11 Sat & Sun
☎ (01827) 280013
Batemans XXXB; Morland Old Speckled Hen; Wychwood Hobgoblin [H]
Visitors are always given a friendly welcome by staff and customers alike at this true locals' two-roomed pub with a traditional bar. It can get quite busy at weekends, but for those who like a quieter pint there is a very comfortable lounge. A popular quiz night is held every Wednesday. The pub is also the headquarters of the local Royal British Legion.
Q🚌(8,9)♣

Wolstanton

New Smithy

21 Church Lane, ST5 0EH
12 (11 Sat)-11; 12-10.30 Sun
☎ (01782) 740467
Everards Tiger; Hop Back Summer Lightning; Marston's Pedigree; guest beers [H]
Ever-popular pub located on the main road through Wolstanton. Despite the Everards signage on the outside, the pub is now owned by Hop Back Brewery, and its beers are always available; guests can hail from any number of breweries and Westons Old Rosie cider is served on draught. Saved from being turned into a car park a number of years ago, the pub continues to thrive.
❀🚌♣P

Yoxall

Golden Cup

Main Street, DE13 8NQ (on A515) SK142191
12-3, 5-midnight; 12-1am Fri & Sat; 12-midnight Sun
☎ (01543) 472295
Marston's Pedigree; guest beer [H]
Impressive, family-run, 300-year-old inn at the centre of the village, opposite St Peter's church and bedecked with attractive floral displays for much of the year. The pub features a smart L-shaped lounge with beamed ceiling, primarily catering for diners, and a plainer public bar with Sky Sports TV. Colourful murals with a classical theme enhance both the ladies and gents toilets. The award-winning pub gardens stretch down to the River Swarbourn and include a camping area (for caravans and motor homes only).
Q❀♿Λ🚌(7,7E)♣P

Join CAMRA

The Campaign for Real Ale has been fighting for over 35 years to save Britain's proud heritage of cask-conditioned ales, independent breweries, and pubs that offer a good choice of beer. You can help that fight by joining the Campaign: use the form at the back of the guide or visit **www.camra.org.uk**

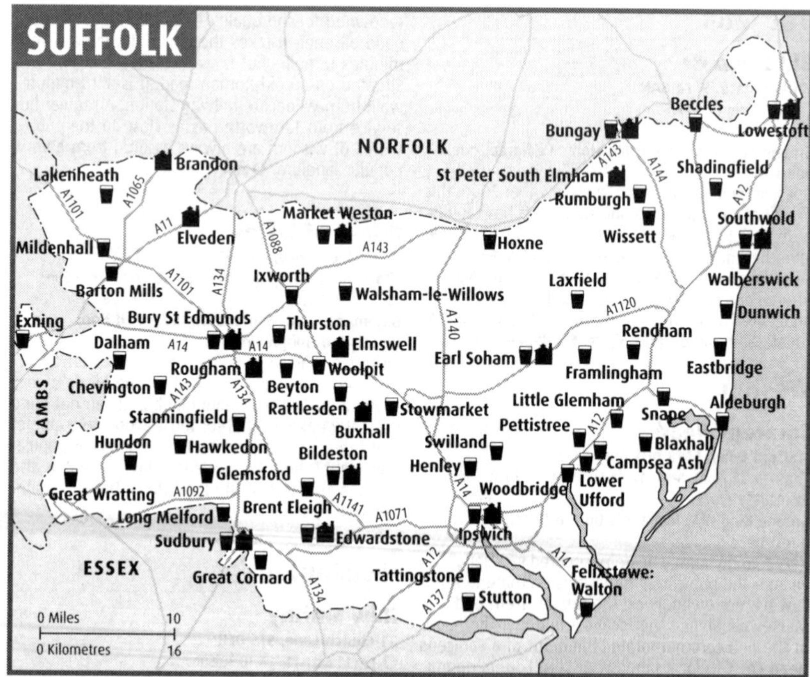

Aldeburgh

Mill Inn

Market Cross Place, IP15 5BJ (opp Moot Hall)
11-11; 11-3, 6-11 winter; 12-10.30 Sun
(01728) 452563
Adnams Bitter, Broadside, seasonal beers; guest beers

A centrally positioned inn in this attractive coastal town, with a snug and restaurant overlooking the seafront. Locally caught fish is a speciality and themed food evenings a highlight. The famous 'fish sheds' can be seen from the pub. A seating area close to the Moot Hall is busy on summer days. Folk music sessions are held monthly on Sunday afternoon. No food is served Monday or Sunday evening. Q

White Hart

222 High Street, IP15 5AJ
11.30-11; 12-10.30 Sun
(01728) 453205
Adnams Bitter, Explorer, Broadside; guest beers, seasonal beers

Formerly a public reading room, this lively single room is decorated with hops and nautical pictures. The pub is adjacent to the town's renowned fish and chip shop and is a popular meeting place for locals and visitors in this popular coastal town. A diverse selection of live music plays every Saturday and Sunday evening.

Barton Mills

Olde Bull Inn

The Street, IP28 6AA
11-11
(01638) 711001 bullinn-bartonmills.com
Adnams Bitter, Broadside; Greene King IPA

Welcoming, family-owned and managed pub with a cosy log fire for cold winter days and a fantastic courtyard for the summer. Four ales are on offer ranging from Greene King and Adnams brews to great beers from local micros such as Brandon and Humpty Dumpty. Alongside the ale you can enjoy a delicious home-made meal, with food served in the bar and also the award-winning restaurant.

Beccles

Caxton Club

Gaol Lane, NR34 9SJ
12-1.30, 7-11 (not Wed); closed Tue; 12-2, 6.30-11 Fri; 12-11 Sat; 12-10.30 Sun
(01502) 712828
John Smith's Bitter; Theakston Black Bull; guest beers

INDEPENDENT BREWERIES

Adnams Southwold
Bartrams Rougham
Brandon Brandon
Cliff Quay Ipswich (NEW)
Cox & Holbrook Buxhall
Earl Soham Earl Soham
Elveden Elveden
Green Dragon Bungay
Green Jack Lowestoft
Greene King Bury St Edmunds
Kings Head Bildeston
Mauldons Sudbury
Mill Green Edwardstone (NEW)
Old Cannon Bury St Edmunds
Old Chimneys Market Weston
Red Rat Elmswell
St Jude's Ipswich
St Peter's St Peter South Elmham

In 1890 this was a club for gentlemen only. Today, all members and guests are welcome at this spacious club building with a central bar, pool table, TV and darts room, and snooker room. There is also a large function room with its own bar hosting music events on Friday and Saturday evenings. Outside is a garden and bowls green. Show this Guide or your CAMRA membership card to be signed in as a guest. CAMRA East Anglian Club of the Year 2009. 🐎❀♿⇌(Beccles)🚌♣⚲

Beyton

Bear Inn

Tostock Road, IP30 9AG

⏲ 12-2, 5-11; 12-4, 7-10.30 Sun

☎ (01359) 270249 🌐 thebearinn.net

Brandon Rusty Bucket; Earl Soham Victoria; Greene King IPA; Woodforde's Wherry Best Bitter ⒽＨ

The building was rebuilt in 1900 after the original thatched Bear burned down in a July thunderstorm – you can read a full account of this event in the bar. The inn has been run by the same family since 1922. The current landlord has updated the building without spoiling a very traditional inn, with two bars and a separate dining room (for residents only at present). There is easy access from the A14 as the pub was originally on the main Ipswich to Cambridge road. ⛰Q❀🛏🍽⛺🚌♣P⚲

Bildeston

Kings Head

132 High Street, IP7 7ED (On B1115 Stowmarket to Hadleigh road)

⏲ 6-midnight Wed & Thu; 4 (12 summer)-midnight Fri; 12-midnight Sat; closed Mon & Tue; 12-10.30 Sun

☎ (01449) 741434

Earl Soham Victoria; Kings Head Brettvale, Landlady; Mill Green Bulls Cross ⒽＨ

The home of the Kings Head Brewery since 1996, this large former coaching inn now has just one bar which retains exposed carved timbers and an inglenook fireplace. A friendly drinking house atmosphere has evolved in the new bar, with food available at weekends only. There is an enclosed rear garden with covered patio area, lawns and play equipment. The May bank holiday beer festival is well established. ⛰❀◐◑🍎

Blaxhall

Ship

School Road, IP12 2DY

⏲ 12-3, 6-midnight

☎ (01728) 688316 🌐 blaxhallshipinn.co.uk

Adnams Bitter; Taylor Landlord; Woodforde's Wherry Best Bitter; guest beers ⒽＨ

Traditional 16th-century pub on the edge of Suffolk Sandlings with a long reputation for singing in the bar. It is also renowned for locally sourced and home cooked food (served 12-2.30pm, 6-9.30pm). The bar is reputed to be visited by friendly ghosts of former regulars, who may share the settles and simple furnishings with today's drinkers. Regular folk music plays, and occasional country and western, too. Eight chalets provide B&B accommodation for those with more time to explore this rural area. ⛰Q❀🛏◐◑🚌♣P

Brent Eleigh

Cock Inn ★

Lavenham Road, CO10 9PB

⏲ 11-4, 6-11; 12-11 Sat; 12-10.30 Sun

☎ (01787) 247371

Adnams Bitter; Greene King Abbot; Nethergate Priory Mild ⒽＨ

An absolute gem, this pub will transport you back in time. In winter both bars are snug and warm; in summer, with the doors open, the bar is at one with its surroundings. Good conversation is guaranteed. The Scottish-born landlord has introduced a range of single malts to complement the excellent ales. Close to Lavenham and the Brett Valley, comfortable accommodation is recommended. CAMROT (Campaign for Real Outside Toilets) approved. ⛰Q❀🛏◐🍽♣🍎P

Bungay

Green Dragon

29 Broad Street, NR35 1EE

⏲ 11-3, 5-11; 11-midnight Fri; 12-midnight Sat; 12-3, 7-11 Sun

☎ (01986) 892681

Green Dragon Chaucer Ale, Gold, Bridge Street, seasonal beers ⒽＨ

Home of the Green Dragon Brewery, this is a lively town pub with a public bar and lounge plus a side room where families are welcome, leading to a side garden surrounded by a hop hedge. Up to four beers are on handpump and sometimes bottle-conditioned beers are also available. A strong, dark mild is brewed in the winter months. ⛰🐎❀🍽⛺🚌P

Bury St Edmunds

Nutshell ★

17 The Traverse, IP33 1BJ

⏲ 11-11; 12-10.30 Sun

☎ (01284) 764867

Greene King IPA, Abbot ⒽＨ

Situated in the historic town centre of the large market town, this tiny bar has been serving beer for 135 years. At just over 15ft by 7ft (4.5m x 2.1m), it is easily Britain's smallest pub. With just 20 people needed to fill the single bar, it is no surprise that the record of 102 customers at one time remains unbroken since 1984. This unique pub is full of curiosities including a 400-year-old cat, a three-legged chicken and a human lower leg.

Old Cannon Brewery

86 Cannon Street, IP33 1JR

⏲ 12-3, 5-11; 12-4, 7-10.30 Sun

☎ (01284) 768769 🌐 oldcannonbrewery.co.uk

Adnams Bitter; Old Cannon Best Bitter, Black Pig, Gunner's Daughter; guest beers ⒽＨ

Formerly the St Edmunds Head, this brew pub is on the site of the original Cannon Brewery. It is regarded as the best place in town for real ale, with beers brewed on site and a good range of guest and foreign ales. Food is served most days (not Sun eve or Mon lunch) and accommodation is available (booking essential). ⛰Q❀🛏◐◑♿⇌🚌P⚲🍺

Rose & Crown ✔

48 Whiting Street, IP33 1NP

⏲ 11.30-11 (11.30 Thu & Fri); 11.30-3, 7-11.30 Sat; 12-2.30, 7-11 Sun

☎ (01284) 755934
Greene King XX Mild, IPA, Abbot; guest beers [H]
Listed red-brick, street-corner pub with two bars and a rare off-sales counter, run by the same family for more than 30 years. Good value lunches are available Monday to Saturday in this homely hostelry. The pub is in sight of Greene King's Westgate Brewery. Suffolk CAMRA Pub of the Year in 2005. Q❀◐⊟♣⅟

Campsea Ash

Dog & Duck
Station Road, IP13 0PT
⏲ 11-2.30 (not Wed), 7-11; 12-2.30, 7-10.30 Sun
☎ (01728) 748439
Adnams Bitter; Woodforde's Mardlers, Wherry Best Bitter [G]
Large, welcoming single bar with a high ceiling, divided into two areas by a fireplace. The handpumps are for display only. Located close to Wickham Market station, this is a great place to start or finish a summer ramble or cycle, with good accommodation for those wishing to stay longer. The food is all home cooked and locally sourced, with seasonal game and vegetarian options (served 12-2.30pm, 7-9pm). There is also a separate restaurant for more formal dining. 'Diddley diddley' music plays on alternate Wednesdays.
♨❀⊨◐◑♿≑(Wickham Market)♣P

Chevington

Greyhound
2 Chedburgh Road, IP29 5QS
⏲ 12-3, 7-11; 7-10.30 Sun
☎ (01284) 850765
Adnams Bitter, Broadside; guest beer [H]
This pub is in its 21st year serving excellent Indian cuisine, with authentic recipes from India. It also has an extensive alternative menu for the non curry lover, with home-cooked lunches plus evening meals and Sunday roasts. A takeaway service is available. Regular guest ales vary from the traditional to the more unusual. The bar has a log-burning fireplace and outside there is a beer garden with swings, slide and climbing frame.
♨Q❀◐◑⊟♣P⅟

Dalham

Affleck Arms ✔
Brookside, CB8 8TG
⏲ 12-2.30 (not Mon), 5-11; 12-11 Sun
☎ (01638) 500306
Adnams Bitter; Greene King IPA [H]
Situated in the thatched village of Dalham, dating back to the 16th century, this friendly pub offers a cosy restaurant and a sleepy bar with original beams and a prominent inglenook fireplace. Two cask ales come from local micro breweries and annual beer fests are hosted every June. The home-cooked food is exceptional and very well priced, catering for families and walkers. There is a rear patio and a garden for diners and drinkers overlooking the river. ♨Q❀⊨◐◑♿⊟♣P⅟

Dunwich

Ship
St James Street, IP17 3DT
⏲ 11-11; 12-10 Sun
☎ (01728) 648219 🌐 shipinndunwich.co.uk
Adnams Bitter, Broadside, guest ales [H]
Cosy and friendly bar in a large building just a short walk from the beach. It has several rooms also used for dining, and can be very busy, particularly at weekends and in the summer when it is popular with visitors to the area walking the historic coastline. Food is locally sourced and prepared on the premises, with many specials (served 12-3pm, 6-9pm). Crib is played on Wednesday evening. A local taxi/bus service is provided. Accommodation is in 10 rooms, some dog friendly and others suitable for wheelchairs.
♨Q❀⊨◐◑⊟♿⊟♣P⅟

Earl Soham

Victoria
The Street, IP13 7RL (on A1120)
⏲ 11.30-3, 6-11; 12-3, 7-10.30 Sun
☎ (01728) 685758
Earl Soham Victoria, Albert, Sir Roger's Porter, seasonal beers [H]
Traditional Victorian two-bar pub on the outskirts of this pleasant village, with the Earl Soham Brewery just 150m away. It offers an interesting, ever-changing food menu alongside locally-brewed beers. The basic decor and friendly, relaxed ambience have not changed much in years. The pub gets busy at weekends and on warm summer days when even a seat in the garden may be difficult to find. A rare gem and a must for visitors to the area who appreciate good pubs – it still has an outside loo, too! ♨Q❀◐◑⊟♣P

Eastbridge

Eels Foot Inn
Leiston Road, IP16 4SN (close to Minsmere nature reserve)
⏲ 12 (11 Sat)-11; 12-10.30 Sun
☎ (01728) 830154 🌐 theeelsfootinn.co.uk
Adnams Bitter, Broadside, seasonal beers [H]
A wonderfully cosy, split-level, single bar with a good reputation for mainly locally-sourced, home-cooked food (served 12-2.30pm, 7-9pm) and good beers. The pub has a long tradition of live music, with regular sessions in the round on Thursday evening and folk on the last Sunday of the month. An adjacent building provides high quality accommodation at reasonable rates – ideal for visitors to the nearby Minsmere RSPB reserve and exploring the heritage coastline. Cycle hire is also available. A Coastlink bus/taxi runs from Saxmundham or Darsham railway.
♨Q❀⊨◐◑⊟♣P

Edwardstone

White Horse
Mill Green, CO10 5PX TL951426
⏲ 12-3, 5-11; 12-midnight Fri-Sun
☎ (01787) 211211 🌐 edwardstonewhitehorse.co.uk
Adnams Bitter [H]**; Crouch Vale Gold** [G]**; Mill Green Mawkin Mild, Loveley's Fair, Bulls Cross** [H]
Well off the beaten track, this lovely rural free house is an ideal holiday base. Recently extended and refurbished, it is Camping & Caravan Club approved and has two self-catering chalets. The owner has erected a windmill to supply power to the pub, chalets and a new green eco-brewery.

Delicious home-made food uses locally sourced and seasonal organic ingredients when available. Regular beer festivals are popular locally and the pub has a late licence when trade demands. Regular live music plays. Award-winning ciders are stocked. ⌂Q❀⇌◐◑▲●P▯

Exning

White Horse

Church Street, CB8 7EH
⏲ 12-11
☎ (01638) 577323
Wells Bombardier; Woodforde's Wherry Best Bitter Ⓗ
The White Horse has been run by the same family since 1923 and is mentioned in the Domesday Book. A genuine village pub, it prides itself on its thriving restaurant and public bar. The restaurant serves home-cooked food specialising in seafood, steaks and classic British dishes (booking is advisable). Happy hour is 5.30-6.30pm daily, extended to 7.30pm on Friday. ❀♿⊟♣P⅟

Felixstowe: Walton

Half Moon

303 Walton High Street, IP11 9QL
⏲ 12-2.30, 5-11; 12-11 Sat; 12-3, 7-10.30 Sun
☎ (01394) 216009 🌐 felixstowe-halfmoon.co.uk
Adnams Bitter, Broadside; Woodforde's Wherry Best Bitter, seasonal beers; guest beer Ⓗ
Traditional two-bar drinkers' pub on the outskirts of Felixstowe away from the drama and bustle of this popular seaside town. The small, basic public bar retains the air of a bygone era, with local dart teams and a welcoming fire on winter evenings. There is a large garden for sunny days. The only food available is pickled eggs, but you can order in a takeaway from the local curry house. Buses stop outside door. ⌂Q♘❀⊡⊟♣P

Framlingham

Station

Station Road, IP13 9EE (on B1116)
⏲ 11-2.30, 5-11; 12-2.30, 7-10.30 Sun
☎ (01728) 723455 🌐 thestationhotel.net
Earl Soham Gannett Mild, Victoria, Albert; guest beers Ⓗ
This small bar and restaurant is full of character with a wealth of ambience and is often very busy with drinkers and diners. It is set in a former station buffet built in 1859 – the branch line closed in 1963. A small second snug bar leads to an enclosed patio area. The menu is displayed on chalkboards and the beers are dispensed from a set of Edwardian German silver handpumps. A beer festival is held on the last weekend in July. Q♘❀◐◑⊟♣P

Glemsford

Angel ✔

Egremont Street, CO10 7SA
⏲ 5-midnight; 12-1am Fri & Sat; 12-midnight Sun
☎ (01787) 281671
Greene King IPA, Abbot Ⓗ
One of the oldest buildings in the village, the Angel breathes history inside and out. Dating in parts from the 15th-century, the exterior is worth more than a second glance before enjoying the two cosy bars inside. Very much a community local, there are teams for darts, quiz and cribbage. A friendly welcome is ensured, with a log fire blazing in winter. And what a pleasure to sit in a pub with no foods smells. A refreshing experience. ⌂❀♣⅟

Great Cornard

Five Bells

63 Bures Road, CO10 0HU (next to church)
⏲ 11-midnight (1am Sat); 11-11.30 Sun
☎ (01787) 379016 🌐 5bells.co.uk
Greene King XX Mild, IPA, Abbot Ⓗ
Friendly community-led ale house next to Great Cornard church (home of the five bells). The pub fields several teams playing traditional games, plus some rarer ones including petanque and uckers. The landlord has invested in a large adventure playground which is large enough for adults and was used in the 2008 Pub Olympics. The chef from Jimmy's Farm has hosted fundraising events here. Live music usually plays on a Friday. ⌂Q♘❀⊡♿⊟♣P⅟

Great Wratting

Red Lion

School Road, CB9 7HA (on B1061 2 miles N of Haverhill)
⏲ 11-2.30, 5-11; 11-1am Fri & Sat; 12-3, 7-10.30 Sun
☎ (01440) 783237
Adnams Bitter, Broadside, seasonal beers; guest beers Ⓗ
Good beer, food and conversation are the mainstays of this traditional village local. Ideal for families in the summer months, it has a huge back garden with plenty to keep children occupied. Take a look at the amazing collection of copper and brass while sampling the Adnams beers or perhaps an occasional guest. Good food is served in the bar and restaurant. Look out for the whale's jawbone that you pass through as you enter the front door. ⌂❀◐◑P⅟

Hawkedon

Queen's Head

Rede Road, IP29 4NN
⏲ 4 (12 Fri-Sun)-11
☎ (01284) 789218
Adnams Bitter; Woodforde's Wherry Best Bitter; guest beers Ⓗ/Ⓖ
You can be sure of a warm and friendly welcome at this village pub. The 15th-century free house has an unspoilt interior and an enormous open fire in the bar. It was voted West Suffolk CAMRA Pub of the Year in 2007 and holds an excellent beer festival in July. As well as the quality beers it also serves traditional cider and perry. The food is home cooked and of excellent quality. ⌂Q❀◐◑▲♣●P⅟

Henley

Cross Keys ✔

Main Road, IP6 0QP
⏲ 11-11 (midnight Thu-Sat); 12-10.30 Sun
☎ (01449) 760229 🌐 henleycrosskeys.co.uk
Brandon Cross Keys; Woodforde's Wherry Best Bitter; guest beers Ⓖ
A sizable and much revived rural pub just three miles north of Ipswich, the Cross Keys is well worth seeking out. The building has three drinking areas, two with real fires, plus a large garden. Open all

day every day, it offers traditional food (available 12-9pm daily) including a popular roast lunch on Sunday. A selection of up to five local ales is served directly from the cask. Seasonal beer festivals are held and music is hosted once a month.
⛰🐴❀◑◐🚭♿🚌🍎P

Hoxne

Swan ✔

Low Street, IP21 5AS
⏲ 12-3, 6-11; 12-11 Sun
☎ (01379) 668275 🌐 hoxneswan.co.uk
Adnams Bitter, Broadside Ⓖ; **Woodforde's Wherry Best Bitter; guest beers** Ⓗ
Fine timber-framed, Grade II-listed building with a mix of rooms including a splendid bar with large carved beams and an impressive fireplace. Originally built for the Bishop of Norwich (c1480), it served as a brothel for many years afterwards. Fresh, seasonal, locally-sourced food is cooked to order including game and vegetarian dishes. Outside there is a large garden beside the river. A quiz night is held monthly and open-mike nights are hosted. The annual beer festival is a highlight in summer (check website). ⛰Q🐴❀◑◐♿🚌♣P⁄–

Hundon

Plough Inn

Brockly Green, CO10 8DT (follow brown signs from Hundon village)
⏲ 12-3, 6-11; 12-7 Sun
☎ (01440) 786789 🌐 theploughhundon.co.uk
Beer range varies Ⓗ/Ⓖ
Set high above Hundon with wonderful views, this is a traditional inn with great character, run by a CAMRA member. Serving two cask ales in winter and up to four in summer, you are assured of a good range of exceptional beers. The menu provides a choice of delicious home-cooked food. Diners can eat in the bar or more formal restaurant, and the large back garden in summer. Beer festivals are held in April and September.
⛰❀🛏◑◐♿🚌P⁄–

Ipswich

Brewery Tap

Cliff Quay, IP3 0AZ (close to former Tolly Cobbold brewery)
⏲ 11-3, 5-11; 11-11 Sat; 12-10.30 Sun
☎ (01473) 225501 🌐 thebrewerytap.org
Earl Soham Gannet Mild, Victoria; Cliff Quay Bitter, Tolly Roger, seasonal beers Ⓗ
After closure in August 2008, this pub was taken over by the Earl Soham Brewery and reopened a couple of months later. The micro-brewery Cliff Quay (formerly Church End) has been installed adjacent to the derelict Tolly Cobbold brewery complex. A selection of new beers will be created as the site is re-established, together with Earl Soham brews. The bar itself remains unchanged with wooden floors, fine decor and stunning views of the River Orwell through a massive bay window. A full food menu is available 12-2pm, 6-9pm.
⛰Q🐴❀◑◐♿♣P⁄–

Dove Street Inn 🏆

St Helens Street, IP4 2LA
⏲ 12-10.45 (last entry – pub open until midnight); 12-10.30 Sun
☎ (01473) 211270 🌐 dovestreetinn.co.uk
Adnams Broadside; Crouch Vale Brewers Gold; Fuller's London Pride Ⓗ; **Woodforde's Wherry Best Bitter** Ⓖ; **guest beers** Ⓗ/Ⓖ
Busy Grade II-listed, timber-framed building with a large new conservatory adding more space. Up to 20 beers including a mild and four ciders are available, served in over-sized beer glasses. Good home-made food and snacks are also on offer. Three popular beer festivals are held annually, each with 60 plus beers. Children and dogs are welcome. A loyalty card scheme was introduced in January 2009. There are plans for accommodation and a house micro-brewery. East Anglian CAMRA Pub of the Year 2006/07, and a former nationwide runner up. 🐴❀◑🚭♿🚌♣🍎⁄–🍺

Emperor

293 Norwich Road, IP1 4BP
⏲ 12-midnight
☎ (01473) 743600 🌐 emperorinn.co.uk
Young's Bitter; guest beers Ⓗ
An open plan pub with three large leather sofas warmed by a real wood fire. Restaurant seating and a large split-level area with a pool table take up the rest of the room. Beer is sometimes served on gravity, with a mild always available (usually Ansells). Pub food includes some vegetarian options. Outside is a seated patio area and beer garden, with steel quoit beds regularly in use in the summer months. Darts and shove ha'penny are played in the bar. ⛰❀◑◐🚌♣P

Fat Cat

288 Spring Road, IP4 5NL
⏲ 12-11 (midnight Fri); 11-midnight Sat
☎ (01473) 726524 🌐 fatcatipswich.co.uk
Crouch Vale Brewers Gold; Fuller's London Pride Ⓖ; **Woodforde's Wherry Best Bitter** Ⓗ; **guest beers** Ⓖ
This ever-popular pub offers up to 14 gravity beers. With no music and no games machines, the intimate inn is always a joy to visit. Original enamel signs, posters and other artefacts are scattered around the walls. Snacks are available and plates can be provided for takeaway meals (not Fri or Sat eve). In summer visitors can also relax in the garden or on the patio. Children under 16 and dogs are not permitted. Dave the pub cat can also be found on Facebook.
Q❀⇌(Derby Rd)🚌(2,75)🍎⁄–

Greyhound

9 Henley Road, IP1 3SE
⏲ 11-2.30, 5-11; 11-11 Fri & Sat; 12-10.30 Sun
☎ (01473) 252862 🌐 greyhound-ipswich.com
Adnams Bitter, Explorer, Broadside, seasonal beers; guest beers Ⓗ
Welcoming traditional pub, close to the town centre and popular with workers at lunchtime and a wide clientele of all ages in the evening. It has a small and cosy public bar at the front and a larger drinking and dining area to the rear. Fresh home-made food from a blackboard menu is served daily. Outside is a small patio and garden. Q❀◑◐🚭P⁄–

Mannings

8 Cornhill, IP1 1DD (next to town hall)
⏲ 11-11; 12-5 Sun
☎ (01473) 254170
Adnams Bitter, Broadside; Fuller's London Pride; Woodforde's Wherry Best Bitter Ⓗ
Although it can be busy, the pub usually offers a small oasis of calm in the town centre, especially

on Friday or Saturday evenings. Outdoor tables and chairs in the summer provide the ideal place to sit and watch the world go by. There is also a small enclosed patio and garden at the back. A popular provisions market is held on Corn Hill four times per week. ✿◐♿⇌🚌⁵—

Woolpack ✔

1 Tuddenham Road, IP4 2SH

11.30-5, 7-midnight; 11.30-1am Fri & Sat; 12-10.30 Sun

☎ (01473) 253059

Adnams Bitter, Broadside; Black Sheep Best Bitter; Caledonian Deuchars IPA; Young's Bitter; guest beer Ⓗ

Attractive village-style local with three bars including a tiny snug, public bar and separate lounge with a welcoming fire in the winter months. At the front of the building the ever-popular paved garden area has wooden benches and umbrellas. Located close to Christchurch Park (with its museum in the famous Tudor mansion), this pub is just a short walk from town centre. An extensive menu of home-cooked food is served daily (except Sun eve), with fish and seafood dishes as specialities. 🏠Q✿◐◑⊟🚌P⁵—

Ixworth

Greyhound

High Street, IP31 2HJ

11-3, 6-11; 12-3, 7-11 Sun

☎ (01359) 230887

Greene King XX Mild, IPA, Ruddles Best, Abbot; guest beers Ⓗ

Situated on the town's pretty High Street, this traditional inn has three bars including a lovely central snug. The heart of the building dates back to Tudor times. The pub is a rare outlet for XX Mild. Good value lunches and early evening meals are served in the restaurant. A beer festival is held in November. Dominoes, crib, darts and pool are played in leagues and for charities. ✿◐◑⊟🚌♣P⁵—

Lakenheath

Brewer's Tap

54 High Street, IP27 9DS

12-midnight; 12-4.30, 7-12 Sun

☎ (01842) 862328

Beer range varies Ⓗ

A true free house, this village pub is full of character. Bigger than it looks from the outside, there is a patio area at the back. Three or four handpumps offer local and national beers, and traditional Sunday lunches are popular. Crib, darts and poker are played. A public car park is nearby. Q✿◐🚌♣⁵—

Laxfield

King's Head (Low House) ★

Gorams Mill Lane, IP13 8DW (behind churchyard)

12-3, 6-midnight; 11-12 Fri & Sat summer; 12-4, 7-10.30 Sun

☎ (01986) 798395 🌐 laxfield-kingshead.co.uk

Adnams Bitter, Broadside, Explorer, seasonal beers Ⓖ**; guest beer** Ⓗ

A listed, multi-roomed and thatched pub with historic high-back settles, quarry-tiled floors and low ceilings. Beer is dispensed by gravity from the tap room. An interesting menu sourced from local ingredients is on offer in the dining room (12-2pm, 7-9.30pm). Set in a village in the heart of countryside, Morris dancers, plays and live music in the garden add to the magic of this hidden gem. Live music plays on the second Thursday of the month and there are beer festivals in May and September. 🏠Q✿🛏◐◑🚌♣P

Little Glemham

Lion Inn ✔

Main Road, IP13 0BA

12-2.30, 6-11; closed Mon; 12-3, 7-10.30 Sun

☎ (01728) 746505 🌐 lioninnlittleglemham.co.uk

Adnams Bitter; Woodforde's Wherry Best Bitter; guest beers Ⓗ

Friendly pub on the main A12 – an ideal stopping point for visitors to the Suffolk heritage coast. Food is traditional, home cooked and mainly locally sourced, with vegetarian options and a special menu for children. Popular themed food evenings and quiz sessions are hosted. 🏠✿◐◑🚌P

Long Melford

Crown

Hall Street, CO10 1JL

11.30-11; 12-10.30 Sun

☎ (01787) 377666 🌐 thecrownhotelmelford.co.uk

Adnams Bitter; Greene King IPA; Nethergate seasonal beers; Taylor Landlord Ⓗ

In the antiques centre of Long Melford, the Crown is a family-run free house dating back to the 17th century. The bar area is set around a central servery and excellent food can be enjoyed in the bar, restaurant and attractive garden area. The last reading of the Riot Act in West Suffolk took place here in 1885. The quality of the beer is excellent, with regulars from Greene King, Adnams and Taylor, plus guests from Nethergate. 🏠✿🛏◐◑♿🚌P⁵—

Lower Ufford

White Lion

Lower Street, IP13 6DW

11.30-2.30, 6-11; 12-3 Sun

☎ (01394) 460770

Adnams Bitter; guest beers Ⓖ

Cosy, small pub close to the church on the edge of this tiny settlement, with a large garden that leads to the River Deben. Special events are held in the evenings including highly popular bingo sessions and themed food events such as hog roasts. Food is available 12-2pm, 6.30-9pm daily except Monday. Weddings and parties are hosted in a large marquee on summer days. The garden also provides space for local riders to rest their horses while enjoying gravity beers in the quarry-tiled bar. 🏠Q♉✿◐◑♣P

Lowestoft

Norman Warrior ✔

Fir Lane, NR32 2RB

11-midnight (12.30am Fri & Sat); 12-10.30 Sun

☎ (01502) 561982 🌐 thenormanwarrior.co.uk

Greene King IPA, Old Speckled Hen; Woodforde's Wherry Best Bitter; guest beers Ⓗ

Popular twin-bar community pub situated between Lowestoft town centre and Oulton Broad. It has a public bar with a pool table and dartboard, a comfortable lounge and a spacious restaurant.

Outside is a large beer garden and terrace. Home-cooked food is served daily, with a comprehensive menu ranging from bar snacks to full meals. A well attended beer festival is held on the August bank holiday weekend. Guest beers are usually supplied by local brewers and traditional cider is available. ❀◐◑⊟≹(Oulton Broad North)⊟♣●P⁵–

Oak Tavern

Crown Street West, NR32 1SQ

☉ 10.30-11; 12-10.30 Sun

☎ (01502) 537246

Adnams Bitter; Greene King Abbot; guest beers Ⓗ

Popular with all ages, this back-street local is on the northern side of town. The jovial open-plan pub has recently been redecorated, and has pool, darts and a large screen TV at one end and a display of Belgian brewery memorabilia at the other. An extensive range of Belgian bottled beers is available, served in the appropriate glasses, to complement the four real ales always on offer. It has a patio and car park at the rear. ❀≹⊟♣P⁵–

Plough & Sail

212 London Road South, NR33 0BB

☉ 11-midnight (1am Fri & Sat); 12-11 Sun

☎ (01502) 566695

Adnams Bitter; Greene King IPA; guest beers Ⓗ

Close to South Lowestoft beach, this locals' pub is set back from the road with a small frontage, but inside there is a large bar area with wooden flooring and panelling throughout. Live music and quiz evenings are held weekly and a large-screen TV shows sporting events. A Greene King beer is always available, plus guests from its portfolio. There is also a private function room adjacent to a secluded courtyard with a canvas-covered smoking area. ❀≹⊟P⁵–

Triangle Tavern 🏆

29 St Peters Street, NR32 1QA

☉ 11-11 (midnight Thu; 1am Fri & Sat); 12-10.30 Sun

☎ (01502) 582711 🌐 thetriangletavern.co.uk

Green Jack Canary, Orange Wheat, Grasshopper, Mahseer IPA, seasonal beers; guest beers Ⓗ

Advertised as England's most easterly brew pub, this lively town tavern has a cosy front bar with a wood burner. A corridor leads to an open-plan back bar with pool table. Both bars are decorated with brewery awards and memorabilia. The full range of Green Jack beers is usually available, with guest beers and cider. Quarterly beer festivals are held. Live music plays on Thursday and Friday evenings. No food is served but customers are welcome to bring their own. ♨⊟≹⊟●⁵–

Market Weston

Mill Inn

Bury Road, IP22 2PD (on B1111)

☉ 12-3 (not Mon), 5-11; 12-3, 7-11 Sun

☎ (01359) 221018

Adnams Bitter; Greene King IPA; Old Chimneys Military Mild, Great Raft; guest beer Ⓗ

This striking white brick-and-flint faced inn stands at a crossroads and is the closest outlet to the Old Chimneys Brewery, located on the other side of the village. It has been run by the same landlady for more than 12 years. An excellent choice of beers is complemented by a good menu of home-cooked meals (no food Mon eve). ♨Q◐◑♣P

Mildenhall

Queens Arms

42 Queensway, IP28 7JY

☉ 12-2.30, 5-11.30; 12-11.30 Fri-Sun

☎ (01638) 713657

Woodforde's Wherry; guest beers Ⓗ

Comfortable and homely pub, used as a community centre by locals. Extremely popular with real ale drinkers since being taken over by Admiral Taverns, four handpumps are in constant use. The landlord is very keen on real ale and holds an annual beer festival on the August bank holiday to coincide with a cycle rally in the town. A range of alternating Belgian beers is stocked and real cider is occasionally available. Q❀⇌♣P⁵–

Pettistree

Greyhound

The Street, IP13 0HP

☉ 11-2.30, 6-11; 12-3, 7-10.30 Sun

☎ (01728) 746451 🌐 pettistreepub.co.uk

Crouch Vale Brewers Gold; Earl Soham Victoria; Woodfordes Wherry Best Bitter; guest beers Ⓗ

This historic inn dating from 1349 was extensively refurbished in 2008 after closure for three years. Thanks to the efforts of the current owners, it now offers good food and beer in two comfortable bars. Food is available 12-2pm, 6-9pm. The garden is popular on summer evenings and occasionally hosts car rallies and other events. The owners are gradually rebuilding links and associations with local community groups. Folk music plays on the second Monday evening of the month. The traditional outdoor toilets remain – CAMROT lives on! ♨☕❀◐◑♿⊟♣P

Rattlesden

Five Bells

High Street, IP30 0RA

☉ 12-12.30am; 12-11.30 Sun

☎ (01449) 737373

Beer range varies Ⓗ

Set beside the church on the high road through the village, this is a good old Suffolk drinking house – few of its kind still survive. The cosy single room has a games room on a lower level. Three well chosen ales on the bar are usually sourced direct from the breweries. ♨Q❀●

Rendham

White Horse

Bruisyard Road, IP17 2AF

☉ 12-2.30, 6-11; 12-3, 7-10.30 Sun

☎ (01728) 663497 🌐 whitehorserendham.co.uk

Earl Soham Victoria; Mauldons Suffolk Pride; Taylor Landlord; guest beers Ⓗ

Cosy, traditional, single bar pub with two comfortable seating areas divided by a central fireplace. The varied menu changes every five or six weeks, offering a selection of locally-sourced produce including a fish and chip takeaway on Friday evening. Regular quiz nights are held on the first Monday of the month plus various other themed evenings. Petanque is occasionally played by locals on warm summer evenings. A beer festival is held during the August bank holiday weekend. ♨☕❀◐◑⊟♣P

Rumburgh

Buck

Mill Road, IP19 0NS
11.45-3, 6.30-11; 12-3, 7-10.30 Sun
(01986) 785257
Adnams Bitter, seasonal beers; guest beers [H]
A popular local at the heart of village life, this inn and the parish church were once part of a Benedictine priory. Interlinked rooms have been added to the original historic core. Today it consists of two dining rooms, a bar and a games room. The bar is timber framed with a flagstone floor. The pub has a good reputation for food (booking advisable). Outside there is a small, enclosed garden with an aviary. P

Shadingfield

Fox

London Road, NR34 8DD (on A145)
12-3, 6-11.30; 12-5 Sun
(01502) 575100 shadingfieldfox.co.uk
Adnams Bitter; guest beers [H]
This 16th-century inn has been refurbished to the highest standards while maintaining traditional surroundings. The original arched doors and carved fox heads on beams have been retained. The interior comprises a conservatory, a bar with comfortable seating and a further dining area. Outside, a sun terrace has umbrellas and chimera heaters. The landlord is keen to hold regular small beer festivals. Excellent food is available, especially Sunday lunch (booking advisable). QP

Snape

Golden Key

Priory Lane, IP17 1SA
12-3.30, 6 (7 Sun)-11
(01728) 688510 snape-golden-key.co.uk
Adnams Bitter, Broadside, a seasonal beer [H]
Single bar with a tiled floor, large open fireplace and low back settle. There is also a small, secluded 'grotto'. Elsewhere, the building is mainly used for dining. It has two restaurant areas, one with a low beamed ceiling. Good, locally-sourced food is prepared on the premises (served 12-2pm, 6.30-9pm). The pub is popular with ramblers in summer. There is a large car park to the rear. P

Southwold

Lord Nelson

42 East Street, IP18 6EJ
10.30-11; 12-10.30 Sun
(01502) 722079
Adnams Bitter, Explorer, Broadside, seasonal beers [H]
Always a busy and lively pub, popular with locals and visitors enjoying the coastal views from the nearby cliff top. The pub has three drinking areas. Children and dogs are welcome in the side room and patio area to the rear. Decorated throughout with naval artefacts, the main bar has a flagstone floor and a welcoming open fire in winter. The pub is renowned for its good food and a full range of Adnams beers which are brewed nearby. Dogs are welcome.

Red Lion

2 South Green, IP18 6ET
11-11 (10.30 Sun)
(01502) 722385
Adnams Bitter, Explorer, Broadside, seasonal ales [H]
A 17th-century inn next to South Green and overlooking the sea. The interior is full of character, with a central wood-panelled bar and flagstone flooring. To one side is a spacious dining area serving good food. It also has a family room with Adnams memorabilia adorning the walls. Outside is an enclosed and covered patio garden. Regular live music and quiz nights are held. Dogs are allowed but must be kept on a lead.

Stanningfield

Red House

Bury Road, IP29 4RR
12-11.30; closed Wed
(01284) 828330 theredhouse.zoomshare.com
Greene King XX Mild, IPA; guest beers [H]
Built in 1866 in Victorian red brick, the building was originally a cobbler's workshop, but licensed by 1900 and now a free house. It was named after the red tunics of the Suffolk regiment. Neat and clean inside and out, this single-bar local has a relaxed and comfortable atmosphere. Live music plays monthly and pub games and sports are well supported. Food is served 12-2pm, 6-8pm (not Sun). The pub plans to offer accommodation. P

Stowmarket

Royal William

53 Union Street, IP14 1HP
11-11; 12-10.30 Sun
(01449) 674553
Greene King IPA; guest beers [G]
A rare find, this is an end-of-terrace, back-street boozer in the finest traditions, with beers served straight from the casks that are kept in a small tap room behind the bar. Always popular, the lively pub has active darts and crib teams. Football is occasionally shown on a TV screen. Thai food is available at the weekend, otherwise you can order in a takeaway. A friendly and welcoming gem.

Stutton

Gardeners Arms

Manningtree Road, IP9 2TG
12-3, 6-11 (10 Sun)
(01473) 328868
Adnams Bitter; guest beers [H]
Cosy two-bar pub, close to the River Stour and just four miles from the historic Flatford Mill. An eclectic selection of artefacts on display includes musical instruments, framed posters, old sports equipment plus a huge bellows and a crossbow. A large patio and garden feature a raised ornamental fish pond. An interesting menu is available, with specials on chalkboards. Trad/New Orleans jazz plays on the second Thursday evening of the month, plus occasional folk/shanty singing. Children and dogs are welcome. QP

Sudbury

Brewery Tap

21 East Street, CO10 2TP
11-11 (midnight Fri & Sat); 12-10.30 Sun
(01787) 370876

Mauldons Moletrap, Silver Adder, Suffolk Pride Ⓗ
Mauldons Brewery's first pub, after many years of searching. Formerly the Black Horse, this street corner local has been transformed in ale house style. Up to six Mauldons beers are on offer, with four or more on gravity dispense, as well as guest beers. Soup and snacks are served, otherwise takeaway meals can be ordered in.

Waggon & Horses
Church Walk, Acton Square, CO10 1HJ
11-3, 7 (5 Wed-Fri)-11
(01787) 312147
Greene King IPA; guest beers Ⓗ
Set just behind Market Hill, this back street pub is worth seeking out. With one regular and two guest beers to accompany the home cooked, great value food, it is a timeless gem. Regular special menus are on offer in the bar, restaurant or courtyard. Look for the collections of old photographs, miniature spirits, water jugs, cigarette cards and tin tobacco signs. A cosy open fire in winter makes this a great place to sample well kept beers.

Swilland

Moon & Mushroom
High Road, IP6 9LR
11-2.30 (not Mon), 6-11; 12-3, 7-10.30 Sun
(01473) 785320
Buffy's Norwich Terrier, Hopleaf; Crouch Vale Brewers Gold; Nethergate Suffolk County; Wolf Bitter, Ⓖ**; Golden Jackal** Ⓗ**; Woodforde's Wherry Best Bitter, Nelson's Revenge** Ⓖ
Attractively decorated throughout with local pictures, tiled floors and scrubbed tables, the pub offers a wide range of beers on gravity from independent brewers, served from the tap room. Home-cooked food, usually including game dishes, is available in the bar and adjoining dining room (not Mon). Occasional live music and themed nights are hosted.

Tattingstone

White Horse
White Horse Hill, IP9 2NU
12-3, 6-11; 12-11 Fri & Sat; 12-10.30 Sun
(01473) 328060 whitehorsetattingstone.co.uk
Adnams Bitter; Crouch Vale Brewers Gold; Woodforde's Wherry Best Bitter; guest beers Ⓗ
Located just north of Alton Water Reservoir, this 17th-century Grade II-listed inn includes a lounge and snug where folk singers perform. A main bar with large black beams, tiled floor and inglenook fireplace leads to a restaurant area with bare floorboards. Food is served all day (booking recommended Sun eve). The increasingly varied menu includes gluten-free options and a monthly curry night on the last Thursday of the month. The wonderfully preserved outside toilets have under-floor heating in the Ladies. Beers include a changing mild.

Thurston

Fox & Hounds
Barton Road, IP31 3QT
12-2.30, 5-11; 12-midnight Fri & Sat; 12-10.30 Sun
(01359) 232228 thurstonfoxandhounds.co.uk
Adnams Bitter; Greene King IPA; guest beers Ⓗ
Dating from 1800, this listed building is now a regular entry in the Guide. A busy village local, it offers a good selection of ever-changing real ales on handpump, served by the ever-cheerful landlord and staff. Good home-cooked food is available. The public bar has a pool table, darts and Sky TV, while the lounge is quieter and more comfortable. Local CAMRA Pub of the Year 2007/08.

Walberswick

Anchor
Main Street, IP18 6UA
11-4, 6-11; 11-11 Sat; 12-11 Sun
(01502) 722112 anchoratwalberswick.com
Adnams Bitter, Broadside, seasonal beers Ⓗ
Comfortable hotel bar with a good local feel. It has two cosy alcove areas, heated by a real fire on both sides, and wooden flooring and panelling throughout. Excellent meals are served in the spacious dining area to the rear (booking recommended). A side room caters for families, leading to a large patio and garden. An outbuilding has been converted to a function room with its own cinema screen. Summer and winter beer festivals are hosted.

Walsham-le-Willows

Blue Boar
The Street, IP31 3AA
12-2.30, 5-midnight; 12-1am Fri & Sat; 12-11.30 Sun
(01359) 258533
Adnams Bitter Ⓗ**; Woodforde's Wherry Best Bitter; guest beers** Ⓗ/Ⓖ
An ale house most of the time since 1420, this true free house offers a fine selection of beers on handpump and gravity and is a supporter of local breweries. Regular themed food nights and live music evenings are hosted. A May bank holiday beer festival is held in a marquee in the garden.

Wissett

Plough
The Street, IP19 0JE
10.30-12.30am; 11.30-11.30 Sun
(01986) 872201
Adnams Bitter; guest beers Ⓗ
Popular village local with an enterprising landlord, well-supported by the local community. This 17th-century inn has a central bar area with wood flooring and original beams throughout. The walls are adorned with garden and farm implements. To one side is an area known as the 'potting shed'. The pub hosts quiz nights, charity events and an annual beer festival in summer. Camping is available in the large garden.

Woodbridge

Cherry Tree Inn
73 Cumberland Street, IP12 4AG
7.30am-11; 9am-11 Sat & Sun
(01394) 384627 thecherrytreepub.co.uk
Adnams Bitter, Explorer, Broadside, seasonal beers; Taylor Mild; guest beers Ⓗ
Open-plan single bar with several seating areas and a reputation for quality real ale. Good, traditional food is served all day from breakfast

onwards. Informal card games and quiz nights are popular, with various family games available to play. A mild is always among the eight beers on offer and a beer festival is held twice a year in May and September. Accommodation is in a converted barn, set back from the pub beside the pretty garden. Child, wheelchair and dog friendly.
Q🐎❀🛏◐◑♿≋🚌♣P

Old Mariner ✔

26 New Street, IP12 1DX

⏲ 11-3.30, 5 (6 Sat)-11; 12-10.30 Sun

☎ (01394) 382679

Adnams Bitter; Fuller's London Pride; Shepherd Neame Spitfire; Young's Bitter Ⓗ

Cosy, small, two-bar pub with a separate restaurant area to the rear. The decor is simple and traditional throughout, with quarry-tiled floors and scrubbed wooden tables. The only concession to the 21st century is a large TV which temporarily replaces a picture of the Battle of Trafalgar on rugby international days, when enthusiasts gather in the front bar. Food is served 12-2pm, 7-9pm, freshly prepared on the premises. The casseroles, stews and roasts are especially recommended (book early for Sunday lunch). 🔥Q❀◐◑≋🚌P⁄–

Sekforde Tap

76 Seckford Street, IP12 4LZ

⏲ 12-2, 5.30-11; 12-2.30, 6-11 Sat; 12-2.30, 7-10.30 Sun

☎ (01394) 384446 🌐 thesekfordetap.com

Earl Soham Victoria; Greene King IPA; guest beers Ⓗ

Comfortable and well furnished multi-roomed pub away from the busy town centre, offering an interesting and changing selection of up to eight beers. The front bar is accessed via a few steps from the roadside patio. The back bar leads to a series of secluded rooms, including a restaurant and, outside, a hidden garden. Tuesday is quiz night. Food options include tapas and Sunday roast. A good place to get to know the locals, especially at the weekend. 🐎❀◐◑♿♣

Woolpit

Bull ✔

The Street, IP30 9SA

⏲ 11-3, 6-11 (midnight Fri); 12-4, 6-midnight Sat; 12-4, 7-10.30 Sun

☎ (01359) 240393 🌐 bullinnwoolpit.co.uk

Adnams Bitter; guest beers Ⓗ

Large village inn on the old Ipswich to Cambridge road. Inside, choose between the community-minded front bar which hosts various charity events thoughout the year, games room, comfortable conservatory and the spacious restaurant to the rear. Wholesome, home-cooked food is served (not Sun). A garden with children's play area leads off the car park beside the pub.
🐎❀🛏◐◑🚏♣P⁄–

Olde Bull Inn, Barton Mills.

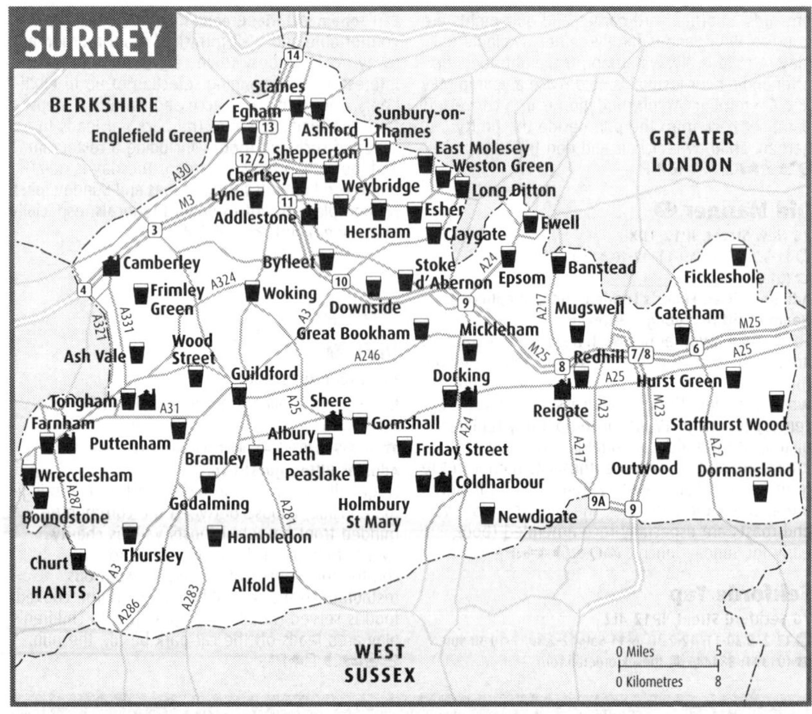

Albury Heath

William IV

Little London, GU5 9DG TQ066467

11-3, 5.30-11; 12-3, 7-10.30 Sun

(01483) 202685 williamivalbury.com

Flowers IPA; Hogs Back TEA; Surrey Hills Ranmore Ale, Shere Drop; guest beer Ⓗ

Dating from the 16th century, the cosy main bar of this secluded and unspoilt country pub has a flagstone floor and wood beams, with a magnificent wood-burning fire. Meals served in the restaurant include Gloucestershire Old Spot pork from the pigs kept in the field behind the pub (no food Sun eve). Real cider is sold in winter, usually replaced with another local beer in summer, when the tables in the front garden are well used. ⛫Q❀◑●P⅟

Alfold

Three Compasses

Dunsfold Road, GU6 8HY (off B2133) TQ035359

10-11

(01483) 275729

Courage Best Bitter; Gale's HSB; Ringwood Fortyniner; guest beers Ⓗ

Dating in parts back to the 17th century, the pub is off the beaten track near Lord Egremont's Wey & Arun Canal which opened in 1816. Inside, the large main bar with stone floors and wooden seats and tables is warmed by a log fire in winter. Outside there are benches on the forecourt (and sometimes a fire on winter evenings), a beer garden and play area. Dunsfold aerodrome, where Top Gear is filmed, is nearby. ⛫Q❀◑▲♣P⅟

Ash Vale

Napiers ✔

72 Vale Road, GU12 5HS (on B3411)

12-11 (midnight Fri & Sat); 12-10.30 Sun

(01252) 314212 napiers.biz

Fuller's London Pride; Taylor Landlord; guest beer Ⓗ

Unassuming locals' pub on the main road between Ash Vale and Aldershot, about 100m from the Basingstoke Canal. The original bar area has been extended to add a room by the entrance with a dartboard and a room at the back with a pool table. Sport is shown on TV but not to the exclusion of those wanting a quiet drink. The pub is home to darts and pool teams and hosts monthly events on Saturdays including race nights and live music. No food is available on Sunday evening or Monday. ❀◑(3,41)♣P⅟

Ashford

Kings Fairway ✔

91 Fordbridge Road, TW15 2SS (on B377)

11-11 (midnight Fri & Sat); 11.30-11 Sun

(01784) 423575 emberinns.co.uk

Adnams Broadside; Caledonian Deuchars IPA; Fuller's London Pride; guest beers Ⓗ

INDEPENDENT BREWERIES

Ascot Camberley
Dorking Dorking (NEW)
Farnham Farnham
Hogs Back Tongham
Leith Hill Coldharbour
Pilgrim Reigate
Surrey Hills Shere
Wayland's Addlestone

This comfortable Ember Inns pub, popular with all ages, offers relaxed seating partitioned into a number of areas on two levels. The real ale-friendly staff manage six handpumps dispensing three constantly-changing guests from around the UK. Food is served daily until 9pm. Quiz nights are Wednesday and Sunday. Real ale, world lager and wine festivals feature throughout the year. There is a covered smoking area and patio seating outside for warmer weather. ❀◐◑♿🚌(290)P⚟

Banstead

Woolpack ✔

186 High Street, SM7 2NZ (on B2217)
⌚ 11-11; 12-10.30 Sun
☎ (01737) 354560
Adnams Bitter; Courage Best Bitter; Youngs Bitter; guest beers Ⓗ
Single bar pub in Banstead centre, with lounge and restaurant areas to the left and a log burner in an open area to the right. Food is available until 9pm (9.30pm Thu-Sat, 6pm Sun), featuring daily specials, grill nights and midweek roasts. Thursday is quiz night and jazz evenings are held on the first Tuesday of the month. There are smokers' areas to the front and rear. Two guest beers are available, one from Punch's Finest Cask range and one which may well be more local. ❀◐◑♿🚌P⚟

Boundstone

Bat & Ball

Bat & Ball Lane, GU10 4SA (via Upper Bourne Lane off Sandrock Hill Rd)
⌚ 11-11; 12-10.30 Sun
☎ (01252) 792108 🌐 thebatandball.co.uk
Harvey's Sussex Best Bitter; Young's Bitter; guest beers Ⓗ
Superb pub that is really part of suburbia, but hidden away on the Bourne stream and at the hub of several footpaths, making it easier to find by foot than by car. Six beers are generally available with guests often from local Surrey/Hampshire breweries. As its name might suggest, there is a strong cricketing theme with photographs and memorabilia, plus a large open fire and robust furniture. There is also a conservatory/family room and a spacious garden with play equipment. ⌂Q♉❀◐◑♿🚌(16)P

Bramley

Jolly Farmer

High Street, GU5 0HB (on A281)
⌚ 11 (12 Sun)-11
☎ (01483) 893355 🌐 jollyfarmer.co.uk
Hogs Back HBB; guest beers Ⓗ
Originally an 18th-century coaching inn on the route from Oxford to Littlehampton, this exceptional free house has eight handpumps dispensing a diverse range of guest beers from all over the country. Character and atmosphere abound, with an esoteric range of artefacts ranging from stuffed animals, cigarette cards, plates and paintings on the walls to agricultural implements, bank notes and beer mats from defunct breweries on the the ceilings. Excellent quality food is served in the bar and rear restaurant. ⌂Q❀🛏◐◑🚌(53,63)♣●P⚟

Byfleet

Plough ✔

104 High Road, KT14 7QT (off A245)
⌚ 11 (12 Sat) -3, 5-11; 12-10.30 Sun
☎ (01932) 354895
Courage Best Bitter; Fuller's London Pride; guest beers Ⓗ
An enduring bastion of real ale discernment with seven guest beers. Local micro-breweries are well represented but quality beers from further afield are never ignored. Two magnificent fireplaces, 18th-century timbers and solid furniture for groups to gather around make this ideal for friends to meet and converse. However, you are warned that mobile phones will not be allowed to intrude or disturb Tinkerbelle the cat. The haven of tranquillity also extends into the hidden garden. ⌂Q❀◐🚌P

Caterham

King & Queen ✔

34 High Street, CR3 5UA (on B2030)
⌚ 11-11; 12-10.30 Sun
☎ (01883) 345438
Fuller's Chiswick, London Pride, ESB, seasonal beers; guest beers Ⓗ
A drinkers' pub, this welcoming 400-year-old red brick-and-flint inn has evolved since the 1840s from three former cottages and was one of Caterham's early ale houses. It retains three distinct areas —a front bar facing the high street, a high-ceilinged middle room with inglenook and log fire, and a small lower-level rear area leading to a patio garden. A side room has a dartboard.Its name refers to Britain's only joint monarchy, William and Mary. No meals Sun. ⌂Q❀◐🚌♣P⚟

Chertsey

Coach & Horses ✔

14 St Ann's Road, KT16 9DG (on B375)
⌚ 12-11; 12-4, 7-10.30 Sun
☎ (01932) 563085 🌐 coachandhorseschertsey.co.uk
Fuller's Chiswick, London Pride, ESB Ⓗ
Attractive, tile-hung long-standing Guide entry dedicated to Fuller's three traditional cask ales. It is near to the town's football and cricket clubs (the third stump is reputed to have been introduced at Chertsey) and also the historic Abbey site and the town museum. Good value English food is available on weekdays. Quiz night is the first Thursday of the month. A seating area at the front has a large awning for smokers. Frequent daytime buses to Staines and Addlestone stop nearby. ⌂❀🛏◐◑🚌♣P⚟

Churt

Crossways 🏆

Churt Road, GU10 2JE (on A287)
⌚ 11-3.30, 5-11; 11-11 Fri & Sat; 12-4, 7-10.30 Sun
☎ (01428) 714323
Courage Best Bitter; Hop Back Crop Circle; Ringwood Fortyniner Ⓗ**; guest beers** Ⓗ/Ⓖ
A village pub where local drinkers happily rub shoulders with ramblers and car travellers in the comfortable saloon and the smaller public bar with its striking chequerboard floor tiling. Five changing guest beers and four ciders have helped the pub win local CAMRA awards for Pub of the Year and Cider Pub of the Year. Lunchtime food is excellent

value and there is a weekly fish and chip evening. A popular beer festival is held in July.
Q❀◖⊟▲⊟(19)♣●P⅃

Claygate

Griffin

50 Common Road, KT10 0HW TQ160635
⏲ 11-11 (midnight Wed-Sat); 12-11 Sun
☎ (01372) 463799
Fuller's London Pride; Young's Bitter; guest beers Ⓗ
Small two-bar back-street freehouse in a residential area. The front windows advertise fomer ownership by Mann, Crossman and Paulin. The public bar is lively with TV and darts, separated from the quieter saloon by a glass leaded light partition with a small door. Guest beers are from a mixture of regional and local brewers. There is a small rear garden and larger fenced front patio with heaters. No food is served Sunday or Monday evenings. ⌂Q❀◖◗⊟⊟(K3)♣P⅃

Coldharbour

Plough Inn

Coldharbour Lane, RH5 6HD TQ152441
⏲ 11.30-11; 12-10.30 Sun
☎ (01306) 711793 🌐 ploughinn.com
Leith Hill Crooked Furrow, Tallywhacker; Ringwood Old Thumper; Shepherd Neame Spitfire; guest beer Ⓗ
Charming old-fashioned village brewpub reached by narrow country lanes, handy for Leith Hill, the highest point in south-east England. The pub is popular with ramblers and cyclists, and opens at 8.45am at the weekend for snacks and soft drinks. There are two small bars with a real fire between them, plus a restaurant selling excellent home-cooked food. The pub also offers good quality accommodation. In summer the large garden is an attraction. ⌂Q❀⊨◖◗♣●P

Dorking

Cricketers ✔

81 South Street, RH4 2JU (on A25 one-way system westbound)
⏲ 12-11 (midnight Thu & Sat, 1am Fri)
☎ (01306) 889938
Fuller's Chiswick, London Pride, ESB; guest beer Ⓗ
Family-run one-bar pub with a Georgian walled patio garden at the back. Monthly music nights alternate between open mike and live acoustic sets. Sandwiches and ploughmans are available weekday lunchtimes, with occasional barbecues in summer. As well as the regular beers there is often a fourth which may be a Fuller's seasonal beer or a guest, usually from an independent brewery. The upper part of the garden has a large umbrella heated for smokers when it is cold. ❀◖⊟♣⅃

Watermill ✔

Reigate Road, RH4 1NN (on A25, 1 mile E of town)
⏲ 11-11; 12-10.30 Sun
☎ (01306) 883248
Courage Best Bitter, Directors; guest beers Ⓗ
Large and comfortable Chef & Brewer bar and restaurant which makes good use of the company's guest beer list – two or three guest ales are usually available, changing frequently. Food is served throughout the day from a regularly changing menu, with fish and other specials always available, and various themed nights. Full table service is offered, even if you only want a drink. The patio garden has fine views across to Box Hill, with a heated area for smokers. ❀◖◗♿⊟P⅃

Dormansland

Old House at Home

63 West Street, RH7 6QP TQ402422
⏲ 11.30-3.30, 6-midnight; 12-4, 7-midnight Sun
☎ (01342) 832117
Shepherd Neame Master Brew Bitter, Ⓗ**; Kent's Best,** Ⓖ**; Spitfire** Ⓗ
Traditional and friendly old pub hidden on the western side of the village but signposted from surrounding roads. The main bar dates from the 16th century but there are later additions. A smaller bar has a dartboard. The pub is renowned for its good quality home-made food, available both in the restaurant and bar (not Sun eve). There is a patio for outdoor drinking. Occasional live music plays. ⌂Q❀◖◗⊟(409)♣P

Plough Inn

44 Plough Road, RH7 6PS (just off B2028) TQ406427
⏲ 12-11 (midnight Fri & Sat; closed 3-5 Mon)
☎ (01342) 832933
Fuller's London Pride; Harveys Sussex Best Bitter Ⓗ
Large, traditional 18th-century country pub with plenty of low wood beams and an inglenook with log fire. One side is set aside for diners, with a choice of genuine Thai or traditional British pub food. The large and pleasant garden is popular in summer. Conveniently situated for the nearby Lingfield racecourse. Occasional beer festivals are held. ⌂Q❀◖◗⊟(236,409)P⅃

Downside

Plough

Plough Lane, KT11 3LT TQ107582
⏲ 11-11
☎ (01932) 589790
Courage Best Bitter; Hogs Back TEA; guest beers Ⓗ
Traditional English pub with facilities for both the diner and the drinker, overlooking meadows surrounding the River Mole. Parts of the pub are 450 years old. It has been a funeral parlour and a butcher's shop in its time. The lounge area has low beams and a large open fireplace. Graffiti from the 1700s has been uncovered in the public bar, in which sports events are screened. There is a garden for summer use. ⌂Q☺❀◖◗⊟♿⊟(513)P

East Molesey

Europa

171 Walton Road, KT8 0DX (on B369)
⏲ 11-11 (midnight Fri & Sat); 12-11 Sun
☎ (020) 8979 8838
Caledonian Deuchars IPA; Courage Best Bitter; Fuller's London Pride; Greene King Abbot; Harveys Sussex Best Bitter; Young's Bitter Ⓗ
Rather good labyrinthine three-bar locals' pub not far from East Molesey shops. The public bar has a dartboard and TV and the saloon features stained glass signs and ceiling skylights. The cosy Cabin bar has photographic memories of Hurst Park racecourse which closed in 1962. A popular jazz night is hosted on Sunday and a jam session on Wednesday evening. The large garden has a covered patio with heaters for smokers.
❀⊨◖⊟♿⊟(411,514)♣P⅃

Egham

Compasses

158 Thorpe Lea Road, Pooley Green, TW20 8HA (on B376)
12 (3 Mon) -11 (midnight Thu-Sat); 12-10.30 Sun
(01784) 454354 compassespub.com
Hogs Back HBB, TEA; Waylands Addlestone Ale; guest beer H
The enthusiastic and enterprising landlord has done wonders for this pub. A wide front bar with a restored real fire is complemented by a side snug area and a pool/function room at the rear. The pub's 100th birthday was in 2009 – the original pub burned down in 1908. Look for signs and lamps of former owners Hodgson's of Kingston and Trumans of London. The front bar has photos of Egham past. The guest beer is mainly from a local micro-brewery. LocAle accredited. (71,441)P

United Services Club

111 Spring Rise, TW20 9PE
12-2.45, 6-11; 12-midnight Fri & Sat; 12-11 Sun
(01784) 435120 eusc.co.uk
Rebellion Mild, IPA; guest beers H
Finalist in CAMRA's 2009 Club of the Year competition, this LocAle accredited club ticks all the boxes. The five handpumps offer an ever-changing range of eclectic beers from near and far. Quarterly beer festivals strive to offer beers for the long distance ale enthusiast. Real ciders come from Mr Whitehead's. All satellite sports channels are available along with a full sized snooker table plus darts, crib and dominoes. The club hosts summer barbecues and live music every Saturday. For entry show a CAMRA membership card or a copy of the Guide. P

Englefield Green

Happy Man

12 Harvest Road, TW20 0QS (off A30)
11-11 (midnight Fri & Sat); 12-10.30 Sun
(01784) 433265
Hop Back Summer Lightning; guest beers H
Originally two Victorian cottages, the internal layout has barely changed since the building was converted to a pub to serve workers building Royal Holloway College (now a regular student haunt). There are separate rooms either side of the bar and a back room for darts. Four handpumps dispense an ever-changing range of guest beers from micro-breweries. Beers on gravity from the cellar are also on offer at times, and up to three real ciders. The rear smokers' refuge is heated. Local CAMRA Pub of the Year 2008.

Epsom

Barley Mow

12 Pikes Hill, KT17 4EA (off A2022)
12-11.30 (midnight Fri & Sat); 12-10.30 Sun
(01372) 721044
Fuller's Discovery, London Pride, ESB; guest beer H
Well-run pub, originally three cottages, tucked away down a narrow side road. Smart in a rustic way, it has various alcoves and seating areas around a central bar. Old style wooden furnishings, two wood surround fireplaces and ornate leaded windows add to the traditional ambience. The guest beer is supplied by Fuller's and may be from another family brewer. Food is served all day at weekends and barbecues are held in summer. Quiz night is Monday. An alley from pub's garden entrance leads to Upper High Street public car park.

Esher

Albert Arms

82 High Street, KT10 9QS (on A307)
10.30-11 (midnight Thu-Sat); 12-10.30 Sun
(01932) 465290 albertarms.com
Black Sheep Best Bitter; Fuller's London Pride; Hogs Back TEA; Surrey Hills Shere Drop; guest beers H
Contemporary town-centre pub with a large restaurant area and smaller drinking space. Six real ales are on at any one time, the majority supplied by smaller breweries. The pub operates a unique pigeonhole system where regulars can collect mail. Major sporting events are screened on TV in the bar and there is an area for hire for private functions. Evening meals are not available on Sunday. Local CAMRA Pub of the Year 2008.

Ewell

Wheatsheaf

34 Kingston Road, KT17 2AA (off A240)
11 (12 Sun)-11
(020) 8393 2879
Wells Bombardier; Young's Bitter; guest beer H
This cosy traditional locals' pub built in 1858 stands opposite the Hogsmill River. It has a small single bar with an adjoining lounge area through an archway. Carpeted throughout, there are red upholstered benches in both areas. Note the leaded Isleworth Brewery windows behind the bar. Photographs of old Ewell decorate the walls and there are two bare brick fireplaces. Beware sitting in the Longhurst Lounge with its connection to the nearby undertakers! Live music plays on Saturday evening.

Farnham

Lamb

43 Abbey Street, GU9 7RJ (off A287)
11-2.30, 5-11; 11-11 Sat; 12-10.30 Sun
(01252) 714133
Shepherd Neame Kent's Best, H**; Spitfire,** G**; seasonal beers** H/G
A dedicated landlord ensures that this pub remains a bastion of quality. Slightly out of the town centre, on the way to the railway station, it caters for both locals and 'those in the know'. Usually an ideal place to enjoy relaxed conversation, it gets noisier on match days and when live music is playing, but escape is possible in the upper garden reached by a metal staircase. The food is excellent (not available Tue eve or all day Sun). Q

Plough

74 West Street, GU9 7EH (on A325)
11.30-11 (11.30 Fri); 12-10.30 Sun
(01252) 728057
Shepherd Neame Master Brew Bitter, Spitfire, seasonal beers H
Originally a pub and dairy dating from 1860, the Plough was renovated and reopened in November 2007. Split level with a raised bar, fireplace, piano, wood panelling and comfortable armchairs, it has a gentle, restrained and reflective ambience. Children are welcome and it has Wi-Fi access and

numerous board games to keep all happy. Dogs are permitted. The garden is a pleasant surprise and has a smokers' area. Well worth the short walk from the town centre. ⛫Q❀◖🚌⁻

Shepherd & Flock

Moor Park Lane, GU9 9JB (centre of roundabout at A325/A31 jct E of town)
⏲ 11-11.30; 12-11 Sun
☎ (01252) 716675
Hogs Back TEA; Ringwood Old Thumper; Sharp's Doom Bar; Triple fff Moondance; guest beers Ⓗ
Located at the eastern end of town, just off the bypass, it is always worth a trip out to sample the choice of seven beers. A genuine free house, a range of changing guest beers from local micros is always on offer. Despite being surrounded by busy roads, the pub has a relaxed feel to it. Outside, there is a choice of drinking areas – the larger, to the front, to watch the kamikaze motorists on the roundabout or a more secluded area to the rear with a heated smokers' space. No food is available on Sunday evening. ⛫Q❀◖◗🚌(14,X65)P⁻

William Cobbett

4 Bridge Square, GU9 7QR (on A287)
⏲ 11-11 (12.30 Fri; midnight Sat); 12-11 Sun
☎ (01252) 726281
Courage Best Bitter; Fuller's London Pride; guest beers Ⓗ
Just off the town centre, the pub is named after the radical MP and author of Rural Rides who is buried in the nearby churchyard. It has a cottage style exterior and inside a number of drinking areas both intimate and more public, with exposed brickwork in parts. To the rear is a large area for drinking and outside a covered smokers' space with comfortable sofas. Three guest beers are often from local micros. Entertainment includes table football, pool and live music on Wednesday night. ❀◖⇌🚌P⁻

Fickleshole

White Bear

Fairchildes Lane, CR6 9PH TQ389603
⏲ 11-11; 12-10.30 Sun
☎ (01959) 573166 🌐 the-whitebear.com
Fuller's London Pride; Harveys Sussex Best Bitter; guest beers Ⓗ
Large 16th-century free house which although on the edge of Greater London, is in some ways a hundred miles from it. Hidden away down narrow country lanes, the building has been extended into adjoining cottages and is now quite a maze of interconnected rooms. The origins of the eponymous stone bear outside the pub are unclear, although there are rumours of auctions, theft and kidnapping. Although food oriented, drinkers are well catered for. Plane spotters will appreciate the garden. ⛫Q❀◖◗P⁻

Friday Street

Stephan Langton

RH5 6JR TQ128456
⏲ 11-3 (not Mon), 5-11; 11-11 Sat; 12-9 Sun
☎ (01306) 730775 🌐 stephan-langton.co.uk
Dorking DB No 1; Fuller's London Pride; Surrey Hills Shere Drop Ⓗ
This hidden-away pub and restaurant is named after a local man who became the Archbishop of Canterbury in 1206 and was a signatory of the Magna Carta. Beautifully situated in good walking country, by an old hammer pond, it gets especially busy in the summer when it might be best to use the nearby walkers' car park to the west. The high quality food is all freshly cooked and locally sourced (not Sun eve or all day Mon). The cider is Westons Old Rosie. ⛫Q❀◖◗🍎P⁻

Frimley Green

Rose & Thistle ✔

1 Stuart Road, GU16 6HT (on B3411)
⏲ 12-midnight (1am Fri & Sat)
☎ (01252) 834942
Fuller's London Pride; St Austell Tribute; Taylor Landlord; guest beers Ⓗ
The arrival of the real ale enthusiast manager has resulted in a tremendous uplift in the sale of cask ale since 2008 – the three guest beers include those from local breweries in line with CAMRA's LocAle initiative. The large conservatory can be reserved, free of charge, for private functions. No food is available on Sunday evening. ❀◖◗🚌♣P⁻

Godalming

Jack Phillips ✔

48-56 High Street, GU7 1DY
⏲ 9-11 (midnight Thu; 1am Fri & Sat)
☎ (01483) 521750
Courage Best Bitter; Greene King IPA, Abbot; Marston's Pedigree; guest beers Ⓗ
A converted supermarket, this town-centre Wetherspoon's was named after the Titanic's radio operator, who was from Godalming. Ten handpumps feature at least three changing guests including ales from local breweries such as Hog's Back. The interior is narrow but deep, broken up by pillars and decorated in pastel shades. In the summer the front opens up with alfresco seating on the pavement. The cider is Westons Old Rosie. Q🛝❀◖◗♿⇌🚌🍎

Star

17 Church Street, GU7 1EL
⏲ 11 (11.45 Mon)-midnight (1am Fri & Sat); 12-midnight Sun
☎ (01483) 417717 🌐 thestargodalming.co.uk
Greene King IPA, H&H Olde Trip Ⓗ**; guest beers** Ⓗ/Ⓖ
17th-century inn situated in an historic part of town. Despite a narrow exterior the pub is remarkably spacious inside, with a beamed, traditional area that leads to a conservatory and a heated outdoor space for smokers. Up to eight real ales are available, including four on gravity, and up to three real ciders are also stocked. Themed beer festivals are held in a marquee in the garden at Easter and Halloween. May close at 11pm Monday-Wednesday if trade is slow. ❀◖⇌🚌♣🍎⁻

Gomshall

Compasses

50 Station Road, GU5 9LA (on A25)
⏲ 11-11; 12-10.30 Sun
☎ (01483) 202506 🌐 thecompassesinn.co.uk
Surrey Hills Ranmore Ale, Shere Drop, seasonal beers Ⓗ
Originally God Encompasses, the name of this early Victorian pub has contracted over time. The bar and restaurant serve the same food menu all day (not Sun eve). Ingredients for the home-made meals are locally sourced. There is a large garden just the

other side of the Tillingbourne Stream and a covered smoking area. The pub is reputed to be home to a friendly ghost who plays with the beer taps. Live music plays on Friday night. Accommodation is in two en-suite twin rooms.

Great Bookham

Royal Oak

16 High Street, KT23 4AG (off A246) TQ144552
11-11; 12-10.30 Sun
(01372) 452533
Caledonian Deuchars IPA; Greene King Abbot; Sharp's Doom Bar; guest beers H
Small two-bar village pub with a very friendly welcome. A pub has been on this site since 1450. The parlour has inviting inglenook fireplace, original beams and flagstone floor. The public bar is more basic with TV and dartboard. A dining room at the rear serves good quality meals made with locally sourced ingredients. Guest beers are selected from the S&N list plus local breweries, and three beer festivals are held yearly. There is a poker tournament on Sunday evening and skittles is played monthly in the restaurant. Folk & Ale Night is the last Saturday of the month. Local CAMRA Pub of the Year 2009.
Q(479)P

Guildford

Keep

29 Castle Street, GU1 3UW
12-11 (midnight Fri & Sat)
(01483) 450600 thekeepguildford.co.uk
Surrey Hills Shere Drop; guest beer H
A pub for 140 years, mostly called the Two Brewers, in recent times it had lost its way with a number of management and name changes. Now the Keep is back on its feet with a name reflecting its proximity to the castle and a wine bar appearance as a result of the last refurbishment. The guest beer comes from a local micro. No food is served on Sunday or Thursday and Friday evenings. A small haven of retreat from the nearby bustling town centre.

Rowbarge

7 Riverside, GU1 1LW (off A320 via Stoughton Rd)
12-midnight (11 Sun)
(01483) 573358
Ascot Posh Pooch; guest beers H
After many years in the doldrums, this three-bar pub has been revitalised by a new and enthusiastic landlord serving beers from local micro-breweries. Situated on the north side of the River Wey, the pub has its own moorings which are free to customers. Alternatively, take a pleasant one and a half mile stroll along the towpath from Guildford Station. There is a covered and heated area for smokers. No food is available on Sunday evening.
P

Varsity Bar

Egerton Road, University of Surrey, GU2 7XU (off A3 near hospital)
11-11 (8.30 Sat); 12-10.30 Sun
(01483) 683226
Beer range varies H
This university sports bar offers an excellent range of ever-changing ales on three handpumps and on gravity for special events. Situated near the hospital (not the main campus), it can be busy on match days (Wed and Sat) although quiet the rest of the time. The last Friday of the month celebrates one brewery and its ales, and an annual beer festival is held. Good food is excellent value. Drinks can be enjoyed outside by the pitches in summer months. P

Hambledon

Merry Harriers

Hambledon Road, GU8 4DR SU968392
12-3 (not Mon), 5.15-10.30 (midnight Fri & Sat); 12-8 Sun
(01483) 682883
Hogs Back TEA; Hop Back Crop Circle; Triple fff Alton's Pride; guest beers H
16th-century pub off the beaten track and recently updated but retaining three separate bar areas, a large open fire, panelled walls and a wooden floor. Six beers are generally available with the guests from local micros. Food is also locally sourced. Quiz night is Thursday and live music plays on the last Saturday of the month. In summer plays are performed in the large car park opposite. Surrey Hills Llamas is nearby. P

Hersham

Royal George

130 Hersham Road, KT12 5QJ (off A244)
11-11 (midnight Fri & Sat); 12-11 Sun
(01932) 220910
Young's Bitter, Special H
Popular two-bar local built in 1964 with a spacious main bar. The public bar has an interesting plan of a Napoleonic Wars ship-of-the-line – the pub is named after one of these ships. There is an extensive English and Thai lunch menu and excellent Thai food in the evening Monday to Saturday. Roast lunches are served on Sunday. Quiz night is Tuesday. Occasional live music plays on Saturday. Outside is a heated awning for smokers. Local CAMRA Pub of the Year 2007.
(218)P

Holmbury St Mary

King's Head

Pitland Street, RH5 6NP (off B2126) TQ112442
12 (4 Mon)-11; 12-10.30 Sun
(01306) 730282
Greene King IPA; King Horsham Best Bitter; Surrey Hills Ranmore Ale; guest beers H
Just off the main road, this wonderful unspoilt pub proudly serves locally sourced beers and food. The wooden-floored bar has a bar billiards table, real fire and some interesting old shooting photos on the walls. Excellent food is served in the restaurant including daily specials and a changing fish menu in the evening (no food Sun eve or Mon). The pub is popular with ramblers and mountain bikers exploring the lovely Surrey Hills countryside. Beer festivals are held on the spring and August bank holidays. Q(21)P

Hurst Green

Diamond

Holland Road, Holland, RH8 9BQ TQ407503
11-11; 12-10.30 Sun
(01883) 716040

Fuller's London Pride; Harveys Sussex Best Bitter; Young's Bitter; guest beer Ⓗ
This dog-friendly community pub on the southern end of Hurst Green has gained many new customers due to its reputation for fine ale and good food (not served Sun eve). There is a large collection of clocks throughout, so not knowing the time is not a valid excuse for staying here too long! Note Morag, who keeps a watchful eye on the bar from above the fireplace. Card carrying CAMRA members receive a discount on cask beers.
(594)P

Long Ditton

City Arms

5-6 Portsmouth Road, KT7 0XE (on A307)
11-11; 12-10.30 Sun
(020) 8398 3552 thecityarms.net
Courage Best Bitter; Fuller's London Pride; guest beers Ⓗ
Welcoming local on the main road between Kingston and Esher. The long front bar is for drinkers, with a real fire at one end that adds to the cosy atmosphere. A quieter back bar and side room are used for dining. Two regular ales are complemented by a weekly changing guest beer from the S&N list. Good value home-made traditional English food is served (not Sun eve). Quiz night is every other Wednesday and board games are available. P

Lyne

Royal Marine

Lyne Lane, KT16 0AN (off B386) TQ012663
12-2.30, 5.30-11 (6.30-11.30 Sat); 12-3 Sun
(01932) 873900
Courage Best Bitter; guest beers Ⓗ
Converted from two cottages 160 years ago, this small, cosy country pub in a quiet village was local CAMRA branch Pub of the Year in 2006. The name is said to commemorate Queen Victoria reviewing her troops nearby. The landlord supports local breweries and sometimes offers a mild. All food is freshly cooked and the portions are generous. The Lyne Mountain Resue Team based at the pub organises events in support of local charities. Darts, cards, crib and dominoes are played.
QP

Mickleham

King William IV

Byttom Hill, RH5 6EL (off A24 southbound) TQ174538
11-3, 6-11; 12-10.30 Sun
(01372) 372590
Hogs Back TEA; Surrey Hills Shere Drop; Triple fff Alton's Pride; guest beer Ⓗ
Built in 1790 as accommodation for workers on the nearby Beaverbrook Estate, this rural pub has a strong focus on local ales. There are two separate drinking and dining areas and a large garden with panoramic views of the surrounding countryside. An extensive menu of freshly prepared food is served using mainly local produce, with a good range of vegetarian options. Parking is available at the bottom of the hill and in the nearby village. Children are welcome at all times. Note the pub sometimes closes on Sunday and Monday evenings in winter. Q(465)

Mugswell

Well House Inn

Chipstead Lane, CR5 3SQ (off A217) TQ259552
12-11 (10.30 Sun)
(01737) 830640 wellhouseinn.co.uk
Adnams Bitter; Fuller's London Pride; Surrey Hills Shere Drop; guest beers Ⓗ
A fine multi-roomed Grade II-listed pub with two drinking areas, a conservatory and a restaurant serving generous portions of good food made with local ingredients (not Sun eve and Mon). A snack menu is available throughout the afternoon (Tue-Sat). The main bar displays an excellent collection of pewter and ceramic tankards. The Domesday Book mentions the well outside which is still monitored today for its water level. Harry the monk's ghost is a pub regular. QP

Newdigate

Surrey Oaks

Parkgate Road, RH5 5DZ (on road to Leigh from Newdigate) TQ205436
11.30-2.30 (3 Sat), 5.30 (6 Sat)-11; 12-10.30 Sun
(01306) 631200 surreyoaks.co.uk
Harveys Sussex Best Bitter; Surrey Hills Ranmore Ale; guest beers Ⓗ
The Soaks, a strong supporter of micro-breweries from near and far, sells more than 300 different beers each year. The 16th-century bar features low beams, flagstones and an inglenook, and has a number of drinking areas. Good home-made food is served in the bar and restaurant (not eves Sun or Mon). Outside is a lovely garden with a boules pitch. Beer festivals are held on the late spring and August bank holidays. Local CAMRA Pub of the Year for the last seven years. QP

Outwood

Bell

Outwood Lane, RH1 5PN TQ328457
12-11 (10.30 Sun)
(01342) 842989
Fuller's London Pride, ESB; guest beer Ⓗ
Dating from 1635, the Bell was previously a coaching stop on the route from London to Brighton. The quarter of a ton bell from which the pub takes its name is displayed by the front door. Although the emphasis is definitely on food, especially fresh fish, drinkers are always made to feel welcome. The comfortable bar includes a large inglenook complete with warming fire. Outside is an umbrella with heaters for smokers. P

Peaslake

Hurtwood Inn

Walking Bottom, GU5 9RR TQ086446
12-3, 5.30-11 (midnight Fri); 12-11 Sat & Sun
(01306) 730851 hurtwoodinnhotel.com
Hogs Back TEA; Surrey Hills Shere Drop; guest beers Ⓗ
The recently refurbished bar at this hotel acts as a local for the village as well as the bar for hotel guests and a lunch stop for walkers in the beautiful surrounding countryside. An enthusiastic purveyor of local beer and produce, two guest beers are available, one often from a nearby brewer. Excellent food is served in the bar as well as the restaurant. (25)P

Puttenham

Good Intent ✓

The Street, GU3 1AR (off B3000) SU931478
12-3, 6-11; 12-11 Sat; 12-10.30 Sun
(01483) 810387 thegoodintent-puttenham.co.uk
Harveys Sussex Best Bitter; Ringwood Best Bitter; Taylor Landlord; guest beers H
Welcoming 16th-century former coaching inn situated on the North Downs and Pilgrims Way and National Cycle Route 22. Popular with walkers and cyclists, and families and dogs are welcome. The last field growing hops in Surrey is situated in the village – the hops are used in Harveys Best. Fish and chips night is Wednesday (no food Sun and Mon eves). Guest beers from local breweries regularly feature and an annual beer festival is held over the late May bank holiday weekend. ⌂Q❀◐▲♣P⁄–

Redhill

Garland ✓

5 Brighton Road, RH1 6PP (on A23)
11.30-midnight (1am Fri & Sat); 12-midnight Sun
(01737) 760377
Harveys Sussex XX Mild, Hadlow Bitter, Sussex Best Bitter, Armada Ale, seasonal beers H
This classic Victorian street-corner local just south of the town centre has the atmosphere of a country pub, and is home to a number of darts and quiz teams. The eight handpumps are often all in use supplying the full range of Harveys beers, including seasonal and one-off brews. There is a side room available for private use and well behaved children are welcome until 7.30pm. An outside smoking area is covered and heated. Lunches are served during the week only. ❀◐⇌▣♣P⁄–

Home Cottage

3 Redstone Hill, RH1 4AW (on A25)
11-11.30; 12-10.30 Sun
(01737) 762771
Wells Bombardier; Young's Bitter, Special, seasonal beers H
Large, mid-19th century community pub with three distinct drinking areas. The front bar, warmed by a real fire, has a relaxing atmosphere and offers an interesting bank of five handpumps. The conservatory is a family room where children are welcome. A separate room at the rear is the venue for comedy nights on the last Friday of the month. Good food is available lunchtimes and evenings (until 8pm Sun). The pub is situated opposite the rear exit of Redhill Station and uphill from the bus station. ⌂❀◐◑⇌▣♣P⁄–

Shepperton

Barley Mow 🏆

67 Watersplash Road, TW17 0EE (off B376)
12-11 (10.30 Sun)
(01932) 225326
Hogs Back TEA; Hop Back Summer Lightning; guest beers H
This friendly community pub in Shepperton Green, known locally as the Barmy Mow, is a five handpump tenanted free house whose landlord is a keen supporter of local micro-breweries and real cider. Live jazz is performed on Wednesday, rhythm 'n' blues on Friday and Saturday. Food includes a Sunday roast. The local special needs school is supported with a Sunday afternoon meat raffle. Well-behaved dogs are welcome. North Surrey CAMRA Pub of the Year 2007 and 2009 and LocAle accredited. ❀◐◑▣●P⁄–

Staffhurst Wood

Royal Oak ✓

Caterfield Lane, RH8 0RR TQ407485
11-11 (closed 3-5 Mon & Tue winter); 12-10.30 Sun
(01883) 722207
Adnams Bitter; Harveys Sussex Best Bitter; Larkins Traditional H**; guest beers** H/G
Hidden away rural free house with guest beers usually coming from local micro-brewers. It also offers a selection of bottled British and Belgian beers and a variety of ciders. The landlord runs a vintage port club. Excellent quality meals made from locally-sourced ingredients are available in the bar and restaurant (not Sun eve). Views from the garden over the surrounding counties are superb and dogs are welcome. Card-carrying CAMRA members receive a discount on cask beers and bar meals. ⌂❀◐◑●P⁄–

Staines

George ✓

2-8 High Street, TW18 4EE (on A308)
9-midnight (1am Fri & Sat)
(01784) 462181
Courage Best Bitter; Greene King IPA, Abbot; Marston's Pedigree; Shepherd Neame Spitfire; guest beers H
Large two-storey Wetherspoon's pub built in the 1990s on the site of a former supermarket. The large downstairs bar with its mixture of tables and intimate booths is always busy but a quieter bar can be reached via a spiral staircase. Up to six guest ales, often from local breweries such as Waylands, Twickenham and Loddon, are provided from the bank of handpumps nearest the main doors, with the national brands and up to two real ciders from Westons at the rear. ◐◑♿⇌▣●⁄–

Swan Hotel

The Hythe, TW18 3JB (off A308/A320 roundabout)
12-11.30 (midnight Fri & Sat)
(01784) 452494 fullersenglishinns.co.uk/swan-hotel
Fuller's Discovery, London Pride, ESB, seasonal beers H
This 18th-century flagship Fuller's hotel is on a site which has been home to a 'Swan' since at least the 15th century. It is well-named with its long riverside terrace overlooking a stretch of the Thames where numerous swans congregate. A number of refurbishments and enlargements have been carried out over the years. The hotel has its own moorings and in centuries past bargemen would tie up here to exchange part of their wages in tokens for food and drink. ⌂❀◐◑♿▣⁄–

Stoke D'Abernon

Old Plough ✓

2 Station Road, KT11 3BN (off A245)
11-11; 12-10.30 Sun
(01932) 862364 theoldplough.net
Courage Best Bitter; guest beers H
Large pub with a strong emphasis on SIBA-listed beers from the surrounding area. The interior has several distinct areas and diners are catered for with light meals or a full restaurant menu. Food is

served lunchtimes and evenings (not Mon) and all day until 9pm Saturday and 6pm Sunday. The location is handy for returning commuters using the nearby station. Families and dogs (on a lead) are welcome. The garden is popular in the summer months. (408)P

Sunbury-on-Thames

Grey Horse

63 Staines Road East, TW16 5AA (on A308)
11-11; 12-10.30 Sun
(01932) 782981
Fuller's London Pride; Twickenham Original; guest beer [H]
Friendly, comfortably furnished little community pub on the way to Kempton Park racecourse. It started life as a beer house in the 1840s and from 1876 changed hands from Ashby's to Simonds to Courage breweries, following a pattern common to other local pubs. It is now part of Enterprise Inns. The guest beer changes regularly and is often from Twickenham Ales. Live sports are shown on TV. The large beer garden has a covered and heated smoking area. There are rumours of resident ghosts including a woman burnt to death.

Phoenix

26-28 Thames Street, Lower Sunbury, TW16 6AF
11-11; 12-10.30 Sun
(01932) 785358 thephoenixsunbury.co.uk
Black Sheep Best Bitter; Fuller's London Pride; Taylor Landlord; guest beer [H]
This former Ashby's of Staines pub has recently undergone a major refurbishment. A popular village local, it has three distinct drinking and dining areas – drinkers mainly congregate to the right of the bar around the open fireplace. The pub is dog friendly and popular with dog walkers. It has a pleasant garden facing Sunbury Lock and Weir with its own landing stage for patrons arriving by boat. (216)

Thursley

Three Horseshoes

Dye House Road, GU8 6QD (off A3)
12-3, 5.30-11; 12-11 Sat; 12-10.30 Sun
(01252) 703268
Gale's HSB; Hogs Back TEA; guest beers [H]
Friendly and welcoming single bar pub dominated by two magnificent fireplaces with a separate restaurant area popular with families. Saved from closure and bought out by local supporters in 2004, it is now a thriving concern offering an excellent combination of good real ale and high-quality home-made food (not Sun eve). Set in the heart of excellent walking territory it has a real rural feel yet is easily accessible from the nearby A3. A changing cider or perry is on handpump.
QP

Tongham

Hogs Back Brewery Shop

Manor Farm Business Centre, The Street, GU10 1DE (off A31)
9-6 (8.30 Wed-Fri); 10-4.30 Sun
(01252) 784495 hogsback.co.uk/breweryshop.htm
Hogs Back HBB, TEA, Hop Garden Gold, seasonal beers [G]
Situated in a barn partially overlooking the brewery, the shop sells the full range of Hogs Back draught beers and bottle-conditioned ales. It also stocks a large selection of bottled beers from Britain and all over the world and a good choice of country wines, plus some excellent Hogs Back souvenir merchandise. Either Westons or Mr Whitehead's cider is also available. Show your CAMRA membership card to receive a 5% discount on Hogs Back products. P

White Hart

76 The Street, GU10 1DH (off A31)
12-11 (midnight Fri & Sat); 12-10.30 Sun
(01252) 782419 whiteharttongham.co.uk
Beer range varies [H]
A family-run pub offering up to nine real ales plus Westons Old Rosie, and hosting occasional beer festivals. The Village Bar and lounge are complemented by a sports bar with pool, TV, darts and a jukebox. Meals are served most lunchtimes and evenings and a snack menu is usually available at other times. Several clubs meet here and events including a regular meat raffle are held in aid of the Surrey Air Ambulance. (3,20)P

Weston Green

Marney's Village Inn

Alma Road, KT10 8JN (off A309)
11-11; 12-10.30 Sun
(020) 8398 4444 marneys.com
Courage Best Bitter; Fuller's London Pride; Wells Bombardier [H]
This 18th-century hunting lodge became a public house in the mid 1800s and was originally called the Alma Arms. The pub is attractively located by Marney's duck pond. Inside, the smaller lower area to the right is the place for a cosy chat, with several wooden tables located up a couple of stairs to the left. Home-made food is served at lunchtime. A vintage car club meets on the first Monday of the month. (515)P

Weybridge

British Volunteer

24 Heath Road, KT13 8TJ (on B374)
11 (12 Sun)-11
(01932) 847733 thebritishvolunteer.com
Fuller's London Pride; Taylor Landlord; Wells Bombardier; guest beer [H]
Traditional community pub with a single L-shaped bar serving a lounge, conservatory and games area. The name refers to the 40,000 volunteers who defended England against the threat of a French invasion in the early 19th century. Major football matches are shown on a large screen in the lounge and there is occasional live music, stand-up comedy and quiz nights (see website for details). A good range of home-cooked food is available (not Sun or Mon eves). Children are welcome before 7pm. A covered and heated area is available for smokers. (451)

Woking

Herbert George Wells

51-57 Chertsey Road, GU21 5AJ
9am-midnight (1am Fri & Sat)
(01483) 722818

Courage Directors; Greene King Abbot; Hogs Back TEA; Ruddles Bitter; guest beers Ⓗ
Town-centre pub in a vibrant area attracting a mixed clientele including office workers, shoppers, a younger set socialising in the town, and, of course, real ale drinkers devouring four ever-changing guest beers. Strong on HG Wells artefacts including a time machine clock and enigmatic invisible man figure, and other local history is well represented in numerous old photographs. A little too handy for rail and bus connections, as the temptation to linger is ever present.
Q❀◑♿⇌🚌🍎

Sovereigns ✔
Guildford Road, GU22 7QQ (on A320)
⏲ 11.30-11 (midnight Fri & Sat)
☎ (01483) 751426
Adnams Broadside; Caledonian Deuchars IPA; guest beers Ⓗ
Six handpumps greet the drinker at this large, comfortable Ember Inn, the oldest pub in Woking, dating from 1840. Food is served daily until 9pm, with a grill night on Tuesday and curry night on Thursday. Quizzes are held on Monday and Wednesday evenings. There is outside seating to the front and side with patio heaters and umbrellas. Local CAMRA Pub of the Year in 2007, it provides tasting notes for its guest beers and hosts occasional beer festivals. ♨❀◑♿⇌🚌♣P⁄—

Woking Railway Athletic Club
Goldsworth Road, GU21 6JT (behind bar Barcelona)
⏲ 10.30-11; 12-10.30 Sun
☎ (01483) 598499
Beer range varies Ⓗ
Welcoming and enterprising working men's club with a mixed clientele enjoying beers from local micros including Bowman and Waylands, and as far afield as Cornwall. A meeting place for many different groups including the Royal Naval Association, railway trade unions and the organisers of Woking Beer Festival, it is often dominated by football on a large screen. Children friendly and there is disabled access via a side ramp. For entry show a CAMRA membership card or this edition of the Guide. ♿⇌🚌♣⁄—

Wood Street

Royal Oak
89 Oak Hill, GU3 3DA
⏲ 11-3, 5-11; 12-3, 7-10.30 Sun
☎ (01483) 235137
Courage Best Bitter; Surrey Hills Shere Drop; guest beers Ⓗ
Ever popular and genuine free house with an imaginative range of guest beers, including an ever-changing mild, and pump clips for 'coming on' beers displayed over the top of the bar. Testimony to the pedigree of this establishment is the large number of framed awards hung around the bar and the numerous CAMRA newsletters from around the country. Q❀◑🚌(17)♣P

Wrecclesham

Sandrock
Sandrock Hill, Boundstone, GU10 4NS (off B3384)
SU830444
⏲ 12-11 (10.30 Sun)
☎ (01252) 715865 🌐 thesandrock.com
Beer range varies Ⓗ
Small, semi-rural and tucked away in the Farnham suburbs, this legendary free house is known by real ale enthusiasts for miles around. The cottage-style building is entered via a narrow door, with a choice of drinking areas. Eight handpumps vie for attention, concentrating on local micros with beers from Bowman usually available. Friendly and unpretentious, excellent food (not available Sat lunch or Sun eve) complements, rather than dominates, the beer. ♨Q❀◑🚌(16)P

Hops: the essential flavouring

Hops are famous for adding bitterness to beer. But this remarkable perennial climbing plant – a member of the hemp family, Cannabinaceae – also contains acids, oils and resins that impart delightful aromas and flavours to beer.

These can be detected in the form of pine, spice, sap and tart, citrus fruit. Fruit is often similar to lemon and orange, while some English hop varieties give powerful hints of apricots, blackcurrants and damsons. American hop varieties, the Cascade in particular, are famous for their grapefruit aroma and flavour.

Many British brewers now use hops from mainland Europe – such as Styrian Goldings from Slovenia and Saaz from the Czech Republic – that have been developed primarily for lager brewing. They impart a more restrained aroma and flavour, with a gentle, resinous character. Lager hops used in ale brewing are usually added late in the copper boil to give a fine aroma to the finished beer.

Kent is often thought of as the main hop-growing area of Britain but, in 2004, it was overtaken by Herefordshire. The main hop varieties used in cask beer production are the Fuggle and Golding, but First Gold, introduced in the 1990s, is now a major variety. First Gold was one of the first dwarf or hedgerow hops that grow to only half the height of conventional varieties. As a result, they are easier to pick, are less susceptible to disease and aphid attack and, therefore, use fewer agri-chemicals. In 2004, a new hop variety called Boadicea was introduced: it is the first aphid-resistant hop and therefore needs fewer pesticides. The hop industry is working on trials of new varieties that need no pesticides or fertilisers and should gain Soil Association approval as organic hops.

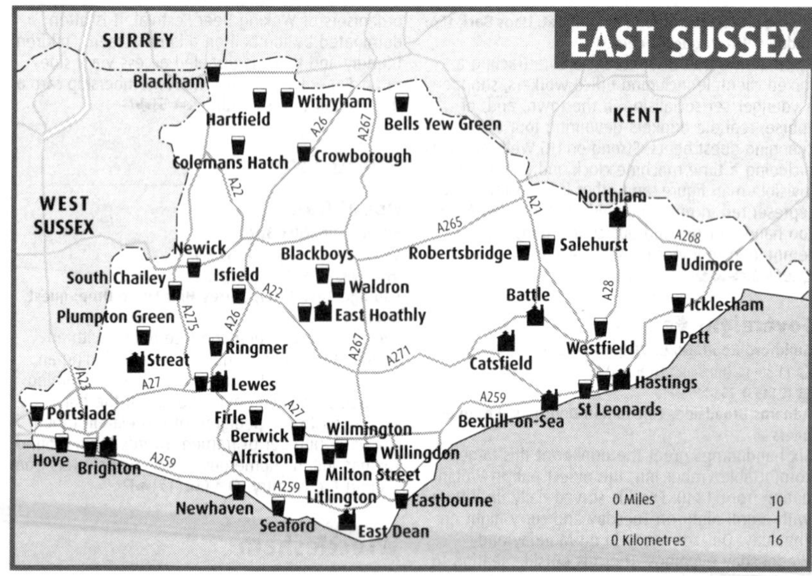

SUSSEX (EAST)

Alfriston

Olde Smugglers Inne

Waterloo Square, BN26 5UE (by market cross)
11-11; 12-10.30 Sun
(01323) 870241 yeoldesmugglersinne.co.uk
Harveys Sussex Best Bitter; Taylor Landlord; guest beers H
Ye Olde Smugglers Inne was built in 1358, and stills holds its character today with an impressive, dominating inglenook fireplace, oak beams, horse brasses and all sorts of interesting iron implements adorning the walls. Along with an extensive pub food menu it offers B&B. The newly revamped beer garden plays host to beer festivals in the barn over bank holiday weekends. Live music is played, in keeping with the pub. Q (126)

Bells Yew Green

Brecknock Arms

TN3 9BJ
12-3, 6-11; closed Mon; 12-11 Fri & Sat
(01892) 750237
Harveys XX Mild, Sussex Best Bitter, seasonal beers H
This traditional ale house dating from the 1850s has a welcoming open fire in its recently refurbished main bar. It is a tied house and pictures of Harveys Brewery adorn the walls. Very much the hub of the community, the pub has a number of local cricket teams visiting regularly. There is a full menu available.
Q (Frant) (256) P

Berwick

Cricketers' Arms

Berwick Village, BN26 6SP (S of A27, W of Drusilla's roundabout)
11-3, 6-11; 11-11 Sat & summer; 12-10.30 Sun
(01323) 870469 cricketersberwick.co.uk
Harveys Sussex Best Bitter, Armada Ale, seasonal beers G
Once two cottages, and a pub since the 18th century, it was extended in 1981 in keeping with its original character. Harvey's beers are served straight from the cask. There is plenty of room to sit in the pleasant gardens in summer or by the real fires in the bars in the winter. A popular stop for walkers on the nearby South Downs, toad in the hole can be played here. Meals are served all day at the weekend. Q P

Blackboys

Blackboys Inn

Lewes Road, TN22 5LG (on B2192 S of village)
11-11
(01825) 890283 theblackboysinn.co.uk
Harveys Hadlow Bitter, Sussex Best Bitter, seasonal beers H
This 14th-century village pub is set back from the road, opposite the pond. Two bars and two restaurant rooms are tastefully decorated with old prints, hop bines and interesting artefacts. Outside is a large terrace plus a covered smoking area, together with an intimate garden set aside for adults. Harveys Old Ale is available in winter, and there is an extensive food menu, from bar snacks to restaurant meals. Q P

Blackham

Sussex Oak

TN3 9UA (on A264)
11 (12 Sun)-11 (closed winter Tue)
(01892) 740273
Fuller's London Pride; Harveys Sussex Best Bitter; Larkins Chiddingstone; guest beers H
Formerly owned by Shepherd Neame, this roadside pub has recently become a free house, and is being carefully refurbished by the new owners. A very friendly pub where customers are immediately made welcome, a good range of home-cooked pub food is available. Local CAMRA Pub of the Year in 2003. Q (Ashurst) (234) P

Brighton

Basketmakers Arms ✔

12 Gloucester Road, BN1 4AD
⏲ 11-11 (midnight Fri & Sat); 12-11 Sun
☎ (01273) 689006 🌐 fullers.co.uk
Fuller's Discovery, ESB, London Pride; Gales HSB; Fuller's seasonal beers; guest beers Ⓗ
This Fuller's tied house has been run by the same landlord for over 20 years. A street-corner local in the busy North Laine area of the city, it is popular with shoppers and office workers. It has a good reputation for inexpensive home-cooked food made using organic, locally-sourced ingredients wherever possible. The walls are covered with old metal advertising signs and containers. It stocks a large selection of malt whiskies. ❀◐◑⇌🚌⅃

Battle of Trafalgar

34 Guildford Road, BN1 3LW
⏲ 12-11 (midnight Fri & Sat)
☎ (01273) 327997
Fuller's London Pride; Harveys Sussex Best Bitter; guest beers Ⓗ
Situated a short walk uphill from Brighton station, this popular pub serves two regular and two guest ales from its four handpumps. The pub, close to the Brighton Toy Museum in Trafalgar Street below the station, has a nautical feel and displays a collection of old beer bottles above the bar. Find the playing card on the ceiling. Good quality food is available lunchtimes and evenings (not Sat and Sun). Occasional live music plays on the last Sunday of the month. Q❀◐◑⇌🚌⅃

Constant Service ✔

96 Islingword Road, BN2 9SJ
⏲ 3-midnight (1am Fri); 12-1am Sat; 12-midnight Sun
☎ (01273) 607058
Harveys Sussex Best Bitter, Armada Ale, seasonal ales; guest beers Ⓗ
This very friendly pub, named after the Constant Service Water Company (the first water company to supply fresh piped water to the residents of Brighton), is a traditional street-corner local in the Hanover area of the city. It is a one-bar pub with, unusually for today, music provided by a record deck with a fine selection of LPs. Among the amenities is a walled garden with overhead heaters. Good value lunches are available on Sunday only. ❀◐🚌(25C,37)⅃

Evening Star

55-56 Surrey Street, BN1 3PB (200m S of station)
⏲ 12-11 (midnight Fri); 11.30-midnight Sat
☎ (01273) 328931 🌐 eveningstarbrighton.co.uk
Dark Star Hophead, seasonal beers; guest beers Ⓗ
The Evening Star is simply the most important real ale pub in Brighton. It is operated by the Dark Star brewery and up to four of its beers will be found alongside three guests, plus cider or perry. If these fail to meet your needs there are continental beers on tap and a large range of worldwide bottled ales. The pub holds regular beer festivals and is, needless to say, very popular and often crowded, particularly at weekends. ❀♿⇌🚌🍎⅃

Greys

105 Southover Street, BN2 9UA (500m E of A270 opp The Level)
⏲ 4-11 (12.30am Fri); 12-12.30am Sat; 12-11 Sun
☎ (01273) 680734 🌐 greyspub.com
Harveys Sussex Best Bitter; Taylor Landlord Ⓗ
Single-bar street-corner Victorian pub situated half way up a steep hill in the Hanover district. The L-shaped room has a wooden floor, with a mixture of benches and settles. Look out for the stuffed crow. Food is available Tuesday-Thursday, Saturday evenings and weekend lunchtimes. Bottled Belgian beers are stocked and an annual Belgian beer festival is held. Live music is performed by artists from the UK and the USA. Check the website for details of food and events. ❀◐◑🚌(37,37B)⅃

Lion & Lobster

24 Sillwood Street, BN1 2PS (jct of Bedford Square and Bedford Place)
⏲ 11-11 (2am Fri & Sat); 12-midnight Sun
☎ (01273) 327299
Dark Star Festival, Hophead; Greene King Abbot; Harveys Sussex Best Bitter; guest beers Ⓗ
Popular back-street pub situated between the seafront and Western Road about a mile from the city centre. The dark interior with subdued lighting gives the pub a relaxing atmosphere. All available wall space is covered with old prints and photographs. The bar is close to the door and can get a little crowded at times but a spacious back room gives extra seating. The upstairs restaurant serves good quality home-made food. There is also a rooftop smoking terrace. Dog friendly. ❀◐◑🚌⅃

Lord Nelson Inn ✔

36 Trafalgar Street, BN1 4ED (200m S of station)
⏲ 12-11 (midnight Fri & Sat); 12-10.30 Sun
☎ (01273) 695872 🌐 thelordnelsoninn.co.uk
Harveys XX Mild, Hadlow Bitter, Sussex Best Bitter, Armada Ale, seasonal beers Ⓗ
Two-bar back-street local in Brighton's North Laine area. The back bar area and conservatory beyond are used for meetings, as a gallery and function room, with a heated patio smoking area off the conservatory. A folk club entertains on the first Monday of the month and there is a quiz night on Tuesday as well as occasional live music (see website). The pub is a local Ale Trail and Guide regular. Food is served daily with pizzas and pasta in the evenings (not Sun). Thatchers organic bottled cider and perry are available. ❀◐⇌🚌🍎⅃

Mitre Tavern ✔

13 Baker Street, BN1 4JN
⏲ 10.30-11; 12-10.30 Sun
☎ (01273) 683173 🌐 mitretavern.co.uk
Harveys XX Mild, Sussex Best Bitter, Armada Ale, seasonal beers Ⓗ
You will find this Harvey's tied house in a side street close to the London Road shops and the Open Market. The traditional pub, which attracts a more mature customer, is divided into a long narrow bar with a TV at one end and a cosy snug. Smokers can use the outside courtyard at the rear. Hadlow IPA and Old Ale (in winter), as well as

INDEPENDENT BREWERIES

1648 East Hoathly
Beachy Head East Dean
Fallen Angel Battle
FILO Hastings
Full Moon Catsfield (NEW)
Harveys Lewes
Kemptown Brighton
Rectory Streat
Rother Valley Northiam
White Bexhill-on-Sea

other Harvey's seasonal beers, regularly complement the three regulars on the pub's five handpumps. ❀⇛(London Rd)🚌♣⛳

Prestonville Arms ✔

64 Hamilton Road, BN1 5DN (between Preston Circus and Seven Dials)

✪ 5-11; 12-midnight Fri & Sat; 12-11 Sun

☎ (01273) 701007 🌐 theprestonvillearms.co.uk

Fuller's London Pride, seasonal beers; Gale's Butser, HSB; guest beers Ⓗ

This traditional local pub has a horseshoe-shaped bar and is situated on a hilly corner in a residential area. A Fuller's tied house, it has wood-panelled walls covered with pictures of historic Brighton. There is plenty of seating indoors and a patio garden outside. Special nights include Tuesday music quiz, Wednesday curry night and Sunday general knowledge quiz. Good pub food is served along with up to five real ales. 🏠❀◑⇛⛳

Pump House ✔

46 Market Street, BN1 1HH

✪ 10-11 (midnight Fri & Sat)

☎ (01273) 827421

Caledonian Deuchars IPA; Fuller's London Pride; Harveys Sussex Best Bitter; Shepherd Neame Spitfire; guest beers Ⓗ

One of the oldest buildings in the renowned Laines area of Brighton, it is named after the original 19th-century sea water pump house. This comfortable pub now offers five hand-pulled real ales. A sampling tray of one-third pint measures of all five beers can be purchased. Excellent food is served all day including 11 types of sausage. There is also an upstairs bar and dining area. A weekly pub quiz is held. ❀◑🚌⛳

Sir Charles Napier ✔

50 Southover Street, BN2 9UE

✪ 4-11; 3-midnight Fri; 12-midnight Sat; 12-11 Sun

☎ (01273) 601413 🌐 fullers.co.uk

Fuller's London Pride, seasonal beers; Gale's HSB; guest beers Ⓗ

One of the last truly traditional pubs in the newly trendy Hanover area, the Napier appeals to a varied cross section of customers. The walls provide a pictorial history of the area plus local maps and items relating to Admiral Sir Charles Napier of Crimean War fame. Pizzas are usually available, along with roast lunches on Sunday. A sheltered, walled garden at the rear is popular, not just with smokers. Q❀◑🚌(37,37B)⛳

Station

1 Hampstead Road, BN1 5NG (opp Preston Park Station)

✪ 11-11 (midnight Thu-Sat); 12-11 Sun

☎ (01273) 501318

Harveys Sussex Best Bitter; guest beers Ⓗ

Imposing Victorian corner pub opposite Preston Park Station, very busy on Brighton & Hove Albion home match days. A single bar serves a raised seating area with real fire, main bar and pool table. Etched windows read 'The Station' and 'Spirits, Beers, Wines'. Small watercolours, railway and brass paraphernalia adorn the walls and two cats and a dog are in residence. Pizzas are served to accompany the regular Harveys, and up to five guest ales. Bottled Westons cider is usually available. 🏠❀◑⇛(Preston Park)🚌●⛳

Colemans Hatch

Hatch Inn

TN7 4EJ (400m S of B2110)

✪ 11.30-3, 5.30-11; 12-10.30 Sun

☎ (01342) 822363 🌐 hatchinn.co.uk

Harveys Sussex Best Bitter; Larkins Traditional; guest beers Ⓗ

Originally three 15th-century cottages, this building has been an inn for the last 200 years. An attractive low-beamed pub, it is extremely popular with visitors to the nearby Ashdown Forest and has two large gardens for summer dining. The meals of locally sourced food are renowned and have earned several accolades. Close by is (Winnie the) Pooh Bridge, Ashdown Forest Visitor Centre and the llama farm. The pub has featured in many TV adverts. 🏠❀◑♿⛺🚌P

Crowborough

Cooper's Arms

Coopers Lane, TN6 1SN (follow St John's Rd from Crowborough Cross)

✪ 12-2.30 (not Mon), 6 (5 Fri)-11; 12-10.30 Sun

☎ (01892) 654796

Greene King IPA; guest beers Ⓗ

A free house well worth visiting for its ever changing range of beers, including many from Sussex breweries. The simply-furnished interior includes a main bar, a small bar with a dartboard and TV, and a separate dining room. Food is served lunchtimes, and Wednesday to Saturday evenings. Thursday is quiz night. Petanque is played. Beer festivals are held at Easter, the August bank holiday and the end of November, as well as some themed weekends. Q❀◑🚌♣P

Wheatsheaf ✔

Mount Pleasant, Jarvis Brook, TN6 2NF

✪ 12-11 (10.30 Sun)

☎ (01892) 663756 🌐 wheatsheafcrowborough.co.uk

Harveys XX Mild, Hadlow Bitter, Sussex Best Bitter, seasonal beers Ⓗ

Most Harvey's regular and seasonal beers are available here, while beer festivals at the end of May and October concentrate mainly on ales from micro-breweries from around the country. Live music is performed twice a month on a Saturday. Lunches are served daily except Sunday and evening meals Tuesday to Thursday only. Dating from 1750, this pub has three separate drinking areas located around a square bar, each with an open fire. 🏠❀🛏◑⇛🚌♣●P⛳

East Hoathly

King's Head

1 High Street, BN8 6DR

✪ 11-11 (midnight Fri & Sat); 12-11 Sun

☎ (01825) 840238 🌐 kingshead1648.co.uk

1648 Signature, Original, seasonal beers; Harveys Sussex Best Bitter; guest beers Ⓗ

Once the village school, and mentioned in Thomas Turner's Diary, this traditional 17th-century pub serves a choice of beers from the adjoining 1648 Brewery. A restaurant area offers an extensive menu of good home-cooked food lunchtimes and evenings. There are also function rooms and a family area. Old prints of the pub and local events decorate the walls. At the rear there is an ancient walled beer garden with further seating at the front. 🏠Q🍼❀◑🚌●P⛳

Eastbourne

Dewdrop Inn

37-39 South Street, BN21 4UP (E of town hall)
11-midnight (1am Fri & Sat); 12-midnight Sun
(01323) 723313
Greene King IPA, H&H Olde Trip; guest beers H
Situated in the 'Little Chelsea' area, close to the Saffrons football and cricket grounds, this pub is popular with drinkers of all ages. One central bar serves the horseshoe-shaped drinking area which is split into two. There is a small garden to the rear, occasional live music and food is served from 12-6pm.

Hurst Arms

76 Willingdon Road, BN21 1TW (on A2270)
11-11; 12-10.30 Sun
(01323) 721762
Harveys Sussex Best Bitter, Armada Ale, seasonal beers H
This welcoming Victorian local has two widely differing bars: an inviting cosy lounge and a lively public bar with two wide-screen TVs, a jukebox, dartboard and pool table. There is a rear garden and a front patio. Harveys beers are served in excellent condition. Two beer festivals are held each year.

Lamb

36 High Street, BN21 1HH (on A259 in Old Town)
10.30-11 (midnight Fri & Sat)
(01323) 720545
Harveys Hadlow Bitter, Sussex Best Bitter, Armada Ale, seasonal beers H
This 12th-century pub situated next to St Mary's Church in the old town is a Harvey's tied house of great character, with wooden beams and unusual features. Two traditional bars and a third sunken area have access to the U-shaped servery. A folk club and Sussex Story Tellers meet here regularly in an upstairs function room with its own bar. Generally four Harvey's beers are available.
Q

Ship

33-35 Meads Street, BN20 7RH
10-11 (midnight Sat); 10-10.30 Sun
(01323) 733815 shipatmeads.co.uk
Beachy Head Original; Draught Bass; Harveys Sussex Best Bitter; Shepherd Neame Kent's Best H
The large single bar has separate comfortable seating and dining areas. Outside is a large garden with two split decked areas and a garden bar used during events and in the summer. There is also a conservatory mainly set for dining. The varied food menu is complemented by a consistent beer range.
Q

Terminus Hotel

153 Terminus Road, BN21 3NU
10-midnight (1am Fri & Sat)
(01323) 733964
Harveys XX Mild, Hadlow Bitter, Sussex Best Bitter, Armada Ale, seasonal beers H
This Victorian building is situated in a pedestrian area with tables and chairs set out in front. It has a conservatory-style extension at the side for dining and drinking. Inside, the single bar benefits from natural light from front windows and a large skylight. The restaurant area is to the rear. Upstairs is a pool lounge and function room. Wi-Fi Internet access is available.

Victoria Hotel

27 Latimer Road, BN22 7BU (behind TAVR Centre, off A259)
11-11 (1am Fri & Sat); 12-10.30 Sun
(01323) 722673 victoriaeastbourne.co.uk
Harveys XX Mild, Sussex Best Bitter, Armada Ale, seasonal beers H
Friendly family-run local situated close to the seafront and the Redoubt fortress. The large front bar has two TVs with an emphasis on sport, while the smaller back room has pool and toad in the hole tables, a dartboard and TV. A beer festival is hosted over the Easter weekend in the secluded rear garden. Good value pub food is served Thursday to Sunday, lunchtimes and evenings. A meat raffle is held on Sunday.

Firle

Ram Inn

The Street, BN8 6NS
11.30-11; 12-10.30 Sun
(01273) 858222 theram-inn.com
Harveys Sussex Best Bitter, seasonal beers; guest beers H
A rambling old country pub with dark painted walls and low-beamed ceilings made cosy with roaring fires in two of its many rooms. It is reputed to be haunted. Locally sourced quality food is served every day except Monday evening, with the menu changing daily (booking recommended, especially Sun lunch). Regular and seasonal beers are from Harveys of Lewes with other handpumps used for guest beers and real cider or perry.
Q (25,125)P

Hartfield

Anchor

Church Street, TN7 4AG (on B2110)
11-11; 12-10.30 Sun
(01892) 770424
Harveys Sussex Best Bitter; Larkins Traditional; guest beers H
A basic village local dating from the 14th-century with two bars and a separate restaurant. It is situated in the centre of the historic village of Hartfield, famous for Pooh Bridge, and an ideal base for exploring the attractions of Ashdown Forest. The guest beers usually come from local breweries. Q P

Hastings

First In Last Out

14-15 High Street, TN34 3EY (in Old Town, near Stables Theatre)
12 (11 Sat)-11 (midnight Fri & Sat)
(01424) 425079 thefilo.co.uk
FILO Mike's Mild, Crofters, Ginger Tom, Cardinal, Gold; guest beers H
Situated in the old town of Hastings and home of the FILO brewery since 1985, the pub has a large bar, heated by an attractive central open fire. Four beers are usually available, sometimes including guests. Organic, freshly cooked food is served Tuesday to Saturday lunchtimes and tapas on Monday lunchtime and evening. Beer festivals are held in the garden at the rear of the pub on most bank holiday weekends. Q

Jenny Lind

69 High Street, TN34 3EW
⊙ 11-midnight (2am Fri & Sat); 12-11 Sun
☎ (01424) 421392
Courage Directors; Sharp's Doom Bar; Young's Bitter; guest beers Ⓗ
A popular two bar pub in the heart of Hastings historic old town serving a good range of beers from five handpumps. It hosts live music at weekends and holds a monthly quiz night. Both bars have warming log fires in the winter. The pub is next door to Hastings historic museum.
⩩Q❀⛟◐⊟♿⊟♣⊱–

White Rock Hotel

1-10 White Rock, TN34 1JU (on A259 opp pier)
⊙ 10 (12 Sun)-11
☎ (01424) 422240 ⊕ thewhiterockhotel.com
Beer range varies Ⓗ
The hotel next door to the White Rock Theatre has a stylish, recently refurbished contemporary bar, serving four ever changing beers, all from independent Sussex breweries. A good range of freshly prepared food is available throughout the day. The large bar area has ample seating and a spacious outside terrace that overlooks the seafront. The hotel has many rooms with sea views. Q❀⛟◐⇌⊟●

Hove

Cliftonville Inn ✔

98-101 George Street, BN3 3YE
⊙ 9-11 (midnight Fri & Sat)
☎ (01273) 726969
Beer range varies Ⓗ
Unprepossessing former furniture store on a busy part-pedestrianised shopping street in the heart of Hove. The walls of this single room bar are decorated with framed panels on local historic topics, with a coal-effect gas fire at one end. As well as Wetherspoon's usual selection of national beers, it offers a changing range of local guest ales often coming from Arundel, WJ King and Weltons. Two Westons ciders also available on handpump.
◐⇌⊟●

Downsman

189 Hangleton Way, BN3 8ES (N of Hangleton)
⊙ 11.30-4, 6-11; 12-4.30, 7-11 Sun
☎ (01273) 711301
Harveys Sussex Best Bitter; guest beers Ⓗ
Friendly two-bar pub on the northern edge of Hangleton, next to the start of the Dyke Railway Trail. The saloon bar is decorated with rural prints and is cosy in winter, with a roaring real fire. There is a separate dining area and Sunday roasts are popular; meals are available at lunchtime every day and Monday to Friday evenings. Smokers are well catered for in a substantial shelter with heating and lighting. Two guest beers are usually available. ⩩❀◐⊟⊟(5,16)P⊱–

Neptune Inn

10 Victoria Terrace, Kingsway, BN3 2WB (on Coast Road)
⊙ 12-1am (2am Fri & Sat); 12-midnight Sun
☎ (01273) 736390 ⊕ theneptunelivemusicbar.co.uk
Dark Star Hophead; Greene King Abbot; Harveys Sussex Best Bitter, seasonal beers; guest beers Ⓗ
A traditional local free house on the Brighton to Shoreham seafront road, close to Hove's shopping area. There is a strong live music theme, with gigs on Friday and Sunday – blues and rock acts being the most regular. The narrow single bar interior has wood-panelled walls covered with pictures of musicians. There are up to five real ales available.
⊟(20)

Icklesham

Queen's Head 🏆

Parsonage Lane, TN36 4BL (off A259, opp village hall)
⊙ 11-11; 12-10.30 Sun
☎ (01424) 814552 ⊕ queenshead.com
Greene King IPA; guest beers Ⓗ
This Guide regular is always worth a visit. A busy pub all year round, it serves five to six beers of varied strength and style, complemented by an interesting, affordable menu. Local cider is also available. It hosts a mini beer festival in the autumn and live music most Sundays. The interior is split into five areas, with an eclectic mix of decorations and memorabilia. A spacious garden offers great views towards Rye. CAMRA branch Pub of the Year 2009. ⩩❀◐⊟♣●P⊱–⊓

Robin Hood

Main Road, TN36 4BD
⊙ 11.30-3, 7-11; 11.30-11 Fri & Sat; 12-5, 7-10.30 Sun
☎ (01424) 814277
Greene King IPA; guest beers Ⓗ
A family-run pub dating from 1607 with parts rebuilt in 1812 following fire damage. There are two bars, one with a pool table and open fire, the other leading to a dining area where excellent home-cooked food is served (not Tue eve). There is a children's play area in the garden. In July the pub hosts the village beer festival and in November the Robin Hood Bonfire Society. ⩩❀◐⊟♿⊟♣P⊱–

Isfield

Laughing Fish ✔

Station Road, TN22 5XB (off A26 between Lewes and Uckfield)
⊙ 11.30-11
☎ (01825) 750349 ⊕ laughingfishonline.co.uk
Greene King IPA, H&H Olde Trip, seasonal beers; guest beers Ⓗ
Victorian village local situated next to the preserved Lavender Line Railway. It has a large, well-kept garden that includes a children's play area plus a heated, covered patio area for smokers. Good food is served (not Sun eve) with smaller portions available for senior citizens and children. A fish and chips takeaway service is also on offer Monday to Thursday. The pub runs numerous themed events and has popular bar games including darts and bar billiards. A regular on the Brighton and South Downs Ale Trail.
⩩❀◐⊟♿⛺⊟(29)♣P⊱–

Lewes

Brewers Arms

91 High Street, BN7 1XN (near Lewes Castle)
⊙ 10-11; 12-10.30 Sun
☎ (01273) 475524 ⊕ brewersarmslewes.co.uk
Harveys Sussex Best Bitter; guest beers Ⓗ
There has been a tavern on this site for at least 350 years but the current Overton and Page pub dates from 1906 (see the original architect's drawings in the front bar). Note the terracotta tiling on the

frontage and 'Shirley Brewery' etched windows at the side. The back bar is dedicated to sport with pool, darts and toad-in-the-hole available, sports-themed artwork on the walls and screens showing major events. The front bar is quieter and attracts more conversationally-minded customers. Biddenden dry cider is on handpump.
Q❀◖⊟≠🚌(28,29)♣🍎⁻

Elephant & Castle

White Hill, BN7 2DJ (off Fisher Street, near police station)
⏲ 11.30-11 (midnight Fri & Sat); 12-11 Sun
☎ (01273) 473797 🌐 elephantandcastlelewes.co.uk
Harveys Sussex Best Bitter; guest beers Ⓗ
Popular community pub catering for all ages, particularly younger drinkers in the evenings. Food is available lunchtimes and Tuesday to Thursday evenings. Games include pool, table football and darts. Lewes Saturday Folk Club, relocated here from the Lewes Arms, meets most weeks in the upstairs function room. Soul and reggae nights are held regularly. Comedy night is the first Friday of the month. The pub has its own Sunday League football team. Westons Old Rosie cider is on handpump. ⛫❀◖◗🚌(127)♣🍎⁻

Gardener's Arms

46 Cliffe High Street, BN7 2AN
⏲ 11-11; 12-10.30 Sun
☎ (01273) 474808
Harveys Sussex Best Bitter; guest beers Ⓗ
A compact, genuine two-bar corner free house. Harveys Best is always stocked and the many guest beers come from small independent breweries. Westons Organic and Black Rat ciders are available on handpump. The bar is decorated with pictures of scenes of Lewes from bygone days; note also the collection of Archers pump clips. The pub's sporting teams include cricket, stoolball and the Sussex game of toad-in-the-hole. Locally sourced pies, sausage rolls and pasties are available.
≠🚌(28,29)♣🍎

John Harvey Tavern ✔

Bear Yard, Cliffe High Street, BN7 2AN (opp Harveys Brewery)
⏲ 11-11; 12-10.30 Sun
☎ (01273) 479880 🌐 johnharveytavern.co.uk
Harveys Hadlow Bitter, Sussex Best Bitter, Armada Ale, seasonal beers Ⓗ
A two-room Harvey's tied house located opposite the entrance to the brewery. The main bar is busy, however there is a quieter side room decorated with pictures of old Lewes. The interior is bright with slate floors and wood-panelled walls. A good selection of food and wines is available together with at least four Harveys beers. An upstairs room is available for meetings. No meals Sunday evening. ⛫Q🛏❀◖◗≠🚌(28,29)

Litlington

Plough & Harrow

The Street, BN26 5RE
⏲ 12-3, 6.30-11; 12-11 Sat & Sun
☎ (01323) 870632
Dark Star Hophead; Harveys Sussex Best Bitter, seasonal beer; guest beer Ⓗ
Dating from the 17th century, this beamed village pub has a main bar leading to an unusual snug with a large open fireplace and a separate dining area. An interesting menu is available at all sessions featuring locally-sourced food. Darts is played and the pub has its own toad-in-the-hole team, the Long Man, named after the local downland chalk figure. ⛫❀◖◗♣P

Milton Street

Sussex Ox ✔

BN26 5RL (signed off A27)
⏲ 11.30-3, 6-11; 12-3, 6-10.30 (12-5 winter) Sun
☎ (01323) 870840 🌐 thesussexox.co.uk
Dark Star range; Harveys Sussex Best Bitter; guest beers Ⓗ
Located at the end of a meandering country lane, the pub sits in two acres of garden with pleasant country views. It has a small beamed and stone-floored bar, a good sized seating area and a restaurant. This is a popular pub due to a good selection of well-kept ales and home-cooked food of a high standard. ⛫Q❀◖◗P

Newhaven

Jolly Boatman

133-135 Lewes Road, BN9 9SJ (N of town centre)
⏲ 11-11 (midnight Fri & Sat); 11-10.30 Sun
☎ (01273) 510030
Harveys Sussex Best Bitter; guest beers Ⓗ
A welcoming street-corner. The single bar is on two levels, offering an ever-changing range of three guest beers, usually from local breweries, plus Harveys Best as a regular. Real cider is also available in summer. Crib and darts are played and the pub hosts a quiz twice a month and regular slide shows in winter. A wide range of snacks, chocolate and sweets is stocked.
⛫≠(Town)🚌(123)♣🍎⁻

Newick

Royal Oak

1 Church Road, BN8 4JU
⏲ 11-11 (10.30 Sun)
☎ (01825) 722506
Fuller's London Pride; Harveys Sussex Best Bitter Ⓗ
A low, wide, brick interior welcomes you at this pub which has two rooms, one with an attached dining area. The cosy fire by the bar is popular with locals in winter and a plethora of ceramic mugs hangs over diners. The public or games bar has a pool table and a little nook to park any children behind the fireplace. Dogs appear to be welcome to romp around and beg for beer mats. Cider is available in summer. ⛫❀◖◗⊟🚌(31,121)🍎P

Pett

Two Sawyers

TN35 4HB
⏲ 11-11; 12-10.30 Sun
☎ (01424) 812255 🌐 twosawyers.co.uk
Harveys Sussex Best Bitter; guest beers Ⓗ
Following a long closure, this 16th-century pub, once a regular in the Guide, now has new owners and once more welcomes real ale drinkers. Serving mostly local beers and providing an excellent menu, it is popular with locals, walkers and campers. Situated in the heart of the village, it comprises two main bars, real fires and a restaurant with several dining areas. The bars are decorated with an interesting array of saws.
⛫Q❀◖◗⊟♿⛺🚌(347)♣🍎P⁻

Plumpton Green

Plough Inn ✔

South Road, BN7 3DF (N of village)
⏲ 12-11 (10.30 Sun)
☎ (01273) 890311 🌐 harveys.org.uk
Harveys Sussex Best Bitter, seasonal beers Ⓗ
Now in the hands of a family experienced in managing pubs to a CAMRA award-winning standard, this pub offers a range of Harvey's cask and bottled beers in two comfortable bars, both warmed by open fires, or in a pleasant garden. Meals can be selected from an imaginative menu. A memorial to Polish Spitfire crews stands in the car park while other war memorabilia adorns the interior walls. Families are welcome.
♨❀◖◗⊟♿🚌(166)♣●P⚟

Portslade

Stanley Arms 🏆

47 Wolseley Road, BN41 1SS
⏲ 3 (4 Mon)-11; 12-11 Sat; 12-10.30 Sun
☎ (01273) 430234 🌐 thestanley.com
Beer range varies Ⓗ
A genuine family-run free house, five handpumps provide a constantly varying selection of beers from all over the UK, real cider and perry, plus an extensive range of British and Belgian bottled beers. Beer festivals are held in spring, summer and autumn, and evening cellar tours are held on the last Monday of the month with reduced price beer and free nibbles. Various hot and cold snacks are served. The pub organises quiz evenings and has a football team. Local CAMRA Pub of the Year 2009. ♨❀⊟⇌(Fishersgate)🚌(2,46)♣●⚟⊔

Ringmer

Cock Inn

Uckfield Road, BN8 5RX (on slip road off A26)
⏲ 11-3, 6-11; 11-11 Sun
☎ (01273) 812040 🌐 cockpub.co.uk
Fuller's London Pride; Harveys Sussex Best Bitter, seasonal beers; guest beers Ⓗ
Hidden on a bypassed section of the A26, this 16th-century pub is renowned locally for the quality of its food and drink. The delightful bar area has exposed beams, a stone floor and an inglenook fireplace. The main dining areas are housed in newer extensions. The regular beers are supplemented in winter by Harveys Old and in summer by locally brewed guest beers such as Dark Star Hophead. Real cider is available in summer. ♨❀◖◗🚌(29,29A)●P⚟

Robertsbridge

George Inn

High Street, TN32 5AW
⏲ 11-3, 6-11; 11-11 Fri & Sat; closed Mon; 12-10 Sun
☎ (01580) 880315
Harveys Sussex Best Bitter; Rother Valley beer range; guest beers Ⓗ
Here customers are given a warm welcome by Stanley the Bassett Hound as well as the staff. Three handpumps supply an ever-changing range of beers. There is a small bar next to an inglenook fireplace at the head of a long dining area which serves home-cooked food, locally supplied within a 30 mile radius. A dog-friendly pub.
♨Q❀◖◗♿⇌(Robertsbridge)🚌P⚟

St Leonards

Bull

530 Bexhill Road, TN38 8AY (on A259, W of St Leonards)
⏲ 11-11; 12-10.30 Sun
☎ (01424) 424984 🌐 the-bull-inn.com
Shepherd Neame Master Brew Bitter, Kent's Best, Spitfire, seasonal beers Ⓗ
Welcoming roadside pub noted for its range of Shepherd Neame beers and voted best pub in the Hastings area in 2006 and 2007 by local newspaper readers. It offers an excellent menu of home-cooked food. The large rear garden has barbecue facilities and a covered smoking area. The pub is convenient for the Glynde Gap shopping centre.
♨Q❀◖◗♿🚌♣P⚟

Dripping Spring

34 Tower Road, TN37 6JE
⏲ 11.30-11 (midnight Fri & Sat)
☎ (01424) 436222
Beer range varies Ⓗ
This small back-street pub in the Bohemia area is once again rising to the fore with its interesting selection of real ales. Robin and Joan have established a warm and friendly atmosphere in this two-bar pub. Four to six beers are regularly available to suit all palates, as well as real cider. Food is served at lunchtime and by request on some evenings. The walled garden to the rear is very popular in summer.
Q❀◖⊟⇌(Warrior Square)🚌♣●⚟

Horse & Groom

4 Mercatoria, TN38 0EB
⏲ 11-11; 12-10.30 Sun
☎ (01424) 420612 🌐 sussex200.com
Adnams Broadside; Fuller's ESB; Greene King IPA; Harveys Sussex Best Bitter; guest beers Ⓗ
A first-class free house, at the heart of Old St Leonards, serving a good range of beers. The unusual horseshoe-shaped bar forms two areas, with a quiet room at the rear. An adjoining restaurant is open Tuesday to Saturday evenings and Sunday lunchtime. The pub is a short walk from the sea and Warrior Square station.
♨Q❀♿⇌(Warrior Sq)♣⚟

Salehurst

Halt

Church Lane, TN32 5PH (by church)
⏲ 12-3, 6-11; 12-11 Fri-Sun; closed Mon
☎ (01580) 880620
Harveys Sussex Best Bitter; guest beers Ⓗ
Originally a steam railway stop on a hop-picking line, this historic, community-led free house was saved from redevelopment by two local families who now own and run it. The traditional single bar features an open fire, low beams, oak floors, wooden furniture and a comfortable snug, while the rear patio and garden afford views over the Rother Valley. The menu includes dishes made from locally reared meat. Live music plays on alternate Sundays from 4pm. Draught cider is often available. ♨Q❀◖◗♣●⚟

Seaford

Cinque Ports ✔

49 High Street, BN25 1PP
⏲ 11-midnight; 12-11.30 Sun

(01323) 892391
Harveys Sussex Best Bitter; Wychwood Hobgoblin; Young's Special; guest beers H
Traditional family-run pub situated in central Seaford within walking distance of the station. The single bar has a real log fire in winter and comfy leather sofas. Food is available daily. A good range of beers includes regulars from Harveys, Hobgoblin and Young's as well as a guest ale. Various sports channels are shown on two TVs. A wide age range of customers and dogs are welcome. Darts and poker are played and there are quiz and charity nights.

South Chailey

Horns Lodge
South Street, BN8 4BD (on A275)
11.30-2.30 (not Tue), 5.30-11; 11.30-11 Sat; 12-10.30 Sun
(01273) 400422 hornslodge.com
Harveys Sussex Best Bitter; guest beers H
This 200-year-old coaching inn is a former Guide entry, now happily restored to its former glory. From its roadside location the pub offers good ales to enjoy in a comfortable bar warmed by log fires in winter or the pleasant garden in summer. Home-cooked meals are available in the restaurant, with pizzas a feature. Traditional pub games are well supported here as are the speciality evenings held throughout the year. Westons perry is available on handpump.
(121)P

Udimore

Kings Head
Rye Road, TN31 6BG (on B2089, W of village)
11-3.30 (not Mon), 6-11; 11-3.30, 6-11 Sun
(01424) 882349
Harveys Sussex Best Bitter; guest beers H
Built in 1535, then extended in the 17th century, this traditional village ale house features exposed beams, two open fires and a very long bar. The pub serves excellent home-cooked food (lunch Tue-Sun, eves Mon-Sat). Trevor and Anita have run the pub for 21 years and this year marks its 15th consecutive year in the Guide. Situated in an area of outstanding natural beauty, there are many scenic walks nearby, while pleasant views over the surrounding countryside unfold from the garden.
QP

Waldron

Star Inn
TN21 0RA
11-3, 6-11; 12-11 Sun
(01435) 812495
Draught Bass; Harveys Sussex Best Bitter; guest beers H
A friendly, busy old traditional village pub dating back to the 17th century with an inglenook fireplace, wood and tiled flooring, oak panelling and beams helping to maintain its true character. There are highly polished horse brasses, artefacts and old pictures of the pub adorning the walls, and even a list of licensees since 1750. A separate restaurant serves good quality food. Outside is a large beer garden with plenty of seating. Toad-in the-hole is played here. QP

Westfield

Old Courthouse
Main Road, TN35 4QE TQ812154
12-11 (10.30 Sun)
(01424) 751603 oldcourthousepub.com
Harveys Sussex Best Bitter; guest beers H
Located in the centre of the village, the pub is very community focused. The main bar has an open fire and low ceilings and there is a smaller second bar. Traditional games are played including bar billiards and darts. Hot food is served until 9pm every day, plus a roast on Sunday lunchtime. The first Friday of the month is curry night. A mini beer festival is held on the August bank holiday weekend. CAMRA South East Sussex Pub of the Year 2007.
QP

Willingdon

Red Lion
99 Wish Hill, BN20 9HQ (S end of village)
11-3, 5-11; 11-11 Fri-Sun
(01323) 502062
Badger K&B Sussex, First Gold, Tanglefoot, seasonal beers H
A popular village pub with new tenants who have plenty of experience. There are two brick fireplaces in the main bar, and bar billiards and darts are played. The dining area at the rear leads to a well-used split-level garden with good, solid wooden garden furniture. Excellent home-cooked food is on offer. An annual beer festival takes place over the August bank holiday weekend. No food Sunday evening after 6pm. P

Wilmington

Giant's Rest
The Street, BN26 5SQ (off A27)
11-3, 6-11; 11.30-11 Sat; 12-10.30 Sun
(01323) 870207 giantsrest.co.uk
Harveys Sussex Best Bitter; Hop Back Summer Lightning; Taylor Landlord H
This Victorian building can be seen from the main road. The interior is wooden, with wooden table games distributed round the pub. Occasionally a seasonal beer may replace one of the three regulars. A varied and interesting menu is available, featuring mainly local produce. The outside seating area is ideal for walkers visiting the Long Man, a nearby chalk figure cut into the Downs. (126)P

Withyham

Dorset Arms
TN7 4BD (on B2110)
11.30-3 (not Mon), 6-11; 12-3, 7-10.30 Sun
(01892) 770278 dorset-arms.co.uk
Harveys Hadlow Bitter, Sussex Best Bitter, seasonal beers H
This attractive 16th-century Harvey's pub set back from the B2110 is a regular entry in the Guide. Close to Ashdown Forest, it is an ideal calling point for those on a Wealden Tour. The large dining area is separate from the bar, which has bare floorboards and a large open fireplace. A varied choice of meals is available (not Sun eve or Mon) and booking is advisable. Dogs are welcome.
(291)P

SUSSEX (WEST)

Amberley

Sportsman

Rackham Road, Cross Gates, BN18 9NR
⏲ 11 (12 Sun)-11
☎ (01798) 831787
Dark Star Hophead; Fuller's London Pride; Harveys Sussex Best Bitter; guest beers 🄷
The genial hosts here offer a warm welcome to drinkers, diners and walkers. The cosy central bar is decorated with Guinness posters and the games room has an old brick floor, while the sun lounge and open decking have magnificent views of the Arun Valley Wild Brooks. The guest beers and ingredients for the excellent food are mostly obtained locally, except the delicious Salcombe ice cream. Local CAMRA Country Pub of the Year 2009.
⛫Q❀🛏◑◐⊟♿♣P

Arundel

King's Arms

36 Tarrant Street, BN18 9DN
⏲ 11-11; 12-10.30 Sun
☎ (01903) 882312 🌐 tinyurl.com/2axe8p
Fuller's London Pride; Young's Special; guest beers 🄷
The King's Arms is situated in one of Arundel's more Bohemian streets, just below the cathedral. This reputedly 500-year-old free house comprises a lounge, separate public bar with jukebox, snug and a heated rear patio with awning for smokers. No food is available, just bring your own (no chips and vinegar, please). If you use your mobile phone you get fined and the RNLI profits. Tuesday is quiz night. A Wi-Fi and dog friendly pub.
❀⊟⛺⇌🚌(84,700)♣⚐

Bepton

Country Inn

Severals Road, GU29 0LR (1 mile SW of Midhurst)
SU870206
⏲ 11.30-3, 5-11; 11.30-11.30 Fri & Sat; 12-10.30 Sun
☎ (01730) 813466 🌐 thecountryinn.co.uk
Ballard's Midhurst Mild; Sharp's Doom Bar; Young's Bitter; guest beer 🄷
Popular local in a quiet spot, an easy walk down the lane from Midhurst and the bus stop for Chichester. A single bar serves two distinct drinking areas on one side, with a log fire opposite. The changing guest beer comes from a small brewer. The dining area enjoys a busy trade (not Sun eve). Outside at the front there are tables, while the extensive rear garden has children's play equipment. Closing time may be later on busy nights. ⛫Q❀◑◐🚌(60)♣P⚐

Bognor Regis

Alex

56 London Road, PO21 1PU (150m SE of railway station)
⏲ 10-11 (midnight Fri & Sat); 12-5 Sun
☎ (01243) 863308
Courage Best Bitter; Greene King Old Speckled Hen; guest beer 🄷
A pleasant and friendly town pub, basically one bar, with seating at the rear, a dining area to the right and a snug to the left. The pub is festooned with mugs hanging from the ceiling and there is always a vase of flowers on the bar. The single guest beer is often from an unusual independent brewery for the area. The attractive rear patio has a sheltered, heated area for smokers.
Q❀◑⇌🚌(700)⚐

Burgess Hill

Watermill Inn

1 Leylands Road, RH15 0QF
⏲ 11 (12 Sun)-11
☎ (01444) 235517
Fuller's London Pride; Goddards Ale of Wight, Fuggle-De-Dum; guest beers 🄷
This regular on the CAMRA Ale Trail is a single bar community local in the World's End area of Burgess Hill. The guest beer is usually from a southern-based independent brewery and changes every month. The walled garden is ideal for families in summer and has an adjacent covered smoking area. A quiz is held every Thursday and varied live music is provided on Friday evening.
⛫❀⇌(Wivelsfield)🚌(40,40X)♣P⚐

Byworth

Black Horse

GU28 0HL (150m off A283, 1 mile SE of Petworth)
⏲ 11 (12 Sun)-11
☎ (01798) 342424 🌐 blackhorsebyworth.com
Dark Star Hophead; Flowerpots Bitter; Fuller's London Pride; guest beers 🄷
A welcoming Georgian-fronted pub, set in a rural hamlet of character, it was once part of the adjacent former tannery. The rustic front bar features a large open log fire. In several cosy areas to the rear, diners can enjoy dishes such as wild venison tartlet from a menu featuring locally-sourced produce. An attractive terraced garden leads down to a stream below and the nearby Virgin Mary spring. Daily Stagecoach buses link Worthing, Midhurst and nearby Petworth House.
⛫Q❀◑◐⊟🚌(1)♣P

Chichester

Bell Inn

3 Broyle Road, PO19 6AT (opp Festival Theatre)
⏲ 11.30-2.30, 5-midnight; 12-3, 7-midnight Sun
☎ (01243) 783388 🌐 thebellinnchichester.com
Beer range varies 🄷
Cosy, comfortable city local which is especially popular with theatre-goers. The ambience is enhanced by exposed brickwork, wooden panelling and beams. An extensive blackboard menu includes several vegetarian options (no food Sun eve). The beer range usually comprises two beers from the Enterprise range and one from a local micro. The rear suntrap garden has a covered smoking area heated by a coal stove.
Q❀◑◐⇌🚌(60)♣P⚐

Eastgate Inn

4 The Hornet, PO19 7JG (500m E of Market Cross, off Eastgate Square)
⏲ 12 (11 Wed; 10 Sat)-11 (midnight Fri & Sat); 12-11 Sun
☎ (01243) 774877
Fuller's Chiswick, London Pride, ESB; Gale's HSB; guest beer 🄷
A fine town pub that featured in the first edition of this Guide in 1973. Dating from 1793, the bar is now open plan, with an area for diners. At the rear

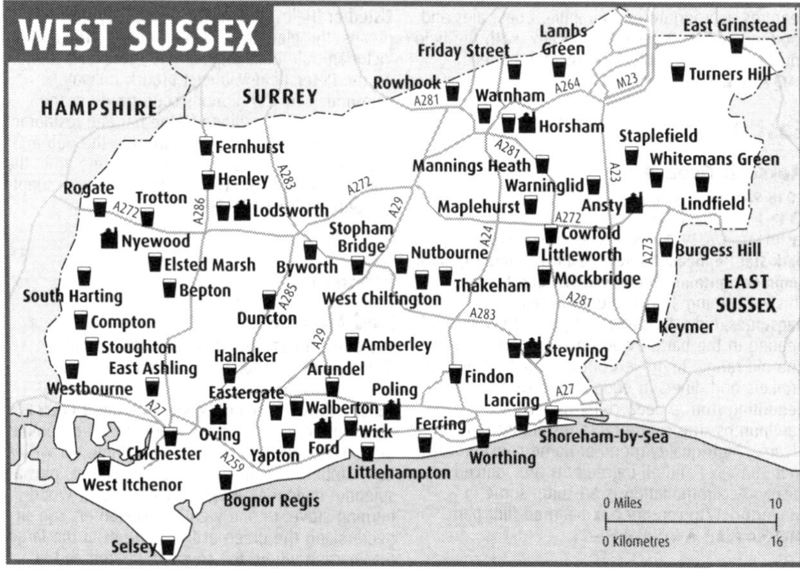

is a pool room and a patio garden. Good value traditional pub meals are served from the specials board at lunchtime and on summer evenings. Customers include locals, holidaymakers and visitors to the nearby market. A midsummer beer festival is hosted each year.

Four Chesnuts

234 Oving Road, PO19 7EJ (900m E of Market Cross)
12-11 (midnight Fri & Sat); 12-10.30 Sun
(01243) 779974
Arundel Sussex Mild; Langham Hip Hop; Oakleaf Hole Hearted; Taylor Landlord
Traditional town hostelry and local CAMRA Pub of the Year 2007, the Chesnuts has been converted to a single bar but retains its distinct drinking areas. The skittle alley doubles as a dining room at busy times and occasionally serves as a venue for successful beer festivals. The menu of good hearty meals includes a 'pie of the moment' (no food Sun eve). The pub has a Saturday music night and hosts the local folk club on Tuesday plus a regular quiz night on Wednesday. Football and rugby matches are often shown on TV. (700)P

Compton

Coach & Horses

The Square, PO18 9HA (on B2146)
12-3, 6-11; 12-4, 7-10.30 Sun
(02392) 631228
Dark Star Hophead; Harveys Sussex Best Bitter; guest beers
Sixteenth-century pub in a remote but charming village, close to lovely local walks. The front bar is warm and welcoming, with two open fires and internal window shutters. The rear bar is a restaurant (reservation required) – this is the oldest part of the pub and features plenty of exposed beams and another open fire. Up to five beers from independent breweries are usually available. There is a bar billiards table, and seats outside in the village square. Food is served Tuesday to Saturday.
Q(54)

Cowfold

Hare & Hounds

Henfield Road, RH13 8DR
11-3, 5-11.30; 11-midnight Sat & Sun
(01403) 865354 hare-and-hounds.co.uk
Fuller's London Pride; Harveys Sussex Best Bitter; WJ King seasonal ales; Weltons Pride 'n' Joy
This Victorian building was refurbished in 1995 from timber fallen in the 1987 Great Storm. In the bar area agricultural implements are displayed over a wood-burning fireplace. There are wooden settles and tables, comfy sofas and a flagstone floor. A step up takes you to a carpeted dining/drinking area. Very friendly staff and customers.
QP

Duncton

Cricketers

High Street, GU28 0LB
11 (12 Sun)-11
(01798) 342473 tinyurl.com/2bm4lv
King Horsham Best Bitter; Skinners Betty Stogs; guest beers
This listed 16th-century coaching inn featuring a large inglenook and wooden panelling was the last stop for the horses before Duncton Hill, on the London to Chichester route. The pub has recently been renovated by the new owner and has strong links with cricket. It was purchased by WG Grace for the famous Victorian cricketer James Dean, and

INDEPENDENT BREWERIES

Adur Steyning (NEW)
Arundel Ford
Ballard's Nyewood
Dark Star Ansty
Gribble Oving
Hammerpot Poling
Hepworth Horsham
King Horsham
Langham Lodsworth
Welton's Horsham

features appropriate memorabilia. Guest ales and food ingredients are sourced locally, with the field mushroom stack particularly recommended.
⛫Q❀◑●P

East Ashling

Horse & Groom

PO18 9AX (on B2178)
⏲ 12-3, 6-11; 12-6 Sun
☎ (01243) 575339 🌐 thehorseandgroomchichester.co.uk
Dark Star Hophead; Harveys Hadlow Bitter; Hop Back Summer Lightning; Young's Bitter; guest beer Ⓗ
This welcoming 17th-century inn features flagstones, old settles and half-panelled walls, with heating in the bar provided by an open fire and a fine old range. Improved but not spoilt, it attracts drinkers and diners in equal measure, the beers benefiting from a deep cellar under the handpumps. The comfortable restaurant offers a diverse, high-quality menu of home-cooked dishes (not Sun eve) and all ingredients are sourced locally. Accommodation is en-suite, some in a converted 17th-century oak-beamed flint barn.
⛫Q❀🛏◑♿▲🚌(54)♣P⍁

East Grinstead

Old Mill ✔

Dunnings Road, RH19 4AT (½ mile from town centre on road to West Hoathly)
⏲ 11-midnight; 12-11 Sun
☎ (01342) 326341 🌐 theolddunningsmill.co.uk
Harveys Hadlow Bitter, Sussex Best Bitter, seasonal beers Ⓗ
Formerly the Dunnings Mill, the interior of the pub has been divided into several areas, with a drinking space away from the dining area. Harvey's seasonal ales are usually available. A comprehensive menu features traditional pub food. Children are welcome in the pub and dog owners may bring their dogs into the drinking area. The old 16th-century water wheel has been restored to working order. Food is served all day.
⛫Q❀◑♿🚌P⍁

Eastergate

Wilkes' Head ✔

Church Lane, PO20 3UT (off A29)
⏲ 12-3, 5-11; 12-midnight Fri & Sat; 12-11 Sun
☎ (01243) 543380
Adnams Bitter; Fuller's London Pride; guest beers Ⓗ
New to the Guide, this small red-brick pub dating from 1803 was named after 18th-century radical John Wilkes. The traditional two-room layout survives, with a cosy lounge lying to the left of the central bar and a larger public bar with inglenook and low beams to the right. A restaurant has been added in a modern extension and there is a large garden with tables for outdoor drinking.
⛫Q❀◑⊞🚌(66,66A)♣P⍁

Elsted Marsh

Elsted Inn

Elsted Road, GU29 0JT (2 miles S of A272 between Midhurst & Petersfield) SU834206
⏲ 5-7 Mon; 12-3, 5-11; 12-11 Sat; 12-5 Sun
☎ (01730) 813662 🌐 theelstedinn.co.uk
Ballard's Best Bitter, Nyewood Gold; Otter Bitter; Skinner's Betty Stogs Ⓗ
Elsted or 'Halesteed' in the Domesday Record means 'the place where elder grows'. Today this Victorian pub, built originally to cater for a station on the Petersfield-Midhurst branch railway, is surrounded by the glorious countryside of the South Downs. In addition to the bar and restaurant it has four en-suite rooms alongside the pub in a detached coach house which was, at one time, the home of Ballard's Brewery, who continue to supply the pub. ⛫Q❀🛏◑🚌(91)P

Fernhurst

Red Lion ✔

The Green, GU27 3HY (N end of village green)
⏲ 11.30-3, 5-11; 11.30-11 Thu-Sat; 11.30-10.30 Sun
☎ (01428) 653304
Fuller's Chiswick, London Pride, ESB; guest beers Ⓗ
Idyllically set by the village green, the Red Lion has been a pub since 1592. Inside is a single bar with a low, timbered ceiling and two side rooms, plus a splendid inglenook fireplace with a large wood-burning stove. In fine weather, customers can sit overlooking the green at the front, or in the large rear garden where the covered, heated and lit smokers' shelter is situated. The pub is popular with both locals and diners.
⛫Q👶❀◑🚌(70,71)♣P⍁

Ferring

Henty Arms ✔

2 Ferring Lane, BN12 6QY (just N of level crossing)
⏲ 11-11 (midnight Fri & Sat); 12-11 Sun
☎ (01903) 241254 🌐 hentyarms.co.uk
Caledonian Deuchars IPA; Fuller's London Pride; Shepherd Neame Spitfire; Young's Bitter; guest beers Ⓗ
Friendly two-bar community pub offering a warm welcome with good value home-cooked food (all day Sat and Sun) including breakfast. The public bar houses a jukebox, TV and a variety of games, including shuffleboard. Well-behaved children are welcome until 9pm. A three-day beer festival is held in July coinciding with Worthing's annual seafront fair and preserved bus rally. Quiz night is Sunday, followed by a game of bingo. Goring station is 10 minutes' walk away along a path on the north side of the railway.
⛫Q❀◑⊞♿⇌(Goring-by-Sea)🚌(700)♣P⍁

Findon

Snooty Fox

High Street, BN14 0TA (just S of village centre)
⏲ 12-2.30, 6-11; 12-10.30 Sun
☎ (01903) 872733 🌐 findonmanor.com
Fuller's London Pride; Harveys Sussex Best Bitter; Wells Bombardier; guest beers Ⓗ
Part of the 16th-century Findon Manor Hotel, and under the care of the same manager for the past 15 years, this establishment serves both excellent real ale and top quality meals. The small, comfortable bar offers a cosy, convivial atmosphere in which to relax and is much appreciated by a varied clientele. With easy access to the South Downs, it is a popular stop off for walkers. Children are welcome, but no dogs are allowed in the bar. ⛫Q❀🛏◑🚌(1)P⍁

Friday Street

Royal Oak 🏆

RH12 4QA (on Rusper to Capel road, signed down side road) TQ183367
12-3, 5-11 (9 Mon); 12-11 Sat; 12-9 Sun
☎ (01293) 871393
Dark Star Best; Surrey Hill Ranmore Ale; guest beers H
A lovely, isolated, low-beamed, narrow free house that is well worth finding, with seven handpumps for real ale, three for cider and two for perry. Ales are usually from local micro-breweries and are constantly changing. Community events include a pantomime horse race, snail race and a weed show together with special food nights featuring home-cooked food made with local ingredients. CAMRA Surrey/Sussex Pub of the Year 2008, and National Pub of the Year Runner-up in 2009. This is a real gem. ⅏Q❀◐◑♣●P⁵–

Halnaker

Anglesey Arms

Stane Street, PO18 0NQ (on A285)
11-3, 5.30-11.30; 11-11 Sat; 12-10.30 Sun
☎ (01243) 773474 ⊕ angleseyarms.co.uk
Black Sheep Best Bitter; Draught Bass; Hepworth's Prospect Organic; Young's Bitter; guest beer H
Family-run listed Georgian pub with a wooden and flagstone-floored public bar, complete with roaring fire, plus a comfortable restaurant renowned for good food using local organic produce (reservations essential). Three of the regular beers plus one hoppy SIBA guest beer are usually available, along with several Belgian beers. Hepworth Prospect Organic is badged Goodwood Organic as the pub belongs to the Estate. Cribbage, darts and cricket are played by pub teams. A two-acre rear garden and numerous flowering baskets make this a pub not to be missed.
⅏Q❀◐◑♿▲🚌(55,99)♣P

Henley

Duke of Cumberland Arms 🏆

Henley Village, GU27 3HQ (off A286, 3 miles N of Midhurst) SU894258
12-3, 5-7; 12-11 Fri-Sun
☎ (01428) 652280
Harveys Sussex Best Bitter; Langham Best Bitter, Hip Hop; guest beers G
Stunning 15th-century inn nestling against the hillside and set in three and a half acres of terraced gardens with extensive views. Often threatened with redevelopment, it was rescued in 2007 by a band of locals who have vowed it will not be spoilt. The single bar has scrubbed-top tables and benches plus a log fire at each end. Real outside toilets and a smokers' shelter with its own wood burner are features of this rural gem. Up to two guest beers come from local micros. Local CAMRA Pub of the Year 2009. ⅏Q❀◐◑🚌(70)P⁵–

Horsham

Bar Vin ✔

3 Market Square, RH12 1EU (E side of Market Square)
12-11 (11.30 Fri & Sat); 12-10.30 Sun
☎ (01403) 250640
Harveys Sussex Best Bitter; Greene King IPA H
This large pub originally opened as the Anchor Hotel in 1899. It became the town hall in 1920, and was in use much later as a bank before conversion to a pub in the early 2000s. It has a large interior with a long bar down one side, with brass overhead light fittings. Opposite the bar is an imposing staircase leading to an upper floor/balcony which can be used for private parties. The yard outside has a smoking area and features a Gilbert Scott red telephone box. ❀◐◑♿🚌⁵–

Beer Essentials

30A East Street, RH12 1HL
10-6 (7 Fri & Sat); closed Sun & Mon
☎ (01403) 218890 ⊕ thebeeressentials.co.uk
Beer range varies G
Specialist beer shop with a constantly changing selection of ales drawn straight from the cask. An extensive range of bottled beers from around the UK plus some foreign beers are always in stock. JB medium cider is available, along with bottled ciders and lagers. The draught products come in minipins, polypins and two-pint containers. The proprietor runs a popular autumn beer festival in a local hall. 🚌●

Black Jug

31 North Street, RH12 1RJ
11.30-11.30; 12-10.30 Sun
☎ (01403) 253526 ⊕ blackjug-horsham.co.uk
Caledonian Deuchars IPA; Harveys Sussex Best Bitter; guest beers H
With easy access from the town centre and railway station, this popular pub has an extensive food menu and is busy at lunchtimes and evenings. Three guest ales are always available. The spacious conservatory leads to the courtyard garden which is always a favourite on summer afternoons. A real fire burns during the winter months. A small library of books is available for the casual reader. The pub has an extensive range of wines and malt whiskies. Over 21s only in the evening.
⅏Q❀◐◑⇌(Horsham)🚌●⁵–

Malt Shovel

15 Springfield Road, RH12 2PG
11-11 (midnight Fri & Sat)
☎ (01403) 254543 ⊕ maltshovel.com
Brakspear Bitter; Fuller's London Pride; Harveys Sussex Best Bitter; Hepworth Pullman H**; guest beers** H/G
A large bar with three distinct drinking areas where a real fire and bare floorboards add to the welcoming feel. There is a good selection of ever-changing guest beers, some on gravity, which often includes locally-brewed ales. Food is available at lunchtime. TV screens in the bar are often tuned to sporting events. A beer festival takes place annually in August. ⅏❀◐♿⇌🚌♣P⁵–

Keymer

Greyhound Inn

Keymer Road, BN6 8QT (on B2116 between Hassocks & Ditchling opp church)
11-midnight (11-3, 6-midnight Mon-Wed winter); 12-10.30 Sun
☎ (01273) 842645
Gale's HSB; Harveys Sussex Best Bitter; guest beers H
Situated in the old part of the village, the pub is thought to date back at least 450 years and is split into two bars. The comfortable main bar features an inglenook fireplace with a dining area behind it,

and the smaller public bar has a bar billiard table and dartboard. The seating is a mixture of settles and stools with an array of tankards and mugs hanging from the beamed ceiling. Families and dogs are welcome. Q❀⊂▸⊟⊟(33,41)♣P⁄–

Lambs Green

Lamb Inn

RH12 4RG (2 miles N of A264)

⊙ 11.30-3, 5.30-11; 11.30-11 Sat; 12-10.30 Sun

☎ (01293) 871336 ⊕ thelambinn.info

Beer range varies H

Until autumn 2007 this was WJ King's only tied house. Now a free house, rotating guest ales abound, though King's beers are normally present, along with other Sussex brewers. This is a delightful country pub where visitors are surrounded by oak beams and cosy nooks, and a real log fire adds to the timeless atmosphere in winter. Home-cooked food is available daily (all day Sat and Sun), and a large conservatory provides an extension to the dining area. Biddenden cider is served. ⊞❀⊂▸●P

Lancing

Crabtree Inn

140 Crabtree Lane, BN15 9NQ (10 mins walk from town centre and station)

⊙ 12 (2 Mon)-11; 12-midnight Fri & Sat; 12-11 Sun

☎ (01903) 755514 ⊕ aaa-camra.org.uk

Fuller's London Pride; guest beers H

An unexpected oasis to the north of Lancing, the traditional Kemp Town House design has a large public bar where pool and darts can be played, while the smaller lounge bar offers a quieter area to enjoy the ever-changing range of guest beers. To the rear is a large child and dog friendly garden with a covered and heated smoking area. Runner-up CAMRA Pub of the Year 2007 and 2008. ❀⊂▸⊟♿⇌⊟(7)♣P⁄–

Lindfield

Stand Up Inn

47 High Street, RH16 2HN

⊙ 11.30-11.30 (midnight Fri & Sat); 12-11.30 Sun

☎ (01444) 482995 ⊕ standupinn.co.uk

Dark Star Best, Hophead, seasonal beers; guest beers H

Conveniently situated in the village high street, this pub has a shop-like bow window frontage. The real fire provides a warm and comfortable presence in the winter, matched by the welcome from the staff. Evidence of the former Durrant's Brewery includes the rescued sign above the bar and the old brewery outbuildings visible from the beer garden. Three beer festivals and one cider/perry event are held annually. Regular live music is also staged (see posters for details). Pasties are available at lunchtime. ⊞Q❀⊟(30,270)♣●⁄–

Littlehampton

New Inn

5 Norfolk Road, BN17 5PL (just off seafront, 20 mins walk from station)

⊙ 11 (12 Sun)-11

☎ (01903) 713112

Arundel Gold; Courage Best Bitter; Gale's HSB H

A prominent street-corner establishment with a Regency facade, behind which lurks a venerable Grade II-listed flint building. Most pubs in Littlehampton are dying on their feet but the New Inn has bucked the trend – a very good locals' pub with two bars, one only recently reopened. There is plenty going on here, with live music on Friday night that sometimes continues all weekend. ⊞❀⊭⊂⊟⊟(9,700)♣⁄–

Littleworth

Windmill

Littleworth Lane, RH13 8EJ (E of B2135)

⊙ 11.30-3, 5-midnight; 12-3.30, 7-11.30 Sun

☎ (01403) 710308

Badger K&B Sussex, Tanglefoot, seasonal beers H

This unspoilt country pub still displays the old King & Barnes signage. The public bar was built over 400 years ago to provide the builders of the nearby monastery with somewhere to drink. Agricultural implements hang from the ceiling. It hosts darts and bar billiards teams. The comfortable saloon bar is newer and is adorned with a collection of ornamental windmills. There is a pleasant garden to the side. The menu is based on home-cooked food. No food Sunday evening. ⊞Q❀⊂▸⊟♣P⁄–

Lodsworth

Hollist Arms

Lodsworth Street, GU28 9BZ

⊙ 11-midnight; 12-11 Sun

☎ (01798) 861310

King's Horsham Best Bitter; Langham Hip Hop; Taylor Landlord H

Set in the village centre and overlooking the green, with its chestnut tree planted in 1897 to mark Queen Victoria's diamond jubilee, the Hollist Arms was created in 1825 from two former cottages. There is a small bar leading to a larger restaurant area, and also a small snug with an ancient inglenook fireplace. At the rear is a raised beer garden with a barbecue area and in front there are seats on the green. Good home-cooked food is served seven days a week. ⊞Q❀⊂▸⊟(1)♣⁄–

Mannings Heath

Dun Horse

49 Brighton Road, RH13 6HZ

⊙ 11-11 (10.30 Sun)

☎ (01403) 265783 ⊕ dunhorseinn.co.uk

Harveys Sussex Best Bitter; guest beers G

Roadside pub on the A281 Horsham-Brighton road which has recently undergone sensitive refurbishment. The present building, dating from 1926, replaced an earlier inn which stood on the site. An unspoilt interior has many original features and a large fireplace. Beer is served straight from the cask. A pool table and TV are in a separate room, which keeps the main bar peaceful. Music and theme nights take place regularly; Wi-Fi Internet access is provided and en-suite accommodation is available. ⊞❀⊭⊂▸⊟♣P

Maplehurst

White Horse

Park Lane, RH13 6LL

⊙ 12-2.30, 6-11 (11.30 most Fridays); 12-3, 7-11 Sun

☎ (01403) 891208

Harveys Sussex Best Bitter; Hogs Back HBB; Welton's Pride & Joy; guest beers Ⓗ
Now in its 23rd year in the Guide, this delightful country pub never fails to impress. The roomy interior oozes character with its imposing timber bar and different drinking areas including a large conservatory opening on to an attractive garden. Food is served, but the emphasis is firmly on conversation. Numerous ales and real cider are on offer, with guests often sourced from small independents. The pub has been local CAMRA Pub of the Year on many occasions, most recently in 2007, as well as Regional Pub of the Year.
Q P

Mockbridge

Bull Inn

London Road, BN5 9AD (on A281 1½ miles N of Henfield)
12-3 (3.30 Sat), 6-11; 12-10.30 Sun
☎ (01273) 492232 thebullinnhenfield.co.uk
Fuller's London Pride; Harveys Sussex Best Bitter; guest beers Ⓗ
The Bull is everything a country pub should be. A separate restaurant serves good food, with pizzas a speciality, and takeaways are available. The skittle alley also serves as a function room which can be hired (see website for details). Log fires are lit in winter time and there is a large garden at the rear with a children's play area for the summer. Guest beers are from the WJ King range.
Q (17)P

Nutbourne

Rising Sun

The Street, RH20 2HE (2 miles E of Pulborough, off A283)
11-3, 6-11; 12-3, 7-10.30 Sun
☎ (01798) 812191 therisingsunnutbourne.co.uk
Fuller's London Pride; guest beers Ⓗ
This 16th-century free house has been in the same family for over 30 years. There are old advertising signs near the courtyard and the front bar is full of character with wooden flooring and a large stone owl on the counter. Guest beers often come from Cottage, Skinner's, Sharp's and Oakleaf. The wide selection of food is recommended.

Rogate

White Horse Inn

East Street, GU31 5EA (on A272)
11-3, 6-11.30 (midnight Fri); 11-midnight Sat; 12-10.30 Sun
☎ (01730) 821333
Harveys Hadlow Bitter, Sussex Best Bitter, Armada Ale, seasonal beers Ⓗ
Dating from the 16th century, this old coaching inn has oak beams, flagstone floors and a huge log fire. A Harvey's tied house, you can expect up to five of its draught beers, including seasonal brews. Half the pub is used for dining and it offers a large range of meals includes steaks and vegetarian choices, plus specials on the blackboard (no food Sun eve). The car park overlooks the village sports field behind the pub. Q (91,92)P

Rowhook

Chequers

Rowhook Road, RH12 3PY
11.30-3, 6-11; 12-3.30 Sun
☎ (01403) 790480 nealsrestaurants.biz
Fuller's London Pride; Harveys Sussex Best Bitter; guest beers Ⓗ
You will find friendly staff at this 15th-century pub with low ceilings, oak beams and Horsham flagstones in the Flagstone Bar. There are wooden floors in the Upper Bar plus wooden tables and settles. Two real fires have seats alongside them. Chef Tim gained three AA rosettes while at the famous South Lodge Hotel and the pub is in the Top 50 Gastro Pubs and 2008 Michelin Guide. There is a separate menu for the Flagstone and Upper Bars and meals are prepared using locally sourced meat and game. QP

Selsey

Seal Hotel

6 Hillfield Road, PO20 0JX (on B2145)
10.30-12.30am; 12-11 Sun
☎ (01243) 602461 the-seal.com
Dark Star Hophead; Greene King Old Speckled Hen; Hop Back Summer Lightning; Young's Bitter; guest beers Ⓗ
Family-run for 38 years, this spacious free house has an enduring popularity with locals and visitors alike. Quality home-cooked food and locally-caught fish await in the restaurant (booking advised). Guest beers are mostly from local micros, and acoustic live music is often played on Sunday. The front patio caters for smokers, with its umbrellas and seating. Upstairs, 12 en-suite B&B rooms are a recent addition, reinstating the pub's former hotel status. Local CAMRA Pub of the Year 2008.
Q (51)

Shoreham-by-Sea

Buckingham Arms

35 Brunswick Road, BN43 5WA (opp railway station)
11-11 (10.30 Sun)
☎ (01273) 453660
Greene King Abbot; Harveys Sussex Best Bitter; Hop Back Summer Lightning; Sharp's Doom Bar; Taylor Landlord; guest beers Ⓗ
In this Guide and Local Ale Trail regular, 11 handpumps dispense six permanent and five ever-changing cask ales. The L-shaped bar is decorated with a collection of mirrors from breweries past and present, together with prints of military and pastoral scenes. Beer festivals are held each February and August. TV and occasional live music are offered. Keith, the landlord, is proud of his record sales of Harveys Tom Paine over the last four years, exceeding even those of Harveys' tied houses. Food is available Monday-Saturday lunchtimes. (2,9)

Duke of Wellington

368 Brighton Road, BN43 6RE (on A259 opp Sussex Yacht Club)
10-11.30; 12-midnight Fri & Sat; 12-10.30 Sun
☎ (01273) 389818 thedukeofwellington.co.uk
Dark Star Hophead, seasonal beers; guest beers Ⓗ
Under enthusiastic new management, this Dark Star house offers a range of its own ales plus guests and Thatchers real cider. Behind a large frontage with an unusual pub sign lies a smart

interior with a patio area, featuring a purpose-built barbecue at the rear. Live music and themed evenings are advertised in advance. Look out for the popular beer festivals. Simple hot bar snacks are available at lunchtime. ❀≹⊟(2,700)♣●⁵–

Red Lion

Old Shoreham Road, BN43 5TE
⊕ 12-11 (10.30 Sun)
☎ (01273) 453171 🌐 theredlionshoreham.co.uk
Beer range varies Ⓗ
Situated at the southern end of the Downs Link Trail, this 16th-century pub is popular with walkers and cyclists, with pleasant views of the old Toll Bridge and over Shoreham Airfield to Lancing College. Inside, beware of low ceilings in the main bar. Excellent food is served in a separate restaurant area. An ever-changing range of real ales, mainly from micro-breweries, is dispensed from five handpumps, and the pub hosts the annual Adur Beer Festival over the Easter weekend.
⩕Q❀◑▷⊟(2A)♣P⁵–

South Harting

Ship Inn

North Lane, GU31 5PZ
⊕ 11.30-11.30; 12-11 Sun
☎ (01730) 825302
Ballard's Nyewood Gold Ⓖ**; Bowman Swift One; Dark Star Hophead; Palmer Best Bitter** Ⓗ
Friendly 17th-century free house built using old ships' timbers that are exposed in the lounge. The pub has a small basic public bar where darts is played and a larger lounge and restaurant where good-value meals are served (not Tue or Sun eve). Booking is recommended at weekends. An enclosed garden flanks the B2146 road.
⩕Q❀◑▷⊟(54,91)♣P

Staplefield

Jolly Tanners

Handcross Road, RH17 6EF
⊕ 11-3, 5.30-11; 11-11 Sat; 11-10.30 Sun
☎ (01444) 400335
Fuller's London Pride; Harveys Sussex Best Bitter; guest beers Ⓗ
Superlative, welcoming village pub opposite the green. The large bar is split into two distinct areas and a log fire adds to the cosy feel. The large range of ever-changing guest beers always includes a mild. Real cider is also served. A good range of tasty food is available at all sessions, however, this is still very much a locals' pub. Beer festivals are held during May and November. A gem, which is not to be missed. ⩕Q❀◑⊟(271)♣●P

Steyning

Chequer Inn ✔

41 High Street, BN44 3RE
⊕ 10-11 (midnight Fri; 12.30am Sat)
☎ (01903) 814437 🌐 chequerinnsteyning.co.uk
Dark Star Best Bitter; Fuller's London Pride; Gale's HSB; Taylor Landlord; guest beers Ⓗ
Superb 15th-century former market town coaching inn of character with many original features and items of historical interest. Two separate bars, one with a full-size snooker table, are connected by a rear drinking corridor with a snug and courtyard garden leading off. The cosy saloon bar has two distinct areas, each with an open log fire. Guest ales and food produce are sourced locally, with a tantalising breakfast menu served until 11.30am.
⩕Q❀⊨◑▷ⴽ⊟(2a,100)P⁵–

Stopham Bridge

White Hart

Stopham Road, RH20 1DS (off A283 W of Pulborough, E of River Arun bridge)
⊕ 11.30-11; 12-10.30 Sun
☎ (01798) 873321 🌐 whitehartstophambridge.co.uk
Arundel Gold; Hogs Back TEA; King Horsham Best Bitter; guest beers Ⓗ
A small central bar serves four separate oak-beamed rooms on two levels in this former coaching inn. The main building dates back to the 16th century but some parts are 300 years older. The pub sits next to the River Arun and the large outdoor drinking area commands an outstanding view across the valley. The restaurant is open all day at the weekend, with the daily specials worthy of investigation. Quiz night is Thursday and occasional musical jam sessions take place.
⩕Q❀◑⊟(1)P⁵–

Stoughton

Hare & Hounds

PO18 9JQ (off B2146, through Walderton) SU802115
⊕ 11-3, 6-11; 11-11 Fri & Sat; 12-10.30 Sun
☎ (02392) 631433 🌐 hareandhoundspub.co.uk
Ballard's Best Bitter; Harveys Sussex Best Bitter; Taylor Landlord; guest beers Ⓗ
Traditional country pub in a beautiful downland valley – an ideal base for walking. A large dining room serves fresh local produce, while the public bar, warmed by an open fire, is the locals' choice. Three open fires, along with stone-flagged floors, beams and simple furniture, help to create a wonderful atmosphere. Outside is a paved drinking area at the front and a garden at the back.
⩕Q❀◑▷&ⴽ⊟(54)♣●P

Thakeham

White Lion Inn

The Street, RH20 3EP (just off B2139)
⊕ 11-11; 12-10.30 Sun
☎ (01798) 813141
Caledonian Deuchars IPA; Fuller's London Pride; Harveys Sussex Best Bitter; guest beers Ⓗ
An unspoilt village pub in an idyllic setting. This is a genuine free house, opened in 1640 and thankfully little changed in the subsequent 370 years. A rambling interior features a central bar, three drinking areas and a separate dining room. The atmosphere is friendly and the food highly regarded. The dining room fireplace is used for smoking ham, cheese and sausages.
⩕Q❀◑▷ⴽ⊟(74)♣P⁵–

Trotton

Keepers Arms

Terwick Lane, GU31 5ER (on A272, 3 miles W of Midhurst)
⊕ 12-3, 6-11; 12-4, 7-10.30 Sun
☎ (01730) 813724 🌐 keepersarms.co.uk
Ballard's Best Bitter; Dark Star Hophead; King Horsham Best Bitter; Ringwood Best Bitter Ⓗ

Set high above the road and the River Rother near Trotton Bridge, this 17th-century inn features low ceilings, bare wood floors and comfortable sofas surrounding an open log fire. There are smart dining areas to complement the adventurous menu, but the bar remains welcoming to drinkers. The elevated patio around two sides of the pub is popular in fine weather. There are three handpumps – Hophead is permanent and the other beers are rotated. Cider or perry is from Westons. ♨Q❀◐◑♿🚌(91,92)●P

Turners Hill

Red Lion ✔

Lion Lane, RH10 4NU (off North St, B2028)

⏲ 11-3, 5-11; 11-11.30 Fri (11 Sat); 12-10 (8 winter) Sun

☎ (01342) 715416

Harveys XX Mild, Sussex Best Bitter, seasonal beers Ⓗ

Still very much the village local, a friendly welcome is assured at this split-level pub with an inglenook fireplace. Mild ale is now available as a result of customer demand. Twice monthly quiz nights are held in aid of local charities. Occasional live music is played in the garden during the summer months. Wi-Fi Internet access is available. Children and dogs are welcome. ♨Q❀◐🚌(82)♣P⚟

Walberton

Holly Tree

The Street, BN18 0PH

⏲ 12-3, 6-11; 12-10.30 Sun

☎ (01243) 554023

Fuller's London Pride; Harveys Sussex Best Bitter; Wells Bombardier; guest beer Ⓗ

A comfortable pub in an attractive coastal plain village with two bright bars, one with a public snug. Three real ales are always available, and there are scrubbed pine tables and a large range of home-cooked meals prepared by a long-serving landlady/cook, all in pleasant surroundings. The pub exterior is a feature of the village with its display of flowers, enhanced by a large seating area perfect for watching the world go by. Quiz night is Wednesday. Convenient for Fontwell or Goodwood races.

♨Q❀◐◑🀫♿⇌(Barnham)🚌(66,66A)♣P⚟

Warnham

Sussex Oak ✔

2 Church Street, RH12 3QW

⏲ 11-11; 12-10.30 Sun

☎ (01403) 265028 🌐 thesussexoak.co.uk

Adnams Bitter; Fuller's London Pride; Taylor Landlord; Young's Bitter; guest beers Ⓗ

A large pub, dating back to the 16th century in parts, situated in the centre of the village. Welcoming to locals and visitors alike, a large L-shaped bar area is broken up by pillars and partitions, giving the appearance of smaller rooms. There is a separate restaurant and outside a large garden. See the blackboards for a wide selection of good food including daily specials and roast lunches on Sunday. The outside smoking area is heated. Families and dogs are welcome.

♨❀◐◑🚌(93)♣●P⚟

Warninglid

Half Moon

The Street, RH17 5TR (on B2115 crossroads, 1 mile W of A23)

⏲ 11.30-2.30, 5.30-11; 12-10.30 Sun

☎ (01444) 461227 🌐 thehalfmoonwarninglid.co.uk

Harveys Sussex Best Bitter; Greene King Old Speckled Hen; guest beers Ⓗ

A popular village freehouse with a thriving food trade based on locally-sourced ingredients as well as a good range of well-kept cask ales – beer and food take equal billing. A large new conservatory features a covered well. Once a year, customers are invited to donate apples to the pub's own cider press for cider sold to raise funds for charity. Children are not allowed inside the pub but dogs are permitted in the bar. The garden is pleasant in summer. ♨Q❀◐◑🚌♣P⚟

West Chiltington

Five Bells

Smock Alley, RH20 2QX (1 mile S of West Chiltington) TQ091170

⏲ 12-3, 6-11; 12-3, 7-10.30 Sun

☎ (01798) 812143 🌐 westchiltington.com/five_bells.htm

Arundel Sussex Mild; Harveys Sussex Best Bitter; Palmer Copper Ale; guest beers Ⓗ

A warm welcome awaits you at this traditional, award-winning pub which offers an excellent choice of beers, plus a local draught cider. Hearty appetites will appreciate fresh, home-cooked and locally sourced fare (not Sun or Mon eve). B&B accommodation is available in five double en-suite bedrooms. Dogs are warmly welcomed throughout. Local CAMRA Pub of the Year 2007 and 2008. ♨Q❀🛏◐◑♣●P

West Itchenor

Ship Inn

The Street, PO20 7AH

⏲ 11-11; 12-10.30 Sun

☎ (01243) 512284 🌐 theshipinn.biz

Ballard's Best Bitter; Itchen Valley Godfathers; King Horsham Best Bitter; Ringwood Fortyniner Ⓗ

Attractive 1930s-built pub in the main street of the village, leading down to the picturesque harbour. Homely wood-panelled bars decorated with yachting memorabilia add to its character and the wide front patio is a sun-trap in summer. Two rooms are dedicated to dining, offering a wide range of traditional meals, often including locally-landed fish. Up to four beers from the smaller local breweries are normally available, with session beers competitively priced.

♨Q❀🛏◐◑🀫🚌(52,53)♣P⚟

Westbourne

Cricketers

Commonside, PO10 8TA (N from The Square, turn E at Lashley's Garage) SU758082

⏲ 5-11; 12-midnight Thu-Sun

☎ (01243) 372647

Fuller's London Pride; Ringwood Fortyniner; Suthwyk Liberation; guest beers Ⓗ

This 300-year-old local is the only free house in a village of good pubs. Situated on the northern outskirts, it is hard to find but well worth the effort. Conversation abounds in the single L-shaped, half-panelled bar. There is a sun-trap garden to the side, with a covered and heated smoking area. The guest beers mainly come from Hants and Sussex micros. Food is served seven days a week except Sunday evening. ⛼Q❀◐◑🚌(11,36)♣P⁝–

Whitemans Green

Ship Inn

RH17 5BY (N of Cuckfield at B2115/B2036 jct)
⏲ 12-2.30 (not Wed), 5.30-11; 12-11 Sat; 12-3 Sun
☎ (01444) 413219
Harveys Sussex Best Bitter; guest beers Ⓖ
This family-run pub is located close to Haywards Heath's rugby club ground. The handpumps are for decorative purposes only and the beers are served by gravity from a cooled back room. The bar features a double-sided fireplace and has a dining area at one end. The pool table and darts are tucked away in a separate games room. Food is served lunchtimes (not Wed) and evenings (not Sun), with a changing range of specials in addition to the regular menu. ⛼Q❀🛏◐◑🚌(271,272)P⁝–

Wick

Dew Drop Inn

96 Wick Street, BN17 7JS (opp Wick Parade shops)
⏲ 10.30-3, 5.30-11; 10.30-11 Sat; 10.30-10.30 Sun
☎ (01903) 716459 🌐 tinyurl.com/2ea78z
Arundel Sussex Gold; Gale's Butser; guest beers Ⓗ
A warm welcome is assured at this classic unspoilt boozer. The very competitively priced beer range changes with the seasons and local bottled beers are available. The no-frills public bar has bar billiards and darts, while the comfortable lounge has probably the shortest bar in the area at just 5ft 1in. Situated just south of the A259, the Dew Drop is one of only two pubs remaining in Wick.
Q🐎🗔⇌(Littlehampton)🚌(12,700)♣

Worthing

George & Dragon

1 High Street, Tarring, BN14 7NN
⏲ 11-11 (midnight Fri & Sat); 12-10.30 Sun
☎ (01903) 202497 🌐 cox-inns.co.uk
Courage Directors; Greene King Abbot; Harveys Sussex Best Bitter; Hop Back Summer Lightning; Young's Bitter; guest beers Ⓗ
Busy 17th-century neighbourhood pub at the southern entrance to the historic high street in Tarring, a village of Saxon origins. The single, low-beamed narrow bar has several distinct drinking areas and a cosy snug. Darts and traditional card games are popular, as is the golf society, while other local sports teams are regulars here. Food is served Monday-Saturday lunchtimes. The sun-trap patio and small garden are the setting for beer festivals. Q❀◐⇌(W Worthing)🚌(6,6a)♣P⁝–

Richard Cobden ✔

2 Cobden Lane, BN11 4BD (5 mins walk S from Worthing station)
⏲ 11-11 (11.30 Fri & Sat); 12-10.30 Sun
☎ (01903) 236856 🌐 therichardcobden.co.uk
Harveys Sussex Best Bitter; Hop Back Summer Lightning; guest beers Ⓗ
This street-corner pub has been at the heart of the local community for more than 140 years. The local Morris men and Sompting Tipteerers dance and perform the Mummers Play here on New Year's Day. The comfortable L-shaped bar hosts folk music on Thursday and jazz on Sunday evening. A beer festival celebrates St George's Day. The small garden has won many awards for its floral displays.
❀◐♿⇌🚌♣⁝–

Selden Arms 🏆

41 Lyndhurst Road, BN11 2DB (near Worthing Hospital)
⏲ 11 (12 Sat)-11; 12-10.30 Sun
Dark Star Hophead; Ringwood Fortyniner; guest beers Ⓗ
A small, single bar 19th-century free house that's a haven for real ale drinkers. There are six handpumps, one dispensing a dark beer, and bottled Belgian beers are also available. A beer festival is held at the end of January and there is occasional live music. The walls are adorned with photographs of old Worthing hostelries. A chalkboard displays a list of forthcoming beers. Dogs are welcome. No food served Sunday. Local CAMRA Pub of the Year 2009. ◐⇌🚌

Swan Inn

79 High Street, BN11 1DN
⏲ 11-11 (midnight Fri & Sat); 12-11 Sun
☎ (01903) 232923
Greene King Abbot; Harveys Sussex Best Bitter; Hop Back Summer Lightning; Shepherd Neame Spitfire; guest beers Ⓗ
Comfortable 19th-century pub just five minutes' walk from Worthing centre, with decor reminiscent of a village local, including Sussex flint walls, beams, agricultural implements and myriad brasses. Two stained glass windows proclaim that this was once a Kemp Town Brewery pub. Good value quality food is served at lunchtime. Beers include probably the finest pint of Harveys Best Bitter in Worthing. By day, the pub attracts both locals and shoppers; evening attractions include darts, bar billiards, quiz and music including folk night on the last Tuesday of every month.
⛼❀◐⇌🚌♣⁝–

Yapton

Maypole Inn

Maypole Lane, BN18 0DP (off B2132 N of village)
SU978042
⏲ 11.30-11 (midnight Fri & Sat); 12-11 Sun
☎ (01243) 551417 🌐 themaypoleinn.co.uk
Dark Star Hophead, Over the Moon; Skinner's Betty Stogs; guest beers Ⓗ
This small flint-built inn is hidden well away from the village centre. Maypole Lane was cut off by the railway in 1846 and the pub has enjoyed its quiet isolation ever since. The cosy lounge boasts two open fires and an imposing row of seven handpumps, dispensing up to three constantly-changing guest beers from small breweries. The larger public bar has a jukebox, darts, pool and a TV for sports events. A skittle alley/function room can be booked and there is a covered verandah for smokers.
⛼Q❀◐🗔⛺⇌(Barnham)🚌(66,66A)♣●P⁝–

A fine beer may be judged with only a sip, but it's better to be thoroughly sure.
Czech proverb

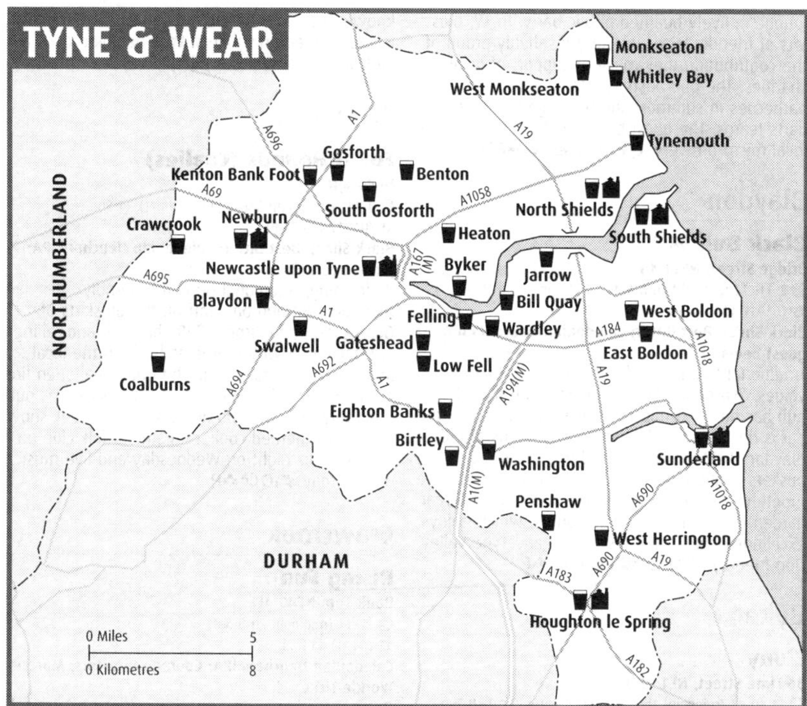

Benton

Benton Ale House

Front Street, NE7 7XE

11-11 (11.30 Wed; midnight Fri & Sat); 12-11 Sun

☎ (0191) 266 1512

Banks's Bitter; Jennings Cumberland Ale; Marston's Pedigree; guest beers Ⓗ

Traditional pub with a horseshoe-shaped bar and large bay windows giving a light and airy feel. There is plenty of good quality seating throughout. Be sure to check the monthly beer menu on the bar. Reasonably priced, good quality food is popular – booking is essential for Sunday lunch. Family friendly. (Four Lane Ends)**P**

Bill Quay

Albion Inn

10 Reay Street, NE10 0TY

4-11 (midnight Fri); 12-midnight Sat; 12-11 Sun

☎ (0191) 469 2418

Jarrow Bitter, Joblings Swinging Gibbet, Rivet Catcher Ⓗ

Owned by the CAMRA award-winning Jarrow Brewery, this well-furnished lounge bar has the feel of a village local, despite its urban setting with views of industrial Tyneside. It has a pleasant conservatory and a vine-covered heated smoking shelter at the back. There are regular busker and Irish music nights, table football is played and free WiFi access is provided. The Coast-to-Coast cycle route and the Keelmans Way Walk both pass the pub. (Pelaw)♣**P**

Birtley

Barley Mow Inn ✔

Durham Road, DH3 2AG

11.30-midnight (12.30am Fri & Sat); 10-midnight Sun

☎ (0191) 410 4504 thebarleymowinn.co.uk

Black Sheep Best Bitter; guest beers Ⓗ

At the southern edge of town, this former roadhouse offers the widest choice of real ales in the area. Its enterprising landlord has increased the number of handpulls to four in the bar and five in the lounge, including a real cider, rare for the county. Guest beers often come from north of England micro-breweries. The pub has a separate dining room. Dominoes and darts are played, there is weekend live music, a weekly quiz and a music and beer festival in February. Dogs are welcome – Saturday afternoon is an informal dog club in the bar! **Q**(21,22)♣**P**

Moulders Arms

Peareth Terrace, Birtley Lane, DH3 2LW

11.30-3.30, 5.30-11.30

☎ (0191) 410 2949

Boddingtons Bitter; Greene King Old Speckled Hen; guest beers Ⓗ

Just away from the main road and close to residential areas, this Guide regular is named after a skilled ironworker. It has a food-led, split-level

INDEPENDENT BREWERIES

Big Lamp Newburn
Bull Lane Sunderland
Darwin Sunderland
Double Maxim Houghton le Spring
Hadrian & Border Newcastle upon Tyne
Jarrow South Shields
Mordue North Shields

lounge, a lively beamed public bar with TV, plus lots of friendly locals who are justifiably proud of the contribution they make in support of local charities. The pub hosts weekly quizzes and barbecues in summer, and has a golf society and darts teams. The guest beer usually comes from a local micro-brewery. Q❀◐♿♣P

Blaydon

Black Bull ✔

Bridge Street, NE21 4JJ
2-11; 12-midnight Fri & Sat; 12-11 Sun
☎ (0191) 414 2816
Black Sheep Best Bitter; Caledonian Deuchars IPA; guest beers H
Traditional two-roomed pub with old-fashioned values: 'No pool table, no jukebox, no bandit,'. A pub has been on this site since the 1800s and the bar is decorated with many photographs of old Blaydon. Folk nights are held weekly and a buskers' night, quiz night and live bands all feature monthly. Barbecues are hosted in the superb rear garden during the summer months, which enjoys excellent views of the River Tyne and Tyne Valley. Dog friendly. Q(10,602)♣P

Byker

Cluny

36 Lime Street, NE1 2PQ
11.30-11 (midnight Thu; 1am Fri & Sat); 12-10.30 Sun
☎ (0191) 230 4474 theheadofsteam.com
Beer range varies H
Large, former industrial building converted into a pub, art gallery and live music venue. The pub runs frequent themed beer festivals and always has a good selection of British and foreign draught and bottled products available. The art gallery shows work of all kinds ranging from final degree shows to local independent established artists in all media, with displays changing monthly. Live music sessions are held most evenings and include a wide range of British, European and American musicians. ❀◐♿⊖

Cumberland Arms ★

James Place Street, NE6 1LD (off Byker Bank)
4.30 (3.30 Fri; 12.30 Sat & Sun)-closing times vary
☎ (0191) 265 6151 thecumberlandarms.co.uk
Wylam Rapper; guest beers H
Three-storey pub rebuilt more than 100 years ago and relatively little changed since then. It stands in a prominent position looking down and across the lower Ouseburn Valley. Home to local dance and music groups, the house beer Rapper from Wylam Brewery is named after a traditional dance. A winner of CAMRA's regional Cider Pub of the Year award, it usually offers up to six ciders and perries. Winter and summer beer festivals are held each year. Q⊖♣P

Free Trade Inn

St Lawrence Road, NE6 1AP
11-11 (midnight Fri & Sat); 12-midnight Sun
☎ (0191) 265 5764 freetradeinn.com
Mordue IPA; guest beers H
Renowned for its splendid views up river to the Tyne bridges and the Newcastle city skyline, this pub offers a changing selection of beers, with local independent breweries well represented. The pub is reassuringly basic and homely, with friendly, knowledgeable staff and a high standard of graffiti in the gentlemen's toilets. Well-behaved dogs are welcome. ❀⊖(Byker)(Q2,106)

Coalburns

Fox & Hounds (Coalies)

NE40 4JN
4-11; 1-midnight Sat; 2 (11 summer)-11 Sun
☎ (0191) 413 2549
Black Sheep Best Bitter; Caledonian Deuchars IPA; guest beers H
Welcoming, traditional pub with friendly management and bar staff on the outskirts of Greenside. Dating from 1795, the walls and ceilings are decorated with memorabilia from the local industries of centuries ago.The traditional open fire is complete with granny's oven and gives this pub a homely feel. The pub holds an annual leek show as well as themed cookery nights, a folk club on Sunday, quiz night on Wednesday and live music on Saturday. Q◐♣P

Crawcrook

Rising Sun

Bank Top, NE40 4EE
12-11 (midnight Fri & Sat)
☎ (0191) 413 3316
Caledonian Deuchars IPA; Courage Directors; Mordue Workie Ticket H
Once a coaching inn, now a popular, spacious pub with a large conservatory. The interior has a comfortable, light and airy feel, with a large-screen TV, pool table and jukebox, but plenty of space for drinkers and diners. Reasonably priced, good food is available. ❀◐(10,11)♣P

East Boldon

Grey Horse

Front Street, NE36 0SJ
11 (12 Sun)-11
☎ (0191) 536 3969
Caledonian Deuchars IPA; guest beer H
Large pub with a mock Tudor facade on the main Sunderland road. The interior is now a single large lounge room, with a number of separate drinking areas and a first-floor function room. The bar area has a low ceiling with subdued lighting and exposed beams. The walls are adorned with bric-a-brac. Sunday is quiz night. ❀◐⊖(9,9A,30)P

Eighton Banks

Ship

The Mount, NE9 7YP
11 (12 Sun)-11
☎ (0191) 416 0273
Beer range varies H
This ancient pub is now a bar-lounge with attractive coloured glasswork, woodwork, an olden-style stove and lots of nautical bric-a-brac – note the fine model sailing ship behind the bar. It has a separate dining room and lovely panoramic views to the southwest, plus a sundial on the front wall. The four handpulls often dispense beers rare for the area, as well as ales from local micro-breweries. Live bands perform on Sundays. Situated close to the road crossing over the Bowes Railway. ❀◐(25,25A,184)P

Felling

Old Fox

10-14 Carlisle Street, NE10 0HQ
3 (1 Fri-Sun)-11
(07941) 393075
Camerons Castle Eden Ale; guest beers H
Pleasant real ale pub just a short walk from Felling Metro. The open fire gives the bar a homely feel. A live band plays on the first Saturday of the month and Monday is local buskers' night. The landlord is very keen on real ale and will happily chat to customers about his beer menu.

Wheatsheaf

26 Carlisle Road, NE10 0HQ
5-11; 12-10.30 Sun
(0191) 420 0659
Big Lamp Bitter, Prince Bishop, Sunny Daze H
Big Lamp's first tied house is well worth the short Metro journey from Newcastle city centre. This is an honest, no nonsense, street-corner local where loyal regulars enjoy darts and dominoes schools. Original features add interest – note the fine gantry and windows. An impromptu folk night is a long-standing tradition every Tuesday.

Gateshead

Borough Arms

82 Bensham Road, NE8 1PS
12-11 (midnight Fri & Sat)
(0191) 478 1323
Wells Bombardier; Wylam Gold Tankard; guest beers H
Reputedly the oldest inn in the area, this bare-boards local is the nearest real ale pub to the town centre and public transport interchange. The landlord supports the SIBA direct delivery scheme and his guest beers usually come from local micro-breweries. There is a welcoming coal fire in winter, TVs, darts and toasties, plus quiz and buskers' nights weekly, and local bands monthly. The pub is on the Town Trail and next to Windmill Hills Park, the site of a Civil War skirmish. P

Gosforth

Brandling Arms

176 High Street, NE3 1HD
(0191) 285 4023 thebrandlingarmsgosforth.co.uk
Caledonian Deuchars IPA; Mordue Workie Ticket; guest beers H
Set back on Gosforth High Street, this is a large pub where the emphasis is on food. It is believed that the name comes from the wealthy Brandlings family of local merchants, land and coal owners. Tastefully refurbished, it has distinctive areas for dining while remaining drinker-friendly. Mordue Workie Ticket and Deuchars IPA are the regular beers, along with two rotating guests. Quiz night is Wednesday. (Regent Centre)

Job Bulman

St Nicholas Avenue, NE3 1AA
9am-11 (10.30 Sun)
(0191) 223 6230
Greene King IPA, Abbot; Marston's Pedigree; guest beers H
Impressive Wetherspoon's conversion of the old post office building just off busy Gosforth High Street. Catering equally for food and drink, the unusual horseshoe-shaped interior houses a large bar area in the centre, with discrete dining areas to each side. Opposite the bar is an outside courtyard with smoking area. Three regular beers are complemented by a constantly rotating guest list, with up to eight ales on at any one time. At least two guest beers are usually from local micro-breweries. (Regent Centre)

Heaton

Chillingham

Chillingham Road, NE6 5XN
11-11 (midnight Fri & Sat); 12-10.30 Sun
(0191) 265 5915
Black Sheep Best Bitter; Jarrow Bitter; Mordue Workie Ticket; guest beers H
A large pub with two rooms in contrasting styles. The traditional public bar has dark wood panelling and a historic mirror recalling the past glories of nearby Wallsend, while the lounge has a contemporary feel with excellent artwork depicting the sights of Newcastle, plus flat screen TVs showing sport. Look out for bottled beer, whisky and wine of the month. The upstairs function room hosts live music and comedy nights.
(Chillingham Rd)(62,63)

Houghton le Spring

Copt Hill

Seaham Road, DH5 8LU (on B1404)
11-midnight; 11.30-11.30 Sun
(0191) 5844485
Maxim Ward's Bitter, Samson, Double Maxim; guest beer H
In a rural setting with views of Houghton below. Sunderland's last real ale desert now has an oasis, with the welcome return of Maxim beers to this former Vaux pub. Newly refurbished, it is the closest outlet to the Maxim Brewery and is its unofficial tap. There are two bars and a separate function room. Live music plays on the first Sunday of the month. (20,148)P

Jarrow

Robin Hood

Primrose Hill, NE32 5UB (on A194, half mile S of A19)
12-11 (11.30 Fri & Sat; 10.30 Sun)
(0191) 428 5454 jarrowbrewery.co.uk
Jarrow Bitter, Rivet Catcher, Joblings Swinging Gibbet, seasonal beers; guest beers H
Since opening in 2002 and winning CAMRA North East Pub of the Year in 2006, this Jarrow Brewery-owned pub has gone from strength to strength. It now offers weekend entertainment in the impressive newly-opened music hall room. Photographs of the Jarrow Crusade adorn the bar walls. Guest beers change regularly and regular beer festivals are held. Jarrow's brewing now takes place elsewhere. Q(Fellgate)P

Kenton Bank Foot

Twin Farms

22 Main Road, NE13 8AB
11.30-11; 11.30-10.30 Sun
(0191) 286 1263
Black Sheep Bitter; Taylor Landlord; guest beers H
Large stone farmhouse building standing in its own grounds. Comfortable and relaxed, it has various areas inside and out to sit and enjoy the extensive

selection of beers on offer. The management runs various events for regulars, including brewery visits and 'meet the brewer' sessions. The pub aims to reduce food miles and offers excellent meals made with locally-sourced ingredients from named suppliers.
⛰Q♉❀◐▶♿⊖(Bank Foot)🚌(X77,X78)P

Low Fell

Aletaster

706 Durham Road, NE9 6JA
✪ 12-11 (midnight Fri); 11-midnight Sat
☎ (0191) 487 0770
Durham White Amarillo; Everards Tiger; Jennings Cumberland Ale; Taylor Landlord; Theakston Best Bitter, Old Peculier; guest beers Ⓗ
With 11 handpulls providing the widest selection of real ales for some distance, this long-time Guide entry also has real cider and hosts occasional beer festivals. Guest beers generally come from north of England micro-breweries. It has an L-shaped public bar and snug decorated in alehouse style. Note the stained-glass window depicting King George IV, who the pub was once named after. Entertainment includes a weekly quiz and live music from time to time. Reputedly home to a ghost! ❀⊟🚌♣P

Monkseaton

Black Horse

68 Front Street, NE25 8DP
✪ 11-midnight; 12-11.30 Sun
☎ (0191) 2536931
Caledonian Deuchars IPA; Durham Magus; Jarrow Rivet Catcher; guest beers Ⓗ
Active town pub with darts, dominoes, football, cricket and even a whist team. The bar area is decked out in signed Newcastle United and Whitley Bay FC shirts. Young actors practise in a room upstairs and perform a live show on the second Saturday of the month. Occasional free Sunday barbecues are hosted in the summer months. A happy pub with a jolly landlord and a cheerful atmosphere. Q♉◐▶⊟♿⊖(Monkseaton)♣⚐

Newburn

Keelman

Grange Road, NE15 8NL
✪ 11-11; 12-10.30 Sun
☎ (0191) 267 0772 🌐 petersen-stainless.co.uk/blb/index.html
Big Lamp Bitter, Sunny Daze, Summerhill Stout, Prince Bishop Ⓗ
This tastefully converted Grade II-listed former pumping station is home to the Big Lamp Brewery and brewery tap. A conservatory has been added to accommodate the growing band of diners and drinkers who come to sample the full range of Big Lamp beers. Quality accommodation is provided in the adjacent Keelman's Lodge and Salmon Cottage. Attractively situated by the Tyne Riverside Country Park, Coast to Coast cycleway and Hadrian's Wall National Trail. ❀◐▶🚌(22)P

Newcastle upon Tyne

Bacchus

42-48 High Bridge, NE1 6BX
✪ 11.30-11 (midnight Fri & Sat); 7-10.30 Sun
☎ (0191) 261 1008
Jarrow River Catcher; guest beers Ⓗ
A local CAMRA Pub of the Year, this smart, comfortable city-centre pub offers a wide range of rapidly changing guest beers. Regular brewery weekends are held when all eight handpumps are given over to ales from a single brewery and food is matched to individual beers. Photographs and posters showing the industries in which this region used to lead the world cover the walls. Ciders are served direct from the cellar. ◐♿⇌⊖(Monument)

Bodega

125 Westgate Road, NE1 6BX
✪ 11-11 (midnight Fri & Sat); 12-10.30 Sun
☎ (0191) 221 1552
Big Lamp Prince Bishop; Durham Magus; Mordue Workie Ticket; guest beers Ⓗ
Two fine stained glass domes are the architectural highlights of this pub, which stands next to the Tyne Theatre and attracts football and music fans. The interior offers a number of standing and seating areas with separate booths for more intimate drinking. A number of old brewery mirrors adorns the walls. TVs show sporting events and the pub can be busy on match days. ◐⇌⊖(Central)

Bridge Hotel

Castle Garth, NE1 1RQ
✪ 11.30-11 (midnight Fri & Sat); 12-10.30 Sun
☎ (0191) 232 6400
Black Sheep Best Bitter; Caledonian Deuchars IPA; guest beers Ⓗ
Situated next to the High Level Bridge, built by Stephenson, and facing the Keep of the New Castle which gave the city its name. The hotel's rear windows and patio have views of the city walls, River Tyne and Gateshead Quays. The main bar area is adorned with many stained glass windows and divided into a number of seating areas, with a raised section at the rear used for serving meals at lunchtime. Among the live music events held in the upstairs function room is what is claimed to be the oldest folk club in the country.
❀◐⇌⊖(Central)

Crown Posada ★

33 Side, NE1 3JE
✪ 12 (11 Thu)-11; 11-midnight Fri; 12-midnight Sat; 7-10.30 Sun
☎ (0191) 232 1269
Hadrian Gladiator; Jarrow Bitter; Taylor Landlord; guest beers Ⓗ
An architecturally fine pub, listed in CAMRA's National Inventory of historic interiors. Behind the narrow street frontage with its two impressive stained glass windows lies a small snug, bar counter and longer seating area. Look for the interesting coffered ceiling, local photographs and cartoons of long gone customers and staff on the walls. Small, local brewers are enthusiastically supported. The pub has been sympathetically refurbished over the years by the owners and is an oasis of calm and peace near the busy Quayside drinking, dining and clubbing circuit.
Q⇌⊖(Central)🚌(Q1,Q2)⚐

Duke of Wellington ✔

High Bridge, NE1 1EN
✪ 11-11; 12-10.30 Sun
☎ (0191) 261 8852
Caledonian Deuchars IPA; guest beers Ⓗ
This pub sits on a street rapidly gaining a reputation as the home of alternative and independent

clothing, music and art retailers, and draws a mixed crowd of drinkers attracted by the selection of beers from all over England. The pub is near the infamous Bigg Market area but just far enough away to ensure that it is off the young revellers' circuit. Home-made lunchtime food is simple and good value. ⇌⊖(Monument)

New Bridge

2 Argyle Street, NE1 6PF
11-11 (11.30 Thu); 12-10.30 Sun
☎ (0191) 232 1020
Beer range varies Ⓗ
Just east of Newcastle city centre, next to a business park and facing a large new extension to Northumbria University, the pub is well served by buses and the Metro. It is very much a locals' pub but all are made welcome, and it attracts a mixed lunchtime and early evening crowd enjoying the beer and home-made food. The ever-changing choice of beers comes from independent brewers. ⊖(Manors)

Newcastle Arms

57 St Andrew's Street, NE1 5SE
11-11; 12-10.30 Sun
☎ (0191) 260 2490 newcastlearms.co.uk
Caledonian Deuchars IPA; guest beers Ⓗ
Popular single-roomed pub near Newcastle United's football ground and the city's Chinese restaurants. A frequent winner of local CAMRA Pub of the Year, the staff are committed to giving the customer what they want. Beer festivals are held every few months when a portable bar brings the number of beers up to 13.
Q♿⇌⊖(Monument/St James)

Strawberry

7 Strawberry Place, NE1 4SF
☎ (0191) 232 6865
Caledonian Deuchars IPA; Mordue No. 9; guest beers Ⓗ
A single-roomed pub situated directly opposite St James' Park, the Strawberry tends to be very busy on match days. The walls are covered in Newcastle United memorabilia, and silent TV screens show sporting events. A new roof terrace with canopies and heaters overlooks the city centre. Two guest beers are available. Above average food at below average prices is served all day - check out the giant filled Yorkshire puddings.
⇌⊖(Monument/St James)P

Tilley's

105-109 Westgate Road, NE1 4AG
12-11 (10.30 Sun)
☎ (0191) 232 0692 theheadofsteam.com
Beer range varies Ⓗ
Regular beer festivals are held in this street-corner pub near the Tyne Theatre, Carling Academy and Dance City in the Theatre Village area of the city. The main bar can get very busy but as quiet alternative there is a smaller sitting room. The beer selection is often themed - a particular area of the country or style of beer - and can include some unusual examples. ⇌⊖(Central/St James)

North Shields

Oddfellows

7 Albion Road, NE30 2RJ
11 (12 Sun)-11
☎ (0191) 257 4288 oddfellowspub.co.uk
Greene King Abbot; Jarrow Bitter; guest beers Ⓗ
The walls of this small, friendly, single room lounge bar are covered with historic maps and photographs of pre-war North Shields, complemented by a slideshow of images shown on the large flat screen TV and relayed to the outside smoking area. The pub has strong sporting links with past boxing champions and current national darts players. Home to football and darts teams, it also fundraises for charity. A beer festival is held annually in May. ♿⊖(306)

Prince of Wales

2 Liddell Street, NE30 1HE
3 (12 Wed-Sat)-11; 12-10.30 Sun
☎ (0191) 296 2816
Samuel Smith OBB Ⓗ
Records for this pub go back to 1627, but the current building faced with green glazed brick dates from 1927. The premises lay empty for some years before a restoration in traditional style by Sam Smith's, reopening in 1992. A rare outlet for Sam Smith's this far north, it is well worth a visit. Close to the Fish Quay where the fish and chips are renowned, there is a replica wooden doll outside which gives the pub its 'Old Wooden Dolly' nickname. Q⊖(North Shields)(333)

Penshaw

Monument

Old Penshaw Village, DH4 7ER (off A183 signed Old Penshaw)
11 (12 Sun)-11
☎ (0191) 584 1027
Beer range varies Ⓗ
A warm and welcoming atmosphere is guaranteed at this cosy and compact village pub located at the foot of the famous local folly Penshaw Monument. The two-roomed pub has lots of pictures of old Penshaw and there is a separate games room. Food is limited to simple snacks. Handy for Herrington Country Park. ♿(78,78A)

South Gosforth

Victory

43 Killingworth Road, NE3 1SY
12-11 (midnight Fri & Sat); 12-10.30 Sun
☎ (0191) 285 1254
Caledonian Deuchars IPA; Courage Directors; Taylor Landlord; Theakston Best Bitter; Wells Bombardier Ⓗ
Established on this site since 1861, the pub takes its name from Nelson's flagship and once served the local mining community. Essentially a single room, the bar has different levels and areas with wood ceilings, traditional decor and two fireplaces. A range of malt whiskies complements the quality beers. Busy at weekends, there are tables outside during the summer, and a covered and heated area for smokers. ♿⊖P

South Shields

Alum Ale House ✔

River Drive, NE33 1JR
11-11 (midnight Thu-Sat); 12-11 Sun
☎ (0191) 427 7745
Banks's Original, Bitter; Marston's Pedigree; guest beers Ⓗ
The number of beers on sale at the Alum has increased to eight since last year's Guide, all from

the Marston's range. The single room pub has bare floorboards and seating around the walls. An ideal place to wait for the ferry across the Tyne to North Shields, it is just a short walk from the Market Place. The cellar bar has recently been reopened and offers a good range of whiskies. ❀⊖

Bamburgh ✔
175 Bamburgh Avenue, NE33 1JR (on coast rd)
11 (12 Sun)-11
☎ (0191) 454 1899
Greene King IPA, Abbot; guest beers Ⓗ
Greene King-managed pub a stone's throw from the coast and the finishing point of the Great North Run. The spacious, open plan pub has a raised dining area at one end and a games area at the other. Mainly a locals pub but also popular with families who come to enjoy the extensive food menu. ❀◑♿⚠🚌(E1)P⁵⁻

Dolly Peel ✔
137 Commercial Road, NE33 1SH
12-11 (midnight Thu-Sat)
☎ (0191) 427 1441
Black Sheep Best Bitter; Courage Directors; Taylor Landlord Ⓗ
Named after a local fishwife and smuggler whose husband and sons were press ganged into the navy. This is a local riverside pub not far from the Mill Dam and attracts a more mature clientele. The interior is divided into two areas, with large-screen TVs for sporting events. Wednesday is buskers' night. Q⊖(Chichester)

Maltings
Claypath Lane, NE3 4PG (off Westoe Rd)
12- 11.30 (10.30 Sun)
☎ (0191) 427 7147 🌐 jarrowbrewery.co.uk
Jarrow Bitter, Joblings Swinging Gibbet, Rivet Catcher, Westoe IPA, seasonal beers; guest beer Ⓗ
Built on the first floor of a former dairy, the Maltings is the home of Jarrow Brewery's second plant, the Westoe Brew House on the ground floor. The full range of Jarrow beers is complemented by an excellent range of imported ales. The large wood-panelled bar is reached by an imposing staircase and has a number of separate seating areas. Wednesday is quiz night when there is a free buffet. Children are welcome until 9pm.
Q❀♿⊖🚌●⁵⁻

Stag's Head ☆
45 Fowler Street, NE33 1NS
11-11 (midnight Fri & Sat); 12-midnight Sun
☎ (0191) 427 2911
Draught Bass; Houston Killelan Bitter Ⓗ
Featuring in CAMRA's Regional Inventory, this small, traditional town centre pub is one of the oldest in South Shields and has changed little over the years. It has a very busy afternoon trade and at the weekend the upstairs function room opens to provide extra space for visitors. Karaoke is a firm favourite on Thursday evening. ⊖♣

Steamboat 🍷 ✔
Coronation Street, Mill Dam, NE33 1EQ
12-11 (10.30 Sun)
☎ (0191) 454 0134
Caledonian Deuchars IPA; Greene King Abbot; Wells Bombardier; guest beers Ⓗ
The Steamboat is one of South Shields' oldest pubs and has undergone a real ale revolution, with the enthusiastic manager doubling the number of cask beers on offer to eight. Four guest beers complement the regulars. The main bar has a nautical and local industry theme, and there is a small, comfortable lounge on the upper level. Local CAMRA Pub of the Year 2009. ⊖🚌

Sunderland

Clarendon
143 High Street, SR1 2BL
12-11
☎ (0191) 510 3200 🌐 bull-lane-brewing.co.uk
Bull Lane Nowtsamatta, Ryhope Tug, Jacks Flag, Jasons Jinja, Sauce o The Niall, Double Barrel Ⓗ
A classic, old-fashioned brew pub with all the character you would expect from a local bar. The single room interior has a large window overlooking the River Wear. Buskers' night is Thursday and live music plays occasionally on a Sunday afternoon. Up to six Bull Lane beers are available. A little out of the way but definitely worth a visit. ♿🚌(5,5A)

Dun Cow ☆
9 High Street West, SR1 3HA
12-12.30 (11.30 Sun)
☎ (0191) 5672984
Beer range varies Ⓗ
One of the oldest pubs in the city. This Grade II-listed building is an architectural gem and features in CAMRA's National Inventory. Real ales usually come from local Bull Lane and Maxim Breweries. The pub is next to the Empire Theatre and can get very busy around performance times. Note the impressive back bar fitting. ⇌⊖🚌♣

Fitzgerald's
10-12 Green Terrace, SR1 3PZ
11-11 (midnight Fri & Sat); 12-10.30 Sun
☎ (0191) 567 0852 🌐 sjf.co.uk
Black Sheep Best Bitter; Taylor Landlord, Ⓗ
A real ale oasis among the city's newer bars. The pub attracts customers of all ages and is very busy at weekends, although the smaller Chart Room is usually quieter. This Guide regular has the largest range of beers in the area with 11 handpumps. Rotating Bull Lane and Durham beers are on offer together with seven guest beers from independent breweries and beers from North East micros. The pub is a former winner of both local and regional CAMRA Pub of the Year awards.
❀◑⇌⊖(University)🚌●⁵⁻

Harbour View
Benedict Road, Roker, SR6 0NL
10.30-11.30 (7 Fri; 12.30am Sat)
☎ (0191) 567 1402
Caledonian Deuchars IPA; Taylor Landlord; guest beers Ⓗ
Smart lounge bar situated just off Roker seafront with views over the marina. It features a central bar with five handpumps and offers the largest range of cask ale on the north side of the city. Beers are often from local breweries. Benedict's bar on the first floor is open at weekends and used as a restaurant during the week. Very popular when Sunderland are at home.
◑⊖(Stadium of Light)🚌(E1)

King's Arms
Beach Street, Deptford, SR4 6BU
11-11 (midnight Fri & Sat); 12-10.30 Sun
☎ (0191) 567 9804

Taylor Landlord; guest beers H
A former local CAMRA and regional Pub of the Year winner, the King's Arms is an old-fashioned pub with an unspoilt timber-panelled interior. A real fire at one end of the bar helps to create the ambience of a traditional pub. Taylor Landlord is the regular ale, served alongside seven ever-changing guests plus a real cider. Large-screen TVs show sport and a marquee at the back of the pub is home to live music during the summer months. (Millfield)(18,11)

Rosedene
Queen Alexandra Road, SR2 9BT
11-11; 12-10.30 Sun
(0191) 528 4313
Greene King IPA, Old Speckled Hen, Abbot, seasonal beers H
Now part of the Greene King chain, the building was originally a Georgian mansion built in 1830, pulled down in 1876 and rebuilt in its current location brick by brick. It was eventually converted to a pub by Vaux in 1964. The pub has a bar area, function room and outside smoking area with TV. It has gained a reputation for quality food, served in the separate restaurant. The function room is licensed for weddings. (10)P

TJ Doyles
Hanover Place, Deptford, SR4 6BY
11-11; 12-10.30 Sun
(0191) 5101554 tjdoyles.com
Bull Lane Neck Oil; guest beers H
Tastefully refurbished former Vaux pub. Now an Irish bar, it champions beers from local micro-breweries – ales from Bull Lane and Maxim are regularly available as well as two guest beers. The bar is large and comfortable with live music playing at weekends. It opens early for an impressive Irish breakfast.
(Millfield)(11)

Wolsey
40 Millum Terrace, Roker, SR6 0ES
11-11 (midnight Fri & Sat)
(0191) 567 2798
Theakston Best Bitter; guest beers H
The Wolsey is one of two buildings left on Millum Terrace and a short walk from Roker Beach and Marina. Recently refurbished, it serves competitively priced meals with a curry night on Wednesday, steak night on Thursday and Sunday carvery. Thursday evenings are especially popular, with a free quiz and Lucky 13 – bingo played with cards. The quizmaster is a bit of a character who claims to be susceptible to bribery! Q(E1)P

Swalwell

Sun Inn
Market Lane, NE16 3AL
11 (12 Sun)-11
Jennings Cocker Hoop; guest beers H
Situated in the modern village of Swallwell, just a stone's throw from the Metrocentre shopping complex, this pub has been in existence for more than 100 years. The central bar divides the interior into two rooms, with an additional room open for buskers' night on Saturday. The enthusiastic landlord has increased the handpulls from one to four and also has real cider on draught. Bar food and snacks are available and free on Sunday.
(Metro Centre)

Tynemouth

Cumberland Arms
17 Front Street, NE30 4DX
12-11 (10.30 Sun)
(0191) 2571820 cumberlandarms.co.uk
Courage Directors; Jennings Cumberland Ale; Tetley Bitter; guest beers H
A friendly welcome awaits you at this cosy split level pub, with attractive stained glass windows and historic artefacts on display. Two bars each dispense three regular ales and up to three guests. Quiet background music plays and large-screen TVs show live football matches. Families are welcome in the dining area at the rear, where good value meals are available. (306)

Turks Head
41 Front Street, NE30 4DZ
12-11 (midnight Fri & Sat; 10.30 Sun)
(0191) 257 6547
Caledonian Deuchars IPA; Courage Directors; Wells Bombardier H
An architecturally interesting pub with a white tiled exterior and stained glass windows. The interior comprises two linked rooms – families are welcome in the rear room until 7pm. Up to eight real ales are on handpump and food is served all day. TVs screen live sports. Look for the famous stuffed dog. (306)

Tynemouth Lodge Hotel
Tynemouth Road, NE30 4AA
11-11; 12-10.30 Sun
(0191) 257 7565 tynemouthlodgehotel.co.uk
Belhaven 80/-; Caledonian Deuchars IPA; Draught Bass H
This attractive, externally tiled free house was built in 1799 and has featured in every issue of the Guide since 1983 when the current owner took over. The comfortable U-shaped lounge has a bar on one side and a hatch on the other. The pub is noted in the area for its Scottish ales and for selling reputedly the highest volume of draught Bass on Tyneside. It is next to Northumberland Park and near the Coast to Coast cycle route. QP

Wardley

Green
White Mare Pool, NE10 8YB (at Leam Lane B1288/A184 jct)
11-11 (10.30 Sun)
(0191) 495 0171
Black Sheep Best Bitter; guest beers H
This bar and brasserie is part of the highly respected Sir John Fitzgerald group. It has eight handpulls dispensing four different real ales sourced from throughout the British Isles, and a CAMRA Good Pub Food Guide-listed restaurant that cooks with locally-sourced ingredients. Furnished throughout to a very high standard, the lounge is in hunting lodge style while the public bar features a large-screen TV and many stylish black and white motor-racing photographs. Weekly quizzes are hosted. P

Washington

Courtyard
Arts Centre, Biddick Lane, Fatfield, NE38 8AB
11-11 (midnight Fri & Sat); 12-11 Sun
(0191) 417 0445

Taylor Landlord; guest beers Ⓗ
Located within the council run Arts Centre, this open plan cafe/bar has a light, airy feel and a friendly welcome awaits visitors. Eight handpumped beers are on offer, with guest ales from independent and micro-breweries from all over the country. Beer festivals are held on the Easter and August bank holidays. There is an outside seating area. Home of the famous Davy Lamp Folk Club. Q❀◐◑♿🚌(M1,M3)♣●P

William de Wessyngton ✔

2-3 Victoria Terrace, Concord, NE37 2SY (opp bus station)
⏲ 9-11.30
☎ (0191) 4180100
Greene King IPA, Abbot; Marston's Pedigree; guest beers Ⓗ
This large, open-plan Wetherspoon's pub is a real ale oasis and the only cask beer outlet in Concord. It is named after an ancestor of George Washington and is housed in a former snooker hall and ice cream parlour. The 10 handpumps offer an excellent range of beers including at least one north east ale. Ale prices are good value and the pub can get very busy when live football is shown. Q🐎◐◑♿🚌●⚐

West Boldon

Black Horse

Rectory Bank, NE36 0QQ (off A184)
⏲ 11-11; 12-10.30 Sun
☎ (0191) 536 1814
Black Sheep Best Bitter Ⓗ
This two-roomed pub has an L-shaped bar and restaurant. The walls are adorned with bric-a-brac and the tables are candle-lit. Live music plays on Sunday evening. 🐎◐◑🚌(9,9A)⚐

West Herrington

Stables

McLaren Way, DH4 4ND (off B1286)
⏲ 12-11 (midnight Fri & Sat)
☎ (0191) 584 9226
Black Sheep Best Bitter; Taylor Landlord; guest beers Ⓗ
From the outside this looks like a private house because there is no pub sign, but it is easy to find in this small village. A tasteful conversion of an old riding school stables, the long, narrow interior has a stone floor, low ceiling and subdued lighting. The introduction of good food means the pub is always busy. Well worth seeking out. 🔥Q🐎❀◐♿🚌(35)P

West Monkseaton

Beacon Hotel ✔

Earsdon Road, NE25 9PT
⏲ 11.30-11 (midnight Fri & Sat); 11-11.30 Sun
☎ (0191) 253 6911
Caledonian Deuchars IPA; guest beers Ⓗ
Superb modern pub, offering excellent food at reasonable prices. The cellar has been updated to dispense ale at the correct temperature. Guest beers change monthly. Look out for the rack of ale – a wooden rack that serves a third of a pint of three different ales chosen by the customer. Food themed nights are popular – Tuesday is grill, Thursday curry. Quiz nights are Sunday and Wednesday. Children over 14 are welcome with an adult. 🔥◐◑♿⊖P

Whitley Bay

Briar Dene

71 The Links, NE26 1UE
⏲ 11-11; 12-10.30 Sun
☎ (0191) 252 0926
Black Sheep Ale; guest beers Ⓗ
This Fitzgerald's pub has a large, attractive lounge with sea views to the links and St Mary's lighthouse, and a more compact rear bar with widescreen TV, pool and darts. The pub is well known for its food, with local fish and chips a speciality. Guest beers change regularly. Children are welcome in a family area in the lounge. There is seating outside at the front of the pub. 🐎❀◐◑♿♣P

Fitzgeralds

2 South Parade, NE26 2RG
⏲ 11-11; 12-10.30 Sun
☎ (0191) 251 1255
Beer range varies Ⓗ
Large, friendly town-centre pub near the Metro and local bus services. Three frequently-changing beers are usually available, with a wider range on offer at the weekend when the pub can be very busy. Like most of the Fitzgerald's chain, the pub offers good value and popular food. ◐◑♿⊖

Rockcliffe Arms

Algernon Place, NE26 2DT
⏲ 11-11 (11.15 Fri & Sat); 12-11 Sun
☎ (0191) 253 1299
Beer range varies Ⓗ
Outstanding back-street Fitzgerald's pub, a few minutes' walk from the Metro station. This one-room establishment has distinct bar and lounge areas with a snug in between. There are four constantly changing guest ales, with beer notes on notices above the dividing arch. Regular darts and dominoes matches are held in the snug. ❀⊖♣⚐

Your shout

We would like to hear from you. If you think a pub not listed in the Guide is worthy of consideration, please let us know. Send us the name, full address and phone number (if known). If a pub in the Guide has given poor service, we would also like to know.

Write to Good Beer Guide, CAMRA, 230 Hatfield Road, St Albans, Herts, AL1 4LW or email **gbgeditor@camra.org.uk**

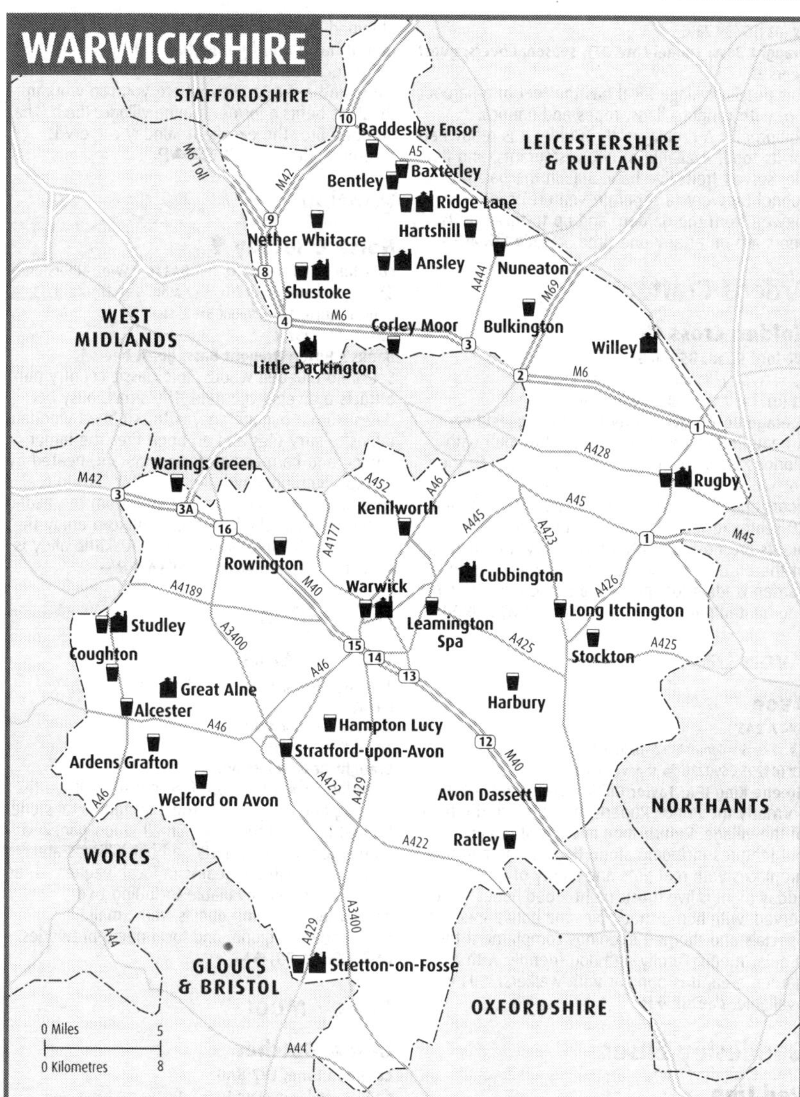

Alcester

Holly Bush

37 Henley Street, B49 5QX

12-11 (10.30 Sun)

☎ (01789) 762482

Black Sheep Best Bitter; Purity Pure Gold, UBU; Uley Bitter; guest beers Ⓗ

This traditional 17th-century local in an historic market town is a frequent CAMRA branch Pub of the Year. Restoration has preserved its five rooms and many original features. Four regular ales and up to four guests are available, and a beer festival is held in June. The food menu offers traditional English and a la carte (not Sun eve). A regular folk session is held monthly and spontaneous music may strike up at any time. The White Hart Morris Men practise here on Monday evening. The pretty walled garden is lovely in summer.
(26,246,247)

Three Tuns

34 High Street, B49 5AB

12-11

☎ (01789) 762626

Hobsons Best Bitter; guest beers Ⓗ

This local CAMRA award-winning pub is a 'must visit'. No music, no pool and no food – just how a real pub should be. The single room interior has low beams, a stone flagged floor and an exposed area of wattle and daub. Up to eight ales from micros and independents provide a permanent yet ever-changing mini beer festival. The pub may close on winter afternoons if there are no customers. Q(26,246,247)

Ansley

Lord Nelson Inn

Birmingham Road, CV10 9PQ

12-11 (10.30 Sun)

☎ (024) 7639 2305
Draught Bass; Tunnel Late OTT, seasonal beers; guest beers Ⓗ
This popular village local has the feel of a harbour inn, with cannon, flags, ropes and nautical equipment. A regular in the Guide, it is renowned for its food, available in two restaurants, and its ale, served from five handpulls in the bar. The Tunnel Brewery (a separate venture) can be viewed from the garden, and up to three of its beers are on at any one time. ♨❀◐◑⊟⊞♣P⁄–

Ardens Grafton

Golden Cross ✔
Wixford Road, B50 4LG
⊙ 11-3, 6-11; 11-midnight Sat; 11.30-11 Sun
☎ (01789) 772420 ⊕ thegoldencross.net
Courage Best Bitter; Purity Pure UBU; guest beer Ⓗ
A beautiful, stone-built, 18th-century pub with glorious views over the Vale of Evesham to the Cotswolds. The interior features stone-flagged floors and a real fire in interlinked bar areas, and a 40-seater restaurant. Regular music and theme nights are hosted, with 'Graftonbury' the highlight of the outdoor music calendar. The large, safe garden is ideal for children, and there is a covered and heated patio area for smokers. ♨Q❀◐◑♿P⁄–

Avon Dassett

Avon
CV47 2AS
⊙ 12-3, 5-midnight; 12-midnight Sat; 12-10.30 Sun
☎ (01295) 690270 ⊕ theavon.co.uk
Greene King IPA; Taylor Golden Best, Landlord Ⓗ
Formerly the Prince Rupert, this pub is in the heart of the village. Refurbished in 2008, it retains many old features including stone flags in the bar area, fireplaces with real fires and plenty of timberwork. Friday night is live music night. Good honest food is served, with home-made pies the house speciality. Specials and themed evenings complement the regular menu. Family and dog friendly with a garden area, it is popular with walkers. WiFi is available. ♨❀◐◑♣P

Baddesley Ensor

Red Lion
The Common, CV9 2BT
⊙ 7 (4 Fri)-11; 12-3, 7-11 Sat; 12-3, 7-10.30 Sun
☎ (01827) 718186
Everards Tiger; Marston's Pedigree; guest beers Ⓗ
Popular community local with a sound trade in real ale. Unusually, it does not feature food. Enjoy instead the open fire and the buzz of conversation in a cosily decorated, music-free environment. Three to four guest ales are available, and the landlord willingly removes the sparkler. There is off-street parking opposite the pub. Note the restricted opening hours. ♨Q⊞(765)♣●

Baxterley

Rose Inn ✔
Main Road, CV9 2LE
⊙ 12-3, 7-11; 12-11 Sat; 12-10.30 Sun
☎ (01827) 713939 ⊕ roseinnbaxterley.com
Draught Bass; St Austell Tribute; guest beers Ⓗ
A classic, rambling pub with a picturesque duck pond. The Rose was originally a bakery but obtained a licence around 1840. A true drinkers' pub, it has a dog-friendly bar and three further intimate areas, plus a restaurant with a scenic view, and a skittle alley where you can work up a thirst. As befits a former mining village, the bar has an open fire. The excellent Sunday carvery is recommended. ♨❀◐◑⊟⊞♣P

Bentley

Horse & Jockey 🏆
Coleshill Road, CV9 2HL (on B4116, SW of Atherstone)
⊙ 12-3 (not Mon, 2.30 Fri), 6 (7 Mon, 5.30 Fri)-11; 12-3, 5-midnight Fri; 12-midnight Sat & Sun
☎ (01827) 715236
Banks's Bitter; Draught Bass; guest beers Ⓗ
Set amid bluebell woods, this classic country pub attracts a diverse clientele. The small, busy bar dates from a bygone age, with scrubbed wooden tables, quarry tiles and an open fire. The larger lounge and barn-conversion restaurant, heated by a wood-burning stove, are more modern in feel. Free of tie, the guest beers range from the exotic to the familiar. Children and adults can enjoy the spacious, attractive beer garden. A skittle alley is available for hire. ♨☕❀◐◑⊟▲♣P⁄–

Bulkington

Weavers Arms
12 Long Street, Ryton, CV12 9JZ (off Wolvey Road B4109)
⊙ 1 (12 Sun)-midnight
☎ (024) 7631 4415
Draught Bass; guest beers Ⓗ
Friendly, cosy, two-room free house well worth seeking out. A log fire warms the traditional stone-floored bar, and there is a small wood-panelled games room where darts and bar billiards are played. The pub has teams in local leagues. Three beers are usually available including two constantly- changing guests from small independent regional and local micro-breweries. ♨❀⊟⊞(56,75)♣⁄–

Corley Moor

Bull & Butcher
Common Lane, CV7 8AQ
⊙ 10am-midnight (1am Fri & Sat); 10am-11 Sun
☎ (01676) 540241
Draught Bass; Greene King Abbot; M&B Brew XI; guest beer Ⓗ
A popular village pub, adorned with hanging baskets in summer, on the outskirts of west Coventry. The wood-beamed and flagstoned bar leads to a cosy snug, both with open fires. There is a pleasant restaurant in the back room, with

INDEPENDENT BREWERIES

Atomic Rugby
Church End Ridge Lane
Discovery Little Packington
Griffin Inn Shustoke
North Cotswold Stretton-on-Fosse
Purity Great Alne
Rugby Willey
Slaughterhouse Warwick
Tunnel Ansley
Warwickshire Cubbington
Weatheroak Studley

decking for summer and good views. Food is served all day from breakfast onwards – the menu includes excellent pies and a Sunday carvery. An attractive family garden is equipped for children. The guest beer changes frequently.
⛰Q❀◑◐⊟♿⛺P⊱

Coughton

Throckmorton Arms

Coughton Hill, B49 5HX (on A435 between Studley and Alcester) SP079609
⏲ 12-11 (10.30 Sun)
☎ (01789) 766366 🌐 thethrockmortonarms.co.uk
Hobsons Best Bitter; St Austell Tribute; guest beers Ⓗ
Situated opposite Coughton Court with its Gunpowder Plot connections, this large roadside hotel offers a smart and comfortable environment to enjoy a pint or a meal. An L-shaped bar serves the open-plan interior, which has distinctive areas creating a feeling of privacy. A separate restaurant overlooks the large patio, with commanding views of the Warwickshire countryside. The hotel is popular with business people during the week and visitors to the area at the weekend. Two guest beers come from local breweries.
⛰❀🛏◑◐⊟♿🚌P⊱

Hampton Lucy

Boars Head 🏆

Church Street, CV35 8BE
⏲ 11.30-3, 5-11; 11-11 Fri & Sat; 11-11 (6 winter) Sun
☎ (01789) 840533 🌐 theboarsheadhamptonlucy4food.co.uk
Beer range varies Ⓗ
Friendly, comfortable village pub dating back to the 17th century – the present kitchen was originally a mortuary. Situated on a Sustrans cycle route, and close to the River Avon, it is popular with cyclists, walkers and visitors to nearby Charlecote Park (NT), as well as the local Young Farmers. A sheltered rear garden hosts Sunday afternoon barbecues in summer. Up to six beers are available including at least one from a small local or independent brewery. ⛰❀◑◐P⊱

Harbury

Old New Inn

Farm Sreet, CV33 9LS
⏲ 3 (11 Fri & Sat)-12.30am; 11-12.30am Sun
☎ (01926) 614023
Beer range varies Ⓗ
Large country village pub built from local Jurassic white lias limestone. Originally several small rooms, over the years these have become the main bar, TV area and pool room. This has resulted in varying ceiling heights – tall folk watch your head! A homely lounge is used by the dominoes and crib teams. The rear garden is a mass of colour in summer. One Church End real ale is available during the week, two at weekends.
⛰Q⚇❀⊟♿⛺🚌(64)♣P⊱

Hartshill

Anchor Inn

Mancetter Road, CV10 0RT (on A4131)
⏲ 5 (12 Sat & Sun)-11
☎ (024) 7639 8839
Everards Tiger Best Bitter, Original; guest beers Ⓗ
The Anchor was thought to be a trading post and mail collection point for narrowboat workers following completion of the canal in 1790. It has a cosy feel in winter, with wooden beams and open fires. In summer there are plenty of outdoor areas including a children's playground. Three restaurants and a carvery are on different levels (no evening meals Sun). Up to four guest beers complement the Everards. ⛰❀◑◐♿P⊱

Kenilworth

Engine ✔

8 Mill End, CV8 2HP
⏲ 4 (12 Thu & Fri)-midnight; 11-1am Sat; 11-midnight Sun
☎ (01926) 853341
M&B Brew XI; guest beers Ⓗ
As its name suggests, this pub is near the railway line, but there is no longer a station in Kenilworth. Situated away from the main part of town, the friendly pub has a single-room, wood-beamed interior. Food is only served on a Thursday lunchtime – originally just for OAPs but now available to all. The guest beers are from the Punch Taverns list. ❀🚌(16,X17)♣⊱

Old Bakery

12 High Street, CV8 1LZ (near A429/A452 jct)
⏲ 5.30 (5 Fri & Sat)-11; 12-2, 7-10.30
☎ (01926) 864111 🌐 theoldbakeryhotel.co.uk
St Austell Tribute; Wye Valley Bitter; guest beers Ⓗ
Attractively restored former bakery in a 400-year-old building in the centre of the old town, with two rooms plus a small outside patio. Monday night's fish and chip suppers are always popular. Disabled access is via the rear car park. Located near Abbey Fields and a 10-minute walk from the castle.
Q❀🛏♿🚌(12)P

Royal Oak

36 New Street, CV8 2EZ
⏲ 4 (12 Sat & Sun)-11
☎ (01926) 856906
Adnams Bitter; Black Sheep Best Bitter; Fuller's London Pride; Taylor Landlord Ⓗ
Pleasant, traditional pub on the main Coventry road into Kenilworth with an extended main bar and separate pool room. Outside, the decked patio is attractive in summer, with a heated and covered smoking area beyond. The pub has a strong local following with men's and ladies' darts teams. Sky Sports is shown on multiple TVs, with large screens for special events. Four regular beers may change occasionally. Excellent pork pies are served on Sunday lunchtime only. ❀🚌(12,X17)♣⊱

Virgins & Castle

7 High Street, CV8 1LY (A429/A452 jct)
⏲ 11-11.30 (midnight Fri & Sat); 12-10.30 Sun
☎ (01926) 853737
Everards Beacon Bitter, Sunchaser, Tiger Best Bitter, Original; Fuller's London Pride; guest beer Ⓗ
The oldest pub in the town, dating from 1563. The interior comprises many separate drinking areas, with an L-shaped central bar. English, Japanese and Filipino food is available lunchtimes and evenings. This is the only Everard's pub in Kenilworth. There is limited parking at the front, but a public car park is close by. Served by buses from Coventry, Leamington Spa and Warwick University.
⛰Q❀◑◐🚌(12)⊱

Wyandotte Inn 🏆

Park Road, CV8 2GF

11-midnight; 11.30-10.30 Sun

(01926) 859076

Banks's Original; Jennings Cocker Hoop; Marston's Burton Bitter; guest beers H

The pub is named after a tribe of native Americans from Canada. One branch of the tribe came to England in 1885 and settled in Kenilworth. They eventually took over the area and many local inhabitants can trace their ancestry back to the Wyandotte. The current landlord and his son have both been elected honorary chiefs of the tribe. Guest beers come from the Marston's portfolio. (16,X17)P

Leamington Spa

Newbold Comyn Arms

Newbold Terrace East, CV32 4EW

5 (12 Fri-Sun)-midnight

(01926) 338810 newboldcomynarms.co.uk

Beer range varies H

Genuine free house situated in Newbold Comyn Park near the leisure centre. The Stables bar was converted from farm buildings and features beamed ceilings, booth seating and lots of brickwork. A wood burner set in the large fireplace provides a focal point. The function room in the main building with its own small bar is available for hire. The south-facing terrace overlooks lawns and a children's play area. Closed Monday to Wednesday in winter. P

Talbot Inn 🏆

34 Rushmore Street, CV31 1JA

12-11 (midnight Fri & Sat)

(01926) 428883

Beer range varies H

Tucked away down back streets, this pub is easier to find by canal. Look for the building with the large mural between Clapham Terrace and St Mary's bridges. This free house is very popular with boaters and towpath walkers as well as locals. It has been recently modernised but retains a traditional close-knit atmosphere. Three regularly-changing real ales are on offer, one usually from a local brewery, plus a Thatchers cider. Still known as Hector's after a previous landlord. Q(12,63,64,U1)

Long Itchington

Green Man

Church Road, CV47 9PW

5 (12 Sun)-midnight

(01926) 812208

Batemans XB; Tetley Bitter; guest beer H

Popular village local with three drinking areas and a lounge/function room. The interior is an interesting mix of low ceilings, beams, quarry tiles, carpet and artex that somehow works. The games room has a display of trophies and photos of past teams. Note, also, the fascinating map of the old Davenport's pub estate plus a framed letter from 1940 stating that the pub is unsafe following bomb damage. A guest beer is always available, with many more during the village May Day beer festival. Q(64)P

Harvester Inn

6 Church Road, CV47 9PG (off A423 at village pond, then first left)

12-2.30, 6-11; 12-3, 7-10.30 Sun

(01926) 812698 theharvesterinn.co.uk

Hook Norton Best Bitter; guest beers H

Unchanging locals' pub in the centre of the village, next to a small square, with two distinct drinking areas plus a popular restaurant. The food is traditional, good quality, value fare. Two changing guest beers are on the bar plus a few surprises including both regular and dark Budvar and a changing draught Belgian beer. A modest range of Belgian bottled beers is also stocked. The pub takes part in the annual village beer festival each May Day bank holiday. Q(64)P

Two Boats Inn ✔

Southam Road, CV47 9QZ

12-11

(01926) 812640 2boats.co.uk

Adnams Bitter, Broadside; Greene King Abbot; guest beer H

This large brick-built pub once offered stabling for canal horses. Recently refurbished by the current licensees, this welcoming pub now has a comfortable lounge with a real fire and a public bar with games area. For sunny days there are plenty of outside seats by the towpath. A live music event is staged most weekends. Good value food ranges from snacks to full meals. An additional guest beer is available in summer and for the May Day village beer festival. (64)P

Nether Whitacre

Dog Inn

Dog Lane, B46 2DU (follow brown sign from B4098)

12-3, 6-11; 12-11 Sat & Sun

(01675) 481318

Adnams Bitter; Marston's Pedigree; Taylor Landlord; Wells Bombardier; guest beers H

Well-hidden, black-and-white rural pub with a countryside theme throughout its four rooms. The gorgeously elaborate carved frontage to the bar, including two pairs of stuffed jays, came from Whitacre Hall. Brass knick-knacks abound, and seating includes a church pew and two overly snug sofas. Two cosy, intimate dining rooms are to the rear. Guest beers usually include a mild. P

Nuneaton

Crown

10 Bond Street, CV11 4BX

12-11 (midnight Fri & Sat)

(024) 7637 3343 thecrownnuneaton.com

Oakham JHB; guest beers H

Seven ales and three ciders and perries are on offer at this popular town-centre, split-level bar. Live bands play on Saturday night, and the first Tuesday of the month is open mike night. You may think you are back in the Blitz when you see the half-built walls inside. An interesting collection of photographs ranges from John Lennon to George Eliot. There is an outside drinking area and a function room for hire. Two beer festivals are held in June and December. P

Hearty Goodfellow

285 Arbury Road, Stockingford, CV10 7NQ

11-11; 12-10.30 Sun

☎ (024) 7638 8152
Marston's Burton Bitter; guest beers H
Large sports-oriented community local where darts, pool and football teams flourish. Sports memorabilia, trophies, pennants and shirts adorn the walls. Several large screen TVs ensure you will not miss your favourite sport from any part of the L-shaped room. There are four handpulls offering the regular Burton Bitter and guests from the Marston's group. The clientele covers all age groups and visitors are made to feel welcome. ❀🚌♣⚡

Rose Inn
Coton Road, CV11 5LY (opp Our Lady of the Angels Catholic Church)
🕐 11-11.30 (11 Sun)
☎ (024) 7674 2991
Marston's Burton Bitter, Pedigree; guest beer H
The Rose was the venue for CAMRA's first AGM, and an account of this occasion hangs on the wall. Landlord Tony is passionate about his ales and also his clock collection on display around the L-shaped lounge. The bar at the front has a pool table and dartboard. There is a covered and heated area for smokers. The pub is handy when visiting Nuneaton Museum across the road in Riversley Park. ❀♿🚌♣P⚡

Ratley

Rose & Crown
OX15 6DS
🕐 12-2.30, 6-11; 12-4, 7-11 Sun
☎ (01295) 678148
Greene King Abbot; St Austell Tribute; Wells Bombardier; Wye Valley Butty Bach, HPA H
A superb country pub in a small secluded village. Dating back to the 11th century, it is stone built with exposed beams and a carpeted bar. Two log fires warm you in winter and candlelit tables await you in the evening. The cosy snug serves as a children's room and can be used for functions. Aunt Sally is played in the summer and there is disabled access from the front of the pub. Newspapers are on offer on Sunday. 🔥Q❀♿🚌(269)♣⚡

Ridge Lane

Church End Brewery Tap
109 Ridge Lane, CV10 0RD SP295947
🕐 6 (12 Fri & Sat)-11; closed Mon-Wed; 12-10.30 Sun
☎ (01827) 713080 🌐 churchendbrewery.co.uk
Beer range varies H
Ever-popular Church End tap, usually offering eight beers from the adjoining brewery, visible through a large glass panel. You can try a 'coffin' of one-third pint tasters. Keg beers are banned here, but there is a good range of Belgian bottled beers plus at least one real cider. A mild is always available. Dogs are welcome inside but children and smokers are relegated to the extensive rural beer garden. Customers are welcome to bring their own food. Q❀♿♣P

Rowington

Rowington Club
Rowington Green, CV35 7BX (E of B4439) SP 199701
🕐 2 (12 Sat & Sun)-11
☎ (01564) 782087 🌐 rowington.org/Rowington/rowington_club.html
Flowers IPA; Wye Valley HPA; guest beers H
Overlooking the village cricket club, this refurbished community club is in an idyllic location. Two guest beers and a cider change frequently. Visitors are warmly welcomed, with day membership for a nominal fee or free for card-carrying CAMRA members. Live music and other social events are held during the week, and family-friendly events including barbecues in summer at the weekend. The pleasant secluded garden hosts a popular beer and cider festival on the August bank holiday. Q❀♿♣P⚡

Rugby

Alexandra Arms
72 James Street, CV21 2SL (next to multi-storey car park)
🕐 11.30-11 (11.30 Fri & Sat); 12-11 Sun
☎ (01788) 578660 🌐 alexandraarms.co.uk
Alexandra Petit Blonde; Greene King Abbot; guest beers H
The pub has a comfortable L-shaped lounge where lively debate flourishes among an eclectic group, and a louder back room which features a fabulous rock jukebox along with pool, skittles and table football. At the rear of the pub is a micro-brewery producing Alexandra and Atomic ales. A large garden with covered seating serves as a venue for summer beer festivals. Guest beers include milds, stouts and porters. Winner of Rugby CAMRA Pub of the Year seven times. Q❀♿(Rugby)♣⚡

Bull
28 Sheep Street, CV21 3BX
🕐 10-midnight; 12-11 Sun
☎ (01788) 543023
Beer range varies H
A new entry to the Guide for 2010, this pub is a short walk from the famous Rugby School. The landlord is keen to promote real ale and offers three beers on handpump which change every week. There is always a range of drink and food promotions on offer to entice customers and the pub is popular with a mixed clientele of all ages. An over-20s policy is enforced. 🚌(200)♣

Merchants Inn
5-6 Little Church Street, CV21 3AW (behind Marks & Spencer)
🕐 12-midnight (1am Fri & Sat); 12-11 Sun
☎ (01788) 571119 🌐 merchantsinn.co.uk
B&T Shefford Bitter; Everards Tiger Best Bitter; Purity Mad Goose; guest beers H
Close to Rugby School, this 'must visit' pub boasts 10 regularly-changing real ales, two on gravity dispense, plus a large range of Belgian beers and traditional cider. One of the country's largest collections of breweriana adorns the interior, adding to the warm, cosy atmosphere, with comfortable sofas, flagstone floors and an open fireplace. Home-cooked food is served at lunchtime seven days a week. Beer festivals are held in April and October, plus an annual Belgian night in February. Warwickshire CAMRA pub of the year 2003 and 2007. 🔥♿🚌♣⚡

Raglan Arms 🏆
50 Dunchurch Road, CV22 6AD
🕐 4-midnight; 12-1am Fri & Sat; 12-midnight Sun
☎ (01788) 544441
Ansells Mild; Fuller's London Pride; Greene King Abbot; Raglan Original Bitter; guest beers H

Since being rescued from closure, this three-roomed town pub has had a tasteful refurbishment and in 2008 was awarded Rugby CAMRA Pub of the Year. The interior has a comfy feel and a friendly atmosphere. Up to 10 beers are available from across the country. Regular poker nights and music are hosted, and major sporting events screened on TV. A cosy room with a fire is available for meetings. Good-value Sunday lunch is served, and an outdoor heated area is open for smokers. ❀◐◑⊟⊡♣P⚟

Seven Stars ✔

40 Albert Square, CV21 2SH (behind Rugby Citroen showroom)
⌚ 12-11 (10.30 Sun)
☎ (01788) 561402
Wells Bombardier; Young's Bitter; guest beers Ⓗ
Excellent back-street local within easy reach of the town centre. The layout comprises three interlinked rooms around a central bar. There is also a conservatory/family room which leads to a patio garden. The pub is committed to local sports leagues, with pool, darts and skittles played. Guest ales come from regional breweries, real cider features occasionally and a beer festival is hosted in March or October. **Q**♘❀🛏◐◑⊟⇌⊡♣●⚟

Squirrel Inn

33 Church Street, CV21 3PU
⌚ 12-11 (10.30 Sun)
☎ (01788) 544154
Dow Bridge Ratae'd; Marston's Pedigree, Old Empire; guest beer Ⓗ
A rare true town local, this tiny single-roomed pub is definitely a pub to squeeze into on any discerning pub crawl of Rugby. The town's oldest licensed inn, it dates from the 18th century, and pictures of 'old' Rugby adorn the walls. The pub supports darts teams and offers all manner of games to visitors including scrabble, chess and table skittles. Live music plays every Wednesday (yes, bands do fit in!). ⌂**Q**⇌⊡♣●

Three Horse Shoes Hotel ✔

22-23 Sheep Street, CV21 3BX (in pedestrian precinct)
⌚ 11-midnight; 12-11 Sun
☎ (01788) 544585 🌐 threehorseshoesrugby.co.uk
Greene King IPA, Abbot; guest beer Ⓗ
Dating back to the 17th century, the hotel has been sensitively restored to reveal original oak beams and an open fireplace. The bar is cosy and welcoming, and offers a reasonably-priced and popular food menu. The hotel is conveniently situated in the town centre, a 20-minute walk from the railway station. ⌂**Q**❀🛏◑⊟♿⇌⊡⚟

Victoria Inn

1 Lower Hillmorton Road, CV21 3ST
⌚ 4-midnight; 12-1am Sat; 12-11 Sun
☎ (01788) 544374 🌐 downthevic.com
Atomic Bomb, Fission, Fusion, Strike, Half Life; guest beers Ⓗ
A fine example of a Victorian hostelry, with an ornately decorated lounge, snug and traditional bar with bar games including pool. The Atomic Ales brewery tap, its 14 handpumps dispense a full range of Atomic beers as well as guest ales from micro-breweries. A large selection of Belgian beers is also available. Regular beer festivals promoting small breweries are held throughout the year. Quiz nights are held and Sky Sports screened (on request). **Q**❀⊟⊡♣●⚟

Shustoke

Griffin Inn

Church Road, B46 2LB (on B4116)
⌚ 12-2.30, 7-11; 12-3, 7-10.30 Sun
☎ (01675) 481205
Jennings Dark Mild; Hook Norton Old Hooky; Marston's Pedigree; RCH Pitchfork; Theakston Old Peculier; guest beers Ⓗ
Long-standing Guide regular which has now opened an on-site brewery. A Griffin Inn Brewery beer is usually available as well as the regular ales and four guests. The music and TV-free interior features low beams and inglenooks with wood-burning stoves, while outside there is patio seating and a large grassy play area. Children are welcome in the conservatory. Food is served Monday to Saturday lunchtimes and local eggs and cheeses are on sale at the bar. ⌂**Q**♘❀◐**Δ**P⚟

Stockton

Crown

8 High Street, CV47 8JZ SP436638
⌚ 11-midnight (1am Fri & Sat)
☎ (01926) 812255
Adnams Broadside; Ansells Mild, Bitter Ⓗ
Popular Victorian brick-built village local. The main drinking area is divided, with seating around the fire on one side and a games area on the other. The landlord's Irish roots are reflected in the collection of Guinness memorabilia and a wide range of whiskies. A petanque pitch at the rear draws teams from a wide area during the summer. A recent extension into the old stables hosts live music events. ⌂❀◐◑⊟♿⊡(63,64)♣P⚟

Stratford-upon-Avon

Old Thatch Tavern

23 Greenhill Street, CV37 6LE
⌚ 11-11
☎ (01789) 295216
Purity Mad Goose, UBU; guest beer Ⓗ
Situated on the corner of the market place, Stratford's second oldest pub is a Grade II-listed building, with the only thatched roof in the town centre. The decor is traditional and relaxed, with a log fire blazing during the winter months. The building was the original home of the 16th-century Stratford Brewery. Food is available lunchtimes and evenings and cider is served from the cask. There are rumours of two ghosts. ⌂❀◐◑⇌⊡●⚟

Stretton-on-Fosse

Plough Inn

GL56 9QX
⌚ 11.30-3, 6 (7 Sun)-11
☎ (01608) 661053
Ansells Mild; Hook Norton Hooky Bitter; guest beers Ⓗ
Delightful 17th-century stone-built inn with oak beams and a flagstoned bar. The large inglenook fireplace is used on winter Sundays to slow-roast a joint of meat. Delicious food is home cooked by the owner (no food Sun eve). Traditional pub games are played in the bar and Aunt Sally in the garden. Quizzes and folk music are hosted on Sunday nights. Traditional cider is available. Winner of CAMRA Warwickshire Pub of the Year 2008. ⌂**Q**❀◐◑♣P⚟

Studley

Little Lark

108 Alcester Road, B80 7NP (Tom's Town Lane jct with A435) SP075632
12-3, 6-11; 12-midnight Sat; 12-3, 6.30-10.30 Sun
(01527) 853105
Ansells Mild; Adnams Bitter; guest beers H
This popular village local serves a great selection of traditional fruit wines and single malt whiskies as well as real ale. The interior is divided into four sections surrounding a central bar, with a patio smoking area towards the rear. The Lark used to publish its own newspaper and the walls are decorated with framed front pages. Food is served lunchtimes and evenings – the Desperate Dan Cow Pie a speciality. The pub also runs an annual cheese festival. **Q**(67,246,247)

Warings Green

Blue Bell Cider House

Warings Green Road, B94 6BP (S of Cheswick Green, off Ilshaw Heath Road) SP128742
11.30-11; 12-10.30 Sun
(01564) 702328
Beer range varies H
Friendly canalside free house offering three regularly changing real ales and two draught ciders usually from Thatchers. A pleasant area for walking, cycling and fishing, temporary moorings make it popular with boaters. The large lounge and cosy bar have real fires in winter, and a large conservatory serves as a family room. Reasonably priced food includes children's and vegetarian menus (no food Mon). Quiz night is Wednesday and live music plays on bank holidays during the warmer months. **Q P**

Warwick

Cape of Good Hope

66 Lower Cape, CV34 5DP (off Cape Road)
12-11
(01926) 498138 capeofgoodhope.co.uk
Greene King IPA, Abbot; Tetley Bitter; Weatheroak Keystone Hops; guest beer H
Canalside pub, easier to reach by boat than road, with a very friendly welcome. The front bar overlooks the water and is the venue for live music evenings. The quieter lounge at the rear is ideal for enjoying good value meals – Sunday lunches are served until 8.30pm. Note the painting in the lounge explaining the origin of the name. The house beer, Two LLocks, is brewed by Church End. **Q**(G1)**P**

Oak

27 Coten End, CV34 4NT
12-midnight (1am Fri & Sat)
(01926) 493774
Fuller's ESB; Taylor Landlord; guest beers H
Despite appearances, this pub is not a recent shop conversion, it dates back to at least 1874. Long and narrow, the bar hides behind a staircase. Beyond the bar are a pool table and dartboard. At the rear is a small patio garden. The house beer is Oak Bitter but its brewer is kept a secret. Food is available only on Sunday lunchtime. The friendly welcome make this an ideal stopping point between town and railway station. (X17)

Welford on Avon

Bell

Binton Road, CV37 8EB
11.30-3, 6-11; 11.30-11 Fri; 11.30-midnight Sat; 11.30-11 Sun
(01789) 750353 thebellwelford.co.uk
Flowers Original; Hobsons Best Bitter; Hook Norton Hooky Bitter; Purity Pure Gold, UBU H
A 17th-century inn facing the village green, with flagstone floors, exposed beams and open fires in winter. The award-winning restaurant hosts monthly theme nights, and the five real ales are complemented by ciders and wines from local producers. The large garden has water features and a covered and heated smoking area.
Q P

The language of beer

Nose: the aroma. Gently swirl the beer to release the aroma. You will detect malt: grainy and biscuity, often likened to crackers or Ovaltine. When darker malts are used, the nose will have powerful hints of chocolate, coffee, nuts, vanilla, liquorice, molasses and such dried fruits as raisins and sultanas. Hops add superb aromas of resins, herbs, spices, fresh-mown grass and tart citrus fruit – lemon and orange are typical, with intense grapefruit notes from some American varieties. Sulphur may also be present when waters are Burtonised : i.e. gypsum and magnesium salts have been added to replicate the famous spring waters of Burton-on-Trent.
Palate: the appeal in the mouth. The tongue can detect sweetness, bitterness and saltiness as the beer passes over it. The rich flavours of malt will come to the fore but hop bitterness will also make a substantial impact. The tongue will also pick out the natural saltiness from the brewing water and fruit from darker malts, yeast and hops. Citrus notes often have a major impact on the palate.
Finish: the aftertaste, as the beer goes over the tongue and down the throat. The finish is often radically different to the nose. The aroma may be dominated by malt whereas hop flavours and bitterness can govern the finish. Darker malts will make their presence felt with roast, chocolate or coffee notes; fruit character may linger. Strong beers may end on a sweet or biscuity note but in mainstream bitters, bitterness and dryness come to the fore.

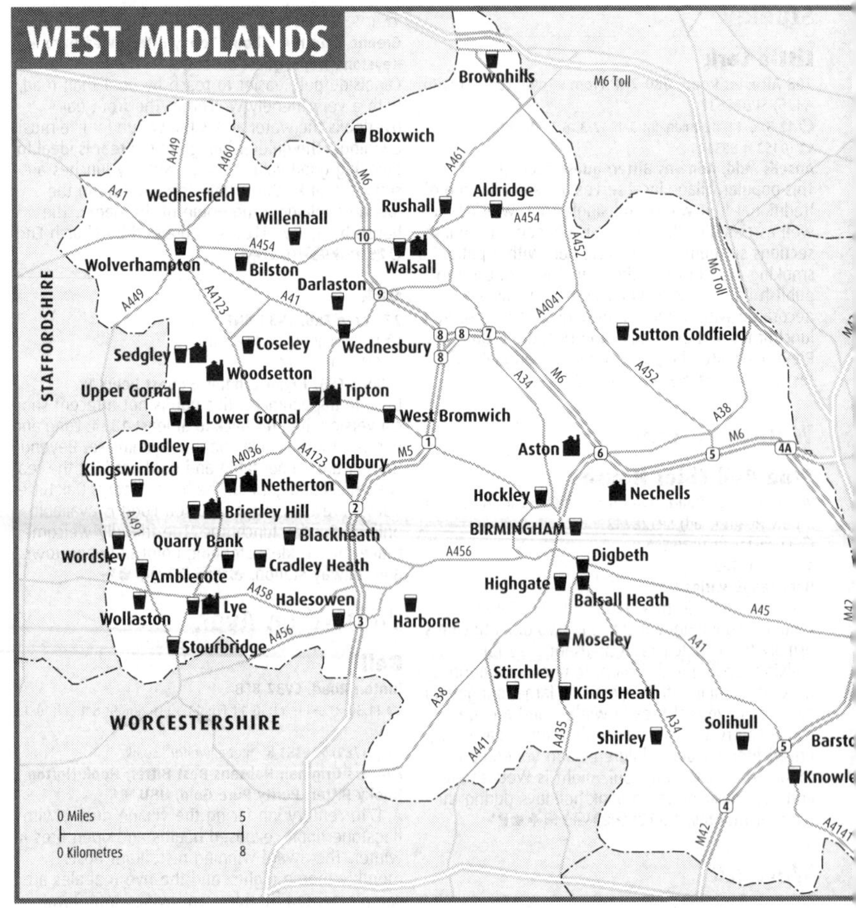

Aldridge

Lazy Hill Tavern

196 Walsall Wood Road, WS9 8HB

12-2.30 (Sat), 6-11; 12-2.30, 7-10.30 Sun

(01922) 452040

Caledonian Deuchars IPA; Courage Best Bitter; Greene King Abbot; Marston's Pedigree; Theakston Mild; Wells Bombardier; guest beer H

Large, welcoming, family-run free house with the same licensee for 30 years. Originally a farmhouse, it became a country club, then finally a pub in 1986. Four separate rooms are all similarly and comfortably furnished with original beams exposed in the middle two. The large 160-seater function room is used mid-week by local sports organisations and can be booked for private parties. Live music plays fortnightly on Tuesday. Q(56,367)P

Amblecote

Maverick

Brettell Lane, DY8 4BA (jct of A491/A461)

12-midnight (1am Wed, Fri & Sat); 12-11 Sun

(01384) 824099

Jennings Cumberland Ale; guest beers H

Large street-corner pub with access from both sides leading to the main bar. A Wild West room doubles as a live music venue catering for a variety of tastes including folk, blues, roots and bluegrass. There is also a small Mexican-themed room. A corridor leads to a covered smoking area outside with a small garden. Four real ales are always available, usually including two from micro-breweries. Several screens show Sky Sports when no live music is playing. The Maverick is CAMRA Stourbridge & Halesowen branch Pub of the Year 2009. (100)

Robin Hood

196 Collis Street, DY8 4EQ (on A4102, off A461 Brettell Lane)

12-3 (Wed & Thu), 5-11; 12-midnight Fri & Sat; 12-10.30 Sun

(01384) 821120

Bathams Best Bitter; Enville Ale, Ginger; guest beers H

In the Glass Quarter and close to the canal network, this family-owned and run free house prides itself on the range and quality of its Cask Marque award-winning beer, regularly offering four guest ales. The restaurant is open seven days, featuring good home-made food that has earned the pub plaudits. A lively quiz takes place on the first Tuesday of the month. En-suite accommodation is available, including a family room, and guests are served a hearty breakfast. (311)P

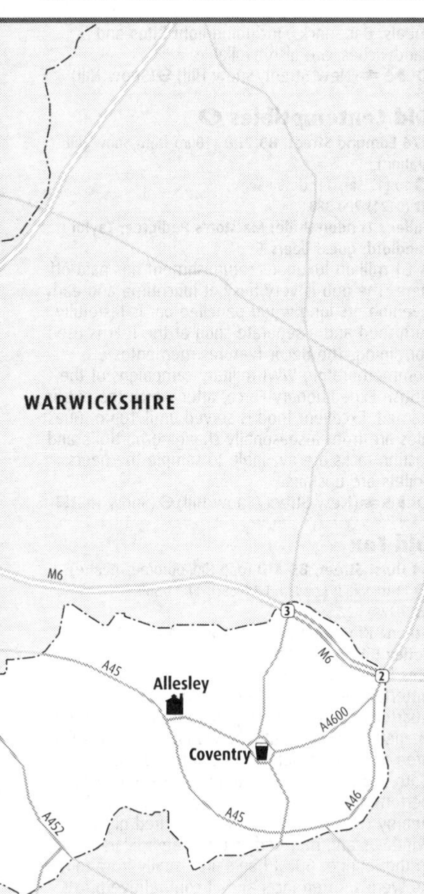

Swan

10 Brettell Lane, DY8 4BN (on A461, ⅓ mile after A491)
12-2.30 (not Tue-Thu), 7-11; 12-11 Sat & Sun
(01384) 76932
Beer range varies H
This free house boasts a comfortable lounge, a separate public bar and a delightful garden. There is a TV in the bar for watching sporting events. A friendly neighbourhood pub, it supports several local charities including the Air Ambulance. Drinkers can choose from the three ever-changing real ales on offer. ❀⊞🚌(311,313)♣⅟–

Barston

Bull's Head 🏆 ✔

Barston Lane, B92 0JU SP2073378090
11-2.30, 5-11; 11-11 Fri & Sat; 12-10.30 Sun
(01675) 442830 thebullsheadbarston.co.uk
Adnams Bitter; Hook Norton Hooky Bitter; guest beers H
Genuine, unspoilt village local in a tranquil part of the country. A former coaching inn, it was local CAMRA pub of the year in 1998, 2002, 2003 and 2009, and has been in the Guide for 17 consecutive years. It has two comfortable bars with log fires in winter and both the regular menu and the ever-changing seasonal specials can be ordered in either bar or the intimate restaurant (no meals Sun eve). The pub boasts a secluded beer garden in pleasant surroundings and hosts the annual Barston fete in its fields, watched over by the resident donkey. Popular with walkers, always welcoming, with regular quizzes, you would go far to find a better pub or a better pint. ⌂Q❀◐◑♣P⅟–

Bilston

Olde White Rose

20 Lichfield Street, WV14 0AG
10-11 (11.30 Fri & Sat); 12-11 Sun
(01902) 498339
Beer range varies H
A Grade II-listed frontage leads to a long, narrow pub which offers up to 12 real ales along with cider and perry from Westons. It offers a standard menu, a specials board and a carvery on some days served 12-9pm. For early arrivals, a breakfast menu operates 10-12 daily. Quiz nights are held every Tuesday and Wednesday. A bierkeller is used for occasional music and can be hired for private parties. Accommodation may be available, ring for details. ❀◐◑♿⊖(Central)🚌🍎⅟–

Trumpet

58 High Street, WV14 0EP
11 (11.30 Mon)-3.30 (4 Sat), 7.30-11.30; 12-4, 7.30-11.30 Sun
(01902) 493723 trumpetjazz.org.uk
Holden's Mild, Bitter, Golden Glow, seasonal beers H
Busy, compact, one-room local serving Holden's award-winning ales at reasonable prices. Plenty of musical memorabilia is on display, including concert tickets for artists from Stephane Grappelli to Miles Davis, and musical instruments on the walls and ceiling. Live jazz and blues plays seven nights a week. A collection plate is passed around for the bands. There is a drinking and smoking area outside. ❀⊖(Central)🚌⅟–

Birmingham: Balsall Heath

Old Moseley Arms

53 Tindal Street, B12 9QU
12-11 (10.30 Sun)
(0121) 440 1954
Black Sheep Best Bitter; Enville Ale; guest beers H
A hidden back-street gem where gaffer Suki has been at the helm for more than 10 years. The pub regularly stocks Bathams which sells out quickly. Other guests include Enville and Purity among others. Recent successful beer festivals will pave the way for more. A regular acoustic night is held on Sunday, while home-made curry is served and a quiz held on Tuesday. Pakoras, pies and other snacks are served daily until 10pm. Live sports events are shown on two large screens. A covered, heated, smoking area out the back has a further screen. ❀⊞🚌(50)⅟–

Birmingham: City Centre

Briar Rose ✔

25 Bennetts Hill, B2 5RE
7-midnight (1am Fri & Sat); 8-midnight
(0121) 634 8100
Greene King IPA, Abbot; Marston's Pedigree; guest beers H
Large city-centre Wetherspoon pub that was formerly the first branch of the Abbey National. This simple, attractively-decorated pub has a 40-

room Wetherlodge next to it. There is also an upstairs function room. Children are allowed before 9pm providing they are having a meal. The guest beer range can feature one brewery at a time or carry a common theme, and often includes local micro-breweries. The food is standard Wetherspoon's fare. Westons Old Rosie and organic cider are available.
(New Street/Snow Hill) (Snow Hill)

Bull

1 Price Street, B4 6JU (off St Chads Queensway)
12-11; closed Sun
(0121) 333 6757 thebull-pricestreet.com
Adnams Broadside; Marston's Pedigree; guest beer H
One of Birmingham's oldest pubs, this popular and friendly back-street local is in the Gun Quarter, close to Aston University and the Childrens' Hospital. Two main rooms are served by a central bar, and there is a quiet room with easy chairs at the rear. Traditional food is served until 9.30pm (children welcome). There is a vast collection of jugs and plates, along with photos, on the shelves and walls around the pub bar. The windows have etched Ansells insignia. Guest beers are often from micros. Q (Snow Hill) (Snow Hill)

Canalside Café

35 Worcester Bar, B1 2JU (situated on canalside parallel to Gas Street)
10-11 (10.30 Sun)
(0121) 248 7979
Beer range varies H
The smallest pub in Birmingham, adjacent to Gas Street Basin which is a major mooring point for canal boats. The pub is full of history and was the fictional home of the character Stan Harvey of Crossroads fame. It is a nice, cosy, intimate pub that usually stocks guest beers from micro-breweries. A range of bottled beers and cider is also available and the extensive food range is of particular note, with a large selection of vegetarian options.

Edmunds

106-110 Edmund Street, B3 2ES
11-midnight (1am Fri; 2am Sat); 11-10.30 Sun
(0121) 200 2423 edmundsbar.co.uk
Sharp's Doom Bar; guest beers H
Edmunds is a trendy, upmarket pub, independently operated and situated at the heart of the business quarter. The interior is comfortably furnished with a contemporary feel. Three real ales are stocked and guest beers are often from Wye Valley or Purity. There is a quieter room at the back which can be hired out for functions. Food is served all day, including an interesting tapas menu. Good disabled access.
(New Street/Snow Hill) (Snow Hill)

Metro Bar & Grill

94 Cornwall Street, B3 2DF
10am-11; closed Sun metrobarandgrill.co.uk
Davenports IPA; Enville White; guest beer H
Wooden-floored, glass-fronted wine bar located in a red-brick building behind Colmore Row and close to offices, so it can get busy with suits of both sexes in the evening. It has a large wooden bar to one side, with bar stalls around and U-shaped seating areas along the wall. The main bar area extends through to a large mirrored wall and then onto a main dining area serving restaurant style meals. Bar snacks, including light bites and sandwiches, are also available.
Q (New Street/Snow Hill) (Snow Hill)

Old Contemptibles

176 Edmund Street, B3 2HB (100m from Snow Hill Station)
10 (12 Sat)-11; closed Sun
(0121) 200 3831
Fuller's London Pride; Marston's Pedigree; Taylor Landlord; guest beers H
A £1 million luxurious refurbishment has paid off here. The pub is very busy at lunchtime and early evening. Its long wood-panelled bar is tastefully furnished and a separate snug at the rear is used for dining. The decor features mementos commemorating WWI military campaigns of the British Expeditionary Force, after which the pub is named. Excellent food is served until 10pm. Guest ales are from a seasonally changing portfolio and tasting racks are available to sample the beers. Toilets are upstairs.
Q (New Street/Snow Hill) (Snow Hill)

Old Fox

54 Hurst Street, B5 4TD (opp Hippodrome Theatre)
11-midnight (2.30am Fri & Sat); 11-11 Sun
(0121) 622 5080
Greene King Old Speckled Hen; St Austell Tribute; Tetley Bitter; guest beers H
This two-roomed pub is situated by the entertainment district and Chinese and gay quarters, opposite the Hippodrome Theatre. The U-shaped bar serves both the wooden floored 'public' area and the carpeted and seated 'lounge' area. Both can get busy with a mixed clientele when performances are on at the Hippodrome or the nearby Glee Club. Impressive coloured glass windows and mirrored columns and pillars feature in the lounge. Guest beers are usually from micro-breweries, often local and at competitive prices.
(New Street)

Old Joint Stock

4 Temple Row, B2 5NY (opp St Philip's Cathedral)
11-11; closed Sun
(0121) 200 1892 fullers.co.uk
Fuller's Chiswick, Discovery, London Pride, ESB, seasonal beers; guest beer H
Fuller's most northern outpost is a Grade II-listed building, formerly the Old Joint Stock Bank. The striking interior is of neo-classic and Victorian design. There is a central island bar with a quieter Club Room at the rear and a balcony area for dining at lunchtimes. A theatre is located upstairs which hosts performances by local acts and comedy nights. A large function room is available for hire.

INDEPENDENT BREWERIES

A.B.C. Birmingham: Aston (NEW)
Backyard Walsall (NEW)
Batham Brierley Hill
Birmingham Nechells (NEW)
Black Country Lower Gornal
Broughs Netherton (NEW)
Highgate Walsall
Holden's Woodsetton
Olde Swan Netherton
Rainbow Allesley
Sarah Hughes Sedgley
Toll End Tipton
Windsor Castle Lye

Poker night is Monday. The guest beer varies. ⇌(New Street/Snow Hill)⊖(Snow Hill)

Old Royal

53 Church Street, B3 2DP (behind Colmore Row)
9am (8am Fri; 12 Sat & Sun)-11
☎ (0121) 200 3841
Fuller's London Pride; Taylor Landlord; guest beer Ⓗ
This large red-brick street-corner pub is popular with a wide range of customers including local office workers and builders, and can get busy. Open at 9am for breakfast and morning coffee, the pub boasts stained glass windows, a wooden L-shaped bar with mirrored columns and impressive bar back, and original tiling on the staircase leading to the upstairs function room. A heated, covered smoking area is accessed from a passage to the side of the stairs.
Q⇌(New Street/Snow Hill)⊖(Snow Hill)

Prince of Wales

84 Cambridge Street, B1 2NP (behind ICC/NIA and Rep Theatre)
12-11 (10.30 Sun)
☎ (0121) 643 9460
Adnams Broadside; Ansells Mild; Everards Tiger; Taylor Landlord; Wells Bombardier; guest beers Ⓗ
Located behind the International Convention Centre and Rep Theatre and close to National Indoor Arena, this is one of the last remaining community locals in the centre of Birmingham; it is therefore prone to surges of custom when events are held. Run by the same landlord for many years, some regulars are local characters – one even has a plaque on his own seat. Eight handpumps sell mainly national brands, but one beer comes from the Punch portfolio. Live music plays most Sunday afternoons. ⇌(New Street)⊖(Snow Hill)

Wellington

37 Bennetts Hill, B2 5SN
10-midnight
☎ (0121) 200 3115 thewellingtonrealale.co.uk
Black Country BFG, Fireside, Pig On The Wall; Purity Mad Goose; Wye Valley HPA; guest beers Ⓗ
Birmingham CAMRA Pub of the Year for three of the past four years, this pub has 15 handpumps and three real ciders. Close to New Street and Snow Hill stations, it has built a reputation as a must-visit among real ale enthusiasts and thus can get busy, but this ensures a quick turnaround of ales. Quarterly beer festivals and regular cheese and quiz evenings are held. No food is provided but you can bring your own (cutlery provided).
Q⇌(New Street/Snow Hill)⊖(Snow Hill)

Birmingham: Digbeth

Anchor ★

308 Bradford Street, B5 6ET
10 (11 Sat)-11; 12-10.30 Sun
☎ (0121) 622 4516 anchorinndigbeth.co.uk
Hobsons Mild; Tetley Bitter; guest beers Ⓗ
Many times local CAMRA Pub of the Year, the Anchor has been in the Keane family for 36 years. Situated in the heart of the Irish Quarter, it looks rather lonely as most of its neighbours have been demolished. Up to eight guest beers served by friendly staff are supplemented by regular themed weekends and beer festivals. The lively public bar at the front complements the quieter rooms and lounge, while the yard provides designated smoking and non-smoking areas. Sporting events are shown on large-screen TVs.
Q⇌(New Street/Moor Street)

Spotted Dog

104 Warwick Street, B12 0NH
7-11; 4-midnight Fri; 12-midnight Sat; 7-12.30am Sun
☎ (0121) 772 3822 birminghamirish.com
Ansell Mild; guest beers Ⓗ
Relatively unspoilt, this multi-roomed pub is known as the spiritual home of Irish music. The surrounding area has been regenerated and the pub is now next to apartments. The same landlord has been at the helm since 1985 and sport is shown on large screen TVs with rugby internationals being especially popular. The pub can be very busy when Birmingham City are playing at home. There is a spacious patio garden and smoking area area to the rear. Guest beers are often from Warwickshire Brewery.

White Swan ★

276 Bradford Street, B12 0QY
12-11 (1am Fri & Sat)
☎ (0121) 622 2586
Banks's Original, Bitter; Jennings Cocker Hoop, Cumberland Ale; guest beer Ⓗ
This welcoming, unspoilt Victorian red-brick pub in the Irish Quarter is 100 metres up from the Anchor. Both pubs are in sight of each other, as everything in between has been demolished for a new riverside development. A long, narrow bar with bench seats and bar stalls opens onto an impressive ornately tiled hallway leading to a small lounge. Both bars have large-screen TVs showing sporting events and can be crowded at times. Guest beers are from the Marston's/Jennings portfolio. ⇌(New Street/Moor Street)

Birmingham: Harborne

Green Man

2 High Street, B17 9NE
12-11 (1am Fri & Sat)
☎ (0121) 427 0961
M&B Brew XI; Taylor Landlord; guest beers Ⓗ
Refurbished Ember Inn which is popular and busy most nights. The interior is typical of the chain but it now has a real fire. A good value food menu is served daily until 9pm. Seating is available outside on a patio area at the front and a covered heated area by the rear car park. Quiz nights are held Sunday and Wednesday. Because of its location on the High Street it is the start of many a pub crawl.
(21,22,29)P

Junction

212 High Street, B17 9PT
12-11 (midnight Thu-Sat); 12-10.30 Sun
☎ (0121) 428 2635 thejunctionharborne.co.uk
Beer range varies Ⓗ
Situated in the heart of Harborne, the Junction, with its imposing Edwardian exterior and quirky, eclectic interior, stands out. An interesting changing beer range is supplemented by a traditional cider and a range of continental lagers. Good food is served from an open kitchen and there is always a lively atmosphere, with a clientele ranging from locals to students. Quiz night is Monday and occasional beer festivals take place. A large heated and covered smoking shelter is at the rear. Board games are available.

Birmingham: Highgate

Lamp

257 Barford Street, B5 7EP (500m from Pershore Road)
12-11
(0121) 622 2599
Church End Gravediggers Mild; Everards Tiger; Stanway Stanney Bitter; guest beers Ⓗ
A friendly back-street local which attracts visiting beer enthusiasts from far and wide. This basic one-roomed pub can get busy in the evenings and at weekends. There is a large function room at the back which is used by local societies and also serves as a music venue. Still the only regular outlet for Stanway beers, including specials, the guest beers come from smaller, often local breweries. A late licence can sometimes be available. ♿⇌(New Street)🚌(35,45,47)

Birmingham: Hockley

Black Eagle

16 Factory Road, B18 5JU (in Jewellery Quarter)
11-3, 5.30-11; 11-11 Fri; 12-3, 7-11 Sat; 12-3 Sun
(0121) 523 4008 blackeaglepub.co.uk
Bathams Bitter; Holden's Bitter; Taylor Landlord; guest beers Ⓗ
This four-times local CAMRA Pub of the Year back-street hostelry retains many of its original features, including Minton tiles. It has two smallish rooms at the front, with a larger room to the rear for relaxed seating. At the back is a restaurant offering food, from sandwiches and light meals to more substantial dishes. The pub holds a beer festival in July in the garden, which has a patio and grassed area and a covered smoking section to the front. **Q**❀◐◑♿⊖(Soho Benson Road)🚌(11,101)

Lord Clifden

34 Great Hampton Street, B18 6AA
9am-1am
(0121) 523 7515 thelordclifden.co.uk
Bathams Bitter; Wye Valley HPA; guest beer Ⓗ
One of very few truly free houses in Birmingham, this pub is owned by a former London hotel chef who is making an impact on the local beer scene, and whose excellent, reasonably priced food reflects his status. The pub has been transformed from 'run down' to one of which the wife would approve. A separate front bar caters for sport, while the rear lounge is for diners and a quiet drink. Outside is a covered smoking area and a suntrap garden.
❀◐◑♿⇌(Jewellery Quarter)⊖(Jewellery Quarter)🚌♣

Red Lion

94/95 Warstone Lane, B18 4NG
10am-midnight
(0121) 233 9144 theredlionbirmingham.com
Purity Mad Goose; Wye Valley Butty Bach; guest beers Ⓗ
Excellent traditional pub near the heart of the Jewellery Quarter. Closed for two years, the pub has now been given a new lease of life with an urban art theme, where eclectic art blends well with traditional furnishings. Four ales are complemented by a superb quality menu served daily. A well appointed function room is available for hire as well as playing host to various pub events. An enclosed patio to the rear is a summer suntrap and also has a smoking shelter.
❀◐◑♿⇌(Jewellery Quarter)⊖🚌(8,101)♣

Birmingham: Kings Heath

Kings Heath Cricket Club

Charlton House, 247 Alcester Road South, B14 6DT
12-midnight
(0121) 444 1913
Fuller's London Pride; Wye Valley Butty Bach, HPA; guest beers Ⓗ
This well-run and friendly sports club is split into two bar areas with the main one housing two full-size snooker tables, seating areas and two large-screen TVs for sporting events including Sky Sports. A lounge area is for more relaxed drinking. Two beer festivals are held in April and November, as well as other social events including live music in the large function room. CAMRA members are welcome on production of a membership card (maximum 10 visits per year).
Q❀◐◑♿🚌(50)♣**P**

Birmingham: Moseley

Prince of Wales

118 Alcester Road, B13 8EE
12-11 (12.30am Fri & Sat); 12-10.30 Sun
(0121) 449 8284
Caledonian Deuchars IPA; Greene King Abbot; Wells Bombardier; guest beers Ⓗ
Large pub in the heart of Moseley undergoing a revival, with an increased beer range and interesting guest beers. Events and live music make use of an extensive covered and heated outdoor area that includes a dance floor and ample seating. The front bar remains popular with regulars and one of the two snugs is often used for dining. Good food has been introduced, including cheese platters and hog roasts on summer Saturdays. Traditional board games are available, but be prepared to end up in conversation with jovial strangers. **Q**❀◐◑♿🚌(50)♣

Birmingham: Stirchley

British Oak ★

1364 Pershore Road, B30 2XS (on main A441 close to Bournville station)
11 (12 Sun)-11 (1am Fri-Sat)
(0121) 458 1758
M&B Mild; Black Sheep Best Bitter; guest beers Ⓗ
This fine example of a roadside 1920s-style ale house has a splendid interior and features in CAMRA's National Inventory of pub interiors. The front bar can be very boisterous at times with large-screen TV for sports, while the rear rooms are more peaceful. Notice the fine wood panelling and superb fireplace in the rear bar. There is a large smoking area and a garden for alfresco dining in the summer months. Guest beers come from a seasonal portfolio.
❀◐◑♿⇌(Bournville)🚌(45,47)**P**

Blackheath

Bell & Bear Inn ✔

71 Gorsty Hill Road, B65 0HA (on A4099)
11.30-11 (11.30 Fri & Sat); 12-11 Sun
(0121) 561 2196
Taylor Landlord; guest beers Ⓗ
Cracking 400-year-old pub with a distinct community feel. The pub was formerly a farmhouse and it maintains a rustic atmosphere in an open-plan, U-shaped bar with discrete separate

areas for dining and drinking. Food is served 12-9pm every day and includes a good mix of traditional home-cooked fare and specials. Three beer festivals are organised per year in April, May and October, as are many themed weekends, along with quizzes on Thursday and Sunday. The beer range features up to six guests from regional breweries. Views of the Black Country vales from the garden are spectacular.
(Old Hill)(230,417)P

Britannia

124 Halesowen Street, B65 0EG
9-midnight (1am Fri & Sat)
(0121) 559 0010
Greene King IPA, Abbot; Marston's Pedigree; guest beers H
Smart JD Wetherspoon conversion conveniently located opposite Sainsbury's in the centre of Blackheath, with a wide customer mix. The pub is open plan but with a homely feel. Typical Wetherspoon fare is served until 10pm daily and a range of up to seven adventurous guest beers is available. The rear garden is a pleasant, secluded location in which to drink during the summer. The pub is reasonably close to Rowley Regis station and buses from Birmingham, West Bromwich and Dudley stop nearby.
Q(Rowley Regis)(128,140,241)
P

Malt Shovel

61 High Street, B65 0EH
11-11 (2am Fri); 10-2am Sat; 12-11 Sun
(0121) 5612321
Enville Ale; Holden's Golden Glow; guest beer H
A small pub five minutes from Blackheath town centre with a distinct community feel and a good customer mix. There is a pronounced sports theme in this L-shaped, one-roomed bar which has four sports screens showing many live events. The guest beer varies and the cider is Thatchers Cheddar Valley. A marquee is erected several times a year in the garden to host various events such as live music and children's events. Many buses pass the pub or stop nearby.
(Rowley Regis)(404,258)

Bloxwich

Turf Tavern ★

13 Wolverhampton Road, WS3 2EZ (opp Bloxwich Park)
12-3, 7-11
(01922) 407745
Titanic Mild, Iceberg; guest beers H
Grade II-listed building, known locally as Tinky's, which has been in the same family for 135 years. The three rooms are dominated by the bar with its splendid tiled floor. The building is steeped in nostalgia and is a haven for quiet conversation, which adds to its traditional appeal. Outside, the charming courtyard serves as a pleasant spot for the summer drinker. Not to be missed.
Q(301)

Wheatsheaf

35 Pinfold, WS3 3JL
11-midnight
(01922) 449292
Banks's Original, Bitter; guest beers H
Once farm cottages, now a good local pub with a friendly atmosphere, close to the main shopping centre, bus and rail links. The bar area has two coal fires, with two more in the lounge area and separate snug. Sandwiches and rolls are often available. There is a dartboard in the lounge area with darts, crib and dominoes teams meeting regularly. Host to Bescot FC supporters club, the pub is reputed to be haunted by three ghosts.
Q(301,370)

Brierley Hill

Rose & Crown

161 Bank Street, DY5 3DD (B4179)
12-2, 6-11; 12-11 Fri & Sat; 12-3.30, 7-11 Sun
(01384) 77825 roseandcrownbrierleyhill.co.uk
Holden's Mild, Bitter, Special, Golden Glow; guest beer H
This traditional pub was originally two terraced properties. The lounge has a cosy, relaxed atmosphere and one end of the bar is dominated by the dartboard. A conservatory extension has added extra space and is used as a dining area in the evening. It opens onto a small garden with tables and benches. A large selection of good value quality food is served lunchtimes and evenings Monday-Saturday. The ever-changing guest beer comes from a variety of small breweries. Five minutes' walk from Brierley Hill High Street which is served by several bus routes.
Q(138,222)P

Vine (Bull & Bladder)

10 Delph Road, DY5 2TN
12-11 (10.30 Sun)
(01384) 78293
Bathams Mild, Best Bitter, XXX (winter) H
Classic, unspoilt brewery tap with an ornately decorated facade proclaiming the Shakespearian quotation: 'Blessing of your heart, you brew good ale'. Step inside and you enter an elongated pub with a labyrinthine feel. The rooms have contrasting characters. The front bar is small and staunchly traditional, while the larger rear bar, with its own servery and leather seating, houses the dartboard at the far end. On the other side of the central passageway is a homely lounge partly converted from former brewery offices. Good value Black Country lunches are served.
Q(99,138)P

Brownhills

Royal Oak

68 Chester Road, WS8 6DU (on A452)
12 (11 Sat)-11 (midnight Thu-Sat); 11-11 Sun
(01543) 452089 theroyaloakpub.co.uk
Caledonian Deuchars IPA; Greene King Abbot; Taylor Landlord; Tetley Bitter; Titanic Iceberg; guest beers H
Set back from the main road, this beautifully decorated Art Deco-style pub is known locally as the Middle Oak. The traditional bar plays host to darts and dominoes teams, while the comfortable lounge provides a more relaxed atmosphere. The pub also boasts a separate dining room and a patio drinking area which leads down to a large garden at the rear. Q(394)

Coseley

New Inn

Birmingham New Road, Ward Street, WV14 9LQ (on A4123)
4-11; 12-11.30 Fri & Sat; 12-10.30 Sun

☎ (07927) 459470 🌐 holdensbrewery.co.uk
Holden's Mild, Bitter, seasonal beers; guest beer Ⓗ
Recently refurbished, cosy one-roomed local, best approached from the Birmingham New Road. The lounge is housed in a late 20th-century extension and the bar in the older 19th-century part of the building separated by the modern bar counter that is the hub of the establishment. An extensive menu is offered Tuesday-Friday evenings, with hot pork sandwiches available Saturday lunchtime. Family parties and events can be catered for. There is a covered, heated outside patio area.
⛰Q🐴◗♿⇌🚌(126)♣P⁼

Coventry

Beer Engine

35 Far Gosford Street, CV1 5DW (off A4600)
⏲ 12-11 (2am Fri & Sat)
☎ (024) 7627 0015 🌐 beerengine.net
Fuller's London Pride; guest beers Ⓗ
An ever-changing selection of five guest ales is always available, together with a range of continental bottled beers, plus Leffe and Hoegaarden on tap. A single room pub, the front is adorned with film posters and the back includes a gallery of work by local artists. A pleasant courtyard has heated shelters for smokers. Sunday roasts are served and at all other times you can bring your own food. No children allowed. Live, usually loud, music plays on Friday and Saturday evening and traditional folk music on Monday evening.
⛰❀🚌(27,32)♣⁼

Burnt Post ✔

Kenpas Highway, CV3 6AW (jct of A45/Wainbody Avenue)
⏲ 12-11 (midnight Thu-Sat); 12-midnight Sun
☎ (024) 7669 2671
Beer range varies Ⓗ
Former Bass local, now one of several Ember Inns pubs, with an open-plan bar and lounge shared by drinkers and diners. An extensive food menu accompanies six changing cask beers, with comprehensive beer tasting notes issued every month. Beer tasting trays offering three third-of-a-pint measures are available for those wishing to sample the widest range of beers.
⛰❀◖◗♿🚌(15)P⁼

City Arms ✔

1 Earlsdon Street, CV5 6EP
⏲ 9-midnight (1am Fri & Sat)
☎ (024) 7671 8170
Greene King IPA, Abbot; Marston's Pedigree; guest beers Ⓗ
Popular Wetherspoon pub, part of the busy Friday and Saturday night Earlsdon scene. Food is served all day until 10pm and children are permitted until 9pm if dining. Curry night is popular on Thursday. A good choice of guest beers includes regular offerings from local breweries such as Purity, Church End and Rugby. TV screens show major football and rugby matches. The pub gets busy mid evening but thins our later with a change of clientele. Well served by public transport from the city centre and Warwick University.
❀◖◗♿🚌(12,19)🍎P⁼

Craven Arms

58 Craven Street, Chapelfields, CV5 8DW (1 mile W of city centre, off Allesley Old Road)
⏲ 12-11.30 (midnight Fri & Sat); 12-11 Sun
☎ (07738) 710057
Flowers Original; Holden's Golden Glow; Oakham JHB; Sarah Hughes Dark Ruby; guest beers Ⓗ
Guest ales often come from the same breweries as the regular beers, often stronger ones during the winter. A perry is also usually available in the summer. The Craven Arms is in a conservation area, with many other interesting pubs nearby. Decorations include a number of posters featuring Lambretta and Vespa scooters, and on summer Wednesdays a number of scooter enthusiasts meets here. Live music is played on Sunday evenings and there is a heated and covered smoking area. ⛰❀🚌(10,32)♣⁼

Gatehouse Tavern 🏆

46 Hill Street, CV1 4AN (jct 8 of ring road)
⏲ 11-3, 5-11; 11-midnight Thu-Sat; 12-10.30 Sun
☎ (024) 7625 6769 🌐 gatehousetavern.com
Beer range varies Ⓗ
This pub was converted from the old gate house of the Leigh Mill by the landlord, with stained glass windows depicting the six nations rugby teams. A popular free house, it has the largest pub garden in the city centre. A fifth handpump has recently been added to provide even more beer choice. Food is served lunchtimes Monday to Saturday and evenings Monday to Friday. ❀◖◗⇌🚌(10,32)🍎⁼

Greyhound Inn

Sutton Stop, Hawkesbury Junction, CV6 6DF
⏲ 11-11; 12-10.30 Sun
☎ (024) 7636 3046 🌐 thegreyhoundinn.com
Highgate Dark Mild; Marston's Pedigree; guest beers Ⓗ
Winner of the 2005-2007 CAMRA award for best pub in Warwickshire, this canalside inn dates from 1830 and has many original features. An extensive menu of freshly cooked food is available and regular beer festivals are held on the St George's day weekend and in mid July. The terrace and rear garden have their own outside bar in the summer, with an additional four cask ales served from the barrel. Within a 25-minute pleasant canalside walk of the Ricoh Arena. ⛰Q❀◖◗♣P⁼

Hearsall Inn

45 Craven Street, CV5 8DS
⏲ 12 (11 Sat)-midnight; 12-midnight Sun
☎ (024) 7671 5729
Beer range varies Ⓗ
Beers here usually include two from either Church End or a local micro-brewery and are the cheapest in the area. A real fire is used in the smoking shelter and the garden also features an old red telephone box. The whole street was built in 1847 for watchmaking and the pub was owned by Atkinsons from 1911 but is now one of very few free houses in Coventry. Traditional music is played by a large number of musicians on Tuesday night.
⛰🐴❀◖⊟♿🚌(10,32)♣⁼

Nursery Tavern

38-39 Lord Street, Chapelfields, CV5 8DA (1 mile W of city centre, off Allesley Old Road)
⏲ 12-11.30; 11-midnight Fri & Sat; 12-11 Sun
☎ (024) 7667 4530
Courage Best Bitter; Fuller's London Pride; John Smith's Bitter; Theakston Mild; guest beers Ⓗ
Terraced community pub and a long-standing Guide entry, situated in the historic watchmaking area. Seven ales are stocked, including three guests. A central bar services three rooms – the

room at the back welcomes families and holds social events including live music on the second Wednesday of every month. Beer festivals are hosted in June and December. The pub is the base for thriving rugby union and formula one clubs. Customers are welcome to bring their dogs with them. Q(10,32)

Old Windmill

22-23 Spon Street, CV1 3BA
11-11 (1am Fri & Sat); 12-midnight Sun
(024) 7625 2183
Greene King Old Speckled Hen; Sharp's Doom Bar; Taylor Landlord; Theakston Old Peculier; Wychwood Hobgoblin; guest beers H
Locally known as Ma Brown's, this timber-framed pub is reckoned to be the oldest in the city. A sympathetic extension was built over the former back yard a few years ago bringing in the old brew house, where old brewing equipment is still in situ. Many small rooms cater for a varied clientele. Food is served weekend lunchtimes only.

Rose & Woodbine

40 North Street, Stoke Heath, CV2 3FW
12-11 (11.30 Fri & Sat); 12-5, 7-11.30 Sun
(024) 7645 1480
Draught Bass; guest beers H
Warm, friendly local in an area where real ale pubs are rare. Originally built for the Northampton Brewery Company, it now features a range of beers from regional breweries and some micro-breweries. As well as the usual pub games, it also hosts both the Premier Homing Society and the Barras Green Homing Society (pigeon racing). Children are welcome until 7pm. The pub is well known for its economic steak meal. Lunchtimes are extended a little on Friday and Saturday.
(10,36)

Sovereign

Charter Avenue, CV4 8DA
12-11; 12-3.30, 7-11 Sun
(024) 7669 4314 thesovereign.org.uk
M&B Brew XI; Shepherd Neame Spitfire; Slaughterhouse Saddleback Best Bitter; guest beer H
Modern public house with a friendly atmosphere. Originally three separate rooms, it has been knocked into one U-shaped room with a pool table tucked out of the way at one end. A small alcove contains children's toys. A quiz is run on Sunday night and on alternate Fridays there is a DJ, karaoke and occasional live music. No food is served Monday or evening meals Sunday.
(19)P

Town Wall Tavern ✔

Bond Street, CV1 4AH (behind Belgrade Theatre)
12-midnight (6 Sun)
(024) 7622 0963
Adnams Bitter, Broadside; Draught Bass; Caledonian Deuchars IPA; M&B Brew XI; guest beer H
This is the home of real ale and real food. Six Cask Marque ales includie Bass, Adnams and a guest beer. To complement the range of ales, wines and spirits, there are traditional pub dishes such as Warwickshire-reared mutton, rabbit crumble and the pub's own hams cooked in cider and spices. Wholesome, satisfying food, excellent real ale, a blazing log fire and a warm welcome await at this historic pub tucked away behind the Belgrade Theatre. Evening meals are served until 8.30pm Monday to Thursday. (10,32)

Whitefriars Olde Ale House

114-115 Gosford Street, CV1 5DL
12-midnight (1am Fri & Sat); 12-11 Sun
(024) 7625 1655 whitefriarscov.com
Beer range varies H
The original building dates back to the 14th century and many features are still discernible today; it's worth taking a look upstairs. Six frequently changing guest beers are available and there is also a selection of British bottled beers. Beer festivals are held on many public holidays during the summer in the semi-covered garden at the back, with ciders and perry also on offer. Winter beer festivals are also held inside. Open mike night is Wednesday with occasional live music on Friday or Saturday. Q(27,32)

Cradley Heath

Holly Bush

53 Newtown Lane, B64 5EA
4 (12 Sat)-11; 12-10 Sun
(07949) 594484 ilovethebush.com
Beer range varies H
Two-roomed split-level corner pub just off the High Street. The lower level front bar has an open fireplace and a small raised area just inside the entrance where comedy performances take place on Thursday (check website for details). A larger lounge at the rear provides a comfortable alternative space in which to enjoy the six changing guest beers.
(99,243,404)

Darlaston

Prince of Wales

74 Walsall Road, WS10 9JJ
3 (12 Tue, Fri & Sat)-11; 12-10.30 Sun
(0121) 5266244
Holden's Bitter, Golden Glow; guest beers H
The snug lounge is family friendly, with photos of the town's local football teams and old maps on the wall. The long narrow bar features cigarette and drinks mirrors, with darts played at the far end. There is a play area and benched garden with shelter at the rear, plus a conservatory for hire. The Darlaston community committee meets here. Good value meals including daily lunchtime specials are available, with British and international dishes to eat in or take out. (333,334,339)

Dudley

Full Moon ✔

58-60 High Street, DY1 1PS
9-11.30 (midnight Fri & Sat)
(01384) 212294
Greene King Ruddles Best, Abbot; Marston's Pedigree; guest beers H
The Full Moon is a large, centrally located Wetherspoon pub offering good value food and drink. Originally a large town centre department store and then a pizza restaurant, it opened as a pub in August 1996. Recently refurbished, it has a friendly, comfortable atmosphere. Historic local photographs and facts adorn the walls. Food is served 9am-11pm. It is close to the main Dudley bus station where buses from all over the region terminate. Q

Halesowen

Hawne Tavern

78 Attwood Street, B63 3UG
4.30 (12 Sat)-11; 12-10.30 Sun
(0121) 620 2601
Banks's Bitter; Bathams Bitter; Red Lion White Lion; guest beers Ⓗ
A thriving and traditional free house with a small Victorian-style lounge opposite a stable bar complete with pool table and comfortable seating to the side. Outside is a suntrap garden and smoking area. Three regular beers are complemented by up to six guest ales, many unique to the area. A worthy past winner of CAMRA local branch Pub of the Year, it has been a regular Guide entry for the past 12 years under the expertise of the same landlord. Handy for the town's local football ground, meals are served Monday-Friday evening and Saturday lunchtime.
Q(300)♣P

Somers Sports & Social Club

The Grange, Grange Hill, B62 0JH (A456/B4551 jct)
12-2.30 (3 Sat), 6-11; 7-10.30 Sun
(0121) 550 1645
Bathams Mild Ale, Best Bitter; Enville Ale; Holden's Black Country Bitter; Olde Swan Original; Wye Valley HPA; guest beers Ⓗ
This impressive Grade II-listed building was the home of a local forge-master, set in extensive grounds. The long bar features 12 handpumps, many of which dispense ales from local brewers. The large garden has a children's play area and crown green bowls. The club has won numerous awards including CAMRA National Club of the Year. To gain admission, show a CAMRA membership card or a copy of the current Guide. Groups of five or more should phone ahead. (99)P

Waggon & Horses

21 Stourbridge Road, B63 3TU (on A458, ½ mile from bus station)
12-11.30 (12.30am Fri & Sat)
(0121) 550 4989
Bank Top Dark Mild; Bathams Best Bitter; Holden's Golden Glow; Nottingham EPA; Oakham White Dwarf; Red Lion White Lion; guest beers Ⓗ
The regular beers, including EPA – badged DPA in honour of Don Dykes who sadly passed away in 2008 – are joined by guest ales, real cider and Belgian beers. There are three rooms; a traditional bar plus quieter rooms at each end. Awards include CAMRA County and Branch Pub of the Year. Owner Bob has been here for more than 21 years, and the pub has appeared in the Guide for most of them. The hostelry enjoys a community feel, with many local regulars. Snacks are available until 6.30pm.
Q(9)

Kingswinford

Bridge

110 Moss Grove, DY6 9HH
12-11.30 (11.45 Fri & Sat); 12-11 Sun
(01384) 352356
Banks's Original, Bitter; guest beers Ⓗ
In addition to a healthy local trade, this pub is most welcoming to visitors. The bar, popular for pub games and sports TV, extends across the front of the building, with a cosy lounge behind. Outside is an enclosed garden with children's play equipment. One or two guest beers come from the brewery list. There is occasional live entertainment at weekends. Hot pies and pasties are available with sandwiches made to order.
(256,257)♣P

Knowle

Vaults

St John's Close, B93 0JU (off High Street A4141)
12-2.30, 5-11; 12-11.30 Fri & Sat; 12-11 Sun
(01564) 773656
Ansells Mild; Greene King IPA; Tetley Bitter; Wadsworth 6X; guest beers Ⓗ
This ever-popular drinkers' pub, located just off the High Street, was voted local CAMRA Pub of the Year 2003-2006 and 2008. Guest beers are often from small breweries rarely seen in the area, and the real cider is from the Westons range. Setanta Sports TV is available on request for important sporting events. The pub holds occasional beer festivals, and an annual pickled onion competition. Light meals are served lunchtimes Monday to Saturday.
(S2,S3)

Lower Gornal

Black Bear

86 Deepdale Lane, DY3 2AE
5 (4 Fri)-11; 12-11 Sat; 12-10.30 Sun
(01384) 253333
Kinver Black Bear IPA; guest beers Ⓗ
This charming traditional pub, originally an 18th-century farmhouse, is built on the hillside with views over the south of the Black Country, and supported with massive buttresses. Inside, the L-shaped, split-level room has discrete and comfortable seating areas. Guest beers are usually from smaller micro-breweries. Gornal Wood bus station is about 10 minutes walk away.
(257,297)♣

Five Ways

Himley Road, DY3 2PZ (jct of B4176/4175)
12-midnight (10.30 Sun)
(01384) 252968
Bathams Best Bitter Ⓗ
Warm and welcoming wayside watering hole on the western edge of the West Midlands conurbation. Its one crook-shaped room is just large enough to accommodate a large TV screen for football matches at one end without interrupting the civilised social discourse at the other. There is a raised decking area overlooking the car park at the back of the pub. (257,297)♣P

Fountain

8 Temple Street, DY3 2PE (on B4157)
12-11 (10.30 Sun)
(01384) 242777
Enville Ale; Greene King Abbot; Hook Norton Old Hooky; RCH Pitchfork; guest beers Ⓗ
Twice winner of Dudley CAMRA Pub of the Year, this excellent free house serves nine real ales accompanied by draught and bottled Belgian beers, real cider and 12 fruit wines. The busy, vibrant bar is complemented by an elevated dining area serving excellent food 12-2.30pm Monday to Friday and 6-9pm Saturday plus Sunday lunches until 5pm. During the summer months the rear garden is a suntrap and a pleasant area in which to while away an hour or two. (541)♣

Lye

Shovel

81 Pedmore Road, DY9 7DZ (on A4036)
5.30 (2.30 Sat)-midnight; 12-midnight Sun
☎ (01384) 423998 🌐 theshovelinn.co.uk
Enville Ale; Greene King Old Speckled Hen, Abbot; Holden's Golden Glow; guest beers Ⓗ
Good old-fashioned traditional pub, serving 13 real ales. Home of the Rale Ale Wall, consisting of 800 pump pulls from the last 24 years, its very ornate gates feature two malt shovels intertwined with grape vines. There is a central bar serving three separate seating areas; two TVs ensure most sporting events are covered. There is also a dartboard and a general knowledge quiz machine. Outside there is a partly covered patio area and a heated smoking area. ❀◗♿⇌🚌(9,276,297)♣

Windsor Castle Inn

7 Stourbridge Road, DY9 7DG (at Lye Cross)
12-11
☎ (01384) 897809 🌐 windsorcastlebrewery.com
Sadler's Jack's Ale, Worcester Sorcerer, Mild, Thin Ice, Green Man, seasonal beers Ⓗ
The Windsor Castle Inn is the tap house for the brewer of the same name and has recently been seen on TV. The brewery was rehoused in Lye in 2004 by descendants of the original brewer. The interior is split in to several seated areas in an open space in front of the bar, with brewers' barrels used as tables. The Pub won 2007 local CAMRA Pub of the Year. Most of the Sadler's ranges of beers are sold, plus seasonal specials. Brewery tours are available every Monday evening or by arrangement. Q❀◖◗♿⇌🚌(9,276)P

Netherton

Olde Swan (Ma Pardoe's) ☆

89 Halesowen Road, DY2 9PY
11-11; 12-4, 7-10.30 Sun
☎ (01384) 253075
Olde Swan Original, Dark Swan, 1835, Entire, Bumble Hole, seasonal beers Ⓗ
Characterful pub on CAMRA's National Inventory of historic pub interiors and home to the Olde Swan Brewery. The front bar is an unspoilt gem, with an enamelled ceiling and a solid fuel stove. There is a cosy rear snug and a more modern lounge. Food is available in the lounge lunchtimes Monday to Friday and Monday evening. The upstairs restaurant, open Tuesday-Saturday, is highly regarded for its a la carte menu, and Sunday lunches are also popular (booking essential for all meals). Olde Swan Entire, Bumble Hole and Black Widow beers are now available in bottles.
Q❀◖◗♿🚌(242A,243,283)P

Oldbury

Jolly Collier

43 Junction Street, B69 3HD (off A457)
12-3, 5-11; 12-11 Fri-Sun
☎ (07817) 286827
Beer range varies Ⓗ
A true community pub, popular with all ages. Traditional pub games and comprehensive TV coverage of live sporting events on large screens are all part of this lively and friendly establishment. There is a heated, covered smoking patio and a large elevated decked area overlooking the garden which is ideal for supervising children as they play on the grassed games area. Two real ales on hand pulls are sourced mainly from local breweries.
❀♿⇌(Sandwell & Dudley)🚌(87,120)♣

Waggon & Horses ★

17A Church Street, B69 3AD
12-11 (midnight Fri & Sat); 12-10.30 (7 winter) Sun
☎ (0121) 552 5467
Brains Reverend James; Enville White; Oakham JHB; guest beers Ⓗ
A pub popular with shoppers and office workers, it provides a selection of real ales and reasonably priced, freshly cooked food with a vegetarian option. Its ornate tiled walls, Holts Brewery etched windows and interesting panelled ceiling prompted CAMRA to include it in their National Inventory listing. There is a large public pay and display car park at the rear and Oldbury bus station is just a two-minute walk away.
Q◖◗♿⇌(Sandwell & Dudley)🚌(87,120)

Quarry Bank

Church Tavern

36 High Street, DY5 2AA
12-11 (10.30 Sun)
☎ (01384) 560249
Beer range varies Ⓗ
Friendly, community-centred free house serving an ever-changing range of four guest beers. The pub has a traditional, L-shaped bar contrasting with a quieter, spacious lounge with a real fire where children are welcome. The pub gets very busy at weekends when live music and a disco are organised on alternate Saturdays, as well as an open mike night on Wednesday. Many buses pass the pub en route to Merry Hill. Cobs are available. There is a small car park to the rear.
🚌(99,138)♣P

Rushall

Manor Arms ★

Park Road, off Daw End Lane, WS4 1LG (off B4154)
12-midnight (11 Sun)
☎ (01922) 642333
Banks's Original, Bitter; Jennings Cocker Hoop; Ringwood Old Thumper; guest beers Ⓗ
Listed in the CAMRA National Inventory of Historic Pubs, this pub has exposed beams and many olde worlde charms including open fires in both bars. It is known locally as 'the pub with no bar', as the beer pulls come straight out of the wall. Recently voted best canalside pub in the country by British Waterways, its large beer garden is near to the canal and local country park. It also has a reputation for being haunted. Good food is served winter afternoons and summer evenings. Dogs are welcome. Q❀◖◗🚌(355,356)P

Sedgley

Beacon Hotel 🏆 ★

129 Bilston Street, DY3 1JE (A463)
12-2.30 (3 Sat), 5.30 (6 Sat)-11; 12-3, 7-10.30 Sun
☎ (01902) 883380
Sarah Hughes Pale Amber, Sedgley Surprise, Dark Ruby; guest beers Ⓗ
This classic, beautifully-restored Victorian tap house and tower brewery is the home of Sarah Hughes ales. The heart of this atmospheric, popular pub is the small island bar with hatches serving the

central corridor, a small cosy snug, and the large main room. Off the corridor are a traditional benched tap room and a family room with access to a well-equipped garden and play area. Cobs are available. CAMRA Branch Pub of the Year 2008 and 2009 and West Midlands Regional Pub of the Year 2008. Q🐴❀🚌(541,545,558)P⚊

Bulls Head

27 Bilston Street, DY3 1JA (A463)
⏲ 10 (11 Sun)-11.30
☎ (01902) 661676
Holden's Mild, Ⓗ; Bitter, Ⓗ/Ⓟ; Golden Glow, seasonal beers; guest beer Ⓗ
This is a small, double-fronted, street-corner listed building. Close to the centre of Sedgley village, the pub has a community atmosphere. The front bar is lively with local chatter, pub games and sports screen. To the side is a lounge which can be curtained off to provide a small function room. Children are welcome in this area. Behind the pub the walled yard houses a well-equipped smoking shelter. Cobs are available. Live music plays on occasional Saturdays. ⛫❀🚌(545,558)♣⚊🖵

Mount Pleasant (Stump)

144 High Street, DY3 1RH (A459)
⏲ 6.30 (7 Mon & Tue)-11; 12-3, 7-10.30 Sun
☎ (0795) 0195652
Beer range varies Ⓗ
The mock-Tudor exterior of this sensitively refurbished free house fronts a friendly and cheerful atmosphere inside. The good-sized bar has a convivial feel, while the homely and warm lounge is divided into two rooms on different levels, both with coal stoves. Eight handpumps provide a good range of guest beers. Dog friendly, the pub is a five-minute walk from Sedgley centre. ⛫Q❀🍺🚌(558)♣P⚊

Shirley

Bernie's Real Ale Off-Licence

266 Cranmore Boulevard, B90 4PX
⏲ 11.30-2, 5-10 (9 Sat); 7-9 Sun
☎ (0121) 744 2827
Taylor Landlord; guest beers Ⓗ
This unique gem sells the most interesting and unusual range of beers from micros anywhere in the Solihull area. Diversity and quality are assured and you can try three or four guest beers before you buy. Take-home containers in sizes from 1-40 pints are available. In addition to Rich's draught cider, there is also a vast range of British and Belgian bottled beers to choose from. Bernie's thoroughly deserves its appearance in this Guide over a 25-year period. 🚌🍎P

Woodman's Rest ✔

Union Road, B90 3DB
⏲ 11.30-11 (11.30 Thu; midnight Fri & Sat)
☎ (0121) 7453904
Greene King IPA, Abbot; guest beers Ⓗ
Refurbished in 2000, the pub is now part of the Ember Inns chain. A single central bar serves the spacious, comfortably-furnished area around it, with three large fires: one real, two coal-effect. The pub offers three guest ales from different areas of the country and participates in the Ember Inns beer festivals. It attracts a varied clientele age-wise and can get very busy, but children over 14 are only allowed if dining. ⛫❀◐♿🚌(53,57,58)P⚊

Solihull

Assembly Rooms ✔

21 Poplar Road, B91 3AD
⏲ 9-1am (2am Thu-Sat)
☎ (0121) 711 6990
Greene King IPA; Highgate Old Ale; Purity Gold, Mad Goose, UBU; guest beers Ⓗ
This imposing building was formerly Solihull's Council House and now includes impressive two-level drinking areas, with the best choice downstairs. Sports are shown upstairs, at volume, and a quiet library area is on the ground floor. Special events are held frequently, from 'meet the brewer' to themed evenings. Regularly changing locally-brewed ales include Purity, Springhead and Highgate, complemented by quality national brews. ◐♿⇌🚌(37,57)⚊🖵

Fieldhouse ✔

10 Knightcote Drive, Monkspath, B91 3JU
⏲ 12-11 (11.30 Thu; midnight Fri & Sat)
☎ (0121) 7118011
M&B Brew XI; guest beers Ⓗ
Part of the Ember Inns chain, this large, modern pub is tastefully decorated and comfortably furnished, featuring four large fires (one real, three coal-effect) and pleasant patio areas. It usually serves four guest ales from across the country, often unusual ones, that change frequently. Always busy, it attracts a wide age range, but children must be over 14 and dining. Regular quiz nights are held on Sunday and Tuesday. ⛫❀◐♿⇌🚌P⚊

Stourbridge

Plough & Harrow

107 Worcester Street, DY8 1AX (on A451 jct B4186)
⏲ 12-11 (11.30 Fri & Sat)
☎ (01384) 397218
Black Sheep Best Bitter; Taylor Landlord; Wye Valley HPA; guest beer Ⓗ
A friendly pub with a continuing commitment to real ale and cider. Both are served from the U-shaped bar, where a middle wicket handpull dispenses a regularly-changing guest. A water bowl provides refreshment for four-legged visitors. Three real fires give a cosy ambience. A covered patio and garden afford a pleasant outdoor drinking area. The nearby Mary Stevens park has a public car park, but beware of the early evening closing hours. ⛫Q❀⇌(Town)🚌♣🍎⚊

Royal Exchange

75 Enville Street, DY8 1XW
⏲ 1 (12 Sat)-11; 12-10.30 Sun
☎ (01384) 396726
Bathams Mild Ale, Best Bitter, XXX (winter) Ⓗ
A perennial Guide entry, set in a row of terraced houses. A narrow passageway has an entrance to the bustling public bar and leads to a paved patio/smoking area. A comfortable lounge is at the rear of the building with a function room upstairs. No hot food is served, but cobs are available plus pork pies at the weekend. A December visit might land you the exclusive XXX on draft. There is a public car park opposite. Q❀🍺⇌(Town)🚌♣P⚊

Sutton Coldfield

Bishop Vesey ✔

63 Boldmere Road, B73 5UY
⏲ 9-11 (midnight Fri & Sat)

☎ (0121) 355 5077
Courage Directors; Greene King IPA, Abbot; Marston's Pedigree; guest beers Ⓗ
Situated in the suburb of Boldmere in Sutton Coldfield and named after the town's benefactor, this is a busy and popular Wetherspoon's which attracts a local clientele. It has the usual open plan layout with upstairs seating and a cosy book-lined area at the end of the bar. There is provision for smokers on an outside heated patio area at the rear of the building. Children are allowed in a designated area. Good value food is served, including a breakfast menu until noon.
❀◐◑♿⇌(Wylde Green)🚌(107,451)🚭

Tipton

Port 'n' Ale
178 Horseley Heath, DY4 7DS
🕒 12-11 (11.30 Fri & Sat)
☎ (0121) 5206572
Greene King Abbot; guest beers Ⓗ
Conveniently situated on the 74 bus route from Dudley to Birmingham near to Great Bridge bus station, this friendly pub serves up to 10 ever-changing real ales including at least one dark beer. It also usually stocks two traditional ciders. It has a large central bar area with an open-plan interior, a beer garden and conservatory. Good food is served all day and children are allowed until 9pm. Regular quiz nights take place each Tuesday, with beer festivals in spring and autumn.
🐎❀◐◑♿⇌(Dudley Port)🚌(74)♣🍎P🚭

Upper Gornal

Britannia (Sally's) ☆
109 Kent Street, DY3 1UX
🕒 12-11 (10.30 Sun)
☎ (01902) 883253 🌐 bathams.co.uk
Bathams Mild Ale, Best Bitter, XXX (winter) Ⓗ
The Britannia owes its National Inventory listing to the cosy tap room at the rear named after legendary former landlady Sally Perry. Its wall-mounted handpumps can be seen in action on Friday evenings. At other times service is from the main front bar, itself a very comfortable place to be. There is also a family/games room with a TV occasionally in use. Behind the pub is the former brewhouse, a delightful backyard smoking shelter and garden. Local pork pies are served.
🔥Q🐎❀⊟♿🚌(558)♣🚭

Jolly Crispin
25 Clarence Street, DY3 1UL
🕒 4 (12 Fri & Sat)-11; 12-10.30 Sun
☎ (01902) 672220 🌐 thejollycrispin.co.uk
Titanic Crispy Nail; guest beers Ⓗ
A building dating in part from the 18th century, this vibrant pub is entered down a couple of steps from street level (take care!), leading into the front bar with two distinct cosy areas. At the rear, with an entrance from the car park, is a comfortable lounge with a panoramic view over the northern Black Country. The pub is deservedly popular with locals and visitors and is dog friendly. There are eight ever-changing guest beers. Real fires have recently been reignited. 🔥❀⊟🚌(558)P🚭

Walsall

Arbor Lights ✔
127-128 Lichfield Street, WS1 1SY (off A4148 Arboretum jct towards town centre)
🕒 10-11 (midnight Fri & Sat); 12-11 Sun
☎ (01922) 613361 🌐 arbor-lights.co.uk
Beer range varies Ⓗ
Opened in 2003, this modern open-plan pub in the town centre is popular with drinkers and diners alike. It has a large dining area with good locally-sourced food served from 12-10pm daily including a fixed priced menu. The pub's name is derived from the nearby arboretum illuminations, which are known locally as The Lights, held annually in September. Three handpumps dispense rotating guest ales and hand-pulled cider and perry are served in summer. ◐◑♿⇌🚌(394,997)🍎🚭

Butts Tavern
44 Butts Street, WS4 2BJ
🕒 12-11 (midnight Fri & Sat)
☎ (01922) 629332 🌐 buttstavern.co.uk
Jennings Cocker Hoop; guest beers Ⓗ
A two-roomed, old-fashioned, friendly community local with a pleasant atmosphere. The large main bar features a stage at one end, while a smaller room includes a pool table and dartboard. There are four hand pulls, with one permanent and up to three changing guest beers. Quiz night is Tuesday and live entertainment takes place most Fridays and Saturdays. Sky Sports is screened but is not too intrusive. There is an external smoking area at the rear. Crusty cobs are often available.
🐎♿⇌🚌(322,394,977)♣🚭

King Arthur
59 Liskeard Road, WS5 3EY (off A34)
🕒 12-11 (midnight Sat)
☎ (01922) 631400 🌐 thekingarthurpub.co.uk
Greene King Ruddles Best, Old Speckled Hen, Abbot; Taylor Landlord; Wye Valley HPA; guest beer Ⓗ
An urban gem located in Park Hall estate, which is hard to find but definitely worth the effort. A two-roomed community pub, it has a bar area with a big screen and five TVs boasting comprehensive sports viewing. The front lounge is popular with diners and is famous for steaks (booking required for four or more people). There are six hand pulls and the pub is decorated with sports memorabilia. There is a heated smoking area outside.
❀◐◑⊟♿🚌(274)P🚭

King George V
Wallows Lane, WS2 9BZ (on A4148 ¼ mile from M6 jct 9)
🕒 11 (12 Sat)-11; 12-10.30 Sun
☎ (01922) 626130
Beer range varies Ⓗ
A large three-roomed pub with a friendly atmosphere. Built in 1936, the George has a mainly local clientele and hosts a weekly quiz on Tuesday, with entertainment on most Friday evenings plus many Saturday functions. At least two constantly changing independent or micro-brewery guest beers are available. The pub is handy for Walsall Football Club and visiting supporters are made to feel welcome. Snacks are available upon request.
🔥🐎❀⊟⇌(Bescot)🚌(311,311A,313)♣P🚭

Lyndon House Hotel
9-10 Upper Rushall Street, WS1 2HA
🕒 11-11.30 (2am Fri & Sat); 12-11 Sun

☎ (01922) 612511 🌐 lyndonhousehotel.co.uk
Courage Directors; Greene King Abbot; Highgate Dark Mild; Theakston Best Bitter; guest beers Ⓗ
This pub is part of a complex containing a hotel and an Italian restaurant. The bar (formerly the Royal Exchange) was converted about 15 years ago. It contains old brick and many old timbers to warm and cosy effect. The luxurious hotel was formerly a Salvation Army hostel. Popular with business people, the clientele is drawn from all over the town to give a slice of Walsall life. Live jazz is staged on the first Monday of the month.
⛫Q❀🛏◐⇌🚌(51,377)

Walsall Cricket Club

Gorway Road, WS1 3BE (off A34, by university campus)
✪ 8-11; 7-11.30 Fri; 12-11.30 Sat; 12-10 (8 Winter) Sun
☎ (01922) 622094 🌐 walsallcricketclub.com
Wye Valley HPA; guest beers Ⓗ
Established in 1830, the Club has occupied this site since 1907. The comfortable lounge displays cricket memorabilia and two large-screen TVs show sporting events. The bar is staffed by members. On match days the cricket can be viewed through panoramic windows. In good weather the lounge is opened onto the patio area. beer festivals are held and on summer evenings this is a rural retreat in the heart of town. Entry to the club for non-members is by CAMRA Membership card.
❀♿🚌(51)P📺

Wheatsheaf 🏆

4 Birmingham Road, WS1 2NA
✪ 12-2.30, 4.30-11; 12-midnight Fri & Sat; 12-11 Sun
☎ (01922) 628992 🌐 wheatsheafwalsall.co.uk
Wells Bombardier; guest beers Ⓗ
Walsall CAMRA Pub of the Year 2008, this friendly community local welcomes dogs and children. Real ale festivals take place every third weekend of every third month. Live music plays every Tuesday night, with a mini library and newspapers available at the weekend. A giant outdoor chess set is available during the warmer months. Home-cooked food is served daily, alongside a choice of 15 wines available by the glass or bottle and an excellent range of single malt whiskies. A function room is available for hire. Q🐴◐◑♿🚌(51)♣

White Lion ✔

150 Sandwell Street, WS1 3EQ
✪ 12-11 (midnight Thu-Sat)
☎ (01922) 628542
Adnams Bitter; Greene King IPA, Abbot; Highgate Dark Mild; Sharp's Doom Bar; guest beer Ⓗ
Imposing late Victorian back-street local. The classic sloping bar, with its deep and shallow ends, is the best in town. A plush, comfortable lounge caters for the drinker who wants to languish. This pub is a great community melting pot, with live music on Tuesday, Thursday and Sunday nights. A small walled garden caters for smokers. A popular quiz is held on the first Monday of the month. Thatchers Medium Scrumpy cider is served. No meals on Monday and Tuesday. ⛫❀◐◑🍺♿🚌(404)♣🍎🚬

Wednesbury

Old Blue Ball

19 Hall End, WS10 9ED (off B4200)
✪ 12-3, 5-11; 12-11 Fri; 12-4.30, 7-11 Sat; 12-3.30, 7-11 Sun
☎ (0121) 5560197
Everards Original; Taylor Landlord; guest beers Ⓗ
Friendly back-street local with six handpumps and four changing guest beers. The interior comprises a small bar on the right with a sliding door, a family room on the left with a dartboard, and a quiet snug across the corridor which, like the corridor, has a serving hatch. Chips and hot pork and stuffing sandwiches are served on Friday and Saturday. The pub has crib and darts teams and host the local historians' society. There is a large garden with seating and a children's play area. Dogs are welcome on a leash.
Q🐴❀🍺⊖(Great Western St)🚌(311A,313)♣🚬

Olde Leathern Bottel ✔

40 Vicarage Road, WS10 9DW (off A461)
✪ 12-2.30 (not Mon), 6-11; 12-2, 6-11.30 Fri; 11-11.30 Sat; 12-4, 7-11 Sun
☎ (0121) 505 0230
Beer range varies Ⓗ
Set in cottages dating from 1510, the pub has four rooms including a snug which doubles as a function room, all decorated with old photographs. Drinkers can stand in the passage and there is seating in the rear yard. There are two guest ales which vary in strength – Jennings beers feature regularly. Home-cooked food is available, including vegetarian dishes, and children are welcome. The pub hosts a quiz on Sunday, and a dominoes team and other organisations meet here. Dogs are welcome in the bar. ⛫❀◐◑🍺⊖(Great Western St)🚌(311)♣🚬

Rosehill Tavern

80 Church Hill, WS10 9DU (off A461, near top of Church Hill)
✪ 12-11 (12.30am Fri & Sat)
☎ (0121) 5308128
Banks's Original; guest beers Ⓗ
A welcoming pub attracting a diverse clientele, with two rooms, a family room and bar adorned with sports memorabilia, complete with TV screens showing all sporting events. The landlord has a keen interest in real ale and offers four handpumps with three changing guest beers. Upstairs is a function room and outside is a spacious garden with a covered smoking area including a wall-mounted TV. Many teams are based here including football, crib and dominoes. Cobs are available daily.
⛫🐴❀🍺♿⊖(Great Western St)🚌(311A,313) ♣P🚬

Wednesfield

Pyle Cock ✔

Rookery Street, WV11 1UN (on old Wolverhampton Road)
✪ 10.30 (11 Thu)-11 (11.30 Fri & Sat); 12-11 Sun
☎ (01902) 732125
Banks's Original, Bitter Ⓟ**; guest beers** Ⓗ
A Mild Merit award winner, this pub was also CAMRA Branch Pub of the Year in 2008. Quality beers are assured, with guest ales from the Marston's list. This traditional inn dates back to the 1860s and offers a choice of bar, smoke room and rear lounge. A friendly welcome awaits you and, with its wide mix of regulars and visitors, you will soon be drawn into conversation.
❀🍺🚌(559)♣P🚬

Royal Tiger ✔

41-43 High Street, WV11 1ST
✪ 9am-midnight (1am Fri & Sat)
☎ (01902) 307816

Banks's Original; Greene King IPA; Marston's Pedigree; guest beers Ⓗ
Open since 2000, this lively Wetherspoon's pub is now a firm favourite among the many shoppers in this small town. Many come to take advantage of the full menu and the choice of beers, while smokers can enjoy a patio area at the rear of the pub. Westons cider is sold here. The decor includes an insight into local history. (559)

Vine ★
35 Lichfield Road, WV11 1TN
12-11
☎ (01902) 733529
Black Country BFG, Pig On The Wall, Fireside; guest beers Ⓗ
A rare intact example of a simple inter-war working-class pub. Built in 1938, this National Inventory and Grade II-listed hostelry retains its bar, lounge and snug. An ever-changing selection of guest beers complements the Black Country Brewery's ales. Good value home-cooked food is available lunchtime and evening, with booking recommended for Sunday lunch (no food Sun eve).
Q(559)P

West Bromwich

Greets Green Sports & Bowling Club
101 Whitehall Road, B70 0HG (B4166)
11.30-11 (midnight Fri & Sat)
☎ (0121) 5571388
Beer range varies Ⓗ
Popular local community club set back from the main road in the Greets Green area. There are two large comfortable rooms, one of which can be booked for functions. A third, more intimate room, which was once the local clinic, is where an occasional beer festival is staged. Free and Easy on Thursday, Friday and Saturday nights. Children are allowed access at all times. The cider is Thatchers.
(401,402A)P

Horse & Jockey
49 Stoney Lane, B71 4EZ
12-11 (midnight Fri & Sat)
☎ (0121) 525 3655 thehorseandjockey.org
Banks's Original, Bitter; Jennings Cocker Hoop; Marston's Old Empire; guest beers Ⓗ
Atmospheric two-roomed pub with a conservatory and enclosed patio area to the rear. This is a true drinkers' pub and an institution in the real ale fraternity. Tied to Marston's, it has access to beers from micro-breweries such as Jennings, Ringwood, Wychwood and Brakspear to name but a few. Entertainment includes live music on Sunday evening and popular home-cooked food is served daily.

Old Hop Pole
474 High Street, B70 9LD
12-1am
☎ (07946) 579957
Hop Back Summer Lightning; Wye Valley HPA; guest beer Ⓗ
Traditional old town-centre pub that offers its customers a warm welcome. It has an open-plan design and its walls are adorned with West Bromwich Albion football memorabilia. The pub gets very busy on match days. Saturday nights often feature a disco-karaoke. Children are welcome until 9pm.
(Dartmouth St)(74,79)

Willenhall

Falcon
77 Gomer Street West, WV13 2NR (off B4464)
12-11 (10.30 Sun)
☎ (01902) 633378
Greene King Abbot; Oakham JHB; Olde Swan Dark Swan; RCH Pitchfork; guest beers Ⓗ
Just a few minutes' walk from the market place, the Falcon is the flagship real ale pub in Willenhall. It has been run by the same family for the past 25 years and has established a strong local following. Built in 1936, it has two rooms – a lively bar and a quieter lounge. Seven keenly-priced beers are served and it is home to popular crib and darts teams. It has an outside drinking area and is handy for the Willenhall Lock Museum. Walsall CAMRA Pub of the Year 2005-2007.
Q(525,529)

Robin Hood
54 The Crescent, WV13 2QR (A462/B4464 jct)
4 (11.30 Fri & Sat)-11; 12-11 Sun
☎ (07928) 234819
Banks's Original; Fuller's London Pride Ⓗ**; Greene King Abbot** Ⓗ/Ⓖ**; Taylor Landlord; guest beers** Ⓗ
A small, warm and friendly pub with a single comfortable U-shaped room. The mainly local trade supports the many charity events held throughout the year. It is often frequented by the local archery club which practises in an adjacent field. Disco or karaoke nights are held every other Friday night, and there is the occasional live band. Two guest beers are usually available. (529)P

Wollaston

Foresters Arms
Bridgnorth Road, DY8 3PL (on A458 towards Bridgnorth)
12-2.30 (not Mon), 6-midnight; 12-3, 7-11 Sun
☎ (01384) 394476
Ansells Mild; Enville Ale; Marston's Pedigree; guest beer Ⓗ
Located on the Ridge and ideal for ramblers, this friendly local is on the outskirts of Wollaston next to the countryside. The L-shaped room provides a convenient area where diners can sample good value, quality food. Quizzes are usually held on the first and third Sunday of each month and a poker night is held on Monday. The annual Wollaston Fun Run starts from outside the pub, followed by a barbecue in the beer garden. A great way to spend a Sunday afternoon, and the proceeds go to charity. P

Unicorn
145 Bridgnorth Road, DY8 3NX (on A458 towards Bridgnorth)
12-11; 12-4, 7-10.30 Sun
☎ (01384) 394823
Bathams Mild Ale, Best Bitter, XXX (winter) Ⓗ
This former brewhouse was purchased by Bathams in the early 1990s following the death of the last member of the Billingham family. Since joining the estate it has become widely regarded as one of the pubs that serves the finest pint. The original brewhouse remains at the side, but sadly will never brew again due to the cost of rebuilding. The pub itself is still a two-bar drinking house, popular with all ages. It serves generous cobs and selected hot snacks at lunchtime. It also offers a free Wi-Fi service. QP

Wolverhampton

Chindit ✔

113 Merridale Road, WV3 9SE

4 (2 Fri; 12 Sat)-11; 12-11 Sun

☎ (01902) 425582 thechindit.co.uk

Caledonian Deuchars IPA; Enville Ale; Wye Valley HPA; guest beers Ⓗ

Street-corner local named in honour of the local men who served with the South Staffordshire regiment, taking part in the 1944 Chindit campaign in Burma. The pub comprises two rooms – a comfortable lounge and a bar with a pool table, both with TV screens showing live sport. Up to three guest beers are available, usually from local micros. Live music is staged on Friday evening. See the website for details. ❀(513,543)P

Combermere Arms

90 Chapel Ash, WV3 0TY (on A41 Tettenhall Road)

11-3, 5.30-11; 12-midnight Fri & Sat; 12-10.30 Sun

☎ (01902) 421880

Banks's Original, Bitter; guest beers Ⓗ

A three-room local with a bar and a snug off a corridor and a servery leading to a heated courtyard, beer garden and the outside Gents' toilets, built around a tree. Bands play in the courtyard on Saturday and bar meals are available weekday lunchtimes only. Popular with Wolves fans on match days, it is also an 'official Swedish Wolves pub', as stated on a certificate in the bar. ❀P

Dog & Gun ✔

1 Wrottesley Road, Tettenhall, WV6 8SB (off A41 Wergs Road)

12-11 (midnight Thu-Sat)

☎ (01902) 747943

Banks's Bitter; Wells Bombardier; guest beers Ⓗ

Recently refurbished by Ember Inns, the pub has individual seating areas around a large U-shaped bar. Comfortable and welcoming, it attracts a wide age range, although children must be over 14 and dining with an adult. Food quality and a varying range of beers ensure a busy, friendly atmosphere. A local writers' group and a rambling club meet here regularly. There is a patio for outside drinking and a covered, heated area for smokers. ❀♿(501,891)P

Great Western

Sun Street, WV10 0DJ

11-11 (10.30 Sun)

☎ (01902) 351090

Bathams Best Bitter; Holden's Mild, Bitter, Golden Glow, Special; guest beer Ⓗ

A historic Grade II-listed, 150-year-old pub which has been extended twice in the 1990s. Although comprising only one room, it offers different areas all served by a central bar. The pub has been enhanced recently by the restoration of three real fires, wonderfully warming on a cold winter's day. The interior features both railway and Wolves memorabilia and is always busy when Wolves are at home. ❀(St George's)P

> The train was over half an hour behind its time and the Traveller complained to the Guard of the train; and the Guard spoke to him very bitterly. He said: 'You must have a very narrow heart that you wouldn't go down to the town and stand your friends a few drinks instead of bothering me to get away'.
> **Jack B Yeats**, 1871-1957

Hog's Head

186 Stafford Street, WV1 1NA

11-11 (midnight Fri; 1am Mon & Sat)

☎ (01902) 717955

Beer range varies Ⓗ

Built in 1894, the Vine Hotel's superb terracotta exterior has led to its local list status. Closed in 1984, the building was used as offices until reopening in 1998 as the Hogshead. It attracts a wide mix of customers, including students from the nearby university. Its single room is split into various areas and features pool tables and TV screens for major sporting events and music. Monday night is now student night, with live music. ❀(St George's)

Horse & Jockey ✔

64 Robert Wynd, Woodcross, WV14 9SB

12-11 (11.30 Fri & Sat)

☎ (01902) 662268

Banks's Original; Draught Bass; guest beers Ⓗ

A welcome return to the Guide for this community pub, last making an appearance in 1998. In the bar is an old Belle portable stove and there is an open fire in the lounge. Good value food is served every day except Sunday evening, with vegetarian options. Families are welcome until 8.30pm. Tuesday is quiz night and Wednesday is curry night. Check out the chalkboard for forthcoming guest ales. ❀(581)P

Moon under Water ✔

53-55 Lichfield Street, WV1 1EQ (opp Grand Theatre)

9am-midnight (1am Fri & Sat)

☎ (01902) 422447

Banks's Original; Greene King IPA; Holden's Golden Glow; Marston's Pedigree; guest beers Ⓗ

Open since 1995, this typical city-centre Wetherspoon's attracts a range of customers. The pub can be very busy pre-theatre due to its close proximity to the Grand Theatre and is popular with young clubbers at weekends. Sofas and large-screen TVs generally show the news with subtitles help to create a relaxed and informal atmosphere. A full Wetherspoon's food menu is served. Westons cider is available. Close to bus, rail and tram connections. ♿(St George's)

Newhampton

19 Riches Street, Whitmore Reans, WV6 0DW

11-11 (midnight Fri & Sat); 12-11 Sun

☎ (01902) 745773

Caledonian Deuchars IPA; Courage Best Bitter, Directors; Taylor Landlord; Wye Valley HPA; guest beers Ⓗ

Multi-roomed local with an unexpectedly large garden where games facilities include a bowling green, boules piste and a children's play area. An upstairs function room is a thriving venue for folk and other music, and there is also a pool room and bowls pavilion. Beers from two local breweries, Enville and Kinver, alternate as guests, and Thatchers cider is sold. ❀(501)♣

Posada

48 Lichfield Street, WV1 1DG (opp art gallery)

12-11 (midnight Thu-Sat); closed Sun

Adnams Broadside; Caledonian Deuchars IPA; Greene King Abbot; Wells Bombardier; guest beers Ⓗ
Built in 1884 and visited by Lawrence of Arabia in 1934, this superb Grade II listed pub boasts up to six ales. Marvel at the original tiling and a superb bar back with snob screens opening into the corridor. This small one-roomed pub attracts a wide mix of customers. Just a five-minute walk from Wolverhampton railway station, it is also conveniently close to both Civic and Wulfrun Halls. A discount on real ales is available to CAMRA members. ❀⇌⊖(St George's)🚌⍿

Swan (at Compton)

Bridgnorth Road, Compton, WV6 8AE
🕘 11-11 (11.30 Thu; midnight Fri & Sat); 12-11 Sun
☎ (01902) 754736
Banks's Original, Bitter; guest beer Ⓗ
A Grade II-listed inn, this basic unspoilt gem has a convivial atmosphere. The traditional bar features wooden settles, exposed beams and a faded painting of a swan dating from 1777. The bar and L-shaped lounge are supplied from a central servery and the lounge doubles as a games room. Local cycling, angling and pigeon clubs meet here. The patio is heated and partially covered for smokers. Dogs are welcome in the bar. Q❀⊟🚌(510,890)♣P⍿

Tap & Spile

35 Princess Street, WV1 1HD
🕘 10am-11 (10.30 Sun)
☎ (01902) 713319
Beer range varies Ⓗ
Rebuilt in 1889, the Duke of York closed in 1961 and became Williams Deacon's Bank, before reopening as the Tap & Spile in 1996. This no-frills city centre pub has two snugs and a narrow bar. A hotbed of darts, its TV screens show major sporting events and music. Popular with a wide mix of customers, it gets very busy when Wolves are at home. Beers are usually LocAle delivered direct and a Ludlow ale is usually among the range. ❀⇌⊖(St George's)🚌♣●⍿

Wordsley

New Inn

117 High Street, DY8 5QR (on A491, 4 miles from Stourbridge)
🕘 12-11; 12-10.30 (12-4, 7-10.30 winter) Sun
☎ (01384) 295614
Bathams Mild, Best Bitter, XXX (seasonal) Ⓗ
On the main Wolverhampton to Stourbridge road, the building has an imposing three-storey facade. It probably became a pub in the 1820s and is listed as a building of special interest. Acquired by Bathams in April 2008, it has become very popular and is often busy. The decor is traditional and there are no TVs or machines. An L-shaped bar serves a single room with a small annexe at one end, and a patio area outside. Children are not allowed inside but there is an play area outside. Bar snacks are available. Good public transport brings in customers, but the pub largely caters for the surrounding community and has the feel of a proper local. ❀♿🚌(256,257)♣●P⍿

Queens Head

128 High Street, DY8 5QS (A491)
🕘 4-11 (midnight Fri); 12-midnight Sat; 12-11 Sun
☎ (01384) 271917
Enville Ale, Ginger, Phoenix, seasonal beer; Sarah Hughes Dark Ruby; guest beer Ⓗ
A pub with a varied clientele, the atmosphere and service is friendly. Outside is a patio/smoking area and a small car park. Inside, the premises consist of a large room which almost surrounds the central bar with traditional decor. At one end there are games and a large TV screen for sport. Away from the TV is a dining and drinking area with plenty of seating. Food is reasonably priced and the Sunday carvery is particularly popular. Recently appointed an Enville Brewery Tap House, at least four Enville ales will be available, together with Sarah Hughes Mild and a changing guest. ⛰☕◑🚌(256,257)P⍿

Wellington, Birmingham.

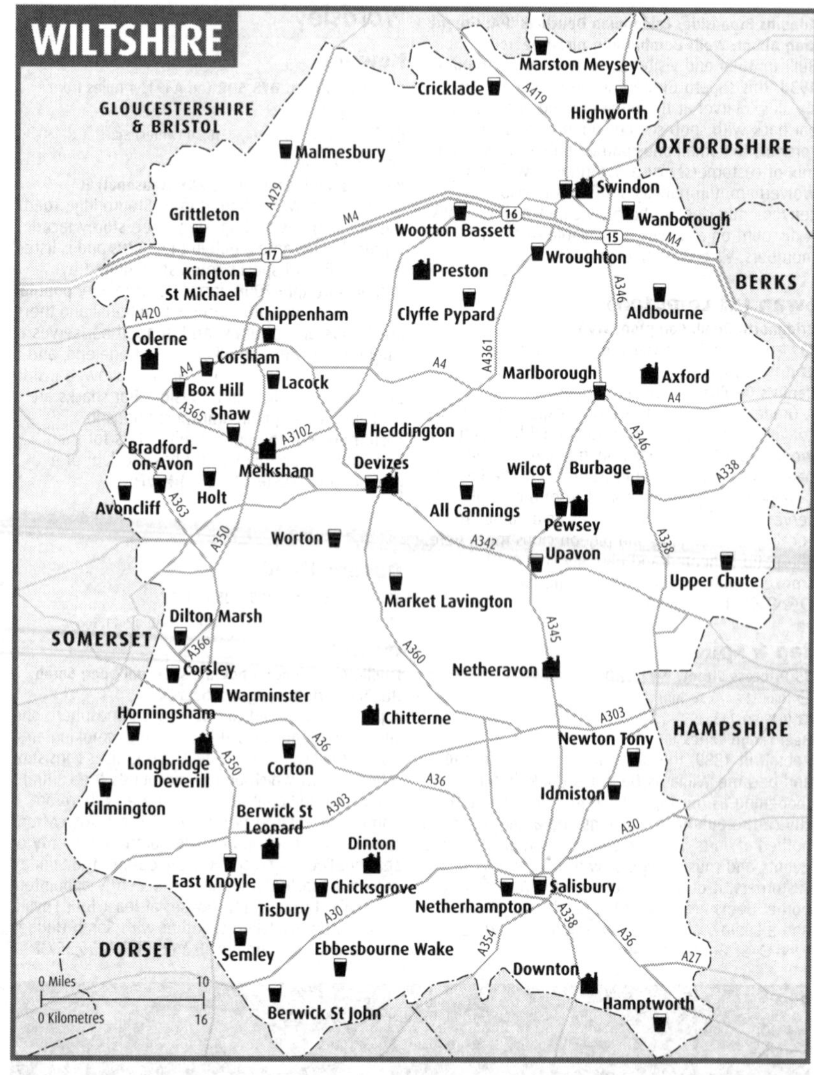

Aldbourne

Blue Boar

20 The Green, SN8 2EN

⏲ 11.30-3, 5.30-11.30; 11.30-midnight Fri & Sat; 12-10.30 Sun

☎ (01672) 540237

Wadworth IPA, 6X; guest beers Ⓗ

Set in an idyllic location by the village green, this friendly pub, with an emphasis on home-cooked food, has a cosy bar and restaurant. Two beer festivals are held annually in April and October, usually featuring well over a dozen beers. The pub is linked to the 101st Airborne Easy Company who were based in Aldbourne in the run up to D-Day. There are mementoes in the bar and veterans still visit. On a lighter note, the pub featured as the Cloven Hoof in a 1970s episode of Dr Who. ⛺Q❀◑▶Ă⊟(46,48)P

> Give my people plenty of beer, good beer and cheap beer, and you will have no revolution among them.
> **Queen Victoria**

All Cannings

Kings Arms Inn ✔

The Street, SN10 3PA SU069618

⏲ 12-3 (not Mon winter), 7-11; 12-10.30 Sun

☎ (01380) 852384 🌐 kingsarmsallcannings.co.uk

Wadworth IPA, Horizon, 6X Ⓗ

A busy, cosy and welcoming village pub, renowned for its excellent Wadworth ales and home-cooked menu. The five handpumps also dispense excellent guest ales that change regularly. Attracting locals and visitors alike, the pub is close to the Kennet & Avon Canal. It is also popular with crop circle aficionados visiting the area. A heated outside seating area caters for smokers and it has a large car park. ⛺❀◑▶Ă♣P⁄–

Avoncliff

Cross Guns

BA15 2HB
10-midnight (1am Fri & Sat)
(01225) 862335 crossguns.net
Box Steam Millworkers; guest beer H
Sixteenth century canalside inn with sloping terraces down to the River Avon, popular with walkers and cyclists. Beers include regular seasonal beers from Box Steam Brewery as well as guests. Food is served all day, with barbecues in the summer. Children and dogs are welcome. The pub is 100m from Avoncliff station and there is a car park nearby. Q

Berwick St John

Talbot

The Cross, SP7 0HA (S of A30, 5 miles E of Shaftesbury)
12-2.30, 6-11; 12-4 Sun
(01747) 828222
Draught Bass; Ringwood Best Bitter; Wadworth 6X; guest beers H
The Talbot opened as a beer house circa 1832, despite vehement opposition from the parson's wife. The building is predominantly stone built with a long, low bar with beams and inglenook fireplace. As well as offering three regular ales, the landlord is keen to promote local micros with a choice of guest ales. The more inquisitive visitor may find the cosy dining room behind the inglenook. The pub is popular with walkers from the local downs. QP

Box Hill

Quarrymans Arms

SN13 8HN (S of A4 between Corsham and Box) ST834693
11-3, 6-11.30; 11-midnight Fri & Sat; 11-11.30 Sun
(01225) 743569 quarrymans-arms.co.uk
Butcombe Bitter; Moles Best Bitter; Wadworth 6X; guest beers H
This pub is tucked away off the main routes, but well worth seeking out (phone for directions if you need to). A 300-year-old miners' pub offering a friendly welcome, it is renowned for high quality food and ales. These can be enjoyed in the bar, restaurant or garden, which has a heated area for smokers. Quiz night, often themed, is held every second Wednesday. Black Rat cider is occasionally on offer. Bed and breakfast accommodation is available in four rooms.
Q(231)P

Bradford-on-Avon

Castle Inn

10 Mount Pleasant, BA15 1SJ (just off A363 at top of Masons Lane)
9-11; 10-10.30 Sun
(01225) 865657 flatcappers.co.uk
Three Castles Barbury Castle, Vale Ale, Knight's Porter; guest beers H
Acquired by pubco Flatcappers in 2006 and transformed by wholesale refurbishment, this quiet, cosy, relaxing pub caters for a wide clientele. The interior comprises a large bar with flagstone floor, lime-washed walls, open fireplace and magnificent reclaimed mahogany bar, and three smaller rooms with elm floorboards, exposed walls and worn club chairs. Food is served throughout the premises. The garden with flagstone terrace has commanding views towards Salisbury Plain. The Three Castles beers are badged as Flatcapper, served alongside three guest beers sourced from local micros. QP

Rising Sun

231 Winsley Road, BA15 1QS
12 (4 Tue)-11; 12-10.30 Sun
(01225) 862354 therisingsunatbradfordonavon.co.uk
Courage Best Bitter; guest beers H
Popular local at the top of a hill with two bars: a small, quiet lounge and a more spacious, livelier saloon with TV screens. There is a walled beer garden with patio. The pub is home to darts, quiz, crib, pool and football teams. It hosts regular live music with a Rhythm & Brews beer festival held on the August bank holiday weekend. Guest beers usually come from local breweries and the cider is Cheddar Valley. The pub's ancient spaniel is ready to welcome you.

Burbage

Three Horseshoes

Stibb Green, SN8 3AE (signed from main road in village)
12-2, 6-11; closed Mon; 12-2, 7-10.30 Sun
(01672) 810324
Wadworth IPA, 6X; guest beer H
A traditional thatched pub near to Savernake Forest and the Kennet & Avon Canal, accessible on foot with care – a walk along part of the A346 is required. Buses between Andover or Pewsey and Marlborough pass through the village. The pub sign is on the village green opposite. There are two rooms, both featuring railway memorabilia (the Berks & Hants main line is nearby). A warm, cosy place on a cold day, with a powerful stove in the bar. Well-behaved dogs are welcome, and the food is highly recommended. One of the best places anywhere to sample Wadworth's IPA and 6X.
QP

Chicksgrove

Compasses Inn

Lower Chicksgrove, SP3 6NB (signed from A30 at Fovant) ST974294
12-3, 6-11 (7-10.30 Sun)
(01722) 714318 thecompassesinn.com
Draught Bass; guest beer H
In the middle of beautiful Wiltshire countryside, the bar is in the cellar of this 14th-century thatched cottage, with flagstone floors, old beams and a

INDEPENDENT BREWERIES

Archers Swindon
Arkell's Swindon
Box Steam Colerne
Braydon Preston (NEW)
Downton Downton
Hidden Dinton
Hop Back Downton
Keystone Berwick St Leonard
Moles Melksham
Plain Ales Chitterne (NEW)
Ramsbury Axford
Stonehenge Netheravon
Three Castles Pewsey
Wadworth Devizes
Wessex Longbridge Deverill

large inglenook fireplace. Local breweries Hidden and Keystone are usually represented among the three guest beers. Once a resting place for smugglers between Poole and Warminster, it now offers visitors a warm welcome, good ale, excellent food, accommodation, wonderful views and some peace and quiet. May be closed on Monday in winter. Q✿♣P

Chippenham

Old Road Tavern

Old Road, SN15 1JA (200m from railway station)
11-11.30 (12.30am Fri & Sat); 11.30-11.30 Sun
(01249) 652094
Fuller's London Pride; Hop Back Summer Lightning; Otter Ale; guest beer H
Good old back-street local with a diverse mix of regulars ensuring lively and friendly conversation. Local folk musicians and Morris dancers frequent the pub and jamming sessions are held on Sunday evenings. There is regular live music on Saturday night. Live sports are sometimes shown on TV. The guest beer is often sourced from a local micro-brewery. The large garden has plenty of seating, providing an attractive but secluded place to drink in summer. The pub is a venue for the annual Chippenham Folk Festival held over the late May bank holiday weekend. ✿♣

Three Crowns

18 The Causeway, SN15 3DB
11.30-2.30, 4.30-11 (midnight Fri); 11.30-midnight Sat; 12-11 Sun
(07811) 665752
St Austell Tribute; Sharp's Doom Bar; Wye Valley HPA; guest beers H
A five-minute walk from the bus station and town centre, this is a popular pub with locals. A recent entry to the Guide, it was discovered by local CAMRA members during a pub crawl one evening – to their surprise. Good quality regular ales are occasionally supplemented with guest beers in the large bar (ring the bell for service in the smaller lounge). Well worth a visit for a curry and a pint on Wednesday evening. P

Clyffe Pypard

Goddard Arms

Wood Street, SN4 7PY (signed from Wootton Bassett to Marlborough Road) SU074769
12-2.30, 7-11; 12-11 Sat; 12-10.30 Sun
(01793) 731386
Beer range varies H
This cosy and friendly community pub recently celebrated 10 years with the same landlord and lady. Three regularly changing beers mainly come from local micro-breweries, and locally-sourced cider is available in the summer. Outside, the large beer garden has a covered area. The White Horse Trail passes nearby, making this village pub a welcoming pit stop for weary cyclists, walkers and dogs. It's also a YHA hostel, open all year round. Q✿♣P

Corsham

Hare & Hounds

48 Pickwick, SN13 0HY
12-11 (10.30 Sun)
(01249) 701106
Bath Ales Gem; Brakspear Oxford Gold; Fuller's HSB; guest beers H
Charles Dickens is reputed to have stayed in this busy coaching inn on the old London to Bath stagecoach route. Five ales are usually available including two constantly changing guest beers, from local breweries. Occasional beer festivals are held. A variety of good food is always on the menu. The pub is divided into three drinking areas and the large lounge can be reserved for private functions. Outside there is plenty of seating for summer drinking. Q✿(231,233)P

Two Pigs

38 Pickwick, SN13 0HY
7-11; 12-2.30, 7-10.30 Sun
(01249) 712515 the2pigs.info
Stonehenge Pigswill; guest beers H
A gem of a pub. This classic free house has featured in the Guide continuously for 20 years. The building dates back to the 18th century, with flagstone floors and wood-panelled walls. Four ales are usually available – Hop Back Summer Lightning alternates with Stonehenge Danish Dynamite and there are two additional guest beers. Live music plays on Monday evening, usually a local Blues band. The covered outdoor drinking area is known as the Sty. A frequent local CAMRA Pub of the Year. ✿(231,233)

Corsley

Cross Keys

Lye's Green, BA12 7PB (off A362 Corsley Heath roundabout) ST821462
12-3, 6.30 (7 Sun)-11; 12-11 Fri & Sat
(01373) 832406
Wadworth IPA, 6X; guest beers H
Always worth a visit, this rural gem has a large open fire and a warm, welcoming ambience. It offers a good portfolio of guest beers along with excellent bar food and restaurant meals. There is a function room and an attractive, award-winning garden for outside drinking. The pub actively supports the local cricket team. Situated in good walking country close to Cley Hill and Longleat House and Safari Park. Q✿♣P

Corton

Dove

BA12 0SZ (On minor Wylye Valley road between Warminster and Wilton) ST 934405
11-3, 6-11; 12-3; 7-10.30 Sun
(01985) 850109 thedove.co.uk
Butcombe Bitter; Hop Back GFB; Shepherd Neame Spitfire; guest beer H
A thriving village pub in the beautiful Wylye Valley. With its huge central log fire, various seating areas and beer garden, a warm, friendly and cosy atmosphere is guaranteed. Excellent food is served from an interesting menu and there is accommodation available in the nearby coach house. The picturesque village of Corton is situated in excellent walking country and lies on the Wiltshire cycle way. Q✿(24)♣P

Cricklade

Red Lion

74 High Street, SN6 6DD
12-11 (10.30 Sun)

☎ (01793) 750776
Moles Best; Ramsbury Gold; Sharp's Doom Bar; Wadworth 6X; guest beers Ⓗ
Friendly 16th-century ale house serving a variety of up to nine real ales from small breweries. Food is served in what used to be the back bar and is now the restaurant (no food Mon). A past winner of CAMRA South West Regional Pub of the Year.
⁂Q❀⇌◑⊟♣P

Devizes

British Lion ✔
9 Estcourt Street, SN10 1LQ
⏲ 11-11 (midnight Fri & Sat); 12-11 Sun
☎ (01380) 720665
Beer range varies Ⓗ
Single bar free house in the centre of town run for years by a committed and enthusiastic landlord. Take this pub as you find it – an eclectic mix of friendly regulars and visitors who are just as likely to be in a three-piece suit as a boiler suit. Four handpumps feature regularly changing ales from southwestern breweries – Abbey Ales, Archers, Bath Ales, Palmer's, Ramsbury, Sharp's, Skinner's and Stonehenge, to name but a few. An essential port of call in the town. ❀⊟(X49)♣●P⊬⊡

Hare & Hounds ✔
Hare & Hounds Street, SN10 1LZ
⏲ 11-2.30 (3 Sat), 7-11; 12-3, 7-10.30 Sun
☎ (01380) 723231
Wadworth 6X, IPA, seasonal ales Ⓗ
A locals' pub just off the town centre with one long comfortable bar and a relaxing atmosphere. Known in the town for its excellent Wadworth ales, it is well worth the extra five minutes walk to get here. Pub games, weekly quiz night, beer garden and small car park make this a cosy enclave in which to enjoy a quiet drink. Some food is served, and well-behaved children are made as welcome as their parents. ⁂Q❀◐⊟(X49)♣P⊬

Dilton Marsh

Prince of Wales
94 High Street, BA13 4DZ
⏲ 12-2.30 (not Mon & Tue, 3 Sat), 7 (6 Fri)-11 (midnight Thu-Sat); 12-3, 7-midnight Sun
☎ (01373) 865487
Wadworth 6X; Young's Bitter; guest beers Ⓗ
Friendly village local with a single bar serving two drinking areas plus a pool table area and skittle alley. Two frequently changing guest ales are on offer, mostly session beers. The pub participates in local skittles, crib and pool leagues and there is a weekly Sunday evening quiz. Moles (not necessarily the beer) are something of a feature at the pub. Can you spot the error on the pub sign?
Q❀◐♿⇌⊟♣P⊬

East Knoyle

Fox & Hounds
The Green, SP3 6BN (signed from B3089) ST871313
⏲ 11.30-3, 5.30-11
☎ (01747) 830573 🌐 foxandhounds-eastknoyle.co.uk
Beer range varies Ⓗ
Attractive old thatched black-and-white pub situated high on a hillside with extensive panoramic rural views. Inside, a comfortable cosy interior is enhanched in winter with a blazing log fire in the huge inglenook fireplace. The three ales always available come in a wide range of ABVs and vary continuously, with local beers given prominence. The real cider is Thatchers Cheddar Valley. Food is served at all sessions. An adjacent skittle alley doubles as a function room.
⁂Q❀◐♣●P

Ebbesbourne Wake

Horseshoe Inn
The Cross, SP5 5JF (just off A30) ST993239
⏲ 12-3 (not Mon), 6.30-11 (11.30 Fri & Sat); 12-4 Sun
☎ (01722) 780474
Bowman Swift One; Otter Bitter; Palmers Copper Ale; guest beer Ⓖ
Unspoilt 18th-century pub in a remote rural setting at the foot of an old ox drove. This friendly pub has two small bars which display an impressive collection of old farm implements, tools and lamps, plus a restaurant, conservatory and pleasant garden. Good local food is served (not Mon) and five beers are served direct from casks stillaged behind the bar. The original serving hatch just inside the front door is still in use. Cider is occasionally available. Q❀⇌◐⊟(29)●P

Grittleton

Neeld Arms
The Street, SN14 6AP (opp school)
⏲ 12-3 (3.30 Sat), 5.30-11; 12.30-3.30, 7-11 Sun
☎ (01249) 782470 🌐 neeldarms.co.uk
Wadworth IPA, 6X; guest beers Ⓗ
Cosy, comfortable 17th-century inn set in a beautiful and unspoilt south Cotswold village with old prints and photographs adorning the walls and a welcoming log fire in winter. A good selection of home-made food is offered and an ever-changing choice of guest beers means there is always something different to try. Popular with locals and visitors, the pub is central to the community. Tourist attractions including Castle Combe, Malmesbury and Bath are close by.
⁂Q❀⇌◐P⊬

Hamptworth

Cuckoo Inn 🏆
Hamptworth Road, SP5 2DU (follow signs from A36 for Hamptworth Golf Club) SU244197
⏲ 11.30-2.30, 5.30-11; 11.30-11 Sat; 12-10.30 Sun
☎ (01794) 390302
Hop Back GFB, Summer Lightning; Ringwood Best Bitter; guest beers Ⓖ
Beautiful thatched pub within the New Forest National Park. Inside are four small rooms, three served from the same bar. Ales are dispensed direct from casks racked in the ground-floor cellar. At least two guest ales and up to six in the summer are available alongside Frams scrumpy cider. The large garden has a quiet adults-only space. An annual beer festival is held in late summer. Pasties and snacks are available. CAMRA branch Pub of the Year 2009. ⁂Q❀♣●P⊬

Heddington

Ivy
Stockley Road, SN11 0PL
⏲ 12-3 (not Mon), 6.30-11; 12-4, 7-10.30 Sun
☎ (01380) 850276

Wadworth IPA, 6X, seasonal beers Ⓖ
At the foot of the Marlborough Downs, this idyllic thatched village local was originally three 15th-century cottages. The Ivy Inn has a reputation for excellent beer from the wood and its home-cooked food (lunches served Tue-Sun, evening meals – reservations advisable – Thu-Sat). The rustic bar is warmed in winter by a large log fire, welcoming users of the local network of footpaths, bridleways, cycleways and numerous equestrian centres.
⚘Q❀◐◑🚌(2)♣P⅃

Highworth

Rose & Crown

19 The Green, SN6 7DB (off A361) OS200922
⏲ 12-midnight (1am Thu-Sat); 12-11.30 Sun
☎ (01793) 766287
Courage Best Bitter; Wadworth 6X; Wells Bombardier; guest beers Ⓗ
A pub since at least 1768 when it was sold for £25, the Rose & Crown has been brewery-owned since 1821, passing through the hands of now-departed breweries Dixons, Bowlys, Simmonds, Courage and Ushers. The bar at the front has five handpumps and there is also a dining area. A wide range of malt whiskies is stocked alongside the well-kept beers. Live music usually plays on Friday and Saturday and a folk evening is hosted on the second Monday of the month. This friendly local has one of the largest gardens in Highworth.
⚘❀◐◑🚌P⅃

Holt

Tollgate Inn

Ham Green, BA14 6PX (on B3105 between Bradford-on-Avon and Melksham) ST 858616
⏲ 11-2.30, 5.30-11; closed Mon; 11.30-2.30 Sun
☎ (01225) 782326 🌐 tollgateholt.co.uk
Beer range varies Ⓗ
This old village pub is a real gem. The main bar area has a wood-burning stove, oak floor and comfy sofas to relax in. The imaginative range of four or five beers, which changes daily, includes a good selection of local beers alongside many from smaller breweries further afield. The food in both the upstairs restaurant and the bar is excellent, while the garden at the rear overlooks a pretty valley. Closed Monday and Sunday evening.
⚘❀🛏◐◑🚌(237)●P⅃

Horningsham

Bath Arms

Longleat Estate, BA12 7LY (near gatehouse to the grounds of Longleat House) ST 810416
⏲ 11-11
☎ (01985) 844308 🌐 batharms.co.uk
Wessex Horningsham Pride; guest beer Ⓗ
17th-century stone building on the edge of Longleat Estate, which became a public house with rooms in 1732. Known then as the New Inn, it became the Marquess of Bath Arms in 1850. It has two bars, a restaurant and accommodation. The house beer Horningsham Pride is brewed locally by Wessex, and one guest ale is always available. The idyllic village of Horningsham is home to the oldest free congregational chapel in England, known as The Old Meeting House, built in 1556 and still in use today. ⚘♘❀🛏◐◑⊟♿⛺🚌♣●P⅃

Idmiston

Earl of Normanton

Tidworth Road, SP4 0AG (on A338) SU195382
⏲ 12-2.30, 6-11; 12-3, 7.45-10.30 Sun
☎ (01980) 610251 🌐 earlofnormanton.co.uk
Flowerpots Bitter; Hop Back Summer Lightning; guest beers Ⓗ
Popular roadside pub with a loyal village clientele and a welcoming atmosphere enhanced by a real fire in winter. Formerly the Plough Inn, the pub was renamed to commemorate previous ownership by the Normanton estate. The guest ales are mostly from local breweries and cider is usually available. Good value home-cooked food is served. There is a small, pleasant garden on the steep hill behind the pub, and a heated, covered smoking area. B&B accommodation is available. A former Salisbury CAMRA Pub of the Year.
⚘Q❀🛏◐◑♿🚌(63,64,66)P⅃

Kilmington

Red Lion Inn ✔

BA12 6RP (on B3092 to Frome)
⏲ 11-2.30, 6.30-11; 12-3, 7-10.30 Sun
☎ (01985) 844263
Butcombe Bitter; Butts Jester; guest beers Ⓗ
Originally a farm worker's cottage, this National Trust-owned pub is more than 400 years old. It is close to Stourhead House and Gardens, next to a coach road and the South Wiltshire Downs. The single bar is mainly stone-flagged with a real fire at both ends and a smaller room to one side. Excellent, value-for-money food is served at lunchtime only. Walkers and dogs are welcome. The large garden has a superb smoking facility. CAMRA Wessex Regional Pub of the Year 2008.
⚘Q❀◐♣●P⅃

Kington St Michael

Jolly Huntsman

80 Kington St Michael, SN14 6JB (signed from A350 between Chippenham and M4 jct 17)
⏲ 11.30-2.30, 6-11 (midnight Fri & Sat); 12-3, 7-10.30 Sun
☎ (01249) 750305 🌐 kingtonstmichael.com
Greene King IPA; Wadworth 6X; guest beers Ⓗ
Situated on the High Street, at the heart of the village, you can be sure of a warm welcome at this free house. A good variety of real ales and ciders is always on offer. The excellent food menu features regularly changing chef's specials and special themed evenings. Quiz night is the first Monday of the month and other entertainment includes live jazz and Blues. Accommodation is in en-suite rooms with free Wi-Fi. ⚘❀🛏◐◑♿🚌(99)♣●P⅃

Lacock

Bell Inn

The Wharf, Bowden Hill, SN15 2PJ
⏲ 11.30-2.30, 5-11; 11.30-11 Sat; 12-10.30 Sun
☎ (01249) 730308
Bath Ales Gem; Wadworth 6X; guest beers Ⓗ
A friendly welcome awaits you at this family run, well-established free house on the edge of the beautiful National Trust village of Lacock. Local CAMRA Pub of the Year for five consecutive years, it has an excellent reputation for its food and constantly-changing stock of real ales. An annual winter beer festival is held in late January/early

February. Originally canal cottages, the pub lies beside the National Cycle Route, with excellent cycle tracks and walks between Chippenham and Melksham. Q❀◐♿♣●P⅟

Rising Sun

32 Bowden Hill, SN15 2PP (1 mile E of Lacock) ST9377680

⏲ 12-3, 6-11 (midnight Wed-Fri); 12-midnight Fri & Sat; 12-11 (5 winter) Sun

☎ (01249) 730363

Moles Tap, Best Bitter, Molecatcher, seasonal beers 🄷

Stone-built 17th-century pub near the top of Bowden Hill with flagstone floors and traditional settles. The spacious conservatory and large terraced garden enjoy spectacular views over the Avon Valley. The brewery tap for the local Melksham brewery Moles, the full range of its beers is available. A good choice of pub food including daily specials and a small appetite menu is cooked to order from fresh local produce. A welcoming and convivial pub with live music on Wednesday evening. ⛫Q❀◐♿♣P⅟

Malmesbury

Whole Hog

8 Market Cross, SN16 9AS

⏲ 11-11; 12-10.30 Sun

☎ (01666) 825845

Archers Best Bitter; Wadworth 6X; Young's Bitter; guest beers 🄷

Located between the 15th-century Market Cross and Abbey, the building has at various times served as a cottage hospital, gas showroom and cafe/restaurant before becoming a licensed premises. With a warm, friendly atmosphere, the pub attracts locals and visitors alike, serving up to five real ales including two guests often from local breweries. Traditional cider comes from Westons. Good food is served in an area adjacent to the bar (no food Sun eve). Q◐🚌●

Market Lavington

Green Dragon

26-28 High Street, SN10 4AG SU017542

⏲ 11-3, 5.15-11;12-midnight Fri-Sun

☎ (01380) 813235 🌐 kollectorskabin.com/greendragon/index.htm

Wadworth IPA, 6X, seasonal beers 🄷

An attractive stone building in the heart of the village, popular with locals and visitors. It offers a warm welcome with an inviting and comfortable interior. The enthusiastic landlord maintains high standards and has held Cask Marque accreditation for several years. There are many pub games including darts, pool and boules. Children and dogs are welcome. Large off-road car park. ❀◐♣⅟

Marlborough

Sun Inn

90 High Street, SN8 1HF

⏲ 12-11.30 (midnight Fri & Sat)

☎ (01672) 515011 🌐 thesunmarlborough.co.uk

Brakspear Oxford Gold; Ringwood Fortyniner; Shepherd Neame Spitfire; Wadworth 6X; guest beer 🄷

Originally a 15th-century coaching inn, this pub has bags of character and a choice of three bars to tempt the visitor. The public bar retains its Tudor wood panelling and has a roaring log fire in winter. For the summer there is a small terraced garden at the back. Good food and recently-refurbished B&B accommodation make this a popular overnight stay. No food is available on Monday or Sunday evening. ⛫Q❀🛏◐🚌♣⅟

Marston Meysey

Old Spotted Cow

SN6 6LQ

⏲ 12-2.30, 5.30-11 (not Mon);12-11 Sat; 12.10.30 Sun

☎ (01285) 810264

Sharp's Doom Bar; Young's Bitter; guest beer 🄷

This former farmhouse made of Cotswold stone is a friendly country pub with large gardens. It has a cosy interior with log fires, beamed ceilings and a restaurant cum family area on the right hand side. Four handpumps deliver three real ales plus a cider, alternating between Black Rat and Stowford. The pub is popular with locals, who usually congregate around the bar, and diners, who sit around the tables. Meals are served daily. The Thames path is one mile away, so the pub is a useful watering hole for hikers. ⛫Q❀◐♿⛺♣●P

Netherhampton

Victoria & Albert

SP2 8PU (opp church) SU108298

⏲ 11-3.30, 5.30-11; 12-3, 7-10.30 Sun

☎ (01722) 743174

Beer range varies 🄷

A classic thatched country pub built in 1540 with a large garden with heated patio. Inside is a real log fire and low beams which add to the atmosphere on a cold night. The four ever-changing real ales are from small independent brewers. The menu ranges from snacks to restaurant meals with all food prepared in the pub. Camping is available at the nearby racecourse. Salisbury CAMRA Pub of the Year 2005 and 2007. Dogs are welcome. ⛫Q❀◐⛺🚌♣P⅟

Newton Tony

Malet Arms

SP4 0HP (opp village green) SU215403

⏲ 11-3, 6-11; 12-3, 7-10.30 Sun

☎ (01980) 629279

Hop Back Summer Lightning, seasonal beers; guest beer 🄷

Traditional village pub named after a local family which is well represented in the village churchyard. There is a spacious main bar and a restaurant. The main bar features a large fireplace and a window reputed to come from an old galleon. Various guest beers usually include at least one local beer and the nearby Stonehenge brewery supplies different beers through the year. The cider is Weston's Old Rosie. The daily-changing menu is based on local produce. ⛫Q❀◐♿🚌(63,64)●P

Pewsey

Crown Inn

60 Wilcot Road, SN9 5EL

⏲ 12-midnight (1am Sat & Sun)

☎ (01672) 562653

Wadworth 6X; guest beers 🄷

Popular inn away from the town centre with a small public bar with pool and darts and a large lounge with seating and more darts. A real ale drinkers' pub, there is a choice of five changing beers, often including an ale from Pewsey's own brewery Three Castles.

Salisbury

Deacons

118 Fisherton Street, SP2 7QT

5-11.30; 4-1am Fri; 12-midnight Sat & Sun

(01722) 504723

Hop Back GFB, Summer Lightning; Sharp's Doom Bar H

Traditional, friendly drinkers' pub, convenient for the city centre and railway station. Popular with a mixture of locals and visitors, the front bar has woodblock flooring and an open gas fire in a traditional hearth. The back bar has table football. Last entry is usually around 10.40pm.

Kings Head Inn

Bridge St, SP1 2ND

7am (8am Sat)-midnight (1am Thu-Sat); 8am-midnight Sun

(01722) 342050

Greene King IPA, Abbot; Marston's Pedigree; guest beer H

This Wetherspoon's Lloyds No1 pub is arranged over two floors of what was once the county hotel. There has been a pub on this site since 1470 when it was known as Bones Place, by 1520 it had changed its name to the Kings Head. The three guest ales usually include one from a local brewery and forthcoming beers are advertised on the bar. The food and selection of foreign bottled beers is Wetherspoon's standard fare. Beer festivals are held twice a year.

Rai d'Or

69 Brown Street, SP1 2AS

5-11; closed Sun

(01722) 327137 raidor.co.uk

Beer range varies H

Historic freehouse dating from 1292 with an open fireplace and panelled benches. This small and cosy pub has a relaxed and casual bar bistro atmosphere. It gets busy at peak times so call ahead if you want to book a table for the excellent and reasonably priced Thai food. Bar space is always available for drinkers to enjoy the warm welcome and CAMRA ale discount. The two beers are usually from local breweries. Salisbury CAMRA Pub of the Year 2008.

Royal George

17 Bedwin Street, SP1 3UT (close to Salisbury Arts Centre)

12-midnight; 12-3, 7-10.30 Sun

(01722) 327782

Hop Back GFB; Ringwood Best Bitter; Sharp's Doom Bar H

Originally a 15th-century inn, this Grade II-listed pub is named after the sister ship of HMS Victory and has a wood beam said to be from that ship. The low beamed bar is decorated with pictures of ships and sea battles. A city pub with the feel of a country local, it is well known for its involvement in crib, darts and pool leagues. Outside is a large secluded garden. P

Village Freehouse

33 Wilton Road, SP2 7EF (on A36 near St Pauls roundabout)

12-midnight

(01722) 329707

Downton Quadhop; Taylor Landlord; guest beers H

This friendly inn serves three ever-changing guest beers, focusing on local micro-breweries and beers unusual for the area. There is a whiteboard for regulars' requests. The only regular outlet in the city for dark beers, a dark ale, mild, porter or stout is always available. Close to the station, it is popular with visitors by rail, and railway memorabilia adorns the walls. Cricket, rugby and football are shown on a small TV. Plates are provided if you bring a takeaway. Salisbury CAMRA Pub of the Year 2001 and 2004.

Winchester Gate

113-117 Rampart Rd, SP1 1JA

12 (2 Mon)-11

(01722) 322834

Beer range varies H

This welcoming freehouse is a former coaching inn on the site of the city's east tollgate. The landlord is a cask beer enthusiast, sourcing beers from local breweries such as Keystone and Three Castles and from further afield. One pump dispenses a Hop Back beer. Beer festivals are held twice a year and there is live music every weekend in the second bar. The large stepped garden features a petanque terrain and attractive lawn area. Food is served 12-7pm Thursday-Saturday and 3-7pm Sunday. P

Wyndham Arms

27 Estcourt Road, SP1 3AS

4.30-11.30; 3-midnight Fri; 12-midnight Sat; 12-11.30 Sun

(01722) 331026

Downton seasonal beers; Hop Back GFB, Crop Circle, Spring Zing, Summer Lightning, seasonal beers H

A carved head of Bacchus greets you as you enter the pub. This is the original home of the Hop Back Brewery although brewing has long since moved to nearby Downton. It offers six real ales, usually five from Hop Back and one from Downton. There is also a selection of bottled ales including Entire Stout. A genuine local, it caters for all – inside is a small bar and two further rooms, one where children are welcome. Salisbury CAMRA Pub of the Year 2006. (57)

Semley

Bennett Arms

SP7 9AS (off A350, 4 miles N of Shaftesbury)

12-3, 5-11; 12-11 Sat & Sun

(01747) 830221

Beer range varies H

A former Gibbs Mew country pub sitting by the village green and pond in this quiet village. It has a single small bar with separate dining areas. The beer choice is varied but regularly includes an offering from the nearest brewery, Keystone, and often Ringwood Best. Excellent home-cooked food is available at all sessions. A warm, friendly welcome is extended to all, including families and dogs in this area popular with walkers.

Shaw

Golden Fleece

Folly Lane, Bath Road, SN12 8HB
12-2.30, 6-11; 12-3, 7-10.30 Sun
(01225) 702050
Fuller's London Pride; Moles Best; Wadworth 6X H
This roadside pub on the A365 is a welcome stop-off for travellers from Bath visiting the nearby National Trust village of Lacock. A warm welcome is assured from the host and hostess and a pleasant mix of locals and visitors ensures good conversation. A good food menu makes use of locally-sourced products, served in a separate dining area. Reservations are advisable for the restaurant. Q (271,272,273)P

Swindon

Beehive

55 Prospect Hill, SN1 3JS
12-midnight (1am Thu-Sat)
(01793) 523187 bee-hive.co.uk
Beer range varies H
Described as 'quirky' on its website, this is a popular, long-established pub, situated on a side street on the periphery of Swindon town centre. Two guest ales and a household brand are available on handpump. A beer festival is hosted in early autumn. There is a programme of live music on Sunday afternoons and mid-week evenings. The Beehive also exhibits for different local artists, rotating on a montly basis. Outside there is a small coutyard.

Glue Pot

5 Emlyn Square, SN1 5BP (behind railway museum on Fleet Street)
12-11; 11-midnight Fri & Sat; 11-10.30 Sun
(01793) 523935
Beer range varies H
A friendly pub with strong links to the local CAMRA branch, situated in the heart of the Great Western Railway workers' village. A range of six Hop Back beers and two guests is sold, with four real ciders alongside. Good pub grub is served at lunchtime including doorstep sandwiches and ham and chips. The pub is usually quiet but gets busy on weekend evenings. Major sporting events are screened but the TV is not obtrusive. (8,54)

Steam Railway

14 Newport Street, SN1 3DX
12-midnight (1am Fri & Sat); 12-10.30 Sun
(01793) 538048
Fuller's London Pride; Wadworth 6X; Wells Bombardier; guest beers H
A former railway hotel, the pub has a traditional real ale bar with a low ceiling and wood panelling, with nine handpumps offering three regular and several guest beers. The bar gets busy when major sporting events are screened on TV; at other times you can enjoy a quiet drink. The largest part of the pub is the roofed-over courtyard where screens show sports and discos take place.

Wheatsheaf

32 Newport Street, SN1 3DP
5-11; 12-midnight Fri & Sat; 12-10.30 Sun
(01793) 523188
Wadworth IPA, Horizon, 6X; guest beers H
Popular two-bar town pub dating back to the 1820s. The larger back bar incorporates what was originally a large courtyard – this is where the students gather, giving it a livelier feel. The front bar is smaller and quieter with a more traditional atmosphere, ideal for a peaceful pint. Traditional cider, or occasionally perry, is stocked. All beers are one price on Real Ale Wednesday. Occasional live music plays. Q

Tisbury

Boot Inn

High Street, SP3 6PS
12-2.30, 7-11; 12-4 Sun
(01747) 870363
Beer range varies G
Fine village pub built of Chilmark stone, licensed since 1768. It has a relaxed, friendly atmosphere appealing to locals and visitors alike. Run by the same landlord since 1976, it became a free house in 2009 – there are plans to increase the range of beers with offerings from local breweries as well as from further afield. Excellent food is served (pizza only on Tuesday) and there is a spacious garden. A former Salisbury CAMRA Pub of the Year.
(25,26)P

Upavon

Ship

10 High Street, SN9 6EA
11-12.30am (1.30am Thu-Sat); 11.30-12.30am
(01980) 630313 upavonpc.co.uk/ship.htm
Wadworth 6X; guest beers H
This free house dating from the 15th century has been completely refurbished, combining traditional wooden beams with a light open appearance. The decorations, including a huge model of the Cutty Sark in the dining room, have a nautical or local theme. A large covered area is available for smokers in the beer garden. There is limited parking outside. Q

Upper Chute

Cross Keys Inn

SP11 9ER (signed from village) SU 295538
12-2.30, 6-11 (midnight Sat)
(01264) 730295 upperchute.com
Fuller's Discovery, London Pride; guest beer H
Situated at the top af a hill, with magnificent views, the building dates from 1705 and became a pub in 1715. In 2006 it was saved from conversion to housing. An old drovers' pub, it now welcomes walkers, cyclists and riders. The two guest beers normally include one from Hop Back and often a dark beer. An extensive menu of freshly prepared meals is available (not Sun eve) and accommodation includes stabling for horses. Families and dogs are welcome. P

Wanborough

Harrow

High Street, SN4 0AE
12-3, 6-11 (5.30-midnight Fri & Sat); 12-3, 7-midnight
(01793) 790622 theharrowinnwanborough.com
Black Sheep Best Bitter; Wadworth 6X; guest beers H
This thatched pub dates back to 1637, making it the oldest in the village. It features two enormous fire grates and many concealed cupboards in the eaves, used by smugglers to hide their illegal goods. Today's more law-abiding visitors can enjoy

good food and fine ale including two guest beers (no food Sun eve). Live music plays on Sunday evening. New accommodation includes three attractively furnished bedrooms.
♨Q❀⛿◑◐⊞⊟♣P⁄

Warminster

Fox & Hounds

6 Deverill Road, BA12 9QP

✪ 11-11

☎ (01985) 216711

Ringwood Best Bitter; Wessex Warminster Warrior; guest beers Ⓗ

Friendly two-bar local just off the town centre. One of the bars is a cosy snug, the other has a pool table and TV at the back. Three real ciders from Rich's and Thatchers are a mainstay of the pub. A regular outlet for the Wessex Brewery, the guest beer is usually sourced from another local micro. Closing time may be later than 11pm.
♨Q❀⊞♿⇌⊟(24,264,265)♣●P⁄

Organ

49 High Street, BA12 9AQ

✪ 11-11

☎ (01985) 211777 ⊕ theorganinn.co.uk

Beer range varies Ⓗ

The Organ was converted from a fish and fruit shop in 2006. The building dates from around 1770 and was a public house up until 1913. New landlords have created a welcoming pub with a traditional feel. There are three rooms including a snug and a games room, and a skittles alley. Two ciders are always stocked and the beer range includes three ever-changing guests usually sourced from local micros. The brewer of Organ Bitter is a closely guarded secret.
♨Q❀⊞♿▲⇌⊟(24,264,265)♣●⁄

Wilcot

Golden Swan ✔

SN9 5NN

✪ 12-3 (not Mon), 6-midnight

☎ (01672) 562289 ⊕ thegoldenswan.co.uk

Wadworth IPA, 6X; guest beer Ⓗ

This friendly mid-19th-century village pub has a tall and steep thatched roof. Inside is a small public bar with an open fire and a lounge where food is served. There is also a barn for private functions and a large field behind for camping. Set in the beautiful Vale of Pewsey, the pub is close to the Kennet & Avon Canal and a Sustrans cycle route. The last Thursday of the month is folk night. The pub has its own darts, cricket and cribbage teams.
♨❀◑◐⊞♿▲⊟(L2)♣

Wootton Bassett

Five Bells

Wood Street, SN4 7BD

✪ 12-3, 5-11.30; 12-midnight Fri & Sat; 12-4, 6.30-11 (all day summer) Sun

☎ (01793) 849422

Black Sheep Best Bitter; Fuller's London Pride; guest beers Ⓗ

Charming thatched pub dating back to 1841, situated just off the high street. The bar area has an open fire and low-beamed ceiling while a second room offers further seating, a dartboard and TV for major sporting events. Outside is a large patio. Three ever-changing guest ales appear alongside two regulars and an Addlestones cider. Excellent home-cooked food is available at lunchtime, with a themed food evening on Wednesday and generous roasts for Sunday lunch. Well-behaved dogs are welcome. An annual beer festival is held in August.
♨❀◑⊟♣●P⁄

Wroughton

Carters Rest 🏆

High Street, SN4 9JU

✪ 5-midnight (1am Fri); 12-1am Sat; 12-11 Sun

☎ (01793) 812288

Cotswold Spring Old English Rose; Hop Back Crop Circle; Sharp's Doom Bar; guest beers Ⓗ

Decorated with photographs of bygone Wroughton, this large two-bar traditional pub situated on the high street offers a genuine warm welcome. There are regular real ales and guest beers displayed on a beer board, with the guests changing frequently. A beer festival is held in December. Live music events are hosted twice a month and a weekly quiz night on Thursday. The pub welcomes children until early evening and permits pets. This is a good honest pub and well worth a visit for real ale buffs.
♨Q❀⊞♿⊟♣P⁄

Compasses Inn, Chicksgrove

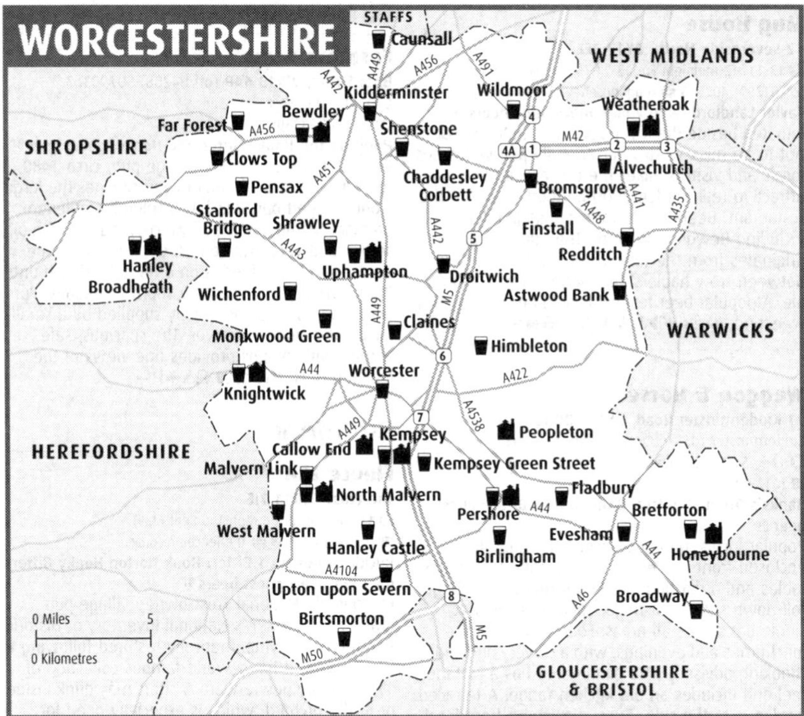

Alvechurch

Weighbridge

Scarfield Wharf, Scarfield Hill, B48 7SQ (follow signs to marina from village) SP022721

12-3 (4 Sat summer), 7-11; 12-4 7-10.30 Sun

(0121) 445 5111 the-weighbridge.co.uk

Kinver Bargees Bitter; guest beers

Popular retreat for walkers, boaters and Morris dancers, with two lounges and a public bar. Good value home-cooked food is served daily. The pleasant garden near the canal has a heated marquee for functions. Two changing guest beers are on offer. Two beer festivals are held annually in the summer and autumn featuring ales from local breweries and live entertainment.

Astwood Bank

Oddfellows Arms

24 Foregate Street, B96 6BW SP043623

12-11.30

(01527) 892806

M&B Brew XI; Wye Valley HPA

Known locally as 'The Oddies', the pub has two rooms with a separate function room for diners. Live sport is shown in the lounge and there is a dartboard in the bar. In the beer garden a large patio is sheltered by a huge canopy which is often heated. The pub holds an annual Oktoberfest in aid of the local carnival charity. Food is served Wednesday and Thursday evenings, plus an all-you-can-eat curry buffet on Friday and roast dinners on Sunday afternoon. (70)

Bewdley

Black Boy

50 Wyre Hill, DY12 2UE (follow Sandy Bank from B4194 at Welch Gate)

12-3, 6-11; 12-11 Fri-Sun

(01299) 403523

Banks's Original, Bitter; Marston's Pedigree; guest beer

Up a steep hill away from the town centre, this long-standing Guide entry is worth the heart-thumping climb. The building dates back several hundred years and has two main rooms served from a single bar. There is an open fire and wooden beams. Many awards for cellarmanship are on display. A small separate room may be used by families at the landlord's discretion. Guest beers come from Banks's list.

(SVR)

Little Pack Horse

31 High Street, DY12 2DH (near Lax Lane, 500 yards from St Annes Church)

12-3.00; 6-11.30. 12-3, 6-12 Fri, 12-12 Sat; 12 - 10.30

(01299) 403762 littlepackhorse.co.uk

Black Sheep Best Bitter; guest beers

Dating from the 15th century, this welcoming pub has a reputation for good beer and great food. Three ales always available with plans for a fourth soon (approx 75 different beers per year). The main eating area is in two rooms behind the bar (booking advisable). Their famous Desperate Dan Pie is a challenge for the hungriest guest while fish and vegetarian choices and specials are on chalk board. There is a red light over the door when it is open.

Mug House
12 Severnside North, DY12 2EE
12-11; 12-midnight Fri; 12-11.30 Sat; 12-1am Sun
(01299) 402543 mughousebewdley.co.uk
Taylor Landlord; Wye Valley HPA; guest beers H
Situated beside the River Severn, the Mug House is not to be missed. This dog-friendly pub welcomes locals and visitors alike. There is a real fire, attractive rear garden and fine food served in the restaurant. Beers are from local independents including Bewdley Brewery. The pub's name originates from the time when deals were struck between trow haulers and carriers over a mug of ale. A popular beer festival is held on the May Day weekend. (SVR)

Waggon & Horses
91 Kidderminster Road, DY12 1DG (on Bewdley to Kidderminster rd, Wribbenhall side of river)
12-3, 5-11; 12-midnight Fri & Sat; 12-11 Sun
(01299) 403170
Banks's Original, Bitter; Batham Best Bitter; guest beer H
Popular locals' pub approached through an enclosed front garden. The small snug has settles, tables and a dartboard; a larger room has a large roll-down screen for major sporting events. A single bar serves all areas. Food is available lunchtimes and evenings, with a carvery on Sunday (booking advised). The dining area has a cottagey feel and includes an old kitchen range. A terraced garden is to the side. Guest ales come from local independents. (SVR)P

Woodcolliers Arms
76 Welch Gate, DY12 2AU
12-3 (Easter-Nov, not Mon), 5-midnight; 12-midnight Sat & Sun
(01299) 400589 woodcolliers.co.uk
Beer range varies H
A short walk from Bewdley centre, this friendly, traditional pub dates from 1870, with open fires and beams. The family-owned free house stocks a constantly changing range of local guest beers as well as bottled real ales. The Cordon Bleu chef offers a speciality Russian menu as well as traditional food – no microwave is used here! Dogs are welcome and the pub stores bikes and fishing tackle for visitiors. Quiz night is Tuesday.
Q(SVR)

Birlingham

Swan
Church Street, WR10 3AQ
12-3, 6.30-11 (10.30 Sun)
(01386) 750485 theswaninn.co.uk
Wye Valley Bitter; guest beers H
Black-and-white thatched free house dating back over 500 years in a quiet village. The open bar/lounge boasts exposed beams and a wood-burning stove. There are two constantly-changing guest beers, two real ciders from Thatchers and Cheddar Valley, and twice-yearly beer festivals in May and September. Traditional home-cooked food is served in the conservatory (not Sun eve). Crib, darts and dominoes are played in the bar. There is a large car park opposite and a pleasant south-facing garden. (382)P

Birtsmorton

Farmers Arms
Birts Street, WR13 6AP (off B4208) SO790363
11-4, 6-11; 12-4, 7-11 Sun
(01684) 833308
Hook Norton Hooky Bitter, Old Hooky; guest beer H
Grade II black-and-white village pub, circa 1480, tucked away down a quiet country lane. The large stone-flagged bar area has a splendid inglenook fireplace, complemented by a cosy lounge with old settles and very low beams. Good value, home-made, traditional food is on offer daily (lunch until 2pm, evening meals until 9.30pm weekdays, 9pm Sun). The guest ale is usually supplied by a small, local, independent brewer. The spacious, safe garden with swings provides fine views of the Malvern Hills. QP

Bretforton

Fleece Inn ★
The Cross, WR11 7JE
11-11 (closed 3-6 Mon-Thu Sept-May)
(01386) 831173 thefleeceinn.co.uk
Buckle Street No 1 Bitter; Hook Norton Hooky Bitter; Uley Pig's Ear; guest beers H
Famous old National Trust-owned village pub featuring in CAMRA's National Inventory of Historic Pub Interiors. Sympathetically restored following a fire in 2005, it has a world-famous collection of 17th-century pewterware. Visitors may drink inside or in the orchard, which is especially good for families in fine weather and hosts the famous asparagus auction in the (very short) season. Buckle Street Brewery in nearby Honeybourne was started in 2008 by the landlord and a fellow Morris dancer. CAMRA Worcestershire County Pub of the Year in 2006. Q(554)

Broadway

Crown & Trumpet
Church Street, WR12 7AE (on road to Snowshill)
11-11 (closed 2.30-5 Mon-Thu winter)
(01386) 853202 cotswoldholidays.co.uk
Stanway seasonal beers; Stroud seasonal beers; guest beers H
Fine 17th-century Cotswold stone inn on the road to Snowshill, complete with oak beams and log fires along with plenty of Flowers Brewery memorabilia. The menu offers specials featuring locally-grown produce, making it popular with locals, tourists and walkers. It offers an unusual range of pub games, and entertainment including jazz and blues on Thursday and live music on Saturday. The Stanway and Stroud seasonal beers rotate throughout the year, some are brewed

INDEPENDENT BREWERIES
Bewdley Bewdley
Blue Bear Kempsey
Brandy Cask Pershore
Buckle Street Honeybourne (NEW)
Cannon Royall Uphampton
Joseph Herbert Smith Hanley Broadheath
Malvern Hills North Malvern
St George's Callow End
Teme Valley Knightwick
Weatheroak Hill Weatheroak (NEW)
Wyre Piddle Peopleton

exclusively for the pub, and guest beers are sourced from the Gloucestershire Ale Trail scheme. (559)P

Bromsgrove

Hop Pole

78 Birmingham Road, B61 0DF
12-11 (11.30 Fri & Sat)
(01527) 870100 hop-pole.com
Worfield Oh Be Joyful; guest beers H
Known as the pub that brought live music back to Bromsgrove, this popular venue features bands covering various music styles every Thursday to Sunday night. The bar area provides an excellent view of the stage while a comfortable home-furnished lounge is situated to the front. At quieter times the pub becomes a community-style local with a brilliant atmosphere. A quiz is hosted on Monday night. There are always three guest beers. The beer garden has a smoking area.

Caunsall

Anchor Inn

DY11 5YL (off A449 Kidderminster-Wolverhampton Rd)
11-4, 7-11; 11-3, 7-10.30 Sun
(01562) 850254 theanchorinncaunsall.co.uk
Hobsons Best Bitter, Town Crier; guest beer H
Welcoming, traditional local run by the same family for 80 years. Little has changed here, with two main rooms served by a long bar and original 1920s tables and chairs. Renowned for its filling cobs served with salad, the pub is easily reached from the nearby canal. The pleasant atmosphere, friendly staff and lovely location attract an impressive mix of customers. QP

Chaddesley Corbett

Fox Inn

Bromsgrove Road, DY10 4QN (on A448 on edge of village) SO892731
11.30-2.30, 5-11; 11.30-11 Sat; 12-10.30 Sun
(01562) 777247 foxinn-chaddesleycorbett.co.uk
Beer range varies H
Situated to the south of the village, this cosy roadside pub offers a large L-shaped lounge bar with adjacent restaurant and carvery as well as bar food. Three guest beers are available from local independents. The old stables and blacksmith's have been converted into a small snug with a pool table and dartboard. Good value food is served and a popular quiz held on Thursday evening. An open beer garden is to the rear. (X3)P

Swan

The Village, DY10 4SD SO892737
11-3, 6-11; 11-11 Fri & Sat; 12-10.30 Sun
(01562) 777302
Bathams Mild Ale, Best Bitter, XXX (winter) H
Superb village pub dating from 1606, with a number of rooms including a snug with an etched glass serving hatch. Jazz nights are held in the lounge on Thursday. Evening meals are served in the restaurant Thursday to Saturday and lunch is available daily, however there is no hot food on Monday. Well-behaved dogs are welcome in the public bar and the pub is well used by walkers. The large garden and play area at the rear are popular with families. The cider is Westons Old Rosie.
QP

Claines

Mug House

Claines Lane, WR3 7RN (next to church) SO852588
12-2.30, 5-11; 12-11 Sat (& Fri summer); 12-11 Sun
(01905) 456649 clainesfriends.org.uk/mughouse.html
Banks's Original, Bitter P**; guest beers** H
One of the original Severn Mug Houses, uniquely situated in a picturesque churchyard. The pub dates from the 15th century and has a classic multi-room layout. Banks's beers are served from electric pumps in lined glasses and the two hand-pulled guests are from the expansive Marston's range. The pub is renowned for its pork pies and popular with early evening drinkers in summer. Occasional jazz nights are hosted. Dog friendly.
Q(32,144,303)

Clows Top

Colliers Arms

Tenbury Road, DY14 9HA (on main A456 Kidderminster-Tenbury road)
11-3, 6-11; 11-11 Sat; 11-6 Sun
(01299) 832242 colliersarms.com
Hobsons Best Bitter; guest beer H
A family-owned and run free house set in Worcestershire countryside with fine views from the restaurant and garden. Open fires are welcoming in winter and the beers are from local independents. Featuring in Michelin and AA food guides, the pub offers excellent home-cooked food made with seasonal, locally-sourced ingredients. A market is held monthly selling local produce. There are regular live music events and quiz nights as well as celebratory specials. See the website for details. P

Droitwich

Hop Pole

40 Friar Street, WR9 8ED SO898634
12-11 (10.30 Sun)
(01905) 770155
Malvern Hills Black Pear; Wye Valley HPA, Butty Bach; guest beer H
Welcoming pub situated in a cul-de-sac close to the town centre. A traditional 18th-century inn, it has a main bar with small areas leading off it which provide quieter seating. The pool room and music on some evenings are popular with younger customers, and the regulars enjoy traditional pub games. Good value food is available at lunchtime and beer festivals are held during the summer months.

Evesham

Old Red Horse

17 Vine Street, WR11 4RE
10 (12 Sun)-11
(01386) 442784
Draught Bass; M&B Brew XI; guest beer H
Friendly local in the heart of town retaining the ambience and character of a traditional old English inn. Award-winning floral displays adorn the exterior while gargoyles and grotesques decorate the public bar and rear courtyard, reflecting the nearby Evesham Abbey. The public bar has a TV and dartboard and there is a separate lounge bar with an area for dining. Traditional home-cooked food is served lunchtimes and evenings, plus an excellent

value weekly steak night. A pub quiz is held on the last Tuesday of the month.
⛫❀⇄◑⊟⇶⊟(50)●⚐

Old Swanne Inne ✔

66 High Street, WR11 4HG (by bus station)
⏲ 9-12 (1 am Fri & Sat)
☎ (01386) 442650
Greene King Abbot; Marstons Pedigree; guest beers ⊞
Busy town-centre Wetherspoons pub situated on the High Street by the bus station, offering a wide range of beers and a traditional cider (Thatchers Heritage). Opened in late 1998 it is now popular and well established with a comfortable family and eating area and a rear courtyard garden and smoking area. Photographs of old Evesham adorn the walls. Cask Marque accredited, it offers three guest beers, although the overall range may be smaller mid-week. The pub hosts several mini-festivals throughout the year. Q❀◑♿⇶⊟⚐

Far Forest

Plough ✔

Cleobury Road, DY14 9TE (½ mile from A456/ B4117 jct)
⏲ 12-11.30; 11-11 Sat
☎ (01299) 266237 🌐 nostalgiainns.co.uk
Wye Valley HPA; guest beers ⊞
Busy, popular country pub and restaurant with open fires and rustic decor in a number of drinking and dining areas served from the main bar. The bar/lounge is at the front and there is a large dining area extending into the conservatory. The beer range varies, with ales from local independents. For diners, there is a renowned carvery and extensive menu. Food is served all day Sunday (booking essential). Children are welcome in the dining areas only. ⛫❀◑♿⛺⊟♣●P⚐

Finstall

Cross Inn

34 Alcester Road, B60 1EW
⏲ 12-15, 16.30-11; 12-11 Sat & Sun
☎ (01527) 872911
Enville White; Taylor Landlord ⊞
In a local village setting on high ground dominating a crossroads, the 350-year-old building has a large interior with a small back room frequently used by local clubs and societies. The landlord has been here for two years after a varied, award-winning career. A real ale drinkers' pub, it is free from jukebox and games machines. Local cider comes from Tardebigge. Hand-made rolls are served at lunchtime and food themed nights are popular.
⛫Q❀◐♿⇶⊟●P⚐

Fladbury

Anchor Inn

Anchor Lane, WR10 2PY
⏲ 11.30-11.30
☎ (01386) 860391 🌐 anchorfladbury.co.uk
Bathams Best Bitter; Fuller's London Pride; M&B Brew XI; Wood Shropshire Lad ⊞
A traditional country pub set on the village green at the heart of picturesque Fladbury. Family owned and run, you can be sure of a warm greeting at this friendly local from the gregarious landlord and cat Charley. The 17th-century wood-beamed pub is at the centre of the local community, with a variety of local groups meeting here. A cosy dining room serves home-made food, and there is a function and pool room. Staff here are rumoured to have witnessed ghostly happenings! ⛫❀◐♿⊟(551)♣

Hanley Broadheath

Fox

B4204, WR15 8QS
⏲ 5-midnight; 3-1 Fri; 12-midnight Sat; 12-11 Sun
☎ (01886) 853189
Bathams Best Bitter; JHS Amy's Rose, Foxy Lady; guest beer ⊞
Black-and-white timbered, 400-year-old, rural free house. Four local real ales are on offer including at least two from the pub's own JHS on-site brewery, plus real cider or perry. The friendly, family-owned pub has a welcoming wood-burning stove lit throughout the winter. An annual August bank holiday beer festival is held in the adjoining field featuring lawnmower racing. Food is served in the evening at weekends, sandwiches during the day. The pub has a games room and hosts live music. Dogs are welcome. ⛫❀◑⛺♣●P⚐

Hanley Castle

Three Kings ☆

Church End, WR8 0BL (signed off B4211) SO838420
⏲ 12-3, 7-11 (10.30 Sun)
☎ (01684) 592686
Butcombe Bitter; Hobsons Best Bitter; guest beers ⊞
Former CAMRA National Pub of the Year and on the National Inventory of Historic Interiors. This unspoilt 15th-century country pub on the village green near the church has been run by the same family since 1911. The three-room interior comprises a small snug with large inglenook, serving hatch and settle wall, a family room and Nell's Lounge, with another inglenook and beams. Three interesting guest ales often come from local breweries. Regular live music sessions are hosted and a popular beer festival is held in November.
⛫Q❀◐⊟(363)●P

Himbleton

Galton Arms

Harrow Lane, WR9 7LQ
⏲ 12-2 (not Mon), 4.30-11; 11-11 Sun
☎ (01905) 391672
Banks's Original, Bitter; Batham Best Bitter; Wye Valley Galton Arms Pale Ale; guest beer ⊞
Popular village local with a welcoming atmosphere. The main bar area has original beams and an open log fire, and there is a separate dining room. Guest beers often come from unusual breweries for the area. Formerly known as the Harrow Inn, the building has been a pub since the 1800s and was renamed for a local family. No food is available on Sunday or Monday nights.
⛫Q❀◑♿P

Kempsey

Walter de Cantelupe ✔

34 Main Road, WR5 3NA
⏲ 12-2, 6-11; closed Mon; 12-3, 7-10.30 (12-10.30 summer) Sun
☎ (01905) 820572 🌐 walterdecantelupeinn.com
Archers Best; Cannon Royall Kings Shilling; Taylor Landlord; guest beer ⊞

Named after the 13th-century Bishop of Worcester, this pub has been in the Guide for more than 10 years. Inside, it has a bar area with a large inglenook and a dining area, outside is an attractive walled garden. Note the settle dating from the 1700s in the top bar. The quality food menu makes use of local food where possible, and ploughmans and sandwiches made with local bread and cheeses are a speciality. Regular events throughout the year include an all-day outdoor paella party in July. ⛫Q❀⛟◖◗⊟(32,372)P⁄–▯

Kempsey Green Street

Huntsman Inn

Green Street, WR5 3QB SO868490
⏲ 12-3.30 (Sat only), 5-11; 12-3.30, 7-10.30 Sun
☎ (01905) 820336
Bathams Best Bitter; Greene King IPA; Wye Valley HPA Ⓗ
A cosy and friendly atmosphere greets visitors to this beamed, 300-year-old ex-farmhouse. A number of rooms are arranged around the central servery – bar, lounge and restaurant serving reasonably-priced home-cooked food. A real fire adds to the pub's character and an attractive garden is situated to the side. The impressive skittle alley has its own bar. Dogs are welcome in the bar and lounge. ⛫Q⛫❀◖◗⊟♣P

Kidderminster

Boar's Head

39 Worcester Street, DY10 1EW
⏲ 12 – 11 (12.30 Thu; 1am Fri & Sat)
☎ (01562) 68776
Banks's Original, Bitter; guest beer Ⓗ
Popular town-centre Victorian pub. The lounge has wood panelling and a wood-burning stove while the snug has an open fire. The main bar leads to a large, covered and heated courtyard where live music is staged on Thursday evening and comedy nights on the last Wednesday of the month. Guest beers are from the Banks's list. Look for the paintings by local artists and the GPO red telephone box. There is a free mineral water dispenser for drivers. ⛫❀◖⊟♿⇌⊟⁄–

King & Castle

SVR Station, Comberton Hill, DY10 1QX (next to mainline station)
⏲ 11-11; 12-10.30 Sun
☎ (01562) 747505
Bathams Best Bitter; Wyre Piddle Royal Piddle; guest beers Ⓗ
A replica of a GWR refreshment room with direct access to the Severn Valley Railway covered concourse and platforms, this Guide regular is popular with both locals and visitors. There is plenty of seating and the carpet has the GWR logo. Food is available in the newly-opened Valley Suite restaurant. A varied selection of guest beers is on offer, many from local independents, including Royal Piddle brewed especially for the pub. A wheelchair WC is available on the platform. ⛫Q♿⇌⊟P

Olde Seven Stars

13-14 Coventry Street, DY10 2BG
⏲ 11 (12 Sun)-11
☎ (01562) 755777 🌐 yeoldesevenstars.co.uk
Caledonian Deuchars IPA; guest beers Ⓗ
Within walking distance of the SVR, this popular town-centre pub is the oldest in Kidderminster, with wood panelling throughout, wooden floors and an inglenook fireplace. Five beers include Deuchars and guests from local independents. The large garden has a covered, heated smoking area and resident hens. Customers are welcome to bring in their own food from local takeaways. Live music plays on some Friday evenings and dogs are welcome. A pub not to be missed. ❀⊟♿⇌⊟♣⁄–▯

Knightwick

Talbot

WR6 5PH (on B4197, 400m from A44 jct)
⏲ 11-midnight; 12-10.30
☎ (01886) 821235 🌐 the-talbot.co.uk
Hobsons Best Bitter; Teme Valley This, That, T'Other Ⓗ
The floods of July 2007 caused the River Teme to flood the pub. A period of hard work to restore it to its former glory followed, which was rewarded when Worcester CAMRA branch declared the Talbot its Pub of the Year. Home of the Teme Valley Brewery, this 14th-century coaching inn is the centre of the local community, often using the surplus from local gardens in the kitchen. The Green Hop beer festival in early October is very popular. A farmers' market is held on the second Sunday of the month. ⛫Q❀◖◗⊟♿⊟(420)♣●P

Malvern Link

Nags Head ✔

21 Bank Street, WR14 2JG
⏲ 11-11.15 (11.30 Fri & Sat); 12-11 Sun
☎ (01684) 574373
Banks's Bitter; Batham Best Bitter; St George's Maidens Saviour, Charger, Dragons Blood; Sharp's Doom Bar; guest beers Ⓗ
The 17 handpumps in this lively town-centre pub are testament to the landlord's dedication to real ale – he also owns the local St George's Brewery. Converted from a row of three cottages, the pub resounds with conversation rather than jukebox or TV. Newspapers are provided for those wanting a quiet read, though the pub gets very busy in the evenings at the weekend. A separate restaurant serves good quality food. There is a no-swearing rule, strictly enforced. Dogs are welcome. ❀◗⇌⊟(44,44A)●⁄–

Monkwood Green

Fox

WR2 6NX (S edge of Monkwood Nature Reserve) SO803601
⏲ 12.30-2.30 (Fri only), 5-11; 12-11 Sat & Sun
☎ (01886) 889123
Cannon Royall Arrowhead; Wye Valley HPA; guest beer Ⓗ
Single-bar village local with long distance views to the south. The guest beer always comes from a local micro, often Malvern Hills Black Pear. The pub is the centre for many events including skittles and indoor air rifle shooting. Live music plays on the last Friday of the month. Monkwood nature reserve is renowned for butterflies and moths. Food can be provided by arrangement for groups and parties. Dogs are welcome. A rare outlet for Barker's cider and perry. ⛫Q⛫❀⛺⊟(308)♣●P⁄–

North Malvern

Star

59 Cowleigh Road, WR14 1QE
4.30-11 (midnight Fri & Sat); closed Mon; 12-10.30 Sun
(01684) 891918
Beer range varies Ⓗ
An unusual fusion of Chinese and English, the Star has a restaurant offering high quality Chinese food (booking essential Fri and Sat) and a comfortable, light and airy bar for drinkers with a fabulously ornate bar back. Outside, the patio has a sheltered area for smokers. Food is served from 4.30pm, Sunday lunches 12-3pm, and a takeaway service is offered. Wye Valley HPA is a regular guest ale. (44,44A,675)P

Pensax

Bell

WR6 6AE (on B4202, Clows Top-Great Witley road)
12-2.30 (not Mon), 5-11; 12-10.30 Sun
(01299) 896677
Hobsons Best Bitter; guest beers Ⓗ
Outstanding, friendly pub serving at least five superbly kept, constantly changing ales, plus local cider and perry. It has wooden floors, hanging hops, open fires and pew seating. There is a separate dining room with superb views and a snug suitable for families. Dogs are welcome. The food menu features local seasonal ingredients. A beer festival is held at the end of June. A consistent Guide regular and CAMRA Pub of the Year winner not to be missed. QP

Pershore

Brandy Cask

25 Bridge Street, WR10 1AJ
11.30-2.30 (3 Fri & Sat), 7-10.30 (11.30 Thu-Sat); 12-3, 7-11 Sun
(01386) 552602
Brandy Cask Whistling Joe, Brandysnapper, John Bakers Original; guest beers Ⓗ
Superb brew pub offering three regular house ales as well as seasonal brews and a wide range of guest beers from around the country. Real cider is also usually available. Food is good and reasonably priced. The rear garden runs down to the River Avon and is delightful in summer. A 'must visit' when in Pershore. Q(382,550,551)

Redditch

Gate Hangs Well

98 Evesham Road, B97 5ES (on main Evesham-Redditch road) SP037659
11-2.30 (not Sat), 6-11 (5.30-11.30 Fri; 6-11.30 Sat); 12-3, 7-11 Sun
(01527) 401293 gatehangswell.com
Ansells Best Bitter; Greene King Old Speckled Hen, Abbot; St Austell Tribute; Tetley Bitter; guest beer Ⓗ
Friendly and cosy local with six beers usually available and future guests advertised in advance. The single room interior is home to darts, sports and games teams. A quiz is held on Sunday and Monday nights. Good value bar snacks are available 12-2pm weekdays. A pub for conversation, there is no loud music and the TVs are only turned on for rugby matches. A free public car park is at the top of nearby Birchfield Road. Q(70)

Rising Sun

4 Alcester Street, B98 8AE (opp town hall)
9am-midnight (1am Sat); 10am-11 Sun
(01527) 62452
Greene King IPA, Abbot; Shepherd Neame Spitfire; guest beers Ⓗ
When the centre of Redditch was redeveloped in 1999, JD Wetherspoon took the opportunity to build its first purpose-built pub. Named after an old pub which once stood on the site, it has a large L-shaped interior with a number of small alcoves for privacy. Local information includes the town's connection with the Gunpowder Plot, needle and fish hook making and Royal Enfield. There is a patio area.

Woodland Cottage

102 Mount Pleasant, Southcrest, B97 4JH
12 (5 Tue)-midnight
(01527) 402299
Greene King Abbot; Taylor Landlord; guest beers Ⓗ
Cosy pub with a warm and friendly welcome. A large open-plan lounge with a single long bar is divided into smaller areas. Parts of the building are believed to date back to Elizabethan times. Artwork by local artists and photographs of old Redditch pubs adorn the walls. Outside is a sheltered seating area for smokers with a patio heater. Local darts teams meet on Tuesday, and live bands play most Saturday evenings. Two guest beers often include ales from St Austell, Purity, Weatheroak and Hobsons. (56,143)P

Shenstone

Plough

Shenstone Village, DY10 4DL (off A450/A448) SO865735
12-3, 6 (7 Sun)-11
(01562) 777340
Bathams Mild Ale, Best Bitter, XXX (winter) Ⓗ
A pub since 1840, this Batham's house is hard to find but well worth seeking out. It was once frequented by members of Led Zeppelin (scenes from The Song Remains The Same were filmed locally). Bar snacks and delicious locally-made pork pies are available. Children are allowed in the courtyard. Harvington Hall, a 16th-century moated manor house, is nearby. QP

Shrawley

New Inn

New Inn Lane, WR6 6TE (on B4196 between Stourport and Worcester)
12-midnight; 12-11.30 Sun
(01299) 822701 newinnshrawley.co.uk
Banks's Original; Mansfield Bitter; guest beers Ⓗ
Olde worlde, traditional pub in the Worcestershire countryside with fantastic open fires in the bar and restaurant. Families are welcome at this child friendly-pub which has a large garden with a play area and many animals including a Shetland pony. Near to Shrawley Woods, walkers and dogs are welcome. Live music plays on Wednesday and Friday, and an annual beer festival is held on the last weekend of July. Old meets new in the contemporary restaurant. The staff are warm and friendly. P

Stanford Bridge

Bridge Hotel

WR6 6RU (off B4203) SO715658
⏲ 12-midnight (1am Wed-Sat)
☎ (01886) 812771
Hobsons Best Bitter; Malvern Hills Black Pear; Wye Valley HPA; guest beer Ⓗ
A former hotel situated just off the B4203 in a pleasant riverside location, this community pub is popular with local residents and has a lively, friendly atmosphere. At least four real ales come from local breweries, and there is always a real cider (Thatchers Heritage) or perry (Westons). Traditional pub games include pool and darts, played in the games room. Food is served Friday to Sunday lunchtimes and Tuesday to Saturday evenings. The August bank holiday beer festival features live bands and lawnmower racing.
❀◑♿♣●P⅟

Uphampton

Fruiterer's Arms

Uphampton Lane, WR9 0JW SO838648
⏲ 12.30-3, 8 (7 Wed & Thu)-11; 12.30-4, 7-midnight Fri; 12-midnight Sat; 12-4.30, 7-11.30 Sun
☎ (01905) 620305
Cannon Royall Fruiterer's Mild, Kings Shilling, Arrowhead, Muzzle Loader, seasonal beers Ⓗ
Although this pub has a rural location it is not far from the A449 Worcester-Kidderminster road, with buses passing during the daytime. Ales are provided by the Cannon Royall Brewery at the rear of the pub, which is a separate business. Beers at very reasonable prices are served in the bar or the oak-beamed lounge decorated with horse memorabilia and pictures. Filled rolls are available Friday to Sunday and children under 14 are welcome until 9pm. ♨Q⊟🚌♣P⅟

Upton upon Severn

White Lion Hotel

High Street, WR8 0HJ
⏲ 10 – 12.30am
☎ (01684) 592551 🌐 whitelionhotel.biz
Greene King Abbot; guest beers Ⓗ
The owners of this historic 16th-century inn ensure that while the facilities and service are high class, the welcome is unstuffy, warm and relaxed. Bar meals are available or you can spoil yourself in the high-quality restaurant. Three guest ales include one from a featured monthly local brewery. The hotel hosts beer events to complement Upton's many riverside music festivals. Local buses to Worcester, Malvern, Tewkesbury and Gloucester stop nearby. The White Lion features in Henry Fielding's novel Tom Jones.
Q♘❀🛏◑♿⛺🚌(351,363,372)P⅟

Weatheroak

Coach & Horses

Weatheroak Hill, B48 7EA (on Alvechurch-Wythall road) SP057741
⏲ 11.30-11; 12-10.30 Sun
☎ (01564) 823386
Hobsons Mild, Best Bitter; Holden's Special; Weatheroak Hill Icknield Pale Ale, WHB; Wood Shropshire Lad; guest beers Ⓗ
This attractive rural pub is now the home of the Weatheroak Hill Brewery. (Note that this is not the same as the Weatheroak Brewery, which has moved to premises in Studley.) It has a quarry-tiled public bar with a real fire, a split level lounge/bar and a modern restaurant. Outside is a large, family friendly garden and patio. Beer festivals, barbecues and Morris dancing are frequent attractions. Children under 14 are not allowed in the bars. Winner of numerous local CAMRA awards.
♨Q♘❀◑⊟●P⅟

West Malvern

Brewers Arms

Lower Dingle, WR14 4BQ (down track by pub sign on B4232) SO76404565
⏲ 12-3, 6-midnight; 12-midnight Fri-Sun
☎ (01684) 568147 🌐 brewersarmswithaview.co.uk
Malvern Hills Black Pear; Marston's Burton Bitter; Wye Valley HPA; guest beers Ⓗ
Comfy, traditional pub, at the centre of the village community as well as an ideal refreshment stop for visitors to the Malvern Hills. The enthusiastic landlord maintains up to eight real ales and holds a festival in October. Home-cooked food is available lunchtimes and evenings. The cosy bar can get busy at times, but extra dining space is available in the function room. The garden has an award-winning view to the Black Mountains. Dog friendly.
♨Q❀◑🚌(675)⅟

Wichenford

Masons Arms

Castle Hill, WR6 6YA (just off B4204)
⏲ 11-11
☎ (01886) 889064 🌐 themasonsarms.uk.com
Wye Valley HPA; guest beers Ⓗ
A fine country pub with a Thai restaurant complementing the traditional bar. The pleasant garden has plenty of space for the kids to roam and stunning views over the Teme Valley. Wednesday is music night with music ranging from folk to rock or swing to blues – see the website for details.
♘❀◑♿P⅟

Wildmoor

Wildmoor Oak

Top Road, B61 0RB
⏲ 5.30-11 Mon; 12-2.30, 3.30-11 Tue-Thu; 12-11.30 Fri & Sat; 12-10.30 Sun
☎ (0121) 453 2696 🌐 wildmooroak.com
Wells Bombardier; guest beers Ⓗ
This rural country inn by a stream is both a local pub and a destination restaurant. Serving traditional British food, international cusine and Caribbean specialities, it has a growing reputation (discount for card-carrying CAMRA members). Diverse themed nights ranging from comedy and quizzes to Chinese buffet or cheese & wine attract a varied clientele. Up to three guest ales often include ales from Hobsons, Weatheroak, Wye Valley and Millstone. Real cider from Tardebigge. A takeaway ale service is also available.
❀◑♿🚌♣●P⅟🍺

Worcester

Bell

35 St Johns, WR2 5AG (W side of the Severn off A44)

10 (11 Sun)-11.30
(01905) 424570
M&B Brew XI; Fuller's London Pride; guest beers H
This community local has the main bar on one side of a corridor running through the centre of the pub, with two small rooms where children are permitted on the other side. At the rear is a skittles alley and a second bar only used at busy times, also available for functions. The guest beers are usually one from Fuller's and two frequently from local independent brewers. Occasional live music plays at weekends.

Berkeley Arms

School Road, WR2 4HF
12-3.30, 5-midnight; 12-12.30am Fri & Sat; 12-3.30, 7.30-11.30 Sun
(01905) 421427
Banks's Original, Bitter P**; Jennings Dark Mild; guest beers** H
A single bar serves two drinking areas. Pub games are popular here, and there is a room at the rear used for meetings or as a children's room. The outside patio has been partially enclosed for the benefit of smokers. Two guest beers are supplied by Marston's, usually from its smaller breweries, seasonal brews or from the larger independents. The draught Thatchers Heritage cider is a recent addition. (44,44A)P

Bridges

Hindlip Lane, WR3 8SB (off B4550 Blackpole Road by Trading Estate West)
12-3, 6-11.30; closed Mon; 12-3 Sun
(01905) 757117 bridgesworcester.co.uk
Blue Bear Roar Spirit; Malvern Hills Black Pear; Wye Valley Butty Bach; guest beer H
A lively, vibrant dining bar and entertainment venue, quieter on Sunday lunchtimes or early doors. Ales are all local and the fanatical landlord has a small beerfest in the early summer. Good home-cooked food is served featuring the popular carvery. Coach parties are welcome. Outside is a large heated gazebo and seating area. Wheelchair friendly. P

Dragon Inn

51 The Tything, WR1 1JT (on A449, 300m N of Foregate St Station)
12-3, 4.30-11 (11.30 Fri); 12-11 Sat; 1-4.30, 7-10.30 Sun
(01905) 25845 thedragoninn.com
Beer range varies H
This real ale paradise offers six ever-changing beers from smaller independent and local brewers. At least one beer from the Little Ale Cart Brewery at the co-owned Wellington in Sheffield is usually available, plus a range of bottle-conditioned Belgian beers. The walls are adorned with pump clips and mementos of life in the pub – note the list of banned conversation topics. A rear patio allows for outdoor drinking and relaxing in warmer weather. Good value lunchtime meals are served on Friday and Saturday.
(Foregate St)(32,144,303)

Plough

23 Fish Street, WR1 2HN (next to fire station)
12-11 (midnight Fri & Sat)
(01905) 21381
Hobsons Best Bitter; Malvern Hills Black Pear; guest beers H
This friendly Grade II-listed pub is a must visit for any visitor to Worcester. Four ever-changing guest ales come from breweries in Worcestershire and surrounding counties, and cider and perry are from local producers. A short flight of stairs leads to two rooms, each with a fire and many original features, and a central bar. A small outside space has views towards the cathedral. Good food is served Friday and Saturday lunchtimes, with roast dinners (including a vegetarian option) on Sunday. Dog friendly. (Foregate St)

Postal Order

18 Foregate Street, WR1 1DN
9am-midnight (1am Fri & Sat)
(01905) 22373
Greene King Ruddles Best, Abbot; Marston's Pedigree; guest beers H
A classic Wetherspoon's pub in what was once the old telephone exchange next to Foregate Street railway station. Up to six guest beers from the group's quarterly list are on offer plus beers from local micros. Local brewers' beers are regularly showcased. Traditional Westons Old Rosie and Vintage Organic cider are also available. Good value food is served daily until 10pm. There is a small heated smoking area. Large screen TVs are prominent but with the sound muted.
Q(Foregate St)(32,144,303)

Swan with Two Nicks

28 New Street, WR1 2DP
11-11 (1am Fri & Sat); 7-10.30 Sun
(01905) 28190 theswanwithtwonicks.co.uk
Boddingtons Bitter; guest beers H
Historic real ale pub with low beams and many original features. Three ever-changing guest beers are on offer, often from Devon and Cornwall or from local micros. Hearty, home-prepared lunchtime meals are served (not Sun) and children are welcome. Upstairs is the retro Lunar '70s cocktail bar and at the rear a heated patio area and Drummonds venue bar with regular live music. Occasional casks of traditional cider or perry are available in summer. (Foregate St)

Before brandy, which has now become common and sold in every little alehouse, came to England in such quantities as it now doth, we drank good strong beer and ale, and all laborious people (which are the greater part of the kingdom), their bodies requiring after hard labour some strong drink to refresh them, did therefore every morning and evening used to drink a pot of ale or a flagon of strong beer, which greatly helped the promotion of our grains and did them no great prejudice; it hindereth not their work, neither did it take away their senses nor cost them much money, whereas the prohibition of brandy would prevent the destruction of his majesty's subjects, many of whom have been killed by drinking thereof, it not agreeing with their constitution.
Petition to the House of Commons, 1673

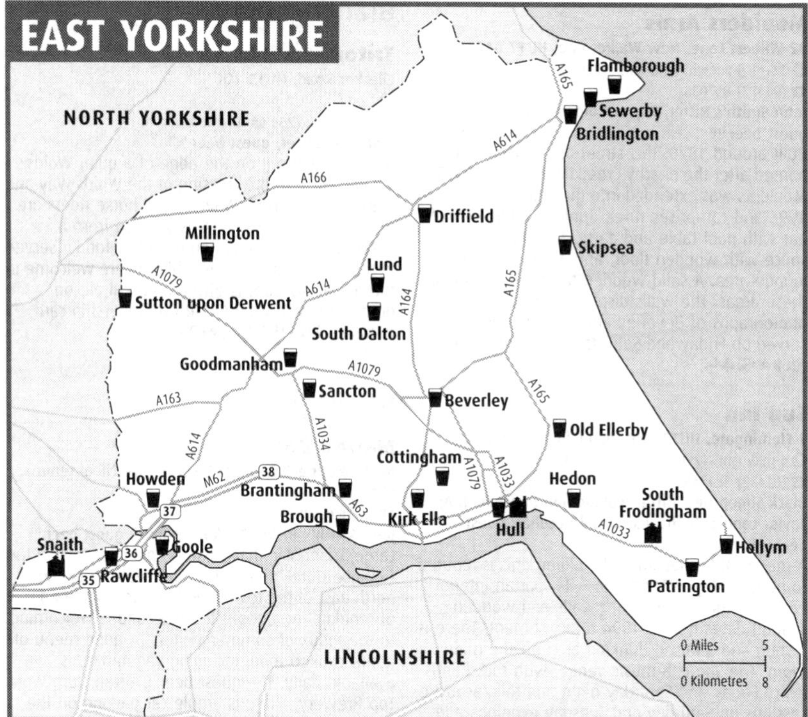

YORKSHIRE (EAST)

Beverley

Dog & Duck

33 Ladygate, HU17 8BH

11-4, 7-midnight; 11-midnight Fri & Sat; 11.30-3, 7-11 Sun

(01482) 862419

Caledonian Deuchars IPA; Copper Dragon Best Bitter; John Smith's Bitter; guest beers H

Situated just off the main Saturday Market, next to the historic Picture Playhouse building. The Dog & Duck, built in the 1930s, has been run by the same family for over 35 years. It comprises three areas: bar with a period brick fireplace and bentwood seating, front lounge and rear snug. The good-value, home-cooked lunches are popular. Guest accommodation is in six purpose-built, self-contained rooms to the rear. CAMRA Hull & East Yorkshire Town Pub of the Year 2008.

Durham Ox

48 Norwood, HU17 9HJ

10.30 (12 Sun)-11

(01482) 679444

John Smith's Bitter; Tetley Bitter; guest beer H

Victorian local on the A1035, 200m east of the bus station. This two-roomed pub has been refurbished after consultation with CAMRA's local pub preservation officer. The lounge was extended to include a games area but retains its original etched windows; the public bar has the old wooden floor, with an off-sales hatch in the entrance lobby. The pub fields five darts and two dominoes teams. Off-street parking is possible directly opposite. Meals are served daily.

Green Dragon

51 Saturday Market, HU17 8AA

11-11 (midnight Thu-Sat); 12-11 Sun

(01482) 889801

Beer range varies H

This historic Tudor-fronted inn was renamed the Green Dragon in 1765. Up to seven beers from Yorkshire breweries and others from throughout the UK are featured. The pub was extensively refurbished and substantially extended 12 years ago; most internal fittings of note were lost, although some wood panelling remains and the bar is incredibly long. Meals are served daily until 10pm; Tuesday and Wednesday are quiz nights and weekends are busy.

Molescroft Inn

75 Molescroft Road, HU17 7EG (1 mile NW of town centre)

11.30-11 (midnight Fri & Sat); 12-11 Sun

(01482) 862968

Jennings Bitter, Sneck Lifter, seasonal beers; guest beer H

A much-enlarged village local dating back to the 18th century, the Molescroft was comprehensively altered in the 1980s with the loss of some small rooms to create a large L-shaped lounge/dining room with a separate bar area around a central servery. There is a dining area adjacent to the pub's large car park. Meals, including specials, are served daily. (121)P

INDEPENDENT BREWERIES

Great Newsome South Frodingham
Old Mill Snaith
Whalebone Hull

Moulders Arms

32 Wilbert Lane, New Walkergate, HU17 0AG
11-11 (midnight Fri & Sat); 12-11 Sun
(01482) 867033
John Smith's Bitter; Taylor Golden Best, Landlord; guest beer H
Built around 1870, this street-corner local was named after the nearby Crosskills Iron Foundry. The Moulders was extended into the adjoining house in 1996 and comprises three drinking areas: a public bar with pool table and darts, a central entrance space with wooden floor, and a comfortable lounge area. A solid wooden bar servery connects these areas. The walls display many old photographs of Beverley and the pub. Meals are served on Friday and Saturday lunch and teatimes.

Sun Inn

1 Flemingate, HU17 0NP (opp E front of Minster)
4-midnight; 12-1am Fri & Sat; 12-11 Sun
(01482) 881245
Black Sheep Best Bitter; Caledonian Deuchars IPA; Taylor Landlord; Theakston Old Peculier; guest beers H
A medieval timber-framed building, this is reputed to be Beverley's oldest pub – its spartan interior with flagstone floors, brick walls and wooden seating dates from a 1994 refurbishment. There is a snug and a raised drinking area off the main room. The Sun is a music venue, with rock bands every Friday and Saturday night and folk/acoustic sessions on Saturday and Tuesday evenings and Sunday 4-7pm. Thursday is quiz night with a pie/fish supper. Meals are served on other days, including Sunday roasts 12-5pm.

Tiger Inn

Lairgate, HU17 8JG (near Memorial Hall)
11-11 (1am Fri & Sat); 12-11 Sun
(01482) 869040
Batemans XXXB; Black Sheep Best Bitter; Tetley Bitter; guest beers H
Attractive 18th-century building refronted in a 1930s brewers' Tudor style by the sadly defunct Darley & Co, which once owned several pubs in Beverley. The Tiger has a multi-roomed interior with a public bar, snug, dining room/lounge and function room. Many local clubs and societies meet here and folk music sessions are held on Friday evening. The large car park to the rear once formed stables and outbuildings. Pub meals are served at lunchtime (not Mon) and 5.30-8pm Tuesday to Saturday. Q (X46,X47) P

Woolpack Inn

37 Westwood Road, HU17 8EN
5-11 (10 Mon; midnight Fri); 12-midnight Sat; 12-11 Sun
(01482) 867095
Jennings Bitter, Cockerhoop, Sneck Lifter, seasonal beers; guest beer H
Located in a Victorian residential street west of the town centre, the Woolpack started life as a pair of cottages and became a public house around 1831, later developing its own brewhouse and stables. Previously a Hull Brewery House, it fell into the hands of Burtonwood and subsequently Marston's. It has been extended slightly to the rear but retains the tiny front snug. Thursday is curry/quiz night. Bar meals are served Friday and Saturday, plus roasts on Sunday 12-4pm. Folk music plays on Tuesday evening. Dog friendly. Q

Brantingham

Triton Inn

Ellerker Road, HU15 1QE
12-11
(01482) 667261 thetritoninn.com
Wold Top Bitter; guest beer H
A pub/restaurant on the edge of a quiet Wolds village, close to the crossing of the Wolds Way and Trans-Pennine Trail. Walkers and horse riders are welcome. The guest beer is sourced from a Yorkshire brewery and home-cooked food is served in the bar and the lounge. Children are welcome in the bar. A discount is offered on real ale on production of a valid CAMRA membership card. (155,156) P

Bridlington

Marine Bar

North Marine Drive, YO15 2LS (1 mile NE of centre)
11-11 (11.30 Sat)
(01262) 675347
John Smith's Bitter; Taylor Landlord; guest beer H
Large, triangular-shaped, open-plan bar, part of the Expanse Hotel, situated on the seafront to the north east of the town. The bar attracts a good mix of regulars throughout the year and is welcoming to the influx of summer visitors. A good menu of home-cooked food, including vegetarian, is available daily. The guest beer is often from Wold Top Brewery. There is ample car parking on the promenade at the front.

Prior John

34-36 The Promenade, YO15 2QD
9-midnight
(01262) 674256
Greene King IPA, Abbot; Marston's Pedigree; guest beers H
Large, busy Wetherspoon's pub in the town centre and close to the bus station. Modern in appearance, the interior is basically one large half-moon shape. To the right of the serving area is a first-floor gallery, reached by a sweeping metal staircase. The downstairs room is a clever mix of metal and wood with a segmented ceiling supported by steel pillars. The decor is plain and bright using mainly pastel colours. Three guest ales are usually available, including a dark beer.
Q

Brough

Buccaneer

47 Station Road, HU15 1DZ
12 -11 (midnight Thu-Sat)
(01482) 667435
Black Sheep Best Bitter; Tetley Dark Mild, Bitter; guest beer H
At the heart of the old village, the pub dates back to 1870 when it was the Railway Tavern. It was renovated in 2000 to provide a rear lounge and a comfortable dining room. The present name was introduced in 1968 in honour of the airplane that was produced locally. The pub has a number of darts teams and a quiz is held on Wednesday night. An extra guest beer may be available at busy times of the year. P

Cottingham

King William IV ✔

152 Hallgate, HU16 4DF

11-11 (11.30 Fri & Sat); 12-11 Sun

☎ (01482) 847320

Jennings Cumberland Ale, seasonal beers; Marston's Pedigree; guest beer Ⓗ

Village centre pub with a traditional bar and lounge that are both free from music. At the rear a former brewery has been converted into a function room offering live music nights and sport on a large-screen TV. The pub also hosts weekly quiz nights and an annual music festival. The rear beer garden and side courtyard have covered smoking areas. Excellent value meals are served in large or small portions. A regular bus service to and from Hull is a short walk away. **Q**

Driffield

Bell Hotel ✔

46 Market Place, YO25 6AN

9.30-11; 12-10.30 Sun

☎ (01377) 256661 bw-bellhotel.co.uk

Beer range varies Ⓗ

This inn has a feeling of elegance, featuring a long, wood-panelled bar and red leather seating, substantial fireplaces, antiques and prints. Two or three real ales are available, usually from Hambleton or Highwood breweries. Over 300 malt whiskies are stocked. A covered courtyard functions as a bistro, and there is a splendid lunchtime carvery buffet Monday to Saturday; Sunday lunch must be booked. Children are welcome until 7.30pm. Runner-up CAMRA East Yorkshire Town Pub of the Year in 2008.

Q(121)**P**

Mariners Arms

47 Eastgate South, YO25 6LR (near old cattle market)

3 (12 Sat & Sun)-midnight

☎ (01377) 253708

Banks's Bitter; Jennings Bitter, seasonal beers; guest beer Ⓗ

A street-corner local that is well worth seeking out as an alternative to the John Smith's outlets that dominate the Capital of the Wolds. Formerly part of the Hull Brewery estate, its four small rooms have now become two: a basic bar and a more comfortable lounge. Live sport is shown and the pub fields various sports teams. The long-standing licensees enjoy a loyal following among locals and offer a friendly welcome to all visitors.

(121)**P**

Tiger Inn

65 Market Place, YO25 6AW

10.30-midnight; 11.30-10.30 Sun

☎ (01377) 257490 thetigeratdriffield.co.uk

Black Sheep Best Bitter; John Smith's Bitter; guest beers Ⓗ

This 18th-century coaching inn was tastefuly refurbished a few years ago and has retained its original tap room at the front. To the rear is a beer garden with a large decked area and children's play area. The pub is one of the venues for the town's annual folk festival. The licensees were presented with a Committed To Cask Award in 2008 by the local CAMRA branch.

Q(121)**P**

Flamborough

Seabirds

Tower Street, YO15 1PD

12-3, 6-midnight; closed Mon winter; 12-3, 6-11 (not winter eve) Sun

☎ (01262) 850242

John Smith's Bitter; guest beer Ⓗ

Originally two rooms, this pub changed hands in 2003 and was refurbished to create a clean, contemporary look. The guest beer often comes from a local brewery. A range of meals, with vegetarian options, is based on local produce whenever possible. The pub is popular with walkers and bird enthusiasts – the spectacular cliffs and Bempton RSPB Sanctuary are close by. Camping is available nearby.

(502,510)**P**

Goodmanham

Goodmanham Arms

Main Street, YO43 3JA

5 (12 Sat & Sun)-11

☎ (01430) 873849

Black Sheep Best Bitter; Theakston Best Bitter; guest beers Ⓗ

Opposite the Saxon church and close to the Wolds Way footpath. There is a small beer garden at the front, and a small car park to the side, with access to the outside gents toilet. The public bar is relatively unspoilt, with a quarry-tiled floor and a warming log fire. The entrance corridor has been combined with an adjacent room and is warmed by a log burner. Hot snacks are served Sunday lunchtime. Runner-up CAMRA East Yorkshire Village Pub of the Year in 2008. **QP**

Goole

City & County ✔

Market Square, DN14 5DR (next to clock tower)

9-midnight

☎ (01405) 722600

Greene King IPA, Abbot; Marston's Pedigree; guest beers Ⓗ

Large, bustling town-centre pub with a welcoming sense of space thanks to its lofty ceiling and open-plan bar. Converted from a former bank by Wetherspoon's, the pub features three regular ales supported by two changing guests, and an extensive food menu. A heated rear courtyard provides a quiet sanctuary away from town centre life. The pub is a short walk from the bus and train stations. **Q**

Macintosh Arms

13 Aire Street, DN14 5QE

10.30-midnight (1am Tue & Thu; 2am Fri & Sat)

☎ (01405) 763850

Marston's Burton Bitter; Tetley Dark Mild, Bitter; guest beers Ⓗ

This Grade II-listed building, originally a magistrate's court, is a gem. Left alone by town planners, it retains a traditional feel, with three rooms set around a central bar, and panelled walls featuring pictures of old Goole. A glass ceiling in the pool bar allows a glimpse of the original plaster ceiling. A motorcycle club meets here. Live music plays on the last Friday of the month and karaoke is hosted on Sunday night. The smokers' area outside is covered and heated. **P**

Hedon

Haven Arms ✓

Havenside, Sheriff Highway, HU12 8HH (½ mile S of A1033 crossroads)

12-11 (midnight Fri & Sat); 12-10.30 Sun

☎ (01482) 897695

Black Sheep Best Bitter; Great Newsome Sleckdust; Taylor Landlord; Tetley Bitter; guest beers Ⓗ

Situated in the historic Haven area of town – once the largest port on the River Humber. The popular bar is divided into a number of areas to cater for all tastes. Traditional, reasonably priced pub food, freshly prepared from local ingredients, is served all day. The concert and cabaret room serves as the focal point for the activities of a large number of community clubs and teams, and children are welcome here during the day. Guest beers come from local micro-breweries.
(75,76,77)♣P

Hollym

Plough Inn

Northside Road, HU19 2RS

12 (5 Mon; 2 Tue-Thu winter)-midnight; 12-midnight (11 winter) Sun

☎ (01964) 612049 theploughinnhollym.co.uk

Tetley Bitter; guest beers Ⓗ

This family-run, 200-year-old, genuine free house of wattle and daub construction has undergone considerable refurbishment. Primarily a locals' pub, it is a haven for discerning holidaymakers in summer. Part of the pub dates from the 16th century, while photographs in the bar depict its role as a WWII ARP station. Good pub food is available – booking is essential on a Sunday. Accommodation comprises three en-suite letting rooms. CAMRA East Yorkshire Village Pub of the Year 2008. (75,76,77)♣P

Howden

Barnes Wallis

Station Road, DN14 7LF

5 (12 Sat)-11; closed Mon; 12-10.30 Sun

☎ (01430) 430639 barneswallisinn.com

John Smith's Bitter; Taylor Landlord; guest beers Ⓗ

The pub in the country that you don't have to drive to. Located beside Howden railway station, this family-run pub has two regular well-known Yorkshire beers, supported by two varying guest beers, one usually dark. The large one-room interior abounds with Barnes Wallis and Dambusters memorabilia, and outside is a spacious beer garden. Good food is cooked in a country style using local produce – the fish only has to travel from Hull. Q P

Hull

Falcon

60 Falkland Road, HU9 5SA

11-11.30 (midnight Fri & Sat); 12-11.30 Sun

☎ (01482) 713721

Lees Bitter; guest beers Ⓗ

Well worth seeking out, this gem is situated on a 1960s council estate deep in the former real ale desert of East Hull, showing what can be achieved with commitment. Up to three guest beers are served in the front bar, usually including a mild, and often including Fuller's London Pride. There is a rear games room. Close to Hull KR rugby ground, the pub gets busy on match days.
(40,42)♣P

Gardeners Arms

35 Cottingham Road, HU5 2PP (100m from A1079/ B1233 jct)

11 (12 Sun & Mon)-midnight

☎ (01482) 342396

Tetley Bitter; guest beers Ⓗ

The original front bar has seen many alterations over the years, but retains the matchboard ceiling that blends with the current ale house style. This room is popular for its choice of four guest beers. The large rear extension is comfortably furnished, housing seven pool tables and large-screen TVs. The pub sponsors local rugby union, football and ten-pin bowling teams and hosts three weekly quizzes. There is a large outdoor drinking area at the front. Food is served daily 12-10pm.
(105)♣P

George Hotel

Land of Green Ginger, HU1 2EA

12-11.30 (midnight Fri & Sat)

☎ (01482) 226373

Adnams Broadside; Fuller's London Pride; Hop Back Summer Lightning; St Austell Tribute; guest beer Ⓗ

Situated in the old town, this traditional pub has beamed ceilings, wood-panelled walls and pictures of old Hull on the walls, with faux gas lamps providing subdued lighting. The bar offers darts and dominoes, TV and piped music. Meals are served until 3pm (6pm Fri-Sun). An upstairs function room is available. The pub is noted for reputedly having England's smallest window, dating back to coaching days and excise searches. ♣

Hop & Vine

24 Albion Street, HU1 3TG

11-11; closed Mon; 4-10 Sun

☎ (07500) 543199 hopandvinehull.co.uk

Beer range varies Ⓗ

Atmospheric basement bar with rare bentwood seating, situated close to Hull New Theatre. The free house serves three changing guest ales from independents, plus rare farmhouse ciders and a perry, together with a good range of Belgian bottled beers. It is also a rare outlet for Budvar Dark and Pilsener Urquell. An interesting menu of freshly-made snacks and hot drinks is served until 9pm (check website for the daily food and drinks menu). The pub hosts a cider festival in October and a mini beer festival in November. Closed between Christmas and New Year.

Three John Scotts ✓

Lowgate, HU1 1XW

9-midnight (1am Fri & Sat)

☎ (01482) 381910

Greene King IPA, Abbot; Marston's Pedigree; guest beers Ⓗ

Converted Edwardian post office, situated opposite St Mary's Church in the old town. Named after three past incumbents of the church, this open-plan Wetherspoon's features modern decor and original works of art. The clientele is mixed at lunchtime, with circuit drinkers appearing at weekends. The covered, heated rear courtyard has seating. Up to five guest beers are available, plus Westons cider and perry. Food is served until 10pm, with a steak club on Tuesday and a curry club on Thursday.

Walters

21 Scale Lane, HU1 1LF
12-11
(01482) 224004
Beer range varies Ⓗ

A contemporary free house that opened in 2007. The name recalls an 1820s barber shop in the same premises. Although modern café bar in style, it is a haven in an area of the old town that is over populated by fashion bars. Up to ten regularly-changing guest beers and up to three ciders and/or perries are sold. Belgian and German draught and bottled beers are also available. An over-21 door policy operates. Runner-up Hull CAMRA Pub of the Year 2008.

Wellington Inn

55 Russell Street, HU2 9AB
4-11; 12-midnight Fri & Sat; 12-11 Sun
(01482) 329486 thewellington-hull.co.uk
Tetley Bitter; guest beers Ⓗ

Hidden free house gem just off Freetown Way, this former Hull Brewery pub dates from 1861 and serves up to six guest beers. It features a walk-in cooler stocking over 100 European bottled beers; note the impressive glass-fronted display in the back bar. Farmhouse ciders and perry can also be found, plus specialist European beers on draught and Lindisfarne fruit wines. Live music plays most Thursdays. No food is served but you can bring your own sandwiches. Hull CAMRA Pub of the Year 2008. P

Whalebone

165 Wincolmlee, HU2 0PA (500m N of North Bridge on W side of river)
11-midnight
(01482) 226648
Copper Dragon Best Bitter; Taylor Landlord; Whalebone Diana Mild, Neckoil Bitter, seasonal beers; guest beer Ⓗ

Built in 1796, the pub is situated in a former industrial area – look for the illuminated M&R Ales sign. The comfortable saloon bar is adorned with photos of bygone Hull pubs, CAMRA awards, and the city's sporting heritage. The adjacent Whalebone Brewery opened in 2003. Two real ciders and a perry, together with European draught and bottled beers, are also stocked. Hot snacks are available. CAMRA Hull & East Yorkshire Cider Pub of the Year 2008, and third place in the Yorkshire Cider Pub of the Year 2008.

Kirk Ella

Beech Tree

Southella Way, HU10 7LY
11.30 (12 Sun)-11
(01482) 654350
Black Sheep Best Bitter; Taylor Landlord; Tetley Bitter; guest beers Ⓗ

Open-plan pub built to serve this community on the western outskirts of Hull. Two or three guest beers are available at any one time. A rack of three third pints can be ordered. Food is available 12-9pm every day. Tuesday is Grill Night and Thursday is Curry Night – both are served from 3pm. Monday and Wednesday are quiz nights, with the theme changing constantly. Children under 14 are not allowed on the premises. (180)P

Lund

Wellington Inn

19 The Green, YO25 9TE
12-3 (not Mon), 6.30-11 (11.30 Fri & Sat); 12-11 Sun
(01377) 217294
Black Sheep Best Bitter; John Smith's Bitter; Taylor Landlord; guest beers Ⓗ

Enjoying a prime location on the green in this award-winning Wold village, most of the pub's trade comes from the local farming community. The building was totally renovated by the present licensee, and features stone-flagged floors, beamed ceilings and three real fires. The multi-roomed interior includes a games room and candlelit restaurant serving evening meals (Tue-Sat). Good food can also be enjoyed at lunchtime from the bar menu and specials board. CAMRA East Yorkshire Village Pub of the Year in 2006. P

Millington

Gait Inn

Main Street, YO42 1TX SE832517
12-2 Fri & Sat, 6.30-11; closed Mon; 12-11 Sun
(01759) 302045
Black Sheep Best Bitter; John Smith's Bitter; Theakston Best Bitter; guest beer Ⓗ

Lovely 16th-century free house set in the Yorkshire Wolds. The pub name refers to the plot of open grazing land on Millington Pastures formerly issued to each villager. There are horse brasses on exposed beams and rural paraphernalia on every shelf. Note the very old Yorkshire map pasted to the ceiling, discoloured from years of smoke from the open fire. There is a separate pool room. Regular varied live music evenings are hosted. P

Old Ellerby

Blue Bell

Crabtree Lane, HU11 5AJ
12-4 Sat, 7-11.30 (midnight Fri & Sat); 12-5, 8-11.30 Sun
(01964) 562364
Greene King Old Speckled Hen; Tetley Bitter; guest beers Ⓗ

This 16th-century inn has an L-shaped bar and a single room split into distinct areas, including a snug to the right and a rear pool area where children are welcome until 8.30pm. The pub has a strong community feel, hosting darts and dominoes teams. Three guest beers in winter increase to four in summer. Outside is a fish pond and a bowling green. Popular with walkers (wipe your shoes please). CAMRA East Yorkshire Village Pub of the Year three times and runner-up in 2006. QP

Patrington

Station Hotel

Station Road, HU12 0NE
12-11 (midnight Sat)
(01964) 630262
Tetley Bitter; guest beers Ⓗ

A family-owned free house on the western edge of the village, this hotel used to service passengers on the Hull-Withernsea railway which closed in the 1960s. The Anglo-German owners have completely refurbished the old building in a welcoming

modern-rustic style, and have added a games room. The hotel is renowned locally for the quality of its food, as well as its interesting guest ales sourced from far and wide.
❀◑◗♿⛺🚌(75,76,77)♣P⁐

Rawcliffe

Jemmy Hirst at the Rose & Crown

26 Riverside, DN14 8RN (down Chapel Lane from the village green)
⏲ 6 (5 Fri; 12 Sat & Sun)-11
☎ (01405) 831038
Taylor Landlord; guest beers Ⓗ
Much loved by visitors across the region, you can be sure of a warm welcome from the owners, locals and Bruno the dog. A constantly changing array of ales suits every taste. A fifth handpump has been fitted recently to satisfy increasing demand. A rustic interior with a real fire and book-lined walls provides a welcome retreat, with lazy summer days on the patio or riverbank. Westons Traditional Cider is available. A real gem. CAMRA branch Pub of the Year 2004-2006/08/09, and Yorkshire runner-up 2007. 🔥Q❀♿🚌(88)●P⁐

Sancton

Star

King Street, YO43 4QP
⏲ 12-2.30, 6.30-11; closed Mon
☎ (01430) 827269 🌐 thestaratsancton.co.uk
Beer range varies Ⓗ
The Star was first licensed in 1710. Following a major refurbishment, it reopened in 2003 as a roadside pub and restaurant. Bar meals are served lunchtimes and evenings. Meals are created from high quality produce, sourced locally. Booking is recomended for the restaurant. The two changing guest beers are sourced from Yorkshire breweries.
❀◑◗P⁐

Sewerby

Ship Inn ✔

Cliff Road, YO15 1EW
⏲ 11-11
☎ (01262) 672374 🌐 shipinnsewerby.co.uk
Banks's Bitter, seasonal beers; guest beers Ⓗ
Village-centre pub serving both locals and those holidaying to the north of Bridlington. One bar is wood panelled with a beamed ceiling, and the beer garden outside has a children's play area. The pub is family friendly, welcoming children and dogs, and the food comprises main meals and snacks. Nearby attractions include a model village, Sewerby Hall and cliff-top walks. The pub sponsors the local cricket club that plays only 100 metres away. 🔥🛝❀◑◗🍷⛺🚌(103,110)♣P⁐

Skipsea

Board Inn

Back Street, YO25 8SU
⏲ 6 (7 winter)-11; 12-midnight Sat; 12-11 Sun
☎ (01262) 468342
Marston's Pedigree, seasonal beers; guest beer Ⓗ
Traditional village local dating from the 17th century with distinct public and lounge bars as well as a recently extended restaurant. The public bar, with its sporting focus (especially rugby league), hosts darts, pool and dominoes teams. The comfortable lounge is home to the landlady's water jug collection. Home-cooked food is served daily from 6pm, and in summer Sunday lunch attracts many holiday makers (booking advisable). Dogs are welcome. 🔥Q❀◑◗🍷⛺♣P⁐

South Dalton

Pipe & Glass

West End, HU17 7PN (follow signs from B1248)
⏲ 12-3, 6.30-11 (not Mon); 12-11 Sat; 12-10.30 Sun
☎ (01430) 810246 🌐 pipeandglass.co.uk
Black Sheep Best Bitter; John Smith's Bitter; guest beers Ⓗ
This delightful pub stands at the site of the original gatehouse to Dalton Hall. Completely renovated by its present owners in 2006, it features exposed beams and custom-made furniture. Food and drink both come from local producers as much as possible. A changing menu offers award-winning high quality meals with a children's menu (check the website for sample menus). Guest beers feature Yorkshire micros. The pub is open on bank holiday Mondays but closes for a week in January.
🔥❀◑◗🍷●P

Sutton upon Derwent

St Vincent Arms

Main Street, YO41 4BN (on B1228 S of Elvington)
⏲ 11.30-3, 6-11; 12-3, 6.30-10.30 Sun
☎ (01904) 608349
Fuller's London Pride, ESB; Old Mill Bitter; Taylor Golden Best, Landlord; Wells Bombardier; York Yorkshire Terrier; guest beer Ⓗ
This pretty white-painted pub on a bend in the road through the village has been family owned and run for many years. The L-shaped bar to the right is popular with locals; note the large Fuller, Smith & Turner mirror. Another small bar with a serving hatch to the left leads to the dining rooms. An excellent restaurant menu includes many fish dishes. Twice York CAMRA Pub of the Year.
Q❀◑◗P🗑

YORKSHIRE (NORTH)

Acomb

Sun Inn

35 The Green, YO26 5LL SE571513
⏲ 12-midnight
☎ (01904) 798500 🌐 .thesuninnacomb.com
John Smith's Bitter; guest beers Ⓗ
This thriving ale house overlooking the village green provides a welcome source of beer variety in the Acomb area of York. The pub is situated opposite the bus stop for links east to York city centre and provides a solid lunchtime menu with regular specials. There are two quiet bars and a comfortable sports bar showing cable channels. Darts and dominoes teams, daily newspapers and a Sunday quiz help to make this a pleasant community pub. ◑🍷♿🚌(4)♣P⁐

Aldbrough St John

Stanwick Inn

High Green, DL11 7SZ (1 mile from B6275)
⏲ 12-3, 5.30 (6.30 Sat)-11; 12-3, 6.30-10.30 Sun
☎ (01325) 374258 🌐 thestanwickinn.co.uk

Daleside Bitter; Black Sheep Best Bitter; guest beers Ⓗ
Set in a picturesque North Yorkshire village on England's second largest village green, this stunning, welcoming 19th-century inn overlooks the meandering beck. It has two bars: one for drinkers and one serving two excellent restaurants which offer good locally-sourced food lunchtimes and evenings seven days a week. The pub demonstrates a passion for real ale, with three guest beers coming from local micros. There is a quiz every third Wednesday. The pub is ideally situated to stay at, and explore, the Yorkshire Dales and Teesdale. ♨Q❀⇔◐◑ ⊟⊟(29)♣P⅟–⊓

Appletreewick

Craven Arms Inn

BD23 6DA
⏲ 11-3, 6-11 Mon & Tue; 11.30-11 Wed-Sat; 11.30-10.30 Sun
☎ (01756) 720270 🌐 craven-cruckbarn.co.uk
Dark Horse Hetton Pale Ale; Taylor Golden Best; Tetley Bitter; guest beer Ⓗ
Built originally in 1548 as a farm, many historic features have recently been returned to this building, including oak beams, stone flagged floors, gas lighting and open fires, to create a charming atmosphere. To the rear is a cruck barn – the first one to be built for 400 years in the Dales, complete with wheelchair access. The menu ranges from a la carte to bar meals and the public bar boasts a rare ring the bull pub game and dartboard. The house beer is from Moorhouses.
♨Q♉❀◐◑ ⊟Ⱥ⊟(74)♣P

New Inn

BD23 6DA (W end of village)
⏲ 12-11
☎ (01756) 720252
Black Sheep Best Bitter; Daleside Bitter, Blonde; John Smith's Bitter; Theakston Old Peculier Ⓗ
Friendly, unspoilt village local with two rooms, both warmed by roaring fires, with a pool table in a third room to the rear. Black and white photographs of bygone Appletreewick adorn the walls. A fine range of bottled beers from around the world is always available. Walkers and cyclists enjoying the surrounding Dales countryside are very welcome, along with their well-behaved dogs. A nearby cycle livery is on hand for any necessary maintenance.
♨Q❀⇔◐◑ Ⱥ⊟(74)♣P⅟–

Askrigg

White Rose Hotel

Main Street, DL8 3HG
⏲ 11.30-midnight (1am Fri & Sat)
☎ (01969) 650515 🌐 thewhiterosehotelaskrigg.co.uk
Black Sheep Best Bitter; John Smith's Bitter; Theakston Best Bitter; Yorkshire Dales Askrigg Ale Ⓗ
A family-run hotel in a picturesque village in the very heart of Wensleydale. The Victorian building was refurbished in 2006, and is a popular base in which to unwind after a day walking in the Dales. It offers a warm welcome to regulars and visitors alike. There is a pleasant beer garden and the nearby Yorkshire Dales Brewery occasionally delivers by wheelbarrow. Good value accommodation is available in 12 letting rooms.
❀⇔◐◑ ♿⊟(157)♣P⅟–

Aysgarth

George & Dragon

DL8 3AD
⏲ 11.30 (12 Sun)-2am
☎ (01969) 663358 🌐 georgeanddragonaysgarth.co.uk
Black Sheep Best Bitter, Ale; Theakston Best Bitter; guest beers Ⓗ
On the main A684 road through Wensleydale close to the tourist hot spot of Aysgarth Falls, this excellent 17th-century inn offers a picturesque location and a fine place in which to slake your thirst on a range of local ales. The local Yorkshire Dales Brewery situated in a nearby village supplies a good range of beers, along with Black Sheep and Theakston ales. For those in need of non-liquid sustenance, the restaurant offers very good food and friendly service. ♨Q♉❀⇔◐◑ Ⱥ⊟(156)♣P⅟–

Beck Hole

Birch Hall Inn ★

YO22 5LE (1½ km N of Goathland)
⏲ 11-11 summer; 11-3, 7.30-11 (closed Mon eve & Tue) winter
☎ (01947) 896245 🌐 beckhole.info
Black Sheep Best Bitter; North Yorkshire Beckwatter; guest beers Ⓗ
This unspoilt rural gem rests in a hamlet of nine cottages and a farm. A CAMRA multi-award winner, it comprises two bars sandwiching a sweet shop. The house ale, Beckwatter, is organically brewed by North Yorkshire Brewing Co. Guest beers are all sourced locally. A painting of the Murk Esk by Algernon Newton, Royal Academy, has been hanging outside the pub since 1944 – donated as a thank you for the village's hospitality during his seven-year residency. Sandwiches, pies and beer cake are always available. ♨Q❀⇔◐◑ ⊟♣●P

INDEPENDENT BREWERIES

Black Sheep Masham
Brown Cow Barlow
Captain Cook Stokesley
Copper Dragon Skipton
Cropton Cropton
Daleside Harrogate
Dark Horse Hetton
East Coast Filey (NEW)
Great Heck Great Heck
Hambleton Melmerby
Litton Litton
Marston Moor Tockwith
Moorview Nesfield (NEW)
Morrissey Fox Marton cum Grafton (NEW)
Naylor's Cross Hills
North Yorkshire Pinchinthorpe
Redscar Redcar
Richmond Richmond
Rooster's/Outlaw Knaresborough
Rudgate Tockwith
Samuel Smith Tadcaster
Storyteller Terrington (NEW)
Theakston Masham
Three Peaks Settle
Wensleydale Bellerby
Wold Top Wold Newton
York York
Yorkshire Dales Askrigg

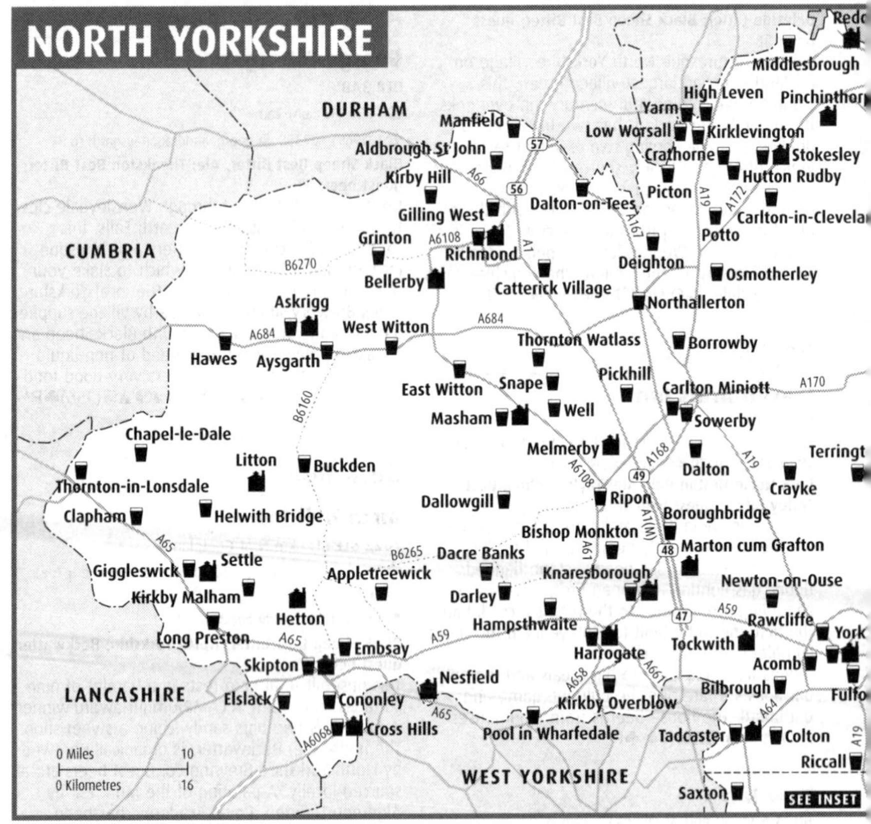

Bilbrough

Three Hares

Main Street, YO23 3PH (off A64, 6 miles W of York) SE530465

12-3 (not Tue), 6-11; closed Mon; 12-8 Sun

☎ (01937) 832128

Beer range varies Ⓗ

Pretty whitewashed village pub with four linked rooms – two for drinking and two for dining – offering a good mix to suit the needs of all customers. The two guest ales are usually from local breweries. An outdoor heated terrace to the rear has a water feature. Live music plays on the second Tuesday of each month. ⌂Q❀◑♿P

Bishop Monkton

Lamb & Flag

Boroughbridge Road, HG4 3QN (off A61)

12-2 (closed Mon & Tue), 5.30-11; 12-3, 7-10.30 Sun

☎ (01765) 677322 lambandflagbarn.co.uk

Tetley Bitter; guest beer Ⓗ

Warm and cosy, this immaculately-kept, traditional village pub supports local charities and fundraising events. Two comfortable rooms adorned with knick-knacks and brasses are served from one central bar, but each has its own open coal/log fire. Good home-cooked food is offered and AA four-star accommodation is available. A garden and a large car park are at the rear, together with tables at the front. May bank holiday sees a duck race and hog roast. ⌂Q❀◑(56)♣P

Boroughbridge

Black Bull Inn

6 St James Square, YO51 9AR

11 (12 Sun)-midnight

☎ (01423) 322413

John Smith's Bitter; Taylor Best Bitter; guest beer Ⓗ

Situated in the main square, this 13th-century Grade II-listed inn, complete with resident ghost, is very popular. A comfortable snug and a larger distinctive bar serve good value beers and there is a wide choice of bar meals. The smart restaurant, converted from old stables, boasts an international menu. This little gem, complete with friendly locals, is well worth a visit. Free town parking is nearby. ⌂Q◑♣P

Borrowby

Wheatsheaf

YO7 4QP (1 mile from A19 trunk route)

5.30 (2 Sat)-11; 12-4, 7-10.30 Sun

☎ (01845) 537274 borrowbypub.co.uk

Daleside Bitter; guest beers Ⓗ

This attractive little 17th-century free house is handy for the A19 trunk route, in a quiet village close to the edge of the North Yorkshire Moors. Inside, a huge stone fireplace dominates the cosy, low-beamed public bar, with a further drinking area behind the bar and a small dining room across the passage. The home-cooked food doesn't dominate what is above all a thriving and friendly locals' pub which focuses on doing things simply

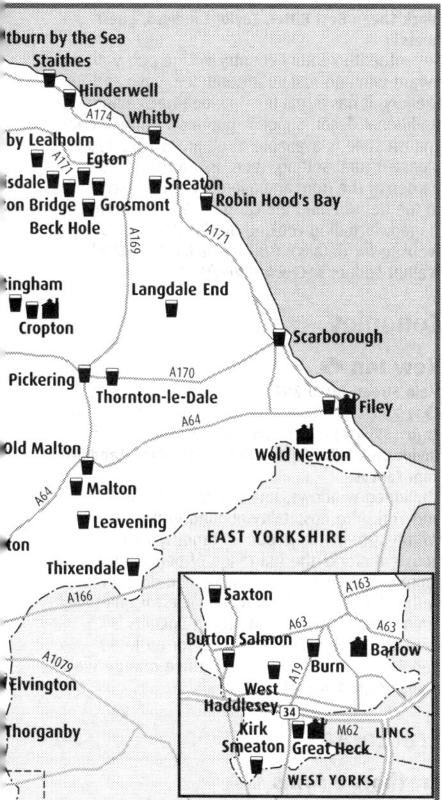

but well. Meals are served Wednesday-Saturday evenings and Sunday lunchtime.
⛰Q🛏❀◑ 🅵⛺♣P

Buckden

Buck Inn

BD23 5JA
⏲ 11-11 (10.30 Sun)
☎ (01756) 760228 🌐 thebuckinnbuckden.co.uk
Black Sheep Best Bitter, Special Ale, Riggwelter; Taylor Landlord Ⓗ
Situated on the Dales Way National Trail, this Georgian coaching inn sits snugly below Buckden Pike among the stunning scenery of Upper Wharfedale. The main room is split between a stone-flagged bar area and a comfortable lounge where up to six beers are on offer. The Courtyard Restaurant is open evenings for home-cooked food made from local ingredients. Accommodation comprises 14 en-suite rooms and the outside seating area offers fantastic views. The house beer is Buckden Pike from Yorkshire Dales.
⛰❀🛏◑🚌(72,74)P

Burn

Wheatsheaf

Main Road, YO8 8LJ (A19 3 miles S of Selby) SE594286
⏲ 12-11
☎ (01757) 270614 🌐 wheatsheafburn.co.uk
John Smith's Bitter; Taylor Best Bitter; guest beers Ⓗ
A renowned roadside free house stocking four reasonably priced guest beers, often from local breweries, especially Brown Cow. A narrow entrance leads to the bar and a spacious lounge with a huge open fire. A collection of bottled beers, artefacts from bygone days and memorabilia of 578 Squadron, stationed at Burn in World War II, adorn the walls. Food is served every lunchtime and Thursday to Saturday evenings. Frequent beer festivals and a monthly jazz night are held.
⛰Q❀◑🚌♣P⚡

Burton Salmon

Plough Inn

Main Street, LS25 5JS (on A162 4 miles N of jct 33 M62) SE492274
⏲ 12-2.30 (not Mon), 4.30-midnight; 12-midnight Sat & Sun
☎ (01977) 672422
Thwaites Original, Wainwright, Lancaster Bomber Ⓗ
Now brewery owned, but still a family-run, 17th-century pub with a family-friendly atmosphere in a quiet village close to the A1. Wood floors, an open fire and a friendly welcome await you. The dining area serves a selection of home-cooked food (not Mon except bank holidays) and is a base for the village cricket team and enthusiastic darts and dominoes teams. A quiz night is held on Sunday.
⛰Q❀◑🚌♣P⚡

Carlton Miniott

Dog & Gun ✔

YO7 4NJ (on A61 1 mile W of Thirsk rail station)
⏲ 12-3, 5.30-midnight; 12-midnight Sat & Sun; closed Mon
☎ (01845) 522150
Theakston Best Bitter; guest beers Ⓗ
A couple of miles west of Thirsk, this village pub has been opened out to form a comfortable lounge but retains a separate bar/games room and a restaurant to the rear. It offers two or three regularly changing guest ales, usually from smaller breweries and often chosen by the regulars. Meals are served daily except Monday, when the pub is closed. The spacious garden includes a caravan park. 🛏❀◑ 🅵⛺🚌(70)♣P⚡

Vale of York

Carlton Road, YO7 4LX (next to Thirsk rail station)
⏲ 12-midnight (11 Sun)
☎ (01845) 523161
Black Sheep Best Bitter; John Smith Bitter; Taylor Landlord; Wold Top Bitter Ⓗ
A large roadside hostelry with 15 letting rooms, it is popular with locals and visitors alike. The main lounge area has been opened out and there is a smaller bar and games room to one side. Handy for the adjacent rail station and less than a mile from Thirsk racecourse, the pub becomes busy on race days. ⛰Q❀🛏◑ 🅵♿⛺⇌🚌♣P⚡

Carlton-in-Cleveland

Blackwell Ox Inn

Main Street, TS9 7DJ
⏲ 11.30-11
☎ (01642) 712287 🌐 theblackwellox.co.uk
Black Sheep Best Bitter; Worthington's Bitter; guest beers Ⓗ
Located in a beautiful area on the edge of the National Park, this previous CAMRA award winner is an impressive and popular multi-roomed village

inn. It is renowned for its first class, good value Thai cuisine, where the winter Monday evening buffet, washed down with several pints, can easily become habit forming. Look out too for early evening year-round specials. But you don't have to eat. Drinkers are also made most welcome. Four handpumps, including two guests, provide an eclectic range of ever-changing beer styles. The garden has an extensive children's play area. ⛰Q❀⛟◐⛺🚌(80,89)P

Catterick Village

Bay Horse ✔

38 Low Green, DL10 7LP

⊙ 12-2.30, 5-midnight; 12-midnight Sat & Sun

☎ (01748) 811383

Jennings Bitter, Cumberland Ale; Wychwood Bitter; guest beers Ⓗ

A comfortable and friendly traditional village pub retaining some original features, conveniently situated close to the A1 and Catterick race course. Benches outside overlook the pretty green, while darts and dominoes are popular in the bar, which stocks a good range of beers from the Marston stable. There is a separate conservatory restaurant, families and dogs are welcome and the garden to the rear has a heated smoking shelter. ❀◐◑🚌♣P⌐

Chapel-le-Dale

Hill Inn

LA6 3AR (on B6255)

⊙ 12-3, 6.30-11; closed Mon; 12-11 Sat

☎ (01524) 241256 🌐 oldhillinn.co.uk

Black Sheep Best Bitter, Ale; Dent Aviator; Taylor Landlord; Theakston Best Bitter Ⓗ

The inn dates from 1615 and is beloved of generations of hikers and potholers. Well-worn paths run from here to both Whernside (Yorkshire's highest peak) and Ingleborough (its best known). Lots of exposed wood and some stonework feature in the bar and the pub is popular with diners (booking advisable); puddings are a speciality and there is a sugarcraft exhibition in an adjoining room. ⛰Q❀⛟◐◑P

Clapham

New Inn

LA2 8HH

⊙ 11-11

☎ (01524) 251203 🌐 newinn-clapham.co.uk

Black Sheep Best Bitter; Copper Dragon Best Bitter, Golden Pippin; Taylor Landlord Ⓗ

Spacious 18th-century coaching inn situated in a major tourist village with two lounge bars. One features oak panelling, the other has photos and cartoons depicting caving on the walls, and is home to pub games. Children are welcome in the restaurant. Guest beers are sometimes available. The railway station is one mile away. ⛰❀⛟◐◑⇌🚌(581)♣P

Colton

Old Sun Inn

Main Street, LS24 8EP (on A64 1 mile S of Bilbrough services) SE542448

⊙ 12-2.30, 6-11; closed Mon; 12-11 Sun

☎ (01904) 744261 🌐 yeoldsuninn.co.uk

Black Sheep Best Bitter; Taylor Landlord; guest beers Ⓗ

Seventeenth-century country village pub with an award-winning restaurant and deli. Cosy and friendly, it has a real fire, low beamed ceilings and traditional decor. Superior pub food in traditional English style is available at all times. Situated in a pleasant rural setting, there is a formal patio garden at the front and a large informal picnic area to the right behind the car park. Special events are staged, including cooking demonstrations (see website for details). B&B is available at nearby Walnut Lodge. ⛰Q❀⛟◐◑♿P⌐▯

Cononley

New Inn ✔

Main Street, BD20 8NR

⊙ 12-2.30, 5.30-midnight; 12-1am Fri & Sat; 12-10.30 Sun

☎ (01535) 636302 🌐 newinncononley.co.uk

Taylor Dark Mild, Golden Best, Best Bitter, Landlord, Ram Tam Ⓗ

Mullioned windows, low ceilings, wooden beams and Yorkshire hospitality abound in this whitewashed village pub. A Timothy Taylor tied house, it stocks the full range of beers. The main room serves as both a drinking and dining area, with a further small room available for quiet dining. The Knowle Spring room upstairs is available for functions, catering for up to 40 people. The railway station is a five-minute walk away. ⛰❀◐◑⇌🚌(78A)♣

Crathorne

Crathorne Arms

TS15 0BA

⊙ 11.30-3, 5-11; 11-11 Sat; 12-4, 6-11 Sun

☎ (01642) 701931 🌐 crathorne-arms.co.uk

Black Sheep Best Bitter; guest beers Ⓗ

The bustling A19 trunk road now bypasses this whitewashed ancient village pub, where a friendly welcome is assured. Close to Crathorne Hall, the pub was once part of Lord Crathorne's estate, as the superb collection of old photographs adorning the walls testifies. While the pub remains the focus of village life, customers are also drawn from far and wide to sample the ales on four handpumps, with guests usually sourced from Hambleton/North Yorkshire. Good value home-cooked food is served (not Sun eve). ⛰Q❀◐◑♿♣P⌐

Crayke

Durham Ox

Westway, YO61 4TE SE562704

⊙ 12-3, 6-11.30; 12-11.30 Sat & Sun

☎ (01347) 821506 🌐 thedurhamox.com

Black Sheep Best Bitter; Taylor Landlord; Theakston Best Bitter Ⓗ

Unashamedly food-oriented but with a good selection of local beers, this renowned pub lies in the beautiful village of Crayke within the Howardian Hills north of York. It comprises characterful cottage-style accommodation, a private dining room, formal dining, bar/restaurant and a public bar. Visitors should note that the best views are at the bottom of the car park from which the Vale of York spreads out wide in front of you. Conveniently located on the Easingwold-York bus route, there are numerous interesting villages nearby. ⛰Q❀⛟◐◑⊟♿P⌐

Cropton

New Inn

Woolcroft, YO18 8HH (5 miles off A170, Pickering-Kirkbymoorside road) SE755888
11-11
(01751) 417330 newinncropton.co.uk
Cropton Endeavour, Old Goat, seasonal beers; guest beers H
Set on the edge of the North Yorkshire Moors National Park, this is the perfect base for walking and cycling. It is the brewery tap for Cropton Brewery and sets the standard for how a rural pub should be run, offering a fantastic ale range, good food and accommodation. An excellent beer festival is held every November, plus a music festival in summer. For those not wanting to drive, the Moors bus service runs regularly from Pickering and Kirkbymoorside. **QP**

Cross Hills

Old White Bear

6 Keighley Road, BD20 7RN (on A6068, close to jct with A629)
11.30-11; 12-10.30 Sun
(01535) 632115
Naylor's Pinnacle Pale Ale, Bitter, Blonde H
Four-room village pub built in 1735 with exposed timbers said to have come from a ship of the same name. The top room is used mainly for dining while two of the remaining three rooms have open real fires. The back room has darts and ring the bull. Quiz night is Thursday and darts and dominoes are played on Monday. A regular outlet for Naylor's Brewery, it was CAMRA Keighley & Craven branch Pub of the Year 2008. (66,66A)**P**

Dacre Banks

Royal Oak Inn

Oak Lane, HG3 4EN
11.30-11; 12-10.30 Sun
(01423) 780200 the-royaloak-dacre.co.uk
Beer range varies H
A family-run Grade II-listed pub built in 1752 close to Brimham Rocks and Upper Nidderdale. Two house beers brewed by HB Clark and Rudgate breweries are usually on offer plus up to two guests. An attractive beer garden overlooks the Nidd Valley. Good quality bar snacks and meals are served in a multi-roomed bar area with a separate restaurant. **P**

Dallowgill

Drovers Inn

HG4 3RH (2 miles W of Laverton on road to Pateley Bridge) OS210720
6.30-11.30 (7-11 winter); closed Mon; 12-3, 6.30-11 Sat & Sun
(01765) 658510
Black Sheep Best Bitter; Hambleton Bitter; Old Mill Mild or Bitter H
This small, homely, single-room pub is adjacent to the Moors and the Old Drovers Road high up in Lower Nidderdale. In winter there is always a roaring open fire and in summer glorious walks in the surrounding countryside beckon. The pub is home to hunting and grouse-shooting parties as well as walkers. Simple home-cooked food is available daily until 8.30pm. **QP**

Dalton

Jolly Farmer

Brookside, YO7 3HY (off A19 or A168)
7-11; 12-3, 6-11 Thu-Sat; 12-3, 7-11 Sun
(01845) 577359
Tetley Bitter; Theakston Mild; guest beers H
Popular with locals, this family-run pub, dating from the mid-1800s, is at the heart of the village, enthusiastically converting customers to real ale. Its six handpumps feature beers from local micros. Freshly prepared home-made dishes using local produce are served from the kitchen, with chips always a favourite. Booking is advisable for Sunday lunch. Three en-suite rooms make an ideal base for exploring the Dales and North Yorkshire moors. Real cider is served in summer.
QP

Dalton-on-Tees

Chequers Inn

DL2 2NT
12-3, 5.30-11; 12-10.30 Sun
(01325) 721213
Banks's Bitter; guest beers H
Traditional inn dating back to the 1840s, comprising a bar, lounge and restaurant, with a warm welcome guaranteed. Formerly known as the Crown & Anchor, this was once part of the now-defunct Fryer's Brewery estate. The landlord is passionate about real ale and at least two guest beers are sourced from micros countrywide. Regular gourmet evenings are hosted and a quiz is held every Wednesday. Overnight accommodation comprises five rooms overlooking the green and its pump. Handy for Croft Circuit.
Q(72,X72)**P**

Danby

Duke of Wellington

2 West Lane, YO21 2LY (200m N of railway station)
12-3 (not Mon), 7-11; 12-11 Fri & Sat; 12-3, 7-10.30 Sun
(01287) 660351 dukeofwellingtondanby.co.uk
Copper Dragon Scotts 1816; Daleside Bitter; guest beer H
This 18th-century inn, a previous local CAMRA Pub of the Season award winner, is set in idyllic countryside and was used as a recruiting post during the Napoleonic War. A cast-iron plaque of the first Duke of Wellington, unearthed during restoration work, hangs above the fireplace in the bar. Both the regular beers and the guest come from local breweries. The blackboard menu offers traditional British meals, using locally-sourced meat, fish and game. The Moors Visitor Centre is nearby. **Q**

Darley

Wellington Inn

HG3 2QQ (on B6451 to W of village)
11.30-11; 12-10.30 Sun
(01423) 780362 wellington-inn.co.uk
Black Sheep Best Bitter; Copper Dragon Golden Pippin; Taylor Landlord; Tetley Bitter H
Spacious stone roadside inn much extended in the 1980s with good views from the beer garden over Nidderdale, an area of outstanding natural beauty. The original bar operates as a tap room. The extension with an impressive inglenook fireplace is

mainly used for dining, and there is a separate restaurant. The pub makes an ideal starting point for exploring the Dales. ♣P

Deighton

White Swan

YO19 6HA SE628441
12-2.30, 5.30-11; 12-11 Sat; 12-10.30 Sun
☎ (01904) 728287 whiteswandeighton.co.uk
Banks's Bitter; Jennings Bitter; Marston's Pedigree; guest beer
An oasis on a busy highway, this spacious pub has a front bar opening up from the entrance, a separate dining area off to one side and a lounge/dining room to the other side. Although now partly open plan, much of the original layout is unchanged. The comprehensive menu of good quality, good value food is the main draw, supplemented by a daily specials board and children's dishes. Q(415)P

East Witton

Cover Bridge Inn

DL8 4SQ (½ mile N of village on A6108) SE144871
11-midnight; 12-11.30 Sun
☎ (01969) 623250 thecoverbridgeinn.co.uk
Black Sheep Best Bitter; John Smith's Bitter; Taylor Landlord; Theakston Best Bitter, Old Peculier; guest beers
A delightful country inn, situated at the convergence of the Rivers Ure and Cover in Wensleydale. A CAMRA multi-award winner, the antique public bar with its low ceilings and homely hearth is reminiscent of a mini beer exhibition, offering eight cask ales if you can work out the quirky door latch. The diminutive lounge leads to a lovely garden, complete with a children's play area overlooking the river. With an enviable reputation for food, this superb pub is ever popular with diners. Q♿(159)♣P

Egton

Wheatsheaf Inn

High Street, YO21 1TZ
11.30-2.30, 5.30-11; closed Mon; 11.30-11 Sat & Sun
☎ (01947) 895271 wheatsheafegton.com
Black Sheep Best Bitter; Caledonian Deuchars IPA; guest beer
Grade I-listed, 19th-century pub, this 2009 CAMRA award winner is entering its tenth year in the Guide under the stewardship of a licensee who has had 23 years of continuous Guide recognition. You can sit on church pews in the cosy bar, where collectables bought at local auctions add to the character. The upmarket food menu is based on local seasonal produce. A grassy area to the front, and table tennis and boules to the rear, are ideal for summer. Six bedrooms and a holiday cottage are available for hire. ♿(99)♣P

Egton Bridge

Horseshoe Hotel

YO21 1XE (down hill from Egton station)
11.30-3, 6.30-11; 11.30-11 Sat; 12-11 Sun
☎ (01947) 895245
Black Sheep Best Bitter; John Smith's Bitter; guest beers
Secluded gem in a natural hollow, easily accessed from the station or across the stepping stones of the River Esk. The bar is furnished with old-fashioned settles and warmed by a large fire. Five handpumps provide a wide beer selection, with guests usually from Copper Dragon and Durham. A large raised grassy area with mature trees makes outdoor drinking a pleasure. The regular menu and specials board offer good-value locally-sourced food.A former CAMRA Pub of the Year award winner. Q♿(Egton)(99)P

Elslack

Tempest Arms

BD23 3AY (off A56 Skipton-Colne road)
11-11; 12-10.30 Sun
☎ (01282) 842450 tempestarms.co.uk
Dark Horse Best Bitter, Hetton Pale Ale; Taylor Landlord; Theakston Best Bitter; Thwaites Wainwrights Ale
Large, popular, up-market country pub, just off the A56, serving good food from an extensive menu in a separate dining area/restaurant. The house beer is from Moorhouses and a range of bottled foreign beers is also served. The decor is a tasteful mix of traditional and contemporary. Conference facilities and a function room are available for hire. ♿(215)P

Elvington

Grey Horse

Main Street, YO41 4AG (on B1228 6 miles SE of York)
12-3 Wed & Thu summer, 5-11; 12-11 Fri-Sun
☎ (01904) 608335 thegreyhorse.com
Black Sheep Best Bitter; John Smith's Bitter; Taylor Landlord; Theakston Best Bitter; guest beers
Situated opposite the village green, complete with maypole, this is a two-roomed local served from a central bar. Recent refurbishment has provided a comfortable lounge area with a glass wall of beer and a collection of old radios. Two guest beers change regularly from a country-wide selection. Food is served in the lounge, or upstairs in the Hayloft if busy (not Mon). An outside area with tables at the front gives a view on passing life, while smokers are well catered for at the back. ♿♣P

Embsay

Elm Tree Inn

5 Elm Tree Square, BD23 6RB
11.30-3, 5.30-11; 11.30-11 Sat (closed 3-5.30 Sat & Sun winter); 12-10.30 Sun
☎ (01756) 790717
Copper Dragon Scotts 1816; Goose Eye No-Eye Deer; Wells Bombardier; Young's Bitter; guest beer
A former coaching inn, this locals' pub is situated in the village square. Inside, it has an open feel with oak beams, a large main bar and a smaller side room mainly used by diners. Look for the worn mounting steps outside at the front. Well situated for walking on the edge of the Yorkshire Dales National Park, with Embsay and Bolton Abbey Steam Railway line nearby. A regular outlet for Westons cider. (214)P

Filey

Bonhommes Bar 🏆

Royal Crescent Court, The Crescent, YO14 9JH
🕐 11 (12 winter)-midnight (1am Fri & Sat); 12-midnight Sun
☎ (01723) 514054
East Coast Bonhomme Richard; guest beers Ⓗ
Situated just off the fine Victorian Royal Crescent Hotel complex, its present name celebrates John Paul Jones, father of the American Navy. His ship, the Bonhomme Richard, was involved in a battle off nearby Flamborough Head during the War of Independence. Five handpumps serve two East Coast beers plus three rotating guests. A fun quiz is held on Saturday, with a main quiz on Sunday. Local CAMRA Rural Pub of the Year 2008 and runner up 2007. ≠🚌●

Flaxton

Blacksmith's Arms

YO60 7RJ (1 mile from A64, opp York Lane Junction) SE678624
🕐 12-2 Thu & Fri, 6-11; closed Mon; 12-3, 6-10.30 Sun
☎ (01904) 468210 🌐 blacksmithsarmsflaxton.co.uk
Black Sheep Best Bitter; Taylor Landlord; Theakston Best Bitter; York Guzzler; guest beer Ⓗ
Family owned and run village pub. The L-shaped main bar has a dining room and a snug off to one side. Four regular ales, all Yorkshire brewed, are served, together with an occasional guest on a fifth pump. The snug has a Yorkshire dartboard (doubles only, no trebles) for darts matches. A welcoming real fire warms the bar in winter months and good food is served evenings and at Sunday lunchtime. ♨🛏◐♣P

Fulford

Saddle Inn

Main Street, YO10 4PJ (A19 2 miles S of York)
🕐 11.30-4, 6.30-midnight; 11.30-midnight Fri & Sat
☎ (01904) 633317
Banks's Bitter; Camerons Bitter; guest beers Ⓗ
A prominent 150-year-old pub on a main road into York, with a comfortable L-shaped lounge and an adjacent dining area where children are welcome. The good-value food is a good accompaniment to the best selection of beers in this part of York. The sports TV, darts and pool are also a draw, as is the unusual petanque terrain in the attractive rear garden, which has open sessions for visitors. ♨♘❀🛏◐🚌(415)♣P⚐

Giggleswick

Black Horse Hotel

Church Street, BD24 0BE (next to church)
🕐 12-2 (not Mon), 5.30-11; 12-11 Sat; 12-10.30 Sun
☎ (01729) 822506
Taylor Golden Best, Landlord; Tetley Bitter; guest beer Ⓗ
Delightful cosy village local close to Giggleswick School. The frontage is interesting architecturally for its Gothic style and fine stained glass windows. Inside there is a long L-shaped bar and a separate restaurant with wood panelling and shelves that are adorned with highly polished traditional brasses. The pub has a well-deserved reputation for excellent home-cooked meals and good value accommodation. ❀🛏◐🚌(580)♣P⚐

Hart's Head Hotel

Belle Hill, BD24 0BA (on B6480 ½ mile N of Settle)
🕐 12-2.30 (not Thu), 5.30-11; 11-11 Sat; 12-10.30 Sun
☎ (01729) 822086 🌐 hartsheadhotel.co.uk
Copper Dragon Golden Pippin; Taylor Landlord; Tetley Bitter; guest beers Ⓗ
A warm welcome is assured at this 18th-century coaching inn. The open-plan bar retains a multi-room feel while the ever-changing guest beers are often sourced from local micro-breweries. Freshly-prepared meals from a varied menu use local ingredients. There is a full size snooker table in the refurbished cellar and an excellent children's play area in the beer garden. Excellent value en-suite accommodation makes the pub an ideal base to explore the Dales. ♨❀🛏◐⊞♿🚌(580)♣P⚐

Gilling West

White Swan Inn

51 High Street, DL10 5JG (2 miles W of Scotch Corner, off A66)
🕐 12-11 (10.30 Sun)
☎ (01748) 821123
Black Sheep Best Bitter; John Smith's Bitter; guest beers Ⓗ
Friendly 17th-century country inn with an open-plan bar with real fire and a dining room offering an extensive menu. This free house sources guest beers from local and national micro-breweries. The bar's beams are covered in bank notes, old and new. The beer garden has tables, chairs and sunshades, and features a collection of unusual objects. There is live acoustic music on alternate Wednesdays, plus local bands at Gilling Gig hosted monthly on Fridays (www.gillinggig.com). ♨Q❀◐⛺🚌(29)♣⚐

Glaisdale

Arncliffe Arms

1 Arncliffe Terrace, YO21 2QL
🕐 12-11 summer; 12-2 (Friday only), 5-11 winter; 12-11 Sat & Sun
☎ (01947) 897555 🌐 arncliffearms.co.uk
Copper Dragon Golden Pippin; guest beers Ⓗ
In a scenic location close to the River Esk and Beggars Bridge, the pub is popular with both locals and holidaymakers. Two guest beers are sourced from local micro-breweries, while upmarket restaurant meals and substantial bar food are sourced from local produce wherever possible. Friday evening features a happy hour. Children are welcome until 9pm. An excellent pub website gives details of a number of circular walks, together with details of the Esk Valley and NYMR train services. Accommodation is in four bedrooms. Dog friendly. ♨Q❀🛏◐≠🚌(99)♣P

Great Heck

Bay Horse

Main Street, DN14 0BE (follow signs from A19)
🕐 12-2, 5-11; 12-11 Sat; closed Mon; 12-10.30 Sun
☎ (01977) 661125
Old Mill Bitter, seasonal beers Ⓗ
An outlet for the local Old Mill Brewery, the pub was converted from cottages some years ago. Although open plan, it has distinct areas including a lounge bar and a raised dining area. An open fire, exposed beams and a display of brasses add traditional character. Excellent home-cooked meals

are served from an extensive menu. Steaks and Sunday roasts are sourced from local farmers. A rear patio is ideal for warm weather. Thursday is quiz night, followed by supper. ⛫❀◑♿♣P⚟

Grinton

Bridge Inn

DL11 6HH (on B6270, 1 mile E of Reeth)
⏲ 12-midnight (1am Fri & Sat); 12-11 Sun
☎ (01748) 884224
Jennings Dark Mild, Cumberland Ale, Cocker Hoop, guest ale Ⓗ
Close to the River Swale beneath the towering Fremington Edge, this carefully renovated old inn retains its traditional character, with a wood-panelled lounge, restaurant and downstairs games room. Food prepared from seasonal produce is served until 9pm daily. Families and pets are welcome but mobile phones are not, and their use incurs a fine. Thursday is musicians' night and the pub hosts mini beer festivals in March and October. ⛫❀◑♿♣P⚟(30)♣P⚟

Grosmont

Crossing Club

Co-operative Building, Front Street, YO22 5QE (opp NYMR car park)
⏲ 8-11 (closed Mon winter)
☎ (01947) 895040
Beer range varies Ⓗ
Directly opposite the NYMR and Esk Valley railway stations, this railway-themed club was converted by volunteers from the Co-operative store's upstairs delivery bay. Five busy handpumps, one usually from Wold Top, have served more than 600 different beers during the club's nine-year existence. Card-carrying CAMRA members are made most welcome. Access is through the ground level glass door (ring the bell). A summer beer festival is held and beer is also supplied for the Music Train that runs on Friday evenings during the summer. Q⇌▣(99)♣

Station Tavern

YO22 5PA (next to NYMR level crossing)
⏲ 11.30 (7 winter)-midnight; 12-11.30 (12-3, 7-11.30 winter) Sun
☎ (01947) 895060 🌐 stationtavern-grosmont.co.uk
Black Sheep Best Bitter; Camerons Strongarm; John Smith's Bitter Ⓗ
Built in 1836, this welcoming family-run pub has a main bar and a separate family room. It offers a good starting point for exploring the surrounding countryside, with both NYMR and Esk Valley railway stations literally next door. Note that it is closed winter afternoons, except during NYMR steam train galas and when the pub is busy with coast-to-coast walkers contemplating the final, or the first, 24 kilometres. Bar food is served at lunchtimes, while packed lunches and evening meals are also available.
⛫Q❀◑♿⇌▣(99)♣P⚟

Hampsthwaite

Joiners Arms

High Street, HG3 2EU (off A59)
⏲ 12-2, 5-11; 12-11 Sat & Sun
☎ (01423) 771673
Rudgate Viking; Tetley Bitter Ⓗ
On entering this popular village local, visitors are presented with a traditional choice of tap room or lounge, but behind the bar these are linked by an unusual snug with stone floor and vaulted ceiling, which was once the cellar. The lounge features an inglenook fireplace and leads to an attractive dining room adorned with a collection of rare gravy boats. Here food is served Wednesday to Saturday evenings, although bar meals are available every lunchtime. Q◑▣(24)P

Harrogate

Coach & Horses

16 West Park, HG1 1BJ (opp The Stray)
⏲ 11-11; 12-10.30 Sun
☎ (01423) 568371 🌐 thecoachandhorses.net
Copper Dragon Golden Pippin; Daleside Bitter; Taylor Landlord; Tetley Bitter; guest beers Ⓗ
A central bar is surrounded by snugs and alcoves, creating a cosy atmosphere. Excellent meals are served at lunchtime and there are frequent themed food evenings. Many of these, together with a Sunday night quiz, raise money for a local children's hospice. Tetley's Bitter and Taylor Landlord are always available, with three other beers sourced from local breweries. A few tables and chairs are placed outside for smokers. Window boxes provide year-round colour, with a quite spectacular display in summer. Q◑⇌▣

Empress

10 Church Square, HG1 4SP (near roundabout at jct of Wetherby & Knaresborough roads)
⏲ 11.30 (12 Sun)-11.30
☎ (01423) 567629
Daleside Bitter; John Smith's Bitter; Tetley Bitter; guest beer Ⓗ
Situated in High Harrogate, the oldest area of this spa town. A central entrance lobby separates the pool table area from the comfortable lounge with tropical fish tank. Guest beers usually include another from the Daleside list. Good food is served every lunchtime. The large upstairs room, overlooking the famous Stray, can be hired for parties and meetings. In the summer rugs are provided for sitting out on The Stray. ◖⇌▣♣

Hales Bar ✔

1-3 Crescent Road, HG1 2RS
⏲ 12-midnight (1am Thu-Sat)
☎ (01423) 725570 🌐 halesbar.co.uk
Daleside Special Bitter; Draught Bass; Taylor Landlord; guest beers Ⓗ
Harrogate's oldest inn, this is on CAMRA's Regional Inventory. It has two rooms – the lounge has a Victorian-style interior with gas lighting over the bar, stuffed birds and old brewery prints and mirrors. There are six handpumps, three serving a changing range of guest beers usually including at least one from Daleside. The pub prides itself on its outdoor floral displays in season. Lunchtime food only. ◑♿⇌▣♣

Old Bell Tavern ✔

6 Royal Parade, HG1 2SZ (500m W of A61)
⏲ 12-11 (10.30 Sun)
☎ (01423) 507930
Black Sheep Best Bitter; Theakston Best Bitter; guest beers Ⓗ
The pub opened in 1999 on the site of the Blue Bell Inn which closed in 1815 and was later demolished. It was expanded in 2001 into the

former Farrah's toffee shop and plenty of Farrah memorabilia is still on show. Guest ales always include Rooster's and Timothy Taylor. A mild is always available as well as a good range of draught and bottled beers. Excellent quality bar food is served every day and a separate upstairs restaurant opens each evening except Sunday. Q

Tap & Spile

Tower Street, HG1 1HS (100m E of A61)
11.30-11; 12-10.30 Sun
(01423) 526785
Fuller's London Pride; Rooster's Yankee; Theakston Old Peculier; guest beers H
Quality ale house with a central bar linking three drinking areas, wood panelling and bare stone walls displaying many photographs of old Harrogate. This well-established pub is popular with all age groups and hosts a folk music session on Tuesday and rock music on Thursday. A quiz is held on Monday evening and darts is played on alternate Tuesdays and Wednesdays. Some outdoor seating is provided. Many of the guest beers are from local brewers.

Winter Gardens

4 Royal Baths, HG1 2WH
9-midnight (1am Fri & Sat)
(01423) 887010
Marston's Burton Bitter, Pedigree; guest beers H
Magnificently recreated main hall of the Victorian Royal Bath Complex, with Harrogate Turkish Baths next door. At least five guest beers are always available at reasonable prices, and a comprehensive range of bottled beers is also stocked. Regular mini beer festivals are hosted. Good food is served all day. Children are welcome until 9pm on weekdays.

Hawes

Fountain Hotel

Market Place, DL8 3RD
11.30-midnight
(01969) 667206 fountainhawes.co.uk
Black Sheep Best Bitter, Ale, Riggwelter; John Smith's Bitter; Theakston Best Bitter; guest beer H
Hawes is the capital of Upper Wensleydale, home to the famous Wensleydale Cheese – the town's creamery, ropeworks and Dales Countryside Museum are all worth a visit. Popular with walkers and anglers, this busy family-run hotel offers a good array of local beers and is particularly busy on Tuesday, when the auction mart and street market operate. The large single-room interior is divided into two areas: the bar to the left and the dining area to the right, where food is served daily, lunchtime and evening.
(156,157)P

Helwith Bridge

Helwith Bridge

BD24 0EH (off B6479, across the river) SD810695
2.30 (12 Fri & Sat)-midnight
(01729) 860220 helwithbridge.com
Caledonian Deuchars IPA, 80 Shilling; Greene King Old Speckled Hen; John Smith's Bitter; Theakston Bitter; Wells Bombardier; guest beers H
The tiny hamlet of Helwith Bridge lies in the shadow of Pen-y-ghent and is a mecca for walkers, climbers and cavers. Despite its relative isolation, the pub is a welcoming, no-frills, thriving community local, run with warmth and a sense of humour. Railway artefacts and humorous material clutter the walls and ceiling. Bar snacks are on offer over and above the main menu times. Bunkhouse accommodation and limited camping facilities are available. The house beer is from Three Peaks Brewery. Q(581,B1)P

High Leven

Fox Covert

Low Lane, TS15 9JW (on A1044, 3 km E of Yarm)
11.30-11 (midnight Fri & Sat); 12-11 Sun
(01642) 760033 thefoxcovert.com
Caledonian Deuchars IPA; Theakston Old Peculier H
Previous CAMRA Pub of the Season award winner, this popular, long-established and uniquely-named inn has been in the same family for more than 20 years. Originally a farmhouse, the pub was built in the traditional longhouse style, with whitewashed walls and a pantiled roof. Inside it is warm and cosy, with two open fires and two drinking areas offering superbly-kept beers. The pub is noted for its food, served all day every day. Conference facilities are available. (507)P

Hinderwell

Brown Cow

55 High Street, TS13 5ET (on A174)
11 (12 Sun)-1am
(01947) 840694
Beer range varies H
Between the moors and the coast, this family-run 2008 CAMRA Pub of the Season award winner has a strong local following, as well as attracting holiday visitors. Two busy handpumps serve weaker beers during the week and stronger beers at weekends. The pub supports darts teams, charity quiz nights, dominoes and whist drives. Smokers are well accommodated. Children and dogs are welcome. Snacks are always available, in addition to lunchtime and evening meals. There is a separate pool room. Accommodation is in three letting bedrooms. (56)P

Hutton Rudby

King's Head

36 North Side, TS15 0DA
12-11.30 (12.30am Fri & Sat); 12-11.30 Sun
(01642) 700342
Camerons Strongarm; Jennings Cockerhoop, Cumberland Ale; guest beers H
Set in a beautiful village, this CAMRA Pub of the Season 2008 award winner is a traditional local with a main bar plus a snug where children are welcome. Five handpumps include two guests. Happy hour on Friday has become a 20-year-old tradition for some. Tapas are served all day, while themed food nights are held regularly. Friendly locals and real fires, together with monthly jazz/blues nights and a Tuesday night quiz, all add to the ambience. Outside is a sheltered, walled beer garden complete with TV. (82)

Kirby Hill

Shoulder of Mutton

DL11 7JH (2½ miles from A66, 4 miles NW of Richmond)

12-3 (Sat only), 6-11.30; 12-3, 6-11 Sun
(01748) 822772 shoulderofmutton.net
Black Sheep Best Bitter; Daleside Bitter; guest beers
Ivy-fronted country inn in a beautiful hillside setting overlooking Lower Teesdale and the ruins of Ravensworth Castle. The pub has an opened-out front bar that links the lounge with a cosy restaurant to the rear. Three guest beers are chosen by the pub's regulars and live music is performed every Monday. A popular pub for walkers, there are five en-suite guest bedrooms available, with meals served Wednesday to Sunday, although the bar area remains for drinkers. QP

Kirk Smeaton

Shoulder of Mutton
Main Street, WF8 3JY
12-2, 6-midnight; 12-1am Fri & Sat; winter hours vary; 12-midnight Sun
(01977) 620348
Black Sheep Best Bitter; guest beer
Traditional village inn offering excellent beers sourced directly from independent breweries. This Doncaster CAMRA District Pub of the Year 2007 comprises a large lounge with open fires and a cosy dark-panelled snug. Outside is a spacious beer garden complete with covered and heated shelter for smokers. Situated near the Went Valley and Brockadale Nature Reserve, this attractive pub is popular with walkers as well as the local community. Ample parking is provided. Quiz night is Tuesday. (409)P

Kirkby Malham

Victoria Inn
BD23 4BS
7 (12 Fri-Sun)-11
(01729) 830499
Bowland Sawley Tempted; Taylor Golden Best, Landlord; Tetley Bitter
Village pub built in 1840 close to a magnificent parish church, popular with both locals and visitors to the nearby tourist honeypot of Malham. The large hostelry has a lounge bar at the front, a tap room at the back and a separate dining room. Outside is a garden at the rear and a patio area by the front door. An extensive range of meals is served, except on Monday. The pub opens at weekday lunchtimes during the holiday season. (210)P

Kirkby Overblow

Shoulder of Mutton
Main Street, HG3 1HD
11.30-3, 6-11; 12-11.30 Sun
(01423) 871205 shoulderatkirkbyoverblow.com
Black Sheep Best Bitter; Taylor Landlord; Tetley Bitter; guest beers
A long-established village hostelry that has gained an enviable reputation for good food. The L-shaped bar covers two servery areas, with welcoming real fires to greet visitors. The chef/proprietor is a real ale enthusiast and has won awards for the quality of his beer. The guest ales are served in special glasses. A converted outbuilding, due to open in Spring 2009, will house a village store. QP

Kirklevington

Crown
Thirsk Road, TS15 9LT (on A67, close to A19 Crathorne jct)
12-11.30 (11 Sun)
(01642) 780044
Black Sheep Best Bitter; John Smith's Magnet
It is hard to believe that this was once a run-down Whitbread pub with few customers. Transformed by the enthusiastic licensee, this cosy village local, which has now featured in the Guide for 10 consecutive years, is warmed throughout the winter by roaring fires. Good-value home-cooked food is served all day (not Sun eve), using locally-sourced produce where possible, and often prepared by the landlady herself. Booking is essential on Sunday lunchtime to avoid disappointment. Q(507)P

Knaresborough

Blind Jack's
18a Market Place, HG5 8AL
4 (5.30 Mon; 3 Fri)-11; 12-11 Sat; 12-10.30 Sun
(01423) 869148 blindjacks.villagebrewer.co.uk
Black Sheep Best Bitter; Taylor Landlord; guest beers
Georgian building with bare brick walls, wooden floorboards and dark wood panelling. This vibrant, award-winning ale house provides a focal point for both locals and the many visitors who appreciate its excellent selection of beers, cosy ambience and lively banter. The ever-changing guest beers often include a Rooster's product, and a mild is usually available. Q(100,101,102)

George & Dragon
9 Briggate, HG5 8BQ (next to Holy Trinity church)
5-11 (midnight Fri); 12-midnight Sat & Sun
(01423) 862792
John Smith's Bitter; guest beers
Traditional local known as the Top House because of its location at the brow of a steep hill. A central bar divides the open plan interior. Up to four guest beers are available, two in quieter times. Hoppy beers are favoured here, with Daleside Blonde, beers from Yorkshire Dales Brewery and Moorhouses featuring regularly. This is a rugby pub, with big games screened live. It also boasts two pool and darts teams. Sunday lunches are served 12-3pm. Excellent B&B. Dogs welcome. P

Mitre Hotel
4 Station Road, HG5 9AA (opp railway station)
12-11
(01423) 868948 themitreinn.co.uk
Black Sheep Ale; Copper Dragon Golden Pippin; Thwaites Wainwright; guest beers
Winner of local CAMRA winter/spring 2008 Pub of the Season, the Mitre comprises a split level lounge, side function room, brasserie/restaurant and an outside drinking area. Five guest ales include a dark beer, rotating beers from the Rooster's/Outlaw label, Timothy Taylor and mainly local brews. Look out for the speciality bottled beer menu, plus some foreign beers also available on draught. Live acoustic music is played on Sunday evening. Dogs (and some of their owners) are welcome.

Langdale End

Moorcock Inn

YO13 0BN SE938912

11-2, 6.30-11; closed Mon; 12-3, 6.30-10.30 Sun

☎ (01723) 882268

Beer range varies Ⓗ/Ⓖ

Sympathetically restored some years ago, the pub is situated in the picturesque hamlet of Langdale End, near the end of the Dalby Forest Drive. The beers are usually from York, Wold Top and Slaters breweries, and served through a hatch to both bars. Bar meals, prepared from local produce, include a popular steak pie. Outside, there is a grassy area for drinking and/or smoking. Winter opening hours may vary, so ring to check.
⛫Q❀◑▲♣P⁄–

Lastingham

Blacksmith's Arms

Front Street, YO62 6TL (4 miles N of A170 between Helmsley and Pickering) SE728904

12 (5 Tue)-11

☎ (01751) 417247 🌐 blacksmithslastingham.co.uk

Theakston Best Bitter; guest beers Ⓗ

Twice winner of York CAMRA Country Pub of the Season, this pretty old stone inn is in a conservation village. Enter through a flagged hallway into the cosy front bar. The adjoining room is served by a hatch. A snug and two dining rooms complete the interior, but do not miss the secluded rear beer garden. Food is served lunchtime and evening every day except Tuesday lunch in winter. This pub is popular with walkers and locals alike.
⛫Q❀🛏◑

Lealholm

Board Inn

Village Green, YO21 2AJ (by River Esk)

9-midnight (2am Fri & Sat)

☎ (01947) 897279 🌐 theboardinn.com

Black Sheep Best Bitter; Camerons Strongarm; guest beers Ⓗ

This family-run, picturesque and increasingly popular 17th-century free house has four handpumps, three ciders and a huge selection of whiskies. Breakfasts are served from 9am, while the restaurant stays open all day. A wide-ranging chalkboard menu reflects the seasons, offering real food virtually all sourced from less than 500m from the pub. And how many licensees still air-cure their own hams, keep 45 laying hens and their own herd of prime beef, as well as having local fishing rights? The riverside patio is used for occasional 12-cask beer festivals. Five letting bedrooms.
⛫Q♘❀🛏◑⊟♿▲⇌🚌(99)♣●P⁄–

Leavening

Jolly Farmer

Main Street, YO17 9SA SE785631

7 (6 Fri)-midnight; 12-midnight Sat & Sun

☎ (01653) 658276

Black Sheep Best Bitter; Taylor Landlord; Tetley Bitter; guest beers Ⓗ

This 17th-century pub is on the edge of the Yorkshire Wolds between York and Malton. The multi-room interior has been extended but still retains a cosiness in two small bars, a family room and dining rooms. Former York CAMRA Pub of the Year, the availability of varied guest beers from independent breweries and an annual beer festival make this an essential visit. The extensive menu includes locally-caught game dishes in season.
⛫♘◑♿♣P⁄–⊓

Long Preston

Maypole Inn

Main Street, BD23 4PH

11-2.30, 6-midnight; 11-midnight Sat; 12-11 Sun

☎ (01729) 840219 🌐 maypole.co.uk

Moorhouses Premier Bitter; Taylor Landlord; guest beers Ⓗ

Situated adjacent to the village green and eponymous maypole, the welcoming licensees have been in charge of this friendly local for 25 years. The cosy lounge displays old photographs of the village and surrounding area and a list of all the licensees since 1695. Good-quality, home-cooked food from locally-sourced suppliers can be enjoyed in the lounge or dining room. Westons cider is served in summer. Winner of Keighley and Craven CAMRA Pub of the Season Spring 2009.
⛫Q❀🛏◑⊟▲⇌🚌(580)♣P⁄–

Low Worsall

Ship

TS15 9PH

12-11 (10.30 Sun)

☎ (01642) 780314

Greene King Old Speckled Hen; guest beers Ⓗ

Situated beside the old Richmond to Yarm turnpike and near a disused quay that marks the centuries-old limit of navigation for commercial boats on the River Tees. Guest beers are usually premium bitters and the pub is known for the quality of its good value food, served all day every day. Smaller portions are available for those unable to tackle the impressively large helpings. The pub is child friendly, with a small play area in the garden.
Q❀◑♿P⁄–

Malton

Crown Hotel (Suddaby's)

12 Wheelgate, YO17 7HP

11-11 (11.30 Fri & Sat); 12-10.45 Sun

☎ (01653) 692038 🌐 suddabys.co.uk

Black Sheep Best Bitter; John Smith's Bitter; Suddaby's Double Chance, seasonal beers; Theakston Best Bitter; guest beers Ⓗ

Grade II-listed, market town-centre pub that has been in the same family for 138 years. No brewing now takes place on the premises – Suddaby's beers are specially brewed by Brown Cow. Beer festivals are held at Easter, summer and Christmas. The on-site shop stocks over 200 different beers, specialising in Belgian and German brews and British micro-breweries, wine and breweriana. A covered smoking patio is at the rear. Accommodation includes two en-suite family rooms, with a small discount available for CAMRA members. ⛫Q❀🛏▲⇌🚌♣P⁄–

Manfield

Crown Inn

Vicars Lane, DL2 2RF (500m from B6275)

5 (12 Sat)-11.30; 12-11 Sun

☎ (01325) 374243 🌐 crowninn.villagebrewer.co.uk

Village White Boar, Seasonabull; guest beers Ⓗ
Yorkshire CAMRA Pub of the Year 2005 and a regular local award winner, this attractive 18th-century pub sits in a quiet village. It has two bars, a games room and a trellised heated smoking area. A mix of locals and visitors creates a friendly atmosphere. Up to six guest beers come from micro-breweries countrywide, along with up to two ciders or perries. Three beer festivals and a cider festival are held annually. Dogs are welcome in this rural gem. Q(29)P

Masham

Black Sheep Brewery Visitors Centre ✓

Wellgarth, HG4 4EN
10-4.30 (11 Thu-Sat)
☎ (01765) 680101 blacksheepbrewery.com
Black Sheep Best Bitter, Ale, Riggwelter Ⓗ
This popular tourist attraction is housed in the spacious former maltings. As well as offering the opportunity to sample the breweries products at the 'Baaar', there is a high quality cafe/bistro serving snacks and full meals with an emphasis on local ingredients. A 'sheepy' shop stocks the bottled product and Black Sheep souvenirs. Visitors can book a 'shepherded' tour of the brewery. A small garden overlooks scenic lower Wensleydale and the River Ure. QP

White Bear ✓

12 Crosshills, HG4 4EN (follow brown tourist signs on A6108)
12-11 (10.30 Sun)
☎ (01765) 689319 thewhitebearhotel.co.uk
Caledonian Deuchars IPA; Theakston Best Bitter, Black Bull Bitter, XB, Old Peculier; guest beers Ⓗ
This recently refurbished brewery tap has been extended into the old brewery offices to make extra room for diners, as well as adding 14 bedrooms and conference facilities. Although the changes have cost £1.5m, the pub has not lost any of its charm as an award-winning hostelry. It is a great favourite with the locals, and directors and staff from the Theakston Brewery too. P

Middlesbrough

Star

14 Southfield Road, TS1 3BX
11-11 (1am Fri & Sat); 12-11 Sun
☎ (01642) 245307 sjf.co.uk
Beer range varies Ⓗ
This large, popular pub opposite the university campus has recently been sympathetically modernised. With a licensee dedicated to promoting a wide variety of real ales, four beers are usually available, together with Westons Old Rosie cider. A contemporary, relaxed atmosphere prevails, with sofas and easy chairs adding to the ambience. The pub attracts a wide-ranging clientele and can get extremely busy at weekends. Good value pub food is on offer. The smoking area is heated and covered.

Newton-on-Ouse

Dawnay Arms

YO30 2BR SE510601
12-2.30, 6-11; 12-11 Sat; closed Mon; 12-10 Sun
☎ (01347) 848345 thedawnayatnewton.co.uk
Black Sheep Best Bitter; Hambleton Bitter; Taylor Golden Best; guest beers Ⓗ
Smartly refurbished pub in an attractive riverside village serving four beers from Yorkshire breweries and gastro-style high quality food using local ingredients where possible. The pub has a rustic feel with wooden furniture, flagstone and wood floors, exposed brickwork around the fireplaces and kitchen implements on the walls and ceiling. The large garden leads to a landing stage on the River Ouse. Q(29)P

Northallerton

Standard

24 High Street, DL7 8EE (on A167 N of town centre)
12-2.30, 5-midnight; 12-midnight Fri-Sun
☎ (01609) 772719
Caledonian Deuchars IPA; John Smith's Bitter; Marston's Pedigree; guest beers Ⓗ
On the A167 just north of the town centre, and named after the nearby Battle of the Standard of 1138, this a real community pub which offers good value food every day. The beer garden features a Jet Provost aircraft, now restored for display. The opened-out stone-flagged bar retains distinct drinking areas and is the unofficial home of the local rugby league club. Spring bank holiday sees an annual beer festival.

Station Hotel

2 Boroughbridge Road, Romanby, DL7 8AN (outside railway station)
12-2 (3 Sat), 5-11; 12-3, 7-10.30 Sun
☎ (01609) 772053
Caledonian Deuchars IPA; Tetley Bitter; guest beer Ⓗ
An imposing Edwardian building prominently located near the railway station. Previously known as the Railway Hotel, as can be seen from the impressive etched windows. Other period features include a lovely tiled entrance hall, while the bar has been sympathetically renovated. Ten rooms are available for accommodation and food is available every evening except Sunday, when there is a regular quiz night. Sunday lunch is also very popular. P

Tithe Bar & Brasserie ✓

2 Friarage Street, DL6 1DP
12-11 (midnight Fri & Sat)
☎ (01609) 778482 markettowntaverns.co.uk
Taylor Landlord; guest beers Ⓗ
A popular bar of character just off the town's busy High Street, this beacon for real ale is part of the renowned Market Town Taverns chain and strongly committed to cask beer. The six ales usually include guests from the Yorkshire area and there is also a fine array of foreign beers. A multi CAMRA award winner, the bar has the feel of a continental beer café downstairs, with good value bar meals, and a brasserie upstairs, open evenings Tuesday-Saturday. Q

Old Malton

Royal Oak

47 Town Street, YO17 7HB (400m off A64 Malton bypass)
5-midnight; 12-1am Fri & Sat; closed Mon Jan & Feb; 12-midnight Sun
☎ (01653) 699334

Tetley Bitter; York Guzzler; guest beers Ⓗ
Friendly and popular pub set in a picturesque village close to the Eden Camp Military Museum. A welcoming atmosphere prevails. There is a cosy snug at the front, with a larger rear room leading to an extensive beer garden with a covered smoking area. Guest beers are usually from York, Moorhouses and Wold Top. Traditional meals featuring locally-sourced produce are served weekend lunchtimes, Thursday night is pie night. Functions can be catered for. Yorkshire Coastliner buses stops outside. Local CAMRA Pub of the Season. ⛼Q❀◖Å⇌🚌(843)♣P⁻

Osmotherley

Golden Lion

6 West End, DL6 3AA (1 mile off A19 at A684 jct)
⏲ 12-3 (not Mon & Tue), 6-11; 12-midnight Sat; 12-10.30 Sun
☎ (01609) 883526 🌐 goldenlionosmotherley.co.uk
Taylor Best Bitter, Landlord; guest beers Ⓗ
Just inside the National Park and handy for the A19, this popular centre for walking on the nearby moors is the start of the famous Lyke Wake Walk and there is a Youth Hostel nearby. Many customers are diners enjoying the fine food but drinkers are equally welcome and there is a beer festival each November. Mirrors make the simple but attractive interior appear larger than it is and there are magnificent views from the tables outside. Guest ales are sourced from local Yorkshire breweries. ⛼❀🛏◖◗Å🚌(80,89)

Pickering

Rose

Bridge Street, YO18 8DT (opp Beck Isle Museum)
⏲ 12-midnight (1am Fri & Sat)
☎ (01751) 475366
Taylor Landlord; Tetley Bitter; guest beers Ⓗ
A friendly welcome awaits locals and visitors to this comfortable pub. It has been fully refurbished since the 2007 floods but retains its charm with low beams and a cast iron stove alongside modern furniture. The food is locally sourced. Children are welcome until 8pm. There is a large drinking area next to the attractive Pickering Beck. The pub is situated very close to the Beck Isle Museum and North York Moors steam railway station, and the market and shops are nearby.
⛼❀◖◗⇌🚌(128)♣P⁻

Pickhill

Nag's Head

YO7 4JG (1 mile off A1 just N of jct with B6261 Masham-Thirsk road) SE345833
⏲ 11 (12 Sun)-11
☎ (01845) 567391 🌐 nagsheadpickhill.co.uk
Black Sheep Best Bitter; Theakston Black Bull; guest beers Ⓗ
Renowned both for its food and allegiance to locally-brewed beers, this long-standing entry in the Guide finds the right balance between a village pub and dining establishment and is also a handy stopping-off point from the busy A1. It offers a warm, friendly and relaxed atmosphere, as well as a splendid range of food served in the restaurant, lounge and bar. There is also high class accommodation, making this an ideal base to explore the Yorkshire Moors and Dales or take in the local race meetings. ⛼Q❀🛏◖◗⊟Å♣P⁻

Picton

Station

TS15 0AE (at level crossing on Kirklevington-Picton road)
⏲ 11-2.30 Sat, 6-11; 11-11.30 Sun
☎ (01642) 700067
John Smith's Magnet Ⓗ
Situated beside the Middlesbrough to York railway, this remote pub is well worth the journey, though sadly not by train as the adjacent station was closed in the 1960s. One superb real ale is served alongside an impressive and varied food menu, using local produce where possible. The portions are of such a size that going home hungry is not an option. Cool in the summer, warm and inviting in the winter, this is a pub for everyone. ⛼Q❀◖◗P

Pool in Wharfedale

Hunters Inn

Harrogate Road, LS21 2PS (on A658 between Otley and Harrogate)
⏲ 11-11; 12-10.30 Sun
☎ (0113) 2841090
Tetley Bitter; Theakston Best Bitter; guest beers Ⓗ
When you first enter this welcoming roadside pub, don't forget to check out the impressive range of up to nine cask ales which are shown on the board to the right. The pub has all the feel of a country lodge with a large single room incorporating a raised area with a real fire during colder months. Well-behaved children are allowed in the pub until 9pm, accompanied by an adult. ⛼❀◖🚌♣P⁻

Potto

Dog & Gun

2 Cooper Lane, DL6 3HQ
⏲ 12-3, 5.30-midnight; 12-midnight Sat; 12-11.30 Sun
☎ (01642) 700232 🌐 thedogandgunpotto.com
Black Sheep Best Bitter; guest beers Ⓗ
Recently refurbished, this large country ale house is under the stewardship of an enthusiastic licensee who is committed to providing only the very best food, drink and accommodation. Inside is a comfortable main bar, a classy restaurant and private dining rooms, as well as five luxury bedrooms and conference facilities. Friendly staff ensure that a welcoming, laid-back ambience prevails in a contemporary setting while outside, open terraces are ideal for summer drinking. Sunday lunches are served until 6pm. Card-carrying CAMRA members receive a 25% discount across the range of real ales. ⛼❀🛏◖◗♿P

Rawcliffe

Lysander Arms

Manor Lane, YO30 5TZ (opp Park & Ride site on A19 N) SE582550
⏲ 11-11 (12.30 Sat)
☎ (01904) 640845 🌐 lysanderarms.co.uk
John Smith's Bitter; Theakston Bitter; York Guzzler Ⓗ
A little gem hidden away at the end of a new housing estate, this new building replaces the original caravan site clubhouse. The pub still has a 10-pitch caravan site and is popular with Dutch and German caravanners. It offers good pub food and well-kept LocAle. The lounge is big enough to have two different sports showing on large screen TVs, or to leave a quiet area. Free Wi-Fi is available.
❀◖◗♿Å♣P⁻

Riccall

Greyhound Inn ✔

Main Street, YO19 6TE (A19 10 miles S of York) SE620380

⏲ 12-midnight (11.30 Sun)

☎ (01757) 249101 🌐 thegreyhoundriccall.co.uk

Black Sheep Best Bitter; John Smith's Bitter; Tetley Bitter; guest beer 🄷

A quiet village pub between Selby and York with a friendly welcome and enthusiastic guest beer policy. Home-made food produced by the landlord is available weekdays except Monday (lunchtime only Sat & Sun). Home to keen darts and dominoes teams, it also attracts cyclists and walkers using the York-Selby cycle path (note the old Cyclist's Touring Club emblem on the front). There is a large garden to the rear for summer meals and drinks. **♨Q❀⛟◐◑🚌♣P⚐**

Richmond

Ralph Fitz Randal ✔

6 Queens Road, DL10 4AE (on main Scotch Corner Rd)

⏲ 9am-midnight (1am Fri & Sat)

☎ (01748) 828080

Greene King Ruddles Bitter, Abbot; Marston's Pedigree; guest beers 🄷

Opening as a Wetherspoon's in 2002, this former post office is named after the 13th-century benefactor of the Friary, formerly located in the gardens opposite. Behind the 20th-century brick frontage is a spacious interior on three levels, with comfy seating in the front lounge area. The bar area below and, beyond that, a popular family area, all have large-screen sports TV. Up to seven guest beers showcase individual breweries and there are themed beer festivals. Food is served all day. **Q♘❀◐◑♿🚌●⚐**

Ripon

Magdalens

26 Princess Road, HG4 1HW

⏲ 4 (1 Tue & Wed)-midnight; 12-midnight Thu-Sun

☎ (01765) 604746

Caledonian Deuchars IPA; John Smith's Magnet; guest beers 🄷

A gem tucked away at the north end of the town, this proper community pub has a Ripon in Bloom award-winning beer garden and a large outdoor children's play area. As well as the two regular beers there are three ever-changing guests. Beer festivals are held in summer in a large marquee in the garden. **❀◐🚌♣P⚐**

One-Eyed Rat ✔

51 Allhallowgate, HG4 1LQ

⏲ 5 (12 Fri & Sat)-11; 12-10.30 Sun

☎ (01765) 607704 🌐 oneeyedrat.com

Black Sheep Best Bitter; guest beers 🄷

Characterful local situated in a terrace in one of the oldest parts of the city. With hops over the bar and a welcoming fire in winter, it has a warm, intimate feel. There are always six guest beers and a draught cider on handpump. A beer garden complete with a covered and heated smoking area is at the rear. Dogs are welcome. **♨Q❀⛺🚌♣●⚐**

Royal Oak ✔

36 Kirkgate, HG4 1PB (off Market Square)

⏲ 11-11 (midnight Fri & Sat); 12-10.30 Sun

☎ (01765) 602284 🌐 royaloakripon.co.uk

Taylor Golden Best, Best Bitter, Landlord 🄷

Although a listed building, this large and airy pub has had a total interior revamp to create a light and modern interior. Emphasis is placed on food and a large menu makes good use of locally-sourced produce. Meals are served lunchtimes and evenings (until 9pm) Monday to Saturday and 12-4pm Sunday. There are six en-suite bedrooms above the pub. **♨Q❀⛟◐◑🚌⚐**

Robin Hood's Bay

Victoria Hotel

Station Road, YO22 4RL (at top of cliff)

⏲ 12-11 Fri-Sun & summer; 12-2, 6-11 winter

☎ (01947) 880205 🌐 thevictoriahotelrobinhoodsbay.co.uk

Camerons Bitter, Strongarm; Daleside Old Leg Over; guest beers 🄷

A warm welcome awaits you at this impressive family-run 19th-century hotel, set in a superb location on the edge of the cliffs, overlooking the bay of this picturesque seaside resort. The large, busy and friendly bar, popular with regulars and visitors alike, serves six beers including three guests. A good value, highly regarded menu, including daily specials, is available lunchtimes and evenings (not winter Sun eve). Stunning views are afforded from the comfortable family room, restaurant and gardens. **♨Q♘❀⛟◐◑🚌(56,93)P🀫**

Saltburn-by-the-Sea

Saltburn Cricket, Bowls & Tennis Club

Marske Mill Lane, TS12 1HJ (next to leisure centre)

⏲ 8-midnight (1am Fri & Sat); 2-midnight Sat match days; 11.30-3, 8-midnight Sun

☎ (01287) 622761

Beer range varies 🄷

This private sports club, well supported by the local community, fields cricket, tennis and bowls teams, and acts as the watering hole for the local diving club. A spacious lounge can be divided for different functions and social events. The balcony, ideal for those lazy sunny afternoons, overlooks the cricket field. Two continually rotating beers are served. Casual visitors are made most welcome – no need to join the club. **❀♿⇌🚌(X4, 48)♣P⚐**

Saxton

Greyhound

Main Street, LS24 9PY (W of A162, 5 miles S of Tadcaster) SE475367

⏲ 11.30-3, 5.30-11; 11-11 Sat; 12-10.30 Sun

☎ (01937) 557202

Samuel Smith Old Brewery Bitter 🄷

This picturesque, Grade II-listed, 13th-century village inn nestles by the village church. It was originally a teasel barn and formerly listed in CAMRA's National Inventory for pubs with outstanding interiors. A low-ceilinged, stone-flagged corridor leads to a tiny bar. Real fires blaze in two of the three rooms in winter and the extensive collection of colourful plates and paraphernalia create a cosy atmosphere. The pub is popular with locals and walkers. **♨Q❀🀫**

Scarborough

Angel
46 North Street, YO11 1DF
11-midnight
(01723) 365504
John Smith's Bitter; Tetley Bitter; Wells Bombardier H
Friendly town-centre local, close to the main shopping area, with a single-room horseshoe bar displaying an excellent collection of saucy seaside postcards. An interest in sport and games is reflected in the impressive array of trophies won by various pub teams and the large-screen TVs used for sporting events. Occasional guest beers are added in summer. Note the Tardis-like quality of the surprisingly large and well appointed patio garden at the rear.

Cellars
35-37 Valley Road, YO11 2LX
12-midnight; 4-11 Mon & Tue winter; 12-10.30 Sun
(01723) 367158 scarborough-brialene.co.uk
Beer range varies H
Family-run pub converted from the cellars of an elegant Victorian house. The bar keeps six beers coming from Archers, Black Sheep and Durham breweries and guests mainly from Yorkshire micros. Excellent, good value, home-cooked food made with locally-sourced produce is served lunchtime and evening. Live music night is Saturday, with an open mike night on Wednesday. Beer festivals are an occasional feature. The patio gardens are popular for alfresco drinking. Children and dogs are welcome. P

Golden Ball
31 Sandside, YO11 1PG
11-11; 12-4, 7-11 winter; 12-10.30 Sun
(01723) 353899
Samuel Smith OBB H
Pub with striking mock-Tudor appearance situated on the seafront, with fabulous views from the Harbour Bar across the harbour to the lighthouse and South Bay. The only Sam Smith's pub in Scarborough, it is multi-roomed, with a family room and a popular summer garden. It becomes a cosy gem in winter, warmed by a real fire. Lunches are served all year round. Free of music, for those who prefer a quiet drink. Dogs are welcome.
Q

North Riding Hotel
161-163 North Marine Road, YO12 7HU
12-midnight (1am Fri & Sat)
(01723) 370004 northridinghotel.co.uk
Taylor Landlord; Tetley Bitter; York Guzzler; guest beers H
Friendly, popular, family-run pub voted local CAMRA Town Pub of the Year 2008 and 2006, located near the cricket ground and opposite Scarborough bowls centre on the North Bay. The pub has a public bar, a refurbished quiet lounge and an upstairs dining room serving home-cooked food. It stocks two or more guest beers from micro-breweries (Yorkshire Dales beers appear regularly), continental bottled beers, plus Edelweiss and Sierra Nevada on draught. Feature brewery weekends are held monthly. Quiz night is Thursday.
Q

Old Scalby Mills
Scalby Mills Road, YO12 6RP
11 (12 winter)-11
(01723) 500449
Copper Dragon Black Gold; Wold Top Premium; guest beers H
Popular seafront local, this building was originally a watermill but has seen many uses over the years – old photographs and prints chart its history. Admire the superb views of the North Bay from the sheltered patio or lounge. The Cleveland Way reaches the seafront here and there is a Sealife Centre nearby. Children are welcome in the lounge. Premium beer from the local Wold Top Brewery is only available here; guest ales invariably include a stout, porter or mild. Q (3A)

Scholars
Somerset Terrace, YO11 2PW
4.30 (12 Sat)-11; 12-10.30 Sun
(01723) 360084
Copper Dragon Golden Pippin; Hambleton Nightmare; Theakston Black Bull; guest beers H
A warm, friendly atmosphere prevails in this town centre pub located at the rear of the main shopping centre. It has a large front bar and a games room. Three handpumps serve rotating beers from Rooster's, Ossett and York breweries. Numerous screens show Sky and other major sporting events. Thursday is quiz night when 28 pints can be won, and free beer is also the prize for rolling dice on Monday, Tuesday, Wednesday and Sunday nights.

United Sports Bar
94-100 St Thomas Street, YO11 1DU
4-midnight; 12-1am Fri & Sat; 12-midnight Sun
(01723) 503350
John Smith's Bitter; Wells Bombardier; guest beers H
This former social club is now open to all, offering a warm welcome to locals and tourists alike. The comfortable bar is found on the first floor via a door opposite the YMCA stage entrance. The bar plays host to a number of indoor sports teams as well as a Sunday football team. Most major sports events are shown on TV. A quiz is held on Wednesday and live music is played on some Saturdays.

Valley
51 Valley Road, YO11 2LX
12-midnight (1am Thu-Sat)
(01723) 372593 valleybar.co.uk
Theakston Best Bitter; Wold Top Mars Magic; guest beers H
CAMRA National Cider Pub of the Year 2007 and local CAMRA Town Pub of the Year 2005 and 2007. This family-run multi-roomed pub has a popular cellar bar. Seven handpumps feature beers mainly from micro-breweries, plus eight real ciders and perries. A hundred different bottled Belgian beers and gluten-free bottled beers and lager are also stocked. The kitchen prepares freshly-cooked bar meals including fresh fish at very reasonable prices.

Skipton

Devonshire
Newmarket Street, BD23 2HR
9-midnight (1am Fri & Sat)
(01756) 692590
Greene King IPA, Abbot; Marston's Pedigree; guest beers H
Built in the 1870s, this establishment has an impressive period frontage, set back from the road with an open patio area. The interior has a large

main bar with several areas for drinking and an area predominantly used for dining off to the side. Note the Grade II-listed staircase to the toilets. The beer range is Wetherspoon's usuals, plus ales from local micros. ♔Q♉❀◐◑♿⇌🚌●

Narrow Boat ✔

38 Victoria Street, BD23 1JE

12-11

☎ (01756) 797922 🌐 markettowntaverns.co.uk

Black Sheep Best Bitter; Copper Dragon Best Bitter, Golden Pippin; Taylor Landlord; guest beers Ⓗ

Popular free house near the canal basin. The bar is furnished with old church pews and decorated with canal-themed murals, old brewery posters and mirrors. No piped music, jukebox or gaming machines disturb the conversation. Guest ales, mostly from northern independent breweries, always include a dark beer, and there is a good selection of continental bottled beers. Folk club is on Monday evening, live jazz on the first Tuesday of the month. Quiz night is Wednesday. Children under 14 are only admitted when dining. Well-behaved dogs welcome. Q❀◐◑⇌🚌⁵—

Snape

Castle Arms

DL8 2TB (off B6268 Bedale-Masham road)

12-3, 6-midnight (1am Thu-Sat)

☎ (01677) 470270 🌐 castlearmsinn.com

Banks's Bitter; Jennings Bitter; Marston's Pedigree; guest beer Ⓗ

Historic pub in a picturesque village and close to Snape Castle (no public access), home to Henry VIII's final wife, Catherine Parr. It is also handy for the beautiful Thorpe Perrow Arboretum, a mile away. An open fire dominates the cosy bar area with its stone-flagged floor, and locally-renowned food is served here and in the restaurant (except Sun eve winter). Nine letting rooms and a small caravan park to the rear add to a thriving local trade. ♔Q❀🛏◐◑Å♣P

Sneaton

Wilson Arms

Beacon Way, YO22 5HS (400m off B1416)

12-2 Sat, 6.30-11; closed Mon winter; 12-4.30, 6.30-11 (not winter eve) Sun

☎ (01947) 602552 🌐 thewilsonarms.co.uk

Black Sheep Best Bitter; John Smith's Bitter; guest beers Ⓗ

Historic Grade II-listed, 18th-century pub situated in a very quiet village just a couple of miles from Whitby and close to the Monks' Pathway, Sneaton Beacon and Beacon Farm, deservedly famous for its ice cream. A warm welcome is guaranteed in this single bar with beamed ceilings and roaring fires. Three handpulled beers, including a guest (usually from Timothy Taylor), and a fine selection of whiskies complement the excellent, traditional home-cooked meals. There is a pool room and seven letting bedrooms. Quiz night is Tuesday. ♔Q♉❀🛏◐◑♣P⁵—

Sowerby

Crown & Anchor

138 Front Street, YO7 1JN

12-midnight (1am Thu-Sat)

☎ (01845) 522448 🌐 crownandanchorsowerby.co.uk

John Smith's Bitter; guest beers Ⓗ

This enterprising and recently refurbished village local just outside Thirsk offers at least three cask guest ales, a range of continental beers and, in summer, real cider. Good no-nonsense food ranges from sandwiches and bar snacks to Sunday lunch with all the trimmings (booking advised). There is occasional live music, a beer garden and covered outdoor smoking area. An annual beer festival each September makes the most of the recently overhauled cellar. ❀◐◑⊟♿🚌♣P⁵—

Staithes

Captain Cook Inn

60 Staithes Lane, TS13 5AD (off A174, by village car park)

11-midnight

☎ (01947) 840200 🌐 captaincookinn.co.uk

Bank Top Bitter; guest beers Ⓗ

CAMRA multi award-winning pub, close to the site of the Staithes railway viaduct and Boulby Cliffs. Six ever-changing handpumps provide an eclectic mix of beer styles, including milds, porters and stouts. The house bitter, Bank Top, is brewed by Tower. The beer range extends to 12 handpumps during the pub's beer & sausage festivals, held to celebrate St George's Day/Jazz Festival, Lifeboat Week, Hallowe'en/Guy Fawkes and Winter Warmers/Pork Pie Week. Four letting bedrooms and a holiday cottage are available. ♔Q❀🛏◐◑🚌(56)♣P

Staxton

Hare & Hounds

Main Street, YO12 4TA

12-11.30

☎ (01944) 710243

Black Sheep Best Bitter; Stones Bitter; Theakston Old Peculier; guest beers Ⓗ

Imposing former coaching inn on the A64 – an excellent stopping-off point when travelling to the East Coast. The bar and lounge/dining area feature low beams and real fires. Guest beers are usually sourced from the Enterprise/SIBA scheme and often come from Wold Top and Copper Dragon breweries. Home-cooked meals are available all day every day, with seafood sourced from Flamborough a speciality in summer. There are large grassed drinking areas at the front and rear of the pub. ♔Q❀◐◑Å🚌P⁵—

Stokesley

Spread Eagle

39 High Street, TS9 5BL

11-1am; 12-12.30am Sun

☎ (01642) 710278

Camerons Strongarm; Marston's Pedigree; guest beers Ⓗ

A fine welcome is assured at this small, unspoilt market-town pub. Friendly regulars drink at one end and an open fire welcomes diners at the other. Excellent, good value home-cooked food, complete with details of where the food has been sourced, is served all day. Two interesting and stronger guest beers are always available. Children are welcome. A rear garden leads down to the tranquil River Leven, where over-fed ducks amuse children and adults alike. Tuesday is live music night. ♔Q❀◐◑Å🚌(29,81)⁵—

White Swan

1 West End, TS9 5BL
11.30 (12 Sun)-11
(01642) 710263 thecaptaincookbrewery.co.uk
Captain Cook Sunset, Slipway, Black Porter; Consett Ale Works White Hot, Red Dust; guest beers H
CAMRA Pub of the Year 2008, this traditional one-room 18th-century local has a single bar with seven handpumps. It is the brewery tap for both the prize-winning Captain Cook Brewery and Consett Ale Works. Two guest ales are also served. Well supported by the local community, the pub holds a quiz on Wednesday, while music nights are hosted monthly. A cheese and beer festival is held at Easter and a beer festival in October. Ploughman's lunches are served Wednesday to Saturday. Children are not allowed in the pub. (29,81)

Tadcaster

Angel & White Horse

23 Bridge Street, LS24 9AW
11-3, 5-11; 12-4, 7-11 Sat; 12-10.30 Sun
(01937) 835470
Samuel Smith OBB H
This old limestone coaching inn is a warm and welcoming town-centre pub, and the brewery tap for Samuel Smith, one of the oldest breweries in England. The interior is wood panelled with a log fire in the winter. A rear door leads to a courtyard with the brewery behind and, in front, the stables for the grey dray Shire horses which are still used to deliver beer to local hostelries. The bitter is pulled from wooden casks.

Terrington

Bay Horse Inn

Main Street, YO60 6PP SE668706
7-11 Tue (not winter); 12-3, 6.30 (6 Fri)-11 Wed & Thu; 12-11 Sat; closed Mon; 12-3 Sun
(01653) 648416
Beer range varies H
Welcoming village free house in the Howardian Hills, home of the Storyteller Brewery, with at least one beer available from the brewery's range, together with guests from micro-breweries. Excellent food made from local produce is served during all sessions. The pub features distinct areas for drinkers and diners and is ideally situated for refreshment when visiting local tourist attractions including Castle Howard and the Yorkshire Lavender Centre. Children and dogs are welcome. P

Thixendale

Cross Keys

YO17 9TG SE843610
12-3, 6-11; 12-3, 7-10.30 Sun
(01377) 288272
Jennings Bitter; Tetley Bitter; guest beer H
The village, dating from 1156, at the junction of many dry Wolds valleys, attracted monastic interest long before the many hikers on the Wolds Way. Owned by the same family for many years, the pub has a single bar with a real fire, interesting guest ales and good value simple food. Remote, but this traditional village local is well worth seeking out.

Thorganby

Ferryboat Inn

Ferry Lane, YO19 6DD (1 mile NE of village, signed from main road) SE697427
7-11; closed Mon; 12-midnight Sat; 12-4, 7-11 Sun
(01904) 448224
Beer range varies H
This warm and welcoming pub in a beautiful rural setting is definitely worth a visit. Its large beer garden runs down to the River Derwent. The river attracts fishermen and boaters and the quiet roads bring cyclists too. It has been run by the same family for more than 60 years. The landlady makes beautiful sandwiches and the landlord gives meticulous attention to his guest beers. Dogs are welcome in the garden. There is a small caravan site. P

Thornton Watlass

Buck Inn

The Village Green, HG4 4AH (off B6268 between Bedale and Masham)
11-11
(01677) 422461 thebuckinn.net
Black Sheep Best Bitter; Theakston Best Bitter, Black Bull Bitter; guest beers H
Overlooking the village green, this traditional country inn features a cosy bar room with real fire, a lounge/function room and separate dining area. Regular beers are from Black Sheep and Theakston breweries just down the road in Masham, with two rotating guests usually from northern micros. The pub hosts regular jazz sessions, and has an attractive tree-lined beer garden. Food is sourced locally and served lunchtime and evening. P

Thornton-in-Lonsdale

Marton Arms

LA6 3BP (¼ mile from A65/A687 jct)
12-11; 12-3, 6-11 Mon-Thu winter; 12-10.30 Sun
(01524) 241281 martonarms.co.uk
Black Sheep Best Bitter; Sharp's Doom Bar; Taylor Golden Best; Theakston Best Bitter; Thwaites Wainwright; guest beers H
In a hamlet that boasts a parish church, old stocks and little else, the pub relies almost entirely on tourists drawn by the 16 handpumps, although there are other interesting beverages, such as the stunning range of malt whiskies. Behind the 1679 datestone and old oak door, a flagged passage leads to a modern bar dominated by white wood. Ten minutes' walk from the start of the Waterfalls Walk. P

Thornton-le-Dale

New Inn

The Square, YO18 7LF
11-11; 11-2.30, 5-11 winter; 12-10.30 Sun
(01751) 474226 the-new-inn.com
Theakston Black Bull; guest beers H
Friendly family-run pub in the centre of this picturesque village in the North York Moors National Park. The comfortable bar is cosy yet bright, with beams and traditional tables and chairs. Two guest beers are available mainly from regional breweries. Walkers, cyclists and dogs (with drinkers) are very welcome. Bar meals and a

candle-lit restaurant serve freshly prepared and locally sourced food. Booking is recommended at weekends and busy holiday periods. Children are welcome until 9pm. Accommodation available. (128,840)P

Well

Milbank Arms

Bedale Road, DL8 2PX (off B6267 2 miles E of Masham)
7-11 Mon; 12-2, 6-11
(01677) 470411
Black Sheep Best Bitter; Theakston Best Bitter; guest beer H
Small but attractive inn in a tiny village on the edge of a limestone scarp. The views from further up the hill are spectacular. A renovated bar area has retained the character of a cosy local rather than an extension of the restaurant, despite a fine reputation for food (not served Mon) which uses locally-sourced produce as much as possible. Guest beers tend to be from a local area of Yorkshire, often from the Wensleydale Brewery.
P

West Haddlesey

George & Dragon

Main Street, YO8 8QA (1 mile W of A19, 5 miles S of Selby) SE565266
5-midnight (1am Fri); 2-1am Sat; 12-10.30 Sun
(01757) 228198
Beer range varies H
Privately-owned free house with an enthusiasm for local micro-brewery beers – the house beer White Dragon is from Brown Cow. Low-ceilinged and cosy bars include a separate area for restaurant users (no meals Sun eve). The large-screen TV stands over a well, providing proof that there has always been liquid refreshment here. Quiz night and jazz music nights are held weekly. Beer festivals are regular events including the annual April festival, close to St George's Day. QP

West Witton

Fox & Hounds

Main Street, DL8 4LP (on A684 in village centre)
12-4, 6-midnight; 12-midnight Sat & Sun
(01969) 623650 foxwitton.com
Black Sheep Best Bitter; John Smith's Bitter; guest beers H
In the same family for over a decade, this CAMRA award-winning free house dates from 1400 and was originally a resthouse for monks from Jervaulx Abbey. A central fireplace divides the friendly bar from the back room, while the dining room retains an inglenook fireplace and beehive oven. To the rear of the Grade II-listed building is a pleasant patio and garden with a quoits pitch. One guest beer is usually from the Yorkshire Dales Brewery. Good value meals are served all week, with a roast on Sunday. (156)P

Whitby

Black Horse

91 Church Street, YO22 4BH (E side of bridge on approach to Abbey steps)
11-11; 12-10.30 Sun
(01947) 602906 the-black-horse.com
Adnams Bitter; Black Dog Rhatas; Taylor Landlord; guest beers H
Dating from the 1600s, this previous CAMRA award winner always offers a warm welcome. The frontage, with its frosted glass windows, together with one of Europe's oldest public serving bars, was built in the 1880s and remains largely unchanged to this day. Alongside beer served from five handpumps, a hot meal is available during winter months, while snuff, tapas, olives, Yorkshire cheeses and hot drinks are on offer all year round. The cider is Westons Traditional Scrumpy. Accommodation comprises four bedrooms and an apartment. Q(56,93)

First In Last Out

1 York Terrace, Fishburn Park, YO21 1PT (300m S of railway station)
12-midnight; 12-11.30 Sun
(01947) 602149 firstinlastoutpub.co.uk
Camerons Strongarm; Tetley Bitter H
One of only three pubs with this name in the country, mortgage documents dating from 1868 show that this street-corner gem of a local was once a fruit and vegetable shop. It is popular with locals and those canny holidaying visitors who have discovered its whereabouts. Tuesday is folk night, while on Friday live bands play. The pub supports darts and dominoes teams. There is no food, but one of Whitby's finest fish and chip shops, the Railway Chippy, is directly opposite.
(56,93)P

Station Inn

New Quay Road, YO21 1DH
10-midnight (11.30 Sun)
(01947) 603937
Black Dog Whitby Abbey Ale; Copper Dragon Challenger IPA; Taylor Golden Best; guest beers H
Next to the harbour and marina, a warm welcome awaits you at this popular multi-roomed pub, where you can have your very own beer festival. Enthusiastic licensees ensure that the eight real ales always represent a superb range of varying beer styles, while Westons cider and a dozen fruit wines also mean there's something for everyone. Now the discerning traveller's waiting room, the pub is ideally situated opposite the bus station and the NYMR and Esk Valley railway terminus. Live entertainment is hosted on Wednesday, Friday and Saturday. (56,93)

Yarm

Black Bull

42 High Street, TS15 9BH
10-midnight (1am Fri-Sun)
(01642) 791251
Black Sheep Best Bitter; Draught Bass; guest beers H
With the best beer garden in the area, this much-extended 17th-century hostelry is one of the area's most popular and well-known venues – the favourite haunt of Teesside's 30-somethings, and older, for decades. It is busy most evenings, but absolutely manic at weekends, when the clientele queues to gain entry. There are two bars inside and a third outside on the large heated patio. Good value pub food is served all day plus summer barbecues on Friday and Saturday evenings. A plaque commerates Bob Tillson, who decided to climb up the pub's chimney – from the inside.
(7)

York

Blue Bell ★

53 Fossgate, YO1 9TF
11-11; 12-10.30 Sun
☎ (01904) 654904
Adnams Bitter; Black Sheep Best Bitter; Caledonian Deuchars IPA; Taylor Landlord; Tetley Dark Mild; guest beers H
A real gem in York, this small, glazed, brick-clad building dating from 1798 is a friendly award-winning community local. It has been recognised regionally and nationally, as well as locally, and is well known for its charity fundraising. The early 1900s wood panelling has been entered in CAMRA's National Inventory. There are two small rooms and the corridor servery which are all equally comfortable places in which to enjoy a well-kept range of beers plus two changing guests. Q

Brigantes Bar & Brasserie ✔

114 Micklegate, YO1 6JX
12-11
☎ (01904) 675355 marketowntaverns.co.uk
Taylor Landlord; guest beers H
A cask beer oasis in a street better known for night clubs and stag nights. Difficult to beat for the sheer scale of its beer range, it offers a wide choice of continental beers and lagers to supplement the traditional ales. Do not expect to find the usual mass market lagers. Food matches the beer styles, as can be expected from the acclaimed Market Town Tavern chain. One open bar provides a good variety of seating. The continent meets Yorkshire and it works well. Q

Golden Ball ★

2 Cromwell Road, YO1 6DU
4-11 Mon-Wed; 5-11.30 Thu; 4.30-11.30 Fri; 12-11.30 Sat; 12-11 Sun
☎ (01904) 652211 goldenball-york.co.uk
Caledonian Deuchars IPA; Greene King Ruddles County; Marston's Pedigree; John Smith's Bitter; Wells Bombardier; guest beers H
Winner of York CAMRA 2004 Pub of the Year, this street-corner hostelry in the residential Bishophill district is a fine community local. Victorian-built, it has an impressive glassed brick exterior. Extensively refurbished in 1929 by John Smith's, it merits an entry on CAMRA's National Inventory of pubs with interiors of outstanding interest. There are four rooms, each with its own atmosphere, one with bar billiards and TV, and a hidden garden. Live music is staged on Thursday and Sunday. Q

Maltings

Tanners Moat, YO1 6HU (below Lendal Bridge)
11-11; 12-10.30 Sun
☎ (01904) 655387 maltings.co.uk
Black Sheep Best Bitter; York Brewery Guzzler; guest beers H
Seven ales and four ciders make this a must visit ale house. The no-frills but quirky decor is matched by the midday menu of home cooked and filling food. Porters and stouts can often be found and are a good thing to wash down the incendiary chilli. Very handy for the railway station, some folk have been known to get no further into York than here. It can be crowded in late evening. Sean and Maxine are legends of the York pub trade and run one of the best ale houses around.

Minster Inn

24 Marygate, YO30 7BH
2-11; 11-midnight Fri & Sat; 12-10.30 Sun
☎ (01904) 624499
Jennings Sneckllifter; Marston's Burton Bitter; guest beers H
This is everyone's idea of what a local pub should be. A warm welcome from Dave and Sally, especially for dogs and families. Guest beers usually include Wychwood, Ringwood and Jennings. Tucked away a short walk from the busy Bootham Bar, this is a haven for visitors and friendly locals alike. Its traditional multi-roomed layout has been retained and games and puzzles to occupy idle fingers and minds are dotted around. One visit and you will want to return many times. Q

Rook & Gaskill

12 Lawrence Street, YO10 3WP (nr Walmgate Bar)
3-11; 12-midnight Fri & Sat; 12-11 Sun
☎ (01904) 674067 castlerockbrewery.co.uk
Castle Rock Harvest Pale, seasonal beers; guest beers H
The beer range is excellent – one of the best in York – and there is always a good choice of styles, including a porter or stout and a mild, from a great selection of local and regional breweries. The atmosphere is friendly and traditional, with pump clips covering the ceiling testimony to the beers that have been and gone. But no need to worry about what has been missed – with 12 handpumps and a choice of eight or nine ales plus a real cider, there is always plenty more to come.

Swan Inn ★

16 Bishopgate Street, YO23 1JH
4-11 (11.30 Thu); 4-midnight Fri, 12-midnight Sat; 12-10.30 Sun
☎ (01904) 634968
Copper Dragon Golden Pippin; Taylor Landlord; Tetley Bitter H
York CAMRA Branch Pub of the Year 2009, this unspoilt Tetley Heritage Inn is a classic street corner local featuring a West Riding layout. The friendly staff serve three regular and three rapidly changing guest beers from the central servery to the drinking lobby, lounge and public bar. One of only three York pubs included in CAMRA's National Inventory of pub interiors of outstanding historic importance, there is a comfortable paved and walled garden to the rear that includes a large covered and heated smoking area.

Tap & Spile

29 Monkgate, YO31 7PB
12-11 (midnight Fri & Sat); 12-10.30 Sun
☎ (01904) 656158 tapandspileyork.co.uk
Rooster's Yankee; guest beers H
Imposing Flemish-style house dating from 1897. Formerly known as the Black Horse, the pub was renamed in 1988 when it became one of the first in the Tap & Spile's chain. The spacious interior has a raised bar area at one end and a separate library-style lounge with an imposing fireplace at the other. Five guest ales come mainly from the SIBA scheme. Regular music nights are held and the annual pork pie festival is a highlight. P

Three-Legged Mare

15 High Petergate, YO1 7EN
11-11 (midnight Fri & Sat); 12-11 Sun

☎ (01904) 638246 🌐 yorkbrew.demon.co.uk/three_legged.html
York Guzzler, Constantine, Wonkey Donkey, Centurion's Ghost; guest beers Ⓗ
York Brewery's second pub, converted from a shop in 2001, situated close to the Minster in the heart of the city centre. With nine handpumps, it is able to offer a good selection of guest beers in addition to the York range. The pub's name comes from a triangular structure for hanging three criminals simultaneously – a replica can be seen in the small beer garden. **Q❀◑⇌🚌⚡**

Yorkshire Terrier

10 Stonegate, YO1 8AS
✪ 11-11 (midnight Fri & Sat); 12-11 Sun
☎ (01904) 676722 🌐 yorkbrew.demon.co.uk/yorkshire_terrier
York Guzzler, Constantine, Yorkshire Terrier, Centurion's Ghost; guest beers Ⓗ
Found behind the York Brewery's city centre shop is a little gem of a pub, where they have definitely squeezed a quart into a pint pot. Imaginative use of space has placed a bar with nine handpumps within a two-roomed drinking area, with a conservatory as well as an upstairs room. There is always plenty of choice of real ales, as well as wholesome daytime meals. Quiz night is Thursday, live music plays on Sunday. **Q🐴◐♿⇌🚌**

YORKSHIRE (SOUTH)

Auckley

Eagle & Child

24 Main Street, DN9 3HS (on B1396)
✪ 11.30-3, 5-11; 11.30-11.30 Fri & Sat; 11.30-11 Sun
☎ (01302) 770406
Black Sheep Best Bitter; John Smith's Bitter; Theakston XB; guest beers Ⓗ
A gem of a village pub, with a long tradition of offering a good range of quality ales. Five cask beers are always available, including two guests usually sourced from micro-breweries. The pub also offers a fine and varied choice of meals at reasonable prices. Robin Hood Airport is nearby. The smoking area is covered and heated. Winner of several CAMRA awards including Pub of the Year in 2006 and 2007. **Q❀◑🚌P⚡**

Barnsley

Dove Inn

102 Doncaster Road, S70 1TP
✪ 12-11 (midnight Fri & Sat)
☎ (01226) 288351
Old Mill Bitter, seasonal beers Ⓗ
A bright, wood-panelled interior gives a warm, cosy feeling as you enter this well cared for pub. Always clean and welcoming, the Old Mill brewery house has a games/TV room, bar area and a small back room which leads to a semi-covered veranda overlooking the neat garden. Keeping both smokers and drinkers happy is what the Dove Inn is all about and you'll find it at its busiest on match days when the friendly hum of conversation is inviting to home and away fans alike.
❀⇌(Interchange)🚌♣⚡

Joseph Bramah ✔

15 Market Hill, S70 2PX
✪ 9-midnight (1am Wed, Fri & Sat)
☎ (01226) 320890
Greene King IPA, Abbot; Marston's Pedigree; guest beers Ⓗ
This Lloyds No. 1 provides the standard Wetherspoon's fare of permanent beers, with up to four additional changing micro-brewery guests, plus one real cider, as well as value for money meals, to ensure a very busy pub. Set over two floors, the T-shaped layout allows for some quieter areas, especially in the smaller upstairs bar. There is good disabled access, including a lift. Outside is a sheltered and heated smoking courtyard. This popular watering hole caters for all.
❀◑♿⇌(Interchange)🍎⚡

Keel Inn

18 Canal Street, S71 1LJ (off A61 near Asda)
✪ 7 (6 Fri)-midnight; 12-11 Sun
☎ (01226) 284512
Beer range varies Ⓗ
This true free house was a former boatmen's pub situated next to the now filled in Barnsley Canal. Two changing guest beers from nearby local micro-breweries, often Acorn and Bradfield, are on offer. The pub has been extended and a variety of areas allows for games, TV and functions. There is a real fire in the winter months. There are active pool and darts teams and frequent folk music events.
🔥❀⇌(Interchange)🚌(11,59)♣P⚡🗑

Shaw Lane Sports Club (Barnsley RUFC)

Shaw Lane, S70 6HZ (200m up lane from Holgate School)
✪ 5 (11.30 Sat & Sun)-11.30
☎ (01226) 203509 🌐 barnsleyrufc.co.uk
Acorn Barnsley Bitter; Black Sheep Best Bitter; guest beer Ⓗ
Take a narrow lane at the war memorial to find this real ale haven set among many sports facilities. A neat brick exterior contains a two-roomed clubhouse with a lounge bar overlooking the cricket pitch and a larger function room housing the three handpumps. Focusing on micro-breweries, the club features at least one LocAle as a permanent beer and one rotating guest. This very busy venue welcomes sportsmen and women as well as spectators. Caravans are permitted on site but no tents. **❀◑♿⛺♣P⚡**

Silkstone Inn ✔

64 Market Street, S70 1SN (160m from Peel Square up Market St)
✪ 9-midnight (1am Wed, Fri & Sat)
☎ (01226) 320860

INDEPENDENT BREWERIES

Abbeydale Sheffield
Acorn Wombwell
Bradfield High Bradfield
Brew Company Sheffield (NEW)
Concertina Mexborough
Crown Sheffield
Glentworth Skellow
Kelham Island Sheffield
Little Ale Cart Sheffield
Oakwell Barnsley
Sheffield Sheffield
Thorne Thorne (NEW)
Wentworth Wentworth

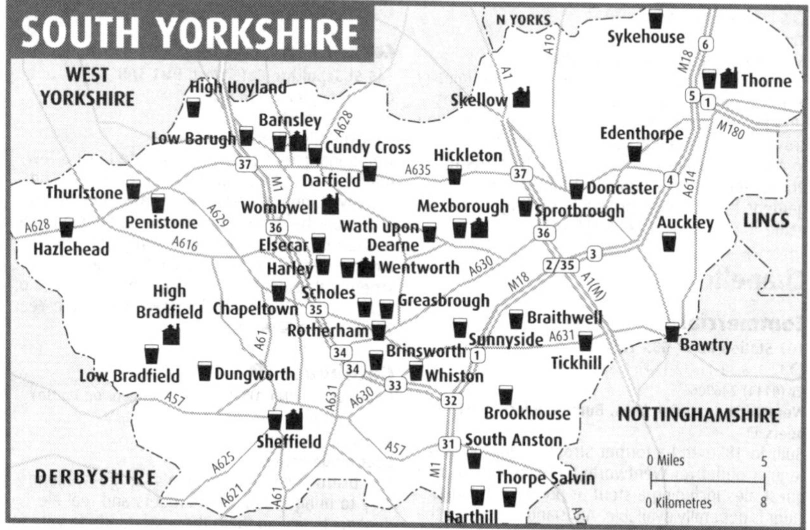

Greene King IPA, Abbot; Marston's Pedigree; guest beers Ⓗ
Situated in the heart of the town centre is the 700th pub in Wetherspoon's arsenal. This redevelopment of an old Co-op store has become a very popular watering hole for the over-30s in town. The name reflects the high quality coal seam that runs from Cawthorne to Chapeltown which was mined in and around Barnsley. The pub's wonderful decor is coal-themed, from the lampshades to the open gas fire, to reflect the history of mining here in Barnsley.
Q❀◑♿⇌(Interchange)●⚡—

Bawtry

Ship ✔

Gainsborough Road, DN10 6HT (on A631 near traffic lights)
✪ 12-11 (10.30 Sun)
☎ (01302) 710275 🌐 theship-bawtry.com
Marston's Burton Ale; guest beers Ⓗ
Probably the most improved pub in Doncaster CAMRA's branch area. New licensees took over in September 2007 and transformed this once run-down roadside pub. Refurbished inside and out, the Ship offers high quality meals at reasonable prices. Four cask ales are available, with Marston's and Jennings' ranges always represented. Quizzes and theme nights are popular. Winner of Doncaster CAMRA Pub of the Season for Autumn 2008 and Cask Marque accredited since October 2008.
❀◑⊟♿🚌♣P⚡—

Turnpike

28-30 High Street, DN10 6JE (on A638)
✪ 11-11; 12-10.30 Sun
☎ (01302) 711960
Caledonian Deuchars IPA; Greene King Ruddles Best; John Smith's Bitter; guest beers Ⓗ
Opened in 1986 and still with the original licensee, the Turnpike celebrates 22 years in this Guide. Situated opposite the old market place, it is arranged over three levels, and features glass and wood panelling together with flagstone floors. The decor includes a county cricket tie collection and photographs of the former RAF Finningley, now Robin Hood Airport. The venue has been local CAMRA Pub of the Season on four occasions. A good selection of lunchtime food is served. ❀◐🚌⚡—

Braithwell

Red Lion

Holywell Lane, S66 7AF (2 miles N of Maltby on B6376)
✪ 12-3, 5-11; 12-11 Fri-Sun
☎ (01709) 812886
Bradfield Farmers Blonde; John Smith's Bitter; Taylor Golden Best; guest beers Ⓗ
A thriving village local with a friendly staff and clientele. The pub has an ever-changing guest beer, as well as an annual mini beer festival. The interior is multi-roomed, with a quiet family room as well as public and lounge bars. The landlord is CAMRA-friendly and won the local branch Pub of the Season award for summer 2008. A whist drive takes place on the first Wednesday of the month.
🔥🐎❀⊟♿🚌♣⚡—

Brinsworth

Phoenix Sports & Social Club ✔

Pavilion Lane, S60 5PA (off Bawtry Road)
✪ 11-11; 12-10.30 Sun
☎ (01709) 363788
Fuller's London Pride; Stones Bitter; Wentworth seasonal beers; Worthington's Bitter; guest beer Ⓗ
Members of the public are very welcome at the Phoenix. A regular outlet for local Wentworth beers, the comfortable refurbished lounge now offers four cask ales, all expertly kept by the enthusiastic stewards. A family room, TV room and snooker room with two full-sized tables are also popular. Lunchtime and evening meals are available. The club boasts numerous local CAMRA awards including Pub of the Season and Pub of the Year. 🐎❀◑♿♣P⚡—

Brookhouse

Travellers' Rest

Main Street, S25 1YA (just over a mile from Dinnington near viaduct)

⏲ 5 (12 Sat & Sun)-11
☎ (01909) 562661
Greene King IPA, H&H Bitter, Abbot Ⓗ
Bungalow-style pub in a farming village, originally a house built using stone from a watermill that stood on the site until the 1960s. The pub has been crowned local CAMRA Rural Pub of the Year 2008. In a handy location for walkers, with access to Roche Abbey and Laughton, it has extensive gardens by the brook providing seating. Good value food is served. ❀◐◑⊟♿♣P⁄–

Chapeltown

Commercial
107 Station Road, S35 2XF
⏲ 12-3, 5.30-11; 12-11 Fri & Sat; 12-10.30 Sun
☎ (0114) 2469066
Wentworth Imperial, WPA, Bumble Beer; guest beers Ⓗ
Built in 1890 and a former Stroutts pub, this is a regular outlet for Wentworth beers as well as five guest ales including a stout or porter. A rotating cider is generally available. An island bar serves the lounge, public/games bar and the snug. Beer festivals are held during the last weekends of May and November with emphasis on beers new to the pub. Outdoor drinking facilities are to the side and rear with a stream at the bottom of the garden. Children are welcome. Hot roast pork sandwiches are available from 10pm on Saturday (no meals Sun eve). ♨Q❀◐◑⊟♿⇌🚌(265)♣●P⁄–

Cundy Cross

Mill of the Black Monk
81 Grange Lane, S71 5QF
⏲ 12-11
☎ (01226) 242244
Acorn Barnsley Bitter; guest beers Ⓗ
Built in 1154 by Cluniac Monks as a water mill to St Mary Magdalene of Lund Priory, the building has been in the hands of Benedictine monks and Quakers, and has spent time as an Almshouse. It won a CAMRA pub design award in 1991 in the special conservation category. Renovations include raising the whole building by 4ft on a float made from silt. Modern features blend with original beams, stonework and doors. Three rooms are over three levels. Reputed to be haunted, paranormal groups carry out overnight huntings here. ❀◐◑♿🚌(32,35,36A)P

Darfield

Station Inn 🏆
128 Doncaster Road, S73 9JA
⏲ 5-11.30; 12-2.30, 5-11.30 Thu-Sat; 12-11.30 Sun
☎ (01226) 752096 🌐 thestationinn.org
John Smith's Bitter; Oakwell Barnsley Bitter; Tom Wood's Old Chuffa; guest beers Ⓗ
A traditional local situated on the fringe of the village. The pub comprises a large bar area with an open fire and a large dining room. The walls are adorned with local photographs. Up to eight real ales are sourced from local and national breweries. One of the house beers, Old Chuffa, is produced specially for the pub by Tom Wood's. Tuesday night is quiz night and other occasional entertainment includes folk nights. Good value meals and Sunday lunch are available, as is a courtesy bus. ♨Q❀◐◑🚌(218,219)♣P⁄–🗍

Doncaster

Corner Pin
145 St Sepulchre Gate West, DN1 3AH
⏲ 12-midnight (1am Fri & Sat)
☎ (01302) 340670
John Smith's Bitter; guest beers Ⓗ
Traditional street-corner pub situated just a few minutes' walk from the Travel Interchange and railway station. It comprises a smart lounge area and public bar area, with an outside drinking space to the rear. Guest beers are mainly from small independent breweries, sourced via the SIBA scheme. Reasonably-priced lunches are served on Sunday 12-2.30pm. Local CAMRA Pub of the Year 2008. ❀⊟⇌🚌♣⁄–🗍

Gatehouse ✔
Priory Walk, DN1 3EF (close to the Mansion House)
⏲ 9am-midnight (1am Fri & Sat)
☎ (01302) 554540
Beer range varies Ⓗ
This bistro-style Wetherspoon's bar goes a long way to bring in CAMRA members and real ale drinkers by giving them the opportunity to vote for beers they would like to see available. Breweries from South Yorkshire are often featured, together with those from further afield. Do not overlook the bank of handpumps at the far end of the bar. ◐◑♿⇌🚌

Plough ★
8 West Laith Gate, DN1 1SF
⏲ 11-11; 11-3, 7-10.30 Sun
☎ (01302) 738310
Acorn Barnsley Bitter; Draught Bass Ⓗ
Close to the bustling Frenchgate Centre, the Plough is a haven for shoppers wanting to escape the activity of the town centre. The unchanged interior dates back to 1934, and features in CAMRA's national inventory. There is a basic public bar at the front with a horse-racing theme, and a comfortable lounge at the rear. Note the display of unusual pictures of old agricultural scenes in the lounge. Winner of several CAMRA awards, the Plough is well worth a visit. Q⊟⇌🚌♣⁄–

Red Lion 🏆 ✔
37-38 Market Place, DN1 1NH (S corner of Market Place, near fish market)
⏲ 9-11 (midnight Fri & Sat)
☎ (01302) 732120
Beer range varies Ⓗ
This large, historic pub has been given a new lease of life since it was taken over by Wetherspoon. A lively front drinking area gives way to a quieter area with tables and chairs towards the rear. Although much altered over the years, it was here in 1776 that discussions took place to organise the St Leger Stakes, the oldest Classic horse race. Plaques are on display commemorating the event and listing post-war winners, including many famous jockeys. ◐◑♿🚌

Salutation Hotel ✔
14 South Parade, DN1 2DR
⏲ 12-midnight (1am Fri & Sat)
☎ (01302) 340705
Tetley Bitter; guest beers Ⓗ
Originally a coaching inn on the Great North Road and now a popular pub on the edge of Doncaster town centre. The Sal consists of cosy drinking areas downstairs, a large function room upstairs and a

patio area behind the pub. The bar features seven handpumps and a constantly changing range of beers. Meet the Brewer evenings are one of the regular attractions at local CAMRA's Winter Pub of the Season 2008-9.

Tut 'n' Shive

6 West Laith Gate, DN1 1SF (next to Frenchgate shopping centre)
11-11 (1am Fri & Sat); 12-midnight Sun
(01302) 360300
Black Sheep Best Bitter; Greene King IPA, Old Speckled Hen, Abbot; guest beers H
Up to six real ales are available at this busy town-centre pub with a stone floor, boarded ceiling and walls decorated with pump clips from past beers. Quiz nights are Wednesday and Sunday. Music is supplied by a 25,000 track jukebox featuring rock and indie music, a classic rock DJ appears on Sunday and occasional live bands play. A large-screen TV shows major sporting events. A relaxed but lively atmosphere ensures that all feel welcome.

Dungworth

Royal Hotel

Main Road, S6 6HF SK280898
6 (12 Sat)-11; 12-4, 7-10.30 Sun
(0114) 285 1213 royalhotel-dungworth.pwp.blueyonder.co.uk
Crown Royal Bitter; guest beers H
A small 19th-century rural pub to the north west of Sheffield in the Vale of Bradfield, with panoramic views over the Loxley Valley. Children, walkers and well-behaved pets are welcome. One bar serves two drinking areas, with a separate room to the left. Early evening meals are available on weekdays, lunch and evening meals on Saturday and lunch on Sunday. Try the home-cooked pies. Sunday lunchtime carol singing from mid-November to Christmas is a highlight. Three en-suite rooms are available in the adjoining lodge.
Q (61,62) P

Edenthorpe

Beverley Inn

Thorne Road, DN3 2JE (on A18 E of Doncaster)
12-3, 5-11 (midnight Sat); 12-3, 7-10.30 Sun
(01302) 882724 beverleyinnandhotel.co.uk
John Smith's Bitter; guest beers H
Welcoming village inn with a reputation for good food – the popular Sunday carvery is excellent value. It offers three constantly changing guest beers as well as the regular John Smith's Bitter. The pub has a pleasant outside drinking area adjacent to the car park, and the accommodation stretches to 14 rooms. Children are welcome if taking meals.
P

Elsecar

Market Hotel

2-4 Wentworth Road, S74 8EP
12 (11 Sat)-11
(01226) 742240
Wentworth WPA; guest beers H
Large, friendly, multi-room pub offering an ever-changing array of beers from a wide range of breweries, always including a LocAle brew. All real ales are sold at the same price irrespective of strength. A spacious beer garden is available at the rear of the premises, and the pub is directly adjacent to the Elsecar Heritage Centre, with excellent walking in unspoiled countryside nearby.
Q (66,67,227) P

Milton Arms

Armroyd Lane, S74 8ES
12-3, 7 (6 Thu & Fri)-midnight; closed Wed; 12-5, 7-midnight Sun
(01226) 742278
Stones Bitter; guest beers H
An inviting three-roomed village pub, close to the Heritage Centre and offering a warm welcome to locals and visitors alike. The pub is the start and finish point for the Milton Six race, run during June each year and attracting athletes from around Yorkshire. The landlord is an accomplished chef and presents a range of quality food to suit all tastes, Thursday to Sunday (not Sun eve). Open fires and an award-winning beer garden with aviaries give the pub year-round interest.
(66,227) P

Greasbrough

Prince of Wales

9 Potters Hill, S61 4NU
11-4, 7-11; 12-3, 7-10.30 Sun
(01709) 551358
Beer range varies H
The Prince continues to go from strength to strength as it celebrates its 15th consecutive entry in the Guide. This popular street corner pub has a spacious, well-decorated lounge and tap room. The friendly landlord is approaching his 30th year of tenancy and continues to provide cask beers from a variety of breweries. The guest beer can change up to three times in one day, ensuring its quality. In summer, tables and chairs outside allow customers to watch the world go by. Q

Harley

Horseshoe Inn

9 Harley Road, S62 7UD (off A6135)
4 (2 Sat)-11 (10 Mon); 12-10.30 Sun
(01226) 742204
Phoenix Arizona; Wentworth seasonal beers; guest beers H
This street-corner pub is situated close to the local Wentworth Brewery and stocks at least one Wentworth beer. The hostelry hosts regular events and is home to a pool team. The guest beer changes regularly to ensure its quality, with ales often coming from local breweries. A carvery is held on Sunday 12-3pm. Book to avoid disappointment.

Harthill

Beehive

16 Union Street, S26 7YH (opp church on road from Kiveton crossroads)
12-3 (not Mon), 6-11; 11-11 Sat & Sun
(01909) 770205
Caledonian Deuchars IPA; Taylor Landlord; Tetley Bitter H
A welcoming village inn close to Rother Valley Country Park and on the Five Churches walk. It provides space for drinkers and diners and is home to a number of local clubs. The rear room houses a

full-sized snooker table. There is a function room upstairs with stairlift access which is available to hire. Q❀◑⊞♿♣P

Hazlehead

Dog & Partridge

Bord Hill, S36 4HH (on A628 Flouch roundabout)
SE177011
12-11
☎ (01226) 763173 🌐 dogandpartridgeinn.co.uk
Acorn Barnsley Bitter; guest beers H
This ancient inn, surrounded by the Dark Peak District's stunning scenery, is an ideal base for exploring the wild country. The medieval Saltersbrook Packhorse Trail, linking Cheshire salt mines with Barnsley, runs nearby. Providing succour for travellers (weary and otherwise) is therefore an established tradition here. The pub serves four excellent real ales from local micros. A huge fire blazes in winter and there is often the chance of a helicopter trip from the field beside the car park. ♨❀◑🚌P

Hickleton

Hickleton Village Hall

Castle Hill Lane, DN5 7BG (off A635)
6 (8 Tue)-midnight; 2-midnight Sat; closed Mon; 12-midnight Sun
☎ (01709) 306371
Beer range varies H
Tucked away in a quiet conservation village, this private members' club (the building is owned by Lord Halifax) metamorphosed into a real ale haven in 2007, and won a local CAMRA Pub of the Season award. Beers from Acorn and White Rose are usually on handpump in the very characterful bar. Quality food is available evenings Wednesday to Saturday and Sunday lunchtime. If you enjoy drinking great ale in a relaxed atmosphere you will love it here. Card-carrying CAMRA members welcome. ♨◑🚌(X19,219)♣

High Hoyland

Cherry Tree

Bank End Lane, S75 4BE
12-3, 5.30-11; 12-11 Sat; 12-10.30 Sun
☎ (01226) 382541
Black Sheep Best Bitter; John Smith's Bitter; guest beers H
A pub with spectacular views over open countryside as far as the Peak District and the cooling towers of Drax. Popular with locals and visitors alike, it is also the venue for High Hoyland parish meetings. The two guest beers are from E&S Elland to complement the regular beers. Good value and quality food is available. The interior comprises a central bar with dining and drinking areas to both sides. The bus service runs 10am-5pm (not Sun). ❀◑♿🚌(95)P⁻

Low Barugh

Millers Inn

Dearne Hall Road, S75 1LX (off the A635, follow B6428 for 400m)
5-11; 4-midnight Fri; 12-midnight Sat; 12-11 Sun
☎ (01226) 210280
Beer range varies H
An open-plan pub with a large central walkaround bar and a games room to one side with pool and darts. A raised brick mural depicting a gunman and dog is over the fireplace. Two lounge areas are to the other side of the bar. Conkers and knock the nail are played as well as dominoes. The River Dearne runs directly to the back of the beer garden where duck races are held in summer months. Clubs and societies meet here, including the clay pigeon club. Beers are from the Marston's portfolio. ❀◑♿🚌(92A,95A)♣P

Low Bradfield

Plough Inn ✔

New Road, S6 6HW SK263916
12-3.30, 6 (7 Tue)-midnight; 12-midnight Wed-Sun
☎ (0114) 285 1280 🌐 the-plough-inn.com
Bradfield Plough; guest beers H
Nestled in the heart of the Loxley Valley, this former farm, built in the early 18th century, celebrated 200 years as a pub during 2009. This true free house provides guest beers, with one from Sheffield and others usually sourced from Yorkshire and the north east. Lunch is served all week and evening meals Wednesday to Sunday, made from locally sourced produce, with the pies a speciality. A music evening is held on the first Tuesday of the month. ♨❀◑⊞♿🚌(61,62)♣P⁻

Mexborough

Concertina Band Club

9A Dolcliffe Road, S64 9AZ (off Bank St)
12-4, 7.45 (7 Fri & Sat)-11; 12-3, 7.45-10.30 Sun
☎ (01709) 580841
Concertina Club Bitter, Bengal Tiger, Club Extreme; John Smith's Bitter H
This unique, family-owned club brewery is a regular in this Guide. The Tina, as it is known locally, was originally home to a band for many years. Photographs from previous decades, plus many well-deserved CAMRA awards, are on display. The club has a bar area above the cellar brewery, a small rear TV and pool room with access to the terrace, and a large lounge/concert room. CAMRA members are welcome – show this Guide or a membership card for entry. ❀⇌🚌♣⁻▯

Penistone

Penistone Royal British Legion Club

14 St Mary's Street, S36 6DT
11-3 (4.30 Thu), 7-11; 11-11.30 Sat; 12-11 Sun
☎ (01226) 766911
Beer range varies H
A spacious, comfortable and well-appointed modern private members' club, with a lounge/concert room and a large games/TV room with two snooker tables. One competitively priced real ale is well tended by the enthusiastic steward. The Trans-Pennine Trail (walking/biking/horse-riding route) runs at the rear of the club on a former railway track. Bingo is hosted on Monday evening and regular entertainment on some other days. Show a copy of this Guide or CAMRA membership card for entry – non-members need to be officially signed in. ❀♿⇌🚌(20,22)P⁻

Wentworth Arms

Sheffield Road, S36 6HG (off train station approach)
12.30-11 (midnight Fri & Sat); 12-11 Sun

☎ (01226) 762494
Banks's Bitter; guest beers Ⓗ
This is a no-frills and no-nonsense community local with a lounge and bar serving some of the best beer in Penistone. Conveniently sited by the rail station, with the Trans-Pennine trail running on the disused Sheffield-Manchester line alongside, this pub is a useful watering hole with an adjacent fish and chip shop. As well as the great beers, pool, darts and an old-fashioned jukebox provide the entertainment. The landlord offers a mild here quite regularly. ⛰☋❀⅄⇌🚌(29,23)P⁴–

Rotherham

Bluecoat ✔
The Crofts, S60 2JD (behind town hall)
✪ 9-midnight (1am Fri & Sat)
☎ (01709) 580841
Greene King Ruddles Best, Abbot; Marston's Pedigree; guest beers Ⓗ
This converted school is situated behind the town hall and is well worth seeking out. Winner of the local CAMRA branch Pub of the Year award 2006-2008, it was also Wetherspoon's Pub of the Year 2006. The Bluecoat offers a wide selection of beers from national and local breweries. Westons Old Rosie Cider is also on handpull. ❀ⒹⒹ♿⇌●P⁴–

Scholes

Bay Horse 🏆
Scholes Lane, S61 2RQ (off A629, near M1 jct 35)
✪ 5 (12 Sat & Sun)-11; 12-11 Sun
☎ (0114) 246 8085
Kelham Island Pale Rider; Taylor Landlord; guest beers Ⓗ
Traditional village pub next to the cricket club. It serves good home-cooked food including Dan's cow pie (earn a certificate if you finish everything on the plate), popular curries and Sunday lunches. The pub holds pork pie competitions and hog roasts feature up to four times a year. Further entertainment is provided by a choir on Thursday and two weekly quizzes. Situated on the Rotherham Round Walk and the Trans-Pennine Trail, the pub also won the local CAMRA branch Pub of the Year award in 2009. ⛰Q❀ⒹⒹ♿P

Sheffield: Central

Bath Hotel ★
66 Victoria Street, S3 7QL
✪ 12-11; 7-10.30 Sun
☎ (0114) 249 5151
Abbeydale Moonshine; Acorn Barnsley Bitter; Tetley Bitter; guest beers Ⓗ
The careful restoration of the 1930s interior gave this two-roomed pub the conservation award in CAMRA's 2003 Pub Design Awards and a place on the National Inventory of historic pubs. Visitors have a choice between the clear lines of the tiled lounge and the warmth of the well-upholstered snug. Up to three guest beers from local breweries and micros from further afield are on offer, as well as a good range of malt whiskies. Live music plays most Sundays.
QⒹ⊖(West St/Sheffield University)🚌

Devonshire Cat ✔
49 Wellington Street, S1 4HG
✪ 11.30-11 (midnight Fri & Sat); 12-10.30 Sun
☎ (0114) 279 6700 🌐 devonshirecat.co.uk
Abbeydale Moonshine, Absolution; Caledonian Deuchars IPA; Theakston Old Peculier; Thornbridge Jaipur; guest beers Ⓗ
With 12 handpumps adorning the bar – the house beer comes from the local Kelham Island Brewery – and over a hundred beers from around the world, the Dev Cat is a great place for the discerning drinker. The menu features light snacks through to hearty meals. Throughout the day the clientele is a mix of beer enthusiasts, students and anyone else in need of liquid refreshment. A must if you are on a short visit to the city. ⒹⒹ♿⊖(West St)🚌

Dove & Rainbow
Hartshead Square, S1 2EL
✪ 4-11.30; 12-12.30am Fri, 2.30-12.30 Sat; 7-11 Sun
☎ (0114) 272 1594 🌐 doveandrainbow.com
Adnams Bitter; John Smith's Bitter; Kelham Island Easy Rider; Wychwood Hobgoblin; guest beers Ⓗ
One of the city's leading pubs for rock music, the Dove is hidden away behind the adjoining Wetherspoons, but is only a few yards from the busy High Street. The open plan bar has a stage and DJ box at one end, and is fairly basic in decor and comfort. However it has an amazing turnover of guest beers, both local and national. Real cider from Westons (Scrumpy and Old Rosie). A LocAle pub. Ⓓ⇌⊖(Castle Square)🚌●⁴–

Fagans
69 Broad Lane, S1 4BS
✪ 12-11.30 (11 Sun)
☎ (0114) 272 8430
Abbeydale Moonshine; Tetley Bitter Ⓗ
Away from the main drinking areas but on one of the city's main traffic arteries, this has the feel of a locals' pub. With dark wood panelling and green and red decoration, the three rooms include what must now be the smallest snug in Sheffield. The pub hosts folk music every night and a fiendish quiz on Thursday. Evening meals are available to 7.30pm. ❀ⒹⒹ⊖(City Hall)🚌(51)⁴–

Fat Cat ✔
23 Alma Street, S3 8SA
✪ 12-11 (midnight Fri & Sat)
☎ (0114) 249 4801
Kelham Island Best Bitter, Pale Rider; Taylor Landlord; guest beers Ⓗ
Opened in 1981 and still ferociously independent, the Fat Cat is the pub that started the real ale revolution in the area. Beers from around the country are served alongside those from its sister operation, the Kelham Island Brewery. The pub is famed for its food, with vegetarian and gluten-free dishes featuring heavily (served until 8pm, not Sun). The walls are covered with a large number of awards presented to the pub and brewery. A curry and quiz night is held on Monday.
Q❀ⒹⒹ♿⊖(Shalesmoor)🚌⁴–

Harlequin
108 Nursery Street, S3 8GG
✪ 11.30-11
☎ (0114) 275 8195 🌐 theharlequinpub.co.uk
Bradfield Farmers Blonde; John Smith's Magnet; guest beers Ⓗ
Reopened in 2006 as a free house, the Harlequin (formerly the Manchester) takes its name from another former Wards pub around the corner, sadly now demolished. The large open-plan interior features a central bar, with seating areas on two

levels. As well as local brews, the nine handpumps serve beers from far and wide, with an emphasis on micro-breweries, and the pub hosts regular highly-regarded beer festivals. There is a quiz on Wednesday and live music Tuesday, Thursday and Saturday nights.
Q ❀ ◐ ⇌ ⊖ (Castle Square) ⊟ (47,48,53) ♣ ● ⁱ—

Kelham Island Tavern

62 Russell Street, S3 8RW
12-11 (midnight Fri-Sun)
☎ (0114) 272 2482 ⊕ kelhamislandtavern.co.uk
Acorn Barnsley Bitter; Bradfield Farmers Blonde; Pictish Brewers Gold; Thwaites Nutty Black; guest beers Ⓗ
Selected as CAMRA's National Pub of the Year in 2008 after previously picking up many local and regional awards, this small gem was rescued from dereliction as recently as 2002. An impressive 10 permanent handpumps include two that always dispense a mild and a stout/porter, so you are sure to find something to suit your mood. In the warmer months you can relax in the pub's multi-award winning beer garden. Regular folk music plays on Sunday and quiz night is Monday. No meals Sunday. Q ❀ ◐ ♿ ⊖ (Shalesmoor) ⊟ ● ⁱ— ⊓

Red Deer

18 Pitt Street, S1 4DD
11.30 (12 Sat)-midnight; 4-11 Sun
☎ (0114) 2722890 ⊕ red-deer-sheffield.co.uk
Adnams Broadside; Black Sheep Best Bitter; Caledonian Deuchars IPA; Greene King Abbot; Taylor Landlord; Wells Bombardier Ⓗ
A genuine, traditional local in the heart of the city. The small frontage of the original three-roomed pub hides an open-plan interior extended to the rear with a gallery seating area. The walls are decorated with prints, watercolours and photos of local scenes, some of which are for sale. There is an impressive range of cask ales and also a selection of continental bottled beers. Free food from around the world is on offer Tuesday teatime, and Cask in the City on Wednesday evening. Evening meals served until 7pm; no food Sunday.
Q ❀ ◐◑ ⊖ (West St) ⊟ ⁱ—

Three Tuns

39 Silver Street Head, S1 2DD
11.30-11.30; 7-11.30 Sat; closed Sun
☎ (0114) 272 0646
Taylor Landlord; Tetley Bitter; guest beers Ⓗ
This V-shaped pub is on two levels, with the guest ale usually on the upper part of the bar. Previously used as a nuns' washroom, the building now serves a much better purpose. Frequented by the office workers who work in nearby offices, there is a buzzing atmosphere during the early evening hours. No weekend meals. ◐ ⊖ (Cathedral) ⊟

Wig & Pen

44 Campo Lane, S1 2EG
11-11 (midnight Fri & Sat); closed Sun
☎ (0114) 276 3988 ⊕ wigandpensheffield.com
Sheffield Paradise Pale; guest beers Ⓗ
At the rear of Sheffield Cathedral, this smart city-centre venue unusually offers a good choice of real ales. The main bar runs along the frontage, with relaxed seating, mood lighting and music. Recently extended, the rear of the main bar overlooks the historic Paradise Square, where John Wesley once preached. Quality food is served both in the bar and the restaurant downstairs, while regular food and drink events feature regional and international themes. Guest beers are mainly from local micro-breweries. ❀ ◐◑ ♿ ⊖ (Cathedral) ⊟ ●

Sheffield: East

Carlton

563 Attercliffe Road, S9 3RA
11-9 (11 Thu-Sat); 2-9 Sun
☎ (0114) 244 3287
Beer range varies Ⓗ
Built in 1862, this former Gilmours house, now the only real ale outlet in the area, lies behind a deceptively small frontage. The main room around the bar is comfortably furnished in traditional style. To the rear is a newly extended games room and a recently created garden. A strict no-swearing policy enhances the friendly atmosphere. Beers are mainly from local breweries and often include Clark's and Wentworth, with some from further afield. ❀ ⊖ (Woodbourn Rd) ⊟ (52,69) ♣ ⁱ— ⊓

Sheffield: North

Hillsborough Hotel

54-58 Langsett Road, S6 2UB
12-11 (midnight Fri & Sat)
☎ (0114) 232 2100 ⊕ hillsborough-hotel.com
Crown Middlewood Mild, HPA, Traditional Bitter, Primrose Pale, Stannington Stout, seasonal beers; guest beers Ⓗ
Family-run hotel serving home-cooked food. Ever-changing guest ales are supplemented by beers from the house brewery in the cellar which brews under the Crown name, with four of the listed beers available at all times. Brewery tours can be booked. The conservatory and raised terrace at the rear feature panoramic views along the upper Don Valley. Attractions include seasonal beer festivals, regular themed events, folk music on Sunday and a popular quiz night (with free roast potatoes) on Tuesday. No food Sunday evening.
Q ❀ ⇔ ◐◑ ♿ ⊖ (Langsett Primrose View) ⊟ ♣ ⁱ—

New Barrack Tavern

601 Penistone Road, S6 2GA
11 (12 Sun)-11 (midnight Fri & Sat)
☎ (0114) 234 9148 ⊕ tynemill.co.uk
Acorn Barnsley Bitter; Batemans XXXB; Bradfield Farmers Bitter; Castle Rock Harvest Pale; guest beers Ⓗ
An essential stop-off for football fans travelling to nearby Hillsborough, this pub offers 11 handpumps, pre-match sustenance and a warm welcome. The home-cooked food is popular at all times and available late night Friday and Saturday, with a carvery on Sunday. The small front bar has darts, the main room features live music Friday, Saturday and some Sundays, and folk on Monday. A wide choice of continental beers, single malts plus a real cider are served. Outside is an award-winning heated, covered patio garden.
⋈ Q ❀ ◐◑ ⊖ (Bamforth St) ⊟ (53,77,78) ♣ ● ⁱ—

Rawson Spring

Langsett Road, Hillsborough, S6 2LN
9-11.30 (midnight Fri & Sat)
☎ (0114) 285 6200
Greene King IPA, Abbot; Marston's Pedigree; guest beers Ⓗ
Large Wetherspoon pub in the former Hillsborough swimming baths, popular on match days, with past

Wednesday team photos adorning the walls, along with other historical prints. It takes its name from the local spring that supplied fresh water to the nearby barracks. The eponymous house beer is provided by Bradfield and six other handpumps supply a range of guest ales. Food is available every day until 11pm. Family-friendly throughout, it has a beer garden and a covered, heated patio area. (Hillsborough)

Wellington

1 Henry Street, S3 7EQ
12-11; 12-3.30, 7-10.30 Sun
(0114) 249 2295
Millstone Baby Git; guest beers H
This popular street-corner pub, also known as the Bottom Wellie, champions an ever-changing range of beers from small independent brewers, with ten handpumps always offering a stout or porter and a real cider, plus a range of continental bottled beers. The house brewery, which adjoins the secluded garden at the rear, recommenced brewing late in 2008. It now produces ever changing beers, usually pale and hoppy, under the Little Ale Cart name, with at least two on sale most of the time.
Q(Shalesmoor)

Sheffield: South

Archer Road Beer Stop

57 Archer Road, S8 0JT
11 (10.30 Sat)-10; 5-10 Sun
(0114) 255 1356
Beer range varies H
Well-established corner-shop off-licence. Four real ales are always available dispensed by handpump, as well as dozens of bottle-conditioned beers. An extensive range of Belgian and other continental ales is also stocked. This little gem has received the local CAMRA award for its outstanding contribution to real ale. Unsurprisingly it has also featured in every edition of this Guide since 1997.

Castle Inn

1 Twentywell Road, Bradway, S17 4PT
12-11 (midnight Fri & Sat); 12-10.30 Sun
(0114) 236 2955
Bradfield Farmers Blonde; Oakwell Barnsley Bitter; Taylor Landlord; Tetley Bitter H
Located at the end of a row of stone-built cottages perched above the Bradway Tunnel, the pub has a tap room with piano and a lounge leading into the restaurant housed in a sympathetic extension to the rear. There is live music on the last Saturday night of the month and a quiz night on Wednesday. A retirement lunch menu is offered, with a special price for pensioners. No meals Saturday and Sunday evenings. Member of the LocAle scheme.
(Dore & Totley)(M17)P

Cricket Inn

Penny Lane, Totley Bents, S17 3AZ
11-midnight
(0114) 236 5256 brewkitchen.co.uk
Thornbridge Cricketers, Lord Marples, Jaipur IPA; guest beers H
In a rural location overlooking the village cricket green, yet only five minutes' walk from suburbia. This is a pub of two halves - one a traditional country inn with an open fire and cosy corners, the other an open-plan dining room. The pub is run by Brewkitchen, a partnership between a local restaurateur and Thornbridge Brewery, with the guest beer from the Thornbridge range. Meals are served all day Saturday and Sunday.
P

Sheaf View

25 Gleadless Road, Heeley, S2 3AA
12-11.30
(0114) 249 6455
Bradfield Farmers Blonde; Kelham Island Easy Rider; guest beers H
Built as a grocer's shop around 1865 before doubling as a beer house and owned by Brampton Brewery of Chesterfield by 1891. In recent times John Smith's and Marston's failed to keep the pub open. However, since 2000 it has flourished as a genuine free house following renovation and subsequent extensions. An extensive range of real ales and draught and bottled continental beers is available, and interesting breweriana adorns the walls. Very busy, especially at weekends and on Sheffield United home match days.
Q(20,20A,53)

Union Hotel

1 Union Road, S11 9EF
12-2.30, 5.30-11; 12-2.30, 7-10.30 Sun
(0114) 255 0689
Abbeydale Moonshine; Black Sheep Best Bitter; Taylor Landlord; Tetley Bitter; guest beer H
A charming pub situated within a prosperous part of the Nether Edge suburb. A central bar serves a single lounge although the layout gives the impression of separate rooms. Lots of dark wood panelling, brasses and a low-beamed ceiling provide a country pub style atmosphere. The tree-lined verandah and additional outside seating enhance this impression. A popular quiz is held on Monday evening. Lunches are served weekdays only. Q(22)

White Lion

615 London Road, Heeley, S2 4HT
2-11; 12-11.30 Fri & Sat; 12-11 Sun
(0114) 255 1500
Kelham Island Easy Rider; Taylor Landlord; Tetley Bitter; guest beers H
One of the three award-winning pubs in the small Just Williams chain, the White Lion is largely unspoilt, with many original features. Note the interesting spelling of Windsor Ales on the stained-glass windows. A number of small rooms including a delightful snug lead off the original tiled corridor. The large concert room at the rear is the venue for jazz sessions on the first Tuesday of the month, with live rock and blues music on occasional Thursdays. (20,20A,53)

Sheffield: West

Cobden View

40 Cobden View Road, Crookes, S10 1HQ
1-midnight (1am Fri); 12-1am Sat; 12-midnight Sun
(0114) 266 1273
Black Sheep Best Bitter; Bradfield Farmers Blonde; Caledonian Deuchars IPA; Greene King Old Speckled Hen; Wychwood Hobgoblin H
Off the main Crookes thoroughfare, this busy community pub caters for a varied clientele, ranging from students to retired folk. The original room layout is still apparent, with the bar serving a snug at the front, a games area with pool table to the rear and a lounge to the right of the entrance. Quizzes are held on Sunday and Tuesday evenings

and there is live music most Thursdays and Saturdays. The spacious garden contains a large covered smoking area. ❀♿🚌♣⅃

Fox & Duck

227 Fulwood Road, Broomhill, S10 3BA

11-11.30 (midnight Fri & Sat); 12-11.30 Sun

☎ (0114) 263 1888

Abbeydale Moonshine; John Smith's Magnet; guest beers H

Although owned by the Sheffield University Students Union, this busy pub at the heart of the Broomhill shopping area is popular with locals as well as students. Originally a two-roomed pub, it was converted to its present open-plan format in the 1980s and extended more recently into an adjacent shop. Although no food is served, drinkers may bring in their own from the numerous nearby takeaways. The guest beers are sourced from local and regional brewers. ❀🚌(51,52)⅃

Ranmoor Inn ✔

330 Fulwood Road, S10 3GD

11.30-11; 12-10.30 Sun

☎ (0114) 230 1325

Abbeydale Moonshine; Bradfield Farmers Bitter, Farmers Blonde; Taylor Landlord; guest beers H

This renovated Victorian local with original etched windows lies in the shadow of Ranmoor Church in the leafy suburb of Fulwood. Now open plan, the seating areas reflect the old room layout. A friendly, old-fashioned pub, it has a diverse clientele that includes choirs and football and rugby teams – the piano by the bar is often played by regulars. A small front garden is supplemented by the former stableyard which has been opened as a partly covered and heated drinking area. Lunches are available Tuesday to Saturday. Q❀◐🚌(40,120)♣⅃

Rising Sun

471 Fulwood Road, S10 3QA

12-11

☎ (0114) 230 3855 🌐 risingsunsheffield.co.uk

Abbeydale Absolution, Brimstone, Daily Bread, Matins, Moonshine, seasonal beers; guest beers H

Operated by local brewer Abbeydale, this is a large suburban roadhouse in the leafy western side of the city. The two rooms are comfortably furnished, with a main bar and raised area to the rear. A range of Abbeydale beers is always available, with up to six guests, mainly from micros, on the impressive bank of handpumps. Entertainment includes live music on Monday and quizzes on Sunday and Wednesday. An annual beer festival, Sunfest, is held in July. Q❀◐◑♿🚌(40,120)♣P⅃

University Arms

197 Brook Hill, S3 7HG

12-11; closed Sun

☎ (0114) 222 8969

Thornbridge White Swan; guest beers H

Formerly the staff club for Sheffield University academics, the University Arms became a pub in 2007. The bar is on the left of the main entrance with a small alcove seating area adjoining, and the main lounge area is to the right. A conservatory at the rear leads to the extensive beer garden. Up to four guest beers always include one from Thornbridge with the others mostly sourced locally. Entertainment includes a quiz on Thursday night and occasional live jazz and blues. A LocAle pub. Q❀◐◑⊖(Sheffield University)🚌(51,52)♣⅃

Walkley Cottage

46 Bole Hill Road, S6 5DD

10 (12 Sun)-11

☎ (0114) 234 4968

Adnams Bitter; Caledonian Deuchars IPA; Greene King Abbot; Taylor Landlord; Tetley Bitter; Wells Bombardier H

Recently refurbished, this spacious roadhouse-style suburban local is now open plan, with an L-shaped lounge providing separate seating areas. Built for Gilmours between the wars on a large site, the extensive garden affords panoramic views over the Rivelin Valley. A lively pub, it holds a popular quiz on Thursday. In addition to the six regular cask ales, there is also a rotating guest beer from a wide variety of local and regional brewers. No evening meals Sunday. ❀◐◑⊞🚌(94,95)♣P

South Anston

Loyal Trooper ✔

34 Sheffield Road, S25 5DT (off A57, 3 miles off M1 jct 31)

12-11 (midnight Fri & Sat)

☎ (01909) 562203

Adnams Bitter; Taylor Landlord; Tetley Bitter; guest beers H

A friendly village local dating back to 1690 in parts, this pub sells a range of real ales and serves good wholesome food. It comprises a public bar, snug and lounge with a function room upstairs used by many local groups. The pub stands on the Five Churches Walk. Q❀◐◑⊞P

Sprotbrough

Boat Inn ✔

Nursery Lane, DN5 7NB

11-11 (10.30 Sun)

☎ (01302) 858500

Black Sheep Best Bitter; guest beers H

In a riverside location near the Trans-Pennine Trail, this multi-roomed pub is popular with walkers, diners and the local community. Good-value food is served throughout the day. The menu is extensive and background music is unobtrusive. Outside, there is a large courtyard drinking area. Cask Marque accredited, it was CAMRA's Doncaster Pub of the Season for summer 2007. ⛰❀◐◑♿P⅃

Ivanhoe Hotel

Melton Road, DN5 7NS

11-2, 5-11; 11-11 Fri & Sat; 12-10.30 Sun

☎ (01302) 853130

Samuel Smith OBB H

In an idyllic setting by the village crossroads, this local CAMRA Pub of the Season Autumn 2006 is popular for its well-kept, competitively-priced beer. The pub comprises a spacious lounge and a separate public bar with pool and snooker tables. Good value food can be enjoyed undisturbed by background music (not Sun or Mon eves). Outside there is a large beer garden adjacent to the village cricket pitch. Q❀◐◑⊞♿🚌(224,225)♣P⅃

Sunnyside

Woodman

Woodlaithes Road, S66 3ZL (off A631, 1½ miles from M18 jct 1)

12-11 (midnight Fri & Sat)

☎ (01709) 533854

Marston's Pedigree; guest beers Ⓗ
A new pub situated on the Woodlaithes village estate, opened around two years ago by Marston's. It offers an extensive menu of locally-sourced food, with popular curry nights and quiz nights held regularly. Winner of the local CAMRA branch's Pub of the Season award for summer 2008. ❀◑♿P⍭

Sykehouse

Old George

Broad Lane, DN14 9AU
⏲ 12 (11 summer)-midnight
☎ (01405) 785635
Tetley Bitter; guest beers Ⓗ
This building is about 200 years old and in the past has been a slaughterhouse and shop as well as a pub. Recently saved from demolition, it has several rooms including one with an open fire. Food is available from an extensive menu, served in the restaurant and throughout the pub, plus a Sunday carvery and OAP specials. Outside is a large patio where barbecues and an outside bar are available in summer. There is a superb children's playground, including a swimming pool. ♔❀◑♿⛺🚌♣P⍭

Thorne

Windmill Inn

19 Queen Street, DN8 5AA (near Finkle St shopping precinct)
⏲ 2-11 (midnight Fri); 12-midnight Sat & Sun
☎ (01405) 812866
Black Sheep Best Bitter; John Smith's Bitter; guest beers Ⓗ
A mere stone's throw from the old Darley Brewery Tower, this extremely well-kept and efficiently-run town centre pub is highly popular with the local community. Sports fans are well-catered for on separate TV channels. The clientele includes players from the Thornensians rugby team, and the Windmill has its own golf, football, cricket and pool societies. A new innovation is coffee and croissants for shoppers during the morning. The smokers' area outside is heated and covered.
❀◘♿⛺⇌(Thorne N)🚌♣P⍭

Thorpe Salvin

Parish Oven

Worksop Road, S80 3JU
⏲ 12-2.30 (not Mon), 5.30-11 (11.30 Fri); 12-midnight Sat; 12-10.30 Sun
☎ (01909) 770685
Black Sheep Best Bitter; guest beers Ⓗ
The Parish Oven gets its name from its location on the site of a former communal bakery. This award-winning pub is a popular venue for Sunday lunch (booking advisable) and evening meals, offering a variety of home-cooked dishes. There is a large outside play area and well-behaved dogs are welcome in the bar area. The pub is on the Five Churches and Round Rotherham walks. ❀◑♿P⍭

Thurlstone

Huntsman

136 Manchester Road, S36 9QW (on A628 Penistone to Manchester road)
⏲ 6-11; 12-10.30 Sun
☎ (01226) 764892
Black Sheep Best Bitter; Taylor Landlord; Tetley Bitter; guest beers Ⓗ
This multi award-winning roadside pub oozes charm. With its exposed beams, real fire and great atmosphere it makes a great stopping place. The three guest beers are usually sourced from local micro-breweries. At the heart of the community, the pub offers regular entertainment including quizzes and acoustic music nights. Good value food is available, with themed meals served on Sunday.
♔Q❀◗🚌(23,24)♣⍭

Tickhill

Scarbrough Arms

Sunderland Street, DN11 9QJ (on A631)
⏲ 12-11 (10.30 Sun)
☎ (01302) 742977
Courage Directors; Greene King Abbot; John Smith's Bitter; Shepherd Neame Spitfire; guest beers Ⓗ
A deserving Guide entry since 1990, this three-roomed stone pub has won several local CAMRA awards, including Pub of the Season several times and Pub of the Year. Originally a farmhouse, the building dates back to the 16th century, although structural changes have taken place. The snug is a delight, with its barrel-shaped tables and real fire, while bar billiards can be played in the bar. The covered smoking area is a former garage/stables. Real cider is available in summer, and seasonal beer festivals are planned. ♔❀◘🚌♣●P⍭

Wath upon Dearne

Church House ✔

Montgomery Square, S63 7RZ
⏲ 9-midnight (1am Fri & Sat)
☎ (01709) 879518
Marston's Pedigree; Greene King IPA; guest beers Ⓗ
This impressive Wetherspoon's pub is set in a pedestrian square in the town centre with excellent access to local bus services. In a handy spot for exploring the RSPB Wetlands Centre at Wombwell, it serves a wide variety of beers from both national and local brewers, including the nearby Acorn Brewery. ♔❀◑♿🚌⍭

Wentworth

George & Dragon

85 Main Street, S62 7TN
⏲ 10-11 (10.30 Sun)
☎ (01709) 742440
Taylor Landlord; Wentworth WPA, seasonal beers; guest beers Ⓗ
Situated in the picturesque village of Wentworth, the pub is just 500 metres from Rotherham's only brewery. It takes up to four ales from the brewery, along with other beers from local and national brewers plus a cask cider. Set back from the road, it has generous gardens out front. Home-cooked food is very popular. Private parties can be booked in the upstairs function room. ♔Q❀◑P

Whiston

Chequers Inn

Pleasley Road, S60 4HB (on A618, 1½ miles from M1 jct 33)
⏲ 12 (4 Mon & Tue)-11; 12-11.30 Fri & Sat; 12-11 Sun
☎ (01709) 829168
Taylor Landlord; Tetley Bitter; guest beers Ⓗ

Former coaching inn next to a 13th-century thatched barn, this friendly local returns to the Guide following a change of landlord. One side hosts a tap room, while the large garden features a barbecue area and its own bar in summer. Situated in a picturesque village, this pub is a regular local CAMRA award winner. ❀◑🚌♣P⁻

Golden Ball ✔

7 Turner Lane, S60 4HY (off A618, 1½ miles from M1 jct 33)

⏲ 12-11 (midnight Thu-Sat)

☎ (01709) 726911

Taylor Landlord; Tetley Bitter; guest beers Ⓗ

Small cottage-style pub in the village of Whiston, popular with both drinkers and diners. The pub has returned to the Guide after a year out, during which time it has been fully refurbished and the beer range increased. The interior has several small enclaves and a comfortable snug to the rear. There are large gardens at the back and an ample car park to the front. Some parts of the building are over 500 years old. **Q**❀◑**P**

Hind ✔

285 East Bawtry Road, S60 4ET (on A631 link road between M1 and M18)

⏲ 12-11 (midnight Thu-Sat)

☎ (01709) 704351

Taylor Landlord; Tetley Bitter; guest beers Ⓗ

This large pub was built for the Mappins Brewery in 1936. Originally known as King Edward VIII, it was renamed when the king abdicated. It is popular for its daytime and evening food. Since refurbishment the interior has been opened out, creating good disabled access. There are extensive gardens to the rear and a snooker table upstairs (membership required to play). 🔥◑♿🚌P⁻

Sitwell Arms

Pleasley Road, S60 4HQ (on A618, around 1½ miles from M1 jct 33)

⏲ 12-11 (midnight Thu-Sat)

☎ (01709) 377003

Acorn Barnsley Gold; Greene King Abbot; Tetley Bitter; guest beer Ⓗ

A re-entry to the Guide, this pub benefits from a large garden with a children's play area and a car park. Low ceilings and oak beams indicate the age of the building – it was a farm and ale house before becoming a coaching inn and some parts are centuries old. The pub has a separate bar and restaurant area and hosts regular quiz nights. ❀◑🍴🚌P

YORKSHIRE (WEST)

Ackworth

Angel

Wakefield Road, WF7 7AB (on A638 800m W of A628/A638 roundabout)

⏲ 12-midnight

☎ (01977) 611276

Black Sheep Best Bitter; Taylor Golden Best Ⓗ

A thoughtful and well-designed open-plan layout centred around a large, arched wooden bar. High quality home-made bar meals using local produce are served lunchtime and evening Monday to Saturday, with a very popular carvery on Sunday from 12-4pm. The adjacent Dando Way, which follows the course of a former railway line used to transport stone from a local quarry, provides a good start and finish point for walking/cycling in the nearby Country Park and surrounding area. 🔥❀◑♿🚌(35,245)♣P⁻🍺

Boot & Shoe

Wakefield Road, WF7 7DF (on A638 500m W of A628/A638 roundabout)

⏲ 11.30-midnight (1am Fri & Sat); 11.30-11 Sun

☎ (01977) 610218 🌐 thebootandshoe.co.uk

Marston's Pedigree; John Smith's Bitter; Samuel Smith OBB Ⓗ

Busy, non-food pub next to the cricket field in the village of Ackworth, which once supplied the grindstones for Sheffield's cutlery industry. The building dates back to the late 16th century, retaining some original features including the delightful semi-circular vestibule. The pub is a rare outlet for Sam Smith's in the free trade. The venue has a strong reputation for live music, with special musical events on bank holidays – it has won an award for Best Live Music Venue. 🔥❀♿🚌(35,245)♣P⁻

Armitage Bridge

Armitage Bridge Monkey Club

Dean Brook Road, HD4 7PB (off B6108 Meltham Road)

⏲ 5 (7 Wed & Thu)-11; closed Mon & Tue; 12-11 Sun

☎ (01484) 664891 🌐 freewebs.com/the-monkey-club

Moorhouses Pride of Pendle; guest beers Ⓗ

Follow the stream running by the side of the lane to this quaint, friendly little club, in the middle of the hamlet of Armitage Bridge. Downstairs there is an L-shaped bar lounge with comfortable seating, upstairs is a games room with a pool table and dartboard. Two guest beers are usually available from independent micros – Brass Monkey beers are a favourite. The annual Monkeyfest beer festival is not to be missed. Show this Guide or a CAMRA membership card to be signed in. ❀🚌(321,323,324)♣P

Baildon

Junction 🏆

1 Baildon Road, BD17 6AB (on Otley road, ¾ mile from Shipley)

⏲ 12-midnight (1am Fri & Sat)

☎ (01274) 582009

Dark Star Hophead; Fuller's ESB; Tetley Bitter; guest beers Ⓗ

A friendly community local, this CAMRA multi award winner has three rooms: a main bar, lounge plus a games room with a pool table and a dartboard. The beers change constantly, including ales from micros, and one pump dedicated to the nearby Saltaire Brewery. Home-cooked food is served on weekday lunchtimes. A music jam session is hosted most Sunday evenings. Sporting events are shown on TV. Another attraction here is the annual beer festival in July. ❀◐⇌(Shipley)🚌🍎⁻

Bankfoot

Woodman ✔

1062 Manchester Road, BD5 8NN

⏲ 12-midnight

☎ (01274) 306445

Copper Dragon Golden Pippin; John Smith's Bitter; Tetley Bitter; guest beers Ⓗ

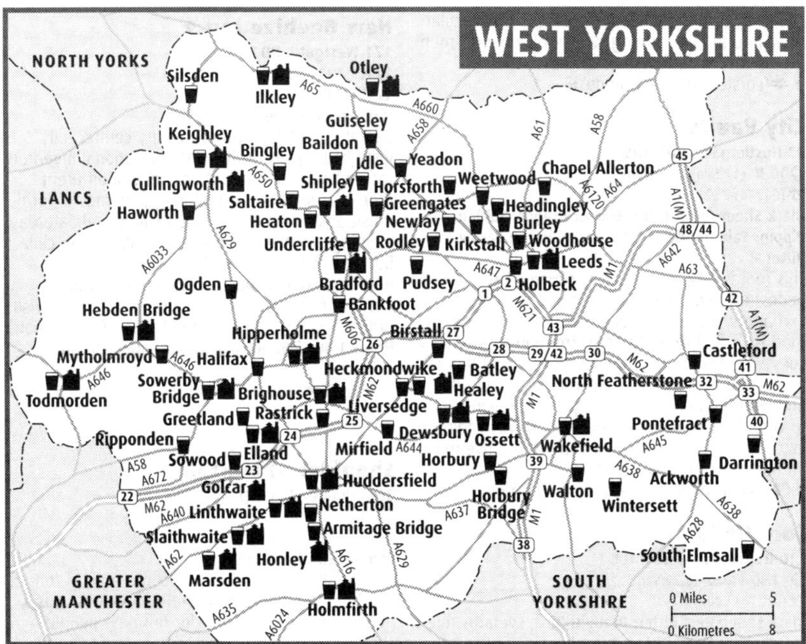

Friendly local with a regular clientele and a reputation for quality ales. Guest beers come from Yorkshire micros including Salamander and Ossett. An L-shaped single room includes a small stage at one end and a pool table at the other. Thursday night is quiz night with a free supper and the pub also hosts pool, darts and domino teams. The outside smoking area includes a heater and a large-screen TV. There is also a children's play area. ❀♿🚌♣P⚡

Batley

Cellar Bar

51 Station Road, WF17 5SU (opp rail station)
❂ 4-11; 12-midnight Fri & Sat; 12-11 Sun
☎ (01924) 423419 🌐 downthecellar.com
Black Sheep Best Bitter; Copper Dragon Golden Pippin; guest beers Ⓗ
Atmospheric, welcoming single-room bar in the basement of a Grade II-listed building in an historic area occasionally used as a film set. Comfortable seating includes two Chesterfield settees, while candles on the tables add to the ambience. A pool table is located on a raised section at the rear. The pub hosts two annual beer festivals. Quiz night is Thursday. Friday evenings often see a DJ in attendance and live music plays on most Saturday evenings. ⇌♣

Bingley

Myrtle Grove ✔

141 Main Street, BD16 1AJ
❂ 9am-midnight
☎ (01274) 568637
Greene King IPA, Abbot; guest beers Ⓗ
A well-established provider of quality real ales, with five guests selected from the likes of Saltaire, Salamander, Ossett, Naylors and Moorhouses. An unusual conversion of a former cinema, the single room interior has a high ceiling with cosy booths along one wall. There is also a raised family area along with award-winning toilets. On a main road, close to car parks and other local amenities, excellent public transport links are very close.
Q◐♿⇌🚌

Birstall

Black Bull

5 Kirkgate, WF17 9PB (off A652/A643)
❂ 12-11 (10.30 Sun)
☎ (01274) 873039 🌐 blackbullbirstall.co.uk
Boddingtons Bitter; John Smith's Bitter; guest beer Ⓗ
Grade II-listed building dating in parts from the 17th century. The upstairs function room with its original wood panelling is a former courtroom, complete with prisoner's dock and witness box. It is thought the last trial was held in 1839. The ground floor comprises several partly opened-out areas and a secluded snug, creating a pleasant ambience. An independent guest beer is fast changing. Lunches are served daily while evening meals are available Wednesday to Saturday. Ask for ramps for wheelchair access to the toilets.
🐴❀◐♿🚌(220,283)P⚡

Bradford

Castle Hotel

20 Grattan Road, BD1 2LU
❂ 11-11; 12-9 Sun
☎ (01274) 393166
Mansfield Cask Ale; guest beers Ⓗ
An established real ale pub in the city centre within easy reach of the transport network, this former Websters house now stocks an ever-changing range of beers from micros up and down the country. A beer from the local Old Spot Brewery is always stocked, and the brewery helps to organise the recently introduced beer festivals at the pub.

The 19th-century building features a semicircular wraparound bar, forming two semi-separate room areas, with a dartboard at one end.
♿⇌(Forster Sq/Interchange)🚌

City Vaults

33 Hustlergate, BD1 1NS
10.30 (11 Sun)-11 (midnight Fri & Sat)
☎ (01274) 739697
Black Sheep Best Bitter; Copper Dragon Golden Pippin; Salamander Golden Salamander; Tetley Bitter Ⓗ
This roomy city centre pub is situated on a pedestrianised area opposite the old Wool Exchange. There are four beers on handpump and food is served from 12-7pm. The pub was converted from former bank premises a number of years ago, and retains a wealth of stained glass and wrought iron. There are upstairs drinking areas to complement the split-level areas downstairs. Jazz plays every Sunday and there is also live music on alternate Saturday evenings.
❀◑♿⇌(Forster square/Interchange)🚌

Corn Dolly

110 Bolton Road, BD1 4DE
11.30-11; 12-10.30 Sun
☎ (01274) 720219
Black Sheep Best Bitter; Draught Bass; Everards Tiger; Moorhouses Dolly Bitter; guest beers Ⓗ
Popular, award-winning local, a short walk from the city centre. This pub has been run by the same family for many years. Opened in 1834 under the name The Wharfe, it originally serviced the thirsts of canal workers. An open-plan layout incorporates a separate games area. Four guest beers complement the regulars and value food is served weekdays. Pump clips adorn the bar and real wood beams can be admired while enjoying the ales.
❀◑♿⇌(Forster Sq/Interchange)
🚌(612,640,641)♣P

Fighting Cock

21-23 Preston Street, BD7 1JE
11.30-11; 12-10.30 Sun
☎ (01274) 726907
Copper Dragon Golden Pippin; Greene King Abbot; Red Lion White Lion; Taylor Best Bitter, Golden Best, Landlord; guest beers Ⓗ
Popular, unassuming pub, just a short walk or bus ride from the city centre. Twelve real ales are usually available including at least one dark beer. Additionally, this regular local CAMRA award winner serves ciders, foreign bottled beers and fruit wines. It attracts a wide variety of customers from loyal locals to well-travelled real ale enthusiasts. Lunches are served Monday to Saturday. ◑♿

Haigy's

31 Lumb Lane, Manningham, BD8 7QU
5 (12 Fri & Sat)-2am; 12-11 Sun
☎ (01274) 731644
Tetley Bitter; guest beers Ⓗ
Friendly locals' pub, a former winner of Bradford CAMRA Pub of the Year, situated on the edge of the city centre. It offers up to four guest ales from northern micros including Phoenix, Newby Wyke and Ossett. The comfortable lounge sports a fine collection of porcelain teapots. The pub is popular with Bradford City fans on match days. Pool players excel on the unusual revolving hexagonal table.
❀⇌(Forster Sq/Interchange)🚌(620,621)♣P

New Beehive Inn ★

171 Westgate, BD1 3AA
12-11 (3am Fri-Sun)
☎ (01274) 721784
Beer range varies Ⓗ
Gas-lit pub at top end of the city centre, fully justifying a place in the CAMRA National Inventory for its historic interior. It has several different rooms – the back bar featuring paintings of local musicians. Live jazz is played Friday and Saturday evenings, with rock, reggae and ska in the cellar bar also at the weekend. Beers come from numerous micros up and down the country. Accommodation is in en-suite rooms, with a Visit Britain 3-star rating from the English Tourist Board. Beers from Saltaire and Salamander feature regularly.
❀⇌(Forster Square)🚌(617,618)♣P

Shoulder of Mutton

28 Kirkgate, BD1 1QL
12-11
☎ (01274) 726038
Samuel Smith OBB Ⓗ
This small multi-roomed city-centre pub, a former coaching inn, dates from the early 1800s. It is a popular lunchtime venue for business people, shoppers and locals, who all appreciate the good value food. Its appeal is enhanced by a large sun-trap garden. The pub has been refurbished without ruining its traditional atmosphere – pictures, photographs and drawings of the old city abound. It is the main base for the Airedale quiz league.
❀⇌(Forster Sq/Interchange)

INDEPENDENT BREWERIES

Anglo Dutch Dewsbury
Atlas Mill Brighouse
Barearts Todmorden
Bob's Healey
Brass Monkey Sowerby Bridge (NEW)
Bridestones Hebden Bridge
Briscoe's Otley
Clark's Wakefield
Eastwood Elland
Elland Elland
Empire Slaithwaite
Fernandes Wakefield
Five Towns Wakefield (NEW)
Fox Beer Leeds (NEW)
Golcar Golcar
Goose Eye Keighley
Halifax Steam Hipperholme
Ilkley Ilkley (NEW)
Leeds Leeds
Linfit Linthwaite
Little Valley Hebden Bridge
Mallinsons Huddersfield
Nook Holmfirth (NEW)
Old Bear Keighley
Old Spot Cullingworth
Ossett Ossett
Riverhead Marsden
Rodham's Otley (brewing suspended)
Ryburn Sowerby Bridge
Salamander Bradford
Saltaire Shipley
Summer Wine Honley
Tigertops Wakefield
Timothy Taylor Keighley

Sir Titus Salt ✔

Unit B, Windsor Baths, Morley Street, BD7 1AQ (behind Alhambra Theatre)
9-midnight (1am Fri & Sat)
☎ (01274) 732853
Greene King IPA, Abbot; Marston's Pedigree; guest beers H
Splendid Wetherspoon conversion of the original swimming baths, now named after a local industrialist and philanthropist. An upstairs seating area overlooks the main bar where framed pictures depict the educational heritage of the city. The pub draws a cosmopolitan clientele including students, theatre-goers, clubbers and diners from nearby Indian restaurants. The location is handy for the National Media Museum.
Q(Forster Sq/Interchange)

Brighouse

Old Ship Inn

34 Bethel Street, HD6 1JN
12-11 (midnight Fri & Sat); 12-10.30 Sun
☎ (01484) 719543 theoldshipinnbrighouse.co.uk
Black Sheep Best Bitter, Riggwelter; Brass Monkey range; Copper Dragon Golden Pippin; guest beers H
A friendly pub in the town centre with a growing reputation for real ale. The main bar area has a stone-flagged floor and wood-panelled walls painted in a light colour. Three constantly-changing beers plus a rotating ale from the local Brass Monkey Brewery complement the regular beers. Good home-cooked food is served at lunchtime, using ingredients sourced from local suppliers. Winner of the local CAMRA Pub of the Season in summer 2008. **Q**(Brighouse)

Red Rooster

123 Elland Road, Brookfoot, HD6 2QR (on A6025)
3 (12 Fri & Sat)-11; 12-10.30 Sun
☎ (01484) 713737
Abbeydale Moonshine; Copper Dragon Golden Pippin; Harviestoun Bitter & Twisted; Taylor Landlord; guest beers H
This small stone-faced pub lies on the inside of a sharp bend. Its former four-roomed layout is still apparent, with a stone-flagged floor throughout. Live music is performed on the last Sunday afternoon of the month. A charity week is held in mid-August and a beer festival in September. There is a small area of decking for outside drinking. Local CAMRA Pub of the Year 2005 and 2007.
(571)

Richard Oastler ✔

Bethell Street, HD6 1JN SE145227
9-midnight (1am Fri & Sat)
☎ (01484) 401756
Greene King IPA, Abbot; Marston's Pedigree; Theakston Old Peculier; guest beers H
A Grade II-listed former Methodist chapel converted to a successful Wetherspoon pub. Inside, the magnificent but inaccessible upper floor with original chapel pews and impressive ceiling has been retained. Up to eight guest beers are served, usually including at least one from a local micro-breweries. Winner of local CAMRA 2009 Winter Pub of the Season.

Burley

Fox & Newt ✔

7-9 Burley Street, LS3 1LD
12-11 (midnight Fri & Sat)
☎ (0113) 245 4505 myspace.com/thefoxandnewt
Beer range varies H
This welcoming, recently refurbished pub is now the home of Fox Beer Company. Of the eight handpumps, two are dedicated to house beers: Nightshade, Fox IPA, Mr Tod or Clarendon Dark Mild. Regular guest beers are from Leeds Brewery, Black Sheep and small northern breweries, with one or two featured each month. A 10 per cent discount on selected lines is offered to CAMRA members and students with an NUS Card.

Castleford

Glass Blower ✔

15 Bank Street, WF10 1JD
9-midnight (1am Fri & Sat)
☎ (01977) 520390
Greene King IPA, Abbot; Marston's Pedigree; guest beers H
Former post office converted to a popular Wetherspoon's in 1998. The pub was to have been called The Glass House, referring to the town's history of glass bottle manufacture, but local people objected because of the link with prison. Pictures of the work of sculptor Henry Moore, who was born in the town, adorn the walls. A selection of guest ales adds to the three regular beers. Excellent value food is served all day and children are welcome. **Q**

Shoulder of Mutton

18 Methley Road, WF10 1LX (on A6032)
12-3 (4 Sat & Sun), 7-midnight (1am Sat & Sun)
☎ (01977) 736039
Tetley Dark Mild, Bitter; guest beer H
This traditional free house started life as a farmhouse in 1632 and is packed with breweriana. The landlord is a fount of knowledge on pub-keeping and a great supporter of micro-brewers, justifiably proud of the many awards he has won for his cellarmanship. Expect lively conversation and a warm welcome from both the landlord and locals. Ring the Bull, Nine Men's Morris and wooden puzzles are played, and it's magic when the George Formby Society meets here on the last Wednesday of the month. Live music plays on Sunday when the pub opens all day.
Q(153,189)**P**

Chapel Allerton

Further North

194 Harrogate Road, LS7 4NZ
5.30-11 (midnight Thu & Fri); 4-midnight Sat; 4-11 Sun
☎ (0113) 237 0962 furthernorth.co.uk
Beer range varies H
Originally a car spares shop, now converted to a single room bar. The beer usually comes from Rooster's plus a good selection of Belgian and other foreign bottles is also offered. Despite its main road location, the fully opening frontage gives a continental feel in summer. The driver is not forgotten, with soft drinks from Fentimans and Looza available. The premises are under the same ownership as North Bar in the city centre. On-street parking is mostly unrestricted.

Three Hulats ✔

13 Harrogate Road, LS7 3NB
⏲ 9-midnight (1am Fri & Sat)
☎ (0113) 262 0524
Greene King IPA, Abbot; Marston's Pedigree; guest beers H
Built in the 1930s, this former Tetley house is now an out-of-town Wetherspoon's, used as a base and meeting place by local community groups. An L-shaped bar boasts 10 handpumps with seven offering changing guest beers from both micros and regionals. The landlord hosts regular themed beer festivals in addition to those held by the chain. Food is served all day and families are welcome until 9pm. Q❀◑♿🚌P

Darrington

Spread Eagle

Estcourt Road, WF8 3AP
⏲ 12-3, 5-11 (midnight Fri, 11.30 Sat); 12-10.30 Sun
☎ (01977) 699698
John Smith's Bitter; Tetley Bitter; guest beers H
Pleasant, friendly pub in the heart of the village. Popular with a wide cross-section of the community, it is very lively in the evenings. Good food is served either in the bar or in a small restaurant-style area. A quiz is held on Monday evening and there is a function room for hire. There are rumours of a ghost – a boy who was shot for horse rustling in 1685. Children are allowed in the pub until 9pm. No food Sunday evening and all day Monday. Q❀◑♿🚌(408,409)P⚐

Dewsbury

Huntsman

Chidswell Lane, Shaw Cross, WF12 7SW (400m from A653/B6128 jct)
⏲ 12-3 (not Mon), 7 (5 Thu-Sat)-11
☎ (01924) 275700
Taylor Landlord; guest beers H
Situated in a semi-rural area, the pub has been tastefully converted from former farmworkers' cottages and enjoys fine views across open fields to the north. There is a warm and friendly atmosphere, welcoming both visitors and locals. A large lounge leads to two further rooms, the smaller has a Yorkshire range and is decorated with militaria and horse brasses. Lunches are served Tuesday-Saturday and evening meals 5-7.30pm Thursday and Friday. The house beer, Chidswell Bitter, is brewed by Highwood.
⛫❀◑⛺🚌(117,205)P

Leggers Inn 🏆

Calder Valley Marina, Mill Street East, WF12 9BD (off B6409, follow brown signs to Canal Basin)
⏲ 10.30-11 (midnight Fri & Sat)
☎ (01924) 502846
Everards Tiger; guest beers H
Once the hayloft of a stable block by the canal basin, the pub has been here for a decade, gaining a wide reputation. Upstairs, mind your head on the low beams which hold many interesting items. Six guest pumps include Leeds and Rooster's beers with a rotating guest cider or perry. Outside, the decked area and tables around the basin make it a fine place for a summer drink. Light meals are served all day and a large function room is available. Bus and rail stations are within a mile.
⛫❀◑♣🍎P⚐

Shepherds Boy ✔

157 Huddersfield Road, WF13 2RP (on A644 half mile from town centre)
⏲ 3 (12 Thu)-11; 12-midnight Fri & Sat; 12-11 Sun
☎ (01924) 454116 🌐 ossett-brewery.co.uk
Ossett Pale Gold, Excelsior; guest beers H
Outside the town centre, this is an excellent pub reconstruction by Ossett Brewery, with many original features retained or reinstated. Four comfortable drinking areas are provided in which to enjoy beers from eight handpumps, and a trademark brick arch separates the front room from the rear. Guest beers include one from Fuller's and a rotating stout or mild. A good selection of draught and bottled foreign beers is also available. Tuesday is quiz night. Beer festivals are hosted twice a year. ❀♿🚌♣P⚐

West Riding Licensed Refreshment Rooms ✔

Railway Station, Wellington Road, WF13 1HF (platform 2 Dewsbury station)
⏲ 11 (12 Mon)-11 (midnight Thu & Fri); 10-midnight Sat; 11-11 Sun
☎ (01924) 459193 🌐 imissedthetrain.com
Black Sheep Best Bitter; Taylor Dark Mild, Landlord; guest beers H
This multi-award winning pub occupies part of the Victorian Grade II-listed building. Eight handpumps include one for Anglo-Dutch Brewery plus a good variety of styles from micro-breweries. The pub was a finalist in the 2006 CAMRA National Pub of the Year contest. Summer and winter beer festivals and live music events are held here; see the website for dates. Lunches and evening specials are renowned. Outside is a large, decked semi-covered patio. Featured in the TV programme Oz and James Drink to Britain. ⛫❀◐♿⇌🚌⚐

Elland

Barge & Barrel ✔

10-20 Park Road, HX5 9HP (on A6025 over Elland Bridge)
⏲ 12-midnight
☎ (01422) 373623
Abbeydale Moonshine; Elland Bargee; Phoenix Wobbly Bob; Shepherd Neame Spitfire; guest beers H
A large roadside pub built to serve the former Elland Station. Its three-sided bar serves the comfortable lounge with its bottle collection and views over the canal and river to Elland town. Opposite, an area warmed by a fireplace is partly divided from the bar by a wall with modern stained glass. The diverse customers includes mountaineers who meet here. Sunday's curry night is popular. The 12 pumps offer mainly micro-brewery beers. ⛫❀◑🚌(537,538)♣P⚐

Greengates

Albion Inn

25 New Line, BD10 9AS
⏲ 12-11
☎ (01274) 613211
Acorn Barnsley Bitter; John Smith's Bitter; guest beers H
A return to the Guide for this busy roadside local on the main Leeds-Keighley bus route. The pub comprises an L-shaped lounge and a separate traditional tap room where pub games are popular. The Albion boasts a thriving social club but

strangers are made very welcome. The current incumbent is keen on traditional values in this friendly pub. ⊟♿♣●P⚟⊓

Greetland

Greetland Community & Sporting Association

Rochdale Road, HX4 8JG (on B6113)
⏲ 5-11; 4-midnight Fri & Sat; 12-11 Sun
☎ (01422) 370140
Coachhouse Duckworth's Delight; Taylor Landlord; guest beers 🄷
Award-winning sports and social club set back from the road at the top of Greetland village. The club is a past winner of both the CAMRA Yorkshire and National Club of the Year awards. It has a wooden decked area outside which in summer affords great views over Halifax. A very warm welcome is offered to all visitors. ❀🚌(343,556,557)P⚟

Guiseley

Coopers ✔

4-6 Otley Road, LS20 8AH (opp Morrisons on A65)
⏲ 12-11
☎ (01943) 878835 🌐 markettowntaverns.co.uk
Black Sheep Best Bitter; Taylor Landlord; guest beers 🄷
One of the Market Town Taverns chain, this light, airy, modern bar-cum-eatery serves eight ales generally from Yorkshire micros and independents. It also stocks a large selection of continental bottled beers. A diverse range of meals is available until 9pm in a separate dining area. The large upstairs function room has regular jazz and musical events and also serves as a dining room.
Q❀◐◑♿⇌🚌(33,33A,97)⚟

Guiseley Factory Workers Club

6 Town Street, LS20 9DT (off A65, near St Oswald's Church)
⏲ 1-4 (5 Mon), 7-11; 11.30 (1 Fri)-midnight Sat; 11-midnight Sun
☎ (01943) 874793
Tetley Bitter; guest beers 🄷
Small, friendly, working men's club, a meeting place for community groups, local clubs and societies. A traditional three-roomed layout includes a lounge, snooker room and concert room hosting Saturday night turns. Quiz night is Sunday; sports are shown on a large-screen TV or in the lounge. There is a large walled and lawned beer garden at the rear. A beer festival is held in April. Show your CAMRA membership card or a copy of this Guide for entry. CAMRA National Club of the Year 2008. ❀⇌🚌(33A,97,737)♣P⚟

Halifax

Big Six

10 Horsfall Street, Saville Park, HX1 3HG (off A646, Skircoat Moor road at King Cross)
⏲ 5-11; 3.30-11.30 Fri; 12-11.30 Sat; 12-11 Sun
☎ (01422) 350169
Adnams Bitter; guest beers 🄷
Busy, friendly mid-terraced pub close to the Free School Lane recreation ground. A through corridor divides two lounges from the bar and games room. Brewery memorabilia plus relics of the former Big Six mineral water company which operated from the premises a century ago are displayed throughout the pub. An ever-changing range of guest beers comes from regional and micro-breweries. There is a small beer garden to the rear. Dogs are welcome. ⛫Q❀🚌♣

Sportsman Inn

Bradford Old Road, Swalesmoor, HX3 6UG (off A647, 1 Mile N of centre)
⏲ 12-2.30 (not Mon), 6-11 (midnight Fri); 12-midnight Sat; 12-11 Sun
☎ (01422) 367000 🌐 ridehalifax.co.uk
Taylor Landlord; Tetley Bitter; guest beer 🄷
Situated on the hillside with stunning views towards Halifax and Queensbury. There are two bars, one serving as a family room, plus a separate restaurant area. Four guest beers, usually from local breweries, are served. The pub is adjacent to a dry ski slope and a children's adventure playground as well as having its own play area.
⛫Q🐎❀◐◑♿🚌(576)♣P⚟

Three Pigeons ★ ✔

1 Sun Fold, South Parade, HX1 2LX
⏲ 3 (12 Fri & Sat)-11.30; 12-11 Sun
☎ (01422) 347001
Ossett Pale Gold, 3 Pigs, Excelsior; guest beers 🄷
This CAMRA National Inventory listed and award-winning pub dates from 1932. Its period features have been restored following its acquisition by Ossett Brewery and the decor is in keeping with the period. It has a central octagonal space with a painted ceiling and three of its four rooms radiate from this space. Usually there are four guest ales on offer including two from the Ossett group and a dark beer. Real cider is stocked, together with a selection of Belgian beers. ⛫❀⇌🚌●⚟

William IV

247 King Cross Road, HX1 3JL
⏲ 11-11; 11.30-10.30 Sun
☎ (01422) 354889
Tetley Bitter 🄷
Popular pub situated in the main shopping street at King Cross. Buses from the town centre stop at the door. The lounge has a standing area and comfortable seating. There is a small public bar to the rear and an extension into a former shop provides further seating at a raised level. Lunches are served Monday to Saturday. Sporting fixtures feature on TV screens in both bars. Benches are provided outside at the rear for smokers and drinkers. ❀◐⊟🚌♣

Haworth

Fleece Inn ✔

67 Main Street, BD22 8DA
⏲ 12 (10 Sat)-11 (11.30 Fri & Sat); 10-10.30 Sun
☎ (01535) 642172 🌐 timothy-taylor.co.uk/fleeceinn
Taylor Dark Mild, Best Bitter, Golden Best, Landlord, Ram Tam 🄷
A three-storey former coaching inn situated halfway up the historic, pretty and steep cobbled Haworth main street. The Haworth brass band can be heard outside on some evenings rehearsing in their band room above the pub; combined with the surroundings, this provides a real traditional Yorkshire atmosphere. The hostelry offers good beer, food and accommodation to visitors, and is also popular with locals. A range of foreign bottled beers is stocked.
⛫🛏◐◑♿⛺⇌(KWVLR)🚌(664,665)

Haworth Old Hall Inn ✔

8 Sun Street, BD22 8BP
⏲ 12-11 (11.30 Thu-Sat)
☎ (01535) 642709 🌐 hawortholdhall.co.uk
Jennings Bitter, Cumberland Ale, Cocker Hoop, Sneck Lifter, seasonal beers; guest beers Ⓗ
On entering this magnificent Yorkshire stone Tudor manor house through the substantial studded oak door, you find stone floors, arches, mullioned windows, two huge fireplaces and a splendid wood-panelled bar serving the full range of Jennings beers, plus guests. Good home-cooked food is served and the pub can get very busy at weekends. Quiz night is Thursday.
⛫❀🛏◐◑♿⛺⇌(KWVLR)🚌(663,665)P⚟

Keighley & Worth Valley Railway Buffet Car

Keighley & Worth Valley Light Railway Ltd, Haworth Station, BD22 8NJ (join at any station on Worth Valley line)
⏲ 11-5.15 Sat & Sun summer (4.30 winter) and Mon-Fri school holidays; other dates as advertised (check timetable)
☎ (01535) 645214 🌐 kwvr.co.uk
Beer range varies Ⓗ
An on-train bar in this famous heritage railway. Beer is cellared and conditioned at Oxenhope then drawn into tea-urn style containers for transfer to the train which serves up to three ever-changing beers. The carriage is warmed with steam pipes from the engine. The line runs every weekend and also weekdays during school holidays. Opening times and facilities vary so it is highly recommended to check before visiting. Please note, a ticket to travel must be purchased.
Q⛺⇌(Keighley)🚌P

Headingley

Arcadia Ale & Wine Bar ✔

34 Arndale Centre, Otley Road, LS6 2UE
⏲ 12-11
☎ (0113) 274 5599 🌐 markettowntaverns.co.uk
Black Sheep Best Bitter; Taylor Landlord; guest beers Ⓗ
Arcadia is an oasis of quality and choice among the surrounding student pubs and bars of Headingley. There is no piped music or fruit machines, just the background noise of animated conversations. Two of the guest beers are normally from Elland Brewery and Copper Dragon; the other four are from reasonably local breweries. Arcadia is a mature drinking environment and humans under the age of 18 are not allowed but well-behaved dogs of all ages are most welcome. Lunchtime food Thursday-Sunday; evening meals Thursday and Friday. Q◐◑🚌

Heaton

Kings Arms

10 Highgate, BD9 4BB (off A650 Keighley Road, opp St Bede's School)
⏲ 12-midnight
☎ (01274) 543165 🌐 kingsarmsheaton.co.uk
Copper Dragon Golden Pippin; guest beers Ⓗ
An imposing Victorian pub located in a prominent position within the urban village of Heaton. Now opened out into a large single-room downstairs drinking area, it also has an upstairs games room and a choice of front or rear outdoor areas. The rear garden has a covered, heated smokers' shelter. The pub is always lively, with weekly quizzes and games nights, plus live music at weekends. Guest beers are from local independents such as Copper Dragon, Saltaire and Elland. ❀🚌(629,680)♣⚟

Hebden Bridge

Fox & Goose

9 Heptonstall Road, HX7 6AZ (on A646)
⏲ 11.30 (7.30 Mon)-midnight; 12-11.30 Sun
☎ (01422) 842649 🌐 foxale.co.uk
Millstone Margery's Tiddlywink; guest beers Ⓗ
Family-owned traditional free house with a hill-side beer garden providing superb views across the Calder Valley. Two beer festivals are held each year and the pub is live music friendly, with regular sessions including a folk club on the first Sunday of the month. The house beer is brewed exclusively for the pub and is now unfined, making it suitable for vegans. Winner of many CAMRA awards.
⛫Q❀⇌🚌♣🍎⚟🥛

Moyles 🏆

4-10 New Road, HX7 8AD (on A646 opp canal marina)
⏲ 12-11
☎ (01422) 845272 🌐 moyles.com
Pictish Brewers Gold; guest beers Ⓗ
An atmosphere of sophistication is created by the state-of-the-art minimalistic interior of this four-room bar/restaurant. The four-star restaurant has been awarded the prestigious AA rosette and the bar was local CAMRA Winter Pub of the Season in 2008. Four guest beers are on offer from micro-breweries – their names are sent by text to tempt customers. The canal marina can be seen from the equally stylish decking area outside.
⛫Q❀🛏◐◑♿⇌🚌(590,591,593)⚟

New Delight Inn ✔

Jack Bridge, Colden, HX7 7HT SD962282
⏲ 12-2.30 (not Mon), 5-11; 12-11 Sat & Sun
☎ (01422) 846178
Bridestones Bottleneck Bride; guest beers Ⓗ
Cosy rural pub whose owners run Bridestones Brewery, based on a nearby farm. The guest beers will usually include other beers from the Bridestones portfolio. Rooms to the left of the main entrance are stone flagged; those to the right are carpeted and have real fires. Ideal for walkers, the pub is just a short detour from the Calderdale and Pennine Ways. Camping is beside the pub car park. The hostelry also provides the beer tent at the local Blackshaw Head village fete. ⛫❀◐◑⊞⛺🚌(E)P

Heckmondwike

New Charnwood

4 Westgate, WF16 0EH (on A638 near green)
⏲ 11-11; closed Mon; 12-10.30 Sun
☎ (01924) 406512 🌐 thenewcharnwood.co.uk
Taylor Landlord; guest beers Ⓗ
An inviting front garden leads to this attractive bay-windowed former Oddfellows Hall, now described as a pub and dining room. Guest beers are mostly from local breweries and usually include a dark mild or an old ale which are also available in the 80-seat function room.Tuesday to Saturday lunch and evening menus both provide high-quality contemporary cuisine. Taylor's Landlord ice cream is available. A Sunday menu served until 5pm offers traditional roasts with a choice of four meats. Good bus links. ❀◐◑♿🚌P⚟

Hipperholme

Cock o' the North

The Conclave, South Edge Works, Brighouse Road, HX3 8EF (on A644)
5 (4 Fri)-11; 12-11 Sat & Sun
☎ (07974) 544980 myspace.com/cockofthenorthbar
Halifax Steam Cock o' the North, Jamaican Ginger, Uncle Jon; guest beers Ⓗ
Situated in a red sectional building next to the imposing Vulcan works, the bar is to the rear of the Cock o' the North Brewery. A single room with polished floors and fittings, the interior is inspired by 1930s Art Deco ocean liners. A showcase for the growing range of Halifax Steam Beers, there are usually 10 to 12 ales on offer, with occasional guests, increasing to 25 during frequent beer festivals. The atmosphere is relaxed, with a friendly, varied clientele. Q (548,549)P

Travellers Inn ✔

53 Tanhouse Hill, HX3 8HN (on A58, back of camping centre)
12-midnight (11 Mon; 11.30 Tue & Wed)
☎ (01422) 202494
Fuller's London Pride; Ossett Pale Gold, Travellers Ale, Excelsior; guest beers Ⓗ
Situated opposite the former railway station, this traditional 18th-century, stone-built local has taken in adjoining cottages to create a series of distinct spaces. Children are welcome until 7pm in the upper area, where a wide selection of board games is available. Dogs are also permitted during quiet periods. There is a small south-facing roadside seating area. A covered yard with heating is provided for smokers. (548,549)♣

Holbeck

Cross Keys

Water Lane, LS11 5WD
12-11 (midnight Fri & Sat); 12-10.30 Sun
☎ (0113) 243 3711 the-crosskeys.com
Beer range varies Ⓗ
Exposed beams, stone flags, tiles and bare brickwork abound in this pub which is under the same ownership as the city-centre North Bar and Reliance. Up to four guest beers are served, with one handpump reserved for a stout or porter. A range of bottled beers from Germany, Belgium and the USA is also available. Downstairs two rooms wrap around a central bar area, each with a wood-burning stove. Upstairs is another bar and function room. Sunday meals are served until 5pm.
♿(Leeds)

Grove Inn

Back Row, LS11 5PL
12-11 (midnight Fri & Sat); 12-10.30 Sun
☎ (0113) 243 9254
Caledonian Deuchars IPA; Daleside Blonde; Moorhouses Black Cat, Pride of Pendle; guest beers Ⓗ
Surrounded by office blocks and situated next to the tallest building in Yorkshire, the inn is an oasis of history in a sea of modernity. A rare surviving example of a traditional West Riding corridor pub, first mentioned in a survey of Leeds in 1850, its four rooms include a concert room and a tap room. A wide variety of live music is played here and there is a dedicated mild handpump. Local CAMRA Pub of the Year 2007-08, the Grove is celebrating its 10th consecutive entry in this Guide.
(Leeds)♣

Midnight Bell

101 Water Lane, LS11 5QN
11.30-11 (midnight Fri & Sat)
☎ (0113) 2445044 midnightbell.co.uk
Leeds Pale, Best, Midnight Bell; guest beers Ⓗ
This is the first pub in the nearby Leeds Brewery estate. Part of the Round Foundry development, the foundry was reputedly the oldest universal industrial building. A beautifully reconditioned old red brick building, it has massive windows, stone floors, pale furniture and white walls, ensuring a light, airy and relaxed ambience. Glass doors to the rear open onto an impressively sized terrace area. A full range of Leeds ales is available, along with its current seasonal offerings. Q♿(Leeds)

Holmfirth

Farmers Arms ✔

2-4 Liphill Bank Road, Burnlee, HD9 2LR (off A635, below Compo's Café)
5 (12 Fri-Sun)-midnight
☎ (01484) 683713
Adnams Bitter; Greene King IPA; John Smith's Bitter; Tetley Bitter; Wells Bombardier; guest beers Ⓗ
Three weavers' cottages were knocked together in the 1920s to create this delightful community pub situated in a quiet corner of 'Summer Wine' country. The pub has a warm, relaxing and welcoming atmosphere and is popular with locals. Home-cooked food is served lunchtime and evenings – Sue's Meat & Potato Pie is a must – to complement the quality range of beers from local and national brewers. A games room hosts local darts teams and folk night is the last Thursday of the month. ♣P

Rose & Crown (Nook)

7 Victoria Square, HD9 2DN (down alley off Hollowgate)
11.30 (12 Sun)-midnight
☎ (01484) 683960 thenookpublichouse.co.uk
Kelham Island Pale Rider; Taylor Best Bitter, Landlord; guest beers Ⓗ
There has been a pub on this site since 1754 and the Nook has featured over 30 times in the Guide. A deceptively spacious pub, it provides home-cooked food all day, including the speciality Nook Burger. The pub features in the local darts league and is renowned for its great live music, with an open mike night every third Wednesday of the month. The Nook has its own micro-brewery and holds an annual beer festival during the August bank holiday. ♿♣

Horbury

Boons ✔

6 Queen Street, WF4 6LP
11-3, 5-11; 11-11 Fri & Sat; 12-10.30 Sun
☎ (01924) 280442
Clarks Classic Blonde; John Smith's Bitter; Taylor Landlord; guest beers Ⓗ
Centrally situated just off the High Street, this Clarks Brewery tied house caters for all age groups and is a real community pub. Three rotating guest beers are always available alongside beers from the Clarks range. At the back of the pub there is a large outdoor drinking area where the annual summer beer festival is held. ♣

Horbury Bridge

Bingley Arms

221 Bridge Road, WF4 5NL (between River Calder and Aire & Calder Canal)
❂ 3 (12 Fri & Sat)-midnight; 12-10.30 Sun
☎ (01924) 281331
Black Sheep Best Bitter; Caledonian Deuchars IPA; Tetley Mild, Bitter; guest beers ⊞
This pub is bordered by the River Calder on one side and by the Aire & Calder Navigation Canal on the other. It has two rooms, both with open fires. The pub is named after the Earl of Bingley who funded the building of the nearby canal; it has its own moorings on the canal, which are popular in the summer months. It also has a good-sized beer garden which gets busy on summer evenings and weekends. The pub is reputed to be haunted – the West Yorkshire Paranormal Society held an all night vigil here, but saw nothing.
⛰❀◐♿🚌(231,232,265)♣P⁵–

Horsforth

Town Street Tavern ✔

16-18 Town Street, LS18 4RJ
❂ 12-11 (10.30 Sun)
☎ (0113) 281 9996 🌐 markettowntaverns.co.uk
Black Sheep Best Bitter; Leeds Pale; Taylor Best Bitter; guest beers ⊞
Part of the popular Market Town Taverns chain, this dog-friendly pub sells eight real ales and a selection of foreign beers on draught and in bottle. Most of the guest ales are from local micro-breweries, with one pump dedicated to dark beers. The upstairs restaurant serves excellent food from 6pm while the downstairs bar also serves food daily. An outdoor patio provides an area for smokers and drinkers. Children are allowed in the main bar until 6pm. Q❀◐◑♿🚌(50,50A)♣⁵–

Huddersfield

Cherry Tree ✔

16-18 John William Street, HD1 1BA
❂ 9-midnight (1am Fri & Sat)
☎ (01484) 448190
Greene King Ruddles Best, Abbot; Marston's Pedigree; guest beers ⊞
This town-centre pub converted from a bed shop in part of a 1960s office block may not be the most elegant building in the Wetherspoon's chain but what it lacks in outward aesthetics it makes up for inside. It has one large room, with a raised area at the back and a small downstairs lounge. There are seven guest beers, many from Yorkshire micros, plus Weston's Old Rosie cider. The management are enthusiastic about real ale and the staff are always happy to advise before you buy.
Q◐◑♿⇌🚌●

Grove

2 Spring Grove Street, HD1 4BP
❂ 12-11 (midnight Thu-Sat)
☎ (01484) 430113 🌐 groveinn.co.uk
College Green Molly's Chocolate Stout; Empire Grove Grog; Fuller's ESB; Marble Ginger Marble; Taylor Golden Best, Landlord; Thornbridge Jaipur IPA; guest beers ⊞
A two-room corner pub, the Grove attracts beer lovers from across the region and beyond. Ten guest ales, many rare for the region and personally selected by the landlord on his many beer expeditions, always include mild, stout and strong ale plus Thatchers Cheddar Valley Cider. There are also nine foreign draughts plus Taddington's Moravka Kvasnicové unpasturised and unfiltered pilsner, as well as 200-plus bottled beers. Enjoy your pint in airy, traditional surroundings featuring interesting artwork, unusual bar snacks and spontaneous folk music. Q❀⊟⇌🚌●⊡

King's Head

St George's Square, HD1 1JF (in station buildings)
❂ 11.30-11; 12-10.30 Sun
☎ (01484) 511058 🌐 the-kings-head-huddersfield.co.uk
Taylor Golden Best, Landlord; guest beers ⊞
Formerly called the Station Tavern, this pub has appeared on television. Displaying a quirky and distinctive individuality, its success is due to its sound management and loyal, friendly staff. The main room has a mosaic-tiled floor which hosts live bands on Sunday afternoon, piano singalongs on Tuesday evening and monthly folk & blues sessions; two smaller rooms provide extra seating. Ten beers are usually on offer, plus sandwiches, in keeping with the homely ethos of this amiable pub. ⛰♿⇌🚌

Marsh Liberal Club

31 New Hey Road, Marsh, HD3 4AL (on A640)
❂ 12-2 (Mon & Fri only), 7-11; 12-11 Sat & Sun
☎ (01484) 420152 🌐 marshlib.co.uk
Taylor Golden Best, Best Bitter, Landlord; guest beers ⊞
Housed in a striking Grade II-listed building, this friendly club celebrated its 150th anniversary during 2008. Two guest beers are normally available, usually from independent micros. Snooker, pool, darts, dominoes and crown green bowls are all played here, and there are regular social events. Finalist in the Club Mirror Cask Club of the Year awards three years running. The building has wheelchair access and a disabled WC. Show this Guide or a CAMRA membership card to be signed in. ❀♿🚌(370,371,538)♣P

Rat & Ratchet ✔

40 Chapel Hill, HD1 3EB (on A616 below ring road)
❂ 12 (3 Mon & Tue)-midnight (12.30am Fri & Sat); 12-11 Sun
☎ (01484) 542400 🌐 ossett-brewery.co.uk
Ossett Pale Gold, Silver King, Excelsior; Fuller's London Pride; guest beers ⊞
A perennial Guide entry and local CAMRA branch Pub of the Year 2008. Twelve handpumps feature Riverhead, Fernandes and guests, including mild, porter and two ciders. It is decorated with brewery adverts and music posters and has a jukebox, pin table and two real fires. There are occasional live music and open mike nights, and a quiz on Wednesday. A dartboard and other games are available. Beer festivals are held in May and September; the former featuring mainly milds. There is an outdoor drinking terrace.
⛰❀◐⇌🚌♣●P⁵–

Star Inn 🏆

7 Albert Street, Folly Hall, HD1 3PJ (off A616)
❂ 5 (12 Sat)-11; closed Mon; 12-10.30 Sun
☎ (01484) 545443 🌐 thestarinn.info
Pictish Brewers Gold; Taylor Best Bitter, Landlord; guest beers ⊞
This is a welcoming pub visited by people from all over the country. There is an emphasis on ever changing guest ales, all individually sourced and researched, including milds, stouts and porters.

There is an open fire during winter months. No jukebox, no pool table, no games machines – just a great atmosphere. A deserved winner of many CAMRA awards, the pub holds three very good beer festivals a year in its marquee, known nationally as some of the best in the country. ⌂Q❀♿🚌⁵–

White Cross Inn

2 Bradley Road, Bradley, HD2 1XD (on A62, 3 miles from town centre)

⏲ 11.45-11; 12-10.30 Sun

☎ (01484) 425728

Copper Dragon Golden Pippin; Taylor Golden Best; guest beers Ⓗ

This busy community pub, located at the busy crossroads of Leeds Road and Bradley Road, offers a warm welcome to both locals and passers-by. The large lounge extends either side of the central bar area where three guest beers are on handpump. Past landlords are recorded from 1806 until the present day. The Cross has won a number of awards for its beer quality, including Huddersfield CAMRA Pub of the Year 2005. An annual beer festival is held in February. ❀◐♿🚌(202,203)♣P⁵–

Idle

Brewery Tap ✔

51 Albion Road, BD10 9QE

⏲ 3-11 (11.30 Thu; midnight Fri); 12-midnight Sat; 12-10.30 Sun

☎ (01274) 613936

Black Sheep Best Bitter; guest beers Ⓗ

Former Trough Brewery pub enjoying a new lease of life under the present tenants. A large central area dominates the single-room interior. The pub is popular with bikers and rock music fans alike who gather on Thursday, Friday and Saturday evenings to listen to live bands. Not a quiet pub, but well worth a visit for the beer. Real cider and sometimes perry are available. ⌂❀♿🚌(640,641)♣●P⁵–

Idle Working Mens Club

23 High Street, BD10 8NB

⏲ 12-4 Mon & Fri, 7-11; 11-5, 7-11 Sat; 12-5, 7-11 Sun

☎ (01274) 613602 🌐 idle-workingmensclub.com

Tetley Bitter; guest beers Ⓗ

Popular club, constantly attracting attention and membership numbers due to its unusual name – and selling suitably branded merchandise. The concert room hosts live entertainment on weekend evenings, while the lounge is a quieter alternative. The downstairs games room has two full-sized snooker tables and a large-screen TV dedicated mainly to sport. Parking is available at the nearby doctors' surgery out of hours. Show this Guide or a current CAMRA membership card to gain admission. ♿🚌(610,611,612)♣

Symposium Ale & Wine Bar ✔

7 Albion Road, BD10 9PY

⏲ 12-2 (not Mon & Tue), 5.30-11; 12-11 Fri & Sat; 12-10.30 Sun

☎ (01274) 616587 🌐 markettowntaverns.co.uk

Beer range varies Ⓗ

At the heart of Idle village, this popular bar and restaurant places equal emphasis on the quality of its food and beer. A member of the Market Town Taverns group, it hosts occasional themed evenings and menus. The beers change constantly in a rolling beer festival, with each brewer's range given a good airing in turn. A wide choice of foreign beers is also available in bottle and draught. The rear snug leads to a terrace which is popular in summer. Q❀◐◑🚌(610,612,640)⁵–

Ilkley

Bar T'at ✔

7 Cuncliffe Road, LS29 9DZ

⏲ 12-11

☎ (01943) 608888 🌐 markettowntaverns.co.uk

Black Sheep Best Bitter; Copper Dragon Golden Pippin; Taylor Landlord; guest beers Ⓗ

Popular side-street pub from the Market Town Taverns group, renowned for the quality of its beer and food. Guest ales usually include a mild or porter, plus brews from Yorkshire micros. A wide choice of good foreign beers is available in bottles and on draught, including Belgian fruit beers. Home-cooked food is on the menu every day. This three-storey building has a music-free bar area. It stands next to the main town centre car park. Q❀◐◑⇌🚌⁵–

Riverside Hotel

Riverside Gardens, Bridge Lane, LS29 9EU

⏲ 10-11 (10.30 Sun)

☎ (01943) 607338 🌐 ilkley-riversidehotel.com

Copper Dragon Best Bitter; Samuel Smith OBB; Tetley Bitter Ⓗ

Family-run hotel with 13 rooms, set by the River Wharfe in a popular park. The adjacent fish and chip shop and ice cream servery, also run by the hotel, are popular in summer. Meals are served until early evening and the bar runs a happy hour on weekdays, 4-8pm. The open fire is a welcome sight in cold weather. The start of the Dales Way is at the old pack horse bridge close to the hotel. ⌂❀🛏◐◑⇌🚌♣P⁵–

Keighley

Boltmakers Arms ✔

117 East Parade, BD21 5HX

⏲ 11-11 (midnight Tue-Sat); 12-11 Sun

☎ (01535) 661936 🌐 timothy-taylor.co.uk/boltmakers

Taylor Dark Mild, Best Bitter, Golden Best, Landlord, Ram Tam; guest beer Ⓗ

Classic Keighley town-centre pub which is the de facto Timothy Taylor Brewery tap. The tiny split-level layout is unfeasibly small but this just serves to add to the character of the place. The licensees take pride in the pub and it is always very welcoming. The guest beer and hand-pulled cider are from various sources at the licensee's whim, also a fine selection of single malts. Quiz night is Tuesday. Occasional live music is held. ⌂❀⇌🚌♣●⁵–

Brown Cow ✔

5 Cross Leeds Street, BD21 2LQ

⏲ 4-11; 12-10.30 Sun 🌐 browncowkeighley.co.uk

Taylor Best Bitter, Golden Best, Landlord, Dark Mild or Ram Tam; guest beers Ⓗ

This popular, friendly, comfortable open-plan pub has gained many CAMRA awards since Carol and Barry Taylor took it over in November 2003. They include Most Improved Pub, Pub of the Season, Pub of the Year and runner-up Yorkshire Pub of the Year in 2008. Bad language is banned. A Timothy Taylor tied house, it offers two regularly changing guest beers, usually from local micros. ⌂❀⇌🚌♣P

Cricketers Arms

Coney Lane, BD21 5JE

11.30-midnight; 12-11.30 Sun

☎ (01535) 669912 cricketersarmskeighley.co.uk

Moorhouses Premier Bitter; guest beers

Back-street pub revitalised by frequent live music sessions featuring bands from near and far. A ground-level bar is now complemented by a downstairs bar (open Friday and Saturday evenings). An interesting montage depicting photographs of regulars hangs at the top of the stairwell. Five guest beers from regional and nationwide micro-breweries are served, together with a range of foreign bottled beers. Occasional beer festivals are held.

Friendly Inn

2 Aireworth Street, BD21 1NS

4 (12 Fri)-11; 2-1am Sat; 12-11 Sun

☎ (01535) 665444

Taylor Dark Mild, Golden Best, Best Bitter, Landlord

Located just outside the town centre, this corner pub retains a slightly old-fashioned feel. A typically small Timothy Taylor hostelry, it has been reinvigorated into a real community town centre local, and is especially busy on its frequent quiz and games nights. No frills, just friendly service and good conversation. It also offers the possibly unique opportunity to compare electric and handpumped Bitter and Golden Best.

Livery Rooms

89-97 North Street, BD21 3AA

9-midnight (1am Fri & Sat)

☎ (01535) 682950

Greene King IPA, Abbot; Marston's Pedigree; guest beers

Opened in June 2004 by Wetherspoon, this pub has become very popular with beer fans and diners alike. The premises has previously been stables, temperance hall, bingo hall and several shops, and this varied history is displayed, using different art forms, on the walls throughout the pub. The guest beer policy gives strong support to ales from local micros. Conveniently located close to the bus station.

Kirkstall

West End House

Abbey Road, LS5 3HS

11-11 (midnight Fri & Sat); 11-10.30 Sun

☎ (0113) 278 6332

Beer range varies

On the A65 out of Leeds towards the famous Kirkstall Abbey, this stone-built pub was first recorded as an ale house in 1867. Four handpumps dispense a variety of ales, usually from the north of England, with a separate pump for real cider. Excellent food is served Monday-Saturday 11.30am-2.30pm and 5.30-7.30pm, as well as 12-4pm on Sunday. The varied menu includes a good range of vegetarian options and traditional pub grub. Sky Sports is available, along with a heated smoking area. (Headingley)

Leeds: City

Horse & Trumpet

51-53 The Headrow, LS1 6LR

10-11 (11.30 Thu; midnight Fri); 9am-midnight Sat; 12-10.30 Sun

☎ (0113) 245 5961

Taylor Landlord; Tetley Bitter; guest beers

Three open rooms head off a lively main bar, comprising a mish-mash of originality with contrasting modern open-plan refurbishment which has rejuvenated the pub, while still leaving it firmly rooted in a bygone era of traditional drinkers' locals. The food menu in the style of modern pub chains remains reasonably priced and available nearly all opening hours. Entertainment is one unobtrusive TV above the bar which can disturb the peace. Dress code (no tracksuits) applies.

Mr Foley's Cask Ale House 🏆

159 The Headrow, LS1 5RG (opp town hall)

11-11 (midnight Fri & Sat)

☎ (0113) 242 9674 yorkbrew.demon.co.uk/Mr_fowleys.html

Beer range varies

Occupying the ground floor of the impressive Pearl Assurance Building, this multi-layered pub offers something for everyone, particularly the discerning real ale fan. A fine array of handpumps – which always dispense a beer from York and Elland breweries – adorns the bar, which is backed by a splendid cabinet and fridges full of bottles of world beers. Sporty TV is popular here, but it is possible to find a quieter corner among the eclectic furniture and squashy chairs. Local CAMRA Pub of the Year 2008-09.

North

24 New Briggate, LS1 6NU

12-2am (1am Mon & Tue); 12-midnight Sun

☎ (0113) 242 4540 northbar.com

Outlaw Wild Mule; guest beers

This small glass-fronted pub has built up a big reputation for quality real ale and a substantial selection of beers from all over the world. Although simply decorated, the walls are often a welcome exhibition space for local artists. The long narrow nature of the pub means it can be busy at peak times. If a great selection of local beers and 60-plus bottles are not enough, then look out for the regular beer festivals: Spring, Belgian Bier, Summer Fete and Oktoberfest.

Palace

Kirkgate, LS2 7DJ

11-11.30 (midnight Fri & Sat); 12-11 Sun

☎ (0113) 244 5882

Draught Bass; Tetley Bitter; guest beers

Adjacent to the old East Bar Stone, which once marked the city boundary and allowed those within the bar special privileges, this spacious two-tiered pub still has traces of its former three-roomed layout, as well as the stone flags in the lower tier. Myriad guest ales are available, including a mild or stout along with Westons Old Rosie for cider lovers.

Scarbrough Hotel

Bishopgate Street, LS1 5DY

11-midnight; 12-10.30 Sun

☎ (0113) 243 4590

Tetley Bitter; guest beers

Rebranded in mid-2008 under the Nicholson's umbrella, with new exterior pub signs and large internal blackboards proclaiming the pub's food offering, available throughout opening hours. All ales on handpump are served in the finest condition, although the range is now restricted due to the pub co's purchasing policy. During the late 1890s what was once the Kings Arms was replaced by a large concert hall and given the present name, and so began the pub's strong association with music hall. Cider and perry are on gravity dispense.

Templar

2 Templar Street, LS2 7NU
11-11; 12-10.30 Sun
(0113) 245 9751
Tetley Mild, Bitter; guest beers
One of the few remaining pubs in Leeds that still has the cream and green glazed Burmantofts exterior tiles and features the Bowing Courtier logo in the leaded upper window panes – a throwback from its days as a Melbourne's pub. The interior is split into two areas, with a corridor to separate them. At one end of the bar there are some drinking booths and at the other an area with an attractive red tiled fireplace.

Town Hall Tavern

17 Westgate, LS1 2RA
11.30-11; closed Sun
(0113) 244 0765
Taylor Golden Best, Best Bitter, Landlord, Ram Tam, seasonal beers
A modern yet traditional city centre local pub with a one-roomed interior decorated with many pictures of Leeds, cartoons and a propeller. Despite being opened out, there are still a couple of cosy areas for a quiet drink and a chat. The friendly, down-to-earth nature of the pub makes for a welcoming contrast to the weekend madness nearby in the city centre. Cider is ever changing from the Westons range, and there are more than a dozen world beers in bottles.

Victoria Family & Commercial

28 Great George Street, LS1 3DL (behind town hall)
10-11 (midnight Thu-Sat); 12-4 Sun
(0113) 245 1386
Acorn Barnsley Bitter; Tetley Bitter; guest beers
The Victoria Hotel was built in 1865 to serve people attending the assize courts newly held at Leeds town hall. The Victoria and Commercial Hotel exterior sign has its origin dating back to the 1890s, and the pub was awarded special recognition for its splendid Victorian features and contribution to city life in 1989. The food menu invites you to choose your sausage and then decide how you want it, from a classic stereotypical pub chain menu. TV and occasional live music events take place. Q

Whitelocks First City Luncheon Bar ★

Turks Head Yard, LS1 6HB (off Briggate)
11-11; 12-5 Sun
(0113) 245 3950 whitelocks.co.uk
Caledonian Deuchars IPA; Leeds Best; Theakston Best Bitter, Old Peculier; guest beers
A classic Leeds alleyway pub, with fans from all across the globe – it even has its own Friends society. The beautiful, and in parts ornate, interior has rightly received appreciation from various quarters, from authors to architectural historians. The restaurant area adjacent to the bar is as much an institution as the pub itself. The smaller bar up the yard is now known as Ma Gamp's and is worth a visit in its own right. Q

Leeds: North

Reliance

76-78 North Street, LS2 7PN
12-11 (midnight Fri & Sat); 12-10.30 Sun
(0113) 295 6060 the-reliance.co.uk
Beer range varies
Traditional yet modern bar occupying a former shop in a Victorian building, with high ceilings and large windows giving a light and airy feel. It has two rooms with wooden floors and mix of furnishings plus a mezzanine dining area. One changing guest beer plus a range of continental bottled and draught beers are available. An extensive menu is offered in the restaurant and bar. The walls display changing art exhibitions from local artists.

Linthwaite

Sair Inn

139 Lane Top, HD7 5SG (off A62) SE100143
5 (12 Fri & Sat)-11; 12-10.30 Sun
(01484) 842370
Linfit Bitter, Gold Medal, Special, Autumn Gold, Old Eli
Brew pub on a hillside above the Colne Valley. Little has altered here over time; staff and brewers have changed, but the same landlord has been in charge for well over 20 years. Linfit beers are available only in the pub itself. The laid-back feel of the place is accentuated by its cluster of small rooms radiating from the central bar; information on local events and attractions is displayed, and socials, meetings and entertainments occasionally take place. Westons 1st Quality cider is available.

Liversedge

Black Bull

37 Halifax Road, WF15 6JR (on A649, near A62)
12-midnight (1am Fri & Sat)
(01924) 403779 ossett-brewery.co.uk
Ossett Pale Gold, Black Bull, Silver King, Fine Fettle, Excelsior; guest beers
This 300-year-old building was the first of Ossett Brewery's chain of pubs in the area. Although it has been opened out slightly, the five rooms have their own styles. The stained glass and woodwork in one has led some regulars to call it 'the chapel'. Most of the nine handpumps have Ossett beers, one always a mild or dark ale. A good range of continental beers is also stocked. Last admission is 30 minutes before closing time.
(254) P

Marsden

Riverhead Brewery Tap

Argyle Street, HD7 6BR (overlooking River Colne in centre of Marsden)
12-11.30 (1am Fri); 11-1am Sat; 12-midnight Sun
(01484) 841270 ossett-brewery.co.uk
Ossett Pale Gold, Silver King; Riverhead Sparth Mild, Butterley Bitter, March Haigh; guest beers
Formerly a Co-op and now part of Ossett Brewery's estate, this pub is at the centre of village life. It offers a relaxed atmosphere and pleasant surroundings. Great pictures of Marsden adorn the walls. Fantastic food is served in the restaurant and there is a riverside terrace for alfresco drinking. The

micro-brewery is visible from the bar – LocAle does not get any more local than this. Up to 10 beers are available, usually six from Riverhead, two from Ossett, London Pride and a guest. Dogs are welcome. Q❀♿⇌🚌(185)

Tunnel End Inn

Waters Road, HD7 6NF

5 (8 Mon)-11; 12-midnight Sat & Sun

☎ (01484) 844636 🌐 tunnelendinn.com

Black Sheep Best Bitter; Taylor Landlord; guest beers Ⓗ

A really friendly family-owned pub set in magnificent Pennine scenery, ideal walking country, in the upper Colne Valley close to the Standedge Tunnel – the longest, deepest and highest canal tunnel in the UK. Keenly-priced guest beers come from both local micros and from further afield. Delicious home-cooked food is served Friday-Sunday, while Wednesday night is Meat and Tatty pie night. Customers are assured of a warm, personable welcome from the friendly proprietors. Dogs are permitted.
Q❀⇌🚌(185)♣

Mirfield

Navigation Tavern

6 Station Road, WF14 8NL (between rail station and canal)

11.30-11 (midnight Fri & Sat); 12-10.30 Sun

☎ (01924) 492476

John Smith's Bitter; Theakston Best Bitter, Black Bull Bitter, XB, Old Peculier; guest beers Ⓗ

Congenial canal-side free house next to a boatyard on the Calder and Hebble Navigation near the centre of Mirfield, and a stone's throw from Mirfield railway station. The pub is popular with all ages, hosting an active sports and pool team, and offering a comprehensive range from Theakston at a competitive price. The pub is registered as an Ambassador for Theakston's Beer. Up to five guest beers are on offer and occasional beer festivals hosted. Ring to check food availability.
❀⇌🚌♣P⁻

Old Colonial Club

Dunbottle Lane, WF14 9JJ (off A644 up Church Lane, 1m NNE of station)

5 (4 Fri, 12 Sat)-midnight; 12-11 Sun

☎ (01924) 496920

Copper Dragon Best Bitter; guest beers Ⓗ

The publican is a cask beer enthusiast supporting mainly Yorkshire breweries, with one-off beers sometimes available on the five guest pumps. A Pub in Bloom winner, there is a Royal British Legion war memorial on site and this is a venue for the National Pie-tasting Championships. The club has one large room plus a spacious conservatory useful for meetings and functions. Good value home-made food is served Thursday to Saturday early evening. Occasional use of large-screen TV for sport. ❀♿🚌(202)P⁻

Mytholmroyd

Shoulder of Mutton

86 New Road, HX7 5DZ (on B6138, near station)

11.30-3, 7-11; 11.30-11 Sat; 12-10.30 Sun

☎ (01422) 883168

Black Sheep Best Bitter; Copper Dragon Best Bitter, Golden Pippin; Greene King IPA; Taylor Landlord Ⓗ

Village inn with a strong community feel and a warm welcome for walkers and other visitors. Excellent value, quality home-cooked food is available lunchtimes and evenings (not Mon and Tue). Major sporting events are shown on a large-screen TV, but there is normally a quiet corner to be found. The bar displays memorabilia relating to the Cragg Vale Coiners, a gang of 18th-century forgers.
❀⇌🚌♣P⁻

Netherton

Beaumont Arms

396 Meltham Road, HD4 7EL (on B6108)

12-2, 4-11 (10 Mon); 12-11 Fri; 2.30-11 Sat; 12-11 Sun

☎ (01484) 661984

Tetley Bitter; guest beers Ⓗ

The Beaumont Arms is a well-known real ale pub in Netherton village, popular with locals and visitors alike. Catering for the whole community, the pub is a meeting place for various clubs and organisations. The pub has won Huddersfield CAMRA Pub of the Season twice. For sports fans there is a large-screen TV. On Wednesday and Sunday evenings a prize quiz takes place. Food is served 12-2pm Monday-Friday lunchtimes and 5-8pm on Monday evening only. ❀🚌(321,324)⁻

Newlay

Abbey

99 Pollard Lane, LS13 1EQ (vehicular access from B6157 only) SE239367

12-11 (10.30 Sun)

☎ (0113) 258 1248 🌐 theabbey-inn.co.uk

Leeds Pale; Tetley's Bitter; guest beers Ⓗ

Grade II-listed building with low ceilings, situated between the River Aire and the Leeds & Liverpool canal with moorings nearby. The pub takes its name from the 12th-century Kirkstall Abbey just over a mile away, and is popular with walkers exploring the valley. The guest beers are mainly from local breweries, with some from further afield. There are jam sessions on Tuesday, live music on Saturday and a quiz night on Sunday. An annual beer festival is held. ❀🚌♣P⁻

North Featherstone

Bradley Arms ✔

98 Willow Lane, WF7 6BG (on B6421 Castleford to Featherstone road)

3.30 (12 Sat & Sun)-midnight

☎ (07833) 762360

Black Sheep Best Bitter; Caledonian Deuchars IPA; John Smith's Bitter; guest beers Ⓗ

Lovely old ex-farm building with several rooms and levels. This inn has a rich history and was a key location in the infamous Featherstone Massacre of 1893, the last time British troops shot and killed British citizens on home soil. The first ever speech on workers' rights by Cunninghame Graham, co-founder of the Scottish Labour Party, was made here and he spoke here again at the time of the Massacre. Candelit evenings in the lounge are a feature, with Sky Sports available in the bar. Much Featherstone Rovers memorabilia is on display.
Q❀🚌(147,157,177)♣P⁻

Ogden

Causeway Foot ✔

13 Causeway Foot, Keighley Road, HX2 8XX (on A629)
12-2.30 (not Mon & Tue), 5.30-11; 12-11 Sun
☎ (01422) 240273 thecausewayfootinn.co.uk
Black Sheep Best Bitter, Ale; Taylor Landlord; guest beers H
A welcoming main road inn near Ogden Water. The comfortable lounge has an adjoining area with settees and a large fireplace. A small dining room lies beyond and there is a separate floorboarded room popular with hikers. Dogs are welcome, as are bikers who sometimes meet and camp on the field next door. The inn is believed to be haunted and a paranormal group meets here. A beer from Goose Eye is usually available.
(502,504)**P**

Ossett

Brewers Pride

Low Mill Road, WF5 8ND (at bottom of Healey Rd, 1½ miles from Ossett town centre)
12-11 (10.30 Sun)
☎ (01924) 273865 brewers-pride.co.uk
Bob's Brewing Co White Lion; Ossett Excelsior; guest beers H
A genuine free house on the outskirts of Ossett, five minutes' walk from the Calder & Hebble Canal. One of the nine handpulls is dedicated to a mild. Good value lunches are served and on Wednesday evening curries, pies, pasta or steaks feature on the menu. Quiz night is Monday, bluegrass is played on Tuesday night with all pickers welcome, and live music is performed on the first and third Sundays of each month. Well-behaved children are allowed. An annual beer festival is held each summer bank holiday. **Q**(102)

Tap ✔

2 The Green, WF5 8JS
3 (12 Thu)-1am; 12-2am Fri & Sat; 12-1am Sun
☎ (01924) 272215 ossett.brewery.co.uk
Ossett Pale Gold, Silver King, Excelsior; guest beers H
Formerly the Mason's Arms, the pub was bought by Ossett Brewery who have turned it into their brewery tap. Alongside the three regular Ossett beers there is usually a special/seasonal beer from Ossett plus four guest ales. A real wood fire and stone-flagged floors give an old-fashioned feel.
Q(117)**P**

Otley

Junction

44 Bondgate, LS21 1AD
11-11 (midnight Fri & Sat); 12-10.30 Sun
☎ (01943) 463233
Taylor Best Bitter, Landlord; Theakston Best Bitter, Old Peculier; guest beers H
Traditional one-roomed pub with a tiled floor and a central fireplace. Ten handpumps provide a mixture of regionals and Yorkshire independents and 30 whiskies should suit all tastes. Live music is performed on Tuesday and Sunday, with a quiz on Wednesday. A cosy, characterful local which welcomes dogs. Food can be brought in from the nearby bakery.

Manor House

Walkergate, LS21 1HB
1-midnight; 12-1am Sat; 12-midnight Sun
☎ (01943) 463807
Thwaites Mild, Original, Lancaster Bomber, Wainwright, seasonal beers H
Comfortable open-plan pub set in a row of terraced houses near Otley's maypole. Four ales are served including the current Thwaites seasonal and either Lancaster Bomber or Wainwright. Live music or the house DJ appear on alternate Thursday nights, with a quiz on Sunday. The darts and dominoes team meet here on Monday night. Dogs are welcome in the bar. There is an outdoor drinking area to the rear with trestle tables, flower tubs and a popular smoking shelter.

Pontefract

Robin Hood

4 Wakefield Road, WF8 4HN (on A645/A639 at traffic lights)
1-4, 7-11.30; 2-11.30 Fri & Sat; 12-4.30, 7-11 Sun
☎ (01977) 702231
John Smith's Bitter; Tetley Bitter; guest beers H
Busy pub near the notorious Town End traffic lights which are known locally as Jenkins Folly. There are three separate drinking areas along with a public bar. Twice-weekly quizzes are held on Tuesday and Sunday evenings. Darts and dominoes teams play in the local charity league. The pub has won many local CAMRA awards and is a former Pub of the Year. There is a rear yard with tables and a covered, heated smoking area.
Q(Tanshelf/Baghill)

Pudsey

Fleece

100 Fartown, LS28 8LU
12-11 (10.30 Sun)
☎ (0113) 236 2748
Taylor Landlord; Tetley Bitter; guest beers H
Situated on the quiet edges of Pudsey, this friendly local pub is smartly decorated and well looked-after. A central bar is surrounded by the classic combination of a comfy lounge with a parquet floor and carpeting, and a more sporty but still cosy tap. Rarely quiet but never too noisy, the pub attracts a mature clientele. The guest ales are often light and hoppy, and frequently from Brown Cow (or Simpson's as it is known here), but can also be from another quality local brewery.
(40,205)**P**

Rastrick

Roundhill Inn ✔

75 Clough Lane, HD6 3QL (on A6107, 400m from jct with A634)
5 (4 Fri)-midnight; 12-midnight Sat; 12-11 Sun
☎ (01484) 713418
Black Sheep Best Bitter; Fuller's London Pride; Taylor Golden Best, Landlord; guest beers H
A two-room genuine free house overlooking a cricket ground and the unusual hill that gives the pub its name. There are spectacular views over Brighouse to the hills beyond. The smaller Maddocks bar may be available for meetings and functions. Guest beers are usually from independent breweries. Monday is quiz night. Limited car parking. **Q**(547,549)**P**

Ripponden

Old Bridge Inn

Priest Lane, HX6 4DF

12-3, 5.30 (5 Fri)-11; 12-11 Sat; 12-10.30 Sun

(01422) 822595 porkpieclub.com

Taylor Golden Best, Best Bitter, Landlord; guest beers H

Very old building, with parts that may date from the 14th or 15th century. It has three rooms – one with a fine exposed cruck beam and another with stud wall panelling. Imaginative menus on blackboards offer buffet lunches from Monday to Friday and excellent home-cooked meals at other times (no eve meals Sat or Sun). The Pork Pie Club meets here on Saturday and holds an annual championship for charity. Impromptu folk music plays on Monday evening. On the route of the Calderdale Way footpath. No dogs please.
Q P

Rodley

Owl

1 Rodley Lane, LS13 1LB (on A657, corner of Bagley Lane)

12-11 (midnight Fri & Sat)

(0113) 256 5242 theowlatrodley.co.uk

John Smith's Bitter; Tetley Bitter; guest beers H

The large lounge has a conservatory which leads to the beer garden and a children's play area. Dogs are welcome in the tap room where pool and darts are played. Guest ales include beers from Copper Dragon and Leeds breweries. Food is served until 7.30pm Monday to Saturday, with a carvery on Sunday until 5pm. A beer festival is held over the August bank holiday weekend. Live music plays on Friday and Saturday with a quiz on Thursday.
(8,9,16A) P

Rodley Barge

182-184 Town Street, LS13 1HP (on A657, by Leeds & Liverpool canal)

12-3, 5-11; 12-11 Fri-Sun

(0113) 257 4606 therodleybarge.wetpaint.com

Clarks Rodley Barge Bitter; Tetley Bitter; guest beers H

This comfortable stone-built pub next to the Leeds & Liverpool Canal offers up to five real ales, with guests mostly from local micro-breweries. There are two rooms served by a central bar. Children are welcome in the back bar. Various quizzes are held throughout the week. A beer festival is held over the August bank holiday weekend. The Barge Anglers angling team meet at the pub once a month. Food is served 12-2pm, Monday to Friday.
(8,9,16A)

Saltaire

Fanny's Ale & Cider House

63 Saltaire Road, BD18 3JN (on A657 opp fire station)

12 (5 Mon)-11 (midnight Fri & Sat); 12 to 11 Sun

(01274) 591419 fannysalehouse.com

Taylor Golden Best, Landlord; Theakston Old Peculier; guest beers H

Near the historic Salts Mill complex and the world heritage site of Saltaire Village, this cosy pub was originally a beer shop. It is now a fully licensed free house stocking an excellent range of beers and also serving a number of draught ciders. A recent extension increased the seating capacity downstairs and added disabled access, while an upstairs room has comfortable seating. The gas-lit lounge is adorned with breweriana and real fires add nicely to the warm welcome. (662)

Shipley

Shipley Club Sports & Social

162 Bradford Road, BD18 3DE

hours vary

(01274) 201842

Beer range varies H

For over a century this thriving club has served its members, going from strength to strength thanks to an enthusiastic stewarding team. Up to three ales are available, often from Yorkshire micros. The local Saltaire Brewery sponsors some club matters and has a dedicated pump on the bar. Bowling is available subject to club commitments, while two snooker tables attract young and old alike to the green baize. Show a current CAMRA card or this Guide for entry. P

Shipley Pride

1 Saltaire Road, BD18 3HH

12-midnight (11.30 Sun)

(01274) 585341

Tetley Bitter; guest beers H

Basically a two-roomed pub with entrances at either side of the front door. To one side there is a tap room leading into a sunken pool room with dartboard. Here is housed a projector-style large-screen TV, with an additional smaller portable TV, both showing various sporting events. On the other side is more comfortable seating with another small TV in one corner. Beers come from a varied range of brewers including some of the lesser known micros of the town. P

Sir Norman Rae

Victoria House, Market Square, BD18 3QB

9-midnight (1am Fri & Sat)

(01274) 535290

Greene King IPA, Old Speckled Hen, Abbot; Marston's Pedigree; guest beers H

Situated in the heart of Shipley town centre, this converted department store opened in 2002 as a Lloyds No.1 bar but is slowly moving towards becoming a more mainstream Wetherspoon outlet. The large open-plan layout provides comfortable surroundings in which to enjoy the wide-ranging food and beer menus. Many ales come from local micros to accompany the regular Greene King line up – Moorhouses is among the regular visiting brewers.

Silsden

Kings Arms

Bolton Road, BD20 0JY

12-midnight

(01535) 653216 kingsarms-silsden.co.uk

Theakston Best Bitter; guest beers H

A vibrant pub featuring regular folk sessions, quizzes and live music. Originally three cottages, the pub is now divided into three rooms, one containing a coal fire. Pub games include darts, dominoes, cards and cribbage. Two regularly changing guest beers are from the Punch Finest Cask list. Gales fruit wines and a real cider are also available. Dogs and well-behaved children are welcome. (70,712,762) P

Slaithwaite

Swan

Carr Lane, HD7 5BQ (off A62, turn right at village centre under viaduct)
⏲ 4-midnight (1am Fri); 12-1am Sat; 12-midnight Sun
☎ (01484) 843225
Taylor Landlord; guest beers 🄷
Homely roadside pub in a quiet corner of Slaithwaite village, run by the same licensees for over two years. Adopting a flexible outlook, their versatility extends to providing quizzes, discos, entertainment, ale festivals and other events, along with the day-to-day running of the bar and cellar. Community events, charities and the like are readily supported. Guest ales are usually all the same price, and a beer from Empire brewery is often available. Beer festivals take place twice a year. ❀⊟⇌🚌P⁄–

South Elmsall

Barnsley Oak

Mill Lane, WF9 2DT (on B6474, off A638 Doncaster-Wakefield road)
⏲ 12-11.30; 11.30-11.30 Sun
☎ (01977) 643427
John Smith's Bitter; guest beers 🄷
This former mining area is fortunate to be served by such a fine community pub. Demand for cask ale continues to grow and the pub often features a guest ale brewed in Yorkshire. Excellent value food is served all day until 7.45pm (4.30pm Sun) and occasional themed food evenings are also hosted. Meals are served in the conservatory which affords panoramic views and children are welcome. Quiz nights are held on Tuesday and Sunday.
❀◐◑⊟⇌(Moorthorpe/S Elmsall)🚌(46,496)P⁄–

Sowerby Bridge

White Horse

Burnley Road, Friendly, HX6 2UG
⏲ 12-11 (10.30 Sun)
☎ (01422) 831173
Tetley Mild, Bitter; guest beer 🄷
White painted pub set back from the busy A646 Burnley Road and on the main bus route from Halifax to Todmorden with a bus stop adjacent. The welcolming local has a tap room and a large lounge partitioned in two. The pub has a strong community following, including members of the friendly football club, brass band and dominoes club. There is a smoking area to the rear and an outside seating area to the front of the pub.
❀🚌(590,591,592)♣P⁄–

Works

12 Hollins Mill Lane, HX6 2QG (opp swimming pool)
⏲ 12-11 (10.30 Sun)
☎ (01422) 834821
Taylor Golden Best, Best Bitter, Landlord; guest beers 🄷
Converted from a former joinery shop, the Works features a simple, open-plan interior with exposed brick walls and wooden floorboards. It is a past winner of the CAMRA pub design award for Conversion to Pub Use and of the local branch Pub of the Season. The L-shaped bar includes nine handpumps. Home-cooked food is served daily, with a curry night on Wednesday. Live blues, jazz and folk music are staged. ♨Q◐◑♿⇌🚌P⁄–

Sowood

Dog & Partridge

Forest Hill Road, HX4 9LP (¼ mile W of B6112)
SE075182
⏲ 12-5 Sun only, 7-11
☎ (01422) 374249
Black Sheep Best Bitter; Taylor Landlord; guest beer 🄷
An unchanged rural pub, run by the same family since 1956. No television, music or gaming machines, just the ticking of a seven-day mill clocking-in clock. Visitors can soon find themselves in conversation with the locals. Other textile mill memorabilia are displayed, including a textile yard quadrant. An impressive collection of Corgi buses is displayed in the side lounge which doubles as the family room. Beware of the witch seemingly hovering over the bar on her broomstick.
Q☕❀♿⛺🚌(537,538)♣P

Todmorden

Barearts Studio Bar

110 Rochdale Road, OL14 7LP
⏲ 5 (12 Sat)-9; closed Mon & Tue; 12-7 Sun
☎ (01706) 839305 🌐 barearts.com
Beer range varies 🄷/🄶
Idiosyncratic off-licence-cum-art gallery close to the town centre; the only outlet for Barearts Brewery's strong bottle-conditioned beers. An ever-changing range of over 20 beers and ciders is available to drink in or take away. The atmosphere is very friendly, the decor quirky; nude paintings and sketches on display are for sale. The regularly updated website gives information on new beers, monthly beer tastings and Sunday music sessions. The bar also has its own Facebook page.
Q⇌🚌(590,592)🍎

Masons Arms

1 Bacup Road, OL14 7PN
⏲ 12-midnight (2am Fri & Sat); 12-11.30 Sun
☎ (01706) 812180
Copper Dragon Black Gold, Best Bitter, Golden Pippin; guest beers 🄷
A Copper Dragon Brewery pub dwarfed by a railway viaduct, and close to the Rochdale Canal. This traditional local has a corridor entrance leading to the bar. There is seating and a pool table in one area and a fireplace in another cosy room. Its tables were once used for laying out bodies. Wednesday night is quiz night and Thursday evening features folk music. The canal towpath provides an interesting walk to Todmorden. Roast lunches are available on Sunday.
♨❀◐⇌(Walsden)🚌(590)♣⁄–

Undercliffe

Milners Arms

126 Undercliffe Road, BD2 3BN (300m from Eccleshill library)
⏲ 4-11 (11.30 Fri); 12-11.30 Sat; 12-11 Sun
☎ (01274) 639938
Beer range varies 🄷
Pleasant and cosy two-roomed community local with a central bar serving both the tap room and lounge. Occasional themed nights and the Wednesday quiz night are popular with a loyal and regular clientele. Three handpumps serve a changing range of beers, with imagination often used in the choices. One guest beer changes every

month. The pub has two distinct drinking areas as well as a separate tap room that enhances the traditional feel. There is a large heated area outside with a log fire. ❀⊟☐(670)♣⁻

Wakefield

Alverthorpe WMC

111 Flanshaw Lane, WF2 9JG (between Dewsbury & Batley roads, 2 miles from city centre)

⏲ 11.30-4, 6.30-11.30; 11.30-11.30 Fri & Sat; 12-3.30, 7-11 Sun

☎ (01924) 374179

Tetley Mild, Bitter; guest beers Ⓗ

Multi-roomed CIU-affiliated club with a cosy interior featuring unusual stained glass and an extensive collection of pot horses. It stocks a wide selection of guest beers, mostly from local micros, and holds an annual beer festival in November. This regular local CAMRA award winner hosts live entertainment on Saturday and Sunday, while snooker and darts are among the traditional games. A large-screen TV is provided for armchair sports enthusiasts. Outside is a floodlit bowling green. ❀⊟♿☐(114)♣P⁻

Black Rock ✔

19 Cross Square, WF1 1PQ (top of Westgate, near the Bull Ring)

⏲ 11-11 (midnight Sat); 12-10.30 Sun

☎ (01924) 375550

Tetley Bitter; guest beers Ⓗ

In the city centre, the Rock has been a bastion of comfort to the ale drinkers of Wakefield for eons. It is an enclave from the surrounding bars and discos of the Yoof Zone. An arched, tiled facade leads into an L-shaped compact local. A warm welcome and comfy interior with many photographs of old Wakefield add to the proper pub feel. A three-minute walk from the bus station.
⇌(Westgate/Kirkgate)☐⁻

Fernandes Brewery Tap & Bier Keller ✔

5 Avison Yard, Kirkgate, WF1 1UA (turn right down lane 100m S of George St/Kirkgate jct)

⏲ 4-11 (midnight Thu); 11-1am Fri & Sat; 12-midnight Sun

☎ (01924) 386348 🌐 ossett-brewery.co.uk

Beer range varies Ⓗ

This pub, a CAMRA award winner, has recently been taken over by Ossett Brewery. The new Bier Keller is a welcome addition (open Wed-Sun, hours vary). The pub has eight handpulls, one dedicated to a mild, stout or porter, and stocks a good selection of bottled Belgian beers. The Bier Keller has 12 premier foreign beers on draught, plus Ossett Silver King and a cider on handpump. The Bier Keller hours are to be standardised shortly (ring to check). ☾⇌(Kirkgate/Westgate)☐●⁻

Harry's Bar

107B Westgate, WF1 1EL

⏲ 5-11.30 (midnight Fri & Sat); 12-11.30 Sun

☎ (01924) 373773

Black Sheep Best Bitter; Bob's Brewing Co Chardonnayle; Ossett Silver King; guest beers Ⓗ

Winner of Wakefield CAMRA branch Pub of the Year for 2007, this small, one-roomed pub has an exposed brick and wood interior complemented by a sun deck and a shady yard. Hidden away down an alley off Westgate, it is secluded from the Fizz and Music Yoof Zone of the city centre. Harry's is a thriving community local with many new friends to meet. Live music plays on Monday and Wednesday. There is a pay and display car park adjacent. ⛼❀⇌(Westgate/Kirkgate)☐⁻

O'Donoghues

60 George Street, WF1 1DL

⏲ 5-11; 12-midnight Fri & Sat; 12-11 Sun

☎ (07877) 520013

East Coast SSB; guest beers Ⓗ

A recent return to the local ale scene after a time in the doldrums. O'Donoghues has already won a Pub of the Season award from the local CAMRA branch for the superb quality of its six ales. Comfy sofas, secluded corners and a real fire complement the warm welcome, while live music on Friday and Saturday gives a kick to the weekend.
⛼⇌(Westgate/Kirkgate)☐(435,443,444)

The Hop ✔

19 Bank Street, WF1 1EH

⏲ 4-midnight; 3 (12 Sat)-1am Fri & Sat; 12-11 Sun

☎ (01924) 367111

Fuller's London Pride; Ossett Pale Gold, Silver King, Excelsior; guest beers Ⓗ

Converted from former Vanguard House offices, this Victorian building has been transformed into a multi-faceted venue for drinking, dining, socialising, music appreciation and conversation. It has bare brick walls with original fireplaces and other features. The 10 draught beers are complemented by an extensive wine list and a selection of bottled Belgian beers. There is live music on Friday and Saturday nights and an open mike night on Monday. Three Wednesdays in each month feature a Live Comedy Store. Rooms are available for hire.
❀☾◗♿⇌(Westgate/Kirkgate)☐⁻

Wakefield Labour Club (The Red Shed)

18 Vicarage Street, WF1 1QX

⏲ 12-4 (Fri only), 7-11; 11-4, 7-11 Sat; 7-11 Sun

☎ (01924) 215626 🌐 theredshed.org.uk

Beer range varies Ⓗ

The Red Shed is a old army hut which has survived the redevelopment of the area. Home to many trade union, community and charity groups, quiz night is Wednesday and live music plays on the second and last Saturday of each month. There are three rooms, with two available for hire for functions. An extensive collection of union plates and badges is displayed over the bar, together with numerous CAMRA awards adorning the walls. The guest ales are usually from northern and Midlands micros. ⇌(Westgate/Kirkgate)☐♣P⊟

Walton

New Inn

144 Shay Lane, WF2 6LA

⏲ 12-midnight

☎ (01924) 255447 🌐 newinnwalton.co.uk

Copper Dragon Best Bitter; John Smith's Bitter; Leeds Pale Ale; Taylor Landlord; guest beer Ⓗ

Traditional 18th-century vernacular stone building with a flagstone roof. Inside it has several areas including a restaurant that offers exceptionally good food (not Mon). This community-focused pub attracts people from all walks of life. Live music is performed each Tuesday from 9pm (see the website for details). It also hosts an annual summer beer festival. An ideal start or finish for rural walks along the route of the former Barnsley Canal. ❀◑♿🚌(194,195,196)P⁄–

Weetwood

Stable Pub

Weetwood Hall, Otley Road, LS16 5PS (just off Leeds ring road on A657 by Weetwood roundabout)
12-11 (midnight Fri & Sat summer); 12-10.30 Sun
☎ (0113) 256 5242 🌐 weetwood.co.uk
Black Sheep Best Bitter; Taylor Landlord; guest beers Ⓗ
Originally the stable block of the manor house, this pub is part of the Weetwood Hotel & Leisure complex. The interior retains an equestrian theme with saddles and harnesses on the walls. Five ales are served including two from Copper Dragon. Food is available until 9pm daily, with regular themed nights and daily specials. Children are allowed in the Stable Stalls until 9pm and outside in the cobbled courtyard. ❀◑♿🚌♣P⁄–

Wintersett

Angler's Retreat 🏆

Ferry Top Lane, WF4 2EB SE382157
12-3, 7-11; 12-11 Sat; closed Tue; 12-3.30, 7-10.30 Sun
☎ (01924) 862370
Acorn Barnsley Bitter; John Smith's Bitter; Samuel Smith OBB; guest beer Ⓗ
This rural ale house is an increasingly rare example of an old-fashioned, no frills community pub. It has a loyal local clientele of many old pitmen and many old tales to be told. Close to the Anglers Country Park, it is also frequented by birdwatchers, walkers and bikers. There are benches and a garden for fine weather drinking, with a large car park opposite. Q❀🚌(194,195,196)♣P⁄–

Woodhouse

Chemic ✓

9 Johnston Street, LS6 2NG (off Woodhouse St)
12-midnight (1am Fri & Sat); 12-11.30 Sun
☎ (0113) 245 7670
Black Sheep Best Bitter; Taylor Landlord; guest beers Ⓗ
An attractive stone-built pub set back above the road. The interior has a cosy country pub feel with dark wood and low ceilings in both the front lounge and rear bar. Two permanent beers and up to three guest ales are available and small beer festivals feature each spring and autumn. There is a grand piano in the bar and live music is played, with jazz on Tuesday, Irish on Wednesday and folk on Thursday and Sunday. A range of board games plus darts are available in the bar.
❀🚌(51,51A)♣P

Yeadon

Tarn

Henshaw Lane, LS19 7RW
12-midnight (11 Sun)
☎ (0113) 210 9536 🌐 thetarn.co.uk
Beer range varies Ⓗ
Traditional post-war functional brick-built pub with one long room divided by a central bar to give a games area and a lounge area at separate ends. Very much a community pub, it is home to darts, dominoes and pool teams, and live music plays on occasional Saturday nights. There are eight handpumps serving a variety of beers from local micro-breweries and from those further afield (see the website for current offerings). An annual beer festival is held each August. ❀◑🚌♣P⁄–

Kelham Island Tavern, Sheffield (Photo: Jon Howard).

Good Beer Guide Belgium

Tim Webb

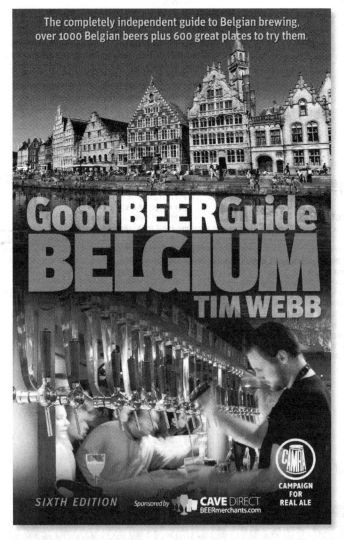

The completely revised and updated 6th edition of the guide so impressive that it is acknowledged as the standard work for Belgian beer lovers, even in Belgium itself. The **Good Beer Guide Belguim** includes comprehensive advice on getting there, being there, what to eat, where to stay and how to bring beers back home. Its outline of breweries, beers and bars makes this book indispensible for both leisure and business travellers a well as for armchair drinkers looking to enjoy a selection of Belgian brews from their local beer store.

£14.99 ISBN 978-1-85249-261-8 Members' price £12.99 368 pages

Wales

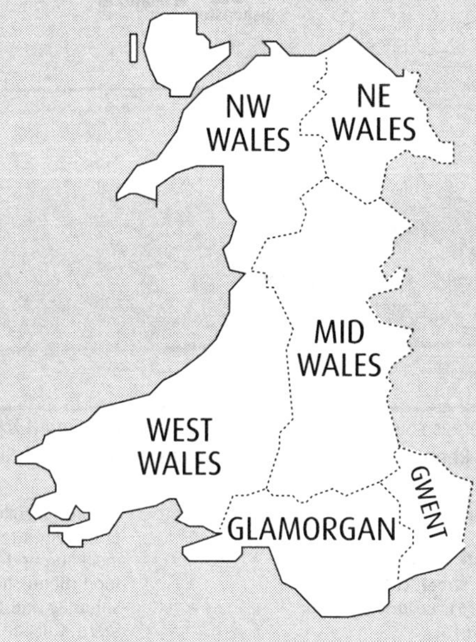
NW
WALES
NE
WALES
MID
WALES
WEST
WALES
GLAMORGAN
GWENT

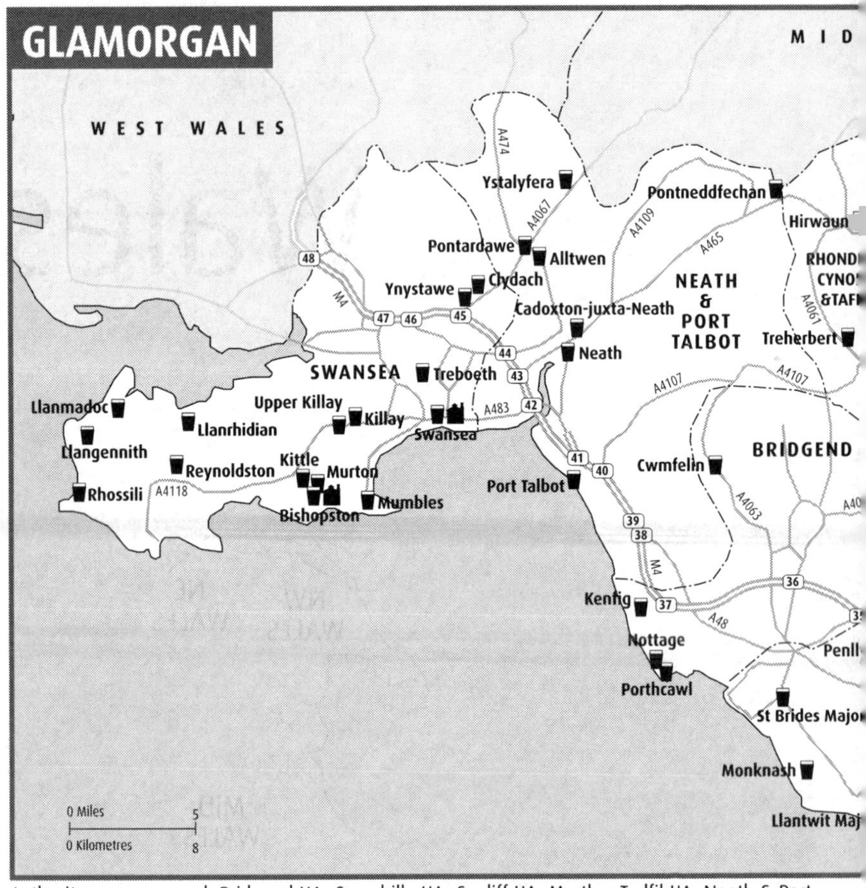

Authority areas covered: Bridgend UA, Caerphilly UA, Cardiff UA, Merthyr Tydfil UA, Neath & Port Talbot UA, Rhondda, Cynon & Taff UA, Swansea UA, Vale of Glamorgan UA

Aberdare

Cambrian Inn

60 Seymour Street, CF44 7DL
12 (11 Sat)-11; 12-10.30 Sun
(01685) 879120
Beer range varies Ⓗ
A short walk from the shops and rail and bus stations, this welcoming town pub has a pleasant atmosphere, its comfortable interior drawing customers from all walks of life. Just one real ale is served, usually sourced from a micro-brewery, but turnover is brisk. Good-value lunches are available. A quiz is held on Wednesday night and there is live acoustic music on Thursday. The pub sign portrays the choral conductor and brewer Caradog (Griffith Rhys Jones), a famous son of Aberdare.

Aberthin

Hare & Hounds

Aberthin Road, CF71 7LG (on A4222)
12 (4 Mon)-midnight
(01446) 774892
Marston's Pedigree, Ⓗ; **Old Empire** Ⓖ; **Ringwood Best Bitter** Ⓗ
A friendly, welcoming and comfortable old village pub. The pleasant bar has wooden settles, an open fire and a collection of historic photographs and prints. An interesting collection of ales is on offer including up to three guests. The extensive, varied food menu changes regularly. Live music plays on Saturday and the pub is home to a thriving darts team. Outside, there is a beer garden and seating for the summer. Well-behaved dogs are welcome in the bar. Q

Alltwen

Butchers at Alltwen

Alltwen Hill, SA8 3BP (off A474 Neath-Pontardawe Road)
12-2.30, 6-11; 12-11 Sun
(01792) 863100
Beer range varies Ⓗ
Newly refurbished pub with a modern feel comprising a bar/dining area and separate restaurant. A melting pot of old and new, it features oak beams, brickwork, various artefacts and an open fireplace. A variety of real ales is on offer, often a reflection of customers' choices. The pub has a good reputation for freshly cooked food, with a la carte and special early bird menus, and steak nights on Monday and Tuesday. A covered, heated veranda on one side gives panoramic views of the Swansea Valley. Q(122)P

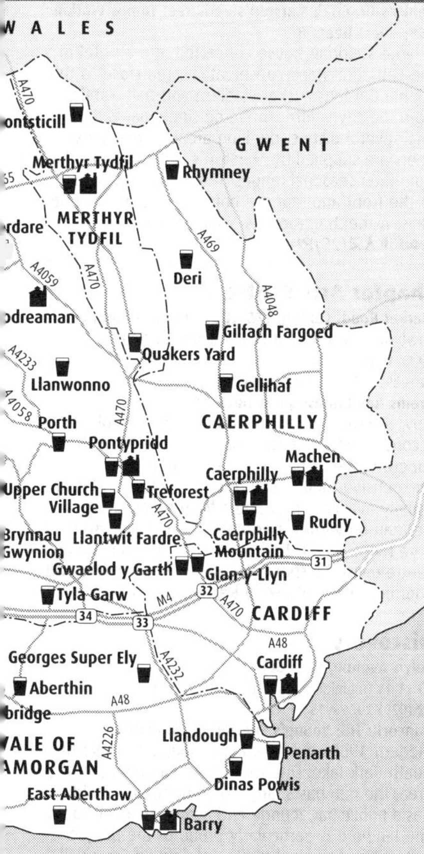

Barry

Barry West End Club

54 St Nicholas Road, CF62 6QY

⏲ 2 (11.30 Sat)-11.30; 12-10.30 Sun

☎ (01446) 735739

Brains Dark, Bitter; guest beer Ⓗ

Set on a hill overlooking Barry Old Harbour, this lively establishment has been voted local CAMRA Club of the Year for the past three years. The club has the feel of a friendly local, with a regular quiz night and snooker, crib, darts and skittles all played. An annual beer festival is held in the autumn. CAMRA members are most welcome. ❀⊟♿⇌🚌♣⛳

Castle Hotel

44 Jewel Street, CF63 3NQ (900m from Barry Dock rail station)

⏲ 12-11.30 (midnight Fri & Sat); 12-11 Sun

☎ (01446) 408916

Brains Bitter, SA; guest beers Ⓗ

Friendly Victorian former hotel close to the historic docks. This is the best place to drink in Barry, with regular changing guest ales. The public bar features live music and large- screen TVs for sports. The quieter lounge bar has many original features and now serves food five nights a week as well as Sunday lunch. There is a skittle alley, snooker room and darts. A local folk club meets regularly upstairs. Previous local CAMRA branch Pub of the Year and regional runner-up in 2008. ❀⊟⇌(Docks)🚌

Bishopston

Joiners Arms

50 Bishopston Road, SA3 3EJ

⏲ 11.30-11; 12-10.30 Sun

☎ (01792) 232658

Courage Best Bitter; Marston's Pedigree; Swansea Bishopswood, Three Cliffs Gold, Original Wood; guest beers Ⓗ

Home of the Swansea Brewing Company and in the heart of the village, this 1860s pub is popular with locals and is always busy in both bars. Beer festivals and music events are held occasionally, adding to the excellent ale range. Good, value-for-money food is served and social events are organised. The pub has won several local CAMRA awards. There is a small car park – if full, try 100 metres down the hill. ⛫Q❀◐◑⊟🚌(14,114)♣P

Brynnau Gwynion

Mountain Hare

Brynna Road, Pencoed, CF35 6PG (off A473 between Pencoed and Llanharan on B4280)

⏲ 5-11.30; 2-midnight Fri & Sat; 12-11 Sun

☎ (01656) 860458 🌐 mountainhare.co.uk

Bullmastiff Welsh Gold; Evan Evans BB; guest beers Ⓗ

Significant refurbishment, including a garden patio area, has taken away none of the character of this family-owned village pub situated where the Vale of Glamorgan meets the former mining valleys. There is a large, comfortable lounge, and a traditional public bar where guest beers are available at all times. An annual Ales of Wales beer festival is hosted here. Q❀⊟♿🚌♣P

Cadoxton-juxta-Neath

Crown & Sceptre Inn

Main Road, SA10 8AP

⏲ 11-11 (10.30 Sun)

☎ (01639) 442145

Greene King Old Speckled Hen; Tomos Watkin OSB Ⓗ

Built in 1835 as a tap for the Vale of Neath brewery, this former coach house has a bar, lounge and refurbished restaurant in the former stables. The popular local has an excellent reputation for its ale and freshly cooked food. As well as the a la carte menus there is a wide range of bar meals on offer. Thai chicken and fillet steak pie are among the favourites. Neath Abbey is nearby. ❀◐◑⊟♿🚌(154,158)P⛳

INDEPENDENT BREWERIES

Artisan Cardiff (NEW)
Brains Cardiff
Bullmastiff Cardiff
Carter's Machen
Celt Experience Caerphilly
Dare Godreaman
Newmans Caerphilly
Otley Pontypridd
Rhymney Merthyr Tydfil
Swansea Bishopston
Tomos Watkin Swansea
Vale of Glamorgan Barry
Zerodegrees Cardiff

Caerphilly

Masons Arms

Mill Road, CF83 3FE (on B4263, N of town centre)
12-11.30 (midnight Fri & Sat)
(029) 208 83353
Brains Bitter; guest beers H
A friendly welcome is assured at this traditional local a short walk from Caerphilly Castle and the town centre. Good value meals are served, mostly in the spacious rear lounge which borders the local park. Cask beers, including two guests, can be found in the lounge – a blackboard in the bar informs drinkers of what is on offer. The smaller front bar sports a pool table and dartboard. The nearest station is Aber, a 15-minute walk.
Q❀◑⊟(C,E)♣P⁻

Caerphilly Mountain

Black Cock Inn

Waunwaelod Way, CF83 1BD (off Watford Road A469)
10.30 (12 Sun)-midnight
(029) 20880534 theblackcockinn.co.uk
Hancock's HB; Theakston Old Peculier; guest beers H
Nicely hidden away, this rural restaurant and bar nestles in the hilltop forest near Castle Heights Golf Club. Access is easiest from Caerphilly Mountain, but also possible via narrow lanes from Pantmawr and Tongwynlais. Two guest beers are stocked, usually from small brewers, with real cider in summer. Food and drink has a Welsh focus. The bar is popular with ramblers and dogs are welcome. The outdoor smoking area is heated and lit.
❀◑♿P⁻

Cardiff

Albany

105 Donald Street, CF24 4TL
12-11 (11.30 Fri); 11-11.30 Sat; 12-10.30 Sun
(029) 20311075
Brains Dark, Bitter, SA, seasonal beers; guest beers H
This street-corner local continues to attract a good mix of students and locals, and offers a popular range of guest beers. The main area is very lively and has a large-screen TV which can also be used to play Wii games, while the lounge is quieter. The pub now has live music on Saturday in addition to a Sunday night poker league and weekly quiz. It has a covered and heated smoking area, skittle alley and large beer garden. Q❀◑⁻

Butchers Arms

29 Llandaff Road, Canton, CF11 9NG
12-11 (11.30 Fri; 10.30 Sat & Sun)
(029) 202 27927
Brains Dark, Bitter, SA; guest beers H
Friendly street-corner local with a jovial public bar and more comfortable family-friendly lounge. The decor is reminiscent of the Brain's pubs of yesteryear and adds to the cosy feel of the interior. The frequently changing guest ale is always a welcome addition to the regular beers. Two small outside drinking areas cater for bar and lounge customers. Two darts teams are based here. Dogs are welcome. Cardiff CAMRA Pub of the Year 2008.
❀(17,18)♣⁻

Cayo Arms

36 Cathedral Road, CF11 9LL
12-11 (midnight Fri & Sat); 12-10.30 Sun
(029) 20391910
Banks's Original; Marston's Pedigree; Tomos Watkin OSB; guest beers H
A large Victorian house converted into a hotel in the Cathedral Road conservation area close to the Sophia Gardens cricket stadium and half a mile from the city centre. The large single bar is divided into several distinct drinking areas. Three guest beers are supplied by Marston's and Tomos Watkin from their seasonal ranges. The outdoor patio areas to the front and rear are popular suntraps on fine days. A meeting room is available for hire.
❀◑(25)P⁻

Chapter Arts Centre

Market Road, Canton, CF5 1QE (100 yards north of Cowbridge Road East at Canton Police Station)
12-11 (12.30am Fri, 12.00 Sat); 12-10.30
(029) 203 13431 chapter.org
Brains Rev James; guest beers H
Now returned to Chapter's main building following reconstruction, this café bar continues to offer a superb range of beers plus good quality inexpensive food. Three or four guest real ales are usually available plus beers from many small German breweries. German beer festivals are held here twice a year. The fact that the bar is in an arts centre gives it a special character with works of art adorning the walls. ❀◑♿≷(17,18)P⁻

Discovery

Celyn Avenue, CF23 6EH
11-11 (midnight Fri & Sat); 12-10.30 Sun
(029) 20755015
Hancocks HB; Young's Special; guest beers H
Modern 1960s pub in a residential area close to Roath Park lake. Due to a Quaker influence in the area, the pub has a large catchment area. Inside, it has a public bar, lounge and a large function room. The landlord is particularly proud of the unique collection of original photos of Captain Scott's ill-fated expedition to the Antarctic on the walls.
Q❀◑♿≷(Heath Halt)P⁻

Gatekeeper ✔

Westgate Street, CF10 1DD
9-midnight (1am Fri & Sat)
(029) 20646020
Brains Bitter; Greene King Abbot; Marston's Pedigree; guest beers H
Large, two-bar Wetherspoon's pub which won a design award when it opened in 2001. Situated opposite the entrance to the Millennium Stadium, it is extremely busy on match days. The paintings on the walls relate to sporting history and Cardiff Arms Park. The pub supports local brewers and holds a Welsh beer festival during St David's Day as well as the bi-annual Wetherspoon's beer festivals.
◑♿≷(Central)

Goat Major ✔

33 High Street, CF10 1PU
11-midnight; 12-11 Sun
(029) 203 37161
Brains Dark, Bitter, SA, Rev James, SA Gold H
This small but popular city-centre Brain's pub is renowned for its traditional appearance and friendly atmosphere, attracting a brisk trade from both locals and visitors. It is named for the mascot of the Royal Welsh Regiment, a fact that is proudly illustrated in the many photographs that adorn the interior. Traditional Welsh food is served into the early evening. ◑♿≷(Central)

Heathcock ✔

58 Bridge Street, Llandaff, CF5 2EN

12-11 (midnight Fri & Sat)

☎ (029) 205 75005

Hancocks HB; St Austell Tribute; guest beers Ⓗ

Near the BBC studios at a busy road junction, the pub has two distinct public areas separated by a central bar. At the rear is a skittle alley that runs the length of the substantial garden, which is very popular during the summer months. There is a covered, heated area outside for smokers. Pub meals include a range of curries. Live music plays on Wednesday evenings. A guest beer often comes from a local brewery.

Mochyn Du

Sophia Close, CF11 9HW

12-11 (midnight Fri & Sat); 12-10.30 Sun

☎ (029) 203 71599

Beer range varies Ⓗ

One of Cardiff's few independently-owned free houses, the name means 'black pig' and comes from a folk song. This converted Victorian gate lodge close to Sophia Gardens has recently been extended to create a larger conservatory-style bar and restaurant area and an additional outdoor space. The pub emphasises its Welshness with bilingual staff and Welsh dishes on the menu. Beers are sourced from Welsh breweries, including local micros, with a house beer supplied by the Vale of Glamorgan Brewery. (25)P

Pen & Wig ✔

1 Park Grove, CF10 3BJ

9-midnight; 10-1am Fri & Sat; 10-11.30 Sun

☎ (029) 20371217

Brains Bitter; Hancocks HB; guest beers Ⓗ

Popular pub located close to the centre of town and particularly busy after work. Furnishings are traditional, with a variety of seating including settles, chairs and stools. Extra facilities include the provision of popular board games and a bike rack. The guest ale range changes weekly. The attractive beer garden is pleasant in summer.
(Queen St)

Pendragon ✔

Excalibur Drive, Thornhill, CF14 9BB

11.30-11.30 (midnight Fri & Sat); 11.30-11 Sun

☎ (029) 206 10550

Brains Dark, Bitter, SA, Rev James, SA Gold Ⓗ

Situated on the slopes of the Caerphilly Mountain on the northern edge of Cardiff, the pub has extensive views across the city from the covered patio. It is approached via a long drive leading to a large car park. The welcoming staff and cordial atmosphere have taken the pub into a customer service awards final. A varied menu of food is served Monday to Saturday, with a traditional Sunday lunch. Charities are well supported by the pub and its regulars. P

Yard ✔

42-43 St Mary Street, CF10 1AD

11-midnight (1am Fri & Sat)

☎ (029) 20227577

Brains Dark, Bitter, SA, Rev James Ⓗ

Situated on the site of the former Brains Brewery, the building has now been converted into Brain's flagship pub in the redeveloped Brewery Quarter. This lively venue is open plan but with distinct areas, and makes use of steel, copper and aluminium to reflect its past history as a brewery. It is centrally located in town and very close to the station. The pub provides Brain's bottles and beers to take home. (Central)

Clydach

New Inn

The Lone, SA6 5SU (on road to Craig-Cefn-Parc)

11-3 (not Mon & Tue), 6-11; 11-11 Fri-Sun

☎ (01792) 842839

Beer range varies Ⓗ

Friendly country pub with a public bar with a log-burning fire in winter, games room and lounge. Good food is served in the bar and lounge. Outside is a children's play area and beer garden. The pub is close to the Cwm Clydach RSPB nature reserve, and is a popular stop-off for walkers.
Q(121)P

Cowbridge

Duke of Wellington ✔

48 High Street, CF71 7AG

11-11; 12-10.30 Sun

☎ (01446) 773592

Brains Dark, Bitter, SA, SA Gold, Rev James Ⓗ

Historic pub at the centre of this market town with a proud history. The well-run Brain's house hosts an annual cider festival. The Duke's best kept secret is a medieval function room with a minstrels' gallery, and the lounge bar features an original Roman wall. The enclosed beer garden is a pleasant spot to relax in summer.
Q(X1,X2)P

Vale of Glamorgan Inn

53 High Street, CF71 7AE

11.30-11 (midnight Fri & Sat); 12-10.30 Sun

☎ (01446) 772252

Celt Experience Bronze; Hancock's HB; Shepherd Neame Bishops Finger; Wye Valley HPA; guest beers Ⓗ

Friendly pub in the centre of town. This one-room bar has a comfortable carpeted lounge area and a wooden-floored bar area with a warming fire. There is no background music or games machines. Excellent home-cooked lunches are on offer (not Sun). The outbuildings were once the home of the Vale of Glamorgan Brewery (no connection with the current business of that name) which was taken over by Hancock's in 1913. A beer festival is hosted in autumn. Q(X1,X2)

Cwmfelin

Cross Inn

Maesteg Road, CF34 9LB (on A4063)

11.45-midnight (1am Fri & Sat); 11-midnight Sun

☎ (01656) 732476

Brains Bitter; Wye Valley Butty Bach; guest beers Ⓗ

A genuine locals' pub where you are sure to get a friendly welcome, in an area where a decent pint is hard to find. This multi-roomed hostelry is situated on the main Bridgend to Maesteg road, with excellent public transport. Children are welcome until 7pm, well-behaved dogs are permitted too (please ask first). The back room displays some interesting photographs. Q(Garth)

WALES

Deri

Old Club ✔

93 Bailey Street, CF81 9HX

5 (12 Sat & Sun)-midnight

(01443) 830278

Beer range varies H

The Old Club is an ideal reason to explore this little corner of Wales. Two guest beers are always available, rising to three at weekends. Variety is the watchword, with local craft brewers featuring, supported by some of the more interesting regionals. Access is easy by bus from Bargoed, or on foot or cycle along the former railway path – much easier going than the road. A little further on is Cwm Darran country park and hill tops popular with paragliders. The Old Club always welcomes visitors – just show this Guide on entry. (1,4)

Dinas Powys

Star ✔

Station Road, CF64 4DE

11.30-11 (midnight Fri & Sat); 12-10.30 Sun

(029) 2051 4245

Brains Dark, Bitter, SA, SA Gold; guest beers H

Comfortable, spacious Brain's house in the village centre, full of character, welcoming and cheerful. Open plan and recently refurbished, it has cosy seating and dining areas where good home-cooked food is available. There is a large car park and patio to the rear with disabled access by wheelchair lift. P

East Aberthaw

Blue Anchor

CF62 3DD (on B4265)

11-11; 12-10.30 Sun

(01446) 750329 blueanchoraberthaw.com

Brains Bitter; Theakston Old Peculier; Wadworth 6X; Wye Valley HPA; guest beer H

Fourteenth-century, family-run pub with an adjoining restaurant, rebuilt and restored after a serious fire. Beneath the thatched roof lies a multi-room, flagstone-floored building with thick stone walls that defeat most mobile phones. The guest beer is often from a local brewery. The car park is across the road and the pub is on regular bus routes. QP

Gellihaf

Coal Hole

Bryn Road, NP12 2QE (on A4049 S of Fleur-de-Lys)

12-3, 6.30-11; 11-11 Fri & Sat; 12-10.30 Sun

(01443) 830280

Greene King Old Speckled Hen; guest beers H

Set back from the road, this friendly one-bar pub was converted from farm buildings during the 19th century – the bar occupies the former stables. Up to two guest beers are stocked. Excellent food is available daily, served in the bar and restaurant, with traditional Sunday lunch a highlight. Extensive views of the Rhymney Valley can be enjoyed, with good ale and a warm welcome. P

Gilfach Fargoed

Capel Hotel

Park Place, CF81 8LW

12-11 (11.30 Fri & Sat); 12-10.30 Sun

(01443) 830272

Brains SA; John Smith's Bitter; guest beers H

This impressive Edwardian hotel retains much of its original character, and is renowned for its warm welcome. Guest beers and ciders are from smaller, often local, producers, and choices of the day are listed on notice-boards. Gravity cider and perry are served from a cold cabinet. An annual beer festival is held in May. Many visitors arrive by rail, alighting at the tiny station that has changed little since the era of steam rail. Take care to select a journey that stops here. Q(X38,50)

Glan-y-Llyn

Fagins Ale & Chop House

9 Cardiff Road, CF15 7QD

11-midnight (1am Fri); 12-1am Sat; 12-11 Sun

(029) 208 11800 faginsalehouse.co.uk

Otley 01, OF H**; guest beers** G

Local CAMRA Pub of the Year 2008, this is one of the best pubs in the area. Set in a typical valleys terrace, the flagstone floor and welcoming log burner greet you on chilly days. A range of craft ales is on offer, with three gravity guest beers usually available. Otley OF is exclusively brewed for Fagins – the landlord has a hand in its recipe. Two handpumped ciders are Gwynt y Ddraig Happy Daze and Farmhouse. Excellent value meals are served (not Sun or Mon eve). Outside drinking is on roadside tables. (26,132)

Gwaelod y Garth

Gwaelod y Garth

Main Road, CF15 9HH

11-11 Mon-Thur, 11-1AM Fri-Sat

(029) 20870408

Felinfoel Double Dragon; Hancock HB; guest beers H

Friendly, atmospheric pub with separate lounge and saloon bars, and an upstairs restaurant. Three to four changing real ales are on handpump. Inside, there are real fires to keep you warm in the cooler months, and outside a lovely view of the surrounding valley from the beer garden. High-quality restaurant food is served. This popular community pub is well worth a visit. Dog-friendly. Q(26B)

Hirwaun

Glancynon Inn

Swansea Road, CF44 9PH

11-11; 12-10.30 Sun

(01685) 811043 glancynoninn.co.uk

Greene King Abbot; guest beers H

The main outlet for real ale in the area, this large country pub with oak beams and a congenial atmosphere is popular with both drinkers and diners. Guest beers are usually sourced from Welsh breweries and the restaurant uses local organic produce wherever possible. The pub features a pleasant lounge with a split-level bar leading to a well-kept beer garden. A little off the beaten track, it is nevertheless easy to find. Lunch is served on Sunday only (booking essential). P

Kenfig

Prince of Wales

Ton Kenfig, CF33 4PR

12-11

☎ (01656) 740356
Draught Bass; Worthington Bitter G
A welcome return to the Guide for this historic, Grade II-listed pub, with a famous old council chamber. Reputed to be one of the most haunted pubs in Wales, ask the landlord to show you around. In the past the building has been used as a church, court house, school and mortuary, as well as a police incident centre. The present landlord is only the 11th since 1820.The Bass served is known locally as Jack's Bass. ⌂Q❀ⒸⒹ⊟⊟P⁄–

Killay

Black Boy
444 Gower Road, SA2 7AL
✪ 11-11 (midnight Fri & Sat); 12-11 Sun
☎ (01792) 299469
Brains Bitter, SA, Rev James H
The single L-shaped room in this large, popular Brain's pub is divided into several distinct areas, some mostly for dining – food is available all day until 9pm. The decor is traditional, with several TV screens used mainly for sporting events. Monday is quiz night. Bus routes 20 and 21 are the main routes from Swansea, others will take you on into Gower. ❀Ⓒ♿⊟(20,21)♣P

Village Inn
5-6 Swan Court, Gower Road, SA2 7BA
✪ 10.30-11.30; 12-11 Sun
☎ (01792) 203311
Evan Evans Warrior; Fuller's London Pride; Taylor Landlord; Worthington's Bitter H
Split-level, L-shaped, single room bar tucked away in the shopping precinct of a suburban Swansea village. The room is divided into several nooks and crannies, some with an extensive display of plates and sporting memorabilia. Quiz nights are Sunday and Tuesday. Food is served lunchtimes and occasionally on special themed evenings. There is free public parking nearby. Ⓒ♿⊟(20,21)P

Kittle

Beaufort Arms ✔
18 Pennard Road, SA3 3JS
✪ 11-11 (11.30 Mon, Fri & Sat); 11-10.30 Sun
☎ (01792) 234521
Brains Buckley's Best Bitter, Rev James H
Reputedly the oldest pub in Gower, the original part of the building boasts a beamed ceiling and early stonework. The pub, with three bars and a function room, has won a number of awards for community focus and 'Gower In Bloom' competitions. There is a large car park, outdoor seating and a children's play area. A quiz is held on Monday. Food hours and the beer range are often extended during holiday periods.
❀ⒸⒹ⊟⊟(14)♣P

Llandough

Merrie Harrier ✔
117 Penlan Road, CF64 2NY
✪ 12-11; 11.30-11.30 Fri; 11-11.30 Sat
☎ (029) 2030 3994
Brains Bitter, SA; guest beers H
One of the Cardiff area's best known landmarks, this large and traditionally styled road house lies on a busy road junction between Cardiff, Penarth and Dinas Powys. It has a spacious, comfortable lounge bar where major sporting events are screened live. The extensive menu of freshly-cooked food is available all day. A friendly and relaxing stop at any time. ❀ⒸⒹ⇌(Cogan)⊟(X45,95)P

Llangennith

Kings Head
SA3 1HX
✪ 11 (12 Sun)-11
☎ (01792) 386212 🌐 kingsheadgower.co.uk
Draught Bass; Hancock's HB; guest beers H
Large and historic stone-built pub and hotel extended over the years to incorporate adjoining farm buildings. The pub is popular with locals, visitors and surfers. It has two rooms, one for games, the other with a large display of images of local scenes and historic characters. Food is served all day from an enticing blackboard menu. There are impressive views of nearby beaches from the superb garden. Note the unusual pub sign. Guest beers are added in summer only.
⌂❀⊨ⒸⒹ⊟Ⓐ⊟(115,118)P

Llanmadoc

Britannia Inn
Llanmadoc, SA3 1DB
✪ 12-11
☎ (01792) 386624 🌐 britanniainngower.co.uk
Marston's Pedigree; Tomos Watkins OSB, H
Timbers from ships wrecked on the nearby coast were used in the construction of this pretty and popular 17th-century pub set in a quiet corner of Gower. There is a cosy bar at the entrance serving good food and beer; the rear bar area has been converted into a fine restaurant. Beer gardens front and rear offer stunning views over the nearby estuary, with an aviary and pet area popular with children. ⌂Q❀⊨ⒸⒹⒶ⊟(116)♣P⁄–

Llanrhidian

Dolphin Inn
SA3 1EH
✪ 5 (1 Fri, Sat & summer)-11; 12-10.30 Sun
☎ (01792) 391069
Brain's Rev James; Fuller's London Pride H
Real ale outsells lager in this cosy village pub, reopened in March 2007 after 12 years' closure. Close to the Loughor estuary, it commands panoramic views of the water from the pleasant garden. Recently refurbished in traditional style, it has a long single room and a stone-faced bar. Local artwork and photography are on display. Light snacks such as a classic local lava bread and cockles are available. Q❀ⒸⒹⒶ⊟(116)♣P

Greyhound Inn
Old Walls, SA3 1HA
✪ 11-11; 12-10.30 Sun
☎ (01792) 391027
Draught Bass; Marston's Pedigree; guest beers H
Welcoming to locals and visitors alike, this large and popular inn usually has up to five real ales available. Families are well catered for and there are separate games and function rooms, as well as a pleasant garden with fine views. The pub has a reputation for good food, which is served in all its bars. The Sunday carvery is very popular. There is a large car park. ⌂Q❀ⒸⒹ⊟Ⓐ⊟(116)♣P⁄–

Llantwit Fardre

Bush Inn
Main Road, CF38 2EP
✪ 11-11; 12-10.30 Sun
☎ (01443) 203958
Tomos Watkin OSB; guest beers Ⓗ
A lively, comfortable village local with a separate games area. Something is going on most nights here, including darts and quizzes. It may stay open later on music evenings – open mike on Thursday night, band on Saturday. The guest ales on offer are usually from smaller Welsh breweries but may include others unusual for the area. Forthcoming beers and bands are listed outside.
❀🚌(100,400)♣P

Crown Inn
Main Road, CF38 2HL
✪ 12 (4 Tue)-midnight; 12-3, 7-midnight Sun
☎ (01443) 218277
Hancocks HB; guest beers Ⓗ
A bright, one-room pub with a comfortable lounge area. Outside chalk boards tell customers which beers and activities are on offer. The guest ales frequently include offerings from the Otley stable but may be beers unusual to the area. Bar food is prepared with Welsh-Italian flair, including Sunday lunches and special event dinners. Live music plays on Friday or Saturday, usually country, blues or folk.
❀◑◗🚌(100,400)P

Llantwit Major

Kings Head
East Street, CF61 1XY
✪ 11.30-11; 12-10.30 Sun
☎ (01446) 792697
Brains Dark, Bitter, SA; guest beers Ⓗ
Well-established local with a reputation for the quality of its ale and excellent lunchtime meals. The large and popular bar has pool, darts, dominoes and a large-screen TV for sport. The quieter lounge is comfortably furnished and retains the character cherished by locals for many years. A rare outlet in the Vale of Glamorgan for Brains Dark, avaiilable in the front bar.
⛰Q🐴❀◑⊟⋀⇌🚌♣P⸗

Old Swan Inn
Church Street, CF61 1SB
✪ 12-11 (10.30 Sun)
☎ (01446) 792230
Beer range varies Ⓗ
The oldest pub in a historic town, this excellent hostelry has won numerous awards for its fine ales and excellent food. Two real ales are on offer during the week, four at weekends, with an emphasis on South Wales breweries alongside regular supplies from Cottage in Somerset. The lively back bar has pool and a jukebox, while the traditional front lounge is quieter and attracts diners and drinkers. The smoking area is heated.
⛰❀◑◗⊟⋀⇌🚌♣●⸗

Llanwonno

Brynffynon Hotel
CF37 3PH ST030955
✪ 12-11 (10.30 Sun)
☎ (01443) 790272
Draught Bass; Greene King Abbot; guest beers Ⓗ
This isolated country inn nestles in the forest between the Cynon and Rhondda Fach valleys. Situated in a tiny village – just the pub and St Gwynno's church – the pub welcomes locals and visitors alike. It serves a range of up to five ales alongside a varied choice of food, and also holds occasional beer festivals. Surprisingly busy for such a remote pub, booking is a must for meals, especially Sunday lunch. ⛰❀🛏◑◗⋀♣P

Machen

White Hart
Nant-y-Ceisiad, CF83 8QQ ST441005
✪ 12-2.30 (not Wed), 6-11.30; 7-11 Sun
☎ (01633) 441005
Beer range varies Ⓗ
A quirky mix of old and new, the interior of this inn is adorned with fittings from the liner Empress of France. Although close to the main road, the pub was built to serve the old Rumney Tramroad which now forms part of national cycle route 4. An independent free house, it stocks up to three guest beers, mainly from smaller breweries, and holds occasional beer festivals. Booking is advisable for Sunday lunch. ❀🛏◑◗🚌(50)♣P

Merthyr Tydfil

Rose & Crown
20 Morgan Street, The Quarr, CF47 8TP (off A4102 Brecon Rd S of Cyfarthfa Park)
✪ 12 (11.30 Sun)-midnight
☎ (01695) 723743
Brains Bitter; Greene King Abbot; Wye Valley Bitter; Young's Bitter; guest beers Ⓗ
This comfortable, back-street local is just a whisker from Brecon Road, easiest approached on foot via Mount Street. It is well worth finding for the warm welcome and good range of beers for the area, kept by an enthusiastic landlord. The interior remains divided into separate rooms, each with a different character. Historic maps and photographs proudly illustrate how the iron-making industry shaped Merthyr Tydfil and Dowlais. ◗⊟🚌(26)♣⸗

Monknash

Plough & Harrow
CF71 7QQ (off B4265 between Wick and Marcross)
✪ 12-11 (10.30 Sun)
☎ (01656) 890209 🌐 theploughmonknash.com
Draught Bass Ⓗ/Ⓖ**; Otley O1; Worthington's Bitter; Wye Valley HPA** Ⓗ
Renowned throughout Wales, this historic pub serves up the finest of foods to complement an excellent choice of ales. Customers in the lounge should note that the beer and cider range is displayed in the bar. The large garden is perfect in summer, especially for the annual July beer festival. Proudly supporting Welsh brewers and cider makers, the pub offers a home delivery service. CAMRA branch Cider Pub of the Year 2008 and 2009. ⛰❀◑◗⊟🚌♣●P⸗

Mumbles

Park Inn
23 Park Street, SA3 4AD
✪ 4 (12 Fri-Sun)-11
☎ (01792) 366738
Beer range varies Ⓗ

A regular Swansea CAMRA Pub of the Year, its five handpumps dispense an ever-changing range of beers, with particular emphasis on independent breweries from Wales and the west of England. The convivial atmosphere in this small establishment attracts discerning drinkers of all ages, though the games room is particularly popular with younger people. On the walls, alongside a fine display of pump clips, are pictures of old Mumbles and its pioneering railway. Q(2,3)

Victoria Inn

21 Westbourne Place, SA3 4DB
12 (11.30 Sat)-11; 12-10.30 Sun
(01792) 360111
Draught Bass; Greene King Old Speckled Hen; Worthington's Bitter; guest beers H
This traditional back-street corner local dates from the mid-19th century. Recently refurbished in comfortable style, it retains many original features of historic interest including a well in the bar area, the source of water in the days when the pub brewed its own beer. Popular with locals, there is live music on alternate Fridays. Quiz night is Monday. (2,3)

Murton

Plough & Harrow

88 Oldway, SA3 3DJ
11-11; 12-10.30 Sun
(01792) 234459
Courage Best Bitter, Directors; guest beers H
One of Gower's oldest inns, the Plough & Harrow has been enlarged and renovated in recent times, but retains its character and popularity. The pub combines a busy food trade with the traditions of a local. The bar area has TV and pool, and there is a quieter space for conversation or a meal. Tuesday is quiz night. Heaters are used to warm the large, covered and decked outdoor area, which unusually also has a pool table. Q(14,114)P

Neath

Borough Arms

2 New Henry Street, SA11 1PH
4 (12 Sat)-11; 12-3, 6-10.30 Sun
(01639) 644902
Beer range varies H
A former regional CAMRA Pub of the Year, it has retained its warm and friendly atmosphere. As you enter you are greeted by the warm conversation of the locals and the welcoming sight of five working handpumps. Although not in the town centre, the pub is worth regular visits for the constantly changing beers on offer. Q

David Protheroe

7 Windsor Road, SA11 1LS
9-midnight (1am Fri & Sat)
(01639) 622130
Beer range varies H
This popular Wetherspoon's is situated opposite the railway station and bus stop so is easily accessible, and has an open plan bar with a family area at the rear. A wide range of food is available and steak and curry nights are held regularly. Drinks prices are reduced on Monday. Two guest ales are usually available. A former police station, the pub is named after the first policeman posted here.

Nottage

Farmers Arms

Lougher Row, CF36 3TA
11-midnight; 11.30-11 Sun
(01656) 784595
Brains SA; Draught Bass; Greene King Abbot; Worthington's Bitter H
Traditional stone-built pub overlooking the village green with benches for outside drinking. Inside, the comfortable lounge has a long bar down one side and a large-screen TV for sport. Live entertainment draws a crowd, with music events regularly throughout the week. There is a separate restaurant at the back. Nottage is now effectively part of Porthcawl, but retains a village atmosphere of its own. P

Rose & Crown Hotel

Heol y Capel, CF36 3ST
11-11.30
(01656) 784850
Brains Bitter, SA, Rev James H
A traditional pub in a small, picturesque village. Three bars including the cosy real ale bar offer up to two guest beers. Very popular with local residents, children are welcome. The restaurant provides a good selection of food throughout the week. For overnight guests, four doubles and four twin rooms are available. QP

Penarth

Albion

28 Glebe Street, CF64 1EF
11-11 (midnight Fri & Sat); 12-11 Sun
(029) 2030 3992
Brains Dark, Bitter, SA, SA Gold; guest beer H
Traditional two-roomed, street-corner local with a lively bar and comfortable lounge. Run by a landlady who is a real ale and music fan, you are guaranteed a warm welcome here, and children are permitted. A pub for the community, most of the musicians of Penarth play here, including the ukelele band, and poetry readings; other activities and classes are hosted. Regular beer festivals are popular. Local CAMRA Pub of the Year 2009.
(92,93,94)

Windsor

93 Windsor Road, CF64 1JF (on A4160 N of town centre)
9-11.30 (11 Sun)
(029) 2070 2871
Brains Bitter, SA Gold; Greene King Abbot; Taylor Landlord; guest beers H
Lively, traditional pub offering a beer exhibition every day, with up to seven real ales. A good range of food is served all day including breakfast. Home to a jazz club on Wednesday and a poker school on many evenings, the pub is also frequented by other clubs and social groups including Morris dancers. A separate function room/restaurant is available. (Dingle Road)(92,93,94)

Penllyn

Red Fox

CF71 7RQ (off A48) SS973763
12-11
(01446) 772352
Hancock's HB; Tomos Watkin OSB; guest beers H
Popular with the residents of this scattered community as well as visitors enjoying nearby

WALES

walks, the pub offers quality food and drink in a friendly atmosphere. The main room, with its flagstone floor and nooks and crannies, has a large log fire, while a separate room is used as a dining area. Exposed stone walls are decorated with pictures, mostly relating to the red fox and its pursuit. An attractive patio to the front and a rear garden are pleasant for outdoor drinking. Quiz night is the last Thursday of the month.
Q (V3)P

Pontardawe

Pink Geranium

31-33 Herbert Street, SA8 4EB
10-midnight (1am Sat & Sun)
(01792) 862255
Beer range varies H
Busy town-centre pub, handy for the Arts Centre. The L-shaped main bar is to the right of the entrance, and there is a lounge and music room with a stage where live bands play on Friday and Saturday nights. Outside is a large, covered patio, popular with smokers and drinkers in the summer. Up to three ales are usually available, including a Welsh beer, often Brains Reverend James or Celt Bronze. Children are permitted in the lounge.
(120,125)

Pontardawe Inn

123 Herbert Street, SA8 4ED
12 (3 winter)-midnight (1am Fri & Sat); 12-11.30 Sun
(01792) 830791 pontardaweinn.co.uk
Banks's Original; Marston's Pedigree; guest beers H
Situated on route 43 of the national cycle track network near the old bridge over the River Tawe. The locals' bar and lounge share a central servery, and there is a side room with a pool table. Live music is hosted on Wednesday and Saturday evenings, and there is a big screen for rugby. Known locally as the Gwachel, the pub is a past winner of CAMRA Neath & Bridgend Pub of the Year. Outside are three boules pistes. Home-cooked Sunday lunches are a highlight, with a curry and a pint offer on Monday evening.
Q (120,122,132)P

Pontneddfechan

Angel Inn

Pontneathvaughan Road, SA11 5NR (on B4242 nr A465 jct)
11.30-11.30 summer; 11.30-4, 6.30-11.30 winter; 12-11.30 Sun
(01639) 722013
Draught Bass; Rhymney Bitter H
Situated near the famous waterfalls, this is a popular stop off point for visitors and walkers. A mainly food-led establishment, it offers a wonderful selection of quality home-cooked meals. The large dining area has a great collection of old jugs and other household artefacts. The outside seating area is very popular in summer months. There is a quaint locals' and walkers' bar behind a curtain next to the main bar. Q (X56)P

Pontsticill

Red Cow

CF48 2UN (follow signs for Brecon Mountain Railway)
11-midnight
(01685) 384828
Wye Valley Bitter; guest beers H
Set within the Brecon Beacons National Park, this traditional pub has flagstone floors and a landlord whose enthusiasm for real ale shines through. With strong local trade, the pub is also popular with walkers and visitors to the nearby Dolygaer outdoor pursuits centre. The Brecon Mountain Railway is within walking distance and there are two golf courses nearby. (24)P

Pontypridd

Bunch of Grapes

Ynysangharad Road, CF37 4DA (off A4054 just N of A470 jct)
12-midnight
(01443) 402934 bunchofgrapes.org.uk
Otley 01 H**; guest beers** H/G
Just a few minutes' walk from the town centre stands this multi award-winning flagship for Otley Brewery. The eclectic range of beers on offer may include guests from near and far – often other Welsh craft breweries – and an interesting range of continental beers. Real cider is available on gravity. This Tardis-like pub also houses a high-class restaurant (booking advisable). Allow plenty of time to experience the fabulous atmosphere here – this is a hostelry you will not want to leave. Note that last admission is 10.30pm. P

Llanover Arms

Bridge Street, CF37 4PE (opp N entrace to Ynysangharad Park)
12-midnight (11 Sun)
(01443) 403215
Brains Bitter; Felinfoel Double Dragon; guest beer H
This free house stands opposite the park and is just a short stroll from Pontypridd's historic Old Bridge and Museum. The pub's three rooms and passageway each attract their own loyal clientele and are festooned with a variety of artefacts including old mirrors, maps and clocks. But for many, the major attraction here is the constantly changing guest beer. There is outside drinking on the patio. P

Port Talbot

Lord Caradoc

69-73 Station Road, SA13 1NW
9-midnight (1am Fri & Sat)
(01639) 896007
Brains SA, Rev James; Greene King Abbot; guest beers H
Typical Wetherspoon's pub situated in the centre of town a short distance from the railway station.The bar has an L-shaped layout with a raised drinking area. Children are welcome in the family area towards the rear of the pub. There is a patio area outside. The usual value-for-money fare is on offer including popular steak and curry nights.

Porth

Rheola

Rheola Road, CF39 0LF
2-midnight; 1-1am Fri; 12-1am Sat; 12-midnight Sun
(01443) 682633
Brains SA Gold; Draught Bass; guest beers H
Comfortable and friendly free house with a lively bar and cosy lounge. A new guest beer is added every weekend to supplement the regulars.

Situated at the gateway to the Rhondda and only a short distance from the Rhondda Heritage Park, this is a pub not to be missed. Occasional beer festivals are held. Note that last admission is 10.30pm. The outdoor smoking area is covered. P

Porthcawl

Lorelei Hotel

36-38 Esplanade Avenue, CF36 3YU

5 (12 Sat)-11; 12-10.30 Sun

(01656) 788342 loreleihotel.co.uk

Draught Bass G; Rhymney Export H; guest beers H/G

This inconspicuous hotel in a terraced street is a real ale oasis. The number of pump clips on display reflects the commitment to a wide range of interesting guest ales, further enhanced by beer festivals at Grand National Weekend and Halloween. Czech Budvar is served on draught along with other European beers. Real cider is available in summer. Q

Quakers Yard

Glantaff Inn

Cardiff Road, CF46 5AH

11-4, 6-1am; 11-1am Fri & Sat; 11-midnight Sun

(01443) 410822

Courage Directors; guest beers H

Comfortable pub featuring a large collection of water jugs, boxing memorabilia and old photographs of local interest. Guest beers are frequently from the local Otley and Rhymney breweries, bringing in the locals as well as walkers and cyclists on the Taff Trail from Cardiff to Brecon. The village's name comes from an old Quaker burial ground. (7,78)

Reynoldston

King Arthur Hotel

Higher Green, SA3 1AD

11-11; 12-10.30 Sun

(01792) 390775 kingarthurhotel.co.uk

Draught Bass; Felinfoel Double Dragon; guest beers H

Set in the heart of Gower's beautiful countryside, this splendid pub, hotel and restaurant is deservedly popular with locals, walkers and tourists. During the summer the large outside area offers idyllic surroundings for drinking and dining, and in winter the cosy atmosphere in the bar is enhanced by a roaring fire. An excellent menu features local produce served in a choice of attractive dining areas. This a pub not to be missed if you are in the area.
Q (115,118) P

Rhosilli

Worm's Head Hotel

SA3 1PP

11 (12 Sun)-11

(01792) 386212 thewormshead.co.uk

Tomos Watkin Worm's Head Ale, OSB H

Perched on the cliffs at the extreme western end of Gower, the hotel enjoys stunning views of Rhosilli's magnificent beach and the headland that gives it its name. This friendly hotel, popular with walkers and tourists, has a spacious, comfortable public bar with a large TV often showing sport, and a separate dining area. Good food is available all day. The large outside terrace is busy during fine weather due to the views and sunsets. A separate car park is nearby. Q (118)

Rhymney

Farmers Arms

Old Brewery Lane, NP22 5EZ

12-11; 12-3.30, 7-11 Sun

(01685) 840257

Brains Bitter, Rev James; Greene King Abbot; guest beer H

Open-plan pub close to the site of the original Andrew Buchan/Rhymney Brewery, whose memory is kept alive by old photographs and breweriana. The bar retains a traditional atmosphere with its flagstone floor and a real fire. An easy walk from Rhymney station, the Farmers is an ideal place to start a tour of the pubs in the valley. A function room is available for up to 40 people. Quiz night is Thursday. No evening meals Sunday and Monday. Q P

Rudry

Maenllwyd Inn

CF83 3EB

12-11 (10.30 Sun)

(029) 208 82372

Beer range varies H

Popular and often busy Chef & Brewer dining pub in a rural setting just beyond the urban sprawl of north east Cardiff – a pleasant sanctuary from the bustle of the capital and nearby towns. The Maenllwyd has won many awards for its food and drink, all proudly displayed near the bar. Four beers are stocked, two frequently changing, all typically sourced from regional and family brewers.
Q P

St Brides Major

Farmers Arms

Wick Road, Pitcot, CF32 0SE

12-3, 6-11; 12-10.30 Sun

(01656) 880224

Brains Rev James; Greene King Abbot; Hancock's HB; Wadworth 6X; Wychwood Hobgoblin H

Known as 'the pub by the pond', this spacious, attractive roadside hostelry on the edge of the village enjoys a good reputation for food and beer. The lounge bar is comfortably furnished and has china jugs hanging from the wood beams; there is also a separate restaurant. Live entertainment is hosted at the weekend. Q P

St Georges Super Ely

Greendown Inn

Drope Road, CF5 6EP

12-2, 6-11; 12-11 Sat & Sun

(01446) 760310 greendownhotel.co.uk

Beer range varies H

The pub dates back to the 15th century, set in beautiful scenery on the edge of a small village close to the city of Cardiff. A single handpump dispenses an ever-changing rotation of often local Welsh beers, making the bar always worth coming back to for another visit. Real cider and perry are also on offer. Look for the darts score ready reckoner – no need for mental arithmetic in this pub. Q P

Swansea

Brunswick

3 Duke Street, SA1 4HS

11-11; 12-10.30 Sun

(01792) 465676 brunswickswansea.co.uk

Courage Best Bitter; Greene King Old Speckled Hen; Wadworth 6X H; guest beer G

This well-run side street pub has the air of a country inn in the city. Wooden beams and comfortable seating create a traditional, relaxing atmosphere. The walls are adorned with an interesting, ever-changing display of artwork, with pictures for sale. Food is available until 8pm (6pm Sat; 3pm Sun). A quiz is held on Monday evening and live, acoustic music can be enjoyed on Sunday, Tuesday and Thursday. The frequently-changing guest beer is gravity dispensed, often from a local micro-brewery.

Eli Jenkins

24 Oxford Street, SA1 3AQ

8am – 11 (midnight Fri & Sat); 11-10.30 Sun

(01792) 641067

Badger Tanglefoot; Brains Bitter; guest beers H

City-centre pub, near the bus station, named after the chapel minister in Swansea-born Dylan Thomas' Under Milk Wood. The interior features wooden alcoves with various seating layouts and prints of local views on the walls. Popular from the moment it opens for early breakfast, it is particularly busy at lunchtime and early evening. Two guest beers are available, occasionally including Fuller's ESB. (High St)

Potters Wheel

85 The Kingsway, SA1 5JE

9am -midnight (1am Fri & Sat)

(01792) 465113

Brains SA; Greene King Ruddles Best, Abbot; Marston's Pedigree; guest beers H

This city-centre Wetherspoon outlet, named after the local industry, displays a greater than usual commitment to a wide range of beers from micro-breweries, and an interesting selection of guest beers has boosted sales of real ale. A long, sprawling bar area has various seating layouts and attracts customers of diverse ages and backgrounds. A real cider from Weston's is often available. (High St)

Queens Hotel

Gloucester Place, SA1 1TY

11-11; 12-10.30 Sun

(01792) 521531

Brains Buckley's Best Bitter; Theakston Best Bitter, Old Peculier; guest beers H

This vibrant free house, local CAMRA Pub of the Year 2008, is located near the Dylan Thomas Arts Centre, City Museum, National Waterfront Museum (featuring science and industry) and marina. The walls display photographs depicting Swansea's rich maritime heritage. The pub enjoys strong local support and the home-cooked lunches are popular. Evening entertainment includes live music on Saturday and a Sunday quiz. A rare local outlet for Theakston Old Peculier as well as a seasonal guest beer from a local micro-brewery.

Wig

134-136 St Helen's Road, SA1 4BL

12-11 (midnight Fri & Sat); 12-11.30 Sun

(01792) 466519 thewigswansea.co.uk

Beer range varies H

A short walk from the city centre near the Guildhall, the Wig is approached by a number of steps, with disabled access to the right. The L-shaped interior includes a bright, comfortable open-plan area to the front and a smaller games area with darts and pool to the rear. Outside seating is popular in summer. Five handpumps serve a rotating range of beers, often from Adnams, Cottage and Rhymney breweries. High quality food is available until 8pm (6pm Sun). (2,3)

Treboeth

King's Head

Llangyfelach Road, SA5 9EL

12-11 (midnight Fri-Sun)

(01792) 773727

Beer range varies H

Pleasant roadside pub with patio tables at the front. The two-tier lounge is decorated in mock-Tudor style, with an upper area that can be used separately. There is also a function room/restaurant with its own bar available for private hire. A large chalk board lists the reasonably-priced bar meals. Quiz nights are Sunday and Tuesday. Two beers are available under the SIBA direct delivery scheme, usually from Welsh or West Country brewers. (36)P

Treforest

Otley Arms

Forest Road, CF37 1SY

11-12.30am (1.30am Fri & Sat); 12-12.30am Sun

(01443) 402033

Otley 01, OG; guest beers H

This much-extended end of terrace hostelry has a number of drinking areas, always in demand by the mixed clientele of locals and Glamorgan University students – as is the range of beers, which may include others from Otley Brewery. A beer festival is held in October. There is a large following for sport on multiple TV screens. A good local rail service makes the pub easily accessible from Cardiff and many valley towns. The outdoor smoking area is heated and covered. (100,244)

Treherbert

Baglan Hotel

30 Baglan Street, CF42 5AW

12 (3 Mon)-11 (1am Sat); 11-11 Sun

(01443) 776111

Brains Rev James; guest beers H

This welcome oasis for real ale has been in the same family for more than 60 years. Photos of well-known visitors adorn the walls. Its location at the head of the Rhondda valley makes the hotel a good base for the more active visitor, particularly followers of outdoor pursuits such as hill walking or mountain biking. Guest beers frequently come from local Welsh breweries. Breakfast is available from 7.30am. (Ynyswen)(120,130)

Tyla Garw

Boar's Head 🏆

Coedcae Lane, CF72 9EZ (600m from A473 over level crossing) ST029815

12-11

☎ (01443) 225400

Beer range varies H

A very friendly hostelry where beer lovers and diners are well catered for. The talk in the compact bar is frequently beer-oriented, as the six ales on offer are compared and contrasted with each other (and with what may lurk in the cellar). The restaurant is extremely popular, especially for Sunday lunch (booking a must) and on Tuesday steak and Wednesday curry nights. Local CAMRA Pub of the Year 2009 and a former regional Pub of the Year. (Pontyclun)P

Upper Church Village

Farmers Arms

St Illyd Road, CF38 1EB

3-11; 12-midnight Thu-Sat; 12-10.30 Sun

☎ (01443) 205766

Black Sheep Best Bitter; Brains Rev James H

Lively, one-roomed village local with a welcome for all. Tuesday's quiz draws the crowds and Thursday's live music – usually singing – is also popular. However, beer and conversation are the main attractions, unless there is a major rugby match showing on TV. Outside, drinkers enjoy the sizeable two-level beer garden. Meals are not served on Monday evening. P

Upper Killay

Railway Inn 🏆

553 Gower Road, SA2 7DS

12-11 (10.30 Sun)

☎ (01792) 203946

Swansea Deep Slade Dark, Bishopswood, Three Cliffs Gold, Original Wood; guest beers H

Built in 1864, this friendly pub is a popular local offering a warm welcome to visitors. Various social events are held, mainly in the summer. The old railway route that runs alongside this former station house is now a footpath and cycleway forming part of the Swansea Bay and South Wales cycle network. Good value food is served at lunchtimes. No children are permitted inside. A former local and regional CAMRA Pub of the Year. (20,21)♣P

Ynystawe

Millers Arms

634 Clydach Road, SA6 5AX (on B4603, half mile N of M4, jct 45)

11-3, 6-11; 12-3, 7-10.30 Sun

☎ (01792) 842614 millers-arms.co.uk

Greene King Abbot; guest beers H

This hospitable roadside pub makes a welcome return to the Guide, thanks to its quietly enthusiastic landlord. A well-presented bar displays an amusing teapot collection and historic local photographs. Reasonably-priced meals are served in the bar, dining room or pleasant beer garden, where there is a heated shelter for smokers. One of the three ales is usually from a Welsh brewery. Meals are not served on Sunday evening. ♣

Ystalyfera

Wern Fawr

47 Wern Road, SA9 2LX

7 (6.30 Fri)-11; 2-10.30 Sun

☎ (01639) 843625 bryncelynbrewery.org.uk

Bryncelyn Buddy Marvellous, Holly Hop, Oh Boy, seasonal beers H

This fascinating establishment is the brewery tap for the Bryncelyn Brewery, renowned for its Buddy Holly-themed ales. The bar is an Aladdin's cave of old domestic, industrial and mining artefacts. There is also a comfortable lounge. CAMRA regional Pub of the Year 2005, it is a popular venue for local cycling and walking groups at the weekend. Q♣

WALES

Of Ale... of Bere...

Of Ale

Ale is made of malte and water, and they the which do put any other thynge to ale than is rehersed, except yest, barme or godisgood (other forms of yeast) do sofysticat (adulterate) theyr ale. Ale for an Englysshe man is a natural drynke. Ale must have these propertyes, it must be freshe and cleare, it must not be ropy (cloudy) or smoky, nor it must have no welt nor tayle (sediment or dregs). Ale should not be dronke under V days olde. Newe ale is unholsome for all men. And soure ale and deade ale the which doth stande a tylt is good for no man. Barley malte maketh better ale then oten malte or any other corne doth, it doth engender grosse humoures, but yette it maketh a man stronge.

Of Bere

Bere is made of malte, of hoppes, and water, it is a natural drinke for a dutche man. And nowe of late dayes it is moche used in Englande to the detryment of many Englysshe men, specyally it kylleth them the which be troubled with the colycke and the stone & strangulion (quinsy), for the drynke is a colde drynke: yet it doth make a man fat and doth inflate the bely, as it doth appere by the dutche mens faces & belyes. If the beer be well served and be fyned & not newe, it doth qualify ye heat of the lyver.

Andrew Boorde (c.1490-1549), A 'Compendyous Regyment' or 'a Dyetary of Helth', 1542

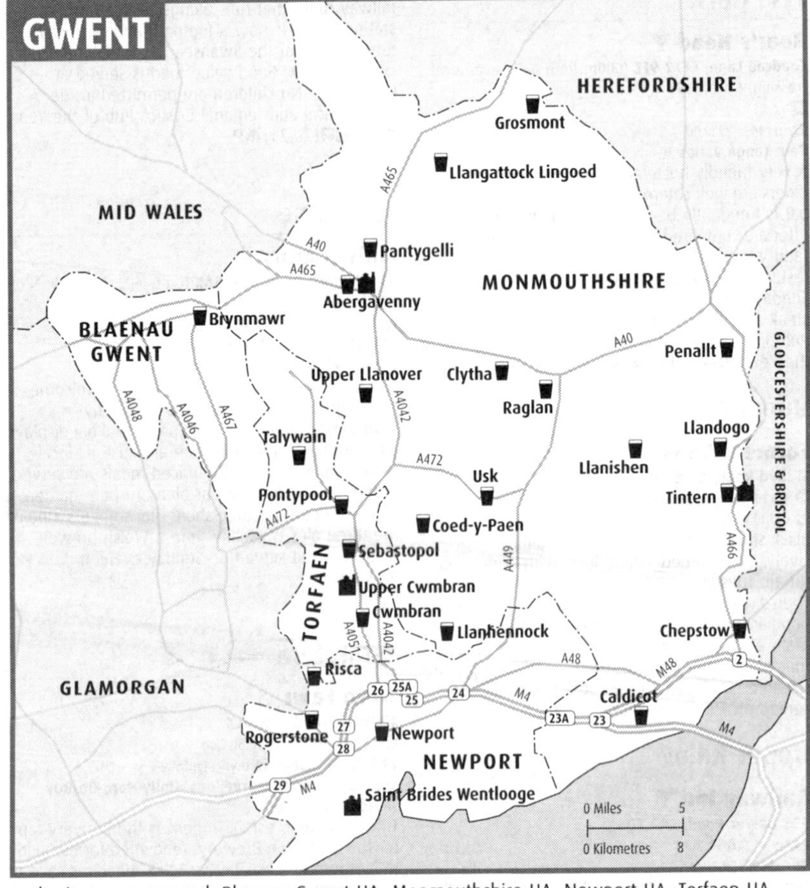

Authority areas covered: Blaenau Gwent UA, Monmouthshire UA, Newport UA, Torfaen UA

Abergavenny

Angel Hotel

15 Cross Street, NP7 5EN

10-3, 6-11 (11.30 Fri & Sat); 12-3, 6-10.30 Sun

(01873) 857121 angelhotelabergavenny.com

Fuller's London Pride; Wye Valley HPA; guest beer Ⓗ

The town's largest hotel shows a clear commitment to serving good quality draught beers. The large main bar has comfortable leather settees and large tables, while a much smaller side lounge provides a quiet haven in a room containing pieces of art. As expected in a quality hotel, there is also a good restaurant offering a wide range of food, from the wonderful afternoon tea to excellent main meals, also served in the bar.

Q (X3,X4,X43)P

Kings Head Hotel

60 Cross Street, NP7 5EU

10.30-11; 12-4, 7-10.30 Sun

(01873) 853575

Wells Bombardier; guest beer Ⓗ

Situated alongside the town hall and market, this pleasant bar has a steady daytime trade and in the evening becomes a popular venue for those who enjoy music. Check out the etched windows featuring the names of old breweries and beverages. Inside, beneath a ceiling of thick wooden beams, there are areas either side of the door, one with screens for sport, the other with a large old fireplace. (X3,X4,X43)♣

Station

37 Brecon Road, NP7 5UH

5 (1 Wed & Thu)-midnight; 12.30 (12 Sat) -1am Fri (no entry after 11pm); 11.30-11 Sun

(01873) 854759

Draught Bass; Fullers London Pride; Wye Valley HPA; Rhymney Bitter; guest beers Ⓗ

Once a tied pub, but for many years now a prominent free house, the place has changed little over time, concentrating on serving a well-balanced range of draught beers to an enthusiastic clientele. There is a large and popular bar – packed on rugby international days – and a much smaller, quieter lounge. Railway pictures reflect the fact that this was once one of several pubs serving the long gone station, part of the line up to the valleys.

(X4,X43)♣P

INDEPENDENT BREWERIES

Cwmbran Upper Cwmbran
Kingstone Tintern
Tudor Abergavenny
Warcop Saint Brides Wentlooge

Brynmawr

Hobby Horse Inn

30 Greenland Road, NP23 4DT (off Alma St)
12-3, 7-midnight; 11.30-midnight Sat & Sun
☎ (01495) 310996 hobbyhorse.cjb.net
Beer range varies H

An attractive frontage features the hobby horse, former trademark of the defunct Rhymney Brewery (not to be confused with the modern brewery of the same name). The availability of two changing draught beers is the current trademark of this free house, a vibrant community pub with a warm welcome. The inn's unusual feature is that it is a meeting point for cavers emerging from the extensive cave systems nearby. The pub offers good value food and accommodation.
❀🛏◐◑🚌♣

Caldicot

Castle

64 Church Road, NP26 4HN (opp St Mary's Church)
12-11 (midnight Fri & Sat)
☎ (01291) 420509
Beer range varies H

Attractive pub that draws a wide clientele including visitors to the neighbouring 12th-century Caldicot Castle and Country Park. The interior has plenty of low beams and is broadly divided either side of the servery between a spacious dining room and a smaller area with plenty of seating for drinkers. Becoming a non-smoking pub ahead of the national ban helped it build a reputation for good, tasty food with an extensive menu.
❀◐◑🚌(X11/14,74)P

Chepstow

Beaufort Hotel

Beaufort Square, NP16 5EP
12-11 (1am Sat); 12-10.30 Sun
☎ (01291) 622497 beauforthotelchepstow.com
Draught Bass; Rhymney Bitter H

This relaxed town-centre hotel and pub sports a single bar with a large side room for busy times. A wide range of simple bar meals is supplemented by a daily-changing menu served in the restaurant. Handy for Chepstow station, the Beaufort also makes a good venue for thirst-slaking before or after walking Offa's Dyke – the national footpath's southern end is just across the border in England.
❀🛏◐◑≋🚌P

Chepstow Athletic Club

Mathern Road, NP16 5JJ (off Bulwark Road)
7-11; 12-midnight Sat; 12-3, 7-10.30 Sun
☎ (01291) 622126
Brains SA; Flowers IPA; Rhymney Bitter; guest beers H

Here real ale, conversation and sport cheerfully blend to create a popular community club where CAMRA members are always welcome. Thirsty customers in the large, comfortable, family-run bar include cricketers, tennis and bowls players, archers and footballers, plus members of many local groups including the Chepstow Male Voice Choir. Local ales feature strongly among the six-strong range, all kept in superb condition. Low prices keep everyone smiling. Real ale is also available in the function room upstairs. ❀≋♣P

Coach & Horses

Welsh Street, NP16 5LN
12-11 (10.30 Sun)
☎ (01291) 622626 coachandhorsesinn.co.uk
Brains Dark, SA, Rev James; guest beers H

This thriving, family-run pub is a haven for people of all ages who enjoy good conversation with ale to match. Five ales from Brains (four in summer, when a Westons cider replaces the Dark) complement one guest, usually from a small independent brewer. Home-prepared food varies daily, available every lunchtime and midweek evening. Frequent charity events and an annual summertime beer festival help make the Coach an enduringly happy place. ❀🛏◐◑≋🚌🍎

Clytha

Clytha Arms

NP7 9BW (on B4598 Old Road between Raglan & Abergavenny) SO366088
12-3 (not Mon), 6-11; 12-11 Sat; 12-10.30 Sun
☎ (01873) 840206 clytha-arms.com
Beer range varies H

A former dower house set in spacious gounds, the Clytha always offers a wide range of local beers and one or two guests from afar. Table skittles, darts, chess and crib can all be played in the attractive bar which is furnished with wooden seats and tables. An extensive selection of interesting food is available in the bar or adjoining restaurant. Westons Old Rosie and Hereford Country Perry are available on draught. The pub is the venue for the Welsh Cider & Perry Festival held in May. Q❀🛏◐◑♣🍎P

Coed-y-Paen

Carpenters Arms

NP4 0TH SO334986
12-3 (not Mon), 6-11; 12-11 Sat; 12-10.30 Sun
☎ (01291) 672621 thecarpenterscoedypaen.co.uk
Beer range varies H

Welcoming and cosy village pub where the emphasis is on providing locally-sourced food and drink. Close to Llandegveth reservoir with facilities for sailing and wind surfing, the area is good walking country – ask the landlord for details of local walks as he has tried them all. There is a large beer garden with limited camping facilities. Note the list of 'feminist' rules in the bar. Q❀◐◑P

Cwmbran

Queen Inn

Upper Cwmbran Road, NP44 5AX
12-midnight (11 Sun)
☎ (01633) 484252
Beer range varies H

This is a town pub in a rural setting, with wildfowl swimming in a stream at the front and hills at the back. The building was originally three miners' cottages, now knocked together. The interior has three areas: a lounge to the right, a small bar to the left and a dining room separated from the bar by a fireplace. There is a wonderful play area outside for children including a tree house and a slide. No food served on Monday. ❀◐◑🚌(1,25)🍎P

Grosmont

Angel Inn

Main Street, NP7 8EP

12-2.30 (not Mon), 6-11; 12-2am Sat; 12-2.30, 7-11 Sun

(01981) 240646

Beer range varies Ⓗ

In danger of closing five years ago, the pub was saved by villagers forming a syndicate and buying it. Since then it has thrived and can truly be said to be at the heart of the community. It is situated right in the topmost corner of Gwent, almost on the border with England and even closer to the historic Grosmont castle. Regular entertainment and events are hosted, including beer and cider festivals in the summer. P

Llandogo

Sloop Inn

NP25 4AJ

12-2.30, 7-11; 12-11 Sat; 12-3, 6-10.30 Sun

(01594) 530291 thesloopinn.co.uk

Sharp's Doom Bar; guest beer Ⓗ

Trow-sailing traders on the nearby and once-busy River Wye gave the Sloop its name and the pub still provides a welcoming and thirst-quenching berth for visitors pausing in their travels through this richly scenic vale. The large main bar at the front is complemented by a quieter, comfortable rear bar where drinkers can also enjoy pub meals. Recently-refurbished bedrooms, including one with a four-poster bed, have fine views across the valley. Motorcyclists appreciate the safe and handy car park. (69)P

Llangattock Lingoed

Hunter's Moon

NP7 8RR (right off the unclassified Llanfihangel Crucorney to Grosmont road, or left off the B4521 at Llanvetherine) SO363201

12-3 (not Mon-Fri Oct-March), 6.30-midnight; 12-3, 6.30-11 Sun

(01873) 821499 hunters-moon-inn.co.uk

Wye Valley HPA Ⓗ**; guest beers** Ⓖ

Ancient pub in a small hamlet a stone's throw from Offa's Dyke long distance path and next to a restored medieval church. The small bar and adjacent dining room dispense good quality beer and food to sustain drinkers, including walkers enjoying this beautiful part of the country. There are two outside areas – a grassy area with a pool, waterfall and ducks, and a decked area overlooking the church and rolling countryside. P

Llanhennock

Wheatsheaf

NP18 1LT ST353927

11-11; 12-3, 7-10.30 Sun

(01633) 420468 thewheatsheafllanhennock.co.uk

Fuller's London Pride; guest beers Ⓗ

Unspoilt rural pub near the top of the old coaching road from Caerleon to Usk, with a pleasant garden for summer drinking. The entrance retains the old bottle servery. To the right is the public bar featuring brewery memorabilia including a vintage electric clock. To the left lies the comfortable lounge where food is served, with a roaring open fire in winter. Boules and darts have a keen local following here. P

Llanishen

Carpenters Arms

NP16 6QH (on B4293 between Monmouth and Devauden) SO478032

12-3 (not Tue), 5.30 (6 Tue)-11; closed Mon; 12-3, 7-10.30 Sun

(01600) 860812

Wadworth 6X; guest beers Ⓗ

Four centuries old, this warm and welcoming free house serves impeccable ale matched by exceptionally fine home-cooked food made with fresh locally-sourced produce. A semi-partition separates diners from the pool table and dartboard area, while a cosy side room creates extra space at busy times. The pub's two self-catering flats, new for 2009, provide an ideal base for exploring the superbly scenic surrounding countryside. The guest ale is often from the local Kingstone Brewery. Q(65)P

Newport

John Wallace Linton

10-12 The Cambrian Centre, Cambrian Road, NP20 1GA

9-midnight (1am Fri & Sat)

(01633) 251752

Brains SA; Greene King IPA, Abbot; Marston's Pedigree; guest beers Ⓗ

World War II hero, submarine commander 'Tubby' Linton VC who did serious damage to enemy shipping, gave his name to this busy Wetherspoon pub after a local campaign. Discerning drinkers make for the first bank of five handpumps which is usually where you will find all kinds of interesting beery treats; the second five offer the core range. The pub is usually busy, being well placed for the railway station, shops and evening entertainment venues. Examples of local history and personalities are depicted around the walls. Q

Old Murenger House

53 High Street, NP20 1GA

11-11; 7-10.30 Sun

(01633) 263977

Samuel Smith OBB Ⓗ

Characterful pub strongly linked to Newport's medieval past, with an ambience to match thanks to Sam Smith's sympathetic treatment of this Tudor building. There is no music or TV but who cares? Settle down in one of several comfortable areas and enjoy the cosy, dark wooded, low-beamed interior and general hubbub of a traditional pub. Dotted around the walls are pictures depicting mainly local scenes and personalities of bygone days. A haven in a 'super-pub' ghetto. Q

Red Lion

47 Charles Street, NP20 1JH

12 (11 Wed & Thu)-midnight (1am Fri & Sat); 12-10.30 Sun

(01633) 264398

Beer range varies Ⓗ

Not much has changed in this city-centre pub for some years and that is what makes it so special. A traditional bar, the emphasis is on conversation, usually dominated by Rugby Union and other sports. Shove-ha'penny has a strong local following and is played most evenings. The guest beers are interesting for the area and carefully chosen for their popularity. A pleasant alternative to the Wetherspoon outlets in the city and well worth finding.

St Julian Inn ✔

Caerleon Road, NP18 1QA
11.30-11.30 (midnight Thu-Sat); 12-11 Sun
☎ (01633) 243548 stjulian.co.uk
John Smith's Bitter; Wells Bombardier; Young's Bitter; guest beers H
The St Julian continues to be a flag bearer for excellent quality ale. A guest beer from a micro-brewery is usually available, with ales from local brewers such as Celt and Rhymney appearing regularly. Several distinct drinking areas are arranged around a central bar. Beautiful views over the River Usk are a major plus point and the terrace is a wonderful place to relax and soak up the sun. The Celtic Manor Resort is nearby – the venue for the Ryder Cup 2010. (28,29,60)P

Pantygelli

Crown

Old Hereford Road, NP7 7HR SO302178
12-2.30 (3 Sat, not Mon), 6-11; 12-3, 6-10.30 Sun
☎ (01873) 853314 thecrownatpantygelli.com
Draught Bass; Rhymney Best, Bitter; Wye Valley HPA; guest beers H
Situated not far from Abergavenny and handy for visiting the ancient Llanthony Abbey, this free house has a high reputation locally for its food and drink. It is a popular destination for walkers and cyclists. Sit outside in good weather and enjoy the view of the Skirrid Mountain. Inside, have a look at the paintings and drawings by local artists decorating the walls. It is advisable to book meals at weekends. P

Penallt

Boat Inn

Lone Lane, NP25 4AJ (take footbridge over river from Redbrook) SO535098
11-3, 5-11; 11-11 Sat; 12-10.30 Sun
☎ (01600) 712615 theboatpenallt.co.uk
Beer range varies G
Perched beside the River Wye with densely-wooded hills as its backdrop, the Boat's superb location and variety of ales, usually including one or more from the Wye Valley Brewery, plus up to 12 bottled ciders ensure its popularity. The homely stone-floored main bar with its small side room hosts twice-weekly music evenings. Tasty food and the valley view from the pub's terrace and hillside garden make the Boat well worth seeking out – access from the A466 is via a footbridge from Redbrook. Q(69)P

Pontypool

John Capel Hanbury ✔

130-131 Osborne Road, NP4 6LT
9am-midnight (1am Fri & Sat)
☎ (01495) 767080
Brains Bitter; Greene King IPA, Abbot; guest beers H
This Wetherspoon Lloyds No.1 outlet has refreshed a jaded pub scene. Attracting a good, mixed clientele, boosted by rugby supporters on match days, it offers a limited beer range that often surprises with an usual guest or two. The interior is open plan with a couple of cosy sofa areas, with several large pictures depicting old town scenes and a local industrial heritage that put Pontypool on the map. The pub is named after a former Lord Lieutenant of the county.

Raglan

Beaufort Arms ✔

High Street, NP15 2DY
11-11; 12-10.30 Sun
☎ (01291) 690412 beaufortraglan.co.uk
Brains Buckleys Best, Rev James; Fuller's London Pride; guest beers H
Former coaching inn opposite the large parish church. The hotel is family owned and imposing without losing its cosy feel, and knowledgeable staff make visitors feel welcome. Good food made with locally sourced produce when possible supplements the beers. The stone-flagged Stable Bar and a separate lounge provide comfortable areas for drinking and dining. Tradition has it that there is a long-lost tunnel connecting the hotel to the nearby castle. Q(60,83)P

Risca

Commercial ✔

Commercial Street, Pontymister, NP11 6BA
11 (12 Sun)-11.30
☎ (01633) 612608
Beer range varies H
Gwent CAMRA Town Pub of the Year 2009, the pub started with two handpumps and now has five – testament to the growing popularity of real ales at the Commercial, which offers the best variety of any in the area. The manager tries to get beers his customers request – mostly from micros. Good, tasty food is available lunchtimes and evenings. Sport has a keen following, with numerous TVs screening various events. The covered and heated patio is very popular. (X15,56,151)

Rogerstone

Tredegar Arms

157 Cefn Road, NP10 9AS
12-3, 5.30-11; 12-11 Fri-Sat; 12-10.30 Sun
☎ (01633) 664999
Courage Best Bitter; Draught Bass; guest beer H
The 'top TA' has an attractive interior with a cosy public bar and a homely lounge. The large fireplace has pictures of the pub in bygone days on the mantel. The pleasant dining room offers a good choice of tasty food, including specials, from a wide ranging menu (no meals Sun eve). The pub has a long association with the former Courage Brewery, hence the presence of Courage Best. The guest beer is usually sourced locally. (56)P

Sebastopol

Open Hearth

Wern Road, NP4 5DR
11.30-midnight (1.30am Fri & Sat); 12-11.30 Sun
☎ (01495) 763752
Wye Valley HPA; guest beers H
Formerly a cowman's cottage, wash house and hotel extended by the Great Western Railway, it is now a welcoming canalside pub with a multi-roomed interior that includes a downstairs bar and function room. The large garden and play area plus the canal towpath are hugely popular in fine weather, particularly when outside events are held. The beer range is drawn from established regional and family brewers and regularly features Welsh brews. Tasty food is served from an appetising menu. P

Sebastopol Social Club

Wern Road, NP4 5DU

12-11.30 (12.30am Fri & Sat); 12-11 Sun

(01495) 763808

M&B Brew XI; guest beers H

Well-run club that includes CAMRA's national title among its many awards, all displayed in the main room which hosts bingo, league darts and live weekend entertainment. A wide-screen TV shows major sporting events and there is another TV in the cosy bar. Skittles and pool are played in the downstairs games room. The competitively priced beer range is always interesting, with ales sourced from all over the UK. Guests are welcome subject to normal visitor rules. P

Talywain

Globe Inn

Commercial Road, NP4 7JH (off B4246 at Abersychan)

5 (1 Sat)-11; 12-10.30 Sun

(01495) 772053

Breconshire Brecon County Ale; guest beers H

A stalwart supporter of Welsh independent brewers, this traditional community pub was one of the first to gain Gwent CAMRA's LocAle accreditation as it usually sells two locally-produced beers. A striking three-dimensional Globe sign is at the front of the premises. The cosy public bar has a real fire in cold weather while the lounge hosts occasional live entertainment at weekends. The area's former industrial heritage including local railway stations is captured in pictures on the walls. (23,X24)

Tintern

Moon & Sixpence

NP16 6SG

12-11

(01291) 689284

Wye Valley Bitter, Butty Bach; guest beer H

Perched above the main road and set into a steep wooded hillside, inside you will find a charmingly bewildering range of small rooms on different levels, complete with a small and entirely real indoor waterfall. The split-level terrace outside is the ideal place for admiring the beautiful Wye Valley. Good-value food is available daily, attracting visitors including hungry explorers from the nearby Offa's Dyke and Wye Valley Walk routes. (69)P

Upper Llanover

Goose & Cuckoo

NP7 9ER SO292073

11.30-3, 7-11; closed Mon; 11.30-11 Fri & Sat; 12-10.30 Sun

(01873) 880277 gooseandcuckoo.co.uk

Newman's Red Stag; guest beers H

Situated in a popular walking area, mobile phones must be turned off at this refreshingly unchanged pub where a welcoming pint and good conversation are the order of the day. A Grade II-listed building, it avoided closure in the 19th century as it was just out of reach of Lady Llanover, who refused to allow alcohol to be dispensed on her land. On a clear day it enjoys glorious views towards the Skirrid. Cottage beers are often among the guests. Local CAMRA Country Pub of the Year 2009. QP

Usk

Kings Head Hotel

18 Old Market Street, NP15 1AL

11-11; 12-10.30 Sun

(01291) 672963

Fuller's London Pride; Taylor Landlord H

A short corridor leads to a cosy bar on two levels, with much hunting and fishing memorabilia scattered about. The pub has plenty of olde worlde charm with its low-beamed ceilings and a good selection of books adorning the walls. An excellent range of food is available in the bar and adjoining Lionel Sweet room. A mix of en-suite and budget accommodation makes this a useful base for exploration of the area. (60,63)P

Nags Head Inn

Twyn Square, NP15 1BH

11-2.30, 5-11; 12-2.30, 5-10.30 Sun

(01291) 672820

Brains Rev James; guest beers H

A fascinating old multi-roomed pub dating back to 1641, in the same family for more than 40 years. Situated in the main town square, this long time Guide entry is well known for a good range of locally sourced produce. Note the unusual brass taps on the front panel of the bar, and the fine collection of old signs from businesses, advertisements and photographs that adorn the walls. Q(60,63)

Royal Hotel

26 New Market Street, NP15 1AT

12-3, 7-11; closed Mon; 12-10.30

(01291) 672931

Draught Bass; guest beers H

A cosy, two-roomed pub, famous for its steaks, and popular with locals and visitors alike. The front door takes you straight into the bar, with a dining area to the left and a drinking space to the right with a high-backed settle. The excellent food is cooked to order, so may take a little longer to appear. (60,63)P

Usk Conservative Club

The Grange, 16 Maryport Street, NP15 1AB

12-3, 7-11 (10.30 Sun)

(01291) 672634

Beer range varies H

Well-appointed private members club set in its own grounds. When you enter, you are greeted with the welcome sight of three handpulls on an elegant bar at the centre of a comfortably furnished lounge, with a games area on one side and a dining room on the other. A large function room is at the rear. An air of old-fashioned gentility prevails at this friendly club. Guests are welcome but club entry rules may apply. Q(60,63)P

I never drink water. I'm afraid it will become habit-forming. **W C Fields**

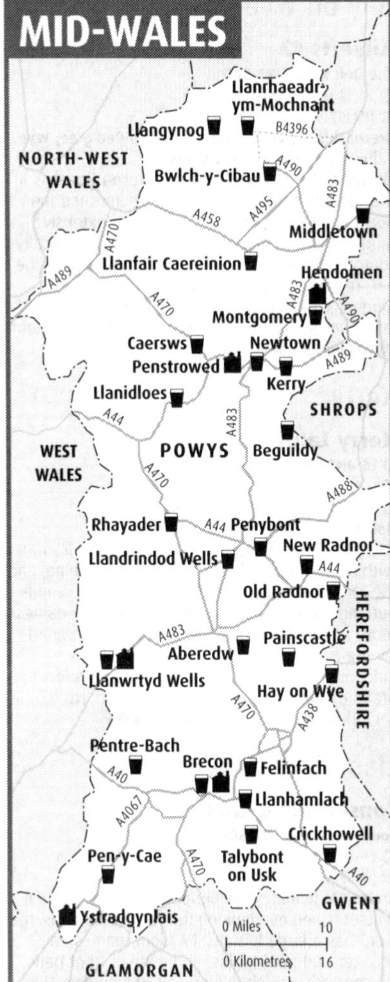

Authority area covered: Powys

Aberedw

Seven Stars

LD2 3UW (off B4567)
⏲ 9am-3, 6.30 (6 Fri & Sat)-11; 12-3.30, 6.30-10.30 Sun
☎ (01982) 560494 🌐 7-stars.co.uk
Beer range varies Ⓗ
Cosy pub with exposed beams, open stonework and flagstone floors. Legend has it that Llywelyn ap Gruffudd, the last true Prince of Wales, had his horse shod with reversed shoes here, to enable him to escape his pursuers. Tragically the ruse was unsuccessful and Llywelyn was killed at nearby Cilmeri. The smithy is now part of the inn. The pub opens around 9am most mornings for tea and coffee. Real cider, and often perry, are now available. ⩕Q❀⊨◑◐⊟♿⅄♣●P⁻

Beguildy

Radnorshire Arms ✔

LD7 1YE (on B4355)
⏲ 7-midnight (1am Fri & Sat); closed Mon; 12-3, 7-midnight Sun
☎ (01547) 510354
Fuller's London Pride; Wye Valley Beguildy Bitter; guest beers Ⓗ
Picturesque 16th-century roadside inn very close to the English border, which would have been used by drovers. The cosy bar has an inglenook and there is an equally small, appealing dining area. The guest beers are sourced from a range of breweries including Breconshire, Hobsons, Six Bells and Wye Valley. No meals are served on Sunday evening. The outdoor smoking area is heated. Q❀◑◐⊟⊡(41)♣P⁻

Brecon

Boar's Head

Ship Street, LD3 9AL
⏲ 11-midnight (2am Fri & Sat); 12-1am Sun
☎ (01874) 622856
Breconshire Welsh Pale Ale, Golden Valley, Cribyn, Ramblers Ruin, seasonal beers Ⓗ
The Breconshire Brewery tap is a popular and lively town-centre pub with two distinct bars – the wood-panelled front bar houses the majority of the handpumps and tends to be a little quieter than the larger back bar, which has a pool table and gets very busy on match days when rugby internationals are shown on TV. Live music evenings and quiz nights are held throughout the year, and the pub is a favourite spot during the Jazz Festival. The riverside patio garden enjoys superb views over the river and up to the Brecon Beacons. ⩕❀◑◐⊟♿⊡♣●P⁻

Bulls Head

86 The Street, LD3 7LS
⏲ 12-midnight (may vary)
☎ (01874) 623900
Evan Evans BB, Cwrw, Warrior, seasonal beer Ⓗ
A friendly and welcoming ale house, the Bulls Head has reverted to its original name after a brief spell as the Black Bull. The central bar and large pillars create three separate drinking and dining areas, but with plenty of wood and good lighting the interior has a spacious, airy feel. Thursday quiz night is well supported and food is served until 9pm every evening except Monday. Real cider is occasionally sold. ⩕❀◑◐⅄⊡●⁻

Clarence

25 The Watton, LD3 7ED
⏲ 12-midnight (2am Fri & Sat)
☎ (01874) 622810
Beer range varies Ⓗ
Two-roomed, town-centre community pub with a relaxed atmosphere. The welcoming front bar tends to be frequented by locals, while the larger back bar is more popular with diners, and the large screen draws a crowd for big sporting events. The spacious garden is a major attraction, especially during the Jazz Festival. Beers are generally sourced from local breweries. ❀◑◐⊟⊡♣●⁻

INDEPENDENT BREWERIES

Breconshire Brecon
Bryncelyn Ystradgynlais
Heart of Wales Llanwrtyd Wells
Monty's Hendomen (NEW)
Waen Penstrowed (NEW)

Bwlch-y-Cibau

Stumble Inn

SY22 5LL
11-11 summer; 6-11 Mon & Tue; closed Wed; 11-11 Thu-Sat winter; 12-3 Sun
☎ (01691) 648860
Beer range varies H
This roadside pub, originally called the Cross Keys, has a public bar and a cosy lounge with a large, well-appointed restaurant. Two changing guest beers and a varied food menu make this a popular venue. The bar features a large twin-bladed propeller with a plaque bearing the name EW Alcock, which came from the Air Force Club in Manchester. P

Caersws

Red Lion

Main Street, SY17 5EL (on B4569)
3-11 (midnight Fri, Sat & summer)
☎ (01686) 688023
Beer range varies H
Friendly, wood-beamed village pub comprising two bars attracting a varied clientele. Early evening can be busy as many villagers call in on the way home from work. The four changing ales usually include two locally produced beers. Accommodation is available in three en-suite rooms. A summer beer festival is held and there is an attractive drinking area outside for warmer weather. (X75,X85)P

Crickhowell

Bear Hotel

High Street, NP8 1BW
11-3, 6-11; 11-3, 7-10.30 Sun
☎ (01873) 810408 bearhotel.co.uk
Brains Rev James; Draught Bass; guest beer H
Originally a 15th-century coaching inn, this is now an award-winning hotel. The multi-roomed bar enjoys grand surroundings with exposed beams, wood panelling, feature fireplaces and fine settles, and an eclectic selection of furnishings and decorations. Food is available from an excellent and varied menu, featuring much local produce. The Bear is an excellent base for exploring the surrounding Black Mountains and Brecon Beacons National Park. QP

Felinfach

Griffin

LD3 0UB (just off A470 3 miles NE of Brecon)
12-11.30
☎ (01874) 620111 eatdrinksleep.ltd.uk
Breconshire Cribyn; Wye Valley Bitter, Butty Bach H
The pub's motto – 'the simple things in life – done well' – says it all. A welcoming country pub, restaurant and hotel, the emphasis here is on good beer and excellent food. The multi-roomed layout allows for discrete areas for drinking and dining. The huge fireplace between the bar and the main dining area dominates during the winter, while a full-sized Aga lurks in a side room, providing warmth throughout the building. The large garden, very popular in summer, affords superb views of the Brecon Beacons and Black Mountains. QP

Hay on Wye

Kilverts

The Bull Ring, HR3 5AG
11-11 (midnight Fri & Sat)
☎ (01497) 821042 kilverts.co.uk
Breconshire Kilverts Gold; Marston's Pedigree; Wye Valley Butty Bach; guest beers H
Nestling at the foothills of the Brecon Beacons in the famous book town, this 12-bedroomed inn boasts five handpumps alongside an extensive range of wines, ciders and malt whiskies. Locally-sourced, home-made food can be enjoyed in the bar, restaurant, front patio or extensive beer garden, which also hosts beer festivals and live jazz. Tuesday is the ever-popular open mike night.

Kerry

Kerry Lamb

SY16 4NP (on A489)
5-11 (midnight Fri & Sat); 12-midnight Sun
☎ (01686) 670226 thekerrylamb.co.uk
Hobsons Best Bitter; guest beers H
This popular village pub has two bars: the front bar with comfortable sofas, mainly used for dining, and the large wooden floored rear bar with a wood-burning stove creating a homely feel. The games room has a pool table. The inn attracts a varied clientele of all ages. Guest beers are from independent breweries. The pub's name refers to a breed of sheep named after the village. No food is served on Monday evening. P

Llandrindod Wells

Conservative Club

South Crescent, LD1 5DH
11-2, 5.30-11; 11-11.30 Fri & Sat; 11.30-10.30 Sun
☎ (01597) 822126
Brains SA; Jennings Cumberland Ale; guest beers H
A quiet haven overlooking the Temple Gardens, the 'Con' has a large lounge, TV room, games bar, snooker and pool tables, and a small front patio. Lunches are available Thursday to Saturday. Live entertainment is sometimes hosted in the evening. CAMRA members are welcome but non-members must be signed in. Q(704)

Llanfair Caereinion

Goat Hotel

High Street, SY21 0QS (off A458)
11-11 (midnight Fri & Sat)
☎ (01938) 810428
Beer range varies H
This excellent inn has a welcoming atmosphere and attracts both locals and tourists. The plush lounge, dominated by a large inglenook with an open fire, has comfortable leather armchairs and sofas, complemented by a dining room serving home-cooked food and a games room at the rear. The choice of three real ales always includes one from the Wood Brewery. P

Llangynog

Tanat Valley Hotel

SY10 0EX (on B4391)
6-midnight; 12-11 Fri-Sun
☎ (01691) 860227

Beer range varies Ⓗ
This popular village pub has a friendly, relaxed feel. The pleasant wood-beamed interior has a stone fireplace, tiled floor and wood-burning stove. Downstairs from the lounge is an additional drinking area with a pool table. The B4391 north-west to Bala is the only road crossing the Berwyns – most unspoilt of Wales' mountain ranges. P

Llanhamlach

Old Ford Inn
LD3 7YB (on A40 3 miles E of Brecon)
12-11
☎ (01874) 665220
Beer range varies Ⓗ
This 12th-century coaching inn has been much extended but retains its original character. The central bar features some unusual copper work and a collection of nip bottles. A larger room beyond the bar, used mainly by diners, has panoramic views of the Brecon Beacons. The excellent food includes regional dishes. Beers are usually sourced from local breweries. QP

Llanidloes

Angel Hotel
High Street, SY18 6BY (off A470)
11.30-2.30, 5-1am (not Wed); 12-3 , 7-midnight
☎ (01686) 412381
Everards Tiger; Greene King Abbot; Thwaites Lancaster Bomber; guest beer Ⓗ
Friendly edge of town pub with two comfortable bars. The larger of the two bars has a stone fireplace and old photographs on the wall. The smaller room has an interesting bar inlaid with old pennies. There is a restaurant at the rear with seating for 40 people (booking recommended). The pub was built in 1748 and Chartists held meetings on the site from 1838 to 1839. (X75,525)♣

Crown & Anchor Inn ★
41 Long Bridge Street, SY18 6EF (off A470)
11-11; 12-10.30 Sun
☎ (01686) 412398
Brains Rev James; Worthington's Bitter Ⓗ
Wonderful, unspoilt town-centre gem with a relaxed and friendly atmosphere, featuring in CAMRA's National Inventory of historic pub interiors. Landlady Ruby has been in charge since 1965 and throughout that time the pub has remained unchanged, retaining its public bar, lounge, snug and two further rooms, one with a pool table and games machine. A central hallway separates the rooms. (X75,525)♣

Red Lion Hotel
Long Bridge Street, SY18 6EE (off A470)
11-midnight (1am Fri & Sat)
☎ (01686) 412270
Greene King Ruddles County; Taylor Landlord; guest beer Ⓗ
Wood-beamed, town-centre hotel with a plush lounge with red leather sofas. The public bar divides into two areas – the front space has an interesting wood-panelled fireplace, the rear area has a pool table and games machines. Three real ales are usually available. In warmer weather there is drinking outside on the patio at the rear of pub. (X75,525)♣

Llanrhaeadr-ym-Mochnant

Plough Inn
SY10 0JR (on B4580)
12-midnight (1.30am Fri; 2.30am Sat)
☎ (01691) 780654
Beer range varies Ⓗ
This true community local was converted from a private house. The multi-roomed interior retains the timber beams and tiled floors, and the front bar has a large open fireplace. A games area at the rear features pool and table football. The range of beers often includes Brains Rev James and Black Sheep Best Bitter. Wales' highest waterfall Pistyll Rhaeadr is close to the village. ♣

Llanwrtyd Wells

Neuadd Arms Hotel
The Square, LD5 4RB
11-midnight (2am Fri & Sat); 11-11 Sun
☎ (01591) 610236 neuaddarmshotel.co.uk
Heart of Wales Aur Cymru, Bitter, Noble Eden, Welsh Black, Innstable, seasonal beers Ⓗ
This large Victorian hotel serves as the tap for the Heart of Wales Brewery, situated behind the building in the old laundry. The Bells Bar features a large fireplace and range, and an eclectic mix of furniture. The bells formerly used to summon servants remain on one wall, along with the winners' boards from some of the town's more unusual competitions such as bog-snorkelling or man vs horse. The lounge bar is a little more formal with deep carpets, sofas and paintings on the walls. The hotel takes part in the town's annual events including the beer festival in November and food festivals. Q♣P

Stonecroft Inn
Dolecoed Road, LD5 4RA
5-midnight; 12-1am Fri-Sun
☎ (01591) 610332 stonecroft.co.uk
Brains Rev James; guest beers Ⓗ
This warm and friendly community pub acts as a hub for the town's many and varied festivities – bog-snorkelling, beer and food festivals, real ale rambles and much more. The hostelry has three main areas for drinking, dining and games, plus a large riverside garden with an aviary. Excellent food complements the fine range of beers. Lodge accommodation is popular with walkers and mountain bikers. ♣P

Middletown

Breidden Hotel
SY21 8EL (on A458)
12-2.30, 5-11; 12-midnight Sat; 11-midnight Sun
☎ (01938) 570250
Beer range varies Ⓗ
This village local has a large wood-beamed L-shaped bar with comfortable seating, a pool table and games machines. At one end of the bar is a small, cosy restaurant area – the pub has a good reputation for eastern cuisine. The hotel takes its name from Breidden Hill, topped by the 18th-century Admiral Rodney's Pillar, which dominates the neighbourhood. The large outside drinking area is partly covered. (X75)♣P

WALES

Montgomery

Dragon Hotel

Market Square, SY15 6PA

11-3, 6-11; 12-3, 7-10.30 Sun

(01686) 668359 dragonhotel.com

Beer range varies H

Small, cosy bar in a 17th-century coaching inn at the centre of a tiny and charming town. The beams are reputedly from Montgomery Castle, which was destroyed by Cromwell. Bric-a-brac adorns the walls. The hotel is well appointed and has a function room. The beer range usually includes an ale from Wood Brewery. Q (81) P

New Radnor

Radnor Arms

Broad Street, LD8 2SP

12-2.30, 5-11; 12-midnight Sat; 12-11 Sun

(01544) 350232

Beer range varies H

Set in the Welsh Marches close to the English border, this cosy pub is an ideal base for an away-from-it-all break. The area offers excellent walking, trekking and cycling; Offa's Dyke is nearby and Hereford 25 miles away by car or bus. Food, served every day, includes a takeaway service and a popular Sunday carvery (booking advisable). Guest beers are mainly from smaller breweries including Cottage, Six Bells and Wye Valley. Real cider and perry are available. Q P

Newtown

Bell Hotel

Commercial Street, SY16 2DE (on B4568)

4 (12 Sat & Sun)-midnight

(01686) 625540

Beer range varies H

Edge of town local with a comfortable lounge and dining area. The public bar has a pool table, and live music is hosted at the weekend. The bar is separated from the lounge by an archway. Three beers are available, usually one from the Six Bells Brewery. (41,704,X75) P

Exchange

Broad Street, SY16 2NA (off A483)

11 – 11 (1am Fri & Sat); 12-10.30 Sun

(01686) 621814

Courage Directors; guest beer H

Town-centre, open-plan pub in what was once the cellar of the local nightclub and cinema. The pub has a wooden floor and a choice of drinking areas, one with a number of wooden settles. A games area at one end of the pub has a pool table and games machines. The guest beer is often from Wem. A beer festival is planned for the spring. (41,704,X75)

Pheasant Inn

Market Street, SY16 2PQ

11-11; 1-midnight Sun

(01686) 625383

Banks's Bitter; guest beer H

Town-centre local with a front bar that is popular with darts players. At the rear is a comfortable lounge and a separate games room with a pool table and more dartboards. There is a large drinking space outside. The guest beer is from the Marston's stable, often Jennings or Wychwood. (41,704,X75)

Railway Tavern

Old Kerry Road, SY16 1BH (off A483)

12-2.30, 6-midnight Mon, Wed & Thu; 11-1am Tue, Fri & Sat; 12-11 Sun

(01686) 626156

Draught Bass; Worthington's Bitter; guest beer H

On the edge of the town centre and handy for the railway station, this friendly one-bar local has a traditional feel. The pub owes its welcoming atmosphere and large following to the long-serving landlord and landlady who have run it for more than 25 years. It is home to a successful darts team and match nights can get busy. Guest beers come from a wide range of independent breweries. (X75)

Old Radnor

Harp Inn

LD8 2RH

12-3 (Sat & Sun only), 6-11; closed Mon

(01544) 350655 harpinnradnor.co.uk

Beer range varies H

This early 15th-century Welsh longhouse commands a fine view over the Radnor Valley. The interior is a tasteful mix of old and new – slate-flagged floors, beamed ceilings, open fireplace, settles, a modern restaurant and en-suite accommodation. The beers are sourced mainly from micro-breweries both local (Hobsons, Three Tuns, Wye Valley) and far-flung (Bath, Leadmill, Millstone). There is also a good range of malt whiskies. Q P

Painscastle

Roast Ox

LD2 3JL

(01497) 851398 roastoxinn.co.uk

Hook Norton Best Bitter H

At the centre of the village, the pub specialises in both cask ales and real ciders – up to five ciders are on offer at most times. Completely renovated and refurbished following a fire some years ago, the inn is steeped in history and has been in existence for at least 500 years. Retaining a number of original features and with stone-flagged floors and a wooden bar, it has the feel of an old and well-loved premises. In the corner there is a well – an unusal feature for any bar. P

Pen-y-Cae

Ancient Briton

Brecon Road, SA9 1YY (on A4067 between Ystradgynlais and Dan-yr-Ogof caves)

11 (12 Sun)-midnight

(01639) 730273

Wye Valley Butty Bach; guest beers H

Fantastic rural real ale pub dating from 1835, offering up to six ales and one cider. Situated on the Swansea to Brecon road, it is frequented by hikers, cavers and climbers visiting the spectacular Brecon Beacons. The historic Craig-y-Nos Castle and Dan-yr-Ogof caves are nearby. Set in large grounds, the pub has a children's play area and beer garden. A good range of quality home-produced food is available lunchtimes and evenings. Local CAMRA Pub of the Year 2006. Q P

Pentre-Bach

Tafarn y Crydd (Shoemakers Arms)

LD3 8UB (signed Country Pub from A40 in Sennybridge) SN909329

11.30-3 (not Tue), 5.30-11; 12-3, 6-11 Sun

☎ (01874) 636508

Brains Rev James; guest beers Ⓗ

Community-owned country pub situated on the edge of the Epynt firing ranges. A warm welcome, excellent food and well-kept ales await you at this previous local CAMRA Pub of the Year. The garden offers superb views of the Brecon Beacons and Mynydd Epynt in an area abundant with wildlife – look out for the red kites. Well worth seeking out – but opening times may vary with the season, so it is a good idea to phone ahead. ⌂Q❀◑◐♿P

Penybont

Severn Arms

LD1 5UA

11-2.30 (3 Sat); 5.30-midnight (1am Fri & Sat); 12-3, 7-10.30 Sun

☎ (01597) 851224 🌐 severn-arms.co.uk

Beer range varies Ⓗ

This 18th-century coaching inn was built to serve the route between Hereford and Aberystwyth (today's A44). The spacious bar with its large open fireplace leads to gardens overlooking the River Ithon – six miles of free fishing is available for residents. There is also a quiet, secluded restaurant and a games room. Guest beers are sourced from a wide range of breweries and there is an above average selection of malt whiskies on offer. ⌂Q❀🛏◑◐⊞▲🚌♣P⚟

Rhayader

Crown Inn

North Street, LD6 5BT

11 (6 Mon Jan & Feb)-11 (midnight Fri & Sat); 12-10.30 Sun

☎ (01597) 811099 🌐 thecrownrhayader.co.uk

Brains Dark, Bitter, Rev James, seasonal beers Ⓗ

This 16th-century beamed pub has an open-plan bar crammed with photographs of local inhabitants and scenes, nearly all with written descriptions – look for the item referring to the eccentric Major Stanscombe, a former owner. This is a rare outlet locally for real mild (recommended), and the current Brain's seasonal or one-off beer is usually available. The outdoor smoking area is covered. Q❀🛏◑◐⊞▲🚌♣⚟

Triangle Inn

Llansantffraed-Cwmdeuddwr, LD6 5AR

12-3 (not Mon), 6.30-midnight (1am Fri & Sat); 12-3, 6.30-11 Sun

☎ (01597) 811099

Brains Rev James; Hancocks HB; Greene King Abbot Ⓗ

An old drovers' inn dating from the 16th-century, the 'Angle' overlooks the River Wye below the falls that gave Rhayader its name (Rhaeadr is Welsh for waterfall). L-shaped, cosy and bijou, the tile-floored bar area is down a step from the small dining area, with the Wye as a backdrop. Headroom is at a premium – darts players have to stand in a hole, which is covered when not in use. ⌂Q🛏◑◐♣⚟

Talybont on Usk

Star Inn 🏆

LD3 7YX (on B4558 between Brecon and Crickhowell) SO114226

11-3, 6-11; 12-3, 7-11 Sun

☎ (01874) 676635

Beer range varies Ⓗ

Large and lively pub with an excellent reputation, situated alongside the Brecon and Monmouth Canal. The spacious garden is extremely popular in summer. The beer range is mostly drawn from local breweries, with some better-known ales added from time to time. Locally produced cider is also available. Live music evenings are held regularly, and quiz nights are popular. The excellent food makes good use of local produce. ⌂❀🛏◑◐⊞▲🚌♣●

Neuadd Arms Hotel, Llanwrtyd Wells.

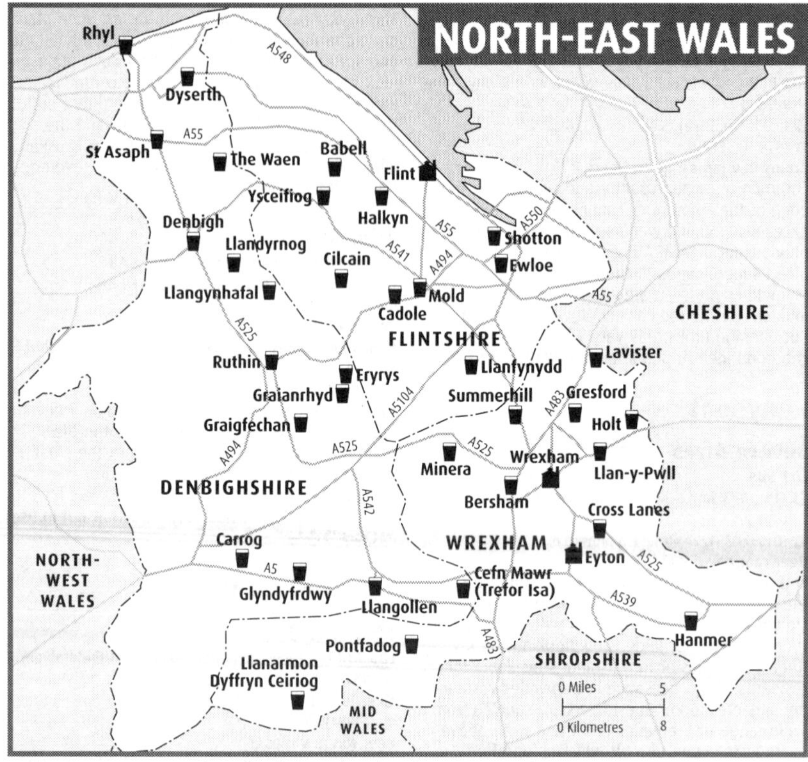

Authority areas covered: Denbighshire UA, Flintshire UA, Wrexham UA

Babell

Black Lion

CH8 8PZ (village signed from B5121 between Brynford and Lixum)
6-11; 12-midnight Sat; 12-11 Sun
(01352) 720239
Facer's Black Lion Bitter; guest beer H
Thirteenth-century coaching inn with a single bar serving several drinking areas and a separate room known as the Liszt. The pub is quiet with music playing in the background. There is also a restaurant which is busy at weekends. The regular beer is from the local Facer's Brewery in Flint and guest beers are usually from north Wales micro-breweries. The inn is said to be haunted.

Bersham

Black Lion

LL14 4HN (off B5099 near Bersham Heritage Centre)
12-12.30am (1am Fri-Sun)
(01978) 365588
Hydes Original Bitter, seasonal beers H
Known locally as the Hole in the Wall, this very friendly pub with a long-serving landlord overlooks the delightful Clwyedog River and is adjacent to the Clwyedog Industrial Trail. It is popular with locals, walkers and visitors to the nearby Heritage Centre. The wood-panelled bar serves two rooms, both with real fires in winter, and a games room. There is a play area in the garden and an outside drinking area. Basic hot bar food is available all day. P

Cadole

Colomendy Arms

Village Road, CH7 5LL (off A494 Mold-Ruthin road)
7 (6 Thu; 4 Fri; 2 Sat)-11; 2-10.30 Sun
(01352) 810217
Beer range varies H
Delightful, traditional village local on the edge of Loggerheads Country Park. This frequent local CAMRA Pub of the Year winner is popular with families, walkers, cavers and runners. Friendly conversation is the main entertainment. The cosy single bar has a roaring fire in winter. Five handpumps provide an ever-varying range of ales, many from local breweries. QP

Carrog

Grouse Inn

Near Corwen, LL21 9AT (on B5437) SJ113435
12-1am
(01490) 430272 thegrouseinn.co.uk
Lees Bitter, seasonal beers H
Situated in a beautiful location alongside the River Dee, with spectacular views of the Dee Valley and Berwyn Mountains, the Grouse is a long-standing Guide entry and was originally a farm and brew-

INDEPENDENT BREWERIES

Facer's Flint
Jolly Brewer Wrexham
McGivern Wrexham
Plassey Eyton
Sandstone Wrexham (NEW)

house. Today, the single bar serves two cosy and separate dining rooms, a games room and an outside covered patio area. The western terminus of the Llangolen Railway is a short walk away. JW Lees seasonal beers are available occasionally. **Q❀◑▲⇌🚌(X94)P⁄–**

Cefn Mawr (Trefor Isa)

Mill

Mill Lane, LL14 3NL SJ275424
✪ 12-midnight (1am Fri & Sat)
☎ (01978) 821799
Greene King Old Speckled Hen; Hydes 1863; guest beer Ⓗ
An unaltered, welcoming, genuine locals' pub with a free jukebox for music aficionados. The smoking area outside has good views of the millstream, with a welcoming brazier for the winter months. Close to the famous Pontcysyllte Aqueduct and Trevor Basin on the Llangollen Canal and River Dee. Dog friendly. **♘❀⊟♣P⁄–**

Cilcain

White Horse

The Square, CH7 5NN (signed from A451 Mold to Denbigh Road) SJ177651
✪ 12-3, 6.30-11; 12-11 Sat; 12-10.30 Sun
☎ (01352) 740142
Banks's Bitter; guest beers Ⓗ
Picturesque, whitewashed pub in an attractive village beside the foothills of Moel Famau, part of the Clwydian range. The public bar has a traditional quarry-tiled floor, where walkers and dogs are welcome. Meals are served in a cosy, split-level lounge (12-2pm, 6.30-9pm). There is an imaginative menu with changing specials. Four log fires keep the pub warm in winter. Children over 14 are allowed in the inn. **♨Q◑⊟♣**

Cross Lanes

Cross Lanes Hotel (Kagan's Brasserie)

Bangor Road, Marchwiel, LL13 0TF (on A525 1 mile from Marchwiel)
✪ 11-midnight (11 Sun)
☎ (01978) 780555 🌐 crosslanes.co.uk
Plassey Bitter; guest beer Ⓗ
This upmarket hotel/lounge bar in a pleasant rural setting is an outlet for the local Plassey brewery. Served by a central bar, the drinking area comprises an airy, well-lit and comfortably furnished front room along with a more rustic back room featuring slate floors, solid oak tables and a superb log fire. The adjoining dining area is decorated with old prints and photographs. Note the magnificent 17th-century oak panelling in the front hall. **♨Q♘❀⛟◑⊟♿P⁄–**

Denbigh

Brookhouse Mill

Ruthin Road, LL16 4RD
✪ 11.30-2.30, 5.30-11.30; 11-midnight Sun
☎ (01745) 813377 🌐 brookhousemill.co.uk
Conwy Welsh Pride; guest beer Ⓗ
This 17th-century building, set in a water-feature garden, was once a flour mill and many artefacts from those times remain, including an external water wheel and much of the internal machinery. In family ownership for 30 years, guest beers from north Wales predominate, while the food menu ranges from bar snacks to full meals. The interior is modern yet cosy, with a copper-topped bar counter and comfortable seating areas. A complimentary minibus operates within a 15-mile radius. **❀◑🚌(X51)P⁄–**

Hand ✔

Lenten Pool, LL16 3PF (opp bus terminus)
✪ 10am-1am (2am Fri & Sat)
☎ (01745) 814286
Jennings Bitter; guest beers Ⓗ
Both the name of the pub and its build date of 1924 can be seen in the exterior dressed stonework. Pass through the pub's distinctive entrance porch and the interior of the building features some period glazed panelling. A central bar serves three distinct sections, including the games area with its pool table. Sporting fixtures are shown on large TV screens. Guest beers from the Marston's list are available. **❀◑🚌(51,76)♣P⁄–**

Railway

2 Ruthin Road, LL16 3EL (by traffic lights at intersection of Vale Road and Ruthin Road)
✪ 12-midnight
☎ (01745) 812376
Beer range varies Ⓗ
The Railway is a basic but cosy locals' pub on the edge of town. It has five rooms: bar, snug, lounge, sports room with pool table and an entrance hall with a serving hatch. The landlord is keen to support local beers and usually has two on handpump. Denbigh is an historic town overlooked by the Castle, built by Edward I. The pub is well served by buses. **▲🚌(51,76)♣P⁄–**

Dyserth

New Inn

Waterfall Road, LL18 6ET (on B5119 close to Dyserth Waterfall) SJ055794
✪ 12-11
☎ (01745) 570482 🌐 thenewinndyserth.co.uk
Banks's Original, Bitter; Marston's Burton Bitter, Pedigree; guest beer Ⓗ
Close to the foot of Dyserth Waterfall tourist attraction, this old pub, now greatly modernised and extended, focuses on food. Nevertheless, five real ales are a good reason to call for a drink in this TV-free zone. Pictures of days gone by attest to the age of the pub and village. There is a pleasant outdoor area. **♨♘❀◑🚌(35,36)P⁄–**

Eryrys

Sun Inn

Village Road, CH7 4BX
✪ 3.30 (5.30 Wed)-11
☎ (01824) 780402
Theakston Best Bitter; guest beers Ⓗ
Built of local stone, the Sun is situated in the centre of the village in an attractive area on the Flintshire-Denbighshire border, and attracts both locals and walkers. The cosy interior, with low beamed ceilings, has an open fire in winter and – bizarrely – a gravestone in the floor. One or two guest ales, frequently from local brewers, are available. Good-quality, home-produced food, including locally-sourced meat, is cooked to order. **♨♘◗⊟P⁄–**

Ewloe

Boars Head

Holywell Road, CH5 3BS (jct of B5125/B5127, just off A55 expressway)
5.30-11; 4-midnight Sat; 12-midnight Sun
☎ (01244) 531065
Draught Bass; Black Sheep Best Bitter H
Cosy, old-fashioned pub, built in 1704. Brasses and an inglenook fireplace dominate the small, half-timbered front bar. More seats are provided in the mezzanine restaurant and the beer garden/smoking area. Food is also served in the dining room at the rear of the pub (not Sat lunch or Sun/Mon eve). There are no buses in the evening. Quiz night is Wednesday. **Q❀◐◑♣P**

Glyndyfrdwy

Sun

LL21 9HG (on A5) SJ150426
12-3.30 (Sat & Sun summer), 6-11
☎ (01490) 430517
Beer range varies H
Traditional roadside free house in the Dee Valley and on the main A5 between Llangollen and Corwen, also handy for Glyndyfrdwy station on the Llangollen Railway. The spacious interior has three drinking areas, a games room and garden. Up to three beers are available including a mild, bitter and a premium ale from an independent brewery. Pub food is available weekends only in summer. Lunchtime openings are restricted in winter – phone ahead to check. **Q❀◐◑(X94)P**

Graianrhyd

Rose & Crown

Llanarmon Road, CH7 4QW SJ218560
4 (12 Fri & Sat)-11; 12-10.30 Sun
☎ (01824) 780727 theroseandcrownpub.co.uk
Flowers IPA; guest beers H
Friendly, welcoming, traditional inn, winner of many CAMRA awards. Popular with locals and walkers, the pub is split into two rooms served by a single bar: one with an open fire, the other with a wood burner. Two ever-changing guest beers are sourced from local breweries and real cider is occasionally on offer. The cheery landlord is justifiably proud of his excellent pub food and fine ales. Snacks are served at lunchtime, no evening meals on Monday. **Q❀◐◑P**

Graigfechan

Three Pigeons

LL15 2EU (on B5429 about 3 miles from Ruthin) SJ145545
12-3, 5.30-11; 12-11 Sat; 12-10.30 Sun
☎ (01824) 703178 threepigeonsinn.co.uk
Hancock's HB H**; guest beers** H/G
The pub is situated on a old drovers' route with picturesque views. The main bar serves a nautically-themed area, with the beer available by handpump or direct from the cask in a jug. A second bar serves the restaurant, where diners can enjoy good food made with locally-sourced produce (booking advisable weekends). A beer festival is held for St David's Day and the pub takes part in the July Route 76 event. Children are not allowed in the bar after 8pm. Dogs welcome. **Q❀◐◑Å(76)♣P**

Gresford

Griffin

Church Green, LL12 8RG
4-11
☎ (01978) 852231
Adnams Bitter; guest beers H
Welcoming community pub adjacent to the 15th-century All Saints Church – its bells are one of the Seven Wonders of Wales. The pub is a picturesque, white building just off the road in an attractive part of the village. Pictures of the Gresford mining disaster adorn the walls, offering some historical perspective. There is a lawned area to the side of the building with seating. Children are welcome in some areas of the pub until 8pm. **Q❀(1)♣P**

Pant-yr-Ochain

Old Wrexham Road, LL12 8TY (off A5156, follow signs to The Flash) SJ347534
12-11 (10.30 Sun)
☎ (01978) 853525 pantyrochain-gresford.co.uk
Flowers Original; Taylor Landlord; Thwaites Original; guest beers H
Converted manor house set in award-winning landscaped gardens and overlooking a small lake to the rear. Inside, a central bar serves two main areas but a walk around will reveal numerous other rooms plus various nooks and crannies for more intimate seating. You could sit by the splendid 16th-century inglenook fireplace in winter or relax in the modern garden room in summer. Half a dozen real ales are on offer and the food is very popular. Real ciders are available in summer only. **Q❀◐◑♿P**

Halkyn

Blue Bell ✔

Rhosesmor Road, CH8 8DL (on B5123) SJ209703
5-11 (midnight Fri); 12-midnight Sat; 12-11 Sun
☎ (01352) 780309 bluebell.uk.eu.org
Facer's Blue Bell Bitter, Dark Blue Bitter; guest beers H
Situated on Halkyn Mountain with spectacular views, this pub is a focal point for community activities, including walks, games nights, Welsh classes and traditional Sunday afternoon jazz (see website). The LocAle house beers, brewed by Facer's, are accompanied by two guest beers, usually from small independent breweries. The pub has won several CAMRA awards including 2007 regional Cider Pub of the Year and 2008 regional Pub of the Year for Merseyside, Cheshire and North Wales. Two ciders and a perry are often available. **Q❀◐Å♣P**

Britannia Inn

Pentre Road, CH8 8BS (off A55 jct 32B)
12 (4 Mon winter)-midnight; 12-11.30 Sun
☎ (01352) 781564 thebritanniainnhalkyn.co.uk
Lees Bitter, seasonal beer H
Situated 400 metres from the main westbound A55 expressway, with views over the Dee estuary, this four-roomed village pub has a relaxed, homely atmosphere. A small rear bar, cosy front lounge and pool room surround the central bar, and the conservatory dining area provides good-value, home-cooked food. Children are welcome in the conservatory until 9pm. Dogs are permitted in the bar area. **Q❀◐◑Å(126)P**

Hanmer

Hanmer Arms Hotel

near Whitchurch, SY13 3DE
⏲ 11-11
☎ (01948) 830532 🌐 hanmerarms.co.uk
Adnams Bitter; Stonehouse Station Bitter; Taylor Landlord Ⓗ
Situated on the borders of Shropshire, Wrexham and Cheshire, this picturesque hotel is only five miles from Whitchurch and 10 miles from Wrexham. A traditional inn with a warm ambience, it offers fresh produce, a good choice of quality ales, friendly service and a great welcome. A full a la carte menu and light snacks are served lunchtimes and evenings, plus a Sunday carvery. Accommodation is in 12 en-suite bedrooms and one suite. ⛺Q❀🛏◑◐⊞♿🚌🍎P⚋

Holt

Peal O' Bells

12 Church Street, LL13 9JP (400m S of Holt-Farndon bridge)
⏲ closed Mon; 4-11 Tue & Wed; 4-11.30 Thu; 4-12.30am Fri; 12-12.30am Sat; 12-10.30 Sun
☎ (01829) 270411 🌐 pealobells.co.uk
Adnams Bittter; Marston's Pedigree; Stonehouse Station Bitter; guest beer Ⓗ
Popular family-friendly village pub next to St Chads Church on the English border. Good-value home-cooked food is served in the restaurant Saturday and Sunday lunchtime and Thursday to Saturday evening (booking essential at the weekend). The sizeable, fully-enclosed garden has a small play area and excellent views of the Dee Valley and Peckforton Hills. Real perry is on handpump.
⛺❀◑◐♿🚌🍎P⚋

Lavister

Nag's Head

Old Chester Road, LL12 0DN (on Old Chester-Wrexham road)
⏲ 5.30-midnight; 12-2am Fri & Sat; 12-midnight Sun
☎ (01244) 570486
Boddingtons Bitter; Everards Tiger; Flowers IPA; Purple Moose Snowdonia Ale; guest beers Ⓗ
Large roadside pub with a single central bar. The spacious central area has tables and several alcoves, and there is a separate area for pool and darts. The pub has connections with the origins of CAMRA. The lively clientele is a good mix of locals and visitors. Food is available Friday to Sunday, including the popular Sunday lunch. Guest beers usually include at least one from a local micro. Outside is a covered, heated smoking area and a children's play space. ⛺❀◐⊞♿🚌♣P⚋

Llan-y-Pwll

Gredington Arms ✔

Holt Road, LL13 9SD (on A534)
⏲ 12-2.30, 5-11; 12-11 Sat & Sun
☎ (01978) 661728 🌐 gredingtonarms.co.uk
Hydes Original Bitter, seasonal beers; guest beers Ⓗ
Modernised bar and bistro on the outskirts of Wrexham with a relaxing atmosphere and a reputation for good-quality locally-sourced food. The owner is proud of his cask ale and also offers an extensive wine list. The Hyde Out bar is in a separate room above the stables and is a good place to watch sport on TV – it can also be hired for functions. No evening or Sunday buses.
❀◑◐⊞🚌(C56)P⚋

Llanarmon Dyffryn Ceiriog

Hand Hotel

LL20 7LD (at end of B4500) SJ157328
⏲ 11-11 (12.30am Fri & Sat); 12-11 Sun
☎ (01691) 600666 🌐 thehandhotel.co.uk
Weetwood Cheshire Cat Ⓗ
Welcoming, comfortable and cosy hotel set at the head of the Ceiriog Valley. A public bar/games room, lounge and restaurant cater for all tastes, with real fires and a wood-burning stove in the dining room adding to the ambience. The pub is best known for its excellent food, justly deserving an AA rosette award. The Weetwood beer is usually complemented by a guest ale from a local brewery during the summer months and at other busy times. This popular destination for cyclists and walkers is also dog friendly. ⛺🐎❀🛏◑◐⊞♿🚌P⚋

West Arms

LL20 7LD
⏲ 12-11 (10.30 Sun)
☎ (01978) 869555 🌐 thewestarms.co.uk
Beer range varies Ⓗ
Well-appointed hotel in a stunning village location. The cosy lounge bar with its period furniture and inglenook fires is an ideal place to relax after a day exploring the surrounding Berwyn mountains. The adjacent public bar is frequented by locals, and dogs are welcome. Two cask ales are usually on offer including at least one from a local independent such as Facer's. High quality meals are served and there is a delightful garden which runs down to the River Ceriog.
⛺Q❀🛏◑◐⊞♿🚌(65)P⚋

Llandyrnog

Golden Lion

LL16 4HG (on B5429 opp village stores)
⏲ 4-11 (12.30am Thu); 2-1am Fri & Sat; 2-11 Sun
☎ (01824) 790373
Facer's DHB; Tetley Bitter; guest beer Ⓗ
A listed building at the heart of the village, the pub has strong links with the local football team who, with its supporters, like to drink here after home matches. Tastefully refurbished, the central bar serves both the lounge area at the front and a public bar to the rear. A carefully-maintained beer garden is popular with customers, as is free Wi-Fi access. ⛺❀◑⊞🚌(76)♣⚋

White Horse (Ceffyl Gwyn)

LL16 4HG (B5429 next to church)
⏲ 12-3, 6-11.30; closed Mon & winter Tue
☎ (01824) 790582
Facer's Flintshire Bitter; guest beer Ⓗ
This village pub has a reputation for good food and fine ale. It is linked with the Golden Lion (see above) and tends to be the preferred location for those in search of a quieter venue with a comfortable fireside seat. The front door opens directly into the bar area; beyond, a restaurant offers quality, home-cooked food. Photographs of both local and historic interest adorn the walls.
⛺❀◑◐🚌(76)P⚋

Llanfynydd

Cross Keys

LL11 5HH

5 (12 Sun)-11; closed Mon

(01978) 760333

Beer range varies H

Attractive, traditional hostelry with a black-and-white exterior – the perfect place to end a visit up Hope Mountain. A basic quarry-tiled bar leads to the restaurant, while a small, cosy lounge, once the village blacksmith's, features carved settles and a real fire. An intimate snug is ideal for meetings. Good-quality meals are served in the evening and Sunday lunchtime. Guest beers are often from a local micro. The pub may close early if quiet.

Llangollen

Corn Mill

Dee Lane, LL20 8PN (off Castle St) SJ214421

12-11 (10.30 Sun)

(01978) 869555 brunningandprice.co.uk/cornmill

Beer range varies H

This conversion of an old mill adjacent to the River Dee incorporates a giant water wheel within the building. From the outside decking you can admire the steam locomotives of the Llangollen Railway across the river. The light and airy interior has two bars on different levels with up to five cask ales on offer, often coming from local independent breweries. Real cider is also available. Imaginative, high-quality food is served until about an hour before closing time. Q

Sun Inn

49 Regent Street, LL20 8HN (on A5 about ½ mile E of town centre)

12-1am (2am Fri & Sat)

(01978) 860079

Salopian Shropshire Gold; Thwaites Original; guest beers H

Splendid, dimly-lit, slate-floored free house with three real fires. It serves six cask ales – four ever changing – plus a wide selection of continental beers, rums and single malt whiskies. From Wednesday to Saturday the games area makes way for extremely popular blues, jazz and rock bands. Covered outside seating and a rear snug offer some relief should you wish to escape the diverse sounds and Bohemian atmosphere. Dogs are welcome. (64)

Llangynhafal

Golden Lion Inn

LL16 4LN OS131634

closed Mon; 6-midnight Tue-Thu; 12-midnight Fri & Sun; 12-2am Sat

(01824) 790451 thegoldenlioninn.com

Bathams Best Bitter; Coach House Gunpowder Mild; Holt Bitter; guest beer H

Situated in a hamlet at a pleasant rural crossroads, this pub has been successful in recent branch and regional Pub of the Year activities. The licensee has organised an innovative inter-pub beer festival along the local 76 bus route, and the pub hosts regular music evenings and whisky-tasting events. A consistently good choice of beer and cider is always served in lined glasses, and a selection of bottled beers is usually on sale. En-suite B&B is available. (76)P

Minera

Tyn-y-Capel

Church Road, LL11 3DA (off B5426) OS268519

12-11 (midnight Sat); closed Mon-Wed winter, Mon summer; 12-11 Sun

(01978) 757502 tyn-y-capel.co.uk

Beer range varies H

The Tyn-y-Capel or Chapel House, hidden in the hills west of Wrexham, was first listed as an ale house in 1764. The attractive whitewashed exterior, with sturdy stone-flanked windows, belies a modern but reputably haunted interior. Step down through the pool room to the modern bar and dining area and enjoy the stunning views across the valley, or bask in the sun out on the terrace and deck.

Mold

Glasfryn

Raikes Lane, CH7 6LR (off A5119) SJ240649

11.30-11; 12-10.30 Sun

(01352) 750500 glasfryn-mold.co.uk

Facer's Fintshire Bitter; Flowers Original; Purple Moose Snowdonia Ale; Thwaites Original; guest beer H

The Glasfryn is situated in its own grounds near Theatr Clwyd and the Civic Centre, with views of the town and surrounding hills. Originally a residence for circuit judges attending the court opposite, it was converted to its present use by Brunning & Price in 1999. The spacious interior is popular with diners but real ale fans also come here for the wide range of beers on offer. Guest beers from local breweries are served regularly – see the blackboards for tasting notes.

Gold Cape

8 Wrexham Road, CH7 1ES (near Market Square crossroads)

9am-midnight (1am Fri & Sat)

(01352) 705920

Greene King Abbot; Marston's Pedigree; guest beers H

The staff are keen to promote real ale at this excellent Wetherspoon pub, with local beers usually available from Facer's and Spitting Feathers. The Gold Cape is named after a Bronze Age artefact unearthed near Mold in 1833 – a replica of the cape is on display in the foyer. The pub walls depict the history of Mold and a tribute to its most famous son, the writer Daniel Owen, who was born locally in 1836. A small outdoor area caters for smokers. Q

Pontfadog

Swan

LL20 7AR (on B4500)

12-2.30 (3 Sat), 6-11; closed Mon and Tue lunch winter; 12-3, 7.30-10.30 Sun

(01691) 718273

Beer range varies H

Sociable village free house in the scenic Ceiriog valley. The homely red-tiled bar features a central fireplace which separates the unobtrusive TV and darts area from the servery where the locals gather. A side dining room often offers themed food nights. An occasional house beer, Swan for the Road, is supplied by a Wrexham micro-brewer, otherwise the ales come from tried and trusted regionals. Q(60,64,65)P

Rhyl

Sussex ✔

26 Sussex Street, LL18 1SG
⌚ 9am-midnight (1am Fri & Sat)
☎ (01745) 362910
Greene King Abbot; Marston's Pedigree; guest beers Ⓗ
Medium-sized Wetherspoon outlet divided into three areas. Originally, this building was a Welsh Wesleyan chapel before becoming the Old Comrades Club; it was then converted to the Sussex in 1992. The walls feature pictures of Rhyl's past, including references to Laurel & Hardy's visit to the resort in 1953 and the pioneering hovercraft service from Rhyl to Wallasey in 1962. Guest beers often include ales from local north Wales breweries. Q♞◐◑♿≠🚌●

Swan ✔

13 Russell Road, LL18 3BS
⌚ 11-11 (11.30 Fri & Sat); 12-10.30 Sun
☎ (01745) 336694
Thwaites Nutty Black, Original, Lancaster Bomber Ⓗ
The Swan is an historic pub, popular with locals, tucked away just off the town centre. The lounge has a dining area to the rear while the public bar is sports oriented with darts, dominoes and pool, plus widescreen TVs for sports events. The outside smoking area also has a TV. The front of the pub displays the name Wilderspool – a long defunct brewery from Warrington. Photographs of old Rhyl adorn the walls. ◐🍺≠🚌🚬

Ruthin

Boars Head

Clwyd Street, LL15 1HW
⌚ 12-11 (midnight Thu; 1am Fri & Sat)
☎ (01824) 703355
Marston's Burton Bitter; guest beer Ⓗ
Traditional former Burtonwood town-centre pub with two drinking areas served from a central bar and a raised section, with a pool table to the rear, which leads to a heated smoking area. A wide-screen TV is turned on for sporting fixtures. Pictures showing local scenes decorate the walls. There is live music on a Friday evening usually once a month. ❀🚌(X51)♣🚬

St Asaph

Plough

The Roe, LL17 0LE (on A525 off A55 jct 27) SJ033744
⌚ 12-11 (1am Fri & Sat)
☎ (01745) 585080
Plassey Bitter; guest beer Ⓗ
Large hostelry with exposed original brickwork. A single bar serves several drinking spaces, including an area with a TV for sports fans where live music plays on Fridays. The first floor houses a restaurant on one side and a cocktail bar with meeting room on the other. Meals are served 12-9pm. There is background music and good wheelchair access. ♨❀◐◑♿🚌(51,52)P🚬

Shotton

Castle Inn

Brookside, Brook Road, CH5 1HL (off B5129)
⌚ 12-11
☎ (01244) 813317
Jennings Cumberland Ale, Cocker Hoop; Marston's Pedigree Ⓗ
Part brick, part whitewashed community-based pub, tucked away at the end of a narrow lane, a large open-plan room is separated by the bar, which serves both the TV viewing area at one end and the seated dining room at the other. Popular with the horse-racing fraternity, the walls display prints and photographs of horses. Sensibly priced meals are served. ❀◐◑🍺♿≠🚌P🚬

Summerhill

Crown ✔

Top Road, LL11 4SR (off Summerhill Road, 1 mile from A483/A541 jct)
⌚ 12-midnight
☎ (01978) 755788
Hydes Original Bitter, seasonal beers; guest beer Ⓗ
The entrance is through a porch facing the car park or a smaller adjacent door. Turn left for the large lounge or straight on for the bar which has a pool/darts area and a drinking space to the left. Unusual pictures of some of the locals can be found in the bar – see how many you can identify. The smoking area outside leads to an area with picnic tables. ♨Q❀◐◑🍺≠(Gwersyllt)🚌♣P🚬

The Waen

Farmers Arms

Near St Asaph, LL17 0DY (S of A55 jct 28, signed for Trefnant) SJ061730
⌚ 12-2, 5.30-midnight; closed Mon
☎ (01745) 582190 🌐 the-farmers-arms.co.uk
Facer's Farmer's Ale, Cwrw y Waen Ⓗ
Once known as the Waen Tavern and sympathetically extended during the mid-20th century, parts of this inn date back to the 1700s. Artefacts and pictures on display within the bar help to reinforce its historic and rural pedigree. The pub was popular with American servicemen, stationed nearby during WWII. Private parties can be catered for. Q❀◐◑⛺P🚬

Ysceifiog

Fox ★

Village Road, CH8 8NJ (village signed from B5121 between Brynford and Lixwm) SJ153714
⌚ 6-11; closed Wed; 12 (4 winter)-11 Sat; 2 (4 winter)-11 Sun
☎ (01352) 720241
Beer range varies Ⓗ
Unspoiled by progress, this three-roomed village pub was built circa 1730 and named after the local landowner, Ignatius Fox. The small front bar is warm and welcoming with a long seat under the counter. The sliding door opens to a bar festooned with hops, and whisky jugs hang from the ceiling. There is another large room, also with a log fire, and a small games room. ♨Q♞❀🍺

Beer makes you feel the way you ought to feel without beer. **Henry Lawson**

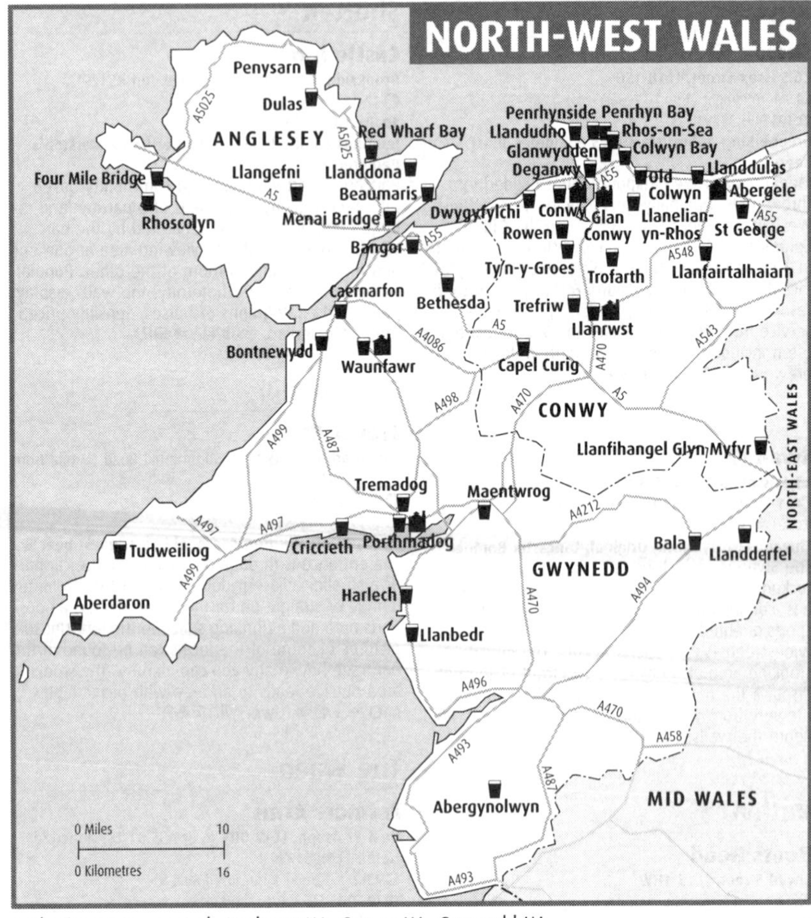

Authority areas covered: Anglesey UA, Conwy UA, Gwynedd UA

Aberdaron

Ship Hotel

LL53 8BE

11-11

(01758) 760204 theshiphotelaberdaron.co.uk

Beer range varies H

The Ship is situated in the centre of the village, at the tip of the Lleyn Peninsula. You can be sure of a friendly welcome in the two bars, one with a games area. Excellent food made with fresh, locally-sourced ingredients is recommended. Two handpumps in summer and one in winter dispense local Welsh beer. The village has a bus service but check times first.

Abergynolwyn

Railway Inn

LL36 9YN (on B4405)

12-midnight (11 Sun)

(01654) 782279

Beer range varies H

Friendly local in the centre of the village not far from the Talylln Railway. You can still see the remains of the old incline that brought goods traffic down from the railway to the village. Excellent food is served alongside a good range of real ale. The pub has stunning views of the surrounding hills. Q (Talyllyn Railway)

Bala

Olde Bulls Head

78 High Street, LL23 7AD (on A494 main street)

12-11 (2am Fri & Sat)

(01678) 520438

Greene King Abbot; Purple Moose Glaslyn H

Friendly two-roomed pub in the town centre with a spacious lounge and separate public bar with pool table. The walls are adorned with photographs of historic local interest, some relating to Royal Welsh Whisky, which was produced at a nearby distillery in the 1890s. The pub is a popular destination for locals, walkers and visitors looking for cask ale in the town. (X94)P

INDEPENDENT BREWERIES

Conwy Conwy
Great Orme Glan Conwy
Nant Llanrwst
North Wales Abergele
Purple Moose Porthmadog
Snowdonia Waunfawr

Bangor

Abbeyfield Hotel
LL57 3UR
12-3, 6.30-midnight; 12-midnight Sat & Sun
☎ (01248) 352219 abbeyfieldhotel.co.uk
Great Orme Orme, Merlyn Ⓗ
Originally a 17th-century farmhouse, this is now a popular country hotel and pub, renowned for its restaurant and fine cuisine. The pub is a free house offering local beer from Llandudno's Great Orme Brewery as well as occasional seasonal beers. The hotel, with 11 en-suite bedrooms, is ideally located for Snowdonia and the resorts of Anglesey.
❀◑♣P

Black Bull (Tarw Du) ✔
107 High Street, LL57 1NS
9-midnight (1am Fri & Sat); 10-midnight Sun
☎ (01248) 387900
Greene King IPA, Abbot; Marston's Pedigree; guest beers Ⓗ
Wetherspoon's pub in a converted church and presbytery at the top of the High Street. It has spacious drinking areas and an outside patio overlooking upper Bangor and the university. Popular with students, it is very busy during term time. Draught cider is regularly available. A lift provides disabled access. ❀◑♿⇌

Mostyn Arms
27 Ambrose Street, LL57 1BH (off Beach Road)
3 (1 Sat & Sun)-midnight
☎ (01248) 364752
Draught Bass; guest beer Ⓗ
Small back-street pub close to Bangor Pier and the swimming pool. It has been completely refurbished with a pool area, lounge area with Sky Sports and a small bar. The Bass alternates with Brains SA plus a guest beer usually from Purple Moose. No food is served. Very friendly and well worth a visit.

Tap & Spile
Garth Road, LL57 2SW (off old A5, follow pier signs)
12-11 (11.30 Tue, Fri & Sat)
☎ (01248) 370835
Beer range varies Ⓗ
Popular split-level pub overlooking the renovated Victorian pier, offering superb views of the Menai Straits. The pub has a back to basics feel with old wooden tables, chairs and several church pews, but the large-screen TV and fruit machines can dominate. Food is served daily except Sunday evening. Local CAMRA Pub of the Year 2004/06/07. ◑♣

Beaumaris

Olde Bulls Head Inn
Castle Street, LL58 8AA
11-11; 12-10.30 Sun
☎ (01248) 810329 bullsheadinn.co.uk
Draught Bass; Hancock's HB; guest beer Ⓗ
Grade II-listed building that was the original posting house of the borough. In 1645 General Mytton, a parliamentarian, commandeered the inn while his forces lay siege to the nearby castle. The Royalists surrendered on 25th June 1646. Dr Johnson and Charles Dickens were famous guests and each bedroom is named after a Dickens character. The beamed bar has a large open fire. Parking is limited. Q◑P

Bethesda

Douglas Arms Hotel ★
London Road, LL57 3AY
6-11; 3.30-midnight Sat; 1-3, 7-11 Sun
☎ (01248) 600219
Marston's Burton Bitter, Pedigree; guest beer Ⓗ
This Grade II-listed building features in CAMRA's National Inventory. Built in 1820, it was an important coaching inn on the historic Telford post route from London to Holyhead. The four-room interior has not changed since the 1930s and includes a snug, lounges and a large tap room with a full-sized snooker table. Bethesda, originally a town built on slate quarries, is convenient for buses to the Ogwen Valley and the surrounding mountains. Q♣

Bontnewydd

Newborough Arms
LL55 2UG
12-11 Fri; 12-11.30 Sat; 12-10.30 Sun
☎ (01286) 673126
Beer range varies Ⓗ
Welcoming locals' pub just off the main road with a separate restaurant offering a good menu and Sunday carvery. The beer range always includes a mild and a Purple Moose ale. Quiz night is Tuesday and live sport is often shown on TV. Families are welcome and there is a beer garden with a children's play area to the rear. The station nearby is on the Welsh Highland Railway.
❀◑♿⇌P

Caernarfon

Black Boy Inn ✔
Northgate Street, LL55 1RW (near the marina)
11-11 (11.30 Fri & Sat); 12-10.30 Sun
☎ (01286) 673604
Brains Rev James; Draught Bass; Hancock's HB; guest beer Ⓗ
Sixteenth-century pub within the town walls between the marina and the castle. A public bar and small lounge are warmed by roaring fires. Good value food is served. This historic town, a world heritage site, is well worth a visit, ending with a welcome pint at the Black Boy. The guest beer usually comes from Purple Moose. There is an outdoor drinking area on the traffic-free street. Limited parking is available. The Welsh Highland Railway starts in Caernarfon. ❀◑⇌P

Capel Curig

Cobdens Hotel
London Road, LL24 0EE SH731576
11-11; 12-10.30 Sun
☎ (01690) 72043 cobdenshotelsnowdonia.co.uk
Conwy Cobden's Ale; guest beers Ⓗ
This 200-year-old hotel is popular with walkers and climbers. The 17-bedroom hotel has a large lounge, a comfortable restaurant and a fascinating bar area built into the side of the adjacent mountain. The hotel has built up a good reputation for its comfortable rooms and hospitality. Lamb shank in Cobden's Ale is one of the many excellent meals on the menu made with local produce. A guest mild and cider are always available.
Q❀◑(S6)♣P

WALES

Colwyn Bay

Pen-y-Bryn

Pen-y-Bryn Road, Upper Colwyn Bay, LL29 6DD (top of King's Rd) SH842782
11.30-11; 12-10.30 Sun
(01492) 533360
Thwaites Original; guest beers H
Open-plan pub popular with all ages, with large bookcases, old furniture and open fires in the winter months. The walls are decorated with old photographs and memorabilia from the local area. Panoramic views of Colwyn Bay and the Great Orme can be admired from the terrace and garden. Excellent imaginative bar food is served – the menu is updated daily on the website. There are five guest beers mainly from local and independent breweries. A former local CAMRA Pub of the Year. **QP**

Picture House

24-26 Princes Drive, LL29 8LA SH849791
9-midnight (1am Fri & Sat)
(01492) 535286
Courage Directors; Greene King Abbot; Marston's Pedigree; guest beers H
Grade II-listed building, once the Princess Cinema, now a Wetherspoon's pub set on three levels with an upper balcony. Theatre memorabilia adorns the walls. There are eight handpumps featuring at least one beer from a local brewery such as Conwy. Local beer festivals, in addition to Wetherspoon's national events, are held throughout the year. This popular pub attracts a wide range of locals and holidaymakers. Quiz night is Monday at 8pm. **Q**(12,14,15)

Conwy

Bridge Inn (Y Bont)

Rosehill Street, LL32 8LD SH783775
11-11 (midnight Fri & Sat); 12-11 Sun
(01492) 573482 bridge-conwy.com
Banks's Bitter; Jennings Dark Mild, Cocker Hoop; Marston's Pedigree; guest beers H
Busy, traditional corner pub inside the town walls within sight of the historic Conwy Castle. It has an open-plan lounge with a central bar area and a separate dining area behind the two-sided fireplace. Here you can order excellent quality home-cooked meals made with locally-sourced ingredients – daily specials are written on the blackboard. Up to two guest beers are on offer and a good selection of malt whiskies. En-suite accommodation is available in a range of pleasant rooms. Y Bedol in Tal-y-Bont is under the same management.

Olde Mail Coach

High Street, LL32 8DE SH781776
11-11 (11.30 Fri & Sat); 12-10.30 Sun
(01492) 593043
Beer range varies H
A warm welcome awaits locals and holidaymakers alike at this former coaching inn with friendly, multi-lingual bar staff. The open-plan lounge features a real fire and a TV for sports, with a raised drinking area at the rear. Outside is a walled beer garden. Meals feature produce from local butchers Edwards of Conwy next door. Quiz nights are Monday and Wednesday. Beers mainly come from local breweries such as Conwy, Purple Moose and Nant. Families are welcome.

Criccieth

Castle Inn

LL52 0RW
12-11
(01766) 523515
Beer range varies H
Traditional three-roomed pub just off the A497 Porthmadog to Pwllheli road, catering for locals and tourists alike. Three handpumps dispense an ever-changing range of beers from regional and small breweries, as well as cider in summer. Well served by public transport, the Cambrian Coast railway station is less than 100 metres away. There is a small outdoor area for enjoying a pint on a warm summer evening.

Deganwy

Castle View

Pentywyn Road, LL31 9TH SH786786
12-11 (midnight Fri & Sat)
(01492) 583777 castleviewpub.com
Black Sheep Best Bitter; Greene King Old Speckled Hen; Marston's Pedigree; Tetley Bitter; guest beer H
Formerly Maggie Murphys, the pub has been extensively refurbished. The interior is divided into various wood-panelled rooms and alcoves with comfortable seating. At the centre is a large, impressive fireplace, sadly gas-fired. Picture windows and a raised terrace afford breathtaking views across the Conwy estuary to the castle and bridges. To the rear is a heated patio. An extensive menu features locally-sourced produce where possible. Monday is quiz night. **P**

Dulas

Pilot Boat Inn

LL70 9EX (on A5025)
11 (12 Sun)-11
(01248) 410205
Robinson's Unicorn H
Friendly, rural, family pub with a play area and converted double decker bus to keep children amused. Originally a cottage-type building, now much extended, the lounge features an unusual bar created from half a boat. The pub is much used by walkers – the coastal path passes through the car park. It is worth visiting Mynydd Bodafan for its spectacular views and Traeth Lligwy for the sands. Meals are served all day. **QP**

Dwygyfylchi

Gladstone

Ysgubor Wen Road, LL34 6PS (off jct 16 A55) SH730772
12-11 (midnight Fri & Sat)
(01492) 623231
Black Sheep Best Bitter; Caledonian Deuchars IPA; Tetley Bitter; guest beer H
The pub was refurbished by the current owners but it retains many original features including the alcoves and wood panelling. A central bar serves both dining and drinking areas. Comfortable sofas surround a wood-burning stove and a galleried balcony with tables and booths overlooks the bar. Beers are served in the correct glasses. Imaginative food is sourced locally. There are magnificent sea views from the outdoor space. Function rooms and luxury accommodation are also available. **P**

Four Mile Bridge

Anchorage Hotel

LL65 3EZ (on B4545, just past bridge to Holy Island)
11 (12 Sun)-11
(01407) 740168
Draught Bass; Taylor Landlord; Theakston XB; guest beer H

This family-run hotel is situated on Holy Island close to Trearddur Bay. There is a large, comfortable lounge bar and a dining area serving a wide selection of meals. The hotel is near some fine sandy beaches and coastal walks. Its proximity to the A55 makes it a useful stopping off point for Holyhead Port. **Q P**

Glanwydden

Queen's Head

LL31 9JP SH817804
11.30-3, 6-10.30; 11.30-10.30 Sat; 11.30-10.30 Sun
(01492) 546570 queensheadglanwydden.co.uk
Adnams Bitter; Great Orme Orme; Weetwood Old Dog Bitter H

This former wheelwright's cottage in the centre of the village welcomes locals and holidaymakers alike. Run by the same owner for more than 20 years, the olde-worlde pub has a traditional front bar with a cosy atmosphere and a rear bar with a dining area. Excellent quality, locally-sourced food includes Fish & Chips in Great Orme Beer Batter and Steak & Ale Pie with Great Orme Ale. There is a heated seating area outside. Guest beers feature occasionally. **Q P**

Harlech

Branwen Hotel

Ffordd Newydd, LL46 2UB (on A462 below Harlech Castle) SH583312
11-11
(01766) 780477 branwenhotel.co.uk
Beer range varies H

Warm and welcoming family-run hotel and bar overlooked by Harlech Castle. The hotel is named after a princess whose tales feature in a collection of Welsh myths known as Y Mabinogion. The popular and stylish bar offers a wide range of cask ales as well as foreign beers. A large selection of wines and malt whiskies is also stocked. Ask for your favourite malt – they are sure to have it. **P**

Llanbedr

Ty Mawr Hotel

LL45 2HH
11-11
(01341) 241440
Worthington's Bitter; guest beers H

Small country hotel set in its own grounds. The modern lounge bar has a slate-flagged floor and cosy wood-burning stove. Unusual flying memorabilia reflect connections with the local airfield. French windows lead out to a verandah and landscaped terrace with seating. A beer festival is held in a marquee on the lawn each year. Popular with locals and walkers, dogs and children are welcome. Meals are served all day. **P**

Llandderfel

Bryntirion Inn

LL23 7RA (on B4401, 4 miles E of Bala)
11 (12 Sun)-11
(01678) 530205
Jennings Cumberland Ale; guest beer H

Old coaching inn in a rural setting with views to the River Dee. Off the pleasant public bar is a family room; there is also a lounge where meals are served in a quiet environment. Bar snacks are also available. There is outdoor seating in the front car park, and at the rear is a courtyard and larger car park. Three bedrooms offer good value accommodation. **Q P**

Llanddona

Owain Glyndwr

Beaumaris, LL58 8UF (signed off B5109, Pentraeth-Beaumaris road)
12 (5 Mon)-midnight; winter hours vary
(01248) 810710
Beer range varies H

Originally cottages and a shop, this multi-room pub opened in 1981. It has a bar area, games room, lounge and dining area, and hosts live music every other Saturday. One beer is available in winter and two in summer, all from micro-breweries. Dogs are welcome in the drinking areas. The pub is in the centre of the village, close to the beach and the Anglesey Coastal Path. **Q P**

Llanddulas

Valentine

Mill Street, LL22 8ES SH908781
4-11; 3-midnight Fri; 12-midnight Sat & Sun
(01492) 518189
Thwaites Lancaster Bomber; guest beers H

Local CAMRA's Most Improved Pub 2008, this traditional village inn dates from the 18th century. It has a well-furnished, comfortable lounge with an open fire in winter, and a separate public bar with a TV. Two beer festivals are held annually – Ales in Wales on the Spring bank holiday and Celtic Ales on the August bank holiday. Brewery memorabilia and many old framed photographs relating to the Valentine decorate the walls. Quiz night is Thursday. Dogs are welcome.
Q (12,13)

Llandudno

King's Head

Old Road, LL30 2NB (next to Great Orme Tramway) SH778827
12-midnight (11 Sun)
(01492) 877993
Greene King IPA, Abbot; guest beers H

The 300-year-old King's Head is the oldest pub in Llandudno and has a traditional split-level bar dominated by a large open fire. There is a grill restaurant at the rear serving good quality food. The pub makes an ideal stop after walking on the Great Orme or riding on Britain's only cable-hauled tramway, and the sun-trap patio with its award-winning flower display is the perfect place to watch the trams pass by. There is a quiz most Wednesdays and acoustic folk plays on the first Sunday of the month. **P**

Llanelian-yn-Rhos

White Lion

LL29 8YA (off B583) SH863764
11.30-3, 6-midnight; closed Mon; 12-4, 6-11 Sun
(01492) 515807 whitelioninn.co.uk
Marston's Burton Bitter, Pedigree; guest beer H
Traditional 16th-century inn next to St Elian's Church in the hills above Old Colwyn. There is a slate flagstoned bar area with a real log fire, antique settles and large, comfortable chairs. Decorative stained glass is mounted above the bar of the tiny snug. The spacious restaurant has a collection of jugs hanging from the ceiling. Two white stone lions guard the door of this attractive family-run inn which has been in the Guide for 18 years. Q P

Llanfairtalhaiarn

Swan Inn

Swan Square, LL22 8RY SH928702
12-3, 6-11 Mon, Tue & Thu; 6-11 Wed; 12-3, 6-midnight Fri; 12-11.30 Sun
(01745) 720233
Marston's Burton Bitter; Thwaites Lancaster Bomber; guest beer H
Located in a peaceful village, this is a good example of an unspoilt traditional village inn, dating from the 16th century. Exuding warmth and hospitality, it has a front dining room/bar and a separate lounge with an open fire. There is also a family room with pool table, dartboard and jukebox, conservatory area and beer garden. Children are welcome until 9.30pm. For warmer weather there is outdoor seating at the front in the square. Occasional entertainment is hosted on Saturday evening. Water colour paintings of village scenes adorn the dining room walls and are for sale.

Llanfihangel Glyn Myfyr

Crown Inn

LL21 9UL (on B5105, 3 miles E of Cerrig-y-Drudion) SH992493
7-11; closed Mon & Tue; 12 (4 winter)-11 Sat & Sun
(01490) 420209
Beer range varies H
Lovely old inn, a rural gem, situated beside the Afon Alwen. The unspoilt interior of the front bar with slate flooring and an open fire provides a warm welcome. The games room is across the corridor with darts, pool and TV. Children are welcome in the pub and there are terraced gardens beside the river. Camping is permitted in the grounds and permits are available for trout fishing – the licensee owns the rights. Beers, one or two, come from small independent breweries. A frequent winner of CAMRA awards. Q P

Llangefni

Railway Inn

48-50 High Street, LL77 7NA
4 (3 Thu & Fri)-11; 12-midnight Sat; 12-11 Sun
(01248) 722166
Lees Bitter H
Classic, friendly, small town pub with a warm welcome, next to the old railway station, displaying photographs of the railway and old Llangefni. The main bar is hewn out of the stone wall. Near the centre of this county town, the pub is also close to Oriel Mon (museum) where you can find out about the history of Anglesey, see Tunnicliffe's bird books and pictures and view Sir Kyffin Williams' paintings.

Llanrwst

Pen-y-Bryn

Ancaster Square, LL26 0LH SH798617
4.30-11; 12-midnight
(01492) 640678
Beer range varies H
Traditional stone-built pub much favoured by locals. The hospitable landlord and friendly regulars offer a warm welcome. A long bar serves a large, comfortable open-plan lounge area containing an original inglenook fireplace, sadly not in use. There is a games room at the rear for pool and darts. Traditional pub games are featured and there is a TV for sporting events. Tuesday is poker night. The two handpumps feature mainly local beers, often from the local Nant Brewery.

Maentwrog

Grapes Hotel

LL41 4HN (on A496)
12-late
(01766) 590365 grapes-hotel.co.uk
Evans Evans Cwrw, Best, Warrior, seasonal beers H
A former coaching inn, this hotel dates back to the 17th century. Situated in a picturesque village, it overlooks the vale of Ffestiniog. The interior comprises a lounge, public bar, verandah and large dining room. All the beers come from the Evan Evans Brewery in Llandeilo, including the full seasonal range. Good value food is a feature, especially the ribs. The railway station nearby is on the Ffestiniog line.
Q (yes) (yes) P

Menai Bridge

Auckland Arms

Water Street, LL59 5DD
12-3, 5-midnight (1am Fri & Sat)
(01248) 712545 anglesey-hotel.co.uk
Beer range varies H
Around 120 years old, the hotel is in a superb location, close to the pier and the Strait. The busy bar, popular with students, has two pool tables and a range of pub games including a popular Monday night quiz. Open mike night is Thursday. Food is available lunchtimes and evenings seven days a week. Beers change constantly but often come from Greene King. There is a patio and garden, and comfortable B&B accommodation. Check opening hours out of term time.

Bridge Inn (Tafarn y Bont)

Telford Road, LL59 5DT
11-midnight; 12-10.30 Sun
(01248) 716888
Banks's Bitter; Marston's Pedigree; guest beers H
Mid 19th-century former shop and tea rooms, close to the famous bridge, now a brasserie-style pub with an excellent restaurant. A beamed interior, log fires and numerous hideaway rooms give the pub an olde-worlde feel. Snowdonia is a short drive away and the Anglesey Coastal Path is very close by.

Victoria Hotel

Telford Bridge, LL59 5DR (between bridge and town centre)
11-11; 12-10.30 Sun
(01248) 712309
Draught Bass; guest beers

Situated 300 metres from the Menai Suspension Bridge, this 19-room hotel overlooks the Straits and affords delightful views from the garden and patio. It is licensed for weddings and has a spacious function room with widescreen HD TV for sports. Live music is a regular added attraction. There is easy access to Snowdonia and the hotel is near the Anglesey Coastal Path.

Old Colwyn

Red Lion

385 Abergele Road, LL29 9PL (on main Colwyn Bay to Abergele road) SH868783
5-11; 4-midnight Fri; 12-midnight Sat; 12-11 Sun
(01492) 515042
Marston's Burton Bitter; guest beers

This ever-popular local serves up to six guest beers from independent and local brewers including a regular guest mild. The free house has won many CAMRA awards and is a former local branch Pub of the Year. The cosy L-shaped interior is warmed by a real coal fire and features antique brewery mirrors and other memorabilia. The traditional public bar has a pool table, darts and TV. To the rear is a covered and heated smoking area. Westons Old Rosie cider is available.

Penrhyn Bay

Penrhyn Old Hall

LL30 3EE SH816815
12-3, 5.30-11; 12-3, 7-10.30 Sun
(01492) 549888
Draught Bass; guest beer

This medieval hall, dating from the 12th century, has been in the Marsh family since 1963. The main Tudor lounge dates back to 1420 and features a wood-panelled bar and a large fireplace concealing a priest hole. Good value meals are served daily in the restaurant at the rear – Sunday lunches are a speciality. A jazz night is held on the first Sunday of the month and the Penrhyn Bay Players stage occasional pub theatre here.

Penrhynside

Penrhyn Arms

Pendre Road, LL30 3BY (off B5115) SH814816
5.30 (4.30 Thu)-midnight; 12-1am Fri & Sat; 12-11 Sun
(07780) 678927 penrhynarms.com
Banks's Bitter; Marston's Pedigree; guest beers

This welcoming local is a real gem and has won many CAMRA awards including local branch Pub of the Year and regional and Welsh Cider Pub of the Year in 2008. It has a spacious L-shaped bar where pool and darts are played and a wide-screen TV for sport. Framed pictures of notable drinkers and brewery memorabilia adorn the walls. Real ciders and perries are on offer plus up to four guest beers including mild and winter ale on gravity at Christmas.

Penysarn

Bedol

LL69 9YR
12 (2 Mon-Fri winter)-11; 12-11 Sat; 12-11 (2-10.30 winter) Sun
(01407) 832590
Robinson's Hartleys XB, seasonal beers

The Bedol (Horseshoe) was built in 1985 to serve a small village, but the regulars now come from a much wider area. This Robinson's tied house hosts regular live entertainment. Food is available all day except midweek lunchtimes in winter. Some of Anglesey's beautiful beaches and the coastal path are nearby.

WALES

Porthmadog

Spooner's Bar

Harbour Station, LL49 9NF
10-11; 12-10.30 Sun
(01766) 516032 festrail.co.uk
Beer range varies

An all-year-round mini beer festival – Spooner's has built its reputation on an ever-changing range from small breweries, including the local Purple Moose. Situated in the terminus of the world famous Ffestiniog Railway, steam trains are outside the door most of the year. Food is served every lunchtime, but out of season only Thursday to Saturday in the evening. Local CAMRA Pub of the Year 2005 and 2007.

Station Inn

LL49 9HT (on mainline station platform)
11-11 (midnight Thu-Sat); 12-11 Sun
(01766) 512629
Brains Rev James; Purple Moose Snowdonia; guest beer

Situated on the Cambrian Coast railway platform, this pub is popular with locals and visitors alike. There is a large lounge and smaller public bar. It can get very busy at the weekend and on nights when live football is shown on TV. A range of pies and sandwiches is available all day.

Red Wharf Bay

Ship Inn

LL75 8RJ (off A5025 between Pentraeth and Benllech)
11-11 (10.30 Sun)
(01248) 852568 shipinnredwharfbay.co.uk
Adnams Bitter; Brains SA; guest beers

Red Wharf Bay was once a busy port exporting coal and fertilisers in the 18th and 19th centuries. Previously known as the Quay, the Ship enjoys an excellent reputation for its bar and restaurant, with meals served lunchtimes and evenings. It gets busy with locals and visitors in the summer. The garden has panoramic views across the bay to south-east Anglesey. The resort town of Benllech is two miles away and the coastal path passes the front door. Beer can be expensive.

Rhos-on-Sea

Toad

West Promenade, LL28 4BU SH847795
11-11.30 (10.30 Sun)
(01492) 532726
Jennings Cumberland Ale; guest beers

This recently refurbished traditional pub situated on the Colwyn Bay promenade offers stunning sea views. Winner of local CAMRA Pub Food of the Year Award in 2009, it serves modern British cuisine freshly prepared with quality local produce, and excellent value Sunday lunches. The downstairs pool room is enjoyed by people of all ages. Professional and friendly staff offer a warm welcome to locals and visitors. P

Rhoscolyn

White Eagle

LL65 2NJ (off B4545 signed Traeth Beach) SH271755
12-3, 6-11; 12-11 Sat; 12-10.30 Sun
(01407) 860267 white-eagle.co.uk
Marston's Burton Bitter, Pedigree; Weetwood Eastgate Ale; guest beers H
Saved from closure by new owners, this pub has been renovated and rebuilt to create an airy, brasserie-style atmosphere. The fine patio enjoys superb views over Caernarfon Bay and the Lleyn Peninsula. The nearby beach offers safe swimming, with a warden on duty in the summer months. The pub is near to the coastal footpath. Excellent food is available lunchtimes and evenings, all day during the school holidays. Q P

Rowen

Ty Gwyn Hotel

LL32 8YU SH759720
12-1am (2am Fri & Sat)
(01492) 650232 tygwynhotelconwy.co.uk
Lees Brewer's Dark, Bitter H
Community village pub in an idyllic setting with a warm welcome for locals and visitors alike. The comfortable lounge has horse brasses and old pictures on the walls; there is also a bar with a pool table and a cosy restaurant. Outside, the walled garden has a river running by. Good food is made with locally-sourced ingredients. The pub hosts traditional Welsh singing on Friday, live entertainment most Saturdays and occasional quiz nights for charity. (19a) P

St George

Kinmel Arms

LL22 9BP SH974758
12-3, 6-11; closed Mon; 11.30 Fri & Sat; closed Sun
(01745) 832207 thekinmelarms.co.uk
Facer's Flintshire Bitter; guest beers H
CAMRA local branch Pub of the Year 2009, this 17th-century coaching inn is set on the hillside overlooking the sea. An L-shaped bar serves a large combined dining and drinking area with a real log fire in one corner and a spacious conservatory at the rear. Two guest beers including a changing mild come from independent breweries, and there is a local cider and a selection of Belgian beers. The pub is renowned for good food. Luxury accommodation is available. Q P

Black velvet, equal parts of Guinness and Champagne, was created in memory of Prince Albert, husband of Queen Victoria, who died in 1861. The Champagne represented the nobility, the stout the 'common classes'.

Trefriw

Old Ship (Yr Hen Long)

LL27 0JH (on B5106) SH781632
12-3, 6-11; closed Mon; 12-11 Sat; 12-10.30 Sun
(01492) 640013 the-old-ship.co.uk
Banks's Bitter; Marston's Pedigree; guest beers H
Dating from the 16th century, this former customs house is now a busy village local. A small central bar serves a cosy L-shaped lounge with an open fire, brass ornaments and pictures of historic and nautical interest. The dining room features an inglenook. This genuine free house serves a good range of guest beers, many from local micro-breweries, and home-cooked food. There is a popular Sunday quiz night. P

Tremadog

Golden Fleece

Market Square, LL49 9RB (on A487)
11.30-3, 6-11; 12.30-3, 6-10.30 Sun
(01766) 512421
Draught Bass; Purple Moose Glaslyn Ale; guest beer H
Situated in the old market square, this former coaching inn is now a friendly local. The pub has a lounge bar, snug and a covered area outside with decking and bench seats. Bar meals are good value and there is a bistro upstairs (booking advisable). Guest beers come from small breweries. Rock climbing and narrow gauge railways are nearby. Q

Trofarth

Holland Arms

Llanrwst Road, LL22 8BG SH840708
12 (6 Tue & Thu)-11; closed Wed; 12-10.30 Sun
(01492) 650777 thehollandarms.co.uk
Beer range varies H
Eighteenth-century coaching house set in a country landscape within sight of Snowdonia. The interior, comprising a pleasantly furnished bar, lounge and restaurant, has been sympathetically refurbished in keeping with the building's original features. Excellent, good value meals are served lunchtimes and evenings. The family-run pub is a big supporter of CAMRA's LocAle scheme, featuring beers from Conwy, Great Orme and Purple Moose. Well worth seeking out, although this is the only pub in the area not accessible by public transport. Q P

Tudweiliog

Lion Hotel

LL53 8ND (on B4417)
11-11 (12-2, 6-11 winter); 11.30-11 Sat; 11-10.30 (12-3 winter) Sun
(01758) 770244
Beer range varies H
Village pub on the glorious, quiet north coast of the Lleyn Peninsula. The cliffs and beaches are a mile away by footpath, a little further by road. The origins of this free house go back over 300 years. Up to three beers are served depending on the season, with Purple Moose a firm favourite. The pub is accessible by No 8 bus from Pwllheli – but not in the evening. Closed Monday lunchtime in winter. Q (8)P

Ty'n-y-Groes

Groes Inn

LL32 8TN (2 miles from Conwy on B5106) SH777740
12-3, 6.30 (6 Sat)-11; 12-10.30 Sun
☎ (01492) 650545 groesinn.com
Great Orme Orme's Best; Tetley Burton Ale Ⓗ
The first licensed house in Wales, dating back to 1573, the Groes Inn has been in the Humphreys family for 23 years. This multi-roomed inn has retained its original architectural features and there is a function room available on the upper floor. Excellent food using local produce is available in the bar or restaurant. You can stay at the inn, a luxury cabin in the hills or a cottage in Conwy. **Q(19)P**

Waunfawr

Snowdonia Park

Beddgelert Road, LL55 4AQ
11-11 (10.30 Sun)
☎ (01286) 650409 snowdonia-park.co.uk
Marston's Mansfield Dark Mild, Burton Bitter, Pedigree; guest beers Ⓗ
Home of the Snowdonia Brewery. The pub has children's play areas inside (separate from the bars) and outside. Meals are served all day. The large campsite gives a discount to CAMRA members. The pub adjoins Waunfawr station on the Welsh Highland Railway – stop off here before going on to Rhyd Ddu (soon to be Beddgelert) on one of the most scenic sections of narrow gauge railway in Britain. **QP**

WALES

Kinmel Arms, St George.

WEST WALES

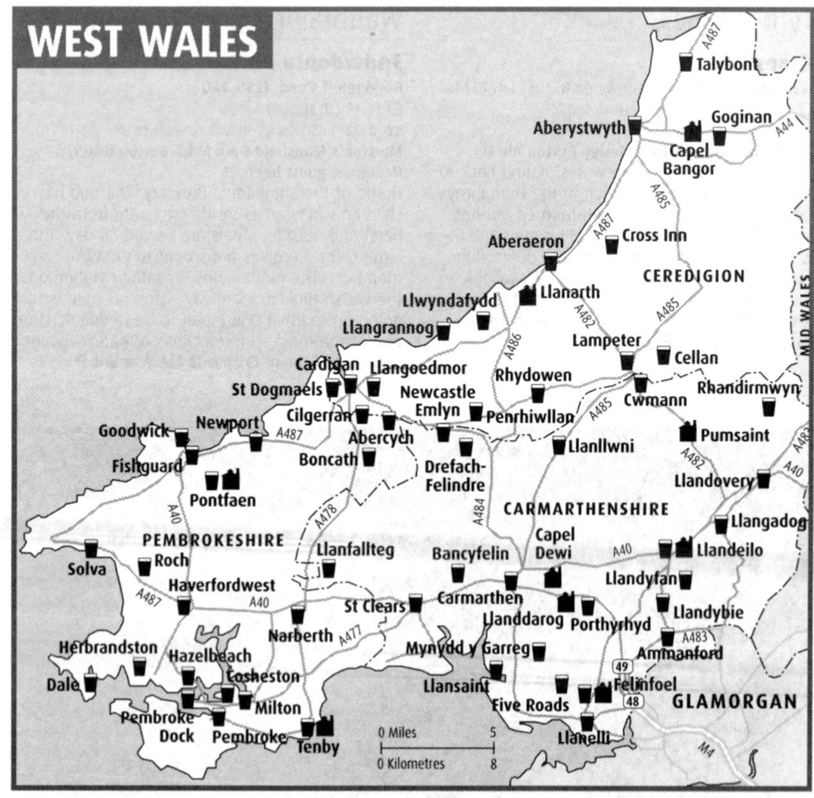

Authority areas covered: Carmarthenshire UA, Ceredigion UA, Pembrokeshire UA

Aberaeron

Harbourmaster

2 Quay Parade, SA46 0BT (off A487, overlooking harbour)
10-11.30
(01545) 570755 harbour-master.com
Evan Evans BB; guest beers
This stylish, comfortable bar, originally a grain warehouse, overlooks Aberaeron harbour. The strong Welsh ethos is reflected in the decor, with paintings by local artists adorning the walls. Staff and signage are bilingual and the excellent menu offers the best of seasonal local produce (no meals Mon lunch). Up to two guest beers invariably come from Welsh breweries, with Purple Moose and Tomos Watkin's often featuring. In the summer, pints can be enjoyed outside overlooking the harbour. Q (X40,X50,550)

Monachty

Market Street, SA46 0AS
12-3, 5-11; 12-11 Sat; 12-3, 5-10.30 Sun
(01545) 570389 monachtyaberaeron.com
Brains Bitter, Reverend James
Situated next to the inner harbour, this Brain's tied house has a comfortable front bar with a wood-burning stove. Linked drinking areas lead through to a restaurant at the rear offering an excellent menu featuring seasonal local produce. The spacious beer garden enjoys stunning views of the harbour and is a must on a summer's day. (X40,X50,550)

Abercych

Nags Head

SA37 0HJ (on B4332 between Cenarth and Eglwyswrw)
11-3 (not Mon), 6-11; 12-10.30 Sun
(01239) 841200
Beer range varies
This well-restored old smithy boasts a beamed bar and riverside garden. The bar area is furnished with collections of old medical instruments, railway memorabilia, and timepieces showing the time in various parts of the world. Space is also found for an extensive display of beer bottles. House beer Old Emrys is brewed for the pub. P

Aberystwyth

Belle Vue Royal Hotel

Marine Terrace, SY23 2BA
11-11 (10.30 Sun)
(01970) 617558 bellevueroyalhotel.co.uk

INDEPENDENT BREWERIES

Coles Llanddarog
Evan Evans Llandeilo
Felinfoel Felinfoel
Ffos y Ffin Capel Dewi
Gwaun Valley Pontfaen (NEW)
Gwynant Capel Bangor (brewing suspended)
Jacobi Pumsaint
Penlon Cottage Llanarth
Preseli Tenby (NEW)

Beer range varies Ⓗ
In an enviable location on the promenade, the bar of this elegant three-star hotel is the perfect place to enjoy a relaxing drink while viewing the headland of Constitution Hill, with its cliff railway and camera obscura, or watching the sun go down over the bay. Up to two real ales are offered, ranging from brews from the nationals (often represented by niche brands such as Young's Winter Warmer), to Welsh micro-breweries. Parking is limited. The hotel entrance has steps, but access ramps are available on request.
🛏◑♿▲⇌🚌P

Nags Head
23 Bridge Street, SY23 1PZ
✪ 12 (11 Sat)-midnight (1am Thu-Sat); 12-11.30 Sun
☎ (01970) 624725
Banks's Original, Bitter Ⓗ
This popular town-centre local is the least altered of Aberystwyth's Banks's pubs. The main bar, with quarry-tiled floor, is dominated by a pool table, but there is a quieter lounge up a step to the right. At the rear, a corridor lined with photos of bygone darts teams leads to a large games room and suntrap outdoor drinking area where smokers are accommodated. Handled glasses are available for those who prefer them. ❀⊟▲⇌🚌♣⚐

Ship & Castle
1 High Street, SY23 1JG
✪ 2-midnight
Wye Valley HPA; guest beers Ⓗ
This friendly town pub is a mecca for the area's real ale drinkers. First mentioned in 1822, it would have been a popular inn with mariners and shipbuilders from the nearby harbour. Today's customers are an interesting mix of students and townsfolk of all ages. A varied range of up to five draught beers comes mainly from micro-breweries from Wales and beyond; the real cider is usually Westons Old Rosie. Beer festivals are held in the spring and autumn, folk music plays on Wednesday night, and occasional quiz nights are run by local CAMRA members. ▲⇌🚌♣🍎

Ammanford

Ammanford Hotel
Wernolau House, 31 Pontamman Road, SA31 2JB
✪ 5.30 (1 Sat)-11; 12-10.30 Sun
☎ (01269) 592598
Beer range varies Ⓗ
Originally a colliery manager's house, this pleasant hotel stands on the outskirts of the town, set in five acres of landscaped grounds and woodland. It is renowned not only for the choice and quality of its beer but also for the warm welcome. Log fires burn in winter and there is a large function room catering for weddings and private events.
🔥Q❀🛏◑▲🚌P

Bancyfelin

Fox & Hounds
SA33 5ND
✪ 11-midnight summer; 11-3, 5.30-midnight winter
☎ (01267) 211341 🌐 foxandhounds-bancyfelin.co.uk
Beer range varies Ⓗ
Family-run village pub nestling in the countryside, offering a real Welsh welcome. Food is served in the lounge/dining area and there is a separate bar with a pool table, jukebox and fruit machines for those who prefer a more traditional bar atmosphere. Q🚸❀◑⊟♿🚌♣P

Boncath

Boncath Inn
SA37 0JN (on B4332 between Cenarth and Eglwyswrw)
✪ 11-11; 12-8.30 Sun
☎ (01239) 841241
Worthington's Bitter; guest beers Ⓗ
Pembrokeshire CAMRA Pub of the Year 2006 and 2007, this pub dates back to the 18th century and is the centre of village life. The interior is divided into several seating areas creating an intimate atmosphere, and the walls display items of local historic interest. Good, home-cooked meals are recommended. A beer festival is held each August bank holiday weekend. 🔥❀◑♿▲🚌♣P⚐

Cardigan

Grosvenor
Bridge Street, SA43 1HY
✪ 11-11; 12-10.30 Sun
☎ (01239) 613792
Greene King Abbot; Worthington's Bitter; guest beer Ⓗ
Situated at the southern entrance to Cardigan, next to Cardigan Castle and the River Teifi, this large pub provides the best choice of beers in town. Recently refurbished, the large open-plan bar/lounge has various areas to relax, eat and drink. There is an extra room upstairs for dining or functions. Good value food is served. ❀◑🚌♣⚐

Red Lion (Llew Coch)
Pwllhai, SA43 1DB (hidden away behind the bus station)
✪ 11-11; 12-10.30 Sun
☎ (01239) 612482
Brains Buckley's Best Bitter, SA Ⓗ
Visitors are made most welcome in this homely local where Welsh is the first language. A smaller private lounge and restaurant area complement the main bar. Live music is a regular feature, and snacks are available at most times. Although tucked away in a quiet corner of town, this pub is well worth seeking out. ❀◑🚌♣⚐

Carmarthen

Queen's Hotel
Queen Street, SA31 1JR
✪ 11-11
☎ (01267) 231800
Beer range varies Ⓗ
Town-centre pub near Carmarthenshire County Hall with a bar, lounge and small function room. The public bar is used by locals and has TV for sporting events. Local ales are usually among the beer range. The patio nestles beneath the castle walls and is a suntrap during the summer months. Food is served daily with a 'two meals for the price of one' offer. ❀⇌🚌⚐

Stag & Pheasant
34 Spilman Street, SA31 1LQ
✪ 11-11; 12-10.30 Sun
☎ (01267) 236278
Beer range varies Ⓗ

Extensively refurbished in 2007, this single-bar pub serves three real ales from Marston's range. There is a terraced area to the rear, and a covered smoking area. The pub can get very busy for food at lunchtime, with mostly local trade in the evenings. There are large TVs at both ends of the room. The pub is near County Hall and a 10-minute walk from the railway and bus stations.

Cellan

Fishers Arms

SA48 8HU (on B4343)
4.30 (12 summer)-11; 12-11 Sun
(01570) 422895
Tetley Bitter; guest beer H
Situated close to the River Teifi, one of Wales' premier trout and salmon rivers, the pub dates from 1580 and was first licensed in 1891. The main bar has a log burner and flagstone floor. The guest beer changes weekly and is usually from a Welsh micro-brewery, though the house beer is from Tetley. The pub is served by two-hourly buses from Aberystwyth and Lampeter Monday-Friday daytimes only. Q(585)P

Cilgerran

Pendre Inn

High Street, SA43 2SL
12-11 (10.30 Sun)
(01239) 614223
Shepherd Neame Spitfire; guest beers H
Welcoming, traditional, unspoilt 14th-century pub standing at the heart of a large village whose attractions include a castle, wildlife centre and the Teifi Gorge. The public bar leads to a lounge area and a separate restaurant. Up to two guest beers change regularly and real cider often appears. Though bar snacks are generally available, evening meals are served Wednesday to Saturday only. Sunday lunch is popular (booking advisable). P

Cosheston

Brewery Inn

SA72 4UD
12-3, 6-11; closed Mon; 12-4, 7-11 Sun
(01646) 686678
Courage Best Bitter; guest beers H
Set between Cosheston Pill and the Carew Estuary just north east of Pembroke, this light and airy stone-built inn boasts a traditional slate floor and bar, roof beams and comfortable seating with old tables. Paintings and drawings by local artists adorn the walls. The outdoor smoking area is heated in winter. QP

Cross Inn

Rhos yr Hafod Inn

SY23 5NB (at B4337/B4577 crossroads)
5-11; closed Mon winter; 12-3, 6-11 Sun
(01974) 272644 rhos-yr-hafod-inn.co.uk
Beer range varies H
This quiet, friendly pub in a small village offers a choice of two real ales, with beer from Welsh micro-breweries increasingly featuring alongside more mainstream fare (often Young's Bitter). Linked drinking areas cluster around a central bar, with some attractive paintings and photographs of local scenes in the back room. Background music plays quietly, but the predominant sound is of conversation. Meals are served Sunday lunchtime and every evening. P

Cwmann

Cwmann Tavern

SA48 8DR (jct of A482/A485)
4-midnight; closed Mon; 12-midnight Sun
(01570) 423861
Beer range varies H
Built in 1720 on a drovers' route, a short walk from Lampeter, the pub is popular with locals and students. Three drinking areas around the central bar feature wooden beams, posts and floors. Beers are from small breweries and Westons Old Rosie cider is always available, backed up with a good range of bottled beers. Tuesday is quiz night, Thursday night a folk session, Friday live band and Saturday karaoke or DJ. (X40)P

Tafarn Jem

SA48 8HF (on A482 4 miles SE of Cwmann) SN615438
12 (closed Wed; 6.30 Thu winter)-10.30
(01558) 650633
Breconshire Ramblers Ruin, Brecon County H
Welcoming 19th-century pub, originally an old drovers' ale house, with stunning views over the valley from outside. There is excellent access for wheelchair users off the car park. Although the interior is open plan there are two distinct areas – the bar and the lounge/restaurant. Food is served daily except Tuesday and Wednesday until 9.30pm. The menu changes every six weeks. P

Dale

Griffin Inn

SA73 3RB
12-11 (12-2, 5.30-11 winter); 12.30-2.30, 5.30-10.30 Sun
(01646) 636227
Brains Rev James; Fuller's London Pride; Worthington's Bitter; guest beers H
In an enviable location at the water's edge and close to the slipway on the Milford Haven waterway, the Griffin is popular with locals and visitors, including those to the Pembrokeshire Coast Path. Some of the outside seats are right by the water. Inside you can have some fun with table skittles. The village is the centre for a thriving sailing club. Q

Drefach-Felindre

Tafarn John y Gwas

SA44 5XG
12-11
(01559) 370469 johnygwas.co.uk
Beer range varies H
This traditional village inn was built in the early 1800s. A locals' pub, there is always a friendly welcome for tourists – and their pets. Two real ales are on offer in winter, three in summer. Home-cooked food is available until 9pm every day, with a roast on Sunday. The food is reasonably priced with children under 12 eating for free. The beer garden has a covered area for smokers. You can play pool or darts, or take part in quiz night on the last Sunday of the month. CAMRA South and Mid Wales Pub of the Year 2008. (460)P

Felinfoel

Harry Watkins

2 Millfield Road, SA14 8HY (on A476)
⏲ 12-11; closed Mon
☎ (01554) 776644
Beer range varies Ⓗ
Renamed after a local rugby hero of yesteryear who features on the pub walls, the pub was originally called the Bear. The open-plan, split-level, family-friendly pub has defined dining areas and a function room. There are covered and open drinking areas outside. Although there is no car park, there is usually ample room for parking on the roadside. National cycle and walking paths to the Swiss Valley and beyond are nearby.
🐴❀◑🚌⁂

Fishguard

Pendre Inn

High Street, SA65 9AT (on A487 300m SW of market square)
⏲ 11 (4 Mon)-midnight; 12-11.30 Sun
☎ (01348) 874128
Worthington's Bitter; guest beers Ⓗ
This friendly, traditional pub on the outskirts of town has a good local following, with pool and darts in the big back bar and a growing reputation for its beer. Two guest beers change regularly and may come from anywhere in the UK. No food is served except packet snacks.
⛼❀🂠🚌(411,412)P⁂

Royal Oak Inn

Market Square, SA65 9HA
⏲ 11-11; 12-10.30 Sun
☎ (01348) 872514
Beer range varies Ⓗ
This charming, friendly, comfortable pub has connections with the last invasion of mainland Britain by a French force at nearby Carregwastad Point in 1797, and displays some fascinating memorabilia from the period. Full of character, it has a bustling public bar and pleasant beer garden. Home-cooked meals are served at affordable prices from a varied menu. Two changing Brain's beers are served alongside one or more guests. A beer and folk festival takes place over the Spring bank holiday weekend with 18 real ales on offer.
❀◑♿▲🚌(411,412)♣⁂

Five Roads

Waun Wyllt Inn

Horeb Road, SA15 5AQ (off B4329)
⏲ 11-11
☎ (01269) 860209 🌐 waunwyllt.com
Greene King Abbot; guest beers Ⓗ
Situated just off National Cycle Trail 47 (the Celtic trail), the Waun Wyllt is set in the heart of the Carmarthenshire countryside. It was built in the 18th century and although recently refurbished retains many original features. The inn is owned by the Great Old Inns group and has become its flagship. It offers a warm welcome, good food and beer including a range of bottled real ales.
⛼Q❀🛏◑♿▲P

Goginan

Druid Inn 🏆

High Street, SY23 3NT (on A44 6 miles E of Aberystwyth)
⏲ 12-midnight (1am Fri & Sat)
☎ (01970) 880650 🌐 goginan.com/druid
Banks's Bitter; Wye Valley Butty Bach; guest beer Ⓗ
This popular pub has gone from strength to strength since its chef became the licensee in 2007. A true community local which also attracts passing trade, it hosts live music nights showcasing local bands. The locally-sourced guest beer is drawn from a wide range of mainly micro-breweries. Food, served 12-9.30pm daily, is excellent and good value. The B&B next door, no longer part of the pub business, is useful for visitors wishing to stay in this glorious area. Local CAMRA Pub of the Year 2008/09. 🐴❀◑🚌(525)♣P⁂

Goodwick

Rose & Crown

SA64 0BP
⏲ 11-12.30am; 12-midnight Sun
☎ (01348) 874449
Marston's Pedigree; guest beers Ⓗ
Picturesque inn close to the ferry port with good views of the harbour and beach. The dining area offers food at lunchtimes and evenings, specialising in pizzas and Mexican dishes. The local lifeboat crew uses the pub as a meeting place. Two guest beers are served. Trains to Fishguard Harbour are infrequent and timed to connect with Irish Ferries. ⛼Q❀◑▲⇌(Fishguard Harbour)🚌♣P

Haverfordwest

Bristol Trader

Quay Street, SA61 1BE
⏲ 11-11 (1am Sat); 12-10.30 Sun
☎ (01437) 762122
Worthington's Bitter; guest beers Ⓗ
Dating back to Haverfordwest's days as a port, this pub retains some character despite recent modernisation. A quiet venue in the daytime, popular for dining, food is served in a large dining area or at outside tables overlooking the river. It gets lively in the evening. Two guest ales are served – beers can be dispensed without tight sparkler on request. ◐♿🚌P

Pembroke Yeoman

11 Hill Street, SA61 1QQ
⏲ 11-11
☎ (01437) 762500
Draught Bass; Flowers IPA; guest beers Ⓗ
In this local pub conversation is king, though there is a well-stocked jukebox should it flag. Two guest ales change often and come from small breweries. Food is served in large portions. Known as the Upper Three Crowns until the 1960s, the pub's name was changed to reflect the presence of the local yeomanry headquarters nearby. ⛼Q◑🚌♣

Hazelbeach

Ferry House Inn

SA73 1EG (signed Llanstadwell from A477 in Neyland)
⏲ 12-3 (2 Sun), 6-11
☎ (01646) 600270
Brains Rev James; guest beers Ⓗ

Situated on the Milford Haven waterway, this pub is convenient for Neyland, with its marina and Brunel connections, and lies on the Pembrokeshire Coast Path. The conservatory restaurant overlooks the river, with fresh local fish featuring on the menu. Three guest beers are served. Good-quality accommodation makes this an ideal base for exploring the area. Q❀⇔◑◐⊞♿P⚟

Herbrandston

Taberna Inn

SA73 3TD (3 miles W of Milford Haven)
⌚ 12-11
☎ (01646) 693498
Hop Back Summer Lightning; guest beers Ⓗ
Built in 1963 in a village dominated by a large oil refinery, this pub has a pleasant atmosphere and welcoming locals. Two guest beers are served alongside Westons and Moles Black Rat cider, and the pub issues its own listing of all the guest beers sold throughout the year. ♨Q❀⇔◑◐⊞♿🚌●P⚟

Lampeter

Kings Head

14 Bridge Street, SA48 7HG
⌚ 12- 2.30, 6-12.30am; 12-1.30am Fri-Sun
☎ (01570) 421498
Jennings Cumberland Ale; Marston's Old Empire; guest beer Ⓗ
This town-centre pub has two bars and a large function room, with a good mix of customers – locals, students and tourists. Good food is served all day with unusual dishes such as rabbit stew on the menu. The pub is tied to Marston's and the guest ale changes frequently, coming from Ringwood and Jennings. The university town is home to the oldest established rugby club in Wales.
♨❀◑◐⊞Å🚌♣P⚟

Llandeilo

Salutation

New Road, SA19 6DF
⌚ 12-midnight (11 Sun)
☎ (01558) 823325
Greene King Abbot; guest beers Ⓗ
Vibrant and welcoming pub, just off the centre of the town, with a central bar area serving an open plan room. Live music plays on a monthly basis – telephone to check bands and dates. Major sporting events are screened. The pub has an extensively renovated restaurant area and a covered space outside at the back. ♨❀♿🚌⚟

White Horse

Rhosmaen Street, SA19 6EN
⌚ 11-11; 12-10.30 Sun
☎ (01558) 822424
Evan Evans Cwrw, seasonal beers; guest beers Ⓗ
Grade II-listed coaching inn dating from the 16th century. This multi-roomed pub is popular with all ages. It has a small outdoor drinking area to the front and a large council car park to the rear with access to the pub down a short flight of steps. The covered area for smokers has its own TV to watch the sport. ❀🚌♣⚟

Llandovery

Red Lion ★

2 Market Square, SA20 0AA
⌚ 5.30-10.30 Fri; 12-2, 7-11 Sat; closed Sun-Thu
☎ (01550) 720813
Beer range varies Ⓖ
You are assured of a warm welcome at this superb old pub which features in CAMRA's National Inventory of historic interiors. The landlord is semi-retired, hence the short opening hours. He is a mine of information about the town and its rugby team – note that Saturday lunchtime hours may vary depending on rugby fixtures. ♨⇌🚌

Llandybie

Ivy Bush

Church Road, SA18 3HZ
⌚ 12-midnight (11 Mon); 11-midnight Sat & Sun
☎ (01269) 850272
Taylor Landlord; guest beer Ⓗ
The oldest pub in the village – this friendly local dates back nearly 300 years. The single bar interior has two comfortable seating areas. It is close to the station on the Heart of Wales line. Pub games and quizzes are run weekly. A large screen TV is available for sport. The guest beer changes regularly. ❀⇌🚌(X13)♣●P⚟

Llandyfan

Square & Compass

SA18 2UD (between Ammanford and Trap)
⌚ 12 (1 Sat)-11 summer; 5-11 winter (hours may vary); 12-6 Sun
☎ (01269) 850402
Beer range varies Ⓗ
This 18th-century building was originally the village blacksmith's, and was converted into a pub in the '60s. Nestling on the western edge of the Brecon Beacons National Park, it offers magnificent local views and plenty of walking opportunities. A traditional family pub, it has a wonderful rustic charm and warm friendly welcome. Up to three guest beers are available, at least one from a local brewery. Q◐♿ÅP⚟

Llanelli

Lemon Tree

2 Prospect Place, SA15 3PT
⌚ 12-11 (10.30 Sun)
☎ (01554) 775121
Evan Evans Best Bitter; guest beer Ⓗ
A no-frills bar with a true local atmosphere. There is a major sports theme to this pub, with many mementos adorning the walls. A pool room adjoins the main bar. The outside area has a covered roof to allow smokers to stay dry. There are also tables outside which are popular in the summer. The pub is situated on a side road on the roundabout entering the town from Felinfoel. ❀♣⚟

Llanfallteg

Plash

SA34 0HN (N off A40 at Llanddewi Velfrey)
⌚ 5-11; 12-midnight Wed-Sun
☎ (01437) 563472
Brains Bitter; Wye Valley Butty Bach; guest beer Ⓗ

Terrace-style cottage pub with a garden. An inn for more than 180 years, it has had four different names in that time. The pub is the centre of village life, with welcoming locals who will talk to anyone who wishes to join in. The attractive bar was rescued from a local outfitter's shop. Traditional home-made dishes are served in the small restaurant. The guest beer is usually from a small, independent brewery. A disabled entrance is to the rear. ⌂Q❀🛏◐◑♿♣P

Llangadog

Red Lion

Church Street, SA19 9AA

⏲ 12-midnight

☎ (01550) 777357 🌐 redlioncoachinginn.co.uk

Evan Evans Cwrw; guest beers Ⓗ

Refurbishment of this Grade II-listed, 16th-century coaching inn has taken it back to its origins. It was reputed to be a safe house for royalist soldiers during the Civil War. Family friendly, it is full of character and atmosphere. Excellent, fresh, locally-sourced food attracts locals and tourists alike. Guest beers include Welsh ales as well as those from across the border. Car parking is through the arch. Carmarthenshire CAMRA Pub of the Year 2008. ⌂❀🛏◐◑♿⛺⇌🚌P

Telegraph Inn

Station Road, SA19 9LS

⏲ 4 (12 Sat)-midnight; 12-11 Sun

☎ (01550) 777727

Black Mountain Black 5; guest beers Ⓗ

On the edge of the village, the inn is next to the railway station on the spectacular Heart of Wales line. Built around 1830, the welcoming pub has a basic bar area and comfortable lounge. It serves three rotating guest beers and food is served Wednesday to Saturday, including takeaways. Curry night is Wednesday. Self-catering accommodation sleeps five. ⌂❀◑⛺⇌🚌(280)P🚬

Llangoedmor

Penllwyndu

SA43 2LY (on B4570, 4 miles E of Cardigan) SN241458

⏲ 3.30 (12 Sat)-11; 12-10.30 Sun

☎ (01239) 682533

Brains Buckleys Best Bitter; guest beers Ⓗ

This is an old-fashioned ale house standing at an isolated crossroads where Cardigan's evil-doers were once hanged – the pub sign is worthy of close inspection. The cheerful and welcoming public bar has a slate floor and inglenook with wood-burning stove. Snacks are usually available and there is a separate dining area where good value home-cooked meals are served. The guest beer is often from Cottage Brewery. ⌂❀◑♣P🚬

Llangrannog

Pentre Arms

SA44 6SP (at seaward end of B4321/B4334)

⏲ 12-midnight

☎ (01239) 654345 🌐 pentrearms.co.uk

St Austell Tribute; guest beer Ⓗ

Right on the shore, in arguably Ceredigion's finest seaside village, this traditional pub offers stunning sea views. Built of local stone, it has a comfortable bar with a separate games room. Its welcoming atmosphere makes it popular with both locals and tourists. Llangrannog has produced generations of seafarers and poets, whose memory is still honoured. Eight letting bedrooms are available. 🐴🛏◐◑⛺♣

Ship

SA44 6SL (At seaward end of B4321/B4334)

⏲ 11-11 (1am Fri & Sat)

☎ (01239) 654510

Tomos Watkin Cwrw Braf; guest beers Ⓗ

Slightly set back from the seafront, the larger of Llangrannog's two pubs is enthusiastically run with a focus on locally-sourced produce and Welsh beers. One guest ale is available in winter, two in summer. A stylish refurbishment featuring bare stone and wood has created a bright modern atmosphere in a pub which is popular with locals and tourists alike. ⌂Q🐴❀◐◑⛺P

Llanllwni

Belle Vue Inn

SA40 9SQ (on A485 2 miles N of B4336 jct)

⏲ 12-2.30 (Sat only), 5-10.30 (11 Fri & Sat); closed Tue; 12-2.30, 6-10.30 Sun

☎ (01570) 480495 🌐 bellevueinn.co.uk

Beer range varies Ⓗ

Set on the main road in a long and straggling village, this 17th-century farmhouse and smithy was converted to an inn in the 1800s. Both licensees are classically trained chefs and have gained a well deserved reputation for excellence, with the emphasis on local produce – special themed evenings are very popular. With two rotating guest ales plus bottled beers, this friendly family-run free house is a magnet for locals and visitors alike – an oasis in a desert of blandness. Q❀◐◑🚌(X40)P🚬🍺

Llansaint

King's Arms

13 Maes yr Eglwys, SA17 5JE

⏲ 12-2.30, 6-11; closed Tue; 12-2.30, 6.30-10.30 Sun

☎ (01267) 267487

Brains Buckley's Best Bitter; guest beer Ⓗ

This friendly village local, a former Carmarthenshire CAMRA Pub of the Year, has been a pub for more than 200 years. Situated near an 11th-century church, it is reputedly built from stone recovered from the lost village of St Ishmaels. Music and poetry nights are held on the third Friday of the month. Good value home-cooked food is served. Carmarthen Bay Holiday Park is a few miles away. ⌂Q❀🛏◐◑⛺🚌♣P

Llwyndafydd

Crown Inn

SA44 6BU (off A487 at Gwenlli chapel, 1 mile S of A486 jct, signed Caerwedros) SN371554

⏲ 12-11 (10.30 Sun)

☎ (01545) 560396 🌐 the-crown-inn.moonfruit.com

Enville Ale; Flowers IPA; guest beers Ⓗ

Among the loveliest pubs in Wales, the Crown offers good food, great beer and a garden play area in an idyllic village setting. A stop on the Dylan Thomas Trail, this is a friendly place in which to savour expertly prepared local produce and enjoy a range of activities including belly dancing and a Thursday evening quiz. Other Enville beers sometimes replace the Ale; guests (one in winter, two in summer) are usually from regional brewers. The coastal Cardi Bach bus comes this way from June to October; more frequent buses ply the main A487. Q P

Milton

Milton Brewery

SA70 8PH (on A477)
12-3, 4.30-11; 12-11 Sun
(01646) 651202 themiltonbrewery.com
Courage Directors; guest beer H
Attractive and substantial ivy-covered pub set on a millstream flowing into the Carew River. It ceased brewing in the early 1900s but there are plans to start again, using water from a capped well which can be seen inside the pub. There is a large caravan park at the rear. Q P

Mynydd y Garreg

Prince of Wales

SA17 4RP
5-11; 12-3 Sun
(01554) 890522
Bullmastiff Brindle, Son of a Bitch; guest beers H
This little gem of a pub, a former Carmarthenshire CAMRA Pub of the Year, is well worth seeking out for both its beer range and its ambience. As well as the two regular Bullmastiff beers, there are up to four rotating guest ales usually from smaller breweries. The cosy single-room bar is packed with movie memorabilia, and the small restaurant offers good, reasonably priced food. Q P

Narberth

Dragon Inn

5 Water Street, SA67 7AT
9am-11 (12.30am Fri & Sat)
(01834) 861667
Marston's Pedigree; guest beers H
Set in an attractive town 10 miles north of Tenby with a prominent place in Welsh mythology, this pub has a split-level bar leading to dining areas. The whitewashed walls display horseracing photographs. Narberth railway station is a mile from the town. Visit the Landsker Visitor Centre to find out more about this fascinating area.

Newcastle Emlyn

Pelican Inn

Sycamore Street, SA38 9AP
2.30 (12 Fri & Sat)-11.30
(01239) 710606
Draught Bass; guest beer H
If you want to enjoy a decent pint while you watch the rugby, this friendly local in the heart of town is the place to be. It has an inviting open fire and there are plenty of cosy nooks for a quiet chat. The bar has Sky TV, a dartboard and pool table.
(460)

Newport

Castle Hotel

Bridge Street, SA42 0TB
11-11; 12-10.30 Sun
(01239) 820472
Greene King Old Speckled Hen; Theakston Best Bitter, XB; guest beer H
This friendly, popular local in a small town full of character has an attractive bar with some impressive wood panelling. Food is served at lunchtimes and evenings in the extensive dining area. An off-street car park is situated behind the hotel. A wealth of prehistoric remains adds interest to the many local walks. (412)P

Golden Lion

East Street, SA42 0SY (on A487)
12-midnight (11 Sun)
(01239) 820321
Brains Rev James; Draught Bass; guest beers H
Another of Newport's sociable locals, this one is reputed to have its own resident ghost. A number of internal walls have been removed to form a spacious open-plan bar area with distinct sections, helping to retain a cosy atmosphere. Car parking space is available on the opposite side of the road.
Q (412)P

Pembroke

Royal George Hotel

9 Northgate, SA71 4NR
11-12.30am (1am Fri & Sat)
(01646) 682751
Banks's Original; guest beers H
Pleasant, cheery riverside local standing directly below Pembroke Castle at what used to be the town's north gate, forming part of the old town wall. The large, split-level, L-shaped room has a single bar serving two guest beers; current and future guests are listed beside the bar.
P

Pembroke Dock

Flying Boat Inn

6 Queen Street, SA72 6JL
10-12.30am; 12-10.30 Sun
(01646) 682810
Beer range varies H
Featuring exposed stone and black beams, the bar of this relaxed and friendly pub displays memorabilia from the heyday of flying boats stationed locally. Sky Sports is shown on the large screen, a beer festival is held annually, and the local folk club meets every Friday evening. Irish Ferries sails twice daily from Pembroke Dock to Rosslare. Q

Station Inn

Hawkestone Road, SA72 6JL (in station building)
7-11 Mon; 11-3, 6-midnight (12.30am Fri & Sat); 12-3, 7-10.30 Sun
(01646) 621255
Beer range varies H
Housed in the town's railway station where trains still depart for Carmarthen and Swansea, this town-centre pub is close to the Irish Ferries terminal and Pembrokeshire Coast Path. Meals are excellent value (no lunches Mon, evening meals Wed-Sat only). Three real ales are generally on sale, drawn from an eclectic range, with Young's Bitter a frequent visitor and a new beer coming on every Tuesday. The June beer festival offers around 20 beers. Live music is performed on Saturday evening. Q P

Penrhiwllan

Daffodil

SA44 5NG (on A475)

⏲ 11.30-midnight

☎ (01559) 370343

Beer range varies Ⓗ

A much-deserved and welcome new entry to the Guide, the Daffodil, formerly the Penrhiwllan Inn, is a family-run pub/restaurant dating from 1750 in a country village 20 minutes from Newquay on the Ceredigion coast. It has been modernised in an elegant style to provide separate, intimate dining areas and cosy drinking areas to cater for all. Two handpumps (three in summer) dispense beers mostly from nationals, with Welsh guest ales. Occasional live music nights are hosted. Disabled facilities are excellent. ⌂Q♘❀◐◑♿♣P⍀

Pontfaen

Dyffryn Arms ★

SA65 9SG (off B4313)

⏲ hours vary

☎ (01348) 881305

Draught Bass; Tetley Burton Ale Ⓖ

This much-loved pub, run by a landlady in her 80s, resembles a 1920s front room where time has stood still. The beer is still served by jug through a sliding serving hatch. Conversation is the main form of entertainment, and the pub's relaxed atmosphere is captivating. Set in the beautiful Gwaun Valley between the Preseli Hills and Fishguard, the Dyffryn Arms is at the heart of almost all local community activity. ⌂Q❀⛺♣

Porthyrhyd

Mansel Arms 🏆

Banc y Mansel, SA32 8BS (on B4310 between Porthyrhyd and Drefach)

⏲ 5-11; 3-midnight Sat; 12-6 Sun

☎ (01267) 275305

Beer range varies Ⓗ

Friendly 18th-century former coaching inn with wood fires in each room. To the rear is a games room for pool and darts which was once used for slaughtering pigs. The original limestone flags have been broken up and used in the fireplace. Low beams have been added to create atmosphere and numerous jugs hang from beams in the bar. Food is served Friday and Saturday evenings and Sunday lunch. ⌂Q◐◑⛺🚌♣🍎

Rhandirmwyn

Royal Oak

SA20 0NY

⏲ 12-3 (2 winter), 6-11; 12-2, 7-10.30 Sun

☎ (01550) 760201 🌐 theroyaloakinn.co.uk

Beer range varies Ⓗ

Remote, stone-flagged inn with excellent views of the Tywi Valley and close to an RSPB bird sanctuary. Originally built as a hunting lodge for the local landowner, it is now a focal point for community activities and popular with fans of outdoor pursuits. A fine range of bottled beers and whiskies is stocked, and the good wholesome food is recommended. The pub has been voted Carmarthenshire CAMRA Pub of the Year four times. ⌂Q❀🛏◐◑⛺♣P

Rhydowen

Alltyrodyn Arms

SA44 4QB (at A475/B4459 crossroads)

⏲ 3 (12 Sat)-midnight; closed Mon; 12-8 Sun

☎ (01545) 590319

Beer range varies Ⓗ

This 400-year-old family-run country pub has an excellent reputation for both food and real ales (no keg beer sold), with an extended range stocked for its August bank holiday beer festival. A games room with pool and darts complements the main bar, and home-made food, including a peasants menu, is served in the dining room. The beer garden and covered decking area have lovely valley views. Families and dogs are always welcome. ⌂❀◐◑🚌(551)♣P⍀

Roch

Victoria Inn

SA62 6AW (on A487)

⏲ 12-2.30am; 12-10.30

☎ (01437) 710426

Beer range varies Ⓗ

A little gem with views across St Brides Bay, this locals' pub offers a warm welcome to all. The inn was established in 1851 although some parts of the building date back to the 18th century. It has retained much of its olde-worlde charm with beamed ceilings and low doorways. The menu features home-made local specialities using Welsh produce, such as Rev James' steak and ale pie. Curry and a pint night is Friday. For those in a hurry there is a beer carry-out service. Occasional live music plays. ⌂Q♘❀🛏◐◑🍺♿🚌(411)♣P

St Clears

Corvus Hotel

Station Road, SA33 4BG (corner of Pentre Road and High Street)

⏲ 11-1am (2am Sat); 12-1am Sun

☎ (01994) 230965

Brains SA; Fuller's London Pride; guest beers Ⓗ

The pub is warm and comfortable with friendly staff. Bar snacks are available all day. There is Sky Sports on TV. Regular events are held such as karaoke, and singers and comedians feature. The beer is well kept and rotated regularly. There is a selection of bottled real ales available. On street parking is freely available. Q♘❀◐◑🍺♿🚌♣⍀

St Dogmaels

White Hart

Finch Street, SA43 3EA

⏲ 10 (11 Sun)-11 (later in summer)

☎ (01239) 612099

> Up the street, in the Sailors Arms, Sinbad Sailors, grandson of Mary Ann Sailors, drew a pint in the sunlit bar. The ship's clock in the bar says half past eleven. Half past eleven is opening time. The hands of the clock have stayed still at half past eleven for fifty years. It is always opening time in the Sailors Arms.
>
> **Dylan Thomas**, Under Milk Wood

Felinfoel Double Dragon; Greene King IPA; guest beers Ⓗ

Set in Pembrokeshire's northernmost village, this small, cheery community pub enjoys a good local following. Guest beers (three in summer, two in winter) change regularly and are often from breweries rarely seen locally. The landlord is a rugby enthusiast. The beach at nearby Poppit Sands marks the northern terminus of the Pembrokeshire Coast Path. ⛫Q◐◑Å🚌P⚐

Solva

Cambrian Inn

SA62 6UU (on A487 by bridge)

⏲ 11-11

☎ (01437) 721210

Tomos Watkin OSB; guest beers Ⓗ

Situated in a popular coastal village, renowned as one of the most delightful places in Pembrokeshire, this sympathetically restored local pub has a high reputation for both beer and food. The bar area has been decorated with local crafts, creating a cosy atmosphere enjoyed by village residents and visitors alike. Q◐◑🚌(411)P⚐

Harbour Inn ✔

SA62 6UU (on A487 next to harbour)

⏲ 11-11

☎ (01437) 720013

Brains Dark, SA; guest beers Ⓗ

This delightful seaside inn, next to the harbour where emigrants once left for North America, remains the same from year to year. A community pub with a traditional atmosphere, it serves as a base for many village activities and is popular with locals who come to enjoy a quiet, relaxing pint. The nearby camping facilities cater for both caravans and tents. ⛫Q❀🛏◐◑♿🚌(411)P⚐

Ship

15 Main Street, SA62 6UU (on A487)

⏲ 12 (11 Fri & Sat summer)-11.30 (midnight Fri & Sat)

☎ (01437) 721247

Banks's Bitter; Jennings Cocker Hoop; Marston's Pedigree; guest beer Ⓗ

Families are made particularly welcome in this traditional pub. The Sunday roast is popular and authentic Indian curries are served in the evening with a free delivery service available subject to a minimum order value. An outdoor smoking area is covered and heated, and ample parking is available nearby at the harbour.
⛫❀🛏◐◑♿Å🚌(411)⚐

Talybont

White Lion (Llew Gwyn) ✔

SY24 5ER (7 miles N of Aberystwyth on A487)

⏲ 11-1am; 12-midnight

☎ (01970) 832245

Banks's Original, Bitter; guest beer Ⓗ

This dog-friendly community pub faces the village green. The front bar retains its flagstone floor and houses a fascinating display of local history in a snug area, the family/games room is at the rear, and a large dining room is to the left of the entrance. Local seafood is a speciality on the food menu. A guest or seasonal beer is usually available, drawn from the Marston's list. Bus times to nearby towns Aberystwyth and Machynlleth are pinned up in the bar. ⛫👪❀🛏◐◑Å🚌(28,X32)♣P⚐

Tenby

Hope & Anchor

St Julian Street, SA70 7AS

⏲ 11-11; 12-10.30 Sun

☎ (01834) 842131

Brains Rev James; Worthington's Bitter; guest beers Ⓗ

Near the harbour and close to the beaches, this pub caters for locals and tourists alike. A range of bar snacks, which may be enjoyed inside or out, makes it an ideal place to take a break when exploring the area. Impressive stretches of the medieval town walls can be seen nearby. ⛫❀◐◑♿Å⇌🚌⚐

Harbourmaster, Aberaeron.

Scotland

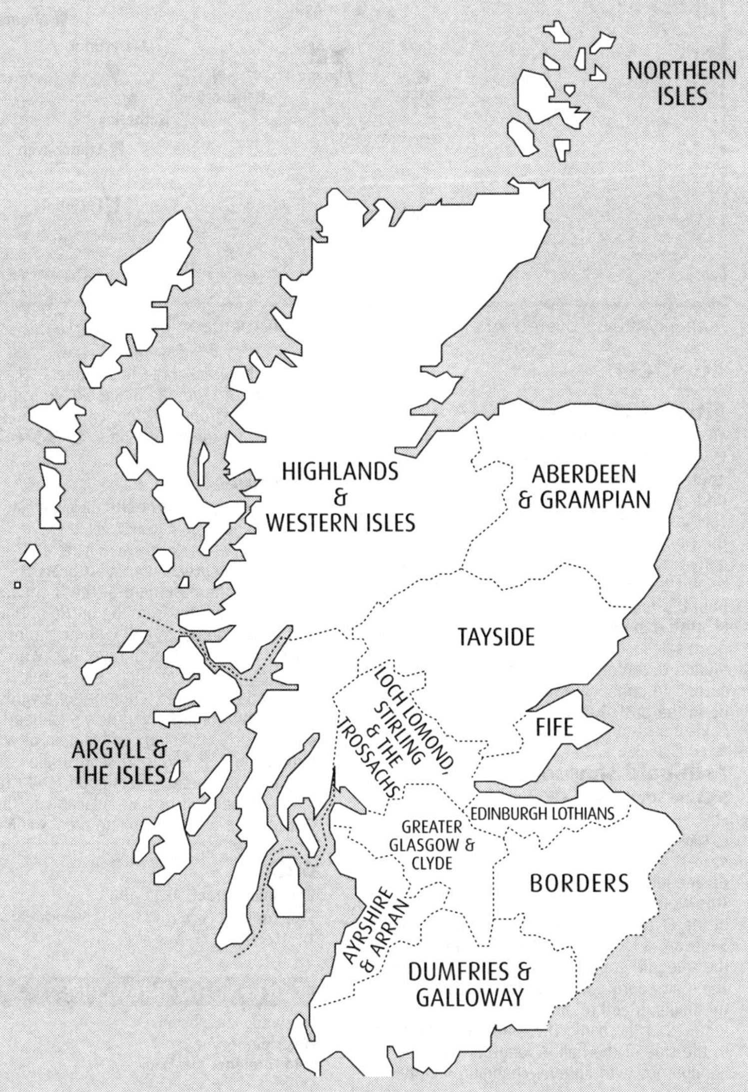
NORTHERN ISLES
HIGHLANDS & WESTERN ISLES
ABERDEEN & GRAMPIAN
TAYSIDE
LOCH LOMOND, STIRLING & THE TROSSACHS
FIFE
ARGYLL & THE ISLES
EDINBURGH LOTHIANS
GREATER GLASGOW & CLYDE
BORDERS
AYRSHIRE & ARRAN
DUMFRIES & GALLOWAY

ABERDEEN & GRAMPIAN

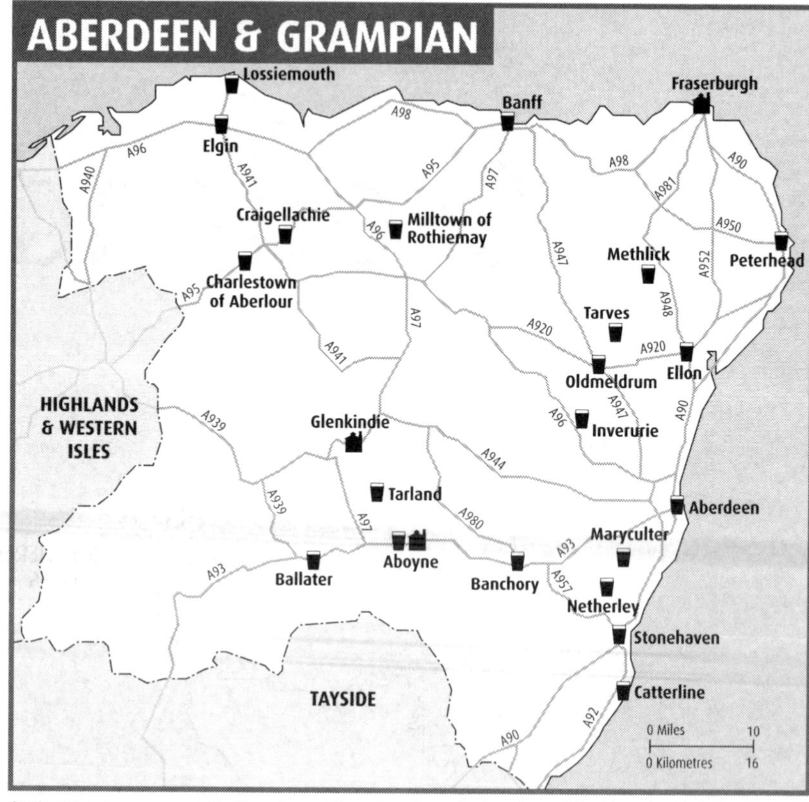

Authority areas covered: Aberdeenshire UA, City of Aberdeen UA, Moray UA

Aberdeen

Aitchies Ale House

10 Trinity Street, AB11 5LY

8am-10 (11 Fri & Sat); closed Sun

(01224) 581459

Orkney Dark Island H

This small corner bar is the closest real ale outlet to the city rail and bus stations, with hours to suit the early traveller. Although renovated in 1994, it retains the flavour of an old-fashioned Scottish pub. Bar food may be described as traditional Scottish pub grub, including roast beef stovies. A good selection of whiskies includes Bell's special edition decanters. The friendly service here is second to none – a reminder of how pubs used to be in the past.

Archibald Simpson ✔

5 Castle Street, AB11 5BQ (corner of Union St and King St)

9am-midnight (1am Fri & Sat); 9am-11 Sun

(01224) 621365

Greene King Abbot; guest beers H

This Wetherspoon's was the former Aberdeen HQ of the Clydesdale Bank, designed by Archibald Simpson, a local architect who designed many of the splendid granite buildings in central Aberdeen. The main room is the high- ceilinged central hall of the building and retains many architectural features of the bank. There are also seating areas to the side of the hall. A long bar features 12 handpumps with an ever-changing variety of beers. There are three house beers —Castlegate from Isle of Skye and Archibald Simpson and Granite City from Houston. CAMRA local Pub of the Year for Aberdeen City 2009.

Carriages

101 Crown Street, AB11 6HH (below Brentwood Hotel)

11-2.30 (not Sat), 4.30-midnight; 6-11 Sun

(01224) 595440 brentwood-hotel.co.uk

Caledonian Deuchars IPA; guest beers H

Located in the basement of the Brentwood Hotel just a few minutes from the bustle of Union Street, this is a comfortable pub with an atmosphere that goes beyond the typical hotel bar. With 10 handpumps, the bar offers a wide selection of real ales, and has earned a number of awards from the local CAMRA branch over the years. Beers include a continuously changing combination of well-known national brands and local Scottish ales. The adjoining restaurant offers good food (from 5.30pm), and lunches are available in the bar. Outside is a heated smoking area. P

Grill ★

213 Union Street, AB11 6BA

10-midnight (1am Fri & Sat); 12.30-midnight Sun

(01224) 573530 thegrillaberdeen.co.uk

INDEPENDENT BREWERIES

Brewdog Fraserburgh
Deeside Aboyne
Old Foreigner Glenkindie

Caledonian 80; Harviestoun Bitter & Twisted; Isle of Skye Red Cuillin; guest beers
With an exquisite interior dating back to a redesign in 1926, and remaining largely unchanged since then, this is the only CAMRA National Inventory pub in the Aberdeen area. A men-only bar until 1975, ladies toilets were eventually provided in 1998. Situated across from the Music Hall, musicians often visit during concert breaks. Guest beers may include Landlord and Isle of Skye. UK Whisky Bar of the Year 2009, an extensive collection of malt whiskies is offered. Bar snacks are served. There is disabled access to the ladies toilet only.

Howff

365 Union Street, AB11 6BT
11-11 (midnight Wed & Thu; 1am Fri & Sat); 12.30-11 Sun
(01224) 580092
Courage Directors; guest beer
Small, friendly basement bar situated in the heart of the city centre at the west end of Union Street. It is easy to find – look for the bandsman clock above Bruce Millers music store next door. A good range of guest beers ensures that very few ales make a return visit. The food is home-made with a healthy outlook (no chips) and served all day until 9pm Monday to Saturday (5pm Sunday).

Ma Camerons

6-8 Little Belmont Street, AB10 1JG (beside St Nicholas churchyard)
11-midnight (1am Fri & Sat); 12.30-midnight Sun
(01224) 644487
Belhaven 80/-; Greene King IPA; guest beers
Known simply as Ma's, this is one of the oldest pubs in Aberdeen. It has a listed, unspoilt snug bar with serving hatch and modern, expansive lounge to the rear where meals are served daily. Part of the Belhaven empire, three handpumps in both bars sell mainly Greene King beers plus an ale from Inveralmond. A quiz is held on the first Monday of the month and sports are shown on TV in the lounge. The snug may close early during the week. Free Wi-Fi.

Moorings

2 Trinity Quay, AB11 5AA (opp quayside at bottom of Market St)
12-midnight (1am Fri & Sat); 12.30-midnight Sun
(01224) 587602
Beer range varies
Hard rock meets real ale in this unique laid-back dockside haven, CAMRA City Pub of the Year 2008/09. The pub has a friendly welcome for all, with relatively low prices for the city centre. Five handpumps dispense an ever-changing selection of ales, usually from Scottish breweries (often BrewDog) and a cider (Thatchers). Note the unusual 'elastic band' method of quality control. More than 60 bottled beers from around the world are also on offer. Frequent live rock bands play, particularly at weekends, for which there may be a charge, and the jukebox tends to be in constant use.

Northern Hotel

1 Great Northern Road, AB24 3PS
11-midnight; 12-10 Sun
(01224) 483342 aberdeennorthernhotel.com
Beer range varies
Located at Kittybrewster just north of the city centre, this imposing A-listed Art Deco building dates from 1939. The public Clifton Bar, with a separate entrance from Clifton Road, is a friendly neighbourhood local with darts teams and pool tables, as well as large-screen TVs for sport. The Ellington Bar & Diner, accessed through the hotel lobby, is a quiet hotel bar and restaurant. Both bars serve up to two ales from mainly from Scottish independent breweries. There is seating outside the Clifton Bar for alfresco drinking.
(17,21,23)

Number 10

10 Queens Terrace, AB10 1XL (by Rubislaw Terrace Gardens)
11-midnight; 12.30-11 Sun
(01224) 631928
Caledonian Deuchars IPA, 80; Fuller's London Pride; Taylor Landlord
Ten minutes' walk from the West End, this low, bricked vaulted cellar bar is popular with the local business community. There is a quiet, seated area to the right as you enter and another area to the left which can be slightly noisier due to the wide-screen TVs showing sport when appropriate. For the lazy cooks among you, breakfasts are served from 9am daily and lunches from 2pm.

Old Blackfriars

52 Castle Street, AB11 5BB
11-midnight (1am Fri & Sat); 12.30-11 Sun
(01224) 581922
Caledonian Deuchars IPA; Greene King Abbot; Inveralmond Ossian Ale; guest beers
Split-level pub, with bars on both levels, located on Castlegate in the historic centre of the city. Unobtrusive background music plays, but there is no TV. Owned by Belhaven, the Scottish arm of the Greene King chain, two guest beers are usually from the Greene King/Belhaven portfolio and two are independents, mainly from Scottish micro-breweries. The pub has a reputation for good pub food served daily until 9.30pm. Quiz night is the first Tuesday of the month and Wi-fi is free. Occasional themed beer festivals are held. Local CAMRA Pub of the Year 2007.

Prince of Wales

7 St Nicholas Lane, AB10 1HF
10-midnight (1am Fri & Sat); 12-midnight Sun
(01224) 640597
Caledonian 80; Inveralmond Prince of Wales; Theakston Old Peculier; guest beers
A frequent winner of CAMRA's City Pub of the Year and listed in Scottish Heritage Pubs, this is one of the oldest pubs in Aberdeen, with possibly the longest bar in the city. It has a friendly atmosphere and traditional feel. Part of the Belhaven/Greene King empire, the usual suspects are supplemented by a varied selection of Scottish and English ales. Folk music plays on Sunday evening and Monday is quiz night. Good value food is served every lunchtime (until 5pm Sat & Sun) and Monday to Thursday evenings until 8pm. Free Wi-Fi. Q

Quarter Deck Bar Diner

Salvesen Tower, Blaikies Quay, AB11 5PW (next to NorthLink ferry)
11-midnight (8 Sat); closed Sun
(01224) 571523 quarterdeckaberdeen.com
Inveralmond Ossian Ale; guest beer
Next to the ferry terminal for the Orkney and Shetland ferries, this dull brick building at the foot of an office tower block conceals a friendly, well-

SCOTLAND

stocked bar. The two handpumps feature a range of beers, often including one from Timothy Taylor. The pub is busy at lunchtime with workers from harbourside offices and also a popular waiting room prior to ferry departures. It has a pool table and plasma screens for sport. Good value food is served and the pub caters for functions. Wi-Fi available. ❀◐⇌⊟

Under The Hammer

11 North Silver Street, AB10 1RJ (off Golden Square)
✪ 5 (4 Fri, 2 Sat)-midnight (1am Thu-Sat); 5-11 Sun
☎ (01224) 640253
Caledonian Deuchars IPA; Inveralmond Ossian Ale; guest beer Ⓗ
Atmospheric, comfortable and inviting basement pub, next door to an auction house —hence the name. Paintings by local artists are displayed on the walls and for sale if they take your fancy. Convenient for the Music Hall and His Majesty's Theatre, the large noticeboard has posters advertising forthcoming events in town. Guest beers such as Caledonian 80 or Old Speckled Hen tend to contrast in style with the two regulars. Tasteful, quiet background music. ⇌⊟

Aboyne

Boat Inn

Charleston Road, AB34 5EL (N bank of River Dee next to Aboyne Bridge)
✪ 11-2.30, 5-11 (midnight Fri); 11-midnight Sat; 11-11 Sun
☎ (01339) 886137 🌐 boatinnaboyne.co.uk
Taylor Landlord; guest beers Ⓗ
Popular riverside inn with a food-oriented lounge featuring a log-burning stove and spiral staircase leading to the upper dining area. Junior diners (and adults!) may request to see the model train, complete with sound effects, traverse the entire pub at picture-rail height upon completion of their meal. The local Rotary Club regularly meets here. Two guest beers usually come from Scottish micros. Vintage E-type Jaguar hire is available in summer. ⌂❀⊨◐◑⊟♿⛺♣P

Ballater

Prince of Wales

2 Church Square, AB35 5NE
✪ 12-11 (1am Fri & Sat)
☎ (01339) 755877
Caledonian Deuchars IPA; guest beers Ⓗ
Cosy, well-maintained bar in the centre of a tourist village. A wood-burning stove keeps the main bar and adjacent pool room warm on a cold winter's evening. Deuchars is served all year round and two guest ales are added in the peak summer tourist season. Camping and caravanning sites and the golf club are nearby. The bus terminus is next door. The renovated Victorian railway station and museum where the Queen used to alight on her way to Balmoral is one of many local tourist attractions. ⌂◐◑♿⛺⊟

Banchory

Douglas Arms Hotel

22 High Street, AB31 5SR (opp West church)
✪ 11-midnight (1am Fri & Sat); 11-11 Sun
☎ (01330) 822547 🌐 douglasarms.co.uk
Beer range varies Ⓗ
Small hotel offering inexpensive accommodation. The public bar is a classic Scottish long bar with etched windows and vintage mirrors, listed in CAMRA's Scottish Inventory. The separate lounge area is in three parts, divided by former exterior and internal walls. It has recently been upgraded and is primarily used for bar suppers. The bar, pool area and snug all feature plasma TV systems where different sports can be watched. Outside is a large, south-facing decking area, ideal for summer. Two or three guest ales usually come from Scottish micros. ⌂Q♨❀⊨◐◑⊟♿⛺⊟(201,202)♣P

Ravenswood Club (Royal British Legion)

25 Ramsay Road, AB31 5TS
✪ 11-11 (midnight Fri & Sat)
☎ (01330) 822347 🌐 banchorylegion.com
Beer range varies Ⓗ
Large British Legion Club with a comfortable lounge adjoining the pool and TV room and a spacious function room used by local clubs and societies as well as members. Darts and snooker are popular and played most evenings. Two handpumps offer a constantly-changing choice of beers. An elevated terrace has fine views of the Deeside hills. Show your CAMRA membership card or a copy of this Guide for entry as a guest. ❀⊨◐◑♿⛺⊟♣P

Banff

Ship Inn

8 Deveronside, AB45 1HP
✪ 12-midnight (1am Fri & Sat); 12.30-midnight Sun
☎ (01261) 812620
Beer range varies Ⓗ
Historic nautically-themed inn whose interior featured in the film Local Hero. The wood-panelled bar and lounge have sea views through the small windows. A blocked carriage arch hints at the earlier history of the building. A rotating selection of beers comes from major regionals including Greene King, Timothy Taylor and Fuller's. Banff Marina, Duff House Gallery (National Gallery of Scotland) and the Macduff Aquarium are close by, and several golf courses. The pub has fine views across the mouth of the Deveron to Macduff. Nowadays a board suggests the pub is a creche for husbands while wives go shopping. ⌂Q⊟

Catterline

Creel Inn

AB39 2UL (on coast off A92, 5 miles S of Stonehaven) NO868782
✪ 12-3, 6-midnight (1am Fri & Sat); 12-midnight Sun
☎ (01569) 750254 🌐 thecreelinn.co.uk
Beer range varies Ⓗ
Compact village inn in a stunning clifftop location, built in 1838, now incorporating a neighbouring row of fishermen's cottages. Locally caught seafood is a speciality and reservations are recommended if dining. The pub may appear food-oriented, but drinkers are always welcome in the bar, which is a popular local for the surrounding area. A selection of more than 100 specialist bottled beers is available and an extensive selection of whiskies. Crawton Bird Sanctuary lies two miles to the north, and the St Cyrus National Nature Reserve is eight miles to the south. ⌂Q❀◐◑P⊱

Charleston of Aberlour

Mash Tun

8 Broomfield Square, AB38 9QP (follow sign for Speyside Way visitor centre)
12-midnight (12.30am Thu-Sat); 12.30-midnight Sun
(01340) 881771 mashtun-aberlour.com
Cairngorm Trade Winds; guest beer H
Built in 1896 as the Station Bar, this unusual, round-ended building has a light interior featuring extensive use of timber. A pledge in the title deeds allowed a name change if the railway closed but it must revert to Station Bar if a train ever pulls up again outside. The Speyside Way now runs past the door and patrons may drink their ales and enjoy the view on the former station platform. Two beers are served during the high season (July and Aug), otherwise just one, mainly from a Scottish micro. Q

Craigellachie

Highlander Inn

10 Victoria Street, AB38 9SR (on A95)
12-11 (12.30am Fri & Sat)
(01340) 881446 whiskyinn.com
Cairngorm Trade Winds; guest beers H
Picturesque whisky and cask ale bar on Speyside's Whisky Trail, close to the Speyside Way, offering a fine selection of malts and good-value tasting sessions with occasional special promotions. CRAC (Craigellachie Real Ale Club) meets monthly and its members, whose special tankards hang up above the bar, help to choose the pub's guest ales, with the full support of the owners and staff. The area is good for fishing and walking. Opens at 11am for coffee. Q(336)P

Elgin

Muckle Cross

34 High Street, IV30 1BU
11-midnight (1am Fri & Sat); 12.30-11.45 Sun
(01343) 559030
Greene King Abbot; guest beers H
Typical small Wetherspoon's outlet converted from a bicycle repair shop, latterly a Halfords branch. A pleasant long room with ample seating, a family area and a long bar, it can get very busy, particularly at weekends. Five handpumps offer a wide range of beers from national and micro-breweries, including Scottish (particularly Isle of Skye, who brew the house beer). The pub also offers a wide range of malt whiskies from more than 20 local distilleries. Opens at 9am for coffee and breakfast. Q

Sunninghill Hotel

Hay Street, IV30 1NH
12-2.30, 5-11 (12.30am Fri & Sat)
(01343) 547799 sunninghillhotel.com
Beer range varies H
Friendly family-run hotel set in its own grounds in a quiet residential area, very close to the town centre and the railway station. A comfortable lounge includes a dining area and there are additional tables in the conservatory, making it a popular venue for families. Four handpumps serve a variety of beers, often from Scottish micros, and a large selection of whiskies is also on offer. Outside seating is available on the patio.
P

Thunderton House

Thunderton Place, IV30 1BG (off High St)
10-11 (12.30am Fri & Sat); 12.30-11 Sun
(01345) 554920
Caledonian Deuchars IPA; Courage Directors H
Parts of this historic townhouse can be traced back to the 11th century, but most of the building dates from the 17th century. Bonnie Prince Charlie stayed here in 1746 before the Battle of Culloden and his ghost is said to still haunt the house. The bar has ample seating and a big screen TV for sports.

Ellon

Tolbooth

21-23 Station Road, AB41 9AE
12-11 (midnight Thu; 12.30am Fri & Sat); 12.30-11 Sun
(01358) 721308
Greene King Abbot; guest beers H
Large pub popular with a mature clientele, close to the centre of town and refurbished in recent years. It has separate seating areas on split levels and includes an airy conservatory. The range of ales varies depending on availability, but often includes Caledonian Deuchars IPA, Harviestoun Bitter & Twisted and Orkney Dark Island, alongside beers from some larger English breweries. No food is served. A small attic bar is available for meetings. (X50,260)

Inverurie

Edwards

2 West High Street, AB51 3SA
10-11 (midnight Thu; 1am Fri & Sat); 12-11 Sun
(01467) 629788 edwardsinverurie.co.uk
Greene King Abbot; guest beers H
Modern café bar converted from an old hotel several years ago, which has quickly become part of the town circuit. The decor is light and modern with a hint of Art Deco. There is a series of comfortable snugs to relax in while enjoying a snack and browsing the newspapers. Up to two guest beers are available, mainly from Scottish breweries. The upstairs function room doubles as a disco at weekends. Extremely close to the railway station, and buses stop nearby.
(10,305,737)

Lossiemouth

Skerry Brae Hotel

Stotfield Road, IV31 6QS
11-11 (12.30am Fri & Sat); 12-11 Sun
(01343) 812040 skerrybrae.co.uk
Beer range varies H
Modern lounge bar in an old hotel building overlooking the Moray Firth and adjacent to the golf course. Very much a food-based venue, it is popular with families, especially from the nearby RAF base, and the bar walls are adorned with a collection of squadron insignia. The range of three beers tends to come from Scottish micros.
(329)P

Maryculter

Old Mill Inn

South Deeside Road, AB12 5FX (B979/B9077 jct)
11 (12 Sun)-11

SCOTLAND

☎ (01224) 733212 🌐 oldmillinn.co.uk
Caledonian Deuchars IPA; Draught Bass; Taylor Landlord Ⓗ
Small privately-owned hotel dating from 1797 in a rural location close to the river Dee, five miles west of Aberdeen city centre. Real ale is served in the cosy lounge bar, furnished with comfortable sofas, and the adjacent restaurant. The large function room is a popular location for weddings. Close by is the children's attraction Storybook Glen and Blairs College Museum of Catholic history. Fishing may be arranged on the river Dee. A camping and caravan site is at the rear of the hotel. ❀🛏◑⊟⅄P

Methlick

Ythanview Hotel

Main Street, AB41 7DT
11-2.30, 5-11 (1am Fri); 11-12.30am Sat; 11-11 Sun
☎ (01651) 806235 🌐 ythanviewhotel.co.uk
Beer range varies Ⓗ
Comfortable village local with a relaxing restaurant and a welcoming fire. Fundraising events are held here for various community teams, including the famous MCC (Methlick Cricket Club). Good quality local ingredients are used in the competitively priced food, and Jay's special curry with whole chillies is still a challenge worth trying. Beer is mainly from Scottish micros and from the Waverley guest list. Live bands play on the first Saturday of the month and Sky Sports is screened in the public bar. Food is available all day at the weekend.
⛼❀🛏◑⊟🚌⚟

Milltown of Rothiemay

Forbes Arms Hotel

AB54 7LT
12-2.30 (not Mon & Tue), 5-11
☎ (01466) 711248 🌐 forbesarms.co.uk
Beer range varies Ⓗ
Small family-run hotel in a remote, pleasant country location near the River Deveron, with public and lounge bars and a separate dining area. Fishing and shooting activities are nearby. The local folk club host a live session on the second Thursday of the month. Two ales are usually available from various breweries including Brains and Fyne Ales, alongside beers from local supplier Ardo Ales. A smoking area has recently been recently added.
❀🛏◑⊟♿P⚟

Netherley

Lairhillock Inn

AB39 3QS (¥ mile E of B979, signed from B979 and A90)
11-11 (midnight Fri & Sat)
☎ (01569) 730001 🌐 lairhillock.co.uk
Taylor Landlord; guest beer Ⓗ
Rambling building in attractive open countryside. Look out for the INN sign on the roof. The traditional wood-panelled bar is warmed by a large log fire in winter. The lounge has a large conservatory area, popular with families for dining, with breathtaking views whatever the season. A Greene King beer rotates between Abbot, Ruddles and Old Speckled Hen, and the guest beer usually comes from the Cairngorm range. Convenient for the attractions of Aberdeen, Stonehaven and Royal Deeside. ⛼Q❀◑⊟♿P

Oldmeldrum

Redgarth Hotel

Kirk Brae, AB51 0DJ (off A947 towards golf course)
11-2.30, 5-midnight; 12-2.30, 5-11 Sun
☎ (01651) 872353 🌐 redgarth.com
Beer range varies Ⓗ/Ⓖ
Winner of many local CAMRA awards, this renowned hotel has imposing views over the eastern Grampian mountains. A successful blend of popular family restaurant with a marvellous real ale pub, it is appreciated by a dedicated core of regulars who come from miles around to sample the imaginatively chosen beers on offer. During occasional Brewers in Residence evenings, three handpumped ales may be supplemented by many more on gravity. ❀🛏◑⅄🚌(305,325)♣

Peterhead

Cross Keys ✔

23-27 Chapel Street, AB42 1TH
9am-11 (midnight Fri & Sat); 12.30-11 Sun
☎ (01779) 483500
Caledonian Deuchars IPA; Greene King Abbot Ⓗ
A new Wetherspoon's outlet, opened in April 2008. The name comes from a chapel which previously stood on the site, dedicated to St Peter, whose traditional symbol is two crossed keys, symbolising the keys to heaven. Inside, the single long room has the bar towards the front and a large seating area to the rear. There is sheltered outdoor seating with heating. The house beer is Cross Keys, brewed by Isle of Skye brewery, complemented by two guest ales. ❀◑♿🚌🍎⚟

Stonehaven

Marine Hotel 🏆

9-10 Shorehead, AB39 2JY
11-midnight (1am Fri & Sat; 11 winter); 11-midnight (11 winter) Sun
☎ (01569) 762155 🌐 marinehotelstonehaven.co.uk
Caledonian Deuchars IPA; Inveralmond Dunnottar Ale; Taylor Landlord; guest beers Ⓗ
Scottish CAMRA Pub of the Year 2008, and branch Pub of the Year 2009, the hotel is situated on the picturesque harbour front, with an outdoor seating area for drinkers. There is an upstairs restaurant with its own handpumps. The house beer is supplemented by an impressive range of up to five guest beers, mostly from Scottish micros, with some Southern imports, often from Timothy Taylor. An impressive range of imported Belgian bottled beers and continental ales on tap add to the attraction. ⛼❀🛏◑⅄🚌(107,117)⚟

Ship Inn

5 Shorehead, AB39 2JY
11-midnight (1am Fri & Sat)
☎ (01569) 762617 🌐 shipinnstonehaven.com
Beer range varies Ⓗ
Traditional old pub facing the harbour front with an outside seating area providing a good view of the harbour. The wood-panelled bar has a maritime theme, with an original mirror from the long defunct Devanha Brewery on the wall at one end. One pump serves an Inveralmond beer and the other an ever-changing selection. An extensive collection of malt whiskies is also on offer. Food is served in the restaurant and bar, all day at the weekend. ❀🛏◑🚌(107,117)⚟

Tarland

Aberdeen Arms

The Square, AB34 4TX (in village square)
11-1am
(01339) 881225
Beer range varies Ⓗ
Three-hundred-year-old listed building with a roaring coal fire in the public/lounge bar. Pool is played in a side room. Music evenings in the bar on a Tuesday often feature star fiddler and resident of the village, Paul Anderson. Three ales are usually on tap, mostly from Scottish micros, with occasional southern beers making a guest appearance. The pub is now run by the owners of local real ale distributor Ardo Ales, who have plans to further develop the establishment and hold an annual beer festival in spring in the back hall.
♣P

Tarves

Aberdeen Arms Hotel

The Square, AB41 7GX
12-2, 5-11 (1am Fri); 12-12.30 Sat; 12.30-11 Sun
(01651) 851214 geocities.com/aberdeenarmshotel
Beer range varies Ⓗ
Previously a farm, the building became a hotel around the 1860s, and is now a small, family-run community local in the middle of a conservation area. Very much a cheery regulars' establishment, it is renowned for its warm welcome to visitors. A wide range of good value, home-cooked food is available. The location is convenient for visiting Tolquhon Castle and Pitmedden Gardens which were laid out in the 17th century by Sir Alexander Seddon, with elaborate flower beds, fountains and pavilions. Beers may be from Cairngorm and Highland breweries. Q(290,291)♣

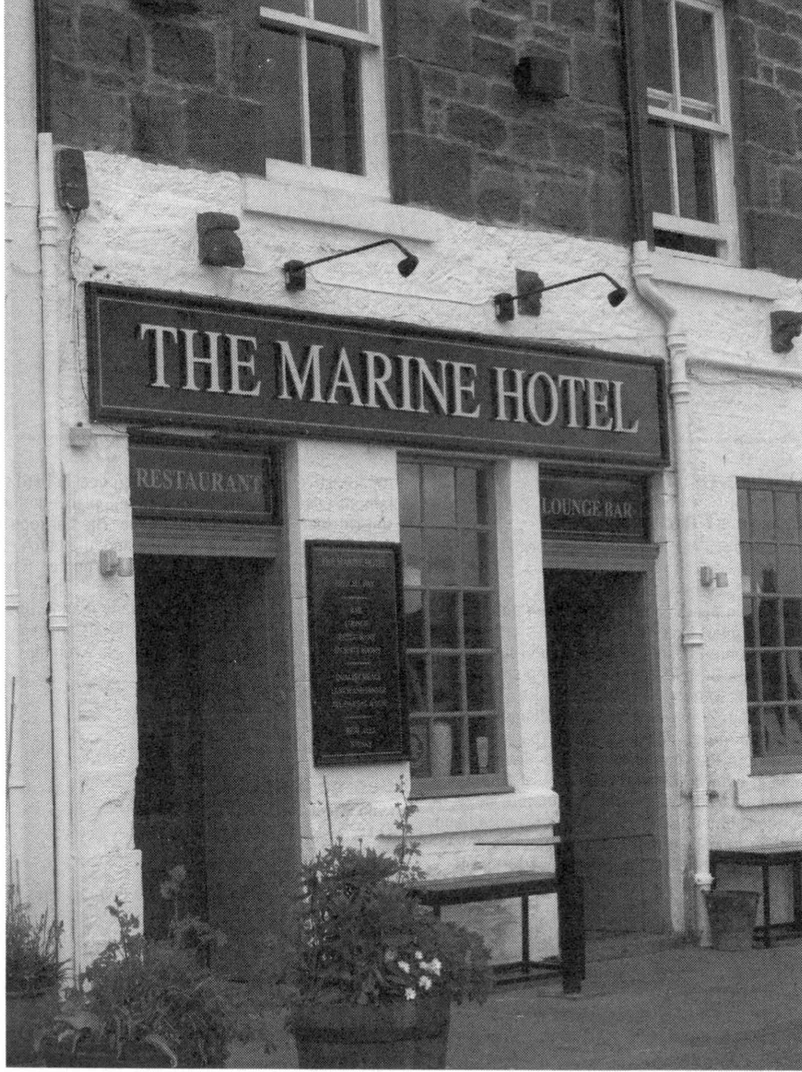

Marine Hotel, Stonehaven.

ARGYLL & THE ISLES

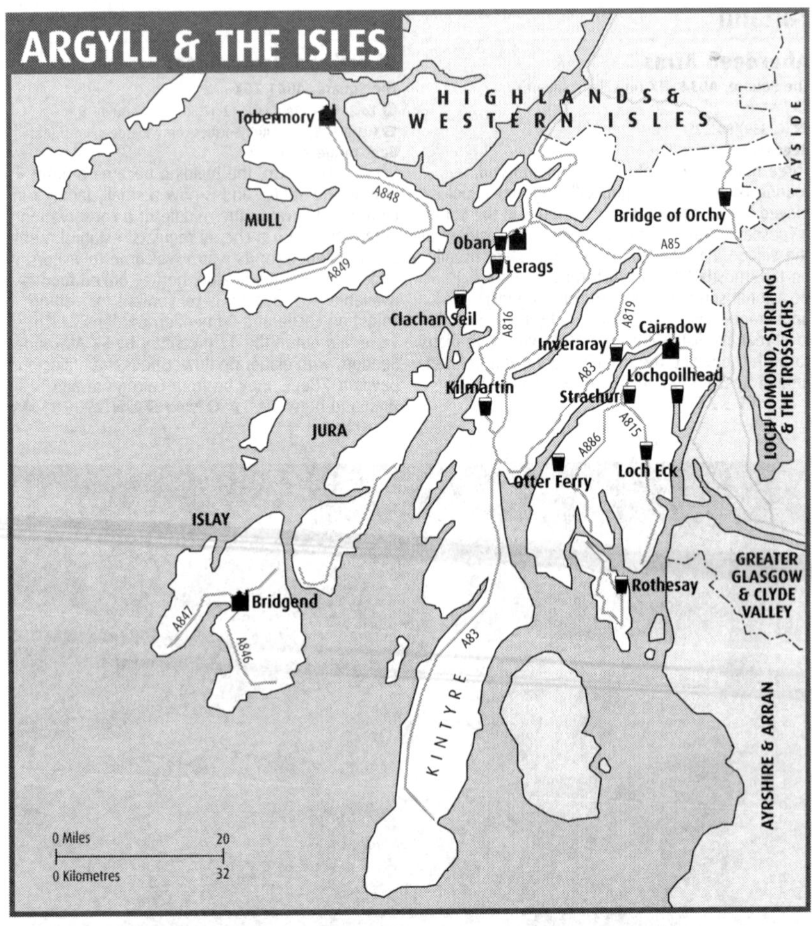

Bridge of Orchy

Bridge of Orchy Hotel ✔

PA36 4AD (on A82 at N end of Glen Orchy) NN298395
11-11 (midnight Fri & Sat); 12.30-11 Sun
☎ (01838) 400208 bridgeoforchy.co.uk
Caledonian Deuchars IPA; Harviestoun Bitter & Twisted; guest beers Ⓗ
White-fronted building on the main route to the Highlands. Despite being set among stunning mountain scenery, it is well served by buses and trains from Glasgow. An archway leads from the front room overlooking the main road to the rear bar where the counter sports three handpumps serving two regular ales plus a guest. The rear restaurant windows provide panoramic views. A hub for numerous outdoor activities and a handy stop for tourists. It may close temporarily in winter so phone ahead. Q(914)**P**

Clachan Seil

Tigh an Truish

Isle of Seil by Oban, PA34 4QZ (on B844 5 miles W of A816 jct, by Clachan Bridge) NM785197
11-11 summer and winter Sat; 11-2.30, 5-11 winter; 12-11 Sun
☎ (01852) 300242 tighantruish.co.uk
Beer range varies Ⓗ
An attractive pub in an idyllic setting near Telford's famous Clachan Bridge, with climbing plants and a sun-catching beer garden and patio. The bar room is rustic with much wood, a piano and 'the perch' – an unusual style of seating – near the counter. Bay windows overlook the bridge and sound. There is also a snug room. Fyne Ales regularly feature on the two handpumps. Popular with locals and a 'must stop' for visitors to the area. No evening meals are available in winter.
Q(418)**P**

Inveraray

George Hotel

Main Street East, PA32 8TT
11-midnight (12.30am Fri & Sat); 12-midnight Sun
☎ (01499) 302111 thegeorgehotel.co.uk
Beer range varies Ⓗ
As full of character as picturesque Inverary, this whitewashed hotel has a number of separate rooms with wood panelling and stone floors. 2010

INDEPENDENT BREWERIES

Fyne Cairndow
Islay Bridgend
Isle of Mull Tobermory
Oban Bay Oban (NEW)

marks the 150th anniversary of ownership in the same hands, with the fifth, sixth and seventh generations of the family currently running it. In the past it has also doubled as a church, with a Gaelic congregation in the lounge and English in the bar! The local Fyne Brewery ales feature strongly among the guest beers.
Q(926,976)P

Kilmartin

Kilmartin Hotel

PA31 8RQ (on A816 10 miles N of Lochgilphead) NR 835 989
12 (5pm winter)-11 (1am Fri & Sat); 12-midnight Sun
(01546) 510250 kilmartin-hotel.com
Caledonian Deuchars IPA, 80; guest beers H
A gem in the glen, this charming family-run hotel is an ideal base to explore the history and location. It is surrounded by stunning scenery, standing stones, burial mounds and stone carvings dating from 5000 years ago – all is explained at the local museum. The cosy bar serves two regular ales plus, in summer, a guest from a local micro. There are separate rooms for dining and playing pool. Food is available 12-2.20pm and 6-9pm.
Q(423)P

Lerags

Barn

Cologin, Lerags, Argyll, PA34 4SE (down minor road off A816, 2 miles S of Oban) NM854260
12 (5 winter Thu, Fri & Mon)-midnight; closed winter Tue & Wed; 12-midnight Sun
(01631) 571313
Fyne Highlander; guest beers H
Although within walking distance of the bustling town of Oban in good weather, this converted farm building has an isolated, almost wilderness feel to it. Yet, as well as being extremely popular with summer visitors, it has a surprisingly large local trade. Set amongst attractive Highland scenery and close to a rugged, rocky coastline, it is a centre for fishing, forestry walks and wildlife trails. The Highlander is usually accompanied by another Fyne beer or Caledonian Deuchars IPA. P

Loch Eck

Coylet Inn

PA23 8SG (on A815 near S end of Loch Eck) NS143885
11-11 (midnight Fri & Sat); closed Mon & Tue winter; 12-10.30 Sun
(01369) 840426 coylet-locheck.co.uk
Beer range varies H
The cosy bar room has a wooden corner counter serving Fyne Ales on up to three handpumps and a stone, log-burning fireplace. Old black and white and sepia photographs decorate the walls. The strong-armed might like to attempt the 'kettle challenge'. Varied food menus offer local game, seafood, traditional and modern, gluten-free and children's dishes in the bar and more formal restaurant which has views of the scenic loch and mountains. The restaurant can be busy so ring ahead if dining. (484)P

Whistlefield Inn

Loch Eck, Argyll & Bute, PA23 8SG NS144933
12.30-11
(01369) 860440 whistlefield.com
Beer range varies H
This inn, on a minor road off the A815, attracts 'locals' from 60 miles away. The cellar dates from the 15th century and the beers in the bar come from Fyne, Kelburn, Atlas and Orkney, on up to three handpumps. A large cow's head looms over the stove. Seating is bench style plus bar stools, while a side room provides comfy sofas. The windows in the large restaurant and family room provide views over Loch Eck. A folk band plays on the first Friday of the month. P

Lochgoilhead

Shore House Inn

PA24 8AD (at head of Loch Goil) NN198015
12 (12.30 Sun)-midnight (hours vary in winter)
(01301) 703340 theshorehouse.net
Fyne Highlander; guest beers H
An old manse building at the head of Loch Goil. Beer is served from two handpumps in the cosy bar, which often hosts local musicians. Pints can be taken out to the terrace and lawn right on the loch shoreline to watch sailing, fishing and wildlife in a magnificent landscape. Or enjoy the same views from a window seat in the modern restaurant, which serves excellent freshly-cooked meals, including pizzas from a wood-fired oven.
Q(484,486)P

Oban

Tartan Tavern

Albany Terrace, George Street, PA34 5NY
11-midnight (1am Fri & Sat)
(01631) 562118
Beer range varies H
This cosy locals' bar is situated in a small street, set back from the north harbour waterfront. It certainly lives up to its name, with tartan carpets and tartan upholstered walls, square column and seats around the walls. In addition there are stools for the bar and windowsills, allowing views of the street. Two TVs show sporting fixtures, otherwise there is low level music.

Otter Ferry

Oystercatcher

Tighnabruaich, PA21 2DH (on B8000 on E coast of Loch Fyne) NR930845
11-1am; closed Tue & Wed winter
(01700) 821229 theoystercatcher.co.uk
Fyne Highlander; guest beers H
Attractive pub near a former ferry dock. Patrons can play chess or giant Jenga in the light, spacious bar with a divided snug area. Up to three beers come from Fyne Ales plus guests. Large windows here and in the restaurant provide scenic views of Loch Fyne and the Knapdale/Kintyre peninsula beyond. The garden leads to a beach, popular for swimming and boating in the summer. The food and leisure facilities draw visitors from near and far.
P

Rothesay: Isle of Bute

Black Bull Inn

3 West Princess Street, PA20 9AF (on promenade opp marina)
11 -11 (midnight Fri,Sat); 12.30-11 Sun
(01700) 502366

Caledonian Deuchars IPA; Greene King Abbot Ⓗ
Situated opposite the new marina, the pub is popular with yachtsmen and the first point of call for ale-thirsty arrivals. The front entrance is handy to quaff one more pint before a ferry dash, though do not miss the luxuriously restored Victorian public conveniences en route. An olden-days inn with many charming features, the pub is loosely divided into separate rooms where you can sit or stand to enjoy a beer and good food. Well worth a day trip from Wemyss Bay.

Strachur

Creggans Inn

PA27 8BX (on A815 Cairndow-Dunoon road, near A886 jct) NN087022

11 (12 Sun)-midnight
(01369) 860279 creggans-inn.co.uk
Beer range varies Ⓗ
This whitewashed inn is a convenient stopping place along Loch Fyne. The main room is divided by a stone wall and has a wood burning fire. On one side the corner bar serves two beers mainly from Fyne Ales and has a TV for sports. On the other, upholstered furniture creates a lounge feel, and a pool room lies beyond. The pub is the HQ for local shinty teams and photographs line the walls. There is a restaurant to the rear.
(484,486)P

Scottish beer

Just as monks call their Lenten beers 'liquid bread', it's tempting to call traditional Scottish ales 'liquid porridge'. They are beers brewed for a cold climate, a country in which beer vies with whisky (uisge breatha – water of life) for nourishment and sustenance.

Brewers blend not only darker malts such as black and chocolate with paler grains, but also add oats, that staple of many foodstuffs in the country. In common with the farmer-brewers of the Low Countries and French Flanders in earlier centuries, domestic brewers in Scotland tended to use whatever grains, herbs and plants were available to make beer. The intriguing use of heather in the Fraoch range of ales recalls brewing practice in Scotland from bygone times.

Domestic: The industrial revolution arrived later in Scotland than in England, and industry tended to concentrate in the Lowland belt around Alloa, Edinburgh and Glasgow. As a result, brewing remained a largely domestic affair for much longer and – as with early Irish ales – made little use of the hop, which could not grow in such inhospitable climes.

Brewing developed on a commercial scale in the Lowlands in the early 19th century at the same time as many French emigres, escaping the revolution, settled in the Scottish capital. They dubbed the rich, warming local ales 'Scottish Burgundy'. Real wine from France, always popular in Scotland as a result of the Auld Alliance, become scarce during the Napoleonic Wars, and commercial brewing grew rapidly to fill the gap and to fuel the needs of a growing class of thirsty industrial workers.

Different: Traditionally, Scottish ales were brewed in a different manner to English ones. Before refrigeration, beer was fermented at ambient temperatures far lower than in England. As a result, not all the sugars turned to alcohol, producing rich, full-bodied ales. As hops had to be imported from England at considerable cost, they were used sparingly. The result was a style of beer markedly different to English ones: vinous, fruity, malty and with only a gentle hop bitterness.

Many of the new breed of ales produced by micro-brewers in Scotland tend to be paler and more bitter than used to be the norm. For the true taste of traditional Scottish ales you will have to sample the products of the likes of Belhaven, Broughton, Caledonian and Traquair.

Complexities: The language of Scottish beers is different, too. The equivalent to English Mild is called Light (even when it's dark in colour), standard Bitter is called Heavy, Premium Bitter, Export; while strong old ales and barley wines (now rare) are called Wee Heavies.

To add to the complexities of the language differences, many traditional beers incorporate the word Shilling in their names. A Light may be dubbed 60 Shilling, a Heavy 70 Shilling, an Export 80 Shilling, and a Wee Heavy 90 Shilling. The designations stem from a pre-decimalisation method of invoicing beer in Victorian times. The stronger the beer, the higher the number of shillings.

Until recent times, cask-conditioned beer in Scotland was served by air pressure. In the pub cellar a water engine, which looks exactly the same as a lavatory cistern but works in reverse, used water to produce air pressure that drove the beer to the bar. Sadly, these wonderful Victorian devices are rarely seen, and the Sassenach handpump and beer engine dominate the pub scene.

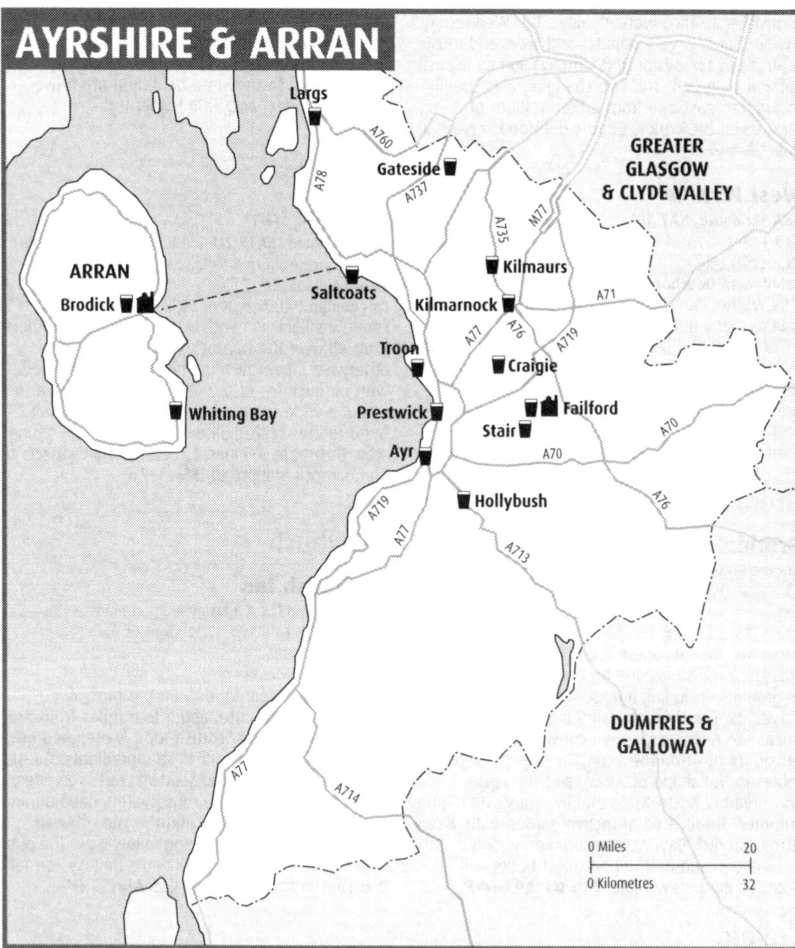

Ayr

Chestnuts Hotel

52 Racecourse Road, KA7 2UZ (A719, 1 Mile S of centre)
11-midnight (12.30am Sat); 12-midnight
(01292) 264393 chestnutshotel.com
Beer range varies H
This hotel was once a centre for the town's Jewish community. It has a warm, comfortable lounge bar with a wood-panelled ceiling and an unusual collection of water jugs. The two real ales vary constantly, from both local and national breweries. The meals are of a very high standard, served in the bar area or restaurant. Handy for the seafront and golf courses. (A9)P

Geordie's Byre

103 Main Street, KA8 8BU
11-11 (midnight Thu-Sat); 12.30-11 Sun
(01292) 264925
Beer range varies A
This CAMRA award-winning gem of a pub serves up to four guest ales sourced from far and near. The owners have reigned supreme for more than 30 years. Both the public bar and the lounge feature a wealth of memorabilia. A wide range of malt whiskies and rums is also available. (Newton-on-Ayr)

Glen Park Hotel

5 Racecourse Road, KA7 2DG
10-12.30; 12-midnight Sun
(01292) 263891 glenparkhotel.com
Beer range varies H
This hotel is in an 1860s B-Listed Victorian residence at the corner of Miller and Racecourse roads, midway between the seafront and the station. The lounge bar has an open fire within a magnificent mahogany surround. There is a restaurant and 21 en-suite rooms. The two cask ales vary, with an emphasis on English bitters. (A9)P

Wellingtons Bar

17 Wellington Square, KA7 1EZ
11-12.30; 12.30-midnight Sun
(01292) 262794 wellingtonsayr.co.uk
Beer range varies H
A large Wellington boot advertises the location of this basement bar. Close to the seafront, bus station and local government offices, it attracts

INDEPENDENT BREWERIES

Arran Brodick
Windie Goat Failford

tourists and office workers alike. The Wednesday evening quiz is very popular and weekend music features live bands or DJ (Saturday) and an acoustic session (Sunday). The two changing ales usually include at least one from either Kelburn or Strathaven breweries. Good value food served all day.

West Kirk

58A Sandgate, KA7 1BX
9-12.30am; 9-midnight Sun
(01292) 880416
Caledonian Deuchars IPA; guest beers H
This Wetherspoon's conversion of a former church retains many of the original features – access to the toilets is via the pulpit. Up to six changing guest ales are offered and local micros are usually well represented. Meals are available all day, with breakfast from 9am. The pub is centrally located and close to the bus station. The front patio drinking area has a smoking shelter.

Brodick: Isle of Arran

Ormidale Hotel

Knowe Road, KA27 8BY (off A841 at W end of village)
12-2.30 (not winter), 4.30-midnight; 12-midnight Sat & Sun
(01770) 302293 ormidale-hotel.co.uk
Arran Ale, Blonde; guest beers A
This large red sandstone hotel is set in seven acres of grounds, including a large wooded area. The bar serves its ales through traditional tall founts. Beer prices are rather expensive considering the proximity of Arran Brewery. The public bar has tables in the shape of Arran, and the large conservatory hosts discos and live music during the summer. There is an attractive garden with views across Brodick Bay. Accommodation is only available in summer, when guest beers will occasionally be available. P

Craigie

Craigie Inn

5 Main Street, KA1 5LY (signed off B730)
12-2, 5-midnight (11 Sat & Sun)
(01563) 860286
Beer range varies H
Built in 1604, this welcoming village inn is a listed building still maintaining some of the original features. Both the real ales and the food are sourced locally – the beer comes from the Strathaven and Houston breweries, and the food menu features imaginative dishes. A folk club meets monthly, featuring jam sessions with local musicians and singers. There is a pool table and dartboard. The pub is not accessible by public transport. Q P

Failford

Failford Inn

KA5 5TF (on B743 Mauchline-Ayr road)
12-11 (12.30am Fri & Sat); 12-midnight Sun
(01292) 540117 failfordinn.co.uk
Beer range varies H
Small country inn with two rooms featuring low ceilings and an old tiled range, a dining room and a garden overlooking the River Ayr. Meals are prepared by the owner, with an emphasis on freshly-cooked local produce, while his wife brews the award-winning Windie Goat beers – at least one is available in the bar. A good starting point for the River Ayr Walk through a dramatic gorge. Regular beer festivals are held, and often live music on Friday. Q (43)

Gateside

Gateside Inn

39 Main Road, KA15 2LF (on B777 1 mile E of Beith)
11-11 (midnight Fri & Sat); 12.30-11
(01505) 503362
Caledonian Deuchars IPA, 80 H
Friendly village inn with a wide mix of customers from all over the Garnock Valley, which is otherwise a beer desert. The walls are adorned with old pictures of the village and the pub also stocks a wide range of bottled beers and malts. Good food is served all day in the bar and dining area. Bus route 337 passes nearby and connects to Glengarnock Station. (337)P

Hollybush

Hollybush Inn

KA6 6EY (on A713 Ayr-Dalmellington road)
11-11 (1am Fri & Sat); 12.30-midnight Sun
(01292) 560580
Beer range varies H
A modernised country pub on the main Ayr-Galloway tourist route, about four miles from Ayr Hospital. Traditional Scottish food is prepared on the premises made with fresh ingredients. Guest beers are normally from Scottish craft breweries, particularly Houston. The conservatory has stunning views of the Carrick Hills and the Isle of Arran. There is a strong motor racing following in the pub, with memorabilia in the bar and a fantasy Formula One season for locals. (52)P

Kilmarnock

Brass & Granite

53 Grange Street, KA1 2DD
11-midnight (12.30am Thu-Sat); 12.30-midnight Sun
(01563) 523431
Beer range varies H
Open-plan town centre pub in a quiet street behind the main post office, popular with a varied clientele. Guest beers tend to be from Scotland or Cumbria, and Belgian fruit beers are available on draught as well as a variety of bottled ales. Food is served all day. There are several large-screen TVs showing sporting events. A pub quiz is held on Sunday, Monday and Wednesday.

Wheatsheaf Inn

70 Portland Street, KA1 1JG
9-11 (midnight Thu & Sun; 1am Fri & Sat)
(01563) 572483
Caledonian Deuchars IPA; Greene King Abbot; guest beers H
Large town-centre Lloyd's No.1 pub situated a short walk from the bus and rail stations. It has various seating areas including booths, sofas and a raised dining space. No music plays daytime Monday to Wednesday, but a live DJ entertains on Friday and Saturday.

Kilmaurs

Weston Tavern

27 Main Street, KA3 2RQ
⏲ 11-midnight (1am Fri & Sat); 12.30-midnight Sun
☎ (01563) 538805 🌐 westontavern.co.uk
Beer range varies Ⓗ
Housed in the former manse of noted reformist minister David Smeaton, a contemporary of Robert Burns, this is a classic country pub and restaurant. It sits beside the jougs (an iron collar padlocked around an offender's neck), the distinctive former jailhouse and tollbooth. The public bar features a tiled floor, stone walls and a wood-burning fire, and hosts live music on the last Saturday of the month. ⛰❀◐◑⊟♿⇌🚌(1,337)♣

Largs

MacAulays

85-87 Main Street, KA30 8AJ
⏲ 11-midnight (1am Fri & Sat); 12.30-midnight Sun
☎ (01475) 687359
Beer range varies Ⓗ
Situated on the main street of this popular Clyde Coast town, this is a friendly one-room pub opposite the railway station. It is also on main bus routes and close to the ferry to Cumbrae. Real ales are from the Belhaven guest list. There is also a good range of malt whiskies on offer. A simple menu of good, honest home-cooked food is available all day. The pub gets lively at weekends. ◐◑♿⇌🚌(585,901)♣⚡

Prestwick

Central Bar

56-58 Main Street, KA9 1NX
⏲ 10-midnight (12.30am Fri & Sat)
☎ (01292) 670454
Beer range varies Ⓗ
Traditional local on the main road through Prestwick. The small bar is adorned with photographs depicting Prestwick in a bygone era, and there is a lounge to the rear. The pub is handy for Prestwick Airport and Prestwick Golf Club where the first Open Championship was held. It is popular with visiting golfers and locals alike.
♞⊟♿⛺⇌🚌♣

Saltcoats

Salt Cot ✔

7 Hamilton Street, KA21 5DS
⏲ 10-11 (midnight Thu-Sat); 12.30-11 Sun
☎ (01294) 465924
Caledonian Deuchars IPA; Greene King Abbot; guest beers Ⓗ
An excellent Wetherspoon's conversion of a former cinema, decorated with photos of the cinema in its heyday and old Saltcoats. Children are allowed in one area and there is a family menu. The pub's name comes from the original cottages at the salt pans. Licensed from 10am, it opens at 9am for breakfast. Q◐◑♿⇌🚌

Stair

Stair Inn

KA5 5HW (B730, 7 miles E of Ayr)
⏲ 12-11 (1am Fri & Sat); 12.30-11 Sun
☎ (01292) 591650 🌐 stairinn.co.uk
Beer range varies Ⓗ
Family-run inn nestling at the foot of a glen on the banks of the River Ayr. The bar, with an open log fire, and restaurant have bespoke hand-made furniture and the bedrooms are furnished in similar style. Built around 1700, it serves a widespread area and is very close to the historic Stair Bridge. The food is locally sourced and the home-smoked fish platter is recommended. Houston beers are regulars. ⛰Q❀🛏◐◑♿P⚡

Troon

Ardneil Hotel

51 St Meddans Street, KA10 6NU (next to station)
⏲ 11-midnight (11 Sun)
☎ (01292) 311611 🌐 ardneil-hotel.co.uk
Fuller's London Pride; guest beers Ⓗ
Family-run hotel next to Troon station and a three-wood drive from three municipal golf courses and the town centre. The two guest ales are often from local micro-breweries. The bar hosts a Wednesday night quiz and regular inter-pub pool competitions. The hotel is popular with locals, tourists and golfers from across Europe who arrive via nearby Prestwick Airport. There is a large beer garden.
❀🛏◐◑⇌🚌(14,110)P⚡

Bruce's Well

91 Portland Street, KA10 6QN
⏲ 12-12.30am; 12.30-midnight Sun
☎ (01292) 311429
Caledonian Deuchars IPA; guest beers Ⓗ
Friendly, spacious and comfortable lounge bar close to Troon town centre, serving two guest ales from the Belhaven list. The bar benefits from a temperature-controlled cellar, situated next door. Major sporting events are shown on a number of flat-screen TVs and the pub gets extremely busy during big matches. Live music nights are hosted occasionally. ⇌🚌(10,14/14E,110)⚡

Harbour Bar

169 Templehill, KA10 6BH (opp P&O ferry terminal)
⏲ 11-12.30; 12.30-midnight Sun
☎ (01292) 312668
Beer range varies Ⓗ
Overlooking Troon's North Bay, a central bar serves the nautically-themed lounge and public bars, decorated with pictures and artefacts from the now closed Ailsa shipyard. Two real ales are served, mostly from local breweries. A good range of malt whiskies and rums is also available. The public bar has a pool table and a well-stocked jukebox, the lounge bar has a dartboard. Popular meals are served throughout the day. CAMRA Branch Pub of the Year 2007. ◐◑⊟♿🚌(10,15,110)♣P

Whiting Bay: Isle of Arran

Eden Lodge Hotel

KA27 8QH
⏲ 12-midnight (1am Thu-Sat); 12.30-midnight Sun
☎ (01770) 700357 🌐 edenlodgehotel.co.uk
Caledonian Deuchars IPA Ⓗ
Bar Eden is the hotel's large, bright public bar with superb views across the bay to Holy Island. Home-cooked bar meals featuring local produce are available all day until 9pm except mid-week winter afternoons. A basement area has pool, TV and juke box. Winter hours may be restricted.
⛰♞❀🛏◐◑⊟🚌(323)♣P⚡

SCOTLAND

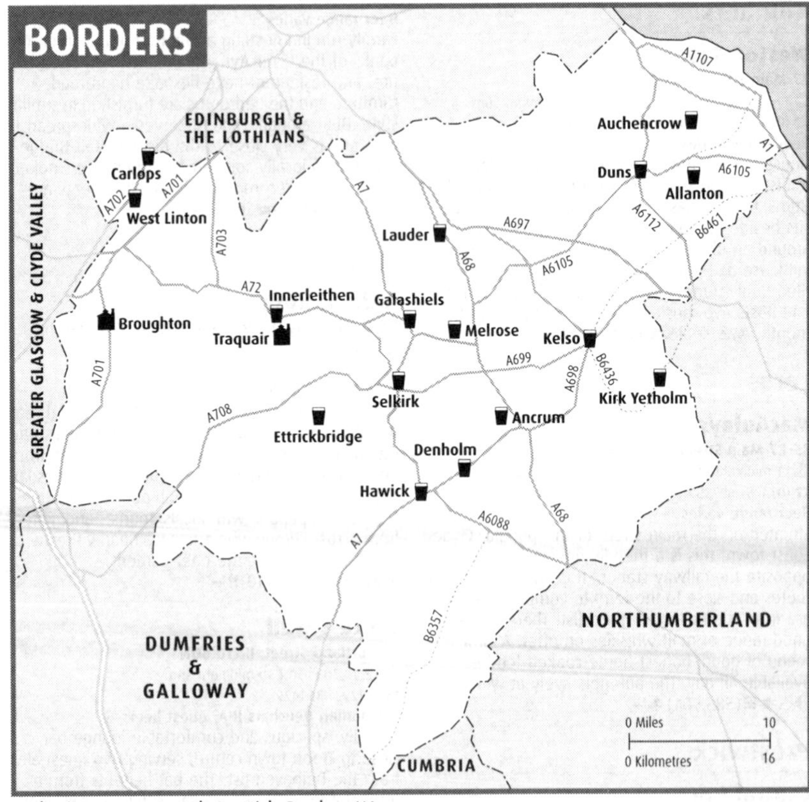

Authority area covered: Scottish Borders UA

Allanton

Allanton Inn

TD11 3JZ

12-2 (not Mon & Tue), 6-10.30 (11 Tue, Fri & Sat; not Sun & Mon)

(01890) 818260 allantoninn.co.uk

Beer range varies Ⓗ

A friendly welcome is assured at this Borders coaching inn dating back to the 18th century – for those arriving by horse there are hitching rings by the door. The front rooms are used for dining and offer good quality food. The bar at the back has recently been refurbished in a unique lounge style and always offers an interesting real ale or two. Accommodation is available for those looking for a base to explore Berwickshire and Northumbria. Dogs are welcome. Q P

Ancrum

Cross Keys Inn

The Green, TD8 6XH (on B6400, off A68)

12-2.30 (not Mon), 6-11 (5-1am Fri); 12-midnight Sat; 12.30-11 Sun

(01835) 830344 ancrumcrosskeys.co.uk

Beer range varies Ⓗ

Friendly village local with a tiny bar that remains almost untouched since 1908. It retains the original pine panelling through onto the gantry, has compact seating and tables made from old sewing machines. The two back lounges have been sympathetically refurbished, one retaining overhead tramlines from the former cellar. Beers from Broughton and An Teallach feature regularly. Children are welcome and dogs are permitted in the bar. Free Wi-Fi access.

Q (25,68) P

Auchencrow

Craw Inn

TD14 5LS (signed from A1)

12-2.30, 6-11 (midnight Fri); 12-midnight Sat; 12.30-11 Sun

(01890) 761253 thecrawinn.co.uk

Beer range varies Ⓗ

This friendly 17th-century village inn is very much the hub of the community. The traditional single bar features beams festooned with pump clips, a wood-burning stove, numerous tables and ample seating. Excellent home cooked food is served every day in both the bar and restaurant. Summer drinking and dining can be enjoyed on the new decking. Children are welcome. Joint winner of local CAMRA Pub of the Year 2009, it holds a beer festival in November. Q P

INDEPENDENT BREWERIES

Broughton Broughton
Traquair Traquair

Carlops

Allan Ramsay Hotel
Main Street, EH26 9NF
12-11 (1am Fri & Sat); 12.30-midnight Sun
☎ (01968) 660258 allanramsayhotel.com
Caledonian Deuchars IPA; guest beer
Hotel in a small village beside the Pentland Hills, dating from 1792. Several rooms have been knocked through into a single area, retaining many original features. Tartan upholstery gives a Scottish feel. One end is a restaurant, the central part is a bar area and a pool table occupies the far end. The bar is inlaid with pre-decimal pennies. Children and dogs are welcome and food is served all day. Free Wi-Fi access available. ♣P

Denholm

Auld Cross Keys Hotel
Main Street, TD9 8NU
11 (12.30 Sun)-11 (1am Fri & Sat)
☎ (01450) 870305 crosskeysdenholm.co.uk
Beer range varies
Overlooking the village green, this small hotel retains the character of an inn. The plain and functional public bar is favoured by drinkers, however there is also a more comfortable lounge bar for relaxed drinking. The beer is from either Hadrian & Border, Northumberland or Inveralmond. Folk music sessions and concerts are regular events. Children are welcome, but dogs only permitted in the bar. Bedrooms are of a good standard. Q(20)♣P

Duns

Black Bull Hotel
15 Black Bull Street, TD11 3AR
11 (12 Sun)-midnight (1am Fri & Sat)
☎ (01361) 883379 blackbullhotelduns.com
Caledonian Deuchars IPA; guest beers
Family-run 200-year-old hotel just off the town square. The cosy wood-panelled front bar is popular with locals and the lounge area, with bench seating, is more suited to families. There is also a traditional restaurant, specialising in fresh fish, which has an intimate, relaxed and candlelit atmosphere. The secluded beer garden is pleasant in summer. Dogs are welcome in bar. Free Wi-Fi access. The letting rooms are all named after local historical figures. ♣P

Ettrickbridge

Cross Keys Inn
TD7 5JN
12 (12.30 Sun)-2.30, 6.30-10.30 (11 Thu-Sat); closed Mon-Wed winter
☎ (01750) 52224 cross-keys-inn.co.uk
Beer range varies
Seventeenth-century inn located in the historic Ettrick valley. The cosy and welcoming bar and adjacent dining room are decorated with old photographs, water jugs and the odd stuffed animal. There is a strong emphasis on quality food so tables are set for meals. However the bar stools remain popular and there is a smaller room available for drinkers. The real ales are often from smaller Scottish breweries such as Broughton and Inveralmond. Children are welcome.
Q♣P

Galashiels

Hunter's Hall
56 High Street, TD1 1SE
9 (12.30 Sun)-midnight (1am Thu-Sat)
☎ (01896) 759795 jdwetherspoon.co.uk
Caledonian Deuchars IPA; Greene King Abbot; guest beers
Originally built as a church, this is now a typical Wetherspoon's pub. Set on two levels, at the front is a family area with paintings by local artists on the walls. (Note that children are only welcome if they are eating.) The spacious main bar area has a bare stone wall, trellis ceiling and historic photos of Galashiels. There is some booth seating as well as high tables and stools. Food is served all day and Wi-Fi access is free.

Salmon Inn
54 Bank Street, TD1 1EP
11-11 (midnight Thu; 1am Fri & Sat); 12.30-midnight Sun
☎ (01896) 752577
Caledonian Deuchars IPA; guest beers
A comfortable, friendly, centrally situated pub which can be very lively when sports events are screened on TV. The L-shaped room is decorated with historic photographs of the Galashiels area. Guest beers are often from smaller Scottish and English breweries. Good home-cooked meals are popular (no food Sun or Tue and Sat eves). Children are welcome at lunchtime only. Dogs are also permitted. ♣

Hawick

Callaghan's Sports Bar
20-22 High Street, TD9 9EH
12 (12.30 Sun)-midnight (1am Fri & Sat)
☎ (01450) 379679
Beer range varies
Bare wooden floors and sturdy wooden furniture give this popular high street pub a rustic feel. The half-panelled walls are decorated with rugby and football jerseys. TV screens favour horse racing, but other sports are also shown. There is live music at weekends and a quiz on Thursday. The beer range varies but Taylor Landlord is a favourite. Children are welcome until 8pm and dogs are permitted.
(72,X95)♣

Innerleithen

St Ronan's Hotel
High Street, EH44 6HF
11 (12 Sun)-midnight (12.45am Fri & Sat)
☎ (01896) 831487 stronanshotel.co.uk
Beer range varies
This village hotel takes its name from a local Saint. The functional public bar is long and thin and has a brick and wooden fireplace. There are two alcoves, one with seating, the other with a dartboard and a photograph of the village on the wall. A room with a pool table leads off from the bar. Food is served in summer only. A pick-up service is available for Southern Upland Way walkers. Children and dogs are welcome and there is Wi-Fi access.
(62)♣

Traquair Arms Hotel
Traquair Road, EH44 6PD (B709, off A72)
11-11 (midnight Fri & Sat); 12-11.30 Sun
☎ (01896) 830229 traquairarmshotel.co.uk

SCOTLAND

Caledonian Deuchars IPA; Taylor Landlord; Traquair Bear Ale Ⓗ
Elegant 18th-century hotel in the scenic Tweed Valley. The comfortable lounge bar features a welcoming real fire in winter and a relaxing tropical fish tank. An Italian bistro area and restaurant provide plenty of room for diners. Food is served all day at weekends. One of the few outlets for draught ales from Traquair House. Children are welcome. ⛰❀🛏◐◑⛺🚌(62)P

Kelso

Cobbles Inn

7 Bowmont Street, TD5 7JH (off NE side of town square)
11 (12.30 Sun)-3, 5-10 (1am Fri); 11-midnight Sat
☎ (01573) 223548 🌐 thecobblesinn.co.uk
Beer range varies Ⓗ
Completely refurbished in 2008, this award-winning gastro pub has a main dining area and a small lounge bar with a huge fireplace. The two handpumps offer a choice of interesting ales from both sides of the border. Menus feature an eclectic mix of British gastro pub classics, Pacific Rim and modern European cuisine, made with the finest locally sourced and seasonal ingredients. Private functions are catered for upstairs. Children are welcome. ⛰❀◐◑♿🚌(20,55,67)

Kirk Yetholm

Border Hotel 🏆

The Green, TD5 8PQ
11 (12 Sun)-midnight (1am Fri & Sat); 12-11 winter
☎ (01573) 420237 🌐 theborderhotel.co.uk
Beer range varies Ⓗ
This 260-year-old coaching inn is a mecca for walkers, situated at the beginning/end of the Pennine Way and on the ancient St Cuthbert's Way. The walls of the wood-beamed bar are adorned with photographs of local gypsies and friezes showing country pursuits. There are also some smaller rooms and a conservatory dining area. Bedrooms have been rebuilt following a fire in 2006. Dogs (in the bar only) and children are welcome. CAMRA Edinburgh & SE Scotland Pub of the Year 2009. ⛰❀🛏◐◑⛺🚌♣P

Lauder

Black Bull Hotel

Market Place, TD2 6SR
11 (12.30 Sun)-11 (midnight Fri & Sat)
☎ (01578) 722208 🌐 blackbull-lauder.com
Beer range varies Ⓗ
A changing range of beers, including some rare for the area from breweries south of the border, can be enjoyed along with excellent food at this well-appointed coaching inn. The small wood-panelled bar, adorned with artefacts and retaining much of the character of yester-year, leads to a lounge and various dining areas. Dogs and children are welcome. Free Wi-Fi access.
Q❀🛏◐◑♿⛺🚌(29)♣P

Melrose

George & Abbotsford Hotel

High Street, TD6 9PD
11 (12 Sun)-11 (midnight Fri & Sat)
☎ (01896) 822308 🌐 georgeandabbotsford.co.uk
Beer range varies Ⓗ
Spacious hotel overlooking the main street. The comfortable bar and lounges offer real ales from a wide selection of Scottish and lesser known English breweries. There is also a small shop selling a range of bottled beers. Look out for the hotel's summer beer festival. Meals are served all day until 8.30pm. Children are welcome but not dogs.
❀🛏◐◑🚌♣P

Selkirk

Heatherlie House Hotel

Heatherlie Park, TD7 5AL (W of centre, off Peebles Rd)
12-11 (midnight Fri & Sat); 12.30-midnight Sun
☎ (01750) 721200
Beer range varies Ⓗ
A family run hotel set in secluded grounds, this Victorian villa retains a quiet air of grandeur, with a magnificent hand- carved fireplace depicting barn owls in the entrance and beautiful cornices. The bar, which is also a dining room, is comfortable and airy and has views through the large bay windows to the gardens. The real ale is mainly from Inveralmond or Stewart Brewing. Children are welcome until 8pm. ⛰Q❀🛏◐◑⛺🚌♣P

West Linton

Gordon Arms Hotel

Dolphinton Road, EH46 7DR (on A702)
11-11 (midnight Tue; 1am Fri & Sat); 12-11 Sun
☎ (01968) 660208 🌐 gordonarms.co.uk
Stewart Pentland IPA; guest beer Ⓗ
Situated in a village close to the Pentland Hills, the pub has an L-shaped public bar with stone walls and interesting cornices. A homely feel is created by a real fire and a collection of sofas and chairs. The attractive, comfortable restaurant has wooden floors and neatly arranged dining tables. Meals are served all day at the weekend. Children and dogs are welcome. An excellent outdoor smoking area and covered extension to the restaurant have recently been added.
⛰❀🛏◐◑🂠⛺🚌(100,101)♣P⅟

Your shout

We would like to hear from you. If you think a pub not listed in the Guide is worthy of consideration, please let us know. Send us the name, full address and phone number (if known). If a pub in the Guide has given poor service, we would also like to know. Write to Good Beer Guide, CAMRA, 230 Hatfield Road, St Albans, Herts, AL1 4LW or email **gbgeditor@camra.org.uk**

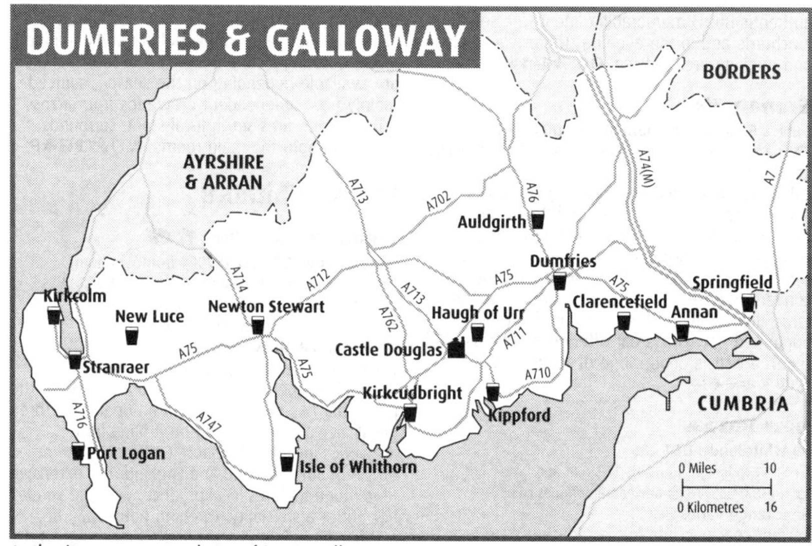

Authority area covered: Dumfries & Galloway UA

Annan

Bluebell Inn

10 High Street, DG12 6AG
11-11 (midnight Thu-Sat); 12.30-11 Sun
(01461) 202385
Caledonian Deuchars IPA; Greene King IPA; guest beers H

Former coaching inn on the entrance to the town from the west side – a long-time CAMRA favourite and award-winning real ale pub. The busy, friendly pub offers a selection of beers drawn from throughout the UK. The wood-lined interior has traditional features retained from its time as a Gretna District State Management Scheme House. Outside, the courtyard to the rear provides a pleasant seated area in summer.

Auldgirth

Auldgirth Inn

DG2 0XJ (adjacent to A76 Dumfries to Kilmarnock road, about 8 miles N of Dumfries)
12-midnight (1am Sat)
(01387) 740250
Beer range varies H

Traditional former coaching inn adjacent to the main Dumfries to Kilmarnock road, offering excellent meals and accommodation. The menu features an impressive range of freshly-prepared food made with ingredients from local sources. Two cask ales are usually available from a range of UK breweries. The hotel is popular with locals and outdoor enthusiasts including cyclists, anglers and shooters. Q P

Clarencefield

Farmers Inn

Main Street, DG1 4NF (on B724)
11-2.30, 6-11.30 (12.30am Fri); 12-12.30am Sat; 12.30-11.30 Sun
(01387) 870675 farmersinn.co.uk
Beer range varies H

Nine miles east of Dumfries, this small village pub offers a good atmosphere and service. The interior comprises a cosy bar and lounge with a separate games room. A good mix of freshly prepared food is available. Well placed for a range of activities – bird watching, golf, fishing and shooting – it also has some interesting tourist attractions nearby, including the eighth-century Ruthwell Cross and the world's first Savings Bank (now a museum). There is a smoking area outside. P

Dumfries

Cavens Arms

20 Buccleuch Street, DG1 2AH
11-11 (midnight Thu-Sat); 12.30-11 Sun
(01387) 252896
Beer range varies H

Lively town-centre pub which fully reflects its success in the quality of its ales and service, featuring a good balance of regular and guest beers. Customers can request the ales they would like to see on handpump. A superb range of great-value meals is served 11.30am (12.30 Sun) to 9pm daily except Monday. Occasional themed nights are hosted. Local CAMRA Pub of the Year 2006-09 inclusive.

Globe Inn

56 High Street, DG1 2JA (opp Loreburn Centre)
11-11 (midnight Thu-Sat); 12.30-midnight Sun
(01387) 252335
Caledonian Deuchars IPA; Sulwath Criffel; Theakston XB H

A busy town-centre pub, the Globe is situated down an alley off the High Street. One of the oldest pubs in Dumfries, it is steeped in tradition and has a large public bar with an adjoining small Burns Room snug bar. The poet Robert Burns was a frequent visitor and the pub boasts a wealth of

INDEPENDENT BREWERIES

Sulwath Castle Douglas

authentic Burns memorabilia. Meals are served at lunchtime and in the evening. There is a smoking and drinking area outside. Q

Granary

Dobies Building, Loreburn Street, DG1 1HN
11-1am (midnight Thu; 2am Fri & Sat); 12.30-midnight Sun
(01387) 250534
Caledonian Deuchars IPA; Greene King IPA
A welcome addition to the Good Beer group of pubs in the town, the Granary shows a real willingness to encourage cask ale. Part of the Greene King/Belhaven group, it is a recent conversion from a former seed warehouse. It has a large club facility upstairs and now features a well-appointed downstairs bar offering two beers. Well worth a visit, a good range of food is served.

New Bazaar

39 Whitesands, DG1 2RS
11-11 (midnight Thu-Sat); 12.30-11 Sun
(01387) 268776 newbazaardumfries.co.uk
Beer range varies
Former coaching inn with a pleasing Victorian gantry in the small, welcoming bar. The pub also has a cosy, quiet lounge with a warming coal fire in winter and a separate room available for meetings. Beside the River Nith in the town centre, it is ideally situated for car parking and local tourist attractions. It gets busy with football fans on match days. There is an outside smoking area.

Robert the Bruce

81-83 Buccleuch Street, DG1 1DJ
11-midnight (1am Fri & Sat); 12.30-midnight Sun
(01387) 270320
Caledonian Deuchars IPA; guest beers
A former Methodist church which has been sympathetically converted by Wetherspoon's. Since opening in 2001 it has established itself as a favourite meeting place in the town centre, with a relaxed and comfortable atmosphere. It offers four changing guest beers, including the house beer Robert the Bruce brewed by the Strathaven Brewery. The menu provides a good range of meals served all day every day. There is a smoking area and seating in the garden.

Ship Inn

97-99 St Michael Street, DG1 2PY (opp St Michael's churchyard)
11 (12.30 Sun)-11
(01387) 255189
Caledonian Deuchars IPA; Greene King Abbot, Old Speckled Hen; Theakston XB; Wells Bombadier
Nice to see this pub returning to form after a few years uncertainty following changes of ownership – it is now owned by Belhaven/Greene King. A long-time favourite for real ale enthusiasts in Dumfries, this small traditional pub gives a cheery welcome to visitors. No meals are served but there are toastie snacks. Q

Haugh of Urr

Laurie Arms Hotel

11-13 Main Street, DG7 3YA (on B794, 1 Mile S of A75)
12 (12.30 Sun)-3, 5.30-midnight
(01556) 660246
Beer range varies
Welcoming family-run pub and restaurant on the main street of this quiet village in the scenic valley of the River Urr. It is popular with locals and visitors alike for its range of well-kept beer and good food, often featuring local produce. Up to four real ales are available depending on the season, sourced mainly from independent breweries from across Britain. Open fires set in local stone surrounds feature in both the main rooms. QP

Isle of Whithorn

Steam Packet Inn

Harbour Row, DG8 8LL (B7004 from Whithorn)
11-11 (1am Fri; 12.30am Sat) summer; 11-2.30, 6 (5 Mon)-11 Mon-Thu winter; 12-11 Sun
(01988) 500334 steampacketinn.com
Theakston XB; guest beers
Traditional and historic family-run hotel overlooking the harbour and surrounding area. The public bar has stone walls and an open fire. Three guest ales are available in both bars, from breweries including Houston, Caledonian and many others in both Scotland and England. The extensive food menu features local produce, with the Sunday hot buffet a speciality. Opening hours may be restricted in winter. Local CAMRA branch Pub of the Year 2008. Q(415)

Kippford

Anchor Hotel

DG5 4LN
11-3, 6-11 (midnight summer); 12.30-11 (midnight summer) Sun
(01556) 620205
Beer range varies
Situated on the main street in the heart of this popular sailing centre, this friendly inn has fine views over the Urr estuary. The varied menu includes meals made with local produce as well as good vegetarian options. There is usually one beer available throughout the year with one more during the tourist season – the ale often comes from the local Sulwath Brewery. The village is served by an infrequent daytime bus service. P

Kirkcolm

Blue Peter Hotel

23 Main Street, DG9 0NL (A718 5 miles N of Stranraer)
6-11.30; 4-midnight Fri; 12-midnight Sat; 12-11.30 Sun
(01776) 853221 bluepeterhotel.co.uk
Beer range varies
A very attractive village pub with two bars and a decked outdoor drinking area where you may catch a glimpse of a red squirrel as well as a wide variety of birds. Two handpumps serve a choice of real ales, sometimes including a local Sulwath beer. Excellent pub food is served on Friday and Saturday evenings and Saturday and Sunday lunchtimes. The pub runs an annual beer festival in central Stranraer in May or June. B&B is available with a discount for CAMRA members. Scotland & Northern Ireland CAMRA Pub of the Year 2007. Q(408)

Kirkcudbright

Masonic Arms

19 Castle Street, DG6 4JA
11 (12.30 Sun)-midnight
(01557) 330517

Beer range varies Ⓗ
This small, sociable bar is welcoming to both locals and visitors. The tables and bar fronts are made from old malt whisky casks from Islay's Bowmore Distillery. One beer is available throughout the year with up to two more during the summer months. The Masonic also offers draught Budvar, a selection of 30 bottled beers from all over the world, and 100 malt whiskies. ⛰Q⛺🚌♣

Selkirk Arms

High Street, DG6 4JQ
11-11 (midnight Fri & Sat); 12.30-11 Sun
☎ (01557) 330402 🌐 selkirkarmshotel.co.uk
Sulwath The Grace; guest beers Ⓗ
Traditional hotel renowned for its quality accommodation and meals. Robert Burns is reputed to have written his famous 'Selkirk Grace' while visiting the hotel. It serves two cask ales, with pumps in the lounge bar; and service to the public bar on request. Kirkcudbright has much to offer the tourist, with its picturesque harbour and houses. The town is notable for its artistic heritage and has a number of interesting galleries and museums. Q❀🛏◐◑🅱♿🚌P⚡

New Luce

Kenmuir Arms Hotel

31 Main Street, DG8 0AJ (8 miles N of Glenluce along old military road)
10-midnight
☎ (01581) 600218 🌐 kenmuirarmsnewluce.com
Beer range varies Ⓗ
Situated in a beautiful village close to the Southern Upland Way, this picturesque hotel has well-kept gardens by the River Luce. The public bar serves one real ale all year round and sometimes two in summer, and occasional beer festivals are held. This is an attractive stopping point for walkers and the pub offers a luggage transfer service. Q❀🛏◐◑♿⛺♣P⚡

Newton Stewart

Creebridge House Hotel

Minigaff, DG8 6NP (on old main road, E of river)
12-2.30, 6-11.30 (midnight Sat); 12.30-11 Sun
☎ (01671) 402121 🌐 creebridge.co.uk
Caledonian Deuchars IPA; Taylor Landlord; guest beers Ⓗ
Traditional country house hotel with three acres of idyllic gardens and woodland, next to the River Cree and close to the town centre. The bar serves two real ales, with an occasional guest beer from the local Sulwath Brewery. There are 18 bedrooms and a separate restaurant and brasserie, plus a large lounge area attached to the main bar. The hotel has a good reputation for freshly prepared food. It also sells very fine walking sticks and crooks. ⛰Q❀🛏◐◑♿🚌(420)♣P⚡

Port Logan

Port Logan Inn

Laigh Street, DG9 9NG
12-midnight
☎ (01776) 860272 🌐 portloganinn.co.uk
Beer range varies Ⓗ
This pleasant pub is situated in an attractive seaside village that was used as the setting for the TV series 2000 Acres of Sky, as was the inn itself. There is a large, cosy bar, a restaurant that is used mainly in summer and a beer garden overlooking the beach. The varied menu of excellent bar meals uses locally sourced food where possible. One varying real ale is on offer in winter, two in summer. ⛰❀🛏◐◑🚌(407)♣P⚡

Springfield

Queens Head

Main Street, DG16 5EH
5 (12 Sat)-11 (midnight Thu & Fri); 12.30-11 Sun
☎ (01461) 337173
Caledonian Deuchars IPA Ⓗ
This single-room village pub, although slightly off the beaten track, is actually little more than a stone's throw from Gretna, wedding capital of the country. It is very close to the A74(M) and about a mile from Gretna Green railway station. Just one real ale is served in this friendly, unpretentious local. Note there is no lunchtime opening on weekdays. ❀🚌♣P

Stranraer

Grapes

4-6 Bridge Street, DG9 7HY
11-11.30 (midnight Fri & Sat); 12.30-11.30 Sun
☎ (01776) 703386
Beer range varies Ⓗ
This traditional 1940s-style town centre bar with a warm and welcoming atmosphere features in Scotland's True Heritage Pubs. One real ale is sold in the bar, as well as a wide selection of malt whiskies, rums and vodkas. A function room is available. The pub runs an annual mini real ale festival in May, with up to 10 ales. ❀🅱⇌🚌♣⚡

Learned drinker

He was a learned man, of immense reading, but is much blamed for his unfaithful quotations. His manner of studie was thus: he wore a long quilt cap, which came two or rather three inches at least over his eies, which served him as an umbrella to defend his eies from the light. About every three houres his man was to bring him a roll and a pot of ale to refocillate [refresh] his wasted spirits, so he studied, and dranke, and muched some bread and this maintained him till night, and then he made a good supper.
An Oxford man, William Prynne (1600-69), as described by **John Aubrey** in Brief Lives, ed. John Buchanan-Brown, 2000

SCOTLAND

EDINBURGH & THE LOTHIANS

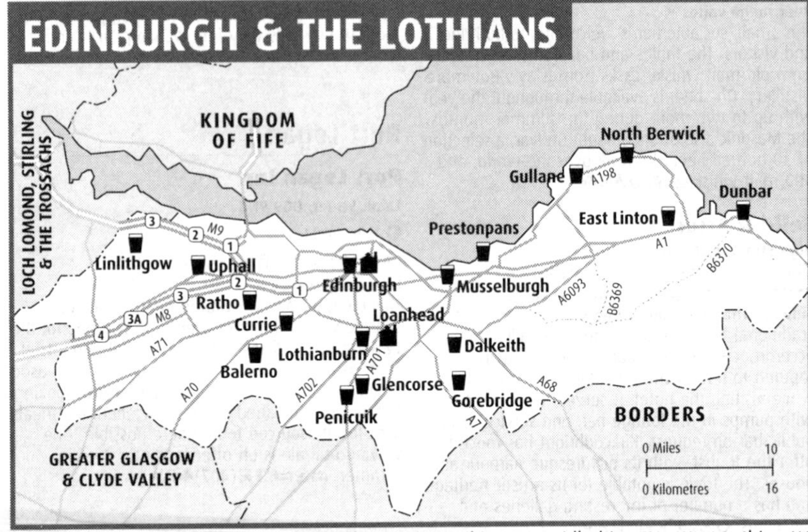

Authority areas covered: City of Edinburgh UA, East Lothian UA, Midlothian UA, West Lothian UA

Balerno

Grey Horse

20 Main Street, EH14 7EH (off A70, in pedestrian area)
10 (12.30 Sun)-1am
(0131) 449 2888 greyhorseinn.co.uk
Caledonian Deuchars IPA; guest beer

Traditional stone-built, village-centre pub dating from 200 years ago. The public bar retains some original features with wood panelling and a fine Bernard's mirror. The pleasant lounge has green banquette seating. The café next door is part of the pub so you can have a drink with your meal. There is an outdoor heated shelter for smokers. Children are permitted in the lounge until 8pm. Dogs are welcomed with water and biscuits.
(44)

Currie

Riccarton Arms Inn

198 Lanark Road West, EH14 5NX
11-11 (midnight Fri & Sat)
(0131) 449 2230
Caledonian Deuchars IPA; guest beer

Over a century old, the pub has a long, narrow lounge bar with half-timbered walls and ceilings. A true community inn, it holds a variety of events including quiz nights and live entertainment. Televised sport is very popular. There is a quieter restaurant area where home-cooked food is available. The landlord is a qualified chef and takes pride in his meals, but above all this is a drinkers' pub. Dogs are welcome. Wi-Fi access is available.
(Currie Hill)

Dalkeith

Blacksmith's Forge

Newmills Road, EH22 1DU
9am-midnight (1am Fri & Sat)
(0131) 561 5100
Caledonian Deuchars IPA; Greene King Abbot; guest beer

Wetherspoon's establishment with a mixture of seating areas. It has a reasonably quiet atmosphere despite the two small TVs and a gaming machine. Dimmed lighting helps to produce a soothing ambience, although the pub does tend to be busy at weekends. Meals are served all day. Children are welcome, but not dogs. (3,86)P

Dunbar

Rocks

Marine Road, EH42 1AR (on clifftop, W of centre)
11 (12.30 Sun)-11
(01368) 862287 experiencetherocks.co.uk
Beer range varies

Imposing red stone villa, now a hotel, set back from the cliffs but with panoramic views across Dunbar Bay. The bar has a high ceiling and dark wood decor, with several dining areas leading off it. Friendly staff are happy to offer advice on the adventurous seafood oriented menu. Some items are expensive, but expect excellent quality. A wide variety of real ales is served on two handpumps. Children are welcome.

Volunteer Arms

17 Victoria Street, EH42 1HP
12-11 (midnight Thu; 1am Fri & Sat); 12.30-midnight Sun
(01368) 862278
Beer range varies

Close to Dunbar harbour, this is a friendly, traditional locals' pub. The cosy panelled bar is decorated with lots of fishing and lifeboat memorabilia. Two real ales are usually from smaller breweries and local real cider is occasionally available. Upstairs is a restaurant serving an excellent, good value menu with an emphasis on seafood. In summer, meals are served all day until 9.30pm. Children are welcome until 8pm and dogs after 9pm.

INDEPENDENT BREWERIES

Caledonian Edinburgh
Stewart Loanhead

East Linton

Crown

25-27 Bridge Street, EH40 3AG
11 (12 winter)-11 (1am Thu-Sat); 11-midnight Sun
(01620) 860335 thecrowneastlinton.co.uk
Adnams Broadside; Caledonian Deuchars IPA; guest beers H
Small 18th-century stone-built hotel in the centre of a historic conservation village. The functional, cosy bar has a real log fire, lots of wood panelling and original Dudgeon windows. To the rear is a large lounge and restaurant that serves good quality pub food from an imaginative menu (food available all day summer, not Sun-Wed eve winter). One of the guest beers is usually from Stewart Brewing. Children are welcome in the lounge and family room. Dogs are also permitted.

Edinburgh

Abbotsford Bar & Restaurant ★

3 Rose Street, EH2 2PR
11-11 (midnight Fri & Sat); 12.30-11 Sun
(0131) 225 5276 theabbotsford.com
Beer range varies A
A traditional Scottish bar listed in CAMRA's National Inventory of historic interiors. The magnificent island bar and gantry in dark mahogany have been a fixture since 1902. The ornate plasterwork and corniced ceiling are outstanding and highlighted by subdued lighting. Beers are normally from Scottish micro-breweries. Evening meals are served in the upstairs restaurant, but you may ask for beer from downstairs. Children are welcome in the restaurant. Q (Waverley)

Athletic Arms (Diggers)

1-3 Angle Park Terrace, EH11 2JX
11 (12.30 Sun)-1am
(0131) 337 3822 theathleticarms.co.uk
Caledonian Deuchars IPA, 80; Stewart Diggers 80/- A**; guest beers** H
Situated between two graveyards, the name 'Diggers' became synonymous with this legendary Edinburgh pub, which opened in 1897. Banquette seating lines the walls, and a compass drawing in the floor aids the geographically challenged. A smaller back room has a dartboard and further seating. Quieter now than in its heyday, though packed when Hearts are at home, it continues to extend a warm welcome to local characters and visitors alike. Dogs are welcome.
(Haymarket)

Auld Hoose

23/25 St Leonards Street, EH8 9QN
12 (12.30 Sun)-12.45am
(0131) 668 2934 theauldhoose.co.uk
Caledonian Deuchars IPA; Wychwood Hobgoblin; guest beer H
Traditional pub dating back to the 1860s with a large central U-shaped bar and lots of pictures of old Edinburgh. Located in the student quarter, this is a friendly pub with a wide clientele. Try the alternative jukebox, have a game of darts with the locals or enter the quiz on Tuesday evening. Good pub food is served all day and includes vegetarian and vegan options. The guest beer is usually from a Scottish micro. Dogs are welcome, and there is free Wi-Fi access. (2)

Barony Bar ☆

81-85 Broughton Street, EH1 3RJ (E edge of New Town)
11-midnight (1am Fri & Sat); 12.30-midnight Sun
(0131) 558 2874
Black Sheep Best Bitter; Caledonian Deuchars IPA, 80; Theakston Old Peculier; guest beers H
Characterful city pub, listed in CAMRA's Scottish pub inventory due to its many fine internal features. Splendid tilework and stained wood are much in evidence, while the bar and gantry are also noteworthy. Detailed cornices and a wooden floor add to the atmosphere of the L-shaped bar. Magnificent whisky mirrors adorn the walls. Food is served all day until 10pm (7pm Sun).
Q (Waverley)

Bennet's Bar

1 Maxwell Street, Morningside, EH10 5HT
11-midnight; 12.30-10 Sun
(0131) 447 1903
Harviestoun Bitter & Twisted; Inveralmond Ossian; Stewart Pentland IPA; guest beers A
Couthy back-street boozer in the wealthy suburb of Morningside, yet just yards from one of the city's main trunk roads south. The pub has been owned by the eponymous family for generations and retains many features from the last major refurbishment some 50 years ago. The walls are adorned with photographs of old Edinburgh. Three regular and three guest beers are usually on. Dog friendly. An outdoor drinking area is available.

Bert's Bar

29-31 William Street, EH3 7NG
11-11 (1am Thu-Sat); 12.30-midnight Sun
(0131) 225 5748
Caledonian Deuchars IPA, 80; Harviestoun Schiehallion; Taylor Landlord; guest beers H
Re-creation of a traditional Scottish single-room bar with quality wood and tilework. There is ample standing room and plenty of seating areas with tables. An excellent Edwardian gantry is complemented by brewery mirrors. Good food is served all day – why not try one of the famous pies? Up to 10 beers are regularly available. Dogs on lead are welcome. Free Wi-Fi access.
(Haymarket)

Blue Blazer

2 Spittal Street, EH3 9DX
11 (12.30 Sun)-1am
(0131) 229 5030
Cairngorm Trade Winds; Stewart Pentland IPA, 80/-; guest beers H
Wood floors and panels, high ceilings and frosted glass windows give this two-room city-centre pub a traditional feel, though wee candles along the bar and unobtrusive background music are nice modern touches. It's often busy, but competent staff keep things moving well. Find details of the eight real ales, often from small Scottish breweries, on Facebook (I Love The Blue Blazer). Try the wide range of whiskies, or the monthly rum tasting. Dogs are welcome. (Haymarket)

Bow Bar

80 West Bow, EH1 2HH (Old Town, off Grassmarket)
12-11.30; 12.30-11 Sun
(0131) 226 7667
Caledonian Deuchars IPA; Stewart 80/-; Taylor Landlord; guest beers A

SCOTLAND

A classic Scottish one-roomed alehouse dedicated to traditional Scottish air pressure dispense and perpendicular drinking. The five guest beers can be from anywhere in the UK. The walls are festooned with original brewery mirrors and the superb gantry does justice to an award-winning selection of single malt whiskies. A map of the original 33 Scottish counties hangs above the fireplace. Bar snacks are available at lunchtime. Dogs are welcome. Q≷(Waverley)

Café Royal ☆ ✔

19 West Register Street, EH2 2AA (off E end of Princes St)
11-11 (midnight Thu; 1am Fri & Sat); 12.30-11 Sun
☎ (0131) 556 1884
Caledonian Deuchars IPA; guest beers Ⓗ
One of the finest Victorian pub interiors in Scotland, listed on CAMRA's National Pub Inventory. It is dominated by an impressive oval island bar with ornate brass light fittings and magnificent ceramic tiled murals of innovators made by Doulton from pictures by John Eyre. The superb sporting windows of the Oyster Bar were made by the same firm that supplied windows for the House of Lords. The Gents features an unusual hand basin. Meals are served all day. Children are welcome in the restaurant. Dogs permitted. ≷(Waverley)

Cask & Barrel

115 Broughton Street, EH1 3RZ (E edge of New Town)
11-12.30am (1am Thu-Sat); 12.30-12.30am Sun
☎ (0131) 556 3132 caskandbarrel.co.uk
Draught Bass; Caledonian Deuchars IPA, 80; Hadrian & Border Cowie; Harviestoun Bitter & Twisted; guest beers Ⓗ
Spacious and busy alehouse drawing a varied clientele of all ages, ranging from business people to football fans. The interior features an imposing horseshoe bar, bare floorboards, a splendid cornice and a collection of brewery mirrors. Old barrels act as tables for those who wish to stand up, or cannot find a seat. The guest beers, often from smaller Scottish breweries, come in a range of strengths and styles. Sparklers can be removed on request. ≷(Waverley)

Cloisters Bar

26 Brougham Street, EH3 9JH
12-midnight (1am Fri & Sat); 12.30-midnight Sun
☎ (0131) 221 9997
Cairngorm Trade Winds; Caledonian Deuchars IPA; Stewart Holy Grail; Taylor Landlord; guest beers Ⓗ
A former parsonage, this bare-boarded ale house is popular with a broad cross-section of drinkers. Large bench seats give the pub a friendly feel. A fine selection of brewery mirrors adorns the walls and the wide range of single malt whiskies does justice to the outstanding gantry. A spiral staircase makes visiting the loo an adventure. Food is served lunchtimes and evenings during the week, 12-6pm on Friday and Saturday. Dogs are welcome.
Q

Dagda Bar

93-95 Buccleuch Street, EH8 9NG
12 (12.30 Sun)-1am
☎ (0131) 667 9773 dagdabar.co.uk/index.php
Beer range varies Ⓗ
Convivial, cosy bar in the university area attracting a wide ranging clientele. The single room has banquette seating on three sides and the bar counter on the other. The stone flagged floor is a little uneven in places. The staff are happy to let you sample the three real ales, which are usually from smaller breweries. Fresh ground coffee and quality tea are also available. Dogs are welcome.
≷(Waverley)(41,42)

Dalriada

77 Promenade, Joppa, EH15 2EL (off Joppa Rd)
12-midnight (closed Mon & Tue Jan and Feb); 12.30-midnight Sun
☎ (0131) 454 4500
Beer range varies Ⓗ
Located on the Portobello/Joppa promenade, you can enjoy a pint and look out for seals. The imposing entrance of this stone-built villa has an original tiled floor and fireplace. There are three bar areas with wooden flooring and furniture. The bar counter has a polished Italian granite top. An extensive snack menu is available 12-3pm (not Mon). Children are welcome until 8pm. Dogs are also welcome on a lead and bowls are provided. Live music plays at weekends.
(15/15A,26)P

Halfway House

24 Fleshmarket Close, EH1 1BX (up steps opp station's Market St entrance)
11-midnight (1am Fri & Sat); 12.30-midnight Sun
☎ (0131) 225 7101 halfwayhouse-edinburgh.com
Beer range varies Ⓗ
Cosy, characterful bar hidden halfway down an old town 'close'. Railway memorabilia and current timetables adorn the interior of this small, often busy, bar. Usually there are four interesting beers on offer from smaller Scottish breweries. Over the summer a different brewery is showcased each week. CAMRA members get a discount on their first pint. Good quality, reasonably priced food is served all day. The bar may stay open until 1am at busy times of the year. Dogs and children are welcome.
≷(Waverley)

Kay's Bar

39 Jamaica Street, EH3 6HF (New Town, off India St)
11-midnight (1am Fri & Sat); 12.30-11 Sun
☎ (0131) 225 1858
Caledonian Deuchars IPA; Theakston Best Bitter; guest beers Ⓗ
This small, cosy and convivial pub is a popular haunt for lawyers in the early evening. It offers an impressive range of beers for the size of the bar. One wall is decorated with whisky barrels, and there is also a good whisky selection behind the bar. Lunches consist of mainly traditional Scottish fare. The building was once used as a wine merchant's and the remains of the pipes can still be seen around the light rose. Dogs are welcome after 2.30pm. Q

Leslies Bar ★

45 Ratcliffe Terrace, EH9 1SU
11-11 (11.30 Thu; 12.30am Fri & Sat); 12.30-11.30 Sun
☎ (0131) 667 7205 lesliesbar.com
Caledonian Deuchars IPA; Stewart 80/-; Taylor Landlord; guest beers Ⓗ
Outstanding Victorian pub, listed on CAMRA's National Pub Inventory. It retains its fine ceiling, cornice, leaded glass and half wood panelling. The island bar has a spectacular snob screen which divides the pub. Small 'ticket window' hatches allow customers to order drinks. A plaque near the fireplace gives further details of this busy, orderly pub. The two guest beers are usually from smaller

breweries. Simple bar snacks are served. Regular live jazz plays on Monday evening. Dogs are welcome. (42)

Malt & Hops

45 The Shore, Leith, EH6 6QU
12-11 (midnight Wed & Thu; 1am Fri & Sat); 12.30-11 Sun
(0131) 555 0083
Caledonian Deuchars IPA; guest beers H
One-roomed public bar dating from 1749 in the heart of 'new' Leith's riverside restaurant district. Wood panelling creates an intimate feel with numerous mirrors, artefacts and a large oil painting adding interest. The superb collection of pump clips, many from now defunct breweries, is evidence of an ever-changing interesting range of guest beers, often from Scottish breweries. No meals are available at the weekend. Children and dogs are welcome.

Oxford Bar ★

8 Young Street, EH2 4JB (New Town, off Charlotte Sq)
11-midnight (1am Thu-Sat); 12.30-11 Sun
(0131) 539 7119 oxfordbar.com
Caledonian Deuchars IPA; guest beers H
Small, basic, vibrant New Town drinking shop unchanged since the late 19th century. It is renowned as one of the favourite pubs of Rebus and his creator Ian Rankin, and a haunt of many other famous and infamous characters over the years, so you never know who you might bump into. Guest beers are normally from Scottish micro-breweries. A real taste of New Town past, and listed on CAMRA's National Pub Inventory. Pies and sausage rolls are available. Dogs are welcome.

Regent

2 Montrose Terrace, EH7 5DL
11 (12.30 Sun)-1am
(0131) 661 8198
Caledonian Deuchars IPA; guest beers H
Large tenement bar with two rooms, one music free. The comfortable seating consists of banquettes, leather sofas and armchairs. Popular with gay and lesbian real ale drinkers, it offers an interesting range of three guest beers. Bar snacks and meals are served all day. A novel slant on pub games is the gymnastic pommel horse by the toilets. CAMRA Edinburgh Pub of the Year 2008. Dogs are welcome. Free Wi-Fi access is available.

Sandy Bells

25 Forrest Road, EH1 2QH
11.30 -1am; 12.30-11 Sun
(0131) 225 2751
Caledonian Deuchars IPA, 80; Courage Directors; Inveralmond Ossian Ale H
Very much a part of Edinburgh folklore, this pub has been part of the traditional music scene for many years. An arch, the gantry bar counter and wall panelling are all in dark wood, in marked contrast to the atmosphere which is far from gloomy. Folk music plays every night and on Saturday and Sunday afternoons. Bring along an instrument and join in! Dog friendly. (Waverley)

Stable Bar

Mortonhall Park,, 30 Frogston Road East, EH16 6TJ
11-11 (midnight summer); 12.30-11 Sun
(0131) 664 0773 mortonhall.co.uk/home/bar/stablebar.htm
Caledonian Deuchars IPA; Stewart Pentland IPA, Copper Cascade H
A real country pub on the edge of the city. Numerous paths are ideal for exploring the surrounding woods. The comfortable bar is dominated by a large stone fireplace, which boasts a roaring log fire in the winter. Food is served all day until 9pm (10pm summer). With real ales coming from breweries less than three miles away, this is a true locale pub. Watch out for the Little Miss Muffet seat. Children and dogs are welcome. Wi-Fi access is available. (11,18)P

Standing Order ✔

62-66 George Street, EH2 2LR
9 (12.30 Sun)-1am
(0131) 225 4460 jdwetherspoon.co.uk
Caledonian Deuchars IPA, 80; Greene King Abbot; guest beers H
Built in 1879 to a Robert Adam design and once the head office of the British Linen Bank, the building was converted into a vast pub in 1997 by JD Wetherspoon. The main bar has a superb high ceiling and polished granite pillars. Smaller rooms lead off, one containing the old Chubb vault door. Despite its size it can be very busy at times. Meals are served all day. Disabled access is via the Rose Street entrance. Children are welcome until 8pm. Free Wi-Fi access. (Waverley)

Starbank Inn

64 Laverockbank Road, EH5 3BZ
11-11 (midnight Thu-Sat); 12.30-11 Sun
(0131) 552 4141 starbankinn.co.uk
Belhaven 80/-; Caledonian Deuchars IPA; Taylor Landlord; guest beers H
Bright, airy, bare-boarded ale house, with a U-shaped layout extending into a conservatory dining area. The walls sport several rare brewery mirrors. Enjoy the superb views across the Firth to Fife. Up to five interesting guest ales, often from Scottish independent breweries, are usually available. Meals are served all day at the weekend. Children are welcome until 8.30pm and dogs are allowed if on a lead. Occasional jazz plays on Sunday. Free Wi-Fi access. Q

Stockbridge Tap ✔

2-4 Raeburn Place, EH4 1HN
12-midnight (1am Fri & Sat); 12.30-midnight Sun
(0131) 343 3000
Cairngorm Trade Winds; Caledonian Deuchars IPA; Stewart 80/-; guest beers H
Very much a specialist real ale house, the Stockbridge offers unusual and interesting beers from all over the UK and holds occasional beer festivals. The L-shaped room, with bright bar area, boasts mirrors from lost breweries including Murray's and Campbell's. The seating is a mixture of soft chairs and church pew style benches, with ample room for vertical drinking. The food menu is excellent, available all day Saturday and Sunday. Dogs are welcome.

Thomson's ✔

182/184 Morrison Street, EH3 8EB
12 (4 Sun)-11.30 (midnight Thu & Sat; 1am Fri)
(0131) 228 5700 thomsonsbar.co.uk
Caledonian Deuchars IPA; guest beers A
Modelled on the architectural style of Glasgow's Alexander 'Greek' Thomson, this award-winning pub is dedicated to traditional Scottish air pressure dispense. The superb, custom built gantry features

SCOTLAND

mirrors inlaid with scenes from Greek mythology. The walls are a veritable history of Scottish brewing, with rare mirrors from long defunct Scottish breweries. Guest beers are often from Pictish, Hop Back or Oakham. No food is available on Sunday and pies only on Saturday. Dogs are welcome. Q❀◐⇌(Haymarket)🚌⁵–

Glencorse

Flotterstone Inn

Milton Bridge, EH26 0PP (off A702 near Pentlands visitor centre)

🕘 11.30 (12.30 Sun)-11

☎ (01968) 673717 🌐 flotterstoneinn.com

Stewart Pentland IPA; guest beers Ⓗ

The large rectangular lounge bar has church pew seating and numerous toby jugs and plates around the walls. A modern timber-clad extension provides additional space overlooking the enclosed garden. Good food is served all day in two dining rooms, which have bare stone walls and wooden ceilings. A handy place to recover from a day on the Pentland Hills, it can be busy at weekends. Children are welcome. Dogs are also welcome in the bar. ❀♿🚌(100)♣P

Gorebridge

Stobbs Mill Inn

25 Powdermill Brae, EH23 4HX

🕘 11-11 (11.30 Thu; midnight Fri & Sat); closed 3-6 Tue & Thu; 12.30-11.30 Sun

☎ (01875) 820202

Beer range varies Ⓗ

Built in 1866 as a public house, this two-storey detached building looks more like a private dwelling. The bar has engraved wooden panels with sporting scenes, which separate it from an intriguingly tiny snug. Old photos of the town adorn the walls along with a selection of water jugs and bottles. The lounge is only open when food is served on Friday and Saturday evenings and Sunday lunchtime. Simple bar snacks are available at all times. Dogs are welcome.
❀◐◑🀫🚌(3A,29)♣P

Gullane

Old Clubhouse

East Links Road, EH31 2AF (W end of village, off A198)

🕘 11-11 (midnight Thu-Sat); 12.30-11 Sun

☎ (01620) 842008 🌐 oldclubhouse.com

Caledonian Deuchars IPA; Taylor Landlord; guest beers Ⓗ

There's a colonial touch to this pub, which looks out over the golf links to the Lammermuir Hills. The half-panelled walls are adorned with historic memorabilia and stuffed animals. Caricature style statuettes of the Marx Brothers and Laurel and Hardy look down from the gantry. Food features highly and is served all day. The extensive menu includes seafood, pasta, barbecue, curries, salads and burgers. Children are welcome until 8pm. Dogs are also permitted. 🔥Q❀♿🚌(X5,124)🍎⁵–

Linlithgow

Four Marys 🏆 ✔

65-67 High Street, EH49 7ED

🕘 12-11, (midnight Thu-Sat); 12.30-11 Sun

☎ (01506) 842171 🌐 thefourmarys.co.uk

Belhaven 80/-, St Andrews Ale; Caledonian Deuchars IPA; guest beers Ⓗ

Much commended hostelry in the main street opposite Linlithgow Palace, the birthplace of Mary Queen of Scots – it is named after her ladies-in-waiting. The pub walls are decked with mementoes of Mary. The building has seen many uses in its 500 year history, from dwelling house to shop. It holds very popular beer festivals in May and October when 20 or more beers from around the UK are available in two bars. Forth Valley CAMRA Pub of the Year 2009. ❀◐◑🀫⇌🚌⁵–

Platform 3 ✔

1A High Street, EH49 7AB (next to railway station)

🕘 10.30-midnight (1am Fri & Sat); 12.30-midnight Sun

☎ (01506) 847405 🌐 platform3.co.uk

Caledonian Deuchars IPA; guest beers Ⓗ

Small, friendly hostelry on the railway station approach. Originally the public bar of the hotel next door, it was purchased and renovated in 1998 as a pub in its own right. Note the interesting memorabilia displayed on the walls and look out for the train running above the bar. The guest ale rotates on one pump and is from either Cairngorm or Stewart breweries. Occasional live music is staged. Dogs are welcome. ⇌🚌♣

Lothianburn

Steading

118-120 Biggar Road, EH10 7DU (on A702, just S of bypass)

🕘 11 (12.30 Sun)-midnight (earlier if quiet)

☎ (0131) 445 1128

Caledonian Deuchars IPA; Taylor Landlord; guest beer Ⓗ

The pub was converted from farm cottages and has distinct areas for drinkers and diners. The popular restaurant includes a large conservatory extension and food is served all day. A simple food menu is also available in the bar. The outside drinking area has excellent views of the Pentland Hills and the pub is ideally placed for a relaxing pint after walking in the hills. Children and dogs are welcome. 🔥❀🚌(4,15/15A)P

Musselburgh

Levenhall Arms

10 Ravensheugh Road, EH21 7PP (B1348, 1m E of centre)

🕘 12 (1 Fri & Sat; 3 winter)-11 (midnight Thu; 1am Fri & Sat); 12.30-midnight Sun

☎ (0131) 665 3220

Stewart Pentland IPA Ⓟ**; guest beers** Ⓗ

This three-roomed hostelry dates from 1830 and is popular with locals and race-goers. The lively, cheerfully decorated public bar is half-timber panelled and carpeted, with a smaller area leading off, with a dartboard and pictures of old local industries. The quieter lounge area, with vinyl banquette seating, is used for food, which is served all day until 8pm. Dogs are welcome in the bar. Children are permitted until 8.30pm in the lounge. Opening times and the menu may vary in winter.
Q❀🀫⛺⇌(Wallyford)🚌♣P⁵–

Volunteer Arms (Staggs)

81 North High Street, EH21 6JE (behind Brunton Hall)

🕘 11-11 (midnight Thu; 12.30am Fri & Sat); 12.30-midnight Sun

☎ (0131) 665 9654 🌐 staggsbar.com
Caledonian Deuchars IPA; guest beers Ⓗ
Superb pub run by the same family since 1858. The bar and snug are traditional with a wooden floor, wood panelling and mirrors from defunct local breweries. The superb gantry is topped with old casks. The snug has a nascent history collection featuring local breweries. The more modern lounge opens at the weekend. Three guest beers, often pale and hoppy, change regularly. Dogs are welcome in the bar, but don't bring the kids. CAMRA Lothian Pub of the Year 2009.

North Berwick

Nether Abbey Hotel
20 Dirleton Avenue, EH39 4BQ (on A198, W of town centre)
11-11 (midnight Thu; 1am Fri & Sat)
☎ (01620) 892802 🌐 netherabbey.co.uk
Caledonian Deuchars IPA; guest beers Ⓐ
Family-run hotel in a stone built villa offering a bright, contemporary interior comprising one open plan, split level room. The lower area is a bar and the upper a restaurant. The marble topped bar counter has a row of modern chrome founts. The middle ones, with horizontally moving levers, dispense the real ales. Food is served all day at weekends. Children are permitted until 9pm. Dogs are also welcome. (X5,124)P

Ship
7-9 Quality Street, EH39 4HJ
11-11 (midnight Thu-Sat)
☎ (01620) 890676 🌐 shipinnnorthberwick.co.uk
Caledonian Deuchars IPA Ⓗ**; guest beers** Ⓐ
Open-plan bar, divided into three areas by a glass partition and a twice pierced wall, with pine floorboards, a mahogany counter and dark stained wooden gantry. Real ale is dispensed from founts, which look similar to those dispensing the keg beers, so check the pump clips before ordering. The pub is popular for food, which is served until 3pm (4pm at weekends). Children are welcome until 8pm and dogs are also permitted. Live music plays regularly on Saturday night. Free Wi-Fi access. (X5,124)

Penicuik

Navaar
23 Bog Road, EH26 9BY
12-1am (midnight Sun)
☎ (01968) 672693
Stewart Pentland IPA Ⓗ
A lively pub with a strong community spirit, situated in an old private house, circa 1870. The large bar is open plan with a log and coal fire and TV screens. The restaurant, with an extensive a la carte menu, serves meals all day. Snacks are available in the bar. A large patio and decked area is popular in summer. Dogs are welcome. P

Prestonpans

Prestoungrange Gothenburg ☆
227 High Street, EH32 9BE
12-3, 5-11; closed Mon; 12-midnight Fri & Sat; 12.30-11 Sun
☎ (01875) 819922 🌐 thegoth.co.uk
Stewart Pentland IPA, 80/- Ⓗ
Superb Gothenburg pub that won the 2005 English Heritage pub refurbishment award and is on CAMRA's National Pub Inventory. The magnificent painted ceiling in the bar has to be seen to be appreciated. Fowler's mothballed micro-brewery can be viewed. There is also a bistro and upstairs is a lounge and function room with superb views over the Forth. The walls throughout are covered in murals and paintings depicting past local life. Meals are served all day Friday to Sunday. Children are welcome. Wi-Fi access. (26,129)P

Ratho

Bridge Inn
27 Baird Road, EH28 8RA (by canal, bridge 15)
11.30-11 (midnight Fri & Sat); 12.30-11 Sun
☎ (0131) 333 1320 🌐 bridgeinn.com
Caledonian Deuchars IPA; guest beers Ⓗ
Food oriented canalside inn. The older part, originally a farmhouse dating from around 1750 and predating the canal, is used as a restaurant. A modern extension houses the lounge bar and dining area with views over the canal. The inn was a focal point during the long campaign to restore the canal, part of the Millennium Link project. Meals are served all day and children are welcome. Cruises on the restaurant barge can be pre-booked throughout the year. Wi-Fi is available. (X48)P

Uphall

Volunteer Arms ✔
103-105 East Main Street, EH52 5JA
11-11.30 (12.30am Fri; 1am Sat); 12.30-11.30 Sun
☎ (01506) 856478
Beer range varies Ⓗ
This simple local, first opened in 1895, has been revitalised by a recent refurbishment and the introduction of real ale. The original landlord, William Paterson, was a member of the local militia/volunteers, hence the name. The beer comes from Stewart and Cairngorm breweries. A comfortable lounge area near the bar is the place for conversation; the darts and pool area is away from the bar. Poker and quiz nights are hosted and occasional live music.

SCOTLAND

Join CAMRA

The Campaign for Real Ale has been fighting for over 35 years to save Britain's proud heritage of cask-conditioned ales, independent breweries, and pubs that offer a good choice of beer.

You can help that fight by joining the Campaign: use the form at the back of the Guide or visit **www.camra.org.uk**

GREATER GLASGOW & CLYDE VALLEY

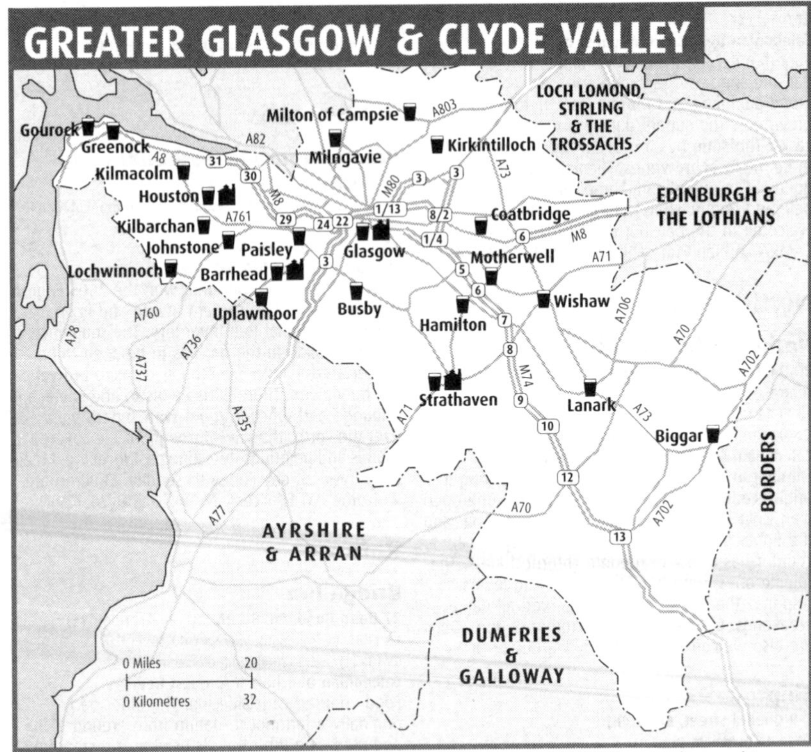

Authority areas covered: Argyll & Bute UA, Ayrshire UAs, City of Glasgow UA, Dunbartonshire UAs, Inverclyde UA, Lanarkshire UAs, Renfrewshire UAs

Barrhead

Cross Stobs Inn

4 Grahamston Road, G78 1NS (on B7712)

11-11 (midnight Thu; 1am Fri; 11.45 Sat); 12.30-11 Sun

(0141) 881 1581

Kelburn Misty Law; guest beers H

Eighteenth-century coaching inn on the road to Paisley. The public bar has a real coal fire and retains much of its original charm with antique furniture and service bells. The lounge is spacious and leads to an enclosed rear garden, and there is also an outside drinking area at the front. The pub also has a pool room and a function suite that can be hired privately. The guest beer is always from the nearby Kelburn Brewery.

Waterside Inn

Glasgow Road, The Hurlet, G53 7TH (A736 near Hurlet)

11-11 (midnight Fri & Sat); 12.30-11 Sun

(0141) 881 2822

Kelburn Carte Blanche; guest beers H

Comfortable bar/restaurant near Levern Water. Although the emphasis is on food, there is a cosy area around the log fire where visitors are welcome to relax with a drink. The restaurant holds theme nights, some with musical accompaniment. Local pictures adorn the walls and, along with souvenirs that staff bring back from their holidays to decorate the gantry, add to the ambience of the inn. The guest beer is always from the nearby Kelburn Brewery. P

Biggar

Crown Inn

109-111 High Street, ML12 6DL

11 (12.30 Sun)-1am

(01899) 220116

Beer range varies H

This former hotel is around 200 years old and lies on the main road to Edinburgh. It caters for locals and tourists plus visitors, especially during the Edinburgh Festival. The main front bar is divided into three areas by the central counter. There is also a snug/dining room, lounge bar and family room, plus a small conservatory. Once frequented by Norman MacCaig and Hugh McDermid, these days karaoke, quizzes and poker have replaced poetry. (191,100)P

Busby

White Cart ✓

61 East Kilbride Road, G76 8HX (on A726 near station)

11 (12.30 Sun)-11

(0141) 644 2711

Beer range varies H

A Chef & Brewer establishment with friendly and attentive staff situated directly across from the train station. Although the emphasis here is on food, ale is dispensed from two handpulls – the pub is LocAle affiliated and one of the beers is always from the Kelburn Brewery. A patio area at the front is popular in summer for alfresco dining. The pub has been awarded a gold award for beautiful beer by Cask Marque. P

Coatbridge

St Andrews Bar

37 Sunnyside Road, ML5 3DG (near Summerlee Heritage Museum)
11-midnight (1am Fri & Sat); 12.30-midnight Sun
(01236) 423773 standrewsbar.com
Beer range varies H
A small, lively public bar with a good local following, probably best known for its wide range of malt whiskies. An even smaller lounge/snug to the rear offers a quieter retreat from the busy main area. The bar features one of the finest surviving brewery mirrors in the country, depicting the former Campbell Hope & King brewery. The beer tends to alternate between Caledonian Deuchars IPA and a guest. The famous Summerlee Industrial Museum is close by. ⇌(Sunnyside)

Glasgow

1901 Bar & Bistro

1534 Pollokshaws Road, G43 1RF
11-11 (midnight Fri & Sat); 12.30-11 Sun
(0141) 632 0161
Caledonian Deuchars IPA; guest beers H
This corner tenement pub opened in 1901 as the White Swan and still retains two of the original etched windows. The curved counter serves two areas of an L-shaped room with ample seating. The guest beer varies between Taylor Landlord and a selection from a local brewery. Meals are available in the bar and Mediterranean bistro, with a reputation for good food. Buses from the city stop outside and the world-famous Burrell Collection is a short walk away through Pollok Park.
⇌(Pollokshaws West/Shawlands)

Babbity Bowster

16-18 Blackfriars Street, Merchant City, G1 1PE (between High St and Walls St/Albion St)
11 (12.30 Sun)-midnight
(0141) 552 5055
Caledonian Deuchars IPA; Kelburn Misty Law; guest beers P
The bar of this hotel/restaurant offers a welcome retreat from Glasgow's increasingly busy Merchant City, with simple furnishings providing an adaptable, comfortable environment. Paintings and photographs are illuminated by large windows overlooking the pedestrianised street. Scottish traditional tall founts dispense a guest ale plus two regulars. Quality bar and restaurant meals are made with local produce including game, fish and seafood. Patrons are warmed by a peat-burning fire in winter and can enjoy a game of boules in the garden in summer.
Q⇌(High St/Argyle St/Queen St)
⊖(Buchanan St)P

Blackfriars

36 Bell Street, Merchant City, G1 1LG (corner of Albion St)
11 (12.30 Sun)-midnight
(0141) 552 5924 blackfriarsglasgow.com
Beer range varies H
Increasingly popular cosmopolitan pub with a raised corner overlooking the bustling Merchant City and a quieter area to the rear. Between lies the main bar where five pumps dispense a changing selection of Scottish and English beers, with the local Kelburn Brewery always represented. There is a selection of bottled beers plus draught foreign beers and occasional farmhouse ciders. Food is served until 8pm (10pm in summer). Live music plays on Sunday and Tuesday, comedy is hosted on Thursday and quiz night is Monday. The pub can be hectic on Friday and Saturday nights.
⇌(High St/Argyll St/Queen St)
⊖(Buchanan St)

Bon Accord

153 North Street, G3 7DA (between Mitchell Library and Argyle St)
11-midnight; 12.30-11 Sun
(0141) 248 4427 thebonaccord.freeserve.co.uk
Caledonian Deuchars IPA; Harviestoun Bitter & Twisted; Marston's Pedigree; guest beers H
The pub that introduced real ale to Glasgow when CAMRA was young. Still going strong, it draws enthusiasts from near and far to sample 10 ales from local, Scottish and English breweries plus real cider. A long counter divides the large split-level room, with comfy sofas accompanying benches and stools, and a dining area to the rear. Good home-made meals are served until 7.30pm. Outside, there is seating under an awning at the front and sun-catching tables at the back.
⇌(Charing Cross/Anderston)

Clockwork Beer Co.

1153-1155 Cathcart Road, Mount Florida, G42 9HB (Kings Park Rd jct, by rail bridge)
11-11 (midnight Thu-Sat); 12.30-11 Sun
(0141) 649 0184 maclay.co.uk
Caledonian Deuchars IPA; guest beers P
Large open-plan brew pub with the brewery visible from the spacious bar. To the rear lies a raised dining area (ring for dining times) and a spiral staircase leads to the upstairs mezzanine room. Five guest beers and the strongest own brews are cask conditioned. Other beers are stored in cellar tanks with a unique gas bag that retains the CO_2 from secondary fermentation. A good selection of foreign bottled beers and whiskies is also on offer. Near Hampden Park, the pub is busy on match days. ⇌(Mount Florida/Cathcart)P

Crystal Palace ✔

36 Jamaica Street, G1 4QD
8 (12.30 Sun)-midnight
(0141) 221 2624
Caledonian Deuchars IPA; Greene King Abbot; guest beers H
This large Wetherspoon's gets its name from the massive windows of the bars on two floors, making the south-east corner a lunchtime suntrap. In summer, there are tables outside on the wide pavement. The original cage lift operates between floors, where you will usually find different beer ranges. Six guest beers augment the two regulars and some local breweries are featured. Popular with a varied customer base, upstairs and a downstairs rear area are family friendly, with children welcome until 7pm. Between 8-11am (12.30 Sun) alcohol is only served when purchasing a meal. Q⇌(Central)⊖(St Enoch)

INDEPENDENT BREWERIES

Clockwork Glasgow
Houston Houston
Kelburn Barrhead
Strathaven Strathaven

SCOTLAND

Esquire House ✔
1487 Great Western Road, Anniesland, G12 0AU
11-11 (midnight Fri & Sat); 12.30-11 Sun
☎ (0141) 341 1130
Caledonian Deuchars IPA; Greene King Abbot; guest beers H
A rare example of a real ale outlet quenching the thirst of drinkers west of Glasgow's West End. Unusually for Wetherspoon's it is a new build – the large split-level room has several distinct areas, some reserved for families, and the decor is smart and modern. Guest ales often include the house ale, Esquire House Red Ale, brewed by Strathaven. Large windows overlook the patio garden, with table parasols in summer. Though out of the city the pub is easily accessible by several buses and by rail. ❀◑♿⇌(Anniesland)🚌(20,66)**P**

Ingram Bar ✔
136-138 Queen Street, G1 3BX
11-11 (midnight Fri & Sat); 12.30-11 Sun
☎ (0141) 221 9330
Greene King IPA; guest beers H
Neat bar off George Square, used by city workers and visitors and known for its selection of malt whiskies which line the gantry of the oval island bar. Pillars, alcoves and raised corners create different areas, some with a reading room feel. The brass-topped stone counter has three handpumps offering a choice of ales, always including one Scottish micro brew, to accompany the home-made meals, available 12-3pm Monday to Friday (6pm Sat). Note the original stained glass panels in the windows. ◐⇌(Queen St)⊖(Buchanan St)🚌

Mulberry Street
778 Pollokshaws Road, G41 2AE
11-11 (midnight Fri & Sat); 12.30-11 Sun
☎ (0141) 424 0858
Caledonian Deuchars IPA; Harviestoun Bitter & Twisted H
Previously known as the Taverna, this is now a popular family-run café bar and restaurant. Large windows catch the sun and provide views to Queen's Park and the busy Pollokshaws Road which has regular buses to the city centre. The pub is located in the Strathbungo conservation area, where the work of the famous Glasgow architect Alexander 'Greek' Thompson can be seen. A good selection of imported bottled beers accompanies the two regular ales. Meals are served in the bar and restaurant.
◐◑♿⇌(Queens Park/Pollokshields West)🚌

Pot Still
154 Hope Street, G2 2TH
11-11 (midnight Thu-Sat); 6-11 Sun
☎ (0141) 333 0980 🌐 thepotstill.co.uk
Caledonian Deuchars IPA; guest beers H
Situated in the heart of the city, close to both main railway stations, this popular and friendly pub caters for a wide range of customers, including office workers, shoppers and visitors. The dark wood decor and upholstered seating create a comfy environment, and a mezzanine corner affords views over the main bar. There are usually two guest beers from Scottish micros, often local breweries Houston and Kelburn. For whisky aficionados, there is a large and renowned collection of malts.
⇌(Central/Queen St)⊖(Buchanan St)🚌

Samuel Dow
69 Nithsdale Road, G41 2PZ
11-11 (midnight Fri & Sat); 12.30-11 Sun
☎ (0141) 423 0107
Beer range varies H
Better known as Sammy Dow's, this fairly small but friendly bar has plenty of seating, including comfortable couches in front of a wood and glass partition opposite the bar. A corridor behind the partition leads to a function suite where rock bands play at the weekend. The bar seems little changed since the '60s, with old Ind Coope mirrors on the wall. The three guest beers come from a wide variety of breweries, but usually includes at least one from a local micro.
⇌(Pollokshields West/Queen's Pk)🚌

Sir John Stirling Maxwell ✔
Unit 14B, 140 Kilmarnock Road, Shawlands, G41 3NN
11-11 (midnight Fri & Sat); 12.30-11 Sun
☎ (0141) 636 9024
Caledonian Deuchars IPA; Greene King Abbot; guest beers H
The only Wetherspoon's on the south side, this former Safeway store lies at the south end of Shawlands shopping centre. It is named after the former owner of Pollok House and grounds, now Pollok Park, where the famous Burrell Collection is located. There is usually a Strathaven house beer among the guests. TVs show occasional sports in the main bar, and there is a raised family area to the rear. Open at 9am for breakfast, the pub can get busy at weekends. ◐◑⇌(Pollokshaws East)🚌

State Bar
148 Holland Street, G2 4NG
11 (12.30 Sun)-midnight
☎ (0141) 332 2159
Caledonian Deuchars IPA, 80; Houston Killellan; Stewart Edinburgh No.3 Premium Scotch Ale; guest beers H
A busy, cosmopolitan, city pub just off Sauchiehall Street and near King's Theatre, featuring an island bar with high gantry and brass rail, and an impressive woodcut of the Glasgow coat of arms on the wall. The ample seating includes stools at the bar and windows, plain and comfy chairs and benches. Partitions and alcoves provide diverse areas for drinkers and diners. Three guests accompany the four regular beers and good value meals results in a flourishing lunchtime trade. Live blues plays on Tuesday night. Glasgow CAMRA Pub of the Year 2007.
◐⇌(Charing Cross)⊖(Cowcaddens)🚌

Station Bar
55 Port Dundas Road, G4 0HF
11 (12.30 Sun)-midnight
☎ (0141) 332 3117
Caledonian Deuchars IPA; Greene King IPA; guest beers H
Traditional street-corner pub a short walk from the city centre, offering an alternative to the glitzy cafes and wine bars prevailing there. Popular with office workers, shoppers and concert goers (the Royal Concert Hall and Pavilion Theatre are nearby), it has the friendly and convivial feel of a real local. Two ever-changing guest beers supplement the regular ales. The bar area can get very busy, especially on Friday after work, but there is an additional quieter area at the back.
⩩◐⇌(Queen St)⊖(Cowcaddens)🚌♣

Tennents ✓

191 Byres Road, G12 8TN
11-11 (midnight Thu-Sat); 12.30-11 Sun
(0141) 339 7203
Broughton Old Jock; Caledonian Deuchars IPA; Fuller's London Pride; Harviestoun Bitter & Twisted; Orkney Dark Island; Taylor Landlord; guest beers H
Since its establishment in 1884, Tennents has been integral to the West End community. The many locals frequenting the large U-shaped bar are joined by workers and customers from nearby shops and offices as well as staff from the adjacent university. Sports fans enjoy several TV screens and the pub can get very busy when big games are shown. Good value meals are served all day. There are six regular beers on offer, joined by four guests. (Hillhead/Kelvinhall)(44)

Three Judges ✓

141 Dumbarton Road, G11 6PR
11-11 (midnight Thu-Sat); 12.30-11 Sun
(0141) 337 3055
Beer range varies P
The pub's name derives from the boxing fraternity rather than the legal profession. A fine example of a corner tenement pub, it is well worth seeking out to discover why it was awarded Glasgow CAMRA Pub of the Year in 2008. Nine beers are displayed on a chalk board along with the current real cider. Guest ales are sourced from a range of small breweries from Scotland and England. A friendly locals' bar where visiting ale fans can easily strike up a conversation.
(Partick)(Kelvinhall)(9,16,62)

Gourock

Spinnaker Hotel

121 Albert Road, PA19 1BU
11-midnight (12.30am Thu; 1am Fri & Sat); 12.30-midnight Sun
(01475) 633107 spinnakerhotel.co.uk
Belhaven 80/-; guest beers H
Family-run hotel situated in a listed sandstone Victorian building on the coast road heading west out of Gourock. Three ever-changing guest ales supplement the regular beer. All food is home made with an accent on local produce. A highlight for any first time visitor to this pub is the view from the large bay windows and front patio looking out across the Firth of Clyde to Dunoon and the beginning of the Highlands. Q

Greenock

James Watt ✓

80-92 Cathcart Road, PA15 1DD
11-11 (midnight Thu; 1am Fri & Sat); 12.30-midnight Sun
(01475) 722640
Caledonian Deuchars IPA; Greene King Abbot; guest beers H
Easy to find near the Central train station, this is a roomy, town centre Wetherspoon's with typical JDW trimmings. It has good wheelchair access and a separate area for families. Food is popular and served all day. Guest beers come from local breweries as well as further afield. Outside is a heated patio. (Central)

Hamilton

George Bar

18 Campbell Street, ML3 6AS (off Cadzow St)
12-11.45 (1am Fri; 11.45 Sat); 12.30-11.45 Sun
(01698) 424225 thegeorgebar.com
Beer range varies H
Local CAMRA branch Lanarkshire Pub of the Year, the George's many awards are proudly displayed on the wall. It is a perfect example of a community pub, welcoming customers of all ages and from all walks of life. There is one main room with a traditional wooden decor. The bar area is quite small but there are two high tables in the centre of the room to allow those standing room to rest their drinks and elbows. (Central)

Houston

Fox & Hounds

South Street, PA6 7EN
11-midnight (12.30am Fri & Sat); 12.30-midnight Sun
(01505) 612448 houston-brewing.co.uk
Houston Killellan, Peter's Well, Texas, Warlock Stout, seasonal beers; guest beers H
Established in 1779, this coaching inn is home to the Houston Brewing Company. The Fox & Vixen lounge has a viewing window to the brewery and serves the full range of Houston beers. The Stables Bar serves three Houston ales and has multiple TV screens for all sporting occasions. The Huntsman's Bar and a la carte restaurant are upstairs. Beer festivals are held in May and August, with guest beers available. P

Johnstone

Coanes

26-28 High Street, PA5 8AH
11-11.30 (midnight Fri & Sat); 12.30-11.30 Sun
(01505) 322925
Caledonian Deuchars IPA; guest beers H
Easy to find pub across the High Street from the only high-rise flats in Johnstone. This popular town centre pub has a separate lounge that doubles as restaurant. Seven beers are on offer, always including one from the Kelburn Brewery. A regular Pub of the Year candidate for the local CAMRA branch. Q

Kilbarchan

Glen Leven Inn

25 New Street, PA10 2LN
12.15-11 (midnight Thu; 1am Fri & Sat); 12.30-11 Sun
(01505) 702481
Beer range varies H
Situated in a conservation village, this friendly pub offers a warm welcome to locals and visitors alike. Live music plays on Saturday from 9pm and Sunday from 4pm. Sunday evening is quiet and a ladies quiz is hosted on the first Tuesday of the month.
(35)

Trust Inn

8 Low Barholm, PA10 2ET
11.45-11.30; 11-1am Fri & Sat; 12.30-11.30 Sun
(01505) 702401
Caledonian Deuchars IPA; Greene King Old Speckled Hen; guest beers H
This is a spacious single-room pub where children are allowed until 8pm. Enthusiastic staff generally

SCOTLAND

check with regulars to see which ales they would like to see on the guest list – Kelburn brews are always popular. Bands and quizzes are regular attractions – quiz night is Tuesday and music plays on Friday. Close to the National Trust for Scotland's Weaver's Cottage. (36)

Kilmacolm

Pullman Tavern

Eithinstone Court, Lochwinnoch Road, PA13 4LG
11-11 (midnight Wed; 1am Fri & Sat); 12.30-11 Sun
(01505) 874501
Beer range varies H
The only pub in the village, this Mitchells & Butlers pub is a converted railway station on the Sustrans cycle path from Paisley to Gourock. The outside seating area is popular with families, walkers and cyclists during the summer. Although the beer range varies, Timothy Taylor Landlord is a regular choice. P

Kirkintilloch

Kirky Puffer

1-11 Townhead, G66 1NG next to canal
11 (12.30 Sun)-midnight
(0141) 775 4140
Caledonian Deuchars IPA; Greene King Abbot; guest beers H
Large Wetherspoon's pub which was formerly a police station – some rooms to the rear were probably once cells. Located at the side of the Forth & Clyde Canal, the pub gets its name from the old puffer steamboats, and there are pictures of them on the walls. The house beer Kirky Puffer Red is brewed by Strathaven and there are up to three additional guests. With views of the tow path and water traffic, plus proximity to the Roman Antonine Way, the pub attracts walkers, cyclists and boaters as well as locals. Q

Lanark

Horse & Jockey

56 High Street, ML11 7ES
11-1am (midnight Sat); 12.30-1am Sun
(01555) 664825
Beer range varies H
A friendly locals' pub on the main street of an historic town. The corner counter has brass handrails and coat hooks and a TV is visible from the upholstered bench side seats and chairs. Lunches are available daily and on Saturday the upstairs restaurant also serves evening meals. In summer the pub attracts visitors to Lanark, who can also take a bus to the heritage village of New Lanark and view the impressive Falls of Clyde, a short journey away. (41)

Wallace Cave

11 Bloomgate, ML11 9ET
11-1am (midnight Sat); 12.30-1am Sun
(01555) 663662
Beer range varies H
Compact pub with a William Wallace theme. Swords and saltires adorn the plastered walls of the main bar room, divided by a square central counter. Windows in the grey stone front wall look to the main street. There is a small, cosy lounge area to the right of the bar, with wood-panelled walls and tartan carpet and upholstery. Popular with locals, this is also a handy watering-hole for visitors to New Lanark heritage village and the Falls of Clyde.

Lochwinnoch

Brown Bull

33 Main Street, PA12 4AH
12-11 (midnight Fri; 11.45 Sat); 12.30-11 Sun
(01505) 843250
Caledonian Deuchars IPA; guest beers H
Now in its 200th year, this traditional village free house is ever popular with locals and visitors to the area. The three guest ales are usually of differing styles and all are hand-picked by the owners. A well-appointed smoking area is at the rear of the bar. The upstairs restaurant makes good use of local produce.

Milngavie

Talbot Arms

30 Main Street, G62 6BU
11-11 (midnight Thu-Sat); 12.30-11 Sun
(0141) 955 0981
Caledonian Deuchars IPA, 80; guest beers H
A traditional corner pub comprising one long room with large TV screens at both ends, often showing football. Located at the southern end of the West Highland Way, the pub is ideally placed to refresh walkers in need of a pint. The two regular beers are joined by a guest ale from the Belhaven list. On warm summer days the tables outside are welcome, as is the home-made ice cream sold nearby. (8,10)

Milton of Campsie

Kincaid House Hotel

Birdston Road, G66 8BZ (signed off B757, just S of village at end of long, wooded drive) NS650759
11-midnight (1am Fri); 12.30-midnight Sun
(0141) 776 2226 kincaidhouse.com
Beer range varies H
This imposing stone hotel lies at the end of a long driveway. The ales are served in a building to the rear, formerly the stables. A long central counter lies between the comfy lounge and dining area and the bar area which has a pool table. Two handpumps serve the beers, usually from Houston and Caledonian. Excellent meals and a safe garden attract locals, families and visitors.
(85)P

Motherwell

Brandon Works

54-60 Merry Street, ML1 1JJ
11-midnight (1am Fri & Sat); 12.30-midnight Sun
(01698) 210280
Caledonian Deuchars IPA; Greene King Abbot; guest beers H
Wetherspoon's pub with a single room interior divided into several levels. Its popularity among local real ale fans is due not only to the beer, but the fact that it rescued Motherwell from the infamy of being Britain's biggest town without real ale. Conveniently sited in a shopping centre, it is named after the former ironworks that once occupied the site of the car park behind the pub. Up to three guest beers accompany the regulars.
Q

Paisley

Bull Inn ★ ✔

7 New Street, PA1 1XU
11-11 (1am Fri & Sat); 12.30-11 Sun
☎ (0141) 8490472
Caledonian Deuchars IPA; guest beers H
A change of management has brought about a vast improvement in this popular town-centre pub. An A-listed pub on CAMRA's National Inventory, the interior is well worth a look, with its three small snugs to the rear. Sport is shown on a large screen TV. Food is served 12-2.45pm Monday to Thursday and 12-4.45pm Friday and Saturday. Guest beers are often from the local Kelburn and Houston breweries. ≠(Gilmour St)

Harvies Bar

86 Glasgow Road, PA1 3NU
11-midnight (1am Fri & Sat); 12.30-midnight Sun
☎ (0141) 889 0911
Caledonian Deuchars IPA H
Well-run, friendly, comfortable local 15 minutes walk from the centre of town, on the main road to Glasgow. Frequent buses pass the door. It has a large, open plan, split level layout with a quiet corner. Two large TV screens show popular sporting events, at other times background music plays. Good-value food is served all day until 8.45pm. ≠(Hawkhead)

Last Post ✔

2 County Square, PA1 1BN
11-midnight (1am Fri & Sat); 12.30-midnight Sun
☎ (0141) 849 6911
Caledonian Deuchars IPA; Greene King Old Speckled Hen, Abbot; guest beers H
Large Wetherspoon's hostelry situated in a building that used to be the main post office. It has an open plan design, plenty of seating downstairs and more on the upstairs balcony. The standard food menu is available. Situated next to the entrance to Gilmour Street station, the pub is handy for a pint between trains. Q≠(Gilmour St)

Wee Howff

53 High Street, PA1 2AN
12-11 (1am Fri & Sat); closed Sun
☎ (0141) 889 2095
Beer range varies H
Small, traditional Scottish pub frequented by a regular local clientele. There is a open-mike night on the first Monday of the month and a pub quiz every Thursday. Three TVs screen regular football fixtures and a jukebox provides the music. The friendly staff will give you a warm welcome and there is a selection of books to read. The pub has appeared in every edition of this Guide for the last 20 years. ≠(Gilmour St)

Strathaven

Weavers

1-3 Green Street, ML10 6LT
11 (4.30 Wed & Thu)-midnight (1am Thu-Sat); 7-1am Sun
Beer range varies H
This family-run pub takes its name from the traditional trade of the town – Strathaven was a major centre of the weavers' rebellion in 1820. A popular meeting place for local clubs, badminton players, mountaineers and pipers can all be found here. The pub is the closest thing to a brewery tap for the local Strathaven brewery – one of its beers is always available along with three guests. A former local CAMRA Pub of the Year, reached by the No 13 bus from Hamilton. (13)

Uplawmoor

Uplawmoor Hotel

66 Neilston Road, G78 4AF (off A736)
11-11 (midnight Sat); 12.30-11 Sun
☎ (01505) 850565 uplawmoor.co.uk
Kelburn Red Smiddy; guest beer H
The hotel is located in the tranquil setting of Uplawmoor village, just over 10 miles from Glasgow. The building dates back to the 18th century when it was a coaching inn used by travellers and customs officers, chasing smugglers en-route between Glasgow and the south west coast of Scotland. Today the hotel continues to offer travellers the opportunity to relax and explore while providing easy access to urban sites and Burns country. The interior is rustic and cosy, serving bar meals from 12-9.30pm. The guest beer is from Houston. QP

Wishaw

Wishaw Malt ✔

62-66 Kirk Road, ML2 7BL
11-11 (midnight Thu; 1am Fri & Sat); 12.30-midnight Sun
☎ (01698) 358806
Caledonian Deuchars IPA; guest beers H
A very popular pub with an excellent real ale range which draws a wide custom from the local area and much further afield. The single large room is split into several separate areas on different levels, each with its own character. A former CAMRA Lanarkshire Pub of the Year, the 10th anniversary of its opening coincides with the publication of this Guide. Over the decade since it was opened by Wetherspoon's, it has done more than most to irrigate the Lanarkshire beer desert.
≠(240,267)

The discreet barman

Over the mahogany, jar followed jorum, gargle, tincture and medium, tailor, scoop, snifter and ball of malt, in a breathless pint-to-pint. Discreet barman, Mr Sugrue thought, turning outside the door and walking in the direction of Stephen's Green. Never give anything away – part of the training. Is Mr so-and-so there, I'll go and see, strict instructions never to say yes in case it might be the wife. Curious now the way the tinge of wickedness hung around the pub, a relic of course of Victorianism, nothing to worry about as long as a man kept himself in hand. **Jack White**, The Devil You Know

SCOTLAND

Authority areas covered: Highland UA, Western Isles UA

Applecross

Applecross Inn

Shore Street, IV54 8LR (off A896) NG710444
11-11.30 (midnight Fri); 12.30-11.30 Sun
(01520) 744262 applecross.uk.com/inn
Beer range varies H

Owned by the same family since 1989, the inn is spectacularly situated on the shore of the Applecross Peninsula, enjoying views of the Isles of Skye and Raasay. It is reached by a single track road over the highest vehicular ascent in Britain, or by a longer scenic route. Two handpumps dispense beers from the Isle of Skye Brewery. Comfortable accommodation is available and local seafood is a speciality on the food menu. Regular ceilidhs feature.

Aviemore

Cairngorm Hotel

Grampian Road, PH22 1PE (opp train station)
11-midnight (1am Fri & Sat); 12.30-midnight Sun
(01479) 810233 cairngorm.com
Cairngorm Stag H

The lounge bar of this 31-room privately owned hotel, though large, has a cosy feel, enhanced by two bay windows, distressed wooden furniture and a large coal-effect fire. Though the trade is mainly holidaymakers, the bar is very popular with locals, and has a large-screen TV showing only sport.

Dalfaber Golf & Country Club

Dalfaber Drive, Dalfaber, PH22 1ST
11 (12.30 Sun)-midnight
(01479) 811244 macdonaldhotels.co.uk
Cairngorm Tradewinds; guest beers H

Dalfaber Lounge Bar serves Tradewinds and one other guest ale from the local Cairngorm Brewery. With live entertainment most evenings and a Sunday night pub quiz, the bar has a lively, friendly and informal atmosphere where families are most welcome. It has two full size snooker tables and there is a leisure club attached with swimming pool and sports hall regularly hosting tournaments for local teams. All major sports are screened on TV.

Old Bridge Inn

Dalfaber Road, PH22 1PU
12-11 (midnight Thu-Sat); 12.30-11 Sun
(01479) 811137 oldbridgeinn.co.uk
Beer range varies H

Busy pub, popular with outdoor enthusiasts, serving good quality food. Originally a cottage and now greatly enlarged, it lies on the road to the Strathspey Steam Railway, overlooking the River Spey. One of the three handpumps usually serves a Scottish beer. Children are welcome and there is a modern bunkhouse attached, accommodating 40.

Brora

Sutherland Inn

Fountain Square, KW9 6NX
11 (12.30 Sun)-midnight
(01408) 621209 sutherlandinn.co.uk
Beer range varies H

Dating from 1853, the Sutherland Inn is an original coaching inn offering original Highland hospitality. There are local beers available all year round, mainly from the Isle of Skye Brewery, along with a collection of over 170 malt whiskies to explore. Locally-sourced food can be enjoyed in the restaurant or lounge bar next to the real open fire. Free wireless internet is available throughout the building.

Carrbridge

Cairn Hotel

PH23 3AS (on B9153)
11-midnight (1am Fri & Sat); 12.30-11 Sun
(01479) 841212 cairnhotel.co.uk
Beer range varies H

In the centre of a pleasant village, just off the A9 and close to the Landmark Heritage Park, this busy pub is part of the hotel. It is popular with locals and visitors, particularly walkers and cyclists. The two handpumps dispense mainly Scottish ales including brews from Cairngorm, Isle of Skye, Caledonian, Orkney and Atlas. Bar meals, soup and toasties are available all day.

Cawdor

Cawdor Tavern

The Lane, IV12 5XP
11-11 (midnight Fri & Sat); 11-3, 5-11 Oct-Apr; 12.30-11 Sun
(01667) 404777 cawdortavern.com
Orkney Dark Island; guest beers H

At the heart of this conservation village, the pub is a short walk from the famous castle and within easy reach of Fort George and Culloden battlefield. A pub full of character, it has a spacious lounge bar, cosy public bar and large restaurant. Both bars are wood panelled with log fires, the public bar featuring a splendid antique mahogany bar and a ceiling covered in old maps. Up to four handpumps dispense ales from Atlas and Orkney – breweries owned by the family that own the pub.

Cladach Chireboist: North Uist

Westford Inn

HS6 5EP (5km NW of A867/865 jct) NF781655
12 (4 Oct-Mar)-midnight (1.30am Fri & Sat); 12.30-midnight Sun
(01876) 580653
Isle of Skye Red Cuillin H

This Georgian listed building is situated on the edge of the Atlantic in a working crofting community with grazing highland cattle. Popular with local fishermen and tourists, the slightly eccentric and dog-friendly pub has a traditional atmosphere where a quick drink can turn into a ceilidh. Live music, both traditional and modern, is hosted and home-cooked pub food is available late into the evening. Real fires are fuelled by peat from the pub's own peat cutting.

Drumnadrochit

Benleva Hotel

Kilmore Road, IV63 6UH (signed from A82)
12-midnight (1am Fri); 12.30-11 Sun
(01456) 450080 benleva.co.uk
Beer range varies H/G

Popular, friendly village inn catering for locals and visitors. A 400-year-old former manse, the sweet chestnut outside was once a hanging tree. Four handpumps dispense mainly Highlands beers, including Isle of Skye, with an occasional beer from the wood. Westons cider is on handpump. Good evening meals, lunches and Sunday roasts are available all year. The pub hosts the Loch Ness Beer Festival in September, occasional quiz nights and traditional music. A former local CAMRA Pub of the Year.

Fort William

Ben Nevis Inn

Claggan, Achintee, PH33 6TE (at start of Ben Nevis footpath) NN125729
12-11 (closed Mon-Wed Nov-Mar); 12.30-11 Sun
(01397) 701227 ben-nevis-inn.co.uk
Beer range varies H

Located in the beautiful Glen Nevis, the inn sits at the very foot of Ben Nevis, Britain's highest mountain at 1,344m. The characterful building is more than 200 years old and is famous for its informal and friendly atmosphere. Food is served all day, offering a mix of traditional favourites and international dishes, all featuring fresh local produce. The three real ales come from local breweries. Regular live music is hosted.

Grog & Gruel

66 High Street, PH33 6AE
12-11.30 (12.30am Thu-Sat); 12.30 (5 winter)-11.30 Sun
(01397) 705078 grogandgruel.co.uk
Beer range varies H

In the shadow of Britain's highest mountain, this bare-floored traditional ale house keeps up to six beers in summer, fewer in winter. Owned by the same family as the Clachaig Inn in Glencoe, it holds regular live music and beer festivals. The beers are predominantly Scottish, often featuring the local Glenfinnan Brewery, and the bar is busy with locals, outdoor enthusiasts and tourists. Home-cooked food is available in the upstairs dining room or from the limited bar menu.

Nevisport Bar

Airds Crossing, High Street, PH33 6EU NN104741
11-11 (1am Fri & Sat); 12.30-11 Sun
(01397) 704790
Beer range varies H

INDEPENDENT BREWERIES

An Teallach Dundonell
Atlas Kinlochleven
Black Isle Munlochy
Cairngorm Aviemore
Cuillin Sligachan
Glenfinnan Glenfinnan
Hebridean Stornoway
Isle of Skye Uig
Plockton Plockton

At the end of the West Highland Way and start of the Great Glen Way, close to Glen Nevis and the Ben Nevis mountain range, this cosy and informal lounge-style bar has been a favourite meeting place for outdoor enthusiasts for many years. Up to four handpumps dispense mostly Scottish beers, often from the Isle of Skye and Atlas breweries. Food is served in the bar or upstairs restaurant where children are welcome. Five minutes' walk from the railway station.

Fortrose

Anderson

Union Street, IV10 8TD
4 (11.30 Sat)-11.30; 12.30-11.30 Sun
(01381) 620236 theanderson.co.uk
Beer range varies H
Homely bar in a quiet seaside village, part of a nine-bedroom hotel. The owners are an international beer writer and self-confessed 'beer geek' and his wife, a New Orleans-trained chef. Serving beers and ciders from independent breweries, this eclectic beer drinkers' mecca also offers more than 200 malts and 100 Belgian beers, earning it a prestigious UK award and the Belgian Ambassadeur d'Orval 2009. In the winter there is a barley wine festival. The food is reasonably priced, high-quality international cuisine. CAMRA members are offered a discount on accommodation. P

Gairloch

Old Inn

Flowerdale, IV21 2BD (opp harbour) NG811751
11-1am (11.45 Sat); 12.30-11.15 Sun
(0800) 542 5444 theoldinn.net
An Teallach Ale; Greene King Abbot; Isle of Skye Red Cuillin; guest beers H
The Old Inn is a traditional, family-run coaching inn, with a river flowing beneath its charming old stone footbridge. Nestling at the foot of Flowerdale Glen, it is in a picturesque setting with spectacular views across Gairloch harbour to Skye and the Outer Isles. Up to eight real ales (three in winter) accompany the enticing menu of home-cooked Highland game dishes and Scottish west coast seafood. The Blind Piper Ale from the Isle of Skye Brewery commemorates a famous local 17th-century piper. P

Glencoe

Clachaig Inn

PH49 4HX (on slip road ½ mile off A83) NN128567
11-11 (12.30 Fri; 11.30 Sat); 12.30-11 Sun
(01855) 811 252 clachaig.com
Beer range varies H
A favourite haunt of climbers and walkers, approached by journeying either through impressive moorlands and mountains, or along the attractive Argyll coast. The main bar has a stone floor, rustic wooden tables and benches, and a warming iron stove. A quieter lounge bar and snug can also be found. Generally five, but up to 15 ales during beer festivals, can be available, predominantly from Scottish micros. Well worth the walk through awe-inspiring scenery, for a fine beer and good, hearty food.
Q (916) P

Inverie

Old Forge

PH41 4PL (100m from ferry terminal)
11 (Tue & Thu 4, 12 winter Sat)-midnight; 11 (12 winter)-midnight Sun
(01678) 462267 theoldforge.co.uk
Beer range varies H
The most remote pub in mainland Britain can be reached only by ferry from Mallaig or a 15-mile hilly walk. In a spectacular setting on the shore of Loch Nevis, it provides an ideal location for walking the rough bounds of Knoydart. Moorings welcome waterborne visitors. Two handpumps usually have an Isle of Skye or Glenfinnan beer on. Excellent food is served all day featuring locally caught seafood specials. Winner of Scottish Licensed Trade News Best Independent Pub in Scotland in 2008.
Q

Inverness

Blackfriars

93-95 Academy Street, IV1 1LU
11-midnight (1am Fri; 12.30 Sat); 12.30-11 Sun
(01463) 233881 blackfriarshighlandpub.co.uk
Caledonian Deuchars IPA; guest beers H
Across the road from the Ironworks music venue, this traditional town-centre pub has a spacious single room interior with a large standing area by the bar and ample seating in comfortable alcoves. Up to seven handpumps are split between English and Scottish breweries, with Scottish beers often from Inveralmond and Highland. Good value meals feature home-cooked Scottish fare with daily specials. A welcoming, music oriented pub, it hosts ceilidh, folk, country and a singing landlord, with local bands often performing at weekends.

Castle Tavern

1 View Place, IV2 4SA (top of Castle Street) NH666449
11-1am (12.30 Sat); 12.30-midnight
(01463) 718178 castletavern.net
Beer range varies H
Small, welcoming bar in a listed building facing Inverness Castle and boasting fine views across the River Ness towards Inverness Cathedral. A five-minute stroll from the city centre, or a 73-mile hike along the Great Glen Way, bring you to a Victorian-style canopy at the entrance. Four handpumps dispense an Isle of Skye house beer plus changing guests, mostly from Scottish independents. Good value meals are served all day in the bar and first floor restaurant. Holds the Inverness Beer Festival.

Clachnaharry Inn

17-19 High Street, Clachnaharry, IV3 8RB (on A862 Beauly road) NH648466
11-11 (midnight Thu-Sat); 12.30-11.45 Sun
(01463) 239806
Beer range varies H
Popular with both locals and visitors, food is served all day, every day at this friendly 17th-century coaching inn where families are made welcome. Ales from Scottish breweries regularly feature on the five handpumps, with ever-changing guest beers. The large patio area, a summer sun-trap, affords fine views over the Caledonian Canal sea lock and Beauly Firth towards the distant Ben Wyvis. Q (19A)P

Number 27

27 Castle Street, IV2 3DU
11-11 (12.30am Fri & Sat); 12.30-11 Sun
(01463) 241999
Beer range varies H

Alongside the two handpumps, this popular city centre bar/restaurant offers 17 draught keg lagers and ciders, together with a bottled range including many continental brews. Real ales are usually from Scottish micros, with beers from Orkney Brewery always popular. There is also a good range of malt whiskies. Lunchtime food ranges from sandwiches to light bites. The comprehensive evening menu features more traditional main courses made with locally sourced ingredients including venison and steak. Free Wi-Fi access is provided.

Snowgoose

Stoneyfield, IV2 7PA (on A96)
12-10.30 (11 Easter-Oct); 12.30-10.30 Sun
(01463) 701921
Caledonian Deuchars IPA; Taylor Landlord H

This traditional dining house supports a popular bar trade, with an area reserved for customers who are not eating. Situated next to a Holiday Inn and a Travelodge, most of the custom comes from the local area. A converted 1788 coach house, the single large L-shaped room has alcoves and log fires to give it a more cosy and intimate feel. A wide variety of food is offered all day at reasonable prices. An extremely well run Mitchells and Butler's Vintage Inn. (1,10)

Kincraig

Suie Hotel

PH21 1NA
5-11 (1am Fri & Sat)
(01540) 651344 suiehotel.com
Cairngorm Tradewinds; guest beer H

This cosy wooden extention to a seven-bedroomed Victorian character hotel has had just two owners in 105 years. The wooden floored bar features a large stove/open fire and has an alcove with pool table and jukebox. Situated between the Cairngorms and Monadhliath mountain ranges and close to the River Spey and Loch Insh, it is popular with locals, hillwalkers, skiers and cyclists. Traditional Scottish music features occasionally. A second handpump usually serves another Cairngorm brew. Very good food is served.

Nairn

Braeval Hotel

Crescent Road, IV12 4NB
12-midnight (12.30am Thu-Sat); 12.30-midnight Sun
(01667) 452341 braevalhotel.co.uk
Beer range varies H

Real ale is served in the Bandstand Bar in this 10-bedroom hotel overlooking the Moray Firth close to Nairn beach. A comfortable, family run hotel renowned for its food, it offers traditional Scottish dishes and seafood specials made with fresh local ingredients. Up to five handpumps dispense a range of ales from near and far – with Scottish ales usually from Isle of Skye or Highland, and Timothy Taylor beers often among the English choices. The pub held its first beer festival recently and is CAMRA Highlands & Western Isles Pub of the Year 2009. (10,305)

Newtonmore

Glen Hotel

Main Street, PH20 1DD
11 (12.30 Sun)-midnight
(01540) 673203 theglenhotel.co.uk
Beer range varies H

Small, welcoming hotel in Monarch of the Glen country in the Cairngorms National Park. It has a good local trade and is also popular with walkers and tourists and holds regular quiz and games nights. There is a large bar with separate games and dining rooms. Four handpumps dispense at least one English and one Scottish beer plus a Westons cider or perry. An extensive menu includes a good selection of vegetarian dishes. The hotel holds the prestigious Eat Safe award.

Plockton

Plockton Hotel

Harbour Street, IV52 8TN NG803335
11-midnight; 12.30-11 Sun
(01599) 544274 plocktonhotel.co.uk
Beer range varies H

Set among an attractive row of traditional waterfront buildings in the picturesque village of Plockton, this popular hotel boasts spectacular views over Loch Carron. The award-winning menu on offer in the comfortable lounge bar includes locally landed fish and shellfish. Brews from the local Plockton Brewery are often on handpump. Close to the Isle of Skye, Eilean Donan Castle and the mountains of Torridon, the village has much to offer and is always bustling in season.

Plockton Inn

Innes Street, IV52 8TW NG803333
11-1am (12.30am Sat); 11-11 Sun
(01599) 544222 plocktoninn.co.uk
Beer range varies H

Nothing is too much trouble at this popular village inn, owned and run by a local family for many years. Locally-caught fish and shellfish take pride of place on the menu and the seafood platter includes fish smoked on the premises. Lively music sessions often feature young musicians from the National Centre of Excellence for Traditional Music which is based in the village. The beer range includes local Plockton and Isle of Skye brews, as well as national ales.

Portree: Isle of Skye

Royal Hotel

Bank Street, IV51 9BU
11 (12.30 Sun)-11
(01478) 612525 royal-hotel-skye.com
Beer range varies H

The Royal Hotel has an enviable location, in the town centre overlooking Portree's picturesque harbour, with 21 bedrooms, two bars, a restaurant and fitness centre. Three handpumps dispense the house special MacNab's Ale and other Isle of Skye beers with occasional guests. Live, traditional music is hosted regularly in the bars, and excellent food is served all year round.

SCOTLAND

Roy Bridge

Stronlossit Hotel

PH31 4AG

11-11.45 (1am Thu-Sat); 12.30-11.45 Sun

☎ (01397) 712253 stronlossit.co.uk

Beer range varies H

Traditional Scottish inn situated at the foot of the Nevis mountain range surrounded by landscaped gardens, making it an ideal base for outdoor activities or touring in the Highlands. Bar meals featuring local produce are available all day. The three handpumps dispense a selection of Scottish beers often from Highland breweries and an occasional cider. Opening times may vary in December and January. ⛰❀🛏◐♿Å≥🚌♠P

Scourie

Scourie Hotel

IV27 4SX (on A894 between Laxford Bridge and Kylesku)

11-2.30, 5-11 summer; winter hours vary; 12-2.30, 6-10.30 Sun

☎ (01971) 502396 scourie-hotel.co.uk

Beer range varies H

Popular with fishermen, this converted 1640 coaching inn overlooks Scourie Bay, handy for the bird reserve of Handa Island and the peaks of Arkle and Foinavon. The bar has a fishing theme with 1940s fishing nets as decoration. In addition to a fixed bar menu, the hotel dining room serves high quality four-course meals featuring seafood, with the menu changing daily. Four handpumps dispense mainly Scottish beer, usually from Cairngorm in winter, and one or two ciders. Q❀🛏◐Å♣♠P⊱

Thurso

Central Hotel

3 Traill Street, KW14 8EJ

11-11.45 (1am Fri & Sat); 12.30-11.45 Sun

☎ (01847) 893129

Beer range varies H

Lively town-centre hotel, two miles from the Orkney Ferry terminal at Scrabster, on the Pentland Firth coast. Four handpumps are located in the downstairs bar with up to three ales available all year round. The main supplier is Rob Hill's Highland Brewing Company, but there is also a wide range of beers from other breweries. Children are not permitted in the downstairs bar but are most welcome in the popular upstairs play area. ❀🛏◐♿Å≥🚌♣⊱

Uig: Isle of Skye

Bakur Bar

The Pier, IV51 9XX

11.30-11 (midnight Thu; 1am Fri; 12.30am Sat); 12.30-11.30 Sun

☎ (01470) 542212

Beer range varies H

Traditional west coast bar situated in a convenient location on the Pier at Uig adjacent to the Western Isles Ferry Terminal, and a stone's throw from the Isle of Skye Brewery, which supplies most of the ales. During the summer months three ales are available, with a more limited range in the quieter winter season. The Bakur has a pool table and is popular with the locals. ❀◐♿Å🚌P⊱

Uig Hotel

IV51 9YE

11 (5 winter, 12.30 Sun)-midnight (11 Sun); closed Jan

☎ (01470) 542205 uighotel.com

Beer range varies H

This attractive and imposing family-run old coaching inn has spectacular views across Uig Bay to the ferry terminal for the Western Isles. The cosy lounge bar dispenses Isle of Skye beers from two handpulls in summer and one in winter. The friendly staff provide excellent service and meals are available in both the bar and adjoining restaurant. The hotel keeps its own highland cattle. Handy for a visit to the Isle of Skye Brewery. ⛰Q❀🛏◐♿🚌P

Ullapool

Morefield Motel

North Road, IV26 2TQ (off A835) NH125947

12 (12.30 Sun)-11

☎ (01854) 612161 morefieldmotel.co.uk

Beer range varies H

Locally-caught seafood is the speciality on the menu at this friendly and welcoming hostelry. Three ales are predominantly from local Highland breweries. Landlord Tony organises the annual Ullapool Beer Festival, held at the Morefield in October. Comfortable motel accommodation provides an excellent base for discovering the surrounding area. Q❀🛏◐♿Å♣P⊱

Waternish: Isle of Skye

Stein Inn ✔

Waternish, IV55 8GA (N of Dunvegan, on B886) NG263564

11-midnight (1am Fri; 12.30am Sat); 12-11 (midnight Fri & Sat) winter; 12.30-11 Sun

☎ (01470) 592362 steininn.co.uk

Isle of Skye Red Cuillin; guest beers H

Family-run 18th-century inn, nestling in a charming fishing village on the shores of Loch Bay, with an intimate, traditional bar. The ever-changing menu features the freshest of local produce from land and sea, transformed into mouth-watering, home-cooked dishes, served in the bar or dining room. Three real ales include an Isle of Skye Brewery house beer. The waterside beer garden enjoys stunning views. ⛰Q❀🛏◐♿♣P⊱

Whitebridge

Whitebridge Hotel

IV2 6UN

11-11 Apr-Oct; 11-2.30, 5-11 Nov-Mar; 12.30-11 Sun

☎ (01456) 486226 whitebridgehotel.co.uk

Caledonian 80; guest beers H

Built in 1899, this hotel is situated on an original military road through the foothills of the Monadhliath mountains. There is a classic Wade Bridge nearby and the famous Falls of Foyers are close. The hotel has fishing rights on two local lochs. The attractive pitch pine panelled main bar has an alcove with a pool table. The second handpump sells a variety of Scottish ales in summer. Most of the traditional pub food is home cooked. ⛰Q❀🛏◐🚌♣P

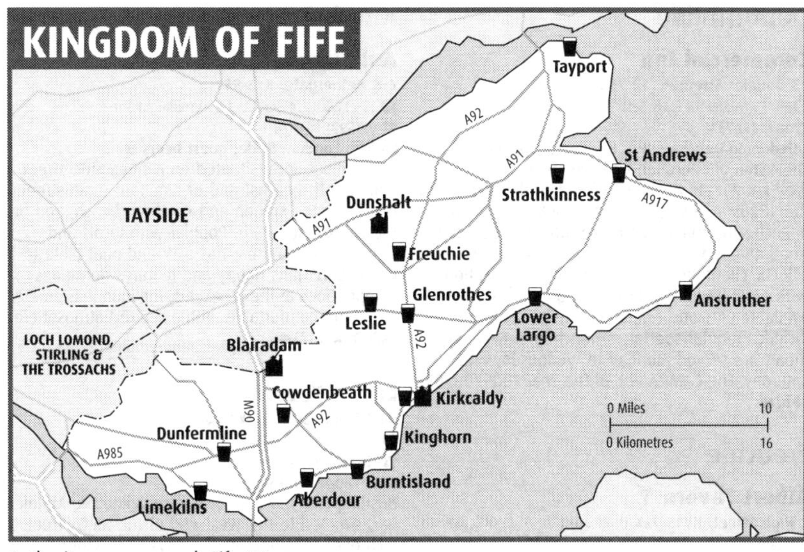

Authority area covered: Fife UA

Aberdour

Aberdour Hotel

38 High Street, KY3 0SW

⌚ 4-11; 3-11.45 Fri; 11-11.45 Sat & Sun

☎ (01383) 860325 🌐 aberdourhotel.co.uk

Caledonian Deuchars IPA; guest beers Ⓗ

Small, friendly, family-run hotel in a popular town overlooking the Forth, handy for the golf course and beaches. The hotel started life as a coaching inn and the old stables are still evident to the rear. The cosy bar with a real coal fire has one real ale during the winter, two in spring and summer. Excellent meals are available in the evening and at weekends, made with fresh local produce.
⛰♨⇌◐◑♿⇌🚌(7)P

Anstruther

Dreel Tavern

16 High Street, KY10 3DL

⌚ 11 (12.30 Sun)-midnight

☎ (01334) 310727 🌐 thedreeltavern.co.uk

Caledonian Deuchars IPA; guest beer Ⓗ

Previously a Fife CAMRA Pub of the Year, the Dreel is housed in an old stone building in a fishing village on the Forth with traditional crow step gables and pantile roof. The public and lounge bars are separated by an open fire. Wood panelling and stone walls with an ornamental stove at one end of the bar all add to a cosy atmosphere. The games room has a pool table. A conservatory to the rear provides a pleasant dining area.
⛰Q❀◐◑🚌(X26,95)♣⊱

Ship Tavern

49 Shore Street, KY10 3AQ

⌚ 11-midnight (1am Fri & Sat); 12.30-midnight Sun

☎ (01333) 310347

Beer range varies Ⓗ

Old, traditional pub on the harbour front. The main bar has a picture window overlooking the harbour, which provides berths for around 100 boats. Above the mirror behind the bar, a mural of the harbour covers two walls. The flagstone floor leads you to a back room which has a pool table. The bar is the office for the Reaper, a herring drifter over 100 years old which still sails to sea festivals during the summer. ⊞🚌♣

Burntisland

Crown Tavern

17 Links Place, KY3 9DY

⌚ 11 (12.30 Sun)-midnight

☎ (01592) 873697

Beer range varies Ⓗ

Two-roomed traditional small-town pub with a lively, spacious public bar with two plasma screens for sports. An attractive gantry, wood panelling and splendid etched glass windows overlooking the links create an old fashioned, traditional feel in the bar. There is also a large lounge with pool table. One beer from a Scottish independent is on handpump, with a second at weekends and busy times. The pub is on the Fife Coastal Path.
⊞♿⇌🚌(6,7)♣

Cowdenbeath

Woodside Hotel

109 Broad Street, KY4 8JR

⌚ 11 (12.30 Sun)-midnight

☎ (01383) 510475

Beer range varies Ⓗ

Large single-roomed bar with two handpumps dispensing changing Inveralmond beers. At one side of the room there is a pool table and dartboard, and around the room there are four plasma screens for sport. A warm, friendly atmosphere prevails, with poker played on Wednesday and Thursday and live entertainment at weekends. A lounge is available for small functions. There is a covered, outdoor decked area with seating at the rear.
❀⇌⊞♿⇌🚌(19,19a,30)♣P⊱

Dunfermline

Commercial Inn

13 Douglas Street, KY12 7EB

11-11 (midnight Fri & Sat); 12.30-11 Sun

(01383) 733876

Caledonian Deuchars IPA, 80; Courage Directors; Theakston Old Peculier; guest beers

Well-known ale house in a building dating back to the 1820s. A cosy town-centre pub, it is situated opposite the main post office off the High Street. Good quality food and friendly service attract an eclectic clientele. This is a pub for conversation, with quiet background music. Eight ales are always available plus one cider. An extensive food menu includes regular specials at lunchtime. Evening meals are served Monday to Wednesday and Saturday. Fife CAMRA Pub of the Year 2005/06/08.

Freuchie

Albert Tavern

2 High Street, KY15 7EX (half km E of A92 Kirkcaldy to Dundee rd)

5 (12 Fri & Sat)-midnight; 12.30-midnight Sun

(07765) 169342

Beer range varies

Family-friendly village local, reputedly a coaching inn when nearby Falkland Palace was a royal residence. An old photograph shows the property as a tavern some time in the 19th century. Both bar and lounge have beamed ceilings and the bar has wainscot panelling. The lounge has TV for sports. Three handpumps offer guest beers. Outside is a small patio area beside the east gable. Scottish CAMRA Pub of the Year 2002 and runner up 2008. National Pub of the Year runner up 2002.
Q

Lomand Hills Hotel

High Street, KY15 7EY

11-2, 5-midnight; 11-midnight Fri & Sat; 12.30-midnight Sun

(01337) 857180 lomondhillshotel.com

Beer range varies

Comfortable country hotel with a marvellous view of the Lomand Hills. The owner has previous experience running ale houses. The small welcoming public bar sports a newly carved bar top. Two beers are always available, usually from Scottish micros. The leisure centre, with heated pool and sauna, is available to guests.
P

Glenrothes

Golden Acorn

1 North Street, KY7 5NA

11 (12.30 Sun)-midnight

(01592) 751175

Beer range varies

Large Wetherspoon's bar with its own accommodation. In the bar, scenes of the local area in days gone by decorate various pillars. Real ale on four handpumps and an occasional cider are on offer, as well as the usual Wetherspoon's festivals and special offers. The house beer is from the local Fyfe Brewing Company. Families are welcome until 6pm if dining. Outside is a seating and smoking area. The bus station is nearby.
P

Kinghorn

Auld Hoose

6-8 Nethergate, KY3 9SY

12 (11 Sat)-midnight; 12.30-midnight Sun

(01592) 891074

Fuller's Londion Pride; guest beers

Busy village local situated on a steep side street leading off the east end of Kinghorn main street, handy for the station and Kinghorn beach, and on the Fife Coastal Path. Popular with locals and visitors, the main bar has a TV and pool table to keep sports fans happy and features dominoes competitions at the weekend. The lounge is quieter and more comfortable with a relaxed atmosphere.
(6,7)

Crown Tavern

55-57 High Street, KY3 9UW

11 (12.30 Sun)-11.45

(01592) 890340

Beer range varies

Bustling two-roomed local, also called the Middle Bar, situated to the west end of the High Street. Two ever-changing ales, always from Scottish independents, are dispensed by cheery bar staff. Attractive stained glass panels feature on the windows and the door. Mainly a sports bar, a large screen shows major events, and there are two TVs and a pool table in a side room. A collection of footballs autographed by SPL players is on show at the end of bar. (6,7)

Kirkcaldy

Harbour Bar

471-475 High Street, KY1 1JL

11-3, 5-midnight; 11-midnight Thu-Sat; 12.30-midnight Sun

(01592) 264270 fyfebrewery.co.uk

Beer range varies

Situated on the ground floor of a tenement building, this unspoilt local has been described by regulars as a 'village local in the middle of town'. Memorabilia featuring the town's past shipping history adorns the walls. Six handpumps offer up to 20 different beers each week from micros all over Britain including those from Fyfe Brewery which is situated to the rear of the pub. CAMRA Fife Pub of the Year on numerous occasions and Scottish Pub of the Year runner up in 2000. Q

Robert Nairn

2-6 Kirk Wynd, KY1 1EH

11 (12.30 Sun)-midnight

(01592) 205049

Beer range varies

A Lloyds No 1 with a split-level lounge and separate family area. Bookcases are dotted around and there are pictures of old Kirkcaldy on the walls. Six handpumps sell a variety of ales, including brews from the local Fyfe Brewery. There is a good selection of bottled ciders. Frequent beer festivals are held throught the year. Meals are served until 10pm.

INDEPENDENT BREWERIES

Fyfe Kirkaldy
Loch Leven Blairadam (NEW)
Luckie Dunshalt (NEW)

Leslie

Burns Tavern

184 High Street, KY6 3DB

12 (11 Fri & Sat)-midnight; 12.30-midnight Sun

(01592) 741345

Taylor Landlord; guest beers H

Typical Scottish two-room main street local in a town once famous for paper making. The public bar is on two levels, the lower lively and friendly, the upper with a large-screen TV, pool table and football memorabilia on the walls. The lounge bar is quieter and more spacious. A quiz is held on Thursday and karaoke in the lounge on Saturday. Leslie Folk Club meets here and plays on a Sunday. Two beers are usually available, one from a Scottish micro. This is a real gem. (X1,201)

Limekilns

Ship Inn

Halkett's Hall, KY11 3HJ (on the promenade)

11-11 (midnight Fri & Sat)

(01383) 872247

Beer range varies; H

Traditional white coastal building near the harbour with a single room interior with a fresh maritime themed decor. Well placed seats outside provide superb views of the River Forth. Three guest ales on handpump are looked after by a knowledgeable owner. Full lunches are served with fish and other seafood a speciality. Bar snacks are available outside lunchtime hours. (73,76)

Lower Largo

Crusoe Hotel

Main Street, KY8 6BT

11-midnight (1am Fri & Sat); 12-midnight Sun

(01333) 320759 crusoehotel.co.uk

Caledonian Deuchars IPA; guest beer H

Very clean and tidy bar with lovely polished brasses and a wood-beamed ceiling. There are three handpulls, one with a regular beer and two guests. The gantry is also well stocked. There is a separate lounge bar. Lunchtime and evening meals are served. Situated on the Fife Coastal Path, this bar is well worth a visit. P

Railway Inn

1 Station Wynd, KY8 6BU

11 (12.30 Sun)-midnight

(01333) 320239

Beer range varies H

Small two-room pub close to the picturesque harbour. The bar has a railway theme and displays photographs of the last trains to pass on the viaduct overhead before the Beeching measures of the 1960s. The four handpumps serve various beers from all over Britain. Q

St Andrews

Central Bar

77-79 Market Street, KY16 9NU

11-11.45 (1am Fri & Sat); 12.30-11.45 Sun

(01334) 478296

Beer range varies H

Student oriented town centre pub, also popular with locals. It has a Victorian style island bar, large windows and ornate mirrors creating a late 19th-century feel. The bar manager is dedicated to his ales and the staff are very friendly. A good mix of students, local business folk and tourists makes this an interesting, bustling hostelry. The only pub in town that serves food until 10pm, pavement tables are available, weather permitting. Ten minutes' walk from the bus station.

Whey Pat Tavern

2 Argyle Street, KY16 9EX

11-11.30 (11.45 Fri & Sat); 12.30-11.30 Sun

(01334) 477740

Greene King IPA; guest beers H

Town-centre pub on a busy road junction just outside the old town walls and three minutes from the bus station. There has been a hostelry on this site for a few centuries. It was taken over by Belhaven in 2002 but has changed little since then, with four beers on handpump, one regular, three guests. The front bar is L-shaped with a dartboard and TV, and there is an airy lounge/meeting room to the rear. A mixed clientele of all ages frequents this busy venue.

Strathkinness

Tavern

4 High Road, KY16 9RS

12-2.30, 5-midnight; 12-midnight Sat; 12.30-midnight Sun

(01334) 850085 strathkinnesstavern.co.uk

Beer range varies H

Public bar with seating and a comfortable lounge at one end, offering a choice of two handpulls with changing guest ales. There is a separate room with a pool table and brain teaser games to test your sobriety. Lunches and suppers are available in the bar or you can dine in the restaurant. (Lunches served 12 -2pm Wed-Fri, all day Sat, 12-4pm Sun; evening meals from 5pm.) There is a beer garden at the rear. Q (96)P

Tayport

Bellrock Tavern

4-6 Dalgleish Street, DD6 9BB

11-midnight (1am Thu-Sat); 12.30-midnight Sun

(01382) 552388

Beer range varies H

Friendly small-town local opposite the picturesque harbour, with wonderful views across the Tay to Dundee and Broughty Ferry. The bar is on three levels, each with a mainly nautical theme, including old charts, photographs of ships and aircraft, old Dundee and the Tay Ferries. One beer is on handpump with a second at busy times. Good value home cooking is served at lunchtimes Monday to Saturday. Evening meals are available Friday and Saturday, with high teas on a Sunday. Close to the Fife coastal path. Q

How easy can the barley-bree
Cement the quarrel.
It's aye the cheapest lawyer's fee
To taste the barrel. **Robert Burns**

LOCH LOMOND, STIRLING & THE TROSSACHS

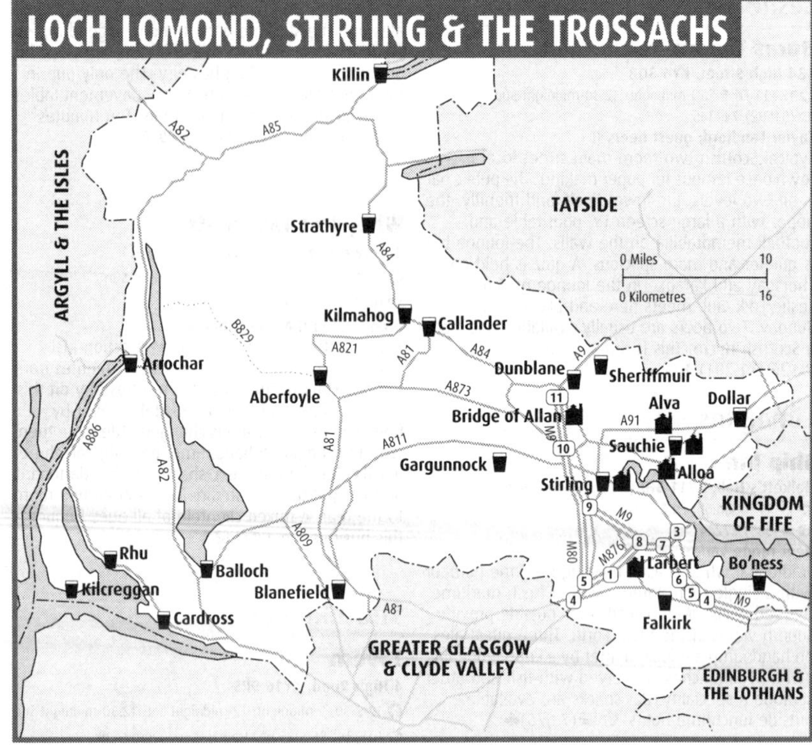

Aberfoyle

Forth Inn Hotel

Main Street, FK8 3UQ
11-midnight (1am Fri & Sat)
(01877) 382372 forthinn.com
Beer range varies

This 100-year-old, family-run hostelry, popular with locals and tourists alike, is situated within Scotland's first National Park. Wood-panelled walls feature in the bar and lounge. There is also a separate restaurant and accommodation. The food and ales make this a must-see location for visitors to the Trossachs. Three handpumps are in use, with beers from Belhaven among the range.

Arrochar

Village Inn

Shore Road, G83 7AX (on A814) NN293034
11-midnight (1am Fri & Sat); 12-midnight Sun
(01301) 702279 maclay.com/village-inn-arrochar.html
Beer range varies

Set back from the road by a sizeable lawn with trees, it is easy to miss this welcoming real ale oasis. The bar has a bay window to view Loch Long and the Arrochar Alps, while three handpumps serve beers mostly from the local Fyne Ales brewery. Good food is available in the bar and restaurant. A 'must visit' for those touring or walking in the area.

Balloch

Tullie Inn

Balloch Road, G83 8SW (next to railway station)
11-midnight (1am Fri & Sat); 12-midnight Sun
(01389) 752052 maclay.com/tullie-inn-balloch.html
Caledonian Deuchars IPA; Fyne Highlander; Greene King Old Speckled Hen, Abbot; guest beers

Contemporary inn serving mainly young locals in the spacious bar, and diners in an older building. Five pumps serve two English and up to three Scottish beers – the guest is often from Fyne Ales. Conveniently situated next to Balloch rail station, with frequent trains from Glasgow, it has a well furnished beer garden and covered and heated smoking area. The pub runs a quiz and musical entertainment at weekends. The restaurant offers good, modern food.

Blanefield

Carbeth Inn

Stockiemuir Road, G63 9AY (on A809 N of Milngavie, near B821 jct) NS524791
11-11 (midnight Thu-Sat); 12.30-11 Sun
(01360) 770002
Beer range varies

INDEPENDENT BREWERIES

Bridge of Allan Bridge of Allan
Devon Sauchie
Harviestoun Alva
Traditional Scottish Ales Stirling
Tryst Larbert
Williams Alloa

An old inn on the road between Milngavie and Drymen. Situated at the edge of Mugdock Country Park on the West Highland Way, the pub provides a welcome resting spot for walkers and those on a day out, as well as fishermen and bikers. The bar has a snug/lounge to one side, with a handpump secreted at the end of the counter serving beers from the Belhaven list. The garden is a real sun trap. (No 8)P

Bo'ness

Riverview

16 Church Wynd, EH51 0EQ

5 (12 Sat)-midnight (1am Fri & Sat); 12.30-midnight Sun

(01506) 826450 riverview.bo-ness.org.uk

Beer range varies H

Bo'ness or Borrowstouness is at the eastern end of the Antonine Wall, built by the Romans and stretching across central Scotland. From the shores of the Forth, Bo'ness rises up a steep slope; halfway up is the Riverview with spectacular views over the Forth. It has a bar area away from the restaurant, where two handpumps serve a varied range of beers from Scotland and England. Although the TV is on for sporting events, conversation is the key to the pub's character. P

Callander

Waverley Hotel

88-92 Main Street, FK17 8BD

11-midnight (1am Fri & Sat); 12.30-midnight Sun

(01877) 330245 thewaverley.co.uk

Beer range varies H

Renowned for the range and quality of its ales, the pub holds two beer festivals in September and December. Four handpumps are in use during the winter, rising to eight in summer. Food and accommodation are available and a beer garden was recently added to the hotel's facilities. An ideal base for visitors to the area, it is situated on the Perthshire whisky trail and at the edge of the Trossachs National Park. Q

Cardross

Coach House Inn

Main Road, G82 5JX NS347775

12-midnight (1am Thu-Sat)

(01389) 841358 coachhousecardross.com

Caledonian Deuchars IPA; guest beers H

A half-hour train ride from Glasgow will find you in the leafy lanes of Cardross, home to this welcoming inn. Divided into dining, bar and pool areas, there is always a free corner to sit and relax. You should find Deuchars on handpump and at the weekend a varying guest ale from anywhere in Britain. With good food and rooms, the pub is well located to enjoy the great scenery. Amble down to the Clyde or walk over to Loch Lomond on the Stoneymollan Trail. (216)P

Dollar

Kings Seat

19-23 Bridge Street, FK14 7DE

11-11 (midnight Fri & Sat); 12.30-11 Sun

(01259) 742515

Caledonian Deuchars IPA; Harviestoun Bitter & Twisted; guest beers H

Popular with locals, and visitors during the tourist season, this old coaching inn has low ceilings and a cosy, comfortable feel. Located on the main street in this historic and attractive village on the southern edge of the Ochil Hills, the pub is well placed for rambling, golf and fishing, with Stirling just 15 miles away. Up to four ales are available, with guests usually including a Harviestoun seasonal beer. The restaurant serves quality meals at reasonable prices. Q(23,65,70)

Dunblane

Dunblane Hotel

10 Stirling Road, FK15 9EP

11-midnight (1am Fri & Sat)

(01786) 822178

Greene King Abbot; Taylor Landlord; guest beers H

Cask ales from local brewers are a regular feature here, with four beers always available. The bar is decorated with brewery mirrors, while the comfortable lounge features pictures with an angling theme. An excellent view of the River Allan can be enjoyed from the rear window, which overlooks the patio. A very popular pub quiz is held every other Thursday. There is an upstairs meeting room for hire and B&B is available. Last orders for food is 8pm. P

Tappit Hen

Kirk Street, FK15 0AL

11-11.45 (1am Fri & Sat); 12.30-midnight Sun

(01786) 825226

Caledonian Deuchars IPA; guest beers H

An ever-changing range of cask ales from north and south of the border is served from five handpumps. Locals and tourists alike are welcomed to this single roomed pub, in the shadows of Dunblane's famous cathedral. All are encouraged to bring an instrument to the folk music night every Tuesday. Building on the success of recent years, real ale festivals are held in May and October. Forth Valley CAMRA Pub of the Year finalist 2009.

Falkirk

Wheatsheaf Inn

16 Baxters Wynd, FK1 1PF

11-11 (1am Fri & Sat); 12.30-11 Sun

(01324) 638282

Caledonian Deuchars IPA; guest beers H

Popular with locals and real ale enthusiasts, this pub dates from the 18th century and retains much of its original character. The bar is wood panelled and furnished in traditional style with plenty of interesting features from the past. Two guest beers are offered midweek and three at the weekend. Quality bar snacks are served until 6pm and tea and coffee are always on offer. A private room is available for hire. A regular local CAMRA Pub of the Year finalist, and winner in 2008. (Grahamston/Falkirk High)

Gargunnock

Gargunnock Inn

Main Street, FK8 3BW

5-11 (1am Fri); 12-1am Sat; 12-11 Sun

(01786) 860333

Beer range varies H

Managed by a keen CAMRA member, the original building was an 18th-century staging inn, since extended to provide a restaurant and a function room. A true village pub, it serves both the local community and passing tourists. The bar offers a rotating range of local and guest ales on handpump, with sparkler option. Bar billiards and a jukebox provide entertainment. The pub holds its own beer festival on the second Sunday in August in a marquee in the car park. ❀♿🚌P

Kilcreggan

Kilcreggan Hotel 🏆

Argyll Road, G84 0JP (At tip of Rosneath Peninsula approx 200m off B833) NS238805

⏲ 11.30-midnight (1am Fri & Sat); 12.30-midnight Sun

☎ (01436) 842 243 🌐 kilcregganhotel.com

Beer range varies Ⓗ

Travel here by ferry from Gourock and it is just a short walk from the pier to reach this Victorian hotel. The elevated bar, decorated with nautical ephemera, has fabulous views of the Clyde. Up to four ales are usually available, often supplied by local micros, but there are beers from all over Britain here too. Good food is served and if you have lingered too long you can return to Glasgow by bus and train. ❀🛏◐🚌(316)P⁻

Killin

Falls of Dochart Inn

Gray Street, FK21 8SL

⏲ 12-midnight

☎ (01567) 820270 🌐 falls-of-dochart-inn.co.uk

Caledonian Deuchars IPA; guest beers Ⓗ

This pub is situated at the end of a bridge overlooking the Falls. The atmospheric bar has a large hearth and log-burning grate. Up to three cask ales may be on offer but often just one in winter. Food is served all day, made with fresh local produce wherever possible. There is a small separate dining room adjoining a tea shop. B&B and self- catering accommodation are available in this pet-friendly establishment. 🔥Q❀🛏◐P

Kilmahog

Lade Inn

FK17 8HD (A84/A821 jct, 1 mile W of Callander)

⏲ 12-11 (1am Fri & Sat); 12.30-11 Sun

☎ (01877) 330152 🌐 theladeinn.com

Trossachs Waylade, Ladeback, Ladeout; guest beers Ⓗ

The Lade Inn goes from strength to strength, ever popular with locals and tourists. Its three cask ales are unique to the pub, which has LocAle accreditation. The food also uses locally-sourced ingredients where possible. The pub offers a public bar, restaurant and beer garden. Live entertainment is provided most weekends, year round, and a beer festival is held during the summer. The Scottish Real Ale shop is adjacent to the inn, with over 120 Scottish bottled beers on sale. 🔥Q👶❀◐🅱♿⛺🚌P

Rhu

Rhu Inn

49 Gareloch Road, G84 8LA

⏲ 11-11.45 (12.45am Fri & Sat); 12.30-11 Sun

☎ (01436) 821048 🌐 therhuinn.co.uk

Caledonian Deuchars IPA Ⓗ

A little gem overlooking Rhu Bay and its yachts on the Gareloch, patronised by locals and yachtsmen. As you take in the sun and scenery, a passing submarine may add further interest. The cosy interior of this village pub features wood panelling, an open fire and some historical pictures, all adding to the charm of an inn that dates back to 1684. A warm welcome is assured. Live music often plays at weekends. 🔥🛏♿🚌(316)♣P

Sauchie

Mansfield Arms ✔

7 Main Street, FK10 3JR

⏲ 11-11.30 (12.30am Fri & Sat); 12.30-11.30 Sun

☎ (01259) 722020 🌐 devonales.com

Devon Original, Thick Black, Pride Ⓟ

This brew-pub, manufacturing the glorious Devon ales, is the oldest operating brewery in the county. The pub is very popular with locals in this ex-mining community, and families come to enjoy good value meals, served in the lounge. Situated close to the once-famous brewing town of Alloa, the pub is on a frequent bus route to Stirling. Golf and fishing are available close by. ◐🅱♿⇌(Alloa)🚌(60,62,63)P🍺

Sheriffmuir

Sheriffmuir Inn

FK15 0LN NN827022

⏲ 12-2, 5.30-11; closed Tue; 12-11 Sat; 12.30-10.30 Sun

☎ (01786) 823285 🌐 sheriffmuirinn.co.uk

Beer range varies Ⓗ

This late 18th-century droving inn features flagstone floors and an open fire in the restaurant. One handpump is in use during the winter months, two in summer. This hostelry is off the beaten track but is very popular with locals, hillwalkers and tourists. Outside is a children's play area and an ancient well, still in use today. Good locally-sourced food and accommodation in two rooms. 🔥Q❀🛏◐🅱♿P⁻

Stirling

Portcullis Hotel

Castle Wynd, FK8 1EG (close to Stirling Castle esplanade)

⏲ 11.30 (12.30 Sun)-midnight

☎ (01786) 472290 🌐 theportcullishotel.com

Beer range varies Ⓗ

Situated close to Stirling Castle, the Portcullis is a former 18th-century grammar school. It is renowned for its food and regularly-changing Scottish real ales and attracts a mix of diners, tourists and regulars. Always busy, diners are advised to reserve a table. 🔥Q❀🛏◐⇌

Strathyre

Inn & Bistro

Main Street, FK18 8NA (on A84)

⏲ 12 (12.30 Sun)-11

☎ (01877) 384224 🌐 innatstrathyre.com

Beer range varies Ⓗ

This pub has a main bar with an open fire and cosy atmosphere. Meals and snacks made with local produce are available in both the bar and bistro. One of the handpumps is used to rotate ales from local breweries on a monthly basis, and a beer festival is held in the summer. A spacious beer garden has been recently added. Accommodation is available, with families and dogs welcome. 🔥Q❀🛏◐♿⛺🚌♣P⁻

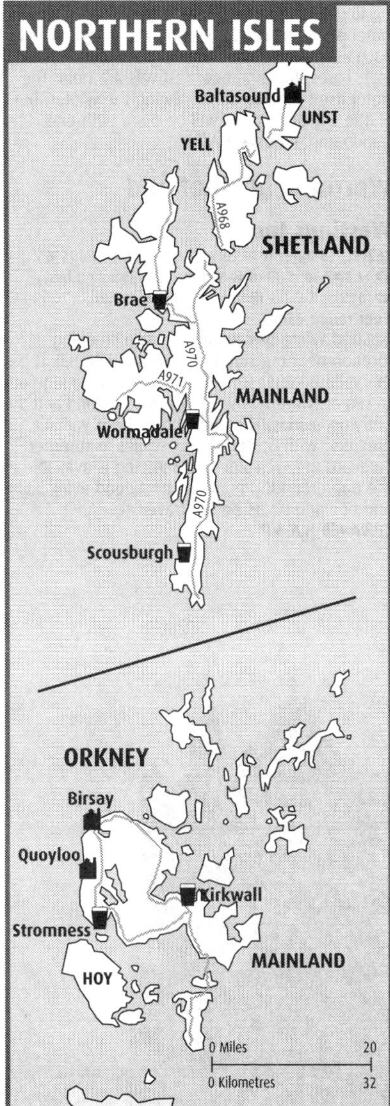

Authority area covered: Highland

Brae: Shetland

Busta House Hotel

ZE2 9QN (signed Busta and Muckle Roe from A970) HU345669

11-11 (midnight Sun)

(01806) 522506 bustahouse.com

Beer range varies H

Rambling mansion house on many levels, dating from 1588 with numerous later additions, sympathetically converted to a country house hotel. Its extensive grounds run down to the seashore. Beer usually comes from local brewery Valhalla. An extensive range of more than 150 malt whiskies is on offer in the lounge bar. Its location is near the centre of Shetland Mainland and Mavis Grind where the Atlantic and the North Sea are separated only by the width of the road. Said to be haunted by the ghost of a young lady, Barbara Pitcairn. **Q P**

Kirkwall: Orkney

Bothy Bar (Albert Hotel)

Mounthoolie Lane, KW15 1HW

11-midnight (1am Thu-Sat); 12-midnight Sun

(01856) 876000 alberthotel.co.uk

Highland Scapa Special; Orkney Red MacGregor, Dark Island, seasonal beers H

Risen from the ashes of a fire around four years ago, the bar has been rebuilt using a lot of the original timber. It is now on just one level and, as a result, is more spacious than before and popular as ever. Ideally located in the centre of town, it is handy for shops, buses and ferries to the outer isles. A popular bar after work and part of the night scene at weekends. Meals are served daily. Beware of the premium price when buying half pints.

Helgi's Bar

14 Harbour Street, KW15 1LE

11-midnight (1am Thu-Sat); 12.30-midnight

(01856) 879273

Highland Scapa Special H

Converted from a former shipping office, this small, modern, smart bar has the look of a modern cafe. Take your drinks to the cosy, upstairs room and overlook the harbour while filling in time before island hopping on the many ferries to the outlying parts. May have installed a second pump by the time this Guide is printed.

Shore

6 Shore Street, KW15 1LG

11.30 (10 Sat)-11 (midnight Fri & Sat); 10-11

(01856) 872200

Highland Scapa Special H

Smart, modern bar in recently re-furbished hotel overlooking the harbour where one can island hop using the many ferries available to Wetray, Sanday and most of the other Orkney Islands. A darts player's haven with, unusually, a dart board at either end of the pub.

Scousburgh: Shetland

Spiggie Hotel

ZE2 9JE (signed from A970 off B9122) HU379174

12-2, 5-11 (midnight Fri); 12-midnight Sat; closed Mon & Tue winter; 12.30-11 Sun

(01950) 460409 thespiggiehotel.co.uk

Beer range varies H

Small family-run hotel built as the original terminus of the Northern Isles ferries. It has a small stone-floored bar and adjacent restaurant with views of St Ninian's Isle and the Loch of Spiggie. Birdwatching and trout fishing on the loch may be arranged. The beer comes from Valhalla brewery, with two guests in summer. There are tables in the car park for outdoor drinking. **Q P**

INDEPENDENT BREWERIES

Highland Birsay
Orkney Quoyloo
Valhalla Baltasound

SCOTLAND

Stromness: Orkney

Ferry Inn

John Street, KW16 3AA (100m from ferry terminal)
⌚ 9 (9.30 Sun)-midnight (1am Thu-Sat)
☎ (01856) 850280 🌐 ferryinn.com
Highland Scapa Special, seasonal beers; Orkney Red MacGregor, Dark Island, seasonal beers; guest beer Ⓗ
A former temperance hotel, this is a welcome sight after the ferry crossing from Scrabster. The hostelry is popular with locals and visitors, particularly the divers who come to Orkney to explore the wrecks of Scapa Flow. Local folk musicians meet regularly. Music features throughout the year and the pub hosts annual blues and folk festivals in conjunction with Stromness Hotel. ❀🛏◑ ⛺🚌

Stromness Hotel

15 Victoria Street, KW16 3AA (opp pier head)
⌚ 12-2, 5-midnight (1am Fri & Sat)
☎ (01856) 850298 🌐 stromnesshotel.com
Highland Scapa Special, seasonal beers; Orkney Red MacGregor, Dark Island, seasonal beers; guest beers Ⓗ
On the first floor of this imposing hotel is a large bar, the Hamnavoe Lounge, with windows and a small balcony overlooking the harbour. In winter (if open) a roaring fire and comfy settees welcome the visitor; during the season more space is given up to dining. Used as an Army HQ during WWII, the hotel is well placed for visiting world heritage sites such as Scara Brae and the Ring of Brodgar. Annual jazz, blues, folk and beer festivals are held. The hotel itself may be closed during the winter, but Flattie Bar downstairs will be open with one handpump. 🔥❀🛏◑ ⛺🚌P

Wormadale: Shetland

Westings Inn

ZE2 9LJ (8 miles N of Lerwick on A 971) HU403465
⌚ 12.30-2.30, 5.30 (6.30 Sun)-10.30 (midnight if busy)
☎ (01595) 840242 🌐 westings.shetland.co.uk
Beer range varies Ⓗ
Isolated white-painted inn set in a stunning location near the summit of Wormadale Hill. It has marvellous views from the comfortable lounge out to sea of Whiteness Voe, western Shetland and the outlying islands. The beer comes from Valhalla brewery, with up to two guest ales in summer. Caravans are welcome and camping is available in the pub grounds. Phone to check food availability and opening hours before travelling.
Q❀🛏◑♿⛺♣P

Stromness Hotel, Stromness: Orkney (Photo: Helge Nareid).

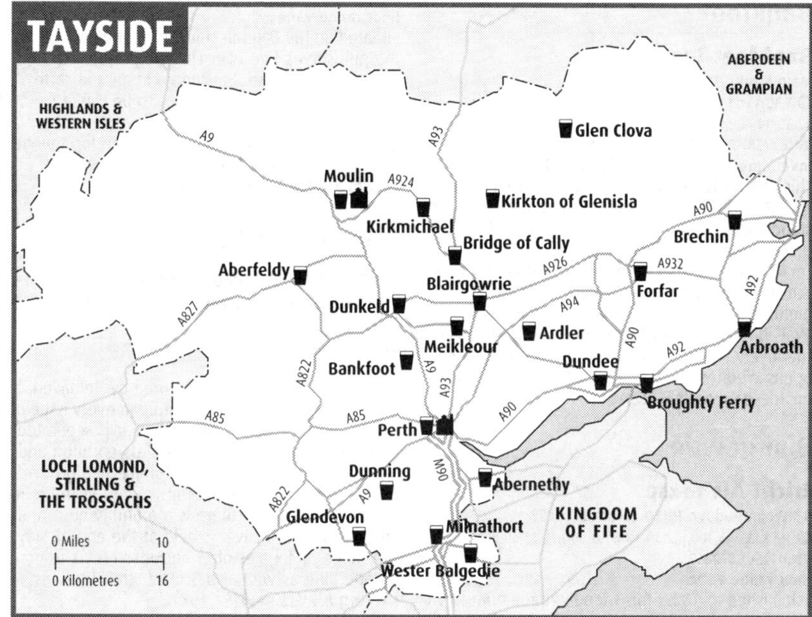

Authority areas covered: Angus UA, City of Dundee UA, Perth & Kinross UA

Aberfeldy

Black Watch Inn

Bank Street, PH15 2BB
11-11 (11.45 Thu; 12.30am Fri & Sat); 12.30-11.30 Sun
☎ (01887) 820699 theblackwatchinn.co.uk
Beer range varies H
Situated on a crossroads at the western end of the village, this hostelry offers two ales, usually from Caledonian and Sinclair breweries. The innovative publican has produced beer descriptions describing the taste and aroma of the beers regularly on offer. For smokers there is a covered and heated shelter outside. This area of Perthshire attracts many tourists and is popular with hill walkers from Britain and abroad. (23)

Abernethy

Crees Inn

Main Street, PH2 9LA
11-2, 5-11; 11-11 Sat & Sun
☎ (01738) 850714 creesinn.co.uk
Beer range varies H
A picturesque former farmhouse lying in the shadow of the imposing Abernethy Tower, one of only two Pictish watch towers in Scotland. A free house, the timber panels and beams display an impressive collection of pumb clips reflecting the varied beer range. Up to six ales are available, often from English breweries. A good selection of meals is served lunchtimes and evenings made with fresh local produce. Q(36)P

Arbroath

Corn Exchange

Market Place, DD11 1HR
11-midnight (1am Fri & Sat); 12.30-midnight Sun
☎ (01241) 432430
Courage Directors; Greene King Abbot; guest beer H
One of the best Wetherspoon's in the Tayside area, with friendly, efficient staff and rapidly-changing guest beers. The long bar usually has two or three guest beers in addition to the regulars and Old Rosie cider. Beer festivals are held in spring and autumn when all eight handpumps are used. Good value meals are served from 9am.

Lochlands Bar

14 Lochlands Street, DD11 3AB
11-midnight (1am Fri & Sat); 12.30-midnight
☎ (01241) 873286
Beer range varies; H
Independently owned, street-corner pub renowned for friendly staff and excellent service. The public bar has a selection of sporting memorabilia adorning the walls, and two satellite TVs that dominate when football (and some rugby) matches are shown. A small lounge is next door with a jukebox and a less obtrusive TV.

Ardler

Tavern

Main Street, PH12 8SR (1 mile S of A94)
6-11; 5-midnight Fri; 11-12.30am Sat; 12.30-midnight Sun
☎ (01828) 640340
Beer range varies; H
This village local has been refurbished to an extremely high standard yet retains the feel of a cosy pub owing to the dedication of the licencee. Beers from Inveralmond and Sinclair breweries are regularly served and light snacks are available. The smoking area is covered. A nearby disused railway line forms part of a rural path network in this scenic part of Perthshire. QP

INDEPENDENT BREWERIES

Inveralmond Perth
Moulin Moulin

SCOTLAND

Bankfoot

Bankfoot Inn

Main Street, PH1 4AB NO067354

⏲ 5.30-11 (11.45 Thu; 12.30am Fri); 12-12.30am Sat; 12.30-11.30 Sun

☎ (01738) 787243 🌐 bankfootinn.co.uk

Inveralmond Ossian, Lia Fail; guest beer Ⓗ

This old inn is situated in the main street of a quaint Scottish village. Refurbished to an excellent standard, the bar and restaurant sell locally-brewed Inveralmond ales as part of the CAMRA LocAle scheme. There are three handpumps, and a Scottish guest ale is also usually on offer. Music nights are held monthly. Accommodation is available allowing guests more time to discover the lovely Perthshire countryside. The restaurant opens Wednesday to Sunday and the bar is closed on Tuesday. 🛏◑🚌(22)

Blairgowrie

Ericht Alehouse

13 Wellmeadow, PH10 6ND NO180452

⏲ 1-11 (11.45 Thu; 12.30am Fri & Sat); 1-11.30 Sun

☎ (01250) 872469

Beer range varies Ⓗ

Established in 1802, this friendly, traditional town-centre pub has two seating areas divided by a well-stocked bar. A log-burning fire provides a warm welcome as you enter the lounge. Six beers vary all the time, complemented by a good selection of bottled beers. Occasionally, live music plays at weekends. Several times winner of Tayside CAMRA Pub of the Year. ♨Q♿🚌(57,59)⛃

Old Cross Inn & Restaurant

Alyth Road, Rattray, PH10 7DY NO191457

⏲ 12-11 (midnight Fri & Sat); 11-11 Sun

☎ (01250) 875502

Inveralmond Ossian Ale; Stewart Edinburgh No 3 Ⓗ

The Old Cross is part of a Victorian building which has been an inn since 1865. Originally called the Rattray Hotel, it has gone through two further name changes before finally settling on its current name in 2004. The cosy bar serves two real ales and a good choice of bar food, while the restaurant offers an a la carte alternative. ❀◑🍽🚌

Brechin

Caledonian Hotel

43-47 South Esk Street, DD9 6DZ

⏲ 5-11 (4.30-midnight Fri; 11.30-midnight Sat); 12.30-11 Sun

☎ (01356) 624345

Beer range varies Ⓗ

Extensively refurbished, this hotel has a large bar and function room/restaurant. The landlord stocks beers from Inveralmond and Houston with occasional English guests. A range of Belgian bottled beers is also offered. The Caledonian Railway terminus is opposite, with steam trains running on summer weekends. Live folk music on the last Friday of the month is popular. ♨Q❀🛏◑🚌(34,140)♣⊢

Bridge of Cally

Bridge of Cally Hotel

PH10 7JJ NO140513

⏲ 11-11 (12.30am Fri & Sat); 12-11 Sun

☎ (01250) 886231 🌐 bridgeofcallyhotel.com

Beer range varies Ⓗ

Situated on the Cateran Trail beside the River Ardle, the pub serves two ever-changing ales, with Houston a favourite. Bar food and an a la carte menu in the restaurant are not to be missed. Popular with locals and visitors, friendly and efficient staff make this an ideal place for anyone wishing to visit this lovely part of the world. ♨Q🐴❀🛏◑🍽♿🚌(71)♣P

Broughty Ferry

Fisherman's Tavern Hotel

10-16 Fort Street, DD5 2AD (by lifeboat station)

⏲ 11-midnight (1am Fri & Sat); 12.30-midnight Sun

☎ (01382) 775941 🌐 fishermanstavern.co.uk

Beer range varies Ⓗ

This 19th-century inn, now owned by Belhaven, is the only pub in Scotland to feature in every issue of the Guide since 1975. The public bar is separated from the snug by a wood and glass partition and has a ship's corner table and tongue and groove panelled walls. Traditional music plays in the rear lounge on Thursday, there is a monthly quiz, and an annual beer festival is held at the end of May. The range of six ales often includes brews from Greene King as well as a Scottish craft brewery. ♨Q❀🛏◑🍽♿⇌🚌(9X,10X)

Royal Arch ✔

258 Queen Street, DD5 2DS

⏲ 11-midnight; 12.30-11 Sun

☎ (01382) 779741 🌐 royal-arch.co.uk

Caledonian Deuchars IPA; guest beers Ⓗ

A strikingly refurbished local with Masonic associations in its name, this pub has three ales in the bar. Meals are served in the lounge. Sport, especially football, is screened on two TVs in the bar, where there is a range of sporting photos and cartoons of local characters. The fine gantry was taken from a demolished Dundee bar, the Craigour. The bus passes the door. ◑🍽⇌🚌(9X,10X)

Dundee

Counting House ✔

67-71 Reform Street, DD1 1SP

⏲ 9am (11 Sun)-midnight

☎ (01382) 225251

Caledonian Deuchars IPA; Greene King IPA; guest beers Ⓗ

A bank conversion by Wetherspoon's in 1998, this is a large open-plan establishment with a long bar. It operates long hours of opening (including food provision), attracting customers at all times of day. There are usually five or six real ales on handpump, with a good variety on the guest fonts. Real ale festivals and special price offers pull in the punters, as do the low prices generally. ◑⇌🚌

Phoenix

103 Nethergate, DD1 4DH

⏲ 11 (12.30 Sun)-midnight

☎ (01382) 200014

Caledonian Deuchars IPA; Tayor Landlord; guest beers Ⓗ

A pub with a striking and imaginative interior – the ceiling and pillars are original, the bar and gantry reputedly came from a demolished Welsh pub. Unusual metal adverts, brewery mirrors (including a rare Ballingall's of Dundee), bric-a-brac, 12-pointer stag's head and secluded seating alcoves all contribute to a place of great character, deservedly popular. Five new fonts of special design have recently been installed by the owner, Alan Bannerman, who will discuss them with customers at the drop of a hat. Several draught foreign beers are also available. ◑⇌🚌

Speedwell (Mennies) ★ ✔
165-167 Perth Road, DD2 1AS
11 (12.30 Sun)-midnight
☎ (01382) 667783 mennies.co.uk
Caledonian Deuchars IPA; guest beer H
One of the finest examples of an Edwardian pub interior in the country and featuring in CAMRA's True Scottish Heritage Pubs, this bar was built for James Speed in 1903. It is known as Mennie's, after the family who ran it for more than 50 years. The L-shaped bar is divided by a part-glazed screen, and has a magnificent mahogany gantry and counter and an anaglypta Jacobean ceiling. Two sitting rooms, separated by a glass screen, include more than 20 fonts serving many different lagers alongside two real ale handpulls. Q🚌

Dunkeld

Royal Dunkeld Hotel
Athol Street, PH8 0AR NO026428
11-11 (12.15am Fri & Sat); 12-11 Sun
☎ (01350) 727322 royaldunkeld.co.uk
Cairngorm Trade Winds; Stewart Pentland IPA; guest beer H
This former coaching inn is now a comfortable hotel on the main street of this historic town. A good sized bar with a real fire welcomes customers as they choose between two real ales from Scottish breweries. A bar menu is on offer in the bar and adjoining lounge, while an a la carte menu is available in the restaurant. The large outdoor seating area is a real sun-trap in the summer months. ◑⇌🚌P

Taybank
Main Street, PH2 9LA NO191164
11-midnight (1am Fri & Sat); 12.30-midnight Sun
☎ (01350) 727340 thetaybank.com
Orkney Northern Lights; guest beer H
This stovie house is a haven for lovers of traditional Scottish and Irish music. The public bar is full of character with an open fire and a large range of musical instruments. There is a small music room where live events are regularly held. The beer garden overlooks the River Tay with Birnam Hill beyond. Q◑⇌🚌♣P

Dunning

Kirkstyle Inn ✔
Kirkstyle Square, PH2 0RR
11-2.30 (not Mon Oct-Mar), 5-11 (midnight Fri); 11-midnight Sat; 12.30-11 Sun
☎ (01764) 684248 kirkstyle-dunning.co.uk
Beer range varies H
This traditional village inn is situated in the centre of Dunning near the historic St Serf's Church which contains the ancient Dupplin Cross and other Pictish relics. Up to three ales are available in the small public bar, often including beers from Harviestoun, Cairngorm and Greene King. There is also a restaurant and snug. Sadly there is no trace of a 19th century brewery which once stood here. Q◑🚌(17)

Forfar

Plough Inn
48 Market Street, DD8 3EW
11-midnight (1am Fri & Sat); 12.30-midnight Sun
☎ (01307) 469288
Inveralmond Ossian Ale, Thrappledouser; guest beers H
A traditional local serving up to three beers, with an emphasis on Scottish micros. Frequent live music events are held as well as occasional beer festivals. Pub games are popular including backgammon and foosball. Good food is served, with high teas daily. Remember that no visit to Forfar would be complete without tasting the legendary Forfar Bridie which is baked in the same street. A good place to stop off if you are heading for the Cairngorms National Park. ◑🚌(20)♣

Glen Clova

Glen Clova Hotel
DD8 4QS NO327731
11-11 (1am Fri & Sat); 12-11 Sun
☎ (01575) 550350 clova.com
Beer range varies H
Comfortable country hotel set within the Cairngorms National Park – a popular destination for walkers, climbers, fishermen and other outdoor types. There is a tourist path from the hotel to Loch Brandy and paths over the hills to Ballater and Braemar for the more adventurous. Beers from Houston and Stewart are served in the Climbers' Bar. A beer festival is held in early August. Recently upgraded, it now offers accommodation ranging from bunkhouse to en-suite rooms plus two luxury lodges. Q◑♣P

Glendevon

An Lochan Tormaukin
FK14 7JY NN993044
11-11 (midnight Sun)
☎ (01259) 781252 anlochan.co.uk
Beer range varies H
This former 18th-century drovers' inn is located in a peaceful setting surrounded by the Ochil Hills. Up to three ales are available including one from the new Luckie Brewery in nearby Auchtermuchty. The owners pride themselves on supporting local businesses. A comfortable, relaxed atmosphere awaits. Traditional Scottish fare and international dishes are offered. Q◑P

Kirkmichael

Strathardle Inn
PH10 7NS (on A924 Bridge of Cally to Pitlochry road) NO082599
12-2, 6-11 (11.30 Fri & Sat)
☎ (01250) 881224 strathardleinn.co.uk
Beer range varies H
The Strathardle is an old coaching inn dating back to the late 1700s, retaining the original barn and stables. It has an attractive woodland garden along with a 700 metre beat of the river Ardle, offering salmon and trout fishing. An excellent base for exploring the Southern Highlands, the Cateran Trail passes in front of the hotel. Up to three ales are available, with a strong commitment to Scottish micros. Good food is available in a relaxed setting. Q◑P

Kirkton of Glenisla

Glenisla Hotel

PH11 8PH (on B951, 10 miles N of Alyth) NO215605
🕘 12-2, 5-11; closed Mon; 12-1am Sat; 12-11 Sun
☎ (01575) 582223 🌐 glenisla-hotel.com
Beer range varies Ⓗ
An oasis for thirsty and hungry travellers, this 17th-century ex-coaching inn is a centre for a large selection of outdoor activities including cycling, fishing, shooting, skiing and pony trekking. Special Cateran Trail walking packages are available. The hotel's cosy oak-beamed bar with a wood-burning fire welcomes locals and visitors, offering one or two real ales from Scottish micros. The hotel is a social centre for the glen with occasional traditional music sessions. Out of season, please phone to confirm opening hours. ♨❀🛏◑◐♿♣P⚡

Meikleour

Meikleour Hotel

PH2 6EB
🕘 11-3, 6-11 (midnight Fri); 11-midnight Sat; 12-11 Sun
☎ (01250) 883206 🌐 meikleour-inn.co.uk
Beer range varies Ⓗ
Warm, welcoming up-market village inn with a stone-flagged bar and comfortable lounge offering up to three cask ales. It is a popular venue for walkers and fishermen as well as those wanting a good meal or drink in a relaxing environment. The house beer, Lure of Meikleour, is brewed by Inveralmond. Nearby is the Meikleour Beech Hedge (100ft high and a third of a mile long), which was planted in 1745 and is recognised in the Guinness Book of Records as the tallest hedge in the world. ♨Q❀🛏◑◐🍺♿🚌(58)P

Milnathort

Village Inn

36 Westerloan, KY13 9YH
🕘 2-11; 11-11.30 Fri & Sat; 12.30-11 Sun
☎ (01577) 863293
Inveralmond Thrappledouser; guest beers Ⓗ
Welcoming village local with a split-level interior – a comfortable lounge area is on the lower level and on the higher level the bar has a low ceiling, exposed joists and stone walls, with an open fire and unobtrusive piped music. The rear games area has a pool table. ♨❀♿🚌(56,56B)♣

Moulin

Moulin Inn

11-13 Kirkmichael Road, PH16 5EH
🕘 11-11 (11.45 Fri & Sat); 12-11.45
☎ (01796) 472196 🌐 moulininn.co.uk
Moulin Light, Braveheart, Ale of Atholl, Old Remedial Ⓗ
This country inn dominates the square in the centre of the village. Located one mile from the town of Pitlochry, the 'Gateway to the Highlands', this 17th-century hostlery brews its range of four beers in the old coach house next door. Extended and refurbished, the pub retains its original character and charm, furnished in traditional style with two log fires. A good choice of home-prepared local fare is served. ♨Q👶❀🛏◑◐♣P

Perth

Capital Asset ✔

26 Tay Street, PH1 5LQ (On W bank of River Tay)
🕘 11-11 (11.45 Thu; 12.30am Fri & Sat); 12.30-11 Sun
☎ (01738) 580457
Caledonian Deuchars IPA; Greene King Abbot; guest beers Ⓗ
A former TSB bank overlooking the River Tay between the town's two bridges, the building was converted by Wetherspoon into a large open plan lounge bar. The original high ceilings and ornate cornices have been retained along with the large safe. Up to five ales are available. Food is served all day. The pub is popular for pre-show refreshments for visitors to the nearby repertory theatre and modern concert hall. It gets very busy at weekend evenings. 👶◑◐♿⇌🚌(7)⚡

Cherrybank Inn

210 Glasgow Road, PH2 0NA
🕘 11-11 (11.45 Sat & Sun)
☎ (01738) 624349 🌐 cherrybankinn.co.uk
Inveralmond Independence, Ossian Ale; guest beers Ⓗ
This former drovers' inn is located on the western outskirts of Perth. A popular local, it is also ideal for travellers, with comfortable accommodation in seven en-suite rooms. Thought to be one of the oldest public houses in the town, it has a small public bar with two adjacent rooms and a comfortable lounge where meals are served. The nearby Cherrybank Gardens are well worth a visit, with the UK's largest collection of heathers. Up to four ales are available from Scottish micros. Q🛏◑◐🍺🚌(7)P⚡

Greyfriars

15 South Street, PH2 8PG
🕘 11-11 (11.45 Fri & Sat); 3-11 Sun
☎ (01738) 633036 🌐 greyfriarsbar.com
Beer range varies Ⓗ
Greyfriars may well be the smallest lounge bar in Perth, but it has an enviable reputation among locals and visitors alike as one of the friendliest pubs in the 'Fair City'. Up to four cask ales are on offer including the house ale Friars Tipple brewed locally by Inveralmond. 'Aite blath agus cardiel' – a warm and friendly place. ◑⇌🚌

Wester Balgedie

Balgedie Toll Tavern

KY13 9HE
🕘 11-11 (11.30 Thu; 12.30am Fri & Sat); 12.30-11.30 Sun
☎ (01592) 840212
Harviestoun Bitter & Twisted; guest beer Ⓗ
A welcoming, comfortable tavern with an emphasis on food. This former toll house has three seating areas and a small bar. Oak beams, horse brasses, low ceilings and an open gas fire contribute to the good old-fashioned ambience. Bar snacks and full meals of a high standard are served. The guest beer is usually from Inveralmond. ❀◑◐🚌(201,205)P⚡

Northern Ireland
Channel Islands
Isle of Man

NORTHERN IRELAND

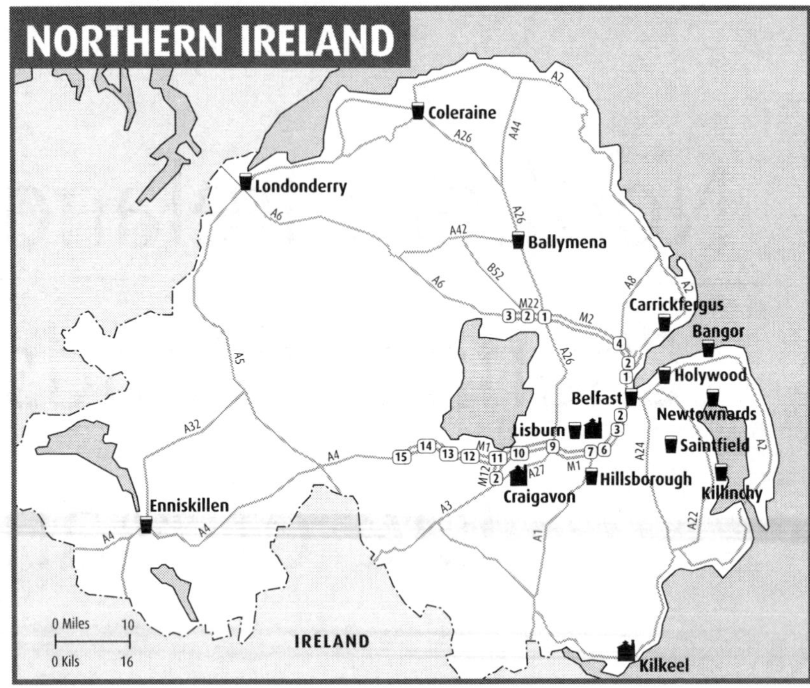

Ballymena

Spinning Mill

17-21 Broughshane Street, BT43 6EB

9-11 (12.30am Fri & Sat)

(028) 2563 8985

Greene King IPA, Abbot; guest beer

This is a town-centre Wetherspoon's pub full of character, with friendly, knowledgeable staff. It boasts an open fire with ornate wooden surrounds and comfortable sofas. Wetherspoon's pricing policy makes this probably the cheapest pub in town, but it maintains a local ambience. Guest beers are whatever is delivered, so it is an adventure every time you visit. The restaurant offers a good value menu. Alcohol is served from 11.30am (12.30 Sun).

Bangor

Esplanade

12 Ballyhome Esplanade, BT20 5LZ

11.30-11 (1am Fri & Sat); 12.30-10 Sun

(028) 9127 0954

Whitewater Belfast Ale, Glen Ale; guest beer

Large corner site comprising bar, lounge, off sales and restaurant, situated opposite the beach in the suburbs of Bangor. A heated garden at the front has wonderful views of Belfast Lough and over to Scotland. The bar has two screens showing sport. Three handpumps dispenses the ale, which can be served in the lounge or garden. The pub runs a quiz night and golfing society. A separate restaurant opens in the evening. (302A)

Keep your Good Beer Guide up to date by consulting the CAMRA website **www.camra.org.uk**

Belfast

Botanic Inn

23-27 Malone Road, BT9 6RU

11.30-1am; 12-midnight Sun

(028) 9050 9740 botanicinns.com

Whitewater Belfast Ale

A large pub with two distinct drinking and dining areas. There is just one handpump in the larger area dispensing Belfast Ale. The other area is a traditional public bar, where the ale is slightly cheaper. The pub attracts a mixture of locals, university students and sports fans. Screens magically appear from the ceiling to show major sporting events. Regular live music plays and food is available untill 7.45pm.

Bridge House

37-43 Bedford Street, BT2 7EJ

8-midnight (1am Thu-Sat)

(028) 9072 7890

Greene King IPA, Abbot; guest beer

Lloyd's No.1 bar just a few minutes walk from the city centre. A large L-shaped downstairs bar is complemented by a smaller, more family-friendly bar and dining area upstairs. All the handpumps are downstairs, dispensing the usual range and, occasionally, local ale from Hilden. The bar gets very busy in the evening. Sky Sports and News play on screens with the volume turned down. Breakfast is available from 8am, alcohol served from 11.30am (12.30 Sun).
(Gt Victoria St)

INDEPENDENT BREWERIES

Clanconnel Craigavon (NEW)
Hilden Lisburn
Whitewater Kilkeel

Crown ★

46 Great Victoria Street, BT2 7BA (opp Europa Hotel and Great Victoria Street station)
11.30-midnight; 12.30-11 Sun
☎ (028) 90243187 crownbar.com
Whitewater Belfast Ale, Crown Glory; guest beer Ⓗ
This is the finest example of Victorian pub architecture you will find in Belfast. The interior, which has not changed since 1885, has snob screens, tiled floor, ornate ceiling, stained glass windows, elaborate woodwork, gas lighting, a Victorian calling system and nine snugs. The exterior tiling is also worth admiring. Whitewater Brewery provides all three ales. Food is served in the bar at lunchtime and upstairs from early evening. A national treasure.
◑♿⇌(Gt Victoria St)🚌

John Hewitt

51 Donegal Street, BT1 2FH (100m from St Anne's Cathedral)
11.30 (12 Sat)-1am; 7-midnight Sun
☎ (028) 9023 3768 thejohnhewitt.com
Hilden Ale; guest beer Ⓗ
Located in Belfast's Cathedral Quarter, the John Hewitt is a five minute walk from the city centre. The pub is owned by the Unemployed Resource Centre and all profits go to fund its work with the unemployed and other projects. The guest beer is usually from the Hilden brewery but, occasionally, other brewery beers feature. The bar can be very busy, particularly on music nights. There are live acts six nights a week and various events such as art exhibitions are also hosted. Q◑♿🚌

King's Head

829 Lisburn Road, BT9 7GY (opp Kings Hall at Balmoral)
12-1am (midnight Sun & Mon)
☎ (028) 9050 9950
Whitewater Belfast Ale; guest beer Ⓗ
Popular drinking, dining and music venue, about three miles south of the centre of Belfast, on the main bus and train routes. Refurbished in recent years, the pub has a modern feel to it. It has three drinking areas and a restaurant upstairs. The handpumps are in the public bar area and usually dispense Whitewater ales. There is live music in the bar and in the adjacent Live Lounge, which also holds an occasional beer festival.
Q❀◑🀫♿⇌(Balmoral)P⚽

Kitchen Bar

1 Victoria Square, BT1 4QG (access off Ann St via Upper Church St)
11.30-11.30 (midnight Mon; 1am Fri & Sat); 12-6 Sun
☎ (028) 90245368 thekitchenbar.com
Whitewater Belfast Ale; guest beer Ⓗ
The Kitchen Bar has had a new lease of life in the past year, now that building work on the Victoria Shopping Centre is complete. It is often very busy during the day with shoppers and after-work drinkers. There are two handpumps mainly dispensing Whitewater ales, with the occasional guest. Food is a major feature of the bar, along with screens for sport. Music plays four nights a week. ◑♿🚌⚽

McHugh's

29-31 Queens Square, BT1 3FG (near Albert Clock)
12-1am (midnight Sun)
☎ (028) 9050 9999 botanicinns.com
Whitewater Belfast Ale; guest beer Ⓗ
One of five Botanic Inns in Belfast serving real ale. It has two handpumps dispensing mainly Whitewater ales. The pub has a large main bar area, an upstairs restaurant and another bar downstairs. Northern Ireland CAMRA branch hold its meetings here every month. It is frequently very busy, especially when local music acts play. The pub has large windows with good views of nearby historic landmarks such as the Albert Clock and the Customs House. 🏔◑♿⇌(Central)🚌⚽

Molly's Yard

1 College Green Mews, Botanic Avenue, BT7 1LN
12-9 (9.30 Fri & Sat); closed Sun
☎ (028) 9032 2600
College Green Molly's Chocolate Stout, Headless Dog Ⓗ
Molly's Yard is a restaurant in the heart of Belfast's University area, situated in the restored stables of College Green House. It has a dining area and bar downstairs with an larger dining area upstairs. Hilden Brewery's second restaurant, it serves College Green ales, currently brewed at the Hilden Brewery and not on the premises. Note that ales can only be ordered if dining.
Q❀◑♿⇌(Botanic)🚌⚽

Ryan's

116-118 Lisburn Road, BT9 6AH
11.30-1am; 12-midnight Sun
☎ (028) 9050 9850 botanicinns.com
Whitewater Belfast Ale Ⓗ
A popular, modern pub situated about a mile from the city centre, attracting mainly students and locals. It features a downstairs bar and an upstairs bistro/restaurant. The bar has one handpump exclusively dispensing Whitewater Belfast Ale. It hosts two quizzes a week and screens some sporting events. Ryan's is part of the Botanic Inns group and like the nearby 'Bot' can be very busy.
◑♿🚌⚽

Carrickfergus

Central Bar

13-15 High Street, BT38 7AN (opp Carrickfergus Castle)
9am-11 (1am Fri & Sat)
☎ (028) 9335 7840
Greene King Abbot; guest beers Ⓗ
Lively town-centre pub, not far from bus and train stops. Inside there are two bars, one upstairs and one down, usually serving a variety of ales from the Wetherspoon's guest list. The beer garden is worth visiting for its views of nearby Carrickfergus Castle. In common with all of the chain's pubs in the province, it opens early for breakfast but alcohol is not served until 11.30am, 12.30 on Sunday. ☕❀◑🀫♿⇌🚌(563)🍏⚽

Coleraine

Old Courthouse ✔

Castlerock Road, BT51 3HP
9am-11 (1am Fri & Sat)
☎ (028) 7032 5820
Greene King Abbot; guest beers Ⓗ
Large, imposing Wetherspoon's conversion, not far from the bridge over the River Bann that runs through Coleraine. The pub retains the look of the former courthouse it once was. Five handpumps dispense an array of ales. Food is available from 9am but alcohol is not served until 11.30am (12.30

Sun). Food and drink can be consumed in the bar, outside on the patio, or in the upstairs balcony dining area.

Enniskillen

Linen Hall

11-13 Townhall Street, BT74 7BD
9-11 (1am Fri & Sat)
(028) 6634 0910
Greene King Abbot, IPA; guest beers H

A welcoming Wetherspoon's in the town centre opposite the bus station and handy for the express bus to/from Belfast. Formerly the Vintage Bar, it is very popular with locals and tourists. There are four distinct drinking areas with five handpumps dispensing two regular and up to three beers from the guest list. A selection of foreign bottled beers and Westons cider on draught are also available. Breakfast is served from 9am, beer from 11.30am (12.30 Sun). Sport is screened on TVs with the sound turned off.

Hillsborough

Hillside

21 Main Street, BT26 6AE
12-11.30 (1am Fri & Sat); 12-11 Sun
(028) 9286 9233
Whitewater Belfast Ale; guest beers H

The Hillside was among the first pubs to sell real ale in the province. These days its three handpumps serve a selection of ales mainly from the Whitewater Brewery. The pub has two drinking areas and a dining area at the back called the Refectory. Paintings depicting countryside pursuits decorate the walls, and there is a heated beer garden. Hillsborough is about 12 miles from Belfast, and well worth a visit.
Q (38,238)

Holywood

Dirty Duck Ale House

3 Kinnegar Road, BT18 9JW
11.30-11.30 (1am Thu-Sat); 12.30-midnight Sun
(028) 9059 6666 thedirtyduckalehouse.co.uk
Beer range varies H

This cheerful pub on the County Down side of Belfast Lough is a previous CAMRA Northern Ireland Pub of the Year. From the picture windows in the bar and upstairs restaurant there are superb views of shipping and County Antrim. Four handpumps dispense a wide variety of beers and the pub won Gastro Pub of the Year in 2008. Live music plays nightly from Thursday to Sunday and there is a quiz on Tuesday. The pub has a golf society.

Killinchy

Daft Eddy's

Sketrick Island, BT23 6QH (2 miles N of Killinchey at Whiterock Bay)
11.30-11.30 (1am Fri); 12-10.30 Sun
(028) 9754 1615
Beer range varies H

A remarkable pub in many ways – real ale, beautiful location, renowned restaurant, and a castle just outside the grounds. There is one handpump in the lounge serving a beer from the Whitewater Brewery. The pub is on Sketrick Island about two miles from Killinchy on the Whiterock Road. The restaurant specialises in seafood (booking recommended). Situated on Strangford Lough, the area has a seafaring aspect with a yacht club nearby. Q P

Lisburn

Tap Room

Hilden Brewery, Hilden, BT27 4TY
12-2.30, 5.30-9; closed Mon; 12.30-3 Sun
(028) 9266 3863 hildenbrewery.co.uk
Hilden Molly Malone; guest beer H

Uniquely for Northern Ireland, this is a restaurant with a brewery next door. The Tap Room's bar has handpumps serving Hilden ales exclusively. This is a popular venue for many functions including music nights and the August bank holiday beer festival, all in the historic surroundings of a mansion dating from 1824. Worth visiting, it is not far from the Belfast to Lisburn road, and the Hilden train halt is a five-minute walk.
Q (Hilden) (325H) P

Tuesday Bell

Unit 4, Lisburn Square, BT28 1TS
9-11.30 (1am Fri & Sat); 9-11 Sun
(028) 9262 7390
Greene King IPA, Abbot; guest beers H

The only outlet for real ale in Lisburn city centre. Named after the bell that used to open the Tuesday market, this Wetherspoon's pub has two floors, each with a bar featuring three handpumps. Occasionally ale from the local Hilden Brewery is offered in addition to the usual guests. Like most Wetherspoon's pubs in the province it screens Sky Sports and News with the sound off. Alcohol is served from 11.30am (12.30 on Sun).

Londonderry

Diamond

23-24 The Diamond, BT48 6HP (centre of the walled city)
9-11 (midnight Wed, Thu; 1am Fri, Sat); 9-midnight
(028) 7127 2880
Greene King IPA, Abbot; guest beers H

This is the largest of the Maiden City's two Wetherspoon pubs. It has a good vantage point, situated in the Diamond that overlooks the city. This former department store has two bars dispensing a number of real ales. Although the pub is very large it can get busy. It opens early for breakfast but alcohol is not served until 11.30am (12.30 Sun).

Ice Wharf

Strand Road, BT48 7AB
9-midnight (1am Thu-Sat)
(028) 7127 6610
Greene King IPA, Abbot; guest beers H

One of two Wetherspoon pubs in the city. Another conversion, it was originally the Strand Hotel, located near the historic Guildhall Square. Inside the wide single room, the bar area is separated from the rest of the interior. A range of guest ales is offered. Breakfast is available early but alcohol is only served from 11.30am (12.30 Sun).

Newtownards

Spirit Merchant ✓

54-56 Regent Street, BT23 4LP (opp bus station)
9-midnight (1am Thu-Sat)
☎ (028) 9182 4270
Greene King IPA, Abbot; guest beers Ⓗ
Friendly, helpful and knowledgeable staff welcome you to this Wetherspoon's close to the town centre, formerly the Jolly Judge bar. Two regular ales and up to three guests are available as well as a selection of foreign bottled beers and Westons cider on draught. Three TV screens play, with the sound turned off. Breakfast is served daily from 9am, beer from 11.30am (12.30 Sun). The standard Wetherspoon food menu includes daily specials. There is a smoking area at the front and a heated courtyard at the side. ❀ ◐ ♿ (5,7,9) P

Saintfield

White Horse 🏆

49 Main Street, BT24 7AB
11.30-11.30; 12-10.30 Sun
☎ (028) 9751 1143
Whitewater Belfast Ale, Mill Ale, Crown Glory; guest beers Ⓗ
CAMRA NI's Pub of the Year 2009, a popular community pub in the historic village of Saintfield. The pub is on two levels with a bar and restaurant upstairs, and downstairs a function room with pool table plus a beer garden. The White Horse is owned by Whitewater Brewery and the bar has four handpumps dispensing its award-winning ales. There are two screens showing sporting events, and live music plays in the bar monthly. The White Horse beer festival is hosted during the spring. ❀ ◐ ♿ (15,215)

Old Courthouse, Coleraine.

NORTHERN IRELAND

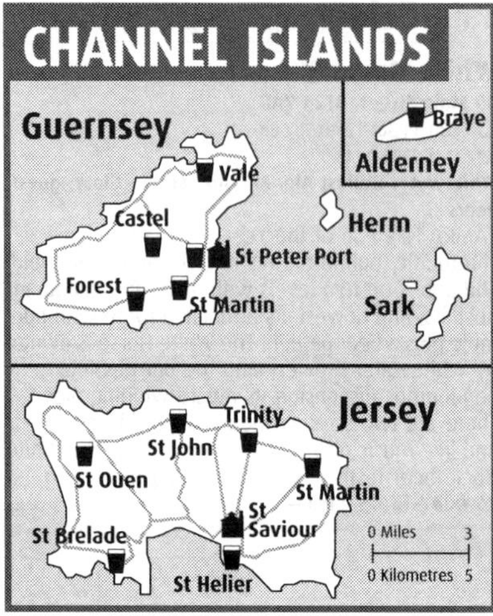

ALDERNEY

Braye

The Coxwain Bar
Braye Street, GY9 3XT
9-11
(01481) 823954
Randalls Patois; guest beers
A small bar attached to the Boathouse restaurant, which together form The Moorings. The harbour, just 100 metres away, makes a delightful vista from the bar windows. The bar's welcoming landlords are enthusiastic about real ale and the pub attracts locals and visitors. Good value food is served from April to October.

GUERNSEY

Castel

Fleur du Jardin
Kings Mills, GY5 7JT
10.30-11.45
(01481) 257996 fleurdujardin.com
Fuller's London Pride; guest beer
A building of unique charm with two bars: one traditional, small and cosy attached to the restaurant, the other recently renovated in a more contemporary style to create a comfortable, relaxing area to enjoy a beer. A door from this area leads to a large covered patio and out to the garden. Menus in both the bar and restaurant feature fresh local produce.

Rockmount Hotel
Cobo, GY5 7HB
10.30-midnight (12.45am Fri & Sat)
(01481) 256757
Randalls Patois
A pub for all seasons, it has two bars: a public to the rear by the large car park and a newly refurbished front bar by the road. A warming fire in winter makes it a cosy retreat from the gales. The old snooker room has been opened up to create a sports-themed area to one side. A good range of tasty food is served and the pub is just across the road from a sandy beach, providing a refreshing pint on a hot summer day. The perfect place to relax with a good pint and enjoy one of the island's best views of Guernsey's legendary sunsets.

Forest

Deerhound
Le Bourg, GY8 0AN
11-11
(01481) 238585
Beer range varies
Modern bar on the main road to the airport. There is an emphasis on food here, with a good choice of tasty meals (booking recommended at weekends). The large, sunny, decked patio is perfect for summer dining and there are also benches dotted about on the grass. The car park fills up quickly when the bar is busy.

St Martin

Ambassador Hotel
Route de Sausmarez, GY4 6SQ
12-3, 6-11.45; 12-3.30 Sun
(01481) 238356 ambassadorguernsey.co.uk
Randalls Patois
The hotel is situated just down from Sausmarez Manor on the main road from St Peter Port to St Martin. A delicious range of meals is available, served in the bar, the restaurant or the Old Guernsey conservatory. There is a patio area to the rear of the bar for sunny days. Accommodation is good value. The car park to the front is quite small and can be busy.

Captain's Hotel
La Fosse, GY4 6EF
11-11 (midnight Fri & Sat); 12-4 Sun
(01481) 238990
Fuller's London Pride; guest beers
In a secluded location down a country lane, this is a popular locals' pub with a lively, friendly atmosphere. There is a small, raised area in front of the bar furnished with a sofa to make a 'comfy zone'. Meals can be eaten in the bar or the newly refurbished bistro area at the rear. A meat draw is held on Friday. There is a car park to the rear which can fill up quickly.

St Peter Port

Cock & Bull
Lower Hauteville, GY1 1LL
11-2.30, 4-12.45am; 11-12.45am Fri & Sat; 4-11 Sun
(01481) 722660
Beer range varies
Popular pub, just up the hill from the town church, with five handpumps providing a changing range of beers. Live music plays on different nights of the week, ranging from salsa, baroque or jazz on a Monday, open mike on Tuesday, to Irish on Thursday. Seating is on three levels and there are several TVs and a large screen for sporting events, particularly rugby and football. Local CAMRA Pub of the Year for 2008.

INDEPENDENT BREWERIES

Jersey St Saviour: Jersey
Randalls St Peter Port: Guernsey

Cornerstone Café

La Tour Beauregard, GY1 1LQ
⏲ 10 (8am Thu & Fri)-midnight
☎ (01481) 713832 🌐 cornerstoneguernsey.co.uk
Randalls Patois; guest beer [H]
Situated across the road from the States Archives, the café has a small bar area to the front with bar stools, and further seating to the rear. Regular quiz evenings are held. The menu offers a wide range of good quality hot and cold meals with a daily specials board (no food Sun). There is a large screen for sporting events and you can top up your mobile here. Occasional Sunday opening. ◐

Randy Paddle

North Esplanade, GY1 2LQ
⏲ 10-11.45 (12.45am Fri & Sat); closed Sun
☎ (01481) 725610
Fuller's London Pride; Wadworth 6X [H]
Across the road from the harbour and next door to the tourist board, the pub is in a perfect position for a drink before a meal at one of the varied restaurants surrounding it. The bar has a nautical theme and although small, makes good use of space, attracting a mixed crowd of regulars and visitors to the island.

Ship & Crown

North Esplanade, GY1 2NB (opp Crown Pier car park)
⏲ 10-12.45am; 12-10 Sun
☎ (01481) 721368
Beer range varies [H]
Now a free house, the pub has a nautical theme, with pictures of ships and a model of the Seven Seas, complete with tiny cannon balls, in a glass case. Situated across the road from Victoria Pier (known locally as Crown Pier), this busy pub attracts a varied clientele of all ages. Real cider – Westons First Quality – is available on handpump. Excellent bar meals are served in generous portions throughout the day, with a daily changing range of specials. The pub's new Crows Nest brasserie has recently opened above the pub. ◐🍎

Vale

Houmet Tavern

Rousse, GY6 8AR (between church and Rousse Tower)
⏲ 10am-12.45am (11.45 if quiet); 10am-6 Sun
☎ (01481) 242214
Beer range varies [H]
The pub has a public bar to the rear, popular with locals. Pub games are played and there is a TV screening sporting events. To the front, there is a large lounge leading to a conservatory, with fabulous views of the bay and local fishing boats. Bar meals are served in the lounge lunchtimes and evenings (not Sun eve). ◐🍺🚌P⚋

JERSEY

St Brelade

Old Court House

Le Boulevard, St Aubin's Harbour, JE3 8AB
⏲ 11-11
☎ (01534) 746433
Draught Bass; Wells Bombardier [H]**; guest beer** [H]/[G]
Situated on the bulwarks of St Aubins harbour, the Old Court House featured prominently in the TV series Bergerac, under the pseudonym of the Royal Barge. It is primarily a restaurant and hotel, but the granite bar and conservatory are popular for drinking. A real ale from Skinner's is usually available on gravity. There is a regular bus service from Jersey town centre, and it is a short walk over the hill to the Smugglers at Ouaisne.
Q🐾❀🛏◐🚌(15)⚋

Old Smugglers Inn

Le Mont du Ouaisne, JE3 8AW
⏲ 11-11 (winter opening hours vary)
☎ (01534) 741510 🌐 oldsmugglersinn.com
Draught Bass [H]**; Greene King Abbot** [G]**; Wells Bombardier; guest beers** [H]
Perched on the edge of Ouaisne Bay, the Smugglers has been the jewel in the crown of the Jersey real ale scene for many years. One of just a few free houses on the island, it is set on several levels within granite-built fishermen's cottages dating back hundreds of years. Up to four real ales are usually available including one from Skinner's, and mini beer festivals are regularly held. The pub is well known for its good food and fresh daily specials. ♨Q◐

St Helier

Lamplighter 🏆 ✔

9 Mulcaster Street, JE2 3NJ
⏲ 11-11
☎ (01534) 723119
Ringwood Best Bitter, Fortyniner, [H]**; Old Thumper** [G]**; Wells Eagle IPA, Bombardier** [H]**; guest beers** [G]
A traditional pub with a modern feel. The gas lamps that gave the pub its name remain, as does the original antique pewter bar top. An excellent range of up to eight real ales and sometimes a real cider are available including one from Skinner's – four are served direct from the cask. Local CAMRA Pub of the Year in 2008. ◐🚌(5)🍎

St John

L'Auberge du Nord

La Route du Nord, JE3 4AJ
⏲ 11-11
☎ (01534) 861697
Ringwood Best Bitter [H]
A 10-minute walk towards the North Coast from St John village centre, this 16th-century farm house was converted to a pub in the 1950s. Under new ownership since 2008, the restaurant has undergone refurbishment. A Skinner's ale often replaces the Ringwood on the bar. Extensive parking and outside seating make the pub a useful meeting place for the North Coast. ♨Q❀◐🚌P⚋

St Martin

Rozel

La Vallee de Rozel, JE3 6AJ
⏲ 11-11
☎ (01534) 869801
Courage Directors; Greene King Abbot; Ringwood Best Bitter; guest beers [H]
Charming little hostelry tucked away in the north-west corner of the island. The pub has a delightful beer garden and there is an excellent restaurant upstairs. Bar meals are served in the public bar and snug, where there is a real fire in winter. A Skinner's beer is often available. The locals are very friendly if sometimes a little rumbustious!
♨Q❀◐🍺🚌(3)P⚋

St Ouen

Moulin de Lecq

Le Mont de la Greve de Lecq, JE3 2DT

⏲ 11-11 (winter opening varies)

☎ (01534) 482818 🌐 moulindelecq.com

Greene King Old Speckled Hen, [H]; Abbot, [G]; seasonal beers; Wells Bombardier; guest beers [H]

The only other free house on the island to offer a range of real ales, the Moulin is a converted 12th-century watermill situated in the valley above the beach at Greve de Lecq. The waterwheel is still in place and the turning mechanism can be seen behind the bar. A newly-built restaurant adjoins the mill. There is a children's play space and a barbecue area used extensively in the summer.

⛰Q❀◐◑🚌(9)🍎P⚡

Trinity

Trinity Arms

La Rue Es Picots, JE3 5JX

⏲ 11-11

☎ (01534) 864691

Jersey Jimmy's, [H]; Best [A]

Sporting the parish's ancient symbol of the Trinity, this 1976-built pub is modern by Jersey country pub standards but has plenty of its own character. Owned by the Jersey Brewery, it is the hub of village community life. Recently refurbished, it has a smart public bar and restaurant where food is served lunchtimes and evenings. Outside is a children's play area, extensive seating and parking.

❀◐◑♿🚌(4)♣P⚡

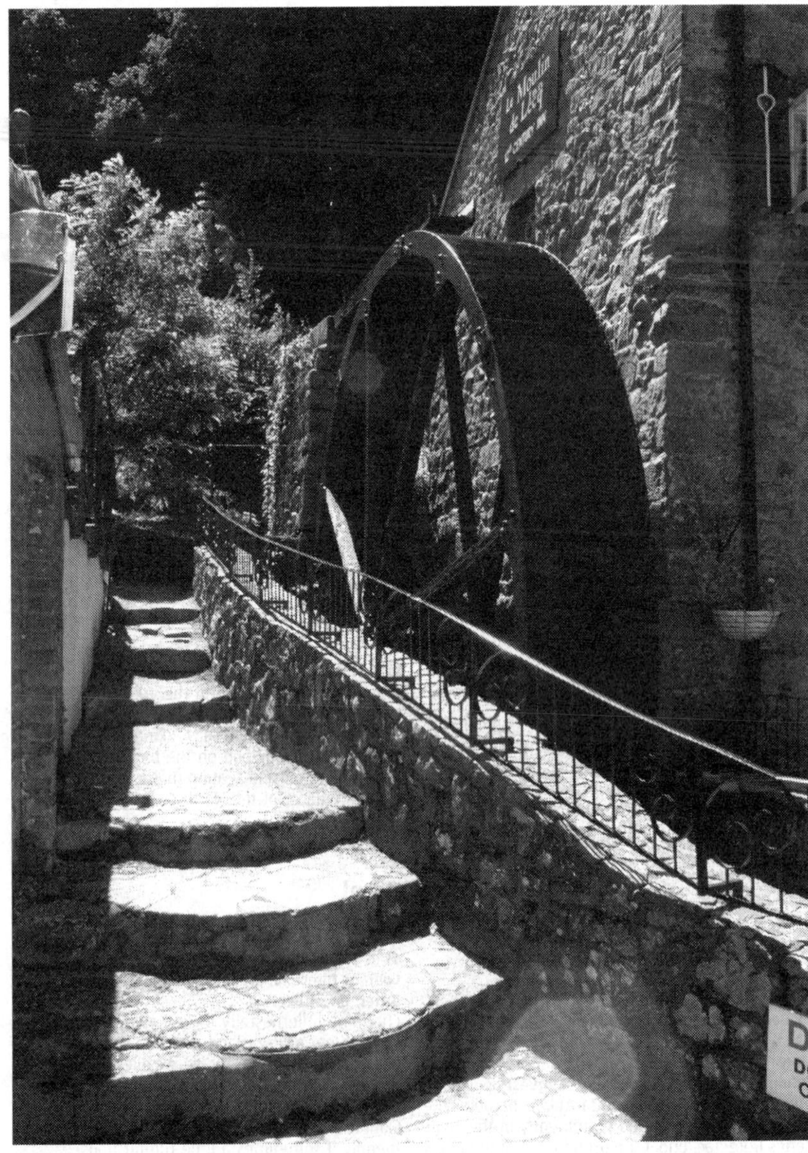

Moulin de Lecq, St Ouen.

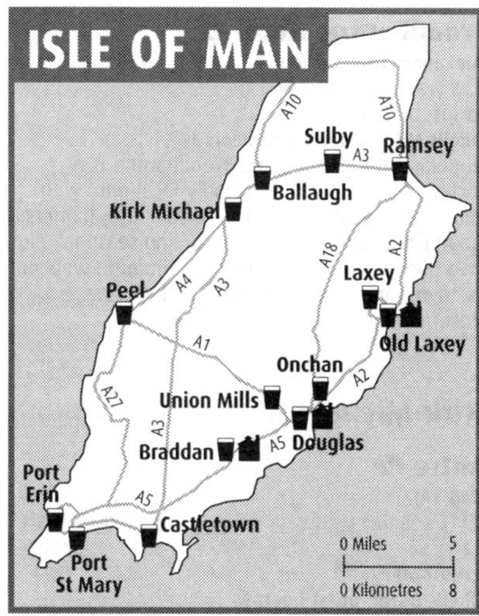

Ballaugh

Raven ✔

The Main Road, IM7 5EG
⌚ 12-11 (midnight Sat)
☎ (01624) 896128
Okells Bitter; guest beer Ⓗ
Situated on the famous Ballaugh Bridge, the Raven provides an excellent vantage point for viewing the TT motorbike races. It now carries up to three guest ales, along with house brew Raven's Claw brewed by Okells. Recently refurbished, it retains the traditional, cosy feel of a village inn, welcoming locals and visitors alike.
Q❀◐◑🚌(5)**P**⚟

Braddan

Hop Garden

Mount Murray, Santon, IM4 1JE (on main Douglas-Castletown road)
⌚ 11-11
☎ (01624) 619527 🌐 hop-garden.com
Bushy's Bitter; guest beers Ⓗ
The Hop Garden is situated in front of Bushy's Brewery. Popular for food, the traditional dining area has been extended into the attractive conservatory. For drinkers there is a comfortable side lounge, with guest beers added in summer. There are beautiful gardens where you can relax, drink and dine during warmer months. Beware, however, the food is too good to share and the ducks are very persistent. 🔥❀◐◑⊟♿🚌(1)**P**⚟

Castletown

Castle Arms (Gluepot) ✔

The Quay, IM9 1LD
⌚ 12-11 (midnight Fri); 10-midnight Sat
☎ (01624) 824673
Okells Bitter; guest beers Ⓗ
An attractive, historic pub, the Castle Arms is also known as the Gluepot due to a less salubrious past. Situated next to Castletown harbour and opposite Castle Rushen, inside, the two small ground floor rooms have a nautical theme. There is also an upstairs seating area, however this is rarely used. The bar now features up to five guest ales. On warm days the patio is ideal for watching the quayside vessels and waterfront wildlife.
❀◐🚌(1)⚟

Sidings

Victoria Road, IM9 1EF (next to railway station)
⌚ 11.30-11 (midnight Fri & Sat)
☎ (01624) 823282 🌐 thesidings.im
Bushy's Mild, Bitter, Castletown Bitter; guest beers Ⓗ
The Sidings is a welcome sight as you arrive in the Island's ancient capital by train. Its impressive and ornate wooden counter dispenses three regular ales at reasonable prices, plus an ever-changing variety of up to seven cask ales from all over the British Isles. No food is served on Sunday. Local CAMRA Pub of the Year in 2003 and 2005.
🔥❀◐⇌(IMR)🚌(1, 2)♣⚟

Douglas

Albert Hotel ✔

3 Chapel Row, IM1 2BJ (next to bus station)
⌚ 10-11 (11.45 Fri & Sat); 12-11 Sun
☎ (01624) 673632
Okells Mild, Bitter; guest beers Ⓗ
The Albert is the nearest real ale pub to the sea terminal. A busy, unspoilt local, it has a traditionally laid out central bar and dark wood panelling. Sport on TV is a constant feature but never loud enough to spoil a conversation. The three resident beers include a house beer brewed by Okells, Jough Manx Ale (jough is Manx Gaelic for beer). Bushy's Castletown Bitter is a regular guest.
Q⊟⇌(IMR)🚌

Cat With No Tail ✔

Hailwood Court, Hailwood Avenue, Governors Hill, IM2 7EA
⌚ 12-11 (midnight Fri & Sat)
☎ (01624) 616364
Okells Bitter; guest beers Ⓗ
A modern building on a relatively new housing estate, with two bars – a lounge and a public. The main beer is Okells Bitter and various guest beers are served, including Shepherd Neame Spitfire. Quizzes are held on Sunday and Thursday evenings and there is monthly karaoke. The public bar has a pool table and dartboard. Children are allowed in the conservatory and food is served in the lounge bar lunchtimes and evenings except Sunday evening. 🐴❀◐◑⊟🚌(25A,28)**P**⚟

Manor Hotel

School Road, Willaston, IM2 6PQ
⌚ 12-11 (midnight Fri & Sat)
☎ (01624) 676957
Okells Bitter; guest beers Ⓗ
A true community pub in the heart of the Willaston Estate, this popular venue is close to the TT Grandstand. There is a large lounge area with dark wood panelling. Corporation owned but on a long term lease, the pub hosts live music and has separate darts and pool rooms. Upstairs is a meeting room widely used by many local clubs and societies. Four dartboards are used for local tournaments. **Q**⊟🚌(22)♣**P**⚟

INDEPENDENT BREWERIES

Bushy's Braddan
Okells Douglas
Old Laxey Old Laxey

Prospect Hotel ✓
Prospect Hill, IM1 1ET
12-11 (midnight Fri); 6-midnight Sat; closed Sun
(01624) 616773
Okells Bitter; guest beers H
Spacious, stylish pub in the financial centre of Douglas, popular with office workers. The single bar interior has a traditional feel, displaying old law court photographs. The Prospect is a tied house with a blackboard outside listing the guest beers available. Food is served at lunchtime only. There is a quiz night on Wednesday. (IMR)

Queens Hotel
Queens Promenade, IM2 4NL (on seafront)
12-midnight (1am Fri & Sat)
(01624) 674438 thequeensdouglas.im
Okells Bitter; guest beers H
Popular with locals and holidaymakers, this is a cheery and friendly open-plan pub. The interior has three distinct areas including a games space. The lounge features a large-screen TV for sporting events. Outside, there is a very good area under awnings with heaters and a great view of Douglas Bay, with the steam packet ferries coming and going. Horse trams stop right outside.
Q (IMR)

Railway Hotel
North Quay, IM1 5AB (opp railway station)
12-2.30, 5-10 (11 Tue & Wed); 12-11.30 Thu; 12-midnight Fri; 6-midnight Sat; closed Sun
(01624) 670773
Okells Bitter; guest beer H
A popular harbourside pub, with guest beers served alongside several world beers, both on draught and in bottles. The modern, comfortable lounge is split into three areas – a raised space with impressive views of the quayside, a central seating area and a games area with dartboard and pool table. In the evenings, office workers mingle with youngsters out celebrating. (IMR)

Rovers Return
11 Church Street, IM1 2AG (behind town hall)
12-11 (midnight Fri & Sat)
(01624) 676459
Bushy's Mild, Bitter, seasonal beers; guest beers H
A popular back-street pub with a mixed clientele. Following a change of licensee, the Rovers has gone from strength to strength, and now has two more handpumps dispensing ever-changing guest beers, alongside the regular ales. Well known for its shrine-room to Blackburn Rovers FC, there are eight further rooms, two with real fires in winter, and an outside seating area for smokers. Occasional live music. (IMR)

Terminus Tavern ✓
Strathallan Crescent, IM2 4NR
12-11 (midnight Fri & Sat)
(01624) 624312
Okells Bitter; guest beer H
The refurbished Terminus Tavern now has a regular guest beer alongside the Okells Bitter. The large front bar is comfortable, with cosy alcove areas around the front windows. There is a separate games room. Horse trams, electric trams and views from the large bay window feature in the black and white photos of bygone times that adorn the lounge walls. Outdoor seating areas cater for smokers and alfresco diners.
(MER)P

Woodbourne Hotel ✓
Alexander Drive, IM2 3QF
5 (12 Fri-Sun)-midnight
(01624) 676754
Okells Mild, Bitter; guest beers H
Popular with all ages, the Woodbourne is a Victorian-built, no frills, friendly local pub, with three bars and a pool room. A tied house, it offers a good choice of local beers, including seasonal, plus two guest ales. It is situated a 10-minute walk out of town, and a quarter of a mile from the Rosemount Terrace shops. Q

Kirk Michael

Mitre ✓
IM6 1AJ
12-2.30 (not Mon), 5-11 (midnight Fri); 12-midnight Sat; 12-11 Sun
(01624) 878244
Okells Bitter; guest beers H
Cosy village pub with plenty of charm, enhanced by a real fire in the winter months. A small room off the main lounge area has numerous photos of motorcycles and bikers of bygone eras that will impress motorbike enthusiasts and historians alike – just ask your hosts for a viewing. Quality beer, good value meals and views of the hills from the rear garden make the Mitre well worth a visit.
P

Laxey

Queen's Hotel
New Road, IM4 7BP
12-11 (midnight Fri & Sat)
(01624) 861195
Bushy's Mild, Bitter; guest beers H
In this busy local every wall is covered with pictures, photos and memorabilia of the local area. Many feature bikes and bikers including several photos of the famous TT rider the late Joey Dunlop. Seating areas include the bar space with comfortable button back benches, a snug porch and several sturdy benches outside where you can sit and watch the world go by. But beware, you may just get too comfortable in the relaxing, friendly atmosphere and watch your bus go by.
(3,3A,3B)P

Old Laxey

Shore Hotel
IM4 7DA
12-midnight
(01624) 861509 shorehotel.im
Old Laxey Bosun Bitter H
This is the island's sole brew pub, with the landlord acting as assistant brewer. A welcoming community hostelry, its convivial atmosphere makes it a pleasant destination all year round. As the name suggests, it is located close to the beach and has a nautical theme. The pub now has permission for a permanent marquee and hosts special themed music weekends. More than 120 whiskies are on offer here – a card is available so you can tick them off as you go.
(3C)P

Onchan

Creg-Ny-Baa

Mountain Road, IM4 5BP (on A18 mountain road, Douglas-Ramsey)
12-10.45 (11 Fri & Sat); 12-10 Sun
(01624) 676948 creg-ny-baa.com
Beer range varies H
The Creg-Ny-Baa (Manx Gaelic for 'rock of the cow') is steeped in history as one of the well-known landmarks on the world famous TT course. It enjoys fantastic views of the course and plays host to thousands of spectators every year for the TT and Manx Grand Prix races. Outside of the races the Creg is renowned for good food, and offers a choice of ales all year round. P

Peel

Creek Inn

Station Place, IM5 1AT (by harbour)
10-midnight
(01624) 842216
Okells Bitter; guest beers H
Two-room pub overlooking the recently modernised quayside, adjacent to the House of Manannan museum and offering excellent views. Much improved in recent years, there is ample seating inside and out. Food is served all day and up to four guest ales are on handpump. Beer festivals are held throughout the year as well as occasional food festivals. The lively, revamped rear bar is a popular venue for regular live music. (5,6)

White House Hotel

Tynwald Road, IM5 1LA (150m from bus station)
11-midnight
(01624) 842252
Bushy's Bitter; Flowers Original; Okells Mild, Bitter; Taylor Landlord; guest beers H
Popular, family-run free house with many rooms converging on a central bar. The additional Captain's Cabin snug has its own bar. The pub has remained largely unchanged since the 1930s and the landlord is one of the longest serving on the Island, having supplied more than 1,000 guest ales during his tenure. Live local music plays on Friday and Saturday. CAMRA IOM Pub of the Year 2009. Q(5,6)P

Port Erin

Bay Hotel

Shore Road, IM9 6HL
12-midnight (1am Fri & Sat)
(01624) 832084
Bushy's Bitter; Bushy's Ruby Mild; Bushy's Castletown Bitter, Old Bushy Tail, seasonal beers; guest beers H
This Bushy's Brewery-owned pub has been carefully refurbished since the brewery acquired it as a dry-rot ridden wreck in 2002. Subdivided into three rooms, one for dining, the Bay is a magnet for beer and food lovers. Located on the shore in the attractive seaside resort of Port Erin, the Bay is the perfect destination after a cliff top walk or a paddle in the sea. In late August the pub is host to a rhythm and blues festival, and various other events are held during the year. A regular CAMRA Pub of the Year finalist, and winner in 2004. (IMR)

Falcon's Nest Hotel

Station Road, IM9 6AF
11-midnight
(01624) 834077 falconsnesthotel.co.uk
Bushy's Bitter; Okells Bitter; guest beers H
Family-run hotel with a lounge bar and a public bar open to all, dispensing local ales including at least one guest beer. The bar has been sympathetically extended with a full-length conservatory where you can enjoy spectacular elevated views over Port Erin Bay, Bradda Head, and on a clear day the distant hills of Northern Ireland. A wide variety of meals are available including a popular carvery served on Sunday. Q(IMR)

Port St Mary

Albert Hotel

Athol Street, IM9 5DS (next to bus terminal)
11.30-midnight; 12-1am Fri & Sat; 12-midnight Sun
(01624) 832118
Bushy's Ruby Mild, Old Bushy Tail; Okells Bitter; guest beers H
This traditional pub has impressive views over the inner harbour of Port St Mary. There are three rooms including a spacious games room with a real fire and a separate entrance. The comfortable, traditional lounge area is even cosier in colder months when the fire is lit, making the Albert an ideal stop-off after a fishing trip. P

Shore Hotel

Shore Road, Gansey, IM9 5LZ (on main Castletown-Port St Mary road)
12-midnight (1am Fri & Sat)
(01624) 832269
Bushy's Bushy Tail; Okells Bitter; guest beers H
Busy, friendly local which has grown in popularity in recent years, with good views of Carrick Rock and Bay. A large TV screen shows sport and there is a pool table in the main bar. The dining room is modern and informal. On the walls are many high quality photographs, taken by the landlady's father-in-law, featuring both local scenes and pictures from around the world. Four rooms are available for B&B accommodation.
(2,2A)P

Ramsey

Swan

Parliament Square, IM8 1AH
12-11.30 (12.30am Fri & Sat)
(01624) 814236
Okells Mild, Bitter H
Friendly pub refurbished in 2007. The larger of the two bars has a dartboard and pool table plus two plasma TVs. Food is served lunchtimes and evenings including some specials. There are two outdoor heated drinking areas. Well situated on the TT course and close to the bus station, high street and harbour. The terminus for the electric railway is a five-minute walk away. Guest ales are served at Christmas, during TT fortnight and the week of the Grand Prix races.

Trafalgar Hotel

West Quay, IM8 1DW (on quayside)
11-11 (midnight Fri & Sat); 12-4, 8-11 Sun
(01624) 814601
Black Sheep Best Bitter; Moorhouses Black Cat; Okells Bitter; guest beers H

The Trafalgar is a comfortable free house situated on the quayside, a short walk from the main shopping area and the parliament square section of the TT course. Popular, friendly and always busy, the pub offers a good selection of well-kept real ales, with guests sourced from all over the UK including interesting and unusual beers. A CAMRA Isle of Man Pub of the Year finalist on many occasions. ≷(MER)🚌♣⁵⁻

Sulby

Sulby Glen Hotel ✔

Main Road, IM7 2HR

⏲ 12-midnight (1am Fri & Sat); 12-11 Sun

☎ (01624) 897240 🌐 sulbyglen.net

Bushy's Bitter; Okells Bitter; guest beers Ⓗ

Long-serving hosts Eddie and Rosie offer a warm welcome to visitors to this large open-plan lounge and bar with a friendly atmosphere. Situated on the Sulby Straight, a fast section of the TT course, this is a popular hostelry for continental TT and Manx Grand Prix motorbike fans. Excellent home-cooked food made with locally-sourced ingredients is served from a varied menu. Live bands and themed nights are hosted regularly. Accommodation is high quality in well-appointed en-suite rooms. ♨Q❀🛏◐◑⊞♿⛺🚌♣🍎P⁵⁻

Union Mills

Railway Inn

Main Road, IM4 4NE (on main A1 Douglas-Peel road)

⏲ 12-11 (midnight Fri & Sat)

☎ (01624) 853006

Okells Mild, Bitter, seasonal beers; guest beers Ⓗ

This busy village inn, dating back to 1841, has been in the same family for five generations. Now open plan, it has three separate seating areas, the back room providing a comfortable lounge space. The historic hostelry is located on part of the famous TT course and is a favourite spot for viewing the races. It displays an interesting collection of TT photos on the walls. A choice of at least two guest ales is on offer, often from Bushy's. Local CAMRA Pub of the Year twice, most recently in 2007.
❀⛺🚌(5,5A,6)♣P⁵⁻

Falcon's Nest Hotel, Port Erin.

The Breweries

How beer is brewed

Real ale is made by taking raw ingredients from the fields, the finest malting barley and hops, along with pure water from natural springs or the public supply, and carefully cultivated strains of brewers' yeast; in this exploded drawing by Trevor Hatchett of a classic British ale brewery, it is possible to follow the process that begins with raw grain and finishes with natural, living cask beer.

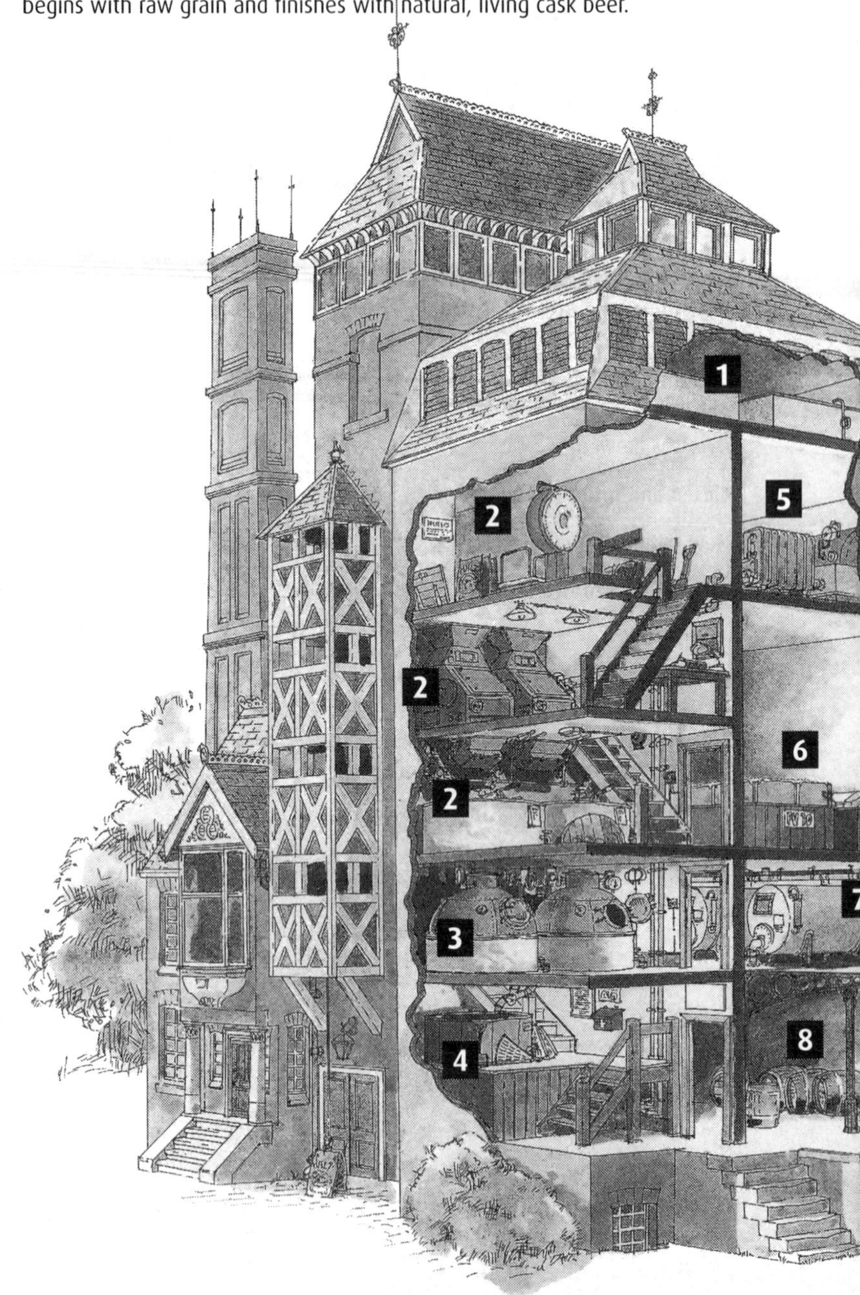

1. On the top floor, in the roof, are the tanks where pure water – called liquor by brewers – is stored. Soft water is not suited to ale brewing, and brewers will add such salts as gypsum and magnesium to replicate the hard, flinty waters of Burton-on-Trent, home of pale ale.

2. In the malt store, grain is weighed and kept until needed.The malt drops down a floor to the mills, which grind it into a coarse powder suitable for brewing. From the mills, the ground malt or grist is poured into the mash tuns along with heated liquor. During the mashing period, natural enzymes in the malt convert starches into fermentable malt sugars.

3. On the same floor as the conditioning tanks are the coppers, where after mashing, the wort is boiled with hops, which add aroma, flavour and bitterness.

4. At the end of the boil, the hopped wort is clarified in a vessel called the hop back on the ground floor. The clarified wort is pumped back to the malt store level where it is passed through a heat exchange unit. See 5.

5. The heat exchange unit cools the hopped wort prior to fermentation.

6. The fermenters are on the same floor as the mash tuns.The house yeast is blended or pitched with the wort.Yeast converts the malt sugars in the wort into alcohol and carbon dioxide. Excess yeast is skimmed off by funnels called parachutes.

7. Fermentation lasts for a week and the 'green' beer is then stored for a few days in conditioning tanks.

8. Finally, the fresh beer is run into casks on the ground floor, where additional hops for aroma and sugar to encourage a secondary fermentation may be added.The casks then leave for pubs, where the beer reaches maturity in the cellars.

How to use the Breweries section

Breweries are listed in alphabetical order. The independents (regional, smaller craft brewers and brew-pubs) are listed first, followed by the nationals and the globals. Within each brewery entry, beers are listed in increasing order of strength. Beers that are available for less than three months are described as 'occasional' or 'seasonal' brews. If a brewery also produces bottle-conditioned beers, this will be mentioned in the main description: these are beers that have not been pasteurised and contain live yeast, allowing them to continue to ferment and mature in the bottle as a draught real ale does in its cask.

Symbols

A brew-pub: a pub that brews beer on the premises.

CAMRA tasting notes, supplied by a trained CAMRA tasting panel. Beer descriptions that do not carry this symbol are based on more limited tastings or have been obtained from other sources.

Tasting notes are not provided for brew-pub beers that are available in fewer than five outlets, nor for other breweries' beers that are available for less than three months of the year.

A CAMRA Beer of the Year in 2008.

One of the 2009 CAMRA Beers of the Year: a finalist in the Champion Beer of Britain competition held during the Great British Beer Festival in London in August 2009, or the Champion Winter Beer of Britain competition held earlier in the year.

The brewery's beers can be acceptably served through a 'tight sparkler' attached to the nozzle of the beer pump, designed to give a thick collar of foam on the beer.

The brewery's beer should NOT be served through a tight sparkler. CAMRA is opposed to the growing tendency to serve southern-brewed beers with the aid of sparklers, which aerate the beer and tend to drive hop aroma and flavour into the head, altering the balance of the beer achieved in the brewery. When neither symbol is used it means the brewery in question has not stated a preference.

Abbreviations

OG stands for original gravity, the measure taken before fermentation of the level of 'fermentable material' (malt sugars and added sugars) in the brew. It is a rough indication of strength and is no longer used for duty purposes.

ABV stands for Alcohol by Volume, which is a more reliable measure of the percentage of alcohol in the finished beer. Many breweries now only disclose ABVs but the Guide lists OGs where available. Often the OG and the ABV of a beer are identical, ie 1035 and 3.5 per cent. If the ABV is higher than the OG, ie OG 1035, ABV 3.8, this indicates that the beer has been 'well attenuated' with most of the malt sugars turned into alcohol. If the ABV is lower than the OG, this means residual sugars have been left in the beer for fullness of body and flavour: this is rare but can apply to some milds or strong old ales, barley wines, and winter beers.

NOTE: The Breweries section was correct at the time of going to press and every effort has been made to ensure that all cask-conditioned beers are included.

The independents

SIBA indicates a member of the Society of Independent Brewers; IFBB indicates a member of the Independent Family Brewers of Britain; EAB indicates a member of the East Anglian Brewers Co-operative. See feature on page 845.

1648 SIBA

1648 Brewing Co Ltd, Old Stables Brewery, Mill Lane, East Hoathly, East Sussex, BN8 6QB
☎ (01825) 840830
✉ brewmaster@1648brewing.co.uk
🌐 1648brewing.co.uk
Tours by arrangement

The 1648 brewery, set up an the old stable block at the King's Head pub in 2003, derives its name and some of the beer names from the time of the deposition of King Charles I. One pub is owned and more than 30 outlets are supplied. Additional fermenting vessels were installed in 2007 doubling capacity to 884 barrels. Seasonal beers: see website. Bottle-conditioned beers are also available.

Hop Pocket (OG 1038, ABV 3.7%)

Original (OG 1040, ABV 3.9%)
Light, quaffable and easy drinking.

Triple Champion (OG 1041, ABV 4%)

Signature (OG 1044, ABV 4.4%)
Light, crisp, medium hoppy clean beer with a bitter finish.

Gold Angel (OG 1049, ABV 5%)

Old Disreputable (OG 1054, ABV 5.4%)
Dark malty brew with distinctive coffee and chocolate hints and a lasting bitter finish.

Suitably Irish (ABV 5.6%)
Full-bodied black stout.

3 Rivers SIBA

3 Rivers Brewery Ltd, Delta House, Greg Street, Reddish, Stockport, Cheshire, SK5 7BS
☎ (0161) 477 3333
✉ contacts@3riversbrewing.co.uk
🌐 3riversbrewery.co.uk
Tours by arrangement

3 Rivers was launched in 2004 on a 2-barrel plant and has since expanded to a 20-barrel one. There is a private members' club on site and consultancy and installation work is undertaken. More than 200 outlets are supplied. Seasonal beers: phone for details. Bottle-conditioned beer is also available.

Old Smokey (ABV 3.7%)

GMT (OG 1038, ABV 3.8%)
Golden bitter with an underlying malt character supported by moderate hop bitterness and a light floral finish.

Harry Jacks (ABV 4.1%)

Manchester IPA (OG 1041, ABV 4.2%)
Light russet/amber colour with a refreshing biscuit-like flavour, supplemented by a complex citrus finish.

Pilgrim's Progress (ABV 4.2%)

Fathers Favourite (OG 1045, ABV 4.5%)
Light amber-coloured ale with hints of coffee and caramel, complemented by a spicy hop character and a complex aroma.

Hillary Gold (OG 1044, ABV 4.5%)

Delta Dark Mild (ABV 4.8%)

Crystal Wheat (OG 1048, ABV 5%)

Abbey Ales SIBA

Abbey Ales Ltd, Abbey Brewery, Camden Row, Bath, Somerset, BA1 5LB
☎ (01225) 444437
✉ enquiries@abbeyales.co.uk
🌐 abbeyales.co.uk
Tours by arrangement

Abbey Ales is the first and only brewery in Bath for nearly 50 years. It supplies more than 80 regular accounts within a 20-mile radius of Bath, while selected wholesalers deliver beer nationally. One tied house, the Star Inn, Bath, is listed on CAMRA's National Inventory of heritage pubs. Seasonal beers: Bath Star (ABV 4.5%, spring), Mild (ABV 4%, May), Chorister (ABV 4.5%, autumn), White Friar (ABV 5%), Black Friar (ABV 5.3%, winter), Twelfth Night (ABV 5%, Xmas).

Bellringer (OG 1042, ABV 4.2%)
A notably hoppy ale, light to medium-bodied, clean-tasting, refreshingly dry, with a balancing sweetness. Citrus, pale malt aroma and dry, bitter finish.

Abbeydale SIBA

Abbeydale Brewery Ltd, Unit 8, Aizlewood Road, Sheffield, South Yorkshire, S8 0YX
☎ (0114) 281 2712
✉ info@abbeydalebrewery.co.uk
🌐 abbeydalebrewery.co.uk

Since starting in 1996, Abbeydale Brewery has grown steadily; it now produces upwards of 70 barrels a week, and the gradual expansion programme is set to continue. The regular range is complemented by ever-changing seasonals, each of which is available for two months – see website for details. It also produces beers under the 'Beer Works' name.

Matins (OG 1034.9, ABV 3.6%)
Pale and full flavoured; a hoppy session beer.

Daily Bread (OG 1037, ABV 3.8%)

Brimstone (OG 1039, ABV 3.9%)
A russet-coloured bitter beer with a distinctive hop aroma.

Moonshine (OG 1041.2, ABV 4.3%)
A beautifully balanced pale ale with a full hop aroma. Pleasant grapefruit traces may be detected.

Absolution (OG 1050, ABV 5.3%)
A fruity pale ale, deceptively drinkable for its strength. Sweetish but not cloying.

Black Mass (OG 1065, ABV 6.7%)
A strong black stout with complex roast flavours and a lasting bitter finish.

Last Rites (OG 1097, ABV 11%)
A pale, strong barley wine.

A.B.C. (NEW)

A.B.C. Pride of Aston, Unit 21, Birch Road, Witton, Aston, Birmingham, West Midlands, B6 7DD
☎ (0121) 328 2655
✉ abcprideofaston@hotmail.co.uk
🌐 abcprideofaston.co.uk
Tours by arrangement

A.B.C. started brewing in 2008, near to Villa Park football ground. A bottling plant has been purchased and there are plans to bottle a variety of beers, including a lager. Around five outlets are supplied.

Aston Dark (ABV 3.6%)

Heartlands Bitter (ABV 4.2%)

Rotunda Red (ABV 4.8%)

Pride of Aston (ABV 5%)

Acorn SIBA

Acorn Brewery of Barnsley Ltd, Unit 3, Mitchell Road, Aldham Industrial Estate, Wombwell, Barnsley, South Yorkshire, S73 8HA
☎ (01226) 270734
✉ sales@acorn-brewery.co.uk
🌐 acorn-brewery.co.uk
Shop Mon-Fri 9am-5pm
Tours by arrangement

Acorn Brewery was set up in 2003 with a 10-barrel ex-Firkin plant. Expansion to a 20-barrel plant was completed in 2007 when demand outgrew capacity. All beers are produced using the original Barnsley Bitter yeast strain, dating back to the 1850s. The brewery currently has a 100-barrel a week capacity. Seasonal beers: see website. Bottle-conditioned beers are also available.

Barnsley Bitter (OG 1038, ABV 3.8%)
A complex aroma of malt and hops. A hint of chocolate with a fresh fruit and bitter taste.

Barnsley Gold (OG 1041.5, ABV 4.3%)
Fruit in the aroma and taste. There is also a hoppy flavour throughout. A well-hopped, clean, dry finish.

Old Moor Porter (OG 1045, ABV 4.4%)
A rich roast malt aroma with chocolate, cherry and liquorice flavours. A creamy mouthfeel leads to a dry finish.

Sovereign (OG 1044, ABV 4.4%)
Well-balanced bitter with plenty of fruit and malt. Excellent mouthfeel.

IPA (OG 1047, ABV 5%)
Full of hoppy and fruit aroma, a hoppy dry and fresh citrus fruit and bitter flavour that leads to a crisp citrus, hoppy finish.

Gorlovka Imperial Stout (OG 1058, ABV 6%)
A deep malt and hoppy aroma with liquorice throughout. Roast, fruit and hops also carry through this full-bodied stout.

Adkin

Adkin Brewery, c/o 52 Adkin Way, Wantage, Oxfordshire
☎ 07709 086149
✉ info@adkinbrewery.co.uk
🌐 adkinbrewery.co.uk
Tours by arrangement

Adkin was established in 2007 and supplies beer festivals and local pubs. No beer list is available at present.

Adnams IFBB

Adnams plc, Sole Bay Brewery, East Green, Southwold, Suffolk, IP18 6JW
☎ (01502) 727200
✉ info@adnams.co.uk
🌐 adnams.co.uk
Shop 10am-6pm daily
Tours by arrangement

The company was founded by George and Ernest Adnams in 1872, who were joined by the Loftus family in 1902; a member of each family is still a director of the company. New fermenting vessels were installed in 2001, 2003 and 2005 to cope with demand while a new eco-friendly distribution centre has opened in neighbouring Reydon. Real ale is available in all 70 pubs and there is national distribution. All beers are now from a new energy efficient 300-barrel brewery, built within the confines of the present site. Seasonal beers: see website.

Bitter (OG 1037, ABV 3.7%)
Hops dominate this classic bitter, from the almost overpowering aroma to the dry, lingering aftertaste.

East Green Cask (OG 1040, ABV 4%)
Light gold in colour with subtle citrus and grassy hop aromas. Dry and refreshing.

Explorer (OG 1042, ABV 4.3%)
Brewed with American hops, hence the name. Citrus fruit in the mouth, with a long, sweet aftertaste.

Broadside (OG 1049, ABV 4.7%)
The aroma and initial taste boom with prunes. Malt and sultanas with a trace of pepper in the mouth. The finish is long, turning drier.

Adur SIBA (NEW)

Adur Brewery Ltd, Charlton Court Farm, Mouse Lane, Steyning, West Sussex, BN44 3DG
☎ (01273) 467527

Office: Adur Business Centre, Little High Street, Shoreham-by-Sea, West Sussex, BN43 5EG
✉ info@adurbrewery.com
🌐 adurbrewery.com

Adur Brewery was launched in 2008 on a 5.5-barrel plant, marking the return of brewing to the Adur Valley after an interval of nearly 100 years. A large part of the output is sold as bottle-conditioned beer and plans are underway for online sales.

Ropetackle Golden Ale (OG 1036, ABV 3.4%)
A light, golden ale with an initial sweetness and delicate aroma balanced by a dry finish.

Velocity (OG 1044, ABV 4.5%)
Traditional best bitter with a hoppy aroma and a hint of marmalade in the taste.

Black William (OG 1055, ABV 5%)
A rich, black stout with dark chocolate aromas and roasted flavours.

Merry Andrew (OG 1062, ABV 6.2%)
Dark, strong ale with complex aroma and a rounded, fruity flavour. The initial sweetness is balanced by a dry finish.

St Cuthman's Red Wheelbarrow (OG 1082, ABV 10.5%)
A Belgian Abbey-style Triple. The complex flavour has hints of caramel, fruit and spice with a long, warming aftertaste.

Alcazar SIBA

Sherwood Forest Brewing Co Ltd, Alcazar Brewery, Church Street, Old Basford, Nottingham, NG6 0GA
☎ (0115) 978 5155/2282
✉ alcazarbrewery@tiscali.co.uk
alcazarbrewery.co.uk
Tours by arrangement

Alcazar was established in 1999 and is located behind its brewery tap, the Fox & Crown. The brewery is full mash with a 10-barrel brew length. Production is mainly for the Fox & Crown and other freehouses within the Turnstone Taverns estate. Seasonal beers: see website.

Sheriffs Gold (OG 1036, ABV 3.6%)
A golden ale made with First Gold and Goldings hops.

Alcazar Ale (OG 1040, ABV 4%)
A session ale made with a blend of English and North American hops; pale, full-flavoured with a fruity aroma and finish.

New Dawn (OG 1045, ABV 4.5%)
Golden ale made with North American hops that give a unique fruity aroma and crisp, malty taste.

Foxtale Ale (OG 1050, ABV 4.9%)
A classic bitter, amber in colour with full malt flavour and a slight sweet edge.

Vixen's Vice (OG 1052, ABV 5.2%)
A pale, strong ale with a malt flavour balanced by a clean, crisp, hop taste.

Windjammer IPA (OG 1060, ABV 6%)
Traditional IPA brewed with five varieties of North American hops. Strong and hoppy.

Bombay Castle IPA (OG 1065, ABV 6.5%)
Traditional IPA brewed with English hops.

Alehouse

Alehouse Pub & Brewing Co Ltd, Verulam Brewery, Farmers Boy, 134 London Road, St Albans, Hertfordshire, AL1 1PQ
☎ 07872 985918
✉ alehousebeer@tiscali.co.uk
alehousebrewery.co.uk
Tours by arrangement

Alehouse took over the Verulam Brewery in 2006. As well as brewing two of the original house beers for the Farmers Boy next door, numerous ales are produced under the Alehouse banner including many seasonal and one-off brews. Beers are supplied direct to local outlets, the West Midlands and Yorkshire.

Simplicity (OG 1039, ABV 3.6%)

I Can't Believe It's Not GBH (OG 1038, ABV 3.8%)

Commercial Mild (OG 1039, ABV 3.9%)

Sauvin So Good! (OG 1038, ABV 4%)

Robust Porter (OG 1044, ABV 4.3%)

Technician's Pale (OG 1040, ABV 4.3%)

For Farmers Boy, St Albans:

Clipper IPA (OG 1039, ABV 4%)

Farmers Joy (OG 1043, ABV 4.5%)

Ales of Scilly SIBA

Ales of Scilly Brewery, 2b Porthmellon Industrial Estate, St Mary's, Isles of Scilly, Cornwall, TR21 0JY
☎ (01720) 423233
✉ mark@alesofscilly.co.uk
Tours by arrangement

Opened in 2001 as a two-barrel plant and expanded in 2004 to five barrels, Ales of Scilly is the most south-westerly brewery in Britain. Nine local pubs are supplied, with regular exports to mainland pubs and beer festivals. The brewery moved to new premises in 2007. Seasonal beers: Firebrand (ABV 4.2%, Easter-Sep). Bottle-conditioned beer is also available.

Scuppered (ABV 4.6%)
The aroma is of fruit and hops, leading to a rich, malty, creamy taste balanced by hops. An initial burst of sweetness is followed by an increasing bitterness on the tongue.

Alexandra Ales

See Atomic

Allendale

Allendale Brew Co Ltd, Allen Mills, Allendale, Hexham, Northumberland, NE47 9EQ
☎ (01434) 618686
✉ tom@allendalebrewco.co.uk
allendalebrewco.co.uk
Shop Mon-Sat 9am-5pm
Tours by arrangement

Allendale was set up in 2006 and is run by father and son team, Jim and Tom Hick. Their locally themed ales are on sale in nearby free houses and also in Newcastle, Durham and surrounding areas. Seasonal beers: Black Grouse Bitter (ABV 4%, Aug-Jan), Curlew's Return (ABV 4.2%, Feb-Jul). All beers are also available bottle conditioned.

Best Bitter (OG 1037, ABV 3.8%)
Amber bitter with spicy aromas and a long, bitter finish.

Golden Plover (OG 1039, ABV 4%)
Light, refreshing, easy-drinking blond beer with a clean finish.

Wolf (OG 1053, ABV 5.5%)
Full-bodied red ale with bitterness in the taste giving way to a fruity finish.

All Gates SIBA

All Gates Brewery Ltd, The Old Brewery, Brewery Yard, off Wallgate, Wigan, WN1 1JU
☎ (01942) 234976
✉ information@allgatesbrewery.com
allgatesbrewery.com
Tours by arrangement

All Gates started brewing in 2006 in a Grade II listed building at the rear of Wigan Main Post

THE BREWERIES

Office. The building is an old tower brewery that has been lovingly restored, but with a new five-barrel plant. Beers are distributed regionally and to its own estate of five pubs. Beers are available nationally through selected wholesalers. A brewery shop and bottling plant are being considered. Seasonal beers: Hung, Drawn & Portered (ABV 5.2%, Nov-Dec). Other seasonal beers available throughout the year.

California (OG 1037, ABV 3.8%)
Well-balanced, straw-coloured ale. Easy-drinking with a berry/herbal aroma.

Mild at Heart (OG 1037, ABV 3.8%) ◆
Dark brown beer with a malty, fruity aroma. Creamy and malty in taste, with blackberry fruits and a satisfying aftertaste.

Young Pretender (OG 1037, ABV 3.8%) ◆
There are hops and fruit on the nose of this yellow beer. Hops, lemon fruit and a touch of sweetness to the taste, with a hoppy, fruity and bitter finish.

Pretoria (OG 1038, ABV 3.9%)
Refreshing golden ale with a distinctive bitterness and aroma.

Bright Blade (OG 1039, ABV 4%)
Light golden ale with a hint of ginger and a lemon nose.

Porteresque (OG 1043, ABV 4.4%)
Classic style porter, dark and rich, bursting with roasted malt flavours.

All Nations

See Shires

All Saints

See Keltek

Alnwick

See Hadrian & Border

Amber

Amber Ales Ltd, Unit A, Asher Lane Business Park, Pentrich, Ripley, Derbyshire, DE5 3RE
☎ (01773) 512864
✉ info@amberales.co.uk
🌐 amberales.co.uk
Shop Thu-Fri 2-6pm; Sat 10am-2pm
Tours by arrangement

⊗ Amber Ales began production in 2006 on a five-barrel plant from the Firkin brewpub chain. Part-time at first, it switched to full-time ahead of plan due to strong local interest. Amber produces four core beers plus one seasonal at any one time. Around 100 outlets are supplied direct. Bottle-conditioned beers are available.

Original Black Stout (OG 1040, ABV 4%)

Barnes Wallis (OG 1036, ABV 4.1%)

Samuel Slater (OG 1038, ABV 4.2%)

Imperial IPA (OG 1060, ABV 6.5%)

Andwell (NEW)

Andwell Brewing Co LLP, Lodge Farm, North Warnborough, Hampshire, RG29 1HA
☎ (01256) 704412
✉ beer@andwells.com
🌐 andwells.com

Brewing commenced in late 2008 on a 10-barrel plant. Beer is distributed within a 30-mile radius of the brewery and more than 150 outlets are supplied.

Resolute Bitter (OG 1036, ABV 3.8%)
A light amber bitter with a balanced aroma.

Gold Muddler (OG 1038, ABV 3.9%)
A golden ale with a fresh taste and light, citrus aroma.

King John (OG 1042, ABV 4.2%)
An amber beer with a rounded flavour and fruity aroma.

Anglo Dutch SIBA

Anglo Dutch Brewery, Unit 12, Saville Bridge Mill, Mill Street East, Dewsbury, West Yorkshire, WF12 9AF
☎ (01924) 457772
✉ angdutchbrew@yahoo.co.uk
🌐 anglo-dutch-brewery.co.uk
Tours by arrangement

Paul Klos (Dutch) set up the brewery with Mike Field (Anglo), who also runs the Refreshment Rooms at Dewsbury Station. Most beers contain wheat except for Spike and Tabatha, which contain lager malt. A bottle-conditioned fruit beer range is also available. Seasonal beers: Devil's Knell (ABV 4.8%, Jan), Wild Flower (ABV 4.2%, Sep).

Best Bitter (ABV 3.8%)

Kletswater (OG 1039, ABV 4%)
Pale-coloured beer with a hoppy nose and a good hop and citrus fruit flavour.

Spike's on 't' Way (OG 1040.5, ABV 4.2%) ◆
Pale bitter with citrus/orange flavour and dry, fruity finish.

Spikus (OG 1040.5, ABV 4.2%)
Made with organic lager malt and New Zealand hops.

Ghost on the Rim (OG 1043, ABV 4.5%)
Pale, dry and fruity.

Yorkshire Wit (ABV 4.5%)

Tabaa-tje (OG 1047.5, ABV 5%)

At 't' Ghoul and Ghost (OG 1048, ABV 5.2%) ◆
Pale golden bitter with a strong citrus and hoppy aroma and flavour. The finish is long, dry, bitter and citrus.

Tabatha the Knackered (OG 1054, ABV 6%) ◆
Golden Belgian-style Tripel with a strong fruity, hoppy and bitter character. Powerful and warming, slightly thinnish, with a bitter, dry finish.

Ann Street

See Jersey

An Teallach

An Teallach Ale Co Ltd, Camusnagaul, Dundonnell, Garve, Ross-shire, IV23 2QT

☎ (01854) 633306
✉ ataleco1@yahoo.co.uk
Tours by arrangement

An Teallach was formed in 2001 by husband and wife team David and Wilma Orr on Wilma's family croft on the shores of Little Loch Broom, Wester Ross. The business has grown steadily each year. 60 pubs are supplied. All beers are also available bottled.

Beinn Dearg Ale (OG 1038, ABV 3.8%) ◆
This malty, sweetish beer has a distinct yeasty background.

An Teallach Ale (OG 1042, ABV 4.2%) ◆
A sweetish pint in the Scottish 80/- tradition. Malt and blackcurrant feature in the taste, which can also have a yeasty background.

Crofters Pale Ale (OG 1042, ABV 4.2%) ◆
A good quaffing golden ale with no strong flavours. Meaty, with yeast often to the fore.

Suilven (OG 1043, ABV 4.3%)

Brew House Special (OG 1044, ABV 4.4%) ◆
A golden ale with some hoppy bitterness and often with yeast and sulphur background.

Kildonan (OG 1044, ABV 4.4%) ◆
Some fruit and a good smack of bitterness.

Appleford SIBA

Appleford Brewery Co Ltd, Unit 14, Highlands Farm, High Road, Brightwell-cum-Sotwell, Wallingford, Oxfordshire, OX10 0QX
☎ (01235) 848055
✉ sales@applefordbrewery.co.uk
🌐 applefordbrewery.co.uk

⊗ Appleford Brewery opened in 2006 when two farm units were converted to house an eight-barrel plant. Deliveries are made to a number of local outlets as well as nationally, via the brewery or wholesalers. Bottle-conditioned beers are available.

River Crossing (ABV 3.8%)
A dark, hoppy session beer

Brightwell Gold (ABV 4%)

Power Station (ABV 4.2%)
A copper-coloured slightly malty bitter.

Arbor

Arbor Ales Ltd, Unit 10a, Bridge Road Industrial Estate, Bridge Road, Kingswood, Bristol, BS15 4TA
☎ (0117) 957 0899
✉ beer@arborales.co.uk
🌐 arborales.co.uk

⊗ Arbor Ales opened in 2007 in the back of the Old Tavern pub in the building that housed the original Old Tavern Brewery, which is believed to have been brewing until around 1930. In 2008 it moved and expanded to a 5.5-barrel plant. Seasonal beers: Mild Nest (ABV 3.6%, spring), Slumberjack (ABV 6.9%, winter). Around 100 outlets are supplied direct.

Brigstow (OG 1043, ABV 4.3%)

Old Knobbley (OG 1043.5, ABV 4.5%) ◆
Brown, malty and complex best bitter.

Oyster Stout (OG 1046.5, ABV 4.6%)

Beech Blonde (OG 1046, ABV 4.9%)

Archers

Archers the Brewers Ltd, Penzance Drive, Swindon, Wiltshire, SN5 7JL
☎ (01793) 879929
✉ sales@archersbrewery.co.uk
🌐 archersbrewery.co.uk
Shop Mon-Fri 9.30am-4.30pm
Tours by arrangement

⊗ Archers Brewery was founded in 1979. In July 2009 it was bought by Wiltshire Ales, owned by Simon Buckley of Evan Evans of Llandeilo. He plans to close the Swindon plant and build a new brewery in Wiltshire. The beer range will change. Seasonal beers: Dark Mild (ABV 3.4%), Special Bitter (ABV 4.7%) plus up to six speciality beers per month.

Pride (OG 1038, ABV 3.6%)
Blonde in colour, light and fresh.

Village (OG 1035, ABV 3.6%) ◆
A dry, well-balanced beer with a full body for its gravity. Malty and fruity in the nose, then a fresh, hoppy flavour with balancing malt and a hoppy, fruity finish.

Best Bitter (OG 1040, ABV 4%) ◆
Slightly sweeter and rounder than Village Bitter, with a malty, fruity aroma and pronounced bitter finish.

IPA (OG 1042, ABV 4.2%)
Pale golden, rich in citrus and grapefruit aroma and flavour with a crisp, bitter finish.

Golden (OG 1046, ABV 4.7%) ◆
A full-bodied, hoppy, straw-coloured brew with an underlying fruity sweetness. A gentle aroma, but a strong, distinctive bitter finish.

Crystal Clear (OG 1050, ABV 5%)
Blond, packed with hop aroma with a subtle, balanced finish.

Arkell's IFBB SIBA

Arkell's Brewery Ltd, Kingsdown, Swindon, Wiltshire, SN2 7RU
☎ (01793) 823026
✉ arkells@arkells.com
🌐 arkells.com
Brewery merchandise can be purchased at reception
Tours by arrangement

⊗ Arkells Brewery was established in 1843 and is still run by the family. The brewery owns 105 pubs in Berkshire, Gloucestershire, Oxfordshire and Wiltshire. Seasonal beers: Summer Ale (ABV 4%), JRA (ABV 3.6%), Noel Ale (ABV 5%). Bees Organic Beer (ABV 4.5%) is suitable for vegetarians.

2B (OG 1032, ABV 3.2%) ◆
Light brown in colour, malty but with a smack of hops and an astringent aftertaste. It has good body for its strength.

3B (OG 1040, ABV 4%) ◆
A medium brown beer with a strong, sweetish malt/caramel flavour. The hops come through strongly in the aftertaste, which is lingering and dry.

Moonlight Ale (OG 1046, ABV 4.5%)

Kingsdown Ale (OG 1051, ABV 5%) ◆
A rich, deep russet-coloured beer, a stronger version of 3B. The malty/fruity aroma continues in

the taste, which has a hint of pears. Hops come through in the aftertaste.

Arran SIBA

Arran Brew Ltd t/a The Arran Brewery, Cladach, Brodick, Isle of Arran, Strathclyde, KA27 8DE
☎ (01770) 302353
✉ info@arranbrewery.co.uk
arranbrewery.com
Shop Mon-Sat 10am-5pm; Sun 12.30-5pm in summer, reduced hours in winter
Tours by arrangement

The brewery opened in 2000 with a 20-barrel plant. Production is up to 100 barrels a week with additional bottling capability. 50 outlets are supplied. Bottle-conditioned beer is available occasionally. Seasonal beers: Sunset (ABV 4.4%, Feb-Mar), Fireside (ABV 4.7%, Oct/Nov-Feb/Mar).

Ale (OG 1038, ABV 3.8%)
An amber ale where the predominance of the hop produces a bitter beer with a subtle balancing sweetness of malt and an occasional hint of roast.

Dark (OG 1042, ABV 4.3%)
A well-balanced malty beer with plenty of roast and hop in the taste and a dry, bitter finish.

Blonde (OG 1048, ABV 5%)
A hoppy beer with substantial fruit balance. The taste is balanced and the finish increasingly bitter. An aromatic strong bitter that drinks below its weight.

Arrow

Arrow Brewery, c/o Wine Vaults, 37 High Street, Kington, Herefordshire, HR5 3BJ
☎ (01544) 230685
✉ deanewright@yahoo.co.uk

Former Bridge Street brewer Deane Wright has built his five-barrel brewery at the rear of the Wine Vaults and re-started brewing in 2005.

Bitter (OG 1042, ABV 4%)

Art Brew (NEW)

Art Brew, The Art Brew Barn, Northend Farm, off Venn Lane, North Chideock, Dorset, DT6 6JY
☎ 07881 783626
✉ artbrewdorset@googlemail.com
artbrew.co.uk

Brewing started in 2008 on a five-barrel plant with its own water source near the Jurassic Coast. Head Brewer John Whinnerah and his wife Becky also own the Royal Oak in Bath, which serves as the brewery tap. Around 60 outlets are supplied, mostly in Dorset, Devon and Somerset. Seasonal beer: Born in A Barn (ABV 6%, Xmas).

Art Nouveau (OG 1039, ABV 3.9%)
Golden and hoppy.

iBeer (OG 1039, ABV 4%)
Speciality vanilla beer.

Art Brut (OG 1044, ABV 4.4%)
A mid-brown bitter.

Dark Brut (OG 1055, ABV 5.2%)

Artisan (NEW)

Artisan Brewing Co Ltd, 183a Kings Road, Cardiff, Glamorgan, CF11 9DF
☎ 07505 401939
✉ info@artisanbeer.co.uk
artisanbeer.co.uk
Tours by arrangement (small groups only)

Artisan was established in 2008. All beers are unfiltered and without additives or preservatives. Bottle-conditioned beers are available.

Bavarian Style Wheat Beer (ABV 4.6%)

Kolsch (ABV 4.9%)

Bohemian Style Pils (ABV 5%)

Helles Style Lager (ABV 5%)

The 'Real' IPA (ABV 5.6%)

Baltic Porter (Espresso) (ABV 6%)
Infused with coffee beans.

Arundel SIBA

Arundel Brewery Ltd, Unit C7, Ford Airfield Industrial Estate, Ford, Arundel, West Sussex, BN18 0HY
☎ (01903) 733111
✉ arundelbrewery@dsl.pipex.com
arundelbrewery.co.uk
Off-sales available Mon-Fri 9am-4pm at brewery

Founded in 1992, Arundel Brewery is the historic town's first brewery in more than 70 years. A range of occasional brands is available in selected months. Seasonal beers: Footslogger (ABV 4.4%, spring), Summer Daze (ABV 4.7%, summer), Autumn Fall (ABV 4.1%, autumn), Black Beastie (ABV 4.9%, winter).

Sussex XXXX (OG 1037, ABV 3.7%)
A dark mild. Strong chocolate and roast aromas, which lead to a bitter taste. The aftertaste is not powerful but the initial flavours remain in the dry and clean finish.

Castle (OG 1038, ABV 3.8%)
A pale tawny beer with fruit and malt noticeable in the aroma. The flavour has a good balance of malt, fruit and hops, with a dry, hoppy finish.

Sussex Gold (OG 1042, ABV 4.2%)
A golden-coloured best bitter with a strong floral hop aroma. The ale is clean-tasting and bitter for its strength, with a tangy citrus flavour. The initial hop and fruit die to a dry and bitter finish.

ASB (OG 1045, ABV 4.5%)
A special bitter with a complex roast malt flavour leading to a fruity, hoppy, bittersweet finish.

Old Knucker (OG 1046, ABV 4.6%)
A very dark old ale. Malt dominates the initial taste but leads on to a bittersweet coffee finish.

Stronghold (OG 1047, ABV 4.7%)
A smooth, full-flavoured premium bitter. A good balance of malt, fruit and hops comes through in this rich, chestnut-coloured beer.

Ascot

Ascot Ales Ltd, Unit 5, Compton Place, Surrey Avenue, Camberley, Surrey, GU15 3DX
☎ (01276) 686696
✉ info@ascot-ales.co.uk
ascot-ales.co.uk
Tours by arrangement

Ascot Ales began production in 2007 on a four-barrel plant. Current owners Chris & Suzanne Gill took over the brewery in late 2007. Since adding a third fermenter the extra capacity has given scope for more seasonal/one off brews in addition to their four regular ales. Seasonal beers: Double Trouble (ABV 5.4%, summer-winter), Wheatsheaf (ABV 4.9%, summer), Oktoberfest (ABV 4.8%, Sep-Oct), Winter Reserve (ABV 5.2%, winter). Bottle-conditioned beers are also available.

On the Rails (OG 1039, ABV 3.8%)
Dark, roasty mild with a good hop character throughout. Bittersweet in the taste and aftertaste. Notably dry finish.

Posh Pooch (OG 1042, ABV 4.2%)
A hoppy best bitter with balancing biscuity malt sweetness. The citrus fruitiness lasts throughout. A clean hoppy aftertaste.

Alligator Ale (OG 1047, ABV 4.6%)
American hops provide grapefruit notes in this golden ale. The biscuit in the aroma fades as hop and bitterness dominate the taste, but a residual sweetness remains even in the sharp dry finish.

Anastasia's Exile Stout (OG 1049, ABV 5%)
Burnt coffee aromas lead to a roast malt flavour in this black beer. Notably fruity throughout. The presence of some hop feeds into the bittersweet aftertaste.

Ashover

Ashover Brewery, 1 Butts Road, Ashover, Chesterfield, Derbyshire, S45 0EW
07803 708526
ashoverbrewery@googlemail.com
ashoverbrewery.com
Tours by arrangement

Ashover Brewery first brewed in early 2007 on a 3.5-barrel plant in the garage of the cottage next to the Old Poet's Corner pub. The brewery caters mainly for this and its sister pub, the Poet & Castle in Codnor, but other local free houses and festivals are also supplied. Seasonal beer: Winter Warmer (ABV 7%).

Light Rale (OG 1038, ABV 3.7%)
Light in colour and taste, with initial sweet and malt flavours, leading to a bitter finish and aftertaste.

Poets Tipple (OG 1041, ABV 4%)
Complex, tawny-coloured beer that drinks above its strength. Predominantly malty in flavour, with increasing bitterness towards the end.

Rainbows End (OG 1045, ABV 4.5%)

Coffin Lane Stout (OG 1050, ABV 5%)
Excellent example of the style, with a chocolate and coffee flavour, balanced by a little sweetness. Finish is long and quite dry.

Butts Pale Ale (OG 1055, ABV 5.5%)

Aston Manor

Aston Manor Brewery Co Ltd, 173 Thimble Mill Lane, Aston, Birmingham, West Midlands, B7 5HS
(0121) 328 4336
sales@astonmanor.co.uk
astonmanor.co.uk

Aston Manor is the former owner of the Highgate Brewery in Walsall (qv). Its own plant concentrates on cider. Beer is bottled at Highgate but is not bottle-conditioned.

Atlantic

Atlantic Brewery, Treisaac Farm, Treisaac, Newquay, Cornwall, TR8 4DX
(0870) 042 1714
stuart@atlanticbrewery.com
atlanticbrewery.com

Atlantic started brewing in 2005. All beers are organic, Soil Association certified and suitable for vegetarians and vegans. It concentrates on bottle-conditioned beers: Gold (ABV 4.6%, summer), Blue (ABV 4.8%), Red (ABV 5%), Fistral (ABV 5.2%), Black (ABV 5.5%), Blackcurrant Porter (ABV 5.5%).

Atlas SIBA

Atlas Brewery, Sinclair Breweries Ltd, Lab Road, Kinlochleven, Argyll, PH50 4SG
(01667) 404555
info@sinclairbreweries.co.uk
atlasbrewery.com
Shop open office hours
Tours by arrangement

Founded in 2002, Atlas is a 20-barrel brewery in a 100 year-old listed Victorian industrial building on the banks of the River Leven. It merged in 2004 with Orkney (qv) and now forms part of Sinclair Breweries. Production remains at both sites. Around 250 outlets in Scotland are supplied direct and via wholesalers to the rest of Britain. Seasonal beers: Equinox (ABV 4.5%, spring), Wayfarer (ABV 4.4%, summer), Tempest (ABV 4.9%, autumn), Blizzard (ABV 4.7%, winter).

Latitude (OG 1036, ABV 3.6%)
This golden ale has a light citrus taste with a hint of hops in the light, bitter finish.

Three Sisters (OG 1043, ABV 4.2%)
Full of malt and summer fruits in the nose and taste, followed by a short, hoppy bitter finish.

Nimbus (OG 1050, ABV 5%)
A full-bodied golden beer using some wheat malt and three types of hops. Dry and fruity at the front, it becomes slightly astringent with lasting fruit and a pleasant, dry finish.

Atlas Mill

Atlas Mill Brewery Ltd, The Tipp Inn, Atlas Mill Road, Brighouse, West Yorkshire, HD6 1ES
(01484) 720440
enquiries@atlasmillbrewery.com
atlasmillbrewery.com
Tours by arrangement

Atlas Mill opened in early 2007 on the first floor of a converted mill. The Brewery Tap, the Tipp Inn, is situated on the ground floor of the mill and was opened in September 2007.

Dark Mild (ABV 3.6%)
Grainy dark red mild. It has a roast and sulphurous aroma followed by a well-balanced, light, hoppy, fruity and malty taste.

Gold (ABV 3.6%)
Lightly-flavoured and refreshing thirst-quencher with a subtle fruity palate and a delicate aftertaste.

Bitter (ABV 3.8%)

THE BREWERIES

Pale brown grainy session bitter. A sulphurous aroma precludes a fruity taste with light hop levels.

Basset Brown Ale (ABV 4.4%)

Gwinness (ABV 4.4%) ◆
Creamy dark brown stout with a chocolate roast aroma. Complex, rich, fruity roast flavours develop in the mouth. It has a long, bittersweet aftertaste.

Hercules (ABV 4.5%) ◆
A distinctly sulphurous best bitter in both taste and aroma. Grainy and pale brown in colour it has a malty, bitter aftertaste.

Irish Gold (ABV 4.8%) ◆
Grainy golden ale with a floral, hoppy aroma. Fruity on the tongue with a strong, bitter aftertaste.

IPA (ABV 5%) ◆
Amber-coloured strong beer with a creamy smoothness. It has a fruity rich flavour with a hoppy character. Bitterness develops in the aftertaste.

Atomic

Atomic Brewery, c/o Sounds Expensive, 12 Regent Street, Rugby, Warwickshire, CV21 2QF
☎ (01788) 542170
✉ sales@atomicbrewery.com
🌐 atomicbrewery.com
Tours by arrangement

⊗ Atomic Brewery started production in 2006 and is run by CAMRA members Keith Abbis and Nick Pugh. They own one pub, the Victoria Inn in Rugby, which acts as the brewery tap. Future plans include new beers and purchasing more pubs.

Strike (OG 1039, ABV 3.7%)

Fission (OG 1040, ABV 3.9%)

Fusion (OG 1042, ABV 4.1%)

Reactor (OG 1047, ABV 4.5%)

Half-Life (OG 1051, ABV 5%)

Bomb (OG 1054, ABV 5.2%)

Avon

Avon Brewing Co Ltd, Unit 4, Russell Town Avenue Industrial Centre, Russell Town Avenue, Bristol, BS5 9LT
☎ (0117) 955 3353
🌐 avonbrewing.co.uk

Avon began brewing in 2008 on an eight-barrel plant. Around 12 outlets are supplied direct.

Re-Session (OG 1040, ABV 3.8%)
An amber bitter berwed with organic malt and hops.

Gurt Lush (OG 1046, ABV 4.5%)
A rich golden ale brewed with organic malt and hops.

AVS

See Loddon

B&T SIBA EAB

B&T Brewery Ltd, The Brewery, Shefford, Bedfordshire, SG17 5DZ
☎ (01462) 815080
✉ brewery@banksandtaylor.com
🌐 banksandtaylor.com
Tours by arrangement

⊗ Banks & Taylor – now just B&T – was founded in 1982. It produces an extensive range of beers, including monthly special brews together with occasional beers: see website for details. Four tied houses, all operated with guest beers as well as B&T beers.

Two Brewers (OG 1036, ABV 3.6%) ◆
Bronze-coloured bitter with citrus hop aroma and taste with a dry finish.

Shefford Bitter (OG 1038, ABV 3.8%) ◆
A pale brown beer with a light hop aroma and a hoppy taste leading to a bitter finish.

Shefford Dark Mild (OG 1038, ABV 3.8%) ◆
A dark beer with a well-balanced taste. Sweetish, roast malt aftertaste.

Golden Fox (OG 1041, ABV 4.1%)
A golden, hoppy ale, dry tasting with a fruity aroma and citrus finish.

Black Dragon Mild (OG 1043, ABV 4.3%) ◆
Black in colour with a toffee and roast malt flavour and a smoky finish.

Dunstable Giant (ABV 4.4%)

Dragonslayer (OG 1045, ABV 4.5%) ◆
A golden beer with a malt and hop flavour and a bitter finish. More malty and less hoppy than is usual for a beer of this style.

Edwin Taylor's Extra Stout (OG 1045, ABV 4.5%) ◆
A complex black beer with a bitter coffee and roast malt flavour and a dry bitter finish.

Fruit Bat (OG 1045, ABV 4.5%) ◆
A warming straw-coloured beer with a generous taste of raspberries and a bitter finish.

Shefford Pale Ale (SPA) (OG 1045, ABV 4.5%) ◆
A well-balanced beer with hop, fruit and malt flavours. Dry, bitter aftertaste.

SOD (OG 1050, ABV 5%)
SOS with caramel added for colour, often sold under house names.

SOS (OG 1050, ABV 5%) ◆
A rich mixture of fruit, hops and malt is present in the taste and aftertaste of this beer. Predominantly hoppy aroma.

Backyard (NEW)

Backyard Brewhouse, Unit 8a, Gatehouse Trading Estate, Lichfield Road, Brownhills, Walsall, West Midlands, WS8 6JZ
☎ 07591 923370
✉ enquiries@thebackyardbrewhouse.com
🌐 thebackyardbrewhouse.com

Backyard began brewing in 2008 on a five-barrel plant. Seasonal beers are planned.

Shire Oak (ABV 3.5%)

GB (ABV 4%)

Blonde (ABV 4.1%)

Big Red (ABV 4.5%)

Nipin (ABV 4.6%)

Boadicea (ABV 4.8%)

Pipin (ABV 5.1%)

Badger

See Hall & Woodhouse

Ballard's SIBA

Ballard's Brewery Ltd, Unit 3, The Old Sawmill, Nyewood, Rogate, Petersfield, Hampshire, GU31 5HA
☎ (01730) 821301/821362
✉ info@ballardsbrewery.org.uk
🌐 ballardsbrewery.org.uk
Shop Mon-Fri 8am-4pm
Tours by arrangement

Launched in 1980 by Mike and Carola Brown at Cumbers Farm, Trotton, Ballard's has been trading at Nyewood since 1988 and now supplies around 60 free trade outlets. Seasonal beers: Trotton Bitter (ABV 3.6%, spring), Wheatsheaf (ABV 5%, summer), On the Hop (ABV 4.5%, autumn), Old Bounder Series (ABV over 9%, winter). Bottle-conditioned beers are also available.

Midhurst Mild (OG 1034, ABV 3.5%)
Traditional dark mild, well-balanced, refreshing, with a biscuity flavour.

Golden Bine (OG 1038, ABV 3.8%)
Amber, clean-tasting bitter. A roast malt aroma leads to a fruity, slightly sweet taste and a dry finish.

Best Bitter (OG 1042, ABV 4.2%)
A copper-coloured beer with a malty aroma. A good balance of fruit and malt in the flavour gives way to a dry, hoppy aftertaste.

Wild (ABV 4.7%)
A blend of Mild and Wassail.

Nyewood Gold (OG 1050, ABV 5%)
Robust golden brown strong bitter, hoppy and fruity throughout, with a tasty balanced finish.

Wassail (OG 1060, ABV 6%)
A strong, full-bodied, tawny-red, fruity beer with a predominance of malt throughout, but also an underlying hoppiness.

Bank Top SIBA

Bank Top Brewery Ltd, The Pavilion, Ashworth Lane, Bolton, Lancashire, BL1 8RA
☎ (01204) 595800
✉ dave@banktopbrewery.com
🌐 banktopbrewery.com
Tours by arrangement

Bank Top was established in 1995 by John Feeney. Since 2002 the brewery has occupied a Grade II listed pavilion. In 2007 the brewing capacity was doubled with the installation of a new 10-barrel plant and in 2008 David Sweeney became the sole proprietor. Bottle-conditioned beers are available.

Bowl Town Bitter (OG 1038, ABV 3.8%)
A straw-coloured, hoppy session beer.

Bad to the Bone (OG 1040, ABV 4%)

Dark Mild (OG 1040, ABV 4%)
Dark brown beer with a malt and roast aroma. Smooth mouthfeel, with malt, roast malt and hops prominent throughout.

Flat Cap (OG 1040, ABV 4%)
Amber ale with a modest fruit aroma leading to a beer with citrus fruit, malt and hops. Good finish of fruit, malt and bitterness.

Gold Digger (OG 1040, ABV 4%)
Golden coloured, with a citrus aroma, grapefruit and a touch of spiciness on the palate; a fresh, hoppy citrus finish.

Pavilion Ale (OG 1045, ABV 4.5%)
A yellow beer with a citrus and hop aroma. Big fruity flavour with a peppery hoppiness; dry, bitter yet fruity finish.

Volunteer Bitter (OG 1045, ABV 4.5%)

Blonde (ABV 5%)
An extremely pale ale made with New Zealand hops resulting in a pleasant woody flavour and distinct berry aroma.

Port O Call (OG 1050, ABV 5%)
Dark brown beer with a malty, fruity aroma. Malt, roast and dark fruits in the bittersweet taste and finish.

Banks's

See Wolverhampton & Dudley in New Nationals section

Barearts

Barearts Brewery, Studio Bar & Gallery: 108-110 Rochdale Road, Todmorden, West Yorkshire, OL14 7LP
☎ (01706) 839305
✉ info@barearts.com
🌐 barearts.com
Shop & Bar: Wed-Thu 7-9.30pm; Fri 4-8pm, Sat 11am-7pm; Sun 3-7pm
Tours by arrangement

A four-barrel craft brewery that began production in 2005 and is owned by Kathryn and Trevor Cook. It is named after their gallery, which is dedicated to nude art work. Ciders and perries are also produced. Their real ales are available in bottles and five litre mini casks. Barearts beers are only available to drink in the studio bar, from the brewery shop or by mail order. All beers are bottle-conditioned, even those sold to drink on the premises: Brown Ale (ABV 5.2%), India Pale Ale (ABV 7%), Cascade (ABV 7.3%), Oat Stout (ABV 8.2%), Dark Barley Wine (ABV 9.6%), Pale Barley Wine (ABV 9.8%).

Barge & Barrel

See Eastwood

Barngates SIBA

Barngates Brewery Ltd, Barngates, Ambleside, Cumbria, LA22 0NG
☎ (015394) 36575
✉ info@barngatesbrewerytrade.co.uk
🌐 barngatesbrewerytrade.co.uk
Tours by arrangement

Barngates Brewery started brewing in 1997 and initially provided only the Drunken Duck Inn. The brewery became a limited company in 1999 upon expansion to a five-barrel plant. Further expansion in 2008 included a brand new, purpose-built 10-barrel plant enabling production to keep pace with

THE BREWERIES

demand. Around 60-80 outlets are supplied direct throughout Cumbria, Lancashire, Yorkshire and Northumberland. Occasional beer: 1077 10th Anniversary Ale (ABV 3.9%).

Mothbag (OG 1037, ABV 3.6%) ◆
Mouth-puckeringly bitter and estery gold-coloured beer. Its saltiness is predominant in the aftertaste.

Cracker Ale (OG 1038, ABV 3.9%)
Copper-coloured with a subtle hoppy aroma, clean, smooth and refreshing, developing into a long bitter finish.

Pride of Westmorland (OG 1042, ABV 4.1%) ◆
A well-crafted pale brown beer with bitterness dominant throughout.

Westmorland Gold (OG 1043, ABV 4.2%) ◆
A golden ale with a good balance of malt and hops, perhaps not as intense as previously.

Tag Lag (OG 1044, ABV 4.4%) ◆
A pale amber beer, smooth and sweetly malty to begin but a lasting, bitter finish.

Red Bull Terrier (OG 1048, ABV 4.8%)
A deep red tone and a complex hop nose are complemented by tangy fruit and malt flavours with a spicy aftertaste.

Chester's Strong & Ugly (OG 1052, ABV 5.2%) ◆
Complex and well-balanced, a richly satisfying dark beer with plenty of roast and hop bitterness.

Barrowden SIBA

Barrowden Brewing Co, c/o Exeter Arms, 28 Main Street, Barrowden, Rutland, LE15 8EQ
☎ (01572) 747247
✉ exeterarms@btconnect.com

⊗ The brewery was established by Peter Blencowe in 1998. Martin Allsopp bought the pub and brewery in 2005, which is situated in a barn at the back of the Exeter Arms.

Beech (OG 1038, ABV 3.8%)

Own Gear (ABV 4%)

Hop Gear (OG 1044, ABV 4.4%)

Bevin (OG 1045, ABV 4.5%)

Black Five (ABV 5%)

Bartrams SIBA EAB

Bartrams Brewery, Rougham Estate, Ipswich Road (A14), Rougham, Suffolk, IP30 9LZ
☎ (01449) 737655
☎ 07768 062581
✉ marc@bartramsbrewery.co.uk
bartramsbrewery.co.uk
Shop Tue & Sat 12-6pm
Tours by arrangement

The brewery was set up in 1999. In 2005 the plant was moved to a building on Rougham Airfield, the site of Bartram's Brewery between 1894 and 1902 run by Captain Bill Bartram. His image graces the pump clips. Beers are available in a selection of local pubs and there is a large amount of trade through local farmers' markets. Marld, Beltane Braces and all porters and stouts are suitable for vegetarians and vegans, as are all bottled beers. Seasonal beers: see website.

Marld (ABV 3.4%)
A traditional mild. Spicy hops and malt with a hint of chocolate, slightly smoky with a light, roasted finish.

Rougham Ready (ABV 3.6%)
A light, crisp bitter, surprisingly full bodied for its strength.

Trial and Error (ABV 3.6%)
A full malty bitter, fruity with a lot of character.

Premier (ABV 3.7%)
A traditional quaffing ale, full-flavoured but light, dry and hoppy.

Little Green Man (ABV 3.8%)
A golden bitter with the peppery and delicate citrus tones of subtle coriander. Dry and bitter.

Red Queen (ABV 3.9%)
Typical IPA style, chocolate malt in the foreground while the resiny hop flavour lingers.

Cats Whiskers (ABV 4%)
A straw-coloured beer with ginger and lemons added; a unique flavour experience.

Grozet (ABV 4%)
Using Little Green Man as the base beer, gooseberries are added to give an appealing extra dimension.

Bees Knees (ABV 4.2%)
An amber beer with a floral aroma; honey softness on the palate leads to a crisp, bitter finish.

Catherine Bartram's IPA (ABV 4.3%)
A full-bodied malty IPA style; tangy hops lead the malt throughout and dominate the dry, hoppy aftertaste.

Mother McCleary's Milk Stout (ABV 4.3%)

Jester Quick One (ABV 4.4%)
A sweet reddish bitter using fruity American Ahtanum hops.

Beltane Braces (ABV 4.5%)
Smooth and dark.

Coal Porter (ABV 4.5%)
Plenty of body in this ruby beer, supported by ample hops.

Stingo (ABV 4.5%)
A sweetish, fruity bitter with a hoppy nose. Light honey softens the bitter finish.

Beer Elsie Bub (ABV 4.8%)
Originally brewed for a Pagan wedding, this strong honey ale is now brewed all year round.

Captain Bill Bartram's Best Bitter (ABV 4.8%)
Modified from a 100-year old recipe, using full malt and traditional Kentish hops.

Captain's Stout (ABV 4.8%)
Biscuity dark malt leads to a lightly smoked aroma, plenty of roasted malt character, coffee notes and a whiff of smoke.

Cherry Stout (ABV 4.8%)
Sensuous hints of chocolate lead to a subtle suggestion of cherries.

Damson Stout (ABV 4.8%)
A robust, full-bodied stout with the chocolate and smoky aroma giving way to a lingering finish.

Trafalgar Squared (ABV 4.8%)
Brewed using malt grown a few miles from Nelson's birthplace and Goldings hops.

Suffolk 'n' Strong (ABV 5%)

A light, smooth and dangerously potable strong bitter, well-balanced malt and hops with an easy finish.

Comrade Bill Bartram's Egalitarian Anti-Imperialist Soviet Stout (ABV 6.9%)
A Russian stout by any other name, a luscious easy-drinking example of the style.

Barum SIBA

Barum Brewery Ltd, c/o Reform Inn, Pilton, Barnstaple, Devon, EX31 1PD
☎ (01271) 329994
✉ info@barumbrewery.co.uk
barumbrewery.co.uk
Tours by arrangement

Barum was formed in 1996 by Tim Webster and is housed in a conversion attached to the Reform Inn which acts as the brewery tap and main outlet. Distribution is exclusively within Devon. Seasonal beers: Mild (ABV 4.2%, spring), Gold (ABV 4%, summer), Barnstablasta (ABV 6.6%, winter), Agincourt (ABV 4.5%, St Crispins Day).

Basil's Best (OG 1040, ABV 4%)

Original (OG 1044, ABV 4.4%)

Breakfast (OG 1048, ABV 5%)

Bateman IFBB SIBA

George Bateman & Son Ltd, Salem Bridge Brewery, Mill Lane, Wainfleet, Lincolnshire, PE24 4JE
☎ (01754) 880317
✉ enquiries@bateman.co.uk
bateman.co.uk
Visitor Centre & Shop 11.30am-3.30pm daily
Daily tours 12pm (Apr-Sep) & 2.30pm (no booking necessary); Evening tours by arrangement

Bateman's Brewery is one of the few remaining independent family-owned brewers. Established in 1874 it has been brewing award-winning beers by four generations of the family. All but one of the 65 tied houses serve cask-conditioned beer. See website for seasonal and speciality beers.

Dark Mild (OG 1030, ABV 3%)
Characteristic orchard fruit and roasted nut nose with hops evident. One of the classic mild ales, although the lasting bitter finish may not be entirely true to type; nevertheless, a ruby-black gem.

XB Bitter (OG 1037, ABV 3.7%)
A mid-brown balanced session bitter with malt most obvious in the finish. The taste is dominated by the house-style apple hop, which also leads the aroma.

GHA Pale Ale (OG 1042, ABV 4.2%)

Salem Porter (OG 1048, ABV 4.7%)
A black and complex mix of chocolate, liquorice and cough elixir.

XXXB (OG 1048, ABV 4.8%)
A brilliant blend of malt, hops and fruit on the nose with a bitter bite over the top of a faintly banana maltiness that stays the course. A russet-tan brown classic.

Bath Ales SIBA

Bath Ales Ltd, Units 3-7, Caxton Business Park, Crown Way, Warmley, Bristol, BS30 8XJ
☎ (0117) 947 4797
✉ hare@bathales.co.uk
bathales.com
Shop Mon-Fri 9am-5pm; Sat 9am-12pm
Tours by arrangement

Bath Ales started brewing in 1995 and moved in 1999 to new premises with a 15-barrel plant. The company now has a purpose-built site on the edge of east Bristol, and can brew 300 barrels a week. Around 350 outlets are supplied direct. Ten pubs are owned, all serving cask ale. Seasonal beers: Festivity (ABV 5%), Rare Hare (ABV 5.2%). Most beers are available for purchase from the website or shop.

SPA (OG 1037, ABV 3.7%)
Gold/yellow colour, this is a light-bodied dry, bitter beer with a citrus hop aroma. Long malty, dry and bitter finish with some fruit.

Gem Bitter (OG 1042, ABV 4.1%)
This well-balanced, medium-bodied bitter is malty (pale and crystal with caramel), fruity and hoppy throughout. Amber-coloured, it is dry and bitter at the end.

Barnstormer (OG 1047, ABV 4.5%)
Malt, hops and fruit aroma with a faint hint of roast, with toffee sweetness. Dark brown, well balanced and smooth with a malty, bitter, dry finish.

Wild Hare (OG 1048, ABV 5%)
Pale, strong bitter. Grapefruit aroma, hoppy/fruity taste developing into a long-lasting dry, fruity finish. Refreshing and clean on the palate.

Batham IFBB

Daniel Batham & Son Ltd, Delph Brewery, Delph Road, Brierley Hill, West Midlands, DY5 2TN
☎ (01384) 77229
✉ info@bathams.com
bathams.com

A classic Black Country small brewery established in 1877. Tim and Matthew Batham represent the fifth generation to run the company. The Vine, one of the Black Country's most famous pubs, is also the site of the brewery. The company has 11 tied houses and supplies around 30 other outlets. Batham's Bitter is delivered in 54-gallon hogsheads to meet demand. Seasonal beer: XXX (ABV 6.3%, Dec).

Mild Ale (OG 1036.5, ABV 3.5%)
A fruity, dark brown mild with malty sweetness and a roast malt finish.

Best Bitter (OG 1043.5, ABV 4.3%)
A pale yellow, fruity, sweetish bitter, with a dry, hoppy finish. A good, light, refreshing beer.

Battledown

Battledown Brewery llp, Keynsham Works, Keynsham Street, Cheltenham, Gloucestershire, GL52 6EJ
☎ (01242) 693409
☎ 07734 834104
✉ roland@battledownbrewery.com
battledownbrewery.com
Shop open Wed/Thu/Sat am
Tours by arrangement

Established in 2005 by Roland and Stephanie Elliott-Berry, and joined in 2006 by Ben Jennison-Phillips (ex-Whittingtons), Battledown operates an eight-barrel plant from an old engineering works and supplies more than 150 outlets. Visitors are always welcome. There is an online shop for mail order purposes.

Saxon (OG 1036, ABV 3.8%)
Fresh and crisp with a hoppy finish.

Sunbeam (OG 1039, ABV 4%)
A smooth and light gold California Common beer, using a lager yeast at ale temperatures.

Tipster (OG 1041, ABV 4.2%)
A golden beer, the malts evident but giving way to the triple hop addition to give a spicy and slightly citrus finish.

Turncoat (OG 1046, ABV 4.5%)
A deep red and smooth porter, coffee notes and a hint of bitterness.

Brigand (OG 1046, ABV 4.7%)
Rich in malt with a hint of spice from Challenger hops.

Cheltenham SPA (OG 1050, ABV 5.2%)
A traditional IPA, crisp with plenty of hops.

Four Kings (OG 1066, ABV 7.2%)
Strong ale. Rich and smooth.

Battlefield

See Tunnel

Bays

Bays Brewery Ltd, Aspen Way, Paignton, Devon, TQ4 7QR
☎ (01803) 555004
✉ info@baysbrewery.co.uk
baysbrewery.co.uk
Shop Mon-Fri 8am-5pm
Tours by arrangement

Bays Brewery opened in early 2007 in an old steel fabrication unit in Paignton on a 20-barrel plant. Over 200 outlets are supplied direct. Seasonal beer: Merry Bays (ABV 5.2%).

Best (OG 1037, ABV 3.7%)

Gold (OG 1042, ABV 4.3%)

Breaker (OG 1046, ABV 4.7%)

Devon Dumpling (ABV 5.2%)

Bazens' SIBA

Bazens' Brewery, Rees Bazen Brewing Co Ltd, Unit 6, Knoll Street Industrial Park, Knoll Street, Salford, Greater Manchester, M7 2BL
☎ (0161) 708 0247
✉ bazensbrewery@mac.com
bazensbrewery.co.uk
Tours by arrangement for CAMRA groups

Run by husband and wife Richard and Jude Bazen, Bazens' Brewery was established in 2002 and moved to its present location a year later. Around 50 pubs are supplied direct.

Black Pig Mild (OG 1037, ABV 3.6%)
A dark brown beer with malt and fruit aromas. Roast, chocolate and fruit flavours, with an underlying bitterness, lead to a dry, malty and slightly smoky aftertaste.

Pacific Bitter (OG 1039, ABV 3.8%)
Gold-coloured bitter with a fruity nose. Hops and citrus fruit dominate the taste and there is a bitter, hoppy finish.

Flatbac (OG 1042, ABV 4.2%)
Well-balanced, distinctive and refreshing blonde beer. A full hop character has pronounced citrus/floral notes.

Zebra Best Bitter (OG 1043, ABV 4.3%)
A complex premium bitter, loaded with full malt flavour and crisp fruity hop character.

Blue Bullet (OG 1045, ABV 4.5%)
Yellow in colour, this golden ale has a fruity aroma. Hops, fruit and bitterness are in the taste and linger in the finish.

Knoll Street Porter (OG 1055, ABV 5.2%)
Dark brown beer with a chocolaty and malt aroma. Roast and chocolate malt, hops and fruit to taste, with a satisfying complex finish.

Beachy Head

Beachy Head Brewing Co Ltd, Seven Sisters Sheep Centre, Birling Manor Farm, Birling Gap Road, East Dean, East Sussex, BN20 0AA
☎ (01323) 423906
✉ charlie@beachyhead.org.uk
beachyhead.org.uk
Tours by arrangement

The 2.5-barrel brew plant was installed at the rear of the Seven Sisters Sheep Centre in late 2006. Beachy Head Brewery produces both cask and bottle-conditioned ales, supplied regularly to around 15 outlets, three of which are local pubs. The full range of ales (including seasonals) can be sampled at the Tiger Inn in East Dean village, which is the brewery tap.

Parson Darbys Hole (ABV 4%)

Beachy Original (ABV 4.5%)

Legless Rambler (ABV 5%)

Beartown SIBA

Beartown Brewery Ltd, Bromley House, Spindle Street, Congleton, Cheshire, CW12 1QN
☎ (01260) 299964
✉ headbrewer@beartownbrewery.co.uk
beartownbrewery.co.uk
Tours by arrangement

Congleton's links with brewing can be traced back to 1272. Two of its most senior officers at the time were Ale Taster and Bear Warden, hence the name of the brewery. Both the brewery's Navigation in Stockport and the Beartown Tap have been named CAMRA regional pubs of the year. There are plans to extend the tied estate to 15 outlets over the next two years. Beartown supplies 250 outlets and owns five pubs. A new 25-barrel plant has been installed.

Bear Ass (OG 1040, ABV 4%)
Dark ruby-red, malty bitter with good hop nose and fruity flavour with dry, bitter, astringent aftertaste.

Ginger Bear (OG 1040, ABV 4%)
The flavours from the malt and hops blend with the added bite from the root ginger to produce a quenching finish.

Kodiak Gold (OG 1040, ABV 4%)
Hops and fruit dominate the taste of this crisp yellow bitter and these follow through to the

dryish aftertaste. Biscuity malt also comes through on the aroma and taste.

Bearskinful (OG 1043, ABV 4.2%)
Biscuity malt dominates the flavour of this amber best bitter. There are hops and a hint of sulphur on the aroma. A balance of malt and bitterness follow through to the aftertaste.

Bearly Literate (OG 1045, ABV 4.5%)

Polar Eclipse (OG 1048, ABV 4.8%)
Classic black, dry and bitter stout, with roast flavours to the fore. Good hop on the nose follow through the taste into a long dry finish.

Black Bear (OG 1050, ABV 5%)
Advertised as a strong mild, this beer is rather bitter for the style. Bitter and malt flavours are balanced and there is also a good roast character along with a hint of liquorice. Aftertaste is short and reasonably dry.

Bruins Ruin (OG 1050, ABV 5%)

Beckstones SIBA

Beckstones Brewery, Upper Beckstones Mill, The Green, Millom, Cumbria, LA18 5HL
☎ (01229) 775294
david@beckstonesbrewery.com
beckstonesbrewery.co.uk

Beckstones started brewing in 2003 on the site of an 18th-century mill with its own water supply. It's a five-barrel, one-man operation and the plant is always working to capacity. The beer names often have a connection to the long-closed Millom Iron Works or local characters.

Leat (OG 1038, ABV 3.6%)
A refreshing golden bitter with tangy fruit and a rising hop finish.

Black Gun Dog Freddy Mild (OG 1040, ABV 3.8%)
A full-bodied, beautifully balanced ruby dark mild, replete with fruit and roast malt.

Iron Town (OG 1040, ABV 3.8%)
A well-balanced, malt and hops session ale.

Beer O'Clock (OG 1040, ABV 3.9%)
A golden, hoppy beer.

Border Steeans (OG 1042, ABV 4.1%)
Scottish Borders style, bittersweet with berry fruit undertones.

Rev Rob (OG 1046, ABV 4.6%)
A strong, golden, hoppy bitter.

Hematite (OG 1058, ABV 5.5%)
A luscious strong dark mild, mellow but punchy, full of dark fruit and a hint of liquorice.

Beer Engine SIBA

Tuttles Unique Co Ltd t/a The Beer Engine, Newton St Cyres, Devon, EX5 5AX
☎ (01392) 851282
info@thebeerengine.co.uk
thebeerengine.co.uk
Tours by arrangement

Beer Engine was developed in 1983 and in 2008 celebrated 25 years as the oldest working microbrewery in Devon, still employing the original brewer, Ian Sharp. The brewery is visible behind glass downstairs in the pub. Three outlets are supplied as well as all local beer festivals.

Rail Ale (OG 1037, ABV 3.8%)
A straw-coloured beer with a fruity aroma and a sweet, fruity finish.

Silver Bullet (OG 1040, ABV 4%)
A light, medium-strength summer beer with a smack of hops.

Piston Bitter (OG 1043, ABV 4.3%)
A mid-brown, sweet-tasting beer with a pleasant, bittersweet aftertaste.

Sleeper Heavy (OG 1052, ABV 5.4%)
A red-coloured beer with a fruity, sweet taste and a bitter finish.

Bees

Bees Brewery, c/o Branstons, 1487 Melton Road, Queniborough, Leicester, LE7 3FP
☎ (0116) 260 7715
☎ 07971 577526
Tours by arrangement

Brewing started in 2008 on a 9.5-barrel plant. More beers are planned in the near future including an organic and a gluten-free beer. Both regular beers are also available bottle conditioned.

Navigator (OG 1045, ABV 4.5%)

Wobble (OG 1050, ABV 5%)

Beeston

Beeston Brewery Ltd, Fransham Road Farm, Beeston, Norfolk, PE32 2LZ
☎ (01328) 700844
☎ 07768 742763
mark_riches@tesco.net
beestonbrewery.co.uk
Tours by arrangement

The brewery was established in 2007 in an old farm building using a five-barrel plant. Brewing water comes from a dedicated borehole and raw ingredients are sourced locally whenever possible. Both cask beers are also available bottle conditioned and in 5 litre mini casks.

Afternoon Delight (OG 1036, ABV 3.7%)
A blonde ale, suitable for lunchtime refreshment or as an evening session beer.

Worth the Wait (OG 1041, ABV 4.2%)
A well-balanced golden bitter with a grainy feel. The initial hoppiness is underpinned with bittersweet notes and a consistent maltiness. The finish slowly fades into dryness.

On the Huh (OG 1048, ABV 5%)
Deceptively smooth bitter with a fruity raisin aroma. A bittersweet maltiness jousts with caramel and roast. A dry hoppiness gives depth to a strong finale.

Norfolk Black (OG 1060, ABV 6%)
A warming, full-bodied stout.

Belhaven

See Greene King in New Nationals section

Belvoir SIBA

Belvoir Brewery Ltd, Crown Park, Station Road, Old Dalby, Leicestershire, LE14 3NQ
☎ (01664) 823455

colin@belvoirbrewery.co.uk
belvoirbrewery.co.uk
Tours by arrangement

Belvoir (pronounced 'beaver') Brewery was set up in 1995 by former Shipstone's brewer Colin Brown. Long-term expansion has seen the introduction of a 20-barrel plant that can produce 50 barrels a week. There is also a visitor centre. Bottle-conditioned beers are produced using in-house bottling equipment. Up to 150 outlets are supplied. Seasonal beers: Whippling Golden Bitter (ABV 3.6%, spring/summer), Peacock's Glory (ABV 4.7%, spring/summer), Old Dalby (ABV 5.1%, winter). Bottle-conditioned beers are also available.

Star Mild (OG 1034, ABV 3.4%)
Reddish/black in colour, this full-bodied and well-balanced mild is both malty and hoppy with hints of fruitiness leading to a long, bittersweet finish.

Star Bitter (OG 1039, ABV 3.9%)
Reminiscent of the long-extinct Shipstone's Bitter, this mid-brown bitter lives up to its name as it is bitter in taste but not unpleasantly so.

Beaver Bitter (OG 1043, ABV 4.3%)
A light brown bitter that starts malty in both aroma and taste, but soon develops a hoppy bitterness. Appreciably fruity.

Melton Mowbray Oatmeal Stout (OG 1044, ABV 4.3%)

Beowulf SIBA

Beowulf Brewing Co, Chasewater Country Park, Pool Road, Brownhills, Staffordshire, WS8 7NL
(01543) 454067
beowulfbrewing@yahoo.co.uk
beowulfbrewery.co.uk
Tours by arrangement

Beowulf Brewing Company beers appear as guest ales predominantly in the central region but also across the country. The brewery's dark beers have a particular reputation for excellence. Seasonal beers: Hurricane (ABV 4%, autumn), Glutlusty (ABV 4.5%, autumn), Blizzard (ABV 5%, winter), Grendel's Winter Ale (ABV 5.8%, winter), Wergild (ABV 4.3%, spring/summer), Wuffa (ABV 4.4%, spring/summer), Gold Work (ABV 5.1%, spring/summer). Bottle-conditioned beer is also available.

Beorma (OG 1038, ABV 3.9%)
A pale session ale with a malty hint of fruit giving way to a lingering bitterness.

Noble Bitter (OG 1039, ABV 4%)
Golden with a sweet malty aroma. Malty start becomes very hoppy then bitter, but not an over-long finish.

Wiglaf (OG 1043, ABV 4.3%)
A golden bitter, with a malty flavour married to a pleasing bitterness, with three hop varieties used.

Chasewater Bitter (OG 1043, ABV 4.4%)
Golden bitter, hoppy throughout with citrus and hints of malt. Long mouth-watering, bitter finish.

Dark Raven (OG 1048, ABV 4.5%)

Swordsman (OG 1045, ABV 4.5%)
Pale gold, light fruity aroma, tangy hoppy flavour. Faintly hoppy finish.

Dragon Smoke Stout (OG 1048, ABV 4.7%)
Black with a light brown, creamy head. Roast aromas of tobacco, charcoal, liquorice with raisins and mixed fruity tangs. Hints of a good port emerge.

Finn's Hall Porter (OG 1049, ABV 4.7%)
Complex tasting porter with strong hints of coffee and a sweet roasty nose. Maltiness comes out strongly on the palate, with a vinous aftertaste.

Heroes Bitter (OG 1046, ABV 4.7%)
Gold colour, malt aroma, hoppy taste but sweetish finish.

Mercian Shine (OG 1048, ABV 5%)
Amber to pale gold with a good bitter and hoppy start. Plenty of caramel and hops with background malt leading to a good bitter finish with caramel and hops lingering in the aftertaste.

Berrow SIBA

Berrow Brewery, Coast Road, Berrow, Burnham-on-Sea, Somerset, TA8 2QU
(01278) 751345
Tours by arrangement

The brewery opened in 1982 and production is now around five barrels a week. It celebrated its silver jubilee in 2007. All the beers have won prizes at beer festivals. 15-20 outlets are supplied. Seasonal beers: Carnivale (ABV 4.7%, Oct-Nov), Christmas Ale (ABV 4.7%, Nov-Dec), Winter Sport (ABV 4.7%).

Best Bitter/4Bs (OG 1038, ABV 3.9%)
A pleasant, pale brown session beer, with a fruity aroma, a malty, fruity flavour and bitterness in the palate and finish.

Berrow Porter (OG 1046, ABV 4.6%)
A ruby-coloured porter with a pronounced hop character.

Silver Berrow (OG 1047, ABV 4.7%)
A pale ale with good hop character, created to celebrate the brewery's silver jubilee.

Topsy Turvy (OG 1055, ABV 5.9%)
A gold-coloured beer with an aroma of malt and hops. Well-balanced malt and hops taste is followed by a hoppy, bitter finish with some fruit notes.

Best Mates

Best Mates Brewery Ltd, Sheep House Farm, Ardington, Wantage, Oxfordshire, OX12 8QB
(01235) 835684
bestmatesbrewery@btconnect.com
bestmatesbrewery.co.uk
Tours by arrangement

Best Mates Brewery was established in 2007 on a five-barrel plant and uses locally sourced water. Bottle-conditioned beers are available.

Scutchaman's Knob (OG 1036, ABV 3.6%)

Vicar's Daughter (OG 1037, ABV 3.7%)

Alfie's (OG 1044, ABV 4.4%)

Satan's Sister (OG 1045, ABV 4.5%)

Betwixt

Betwixt Beer Co Ltd, The Brewery, 8 Pool Street, Birkenhead, Merseyside, CH41 3NL
(0151) 647 7688

✉ **brewer@betwixtbeer.co.uk**
🌐 **betwixt.co.uk**
Tours by arrangement (groups only)

⊗The company was created in 2005 and is situated on the Wirral peninsula 'Betwixt the Mersey and the Dee'. After a few years of 'cuckoo-brewing' at a local micro-brewery (Northern), Wirral-born founder Mike McGuigan joined forces with local businessman Steve Briscoe to build a brewplant to return brewing to Birkenhead for the first time in over 40 years. The beers are sold through farmers markets, festivals and in local pubs. In addition to cask ales, continental lagers and wheat beers are also brewed (available in cask and bottle). Seasonal beers: Hazy Days (ABV 3.8%, Jun-Aug), BeWilder (ABV 4.3%, Sep-Nov), IceBreaker (ABV 6%, Nov-Dec). Bottle-conditioned beers: as for cask beer range including seasonals. All bottled beers are suitable for vegetarians and vegans.

Skyline Bitter (OG 1035, ABV 3.5%)
Hoppy, copper-coloured quaffing bitter.

Dark Matter (OG 1040, ABV 4%)
Based on a black lager. Chocolate and coffee flavours.

Sunlight (OG 1043, ABV 4.3%)
Hoppy golden ale.

Storr Lager (OG 1048, ABV 4.8%)
Crisp, clean, authentic golden cask lager. Hoppy and dry.

Red Rocks (OG 1050, ABV 5%)
Rich, ruby ale.

Bewdley SIBA

Bewdley Brewery Ltd, Unit 7, Bewdley Craft Centre, Lax Lane, Bewdley, Worcestershire, DY12 2DZ
☎ **(01299) 405148**
✉ **bewdleybrewery@hotmail.co.uk**
🌐 **bewdleybrewery.co.uk**
Tours by arrangement

⊗Bewdley began brewing in 2008 on a six-barrel plant in an old school. Seasonal beers: Bah Humbug (ABV 4.6%, Xmas), Festival Ale (ABV 4.3%, Oct), William Mucklow Dark Mild (ABV 6%, May). Bottle-conditioned beers are available.

Junior School Bitter (ABV 3.4%)
A light summer pale ale.

Worcestershire Way (ABV 3.6%)
A light beer with citrus notes.

Old School Bitter (ABV 3.8%)
Session bitter with a hoppy finish.

Leg'End of St George (ABV 4.1%)
Well-balanced, amber-coloured bitter with a malty taste and hoppy finish.

Senior School Bitter (ABV 4.1%)
A premium bitter, amber-coloured with malty taste and hoppy finish.

Big Lamp

Big Lamp Brewers, Grange Road, Newburn, Newcastle upon Tyne, Tyne & Wear, NE15 8NL
☎ **(0191) 267 1689**
✉ **admin@biglampbrewers.co.uk**
🌐 **biglampbrewers.co.uk**
Tours by arrangement

Big Lamp started in 1982 and relocated in 1997 to a 55-barrel plant in a former water pumping station. It is the oldest micro-brewery in the north-east of England. Around 35 outlets are supplied and two pubs are owned. Seasonal/occasional beers: Old Genie (ABV 7.4%), Blackout (ABV 11%), Embers (ABV 5.5%, Nov-Apr).

Sunny Daze (OG 1036, ABV 3.6%)
Golden hoppy session bitter with a clean taste and finish.

Bitter (OG 1039, ABV 3.9%)
A clean tasting bitter, full of hops and malt. A hint of fruit with a good hoppy finish

One Hop (OG 1040, ABV 4%)
Dark amber beer with a smooth finish and a hint of hazelnut.

Summerhill Stout (OG 1044, ABV 4.4%)
A rich tasty stout, dark in colour with a lasting rich roast character. Malty mouthfeel with a lingering finish.

Prince Bishop Ale (OG 1048, ABV 4.8%)
A refreshing, easy-drinking bitter, golden in colour, full of fruit and hops. Strong bitterness with a spicy dry finish.

Premium (OG 1052, ABV 5.2%)
Hoppy ale with a good bitter finish.

Keelman Brown (OG 1057, ABV 5.7%)
A full-bodied ale with a hint of toffee.

Birmingham SIBA (NEW)

Birmingham Brewery Ltd, Unit 45, Mount Street Business Centre, Nechells, Birmingham, West Midlands, B7 5RD
☎ **(0121) 328 2120**
✉ **sales@birminghambrewery.co.uk**
🌐 **birminghambrewery.co.uk**

The brewery was opened in 2008 by novice brewers Mark Norridge and Tim Watson. A six-barrel brew plant is operated and around 20 outlets are supplied direct.

Dark Mild (BDM) (OG 1038, ABV 3.8%)
Dark-brown, traditional Midlands mild with balanced sweet and roast malt flavours.

Pale Ale (OG 1041, ABV 4.1%)
A traditional, lightly-hopped English pale ale with a dry aftertaste.

Bitter End

Bitter End Pub & Brewery, 15 Kirkgate, Cockermouth, Cumbria, CA13 9PJ
☎ **(01900) 828993**
✉ **info@bitterend.co.uk**
🌐 **bitterend.co.uk**
Tours by arrangement

The brewery was established by Mike Askey in 1995 behind glass at the back of the Bitter End pub and was upgraded in 2004 to a four-barrel copper clad system imported from the US. Three beers and a seasonal range of traditional English beer styles are brewed with distribution to the free trade – see website for details. One-off and festival beers are also produced.

Lakeland Bitter (ABV 3.8%)

Lakeland Pale Ale (ABV 4%)

Lakeland Best Gold (ABV 4.3%)

THE BREWERIES

Blackawton SIBA

Blackawton Brewery, Unit 7, Peninsula Park, Moorlands Trading Estate, Saltash, Cornwall, PL12 6LX
☎ (01752) 848777
✉ steve@blackawtonbrewery.eclipse.co.uk
🌐 blackawtonbrewery.com

⊗ Blackawton was once Devon's oldest operating brewery, but relocated to Cornwall in 2000 and ownership changed in 2004. Around 30 outlets are supplied. Seasonal beers: Saltash Sunrise (ABV 5%, summer), Winter Fuel (ABV 5%). Bottle-conditioned beers are also available.

Original Bitter (OG 1037, ABV 3.8%)
A copper-coloured bitter; an ideal session beer with a fresh floral hop aroma.

Westcountry Gold (OG 1039, ABV 4.1%)
A light, golden, fresh-tasting summer beer with sweet malt flavours and delicate vanilla and fruit hints from Styrian Goldings hops.

44 Special (OG 1044, ABV 4.5%)
A premium, full-strength bitter that is rich and sweet with the aroma of ripe hops and fruit.

Peninsula Ale (OG 1046, ABV 4.6%)
A dark amber-coloured premium bitter with a hoppy, bitter finish.

Exhibition Ale (OG 1047, ABV 4.7%)

Headstrong (OG 1048, ABV 5.2%)
A deceptively smooth beer with a bitter malt taste.

Blackbeck (NEW)

Blackbeck Brewery, Blackbeck Inn, Egremont, Cumbria, CA22 2NY
☎ (01946) 841661
✉ drink@blackbeckbrewery.co.uk
🌐 blackbeckbrewery.co.uk

Blackbeck Brewery is owned and run by Tommy Taylor and Kenny O'Hara. It was established in 2009 using a five-barrel, purpose-built, solar-powered brewery behind the hotel.

Trial Run (ABV 3.4%)

Black Country

Black Country Ales, Old Bulls Head, 1 Redhall Road, Lower Gornal, Dudley, West Midlands, DY3 2NU
☎ (01384) 480156
☎ 07946 454150
✉ info@blackcountryales.co.uk
🌐 blackcountryales.co.uk
Tours by arrangement

Brewing started on the site around 1834. In 1900, oak vessels were installed that have now been refurbished and brought back into production. The brewery was closed down in 1934 but re-opened in 2004, with many original features still remaining. Seasonal beers: English Summer (ABV 4.1%), English Winter (ABV 5.5%).

Bradley's Finest Golden (OG 1041, ABV 4.2%)

Pig on the Wall (OG 1042, ABV 4.3%)

Fireside (OG 1047, ABV 5%)

Black Dog

Black Dog Brewery, Foulsyke Farm, Fylingdales, Whitby, North Yorkshire, YO22 4QL
☎ (0845) 301 2337
🌐 blackdogbrewery.co.uk

Black Dog started brewing in 1997 in the centre of Whitby, but closed in 2000. In 2006 Tony Bryars purchased the original Black Dog five-barrel plant, together with recipes, and re-established the brewery on his farm, using local spring water. The beers are now contract brewed by Hambleton Ales (qv).

Blackfriars

Blackfriars Brewery Ltd, The Courtyard, Main Cross Road, Great Yarmouth, Norfolk, NR30 3NZ
☎ (01493) 850578
✉ pints@blackfriars-brewery.co.uk
🌐 blackfriars-brewery.co.uk
Shop: Mon-Fri 9am-4.30pm
Tours by arrangement

⊗ The brewery was established in 2004 using a purpose-built five-barrel plant and was extended in 2007. In 2008 the brewery relocated and now has a shop, visitor centre and fully-licensed bar. More than 50 outlets are supplied. All beers (with the exception of specials) are available in bottle-conditioned form. Special beers: Holy Smoke (ABV 6.7%), Audit Ale (ABV 8%).

Mild (ABV 3.4%) ◆
Sweet and malty in true Norfolk fashion. Red-hued with a gentle roast malt aroma. Stewed prunes and caramel lurk in the background as the finish lingers long and sweet.

Yarmouth Bitter (OG 1036, ABV 3.8%) ◆
A malt-dominated brew. Pale brown and smooth drinking with a distinctly malty nose. A bittersweet fruitiness in the taste turns to an increasing bitterness to rival the malt character.

Mitre Gold (OG 1044, ABV 4%)

Springtide (ABV 4.2%)
Traditional, well-hopped bitter.

Whyte Angel (ABV 4.5%) ◆
Fragrant hoppy aroma leads to a strong bitter first taste. Golden hued with honey notes softening the dryness of the bitter hops. Gentle malt background throughout.

St Georges Honey (ABV 4.7%)
Rich, smooth beer with Norfolk honey.

Maritime (ABV 5%) ◆
Copper-coloured, rich, heavy and malty brew. Vinous, fruitcake characteristics supplement the richness of taste. A muted hoppy bitterness can be detected in the long finish.

Old Habit (OG 1052, ABV 5.6%) ◆
Old-fashioned mix of roast, malt and plummy fruitiness. Smooth and aromatic with coffee notes and a heavy mouthfeel. Finish softens to a malty character.

Black Hole SIBA

Black Hole Brewery Ltd, Unit 63, Ground Floor, Imex Business Park, Shobnall Road, Burton upon Trent, Staffordshire, DE14 2AU
☎ (01283) 534060
✉ beer@blackholebrewery.co.uk
🌐 blackholebrewery.co.uk
Tours by arrangement

The brewery was established in 2007 on a purpose-built, 10-barrel plant in the former Ind Coope bottling stores. Fermenting capacity is being progressively increased with the aim of producing a brew per day. Occasional beers are brewed to mark special occasions such as Halloween and Xmas. Around 250 outlets are supplied.

Bitter (OG 1040, ABV 3.8%)
Gentle malt and hop aroma from this amber beer. After a grassy start the bitterness develops into a satisfying hop bite. There is a dry finish with some fruitiness and malt.

Stargazer (OG 1042, ABV 4%)

Cosmic (OG 1044, ABV 4.2%)

Red Dwarf (OG 1046, ABV 4.5%)

Supernova (OG 1048, ABV 4.8%)

No Escape (OG 1053, ABV 5.2%)

Milky Way (OG 1059, ABV 6%)

Black Isle SIBA

Black Isle Brewery Ltd, Old Allengrange, Munlochy, Ross-shire, IV8 8NZ
☎ (01463) 811871
greatbeers@blackislebrewery.com
blackislebrewery.com
Shop: Mon-Sat 10am-6pm; Sun 11am-6pm (Apr-Sep)
Tours offered between 10am-5pm

Black Isle Brewery was set up in 1998 in the heart of the Scottish Highlands. The five-barrel plant was upgraded to a 30-barrel plant in 2009. All beers are organic, suitable for vegetarians and vegans and have Soil Association certification. Bottled (including bottle-conditioned) beers are available by mail order to anywhere in mainland Britain. Seasonal beers: See website.

Yellowhammer (OG 1038, ABV 3.9%)
A refreshing hoppy, golden ale with light hop and passion fruit throughout. A short bitter finish with a yeasty background.

Red Kite (OG 1042, ABV 4.2%)
Tawny ale with light malt on the nose and some fruit on the palate. Slight sweetness in the taste and a short bitter finish.

Porter (OG 1046, ABV 4.6%)
A hint of liquorice and burnt chocolate on the nose and a nice creamy mix of malt and fruit in the taste.

Blonde (OG 1046, ABV 5%)

Black Sheep SIBA

Black Sheep Brewery plc, Wellgarth, Masham, Ripon, North Yorkshire, HG4 4EN
☎ (01765) 689227
blacksheepbrewery.com
Shop 10am-5pm daily
Tours by arrangement

Black Sheep was established 1992 by Paul Theakston, a member of Masham's famous brewing family, in the former Wellgarth Maltings. The company has enjoyed continued growth and now supplies a free trade of around 700 outlets, but owns no pubs. The brewery specialises in cask ale (70% of production). Occasional beer: Emmerdale Ale (ABV 4.2%).

Best Bitter (OG 1038, ABV 3.8%)
A hoppy and fruity beer with strong bitter overtones, leading to a long, dry, bitter finish.

Ale (OG 1044, ABV 4.4%)
A premium bitter with robust fruit, malt and hops.

Riggwelter (OG 1059, ABV 5.9%)
A fruity bitter, with complex underlying tastes and hints of liquorice and pear drops leading to a long, dry, bitter finish.

Blackwater

Blackwater Brewery, Brewers Wholesale, Unit 2b Gainsborough Trading Estate, Rufford Road, Stourbridge, West Midlands, DY9 7ND
☎ (01384) 374050
enquiries@thebrewerswholesale.co.uk
thebrewerswholesale.co.uk

Beers are contract brewed by Salopian Brewery (qv).

Blakemere

See Northern

Blencowe

See Barrowden

Blindmans SIBA

Blindmans Brewery Ltd, Talbot Farm, Leighton, Frome, Somerset, BA11 4PN
☎ (01749) 880038
info@blindmansbrewery.co.uk
blindmansbrewery.co.uk
Tours by arrangement

Blindmans Brewery was established in 2002 in a converted milking parlour. In 2004 the brewery was bought by Paul Edney and Lloyd Chamberlain. The brewery has its own exclusive water spring. They opened their first pub in early 2008, the Lamb Inn in Frome, serving several exclusively brewed ales. Seasonal beers: Siberia (ABV 4.7%), Bah Humbug! (ABV 4.5%).

Buff (ABV 3.6%)
Amber-coloured, smooth session beer.

Golden Spring (ABV 4%)
Fresh and aromatic straw-coloured beer, brewed using selected lager malt.

Eclipse (ABV 4.2%)
A porter full of chocolate flavours and subtle bitterness

Mine Beer (ABV 4.2%)
Full-bodied, copper-coloured, blended malt ale.

Icarus (ABV 4.5%)
Fruity, rich, mid-dark ruby ale.

Blorenge

See Tudor

Blue Anchor SIBA

Blue Anchor Inn Brewery, 50 Coinagehall Street, Helston, Cornwall, TR13 8EL
☎ (01326) 565765

THE BREWERIES

✉ theblueanchor@btconnect.com
🌐 spingoales.com
Tours by arrangement

Dating back to the 15th century, this is the oldest brewery in Cornwall and was originally a monks' hospice. After the dissolution of the monasteries it became a tavern brewing its own uniquely flavoured beer called Spingo at the rear of the premises. Brewing has continued to this day and people travel from all over the world to sample the delights of this wonderful inn, untouched by time. Five outlets are supplied. Seasonal beers: Spingo Bragget (ABV 6.1%, Apr-Oct), Spingo Easter Special (ABV 7.6%), Spingo Christmas Special (ABV 7.6%). All draught beers are available in bottle-conditioned form. Bragget is a recreation of a medieval beer style.

Spingo Jubilee/IPA (OG 1045, ABV 4.6%)

Spingo Middle (OG 1050, ABV 5.1%)
A copper-red beer with a fruity aroma, a hint of vanilla and a peppery note from the hops. The palate is nutty, with a fruit cake note. The complex bittersweet finish is fruity and dry.

Spingo Special (OG 1066, ABV 6.7%)
Darker than Middle with a pronounced earthy character on the nose balanced by rich fruit. Fruit and peppery hops dominate the mouth, followed by a finish with malt, fruit and hops.

Blue Bear

Blue Bear Brewery Ltd, Unit 1, Open Barn Farm, Kempsey, Worcestershire, WR5 3LW
☎ (01905) 828258
✉ sales@bluebearbrewery.co.uk
🌐 bluebearbrewery.co.uk
Tours by arrangement (for 12 people or more)

Blue Bear is run by a husband and wife team and started production in 2006 in an old potato store. Bottle-conditioned beers are available. More than 250 outlets are supplied direct. Seasonal beers: See website.

Wanderlust (ABV 3.8%)
A hoppy, straw-coloured beer with biscuit tones on the palate and a floral finish.

Roar Spirit (OG 1040, ABV 4.2%)
An amber-coloured beer with a rounded, malted flavour and a spicy, blackcurrant aftertaste.

White Bear (OG 1043, ABV 4.5%)
A golden premium ale with a fruit character that leaves a smooth mouth feel of citrus on the palate.

Blue Bell

Blue Bell Brewery, Sycamore House, Lapwater Lane, Holbeach St Marks, Lincolnshire, PE12 8EX
☎ (01406) 701000
✉ enquiries@bluebellbrewery.co.uk
🌐 bluebellbrewery.co.uk
Tours by arrangement

The Blue Bell Brewery was founded in 1998 in a former potato shed located behind the Blue Bell pub, Whaplode St Catherine, and is run by Emma Bell and Pat Sage. The brewery operates as a separate business from the Blue Bell pub but the pub does act as the brewery tap. Around 30 outlets are supplied.

Old Honesty (OG 1040, ABV 4.1%)

Old Resurgence (ABV 4.3%)

Old Gold (OG 1045, ABV 4.5%)

Old Fashioned (OG 1045, ABV 4.8%)

Old Comfort (OG 1050, ABV 5%)

For Blue Bell Inn, Whaplode St Catherine:

Ingle Dingle (OG 1054, ABV 5.1%)

Blue Cow

Blue Cow Inn & Brewery, High Street, South Witham, Lincolnshire, NG33 5QB
☎ (01572) 768432
✉ enquiries@bluecowinn.co.uk
🌐 bluecowinn.co.uk
Tours by arrangement

Owned by Simon Crathorn since 2005, Blue Cow is a traditional 13th-century pub with a brewery. The beer is only available in the pub.

Best Bitter (OG 1038, ABV 3.8%)

Blue Monkey (NEW)

Blue Monkey Brewing Ltd, Unit 1, Enterprise Court, Manners Industrial Estate, Ilkeston, Derbyshire, DE7 8EW
☎ 07500 555595
✉ john@bluemonkeybrewery.com
🌐 bluemonkeybrewery.com

Blue Monkey was established in 2008 by John Hickling. There are plans to double brewing capacity and to complement the current range of two beers with stronger seasonal brews. 100 outlets are supplied direct.

Original (OG 1039, ABV 3.6%)
A classic, copper-coloured session ale.

Evolution (OG 1043, ABV 4.3%)
A premium pale ale, golden in colour. Fruity with a pronounced citrus aroma.

Blue Moon

Blue Moon Brewery, Cock Inn, Watton Road, Barford, Norfolk, NR9 4AS
☎ (01603) 757646

The brewery supplies the Cock Inn and around 40 other free trade outlets. Seasonal beer: Moon Dance (ABV 4.7%, summer).

Easy Life (OG 1040, ABV 3.8%) ◆
Light, refreshing bitter with hop notes in both aroma and taste. Soft fruit and a sweet toffeeness provide balance but do not detract from the crisp, hoppy finish.

Dark Side (OG 1048, ABV 4%)

Sea of Tranquility (OG 1042, ABV 4.2%) ◆
An undemanding malty bitter with fruity undertones. A hint of banana on the nose continues into the initial taste but is lost in the short, malty finish.

Hingham High (OG 1050, ABV 5.2%) ◆
A complex, multi-layered reddish brew. A rich, malty nose leads into a suprisingly bitter first taste. Early hints of malt and fruit subside into a long, increasingly dry finish.

Milk of Amnesia (OG 1055, ABV 5.2%) ◆

A complex, mid-brown beer. The taste has a port-like note; cinnamon and ginger jostle with pepper and citrus as the flavours continue to hold up well.

Liquor Mortis (OG 1075, ABV 7.5%)
A heavy blackcurrant signature introduces this dark brown barley wine. A mature roast beginning counter-balances the fruity sweetness that carries through to a long, filling finish.

Total Eclipse (ABV 9%)

Blythe SIBA

Blythe Brewery, Blythe Farm House, Lichfield Road, Hamstall Ridware, Rugeley, Staffordshire, WS15 3QQ
☎ 07773 747724
info@blythebrewery.plus.com
blythebrewery.co.uk
Tours by arrangement

Robert Greenway started brewing in 2003 using a 2.5-barrel plant in a converted barn on a farm. As well as specials, seasonal beers are produced on a quarterly basis. Fifteen outlets are supplied.
Seasonal beer: Old Horny (ABV 4.6%, Sep-Nov).
Bottle-conditioned beers: as for cask beers listed below.

Bitter (OG 1040, ABV 4%)
Amber with a full hoppy aroma and sweet touch. Immediate full hoppy taste that develops into an intense hoppy, lingering finish.

Ridware Pale (OG 1042, ABV 4.3%)
Bright and golden with a bitter floral hop aroma and citrus taste. Good and hop-sharp, bitter and refreshing. Long, lingering bite with ripples of citrus across the tongue.

Chase Bitter (OG 1044, ABV 4.4%)
Slight smoky aroma and traditional colour. Sweetish with malt, fruit and developing hops. Good mouthfeel and hoppiness to finish.

Staffie (OG 1044, ABV 4.4%)
Hoppy and grassy aroma with hints of sweetness from this amber beer. Caramel start is soon overwhelmed by mouth-watering hops.

Palmer's Poison (OG 1045, ABV 4.5%)
Mid-brown with spicy tastes amid the fruit and hops. Bittersweet balance with hops developing. Sweet caramel holds back the long, hedgerow hoppy taste.

Johnson's (OG 1056, ABV 5.2%)
Black with thick aroma. Full-bodied with lingering bitterness of chocolate, dates and coal smoke.

BMG Brewing

BMG Brewing Ltd, c/o Tower Brewery, Old Water Tower, Walsitch Maltings, Glensyl Way, Burton upon Trent, Staffordshire, DE14 1LX
☎ (01283) 561330

Beers are contract brews by Tower Brewery (qv) for Beer My Guest distributors.

Bob's

Bob's Brewing Co Ltd, The Healey Brewery, Low Mill Road, Healey, West Yorkshire, WF5 8ND
☎ 07789 693597

The brewery was founded in 2002 by Bob Hunter, a former partner in Ossett Brewery, in outbuildings behind the Red Lion pub. During 2009 brewing relocated to a new eight-barrel plant. The beers appear regularly in around 25 freehouses across West Yorkshire and in the West Midlands via wholesalers.

White Lion (OG 1043, ABV 4.3%)
Pale, flowery, lager-style beer using American Cascade hops.

Yakima Pale Ale (OG 1045.5, ABV 4.6%)
A hoppy and bitter yellow beer that uses hops from the Yakima Valley in Washington State, U.S.

Chardonnayle (OG 1051.5, ABV 5.1%)
Complex, stylish strong pale ale with hints of lemongrass and fruits, with Willamette hops for aroma.

Boggart Hole Clough

Boggart Hole Clough Brewing Co, Unit 13, Brookside Works, Clough Road, Moston, Manchester, M9 4FP
☎ (0161) 277 9666
boggartoffice@btconnect.com
boggart-brewery.co.uk

The brewery was set up by Mark Dade in 2001 next to Boggart Hole Clough Park in former engineering works. The site also houses Boggart Beer Distribution, launched in 2003 delivering to more than 250 outlets throughout the country. Monthly specials are produced as are bottle-conditioned beers. In 2009 the brewery opened its first outlet, The Micro Bar, in the Arndale Market in Manchester's Arndale Centre.

Ruby Tuesday (ABV 3.8%)
A reddish-coloured hoppy session ale.

Ray of Sunshine (ABV 3.9%)
A pale session bitter.

Bog Eyed (ABV 4%)
A light-coloured session ale with pronounced hoppiness and aroma.

Dark Mild (ABV 4%)
A classic dark mild.

Standard Pioneer (ABV 4%)
A light-coloured session ale with lemon citrus taste and aroma.

Angel Hill (OG 1042, ABV 4.2%)
A premium, golden pale ale with an aromatic explosion of flavour.

Boggart Brew (OG 1043, ABV 4.3%)
A quaffable ruby-red beer.

Dark Side (OG 1044, ABV 4.4%)
A classic porter with a smooth roast finish and subtle hop aftertaste.

Sun Dial (OG 1047, ABV 4.7%)
A pale beer with a refreshing, fruity hop taste and aroma.

Waterloo Sunset (ABV 5%)
Traditional porter with an oak roast finish.

Bollington (NEW)

Bollington Brewing Co Ltd, Adlington Road, Bollington, Cheshire, SK10 5JT
☎ (01625) 575380
lee@bollingtonbrewing.co.uk
bollingtonbrewing.co.uk
Tours by arrangement

Lee Wainwright bought the Vale Inn, a closed freehouse in Bollington in 2005. His love of real ale became the focus of the pub and he started brewing in 2008. At present beer is only available in the Vale Inn.

Bollington Nights (ABV 3.9%)

Ruby Nights (OG 1040, ABV 3.9%)

Happy Valley (OG 1040, ABV 4%)

White Nancy (OG 1041, ABV 4.1%)

Bollington Best (OG 1042, ABV 4.2%)

Dinner Ale (OG 1043, ABV 4.3%)

Winter Reserve (OG 1046, ABV 4.6%)

Borough Arms

Borough Arms, 33 Earle Street, Crewe, Cheshire, CW1 2BG
(01270) 254999
info@borougharmscrewe.co.uk
borougharmscrewe.co.uk
Tours by arrangement

A two-barrel brewery opened in 2005 to supply the pub. After a brief suspension German master brewer Rainer Dresselhays has been brewing regularly since 2008. All beers are only available at the pub. Seasonal beer: Leaves on the Line (ABV 4.7%, autumn).

Blonde Temptation (ABV 3.8%)
A light session ale.

Borough Gold (ABV 4%)
A hoppy, golden ale.

Earle St Stout (ABV 4.3%)

Befuggled (ABV 5.2%)
A strong, light ale.

Bottle Brook

Bottle Brook Brewery, Church Street, Kilburn, Belper, Derbyshire, DE56 0LU
(01332) 880051
07971 189915

Bottle Brook was established in 2005 using a 2.5-barrel plant on a tower gravity system. The traditional brewery specialises in using rare and unusual hop varieties and at one point there was no range of permanent beers – most are now repeated occasionally. New fermenters were added in 2008 to boost output. Around 30 outlets are supplied.

Two Tuns Pale Ale (OG 1037, ABV 3.6%)

Columbus (OG 1040, ABV 4%)

Pot of Gold (OG 1042, ABV 4.1%)

Full Moon (OG 1045, ABV 4.6%)

Hallucination (OG 1046, ABV 4.7%)

Midnight Mash (OG 1050, ABV 5.1%)

Bow House (NEW)

See Plain Ales

Bowland SIBA

Bowland Beer Co Ltd, Bashall Town, Clitheroe, Lancashire, BB7 3LQ
(01200) 443592
07952 639465
richardbakerbb@btconnect.com
bowlandbrewery.com
Shop Mon-Sun 10.30am-5pm
Tours by arrangement

Bowland started brewing in 2003 and has steadily expanded capacity to 50 barrels per week, supplying more than 100 outlets in the north west. Five litre mini-casks are sold through the on-site shop and visitor centre. A new range of quirky bottled beers was launched in 2008. At least one new cask ale is brewed each month. Seasonal beers include: Patriot, Sorceress, Headless Peg and Sleigh Belle.

Hunters Moon (OG 1039, ABV 3.7%)
A dark mild with chocolate and coffee flavours.

Sawley Tempted (OG 1038, ABV 3.7%)
A copper-coloured fruity session bitter with toffee in the mouth and a spicy finish.

Bowland Gold (OG 1039, ABV 3.8%)
A hoppy golden bitter with intense grapefruit flavours.

Chipping Steamer (OG 1040, ABV 3.9%)
A mid-gold bitter with hints of orange and a slightly floral finish.

Hen Harrier (OG 1040, ABV 4%)
A pale gold bitter with soft citrus, peach and apricot flavours throughout.

Oak (OG 1041, ABV 4%)
A light chestnut coloured bitter with generous maltiness balanced by lime-marmalade hop flavours.

Dragon (OG 1043, ABV 4.2%)
A golden bitter with rounded fruit in the mouth and a refreshing finish.

Black Dragon Porter (OG 1046, ABV 4.5%)
A deep, dark porter with chocolate and dark fruit flavours.

Bowman

Bowman Ales Ltd, Wallops Wood, Sheardley Lane, Droxford, Hampshire, SO32 3QY
(01489) 878110
info@bowman-ales.com
bowman-ales.com
Tours by arrangement

Brewing started in 2006 on a 20-barrel brew plant in converted farm buildings. The brewery supplies more than 75 outlets. Future plans include bottling and a range of unusual celebratory and occasional brews. Seasonal beer: Nutz (ABV 5%, winter).

Elderado (OG 1035, ABV 3.5%)
Yellow-coloured beer containing elderflower. A citrus aroma with a fruity, bitter taste and good hoppiness. A dry, bitter finish.

Swift One (OG 1038, ABV 3.8%)
A glorious golden ale characterised by strong hoppiness throughout. Aroma of grapefruit leads to a pleasing bitterness and a long dry finish.

Wallops Wood (OG 1040, ABV 4%)
Well-balanced bitter, with no particular flavour dominating this well crafted beer. Malt flavours throughout are balanced by toffee notes in the flavour and a slightly dry finish.

Quiver Bitter (OG 1045, ABV 4.5%)
A drinkable golden best bitter, with a strong hoppy aroma, leading through a bittersweet taste to a refreshing hoppy finish.

Box Steam

Box Steam Brewery, Oaks Farm, Rode Hill, Colerne, Wiltshire, SN14 8AR
☎ (01225) 858383
info@boxsteambrewery.com
boxsteambrewery.com
Tours by arrangement

The brewery was founded in 2004 and boasts a Fulton steam-fired copper, hence the name. Under present ownership since 2006, the brewery has undergone a series of expansion work to increase production capacity. Two pubs are owned and more than 100 outlets are supplied. Seasonal beer: Figgy Pudding (ABV 5%, Xmas).

Reverend Awdry's Ale (OG 1037.5, ABV 3.8%)
A light, straw-coloured bitter with a hoppy aftertaste.

Box Best Bitter (OG 1040, ABV 4%)
A traditional best bitter with a light, fragrant nose and hoppy character.

Tunnel Vision (OG 1040.5, ABV 4.2%)
A well-rounded traditional bitter. Clean-tasting with a slight bitterness on the palate.

Blindhouse (OG 1044.5, ABV 4.6%)
A dark, hoppy, full-bodied beer with hints of red wine and cinnamon.

Dark & Handsome (OG 1047.5, ABV 5%)
Brewed in the style of a traditional old ale, this is a smooth, creamy beer with hints of lemon and subtle blackcurrant and liquorice undertones with a sweet start and finish.

Piston Broke (OG 1047.5, ABV 5%)
A subtle, single-hopped, golden-coloured beer with a hoppy aroma and a dry finish.

Bradfield

Bradfield Brewery, Watt House Farm, High Bradfield, Sheffield, South Yorkshire, S6 6LG
☎ (0114) 285 1118
info@bradfieldbrewery.com
bradfieldbrewery.co.uk
Shop Mon-Sat 10am-4pm

Bradfield Brewery is a family-run business, based on a working farm in the Peak District. Only the finest ingredients are used, along with pure Milstone Grit spring water from a borehole. More than 200 outlets are supplied. In January 2009 the brewery bought its first brewery tap – the Nags Head, Loxley. Seasonal beer: Farmers Irish Dexter (ABV 4.8%), Bradfield Ye Olde English Ale (ABV 4.6%), Farmers Wim-Bull-Don (ABV 4.5%), Farmers Jack O'Lantern (ABV 4.5%), Farmers Belgian Blue (ABV 4.9%, Xmas). Bottle-conditioned beers are also available along with five-litre mini kegs.

Farmers Bitter (OG 1039, ABV 3.9%)
A traditional copper-coloured malt ale with a floral aroma.

Farmers Blonde (OG 1041, ABV 4%)
Pale, blonde beer with citrus and summer fruits aromas.

Farmers Brown Cow (OG 1042.5, ABV 4.2%)
Deep chestnut-coloured ale with a smooth, creamy head. A citrus taste gives way to a long, dry finish.

Farmers Stout (OG 1045, ABV 4.5%)
A dark stout with roasted malts and flaked oats and a subtle, bitter hop character.

Farmers Pale Ale (OG 1049, ABV 5%)
A full-bodied pale ale with a powerful floral bouquet leaving a predominantly dry aftertaste.

Farmers Sixer (OG 1056, ABV 6%)
A strong, lager-type ale with a fruity, pleasant finish.

Brains IFBB

S A Brain & Co Ltd, Cardiff Brewery, PO Box 53, Crawshay Street, Cardiff, CF10 1SP
☎ (029) 2040 2060
brains@sabrain.com
sabrain.com

Brains began trading at the Old Brewery in Cardiff in 1882 when Samuel Arthur Brain and his uncle Joseph Benjamin Brain purchased a site founded in 1713. The company has remained in family ownership ever since. The full range of Brains ales is now produced at the company's Cardiff Brewery (formerly Hancock's), bought from Bass in 1999. The company owns more than 270 pubs, spread throughout Wales, the West Country and the Midlands. Brains is the official sponsor of the Wales Rugby Union Team, the Football Association of Wales and Glamorgan County Cricket Club. Seasonal beers: see website.

Dark (OG 1035.5, ABV 3.5%)
A tasty, classic dark brown mild, a mix of malt, roast, caramel with a background of hops. Bittersweet, mellow and with a lasting finish of malt and roast.

Bitter (OG 1036, ABV 3.7%)
Amber coloured with a gentle aroma of malt and hops. Malt, hops and bitterness combine in an easy-drinking beer with a bitter finish.

SA (OG 1042, ABV 4.2%)
A mellow, full-bodied beer. Gentle malt and hop aroma leads to a malty, hop and fruit mix with a balancing bitterness.

Rev James (OG 1045.5, ABV 4.5%)
A faint malt and fruit aroma with malt and fruit flavours in the taste, initially bittersweet. Bitterness balances the flavour and makes this an easy-drinking beer.

SA Gold (OG 1047, ABV 4.7%)
A golden beer with a hoppy aroma. Well balanced with a zesty hop, malt, fruit and balancing bitterness; a similar satisfying finish.

Brakspear

See Marston's in New Nationals section

Brampton

Brampton Brewery Ltd, Unit 5, Chatsworth Business Park, Chatsworth Road, Chesterfield, S40 2AR
☎ (01246) 221680
info@bramptonbrewery.co.uk
bramptonbrewery.co.uk
Shop via website
Tours by arrangement

THE BREWERIES

The old Brampton Brewery existed in the town for more than 100 years before being taken over in 1955. After a lapse of 52 years the Brampton name was re-registered for a new brewery a stone's throw away from the original. The first commercial brew took place in 2007 on the eight-barrel plant. Around 30 outlets are supplied. Seasonal beer: Jerusalem (ABV 4.6%, St George's Day), Golden Bud Speciale (ABV 5.8%). Bottle-conditioned beers are also available.

Aspire (OG 1038, ABV 3.7%)

Golden Bud (OG 1037, ABV 3.8%)
Light, balanced session beer with hop and fruit flavours. Becomes increasingly bitter towards to finish.

Best (OG 1041, ABV 4.2%)
Classic malty and fruity best bitter. Bittersweet taste leads to a lingering bitter fruit finish.

Impy Dark (OG 1047, ABV 4.3%)

Mild (OG 1054, ABV 4.9%)

Wasp Nest (OG 1049, ABV 5%)
Strong and complex tawny-coloured brew with bags of flavour and a smooth mouthfeel. Balanced malt and fruit flavours make this a deceptively drinkable beer.

Brancaster EAB

Brancaster Brewery, Jolly Sailors, Main Road, Brancaster Staithe, Norfolk, PE31 8BJ
☎ (01485) 210314
info@brancasterbrewery.co.uk
brancasterbrewery.co.uk

Brancaster opened in 2003 with a five-barrel plant squeezed into a converted ocean-going steel container adjacent to its own pub/restaurant. The brewery closed in 2008 but has been resurrected by the current licensee, James Nye. Both beers are also available bottle conditioned.

Best (ABV 3.8%)

Oystercatcher (ABV 4.2%)

Brandon

Brandon Brewery, 76 High Street, Brandon, Suffolk, IP27 0AU
☎ (01842) 878496
☎ 07876 234689
enquiries@brandonbrewery.co.uk
brandonbrewery.co.uk
Shop Mon-Sat 9am-5pm (please ring before visiting)
Tours by arrangement

Brandon started brewing in 2005 in the old dairy of a 15th-century cottage. Visitors are welcome and encouraged to sample from the beer shop. 60 outlets are supplied. The entire range of beers is also available bottle conditioned.

Breckland Gold (OG 1037, ABV 3.8%)
A combination of Goldings and Fuggles hops give a delicate, smooth, slightly spicy taste and a dry, lingering, malty finish.

Bitter (OG 1040, ABV 4%)
A full-bodied but balanced bitterness with pleasant floral and spicy notes and a gentle, hoppy, dry aftertaste.

Saxon Gold (ABV 4%)
A pale, golden beer with a subtle aroma of hops. The taste is a clean, crisp mix of spice and bitter fruits with a dry, hoppy finish.

Molly's Secret (ABV 4.1%)
A pale ale based on an old recipe.

Norfolk Poacher (ABV 4.1%)
A reddish amber beer. Full-bodied and malty with a hoppy, fruit flavour.

Royal Ginger (ABV 4.1%)
A refreshing summer ale with a distinctive mix of malt and hoppy spice, balanced with a gentle ginger flavour and finish.

Gun Flint (OG 1041, ABV 4.2%)
Roasted malts are used to produce a malty, chocolate flavour. This combines well with spicy, citrus hops to give a dry, bittersweet, roasted malt finish.

Wee Drop of Mischief (ABV 4.2%)
An amber-coloured premium bitter. Gentle malt flavours give way to a delightful hop character and a dry, increasingly bitter aftertaste.

Rusty Bucket (OG 1043, ABV 4.4%)
Based on a traditional best bitter brew, this beer is smooth on the palate with a soft and fruity flavour.

Slippery Jack (OG 1044, ABV 4.5%)
A dark brown stout. Complex but well-balanced flavours of roasted grain and hop bitterness. Dry with a lingering, pleasantly bitter finish.

Nappertandy (OG 1047, ABV 4.8%)
A reddish amber beer, full-bodied with a malty aroma. Crisp and spicy with an underlying citrus flavour and a dry, malty, bitter fruit finish.

Grumpy Bastard (OG 1048, ABV 5%)

Brandy Cask SIBA

Brandy Cask Pub & Brewery, 25 Bridge Street, Pershore, Worcestershire, WR10 1AJ
☎ (01386) 552602
Tours by arrangement

Brewing started in 1995 in a refurbished bottle store in the garden of the pub. Brewery and pub now operate under one umbrella, with brewing carried out by the owner/landlord.

Whistling Joe (ABV 3.6%)
A sweet, fruity, copper-coloured beer that has plenty of contrast in the aroma. A malty balance lingers but the aftertaste is not dry.

Brandy Snapper (ABV 4%)
Golden brew with low alpha hops. Plenty of fruit and hop aroma leads to a rich taste in the mouth and a lingering aftertaste.

Ale Mary (ABV 4.8%)
A rich malt and fruit aroma leads to an equally complex taste with no one flavour dominating. A dry finish.

John Baker's Original (ABV 4.8%)
A superb blend of flavours with roasted malt to the fore. The rich hoppy aroma is complemented by a complex aftertaste.

Branscombe Vale SIBA

Branscombe Vale Brewery Ltd, Branscombe, Devon, EX12 3DP
☎ (01297) 680511
branscombebrewery@yahoo.co.uk

The brewery was set up in 1992 by former dairy workers Paul Dimond and Graham Luxton in cowsheds owned by the National Trust. Paul and Graham converted the sheds and dug their own well. The NT built an extension for the brewery to ensure future growth. In 2008 a new 25-barrel plant was added to the brewhouse. Around 80 outlets are supplied. Seasonal beers: Anniversary Ale (ABV 4.6%, Feb-Mar), Hells Belles (ABV 4.8%), Yo Ho Ho (ABV 6%, Xmas). Bottle-conditioned beer is also available.

Branoc (OG 1038, ABV 3.8%)
Pale brown brew with a malt and fruit aroma and a hint of caramel. Malt and bitter taste with a dry, hoppy finish.

Draymans Best Bitter (OG 1042, ABV 4.2%)
A mid-brown beer with hop and caramel notes and a lingering finish.

BVB Best Bitter (OG 1045, ABV 4.6%)
Reddy/brown-coloured beer with a fruity aroma and taste, and bitter/astringent finish.

Summa That (OG 1049, ABV 5%)
Light golden beer with a clean and refreshing taste and a long hoppy finish.

Brass Monkey (NEW)

Brass Monkey Brewery Co Ltd, Unit 25, Asquith Bottom Mill, Sowerby Bridge, West Yorkshire, HX6 3BS
☎ (01422) 316040
sales@thebrassmonkeybrewery.co.uk
thebrassmonkeybrewery.co.uk
Tours by arrangement

Brass Monkey was established in 2008 on a seven-barrel brew plant and is distributed nationwide through a sister company. Around 70 outlets are supplied. Seasonal beer: Capuchin (ABV 4.4%, winter).

Bitter (ABV 3.8%)

Golden Monkey (ABV 4.1%)

Mandrill (ABV 4.2%)

Silverback (ABV 5%)

Braydon (NEW)

Braydon Ales Ltd, Preston West Farm, Preston, Chippenham, Wiltshire, SN15 4DX
☎ (01249) 892900
info@braydonales.co.uk
braydonales.co.uk

Braydon began brewing in 2009 on a five-barrel plant. Further beers are planned.

Yertiz (ABV 4.1%)

Breconshire SIBA

Breconshire Brewery Ltd, Ffrwdgrech Industrial Estate, Brecon, Powys, LD3 8LA
☎ (01874) 623731
sales@breconshirebrewery.com
breconshirebrewery.com
Shop Mon-Fri 8.30am-4.30pm
Tours by arrangement

Breconshire Brewery was founded by Howard Marlow in 2002 as part of C H Marlow, a wholesaler and distributor of ales, beers, wines and spirits in the south Wales area for more than 30 years. The 10-barrel plant uses British Optic malts blended with a range of British whole hops. The beers are distributed throughout mid, south and west Wales and the west of England. Seasonal beers include: Winter Beacon (ABV 5.3%, Nov-Feb). Bottle-conditioned beers are also available. Beers are bottled on site.

Brecon County Ale (OG 1037, ABV 3.7%)
A traditional amber-coloured bitter. A clean hoppy flavour, background malt and fruit, with a good thirst-quenching bitterness.

Welsh Pale Ale (OG 1037, ABV 3.7%)
Pale golden, mildy hopped session ale. Brewed to an old Welsh style of pale ale.

Golden Valley (OG 1042, ABV 4.2%)
Golden in colour with a welcoming aroma of hops, malt and fruit. A balanced mix of these flavours and moderate, building bitterness lead to a satisfying, rounded finish.

Cribyn (OG 1045, ABV 4.5%)
A pale, straw-coloured aromatic best bitter. Brewed with Northdown, Challenger and Bramling Cross hops.

Red Dragon (OG 1047, ABV 4.7%)
A red-hued premium ale brewed with a complex grist of Optic and wheat malts and a blend of hedgerow hops.

Ramblers Ruin (OG 1050, ABV 5%)
Dark amber, full-bodied with rich biscuity malt and fruit flavours; background hops and bitterness round off the beer.

Brentwood SIBA

Brentwood Brewing Co Ltd, Frieze Hall Farm, Coxtie Green Road, South Weald, Essex, CM14 5RE
☎ (01277) 375577
brentwoodbrewing@aol.com
brentwoodbrewing.co.uk
Tours by arrangement

Since its launch in 2006 Brentwood has steadily increased its capacity and distribution. A major expansion and relocation in 2007/08 means an 18-barrel plant is now being used. It supplies more than 50 local outlets as well as beer festivals and selected tied houses through its own distribution and the SIBA Direct Distribution Scheme. Bottle-conditioned beers should be available in the near future. Seasonal/occasional beers: see website.

Roy Rogers (OG 1040, ABV 3.8%)

Spooky Moon (OG 1040, ABV 3.8%)
Well-balanced session bitter. The sweet marmalade aroma hints at the citrus bitterness to be found in the finish.

Best (OG 1042, ABV 4.2%)

Heavenly Body (OG 1043, ABV 4.3%)

Hope & Glory (OG 1046, ABV 4.5%)

Lumberjack (OG 1052, ABV 5.2%)

Brew Company (NEW)

Brew Company Ltd, G4, 19-21 Carlisle Street East, Sheffield, South Yorkshire, S4 7QN
☎ (0114) 270 9991
thebrewcompany@gmail.com
thebrewcompany.co.uk

Tours by arrangement

Brewer Pete Roberts set up this eight-barrel plant in part of a former factory in Sheffield's industrial east end in 2008. Seasonal beers include St Petrus Stout (ABV 5%), Bock (ABV 5%) and Spring Bock (ABV 3.8%). A monthly special is also brewed exclusively for the nearby Harlequin pub.

Slaker Pale Ale (ABV 3.8%)
Pale, crisp and fruity.

Elixir (ABV 4%)
Amber-coloured traditional English bitter with a dry roasted flavour.

Abyss (ABV 4.2%)
A best bitter, dark walnut in colour and full of malty bitter flavours.

Eclipse (ABV 4.7%)
A traditional, heavy-bodied, dark, malty porter with a thick mouthfeel, a dry palate and a delicate toasted coffee grain finish.

Frontier IPA (ABV 4.7%)
Straw-coloured, crisp and dry with a bitter aftertaste.

BrewDog

BrewDog Ltd, Unit 1, Kessock Workshops, Kessock Road, Fraserburgh, AB43 8UE
☎ (01346) 519009
✉ info@brewdog.com
🌐 brewdog.com
Tours by arrangement

BrewDog was established in 2007 by James Watt and Martin Dickie. Most of the production goes into bottles but a limited amount of cask ale is available.

Physics (OG 1050, ABV 5.2%)

Hop Rocker (ABV 5.5%)

Punk IPA (OG 1058, ABV 6.2%)

Rip Tide (OG 1075, ABV 8%)

Paradox (OG 1075, ABV 10%)
Matured in whisky barrels.

Brewster's SIBA

Brewster's Brewing Co Ltd, Burnside, Turnpike Close, Grantham, Lincolnshire, NG31 7XU
☎ (01476) 566000
✉ sara@brewsters.co.uk
🌐 brewsters.co.uk
Tours by arrangement

Brewster is the old English term for a female brewer and Sara Barton is a modern example. Brewster's Brewery was set up in the heart of the Vale of Belvoir in 1998 and moved in 2006 to its current premises. Beer is supplied to some 250 outlets throughout central England and further afield via wholesalers. Seasonal beers: see website.

Hophead (OG 1036, ABV 3.6%)
This amber beer has a floral/hoppy character; hops predominate throughout before finally yielding to grapefruit in a slightly astringent finish.

Marquis (OG 1038, ABV 3.8%)
A well-balanced and refreshing session bitter with maltiness and a dry, hoppy finish.

Daffys Elixir (OG 1042, ABV 4.2%)
A pale golden best bitter, well-balanced with a big hop finish.

Hop A Doodle Doo (OG 1043, ABV 4.3%)
A copper-coloured ale with a rich, full-bodied feel and fruity hop character.

Decadence (ABV 4.4%)
Well-balanced, full-flavoured golden ale with pronounced hop notes.

Rutterkin (OG 1046, ABV 4.6%)
A premium bitter with a golden appearance. A zesty hop flavour from American Mount Hood hops combines with a touch of malt sweetness to give a rich, full-bodied beer.

Wicked Women Range (OG 1048, ABV 4.8%)
(Varies seasonally)

Porter (ABV 5%)
Rich and roasty.

Belly Dancer (OG 1050, ABV 5.2%)
Well-balanced, ruby-red ale with a full-bodied taste from crystal and roast malts, with a subtle hop finish from Bramling Cross and Fuggles.

Brew Wharf

Brew Wharf Co Ltd, Brew Wharf Yard, Stoney Street, London, SE1 9AD
☎ (020) 7378 6601
✉ brewer-brewwharf@vinopolis.co.uk
🌐 brewwharf.com

Brew Wharf opened in 2005 and has a bar plus a restaurant where dishes are matched with beer. Wharf Best is the permanent cask ale with a changing special beer brewed each month.

Wharf Best (OG 1041, ABV 4.2%)

Bridestones

Bridestones Brewery, The Brewery, Smithy Farm, Blackshaw Head, Hebden Bridge, West Yorkshire, HX7 7JB
☎ (01422) 847104
☎ 07921 211870
✉ dan@newdelight.freeserve.co.uk

Bridestones started brewing in 2006 and supplies around 20 outlets. There are plans to bottle beer in the near future. Seasonal beer: Pennine Stout (ABV 4.8%, Sep-Mar) plus monthly specials.

Pennine Best (OG 1041, ABV 4%)

Pennine Gold (OG 1043, ABV 4.3%)

Pennine Bier (OG 1045, ABV 4.4%)

Pennine Pale Ale (OG 1048, ABV 5%)

Bridge of Allan SIBA

Bridge of Allan Brewery, The Brewhouse, Queens Lane, Bridge of Allan, Stirlingshire, FK9 4NY
☎ (01786) 834555
✉ brewery@bridgeofallan.co.uk
Shop 12-5pm daily

Beer is now brewed by Traditional Scottish Ales at Stirling (qv). Bridge of Allan beer, however, is still available from the Brewhouse. The Brewhouse also showcases a range of Scottish bottled beers, which includes both bottle-conditioned and organic beers.

Bridgetown

Bridgetown Brewery, Albert Inn, Bridgetown Close, Totnes, Devon, TQ9 5AD
☎ (01803) 863214

Bridgetown started brewing in 2008 on a 2.5-barrel plant. Seasonal beers are available.

AA (The Real Emergency Service) (ABV 3.8%)

Realaleativity (ABV 4.8%)

Bridgnorth

Bridgnorth Brewing Co Ltd, The Old Brewhouse, Kings Head Courtyard, Whitburn Street, Bridgnorth, Shropshire, WV16 4QN
☎ (01746) 762889
info@bridgnorthbrewing.com
bridgnorthbrewing.com
Tours by arrangement

Brewing started in 2007 with the original four-barrel plant expanding to 16 barrels by 2008. The King's Head Stable Bar opened next door as the brewery tap, serving real ale and fine wines. It supplies to over 30 outlets all over Shropshire and through SIBA. Brewing is temporarily suspended. Beers are currently brewed by Holdens under licence.

Brimstage

Brimstage Brewing Co Ltd, Home Farm, Brimstage, Wirral, CH63 6HY
☎ (0151) 342 1181
☎ 07870 968323
info@brimstagebrewery.com
brimstagebrewery.com
Tours by arrangement (max of 20 people)

Brewing started in 2006 on a 10-barrel plant in a redundant farm dairy in the heart of the Wirral countryside. This is Wirral's first brewery since the closure of the Birkenhead Brewery in the late 1960s. Around 60 outlets are supplied. Seasonal beers: Sandpiper Light Ale (ABV 3.4%, spring/summer), Frosty Ferret Winter Warmer (ABV 5%, winter).

Trappers Hat Bitter (ABV 3.8%)
Gold-coloured with a complex bouquet. It provides a mouthful of fruit zest, with hints of orange and grapefruit. A refreshingly hoppy session brew.

Rhode Island Red Bitter (ABV 4%)
Red, smooth and well-balanced malty beer with a good dry aftertaste. Some fruitiness in the taste.

Scarecrow Bitter (ABV 4.2%)
Orange marmalade in colour, this well-balanced session brew has a distinct citrus fruit bouquet.

Oyster Catcher Stout (ABV 4.4%)
A smooth easy drinking stout with rich chocolate aromas leading to a mellow roasted coffee flavour and lingering bitter finish.

Briscoe's

Briscoe's Brewery, 16 Ash Grove, Otley, West Yorkshire, LS21 3EL
☎ (01943) 466515
briscoe.brewery@virgin.net

The brewery was launched in 1998 by microbiologist/chemist Dr Paul Briscoe in the cellar of his house with a one-barrel brew length. Following a spell brewing on a larger scale at the back of a local pub, Dr Briscoe is currently producing two occasional brews on his original plant.

Chevin Chaser (OG 1043, ABV 4.3%)
A refreshing, pale-coloured, all-malt bitter with a distinct hop finish.

Three Peaks Ale (OG 1045, ABV 4.5%)
A strong, pale premium bitter brewed with only pale malt and traditional hops.

Bristol Beer Factory

Bristol Brewing Co Ltd, t/a Bristol Beer Factory, Unit A The Old Brewery, Durnford Street, Ashton, Bristol, BS3 2AW
☎ (0117) 902 6317
enquiries@bristolbeerfactory.co.uk
bristolbeerfactory.co.uk
Tours by arrangement

The Beer Factory is a 10-barrel micro-brewery in a part of the former Ashton Gate Brewing Co, which closed in 1933. 50 outlets are supplied.

Red (OG 1038, ABV 3.8%)
Dark ale with slight roast barley taste, fruity aroma and ruby red tint.

No. 7 (OG 1042, ABV 4.2%)
Mid-brown, old-fashioned style, malty best bitter. Good body and mouthfeel, some apple-type fruit flavours, with a drying bitter and astringent finish.

Sunrise (OG 1044.5, ABV 4.4%)
Light, gold-coloured best bitter, with a strong hoppy finish.

Milk Stout (OG 1059, ABV 4.5%)
Dark creamy stout, reviving an old Bristol tradition. Black colour with a creamy mouthfeel.

Exhibition (OG 1051, ABV 5.2%)
A classic, strong, dark ale. Crystal and chocolate malts give a full rich, estery flavour.

Brodie's SIBA (NEW)

Brodie's Brewery, 816a High Road, Leyton, London, E10 6AE
☎ 07828 498733
james@brodiesbeers.com
brodiesbeers.com
Tours by arrangement

Siblings James and Lizzie began commercial brewing in 2008 on a five-barrel plant at the back of the William IV pub in East London. Beers are available at the William IV and their small chain of family-owned pubs as well as other local outlets. All cask ales are available bottle conditioned. Seasonal ales and festival specials are also brewed regularly – see website for more information.

Mild (OG 1038, ABV 3.6%)
A well balanced sweetish dark mild with some roast notes including a little burnt bitterness on the aftertaste. Caramelised fruit on nose and palate.

English Best (OG 1040, ABV 3.9%)

IPA (OG 1040, ABV 4%)
A light drinking beer with a citrus flavour and finish that is balanced by a little dry bitterness. Aroma has traces of fruit and malt.

Sunshine (OG 1040, ABV 4%)

THE BREWERIES

Red (OG 1042, ABV 4.3%)

Brothers

See Freedom

Broughs (NEW)

Broughs Brewing, c/o Olde Swan Brewery, 89 Halesowen Road, Netherton, West Midlands, DY2 9PY

Broughs is currently using spare capacity at the Olde Swan Brewery in Netherton. Head Brewer is Andy Brough, former brewer at Sarah Hughes in Sedgley.

Pale Ale (OG 1048, ABV 4.8%)

Broughton SIBA

Broughton Ales Ltd, Broughton, Biggar, Peebles-shire, ML12 6HQ
☎ (01899) 830345
✉ beer@broughtonales.co.uk
🌐 broughtonales.co.uk
Shop Mon-Fri 8am-5pm
Tours by arrangement

Founded in 1979 in Scottish Border country, Broughton Ales has been brewing cask beers for more than 25 years but more than 60% of production goes into bottle for sale in Britain and export markets. Seasonal beers: Summer Ale (ABV 3.5%), Champion Double Ale (ABV 5%), Winter Fire (ABV 4.2%), Scottish Oatmeal Stout (ABV 4.2%), The Ghillie (ABV 4.5%), Dr Johnson's Definitive (ABV 5%). All bottled beers are suitable for vegetarians and vegans.

Coulsons EPA (OG 1034, ABV 3.5%)
A light, yellow-coloured ale with a mellow lingering flavour and tangy aftertaste.

The Reiver (OG 1038, ABV 3.8%)
A light-coloured session ale with a predominantly hoppy flavour and aroma on a background of fruity malt. The aftertaste is crisp and clean.

Bramling Cross (OG 1041, ABV 4.2%)
A golden ale with a blend of malt and hop flavours followed by a hoppy aftertaste.

Clipper IPA (OG 1042, ABV 4.2%)
A light-coloured, crisp, hoppy beer with a clean aftertaste.

Merlin's Ale (OG 1042, ABV 4.2%)
A well-hopped, fruity flavour is balanced by malt in the taste. The finish is bittersweet, light but dry.

Exciseman's 80/- (OG 1045, ABV 4.6%)
A traditional 80/- cask ale. A dark, malty brew. Full drinking with a good hop aftertaste.

Old Jock (OG 1070, ABV 6.7%)
Strong, sweetish and fruity in the finish.

Brown Cow

Brown Cow Brewery, Brown Cow Road, Barlow, Selby, North Yorkshire, YO8 8EH
☎ (01757) 618947
✉ susansimpson@browncowbrewery.co.uk
🌐 browncowbrewery.co.uk

Established in 1997 by Susan Simpson and joined by husband Keith in 2004, the brewery has steadily expanded, the five-barrel plant now brewing at its capacity of 15 barrels per week. In addition to the six regular beers, an innovative range of seasonal, occasional and one-off brews is crafted. Beers are supplied throughout Yorkshire and to outlets in southern counties.

Bitter (OG 1038, ABV 3.8%)
A well-hopped, traditional session bitter.

Suddaby's Double Chance (OG 1038, ABV 3.8%)
A hoppy session bitter.

White Dragon (OG 1039, ABV 4%)
A pale, aromatic best bitter.

Captain Oates Dark Oat Mild (OG 1044, ABV 4.5%)
A satisfying dark beer with fruit and mild hop flavours throughout.

IPA (OG 1047, ABV 5%)
A full-bodied, classic IPA, packed with hop and malt flavour.

Suddaby's After Dark Coffee Porter (OG 1052, ABV 5%)
A full-flavoured porter with a complex mix of malts and a hint of coffee.

Brunswick SIBA

Brunswick Brewery Ltd, 1 Railway Terrace, Derby, Derbyshire, DE1 2RU
☎ (01332) 290677
🌐 brunswickinn.co.uk
Tours by arrangement

The Brunswick is a purpose-built tower brewery that started brewing in 1991. A viewing area allows pub users to watch production. Bought by Everards in 2002, it is now a tenancy supplying beers to local outlets and the Everard's estate. Seasonal beer: Rambo (ABV 8%, winter).

White Feather (OG 1038, ABV 3.6%)
Very pale citrus/floral session beer. Full-bodied with a grassy finish.

Midnight Express (OG 1040, ABV 3.9%)
A classic dark mild, lightly-hopped, slightly sweet and full of roast chocolate notes.

Triple Hop (OG 1038, ABV 4%)
A pale gold colour and citrus hop bouquet promise sweetness but the hops deliver a firm, dry, lasting bitterness.

Second Brew (OG 1042, ABV 4.2%)
This tawny best bitter, also known as The Usual, presents an aroma of sulphur and hops that continue throughout, accompanied by a striking bitterness and astringency.

Porter (OG 1045, ABV 4.3%)
Typical English porter – dark black chocolate and caramel with deep bitter undertones.

Station Approach (OG 1048, ABV 4.7%)
Straw-coloured bitter with lingering hints of citrus, with a hoppy aftertaste.

Old Accidental (OG 1050, ABV 5%)
A well-balanced, malty beer leading to a bitter finish with warming aftertaste. A light, vinous floral hop has underlying malt notes.

Father Mike's Dark Rich Ruby (OG 1055, ABV 5.8%)
A smooth, near black mild with a hint of red. Well-balanced and filled with sweet roast flavours that conceal its strength.

Black Sabbath (OG 1058, ABV 6%)

A genuine mild with a voluptuous feast of coffee, chocolate and caramel flavours. High alcohol balanced with fine body.

Bryncelyn

Bryncelyn Brewery, Unit 303, Ystradgynlais Workshops, Trawsffordd Road, Ystradgynlais, SA9 1BS
☎ (01639) 841900
✉ bryncelynbrewery@hotmail.co.uk
🌐 bryncelynbrewery.org.uk

A one-quarter barrel brewery was opened in 1999 by William Hopton (owner) and Robert Scott (brewer) and capacity was increased to a three-quarter barrel plant in the same year. The brewery relocated to its present premises in 2008 with a six-barrel plant acquired from the old Webb's Brewery of Ebbw Vale. As the beer names imply, the owner is fond of Buddy Holly: Feb 59 (seasonal) commemorates the singer's death. Seasonal beers: see website.

Everyday Ale (OG 1038, ABV 3.8%)

Holly Hop (ABV 3.9%)
Pale amber with a hoppy aroma. A refreshing hoppy, fruity flavour with balancing bitterness; a similar lasting finish. A beer full of flavour for its gravity.

Buddy Marvellous (OG 1040, ABV 4%)
Dark brown with an inviting aroma of malt, roast and fruit. A gentle bitterness mixes roast with malt, hops and fruit, giving a complex, satisfying and lasting finish.

Buddy's Delight (OG 1042, ABV 4.2%)

Cwrw Celyn (OG 1044, ABV 4.4%)

CHH (OG 1045, ABV 4.5%)
A pale brown beer with hints of red malt and an inviting hop aroma, with fruit and bitterness adding to the flavour. The finish is clean and hoppy-bitter.

Oh Boy (OG 1045, ABV 4.5%)
An inviting aroma of hops, fruit and malt, and a golden colour. The tasty mix of hops, fruit, bitterness and background malt ends with a long, hoppy, bitter aftertaste. Full-bodied and drinkable.

Buddy Confusing (OG 1050, ABV 5%)

Rave On (OG 1050, ABV 5%)

Brysons

Brysons Brewery, Newgate Brewery, White Lund Industrial Estate, Morecambe, Lancashire, LA3 3PT
☎ (01524) 39481
✉ petermcross@msn.co.uk
🌐 brysonsbrewery.co.uk

Established in 2000 by George Palmer, the four-barrel plant is due to be expanded in the near future. Around 60 outlets are supplied.

Westmorland Bitter (OG 1036, ABV 3.6%)

Lifesaver Bitter (OG 1039, ABV 3.8%)
A golden bitter brewed for charity (RNLI).

Union Flag (OG 1040, ABV 3.9%)
A full-bodied, fruity blonde ale.

Hurricane Bitter (OG 1040.5, ABV 4.1%)
A pale, hoppy bitter.

John McGuinness Bitter (OG 1042, ABV 4.2%)
A classic North West bitter.

Patrick's Porter (OG 1050.5, ABV 5%)
A rich, complex porter.

Buckle Street (NEW)

Buckle Street Brewery Ltd, Unit 11, 2 Shires Industrial Estate, Buckle Street, Honeybourne, Evesham, Worcestershire, WR11 7QE
☎ (01386) 831173 (Fleece Inn)
✉ info@bucklestreetbrewery.co.uk
🌐 bucklestreetbrewery.co.uk
Tours by arrangement

Buckle Street was set up in 2008 by Andy Davies and Nigel Smith (Fleece Inn, Bretforton). It is named after the adjacent Roman road. It currently only supplies the Fleece but there are plans for expansion. Bottle-conditioned beer is available.

No. 1 Bitter (OG 1034, ABV 3.8%)

Dog in the Fog (OG 1040, ABV 4.3%)

Pandora's Box (OG 1040, ABV 4.3%)

Buffy's SIBA EAB

Buffy's Brewery Ltd, Rectory Road, Tivetshall St Mary, Norfolk, NR15 2DD
☎ (01379) 676523
✉ buffysbrewery@gmail.com
🌐 buffys.co.uk

Buffy's was established in 1993. The brewing capacity is 45 barrels, but a move to bigger premises is in hand with plans for a bottling plant. The brewery owns two pubs, the Cherry Tree at Wicklewood and the White Hart at Foulden. Barley for all brewing is grown in Norfolk. Around 150 outlets are supplied. Seasonal beers: Sleigher (ABV 4.1%, Dec-Jan), Hollybeery (ABV 5.5% Dec-Jan). Bottle-conditioned beers are also available.

Norwich Terrier (OG 1036, ABV 3.6%)
A fragrant peachy aroma introduces this refreshing, gold-coloured bitter. Strong bitter notes dominate throughout as hops mingle with grapefruit to produce a long, increasingly dry finish.

Bitter (OG 1039, ABV 3.9%)
The strong malty aroma contrasts totally with the dry bitterness of the taste. A pale brown beer with an increasingly hoppy finish that grows and grows.

Mild (OG 1042, ABV 4.2%)
A complex brew, deep red with a smooth but grainy feel. Caramel and blackcurrant bolster the heavy malt influence that is the main characteristic of this understated, deceptively strong mild.

Polly's Folly (OG 1043, ABV 4.3%)
A mixture of hoppiness, citrus fruit and malt gives this well-balanced offering a lively, satisfying feel. Grapefruit creeps into the flavour towards the end as the overall character becomes biscuity dry.

Hopleaf (OG 1044.5, ABV 4.5%)
Pale brown beer with a gentle hop nose. Strawberries mingle with the hops and malt, remaining as the malt gently subsides to leave a bittersweet, dry finish.

Mucky Duck (OG 1044, ABV 4.5%)
Porter style beer. Slightly sweet but with a good bitter edge.

Norwegian Blue (OG 1049, ABV 4.9%)
A gentle hoppy nose belies the rich warming character of the taste explosion. A complex, ever-

changing mix of malt, hops, bitterness and fruit. A long, lingering, bittersweet ending.

Buffy's Ale (OG 1055, ABV 5.5%)

Roger's Ruin (OG 1063, ABV 6.2%)
A warming, full-bodied, satisfying beer with a spicy kick. Deep copper in colour.

Bull Box

Bull Box Brewery, c/o 3 Trafalgar Road, Downham Market, Norfolk, PE38 9JP
☎ 07920 163116
✉ bullboxinfo@msn.com

Bull Box Brewery was launched in 2006 and operates on a two-barrel plant based in Stradsett. Bottle-conditioned beers are available.

Bitter (ABV 4%)

Bagge's Bitter (ABV 4.5%)

Brewers Drop (ABV 4.5%)

Mid Life Crisis (ABV 4.5%)
Red-coloured with a rich coffee character. Hop notes with a background of roast and malt give some depth to a somewhat light, uncomplicated brew.

Kerb Crawler (ABV 5.2%)

Tangerine Dream (ABV 5.2%)

Moot Point (ABV 6.5%)

Bull Lane

Bull Lane Brewing Co, Clarendon Hotel, 143 High Street East, Sunderland, Tyne & Wear, SR1 2BL
☎ (0191) 510 3299
✉ bulllanebrewingco@hotmail.co.uk
bull-lane-brewing.co.uk
Tours by arrangement

Sunderland's first brew-pub started production in 2005 in the cellar of the Clarendon pub. The beers are supplied direct to pubs within a 30-mile radius of Sunderland and are regularly available in Sir John Fitzgerald's pubs.

Nowtsa Matta BB (OG 1037, ABV 3.7%)

Sun Inn Light (OG 1038, ABV 3.8%)

Ryhope Tug (OG 1039, ABV 3.9%)

Terry's All Gold (OG 1042, ABV 4.3%)

Mutt's Nutts (OG 1044, ABV 4.4%)

Jack's Flag (OG 1045, ABV 4.5%)

Jason's Jinja Ale (OG 1045, ABV 4.5%)

Nowtsa Matta XB (OG 1045, ABV 4.5%)

Sauce of the Niall (OG 1045, ABV 4.5%)

Double Barrel (OG 1052, ABV 5.5%)

For TJ Doyles, Sunderland:

Neck Oil (ABV 4.3%)

Bullmastiff SIBA

Bullmastiff Brewery, 14 Bessemer Close, Leckwith, Cardiff, CF11 8DL
☎ (029) 2066 5292

An award-winning small craft brewery run by brothers Bob and Paul Jenkins since 1987. The name stems from their love of the bullmastiff breed. They have no ambitions for expansion or owning any pubs, preferring to concentrate on quality control. 30 outlets are supplied. Seasonal beers: Summer Moult (ABV 4.3%), Mogadog (ABV 10%, winter).

Welsh Gold (OG 1039, ABV 3.8%)
A hoppy and fruity aroma leads into the same juicy blend of flavours. Bittersweet initially, an easy-drinking and refreshing beer.

Jack the Lad (OG 1041, ABV 4.1%)

Thoroughbred (OG 1046, ABV 4.5%)
A good hop aroma leads to a hoppy flavour with accompanying fruit, malt and balancing bitterness. There is a quenching hoppy bitterness in the finish.

Welsh Black (OG 1050, ABV 4.8%)

Welsh Red (OG 1048, ABV 4.8%)

Brindle (OG 1050, ABV 5.1%)
A full-bodied, flavoursome pale beer. Good hop aroma with a mix of malt, hops, fruit and bitterness in the taste. A lasting and satisfying finish.

Son of a Bitch (OG 1062, ABV 6%)
A complex, warming amber ale with a tasty blend of hops, malt and fruit flavours, with increasing bitterness.

Buntingford SIBA

Buntingford Brewery Co Ltd, Greys Brewhouse, Therfield Road, Royston, Hertfordshire, SG8 9NW
☎ (01763) 250749
☎ 07879 698541
✉ contact@buntingford-brewery.co.uk
buntingford-brewery.co.uk
Tours by arrangement

Production started in 2005 using a 15-barrel plant capable of producing up to 45 barrels a week. Beers are brewed with traditional floor malted barley from Warminster Maltings. The brewery is located on a conservation farm: all brewery waste liquids are treated in a reedbed and plans are in hand to make full use of green energy sources. Beers are sold mostly within a 35-mile radius. Occasional beers: Pargeters (ABV 3.7%), Britannia (ABV 4.4%), 92 Squadron (ABV 4.5%). Seasonal beer: Oatmeal Stout (ABV 4.4%, winter).

Highwayman IPA (ABV 3.6%)

Golden Plover (ABV 3.8%)
Golden session bitter with citrus flavours.

Polar Star (ABV 4.4%)
Pale blonde beer with a strong citrus character.

Burton Bridge SIBA

Burton Bridge Brewery Ltd, Bridge Street, Burton upon Trent, Staffordshire, DE14 1SY
☎ (01283) 510573
✉ bbb@burtonbridgebrewery.fsnet.co.uk
burtonbridgebrewery.co.uk
Shop at Bridge Inn 11.30am-2.15pm, 5-11pm
Tours by arrangement (Wed evenings)

A brewery established in 1982 by Bruce Wilkinson and Geoff Mumford. The brewery owns five pubs in the town, including its CAMRA award-winning brewery tap. More than 300 outlets are supplied direct. An ever-changing range of seasonal/monthly beers is available. Bottle-conditioned beers are also available.

Golden Delicious (OG 1037, ABV 3.8%)
A Burton classic with sulphurous aroma and well-balanced hops and fruit. A crisp start leads to a apple fruitiness then proceeds to a lingering, mouth-watering bitter finish with a hint of astringency. Light, crisp and refreshing.

Sovereign Gold (OG 1040, ABV 4%)

XL Bitter (OG 1039, ABV 4%)
Another Burton classic with sulphurous aroma. Golden with fruit and hops and characteristic lingering aftertaste.

Bridge Bitter (OG 1041, ABV 4.2%)
Pale brown and hoppy with a hint of roast and caramel. Complex taste with hops just dominating to provide a lingering hoppy finish.

Burton Porter (OG 1044, ABV 4.5%)
Quite malty throughout but with plenty of roast, fruit and liquorice, and a long bitter aftertaste.

Stairway to Heaven (OG 1049, ABV 5%)
Golden bitter. A perfectly balanced beer. The malty and hoppy start leads to a hoppy body with some astringency.

Top Dog Stout (OG 1049, ABV 5%)
Black and rich with a roast and malty start. Fruity and abundant hops give a fruity, bitter finish with a mouth-watering edge. Also available as Bramble Stout.

Festival Ale (OG 1054, ABV 5.5%)
Pale brown with a fruity aroma. Fruity start reminiscent of Xmas pudding ingredients; sweet fruity finish that develops to bitterness.

Thomas Sykes (OG 1095, ABV 10%)
Rich and warming, fruity, heady and hoppy. A true barley wine to be handled with caution.

Burton Old Cottage

Burton Old Cottage Beer Co Ltd, Unit 10, Eccleshall Business Park, Hawkins Lane, Burton upon Trent, Staffordshire, DE14 1PT
☎ 07909 931250
✉ jwsaville@tiscali.co.uk
oldcottagebeer.co.uk
Tours by arrangement

Old Cottage was originally installed in the old Heritage Brewery, once Everard's production plant in Burton. When the site was taken over, the brewery moved to a modern industrial unit. The brewery was sold in 2005 and 2006 saw heavy investment in new production and storage facilities by the new owners. Around 10 outlets are supplied. Seasonal beer: Snow Joke (ABV 5.2%, winter), Prancers Pride (ABV 4.7%, winter).

Pail Ale (OG 1040, ABV 3.8%)
A well-balanced, light-coloured ale with a full measure of maltiness and hop aroma.

Oak Ale (OG 1044, ABV 4%)
Tawny, full-bodied bitter. A sweet start gives way to a slight roast taste with some caramel. A dry, hoppy finish.

Chestnut (ABV 4.2%)
A dark session ale with a touch of bitterness and a pleasant, full aftertaste.

Cottage IPA (OG 1047, ABV 4.4%)
An intense, complex brew with elegant hop flavours.

Redwood (OG 1046, ABV 4.6%)
A unique flavour of fruit and hops with a slightly malty background and aftertaste.

Cloughy's Clout (OG 1047, ABV 4.7%)
A chestnut-coloured ale with light malty undertones and a touch of bitterness.

Stout (OG 1047, ABV 4.7%)
Dense black but not heavy. Sweet with lots of caramel, hints of liquorice and a roast and bitter finish.

Pastiche (OG 1050, ABV 5.2%)
A smooth, balanced ale with a complex taste and aroma.

Halcyon Daze (OG 1050, ABV 5.3%)
Tawny and creamy with touches of hop, fruit and malt aroma. Fruity taste and finish.

Burtonwood

Thomas Hardy Burtonwood Ltd, Bold Lane, Burtonwood, Warrington, Cheshire, WA5 4TH
☎ (01925) 220022
thomashardybrewery.co.uk

Following the sale of 60% of its brewing operation to Thomas Hardy in 1998, Burtonwood PLC sold the remaining 40% in 2004 to become solely a pub-owning group that was bought by Marston's (qv) in 2005. Burtonwood is now Thomas Hardy's only brewery, run by Peter Ward as a contract operation, principally for Scottish & Newcastle. It also brews Websters Green Label (ABV 3.2%) and Websters Yorkshire Bitter (ABV 3.5%), which are no longer owned by S&N. The beers have been sold to an unnamed holding company.

Bushy's SIBA

Mount Murray Brewing Co Ltd, Mount Murray Brewery, Mount Murray, Braddan, Isle of Man, IM4 1JE
☎ (01624) 661244
✉ bushys@manx.net
bushys.com
Tours by arrangement

Set up in 1986 as a brew-pub, Bushy's moved to its present site in 1990 when demand outgrew capacity. It owns four tied houses and the beers are also supplied to 25 other outlets. Bushy's goes one step further than the Manx Pure Beer Law, which permits only malt, hops, sugar and yeast, preferring the German Reinheitsgebot (Pure Beer Law) that excludes sugar. Seasonal beers are numerous and include Oyster Stout (ABV 4.2%) – see website.

Castletown Bitter (OG 1035, ABV 3.5%)
A light, golden beer full of floral and citrus hints. A refreshing session beer.

Ruby (1874) Mild (OG 1035, ABV 3.5%)
An authentic malt brewed Mild with a fine aroma of crystal malt and Fuggles.

Bitter (OG 1038, ABV 3.8%)
An aroma full of pale malt and hops introduces a beautifully hoppy, bitter beer. Despite the predominant hop character, malt is also evident. Fresh and clean-tasting.

Old Bushy Tail (OG 1045, ABV 4.5%)
A reddish-brown beer with a pronounced hop and malt aroma, the malt tending towards treacle. Slightly sweet and malty on the palate with distinct

THE BREWERIES

orangy tones. The full finish is malty and hoppy with a hint of toffee.

Piston Brew (OG 1045, ABV 4.5%)
A ruby-coloured ale, slightly sweet with subtle hop flavours coming through from the late addition of Challenger and Fuggles hops. Malty with hints of toffee.

Weiss Beer (OG 1040, ABV 4.5%)
A light, refreshing, cloudy wheat beer.

Butcombe SIBA

Butcombe Brewery Ltd, Cox's Green, Wrington, Bristol, BS40 5PA
☎ (01934) 863963
✉ info@butcombe.com
🌐 butcombe.com
Shop Mon-Fri 9am-5pm; Sat 9am-12pm
Tours by arrangement

Established in 1978 by Simon Whitmore and sold to Guy Newell and friends in 2003, Butcombe moved to a new purpose-built brewery in 2004. It supplies about 500 outlets and similar numbers via wholesalers and pub companies. Butcombe has an estate of 15 freehouses. Seasonal beers: Blond (ABV 4.3%, Apr-Sep), Brunel IPA (ABV 5%, Oct-Mar).

Bitter (OG 1039, ABV 4%)
Amber-coloured, malty and notably bitter beer, with subtle citrus notes. Hoppy, malty, citrus and a slight sulphur aroma, and a long, dry, bitter finish.

Gold (OG 1044, ABV 4.4%)
Aroma of pale malt, citrus hops and fruit. Medium bodied, well-balanced, with good pale malt, hops and bitterness. It is fruity, slightly sweet, with an abiding dryness.

Butts SIBA

Butts Brewery Ltd, Northfield Farm, Wantage Road, Great Shefford, Hungerford, Berkshire, RG17 7BY
☎ (01488) 648133
✉ sales@buttsbrewery.com
🌐 buttsbrewery.com

The brewery was set up in a converted Dutch barn in 1994. In 2002, the brewery took the decision to become dedicated to organic production: all the beers brewed use organic malted barley and organic hops when suitable varieties are available. All beers are certified by the Soil Association. Around 60 outlets are supplied. Seasonal beers: Mudskipper (ABV 4.5%, summer), Bit o'Posh (ABV 4.2%, autumn). Bottle-conditioned beers are also available.

Jester (OG 1036, ABV 3.5%)
A pale brown session bitter with a hoppy aroma and a hint of fruit. The taste balances malt, hops, fruit and bitterness with a hoppy aftertaste.

Traditional (OG 1040, ABV 4%)
A pale brown bitter which is quite soft on the tongue with hoppy citrus flavours accompanying a gentle bittersweetness. A long, dry aftertaste is dominated by fruity hops.

Blackguard (OG 1045, ABV 4.5%)
A porter with caramel, malt, roast and fruit dominating the aroma. The taste is a combination of sweet malt and roast with caramel undertones.

Barbus Barbus (OG 1046, ABV 4.6%)
Golden ale with a fruity hoppy aroma and a hint of malt. Hops dominate taste and aftertaste, accompanied by fruitiness and bitterness, with a hint of balancing sweetness.

Golden Brown (OG 1050, ABV 5%)
A golden brown ale with malt and caramel dominating the aroma. A malty, bittersweet taste lingers on into the subtle aftertaste.

Le Butts (OG 1050, ABV 5%)
Brewed with lager yeast and hops resulting in a crisp and refreshing European-style beer.

Coper (OG 1059, ABV 6%)

Buxton (NEW)

Buxton Brewery Co Ltd, t/a Buxton Real Ale, The Old Cowshed, Staden Grange, Buxton, Derbyshire, SK17 9RZ
☎ (01298) 72208
☎ 07754 015743
✉ geoff@buxtonrealale.co.uk
🌐 buxtonrealale.co.uk

The brewery was set up in late 2009 by two partners supplying the local free trade and outlets further afield. All beers are brewed using natural spring water from the Buxton Spring Water Company. Bottle-conditioned beers are available.

Festival (OG 1037, ABV 3.8%)

Rock Head Pale (OG 1042, ABV 4.2%)

Kinder Sunset (OG 1046, ABV 4.8%)

Robert Cain SIBA

Robert Cain Brewery, Stanhope Street, Liverpool, Merseyside, L8 5XJ
☎ (0151) 709 8734
✉ info@cains.co.uk
🌐 cains.co.uk
Shop 12-10pm daily
Tours by arrangement

The Dusanj brothers, Ajmail and Sudarghara, bought the brewery in 2002, but after investing heavily and following a reverse takeover of the Honeycombe leased pubs estate, Cains Beer Co went into administration in 2008. The brewing operation was then sold back to the Dusanj family. Nine pubs are owned all serving cask beer and around 300 outlets are supplied. Seasonal beers: see website.

Dark Mild (OG 1034.5, ABV 3.2%)
Sweetish, fruity mild with roast notes throughout and a dry aftertaste.

IPA (OG 1036, ABV 3.5%)
A light, full-flavoured session beer with a subtle hop aroma.

Finest Bitter (OG 1041, ABV 4%)
Blackcurrant fruit and malt dominate the aroma. A sweetish malty bitter with hints of roast and caramel. Hops come through in the dry, bitter aftertaste.

Formidable Ale/FA (OG 1049, ABV 5%)
A bitter and hoppy beer with a good dry aftertaste. Sharp, clean and dry.

Cairngorm SIBA

Cairngorm Brewery Co Ltd, Unit 12, Dalfaber Industrial Estate, Aviemore, Highlands, PH22 1ST
☎ (01479) 812222
✉ info@cairngormbrewery.com
🌐 cairngormbrewery.com
Shop Mon-Sat 9am-5pm (online shop also available)
Tours: Mon-Fri 10.30am & 2.30pm by arrangement

The brewery has enjoyed much success since winning Champion Beer of Scotland in 2004 and 2005, and gold medals at GBBF in 2004-2006. Seven regular cask beers are produced along with a rolling programme of seasonal ales throughout the year. Expansion continued during 2008, taking weekly capacity to 110 barrels. The free trade is supplied as far as the central belt with national delivery via wholesalers. Seasonal beers: See website.

Stag (OG 1040, ABV 4.1%)
A drinkable best bitter with plenty of hop bitterness throughout. This tawny brew has some malt in the lingering bitter aftertaste.

Trade Winds (OG 1043, ABV 4.3%)
A massive citrus fruit, hop and elderflower nose leads to hints of grapefruit and apricot in the mouth. The exceptional bittersweetness in the taste lasts through the long, lingering aftertaste.

Black Gold (OG 1044, ABV 4.4%)
Worthy Championship-winning beer with many accolades. Roast malt dominates but the liquorice and blackcurrant in the taste and nose give it a background sweetness. Very long, dry, bitter finish.

Nessies Monster Mash (OG 1044, ABV 4.4%)
A good, traditional, English-type bitter with plenty of bitterness and light malt flavour. Lingering bitterness in the aftertaste with diminishing sweetness.

Cairngorm Gold (OG 1044, ABV 4.5%)

Sheepshaggers Gold (OG 1044, ABV 4.5%)
A golden amber brew with faint aromas and tastes of grapefruit and passion fruit. Some light bitterness in the otherwise sweet aftertaste.

Wildcat (OG 1049.5, ABV 5.1%)
A full-bodied strong bitter. Malt predominates but there is an underlying hop character through to the well-balanced aftertaste.

Caledonian

See S&N/Heineken in Global Giants section

Callow Top

See Haywood Bad Ram

Calvors

Calvors Brewery Ltd, Home Farm, Coddenham, Ipswich, Suffolk, IP6 9UN
☎ (01449) 711055
✉ info@calvors.co.uk
🌐 calvors.co.uk

No real ale. Calvors Brewery was established in early 2008 and brews two bottled real lagers, Calvors Suffolk Lager (ABV 3.8%) and Calvors Premium (ABV 5%), which are available bottled and on draught.

Cambridge Moonshine

Cambridge Moonshine Brewery, Hill Farm, Shelford Road, Fulbourn, Cambridgeshire, CB21 5EQ
☎ (01223) 514366
☎ 07906 066794
✉ mark@moonshinebrewery.co.uk

Established in 2004, the brewery has recently moved to larger premises incorporating a five-barrel plant. Locally produced ingredients are used including water from their own well. The brewery mainly concentrates on supplying CAMRA beer festivals, with two outlets supplied direct. Bottle-conditioned beers are available.

Sparkling Moon (ABV 3.6%)
A light blond lager beer with a delicate hop aroma and a crisp, clean taste with hints of vanilla.

Harvest Moon Mild (OG 1040, ABV 3.9%)
Smooth fruit notes combine with coffee and chocolate flavours, lightly hopped. A well-balanced beer, slightly sweet with plenty of character.

Barton Bitter (ABV 4%)
Pale brown with red and amber highlights, balanced malt and hops and a fruity backdrop on both nose and palate. A bittersweet flavour dries as fruit and sweetness diminish.

Thunder Moon (ABV 4.1%)
A light-bodied golden ale with a citrus fruit bouquet and taste that contines through to a pleasantly refreshing, clean and dry finish.

CB1 (ABV 4.2%)
Amber-coloured traditional best bitter with a good blend of malt and hops with a rounded, hoppy finish.

Red Watch (ABV 4.2%)
A red-coloured beer brewed with fresh blueberries. A thirst-quenching, refreshing, fruity summer ale.

Pigs Ear Porter (ABV 4.5%)
Five types of malts, four varieties of hops plus black honey from the Cambridge Beekeepers Association are blended together to create a unique and rounded flavour.

Minion of the Moon (ABV 4.6%)
A premium, light-coloured, full-flavoured fruity beer. Rich malt, fruit and hops dominate the taste, the fullness of flavour is sustained throughout leading to an uplifting and satisfying bittersweet finish.

Black Hole Stout (ABV 5%)
Full-bodied stout with a complex malt and caramel profile, dry-roasted bitter flavour that is rich, smooth and long lasting.

Budding Moon (ABV 5.1%)
A smooth, refreshing golden wheat beer. With a citrus hop bouquet and a rich, malty fruit flavour. The addition of locally produced honey gives a moderately bittersweet finish.

Chocolate Orange Stout (ABV 6.7%)
Full-bodied, rounded soft stout. Loaded with chocolate and coffee flavours with a good hop balance that has a hint of orange on the nose.

THE BREWERIES

Cambrinus SIBA

Cambrinus Craft Brewery, Home Farm, Knowsley Park, Knowsley, Merseyside, L34 4AQ
☎ (0151) 546 2226

⊗ Established in 1997, Cambrinus is housed in part of a former farm building on a private estate. It produces around 250 hectolitres a year on a five-barrel plant. Some 45 outlets are supplied on a regular basis in and around Lancashire, Cheshire and Cumbria. Seasonal beers: Bootstrap (ABV 4.5%, spring), Fruit Wheat Beer (summer), St Georges Ale (ABV 4.5%, Apr), Clogdance (ABV 3.6%, May), Solstice (ABV 3.8%, Jun), Honeywheat (ABV 3.7%, Jul), Dark Harvest (ABV 4%, autumn), Hearts of Oak (ABV 5%, Oct), Parkin (ABV 3.8%, Nov), Lamp Oil (ABV 4.5%, winter), Celebrance (ABV 5.5%, Xmas).

Herald (OG 1036, ABV 3.7%)
Light summer drinking bitter, pale and refreshing.

Yardstick (OG 1040, ABV 4%)
Mild, malty and lightly hopped.

Deliverance (OG 1040, ABV 4.2%)
Pale premium bitter.

Endurance (OG 1045, ABV 4.3%)
IPA-style, smooth and hoppy, fermented in oak.

Camerons

Camerons Brewery Ltd, Lion Brewery, Stranton, Hartlepool, Co Durham, TS24 7QS
☎ (01429) 852000
✉ martindutoy@cameronsbrewery.com
cameronsbrewery.com
Shop Mon-Sat 12-4pm
Tours by arrangement

Founded in 1865, Camerons was bought in 2002 by Castle Eden brewery, which moved production to Hartlepool. In 2003 a 10-barrel micro-brewery, the Lions Den, opened to produce and bottle small brews of guest ales and to undertake contract brewing and bottling. Around 75 pubs are owned, with five selling real ale. Seasonal beers have been dropped in favour of monthly guest beer production.

Bitter (OG 1036, ABV 3.6%) ◆
A light bitter, but well-balanced, with hops and malt.

Strongarm (OG 1041, ABV 4%) ◆
A well-rounded, ruby-red ale with a distinctive, tight creamy head; initially fruity, but with a good balance of malt, hops and moderate bitterness.

Castle Eden Ale (OG 1043, ABV 4.2%) ◆
A light, creamy, malty sweet ale with fruit notes and a mellow dry bitterness in the finish.

Nimmo's XXXX (OG 1045, ABV 4.4%) ◆
Light golden beer with a well-balanced character derived from English malt and Goldings hops.

For Scottish & Newcastle/Heineken:

John Smith's Magnet (OG 1039.8, ABV 4%)
Ruby-red ale with good balance between malt and hops

Cannon Royall SIBA

Cannon Royall Brewery Ltd, Fruiterer's Arms, Uphampton Lane, Uphampton, Worcestershire, WR9 0JW
☎ (01905) 621161
✉ info@cannonroyall.co.uk
cannonroyall.co.uk

Cannon Royall's first brew was in 1993 in a converted cider house behind the Fruiterer's Arms. It has increased capacity from five barrels to more than 16 a week. The brewery supplies a number of outlets throughout the Midlands. Seasonal beers are regularly produced. Bottle-conditioned beers are also available.

Fruiterer's Mild (OG 1037, ABV 3.7%) ◆
This black-hued brew has rich malty aromas that lead to a fruity mix of bitter hops and sweetness, and a short balanced aftertaste.

King's Shilling (OG 1038, ABV 3.8%) ◆
A golden bitter that packs a citrus hoppy punch throughout.

Arrowhead Bitter (OG 1039, ABV 3.9%) ◆
A powerful punch of hops attacks the nose before the feast of bitterness. The memory of this golden brew fades too soon.

Muzzle Loader (OG 1042, ABV 4.2%) ◆
The lingering aftertaste bears witness to this amber liquid's agreeable balance of malt and hoppy flavours that is evident in the aroma and palate.

Arrowhead Extra (OG 1043, ABV 4.3%)
An intense hop aroma with some sweetness on the palate. The finish is long and bitter.

Captain Cook SIBA

Captain Cook Brewery Ltd, White Swan, 1 West End, Stokesley, North Yorkshire, TS9 5BL
☎ (01642) 710263
✉ jeff.hind@thewynyardrooms.com
thecaptaincookbrewery.co.uk
Tours by arrangement

The Captain Cook Brewery is located within the 18th-century White Swan pub. The brewery celebrated its 10th anniversary in 2009. With a four-barrel plant it is brewing up to 12 barrels a week in order to supply other local outlets. Seasonal beer: Easter Island (ABV 4.1%, spring).

Sunset (OG 1040, ABV 4.1%)
An extremely smooth light ale with a good balance of malt and hops.

Slipway (OG 1042, ABV 4.2%)
A light-coloured hoppy ale with bitterness coming through from Challenger hops. A full-flavoured ale with a smooth malt aftertaste.

Endeavour (OG 1043, ABV 4.3%)
Mid brown ale with a bitter finish.

Black Porter (OG 1044, ABV 4.4%)
Chocolate notes and dominant roast flavours lead to a dry, bitter finish.

Carter's

Carter's Brewery, White Hart Inn, White Hart Lane, Machen, CF83 8QQ
☎ (01633) 441005

Carter's started in 2002 on a 1.5-barrel plant and only brews for special occasions and local beer festivals. There are plans to step up production and brew more regularly in the future.

Castle Rock SIBA

Tynemill Ltd t/a Castle Rock Brewery, Queensbridge Road, Nottingham, Nottinghamshire, NG2 1NB
☎ (0115) 985 1615
✉ admin@castlerockbrewery.co.uk
castlerockbrewery.co.uk
Tours by arrangement (groups of 10 or more)

Established in 1998 producing 30 barrels weekly, since then capacity has steadily increased and a fifth fermenting vessel installed during 2008 saw capacity reach 120 barrels. Beers are distributed through its own estate of 23 pubs and further afield through wholesalers. A different beer is brewed monthly to support the Nottinghamshire Wildlife Trust. Harvest Pale now accounts for over 50% of production. Seasonal beers: see website. Bottle-conditioned beers are also available.

Black Gold (OG 1038, ABV 3.8%)
Dark ruby mild with subtle sweetness.

Harvest Pale (OG 1038, ABV 3.8%)
Blonde and refreshing with distinctive citrus hop.

Hemlock (OG 1040, ABV 4%)
A well-hopped session bitter.

Preservation Fine Ale (OG 1044, ABV 4.4%)
A full-flavoured beer with some residual sweetness that is well-balanced with a resinous hop character.

Elsie Mo (OG 1047, ABV 4.7%)
Blond beer with a subtle floral nose and lemongrass freshness delivering a clean finish.

Screech Owl (OG 1055, ABV 5.5%)
A traditional, well-hopped India Pale Ale.

Castle

Castle Brewery, Unit 9a-7, Restormel Industrial Estate, Liddicoat Road, Lostwithiel, Cornwall, PL22 0HG
☎ (01726) 871133
☎ 07800 635831
✉ castlebrewery@aol.com

Castle started brewing in early 2008 on a two-barrel plant. Only bottle-conditioned ales are produced; Moat Mild (ABV 4.4%), Battle Stout (ABV 4.6%), Once A Knight (ABV 5%), Lostwithiale (ABV 7%), Hung, Drawn & Slaughtered (ABV 10%).

Cathedral

Cathedral Ales, c/o Green Dragon, Magpie Square, Broadgate, Lincoln, Lincolnshire, LN2 5DH
☎ (01522) 567155
✉ info@greendragonpub.co.uk
greendragonpub.co.uk
Tours by arrangement

Cathedral Ales began brewing in January 2009 on a five-barrel plant in the basement of the Green Dragon – a 14th-century timber framed pub. Six regular ales are brewed. Cathedral is a sister brewery to Milestone.

Red Imp (ABV 4.2%)

Golden Imp (ABV 4.3%)

Black Imp (ABV 4.7%)

Eight Bells (ABV 4.8%)

Magna Carta (ABV 5%)

Bishops Tipple (ABV 5.2%)

Caythorpe SIBA

Caythorpe Brewery Ltd, c/o Black Horse, 29 Main Street, Caythorpe, Nottinghamshire, NG14 7ED
☎ (0115) 966 4933
☎ 07913 434922
✉ caythorpebrewery@btinternet.com
Tours by arrangement

Caythorpe was set up using a 2.5-barrel brewery in a building at the rear of the Black Horse pub in 1997. Ownership changed in 2005 but the brewery continues to produce its small range of beers that have a big reputation in the local area. Seasonal beers: Winter Light (ABV 3.6%, autumn/winter), One Swallow (ABV 3.6%, spring/summer).

Bitter (OG 1034.7, ABV 3.7%)

Dover Beck (OG 1037, ABV 4%)

Stout Fellow (OG 1038.6, ABV 4.2%)

Cellar Rat

Cellar Rat Brews, c/o 3 Rivers Brewery, Delta House, Gregg Street, Reddish, Cheshire, SK5 7BS
☎ 07971 363107
✉ cellarratbrews@yahoo.com

Established in 2007, Cellar Rat beers only appeared at local festivals and the Crown in Stockport until 2009 when Head Brewer Sarah Bergin showcased beers at the National Winter Ales Festival. Spare capacity is used at 3 Rivers Brewery. An imaginative range of one-off brews are also produced. Seasonal beers: Rosie Rat (ABV 5.9%, Jun-Jul), Fat Rat (ABV 5%, Oct-Nov).

City Life (ABV 3.9%)

Celt Experience

Celt Experience Brewery Ltd, Unit 2E, Former Hill Buildings, Pontygwindy Industrial Estate, Caerphilly, CF83 3HU
☎ 0870 803 3876
✉ celt@theceltexperience.co.uk
theceltexperience.co.uk

Celt Experience first brewed in late 2007. A sister brewery to Newmans (qv), they share the 40-barrel plant. A bottling plant was installed in 2009.

Celt Golden (ABV 4.2%)

Native Storm (OG 1045, ABV 4.4%)

Celt Bronze (ABV 4.5%)

Cwrw Celt (ABV 5%)
A real lager.

Chalk Hill

Chalk Hill Brewery, Rosary Road, Norwich, Norfolk, NR1 4DA
☎ (01603) 477078
✉ chalkhillinns@ntlworld.com
Tours by arrangement

Chalk Hill began production in 1993 on a 15-barrel plant. It supplies local pubs and festivals.

Tap Bitter (OG 1036, ABV 3.6%)
A light, fruity beer with underlying hop notes. A malty bitterness and a slightly resinous feel to the initial taste. The balance of flavour remains to the end of the short, light finish.

CHB (OG 1042, ABV 4.2%)

A copper-coloured brew with a dominant bitter flavour. Hops in the bouquet continue through and give a dry, lingering aftertaste. Background maltiness gives balance.

Gold (ABV 4.3%)
A well-balanced golden ale. Malt, hops, citrus notes and bitterness can all be found in subtle amounts in both the aroma and taste. Surprisingly long finish develops a slight dryness.

Dreadnought (OG 1049, ABV 4.9%)
A rich plummy fruitiness pervades the nose and taste of this mid-brown strong bitter. Malt joins with a caramel and roast background to give depth. Sweetness outlasts a quick finish.

Flintknapper's Mild (OG 1052, ABV 5%)
Chocolate, stewed fruits, liquorice, hops and malt can all be found in this rich, red-coloured brew. The light malt nose belies the variety of flavours.

Old Tackle (OG 1056, ABV 5.6%)
Red hued with a blackcurrant bouquet, this rich malty brew slowly subsides to a long dryish end. Roast notes remain consistent.

Cheddar Ales

Cheddar Ales Ltd, Winchester Farm, Draycott Road, Cheddar, Somerset, BS27 3RP
☎ (01934) 744193
brewery@cheddarales.co.uk
cheddarales.co.uk
Shop Mon-Fri 8am-4pm; Sat-Sun by appointment
Tours by arrangement

Cheddar Ales is a 20-barrel brewery set up in 2006 with a capacity of 17,000 pints per week. It is a local brewery serving a local market and has received many awards during its short history. Around 50 outlets are supplied regularly. Bottle-conditioned beers are available.

Mild Cheddar (OG 1036.5, ABV 3.6%)
A dark brown ale with a rounded blend of rich malt flavours, balanced with a light hop bitterness.

Gorge Best Bitter (OG 1040, ABV 4%)
A best bitter with warm malt flavours and a clean, bitter finish.

Potholer (OG 1043.5, ABV 4.3%)
Amber malty best bitter, biscuity aroma and citrus in the mouth. Bitter fruit finish.

Totty Pot (OG 1043.5, ABV 4.5%)
A rich, dark porter with hints of roasted coffee and a creamy malt finish.

Goat's Leap (OG 1054.5, ABV 5.5%)
A contemporary IPA that stays close to the style's traditional roots. Full-bodied, strong and with a striking bitter finish. Brimming with hop character.

Cherwell Valley

Cherwell Valley Brewery Ltd, Unit 2, St David's Court, Top Station Road, Brackley, Northamptonshire, NN13 7UG
☎ (01280) 706888
tythinggraham@aol.com
cherwellvalleybrewery.com

Cherwell Valley commenced brewed in early 2008 using a 2.5-barrel plant. Seasonal beers: Larkrise (ABV 4%, summer), Old Noll (ABV 4.9%, winter). Bottle-conditioned beers are also available.

Kineton Flight (ABV 3.6%)

Cropredy Bridge 1844 (ABV 4.2%)

Chiltern SIBA

Chiltern Brewery, Nash Lee Road, Terrick, Aylesbury, Buckinghamshire, HP17 0TQ
☎ (01296) 613647
info@chilternbrewery.co.uk
chilternbrewery.co.uk
Shop Mon-Sat 9am-5pm
Tours by arrangement

Founded in 1980, the brewery is one of the first dozen micro-breweries to have been established in the country and is the oldest independent brewery in the Chilterns. This second generation family brewery produces a broad range of award-winning beers with English ingredients. The brewery tap is the Farmers' Bar at the King's Head in Aylesbury. Seasonal beers: Chiltern's Nut Brown Mild (ABV 3.9%, spring), Cobblestones (ABV 3.5%, summer), Copper Beech (ABV 4.4%, autumn), Three Hundreds Old Ale (ABV 4.9%, winter), Oatmeal Stout (ABV 4.3%, winter). Bottle-conditioned beers are also available.

Chiltern Ale (OG 1037, ABV 3.7%)
An amber, refreshing beer with a slight fruit aroma, leading to a good malt/bitter balance in the mouth. The aftertaste is bitter and dry.

Beechwood Bitter (OG 1043, ABV 4.3%)
This pale brown beer has a balanced butterscotch/toffee aroma, with a slight hop note. The taste balances bitterness and sweetness, leading to a long bitter finish.

Chough SIBA

Chough Brewery, Unit 1, Higher Bochym, Cury Cross Lanes, Helston, Cornwall, TR12 7AZ
☎ (01326) 241555
Tours by arrangement

Established in 2000 and formerly known as Organic Brewery, its mini tower system was exclusively organic. The brewery now produce six regular beers in either standard or organic styles, hence the name change. The beers can be found locally in more than 20 outlets and further afield through wholesalers. They are still produced using the brewery's own source of natural mineral water. All organic beers are Soil Association certified and suitable for vegetarians. Bottle-conditioned beers are available.

Halzephron Gold (OG 1033, ABV 3.6%)

Lizard Point (OG 1036, ABV 4%)

Serpentine (OG 1042, ABV 4.5%)
A big malty nose, a bittersweet palate and a finish balanced by rich malt and tangy hops.

Black Rock (OG 1043, ABV 4.7%)
Hop and apple aroma masked by complex roast overtones.

Wolf Rock (OG 1046, ABV 5%)

Charlie's Pride Lager (OG 1048, ABV 5.3%)

Julian Church (NEW)

Julian Church Brewery, c/o Alexandra Arms, 39 Victoria Street, Kettering, Northamptonshire, NN16 0BU

Julian Church started brewing on Nobby's Brewery plant. When Nobby's moved, Julian took over the brewery in January 2009. Parson's Nose is rebadged as Father Nip for the Alexandra Arms.

Parson's Nose (ABV 3.9%)

Midnight Mass (ABV 4.2%)

Wonky Spire (ABV 4.7%)

Headstone (ABV 5.8%)

Church End SIBA

Church End Brewery Ltd, Ridge Lane, Nuneaton, Warwickshire, CV10 0RD
☎ (01827) 713080
✉ stewart@churchendbrewery.co.uk
🌐 churchendbrewery.co.uk
Shop during tap opening hours
Tours by arrangement

⊗ Stewart Elliot started brewing in 1994 in an old coffin shop in Shustoke. He moved to the present site and upgraded to a 10-barrel plant in 2001 with further expansion to a 20-barrel plant in 2008. The brewery tap was opened in 2002. A portfolio of around 60 non-regular beers are produced as well as many one-off specials, including fruit, herb and spice beers. Some 500 outlets are supplied. Seasonal beers: Without-a-Bix (ABV 4.2%), Pews Porter (ABV 4.5%), Old Pal (ABV 5.5%), Arthurs Wit (ABV 6%), Rest-in-Peace (ABV 7%). Bottle-conditioned beers are also available.

Poachers Pocket (ABV 3.5%)

Pheasant Plucker (ABV 3.7%)

Cuthberts (ABV 3.8%) ◆
A refreshing, hoppy beer, with hints of malt, fruit and caramel taste. Lingering bitter aftertaste.

Goat's Milk (ABV 3.8%)

Gravediggers Ale (ABV 3.8%) ◆
A premium mild. Black and red in colour, with a complex mix of chocolate and roast flavours, it is almost a light porter.

Hop Gun (ABV 4.1%)

What the Fox's Hat (ABV 4.2%) ◆
A beer with a malty aroma, and a hoppy and malty taste with some caramel flavour.

Pooh Bear (ABV 4.3%)

Vicar's Ruin (ABV 4.4%) ◆
A straw-coloured best bitter with an initially hoppy, bitter flavour, softening to a delicate malt finish.

Stout Coffin (ABV 4.6%)

Fallen Angel (ABV 5%)

For Cape of Good Hope, Warwick:

Two Llocks (ABV 4%)

City of Cambridge EAB

City of Cambridge Brewery Co Ltd, Ely Road, Chittering, Cambridge, CB5 9PH
☎ (01223) 864864
✉ sales@cambridge-brewery.co.uk
🌐 cambridge-brewery.co.uk

⊗ City of Cambridge opened in 1997 and moved to its present site in 2002. The brewery site is in the process of being redeveloped, with the intention of keeping the brewery on the site. At present all brewing is being done under contract by Wolf Brewery (qv). In addition to prizes for its cask beers, the brewery holds a conservation award for the introduction of native reed beds at its site to treat brewery water. Seasonal beers: Mich'aelmas (ABV 4.5%, Xmas), Holly Heaven (ABV 4.8%, Xmas).

City of Stirling

See Traditional Scottish Ales

Clanconnel (NEW)

Clanconnel Brewing Co Ltd, PO Box 316, Craigavon, Co Down, BT65 9AZ
☎ 07711 626770
✉ info@clanconnelbrewing.com
🌐 clanconnelbrewing.com

Clanconnel started producing bottled beer in late 2008: Weaver's Gold (ABV 4.5%).

Clark's SIBA

HB Clark & Co (Successors) Ltd, Westgate Brewery, Wakefield, West Yorkshire, WF2 9SW
☎ (01924) 373328 Ext 211
✉ rickp@hbclark.co.uk
🌐 hbclark.co.uk
Tours by arrangement

◎ Founded in 1906, Clark's recently celebrated its centenary. It ceased brewing during the 1960s/70s but resumed cask ale production in 1982 and now delivers to around 220 outlets. Four pubs are owned, all serving cask ale. Seasonal beers: see website.

Classic Blonde (OG 1039, ABV 3.9%)
A light-coloured ale with a citrus and hoppy flavour, a distinctive grapefruit aroma and a dry finish.

No Angel (OG 1040, ABV 4%)
A bitter with a dry hop finish, well-balanced and full of flavour. Pale brown in colour with hints of fruit and hops.

Westgate Gold (OG 1042, ABV 4.2%)
A light-coloured, fruity beer with a full body and rich aroma.

Rams Revenge (OG 1046, ABV 4.6%) ◆
A rich, ruby-coloured premium ale, well-balanced with malt and hops, with a deep fruity taste and a dry hoppy aftertaste, with a pleasant hoppy aroma.

Clearwater SIBA

Clearwater Brewery, 2-4 Devon Units, Hatchmoor Industrial Estate, Torrington, Devon, EX38 7HP
☎ (01805) 625242
✉ brian@clearwaterbrewery.co.uk

⊗ Clearwater took over the closed St Giles in the Wood brewery in 1999 and has steadily grown since. Many of the beers have names on the Civil War theme following the great battle of Torrington in 1646. Around 40 outlets are supplied. Seasonal/occasional beer: Ebony & Ivory (ABV 4.2%, winter). Bottle-conditioned beers are also available.

Village Pride (OG 1036, ABV 3.7%)
Golden, hoppy ale.

Cavalier (OG 1041, ABV 4%) ◆
Mid-brown, full-bodied best bitter with a burnt, rich malt aroma and taste, leading to a bitter, well-rounded finish.

High Tide (OG 1046, ABV 4.5%)
Copper-coloured ale with a malt flavour.

Olivers Nectar (OG 1052, ABV 5.2%)
Dark ruby beer with a rich, malt flavour.

Cliff Quay (NEW)

Cliff Quay Brewery, Cliff Road, Ipswich, Suffolk, IP3 0BS
☎ (01473) 225501
✉ brewerytap@cliffquay.co.uk
cliffquay.co.uk
Tours by arrangement

Cliff Quay was established in 2008 by former Wychwood brewer Jeremy Moss and John Bjornson on part of the historic Tolly Cobbold riverside site. Cliff Quay also operates the adjoining pub, which acts as the brewery tap.

Bitter (ABV 3.5%)

Tolly Roger (ABV 4.2%)

Black Jack Porter (ABV 4.5%)

Tumblehome (ABV 4.7%)

Clockwork

The Clockwork Beer Co, Maclay Inns PLC, 1153-5 Cathcart Road, Glasgow, G42 9HB
☎ (0141) 649 0184
✉ clockwork@maclay.co.uk
maclay.com
Tours by arrangement

The brewpub, the oldest in Glasgow, was established in 1997. The beers are kept in cellar tanks where fermentation gases from the conditioning vessel blanket the beers on tap (but not under pressure). A wide range of ales, lagers and specials are produced. Most beers are naturally gassed while the Original Lager and Seriously Ginger, are pressurised. Having taken ownership of the Maclay's cookbook when Maclay Inns took over two years ago, some old recipes including Wallace IPA (ABV 4.5%), Oat Malt Stout (ABV 4.4%), Honey Weizen (ABV 4.6%) and Maclay's 90/- (ABV 6%) have been brewed with more to come.

Amber IPA (ABV 3.8%)

Red Alt (ABV 4.4%)

Gosch (ABV 4.8%)

Original Lager (ABV 4.8%)

Hazy Daze Seriously Ginger (ABV 5%)

Oregon IPA (ABV 5.5%)

Strong Ale (ABV 6%)

Thunder & Lightning (ABV 6%)

Coach House SIBA

Coach House Brewing Co Ltd, Wharf Street, Warrington, Cheshire, WA1 2DQ
☎ (01925) 232800
✉ info@coach-house-brewing.co.uk
coach-house-brewing.co.uk
Tours by arrangement for CAMRA groups

The brewery was founded in 1991. In 1995 Coach House increased its brewing capacity to cope with growing demand and it now delivers to around 250 outlets throughout Britain, either from the brewery or via wholesalers. The brewery also brews a large number of one-off and special beers. Its visitor centre opened in 2008. Seasonal beers: see website.

Coachman's Best Bitter (OG 1037, ABV 3.7%) ◆
A well-hopped, malty bitter, moderately fruity with a hint of sweetness and a peppery nose.

Gunpowder Mild (OG 1037, ABV 3.8%) ◆
Biscuity dark mild with a blackcurrant sweetness. Bitterness and fruit dominate with some hints of caramel and a slightly stronger roast flavour.

Honeypot Bitter (OG 1037, ABV 3.8%)

Farrier's Best Bitter (OG 1038, ABV 3.9%)

Dick Turpin (OG 1042, ABV 4.2%) ◆
Malty, hoppy pale brown beer with some initial sweetish flavours leading to a short, bitter aftertaste. Sold under other names as a pub house beer.

Flintlock Pale Ale (OG 1044, ABV 4.4%)

Innkeeper's Special Reserve (OG 1045, ABV 4.5%) ◆
A darkish, full-flavoured bitter. Quite fruity, with a strong, bitter aftertaste.

Postlethwaite (OG 1045, ABV 4.6%) ◆
Thin bitter with a short, dry aftertaste. Biscuity malt dominates.

Gingernut Premium (OG 1050, ABV 5%)

Posthorn Premium (OG 1050, ABV 5%) ◆
Dry golden bitter with a blackcurrant fruitiness and good hop flavours leading to a strong, dry finish. Well-balanced but slightly thin for its gravity.

For John Joule of Stone:

Old Knotty (ABV 3.6%)

Old Priory (ABV 4.4%)

Victory (ABV 5.2%)

Coastal SIBA

Coastal Brewery, Unit 9B, Cardrew Industrial Estate, Redruth, Cornwall, TR15 1SS
☎ 07875 405407
✉ coastalbrewery@tiscali.co.uk
coastalbrewery.co.uk

Coastal was set up in late 2006 on a five-barrel plant by Alan Hinde, former brewer and owner of the Borough Arms in Crewe, Cheshire. Around 30 outlets are supplied. Seasonal beers: Frosty (ABV 4.2%, Dec-Jan), Shine On (ABV 3.8%, summer). Bottle-conditioned beers are also available.

Hop Monster (OG 1038, ABV 3.7%)

Handliner (OG 1040, ABV 4%)

Merry Maidens Mild (OG 1040, ABV 4%)

Angelina (OG 1042, ABV 4.1%)

Golden Hinde (OG 1044, ABV 4.3%)

St Pirans Porter (ABV 6%)

Erosion (OG 1080, ABV 8%)

Coles

Coles Family Brewery, White Hart Thatched Inn & Brewery, Llanddarog, Carmarthen, SA32 8NT
☎ (01267) 275395
✉ marcusrcoles@aol.com
thebestpubinwales.co.uk

The brewery is based at the ancient White Hart Inn, built in 1371. Centuries ago beer was brewed on site, but brewing only started again in 1999 on a nine-gallon plant. A one-barrel plant was fitted in 2000. Coles produces many unique ales throughout the year, style depends on the season.

Roasted Barley Stout (ABV 4%)

Golden Ale (ABV 4.2%)

Llanddarog (ABV 4.2%)

Swn y Dail (ABV 4.2%)

White Stag (ABV 4.2%)

Cwrw Blasus (ABV 4.4%)

College Green

College Green Brewery, 1 College Green Mews, Botanic Avenue, Belfast, BT7 1LW
☎ (02892) 660800/(02890) 322600
✉ irishbeers@hildenbrewery.co.uk
hildenbrewery.co.uk

College Green was set up in 2005 by Owen Scullion as a sister brewery to Hilden Brewery. Located in Belfast's lively university area, College Green (the city's only brewery) is housed in a tiny 19th-century coach house and brews for Molly's Yard Restaurant in the adjoining stables building. Bottle-conditioned beer is available. All beers are brewed at the Hilden Brewery.

Colonsay

Colonsay Brewery, The Brewery, Isle of Colonsay, PA61 7YT
☎ (01951) 200190
✉ info@colonsaybrewery.co.uk
colonsaybrewery.co.uk

Colonsay began brewing in 2007 on a five-barrel plant. Beer is mainly bottled or brewery conditioned for the local trade: Lager (ABV 4.4%), 80/- Ale (ABV 4.2%), IPA (ABV 3.9%).

Concertina SIBA

Concertina Brewery, 9a Dolcliffe Road, Mexborough, South Yorkshire, S64 9AZ
☎ (01709) 580841
Tours by arrangement

The brewery started in 1992 in the cellar of a club once famous as the home of a long-gone concertina band. The plant produces up to eight barrels a week for the club and other occasional outlets. Other beers are brewed on a seasonal basis, including Room at the Inn at Xmas.

Club Bitter (ABV 3.9%)
A fruity session bitter with a good bitter flavour.

Old Dark Attic (OG 1038, ABV 3.9%)
A dark brown beer with a fairly sweet, fruity taste.

One Eyed Jack (OG 1039, ABV 4%)
Fairly pale in colour with plenty of hop bitterness. Brewed with the same malt and hop combination as Bengal Tiger, but more of a session beer. Also badged as Mexborough Bitter.

Bengal Tiger (OG 1043, ABV 4.6%)
Light amber ale with an aromatic hoppy nose followed by a combination of fruit and bitterness.

Dictators (OG 1044, ABV 4.7%)

Ariel Square Four (OG 1046, ABV 5.2%)

Concrete Cow

Concrete Cow Brewery, 59 Alston Drive, Bradwell Abbey, Milton Keynes, Buckinghamshire, MK13 9HB
☎ (01908) 316794
✉ dan@concretecowbrewery.co.uk
concretecowbrewery.co.uk

Concrete Cow opened in 2007 on a 5.5-barrel plant. The beers are named after aspects of local history and all are available bottle conditioned as well as in casks. The brewery supplies pubs, farmers markets, local shops and restaurants. Seasonal beers: Black Monk (ABV 3.6%, May), Cowzat! (ABV 3.9%, summer), Winter Ale (ABV 5%).

Midsummer Ale (OG 1039, ABV 3.8%)

Iron Bridge Brew (ABV 3.9%)

Fenny Popper (OG 1039, ABV 4%)

Cock 'n' Bull Story (OG 1041, ABV 4.1%)

Watling Gold (OG 1044, ABV 4.5%)

Old Bloomer (OG 1045, ABV 4.7%)

Coniston SIBA

Coniston Brewing Co Ltd, Coppermines Road, Coniston, Cumbria, LA21 8HL
☎ (01539) 441133
✉ beer@conistonbrewery.com
conistonbrewery.com
Shop (in Black Bull Inn) 11am-11pm
Tours by arrangement

A 10-barrel brewery set up in 1995 behind the Black Bull inn, Coniston. It now brews 40 barrels a week and supplies 70 local outlets while the beers are distributed nationally by wholesalers. One pub is owned. Some bottle-conditioned Coniston beers are brewed by Refresh UK using Hepworth's Horsham plant: Bluebird (ABV 4.2%), Bluebird XB (ABV 4.4%), Oldman Ale (ABV 4.8%). Others are bottled on site.

Olivers Light Ale (OG 1035, ABV 3.4%)
A light, straw-coloured light mild with subtle hops and Demerera sugar.

Bluebird Bitter (OG 1036, ABV 3.6%)
A yellow-gold, predominantly hoppy and fruity beer, well-balanced with some sweetness and a rising bitter finish.

Bluebird XB (OG 1040.5, ABV 4.2%)
Well-balanced, hoppy and fruity golden bitter. Bittersweet in the mouth with dryness building.

Oldman Ale (OG 1040.5, ABV 4.2%)
Delicious fruity, winey beer with a complex, well-balanced richness.

Quicksilver (OG 1044, ABV 4.3%)
A golden amber ale, smooth and fruity with malt and hop tones.

Special Oatmeal Stout (OG 1044, ABV 4.5%)

Blacksmiths Ale (OG 1047.5, ABV 5%)
A well-balanced strong bitter with hints of Xmas pudding.

Consett Ale Works

Consett Ale Works Ltd, Grey Horse Inn, 115 Sherburn Terrace, Consett, Co Durham, DH8 6NE
☎ (01207) 591540
✉ jeffhind@aol.com
thegreyhorse.co.uk
Tours by arrangement

The brewery opened in 2006 in the stables of a former coaching inn, the Grey Horse, Consett's oldest pub. It expanded in 2007 to cope with demand. More than 100 outlets are supplied direct.

Steel Town Bitter (ABV 3.8%)

White Hot (ABV 4%)

Cast Iron (ABV 4.1%)

Last Tap (ABV 4.3%)

Stout (ABV 4.3%)

Red Dust (ABV 4.5%)

Conwy

Conwy Brewery Ltd, Unit 3, Morfa Conwy Enterprise Park, Parc Caer Selon, Conwy, LL32 8FA
☎ (01492) 585287
✉ enquiries@conwybrewery.co.uk
conwybrewery.co.uk
Shop Mon-Fri 9am-5pm (please ring if making special trip)
Tours by arrangement

Conwy started brewing in 2003 and was the first brewery in Conwy for at least 100 years. Due to steady growth it has recently moved premises. Around 50 outlets are supplied. Seasonal beers: Gold 'n' Delicious (ABV 3.6%, Apr-Sep), Telford Porter (ABV 5.6%, autumn), Hoppy Xmas/Nadolig Hopus (ABV 4.3%, Dec). Bottle-conditioned beers are also available.

Castle Bitter/Cwrw Castell (OG 1037, ABV 3.7%)

Mulberry Dark (ABV 3.8%)

Welsh Pride/Balchder Cymru (OG 1040, ABV 4%)
A clean-tasting, malty bitter. Fruit in aroma and taste with a crisp, grainy mouthfeel and a lingering hoppy bitter aftertaste.

Celebration Ale (OG 1041, ABV 4.2%)
Sweetish best bitter with a fruity nose and palate, and a good hoppy finish.

Honey Fayre/Cwrw Mel (OG 1044, ABV 4.5%)
Amber best bitter with hints of honey sweetness in the taste balanced by an increasingly hoppy, bitter finish. Slightly watery mouthfeel for a beer of this strength.

Rampart (OG 1045, ABV 4.5%)

For Cobdens Hotel, Capel Curig:

Cobdens Hotel Bitter/Cwrw Gwesty Cobdens (OG 1040, ABV 4.1%)

Copper Dragon SIBA

Copper Dragon Brewery Ltd, Snaygill Industrial Estate, Keighley Road, Skipton, North Yorkshire, BD23 2QR
☎ (01756) 702130
✉ post@copperdragon.uk.com
copperdragon.uk.com
Bistro/Bar/Shop Mon-Sat 9am-6pm
Tours by arrangement

Copper Dragon began brewing in 2003. Commissioned during October 2008, the purpose built 'double 60' brewhouse is the centrepiece of an impressive and technologically advanced operation. The site also boasts a visitor centre, shop, conference facilities and a bar/bistro. Beer distribution is widespread across northern England. Ten pubs are owned.

Black Gold (OG 1036, ABV 3.7%)
This dark ale has a roast character throughout with coffee flavours and a tangy fruit note in the background. The finish is bitter and malty.

Best Bitter (OG 1036, ABV 3.8%)
A traditional Yorkshire bitter with a gentle hoppy, fruity aroma. Bitterness in the taste is balanced by malt, hops and hints of fruit, followed by a bitter, hoppy finish.

Golden Pippin (OG 1037, ABV 3.9%)
This golden ale has an intense citrus aroma and flavour, characteristic of American Cascade hops. The dry, bitter astringency increases in the aftertaste.

Scotts 1816 (OG 1041, ABV 4.1%)
A well-balanced, full-bodied, copper-coloured premium bitter with a tropical fruit character. Bitterness continues in the finish and leaves a dry, hoppy fruitiness.

Challenger IPA (OG 1042, ABV 4.4%)
Amber-coloured, this is more of a best bitter than a traditional IPA, with a fruity hoppiness in the aroma and taste and a growing dry bitter finish.

Corvedale SIBA

Corvedale Brewery, Sun Inn, Corfton, Craven Arms, Shropshire, SY7 9DF
☎ (01584) 861239
✉ normanspride@aol.com
corvedalebrewery.co.uk
Tours by arrangement

Brewing started in 1999 in a building behind the pub. Landlord Norman Pearce is also the brewer and he uses only British malt and hops, with water from a local borehole. One pub is owned and 100 outlets are supplied. Seasonal beers: Green Hop (ABV 4.5%, autumn), Teresa's Pride (ABV 4.8%, Jan). All beers are on sale in the pub in bottle-conditioned form and are suitable for vegetarians and vegans.

Molly Morgan (OG 1041, ABV 4%)

Katie's Pride (OG 1040, ABV 4.3%)

Norman's Pride (OG 1043, ABV 4.3%)
A golden amber beer with a refreshing, slightly hoppy taste and a bitter finish.

Farmer Ray Ale (OG 1045, ABV 4.5%)
A clear, ruby bitter with a smooth malty taste. Customers are invited to guess the hop!

Dark and Delicious (OG 1045, ABV 4.6%)
A dark ruby beer with hops on the aroma and palate, and a sweet aftertaste.

Cotleigh SIBA

Cotleigh Brewery Ltd, Ford Road, Wiveliscombe, Somerset, TA4 2RE
☎ (01984) 624086
✉ sales@cotleighbrewery.com
🌐 cotleighbrewery.co.uk
Shop Mon-Fri 9am-4pm
Tours by arrangement for select CAMRA groups

Situated in the historic brewing town of Wiveliscombe, Cotleigh has become one of the most successful independent breweries in the West Country. The brewery, which started trading in 1979, is housed in specially converted premises with a modern plant capable of producing 165 barrels a week. 300 pubs and 250 retail outlets are supplied; the beers are also widely available through select wholesalers. Cotleigh's charitable partner is The Hawk and Owl Trust. Seasonal beers: See website. Bottle-conditioned beers are also available.

Harrier (OG 1035, ABV 3.5%)
A delicate floral and fruity aroma with a refreshing, sweet and lightly hopped finish.

Tawny Owl (OG 1038, ABV 3.8%) ◆
Well-balanced, tawny-coloured bitter with plenty of malt and fruitiness on the nose, and malt to the fore in the taste, followed by hop fruit, developing to a satisfying bitter finish.

25 (ABV 4%)

Golden Seahawk Premium Bitter (OG 1042, ABV 4.2%) ◆
A gold, well-hopped premium bitter with a flowery hop aroma and fruity hop flavour, clean mouthfeel, leading to a dry, hoppy finish.

Peregrine Porter (ABV 4.4%)
An old-style porter – smooth and dark with a dry, well-hopped finish.

Barn Owl Premium Ale (OG 1045, ABV 4.5%) ◆
A pale to mid-brown beer with a good balance of malt and hops on the nose; a smooth, full-bodied taste where hops dominate, but balanced by malt, following through to the finish.

Buzzard Dark Ale (ABV 4.8%)
An old ale brewed with roasted malts. Dark and satisfying with a dry, hoppy finish.

Cotswold

Cotswold Brewing Co Ltd, Foxholes Lane, Foscot, Oxfordshire, OX7 6RL
☎ (01608) 659631
☎ 07971 902385
✉ lager@cotswoldbrewingcompany.com
🌐 cotswoldbrewingcompany.com
Tours by arrangement

Cotswold Brewing Co is an independent producer of lager and speciality beers. The brewery was established in 2005 with the intention of supplying quality lagers to the local Cotswold market. Inspiration is drawn from continental Europe. The brewery is housed in an old Cotswold stone barn, part of a working farm estate. More than 60 outlets are supplied. Seasonal beer: Autumn Ale (ABV 4.3%), Winter Lager (ABV 5.3%). Bottle-conditioned beer is also available.

Three Point Eight Lager (OG 1035, ABV 3.8%)

Wheat Beer (OG 1040, ABV 4.2%)

Premium Lager (OG 1044, ABV 5%)

Cotswold Spring

Cotswold Spring Brewery Ltd, Dodington Ash, Chipping Sodbury, Gloucestershire, BS37 6RX
☎ (01454) 323088
✉ info@cotswoldbrewery.com
🌐 cotswoldbrewery.com
Shop Mon-Fri 9am-6pm; Sat 10am-1pm
Tours by arrangement

Cotswold Spring opened in 2005 with a 10-barrel refurbished plant that produces beers brewed using only the finest malted barley, subtle blends of hops and natural Cotswold spring water. All the beers are fermented in traditional vessels using specialist strains of yeast. They contain no artificial preservatives, flavourings or colourings. Seasonal beers: see website.

Old English Rose (OG 1040, ABV 4%) ◆
Beautifully balanced quaffing ale with delicate floral aroma and hints of tropical fruit. Bittersweet finish.

Gloucestershire's Glory (OG 1041, ABV 4.1%)
A golden beer with a distinctive citrus hop nose, mouth-filling malt and fruit and a deep, dry finish. Brewed to celebrate the 1000th anniversary of Gloucestershire becoming a county.

Codrington Codger (OG 1042, ABV 4.2%) ◆
Mid-brown best bitter with the emphasis on malt. Nutty character.

Codrington Royal (OG 1045, ABV 4.5%) ◆
Ruby in colour with dark, sweet malt. Fruity with a hint of dandelion and burdock.

Cottage SIBA

Cottage Brewing Co Ltd, The Old Cheese Dairy, Hornblotton Road, Lovington, Somerset, BA7 7PS
☎ (01963) 240551
Tours by arrangement

The brewery was established in 1993 in West Lydford and moved to larger premises in 1996, doubling brewing capacity at the same time. In 2001, Cottage installed a 30-barrel plant. 1,500 outlets are supplied. The names of beers mostly follow a railway theme. Seasonal beers: Goldrush (ABV 5%), Santa's Steaming Ale (ABV 5.5%, Xmas).

Southern Bitter (OG 1039, ABV 3.7%) ◆
Gold-coloured beer with malt and fruity hops on the nose. Malt and hops in the mouth with a long fruity, bitter finish.

Broadgauge Bitter (OG 1040, ABV 3.9%)
A light tawny-coloured session bitter with a floral aroma and a balanced bitter finish.

Champflower Ale (OG 1041, ABV 4.2%) ◆
Amber beer with a fruity hop aroma, full hop taste and powerful bitter finish.

Somerset & Dorset Ale (OG 1044, ABV 4.4%)
A well-hopped, malty brew, with a deep red colour.

Golden Arrow (OG 1043, ABV 4.5%) ◆
A hoppy golden bitter with a powerful floral bouquet, a fruity, full-bodied taste and a lingering dry, bitter finish.

Goldrush (OG 1051, ABV 5%)

A deep golden strong ale brewed with Cascade hops.

Norman's Conquest (OG 1066, ABV 7%) ◆
A dark strong ale, with plenty of fruit in the aroma and taste; rounded vinous, hoppy finish.

Country Life SIBA

Country Life Brewery, The Big Sheep, Abbotsham, Bideford, Devon, EX39 5AP
☎ **(01237) 420808**
☎ **07971 267790**
✉ **simon@countrylifebrewery.co.uk**
🌐 **countrylifebrewery.co.uk**
Shop 12-4pm daily
Tours by arrangement

The brewery is based at the Big Sheep tourist attraction that welcomes more than 100,000 visitors in the summer. The brewery offers a beer show and free samples in the shop during the peak season (Apr-Oct). A 15.5-barrel plant was installed in 2005, making Country Life the biggest brewery in north Devon. Bottling is now carried out on site. Around 100 outlets are supplied. All cask ales are also available in bottle-conditioned form plus Devonshire Ten-der (ABV 10%). Seasonal beer: Black Boar (ABV 5%, winter).

Old Appledore (OG 1037, ABV 3.7%)

Lacey's Ale (OG 1042, ABV 4.2%)

Pot Wallop (OG 1044, ABV 4.4%)

Golden Pig (OG 1046, ABV 4.7%)

Country Bum (OG 1058, ABV 6%)

Cox & Holbrook EAB

Cox & Holbrook, Manor Farm, Brettenham Road, Buxhall, Suffolk, IP14 3DY
☎ **(01449) 736323**
Tours by arrangement

First opened in 1997, the brewery concentrates on producing a range of bitters, four of which are available at any one time, along with more specialised medium strength beers and milds. There is also a strong emphasis on the preservation and resurrection of rare and traditional styles. Bottle-conditioned versions of draught beers are available at varying times of the year.

Crown Dark Mild (OG 1037, ABV 3.6%) ◆
Thin tasting at first but plenty of malt, caramel and roast flavours burst through to give a thoroughly satisfying beer.

Shelley Dark (OG 1036, ABV 3.6%)
Full-flavoured and satisfying.

Beyton Bitter (OG 1038, ABV 3.8%)
A traditional bitter, pale tawny in colour, malty with Fuggles and Goldings hops.

Old Mill Bitter (OG 1038, ABV 3.8%)
Pale, hoppy and thirst quenching.

Rattlesden Best Bitter (OG 1043, ABV 4%)
A full-bodied and malty best bitter.

Albion Pale Ale (OG 1042, ABV 4.2%)
Refreshingly clean, hoppy ale.

Goodcock's Winner (OG 1050, ABV 5%)
An amber ale, rather malty yet not too heavy, with a sharp hop finish.

Ironoak Single Stout (OG 1051, ABV 5%)
Full-bodied with strong roast grain flavours and plenty of hop bitterness plus a distinct hint of oak.

Remus (OG 1051, ABV 5%)
An amber ale, soft on the palate with full hop flavours but subdued bitterness.

Stormwatch (OG 1052, ABV 5%)
An unusual premium pale ale with a full, slightly fruity flavour.

Stowmarket Porter (OG 1056, ABV 5%) ◆
Strong caramel flavour and lingering caramel aftertaste, balanced by full malt and roast flavours. The overall impression is of a very sweet beer.

Uncle Stan Single Brown Stout (OG 1053, ABV 5%)
Unusual soft malt and fruit flavours in a full and satisfying bit of history.

East Anglian Pale Ale (OG 1059, ABV 6%)
Well-matured, pale beer with a strong Goldings hops character.

Prentice Strong Dark Ale (OG 1083, ABV 8%)
A strong porter.

Crondall

Crondall Brewing Co Ltd, Lower Old Park Farm, Dora's Green Lane, Dora's Green, Nr Crondall, Hampshire, GU10 5DX
☎ **(01252) 319000**
✉ **crondallbrewery@btinternet.com**
🌐 **crondallbrewery.co.uk**
Shop Fri 3-7pm; Sat 10am-4.30pm

Crondall was established in 2005 using a 10-barrel plant in a converted granary barn. The company sells to the general public and to local free houses in the area, and supplies around 75 outlets. Seasonal beers include Easter Gold, Mr T's Wedding Ale, Ghoulies, Rocket Fuel, Crondall's Stocking Filler.

Best (ABV 4%) ◆
A pleasant and uncomplicated bitter. A modest hoppy bouquet and initially bitter palate lead to a satisfying dry, bitter aftertaste.

Sober as a Judge (ABV 4%) ◆
A complex brown bitter, with a noticeably malty aroma. Toffee characteristics combine with a sharp flavour, which leads to an astringent finish but remaining noticeably biscuity throughout.

Mitchell's Dream (ABV 4.5%) ◆
Sweet bitter with a pronounced malty nose. Maltiness remains present throughout with roast and caramel flavours building into a rich rounded aftertaste

Cropton SIBA

New Inn & Cropton Brewery, Woolcroft, Cropton, North Yorkshire, YO18 8HH
☎ **(01751) 417330**
✉ **info@croptonbrewery.co.uk**
🌐 **croptonbrewery.com**
Tours by arrangement

Cropton was established in the cellars of the New Inn in 1984 on a five-barrel plant. This was extended in 1988, but by 1994 it had outgrown the cellar and a purpose-built brewery was installed behind the pub. A brand new state of the art brewery was opened in 2006 that can produce 100 barrels per week. All the beers are available bottle conditioned and are suitable for vegetarians and vegans. Seasonal beer: Rudolph's Revenge (ABV 4.6%, winter).

Endeavour Ale (OG 1038, ABV 3.6%)
A light session ale, made with best quality hops, providing a refreshing drink with a delicate fruity aftertaste.

Two Pints (OG 1040, ABV 4%) ◆
A good, full-bodied bitter. Malt flavours initially dominate, with a touch of caramel, but the balancing hoppiness and residual sweetness come through.

Honey Gold (OG 1042, ABV 4.2%) ◆
A medium-bodied beer, ideal for summer drinking. Honey is apparent in both aroma and taste but does not overwhelm. Clean finish with a hint of hops.

Scoresby Stout (OG 1042, ABV 4.2%)

Balmy Mild (OG 1044, ABV 4.4%)

Uncle Sam's (OG 1046, ABV 4.4%)

Yorkshire Moors Bitter (OG 1046, ABV 4.6%)
A fine ruby beer brewed with Fuggles and Progress hops. A hoppy beer with a fruity aftertaste.

Monkmans Slaughter (OG 1060, ABV 6%) ◆
Rich tasting and warming; fruit and malt in the aroma and taste, with dark chocolate, caramel and autumn fruit notes. Subtle bitterness continues into the aftertaste.

Crouch Vale SIBA

Crouch Vale Brewery Ltd, 23 Haltwhistle Road, South Woodham Ferrers, Essex, CM3 5ZA
☎ (01245) 322744
✉ info@crouchvale.co.uk
🌐 crouchvale.co.uk
Shop Mon-Fri 8.30am-5pm
Tours by arrangement

Founded in 1981 by two CAMRA enthusiasts, Crouch Vale is now well established as a major craft brewer in Essex, having moved to larger premises in 2006. The company is also a major wholesaler of cask ale from other independent breweries, which they supply to more than 100 outlets as well as beer festivals throughout the region. One tied house, the Queen's Head in Chelmsford, is owned. Seasonal beers: one beer available each month, details on website.

Essex Boys Bitter (OG 1035, ABV 3.5%) ◆
Light-bodied bitter with a malty, biscuity taste and an astringent finish.

Blackwater Mild (OG 1037, ABV 3.7%) ◆
A dark bitter rather than a true mild. Roasty and very bitter towards the end.

Brewers Gold (OG 1040, ABV 4%) ◆
Pale golden ale with a striking citrus nose. Sweet fruit and bitter hops are well matched throughout.

Crouch Best (OG 1040, ABV 4%) ◆
Dry, fruity session bitter with biscuity malt taste and pronounced bitterness in the finish.

Amarillo (OG 1050, ABV 5%)
A strong golden ale with a spicy aroma, juicy malt mouthfeel and an extremely long and bitter hop finish.

Crown

Crown Brewery, Hillsborough Hotel, 54-58 Langsett Road, Sheffield, South Yorkshire, S6 2UB
☎ (0114) 232 2100
✉ crown-brewery@btconnect.com
🌐 crownbrewery.co.uk
Tours by arrangement

The brewery was set up in 2001 with a four-barrel plant in the cellar of the hotel. It was sold to Edale Brewery in 2004 and has been owned by the Walker family since 2006. Around 25 outlets are supplied direct. Seasonal beer: Wheetie-Bits (ABV 4.4%), Middlewood Mild (ABV 3.8%), Primrose Pale Ale (ABV 4.2%). Bottle-conditioned beers are also available.

Middlewood Mild (OG 1039, ABV 3.8%) ◆
A dark traditional mild with flavours of chocolate and liquorice, and toffee in the aftertaste.

Hillsborough Pale Ale/HPA (OG 1038, ABV 3.9%) ◆
A straw-coloured bitter with a citrus nose, flowery head and petal undertones.

Traditional Bitter (OG 1039, ABV 4%) ◆
A traditional style, amber-coloured malty bitter.

Primrose Pale Ale (OG 1042, ABV 4.2%) ◆
Fairly bitter yellow ale with medium hoppiness and hints of grapefruit in the aftertaste.

Loxley Gold (OG 1043, ABV 4.5%) ◆
Golden coloured premium pale ale, hoppy with a clean, dry finish.

Stannington Stout (OG 1050, ABV 5%) ◆
Jet black, rich tasting, bitter yet smooth.

Samuel Berry's IPA (OG 1049, ABV 5.1%) ◆
Fairly dark IPA style fruity bitter, with some sweetness in the aftertaste.

Cuillin

Cuillin Brewery Ltd, Sligachan Hotel, Sligachan, Carbost, Isle of Skye, IV47 8SW
☎ (01478) 650204
☎ 07795 250808
✉ steve@cuillinbrewery.co.uk
🌐 cuillinbrewery.co.uk
Tours by arrangement

The five-barrel brewery opened in 2004 and is situated in central Skye, close to the famous Cuillin mountain. The water provides a distinctive colour and taste to the ales. Specials are brewed throughout the year. The brewery is closed in winter. Seasonal beers: Black Face (Easter-Aug), Eagle Ale (Easter-Aug).

Skye Ale (ABV 4.1%)

Glamaig (ABV 4.5%)

Pinnacle (OG 1047, ABV 4.7%) ◆
Amber-gold sweet brew with a light nose and syrupy background.

Cumberland (NEW)

Cumberland Breweries Ltd, The Green, Great Corby, Carlisle, Cumbria, CA4 8LR
☎ (01228) 560899
✉ enquiries@cumberlandbreweries.co.uk
🌐 cumberlandbreweries.co.uk
Tours by arrangement

THE BREWERIES

Cumberland was established in 2009.

Corby Ale (ABV 3.8%)

Cumbrian SIBA

Cumbrian Legendary Ales Ltd, Old Hall Brewery, Hawkshead, Cumbria, LA22 0QF
☎ (015394) 36436
✉ info@cumbrianlegendaryales.com
🌐 cumbrianlegendaryales.com

Old Hall Brewery and its 10-barrel brewhouse were established in 2006 in a renovated Tudor farmstead on the western shores of Esthwaite Water. The brewery was taken over in March 2009 by the Loweswater Brewery with Hayley Barton as head brewer. 50 outlets are supplied. The brewery is currently concentrating on a smaller number of beers while introducing Loweswater's Kirkstile Gold to a wider audience. Other Loweswater beers will be produced at this site in due course. Seasonal beers are available.

LPA (ABV 3.6%)

Melbreak Bitter (ABV 3.7%)

Dickie Doodle (OG 1040, ABV 3.9%)
A golden bitter with distinctive flavour and aroma of American Cascade hops.

Grasmoor Dark Ale (ABV 4.3%)

Buttermere Beauty (OG 1047, ABV 4.8%)
A creditable English lager, full-bodied and fruity with a clean finish.

For Loweswater Brewery:

Gold (ABV 4.3%)

Cwmbran SIBA

Cwmbran Brewery, Gorse Cottage, Graig Road, Upper Cwmbran, Torfaen, NP44 5AS
☎ (01633) 485233
✉ cwmbranbrewery@talktalkbusiness.net
🌐 cwmbranbrewery.co.uk

Cwmbran is a craft brewery on the slopes of Mynydd Maen in Upper Cwmbran in Gwent's eastern valley. Founded in 1994, it is sited alongside the brewer's cottage home. A mountain spring supplies the water used for brewing liquor. An extension to the brewery has increased both capacity and flexibility. Seasonal beers: See website.

Crow Valley Bitter (OG 1042, ABV 4.2%)
Faint malt and hops aroma. Amber coloured with a clean taste of malt, hops and fruit flavours. Bitterness builds with a lasting bitter finish.

Golden Wheat Beer (OG 1045, ABV 4.5%)

Nut Brown Premium Ale (OG 1044, ABV 4.5%)

Pure Welsh (OG 1045, ABV 4.5%)

Four Season (OG 1048, ABV 4.8%)

Full Malty (OG 1048, ABV 4.8%)

Daleside

Daleside Brewery Ltd, Camwal Road, Starbeck, Harrogate, North Yorkshire, HG1 4PT
☎ (01423) 880022
✉ enquiries@dalesidebrewery.com
🌐 dalesidebrewery.com
Shop Mon-Fri 9am-4pm (Off sales only)

Opened in 1991 in Harrogate with a 20-barrel plant, beer is now supplied to around 200 local outlets, via wholesalers nationally and through SIBA's direct delivery scheme. Seasonal beers: see website.

Bitter (OG 1039, ABV 3.7%)
Pale brown in colour, this well-balanced, hoppy beer is complemented by fruity bitterness and a hint of sweetness, leading to a long, bitter finish.

Blonde (OG 1040, ABV 3.9%)
A pale golden beer with a predominantly hoppy aroma and taste, leading to a refreshing hoppy, bitter but short finish.

Old Leg Over (OG 1043, ABV 4.1%)
Well-balanced mid brown refreshing beer that leads to an equally well-balanced fruity bitter aftertaste.

Special Bitter (OG 1043, ABV 4.1%)
A mid-amber beer with a malty nose and a hint of fruitiness. Hops and malt carry over to leave a clean, hoppy aftertaste.

Dane Town

Dane Town Brewery, Lowes Arms, 301 Hyde Road, Denton, Manchester, M34 3FF
☎ (0161) 336 3064
🌐 lowesarms.co.uk

Formerly the Lowes Arms Brewery, re-opened in 2007 as Dane Town, harking back to Denton's Viking roots with the beers named appropriately. Only the pub is supplied. Brewing was being carried out by the nearby Hornbeam Brewery (qv) but the decision has been taken to continue brewing at the pub in the future and all brewing is currently suspended.

Dare

Dare Brewery Ltd, Falcon Inn, 1 Incline Row, Godreaman, Aberdare, CF44 6LU
☎ 07812 366369
✉ info@darebrewery.co.uk
🌐 darebrewery.co.uk
Tours by arrangement

Dare Brewery opened in 2007 using a 5.5-barrel plant in a refurbished barn at the Falcon Inn (run as a separate operation from the pub). Falcon Inn keeps Dare Brewery beers on the bar whenever possible. All cask beers are also available bottle conditioned. Seasonal and occasional beers are also brewed.

Dat Dare (ABV 4.1%)
A reddish-brown beer with good malt and hop character. A rounded flavour with a bitter finish and a hint of chocolate.

Dare Too (ABV 4.7%)
A smooth copper-coloured premium beer with balanced malt and hop flavours. Dry hopped in the cask for aroma.

Falcon Flyer (ABV 5.2%)
Distinctive Sovereign variety hop finish to this full-bodied tawny ale. Strong and satisfying.

Dark Horse

Dark Horse Brewery, Coonlands Laithe, Hetton, Skipton, North Yorkshire, BD23 6LY

☎ (01756) 730555
✉ richard@darkhorsebrewery.co.uk
🌐 darkhorsebrewery.co.uk

Formerly the Wharfedale Brewery, Dark Horse opened in late 2008 with new owners. The brewery is based in an old hay barn within the Yorkshire Dales National Park.

Best Bitter (ABV 3.8%)
This mid-brown bitter has dark malts and fruit on the nose, which continue into the taste. Bitterness increases in the finish, with a spicy hint. Background roast throughout.

Hetton Pale Ale (ABV 4.2%)
A well-balanced and full-bodied golden pale ale, with bitterness on the palate overlaying a malty base. Look for peach, grapefruit and white wine in the estery aroma.

Whip Cracker (ABV 5%)

Dark Star SIBA

Dark Star Brewing Co Ltd, Moonhill Farm, Burgess Hill Road, Ansty, West Sussex, RH17 5AH
☎ (01444) 412311
✉ info@darkstarbrewing.co.uk
🌐 darkstarbrewing.co.uk
Shop Mon-Fri 8.30am-5pm; Sat 9am-12pm
Tours by arrangement

Originally set up in the cellar of the Evening Star in Brighton, Dark Star moved operations to its current site in 2001 on a 15-barrel plant. Three pubs are now owned. The brewery takes it name from a former Champion Beer of Britain winner, which was brewed by one of the founder directors. The range of beers is divided between permanent, seasonal and monthly specials. Around 80 outlets are supplied. Seasonal beers: See website. Bottle-conditioned beer is also available.

Hophead (OG 1040, ABV 3.8%)
A golden-coloured bitter with a fruity/hoppy aroma and a citrus/bitter taste and aftertaste. Flavours remain strong to the end.

Best Bitter (OG 1041, ABV 4%)
A slight malty flavour is complemented by East Kent Goldings hops.

Espresso (OG 1043, ABV 4.2%)

Festival (OG 1050, ABV 5%)
A chestnut, bronze-coloured bitter with a smooth mouthfeel and freshness.

Original (OG 1052, ABV 5%)
Dark, full-bodied ale with a roast malt aroma and a dry, bitter, stout-like finish.

DarkTribe

DarkTribe Brewery, Dog & Gun, High Street, East Butterwick, Lincolnshire, DN17 3AJ
☎ (01724) 782324
✉ dixie@darktribe.co.uk
🌐 darktribe.co.uk
Tours by arrangement

A small brewery was built during the summer of 1996 in a workshop at the bottom of his garden by Dave 'Dixie' Dean. In 2005 Dixie bought the Dog & Gun pub and moved the 2.5-barrel brewing equipment there. The beers generally follow a marine theme, recalling Dixie's days as an engineer in the Merchant Navy and his enthusiasm for sailing. Local outlets are supplied. Seasonal beers: Dixie's Midnight Runner (ABV 6.5%, Dec-Jan), Dark Destroyer (ABV 9.7%, Aug onwards), Daft Bat (ABV 4.9%, Halloween), Starburst (ABV 5.1%, Bonfire Night), Ruddy Christmas (ABV 4.3%, Dec).

Dixie's Mild (ABV 3.6%)

Honey Mild (ABV 3.6%)

Admiral Sir Sidney Smith (ABV 3.8%)

Full Ahead (ABV 3.8%)
A malty smoothness is backed by a slightly fruity hop that gives a good bitterness to this amber-brown bitter.

Albacore (ABV 4%)

Red Duster (ABV 4%)

Red Rock (ABV 4.2%)

Sternwheeler (ABV 4.2%)

Intelligent Whale (ABV 4.3%)

RAMP (Richard's Amazing Magical Potion) (ABV 4.3%)

Bucket Hitch (ABV 4.4%)

Dixie's Bollards (ABV 4.5%)

Dr Griffin's Mermaid (ABV 4.5%)

Old Gaffer (ABV 4.5%)

Galleon (ABV 4.7%)
A tasty, golden, smooth, full-bodied ale with fruity hops and consistent malt. The thirst-quenching bitterness lingers into a well-balanced finish.

Twin Screw (ABV 5.1%)
A fruity, rose-hip tasting beer, red in colour. Good malt presence with a dry, hoppy bitterness coming through in the finish.

Dartmoor SIBA

Dartmoor Brewery Ltd, The Brewery, Station Road, Princetown, Dartmoor, Devon, PL20 6QX
☎ (01822) 890789
🌐 jailale.com

Established in 1994, it is the highest brewery in England at 1,400 feet above sea level. It moved into a new purpose-built building in 2005 with equipment manufactured in Germany. The capacity is now 180 barrels a week with scope for further expansion. The brewery changed name from Princetown to Dartmoor in May 2008 with no change to the structure or ownership of the company. Bottle-conditioned ales are available.

Dartmoor IPA (OG 1039, ABV 4%)
There is a flowery hop aroma and taste with a bitter aftertaste to this full-bodied, amber-coloured beer.

Jail Ale (OG 1047, ABV 4.8%)
Hops and fruit predominate in the flavour of this mid-brown beer, which has a slightly sweet aftertaste.

Dartmouth

Dartmouth Brewery, Dartmouth Inn, 63 East Street, Newton Abbot, Devon, TQ12 2JP
☎ 07969 860184
✉ kieran.aylward@ntlworld.com
Tours by arrangement

Dartmouth Brewery was established in 2007. Around 15 outlets are supplied direct. More beers are planned.

Ranger (OG 1042, ABV 4.2%)

Golden Showers (OG 1045, ABV 4.5%)

Big 5 (OG 1050, ABV 5%)

Summer Solstice (OG 1080, ABV 8%)

Darwin SIBA

Darwin Brewery Ltd, 63 Back Tatham Street, Sunderland, Tyne & Wear, SR1 2QE
☎ (0191) 514 4746
✉ info@darwinbrewery.com
🌐 darwinbrewery.com
Tours by arrangement (based at Brewlab)

The Darwin Brewery first brewed in 1994 and expanded with the construction of its Wearside brewery in central Sunderland in 2002 after a move from the Hodges brewhouse in Crook, Co Durham. Darwin specialises in recreations of past beers and also produces trial beers from the Brewlab training and research unit at the University of Sunderland, and experiments in the production of novel and overseas styles for occasional production. Output from the brewery grew significantly in 2005. The brewery also produces the beers of the closed High Force Brewery in Teesdale. A changing portfolio of unique brews (developed by Brewlab) is available in limited edition bottles.

Sunderland Best (OG 1041, ABV 3.9%)
A light and smooth-tasting session bitter, full of hop character and moderate bitterness. Amber malt provides a smooth body and creamy character.

Evolution Ale (OG 1041, ABV 4%)
A dark amber, full-bodied bitter with a malty flavour and a clean, bitter aftertaste.

Ghost Ale (OG 1041, ABV 4.1%)

Richmond Ale (OG 1047, ABV 4.5%)

Rolling Hitch (OG 1055, ABV 5.2%)

Killer Bee (OG 1065, ABV 6%)
A strong but light ale matured with honey.

Extinction Ale (OG 1084, ABV 8.3%)

For High Force Hotel:

Forest XB (OG 1044, ABV 4.2%)

Cauldron Snout (OG 1056, ABV 5.6%)

Deeside

Deeside Brewery, Deeside Activity Park, Dess, Aboyne, Aberdeenshire, AB34 5RD
☎ (01339) 883536
☎ 07966 033457
✉ info@deesidebrewery.com
🌐 deesidebrewery.co.uk
Tours by arrangement

Formerly Hillside Brewery. Business consultant and home brewer Rob James established Hillside Brewery in 2005 and began selling his bottle-conditioned beers into local food outlets in early 2006. Installation of a 10-barrel plant at Deeside Activity Park means the beers can now reach a wider audience. 40 outlets are supplied direct. Seasonal beer: Lady Macbeth (ABV 3.7%, summer). Bottle-conditioned beers are also available and are suitable for vegetarians and vegans.

Brude (OG 1032, ABV 3.5%)

Lulach (OG 1036, ABV 4%)

Macbeth (OG 1039, ABV 4.3%)

Talorcan (OG 1047, ABV 4.5%)

Broichan (OG 1047, ABV 5.2%)

Dent SIBA

Dent Brewery Ltd, Hollins, Cowgill, Sedbergh, Cumbria, LA10 5TQ
☎ (015396) 25326
✉ paul@dentbrewery.co.uk
🌐 dentbrewery.co.uk

Dent was set up in 1990 in a converted barn next to a former farmhouse in the Yorkshire Dales National Park. In 2005 the brewery was completely refurbished and capacity expanded. Two pubs are owned. Monthly specials are produced, all at ABV 4.5%.

Bitter (OG 1036, ABV 3.7%)
Fruity throughout and lightly hopped. This beer has a pervading earthiness. A short, bitter finish.

Aviator (OG 1038, ABV 4%)
This medium-bodied amber ale is characterised by strong citrus and hoppy flavours that develop into a long bitter finish.

Rambrau (OG 1039, ABV 4.2%)
A cask-conditioned lager.

Ramsbottom Strong Ale (OG 1044, ABV 4.5%)
This complex, mid-brown beer has a warming, dry, bitter finish to follow its unusual combination of roast, bitter, fruity and sweet flavours.

Kamikaze (OG 1048, ABV 5%)
Hops and fruit dominate this full-bodied, golden, strong bitter, with a dry bitterness growing in the aftertaste.

T'Owd Tup (OG 1058, ABV 6%)
A rich, full-flavoured, strong stout with a coffee aroma. The dominant roast character is balanced by a warming sweetness and a raisiny, fruitcake taste that linger on into the finish.

Derby SIBA

Derby Brewing Co Ltd, Masons Place Business Park, Nottingham Road, Derby, Derbyshire, DE21 6AQ
☎ (01332) 242888
☎ 07887 556788
✉ sales@derbybrewing.co.uk
🌐 derbybrewing.co.uk
Tours by arrangement

A purpose-built brewery, established 2004, in the varnish workshop of the old Masons Paintworks by owner/brewer Trevor Harris, former brewer at the Brunswick Inn, Derby. The business has grown massively over the years and the brewery has recently purchased its first pub, the Brewery Tap, Derby's Royal Standard, which was local CAMRA City Pub of the Year 2009. More than 180 outlets are supplied. Seasonal beer: White Christmas (ABV 5.5%), Christmas Porter (ABV 5%). Two new beers are brewed each month.

Hop Till You Drop (OG 1039, ABV 3.9%)

Triple Hop (OG 1041, ABV 4.1%)

Business As Usual (OG 1044, ABV 4.4%)

Dashingly Dark (OG 1045, ABV 4.5%)

Double Mash (OG 1046, ABV 4.6%)

Penny's Porter (OG 1046, ABV 4.6%)

Old Intentional (OG 1050, ABV 5%)

Derventio

Derventio Brewery Ltd, The Brewhouse, Trusley Brook Farm, Trusley, Derbyshire, DE6 5JP
☎ (01283) 733111
✉ enquiries@derventiobrewery.co.uk
🌐 derventiobrewery.co.uk
Shop Mon-Fri 10am-4pm; Sat 10am-2pm
Tours by arrangement

Derventio Brewery was established in 2005 and first brewed in early 2006. A shop and management training centre opened in 2008, followed by a brewery tap, which is available for hire. The brewery is involved in sponsorship of local cricket teams as well as numerous outside events. Derventio are also one of the founder members of the Derbyshire Brewers Collective. Seasonal beers: Barbarian (ABV 5.5%), Winter Solstice (ABV 5%), Summer Solstice (ABV 4%), Cleopatra (ABV 5%).

Roman Pale Ale (ABV 3.6%)

Aquilifer (ABV 3.8%)

Maia Mild (ABV 4%)

Cupid (ABV 4.1%)

Emperors Whim (ABV 4.2%)

Centurion (OG 1042, ABV 4.3%)

Arminius (ABV 5%)

Venus (OG 1048, ABV 5%)

Caesar (ABV 6%)

Vesuvius (ABV 6.5%)

Derwent Rose

See Consett Ale Works

Derwent

Derwent Brewery Co, Units 2a/2b, Station Road Industrial Estate, Silloth, Cumbria, CA7 4AG
☎ (01697) 331522
Tours by arrangement

Derwent was set up in 1996 in Cockermouth and moved to Silloth in 1998. Derwent supplies beers throughout the north of England, with outlets in Cheshire, Cumbria, Lancashire, Yorkshire and the North-east. It is involved with the Silloth Beer Festival every September and has supplied Carlisle State Bitter to the House of Commons, a beer that recreates one produced by the former state-owned Carlisle Brewery. Seasonal beers: Summer Rose (ABV 4.2%, Jun-Aug), Spring Time (ABV 4.3%, Mar-May), Harvester (ABV 4.3%, Sep), Winter Gold (ABV 4.1%, Oct-Dec), Auld Kendal (ABV 5.7%, Dec).

Carlisle State Bitter (OG 1037, ABV 3.7%)
Amber bitter with a fruity mouthfeeel and slightly astringent bitterness that fades in the finish.

Parsons Pledge (OG 1040, ABV 4%)

Hofbrau (OG 1040, ABV 4.2%)

W&M Pale Ale (OG 1042, ABV 4.4%)
A sweet, fruity, hoppy beer with a bitter finish.

Devil's Dyke

Devil's Dyke Brewery, Dyke's End, 8 Fair Green, Reach, Cambridgeshire, CB25 0JD
☎ (01638) 743816
Tours by arrangement

Devil's Dyke came on stream in 2007 using a plant bought from the Red Rose Brewery. It is situated in outbuildings to the rear of the Dyke's End pub, the freehold of which was bought by the village in the late 1990s to save it from being turned back into a private house. Several outlets are supplied in the area. Seasonal beer: IPA (ABV 5.5%).

Bitter (OG 1036.7, ABV 3.8%)

No. 7 Pale Ale (OG 1039.8, ABV 4.1%)

Victorian (OG 1044, ABV 4.7%)

Strong Mild (OG 1049, ABV 5%)

Devon

Devon Ales Ltd, Mansfield Arms, 7 Main Street, Sauchie, Clackmannanshire, FK10 3JR
☎ (01259) 722020
✉ info@devonales.com
🌐 devonales.com
Tours by arrangement

Established in 1992 to produce high quality cask ales for the Mansfield Arms, Sauchie, Devon is the oldest operating brewery in the county. A second pub, The Inn at Muckhart, was purchased in 1994.

Original (OG 1038, ABV 3.8%)

Thick Black (OG 1042, ABV 4.2%)

Pride (OG 1046, ABV 4.8%)

Devon Earth

Devon Earth Brewery, 7 Fernham Terrace, Torquay Road, Paignton, Devon, TQ3 2AQ
☎ (01803) 525778
✉ info@devonearthbrewery.co.uk
🌐 devonearthbrewery.co.uk

Devon Earth was launched in 2008 on a 2.5-barrel plant and supplies local pubs and beer festivals. Seasonal specials are also available, bottle conditioned or in cask.

Devon Earth (ABV 4%)

Lost in the Woods (ABV 4.7%)

Grounded (ABV 5.2%)

Digfield

Digfield Ales, North Lodge Farm, Barnwell, Peterborough, Cambridgeshire, PE8 5RJ
☎ (01832) 293248
🌐 digfield-ales.co.uk

With equipment from the Cannon Brewery, Digfield Ales started brewing in 2005 as part of a farm diversification scheme. Digfield operates on a 7.5-barrel plant run by three partners. It supplies the local Barnwell pub, the Montagu Arms, as well as 30 other outlets.

Fools Nook (OG 1037, ABV 3.8%)
The floral aroma, dominated by lavender and honey, belies the hoppy bitterness that comes through in the taste of this golden ale. A fruity balance lasts.

Barnwell Bitter (OG 1039, ABV 4%)
A fruity, sulphurous aroma introduces a beer in which sharp bitterness is balanced by dry, biscuity malt.

March Hare (OG 1043, ABV 4.4%)
A straw-coloured premium ale with a subtle fruit flavour throughout.

Shacklebush (OG 1044, ABV 4.5%)
Dry tawny bitter with a roasty, astringent finish.

I.P.A. (OG 1046, ABV 4.7%)
A strong flavoured pale ale with a hoppy aroma and a dry, lingering finish.

Mad Monk (OG 1047, ABV 4.8%)
Fruity beer with bitter, earthy hops in evidence.

Discovery

Discovery Ales, Brook Farm, Packington Lane, Little Packington, Warwickshire, CV7 7HN
☎ (01675) 463809

Correspondence: 52 Doris Road, Coleshill, Birmingham, 39, B46 1EJ
✉ simonamanda@btinternet.com

Discovery Ales began brewing on a part-time basis in 2007 on a 2.5-barrel plant.

Pioneer (OG 1039.6, ABV 4.2%)

Darwin's Delight (OG 1041.1, ABV 4.4%)

Lightening Frank (ABV 4.5%)
Light brown in colour with a gently sharp bitterness and clean finish.

Colombus (OG 1043.4, ABV 4.7%)
A copper-coloured, well-balanced beer with a pleasant mouthfeel and smooth bitterness.

Newton's Cream (OG 1044.2, ABV 4.8%)
A pale ale made using only pale malt and hopped with First Gold. An uncomplicated, satisfying ale.

Dynamite (OG 1045.8, ABV 5%)
A copper-coloured beer with a pleasant aroma that drinks below its gravity.

Dolphin

Dolphin Brewery Ltd, The Dolphin, 48 St Michael Street, Shrewsbury, Shropshire, SY1 2EZ
☎ (01743) 350419
✉ mark@dolphin-shrewsbury.co.uk
dolphin-shrewsbury.co.uk

Dolphin was launched in 2000 and upgraded to a 4.5-barrel plant in 2001. In 2006 both the pub and brewery were taken over by present owner Mark Oseland. After pub alterations the brewery was re-opened with a new range of beers.

Dizzy Lizzy (OG 1042, ABV 4.2%)

Ollie Dog (OG 1042, ABV 4.2%)

Donnington IFBB

Donnington Brewery, Upper Swell, Stow-on-the-Wold, Gloucestershire, GL54 1EP
☎ (01451) 830603
✉ info@donnington-brewery.com
donningtonales.com

Thomas Arkell bought a 13th-century watermill in 1827 and began brewing on the site in 1865; the waterwheel is still in use. Thomas' decendent Claude owned and ran the brewery until his death in 2007, supplying 20 outlets direct. It has now passed to Claude's cousin, James Arkell, also of Arkells Brewery, Swindon (qv). He plans to continue brewing Donnington beers at this unique site. Bottle-conditioned beer is available.

BB (OG 1035, ABV 3.6%)
A pleasant amber bitter with a slight hop aroma, a good balance of malt and hops in the mouth and a bitter aftertaste.

SBA (OG 1045, ABV 4.4%)
Malt dominates over bitterness in the subtle flavour of this premium bitter, which has a hint of fruit and a dry malty finish.

Dorking (NEW)

Brewery at Dorking Ltd, Engine Shed, Dorking West Station Yard, Station Road, Dorking, Surrey, RH4 1HF
☎ (01306) 877988
✉ info@dorkingbrewery.com
dorkingbrewery.com
Tours by arrangement

Dorking started brewing in July 2008 and supplies an increasing number of local pubs and clubs. Seasonal beers are planned.

Dry Hop Gold (ABV 3.8%)
A hoppy bitterness dominates this golden-coloured ale but balancing malt is also present. New Zealand hops result in a green hop character. Dry, bitter finish.

Number One (ABV 4.2%)
Hoppy best bitter with underlying orange fruit notes. Some balancing malt sweetness in the taste leads to a dry, bitter finish.

Winter Ruby (ABV 5.2%)
Fruity dark old ale with roast malt evident throughout and raisin and banana notes. Slightly sweet but with dryness coming through.

Dorset SIBA

Dorset Brewing Co, Hope Square, Weymouth, Dorset, DT4 8TR
☎ (01305) 777515
✉ info@dbcales.com
dbcales.com
Shop at Brewers Quay 10am-5.30pm daily
Tours by arrangement via Timewalk at Brewers Quay

The Dorset Brewing Company, formerly the Quay Brewery, is the most recent in a long succession of breweries in Hope Square. Brewing first started there in 1256 but in more recent times it was famous for being the home of the Devenish and Groves breweries. Brewing stopped in 1986 but restarted in 1996, when Giles Smeath set up Quay in part of the old brewery buildings. His beers are available in local pubs and selected outlets throughout the South-west. In 2008 Dorset took over the running of Dorchester's brewpub, Tom Brown's (Goldfinch Brewery). Seasonal beers: Coastguard (ABV 4.1%, spring), Chesil (ABV 4.1%, summer), Ammonite (ABV 3.8%, autumn), Silent Knight (ABV 5.9%, winter).

Weymouth Harbour Master (OG 1036, ABV 3.6%) ◈
Light, easy-drinking session beer. Well-balanced, with a long, bittersweet, citrus finish.

Weymouth Best Bitter (OG 1038, ABV 4%) ◈
Complex bitter ale with strong malt and fruit flavours despite its light gravity.

Jurassic (OG 1040, ABV 4.2%) ◈
Clean-tasting, easy-drinking bitter. Well balanced with lingering bitterness after moderate sweetness.

Steam Beer (OG 1043, ABV 4.5%) ◈
Citrus fruit and roasted malt dominate this complex best bitter, from the first aroma through to the long, lingering finish.

Durdle Door (OG 1046, ABV 5%) ◈
A tawny hue and fruity aroma with a hint of pear drops and good malty undertone, joined by hops and a little roast malt in the taste. Lingering bittersweet finish.

For Goldfinch Brewery (qv):

Stormbroker (ABV 4%)

Tom Brown's (ABV 4%)

Flashman's Clout (ABV 4.5%)

Midnight Sun (ABV 4.5%)

Dorset Piddle

Dorset Piddle Brewery Ltd, Unit 7, Enterprise Park, Piddlehinton, Dorchester, Dorset, DT2 7UA
☎ (01305) 849336
🌐 dorsetpiddlebrewery.co.uk

Dorset Piddle began brewing in late 2007 on an eight-barrel plant. Monthly seasonals are available as are bottle conditioned beers.

Jimmy Riddle (ABV 3.7%) ◈
Pale brown session beer with a good depth of malty flavours for its strength.

Piddle (ABV 4.1%) ◈
An enjoyable, well-balanced bitter with a lingering bitter finish.

Cocky Hop (ABV 4.7%)

Yogi Beer (ABV 4.9%)

Silent Slasher (ABV 5.1%)

Double Maxim

Double Maxim Beer Co Ltd, Maxim Brewery, 1 Gadwall Road, Rainton Bridge South, Houghton le Spring, County Durham, DH4 5NL
☎ (0191) 584 8844
✉ admin@dmbc.org.uk
🌐 maximbrewery.co.uk
Tours by arrangement

⊗ Initially the former Vaux beer, Double Maxim, was contract brewed by Robinsons for this company but in summer 2007 it opened its own 20-barrel plant on the site of the old Canongate Brewery. 100 outlets are supplied direct and four pubs are owned, three serving cask ales.

Maxim Sladek (OG 1038, ABV 3.8%)
A deep golden beer that has a classic hop aroma with a touch of citrus, a full-bodied taste with residual malt flavour and subtle hop bitterness that leaves a lingering, balanced aftertaste.

Samson (OG 1040, ABV 4%)
A distinctive, well-balanced beer with a lingering, smooth flavour.

Ward's Best Bitter (OG 1040, ABV 4%)
A subtle aroma with hop overtones complements the taste of this malty, full-flavoured traditional Yorkshire Bitter.

Double Maxim (OG 1048, ABV 4.7%)
A brown ale with a well-balanced, smooth flavour leaving a pleasant, slightly sweet aftertaste.

Maximus (OG 1062, ABV 6%)
A strong premium ale, dark ruby in colour, with a sweet liquorice taste. Warming and easy to drink.

Dow Bridge

Dow Bridge Brewery, 2-3 Rugby Road, Catthorpe, Leicestershire, LE17 6DA
☎ (01788) 869121
✉ dowbridge.brewery@virgin.net
🌐 dowbridgebrewery.co.uk
Tours by arrangement

⊗ Dow Bridge commenced brewing in 2001. The brewery adheres to using English whole hops and malt with no adjuncts or additives. More than 140 outlets are supplied direct through its own distribution company. The brewery name is derived from a local bridge where Watling Street spans the River Avon; hence beer names given a Roman connotation. Beers are also contract brewed for Morgan Ales. Seasonal beer: Praetorian Porter (ABV 5%, winter). Bottle-conditioned beers are also available.

Bonum Mild (OG 1035, ABV 3.5%) ◈
Complex dark brown, full-flavoured mild, with strong malt and roast flavours to the fore and continuing into the aftertaste, leading to a long, satisfying finish.

Acris (OG 1037, ABV 3.8%)

Centurion (OG 1039, ABV 4%)

Ratae'd (OG 1042, ABV 4.3%) ◈
Tawny-coloured, bitter beer in which bitter and hop flavours dominate, to the detriment of balance, leading to a long, bitter and astringent aftertaste.

Fosse Ale (OG 1046, ABV 4.8%)

For Morgan Ales:

Chedhams Ale (OG 1039, ABV 3.8%)

Downton

Downton Brewery Co Ltd, Unit 11 Batten Road, Downton Industrial Estate, Downton, Wiltshire, SP5 3HU
☎ (01725) 513313
✉ martins@downtonbrewery.com
🌐 downtonbrewery.com

⊗ Downton was set up in 2003 with equipment leased from the Hop Back Brewery (qv). The brewery has a 20-barrel brew length and has recently expanded its capacity by installing a third 20-barrel fermenting vessel. A different monthly special is brewed every month as well as regular and seasonal beers. Specials often include fruit or spiced beers. Around 30 outlets are supplied direct. Seasonal beers: Honey Blonde (ABV 4.3%, spring/summer), Honey Porter (ABV 4.4%, Nov-Dec). Bottle-conditioned beers are also available.

Quadhop (OG 1038, ABV 3.9%)

Elderquad (OG 1039, ABV 4%)

Dark Delight (OG 1052, ABV 5.5%)

IPA (OG 1063, ABV 6.8%)

Driftwood

Driftwood Brewery, Driftwood Spars Hotel, Trevaunance Cove, St Agnes, Cornwall, TR5 0RT
☎ (01872) 552428
✉ driftwoodspars@hotmail.com
driftwoodspars.com
Tours by arrangement

Brewing commenced in 2000 in this famous 17th-century pub. The brewery is based in the former Flying Dutchman café across the road. The original one-barrel plant has been replaced by a customised, five-barrel kit. On changing hands in 2007, Peter Martin, formerly of Bathtub Brewery, was appointed Head Brewer. The range has expanded to six regular beers and an alcoholic ginger beer called Furnace is also produced. Expansion in 2009 means that the beers are more widely available.

Bawden Rocks (OG 1037, ABV 3.8%)

Blackheads Mild (OG 1037, ABV 3.8%)

Blue Hills Bitter (OG 1039, ABV 4%)

Badlands Bitter (OG 1047, ABV 4.8%)

Bolster's Blood Porter (OG 1049, ABV 5%)

Lou's Brew (OG 1049, ABV 5%)

Alfie's Revenge (ABV 6.5%)

Dunham Massey

Dunham Massey Brewing Co, 100 Oldfield Lane, Dunham Massey, WA14 4PE
☎ (0161) 929 0663
✉ info@dunhammasseybrewing.co.uk
dunhammasseybrewing.co.uk
Shop Mon-Fri 10am-5pm; Sat-Sun 11am-4pm

Dunham Massey commenced brewing in late 2007, brewing traditional North-western ales using only English ingredients and no added sugars. The beer range is also available bottle conditioned, which are suitable for vegetarians and vegans. Around 30 outlets are supplied direct. Seasonal beers: Brown Ale (ABV 5.1%, spring), Treacle Treat (ABV 4.1%, autumn), Winter Warmer (ABV 6.6%, winter), Summer Meadow (ABV 4.3%, summer).

Little Bollington Bitter (OG 1036.5, ABV 3.7%)

Chocolate Cherry Mild (OG 1040.5, ABV 3.8%)

Dark Mild (OG 1040.5, ABV 3.8%)

Light Mild (OG 1040.5, ABV 3.8%)

Big Tree Bitter (OG 1040.5, ABV 3.9%)

Milk Stout (OG 1051, ABV 4%)

Stamford Bitter (OG 1044, ABV 4.2%)

Stout (OG 1046, ABV 4.2%)

Deer Beer (OG 1047, ABV 4.5%)

Cheshire IPA (OG 1047, ABV 4.7%)

Porter (OG 1056, ABV 5.2%)

Durham SIBA

Durham Brewery Ltd, Unit 5a, Bowburn North Industrial Estate, Bowburn, Co Durham, DH6 5PF
☎ (0191) 377 1991
✉ steve@durham-brewery.co.uk
durham-brewery.co.uk
Shop Mon-Fri 8am-4pm; Sat 10am-12.00pm
Tours by arrangement

Established in 1994, Durham now has a portfolio of around 20 beers. These are not all available as regular beers – please see website for full list. Bottles and five litre mini-casks can be purchased via the online shop and an own label/special message service is available. 70-80 outlets are supplied direct. Seasonal beers are brewed. Bottle-conditioned beers are also available and suitable for vegans.

Magus (ABV 3.8%)
Pale malt gives this brew its straw colour but the hops define its character, with a fruity aroma, a clean bitter mouthfeel, and a lingering dry, citrus-like finish.

Earl Soham SIBA

Earl Soham Brewery, The Street, Earl Soham, Woodbridge, Suffolk, IP13 7RT
☎ (01728) 684097
✉ info@earlsohambrewery.co.uk
earlsohambrewery.co.uk
Shop is village store next to brewery
Tours by arrangement

Earl Soham was set up behind the Victoria pub in 1984 and continued there until 2001 when the brewery moved 200 metres down the road. The Victoria and the Station in Framlingham both sell the beers on a regular basis, as does the Brewery Tap in Ipswich. When there is spare stock beer is supplied to local free houses and as many beer festivals as possible. 30 outlets are supplied and three pubs are owned. Seasonal beer: Jolabrugg (ABV 5%, Dec). Most of the beers are bottle conditioned for the shop next door and other selected outlets.

Gannet Mild (OG 1034, ABV 3.3%)
A beautifully balanced mild, sweet and fruity flavour with a lingering, coffee aftertaste which will have you coming back for more.

Victoria Bitter (OG 1037, ABV 3.6%)
A light, fruity, amber session beer with a clean taste and a long, lingering hoppy aftertaste.

Sir Roger's Porter (OG 1042, ABV 4.2%)
Smooth and easy drinking porter with an initial roasty flavour which is soon replaced by a sweet, lingering aftertaste.

Albert Ale (OG 1045, ABV 4.4%)
Hops dominate every aspect of this beer, but especially the finish. A fruity, astringent beer.

Brandeston Gold (OG 1045, ABV 4.5%)
A burnished gold coloured beer, full-bodied with a bitter tang.

East Coast (NEW)

East Coast Brewing Co, 3 Clayhouse Yard, Off Mitford Street, Filey, North Yorkshire, YO14 9DX
☎ (01723) 514865
eastcoastbrewingcompany.co.uk
Tours by arrangement

The brewery is a converted stable and coach house. Six beers are produced and around 20 outlets are supplied direct. Beers are also available via wholesalers.

Bonhomme Richard (ABV 3.6%)

Commodore (ABV 4.1%)

John Paul Jones (ABV 4.3%)

High Tide (ABV 5.2%)

Alfred Moodies Mild (ABV 6%)

Empress of India (ABV 6%)

Eastwood

Eastwood the Brewer, Barge & Barrel, 10-12 Park Road, Elland, West Yorkshire, HX5 9HP
☎ 07949 148476
✉ taggartkeith@yahoo.co.uk
Tours by arrangement

The brewery was founded by John Eastwood at the Barge & Barrel pub. 50-70 outlets are supplied direct. Seasonal beers are produced.

Stirling (ABV 3.8%)
An amber-coloured session beer with a pleasant, long-lasting, fruity finish.

Best Bitter (ABV 4%)
Creamy, yellow, hoppy bitter with hints of citrus fruits. Pleasantly strong bitter aftertaste.

Gold Award (ABV 4.4%)
Complex copper-coloured beer with malt, roast and caramel flavours. It has a hoppy and bitter aftertaste.

Black Prince (ABV 5%)
A distinctive strong black porter with a blend of pale and chocolate malts and roasted barley.

Eccleshall

See Slater's

Edinburgh

See Greene King in New Nationals section

Elgood's IFBB SIBA

Elgood & Sons Ltd, North Brink Brewery, Wisbech, Cambridgeshire, PE13 1LN
☎ (01945) 583160
✉ info@elgoods-brewery.co.uk
elgoods-brewery.co..uk
Shop Tue-Thu 11.30am-4.30pm daily (May-Sep)
Tours by arrangement

The North Brink Brewery was established in 1795 and was one of the first classic Georgian breweries to be built outside London. In 1878 it came under the control of the Elgood family and is still run today as one of the few remaining independent family breweries, with the fifth generation of the family now helping to run the company. The beers go to 42 Elgood's pubs within a 50-mile radius of Wisbech and free trade outlets throughout East Anglia, while wholesalers distribute nationally. Elgood's has a visitor centre, offering a tour of the brewery and the gardens. Seasonal beers: see website.

Black Dog (OG 1036.8, ABV 3.6%)
Roast malt and underlying caramel characterise the aroma of this dark brown/red mild. Roast and malt are supported by hints of fruit on a bittersweet palate ending with roast bitterness.

Cambridge Bitter (OG 1037.8, ABV 3.8%)
Malt and hops dominate the aroma of this copper-coloured beer. Well-balanced malt and hops on the palate and in the aftertaste. Long, dry finish.

Golden Newt (OG 1041.5, ABV 4.1%)
Golden ale with floral hops and sulphur aroma. Floral hops and a fruity presence on a bittersweet background lead to a short, muted hoppy and fruity finish.

Greyhound Strong Bitter (OG 1052.8, ABV 5.2%)
A tawny/brown beer with a malty aroma. Malt and raisin fruit on the palate balanced by pleasing dryness. Dry finish with faint malt and hops.

Elland SIBA

Elland Brewery Ltd, Units 3-5, Heathfield Industrial Estate, Heathfield Street, Elland, West Yorkshire, HX5 9AE
☎ (01422) 377677
✉ eands@btconnect.com
eandsbrewery.co.uk
Tours by arrangement

The brewery was originally formed as Eastwood & Sanders in 2002 by the amalgamation of the Barge & Barrel Brewery and West Yorkshire Brewery. The company was renamed Elland in 2006 to reinforce its links with the town of Elland. The brewery has a capacity to brew 50 barrels a week and offers more than 25 seasonal specials as well as a monthly Head Brewer's Reserve range of beers. More than 150 outlets are supplied.

Bargee (OG 1038, ABV 3.8%)
Amber, creamy session bitter. Fruity, hoppy aroma and taste complement a bitter edge in the finish.

Best Bitter (OG 1041, ABV 4%)
Creamy, yellow, hoppy ale with hints of citrus fruits. Pleasantly strong bitter aftertaste.

Beyond the Pale (OG 1042, ABV 4.2%)
Gold-coloured, robust, creamy beer with ripe aromas of hops and fruit. Bitterness predominates in the mouth and leads to a dry, fruity and hoppy aftertaste.

Eden (OG 1042, ABV 4.2%)
A golden, hoppy, citrussy beer.

Nettlethrasher (OG 1044, ABV 4.4%)
Grainy amber-coloured beer. A rounded nose with some fragrant hops notes followed by a mellow nutty and fruity taste and a dry finish.

1872 Porter (OG 1065, ABV 6.5%)
Creamy, full-flavoured porter. Rich liqourice flavours with a hint of chocolate from roast malt. A soft but satisfying aftertaste of bittersweet roast and malt.

Elmtree

Elmtree Beers, Snetterton Brewery, Unit 10, Oakwood Industrial Estate, Harling Road, Snetterton, Norfolk, NR16 2JU
☎ (01953) 887065
☎ 07939 549241
✉ sales@elmtreebeers.co.uk

THE BREWERIES

elmtreebeers.co.uk
Shop Sat-Sun 11am-4pm

Elmtree was established in 2007 using a five-barrel plant and moved in 2008 to new premises. 40 outlets are supplied direct.

Bitter (OG 1041, ABV 4.2%)

Dark Horse (OG 1048, ABV 5%)

Golden Pale Ale (OG 1048, ABV 5%)

Nightlight Mild (OG 1057, ABV 5.7%)
A complex and creamy brew. Strong hints of Irish coffee and kirsch on the palate while the finish combines roast and blackberries.

Elveden EAB

Elveden Ales, The Courtyard, Elveden Estate, Elveden, Thetford, Norfolk, IP24 3TA
(01842) 878922

Elveden is a five-barrel brewery based on the estate of Lord Iveagh, a member of the ennobled branch of the Guinness family. The brewery is run by Frances Moore, daughter of Brendan Moore at Iceni Brewery (qv) and produces three ales: Elveden Stout (ABV 5%) and Elveden Ale (ABV 5.2%), which are mainly bottled in stoneware bottles. The third is Charter Ale (ABV 10%) to mark the celebrations for the award of a Royal Charter for Harwich in 1604. The beer is available in cask and bottle-conditioned versions. The phone number listed is shared with Iceni. The majority of sales take place through the farm shop, adjacent to the brewery. During 2007 the brewery building was restored as part of the development of the outbuilding of the Elveden estate as a tourist attraction. The visitor centre re-opened in summer 2008, giving regular tours – please phone for details.

Empire

Empire Brewing, The Old Boiler House, Unit 33, Upper Mills, Slaithwaite, Huddersfield, West Yorkshire, HD7 5HA
(01484) 847343
07966 592276
empirebrewing.com
Tours by arrangement

Empire Brewing was set up 2006 in a mill on the bank of the scenic Huddersfield Narrow Canal, close to the centre of Slaithwaite. The five-barrel plant produces 20 barrels a week. Beers are supplied to local free houses and through independent specialist beer agencies and wholesalers. Seasonal beers are available, as are bottle conditioned ales.

Golden Warrior (ABV 3.8%)
Pale bitter, quite fruity with a sherbet aftertaste, moderate bitterness.

Ensign (ABV 3.9%)
Pale, straw-coloured bitter made with lager malt, quite floral on the nose with a pine/lemon flavour.

Strikes Back (ABV 4%)
Pale golden bitter with a hoppy aroma and good hop and malt balance with a citrus flavour, very light on the palate. Good session beer.

Valour (ABV 4.2%)

Longbow (ABV 4.3%)
Golden bitter with a well-balanced malt, floral citrus hop aroma. Spicy yet smooth tasting.

Crusader (ABV 5%)
Light coloured ale with distinctive pine/lemon citrus flavour, good hoppy nose with moderate bitterness.

Enville SIBA

Enville Ales Ltd, Enville Brewery, Coxgreen, Hollies Lane, Enville, Stourbridge, West Midlands, DY7 5LG
(01384) 873728
info@envilleales.com
envilleales.com
Tours by arrangement for small groups only

Enville Brewery is sited on a picturesque Victorian, Grade II listed farm complex. Using natural spring water, traditional steam brewing and a reed and willow effluent plant, Enville produce a full range of award-winning beers in an eco-friendly environment. Enville Ale is infused with honey and is from a 19th century recipe for beekeeper's ale passed down from the former proprietor's great-great aunt. Seasonal beers: see website.

LPA (Light Pale Ale) (ABV 4%)
Traditional session bitter; dry and golden with a mellow, hoppy flavour.

Nailmaker Mild (OG 1041, ABV 4%)
A well-defined hop aroma and underlying sweetness give way to a dry finish.

Simply Simpkiss (ABV 4%)

Saaz (OG 1042, ABV 4.2%)
Golden lager-style beer. Lager bite but with more taste and lasting bitterness. The malty aroma is late arriving but the bitter finish, balanced by fruit and hops, compensates.

White (OG 1041, ABV 4.2%)
Yellow with a malt, hops and fruit aroma. Hoppy but sweet finish.

Ale (OG 1044, ABV 4.5%)
Golden ale with a sweet, hoppy aroma. Sweet start when the honey kicks in, but a hoppy ending with a whisky and heather blend; thirst-quenching.

Porter (OG 1044, ABV 4.5%)
Black with a creamy head and sulphurous aroma. Sweet and fruity start with touches of spice. Good balance between sweet and bitter, but hops dominate the finish.

Ginger Beer (OG 1045, ABV 4.6%)
Golden bright with gently gingered tangs. A drinkable beer with no acute flavours but a satisfying aftertaste of sweet hoppiness.

Epping

See Pitfield

Evan Evans

Evan Evans Brewery, The New Brewery, 1 Rhosmaen Street, Llandeilo, Carmarthenshire, SA19 6LU
(01558) 824455
info@evan-evans.com
evan-evans.com
Shop Mon-Fri 10am-4pm
Tours by arrangement

Evan Evans opened in 2004 with a brand new Canadian brewing plant. Additional fermenting capacity was added in 2009, taking brewing capacity to 8,000 barrels per annum. Contract suppliers to Carlsberg Tetley and Marstons. Eight pubs are owned. It is Wales' first Soil Association organic approved brewery. A large range of seasonal ales is available.

BB (OG 1038, ABV 3.8%)

Hwoc Bitter (ABV 4%)

Cwrw (OG 1043, ABV 4.2%)

Organic Export Stout (ABV 4.2%)

Organic Gold (ABV 4.2%)

Golden Hop (ABV 4.3%)

Warrior (OG 1046, ABV 4.6%)

1767 (ABV 4.7%)

Everards IFBB

Everards Brewery Ltd, Castle Acres, Narborough, Leicestershire, LE19 1BY
☎ (0116) 201 4100
mail@everards.co.uk
everards.co.uk
Shop Sat 10am-2pm
Tours by arrangement for parties of 8-12

Established by William Everard in 1849, Everards brewery remains an independent family-owned brewery. Four core ales are brewed as well as a range of seasonal beers – see website for more details. Everards owns a pub estate of more than 160 tenanted houses throughout the Midlands.

Beacon Bitter (OG 1036, ABV 3.8%)
Light, refreshing, well-balanced pale amber bitter in the Burton style.

Sunchaser Blonde (ABV 4%)
A golden brew with a sweet, lightly-hopped character. Some citrus notes to the fore in a quick finish that becomes increasingly bitter.

Tiger Best Bitter (OG 1041, ABV 4.2%)
A mid-brown, well-balanced best bitter crafted for broad appeal, benefiting from a long, bittersweet finish.

Original (OG 1050, ABV 5.2%)
Full-bodied, mid-brown strong bitter with a pleasant rich, grainy mouthfeel. Well-balanced flavours, with malt slightly to the fore, merging into a long, satisfying finish.

Exe Valley SIBA

Exe Valley Brewery, Silverton, Exeter, Devon, EX5 4HF
☎ (01392) 860406
exevalley@supanet.com
Tours by arrangement (for a charge)

Exe Valley was established as Barron's Brewery in 1984. Guy Sheppard, who joined the business in 1991, continues to run the company. The brewery is located in a converted barn overlooking the Exe Valley and Dartmoor hills. Locally sourced malt and English hops are used, along with the brewery's own spring water. Around 100 outlets are supplied within a 45-mile radius of the brewery. Beers are also available nationally via wholesalers. Seasonal beers: Devon Summer (ABV 3.9%, Jun-Aug), Spring Beer (ABV 4.3%, Mar-May), Autumn Glory (ABV 4.5%, Sep-Nov), Devon Dawn (ABV 4.5%, Dec-Jan), Winter Glow (ABV 6%, Dec-Feb). Bottle-conditioned beer is also available.

Bitter (OG 1036, ABV 3.7%)
Mid-brown bitter, pleasantly fruity with underlying malt through the aroma, taste and finish.

Barron's Hopsit (OG 1040, ABV 4.1%)
Straw-coloured beer with strong hop aroma, hop and fruit flavour and a bitter hop finish.

Dob's Best Bitter (OG 1040, ABV 4.1%)
Light brown bitter. Malt and fruit predominate in the aroma and taste with a dry, bitter, fruity finish.

Devon Glory (OG 1046, ABV 4.7%)
Mid-brown, fruity-tasting pint with a sweet, fruity finish.

Mr Sheppard's Crook (OG 1046, ABV 4.7%)
Smooth, full-bodied, mid-brown beer with a malty-fruit nose and a sweetish palate leading to a bitter, dry finish.

Exeter Old Bitter (OG 1046, ABV 4.8%)
Mid-brown old ale with a rich fruity taste and slightly earthy aroma and bitter finish.

Exeter

Exeter Brewery Ltd, 5 Lions Rest, Station Road, Exminster, Exeter, Devon, EX6 8DZ
☎ (01392) 823013
sales@theexeterbrewery.co.uk
theexeterbrewery.co.uk

The Exeter Brewery, formerly named the Topsham & Exminster, remains on the same site amid the beautiful Exminster marshes, where it has brewed since 2003. The brewery has been completely refurbished and re-equipped, providing much greater production capacity and enabling a greater range of ales. More beers are planned in the near future.

Avocet (ABV 3.7%)

Ferryman (ABV 4.2%)

Exmoor SIBA

Exmoor Ales Ltd, Golden Hill Brewery, Wiveliscombe, Somerset, TA4 2NY
☎ (01984) 623798
info@exmoorales.co.uk
exmoorales.co.uk
Tours by arrangement

Somerset's largest brewery was founded in 1980 in the old Hancock's brewery, which closed in 1959. Around 250 outlets in the South-west are supplied and others nationwide via wholesalers and pub chains. Seasonal beers: see website.

Ale (OG 1039, ABV 3.8%)
A pale to mid-brown, medium-bodied session bitter. A mixture of malt and hops in the aroma and taste lead to a hoppy, bitter aftertaste.

Fox (OG 1043, ABV 4.2%)
A mid-brown beer; the slight maltiness on the tongue is followed by a burst of hops with a lingering bittersweet aftertaste.

Gold (OG 1045, ABV 4.5%)
A yellow/golden best bitter with a good balance of malt and fruity hop on the nose and the palate. The sweetness follows through an ultimately more bitter finish.

Hart (OG 1049, ABV 4.8%)

A mid-to-dark brown beer with a mixture of malt and hops in the aroma. A rich, full-bodied malt and fruit flavour follows through to a clean, hoppy aftertaste.

Stag (OG 1050, ABV 5.2%) ◆
A pale brown beer, with a malty taste and aroma, and a bitter finish.

Beast (OG 1066, ABV 6.6%)
A dark beer brewed with chocolate and crystal malts.

Facer's SIBA

Facer's Flintshire Brewery, A8-9, Ashmount Enterprise Park, Aber Road, Flint, North Wales, CH6 5YL
☎ 07713 566370
✉ dave@facers.co.uk
🌐 facers.co.uk
Tours by arrangement for CAMRA groups only

Bragdy Sir y Fflint Facer's (Facer's Flintshire Brewery) is the only brewery in Flintshire, having moved west from Salford in 2006. Ex-Boddington's head brewer Dave Facer ran the brewery single-handed from its launch in 2003 until 2007, when the first employee was recruited. The brewery was expanded to twice the floor space in early 2008. Around 70 outlets are supplied.

Clwyd Gold (OG 1034, ABV 3.5%) ◆
Clean tasting session bitter, mid-brown in colour with a full mouthfeel. The malty flavours are accompanied by increasing hoppiness in the bitter finish.

Flintshire Bitter (OG 1036, ABV 3.7%) ◆
Well-balanced session bitter with a full mouthfeel. Some fruitiness in aroma and taste with increasing hoppy bitterness in the dry finish.

North Star Porter (OG 1042, ABV 4%)

Sunny Bitter (OG 1040, ABV 4.2%) ◆
An amber beer with a dry taste. The hop aroma continues into the taste where some faint fruit notes are also present. Lasting dry finish.

DHB (Dave's Hoppy Beer) (OG 1041, ABV 4.3%) ◆
A dry-hopped version of Splendid Ale with some sweet flavours also coming through in the mainly hoppy, bitter taste.

This Splendid Ale (OG 1041, ABV 4.3%) ◆
Refreshing tangy best bitter, yellow in colour with a sharp hoppy, bitter taste. Good citrus fruit undertones with hints of grapefruit throughout.

Landslide (OG 1047, ABV 4.9%) ◆
Full-flavoured, complex premium bitter with tangy orange marmalade fruitiness in aroma and taste. Long-lasting hoppy flavours throughout.

Fallen Angel

Fallen Angel Brewery, PO Box 95, Battle, East Sussex, TN33 0XF
☎ (01424) 777867
✉ custservice@fallenangelbrewery.com
🌐 fallenangelbrewery.com
Tours by arrangement

The brewery was launched in 2004 by Tony Betts and his wife and has been expanded from a one-barrel to a four-barrel plant. The brewery make bottle-conditioned beers for farmers' markets and shops. Cask ales are planned for festivals. Seasonal beers are produced. Bottle-conditioned beers: St Patrick's Irish Stout (ABV 3.1%), Englishman's Nut Brown Ale (ABV 3.2%), Gamekeeper's Bitter (ABV 3.5%), Cowgirl Lite (ABV 3.6%), Fire in the Hole Chilli Beer (ABV 3.9%), Hickory Switch Porter (ABV 4.3%), Angry Ox Bitter (ABV 5.3%), Howlin' Red (ABV 5.5%), Naughty Nun (ABV 5.6%), Black Cat (ABV 6.1%). All beers are suitable for vegetarians.

Fallons

Fallons Exquisite Ales, Unit 15, Darwen Enterprise Centre, Railway Road, Darwen, Lancashire, BB3 3EH
☎ 07905 246810
✉ info@fallonsales.com
🌐 fallonsales.com

Fallons is a small family brewery established in 2008 with a 10-barrel plant in a unit on railway sidings. It now also has a small test brew plant in the Black Horse, the brewery tap. Beers are supplied to local pubs and festivals. Test and experimental beers appear under the name Graffiti Brewery.

T.J. Fallon (OG 1035.9, ABV 3.7%)

Angel Tears (OG 1036.8, ABV 3.8%)

Lancastrian Gold (OG 1038.8, ABV 4%)

Red Merkin (OG 1038.8, ABV 4%)

Original Dark Night (OG 1041.7, ABV 4.3%)

Dark Prince (OG 1047.1, ABV 4.8%)

Hex Original (OG 1048.8, ABV 5%)

Falstaff

Falstaff Brewery, 24 Society Place, Normanton, Derby, Derbyshire, DE23 6UH
☎ (01332) 342902
✉ info@falstaffbrewery.co.uk
🌐 falstaffbrewery.co.uk
Tours by arrangement

Attached to the Falstaff freehouse, the brewery dates from 1999 but was refurbished and re-opened in 2003 under new management and has since doubled capacity to 10 barrels. Since 2005 Falstaff has also brewed themed monthly specials for the Babington Arms in Derby. More than 30 outlets are supplied.

Fist Full of Hops (OG 1044, ABV 4.5%)
An amber ale with lots of hop.

Phoenix (OG 1047, ABV 4.7%) ◆
A smooth, tawny ale with fruit and hop, joined by plenty of malt in the mouth. A subtle sweetness produces a drinkable ale.

Smiling Assassin (OG 1050, ABV 5.2%)
A copper-coloured beer with sweet malt flavours.

Famous Railway Tavern

Famous Railway Tavern Brewing Co, 58 Station Road, Brightlingsea, Essex, CO7 0DT
☎ (01206) 302581
✉ famousrailway@yahoo.co.uk
Tours by arrangement

The brewery started life as a kitchen-sink affair in 1998 but Crouch Vale Brewery assisted the development and increased production. The brewery expanded in 2006 and it is now able to brew up to 135 gallons of beer a week for the pub, other local pubs and beer festivals. Many of the beers are available bottle conditioned. Seasonal beers are also available. Many of the beers are suitable for vegetarians and vegans.

Crab & Winkle Mild (ABV 4%)
Thin-bodied mild with a pear drop aroma and a rather roasty taste. The aftertaste is slightly ash-like with suggestions of bitter chocolate.

Bladderwrack Stout (ABV 5%)
Full-bodied stout with an intense roast grain character that is initially underpinned by subtle sweetness, which subsides to leave a drier finish.

Farmer's Ales EAB

Farmer's Ales, Stable Brewery, Silver Street, Maldon, Essex, CM9 4QE
☎ (01621) 851000
info@maldonbrewing.co.uk
maldonbrewing.co.uk
Shop open for beer sales at the brewery
Tours by arrangement for small parties only

Situated in a restored stable block behind the historic Blue Boar Hotel, this eight-barrel brewery started in 2002 and continues to enjoy success in local pubs and beer festivals. The beers are available at the Blue Boar, selected Gray & Sons houses as well as in a number of local pubs. Other outlets are supplied through Crouch Vale Brewery. All cask beers are available in bottle-conditioned form from the brewery and other local shops. Eight seasonal beers are also produced.

Drop of Nelson's Blood (OG 1038, ABV 3.8%)
Red-brown session bitter. Initially quite sweet and fruity, with a pleasing bite to the aftertaste.

Hotel Porter (OG 1041, ABV 4.1%)
Roast grain dominates this oatmeal stout, but an unusual fresh hop character is evident.

Pucks Folly (OG 1042, ABV 4.2%)
Pale golden ale with spicy notes and sweet fruit. Biscuity malt in the taste fades and the finish is dominated by bitterness.

Captain Ann (OG 1045, ABV 4.5%)
A deep ruby traditional malty best bitter.

Golden Boar (OG 1050, ABV 5%)
Powerful, deep-golden ale. The hop character is initially full and citrus, but becomes more spicy in the aftertaste.

Farnham

Farnham Brewery, Claverton Marketing Ltd, t/a The Ball & Wicket Public House, 104 Upper Hale Road, Farnham, Surrey, GU9 0PB
☎ (01252) 735278
ballwick@ntlworld.com

The Farnham Brewery opened in 2006 and supplies the Ball & Wicket pub as well as around 10 other local outlets. Seasonal beers: Honeymoon (ABV 6.5%, Feb), Elderflower Spring Ale (ABV 6.3%, Apr-May), Rockin' Robin (ABV 6.5%, Aug-Sep).

Bishop Sumner (OG 1040, ABV 3.8%)

William Cobbett (ABV 4.3%)

Mike Hawthorn (OG 1055, ABV 5.3%)

Far North

Far North Brewery, 1 Keoltag Drive, Reay, KW14 7SD
☎ (01847) 811118
info@farnorthbrewery.co.uk
farnorthbrewery.co.uk

Originally at the Melvich Hotel, Far North is now a part-time operation based at the brewer's home. Two bottled beers are contract brewed in Scotland; Real Mackay (ABV 4.5%) and Caithness Gold (ABV 4%).

Fat Cat

Fat Cat Brewing Co, Cider Shed, 98-100 Lawson Road, Norwich, Norfolk, NR3 4LF
☎ (01603) 788508 / 624364
☎ 07816 672397
norfolkcottagebeers@tiscali.co.uk
fatcatbrewery.co.uk
Tours by arrangement

Fat Cat Brewery was founded by the owner of the Fat Cat free house in Norwich. Brewing started in 2005 at the Fat Cat's sister pub, the Shed, under the supervision and management of former Woodforde's owner Ray Ashworth. Seasonal beers: Stout Cat (ABV 4.6%), Fat Cat Porter (ABV 5%), IPA (ABV 7%). Bottle-conditioned beers: Top Cat, IPA, Stout Cat.

Bitter (OG 1038, ABV 3.8%)
Abundantly hoppy with a dry bitter finish. Some citrus notes bulk out the hoppy aroma and continue through to the initial taste. Little complexity in the slightly astringent finish.

Honey Cat (OG 1043, ABV 4.3%)
A malty/hoppy brew with a taste of honey. A pleasant, low key mix of malt and hops bound together with a sweetish honey background. Gold coloured with a grainy mouthfeel.

Top Cat (OG 1048, ABV 4.8%)
Wild flowers mix with fruit and hop in the nose of this golden, well-balanced bitter. Hops stand out from but do not dominate the underlying mix of malt, vanilla, and bitterness.

Marmalade Cat (OG 1055, ABV 5.5%)
A complex beer with a growing malt influence over a dry hoppy beginning. Sweet fruity notes in the nose continue into the taste. A heavy grainy feel for such a complex well balanced brew.

Felinfoel SIBA

Felinfoel Brewery Co Ltd, Farmers Row, Felinfoel, Llanelli, Carmarthenshire, SA14 8LB
☎ (01554) 773357
info@felinfoel-brewery.com
felinfoel-brewery.com
Shop 9am-4pm
Tours by arrangement

Founded in the 1830s, the company is still family-owned and is now the oldest brewery in Wales. The present buildings are Grade II* listed and were built in the 1870s. It supplies cask ale to half its 84 houses, though some use top pressure dispense, and to approximately 350 free trade outlets.

Best Bitter (OG 1038, ABV 3.8%)
A balanced beer, with a low aroma. Bittersweet initially with an increasing moderate bitterness.

Cambrian Best Bitter (OG 1039, ABV 3.9%)

Stout (OG 1041, ABV 4.1%)

Double Dragon (OG 1042, ABV 4.2%) ♦
This pale brown beer has a malty, fruity aroma. The taste is also malt and fruit with a background hop presence throughout. A malty and fruity finish.

Celtic Pride (OG 1043, ABV 4.3%)

Felstar EAB

Felstar Brewery, Felsted Vineyards, Crix Green, Felsted, Essex, CM6 3JT
☎ (01245) 361504
☎ 07973 315503
✉ sales@felstarbrewery.co.uk
🌐 felstarbrewery.co.uk
Shop 10am-dusk daily
Tours by arrangement

⊗ The Felstar Brewery opened in 2001 with a five-barrel plant based in the old bonded warehouse of the Felsted Vineyard. A small number of outlets are supplied. Seasonal beers: Rayne Forest (ABV 4%), Chick Chat (ABV 4.1%), Dark Wheat (ABV 5.4%), Xmas Ale (ABV 6%). Bottle-conditioned beers are also available.

Felstar (OG 1036, ABV 3.4%)

Crix Gold (OG 1041, ABV 4%)

Shalford (OG 1042, ABV 4%)

Hopsin (OG 1048, ABV 4.6%)

Wheat (OG 1048, ABV 4.8%)

Good Knight (OG 1050, ABV 5%)

Lord Essex (OG 1056, ABV 5.4%)

Haunted Hen (OG 1062, ABV 6%)

Fernandes SIBA

Fernandes Brewery, 5 Avison Yard, Kirkgate, Wakefield, West Yorkshire, WF1 1UA
☎ (01924) 291709
Tours by arrangement

The brewery opened in 1997 and is housed in a 19th-century malthouse. Ossett Brewing Company purchased the brewery and tap in 2007, and independent brewing continues. The former home-brew shop has been turned into a Bavarian style 'Bier Keller' and sells continental beers as well as real ale. The tap, which has been local CAMRA's Pub of the Year every year since 1999, sells Fernandes and Ossett beer as well as guest ales. Fernandes beers are more widely available through Ossett's supply chain. Many occasional beers are produced.

Malt Shovel Mild (OG 1038, ABV 3.8%)
A dark, full-bodied, malty mild with roast malt and chocolate flavours, leading to a lingering, dry, malty finish.

Triple O (OG 1041, ABV 3.9%)
A light, refreshing, hoppy session beer with a lingering fruity finish.

Ale to the Tsar (OG 1042, ABV 4.1%)
A pale, smooth, well-balanced beer with some sweetness leading to a nutty, malty and satisfying aftertaste.

Centennial (OG 1043, ABV 4.1%)
Light-coloured extremely hoppy beer with a long, lingering aftertaste.

Great Northern (OG 1050, ABV 5.1%)
Pale, citrussy and extremely hoppy.

Double Six (OG 1062, ABV 6%)
A powerful, dark and rich strong beer with an array of malt, roast malt and chocolate flavours and a strong, lasting malty finish, with some hoppiness.

Festival

A.Forbes Ltd t/a Festival Brewery, Unit 17, Malmesbury Road, Kingsditch Trading Estate, Cheltenham, Gloucestershire, GL51 9PL
☎ (01242) 521444
✉ info@festivalbrewery.co.uk
🌐 festivalbrewery.co.uk
Tours by arrangement

⊗ Festival was established in 2007 on a 10-barrel plant. 150 outlets are supplied direct.

Amber (OG 1036.8, ABV 3.8%)
An amber-coloured session beer with a refreshing balance of hops and malt.

Pride (OG 1039.7, ABV 4.1%)
A classic English best bitter giving a hint of berry with a fruity, herbal aroma.

Gold (OG 1042.6, ABV 4.4%)
Refreshing golden ale with sweet floral aroma and a dry finish.

Ruby (OG 1045.5, ABV 4.7%)
A strong bitter, ruby-coloured with a rich and warming character.

Ffos y Ffin

Ffos y Ffin Brewery, Capel Dewi, Carmarthenshire, SA32 8AG
☎ 07838 384868
✉ info@ffosyffinbrewery.co.uk
🌐 ffosyffinbrewery.co.uk
Tours by arrangement

⊗ Established in 2006, the brewery has its own well to provide brewing liquor. The processes used are traditional with no chemical or mechanical filtering. Around 75 outlets are supplied. All beers are also available bottle conditioned.

Cothi Gold (OG 1038, ABV 3.9%)

Cwrw Caredig (OG 1039, ABV 4.1%)

Dylans Choice (OG 1042, ABV 4.4%)

Three Arches (OG 1046, ABV 4.8%)

Towy Ale (OG 1048, ABV 5%)

Paxtons Pride (OG 1053, ABV 5.5%)

FILO SIBA

FILO Brewing Co Ltd, First In Last Out, 14-15 High Street, Hastings, East Sussex, TN34 3EY
☎ (01424) 425079

Office: Torfield Cottage, 8 Old London Road, Hastings, East Sussex, TN34 3HA
✉ office@thefilo.co.uk
🌐 thefilo.co.uk
Tours by arrangement

⊗ The FILO Brewery was established in 1985, with the current owners taking over in 1988. There is a possibilty of the brewery moving to a barn at Torfield Cottage. Two outlets are supplied direct.

Mike's Mild (ABV 3.4%)

Crofters (ABV 3.8%)

Ginger Tom (ABV 4.5%)

Cardinal (ABV 4.6%)

Gold (ABV 4.8%)

Five Towns (NEW)

Five Towns Brewery, 651 Leeds Road, Outwood, Wakefield, West Yorkshire, WF1 2LU
☎ (01924) 781887
✉ malcolmbastow@gmail.com

Five Towns began production on a 2.5-barrel plant in September 2008 and mostly supplies outlets in Yorkshire. Seasonal beers: Indian Summer Ale (ABV 3.8%, Sep), Jimmy Riddle (ABV 3.7%, Oct), Davy Jones' Locker (ABV 3.9%, Nov), Christmas Ale (ABV 4%, Dec).

Outside Edge (ABV 3.9%)
An easy-drinking, light-coloured, lightly-flavoured beer.

Outwood Bound (ABV 4.2%)
A chestnut beer with a toffee nose and strong, dry, bitter finish.

Callum's Best (ABV 4.6%)
A dark-coloured bitter with a full flavour and bitter finish.

Florence

Florence Brewhouse, The Florence, Capital Pub Co PLC, 133 Dulwich Road, Herne Hill, London, SE24 0NG
☎ (020) 7326 4987
✉ enquiries@florencehernehill.com
florencehernehill.com

The Florence has been brewing since opening in 2007 alongside its sister brewpub, the Cock & Hen in Fulham (now closed). Beer is supplied to three outlets, the Florence itself, the Clarence in Balham and the Merchant of Battersea in Battersea.

Bonobo (ABV 4.5%)

Weasel (ABV 4.5%)

Beaver (ABV 4.8%)

Flowerpots

Flowerpots Brewery, Cheriton, Alresford, Hampshire, SO24 0QQ
☎ (01962) 771534
flowerpots-inn.co.uk
Tours by arrangement (small groups only)

Flowerpots began production in 2006. CAMRA members Iain McIntosh and Steve Haigh are the brewers alongside the owner, Paul Tickner. Two pubs are owned and many local outlets are supplied direct.

Pots Black (OG 1033, ABV 3.2%)
A traditional style dark mild; not too bitter and with a hint of smoky malt.

Bitter (OG 1038, ABV 3.8%)
Dry, earthy hop flavours, balanced by malt and toffee. Good bitterness with a hoppy aroma and a sharp finish.

Elder Ale (OG 1038, ABV 3.8%)
A dry beer, very light in colour with a hint of elderflower; refreshing and fragrant.

Stottidge Stout (OG 1048, ABV 4.5%)
A traditional stout with not too much bitterness or hop character allowing the roasted barley flavour to come through.

Goodens Gold (OG 1048, ABV 4.8%)
A yellow-coloured, full-bodied strong bitter. Bursting with hops and fruit in the aroma and taste, leading to a long dry finish.

Forge (NEW)

Forge Brewery, Ford Hill Forge, Hartland, Devon, EX39 6EE
☎ (01237) 440015
✉ dave@forgebrewery.co.uk
forgebrewery.co.uk
Tours by arrangement

Forge is situated in a coastal village near Bideford in North Devon. Dave Lang began brewing in 2008 on a five-barrel plant. 20 outlets are supplied direct. Seasonal beer: Forged Porter (ABV 4.2%, Sep-Mar).

Hartland Blonde (OG 1040, ABV 4%)
A refreshing ale with a crisp, citrus bite and aromas of fruit with a dry, fresh, hoppy finish.

Maid in Devon (OG 1040, ABV 4%)
Copper-coloured ale with a fresh citrus nose and fruity flavours with a powerful, hoppy finish.

Light House Ale (ABV 4.4%)

Dreckly (OG 1046, ABV 4.8%)
A warm, ruby-coloured strong premium ale fortified with gorse and heather, rich in malt with a spicy aroma and a malty aftertaste.

Forgotten Corner (NEW)

Forgotten Corner Brewery, The Stables, Maker Barracks, Maker Heights, Cornwall, PL10 1LA
☎ (01752) 829363

Postal Address: 64 West Street, Millbrook, Torpoint, Cornwall, PL10 1AE
✉ gibsonb45@yahoo.com
Tours by arrangement

The brewery began production in June 2008 and several local outlets are supplied. There are plans to extend the beer range.

J.P. (OG 1038, ABV 3.7%)
Crisp, clean and refreshing pale beer.

Trust Ale (OG 1040, ABV 4%)
A session bitter, full of malty flavours.

Hunters Porter (OG 1054, ABV 5.5%)
Full-bodied, rich, chocolaty molasses with bitterness to follow.

Four Alls

Four Alls Brewery, Ovington, North Yorkshire, DL11 7BP
☎ (01833) 627302
✉ john.stroud@virgin.net
thefouralls-teesdale.co.uk
Tours by arrangement

The one-barrel brewery was launched in 2003 by John Stroud, one of the founders of Ales of Kent, using that name. In 2004 it became Four Alls, named after the pub where it is based, the only outlet except for two beers supplied twice yearly to Darlington beer festivals. Phone first to check if beer is available.

Iggy Pop (OG 1036, ABV 3.6%)
A honey-coloured beer made from pale, crystal and wheat malts and hopped with First Gold and Goldings.

30 Shillings (OG 1039, ABV 3.8%)
A dark session ale made from pale, crystal and chocolate malts with First Gold and Fuggles hops.

Swift (OG 1038, ABV 3.8%)
A dark mild made with pale, crystal and chocolate malts. Hopped with Fuggles and Goldings to give a smooth, pleasant character.

Red Admiral (OG 1041, ABV 3.9%)
A deep red beer that uses pale and crystal malts and is hopped with Fuggles. A malty beer with flowery notes.

Smugglers Glory (OG 1041, ABV 4%)

Tallyman IPA (OG 1041, ABV 4%)
A citrus bitter foretaste gives way to a biscuity and malty aftertaste with further citrus notes.

Fox EAB

Fox Brewery, 22 Station Road, Heacham, Norfolk, PE31 7EX
☎ (01485) 570345
info@foxbrewery.co.uk
foxbrewery.co.uk
Tours by arrangement

Based in an old cottage adjacent to the Fox & Hounds pub, Fox brewery was established in 2002 and now supplies around 50 outlets as well as the pub. All the Branthill beers are brewed from barley grown on Branthill Farm and malted at Crisp's in Great Ryburgh. A new extension has been built, which should double capacity. All cask beers are also available bottle conditioned. Seasonal beers: Nina's Mild (ABV 3.9%), Fresh as a Daisy (ABV 4.2%), Fox's Willie (ABV 4.4%), Cerberus Stout (ABV 4.5%), Heacham Kriek (ABV 5.1%), Punt Gun (ABV 5.9%).

Branthill Best (OG 1037, ABV 3.8%)
Old-fashioned best bitter.

Heacham Gold (OG 1037, ABV 3.9%)
A gentle beer with light citrus airs. A low but increasing bitterness is the major flavour as some initial sweet hoppiness quickly declines.

LJB (OG 1040, ABV 4%)
A well-balanced malty brew with a hoppy, bitter background. The long finish holds up well, as a sultana-like fruitiness develops. Mid-brown with a slightly thin mouthfeel.

Red Knocker (OG 1043, ABV 4.2%)
Copper coloured and malty.

Branthill Norfolk Nectar (OG 1043, ABV 4.3%)
Slightly sweet. Brewed only with Maris Otter pale malt.

Chinook (OG 1043, ABV 4.4%)
A mid amber-coloured beer with hoppy aroma and orangey citrus fruit flavour.

Grizzly Beer (OG 1048, ABV 4.8%)
Honey wheat beer brewed from an American recipe.

Cascade (OG 1051, ABV 5%)
A very light beer with a hoppy flavour.

Bullet (OG 1050, ABV 5.1%)
Pale golden yellow beer with resinous hop aroma and tropical fruit flavours.

Nelson's Blood (OG 1049, ABV 5.1%)
A liquor of beers. Red, full-bodied; made with Nelson's Blood Rum.

IPA (OG 1051, ABV 5.2%)
Based on a 19th-century recipe. Easy drinking for its strength.

Fox Beer (NEW)

Innporter Ltd t/a The Fox Beer Co, The Fox & Newt, 9 Burley Street, Leeds, West Yorkshire, LS3 1LD
☎ (0113) 245 4505
thefoxandnewt@googlemail.com
Tours by arrangement

The brewery was re-commissioned by the ex-Tetley's Head Brewer, Ian Smith, with the first brew being completed in December 2008. The brewery started as a Whitbread malt extract pub in the 1980s, with the mash tun added in the 1990s. Around eight outlets are supplied direct. More beers are planned.

Mr Tod (OG 1043, ABV 4.3%)

Nightshade (OG 1050, ABV 4.9%)

Foxfield

Foxfield Brewery, Prince of Wales, Foxfield, Broughton in Furness, Cumbria, LA20 6BX
☎ (01229) 716238
princeofwalesfoxfield.co.uk
Tours by arrangement

Foxfield is a three-barrel plant in old stables attached to the Prince of Wales inn. A few other outlets are supplied. Tigertops in Wakefield is also owned. The beer range constantly changes so the beers listed here may not necessarily be available. There are many occasional and seasonal beers. Dark Mild is suitable for vegetarians and vegans.

Sands (OG 1038, ABV 3.4%)
A pale, light, aromatic quaffing ale.

Fleur-de-Lys (OG 1038, ABV 3.6%)

Dark Mild (OG 1040, ABV 3.7%)

Brief Encounter (OG 1040, ABV 3.8%)
A fruity beer with a long, bitter finish.

Freedom

Freedom Brewery Ltd, Bagots Park, Abbots Bromley, Staffordshire, WS15 3ER
☎ (01283) 840721
freedom@freedombrewery.com
freedomlager.com
Shop Mon-Fri 9am-4pm
Tours by arrangement

No real ale. Brothers Brewery was established in 2005 by acquiring Freedom Brewery, and specialises in lagers produced to the German Reinheitsgebot purity law. In 2008 it reverted to the name Freedom Brewery Ltd. It currently produces three beers, Freedom Organic Lager (ABV 4.8%), Freedom Pilsener (ABV 5%) and Freedom

Organic Dark Lager (ABV 4.7%). All are suitable for vegetarians and vegans.

Freeminer SIBA

Freeminer Ltd, Whimsey Road, Steam Mills, Cinderford, Gloucestershire, GL14 3JA
☎ (01594) 827989
✉ don@freeminer.co.uk
🌐 freeminer.com

⊗ Founded by Don Burgess in 1992, Freeminer – previously Freeminer Brewery – has grown to be one of the vanguard of the quality bottled beers revival. It has two major national listings and bottled Fairtrade beers are being developed. These are sometimes released on draught. The brewery changed hands in 2006 but Don Burgess remains in post. Bottle-conditioned beers are available (brewed for Morrisons and Co-op). Co-op beers are now brewed with barley grown on Co-op farms and malted at Warminster. Fairtrade and organic beers are also produced, with limited edition cask versions available for Fairtrade fortnight.

Bitter (OG 1038, ABV 4%) ◆
A light, hoppy session bitter with an intense hop aroma and a dry, hoppy finish.

Strip & At It (OG 1035, ABV 4%)

Slaughter Porter (OG 1047, ABV 4.8%)

Speculation (OG 1047, ABV 4.8%) ◆
An aromatic, chestnut-brown, full-bodied beer with a smooth, well-balanced mix of malt and hops, and a predominately hoppy aftertaste.

Frodsham

Frodsham Brewery incorporating Stationhouse Brewery, Lady Heyes Craft Centre, Kingsley Road, Frodsham, Cheshire, WA6 6SU
☎ (01928) 787917
✉ enquire@frodshambrewery.co.uk
🌐 frodshambrewery.co.uk
Shop 10am-4pm daily
Tours by arrangement

⊗ Stationhouse started trading in 2005 in Ellesmere Port. The brewery moved to Frodsham in 2007 and changed its name in 2009. A 5-7 barrel electric and propane powered unit is used to produce the core range as well as seasonal and celebration brews. 115 outlets are supplied direct. Seasonal/occasional beers: see website. Bottle-conditioned beers are also available.

1st Lite (OG 1037, ABV 3.8%) ◆
Light, hoppy bitter with clean lemon/grapefruit hop flavours and the trademark Station House bitterness and dry aftertaste. Clean and refreshing.

Mynza Mild (ABV 3.9%)
A mahogany mild with fruity aftertaste.

Buzzin' (OG 1042, ABV 4.3%) ◆
Golden fruity bitter dominated by a honey sweetness. Good hop flavours in initial taste and a long, lasting dry finish.

3 Score (OG 1043, ABV 4.5%)
An amber malt beer with a fruity tang and long aftertaste.

Nightmail (ABV 4.7%)
A dry, jet black stout. Sharp with a mellow aftertaste.

Aonach (OG 1047, ABV 4.9%)
A typical Scottish style 80/- beer. Dark amber in colour.

Lammastide (OG 1048, ABV 5%)
An amber English wheat beer with distinct elderflower aromas.

Frog Island SIBA

Frog Island Brewery, The Maltings, Westbridge, St James Road, Northampton, Northamptonshire, NN5 5HS
☎ (01604) 587772
✉ beer@frogislandbrewery.co.uk
🌐 frogislandbrewery.co.uk
Tours by arrangement to licensed trade only

⊗ Started in 1994 by home-brewer Bruce Littler and business partner Graham Cherry in a malt house built by the long-defunct Thomas Manning brewery, Frog Island expanded by doubling its brew length to 10 barrels in 1998. It specialises in beers with personalised bottle labels, available by mail order. Some 40 free trade outlets are supplied, with the beer occasionally available through other micro-brewers. Bottle-conditioned beers are available.

Best Bitter (OG 1040, ABV 3.8%) ◆
Blackcurrant and gooseberry enhance the full malty aroma with pineapple and papaya joining on the tongue. Bitterness develops in the fairly long Target/Fuggles finish.

Shoemaker (OG 1043, ABV 4.2%) ◆
An orangey aroma of fruity Cascade hops is balanced by malt. Citrus and hoppy bitterness last into a long, dry finish. Amber colour.

Natterjack (OG 1048, ABV 4.8%) ◆
Deceptively robust, golden and smooth. Fruit and hop aromas fight for dominance before the grainy astringency and floral palate give way to a long, dry aftertaste.

Fire Bellied Toad (OG 1050, ABV 5%) ◆
Amber-gold brew with an extraordinary long bitter/fruity finish. Huge malt and Phoenix hop flavours have a hint of apples.

Croak & Stagger (OG 1056, ABV 5.6%) ◆
The initial honey/fruit aroma is quickly overpowered by roast malt then bitter chocolate and pale malt sweetness on the tongue. Gentle, bittersweet finish.

Front Street

Front Street Brewery, 45 Front Street, Binham, Fakenham, Norfolk, NR21 0AL
☎ (01328) 830297
✉ steve@frontstreetbrewery.co.uk
🌐 frontstreetbrewery.co.uk
Tours by arrangement

The brewery is based at the Chequers Inn and is probably Britain's smallest five-barrel plant. Brewing started in 2005 and three regular beers are produced as well as seasonal and occasional brews. Both cask and bottled beers are delivered to the free trade and retail outlets throughout East Anglia. Seasonal beers: China Gold (ABV 5%, winter), The Tsar (ABV 8.5%, winter), Old Sid (ABV 10.2%, Oct-Mar). Bottle-conditioned beers are also available.

Binham Cheer (OG 1039, ABV 3.9%)

THE BREWERIES

Callums Ale (OG 1043, ABV 4.3%)

Unity Strong (OG 1051, ABV 5%)

Fugelestou

See Fulstow

Fuller's IFBB SIBA

Fuller, Smith & Turner plc, Griffin Brewery, Chiswick Lane South, London, W4 2QB
☎ (020) 8996 2000
✉ fullers@fullers.co.uk
fullers.co.uk
Shop Mon-Fri 10am-6pm; Sat 10am-5pm
Tours by arrangement

Fuller, Smith & Turner's Griffin Brewery has stood on the same site in Chiswick for more than 350 years. The partnership from which the company now takes its name was formed in 1845 and members of the founding families are still involved in running the company today. Three different Fuller's beers have won the Champion Beer of Britain title, Chiswick Bitter, London Pride and ESB. At the end of 2005 Fuller's announced an agreed acquisition of Hampshire brewer George Gale. The company now operates 356 pubs and hotels. Fuller's stopped brewing at the Gale's Horndean site in 2006 and all of the brands, including some seasonals, are now brewed at Chiswick. Seasonal beers: see website. Bottle-conditioned beers are also available.

Chiswick Bitter (OG 1034.5, ABV 3.5%)
Easy-drinking fruity pale brown bitter with a little malty sweetness balanced by a trace of hops on the palate and in the clean, bitter finish.

Discovery (ABV 3.9%)
Light-drinking golden ale with a low aroma. Flavour is of citrus fruit and malt, which fades quickly on the aftertaste. Designed to be drunk cold.

London Pride (OG 1040.5, ABV 4.1%)
A well-balanced pale brown beer with citrus, malt and hops all in evidence on nose, palate and aftertaste. Sharper when fresh; some pleasant creamy toffee notes when older.

ESB (OG 1054, ABV 5.5%)
Tawny-coloured, complex strong beer with bitter marmalade notes overlaid on hops and raisins. A satisfyingly smooth aftertaste that lingers.

Under the Gale's brand name:

Seafarers Ale (ABV 3.6%)
Well-developed fruity malt flavours and gentle bitterness with a satisfying hoppy finish. A donation from each barrel sold goes to the charity Seafarers UK.

HSB (OG 1050, ABV 4.8%)
Good interpretation of the flagship Gale's beer. A sweet, full-bodied bitter with dark fruit aromas and hints of caramel, leading to a bittersweet finish with a hint of dryness.

Full Mash

Full Mash Brewery, 17 Lower Park Street, Stapleford, Nottinghamshire, NG9 8EW
☎ (0115) 949 9262
✉ fullmashbrewery@yahoo.com

Full Mash started brewing in 2003 with a quarter-barrel plant. The brewery has now expanded to four barrels and, with the addition of extra fermenters, 16 barrels a week are now produced. Trade is expanding with five regular beers supplied to 45 outlets.

Ouija (OG 1043, ABV 3.7%)

ESP (OG 1039, ABV 3.8%)

Seance (OG 1041, ABV 4%)

Spiritualist (OG 1044, ABV 4.3%)

Apparition (OG 1046, ABV 4.5%)

Full Moon (NEW)

Full Moon Brewery Ltd, Sharpes Farm, Henley Down, Catsfield, Battle, East Sussex, TN33 9BN
☎ 07832 220745
fullmoonbrewery.com

Full Moon was established in 2008 by James Pryke and Professor Philip Parsons.

Hopdance (OG 1039, ABV 3.9%)
A hoppy, refreshing bitter.

Darkerside (OG 1045, ABV 4.4%)
A rich porter.

Fulstow

Fulstow Brewery, 13 Thames Street, Louth, Lincolnshire, LN11 7AD
☎ (01507) 608202
✉ fulstow.brewery@virgin.net
fulstowbrewery.co.uk
Tours by arrangement

Fulstow operates on a 2.5-barrel plant and started brewing in 2004 in a garage at the home of the head brewer in Fulstow. The brewery moved to Louth in 2006 and was the first brewery to be established there for more than 100 years. 'Fugelstou Ales' are distributed throughout Britain and one-off brews are produced on a regular basis.

Fulstow Common (OG 1038, ABV 3.8%)
A copper-coloured, medium-bodied beer with a strong hop character and malt discernable in the taste.

Marsh Mild (OG 1039, ABV 3.8%)
Traditional mild with a malty aroma. Chocolate malt on the palate with toffee and caramel overtones.

Village Life (OG 1040, ABV 4%)
Ruby red ale with great depth of malt and hop balance.

Northway IPA (OG 1042, ABV 4.2%)
A clean, crisp ale with a citrus aroma; very hoppy with a dry finish.

Pride of Fulstow (OG 1045, ABV 4.5%)
Copper-coloured bitter with a ripe malt taste in the mouth and a good hop balance. A dry finish with blackcurrant fruit notes.

Sledge Hammer Stout (OG 1077, ABV 8%)
Full-flavoured with rich liquorice flavours with fruit and raisins. A satisfying bitter aftertaste.

Funfair

Funfair Brewing Co, Office: 34 Spinney Road, Ilkeston, Derbyshire, DE7 4GL

☎ 07971 540186
✉ sales@funfairbrewingcompany.co.uk
🌐 funfairbrewingcompany.co.uk

Funfair was launched in 2004 at the Wheel Inn in Holbrook. The brewery relocated to Ilkeston and in 2006 relocated again to its present site. A bottling plant was installed in 2007. Over 50 outlets are supplied. Seasonal beers: Elfer Skelter (ABV 4.3%, Xmas), Christmas Cakewalk (ABV 6.5%), House of Horrors (ABV 4.4%, Oct), Roller Ghoster (ABV 4.7%). Bottle-conditioned beers are also available.

Gallopers (OG 1038, ABV 3.8%)

Waltzer (OG 1045, ABV 4.5%)

Dive Bomber (OG 1047, ABV 4.7%)

Dodgem (OG 1047, ABV 4.7%)

Cakewalk (OG 1060, ABV 6%)

Fuzzy Duck

Fuzzy Duck Brewery, 18 Wood Street, Poulton Industrial Estate, Poulton-le-Fylde, Lancashire, FY6 8JY
☎ 07904 343729
✉ ben@fuzzyduckbrewery.co.uk
🌐 fuzzyduckbrewery.co.uk
Tours by arrangement

Fuzzy Duck was started on a half-barrel plant at the owner's home in 2006. It relocated to an industrial unit and expanded capacity to eight barrels. There are plans to introduce a bottle-conditioned range of beers. 30 outlets are supplied.

Thumb Ducker (OG 1040, ABV 3.9%)

Feathers (OG 1040, ABV 4%)

Stout (OG 1042, ABV 4%)

Cunning Stunt (OG 1044, ABV 4.3%)

Fyfe SIBA

Fyfe Brewing Co, 469 High Street, Kirkaldy, Fife, KY1 2SN
☎ (01592) 246270
✉ fyfebrew@tiscali.co.uk
🌐 fyfebrewery.co.uk
Tours by arrangement

Fyfe was established in an old sailmakers behind the Harbour Bar in 1995 on a 2.5-barrel plant. Most of the output is taken by the pub, the remainder being sold direct to around 20 local outlets, including a house beer for JD Wetherspoon in Glenrothes. Seasonal beer: Cauld Turkey (ABV 6%, winter but can be brewed on request all year round).

Rope of Sand (OG 1037, ABV 3.7%)
A quenching bitter. Malt and fruit throughout, with a hoppy, bitter aftertaste.

19th Hole (OG 1038, ABV 3.8%)

Greengo (OG 1038, ABV 3.8%)
Golden coloured with a hoppy aroma and a citrus/bitter taste and aftertaste. Clean and refreshing.

Auld Alliance (OG 1040, ABV 4%)
A bitter beer with a lingering, dry, hoppy finish. Malt and hop, with fruit, are present throughout, fading in the finish.

Featherie (OG 1041, ABV 4.1%)
A light, refreshing, easy-drinking pale ale with a hoppy, lingering finish.

Lion Slayer (OG 1042, ABV 4.2%)
Amber-coloured ale with malt and fruit on the nose. Fruit predominates on the palate. A slightly dry finish.

Baffie (OG 1043, ABV 4.3%)
A pale coloured beer. Hops and fruit are evident and are balanced by malt throughout. A hoppy, bitter finish.

First Lyte (OG 1043, ABV 4.3%)
Clean tasting, light in colour with a good balance of malt and hops. Dry bitter finish.

Weiss Squad (OG 1045, ABV 4.5%)
Hoppy, bitter wheat beer with bags of citrus in the taste and finish.

Fyfe Fyre (OG 1048, ABV 4.8%)
Pale golden best bitter, full-bodied and balanced with malt, hops and fruit. Hoppy bitterness grows in an increasingly dry aftertaste.

Fyne SIBA

Fyne Ales Ltd, Achadunan, Cairndow, Argyll, PA26 8BJ
☎ (01499) 600238
✉ jonny@fyneales.com
🌐 fyneales.com
Shop Mon-Sat 10am-4pm; Sun seasonal
Tours by arrangement

Fyne Ales has been brewing since 2001. The 10-barrel plant was installed in a redundant milking parlour on a farm in Argyll, set in a beautiful highland glen at the head of Loch Fyne. Around 430 outlets are supplied. The range of beers is supplemented by ale brewed for special events. Seasonal beers: Innishail (ABV 3.6%), Somerled (ABV 4%), Fyne Porter (ABV 4.5%), Holly Daze (ABV 5%).

Piper's Gold (OG 1037.5, ABV 3.8%)
Fresh, golden session ale. Well bittered but balanced with fruit and malt. Long, dry, bitter finish.

Maverick (OG 1040.5, ABV 4.2%)
Full-bodied, roasty, tawny best bitter. It is balanced, fruity and well hopped.

Vital Spark (OG 1042.5, ABV 4.4%)
A rich, dark beer that shows glints of red. The taste is clean and slightly sharp with a hint of blackcurrant.

Avalanche (OG 1043.5, ABV 4.5%)
This true golden ale starts with stunning citrus hops on the nose. Well-balanced with good body and fruit balancing a refreshing hoppy taste, it finishes with a long bittersweet aftertaste.

Highlander (OG 1045.5, ABV 4.8%)
Full-bodied, bittersweet ale with a good dry hop finish. In the style of a Heavy although the malt is less pronounced and the sweetness ebbs away to leave a bitter, hoppy finish.

Gale's

See Fuller's

Gargoyles

Gargoyles Brewery, Court Farm, Holcombe Village, Dawlish, Devon, EX7 0JT
☎ 07773 444501

Gargoyles Brewery was established in 2005. A honey beer is planned in the near future. Around 30 outlets are supplied. Seasonal beers: Summer Ale (ABV 3.8%), Humbug (ABV 5%, winter), Devil's Footprint (ABV 4.4%).

Best Bitter (ABV 4.2%)
An amber-coloured beer with a fresh, hoppy aftertaste.

Garthela (NEW)

Garthela Brewhouse, Garthela, Beardwood Brow, Blackburn, Lancashire, BB2 7AT
☎ 07919 847214
✉ garthelabrewhouse@gmail.com
🌐 garthelabrewhouse.co.uk
Tours by arrangement

Garthela began production in December 2008 on a 2.5-barrel plant. Seasonal beers are planned.

Barm Cake Bitter (OG 1038, ABV 3.8%)
Golden-coloured with a malty nose and a clean bitterness through to the finish.

Eccles Cake Ale (OG 1041, ABV 4.2%)
Rich in colour with a hint of ruby. A touch of roast with a clean-tasting, delicate hoppiness throughout.

Black Pudding Porter (OG 1045, ABV 4.5%)
Dark with a velvety sweetness and creaminess.

Geltsdale

Geltsdale Brewery Ltd, Unit 6, Old Brewery Yard, Craw Hall, Brampton, Cumbria, CA8 1TR
☎ (016977) 41541
✉ geltsdale@mac.com
🌐 geltsdalebrewery.com
Tours by arrangement (max. 15 persons)

◎Geltsdale Brewery was established in 2006 by Fiona Deal and operates from a small unit in Brampton's Old Brewery, dating back to 1785. The beers are named after local landmarks within Geltsdale. Around 70 outlets are supplied direct.

Black Dub (OG 1036, ABV 3.6%)

King's Forest (OG 1038, ABV 3.8%)

Cold Fell (ABV 3.9%)

Bewcastle Brown Ale (ABV 4%)

Brampton Bitter (ABV 4%)

Tarnmonath (OG 1040, ABV 4%)

Hell Beck (OG 1042, ABV 4.2%)

Lager (ABV 4.5%)

George Wright

See under Wright

Gidleys

Gidleys Brewery, Unit 5, Gidleys Meadow, Christow, Exeter, Devon, EX6 7QB
☎ (01647) 252120
✉ beer@gidleysbrewery.co.uk
🌐 gidleysbrewery.co.uk

The brewery was set up in 1998 on the edge of Dartmoor National Park and was taken over by Geoff Mann in 2009. Beer range not available at the time of going to press.

Glastonbury SIBA

Glastonbury Ales, 11 Wessex Park, Somerton Business Park, Somerton, Somerset, TA11 6SB
☎ (01458) 272244
✉ info@glastonburyales.com
🌐 glastonburyale.com
Tours by arrangement

⊗Glastonbury Ales was established in 2002 on a five-barrel plant. In 2006 the brewery changed ownership and has recently grown to a 20-barrel outfit. Organic ales are in the pipeline. Seasonal beers: Love Monkey (ABV 4.2%, Feb & Jun), Solstice (ABV 4%, Jun-Aug), Pomparles Porter (ABV 4.5%, Feb-Mar), Spring Loaded (ABV 4.2%, Mar-Apr), Pilton Pop (ABV 4.2%, May-Jun), Black as Yer 'At (ABV 4.3%, Jan-Nov), FMB (ABV 5%, Sep-Dec), Holy Thorn (ABV 4.2%, Nov-Jan), Festivale (ABV 4.6%, Xmas).

Mystery Tor (OG 1040, ABV 3.8%) ◆
A golden bitter with plenty of floral hop and fruit on the nose and palate, the sweetness giving way to a bitter hop finish. Full-bodied for a session bitter.

Lady of the Lake (OG 1042, ABV 4.2%) ◆
A full-bodied amber best bitter with plenty of hops to the fore balanced by a fruity malt flavour and a subtle hint of vanilla, leading to a clean, bitter hop aftertaste.

Hedgemonkey (OG 1048, ABV 4.6%)
A well-rounded deep amber bitter. Malty, rich and very hoppy.

Golden Chalice (OG 1048, ABV 4.8%)
Light and golden best bitter with a robust malt character.

Glenfinnan

Glenfinnan Brewery Co Ltd, Sruth A Mhuilinn, Glenfinnan, PH37 4LT
☎ (01397) 704309
☎ 07999 261010
✉ info@glenfinnanbrewery.co.uk
🌐 glenfinnanbrewery.co.uk

◎Glenfinnan opened in 2007 and operates on a four-barrel plant. It produces around 600 litres per week during the tourist season. Further expansion is planned. Seasonal beer: Dark Ale (ABV 5.2%, winter).

Gold Ale (OG 1040, ABV 3.8%)

Standard Ale (OG 1044, ABV 4.2%)

Glentworth SIBA

Glentworth Brewery, Glentworth House, Crossfield Lane, Skellow, Doncaster, South Yorkshire, DN6 8PL
☎ (01302) 725555

◎The brewery was founded in 1996 and is housed in former dairy buildings. The five-barrel plant supplies more than 80 pubs. Production is concentrated on mainly light-coloured, hoppy ales. Seasonal beers (brewed to order): Oasis (ABV

4.1%), Happy Hooker (ABV 4.3%), North Star (ABV 4.3%), Perle (ABV 4.4%), Dizzy Blonde (ABV 4.5%), Whispers (ABV 4.5%).

Lightyear (OG 1037, ABV 3.9%)

Globe

Globe Brewpub, 144 High Street West, Glossop, Derbyshire, SK13 8HJ
☎ (01457) 852417
globemusic.org

Globe was established in 2006 on a 2.5-barrel plant in an old stable behind the Globe pub. The beers are mainly for the pub but special one-off brews are produced for beer festivals.

Amber (ABV 3.8%)

Comet (ABV 4.3%)

Eclipse (ABV 4.3%)

Sirius (ABV 5.2%)

Goacher's

P & DJ Goacher, Unit 8, Tovil Green Business Park, Burial Ground Lane, Tovil, Maidstone, Kent, ME15 6TA
☎ (01622) 682112
goachers.com
Tours by arrangement

A traditional brewery that uses only malt and Kentish hops for all its beers. Phil and Debbie Goacher have concentrated on brewing good wholesome beers without gimmicks. Two tied houses and around 30 free trade outlets in the mid-Kent area are supplied. Special is brewed for sale under house names. Seasonal beer: Old 1066 (ABV 6.7%).

Real Mild Ale (OG 1033, ABV 3.4%)
A full-flavoured dark mild with background bitterness.

Fine Light Ale (OG 1036, ABV 3.7%)
A pale, golden brown bitter with a strong, floral, hoppy aroma and aftertaste. A hoppy and moderately malty session beer.

House Ale (OG 1037, ABV 3.8%)

Best Dark Ale (OG 1040, ABV 4.1%)
A bitter beer, balanced by a moderate maltiness, with a complex aftertaste.

Crown Imperial Stout (OG 1044, ABV 4.5%)
A classic Irish-style stout with a clean palate and satisfying aftertaste from Kent Fuggles hops.

Gold Star Strong Ale (OG 1050, ABV 5.1%)
A strong pale ale brewed from 100% Maris Otter malt and East Kent Goldings hops.

Goddards SIBA

Goddards Brewery Ltd, Barnsley Farm, Bullen Road, Ryde, Isle of Wight, PO33 1QF
☎ (01983) 611011
office@goddardsbrewery.com
goddardsbrewery.com

Goddards was established in 1993 on a farmstead on the Isle of Wight. Originally occupying an 18th-century barn, expansion has meant that a new brewery was built in 2008. 300 outlets are supplied. Seasonal beers: Duck's Folly (ABV 5%, early autumn), Iron Horse (ABV 4.8%, late autumn), Inspiration (ABV 5%, spring/summer), Winter Warmer (ABV 5.2%, winter).

Ale of Wight (OG 1037, ABV 3.7%)
An aromatic, fresh and zesty pale beer.

Special Bitter (OG 1038.5, ABV 4%)
Well-balanced session beer that maintains its flavour and bite with compelling drinkability.

Fuggle-Dee-Dum (OG 1048.5, ABV 4.8%)
Brown-coloured strong ale with plenty of malt and hops.

Goff's SIBA

Goff's Brewery Ltd, 9 Isbourne Way, Winchcombe, Cheltenham, Gloucestershire, GL54 5NS
☎ (01242) 603383
brewery@goffsbrewery.com
goffsbrewery.com

Goff's is a family concern that has been brewing cask-conditioned ales since 1994. The ales are available regionally in more than 200 outlets and nationally through wholesalers. The addition of the seasonal Ales of the Round Table provides a range of 12 beers of which four or five are always available: see website for details.

Jouster (OG 1040, ABV 4%)
A drinkable, tawny-coloured ale, with a light hoppiness in the aroma. It has a good balance of malt and bitterness in the mouth, underscored by fruitiness, with a clean, hoppy aftertaste.

Tournament (OG 1038, ABV 4%)
Dark golden in colour, with a pleasant hop aroma. A clean, light and refreshing session bitter with a pleasant hop aftertaste.

White Knight (OG 1046, ABV 4.7%)
A well-hopped bitter with a light colour and full-bodied taste. Bitterness predominates in the mouth and leads to a dry, hoppy aftertaste.

Golcar SIBA

Golcar Brewery, 60a Swallow Lane, Golcar, Huddersfield, West Yorkshire, HD7 4NB
☎ (01484) 644241
☎ 07970 267555
golcarbrewrey@btconnect.com
Tours by arrangement

Golcar started brewing in 2001 and production has increased from 2.5 barrels to five barrels a week. The brewery owns one pub, the Rose & Crown at Golcar, and supplies other outlets in the local area.

Dark Mild (OG 1034, ABV 3.4%)
Dark mild with a light roasted malt and liquorice taste. Smooth and satisfying.

Bitter (OG 1039, ABV 3.9%)
Amber bitter with a hoppy, citrus taste, with fruity overtones and a bitter finish.

Pennine Gold (OG 1038, ABV 4%)
A hoppy and fruity session beer.

Weavers Delight (OG 1045, ABV 4.8%)
Malty best bitter with fruity overtones.

Guthlac's Porter (OG 1047, ABV 5%)
A robust all grain and malty working man's porter.

Golden Valley (NEW)

Golden Valley Ales, Main Street, Kingstone, Hereford, Herefordshire, HR2 9HE
☎ (01981) 252988
✉ pauljkenyon@btinternet.com
Tours by arrangement

Golden Valley was set up in 2009 with equipment from the Dunn Plowman Brewery. The owner, Paul Kenyon, previously ran Flannery's Brewery in Aberystwyth and a microbrewery in Kilkenny, Ireland. His brother, Jim, owns the Spinning Dog Brewery. 20 outlets are supplied. Bottle-conditioned beers are planned.

4-10 (OG 1039, ABV 3.8%)

Hop, Stock & Barrel (OG 1044, ABV 4.4%)

Goldfinch

Goldfinch Brewery, 47 High Street East, Dorchester, Dorset, DT1 1HU
☎ (01305) 264020
✉ info@goldfinchbrewery.com
goldfinchbrewery.com
Shop 11am-11pm daily
Tours by arrangement

Goldfinch has been brewing since 1987 and is situated behind the Tom Brown public house. In 2008 the brewery and pub were purchased by Dorset Brewing Co (qv). Eight outlets are supplied. Seasonal beer: Midnight Blinder (ABV 5%, Nov-Feb). All beers are currently brewed in Weymouth by Dorset Brewing Co (qv).

Goose Eye SIBA

Goose Eye Brewery Ltd, Ingrow Bridge, South Street, Keighley, West Yorkshire, BD21 5AX
☎ (01535) 605807
✉ gooseeyebrewery@btconnect.com
goose-eye-brewery.co.uk

Goose Eye is a family-run brewery supplying 60-70 regular outlets, mainly in Yorkshire and Lancashire. The beers are available through national wholesalers and pub chains. It produces monthly occasional and seasonal beers with entertaining names.

Barm Pot Bitter (OG 1038, ABV 3.8%)
The bitter hop and citrus flavours that dominate this amber session bitter are balanced by a malty base. The finish is increasingly dry and bitter.

Bronte Bitter (OG 1040, ABV 4%)
A golden amber well-hopped best bitter with bitterness increasing to give a lingering, dry finish.

No-Eye Deer (OG 1040, ABV 4%)
A faint fruity and malty aroma. Strong hoppy flavours and an intense, bitter finish characterise this pale brown bitter.

Chinook Blonde (OG 1042, ABV 4.2%)
An increasingly tart bitter finish follows assertive grapefruit hoppiness in both the aroma and taste of this satisfying blonde brew.

Golden Goose (OG 1045, ABV 4.5%)
A straw-coloured beer light on the palate with a smooth and refreshing hoppy finish.

Over and Stout (OG 1052, ABV 5.2%)
A full-bodied stout with a complex palate in which roast and caramel flavours mingle with malt, dark fruit and liquorice. Look also for tart fruit on the nose and a growing bitter finish.

Pommies Revenge (OG 1052, ABV 5.2%)
An extra strong, single malt bitter.

Graffiti

See Fallons

Grafters

Grafters Brewery, The Half Moon, 23 High Street, Willingham by Stow, Lincolnshire, DN21 5JZ
☎ (01427) 788340
✉ phil@graftersbrewery.com
graftersbrewery.com
Tours by arrangement

Brewing started on a 2.5-barrel plant in 2007 in a converted garage adjacent to the owner's freehouse, the Half Moon. Several new beers are planned as well as bottling.

Traditional Bitter (ABV 3.8%)

Over the Moon (ABV 4%)

Brewers Troop (ABV 4.2%)

Grafton

Grafton Brewing & Pub Co, Packet Inn, Bescoby Street, Retford, Nottinghamshire, DN22 6LJ
☎ (01909) 476121
☎ 07816 443581

Head Office: 8 Oak Close, Worksop, Nottinghamshire, S80 1GH
✉ allbeers@oakclose.orangehome.co.uk
Shop open during licensing hours
Tours by arrangement

The brewery became operational in early 2007 and is housed in a converted stable block at the Packet Inn. The recipes for the re-named beers were purchased from Broadstone Brewery when that closed in 2006. Around 200 outlets are supplied. The brewery has recently been expanded to a five-barrel plant. Seasonal beers: Snowmans Folly (ABV 4.2%, Oct-Mar), Winters Dream (ABV 4.5%, Oct-Mar), Summer Bliss (ABV 4.5%), Yule Fuel (ABV 4%).

Two Water Grog (OG 1040, ABV 4%)

Lady Julia (OG 1042, ABV 4.3%)

Lady Catherine (OG 1044, ABV 4.5%)

Blondie (OG 1046, ABV 4.8%)

Lady Mary (OG 1050, ABV 5%)

Grain

Grain Brewery, South Farm, Tunbeck Road, Alburgh, Harleston, Norfolk, IP20 0BS
☎ (01986) 788884
✉ info@grainbrewery.co.uk
grainbrewery.co.uk
Shop Mon-Sat 10am-5pm
Tours by arrangement

Grain Brewery was launched in 2006 by friends, Geoff Wright (former Marketing Manager at Adnams) and Phil Halls. The five-barrel brewery is located in a converted dairy on a farm in the Waveney Valley. 80 local outlets are supplied.

Seasonal beers: Blonde Ash Wheat Beer (ABV 4%), Winter Spice (ABV 4.6%).

Oak (OG 1038, ABV 3.8%)
A pale brown beer with a gentle hoppy aroma. A dry, hoppy beer with an increasing bitterness towards the end. Lacking in subtlety.

Redwood (ABV 4.5%)
A dark and malty traditional ale balanced with light bitterness and fruity sweetness.

Blackwood Stout (OG 1048, ABV 5%)

Ported Porter (OG 1050, ABV 5.2%)
A creamy, vanilla-enhanced brew. Well-rounded maltiness flows through both bouquet and taste and gives depth to the creamy, coffee-like roast character. A big, warming finish.

Tamarind IPA (ABV 5.5%)
A classic IPA style beer with an overtly bitter signature. Hops dominate the nose and combine with the bitterness to give a clean, grapefruit dryness. Malt gives both depth and balance.

Grainstore SIBA

Davis'es Brewing Co Ltd (Grainstore), Grainstore Brewery, Station Approach, Oakham, Rutland, LE15 6RE
☎ (01572) 770065
grainstorebry@aol.com
grainstorebrewery.com
Tours by arrangement

Grainstore, the smallest county's largest brewery, has been in production since 1995. The brewery's curious name comes from the fact that it was founded by Tony Davis and Mike Davies. After 30 years in the industry Tony decided to set up his own business after finding a derelict Victorian railway grainstore building. 80 outlets are supplied. Seasonal beers: Springtime (ABV 4.5%, Mar-May), Tupping Ale (ABV 4.5%, Sep-Oct), Three Kings (ABV 4.5%, Nov-Dec). Bottle-conditioned beer is also available.

Rutland Panther (OG 1034, ABV 3.4%)
This superb reddish-black mild punches above its weight with malt and roast flavours combining to deliver a brew that can match the average stout for intensity of flavour.

Cooking Bitter (OG 1036, ABV 3.6%)
Tawny-coloured beer with malt and hops on the nose and a pleasant grainy mouthfeel. Hops and fruit flavours combine to give a bitterness that continues into a long finish.

Triple B (OG 1042, ABV 4.2%)
Initially hops dominate over malt in both the aroma and taste, but fruit is there, too. All three linger in varying degrees in the sweetish aftertaste of this brown brew.

Gold (OG 1045, ABV 4.5%)
A refreshing, light beer with a complex blend of mellow malt and sweetness, balanced against a subtle floral aroma and smooth bitterness.

Ten Fifty (OG 1050, ABV 5%)
Full-bodied, mid-brown strong bitter with a hint of malt on the nose. Malt, hops and fruitiness coalesce in a well-balanced taste; bittersweet finish.

Rutland Beast (OG 1053, ABV 5.3%)
A strong beer, dark brown in colour. Well-balanced flavours blend together to produce a full-bodied drink.

Nip (OG 1073, ABV 7.3%)
A true barley wine. A good balance of sweetness and bitterness meld together so that neither predominates over the other. Smooth and warming.

Great Gable

Great Gable Brewing Co Ltd, Wasdale Head Inn, Gosforth, Cumbria, CA20 1EX
☎ (019467) 26229
info@greatgablebrewing.co.uk
greatgablebrewing.com
Tours by arrangement

Based at the Wasdale Head Inn, the brewery lies at the foot of England's highest mountain (Scafell Pike), near its deepest lake (Wastwater) and its smallest church (St Olaf's). Howard Christie and Giles Holiday set up the five-barrel brewery in 2002. It uses its own spring water from Yewbarrow Fell. Only the Wasdale Head Inn is supplied. Occasional and seasonal beers: Liar (ABV 3.4%), Wry'nose (ABV 4%, Easter-Oct), Lingmell (ABV 4.1%), Brown Tongue (ABV 5.2%). Bottle-conditioned beer is sometimes available.

Liar (OG 1037, ABV 3.4%)
A light mild, gently hopped with a sweet, malty finish.

Great Gable (OG 1035, ABV 3.7%)
Refreshing hoppy, fruity bitter with a pleasant, bitter aftertaste.

Trail (OG 1036, ABV 3.8%)
A light, bright quaffable ale.

Britain's Favourite View (OG 1038, ABV 3.9%)

Wry'Nose (OG 1039, ABV 4%)
Summer ale with a zesty tingle, which mellows as it lingers.

Burnmoor Pale Ale (OG 1040, ABV 4.2%)
A dry, hoppy bitter, refreshing and clean-tasting. Straw-coloured with a fruity taste and grapefruit overtones. Long, bitter finish.

Wasd'ale (OG 1042, ABV 4.4%)
Ruby-coloured best bitter.

Scawfell (OG 1046, ABV 4.8%)

Illgill IPA (OG 1048, ABV 5%)

Brown Tongue (OG 1050, ABV 5.2%)
Northern-style brown ale.

Golden Gill (OG 1046, ABV 5.2%)
A golden ale with a sweet finish.

Yewbarrow (OG 1054, ABV 5.5%)
Strong, mild dark ale with robust roast flavours, rich and malty. Satisfying, with hints of spice and fruit. Smooth, chocolate and coffee aromas.

Great Heck

Great Heck Brewing Co Ltd, Harwinn House, Main Street, Great Heck, North Yorkshire, DN14 0BQ
☎ (01977) 661430
☎ 07723 381002
denzil@greatheckbrewery.co.uk
greatheckbrewery.co.uk

Great Heck began production in 2008 on a four-barrel plant in a converted slaughterhouse. The brewery is planning to expand. 35 outlets are supplied.

Dave (ABV 3.8%)
A smooth, dark, velvety bitter.

Golden Fleece (ABV 3.8%)
A golden session ale with subtle overtones of roasted malt.

Blooming Heck (ABV 4.2%)
An amber best bitter with a light roasted malt flavour.

Yorkshire Pale Ale (ABV 4.3%)
A premium pale ale with a complex malt character and zesty finish.

Slaughterhouse Porter (ABV 4.5%)
Very black, full-bodied porter with a smooth malt character.

Great Newsome

Great Newsome Brewery Ltd, Great Newsome Farm, South Frodingham, Winestead, East Yorkshire, HU12 0NR
☎ (01964) 612201
☎ 07808 367386
✉ enquiries@greatnewsomebrewery.co.uk
🌐 greatnewsomebrewery.co.uk

Nestled in the Holderness countryside, Great Newsome began production in 2007 on a 10-barrel plant, brewing in renovated farm buildings. Beer is distributed throughout Yorkshire as well as North Lincolnshire. Seasonal beers: see website.

Sleck Dust (OG 1035, ABV 3.8%)
Straw-coloured, refreshingly bitter session beer with floral aroma and subtle dry finish.

Stoney Binks (OG 1040, ABV 4.1%)
'Burton' style amber ale, mildly bitter with a mellow finish.

Pricky Back Otchan (OG 1039, ABV 4.2%)
Hoppy amber bitter with fresh citrus aroma.

Frothingham Best (OG 1041, ABV 4.3%)
Dark amber best bitter with subtle dry finish.

Jem's Stout (OG 1044, ABV 4.3%)
Dark, smooth beer with smoky, roasted malt flavours and aroma.

Great Oakley

Great Oakley Brewery, Bridge Farm, 11 Brooke Road, Great Oakley, Northamptonshire, NN18 8HG
☎ (01536) 744888
✉ tailshaker@tiscali.co.uk
🌐 greatoakleybrewery.co.uk
Tours by arrangement

The brewery started production in 2005 and is housed in converted stables on a former working farm. It is run by husband and wife team Phil and Hazel Greenway. More than 50 outlets are supplied, including the Malt Shovel Tavern in Northampton, which is the brewery tap. Seasonal beers: see website. Bottle-conditioned beers are also available.

Welland Valley Mild (OG 1037, ABV 3.6%)
A dark, traditional mild. Full of flavour.

Wagtail (OG 1040, ABV 3.9%)
Light coloured with a unique bitterness derived from New Zealand hops.

Wot's Occurring (OG 1040, ABV 3.9%)
A mid-golden session bitter with a subtle hop finish.

Marching In (OG 1041, ABV 4.1%)
A golden, clean-tasting beer.

Harpers (OG 1045, ABV 4.3%)
Traditional mid-brown bitter with a malty taste and slight hints of chocolate and citrus in the finish.

Gobble (OG 1046, ABV 4.5%)
Straw-coloured with a pleasant hop aftertaste.

Delapre Dark (OG 1047, ABV 4.6%)
A dark, full-bodied ale made from five different malts.

Tailshaker (OG 1051, ABV 5%)
A complex golden ale with a great depth of flavour.

Great Orme

Great Orme Brewery Ltd, Nant y Cywarch, Glan Conwy, Conwy, LL28 5PP
☎ (01492) 580548
✉ info@greatormebrewery.co.uk
🌐 greatormebrewery.co.uk

Great Orme is a five-barrel micro-brewery situated on a hillside in the Conwy Valley between Llandudno and Betws-y-Coed, with views of the Conwy Estuary and the Great Orme. Established in 2005, it is housed in a number of converted farm buildings. Around 50 outlets are supplied.

Cambria (ABV 3.8%)
A modern IPA with a full hop flavour and dry finish.

Welsh Black (OG 1042, ABV 4%)
Smooth-tasting dark beer with roast coffee notes in aroma and taste. Sweetish in flavour and having some characteristics of a mild ale with hoppiness also present in the aftertaste.

Orme (OG 1043, ABV 4.2%)
Malty best bitter with a dry finish. Faint hop and fruit notes in aroma and taste, but malt dominates throughout.

Celtica (OG 1045, ABV 4.5%)
Yellow in colour with a zesty taste full of citrus fruit flavours. Some initial sweetness followed by peppery hops and a bitter finish.

Merlyn (OG 1051, ABV 5%)
A strong ale with balanced hop bitterness and sweet malt.

Great Western

Great Western Brewing Co Ltd, Stream Bakery, Bristol Road, Hambrook, Bristol, BS16 1RF
☎ (0117) 957 2842
✉ contact@greatwesternbrewingcompany.co.uk
🌐 greatwesternbrewingcompany.co.uk
Shop Mon/Wed/Thu 10am-5pm; Fri 10am-6pm; Sat 10am-4pm
Tours by arrangement

Great Western is a 12-barrel brewery set up in 2008 by Kevin Stone in a former bakery. The property has been renovated resulting in a bespoke showpiece brewery retaining many of the buildings original features. 150 outlets are supplied and one pub is owned.

Maiden Voyage (OG 1040, ABV 4%)

Bees Knees (OG 1041, ABV 4.2%)

Classic Gold (OG 1044, ABV 4.6%)

Old Higby (OG 1045, ABV 4.8%)

Green Dragon

Green Dragon Brewery, Green Dragon, 29 Broad Street, Bungay, Suffolk, NR35 1EF
☎ (01986) 892681
Tours by arrangement

The Green Dragon pub was purchased from Brent Walker in 1991 and the buildings at the rear converted to a brewery. In 1994 the plant was expanded and moved into a converted barn across the car park. The doubling of capacity allowed the production of a larger range of ales, including seasonal and occasional brews. The beers are available at the pub and beer festivals. Seasonal beers: Mild (ABV 5%, autumn/winter), Wynnter Warmer (ABV 6.5%).

Chaucer Ale (OG 1037, ABV 3.7%)

Gold (OG 1045, ABV 4.4%)

Bridge Street Bitter (OG 1046, ABV 4.5%)

Strong Mild (ABV 5.4%)

Greene King

See under New Nationals section

Greenfield SIBA

Greenfield Real Ale Brewery, Unit 8 Waterside Mills, Greenfield, Saddleworth, Greater Manchester, OL3 7PF
☎ (01457) 879789
office@greenfieldrealale.co.uk
greenfieldrealale.co.uk
Shop 9am-5pm daily
Tours by arrangement

Greenfield was launched in 2002 by Peter Percival, former brewer at Saddleworth. Tony Harratt joined Peter in 2005 as a partner. The brewery space was doubled in 2008 to provide extra storage and bottling facilities. 100-120 outlets are supplied. Seasonal beers: see website. Bottle-conditioned ales are also available.

Black Five (OG 1040, ABV 4%)
A dark brown beer in which malt, roast, toffee, fruit and chocolate can all be found in aroma and taste. Smooth, malty aftertaste.

Monkey Business (OG 1041, ABV 4%)
Yellow in colour with a fruit and hop aroma. Hops and grapefruit in the mouth, with a dry, astringent finish.

Delph Donkey (OG 1041, ABV 4.1%)

Dobcross Bitter (OG 1041, ABV 4.2%)

Green Jack

Green Jack Brewing Co Ltd, Argyle Place, Love Road, Lowestoft, Suffolk, NR32 2NZ
☎ (01502) 562863
greenjack.com
Shop 9am-6pm daily
Tours by arrangement

Green Jack started brewing in 2003 and moved to a 35-barrel brew house in 2009. 20 outlets are supplied and two pubs are owned. Seasonal ales: Honey Bunny (ABV 4%, spring), Summer Dream Elderflower Ale (ABV 4%).

Canary Pale Ale (OG 1038, ABV 3.8%)

Orange Wheat Beer (OG 1041, ABV 4.2%)
Beatifully balanced with a golden colour. Slightly bitter on the tongue but with a strong fruit flavour and a complex aroma and aftertaste.

Grasshopper Best (OG 1045, ABV 4.6%)

Lurcher Stout (OG 1046, ABV 4.8%)

Mahseer IPA (OG 1048, ABV 5%)

Gone Fishing ESB (OG 1052, ABV 5.5%)

Ripper Tripel (OG 1074, ABV 8.5%)

Green Mill

Green Mill Brewery, Queensway Snooker Club, Green Mill, Well I' Th' Lane, Rochdale, OL11 2LS
☎ 07967 656887
greenmillbrewery@msn.com
greenmillbrewery.co.uk

Green Mill started brewing in 2007 on a 2.5-barrel plant. A number of seasonal and occasional ales are brewed. Around 30 outlets are supplied either directly or through wholesalers.

Gold (ABV 3.6%)

Bitter T'ale (ABV 4%)

Chief (ABV 4.2%)

Northern Lights (ABV 4.5%)

Green Tye EAB

Green Tye Brewery, Green Tye, Much Hadham, Hertfordshire, SG10 6JP
☎ (01279) 841041
info@gtbrewery.co.uk
gtbrewery.co.uk
Tours by arrangement for small groups

Established in 1999 near Much Hadham, on the edge of the Ash Valley. The local free trade and neighbouring counties are supplied, and further afield via beer agencies and swaps with other micro-breweries. Cask beers are also available bottle conditioned. Seasonal beers: Snowdrop (ABV 3.9%, winter/spring), Mad Morris (ABV 4.2%, summer), Green Tiger (ABV 4.2%, summer), Autumn Rose (ABV 4.2%), Conkerer (ABV 4.7%, autumn), Coal Porter (ABV 4.5%, winter).

Union Jack (OG 1036, ABV 3.6%)
A copper-coloured bitter, fruity with a citrus taste and a hoppy, citrus aroma, with a balanced, bitter finish.

Hertfordshire Hedgehog (OG 1042, ABV 4%)
Traditional, chestnut-coloured bitter with a deep, hoppy nose. Starts soft and full with malt fruit flavours and bitterness, developing through to a full bitter finish.

East Anglian Gold (OG 1042, ABV 4.2%)

Gribble

Gribble Microbrewery Ltd, Gribble Inn, Oving, West Sussex, PO20 2BP
☎ (01243) 786893

✉ dave@thegribble.co.uk
🌐 thegribble.co.uk

The Gribble Brewery is more than 25 years old. Until 2005 it was run as a managed house operation by Hall & Woodhouse (qv) but it is now an independent micro-brewery owned by Dave and Linda Stone, the publicans of the inn on the same site. Seasonal beer: Wobbler (ABV 7.2%, Xmas).

CHI P A (ABV 3.8%)

Gribble Ale (ABV 4.1%)

Puzzle's Pint (ABV 4.1%)

Bashful Beaver (ABV 4.3%)

Fuzzy Duck (ABV 4.3%)

Reg's Tipple (ABV 5%)
Reg's Tipple was named after a customer from the early days of the brewery. It has a smooth nutty flavour with a pleasant afterbite.

Plucking Pheasant (ABV 5.2%)

Pig's Ear (ABV 5.8%)

Griffin

Griffin Brewery, Church Road, Shustoke, Warwickshire, B46 2LB
☎ (01675) 481208
Tours by arrangement

Brewing started in 2008 in the old coffin shop premises adjacent to the pub (formerly occupied by Church End Brewery). The brewery is a venture between Griffin licensee Mick Pugh and his son Oliver. At present the brewery only supplies the Griffin Inn and beer festivals.

Slurcher (OG 1041, ABV 4%)

'Ere It Is (OG 1045, ABV 4.5%)

Black Magic Woman (OG 1047, ABV 4.7%)

Pricklee 'olly (OG 1066, ABV 6.3%)

Gwaun Valley (NEW)

Gwaun Valley Brewery, Kilkiffeth Farm, Pontfaen, Fishguard, SA65 9TP
☎ (01348) 881304

Gwaun Valley began brewing in 2009 on a four-barrel plant. They are open for sampling and visitors during business hours.

Light (ABV 3.8%)

Bitter (ABV 4%)

Dark (ABV 4.2%)

Gwynant

Bragdy Gwynant, Tynllidiart Arms, Capel Bangor, Aberystwyth, Ceredigion, SY23 3LR
☎ (01970) 880248
Tours by arrangement

Brewing started in 2004 in a building at the front of the pub, measuring just 4ft 6ins by 4ft, with a brew length of nine gallons. Beer is only sold in the pub. The brewery has now been recognised as the smallest commercial brewery in the world by the Guinness Book of Records. Brewing is currently suspended.

Cwrw Gwynant (OG 1044, ABV 4.2%)

Hadrian & Border SIBA

Alnwick Ales Ltd t/a Hadrian & Border Brewery, Unit 11, Hawick Crescent Industrial Estate, Newcastle upon Tyne, Tyne & Wear, NE6 1AS
☎ (0191) 276 5302
✉ **hadrianborder@yahoo.co.uk**
🌐 **hadrian-border-brewery.co.uk**
Tours by arrangement

Hadrian & Border is based at the former Four Rivers 20-barrel site in Newcastle. The company's brands are available from Glasgow to Yorkshire, and nationally through wholesalers. They are popular on Tyneside; the Sir John Fitzgerald group stocks them regularly. Around 100 outlets are supplied.

Gladiator (OG 1036, ABV 3.8%)
Tawny-coloured bitter with plenty of malt in the aroma and palate leading to a strong bitter finish.

Tyneside Blonde (OG 1037, ABV 3.9%)
Refreshing blonde ale with zesty notes and a clean, fruity finish.

Farne Island Pale Ale (OG 1038, ABV 4%)
A copper-coloured bitter with a refreshing malt/hop balance.

Flotsam (OG 1038, ABV 4%)
Bronze coloured with a citrus bitterness and a distinctive floral aroma.

Legion Ale (OG 1040, ABV 4.2%)
Well-balanced, amber-coloured beer, full bodied with good malt flavours. Well hopped with a long bitter finish.

Newcastle Pioneer (ABV 4.2%)
Light amber ale, well hopped with only Pioneer hops to give a light spicy/fruity finish.

Secret Kingdom (OG 1042, ABV 4.3%)
Dark, rich and full-bodied, slightly roasted with a malty palate ending with a pleasant bitterness.

Reiver's IPA (OG 1042, ABV 4.4%)
Golden bitter with a clean citrus palate and aroma with subtle malt flavours breaking through at the end.

Centurion Best Bitter (OG 1043, ABV 4.5%)
Smooth, clean-tasting bitter with a distinct hop palate leading to a good bitter finish.

Jetsam (OG 1043, ABV 4.5%)
Light-coloured, refreshing and clean tasting. Dry hopped with Styrian Goldings.

Halfpenny (NEW)

Halfpenny Brewery, Crown Inn, High Street, Lechlade, Gloucestershire, GL7 3AE
☎ (01367) 252198
🌐 **halfpennybrewery.co.uk**
Tours by arrangement

Halfpenny was established in late 2008 on a four-barrel plant. Two more fermentation vessels are planned to keep up with demand as are more beers. Bottle-conditioned beers are available.

Ha'penny Ale (OG 1041.2, ABV 4%)

Old Lech (OG 1043.6, ABV 4.5%)

Halifax Steam

Halifax Steam Brewing Co Ltd, The Conclave, Southedge Works, Brighouse Road, Hipperholme, West Yorkshire, HX3 8EF

☎ 07974 544980
✉ david@halifax-steam.co.uk
🌐 halifax-steam.co.uk

Halifax Steam was established in 2001 on a five-barrel plant and only supplies its brewery tap, the Cock o' the North, which is adjacent to the brewery. Approximately 100 different rotating beers are produced, three of which are permanent. The brewery also produces the only rice beers in the country. 10 Halifax Steam beers are available at any one time, plus occasional guests on a fair trade basis.

Jamaican Ginger (ABV 4%)
Refreshing yellow, grainy speciality beer. The ginger dominates but is not too fiery. It finishes sweet with the ginger receding on the palate.

Uncle John (ABV 4.3%)
Roast predominates in this creamy, dark brown stout. The finish is smooth with no harsh edges.

Cock o' the North (ABV 5%)
Amber-coloured, grainy strong bitter. Predominantly malty nose and taste, with a dry and astringent finish.

Hall & Woodhouse IFBB

Hall & Woodhouse Ltd, Blandford St Mary, Blandford Forum, Dorset, DT11 9LS
☎ (01258) 452141
✉ info@hall-woodhouse.co.uk
🌐 hall-woodhouse.co.uk
Shop Mon-Sat 9am-6pm; Sun 11am-3pm (Easter-Oct)
Tours by arrangement (call to book)

Founded by Charles Hall in 1777, Hall & Woodhouse is an independent family brewer, today run by the fifth generation of the Woodhouse family. The Badger logo was adopted in 1875, one of the oldest registered trademarks on record. The company moved from Ansty to its present site in 1900 and a new brewery is planned on part of the current site. Cask beer is sold in all 263 pubs. Seasonal beers: see website.

K&B Sussex Bitter (OG 1036, ABV 3.5%)
Well-flavoured session bitter with hints of toffee and roast malts. It has the fruitiness common to all Badger beers, but with a drier character than the others.

Badger First Gold (OG 1041, ABV 4%)
Appetising aroma with pear fruitiness that gives way to a more restrained bittersweet flavour. Hops in evidence throughout with fruit returning in the aftertaste.

Tanglefoot (OG 1047, ABV 4.9%)
A complex, satisfying beer that retains an easy drinking balance. Aromas of bananas and caramel and a sweetish, malty and fruity flavour. Long, bittersweet finish with echoes of the fruit aromas.

Hambleton SIBA

Nick Stafford Hambleton Ales, Melmerby Green Road, Melmerby, North Yorkshire, HG4 5NB
☎ (01765) 640108
✉ sales@hambletonales.co.uk
🌐 hambletonales.co.uk
Shop Mon-Fri 7.30am-5pm
Tours by arrangement

Hambleton Ales was established in 1991 on the banks of the River Swale in the heart of the Vale of York. Expansion over the years has resulted in relocation to larger premises on several occasions, the last being December 2007. Brewing capacity has increased to 100 barrels a week and a bottling line caters for micros and larger brewers, handling more than 20 brands. More than 100 outlets are supplied throughout Yorkshire and the North-east. Five core brands are produced along with an additional special brew each month. The company also brew beers under contract for the Village Brewer.

Bitter (ABV 3.8%)
A golden bitter with a good balance of malty and refreshing citrus notes leading to a mellow, tangy finish.

Goldfield (OG 1041, ABV 4.2%)
A light amber bitter with good hop character and increasing dryness. A fine blend of malts gives a smooth overall impression.

Stallion (OG 1041, ABV 4.2%)
A premium bitter, moderately hoppy throughout and richly balanced in malt and fruit, developing a sound and robust bitterness, with earthy hops drying the aftertaste.

Stud (OG 1042.5, ABV 4.3%)
A strongly bitter beer, with rich hop and fruit. It ends dry and spicy.

Nightmare (OG 1050, ABV 5%)
This impressively flavoured beer satisfies all parts of the palate. Strong roast malts dominate, but hoppiness rears out of this complex blend.

For Black Dog Brewery, Whitby:

Whitby Abbey Ale (ABV 3.8%)

Schooner (ABV 4.2%)

Rhatas (ABV 4.6%)

For Village Brewer:

White Boar (OG 1037.5, ABV 3.8%)
A light, flowery and fruity ale; crisp, clean and refreshing, with a dry-hopped, powerful but not aggressive bitter finish.

Bull (OG 1039, ABV 4%)
A pale, full, fruity bitter, well hopped to give a lingering bitterness.

Old Raby (OG 1045, ABV 4.8%)
A full-bodied, smooth, rich-tasting dark ale. A complex balance of malt, fruit character and creamy caramel sweetness offsets the bitterness.

Hammerpot

Hammerpot Brewery Ltd, Unit 30, The Vinery, Arundel Road, Poling, West Sussex, BN18 9PY
☎ (01903) 883338
✉ sales@hammerpot-brewery.co.uk
🌐 hammerpot-brewery.co.uk

Hammerpot started brewing in 2005 and the brew plant has been upgraded to a five-barrel brew-length. The brewery supplies a wide area between Southamptom and Eastbourne and north to the M25. All cask beers are available in bottle-conditioned form. Seasonal beers: Martlet (ABV 3.5%, Apr-Sep), Bottle Wreck Porter (ABV 4.7%, Oct-Mar), Shepherd's Warmer (ABV 5.5%), Vinery Mild (ABV 3.4%, May & Sep), HPA (ABV 4.1%, Jun-Aug).

Meteor (OG 1038, ABV 3.8%)

White Wing (OG 1039, ABV 4%)

Red Hunter (OG 1046, ABV 4.3%)

Woodcote (OG 1047, ABV 4.5%)

Madgwick Gold (OG 1050, ABV 5%)

Hanby

See Wem

Ha'penny (NEW)

Ha'penny Brewing Co Ltd, Cuckoo Hall Brewery, Unit 8, Aldborough Hall Farm, Aldborough Hatch, Ilford, Essex, IG2 7TD
☎ (020) 8262 9712
☎ 07961 161869
info@hapenny-brewing.co.uk
hapenny-brewing.co.uk
Tours by arrangement

Ha'penny was established in 2009 by two CAMRA members in a disused stable block.

Sixteen-String Jack (ABV 4%)

London Stone (ABV 4.5%)

Hardknott

Hardknott Brewery t/a Woolpack Inn, Boot, Cumbria, CA19 1TH
☎ (01946) 723230
enquiries@woolpack.co.uk
woolpack.co.uk
Tours by arrangement

Hardknott Brewery opened in 2005 using a two-barrel plant. The beers are only available at the Woolpack Inn. The beer list constantly changes, therefore beers listed may not be available at any given time and others may also appear. Seasonal beers are also brewed.

Light Cascade (ABV 3.4%)

Stout Tenacity (ABV 3.8%)

Woolpacker (ABV 3.9%)

Pride of Eskdale (ABV 4.3%)
Aggressively attractive darkish bitter with intense bitterness, especially in the aftertaste.

Saazy's Weisse (ABV 4.3%)

Saazy Lamm (ABV 4.6%)

Hardys & Hansons

See Greene King in New Nationals section

Hart

Hart Brewery Ltd, Cartford Inn & Restaurant, Cartford Lane, Little Eccleston, Lancashire, PR3 0YP
☎ (01995) 671686
johnsmith@hartbreweryltd.co.uk
hartbreweryltd.co.uk
Tours by arrangement

The brewery opened 1995 behind the Cartford Hotel on rural Lancashire's Fylde Plain. Hart supplies a number of local outlets and arranges exchanges with other micro-breweries. Monthly specials are also available.

Cartford Gold (ABV 3.6%)

Dishy Debbie (OG 1040, ABV 4%)

Ice Maiden (OG 1040, ABV 4%)
Hoppy, crisp, straw-coloured bitter with floral notes and a dry finish.

Squirrels Hoard (OG 1040, ABV 4%)

Nemesis (OG 1041, ABV 4.1%)

Cait-Lin Gold (OG 1042, ABV 4.2%)

Hart of Stebbing

Hart of Stebbing Brewery Ltd, White Hart, High Street, Stebbing, Essex, CM6 3SQ
☎ (01371) 856383
bobdovey@tiscali.co.uk
hartofstebbingbrewery.co.uk
Tours by arrangement

The brewery was established in summer 2007 by Bob Dovey and Nick Eldred, who is also the owner of the White Hart pub where the brewery is based. More beers are planned, as are bottle-conditioned beers. At present only the White Hart and local beer festivals are supplied.

Hart Throb (OG 1036, ABV 3.8%)

Hart's Content (ABV 3.8%)

Hart and Soul (ABV 4.2%)

Black Hart (ABV 5%)

Harveys IFBB

Harvey & Son (Lewes) Ltd, Bridge Wharf Brewery, 6 Cliffe High Street, Lewes, East Sussex, BN7 2AH
☎ (01273) 480209
maj@harveys.org.uk
harveys.org.uk
Shop Mon-Sat 9.30am-4.45pm
Tours by arrangement (currently two year waiting list)

Established in 1790, this independent family brewery operates from the banks of the River Ouse in Lewes. A major development in 1985 doubled the brewhouse capacity and subsequent additional fermenting capacity has seen production rise to more than 38,000 barrels a year. Harveys supplies real ale to all its 48 pubs and 450 free trade outlets in Sussex and Kent. Seasonal beers: see website. Bottle-conditioned beer is also available.

Sussex XX Mild Ale (OG 1030, ABV 3%)
A dark copper-brown colour. Roast malt dominates the aroma and palate leading to a sweet, caramel finish.

Hadlow Bitter (OG 1033, ABV 3.5%)
Formerly Sussex Pale Ale

Sussex Best Bitter (OG 1040, ABV 4%)
Full-bodied brown bitter. A hoppy aroma leads to a good malt and hop balance, and a dry aftertaste.

Armada Ale (OG 1045, ABV 4.5%)
Hoppy amber best bitter. Well-balanced fruit and hops dominate throughout with a fruity palate.

Harviestoun SIBA

Harviestoun Brewery Ltd, Alva Industrial Estate, Alva, Clackmannanshire, FK12 5DQ
☎ (01259) 769100
info@harviestoun.com

harviestoun.com
Tours by arrangement

Harviestoun started in a barn in the village of Dollar in 1985 with a five-barrel brew plant, but now operate on a state-of-the-art 60-barrel brewery in Alva. The brewery supplies local outlets direct and nationwide via wholesalers. It was bought by Caledonian Brewing Co in 2006 but is now independent following the takeover of Caledonian by Scottish & Newcastle in April 2008. Further expansion is planned. Seasonal beers: see website.

Bitter & Twisted (OG 1036, ABV 3.8%)
Refreshingly hoppy beer with fruit throughout. A bittersweet taste with a long bitter finish. A golden session beer.

Ptarmigan (OG 1045, ABV 4.5%)
A well-balanced, bittersweet beer in which hops and malt dominate. The blend of malt, hops and fruit produces a clean, hoppy aftertaste.

Schiehallion (OG 1048, ABV 4.8%)
A Scottish cask lager, brewed using a lager yeast and Hersbrucker hops. A hoppy aroma, with fruit and malt, leads to a malty, bitter taste with floral hoppiness and a bitter finish.

Harwich Town EAB

Harwich Town Brewing Co, Station Approach, Harwich, Essex, CO12 3NA
(01255) 551155
info@harwichtown.co.uk
harwichtown.co.uk
Shop – see website
Tours by arrangement

Brewing started in 2007 on a five-barrel plant next to Harwich Town railway station. The brewer is a CAMRA member and former customs officer. Beers are named after local landmarks, characters or events. 50 outlets are supplied. Seasonal beers: see website. An annual festival special is brewed for Harwich & Dovercourt Bay Winter Ale Festival in December.

Ha'Penny Mild (ABV 3.6%)

Leading Lights (ABV 3.8%)

Misleading Lights (ABV 4%)

Redoubt Stout (ABV 4.2%)

Parkeston Porter (ABV 4.5%)

Lighthouse Bitter (ABV 4.8%)

Havant (NEW)

Havant Brewery, c/o 29 Gladys Avenue, Cowplain, Waterlooville, Hampshire, PO8 8HT
(023) 9225 2118
07872 959118
mike@thehavantbrewery.co.uk
thehavantbrewery.co.uk

Havant began brewing in 2009 on a one-barrel plant. Seasonal beers are planned.

Started (ABV 4%)

Stopped Dancing (ABV 4.4%)

Finished (ABV 5%)

Hawkshead SIBA

Hawkshead Brewery Ltd, Mill Yard, Staveley, Cumbria, LA8 9LR
(01539) 822644
info@hawksheadbrewery.co.uk
hawksheadbrewery.co.uk
Shop Mon-Tue 12-5pm; Wed-Sun 12-6pm

Hawkshead Brewery is based in Staveley, between Kendal and Windermere in the Lake District. The brewery complex is a showcase for real ale and contains a purpose-built 20-barrel brewery and The Beer Hall, which is the brewery tap, beer shop, visitor centre and dining room. The brewery expanded in 2006, having outgrown its original site (opened in 2002) in a barn at Hawkshead. More than 100 outlets are supplied direct. Bottle-conditioned beers are available.

Windermere Pale (OG 1036, ABV 3.5%)
A fresh, hoppy, blonde beer.

Bitter (OG 1037, ABV 3.7%)
Well-balanced, thirst-quenching beer with fruit and hops aroma, leading to a lasting bitter finish.

Red (OG 1042, ABV 4.2%)
A red ale; malty and spicy, with a long dry finish.

Lakeland Gold (OG 1043, ABV 4.4%)
Fresh, well-balanced fruity, hoppy beer with a clean bitter aftertaste.

Organic Oatmeal Stout (OG 1044, ABV 4.5%)

Lakeland Lager (OG 1045, ABV 4.8%)
A cask-conditioned lager.

Brodie's Prime (OG 1048, ABV 4.9%)
Complex, dark brown beer with plenty of malt, fruit and roast taste. Satisfying full body with clean finish.

Haywood Bad Ram

Haywood Bad Ram Brewery, Callow Top Holiday Park, Sandybrook, Ashbourne, Derbyshire, DE6 2AQ
07974 948427
acphaywood@aol.com
callowtop.co.uk
Shop 9am-5pm (seasonal)
Tours by arrangement

The brewery is based in a converted barn. One pub is owned (on site) and several other outlets are supplied. The brewery is not operational during the winter. Bottle-conditioned beers are available.

Dr Samuel Johnson (ABV 4.5%)

Bad Ram (ABV 5%)

Lone Soldier (ABV 5%)

Woggle Dance (ABV 5%)

Callow Top IPA (ABV 5.2%)

Headless

Headless Brewing Co Ltd, The Flowerpot, 19-25 King Street, Derby, Derbyshire, DE1 3DZ
(01332) 204955
Tours by arrangement

Headless is situated at the rear of the Flowerpot pub in Derby and was established in September 2007 on a 10-barrel plant. Seasonal beer: Ebenezer (ABV 6%, Xmas), Zymosis (ABV 7.5%, Over and Out Stout (ABV 4.5%).

King Street Ale (KSA) (OG 1038, ABV 3.8%)

First Bloom (OG 1040, ABV 4.3%)

Five Gates (OG 1046, ABV 5%)

Heart of Wales

Neuadd Arms Brewing Co t/a Heart of Wales Brewery, Stables Yard, Zion Street, Llanwrtyd Wells, Powys, LD5 4RD
☎ (01591) 610236
✉ Lindsay@heartofwalesbrewery.co.uk
heartofwalesbrewery.co.uk
Shop 10am-6pm daily
Tours by arrangement

The brewery was set up with a six-barrel plant in 2006 in old stables at the rear of the Neuadd Arms Hotel. Selected ales are conditioned in oak barrels prior to being casked. Seasonal brews celebrate local events such as the World Bogsnorkelling Championships and the Man v Horse Marathon. Seasonal and bottle-conditioned beers are available. All bottle-conditioned beers are suitable for vegetarians and vegans.

Irfon Valley Bitter (ABV 3.6%)

Aur Cymru (ABV 3.8%)

Bitter (ABV 4.1%)

Welsh Black (ABV 4.4%)

Noble Eden Ale (ABV 4.6%)

Inn-stable (ABV 6.8%)

Hebridean SIBA

Hebridean Brewing Co, 18a Bells Road, Stornoway, Isle of Lewis, HS1 2RA
☎ (01851) 700123
✉ info@hebridean-brewery.co.uk
hebridean-brewery.co.uk
Shop open in summer months only
Tours by arrangement

The company was set up in 2001 on a steam powered plant with a 14-barrel brew length. A shop is attached to the brewery. Seasonal beers are produced for Mods, Gaelic festivals that are the Scottish equivalent of the Welsh Eisteddfod. These include Pagan Dark Winter Ale (ABV 4.8%, Mar-May).

Celtic Black Ale (OG 1036, ABV 3.9%)
A dark ale full of flavour, balancing an aromatic hop combined with a subtle bite and a pleasantly smooth caramel aftertaste.

Clansman Ale (OG 1036, ABV 3.9%)
A light Hebridean beer, brewed with Scottish malts and lightly hopped to give a subtle bittering.

Seaforth Ale (ABV 4.2%)
A golden beer in the continental style.

Islander Strong Premium Ale (OG 1044, ABV 4.8%)
A malty, fruity strong bitter drinking dangerously below its ABV.

Berserker Export Pale Ale (OG 1068, ABV 7.5%)
This malty, fruity 'winter warmer' is packed full of flavour, with toffee apple and caramel notes right through to the long, satisfying aftertaste.

Hektors

Hektors Brewery Ltd, The Office, Henham Park, Southwold, Suffolk, NR34 8AN
☎ 07900 553426
✉ hektor@henhampark.com
hektorsbrewery.com

Beers are currently brewed under contract by other breweries, including Green Jack and Oakham. However, there are plans to install a brewery in a converted barn at Henham Park in the future. Hektor's beers are provided to Henham Park's 65,000 annual visitors in addition to five other outlets and local events.

Pure (OG 1038, ABV 3.8%)

House (OG 1042, ABV 4.2%)

Scarecrow (OG 1050, ABV 5%)

Hepworth SIBA

Hepworth & Co Brewers Ltd, The Beer Station, Railway Yard, Horsham, West Sussex, RH12 2NW
☎ (01403) 269696
✉ mail@hepworthbrewery.co.uk
hepworthbrewery.co.uk
Sales 9am-6pm daily

Hepworth's was established in 2001, initially bottling beer only. In 2003 draught beer brewing was started with Sussex malt and hops. In 2004 an organic lager was introduced in bottle and on draught. 274 outlets are supplied. Seasonal beers: Summer Ale (ABV 3.4%), Harvest Ale (ABV 4.5%, autumn), Old Ale (ABV 4.8%, winter), Christmas Ale (ABV 7.5%), Cloud 9 (ABV 4.5%, spring).

Traditional Sussex Bitter (OG 1035, ABV 3.6%)
A fine, clean-tasting amber session beer. A bitter beer with a pleasant fruity and hoppy aroma that leads to a crisp, tangy taste. A long, dry finish.

Pullman First Class Ale (OG 1041, ABV 4.2%)
A sweet, nutty maltiness and fruitiness are balanced by hops and bitterness in this easy-drinking, pale brown best bitter. A subtle bitter aftertaste.

Prospect Organic (ABV 4.5%)
A well-balanced and traditional brew.

Classic Old Ale (OG 1046, ABV 4.8%)
A traditional winter brew, rich with a variety of roasted malts balanced with sweetness and the bitterness of Admiral hops.

Iron Horse (OG 1048, ABV 4.8%)
There's a fruity, toffee aroma to this light brown, full-bodied bitter. A citrus flavour balanced by caramel and malt leads to a clean, dry finish.

Blonde (ABV 5%)
Organic lager. Suitable for vegans.

Hereward

Hereward Brewery, 50 Fleetwood, Ely, Cambridgeshire, CB6 1BH
☎ (01353) 666441
✉ michael.czarnobaj@ntlworld.com

A small home-based brewery launched in 2003 on a 10-gallon kit. The brewery supplies mainly beer festivals and also brews festival specials (brewed to order). Seasonal beer: Uncle Joe's Winter Ale (ABV 5%).

Michael's Mild (ABV 3.4%)

Bitter (ABV 3.8%)

St Ethelreda's Golden Bitter (ABV 4%)

Porta Porter (ABV 4.2%)

Oatmeal Stout (ABV 4.5%)

Hesket Newmarket SIBA

Hesket Newmarket Brewery Ltd, Old Crown Barn, Back Green, Hesket Newmarket, Cumbria, CA7 8JG
☎ (01697) 478066
✉ admin@hesketbrewery.co.uk
hesketbrewery.co.uk
Shop Mon-Fri 8.30am-5pm; Sat 10am-2pm (summer)
Tours by arrangement

The brewery was established in 1988 and was bought by a co-operative of villagers in 1999, anxious to preserve a community resource. Most of the original recipes have been retained, all named after local fells except for Doris's 90th Birthday Ale. An 11-barrel plant was installed in 2005 followed by a small-scale bottling plant in 2006. Around 50 regular outlets are supplied. Bottle-conditioned beers are available.

Great Cockup Porter (OG 1035, ABV 3%)
A refreshing, dark and chocolatey porter with a dry finish.

Blencathra Bitter (OG 1035, ABV 3.3%)
A malty, tawny ale, mild and mellow for a bitter, with a dominant caramel flavour.

Haystacks Refreshing Ale (OG 1037, ABV 3.7%)
Light, easy-drinking, thirst-quenching blond beer; very pleasant for its strength.

Skiddaw Special Bitter (OG 1037, ABV 3.7%)
An amber session beer, malty throughout, well-balanced with a dryish finish.

Helvellyn Gold (OG 1039, ABV 4%)
A smooth, golden bitter. light in colour but full-flavoured.

High Pike Dark Amber Bitter (OG 1042, ABV 4.2%)

Doris's 90th Birthday Ale (OG 1045, ABV 4.3%)

Scafell Blonde (OG 1043, ABV 4.3%)
Pale with bags of hop flavour, not too bitter. A good introduction to real ale for lager drinkers.

Catbells Pale Ale (OG 1050, ABV 5%)
Golden ale with a nice balance of fruity sweetness and bitterness, almost syrupy but with an unexpectedly dry finish.

Old Carrock Strong Ale (OG 1060, ABV 6%)
A dark red, powerful ale. Full of fruit flavours with a dry, chocolate finish.

Hexhamshire SIBA

Hexhamshire Brewery, Leafields, Ordley, Hexham, Northumberland, NE46 1SX
☎ (01434) 606577
✉ ghb@hexhamshire.co.uk
hexhamshire.co.uk

Hexhamshire was founded in 1992 and is operated by one of the founding partners and his family. 40 outlets are supplied direct. A relocation to the Dipton Mill Inn is planned.

Devil's Elbow (OG 1036, ABV 3.6%)
Amber brew full of hops and fruit, leading to a bitter finish.

Shire Bitter (OG 1037, ABV 3.8%)
A good balance of hops with fruity overtones, this amber beer makes an easy-drinking session bitter.

Devil's Water (OG 1041, ABV 4.1%)
Copper-coloured best bitter, well-balanced with a slightly fruity, hoppy finish.

Whapweasel (OG 1048, ABV 4.8%)
An interesting smooth, hoppy beer with a fruity flavour. Amber in colour, the bitter finish brings out the fruit and hops.

Old Humbug (OG 1055, ABV 5.5%)

Hidden SIBA

Hidden Brewery Ltd, Unit 1, Oakley Industrial Estate, Wylye Road, Dinton, Salisbury, Wiltshire, SP3 5EU
☎ (01722) 716440
✉ sales@thehiddenbrewery.com
thehiddenbrewery.com
Tours by arrangement

The Hidden Brewery was founded in 2003 by Head Brewer Gary Lumber and partner Michael Woodhouse. The brewery is named after its location, hidden away in the Wiltshire countryside. The brewery has a substantial UK customer base but following the introduction of its range of bottled beers is now focusing heavily on the export markets. The Chough Inn, one of four tied houses, continues to develop into a successful town centre brewery tap. Seasonal beers: Hidden Spring (ABV 4.5%), Hidden Fantasy (ABV 4.6%), Hidden Depths (ABV 4.6%), Hidden Treasure (ABV 4.8%).

Pint (OG 1039, ABV 3.8%)
A clean-tasting, tangy bitter with good hop content, and a citrus fruit and malt balance. Dry finish, mid-brown in colour; light hop aroma.

Old Sarum (OG 1042, ABV 4.1%)
A well-balanced bitter with a complex combination of malts and hops. The aroma is floral and spicy, full-flavoured with a dry bitterness.

Potential (OG 1042, ABV 4.2%)
A traditional bitter with a balanced malty flavour. Clean tasting with slight citrus tones.

Quest (OG 1042, ABV 4.2%)
An amber-coloured bitter with a malt background, fruity aroma and a dry finish.

Pleasure (OG 1049, ABV 4.9%)
A deep golden coloured, strong, dry, traditional IPA with a hoppy finish.

Highgate SIBA

Highgate Brewery Ltd, Sandymount Road, Walsall, West Midlands, WS1 3AP
☎ (01922) 644453
✉ info@highgatebrewery.com
highgatebrewery.com
Tours by arrangement

Built in 1898, Highgate was an independent brewery until 1938 when it was taken over by Mitchells & Butlers and subsequently became the smallest brewery in the Bass group. It was brought back into the independent sector in 1995 as the result of a management buy-out and was subsequently acquired by Aston Manor (qv) in

2000. Highgate has nine tied houses, six of which serve cask beer. In July 2007 Highgate was bought by Global Star, a pub group in Birmingham. Some 200 outlets are supplied. The company also has a contract to supply Mitchells & Butlers pubs as well as contract brewing for Smiles Brewery. Beer range liable to change. Seasonal beer: Old Ale (ABV 5.3%, winter).

Dark Mild (OG 1036.8, ABV 3.4%)
A dark brown Black Country mild with a good balance of malt and hops, and traces of roast flavour following a malty aroma.

Davenports IPA (OG 1040.8, ABV 4%)

Special Bitter (OG 1037.8, ABV 4%)

Davenports Premium (OG 1046.8, ABV 4.6%)

Saddlers Best Bitter (OG 1043.8, ABV 4.6%)

For Coors:

M&B Mild (OG 1034.8, ABV 3.2%)

For Smiles:

Blonde (ABV 3.8%)

Best (ABV 4.1%)

Bristol IPA (ABV 4.4%)

Heritage (ABV 5.2%)

High House Farm SIBA

High House Farm Brewery, Matfen, Newcastle upon Tyne, Tyne & Wear, NE20 0RG
☎ (01661) 886192/886769 (Sales line)
info@highhousefarmbrewery.co.uk
highhousefarmbrewery.co.uk
Shop 10.30am-5pm daily except Wed
Tours by arrangement

The brewery was founded in 2003 on a working farm with visitor centre, brewery shop and exhibition and function room. Over 350 outlets are supplied. Seasonal beers: Sundancer (ABV 3.6%, summer), Red Shep (ABV 4%, autumn/winter), Black Moss (ABV 4.3%, winter).

Auld Hemp (OG 1038, ABV 3.8%)
Tawny coloured ale with malt and fruit flavours and good bitter finish.

Nel's Best (OG 1041, ABV 4.2%)
Golden hoppy ale full of flavour with a clean, bitter finish.

Nettle Beer (OG 1043, ABV 4.5%)

Matfen Magic (OG 1046.5, ABV 4.8%)
Well-hopped brown ale with a fruity aroma; m alt and chocolate overtones with a rich bitter finish.

Cyril the Magnificent (OG 1051, ABV 5.5%)

Highland

Highland Brewing Co Ltd, Swannay Brewery, Swannay by Evie, Birsay, Orkney, KW17 2NP
☎ (01856) 721700
info@highlandbrewingcompany.co.uk
highlandbrewingcompany.co.uk
Tours by arrangement

Brewing began in 2006 and bigger plant was installed a year later. A visitor centre and café are planned. 80 outlets are supplied.

Light Munro (OG 1034, ABV 3%)
Paler and lower in alcohol than Dark Munro with delicate roast malt and a pleasant fruitiness with a hint of hop to balance the sweet finish.

Orkney Best (OG 1038, ABV 3.6%)
A refreshing, light-bodied, low gravity golden beer bursting with hop, peach and sweet malt flavours. The long, hoppy finish leaves a dry, moreish bitterness.

Dark Munro (OG 1040, ABV 4%)
The nose presents an intense roast hit which is followed by summer fruits in the mouth. The strong roast malt continues into the aftertaste. A very drinkable strong mild.

Orkney Stout (OG 1044, ABV 4.2%)

Scapa Special (OG 1042, ABV 4.2%)
A good copy of a typical Lancashire bitter, full of bitterness and background hops, leaving your mouth tingling in the lingering aftertaste.

Saint Magnus Ale (OG 1045, ABV 4.5%)
A complex tawny bitter with a stunning balance of malt and hop, and some soft roast. Full-bodied and very drinkable.

Orkney IPA (OG 1048, ABV 4.8%)
A very drinkable traditional bitter, with light hop and fruit flavour throughout.

Strong Northerley (OG 1055, ABV 5.5%)

Orkney Blast (OG 1058, ABV 6%)
A warming strong bitter. A mushroom and woody aroma blossoms into a well-balanced smack of malt and hop in the taste.

Orkney Porter (OG 1082, ABV 9%)

Highlands & Islands

See Sinclair Breweries

Highwood SIBA

Highwood Brewery Ltd, Grimsby West, Birchin Way, Grimsby, Lincolnshire, DN31 2SG
☎ (01472) 255500
tomwood@tom-wood.com
tom-wood.com

Highwood, best known under the Tom Wood brand name, started brewing in a converted Victorian granary on the family farm in 1995. The brew-length was increased from 10 barrels to 30 in 2001, using plant from Ash Vine brewery. In 2002, Highwood bought Conway's Licensed Trade Wholesalers. It now distributes most regional and national cask ales throughout Lincolnshire and Nottinghamshire. More than 300 outlets are supplied. Seasonal beers: see website.

Best Bitter (OG 1034, ABV 3.5%)
A good citrus, passion fruit hop dominates the nose and taste, with background malt. A lingering hoppy and bitter finish.

Dark Mild (OG 1034, ABV 3.5%)

Hop and Glory (ABV 3.6%)
Hoppy golden bitter made using English-grown Cascade hops.

Shepherd's Delight (OG 1040, ABV 4%)
Malt is the dominant taste in this amber brew, although the fruity hop bitterness complements it all the way.

Harvest Bitter (OG 1042, ABV 4.3%)

A well-balanced amber beer where the hops and bitterness just about outdo the malt.

Old Timber (OG 1043, ABV 4.5%) ◆
Hoppy on the nose, but featuring well-balanced malt and hops. A slight, lingering roast/coffee flavour develops, but this is generally a bitter, darkish brown beer.

Bomber County (OG 1046, ABV 4.8%) ◆
An earthy malt aroma but with a complex underlying mix of coffee, hops, caramel and apple fruit. The beer starts bitter and intensifies to the end.

Hilden

Hilden Brewing Co, Hilden House, Hilden, Lisburn, Co Antrim, BT27 4TY
☎ (02892) 660800
✉ irishbeers@hildenbrewery.co.uk
🌐 hildenbrewery.co.uk
Shop Tue-Sun 12-2.30pm (3pm Sun) – Taproom Restaurant
Tours by arrangement (Tue-Sat 11.30am & 6.30pm)

Hilden was established in 1981 and is Ireland's oldest independent brewery. Now well into the second generation of the family-owned business, the beers are widely distributed across the UK. Around 15 outlets are supplied direct and two pubs are owned. More beers are planned.

Ale (OG 1038, ABV 4%) ◆
An amber-coloured beer with an aroma of malt, hops and fruit. The balanced taste is slightly slanted towards hops, and hops are also prominent in the full, malty finish.

Silver (OG 1042, ABV 4.2%)
A pale ale, light and refreshing on the palate but with a satisfying mellow hop character derived from a judicious blend of aromatic Saaz hops.

Molly Malone (OG 1045, ABV 4.6%)
Dark ruby-red porter with complex flavours of hop bitterness and chocolate malt.

Scullion's Irish (OG 1045, ABV 4.6%)
A bright amber ale, initially smooth with a slight taste of honey that is balanced by a long, dry aftertaste that lingers on the palate.

Halt (OG 1058, ABV 6.1%)
A premium traditional Irish red ale with a malty, mild hop flavour. This special reserve derives its name from the local train stop, which was used to service the local linen mill.

For College Green Brewery:

Molly's Chocolate Stout (OG 1042, ABV 4.2%)
A dark chocolate-coloured beer with a full-bodied character.

Headless Dog (OG 1042, ABV 4.3%)
A well-hopped bright amber ale.

Belfast Blonde (OG 1047, ABV 4.7%)
A natural blonde beer with a clean and refreshing character.

Hill Island

Michael Griffin t/a Hill Island Brewery, Unit 7, Fowlers Yard, Back Silver Street, Durham, County Durham, DH1 3RA
☎ 07740 932584
✉ mike@hillisland.freeserve.co.uk
Tours by arrangement for groups of 10-15 (£10 per head inc beer samples)

Hill Island is a literal translation of Dunholme from which Durham is derived. The brewery began trading in 2002 and stands by the banks of the Wear in the heart of Durham City. Many of the beers produced have names reflecting local history and heritage. Brews can also be made exclusively for individual pubs. Around 40 outlets are supplied. The brewery is open to visitors most weekdays between 10am-2pm, please phone beforehand to confirm. Seasonal beers: Priory Summer Ale (ABV 3.5%), Miner's Gala Bitter (ABV 3.7%), Festive Ale (ABV 4.2%), St Oswald's Xmas Ale (ABV 4.5%).

Peninsula Pint (OG 1036.5, ABV 3.7%)

Bitter (OG 1038, ABV 3.9%)

Dun Cow Bitter (OG 1041, ABV 4.2%)

Cathedral Ale (OG 1042, ABV 4.3%)

Griffin's Irish Stout (OG 1045, ABV 4.5%)

Hillside

See Deeside

Hobden's

See Wessex

Hobsons SIBA

Hobsons Brewery & Co Ltd, Newhouse Farm, Tenbury Road, Cleobury Mortimer, Worcestershire, DY14 8RD
☎ (01299) 270837
✉ beer@hobsons-brewery.co.uk
🌐 hobsons-brewery.co.uk
Tours by arrangement

Established in 1993 in a former sawmill, Hobsons relocated to a farm site with more space in 1995. A second brewery, bottling plant and a warehouse have been added along with significant expansion to the first brewery. It now uses environmentally sustainable technologies where possible. Beers are supplied within a radius of 50 miles. Hobsons also brews and bottles for the local tourist attraction, the Severn Valley Railway (Manor Ale, ABV 4.2%). Seasonal beer: Old Henry (ABV 5.2%, Sep-Apr). Bottle-conditioned beers are also available.

Mild (OG 1034, ABV 3.2%) ◆
A classic mild. Complex layers of taste come from roasted malts that predominate and give lots of flavour.

Twisted Spire (OG 1036, ABV 3.6%)

Best Bitter (OG 1038.5, ABV 3.8%) ◆
A pale brown to amber, medium-bodied beer with strong hop character throughout. It is consequently bitter, but with malt discernible in the taste.

Town Crier (OG 1044, ABV 4.5%)
An elegant straw-coloured bitter. The hint of sweetness is complemented by subtle hop flavours, leading to a dry finish.

Hoggleys SIBA

Hoggleys Brewery, Unit 12, Litchborough Industrial Estate, Northampton Road, Litchborough, Northamptonshire, NN12 8JB
☎ (01604) 831762

THE BREWERIES

☎ 07717 078402
✉ enquiries@hoggleys.co.uk
🌐 hoggleys.co.uk
Tours by arrangement

Hoggleys was established in 2003 as a part-time brewery. It expanded to an eight-barrel plant in 2006, became full-time and moved to larger premises. Around 35 outlets are supplied. Solstice Stout and Mill Lane Mild are suitable for vegetarians and vegans as are all bottle-conditioned beers.

Kislingbury Bitter (OG 1040, ABV 4%)

Mill Lane Mild (OG 1040, ABV 4%)
Brewed from mild, black and crystal malts and hopped with Challenger and Fuggles.

Northamptonshire Bitter (OG 1040, ABV 4%)
A straw-coloured bitter brewed with pale malt only. The hops are Fuggles and Northdown, and the beer is late hopped with Fuggles for aroma.

Reservoir Hogs (OG 1042, ABV 4.3%)
Mid golden, hoppy and refreshing.

Pump Fiction (OG 1045, ABV 4.5%)
Light copper, complex but easy drinking.

Solstice Stout (OG 1050, ABV 5%)

Hogs Back SIBA

Hogs Back Brewery Ltd, Manor Farm, The Street, Tongham, Surrey, GU10 1DE
☎ (01252) 783000
✉ info@hogsback.co.uk
🌐 hogsback.co.uk
Shop – see website
Tours by arrangement

This traditionally-styled brewery, established in 1992, boasts an extensive range of award-winning ales, brewed using the finest malted barley and whole English hops. The shop sells all the brewery's beers and related merchandise plus over 400 beers and ciders from around the world. See website for more info. Around 400 outlets are supplied direct. Seasonal beers: see website. Bottle-conditioned beers also produced for home and export.

HBB/Hogs Back Bitter (OG 1039, ABV 3.7%)
An aromatic session beer. Biscuity aroma with some hops and lemon notes. Well balanced. Plenty of hoppy impact in the mouth with a long-lasting, dry, hoppy bitter aftertaste.

TEA/Traditional English Ale (OG 1044, ABV 4.2%)
A copper-coloured best bitter, with both malt and hops present in the nose. These carry through into a well-rounded bitter flavour, with slightly more fruit and sweetness than bitterness.

Hop Garden Gold (OG 1048, ABV 4.6%)
Pale golden best bitter, full-bodied and well-balanced with an aroma of malt, hops and fruit. Delicate flowery-citrus hop flavours are balanced by malt and fruit. Hoppy bitterness grows in an increasingly dry aftertaste with a hint of sweetness.

A Over T/Aromas Over Tongham (OG 1094, ABV 9%)
A full-bodied, tawny-coloured barley wine that is packed with flavour. The malty aroma, with hints of vanilla, lead to a well-balanced taste, where the hops cut through the underlying sweetness and dominate in the finish.

Holden's IFBB

Holden's Brewery Ltd, George Street, Woodsetton, Dudley, West Midlands, DY1 4LW
☎ (01902) 880051
✉ holdens.brewery@virgin.net
🌐 holdensbrewery.co.uk
Shop Mon-Fri 9am-5pm
Tours by arrangement

A family brewery going back four generations, Holden's began life as a brew-pub in the 1920s. The company continues to grow with 19 tied pubs and supplies around 70 other outlets.

Black Country Mild (OG 1037, ABV 3.7%)
A good, red/brown mild; a refreshing, light blend of roast malt, hops and fruit, dominated by malt throughout.

Black Country Bitter (OG 1039, ABV 3.9%)
A medium-bodied, golden ale; a light, well-balanced bitter with a subtle, dry, hoppy finish.

XB (OG 1042, ABV 4.1%)
A sweeter, slightly fuller version of the Bitter. Sold in a number of outlets under different names.

Golden Glow (OG 1045, ABV 4.4%)
A pale golden beer with a subtle hop aroma plus gentle sweetness and a light hoppiness.

Special (OG 1052, ABV 5.1%)
A sweet, malty, full-bodied amber ale with hops to balance in the taste and in the good, bittersweet finish.

For Bridgnorth Brewery:

Apley Ale (OG 1040, ABV 3.9%)

Best Bitter (OG 1044, ABV 4.4%)

Pale Ale (OG 1045, ABV 4.5%)

Northgate Gold (OG 1046, ABV 4.6%)

Bishop Percy (OG 1048, ABV 4.7%)

Strong Dark Mild (OG 1058, ABV 6%)

Holland

Holland Brewery, 5 Browns Flats, Brewery Street, Kimberley, Nottinghamshire, NG16 2JU
☎ (0115) 938 2685
✉ hollandbrew@btopenworld.com

Len Holland, a keen home-brewer for 30 years, went commercial in 2000, in the shadow of now closed Hardys & Hansons. Seasonal beers: Holly Hop Gold (ABV 4.7%, Xmas), Dutch Courage (ABV 5%, winter), Glamour Puss (ABV 4.2%, spring), Blonde Belter (ABV 4.5%, summer).

Chocolate Clog (OG 1038, ABV 3.8%)

Golden Blond (OG 1040, ABV 4%)

Lipsmacker (OG 1040, ABV 4%)

Cloghopper (OG 1042, ABV 4.2%)

Double Dutch (OG 1045, ABV 4.5%)

Mad Jack Stout (OG 1045, ABV 4.5%)

Holt IFBB

Joseph Holt Ltd, The Brewery, Empire Street, Cheetham, Manchester, M3 1JD

☎ (0161) 834 3285
🌐 joseph-holt.com

The brewery was established in 1849 by Joseph Holt and his wife Catherine. It is still a family-run business in the hands of the great, great-grandson of the founder. Holt's supplies approximately 100 outlets as well as its own estate of 131 tied pubs. It still delivers beer to many of its tied houses in large 54-gallon hogsheads. A dedicated 30-barrel brew plant is used for seasonal beers: see website.

Mild (OG 1033, ABV 3.2%)
A dark brown/red beer with a fruity, malty nose. Roast, malt, fruit and hops in the taste, with strong bitterness for a mild, and a dry malt and hops finish.

Bitter (OG 1040, ABV 4%)
Copper-coloured beer with malt and hops in the aroma. Malt, hops and fruit in the taste with a bitter and hoppy finish.

Hook Norton IFBB

Hook Norton Brewery Co Ltd, The Brewery, Hook Norton, Banbury, Oxfordshire, OX15 5NY
☎ (01608) 737210
🌐 hooky.co.uk
Shop Mon-Fri 9am-5pm; Sat 9am-3pm
Tours by arrangement

Hook Norton was founded in 1849 by John Harris, a farmer and maltster. The current premises were built in 1900 and Hook Norton is one of the finest examples of a Victorian tower brewery, with a 25hp steam engine for most of its motive power. The brewhouse has recently been expanded. Hook Norton owns 47 pubs and supplies approximately 300 free trade accounts. Seasonal beers: see website.

Hooky Dark (OG 1033, ABV 3.2%)
A chestnut brown, easy-drinking mild. A complex malt and hop aroma give way to a well-balanced taste, leading to a long, hoppy finish that is unusual for a mild.

Hooky Bitter (OG 1036, ABV 3.6%)
A classic golden session bitter. Hoppy and fruity aroma followed by a malt and hops taste and a continuing hoppy finish.

Hooky Gold (OG 1042, ABV 4.1%)
A golden, crisp beer with a citrus aroma and a fruity, rounded body.

Old Hooky (OG 1048, ABV 4.6%)
A strong bitter, tawny in colour. A well-rounded fruity taste with a balanced bitter finish.

Hop Back SIBA

Hop Back Brewery plc, Units 22-24, Batten Road Industrial Estate, Downton, Salisbury, Wiltshire, SP5 3HU
☎ (01725) 510986
✉ info@hopback.co.uk
🌐 hopback.co.uk

Started by John Gilbert in 1987 at the Wyndham Arms in Salisbury, the brewery has expanded steadily ever since. It went public via a Business Expansion Scheme in 1993 and has enjoyed rapid continued growth. Summer Lightning has won many awards. The brewery has 11 tied houses and also sells to some 500 other outlets. Seasonal beers are produced on a monthly basis. Entire Stout is suitable for vegans. Bottle-conditioned beers are also produced.

GFB/Gilbert's First Brew (OG 1035, ABV 3.5%)
A golden beer, with a light, clean quality that makes it an ideal session ale. A hoppy aroma and taste lead to a good, dry finish.

Odyssey (OG 1040, ABV 4%)
A darker bitter with toasted malty overtones from the use of four dark malts in the recipe.

Crop Circle (OG 1041, ABV 4.2%)
A refreshingly sharp and hoppy summer beer. Gold coloured with a slight citrus taste. The crisp, dry aftertaste lingers.

Spring Zing (OG 1041, ABV 4.2%)
A dry-hopped version of Crop Circle which gives it a flowery, more rounded palate.

Entire Stout (OG 1043, ABV 4.5%)
A rich, dark stout with a strong roasted malt flavour and a long, sweet and malty aftertaste. A beer suitable for vegans.

Summer Lightning (OG 1048, ABV 5%)
A pleasurable pale bitter with a good, fresh, hoppy aroma and a malty, hoppy flavour. Finely balanced, it has an intense bitterness leading to a long, dry finish.

Hopdaemon

Hopdaemon Brewery Co Ltd, Unit 1, Parsonage Farm, Seed Road, Newnham, Kent, ME9 0NA
☎ (01795) 892078
✉ info@hopdaemon.com
🌐 hopdaemon.com
Tours by arrangement

Tonie Prins opened a 12-barrel plant in 2000 in Canterbury and within six months was supplying more than 30 pubs in the area with his cask ales and bottle-conditioned beers. In 2005 the brewery moved to bigger premises in Newnham and some 100 outlets are now supplied.

Golden Braid (OG 1039, ABV 3.7%)

Incubus (OG 1041, ABV 4%)

Skrimshander IPA (OG 1045, ABV 4.5%)

Green Daemon (OG 1048, ABV 5%)

Dominator (OG 1050, ABV 5.1%)

Leviathan (OG 1057, ABV 6%)

Hopshackle

Hopshackle Brewery Ltd, Unit F, Bentley Business Park, Blenheim Way, Northfields Industrial Estate, Market Deeping, Lincolnshire, PE6 8LD
☎ (01778) 348542
✉ nigel@hopshacklebrewery.co.uk
🌐 hopshacklebrewery.co.uk

Hopshackle was established in 2006 on a five-barrel brew plant. Monthly seasonals are brewed providing variety in styles and ABVs. More than 40 outlets are supplied direct. Bottle-conditioned beers are also available.

Caskadia (OG 1040, ABV 4.3%)

Special Bitter (OG 1040, ABV 4.3%)

Hop and Spicy (OG 1045, ABV 4.5%)

Extra Special Bitter (OG 1045, ABV 4.8%)

Historic Porter (OG 1053, ABV 4.8%)

Shacklers Gold (OG 1048, ABV 5.2%)

Special No. 1 Bitter (OG 1048, ABV 5.2%)

Double Momentum (OG 1065, ABV 7%)

Momentum (OG 1065, ABV 7%)

Hopstar

Hopstar Brewery, 11 Pole Lane, Darwen, Lancashire, BB3 3LD
☎ (01254) 703389
☎ 07849 369798
✉ hopstarbrewery@hotmail.com
Tours by arrangement (for small groups)

Hopstar first brewed in 2004 on a 2.5-barrel kit. 20-50 outlets are supplied around Lancashire and Greater Manchester. Beer Festival organisers are offered a chance to brew beer for their own festival.

Dizzy Danny Ale (OG 1039, ABV 3.8%)

Dark Knight (OG 1041, ABV 4%)

J.C. (OG 1041, ABV 4%)

Lancashire Gold (OG 1041, ABV 4%)

Smokey Joe's Black Beer (OG 1041, ABV 4%)

Hornbeam

Hornbeam Brewery, 1-1c Grey Street, Denton, Manchester, M34 3RU
☎ (0161) 320 5627
☎ 07984 443383
✉ kevin@hornbeambrewery.com
hornbeambrewery.com
Tours by arrangement

Hornbeam began brewing in 2007 on an eight-barrel plant. Regular monthly special beers are brewed.

Lemon Blossom (ABV 3.7%)
Golden, citrussy and light in colour. It makes use of Sorachi Ace, which is a Japanese/New Zealand hop.

Bitter (ABV 3.8%)
A smooth, easy-drinking beer with a rich hop flavour.

Top Hop (ABV 4.2%)
Full-bodied with malt appeal and ample bitterness.

Black Coral Stout (ABV 4.5%)
A smooth, dry roast malt. Dark and full-bodied with a rich, creamy head. Satisfying with a subtle bitterness.

For Dane Town Brewery, Denton:

Valkyrie Bitter (ABV 4.2%)
A session beer with malty aroma and hoppy finish.

Horseshoe

See McLaughlin

Hoskins

Hoskins Brothers Ales, The Ale Wagon, 27 Rutland Street, Leicester, LE1 1RE
☎ (0116) 262 3330
✉ mail@alewagon.com
alewagon.co.uk

Hoskins brothers are not currently brewing pending the building of a new brewery at the Ale Wagon in Leicester. Their beers are currently contract brewed at Tower Brewery, Burton upon Trent. See Tower for beer list.

Houston SIBA

Houston Brewing Co, South Street, Houston, Renfrewshire, PA6 7EN
☎ (01505) 612620
✉ ale@houston-brewing.co.uk
houston-brewing.co.uk
Shop open pub hours, daily
Tours by arrangement

Established by Carl Wengel in 1997, the brewery is attached to the Fox & Hounds pub and restaurant. Brewery tours include dinner and tastings. Houston deliver throughout Britain via a network of distributors and direct. Polypins, bottles and giftpacks are for sale via the website. Seasonal beers: see website.

Killellan Bitter (OG 1037, ABV 3.7%)
A light session ale, with a floral hop and fruity taste. The finish of this amber beer is dry and quenching.

Blonde Bombshell (OG 1040, ABV 4%)
A gold-coloured ale with a fresh hop aroma and rounded maltiness.

Black & Tan (ABV 4.2%)

Peter's Well (OG 1042, ABV 4.2%)
Well-balanced fruity taste with sweet hop, leading to an increasingly bittersweet finish.

Texas (ABV 4.3%)

Tartan Terror (ABV 4.5%)

Warlock Stout (ABV 4.7%)

Howard Town

Howard Town Brewery Ltd, Hawkshead Mill, Hope Street, Glossop, Derbyshire, SK13 7SS
☎ (01457) 869800
✉ beer@howardtownbrewery.co.uk
howardtownbrewery.co.uk
Tours by arrangement

Howard Town was established in 2005 and is the Midlands most northerly brewery. More than 100 outlets are supplied. Seasonal beers: Hope (ABV 4.1%, spring), Dragon's Nest (ABV 4.4%, St George's Day), Snake Ale (ABV 4%, autumn), Robins Nest (ABV 5.2%, winter), Sparrows Nest (ABV 3.6%, winter). Bottle-conditioned beers are also available.

Mill Town (OG 1036, ABV 3.5%)

Bleaklow (OG 1040, ABV 3.8%)

Longdendale Light (OG 1039, ABV 3.9%)

Monks Gold (OG 1041.5, ABV 4%)

Wrens Nest (OG 1043, ABV 4.2%)

Dinting Arches (OG 1045, ABV 4.5%)

Glotts Hop (OG 1049, ABV 5%)

Dark Peak (OG 1061, ABV 6.4%)

Sarah Hughes

Sarah Hughes Brewery, Beacon Hotel, 129 Bilston Street, Sedgley, Dudley, West Midlands, DY3 1JE
☎ (01902) 883381
Tours by arrangement

A traditional Black Country tower brewery, established in 1921. The original grist case and rare open-topped copper add to the ambience of the Victorian brewhouse and give a unique character to the brews. Seasonal beer: Snowflake (ABV 8%, winter).

Pale Amber (OG 1038, ABV 4%)
A well-balanced beer, initially slightly sweet but with hops close behind.

Surprise (OG 1048, ABV 5%)
A bittersweet, medium-bodied, hoppy ale with some malt.

Dark Ruby (OG 1058, ABV 6%)
A dark ruby strong ale with a good balance of fruit and hops, leading to a pleasant, lingering hops and malt finish.

Humpty Dumpty

Norfolk Broads Brewing LLP t/a Humpty Dumpty Brewery, Church Road, Reedham, Norfolk, NR13 3TZ
☎ (01493) 701818
sales@humptydumptybrewery.co.uk
humptydumptybrewery.co.uk
Shop 12-5pm daily (Easter-end Oct); Sat-Sun 12.30-4pm (Nov-Xmas); Jan-Feb closed
Tours by arrangement

Established in 1998, the 11-barrel brewery moved to its present site in 2001. The brewers use local ingredients and many regional outlets are supplied. The on-site shop sells bottled and draught beer from the brewery as well as from other East Anglian micros. Seasonal beers: see website. Bottle-conditioned beers are also available.

Little Sharpie (OG 1040, ABV 3.8%)
A well-balanced golden beer with lemon and grapefruit notes. A light, hoppy nose introduces a lively initial taste with hops again to the fore. Citrus flavours mix well with malt to give depth.

Lemon & Ginger (OG 1041, ABV 4%)
An amber, crisp ale with a ginger and lemon tang.

Swallowtail (OG 1041, ABV 4%)
A pale amber ale with a lively hop finish.

Ale (OG 1043, ABV 4.1%)
An amber-coloured bitter with a predominantly fruity nose. Initial sweetness fades to leave a long, dry finish.

Broadland Sunrise (OG 1044, ABV 4.2%)
A crisp, orange-red ale brewed with additions of rye for a dry finish with American hop notes.

Reedcutter (OG 1046, ABV 4.4%)
A sweet, malty beer, golden hued with a gentle malt background. Smooth and full-bodied with a quick, gentle finish.

The King John (OG 1046, ABV 4.5%)
A golden ale with soft, fruity undertones leading to a complex bittersweet finish.

Cheltenham Flyer (OG 1048, ABV 4.6%)
A full-flavoured golden, earthy bitter with a long, grainy finish. A strong hop bitterness dominates throughout. Little evidence of malt.

Norfolk Nectar (OG 1048, ABV 4.6%)
Honey dominates the aroma and taste of this amber brew. A one dimensional beer with a subtle malt and hop background. A quick, sweet finish with butterscotch notes.

Railway Sleeper (OG 1051, ABV 5%)
Full-bodied tawny brew with a rich, fruity nature. A strong plummy character where sweetness and malt counter balance the background bitterness. A quick, spicy, bitter finish.

Golden Gorse (OG 1054, ABV 5.4%)
A full-bodied, fruity beer. Hints of banana, rhubarb, vanilla, peaches and toffee throughout. Malt is also present and helps suppress a soft, bitter background. A surprisingly short finish.

Porter (OG 1054, ABV 5.4%)
A full-bodied, malty brew. Deeply red hued with a hint of liqourice in the taste. Roast notes come to the fore as the sweet fruitiness slowly diminishes.

Hunter's (NEW)

Hunter's Brewery Ltd, Bulleigh Barton Farm, Ipplepen, Devon, TQ12 5UE
☎ 07530 891862

Office: Glebe Acres, Orley Road, Ipplepen, Devon, TQ12 5SA
huntersbrewery.co.uk

Hunters began brewing in 2008 on a five-barrel brew plant. Seasonal beers are planned.

Crack Shot (ABV 3.8%)

Half Bore (ABV 4%)

Pheasant Plucker (ABV 4.3%)

Gold (ABV 4.8%)

Full Bore (ABV 8%)

Hurns

See Tomos Watkin

Hydes IFBB

Hydes Brewery Ltd, 46 Moss Lane West, Moss Side, Manchester, M15 5PH
☎ (0161) 226 1317
mail@hydesbrewery.com
hydesbrewery.com
Tours by arrangement (Mon-Thu 7pm)

Hydes has been a family-owned regional brewer since 1863 and is currently the biggest volume producer of cask ales in the north west, thanks in part to its contract brewing for InBev and others. The brewery has been on the same site for more than 120 years with the brewery building Grade II listed. Hydes owns over 75 tied pubs, all selling cask ale, and have more than 300 free trade accounts. In addition Hydes beers are supplied to Algates and Greene King pubs. Six seasonal beers are also produced.

Light Mild/1863 (OG 1033.5, ABV 3.5%)
Lightly hopped, pale brown session beer with some hops, malt and fruit in the taste and a short, dry finish.

Owd Oak (OG 1033.5, ABV 3.5%)
Dark brown/red in colour, with a fruit and malt nose. Taste includes biscuity malt and green fruits, with a satisfying aftertaste.

THE BREWERIES

Traditional Mild (OG 1033.5, ABV 3.5%) ◆
A mid-brown beer with malt and citrus fruits in the aroma and taste. Dry, malty aftertaste.

Original Bitter (OG 1036.5, ABV 3.8%) ◆
Pale brown beer with a malty nose, malt and an earthy hoppiness in the taste, and a good bitterness through to the finish.

Jekyll's Gold Premium (OG 1042, ABV 4.3%) ◆
Pale gold in colour, with a fruity nose. A well-balanced beer with hops, fruit and malt in the taste and bitter finish.

XXXX (OG 1070, ABV 6.8%)
Auburn chestnut brown in colour with a sweet malt toffee nose. A strong robust winter ale with a rich toffee taste.

For InBev UK:

Boddingtons Bitter (OG 1038, ABV 4.1%)

Iceni SIBA EAB

Iceni Brewery, 3 Foulden Road, Ickburgh, Norfolk, IP26 5HB
☎ **(01842) 878922**
✉ **icenibrewe@aol.com**
🌐 **icenibrewery.co.uk**
Shop Mon-Fri 8.30am-5pm; Sat 9am-3pm
Tours by arrangement

Iceni was launched in 1995 by Brendan Moore. The brewery has its own hop garden aimed at the many visitors that flock to the shop to buy the 28 different ales, stouts and lagers bottled on-site. 30 outlets are supplied as well as local farmers' markets and a tourist shop in nearby Thetford Forest. The brewery aims to malt its own barley. Special beers are brewed for festivals and many seasonal beers are available.

Elveden Forest Gold (OG 1040, ABV 3.9%) ◆
Forest fruits on the nose give way to strong hop bitterness in the initial taste. Residual maltiness provides balance at first but is swamped by a long, dry, bitter finish.

Celtic Queen (OG 1038, ABV 4%) ◆
A golden brew with a light hoppy nose giving way to distinctly bitter characteristics throughout. A shallow mix of malt and hops adds some depth. A long, lingering finish.

Fine Soft Day (OG 1038, ABV 4%) ◆
The jam nose contrasts with the distinctly bitter character of this quick-finishing brew. Hops and malt can be found initially but soon subside.

Fen Tiger (OG 1040, ABV 4.2%)

It's A Grand Day (OG 1044, ABV 4.5%) ◆
Gentle hop and citrus aroma introduces this pale brown brew. An orange sweetness contrasts with the underlying hoppy bitterness. Long-lasting and creamy but undemanding.

Raspberry Wheat (OG 1048, ABV 5%)

Winter Lightning (ABV 5%)

Men of Norfolk (OG 1060, ABV 6.2%) ◆
Chocolaty stout with roast overtones from initial aroma to strong finish. Malt and vine fruits counterbalance the initial roast character while a caramel undertone remains to the end.

Idle

Idle Brewery, White Hart Inn, Main Street, West Stockwith, South Yorkshire, DN10 4EY
☎ **(01427) 753226**
☎ **07949 137174**
✉ **theidlebrewery@btinternet.com**
Tours by arrangement

The brewery began production in 2007 and is situated in a converted stable at the back of the White Hart Inn alongside the River Idle. Seasonal beers: Idle B (ABV 4.1%, summer), Cricketer (ABV 4.6%, summer).

Boggins Ale (ABV 3.8%)
Tawny with a bitter finish.

Dog (ABV 4.2%)
A copper-coloured ale, moderately hoppy with a good balance of malt and hops leading to a bitter finish.

Sod (ABV 4.2%)

Coopers (ABV 4.3%)

Black Abbot (ABV 4.5%)

Landlord (ABV 4.6%)
A dark brown ale with plenty of body, a malty flavour and a caramel/coffee finish.

Ilkley (NEW)

Ilkley Brewery Co Ltd, Unit 4, Lencia Industrial Estate, East Parade, Ilkley, West Yorkshire, LS29 8JP
☎ **(01943) 604604**
☎ **(07721) 880108**
✉ **info@ilkleybrewery.co.uk**
🌐 **ilkleybrewery.co.uk**

Ilkley began brewing in 2009 on an eight-barrel plant, bringing brewing back to the town after a gap of some 80 years. Beers are brewed traditionally using only the highest quality home-grown malted barley and whole hops with soft Yorkshire water. Seasonal beer: Mary Jane (ABV 3.6%, summer).

Olicana Gold (ABV 3.9%)
A refreshing, light session golden ale with a floral citrus aroma and delicate bitter finish.

Olicana Best (ABV 4%)
A highly hopped golden ale with a strong, bitter finish.

Olicana Original (ABV 4.3%)
A full-bodied, chestnut-coloured Yorkshire ale with rich flavours and aroma.

Innis & Gunn

Innis & Gunn Brewing Co Ltd, PO Box 17246, Edinburgh, EH11 1YR
☎ **(0131) 337 4420**
✉ **dougal.sharp@innisandgunn.com**
🌐 **innisandgunn.com**

Innis & Gunn does not brew but an unnamed Scottish brewer produces one regular bottled (not bottle-conditioned) beer for the company, Oak Aged Beer (ABV 6.6%).

Inveralmond SIBA

Inveralmond Brewery Ltd, 1 Inveralmond Way, Inveralmond, Perth, PH1 3UQ

☎ (01738) 449448
✉ info@inveralmond-brewery.co.uk
🌐 inveralmond-brewery.co.uk

Established in 1997, Inveralmond was the first brewery in Perth for more than 30 years. The brewery has gone from strength to strength, with around 200 outlets supplied and wholesalers taking beers nationwide. In 2005 the brewery expanded ino the next door premises, more than doubling floor space and output. The brewery has since outgrown this and a new brewery has been built on nearby land. Seasonal beers: see website.

Independence (OG 1040, ABV 3.8%)
A well-balanced Scottish ale with fruit and malt tones. Hop provides an increasing bitterness in the finish.

Ossian (OG 1042, ABV 4.1%)
Well-balanced best bitter with a dry finish. This full-bodied amber ale is dominated by fruit and hop with a bittersweet character although excessive caramel can distract from this.

Thrappledouser (OG 1043, ABV 4.3%)
A refreshing amber beer with reddish hues. The crisp, hoppy aroma is finely balanced with a tangy but quenching taste.

Lia Fail (OG 1048, ABV 4.7%)
The Gaelic name means Stone of Destiny. A dark, robust, full-bodied beer with a deep malty taste. Smooth texture and balanced finish.

Ironbridge

Ironbridge Brewery Ltd, Unit 7, Merrythought, The Wharfage, Ironbridge, Telford, Shropshire, TF8 7NJ
☎ (01952) 433910
✉ david@ironbridgebrewery.co.uk
🌐 ironbridgebrewery.co.uk
Tours by arrangement

Ironbridge was established in spring 2008 and operates on a 12-barrel brewery in an old Victorian warehouse alongside the River Severn in the heart of the Ironbridge Gorge. A visitor centre and shop were opened in 2009. All regular beers are also available bottle conditioned. Occasional beer: Shankers Tipple (ABV 4.6%).

Coracle Bitter (OG 1039, ABV 3.8%)

1779 (OG 1043, ABV 4.2%)

Ironbridge Gold (OG 1047, ABV 4.5%)

ISB (OG 1051, ABV 5%)

Irving SIBA

Irving & Co Brewers Ltd, Unit G1, Railway Triangle, Walton Road, Portsmouth, Hampshire, PO6 1TQ
☎ (023) 9238 9988
✉ sales@irvingbrewers.co.uk
🌐 irvingbrewers.co.uk
Shop Thu & Fri 3-6pm
Tours by arrangement

Irving's was set up by former Gale's brewer Malcolm Irving and a small team of ex-Gales employees using a 15-barrel plant. Around 60 outlets are supplied direct. Seasonal beers: see website.

Frigate (OG 1039, ABV 3.8%)

Type42 (OG 1042, ABV 4.2%)

Invincible (OG 1048, ABV 4.6%)
A tawny-coloured strong bitter. Sweet and fruity with an underlying maltiness throughout and a dryness that increases gradually, contrasting well with the sweetness of the finish.

Islay

Islay Ales Co Ltd, The Brewery, Islay House Square, Bridgend, Isle of Islay, PA44 7NZ
☎ (01496) 810014
✉ info@islayales.com
🌐 islayales.com
Shop Mon-Sat 10.30am-5pm
Tours by arrangement

Brewing started on a four-barrel plant in a converted tractor shed in 2004. The brewery shop is next door. Paul Hathaway, Paul Capper and Walter Schobert set up the brewery on an island more famous for its whisky, but it has established itself as a must-see place for those visiting the eight working distilleries on the island. The beers are available in many hotels, pubs and restaurants on the Island. Bottle-conditioned beers are available.

Finlaggan Ale (OG 1039, ABV 3.7%)

Black Rock Ale (OG 1040, ABV 4.2%)

Dun Hogs Head Ale (OG 1044, ABV 4.4%)

Saligo Ale (OG 1044, ABV 4.4%)

Angus OG Ale (OG 1045, ABV 4.5%)

Ardnave Ale (OG 1048, ABV 4.6%)

Nerabus Ale (OG 1046, ABV 4.8%)

Single Malt Ale (OG 1050, ABV 5%)

Isle of Arran

See Arran

Isle of Mull

Isle of Mull Brewing Co Ltd, Ledaig, Tobermory, Isle of Mull, PA75 6NR
☎ (01688) 302821
✉ isleofmullbrewing@btinternet.com

Brewing started in 2005 using a five-barrel plant. Bottled beers are available but are not bottle conditioned.

Island Pale Ale (OG 1038, ABV 3.9%)

Galleon Gold (ABV 4.1%)

Royal Regiment of Scotland (ABV 4.1%)

McCaig's Folly (OG 1042, ABV 4.2%)

Terror of Tobermory (OG 1045, ABV 4.6%)

Isle of Purbeck

Isle of Purbeck Brewery, Manor Road, Studland, Dorset, BH19 3AU
☎ (01929) 450227
✉ info@isleofpurbeckbrewery.com
🌐 isleofpurbeckbrewery.com
Tours by arrangement

Brewing started in 2002 on a 10-barrel plant using brewing equipment from the former Poole Brewery. The brewery is in the grounds of the Bankes Arms Hotel, overlooking Studland Bay on the Jurassic coast. Seasonal beer: Thermal Cheer

(ABV 4.8%, winter). Further seasonal beers are planned and bottle-conditioned beers are available.

Best Bitter (OG 1036, ABV 3.6%) ◆
The latest addition to the range, a classic malty bitter with rich malt aroma and taste and smooth malty, bitter finish.

Fossil Fuel (OG 1040, ABV 4.1%) ◆
Amber bitter with a complex peppery aroma. Rich malts pervade the taste with a smooth dry finish.

Solar Power (OG 1043, ABV 4.3%) ◆
Light golden ale brewed using Continental hops to provide a refreshing mouthfeel. Hop aromas follow into the taste to provide a smooth finish.

Studland Bay Wrecked (OG 1044, ABV 4.5%) ◆
Deep-red ale with a slightly sweet aroma reflecting the mixture of caramel, malt and hops that provide the unique flavour and dry, rich finish.

IPA (OG 1047, ABV 4.8%) ◆
A novel twist on an old style of ale, the complex balance of malt and several hops offer a well-balanced taste and aroma leading to a dry bitter, hoppy finish.

Isle of Skye

Isle of Skye Brewing Co (Leann an Eilein) Ltd, The Pier, Uig, Isle of Skye, IV51 9XP
☎ (01470) 542477
✉ info@skyebrewery.co.uk
🌐 skyebrewery.co.uk
Shop Mon-Sat 10am-6pm; Sun 12.30-4.30pm (Apr-Oct)
Tours by arrangement

The Isle of Skye Brewery was established in 1995, the first commercial brewery in the Hebrides. Originally a 10-barrel plant, it was upgraded to 20-barrels in 2004. Fermenting capacity now stands at 80 barrels, with plans to further increase this and upgrade bottling facilities. Seasonal beers: see website.

Skyelight (OG 1038, ABV 3.8%)

Young Pretender (OG 1039, ABV 4%) ◆
A full-bodied golden ale, predominantly hoppy and fruity. The bitterness in the mouth is also balanced by summer fruits and hops, continuing into the lingering bitter finish.

Red Cuillin (OG 1041, ABV 4.2%) ◆
A light, fruity nose with a hint of caramel leads to a full-bodied, malty flavour and a long, dry, bittersweet finish.

Hebridean Gold (OG 1041.5, ABV 4.3%) ◆
Porridge oats are used to produce this delicious golden speciality beer. Nicely balanced, it has a refreshingly soft, fruity, bitter flavour. Thirst quenching and very drinkable. Could be mistaken for a best bitter.

Black Cuillin (OG 1044, ABV 4.5%) ◆
A complex, tasty brew worthy of its many awards. Full-bodied with a malty richness, malts do hold sway but there are plenty of hops and fruit to be discovered in its varied character. A truly delicious Scottish old ale.

Blaven (OG 1047, ABV 5%) ◆
A well-balanced strong amber bitter with kiwi fruit and caramel in the nose and a lingering, sharp bitterness.

Cuillin Beast (OG 1061.5, ABV 7%) ◆
A fruity 'winter warmer'; sweet and fruity, and much more drinkable than the strength would suggest. Plenty of caramel throughout with a variety of fruit on the nose.

Itchen Valley SIBA

Itchen Valley Brewery Ltd, Prospect Commercial Park, Prospect Road, New Alresford, Hampshire, SO24 9QF
☎ (01962) 735111/736429
✉ info@itchenvalley.com
🌐 itchenvalley.com
Shop Mon-Fri 9am-5pm
Tours by arrangement

Established in 1997, Itchen Valley moved to new premises in 2006. The brewery has a gift shop and offers brewery tours and mini conferencing facilities. More than 300 pubs are supplied, with wholesalers used for further distribution. Seasonal beers: Father Christmas (ABV 5%), Rudolph (ABV 3.8%), Watercress Line (ABV 4.2%). Bottle-conditioned beers are also available.

Godfathers (OG 1038, ABV 3.8%) ◆
A citrus hop character with a malty taste and a light body, leading to an increasingly dry, bitter finish. Pale brown in colour.

Fagin's (OG 1041, ABV 4.1%) ◆
Enjoyable copper-coloured best bitter with a hint of crystal malt and a pleasant bitter aftertaste.

Hampshire Rose (OG 1042, ABV 4.2%)
A golden amber ale. Fruit and hops dominate the taste throughout, with a good mouth feel.

Winchester Ale (OG 1042, ABV 4.2%)
Traditional English bitter, nut brown with a sweet, malty flavour with a good hoppy nose.

Pure Gold (OG 1046, ABV 4.6%) ◆
An aromatic, hoppy, golden bitter. Initial grapefruit flavours lead to a dry, bitter finish.

Jacobi

Jacobi Brewery of Caio, Penlanwen Farm, Pumsaint, Carmarthenshire, SA19 8RR
☎ (01558) 650605
✉ justin@jacobibrewery.co.uk
🌐 jacobibrewery.co.uk

Brewing started in 2006 on an eight-barrel plant in a converted barn. Brewer Justin Jacobi is also the owner of the Brunant Arms in Caio, which is a regular outlet for the beers. The brewery is located 50 yards from the Dolaucothi mines where the Romans dug for gold. A visitor centre and bottling line are planned.

Light Ale (OG 1040, ABV 3.8%)

Original (OG 1044, ABV 4%)

Dark Ale (OG 1052, ABV 5%)

Jarrow SIBA

Jarrow Brewery, The Maltings, 9 Claypath Lane, South Shields, Tyne & Wear, NE33 4PG
☎ (0191) 483 6792
✉ jarrowbrewery@btconnect.com
🌐 jarrowbrewing.co.uk
Tours by arrangement

Real ale enthusiasts Jess and Alison McConnell commenced brewing at the Robin Hood, Jarrow in

2002. In 2008 all brewing was transferred to a larger plant at The Maltings in South Shields. Seasonal beers: Westoe Crown (ABV 4.2%, May, Jul & Sep), Red Ellen (ABV 4.4%, Feb-Mar & Oct-Nov), Venerable Bede (ABV 4.5%, Apr, Jun & Aug), Old Cornelius (ABV 4.8%, Dec-Jan).

Bitter (OG 1037.5, ABV 3.8%)
A light golden session bitter with a delicate hop aroma and a lingering fruity finish.

Rivet Catcher (OG 1039, ABV 4%)
A light, smooth, satisfying gold bitter with fruity hops on the tongue and nose.

Joblings Swinging Gibbet (OG 1041, ABV 4.1%)
A copper-coloured, evenly balanced beer with a good hop aroma and a fruity finish.

Caulkner (ABV 4.2%)

McConnells Irish Stout (OG 1045, ABV 4.6%)

Westoe IPA (OG 1044.5, ABV 4.6%)

Jennings

See Marston's in the New Nationals section

Jersey SIBA

Jersey Brewery, Tregear House, Longueville Road, St Saviour, Jersey, JE2 7WF
☎ (01534) 508151
paulhurley@victor-hugo-ltd.com
Tours by arrangement

Following the closure of the original brewery in Ann Street in 2004, the Jersey Brewery is now located in an old soft drinks factory using a 40-barrel plant along with the eight-barrel plant from the former Tipsy Toad Brewery. Most cask beers are produced on the smaller plant, though the bigger one, which usually produces keg beer, can also be used for cask production. Cask Special was first produced for the 2005 Jersey beer festival but, after receiving the Beer of the Festival award, is now in regular production. The other cask ale, Sunbeam, is produced for the Guernsey market following the closure of the Guernsey Brewery. Up to four seasonal beers are produced each year.

Liberation Ale (ABV 4%)
Golden beer with a hint of citrus on the nose.

Guernsey Sunbeam (OG 1042, ABV 4.2%)

Special (OG 1045, ABV 4.5%)

Jollyboat

Jollyboat Brewery (Bideford) Ltd, The Coach House, Buttgarden Street, Bideford, Devon, EX39 2AU
☎ (01237) 424343

Established in 1995 the brewery is named after a sailor's leave boat and all the beers have a nautical theme. Most outlets supplied are in Devon but a trade route to Bristol has recently been established. Seasonal beers: Buccaneers (ABV 3.7%, summer), Contraband (ABV 5.8%, winter). Bottle-conditioned beers are also available.

Grenville's Renown (OG 1037, ABV 3.8%)

Freebooter (OG 1040, ABV 4%)

Mainbrace (OG 1042, ABV 4.2%)
Pale brown brew with a rich fruity aroma and a bitter taste and aftertaste.

Hart of Oak (OG 1044, ABV 4.4%)

Plunder (OG 1047, ABV 4.8%)

Jolly Brewer

Jolly Brewer, Kingston Villa, 27 Poplar Road, Wrexham, LL13 7DG
☎ (01978) 261884
pene@jollybrewer.co.uk
jollybrewer.co.uk
Tours by arrangement (small groups only)

Jolly Brewer is a well-established cottage industry with the capacity to produce 20 gallons of beer per day. Penelope Coles brews casks to order from her long list of recipes and all beers are also available in bottle-conditioned form. Her beers can be purchased at the Wrexham Farmer's Market on the third Friday of the month and at the Grosvenor Garden Centre Farmer's Market in Chester on the second Friday. All bottle-conditioned beers are suitable for vegetarians and vegans.

Chwerw Cymreig (OG 1042, ABV 4%)

Druid's Ale (OG 1042, ABV 4%)

Festival Ale (OG 1042, ABV 4%)

Taid's Garden (OG 1042, ABV 4%)

Cwrw Du (OG 1043, ABV 4.2%)

Lucinda's Lager (OG 1040, ABV 4.5%)

Porter (Penelope's Secret) (OG 1050, ABV 4.5%)

Suzanne's Stout (OG 1050, ABV 4.5%)

Taffy's Tipple (OG 1045, ABV 4.5%)

Y Ddraig Goch (OG 1045, ABV 4.5%)

Dynes Dywyll (OG 1050, ABV 5%)

Dark Lager (OG 1060, ABV 6%)

Joseph Herbert Smith

Joseph Herbert Smith Trad Brewers, Fox Inn, Hanley Broadheath, Nr Tenbury Wells, Worcestershire, WR15 8QS
☎ (01886) 853189
☎ 07786 220409
jonathansmudge2000@yahoo.co.uk
Tours by arrangement

The brewery was established in 2007 by Jonathan Smith on a 2.5-barrel plant from Danelaw Brewery. In 2008 it relocated from Wombourne in Staffordshire to barns adjacent to the Fox Inn in Tenbury Wells. All equipment is gas fired and ingredients are sourced locally where possible. Seasonal beer: Kinny's Port Stout (ABV 4.5%, Nov-Feb), Elm (ABV 3.9%). Monthly feature beers are also available.

Amy's Rose (OG 1040, ABV 4%)

Foxy Lady (OG 1043, ABV 4.3%)

Kelburn SIBA

Kelburn Brewing Co Ltd, 10 Muriel Lane, Barrhead, East Renfrewshire, G78 1QB
☎ (0141) 881 2138
info@kelburnbrewery.com
kelburnbrewery.com
Tours by arrangement

Kelburn is a family business established in 2002. In the first six years of business, the beers

THE BREWERIES

have won 24 awards. Beers are available bottled and in take-away polypins. Seasonal beers: Ca'Canny (ABV 5.2%, winter), Pivo Estivo (ABV 3.9%, summer), Tartan Army (ABV 4.3%, Easter, autumn & when Scotland football team are playing), Kracker (ABV 6%, Xmas).

Goldihops (OG 1038, ABV 3.8%)
Well-hopped session ale with a fruity taste and a bitter finish.

Misty Law (ABV 4%)
A dry, hoppy amber ale with a long-lasting bitter finish.

Red Smiddy (OG 1040, ABV 4.1%)
This bittersweet ale predominantly features an intense citrus hop character that assaults the nose and continues into the flavour, balanced perfectly with fruity malt.

Dark Moor (OG 1044, ABV 4.5%)
A dark, fruity ale with undertones of liquorice and blackcurrant.

Cart Blanche (OG 1048, ABV 5%)
A golden, full-bodied ale. The assault of fruit and hop camouflages the strength of this easy-drinking, malty ale.

Kelham Island SIBA

Kelham Island Brewery Ltd, 23 Alma Street, Sheffield, South Yorkshire, S3 8SA
(0114) 249 4804
sales@kelhambrewery.co.uk
kelhambrewery.co.uk
Tours by arrangement

The brewery opened in 1990 behind the Fat Cat public house. Due to its success, the brewery moved to new purpose-built premises in 1999 (adjacent to the pub), with five times the capacity of the original brewery. The old building has been converted into a visitor centre. Four regular beers are brewed as well as monthly themed specials and more than 200 outlets are supplied. Seasonal beers: Golden Eagle (ABV 4.2%, summer), Brooklyn Smoked Porter (ABV 6.5%, winter). Bottle-conditioned beers are also available and are suitable for vegetarians.

Kelham Best Bitter (OG 1038, ABV 3.8%)
A clean, characterful, crisp, pale brown beer. The nose and palate are dominated by refreshing hoppiness and fruitiness, which, with a good bitter dryness, lasts in the aftertaste.

Pride of Sheffield (OG 1040.5, ABV 4%)
A full-flavoured amber coloured bitter.

Easy Rider (OG 1041.8, ABV 4.3%)
A pale, straw-coloured beer with a sweetish flavour and delicate hints of citrus fruits. A beer with hints of flavour rather than full-bodied.

Pale Rider (OG 1050, ABV 5.2%)
A full-bodied, straw pale ale, with a good fruity aroma and a strong fruit and hop taste. Its well-balanced sweetness and bitterness continue in the finish.

Keltek SIBA

Keltek Brewery, Candela House, Cardrew Way, Redruth, Cornwall, TR15 1SS
(01209) 313620
sales@keltekbrewery.co.uk
keltekbrewery.co.uk
Shop Mon-Fri 8am-6pm

Keltek Brewery moved to Lostwithiel in 1999 and in 2006 moved again to Redruth and installed a new 25-barrel plant in addition to the original two-barrel plant, which is still used for specials and development. About 20 local pubs in the Redruth area are supplied direct with ales available nationally via wholesalers. All ales are also available bottle conditioned. Keltek took over Doghouse Brewery in 2008. CAMRA members are welcome (by appointment) to try their hand at brewing.

4K Mild (OG 1038, ABV 3.8%)

Golden Lance (OG 1038, ABV 4%)

Magik (OG 1040, ABV 4.2%)
A rounded, well-balanced and complex beer.

Mr Murdoch's Golden IPA (OG 1043, ABV 4.5%)

Natural Magik (OG 1044, ABV 4.5%)

Trevithick's Revenge (OG 1043, ABV 4.5%)

King (OG 1049, ABV 5.1%)

Grim Reaper (OG 1058, ABV 6%)

Beheaded (OG 1068, ABV 7.6%)

Brewed under All Saints Brewery name:

St Pirans Cornish Best Bitter (OG 1039, ABV 4%)
Copper-coloured bitter combining three different malts and hops.

St Arnold (OG 1045, ABV 4.6%)
Golden IPA full of hoppy bitterness.

Kemptown SIBA

Kemptown Brewery Co Ltd, 33 Upper St James's Street, Kemptown, Brighton, East Sussex, BN2 1JN
(01273) 699595
bev@kemptownbrewery.co.uk
kemptownbrewery.co.uk
Tours by arrangement

Kemptown was established in 1989 and built in the tower tradition behind the Hand in Hand, which is possibly the smallest brewpub in England. It takes its name and logo from the former Charrington's Kemptown Brewery, which closed in 1964. Seasonal beers are available.

Kemptown (OG 1040, ABV 4%)
A light session ale. Crisp and hoppy.

Ye Olde Trout (OG 1045, ABV 4.5%)
A golden brown beer with fruity aromas and a dry finish.

Keswick

Keswick Brewing Co, The Old Brewery, Brewery Lane, Keswick, Cumbria, CA12 5BY
(01768) 780700
info@keswickbrewery.co.uk
keswickbrewery.co.uk
Shop – call for details (usually Mon-Fri 9am-5pm)
Tours by arrangement

Phil and Sue Harrison set up their 10-barrel brewery in 2006 with quality and environmental issues at its heart. It is located on the site of a brewery which closed in 1897. More than 70 outlets are supplied. Seasonal beers: see website.

Thirst Rescue (OG 1036, ABV 3.7%)

Thirst Pitch (OG 1037, ABV 3.8%)

Thirst Ascent (OG 1039, ABV 4%)

Thirst Run (OG 1041, ABV 4.2%)

Thirst Fall (OG 1048, ABV 5%)

Thirst Celebration (OG 1065, ABV 7%)

Keystone

Keystone Brewery, Old Carpenters Workshop, Berwick St Leonard, Salisbury, Wiltshire, SP3 5SN
☎ (01747) 820426
✉ info@keystonebrewery.co.uk
🌐 keystonebrewery.co.uk
Shop Mon, Tue & Fri 10am-5pm
Tours by arrangement

⊗ Keystone Brewery was set up in 2006 with a 10-barrel plant. The beers have low food miles to help support a sustainable local community. Around 200 outlets are supplied. Seasonal beers: Bedrock (ABV 3.6%, spring), Porter (ABV 4.5%, autumn), Cheer Up (ABV 4.6%, late winter). Bottle-conditioned beers are also available.

Solar Brew (OG 1037, ABV 3.8%)

Gold Spice (OG 1039, ABV 4%)

Gold Standard (OG 1039, ABV 4%)

Large One (OG 1041, ABV 4.2%)

Cornerstone (OG 1047, ABV 4.8%)

Kilderkin

Kilderkin Brewing Co, 1 Mill Road, Impington, Cambridgeshire, CB24 9PE
✉ sales@kilderkin.co.uk
🌐 kilderkin.co.uk

Kilderkin was founded in 2006 in a village just outside Cambridge. It produces bottle-conditioned ales for sale to a handful of local outlets and cask ales, which are mainly sold on an adhoc basis to local beer festivals.

Porter (OG 1048, ABV 4.8%)

Double (OG 1065, ABV 6%)

King SIBA

W J King & Co (Brewers), 3-5 Jubilee Estate, Foundry Lane, Horsham, West Sussex, RH13 5UE
☎ (01403) 272102
✉ sales@kingbeer.co.uk
🌐 kingbeer.co.uk
Shop Sat 10am-2pm
Tours by arrangement (limited to 15)

⊗ Launched in 2001 on a 20-barrel plant, the brewery had expanded to a capacity of 50 barrels a week by mid-2004. In 2004 premises next door were added to give more cellar space and to enable room to stock more bottle-conditioned beers. Around 200 outlets are supplied. Seasonal beers: Old Ale (ABV 4.5%, winter), Summer Ale (ABV 4%), Merry Ale (ABV 6.5%, Xmas).

Horsham Best Bitter (OG 1038, ABV 3.8%) ◆
A predominantly malty best bitter, brown in colour. The nutty flavours have some sweetness with a little bitterness that grows in the aftertaste.

Red River (OG 1048, ABV 4.8%) ◆
A full-flavoured, mid-brown beer. It is malty with some berry fruitiness in the aroma and taste. The finish is reasonably balanced with a sharp bitterness coming through.

Kings Head

Kings Head Brewery, Kings Head, 132 High Street, Bildeston, Ipswich, Suffolk, IP7 7ED
☎ (01449) 741434
✉ kingshead.bildeston@tiscali.co.uk
🌐 bildestonkingshead.co.uk
Tours by arrangement

⊗ Kings Head has been brewing since 1996 in an old cart lodge at the back of the pub. Under new ownership since 2008, the three-barrel plant brews weekly. Local pubs and beer festivals are supplied. Seasonal beers: see website.

Bildeston Best (OG 1036, ABV 3.6%)
Traditional best. Well-hopped with a malty sweetness and dry finish.

Blondie (OG 1040, ABV 4%)
Cask lager.

Landlady (OG 1040, ABV 4%)
Pale ale, hoppy and fruity with a dry finish.

Dark Vadar (OG 1044, ABV 4.3%)
Porter with chocolate maltyness.

First Gold (OG 1043, ABV 4.3%)

Crowdie (OG 1050, ABV 5%)
An oatmeal stout.

Kingstone

Kingstone Brewery, Meadow Farm, Tintern, Monmouthshire, NP16 7NX
☎ (01291) 680111/680101
✉ shop@kingstonebrewery.co.uk
🌐 kingstonebrewery.co.uk

⊗ Kingstone Brewery is located in the Wye Valley where brewing began on a four-barrel plant in 2005. All cask ales are also available bottle conditioned.

Tewdric's Tipple (ABV 3.8%)

Challenger (ABV 4%)

Gold (ABV 4%)

No. 1 Stout (ABV 4.4%)

Classic (ABV 4.5%)

1503 (ABV 4.8%)

Abbey Ale (ABV 5.1%)

Humpty's Fuddle (ABV 5.8%)

Kinver SIBA

Kinver Brewery, Unit 2, Fairfield Drive, Kinver, Staffordshire, DY7 6EW
☎ 07715 842679/07906 146777
✉ kinvercave@aol.com
🌐 kinverbrewery.co.uk
Tours by arrangement

⊗ Established in 2004 by two CAMRA members, Kinver Brewery consists of a five-barrel plant, producing six regular beers, seasonals and one-off brews. Kinver brews three times a week and supplies more than 30 pubs and clubs throughout the Midlands, including two in Kinver. Seasonal beers: Dudley Bug (ABV 4.8%, May-Aug), Maybug (ABV 4.8%, May-Jun), Sunarise (ABV 4%, summer), Over the Edge (ABV 7.6%, Nov-Mar).

Edge (OG 1041, ABV 4.2%) ◆
Amber with a caramel and biscuit aroma. The sweet start with a little fruitiness develops into a bitterness that elbows out the sweetness and promotes the hops for a lingering, mouth-watering finish.

Pail Ale (OG 1044, ABV 4.4%) ◆
Gold with a hoppy aroma and malty background. Citrus hops dominate but are tempered with fruit for a bittersweet balance. Astringent note at the end.

Crystal (OG 1046, ABV 4.8%)
Pale premium bitter with a dry, citrus finish.

Caveman (OG 1049, ABV 5%) ◆
A malt aroma leads into a malt and hop start that intensifies to a long hoppy aftertaste.

Half Centurion (OG 1048, ABV 5%)
Pale bitter with citrus hop flavours and a bitter finish.

Khyber (OG 1054, ABV 5.8%)
Traditional strength imperial pale ale.

Kirkby Lonsdale (NEW)

Kirkby Lonsdale Brewery Co Ltd, Unit 2F, Old Station Yard, Kirkby Lonsdale, Lancashire, LA6 2HP
☎ (01524) 272221
☎ 07793 149999
✉ info@kirkbylonsdalebrewery.com
🌐 kirkbylonsdalebrewery.com
Tours by arrangement

Kirkby Lonsdale is a family-run business established in 2009 on a six-barrel plant.

Ruskin's Bitter (ABV 3.9%)

Monumental (ABV 4.5%)

Jubilee (ABV 5.5%)

Lancaster SIBA

Lancaster Brewery Co Ltd, 19 Lansil Walk, Caton Road, Lancaster, LA1 3PQ
☎ (01524) 848537
✉ info@lancasterbrewery.co.uk
🌐 lancasterbrewery.co.uk
Tours by arrangement

◎ Lancaster began brewing in 2005. In 2007 the brewery underwent a change in direction with new faciities installed and new brands launched. More than 200 outlets are supplied direct. Seasonal beer: Redder (ABV 5.9%, Dec).

Amber (OG 1038, ABV 3.7%)
Dark gold session beer with a hoppy bouquet and subtle floral and citrus aromas.

Blonde (OG 1042, ABV 4.1%)
Golden bitter with a citrus and delicate earthy aroma. Initial bitterness is followed by good mouthfeel with a long, dry finish.

Slate (ABV 4.2%)
A rich, full-bodied porter. Packed with hop character both in taste and on the nose.

Black (OG 1046, ABV 4.6%)
Traditional stout; rich and full-bodied.

Red (OG 1048, ABV 4.9%)
Robust ale with a malt dominated body.

Langham

Langham Brewery, Old Granary, Langham Lane, Lodsworth, West Sussex, GU28 9BU
☎ (01798) 860861
✉ office@langhambrewery.co.uk
🌐 langhambrewery.co.uk
Shop Tue & Sat 9am-5pm
Tours by arrangement

⊗ Langham Brewery was established in 2006 in an 18th-century granary barn and is set in the heart of West Sussex with fine views to the rolling South Downs. It is owned by Steve Mansley and James Berrow who both brew and run the business. The brewery is a 10-barrel steam heated plant and over 50 outlets are supplied.

Halfway to Heaven (OG 1035, ABV 3.5%)
A chestnut-coloured beer with a balanced biscuit maltiness and citrus and fruit hop character with a hint of spice.

Hip Hop (OG 1040, ABV 4%)
A blonde beer – clean and crisp. The nose is loaded with floral hop aroma while the pale malt flavour is overtaken by a dry and bitter finish.

Best (OG 1042, ABV 4.2%)
A tawny-coloured classic best with well-balanced malt flavours and bitterness.

Sundowner (OG 1042, ABV 4.2%)
A deep golden beer. The nose has tropical fruit, pineapple and citrus notes with a smooth maltiness in the background. There is a balanced dry and bitter finish with floral hop aroma.

Langham Special Draught/LSD (OG 1049, ABV 5.2%)
An auburn beer with rich, complex flavours and a deep red glow. The sweet maltiness is balanced with spicy hop aromas and a dry finish.

Langton

Langton Brewery, Grange Farm, Welham Road, Thorpe Langton, Leicestershire, LE16 7TU
☎ 07840 532826
🌐 langtonbrewery.co.uk

⊗ The Langton Brewery started in 1999 in buildings behind the Bell Inn, East Langton. Due to demand, the brewery relocated in 2005 to a converted barn in Thorpe Langton, where a four-barrel plant was installed. All beers are available to take away in casks, polypins or bottles. 60 outlets are supplied. Seasonal beer: Welland Sunrise (ABV 4.5%). Bottle-conditioned beers are also available.

Caudle Bitter (OG 1039, ABV 3.9%) ◆
Copper-coloured session bitter that is close to pale ale in style. Flavours are relatively well-balanced throughout with hops slightly to the fore.

Inclined Plane Bitter (OG 1042, ABV 4.2%)
A straw-coloured bitter with a citrus nose and long, hoppy finish.

Hop On (ABV 4.4%)

Bowler Strong Ale (OG 1048, ABV 4.8%)
A strong traditional ale with a deep red colour and a hoppy nose.

Larkins SIBA

Larkins Brewery Ltd, Larkins Farm, Hampkin Hill Road, Chiddingstone, Kent, TN8 7BB
☎ (01892) 870328
Tours by arrangement (Nov-Feb)

⊗ Larkins Brewery was founded in 1986 by the Dockerty family, who bought the Royal Tunbridge Wells Brewery. The company moved to Larkins Farm in 1987. Since then the production of three regular brews and Porter in the winter months has steadily increased. Larkins owns one pub, the Rock at Chiddingstone Hoath, and supplies around 70 free houses within a radius of 20 miles. Seasonal beer: Platinum Blonde (ABV 3.6%, summer).

Traditional Ale (OG 1035, ABV 3.4%)
Tawny in colour, a full-tasting hoppy ale with plenty of character for its strength.

Chiddingstone (OG 1040, ABV 4%)
Named after the village where the brewery is based, Chiddingstone is a mid-strength, hoppy, fruity ale with a long, bittersweet aftertaste.

Best (OG 1045, ABV 4.5%) ◆
Full-bodied, slightly fruity and unusually bitter for its gravity.

Porter (OG 1052, ABV 5.2%) ◆
Each taste and smell of this potent black winter beer (Nov-Apr) reveals another facet of its character. An explosion of roasted malt, bitter and fruity flavours leaves a bittersweet aftertaste.

Leadmill

Leadmill Brewery Ltd, Unit 1, Park Hall Farm, Park Hall Road, Denby, Derbyshire, DE5 8PX
☎ (01332) 835609
✉ tlc@leadmill.fsnet.co.uk

⊗ Originally set up in a pig sty in Selston, the brewery moved to Denby in 2002 and now has a four-barrel plant. Its sister brewery, Bottle Brook (qv), sources rare and unusual hops to be incorporated into Leadmill recipes. Its brewery tap is the Old Oak Inn, two miles away. Seasonal beers: Jersey City (ABV 5%, autumn), Ginger Spice (ABV 5%, summer), Autumn Goddess (ABV 4.2%), Get Stuffed (ABV 6.7%, Xmas).

Mash Tun Bitter (OG 1036, ABV 3.6%)

Old Oak Bitter (OG 1037, ABV 3.7%)

Duchess (OG 1041, ABV 4.2%)

Old Mottled Cock (OG 1041, ABV 4.2%)

Dream Weaver (OG 1042, ABV 4.3%)

Frosted Hop (OG 1042, ABV 4.3%)

Strawberry Blonde (OG 1042, ABV 4.4%)

Rolling Thunder (OG 1043, ABV 4.5%)

Curly Blonde (OG 1044, ABV 4.6%)

Maple Porter (OG 1045, ABV 4.7%)

Snakeyes (OG 1045, ABV 4.8%)

Agent Orange (OG 1047, ABV 4.9%)

Born in the USA (OG 1048, ABV 5%)

Rampage (OG 1050, ABV 5.1%)

B52 (OG 1050, ABV 5.2%)

Destitution (OG 1051, ABV 5.3%)

Ghostrider (OG 1052, ABV 5.4%)

Beast (OG 1053, ABV 5.7%)

Nemesis (OG 1062, ABV 6.4%)

WMD (OG 1065, ABV 6.7%)

Leatherbritches

Leatherbritches Brewery, Green Man & Blacks Head Royal Hotel, St John Street, Ashbourne, Derbyshire, DE6 1GH
☎ 07976 279253
✉ leatherbritches@btconnect.com
Shop: Opening times vary – please ring first (01335) 342374
Tours by arrangement

The brewery, founded in 1993 in Fenny Bentley, moved to Ashbourne in 2008 with a new, bigger brewing plant. The hotel and brewery business are separate but the hotel sells beers from the brewery. Bottle-conditioned beers are available. 30-50 outlets are supplied direct.

Goldings (OG 1036, ABV 3.6%)
A light golden beer with a flowery hoppy aroma and a bitter finish.

Ginger Spice (OG 1036, ABV 3.8%)
A light, highly-hopped bitter with the added zest of Chinese stem ginger.

Ashbourne Ale (OG 1040, ABV 4%)
A pale bitter brewed with Goldings hops for a crisp lasting taste.

Doctor Johnsons (ABV 4%)

Belt-n-Braces (OG 1040, ABV 4.4%)
Mid-brown, full-flavoured, dry-hopped bitter.

Belter (OG 1040, ABV 4.4%)
Maris Otter malt produces a pale but interesting beer.

Dovedale (OG 1044, ABV 4.4%)

Ginger Helmet (OG 1047, ABV 4.7%)
As for Hairy Helmet but with a hint of China's most astringent herb.

Hairy Helmet (OG 1047, ABV 4.7%)
Pale bitter, well hopped but with a sweet finish.

Bespoke (OG 1050, ABV 5%)
Full-bodied, well-rounded premium bitter.

Leeds

Leeds Brewery Co Ltd, 3 Sydenham Road, Leeds, West Yorkshire, LS11 9RU
☎ (0113) 244 5866
✉ sales@leedsbrewery.co.uk
🌐 leedsbrewery.co.uk

Leeds Brewery began production in June 2007 using a 20-barrel plant. It is the largest independent brewer in the city and uses a unique strain of yeast originally used by another, now defunct, West Yorkshire brewery. Around 300 outlets are supplied direct. Seasonal beers: see website.

Pale (OG 1037.5, ABV 3.8%)

Best (OG 1041, ABV 4.3%)

Midnight Bell (OG 1047.5, ABV 4.8%)

Leek

Staffordshire Brewing Co t/a Leek Brewery, 12 Churnet Court, Cheddleton, Staffordshire, ST13 7EF
☎ (01538) 361919
☎ 07971 808370
✉ leekbrewery@hotmail.com
🌐 beersandcheese.co.uk
Tours by arrangement

Brewing started in 2002 with a 4.5-barrel plant located behind the owner's house, before moving to the current site in 2004. The brewery was upgraded to a six-barrel plant in 2007. Cask beer is only available to special order as 95% of the beer is now in bottle-conditioned form, suitable for vegetarians. A range of beer cheeses is also made in the dairy, next door to the brewery.

Staffordshire Gold (ABV 3.8%)
Light, straw-coloured with a pleasing hoppy aroma and a hint of malt. Bitter finish from the hops, making it easily drunk and thirst-quenching.

Danebridge IPA (ABV 4.1%)
Full fruit and hop aroma. Flowery hop start with a bitter taste. Finish of hops and flowers.

Staffordshire Bitter (ABV 4.2%)
Amber with a fruity aroma. Malty and hoppy start with the hoppy finish diminishing quickly.

Black Grouse (ABV 4.5%)

Hen Cloud (ABV 4.5%)

St Edwards (ABV 4.7%)

Rudyard Ruby (ABV 4.8%)

Double Sunset (ABV 5.2%)

Rocheberg Blonde (ABV 5.6%)

Cheddleton Steamer (ABV 6%)

Tittesworth Tipple (ABV 6.5%)

Lees IFBB

J W Lees & Co (Brewers) Ltd, Greengate Brewery, Middleton Junction, Manchester, M24 2AX
☎ (0161) 643 2487
✉ mail@jwlees.co.uk
🌐 jwlees.co.uk
Tours by arrangement

Lees is a family-owned brewery founded in 1828 by John Lees and run by the sixth generation of the family. Brewing takes place in the 1876 brewhouse designed and built by John Willie Lees, the grandson of the founder. The brewhouse has been completely modernised in recent years to give greater flexibility. The company has a tied estate of around 170 pubs, mostly in North Manchester, with 30 in North Wales; all serve cask beer. Seasonal beers are brewed four times a year.

Brewer's Dark (OG 1032, ABV 3.5%)
Formerly GB Mild, this is a dark brown beer with a malt and caramel aroma. Creamy mouthfeel, with malt, caramel and fruit flavours and a malty finish. Becoming rare.

Bitter (OG 1037, ABV 4%)
Copper-coloured beer with malt and fruit in aroma, taste and finish.

Scorcher (OG 1038, ABV 4.2%)
A golden, easy-drinking beer with a fruity aroma and a refreshing hop finish.

John Willie's (OG 1041, ABV 4.5%)
A well-balanced, full-bodied premium bitter.

Moonraker (OG 1073, ABV 7.5%)
A reddish-brown beer with a strong, malty, fruity aroma. The flavour is rich and sweet, with roast malt, and the finish is fruity yet dry. Available only in a handful of outlets.

Leila Cottage

Leila Cottage Brewery, The Countryman, Chapel Road, Ingoldmells, Skegness, Lincolnshire, PE25 1ND
☎ (01754) 872268
✉ countryman_inn@btconnect.com
Tours by arrangement

Leila Cottage started brewing in 2007. The brewery is situated at the Countryman pub – Leila Cottage was the original name of the building before it became a licensed club and more recently a pub. In 2009 the brewery upgraded from a 0.5-barrel plant to a 2-barrel one and began bottling. Only the Countryman is supplied at present.

Ace Ale (OG 1040, ABV 3.8%)

Leila's Ale (ABV 3.9%)

Leith Hill

Leith Hill Brewery, c/o Plough Inn, Coldharbour Lane, Coldharbour, Surrey, RH5 6HD
☎ (01306) 711793
✉ theploughinn@btinternet.com
🌐 ploughinn.com
Tours by arrangement

Leith Hill was formed in 1996 using home-made equipment to produce nine-gallon brews in a room at the front of the pub. The brewery moved to converted storerooms at the rear of the Plough Inn in 2001 and increased capacity to 2.5-barrels in 2005. All beers brewed are sold only on the premises.

Crooked Furrow (OG 1040, ABV 4%)
A malty beer, with some balancing hop bitterness. Pale brown in colour with an earthy malty aroma and a long dry and bittersweet aftertaste. Some fruit is also present throughout.

Tallywhacker (OG 1048, ABV 4.8%)
Dark, sweet and fruity old ale with good roast malt character.

Leyden SIBA

Leyden Brewing Ltd, Lord Raglan, Nangreaves, Bury, Greater Manchester, BL9 6SP
☎ (0161) 764 6680
Tours by arrangement

The brewery was built by Brian Farnworth and started production in 1999. Additional fermenting vessels have been installed, allowing a maximum production of 12 barrels a week. One pub is owned and 30 outlets are supplied. In addition to the permanent beers, a number of seasonal and occasional beers are brewed.

Balaclava (ABV 3.8%)

Black Pudding (ABV 3.8%)
A dark brown, creamy mild with a malty flavour, followed by a balanced finish.

Nanny Flyer (OG 1040, ABV 3.8%)

A drinkable session bitter with an initial dryness, and a hint of citrus, followed by a strong, malty finish.

Light Brigade (OG 1043, ABV 4.2%) ◆
Copper in colour with a citrus aroma. The flavour is a balance of malt, hops and fruit, with a bitter finish.

Rammy Rocket (ABV 4.2%)

Forever Bury (ABV 4.5%)

Raglan Sleeve (OG 1047, ABV 4.6%) ◆
Dark red/brown beer with a hoppy aroma and a dry, roasty, hoppy taste and finish.

Crowning Glory (OG 1069, ABV 6.8%)

Lichfield

Lichfield Brewery Co Ltd, Upper St John Street, Lichfield, Staffordshire
robsondavidb@hotmail.com
lichfieldbrewery.co.uk

Does not brew; beers mainly contracted by Blythe, Tower and Highgate breweries (qv).

Linfit

Linfit Brewery, Sair Inn, 139 Lane Top, Linthwaite, Huddersfield, West Yorkshire, HD7 5SG
☎ (01484) 842370

A 19th-century brew-pub that started brewing again in 1982. The beer is only available at the Sair Inn.

Bitter (OG 1035, ABV 3.7%) ◆
A refreshing session beer. A dry-hopped aroma leads to a clean-tasting, hoppy bitterness, then a long, bitter finish with a hint of malt.

Gold Medal (OG 1040, ABV 4.2%)
Very pale and hoppy. Use of the new dwarf variety of English hops, First Gold, gives an aromatic and fruity character.

Special (OG 1041, ABV 4.3%) ◆
Dry-hopping provides the aroma for this rich and mellow bitter, which has a very soft profile and character: it fills the mouth with texture rather than taste. Clean, rounded finish.

Autumn Gold (OG 1045, ABV 4.7%) ◆
Straw-coloured best bitter with hop and fruit aromas, then the bittersweetness of autumn fruit in the taste and the finish.

Old Eli (OG 1050, ABV 5.3%)
A well-balanced premium bitter with a dry-hop aroma and a fruity, bitter finish.

Lion's Tale SIBA

Lion's Tale Brewery, Red Lion, High Street, Cheswardine, Shropshire, TF9 2RS
☎ (01630) 661234
cheslion96@yahoo.co.uk

The building that houses the brewery was purpose-built in 2005 and houses a 2.5-barrel plant. Jon Morris and his wife have owned the Red Lion pub since 1996. Expansion is planned in the near future. Seasonal beer: Chesmas Bells (ABV 5.2%, Xmas).

Blooming Blonde (ABV 4.1%)

Lionbru (ABV 4.1%)

Chesbrewnette (ABV 4.5%)

Little Ale Cart

Little Ale Cart Brewing Co, c/o The Wellington, 1 Henry Street, Sheffield, South Yorkshire, S3 7EQ
☎ (0114) 249 2295

Brewing started in 2001, as Port Mahon, in a purpose-built brewery behind the Cask & Cutler. In 2007 the brewery and pub were taken over and the names of both changed to Little Ale Cart Brewing and the Wellington. The beer range varies as the brewer continues to trial new recipes, but tends to include a 4%, 4.3% and a 5% ABV beer.

Pale & Hoppy (ABV 4%)

Little Valley

Little Valley Brewery Ltd, Turkey Lodge Farm, New Road, Cragg Vale, Hebden Bridge, West Yorkshire, HX7 5TT
☎ (01422) 883888
info@littlevalleybrewery.co.uk
littlevalleybrewery.co.uk
Shop Mon-Fri 9am-5pm
Tours by arrangement

Little Valley Brewery opened in 2005 and is situated in the Upper Calder Valley, high above Cragg Vale in Hebden Bridge, West Yorkshire. The 10-barrel plant is in a converted turkey shed. It is a wholly organic brewery and is approved by the Soil Association. It does not use isinglass in the beers and is approved by the Vegan Society. The brewery is also a licensee of the Fairtrade Foundation for one of its beers, Ginger Pale Ale. All cask beers are also available in bottle-conditioned form. Around 100 outlets are supplied. Several beers are also contract brewed for Suma Wholefoods. A range of monthly specials was introduced in 2007.

Withens IPA (OG 1037, ABV 3.9%) ◆
Creamy, gold-coloured, refreshingly light ale. Floral, spicy hop aroma, lightly flavoured with hints of lemon and grapefruit. Clean, bitter aftertaste.

Ginger Pale Ale (OG 1037, ABV 4%) ◆
Full-bodied speciality ale. Ginger predominates in the aroma and taste. It has a pleasantly powerful, fiery and spicy finish.

Cragg Vale Bitter (OG 1039, ABV 4.2%) ◆
Grainy, pale-brown session bitter. Light on the palate with a delicate flavour of malt and fruit and a bitter finish.

Hebden's Wheat (OG 1043, ABV 4.5%) ◆
A pale yellow, creamy wheat beer with a good balance of bitterness and fruit. A hint of sweetness but with a lasting, dry finish.

Stoodley Stout (OG 1044, ABV 4.8%) ◆
Dark brown, creamy stout with a rich roast aroma and luscious fruity, chocolate roast flavours. Well-balanced with a clean, bitter finish.

Tod's Blonde (OG 1045, ABV 5%) ◆
Bright yellow, grainy speciality beer with a citrus hop start and a dry finish. Fruity, with a hint of spice. Similar in style to a Belgian blonde beer.

Moor Ale (OG 1051, ABV 5.5%) ◆
Tawny in colour with a full-bodied taste. It has a strong, malty nose and palate, with hints of heather and peat-smoked malt. Well-balanced with a bitter finish.

Litton

4-Bottles Ltd t/a Litton Ale Brewery, Queens Arms, Litton, North Yorkshire, BD23 5QJ
(01756) 770208
info@queensarmslitton.co.uk
queensarmslitton.co.uk

Brewing started in 2003 in a purpose-built stone extension at the rear of the pub. Brewing liquor is sourced from a spring that provides the pub with its own water supply. The brew length is three barrels and all production is in cask form. Around 20 outlets are supplied.

Ale (OG 1038, ABV 3.8%)
An easy-drinking, traditional bitter with a good malt/hop balance and a bitter finish.

Leading Light (OG 1038, ABV 3.8%)
A long, bitter aftertaste follows a malty flavour with tart fruit and a rising hop bitterness in this light-coloured beer. Low aroma.

Gold Crest (OG 1039, ABV 3.9%)
A very pale beer with a smooth, creamy head. Heavy, fruity hoppiness with no lingering bitterness.

Dark Star (OG 1040, ABV 4%)
A smooth, creamy dark mild, full-bodied for its strength. The taste is quite bitter with roast coffee and tart dark fruit flavours, complemented by a bitter, roast finish.

Potts Beck (OG 1043, ABV 4.2%)
Malt and hops fight for control in this copper-coloured best bitter with a fruity aroma.

Lizard

Lizard Ales Ltd, The Old Nuclear Bunker, Pednavounder, Nr Coverack, Cornwall, TR12 6SE
(01326) 281135
lizardales@msn.com
lizardales.co.uk
Shop Mon-Fri 9am-5pm

Launched in 2004 by partners Richard Martin and Mark and Leonora Nattrass, Lizard Ales supplies mainly in west Cornwall. Bottle-conditioned beers are a speciality (suitable for vegetarians and vegans). The brewery moved in spring 2008 to larger premises allowing space for expansion.

Helford River (OG 1035, ABV 3.6%)

Bitter (OG 1041, ABV 4.2%)

Frenchman's Creek (OG 1042, ABV 4.6%)

An Gof (OG 1049, ABV 5.2%)

Loch Leven (NEW)

Loch Leven Brewery, Criochan House, Maryburgh, Blairadam, KY4 0JE
(01383) 831751
neilwilkie64@yahoo.co.uk

Loch Leven was established in 2009 on a four-barrel brewery. More beers are planned.

Golden Goose (ABV 4.1%)

Loddon SIBA

Loddon Brewery Ltd, Dunsden Green Farm, Church Lane, Dunsden, Oxfordshire, RG4 9QD
(0118) 948 1111
sales@loddonbrewery.com
loddonbrewery.com
Shop Mon-Fri 8am-5pm; Sat 9am-3pm
Tours by arrangement

Loddon was established in 2003 in a 240-year-old brick and flint barn that houses a 17-barrel brewery able to produce 70 barrels a week. Over 350 outlets are supplied. The brewery site was expanded in 2008-09. Seasonal beers and monthly specials: see website. Bottle-conditioned beers are also available.

Hoppit (OG 1035.5, ABV 3.5%)
Hops dominate the aroma of this drinkable, light-coloured session beer. Malt and hops create a balanced taste and a pleasant bitterness carries through to the aftertaste.

Rin Tin Tin (OG 1042.8, ABV 4.1%)
A well-balanced complex brew. Malt and caramel dominate the aroma with hops entering the taste, leading to a bittersweet finish.

Hullabaloo (OG 1043.8, ABV 4.2%)
A hint of fruit in the initial taste develops into a balance of hops and malt in this well-rounded, medium bodied bitter with a bitter aftertaste.

Ferryman's Gold (OG 1044.8, ABV 4.4%)
Golden coloured with a strong hoppy character throughout, accompanied by fruit in the taste and aftertaste.

Bamboozle (OG 1048.8, ABV 4.8%)
Full-bodied and well balanced. Distinctive bittersweet flavour with hop and caramel to accompany.

Lovibonds

Lovibonds Brewery Ltd, Rear of 19-21 Market Place, Henley-on-Thames, Oxfordshire, RG9 2AA
(01491) 576596
info@lovibonds.com
lovibonds.com
Shop Sat 11am-5pm
Tours by arrangement

Lovibonds Brewery was founded by Jeff Rosenmeier in 2005 and is named after Joseph William Lovibond, who invented the Tintometer to measure beer colour. In addition to cask-conditioned ales, Lovibonds brews beers inspired by the traditions of other brewing nations. Around 50 outlets are supplied. Brewing also takes place on the Old Luxters Brewery plant (qv), 5 miles from Henley-on-Thames.

Henley Amber (OG 1035, ABV 3.4%)
An amber session bitter with a blend of roasted malts that gives a complex profile with a classic hop flavour and bitterness.

Henley Gold (OG 1045, ABV 4.6%)

Henley Dark (OG 1048, ABV 4.8%)

Lowes Arms

See Dane Town

Loweswater

Loweswater Brewery, Kirkstile Inn, Loweswater, Cumbria, CA13 0RU
(01900) 85219
info@kirkstile.com

kirkstile.com
Tours by arrangement

Loweswater Brewery was re-established at the Kirkstile Inn in 2003 by head brewer Matt Webster. The brewery produces six barrels a week for the inn and local beer festivals. Recent refurbishment and extension has increased capacity. In 2009 Loweswater Brewery bought Cumbrian Legendary Ales in Hawkshead.

Loweswater Pale Ale (LPA) (OG 1036, ABV 3.6%)

Melbreak Bitter (OG 1038, ABV 3.7%)
Pale bronze with a tangy fruit and hop resins aroma, and a long, bitter finish.

Rannerdale Best (OG 1042, ABV 4%)
A fruity beer made with Styrian Goldings hops.

Gold (OG 1042, ABV 4.3%)
Pale lager-style beer with masses of tropical fruit flavour. Brewed with German hops.

Grasmoor Dark (OG 1042, ABV 4.3%)
Deep ruby red beer with chocolate malt on the aroma, and hop resins, roast malt and raisin fruit on the palate.

Luckie (NEW)

Luckie Ales, Unit 8, Daubs Farm, Dunshalt, Fife, KY14 7ES
(01333) 352801
info@luckie-ales.com
luckie-ales.com

Luckie Ales was established in 2009. Three outlets are supplied direct. Bottle-conditioned beers are available.

Midnycht Myld (OG 1037, ABV 3.4%)

Scottish 70/- (OG 1038, ABV 3.6%)

Amber Ale (OG 1040, ABV 3.7%)

Ludlow SIBA

Ludlow Brewing Co Ltd, Kingsley Garage, 105 Corve Street, Ludlow, Shropshire, SY8 1DJ
(01584) 873291
gary@theludlowbrewingcompany.co.uk
theludlowbrewingcompany.co.uk
Shop open all hours (not Sun)

The brewery opened in 2006 in a 250-year-old building that was once a malthouse. More than 30 pubs are supplied within a 70-mile radius. The six-barrel plant has been extended with two additional fermenters to cope with increased sales. All beers are also available bottle conditioned.

Best (ABV 3.7%)

Gold (ABV 4.2%)

Boiling Well (ABV 4.7%)

Lymestone (NEW)

Lymestone Brewery Ltd, Unit 5, Mount Street Industrial Estate, Mount Street, Stone, Staffordshire, ST15 8LL
(01785) 817796
lymestonebrewery.co.uk

Lymestone was established in 2008 on a 10-barrel brew plant.

Stoney Broke (ABV 3.2%)
A ruby beer, packed with roast flavours that are balanced by a hoppy bitterness. Full-flavoured for its strength.

Stone Cutter (ABV 3.7%)
A pale brew full of floral and citrus flavours. Crisp on the palate wit a long, bitter yet balanced finish.

Stone Faced (ABV 4%)
Subtle citrus and toffee flavours balanced by a hoppy aroma and bitter finish.

Foundation Stone (OG 1047, ABV 4.5%)
A golden beer bursting with citrus flavours that give way to a long, pleasant bitter finish.

Stone The Crows (OG 1056, ABV 5.4%)
A rich, malty strong bitter full of juicy dark fruit flavours that give way to a long, bitter finish.

Lytham

Lytham Brewery Ltd, Unit 11, Lidun Park Industrial Estate, Boundary Road, Lytham, Lancashire, FY8 5HU
(01253) 737707
info@LythamBrewery.co.uk
LythamBrewery.co.uk
Tours by arrangement

Lytham started brewing in early 2008 at the Hastings Club in Lytham but moved to larger premises soon after due to demand.

Amber (OG 1037, ABV 3.6%)
A traditional malty beer using English hops.

Gold (OG 1042, ABV 4.2%)
A golden beer with a fruity aroma and lasting bitter finish.

Dark (OG 1047, ABV 5%)
Dark chocolate malt with a hint of vanilla and a smooth, dry finish.

McGivern

McGivern Ales, 17 Salisbury Road, Wrexham, LL13 7AS
(01978) 354232
07891 676614
mcgivernmatt@hotmail.com
Tours by arrangement

The brewery was established in early 2008 and brews 10-20 gallons a week for pubs and bottle-conditioned beers for markets. Around 15 outlets are supplied direct. Bottle-conditioned beers are suitable for vegetarians and vegans.

Mild Matt's Mild (OG 1037, ABV 3.6%)

Amber Ale (OG 1040, ABV 4%)

Crest Pale (OG 1041, ABV 4%)

Stout (OG 1042, ABV 4.2%)

No. 17 Pale (OG 1044, ABV 4.4%)

McGuinness

See Offa's Dyke

McLaughlin

McLaughlin Brewhouse, The Horseshoe, 28 Heath Street, Hampstead, London, NW3 6TE
(020) 7431 7206
getlucky@thehorseshoehampstead.com
thehorseshoehampstead.com
Tours by arrangement

THE BREWERIES

A micro-brewery built in 2006 to honour the landlord's late grandfather, who owned Mac's Brewery in Rockhampton, Australia. At present it only supplies its own pub, the Horseshoe.

McLaughlin Summer (OG 1041, ABV 3.6%)
Refreshing golden ale with light, hoppy notes.

McLaughlin Spring (OG 1044, ABV 4%)
Pale, hop-driven ale. Light on malt, big on hops.

McLaughlin Laurie Best Bitter (OG 1048, ABV 4.1%)
Full-bodied copper ale. Smooth, rich and bitter.

McLaughlin Winter (OG 1050, ABV 5%)
Full-bodied dark malt bitter. Smooth with a sweet, moreish aftertaste.

McMullen IFBB

McMullen & Sons Ltd, 26 Old Cross, Hertford, Hertfordshire, SG14 1RD
☎ (01992) 584911
reception@mcmullens.co.uk
mcmullens.co.uk

McMullen is Hertfordshire's oldest independent brewery, celebrating 180 years of brewing in 2007. A new brewhouse opened in 2006, giving the company greater flexibility to produce its regular cask beers and up to eight seasonal beers a year. Cask beer is served in all 136 pubs.

AK (OG 1035, ABV 3.7%)
A pleasant mix of malt and hops leads to a distinctive, dry aftertaste that isn't always as pronounced as it used to be.

Cask Ale (OG 1039, ABV 3.8%)
A light and refreshing beer marked by the use of Styrian Goldings and English Fuggle hops.

Country Bitter (OG 1042, ABV 4.3%)
A full-bodied beer with a well-balanced mix of malt, hops and fruit throughout.

Maclay

See Belhaven

Magpie

Magpie Brewery, Unit 4, Ashling Court, Ashling Street, Nottingham, Nottinghamshire, NG2 3JA
☎ 07738 762897
info@magpiebrewery.com
magpiebrewery.com

Magpie is a six-barrel brewery launched in 2006 by three friends. It is located a few feet from the perimeter of the Meadow Lane Stadium, home of Notts County FC (the Magpies) from which the brewery name naturally derived. Seasonal and occasional beers: see website.

Fledgling (ABV 3.8%)

Magpie Best (ABV 4.2%)

Thieving Rogue (ABV 4.5%)

Monty's Firkin (ABV 4.6%)

Full Flight (ABV 4.8%)

JPA (ABV 5.2%)

Maldon

See Farmers Ales

Mallard SIBA

Mallard Brewery, 15 Hartington Avenue, Carlton, Nottingham, NG4 3NR
☎ (0115) 952 1289
Tours by arrangement

Phil Mallard built and installed a two-barrel plant in a shed at his home and started brewing in 1995. The brewery is only nine square metres and contains a hot liquor tank, mash tun, copper, and three fermenters. Since 1995 production has risen from one barrel a week to between six or eight barrels, which is the plant's maximum. Around 12 outlets are supplied. Seasonal beers: Waddlers Mild (ABV 3.7%, spring), DA (ABV 5.8%, Jan-Mar), Quismas Quacker (ABV 6%, Dec), Owd Duck (ABV 4.8%, winter).

Duck 'n' Dive (OG 1039, ABV 3.7%)
A light, single-hopped beer made from the hedgerow hop, First Gold. A bitter beer with a hoppy nose, good bitterness on the palate and a dry finish.

Quacker Jack (OG 1040, ABV 4%)

Feather Light (OG 1040, ABV 4.1%)
A pale lager-style bitter with a floral bouquet and sweetness on the palate. A light, hoppy session beer.

Duckling (OG 1041, ABV 4.2%)
A crisp refreshing bitter with a hint of honey and citrus flavour.

Webbed Wheat (OG 1043, ABV 4.3%)
A wheat beer with a fruity, hoppy nose and taste.

Spittin' Feathers (OG 1044, ABV 4.4%)
A mellow, ruby bitter with a complex malt flavour of chocolate, toffee and coffee, complemented with a full and fruity/hoppy aftertaste.

Drake (OG 1045, ABV 4.5%)
A full-bodied premium bitter, with malt and hops on the palate, and a fruity finish.

Duck 'n' Disorderly (OG 1050, ABV 5%)

Friar Duck (OG 1050, ABV 5%)
A pale, full malt beer, hoppy with a hint of blackcurrant flavour.

Mallinsons

Mallinsons Brewing Co, Plover Road Garage, Plover Road, Huddersfield, West Yorkshire, HD3 3HS
☎ (01484) 654301
info@drinkmallinsons.co.uk
drinkmallinsons.co.uk
Tours by arrangement

The brewery was set up in early 2008 on a six-barrel plant in a former garage by CAMRA member Tara Mallinson. Tara is Huddersfield's only brewster. A range of seasonal and one-off specials is planned as well as bottle-conditioned beers.

Emley Moor Mild (ABV 3.4%)
Black with a ruby hint. A full-bodied mild with a nutty taste and slightly bitter finish.

Stadium Bitter (ABV 3.8%)
Straw-coloured with a clean, bitter taste and dry, fruity finish.

Station Best Bitter (ABV 4.2%)
An amber-coloured best bitter with a balance of malt and fruity hops.

Castle Hill Premium (ABV 4.6%)
A golden-coloured premium bitter, hoppy with citrus tones.

Malt B

Malt B Brewing Co, Crown Inn, Beesby Road, Maltby le Marsh, Lincolnshire, LN13 0JJ
☎ (01507) 450100
nwalpole@btconnect.com
thecrowninnmaltby.co.uk
Tours by arrangement

Malt B started brewing in early 2008. Until the 1970s the building that houses the brewery was an outside toilet, hence some beer names incorporate toilet humour. Seasonal beer: Tinkle Bells Christmas Beer (ABV 4.4%).

P.E.A. (Proper English Ale) (OG 1037, ABV 3.6%)

Old Reliable (OG 1042, ABV 4.2%)

Smarty's Night Porter (OG 1045, ABV 4.5%)

Malvern Hills SIBA

Malvern Hills Brewery Ltd, 15 West Malvern Road, Malvern, Worcestershire, WR14 4ND
☎ (01684) 560165
beer@tiscali.co.uk
malvernhillsbrewery.co.uk
Tours by arrangement

Founded in 1998 in an old quarrying dynamite store. Now an established presence in the Three Counties and Black Country, the brewery has around 80 regular outlets. Future plans include a 50% expansion of the brewing capacity. Rationalisation of the product range in 2009 created a rolling programme of monthly specials to supplement the core permanent brews.

Santler (ABV 3.6%)

Feelgood (OG 1038, ABV 3.8%)

Swedish Nightingale (OG 1040, ABV 4%)

Priessnitz Plzen (OG 1043, ABV 4.3%)
A mix of soft fruit and citrus give this straw-coloured brew its quaffability, making it ideal for quenching summer thirsts.

Black Pear (OG 1044, ABV 4.4%)
A sharp citrus hoppiness is the main constituent of this golden brew that has a long, dry aftertaste.

Mansfield

See Marston's in New Nationals section

Marble SIBA

Marble Beers Ltd, 73 Rochdale Road, Manchester, M4 4HY
☎ (0161) 819 2694
thebrewers_marblebeers@msn.com
Tours by arrangement

Marble opened at the Marble Arch Inn in 1997 and produces organic and vegan beers as well as some non-organic ales. It is registered with the Soil Association and the Vegetarian Society. Marble currently owns two pubs and supplies around 10 outlets. A number of bottle-conditioned beers are available as well as regular seasonals such as Port Stout (ABV 4.7%, Xmas) and Festival (ABV 4.4%, Oct).

Pint (OG 1038.5, ABV 3.9%)
A pale, dry and extremely hoppy beer.

Manchester (OG 1042, ABV 4.2%)
Yellow beer with a fruity and hoppy aroma. Hops, fruit and bitterness on the palate and in the finish.

JP Best (OG 1043, ABV 4.3%)
Pale tawny in colour. Hoppy with a good malt balance, assertively bitter.

Ginger (OG 1046, ABV 4.5%)
Intense and complex. Full-bodied and fiery with a sharp, snappy bite.

Stouter Stout (OG 1048, ABV 4.7%)
Black in colour, with roast malt dominating the aroma. Roast malt and hops in the mouth, with a little fruit. Pleasant, dry, bitter aftertaste.

Lagonda IPA (OG 1047.5, ABV 5%)
Golden yellow beer with a spicy, fruity nose. Fruit, hops and malt in the mouth, with a dry fruitiness continuing into the bitter aftertaste.

Chocolate (OG 1054.5, ABV 5.5%)
A strong, stout-like ale.

Marston Moor

Marston Moor Brewery Ltd, PO Box 9, York, North Yorkshire, YO26 7XW
☎ (01423) 359641
info@marstonmoorbrewery.co.uk

Established in 1983 in Kirk Hammerton, the brewery had a re-investment programme in 2005, moving brewing operations to nearby Tockwith, where it shares the site with Rudgate Brewery (qv). Two special beers are available each month. Around 250 outlets are supplied.

Cromwell's Pale (OG 1036, ABV 3.8%)
A golden beer with hops and fruit in strong evidence on the nose. Bitterness as well as fruit and hops dominate the taste and long aftertaste.

Matchlock Mild (OG 1038, ABV 4%)
Traditional, full-flavoured dark mild.

Mongrel (OG 1038, ABV 4%)
A balanced bitter with plenty of fruit character.

Fairfax Special (OG 1039, ABV 4.2%)
A full-bodied premium bitter, pale in colour with a well-balanced slightly citrus aroma.

Merriemaker (OG 1042, ABV 4.5%)
A premium straw-coloured ale with a typical Yorkshire taste.

Brewers Droop (OG 1045.5, ABV 5%)
A powerful golden ale with a sweet taste.

Marston's

See Marston's in New Nationals section

Matthews SIBA

Matthews Brewing Co Ltd, Unit 7, Timsbury Workshop Estate, Hayeswood Road, Timsbury, Bath, BA2 0HQ
☎ (01761) 472242
brewery@matthewsbrewing.co.uk
matthewsbrewing.co.uk

Shop – phone for details
Tours by arrangement

Matthews Brewing Company was established in 2005 on a five-barrel plant by Stuart Matthews and Sue Appleby. The emphasis is on the use of traditional techniques and quality ingredients, such as floor-malted barley from the nearby Warminster Maltings. Around 80 outlets are supplied direct and the ales are distributed more widely by wholesalers. Seasonal beers and monthly specials: see website.

Brassknocker (OG 1037, ABV 3.8%)
Well-flavoured pale, hoppy citrus bitter with underlying sweetness; dry, astringent finish.

Green Barrel (OG 1039, ABV 4%)

Bob Wall (OG 1041, ABV 4.2%)
Fruity best bitter; roasty hint with intense forest fruit and rich malt flavour continuing to a good balanced finish.

Mauldons SIBA EAB

Mauldons Ltd, Black Adder Brewery, 13 Church Field Road, Sudbury, Suffolk, CO10 2YA
(01787) 311055
sims@mauldons.co.uk
mauldons.co.uk
Shop Mon-Fri 9.30am-4pm
Tours by arrangement

The Mauldon family started brewing in Sudbury in 1795. The brewery with 26 pubs was bought by Greene King in the 1960s. The current business, established in 1982, was bought by Steve and Alison Sims – both former employees of Adnams – in 2000. They relocated to a new brewery in 2005, with a 30-barrel plant that has doubled production. The brewery tap was bought in 2008. Around 150 outlets are supplied. There is a rolling programme of seasonal beers: see website.

Micawber's Mild (OG 1035, ABV 3.5%)
Fruit and roast flavours dominate the nose, with vine fruit and caramel on the tongue and a short, dry, coffeeish aftertaste. Full-bodied and satisfying.

Moletrap Bitter (OG 1038, ABV 3.8%)
Easy-drinking session bitter. Crisp and refreshing, hoppy and fruity throughout.

Silver Adder (OG 1042, ABV 4.2%)
A light-coloured bitter with five hop and malt combinations giving a refreshing, crisp finish.

Suffolk Pride (OG 1048, ABV 4.8%)
A full-bodied, copper-coloured beer with a good balance of malt, hops and fruit in the taste.

Black Adder (OG 1053, ABV 5.3%)
Superbly balanced dark, sweet ale, but with rich vine fruit throughout. The brewery's flagship beer.

Mayfields

Mayfields Brewery, No. 8 Croft Business Park, Leominster, Herefordshire, HR6 0QF
(01568) 611197
info@mayfieldsbrewery.co.uk
mayfieldsbrewery.co.uk

Established in 2005, the Mayfields Brewery is located in the heart of one of England's major hop growing regions. Only Herefordshire hops are used, many of which are grown on the farm where the brewery was founded and takes its name. 2008 saw a change of location and ownership. Around 25 outlets are supplied. Seasonal beers: Crusader (ABV 4.3%, St George's Day/Trafalgar Day), Conqueror (ABV 4.3%, winter).

Pioneer (ABV 3.9%)
Straw-coloured ale with a fruity finish.

Naughty Nell's (ABV 4.2%)
Smooth, copper-coloured ale with a malty body and citrus hop finish.

Aunty Myrtle's (ABV 4.5%)
Full bodied and fruity.

Mayflower

Mayflower Brewery, c/o Royal Oak Hotel, Standishgate, Wigan, WN1 1XL
07984 404567
info@mayflower-beer.co.uk
mayflower-beer.co.uk

Mayflower was established in 2001 in Standish and relocated to the Royal Oak Hotel in Wigan in 2004. The original vessels and casks are still used. The Royal Oak is supplied as well as a number of other outlets in and around Wigan. Seasonal beers: Autumn Gold (ABV 4.5%, autumn), Hic Bibi (ABV 5%, winter).

Black Diamond (OG 1033.5, ABV 3.4%)

Auldens Amber Ale (OG 1040, ABV 3.7%)

Douglas Valley Ale (OG 1044, ABV 4%)

Wigan Bier (OG 1039.5, ABV 4.2%)

Maypole

Maypole Brewery Ltd, North Laithes Farm, Wellow Road, Eakring, Newark, Nottinghamshire, NG22 0AN
07971 277598
maypolebrewery@aol.com
maypolebrewery.co.uk

The brewery opened in 1995 in a converted 18th-century farm building. After changing hands in 2001 it was bought by the former head brewer, Rob Neil, in 2005. Seasonal beers can be ordered at any time for beer festivals: see website for details and list.

Mayfly Bitter (OG 1038, ABV 3.8%)

Gate Hopper (OG 1040, ABV 4%)

Mayfair (OG 1040, ABV 4.1%)

Maybee (OG 1041, ABV 4.3%)

Mae West/Wellow Gold (OG 1044, ABV 4.6%)

Mayhem (OG 1048, ABV 5%)

Platinum Blonde (OG 1048, ABV 5.1%)

For Olde Red Lion, Wellow:

Olde Lions Ale (ABV 3.9%)

Meantime SIBA

Meantime Brewing Co Ltd, Greenwich Brewery, 2 Penhall Road, London, SE7 8RX
(020) 8293 1111
info@meantimebrewing.com
meantimebrewing.com

Founded in 2000, Meantime brews a wide range of continental style beer and traditional English bottle-conditioned ales. Bottle-conditioned beers:

London Pale Ale (ABV 4.3%), London Stout (ABV 4.5%), Wheat (ABV 5%), Winter Time (ABV 5.4%), Coffee Porter (ABV 6%), Chocolate (ABV 6.5%), London Porter (ABV 6.5%), Raspberry Grand Cru (ABV 6.5%), IPA (ABV 7.5%). All beers are suitable for vegetarians and vegans.

London Pale (ABV 4.3%)

Meesons

See Old Bog

Melbourn

Melbourn Bros Brewery, All Saints Brewery, All Saints Street, Stamford, Lincolnshire, PE9 2PA
☎ (01780) 752186

A famous Stamford brewery that opened in 1825 and closed in 1974. It re-opened in 1994 and is owned by Samuel Smith of Tadcaster (qv). Melbourn brews three handcrafted, organic fruit beers (Cherry, Strawberry and Raspberry) using the antique steam-driven brewing equipment. The beers are all suitable for vegans and are organic.

Mersea Island

Mersea Island Brewery, Rewsalls Lane, East Mersea, Colchester, Essex, CO5 8SX
☎ (01206) 385900
✉ beers@merseawine.com
merseawine.com
Shop 11am-4pm daily (closed Tue)

The brewery was established at Mersea Island Vineyard in 2005, producing cask and bottle-conditioned beers. The brewery supplies several local pubs on a guest beer basis as well as most local beer festivals. The brewery holds its own festival of Essex-produced ales over the four day Easter weekend.

Yo Boy Bitter (OG 1038, ABV 3.8%)
Pale session beer. Peach and orange on the aroma and taste, leading to a pleasantly bitter finish.

Gold (OG 1043, ABV 4.5%)
A lager/Pilsner style.

Skippers Bitter (OG 1047, ABV 4.8%)
Strong bitter, whose full character is dominated by pear drops and juicy malt. A raspberry tartness follows.

Oyster (OG 1048, ABV 5%)

Monkeys (OG 1049, ABV 5.1%)
A porter with deep and lasting malt and hop flavours.

Mighty Oak SIBA

Mighty Oak Brewing Co Ltd, 14b West Station Yard, Spital Road, Maldon, Essex, CM9 6TW
☎ (01621) 843713
✉ sales@mightyoakbrewing.co.uk
Tours by arrangement

Mighty Oak was formed in 1996 and moved in 2001 to Maldon, where capacity was increased to 67.5 barrels a week, increased again in 2009 to 92.5 barrels a week. Around 200 outlets are supplied plus a small number of wholesalers are used. Twelve monthly ales are brewed based on a theme; for 2009 the theme was 'Computers' including 'Spell Checker' and 'X Mouse Ale'. 2010 is 'Bars' including 'Barack Obama', 'Barking Mad' and 'Ilkley Moor Bar T'at'. The brewery also market Buffer Ale (ABV 4.2%) under the 'Goods Shed' label.

IPA (OG 1031.5, ABV 3.5%)
Light-bodied, pale session bitter, Hop notes are initially suppressed by a delicate sweetness but the aftertaste is more assertive.

Oscar Wilde (OG 1039.5, ABV 3.7%)
Roasty dark mild with suggestions of forest fruits and dark chocolate. A sweet taste yields to a more bitter finish.

Maldon Gold (OG 1039.5, ABV 3.8%)
Pale golden ale with a sharp citrus note moderated by honey and biscuity malt.

Burntwood Bitter (OG 1041, ABV 4%)
Full-bodied bitter with an unusual blend of caramel, roast grain and grapefruit.

Simply The Best (OG 1044.1, ABV 4.4%)
Well-balanced, mid-strength bitter with a sweet start and a dry, bitter finish.

English Oak (OG 1047.9, ABV 4.8%)
Strong tawny, fruity bitter with caramel, butterscotch and vanilla. A gentle hop character is present throughout.

Milestone

Milestone Brewing Co Ltd, Great North Road, Cromwell, Newark, Nottinghamshire, NG23 6JE
☎ (01636) 822255
✉ info@milestonebrewery.co.uk
milestonebrewery.co.uk
Shop Mon-Fri 8am-5pm; Sat 9am-3pm
Tours by arrangement

The brewery has been in production since 2005 on a 12-barrel plant. It was founded by Kenneth and Frances Munro with head brewer Dean Penney. Around 150 outlets are supplied. Seasonal beers: Cool Amber (ABV 6%, May-Aug), Donner & Blitzed/Xmas Cracker (ABV 5.4%, Nov-Dec). Bottle-conditioned beers are also available.

Lions Pride (ABV 3.8%)

Cromwell Gold (ABV 4%)

Old Oak (ABV 4%)

Shine On (ABV 4%)

Tucks Tipple (ABV 4%)

Loxley Ale (ABV 4.2%)

Black Pearl (ABV 4.3%)

Maid Marian (ABV 4.3%)

Crusader (ABV 4.4%)

Lion Heart (ABV 4.4%)

Rich Ruby (ABV 4.5%)

Imperial Pale Ale (ABV 4.8%)

Olde Home Wrecker (ABV 4.9%)

Little John (ABV 5%)

Raspberry Wheat Beer (ABV 5.6%)

Milk Street SIBA

Milk Street Brewery Ltd (MSB Ltd), The Griffin, 25 Milk Street, Frome, Somerset, BA11 3DL
☎ (01373) 467766
✉ rjlyall@hotmail.com
milkstreetbrewery.co.uk
Tours by arrangement

Milk Street was started in 1999 in a former pub and porn cinema. The cinema is long gone and now houses the brewery, which expanded in 2005 and is now capable of producing 30 barrels per week. It mainly produces for its own estate of three outlets with direct delivery to pubs in a 30-mile radius. Wholesalers are used to distribute the beers further afield.

Funky Monkey (OG 1040, ABV 4%)
Copper-coloured summer ale with fruity flavours and aromas. A dry finish with developing bitterness and an undertone of citrus fruit.

Mermaid (OG 1041, ABV 4.1%)
Amber-coloured ale with a rich hop character on the nose, plenty of citrus fruit on the palate and a lasting bitter and hoppy finish.

Amarillo (OG 1043, ABV 4.3%)
Brewed with American hops to give the beer floral and spicy notes. Initially soft on the palate, the flavour develops to that of burnt oranges and a pleasant herbal taste.

Zig-Zag Stout (OG 1046, ABV 4.5%)
A dark ruby stout with characteristic roastiness and dryness with bitter chocolate and citrus fruit in the background.

Beer (OG 1049, ABV 5%)
A blonde beer with musky hoppiness and citrus fruit on the nose, while more fruit surges through on the palate before the bittersweet finish.

Mill Green (NEW)

Mill Green Brewery, White Horse, Edwardstone, Sudbury, Suffolk, CO10 5PX
☎ (01787) 211118
✉ enquiries@millgreenbrewery.co.uk
millgreenbrewery.co.uk

Mill Green started brewing in 2008 as an eco brewery in a new build complex behind the White Horse pub. Brewing liquor is heated by solar panels, wood boiler and wind turbine. 20 outlets are supplied. Bottle-conditioned beers are available.

Mawkin Mild (OG 1028, ABV 2.9%)

Bulls Cross Bitter (OG 1034, ABV 3.5%)

Loveleys Fair (OG 1039, ABV 4%)

Millis

Millis Brewing Co Ltd, St Margaret's Farm, St Margaret's Road, South Darenth, Dartford, Kent, DA4 9LB
☎ (01322) 866233

John and Miriam Millis started with a half-barrel plant at their home in Gravesend. Demand outstripped the facility and Millis moved in 2003 to a new site – a former farm cold store – with a 10-barrel plant. They now supply around 40 outlets within a 50-mile radius. Seasonal beer: Winter Witch (ABV 4.8%).

Kentish Dark (OG 1035, ABV 3.5%)
A traditional dark mild with chocolate and roasted notes.

Gravesend Guzzler (OG 1037, ABV 3.7%)

Oast Shovellers (OG 1039, ABV 3.9%)
A copper-coloured ale with a pale and crystal malt base, ending with a distinctive, clean finish.

Hopping Haze (OG 1041, ABV 4.1%)

Kentish Gold (OG 1041, ABV 4.1%)
A pale, full-hopped flavoured beer with a crisp, dry finish.

Dartford Wobbler (OG 1043, ABV 4.3%)
A tawny-coloured, full-bodied best bitter with complex malt and hop flavours and a long, clean, slightly roasted finish.

Kentish Red Ale (OG 1043, ABV 4.3%)
A traditional red ale with complex malt, hops and fruit notes.

Old Kentish Ale (OG 1048, ABV 4.8%)

Millstone SIBA

Millstone Brewery Ltd, Unit 4, Vale Mill, Micklehurst Road, Mossley, nr Oldham, OL5 9JL
☎ (01457) 835835
✉ info@millstonebrewery.co.uk
millstonebrewery.co.uk

Established in 2003 by Nick Boughton and Jon Hunt, the brewery is located in an 18th-century textile mill. The eight-barrel plant produces a range of pale, hoppy beers including five regular and seasonal/occasional beers (including the 'pub name' series). Over 50 outlets are supplied.

Vale Mill (OG 1039, ABV 3.9%)
A pale gold session bitter with a floral and spicy aroma building upon a crisp and refreshing taste.

Three Shires Bitter (OG 1040, ABV 4%)
Yellow beer with hop and fruit aroma. Fresh citrus fruit, hops and bitterness in the taste and aftertaste.

Tiger Rut (OG 1040, ABV 4%)
A pale, hoppy ale with a distinctive citrus/grapefruit aroma.

Grain Storm (OG 1042, ABV 4.2%)
Yellow/gold beer with a grainy mouthfeel and fresh fruit and hop aroma. Citrus peel and hops in the mouth, with a bitter finish.

True Grit (OG 1049, ABV 5%)
A well-hopped strong ale with a mellow bitterness and a citrus/grapefruit aroma.

Milton SIBA EAB

Milton Brewery Cambridge Ltd, 111 Cambridge Road, Milton, Cambridgeshire, CB24 6AT
☎ (01223) 226198
✉ enquiries@miltonbrewery.co.uk
miltonbrewery.co.uk
Tours by arrangement

The brewery has grown steadily since it was founded in 1999. More than 100 outlets are supplied around the Cambridge area and further afield through wholesalers. Four tied houses (Norwich, Peterborough and London) are owned by an associated company, Individual Pubs Ltd. Regular seasonal beers are also brewed including

Mammon (ABV 7%, Dec-Feb). Nero is suitable for vegetarians and vegans.

Minotaur (OG 1035, ABV 3.3%)
Red/brown mild with a defined malt and roast nose, then a sweetish malt and fruit balance with roast adding depth. The malt and sweetness remain in the aftertaste with little bitterness.

Jupiter (OG 1037, ABV 3.5%)
A copper-coloured bitter with malt and hops in balance on nose and palate. Some caramel sweetness, but butterscotch lingers on in the aftertaste.

Neptune (OG 1039, ABV 3.8%)
Delicious hop aromas introduce this well-balanced, nutty and refreshing copper-coloured ale. Good hoppy finish.

Pegasus (OG 1043, ABV 4.1%)
A malty, slightly fruity aroma leads into bitter fruitiness which is complemented by malty richness. An appealing amber brew with a well-rounded, bittersweet finish.

Sparta (OG 1043, ABV 4.3%)
Peach and malt scents, amber and golden hues and a palate of fruity hops on a bittersweet base. Crisp finish of hops, fruit and bitterness with a touch of sweetness.

Nero (OG 1050, ABV 5%)
A creamy black stout. Prunes and raisins on the nose lead in to flavours of sweet chocolate, malt and roast with layers of fruit. The aftertaste develops to chocolaty dryness.

Cyclops (OG 1055, ABV 5.3%)
Deep copper-coloured ale, with a rich hoppy aroma and full body; fruit and malt notes develop in the finish.

Moles SIBA

Moles Brewery (Cascade Drinks Ltd), 5 Merlin Way, Bowerhill, Melksham, Wiltshire, SN12 6TJ
☎ (01225) 704734/708842
✉ sales@moles-cascade.co.uk
molesbrewery.com
Shop Mon-Fri 9am-5pm; Sat 9am-12pm
Tours by arrangement

Moles was established in 1982 by Roger Catte, a former Ushers brewer, using his nickname to name the brewery. It produces traditionally brewed all malt beers with a balanced bitterness from a variety of leaf hops. 12 pubs are owned, all serving cask beer. Around 200 outlets are supplied locally. Seasonal beers: see website.

Tap Bitter (OG 1035, ABV 3.5%)
A session bitter with a smooth, malty flavour and clean bitter finish.

Best Bitter (OG 1040, ABV 4%)
A well-balanced, amber-coloured bitter, clean, dry and malty with some bitterness, and delicate floral hop flavour.

Landlords Choice (OG 1045, ABV 4.5%)
A dark, strong, smooth porter, with a rich fruity palate and malty finish.

Rucking Mole (OG 1045, ABV 4.5%)
A chestnut-coloured premium ale, fruity and malty with a smooth bitter finish.

Molecatcher (OG 1050, ABV 5%)
A copper-coloured ale with a delightfully spicy hop aroma and taste, and a long bitter finish.

Monty's (NEW)

Monty's Brewery, Unit 1, Castle Works, Hendomen, Montgomery, Powys, SY15 6HA
☎ (01686) 668933
✉ Pam@montysbrewery.co.uk
montysbrewery.co.uk
Tours by arrangement

Monty's is the first brewery to produce beer in Montgomeryshire since the closure of the Eagle Brewery in Newtown in 1988. It began brewing in early 2009. Pump clips are available in English and Welsh.

Mojo (OG 1042, ABV 3.8%)
A golden, slightly toasty brew, with a hint of marmalade.

Moonrise (OG 1040, ABV 4%)
A copper-coloured, gently malty, well-balanced traditional brew.

Sunshine (OG 1041, ABV 4.2%)
A golden, hoppy, floral/citrus ale with a pleasantly dry finish.

Moonstone

Moonstone Brewery (Gem Taverns Ltd), Ministry of Ale, 9 Trafalgar Street, Burnley, Lancashire, BB11 1TQ
☎ (01282) 830909
✉ meet@ministryofale.co.uk
moonstonebrewery.co.uk
Tours by arrangement

A small, 2.5-barrel brewery, based in the Ministry of Ale pub. Brewing started in 2001 and beer is only generally available in the pub. Seasonal beer: Red Jasper (ABV 6%, winter).

Black Star (OG 1037, ABV 3.4%)

Blue John (ABV 3.6%)

Tigers Eye (OG 1037, ABV 3.8%)

MPA (ABV 4%)

Darkish (OG 1042, ABV 4.2%)

Moor SIBA

Moor Beer Co Ltd, c/o Chapel Court, Pitney, Somerset, TA10 9AE
☎ 07887 556521
✉ justin@moorbeer.co.uk
moorbeer.co.uk
Tours by arrangement

Moor Beer was founded in 1996. Award-winning brewer Justin Hawke completed his acquisition of the brewery in 2008. The beers are mostly found in Somerset and at select pubs and festivals across the UK via wholesalers. Specials and seasonal beers are available. Contact the brewery for details of bottle-conditioned beers, all hand bottled.

Revival (OG 1038, ABV 3.8%)
An immensely hoppy and refreshing pale ale.

Milly's (OG 1041, ABV 3.9%)
A dark mild with a smooth mouthfeel and a slightly roasty finish.

Merlin's Magic (OG 1045, ABV 4.3%)

THE BREWERIES

Dark amber-coloured, complex, full-bodied beer, with fruity notes.

Peat Porter (OG 1047, ABV 4.5%) ◆
Dark brown/black beer with an initially fruity taste leading to roast malt with a little bitterness. A slightly sweet malty finish.

Confidence (OG 1048, ABV 4.6%)
Ruby-coloured premium bitter with a spicy hoppiness and rich malt profile.

Ported Peat Porter (OG 1049, ABV 4.7%)
Peat Porter with added Reserve Port.

Somerland Gold (OG 1052, ABV 5%)
Hoppy blonde ale with hints of honey and a long, hoppy finish.

Old Freddy Walker (OG 1075, ABV 7.3%) ◆
Rich, dark, strong ale with a fruity complex taste, leaving a fruitcake finish.

JJJ IPA (OG 1090, ABV 9%)
Copper-coloured, new world triple IPA. Immensely hoppy and malty.

Moorhouse's SIBA

Moorhouse's Brewery (Burnley) Ltd, The Brewery, Moorhouse Street, Burnley, Lancashire, BB11 5EN
☎ (01282) 422864/416004
✉ info@moorhouses.co.uk
moorhouses.co.uk
Tours by arrangement

Established in 1865 as a drinks manufacturer, the brewery started producing cask-conditioned ale in 1978 and has achieved recognition by winning more international and CAMRA awards than any other brewery of its size. Two new additional 30-barrel fermenters were installed in 2004, taking production to 320 barrels a week maximum. A new brewhouse is planned that will increase production to 40,000 barrels a year. The company owns six pubs, all serving cask-conditioned beer, and supplies some 250 free trade outlets. There is a selection of seasonal ales throughout the year: see website.

Black Cat (OG 1036, ABV 3.4%) ◆
A dark mild-style beer with delicate chocolate and coffee roast flavours and a crisp, bitter finish.

Premier Bitter (OG 1036, ABV 3.7%) ◆
A clean and satisfying bitter aftertaste rounds off this well-balanced hoppy, amber session bitter.

Pride of Pendle (OG 1040, ABV 4.1%) ◆
Well-balanced amber best bitter with a fresh initial hoppiness and a mellow, malt-driven body.

Blond Witch (OG 1045, ABV 4.5%)
A pale coloured ale with a crisp, delicate fruit flavour. Dry and refreshing with a smooth hop finish.

Pendle Witches Brew (OG 1050, ABV 5.1%) ◆
Well-balanced, full-bodied, malty beer with a long, complex finish.

Moorview (NEW)

Moorview Brewery, Upper Austby Farm, Nesfield, North Yorkshire, LS29 0EQ
☎ 0845 349 3778
✉ johnny@moorviewbrewery.co.uk
moorviewbrewery.co.uk

Moorview began brewing in 2008 using the old brew plant from the Turkey Inn at Goose Eye. Around 20 outlets are supplied direct. Seasonal beer: Bucking Funny (ABV 4%, Easter).

First Born Bitter (OG 1037, ABV 3.4%)

Full Mashings (OG 1038, ABV 3.6%)

Goldilocks & the Three Bears (ABV 3.6%)

Mordue SIBA

Mordue Brewery, Units D1 & D2, Narvic Way, Tyne Tunnel Estate, North Shields, Tyne & Wear, NE29 7XJ
☎ (0191) 296 1879
✉ enquiries@morduebrewery.com
morduebrewery.com
Shop: see website
Tours by arrangement

In 1995 the Fawston brothers revived the Mordue Brewery name (the original closed in 1879). High demand required moves to larger premises and replacing the original five-barrel plant with a 20-barrel one. The beers are distributed nationally and 200 outlets are supplied direct. Seasonal beers: see website.

Five Bridge Bitter (OG 1038, ABV 3.8%) ◆
Crisp golden beer with a good hint of hops, the bitterness carries on in the finish.

Geordie Pride (OG 1042, ABV 4.2%) ◆
Well balanced and hoppy with a long bitter finish.

Workie Ticket (OG 1045, ABV 4.5%) ◆
Complex tasty bitter with plenty of malt and hops, and a long satisfying, bitter finish.

Radgie Gadgie (OG 1048, ABV 4.8%) ◆
Strong, easy-drinking bitter with plenty of fruit and hops.

IPA (OG 1051, ABV 5.1%) ◆
Easy-drinking golden ale with plenty of hops, the bitterness carries on in the finish.

Morrissey Fox (NEW)

Morrissey Fox Breweries Ltd, Ye Olde Punchbowl, Marton cum Grafton, York, North Yorkshire, YO51 9QY
☎ 07949 946007
✉ enquiries@morrisseyfox.co.uk
morrisseyfox.co.uk
Tours by arrangement

Morrissey Fox Breweries was developed in 2008 and filmed by Channel 4. The brewery is now fully operational and supplies Ye Olde Punchbowl. Seasonal beer: Mulled Ale (ABV 4.6%, Dec). Blonde and all bottled beers are contract brewed elsewhere.

Bitter (OG 1040, ABV 3.9%)

Blonde (OG 1043, ABV 4.2%)

Morton

Morton Brewery, Unit 10, Essington Light Industrial Estate, Essington, Wolverhampton, Staffordshire, WV11 2BH
☎ 07988 069647

Office: 96 Brewood Road, Coven, Staffordshire, WV9 5EF
✉ mortonbrewery@aol.com
mortonbrewery.co.uk

Morton was established in 2007 on a three-barrel plant by Gary and Angela Morton, both CAMRA members. The brewery moved to Essington in 2008 to meet demand. 20 outlets are supplied direct plus various beer festivals. Seasonal beers: Irish George (ABV 5%, winter), Forever in Darkness (ABV 4%, spring), Penkside Pale (ABV 3.6%, summer), Gregorys Gold (ABV 4.4%, autumn). See website for special beers.

Merry Mount (OG 1037, ABV 3.8%)

Essington Ale (OG 1041, ABV 4.2%)

Jelly Roll (OG 1041, ABV 4.2%)

Scottish Maiden (OG 1045, ABV 4.6%)

Moulin

Moulin Hotel & Brewery, 2 Baledmund Road, Moulin, Pitlochry, Perthshire, PH16 5EL
☎ (01796) 472196
✉ enquiries@moulinhotel.co.uk
moulinhotel.co.uk
Shop 12-3pm daily
Tours by arrangement

The brewery opened in 1995 to celebrate the Moulin Hotel's 300th anniversary. Two pubs are owned and four outlets are supplied. Bottle-conditioned beer is available.

Light (OG 1036, ABV 3.7%)
Thirst-quenching, straw-coloured session beer, with a light, hoppy, fruity balance, ending with a gentle, hoppy sweetness.

Braveheart (OG 1039, ABV 4%)
An amber bitter, with a delicate balance of malt and fruit and a Scottish-style sweetness.

Ale of Atholl (OG 1043.5, ABV 4.5%)
A reddish, quaffable, malty ale, with a solid body and a mellow finish.

Old Remedial (OG 1050.5, ABV 5.2%)
A distinctive and satisfying dark brown old ale, with roast malt to the fore and tannin in a robust taste.

Muirhouse (NEW)

Muirhouse Brewery, Quantock Road, Long Eaton, Nottinghamshire, NG10 4FZ
☎ 07916 590525
✉ rmuir@muirhousebrewery.co.uk
muirhousebrewery.co.uk

After carrying out several successful test brews at the nearby Full Mash Brewery, Richard Muir produced the first beers on his small 100-litre plant in 2009. The beer range was not finalised at the time of going to press.

Nailsworth

Nailsworth Brewery Ltd, Village Inn, The Cross, Nailsworth, Gloucestershire, GL6 0HH
☎ 07878 448377
✉ jonk@nailsworth-brewery.co.uk
nailsworth-brewery.co.uk
Tours by arrangement

The original Nailsworth Brewery closed in 1908. In 2004, after a gap of 98 years, commercial brewing returned in the form of a six-barrel micro-brewery. This is the brainchild of Messrs Hawes and Kemp, whose aim is to make the town of Nailsworth once again synonymous with quality beer. Around 30 outlets are supplied direct. Seasonal beer: Winter Woolie (ABV 4.9%). Bottle-conditioned beer is also available.

Alestock (ABV 3.6%)

Artist's Ale (OG 1040, ABV 3.8%)
A light-coloured bitter full of citrus flavours.

Dudbridge Donkey (ABV 4%)

Mayor's Bitter (OG 1042, ABV 4.3%)
A best bitter with malt textures complemented by a long-lasting taste of blackcurrant.

Town Crier (OG 1046, ABV 4.5%)
A premium ale with delicate grassy and floral overtones.

Vicar's Stout (ABV 4.5%)

Nant

Bragdy'r Nant, Penrhwylfa, Maenan, Llanrwst, Conwy, LL26 0UA
☎ 07723 036862
✉ postmaster@jonesgw2.demon.co.uk
cwrwnant.co.uk

Nant commenced brewing in late 2007 with a plant purchased from the Yorkshire Dales Brewery. Capacity is currently 10-15 firkins a week. Seasonal and one-off beers are also produced.

Mochyn Hapus (ABV 3.7%)

Cwrw Coryn (ABV 4.2%)

Pen Dafad (ABV 4.2%)

Chawden Aur (ABV 4.3%)

Grans's Lamb (ABV 4.5%)

Mwnci Nell (ABV 5.3%)

Naylor's

Naylor's Brewery, Midland Mills, Station Road, Cross Hills, Keighley, West Yorkshire, BD20 7DT
☎ (01535) 637451
✉ naylorsbrewery@btconnect.com
naylorsbrewery.com
Shop Mon-Fri 10am-5pm; Sat 10am-3pm
Tours by arrangement

Naylors started brewing early in 2005, based at the Old White Bear pub in Crosshills. Expansion required a move to the current site in 2006 and included a rebranding of the beers. Further expansion in 2009 gave better facilities for bottling as well as a shop and bar. Around 110 outlets are supplied. Bottle-conditioned ales are also produced. All bottled beers are suitable for vegetarians.

Pinnacle Mild (ABV 3.4%)
This dark brown, malty mild has complex roast flavours with chocolate and fruity undertones and a roast bitter finish.

Pinnacle Pale Ale (ABV 3.6%)
A clean-tasting pale ale, which starts off sweet against a fruity background. A prickly hoppiness kicks in leading to a bitter, slightly astringent finish.

Pinnacle Bitter (ABV 3.9%)

THE BREWERIES

Predominantly malty, this traditional mid-brown bitter also has subtle fruit and hops in the nose and taste and growing bitterness in the finish.

Pinnacle Blonde (ABV 4.3%)
This hoppy, fruity ale is darker than a typical blonde. Look for hints of peach and mango in the aroma and some spiciness in the bitter finish.

Pinnacle Porter (ABV 4.8%)
An intense roast bitterness characterises this full-bodied black beer. There are also hints of sweetness, chocolate and coffee against a fruity background. Roast dominates the lingering aftertaste.

Nelson SIBA

Nelson Brewing Co UK Ltd, Unit 2, Building 64, The Historic Dockyard, Chatham, Kent, ME4 4TE
☎ (01634) 832828
sales@nelsonbrewingcompany.co.uk
nelsonbrewingcompany.co.uk
Shop Mon-Fri 9am-4.30pm
Tours by arrangement

Nelson started out in 1995 as the Flagship Brewery but changed its name in 2004. It was acquired by the current owner, Piers MacDonald, in 2006. The brewery is based in Chatham's preserved Georgian dockyard, where Nelson's flagship, HMS Victory, was built. 80 outlets are supplied direct. All cask beers are also available bottle conditioned. Seasonal and occasional beers: see website.

Helmsman (OG 1035, ABV 3.4%)

Master Mate Mild (OG 1038, ABV 3.7%)

Pieces of Eight (OG 1039, ABV 3.8%)

Spanker (OG 1040, ABV 4.1%)

Trafalgar Bitter (OG 1039, ABV 4.1%)
A light, easy-drinking ale with balanced malt and hop flavour and hints of honey and nuts to finish.

Powder Monkey (OG 1044, ABV 4.4%)

Dogwatch Stout (OG 1044, ABV 4.5%)

Friggin' in the Riggin' (OG 1048, ABV 4.7%)
Drinkable premium bitter with smooth malt flavour and bittersweet aftertaste.

Purser's Pussy Porter (OG 1049, ABV 5.1%)

Nethergate SIBA EAB

Nethergate Holdings Ltd, The Growler Brewery, The Street, Pentlow, Essex, CO10 7JJ
☎ (01787) 283220
orders@nethergate.co.uk
nethergatebrewery.co.uk
Tours by arrangement

Nethergate Brewery was established in 1986 at Clare, Suffolk. The plant was doubled in 1993 and the brewery moved over the border into Pentlow, Essex in 2005, where it doubled in size again. The brewery is still in the stewardship of one of its founders, Dick Burge, and has won many awards. A large range of individual monthly beers are brewed and most of the permanent and some monthly beers are also available bottle conditioned.

IPA (OG 1036, ABV 3.5%)
Bitter-tasting session beer with some fruit and malt balancing the predominate hop character. Very dry aftertaste.

Priory Mild (OG 1036, ABV 3.5%)
A 'black bitter' rather than a true mild. Strong roast and bitter tastes dominate throughout.

Umbel Ale (OG 1039, ABV 3.8%)
Pleasant, easy-drinking bitter, infused with coriander, which dominates.

Three Point Nine (OG 1040, ABV 3.9%)
Light tasting, sweetish and fruity session beer.

Suffolk County Best Bitter (OG 1041, ABV 4%)
Dark bitter with roast grain tones off-setting biscuity malt and powerful hoppy, bitter notes.

Augustinian Ale (OG 1046, ABV 4.5%)
A pale, refreshing, complex best bitter. A fruity aroma leads to a bittersweet flavour and aftertaste with a predominance of citrus tones.

Essex Border (OG 1049, ABV 4.8%)

Old Growler (OG 1051, ABV 5%)
Well-balanced porter in which roast grain is complemented by fruit and bubblegum.

Umbel Magna (OG 1051, ABV 5%)
Old Growler flavoured with coriander. The spice is less dominant than in Umbel Ale, with some of the weight and body of the beer coming through.

Stour Valley Strong (SVS) (OG 1064, ABV 6.2%)
Massive amounts of blackcurrant and fruit both in aroma and palate, balanced by dark roast grain, smokiness and peppery hops with a hint of sourness in the finish.

Newby Wyke SIBA

Newby Wyke Brewery, Willoughby Arms Cottages, Station Road, Little Bytham, Lincolnshire, NG33 4RA
☎ (01780) 411119
newbywyke.brewery@btopenworld.com
newbywyke.co.uk
Tours by arrangement

The brewery is named after a Hull trawler skippered by brewer Rob March's grandfather. After starting life in 1998 as a 2.5-barrel plant in a converted garage, growth has been steady and the brewery moved to premises behind the Willoughby Arms. Current brewing capacity is 50 barrels a week. Some 180 outlets are supplied. Seasonal beers: see website. The brewery plans to move back to Grantham in the near future but details had not been finalised at time of going to press.

HMS Revenge (OG 1037, ABV 4.2%)
A single-hopped ale with floral undertones.

Kingston Topaz (OG 1037, ABV 4.2%)

Bear Island (OG 1044, ABV 4.6%)
A blonde beer with a hoppy aroma and a crisp, dry citrus finish.

White Squall (OG 1045, ABV 4.8%)
A pale blonde ale with a full hop taste and a citrus finish.

For Nobody Inn, Grantham:

Grantham Gold (OG 1037, ABV 4.2%)

Newmans SIBA

T G Newman t/a Newmans Brewery, Unit 2E, Former Hill Buildings, Pontygwindy Industrial Estate, Caerphilly, CF83 3HU
☎ 0870 803 3876
sales@newmansbrewery.com

newmansbrewery.com
Tours by arrangement

Newmans opened on the day England won the Rugby World Cup in November 2003. It has since expanded from a five-barrel plant to a 20-barrel in 2005 and has re-located the brewery to a 40-barrel plant in South Wales, sharing the brewery with sister brewing company, The Celt Experience Ltd.

Red Stag Bitter (OG 1039, ABV 3.6%)
Dark red session ale, smooth, malty with soft fruit accents; dry fruit finish.

Wolvers Ale (OG 1042, ABV 4.1%)
Well-rounded best bitter with good body for its strength. Initial sweetness with a fine malt flavour is balanced by a slightly astringent, hoppy finish.

Red Castle Cream (ABV 4.7%)

Nobby's

Nobby's Brewery, c/o Ward Arms, High Street, Guilsborough, Northamptonshire, NN6 8PY
(01604) 740785

Office: 3 Pagent Court, Kettering, Northamptonshire, NN15 6GR
info@nobbysbrewery.co.uk
nobbysbrewery.co.uk
Shop Mon-Fri 9am-5pm; Sat 10am-1pm
Tours by arrangement

Paul 'Nobby' Mulliner started commercial brewing in 2004 on a 2.5-barrel plant at the rear of the Alexandra Arms in Kettering, which also served as the brewery tap. In 2007 a 14-barrel plant was also set up at the Ward Arms, Guilsborough. There are plans to install a bottling line. Seasonal beers: see website. The plant at the Alexandra was sold in 2009 and now brews as the Julian Church Brewery.

Claridges Crystal (OG 1035, ABV 3.6%)

Best (OG 1039, ABV 3.8%)

Tressler XXX Mild (OG 1038, ABV 3.8%)

Guilsborough Gold (OG 1041, ABV 4%)

Wild West (OG 1046, ABV 4.6%)

Landlords Own (OG 1050, ABV 5%)

T'owd Navigation (OG 1061, ABV 6.1%)

Nook (NEW)

The Nook Brewhouse, Riverside, 7b Victoria Square, Holmfirth, West Yorkshire, HD9 2DN
(01484) 682373
info@thenookpublichouse.co.uk
thenookpublichouse.co.uk
Tours by arrangement

The Nook Brewhouse is the natural progression for the owners of the Nook public house, with a real ale pedigree including 30 consecutive years in the Good Beer Guide. It supplies two brewery taps and is built on the foundations of a previous brewhouse dating back to 1752, next to the River Ribble. A history room with renovated archives dating back to the 1700s and a brewery shop are planned once brewing is consolidated.

Blonde (ABV 4.5%)

Norfolk Cottage SIBA

Norfolk Cottage Brewing, 98-100 Lawson Road, Norwich, Norfolk, NR3 4LF
(01603) 788508/270520
norfolkcottagebeers@tiscali.co.uk

Launched in 2004 by Ray Ashworth, founder of Woodforde's, Norfolk Cottage undertakes consultancy brewing and pilot brews for the Fat Cat Brewing Co at the same address. One best bitter is available to the trade plus bespoke ales in small quantities to order. Three outlets are supplied direct.

Best (OG 1042, ABV 4.1%)

Norfolk Square

Norfolk Square Brewery LLP, Unit 7, Estcourt Road, Great Yarmouth, Norfolk, NR30 4JQ
(01493) 854484
beer@norfolksquarebrewery.co.uk
norfolksquarebrewery.co.uk

Norfolk Square began brewing in May 2008 on a 2.5-barrel plant. Bottle-conditioned beers are available. Seasonal beers: Sunshiny (ABV 5.5%, summer), Winklepicker (ABV 5%, winter), Square Miled (ABV 4%, spring).

Pi (ABV 3.8%)

Scroby (ABV 4.2%)

Stiletto (ABV 4.5%)

North Cotswold SIBA

North Cotswold Brewery (Pilling Brewing Co), Unit 3, Ditchford Farm, Campden Road, Stretton-on-Fosse, Warwickshire, GL56 9RD
(01608) 663947
ncb@pillingweb.co.uk
northcotswoldbrewery.co.uk
Shop – please ring first
Tours by arrangement

North Cotswold started in 1999 as a 2.5-barrel plant, which was upgraded in 2000 to 10 barrels. A shop and visitor centre are on site. The brewery produces around 30 different ales a year, which includes a monthly special. It also owns the Happy Apple Cider Company, which produces real cider and perry from orchards on the estate of the farm. Further expansion is planned as is the purchasing of a brewery tap. Around 200 outlets are supplied locally and nationally. Bottle-conditioned beer is available. Seasonal beers: see website.

Pig Brook (OG 1038, ABV 3.8%)
Full-flavoured session bitter.

Shag Weaver (OG 1045, ABV 4.5%)
A very pale bitter with New Zealand hops.

Hung, Drawn 'n' Portered (OG 1050, ABV 5%)
A black treacle porter.

North Curry

North Curry Brewery Co, The Old Coach House, Gwyon House, Church Road, North Curry, Somerset, TA3 6LH
07928 815053
thenorthcurrybreweryco@hotmail.co.uk
thenorthcurrybrewerycouk.com
Tours by arrangement

THE BREWERIES

The brewery opened in summer 2006 and is attached to one of the oldest properties in North Curry. Brewing last took place in the village in the 1920s. Five outlets are supplied direct. All beers are available bottle conditioned; Red Heron is organic.

Red Heron (OG 1041, ABV 4.3%)

The Witheyman (OG 1043, ABV 4.6%)

Level Headed (OG 1044, ABV 4.7%)

Northern SIBA

Northern Brewing Ltd, Blakemere Brewery, Blakemere Craft Centre, Chester Road, Sandiway, Northwich, Cheshire, CW8 2EB
☎ (01606) 301000
✉ sales@norbrew.co.uk
norbrew.co.uk
Tours by arrangement

Northern first brewed in 2003 on a five-barrel plant located in Runcorn. It relocated to a larger unit at Blakemere Craft Centre in 2005. A hospitality/bar area is available for brewery tours. Some beer names are Northern Soul themed and at least two specials per month are produced under both the Northern and Blakemere brand names.

All-Niter (ABV 3.8%)
Full-bodied, pale bitter beer with caramel overtones. Good hoppy nose and aftertaste.

Soul Rider (ABV 4%)

Dancer (ABV 4.2%)

'45 (ABV 4.5%)
Soft, light and malty pale brown beer. Fairly sweet with fruit to the fore on the nose and in the flavour. Hop flavour leads into the aftertaste.

Hit and Run (ABV 4.5%)

One-Der-Ful Wheat (ABV 4.7%)

Soul Time (ABV 5%)

Two Tone Special Stout (ABV 5%)

Deep, Dark Secret (ABV 5.2%)

Flaming Embers (ABV 6%)

Northumberland SIBA

Northumberland Brewery Ltd, Accessory House, Barrington Road, Bedlington, Northumberland, NE22 7AP
☎ (01670) 822112
✉ dave@northumberlandbrewery.co.uk
northumberlandbrewery.co.uk
Tours by arrangement

The brewery has been in operation for 11 years using a 10-barrel brew plant. More than 400 outlets are supplied. The Legends of the Tyne and Legends of the Wear series of beers are also produced as regulars. Seasonal beers: see website.

Pit Pony (ABV 3.8%)

Bucking Fastard (ABV 4%)

Fog on the Tyne (ABV 4.1%)

Brown Ale (ABV 4.6%)

Sheepdog (ABV 4.7%)
An old-fashioned tawny beer, with fruit and malt throughout and a hoppy finish.

North Wales SIBA

North Wales Brewery, Tan-y-Mynydd, Moelfre, Abergele, Conwy, LL22 9RF
☎ (0800) 083 4100
✉ northwalesbrewery@uwclub.net
northwalesbrewery.net

North Wales started brewing in June 2007 on a plant transferred from Paradise Brewery's former home in Wrenbury. Bottle-conditioned beers are available as are occasional seasonal brews.

Bodelwyddan Bitter (ABV 3.8%)

Farmers Ale (ABV 4%)

Llew Aur (Golden Lion) (ABV 4.5%)

Abergele Ale (ABV 5%)

Dragon's Wheat (ABV 5%)

Welsh Stout (ABV 5.2%)

North Yorkshire

North Yorkshire Brewing Co, Pinchinthorpe Hall, Pinchinthorpe, North Yorkshire, TS14 8HG
☎ (01287) 630200
✉ sales@nybrewery.co.uk
nybrewery.co.uk
Shop 10am-5pm daily
Tours by arrangement (inc 3 course meal)

The brewery was founded in Middlesbrough in 1989 and moved in 1998 to Pinchinthorpe Hall, a moated and listed medieval estate near Guisborough that has its own spring water. The site also includes a hotel, restaurant and bistro. More than 100 free trade outlets are supplied. A special monthly beer is produced together with four beers in the Cosmic range. All beers are organic and bottle-conditioned beers are available.

Best (OG 1036, ABV 3.6%)

Golden Ginseng (ABV 3.6%)

Prior's Ale (OG 1036, ABV 3.6%)
Light, refreshing and surprisingly full-flavoured for a pale, low gravity beer, with a complex, bittersweet mixture of malt, hops and fruit carrying through into the aftertaste.

Archbishop Lee's Ruby Ale (OG 1040, ABV 4%)

Boro Best (OG 1040, ABV 4%)

Crystal Tips (OG 1040, ABV 4%)

Love Muscle (OG 1040, ABV 4%)

Honey Bunny (OG 1042, ABV 4.2%)

Mayhem (ABV 4.3%)

Cereal Killer (OG 1045, ABV 4.5%)

Blond (ABV 4.6%)

Fools Gold (OG 1046, ABV 4.6%)

Golden Ale (OG 1046, ABV 4.6%)
A well-hopped, lightly-malted, golden premium bitter, using Styrian Goldings and Goldings hops.

Flying Herbert (OG 1047, ABV 4.7%)

Lord Lee's (OG 1047, ABV 4.7%)
A refreshing, red/brown beer with a hoppy aroma. The flavour is a pleasant balance of roast malt and sweetness that predominates over hops. The malty, bitter finish develops slowly.

White Lady (OG 1047, ABV 4.7%)

Dizzy Duck (OG 1048, ABV 4.8%)

Rocket Fuel (OG 1050, ABV 5%)

Nottingham SIBA

Nottingham Brewing Co Ltd, Plough Inn, 17 St Peter's Street, Radford, Nottingham, NG7 3EN
☎ (0115) 942 2649
☎ 07815 073447
✉ philip.darby@nottinghambrewery.com
nottinghambrewery.com
Tours by arrangement

The former owners of the Bramcote and Castle Rock Breweries re-established the Nottingham Brewery in 2000 in a purpose built brewhouse behind the Plough Inn. Philip Darby and Niven Balfour set out to revive the brands of the original Nottingham Brewery, closed by Whitbread in the 50s, with a view to supplying local outlets very much within the LocAle ethos.

Rock Ale Bitter Beer (OG 1038, ABV 3.8%)

Rock Ale Mild Beer (OG 1038, ABV 3.8%)

Legend (OG 1040, ABV 4%)

Extra Pale Ale (OG 1042, ABV 4.2%)

Dreadnought (OG 1045, ABV 4.5%)

Bullion (OG 1047, ABV 4.7%)

Sooty Stout (OG 1048, ABV 4.8%)

Supreme Bitter (OG 1052, ABV 5.2%)

For Finesse Hotels Group:

Cock & Hoop (OG 1043, ABV 4.3%)

Nutbrook

Nutbrook Brewery Ltd, 6 Hallam Way, West Hallam, Derbyshire, DE7 6LA
☎ 0800 458 2460
✉ dean@nutbrookbrewery.com
nutbrookbrewery.com
Shop (by invite only) Mon-Fri 10am-6pm; Sat 10am-1pm
Tours by arrangement

Nutbrook was established in January 2007 on a one-barrel brewery in the owner's garage. Beers are brewed to order for domestic and corporate clients, and customers can design their own recipes. All beers are available bottle conditioned and a range of organic beers is planned. Seasonal beer: Midnight (ABV 4.7%, Xmas).

Or8 (OG 1041.5, ABV 3.8%)

Squirrel (OG 1038.8, ABV 4.1%)

Bitlyke (OG 1040.6, ABV 4.2%)

Responsibly (OG 1044.1, ABV 4.4%)

Banter (OG 1040.9, ABV 4.5%)

Mongrel (OG 1046.9, ABV 4.5%)

More (OG 1047.2, ABV 4.8%)

For Seven Oaks:

Oak's Ale (OG 1039, ABV 4%)

O'Hanlon's SIBA

O'Hanlon's Brewing Co Ltd, Great Barton Farm, Whimple, Devon, EX5 2NY
☎ (01404) 822412
✉ info@ohanlons.co.uk
ohanlons.co.uk

Since moving to Whimple in 2000, O'Hanlon's has continued to expand to cope with ever increasing demand for its prize-winning beers. More than 100 outlets are regularly supplied, with wholesalers providing publicans nationwide with access to the cask products. A new bottling plant has increased production and enabled O'Hanlon's to contract bottle for several other breweries. Export sales also continue to grow but in June 2009 the company said it would stop production of Thomas Hardy's Ale. Bottle-conditioned ales are available.

Firefly (OG 1035, ABV 3.7%)
Malty and fruity light bitter. Hints of orange in the taste.

Golde Blade Wheat (OG 1037, ABV 4%)
1999 and 2002 SIBA Champion Wheat Beer of Britain has a fine citrus taste.

Yellowhammer (OG 1041, ABV 4%)
A well-balanced, smooth pale yellow beer with a predominant hop and fruit nose and taste, leading to a dry, bitter finish.

Dry Stout (OG 1041, ABV 4.2%)
A dark malty, well-balanced stout with a dry, bitter finish and plenty of roast and fruit flavours up front.

Original Port Stout (OG 1041, ABV 4.8%)
A black beer with roast malt in the aroma that remains in the taste but gives way to hoppy bitterness in the aftertaste.

Royal Oak (OG 1048, ABV 5%)
Well-balanced copper-coloured beer with a strong fruit and malt aroma; a malty, fruity and sweet taste; and bitter aftertaste.

Thomas Hardy Ale (OG 1120, ABV 11.7%)
A tawny brown colour. Dark malts dominate with hints of sherry, treacle, molasses, toffee and port. The finish combines red wine, sherry and plenty of rich fruit. Future of the beer is in doubt.

Oakham SIBA EAB

Oakham Ales, 2 Maxwell Road, Woodston, Peterborough, Cambridgeshire, PE2 7JB
☎ (01733) 370500
✉ info@oakhamales.com
oakhamales.com
Tours by arrangement

The brewery started in 1993 in Oakham, Rutland, and expanded to a 35-barrel plant from the original 10-barrel in 1998 after moving to Peterborough. This was the brewery's main brewhouse until 2006 when a new 70-barrel brewery was completed at Maxwell Road. The 35-barrel plant was removed from the brewery tap in 2008 and replaced by a custom-built brewhouse. This allows brewing to continue within the brewery tap on what is effectively Oakham's pilot plant, used for experimental brewing. Around 200 outlets are supplied and four pubs are owned. Seasonal beers: see website.

Jeffrey Hudson Bitter/JHB (OG 1038, ABV 3.8%)
A straw-coloured beer with a smooth mouthfeel. Spicy hop predominates the aroma and there are citrus and grassy hops in the mouth with a little sweetness. Lingering hoppy finish.

THE BREWERIES

Inferno (OG 1040, ABV 4%) ◆
Impressive golden ale with explosive fruity hop fumes. The palate comprises a powerful resiny and spicy hop character with complex fruit flavours and a satisfying bitterness. Strong, dry, hoppy finale.

White Dwarf (OG 1042, ABV 4.3%) ◆
A speciality beer with fruit and hops on the aroma and in the taste. Dry and faintly astringent on the palate, leading to a strong, dry and moderately astringent finish.

Bishops Farewell (OG 1046, ABV 4.6%) ◆
Citrus and grassy hops on the nose of this golden ale. A spirited spicy hop tang is coupled with strong bitterness and leads into an intense, dry, hoppy aftertaste.

Oakleaf SIBA

Oakleaf Brewing Co Ltd, Unit 7, Clarence Wharf Industrial Estate, Mumby Road, Gosport, Hampshire, PO12 1AJ
☎ **(023) 9251 3222**
✉ **info@oakleafbrewing.co.uk**
🌐 **oakleafbrewing.co.uk**
Shop Mon-Fri 9am-5pm; Sat 10am-1pm
Tours by arrangement

⊗ Ed Anderson set up Oakleaf with his father-in-law, Dave Pickersgill, in 2000. The brewery stands on the side of Portsmouth Harbour. Bottled beers are sold in the Victory Shop at the historic dockyard in Portsmouth. Some 150 outlets are supplied. Seasonal beers: see website. Bottle-conditioned beers are also available.

Bitter (OG 1038, ABV 3.8%) ◆
A copper-coloured beer with a hoppy and fruity aroma, which leads to an intensely hoppy and bitter flavour, with balancing lemon and grapefruit and some malt. A long dry finish. Full tasting for its strength.

Maypole Mild (OG 1040, ABV 3.8%) ◆
This dark mild has a full biscuity aroma. A lasting mix of flavours – roast, toffee – leads to a slightly unexpected hoppiness and a roast, bitter finish. Not typical of the style but bags of flavour for its strength.

Nuptu'ale (OG 1042, ABV 4.2%) ◆
A full-bodied pale ale, strongly hopped with an uncompromising bitterness. An intense hoppy, spicy, floral aroma leads to a complex hoppy taste. Well-balanced with malt and citrus flavours make for a refreshing bitter.

Pompey Royal (ABV 4.5%)

Hole Hearted (OG 1048, ABV 4.7%) ◆
An amber-coloured strong bitter, with strong floral hop and citrus notes in the aroma. These continue to dominate the flavour and lead to a long bittersweet finish.

I Can't Believe It's Not Bitter (OG 1048, ABV 4.9%)
Cask-conditioned lager.

Blake's Gosport Bitter (OG 1053, ABV 5.2%) ◆
Packed with berry fruits and roastiness, this is a complex strong bitter. Malt, roast and caramel are prevalent as sweetness builds to an uncompromising vinous finish. Warming, spicy, well balanced and delicious.

For Suthwyk Ales:

Bloomfields Bitter (ABV 3.8%) ◆
Pleasant, clean-tasting pale brown bitter. Easy drinking and well balanced. Beer is brewed by Oakleaf for Suthwyk using ingredients grown on their own farm.

Liberation (ABV 4.2%)

Skew Sunshine Ale (ABV 4.6%) ◆
An amber-coloured beer. Initial hoppiness leads to a fruity taste and finish. A slightly cloying mouthfeel.

Oakwell SIBA

Oakwell Brewery, PO Box 87, Pontefract Road, Barnsley, South Yorkshire, S71 1EZ
☎ **(01226) 296161**
✉ **jstancill@oakwellbrewery.co.uk**

⊛ Brewing started in 1997. Oakwell supplies around 30 outlets.

Old Tom Mild (OG 1033.5, ABV 3.4%) ◆
A dark brown session mild, with a fruit aroma and a subtle hint of roast. Crisp and refreshing with a sharp finish.

Barnsley Bitter (OG 1036, ABV 3.8%)

Oban Bay (NEW)

Oban Bay Brewery, Cuan Mor, 60 George Street, Oban, Argyll, PA34 5DS
☎ **(01631) 565078**

Brewing began in 2009. 20 outlets are supplied.

Kilp Lifter (ABV 3.9%)

Skinny Blonde (ABV 4.1%)

Skelpt Lug (ABV 4.2%)

Fair Puggled (ABV 4.5%)

Odcombe

Odcombe Brewery, Masons Arms, 41 Lower Odcombe, Lower Odcombe, Somerset, BA22 8TX
☎ **(01935) 862591**
✉ **paula@masonsarmsodcombe.co.uk**
🌐 **masonsarmsodcombe.co.uk**
Tours by arrangement

Odcombe Brewery opened in 2000 and closed a few years later. It re-opened in 2005 with assistance from Shepherd Neame. Brewing takes place once a week and beers are only available at the pub. Seasonal beers: Half Jack (ABV 3.8%), Winter's Tail (ABV 4.3%).

No 1 (OG 1040, ABV 4%)

Spring (OG 1041, ABV 4.1%)

Offa's Dyke

Offa's Dyke Brewery Ltd, Barley Mow Inn, Chapel Lane, Trefonen, Oswestry, Shropshire, SY10 9DX
☎ **(01691) 656889**
✉ **realales@offasdykebrewery.com**
🌐 **offasdykebrewery.com**
Shop Mon-Fri 5-11pm; Sat & Sun 12-12
Tours by arrangement

⊛ Offa's Dyke was established in 2006 and changed hands early in 2007. This is the second brewery on this site in the last three years, the first relocating. The brewery and adjoining pub straddle the old England/Wales border, Offa's Dyke. Thomas

McGuinness' five-barrel plant was acquired and brewing commenced in August 2007. The owner grows barley locally and is experimenting with small-scale hop cultivation. Bottle-conditioned beers are planned.

Harvest Moon (OG 1038, ABV 3.6%)

Barley Gold (OG 1038, ABV 3.8%)

Barley Blonde (ABV 4%)

Thirst Brew (OG 1042, ABV 4.2%)

Grim Reaper (OG 1050, ABV 5%)

Okells SIBA

Okell & Son Ltd, Kewaigue, Douglas, Isle of Man, IM2 1QG
☎ (01624) 699400
✉ mac@okells.co.uk
🌐 okells.co.uk
Tours by arrangement

Founded in 1874 by Dr Okell and formerly trading as Isle of Man Breweries, this is the main brewery on the island, having taken over and closed the rival Castletown Brewery in 1986. The brewery moved in 1994 to a new, purpose-built plant at Kewaigue to replace the Falcon Brewery in Douglas. All the beers are produced under the Manx Brewers' Act 1874 (permitted ingredients: water, malt, sugar and hops only). 36 of the company's 48 IoM pubs and four on the mainland sell cask beer and some 70 free trade outlets are also supplied. Seasonal beers: see website.

Mild (OG 1034, ABV 3.4%)
A fine aroma of hops and crystal malt. Red-brown in colour, the beer has a full malt flavour with surprising bitter hop notes and a hint of blackcurrants and oranges.

Bitter (OG 1035, ABV 3.7%)
A golden beer, malty and hoppy in aroma, with a hint of honey. Rich and malty on the tongue, it has a dry, malt and hop finish. A complex but rewarding beer.

Maclir (OG 1042, ABV 4.4%)
Beer with resiny hops and lemon fruit on the aroma, banana and lemon in the mouth and a big, bitter finish, dominated by hops, juicy malt and citrus fruit.

Dr Okells IPA (OG 1044, ABV 4.5%)
A light-coloured beer with a full-bodied taste. The sweetness is offset by strong hopping that gives the beer an overall roundness with spicy lemon notes and a fine dry finish.

Old Bear SIBA

Old Bear Brewery, Unit 4b, Atlas Works, Pitt Street, Keighley, West Yorkshire, BD21 4YL
☎ (01535) 601222
☎ 07713 161224
✉ sales@oldbearbrewery.com
🌐 oldbearbrewery.co.uk
Tours by arrangement

Old Bear is a family business founded in 1993 at the Old White Bear in Crosshills. The brewery moved to Keighley in 2004 to a purpose-built unit to cater for increased production. The original 10-barrel plant was retained and there is now a one-barrel plant for specials. Beers are supplied within a 60-mile radius of Keighley and via wholesalers. All cask beers are also available bottle conditioned.

Bruin (OG 1035, ABV 3.5%)
The combination of hops gives off a sharp wild blackcurrant taste with a smoothness to follow.

Estivator (OG 1037, ABV 3.8%)
A light golden ale with a smooth, creamy, sweet lemon taste followed by buttery smoothness leading to a bitter, hoppy aftertaste.

Original (OG 1039, ABV 3.9%)
A refreshing and easy-to-drink bitter. The balance of malt and hops gives way to a short, dry, bitter aftertaste.

Black Mari'a (OG 1043, ABV 4.2%)
A black stout, smooth on the palate with a strong roast malt flavour and fruity finish.

Honeypot (OG 1044, ABV 4.4%)
Straw-coloured beer enhanced with golden honey.

Goldilocks (OG 1047, ABV 4.5%)
A fruity, straw-coloured golden ale, well-hopped and assertively bitter through to the finish.

Hibernator (OG 1055, ABV 5%)
A complex rich dark ale dominated by roast and bitter flavours against a background sweetness. Look for roast coffee, hints of caramel and dark vine fruit on the nose. The finish is distinctly bitter and quite astringent.

Duke of Bronte (ABV 12.5%)

Old Bog

Old Bog Brewery, Masons Arms, 2 Quarry School Place, Oxford, OX3 8LH
☎ (01865) 764579
✉ theoldbog@hotmail.co.uk
🌐 masonsquarry.co.uk

Brewing started in 2005 on a one-barrel plant. At present Old Bog brews once a week. The beers, when available, are sold at the Masons Arms and occasionally at beer festivals. A number of one-off brews appear throughout the year.

Quarry Gold (OG 1041, ABV 4.1%)

Old Cannon

Old Cannon Brewery Ltd, 86 Cannon Street, Bury St Edmunds, Suffolk, IP33 1JR
☎ (01284) 768769
✉ drink@oldcannonbrewery.co.uk
🌐 oldcannonbrewery.co.uk
Tours by arrangement (small groups only)

The St Edmunds Head pub opened in 1845 with its own brewery. Brewing ceased in 1917, and Greene King closed the pub in 1995. It re-opened in 1999 as the Old Cannon Brewery complete with a unique state-of-the-art brewery housed in the bar area. Brewing takes place on a Monday when the pub is closed. A growing number of local outlets are supplied. Seasonal beers: Brass Monkey (ABV 4.6%, winter), St Edmund's Head (ABV 4.6%, winter), Blonde Bombshell (ABV 4.2%).

Best Bitter (OG 1037, ABV 3.8%)
Session bitter brewed using Styrian Goldings, giving a crisp grapefruit aroma and taste. Refreshing and full of flavour.

Gunner's Daughter (OG 1052, ABV 5.5%)

A well-balanced strong ale with a complexity of hop, fruit, sweetness and bitterness in the flavour, and a lingering hoppy, bitter aftertaste.

Old Chimneys

Old Chimneys Brewery, Hopton End Farm, Church Road, Market Weston, Diss, Norfolk, IP22 2NX
☎ (01359) 221411/221013
oldchimneysbrewery.com
Shop Fri 2-7pm; Sat 11am-2pm
Tours by arrangement

Old Chimneys opened in 1995 and moved to larger premises in a converted farm building in 2001. Despite the postal address, the brewery is in Suffolk. The beers produced are mostly named after endangered local species. Seasonal beers: Polecat Porter (ABV 4.2%, winter), Red Clover (ABV 6%, winter). All cask ales are available bottle conditioned and are suitable for vegetarians and vegans except Black Rat and Hairy Canary.

Military Mild (OG 1035, ABV 3.3%)
A rich, dark mild with good body for its gravity. Sweetish toffee and light roast bitterness dominate, leading to a dry aftertaste.

Great Raft Bitter (OG 1040, ABV 4%)
Pale copper bitter bursting with fruit. Malt and hops add to the sweetish fruity flavour, which is rounded off with hoppy bitterness in the aftertaste.

Black Rat Stout (OG 1048, ABV 4.4%)

Golden Pheasant (OG 1044, ABV 4.5%)

Scarlet Tiger (OG 1046, ABV 4.6%)

Good King Henry (OG 1107, ABV 9%)

Old Cross (NEW)

Old Cross Tavern Brewery, Old Cross Tavern, 8 St Andrew Street, Hertford, Hertfordshire, SG14 1JA
☎ (01992) 583133

The micro-brewery was set up in 2008 and is located within the pub. Owner Nigel Beviss brews solely for the Old Cross Tavern. There are currently two beers, with one usually available at the bar.

Laugh and Titter (ABV 3.7%)

OXT'ale (ABV 4%)

Oldershaw SIBA

Oldershaw Brewery, 12 Harrowby Hall Estate, Grantham, Lincolnshire, NG31 9HB
☎ (01476) 572135
oldershawbrewery@btconnect.com
oldershawbrewery.com

Experienced home-brewer Gary Oldershaw and his wife Diane set up the brewery at their home in 1997. Grantham's first brewery for 30 years, Oldershaw now supplies 60 local free houses. The Oldershaws have introduced small-scale bottling and sell bottle-conditioned beer direct from the brewery. Seasonal beers: Sunnydaze (ABV 4%, May-Aug), Yuletide (ABV 5.2%, Nov-Dec), Grantham Dark (ABV 3.6%), Alma's Brew (ABV 4.1%).

Pearl (ABV 3%)

Mowbrays Mash (OG 1037, ABV 3.7%)

Harrowby Pale Ale (OG 1039, ABV 3.9%)

High Dyke (OG 1039, ABV 3.9%)
Golden and moderately bitter. A predominantly hoppy session beer.

OSB (OG 1040, ABV 4%)

Newton's Drop (OG 1041, ABV 4.1%)
Balanced malt and hops but with a strong bitter, lingering taste in this mid-brown beer.

Caskade (OG 1042, ABV 4.2%)
Pale, golden beer brewed with American Cascade hops to give a distinctive floral, hoppy flavour and aroma, and a clean lasting finish.

Ahtanum Gold (OG 1043, ABV 4.3%)
A gold-coloured, fruity, hoppy beer balanced with some maltiness. Moderately bitter.

Grantham Stout (OG 1043, ABV 4.3%)
Dark brown and smooth with rich roast malt flavour, supported by some fruit and bitterness. A long, moderately dry finish.

Regal Blonde (OG 1043, ABV 4.4%)
Straw-coloured, lager-style beer with a good malt/hop balance throughout; strong bitterness on the taste lingers.

Isaac's Gold (OG 1044, ABV 4.5%)

Old Boy (OG 1047, ABV 4.8%)
A full-bodied amber ale, fruity and bitter with a hop/fruit aroma. The malt that backs the taste dies in the long finish.

Alchemy (OG 1052, ABV 5.3%)
A golden, premium hoppy beer brewed with First Gold hops.

Olde Swan

Olde Swan Brewery, 89 Halesowen Road, Netherton, Dudley, West Midlands, DY2 9PY
☎ (01384) 253075
Tours by arrangement

A famous brew-pub best known as 'Ma Pardoe's' after the matriarch who ruled it for years. The pub has been licensed since 1835 and the present brewery and pub were built in 1863. Brewing continued until 1988 and restarted in 2001. The plant brews primarily for the on-site pub with some beer available to the trade. Seasonal beer: Black Widow (ABV 6.7%, winter). Monthly specials are available together with various commemorative beers for sporting events as well as bottle-conditioned beers from the brewery tap.

Original (OG 1034, ABV 3.5%)
Straw-coloured light mild, smooth but tangy, and sweetly refreshing with a faint hoppiness.

Dark Swan (OG 1041, ABV 4.2%)
Smooth, sweet dark mild with late roast malt in the finish.

1835 (OG 1044, ABV 4.3%)
A pale amber bitter with a distinctive hop character.

Entire (OG 1043, ABV 4.4%)
Faintly hoppy, amber premium bitter with sweetness persistent throughout.

Bumble Hole Bitter (OG 1052, ABV 5.2%)
Sweet, smooth amber ale with hints of astringency in the finish.

Old Foreigner

Old Foreigner Brewery, Glenkindie Arms Hotel, Glenkindie, Aberdeenshire, AB33 8SX
☎ (01975) 641288
eddie@theglenkindiearmshotel.com
theglenkindiearmshotel.com
Tours by arrangement

A one-barrel brew plant was installed in April 2007.

Gartly Nagger (ABV 4.2%)

The Wicked Wickerman (OG 1042, ABV 4.2%)

Sentinel (ABV 4.4%)

Old Forge

See Cumberland

Old Laxey

Old Laxey Brewing Co Ltd, Shore Hotel Brew Pub, Old Laxey, Isle of Man, IM4 7DA
☎ (01624) 863214
shore@mcb.net
Tours by arrangement

Beer brewed on the Isle of Man is brewed to a strict Beer Purity Act. Additives are not permitted to extend shelf life, nor are chemicals allowed to assist with head retention. Most of Old Laxey's beer is sold through the Shore Hotel alongside the brewery.

Bosun Bitter (OG 1038, ABV 3.8%)
Crisp and fresh with a hoppy aftertaste.

Old Luxters SIBA

Old Luxters Farm Brewery, Hambleden, Henley-on-Thames, Oxfordshire, RG9 6JW
☎ (01491) 638330
enquiries@chilternvalley.co.uk
chilternvalley.co.uk
Shop Mon-Fri 9am-6pm (5pm winter); Sat- Sun 11am-6pm (5pm winter)
Tours by arrangement

A traditional, full-mash farm brewery established in 1990 and now with the 'By Royal Appointment' accolade, is situated in a 17th-century barn alongside the Chiltern Valley Vineyard. The brewery is in Buckinghamshire despite the postal address. Several bottle-conditoned beers are brewed under contract. Three winter warmers are brewed for Xmas.

Barn Ale Bitter (OG 1038, ABV 4%)
A fruity, aromatic, fairly hoppy, bitter beer.

Barn Ale Special (OG 1042.5, ABV 4.5%)
Predominantly malty, fruity and hoppy in taste and nose, and tawny/amber in colour. Fairly strong in flavour: the initial, sharp, malty and fruity taste leaves a dry, bittersweet, fruity aftertaste. It can be slightly sulphurous.

Dark Roast Ale (OG 1048, ABV 5%)
The use of chocolate and crystal malts give this ale a nutty, roasty bitter flavour.

Old Mill

Old Mill Brewery, Mill Street, Snaith, East Yorkshire, DN14 9HU
☎ (01405) 861813
sales@oldmillbrewery.co.uk
oldmillbrewery.co.uk
Tours by arrangement to organisations and customers only

Old Mill is a craft brewery opened in 1983 in a 200-year-old former malt kiln and corn mill. The brew-length is 60 barrels. The brewery is building a tied estate, now standing at 19 houses. Beers can be found nationwide through wholesalers and around 80 free trade outlets are supplied direct. There is a rolling programme of seasonal beers (see website) and monthly specials.

Mild (OG 1034, ABV 3.4%)
A satisfying roast malt flavour dominates this easy-drinking, quality dark mild.

Bitter (OG 1038.5, ABV 3.9%)
A malty nose is carried through to the initial flavour. Bitterness runs throughout.

Old Curiosity (OG 1044.5, ABV 4.5%)
Slightly sweet amber brew, malty to start with. Malt flavours all the way through.

Bullion (OG 1047.5, ABV 4.7%)
The malty and hoppy aroma is followed by a neat mix of hop and fruit tastes within an enveloping maltiness. Dark brown/amber in colour.

Old Poet's

See Ashover

Old Spot

Old Spot Brewery Ltd, Manor Farm, Station Road, Cullingworth, Bradford, West Yorkshire, BD13 5HN
☎ (01535) 691144
sales@oldspotbrewery.co.uk
oldspotbrewery.co.uk
Tours by arrangement

Old Spot started brewing in 2005 and is named after a retired sheepdog on Manor Farm. The brewery targets the ever-changing guest ale market and creates new brews every 2-3 weeks, along with the stock beers. Around 35 outlets are supplied.

Darkside Pup (ABV 3.6%)
Full-bodied dark mild with a deep coffee taste with liquorice to finish.

Light But Dark (ABV 4%)
Chestnut-coloured bitter with a slight malty taste and pleasant bitter finish. An ideal session beer.

Inn-Spired (ABV 4.3%)
Light-coloured bitter with a light, hoppy taste and a slight, fruity finish.

Spot O'Bother (ABV 5.5%)
Porter with a chocolate ice cream taste and slight liquorice bitterness to finish. A very complex brew.

Ole Slewfoot (NEW)

Ole Slewfoot Brewing Co Ltd, 3 Pollard Road, Hainford, Norwich, Norfolk, NR10 3BE
☎ (01603) 279927
john@oleslewfootbrewery.co.uk
oleslewfootbrewery.co.uk

Ole Slewfoot was established in 2009. Five outlets are supplied direct.

January 8th (OG 1040, ABV 4.2%)

Fox on the Run (OG 1045, ABV 4.8%)

Devils Dream (OG 1048, ABV 5%)

Opa Hay's (NEW)

Opa Hay's Brewery, Glencot, Wood Lane, Aldeby, NR34 0DA
☎ (01502) 679144
☎ 07916 282729
✉ mail@engelfineales.com
engelfineales.com

Opa Hay's began brewing in late 2008. Seasonal beers: Engel's Porter (ABV 5.2%), Ether Party (ABV 5.2%).

Engel's Best Bitter (ABV 4%)

Engel's Amber Ale (ABV 4.3%)

Engel's Pale Ale (ABV 4.6%)

For King's Head Hotel, Beccles:

Matilda's Revenge (ABV 4.3%)

Organic

See Chough

Orkney SIBA

Orkney Brewery, Sinclair Breweries Ltd, Quoyloo, Stromness, Orkney, KW16 3LT
☎ (01667) 404555
✉ info@sinclairbreweries.co.uk
orkneybrewery.co.uk

Set up in 1988 in an old school building in the remote Orkney hamlet of Quoyloo, the brewery was modernised in 1995. Capacity is now 120 barrels a week, all brewed along strict ecological lines from its own water supply. All waste water is treated through two lakes on the brewery's land, which in turn support fish and several dozen Mallard ducks. Along with Atlas (qv), Orkney is part of Sinclair Breweries; the combined business distributes to some 600 outlets across Scotland and via wholesalers to the rest of Britain. Seasonal beer: Clootie Dumpling (ABV 4.3%, Dec-Jan).

Raven (OG 1038, ABV 3.8%)
A well-balanced, quaffable bitter. Malty fruitiness and bitter hops last through to the long, dry aftertaste.

Dragonhead Stout (OG 1040, ABV 4%)
A strong, dark malt aroma flows into the taste in this superb Scottish stout. The roast malt continues to dominate the aftertaste, and blends with chocolate to develop a strong, dry finish.

Northern Light (OG 1040, ABV 4%)
A very drinkable, well-balanced Golden Ale, with a real smack of fruit and hops in the taste and an increasing bitter aftertaste.

Red MacGregor (OG 1040, ABV 4%)
Generally a well-balanced bitter, this tawny red ale has a powerful smack of fruit and a clean, fresh mouthfeel.

Dark Island (OG 1045, ABV 4.6%)
An excellent brew receiving many awards. The roast malt and chocolate character varies, making the beer hard to categorise as a stout or old ale. Generally a sweetish roast malt taste leads to a long-lasting roasted, slightly bitter, dry finish.

Skull Splitter (OG 1080, ABV 8.5%)
An intense velvet malt nose with hints of apple, prune and plum. The hoppy taste is balanced by satiny smooth malt with fruity spicy edges, leading to a long, dry finish with a hint of nut.

Ossett SIBA

Ossett Brewing Co Ltd, Kings Yard, Low Mill Road, Ossett, West Yorkshire, WF5 8ND
☎ (01924) 261333
✉ brewery@ossett-brewery.co.uk
ossett-brewery.co.uk
Shop Mon-Fri 9am-4.30pm
Tours by arrangement

Brewing began in 1998 but the brewery soon outgrew the premises moving to a new site 50 metres away in 2005. A new 2500 square feet cold store was added in 2008 and brewing capacity currently stands at 160 barrels per week. Ossett delivers between Newcastle and Peterborough and beer is available through wholesalers. The brewery owns 14 pubs, three restaurants and two micro-breweries. The Riverhead Brewery was purchased in 2006 and Fernandes Brewery in 2007. Seasonal and special beers: see website.

Pale Gold (OG 1038, ABV 3.8%)
A light, refreshing pale ale with a light, hoppy aroma.

Big Red Bitter (OG 1042, ABV 4%)
Deep red, malty Yorkshire bitter.

Silver King (OG 1041, ABV 4.3%)
A lager-style beer with a crisp, dry flavour and citrus fruity aroma.

Revolution IPA (OG 1044, ABV 4.5%)
American style pale ale. Bitter and intensely hoppy.

Excelsior (OG 1051, ABV 5.2%)
A strong pale ale with a full, mellow flavour and a fresh, hoppy aroma with citrus/floral characteristics.

Otley

Otley Brewing Co Ltd, Unit 42, Albion Industrial Estate, Pontypridd, Mid Glamorgan, CF37 4NX
☎ (01443) 480555
✉ info@otleybrewing.co.uk
otleybrewing.co.uk
Tours by arrangement

Otley Brewing was set up during the summer of 2005. Since then the brewery has doubled in size and now supplies Mid, West and East Wales. Seasonal beers: see website. Bottle-conditioned beers are also available.

01 (OG 1038, ABV 4%)
A pale golden beer with a hoppy aroma. The taste has hops, malt, fruit and a thirst-quenching bitterness. A satisfying finish completes this beer.

Dark 0 (OG 1039.7, ABV 4.1%)
A medium bodied, easy-drinking mild/stout with chocolate and roasted barley flavours.

02 (OG 1040.7, ABV 4.2%)
Golden-brown in colour, fruity with heavy floral aromas.

Boss (OG 1042.6, ABV 4.4%)

OBB (OG 1043.6, ABV 4.5%)
A tawny-red ale.

O-Garden (OG 1046.5, ABV 4.8%)

OG (OG 1052.3, ABV 5.4%)
A golden, honey-coloured ale, extremely smooth.

O8 (OG 1077.5, ABV 8%)
A pale and strong ale, deceptively smooth.

Otter SIBA

Otter Brewery Ltd, Mathayes, Luppitt, Honiton, Devon, EX14 4SA
☎ (01404) 891285
info@otterbrewery.com
otterbrewery.com
Tours by arrangement

Otter Brewery was set up in 1990 by the McCaig family and has grown into one of the West Country's major producers of beers. The brewery is located in the Blackdown Hills, between Taunton and Honiton. 2009 saw the completion of Otter's 'eco cellar', partly underground and built with clay blocks and a grass roof. The beers are made from the brewery's own springs and are delivered to more than 500 pubs across the south-west including the families first pub, the Holt, in Honiton. Seasonal beer: Witch Otter/Otter Claus/McOtter/Cupid Otter (name varies) (ABV 5%, winter).

Bitter (OG 1036, ABV 3.6%)
Well-balanced amber session bitter with a fruity nose and bitter taste and aftertaste.

Amber (ABV 4%)

Bright (OG 1039, ABV 4.3%)
Pale yellow/golden ale with a strong fruit aroma, sweet fruity taste and a bittersweet finish.

Ale (OG 1043, ABV 4.5%)
A full-bodied best bitter. A malty aroma predominates with a fruity taste and finish.

Head (OG 1054, ABV 5.8%)
Fruity aroma and taste with a pleasant bitter finish. Dark brown and full-bodied.

Outlaw

See Roosters

Outstanding

Outstanding Brewing Co Ltd, Britannia Mill, Cobden Street, Bury, Lancashire, BL9 6AW
☎ (0161) 764 7723
info@outstandingbeers.co.uk
outstandingbeers.com

The brewery was set up as a collaboration between Paul Sandiford, Glen Woodcock and David Porter. The 15-barrel plant went into production in March 2008. Selective free trade accounts are supplied nationally. Lagers (Pilsner, White and Amber Bock) are also available as cask beer on request.

OSB (OG 1042, ABV 4.4%)
A mid range copper-coloured ale with a distinctive hop finish.

Blonde (OG 1044, ABV 4.5%)

Ginger (OG 1044, ABV 4.5%)
Light brown beer with a noticeable hint of ginger.

SOS (OG 1044, ABV 4.5%)
Light brown bitter, dry and intensely bitter.

Smoked Out (OG 1049, ABV 5%)
A brown ale brewed with traditional continental smoked lager malt.

Standing Out (OG 1053, ABV 5.5%)
A pale golden ale, dry and bitter with lots of hop aroma.

Stout (OG 1057, ABV 5.5%)
Thick, jet black and bitter with liquorice overtones.

Pushing Out (OG 1065, ABV 7.4%)
A pale golden ale with a strong, distinctive dry, bitter flavour and a hop aroma.

Oxfordshire Ales

Bicester Beers & Minerals Ltd, 12 Pear Tree Farm Industrial Units, Bicester Road, Marsh Gibbon, Bicester, Oxfordshire, OX27 0GB
☎ (01869) 278765
bicesterbeers@tiscali.co.uk
oxfordshireales.co.uk
Tours by arrangement

The company first brewed in 2005. The five-barrel plant was previously at Picks Brewery but has now been upgraded to a 10-barrel plant with the purchase of a larger copper. It supplies 50-60 outlets as well as several wholesalers. Seasonal beers are produced.

Triple B (ABV 3.7%)
This pale amber beer has a huge caramel aroma. The caramel diminishes in the initial taste, which changes to a fruit/bitter balance. This in turn leads to a long, refreshing, bitter aftertaste.

Pride of Oxfordshire (ABV 4.1%)
An amber beer, the aroma is butterscotch/caramel, which carries on into the initial taste. The taste then becomes bitter with sweetish/malty overtones. There is a long, dry, bitter finish.

Marshmellow (ABV 4.7%)
The slightly fruity aroma in this golden-amber beer leads to a hoppy but thin taste, with slight caramel notes. The aftertaste is short and bitter.

For Plough, Marsh Gibbon:

Ploughmans Pride (ABV 4.2%)

Oyster

Oyster Brewery, Ellenabeich Harbour, Isle of Seil, Oban, PA34 4RQ
☎ (01852) 300121
gascoignea@tiscali.co.uk

The brewery came on stream in 2005. Head brewer Andy Gascoigne brought the brewery north after first installing it in his pub in West Yorkshire. In 2009 the brewery moved back to West Yorkshire (Leeds) but still supplies the Oyster Bar & Restaurant. No address details are available at time of going to press.

Easd'ale (OG 1038, ABV 3.8%)
Golden smooth bitter with a dry aftertaste.

Thistle Tickler (OG 1040, ABV 4%)
Amber, fruity session bitter using Fuggles hops and Vienna malt.

Corryvreckan (OG 1044, ABV 4.4%)

THE BREWERIES

Old Tosser (OG 1050, ABV 5%)
Strong dark ale brewed with roasted barley and American Cascade hops to give a rich, full-bodied character.

Palmer IFBB SIBA

JC & RH Palmer Ltd, The Old Brewery, West Bay Road, Bridport, Dorset, DT6 4JA
☎ (01308) 422396
✉ enquiries@palmersbrewery.com
🌐 palmersbrewery.com
Shop Mon-Sat 9am-6pm
Tours by arrangement (Please ring 01308 427500)

Palmers is Britain's only thatched brewery and dates from 1794. It is situated in Bridport, in the heart of the Jurassic Coast in south-west Dorset. The company continues to make substantial inventment in its 57 tenanted pubs, all serving cask ale. Around 250 outlets are supplied.

Copper Ale (OG 1036, ABV 3.7%)
Beautifully balanced, copper-coloured light bitter with a hoppy aroma.

Traditional Best Bitter (IPA) (OG 1040, ABV 4.2%)
Hop aroma and bitterness stay in the background in this predominately malty best bitter, with some fruit on the aroma.

Dorset Gold (OG 1046, ABV 4.5%)
More complex than many golden ales thanks to a pleasant banana and mango fruitiness on the aroma that carries on into the taste and aftertaste.

200 (OG 1052, ABV 5%)
This is a big beer with a touch of caramel sweetness adding to a complex hoppy, fruit taste that lasts from the aroma well into the aftertaste.

Tally Ho! (OG 1057, ABV 5.5%)
A complex dark old ale. Roast malts and treacle toffee on the palate lead in to a long, lingering finish with more than a hint of coffee.

Parish

Parish Brewery, 6 Main Street, Burrough on the Hill, Leicestershire, LE14 2JQ
☎ (01664) 454801
☎ 07715 369410
✉ barrie@parishbrewery.orangehome.co.uk
Tours by arrangement

Parish began in 1983 and is now located in a 400-year-old building and former stables next to the Stag & Hounds pub. The 20-barrel brewery supplies local outlets with the regular beer range and special one-off brews are produced for beer festivals across Leicestershire, Rutland and Cambridgeshire. Bottle-conditioned beers are also available.

PSB (OG 1038, ABV 3.8%)
Hoppy session beer with malty aftertaste.

Farm Gold (OG 1042, ABV 4.2%)
Light-coloured beer with distinctive hoppy taste and powerful aroma.

Burrough Bitter (OG 1048, ABV 4.8%)
Darker version of PSB with medium to strong bitterness and more pronounced malty aftertaste.

Baz's Bonce Blower (OG 1110, ABV 12%)
Strong, very dark beer with a very rich, malty character.

Peak Ales SIBA

Peak Ales, Barn Brewery, Chatsworth, Bakewell, Derbyshire, DE45 1EX
☎ (01246) 583737
✉ info@peakales.co.uk
🌐 peakales.co.uk
Tours by arrangement

Peak Ales opened in 2005 in converted, former derelict farm buildings on the Chatsworth estate, with the aid of a DEFRA Rural Enterprise Scheme grant, with support from trustees of Chatsworth Settlement. The brewery supplies around 30 local outlets and selected distributors. Seasonal beer: Noggin Filler (ABV 5%, winter).

Swift Nick (OG 1038, ABV 3.8%)
Traditional English session bitter with a slight fruit and hop aroma. Balanced flavours of malt and hops lead to a dry, bitter finish.

Bakewell Best Bitter (OG 1041, ABV 4.2%)
Impressive copper-coloured bitter beer. Little aroma but initial sweetness leads to a complex but balanced hop and malt flavour. Bitterness is present throughout, ending in a dry, fruity finish and aftertaste.

Chatsworth Gold (ABV 4.6%)
Golden beer made with honey from the Chatsworth Estate giving a delicate sweetness which is well balanced by the hoppy bitterness.

DPA (OG 1045, ABV 4.6%)
Golden brown, easy-drinking best bitter with a slight malt and hop aroma. Initial sweetness gives way to a bitter finish and aftertaste.

Peakstones Rock

Peakstones Rock Brewery, Peakstones Farm, Cheadle Road, Alton, Staffordshire, ST10 4DH
☎ 07891 350908
🌐 peakstonesrock.co.uk
Tours by arrangement

Peakstones Rock was established in 2005 on a purpose-built, five-barrel plant in an old farm building. It was expanded to a 10-barrel plant in 2008 and added fermentation vessels to keep up with demand. 60-70 outlets are supplied direct.

Nemesis (OG 1042, ABV 3.8%)
Pale brown with a liquorice aroma; roast but not burnt. Pleasing lingering bitter finish.

Chained Oak (OG 1045, ABV 4.2%)
A copper-coloured beer with a bitter finish and hop aroma.

Alton Abbey (OG 1051, ABV 4.5%)

Black Hole (OG 1048, ABV 4.8%)

Oblivion (OG 1055, ABV 5.5%)

Penlon Cottage

Penlon Cottage Brewery, Penlon Farm, Pencae, Llanarth, Ceredigion, SA47 0QN
☎ (01545) 580022
✉ beer@penlon.biz
🌐 penlon.biz

Penlon opened in 2004 and is located on a working smallholding in the Ceredigion coastal region of West Wales. Hops and malting barley are part of a programme of self-sufficiency, with grain, yeast and beer fed to pigs, sheep and chickens on the holding. It is the only Welsh brewery to have won the prestigious Wales True Taste awards twice for the best alcoholic drinks category. Bottle-conditioned beers: Lambs Gold Light Ale (ABV 3.2%), Tipsy Tup Pale Ale (ABV 3.8%), Heather Honey Ale (ABV 4.2%), Torddu Light Fruit Beer (ABV 4.2%), Chocolate Stout (ABV 4.5%), Torwen Dark Fruit Beer (ABV 4.5%), Stock Ram Stout (ABV 4.6%), Twin Ram IPA (ABV 4.8%), Ewes Frolic Lager (ABV 5.2%), Gimmers Mischief Premium Ale (ABV 5.2%), Ramnesia Strong Ale (ABV 5.6%). All bottled beers are suitable for vegetarians and vegans.

Cardi Bay Best Bitter (OG 1048, ABV 4%)

Pennine

Pennine Ale Ltd, The Rossendale Brewery, The Griffin Inn, 84-86 Hud Rake, Haslingden, Lancashire, BB4 5AF
☎ (01706) 214021
✉ pennine.ale@btconnect.com
Tours by arrangement

Pennine Ale acquired the brew plant previously used by Porter Brewing Co in November 2007. It produces six regular cask ales and supplies mainly to its own three pubs but has now started to supply the local free trade. All beers are suitable for vegetarians and vegans.

Floral Dance (OG 1035, ABV 3.6%)
A pale and fruity session beer.

Hameldon Bitter (OG 1037, ABV 3.8%)
A dark traditional bitter with a dry and assertive character that develops in the finish.

Railway Sleeper (OG 1040, ABV 4.2%)
An amber bitter.

Rossendale Ale (OG 1041, ABV 4.2%)
A malty aroma leads to a complex, malt dominated flavour, supported by a dry, increasingly bitter finish.

Pitch Porter (OG 1050, ABV 5%)
A full-bodied, rich beer with a slightly sweet, malty start, counter balanced with sharp bitterness and a roast barley dominance.

White Owl (ABV 5%)
A cloudy wheat beer.

Sunshine (OG 1050, ABV 5.3%)
A hoppy and bitter golden beer with a citrus character. The lingering finish is dry and spicy.

Penpont (NEW)

Penpont Brewery, Inner Trenarrett, Altarnun, Launceston, Cornwall, PL15 7SY
☎ (01566) 86069
☎ 07933 510461
✉ info@penpontbrewery.co.uk
🌐 penpontbrewery.co.uk

Penpont opened in late 2008. Beers are available in outlets across Cornwall and at beer festivals.

St Nonna's (ABV 3.7%)

Cornish Arvor (ABV 4%)

Roughtor (ABV 4.7%)

Penzance

Penzance Brewing Company, Star Inn, Crowlas, Penzance, Cornwall, TR20 8DX
☎ (01736) 740375

Penzance began brewing in June 2008 on a five-barrel plant. The brewery is situated in the yard of the Star Inn. The beers are produced by owner Peter Elvin, who was head brewer for Cotleigh Brewery for 16 years. Expansion of the range is planned. Beer is mostly produced for the pub but can be found at many beer festivals.

Crowlas Bitter (OG 1037, ABV 3.8%) ◆
Copper session bitter with good balance of malt, hops and citrus in the mouth. The aroma promises hops and malt, while the finish carries malt with dry bitterness.

Potion No 9 (OG 1039, ABV 4%)
Smooth-drinking golden session bitter. Well-balanced with a hoppy finish.

Phoenix

Oak Brewing Co Ltd t/a Phoenix Brewery, Green Lane, Heywood, Greater Manchester, OL10 2EP
☎ (01706) 627009
✉ tony@phoenixbrewery.co.uk

A company established as Oak Brewery in 1982 at Ellesmere Port, it moved in 1991 to the disused Phoenix Brewery and adopted the name. It now supplies 400-500 outlets with additional deliveries via wholesalers. Many seasonal beers are produced throughout the year. Restoration of the old brewery, built in 1897, is progressing well.

Bantam (OG 1035, ABV 3.5%) ◆
Light brown beer with a fruity aroma. Balance of malt, citrus fruit and hops in taste. Hoppy, bitter finish.

Hopsack (OG 1038, ABV 3.8%)
A light-drinking, hoppy session beer.

Navvy (OG 1039, ABV 3.8%) ◆
Amber beer with a citrus fruit and malt nose. Good balance of citrus fruit, malt and hops with bitterness coming through in the aftertaste.

Monkeytown Mild (OG 1039, ABV 3.9%)

Arizona (OG 1040, ABV 4.1%) ◆
Yellow in colour with a fruity and hoppy aroma. A refreshing beer with citrus, hops and good bitterness, and a shortish dry aftertaste.

Spotland Gold (OG 1041, ABV 4.1%)
A pale, hoppy beer with a lingering bitter finish.

Pale Moonlight (OG 1042, ABV 4.2%)

Black Bee (OG 1045, ABV 4.5%)

White Monk (OG 1045, ABV 4.5%) ◆
Yellow beer with a citrus fruit aroma, plenty of fruit, hops and bitterness in the taste, and a hoppy, bitter finish.

Thirsty Moon (OG 1046, ABV 4.6%) ◆
Tawny beer with a fresh citrus aroma. Hoppy, fruity and malty with a dry, hoppy finish.

West Coast IPA (OG 1046, ABV 4.6%) ◆
Golden in colour with a hoppy, fruity nose, Strong hoppy and fruity taste and aftertaste with good bitterness throughout.

Double Gold (OG 1050, ABV 5%)

Wobbly Bob (OG 1060, ABV 6%)
A red/brown beer with malty, fruity aroma and creamy mouthfeel. Strongly malty and fruity in flavour, with hops and a hint of herbs. Both sweetness and bitterness are evident throughout.

Pictish

Pictish Brewing Co Ltd, Unit 9, Canalside Industrial Estate, Rochdale, Greater Manchester, OL16 5LB
☎ (01706) 522227
✉ mail@pictish-brewing.co.uk
pictish-brewing.co.uk

The brewery was established in 2000 by Richard Sutton and supplies 60 free trade outlets in the north-west and west Yorkshire. Seasonal beers: see website.

Brewers Gold (OG 1038, ABV 3.8%)
Yellow in colour, with a hoppy, fruity nose. Soft maltiness and a strong hop/citrus flavour lead to a dry, bitter finish.

Alchemists Ale (OG 1043, ABV 4.3%)
Yellow beer with generous hop and fruit on the nose and palate. Good bitter hop finish.

For Crown Inn, Bacup:

Crown IPA (OG 1050, ABV 5%)

Pilgrim SIBA

Pilgrim Brewery, 11 West Street, Reigate, Surrey, RH2 9BL
☎ (01737) 222651
✉ pilgrimbrewery@hotmail.com
pilgrim.co.uk

Pilgrim was set up in 1982 in Woldingham, Surrey and moved to Reigate in 1985. The original owner, Dave Roberts, is still in charge. Beers are sold mostly in the Surrey area to around 30 outlets. Seasonal beers: Autumnal (ABV 4.5%), Excalibur (ABV 4.5%, Easter), Crusader (ABV 4.9%, summer), Talisman (ABV 5%, winter), Pudding (ABV 5.3%, Xmas). Other beers are also produced occasionally.

Surrey Bitter (OG 1037, ABV 3.7%)
Pineapple, grapefruit and spicy aromas in this well-balanced quaffing beer. Initial biscuity maltiness with a hint of vanilla gives way to a hoppy bitterness that becomes more pronounced in a refreshing bittersweet finish.

Weald Ale (ABV 3.7%)

Moild (ABV 3.8%)

Templar (ABV 3.8%)

Porter (OG 1040, ABV 4%)
Black beer with a good balance of dark malts with hints of berry fruit. Roast character present throughout to give a slightly bitter finish. Some balancing hop in the taste.

Progress (OG 1040, ABV 4%)
A well-rounded, tawny-coloured bitter. Predominantly sweet and malty, with an underlying fruitiness and a hint of toffee. The flavour is well balanced overall with a subdued bitterness. Little aroma and the aftertaste dissipates quickly.

Pitfield

Pitfield Brewery, Ashlyns Farm, Epping Road, North Weald, Epping, Essex, CM16 6RZ
☎ (0845) 833 1492
✉ sales@pitfieldbeershop.co.uk
pitfieldbeershop.co.uk
Shop daily 10am-4pm
Tours by arrangement

After 24 years in London, Pitfield Brewery left the capital in 2006 and moved to new premises in Essex. It has since moved again to an organic farm with 25 acres of organic barley for the brewery's use. The beers are sold at farmers' and organic markets in the south-east of England. Pitfield also produces organic fruit wines, cider and perry. Seasonal beer: St George's Ale (ABV 4.3%), 1896 Stock Ale (ABV 10%, Nov). All beers are organically produced to Soil Association standards and are vegan-friendly. Two further beers are produced using non-organic ingredients under the Epping Brewery name.

Dark Mild (OG 1036, ABV 3.4%)

Bitter (OG 1036, ABV 3.7%)

Lager (OG 1036, ABV 3.7%)

Shoreditch Stout (OG 1038, ABV 4%)
Chocolate and a raisin fruitiness on the nose lead to a fruity roast flavour and a sweetish finish with a little bitterness.

East Kent Goldings (OG 1040, ABV 4.2%)
A dry, yellow beer with bitter notes throughout and a faint hint of honey on the palate.

Eco Warrior (OG 1043, ABV 4.5%)
Golden ale with a vivid, citrus hop aroma. The hop character is balanced with a delicate sweetness in the taste, followed by an increasingly bitter finish.

Red Ale (OG 1046, ABV 4.8%)
Complex beer with a full, malty body and strong hop character.

1850 London Porter (OG 1048, ABV 5%)
Big-tasting dark ale dominated by coffee and forest fruits. The finish is dry but not acrid.

N1 Wheat Beer (OG 1048, ABV 5%)

1837 India Pale Ale (OG 1065, ABV 7%)

1792 Imperial Stout (OG 1085, ABV 9.3%)

For Duke of Cambridge, Islington:

SB Bitter (OG 1036, ABV 3.7%)

For Epping Brewery:

Dark (OG 1039, ABV 3.4%)

Forest Bitter (OG 1036, ABV 3.7%)

Pitstop (NEW)

Pitstop Brewery, Bellingers, Station Road, Grove, Oxfordshire, OX12 0DH
☎ (01235) 770548
✉ peterfowler@bellinger.co.uk
pitstopbrewery.co.uk
Shop Mon-Sat 8am-9pm; Sun 10am-8pm
Tours by arrangement

Pitstop was established in 2008 on a one-barrel plant to supply the existing off-licence (Bellingers). Demand was so great that the brewery expanded to a five-barrel plant in 2009.

Grand Prix (OG 1047, ABV 4.5%)

Penelope (OG 1054, ABV 5%)

Pole Position (OG 1054, ABV 5%)

Brickyard (OG 1067, ABV 6%)

Sump (OG 1076, ABV 7%)

Last Lap (OG 1100, ABV 9%)

Bitumen (OG 1113, ABV 10%)

Plain Ales (NEW)

Bow House Brewery Ltd t/a Plain Ales, Bow House, 44 Chitterne, Warminster, Wiltshire, BA12 0LG
☎ (01985) 851105
✉ james@plainales.co.uk
🌐 plainales.co.uk

Plain Ales started production in 2008 on a 2.5-barrel plant. There are plans for expansion to an eight-barrel plant.

Innocence (ABV 4%)

Innspiration (OG 1038, ABV 4%)

Inndulgence (ABV 4.5%)

Plassey SIBA

Plassey Brewery, Eyton, Wrexham, LL13 0SP
☎ (01978) 781111
☎ 07050 327127
✉ plassey@globalnet.co.uk
🌐 plasseybrewery.co.uk
Shop open office hours
Tours by arrangement

The brewery was founded in 1985 on the 250-acre Plassey Estate, which also incorporates a touring caravan park, craft centres, a golf course, three licensed outlets for Plassey's ales, and a brewery shop. Some 30 free trade outlets are also supplied. Seasonal beer: Ruddy Rudolph (ABV 4.5%, Xmas).

Original Border Mild (ABV 3.6%)

Welsh Border Exhibition Ale (OG 1036, ABV 3.8%)

Bitter (OG 1041, ABV 4%) ◆
Full-bodied and distinctive best bitter. Good balance of hops and fruit flavours with a lasting dry bitter aftertaste.

Offa's Dyke Ale (OG 1043, ABV 4.3%) ◆
Sweetish and fruity refreshing best bitter with caramel undertones. Some bitterness in the finish.

Owain Glyndwr's Ale (OG 1043, ABV 4.3%)

Fusilier (OG 1046, ABV 4.5%)

Cwrw Tudno (OG 1048, ABV 5%) ◆
A mellow, sweetish premium beer with classic Plassey flavours of fruit and hops.

Dragon's Breath (OG 1060, ABV 6%)
A fruity, strong bitter, smooth and quite sweet, though not cloying, with an intense, fruity aroma.

Plockton

Plockton Brewery, 5 Bank Street, Plockton, Ross-shire, IV52 8TP
☎ (01599) 544276
✉ andy@theplocktonbrewery.com
🌐 theplocktonbrewery.com
Tours by arrangement

The brewery started trading in April 2007 and has expanded to a 2.5-barrel capacity. 2 outlets are supplied direct. Seasonal beer: Starboard! (ABV 5.1%), Dall Winter Sunshine (ABV 4.8%, winter). Bottle-conditioned beers are also available.

Crags Ale (OG 1042, ABV 4.3%)

Poachers

Poachers Brewery, 439 Newark Road, North Hykeham, Lincolnshire, LN6 9SP
☎ (01522) 807404
☎ 07959 229638
🌐 poachersbrewery.co.uk
Tours by arrangement

Brewing started in 2001 on a five-barrel plant. In 2006 it was downsized to a 2.5-barrel plant and relocated by brewer George Batterbee at the rear of his house. Regular outlets are supplied throughout Lincolnshire and surrounding counties; outlets further afield are supplied via wholesalers. Seasonal beer: Santas Come (ABV 6.5%, Xmas). Bottle-conditioned beers are also available.

Trembling Rabbit Mild (OG 1034, ABV 3.4%)
Rich, dark mild with a smooth malty flavour and a slightly bitter finish.

Shy Talk Bitter (OG 1037, ABV 3.7%)
Clean-tasting session beer, pale gold in colour; slightly bitter finish, dry hopped.

Poachers Pride (OG 1040, ABV 4%)
Amber bitter brewed using Cascade hops that produce a fine flavour and aroma that lingers.

Bog Trotter (OG 1042, ABV 4.2%)
A malty, earthy-tasting best bitter.

Poachers Trail (OG 1042, ABV 4.2%) ◆
A flowery hop-nosed, mid-brown beer with a well-balanced but bitter taste that stays with the malt, becoming more apparent in the drying finish.

Billy Boy (OG 1044, ABV 4.4%)
A mid-brown beer hopped with Fuggles and Mount Hood.

Black Crow Stout (OG 1045, ABV 4.5%)
Dry stout with burnt toffee and caramel flavour.

Hare Repie (OG 1045, ABV 4.5%)
A golden-coloured, sweet smelling ale; dry in flavour.

Poachers Dick (OG 1045, ABV 4.5%)
Ruby-red bitter, smooth fruity flavour balanced by the bitterness of Goldings hops.

Jock's Trap (OG 1050, ABV 5%)
A strong, pale brown bitter; hoppy and well-balanced with a slightly dry fruit finish.

Trout Tickler (OG 1055, ABV 5.5%)
Ruby bitter with intense flavour and character, sweet undertones with a hint of chocolate.

Porter

See Outstanding

Port Mahon

See Little Ale Cart

Potbelly

Potbelly Brewery Ltd, Sydney Street Entrance, Kettering, Northamptonshire, NN16 0JA
☎ (01536) 410818
☎ 07834 867825
✉ toni@potbelly-brewery.co.uk
🌐 potbelly-brewery.co.uk
Tours by arrangement

Potbelly started brewing in 2005 on a 10-barrel plant. Sawyers in Kettering acts as a brewery tap. Some 200 outlets are supplied. Potbelly has won 25 awards for its beers in only four years of brewing. Seasonal beers: see website.

Best (OG 1036.9, ABV 3.6%)

Aisling (OG 1038.4, ABV 4%)

Beijing Black (OG 1044, ABV 4.4%)

Pigs Do Fly (OG 1041, ABV 4.4%)

Crazy Daze (OG 1050, ABV 5.5%)

Potton SIBA

Potton Brewery Co Ltd, 10 Shannon Place, Potton, Bedfordshire, SG19 2SP
☎ (01767) 261042
✉ info@potton-brewery.co.uk
🌐 potton-brewery.co.uk

⊗ Set up by Clive Towner and Bob Hearson in 1998, it was Potton's first brewery since 1922. The brewery expanded from 20 barrels a week to 50 in 2004 and further expansion is now taking place. Around 150 outlets are supplied. Seasonal beers: Bunny Hops (ABV 4.1%, Mar-Apr), Fallen Angel (ABV 4.8%, Nov-Dec). Bottle-conditioned beers are also available.

Shannon IPA (OG 1035, ABV 3.6%)
A well-balanced session bitter with good bitterness and fruity late-hop character.

Penny Bitter (ABV 4%)
A dark, malty bitter with a light, hoppy character.

Gold (OG 1040, ABV 4.1%)
Golden-coloured, refreshing beer with a spicy/citrus late-hop character.

Shambles Bitter (OG 1043, ABV 4.3%)
A robust pale and heavily hopped beer with a subtle dry hop character imparted by Styrian Goldings.

Village Bike (OG 1042, ABV 4.3%) ◆
Classic English premium bitter, amber in colour, heavily late-hopped.

Pride of Potton (OG 1057, ABV 6%) ◆
Impressive, robust amber ale with a malty aroma, malt and ripe fruit in the mouth, and a fading sweetness.

Prescott (NEW)

Prescott Brewery LLP, Unit 1, The Bramery Business Park, Alstone Lane, Cheltenham, Gloucestershire, GL51 8HE
☎ 07526 934866
✉ info@prescottales.co.uk
🌐 prescottales.co.uk

Prescott started brewing in early 2009 on a 10-barrel plant.

Hill Climb (ABV 3.8%)

Track Record (ABV 4.4%)

Grand Prix (ABV 5.2%)

Preseli (NEW)

Preseli Brewery, Unit 15, The Salterns, Tenby, Pembrokeshire, SA70 8EQ
☎ 07824 512103
🌐 preseli-brewery.co.uk

Preseli began brewing in 2009 on a six-barrel plant.

Rocky Bottom (OG 1040, ABV 4%)

Princetown

See Dartmoor

Prospect SIBA

Prospect Brewery Ltd, 120 Wigan Road, Standish, Wigan, Lancashire, WN6 0AY
☎ (01257) 421329
✉ info@prospectbrewery.com
🌐 prospectbrewery.com

◎Brewing commenced at the end of August 2007 on a five-barrel plant from Bank Top Brewery. The brewery is situated at the top of Prospect Hill – hence the name – and the beers are named along prospecting/mining themes. Over 50 outlets are supplied direct. Seasonal beers: Clementine (ABV 5%, Xmas), Pick Axe (ABV 5%, Oct-Mar), Blinding Light (ABV 4.2%, Mar-Oct). Bottle-conditioned beers are also available.

Silver Tally (OG 1037, ABV 3.7%)

Nutty Slack (OG 1039, ABV 3.9%)

Pioneer (OG 1040, ABV 4%)

Big Brew (OG 1041, ABV 4.1%)

Giants Hall (OG 1041, ABV 4.1%)

Gold Rush (OG 1045, ABV 4.5%)

Big Adventure (OG 1053, ABV 5.5%)

Purity

Purity Brewing Co Ltd, The Brewery, Upper Spernall Farm, Great Alne, Warwickshire, B49 6JF
☎ (01789) 488007
✉ sales@puritybrewing.com
🌐 puritybrewing.com
Shop Mon-Fri 8am-5pm; Sat 10am-1pm
Tours by arrangement

◎ Brewing began in 2005 in a purpose-designed plant housed in converted barns in the heart of Warwickshire. The brewery incorporates an environmentally-friendly effluent treatment system. It supplies the free trade within a 50-mile radius and delivers to over 300 outlets.

Pure Gold (OG 1039.5, ABV 3.8%)

Mad Goose (OG 1042.5, ABV 4.2%)

Pure Ubu (OG 1044.8, ABV 4.5%)

Purple Moose SIBA

Bragdy Mws Piws Cyf/Purple Moose Brewery Ltd, Madoc Street, Porthmadog, Gwynedd, LL49 9DB

☎ (01766) 515571
✉ beer@purplemoose.co.uk
🌐 purplemoose.co.uk
Shop Mon-Fri 9am-5pm
Tours by arrangement

A 10-barrel plant opened in 2005 by Lawrence Washington in a former saw mill and farmers' warehouse in the coastal town of Porthmadog. The names of the beers reflect local history and geography. The brewery now supplies around 100 outlets. Seasonal and monthly special beers: see website.

Cwrw Eryri/Snowdonia Ale (OG 1035.3, ABV 3.6%) ◆
Golden, refreshing bitter with citrus fruit hoppiness in aroma and taste. The full mouthfeel leads to a long-lasting, dry, bitter finish.

Cwrw Madog/Madog's Ale (OG 1037, ABV 3.7%) ◆
Full-bodied session bitter. Malty nose and an initial nutty flavour but bitterness dominates. Well balanced and refreshing with a dry roastiness on the taste and a good dry finish.

Cwrw Glaslyn/Glaslyn Ale (OG 1041, ABV 4.2%) ◆
Refreshing light and malty amber-coloured ale. Plenty of hop in the aroma and taste. Good smooth mouthfeel leading to a slightly chewy finish.

Ochr Tywyll y Mws/Dark Side of the Moose (OG 1045, ABV 4.6%)
A delicious dark ale with a deep malt flavour and a fruity bitterness.

Quantock

Quantock Brewery, Unit E, Monument View, Summerfield Avenue, Chelston Business Park, Wellington, Somerset, TA21 9ND
☎ (01823) 662669
✉ rob@quantockbrewery.co.uk
🌐 quantockbrewery.co.uk

Quantock began brewing in early 2008 on an eight-barrel plant. Bottle-conditioned beers are available.

Ale (ABV 3.8%)

Sunraker (ABV 4.2%)

Stout (ABV 4.5%)

White Hind (ABV 4.5%)

Royal Stag IPA (ABV 6%)

Quartz

Quartz Brewing Ltd, Archers, Alrewas Road, Kings Bromley, Staffordshire, DE13 7HW
☎ (01543) 473965

2nd Brewery: Unit 18, Heart of the Country Village, London Road, Swinfen, Staffordshire, WS14 9QR
✉ scott@quartzbrewing.co.uk
🌐 quartzbrewing.co.uk
Shop Tue-Sun 10am-5pm (Fri 8pm, Apr-Dec)
Tours by arrangement

The brewery was set up on 2005 by Scott Barnett, a brewing engineer previously with Bass, and Julia Barnett, a master brewer from Carlsberg. The brewery produces four main brands plus seasonal specials. A licensed visitor centre has opened at Heart of the Country Craft Centre, Swinfin, and supplies draught beers, bottles and mini-casks. Around 30 outlets are supplied.

Blonde (OG 1038, ABV 3.8%) ◆
Light amber bitter, slightly sweet and fruity with a pleasant bitter finish and an astringent hint.

Crystal (OG 1040, ABV 4.2%) ◆
Sweet aroma with fruit and yeasty, Marmite hints. Sweet start with fruit. Hoppiness dwindles to a gentle, bittersweet finish.

Extra Blonde (OG 1042, ABV 4.4%)
A full, fruity flavour with a continental hop finish.

Heart (OG 1045, ABV 4.6%)
Dark amber in colour with a spicy hop finish and a roasted character.

Quay

See Dorset

Quercus

Quercus Brewery & Beer House, Unit 2M, South Hams Business Park, Churchstow, Kingsbridge, Devon, TQ7 3QH
☎ (01548) 854888
✉ info@quercusbrewery.com
🌐 quercusbrewery.com
Shop Wed-Thu 3-6pm (summer); Fri-Sat 10am-5pm; Sat 10am-3pm

Quercus began trading in summer 2007 and is a small, family-run brewery and specialist beer shop. The brewery has an eight-barrel brew length. 20 outlets are supplied direct. Seasonal beers: Stormbrew (ABV 5%), QPA (ABV 5.8%).

Origin (ABV 3.9%)

Prospect (OG 1039, ABV 4%)

Shingle Bay (OG 1041, ABV 4.2%)

QB (OG 1044, ABV 4.5%)

QPA (ABV 5.8%)

Rainbow

Rainbow Inn & Brewery, 73 Birmingham Road, Allesley Village, Coventry, West Midlands, CV5 9GT
☎ (02476) 402888
Tours by arrangement

Rainbow was launched in 1994. Output is through the pub although nine-gallon casks and polypins can be ordered for home use or beer festivals.

Piddlebrook (OG 1040, ABV 4%)

Ramsbury SIBA

Ramsbury Estates Ltd, Priory Farm, Axford, Marlborough, Wiltshire, SN8 2HA
☎ (01672) 520647/541407
✉ dgolding@ramsburyestates.com
🌐 ramsburybrewery.com
Tours by arrangement

Ramsbury started brewing in 2004. Ramsbury Estates is a farming company covering approximately 5,500 acres of the Marlborough Downs in Wiltshire. It grows malting barley for the brewing industry including Optic, which the brewery also uses. Additional fermenters have been purchased and contract bottling taken on. Some 90 outlets are supplied. Seasonal beer: Deerhunter (ABV 5%, winter).

Bitter (OG 1036, ABV 3.6%)
Amber-coloured beer with a smooth, delicate aroma and flavour.

Kennet Valley (OG 1040, ABV 4.1%)
A light amber, hoppy bitter with a long, dry finish.

Flintknapper (OG 1041, ABV 4.2%)
Rich amber in colour with a malty taste.

Gold (OG 1043, ABV 4.5%)
A rich golden-coloured beer with a light hoppy aroma and taste.

Ramsgate SIBA

Ramsgate Brewery Ltd, 1 Hornet Close, Pyson's Road Industrial Estate, Broadstairs, Kent, CT10 2YD
☎ (01843) 868453
✉ info@ramsgatebrewery.co.uk
🌐 ramsgatebrewery.co.uk
Shop Mon-Fri 9am-5pm
Tours by arrangement

⊗ Ramsgate was established in 2002 in a derelict sea-front restaurant and uses only locally grown hops. In 2006 the brewery moved to its current location, allowing for increased capacity and bottling. Within the brewery is possibly the smallest pub in the world, the Ram's Head, which can only accommodate three people standing. Bottle-conditioned beers are available. Seasonal and monthly specials: see website.

Gadds' No. 7 Bitter Ale (OG 1037, ABV 3.8%)
Satisfying session bitter using local Fuggles hops.

East Kent Pale Ale (OG 1041, ABV 4.1%)

Gadds' Seasider (OG 1042, ABV 4.3%)

Gadds' No. 5 Best Bitter Ale (OG 1043, ABV 4.4%)
Complex, easy-drinking best bitter using East Kent Goldings and Fuggles hops.

Gadds' No. 3 Kent Pale Ale (OG 1047, ABV 5%)
A light and refreshing, full-strength pale ale, brewed with locally-grown East Kent Goldings hops.

Gadds' Faithful Dogbolter Porter (OG 1054, ABV 5.6%)

Randalls SIBA

RW Randall Ltd, La Piette Brewery, St Georges Esplanade, St Peter Port, Guernsey, GY1 2BH
☎ (01481) 720134
Tours by arrangement

Randalls has been brewing since 1868 and was bought in 2006 by a group of private investors. It recently moved to new premises with a 36-barrel brewhouse. 18 pubs are owned and a further 50 outlets are supplied.

Patois (OG 1045, ABV 4.5%)

RCH

RCH Brewery, West Hewish, Weston-Super-Mare, Somerset, BS24 6RR
☎ (01934) 834447
✉ rchbrewery@aol.com
🌐 rchbrewery.com
Shop Mon-Fri 8.30am-4pm

⊗ The brewery was originally installed in the early 1980s behind the Royal Clarence Hotel at Burnham-on-Sea. Since 1993 brewing has taken place in a former cider mill at West Hewish. A 30-barrel plant was installed in 2000. RCH supplies 150 outlets and the award-winning beers are available nationwide through its own wholesaling company, which also distributes beers from other small independent breweries. Seasonal beers: see website. Bottle-conditioned beers are also available.

Hewish IPA (OG 1036, ABV 3.6%) ◆
Light, hoppy bitter with some malt and fruit, though slightly less fruit in the finish. Floral citrus hop aroma; pale/brown amber colour.

PG Steam (OG 1039, ABV 3.9%) ◆
Amber-coloured, medium-bodied with a floral hop aroma. Bitter citrus taste with a hint of sweetness.

Pitchfork (OG 1043, ABV 4.3%) ◆
Yellow, grapefruit-flavoured bitter bursting with citrus with underlying sweetness.

Old Slug Porter (OG 1046, ABV 4.5%) ◆
Chocolate, coffee, roast malt and hops with lots of body and dark fruits. A complex, rich beer, dark brown in colour.

East Street Cream (OG 1050, ABV 5%) ◆
Pale brown strong bitter. Flavours of roast malt and fruit with a bittersweet finish.

Double Header (OG 1053, ABV 5.3%) ◆
Light brown, full-bodied strong bitter. Beautifully balanced flavours of malt, hops and tropical fruits are followed by a long, bittersweet finish. Refreshing and easy-drinking for its strength.

Firebox (OG 1060, ABV 6%) ◆
An aroma and taste of citrus hops and pale crystal malt are followed by a strong, complex, full-bodied, mid-brown beer with a well-balanced flavour of malt and hops.

Rebellion SIBA

Rebellion Beer Co, Marlow Brewery, Bencombe Farm, Marlow Bottom, Buckinghamshire, SL7 3LT
☎ (01628) 476594
✉ info@rebellionbeer.co.uk
🌐 rebellionbeer.co.uk
Shop Mon-Fri 8am-6pm; Sat 9am-6pm
Tours by arrangement (1st Tue of the month 7.15pm – £10 per head)

⊗ Established in 1993, Rebellion has filled the void left when Wethereds ceased brewing in 1987 at Marlow. A steady growth in fortunes led to larger premises being sought and, following relocation in 1999, the brewery has gone from strength to strength and maximised output. Rebellion's nearby Three Horseshoes pub is the brewery tap. Rebellion Mild is exclusive to this pub. Around 200 other outlets are supplied. Seasonal beers: see website. Bottle-conditioned beer is also available.

Mild (OG 1035, ABV 3.5%)

IPA (OG 1039, ABV 3.7%) ◆
Copper-coloured bitter, sweet and malty, with resinous and red apple flavours. Caramel and fruit decline to leave a dry, bitter and malty finish.

Smuggler (OG 1042, ABV 4.1%) ◆

A red-brown beer, well-bodied and bitter with an uncompromisingly dry, bitter finish.

Mutiny (OG 1046, ABV 4.5%)
Tawny in colour, this full-bodied best bitter is predominantly fruity and moderately bitter with crystal malt continuing to a dry finish.

Rectory SIBA

Rectory Ales Ltd, Streat Hill Farm, Streat Hill, Streat, Hassocks, East Sussex, BN6 8RP
☎ (01273) 890570
✉ rectoryales@hotmail.com
Tours by arrangement (Easter-Sep)

Rectory was founded in 1995 by the Rector of Plumpton, the Rev Godfrey Broster, to generate funds for the maintenance of his three parish churches. 107 parishioners are shareholders. The brewing capacity is now 20 barrels a week. All outlets are supplied from the brewery. A different seasonal beer is produced each month – please ring for details.

Rector's Bitter (OG 1040, ABV 4%)

Rector's Best Bitter (OG 1043, ABV 4.3%)

Rector's Strong Ale (OG 1050, ABV 5%)

Red Fox (NEW)

Red Fox Brewery Ltd, The Chicken Sheds, Upphall Farm, Salmons Lane, Coggeshall, Essex, CO6 1RY
☎ (01376) 563123
✉ info@redfoxbrewery.co.uk
redfoxbrewery.co.uk
Tours by arrangement

Red Fox began brewing in August 2008. Head Brewer Russell Barnes previously worked at Crouch Vale Brewery. 20 outlets are supplied direct. Bottle-conditioned beer is available.

Red Fox Mild (OG 1036, ABV 3.6%)

Fox and Hind Bitter (OG 1039, ABV 3.8%)

Hunter's Gold (OG 1040, ABV 3.9%)

Wily Ol' Fox (OG 1048, ABV 5.2%)

Red Rat

Red Rat Craft Brewery, c/o Broadmere Cottages, Troston, Bury St Edmunds, Suffolk, IP31 1EH
☎ (01359) 269742
☎ 07704 817632
✉ enquiries@redratcraftbrewery.co.uk
redratcraftbrewery.co.uk

Red Rat started brewing in summer 2007, and expanded in June 2009 to a 10-barrel plant. Around 30 barrels are produced a week. The brewery also produces one-off customised brews on request. All beers are also available bottle conditioned. The brewery itself is located at Elmswell.

Hadley's (ABV 4.2%)

Rock Ape (ABV 4.5%)

Rutting Buck (ABV 5%)

Talking Bull (ABV 5%)

The Same Again (ABV 5.2%)

Hadley's Gold (ABV 5.5%)

Crazy Dog Stout (ABV 6%)

Jimmy's Flying Pig (ABV 6%)

Jimmy's Large Black Pig (ABV 6%)

Red Rock

Red Rock Brewery Ltd, Higher Humber Farm, Bishopsteignton, Devon, TQ14 9TD
☎ (01626) 879738
☎ 07894 035094
✉ john@redrockbrewery.co.uk
redrockbrewery.co.uk
Shop Mon-Fri 9am-4pm (phone for weekend hours)
Tours by arrangement

Red Rock first started brewing in 2006 with a four-barrel plant. It is based in a converted barn on a working farm using locally sourced malt, English hops and the farm's own spring water. All beers are also hand bottled (bottle conditioned) and labelled. Around 60 outlets are supplied. Seasonal beer: Christmas Cheer (ABV 5.2%, winter).

Back Beach (OG 1038, ABV 3.8%)

Red Rock (OG 1041, ABV 4.2%)

Drift Wood (OG 1042, ABV 4.3%)

Rushy Mede (OG 1043, ABV 4.4%)

Dark Ness (OG 1045, ABV 4.5%)

Break Water (OG 1046, ABV 4.6%)

Red Rose SIBA

Red Rose Brewery, Royal Hotel, Station Road, Great Harwood, Lancashire, BB6 7BA
☎ (01254) 877373/883541
✉ beer@redrosebrewery.co.uk
redrosebrewery.co.uk
Tours by arrangement

Red Rose was launched in 2002 to supply the Royal Hotel, Great Harwood. Expansion has seen several moves, the latest being in January 2008 to the present premises and as a result the beers are now available nationwide. Seasonal beers: Pissed Over Pendle Halloween Ale (ABV 4.4%), 34th Street Miracle Beer (ABV 4.5%). Special beers are available throughout the year.

Bowley Best (ABV 3.7%)
Darkish northern bitter. Malty yet sharp with hoppy citrus finish.

Treacle Miners Tipple (ABV 3.9%)

Target (ABV 4%)

Festival Ale (ABV 4.1%)

Mel'n Collie (ABV 4.1%)

Felix (ABV 4.2%)
Dry, pale and remarkably hoppy with a keen nose, yet rounded and smooth with a lingering finish.

Old Ben (ABV 4.3%)
Pale, clean-tasting, crisp beer with a strong hop presence and no sweetness.

Lancashire & Yorkshire Aleway/ Steaming (ABV 4.5%)
Copper-coloured, strong beer. Initially sweet and malty, with a good hop aroma. Full and fruity.

Paddy O'Hackers Genuine Irish Stout Brewed In Lancashire (ABV 4.6%)

THE BREWERIES

Older Empire (ABV 5.5%)

Care Taker of History (ABV 6%) ◆
A dark, strong ale with a roast malt aroma. The taste is complex, rich and warming. Well-balanced and drinkable.

Redscar

Redscar Brewery Ltd, c/o The Cleveland Hotel, 9-11 High Street West, Redcar, TS10 1SQ
☎ (01642) 484035
✉ chrisappleby@ntlworld.com
🌐 redscar-brewery.co.uk

Redscar first brewed in early 2008 on a 2.5-barrel plant. The brewery supplies the hotel, local pubs and beer festivals.

Sands (ABV 4.2%)

Pier (ABV 4.5%)

Rocks (ABV 4.5%)

Red Shoot

Red Shoot Inn & Brewery, Toms Lane, Linwood, Ringwood, Hampshire, BH24 3QT
☎ (01425) 475792
✉ redshoot@wadworth.co.uk

The 2.5-barrel brewery, owned by Wadworth, was commissioned in 1998. In summer the brewery works to capacity, half the output going to the pub and half elsewhere locally, being distributed by Wadworth. Seasonal beer: Forest Grump (ABV 3.6%, winter).

New Forest Gold (ABV 3.8%)

Muddy Boot (ABV 4.2%)

Tom's Tipple (ABV 4.8%)

Red Squirrel

Red Squirrel Brewery, 14b Mimram Road, Hertford, Hertfordshire, SG14 1NN
☎ (01992) 501100
✉ gary@redsquirrelbrewery.co.uk
🌐 redsquirrelbrewery.co.uk
Tours by arrangement

Red Squirrel started brewing in 2004 with a 10-barrel plant. Several seasonal beers are also produced including Irish, Scottish and strong American ales (produced to original recipes). 40 outlets are supplied. Bottle-conditioned beers ae available.

Dark Ruby Mild (OG 1036, ABV 3.7%)

RSB (ABV 3.9%)

Blonde (ABV 4.1%)

Conservation Bitter (OG 1040, ABV 4.1%)

Gold (OG 1041, ABV 4.2%)

London Porter (ABV 5%)

American IPA (ABV 5.4%)

Reepham

Reepham Brewery, Unit 1, Collers Way, Reepham, Norwich, Norfolk, NR10 4SW
☎ (01603) 871091
✉ t.williams@myportoffice.co.uk
Tours by arrangement

Reepham has completed more than 25 years of continuous brewing in the same premises. A beer in the style of Newcastle Brown Ale was introduced (Tyne Brown), to show support for the Tynesiders' brewery. S&P Best Bitter was launched in 2005 to celebrate Norwich's brewing heritage: the beer is named after Steward & Patteson, bought and closed by Watneys. Some 20 outlets are supplied. Bottle-conditioned beer is available.

Granary Bitter (OG 1038, ABV 3.5%) ◆
A gold-coloured beer with a light hoppy aroma followed by a malty sweetish flavour with some smoke notes. A well-balanced beer with a long, moderately hoppy aftertaste.

S&P Best Bitter (OG 1038, ABV 3.7%)

Rapier Pale Ale (OG 1043, ABV 4.2%) ◆
Complex, amber-coloured brew. Malt and hops in the aroma metamorphose into a distinctly hoppy first taste with smoky bitter overtones. Long drawn-out bitter finale.

Norfolk Wheaten (OG 1044, ABV 4.4%)

Velvet Sweet Stout (OG 1044, ABV 4.5%) ◆
There is a heavy roast influence in aroma and taste. A smoky malt feel produces a combination that is both creamy and well-defined. Fruit and hop indicate a subtle sweetness that soon fades to leave a growing dry bitterness.

Tyne Brown (OG 1046, ABV 4.6%) ◆
Marzipan and fruit cake overtones dominate this rich, malty brown ale. The aroma and taste are malty although a rising bitterness gives the finish a vinous quality.

St Agnes (OG 1047, ABV 4.8%) ◆
Smooth and creamy with bananas to the fore in aroma and taste. Smoky malt overtones subside as increasing bitterness dominates a gently receding finish.

Rhymney

Rhymney Brewery Ltd, Unit A2, Valley Enterprise Centre, Pant Industrial Estate, Dowlais, Merthyr Tydfil, CF48 2SR
☎ (01685) 722253
✉ enquiries@rhymneybreweryltd.com
🌐 rhymneybreweryltd.com
Shop Sat 10am-2pm
Tours by arrangement

Rhymney first brewed in 2005. The 75-hl plant, sourced from Canada, is capable of producing both cask and keg beers. Around 220 outlets are supplied.

Best (OG 1037, ABV 3.7%)

Hobby Horse (OG 1038, ABV 3.8%)

Centenary Ale 1905 (OG 1039, ABV 3.9%)

Dark (OG 1040, ABV 4%)

Bevans Bitter (OG 1042, ABV 4.2%)

Bitter (OG 1043, ABV 4.3%)

General Picton (OG 1043, ABV 4.3%)

Premier Lager (OG 1044, ABV 4.4%)

Silver Drum (OG 1044, ABV 4.4%)

Export Ale (OG 1050, ABV 5%)

Richmond

Richmond Brewing Co Ltd, The Station Brewery, Richmond, North Yorkshire, DL10 4LD
☎ (01748) 828266
✉ andy@richmondbrewing.co.uk
richmondbrewing.co.uk
Shop Tue-Sun 10.30am-5pm
Tours by arrangement

Richmond opened in June 2008 and is situated in a multi million pound re-development of the listed Victorian station. The brewery concentrates on bottled ales with about 20% of their output being cask conditioned.

Sw'Ale (OG 1035, ABV 3.7%)

Station Ale (OG 1039, ABV 4%)

Stump Cross Ale (OG 1046, ABV 4.7%)

Ridgeway SIBA

Ridgeway Brewing, Beer Counter Ltd, South Stoke, Oxfordshire, RG8 0JW
☎ (01491) 873474
✉ peter.scholey@beercounter.co.uk

Ridgeway was set up by ex-Brakspear head brewer Peter Scholey. It specialises in bottle-conditioned beers but equivalent cask beers are also available. At present Ridgeway beers are brewed by Peter using his own ingredients on a plant at Hepworth's of Horsham (qv) and occasionally elsewhere. All beers listed are available cask and bottle-conditioned. Six strong (ABV 6-9%) bottle-conditioned Christmas beers are produced annually, principally for export to the U.S.

Bitter (OG 1040, ABV 4%)

Organic Beer/ROB (OG 1043, ABV 4.3%)

Blue (OG 1049, ABV 5%)

Ivanhoe (OG 1050, ABV 5.2%)

IPA (OG 1055, ABV 5.5%)

Foreign Export Stout (OG 1078, ABV 8%)

For Coniston Brewing:

Coniston Bluebird (ABV 4.2%)

Coniston XB (ABV 4.4%)

Coniston Old Man (ABV 4.8%)

Ridleys

See Greene King in New Nationals section

Ringmore

Ringmore Craft Brewery Ltd, Higher Ringmore Road, Shaldon, Devon, TQ14 0HG
☎ (01626) 873114
✉ geoff@ringmorecraftbrewery.co.uk

Ringmore was established in early 2007 on a one-barrel plant and is the first brewery in Shaldon since 1920. Seasonal beers: Rollocking Christmas (ABV 5.5%), Santa's Little Helper (ABV 5.7%). Bottle-conditioned ales are also available, including seasonal ones.

Rollocks (OG 1044, ABV 4.5%)

Oarsome Ale (OG 1046, ABV 4.6%)

Ringwood

See Marston's in New Nationals section

Riverhead

Riverhead Brewery Ltd, Riverhead Brewery Tap & Dining Room, 2 Peel Street, Marsden, Huddersfield, West Yorkshire, HD7 6BR
☎ (01484) 841270 (Pub)
☎ (01924) 261333 (Brewery)
✉ brewery@ossett-brewery.co.uk
ossett-brewery.co.uk
Tours by arrangement (through Ossett Brewing Co)

Riverhead is a brew-pub that opened in 1995 after conversion from an old grocery shop. Ossett Brewing Co Ltd purchased the site in 2006 but runs it as a separate brewery. It has since opened The Dining Room on the first floor, which uses Riverhead beers in its dishes. All original recipes have been retained with new beers also being added. The core range of beers are named after local reservoirs, with the height of the reservoir relating to the strength of the beer. Rotating beers: Leggers Lite (ABV 3.6%), Deer Hill Porter (ABV 4%), Wessenden Wheat (ABV 4%), Cupwith Special (ABV 4.2%), Marsden Best (ABV 4.2%), Black Moss Stout (ABV 4.3%), Premium Mild (ABV 4.7%). Seasonal beers: Ruffled Feathers (ABV 4.6%, Cuckoo Day), Bandsman's Bitter (ABV 4.5%, for Brass Band Competition), Jazz Bitter (ABV 3.8%, for Marsden Jazz Festival), Marsden Merrymaker (ABV 6.5%, Xmas).

Butterley Bitter (OG 1038, ABV 3.8%)
A dry, amber-coloured, hoppy session beer.

March Haigh (OG 1046, ABV 4.6%)
A golden-brown premium bitter. Malty and full-bodied with moderate bitterness.

Riverside

Riverside Brewery, Bee's Farm, Wainfleet, Lincolnshire, PE24 4LX
☎ (01754) 881288
☎ 07779 280996
wainfleet.info/shops.brewery-riverside.htm

Riverside started brewing in 2003, almost across the road from Bateman's, using a five-barrel plant. In 2008 the brewery moved to new premises. Eight barrels a week are produced, with some 15-20 outlets supplied. Seasonal beers: January's Ale (ABV 4.3%), Hoppy Easter (ABV 4.2%), Witches Wollop (ABV 4.4%), Dixon's Dynamite (ABV 4.5%), Autumn Ale (ABV 4.4%).

Dixon's Major (OG 1038, ABV 3.9%)

Dixon's Hoppy Daze (OG 1041, ABV 4.2%)

Dixon's Old Diabolical (OG 1043, ABV 4.4%)

John Roberts

See Three Tuns

Robinson's IFBB

Frederic Robinson Ltd, Unicorn Brewery, Lower Hillgate, Stockport, Cheshire, SK1 1JJ
☎ (0161) 612 4061
✉ brewery@frederic-robinson.co.uk

🌐 frederic-robinson.com
Tours by arrangement

Robinson's has been brewing since 1838 and the business is still owned and run by the family (5th and 6th generations). It has an estate of just under 400 pubs. Contract beers are also brewed. Seasonal beers: see website.

Hatters (OG 1032, ABV 3.3%)
A light mild with a malty, fruity aroma. Biscuity malt with some hop and fruit in the taste and finish. (A darkened version is available in a handful of outlets and badged Dark Hatters.)

Old Stockport (OG 1034, ABV 3.5%)
A beer with a refreshing taste of malt, hops and citrus fruit, a fruity aroma, and a short, dry finish.

Hartleys XB (OG 1040, ABV 4%)
An overly sweet and malty bitter with a bitter citrus peel fruitiness and a hint of liquorice in the finish.

Cumbria Way (OG 1040, ABV 4.1%)
A pronounced malt aroma with rich fruit notes. Rounded malt and hops in the mouth, long dry finish with citrus fruit notes. Brewed for the Hartley's estate in Cumbria.

Unicorn (OG 1041, ABV 4.2%)
Amber beer with a fruity aroma. Malt, hops and fruit in the taste with a bitter, malty finish.

Double Hop (OG 1050, ABV 5%)
Pale brown beer with malt and fruit on the nose. Full hoppy taste with malt and fruit, leading to a hoppy, bitter finish.

Old Tom (OG 1079, ABV 8.5%)
A full-bodied, dark beer with malt, fruit and chocolate on the aroma. A complex range of flavours includes dark chocolate, full maltiness, port and fruits and lead to a long, bittersweet aftertaste.

Rockingham SIBA

Rockingham Ales, c/o 25 Wansford Road, Elton, Cambridgeshire, PE8 6RZ
☎ (01832) 280722
✉ brian@rockinghamales.co.uk
🌐 rockinghamales.co.uk

A part-time brewery established in 1997 that operates from a converted farm building near Blatherwycke, Northamptonshire (business address as above). The two-barrel plant produces a prolific range of beers and supplies six local outlets. The regular beers are brewed on a rota basis, with special beers brewed to order. Seasonal beers: Fineshade (ABV 3.8%, autumn), Sanity Clause (ABV 4.3%, Dec), Old Herbaceous (ABV 4.5%, winter).

Forest Gold (OG 1039, ABV 3.9%)
A hoppy blonde ale with citrus flavours. Well-balanced and clean finishing.

Hop Devil (OG 1040, ABV 3.9%)
Six hop varieties give this golden ale a bitter start and spicy finish.

A1 Amber Ale (OG 1041, ABV 4%)
A hoppy session beer with fruit and blackcurrant undertones.

Saxon Cross (OG 1041, ABV 4.1%)
A golden-red ale with nut and coffee aromas. Citrus hop flavours predominate.

Fruits of the Forest (OG 1043, ABV 4.2%)
A multi-layered beer in which summer fruits and several spices compete with a big hop presence.

Dark Forest (OG 1050, ABV 5%)
A dark and complex beer, similar to a Belgian dubbel, with malty/smoky flavours that give way to a fruity bitter finish.

Rodham's

Rodham's Brewery, 74 Albion Street, Otley, West Yorkshire, LS21 1BZ
☎ (01943) 464530

Michael Rodham began brewing in 2005 on a one-barrel plant in the cellar of his house. Capacity has gradually increased and is now 2.5 barrels. All beers produced are malt-only, using whole hops. Occasional seasonal and bottle-conditioned beers are available. Brewing is currently suspended.

Rubicon (OG 1039, ABV 4.1%)
Amber-coloured with a nutty, malt and light fruit taste. A dry, peppery and bitter aftertaste.

Wheat Beer (OG 1039, ABV 4.1%)
Naturally cloudy, sharp and refreshing.

Royale (OG 1042, ABV 4.4%)
A golden beer with a citrus, hoppy taste, underlying malt with a bitter finish.

Old Albion (OG 1048, ABV 5%)
Ruby black premium beer with a complex mix of roasted malt, liquorice and tart fruit with a balancing bitterness.

IPA (OG 1053, ABV 5.7%)
Rich malt combines with tart citrus hops giving a long, bitter finish.

Rooster's SIBA

Rooster's Brewing Co Ltd, Unit 3, Grimbald Park, Wetherby Road, Knaresborough, North Yorkshire, HG5 8LJ
☎ (01423) 865959
✉ sean@roosters.co.uk
🌐 roosters.co.uk
Tours by arrangement

Rooster's was opened in 1993 by Sean and Alison Franklin. From 1996 beers were also brewed under the Outlaw Brewery Co label. The brewery moved to larger premises in 2001. Seasonal beer: Rooster's Nector (ABV 5.2%, autumn/winter). Bottle-conditioned beers are also available.

Special (OG 1038, ABV 3.9%)
Yellow in colour, a full-bodied, floral bitter with fruit and hop notes being carried over in to the long aftertaste. Hops and bitterness tend to increase in the finish.

Yankee (OG 1042, ABV 4.3%)
A straw-coloured beer with a delicate, fruity aroma leading to a well-balanced taste of malt and hops with a slight evidence of sweetness, followed by a refreshing, fruity/bitter finish.

YPA (OG 1042, ABV 4.3%)
A pale-coloured beer with pronounced raspberry and flower aromas.

Under Outlaw Brewery name:

Wrangler (ABV 3.7%)

Wild Mule (ABV 3.9%)

Dry Irish Stout (ABV 4.7%)

Dead or Alive (ABV 5%)

Roseland (NEW)

Roseland Brewery, c/o Roseland Inn, Philleigh, Nr St Mawes, Truro, Cornwall, TR2 5NB
☎ (01872) 580254

Roseland was established in 2009 by Phil Heslip at his pub, the Roseland Inn. The beers are named after local birds and are only available in the Roseland or its sister pub, the Victory at St Mawes.

Cornish Shag (ABV 3.8%)

Choughed to Bits (ABV 4.1%)

Rother Valley SIBA

Rother Valley Brewing Co, Gate Court Farm, Station Road, Northiam, East Sussex, TN31 6QT
☎ (01797) 253535
Tours by arrangement

Rother Valley was established in Northiam in 1993 overlooking the Rother Levels. Hops grown on the farm and from Sandhurst are used. Brewing is split between cask and an ever-increasing range of filtered bottled beers. Around 100 outlets are supplied. A monthly seasonal ale is available.

Honeyfuzz (OG 1038, ABV 3.8%)

Smild (OG 1038, ABV 3.8%)
A full-bodied, dark, creamy mild with hints of chocolate.

Level Best (OG 1040, ABV 4%)
Full-bodied tawny session bitter with a malt and fruit aroma, malty taste and a dry, hoppy finish.

Copper Ale (OG 1041, ABV 4.1%)

Hoppers Ale (OG 1044, ABV 4.4%)
A copper-coloured ale. The initial burst of hop is followed by a pleasant caramel taste.

Boadicea (OG 1045, ABV 4.5%)
A straw-coloured beer with a delicate, fruity flavour.

Blues (OG 1050, ABV 5%)
A dark brew full of complex tastes such as chocolate, raisins and a roast finish. Deceptively smooth.

Rowton (NEW)

Rowton Brewery Ltd, Stone House, Rowton, Telford, Shropshire, TF6 6QX
☎ 07746 290995

Rowton was established in July 2008 on a four-barrel plant in an old cow shed on the owner's farm. Water is from a borehole on site. The brewery grows its own organic barley and will be growing hops in the future. Meteorite is named after a meteorite that landed on the farm in the 19th century and is now in a London museum.

Bitter (ABV 3.9%)

Meteorite (ABV 4.7%)

Rudgate SIBA

Rudgate Brewery Ltd, 2 Centre Park, Marston Moor Business Park, Tockwith, York, North Yorkshire, YO26 7QF
☎ (01423) 358382
✉ sales@rudgatebrewery.co.uk
rudgatebrewery.co.uk

Rudgate Brewery was founded in 1992 and is located in an old armoury building on a disused World War II airfield. It has a 15-barrel plant and four open fermenting vessels, producing more than 40 barrels a week. Around 350 outlets are supplied direct. Seasonal beers: Rudolphs Ruin (ABV 4.6%, Xmas). Three seasonal beers are produced every month.

Viking (OG 1036, ABV 3.8%)
An initially warming and malty, full-bodied beer, with hops and fruit lingering into the aftertaste.

Battleaxe (OG 1040, ABV 4.2%)
A well-hopped bitter with slightly sweet initial taste and light bitterness. Complex fruit character gives a memorable aftertaste.

Ruby Mild (OG 1041, ABV 4.4%)
Nutty, rich ruby ale, stronger than usual for a mild.

Special (OG 1042, ABV 4.5%)
Moderately bitter leading to a citrus, hoppy finish.

Well Blathered (OG 1046, ABV 5%)
A premium bitter, golden-coloured with distinctive lemon on the nose.

Rugby

Rugby Brewing Co Ltd, The Brewery, Wood Farm Buildings, Coal Pit Lane, Willey, Rugby, Warwickshire, CV23 0SL
☎ 0845 017 8844
rugbybrewingco.co.uk
Tours by arrangement (max. 20 people)

Rugby started brewing in 2005 and moved to its current farm location in 2008. The brewery obtained organic status in 2010. Seasonal beers: see website.

1823 (ABV 3.5%)

Twickers (ABV 3.7%)

Webb Ellis (ABV 3.8%)

Victorious (ABV 4.2%)

Sidestep (ABV 4.5%)

Union (ABV 4.6%)

No. 8 (ABV 5%)

Winger IPA (ABV 5.2%)

Cement (ABV 6.8%)

Ryburn

Ryburn Brewery, Rams Head Inn, 26 Wakefield Road, Sowerby Bridge, West Yorkshire, HX6 2AZ
☎ (01422) 835413
✉ ryburnbrewery@talk21.com
Tours by arrangement

The brewery was established in 1989 at Mill House, Sowerby Bridge, but has since been relocated to the company's sole tied house, the Rams Head. Some business is done with the local free trade but the main market for the brewery's products is via wholesalers, chiefly JD Wetherspoon.

Best Mild (OG 1033, ABV 3.3%)

THE BREWERIES

A traditional northern-style mild with chocolate in evidence. Smooth, bitter aftertaste.

Best Bitter (OG 1038, ABV 3.8%)
Creamy, amber session beer with a sulphurous aroma. The taste is rich, nutty and malty. Bitterness lingers in the aftertaste.

Numpty Bitter (OG 1044, ABV 4.2%)
Creamy, tawny and sulphurous best bitter. Lightly-hopped nose followed by a well-balanced malty, fruity taste. Dry, bitter finish.

Luddite (OG 1048, ABV 5%)
Intensely flavoured, black, creamy stout. Well-balanced with strong chocolate, caramel and liquorice flavours, tempered by sweetness.

Stabbers (OG 1052, ABV 5.2%)
Amber-coloured, creamy strong ale. Fruity, sweet and vinous in taste. Its drinkability belies its strength.

Saddleworth

Church Inn & Saddleworth Brewery, Church Lane, Uppermill, Oldham, Greater Manchester, OL3 6LW
☎ (01457) 820902/872415
Tours by arrangement

Saddleworth started brewing in 1997 in a brewhouse that had been closed for around 120 years. Brewery and inn are set in a historic location at the top of a valley overlooking Saddleworth and next to St Chads Church, which dates from 1215. Seasonal beers: Bert Corner (ABV 4%, Feb), St George's Bitter (ABV 4%, Apr), Ayrton's Ale (ABV 4.1%, Apr-May), Harvest Moon (ABV 4.1%, Aug-Sep), Robyn's Bitter (ABV 4.6%, Nov-Dec), Christmas Carol (ABV 6.6%, Dec-Jan).

Clog Dancer (ABV 3.6%)

Mild (ABV 3.8%)

More (ABV 3.8%)

Honey Smacker (ABV 4.1%)

Hop Smacker (ABV 4.1%)

Indya Pale Ale (ABV 4.1%)

Shaftbender (ABV 5.4%)

Sadlers

See Windsor Castle

Saffron

Saffron Brewery, The Cartshed, Parsonage Farm, Henham, Essex, CM22 6AN
☎ (01279) 850923
☎ 07747 696901
✉ tb@saffronbrewery.co.uk
saffronbrewery.co.uk
Tours by arrangement

Founded in 2005, Saffron is situated near the historic East Anglian town of Saffron Walden, famous for its malting industry in the 18th century. The brewery was upgraded to a 15-barrel plant in early 2008 and re-located to a converted barn at Parsonage Farm by Henham church, with a purpose built reed bed for environmentally friendly disposal of waste products. 40 outlets are supplied direct. Seasonal beers: see website. Bottle-conditioned beers are also available.

Ramblers Tipple (OG 1040, ABV 3.9%)
A rich, copper-coloured bitter with toffee and caramel flavours.

Saffron Blonde (OG 1044, ABV 4.3%)
A light golden ale with a delicate balance of citrus and smooth, malty flavours and a crisp finish.

Squires Gamble (OG 1044, ABV 4.3%)
Traditional style copper ale; soft, mellow, full-flavoured and hoppy with citrus and biscuit hints.

St Austell IFBB SIBA

St Austell Brewery Co Ltd, 63 Trevarthian Road, St Austell, Cornwall, PL25 4BY
☎ (01726) 74444
✉ info@staustellbrewery.co.uk
staustellbrewery.co.uk
Shop Mon-Fri 9am-5pm; Sat 10am-4pm
Tours by arrangement

St Austell Brewery celebrated 150 years of brewing in 2001. Founded by Walter Hicks in 1851, the company is still family owned, with a powerful commitment to cask beer. Cask beer is available in all 169 licensed houses, as well as in the free trade throughout Cornwall, Devon and Somerset. A visitor centre offers guided tours and souvenirs from the brewery. Bottle-conditioned beers are available.

IPA (OG 1035, ABV 3.4%)
Copper/bronze in colour, the nose blossoms with fresh hops. The palate is clean and full-bodied with a hint of toffee caramel. The finish is short and crisp.

Tinners (OG 1038, ABV 3.7%)
Golden beer with an appetising malt aroma and a good balance of malt and hops in the flavour. Lasting finish.

Dartmoor Best Bitter (OG 1039, ABV 3.9%)
Superbly balanced copper session bitter with a fruity malt nose. Full-bodied and grainy in the mouth but with a noticeable hoppy bite. Short finish of hops and malt.

Black Prince (OG 1041, ABV 4%)
Faint malt and bubblegum aroma of this black mild leads to a complex taste of roast flavours, toffee and fruit esters balanced by bitterness. Liquorice, fudge and bitterness linger on the palate.

Tribute (OG 1043, ABV 4.2%)
Medium-bodied, copper-bronze premium ale. Refreshingly bittersweet with a balance of malt and hops. Aroma of Oregon hops and malt with a trace of tangy ester. The finish is long, bitter and moderately dry.

Proper Job IPA (ABV 4.5%)
Floral aromatic hops greet the nose and persist in the mouth but are mellowed by a sweet, well-rounded and full-bodied palate that disappears in a bittersweet aftertaste.

Hicks Special Draught/HSD (OG 1052, ABV 5%)
An aromatic, fruity, hoppy bitter that is initially sweet with an aftertaste of pronounced bitterness, but whose flavour is fully rounded.

St George's

St George's Brewery Ltd, Bush Lane, Callow End, Worcestershire, WR2 4TF
☎ (01905) 831316

✉ **info@stgeorgesbrewery.co.uk**
🌐 **stgeorgesbrewery.co.uk**
Tours by arrangement

⊗ The brewery was established in 1998 in old village bakery premises. It was acquired in 2006 by Duncan Ironmonger. Andrew Sankey has been the brewer and brewery manager for a number of years. The brewery supplies local freehouses and wholesalers for a wider distribution. At least two monthly specials are usually available.

Order of the Garter (ABV 3.8%)
Light golden beer with a well-hopped, smooth taste.

Friar Tuck (OG 1040, ABV 4%)
A light, golden beer with a citrus fruity flavour.

Worcester Sauce (ABV 4%)
A well-balanced amber beer with a hoppy start and smooth, bitter finish.

Blues & Royals (OG 1043, ABV 4.3%)
Deep copper in colour with a biscuity, hoppy taste.

Charger (OG 1046, ABV 4.6%)
A light, refreshing beer.

Dragons Blood (OG 1048, ABV 4.8%)
A ruby red beer with a citrus flavour.

St Jude's

St Jude's Brewery Ltd, 2 Cardigan Street, Ipswich, Suffolk, IP1 3PF
☎ **(01473) 413334**
☎ **07870 358834**
🌐 **stjudesbrewery.co.uk**
Shop by prior appt Mon-Sat 10am-5pm
Tours by arrangement

⊗ St Jude's was established in 2006 on a seven-barrel plant. It bottles on site and supplies to many outlets in the UK. Bottle-conditioned beers are available. Pagan Path and St Francis are suitable for vegetarians and vegans.

Pagan Path (ABV 4%)
A vanilla wheat pale ale. Light in colour with a pleasant vanilla aftertaste.

St Francis (OG 1049, ABV 4%) ◆
Pale golden. Surprisingly malty aroma but the taste is all fruit and hops. Suitable for vegetarians and vegans.

Gypeswic Bitter (OG 1048, ABV 4.4%) ◆
Beautifully balanced amber bitter with fruity aroma and pleasantly lingering aftertaste.

Ipswich Bright (OG 1042, ABV 4.4%) ◆
A refreshing, golden bitter beer with a long, hoppy aftertaste.

Coachmans Whip (OG 1064, ABV 5.2%)
A well-balanced ale with a bitter, rich flavour.

John Orfords Strong Brown Ale (OG 1064, ABV 6.2%) ◆
Strong caramel and malt aroma and taste.

St Peter's EAB SIBA

St Peter's Brewery Co Ltd, St Peter's Hall, St Peter South Elmham, Suffolk, NR35 1NQ
☎ **(01986) 782322**
✉ **beers@stpetersbrewery.co.uk**
🌐 **stpetersbrewery.co.uk**
Shop Mon-Fri 9am-5pm; Sat & Sun 11am-5pm
Tours by arrangement Sat, Sun & bank holidays 12-4pm (groups of 20+)

⊗ St Peter's was launched in 1996 and concentrates in the main on bottled beer (90% of capacity) but has a rapidly increasing cask market. Two pubs are owned and 75 outlets are supplied. Seasonal beers: Ruby Red (ABV 4.3%), Wheat Beer (ABV 4.7%), Summer Ale (ABV 6.5%), Winter Ale (ABV 6.5%), Strong Ale (ABV 5.1%).

Best Bitter (OG 1038, ABV 3.7%) ◆
A complex but well-balanced hoppy brew. A gentle hop nose introduces a singular hoppiness with supporting malt notes and underlying bitterness. Other flavours fade to leave a long, dry, hoppy finish.

Mild (OG 1037, ABV 3.7%)
Sweetness balanced by bitter chocolate malt to produce a rare but much sought after traditional mild.

Organic Best (OG 1041, ABV 4.1%) ◆
A very dry and bitter beer with a growing astringency. Pale brown in colour, it has a gentle hop aroma which makes the definitive bitterness surprising. One for the committed.

Organic Ale (OG 1045, ABV 4.5%) ◆
A rich toffee apple aroma and a smooth grainy feel. Malt and caramel initially match the dry hoppy bitterness. As the flavours mature, liqourice dryness develops. Full-bodied.

Golden Ale (OG 1047, ABV 4.7%) ◆
Amber-coloured, full-bodied, robust ale. A strong hop bouquet leads to a mix of malt and hops combined with a dry, fruity hoppiness. The malt quickly subsides, leaving creamy bitterness.

Grapefruit Beer (OG 1047, ABV 4.7%) ◆
With a very strong aroma and taste of grapefruit, this refreshing beer is exactly what it says on the tin. A superb example of a fruit beer.

IPA (OG 1055, ABV 5.5%)
A full-bodied, highly hopped pale ale with a zesty character.

Salamander

Salamander Brewing Co Ltd, 22 Harry Street, Bradford, West Yorkshire, BD4 9PH
☎ **(01274) 652323**
✉ **salamanderbrewing@fsmail.net**
🌐 **salamanderbrewing.co.uk**
Tours by arrangement

⊗ Salamander first brewed in 2000 in a former pork pie factory. Further expansion during 2004 took the brewery to 40-barrel capacity. There are direct deliveries to more widespread areas such as Cumbria, East Yorkshire and Lancashire in addition to the established trade of about 100 outlets throughout Lancashire, Manchester, North Yorkshire and Derbyshire.

Axolotl (ABV 3.9%)

Mudpuppy (OG 1042, ABV 4.2%) ◆
A well-balanced, copper-coloured best bitter with a fruity, hoppy nose and a bitter finish.

Golden Salamander (OG 1045, ABV 4.5%) ◆
Citrus hops characterise the aroma and taste of this golden premium bitter, which has malt undertones throughout. The aftertaste is dry, hoppy and bitter.

Stout (OG 1045, ABV 4.5%) ◆

Rich roast malts dominate the smooth coffee and chocolate flavour. Nicely balanced. A dry, roast, bitter finish develops over time.

Salopian SIBA

Salopian Brewing Co Ltd, 67 Mytton Oak Road, Shrewsbury, Shropshire, SY3 8UQ
☎ (01743) 248414
✉ enquiries@salopianbrewery.co.uk
salopianbrewery.co.uk
Tours by arrangement

The brewery was established in 1995 in an old dairy on the outskirts of Shrewsbury and, having grown steadily, now produces 60 barrels a week. Over 200 outlets are supplied.

Shropshire Gold (OG 1037, ABV 3.8%)
A light, copper-coloured ale with an unusual blend of body and dryness.

Oracle (OG 1040, ABV 4%)
A crisp golden ale with a striking hop profile. Dry and refreshing with a long-balanced aromatic finish.

Abbey Gates (OG 1042, ABV 4.3%)
A traditional, copper-coloured ale. Light bodied and refreshing.

Hop Twister (OG 1044, ABV 4.5%)
A premium bitter with a citrus flavour and complex hop finish. Refreshing and crisp.

Lemon Dream (OG 1043.5, ABV 4.5%)
A light gold ale brewed with wheat malt and subtly flavoured with fresh lemons.

Golden Thread (OG 1048, ABV 5%)
A bright gold ale. Strong and quite bitter but well-balanced.

Saltaire

Saltaire Brewery Ltd, Unit 6, County Works, Dockfield Road, Shipley, West Yorkshire, BD17 7AR
☎ (01274) 594959
✉ info@saltairebrewery.co.uk
saltairebrewery.co.uk
Tours by arrangement

Launched in 2006, Saltaire Brewery is an award-winning 20-barrel brewery based in a Victorian industrial building that formerly generated electricity for the local tram system. A mezzanine bar gives visitors views of the brewing plant and the chance to taste the beers. More than 300 pubs are supplied across West Yorkshire and the north of England.

Rye Smile (OG 1038, ABV 3.8%)
Copper-coloured with silky toffee flavours.

Blonde (OG 1040, ABV 4%)
Straw-coloured light ale with soft malt flavours.

Raspberry Blonde (ABV 4%)
Refreshing blonde ale infused with a hint of raspberries.

Blackberry Cascade (ABV 4.8%)
Cascade infused with a hint of blackberries.

Cascade Pale Ale (OG 1047, ABV 4.8%)
American-style pale ale with floral aromas and strong bitterness.

Sambrook's (NEW)

Sambrook's Brewery Limited, Units 1 & 2, Yelverton Road, Battersea, London, SW11 3QG
☎ (020) 7228 0598
✉ sales@sambrooksbrewery.co.uk
sambrooksbrewery.co.uk
Shop Mon-Fri 10am-6pm; Summer Sat 10am-1pm)
Tours by arrangement

Sambrooks was established in 2008 by Duncan Sambrook and David Welsh using a 20-barrel plant. Bottle-conditioned beer is available.

Wandle Ale (OG 1038, ABV 3.8%)
Amber-coloured beer with a smooth mouthfeel. Citrus and a little hop on the nose with fruit becoming stronger in the taste and some bitterness that lingers in the finish.

Sandstone (NEW)

Sandstone Brewery LLP, Unit 5, Wrexham Enterprise Park, Preston Road, Off Ash Road, North Wrexham Industrial Estate, Wrexham, LL13 9JT
☎ 07851 001118
✉ info@sandstonebrewery.co.uk
sandstonebrewery.co.uk

Sandstone Brewery was established in late 2008 by three CAMRA members on a four-barrel brew plant. More than 45 outlets are supplied direct.

Edge (OG 1039, ABV 3.8%)
A light, aromatic session beer.

Postman Prat (OG 1046, ABV 4.4%)
A red/brown fruity, warming ale.

Doctors Orders (OG 1046, ABV 4.5%)
A full-bodied ale with a slightly nutty taste.

Buxom Barmaid (OG 1047, ABV 4.7%)
A rich, golden ale with fruity overtones.

Sawbridgeworth

Sawbridgeworth Brewery, 81 London Road, Sawbridgeworth, Hertfordshire, CM21 9JJ
☎ (01279) 722313
✉ thegatepub@talktalk.net
Tours by arrangement

The brewery was set up in 2000 by Tom and Gary Barnett at the back of the Gate pub. One pub is owned. Tom is a former professional footballer whose clubs included Crystal Palace. Special or one-off beers are regularly brewed. All beers are also available bottle conditioned.

Selhurst Park Flyer (ABV 3.7%)

Viking (ABV 3.8%)

RACS (ABV 4%)

Is It Yourself (ABV 4.2%)

Stout (ABV 4.3%)

Brooklands Express (ABV 4.6%)

Piledriver (ABV 5.3%)

Malt Shovel Porter (ABV 6%)

Scattor Rock

See Gidleys

Severn Vale SIBA

Severn Vale Brewing Co, Woodend Lane, Cam, Dursley, Gloucestershire, GL11 5HS
☎ (01453) 547550
☎ 07971 640244
✉ steve@severnvalebrewing.co.uk
🌐 severnvalebrewing.co.uk
Shop: Please ring first
Tours by arrangement

⊗ Severn Vale started brewing in 2005 in an old milking parlour using a new five-barrel plant. Warminster malted barley is used and mainly Herefordshire hops. Around 50 outlets are supplied. Seasonal beers: Severn Bells (ABV 4.3%, summer), Severn Swans-a-Swimming (ABV 4.7%, Xmas), Severn Nations (ABV 4.4%, Feb-Mar).

Session (ABV 3.4%)

Vale Ale (OG 1039, ABV 3.8%)
A rich amber beer with full-bodied malt flavours and a complex nose and taste.

Dursley Steam Bitter (OG 1043, ABV 4.2%)
A sparkling summer ale full of flowery hops.

Monumentale (OG 1047, ABV 4.5%)
Designed as a porter but not dissimilar to a strong mild with a lingering, malty flavour.

Severn Sins (ABV 5.2%)
A jet-black stout with a dry roast malt flavour with hints of chocolate and liquorice.

Shalford

Shalford Brewery, c/o PO Box 10411, Braintree, Essex, CM7 5WP
☎ (01371) 850925
☎ 07749 658512
✉ nigel@shalfordbrewery.co.uk
🌐 shalfordbrewery.co.uk

⊗ Shalford began brewing in July 2007 on a five-barrel plant at Hyde Farm in the Pant Valley in Essex. Over 20 outlets are supplied direct. Bottle-conditioned beers are available.

Barnfield Bitter (ABV 4%) ◆
Pale-coloured but full-flavoured, this is a traditional, hoppy bitter rather than a golden ale. Malt persists throughout, with bitterness becoming more dominant towards the end.

Levelly Gold (ABV 4%)
Golden, summery bitter with a pleasant finish.

Stoneley Bitter (ABV 4.2%) ◆
Dark amber session beer whose vivid hop character is supported by a juicy, malty body. A dry finish makes this beer very drinkable.

Hyde Bitter (ABV 4.7%) ◆
Stronger version of Barnfield, with a similar but more assertive character.

Levelly Black (ABV 4.8%)
A winter stout; dark, malty and smooth.

Longfield Lager (ABV 5.5%)

Springfield Wheat Beer (ABV 6%)
A refreshing, crisp, clean bitter.

Rotten End (ABV 6.5%)
Strong beer with slightly sweet, nutty undertones and a bitter edge to finish.

Shardlow

Shardlow Brewing Co Ltd, The Old Brewery Stables, British Waterways Yard, Cavendish Bridge, Leicestershire, DE72 2HL
☎ (01332) 799188
✉ kev@shardlowbrewing.co.uk
Tours by arrangement

On a site associated with brewing since 1819, Shardlow delivers to more than 100 outlets throughout the East Midlands. Due to increased sales, two new fermenters have been added. Reverend Eaton is named after a scion of the Eaton brewing family, Rector of Shardlow for 40 years. The brewery tap is the Blue Bell Inn at Melbourne, Derbyshire. Seasonal beers: Frostbite (ABV 5.5%), Stedmans Tipple (ABV 5.1%), Six Bells (ABV 6%). Bottle-conditioned beers are also available.

Chancellors Revenge (OG 1036, ABV 3.6%)
A light-coloured, refreshing, full-flavoured and well-hopped session bitter.

Cavendish Dark (OG 1037, ABV 3.7%)

Special Bitter (OG 1039, ABV 3.9%)
A well-balanced, amber-coloured, quaffable bitter.

Golden Hop (OG 1041, ABV 4.1%)

Kiln House (ABV 4.1%)

Narrow Boat (OG 1043, ABV 4.3%)
A pale amber bitter, with a short, crisp hoppy aftertaste.

Cavendish Bridge (ABV 4.5%)

Cavendish Gold (ABV 4.5%)

Reverend Eaton (OG 1045, ABV 4.5%)
A smooth, medium-strong bitter, full of malt and hop flavours with a sweet aftertaste.

Mayfly (ABV 4.8%)

Five Bells (OG 1050, ABV 5%)

Whistlestop (OG 1050, ABV 5%)
Maris Otter pale malt and two hops produce this smooth and surprisingly strong pale beer.

Sharp's SIBA

Sharp's Brewery Ltd, Pityme Business Centre, Rock, Cornwall, PL27 6NU
☎ (01208) 862121
✉ enquiries@sharpsbrewery.co.uk
🌐 sharpsbrewery.co.uk
Shop Mon-Fri 9am-5pm
Tours by arrangement

⊗ Sharp's Brewery was founded in 1994. Within 10 years the brewery had grown from producing 1,500 barrels annually to selling 35,000. Sharp's has no pubs and delivers beer to more than 1,000 outlets across the south of England. All beer is produced at the brewery in Rock and is delivered via temperature controlled depots in Bristol, Manchester and London. Seasonal beer: Nadelik (ABV 4.6%). Bottle-conditioned beer is also available.

Cornish Coaster (OG 1035.2, ABV 3.6%) ◆
A smooth, easy-drinking beer, golden in colour, with a fresh hop aroma and dry malt and hops in the mouth. The finish starts malty but becomes dry and hoppy.

Cornish Jack (OG 1037, ABV 3.8%)

THE BREWERIES

Light candied fruit dominates the aroma, underpinned with fresh hop notes. The flavour is a delicate balance of light sweetness, fruity notes and fresh spicy hops. Subtle bitterness and dry fruit notes linger in the finish.

Doom Bar (OG 1038.5, ABV 4%) ◆
Faint aroma of flowery, spicy hop leads to fruit and malt in the mouth, with bitterness running through. The bitter finish is long with some sweetness and dryness.

Atlantic IPA (OG 1040, ABV 4.2%)

Eden Pure Ale (OG 1041, ABV 4.3%)
Hops dominate the aroma complemented by light fruit esters. In the mouth hops are again the centrepiece with a dry bitterness and a hint of malty sweetness. The finish is dry and hoppy.

Own (OG 1042.5, ABV 4.4%) ◆
A deep golden brown beer with a delicate hops and malt aroma, and dry malt and hops in the mouth. Like the other beers, its finish starts malty but turns dry and hoppy.

Special (OG 1048.5, ABV 5.2%) ◆
Deep golden brown with a fresh hop aroma. Dry malt and hops in the mouth; the finish is malty but becomes dry and hoppy.

Shaws

Shaws Brewery, The Old Stables, Park Road, Dukinfield, Greater Manchester, SK16 5LX
☎ (0161) 330 5471
✉ sales@windsor-fabrications.co.uk

The brewery is housed in the stables of William Shaws Brewery, established in 1856 and closed by John Smiths in 1941. Brewing re-started in 2002 with a five-barrel plant. Beer is supplied to more than 30 local free trade outlets and beer festivals. Monthly guest beers are produced.

Golden Globe (OG 1040, ABV 4.3%) ◆
Yellow beer with a modest hoppy/fruity aroma. Biscuity malt and tart fruits on the palate and in the bitter aftertaste.

Sheffield SIBA

Sheffield Brewery Co Ltd, Unit 111, J C Albyn Complex, Burton Road, Sheffield, South Yorkshire, S3 8BT
☎ (0114) 272 7256
✉ sales@sheffieldbrewery.com
sheffieldbrewery.com
Tours by arrangement

Sheffield began brewing in January 2007 in the former Blanco polish works on a 10-barrel plant. Building works were completed in autumn 2007 allowing the brewing plant to be relocated on a tower principle. Over 10 outlets are supplied direct. Seasonal beers: Golden Frame (ABV 3.9%), Spring Steel (ABV 4.6%), Top Forge (ABV 4.7%). Bottle-conditioned beers are also available.

Crucible Best (OG 1038, ABV 3.8%)

Five Rivers (OG 1038, ABV 3.8%)

Blanco Blonde (OG 1041, ABV 4.1%)

Seven Hills (OG 1041, ABV 4.1%)

Shepherd Neame IFBB

Shepherd Neame Ltd, 17 Court Street, Faversham, Kent, ME13 7AX
☎ (01795) 532206
shepherd-neame.co.uk
Shop Mon-Sat 10am-4.30pm
Tours by arrangement

Kent's major independent brewery is believed to be the oldest continuous brewer in the country (since 1698), but records show brewing began on the site as far back as the 12th century. The same water source is still used today and 1914 oak mash tuns are still operational. In 2004/2005 investment increased production to more than 200,000 barrels a year. The company has 370 tied houses in the South-east, nearly all selling cask ale. More than 2,000 other outlets are also supplied. All Shepherd Neame ales use locally sourced ingredients. The cask beers are made with Kentish hops, local malted barley and water from the brewery's own artesian well. In 2007 a new micro-plant was installed inside the main brewery to brew speciality ales in small quantities for special occasions. These brews are available for a limited time in selected pubs. In the first year over 50 beers were produced. Seasonal beers: see website. Bottle-conditioned beer is also available.

Canterbury Jack (OG 1033, ABV 3.5%)
A full-bodied, pale beer with a grapefruit aroma. Malty, citrus notes on the palate lead to a crisp, refreshing, bitter aftertaste.

Master Brew Bitter (OG 1032, ABV 3.7%) ◆
A distinctive bitter, mid-brown in colour, with a hoppy aroma. Well-balanced, with a nicely aggressive bitter taste from its hops, it leaves a hoppy/bitter finish, tinged with sweetness.

Kent's Best (OG 1036, ABV 4.1%)
A mellow bitter which merges the biscuity sweetness of English malt with the fruity, floral bitterness of locally grown hops.

Spitfire Premium Ale (OG 1040, ABV 4.2%)
A commemorative Battle of Britain brew for the RAF Benevolent Fund's appeal, now the brewery's flagship ale.

Bishops Finger (OG 1046, ABV 5%)
A cask-conditioned version of a famous bottled beer. A strong ale with a complex hop aroma reminiscent of lemons, oranges and bananas combined with malt, molasses and toffee. Refreshing with a good malt character tinged with a lingering bitterness.

Sherborne

Sherborne Brewery Ltd, 257 Westbury, Sherborne, Dorset, DT9 3EH
☎ (01935) 812094
sherbornebrewery.co.uk

Sherborne Brewery started in late 2005 on a 2.5-barrel plant. It moved in 2006 to new premises at the rear of the brewery's pub, Docherty's Bar. Beer is supplied to the pub and to 15-20 other local outlets as a guest beer.

257 (OG 1039, ABV 3.9%)

Cheap Street (OG 1044, ABV 4.4%)

Ship Inn

Ship Inn Brewery, Ship Inn, The Square, Low Newton by the Sea, Northumberland, NE66 3EL
☎ (01665) 576262
shipinnnewton.co.uk

The Ship Inn started brewing in early 2008. Beers are only produced for the pub – ABVs may vary.

Sandcastle at Dawn (ABV 2.8%)

Sea Coal (ABV 4%)

Sea Wheat (ABV 4%)

Ship Hop (ABV 4.1%)

Dolly Daydream (ABV 4.3%)

Shires

Shires Brewery, All Nations Brewhouse, Coalport Road, Madeley, Shropshire, TF7 6DP
☎ (01952) 580570
info@shiresbrewery.co.uk
shiresbrewery.co.uk

Shires succeeded Worfield Brewery in 2009 to continue the All Nations tradition and produce ale for the pub as well as supplying surrounding counties. Mike Handley continues as head brewer and supervises the 10-barrel plant. Worfield originally began brewing in 1993 at the Davenport Arms and moved to Brignorth in 1998. Following the reopening of the All Nations in Madeley, the brewery produced Dabley Ale for the pub and in 2004 relocated to the All Nations. Seasonal beers: Winter Classic (ABV 4.5%, Jan), Spring Classic (ABV 4.5%, Mar), Summer Classic (ABV 4.3%, Jun), Autumn Classic (ABV 4.5%, Sep), Redneck (ABV 5.5%, Xmas).

Coalport Dodger Mild (OG 1034, ABV 3.5%)
Traditional dark mild, full of nutty flavour from dark malts and full-bodied for its strength.

Best Bitter (ABV 3.8%)
Pale-coloured session beer with a good fruity taste and hop aroma.

Dabley Ale (OG 1039, ABV 3.8%)
Pale, fruit and citrus tasting session beer.

OBJ (Oh Be Joyful) (OG 1043, ABV 4.2%)
A light and sweet bitter; delicate flavour belies the strength.

Shropshire Pride (OG 1045, ABV 4.5%)
A dark bitter, very full-bodied and malty with a pleasant bittersweet balance.

Gold (OG 1050, ABV 5%)
The big borther of Dabley Ale, produced from the same recipe but brewed to a higher gravity giving a sweeter, full flavour.

Shoes SIBA

Shoes Brewery, Three Horseshoes Inn, Norton Canon, Hereford, HR4 7BH
☎ (01544) 318375
Tours by arrangement

Landlord Frank Goodwin was a keen home brewer who decided in 1994 to brew on a commercial basis for his pub. The beers are brewed from malt extract and are normally only available at the Three Horseshoes. Each September Canon Bitter is brewed with 'green' hops fresh from the harvest. Bottle-conditioned beers are available.

Canon Bitter (OG 1038, ABV 3.6%)

Norton Ale (OG 1040, ABV 4.1%)

Peploe's Tipple (OG 1060, ABV 6%)

Farriers Ale (OG 1114, ABV 15.5%)

Shugborough

Shugborough Brewery, Shugborough Estate, Milford, Staffordshire, ST17 0XB
☎ (01782) 823447
shugborough.org.uk
Tours daily Mar-Oct

Brewing in the original brewhouse at Shugborough, home of the Earls of Lichfield, restarted in 1990 but a lack of expertise led to the brewery being a static museum piece until Titanic Brewery of Stoke-on-Trent (qv) began helping in 1996. Brewing takes place every weekend during the visitor season with museum guides in period costume.

Miladys Fancy (OG 1048, ABV 4.6%)

Lordships Own (OG 1054, ABV 5%)

Silverstone (NEW)

Silverstone Brewing Co Ltd, Kingshill Farm, Syresham, Northamptonshire, NN13 5TH
☎ (01280) 850629
mwarren@silverstonebrewingcompany.com
silverstonebrewingcompany.com
Tours by arrangement

The brewery, which is located near the celebrated motor racing circuit, opened in late 2008. In keeping with its motor racing theme the brewery is the proud sponsor of Formula V10. 20 outlets are supplied direct.

Pitstop (OG 1039, ABV 3.8%)

Chequered Flag (OG 1045, ABV 4.5%)

Sinclair

See Atlas and Orkney

Six Bells SIBA

Six Bells Brewery, Church Street, Bishop's Castle, Shropshire, SY9 5AA
☎ (01588) 638930
bishops-castle.co.uk/SixBells/brewery.htm
Tours by arrangement

Neville Richards – 'Big Nev' – started brewing in 1997 with a five-barrel plant and two fermenters. Alterations in 1999 included two more fermenters, a new grain store and mashing equipment. He supplies a number of customers both within the county and over the border in Wales. A new 12-barrel plant opened in April 2007. In addition to the core beer range, 12 monthly specials are produced.

Big Nev's (OG 1037, ABV 3.8%)
A pale, fairly hoppy bitter.

Goldings BB (OG 1041, ABV 4%)
Made entirely with Goldings hops; moderately hoppy with a distinctive aroma.

Cloud Nine (OG 1043, ABV 4.2%)
Pale amber-colour with a slight citrus finish.

Skinner's SIBA

Skinner's Brewing Co Ltd, Riverside, Newham Road, Truro, Cornwall, TR1 2DP
☎ (01872) 271885
✉ info@skinnersbrewery.com
skinnersbrewery.com
Shop Mon-Sat 10am-5pm
Tours by arrangement (ring 01872 254689)

Skinner's brewery was founded by Steve and Sarah Skinner in 1997. To increase production the brewery moved to bigger premises in 2003, opening a brewery shop and visitor centre. Since opening, the brewery has won numerous awards. Merchandise and beer available to purchase online. Seasonal beers: see website.

Ginger Tosser (OG 1038, ABV 3.8%)
Hoppy golden ale fused with Cornish honey. The rounded finish has a hint of ginger.

Spriggan Ale (OG 1038, ABV 3.8%)
A light golden, hoppy bitter. Well-balanced with a smooth bitter finish.

Betty Stogs (OG 1040, ABV 4%)
Light hop perfume with underlying malt. Easy-drinking copper ale with balance of citrus and apple fruit, malt and bitterness, plus a hint of sulphur. Bitter finish is slow to develop but long to fade.

Heligan Honey (OG 1040, ABV 4%)
A slightly sweet amber bitter, brewed with West Country malt and Heligan Garden honey.

Keel Over (OG 1041, ABV 4.2%)
A classic Cornish bitter, amber in colour, beautifully balanced with a smooth finish.

Cornish Knocker Ale (OG 1044, ABV 4.5%)
Refreshing, amber/gold beer full of life with hops all the way through. Spice and fruit in the mouth balanced by bitter and malt undertones, with a clean and lasting bittersweet finish.

Figgy's Brew (OG 1044, ABV 4.5%)
A classic, dark, premium-strength bitter. Full-flavoured with a smooth finish.

Cornish Blonde (OG 1048, ABV 5%)
A combination of wheat malt and English and American hops makes this light-coloured wheat beer deceptively easy to drink.

Slater's SIBA

Eccleshall Brewing Co Ltd, Slater's Brewery, St Albans Road, Common Road Industrial Estate, Stafford, ST16 3DR
☎ (01785) 257976
✉ sales@slatersales.co.uk
slatersales.co.uk
Tours by arrangement

The brewery was opened in 1995 and in 2006 moved to new, larger premises, resulting in a tripling of capacity. It has won numerous awards from CAMRA and SIBA and supplies more than 1,100 outlets. One pub is owned, the George at Eccleshall, which serves as the brewery tap. Seasonal beers are produced bi-annually. Supreme (ABV 4.7%) is brewed occasionally.

Bitter (OG 1036, ABV 3.6%)
Amber with a hop and malt aroma. Hoppiness develops into a long dry finish.

Common Road (ABV 3.8%)

Owzat (ABV 3.8%)

Original (OG 1040, ABV 4%)
Amber bitter. Malty aroma with caramel notes, hoppy taste develops into a dry hoppy finish with a touch of sweetness.

Top Totty (OG 1040, ABV 4%)
Great yellow colour with a fruit and hop nose. Hop and fruit balanced taste leads to citrus hints with mouth-watering edges. Dry finish with tangs of lemon.

Queen Bee (OG 1042, ABV 4.2%)
Golden with a sweet and spicy aroma and hop background. Honey sweet taste followed by a gentle bitter finish on the tongue.

Premium (OG 1044, ABV 4.4%)
Pale brown bitter with malt and caramel aroma. Malt and caramel taste supported by hops and some fruit provide a warming descent and satisfyingly bitter mouthfeel.

Slaughterhouse SIBA

Slaughterhouse Brewery Ltd, Bridge Street, Warwick, CV34 5PD
☎ (01926) 490986
✉ enquiries@slaughterhousebrewery.com
slaughterhousebrewery.com
Tours by arrangement

Production began in 2003 on a four-barrel plant in a former slaughterhouse. Due to its success, beer production now consists mainly of Saddleback, supplemented by monthly special and seasonal beers. Around 30 outlets are supplied. The brewery premises are licensed for off-sales direct to the public. Seasonal beers: see website.

Saddleback Best Bitter (OG 1038, ABV 3.8%)
Amber-coloured session bitter with a distinctive Challenger hop flavour.

For the Waterman, Hatton:

Arkwright's Special Bitter (ABV 3.8%)

Small Paul's

Small Paul's Brewery, 27 Briar Close, Gillingham, Dorset, SP8 4SS
☎ (01747) 823574
✉ smallbrewer@aol.com
Tours by arrangement

The brewery was launched in September 2006 by an enthusiastic home brewer on a half-barrel plant. There are usually two brews a month and half a dozen local free houses and clubs are supplied direct with beers being supplied to festivals further afield. Different beers can be designed and brewed to order.

Gylla's Gold (OG 1039, ABV 3.8%)
Golden session beer with a citrus aroma.

Wyvern (OG 1044, ABV 4.4%)
A dark brown fruity beer with chocolate undertones.

Gillingham Pale (OG 1045, ABV 4.5%)
A pale bitter with floral aroma and dry finish.

Smiles

See Highgate

Samuel Smith

Samuel Smith Old Brewery (Tadcaster), High Street, Tadcaster, North Yorkshire, LS24 9SB
☎ (01937) 832225

A fiercely independent, family-owned company. Tradition, quality and value are important, resulting in traditional brewing without any artificial additives. All real ale is supplied in wooden casks, though nitrokeg has replaced cask beer in some pubs in recent years. An unfiltered draught wheat beer is a recent addition. Around 200 pubs are owned. A bottle-conditioned beer was introduced in 2008 (Yorkshire Stingo, ABV 8%) but is only available in specialist off-licences.

Old Brewery Bitter/OBB (OG 1040, ABV 4%)
Malt dominates the aroma, with an initial burst of malt, hops and fruit in the taste, which is sustained in the aftertaste.

Snowdonia SIBA

Snowdonia Brewery, Snowdonia Parc Brewpub & Campsite, Waunfawr, Caernarfon, Gwynedd, LL55 4AQ
☎ (01286) 650409
info@snowdonia-park.co.uk
snowdonia-park.co.uk

Snowdonia started brewing in 1998 in a two-barrel brewhouse. The brewing is now carried out by the new co-owner, Carmen Pierce. The beer is brewed solely for the Snowdonia Park pub and campsite.

Station Bitter (OG 1040, ABV 4%)

Carmen Sutra (OG 1043, ABV 4.4%)

Snowdonia Gold (OG 1050, ABV 5%)

Welsh Highland Bitter (OG 1048, ABV 5%)

Somerset (Electric)

See Taunton

Son of Sid

Son of Sid Brewery, The Chequers, 71 Main Road, Little Gransden, Bedfordshire, SG19 3DW
☎ (01767) 677348
chequersgransden@btinternet.com

Son of Sid was established in 2007 on a 2.5-barrel plant in a separate room of the pub. The brewery can be viewed from the lounge bar. It is named after the father of the current landlord, who ran the pub for 42 years. His son has carried the business on for the past 17 years as a family-run enterprise. Beer is only sold in the pub.

Muckcart Mild (ABV 3.5%)

South Hams SIBA

South Hams Brewery Ltd, Stokeley Barton, Stokenham, Kingsbridge, Devon, TQ7 2SE
☎ (01548) 581151
info@southhamsbrewery.co.uk
southhamsbrewery.co.uk
Tours by arrangement

The brewery moved to its present site in 2003, with a 10-barrel plant and plenty of room to expand. It supplies more than 60 outlets in Plymouth and south Devon. Wholesalers are used to distribute to other areas. Two pubs are owned. Seasonal beers: Hopnosis (ABV 4.5%), Porter (ABV 5%), Knickadroppa Glory (ABV 5.2%). Bottle-conditioned beers are also available.

Devon Pride (OG 1039, ABV 3.8%)

Re'session Ale (ABV 4%)

XSB (OG 1043, ABV 4.2%)
Amber nectar with a fruity nose and a bitter finish.

Wild Blonde (ABV 4.4%)

Eddystone (OG 1050, ABV 4.8%)

Southport SIBA

Southport Brewery, Unit 3, Enterprise Business Park, Russell Road, Southport, Merseyside, PR9 7RF
☎ 07748 387652
southportbrewery@fsmail.net
southportbrewery.co.uk

The Southport brewery opened in 2004 as a 2.5-barrel plant but moved up to a five-barrel plant due to demand. Around 30 pubs are supplied in the North-west. It also supplies the free trade via Boggart Brewery (qv). Seasonal beers: Old Shrimper (ABV 5.5%, Nov-Feb), Tower Mild (ABV 3.7%, May-Sep), National Hero (ABV 4%, Mar-Apr).

Cyclone (OG 1039.5, ABV 3.8%)
A bronze-coloured bitter with a fruity blackcurrant aftertaste.

Sandgrounder Bitter (OG 1039.5, ABV 3.8%)
Pale, hoppy session bitter with a floral character.

Carousel (OG 1041.5, ABV 4%)
A refreshing, floral, hoppy best bitter.

Golden Sands (OG 1041.5, ABV 4%)
A golden-coloured, triple hopped bitter with citrus flavour.

Natterjack (OG 1043.5, ABV 4.3%)
A premium bitter with fruit notes and a hint of coffee.

For Southport Football Club:

Grandstand Gold (OG 1039.5, ABV 3.8%)
A gold-coloured bitter, available for all home matches.

Spectrum EAB SIBA

Spectrum Brewery, Unit 11, Wellington Road, Tharston, Norwich, Norfolk, NR15 2PE
☎ 07949 254383
info@spectrumbrewery.co.uk
spectrumbrewery.co.uk
Tours by arrangement

Proprietor and founder Andy Mitchell established Spectrum in 2002. The brewery moved premises in 2007 as well as increasing brew length and gaining organic certification for all beers. Seasonal beers: Spring Promise (ABV 4.5%, Jan-Feb), Autumn Beer (ABV 4.5%, Sep-Oct —names and formulations vary), Yule Fuel (ABV 7%). The beers are also available mail order through the website.

Light Fantastic (OG 1035.5, ABV 3.7%)
Golden hued with a refreshing citrus character on nose and taste. Grapefruit notes add depth to the hoppy bitterness in the beginning. Initial malt

background fades to a sharp, slightly astringent finish.

Dark Fantastic (OG 1041, ABV 3.8%)
A rich vine fruit and roast aroma introduces this dark mild. Heavy chocolate notes permeate the malty sweetness, contrasting with the underlying bitterness. A long, rich, tapering ending.

Bezants (OG 1038, ABV 4%)
Dry, somewhat sulphurous golden ale. A one dimensional beer with a direct bitterness that overpowers any other flavours. A minimal maltiness sinks without trace.

42 (OG 1039.5, ABV 4.2%)
Sulphourous notes in the nose do not transfer to the taste. Although bitterness is the outstanding flavour there is more than a trace of both malt and soft fruits. A quick, crisp ending.

Black Buffle (OG 1047, ABV 4.5%)
The deep roast backbone is softened by a blackcurrant fruitiness. Malt is in evidence but is soon masked by a growing bitterness. A satisfying spectrum of aroma and taste.

XXXX (OG 1045.5, ABV 4.6%)
A deep copper strong bitter, first brewed for the proprietor's 40th birthday.

Wizzard (OG 1047.5, ABV 4.9%)
Rich and fruity in nose and taste. A full-bodied, complex brew with raisin and cherry matching the heavy malt overtones. Well-balanced refreshing and creamy with an increasingly bitter finish.

Old Stoatwobbler (OG 1064.5, ABV 6%)
Rich and creamy old ale with a dark chocolate digestive flavour. Roast and vine fruits with a touch of caramel mask a background hoppy bitterness. A long sustained finish.

Trip Hazard (OG 1061.5, ABV 6.5%)
A sweet, fruity brew with bubblegum notes throughout. Smooth bodied and easy drinking. A bitter hop undertow lightens the sweet resinous maltiness towards the sustained end.

Solstice Blinder (OG 1079, ABV 8.5%)
Strong IPA. Brewed twice a year, dry-hopped and left to mature (unfined) for at least three months before release in time for the solstices.

Spinning Dog SIBA

Spinning Dog Brewery, 88 St Owen Street, Hereford, HR1 2QD
☎ (01432) 342125
jfkenyon@aol.com
spinningdogbrewery.co.uk
Tours by arrangement

The brewery was built in a room of the Victory in 2000 by Jim Kenyon, following the purchase of the pub. Initially only serving the pub, it has steadily grown from a four-barrel to a 10-barrel plant. In 2005 the brewery commissioned its own bottling plant, capable of producing 80 cases a day. It now supplies some 300 other outlets as well as selling bottle-conditioned beer via the internet. Seasonal/occasional beers: Mutleys Mongrel (ABV 3.9%), Harvest Moon (ABV 4.5%), Santa Paws (ABV 5.2%), Mutleys Springer (ABV 4.4%), Christmas Cheer (ABV 4.3%), Organic Oatmeal Stout (ABV 4.4%).

Hereford Original Bitter (ABV 3.7%)
Light in colour with a distinctive fruitiness from start to finish.

Herefordshire Owd Bull (ABV 3.9%)
A good session beer with an abundance of hops and bitterness. Dry, with citrus aftertaste.

Hereford Cathedral Bitter (OG 1040, ABV 4%)
A crisp amber beer made with local hops, producing a well-rounded malt/hop bitterness throughout and a pleasing, lingering aftertaste.

Herefordshire Light Ale (ABV 4%)
Brewed along the lines of the award-winning Mutleys Pitstop. Light and refreshing.

Mutleys Dark (OG 1040, ABV 4%)
A dark, malty mild with a hint of bitterness and a touch of roast caramel. A smooth drinkable ale.

Top Dog (OG 1042, ABV 4.2%)
A hoppy beer with both malt and fruit flavours.

Celtic Gold (OG 1045, ABV 4.5%)
A bright gold best bitter, full of fruit and blackcurrant flavours.

Mutleys Revenge (OG 1048, ABV 4.8%)
A strong, smooth, hoppy beer, amber in colour. Full-bodied with a dry, citrus aftertaste.

Mutts Nuts (OG 1050, ABV 5%)
A dark, strong ale, full bodied with a hint of a chocolate aftertaste.

Spire SIBA

Spire Brewery, Units 2-3, Gisborne Close, Ireland Business Park, Staveley, Chesterfield, Derbyshire, S43 3JT
☎ (01246) 476005
info@spirebrewery.co.uk
spirebrewery.co.uk
Tours by arrangement

The brewery was set up by ex-Scots Guards musician and teacher David McLaren in 2006. Having acquired a brewery tap in Tupton, the brewery continues to expand both its outlets and range of beers including monthly specials and a wide selection of bottle-conditioned beers. Over 100 outlets are supplied direct. Seasonal beers: see website.

Overture (OG 1038, ABV 3.9%)
Traditional amber session beer with a little malt and hop aroma. Balanced malt and roast flavours lead to a developing bitterness, ending in a long malty finish.

Good As Gold (OG 1039, ABV 4%)
Pale, straw-coloured session beer with hop and malt flavours and a subtle citrus finish.

80/- Ale (OG 1043, ABV 4.3%)

Dark Side of the Moon (OG 1043, ABV 4.3%)

Chesterfield Best Bitter (OG 1044, ABV 4.5%)
Classic brown strong bitter with malt and fruit flavours and a hint of caramel and chocolate in the finish. There is a little bitterness in the aftertaste.

Land of Hop & Glory (OG 1044, ABV 4.5%)
An excellent example of a clean, crisp-tasting golden ale. Easy to drink with grapefruit and lemon flavours developing. The complex citrus hop flavours lead to a bitter, dry aftertaste.

Twist & Stout (OG 1044, ABV 4.5%)

Sovereign IPA (OG 1051, ABV 5.2%)

Sgt Pepper Stout (OG 1053, ABV 5.5%)
Unique full-flavoured stout brewed with ground black pepper. Liquorice and pepper flavours

dominate this original, complex dark and delicious beer.

Spitting Feathers

Spitting Feathers Brewery, Common Farm, Waverton, Chester, Cheshire, CH3 7QT
☎ (01244) 332052
✉ info@spittingfeathers.org
🌐 spittingfeathers.org
Tours by arrangement

Spitting Feathers was established in 2005 at Common Farm on the outskirts of Chester. The brewery and visitors' bar are in traditional sandstone buildings around a cobbled yard, which is also the setting for the West Cheshire Brewers' Beer Festival in July. Beehives provide honey for the brewery and spent grains are fed to livestock. The brewery opened its first pub in Chester in 2008. Around 200 outlets are supplied. Seasonal beers: see website. Bottle-conditioned beers are also available. All bottled beers are suitable for vegetarians and vegans.

Farmhouse Ale (OG 1035, ABV 3.6%)

Thirstquencher (OG 1038, ABV 3.9%) ◆
Powerful hop aroma leads into the taste. Bitterness and a fruity citrus hop flavour fight for attention. A sharp, clean golden beer with a long, dry, bitter aftertaste.

Special Ale (OG 1041, ABV 4.2%) ◆
Complex tawny-coloured beer with a sharp, grainy mouthfeel. Malty with good hop coming through in the aroma and taste. Hints of nuttiness and a touch of acidity. Dry, astringent finish.

Old Wavertonian (OG 1043, ABV 4.4%) ◆
Creamy and smooth stout. Full-flavoured with coffee notes in aroma and taste. Roast and nut flavours throughout, leading to a hoppy, bitter finish.

Basket Case (OG 1046, ABV 4.8%) ◆
Reddish, complex beer. Sweetness and fruit dominate taste, offset by hops and bitterness that follow through into the aftertaste.

Springhead SIBA

Springhead Fine Ales Ltd, Old Great North Road, Sutton-on-Trent, Newark, Nottinghamshire, NG23 6QS
☎ (01636) 821000
✉ steve@springhead.co.uk
🌐 springhead.co.uk
Tours by arrangement

Springhead Brewery opened in 1990 moving to bigger premises three years later and, to meet increased demand, expanded to a brew length of 50 barrels. Around 500 outlets are supplied. Many of the beer names have a Civil War theme. Puritans' Porter is suitable for vegans.

Liberty (OG 1036, ABV 3.8%)
A pale, straw-coloured beer with hints of lemon and a dry, biscuity finish.

Bitter (OG 1041, ABV 4%)
A clean-tasting, easy-drinking, hoppy bitter.

Puritans' Porter (OG 1041, ABV 4%)

Roundhead's Gold (OG 1042, ABV 4.2%)
Golden beer made with wild flower honey. Refreshing but not sweet.

Rupert's Ruin (OG 1042, ABV 4.2%)

Goodrich Castle (OG 1044, ABV 4.4%)
Brewed following a 17th-century recipe using rosemary: a pale ale, light on the palate with a bitter finish and delicate flavour.

Oliver's Army (OG 1044, ABV 4.4%)

Charlie's Angel (OG 1045, ABV 4.5%)
A pale, golden beer where Cluster hops, oranges and coriander result in a deeply fruity beer with a well-rounded bitterness and dry finish.

Sweetlips (OG 1046, ABV 4.6%)

Leveller (OG 1047, ABV 4.8%)
A dark, smoky intense flavour with a toffee finish. Brewed in the style of Belgian Trappist ale.

Cromwell's Hat (OG 1045, ABV 5%)

Newark Castle Brown (OG 1049, ABV 5%)

Willy's Wheatbeer (OG 1051, ABV 5.3%)

Roaring Meg (OG 1052, ABV 5.5%)
Smooth and sweet with a dry finish and citrus honey aroma.

Stables (NEW)

Stables Brewing Co, Beamish Hall Country House Hotel, Beamish, County Durham, DH9 0YB
☎ (01207) 288750
✉ stables@beamish-hall.co.uk
🌐 beamish-hall.co.uk/stables
Tours by arrangement

Stables was established as part of a three quarter of a million pound development of an old stable block, converting a disused building to a pub, restaurant and micro-brewery.

Beamish Hall Best Bitter (OG 1038, ABV 3.8%)

Old Miner Tommy (OG 1037, ABV 3.8%)

Bobby Dazzler (OG 1042, ABV 4.2%)

Coppy Lonnen (OG 1043, ABV 4.2%)

Silver Buckles (OG 1044, ABV 4.4%)

Beamish Burn (OG 1045, ABV 4.5%)

Bell Tower (OG 1052, ABV 5%)

Stanway

Stanway Brewery, Stanway, Cheltenham, Gloucestershire, GL54 5PQ
☎ (01386) 584320
🌐 stanwaybrewery.co.uk

Stanway is a small brewery founded in 1993 with a five-barrel plant that confines its sales to the Cotswolds area (15 to 20 outlets). The brewery is the only known plant in the country to use wood-fired coppers for all its production. Seasonal beers: Morris-a-Leaping (ABV 3.9%, spring), Cotteswold Gold (ABV 3.9%, summer), Wizard's Brew (ABV 4%, autumn), Lords-a-Leaping (ABV 4.5%, Xmas).

Stanney Bitter (OG 1042, ABV 4.5%) ◆
A light, refreshing, amber-coloured beer, dominated by hops in the aroma, with a bitter taste and a hoppy, bitter finish.

THE BREWERIES

Star

See Wibblers

Stationhouse

See Frodsham

Steamin' Billy

Steamin' Billy Brewing Co Ltd, Registered Office: 5 The Oval, Oadby, Leicestershire, LE2 5JB
☎ (0116) 271 2616
✉ enquiries@steamin-billy.co.uk
🌐 steamin-billy.co.uk

Steamin' Billy was formed in 1995 by licensee Barry Lount and brewer Bill Allingham. Bill originally brewed in Derbyshire but after outgrowing the plant the beers have since been contracted out. Bill is currently brewing at Tower Brewery (qv) in conjunction with John Mills. Four pubs are owned. The beers are named after the owners' Jack Russell dog, which is featured in cartoon form on the pump clips. Seasonal beers: see website. See Tower for regular beers.

Stewart

Stewart Brewing Ltd, Unit 5, 42 Dryden Road, Bilston Glen Industrial Estate, Loanhead, Midlothian, EH20 9LZ
☎ (0131) 440 2442
✉ steve.stewart@stewartbrewing.co.uk
🌐 stewartbrewing.co.uk
Tours by arrangement

Established in 2004 by Steve Stewart, a qualified master brewer and specialising in high-quality premium cask ales, all made from natural ingredients. The beers are widely available in South-east Scotland. Beer for home can be purchased direct from the brewery for collection or delivery in the Edinburgh area. Bottle-conditioned beers are available.

Pentland IPA (OG 1040, ABV 3.9%)

Copper Cascade (OG 1041, ABV 4.1%)

Edinburgh No.3 Premium Scotch Ale (OG 1043, ABV 4.3%)
Traditional dark Scottish ale. The pronounced malt character is part of a complex flavour profile, including fruit and hop. Initial sweetness leads into a dry, bitter, lingering finish.

80/- (OG 1044, ABV 4.4%)
Classic full-bodied, malty, bittersweet Scottish 80/- with plenty of character.

Edinburgh Gold (OG 1048, ABV 4.8%)
Full-bodied golden ale in the continental style. Plenty of hops are enjoyed throughout the drinking experience and give the beer a bitter profile balanced by the sweetness of fruit.

Sticklegs (NEW)

Sticklegs Brewery, Room 2, The Cross Inn, Ardleigh Road, Great Bromley, Essex, CO7 7TL
☎ 07962 012906
✉ tom@sticklegs.co.uk
🌐 sticklegs.co.uk

Sticklegs opened in 2008 and only supplies the Cross Inn. No expansion is planned but the brewery sometimes supplies local beer festivals.

Malt Shovel Mild (OG 1032, ABV 3.4%)

Prizefighter (OG 1042, ABV 4.2%)

Stirling

See Traditional Scottish Ales

Stonehenge SIBA

Stonehenge Ales Ltd, The Old Mill, Mill Road, Netheravon, Salisbury, Wiltshire, SP4 9QB
☎ (01980) 670631
✉ info@stonehengeales.co.uk
🌐 stonehengeales.co.uk
Tours by arrangement

The beer is brewed in a mill built in 1914 to generate electricity from the River Avon. The site was converted to a gravity-fed brewery in 1984 (Bunce's Brewery) and in 1994 the company was bought by Danish master brewer Stig Anker Andersen. More than 300 outlets in the south of England and several wholesalers are supplied. Seasonal beers: Sign of Spring (ABV 4.6%), Eye-Opener (ABV 4.5%), Old Smokey (ABV 5%), Rudolph (ABV 5%).

Spire Ale (OG 1037, ABV 3.8%)
A light, golden, hoppy bitter.

Pigswill (OG 1038, ABV 4%)
A full-bodied beer, rich in hop aroma, with a warm amber colour.

Heelstone (OG 1042, ABV 4.3%)
A crisp, clean, refreshing bitter, deep amber in colour, well balanced with a fruity blackcurrant nose.

Great Bustard (OG 1046, ABV 4.8%)
A strong, fruity, malty bitter.

Danish Dynamite (OG 1048, ABV 5%)
A strong, dry ale, slightly fruity with a well-balanced, bitter hop flavour.

Stonehouse

Stonehouse Brewery, Stonehouse, Weston, Oswestry, Shropshire, SY10 9ES
☎ (01691) 676457
✉ info@stonehousebrewery.co.uk
🌐 stonehousebrewery.co.uk
Shop Mon-Fri 9am-5pm
Tours by arrangement

Stonehouse was established early in 2007 on a 15-barrel plant. The brewery is based in former chicken sheds and is next to the old Cambrian railway line, hence the beer names. 60 outlets are supplied direct, mainly in Wales, Shropshire and South Cheshire. Seasonal beers: Wheeltappers (ABV 4.5%, summer), Off The Rails (ABV 4.8%, winter). Bottle-conditioned beers are also available.

Station Bitter (OG 1041, ABV 3.9%)

Cambrian Gold (OG 1042, ABV 4.2%)

KPA (OG 1047, ABV 4.6%)

Storm SIBA

Storm Brewing Co Ltd, 2 Waterside, Macclesfield, Cheshire, SK11 7HJ
☎ (01625) 431234
✉ stormbrewing@dsl.pipex.com
🌐 stormbrewing.co.uk

Storm Brewing was founded in 1998 and operated from an old ICI boiler room until 2001 when the brewing operation moved to the current location, which until 1937 was a public house known as the Mechanics Arms. More than 60 outlets are supplied in Cheshire, Manchester and the Peak District. Seasonal beers: Summer Breeze (ABV 3.8%), Looks Like Rain Dear (ABV 4.8%, Xmas). Bottle-conditioned beers are also available.

Beauforts Ale (OG 1038, ABV 3.8%)
Golden brown, full-flavoured session bitter with a lingering hoppy taste.

Bitter Experience (OG 1040, ABV 4%)
A distinctive hop aroma draws you into this amber-coloured bitter. The palate has a mineral dryness that accentuates the crisp hop flavour and clean bitter finish.

Desert Storm (OG 1040, ABV 4%)
Amber-coloured beer with a smoky flavour of fruit and malt.

Twister (OG 1041, ABV 4%)
A light golden bitter with a smooth fruity hop aroma complemented by a subtle bitter aftertaste.

Bosley Cloud (OG 1041, ABV 4.1%) ◆
Dry, golden bitter with peppery hop notes throughout. Some initial sweetness and a mainly bitter aftertaste. Soft, well-balanced and quaffable.

Brainstorm (OG 1041, ABV 4.1%)
Light gold in colour and strong in citrus fruit flavours.

Ale Force (OG 1042, ABV 4.2%) ◆
Amber, smooth-tasting, complex beer that balances malt, hop and fruit on the taste, leading to a roasty, slightly sweet aftertaste.

Downpour (OG 1043, ABV 4.3%)
A combination of Pearl and lager malts produces this pale ale with a full, fruity flavour with a hint of apple and sightly hoppy aftertaste.

PGA (OG 1044, ABV 4.4%) ◆
Light, crisp, lager-style beer with a balance of malt, hops and fruit. Moderately bitter and slight dry aftertaste.

Tornado (OG 1044, ABV 4.4%) ◆
Fruity premium bitter with some graininess. Dry, satisfying finish.

Hurricane Hubert (OG 1045, ABV 4.5%)
A dark beer with a refreshing full, fruity hop aroma and a subtle bitter aftertaste.

Windgather (OG 1045, ABV 4.5%)
A gold-coloured beer with a distinctive crisp, fruity flavour right through to the aftertaste.

Silk of Amnesia (OG 1047, ABV 4.7%) ◆
Smooth premium, easy-drinking bitter. Fruit and hops dominate throughout. Not too sweet, with a good lasting finish.

Storm Damage (OG 1047, ABV 4.7%)
A light-coloured, well-hopped and fruity beer balanced by a clean bitterness and smooth full palate.

Typhoon (OG 1050, ABV 5%) ◆
Copper-coloured, smooth strong bitter. Roasty overtones and a hint of caramel and marzipan.

Storyteller (NEW)

Storyteller Brewery Ltd, Bay Horse Inn, Main Street, Terrington, York, North Yorkshire, YO60 6PP
☎ (01653) 648416
✉ rob@thestorytellerb.plus.com
🌐 thestorytellerbrewery.co.uk

Storyteller was established in 2008 and only brews for the Bay Horse Inn.

Genesis (OG 1039, ABV 3.8%)

Telltale (OG 1039, ABV 3.8%)

1402 (OG 1042, ABV 4%)

Fireside (OG 1052, ABV 4.7%)

Stowey

Stowey Brewery Ltd, Old Cider House, 25 Castle Street, Nether Stowey, Somerset, TA5 1LN
☎ (01278) 732228
✉ info@stoweybrewery.co.uk
🌐 stoweybrewery.co.uk
Tours by arrangement

Stowey was established in 2006, primarily to supply the owners' guesthouse and to provide beer to participants on 'real ale walks' run from the accommodation. 2007 saw the introduction of 'Brew your own Beer' breaks to guests. The brewery now supplies beer to two local pubs on a guest beer basis.

Nether Ending (OG 1044, ABV 4%)

Nether Underestimate a Blonde (OG 1044, ABV 4.2%)

Strands

Strands Brewery, Strands Hotel, Nether Wasdale, Cumbria, CA20 1ET
☎ (019467) 26237
✉ info@strandshotel.com
🌐 strandshotel.com
Tours by arrangement

Strands began brewing in early 2007 on a three-barrel plant with a 12-barrel fermenting capacity. The first beer produced was called Errmmm. . . as the owners couldn't think of a name for it.

Errmmm... (OG 1042, ABV 3.8%)

Corrsberg (ABV 4.1%)

Dafydd Ale (ABV 4.2%)

Bersteinale (OG 1047, ABV 4.5%)

Red Screes (OG 1047, ABV 4.5%)

T'Errmmm-inator (ABV 4.9%)

Strangford Lough

Strangford Lough Brewing Co, 22 Shore Road, Killyleagh, Downpatrick, Northern Ireland, BT30 9UE
☎ (028) 4482 1461
✉ contact@slbc.ie
🌐 slbc.ie

Beers for the company are contract-brewed by an unnamed brewery in England, though there are plans to build a plant in Northern Ireland. Bottle-

THE BREWERIES

conditioned beers: St Patrick's Best (ABV 3.8%), St Patrick's Gold (ABV 4.5%), St Patrick's Ale (ABV 6%), Barelegs Brew (ABV 4.5%), Legbiter (ABV 4.8%).

Strathaven

Strathaven Ales, Craigmill Brewery, Strathaven, ML10 6PB
☎ (01357) 520419
✉ info@strathavenales.co.uk
🌐 strathavenales.co.uk
Shop Mon-Fri 9am-5pm (phone at weekend)
Tours by arrangement

⊗ Strathaven Ales is a 10-barrel brewery on the River Avon close to Strathaven and was converted from the remains of a 16th-century mill. The range is distributed throughout Scotland and the north of England. Seasonal beers: Duchess Anne (ABV 3.9%), Trumpeter (ABV 4.2%).

Clydesdale (OG 1038, ABV 3.8%)

Avondale (OG 1048, ABV 4%)

Old Mortality (OG 1046, ABV 4.2%)

Claverhouse (OG 1046, ABV 4.5%)

Stringers (NEW)

Stringers Beer, Unit 3, Low Mill Business Park, Ulverston, Cumbria, LA12 9EE
☎ (01229) 581387
✉ info@stringersbeer.co.uk
🌐 stringersbeer.co.uk
Tours by arrangement

Stringers is a family-run, small craft brewery. Brewing started in 2008 on a five-barrel plant run on 100% renewable energy. A small number of seasonal beers are produced including Genuine Stunning (ABV 6.5%, Nov-Jan). There are plans for bottling. No. 2 Stout is suitable for vegans.

Golden (OG 1037, ABV 3.7%)

No. 2 Stout (OG 1040, ABV 4%)

Best Bitter (OG 1042, ABV 4.2%)

Stroud SIBA

Stroud Brewery Ltd, Unit 7, Phoenix Works, London Road, Thrupp, Stroud, Gloucestershire, GL5 2BU
☎ 07891 995878

Office: 141 Thrupp Lane, Thrupp, Stroud, Gloucestershire, GL5 2DQ
✉ greg@stroudbrewery.co.uk
🌐 stroudbrewery.co.uk
Tours by arrangement

⊗ The brewery was established in 2005 with production commencing in mid 2006 on a five-barrel plant. Stroud supports the local economy and does not sell any beer through supermarkets, delivering direct to around 50 pubs, independent retailers and direct to the public. A draught organic ale is produced and its full range of bottled beers are organic, all certified by the Soil Association. Seasonal beers: see website.

Tom Long (OG 1039, ABV 3.8%)
An amber-coloured bitter with a spicy citrus aroma.

Stroud Organic Ale (ABV 4%)
A fresh, hoppy, golden organic ale.

Budding (OG 1045, ABV 4.5%)
A pale ale with a grassy bitterness, sweet malt and floral aroma.

Stumpy's

Stumpy's Brewery, Unit 4C, Langbridge Business Centre, Newchurch, Isle of Wight, PO36 0NP
☎ (01983) 731731
☎ 07771 557378
✉ info@stumpysbrewery.com
🌐 stumpysbrewery.com
Tours by arrangement

⊗ Stumpy's opened a five-barrel brewery in 2004 in Upper Swanmore in Hampshire. It relocated to the Isle of Wight in summer 2008, sharing premises with Yates' Brewery (qv). Seasonal beer: Silent Night (ABV 5%, Oct-Feb). Bottle-conditioned beers are also available (these account for about 75% of production).

Dog Daze (OG 1040, ABV 3.8%) ◆
A light, golden summer beer with a strong, malty aroma. Tastes rather thin and sweet and lacking in bitterness. A sweet, malty finish.

Hop a Doodle Doo (OG 1040, ABV 4%)

Hot Dog (OG 1045, ABV 4.5%)

Old Ginger (OG 1045, ABV 4.5%)

Old Stumpy (OG 1045, ABV 4.5%) ◆
Grassy best bitter, with a strong hoppy and fruity aroma. Some malt and bitterness in the flavour lead to a harsh finish.

Bo'sun's Call (OG 1050, ABV 5%)

Haven (OG 1050, ABV 5%)

Tumbledown (OG 1050, ABV 5%)

IKB 1806 (OG 1070, ABV 7.2%)

Suddaby's SIBA

Suddaby's Ltd, Crown Hotel, 12 Wheelgate, Malton, North Yorkshire, YO17 7HP
☎ (01653) 692038
✉ enquiries@suddabys.co.uk
🌐 suddabys.co.uk

Suddabys no longer brews on site. The beers are contract brewed by Brown Cow (qv) at Selby and are only sold in bottled form in the Malt'on Hops Beer & Wine Shop located within the Crown Hotel and a few other selected outlets. Suddabys draught beers are also available in the Crown Hotel.

Sulwath SIBA

Sulwath Brewers Ltd, The Brewery, 209 King Street, Castle Douglas, Dumfries & Galloway, DG7 1DT
☎ (01556) 504525
✉ info@sulwathbrewers.co.uk
🌐 sulwathbrewers.co.uk
Tours daily at 1pm or by arrangement

◎ Sulwath started brewing in 1995. The beers are supplied to markets as far away as Devon in the south and Aberdeen in the north. The brewery has a fully licensed brewery tap and off sales open 10am-5pm Mon-Sat. Cask ales are sold to around 100 outlets and four wholesalers. Seasonal beers: Rein Beer (ABV 4.5%, Nov-Dec), Tam O'Shanter (ABV 4.1%, Jan-Feb), Happy Hooker (ABV 4%, Feb),

Woozy Wabbit (ABV 5%, Mar-Apr), Hells Bells (ABV 4.5%, May-Jun), Saltaire Cross (ABV 4.1%, Nov-Dec).

Cuil Hill (OG 1039, ABV 3.6%) ◆
Distinctively fruity session ale with malt and hop undertones. The taste is bittersweet with a long-lasting dry finish.

John Paul Jones (ABV 4%)

The Grace (OG 1044, ABV 4.3%)

Black Galloway (OG 1046, ABV 4.4%)
A robust porter/stout that derives its colour from the abundance of Maris Otter barley and chocolate malts used in the brewing process.

Criffel (OG 1044, ABV 4.6%) ◆
Full-bodied beer with a distinctive bitterness. Fruit is to the fore of the taste with hop becoming increasingly dominant in the taste and finish.

Galloway Gold (OG 1049, ABV 5%) ◆
A cask-conditioned lager that will be too sweet for many despite being heavily hopped.

Knockendoch (OG 1047, ABV 5%) ◆
Dark, copper-coloured, reflecting a roast malt content, with bitterness from Challenger hops.

Solway Mist (OG 1052, ABV 5.5%)
A naturally cloudy wheat beer. Sweetish and fruity.

Summerskills SIBA

Summerskills Brewery, 15 Pomphlett Farm Industrial Estate, Broxton Drive, Billacombe, Plymouth, Devon, PL7 9BG
☎ (01752) 481283
✉ info@summerskills.co.uk
🌐 summerskills.co.uk

⊗ Originally established in a vineyard in 1983 at Bigbury-on-Sea, Summerskills moved to its present site in 1985 and has expanded since then. National distribution is carried out by wholesalers. 20 outlets are supplied by the brewery. Seasonal beers: Whistle Belly Vengeance (ABV 4.7%, Oct-Apr), Indiana's Bones (ABV 5.6%, Oct-Apr), Isambard Kingdom Brunel 1859 (ABV 4.7%, Apr-Oct). Bottle-conditioned beers are also available.

Cellar Vee (OG 1037, ABV 3.7%)

Hopscotch (OG 1042, ABV 4.1%)

Best Bitter (OG 1043, ABV 4.3%) ◆
A mid-brown beer, with plenty of malt and hops through the aroma, taste and finish. A good session beer.

Tamar (OG 1043, ABV 4.3%)
A tawny-coloured bitter with a fruity aroma and a hop taste and finish.

Menacing Dennis (OG 1045, ABV 4.5%)

Devon Dew (OG 1047, ABV 4.7%)

Summer Wine

Summer Wine Brewery Ltd, The Old Furnace, Unit 15, Crossley Mills, New Mill Road, Honley, Holmfirth, West Yorkshire, HD9 6QB
☎ (01484) 665466
✉ info@summerwinebrewery.co.uk
🌐 summerwinebrewery.co.uk

⊗ Summer Wine started brewing in 2006 in the cellar of the home of owner James Farran, using a 10-gallon kit with an emphasis on bottle-conditioned beers. The brewery upgraded in 2007 and again in 2009 when it moved premises. It now operates on a six-barrel plant with 22 barrels per week production capability. Over 30 outlets are supplied direct. Bottle-conditioned beers are available.

Vagabond (ABV 3.6%)
A Yorkshire bitter with flavoursome body and hoppy kick.

Elbow Grease (ABV 3.8%)
A golden ale with a citrus nose, fruity notes and dry finish.

Furnace Gold (ABV 4.2%)

Holmfirth IPA (ABV 4.2%)
A deep, copper-coloured hoppy IPA with an Admiral hop hit.

Surrey Hills SIBA

Surrey Hills Brewery Ltd, Old Scotland Farm, Staple Lane, Shere, Guildford, Surrey, GU5 9TE
☎ (01483) 212812
✉ info@surreyhills.co.uk
🌐 surreyhills.co.uk
Open for beer sales Thu-Fri 12-2pm, 4-5pm; Sat 10am-12pm
Tours by arrangement

⊗ Surrey Hills started in 2005 and is based in an old milking parlour, hidden away down country lanes in the Surrey Hills. The beers are sold in around 150 local outlets – see website for up-to-date list. More than 95% of production is sold in outlets less than 15 miles from the brewery. Seasonal beers (available for six months): Albury Ruby (ABV 4.6%, winter), Gilt Complex (ABV 4.6%, summer).

Hammer Mild (ABV 3.8%) ◆
Fine dark mild with a fruity roast malt character that lasts from the aroma through to the finish. Moderately sweet, but some hop and bitterness are also present.

Ranmore Ale (ABV 3.8%) ◆
A light session beer with plenty of flavour. An earthy hoppy nose leads into a citrus grapefruit and hoppy taste and a clean, bitter finish. Regional bitter of the year 2009.

Shere Drop (ABV 4.2%) ◆
The brewery's flagship beer is hoppy with some balancing malt. There is a pleasant citrus aroma and a noticeable fruitiness in the taste. The finish is dry, hoppy and bitter.

Suthwyk

Suthwyk Ales, Offwell Farm, Southwick, Fareham, Hampshire, PO17 6DX
☎ (02392) 325252
✉ mjbazeley@suthwykales.com
🌐 suthwykales.com/southwickbrewhouse.co.uk

Barley farmer Martin Bazeley does not brew himself. The beers are produced by Oakleaf Brewing (qv) in Gosport.

Bloomfields (ABV 3.8%)

Liberation (ABV 4.2%)

Skew Sunshine Ale (ABV 4.6%)

Palmerston's Folly (ABV 4.8%)

THE BREWERIES

Sutton

See South Hams

Swan on the Green

Swan on the Green Brewery, West Peckham, Maidstone, Kent, ME18 5JW
☎ (01622) 812271
info@swan-on-the-green.co.uk
swan-on-the-green.co.uk
Tours by arrangement

The brewery was established in 2000 to produce handcrafted beers. The beers are not filtered and no artificial ingredients are used. There are plans to expand the plant. One pub is owned and other outlets and beer festivals are occasionally supplied. Seasonal beers are brewed.

Fuggles Pale (OG 1037, ABV 3.6%)
A session bitter, traditionally hoppy, using local Fuggles hops.

Whooper (OG 1037, ABV 3.6%)
Straw coloured and lightly hopped with American Cascade for a subtle fruity aroma.

Trumpeter Best (OG 1041, ABV 4%)
A copper-coloured ale hopped with First Gold and Target.

Cygnet (OG 1048, ABV 4.2%)

Bewick (OG 1052, ABV 5.3%)
A heavyweight premium bitter hopped with Target for bite and softened with Kentish Goldings for aroma.

Swansea SIBA

Swansea Brewing Co, Joiners Arms, 50 Bishopston Road, Bishopston, Swansea, SA3 3EJ
☎ (01792) 232658/290197 (Office)

Office: 74 Hawthorne Avenue, Uplands, Swansea, SA2 0LY
rory@swansea_brewing.co.uk
Tours by arrangement

Opened in 1996, Swansea was the first commercial brewery in the area for almost 30 years and is the city's only brew-pub. It doubled its capacity within the first year and now produces four regular beers and occasional experimental ones. Four regular outlets are supplied along with other pubs in the South Wales area. Seasonal beers: St Teilo's Tipple (ABV 5.5%), Barland Strong (ABV 6%), Pwll Du XXXX (ABV 4.9%).

Deep Slade Dark (OG 1034, ABV 4%)

Bishopswood Bitter (OG 1038, ABV 4.3%) ◆
A delicate aroma of hops and malt in this pale brown colour. The taste is a balanced mix of hops and malt with a growing hoppy bitterness ending in a lasting bitter finish.

Three Cliffs Gold (OG 1042, ABV 4.7%) ◆
A golden beer with a hoppy and fruity aroma, a hoppy taste with fruit and malt, and a quenching bitterness. The pleasant finish has a good hop flavour and bitterness.

Original Wood (OG 1046, ABV 5.2%) ◆
A full-bodied, pale brown beer with an aroma of hops, fruit and malt. A complex blend of these flavours with a firm bitterness ends with increasing bitterness.

Swaton

Swaton Brewery, North End Farm, Swaton, Sleaford, Lincolnshire, NG34 0JP
☎ (01529) 421241
swatonbrewery@hotmail.co.uk
swatonbrewery.com
Shop Tue-Sat 10am-5pm
Tours by arrangement

Swaton commenced brewing in 2007 on a five-barrel plant and is sited in the outbuildings of the owner's farm. It supplies beer festivals and local pubs. A visitor centre/cafe/shop is situated next to the brewery. All beers are also available bottle conditioned.

Happy Jack (OG 1040, ABV 4.2%)

Dozy Bull (OG 1041.8, ABV 4.5%)

Kiss Goodnight (OG 1041.8, ABV 4.5%)

Three Degrees (OG 1043.5, ABV 4.7%)

Sweet William

See Brodie's

Taddington (NEW)

Taddington Brewery Ltd, Blackwell Hall, Blackwell, Buxton, SK17 9TQ
☎ (01298) 85734

No real ale. Taddington started brewing in 2007, and brews one Czech-style unpasteurised lager in two different strengths: Moravka (ABV 4.4% and 5%), which is available on draught.

Taunton

Taunton Brewing Co Ltd, Unit 1F, Hillview Industrial Estate, West Bagbrough, Somerset, TA4 3EW
☎ (01823) 433999
tauntonbrewingco@supanet.com
Tours by arrangement

Formerly Somerset Electric/Taunton Vale Brewery, established in 2003 in the cellar of the New Inn, Halse. Taunton Brewing Co took over in 2006, led by the former head brewer from Exmoor Ales, Colin Green. The brewery relocated in 2007 and now uses a 10-barrel plant. 140 outlets are supplied.

Phoenix (OG 1037, ABV 3.6%)

Ale (OG 1039.8, ABV 3.9%)

Braunton in Steam (OG 1042, ABV 4.2%)

Castle (OG 1043, ABV 4.3%)

Gold (OG 1045, ABV 4.5%)

Mayor (OG 1049, ABV 5%)

Timothy Taylor IFBB

Timothy Taylor & Co Ltd, Knowle Spring Brewery, Keighley, West Yorkshire, BD21 1AW
☎ (01535) 603139
timothy-taylor.co.uk

Timothy Taylor is an independent family-owned company established in 1858. It moved to the site of the Knowle Spring in 1863. Its prize-winning ales, which use Pennine spring water, are served in 28 of the brewery's 29 pubs as well as more than

300 other outlets. Major expansion including land acquisition is underway to meet increased demand.

Dark Mild (OG 1034, ABV 3.5%)
Malt and caramel dominate the aroma and palate with hops and hints of fruit leading to a dry, bitter finish.

Golden Best (OG 1033, ABV 3.5%)
This clean-tasting and refreshing, traditional Pennine light mild is malty throughout. A little fruit in the nose increases to complement the delicate hoppy taste.

Best Bitter (OG 1038, ABV 4%)
Hops and fruit combine well with a nutty malt character in this drinkable bitter. Bitterness increases down the glass and lingers in the aftertaste.

Landlord (OG 1042, ABV 4.3%)
A hoppy, increasingly bitter finish complements the background malt and spicy, citrus character of this full-flavoured and well-balanced amber beer.

Ram Tam (OG 1043, ABV 4.3%)
Caramel combines well with malt and hops to produce a well-balanced black beer with red hints and a coffee-coloured head.

Teignworthy SIBA

Teignworthy Brewery Ltd, The Maltings, Teignworthy, Newton Abbot, Devon, TQ12 4AA
☎ (01626) 332066
sales@teignworthybreweryltd.co.uk
teignworthybrewery.com
Shop 10am-5pm weekdays at Tuckers Maltings
Tours available for trade customers only

Teignworthy Brewery was established in 1994 and is located in part of the historic Tuckers Maltings. The brewery is a 20-barrel plant and production is now up to 65 barrels a week, using malt from Tuckers. It supplies around 300 outlets in Devon and Somerset. A large range of seasonal ales is available: see website. Bottle-conditioned beers are also produced. Martha's Mild is suitable for vegans in bottle-conditioned form.

Neap Tide (OG 1038, ABV 3.8%)

Reel Ale (OG 1039.5, ABV 4%)
Clean, sharp-tasting bitter with lasting hoppiness; predominantly malty aroma.

Springtide (OG 1043.5, ABV 4.3%)
An excellent, full and well-rounded, mid-brown beer with a dry, bitter taste and aftertaste.

Old Moggie (OG 1044.5, ABV 4.4%)
A golden, hoppy and fruity ale.

Beachcomber (OG 1045.5, ABV 4.5%)
A pale brown beer with a light, refreshing fruit and hop nose, grapefruit taste and a dry, hoppy finish.

Teme Valley SIBA

Teme Valley Brewery, The Talbot, Bromyard Road, Knightwick, Worcester, WR6 5PH
☎ (01886) 821235
enquiries@temevalleybrewery.co.uk
temevalleybrewery.co.uk
Tours by arrangement

Teme Valley Brewery opened in 1997. In 2005, new investment enabled the brewery to expand to a 10-barrel brew-length. It maintains strong ties with local hop farming, using only Worcestershire-grown hops. Some 30 outlets are supplied. Seasonal beers: see website. Bottle-conditioned beers are also available. Occasional beer: Heartwarmer (ABV 6%).

T'Other (OG 1035, ABV 3.5%)
Refreshing amber beer offering an abundance of flavour in the fruity aroma, followed by a short, dry bitterness.

This (OG 1037, ABV 3.7%)
Dark gold brew with a mellow array of flavours in a malty balance.

That (OG 1041, ABV 4.1%)
A rich fruity nose and a wide range of hoppy and malty flavours in this copper-coloured best bitter.

Talbot Blond (OG 1042, ABV 4.4%)
A smooth, rich, pale beer.

Theakston

T&R Theakston Ltd, The Brewery, Masham, Ripon, North Yorkshire, HG4 4YD
☎ (01765) 680000
info@theakstons.co.uk
theakstons.co.uk
Tours available daily throughout the year

In July 2009 the brewery welcomed back Best Bitter after a 35-year absence. The brewery's flagship brand had been brewed in Carlisle, Workington Tyne Brewery and then by John Smith's in Tadcaster. All Theakston's cask beers are now brewed at Masham. Theakstons returned to the independent sector in 2003 when the family bought the company back from S&N. It's now owned by four Theakston brothers. The brewery is one of the oldest in Yorkshire, built in 1875 by the brothers' great-grandfather, Thomas Theakston, the son of the company's founder. In 2004 a new fermentation room was added to provide additional flexibility and capacity. Further new capacity was added in 2006, with additional investment in 2009 to allow for the return of Best Bitter. Seasonal beers: see website.

Traditional Mild (OG 1035, ABV 3.5%)
A rich and smooth mild ale with a creamy body and a rounded liquorice taste. Dark ruby/amber in colour, with a mix of malt and fruit on the nose, and a dry, hoppy aftertaste.

Best Bitter (OG 1038, ABV 3.8%)
A golden-coloured beer with a full flavour that lingers pleasantly on the palate. With a good bitter/sweet balance, this beer has a robust hop character, citrus and spicy.

Black Bull Bitter (OG 1037, ABV 3.9%)
A distinctively hoppy aroma leads to a bitter, hoppy taste with some fruitiness and a short bitter finish.

XB (OG 1044, ABV 4.5%)
A sweet-tasting bitter with background fruit and spicy hop. Some caramel character gives this ale a malty dominance.

Old Peculier (OG 1057, ABV 5.6%)
A full-bodied, dark brown, strong ale. Slightly malty but with hints of roast coffee and liquorice. A smooth caramel overlay and a complex fruitiness leads to a bitter chocolate finish.

Abraham Thompson

Abraham Thompson's Brewing Co, Flass Lane, Barrow-in-Furness, Cumbria, LA13 0AD
☎ 07708 191437
✉ abraham.thompson@btinternet.com

Abraham Thompson was set up in 2004 to return Barrow-brewed beers to local pubs. This was achieved in 2005 after an absence of more than 30 years following the demise of Case's Brewery in 1972. With a half-barrel plant, this nano-brewery has concentrated almost exclusively on dark beers, reflecting the tastes of the brewer. As a result of the small output, finding the beers outside the Low Furness area is difficult. The only frequent stockist is the Black Dog Inn between Dalton and Ireleth.

Dark Mild (ABV 3.5%)

Lickerish Stout (ABV 3.8%)
A black, full-bodied stout with heavy roast flavours and good bitterness.

Oatmeal Stout (ABV 4.5%)

Porter (ABV 4.8%)
A deep, dark porter with good body and a smooth chocolate finish.

Letargion (ABV 9%)
Black, bitter and heavily roast but still very drinkable. A meal in a glass.

Lord Marples (OG 1041, ABV 4%)
An easy-drinking, copper-coloured, fruity session beer. Malty, with a citrus finish and long bitter aftertaste.

Ashford (OG 1043, ABV 4.2%)
A brown ale with a floral hoppiness and delicate coffee finish.

Blackthorn Ale (OG 1044, ABV 4.4%)
Clear golden ale, with a slight aroma of floral hops. Nicely balanced flavours of hops, citrus and sweetness lead to a lingering fruit and hop aftertaste.

Kipling (OG 1050, ABV 5.2%)
Golden pale bitter with aromas of grapefruit and passion fruit. Intense fruit flavours continue throughout, leading to a long bitter aftertaste.

Jaipur IPA (OG 1055, ABV 5.9%)
Complex, well-balanced IPA with a lovely blend of citrus and fruit flavours mixed with a slight sweetness and ending with a lingering, bitter finish.

Saint Petersburg (Imperial Russian Stout) (OG 1073, ABV 7.7%)
Full-bodied beer in the style of a Russian imperial stout. A combination of coffee, liquorice and roasted malt flavours gives way to a long bittersweet finish and aftertaste.

John Thompson

John Thompson Inn & Brewery, Ingleby, Melbourne, Derbyshire, DE73 7HW
☎ (01332) 862469
✉ nick@johnthompsoninn.com
🌐 johnthompsoninn.com
Tours by arrangement

John Thompson set up the brewery in 1977. The pub and brewery are now run by his son, Nick. Seasonal beers: Rich Porter (ABV 4.5%, winter), St Nicks (ABV 5%, Xmas).

JTS XXX (OG 1041, ABV 4.1%)

Gold (OG 1045, ABV 4.5%)

Thornbridge SIBA

Thornbridge Brewery, Riverside Business Park, Bakewell, Derbyshire, DE45 1GS
☎ (01629) 641000
✉ alex@thornbridgehallbrewery.co.uk
🌐 thornbridgebrewery.co.uk
Tours by arrangement

The first Thornbridge craft beers were produced in 2005 in a 10-barrel brewery, housed in the grounds of Thornbridge Hall. Around 75 outlets are supplied direct. A new 30-barrel brewery was commissioned in 2009 on the Riverside Trading Estate in Bakewell. Production of specialised, experimental and seasonal beers will remain at the original site, along with administration. Three pubs are owned. Seasonal/occasional beers: Brother Rabbit (ABV 3.7%), Brock (ABV 4.1%, Sep-Mar), Hark (ABV 4.8%, Nov-Feb), McConnells (ABV 5%, Sep-Mar). Bottle-conditioned beers are also available.

Wild Swan (OG 1035, ABV 3.5%)
Extremely light bodied, pale gold beer with subtle lemon and spice aroma. Citrus notes continue in the taste, leading to a bitter aftertaste.

Thorne (NEW)

Thorne Brewery CIC, Unit A2, Thorne Enterprise Park, King Edward Road, Thorne, South Yorkshire, DN8 4HU
☎ (01405) 741685
✉ info@thornebrewery.com
🌐 thornebrewery.com
Tours by arrangement

Thorne Brewery Community Interest Company was set up in 2008 to bring brewing back to Thorne. In early 2009 a 10-barrel brew plant was purchased and the first beers were available shortly after. Profits are re-invested in the local community to help improve the area.

Best Bitter (OG 1039, ABV 3.9%)
Malt dominates the taste with caramel, chocolate and fruitcake flavours. The hops complement this will a full-bodied bitterness and notes of orange peel, pepper and herbal aromas.

Pale Ale (OG 1041, ABV 4.2%)
English hops give a fruity flavour and a resinous, grassy aroma. Well-balanced bitterness gives a clean finish.

Three B's

Three B's Brewery, Laneside Works, Stockclough Lane, Feniscowles, Blackburn, Lancashire, BB2 5JR
☎ (01254) 207686
✉ robert@threebsbrewery.co.uk
🌐 threebsbrewery.co.uk
Tours by arrangement

Robert Bell designed and began building his two-barrel brewery in 1998 and in 1999 he obtained premises in Blackburn to set up the equipment and complete the project. Now, after a move to larger premises, it is a 10-barrel brewery with up to 30-barrel production per week. Over 50 regular outlets are supplied. Seasonal beers: see website.

Stoker's Slake (OG 1038, ABV 3.6%) ♦
Lightly roasted coffee flavours are in the aroma and the initial taste. A well-rounded, dark brown mild with dried fruit flavours in the long finish.

Bobbin's Bitter (OG 1040, ABV 3.8%)
Warm aromas of malt, Goldings hops and nuts; a full, fruity flavour with a light dry finish.

Tackler's Tipple (OG 1044, ABV 4.3%)
A best bitter with full hop flavour, biscuit tones on the tongue and a deep, dry finish. A darker coloured ale with a fascinating blend of hops and dark malt.

Doff Cocker (OG 1045, ABV 4.5%) ♦
Yellow with a hoppy aroma and initial taste giving way to subtle malt notes and orchard fruit flavours. Crisp, dry finish.

Pinch Noggin (OG 1046, ABV 4.6%)
A luscious balance of malt, hops and fruit, with a lively, colourful spicy aroma of citrus fruit. A quenching golden beer.

Knocker Up (OG 1048, ABV 4.8%) ♦
A smooth, rich, creamy porter. The roast flavour is foremost without dominating and is balanced by fruit and hop notes.

Shuttle Ale (OG 1052, ABV 5.2%)
A strong pale ale, light in colour with a balanced malt and hop flavour, a Goldings hops aroma, a long dry finish and delicate fruit notes.

Three Castles SIBA

Three Castles Brewery Ltd, Unit 12, Salisbury Road Business Park, Pewsey, Wiltshire, SN9 5PZ
☎ **(01672) 564433**
☎ **07725 148671**
✉ **sales@threecastlesbrewery.co.uk**
🌐 **threecastlesbrewery.co.uk**
Shop Mon-Fri 9am-4pm; Sat 9am-1pm
Tours by arrangement

⊗ Three Castles is an independent, family-run brewery, established in 2006. Its location in the Vale of Pewsey has inspired the names for its range of ales. The brewery has plans for expansion. Around 175 outlets are supplied. Seasonal beers: see website. Bottle-conditioned beers are also available.

Barbury Castle (OG 1039, ABV 3.9%)
A balanced, easy-drinking pale ale with a hoppy, spicy palate.

Liffington Castle (OG 1042, ABV 4.2%)

Vale Ale (OG 1043, ABV 4.3%)
Golden-coloured with a fruity palate and strong floral aroma.

Knights Porter (OG 1046, ABV 4.6%)

Tanked Up (OG 1050, ABV 5%)
Copper-coloured strong ale.

Three Peaks

Three Peaks Brewery, 7 Craven Terrace, Settle, North Yorkshire, BD24 9DB
☎ **(01729) 822939**

⊗ Formed in 2006, Three Peaks is run by husband and wife team Colin and Susan Ashwell. The brewery is located in the cellar of their home. One beer is brewed at present on their 1.25-barrel plant but more are planned.

Pen-y-Ghent Bitter (OG 1040, ABV 3.8%) ♦
Malt and fruit flavours dominate this mid-brown session bitter, with some bitterness coming through afterwards.

Three Rivers

See 3 Rivers

Three Tuns SIBA

Three Tuns Brewery, 16 Market Square, Bishop's Castle, Shropshire, SY9 5BN
☎ **(01588) 638392**
✉ **tunsbrewery@aol.com**
🌐 **threetunsbrewery.co.uk**
Shop Mon-Fri 9am-5pm
Tours by arrangement

⊗ Brewing started on the site in 1642. In the 1970s the Three Tuns was one of only four brew-pubs left in the country. Nowadays the brewery and Three Tuns pub are separate businesses. Plans to increase the brew length are in progress. Around 125 outlets are supplied. Seasonal beers: see website.

1642 Bitter (OG 1042, ABV 3.8%)
A golden ale with a light, nutty maltiness and spicy bitterness.

XXX (OG 1046, ABV 4.3%) ♦
A pale, sweetish bitter with a light hop aftertaste that has a honey finish.

Cleric's Cure (OG 1059, ABV 5%)
A light tan coloured ale with a malty sweetness. Strong and spicy with a floral bitterness.

Thwaites IFBB

Daniel Thwaites plc, Star Brewery, PO Box 50, Blackburn, Lancashire, BB1 5BU
☎ **(01254) 686868**
✉ **marketing@thwaites.co.uk**
🌐 **thwaites.co.uk**
Tours by arrangement

⊛ Established in 1807, Thwaites is still controlled by the Yerburgh family, decendents of the founder, Daniel Thwaites. The company owns around 400 pubs. Real ale is available in about 60% of these but Nutty Black is hard to find. Seasonal beers appear regularly throughout the year – see website for more information.

Nutty Black (OG 1036, ABV 3.3%) ♦
A tasty traditional dark mild presenting a malty flavour with caramel notes and a slightly bitter finish.

Original (OG 1036, ABV 3.6%) ♦
Hop driven, yet well-balanced amber session bitter. Hops continue through to the long finish.

Wainwright (OG 1042, ABV 4.1%)
A straw-coloured bitter with soft fruit flavours and a hint of malty sweetness.

Lancaster Bomber (OG 1044, ABV 4.4%) ♦
Well-balanced, copper-coloured best bitter with firm malt flavours, a fruity background and a long, dry finish.

Tigertops SIBA

Tigertops Brewery, 22 Oaks Street, Flanshaw, Wakefield, West Yorkshire, WF2 9LN
☎ (01229) 716238 / (01924) 897728
✉ tigertopsbrewery@hotmail.com

Tigertops was established in 1995 by Stuart Johnson and his wife Lynda. They own the brewery as well as running the Foxfield brew-pub in Cumbria (qv) but Tigertops is run on their behalf by Barry Smith. Five outlets are supplied. Seasonal beers: Billy Bock (ABV 7.9%, Nov-Feb), May Bock (ABV 6.2%, May-Jun), 8 Ace (ABV 8%, May).

Axeman's Block (OG 1036, ABV 3.6%)
A malty beer with a good hop finish.

Busy Lizzy (ABV 3.6%)

Dark Wheat Mild (OG 1036, ABV 3.6%)
An unusual mild made primarily with wheat malt.

Tom Tom Mild (ABV 3.7%)
Dark rye mild.

Thor Bitter (OG 1038, ABV 3.8%)
A light, hoppy bitter.

Blanche de Newland (OG 1044, ABV 4.5%)
A cloudy Belgian-style wheat beer.

Ginger Fix (OG 1044, ABV 4.6%)
A mid-amber ginger beer.

White Max (OG 1044, ABV 4.6%)
A light, German-style wheat beer.

Uber Weiss (OG 1046, ABV 4.8%)
A dark, German-style wheat beer.

Big Ginger (OG 1058, ABV 6%)
A strong, amber ginger beer.

Tindall EAB

Tindall Ales Brewery, Toad Lane, Seething, Norfolk, NR35 2EQ
☎ (01508) 483844
☎ 07795 113163
✉ greenangela5@aol.com
Shop Tue & Wed 9.30am-12.30pm
Tours by arrangement

Tindall Ales was established in 1998 and was situated on the edge of the medieval Tindall wood but moved to new premises in 2001. It is a family-run business and now only brews on a seasonal basis, meaning supply is limited. Bottle-conditioned beers are available.

Best Bitter (ABV 3.7%)

Mild (ABV 3.7%)

Alltime (ABV 4%)

Autumn (ABV 4%)

Ditchingham Dam (ABV 4.2%)

Seething Pint (ABV 4.3%)

Norfolk 'n' Good (ABV 4.6%)

Norwich Dragon (ABV 4.6%)

Honeydo (ABV 5%)

Tintagel (NEW)

Tintagel Brewery, Condolden Farm, Condolden, Tintagel, Cornwall, PL34 0HJ
☎ (01840) 216671
✉ john@condolden.wanadoo.co.uk
tintagelbrewery.co.uk

This 7.5-barrel brewery was established in early 2009 in a redundant milk parlour on the highest farm in Cornwall.

Castle Gold (ABV 3.8%)

Gull Rock (ABV 4.2%)

Tipples EAB

Tipples Brewery, Units 5 & 6, Damgate Lane Industrial Estate, Acle, Norwich, Norfolk, NR13 3DJ
☎ (01493) 741007
✉ brewery@tipplesbrewery.com
tipplesbrewery.com

Tipples was established by Jason Tipple in 2004 on a six-barrel brew plant supplied by Porter Brewing Company and produces both cask and bottle-conditioned ales. The brewery expanded in 2007 and opened a brewery shop on Elm Hill in Norwich the same year. There are plans for further expansion with an increase in the product range and diversity. Seasonal beers: Lazy Summer (ABV 4.3%, May-Sep), Crackle (ABV 6.5%, Nov-Feb).

Longshore (OG 1036, ABV 3.6%) ◆
Yellow hued with a soft, peachy aroma and creamy mouthfeel. The initial fruity apricot flavour quickly subsides to a long, dry bitterness.

Ginger (ABV 3.8%) ◆
A spicy aroma introduces this well-balanced yellow-gold brew. Ginger dominates but does not overwhelm the supporting malty bitterness. Quick ginger nut finish.

Hanged Monk (ABV 4%) ◆
Well balanced with the dominant roast notes in both aroma and taste countered by a host of other flavours. A bittersweet maltiness with a hint of caramel at the start gives depth. Long coffee-like finish.

Lady Evelyn (OG 1041, ABV 4.1%) ◆
A crisp hoppy aroma introduces this lively pale ale. Bitterness and hop loom large in the taste throughout. Some malt and sweetness take the edge off as a background smoky flavour becomes apparent.

Redhead (OG 1042, ABV 4.2%) ◆
Malt and hops are well matched in both nose and palate. Toffee in the nose and initial taste soon gives way to an increasing bitterness. A fine finale retains the mix of flavours.

Topper (ABV 4.5%) ◆
Black-hued stout. Coffee and dark chocolate to the fore in all aspects. A roast-flavoured beer with just enough malt sweetness and bitterness to provide a counterpoint. Strong, big-hearted fiinish.

Brewers Progress (ABV 4.6%) ◆
Copper coloured with a fruity character. Plums and raisins in the initial taste add to the hops and malt to give a trio of flavours that flow through to a sustained finale.

Moonrocket (ABV 5%) ◆
A complex golden brew with an earthy aroma. Malt hop bitterness and a fruity sweetness swirl round in an ever-changing kaleidoscope of flavours. A satisfying finish with hops finally emerging on top.

Jacks' Revenge (ABV 5.8%) ◆

An explosion of malt, chocolate, roast and plum pudding fruitiness. Full-bodied with a deep red hue and a strong solid finish that develops into a vinous fruitiness.

Tipsy Toad

See Jersey

Tirril SIBA

Tirril Brewery Ltd, Red House, Long Marton, Appleby-in-Westmorland, Cumbria, CA16 6BN
☎ **(01768) 361846**
✉ **enquiries@tirrilbrewery.co.uk**
🌐 **tirrilbrewery.co.uk / tirrilales.co.uk**
Tours by arrangement

Tirril Brewery was established in 1999 in an abandoned toilet block behind the Queen's Head in Tirril. Since then it has relocated to the 1823 gothic brewing rooms at Brougham Hall and is now at the Red House Barn in Long Marton beneath the Pennines. Capacity has grown from 2.25 barrels to 20 barrels over the years. Around 70 outlets are supplied and one pub is owned. Seasonal beers: Graduate (ABV 4.6%, Dec), Balls Up (ABV 3.9%, summer).

John Bewsher's Best Bitter (OG 1038.5, ABV 3.8%)
A lightly-hopped, golden brown session beer, named after the landlord and brewer at the Queen's Head in the 1830s.

Brougham Ale (OG 1039, ABV 3.9%)
A gently hopped, amber bitter.

Charles Gough's Old Faithful (OG 1040, ABV 4%)
Initially bitter, gold-coloured ale with an astringent finish.

1823 (OG 1041, ABV 4.1%)
A full-bodied session bitter with a gentle bitterness.

Amber's Ale (OG 1041.5, ABV 4.2%)
Rosy golden ale. Light and hoppy.

Thomas Slee's Academy Ale (OG 1041.5, ABV 4.2%)
A dark, full-bodied, traditional rich and malty ale.

Red Barn Ale (OG 1043, ABV 4.4%)
A ruby red ale with a strong hop finish.

Titanic SIBA

Titanic Brewery Co Ltd, Unit 5, Callender Place, Burslem, Stoke-on-Trent, Staffordshire, ST6 1JL
☎ **(01782) 823447**
✉ **titanic@titanicbrewery.co.uk**
🌐 **titanicbrewery.co.uk**
Tours by arrangement

Founded in 1985, the brewery is named in honour of Captain Smith who hailed from the Potteries and had the misfortune to captain the Titanic. A monthly seasonal beer provides the opportunity to offer distinctive beers of many styles, each with a link to the liner. Titanic supplies 300 free trade outlets throughout the country. The brewery has a small, constantly expanding tied house estate. Bottle-conditioned beer is also available.

Mild (OG 1036, ABV 3.5%)
Fruity plum aroma and sweet fruity start. Fruity throughout with roast leading to a dry bitterness.

Steerage (OG 1036, ABV 3.5%)
Hoppy aroma with fruity hints. Gentle start then a developing zesty bitterness. Well balanced for a light session beer with a long, dry finish.

Lifeboat (OG 1040, ABV 4%)
Tawny beer with a roast, caramel and fruity aroma, sweet fruity start with biscuity malt leading to a sweet finish with residual bitterness.

Anchor Bitter (OG 1042, ABV 4.1%)
Spicy, peppery aroma, a sweet fruity start, a mouth-watering and spicy middle, and then a clean dry bitter finish.

Iceberg (OG 1042, ABV 4.1%)
Floral and citrus aroma. Lemon and grapefruit bitterness from the start. Refreshingly hoppy with a dry finish.

Stout (OG 1046, ABV 4.5%)
Roasty, toasty with tobacco, autumn bonfires, chocolate and hints of liquorice; perfectly balanced with a bitter, dry finish reminiscent of real coffee.

White Star (OG 1050, ABV 4.8%)
Honey and spice aroma belies the sharp, crisp and zesty taste leaving a satisfying hop bite and bitter finish.

Captain Smith's Strong Ale (OG 1054, ABV 5.2%)
Lots of apple aroma with a hint of honey. Quite malty throughout but finishing on a bittersweet note.

Toll End

Toll End Brewery, c/o Waggon & Horses, 131 Toll End Road, Tipton, West Midlands, DY4 0ET
☎ **07903 725574**
Tours by arrangement

The four-barrel brewery opened in 2004. With the exception of Phoebe's Ale, named after the brewer's daughter, all brews commemorate local landmarks, events and people. Toll End is brewing to full capacity and produces around 300 gallons a week. Four outlets are supplied. Several specials are also brewed throughout the year.

William Perry (OG 1043, ABV 4.3%)

Phoebe's Ale/PA (OG 1044, ABV 4.4%)

Polly Stevens (OG 1044, ABV 4.4%)

Black Bridge (OG 1046, ABV 4.6%)

Tipton Pride (OG 1046, ABV 4.6%)

Power Station (OG 1049, ABV 4.9%)
Cask-conditioned lager.

Tollgate SIBA

Tollgate Brewery, Unit 8, Viking Business Centre, High Street, Woodville, Swadlincote, Derbyshire, DE11 7EH
☎ **(01283) 229194**
✉ **tollgatebrewery@tiscali.co.uk**
Tours by arrangement

Tollgate, a six-barrel brewery that opened in 2005, is on the site of the old Brunt & Bucknall Brewery, which was bought and closed by Bass in 1927. More than 70 outlets are supplied. Seasonal beer: Woodville Pale (ABV 4%, May-Jun), Summer Pale (ABV 4.2%, Jun-Aug), Stout Porter (ABV 4.3%,

THE BREWERIES

Oct-Jan), Snowy (ABV 4.5%, Dec-Jan), Tollgate Light (ABV 4.5%, Jun-Sep), Billy's Best Bitter (ABV 4.6%, Sep-Mar), Tollgate Cracker (ABV 4.6%, Dec), Portly Porter (ABV 4.8%, Oct-Jan). Bottle-conditioned beers are also available.

Mellow Yellow (OG 1042, ABV 4%)

Mild (OG 1044, ABV 4.2%)

Bitter (OG 1045, ABV 4.3%)

Red Star IPA (OG 1047, ABV 4.5%)

Red McAdy (OG 1052, ABV 5%)

For Harrington Arms, Thulston:

Earl's Ale (OG 1042, ABV 4%)

Tomos Watkin

See under 'W'

Topsham & Exminster

See Exeter

Tower SIBA

Tower Brewery, Old Water Tower, Walsitch Maltings, Glensyl Way, Burton upon Trent, Staffordshire, DE14 1LX
☎ (01283) 530695
✉ towerbrewery@aol.com
Tours by arrangement

Tower was established in 2001 by John Mills, previously the brewer at Burton Bridge, in a converted derelict water tower of Thomas Salt's maltings. The conversion was given a Civic Society award for the restoration of a Historic Industrial Building in 2001. Tower has 20 regular outlets. Seasonal beers: Sundowner (ABV 4%, May-Aug), Spring Equinox (ABV 4.6%, Mar-May), Autumn Equinox (ABV 4.6%, Sep-Nov), Winter Spirit (ABV 5%).

Thomas Salt's Bitter (OG 1038, ABV 3.8%)

Bitter (OG 1042, ABV 4.2%)
Gold coloured with a malty, caramel and hoppy aroma. A full hop and fruit taste with the fruit lingering. A bitter and astringent finish.

Malty Towers (OG 1044, ABV 4.4%)
Yellow with a malty aroma and a hint of tobacco. Strong hops give a long, dry, bitter finish with pleasant astringency.

Pale Ale (OG 1048, ABV 4.8%)

Tower of Strength (OG 1076, ABV 7.6%)

For Castle Rock, Nottingham:

Sheriff's Tipple (OG 1035, ABV 3.5%)
A light-tawny session bitter with distinctive hop character.

For Hoskins Brothers, Leicester:

Hob Best Mild (ABV 3.5%)

Brigadier Bitter (ABV 3.6%)

Hob Bitter (ABV 4%)

White Dolphin (ABV 4%)

Tom Kelly's Stout (ABV 4.2%)

EXS (ABV 5%)

Ginger Tom (ABV 5.2%)

Old Navigation Ale (ABV 7%)

For Steamin' Billy Brewing Co (qv):

Billy's Last Bark (OG 1038, ABV 3.8%)

Grand Prix Mild (OG 1038, ABV 3.8%)

Steamin' Billy Bitter (OG 1043, ABV 4.3%)
Brown-coloured best bitter. Initial malt and hops aromas are superseded by fruit and hop taste and aftertaste, accompanied by a refreshing bitterness.

Lazy Summer (OG 1045, ABV 4.5%)

Skydiver (OG 1050, ABV 5%)
Full-bodied, strong, mahogany-coloured beer in which an initial malty aroma is followed by a characteristic malty sweetness that is balanced by a hoppy bitterness.

Townes SIBA

Townes Brewery, Speedwell Inn, Lowgates, Staveley, Chesterfield, Derbyshire, S43 3TT
☎ (01246) 472252
✉ curly@townes48.wanadoo.co.uk
Tours by arrangement

Townes Brewery started in 1994 in an old bakery on the outskirts of Chesterfield using a five-barrel plant. It was the first brewery in the town for more than 40 years. In 1997, the Speedwell Inn at Staveley was bought and the plant was moved to the rear of the pub, becoming the first brew-pub in north Derbyshire in the 20th century. Seasonal beers: Stargazer (ABV 4.7%, Dec-Jan), Sunshine (ABV 3.7%, Jul-Aug). Bottle-conditioned beers are also available and are suitable for vegetarians and vegans.

Speedwell Bitter (OG 1039, ABV 3.9%)
Well-balanced amber bitter with little aroma. Hints of caramel and hops lead to a bitterness developing in the long aftertaste.

Lowgate Light (OG 1041, ABV 4.1%)

Staveley Cross (OG 1043, ABV 4.3%)
Amber-gold best bitter with a faint caramel aroma. Hoppy with bitterness present throughout, culminating in a very long, dry, slightly astringent aftertaste.

IPA (OG 1045, ABV 4.5%)
Well-crafted flavoursome IPA of little aroma and a good bittersweet balanced taste. This leads to a lingering aftertaste, which is predominantly sweet with hoppy undertones.

Pynot Porter (ABV 4.5%)
Classic red-brown porter with a faint malt and roast aroma. Roast malt flavours combine with vine fruit, becoming increasingly bitter towards the finish.

Staveleyan (OG 1049, ABV 4.9%)

Townhouse

Townhouse Brewery, Units 1-4, Townhouse Studios, Townhouse Farm, Alsager Road, Audley, Staffordshire, ST7 8JQ
☎ 07976 209437/07812 035143
✉ j.nixon2@btinternet.com
Tours by arrangement

Townhouse was set up in 2002 with a 2.5-barrel plant. In 2004 the brewery scaled up to five-barrels. Demand is growing rapidly and in early 2006 two additional fermenting vessels were added. Bottling is planned. Some 30 outlets are supplied.

Audley Bitter (OG 1038, ABV 3.8%)
A pale, well-balanced session bitter with a citrus hop character.

Flowerdew (OG 1039, ABV 4%) ◆
Golden with a wonderful floral aroma. Fabulous flavour of flowery hops delivering a hoppy bite and presenting a lingering taste of flowery citrus waves.

Dark Horse (OG 1042, ABV 4.3%)
A dark ruby ale with malt character and late hoppy finish.

A'dleyweisse (OG 1043, ABV 4.5%)
An English style wheat beer, full-bodied and golden with a strongly defined fruity hop character and a dry finish.

Audley Gold (OG 1043, ABV 4.5%) ◆
Straw colour with a flower hop aroma hinting at lime and grapefruit. A grassy hop start gives plenty of bitterness and a dry but not astringent finish.

Barney's Stout (OG 1043, ABV 4.5%) ◆
Roast chocolate and toffee nose atop this black stout. Sweet start going bitter at the end, with roast throughout.

Armstrong Ale (OG 1045, ABV 4.8%)
A rich, fruity ruby red beer with a hoppy, dry finish.

Monument Ale (OG 1048, ABV 5%)
A copper-coloured, well-balanced strong ale with a pronounced malt character.

Traditional Scottish Ales

Traditional Scottish Ales Ltd, Unit 7c, Bandeath Industrial Estate, Stirling, FK7 7NP
☎ **(01786) 817000**
✉ **brewery@traditionalscottishales.com**
🌐 **traditionalscottishales.com**

◎ A new company set up in 2005 to develop and market the Bridge of Allan, Stirling and Trossach's Craft Brewery products. The brewery is located in a former torpedo factory. A five-barrel plant is used for cask ales and a custom-built 20-barrel plant is dedicated to bottled products. More than 200 outlets are supplied. Bottle-conditioned beer is available. All bottled ales are suitable for vegetarians and vegans.

Stirling Bitter (OG 1039, ABV 3.7%)

Ben Nevis Organic (OG 1042, ABV 4%) ◆
A traditional Scottish 80/-, with a distinctive roast and caramel character. Bittersweet fruit throughout provides the sweetness typical of a Scottish Heavy.

Stirling Brig (OG 1042, ABV 4.1%)

Bannockburn Ale (OG 1044, ABV 4.2%)

Glencoe Wild Oat Stout Organic (OG 1048, ABV 4.5%) ◆
A sweetish stout, surprisingly not dark in colour. Plenty of malt and roast balanced by fruit and finished with a hint of hop.

William Wallace (OG 1050, ABV 4.5%)

Ginger Explosion (OG 1052, ABV 5%)

Lomond Gold Organic (OG 1052, ABV 5%) ◆
A malty, bittersweet golden ale with plenty of fruity hop character.

Red Mist (OG 1052, ABV 5%)
A raspberry beer.

1488 (OG 1075, ABV 7%)

For Trossach's Craft Brewery:

Waylade (OG 1040, ABV 3.9%)

LadeBack (OG 1048, ABV 4.5%)

LadeOut (OG 1055, ABV 5.1%)

Traquair SIBA

Traquair House Brewery, Traquair House, Innerleithen, Peeblesshire, EH44 6PW
☎ **(01896) 830323**
✉ **enquiries@traquair.co.uk**
🌐 **traquair.co.uk/brewery**
Shop Easter-Oct 12-5pm daily (Jun-Aug 10.30am-5pm)
Tours by arrangement

The 18th-century brewhouse is based in one of the wings of the 1,000-year-old Traquair House, Scotland's oldest inhabited house. The brewhouse was rediscovered by the 20th Laird, the late Peter Maxwell Stuart, in 1965. He began brewing again using all the original equipment, which remained intact, despite having lain idle for more than 100 years. The brewery has been run by Peter's daughter, Catherine Maxwell Stuart, since his death in 1990. The Maxwell Stuarts are members of the Stuart clan, and the main Bear Gates will remain shut until a Stuart returns to the throne. All the beers are oak-fermented and 60 per cent of production is exported. Seasonal beer: Stuart Ale (ABV 4.5%, summer), Bear Ale (ABV 5%, winter).

Bear Ale (ABV 5%)

Laird's Liquor (ABV 6%)

Traquair House Ale (ABV 7%)

Jacobite Ale (ABV 8%)

Tring SIBA

Tring Brewery Co Ltd, 81-82 Akeman Street, Tring, Hertfordshire, HP23 6AF
☎ **(01442) 890721**
✉ **info@tringbrewery.co.uk**
🌐 **tringbrewery.co.uk**
Shop 9am-5pm (12pm Sat, 6pm Wed-Fri); closed Sun
Tours by arrangement (evenings only)

Founded in 1992, the Tring Brewery is based on a small industrial estate and brews 50 barrels a week. Most of the beers take their names from local myths and legends. In addition to the regular and seasonal ales, Tring brews a selection of monthly specials. There are plans to move the brewery to larger premises. Seasonal beers: Legless Lal's Winter Ale (ABV 4.5%), Royal Poacher (ABV 4.1%), Fanny Ebbs Summer Ale (ABV 3.9%), Huck-Me-Buck (ABV 4.4%), Santa's Little Helper (ABV 4.8%).

Side Pocket for a Toad (OG 1035, ABV 3.6%)
Citrus notes from American Cascade hops balanced with a floral aroma and a crisp, dry finish in a straw-coloured ale.

Brock Bitter (ABV 3.7%)
A light brown session ale with hints of sweetness and caramel, gentle bitterness and a floral aroma from Styrian hops.

Mansion Mild (ABV 3.7%)

Smooth and creamy dark ruby mild with a fruity palate and gentle late hop.

Blonde (OG 1039, ABV 4%)
A refreshing blonde beer with a fruity palate, balanced with a lingering hop aroma.

Ridgeway (OG 1039, ABV 4%)
Balanced malt and hop flavours with a dry, flowery hop aftertaste.

Jack O'Legs (OG 1041, ABV 4.2%)
A combination of four types of malt and two types of aroma hops provide a copper-coloured premium ale with full fruit and a distinctive hoppy bitterness.

Tea Kettle Stout (OG 1047, ABV 4.7%)
Rich and complex traditional stout with a hint of liquorice and moderate bitterness.

Colley's Dog (OG 1051, ABV 5.2%)
Dark but not over-rich, strong yet drinkable, this premium ale has a long dry finish with overtones of malt and walnuts.

Death or Glory (ABV 7.2%)
A strong, dark, aromatic barley wine.

Triple fff SIBA

Triple fff Brewing Co Ltd, Magpie Works, Station Approach, Four Marks, Alton, Hampshire, GU34 5HN
☎ (01420) 561422
sales-triplefbrewery@tiscali.co.uk
triplefff.com
Shop (ring for opening hours)
Tours by arrangement

The brewery was founded in 1997 with a five-barrel plant. Since then demand has rocketed with the brewery growing in size to a 50-barrel plant. The brewery has two of its own outlets, the Railway Arms in Alton and the White Lion in Aldershot, as well as supplying over 300 other outlets. Four core beers are available all year round, supplemented by some seasonals throughout the year.

Alton's Pride (ABV 3.8%)
This is an excellent, clean-tasting, golden brown session beer, full bodied for its strength with a glorious aroma of floral hops. An initially malty flavour fades as citrus notes and hoppiness take over, leading to a lasting hoppy, bitter finish

Pressed Rat & Warthog (ABV 3.8%)
Complex hoppy and bitter mild not in the classic style but nevertheless delicious. Ruby in colour, a roast malt aroma with hints of blackcurrant and chocolate lead to a well-balanced flavour with roast, fruit and malt vying with the hoppy bitterness and a dry, bitter finish.

Moondance (ABV 4.2%)
A pale brown coloured best bitter, wonderfully hopped with an aromatic citrus hop nose, balanced by bitterness and a hint of sweetness in the mouth. Bitterness increases in the finish as the fruit declines leading to a bittersweet finish.

Stairway (ABV 4.6%)
An aroma of pale and crystal malts introduces this pale brown beer with a flavour of summer fruits. Well-balanced with a dry, strong hoppy finish. Predominantly bitter, but with some sweetness and malt.

Trossach's Craft

See Traditional Scottish Ales

Tryst SIBA

Tryst Brewery, Lorne Road, Larbert, Stirling, FK5 4AT
☎ (01324) 554000
john@trystbrewery.co.uk
trystbrewery.co.uk
Shop Mon-Fri office hours; Sat am
Tours by arrangement

John McGarva, a member of Scottish Craft Brewers, started brewing in 2003 in an industrial unit near Larbert station. Around 50 outlets are supplied. Bottle-conditioned ales are available.

Brockville Dark (OG 1039, ABV 3.8%)

Brockville Pale (OG 1039, ABV 3.8%)
Golden session ale with a refreshing mix of fruit and malt that lingers in the aftertaste.

Bla'than (OG 1041, ABV 4%)
A strong floral nose and refreshing taste enhanced with elderflower and pale malts.

Drovers 80/- (OG 1041, ABV 4%)
Full-bodied with a hint of spice and malt.

Stars & Stripes (OG 1041, ABV 4%)
Golden ale with moderate bitterness and a subtle combination of malts.

Carronade IPA (OG 1043, ABV 4.2%)
Well-balanced with citrus flavours that linger on the palate.

Zetland Wheatbier (OG 1046, ABV 4.5%)
Refreshing with a distinctive banana nose.

RAJ IPA (OG 1055, ABV 5.5%)

Carron Oatmeal Stout (OG 1061, ABV 6.1%)

Tudor

Tudor Brewery, 1 Castle Meadow Park, Merthyr Road, Abergavenny, NP7 7RZ
☎ (01873) 735770
sales@tudorbrewery.co.uk
tudorbrewery.co.uk
Shop open daily 9am-5pm
Tours by arrangement

The Tudor Brewery was established in September 2007 in the Kings Arms pub in Abergavenny. Around 60 outlets are supplied direct. Seasonal beers: Black Mountain Porter (ABV 5%, Nov-Jan), Summer Ale (ABV 3.8%, May-Sep).

Blorenge (ABV 3.8%)

Skirrid (ABV 4.2%)

Sugar Loaf (ABV 4.7%)

Tunnel SIBA

Tunnel Brewery Ltd, c/o Lord Nelson Inn, Birmingham Road, Ansley, Nuneaton, Warwickshire, CV10 9PQ
☎ (02476) 396450
info@tunnelbrewery.co.uk
tunnelbrewery.co.uk
Tours by arrangement

Bob Yates and Mike Walsh started brewing in 2005, taking the name from a rail tunnel that passes under the village. Pub and brewery are independent of one another but the beers are available in the pub as well as being supplied to more than 100 other outlets. Brewing more than doubled in 2008 and a new unit for storage and bottling has been established. Seasonal beers: see website. Tunnel also brews for Battlefield Brewery, which will take over production once the brewery is built at Bosworth Battlefield Visitor Centre in Leicestershire. Bottle-conditioned beers are also available and are suitable for vegans (for both Tunnel and Battlefield).

Linda Lear Beer (OG 1038, ABV 3.7%)
A dark amber, fruity beer with a strong hop finish.

Let Battle Commence (OG 1038, ABV 3.8%)

Late Ott (OG 1040, ABV 4%)
Dark golden session bitter with a fruity nose and perfumed hop edge. The finish is dry and bitter.

Trade Winds (OG 1045, ABV 4.6%)
An aromatic, copper-coloured beer with an aroma of Cascade hops and a clean, crisp hint of citrus, followed by fruity malts and a dry finish full of scented hops.

Parish Ale (OG 1047, ABV 4.7%)
A reddish-amber, malty ale with a slight chocolate aroma enhanced by citrus notes. It becomes increasingly fruity as the English hops kick in. Smooth, gentle hop bitterness in the finish.

Shadow Weaver (OG 1046, ABV 4.7%)

Jean 'Cloudy' Van Damme (OG 1048, ABV 5%)

Stranger In The Mist (OG 1048, ABV 5%)

Nelson's Column (OG 1051, ABV 5.2%)
A ruby red, strong old English ale.

Boston Beer Party (OG 1056, ABV 5.6%)

For Battlefield Brewery:

Let Battle Commence (ABV 3.8%)

Richard III Plantagenet (ABV 4.2%)

Henry Tudor (ABV 5%)

Twickenham SIBA

Twickenham Fine Ales Ltd, Ryecroft Works, Edwin Road, Twickenham, Middlesex, TW2 6SP
☎ (020) 8241 1825
✉ info@twickenham-fine-ales.co.uk
🌐 twickenham-fine-ales.co.uk
Tours by arrangement

The 10-barrel brewery was set up in 2004 and was the first brewery in Twickenham since the 1920s. The brewery supplies around 300 pubs and clubs within ten miles of the brewery and selected outlets in central London. It is looking to expand capacity in 2009. Seasonal/occasional beers: see website.

Sundancer (OG 1037, ABV 3.7%) ◆
A golden beer with a lingering, dry, bitter aftertaste. Malty nose with a trace of fruit. Fruity citrus hops and sweetness on the palate.

Original (OG 1042, ABV 4.2%) ◆
Malt is balanced by fruit on the nose, which follows through into the flavour and aftertaste where hops are also present. Traditionally brown in colour.

Naked Ladies (OG 1044, ABV 4.4%) ◆
Full-bodied, dark golden ale with bitter hops balanced by a malty honey character that lingers. A little citrus can be picked up in the taste and finish.

Tydd Steam

Tydd Steam Brewery, Manor Barn, Kirkgate, Tydd Saint Giles, Cambridgeshire, PE13 5NE
☎ (01945) 871020
☎ 07932 726552
✉ info@tyddsteam.co.uk
🌐 tyddsteam.co.uk
Tours by arrangement

⊗ Tydd Steam opened in 2007 in a converted agricultural barn using a 5.5-barrel plant. A new eight-barrel plant was installed in 2009 to meet demand. The brewery is named after two farm steam engines which were formerly kept in the barn now used for brewing. The steam engines have now been moved to the Museum of Lincolnshire Life. 55 outlets are supplied direct. Seasonal/occasional beers: Summer Ale (ABV 3.8%), The Leveller (ABV 4.7%, winter), Yooligan (ABV 4.7%, Xmas), Iron Brew (ABV 4.2%, autumn), Flatlanders Gold (ABV 4%), Mother-in-Law (ABV 4.5%). Bottle-conditioned beers are also available on an occasional basis.

Barn Ale (OG 1038, ABV 3.9%)

Roadhouse Bitter (OG 1042, ABV 4.3%)

Piston Bob (OG 1044, ABV 4.6%)

Armageddon (OG 1049, ABV 5%)

Ufford

Ufford Ales Ltd, White Hart, Main Street, Ufford, Cambridgeshire, PE9 3BH
☎ (01780) 740250
✉ info@ufford-ales.co.uk
🌐 ufford-ales.co.uk
Tours by arrangement

⊗ Opened in early 2005, the brewery expanded in 2009 to produce 80 firkins of beer per week. It supplies 15 local outlets, 30 further afield and beer festivals. Bi-monthly special beers are produced and bottle-conditioned beer is also available.

White Hart (ABV 3.8%)

Nirvana (ABV 5.7%)

Uley

Uley Brewery Ltd, The Old Brewery, 31 The Street, Uley, Gloucestershire, GL11 5TB
☎ (01453) 860120
✉ chas@uleybrewery.com
🌐 uleybrewery.com

⊗ Brewing at Uley began in 1833 as Price's Brewery. After a long gap, the premises were restored and Uley Brewery opened in 1985. It has its own spring water, which is used to mash in with Tucker's Maris Otter malt and boiled with Herefordshire hops. Uley serves 40-50 free trade outlets in the Cotswold area and is brewing to capacity. Seasonal beers: Reverend Janet (ABV 4.3%), Gilt Edge (ABV 4.5%).

Hogshead Cotswold Pale Ale (OG 1030, ABV 3.5%) ◆
A pale-coloured, hoppy session bitter with a good hop aroma and a full flavour for its strength, ending in a bittersweet aftertaste.

Bitter (OG 1040, ABV 4%) ◆

A copper-coloured beer with hops and fruit in the aroma and a malty, fruity taste, underscored by a hoppy bitterness. The finish is dry, with a balance of hops and malt.

Laurie Lee's Bitter (OG 1045, ABV 4.5%)
A copper-coloured, full-flavoured, hoppy bitter with some fruitiness and a smooth, long, balanced finish.

Old Ric (OG 1045, ABV 4.5%) ◈
A full-flavoured, hoppy bitter with some fruitiness and a smooth, balanced finish. Distinctively copper-coloured, this is the house beer for the Old Spot Inn, Dursley.

Old Spot Prize Strong Ale (OG 1050, ABV 5%) ◈
A distinctive full-bodied, red/brown ale with a fruity aroma, a malty, fruity taste, with a hoppy bitterness, and a strong, balanced aftertaste.

Pig's Ear Strong Beer (OG 1050, ABV 5%) ◈
A pale-coloured beer, deceptively strong. Notably bitter in flavour, with a hoppy, fruity aroma and a bitter finish.

Ulverston

Ulverston Brewing Co, Diamond Buildings, Pennington Lane, Lindal in Furness, Cumbria, LA12 0LA
☎ (01229) 584280
☎ 07840 192022
✉ info.ubc@tiscali.co.uk
🌐 ulverstonbrewing.co.uk

The brewery went into production in 2006, the first beers to be brewed in Ulverston since the closure of Hartleys in 1991. It is situated in the old engine house of the long extinct Lindal Moor Mining Company. Most of the beers are named using a Laurel and Hardy theme after Ulverston's most famous son, Stan Laurel. Seasonal beers: What the Dickens (ABV 4%, Nov), Stout Ollie (ABV 4.3%), Bad Medicine (ABV 6.3%).

Flying Elephants (OG 1037, ABV 3.7%)

Celebration Ale (OG 1039, ABV 3.9%)

Harvest Moon (OG 1039, ABV 3.9%)

Another Fine Mess (OG 1040, ABV 4%) ◈
A refreshing gold-coloured bitter. Initially fruity but with a rising bitterness.

Laughing Gravy (OG 1040, ABV 4%)

Lonesome Pine (OG 1042, ABV 4.2%) ◈
A fresh and fruity pale gold beer; honeyed, lemony and resiny with an increasingly bitter finish.

Uncle Stuarts

Uncle Stuarts Brewery, Wroxham Barns, Tunstead Road, Hoveton, Norwich, Norfolk, NR12 8QU
☎ (01603) 783888
✉ stuartsbrewery@aol.com
Tours by arrangement

The brewery started in 2002, selling bottle-conditioned beers and polypins direct to customers and by mail order. In 2009 the brewery moved to Wroxham Barns Craft Centre. The beers are also available in nine-gallon casks. Seasonal beer: Xmas (ABV 7%).

North Norfolk Beauty (ABV 3.8%)

Pack Lane (OG 1038, ABV 4%)

Excelsior (ABV 4.5%)

Local Hero (ABV 4.7%)

Wroxham Barns Bitter (ABV 4.8%)

Norwich Castle (ABV 5%)

Buckenham Woods (OG 1051, ABV 5.6%) ◈
Spicy with more than a hint of raisin and sultana. Heavy aroma translates into a richly-flavoured ale with a surprisingly light and creamy mouthfeel.

Strumpshaw Fen (ABV 5.7%)

Norwich Cathedral (ABV 6.5%)

Union

Union Brewery, Dartmoor Union, Fore Street, Holbeton, Devon, PL8 1NE
☎ (01752) 830460
🌐 dartmoorunion.co.uk

⊠ The Union Brewery started as a pipe dream. It is now in the hands of very enthusiastic amateurs and is in full (although small) production.

Pride (OG 1037, ABV 3.9%)

Jacks (OG 1045, ABV 4.5%)

Ushers

See Wadworth and Wychwood

Vale SIBA

Vale Brewery Co, Tramway Business Park, Ludgershall Road, Brill, Buckinghamshire, HP18 9TY
☎ (01844) 239237
✉ info@valebrewery.co.uk
🌐 valebrewery.co.uk

Established in 1994 and initially based in Haddenham, Vale moved to Brill in 2007. Four pubs are owned, including brewery tap the Hop Pole in Aylesbury. There is a brewery shop open to the public. Seasonal and monthly specials: see website. A wide range of bottle-conditioned beers are available. Personalised bottling is also undertaken. All beers are suitable for vegans.

Best Bitter (OG 1036, ABV 3.7%) ◈
This pale amber beer starts with a slight fruit aroma. This leads to a clean, bitter taste where hops and fruit dominate. The finish is long and bitter with a slight hop note.

Black Swan Mild (OG 1038, ABV 3.9%)
Dark and smooth with hints of chocolate and coffee on the nose and a malty, dry finish.

Wychert Ale (OG 1038, ABV 3.9%)
A traditional Thames Valley beer. Woody flavours are notable in this malty beer with a finish of port and berries on the nose.

VPA/Vale Pale Ale (OG 1042, ABV 4.2%)
An assertive, dry, hoppy ale with a citrus nose, combined with a pronounced malt background.

Black Beauty Porter (OG 1043, ABV 4.3%) ◈
A very dark ale, the initial aroma is malty. Roast malt dominates initially and is followed by a rich fruitiness, with some sweetness. The finish is increasingly hoppy and dry.

Edgar's Golden Ale (OG 1043, ABV 4.3%) ◈

A golden, hoppy best bitter with some sweetness and a dry, bittersweet finish. An unpretentious and well-crafted beer.

Special (OG 1046, ABV 4.5%)
Premium ale with a rich, complex and satisfying finish.

Grumpling Premium Ale (OG 1046, ABV 4.6%)
A rich, warming ruby brown traditional English bitter with mellow fruity malt flavours accompanied by a subtle dry, hoppy finish.

Gravitas (OG 1047, ABV 4.8%)
A strong, pale ale packed with hop and citrus flavours, rounded off by a dry, malty, biscuit finish. A pronounced hop aroma throughout.

Vale of Glamorgan

Vale of Glamorgan Brewery Ltd, Unit 8a, Atlantic Trading Estate, Barry, Vale of Glamorgan, CF63 3RF
☎ (01446) 730757
✉ info@vogbrewery.co.uk
🌐 vogbrewery.co.uk
Tours by arrangement (max. 15 people)

Vale of Glamorgan Brewery started brewing in 2005 on a 10-barrel plant. More than 40 local outlets are supplied. Occasional beer: Oggy VoG (ABV 4%). Seasonal beers are brewed and bottle-conditioned beers are available.

Grog Y VoG (OG 1043, ABV 4.3%)

VoG Best (OG 1040, ABV 4.3%)

For Mochyn Du, Cardiff:

Cwrw'r Mochyn (ABV 4%)

Valhalla

Valhalla Brewery, Shetland Refreshments Ltd, Baltasound, Unst, Shetland, ZE2 9DX
☎ (01957) 711658
✉ mail@valhallabrewery.co.uk
🌐 valhallabrewery.co.uk
Tours by arrangement

The brewery started production in 1997, set up by husband and wife team Sonny and Sylvia Priest. A bottling plant was installed in 1999 and work on a new brewhouse is proceeding. One outlet is supplied direct.

White Wife (OG 1038, ABV 3.8%)
Predominantly malty aroma with hop and fruit, which remain on the palate. The aftertaste is increasingly bitter.

Old Scatness (OG 1038, ABV 4%)
A light bitter, named after an archaeological dig at the south end of Shetland where early evidence of malting and brewing was found. One of the ingredients is an ancient strain of barley called Bere which used to be common in Shetland until the middle of the last century.

Simmer Dim (OG 1039, ABV 4%)
A light golden ale, named after the long Shetland twilight. The sulphur features do not mask the fruits and hops of this well-balanced beer.

Auld Rock (OG 1043, ABV 4.5%)
A full-bodied, dark Scottish-style best bitter, it has a rich malty nose but does not lack bitterness in the long dry finish.

Sjolmet Stout (OG 1048, ABV 5%)
Full of malt and roast barley, especially in the taste. Smooth, creamy, fruity finish, not as dry as some stouts.

Verulam

See Alehouse

Village Brewer

See Hambleton

Wadworth IFBB

Wadworth & Co Ltd, Northgate Brewery, Devizes, Wiltshire, SN10 1JW
☎ (01380) 723361
✉ sales@wadworth.co.uk
🌐 wadworth.co.uk
Shop Mon-Fri 10am-6pm (4.30pm winter); Sat 10am (11am winter)-4pm
Tours by arrangement

A market town brewery set up in 1885 by Henry Wadworth, it is one of few remaining producers to sell beer locally in oak casks; the brewery still employs a cooper. Though solidly traditional, with its own dray horses, it continues to invest in the future and to expand, producing up to 2,000 barrels per week to supply a wide-ranging free trade, around 300 outlets in the south of England, as well as its own 259 pubs. All tied houses serve cask beer. Wadworth also has a 2.5-barrel micro-brewery used for brewing trials, speciality brews and the production of cask mild. Seasonal beers: see website.

Pint Size Mild (OG 1033, ABV 3.3%)
A classic mild. Deep ruby red with a hint of coffee and smoky flavours.

Henry's Original IPA (OG 1035, ABV 3.6%)
A light copper bitter with a delicate malt aroma and slight hoppiness.

Horizon (OG 1039, ABV 4%)
A pale gold beer with zesty citrus and hop aromas and a crisp, tangy finish on the palate.

6X (OG 1041, ABV 4.3%)
Copper-coloured ale with a malty and fruity nose, and some balancing hop character. The flavour is similar, with some bitterness and a lingering malty, but bitter finish.

JCB (OG 1046, ABV 4.7%)
A well-balanced deep copper beer with a hoppy aroma.

The Bishops Tipple (OG 1048, ABV 5%)
A golden brew giving well-balanced hop bitterness and a clean finish.

Waen (NEW)

Waen Brewery Ltd, Unit 5, Penstrowed, SY17 5SG
☎ (01686) 627042
✉ info@thewaenbrewery.co.uk
🌐 thewaenbrewery.co.uk

Waen Brewery began brewing in 2009 on a five-barrel plant. Special beers are often brewed and bottle-conditioned beers are available.

First of the Summer Waen (OG 1040, ABV 4%)
A light summer beer, full of fruity flavour.

Festival Landmark Waen (OG 1042, ABV 4.2%)

Brewster's Waen (OG 1046, ABV 4.8%)
Dark, rich red ale. Hoppy and malty.

Landmark Waen (OG 1052, ABV 5.5%)
Light-coloured beer with an aroma of hops and lemon balm.

Wagtail

Wagtail Brewery, New Barn Farm, Wilby Warrens, Old Buckenham, Norfolk, NR17 1PF
☎ (01953) 887133
✉ wagtailbrewery@btinternet.com
🌐 wagtailbrewery.com

Wagtail brewery went into full-time production in 2006. All cask-conditioned beers are also available bottle conditioned and are suitable for vegetarians and vegans.

Best Bittern (OG 1040, ABV 4%)

Gold Rush (OG 1040, ABV 4%)
A sulphurous peppery aroma. A rolling mix of hops and bitterness give a spicy taste to this golden ale. A quick finish leaves a fruity sulphurous taste.

King Tut (OG 1040, ABV 4%)
Golden hued with a grainy character. A gentle bittersweet introduction with grapefruit notes. Flavours rub gently together towards a dry slightly astringent finish.

Royal Norfolk (OG 1040, ABV 4%)
A bitter beer with hops and malt giving depth. Pale brown with a slightly sulphurous nose. A softly receding finish with smoky overtones.

English Ale (OG 1042, ABV 4.2%)
Lots of malt and roast notes in the aroma. Chocolate and vine fruit are to the fore in the first taste. Background hop and bitter notes soon fade with the other flavours to leave a single raisin-like taste.

Black Beauty (OG 1044, ABV 4.5%)
Roast is well supported by malt and bitterness throughout. Background traces of hop, raisin and sweetness add character. A dry, bitter ending with roast and malt support.

Black Shuck (OG 1044, ABV 4.5%)
Black and brooding, as befits a Norfolk legend. Deep roast notes hold this classic stout together. A grainy mouthfeel is in keeping with the roast character. Malt and bitterness provide contrasting flavours.

Hornblower (OG 1044, ABV 4.5%)
Dominated by malt in both aroma and taste. Bitterness introduces a different perspective and gives balance. A grainy texture with caramel and soft fruit notes. A tapering, dry finish.

Jumping Jericho (OG 1050, ABV 5.2%)

Wapping

Wapping Beers Ltd, Baltic Fleet, 33a Wapping, Liverpool, Merseyside, L1 8DQ
☎ (0151) 707 2247 (Brewery) / (0151) 709 3116 (Pub)
✉ simon@wappingbeers.co.uk
🌐 wappingbeers.co.uk
Tours by arrangement

Wapping was established in 2002 using the kit from Passageway Brewery, in the cellar of the Baltic Fleet pub on the waterfront in Liverpool. Around 20 new beers are produced each year, the best of which are added to the permanent beers list. Seasonal beers: Tabley Dark (ABV 3.6%, May), Winter Ale (ABV 6.5%, Nov-Feb). Bottle-conditioned beers are also available.

Bitter (OG 1036, ABV 3.6%)
Light, easy-drinking session beer with a good, bitter finish.

Bowsprit (OG 1036, ABV 3.6%)
Dry, hoppy session beer with a satisfyingly dry, bitter aftertaste. Hint of fruitiness on the aroma.

Magna 800 (OG 1037, ABV 3.7%)

Baltic Gold (OG 1039, ABV 3.9%)
Hoppy golden ale with plenty of citrus hop flavour. Refreshing with good body and mouthfeel.

Beckwiths Bitter (OG 1039, ABV 3.9%)

Zebu (OG 1039, ABV 3.9%)

3 Sheets (OG 1040, ABV 4%)

Blonde Wheat (OG 1040, ABV 4%)

Brigantine Pilsner (OG 1040, ABV 4%)

Cutter Pilsner (OG 1040, ABV 4%)

Summer Ale (OG 1042, ABV 4.2%)
Refreshing golden beer with floral hops dominating the nose and taste. Some fruit also on the aroma and in the taste. Good bitterness throughout, leading to a dry, bitter aftertaste.

Smoked Porter (OG 1050, ABV 5%)

Stout (OG 1050, ABV 5%)
Classic dry roasty stout with strong bitterness balanced by fruit and hop flavours. The flavours follow through to a pleasantly dry finish.

Golden Promise IPA (OG 1052, ABV 5.5%)

Warcop

Warcop Country Ales, c/o 9 Nellive Park, Saint Brides Wentlooge, Gwent, NP10 8SE
☎ (01633) 680058
✉ wiliam.picton@tesco.net
🌐 warcopales.com

A small brewery at Newhouse Farm, Saint Brides Wentlooge, based in a converted milking parlour. Cask ales are also available bottle conditioned. The brewery has a portfolio of 28 beers which are made on a cyclical basis, with five to six beers normally in stock at any one time: see website for full range. Seasonal beers: see website.

Warrior

Warrior Brewing Co, c/o Coastal Brewery, Unit 9B, Cardrew Industrial Estate, Redruth, Cornwall, TR15 1SS
☎ (01736) 788586
✉ warrior@warrior.go-plus.net
🌐 jameswarrior.com

James and Jude Warrior started brewing in 2004. James has been a professional actor for 40 years and has to suspend brewing from time to time when he is called away to work in the theatre or appear before the cameras. The brewery moved to Cornwall from Exeter in 2009. Seasonal beer: Sitting Bull (ABV 5%, Dec-Feb).

Golden Wolf (OG 1041, ABV 4%)

A pale golden beer with a biting, clean first taste and a refreshing, floral finish.

Tomahawk (OG 1041, ABV 4%)
A dry, refreshing bitter, full of flavour with a strong, lingering, hoppy taste.

Geronimo (OG 1049, ABV 4.9%)
Full-bodied with a robust and rounded malty flavour and a long, bittersweet finish.

Crazy Horse (OG 1049, ABV 5%)
A light, golden beer with a subtle blend of four different hops and a fresh, dry, distinctive taste.

IPA (OG 1059, ABV 6%)

Warwickshire

Warwickshire Beer Co Ltd, The Brewery, Queen Street, Cubbington, Warwickshire, CV32 7NA
☎ (01926) 450747
✉ info@warwickshirebeer.co.uk
warwickshirebeer.co.uk
Shop open most days inc. Sat am (please ring first)

Warwickshire is a six-barrel brewery operating in a former village bakery since 1998. Brewing takes place four times a week. The cask beers are available in over 100 outlets as well as the brewery's three pubs. Seasonal beers: see website. Bottle-conditioned beers are also available.

Shakespeare's County (OG 1034, ABV 3.4%)
A very light session ale.

Best Bitter (OG 1039, ABV 3.9%)
A golden brown session bitter.

Lady Godiva (OG 1042, ABV 4.2%)
Blond, gentle, and full-bodied.

Falstaff (OG 1044, ABV 4.4%)

Churchyard Bob (OG 1049, ABV 4.9%)

Golden Bear (OG 1049, ABV 4.9%)
Golden in colour with well-balanced bitterness and spicy/fruity notes.

King Maker (OG 1055, ABV 5.5%)

Watermill

Watermill Brewing Co, Watermill Inn, Ings, Nr Windermere, Cumbria, LA8 9PY
☎ (01539) 821309
✉ info@lakelandpub.co.uk
lakelandpub.co.uk
Tours by arrangement

Watermill was established in 2006 in a purpose-built extension to the inn. The five-barrel plant and equipment were originally at the Hops Bar & Grill opposite Daytona International Speedway in Florida. The beers have a doggie theme; dogs are allowed in the main bar of the pub and usually get served with biscuits before their owners. The brewery was extended in 2008. Three local outlets are supplied as well as the pub itself. Malt grains are fed to their own herd of cattle.

Collie Wobbles (OG 1037.5, ABV 3.7%)
A pale gold bitter with a slight citrus taste. A good hop and malt balance gives way to a dry finish.

Black Beard (OG 1038, ABV 3.8%)
A dark mild with bags of fruit and malt flavours.

A Bit'er Ruff (OG 1041.5, ABV 4.1%)
Copper-coloured, balanced fruity beer with a lingering, bitter aftertaste.

Ruff Justice (OG 1041, ABV 4.2%)
A malty golden ale, well-balanced with caramel, light floral hops and a fresh, dry finish.

A Winters Tail (OG 1042, ABV 4.3%)
A warming, ruby-coloured bitter, smooth in the mouth with a subtle hint of ginger and orange. Well-balanced with a small amount of pale chocolate malt.

Isle of Dogs (OG 1044, ABV 4.5%)
A golden bitter with a fresh, malty aroma and a distinctive citrus fruity flavour with an intense, dry aftertaste.

Wruff Night (OG 1047.5, ABV 5%)
Straw-coloured, sweet and fruity, uncomplicated beer with bitterness in a short-lived aftertaste.

Dog'th Vaider (OG 1050, ABV 5.1%)
A dark, hoppy ale with a refreshing, dry finish.

Tomos Watkin SIBA

Hurns Brewing Co Ltd t/a Tomos Watkin, Unit 3, Alberto Road, Century Park, Valley Way, Swansea Enterprise Park, Swansea, SA6 8RP
☎ (01792) 797300
✉ phillparry@tomoswatkin.co.uk
hurns.co.uk
Shop Mon-Fri 9am-5pm
Tours by arrangement

Brewing started in 1995 in Llandeilo using a 10-barrel plant in converted garages. Tomos Watkin moved to bigger premises in Swansea in 2000 and the plant increased to a 50-barrel capacity. HBC Ltd was formed in 2002 when the Brewery was purchased from Tomos Watkin. Over 50% of production is now bottled beers (not bottle conditioned). More than 300 outlets are supplied. Seasonal beers: see website.

Cwrw Braf (OG 1038, ABV 3.7%)
A clean-drinking, amber-coloured ale with a light bitterness and gentle hop aroma.

Chwarae Teg (OG 1041, ABV 4.1%)
A golden ale with malty, nutty flavours.

Old Style Bitter/OSB (OG 1046, ABV 4.5%)
Amber-coloured with an inviting aroma of hops and malt. Full bodied; hops, fruit, malt and bitterness combine to give a balanced flavour continuing into the finish.

Aber Cwrw (ABV 4.7%)
An easy-drinking golden ale with a clean finish and balance.

Waveney

Waveney Brewing Co, Queen's Head, Station Road, Earsham, Norfolk, NR35 2TS
☎ (01986) 892623
✉ lyndahamps@aol.com

Established at the Queens Head in 2004, the five-barrel brewery produces three beers, regularly available at the pub along with free trade outlets. Occasional beers are brewed and there are plans to bottle beers. Seasonal beer: Raging Bullace (ABV 5.1%, Dec-Jan), Sugar Ray (ABV 4.4%, Mar-May), Great White Hope (ABV 4.8%).

East Coast Mild (OG 1037, ABV 3.8%)
A traditional mild with distinctive roast malt aroma and red-brown colouring. A sweet, plummy malt

THE BREWERIES

beginning quickly fades as a dry roasted bitterness begins to make its presence felt.

Lightweight (OG 1039, ABV 3.9%) ◆
A gentle beer with a light but well-balanced hop and malt character. A light body is reflected in the quick, bitter finish. Golden hued with a distinctive strawberry and cream nose.

Welterweight (OG 1042, ABV 4.2%)

Wayland's

Wayland's Brewery, 6 Marley Close, Addlestone, Surrey, KT15 1AR
☎ 07956 531618
✉ mail@waylandsbrewery.co.uk
🌐 waylandsbrewery.co.uk

⊗ Waylands was established in summer 2007 on a 2.5-barrel plant. It expanded quickly to a five-barrel plant to meet local demand. 32 outlets are supplied direct. Seasonal beers: Hare Hill (ABV 4.5%), Olympic Gold (ABV 3.9%), Carolinas Pale Ale (ABV 4%), Marley's Ghost (ABV 5.9%, Xmas), Winter Warmer (ABV 5%), Dark Knight Oatmeal Stout (ABV 4.2%).

Martian Mild (ABV 3.7%) ◆
Light mild with a biscuity aroma. Sweet and slightly bitter initially in the taste, getting increasingly dry in the finish.

Great British Ale (ABV 3.8%)

Addlestone Ale (OG 1043, ABV 4.2%) ◆
The pleasant estery aroma leads to a balanced taste where hops slightly dominate. This continues into the lingering aftertaste of this pale brown best bitter.

Blonde Belle (OG 1044, ABV 4.3%)
A pale golden-coloured ale with a mellow citrus flavour and a good hop character.

Special FX (ABV 4.8%)
A powerful, dark and complex ale with rich chocolate and roasted barley notes and a clean, bittersweet finish.

WC

WC Brewery, 3 Micklegate, Mickle Trafford, Chester, CH2 4TF
✉ thegents@wcbrewery.com
🌐 wcbrewery.com

Founded in 2003 by Ian Williams and Steve Carr, the WC Brewery is one of the smallest commercial breweries in the country. The Gents generally brew to order for local pubs and beer festivals. Seasonal beers: B'Day (ABV 3.8%, Jun), Autumn's Platter (ABV 4.3%), Yellow Snow (ABV 5%, Jan).

IP Ale (ABV 3.8%)
A pale beer, heavily hopped for extra bitterness and a lingering citrus finish.

Golden Cascade (ABV 4%)
A light and refreshing bitter with a distinct hoppy character.

Gypsy's Kiss (ABV 4.1%)
A copper-coloured ale, well-balanced with spicy citrus hops.

Lift a Buttercup (ABV 4.1%)
A refreshing pale ale with floral hop flavours.

SBD (ABV 5%)
A premium ale; rich, fruity and deceptively strong.

Weatheroak Hill (NEW)

Weatheroak Hill Brewery, Coach & Horses, Weatheroak Hill, Warwickshire, B48 7EA
☎ (01564) 823386 (pub)
Tours by arrangement

⊗ Weatheroak Hill started brewing in 2008. At present only the pub and beer festivals are supplied. Seasonal beers: Shires Ale (ABV 4.7%, summer), Radford Ale (ABV 4.7%, winter).

Icknield Pale Ale (OG 1038, ABV 3.8%)

Bitter (OG 1042, ABV 4.2%)

Weatheroak

Weatheroak Brewery Ltd, Unit 7, Victoria Works, Birmingham Road, Studley, Warwickshire, B80 7AP
☎ (0121) 445 4411 (eve)
☎ 07798 773894 (day)

Office: 25 Withybed Lane, Alvechurch, Birmingham, West Midlands, B48 7NX
✉ dave@weatheroakales.co.uk
🌐 weatheroakales.co.uk
Shop Fri & Sat 5.30-8.30pm

⊗ The brewery was set up in 1997 in an outhouse at the Coach & Horses, Weatheroak Hill. The first brew was produced in 1998. In 2008 it moved to Alvechurch (adjacent to the Weatheroak Ales Off-Licence – address to be used for correspondence) and then to a spacious factory unit in Studley, Warks. Weatheroak supplies 40 outlets. Seasonal beers are brewed on a regular basis.

Light Oak (ABV 3.6%) ◆
This straw-coloured quaffing ale has lots of hoppy notes on the tongue and nose, and a fleetingly sweet aftertaste.

Ale (ABV 4.1%) ◆
The aroma is dominated by hops in this golden-coloured brew. Hops also feature in the mouth and there is a rapidly fading dry aftertaste.

Keystone Hops (ABV 5%) ◆
A golden yellow beer that is surprisingly easy to quaff given the strength. Fruity hops are the dominant flavour without the commonly associated astringency.

For Gate Hangs Well, Woodgate:

Scoop (ABV 3.7%)
A honey beer with a pleasing bitter flavour and slightly sweet aftertaste.

Weetwood

Weetwood Ales Ltd, Weetwood Grange, Weetwood, Tarporley, Cheshire, CW6 0NQ
☎ (01829) 752377
✉ sales@weetwoodales.co.uk
🌐 weetwoodales.co.uk

The brewery was set up at an equestrian centre in 1993. In 1998, the five-barrel plant was replaced by a 10-barrel kit. Around 200 regular customers are supplied.

Best Bitter (OG 1038.5, ABV 3.8%) ◆
Pale brown beer with an assertive bitterness and a lingering dry finish. Despite initial sweetness, peppery hops dominate throughout.

Cheshire Cat (ABV 4%) ◆

Pale, dry bitter with a spritzy lemon zest and a grapy aroma. Hoppy aroma leads through to the initial taste before fruitiness takes over. Smooth creamy mouthfeel and a short, dry finish.

Eastgate Ale (OG 1043.5, ABV 4.2%) ◆
Well-balanced and refreshing clean amber beer. Citrus fruit flavours predominate in the taste and there is a short, dry aftertaste.

Old Dog Bitter (OG 1045, ABV 4.5%) ◆
Robust, well-balanced amber beer with a slightly fruity aroma. Rich malt and fruit flavours are balanced by bitterness. Some sweetness and a hint of sulphur on nose and taste.

Ambush Ale (OG 1047.5, ABV 4.8%) ◆
Full-bodied malty, premium bitter with initial sweetness balanced by bitterness and leading to a long-lasting dry finish. Blackberries and bitterness predominate alongside the hops.

Oasthouse Gold (OG 1050, ABV 5%) ◆
Straw-coloured, crisp, full-bodied and fruity golden ale with a good dry finish.

Wellington

See Crown

Wells & Young's

See New Nationals section

Welton's SIBA

Welton's Brewery, 1 Mulberry Trading Estate, Foundry Lane, Horsham, West Sussex, RH13 5PX
☎ **(01403) 242901/251873**
✉ **sales@weltons.co.uk**
🌐 **weltonsbeer.com**
Tours by arrangement

Ray Welton moved his brewery to a factory unit in Horsham in 2003, which has given him space to expand. Many different beers are brewed throughout the year. Around 400 outlets are supplied. Bottle-conditioned beers are available.

Pride 'n' Joy (ABV 2.8%) ◆
A light brown bitter with a slight malty and hoppy aroma. Fruity with a pleasant hoppiness and some sweetness in the flavour, leading to a short malty finish.

Horsham Bitter (ABV 3.8%)
Amber-coloured, bitter but with a huge aroma.

Old Cocky (OG 1043, ABV 4.3%)

Horsham Old (OG 1046, ABV 4.6%) ◆
Roast and toffee flavours predominate with some bitterness in this traditional old ale. Bittersweet with plenty of caramel and roast in a rather short finish.

Export Stout (ABV 4.7%)
Hints of burnt toast, balanced by good levels of hops with a long finish.

Old Harry (OG 1051, ABV 5.2%)

Wem SIBA

Wem Brewing Co Ltd, The Brew House, Aston Park, Soulton Road, Wem, Shropshire, SY4 5SD
☎ **(01939) 232432**
✉ **info@wembrewingcompany.co.uk**
🌐 **wembrewingcompany.co.uk**
Tours by arrangement

A new company formed in late 2008 following the purchase of Hanby Ales by Steven Woodland. Jack Hanby continues as head brewer at the same site, continuing the 200 year old tradition of brewing in the area. 250-300 outlets are supplied. Seasonal beer: Green Admiral (ABV 4.5%, Sep-Oct).

Pure Gold (OG 1037, ABV 3.7%)

Drawwell Bitter (OG 1039, ABV 3.9%) ◆
A hoppy beer with excellent bitterness, both in taste and aftertaste. Beautiful amber colour.

Black Magic Mild (OG 1041, ABV 4%) ◆
A dark, reddish-brown mild, which is dry and bitter with a roast malt taste.

All Seasons (OG 1042, ABV 4.2%)
A light, hoppy bitter, well balanced and thirst quenching, brewed with a fine blend of Cascade and Fuggles hops.

Rainbow Chaser (OG 1043, ABV 4.3%)
A pale beer brewed with Styrian Goldings hops.

Wem Special (OG 1044, ABV 4.4%)
A pale, straw-coloured, smooth, hoppy bitter.

Cascade (OG 1045, ABV 4.5%)
A pale beer, brewed with Cascade hops, producing a clean crisp flavour and a hoppy finish.

Golden Honey (OG 1045, ABV 4.5%)
A beer made with the addition of Australian honey. Not over sweet.

Scorpio Porter (OG 1045, ABV 4.5%)
A dark porter with a complex palate introducing hints of coffee and chocolate, contrasting and complementing the background hoppiness.

Shropshire Stout (OG 1044, ABV 4.5%)
A full-bodied, rich ruby/black coloured stout. A blend of four malts produces a distinct chocolate malt dry flavour, with a mushroom-coloured head.

Premium (OG 1046, ABV 4.6%)
An amber-coloured beer that is sweeter and fruitier than most of the beers above. Slight malt and hop taste.

Old Wemian (OG 1049, ABV 4.9%)
Golden-brown colour with an aroma of malt and hops and a soft, malty palate.

Taverners (OG 1053, ABV 5.3%)
A smooth and fruity old ale, full of body.

Cherry Bomb (OG 1060, ABV 6%)
A splendid rich and fruity beer with maraschino cherry flavour.

Joy Bringer (OG 1060, ABV 6%)
Deceptively strong beer with a distinct ginger flavour.

Nutcracker (OG 1060, ABV 6%)
Tawny beer with a fine blend of malt and hops.

Wensleydale

Wensleydale Brewery Ltd, Manor Road, Bellerby, Leyburn, North Yorkshire, DL8 5QH
☎ **(01969) 622463**
☎ **07939 751130**
✉ **info@wensleydalebrewery.com**
🌐 **wensleydalebrewery.com**
Tours by arrangement

⊗ Wensleydale Brewery (formerly Lidstone's) was set up in 2003 on a two-barrel plant in Yorkshire Dales National Park. A year later the brewery relocated to larger premises six miles away. Most beers are also available bottle conditioned and are suitable for vegetarians. Around 60 outlets are supplied.

Lidstone's Rowley Mild (OG 1037, ABV 3.2%) ◆
Chocolate and toffee aromas lead into what, for its strength, is an impressively rich and flavoursome taste. The finish is pleasantly bittersweet.

Bitter (OG 1038, ABV 3.7%) ◆
Intensely aromatic, straw-coloured ale offering a superb balance of malt and hops on the tongue.

Semer Water (OG 1041, ABV 4.1%)
Golden ale with a hint of banana on the nose. The taste is clean, crisp and hoppy, with grapefruit flavours also present.

Coverdale Gamekeeper (OG 1042, ABV 4.3%)
A light copper best bitter with a spicy aroma and juicy malt leading to a bittersweet finish with citrus notes.

Black Dub Oat Stout (OG 1044, ABV 4.4%)
Black beer brimming with roasted chocolate taste and aroma.

Sheep Rustler's Nut Brown Ale (ABV 4.4%)
A dark, reddish brown beer with a sweetish roast malt taste leading to a long-lasting, roasted, slightly bitter finish.

Coverdale Poacher IPA (OG 1049, ABV 5%) ◆
Citrus flavours dominate both aroma and taste in this pale, smooth, refreshing beer; the aftertaste is quite dry.

Barley Wine (ABV 8.5%)
A dark, rich, ruby colour wiht a thick, creamy head. Vinous and bitter plum aromas blend with rich, fruity sweetness suggesting honey and figs with rum-soaked raisins.

Wentworth SIBA

Wentworth Brewery Ltd, Power House, Gun Park, Wentworth, South Yorkshire, S62 7TF
☎ (01226) 747070
✉ info@wentworth-brewery.co.uk
🌐 wentworth-brewery.co.uk
Tours by arrangement

Brewing started at Wentworth in 1999. In 2006 custom-built brewing kit was installed, increasing production to 30 barrels a day. More than 300 outlets are supplied.

Imperial Ale (OG 1038, ABV 3.8%)
A tawny, bitter beer with a floral nose. There is a slight hint of sweetness on the aftertaste.

WPA (OG 1039.5, ABV 4%) ◆
An extremely well hopped IPA-style beer that leads to some astringency. A very bitter beer.

Best Bitter (OG 1040, ABV 4.1%) ◆
A hoppy, bitter beer with hints of citrus fruits. A bitter taste dominates the aftertaste.

Bumble Beer (OG 1043, ABV 4.3%)
A pale golden beer, made with local honey, which gives it a unique and distinctive flavour throughout the year.

Black Zac (OG 1046, ABV 4.6%)
A mellow, dark ruby-red ale with chocolate and pale malts leading to a bitter taste, with a coffee finish.

Oatmeal Stout (OG 1050, ABV 4.8%) ◆
Black, smooth, with roast and chocolate malt and toffee overtones.

Rampant Gryphon (OG 1062, ABV 6.2%) ◆
A strong, well-balanced golden ale with hints of fruit and sweetness but which retains a hoppy character.

Wessex SIBA

CF Hobden t/a Wessex Brewery, Rye Hill Farm, Longbridge Deverill, Warminster, Wiltshire, BA12 7DE
☎ (01985) 844532
✉ wessexbrewery@tinyworld.co.uk
Tours by arrangement

⊗ The brewery went into production in 2001 and moved to its current location in 2004. 15 local outlets are supplied. Beers are also available through selected wholesalers. Seasonal beers: Burlington Bertie (ABV 3.33%, summer), Farmer's Tan (ABV 4.7%, autumn). Election years: Truth Decay Mild (ABV 4.3%), Electile Dysfunction (ABV 6.66%).

Potter's Ale (OG 1038, ABV 3.8%)

Longleat Pride (OG 1040, ABV 4%)
A pale, hoppy bitter.

Crockerton Classic (OG 1041, ABV 4.1%)
A full-bodied, tawny, full-flavoured bitter; fruity and malty.

Merrie Mink (OG 1041, ABV 4.2%)
A full-flavoured best with a strong hop aroma.

Deverill's Advocate (OG 1046, ABV 4.5%)
A well-balanced golden premium ale.

Warminster Warrior (OG 1045, ABV 4.5%)
Full-flavoured premium bitter.

Russian Stoat (OG 1080, ABV 9%)

West

West Brewery, Bar & Restaurant, Binnie Place, Glasgow Green, Glasgow, G40 1AW
☎ (0141) 550 0135
✉ info@westbeer.com
🌐 westbeer.com
Tours by arrangement

No real ale. West opened in 2006 and produces a full range of European-style beers. The brewery's copper-clad system, visible from the 300-seat bar and restaurant, is a fully-automated German one with an annual capacity of 1.5 million litres. Brewing is in strict accordance with the Reinheitsgebot, the German purity law, importing all malt, hops and yeast from Germany. Five regular beers are produced along with a range of seasonals. Beers: Hefeweizen (ABV 4.9%), St Mungo (ABV 4.9%), Helles Light (ABV 3.9%), Dunkel (ABV 4.9%), Munich Red (ABV 4.9%).

West Berkshire SIBA

West Berkshire Brewery Co Ltd, Old Bakery, Yattendon, Thatcham, Berkshire, RG18 0UE
☎ (01635) 202968/202638
✉ info@wbbrew.co.uk
🌐 wbbrew.co.uk

Shop Mon-Fri 10am-4pm; Sat 10am-1pm
Tours by arrangement

The brewery, established in 1995, has since moved its main site to Yattendon. In 2006 the brewhouse was extended and a new plant installed; the original five-barrel plant at the Potkiln pub in Frilsham has now closed. Around 100 outlets are supplied. One pub is owned, and the brewery hopes to acquire more. A monthly beer is also brewed – the beer names follow an annual theme.

Old Father Thames (OG 1038, ABV 3.4%)
A traditional pale ale with a full flavour despite its low strength.

Mr Chubb's Lunchtime Bitter (OG 1040, ABV 3.7%)
A drinkable, balanced, session bitter. A malty caramel note dominates aroma and taste and is accompanied by a nutty bittersweetness and a hoppy aftertaste.

Maggs' Magnificent Mild (OG 1041, ABV 3.8%)
Silky, full-bodied, dark mild with creamy head. Roast malt aroma is joined in the taste by caramel, sweetness and mild, fruity hoppiness. Aftertaste of roast malt with balancing bitterness.

Good Old Boy (OG 1043, ABV 4%)
Well-rounded, tawny bitter with malt and hops dominating throughout. A balancing bitterness accompaniment in the taste and aftertaste.

Dr Hexter's Wedding Ale (OG 1044, ABV 4.1%)
Fruit and hops dominate the aroma and are joined in the taste by a hint of malt. The aftertaste has a pleasant bitter hoppiness.

Full Circle (OG 1047, ABV 4.5%)
A golden ale with a pleasing aroma and taste of bitter hops with a hint of malt. The aftertaste is hoppy and bitter with a rounding note of malt.

Dr Hexter's Healer (OG 1052, ABV 5%)
An amber strong bitter with malt, caramel and hops in the aroma. Taste is a balance of malt, caramel, fruit, hops and bittersweetness. Caramel, fruit and bittersweetness dominate the aftertaste.

Westbury

See Wessex

Westerham SIBA

Westerham Brewery Co Ltd, Grange Farm, Pootings Road, Crockham Hill, Edenbridge, Kent, TN8 6SA
(01732) 864427
sales@westerhambrewery.co.uk
westerhambrewery.co.uk
Shop Mon-Fri 9am-5pm
Tours by arrangement (min 30 people, charge made)

The brewery was established in 2004 and restored a brewing tradition to Westerham that was lost when the Black Eagle Brewery was taken over by Ind Coope in 1959 and closed in 1965. Two of Black Eagle's yeast strains were deposited at the National Collection of Yeast Cultures and are used to recreate the true flavour of Westerham beers. The new brewery is based at the National Trust's Grange Farm in a former dairy and uses the same water supply as Black Eagle. Around 200 outlets are supplied in Kent, Surrey, Sussex and South London. Single hop varietal beers and occasional brews: see website. Bottle-conditioned beers are also available.

Finchcocks Original (OG 1036.2, ABV 3.5%)
Mid-gold session beer. Citrus notes on the palate with a hint of biscuit and resiny hoppiness.

Grasshopper Kentish Bitter (OG 1039, ABV 3.8%)
A dark, malty bitter with nutty, roasted notes from the chocolate malt.

SPA (Special Pale Ale) (OG 1038.5, ABV 3.8%)

Summer Perle (OG 1038.5, ABV 3.8%)
Golden ale with a spicy, refreshing finish.

British Bulldog (OG 1043.5, ABV 4.3%)
A rich, full-bodied best bitter with a massive aroma and palate of jammy fruit, biscuity malt and bitter hop resins.

William Wilberforce Freedom Ale (OG 1042, ABV 4.3%)
Deep golden ale with a mellow bitterness and long, hoppy finish.

India Pale Ale (OG 1047, ABV 4.8%)
Traditional IPA with plum jam and blackcurrant aroma and palate, balanced by sappy malt and a long, lingering bitter, fruity finish.

1965 – Special Bitter Ale (OG 1047.5, ABV 4.9%)
A clean, refreshing bitter with a full-bodied flavour.

Whalebone

Whalebone Brewery, 163 Wincolmlee, Hull, East Yorkshire, HU2 0PA
(01482) 226648
Tours by arrangement

The Whalebone pub, which dates from 1796, was bought by Hull CAMRA founding member Alex Craig in 2002. He opened the brewery the following year and his beers have names connected with the former whaling industry on the adjoining River Hull. Two or three outlets are supplied as well as the pub. Seasonal beers: Truelove Porter (ABV 4.7%), Joseph Allen (ABV 5%), Moby Dick (ABV 8%), Full Ship (ABV 8.4%).

Diana Mild (OG 1037, ABV 3.5%)

Neckoil Bitter (OG 1039, ABV 3.9%)

Wharfedale

See Dark Horse

Whim SIBA

Whim Ales Ltd, Whim Farm, Hartington, Derbyshire, SK17 0AX
(01298) 84991

A brewery opened in 1993 in outbuildings at Whim Farm. Whim's beers are available in 50-70 outlets and the brewery's tied house, the Wilkes Head in Leek, Staffs. Some one-off brews are produced. Occasional/seasonal beers: Kaskade (ABV 4.3%, lager), Snow White (ABV 4.5%, wheat beer), Easter Special (ABV 4.8%), Stout Jenny (ABV 4.7%), Black Xmas (ABV 6.5%).

Arbor Light (OG 1035, ABV 3.6%)
Light-coloured bitter, sharp and clean with lots of hop character and a delicate light aroma.

Hartington Bitter (OG 1039, ABV 4%)
A light, golden-coloured, well-hopped session beer. A dry finish with a spicy, floral aroma.

Hartington IPA (OG 1045, ABV 4.5%)
Pale and light-coloured, smooth on the palate allowing malt to predominate. Slightly sweet finish combined with distinctive light hop bitterness. Well rounded.

Flower Power (OG 1052, ABV 5.3%)
Light, golden coloured beer with a flowery hop aroma, citrus with mild spice on the palate and a dry, bitter finish.

White SIBA

White Brewing Co, 1066 Country Brewery, Pebsham Farm Industrial Estate, Pebsham Lane, Bexhill-on-Sea, East Sussex, TN40 2RZ
☎ (01424) 731066
✉ whitebrewing@fsbdial.co.uk
🌐 white-brewing.co.uk
Tours by arrangement

The brewery was founded in 1995 to serve local free trade outlets and some wholesalers. White has expanded production threefold with the addition of seasonal and occasional beers. Around 30 outlets are supplied. Seasonal beers: White Gold (ABV 4.9%, summer), Chilly Willy (ABV 5.1%, winter), Old White Christmas (ABV 4%). Bottle-conditioned beers are also available.

1066 Country Bitter (OG 1040, ABV 4%)
Amber-gold in colour, a light, sweetish beer with good malt and hop balance, and a bitter, refreshing finish.

Dark (OG 1040, ABV 4%)

Heart of Rother (ABV 4.5%)

Whitehaven

Whitehaven Brewing Co Ltd, Croasdale Farm Barn, Ennerdale, Cleator, Cumbria, CA23 3AT
☎ (01946) 861755
✉ info@twbcl.co.uk
🌐 twbcl.co.uk
Tours by arrangement

The brewery was established in late 2007 on a 10-barrel plant and brews using spring water. Four regular beers are produced under the brand 'Real Ales' from Ennerdale. Seasonal beers include Mild Ennerdale (ABV 3.9%), Classic Bitter (ABV 4.2%) and Strong Blonde (ABV 4.6%).

Ennerdale Bitter (ABV 3.6%) ◆
Mildly fruity and lightly-hopped amber beer.

Ennerdale Blonde (ABV 3.8%)

Ennerdale Copper (ABV 3.8%)

Darkest Ennerdale (ABV 4.2%)

White Horse

White Horse Brewery Co Ltd, 3 Ware Road, White Horse Business Park, Stanford-in-the-Vale, Oxfordshire, SN7 8NY
☎ (01367) 718700
🌐 whitehorsebrewery.com
Tours by arrangement

⊗ White Horse was founded on a modern industrial estate in 2004. The second-hand brewing plant was manufactured in Belgium and has a brew-length of 7.5 barrels. It uses the continental method of brewing with a lauter tun rather than an infusion mash tun. The brewery now has its own pub in Oxford as well as supplying more than 150 outlets. Seasonal beers: Dragon Hill (ABV 4.2%, autumn), Flibbertigibbet (ABV 4.3%, summer), Saracen IPA (ABV 4.5%, spring), Giant (ABV 4.3%, winter), Rudolf The Red Nosed White Horse (ABV 4.8%, Xmas).

Oxfordshire Bitter (OG 1039, ABV 3.7%)
Golden bitter, well-hopped with a clean, fruity finish.

Village Idiot (OG 1044.5, ABV 4.1%)
A blonde ale with a complex hop aroma and taste.

Wayland Smithy (OG 1049, ABV 4.4%)
A red-brown ale with a nice biscuit flavour that is balanced with a spicy hop finish.

Black Horse Porter (OG 1052, ABV 5%)
Dark red porter with a chocolate character and a fruity/berry hop aroma and taste.

The Guv'nor (OG 1066, ABV 6.5%)
A light golden strong ale with a fruity finish.

For Turf Tavern, Oxford:

Summer Ale (OG 1042, ABV 4.1%)
A golden ale with a dry aftertaste.

White Park

White Park Brewery, Perry Hill Farm, Bourne End Road, Cranfield, Beds, MK43 0BA
☎ (01223) 911357
✉ info@whiteparkbrewery.co.uk
🌐 whiteparkbrewery.co.uk

White Park is a family business established in 2007 on a five-barrel plant. Spent malt is recycled as feed for rare breed cattle. 60 outlets are supplied direct. Seasonal beers: Blonde (ABV 4%, summer), Kelly's Stout (ABV 4.2%, winter), Nightjar (ABV 4.5%, autumn).

White Gold (OG 1037, ABV 3.8%)

Cranfield Bitter (OG 1042.5, ABV 4.4%)

GB (OG 1047, ABV 5%)

White Rose (NEW)

White Rose Brewery Ltd, 119 Chapel Road, Chapeltown, Sheffield, South Yorkshire, S35 1QL

Test beers appeared in late 2007, brewed at Sheffield Brewery. Since 2008 beers are contract brewed by Little Ale Cart.

Whitewater

Whitewater Brewing Co, 40 Tullyframe Road, Kilkeel, Co Down, Northern Ireland, BT34 4RZ
☎ (028) 4176 9449
✉ info@whitewaterbrewing.com
🌐 whitewaterbrewing.co.uk
Tours by arrangement

Set up in 1996, Whitewater is now the biggest brewery in Northern Ireland. Currently, Whitewater supplies 15 outlets and owns one pub, the White Horse, Saintfield, Co. Down. Seasonal beers: see website.

Mill Ale (OG 1038, ABV 3.7%)

Crown & Glory (OG 1038, ABV 3.8%)

Belfast Lager (OG 1040, ABV 4%)

Belfast Ale (OG 1046, ABV 4.5%)

Clotworthy Dobbin (OG 1050, ABV 5%)

Whitstable

Whitstable Brewery, Little Telpits Farm, Woodcock Lane, Grafty Green, Kent, ME17 2AY
☎ (01622) 851007
✉ whitstablebrewer@btconnect.com
🌐 whitstablebrewery.info
Tours by arrangement

Whitstable was launched in 2003 when the Green family purchased the Swale and North Weald Brewery to supply their own outlets (a hotel and three restaurants) in Whitstable, and beer festival orders. In 2006 they opened a bar in East Quay selling their own beers and other micros. The brewery now supplies over 75 outlets in Kent, Surrey and London. Seasonal beers: Winkle Picker (ABV 4.5%), Christmas Cake (ABV 4.6%). Bottle-conditioned beers are also available.

Native Bitter (OG 1037, ABV 3.7%)
A deep amber beer with nutty notes and malt flavours.

East India Pale Ale (OG 1040, ABV 4.1%)
A pale-coloured, sharp, clean beer with well-balanced hop flavours leaving the palate on a bittersweet assertive finish.

Oyster Stout (OG 1042, ABV 4.5%)
Rich, dry deep chocolate and mocha flavours.

Pearl of Kent (OG 1042, ABV 4.5%)
A light-coloured, well-rounded premium beer with tropical fruit flavours.

Kentish Reserve (OG 1045, ABV 5%)
A copper ale with warm plum pudding flavours and a ruby port finish.

Whittington's SIBA

Whittington's Brewery, Three Choirs Vineyards Ltd, Newent, Gloucestershire, GL18 1LS
☎ (01531) 890555
✉ brewery@threechoirs.com
🌐 whittingtonbrewery.co.uk
Shop 9am-5pm daily (later during summer)
Tours by arrangement (for a charge)

Whittington's started in 2003 using a purpose-built five-barrel plant producing 20 barrels per week. Dick Whittington came from the nearby Pauntley, hence the name and feline theme. The beers are currently only available bottle-conditioned from the onsite shop, online and from local outlets.

Why Not

Why Not Brewery, 17 Cavalier Close, Thorpe St Andrew, Norwich, Norfolk, NR7 0TE
☎ (01603) 300786
✉ colin@thewhynotbrewery.co.uk
🌐 thewhynotbrewery.co.uk

Why Not opened in 2006 with equipment located in a shed and custom-made by Brendan Moore of Iceni Brewery. The brewery can produce up to two barrels per brew. All beers are available in bottle-conditioned form and are occasionally put into casks to order.

Wally's Revenge (OG 1040, ABV 4%) ◆
An overtly bitter beer with a hoppy background. The bitterness holds on to the end as an increasing astringent dryness develops.

Roundhead Porter (OG 1045, ABV 4.5%)
A traditional old style London porter.

Cavalier Red (OG 1047, ABV 4.7%) ◆
Explosive fruity nose belies the gentleness of the taste. The summer fruit aroma dominates this red-gold brew. A sweet, fruity start disappears under a quick, bitter ending.

Norfolk Honey Ale (OG 1050, ABV 5%)
A golden beer with a honey nose. A definite hop edge leaves a honey aftertaste.

Chocolate Nutter (OG 1056, ABV 5.5%)

Wibblers

Wibblers Brewery Ltd, Joyces Farm Building, Southminster Road, Mayland, Essex, CM3 6EB
☎ (01621) 789003
☎ 07775 577982
✉ info@wibblers.com
🌐 wibblers.com
Tours by arrangement

Wibblers was established commercially in 2007 after 16 years of home craft brewing. Demand grew the brew length from two-barrel to five-barrel in the first year with a new 18-barrel plant in 2009. Seasonal and one-off beers are brewed every month. Most beers are also available in bottle-conditioned form and are suitable for vegetarians. Seasonal beers: New Dawn (ABV 3.8%, May-Jun), Mayflower (ABV 3.8%, Apr-May), Hop Harvest (ABV 4.1%, Sep-Oct), Santa's Night Off (ABV 4.2%, Nov-Dec).

Dengie Best (OG 1036, ABV 3.6%)

Apprentice (OG 1039, ABV 3.9%)

Hoppy Helper (OG 1041, ABV 4%)

Darker Mild (OG 1044, ABV 4.3%)

Crafty Stoat (OG 1056, ABV 5.3%)

Wicked Hathern

Wicked Hathern Brewery Ltd, 17 Nixon Walk, East Leake, Leicestershire, LE12 6HL
☎ (01509) 559308
✉ sean.oneill@escapade-rs.com
🌐 wicked-hathern.co.uk

Opened in 2000, the brewery generally supplies beer on a guest basis to many local pubs and beer festivals, and brews commissioned beers for special occasions. All beers are available bottled from selected off-licences (see website) and from Hathern Stores. Special cask beer is brewed for the Albion Inn, Loughborough, and special bottled beers for Hathern Stores and Alexander Wines in Earlsdon. The brewery itself is not currently operating and the beers are being produced by the Wicked Hathern brewers at Leek Brewery (qv). Seasonal beer: Gladstone Tidings (ABV 5.1%, Xmas).

Dobles' Dog (OG 1035, ABV 3.5%)
A full-bodied, stout-like dark mild with fruit and nut flavours on the palate. Gently bitter, malty finish with a lingering hint of roasted malts.

WHB/Wicked Hathern Bitter (OG 1038, ABV 3.8%)

A light-tasting session bitter with a dry palate and good hop aroma.

Cockfighter (OG 1043, ABV 4.2%)
A copper-coloured beer with an aroma of fruit, creamy malt and hop resins.

Hawthorn Gold (OG 1045, ABV 4.5%)
A pale golden ale with delicate malt and spicy hop in the aroma. The taste is hoppy and mostly bitter but with good malt support and body. Dry, malt and hops aftertaste.

Derby Porter (OG 1048, ABV 4.8%)
A deep ruby porter with a creamy nose of lightly smoky, chocolatey, nutty dark malts.

Soar Head (OG 1048, ABV 4.8%) ◆
A dark ruby-coloured strong bitter with a cocktail of distinctive flavours.

Swift 'Un (OG 1048, ABV 4.8%)
A light-golden mellow beer with fruity overtones.

For Albion, Canal Bank, Loughborough:

Albion Special (OG 1041, ABV 4%)
A light, copper-coloured bitter with a nutty aroma and smoky malt taste, hops leading through.

For Burleigh Court, Loughborough University Campus:

Burly Court Jester (OG 1038, ABV 3.8%)

Wickwar SIBA

Wickwar Brewing Co, Old Brewery, Station Road, Wickwar, Gloucestershire, GL12 8NB
☎ **0870 777 5671**
✉ **bob@wickwarbrewing.co.uk**
🌐 **wickwarbrewing.co.uk**
Shop Mon-Fri 8am-6pm; Sat 9am-5pm (Tel: 01453 299592)
Tours by arrangement

⊗ Wickwar was established as a 10-barrel brewery in 1990 in the cooper's shop of the former Arnold Perrett Brewery. In 2004 it was expanded to 50 barrels and moved into the original 19th-century brewery. Some 350 local outlets are supplied on a regular basis and the beers are available nationally through most distributors and SIBA. Seasonal beers: see website. Bottle-conditioned beers are also available.

Coopers WPA (OG 1036.5, ABV 3.5%) ◆
Golden-coloured, this well-balanced beer is light and refreshing, with hops, citrus fruit, apple/pear flavour and notable pale malt character. Bitter, dry finish.

Banker$ Draft (OG 1040, ABV 4%)
An amber ale, well-hopped with a pleasant malt flavour.

Brand Oak Bitter (BOB) (OG 1039, ABV 4%) ◆
Amber-coloured, this has a distinctive blend of hop, malt and apple/pear citrus fruits. The slightly sweet taste turns into a fine, dry bitterness, with a similar malty-lasting finish.

Cotswold Way (OG 1043, ABV 4.2%) ◆
Amber-coloured, it has a pleasant aroma of pale malt, hop and fruit. Good dry bitterness in the taste with some sweetness. Similar though less sweet in the finish, with good hop content.

Rite Flanker (OG 1043, ABV 4.3%)
Amber in colour with a big malt taste and fruit notes and a hoppy finish.

IKB (OG 1045, ABV 4.5%)
A ruby-red ale with a complex hop aroma and flavour derived from the use of three hop varieties. Flowery but well balanced.

Old Arnold (OG 1047, ABV 4.8%)
A full-flavoured and well-balanced ale with malt, hops and cherry fruit throughout. Amber/pale brown, it is slightly sweet with a long-lasting, malty, dry, fruity and increasingly bitter finish.

Mr Perretts Traditional Stout (OG 1059, ABV 5.9%) ◆
Aroma and taste of smoky chocolate malts and peppery hops. Dark fruits of black cherry and blackcurrant give hints of sweetness to the dry, quite bitter, slightly spicy, well-balanced taste.

Station Porter (OG 1062, ABV 6.1%) ◆
This is a rich, smooth, dark ruby-brown ale. Starts with roast malt; coffee, chocolate and dark fruit then develops a complex, spicy, bittersweet taste and a long roast finish.

Wild Walker (NEW)

Wild Walker Brewing Co Ltd, Unit 1, Victory Park, Victory Road, Derby, DE24 8ZF
☎ **(01332) 766195**
✉ **enquiry@wildwalker.co.uk**
🌐 **wildwalker.co.uk**
Tours by arrangement

Wild Walker commenced brewing in early 2009 on a five-barrel plant. There are plans to brew seasonal and specials beers as well as to produce bottle-conditioned ales.

Last Orders (ABV 3.8%)
A traditional session bitter.

Old Bighead (OG 1042, ABV 4.1%)
A creamy, amber-coloured beer with rounded bitterness and fruity character

Great Escape (OG 1050, ABV 5%)
Dark and rich, malty bitter with a subtle hoppiness.

Williams SIBA

Williams Brothers Brewing Co/Heather Ale Ltd, New Alloa Brewery, Kelliebank, Alloa, FK10 1NT
☎ **(01259) 725511**
✉ **fraoch@heatherale.co.uk**
🌐 **heatherale.co.uk**
Tours by arrangement

Bruce and Scott Williams started brewing Heather Ale in the West Highlands in 1993. A range of indigenous, historic ales were added over the following 10 years before the brothers invested in a 40-barrel brewery and bottling line in 2003. New beers are branded as 'Williams Bros' of which there are many hoppy and esoteric styles to choose from. Around 50 regular cask ale outlets are supplied. Seasonal beers: Ebulum (ABV 6.5%, winter), Alba (ABV 7.5%, winter).

Gold (OG 1040, ABV 3.9%)

Harvest Sun (OG 1038, ABV 3.9%)

Fraoch Heather Ale (OG 1041, ABV 4.1%) ◆
The unique taste of heather flowers is noticeable in this beer. A fine floral aroma and spicy taste give character to this drinkable speciality beer.

Black (OG 1039, ABV 4.2%)

Roisin-Tayberry (OG 1040, ABV 4.2%)

Good Times (OG 1040, ABV 4.3%)

Red (OG 1045, ABV 4.5%)

Joker IPA (OG 1047, ABV 5%)

Seven Giraffes (OG 1047, ABV 5.1%)

Midnight Sun (OG 1056, ABV 5.6%)

Willoughby

Willoughby Brewing Co, Brockhampton Brewery, Whitbourne, Worcestershire, WR6 5SH
☎ (01885) 482359
✉ wbc@mccallum66.fsnet.co.uk

Willoughby began brewing in June 2008 on a six-barrel plant on part of the National Trust estate at Brockhampton. Bottle-conditioned beers are available.

Trust Gold (ABV 3.8%)

Tried & Trusted (ABV 4.2%)

Willy's SIBA

Willy's Wine Bar Ltd, 17 High Cliff Road, Cleethorpes, Lincolnshire, DN35 8RQ
☎ (01472) 602145
Tours by arrangement

The brewery opened in 1989 to provide beer for its two pubs in Grimsby and Cleethorpes. It has a five-barrel plant with maximum capacity of 15 barrels a week. The brewery can be viewed at any time from pub or street.

Original Bitter (OG 1038, ABV 3.8%)
A light brown 'sea air' beer with a fruity, tangy hop on the nose and taste, giving a strong bitterness tempered by the underlying malt.

Burcom Bitter (OG 1044, ABV 4.2%)
Sometimes known as Mariner's Gold, although the beer is dark ruby in colour. It is a smooth and creamy brew with a sweet chocolate-bar maltiness, giving way to an increasingly bitter finish.

Last Resort (OG 1044, ABV 4.3%)

Weiss Buoy (OG 1045, ABV 4.5%)
A cloudy wheat beer.

Coxswains Special (OG 1050, ABV 4.9%)

Old Groyne (OG 1060, ABV 6.2%)
An initial sweet banana fruitiness blends with malt to give a vanilla quality to the taste and slightly bitter aftertaste. A copper-coloured beer reminiscent of a Belgian ale.

Wincle (NEW)

Wincle Beer Co Ltd, Heaton House, Rushton Spencer, Cheshire, SK11 0RD
☎ (01260) 226166
✉ sales@winclebeer.co.uk
winclebeer.co.uk
Tours by arrangement

Wincle was set up by publicans Giles Meadows and Neil Murphy in an old milking parlour. Brewing began in 2008 on a five-barrel plant purchased from Saffron Brewery. 120 outlets are supplied direct within a 25-mile radius. Bottle-conditioned beers are available.

Wincle Waller (OG 1038, ABV 3.8%)

Sir Phillip (OG 1041, ABV 4.2%)

Wibbly Wallaby (OG 1043, ABV 4.4%)

Undertaker (OG 1044, ABV 4.5%)

Mr Mullin's IPA (OG 1047, ABV 4.8%)

Windie Goat

Windie Goat Brewery, Failford Inn, Failford, South Ayrshire, KA5 5TF
☎ (01292) 540117
✉ beer@windiegoatbrewery.co.uk
windiegoatbrewery.co.uk
Tours by arrangement

Established in 2006 in the old cellar of the Failford Inn using a 2.5-barrel plant, the brewery name comes from Windiegoat Wood downstream from the pub and the beer names are linked to fishing pools along the River Ayr. A range of bottle-conditioned beers is planned and the brewery is looking to increase capacity. Seasonal beers: Gutter Slab (ABV 5.5%, spring/summer), The Dubh (ABV 4.6%, autumn/winter).

Peden's Cove (ABV 3.8%)
Pale-coloured with a light, hoppy aroma, slight vanilla notes and citrus finish.

Priest's Wheel (ABV 4.3%)
Amber ale with full, sweet aroma and flavour. Malty, easy-drinking, clean finish.

Windsor Castle

Windsor Castle Brewery Ltd t/a Sadler's Ales, 7 Stourbridge Road, Lye, Stourbridge, West Midlands, DY9 7DG
☎ (01384) 895230
✉ enquiries@windsorcastlebrewery.com
windsorcastlebrewery.com
Tours by arrangement

Thomas Alexander Sadler founded the original brewery in 1900 adjacent to the Windsor Castle Inn, Oldbury. Fourth generation brewers John and Chris Sadler re-opened the brewery in its new location in 2004. The brewery tap house was built and opened in 2006 next to the brewery. Around 250 outlets are supplied. An extensive range of bottle-conditioned beers are available as well as beer-based cheeses and condiments.

Jack's Ale (OG 1037, ABV 3.8%)
A very pale, hoppy bitter with a crisp and zesty lemon undertone.

Green Man (ABV 4%)
A smooth pale ale, brewed with lager hops.

Mild Ale (OG 1039, ABV 4%)
A Black Country dark mild with hints of chocolate and a dry finish.

Worcester Sorcerer (OG 1043, ABV 4.3%)
Brewed with English hops and barley with hints of mint and lemon, creating a floral aroma and crisp bitterness.

Mellow Yellow (OG 1045, ABV 4.5%)
A pale ale brewed with plenty of hop and honey.

Thin Ice (OG 1045, ABV 4.5%)
A pale ale. Bitter but with an orange and lemon finish.

Stumbling Badger (OG 1049, ABV 4.9%)
A well-balanced strong ale, packed with flavour and aroma with hints of fruit and a hoppy finish.

Mud City Stout (OG 1066, ABV 6.6%)
Rich, full-bodied strong stout brewed with raw cocoa, fresh vanilla pods, oats, wheat and dark malts.

Winter's SIBA

Winter's Brewery, 8 Keelan Close, Norwich, Norfolk, NR6 6QZ
☎ (01603) 787820

⊗ David Winter, who had previous award-winning success as brewer for both Woodforde's and Chalk Hill breweries, decided to set up on his own in 2001. He purchased the brewing plant from the now defunct Scott's Brewery in Lowestoft. The local free trade is supplied.

Mild (OG 1036.5, ABV 3.6%) ◆
Classic dark mild, red-brown with a nutty roast character. A good balance of malt caramel and roast abetted by both sweetness and a light, hoppy bitterness. Lingering finish develops a plummy feel.

Bitter (OG 1039.5, ABV 3.8%) ◆
A well-balanced amber bitter. Hops and malt are balanced by a crisp citrus fruitiness. A pleasant hoppy nose with a hint of grapefruit. Long, sustained, dry, grapefruit finish.

Golden (ABV 4.1%) ◆
Just a hint of hops in the aroma. The initial taste combines a dry bitterness with a fruity apple buttress. The finish slowly subsides into a long, dry bitterness.

Revenge (OG 1047, ABV 4.7%) ◆
Blackcurrant notes give depth to the inherent maltiness of this pale brown beer. A bittersweet background becomes more pronounced as the fruitiness gently wanes.

Storm Force (OG 1053, ABV 5.3%) ◆
A well-defined, sweetish brew. Hops and vine fruit give depth to the malty backbone of this pale brown strong beer. All flavours hold up well as the finish develops a warming softness.

Wirksworth

Wirksworth Brewery, 25 St John Street, Wirksworth, Derbyshire, DE4 4DR
☎ (01629) 824011
✉ wirksworthbrewery@hotmail.co.uk
🌐 wirksworthbrewery.co.uk

◎ Jeff Green started brewing in 2007 with a 2.5-barrel plant installed by David Porter in a converted stone workshop. Wirksworth supplies Derbyshire pubs with four core beers and supplements these with at least one seasonal offering. Every September there is a brew house open weekend giving visitors the opportunity to gain an insight into the brewing process and taste the real ales.

Cruckbeam (OG 1040, ABV 3.9%)

Sunbeam (OG 1040, ABV 4%)

First Brew (OG 1042, ABV 4.2%)

T'owd Man (OG 1050, ABV 4.9%)

Wissey Valley

Wissey Valley Brewery, Clover Club, Low Road, Wretton, Norfolk, PE33 9QN
☎ (01366) 500767
✉ info@wisseyvalleybrewery.com
🌐 wisseyvalleybrewery.com
Tours by arrangement

⊗ The brewery was launched in 2002 as Captain Grumpy's and in 2003 moved to Stoke Ferry and was re-established as Wissey Valley. The brewery re-launched in 2006, moving to the neighbouring village of Wretton. Around 15 outlets are supplied direct as well as wholesalers and beer festivals. Bottle-conditioned beers are available.

Bitter (OG 1036, ABV 3.7%)

Missey Wissey Blackberry Ale (OG 1036, ABV 3.7%)

Old Grumpy Bitter (OG 1043, ABV 4.5%)

Walsingham Ale (OG 1043, ABV 4.5%)

Old Grumpy Porter (OG 1049, ABV 5%)

Tishtash Coriander Ale (OG 1047, ABV 5%)

Wizard SIBA

Wizard Ales, Unit 4, Lundy View, Mullacott Cross Industrial Estate, Ilfracombe, Devon, EX34 8PY
☎ (01271) 865350
✉ mike@wizardales.co.uk
🌐 wizardales.co.uk
Tours by arrangement

⊗ Brewing started in 2003 on a 1.25-barrel plant, since upgraded to five barrels. The brewery moved from Warwickshire to Devon in 2007. Around 20 local outlets are supplied. Seasonal beer: Bah Humbug (ABV 5.8%, Xmas). Bottle-conditioned beers are also available.

Apprentice (OG 1038, ABV 3.6%)

Lundy Gold (OG 1042, ABV 4.1%)

Old Combe (OG 1043, ABV 4.2%)

Druid's Fluid (OG 1048, ABV 5%)

Wold Top SIBA

Wold Top Brewery, Hunmanby Grange, Wold Newton, Driffield, East Yorkshire, YO25 3HS
☎ (01723) 892222
✉ enquiries@woldtopbrewery.co.uk
🌐 woldtopbrewery.co.uk

⊗ Wold Top is a small brewery that commenced brewing in 2003 and is an integral part of Hunmanby Grange, a family farm. It uses home-grown malting barley, chalk-filtered borehole water and some home-grown hops. Over 600 outlets are supplied. Seasonal beers: see website.

Bitter (OG 1037, ABV 3.7%)

Falling Stone (OG 1041, ABV 4.2%)

Mars Magic (OG 1044, ABV 4.6%)

Wold Gold (OG 1046, ABV 4.8%)

Wolf

WBC (Norfolk) Ltd t/a The Wolf Brewery, Rookery Farm, Silver Street, Besthorpe, Attleborough, Norfolk, NR17 2LD
☎ (01953) 457775
✉ info@wolfbrewery.com
🌐 wolfbrewery.com
Shop Mon-Fri 9am-5pm (all year); Sat 10am-3pm (Dec only)

Tours by arrangement

The brewery was founded iin 1996 on a 20-barrel plant, which was upgraded to a 24-barrel one in 2006. Over 200 outlets are supplied. Seasonal beers: see website.

Golden Jackal (OG 1039, ABV 3.7%)
Crisp, fruity, golden ale with hoppy overtones. Citrus notes in the nose. Well-balanced throughout with a trace of vanilla that fades as the finish slowly tapers into a dry, biscuity bitterness.

Wolf In Sheep's Clothing (OG 1039, ABV 3.7%)
A malty aroma with fruity undertones introduce this reddish-hued mild. Malt, with a bitter background that remains throughout, is the dominant flavour of this clean-tasting beer.

Ale (ABV 3.9%)

Coyote Bitter (OG 1044, ABV 4.3%)
A well-balanced golden brew with a hop and citrus aroma. The dominant hoppy bitterness is countered by a malty, slightly sweet backdrop. Complex flavours continue to mix as the dry, bitter ending slowly fades.

Straw Dog (ABV 4.5%)
A sweet fruity aroma leads into a smooth blend of citrus hop and bitterness. The pale yellow colouring matches the delicacy of the flavours. The fruitiness is the mainstay of a lingering, one-dimensional finish.

Granny Wouldn't Like It (OG 1049, ABV 4.8%)
Red-brown with a pronounced malty bouquet. Bitterness increases throughout but is softened by a smoky malt background. Some roast notes and a gentle, fruity sweetness add depth.

For City of Cambridge Brewery:

Boathouse Bitter (ABV 3.7%)
Copper-brown and full-bodied session bitter, starting with impressive citrus and floral hop; grassy fruit notes are present with finally a gentle bitterness.

Hobson's Choice (ABV 4.1%)
This golden ale has a predominantly spicy hop aroma. Bittersweet on the palate with plenty of hops leading through to a dry, hoppy finish.

Atom Splitter (ABV 4.5%)
Robust copper-coloured strong bitter with a hop aroma and taste, and a distinct sulphury edge.

Parkers Porter (ABV 5%)
Impressive reddish brew with a defined roast character throughout, and a short, fruity, bittersweet palate.

Wolverhampton & Dudley

See Marston's in the New Nationals section

Wood SIBA

Wood Brewery Ltd, Wistanstow, Craven Arms, Shropshire, SY7 8DG
☎ (01588) 672523
mail@woodbrewery.co.uk
woodbrewery.co.uk
Tours by arrangement

The brewery opened in 1980 in buildings next to the Plough Inn, still the brewery's only tied house. Steady growth over the years included the acquisition of the Sam Powell Brewery and its beers in 1991. Production averages 70 barrels a week and around 200 outlets are supplied. Seasonal beers: see website. A monthly beer is also brewed.

Quaff (ABV 3.7%)
A pale and refreshing light bitter with a clean, hoppy finish.

Craven Ale (ABV 3.8%)
An attractively coloured beer with a pleasant hop aroma and a refreshing taste.

Parish Bitter (OG 1040, ABV 4%)
A blend of malt and hops with a bitter aftertaste. Pale brown in colour.

Shropshire Lass (OG 1041, ABV 4.1%)
A golden ale with zesty bitterness.

Special Bitter (OG 1042, ABV 4.2%)
A tawny brown bitter with malt, hops and some fruitiness.

Pot O' Gold (OG 1044, ABV 4.4%)

Shropshire Lad (OG 1045, ABV 4.5%)
A strong, well-rounded bitter, drawing flavour from a fine blend of selected English malted barley and Fuggles and Golding hops.

Old Sam (OG 1047, ABV 4.6%)
A dark copper ale with a ripe, rounded flavour and hop bitterness.

Wonderful (OG 1048, ABV 4.8%)
A mid-brown, fruity beer, with a roast and malt taste.

Tom Wood

See Highwood

Wooden Hand

Wooden Hand Brewery, Unit 3, Grampound Road Industrial Estate, Grampound Road, Truro, Cornwall, TR2 4TB
☎ (01726) 884596
mel@woodenhand.co.uk
woodenhand.co.uk

Wooden Hand was founded in 2004 by Anglo-Swedish businessman Rolf Munding. The brewery is named after the Black Hand of John Carew of Penwarne, in the parish of Mevagissey – Carew lost his hand in fighting at the siege of Ostend in the reign of Elizabeth I. The brewery supplies around 50 outlets with a high percentage being sold further afield via wholesalers. A bottling line was installed in 2005, which also bottles for other breweries.

Pirates Gold (OG 1040.6, ABV 4%)
A slightly tart pale session bitter with hop aroma, light fruit yet malty underlying flavour and tangy fruit finish.

Cornish Buccaneer (OG 1043.6, ABV 4.3%)
A golden beer with full flavour hop character, good fruit and hop balance and a long, dry finish.

Black Pearl (OG 1050.6, ABV 4.5%)
A rich, nutty stout with good hop balance and dry chocolate finish.

Cornish Mutiny (OG 1048.6, ABV 4.8%)
Rich, full-bodied strong ale with distinctive full hop character. Slightly biscuity and complex flavour with full mouth finish.

Woodforde's SIBA

Woodforde's Norfolk Ales, Broadland Brewery, Woodbastwick, Norwich, Norfolk, NR13 6SW
☎ (01603) 720353
✉ info@woodfordes.co.uk
🌐 woodfordes.co.uk
Shop Mon-Fri 10.30am-4.30pm; Sat & Sun 11.30am-4.30pm (01603 722218)
Tours by arrangement (Tue & Thu evenings)

Founded in 1981 in Drayton, Woodforde's moved to Erpingham in 1982, and then moved again to a converted farm complex in Woodbastwick, with greatly increased production capacity, in 1989. Major expansion took place in 2001 and 2008 to more than double production and included a new brewery shop and visitor centre. Woodforde's runs two tied houses with around 600 outlets supplied on a regular basis. Bottle-conditioned beers are available. The Woodforde's Club now has over 13,000 members and is free to join: see website for details.

Mardler's (OG 1035, ABV 3.5%)
Chocolate and roast aromas introduce this well-balanced dark mild. Swathes of vanilla, caramel and malt boost the dominant roast and chocolate flavours. A fine, flavoursome finish.

Wherry (OG 1037.4, ABV 3.8%)
A smooth-textured brew with a balanced malt and hop character. Both nose and taste have a significant amount of malt and hops boosted by a bittersweet fruitiness. A gentle finish retains character.

Sundew Ale (OG 1039, ABV 4.1%)
A fruity fusion of citrus and hop with some background malt. A pleasant grainy feel adds to the character of this light-tasting golden ale. A noticeable but increasing bitterness towards the end.

Nelson's Revenge (OG 1042.7, ABV 4.5%)
A rich, fruity copper-coloured brew with a malty aroma. Vine fruits and malt intertwine with hoppy bitterness to give a balanced, full-bodied tasting experience. The grainy character and diminishing sweetness lead to a lingering dry finish.

Norfolk Nog (OG 1046.8, ABV 4.6%)
Echoes of Pontefract cake in all aspects of this red-hued, roast-dominated brew. A plummy sweetness aided by a dry bitterness and a hint of caramel all provide rallying points to counter to the main roast character.

Admiral's Reserve (OG 1050, ABV 5%)
Tawny-coloured strong ale with a gentle malty aroma. A smooth sultana and malt introduction with more than a hint of hop-induced bitterness. Balanced finish with fruit making a noticeably quick retreat.

Headcracker (OG 1065.7, ABV 7%)
Malty, sweet-tasting tawny ale with a satisfyingly sticky mouthfeel. Initially the malt matches the heavy fruity aura. Initial traces of hop and caramel soon disappear as the malty influence recedes.

Norfolk Nip (OG 1076, ABV 8.5%)
Dark mahogany in colour, this intensely flavoured beer has a stunning range of malts and hops enveloped by a warming balanced bitterness.

Woodlands SIBA

Woodlands Brewing Co Ltd, Unit 3, Meadow Lane Farm, London Road, Stapeley, Cheshire, CW5 7JU

Office: Wayside, Dairy Lane, Nantwich, Cheshire, CW5 6DS
☎ (01270) 620101
✉ info@woodlandsbrewery.co.uk
🌐 woodlandsbrewery.co.uk
Shop Mon-Fri 9am-4.30pm
Tours by arrangement

The brewery opened in 2004 with a five-barrel plant from the former Khean Brewery and moved to larger premises in 2008. The beers are brewed using water from a spring that surfaces on a nearby peat field at Woodlands Farm. Over 100 outlets are supplied including the brewery's first tied house, the Globe in Nantwich. Bottle-conditioned beers are available.

Mild (OG 1035, ABV 3.5%)

Drummer (OG 1039, ABV 3.9%)
Clean, malty session bitter with lasting dry finish and increasing bitterness in the aftertaste.

Light Oak (OG 1040, ABV 4%)

Oak Beauty (OG 1042, ABV 4.2%)
Malty, sweetish copper-coloured bitter with toffee and caramel flavours. Long-lasting and satisfying bitter finish.

Bitter (OG 1044, ABV 4.4%)

Midnight Stout (OG 1044, ABV 4.4%)
Classic creamy dry stout with roast flavours to the fore. Well-balanced with bitterness and good hops on the taste and a good dry, roasty aftertaste. Some sweetness.

Bees Knees (OG 1045, ABV 4.5%)
Brewed with honey.

Redwood (OG 1049, ABV 4.9%)

Generals Tipple (OG 1055, ABV 5.5%)

Super IPA (OG 1064, ABV 6.4%)

Worfield

See Shires

George Wright

George Wright Brewing Co, Unit 11, Diamond Business Park, Sandwash Close, Rainford, Merseyside, WA11 8LU
☎ (01744) 886686
✉ sales@georgewrightbrewing.co.uk
🌐 georgewrightbrewing.co.uk
Tours by arrangement

George Wright started production in 2003. The original 2.5-barrel plant was replaced by a five-barrel one, which has since been upgraded again to 25 barrels with production of 200 casks a week.

Black Swan (ABV 3.8%)
A dark, distinctive beer. Very creamy and full of malty flavour.

Drunken Duck (ABV 3.9%)
Fruity gold-coloured bitter beer with good hop and a dry aftertaste. Some acidity.

Longboat (ABV 3.9%)
Good hoppy bitter with grapefruit and an almost tart bitterness throughout. Some astringency in the

aftertaste. Well-balanced, light and refreshing with a good mouthfeel and long, dry finish.

Pipe Dream (ABV 4.3%)
Refreshing hoppy best bitter with a fruity nose and grapefruit to the fore in the taste. Lasting dry, bitter finish.

Pure Blonde (ABV 4.6%)
A premium blonde beer, very light in colour with a herbal nose, floral taste and sweet finish.

Cheeky Pheasant (ABV 4.7%)

Roman Black (ABV 4.8%)

Blue Moon (ABV 4.9%)
Easy-drinking strong, gold-coloured beer. Good malt/bitter balance and well hopped.

Wychwood

See Marston's in New Nationals section

Wye Valley SIBA

Wye Valley Brewery, Stoke Lacy, Herefordshire, HR7 4HG
☎ (01885) 490505
sales@wyevalleybrewery.co.uk
wyevalleybrewery.co.uk
Shop Mon-Fri 10am-4pm
Tours by arrangement

Founded in 1995 in Canon Pyon, Herefordshire, Wye Valley Brewery now occupies the historic Symonds Cider site at Stoke Lacy. Growth and investment continue with a state of the art bottling line commissioned in 2008. Bottle-conditioned beers are available.

Bitter (OG 1037, ABV 3.7%)
A beer whose aroma gives little hint of the bitter hoppiness that follows right through to the aftertaste.

HPA (OG 1040, ABV 4%)
A pale, hoppy, malty brew with a hint of sweetness before a dry finish.

Dorothy Goodbody's Golden Ale (OG 1042, ABV 4.2%)
A light, gold-coloured ale with a good hop character throughout.

Butty Bach (OG 1046, ABV 4.5%)
A burnished gold, full-bodied premium ale.

Dorothy Goodbody's Wholesome Stout (OG 1046, ABV 4.6%)
A smooth and satisfying stout with a bitter edge to its roast flavours. The finish combines roast grain and malt.

Wylam SIBA

Wylam Brewery Ltd, South Houghton Farm, Heddon on the Wall, Northumberland, NE15 0EZ
☎ (01661) 853377
admin@wylambrewery.co.uk
wylambrew.co.uk
Tours by arrangement

Wylam started in 2000 on a 4.5-barrel plant, which increased to nine barrels in 2002. New premises and brew plant (20 barrels) were installed on the same site in 2006. The brewery delivers to more than 200 local outlets and beers are available through wholesalers around the country. Seasonal beers: see website.

Bitter (OG 1039, ABV 3.8%)
A refreshing, copper-coloured, hoppy bitter with a clean, bitter finish.

Gold Tankard (OG 1040, ABV 4%)
Fresh, clean flavour, full of hops. This golden ale has a hint of citrus in the finish.

Magic (OG 1042, ABV 4.2%)
Light, crisp and refreshing. Floral and spicy with a good bitter finish.

Angel (OG 1044, ABV 4.3%)

Northern Kite (OG 1046.5, ABV 4.5%)

Bohemia (OG 1046, ABV 4.6%)
Tawny in colour with a heady bouquet of malt and hops, and a deep finish of fruit.

Haugh (OG 1046, ABV 4.6%)
A smooth velvet porter packed with flavour. Roast malt and a slight fruitiness provide a satisfying beer with a smooth finish.

Locomotion No. 1 (OG 1050, ABV 5%)

Rocket (OG 1048, ABV 5%)
A copper-coloured strong bitter.

Wyre Piddle

Wyre Piddle Brewery Ltd, Highgrove Farm, Peopleton, Nr Pershore, Wiltshire, WR10 2LF
☎ (01905) 841853
strongbow1@btopenworld.com

Wyre Piddle was established in 1992. The brewery relocated and upgraded its equipment in 1997 and moved to its current location in 2002, where it has continued to expand. The beers can be found in pubs throughout the UK and around 100 pubs are supplied directly in the Midlands. It also brews for Green Dragon, Malvern: Dragon's Downfall (ABV 3.9%) and for Severn Valley Railway: Royal Piddle (ABV 4.2%). Seasonal beer: Yule Piddle (ABV 4.5%, Xmas).

Piddle in the Hole (OG 1039, ABV 3.9%)
Copper-coloured and quite dry, with lots of hops and fruitiness throughout.

Piddle in the Dark (ABV 4.5%)
A rich ruby-red bitter with a smooth flavour.

Piddle in the Wind (ABV 4.5%)
This drink has a superb mix of flavours. A hoppy nose continues through to a lasting aftertaste, making it a good, all-round beer.

Piddle in the Sun/Snow (ABV 5.2%)
A dry, strong taste all the way through draws your attention to the balance between malt and hops in the brew. A glorious way to end an evening's drinking.

Yard of Ale

Yard of Ale Brewing Co Ltd, Surtees Arms, Chilton Lane, Ferryhill, County Durham, DL17 0DH
☎ (01740) 655724
surteesarms@btconnect.com
thesurteesarms.co.uk

Established in early 2008, the 2.5-barrel micro supplies ales to its brewery tap, the Surtees Arms, and also to pubs, clubs and beer festivals in surrounding areas. Seasonal ale: Winter's Yard (ABV 4.7%).

First Yard (OG 1040, ABV 3.8%)
A copper-coloured session bitter with malty flavours and a mild roasted finish.

Yard Hopper (OG 1041, ABV 4%)
A pale ale, uniquely brewed using locally-grown hops resulting in delicate hop aromas and a bitter, zesty finish.

Black As Owt Stout (OG 1043, ABV 4.2%)
A traditional, bitter dark stout with distinctive roast coffee nose and smooth chocolate and coffee flavours.

One Foot In The Yard (OG 1044, ABV 4.5%)
Premium golden ale. Fruity on the nose and palate with a sweet finish.

Yates SIBA

Yates Brewery Ltd, Ghyll Farm, Westnewton, Wigton, Cumbria, CA7 3NX
☎ (01697) 321081
✉ enquiry@yatesbrewery.co.uk
yatesbrewery.co.uk
Tours by arrangement

Cumbria's oldest micro-brewery, established in 1986. The brewery was bought in 1998 by Graeme and Caroline Baxter, who had previously owned High Force Brewery in Teesdale. Deliveries are mainly to its Cumbrian stronghold and the A69 corridor as far as Hexham. A brewhouse and reed bed effluent system have been added on the same site. Around 40 outlets are supplied. Seasonal beers: see website.

Bitter (OG 1035, ABV 3.7%)
A well-balanced, full-bodied bitter, golden in colour with complex hop bitterness. Good aroma and distinctive flavour.

Fever Pitch (OG 1039, ABV 3.9%)
Skilful use of lager malt and hops results in a pale beer with a light bitterness; melon fruit and a clean, refreshing finish.

Sun Goddess (OG 1042, ABV 4.2%)
A complex honeyed beer, packed with tropical fruit.

Yates' SIBA

Yates' Brewery, Unit 4C, Langbridge Business Centre, Newchurch, Isle of Wight, PO36 0NP
☎ (01983) 731731 (Office)
✉ info@yates-brewery.co.uk
yates-brewery.co.uk
Tours by arrangement

Brewing started in 2000 on a five-barrel plant at the Inn at St Lawrence. The brewery moved in 2009 to premises in Newchurch. Seasonal beer: Yule B Sorry (ABV 7.6%, Xmas), Wight Winter (ABV 5%), St Lawrence Ale (ABV 5%, summer). Bottle-conditioned beers are also available.

Best Bitter (ABV 3.8%)
Initial sweetness is quickly balanced by subtle fruitiness and moderate hop bitterness. A full-flavoured beer with a bittersweet aftertaste.

Undercliff Experience (OG 1040, ABV 4.1%)
An amber ale with a bittersweet malt and hop taste with a dry, lemon edge that dominates the bitter finish.

Blonde Ale (OG 1045, ABV 4.5%)
A golden beer with a malty aroma, laced with floral, citrus hops. The taste is hoppy and bitter to start, with smooth malt support and light lemon notes. Dry, hoppy aftertaste.

Holy Joe (OG 1050, ABV 4.9%)
Strongly bittered golden ale with pronounced spice and citrus character, and underlying light hint of malt.

Special Draught (OG 1056, ABV 5.5%)
Easy-drinking strong, amber ale with pronounced tart bitterness and a refreshing bite in the aftertaste.

Wight Old Ale (ABV 6%)
A deep ruby ale with a smooth taste.

Yeovil

Yeovil Ales Ltd, Unit 5, Bofors Park, Artillery Road, Lufton Trading Estate, Yeovil, Somerset, BA22 8YH
☎ (01935) 414888
✉ rob@yeovilales.com
yeovilales.com
Sales counter Fri pm only until 5.30pm
Tours by arrangement

Yeovil Ales was established in 2006 with an 18-barrel plant. Production has steadily increased since and up to 350 outlets are supplied direct across six counties in the south west. Seasonal beers: Spring Forward (ABV 4.5%, Mar-May), British Summer Time (ABV 4.5%, May-Sep).

Glory (OG 1039, ABV 3.8%)
A well-balanced bitter with citrus hop notes.

Star Gazer (OG 1042, ABV 4%)
Dark copper bitter with late-hopped floral bouquet.

Summerset (OG 1043, ABV 4.1%)
Blonde ale with fruity hop finish.

Ruby (OG 1047, ABV 4.5%)
Red bitter with rich malt depth.

Yetman's

Yetman's Brewery, Bayfield Farm Barns, Bayfield Brecks Farm, Bayfield, Norfolk, BR25 7DZ
☎ 07774 809016
✉ peter@yetmans.net
yetmans.net

A 2.5-barrel plant built by Moss Brew was installed in restored medieval barns in 2005. The brewery supplies local free trade outlets. Bottle-conditioned beers are available.

Red (OG 1036, ABV 3.8%)

Orange (OG 1040, ABV 4.2%)
A distinctly malty beer in both taste and aroma. Copper coloured with a sustained bitter edge that becomes slightly astringent in the long finish.

Green (OG 1044, ABV 4.8%)

York SIBA

York Brewery Ltd, 12 Toft Green, York, North Yorkshire, YO1 6JT
☎ (01904) 621162
✉ info@yorkbrew.co.uk
yorkbrew.co.uk
Shop Mon-Sat 12-6pm
Tours by arrangement (ring for daily tour times)

York started production in 1996, the first brewery in the city for 40 years. It has a visitor centre with bar and gift shop, and was designed as a show brewery, with a gallery above the 20-barrel plant and viewing panels to fermentation and conditioning rooms. The brewery owns several pubs and in 2006 additional space was acquired to increase production capacity. More than 400 outlets are supplied. Seasonal beers: see website. The brewery was bought by Mitchell's Hotels & Inns in 2008, but no major changes to the brewery or pubs are planned.

Guzzler (OG 1036, ABV 3.6%) ◆
Refreshing golden ale with dominant hop and fruit flavours developing throughout.

Constantine (ABV 3.9%)

Yorkshire Terrier (OG 1041, ABV 4.2%) ◆
Refreshing and distinctive amber/gold brew where fruit and hops dominate the aroma and taste. Hoppy bitterness remains assertive in the aftertaste.

Centurion's Ghost Ale (OG 1051, ABV 5.4%) ◆
Dark ruby in colour, full-tasting with mellow roast malt character balanced by light bitterness and autumn fruit flavours that linger into the aftertaste.

Yorkshire Dales

Yorkshire Dales Brewing Co Ltd, Seata Barn, Elm Hill, Askrigg, North Yorkshire, DL8 3HG
☎ (01969) 622027
☎ 07818 035592
✉ rob@yorkshiredalesbrewery.com
🌐 yorkshiredalesbrewery.com

Situated in the heart of the Yorkshire Dales, brewing started in 2005. Installation of a five-barrel plant and additional fermenters at the converted milking parlour increased capacity to 20 barrels a week. Over 150 pubs are supplied throughout the North of England. Four monthly special are always available, including a dark mild.

Butter Tubs (OG 1037, ABV 3.7%)
A pale golden beer with a dry bitterness complemented by strong citrus flavours and aroma.

Leyburn Shawl (OG 1038, ABV 3.8%)
A crisp, dry, pale ale with an underlying sharpness.

Buckden Pike (OG 1040, ABV 3.9%)
A refreshing blonde beer with a crisp, fruity finish.

Kings' Arms Ale (OG 1041, ABV 4%)
A golden ale brewed with a trio of American hops for citrus and peach flavours throughout.

Muker Silver (OG 1041, ABV 4.1%)
A blonde lager-style ale, very crisp with a sharp, hoppy finish.

Askrigg Ale (OG 1043, ABV 4.3%)
A pale golden ale with intense aroma that generates a crisp, dry flavour with a long, bitter finish.

Yorkshire Penny (OG 1046, ABV 4.5%)
Classic dry stout with rich liquorice and chocolate malt flavours.

Garsdale Smokebox (OG 1057, ABV 5.6%)
A complex ale created by the smoked and dark malts. Deep, rich chocolate and coffee flavours are complimented by the smokiness.

Young's

See Wells & Young's in New Nationals section

Zerodegrees SIBA

Blackheath: Zerodegrees Microbrewery, 29-31 Montpelier Vale, Blackheath, London, SE3 0TJ
☎ (020) 8852 5619

Bristol: Zerodegrees Microbrewery, 53 Colston Street, Bristol, BS1 5BA
☎ (0117) 925 2706

Reading: 9 Bridge Street, Reading, Berkshire, RG1 2LR
☎ (0118) 959 7959

Cardiff: 27 Westgate Street, Cardiff, CF10 1DD
✉ info@zerodegrees.co.uk
🌐 zerodegrees.co.uk
Tours by arrangement

Brewing started in 2000 in London and incorporates a state-of-the-art, computer-controlled German plant, producing unfiltered and unfined ales and lagers, served from tanks using air pressure (not CO2). Four pubs are owned. All beers are suitable for vegetarians and vegans. All branches of Zerodegrees follow the same concept of beers with natural ingredients. There are regular seasonal specials including fruit beers.

Fruit Beer (OG 1040, ABV 4%)
The type of fruit used varies during the year.

Wheat Ale (OG 1045, ABV 4.2%) ◆
Refreshing wheat ale with spicy aroma; banana, vanilla and sweet flavours; dry, lasting finish.

Pale Ale (OG 1046, ABV 4.6%) ◆
American-style IPA with complex fruit aroma and peach flavours. Clean bitter finish with long aftertaste.

Black Lager (OG 1048, ABV 4.8%) ◆
Light, Eastern European-style black lager brewed with roasted malt. Refreshing coffee finish.

Pilsner (OG 1048, ABV 4.8%) ◆
Clean-tasting refreshing Pilsner with a malty aroma and taste, accompanied by delicate bitterness and citrus fruits.

REPUBLIC OF IRELAND BREWERIES

Arainn Mhor

Arainn Mhor Brewing Co, Airainn Mhor Island, Burtinport, Co Donegal 00353 87 630 6856
🌐 ambrewco.com

No real ale but there are two bottle-conditioned beers, Ban and Rua.

Beoir Chorca Dhuibhne/Dark Corner Beer

Beoir Chorca Dhuibhne/Dark Corner Beer, c/o Tig Bhric, Nr Ballyferriter, Co Kerry 00353 66 915 6325
✉ info@tigbhric.com
🌐 tigbhric.com

Beer is brewed on a 400-litre plant in a remote area where Erse/Gaelic is the main language.

Cul Dhorca (ABV 4.1%)

THE BREWERIES

Carlow

Carlow Brewing Co, The Goods Store, Station Road, Carlow, Co Carlow 00353 503 34356
info@carlowbrewing.com
carlowbrewing.com

One of the bigger Irish independents with a sizable range of cask beers.

O'Hara's Irish Stout (ABV 4.3%)

O'Hara's Red Ale (ABV 4.3%)

Druid's Brew Stout (ABV 4.7%)

Wheat Beer (ABV 4.7%)

Lann Follain Stout (ABV 6%)

Franciscan Well

Franciscan Well Brewery, 14 North Mall, Cork City, Co Cork 00353 59 913 4356

Small brewery that brings choice to a city dominated by Beamish and Murphy, both owned by Heineken, which plans to close Beamish. Franciscan Well brews Stout and Red Ale, both keg beers but occasionally produce in cask form for special events.

Galway Hooker

Galway Hooker Brewery, IDA Business Park, Racecourse Road, Roscommon, Co Galway 00353 87 776283
galwayhooker.ie

Galway Hooker produce a filtered keg beer in Ireland but make it in cask form for beer festivals in Britain. It was available at the Great British Beer Festival in 2008.

Pale Ale (ABV 4.4%)

Messrs Maguire

Messrs Maguire Brewing Co, 1-2 Burgh Quay, Dublin 2 00353 16 705 7777
messrsmaguire.ie

Pub, brewery and restaurant in the historic O'Connell Bridge area of the city. It brews a range of keg beers, including stout, plain (porter) and wheat beer.

Best (ABV 4.3%)
Cask-conditioned best bitter.

Porterhouse

Porterhouse Brewing Co, Unit 6D, Rosemount, Park Road, Ballycoolin, Blanchardstown, Dublin 15 00353 18 227417
porterhousebrewco.com

The oldest surviving micro in Ireland. It has three pubs in Dublin, 16-18 Parliament Street, Temple Bar, Dublin 2; Porterhouse North, Cross Guns Bridge, Glasnevin, Dublin 9; Porterhouse Central, 45-47 Nassau Street, City Centre South, Dublin 2; plus Porterhouse Bray, Strand Road, Co Wicklow. There's also a branch in Covent Garden, London. A wide range of keg stouts, porters and red ale.

TSB (ABV 4.3%)
Cask-conditioned bitter.

White Gypsy

White Gypsy Brewing Co, 14 Priory Place, Templemore, Co Tipperary
whitegypsy.ie

White Gypsy also brews for Barrelhead Brewery of Dublin, a new brew-pub not currently in production. A trial beer is Bull Island Pale Ale.

St Cuilan's Ale (ABV 4.6%)

India Pale Ale (ABV 5.2%)

FROM OVERSEAS

De Koninck

Brouwerij De Koninck NV, 291 Mechelsesteenweg, 2018 Antwerp, Belgium
(0032) 3 218 4048
info@dekoninck.com
dekoninck.be

Legendary Belgian brewer of a classic pale ale, founded in 1833. In its home territory the beer is served under pressure but a cask-conditioned version is available in selected Wetherspoon's pubs in Britain. The beer is fined and racked into casks by Shepherd Neame in Faversham. The beer is called Ambrée in Britain but is known simply as De Koninck in Belgium.

Ambree (ABV 5%)

Palm

Brouwerij Palm, 3 Steenhuffeldoorp, 1840 Steenhuffel, Belgium
(0032) 3 52 31 74 11
info@palmbreweries.com
palmbreweries.com

Family-owned since 1747, Palm has grown to become one of Belgium's major independents. Its home base is near Mechelen. It took over Rodenbach in 1998 and has close links with the Boon lambic brewery. Its main brand since 1929 has been Palm Special, an amber beer that became so popular that in 1975 the brewery was named after the beer. The cask-conditioned version, known simply as Palm, is racked into casks by Marston's for selected Wetherspoon's outlets.

Palm (ABV 5%)

Your shout

We would like to hear from you. If you think a pub not listed in the Guide is worthy of consideration, please let us know. Send us the name, full address and phone number (if known). If a pub in the Guide has given poor service, we would also like to know.

Write to Good Beer Guide, CAMRA, 230 Hatfield Road, St Albans, Herts, AL1 4LW or email **gbgeditor@camra.org.uk**

R.I.P.

The following breweries have closed, gone out of business or suspended operations since the 2009 Guide was published:

Abbey Bells, Hirst Courtney, North Yorkshire
Archers, Swindon, Wiltshire
Battersea, Battersea, London
Bells, Broughton Astley, Leicestershire
Blackdown, Honiton, Devon
Black Mountain, Llangadog, Carmarthenshire
Bricktop, Stoke Prior, Worcestershire
Bridgnorth, Bridgnorth, Shropshire (Suspended)
Bunker, Covent Garden, London
Butler's, Mapledurham, Oxfordshire
Burford, Witney, Oxfordshire
Combe Martin, Combe Martin, Devon
Dane Town, Denton, Greater Manchester (Suspended)
Dunn Plowman, Kington, Herefordshire
Fen, Long Sutton, Lincolnshire
Fenland, Little Downham, Cambridgeshire
Fowler's, Prestonpans, East Lothian
Grindleton, Clitheroe, Lancashire
Gwynant, Capel Bangor, West Wales (Suspended)
Hampshire, Romsey, Hampshire
Higson's, Liverpool, Merseyside
Keynsham, Keynsham, Bristol
Marches, Leominster, Herefordshire
Oulton, Oulton Broad, Suffolk
Packfield, Black Notley, Essex
Phipps, Banbury, Oxfordshire
Rodham's, Otley, West Yorkshire (Suspended)
Selby, Selby, North Yorkshire
Ventnor, Ventnor, Isle of Wight
Wear Valley, Bishop Auckland, County Durham
WF6, Altofts, West Yorkshire
Wonky Dog, Brightlingsea, Essex

Future breweries

The following new breweries have been notified to the Guide and will start to produce beer during 2009/2010. In a few cases, they were in production during the summer of 2009 but were too late for a full listing in the Guide:

Albion, Warrington, Cheshire
Ayr, Ayr, Scotland: Ayrshire & Arran
Beverley, Beverley, East Yorkshire
Bird Brain, Howden, East Yorkshire
Buckinghamshire, Aylesbury, Buckinghamshire
Calside, Paisley, Renfrewshire, Scotland: Greater Glasgow & Clyde Valley
Castor, Castor, Cambridgeshire
Dove Street, Ipswich, Suffolk
Ferry House, Burton upon Stather, Lincolnshire
Grove, Huddersfield, West Yorkshire
Heritage, Sowerby Bridge, West Yorkshire
Joules, Market Drayton, Shropshire
Kelda, Keld, North Yorkshire
Kinneil, Bo'ness, West Lothian, Scotland: Edinburgh & The Lothians
Lever, Malpas, Cheshire
Liverpool Organic, Liverpool, Merseyside
Old Farm, Whitebrook, Monmouth
Red Man, Braystones, Cumbria
Scottish Borders, Jedburgh, Scotland: Borders
Shedded, Salford, Greater Manchester
Staughton, Bedford, Bedfordshire
Tatton, Knutsford, Cheshire
Trent Navigation, Nottingham, Nottinghamshire
Trowel, Chesham, Buckinghamshire
Tweedies, Grasmere, Cumbria

New nationals

The rapid growth of Greene King, Marston's and Wells & Young's since 2000 has given them the status of national breweries. Marston's is the new name for Wolverhampton & Dudley Breweries while Wells & Young's was formed when Young & Co of London closed its brewery in 2006 and all production was moved to Bedford. The new nationals do not match the size of the global brewers but they do reach most areas of Britain as a result of both their tied and free trade activities. Unlike the global producers or the old national brewers who disappeared in the 1990s, Greene King, Marston's and W&Y are committed to cask beer production. Greene King IPA is the biggest-selling standard cask beer in the country, closely followed by Young's Bitter, Marston's Pedigree now outsells Draught Bass in the premium sector, and Wells Bombardier is one of the fastest-growing premium cask brands. There is a down-side to this progress: in some parts of the country, the choice of real ale is often confined to the products of Greene King and Marston's, and their continued expansion, seen in the takeovers of Belhaven, Hardys & Hansons, Jennings, Refresh (Brakspear and Wychwood), Ringwood and Ridley's, is cause for concern for drinkers who cherish choice and diversity.

GREENE KING

Greene King

Greene King plc, Westgate Brewery, Bury St Edmunds, Suffolk, IP33 1QT
☎ (01284) 763222
✉ solutions@greeneking.co.uk
🌐 greeneking.co.uk
Shop Mon-Sat 10am-5pm; Sun 12-4pm
Tours 11am, 2pm and evening by arrangement

⊗ Greene King has been brewing in the market town of Bury St Edmunds since 1799. In the 1990s it bought the brands of the former Morland and Ruddles breweries and has given a massive promotion to Old Speckled Hen, which in bottled form is now the biggest ale brand in Britain. As a result of buying the former Morland pub estate, the company acquired a major presence in the Thames Valley region. But it has not confined itself to East Anglia or the Home Counties. Its tenanted and managed pubs, which include Old English Inns and Hungry Horse, total more than 2,100 while the assiduous development of its free trade sales, totalling more than 3,000 outlets, means its beers can be found as far from its home base as Wales and the north of England. In 2005 Greene King bought and rapidly closed Ridley's of Essex. Also in 2005, the group bought Belhaven of Dunbar in Scotland. Belhaven has a large pub estate that has enabled Greene King to build sales north of the border. In 2006 the group bought and closed Hardys & Hansons in Nottingham, taking its pub estate to close to 3,000. Seasonal beers change monthly with sporting or topical names. Bottle-conditioned beer: Hen's Tooth (ABV 6.5%).

XX Mild (OG 1035, ABV 3%)
A dark mild with a sweet and roast flavour.

IPA (OG 1036, ABV 3.6%) ◆
Delightfully hoppy but thin beer with a surprisingly sweet and fruity finish. A good session beer if kept well.

Ruddles Best Bitter (OG 1037, ABV 3.7%) ◆
An amber/brown beer, strong on bitterness but with some initial sweetness, fruit and subtle, distinctive Bramling Cross hop. Dryness lingers in the aftertaste.

H&H Bitter (OG 1038, ABV 3.9%)
A balance of sweetness and bitterness that combines with a subtle hop character. A distinctive beer with a full finish.

Morland Original Bitter (OG 1039, ABV 4%)
A subtle malt and fruit character and a pronounced bitter finish.

H&H Olde Trip (OG 1043, ABV 4.3%)
A rich toffee flavoured beer with a fruity character and a clean, bitter finish.

Ruddles County (OG 1048, ABV 4.3%) ◆
Sweet, malty and bitter, with a dry and bitter aftertaste.

Old Speckled Hen (OG 1045, ABV 4.5%) ◆
Smooth, malty and fruity, with a short finish.

Abbot Ale (OG 1049, ABV 5%)
A full-bodied, distinctive beer with a bittersweet aftertaste.

Belhaven

Belhaven Brewing Co, Spott Road, Dunbar, East Lothian, EH42 1RS
☎ (01368) 862734
✉ info@belhaven.co.uk
🌐 belhaven.co.uk
Shop open during tours
Tours by arrangement

◎ Belhaven is located in Dunbar, some 30 miles east of Edinburgh on the East Lothian coast. The company claimed to be the oldest independent brewery in Scotland but it lost that independence when Greene King bought it. Belhaven owns 275 tied pubs and has around 2,500 direct free trade accounts. Seasonal beers: Fruit Beer (ABV 4.6%, Jul), Fruity Partridge (ABV 5.2%, Dec).

60/- Ale (OG 1030, ABV 2.9%) ◆
A fine but virtually unavailable example of a Scottish light. This bittersweet, reddish-brown beer is dominated by fruit and malt with a hint of roast and caramel, and increasing bitterness in the aftertaste.

70/- Ale (OG 1038, ABV 3.5%) ◆
This pale brown beer has malt and fruit and some hop throughout, and is increasingly bittersweet in the aftertaste.

Sandy Hunter's Traditional Ale (OG 1038, ABV 3.6%) ◆
A distinctive, medium-bodied beer. An aroma of malt and hops greets the nose. A hint of roast combines with the malt and hops to give a bittersweet taste and finish.

80/- Ale (OG 1040, ABV 4.2%) ◆
One of the last remaining original Scottish 80 Shillings, with malt the predominant flavour characteristic, though it is balanced by hop and fruit. Those used to hops as the leaders in a beer's taste may find this complex ale disconcerting.

St Andrew's Ale (OG 1046, ABV 4.9%)
A bittersweet beer with lots of body. The malt, fruit and roast mingle throughout with hints of hop and caramel.

For Edinburgh Brewing Co (qv):

Edinburgh Pale Ale (ABV 3.4%)

For Maclay pub group:

Signature (OG 1038, ABV 3.8%)
A pronounced malty note is followed by a digestive biscuit flavour. The beer has a late addition of Goldings and Styrian hops.

Kane's Amber Ale (ABV 4%)
A hoppy aroma gives way to a malty yet slightly bitter flavour.

Wallace IPA (ABV 4.5%)
A classic IPA in both colour and style, with a long, dry finish.

Golden Scotch Ale (ABV 5%)
Brewed to an original Maclay's recipe, the emphasis is firmly on malt.

MARSTON'S

Marston's plc, Marston's House, Wolverhampton, West Midlands, WV1 4JT
☎ (01902) 711811
✉ enquiries@marstons.co.uk
🌐 wdb.co.uk

Marston's, formerly Wolverhampton & Dudley, has grown with spectacular speed in recent years. It became a 'super regional' in 1999 when it bought both Mansfield and Marston's breweries, though it quickly closed Mansfield. In 2005 it bought Jennings of Cockermouth and has invested £250,000 in Cumbria to expand fermenting and cask racking capacity. In total, Marston's owns 2,537 pubs and supplies some 3,000 free trade pubs and clubs throughout the country. It no longer has a stake in Burtonwood Brewery (qv) but brews Burtonwood Bitter for the pub estate, which is owned by Marston's. It added a further 70 pubs in 2006 when it bought Celtic Inns for £43.6 million. In January 2007 it paid £155 million for the 158-strong Eldridge Pope pub estate. In July 2007 it bought Ringwood in Hampshire and in the same year added Brakspear and Wychwood in Witney, Oxfordshire.

Banks's & Hanson's

Banks's Brewery, Park Brewery, Wolverhampton, West Midlands, WV1 4NY Contact details as above

Banks's was formed in 1890 by the amalgamation of three local companies. Hanson's was acquired in 1943 but its Dudley brewery was closed in 1991. Hanson's beers are now brewed in Wolverhampton, though its pubs retain the Hanson's livery. Banks's Original, the biggest-selling brand, is a fine example of West Midlands mild ale but the name was changed to give it a more 'modern' image. Beers from the closed Mansfield Brewery are now brewed at Wolverhampton. Hanson's Mild has been discontinued.

Original (OG 1036, ABV 3.5%)
An amber-coloured, well-balanced, refreshing session beer.

Bitter (OG 1038, ABV 3.8%)
A pale brown bitter with a pleasant balance of hops and malt. Hops continue from the taste through to a bittersweet aftertaste.

Mansfield Cask Ale (OG 1038, ABV 3.9%)

Brakspear

Brakspear Brewing Co, Eagle Maltings, The Crofts, Witney, Oxfordshire, OX28 4DP
☎ (01993) 890800
✉ info@brakspear-beers.co.uk
🌐 brakspear-beers.co.uk
Merchandise available online
Tours by arrangement

Brakspear, along with Wychwood (see below) was bought by Marston's in March 2007. Brakspear was originally based in Henley-on-Thames and is one of Britain's oldest breweries, founded before 1700 and run by the Brakspear family since 1779. In 2002, the brewery closed and became a pub company. Refresh UK, a company based in Witney and owners of Wychwood, bought the rights to the Brakspear brands and brewed them again from 2004 after moving the Henley equipment, including the famous 'double drop' fermenters, to Witney. NB Pubs that carry the Brakspear name belong to a separate company that has no connection with Brakspear Brewing Co, though the brewery does supply the pub company with beer. Bottle-conditioned beers are available.

Bitter (OG 1035, ABV 3.4%)
A classic copper-coloured pale ale with a big hop resins, juicy malt and orange fruit aroma, intense hop bitterness in the mouth and finish, and a firm maltiness and tangy fruitiness throughout.

Oxford Gold (OG 1040, ABV 4%)

Jennings

Jennings Bros plc, Castle Brewery, Cockermouth, Cumbria, CA13 9NE
☎ 0845 129 7185
🌐 jenningsbrewery.co.uk
Shop Mon-Fri 9am-5pm; Sat 10am-4pm; Sun 10am-4pm (Jul & Aug)
Tours daily (except Sun); 7 days a week Jul & Aug. Booking advised. Other tours by arrangement

Jennings Brewery was established as a family concern in 1828 in the village of Lorton. The company moved to its present location in 1874. Pure Lakeland water is still used for brewing, drawn from the brewery's own well, along with Maris Otter barley malt and Fuggles and Goldings hops. Regular specials reflect the Cumbrian heritage of Jennings and include Crag Rat (ABV 4.3%), Fish King (ABV 4.3%), Golden Host (ABV 4.3%), Tom Fool (4%).

Dark Mild (OG 1031, ABV 3.1%)
A well-balanced, dark brown mild with a malty aroma, strong roast taste, not over-sweet, with some hops and a slightly bitter finish.

Bitter (OG 1035, ABV 3.5%)
A malty beer with a good mouthfeel that combines with roast flavour and a hoppy finish.

Cumberland Ale (OG 1039, ABV 4%)
A light, creamy, hoppy beer with a dry aftertaste.

Cocker Hoop (OG 1044, ABV 4.6%)

THE BREWERIES

A rich, creamy, copper-coloured beer with raisiny maltiness balanced with a resiny hoppiness, with a developing bitterness towards the end.

Sneck Lifter (OG 1051, ABV 5.1%) ◆
A strong, dark brown ale with a complex balance of fruit, malt and roast flavours through to the finish.

Marston's

Marston, Thompson & Evershed, Marston's Brewery, Shobnall Road, Burton upon Trent, Staffordshire, DE14 2BW
☎ (01283) 531131
🌐 wdb.co.uk

Marston's has been brewing cask beer in Burton since 1834 and the current site is the home of the only working 'Burton Union' fermenters, housed in rooms known collectively as the 'Cathedral of Brewing'. Burton Unions were developed in the 19th century to cleanse the new pale ales of yeast. Only Pedigree is fermented in the unions but yeast from the system is used to ferment the other beers.

Burton Bitter (OG 1037, ABV 3.8%) ◆
Overwhelming sulphurous aroma supports a scattering of hops and fruit with an easy-drinking sweetness. The taste develops from the sweet middle to a satisfyingly hoppy finish.

Pedigree (OG 1043, ABV 4.5%) ◆
Sweet beer with a slight sulphur aroma. Has the hoppy but sweet finish of a short session beer.

Old Empire (OG 1057, ABV 5.7%) ◆
Sulphur dominates the aroma over malt. Malty and sweet to start but developing bitterness with fruit and a touch of sweetness. A balanced aftertaste of hops and fruit leads to a lingering bitterness.

For InBev UK:

Draught Bass (OG 1043, ABV 4.4%) ◆
Pale brown with a fruity aroma and a hint of hops. Hoppy but sweet taste with malt, then a lingering hoppy bitterness.

Ringwood

Ringwood Brewery Ltd, Christchurch Road, Ringwood, Hampshire, BH24 3AP
☎ (01425) 471177
✉ enquiries@ringwoodbrewery.co.uk
🌐 ringwoodbrewery.co.uk
Shop Mon-Fri 9.30am-5pm; Sat 9.30am-12pm
Tours by arrangement

Ringwood was bought in 2007 by Marston's for £19 million. The group plans to increase production to 50,000 barrels a year. Some 750 outlets are supplied and seven pubs are owned. Seasonal beers: Boondoggle (ABV 4%, summer), Bold Forester (ABV 4.2%, spring), Huffkin (ABV 4.4%, autumn), XXXX Porter (ABV 4.7%, winter). Bottle-conditioned beers are also available.

Best Bitter (OG 1038, ABV 3.8%)

Fortyniner (OG 1049, ABV 4.9%) ◆
A fruity, biscuity aroma leads to a sweet but well-balanced taste with malt, fruit and hop flavours all present. The finish is bittersweet with some fruit.

Old Thumper (OG 1055, ABV 5.6%) ◆
A powerful, sweet, copper-coloured beer. A fruity aroma preludes a strong sweet malty taste with soft fruit and caramel, which is not cloying, and leads to a surprisingly bittersweet aftertaste.

Wychwood

Wychwood Brewery Ltd, Eagle Maltings, The Crofts, Witney, Oxfordshire, OX28 4DP
☎ (01993) 890800
✉ info@wychwood.co.uk
🌐 wychwood.co.uk
Shop Sat 2-6pm
Tours by arrangement

Wychwood Brewery is located on the fringes of the ancient medieval forest, the Wychwood. The brewery was founded in 1983 on a site dating back to the 1880s, which was once the original maltings for the town's brewery. A range of seasonal beers is produced.

Hobgoblin (OG 1045, ABV 4.5%)
The beer was reduced in strength early in 2008 by the previous owner, Refresh UK.

WELLS & YOUNG'S

Wells & Young's IFBB

Wells & Young's Brewing Co, Bedford Brewery, Havelock Street, Bedford, MK40 4LU
☎ (01234) 272766
✉ postmaster@wellsandyoungs.co.uk

SIBA Direct Delivery Scheme

In 2003 the Society of Independent Brewers (SIBA) launched a Direct Delivery Scheme (DDS) that enables its members to deliver beer to individual pubs rather than to the warehouses of pub companies. Before the scheme came into operation, small craft brewers could only sell beer to the national pubcos if they delivered beer to their depots. In one case, a brewer in Sheffield was told by Punch Taverns that the pubco would only take his beer if he delivered it to a warehouse in Liverpool and then returned to pick up the empty casks. In the time between delivery and pick-up, some of the beer would have been delivered by Punch to...Sheffield.

Now SIBA has struck agreements with Admiral Taverns, Edinburgh Woollen Mills, Enterprise Inns, New Century Inns, Orchard Pubs, and Punch, as well as off-licence chains Asda and Thresher to deliver direct to their pubs or shops. The scheme has been such a success that DDS is now a separate but wholly-owned subsidiary of SIBA. See **www.siba.co.uk/dds**

wellsandyoungs.co.uk
Merchandise available online
Tours by arrangement

Wells & Young's was created in 2006 when Young's of Wandsworth, south London, announced it would close its brewery and transfer production to Bedford. The new company jointly owns the Bedford Brewery, which opened in 1976; the Wells family has been brewing in the town since 1876. Wells & Young's has a combined sales team that has expanded sales of such key brands as Wells Bombardier, the fastest-growing premium cask beer in Britain, and Young's Bitter, the fastest-growing standard cask bitter. Wells and Young's runs separate pub estates. In 2007, Scottish & Newcastle reached an agreement with W&Y to brew Courage beers at Bedford. A new company, Courage Brands Ltd, was created, with W&Y controlling 83% of the shares. The deal added a further 80,000 barrels a year at Bedford, taking volumes to more than 550,000-600,000 barrels and overtaking Greene King in size. The Courage beers are aimed primarily at the free trade. Some Wells' beers are now available in Young's pubs and vice-versa. Wells owns 250 pubs and 245 serve cask beer; Young's owns 222 pubs in London and the Home Counties, all selling real ale. Young's has invested heavily in estate improvement and expansion over the past two years. Seasonal beer: Young's Waggledance (ABV 4%). There are several occasional beers. Bottle-conditioned beers: Young's Bitter (ABV 4.5%). Young's Kew Gold (ABV 4.8%), Young's Special London Ale (ABV 6.4%).

Eagle IPA (OG 1035, ABV 3.6%)
A refreshing, amber session bitter with pronounced citrus hop aroma and palate, faint malt in the mouth, and a lasting dry, bitter finish.

Young's Bitter (OG 1036, ABV 3.7%)
A refreshing amber coloured bitter with a citrus hop character throughout. Finish is dry with some bitterness and a little malt.

Wells Bombardier (OG 1042, ABV 4.3%)
Gentle citrus hop is balanced by traces of malt in the mouth, and this pale brown best bitter ends with a lasting dryness. Sulphur often dominates the aroma, particularly with younger casks.

Young's Special (OG 1044, ABV 4.5%)
Amber in colour, the aroma is of malt and citrus, carrying into the flavour and aftertaste where it is balanced by a lingering bitterness and a dry, but smooth mouthfeel.

Young's Winter Warmer (OG 1055, ABV 5%)
Raisins, dark roast notes (sometimes coffee) are complemented by some hops and malty sweetness on the palate in this dark reddish brown beer. Aftertaste is dryish with a bitter character. Available Nov-Jan in selected pubs.

For Courage Brands:

Courage Best Bitter (OG 1038.3, ABV 4%)

Courage Directors Bitter (OG 1045.5, ABV 4.8%)

All hands to the pumps

British beer is unique and so are the methods used for serving it. The best-known English system, the beer engine operated by a handpump on the pub bar, arrived early in the 19th century. It coincided with and was prompted by the decline of the publican brewer and the rise of commercial companies that began to dominate the supply of beer to public houses. In order to sell more beer, commercial brewers and publicans looked for faster and less labour-intensive methods of serving beer.

In The Brewing Industry in England, 1700-1830, Peter Mathias records that 'most beer had to be stored in butts in the publicans' cellars for the technical reason that it needed an even and fairly low temperature, even where convenience and restricted space behind the bar did not enforce it. This meant, equally inevitably, continuous journeying to and from the cellars by the potboys to fill up jugs from the spigots: a waste of time for the customer and of labour and trade for the publican. Drawing up beer from the cellar at the pull of a handle at the bar at once increased the speed of sale and cut the wage bill.'

The first attempt at a system for raising beer from cellar to bar was patented by Joseph Bramah in 1797. But his system – using heavy boxes of sand that pressed down on storage vessels holding the beer – was so elaborate that it was never used. But his idea encouraged others to develop simpler systems. Mathias writes: 'One of the few technical devices of importance to come into the public house since the publican stopped brewing his own beer was the beer engine. It was, from the first, a simple manually operated pump, incorporating no advances in hydraulic knowledge or engineering skill, similar in design to many pumps used at sea, yet perfectly adapted to its function in the public house.'

By 1801, John Chadwell of Blackfriars, London, was registered as a 'beer-engine maker' and soon afterwards Thomas Rowntree in the same area described himself as a 'maker of a double-acting beer-machine'. By the 1820s, beer engine services had become standard throughout most of urban England and Gaskell & Chambers in the Midlands had become the leading manufacturer, employing more than 700 people in their Birmingham works alone.

Global giants

Eight out of ten pints of beer brewed in Britain come from the international groups listed below. Most of these huge companies have little or no interest in cask beer. Increasingly, their real ale brands are produced for them by smaller regional brewers. The major change at the top of the industry was the takeover of Britain's biggest brewer, Scottish & Newcastle, by Carlsberg and Heineken in 2008. Carlsberg now controls S&N's interests in Russia and the Baltic and owns outright the Baltika breweries, along with Kronenbourg in France. Heineken now owns S&N's British interests including S&N Pub Enterprises, an estate of 1,170 pubs.

A-B InBev

A-B InBev UK Ltd, Porter Tun House, 500 Capability Green, Luton, Bedfordshire, LU1 3LS
☎ (01582) 391166
name.surname@interbrew.co.uk
inbev.com

The biggest merger in brewing history in 2008 created A-B InBev, when InBev of Belgium and Brazil bought American giant Anheuser-Busch, best-known for the world's biggest (but not best) beer brand, Budweiser. The giant is a major player in the European market with such lager brands as Stella Artois and Jupiler. It has some interest in ale brewing with the cask- and bottle-conditioned wheat beer, Hoegaarden, and the Abbey beer Leffe. It has a ruthless track record of closing plants and disposing of brands: it has already announced the closure of the historic Stag Brewery in Mortlake, London, formerly Watney's, where the British version of Budweiser is brewed. It's not known where the brand will be produced following the closure of the Mortlake plant but it's unlikely that many readers of the Good Beer Guide will care. In 2000 Interbrew, as it was then known, bought both Bass's and Whitbread's brewing operations, giving it a 32 per cent market share. The British government told Interbrew to dispose of parts of the Bass brewing group, which were bought by Coors (qv). Draught Bass has declined to around 100,000 barrels a year: it once sold more than two million barrels a year, but was sidelined by the Bass empire. It is now brewed under licence by Marston's (see New Nationals section). Only 30 per cent of draught Boddingtons is now in cask form and this is brewed under licence by Hydes of Manchester (qv Independents section).

Brewed for A-B InBev by Brain's of Cardiff:

Flowers IPA (ABV 3.6%)

Flowers Original (ABV 4.5%)

Carlsberg UK

Carlsberg Brewing Ltd, PO Box 142, The Brewery, Leeds, West Yorkshire, LS1 1QG
☎ (0113) 259 4594
carlsberg.co.uk/carlsberg.com

Tetley, the historic Leeds brewery, now answers to the name of Carlsberg UK: Carlsberg-Tetley was unceremoniously dumped in 2004. A wholly-owned subsidiary of Carlsberg Breweries of Copenhagen, Denmark, Carlsberg is an international lager giant. In Britain its lagers are brewed at a dedicated plant in Northampton, while Tetley in Leeds produces ales and some Carlsberg products. Some 140,000 barrels are produced annually. Tetley's cask brands receive little or no promotional support outside Yorkshire, most advertising being reserved for the nitro-keg version of Tetley Bitter. Carlsberg plans to close the Leeds site in 2011 or 2012 and has already removed the famous Yorkshire Square fermenters. It's not yet known where the Tetley brands will be brewed following the closure.

Tetley Bitter (OG 1035, ABV 3.7%) ◆
A variable, amber-coloured light, dry bitter with a slight malt and hop aroma, leading to a moderate bitterness with a hint of fruit, ending with a dry and bitter finish.

Brewed for Carlsberg by JW Lees:

Ansells Mild (OG 1033, ABV 3.4%)

Ansells Best Bitter (OG 1035, ABV 3.7%)

Greenalls Bitter (ABV 3.8%)

Draught Burton Ale (OG 1047, ABV 4.8%) ◆
A beer with hops, fruit and malt present throughout, and a lingering complex aftertaste, but lacking some hoppiness compared to its Burton original.

Brewed for Carlsberg by Marston's:

Tetley Dark Mild (OG 1031, ABV 3.2%)

Tetley Mild (OG 1034, ABV 3.3%) ◆
A mid-brown beer with a light malt and caramel aroma. A well-balanced taste of malt and caramel follows, with good bitterness and a satisfying finish.

Coors

Coors Brewers Ltd, 137 High Street, Burton upon Trent, Staffordshire, DE14 1JZ
☎ (01283) 511000
coorsbrewers.com

Coors of Colorado established itself in Europe in 2002 by buying part of the former Bass brewing empire, when Interbrew (now A-B InBev) was instructed by the British government to divest itself of some of its interests in Bass. Coors owns several cask ale brands. It brews 110,000 barrels of cask beer a year (under licensing arrangements with other brewers) and also provides a further 50,000 barrels of cask beer from other breweries.

M&B Mild (OG 1034, ABV 3.2%)

Brewed for Coors by Everards:

Hancock's HB (OG 1038, ABV 3.6%) ◆
A pale brown, slightly malty beer whose initial sweetness is balanced by bitterness but lacks a noticeable finish. A consistent if inoffensive Welsh beer.

Worthington's Bitter (OG 1038, ABV 3.6%)
A pale brown bitter of thin and unremarkable character.

M&B Brew XI (OG 1039.5, ABV 3.8%)
A sweet, malty beer with a hoppy, bitter aftertaste.

Worthington's White Shield (ABV 5.6%) ◆

Bottle-conditioned. Fruity aroma with malt touches. Fruity start with hops but the fruit lasts to a classic bitter finish. Due to the success of the beer since it returned to Burton, it was due to move into the main Coors brewery in autumn 2009 where more than 100,000 barrels a year will be produced. The beer has been a major success in Sainsbury's stores and increased production will allow the beer to go on sale in Asda and Waitrose outlets.

Brewed under licence by Highgate Brewery, Walsall:

Stones Bitter (OG 1037, ABV 3.7%)

White Shield Brewery

White Shield Brewery, Horninglow Street, Burton-upon-Trent, Staffordshire, DE14 1YQ
☎ 0845 600 0598
Tours by arrangement

The White Shield Brewery, formerly the Museum Brewing Co, was based in part of the now-closed Museum of Brewing. The brewery opened in 1994 and recreated some of the older Bass beers that had been discontinued. In 2008 Coors announced the visitor centre and museum, formerly the Bass Museum, would close at the end of June. The brewery continues to brew with production divided 50:50 between cask and bottled beers. Imperial Stout and No 1 Barley Wine are now brewed on an occasional basis and in bottle only, though draught versions are supplied to CAMRA festivals when supplies are available.

Worthington's Red Shield (ABV 4.2%)
A new cask beer.

Worthington's St Modwen (OG 1038, ABV 4.2%) ◆
Hop and malt aroma. Delicate taste of hops and orange. Flowery citrus fruity finish.

Brewery Tap (OG 1042, ABV 4.5%)

Worthington E (OG 1044, ABV 4.8%)

Worthington's White Shield (ABV 5%)
A new cask version of the bottled beer.

Czar's Imperial Stout (OG 1078, ABV 8%) ◆
A library of tastes, from a full roast, liquorice beginning, dark toffee, brown sugar, molasses, Christmas pudding, rum, dark chocolate to name but a few. Fruit emerges, blackberry changing to blackcurrant jam, then liquorice root.

No 1 Barley Wine (OG 1105, ABV 10.5%) ◆
Unbelievably fruity! Thick and chewy, with fruit and sugar going in to an amazing complex of bitter, fruity tastes. Brewed in summer and fermented in casks for 12 months.

Guinness

Guinness closed its London brewery in 2005. All Guinness keg and bottled products on sale in Britain are now brewed in Dublin.

Scottish & Newcastle/Heineken

Scottish & Newcastle/Heineken, 2-4 Broadway Park, South Gyle Broadway, Edinburgh, EH12 9JZ
☎ (0131) 528 1000
🌐 scottish-newcastle.com

Scottish & Newcastle/Heineken is Britain's biggest brewing group with close to 30 per cent of the market. Scottish & Newcastle was formed in 1960, a merger between Scottish Brewers (Younger and McEwan) and Newcastle Breweries. In 1995 it bought Courage from its Australian owners, Foster's/Carlton & United. Since the merger that formed Scottish Courage, the group rationalised by closing its breweries in Edinburgh, Newcastle, Nottingham, Halifax and the historic Courage (George's) Brewery in Bristol. The remaining beers were transferred to John Smith's in Tadcaster. It bought the financially stricken Bulmer's Cider group, which included the Beer Seller wholesalers, now part of WaverleyTBS. S&N/Heineken continue to own Bulmer's, WaverleyTBS and the S&N 1,700-strong pub estate. In 2003, S&N sold the Theakston's Brewery in Yorkshire back to the original family (see Theakston's entry in Independents section). In February 2004, S&N entered into an arrangement with the Caledonian brewery in Edinburgh that gave S&N a 30% stake in Caledonian and 100% control of the brewery's assets but in March 2008 S&N bought the whole of the company, which is now a subsidiary of S&N/Heineken. S&N's sole Scottish cask beer, McEwan's 80/-, has been discontinued. The Courage brands are now brewed by Wells & Young's and owned by a new company, Courage Brands Ltd (see New Nationals section).

There are three organisations mentioned in the Breweries section to which breweries can belong.

The Independent Families Brewers of Britain (IFBB) represents around 35 regional companies still owned by families. As many regional breweries closed in the 1990s, the IFBB represents the interests of the survivors, staging events such as the annual Cask Beer Week to emphasise the important role played by the independent sector.

The Society of Independent Brewers (SIBA) represents the growing number of small craft or micro brewers: some smaller regionals are also members. SIBA is an effective lobbying organisation and played a leading role in persuading the government to introduce Progressive Beer Duty. It has also campaigned to get large pub companies to take beers from smaller breweries and has had considerable success with Enterprise Inns, the biggest pubco.

The East Anglian Brewers' Co-operative (EAB) was the brainchild of Brendan Moore at Iceni Brewery. Finding it impossible to get their beers into pub companies and faced by the giant power of Greene King in the region, the co-op makes bulk deliveries to the genuine free trade and also sells beer at farmers' markets and specialist beer shops. EAB also buys malt and hops in bulk for its members, thus reducing costs.

Berkshire

Berkshire Brewery, Imperial Way, Reading, Berkshire, RG2 0PN
☎ (0118) 922 2988

No cask beer. Due to close in 2010.

Caledonian

Caledonian Brewing Co Ltd, 42 Slateford Road, Edinburgh, EH11 1PH
☎ (0131) 337 1286
✉ info@caledonian-brewery.co.uk
caledonian-brewery.co.uk
Tours by arrangement

The brewery was founded by Lorimer & Clark in 1869 and was sold to Vaux of Sunderland in 1919. In 1987 the brewery was saved from closure by a management buy-out. The brewery site was purchased by S&N in 2004 and became a wholly-owned subsidiary of S&N/Heineken in 2008. A rolling programme of seasonal beers is produced. The Harviestoun Brewery (qv), which was a subsidiary of Caledonian, is now independent.

Deuchars IPA (OG 1039, ABV 3.8%)
A tasty and refreshing pale golden session beer. Hops and fruit are evident and are gently balanced by malt. The lingering aftertaste is delightfully bitter and hoppy.

80 (OG 1042, ABV 4.1%)
A predominantly malty, tawny beer with caramel and roast notes throughout. Smooth and rounded with a sweet taste that dries in the finish.

XPA (ABV 4.3%)

Royal

Royal Brewery, 201 Denmark Road, Manchester, M15 6LD
☎ (0161) 220 4371

Massive brewery in Manchester capable of producing 1.3 million barrels of beer a year. No cask beer.

S&N UK Dunston

S&N Dunston Brewery, Lancaster Road, Dunston, Gateshead, Tyne & Wear, NE11 9JR

The former co-operative Federation brewery run by working men's clubs. S&N transferred production to Dunston when it closed its Tyneside plant in 2004 and bought Federation. 'Newcastle' Brown Ale is now brewed in Gateshead. No cask beer.

S&N UK Tadcaster

John Smith's Brewery, Tadcaster, North Yorkshire, LS24 9SA
☎ (01937) 832091
scottish-newcastle.com
Tours by arrangement

The brewery was built in 1879 by a relative of Samuel Smith (qv). John Smith's became part of the Courage group in 1970. Major expansion has taken place, with 11 new fermenting vessels installed. Traditional Yorkshire Square fermenters have been replaced by conical vessels.

John Smith's Bitter (OG 1035.8, ABV 3.8%)
A copper-coloured beer, well-balanced but with no dominating features. It has a short hoppy finish.

Brewed under licence by Cameron's of Hartlepool:

John Smith's Magnet (ABV 4%)

Tetley Brewery, Leeds; due to close in 2011/2012

The beers index

These beers refer to those in bold type in the breweries section (beers in regular production) and so therefore do not include seasonal, special or occasional beers that may be mentioned elsewhere in the text.

BEERS INDEX

C

D

E

F

G

H

BEERS INDEX

BEERS INDEX

M

BEERS INDEX

N

O

P

S

T

X

Y

Z

Readers' recommendations

Suggestions for pubs to be included or excluded

All pubs are surveyed by local branches of the Campaign for Real Ale. If you would like to comment on a pub already featured, or on any you think should be featured, please fill in the form below (or copy it), and send it to the address indicated. Your views will be passed on to the branch concerned. Please mark your envelope with the county where the pub is, which will help us to direct the suggestion efficiently.

Pub name:

Address:

Reason for recommendation/criticism:

Pub name:

Address:

Reason for recommendation/criticism:

Pub name:

Address:

Reason for recommendation/criticism:

Your name and address:

Please send to: [Name of county] Section, Good Beer Guide,
230 Hatfield Road, St Albans, Hertfordshire AL1 4LW

Pub name:

Address:

Reason for recommendation/criticism:

Pub name:

Address:

Reason for recommendation/criticism:

Pub name:

Address:

Reason for recommendation/criticism:

Pub name:

Address:

Reason for recommendation/criticism:

Your name and address:

Please send to: [Name of county] Section, Good Beer Guide,
230 Hatfield Road, St Albans, Hertfordshire AL1 4LW

Have your say

Feedback on the Good Beer Guide

We are always trying to improve the Good Beer Guide for our readers and we welcome your feedback. If you have any suggestions for how the Good Beer Guide, Good Beer Guide Mobile Edition or sat-nav POI could be improved, or made easier to use or navigate, please let us know. Simply fill out the form below (or a copy of it) and send it to the address indicated, or make your comments on our website at: **www.camra.org.uk/gbgfeedback**. Thank you.

Colour section:

Pubs section:

Maps:

Brewery section:

Good Beer Guide sat-nav POI:

Good Beer Guide Mobile Edition:

What other suggestions do you have?

Please send to: Good Beer Guide – Have your say,
230 Hatfield Road, St Albans, Hertfordshire, AL1 4LW

Award winning pubs

Local Camra Pubs of the Year

The Pub of the Year competition is judged by CAMRA members. Each of the CAMRA branches votes for its favourite pub. They are judged on criteria such as customer service, décor, clientele mix, value for money and, most importantly, the quality of the cask beer. The pubs listed below are the winners of the 2009 title, look out for the (🏆) symbol next to the entries in the Guide.

England

🏆 Bedfordshire
Three Cup, Bedford
Golden Pheasant, Biggleswade
Globe, Dunstable

🏆 Berkshire
Victoria Arms, Binfield
Dundas Arms, Kintbury
Nag's Head, Reading

🏆 Buckinghamshire
White Horse, Hedgerley
Whip, Lacey Green
Victoria Inn, Milton Keynes

🏆 Cambridgeshire
West End House, Ely
Mad Cat, Pidley
White Horse, Swavesey
Boat, Whittlesey

🏆 Cheshire
Old Harkers Arms, Chester
Borough Arms, Crewe
Harrington Arms, Gawsworth
Plough, Houghton Green
Weaver Hotel, Weston Point

🏆 Cornwall
Driftwood Spars, Trevaunance Cove

🏆 Cumbria
Cumberland Inn, Alston
Prince of Wales, Foxfield
Watermill Inn, Ings
Kirkstile Inn, Loweswater

🏆 Derbyshire
Old Poets' Corner, Ashover
Brewery Tap – Derby's Royal Standard, Derby
Coach & Horses, Dronfield
Old Oak Inn, Horsley Woodhouse
Dewdrop, Ilkeston
Temple Hotel, Matlock Bath
Devonshire Arms, South Normanton

🏆 Devon
Hunters Inn, Heddon Valley
Fortescue, Plymouth
Royal Oak, South Brent
Tom Cobley Tavern, Spreyton
Trout & Tipple, Tavistock

🏆 Dorset
Stapleton Arms, Buckhorn Weston
Olde George Inn, Christchurch
Blue Raddle, Dorchester

🏆 Durham
Quakerhouse, Darlington
Victoria Inn, Durham
Ship Inn, Middlestone Village
Thomas Sheraton, Stockton-on-Tees

🏆 Essex
Odd One Out, Colchester
White Hart, Grays
Haywain, Little Bromley
Swan, Little, Totham
White Horse Inn, Ridgewell
Horse & Groom, Rochford
Wheatsheaf, Writtle

🏆 Gloucestershire & Bristol
Old Spot, Dursley
Ebrington Arms, Ebrington

🏆 Hampshire
White Hart, Charter Alley
Hole in the Wall, Portsmouth
Guide Dog, Southampton

🏆 Herefordshire
Green Dragon, Bishops Frome

🏆 Hertfordshire
Valiant Trooper, Aldbury
Land of Liberty, Peace & Plenty, Heronsgate
Old Cross Tavern, Hertford
Rising Sun, High Wych
Half Moon, Hitchin

🏆 Isle of Wight
Yarbridge Inn, Brading

Kent
Elephant, Faversham
Rose & Crown, Halstead
Butcher's Arms, Herne
Bull, Horton Kirby
Flower Pot, Maidstone
Montefiore Arms, Ramsgate
Red Lion, Snargate
King's Arms, Upper Upnor
Berry, Walmer

Lancashire
Bridge Bier Huis, Burnley
Top Lock, Heapey
White Cross, Lancaster
Taps, Lytham

Leicestershire & Rutland
Old Crown, Cavendish Bridge
Criterion, Leicester

Lincolnshire
White Swan, Barrowby
Tollemache Inn, Grantham
Yarborough Hotel, Grimsby
Dog & Bone, Lincoln
Boars Head, Louth
White Hart Inn, Ludford
Click'em Inn, Swinhope
Half Moon, Willingham by Stow

Greater London
Britannia, Barking, East London
Dispensary, E1: Aldgate, East London
Beehive, N9: Lower Edmonton, North London
Bree Louise, NW1: Euston, North-West London
Claret Free House, Addiscombe, South-East London
Robin Hood & Little John, Bexleyheath, South-East London
Dog & Bell, SE8: Deptford, South-East London
Bricklayer's Arms, SW15: Putney, South-West London
White Horse, SW6: Parsons Green, South-West London
Roebuck, Hampton Hill, West London
Red Lion, W5: Ealing, West London

Greater Manchester
Pendle Witch, Atherton
Knott, Manchester City Centre
Baum, Rochdale
New Oxford, Salford
Arden Arms, Stockport
Crown Hotel, Worthington

Merseyside
Ship & Mitre, Liverpool: City Centre
Telegraph Inn, New Brighton
Baron's Bar (Scarisbrick Hotel), Southport

Norfolk
Artichoke, Broome
Union Jack, Roydon

Northamptonshire
Coach & Horses, Wellingborough

Northumberland
Boathouse Inn, Wylam

Nottinghamshire
Crown, Bathley
Royal Oak, Car Colston
Bold Forester, Mansfield
Newshouse, Nottingham: Central
Rum Runner, Retford

Oxfordshire
Red Lion, Brightwell-cum-Sotwell
Rose & Crown, Charlbury
Old Bookbinders, Oxford
Royal Oak Inn, Wantage

Shropshire
Salopian Bar, Shrewsbury
Cock Hotel, Telford: Wellington

Somerset
Royal Oak, Bath
Brewers Arms, South Petherton

Staffordshire
Swan, Bignall End
Burton Bridge Inn, Burton upon Trent
Cross Keys Hotel, Hednesford
Vine, Kinver
Barley Mow, Penn Common
Greyhound, Stafford
Sir Robert Peel, Tamworth

Suffolk
Dove Street Inn, Ipswich
Triangle Tavern, Lowestoft
Fox & Hounds, Thurston

Surrey
Crossways, Churt
Royal Oak, Great Bookham
Surrey Oaks, Newdigate
Barley Mow, Shepperton

East Sussex
Queen's Head, Icklesham
Stanley Arms, Portslade

West Sussex
Royal Oak, Friday Street
Duke of Cumberland Arms, Henley
Selden Arms, Worthing

Tyne & Wear
Steamboat, South Shields

Warwickshire
Horse & Jockey, Bentley
Boars Head, Hampton Lucy
Wyandotte Inn, Kenilworth
Talbot Inn, Leamington Spa
Raglan Arms, Rugby

West Midlands
Maverick, Amblecote
Bull's Head, Barston
Wellington, Birmingham: City Centre
Gatehouse Tavern, Coventry
Beacon Hotel, Sedgley
Wheatsheaf, Walsall
Vine, Wednesfield

Wiltshire
Two Pigs, Corsham
Cuckoo Inn, Hamptworth
Carters Rest, Wroughton

Worcestershire
Weighbridge, Alvechurch
Fleece Inn, Bretforton
Bell, Pensax
Plough, Worcester

East Yorkshire
Dog & Duck, Beverley
Plough Inn, Hollym
Wellington Inn, Hull

North Yorkshire
Old White Bear, Cross Hills
Bonhommes Bar, Filey
Mitre Hotel, Knaresborough
Tithe Bar & Brasserie, Northallerton
North Riding Hotel, Scarborough
Swan Inn, York

South Yorkshire
Station Inn, Darfield
Red Lion, Doncaster
Bay Horse, Scholes
Kelham Island Tavern, Sheffield: Central

West Yorkshire
Junction, Baildon
Leggers Inn, Dewsbury
Moyles, Hebden Bridge
Star Inn, Huddersfield
Mr Foley's Cask Ale House, Leeds: City
Angler's Retreat, Wintersett

Wales

Glamorgan
Albion, Penarth
Boar's Head, Tyla Garw
Railway Inn, Upper Killay

Gwent
Commercial, Risca
Goose & Cuckoo, Upper Llanover

Mid-Wales
Ancient Briton, Pen-y-Cae
Star Inn, Talybont on Usk

North-East Wales
Sun Inn, Llangollen
Golden Lion Inn, Llangynhafal

North-West Wales
Spooner's Bar, Porthmadog
Kinmel Arms, St George

West Wales
Pendre Inn, Cilgerran
Tafarn John y Gwas, Drefach-Felindre
Druid Inn, Goginan
Mansel Arms, Porthyrhyd

Scotland

Aberdeen & Grampian
Marine Hotel, Stonehaven

Borders
Border Hotel, Kirk Yetholm

Dumfries & Galloway
Cavens Arms, Dumfries
Steam Packet Inn, Isle of Whithorn

Edinburgh & The Lothians
Four Marys, Linlithgow

Greater Glasgow & Clyde Valley
Brown Bull, Lochwinnoch

Highlands & Western Isles
Braeval Hotel, Nairn

Kingdom of Fife
Albert Tavern, Freuchie

Loch Lomond, Stirling & The Trossachs
Kilcreggan Hotel, Kilcreggan

Tayside
Crees Inn, Abernethy

Northern Ireland

White Horse, Saintfield

Channel Islands

Guernsey
Cock & Bull, St Peter Port

Jersey
Lamplighter, St Helier

Isle of Man

White House Hotel, Peel

Pubs transport – 2010

Hop on a bus, train or tram

Using public transport is an excellent way to get to the pub, but many people use them irregularly, and systems can be slightly different from place to place. This Guide is designed to help you.

Information

First, you need to know the route and time. You should find information at the bus stop timetable case, which usually gives contact telephone numbers and text messaging services. You can also get information from information centres run nationally, regionally or locally. Remember that many operators will not tell you about other operators' services.

Information by phone

The national Traveline system (0871 200 22 23) gives information on all bus and local rail services throughout England, Scotland and Wales. Calls are put through to a local call centre and if necessary your call will be switched through to a more relevant centre. Mobile phone users will be given a series of menu options to locate the relevant centre. In London use Traveline or the Transport for London information line, 020 7222 1234. For National Rail Enquiries telephone 08457 48 49 50.

On the net

Try Transport Direct, **www.transportdirect.info**, or Traveline, **www.traveline.org.uk**. For London try **www.tfl.gov.uk**. National Rail Enquiries are at **www.nationalrail.co.uk/times_fares**. Scotland has its own planner at **www.travelinescotland.com**, with a link from Traveline. Just a tip – it can help to know the post code of the pub(s) you want to visit!

Coach

The two main UK coach sites are:
National Express – telephone 08717 818181 – website **www.nationalexpress.com**
Scottish Citylink – telephone 08705 505050 – website **www.citylink.co.uk**

Using the bus

Bus stops in towns and villages are clearly marked. If there is a number of stops in an area, make sure the service you want is listed on the bus stop plate or timetable case. If no services are listed then all buses should stop there, apart perhaps from some 'express' buses. Give a clear signal to the driver to stop the bus.
Some routes operate on a 'hail and ride' principle where the bus will stop anywhere it is safe to do so. Ask the enquiry service or operator, or, if you use a stop on the outward journey, ask the driver. If you don't know where to get off, ask the driver to let you know. It's often worth asking the driver where your return stop is, as sometimes it's not too obvious.
Some buses run 'on demand' so you'll have to telephone in advance. The information centre should know, and give you the contact number.

Paying your fare

You usually get on at the front and pay the driver. Have some small change ready as some companies operate a 'fast fare' system and don't give change. In central London and on many tram systems you need to buy a ticket in advance from a nearby machine.

Special fares

Where available, return tickets are often cheaper than two singles. Many operators, and some local authorities, offer 'network' tickets for a number of journeys. If buying an operator's multi-journey ticket check that you can use it on other operators' services – important if more than one company operates the route.

On trains, standard and 'saver' return tickets allow you to break your journey, so if you are visiting a number of pubs by train, book to the furthest station. This may not apply to other types of rail ticket – ask in advance.

Concessionary fares

There are concessionary fares schemes for people aged over 60 or with certain disabilities. The English national concessionary fares scheme provides free travel for pass-holders on buses anywhere in England between 9.30am and 11pm, and at any time at weekends or on bank holidays. It does not provide free bus travel outside England, nor is it generally valid on trains, trams or ferries. However, there are local exceptions where the scheme is enhanced, either for local residents or for everyone. It is worth checking locally.

The Scottish, Welsh and Northern Irish schemes are slightly different. Eligible people should enquire locally. As in England, there are local enhancements.

National Express offer half fare discounts for people over 60 or with certain disabilities on most of their services throughout the United Kingdom. If you think you are eligible, ask before you book. If you have a concessionary fares card, this will generally give proof of entitlement. Scottish passes are valid on long distance coaches within Scotland, such as those operated by Scottish CityLink. This entitlement is only for Scottish residents.

National Rail sell a range of rail cards, including ones for people over 60, with certain disabilities, or between the ages of 16 and 25. These give a discount of 34% on most tickets, and there can be other advantages. Either ask at your nearest staffed station, telephone National Rail Enquiries, or look on the National Rail web site

Complaints, problems and lost property

If you have any complaints, problems or lose anything when using public transport, please contact the operator running the service as soon as possible. Keep your ticket. The information is important. If you feel your complaint is not dealt with satisfactorily, contact the relevant Transport Authority who may be able to help. Service reliability is improving rapidly but occasionally things do go wrong and the bus doesn't turn up. If, because of this, you need get a taxi, ask for a receipt and send it in with your complaint. You may get reimbursed.

Outside Mainland UK, but within the area of this Guide, information services are:

NORTHERN IRELAND
Translink, 02890 666630,
www.translink.co.uk or
www.traveline.org.uk

ISLE OF MAN
Isle of Man Transport, 01624 662525,
www.iombusandrail.info

JERSEY
Telephone 01534 877772,
www.thisisjersey.com

GUERNSEY
Island Coachways 01481 720210,
www.buses.gg

NOTE: All information was correct at the time of writing, however CAMRA cannot be held responsible for any changes made since that date.

An offer for CAMRA members

Good Beer Guide annual subscription

Being a CAMRA member brings many benefits, not least a big discount on the Good Beer Guide. Now you can take advantage of an even bigger discount on the Guide by taking out an annual subscription.

Simply fill in the form below and the Direct Debit form on p887 (photocopies will do if you don't want to spoil your book), and send them to CAMRA at 230 Hatfield Road, St Albans, Hertfordshire AL1 4LW.

You will then receive the **Good Beer Guide** automatically every year. It will be posted to you before the official publication date and before any other postal sales are processed.

You won't have to bother with filling in cheques every year and you will receive the book at a lower price than other CAMRA members (for instance, the **2009** Guide was sold to annual subscribers **for just £10**)

So sign up now and be sure of receiving your copy early every year.

Note: This offer is open only to CAMRA members and is only available through using a Direct Debit instruction to a UK bank. This offer applies to the **Good Beer Guide 2010** onwards.

Name

CAMRA Membership No.

Address and Postcode

I wish to purchase the *Good Beer Guide* annually by Direct Debit and I have completed the Direct Debit instructions to my bank which are enclosed.

Signature Date

Books for beer lovers

100 Belgian Beers to Try Before You Die!

Tim Webb & Joris Pattyn

100 Belgian Beers to Try Before You Die! showcases 100 of the best Begian beers as chosen by internationally-known beer writers Tim Webb and Joris Pattyn. Lavishly illustrated throughout with images of the beers, breweries, Belgian beer bars and some of the characters involved in Belgian brewing, the book encourages both connoisseurs and newcomers to Belgian beer to sample them for themselves, both in Belgium and at home.

£12.99 ISBN 987-1-85249-248-9   Members' Price £10.99

300 Beers to Try Before You Die!

Roger Protz

300 beers from around the world, handpicked by award-winning journalist, author and broadcaster Roger Protz to try before you die! A comprehensive portfolio of top beers from the smallest microbreweries in the United States to family-run British breweries and the world's largest brands. This book is indispensible for both beer novices and aficionados.

£12.99 ISBN 978-1-85249-213-7   Members' Price £10.99

A Beer a Day

Jeff Evans

Written by leading beer writer Jeff Evans, **A Beer a Day** is a beer lover's almanac, crammed with beers from around the world to enjoy on every day and in every season, and celebrating beer's connections with history, sport, music film and television. Whether it's Christmas Eve, Midsummer's Day, Bonfire Night, or just a wet Wednesday in the middle of October, **A Beer a Day** has just the beer for you to savour and enjoy.

£12.99 ISBN 978-1-85249-235-9   Members' Price £10.99

A Life on the Hop: Memoirs from a career in beer

Roger Protz

The entertaining highlights and challenging low points of acclaimed beer-writer Roger Protz's busy and influential career in beer. Well known and admired within the world of beer, Protz has written many indispensible books on the subject and travelled to most of the great beer-drinking nations – from Britain, through Europe to Russia, Mexico and the USA – and commentated as microbrewers bring back taste and flavour to countries dominated by bland national brands.

£12.99 ISBN 978-1-85249-256-4   Members' Price £10.99

Cider **Photography by Mark Bolton**

Proper cider and perry – made with apples and pears and nothing but, is a wonderful drink – but there's so much more to it than that. **Cider** is a lavishly illustrated celebration of real cider, and its close cousin perry, for anyone who wants to learn more about Britain's oldest drink. With features on the UK's most interesting and characterful cider and perry makers, how to make your own cider, foreign ciders, and the best places to drink cider – including unique dedicated cider houses, award-winning pubs and year-round CAMRA festivals all over the country – **Cider** is the essential book for any cider or perry lover.

£14.99 ISBN 978-1-85249-259-5   Members' Price £12.99

Good Beer Guide Belgium Tim Webb

The completely revised and updated 6th edition of the guide so impressive that it is acknowledged as the standard work for Belgian beer lovers, even in Belgium itself. The **Good Beer Guide Belguim** includes comprehensive advice on getting there, being there, what to eat, where to stay and how to bring beers back home. Its outline of breweries, beers and bars makes this book indispensible for both leisure and business travellers a well as for armchair drinkers looking to enjoy a selection of Belgian brews from their local beer store.

£14.99 ISBN 978-1-85249-261-8 Members Price £12.99

Good Beer Guide West Coast USA

Ben McFarland & Tom Sandham

Taking in the whole western seaboard of the USA, as well as Las Vegas, Alaska and Hawaii, this is a lively, comprehensive and entertaining tour that unveils some of the most exhilarating beers, breweries and bars on the planet. It is the definitive, totally independent guide to understanding and discovering the heart of America's thriving craft beer scene, and an essential companion for any beer drinker visiting West Coast America or seeking out American beer in the UK, Written with verve and insight by two respected young beer journalists, **Good Beer Guide West Coast USA** is a must – not just for those who find themselves on the West Coast, but for all discerning beer enthusiasts and barflies everywhere.

14.99 ISBN 978-1-85249-244-1 Members' Price £12.99

Good Bottled Beer Guide Jeff Evans

A pocket-sized guide for discerning drinkers looking to buy bottled real ales and enjoy a fresh glass of their favourite beers at home. The 7th edition of the **Good Bottled Beer Guide** is completely revised, updated and redesigned to showcase the very best bottled British real ales now being produced, and detail where they can be bought. Everything you need to know about bottled beers; tasting notes, ingredients, brewery details, and a glossary to help the reader understand more about them.

£12.99 ISBN 978-1-85249-262-5 Members' Price £10.99

London Heritage Pubs – An inside story

Geoff Brandwood & Jane Jephcote

The definitive guidebook to London's most unspoilt pubs. Raging from gloriously rich Victorian extravaganzas to unspoilt community street-corner locals, the pubs not only have interiors of genuine heritage value, they also have fascinating stories to tell. **London Heritage Pubs – An inside story** is a must for anyone interested in visiting and learning about London's magnificent pubs.

£14.99 ISBN 978-1-85249-247-2 Members' Price £12.99

Peak District Pub Walks Bob Steel

A practical, pocket-sized traveller's guide to some of the best pubs and best walking in the Peak District. This book features 25 walks, as well as cycle routes and local attractions, helping you see the best of Britain's oldest national park while never straying too far from a decent pint. Each route has been selected for its inspiring landscape, historical interest and welcoming pubs.

£9.99 ISBN 978-1-85249-246-5 Members' Price £7.99

Order these and other CAMRA books online at **www.camra.org.uk/books**, ask your local bookstore, or contact:

CAMRA, 230 Hatfield Road, St Albans, AL1 4LW. Telephone 01727 867201

Find Good Beer Guide pubs on the move – anytime, anywhere!

CAMRA is pleased to announce two hi-tech services for beer lovers – **Good Beer Guide Mobile** and the **Good Beer Guide POI** sat-nav file. Together, these offer the perfect solution to pub-finding on the move

Good Beer Guide Mobile

FREE 3 day trial with no obligation!

Just £10 for a year's subscription!

Good Beer Guide Mobile provides detailed information on local Good Beer Guide pubs, breweries and beers wherever you are or wherever you're going!

Simple to use, the mobile edition offers the following features:

- Search results with detailed information and pub descriptions.
- CAMRA tasting notes for regular beers.
- Interactive maps help you find your way.
- Search from a postcode, place name or auto locate using GPS.
- Available on a wide range of mobile phones (please check the website for more information).

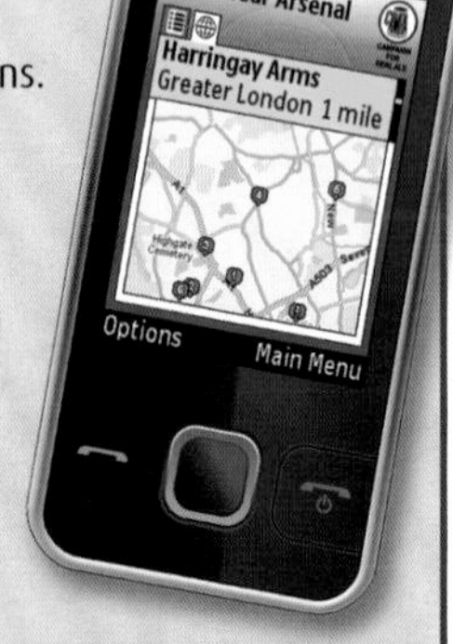

To download Good Beer Guide Mobile visit: **http://m.camra.org.uk** or text **'camra'** to **88080**

(NOTE: Your standard network charge applies)

Find Good Beer Guide pubs using satellite navigation!

The Good Beer Guide POI (Points of Interest) file allows users of TomTom, Garmin and Navman sat-nav systems to see the locations of all the 4,500-plus current Good Beer Guide pubs and plan routes to them. So, now, wherever you are, there is no excuse for not finding your nearest Good Beer Guide pub!

The file is simple to install and use and full instructions are provided. Priced at just £5.00, it is the perfect tool for any serious pub explorer. No more wasting time thumbing through road atlases or getting lost down country lanes. Navigate your way easily, every time, and make the most of Britain's best pubs.

- To download the file vist: **www.camra.org.uk/gbgpoi**

PUB DESIGN AWARDS

Design awards boost for community pubs

FOR 20 YEARS, CAMRA has run the Pub Design Awards as part of its commitment to supporting pubs in the community. The awards, run in conjunction with English Heritage and the Victorian Society, have taken on a new importance as a result of the recession and pub closures.

Announcing the latest results in June 2009, Dr Steven Parissien, the leading architectural historian and one of the judges, said: 'When a pub disappears, so does the heart and soul of the community which it adorns and defines. In the midst of a recession, it's even more important than ever to hang on to what we hold dear – to what has shaped our past and can provide a valuable touchstone for our future.

Etched glass in the Princess Louise

'Communities need pubs as never before, to give us a feeling of identity, belonging and continuity in an ever-changing landscape. We must act to halt the steady erosion of character, choice and uniqueness in our towns, cities and villages.'

Dr Parissien said pub design is crucial in defining not only the pub's own welcome but also what makes its location – its street or its community – so special. He added that the awards have sought to praise pub restorations that celebrate the uniqueness of the building inside and out rather than an 'indiscriminate, irrelevant and all-too-transient corporate theme. Amid the gloom and doom of Recession Britain, this past year has, reassuringly, seen a number of first-rate pub schemes all of which illustrate how pubs can and should be treated.'

The judges' Newbuild Award went to Zero Degrees in Bridge Street, Reading. They praised its 'strikingly modern, glass-fronted design, which, like the three other pubs in the group, makes an architectural virtue of its in-house brewing equipment. The northern facade is assertive but not brash or over-sized, while the side that fronts Bridge Street is expressively glazed yet appropriately scaled. Inside, the various floors and bars are defined with sleek, flowing lines rather than with brusque punctuation. Set on two floors, the interior offers distinctively different bars and eating areas to cater to a diverse audience.'

The Refurbishment Award went to what the judges described as 'two outstanding treatments of famous old pubs. Sam Smith's renowned Princess Louise in Holborn, London, has undergone a comprehensive redesign that has seen the reintroduction of the original multi-bar layout, complete with bar doors and snob screens. This has made what was already an interesting and worthy pub even more of a pubgoers' icon.'

The Newbuild Award-winning Zero Degrees in Reading

The refurbished Princess Louise in London

The pub was built in 1891-2 and is Grade II listed, placing it in the top 10 per cent of historic buildings. The judges said it 'already enjoyed an impressive array of striking tile work, cut-glass mirrors, ornate plasterwork and robust Lincrusta covering the ceiling. Now it also boasts a historical plan. After a six-month closure, this celebrated landmark has re-opened in a guise that reflects both its incarnation of over a century ago and the modern customer's wish to drink and chat in a cosy, quiet and private environment.

The commended White Horse, Overton-on-Dee

This is one instance where gilding the lily can improve the subject.'

The other joint winner was the Castle Inn in Mount Pleasant, Bradford-on-Avon in Wiltshire. The judges said: 'The owners, Flatcappers, have retained this handsome Georgian pub's historic features while gearing the interior to its food-oriented clientele. The Castle shows you don't have to shed pub identity in order to maximise the opportunities to eat.

'The multi-roomed plan has been mostly retained – though some areas have been opened out – appropriate finishes applied to the floors and walls, while on the walls historic browns, creams and greens predominate. The seat furniture is a pleasingly mix-and-match, elderly but comfortable, while outside even the iron railings have won a civic award, a success that demonstrates the great attention to detail at this hilltop site.'

The White Horse, High Street, Overton-on-Dee, Clwyd, on the Welsh border near Wrexham, was Highly Commended for its refurbishment. The judges' opinion was that 'Joules Brewery and Tuns Taverns have treated the building in a very different manner to the Castle Inn. This was a run-down, town-centre hotel that appeared ripe for redevelopment for residential or retail use. Instead, it's been saved in a manner that spirited and individual.

'The enthusiastic provision of bright new stained glass, pristine wooden partitions and salvaged fireplaces is at times a bit over-eager but the original plan has been largely retained and a fine building, at Overton's cultural as well as geographical heart, has been successfully revitalised.'

Julian Hough, CAMRA's Pubs Director, commenting on the awards, said he remained upbeat about the future of the British pub and added that there will be plenty of innovation and flair in the pub industry for years to come.

'It's wonderful to see people invest in pubs and believe wholeheartedly in their future,' he added. 'These winners are successful community pubs and we must do everything we can to support them.'

The revamped Castle Inn, Bradford-on-Avon

Instruction to your Bank or Building Society to pay by Direct Debit

Please fill in the form and send to: Campaign for Real Ale Ltd. 230 Hatfield Road, St. Albans, Herts. AL1 4LW

Name and full postal address of your Bank or Building Society

To The Manager Bank or Building Society

Address

Postcode

Name (s) of Account Holder (s)

Bank or Building Society account number

Branch Sort Code

Reference Number

Originator's Identification Number

9	2	6	1	2	9

FOR CAMRA OFFICIAL USE ONLY
This is not part of the instruction to your Bank or Building Society

Membership Number

Name

Postcode

Instruction to your Bank or Building Society
Please pay CAMRA Direct Debits from the account detailed on this Instruction subject to the safeguards assured by the Direct Debit Guarantee. I understand that this instruction may remain with CAMRA and, if so, will be passed electronically to my Bank/Building Society

Signature(s)

Date

Banks and Building Societies may not accept Direct Debit Instructions for some types of account

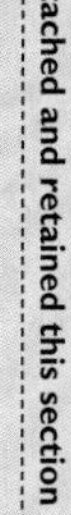

DIRECT Debit

This Guarantee should be detached and retained by the payer.

The Direct Debit Guarantee

- This Guarantee is offered by all Banks and Building Societies that take part in the Direct Debit Scheme. The efficiency and security of the Scheme is monitored and protected by your own Bank or Building Society.
- If the amounts to be paid or the payment dates change CAMRA will notify you 10 working days in advance of your account being debited or as otherwise agreed.
- If an error is made by CAMRA or your Bank or Building Society, you are guaranteed a full and immediate refund from your branch of the amount paid.
- You can cancel a Direct Debit at any time by writing to your Bank or Building Society. Please also send a copy of your letter to us.

It takes all sorts to Campaign for Real Ale

CAMRA, the Campaign for Real Ale, is an independent not-for-profit, volunteer-led consumer group. We promote good-quality real ale and pubs, as well as lobbying government to champion drinkers' rights and protect local pubs as centres of community life.

CAMRA has over 100,000 members from all ages and backgrounds, brought together by a common belief in the issues that CAMRA deals with and their love of good quality British beer. From just £20 a year – that's less than a pint a month – you can join CAMRA and enjoy the following benefits:

- A monthly colour newspaper and quarterly magazine informing you about beer and pub news and detailing events and beer festivals around the country.
- Free or reduced entry to over 140 national, regional and local beer festivals.
- Money off many of our publications including the Good Beer Guide and the Good Bottled Beer Guide.
- A 10% discount on all holidays booked with Cottages4you and a 6% discount on all holidays booked with Thomas Cook.
- £20 worth of JD Wetherspoon real ale vouchers (40 x 50 pence off a pint).
- The opportunity to campaign to save pubs under threat of closure, for pubs to be open when people want to drink and a reduction in beer duty that will help Britain's brewing industry survive.

Do you feel passionately about your pint? Then why not join CAMRA

Just fill in the application form (or a photocopy of it) and the Direct Debit form on the previous page to receive three months' membership FREE!*

If you wish to join but do not want to pay by Direct Debit, please fill in the application form below and send a cheque, payable to CAMRA, to: CAMRA, 230 Hatfield Road, St Albans, Hertfordshire, AL1 4LW. Please note than non Direct Debit payments will incur a £2 surcharge. Figures are given below.

Please tick appropriate box	**Direct Debit**	**Non Direct Debit**
Single membership (UK & EU)	£20 ☐	£22 ☐
Concessionary membership (under 26 or 60 and over)	£14 ☐	£16 ☐
Joint membership	£25 ☐	£27 ☐
Concessionary joint membership	£17 ☐	£19 ☐

Life membership information is available on request.

Title ____________ Surname ____________

Forename(s) ____________

Address ____________

____________ Postcode ____________

Date of Birth ____________ Email address ____________

Signature ____________

Partner's details (for Joint Membership)

Title ____________ Surname ____________

Forename(s) ____________

Date of Birth ____________ Email address ____________

CAMRA will occasionally send you e-mails related to your membership. We will also allow your local branch access to your email. If you would like to opt-out of contact from your local branch please tick here ☐ (at no point will your details be released to a third party).

Find out more at **www.camra.org.uk/joinus** or telephone **01727 867201**

*Three months free is only available the first time a member pays by Direct Debit

NOTE: Membership benefits are subject to change.

REF: GBG2010